BUSINESS AND COMPANY LEGISLATION

Published by
CLP, an imprint of Packhouse,
Packhouse Manor Press House Pear St Handcross, Chittings WD12 2HA

© CLP, an imprint of 2015

British Library Cataloguing-in-Publication Data
A catalogue record for this book is available from the British Library.

Crown copyright material is reproduced with permission of HMSO. The Takeover Code is reproduced with permission of the Takeover Panel.

BUSINESS AND COMPANY LEGISLATION

Trevor Adams BSc, PhD, Solicitor

Published by
College of Law Publishing,
Braboeuf Manor, Portsmouth Road, St Catherines, Guildford GU3 1HA

British Library Cataloguing-in-Publication Data
A catalogue record for this book is available from the British Library.

ISBN 0 905835 92 1

Typeset by Style Photosetting Ltd, Mayfield, East Sussex
Printed in Great Britain by Ashford Colour Press Ltd.

Contents

Note: The text of the legislation incorporates amendments and repeals to 1 March 2005. Repeals and provisions omitted because they are amending only are indicated by an ellipsis and prospective repeals and legislation not yet brought into force are printed in italics.

Merger Control

EC Legislation

INDEX

Companies Act 1985

Arrangement of sections

Companies Act 1985

1985 c. 6

An Act to consolidate the greater part of the Companies Acts

[11th March 1985]

PART I
FORMATION AND REGISTRATION OF COMPANIES;
JURIDICAL STATUS AND MEMBERSHIP

CHAPTER I
COMPANY FORMATION

Memorandum of association

1. Mode of forming incorporated company

(1) Any two or more persons associated for a lawful purpose may, by subscribing their names to a memorandum of association and otherwise complying with the requirements of this Act in respect of registration, form an incorporated company, with or without limited liability.

(2) A company so formed may be either—

    (a) a company having the liability of its members limited by the memorandum to the amount, if any, unpaid on the shares respectively held by them ("a company limited by shares");

    (b) a company having the liability of its members limited by the memorandum to such amount as the members may respectively thereby undertake to contribute to the assets of the company in the event of its being wound up ("a company limited by guarantee"); or

    (c) a company not having any limit on the liability of its members ("an unlimited company").

(3) A "public company" is a company limited by shares or limited by guarantee and having a share capital, being a company—

    (a) the memorandum of which states that it is to be a public company, and

    (b) in relation to which the provisions of this Act or the former Companies Acts as to the registration or re-registration of a company as a public company have been complied with on or after 22nd December 1980;

and a "private company" is a company that is not a public company.

(3A) Notwithstanding subsection (1), one person may, for a lawful purpose, by subscribing his name to a memorandum of association and otherwise complying with the requirements of this Act in respect of registration, form an incorporated company being a private company limited by shares or by guarantee.

(4) With effect from 22nd December 1980, a company cannot be formed as, or become, a company limited by guarantee with a share capital.

2. Requirements with respect to memorandum

(1) The memorandum of every company must state—

    (a) the name of the company;

    (b) whether the registered office of the company is to be situated in England and Wales, or in Scotland;

    (c) the objects of the company.

(2) Alternatively to subsection (1)(b), the memorandum may contain a statement that the company's registered office is to be situated in Wales; and a company whose registered office is situated in Wales may by special resolution alter its memorandum so as to provide that its registered office is to be so situated.

(3) The memorandum of a company limited by shares or by guarantee must also state that the liability of its members is limited.

(4)   The memorandum of a company limited by guarantee must also state that each member undertakes to contribute to the assets of the company if it should be wound up while he is a member, or within one year after he ceases to be a member, for payment of the debts and liabilities of the company contracted before he ceases to be a member, and of the costs, charges and expenses of winding up, and for adjustment of the rights of the contributories among themselves, such amount as may be required, not exceeding a specified amount.

(5)   In the case of a company having a share capital—

     (a)   the memorandum must also (unless it is an unlimited company) state the amount of the share capital with which the company proposes to be registered and the division of the share capital into shares of a fixed amount;

     (b)   no subscriber of the memorandum may take less than one share; and

     (c)   there must be shown in the memorandum against the name of each subscriber the number of shares he takes.

(6)   Subject to subsection (6A), the memorandum must be signed by each subscriber in the presence of at least one witness, who must attest the signature; *and that attestation is sufficient in Scotland as well as in England and Wales.*

(6A)   Where the memorandum is delivered to the registrar otherwise than in legible form and is authenticated by each subscriber in such manner as is directed by the registrar, the requirements in subsection (6) for signature in the presence of at least one witness and for attestation of the signature do not apply.

(7)   A company may not alter the conditions contained in its memorandum except in the cases, in the mode and to the extent, for which express provision is made by this Act.

Note. The words "and that attestation is sufficient in Scotland as well as in England and Wales" in subsection (6) are repealed in relation to Scotland by the Requirements of Writing (Scotland) Act 1995, s. 14(2), Sch. 5.

3.   **Forms of memorandum**

(1)   Subject to the provisions of sections 1 and 2, the form of the memorandum of association of—

     (a)   a public company, being a company limited by shares,

     (b)   a public company, being a company limited by guarantee and having a share capital,

     (c)   a private company limited by shares,

     (d)   a private company limited by guarantee and not having a share capital,

     (e)   a private company limited by guarantee and having a share capital, and

     (f)   an unlimited company having a share capital,

shall be as specified respectively for such companies by regulations made by the Secretary of State, or as near to that form as circumstances admit.

(2)   Regulations under this section shall be made by statutory instrument subject to annulment in pursuance of a resolution of either House of Parliament.

3A.   **Statement of company's objects: general commercial company**

Where the company's memorandum states that the object of the company is to carry on business as a general commercial company—

     (a)   the object of the company is to carry on any trade or business whatsoever, and

     (b)   the company has power to do all such things as are incidental or conducive to the carrying on of any trade or business by it.

4.   **Resolution to alter objects**

(1)   A company may by special resolution alter its memorandum with respect to the statement of the company's objects.

(2)   If an application is made under the following section, an alteration does not have effect except in so far as it is confirmed by the court.

5.   **Procedure for objecting to alteration**

(1)   Where a company's memorandum has been altered by special resolution under section 4, application may be made to the court for the alteration to be cancelled.

(2)   Such an application may be made—
         (a)   by the holders of not less in the aggregate than 15 per cent in nominal value of the
               company's issued share capital or any class of it or, if the company is not limited by shares,
               not less than 15 per cent of the company's members; or
         (b)   by the holders of not less than 15 per cent of the company's debentures entitling the holders
               to object to an alteration of its objects;
         but an application shall not be made by any person who has consented to or voted in favour of the
         alteration.

(3)   The application must be made within 21 days after the date on which the resolution altering the
         company's objects was passed, and may be made on behalf of the persons entitled to make the
         application by such one or more of their number as they may appoint in writing for the purpose.

(4)   The court may on such an application make an order confirming the alteration either wholly or in
         part and on such terms and conditions as it thinks fit, and may—
         (a)   if it thinks fit, adjourn the proceedings in order that an arrangement may be made to its
               satisfaction for the purchase of the interests of dissentient members, and
         (b)   give such directions and make such orders as it thinks expedient for facilitating or carrying
               into effect any such arrangement.

(5)   The court's order may (if the court thinks fit) provide for the purchase by the company of the
         shares of any members of the company, and for the reduction accordingly of its capital, and may
         make such alterations in the company's memorandum and articles as may be required in
         consequence of that provision.

(6)   If the court's order requires the company not to make any, or any specified, alteration in its
         memorandum or articles, the company does not then have power without the leave of the court to
         make any such alteration in breach of that requirement.

(7)   An alteration in the memorandum or articles of a company made by virtue of an order under this
         section, other than one made by resolution of the company, is of the same effect as if duly made
         by resolution; and this Act applies accordingly to the memorandum or articles as so altered.

(7A)   For the purposes of subsection (2)(a), any of the company's issued share capital held as treasury
         shares must be disregarded.

(8)   The debentures entitling the holders to object to an alteration of a company's objects are any
         debentures secured by a floating charge which were issued or first issued before 1st December
         1947 or form part of the same series as any debentures so issued; and a special resolution altering
         a company's objects requires the same notice to the holders of any such debentures as to members
         of the company.
         In the absence of provisions regulating the giving of notice to any such debenture holders, the
         provisions of the company's articles regulating the giving of notice to members apply.

6.   Provisions supplementing ss 4, 5

(1)   Where a company passes a resolution altering its objects, then—
         (a)   if with respect to the resolution no application is made under section 5, the company shall
               within 15 days from the end of the period for making such an application deliver to the
               registrar of companies a printed copy of its memorandum as altered; and
         (b)   if such an application is made, the company shall—
               (i)   forthwith give notice (in the prescribed form) of that fact to the registrar, and
               (ii)   within 15 days from the date of any order cancelling or confirming the alteration,
                      deliver to the registrar an office copy of the order and, in the case of an order confirm-
                      ing the alteration, a printed copy of the memorandum as altered.

(2)   The court may by order at any time extend the time for the delivery of documents to the registrar
         under subsection (1)(b) for such period as the court may think proper.

(3)   If a company makes default in giving notice or delivering any document to the registrar of
         companies as required by subsection (1), the company and every officer of it who is in default is
         liable to a fine and, for continued contravention, to a daily default fine.

(4)   The validity of an alteration of a company's memorandum with respect to the objects of the
        company shall not be questioned on the ground that it was not authorised by section 4, except in
        proceedings taken for the purpose (whether under section 5 or otherwise) before the expiration of
        21 days after the date of the resolution in that behalf.

(5)   Where such proceedings are taken otherwise than under section 5, subsections (1) to (3) above
        apply in relation to the proceedings as if they had been taken under that section, and as if an order
        declaring the alteration invalid were an order cancelling it, and as if an order dismissing the
        proceedings were an order confirming the alteration.

Articles of association

7.   Articles prescribing regulations for companies

(1)   There may in the case of a company limited by shares, and there shall in the case of a company
        limited by guarantee or unlimited, be registered with the memorandum articles of association
        signed by the subscribers to the memorandum and prescribing regulations for the company.

(2)   In the case of an unlimited company having a share capital, the articles must state the amount of
        share capital with which the company proposes to be registered.

(3)   Articles must—
        (a)   be printed,
        (b)   be divided into paragraphs numbered consecutively, and
        (c)   subject to subsection (3A), be signed by each subscriber of the memorandum in the
              presence of at least one witness who must attest the signature *(which attestation is sufficient
              in Scotland as well as in England and Wales).*

(3A)   Where the articles are delivered to the registrar otherwise than in legible form and are
        authenticated by each subscriber to the memorandum in such manner as is directed by the
        registrar, the requirements in subsection (3)(c) for signature in the presence of at least one witness
        and for attestation of the signature do not apply.

        Note. The words "(which attestation is sufficient in Scotland as well as in England and Wales)" in subsection
        (3)(c) are repealed in relation to Scotland by the Requirements of Writing (Scotland) Act 1995, s. 14(2),
        Sch. 5.

8.   Tables A, C, D and E

(1)   Table A is as prescribed by regulations made by the Secretary of State; and a company may for its
        articles adopt the whole or any part of that Table.

(2)   In the case of a company limited by shares, if articles are not registered or, if articles are
        registered, in so far as they do not exclude or modify Table A, that Table (so far as applicable, and
        as in force at the date of the company's registration) constitutes the company's articles, in the
        same manner and to the same extent as if articles in the form of that Table had been duly
        registered.

(3)   If in consequence of regulations under this section Table A is altered, the alteration does not affect
        a company registered before the alteration takes effect, or repeal as respects that company any
        portion of the Table.

(4)   The form of the articles of association of—
        (a)   a company limited by guarantee and not having a share capital,
        (b)   a company limited by guarantee and having a share capital, and
        (c)   an unlimited company having a share capital,
        shall be respectively in accordance with Table C, D or E prescribed by regulations made by the
        Secretary of State, or as near to that form as circumstances admit.

(5)   Regulations under this section shall be made by statutory instrument subject to annulment in
        pursuance of a resolution of either House of Parliament.

8A. ***Table G***

(1)　*The Secretary of State may by regulations prescribe a Table G containing articles of association appropriate for a partnership company, that is, a company limited by shares whose shares are intended to be held to a substantial extent by or on behalf of its employees.*

(2)　*A company limited by shares may for its articles adopt the whole or any part of that Table.*

(3)　*If in consequence of regulations under this section Table G is altered, the alteration does not affect a company registered before the alteration takes effect, or repeal as respects that company any portion of the Table.*

(4)　*Regulations under this section shall be made by statutory instrument which shall be subject to annulment in pursuance of a resolution of either House of Parliament.*

Note. This section is inserted by the Companies Act 1989, s. 128, as from a day to be appointed.

9.　**Alteration of articles by special resolution**

(1)　Subject to the provisions of this Act and to the conditions contained in its memorandum, a company may by special resolution alter its articles.

(2)　Alterations so made in the articles are (subject to this Act) as valid as if originally contained in them, and are subject in like manner to alteration by special resolution.

Registration and its consequences

10.　**Documents to be sent to registrar**

(1)　The company's memorandum and articles (if any) shall be delivered—

　　(a)　to the registrar of companies for England and Wales, if the memorandum states that the registered office of the company is to be situated in England and Wales, or that it is to be situated in Wales; and

　　(b)　to the registrar of companies for Scotland, if the memorandum states that the registered office of the company is to be situated in Scotland.

(2)　With the memorandum there shall be delivered a statement in the prescribed form containing the names and requisite particulars of—

　　(a)　the person who is, or the persons who are, to be the first director or directors of the company; and

　　(b)　the person who is, or the persons who are, to be the first secretary or joint secretaries of the company;

　　and the requisite particulars in each case are those set out in Schedule 1.

(2A)　Where any statement delivered under subsection (2) includes an address specified in reliance on paragraph 5 of Schedule 1 there shall be delivered with the statement, a statement in the prescribed form containing particulars of the usual residential address of the director or secretary whose address is so specified.

(3)　The statement under subsection (2) shall be signed by or on behalf of the subscribers of the memorandum and shall contain a consent signed by each of the persons named in it as a director, as secretary or as one of joint secretaries, to act in the relevant capacity.

(4)　Where a memorandum is delivered by a person as agent for the subscribers, the statement shall specify that fact and the person's name and address.

(5)　An appointment by any articles delivered with the memorandum of a person as director or secretary of the company is void unless he is named as a director or secretary in the statement.

(6)　There shall in the statement be specified the intended situation of the company's registered office on incorporation.

11.　**Minimum authorised capital (public companies)**

When a memorandum delivered to the registrar of companies under section 10 states that the association to be registered is to be a public company, the amount of the share capital stated in the memorandum to be that with which the company proposes to be registered must not be less than the authorised minimum (defined in section 118).

12.   **Duty of registrar**

(1)   The registrar of companies shall not register a company's memorandum delivered under section 10 unless he is satisfied that all the requirements of this Act in respect of registration and of matters precedent and incidental to it have been complied with.

(2)   Subject to this, the registrar shall retain and register the memorandum and articles (if any) delivered to him under that section.

(3)   Subject to subsection (3A), a statutory declaration in the prescribed form by—

      (a)   a solicitor engaged in the formation of a company, or

      (b)   a person named as a director or secretary of the company in the statement delivered under section 10(2),

that those requirements have been complied with shall be delivered to the registrar of companies, and the registrar may accept such a declaration as sufficient evidence of compliance.

(3A)   In place of the statutory declaration referred to in subsection (3), there may be delivered to the registrar of companies using electronic communications a statement made by a person mentioned in paragraph (a) or (b) of subsection (3) that the requirements mentioned in subsection (1) have been complied with; and the registrar may accept such a statement as sufficient evidence of compliance.

(3B)   Any person who makes a false statement under subsection (3A) which he knows to be false or does not believe to be true is liable to imprisonment or a fine, or both.

13.   **Effect of registration**

(1)   On the registration of a company's memorandum, the registrar of companies shall give a certificate that the company is incorporated and, in the case of a limited company, that it is limited.

(2)   The certificate may be signed by the registrar, or authenticated by his official seal.

(3)   From the date of incorporation mentioned in the certificate, the subscribers of the memorandum, together with such other persons as may from time to time become members of the company, shall be a body corporate by the name contained in the memorandum.

(4)   That body corporate is then capable forthwith of exercising all the functions of an incorporated company, but with such liability on the part of its members to contribute to its assets in the event of its being wound up as is provided by this Act and the Insolvency Act.

This is subject, in the case of a public company, to section 117 (additional certificate as to amount of allotted share capital).

(5)   The persons named in the statement under section 10 as directors, secretary or joint secretaries are, on the company's incorporation, deemed to have been respectively appointed as its first directors, secretary or joint secretaries.

(6)   Where the registrar registers an association's memorandum which states that the association is to be a public company, the certificate of incorporation shall contain a statement that the company is a public company.

(7)   A certificate of incorporation given in respect of an association is conclusive evidence—

      (a)   that the requirements of this Act in respect of registration and of matters precedent and incidental to it have been complied with, and that the association is a company authorised to be registered, and is duly registered, under this Act, and

      (b)   if the certificate contains a statement that the company is a public company, that the company is such a company.

14.   **Effect of memorandum and articles**

(1)   Subject to the provisions of this Act, the memorandum and articles, when registered, bind the company and its members to the same extent as if they respectively had been signed and sealed by each member, and contained covenants on the part of each member to observe all the provisions of the memorandum and of the articles.

(2)   Money payable by a member to the company under the memorandum or articles is a debt due from him to the company, and in England and Wales is of the nature of a specialty debt.

15.   Memorandum and articles of company limited by guarantee

(1)   In the case of a company limited by guarantee and not having a share capital, every provision in the memorandum or articles, or in any resolution of the company purporting to give any person a right to participate in the divisible profits of the company otherwise than as a member, is void.

(2)   For purposes of provisions of this Act relating to the memorandum of a company limited by guarantee, and for those of section 1(4) and this section, every provision in the memorandum or articles, or in any resolution, of a company so limited purporting to divide the company's undertaking into shares or interests is to be treated as a provision for a share capital, notwithstanding that the nominal amount or number of the shares or interests is not specified by the provision.

16.   Effect of alteration on company's members

(1)   A member of a company is not bound by an alteration made in the memorandum or articles after the date on which he became a member, if and so far as the alteration—

(a)   requires him to take or subscribe for more shares than the number held by him at the date on which the alteration is made; or

(b)   in any way increases his liability as at that date to contribute to the company's share capital or otherwise to pay money to the company.

(2)   Subsection (1) operates notwithstanding anything in the memorandum or articles; but it does not apply in a case where the member agrees in writing, either before or after the alteration is made, to be bound by the alteration.

17.   Conditions in memorandum which could have been in articles

(1)   A condition contained in a company's memorandum which could lawfully have been contained in articles of association instead of in the memorandum may be altered by the company by special resolution; but if an application is made to the court for the alteration to be cancelled, the alteration does not have effect except in so far as it is confirmed by the court.

(2)   This section—

(a)   is subject to section 16, and also to Part XVII (court order protecting minority), and

(b)   does not apply where the memorandum itself provides for or prohibits the alteration of all or any of the conditions above referred to, and does not authorise any variation or abrogation of the special rights of any class of members.

(3)   Section 5 (except subsections (2)(b) and (8)) and section 6(1) to (3) apply in relation to any alteration and to any application made under this section as they apply in relation to alterations and applications under sections 4 to 6.

18.   Amendments of memorandum or articles to be registered

(1)   Where an alteration is made in a company's memorandum or articles by any statutory provision, whether contained in an Act of Parliament or in an instrument made under an Act, a printed copy of the Act or instrument shall, not later than 15 days after that provision comes into force, be forwarded to the registrar of companies and recorded by him.

(2)   Where a company is required (by this section or otherwise) to send to the registrar any document making or evidencing an alteration in the company's memorandum or articles (other than a special resolution under section 4), the company shall send with it a printed copy of the memorandum or articles as altered.

(3)   If a company fails to comply with this section, the company and any officer of it who is in default is liable to a fine and, for continued contravention, to a daily default fine.

19.   Copies of memorandum and articles to be given to members

(1)   A company shall, on being so required by any member, send to him a copy of the memorandum and of the articles (if any), and a copy of any Act of Parliament which alters the memorandum, subject to payment—

(a)   in the case of a copy of the memorandum and of the articles, of 5 pence or such less sum as the company may prescribe, and

(b)   in the case of a copy of an Act, of such sum not exceeding its published price as the
      company may require.

(2)   If a company makes default in complying with this section, the company and every officer of it
      who is in default is liable for each offence to a fine.

20.   Issued copy of memorandum to embody alterations

(1)   Where an alteration is made in a company's memorandum, every copy of the memorandum
      issued after the date of the alteration shall be in accordance with the alteration.

(2)   If, where any such alteration has been made, the company at any time after the date of the
      alteration issues any copies of the memorandum which are not in accordance with the alteration,
      it is liable to a fine, and so too is every officer of the company who is in default.

21.   ...

A company's membership

22.   Definition of "member"

(1)   The subscribers of a company's memorandum are deemed to have agreed to become members of
      the company, and on its registration shall be entered as such in its register of members.

(2)   Every other person who agrees to become a member of a company, and whose name is entered in
      its register of members, is a member of the company.

23.   Membership of holding company

(1)   Except as mentioned in this section, a body corporate cannot be a member of a company which is
      its holding company and any allotment or transfer of shares in a company to its subsidiary is void.

(2)   The prohibition does not apply where the subsidiary is concerned only as personal representative
      or trustee unless, in the latter case, the holding company or a subsidiary of it is beneficially
      interested under the trust.
      For the purpose of ascertaining whether the holding company or a subsidiary is so interested,
      there shall be disregarded—

      (a)   any interest held only by way of security for the purposes of a transaction entered into by the
            holding company or subsidiary in the ordinary course of a business which includes the
            lending of money;

      (b)   any such interest as is mentioned in Part I of Schedule 2.

(3)   The prohibition does not apply where shares in the holding company are held by the subsidiary in
      the ordinary course of its business as an intermediary.
      For this purpose a person is an intermediary if that person—

      (a)   carries on a bona fide business of dealing in securities;

      (b)   is a member of an EEA exchange (and satisfies any requirements for recognition as a dealer
            in securities laid down by that exchange) or is otherwise approved or supervised as a dealer
            in securities under the laws of an EEA State; and

      (c)   does not carry on an excluded business.

(3A) The excluded businesses are the following—

      (a)   any business which consists wholly or mainly in the making or managing of investments;

      (b)   any business which consists wholly or mainly in, or is carried on wholly or mainly for the
            purpose of, providing services to persons who are connected with the person carrying on the
            business;

      (c)   any business which consists in insurance business;

      (d)   any business which consists in managing or acting as trustee in relation to a pension scheme
            or which is carried on by the manager or trustee of such a scheme in connection with or for
            the purposes of the scheme;

      (e)   any business which consists in operating or acting as trustee in relation to a collective
            investment scheme or is carried on by the operator or trustee of such a scheme in connection
            with or for the purposes of the scheme.

(3B) For the purposes of subsections (3) and (3A)—

(a)   the question whether a person is connected with another shall be determined in accordance with the provisions of section 839 of the Income and Corporation Taxes Act 1988;

(b)   "collective investment scheme" has the meaning given in section 236 of the Financial Services and Markets Act 2000;

(c)   "EEA exchange" means a market which appears on the list drawn up by an EEA State pursuant to Article 16 of Council Directive 93/22/EEC on investment services in the securities field;

(d)   "insurance business" means business which consists of the effecting or carrying out of contracts of insurance;

(e)   "securities" includes—

(i)   options,

(ii)   futures, and

(iii)   contracts for differences,

and rights or interests in those investments;

(f)   "trustee" and "the operator" shall, in relation to a collective investment scheme, be construed in accordance with section 237(2) of the Financial Services and Markets Act 2000.

(3BA)   Subsection (3B) must be read with—

(a)   section 22 of the Financial Services and Markets Act 2000;

(b)   any relevant order under that section; and

(c)   Schedule 2 to that Act.

(3C)   Where—

(a)   a subsidiary which is a dealer in securities has purportedly acquired shares in its holding company in contravention of the prohibition in subsection (1); and

(b)   a person acting in good faith has agreed, for value and without notice of that contravention, to acquire shares in the holding company from the subsidiary or from someone who has purportedly acquired the shares after their disposal by the subsidiary,

any transfer to that person of the shares mentioned in paragraph (a) shall have the same effect as it would have had if their original acquisition by the subsidiary had not been in contravention of the prohibition.

(4)   Where a body corporate became a holder of shares in a company—

(a)   before 1st July 1948, or

(b)   on or after that date and before 20th October 1997, in circumstances in which this section as it then had effect did not apply,

but at any time on or after 20th October 1997 falls within the prohibition in subsection (1) above in respect of those shares, it may continue to be a member of that company; but for so long as that prohibition would apply, apart from this subsection, it has no right to vote in respect of those shares at meetings of the company or of any class of its members.

(5)   Where a body corporate becomes a holder of shares in a company on or after 20th October 1997 in circumstances in which the prohibition in subsection (1) does not apply, but subsequently falls within that prohibition in respect of those shares, it may continue to be a member of that company; but for so long as that prohibition would apply, apart from this subsection, it has no right to vote in respect of those shares at meetings of the company or of any class of its members.

(6)   Where a body corporate is permitted to continue as a member of a company by virtue of subsection (4) or (5), an allotment to it of fully paid shares in the company may be validly made by way of capitalisation of reserves of the company; but for so long as the prohibition in subsection (1) would apply, apart from subsection (4) or (5), it has no right to vote in respect of those shares at meetings of the company or of any class of its members.

(7)   The provisions of this section apply to a nominee acting on behalf of a subsidiary as to the subsidiary itself.

(8)   In relation to a company other than a company limited by shares, the references in this section to shares shall be construed as references to the interest of its members as such, whatever the form of that interest.

24.   Minimum membership for carrying on business

(1)   If a company, other than a private company limited by shares or by guarantee, carries on business without having at least two members and does so for more than 6 months, a person who, for the whole or any part of the period that it so carries on business after those 6 months—

    (a)   is a member of the company, and

    (b)   knows that it is carrying on business with only one member,

    is liable (jointly and severally with the company) for the payment of the company's debts contracted during the period or, as the case may be, that part of it.

(2)   For the purposes of this section references to a member of a company do not include the company itself where it is such a member only by virtue of its holding shares as treasury shares.

CHAPTER II
COMPANY NAMES

25.   Name as stated in memorandum

(1)   The name of a public company must end with the words "public limited company" or, if the memorandum states that the company's registered office is to be situated in Wales, those words or their equivalent in Welsh ("cwmni cyfyngedig cyhoeddus"); and those words or that equivalent may not be preceded by the word "limited" or its equivalent in Welsh ("cyfyngedig").

(2)   In the case of a company limited by shares or by guarantee (not being a public company), the name must have "limited" as its last word, except that—

    (a)   this is subject to section 30 (exempting, in certain circumstances, a company from the requirement to have "limited" as part of the name), and

    (b)   if the company is to be registered with a memorandum stating that its registered office is to be situated in Wales, the name may have "cyfyngedig" as its last word.

26.   Prohibition on registration of certain names

(1)   A company shall not be registered under this Act by a name—

    (a)   which includes, otherwise than at the end of the name, any of the following words or expressions, that is to say, "limited", "unlimited" *or "public limited company" [, "public limited company", "community interest company" or "community interest public limited company"]* or their Welsh equivalents ("cyfyngedig", "anghyfyngedig" *and "cwmni cyfyngedig cyhoeddus" [, "cwmni cyfyngedig cyhoeddus", "cwmni buddiant cymunedol" and "cwmni buddiant cymunedol cyhoeddus cyfyngedig"]* respectively);

    (b)   which includes, otherwise than at the end of the name, an abbreviation of any of those words or expressions;

    (bb)   which includes, at any place in the name, the expressions "investment company with variable capital" or "open-ended investment company" or their Welsh equivalents ("cwmni buddsoddi â chyfalaf newidiol" and "cwmni buddsoddiant penagored" respectively);

    (bbb) which includes, at any place in the name, the expression "limited liability partnership" or its Welsh equivalent ("partneriaeth atebolrwydd cyfyngedig");

    (c)   which is the same as a name appearing in the registrar's index of company names;

    (d)   the use of which by the company would in the opinion of the Secretary of State constitute a criminal offence; or

    (e)   which in the opinion of the Secretary of State is offensive.

(2)   Except with the approval of the Secretary of State, a company shall not be registered under this Act by a name which—

    (a)   in the opinion of the Secretary of State would be likely to give the impression that the company is connected in any way with Her Majesty's Government or with any local authority; or

(b)   includes any word or expression for the time being specified in regulations under section 29. "Local authority" means any local authority within the meaning of the Local Government Act 1972 or the Local Government (Scotland) Act 1973, the Common Council of the City of London or the Council of the Isles of Scilly.

(3)   In determining for purposes of subsection (1)(c) whether one name is the same as another, there are to be disregarded—

(a)   the definite article, where it is the first word of the name;

(b)   the following words and expressions where they appear at the end of the name, that is to say—

"company" or its Welsh equivalent ("cwmni"),

"and company" or its Welsh equivalent ("a'r cwmni"),

"company limited" or its Welsh equivalent ("cwmni cyfyngedig"),

"and company limited" or its Welsh equivalent ("a'r cwmni cyfyngedig"),

"limited" or its Welsh equivalent ("cyfyngedig"),

"unlimited" or its Welsh equivalent ("anghyfyngedig"), ...

"public limited company" or its Welsh equivalent ("cwmni cyfyngedig cyhoeddus"); ...

"community interest company" or its Welsh equivalent ("cwmni buddiant cymunedol");

"community interest public limited company" or its Welsh equivalent ("cwmni buddiant cymunedol cyhoeddus cyfyngedig");

"investment company with variable capital" or its Welsh equivalent ("cwmni buddsoddi a chyfalaf newidiol"); and

"open-ended investment company" or its Welsh equivalent ("cwmni buddsoddiant penagored");

(c)   abbreviations of any of those words or expressions where they appear at the end of the name; and

(d)   type and case of letters, accents, spaces between letters and punctuation marks;

and "and" and "&" are to be taken as the same.

Note. The italicized words in subsection (1)(a) are repealed, the words subsequent to them in square brackets are substituted, and the italicized words in subsection (3)(b) are inserted, by the Companies (Audit, Investigations and Community Enterprise) Act 2004, s. 33(6), Sch. 6, paras. 1, 2, as from 1 July 2005.

27.   Alternatives of statutory designations

(1)   A company which by any provision of this Act is either required or entitled to include in its name, as its last part, any of the words specified in subsection (4) below may, instead of those words, include as the last part of the name the abbreviations there specified as alternatives in relation to those words.

(2)   A reference in this Act to the name of a company or to the inclusion of any of those words in a company's name includes a reference to the name including (in place of any of the words so specified) the appropriate alternative, or to the inclusion of the appropriate alternative, as the case may be.

(3)   A provision of this Act requiring a company not to include any of those words in its name also requires it not to include the abbreviated alternative specified in subsection (4).

(4)   For the purposes of this section—

(a)   the alternative of "limited" is "ltd.";

(b)   the alternative of "public limited company" is "p.l.c.";

(c)   the alternative of "cyfyngedig" is "cyf."; *and*

(d)   the alternative of "cwmni cyfyngedig cyhoeddus" is "c.c.c."; *and*

(e)   *the alternative of "community interest company" is "c.i.c.";*

(f)   *the alternative of "cwmni buddiant cymunedol" is "c.b.c.";*

(g)   *the alternative of "community interest public limited company" is "community interest p.l.c."; and*

(h)   *the alternative of "cwmni buddiant cymunedol cyhoeddus cyfyngedig" is "cwmni buddiant cymunedol c.c.c.".*

Note. The italicized word in subsection (4)(c) is repealed, and subsection (4)(e)–(h) and the word "and" at the end of subsection (4)(d) are added, by the Companies (Audit, Investigations and Community Enterprise) Act 2004, ss. 33(6), 64, Sch. 6, paras. 1, 3, Sch. 8, as from 1 July 2005.

28. Change of name

(1)   A company may by special resolution change its name (but subject to section 31 in the case of a company which has received a direction under subsection (2) of that section from the Secretary of State).

(2)   Where a company has been registered by a name which—

     (a)   is the same as or, in the opinion of the Secretary of State, too like a name appearing at the time of the registration in the registrar's index of company names, or

     (b)   is the same as or, in the opinion of the Secretary of State, too like a name which should have appeared in that index at that time,

the Secretary of State may within 12 months of that time, in writing, direct the company to change its name within such period as he may specify.

Section 26(3) applies in determining under this subsection whether a name is the same as or too like another.

(3)   If it appears to the Secretary of State that misleading information has been given for the purpose of a company's registration with a particular name, or that undertakings or assurances have been given for that purpose and have not been fulfilled, he may within 5 years of the date of its registration with that name in writing direct the company to change its name within such period as he may specify.

(4)   Where a direction has been given under subsection (2) or (3), the Secretary of State may by a further direction in writing extend the period within which the company is to change its name, at any time before the end of that period.

(5)   A company which fails to comply with a direction under this section, and any officer of it who is in default, is liable to a fine and, for continued contravention, to a daily default fine.

(6)   Where a company changes its name under this section, the registrar of companies shall (subject to section 26) enter the new name on the register in place of the former name, and shall issue a certificate of incorporation altered to meet the circumstances of the case; and the change of name has effect from the date on which the altered certificate is issued.

(7)   A change of name by a company under this section does not affect any rights or obligations of the company or render defective any legal proceedings by or against it; and any legal proceedings that might have been continued or commenced against it by its former name may be continued or commenced against it by its new name.

29. Regulations about names

(1)   The Secretary of State may by regulations—

     (a)   specify words or expressions for the registration of which as or as part of a company's corporate name his approval is required under section 26(2)(b), and

     (b)   in relation to any such word or expression, specify a Government department or other body as the relevant body for purposes of the following subsection.

(2)   Where a company proposes to have as, or as part of, its corporate name any such word or expression and a Government department or other body is specified under subsection (1)(b) in relation to that word or expression, a request shall be made (in writing) to the relevant body to indicate whether (and if so why) it has any objections to the proposal; and the person to make the request is—

     (a)   in the case of a company seeking to be registered under this Part, the person making the statutory declaration under section 12(3) or statement under section 12(3A) (as the case may be),

     (b)   in the case of a company seeking to be registered under section 680, the persons making the statutory declaration under section 686(2) or statement under section 686(2A) (as the case may be), and

(c)   in any other case, a director or secretary of the company concerned.

(3)   The person who has made that request to the relevant body shall submit to the registrar of companies a statement that it has been made and a copy of any response received from that body, together with—

(a)   the requisite statutory declaration or statement, or

(b)   a copy of the special resolution changing the company's name,

according as the case is one or other of those mentioned in subsection (2).

(4)   Sections 709 and 710 (public rights of inspection of documents kept by registrar of companies) do not apply to documents sent under subsection (3) of this section.

(5)   Regulations under this section may contain such transitional provisions and savings as the Secretary of State thinks appropriate and may make different provision for different cases or classes of case.

(6)   The regulations shall be made by statutory instrument, to be laid before Parliament after it is made; and the regulations shall cease to have effect at the end of 28 days beginning with the day on which the regulations were made (but without prejudice to anything previously done by virtue of them or to the making of new regulations), unless during that period they are approved by resolution of each House. In reckoning that period, no account is to be taken of any time during which Parliament is dissolved or prorogued or during which both Houses are adjourned for more than 4 days.

30.   Exemption from requirement of "limited" as part of the name

(1)   Certain companies are exempt from requirements of this Act relating to the use of "limited" as part of the company name.

(2)   A private company limited by guarantee is exempt from those requirements, and so too is a company which on 25th February 1982 was a private company limited by shares with a name which, by virtue of a licence under section 19 of the Companies Act 1948, did not include "limited"; but in either case the company must, to have the exemption, comply with the requirements of the following subsection.

(3)   Those requirements are that—

(a)   the objects of the company are (or, in the case of a company about to be registered, are to be) the promotion of commerce, art, science, education, religion, charity or any profession, and anything incidental or conducive to any of those objects; and

(b)   the company's memorandum or articles—

(i)   require its profits (if any) or other income to be applied in promoting its objects,

(ii)   prohibit the payment of dividends to its members, and

(iii) require all the assets which would otherwise be available to its members generally to be transferred on its winding up either to another body with objects similar to its own or to another body the objects of which are the promotion of charity and anything inci- dental or conducive thereto (whether or not the body is a member of the company).

(4)   Subject to subsection (5A), a statutory declaration that a company complies with the requirements of subsection (3) may be delivered to the registrar of companies, who may accept the declaration as sufficient evidence of the matters stated in it …

(5)   The statutory declaration must be in the prescribed form and be made—

(a)   in the case of a company to be formed, by a solicitor engaged in its formation or by a person named as director or secretary in the statement delivered under section 10(2);

(b)   in the case of a company to be registered in pursuance of section 680, by two or more directors or other principal officers of the company; and

(c)   in the case of a company proposing to change its name so that it ceases to have the word "limited" as part of its name, by a director or secretary of the company.

(5A)   In place of the statutory declaration referred to in subsection (4), there may be delivered to the registrar of companies using electronic communications a statement made by a person falling within the applicable paragraph of subsection (5) stating that the company complies with the requirements of subsection (3); and the registrar may accept such a statement as sufficient evidence of the matters stated in it.

(5B)   The registrar may refuse to register a company by a name which does not include the word "limited" unless a statutory declaration under subsection (4) or statement under subsection (5A) has been delivered to him.

(5C)   Any person who makes a false statement under subsection (5A) which he knows to be false or does not believe to be true is liable to imprisonment or a fine, or both.

(6)   References in this section to the word "limited" include (in an appropriate case) its Welsh equivalent ("cyfyngedig"), and the appropriate alternative ("ltd." or "cyf.", as the case may be).

(7)   A company which *under this section* is exempt from requirements relating to the use of "limited" and does not include that word as part of its name, is also exempt from the requirements of this Act relating to the publication of its name and the sending of lists of members to the registrar of companies.

Note. The italicized words in subsection (7) are inserted by the Companies (Audit, Investigations and Community Enterprise) Act 2004, s. 33(6), Sch. 6, paras. 1, 4, as from 1 July 2005.

31.   Provisions applying to company exempt under s 30

(1)   A company which is exempt under section 30 and whose name does not include "limited" shall not alter its memorandum or articles of association so that it ceases to comply with the requirements of subsection (3) of that section.

(2)   If it appears to the Secretary of State that such a company—
  (a)   has carried on any business other than the promotion of any of the objects mentioned in that subsection, or
  (b)   has applied any of its profits or other income otherwise than in promoting such objects, or
  (c)   has paid a dividend to any of its members,
  he may, in writing, direct the company to change its name by resolution of the directors within such period as may be specified in the direction, so that its name ends with "limited".
  A resolution passed by the directors in compliance with a direction under this subsection is subject to section 380 of this Act (copy to be forwarded to the registrar of companies within 15 days).

(3)   A company which has received a direction under subsection (2) shall not thereafter be registered by a name which does not include "limited", without the approval of the Secretary of State.

(4)   References in this section to the word "limited" include (in an appropriate case) its Welsh equivalent ("cyfyngedig"), and the appropriate alternative ("ltd." or "cyf.", as the case may be).

(5)   A company which contravenes subsection (1), and any officer of it who is in default, is liable to a fine and, for continued contravention, to a daily default fine.

(6)   A company which fails to comply with a direction by the Secretary of State under subsection (2), and any officer of the company who is in default, is liable to a fine and, for continued contravention, to a daily default fine.

32.   Power to require company to abandon misleading name

(1)   If in the Secretary of State's opinion the name by which a company is registered gives so misleading an indication of the nature of its activities as to be likely to cause harm to the public, he may direct it to change its name.

(2)   The direction must, if not duly made the subject of an application to the court under the following subsection, be complied with within a period of 6 weeks from the date of the direction or such longer period as the Secretary of State may think fit to allow.

(3)   The company may, within a period of 3 weeks from the date of the direction, apply to the court to set it aside; and the court may set the direction aside or confirm it and, if it confirms the direction, shall specify a period within which it must be complied with.

(4)   If a company makes default in complying with a direction under this section, it is liable to a fine and, for continued contravention, to a daily default fine.

(5)   Where a company changes its name under this section, the registrar shall (subject to section 26) enter the new name on the register in place of the former name, and shall issue a certificate of incorporation altered to meet the circumstances of the case; and the change of name has effect from the date on which the altered certificate is issued.

(6)   A change of name by a company under this section does not affect any of the rights or obligations of the company, or render defective any legal proceedings by or against it; and any legal proceedings that might have been continued or commenced against it by its former name may be continued or commenced against it by its new name.

33.   Prohibition on trading under misleading name

(1)   A person who is not a public company is guilty of an offence if he carries on any trade, profession or business under a name which includes, as its last part, the words "public limited company" or their equivalent in Welsh ("cwmni cyfyngedig cyhoeddus"); *and a community interest company which is not a public company is guilty of an offence if it does so under a name which includes, as its last part, the words "cwmni buddiant cymunedol cyhoeddus cyfyngedig".*

(2)   A public company is guilty of an offence if, in circumstances in which the fact that it is a public company is likely to be material to any person, it uses a name which may reasonably be expected to give the impression that it is a private company.

(3)   A person guilty of an offence under subsection (1) or (2) and, if that person is a company, any officer of the company who is in default, is liable to a fine and, for continued contravention, to a daily default fine.

Note. The italicized words at the end of subsection (1) are added by the Companies (Audit, Investigations and Community Enterprise) Act 2004, s. 33(6), Sch. 6, paras. 1, 5, as from 1 July 2005.

34.   Penalty for improper use of "limited" or "cyfyngedig"

If any person trades or carries on business under a name or title of which "limited" or "cyfyngedig", or any contraction or imitation of either of those words, is the last word, that person, unless duly incorporated with limited liability, is liable to a fine and, for continued contravention, to a daily default fine.

34A.   *Penalty for improper use of "community interest company" etc.*

(1)   *A company which is not a community interest company is guilty of an offence if it carries on any trade, profession or business under a name which includes any of the expressions specified in subsection (3).*

(2)   *A person other than a company is guilty of an offence if it carries on any trade, profession or business under a name which includes any of those expressions (or any contraction of them) as its last part.*

(3)   *The expressions are—*

(a)   *"community interest company" or its Welsh equivalent ("cwmni buddiant cymunedol"), and*

(b)   *"community interest public limited company" or its Welsh equivalent ("cwmni buddiant cymunedol cyhoeddus cyfyngedig").*

(4)   *Subsections (1) and (2) do not apply—*

(a)   *to a person who was carrying on a trade, profession or business under the name in question at any time during the period beginning with 1st September 2003 and ending with 4th December 2003, or*

(b)   *if the name in question was on 4th December 2003 a registered trade mark or Community trade mark (within the meaning of the Trade Marks Act 1994 (c. 26)), to a person who was on that date a proprietor or licensee of that trade mark.*

(5)   *A person guilty of an offence under subsection (1) or (2) and, if that person is a company, any officer of the company who is in default, is liable to a fine and, for continued contravention, to a daily default fine.*

Note. The section is inserted by the Companies (Audit, Investigations and Community Enterprise) Act 2004, s. 33(6), Sch. 6, paras. 1, 6, as from 1 July 2005.

CHAPTER III
A COMPANY'S CAPACITY; FORMALITIES OF CARRYING ON BUSINESS

35.   A company's capacity not limited by its memorandum

(1)   The validity of an act done by a company shall not be called into question on the ground of lack of capacity by reason of anything in the company's memorandum.

(2)   A member of a company may bring proceedings to restrain the doing of an act which but for subsection (1) would be beyond the company's capacity; but no such proceedings shall lie in respect of an act to be done in fulfilment of a legal obligation arising from a previous act of the company.

(3)   It remains the duty of the directors to observe any limitations on their powers flowing from the company's memorandum; and action by the directors which but for subsection (1) would be beyond the company's capacity may only be ratified by the company by special resolution.
       A resolution ratifying such action shall not affect any liability incurred by the directors or any other person; relief from any such liability must be agreed to separately by special resolution.

(4)   The operation of this section is restricted by section 65(1) of the Charities Act 1993 and section 112(3) of the Companies Act 1989 in relation to companies which are charities; and section 322A below (invalidity of certain transactions to which directors or their associates are parties) has effect notwithstanding this section.

35A.   Power of directors to bind the company

(1)   In favour of a person dealing with a company in good faith, the power of the board of directors to bind the company, or authorise others to do so, shall be deemed to be free of any limitation under the company's constitution.

(2)   For this purpose—
       (a)   a person "deals with" a company if he is a party to any transaction or other act to which the company is a party;
       (b)   a person shall not be regarded as acting in bad faith by reason only of his knowing that an act is beyond the powers of the directors under the company's constitution; and
       (c)   a person shall be presumed to have acted in good faith unless the contrary is proved.

(3)   The references above to limitations on the directors' powers under the company's constitution include limitations deriving—
       (a)   from a resolution of the company in general meeting or a meeting of any class of shareholders, or
       (b)   from any agreement between the members of the company or of any class of shareholders.

(4)   Subsection (1) does not affect any right of a member of the company to bring proceedings to restrain the doing of an act which is beyond the powers of the directors; but no such proceedings shall lie in respect of an act to be done in fulfilment of a legal obligation arising from a previous act of the company.

(5)   Nor does that subsection affect any liability incurred by the directors, or any other person, by reason of the directors' exceeding their powers.

(6)   The operation of this section is restricted by section 65(1) of the Charities Act 1993 and section 112(3) of the Companies Act 1989 in relation to companies which are charities; and section 322A below (invalidity of certain transactions to which directors or their associates are parties) has effect notwithstanding this section.

35B.   No duty to enquire as to capacity of company or authority of directors

       A party to a transaction with a company is not bound to enquire as to whether it is permitted by the company's memorandum or as to any limitation on the powers of the board of directors to bind the company or authorise others to do so.

36.   Company contracts: England and Wales

       Under the law of England and Wales a contract may be made—
       (a)   by a company, by writing under its common seal, or

(b)   on behalf of a company, by any person acting under its authority, express or implied;
and any formalities required by law in the case of a contract made by an individual also apply, unless a contrary intention appears, to a contract made by or on behalf of a company.

36A.   Execution of documents: England and Wales

(1)   Under the law of England and Wales the following provisions have effect with respect to the execution of documents by a company.

(2)   A document is executed by a company by the affixing of its common seal.

(3)   A company need not have a common seal, however, and the following subsections apply whether it does or not.

(4)   A document signed by a director and the secretary of a company, or by two directors of a company, and expressed (in whatever form of words) to be executed by the company has the same effect as if executed under the common seal of the company.

(5)   A document executed by a company which makes it clear on its face that it is intended by the person or persons making it to be a deed has effect, upon delivery, as a deed; and it shall be presumed, unless a contrary intention is proved, to be delivered upon its being so executed.

(6)   In favour of a purchaser a document shall be deemed to have been duly executed by a company if it purports to be signed by a director and the secretary of the company, or by two directors of the company, and, where it makes it clear on its face that it is intended by the person or persons making it to be a deed, to have been delivered upon its being executed.
A "purchaser" means a purchaser in good faith for valuable consideration and includes a lessee, mortgagee or other person who for valuable consideration acquires an interest in property.

36B.   Execution of documents by companies

(1)   Notwithstanding the provisions of any enactment, a company need not have a company seal.

(2)   For the purposes of any enactment—
(a)   providing for a document to be executed by a company by affixing its common seal; or
(b)   referring (in whatever terms) to a document so executed,
a document signed or subscribed by or on behalf of the company in accordance with the provisions of the Requirements of Writing (Scotland) Act 1995 shall have effect as if so executed.

(3)   In this section "enactment" includes an enactment contained in a statutory instrument.

36C.   Pre-incorporation contracts, deeds and obligations

(1)   A contract which purports to be made by or on behalf of a company at a time when the company has not been formed has effect, subject to any agreement to the contrary, as one made with the person purporting to act for the company or as agent for it, and he is personally liable on the contract accordingly.

(2)   Subsection (1) applies—
(a)   to the making of a deed under the law of England and Wales, and
(b)   to the undertaking of an obligation under the law of Scotland,
as it applies to the making of a contract.

37.   Bills of exchange and promissory notes

A bill of exchange or promissory note is deemed to have been made, accepted or endorsed on behalf of a company if made, accepted or endorsed in the name of, or by or on behalf or on account of, the company by a person acting under its authority.

38.   Execution of deeds abroad

(1)   A company may, ... by writing under its common seal, empower any person, either generally or in respect of any specified matters, as its attorney, to execute deeds on its behalf in any place elsewhere than in the United Kingdom.

(2)   A deed executed by such an attorney on behalf of the company has the same effect as if it were executed under the company's common seal.

(3)   This section does not extend to Scotland.

39.   Power of company to have official seal for use abroad

(1)   A company which has a common seal whose objects require or comprise the transaction of business in foreign countries may, if authorised by its articles, have for use in any territory, district, or place elsewhere than in the United Kingdom, an official seal, which shall be a facsimile of its common seal, with the addition on its face of the name of every territory, district or place where it is to be used.

(2)   The official seal when duly affixed to a document has the same effect as the company's common seal.

(2A)   Subsection (2) does not extend to Scotland.

(3)   A company having an official seal for use in any such territory, district or place may, by writing under its common seal, or as respects Scotland by writing in accordance with the Requirements of Writing (Scotland) Act 1995 ... authorise any person appointed for the purpose in that territory, district or place to affix the official seal to any deed or other document to which the company is party in that territory, district or place.

(4)   As between the company and a person dealing with such an agent, the agent's authority continues during the period (if any) mentioned in the instrument conferring the authority, or if no period is there mentioned, then until notice of the revocation or determination of the agent's authority has been given to the person dealing with him.

(5)   The person affixing the official seal shall certify in writing on the deed or other instrument to which the seal is affixed the date on which and the place at which it is affixed.

40.   Official seal for share certificates, etc

(1)   A company which has a common seal may have, for use for sealing securities issued by the company and for sealing documents creating or evidencing securities so issued, an official seal which is a facsimile of its common seal with the addition on its face of the word "Securities".
         The official seal when duly affixed to a document has the same effect as the company's common seal.

(2)   Nothing in this section shall affect the right of a company registered in Scotland to subscribe such securities and documents in accordance with the Requirements of Writing (Scotland) Act 1995.

41.   Authentication of documents

A document or proceeding requiring authentication by a company is sufficiently authenticated for the purposes of the law of England and Wales by the signature of a director, secretary or other authorised officer of the company.

42.   Events affecting a company's status

(1)   A company is not entitled to rely against other persons on the happening of any of the following events—

         (a)   the making of a winding-up order in respect of the company, or the appointment of a liquidator in a voluntary winding up of the company, or

         (b)   any alteration of the company's memorandum or articles, or

         (c)   any change among the company's directors, or

         (d)   (as regards service of any document on the company) any change in the situation of the company's registered office,

         if the event had not been officially notified at the material time and is not shown by the company to have been known at that time to the person concerned, or if the material time fell on or before the 15th day after the date of official notification (or, where the 15th day was a non-business day, on or before the next day that was not) and it is shown that the person concerned was unavoidably prevented from knowing of the event at that time.

(2)   In subsection (1)—

         (a)   "official notification" and "officially notified" have the meanings given by section 711(2) (registrar of companies to give public notice of the issue or receipt by him of certain documents), and

(b)   "non-business day" means a Saturday or Sunday, Christmas Day, Good Friday and any other day which is a bank holiday in the part of Great Britain where the company is registered.

PART II
RE-REGISTRATION AS A MEANS OF ALTERING A COMPANY'S STATUS

Private company becoming public

43.   **Re-registration of private company as public**

(1)   Subject to this and the following five sections, a private company (other than a company not having a share capital) may be re-registered as a public company if—

     (a)   a special resolution that it should be so re-registered is passed; and

     (b)   an application for re-registration is delivered to the registrar of companies, together with the necessary documents.

     A company cannot be re-registered under this section if it has previously been re-registered as unlimited.

(2)   The special resolution must—

     (a)   alter the company's memorandum so that it states that the company is to be a public company; and

     (b)   make such other alterations in the memorandum as are necessary to bring it (in substance and in form) into conformity with the requirements of this Act with respect to the memorandum of a public company (the alterations to include compliance with section 25(1), *or section 33 of the Companies (Audit, Investigations and Community Enterprise) Act 2004,* as regards the company's name); and

     (c)   make such alterations in the company's articles as are requisite in the circumstances.

(3)   The application must be in the prescribed form and be signed by a director or secretary of the company; and the documents to be delivered with it are the following—

     (a)   a printed copy of the memorandum and articles as altered in pursuance of the resolution;

     (b)   a copy of a written statement by the company's auditors that in their opinion the relevant balance sheet shows that at the balance sheet date the amount of the company's net assets (within the meaning given to that expression by section 264(2)) was not less than the aggregate of its called-up share capital and undistributable reserves;

     (c)   a copy of the relevant balance sheet, together with a copy of an unqualified report (defined in section 46) by the company's auditors in relation to that balance sheet;

     (d)   if section 44 applies, a copy of the valuation report under subsection (2)(b) of that section; and

     (e)   subject to subsection (3A), a statutory declaration in the prescribed form by a director or secretary of the company—

        (i)   that the special resolution required by this section has been passed and that the conditions of the following two sections (so far as applicable) have been satisfied, and

        (ii)   that, between the balance sheet date and the application for re-registration, there has been no change in the company's financial position that has resulted in the amount of its net assets becoming less than the aggregate of its called-up share capital and undistributable reserves.

(3A)   In place of the statutory declaration referred to in paragraph (e) of subsection (3), there may be delivered to the registrar of companies using electronic communications a statement made by a director or secretary of the company as to the matters set out in sub-paragraphs (i) and (ii) of that paragraph.

(3B)   Any person who makes a false statement under subsection (3A) which he knows to be false or does not believe to be true is liable to imprisonment or a fine, or both.

(4)   "Relevant balance sheet" means a balance sheet prepared as at a date not more than 7 months before the company's application under this section.

(5)   A resolution that a company be re-registered as a public company may change the company name by deleting the word "company" or the words "and company", or its or their equivalent in Welsh ("cwmni", "a'r cwmni"), including any abbreviation of them.

Note. The italicized words in subsection (2)(b) are inserted by the Companies (Audit, Investigations and Community Enterprise) Act 2004, s. 33(6), Sch. 6, paras. 1, 7, as from 1 July 2005.

44.   Consideration for shares recently allotted to be valued

(1)   The following applies if shares have been allotted by the company between the date as at which the relevant balance sheet was prepared and the passing of the special resolution under section 43, and those shares were allotted as fully or partly paid up as to their nominal value or any premium on them otherwise than in cash.

(2)   Subject to the following provisions, the registrar of companies shall not entertain an application by the company under section 43 unless beforehand—

(a)   the consideration for the allotment has been valued in accordance with section 108, and

(b)   a report with respect to the value of the consideration has been made to the company (in accordance with that section) during the 6 months immediately preceding the allotment of the shares.

(3)   Where an amount standing to the credit of any of the company's reserve accounts, or of its profit and loss account, has been applied in paying up (to any extent) any of the shares allotted or any premium on those shares, the amount applied does not count as consideration for the allotment, and accordingly subsection (2) does not apply to it.

(4)   Subsection (2) does not apply if the allotment is in connection with an arrangement providing for it to be on terms that the whole or part of the consideration for the shares allotted is to be provided by the transfer to the company or the cancellation of all or some of the shares, or of all or some of the shares of a particular class, in another company (with or without the issue to the company applying under section 43 of shares, or of shares of any particular class, in that other company).

(5)   But subsection (4) does not exclude the application of subsection (2), unless under the arrangement it is open to all the holders of the shares of the other company in question (or, where the arrangement applies only to shares of a particular class, all the holders of the other company's shares of that class) to take part in the arrangement.

In determining whether that is the case, shares held by or by a nominee of the company allotting shares in connection with the arrangement, or by or by a nominee of a company which is that company's holding company or subsidiary or a company which is a subsidiary of its holding company, are to be disregarded.

(6)   Subsection (2) does not apply to preclude an application under section 43, if the allotment of the company's shares is in connection with its proposed merger with another company; that is, where one of the companies concerned proposes to acquire all the assets and liabilities of the other in exchange for the issue of shares or other securities of that one to shareholders of the other, with or without any cash payment to shareholders.

(7)   In this section—

(a)   "arrangement" means any agreement, scheme or arrangement, including an arrangement sanctioned in accordance with section 425 (company compromise with creditors and members) or section 110 of the Insolvency Act (liquidator in winding up accepting shares as consideration for sale of company's property), and

(b)   "another company" includes any body corporate ...

45.   Additional requirements relating to share capital

(1)   For a private company to be re-registered under section 43 as a public company, the following conditions with respect to its share capital must be satisfied at the time the special resolution under that section is passed.

(2)   Subject to subsections (5) to (7) below—

(a)   the nominal value of the company's allotted share capital must be not less than the authorised minimum, and

(b)   each of the company's allotted shares must be paid up at least as to one-quarter of the nominal value of that share and the whole of any premium on it.

(3)   Subject to subsection (5), if any shares in the company or any premium on them have been fully or partly paid up by an undertaking given by any person that he or another should do work or perform services (whether for the company or any other person), the undertaking must have been performed or otherwise discharged.

(4)   Subject to subsection (5), if shares have been allotted as fully or partly paid up as to their nominal value or any premium on them otherwise than in cash, and the consideration for the allotment consists of or includes an undertaking to the company (other than one to which subsection (3) applies), then either—

(a)   the undertaking must have been performed or otherwise discharged, or

(b)   there must be a contract between the company and some person pursuant to which the undertaking is to be performed within 5 years from the time the resolution under section 43 is passed.

(5)   For the purpose of determining whether subsections (2)(b), (3) and (4) are complied with, certain shares in the company may be disregarded; and these are—

(a)   subject to the next subsection, any share which was allotted before 22nd June 1982, and

(b)   any share which was allotted in pursuance of an employees' share scheme and by reason of which the company would, but for this subsection, be precluded under subsection (2)(b) (but not otherwise) from being re-registered as a public company.

(6)   A share is not to be disregarded under subsection (5)(a) if the aggregate in nominal value of that share and other shares proposed to be so disregarded is more than one-tenth of the nominal value of the company's allotted share capital; but for this purpose the allotted share capital is treated as not including any shares disregarded under subsection (5)(b).

(7)   Any shares disregarded under subsection (5) are treated as not forming part of the allotted share capital for the purposes of subsection (2)(a).

46.   Meaning of "unqualified report" in s 43(3)

(1)   The following subsections explain the reference in section 43(3)(c) to an unqualified report of the company's auditors on the relevant balance sheet.

(2)   If the balance sheet was prepared for a financial year of the company, the reference is to an auditors' report stating without material qualification the auditors' opinion that the balance sheet has been properly prepared in accordance with this Act.

(3)   If the balance sheet was not prepared for a financial year of the company, the reference is to an auditors' report stating without material qualification the auditors' opinion that the balance sheet has been properly prepared in accordance with the provisions of this Act which would have applied if it had been so prepared.

For the purposes of an auditors' report under this subsection the provisions of this Act shall be deemed to apply with such modifications as are necessary by reason of the fact that the balance sheet is not prepared for a financial year of the company.

(4)   A qualification shall be regarded as material unless the auditors state in their report that the matter giving rise to the qualification is not material for the purpose of determining (by reference to the company's balance sheet) whether at the balance sheet date the amount of the company's net assets was not less than the aggregate of its called up share capital and undistributable reserves.

In this subsection "net assets" and "undistributable reserves" have the meaning given by section 264(2) and (3).

47.   Certificate of re-registration under s 43

(1)   If the registrar of companies is satisfied, on an application under section 43, that a company may be re-registered under that section as a public company, he shall—

(a)   retain the application and other documents delivered to him under the section; and

(b)   issue the company with a certificate of incorporation stating that the company is a public company.

(2)   The registrar may accept a declaration under section 43(3)(e) or a statement under section 43(3A) as sufficient evidence that the special resolution required by that section has been passed and the other conditions of re-registration satisfied.

(3)   The registrar shall not issue the certificate if it appears to him that the court has made an order confirming a reduction of the company's capital which has the effect of bringing the nominal value of the company's allotted share capital below the authorised minimum.

(4)   Upon the issue to a company of a certificate of incorporation under this section—

   (a)   the company by virtue of the issue of that certificate becomes a public company; and

   (b)   any alterations in the memorandum and articles set out in the resolution take effect accordingly.

(5)   The certificate is conclusive evidence—

   (a)   that the requirements of this Act in respect of re-registration and of matters precedent and incidental thereto have been complied with; and

   (b)   that the company is a public company.

48.   Modification for unlimited company re-registering

(1)   In their application to unlimited companies, sections 43 to 47 are modified as follows.

(2)   The special resolution required by section 43(1) must, in addition to the matters mentioned in subsection (2) of that section—

   (a)   state that the liability of the members is to be limited by shares, and what the company's share capital is to be; and

   (b)   make such alterations in the company's memorandum as are necessary to bring it in substance and in form into conformity with the requirements of this Act with respect to the memorandum of a company limited by shares.

(3)   The certificate of incorporation issued under section 47(1) shall, in addition to containing the statement required by paragraph (b) of that subsection, state that the company has been incorporated as a company limited by shares; and—

   (a)   the company by virtue of the issue of the certificate becomes a public company so limited; and

   (b)   the certificate is conclusive evidence of the fact that it is such a company.

Limited company becoming unlimited

49.   Re-registration of limited company as unlimited

(1)   Subject as follows, a company which is registered as limited may be re-registered as unlimited in pursuance of an application in that behalf complying with the requirements of this section.

(2)   A company is excluded from re-registering under this section if it is limited by virtue of re-registration under section 44 of the Companies Act 1967 or section 51 of this Act.

(3)   A public company cannot be re-registered under this section; nor can a company which has previously been re-registered as unlimited.

(4)   An application under this section must be in the prescribed form and be signed by a director or the secretary of the company, and be lodged with the registrar of companies, together with the documents specified in subsection (8) below.

(5)   The application must set out such alterations in the company's memorandum as—

   (a)   if it is to have a share capital, are requisite to bring it (in substance and in form) into conformity with the requirements of this Act with respect to the memorandum of a company to be formed as an unlimited company having a share capital; or

   (b)   if it is not to have a share capital, are requisite in the circumstances.

(6)   If articles have been registered, the application must set out such alterations in them as—

   (a)   if the company is to have a share capital, are requisite to bring the articles (in substance and in form) into conformity with the requirements of this Act with respect to the articles of a company to be formed as an unlimited company having a share capital; or

   (b)   if the company is not to have a share capital, are requisite in the circumstances.

(7)   If articles have not been registered, the application must have annexed to it, and request the registration of, printed articles; and these must, if the company is to have a share capital, comply with the requirements mentioned in subsection (6)(a) and, if not, be articles appropriate to the circumstances.

(8)   The documents to be lodged with the registrar are—

(a)   the prescribed form of assent to the company's being registered as unlimited, subscribed by or on behalf of all the members of the company;

(b)   subject to subsection (8A), a statutory declaration made by the directors of the company—

(i)   that the persons by whom or on whose behalf the form of assent is subscribed constitute the whole membership of the company, and

(ii)   if any of the members have not subscribed that form themselves, that the directors have taken all reasonable steps to satisfy themselves that each person who subscribed it on behalf of a member was lawfully empowered to do so;

(c)   a printed copy of the memorandum incorporating the alterations in it set out in the application; and

(d)   if articles have been registered, a printed copy of them incorporating the alterations set out in the application.

(8A)   In place of the lodging of a statutory declaration under paragraph (b) of subsection (8), there may be delivered to the registrar of companies using electronic communications a statement made by the directors of the company as to the matters set out in sub-paragraphs (i) and (ii) of that paragraph.

(8B)   Any person who makes a false statement under subsection (8A) which he knows to be false or does not believe to be true is liable to imprisonment or a fine, or both.

(9)   For purposes of this section—

(a)   subscription to a form of assent by the legal personal representative of a deceased member of a company is deemed subscription by him; and

(b)   a trustee in bankruptcy of a member of a company is, to the exclusion of the latter, deemed a member of the company.

50.   Certificate of re-registration under s 49

(1)   The registrar of companies shall retain the application and other documents lodged with him under section 49 and shall—

(a)   if articles are annexed to the application, register them; and

(b)   issue to the company a certificate of incorporation appropriate to the status to be assumed by it by virtue of that section.

(2)   On the issue of the certificate—

(a)   the status of the company, by virtue of the issue, is changed from limited to unlimited; and

(b)   the alterations in the memorandum set out in the application and (if articles have been previously registered) any alterations to the articles so set out take effect as if duly made by resolution of the company; and

(c)   the provisions of this Act apply accordingly to the memorandum and articles as altered.

(3)   The certificate is conclusive evidence that the requirements of section 49 in respect of re-registration and of matters precedent and incidental to it have been complied with, and that the company was authorised to be re-registered under this Act in pursuance of that section and was duly so re-registered.

Unlimited company becoming limited

51.   Re-registration of unlimited company as limited

(1)   Subject as follows, a company which is registered as unlimited may be re-registered as limited if a special resolution that it should be so re-registered is passed, and the requirements of this section are complied with in respect of the resolution and otherwise.

(2)   A company cannot under this section be re-registered as a public company; and a company is excluded from re-registering under it if it is unlimited by virtue of re-registration under section 43 of the Companies Act 1967 or section 49 of this Act.

(3)   The special resolution must state whether the company is to be limited by shares or by guarantee and—

(a)   if it is to be limited by shares, must state what the share capital is to be and provide for the making of such alterations in the memorandum as are necessary to bring it (in substance and in form) into conformity with the requirements of this Act with respect to the memorandum of a company so limited, and such alterations in the articles as are requisite in the circumstances;

(b)   if it is to be limited by guarantee, must provide for the making of such alterations in its memorandum and articles as are necessary to bring them (in substance and in form) into conformity with the requirements of this Act with respect to the memorandum and articles of a company so limited.

(4)   The special resolution is subject to section 380 of this Act (copy to be forwarded to registrar within 15 days); and an application for the company to be re-registered as limited, framed in the prescribed form and signed by a director or by the secretary of the company, must be lodged with the registrar of companies, together with the necessary documents, not earlier than the day on which the copy of the resolution forwarded under section 380 is received by him.

(5)   The documents to be lodged with the registrar are—

(a)   a printed copy of the memorandum as altered in pursuance of the resolution; and

(b)   a printed copy of the articles as so altered.

(6)   This section does not apply in relation to the re-registration of an unlimited company as a public company under section 43.

52.   Certificate of re-registration under s 51

(1)   The registrar shall retain the application and other documents lodged with him under section 51, and shall issue to the company a certificate of incorporation appropriate to the status to be assumed by the company by virtue of that section.

(2)   On the issue of the certificate—

(a)   the status of the company is, by virtue of the issue, changed from unlimited to limited; and

(b)   the alterations in the memorandum specified in the resolution and the alterations in, and additions to, the articles so specified take effect.

(3)   The certificate is conclusive evidence that the requirements of section 51 in respect of re-registration and of matters precedent and incidental to it have been complied with, and that the company was authorised to be re-registered in pursuance of that section and was duly so re-registered.

Public company becoming private

53.   Re-registration of public company as private

(1)   A public company may be re-registered as a private company if—

(a)   a special resolution complying with subsection (2) below that it should be so re-registered is passed and has not been cancelled by the court under the following section;

(b)   an application for the purpose in the prescribed form and signed by a director or the secretary of the company is delivered to the registrar of companies, together with a printed copy of the memorandum and articles of the company as altered by the resolution; and

(c)   the period during which an application for the cancellation of the resolution under the following section may be made has expired without any such application having been made; or

(d)   where such an application has been made, the application has been withdrawn or an order has been made under section 54(5) confirming the resolution and a copy of that order has been delivered to the registrar.

(2) The special resolution must alter the company's memorandum so that it no longer states that the company is to be a public company and must make such other alterations in the company's memorandum and articles as are requisite in the circumstances.

(3) A company cannot under this section be re-registered otherwise than as a company limited by shares or by guarantee.

54. Litigated objection to resolution under s 53

(1) Where a special resolution by a public company to be re-registered under section 53 as a private company has been passed, an application may be made to the court for the cancellation of that resolution.

(2) The application may be made—
 (a) by the holders of not less in the aggregate than 5 per cent in nominal value of the company's issued share capital or any class thereof;
 (b) if the company is not limited by shares, by not less than 5 per cent of its members; or
 (c) by not less than 50 of the company's members;
 but not by a person who has consented to or voted in favour of the resolution.

(2A) For the purposes of subsection (2)(a), any of the company's issued share capital held as treasury shares must be disregarded.

(3) The application must be made within 28 days after the passing of the resolution and may be made on behalf of the persons entitled to make the application by such one or more of their number as they may appoint in writing for the purpose.

(4) If such an application is made, the company shall forthwith give notice in the prescribed form of that fact to the registrar of companies.

(5) On the hearing of the application, the court shall make an order either cancelling or confirming the resolution and—
 (a) may make that order on such terms and conditions as it thinks fit, and may (if it thinks fit) adjourn the proceedings in order that an arrangement may be made to the satisfaction of the court for the purchase of the interests of dissentient members; and
 (b) may give such directions and make such orders as it thinks expedient for facilitating or carrying into effect any such arrangement.

(6) The court's order may, if the court thinks fit, provide for the purchase by the company of the shares of any of its members and for the reduction accordingly of the company's capital, and may make such alterations in the company's memorandum and articles as may be required in consequence of that provision.

(7) The company shall, within 15 days from the making of the court's order, or within such longer period as the court may at any time by order direct, deliver to the registrar of companies an office copy of the order.

(8) If the court's order requires the company not to make any, or any specified, alteration in its memorandum or articles, the company has not then power without the leave of the court to make any such alteration in breach of the requirement.

(9) An alteration in the memorandum or articles made by virtue of an order under this section, if not made by resolution of the company, is of the same effect as if duly made by resolution; and this Act applies accordingly to the memorandum or articles as so altered.

(10) A company which fails to comply with subsection (4) or subsection (7), and any officer of it who is in default, is liable to a fine and, for continued contravention, to a daily default fine.

55. Certificate of re-registration under s 53

(1) If the registrar of companies is satisfied that a company may be re-registered under section 53, he shall—
 (a) retain the application and other documents delivered to him under that section; and
 (b) issue the company with a certificate of incorporation appropriate to a private company.

(2) On the issue of the certificate—
 (a) the company by virtue of the issue becomes a private company; and

(b)   the alterations in the memorandum and articles set out in the resolution under section 53 take effect accordingly.

(3)   The certificate is conclusive evidence—

     (a)   that the requirements of section 53 in respect of re-registration and of matters precedent and incidental to it have been complied with; and

     (b)   that the company is a private company.

PART III
CAPITAL ISSUES

CHAPTER I
ISSUES BY COMPANIES REGISTERED, OR TO BE REGISTERED, IN GREAT BRITAIN

The prospectus

56, 57. ...

58.   *Document offering shares etc for sale deemed a prospectus*

(1)   *If a company allots or agrees to allot its shares or debentures with a view to all or any of them being offered for sale to the public, any document by which the offer for sale to the public is made is deemed for all purposes a prospectus issued by the company.*

(2)   *All enactments and rules of law as to the contents of prospectuses, and to liability in respect of statements in and omissions from prospectuses, or otherwise relating to prospectuses, apply and have effect accordingly, as if the shares or debentures had been offered to the public for subscription and as if persons accepting the offer in respect of any shares or debentures were subscribers for those shares or debentures.*

This is without prejudice to the liability (if any) of the persons by whom the offer is made, in respect of mis-statements in the document or otherwise in respect of it.

(3)   *For purposes of this Act it is evidence (unless the contrary is proved) that an allotment of, or an agreement to allot, shares or debentures was made with a view to their being offered for sale to the public if it is shown—*

     (a)   *that an offer of the shares or debentures (or of any of them) for sale to the public was made within 6 months after the allotment or agreement to allot, or*

     (b)   *that at the date when the offer was made the whole consideration to be received by the company in respect of the shares or debentures had not been so received.*

(4)   *Section 56 as applied by this section has effect as if it required a prospectus to state, in addition to the matters required by that section—*

     (a)   *the net amount of the consideration received or to be received by the company in respect of the shares or debentures to which the offer relates, and*

     (b)   *the place and time at which the contract under which those shares or debentures have been or are to be allotted may be inspected.*

Note. Repealed for certain purposes by the Financial Services Act 1986, s. 212(3), Sch. 17, Pt. I and for remaining purposes as from a day to be appointed.

59–61. ...

62.   *Meaning of "expert"*

The expression "expert", in both Chapters of this Part, includes engineer, valuer, accountant and any other person whose profession gives authority to a statement made by him.

Note. Repealed for certain purposes by the Financial Services Act 1986, s. 212(3), Sch. 17, Pt. I and for remaining purposes as from a day to be appointed.

63–79. ...

PART IV
ALLOTMENT OF SHARES AND DEBENTURES

General provisions as to allotment

80. **Authority of company required for certain allotments**

(1) The directors of a company shall not exercise any power of the company to allot relevant securities, unless they are, in accordance with this section or section 80A, authorised to do so by—

    (a)   the company in general meeting; or

    (b)   the company's articles.

(2) In this section "relevant securities" means—

    (a)   shares in the company other than shares shown in the memorandum to have been taken by the subscribers to it or shares allotted in pursuance of an employees' share scheme, and

    (b)   any right to subscribe for, or to convert any security into, shares in the company (other than shares so allotted);

    and a reference to the allotment of relevant securities includes the grant of such a right but (subject to subsection (6) below), not the allotment of shares pursuant to such a right.

(3) Authority under this section may be given for a particular exercise of the power or for its exercise generally, and may be unconditional or subject to conditions.

(4) The authority must state the maximum amount of relevant securities that may be allotted under it and the date on which it will expire, which must be not more than 5 years from whichever is relevant of the following dates—

    (a)   in the case of an authority contained in the company's articles at the time of its original incorporation, the date of that incorporation; and

    (b)   in any other case, the date on which the resolution is passed by virtue of which the authority is given;

    but such an authority (including an authority contained in the articles) may be previously revoked or varied by the company in general meeting.

(5) The authority may be renewed or further renewed by the company in general meeting for a further period not exceeding 5 years; but the resolution must state (or restate) the amount of relevant securities which may be allotted under the authority or, as the case may be, the amount remaining to be allotted under it, and must specify the date on which the renewed authority will expire.

(6) In relation to authority under this section for the grant of such rights as are mentioned in subsection (2)(b), the reference in subsection (4) (as also the corresponding reference in subsection (5)) to the maximum amount of relevant securities that may be allotted under the authority is to the maximum amount of shares which may be allotted pursuant to the rights.

(7) The directors may allot relevant securities, notwithstanding that authority under this section has expired, if they are allotted in pursuance of an offer or agreement made by the company before the authority expired and the authority allowed it to make an offer or agreement which would or might require relevant securities to be allotted after the authority expired.

(8) A resolution of a company to give, vary, revoke or renew such an authority may, notwithstanding that it alters the company's articles, be an ordinary resolution; but it is in any case subject to section 380 of this Act (copy to be forwarded to registrar within 15 days).

(9) A director who knowingly and wilfully contravenes, or permits or authorises a contravention of, this section is liable to a fine.

(10) Nothing in this section affects the validity of any allotment.

(11) This section does not apply to any allotment of relevant securities by a company, other than a public company registered as such on its original incorporation, if it is made in pursuance of an offer or agreement made before the earlier of the following two dates—

(a)   the date of the holding of the first general meeting of the company after its registration or re-registration as a public company, and

(b)   22nd June 1982;

but any resolution to give, vary or revoke an authority for the purposes of section 14 of the Companies Act 1980 or this section has effect for those purposes if passed at any time after the end of April 1980.

80A.   Election by private company as to duration of authority

(1)   A private company may elect (by elective resolution in accordance with section 379A) that the provisions of this section shall apply, instead of the provisions of section 80(4) and (5), in relation to the giving or renewal, after the election, of an authority under that section.

(2)   The authority must state the maximum amount of relevant securities that may be allotted under it and may be given—

(a)   for an indefinite period, or

(b)   for a fixed period, in which case it must state the date on which it will expire.

(3)   In either case an authority (including an authority contained in the articles) may be revoked or varied by the company in general meeting.

(4)   An authority given for a fixed period may be renewed or further renewed by the company in general meeting.

(5)   A resolution renewing an authority—

(a)   must state, or re-state, the amount of relevant securities which may be allotted under the authority or, as the case may be, the amount remaining to be allotted under it, and

(b)   must state whether the authority is renewed for an indefinite period or for a fixed period, in which case it must state the date on which the renewed authority will expire.

(6)   The references in this section to the maximum amount of relevant securities that may be allotted shall be construed in accordance with section 80(6).

(7)   If an election under this section ceases to have effect, an authority then in force which was given for an indefinite period or for a fixed period of more than five years—

(a)   if given five years or more before the election ceases to have effect, shall expire forthwith, and

(b)   otherwise, shall have effect as if it had been given for a fixed period of five years.

81.   *Restriction on public offers by private company*

(1)   A private limited company (other than a company limited by guarantee and not having a share capital) commits an offence if it—

(a)   offers to the public (whether for cash or otherwise) any shares in or debentures of the company; or

(b)   allots or agrees to allot (whether for cash or otherwise) any shares in or debentures of the company with a view to all or any of those shares or debentures being offered for sale to the public (within the meaning given to that expression by sections 58 and 742A).

(2)   A company guilty of an offence under this section, and any officer of it who is in default, is liable to a fine.

(3)   Nothing in this section affects the validity of any allotment or sale of shares or debentures, or of any agreement to allot or sell shares or debentures.

Note. Repealed for certain purposes by the Financial Services Act 1986, s. 212(3), Sch. 17, Pt. I.

82.   *Application for, and allotment of, shares and debentures*

(1)   No allotment shall be made of a company's shares or debentures in pursuance of a prospectus issued generally, and no proceedings shall be taken on applications made in pursuance of a prospectus so issued, until the beginning of the third day after that on which the prospectus is first so issued or such later time (if any) as may be specified in the prospectus.

(2) The beginning of that third day, or that later time, is "the time of the opening of the subscription lists".

(3) In subsection (1), the reference to the day on which the prospectus is first issued generally is to the day when it is first so issued as a newspaper advertisement'; and if it is not so issued as a newspaper advertisement before the third day after that on which it is first so issued in any other manner, the reference is to the day on which it is first so issued in any manner.

(4) In reckoning for this purpose the third day after another day—

(a) any intervening day which is a Saturday or Sunday, or is a bank holiday in any part of Great Britain, is to be disregarded; and

(b) if the third day (as so reckoned) is itself a Saturday or Sunday, or a bank holiday, there is to be substituted the first day after that which is none of them.

(5) The validity of an allotment is not affected by any contravention of subsections (1) to (4); but in the event of contravention, the company and every officer of it who is in default is liable to a fine.

(6) As applying to a prospectus offering shares or debentures for sale, the above provisions are modified as follows—

(a) for references to allotment, substitute references to sale; and

(b) for the reference to the company and every officer of it who is in default, substitute a reference to any person by or through whom the offer is made and who knowingly and wilfully authorised or permits the contravention.

(7) An application for shares in or debentures of a company which is made in pursuance of a prospectus issued generally is not recoverable until after the expiration of the third day after the time of the opening of the subscription lists, or the giving before the expiration of that day of the appropriate public notice; and that notice is one given by some person responsible under section 67 to 69 for the prospectus and having the effect under those sections of excluding or limiting the responsibility of the giver.

Note. Repealed for certain purposes by the Financial Services Act 1986, s. 212(3), Sch. 17, Pt. I.

83. No allotment unless minimum subscription received

(1) No allotment shall be made of any share capital of a company offered to the public for subscription unless—

(a) there has been subscribed the amount stated in the prospectus as the minimum amount which, in the opinion of the directors, must be raised by the issue of share capital in order to provide for the matters specified in paragraph 2 of Schedule 3 (preliminary expenses, purchase of property, working capital, etc); and

(b) the sum payable on application for the amount so stated has been paid to and received by the company.

(2) For purposes of subsection (1)(b), a sum is deemed paid to the company, and received by it, if a cheque for that sum has been received in good faith by the company and the directors have no reason for suspecting that the cheque will not be paid.

(3) The amount so stated in the prospectus is to be reckoned exclusively of any amount payable otherwise than in cash and is known as "the minimum subscription".

(4) If the above conditions have not been complied with on the expiration of 40 days after the first issue of the prospectus, all money received from applicants for shares shall be forthwith repaid to them without interest.

(5) If any of the money is not repaid within 48 days after the issue of the prospectus, the directors of the company are jointly and severally liable to repay it with interest at the rate of 5 per cent per annum from the expiration of the 48th day; except that a director is not so liable if he proves that the default in the repayment of the money was not due to any misconduct or negligence on his part.

(6)   *Any condition requiring or binding an applicant for shares to waive compliance with any requirement of this section is void.*

(7)   *This section does not apply to an allotment of shares subsequent to the first allotment of shares offered to the public for subscription.*

Note. Repealed for certain purposes by the Financial Services Act 1986, s. 212(3), Sch. 17, Pt. I.

84. Allotment where issue not fully subscribed

(1)   No allotment shall be made of any share capital of a public company offered for subscription unless—

    (a)   that capital is subscribed for in full; or

    (b)   the offer states that, even if the capital is not subscribed for in full, the amount of that capital subscribed for may be allotted in any event or in the event of the conditions specified in the offer being satisfied;

and, where conditions are so specified, no allotment of the capital shall be made by virtue of paragraph (b) unless those conditions are satisfied.

This is without prejudice to section 83.

(2)   If shares are prohibited from being allotted by subsection (1) and 40 days have elapsed after the first issue of the prospectus, all money received from applicants for shares shall be forthwith repaid to them without interest.

(3)   If any of the money is not repaid within 48 days after the issue of the prospectus, the directors of the company are jointly and severally liable to repay it with interest at the rate of 5 per cent per annum from the expiration of the 48th day; except that a director is not so liable if he proves that the default in repayment was not due to any misconduct or negligence on his part.

(4)   This section applies in the case of shares offered as wholly or partly payable otherwise than in cash as it applies in the case of shares offered for subscription (the word "subscribed" in subsection (1) being construed accordingly).

(5)   In subsections (2) and (3) as they apply to the case of shares offered as wholly or partly payable otherwise than in cash, references to the repayment of money received from applicants for shares include—

    (a)   the return of any other consideration so received (including, if the case so requires, the release of the applicant from any undertaking), or

    (b)   if it is not reasonably practicable to return the consideration, the payment of money equal to its value at the time it was so received,

and references to interest apply accordingly.

(6)   Any condition requiring or binding an applicant for shares to waive compliance with any requirement of this section is void.

Note. The italicized words in subsection (1) are repealed for certain purposes by the Financial Services Act 1986, s. 212(3), Sch. 17, Pt. I and for remaining purposes as from a day to be appointed.

85. Effect of irregular allotment

(1)   An allotment made by a company to an applicant in contravention of section *83 or* 84 is voidable at the instance of the applicant within one month after the date of the allotment, and not later, and is so voidable notwithstanding that the company is in the course of being wound up.

(2)   If a director of a company knowingly contravenes, or permits or authorises the contravention of, any provision of either of those sections with respect to allotment, he is liable to compensate the company and the allottee respectively for any loss, damages or costs which the company or the allottee may have sustained or incurred by the contravention.

(3)   But proceedings to recover any such loss, damages or costs shall not be commenced after the expiration of 2 years from the date of the allotment.

Note. The italicized words in subsection (1) are repealed for certain purposes by the Financial Services Act 1986, s. 212(3), Sch. 17, Pt. I and for remaining purposes as from a day to be appointed.

86, 87. ...

88.   Return as to allotments, etc

(1)   This section applies to a company limited by shares and to a company limited by guarantee and having a share capital.

(2)   When such a company makes an allotment of its shares, the company shall within one month thereafter deliver to the registrar of companies for registration—

(a)   a return of the allotments (in the prescribed form) stating the number and nominal amount of the shares comprised in the allotment, the names and addresses of the allottees, and the amount (if any) paid or due and payable on each share, whether on account of the nominal value of the share or by way of premium; and

(b)   in the case of shares allotted as fully or partly paid up otherwise than in cash—

(i)   a contract in writing constituting the title of the allottee to the allotment together with any contract of sale, or for services or other consideration in respect of which that allotment was made (such contracts being duly stamped), and

(ii)   a return stating the number and nominal amount of shares so allotted, the extent to which they are to be treated as paid up, and the consideration for which they have been allotted.

(3)   Where such a contract as above mentioned is not reduced to writing, the company shall within one month after the allotment deliver to the registrar of companies for registration the prescribed particulars of the contract ....

(4)   ...

(5)   If default is made in complying with this section, every officer of the company who is in default is liable to a fine and, for continued contravention, to a daily default fine, but subject as follows.

(6)   In the case of default in delivering to the registrar within one month after the allotment any document required by this section to be delivered, the company, or any officer liable for the default, may apply to the court for relief; and the court, if satisfied that the omission to deliver the document was accidental or due to inadvertence, or that it is just and equitable to grant relief, may make an order extending the time for the delivery of the document for such period as the court thinks proper.

Pre-emption rights

89.   Offers to shareholders to be on pre-emptive basis

(1)   Subject to the provisions of this section and the seven sections next following, a company proposing to allot equity securities (defined in section 94)—

(a)   shall not allot any of them on any terms to a person unless it has made an offer to each person who holds relevant shares or relevant employee shares to allot to him on the same or more favourable terms a proportion of those securities which is as nearly as practicable equal to the proportion in nominal value held by him of the aggregate of relevant shares and relevant employee shares, and

(b)   shall not allot any of those securities to a person unless the period during which any such offer may be accepted has expired or the company has received notice of the acceptance or refusal of every offer so made.

(2)   Subsection (3) below applies to any provision of a company's memorandum or articles which requires the company, when proposing to allot equity securities consisting of relevant shares of any particular class, not to allot those securities on any terms unless it has complied with the condition that it makes such an offer as is described in subsection (1) to each person who holds relevant shares or relevant employee shares of that class.

(3)   If in accordance with a provision to which this subsection applies—

(a)   a company makes an offer to allot securities to such a holder, and

(b)   he or anyone in whose favour he has renounced his right to their allotment accepts the offer,

subsection (1) does not apply to the allotment of those securities, and the company may allot them accordingly; but this is without prejudice to the application of subsection (1) in any other case.

(4)   Subsection (1) does not apply to a particular allotment of equity securities if these are, or are to be, wholly or partly paid up otherwise than in cash; and securities which a company has offered to allot to a holder of relevant shares or relevant employee shares may be allotted to him, or anyone in whose favour he has renounced his right to their allotment, without contravening subsection (1)(b).

(5)   Subsection (1) does not apply to the allotment of securities which would, apart from a renunciation or assignment of the right to their allotment, be held under an employees' share scheme.

(6)   Where a company holds relevant shares as treasury shares—

     (a)   for the purposes of subsections (1) and (2), the company is not a "person who holds relevant shares"; and

     (b)   for the purposes of subsection (1), the shares held as treasury shares do not form part of "the aggregate of relevant shares and relevant employee shares".

90. Communication of pre-emption offers to shareholders

(1)   This section has effect as to the manner in which offers required by section 89(1), or by a provision to which section 89(3) applies, are to be made to holders of a company's shares.

(2)   Subject to the following subsections, an offer shall be in writing and shall be made to a holder of shares either personally or by sending it by post (that is to say, prepaying and posting a letter containing the offer) to him or to his registered address or, if he has no registered address in the United Kingdom, to the address in the United Kingdom supplied by him to the company for the giving of notice to him.

If sent by post, the offer is deemed to be made at the time at which the letter would be delivered in the ordinary course of post.

(3)   Where shares are held by two or more persons jointly, the offer may be made to the joint holder first named in the register of members in respect of the shares.

(4)   In the case of a holder's death or bankruptcy, the offer may be made—

     (a)   by sending it by post in a prepaid letter addressed to the persons claiming to be entitled to the shares in consequence of the death or bankruptcy by name, or by the title of representatives of the deceased, or trustee of the bankrupt, or by any like description, at the address in the United Kingdom supplied for the purpose by those so claiming, or

     (b)   (until such an address has been so supplied) by giving the notice in any manner in which it might have been given if the death or bankruptcy had not occurred.

(5)   If the holder—

     (a)   has no registered address in the United Kingdom and has not given to the company an address in the United Kingdom for the service of notices on him, or

     (b)   is the holder of a share warrant,

the offer may be made by causing it, or a notice specifying where a copy of it can be obtained or inspected, to be published in the Gazette.

(6)   The offer must state a period of not less than 21 days during which it may be accepted; and the offer shall not be withdrawn before the end of that period.

(7)   This section does not invalidate a provision to which section 89(3) applies by reason that that provision requires or authorises an offer under it to be made in contravention of any of subsections (1) to (6) above; but, to the extent that the provision requires or authorises such an offer to be so made, it is of no effect.

91. Exclusion of ss 89, 90 by private company

(1)   Section 89(1), section 90(1) to (5) or section 90(6) may, as applying to allotments by a private company of equity securities or to such allotments of a particular description, be excluded by a provision contained in the memorandum or articles of that company.

(2)   A requirement or authority contained in the memorandum or articles of a private company, if it is inconsistent with any of those subsections, has effect as a provision excluding that subsection; but a provision to which section 89(3) applies is not to be treated as inconsistent with section 89(1).

92.   **Consequences of contravening ss 89, 90**

(1)   If there is a contravention of section 89(1), or of section 90(1) to (5) or section 90(6), or of a provision to which section 89(3) applies, the company, and every officer of it who knowingly authorised or permitted the contravention, are jointly and severally liable to compensate any person to whom an offer should have been made under the subsection or provision contravened for any loss, damage, costs or expenses which the person has sustained or incurred by reason of the contravention.

(2)   However, no proceedings to recover any such loss, damage, costs or expenses shall be commenced after the expiration of 2 years from the delivery to the registrar of companies of the return of allotments in question or, where equity securities other than shares are granted, from the date of the grant.

93.   **Saving for other restrictions as to offers**

(1)   Sections 89 to 92 are without prejudice to any enactment by virtue of which a company is prohibited (whether generally or in specified circumstances) from offering or allotting equity securities to any person.

(2)   Where a company cannot by virtue of such an enactment offer or allot equity securities to a holder of relevant shares or relevant employee shares, those sections have effect as if the shares held by that holder were not relevant shares or relevant employee shares.

94.   **Definitions for ss 89–96**

(1)   The following subsections apply for the interpretation of sections 89 to 96.

(2)   "Equity security", in relation to a company, means a relevant share in the company (other than a share shown in the memorandum to have been taken by a subscriber to the memorandum or a bonus share), or a right to subscribe for, or to convert securities into, relevant shares in the company.

(3)   A reference to the allotment of equity securities or of equity securities consisting of relevant shares of a particular class includes the grant of a right to subscribe for, or to convert any securities into, relevant shares in the company or (as the case may be) relevant shares of a particular class; but such a reference does not include the allotment of any relevant shares pursuant to such a right.

(3A)   A reference to the allotment of equity securities or of equity securities consisting of relevant shares of a particular class also includes the sale of any relevant shares in the company or (as the case may be) relevant shares of a particular class if, immediately before the sale, the shares were held by the company as treasury shares.

(4)   "Relevant employee shares", in relation to a company, means shares of the company which would be relevant in it but for the fact that they are held by a person who acquired them in pursuance of an employees' share scheme.

(5)   "Relevant shares", in relation to a company, means shares in the company other than—

   (a)   shares which as respects dividends and capital carry a right to participate only up to a specified amount in a distribution, and

   (b)   shares which are held by a person who acquired them in pursuance of an employees' share scheme or, in the case of shares which have not been allotted, are to be allotted in pursuance of such a scheme or, in the case of shares held by the company as treasury shares, are to be transferred in pursuance of such a scheme.

(6)   A reference to a class of shares is to shares to which the same rights are attached as to voting and as to participation, both as respects dividends and as respects capital, in a distribution.

(7)   In relation to an offer to allot securities required by section 89(1) or by any provision to which section 89(3) applies, a reference in sections 89 to 94 (however expressed) to the holder of shares of any description is to whoever was at the close of business on a date, to be specified in the offer and to fall in the period of 28 days immediately before the date of the offer, the holder of shares of that description.

95.   Disapplication of pre-emption rights

(1)   Where the directors of a company are generally authorised for purposes of section 80, they may be given power by the articles, or by a special resolution of the company, to allot equity securities pursuant to that authority as if—

    (a)   section 89(1) did not apply to the allotment, or

    (b)   that subsection applied to the allotment with such modifications as the directors may determine;

and where the directors make an allotment under this subsection, sections 89 to 94 have effect accordingly.

(2)   Where the directors of a company are authorised for purposes of section 80 (whether generally or otherwise), the company may by special resolution resolve either—

    (a)   that section 89(1) shall not apply to a specified allotment of equity securities to be made pursuant to that authority, or

    (b)   that that subsection shall apply to the allotment with such modifications as may be specified in the resolution;

and where such a resolution is passed, sections 89 to 94 have effect accordingly.

(2A)   Subsections (1) and (2) apply in relation to a sale of shares which is an allotment of equity securities by virtue of section 94(3A) as if—

    (a)   in subsection (1) for "Where the directors of a company are generally authorised for purposes of section 80, they" there were substituted "The directors of a company" and the words "pursuant to that authority" were omitted, and

    (b)   in subsection (2), the words from "Where" to "otherwise)," and, in paragraph (a), the words "to be made pursuant to that authority" were omitted.

(3)   The power conferred by subsection (1) or a special resolution under subsection (2) ceases to have effect when the authority to which it relates is revoked or would (if not renewed) expire; but if the authority is renewed, the power or (as the case may be) the resolution may also be renewed, for a period not longer than that for which the authority is renewed, by a special resolution of the company.

(4)   Notwithstanding that any such power or resolution has expired, the directors may allot equity securities in pursuance of an offer or agreement previously made by the company, if the power or resolution enabled the company to make an offer or agreement which would or might require equity securities to be allotted after it expired.

(5)   A special resolution under subsection (2), or a special resolution to renew such a resolution, shall not be proposed unless it is recommended by the directors and there has been circulated, with the notice of the meeting at which the resolution is proposed, to the members entitled to have that notice a written statement by the directors setting out—

    (a)   their reasons for making the recommendation,

    (b)   the amount to be paid to the company in respect of the equity securities to be allotted, and

    (c)   the directors' justification of that amount.

(6)   A person who knowingly or recklessly authorises or permits the inclusion in a statement circulated under subsection (5) of any matter which is misleading, false or deceptive in a material particular is liable to imprisonment or a fine, or both.

96.   Saving for company's pre-emption procedure operative before 1982

(1)   Where a company which is re-registered or registered as a public company is or, but for the provisions of the Companies Act 1980 and the enactments replacing it, would be subject at the time of re-registration or (as the case may be) registration to a pre-1982 pre-emption requirement, sections 89 to 95 do not apply to an allotment of the equity securities which are subject to that requirement.

(2)   A "pre-1982 pre-emption requirement" is a requirement imposed (whether by the company's memorandum or articles, or otherwise) before the relevant date in 1982 by virtue of which the company must, when making an allotment of equity securities, make an offer to allot those securities or some of them in a manner which (otherwise than because involving a contravention

of section 90(1) to (5) or 90(6)) is inconsistent with sections 89 to 94; and "the relevant date in 1982" is—

    (a)   except in a case falling within the following paragraph, 22nd June in that year, and

    (b)   in the case of a company which was re-registered or registered as a public company on an application made before that date, the date on which the application was made.

(3)   A requirement which—

    (a)   is imposed on a private company (having been so imposed before the relevant date in 1982) otherwise than by the company's memorandum or articles, and

    (b)   if contained in the company's memorandum or articles, would have effect under section 91 to the exclusion of any provisions of sections 89 to 94,

has effect, so long as the company remains a private company, as if it were contained in the memorandum or articles.

(4)   If on the relevant date in 1982 a company, other than a public company registered as such on its original incorporation, was subject to such a requirement as is mentioned in section 89(2) imposed otherwise than by the memorandum or articles, the requirement is to be treated for purposes of sections 89 to 94 as if it were contained in the memorandum or articles.

Commissions and discounts

97.   **Power of company to pay commissions**

(1)   It is lawful for a company to pay a commission to any person in consideration of his subscribing or agreeing to subscribe (whether absolutely or conditionally) for any shares in the company, or procuring or agreeing to procure subscriptions (whether absolute or conditional) for any shares in the company, if the following conditions *and any conditions which apply in respect of any such payment by virtue of rules made under section 169(2) of the Financial Services Act 1986* are satisfied.

(2)   The payment of the commission must be authorised by the company's articles; and—

    (a)   the commission paid or agreed to be paid must not exceed *10 per cent of the price at which the shares are issued or the amount or rate authorised by the articles, whichever is the less* [(i)   *any limit imposed on it by those rules or, if none is so imposed, 10 per cent, of the price at which the shares are issued; or*

        (ii)   *the amount or rate authorised by the articles, whichever is the less]; and*

    (b)   *the amount or rate per cent of commission paid or agreed to be paid, and the number of shares which persons have agreed for a commission to subscribe absolutely, must be disclosed in the manner required by the following subsection.*

(3)   *Those matters must, in the case of shares offered to the public for subscription, be disclosed in the prospectus; and in the case of shares not so offered—*

    (a)   *they must be disclosed in a statement in the prescribed form signed by every director of the company or by his agent authorised in writing, and delivered (before payment of the commission) to the registrar of companies for registration; and*

    (b)   *where a circular or notice (not being a prospectus) inviting subscription for the shares is issued, they must also be disclosed in that circular or notice.*

(4)   *If default is made in complying with subsection (3)(a) as regards delivery to the registrar of the statement in prescribed form, the company and every officer of it who is in default is liable to a fine.*

Note. The italicized words from "and any" to "Financial Services Act 1986" in subsection (1) are inserted by the Financial Services Act 1986, s. 212(2), Sch. 16, para. 16, as from a day to be appointed.

The italicized words in subsection (2)(a) are prospectively repealed and the words in square brackets are prospectively substituted by the Financial Services Act 1986, s. 212(2), Sch. 16, para. 16, as from a day to be appointed.

Subsections (2)(b) (and the word "and" immediately preceding it), (3), (4) are repealed for certain purposes by the Financial Services Act 1986, s. 212(3), Sch. 17, Pt. I and repealed for remaining purposes, as from a day to be appointed.

98. **Apart from s 97, commissions and discounts barred**

(1)   Except as permitted by section 97, no company shall apply any of its shares or capital money, either directly or indirectly in payment of any commission, discount or allowance to any person in consideration of his subscribing or agreeing to subscribe (whether absolutely or conditionally) for any shares in the company, or procuring or agreeing to procure subscriptions (whether absolute or conditional) for any shares in the company.

(2)   This applies whether the shares or money be so applied by being added to the purchase money of any property acquired by the company or to the contract price of any work to be executed for the company, or the money be paid out of the nominal purchase money or contract price, or otherwise.

(3)   Nothing in section 97 or this section affects the power of a company to pay such brokerage as has previously been lawful.

(4)   A vendor to, or promoter of, or other person who receives payment in money or shares from, a company has, and is deemed always to have had, power to apply any part of the money or shares so received in payment of any commission, the payment of which, if made directly by the company, would have been lawful under section 97 and this section.

Amount to be paid for shares; the means of payment

99. **General rules as to payment for shares on allotment**

(1)   Subject to the following provisions of this Part, shares allotted by a company, and any premium on them, may be paid up in money or money's worth (including goodwill and know-how).

(2)   A public company shall not accept at any time, in payment up of its shares or any premium on them, an undertaking given by any person that he or another should do work or perform services for the company or any other person.

(3)   If a public company accepts such an undertaking in payment up of its shares or any premium on them, the holder of the shares when they or the premium are treated as paid up (in whole or in part) by the undertaking is liable—

 (a)   to pay the company in respect of those shares an amount equal to their nominal value, together with the whole of any premium or, if the case so requires, such proportion of that amount as is treated as paid up by the undertaking; and

 (b)   to pay interest at the appropriate rate on the amount payable under paragraph (a) above.

(4)   This section does not prevent a company from allotting bonus shares to its members or from paying up, with sums available for the purpose, any amounts for the time being unpaid on any of its shares (whether on account of the nominal value of the shares or by way of premium).

(5)   The reference in subsection (3) to the holder of shares includes any person who has an unconditional right to be included in the company's register of members in respect of those shares or to have an instrument of transfer of them executed in his favour.

100. **Prohibition on allotment of shares at a discount**

(1)   A company's shares shall not be allotted at a discount.

(2)   If shares are allotted in contravention of this section, the allottee is liable to pay the company an amount equal to the amount of the discount, with interest at the appropriate rate.

101. **Shares to be allotted as at least one-quarter paid-up**

(1)   A public company shall not allot a share except as paid up at least as to one-quarter of its nominal value and the whole of any premium on it.

(2)   Subsection (1) does not apply to shares allotted in pursuance of an employees' share scheme.

(3)   If a company allots a share in contravention of subsection (1), the share is to be treated as if one-quarter of its nominal value, together with the whole of any premium on it, had been received.

(4)   But the allottee is liable to pay the company the minimum amount which should have been received in respect of the share under subsection (1) (less the value of any consideration actually applied in payment up, to any extent, of the share and any premium on it), with interest at the appropriate rate.

(5)   Subsections (3) and (4) do not apply to the allotment of bonus shares, unless the allottee knew or ought to have known the shares were allotted in contravention of subsection (1).

102.   Restriction on payment by long-term undertaking

(1)   A public company shall not allot shares as fully or partly paid up (as to their nominal value or any premium on them) otherwise than in cash if the consideration for the allotment is or includes an undertaking which is to be, or may be, performed more than 5 years after the date of the allotment.

(2)   If a company allots shares in contravention of subsection (1), the allottee is liable to pay the company an amount equal to the aggregate of their nominal value and the whole of any premium (or, if the case so requires, so much of that aggregate as is treated as paid up by the undertaking), with interest at the appropriate rate.

(3)   Where a contract for the allotment of shares does not contravene subsection (1), any variation of the contract which has the effect that the contract would have contravened the subsection, if the terms of the contract as varied had been its original terms, is void.

(4)   Subsection (3) applies also to the variation by a public company of the terms of a contract entered into before the company was re-registered as a public company.

(5)   The following subsection applies where a public company allots shares for a consideration which consists of or includes (in accordance with subsection (1)) an undertaking which is to be performed within 5 years of the allotment, but the undertaking is not performed within the period allowed by the contract for the allotment of the shares.

(6)   The allottee is then liable to pay the company, at the end of the period so allowed, an amount equal to the aggregate of the nominal value of the shares and the whole of any premium (or, if the case so requires, so much of that aggregate as is treated as paid up by the undertaking), with interest at the appropriate rate.

(7)   A reference in this section to a contract for the allotment of shares includes an ancillary contract relating to payment in respect of them.

103.   Non-cash consideration to be valued before allotment

(1)   A public company shall not allot shares as fully or partly paid up (as to their nominal value or any premium on them) otherwise than in cash unless—

    (a)   the consideration for the allotment has been independently valued under section 108; and

    (b)   a report with respect to its value has been made to the company by a person appointed by the company (in accordance with that section) during the 6 months immediately preceding the allotment of the shares; and

    (c)   a copy of the report has been sent to the proposed allottee.

(2)   Where an amount standing to the credit of any of a company's reserve accounts, or of its profit and loss account, is applied in paying up (to any extent) any shares allotted to members of the company or any premiums on shares so allotted, the amount applied does not count as consideration for the allotment, and accordingly subsection (1) does not apply in that case.

(3)   Subsection (1) does not apply to the allotment of shares by a company in connection with an arrangement providing for the allotment of shares in that company on terms that the whole or part of the consideration for the shares allotted is to be provided by the transfer to that company (or the cancellation) of all or some of the shares, or of all or some of the shares of a particular class, in another company (with or without the issue to that company of shares, or of shares of any particular class, in that other company).

(4)   But subsection (3) does not exclude the application of subsection (1) unless under the arrangement it is open to all the holders of the shares in the other company in question ("the relevant company") (or, where the arrangement applies only to shares of a particular class, to all

the holders of shares in the relevant company, being holders of shares of that class) to take part in the arrangement.

In determining whether that is the case, the following shall be disregarded—

    (a)   shares held by or by a nominee of the company proposing to allot the shares in connection with the arrangement ("the allotting company");

    (b)   shares held by or by a nominee of a company which is—

        (i)   the holding company, or a subsidiary, of the allotting company, or

        (ii)   a subsidiary of that holding company; and

    (c)   shares held as treasury shares by the relevant company.

(5)   Subsection (1) also does not apply to the allotment of shares by a company in connection with its proposed merger with another company; that is, where one of the companies proposes to acquire all the assets and liabilities of the other in exchange for the issue of shares or other securities of that one to shareholders of the other, with or without any cash payment to shareholders.

(6)   If a company allots shares in contravention of subsection (1) and either—

    (a)   the allottee has not received the valuer's report required by that subsection to be sent to him; or

    (b)   there has been some other contravention of this section or section 108 which the allottee knew or ought to have known amounted to a contravention,

the allottee is liable to pay the company an amount equal to the aggregate of the nominal value of the shares and the whole of any premium (or, if the case so requires, so much of that aggregate as is treated as paid up by the consideration), with interest at the appropriate rate.

(7)   In this section—

    (a)   "arrangement" means any agreement, scheme or arrangement (including an arrangement sanctioned in accordance with section 425 (company compromise with creditors and members) or section 110 of the Insolvency Act (liquidator in winding up accepting shares as consideration for sale of company property)), and

    (b)   any reference to a company, except where it is or is to be construed as a reference to a public company, includes any body corporate ...

104.   Transfer to public company of non-cash asset in initial period

(1)   A public company formed as such shall not, unless the conditions of this section have been complied with, enter into an agreement with a person for the transfer by him during the initial period of one or more non-cash assets to the company or another, if—

    (a)   that person is a subscriber to the company's memorandum, and

    (b)   the consideration for the transfer to be given by the company is equal in value at the time of the agreement to one-tenth or more of the company's nominal share capital issued at that time.

(2)   The "initial period" for this purpose is 2 years beginning with the date of the company being issued with a certificate under section 117 (or the previous corresponding provision) that it was entitled to do business.

(3)   This section applies also to a company re-registered as a public company (except one re-registered under section 8 of the Companies Act 1980 or section 2 of the Consequential Provisions Act), or registered under section 685 (joint stock company) or the previous corresponding provision; but in that case—

    (a)   there is substituted a reference in subsection (1)(a) to a person who is a member of the company on the date of registration or re-registration, and

    (b)   the initial period is then 2 years beginning with that date.

In this subsection the reference to a company re-registered as a public company includes a private company so re-registered which was a public company before it was a private company.

(4)   The conditions of this section are as follows—

    (a)   the consideration to be received by the company, and any consideration other than cash to be given by the company, must have been independently valued under section 109;

(b) a report with respect to the consideration to be so received and given must have been made to the company in accordance with that section during the 6 months immediately preceding the date of the agreement;

(c) the terms of the agreement must have been approved by an ordinary resolution of the company; and

(d) not later than the giving of the notice of the meeting at which the resolution is proposed, copies of the resolution and report must have been circulated to the members of the company entitled to receive the notice and, if the person with whom the agreement in question is proposed to be made is not then a member of the company so entitled, to that person.

(5) In subsection (4)(a)—

(a) the reference to the consideration to be received by the company is to the asset to be transferred to it or the advantage to the company of the asset's transfer to another person; and

(b) the specified condition is without prejudice to any requirement to value any consideration for purposes of section 103.

(6) In the case of the following agreements, this section does not apply—

(a) where it is part of the company's ordinary business to acquire, or arrange for other persons to acquire, assets of a particular description, an agreement entered into by the company in the ordinary course of its business for the transfer of an asset of that description to it or to such a person, as the case may be;

(b) an agreement entered into by the company under the supervision of the court, or of an officer authorised by the court for the purpose, for the transfer of an asset to the company or to another.

105.   Agreements contravening s 104

(1) The following subsection applies if a public company enters into an agreement contravening section 104, the agreement being made with the person referred to in subsection (1)(a) or (as the case may be) subsection (3) of that section, and either—

(a) that person has not received the valuer's report required for compliance with the conditions of the section, or

(b) there has been some other contravention of the section or of section 108(1), (2) or (5) or section 109, which he knew or ought to have known amounted to a contravention.

(2) The company is then entitled to recover from that person any consideration given by it under the agreement, or an amount equal to the value of the consideration at the time of the agreement; and the agreement, so far as not carried out, is void.

(3) However, if the agreement is or includes an agreement for the allotment of shares in the company, then—

(a) whether or not the agreement also contravenes section 103, subsection (2) above does not apply to it in so far as it is for the allotment of shares; and

(b) the allottee is liable to pay the company an amount equal to the aggregate of the nominal value of the shares and the whole of any premium (or, if the case so requires, so much of that aggregate as is treated as paid up by the consideration), with interest at the appropriate rate.

106.   Shares issued to subscribers of memorandum

Shares taken by a subscriber to the memorandum of a public company in pursuance of an undertaking of his in the memorandum, and any premium on the shares, shall be paid up in cash.

107.   Meaning of "the appropriate rate"

In sections 99 to 105 "the appropriate rate", in relation to interest, means 5 per cent per annum or such other rate as may be specified by order made by the Secretary of State by statutory instrument subject to annulment in pursuance of a resolution of either House of Parliament.

Valuation provisions

108.   Valuation and report (s 103)

(1)   The valuation and report required by section 103 (or, where applicable, section 44) shall be made by an independent person, that is to say a person qualified at the time of the report to be appointed, or continue to be, an auditor of the company.

(2)   However, where it appears to the independent person (from here on referred to as "the valuer") to be reasonable for the valuation of the consideration, or part of it, to be made (or for him to accept such a valuation) by another person who—

(a)   appears to him to have the requisite knowledge and experience to value the consideration or that part of it; and

(b)   is not an officer or servant of the company or any other body corporate which is that company's subsidiary or holding company or a subsidiary of that company's holding company or a partner or employee of such an officer or servant,

he may arrange for or accept such a valuation, together with a report which will enable him to make his own report under this section and provide the note required by subsection (6) below.

(3)   The reference in subsection (2)(b) to an officer or servant does not include an auditor.

(4)   The valuer's report shall state—

(a)   the nominal value of the shares to be wholly or partly paid for by the consideration in question;

(b)   the amount of any premium payable on the shares;

(c)   the description of the consideration and, as respects so much of the consideration as he himself has valued, a description of that part of the consideration, the method used to value it and the date of the valuation;

(d)   the extent to which the nominal value of the shares and any premium are to be treated as paid up—

(i)   by the consideration;

(ii)   in cash.

(5)   Where the consideration or part of it is valued by a person other than the valuer himself, the latter's report shall state that fact and shall also—

(a)   state the former's name and what knowledge and experience he has to carry out the valuation, and

(b)   describe so much of the consideration as was valued by the other person, and the method used to value it, and specify the date of the valuation.

(6)   The valuer's report shall contain or be accompanied by a note by him—

(a)   in the case of a valuation made by a person other than himself, that it appeared to himself reasonable to arrange for it to be so made or to accept a valuation so made;

(b)   whoever made the valuation, that the method of valuation was reasonable in all the circumstances;

(c)   that it appears to the valuer that there has been no material change in the value of the consideration in question since the valuation; and

(d)   that on the basis of the valuation the value of the consideration, together with any cash by which the nominal value of the shares or any premium payable on them is to be paid up, is not less than so much of the aggregate of the nominal value and the whole of any such premium as is treated as paid up by the consideration and any such cash.

(7)   Where the consideration to be valued is accepted partly in payment up of the nominal value of the shares and any premium and partly for some other consideration given by the company, section 103 (and, where applicable, section 44) and the foregoing provisions of this section apply as if references to the consideration accepted by the company included the proportion of that consideration which is properly attributable to the payment up of that value and any premium; and—

(a)   the valuer shall carry out, or arrange for, such other valuations as will enable him to determine that proportion; and

(b)   his report shall state what valuations have been made under this subsection and also the reason for, and method and date of, any such valuation and any other matters which may be relevant to that determination.

109.   Valuation and report (s 104)

(1)   Subsections (1) to (3) and (5) of section 108 apply also as respects the valuation and report for the purposes of section 104.

(2)   The valuer's report for those purposes shall—

   (a)   state the consideration to be received by the company, describing the asset in question (specifying the amount to be received in cash) and the consideration to be given by the company (specifying the amount to be given in cash);

   (b)   state the method and date of valuation;

   (c)   contain or be accompanied by a note as to the matters mentioned in section 108(6)(a) to (c); and

   (d)   contain or be accompanied by a note that on the basis of the valuation the value of the consideration to be received by the company is not less than the value of the consideration to be given by it.

(3)   A reference in section 104 or this section to consideration given for the transfer of an asset includes consideration given partly for its transfer; but—

   (a)   the value of any consideration partly so given is to be taken as the proportion of the consideration properly attributable to its transfer;

   (b)   the valuer shall carry out or arrange for such valuations of anything else as will enable him to determine that proportion; and

   (c)   his report for purposes of section 104 shall state what valuation has been made under this subsection and also the reason for and method and date of any such valuation and any other matters which may be relevant to that determination.

110.   Entitlement of valuer to full disclosure

(1)   A person carrying out a valuation or making a report under section 103 or 104, with respect to any consideration proposed to be accepted or given by a company, is entitled to require from the officers of the company such information and explanation as he thinks necessary to enable him to carry out the valuation or make the report and provide a note under section 108(6) or (as the case may be) section 109(2)(c).

(2)   A person who knowingly or recklessly makes a statement which—

   (a)   is misleading, false or deceptive in a material particular, and

   (b)   is a statement to which this subsection applies,

is guilty of an offence and liable to imprisonment or a fine, or both.

(3)   Subsection (2) applies to any statement made (whether orally or in writing) to a person carrying out a valuation or making a report under section 108 or 109, being a statement which conveys or purports to convey any information or explanation which that person requires, or is entitled to require, under subsection (1) of this section.

111.   Matters to be communicated to registrar

(1)   A company to which a report is made under section 108 as to the value of any consideration for which, or partly for which, it proposes to allot shares shall deliver a copy of the report to the registrar of companies for registration at the same time that it files the return of the allotments of those shares under section 88.

(2)   A company which has passed a resolution under section 104 with respect to the transfer of an asset shall, within 15 days of so doing, deliver to the registrar of companies a copy of the resolution together with the valuer's report required by that section.

(3)   If default is made in complying with subsection (1), every officer of the company who is in default is liable to a fine and, for continued contravention, to a daily default fine; but this is subject to the same exception as is made by section 88(6) (relief on application to the court) in the case of default in complying with that section.

(4)   If a company fails to comply with subsection (2), it and every officer of it who is in default is liable to a fine and, for continued contravention, to a daily default fine.

Other matters arising out of allotment, &c

111A.   Right to damages, &c not affected

A person is not debarred from obtaining damages or other compensation from a company by reason only of his holding or having held shares in the company or any right to apply or subscribe for shares or to be included in the company's register in respect of shares.

112.   Liability of subsequent holders of shares allotted

(1)   If a person becomes a holder of shares in respect of which—
   (a)   there has been a contravention of section 99, 100, 101 or 103; and
   (b)   by virtue of that contravention, another is liable to pay any amount under the section contravened,
   that person is also liable to pay that amount (jointly and severally with any other person so liable), unless he is exempted from liability by subsection (3) below.

(2)   If a company enters into an agreement in contravention of section 104 and—
   (a)   the agreement is or includes an agreement for the allotment of shares in the company; and
   (b)   a person becomes a holder of shares allotted under the agreement; and
   (c)   by virtue of the agreement and allotment under it, another person is liable to pay any amount under section 105,
   the person who becomes the holder of the shares is also liable to pay that amount (jointly and severally with any other person so liable), unless he is exempted from liability by the following subsection; and this applies whether or not the agreement also contravenes section 103.

(3)   A person otherwise liable under subsection (1) or (2) is exempted from that liability if either—
   (a)   he is a purchaser for value and, at the time of the purchase, he did not have actual notice of the contravention concerned; or
   (b)   he derived title to the shares (directly or indirectly) from a person who became a holder of them after the contravention and was not liable under subsection (1) or (as the case may be) subsection (2).

(4)   References in this section to a holder, in relation to shares in a company, include any person who has an unconditional right to be included in the company's register of members in respect of those shares or to have an instrument of transfer of the shares executed in his favour.

(5)   As subsections (1) and (3) apply in relation to the contraventions there mentioned, they also apply—
   (a)   to a contravention of section 102; and
   (b)   to a failure to carry out a term of a contract as mentioned in subsections (5) and (6) of that section.

113.   Relief in respect of certain liabilities under ss 99 ff

(1)   Where a person is liable to a company under—
   (a)   section 99, 102, 103 or 105;
   (b)   section 112(1) by reference to a contravention of section 99 or 103; or
   (c)   section 112(2) or (5),
   in relation to payment in respect of any shares in the company, or is liable by virtue of an undertaking given to it in, or in connection with, payment for any such shares, the person so liable may make an application to the court to be exempted in whole or in part from the liability.

(2)   If the liability mentioned in subsection (1) arises in relation to payment in respect of any shares, the court may, on an application under that subsection, exempt the applicant from the liability only—
   (a)   if and to the extent that it appears to the court just and equitable to do so having regard to the matters mentioned in the following subsection,

(b) if and to the extent that it appears to the court just and equitable to do so in respect of any interest which he is liable to pay the company under any of the relevant sections.

(3) The matters to be taken into account by the court under subsection (2)(a) are—

(a) whether the applicant has paid, or is liable to pay, any amount in respect of any other liability arising in relation to those shares under any of the relevant sections, or of any liability arising by virtue of any undertaking given in or in connection with payment for those shares;

(b) whether any person other than the applicant has paid or is likely to pay (whether in pursuance of an order of the court or otherwise) any such amount; and

(c) whether the applicant or any other person has performed in whole or in part, or is likely so to perform, any such undertaking, or has done or is likely to do any other thing in payment or part payment for the shares.

(4) Where the liability arises by virtue of an undertaking given to the company in, or in connection with, payment for shares in it, the court may, on an application under subsection (1), exempt the applicant from the liability only if and to the extent that it appears to the court just and equitable to do so having regard to—

(a) whether the applicant has paid or is liable to pay any amount in respect of liability arising in relation to the shares under any of the provisions mentioned in that subsection; and

(b) whether any person other than the applicant has paid or is likely to pay (whether in pursuance of an order of the court or otherwise) any such amount.

(5) In determining whether it should exempt the applicant in whole or in part from any liability, the court shall have regard to the following overriding principles, namely—

(a) that a company which has allotted shares should receive money or money's worth at least equal in value to the aggregate of the nominal value of those shares and the whole of any premium or, if the case so requires, so much of that aggregate as is treated as paid up; and

(b) subject to this, that where such a company would, if the court did not grant the exemption, have more than one remedy against a particular person, it should be for the company to decide which remedy it should remain entitled to pursue.

(6) If a person brings proceedings against another ("the contributor") for a contribution in respect of liability to a company arising under any of sections 99 to 105 or 112, and it appears to the court that the contributor is liable to make such a contribution, the court may exercise the powers of the following subsection.

(7) The court may, if and to the extent that it appears to it, having regard to the respective culpability (in respect of the liability to the company) of the contributor and the person bringing the proceedings, that it is just and equitable to do so—

(a) exempt the contributor in whole or in part from his liability to make such a contribution; or

(b) order the contributor to make a larger contribution than, but for this subsection, he would be liable to make.

(8) Where a person is liable to a company under section 105(2), the court may, on application, exempt him in whole or in part from that liability if and to the extent that it appears to the court just and equitable to do so having regard to any benefit accruing to the company by virtue of anything done by him towards the carrying out of the agreement mentioned in that subsection

114. Penalty for contravention

If a company contravenes any of the provisions of sections 99 to 104 and 106 the company and any officer of it who is in default is liable to a fine.

115. Undertakings to do work, etc

(1) Subject to section 113, an undertaking given by any person, in or in connection with payment for shares in a company, to do work or perform services or to do any other thing, if it is enforceable by the company apart from this Act, is so enforceable notwithstanding that there has been a contravention in relation to it of section 99, 102 or 103.

(2)   Where such an undertaking is given in contravention of section 104 in respect of the allotment of shares, it is so enforceable notwithstanding the contravention.

116.   **Application of ss 99 ff to special cases**

Except as provided by section 9 of the Consequential Provisions Act (transitional cases dealt with by section 31 of the Companies Act 1980), sections 99, 101 to 103, 106, 108, 110, 111 and 112 to 115 apply—

     (a)   to a company which has passed and not revoked a resolution to be re-registered under section 43 as a public company, and

     (b)   to a joint stock company which has passed, and not revoked, a resolution that the company be a public company,

as those sections apply to a public company.

PART V
SHARE CAPITAL, ITS INCREASE, MAINTENANCE AND REDUCTION

CHAPTER I
GENERAL PROVISIONS ABOUT SHARE CAPITAL

117.   **Public company share capital requirements**

(1)   A company registered as a public company on its original incorporation shall not do business or exercise any borrowing powers unless the registrar of companies has issued it with a certificate under this section or the company is re-registered as a private company.

(2)   The registrar shall issue a company with such a certificate if, on an application made to him by the company in the prescribed form, he is satisfied that the nominal value of the company's allotted share capital is not less than the authorised minimum, and there is delivered to him a statutory declaration complying with the following subsection.

     This subsection is subject to subsection (3A).

(3)   The statutory declaration must be in the prescribed form and be signed by a director or secretary of the company; and it must—

     (a)   state that the nominal value of the company's allotted share capital is not less than the authorised minimum;

     (b)   specify the amount paid up, at the time of the application, on the allotted share capital of the company;

     (c)   specify the amount, or estimated amount, of the company's preliminary expenses and the persons by whom any of those expenses have been paid or are payable; and

     (d)   specify any amount or benefit paid or given, or intended to be paid or given, to any promoter of the company, and the consideration for the payment or benefit.

(3A)   In place of the statutory declaration referred to in subsection (2), there may be delivered to the registrar of companies using electronic communications a statement made by a director or secretary of the company complying with the requirements of subsection (3)(a) to (d).

(4)   For the purposes of subsection (2), a share allotted in pursuance of an employees' share scheme may not be taken into account in determining the nominal value of the company's allotted share capital unless it is paid up at least as to one-quarter of the nominal value of the share and the whole of any premium on the share.

(5)   The registrar may accept a statutory declaration or statement delivered to him under this section as sufficient evidence of the matters stated in it.

(6)   A certificate under this section in respect of a company is conclusive evidence that the company is entitled to do business and exercise any borrowing powers.

(7)   If a company does business or exercises borrowing powers in contravention of this section, the company and any officer of it who is in default is liable to a fine.

(7A)   Any person who makes a false statement under subsection (3A) which he knows to be false or does not believe to be true is liable to imprisonment or a fine, or both.

(8)   Nothing in this section affects the validity of any transaction entered into by a company; but, if a company enters into a transaction in contravention of this section and fails to comply with its obligations in that connection within 21 days from being called upon to do so, the directors of the company are jointly and severally liable to indemnify the other party to the transaction in respect of any loss or damage suffered by him by reason of the company's failure to comply with those obligations.

118.   **The authorised minimum**

(1)   In this Act, "the authorised minimum" means £50,000, or such other sum as the Secretary of State may by order made by statutory instrument specify instead.

(2)   An order under this section which increases the authorised minimum may—

     (a)   require any public company having an allotted share capital of which the nominal value is less than the amount specified in the order as the authorised minimum to increase that value to not less than that amount or make application to be re-registered as a private company;

     (b)   make, in connection with any such requirement, provision for any of the matters from which provision is made by this Act relating to a company's registration, re-registration or change of name, to payment for any share comprised in a company's capital and to offers of shares in or debentures of a company to the public, including provision as to the consequences (whether in criminal law or otherwise) of a failure to comply with any requirement of the order; and

     (c)   contain such supplemental and transitional provisions as the Secretary of State thinks appropriate, make different provision for different cases and, in particular, provide for any provision of the order to come into operation on different days for different purposes.

(3)   An order shall not be made under this section unless a draft of it has been laid before Parliament and approved by resolution of each House.

119.   **Provision for different amounts to be paid on shares**

A company, if so authorised by its articles, may do any one or more of the following things—

     (a)   make arrangements on the issue of shares for a difference between the shareholders in the amounts and times of payment of calls on their shares;

     (b)   accept from any member the whole or a part of the amount remaining unpaid on any shares held by him, although no part of that amount has been called up;

     (c)   pay dividend in proportion to the amount paid up on each share where a larger amount is paid up on some shares than on others.

120.   **Reserve liability of limited company**

A limited company may by special resolution determine that any portion of its share capital which has not been already called up shall not be capable of being called up except in the event and for the purposes of the company being wound up; and that portion of its share capital is then not capable of being called up except in that event and for those purposes.

121.   **Alteration of share capital (limited companies)**

(1)   A company limited by shares or a company limited by guarantee and having a share capital, if so authorised by its articles, may alter the conditions of its memorandum in any of the following ways.

(2)   The company may—

     (a)   increase its share capital by new shares of such amount as it thinks expedient;

     (b)   consolidate and divide all or any of its share capital into shares of larger amount than its existing shares;

     (c)   convert all or any of its paid-up shares into stock, and re-convert that stock into paid-up shares of any denomination;

     (d)   sub-divide its shares, or any of them, into shares of smaller amount than is fixed by the memorandum (but subject to the following subsection);

(e)   cancel shares which, at the date of the passing of the resolution to cancel them, have not been taken or agreed to be taken by any person, and diminish the amount of the company's share capital by the amount of the shares so cancelled.

(3)   In any sub-division under subsection (2)(d) the proportion between the amount paid and the amount, if any, unpaid on each reduced share must be the same as it was in the case of the share from which the reduced share is derived.

(4)   The powers conferred by this section must be exercised by the company in general meeting.

(5)   A cancellation of shares under this section does not for purposes of this Act constitute a reduction of share capital.

122.   Notice to registrar of alteration

(1)   If a company having a share capital has—

    (a)   consolidated and divided its share capital into shares of larger amount than its existing shares; or

    (b)   converted any shares into stock; or

    (c)   re-converted stock into shares; or

    (d)   sub-divided its shares or any of them; or

    (e)   redeemed any redeemable shares; or

    (f)   cancelled any shares (otherwise than in connection with a reduction of share capital under section 135),

it shall within one month after so doing give notice in the prescribed form to the registrar of companies, specifying (as the case may be) the shares consolidated, divided, converted, sub-divided, redeemed or cancelled, or the stock re-converted.

(2)   If default is made in complying with this section, the company and every officer of it who is in default is liable to a fine and, for continued contravention, to a daily default fine.

123.   Notice to registrar of increased share capital

(1)   If a company having a share capital (whether or not its shares have been converted into stock) increases its share capital beyond the registered capital, it shall within 15 days after the passing of the resolution authorising the increase, give to the registrar of companies notice of the increase, and the registrar shall record the increase.

(2)   The notice must include such particulars as may be prescribed with respect to the classes of shares affected and the conditions subject to which the new shares have been or are to be issued.

(3)   There shall be forwarded to the registrar together with the notice a printed copy of the resolution authorising the increase, or a copy of the resolution in some other form approved by the registrar.

(4)   If default is made in complying with this section, the company and every officer of it who is in default is liable to a fine and, for continued contravention, to a daily default fine.

124.   Reserve capital of unlimited company

An unlimited company having a share capital may by its resolution for re-registration as a public company under section 43, or as a limited company under section 51—

    (a)   increase the nominal amount of its share capital by increasing the nominal amount of each of its shares (but subject to the condition that no part of the increased capital is to be capable of being called up except in the event and for the purpose of the company being wound up), and

    (b)   alternatively or in addition, provide that a specified portion of its uncalled share capital is not to be capable of being called up except in that event and for that purpose.

CHAPTER II
CLASS RIGHTS

125.   Variation of class rights

(1)   This section is concerned with the variation of the rights attached to any class of shares in a company whose share capital is divided into shares of different classes.

(2)   Where the rights are attached to a class of shares otherwise than by the company's memorandum, and the company's articles do not contain provision with respect to the variation of the rights, those rights may be varied if, but only if—

(a)   the holders of three-quarters in nominal value of the issued shares of that class (excluding any shares of that class held as treasury shares) consent in writing to the variation; or

(b)   an extraordinary resolution passed at a separate general meeting of the holders of that class sanctions the variation;

and any requirement (howsoever imposed) in relation to the variation of those rights is complied with to the extent that it is not comprised in paragraphs (a) and (b) above.

(3)   Where—

(a)   the rights are attached to a class of shares by the memorandum or otherwise;

(b)   the memorandum or articles contain provision for the variation of those rights; and

(c)   the variation of those rights is connected with the giving, variation, revocation or renewal of an authority for allotment under section 80 or with a reduction of the company's share capital under section 135;

those rights shall not be varied unless—

(i)   the condition mentioned in subsection (2)(a) or (b) above is satisfied; and

(ii)   any requirement of the memorandum or articles in relation to the variation of rights of that class is complied with to the extent that it is not comprised in that condition.

(4)   If the rights are attached to a class of shares in the company by the memorandum or otherwise and—

(a)   where they are so attached by the memorandum, the articles contain provision with respect to their variation which had been included in the articles at the time of the company's original incorporation; or

(b)   where they are so attached otherwise, the articles contain such provision (whenever first so included),

and in either case the variation is not connected as mentioned in subsection (3)(c), those rights may only be varied in accordance with that provision of the articles.

(5)   If the rights are attached to a class of shares by the memorandum, and the memorandum and articles do not contain provision with respect to the variation of those rights, those rights may be varied if all the members of the company (excluding any member holding shares as treasury shares) agree to the variation.

(6)   The provisions of section 369 (length of notice for calling company meetings), section 370 (general provisions as to meetings and votes), and sections 376 and 377 (circulation of members' resolutions) and the provisions of the articles relating to general meetings shall, so far as applicable, apply in relation to any meeting of shareholders required by this section or otherwise to take place in connection with the variation of the rights attached to a class of shares, and shall so apply with the necessary modifications and subject to the following provisions, namely—

(a)   the necessary quorum at any such meeting other than an adjourned meeting shall be two persons holding or representing by proxy at least one-third in nominal value of the issued shares of the class in question (excluding any shares of that class held as treasury shares) and at an adjourned meeting one person holding shares of the class in question or his proxy;

(b)   any holder of shares of the class in question present in person or by proxy may demand a poll.

(7)   Any alteration of a provision contained in a company's articles for the variation of the rights attached to a class of shares, or the insertion of any such provision into the articles, is itself to be treated as a variation of those rights.

(8)   In this section and (except where the context otherwise requires) in any provision for the variation of the rights attached to a class of shares contained in a company's memorandum or articles, references to the variation of those rights are to be read as including references to their abrogation.

126.   Saving for court's powers under other provisions

Nothing in subsections (2) to (5) of section 125 derogates from the powers of the court under the following sections of this Act, namely—

sections 4 to 6 (company resolution to alter objects),

section 54 (litigated objection to public company becoming private by re-registration),

section 425 (court control of company compromising with members and creditors),

section 427 (company reconstruction or amalgamation),

sections 459 to 461 (protection of minorities).

127.   Shareholders' right to object to variation

(1)   This section applies if, in the case of a company whose share capital is divided into different classes of shares—

    (a)   provision is made by the memorandum or articles for authorising the variation of the rights attached to any class of shares in the company, subject to—

        (i)   the consent of any specified proportion of the holders of the issued shares of that class, or

        (ii)   the sanction of a resolution passed at a separate meeting of the holders of those shares,

and in pursuance of that provision the rights attached to any such class of shares are at any time varied; or

    (b)   the rights attached to any class of shares in the company are varied under section 125(2).

(2)   The holders of not less in the aggregate than 15 per cent of the issued shares of the class in question (being persons who did not consent to or vote in favour of the resolution for the variation), may apply to the court to have the variation cancelled; and if such an application is made, the variation has no effect unless and until it is confirmed by the court.

(2A)   For the purposes of subsection (2), any of the company's issued share capital held as treasury shares must be disregarded.

(3)   Application to the court must be made within 21 days after the date on which the consent was given or the resolution was passed (as the case may be), and may be made on behalf of the shareholders entitled to make the application by such one or more of their number as they may appoint in writing for the purpose.

(4)   The court, after hearing the applicant and any other persons who apply to the court to be heard and appear to the court to be interested in the application, may, if satisfied having regard to all the circumstances of the case, that the variation would unfairly prejudice the shareholders of the class represented by the applicant, disallow the variation and shall, if not satisfied, confirm it.

The decision of the court on any such application is final.

(5)   The company shall within 15 days after the making of an order by the court on such an application forward a copy of the order to the registrar of companies; and, if default is made in complying with this provision, the company and every officer of it who is in default is liable to a fine and, for continued contravention, to a daily default fine.

(6)   "Variation", in this section, includes abrogation; and "varied" is to be construed accordingly.

128.   Registration of particulars of special rights

(1)   If a company allots shares with rights which are not stated in its memorandum or articles, or in any resolution or agreement which is required by section 380 to be sent to the registrar of companies, the company shall deliver to the registrar of companies, within one month from allotting the shares, a statement in the prescribed form containing particulars of those rights.

(2)   This does not apply if the shares are in all respects uniform with shares previously allotted; and shares are not for this purpose to be treated as different from shares previously allotted by reason only that the former do not carry the same rights to dividends as the latter during the 12 months immediately following the former's allotment.

(3)   Where the rights attached to any shares of a company are varied otherwise than by an amendment of the company's memorandum or articles or by a resolution or agreement subject to section 380,

the company shall within one month from the date on which the variation is made deliver to the registrar of companies a statement in the prescribed form containing particulars of the variation.

(4)   Where a company (otherwise than by any such amendment, resolution or agreement as is mentioned above) assigns a name or other designation, or a new name or other designation, to any class of its shares, it shall within one month from doing so deliver to the registrar of companies a notice in the prescribed form giving particulars of the name or designation so assigned.

(5)   If a company fails to comply with this section, the company and every officer of it who is in default is liable to a fine and, for continued contravention, to a daily default fine.

129.   Registration of newly created class rights

(1)   If a company not having a share capital creates a class of members with rights which are not stated in its memorandum or articles or in a resolution or agreement to which section 380 applies, the company shall deliver to the registrar of companies within one month from the date on which the new class is created a statement in the prescribed form containing particulars of the rights attached to that class.

(2)   If the rights of any class of members of the company are varied otherwise than by an amendment of the memorandum or articles or by a resolution or agreement subject to section 380, the company shall within one month from the date on which the variation is made deliver to the registrar a statement in the prescribed form containing particulars of the variation.

(3)   If a company (otherwise than by such an amendment, resolution or agreement as is mentioned above) assigns a name or other designation, or a new name or other designation, to any class of its members, it shall within one month from doing so deliver to the registrar a notice in the prescribed form giving particulars of the name or designation so assigned.

(4)   If a company fails to comply with this section, the company and every officer of it who is in default is liable to a fine and, for continued contravention, to a daily default fine.

CHAPTER III
SHARE PREMIUMS

130.   Application of share premiums

(1)   If a company issues shares at a premium, whether for cash or otherwise, a sum equal to the aggregate amount or value of the premiums on those shares shall be transferred to an account called "the share premium account".

(2)   The share premium account may be applied by the company in paying up unissued shares to be allotted to members as fully paid bonus shares, or in writing off—

(a)   the company's preliminary expenses; or

(b)   the expenses of, or the commission paid or discount allowed on, any issue of shares or debentures of the company,

or in providing for the premium payable on redemption of debentures of the company.

(3)   Subject to this, the provisions of this Act relating to the reduction of a company's share capital apply as if the share premium account were part of its paid up share capital.

(4)   Sections 131 and 132 below give relief from the requirements of this section, and in those sections references to the issuing company are to the company issuing shares as above mentioned.

131.   Merger relief

(1)   With the exception made by section 132(8) (group reconstruction) this section applies where the issuing company has secured at least a 90 per cent equity holding in another company in pursuance of an arrangement providing for the allotment of equity shares in the issuing company on terms that the consideration for the shares allotted is to be provided—

(a)   by the issue or transfer to the issuing company of equity shares in the other company, or

(b)   by the cancellation of any such shares not held by the issuing company.

(2)   If the equity shares in the issuing company allotted in pursuance of the arrangement in consideration for the acquisition or cancellation of equity shares in the other company are issued at a premium, section 130 does not apply to the premiums on those shares.

(3)   Where the arrangement also provides for the allotment of any shares in the issuing company on terms that the consideration for those shares is to be provided by the issue or transfer to the issuing company of non-equity shares in the other company or by the cancellation of any such shares in that company not held by the issuing company, relief under subsection (2) extends to any shares in the issuing company allotted on those terms in pursuance of the arrangement.

(4)   Subject to the next subsection, the issuing company is to be regarded for purposes of this section as having secured at least a 90 per cent equity holding in another company in pursuance of such an arrangement as is mentioned in subsection (1) if in consequence of an acquisition or cancellation of equity shares in that company (in pursuance of that arrangement) it holds equity shares in that company (whether all or any of those shares were acquired in pursuance of that arrangement, or not) of an aggregate nominal value equal to 90 per cent or more of the nominal value of that company's equity share capital (excluding any shares in that company held as treasury shares).

(5)   Where the equity share capital of the other company is divided into different classes of shares, this section does not apply unless the requirements of subsection (1) are satisfied in relation to each of those classes of shares taken separately.

(6)   Shares held by a company which is the issuing company's holding company or subsidiary, or a subsidiary of the issuing company's holding company, or by its or their nominees, are to be regarded for purposes of this section as held by the issuing company.

(7)   In relation to a company and its shares and capital, the following definitions apply for purposes of this section—
        (a)   "equity shares" means shares comprised in the company's equity share capital; and
        (b)   "non-equity shares" means shares (of any class) not so comprised;
        and "arrangement" means any agreement, scheme or arrangement (including an arrangement sanctioned under section 425 (company compromise with members and creditors) or section 110 of the Insolvency Act (liquidator accepting shares etc as consideration for sale of company property)).

(8)   The relief allowed by this section does not apply if the issue of shares took place before 4th February 1981.

132.   Relief in respect of group reconstructions

(1)   This section applies where the issuing company—
        (a)   is a wholly-owned subsidiary of another company ("the holding company"), and
        (b)   allots shares to the holding company or to another wholly-owned subsidiary of the holding company in consideration for the transfer to the issuing company of assets other than cash, being assets of any company ("the transferor company") which is a member of the group of companies which comprises the holding company and all its wholly-owned subsidiaries.

(2)   Where the shares in the issuing company allotted in consideration for the transfer are issued at a premium, the issuing company is not required by section 130 to transfer any amount in excess of the minimum premium value to the share premium account.

(3)   In subsection (2), "the minimum premium value" means the amount (if any) by which the base value of the consideration for the shares allotted exceeds the aggregate nominal value of those shares.

(4)   For the purposes of subsection (3), the base value of the consideration for the shares allotted is the amount by which the base value of the assets transferred exceeds the base value of any liabilities of the transferor company assumed by the issuing company as part of the consideration for the assets transferred.

(5)   For the purposes of subsection (4)—
        (a)   the base value of assets transferred is to be taken as—
               (i)   the cost of those assets to the transferor company, or
               (ii)   the amount at which those assets are stated in the transferor company's accounting records immediately before the transfer,
               whichever is the less; and

(b) the base value of the liabilities assumed is to be taken as the amount at which they are stated in the transferor company's accounting records immediately before the transfer.

(6)   The relief allowed by this section does not apply (subject to the next subsection) if the issue of shares took place before the date of the coming into force of the Companies (Share Premium Account) Regulations 1984 (which were made on 21st December 1984).

(7)   To the extent that the relief allowed by this section would have been allowed by section 38 of the Companies Act 1981 as originally enacted (the text of which section is set out in Schedule 25 to this Act), the relief applies where the issue of shares took place before the date of the coming into force of those Regulations, but not if the issue took place before 4th February 1981.

(8)   Section 131 does not apply in a case falling within this section.

133.   Provisions supplementing ss 131, 132

(1)   An amount corresponding to one representing the premiums or part of the premiums on shares issued by a company which by virtue of sections 131 or 132 of this Act, or section 12 of the Consequential Provisions Act, is not included in the company's share premium account may also be disregarded in determining the amount at which any shares or other consideration provided for the shares issued is to be included in the company's balance sheet.

(2)   References in this Chapter (however expressed) to—
(a)   the acquisition by a company of shares in another company; and
(b)   the issue or allotment of shares to, or the transfer of shares to or by, a company,
include (respectively) the acquisition of any of those shares by, and the issue or allotment or (as the case may be) the transfer of any of those shares to or by, nominees of that company; and the reference in section 132 to the company transferring the shares is to be construed accordingly.

(3)   References in this Chapter to the transfer of shares in a company include the transfer of a right to be included in the company's register of members in respect of those shares.

(4)   In sections 131 to 133 "company", except in references to the issuing company, includes any body corporate.

134.   Provision for extending or restricting relief from s 130

(1)   The Secretary of State may by regulations in a statutory instrument make such provision as appears to him to be appropriate—
(a)   for relieving companies from the requirements of section 130 in relation to premiums other than cash premiums, or
(b)   for restricting or otherwise modifying any relief from those requirements provided by this Chapter.

(2)   Regulations under this section may make different provision for different cases or classes of case and may contain such incidental and supplementary provisions as the Secretary of State thinks fit.

(3)   No such regulations shall be made unless a draft of the instrument containing them has been laid before Parliament and approved by a resolution of each House.

CHAPTER IV
REDUCTION OF SHARE CAPITAL

135.   Special resolution for reduction of share capital

(1)   Subject to confirmation by the court, a company limited by shares or a company limited by guarantee and having a share capital may, if so authorised by its articles, by special resolution reduce its share capital in any way.

(2)   In particular, and without prejudice to subsection (1), the company may—
(a)   extinguish or reduce the liability on any of its shares in respect of share capital not paid up; or
(b)   either with or without extinguishing or reducing liability on any of its shares, cancel any paid-up share capital which is lost or unrepresented by available assets; or
(c)   either with or without extinguishing or reducing liability on any of its shares, pay off any paid-up share capital which is in excess of the company's wants;

and the company may, if and so far as is necessary, alter its memorandum by reducing the amount of its share capital and of its shares accordingly.

(3)   A special resolution under this section is in this Act referred to as "a resolution for reducing share capital".

136.   Application to court for order of confirmation

(1)   Where a company has passed a resolution for reducing share capital, it may apply to the court for an order confirming the reduction.

(2)   If the proposed reduction of share capital involves either—

    (a)   diminution of liability in respect of unpaid share capital; or

    (b)   the payment to a shareholder of any paid-up share capital,

and in any other case if the court so directs, the next three subsections have effect, but subject throughout to subsection (6).

(3)   Every creditor of the company who at the date fixed by the court is entitled to any debt or claim which, if that date were the commencement of the winding up of the company, would be admissible in proof against the company is entitled to object to the reduction of capital.

(4)   The court shall settle a list of creditors entitled to object, and for that purpose—

    (a)   shall ascertain, as far as possible without requiring an application from any creditor, the names of those creditors and the nature and amount of their debts or claims; and

    (b)   may publish notices fixing a day or days within which creditors not entered on the list are to claim to be so entered or are to be excluded from the right of objecting to the reduction of capital.

(5)   If a creditor entered on the list whose debt or claim is not discharged or has not determined does not consent to the reduction, the court may, if it thinks fit, dispense with the consent of that creditor, on the company securing payment of his debt or claim by appropriating (as the court may direct) the following amount—

    (a)   if the company admits the full amount of the debt or claim or, though not admitting it, is willing to provide for it, then the full amount of the debt or claim;

    (b)   if the company does not admit, and is not willing to provide for, the full amount of the debt or claim, or if the amount is contingent or not ascertained, then an amount fixed by the court after the like enquiry and adjudication as if the company were being wound up by the court.

(6)   If a proposed reduction of share capital involves either the diminution of any liability in respect of unpaid share capital or the payment to any shareholder of any paid-up share capital, the court may, if having regard to any special circumstances of the case it thinks proper to do so, direct that subsections (3) to (5) of this section shall not apply as regards any class or any classes of creditors.

137.   Court order confirming reduction

(1)   The court, if satisfied with respect to every creditor of the company who under section 136 is entitled to object to the reduction of capital that either—

    (a)   his consent to the reduction has been obtained; or

    (b)   his debt or claim has been discharged or has determined, or has been secured,

may make an order confirming the reduction on such terms and conditions as it thinks fit.

(2)   Where the court so orders, it may also—

    (a)   if for any special reason it thinks proper to do so, make an order directing that the company shall, during such period (commencing on or at any time after the date of the order) as is specified in the order, add to its name as its last words the words "and reduced"; and

    (b)   make an order requiring the company to publish (as the court directs) the reasons for reduction of capital or such other information in regard to it as the court thinks expedient with a view to giving proper information to the public and (if the court thinks fit) the causes which led to the reduction.

(3)   Where a company is ordered to add to its name the words "and reduced", those words are, until the expiration of the period specified in the order, deemed to be part of the company's name.

138.   Registration of order and minute of reduction

(1)   The registrar of companies, on production to him of an order of the court confirming the reduction of a company's share capital, and the delivery to him of a copy of the order and of a minute (approved by the court) showing, with respect to the company's share capital as altered by the order—

    (a)   the amount of the share capital;

    (b)   the number of shares into which it is to be divided, and the amount of each share; and

    (c)   the amount (if any) at the date of the registration deemed to be paid up on each share,

    shall register the order and minute (but subject to section 139).

(2)   On the registration of the order and minute, and not before, the resolution for reducing share capital as confirmed by the order so registered takes effect.

(3)   Notice of the registration shall be published in such manner as the court may direct.

(4)   The registrar shall certify the registration of the order and minute; and the certificate—

    (a)   may be either signed by the registrar, or authenticated by his official seal;

    (b)   is conclusive evidence that all the requirements of this Act with respect to the reduction of share capital have been complied with, and that the company's share capital is as stated in the minute.

(5)   The minute when registered is deemed to be substituted for the corresponding part of the company's memorandum, and is valid and alterable as if it had been originally contained therein.

(6)   The substitution of such a minute for part of the company's memorandum is deemed an alteration of the memorandum for purposes of section 20.

139.   Public company reducing capital below authorised minimum

(1)   This section applies where the court makes an order confirming a reduction of a public company's capital which has the effect of bringing the nominal value of its allotted share capital below the authorised minimum.

(2)   The registrar of companies shall not register the order under section 138 unless the court otherwise directs, or the company is first re-registered as a private company.

(3)   The court may authorise the company to be so re-registered without its having passed the special resolution required by section 53; and where that authority is given, the court shall specify in the order the alterations in the company's memorandum and articles to be made in connection with that re-registration.

(4)   The company may then be re-registered as a private company, if an application in the prescribed form and signed by a director or secretary of the company is delivered to the registrar, together with a printed copy of the memorandum and articles as altered by the court's order.

(5)   On receipt of such an application, the registrar shall retain it and the other documents delivered with it and issue the company with a certificate of incorporation appropriate to a company that is not a public company; and—

    (a)   the company by virtue of the issue of the certificate becomes a private company, and the alterations in the memorandum and articles set out in the court's order take effect; and

    (b)   the certificate is conclusive evidence that the requirements of this section in respect of re-registration and of matters precedent and incidental thereto have been complied with, and that the company is a private company.

140.   Liability of members on reduced shares

(1)   Where a company's share capital is reduced, a member of the company (past or present) is not liable in respect of any share to any call or contribution exceeding in amount the difference (if any) between the amount of the share as fixed by the minute and the amount paid on the share or the reduced amount (if any), which is deemed to have been paid on it, as the case may be.

(2)   But the following two subsections apply if—

    (a)   a creditor, entitled in respect of a debt or claim to object to the reduction of share capital, by reason of his ignorance of the proceedings for reduction of share capital, or of their nature and effect with respect to his claim, is not entered on the list of creditors; and

(b)   after the reduction of capital, the company is unable (within the meaning of section 123 of the Insolvency Act) to pay the amount of his debt or claim.

(3)   Every person who was a member of the company at the date of the registration of the order for reduction and minute is then liable to contribute for the payment of the debt or claim in question an amount not exceeding that which he would have been liable to contribute if the company had commenced to be wound up on the day before that date.

(4)   If the company is wound up, the court, on the application of the creditor in question and proof of ignorance referred to in subsection (2)(a), may (if it thinks fit) settle accordingly a list of persons so liable to contribute, and make and enforce calls and orders on the contributories settled on the list, as if they were ordinary contributories in a winding up.

(5)   Nothing in this section affects the rights of the contributories among themselves.

141.   Penalty for concealing name of creditor, etc

If an officer of the company—

(a)   wilfully conceals the name of a creditor entitled to object to the reduction of capital; or

(b)   wilfully misrepresents the nature or amount of the debt or claim of any creditor; or

(c)   aids, abets or is privy to any such concealment or misrepresentation as is mentioned above,

he is guilty of an offence and liable to a fine.

CHAPTER V
MAINTENANCE OF CAPITAL

142.   Duty of directors on serious loss of capital

(1)   Where the net assets of a public company are half or less of its called-up share capital, the directors shall, not later than 28 days from the earliest day on which that fact is known to a director of the company, duly convene an extraordinary general meeting of the company for a date not later than 56 days from that day for the purpose of considering whether any, and if so what, steps should be taken to deal with the situation.

(2)   If there is a failure to convene an extraordinary general meeting as required by subsection (1), each of the directors of the company who—

(a)   knowingly and wilfully authorises or permits the failure, or

(b)   after the expiry of the period during which that meeting should have been convened, knowingly and wilfully authorises or permits the failure to continue,

is liable to a fine.

(3)   Nothing in this section authorises the consideration, at a meeting convened in pursuance of subsection (1), of any matter which could not have been considered at that meeting apart from this section.

143.   General rule against company acquiring own shares

(1)   Subject to the following provisions, a company limited by shares or limited by guarantee and having a share capital shall not acquire its own shares, whether by purchase, subscription or otherwise.

(2)   If a company purports to act in contravention of this section, the company is liable to a fine, and every officer of the company who is in default is liable to imprisonment or a fine, or both; and, subject to subsection (2A), the purported acquisition is void.

(2A)   Where a company purchases qualifying shares out of distributable profits under section 162, any contravention by the company of any provision of section 162B(1) or (2) shall not render the acquisition void under subsection (2) above.

(3)   A company limited by shares may acquire any of its own fully paid shares otherwise than for valuable consideration; and subsection (1) does not apply in relation to—

(a)   the redemption or purchase of shares in accordance with Chapter VII of this Part,

(b)   the acquisition of shares in a reduction of capital duly made,

(c) the purchase of shares in pursuance of an order of the court under section 5 (alteration of objects), section 54 (litigated objection to resolution for company to be re-registered as private) or Part XVII (relief to members unfairly prejudiced), or

(d) the forfeiture of shares, or the acceptance of shares surrendered in lieu, in pursuance of the articles, for failure to pay any sum payable in respect of the shares.

144. Acquisition of shares by company's nominee

(1) Subject to section 145, where shares are issued to a nominee of a company mentioned in section 143(1), or are acquired by a nominee of such a company from a third person as partly paid up, then, for all purposes—

(a) the shares are to be treated as held by the nominee on his own account; and

(b) the company is to be regarded as having no beneficial interest in them.

(2) Subject to that section, if a person is called on to pay any amount for the purpose of paying up, or paying any premium on, any shares in such a company which were issued to him, or which he otherwise acquired, as the company's nominee and he fails to pay that amount within 21 days from being called on to do so, then—

(a) if the shares were issued to him as subscriber to the memorandum by virtue of an undertaking of his in the memorandum, the other subscribers to the memorandum, or

(b) if the shares were otherwise issued to or acquired by him, the directors of the company at the time of the issue or acquisition,

are jointly and severally liable with him to pay that amount.

(3) If in proceedings for the recovery of any such amount from any such subscriber or director under this section it appears to the court—

(a) that he is or may be liable to pay that amount, but

(b) that he has acted honestly and reasonably and, having regard to all the circumstances of the case, he ought fairly to be excused from liability,

the court may relieve him, either wholly or partly, from his liability on such terms as the court thinks fit.

(4) Where any such subscriber or director has reason to apprehend that a claim will or might be made for the recovery of any such amount from him, he may apply to the court for relief; and the court has the same power to relieve him as it would have had in proceedings for the recovery of that amount.

145. Exceptions from s 144

(1) Section 144(1) does not apply to shares acquired otherwise than by subscription by a nominee of a public company, where a person acquires shares in the company with financial assistance given to him directly or indirectly by the company for the purpose of or in connection with the acquisition, and the company has a beneficial interest in the shares.

(2) Section 144(1) and (2) do not apply—

(a) to shares acquired by a nominee of a company when the company has no beneficial interest in those shares, or

(b) to shares issued in consequence of an application made before 22nd December 1980, or transferred in pursuance of an agreement to acquire them made before that date.

(3) Schedule 2 to this Act has effect for the interpretation of references in this section to a company having, or not having, a beneficial interest in shares.

146. Treatment of shares held by or for public company

(1) Except as provided by section 148, the following applies to a public company—

(a) where shares in the company are forfeited, or surrendered to the company in lieu, in pursuance of the articles, for failure to pay any sum payable in respect of the shares;

(aa) where shares in the company are surrendered to the company in pursuance of section 102C(1)(b) of the Building Societies Act 1986;

(b)   where shares in the company are acquired by it (otherwise than by any of the methods mentioned in section 143(3)(a) to (d)) and the company has a beneficial interest in the shares;

(c)   where the nominee of the company acquires shares in the company from a third person without financial assistance being given directly or indirectly by the company and the company has a beneficial interest in the shares; or

(d)   where a person acquires shares in the company with financial assistance given to him directly or indirectly by the company for the purpose of or in connection with the acquisition, and the company has a beneficial interest in the shares.

Schedule 2 to this Act has effect for the interpretation of references in this subsection to the company having a beneficial interest in shares.

(2)   Unless the shares or any interest of the company in them are previously disposed of, the company must, not later than the end of the relevant period from their forfeiture or surrender or, in a case within subsection (1)(b), (c) or (d), their acquisition—

(a)   cancel them and diminish the amount of the share capital by the nominal value of the shares cancelled, and

(b)   where the effect of cancelling the shares will be that the nominal value of the company's allotted share capital is brought below the authorised minimum, apply for re-registration as a private company, stating the effect of the cancellation.

(3)   For this purpose "the relevant period" is—

(a)   3 years in the case of shares forfeited or surrendered to the company in lieu of forfeiture, or acquired as mentioned in subsection (1)(b) or (c);

(b)   one year in the case of shares acquired as mentioned in subsection (1)(d).

(4)   The company and, in a case within subsection (1)(c) or (d), the company's nominee or (as the case may be) the other shareholder must not exercise any voting rights in respect of the shares; and any purported exercise of those rights is void.

147.   Matters arising out of compliance with s 146(2)

(1)   The directors may take such steps as are requisite to enable the company to carry out its obligations under section 146(2) without complying with sections 135 and 136 (resolution to reduce share capital; application to court for approval).

(2)   The steps taken may include the passing of a resolution to alter the company's memorandum so that it no longer states that the company is to be a public company; and the resolution may make such other alterations in the memorandum as are requisite in the circumstances.

Such a resolution is subject to section 380 (copy to be forwarded to registrar within 15 days).

(3)   The application for re-registration required by section 146(2)(b) must be in the prescribed form and be signed by a director or secretary of the company, and must be delivered to the registrar of companies together with a printed copy of the memorandum and articles of the company as altered by the resolution.

(4)   If the registrar is satisfied that the company may be re-registered under section 146, he shall retain the application and other documents delivered with it and issue the company with a certificate of incorporation appropriate to a company that is not a public company; and—

(a)   the company by virtue of the issue of the certificate becomes a private company, and the alterations in the memorandum and articles set out in the resolution take effect accordingly, and

(b)   the certificate is conclusive evidence that the requirements of sections 146 to 148 in respect of re-registration and of matters precedent and incidental to it have been complied with, and that the company is a private company.

148.   Further provisions supplementing ss 146, 147

(1)   Where, after shares in a private company—

(a)   are forfeited in pursuance of the company's articles or are surrendered to the company in lieu of forfeiture, or

(b)   are acquired by the company (otherwise than by such surrender or forfeiture, and otherwise than by any of the methods mentioned in section 143(3)), the company having a beneficial interest in the shares, or

(c)   are acquired by the nominee of a company in the circumstances mentioned in section 146(1)(c), or

(d)   are acquired by any person in the circumstances mentioned in section 146(1)(d),

the company is re-registered as a public company, sections 146 and 147, and also section 149, apply to the company as if it had been a public company at the time of the forfeiture, surrender or acquisition, but with the modification required by the following subsection.

(2)   That modification is to treat any reference to the relevant period from the forfeiture, surrender or acquisition as referring to the relevant period from the re-registration of the company as a public company.

(3)   Schedule 2 to this Act has effect for the interpretation of the reference in subsection (1)(b) to the company having a beneficial interest in shares.

(4)   Where a public company or a nominee of a public company acquires shares in the company or an interest in such shares, and those shares are (or that interest is) shown in a balance sheet of the company as an asset, an amount equal to the value of the shares or (as the case may be) the value to the company of its interest in them shall be transferred out of profits available for dividend to a reserve fund and are not then available for distribution.

149.   Sanctions for non-compliance

(1)   If a public company required by section 146(2) to apply to be re-registered as a private company fails to do so before the end of the relevant period referred to in that subsection, section 81 (restriction on public offers) applies to it as if it were a private company such as is mentioned in that section; but, subject to this, the company continues to be treated for the purpose of this Act as a public company until it is so re-registered.

(2)   If a company when required to do so by section 146(2) (including that subsection as applied by section 148(1)) fails to cancel any shares in accordance with paragraph (a) of that subsection or to make an application for re-registration in accordance with paragraph (b) of it, the company and every officer of it who is in default is liable to a fine and, for continued contravention, to a daily default fine.

150.   Charges of public companies on own shares

(1)   A lien or other charge of a public company on its own shares (whether taken expressly or otherwise), except a charge permitted by any of the following subsections, is void.

This is subject to section 6 of the Consequential Provisions Act (saving for charges of old public companies on their own shares).

(2)   In the case of any description of company, a charge on its own shares is permitted if the shares are not fully paid and the charge is for any amount payable in respect of the shares.

(3)   In the case of a company whose ordinary business—

(a)   includes the lending of money, or

(b)   consists of the provision of credit or the bailment (in Scotland, hiring) of goods under a hire purchase agreement, or both,

a charge of the company on its own shares is permitted (whether the shares are fully paid or not) if it arises in connection with a transaction entered into by the company in the ordinary course of its business.

(4)   In the case of a company which is re-registered or is registered under section 680 as a public company, a charge on its own shares is permitted if the charge was in existence immediately before the company's application for re-registration or (as the case may be) registration.

This subsection does not apply in the case of such a company as is referred to in section 6(3) of the Consequential Provisions Act (old public company remaining such after 22nd March 1982, not having applied to be re-registered as public company).

CHAPTER VI
FINANCIAL ASSISTANCE BY A COMPANY FOR ACQUISITION OF ITS OWN SHARES

Provisions applying to both public and private companies

151.   Financial assistance generally prohibited

(1)   Subject to the following provisions of this Chapter, where a person is acquiring or is proposing to acquire shares in a company, it is not lawful for the company or any of its subsidiaries to give financial assistance directly or indirectly for the purpose of that acquisition before or at the same time as the acquisition takes place.

(2)   Subject to those provisions, where a person has acquired shares in a company and any liability has been incurred (by that or any other person), for the purpose of that acquisition, it is not lawful for the company or any of its subsidiaries to give financial assistance directly or indirectly for the purpose of reducing or discharging the liability so incurred.

(3)   If a company acts in contravention of this section, it is liable to a fine, and every officer of it who is in default is liable to imprisonment or a fine, or both.

152.   Definitions for this Chapter

(1)   In this Chapter—

    (a)   "financial assistance" means—

        (i)   financial assistance given by way of gift,

        (ii)   financial assistance given by way of guarantee, security or indemnity, other than an indemnity in respect of the indemnifier's own neglect or default, or by way of release or waiver,

        (iii)   financial assistance given by way of a loan or any other agreement under which any of the obligations of the person giving the assistance are to be fulfilled at a time when in accordance with the agreement any obligation of another party to the agreement remains unfulfilled, or by way of the novation of, or the assignment of rights arising under, a loan or such other agreement, or

        (iv)   any other financial assistance given by a company the net assets of which are thereby reduced to a material extent or which has no net assets;

    (b)   "distributable profits", in relation to the giving of any financial assistance—

        (i)   means those profits out of which the company could lawfully make a distribution equal in value to that assistance, and

        (ii)   includes, in a case where the financial assistance is or includes a non-cash asset, any profit which, if the company were to make a distribution of that asset, would under section 276 (distributions in kind) be available for that purpose, and

    (c)   "distribution" has the meaning given by section 263(2).

(2)   In subsection (1)(a)(iv), "net assets" means the aggregate of the company's assets, less the aggregate of its liabilities ("liabilities" to include any provision for liabilities within paragraph 89 of Schedule 4) that is made in Companies Act individual accounts and any provision that is made in IAS individual accounts.

(3)   In this Chapter—

    (a)   a reference to a person incurring a liability includes his changing his financial position by making an agreement or arrangement (whether enforceable or unenforceable, and whether made on his own account or with any other person) or by any other means, and

    (b)   a reference to a company giving financial assistance for the purpose of reducing or discharging a liability incurred by a person for the purpose of the acquisition of shares includes its giving such assistance for the purpose of wholly or partly restoring his financial position to what it was before the acquisition took place.

153.   Transactions not prohibited by s 151

(1)   Section 151(1) does not prohibit a company from giving financial assistance for the purpose of an acquisition of shares in it or its holding company if—

    (a)   the company's principal purpose in giving that assistance is not to give it for the purpose of any such acquisition, or the giving of the assistance for that purpose is but an incidental part of some larger purpose of the company, and

    (b)   the assistance is given in good faith in the interests of the company.

(2)   Section 151(2) does not prohibit a company from giving financial assistance if—

    (a)   the company's principal purpose in giving the assistance is not to reduce or discharge any liability incurred by a person for the purpose of the acquisition of shares in the company or its holding company, or the reduction or discharge of any such liability is but an incidental part of some larger purpose of the company, and

    (b)   the assistance is given in good faith in the interests of the company.

(3)   Section 151 does not prohibit—

    (a)   a distribution of a company's assets by way of dividend lawfully made or a distribution made in the course of the company's winding up,

    (b)   the allotment of bonus shares,

    (c)   a reduction of capital confirmed by order of the court under section 137,

    (d)   a redemption or purchase of shares made in accordance with Chapter VII of this Part,

    (e)   anything done in pursuance of an order of the court under section 425 (compromises and arrangements with creditors and members),

    (f)   anything done under an arrangement made in pursuance of section 110 of the Insolvency Act (acceptance of shares by liquidator in winding up as consideration for sale of property), or

    (g)   anything done under an arrangement made between a company and its creditors which is binding on the creditors by virtue of Part I of the Insolvency Act.

(4)   Section 151 does not prohibit—

    (a)   where the lending of money is part of the ordinary business of the company, the lending of money by the company in the ordinary course of its business,

    (b)   the provision by a company, in good faith in the interests of the company, of financial assistance for the purposes of an employees' share scheme,

    (bb)   without prejudice to paragraph (b), the provision of financial assistance by a company or any of its subsidiaries for the purposes of or in connection with anything done by the company (or a company in the same group) for the purpose of enabling or facilitating transactions in shares in the first-mentioned company between, and involving the acquisition of beneficial ownership of those shares by, any of the following persons—

        (i)   the bona fide employees or former employees of that company or of another company in the same group; or

        (ii)   the wives, husbands, widows, widowers, children or step-children under the age of eighteen of any such employees or former employees,

    (c)   the making by a company of loans to persons (other than directors) employed in good faith by the company with a view to enabling those persons to acquire fully paid shares in the company or its holding company to be held by them by way of beneficial ownership.

(5)   For the purposes of subsection (4)(bb) a company is in the same group as another company if it is a holding company or subsidiary of that company, or a subsidiary of a holding company of that company.

154.   Special restriction for public companies

(1)   In the case of a public company, section 153(4) authorises the giving of financial assistance only if the company has net assets which are not thereby reduced or, to the extent that those assets are thereby reduced, if the assistance is provided out of distributable profits.

(2)   For this purpose the following definitions apply—

    (a)   "net assets" means the amount by which the aggregate of the company's assets exceeds the aggregate of its liabilities (taking the amount of both assets and liabilities to be as stated in the company's accounting records immediately before the financial assistance is given);

(b) "liabilities" includes any amount retained as reasonably necessary for the purpose of providing for any liability the nature of which is clearly defined and which is either likely to be incurred, or certain to be incurred but uncertain as to amount or as to the date on which it will arise.

Private companies

155. Relaxation of s 151 for private companies

(1) Section 151 does not prohibit a private company from giving financial assistance in a case where the acquisition of shares in question is or was an acquisition of shares in the company or, if it is a subsidiary of another private company, in that other company if the following provisions of this section, and sections 156 to 158, are complied with as respects the giving of that assistance.

(2) The financial assistance may only be given if the company has net assets which are not thereby reduced or, to the extent that they are reduced, if the assistance is provided out of distributable profits.
Section 154(2) applies for the interpretation of this subsection.

(3) This section does not permit financial assistance to be given by a subsidiary, in a case where the acquisition of shares in question is or was an acquisition of shares in its holding company, if it is also a subsidiary of a public company which is itself a subsidiary of that holding company.

(4) Unless the company proposing to give the financial assistance is a wholly-owned subsidiary, the giving of assistance under this section must be approved by special resolution of the company in general meeting.

(5) Where the financial assistance is to be given by the company in a case where the acquisition of shares in question is or was an acquisition of shares in its holding company, that holding company and any other company which is both the company's holding company and a subsidiary of that other holding company (except, in any case, a company which is a wholly-owned subsidiary) shall also approve by special resolution in general meeting the giving of the financial assistance.

(6) Subject to subsection (6A), the directors of the company proposing to give the financial assistance and, where the shares acquired or to be acquired are shares in its holding company, the directors of that company and of any other company which is both the company's holding company and a subsidiary of that other holding company shall before the financial assistance is given make a statutory declaration in the prescribed form complying with the section next following.

(6A) In place of the statutory declaration referred to in subsection (6), there may be delivered to the registrar of companies under section 156(5) a statement made by the persons mentioned in subsection (6) above complying with the section next following.

156. Statutory declaration under s 155

(1) A statutory declaration made by a company's directors under section 155(6) shall contain such particulars of the financial assistance to be given, and of the business of the company of which they are directors, as may be prescribed, and shall identify the person to whom the assistance is to be given.

(1A) A statement made by a company's directors under section 155(6A) shall state—
(a) the names and addresses of all the directors of the company,
(b) whether the business of the company is that of a banking company or insurance company or some other business,
(c) that the company or (as the case may be) a company (naming such company) of which it is the holding company is proposing to give financial assistance in connection with the acquisition of shares in the company or (as the case may be) its holding company (naming that holding company),
(d) whether the assistance is for the purpose of that acquisition or for reducing or discharging a liability incurred for the purpose of that acquisition,
(e) the name and address of the person to whom the assistance is to be given (and in the case of a company its registered office),

(f)   the name of the person who has acquired or will acquire the shares and the number and class of the shares acquired or to be acquired,

(g)   the principal terms on which the assistance will be given,

(h)   the form the financial assistance will take (stating the amount of cash or value of any asset to be transferred to the person assisted), and

(i)   the date on which the assistance is to be given.

(2)   The declaration under section 155(6) or (as the case may be) statement under section 155(6A) shall state that the directors have formed the opinion, as regards the company's initial situation immediately following the date on which the assistance is proposed to be given, that there will be no ground on which it could then be found to be unable to pay its debts; and either—

(a)   if it is intended to commence the winding up of the company within 12 months of that date, that the company will be able to pay its debts in full within 12 months of the commencement of the winding up, or

(b)   in any other case, that the company will be able to pay its debts as they fall due during the year immediately following that date.

(3)   In forming their opinion for purposes of subsection (2), the directors shall take into account the same liabilities (including contingent and prospective liabilities) as would be relevant under section 122 of the Insolvency Act (winding up by the court) to the question whether the company is unable to pay its debts.

(4)   The directors' statutory declaration or statement shall have annexed to it a report addressed to them by their company's auditors stating that—

(a)   they have enquired into the state of affairs of the company, and

(b)   they are not aware of anything to indicate that the opinion expressed by the directors in the declaration or statement as to any of the matters mentioned in subsection (2) of this section is unreasonable in all the circumstances.

(5)   The statutory declaration or statement and auditors' report shall be delivered to the registrar of companies—

(a)   together with a copy of any special resolution passed by the company under section 155 and delivered to the registrar in compliance with section 380, or

(b)   where no such resolution is required to be passed, within 15 days after the making of the declaration or statement.

(6)   If a company fails to comply with subsection (5), the company and every officer of it who is in default is liable to a fine and, for continued contravention, to a daily default fine.

(7)   A director of a company who makes a statutory declaration or statement under section 155 without having reasonable grounds for the opinion expressed in it is liable to imprisonment or a fine, or both.

157.   Special resolution under s 155

(1)   A special resolution required by section 155 to be passed by a company approving the giving of financial assistance must be passed on the date on which the directors of that company make the statutory declaration or statement required by that section in connection with the giving of that assistance, or within the week immediately following that date.

(2)   Where such a resolution has been passed, an application may be made to the court for the cancellation of the resolution—

(a)   by the holders of not less in the aggregate than 10 per cent in nominal value of the company's issued share capital or any class of it, or

(b)   if the company is not limited by shares, by not less than 10 per cent of the company's members;

but the application shall not be made by a person who has consented to or voted in favour of the resolution.

(3)   Subsections (3) to (10) of section 54 (litigation to cancel resolution under section 53) apply to applications under this section as to applications under section 54.

(4)   A special resolution passed by a company is not effective for purposes of section 155—

    (a)   unless the declaration or statement made in compliance with subsection (6) of that section by the directors of the company, together with the auditors' report annexed to it, is available for inspection by members of the company at the meeting at which the resolution is passed,

    (b)   if it is cancelled by the court on an application under this section.

158.   **Time for giving financial assistance under s 155**

(1)   This section applies as to the time before and after which financial assistance may not be given by a company in pursuance of section 155.

(2)   Where a special resolution is required by that section to be passed approving the giving of the assistance, the assistance shall not be given before the expiry of the period of 4 weeks beginning with—

    (a)   the date on which the special resolution is passed, or

    (b)   where more than one such resolution is passed, the date on which the last of them is passed,

unless, as respects that resolution (or, if more than one, each of them), every member of the company which passed the resolution who is entitled to vote at general meetings of the company voted in favour of the resolution.

(3)   If application for the cancellation of any such resolution is made under section 157, the financial assistance shall not be given before the final determination of the application unless the court otherwise orders.

(4)   The assistance shall not be given after the expiry of the period of 8 weeks beginning with—

    (a)   the date on which the directors of the company proposing to give the assistance made their statutory declaration or statement under section 155, or

    (b)   where that company is a subsidiary and both its directors and the directors of any of its holding companies made such a declaration or statement, the date on which the earliest of the declarations or statements is made,

unless the court, on an application under section 157, otherwise orders.

CHAPTER VII

REDEEMABLE SHARES; PURCHASE BY A COMPANY OF ITS OWN SHARES

Redemption and purchase generally

159.   **Power to issue redeemable shares**

(1)   Subject to the provisions of this Chapter, a company limited by shares or limited by guarantee and having a share capital may, if authorised to do so by its articles, issue shares which are to be redeemed or are liable to be redeemed at the option of the company or the shareholder.

(2)   No redeemable shares may be issued at a time when there are no issued shares of the company which are not redeemable.

(3)   Redeemable shares may not be redeemed unless they are fully paid; and the terms of redemption must provide for payment on redemption.

159A.   *Terms and manner of redemption*

(1)   *Redeemable shares may not be issued unless the following conditions are satisfied as regards the terms and manner of redemption.*

(2)   *The date on or by which, or dates between which, the shares are to be or may be redeemed must be specified in the company's articles or, if the articles so provide, fixed by the directors, and in the latter case the date or dates must be fixed before the shares are issued.*

(3)   *Any other circumstances in which the shares are to be or may be redeemed must be specified in the company's articles.*

(4)   *The amount payable on redemption must be specified in, or determined in accordance with, the company's articles, and in the latter case the articles must not provide for the amount to be determined by reference to any person's discretion or opinion.*

(5)   *Any other terms and conditions of redemption shall be specified in the company's articles.*

(6)   *Nothing in this section shall be construed as requiring a company to provide in its articles for any matter for which provision is made by this Act.*

Note. This section is inserted by the Companies Act 1989, s. 133(2), as from a day to be appointed.

160.   **Financing etc of redemption**

(1)   Subject to the next subsection and to sections 171 (private companies redeeming or purchasing own shares out of capital) and 178(4) (terms of redemption or purchase enforceable in a winding up)—

     (a)   redeemable shares may only be redeemed out of distributable profits of the company or out of the proceeds of a fresh issue of shares made for the purposes of the redemption; and

     (b)   any premium payable on redemption must be paid out of distributable profits of the company.

(2)   If the redeemable shares were issued at a premium, any premium payable on their redemption may be paid out of the proceeds of a fresh issue of shares made for the purposes of the redemption, up to an amount equal to—

     (a)   the aggregate of the premiums received by the company on the issue of the shares redeemed, or

     (b)   the current amount of the company's share premium account (including any sum transferred to that account in respect of premiums on the new shares),

    whichever is the less; and in that case the amount of the company's share premium account shall be reduced by a sum corresponding (or by sums in the aggregate corresponding) to the amount of any payment made by virtue of this subsection out of the proceeds of the issue of the new shares.

(3)   *Subject to the following provisions of this Chapter, redemption of shares may be effected on such terms and in such manner as may be provided by the company's articles.*

(4)   Shares *redeemed under this section* [*redeemed under this Chapter*] shall be treated as cancelled on redemption, and the amount of the company's issued share capital shall be diminished by the nominal value of those shares accordingly; but the redemption of shares by a company is not to be taken as reducing the amount of the company's authorised share capital.

(5)   Without prejudice to subsection (4), where a company is about to redeem shares, it has power to issue shares up to the nominal value of the shares to be redeemed as if those shares had never been issued.

Note. Subsection (3) and the italicized words in subsection (4) are repealed, and the words in square brackets in subsection (4) are substituted, by the Companies Act 1989, s. 133(3), as from a day to be appointed.

161.   ...

162.   **Power of company to purchase own shares**

(1)   Subject to the following provisions of this Chapter, a company limited by shares or limited by guarantee and having a share capital may, if authorised to do so by its articles, purchase its own shares (including any redeemable shares).

(2)   Sections 159 and 160 apply to the purchase by a company under this section of its own shares as they apply to the redemption of redeemable shares.

    This is subject to subsections (2A) and (2B).

(2A)   The terms and manner of a purchase under this section need not be determined by the articles as required by section 160(3).

(2B)   Where a company makes a purchase of qualifying shares out of distributable profits under this section, section 162A applies to the shares purchased; and accordingly section 160(4) does not apply to those shares.

(3)   A company may not under this section purchase its shares if as a result of the purchase there would no longer be any member of the company holding shares other than redeemable shares or shares held as treasury shares.

(4)   For the purposes of this Chapter "qualifying shares" are shares which—

(a)   are included in the official list in accordance with the provisions of Part 6 of the Financial Services and Markets Act 2000,

(b)   are traded on the market known as the Alternative Investment Market established under the rules of London Stock Exchange plc,

(c)   are officially listed in an EEA State, or

(d)   are traded on a market established in an EEA State which is a regulated market for the purposes of Article 16 of Council Directive 93/22/EEC on investment services in the securities field

and in paragraph (a) "the official list" has the meaning given in section 103(1) of the Financial Services and Markets Act 2000.

162A.   Treasury shares

(1)   Where qualifying shares are purchased by a company out of distributable profits in accordance with section 162, the company may—

(a)   hold the shares (or any of them), or

(b)   deal with any of them, at any time, in accordance with section 162D.

(2)   Where shares are held under subsection (1)(a) then, for the purposes of section 352, the company must be entered in the register as the member holding those shares.

(3)   In this Act, references to a company holding shares as treasury shares are references to the company holding shares which—

(a)   were (or are treated as having been) purchased by it in circumstances in which this section applies, and

(b)   have been held by the company continuously since they were so purchased.

162B.   Treasury shares: maximum holdings

(1)   Where a company has shares of only one class, the aggregate nominal value of shares held as treasury shares must not at any time exceed 10 per cent of the nominal value of the issued share capital of the company at that time.

(2)   Where the share capital of a company is divided into shares of different classes, the aggregate nominal value of the shares of any class held as treasury shares must not at any time exceed 10 per cent of the nominal value of the issued share capital of the shares in that class at that time.

(3)   Where subsection (1) or (2) is contravened by a company, the company must dispose of or cancel the excess shares, in accordance with section 162D, before the end of the period of 12 months beginning with the day on which that contravention occurs.

For this purpose "the excess shares" means such number of the shares, held by the company as treasury shares at the time in question, as resulted in the limit being exceeded.

162C.   Treasury shares: voting and other rights

(1)   This section applies to shares which are held by a company as treasury shares ("the treasury shares").

(2)   The company must not exercise any right in respect of the treasury shares, and any purported exercise of such a right is void.

(3)   The rights to which subsection (2) applies include any right to attend or vote at meetings (including meetings under section 425).

(4)   No dividend may be paid, and no other distribution (whether in cash or otherwise) of the company's assets (including any distribution of assets to members on a winding up) may be made, to the company in respect of the treasury shares.

(5)   Nothing in this section is to be taken as preventing—

(a)   an allotment of shares as fully paid bonus shares in respect of the treasury shares, or

(b)   the payment of any amount payable on the redemption of the treasury shares (if they are redeemable shares).

(6)   Any shares allotted as fully paid bonus shares in respect of the treasury shares shall be treated for the purposes of this Act as if they were purchased by the company at the time they were allotted, in circumstances in which section 162A(1) applied.

162D. Treasury shares: disposal and cancellation

(1)   Where shares are held as treasury shares, a company may at any time—

    (a)   sell the shares (or any of them) for cash,

    (b)   transfer the shares (or any of them) for the purposes of or pursuant to an employees' share scheme, or

    (c)   cancel the shares (or any of them).

(2)   For the purposes of subsection (1)(a), "cash", in relation to a sale of shares by a company, means—

    (a)   cash (including foreign currency) received by the company, or

    (b)   a cheque received by the company in good faith which the directors have no reason for suspecting will not be paid, or

    (c)   a release of a liability of the company for a liquidated sum, or

    (d)   an undertaking to pay cash to the company on or before a date not more than 90 days after the date on which the company agrees to sell the shares.

(3)   But if the company receives a notice under section 429 (right of offeror to buy out minority shareholders) that a person desires to acquire any of the shares, the company must not, under subsection (1), sell or transfer the shares to which the notice relates except to that person.

(4)   If under subsection (1) the company cancels shares held as treasury shares, the company must diminish the amount of the issued share capital by the nominal value of the shares cancelled; but the cancellation is not to be taken as reducing the amount of the company's authorised share capital.

(5)   The directors may take such steps as are requisite to enable the company to cancel its shares under subsection (1) without complying with sections 135 and 136 (resolution to reduce issued share capital; application to court for approval).

162E. Treasury shares: mandatory cancellation

(1)   If shares held as treasury shares cease to be qualifying shares, the company must forthwith cancel the shares in accordance with section 162D.

(2)   For the purposes of subsection (1), shares are not to be regarded as ceasing to be qualifying shares by virtue only of—

    (a)   the suspension of their listing in accordance with the applicable rules in the EEA State in which the shares are officially listed, or

    (b)   the suspension of their trading in accordance with—

        (i)   in the case of shares traded on the market known as the Alternative Investment Market, the rules of London Stock Exchange plc, and

        (ii)   in any other case, the rules of the regulated market on which they are traded.

(3)   For the purposes of this section "regulated market" means a market which is a regulated market for the purposes of Article 16 of Council Directive 93/22/EEC on investment services in the securities field.

162F. Treasury shares: proceeds of sale

(1)   Where shares held as treasury shares are sold, the proceeds of sale shall be dealt with in accordance with this section.

(2)   Where the proceeds of sale are equal to or less than the purchase price paid by the company for the shares, the proceeds shall be treated for the purposes of Part 8 as a realised profit of the company.

(3)   Where the proceeds of sale exceed the purchase price paid by the company for the shares—

    (a)   that part of the proceeds of sale that is equal to the purchase price paid shall be treated for the purposes of Part 8 as a realised profit of the company, and

    (b)   a sum equal to the excess shall be transferred to the company's share premium account.

(4)   The purchase price paid by the company for the shares shall be determined by the application of a weighted average price method.

(5)   Where the shares were allotted to the company as fully paid bonus shares, the purchase price paid for them shall, for the purposes of subsection (4), be treated as being nil.

162G. Treasury shares: penalty for contravention

If a company contravenes any provision of sections 162A to 162F every officer of it who is in default is liable to a fine.

163. Definitions of "off-market" and "market" purchase

(1)   A purchase by a company of its own shares is "off-market" if the shares either—

      (a)   are purchased otherwise than on a recognised investment exchange, or

      (b)   are purchased on a recognised investment exchange but are not subject to a marketing arrangement on that investment exchange.

(2)   For this purpose, a company's shares are subject to a marketing arrangement on a recognised investment exchange if either—

      (a)   they are listed under Part 6 of the Financial Services and Markets Act 2000; or

      (b)   the company has been afforded facilities for dealings in those shares to take place on that investment exchange without prior permission for individual transactions from the authority governing that investment exchange and without limit as to the time during which those facilities are to be available.

(3)   A purchase by a company of its own shares is a "market purchase" if it is a purchase made on a recognised investment exchange, other than a purchase which is an off-market purchase by virtue of subsection (1)(b).

(4)   "Recognised investment exchange" means a recognised investment exchange other than an overseas investment exchange.

(5)   Expressions used in the definition contained in subsection (4) have the same meaning as in Part 18 of the Financial Services and Markets Act 2000.

164. Authority for off-market purchase

(1)   A company may only make an off-market purchase of its own shares in pursuance of a contract approved in advance in accordance with this section or under section 165 below.

(2)   The terms of the proposed contract must be authorised by a special resolution of the company before the contract is entered into; and the following subsections apply with respect to that authority and to resolutions conferring it.

(3)   Subject to the next subsection, the authority may be varied, revoked or from time to time renewed by special resolution of the company.

(4)   In the case of a public company, the authority conferred by the resolution must specify a date on which the authority is to expire; and in a resolution conferring or renewing authority that date must not be later than 18 months after that on which the resolution is passed.

(5)   A special resolution to confer, vary, revoke or renew authority is not effective if any member of the company holding shares to which the resolution relates exercises the voting rights carried by any of those shares in voting on the resolution and the resolution would not have been passed if he had not done so.

      For this purpose—

      (a)   a member who holds shares to which the resolution relates is regarded as exercising the voting rights carried by those shares not only if he votes in respect of them on a poll on the question whether the resolution shall be passed, but also if he votes on the resolution otherwise than on a poll;

      (b)   notwithstanding anything in the company's articles, any member of the company may demand a poll on that question; and

      (c)   a vote and a demand for a poll by a person as proxy for a member are the same respectively as a vote and a demand by the member.

(6)   Such a resolution is not effective for the purposes of this section unless (if the proposed contract is in writing) a copy of the contract or (if not) a written memorandum of its terms is available for inspection by members of the company both—

(a)   at the company's registered office for not less than 15 days ending with the date of the meeting at which the resolution is passed, and

(b)   at the meeting itself.

A memorandum of contract terms so made available must include the names of any members holding shares to which the contract relates; and a copy of the contract so made available must have annexed to it a written memorandum specifying any such names which do not appear in the contract itself.

(7)   A company may agree to a variation of an existing contract so approved, but only if the variation is authorised by a special resolution of the company before it is agreed to; and subsections (3) to (6) above apply to the authority for a proposed variation as they apply to the authority for a proposed contract, save that a copy of the original contract or (as the case may require) a memorandum of its terms, together with any variations previously made, must also be available for inspection in accordance with subsection (6).

165.   Authority for contingent purchase contract

(1)   A contingent purchase contract is a contract entered into by a company and relating to any of its shares—

(a)   which does not amount to a contract to purchase those shares, but

(b)   under which the company may (subject to any conditions) become entitled or obliged to purchase those shares.

(2)   A company may only make a purchase of its own shares in pursuance of a contingent purchase contract if the contract is approved in advance by a special resolution of the company before the contract is entered into; and subsections (3) to (7) of section 164 apply to the contract and its terms.

166.   Authority for market purchase

(1)   A company shall not make a market purchase of its own shares unless the purchase has first been authorised by the company in general meeting.

(2)   That authority—

(a)   may be general for that purpose, or limited to the purchase of shares of any particular class or description, and

(b)   may be unconditional or subject to conditions.

(3)   The authority must—

(a)   specify the maximum number of shares authorised to be acquired,

(b)   determine both the maximum and the minimum prices which may be paid for the shares, and

(c)   specify a date on which it is to expire.

(4)   The authority may be varied, revoked or from time to time renewed by the company in general meeting, but this is subject to subsection (3) above; and in a resolution to confer or renew authority, the date on which the authority is to expire must not be later than 18 months after that on which the resolution is passed.

(5)   A company may under this section make a purchase of its own shares after the expiry of the time limit imposed to comply with subsection (3)(c), if the contract of purchase was concluded before the authority expired and the terms of the authority permitted the company to make a contract of purchase which would or might be executed wholly or partly after its expiration.

(6)   A resolution to confer or vary authority under this section may determine either or both the maximum and minimum prices for purchase by—

(a)   specifying a particular sum, or

(b)   providing a basis or formula for calculating the amount of the price in question without reference to any person's discretion or opinion.

(7)   A resolution of a company conferring, varying, revoking or renewing authority under this section is subject to section 380 (resolution to be sent to registrar of companies within 15 days).

167.   Assignment or release of company's right to purchase own shares

(1)   The rights of a company under a contract approved under section 164 or 165, or under a contract for a purchase authorised under section 166, are not capable of being assigned.

(2)   An agreement by a company to release its rights under a contract approved under section 164 or 165 is void unless the terms of the release agreement are approved in advance by a special resolution of the company before the agreement is entered into; and subsections (3) to (7) of section 164 apply to approval for a proposed release agreement as to authority for a proposed variation of an existing contract.

168.   Payments apart from purchase price to be made out of distributable profits

(1)   A payment made by a company in consideration of—

   (a)   acquiring any right with respect to the purchase of its own shares in pursuance of a contract approved under section 165, or

   (b)   the variation of a contract approved under section 164 or 165, or

   (c)   the release of any of the company's obligations with respect to the purchase of any of its own shares under a contract approved under section 164 or 165 or under a contract for a purchase authorised under section 166,

must be made out of the company's distributable profits.

(2)   If the requirements of subsection (1) are not satisfied in relation to a contract—

   (a)   in a case within paragraph (a) of the subsection, no purchase by the company of its own shares in pursuance of that contract is lawful under this Chapter,

   (b)   in a case within paragraph (b), no such purchase following the variation is lawful under this Chapter, and

   (c)   in a case within paragraph (c), the purported release is void.

169.   Disclosure by company of purchase of own shares

(1)   Within the period of 28 days beginning with the date on which any shares purchased by a company under this Chapter are delivered to it, the company shall deliver to the registrar of companies for registration a return in the prescribed form stating with respect to shares of each class purchased the number and nominal value of those shares and the date on which they were delivered to the company.

(1A)   But in the case of a company which has purchased its own shares in circumstances in which section 162A applies, the requirement to deliver a return under subsection (1) shall apply only where some or all of the shares have been cancelled forthwith after the date of their delivery in accordance with section 162D(1) and in those circumstances the particulars required by that subsection to be stated with respect to the shares purchased shall apply only to such of the shares as have been so cancelled.

(1B)   Where a company has purchased its own shares in circumstances in which section 162A applies, the company shall within the period of 28 days beginning with the date on which such shares are delivered to it (except where all of the shares have been cancelled forthwith after the date of their delivery in the circumstances referred to in subsection (1A)) deliver to the registrar of companies for registration a return in the prescribed form stating with respect to shares of each class purchased (other than any shares which have been cancelled in the circumstances referred to in subsection (1A)) the number and nominal value of each of those shares which are held as treasury shares and the date on which they were delivered to the company.

(2)   In the case of a public company, any return under subsection (1) or (1B) shall also state—

   (a)   the aggregate amount paid by the company for the shares; and

   (b)   the maximum and minimum prices paid in respect of shares of each class purchased.

(3)   Particulars of shares delivered to the company on different dates and under different contracts may be included in a single return under either subsection (1) or (1B) to the registrar; and in such a case the amount required to be stated under subsection (2)(a) is the aggregate amount paid by the company for all the shares to which the return relates.

(4)   Where a company enters into a contract approved under section 164 or 165, or a contract for a purchase authorised under section 166, the company shall keep at its registered office—

(a)   if the contract is in writing, a copy of it; and

(b)   if not, a memorandum of its terms,

from the conclusion of the contract until the end of the period of 10 years beginning with the date on which the purchase of all the shares in pursuance of the contract is completed or (as the case may be) the date on which the contract otherwise determines.

(5)   Every copy and memorandum so required to be kept shall ... be open to inspection without charge—

(a)   by any member of the company, and

(b)   if it is a public company, by any other person.

(6)   If default is made in delivering to the registrar any return required by this section, every officer of the company who is in default is liable to a fine and, for continued contravention, to a daily default fine.

(7)   If default is made in complying with subsection (4), or if an inspection required under subsection (5) is refused, the company and every officer of it who is in default is liable to a fine and, for continued contravention, to a daily default fine.

(8)   In the case of a refusal of an inspection required under subsection (5) of a copy or memorandum, the court may by order compel an immediate inspection of it.

(9)   The obligation of a company under subsection (4) to keep a copy of any contract or (as the case may be) a memorandum of its terms applies to any variation of the contract so long as it applies to the contract.

169A.   Disclosure by company of cancellation or disposal of treasury shares

(1)   Subsection (2) applies in relation to any shares held by a company as treasury shares if—

(a)   the company is or was required to make a return under section 169(1B) in relation to the shares, and

(b)   the shares have—

(i)   been cancelled in accordance with section 162D(1), or

(ii)   been sold or transferred for the purposes of or pursuant to an employees' share scheme under section 162D(1).

(2)   Within the period of 28 days beginning with the date on which such shares are cancelled or disposed of, the company shall deliver to the registrar of companies for registration a return in the prescribed form stating with respect to shares of each class cancelled or disposed of—

(a)   the number and nominal value of those shares, and

(b)   the date on which they were cancelled or disposed of.

(3)   Particulars of shares cancelled or disposed of on different dates may be included in a single return to the registrar.

(4)   If default is made in delivering to the registrar any return required by this section, every officer of the company who is in default is liable to a fine and, for continued contravention, to a daily default fine.

170.   The capital redemption reserve

(1)   Where under this Chapter shares of a company are redeemed or purchased wholly out of the company's profits, the amount by which the company's issued share capital is diminished in accordance with section 160(4) on cancellation of the shares redeemed or purchased, or in accordance with section 162D(4) on cancellation of shares held as treasury shares, shall be transferred to a reserve, called "the capital redemption reserve".

(2)   If the shares are redeemed or purchased wholly or partly out of the proceeds of a fresh issue and the aggregate amount of those proceeds is less than the aggregate nominal value of the shares redeemed or purchased, the amount of the difference shall be transferred to the capital redemption reserve.

(3)   But subsection (2) does not apply if the proceeds of the fresh issue are applied by the company in making a redemption or purchase of its own shares in addition to a payment out of capital under section 171.

(4)   The provisions of this Act relating to the reduction of a company's share capital apply as if the capital redemption reserve were paid-up share capital of the company, except that the reserve may be applied by the company in paying up its unissued shares to be allotted to members of the company as fully paid bonus shares.

Redemption or purchase of own shares out of capital (private companies only)

171.   Power of private companies to redeem or purchase own shares out of capital

(1)   Subject to the following provisions of this Chapter, a private company limited by shares or limited by guarantee and having a share capital may, if so authorised by its articles, make a payment in respect of the redemption or purchase under section 160 or (as the case may be) section 162, of its own shares otherwise than out of its distributable profits or the proceeds of a fresh issue of shares.

(2)   References below in this Chapter to payment out of capital are (subject to subsection (6)) to any payment so made, whether or not it would be regarded apart from this section as a payment out of capital.

(3)   The payment which may (if authorised in accordance with the following provisions of this Chapter) be made by a company out of capital in respect of the redemption or purchase of its own shares is such an amount as, taken together with—

(a)   any available profits of the company, and

(b)   the proceeds of any fresh issue of shares made for the purposes of the redemption or purchase,

is equal to the price of redemption or purchase; and the payment permissible under this subsection is referred to below in this Chapter as the permissible capital payment for the shares.

(4)   Subject to subsection (6), if the permissible capital payment for shares redeemed or purchased is less than their nominal amount, the amount of the difference shall be transferred to the company's capital redemption reserve.

(5)   Subject to subsection (6), if the permissible capital payment is greater than the nominal amount of the shares redeemed or purchased—

(a)   the amount of any capital redemption reserve, share premium account or fully paid share capital of the company, and

(b)   any amount representing unrealised profits of the company for the time being standing to the credit of any reserve maintained by the company in accordance with paragraph 34 of Schedule 4 or paragraph 34 of Schedule 8 (revaluation reserve),

may be reduced by a sum not exceeding (or by sums not in the aggregate exceeding) the amount by which the permissible capital payment exceeds the nominal amount of the shares.

(6)   Where the proceeds of a fresh issue are applied by a company in making any redemption or purchase of its own shares in addition to a payment out of capital under this section, the references in subsections (4) and (5) to the permissible capital payment are to be read as referring to the aggregate of that payment and those proceeds.

172.   Availability of profits for purposes of s 171

(1)   The reference in section 171(3)(a) to available profits of the company is to the company's profits which are available for distribution (within the meaning of Part VIII); but the question whether a company has any profits so available and the amount of any such profits are to be determined for purposes of that section in accordance with the following subsections, instead of sections 270 to 275 in that Part.

(2)   Subject to the next subsection, that question is to be determined by reference to the following items as stated in the relevant accounts for determining the permissible capital payments for shares—

(a)   profits, losses, assets and liabilities,

(b)   the following provisions—

    (i)   in the case of Companies Act individual accounts, provisions of any of the kinds mentioned in paragraphs 88 and 89 of Schedule 4 (depreciation, diminution in value of assets, retentions to meet liabilities, etc), and

    (ii)   in the case of IAS individual accounts, provisions of any kind, and

(c)   share capital and reserves (including undistributable reserves),

...

(3)   The relevant accounts for this purpose are such accounts, prepared as at any date within the period for determining the amount of the permissible capital payment, as are necessary to enable a reasonable judgment to be made as to the amounts of any of the items mentioned in subsection (2)(a) to (c) above.

(4)   For purposes of determining the amount of the permissible capital payment for shares, the amount of the company's available profits (if any) determined in accordance with subsections (2) and (3) is treated as reduced by the amount of any distributions lawfully made by the company after the date of the relevant accounts and before the end of the period for determining the amount of that payment.

(5)   The reference in subsection (4) to distributions lawfully made by the company includes—

(a)   financial assistance lawfully given out of distributable profits in a case falling within section 154 or 155,

(b)   any payment lawfully made by the company in respect of the purchase by it of any shares in the company (except a payment lawfully made otherwise than out of distributable profits), and

(c)   a payment of any description specified in section 168(1) lawfully made by the company.

(6)   References in this section to the period for determining the amount of the permissible capital payment for shares are to the period of 3 months ending with the date on which the statutory declaration of the directors purporting to specify the amount of that payment is made in accordance with subsection (3) of the section next following.

173.   Conditions for payment out of capital

(1)   Subject to any order of the court under section 177, a payment out of capital by a private company for the redemption or purchase of its own shares is not lawful unless the requirements of this and the next two sections are satisfied.

(2)   The payment out of capital must be approved by a special resolution of the company.

(3)   The company's directors must make a statutory declaration specifying the amount of the permissible capital payment for the shares in question and stating that, having made full inquiry into the affairs and prospects of the company, they have formed the opinion—

(a)   as regards its initial situation immediately following the date on which the payment out of capital is proposed to be made, that there will be no grounds on which the company could then be found unable to pay its debts, and

(b)   as regards its prospects for the year immediately following that date, that, having regard to their intentions with respect to the management of the company's business during that year and to the amount and character of the financial resources which will in their view be available to the company during that year, the company will be able to continue to carry on business as a going concern (and will accordingly be able to pay its debts as they fall due) throughout that year.

(4)   In forming their opinion for purposes of subsection (3)(a), the directors shall take into account the same liabilities (including prospective and contingent liabilities) as would be relevant under section 122 of the Insolvency Act (winding up by the court) to the question whether a company is unable to pay its debts.

(5)   The directors' statutory declaration must be in the prescribed form and contain such information with respect to the nature of the company's business as may be prescribed, and must in addition have annexed to it a report addressed to the directors by the company's auditors stating that—

(a)   they have inquired into the company's state of affairs; and

(b)   the amount specified in the declaration as the permissible capital payment for the shares in question is in their view properly determined in accordance with sections 171 and 172; and

(c)   they are not aware of anything to indicate that the opinion expressed by the directors in the declaration as to any of the matters mentioned in subsection (3) is unreasonable in all the circumstances.

(6)   A director who makes a declaration under this section without having reasonable grounds for the opinion expressed in the declaration is liable to imprisonment or a fine, or both.

174. Procedure for special resolution under s 173

(1)   The resolution required by section 173 must be passed on, or within the week immediately following, the date on which the directors make the statutory declaration required by that section; and the payment out of capital must be made no earlier than 5 nor more than 7 weeks after the date of the resolution.

(2)   The resolution is ineffective if any member of the company holding shares to which the resolution relates exercises the voting rights carried by any of those shares in voting on the resolution and the resolution would not have been passed if he had not done so.

(3)   For purposes of subsection (2), a member who holds such shares is to be regarded as exercising the voting rights carried by them in voting on the resolution not only if he votes in respect of them on a poll on the question whether the resolution shall be passed, but also if he votes on the resolution otherwise than on a poll; and, notwithstanding anything in a company's articles, any member of the company may demand a poll on that question.

(4)   The resolution is ineffective unless the statutory declaration and auditors' report required by the section are available for inspection by members of the company at the meeting at which the resolution is passed.

(5)   For purposes of this section a vote and a demand for a poll by a person as proxy for a member are the same (respectively) as a vote and demand by the member.

175. Publicity for proposed payment out of capital

(1)   Within the week immediately following the date of the resolution for payment out of capital the company must cause to be published in the Gazette a notice—

(a)   stating that the company has approved a payment out of capital for the purpose of acquiring its own shares by redemption or purchase or both (as the case may be);

(b)   specifying the amount of the permissible capital payment for the shares in question and the date of the resolution under section 173;

(c)   stating that the statutory declaration of the directors and the auditors' report required by that section are available for inspection at the company's registered office; and

(d)   stating that any creditor of the company may at any time within the 5 weeks immediately following the date of the resolution for payment out of capital apply to the court under section 176 for an order prohibiting the payment.

(2)   Within the week immediately following the date of the resolution the company must also either cause a notice to the same effect as that required by subsection (1) to be published in an appropriate national newspaper or give notice in writing to that effect to each of its creditors.

(3)   "An appropriate national newspaper" means a newspaper circulating throughout England and Wales (in the case of a company registered in England and Wales), and a newspaper circulating throughout Scotland (in the case of a company registered in Scotland).

(4)   References below in this section to the first notice date are to the day on which the company first publishes the notice required by subsection (1) or first publishes or gives the notice required by subsection (2) (whichever is the earlier).

(5)   Not later than the first notice date the company must deliver to the registrar of companies a copy of the statutory declaration of the directors and of the auditors' report required by section 173.

(6)   The statutory declaration and auditors' report—

(a)   shall be kept at the company's registered office throughout the period beginning with the first notice date and ending 5 weeks after the date of the resolution for payment out of capital, and

(b)   shall ... be open to the inspection of any member or creditor of the company without charge.

(7)   If an inspection required under subsection (6) is refused, the company and every officer of it who is in default is liable to a fine and, for continued contravention, to a daily default fine.

(8)   In the case of refusal of an inspection required under subsection (6) of a declaration or report, the court may by order compel an immediate inspection of that declaration or report.

176.   Objections by company's members or creditors

(1)   Where a private company passes a special resolution approving for purposes of this Chapter any payment out of capital for the redemption or purchase of any of its shares—

(a)   any member of the company other than one who consented to or voted in favour of the resolution; and

(b)   any creditor of the company,

may within 5 weeks of the date on which the resolution was passed apply to the court for cancellation of the resolution.

(2)   The application may be made on behalf of the persons entitled to make it by such one or more of their number as they may appoint in writing for the purpose.

(3)   If an application is made, the company shall—

(a)   forthwith give notice in the prescribed form of that fact to the registrar of companies; and

(b)   within 15 days from the making of any order of the court on the hearing of the application, or such longer period as the court may by order direct, deliver an office copy of the order to the registrar.

(4)   A company which fails to comply with subsection (3), and any officer of it who is in default, is liable to a fine and for continued contravention, to a daily default fine.

177.   Powers of court on application under s 176

(1)   On the hearing of an application under section 176 the court may, if it thinks fit, adjourn the proceedings in order that an arrangement may be made to the court's satisfaction for the purchase of the interests of dissentient members or for the protection of dissentient creditors (as the case may be); and the court may give such directions and make such orders as it thinks expedient for facilitating or carrying into effect any such arrangement.

(2)   Without prejudice to its powers under subsection (1), the court shall make an order on such terms and conditions as it thinks fit either confirming or cancelling the resolution; and, if the court confirms the resolution, it may in particular by order alter or extend any date or period of time specified in the resolution or in any provision in this Chapter which applies to the redemption or purchase of shares to which the resolution refers.

(3)   The court's order may, if the court thinks fit, provide for the purchase by the company of the shares of any of its members and for the reduction accordingly of the company's capital, and may make such alterations in the company's memorandum and articles as may be required in consequence of that provision.

(4)   If the court's order requires the company not to make any, or any specified, alteration in its memorandum or articles, the company has not then power without leave of the court to make any such alteration in breach of the requirement.

(5)   An alteration in the memorandum or articles made by virtue of an order under this section, if not made by resolution of the company, is of the same effect as if duly made by resolution; and this Act applies accordingly to the memorandum or articles as so altered.

Supplementary

178.   Effect of company's failure to redeem or purchase

(1)   This section has effect where a company has, on or after 15th June 1982,—

(a)   issued shares on terms that they are or are liable to be redeemed, or

(b)   agreed to purchase any of its own shares.

(2)   The company is not liable in damages in respect of any failure on its part to redeem or purchase any of the shares.

(3)   Subsection (2) is without prejudice to any right of the holder of the shares other than his right to sue the company for damages in respect of its failure; but the court shall not grant an order for specific performance of the terms of redemption or purchase if the company shows that it is unable to meet the costs of redeeming or purchasing the shares in question out of distributable profits.

(4)   If the company is wound up and at the commencement of the winding up any of the shares have not been redeemed or purchased, the terms of redemption or purchase may be enforced against the company; and when shares are redeemed or purchased under this subsection, they are treated as cancelled.

(5)   However, subsection (4) does not apply if—

(a)   the terms provided for the redemption or purchase to take place at a date later than that of the commencement of the winding up, or

(b)   during the period beginning with the date on which the redemption or purchase was to have taken place and ending with the commencement of the winding up the company could not at any time have lawfully made a distribution equal in value to the price at which the shares were to have been redeemed or purchased.

(6)   There shall be paid in priority to any amount which the company is liable under subsection (4) to pay in respect of any shares—

(a)   all other debts and liabilities of the company (other than any due to members in their character as such),

(b)   if other shares carry rights (whether as to capital or as to income) which are preferred to the rights as to capital attaching to the first-mentioned shares, any amount due in satisfaction of those preferred rights;

but, subject to that, any such amount shall be paid in priority to any amounts due to members in satisfaction of their rights (whether as to capital or income) as members.

(7)   ...

179.   Power for Secretary of State to modify this Chapter

(1)   The Secretary of State may by regulations made by statutory instrument modify the provisions of this Chapter with respect to any of the following matters—

(a)   the authority required for a purchase by a company of its own shares,

(b)   the authority required for the release by a company of its rights under a contract for the purchase of its own shares or a contract under which the company may (subject to any conditions) become entitled or obliged to purchase its own shares,

(c)   the information to be included in a return delivered by a company to the registrar of companies in accordance with section 169(1),

(d)   the matters to be dealt with in the statutory declaration of the directors under section 173 with a view to indicating their opinion of their company's ability to make a proposed payment out of capital with due regard to its financial situation and prospects, and

(e)   the contents of the auditors' report required by that section to be annexed to that declaration.

(2)   The Secretary of State may also by regulations so made make such provision (including modification of the provisions of this Chapter) as appears to him to be appropriate—

(a)   for wholly or partly relieving companies from the requirement of section 171(3)(a) that any available profits must be taken into account in determining the amount of the permissible capital payment for shares under that section, or

(b)   for permitting a company's share premium account to be applied, to any extent appearing to the Secretary of State to be appropriate, in providing for the premiums payable on redemption or purchase by the company of any of its own shares.

(3)   Regulations under this section—

(a) may make such further modification of any provisions of this Chapter as appears to the Secretary of State to be reasonably necessary in consequence of any provision made under such regulations by virtue of subsection (1) or (2),

(b) may make different provision for different cases or classes of case, and

(c) may contain such further consequential provisions, and such incidental and supplementary provisions, as the Secretary of State thinks fit.

(4) No regulations shall be made under this section unless a draft of the instrument containing them has been laid before Parliament and approved by resolution of each House.

180. Transitional cases arising under this Chapter; and savings

(1) Any preference shares issued by a company before 15th June 1982 which could but for the repeal by the Companies Act 1981 of section 58 of the Companies Act 1948 (power to issue redeemable preference shares) have been redeemed under that section are subject to redemption in accordance with the provisions of this Chapter.

(2) In a case to which sections 159 and 160 apply by virtue of this section, any premium payable on redemption may, notwithstanding the repeal by the 1981 Act of any provision of the 1948 Act, be paid out of the share premium account instead of out of profits, or partly out of that account and partly out of profits (but subject to the provisions of this Chapter so far as payment is out of profits).

(3) Any capital redemption reserve fund established before 15th June 1982 by a company for the purposes of section 58 of the Act of 1948 is to be known as the company's capital redemption reserve and be treated as if it had been established for the purposes of section 170 of this Act; and accordingly, a reference in any enactment or in the articles of any company, or in any other instrument, to a company's capital redemption reserve fund is to be construed as a reference to the company's capital redemption reserve.

181. Definitions for Chapter VII

In this Chapter—

(a) "distributable profits", in relation to the making of any payment by a company, means those profits out of which it could lawfully make a distribution (within the meaning given by section 263(2)) equal in value to the payment, and

(b) "permissible capital payment" means the payment permitted by section 171;

and references to payment out of capital are to be construed in accordance with section 171.

CHAPTER VIII
MISCELLANEOUS PROVISIONS ABOUT SHARES AND DEBENTURES

Share and debenture certificates, transfers and warrants

182. Nature, transfer and numbering of shares

(1) The shares or other interest of any member in a company—

(a) are personal estate or, in Scotland, moveable property and are not in the nature of real estate or heritage,

(b) are transferable in manner provided by the company's articles, but subject to the Stock Transfer Act 1963 (which enables securities of certain descriptions to be transferred by a simplified process) and to regulations made under section 207 of the Companies Act 1989 (which enable title to securities to be evidenced and transferred without a written instrument).

(2) Each share in a company having a share capital shall be distinguished by its appropriate number; except that, if at any time all the issued shares in a company, or all the issued shares in it of a particular class, are fully paid up and rank *pari passu* for all purposes, none of those shares need thereafter have a distinguishing number so long as it remains fully paid up and ranks *pari passu* for all purposes with all shares of the same class for the time being issued and fully paid up.

183.   Transfer and registration

(1)   It is not lawful for a company to register a transfer of shares in or debentures of the company unless a proper instrument of transfer has been delivered to it, or the transfer is an exempt transfer within the Stock Transfer Act 1982 or is in accordance with regulations made under section 207 of the Companies Act 1989.
This applies notwithstanding anything in the company's articles.

(2)   Subsection (1) does not prejudice any power of the company to register as shareholder or debenture holder a person to whom the right to any shares in or debentures of the company has been transmitted by operation of law.

(3)   A transfer of the share or other interest of a deceased member of a company made by his personal representative, although the personal representative is not himself a member of the company, is as valid as if he had been such a member at the time of the execution of the instrument of transfer.

(4)   On the application of the transferor of any share or interest in a company, the company shall enter in its register of members the name of the transferee in the same manner and subject to the same conditions as if the application for the entry were made by the transferee.

(5)   If a company refuses to register a transfer of shares or debentures, the company shall, within 2 months after the date on which the transfer was lodged with it, send to the transferee notice of the refusal.

(6)   If default is made in complying with subsection (5), the company and every officer of it who is in default is liable to a fine and, for continued contravention, to a daily default fine.

184.   Certification of transfers

(1)   The certification by a company of any instrument of transfer of any shares in, or debentures of, the company is to be taken as a representation by the company to any person acting on the faith of the certification that there have been produced to the company such documents as on their face show a prima facie title to the shares or debentures in the transferor named in the instrument.
However, the certification is not to be taken as a representation that the transferor has any title to the shares or debentures.

(2)   Where a person acts on the faith of a false certification by a company made negligently, the company is under the same liability to him as if the certification had been made fraudulently.

(3)   For purposes of this section—

    (a)   an instrument of transfer is deemed certificated if it bears the words "certificate lodged" (or words to the like effect);

    (b)   the certification of an instrument of transfer is deemed made by a company if—

        (i)   the person issuing the instrument is a person authorised to issue certificated instruments of transfer on the company's behalf, and

        (ii)   the certification is signed by a person authorised to certificate transfers on the company's behalf or by an officer or servant either of the company or of a body corporate so authorised;

    (c)   a certification is deemed signed by a person if—

        (i)   it purports to be authenticated by his signature or initials (whether handwritten or not), and

        (ii)   it is not shown that the signature or initials was or were placed there neither by himself nor by a person authorised to use the signature or initials for the purpose of certificating transfers on the company's behalf.

185.   Duty of company as to issue of certificates

(1)   Subject to the following provisions, every company shall—

    (a)   within 2 months after the allotment of any of its shares, debentures or debenture stock, and

    (b)   within 2 months after the date on which a transfer of any such shares, debentures or debenture stock is lodged with the company, complete and have ready for delivery the certificates of all shares, the debentures and the certificates of all debenture stock allotted or transferred (unless the conditions of issue of the shares, debentures or debenture stock otherwise provide).

(2)   For this purpose, "transfer" means a transfer duly stamped and otherwise valid, or an exempt transfer within the Stock Transfer Act 1982, and does not include such a transfer as the company is for any reason entitled to refuse to register and does not register.

(3)   Subsection (1) does not apply in the case of a transfer to any person where, by virtue of regulations under section 3 of the Stock Transfer Act 1982, he is not entitled to a certificate or other document of or evidencing title in respect of the securities transferred; but if in such a case the transferee—

(a)   subsequently becomes entitled to such a certificate or other document by virtue of any provision of those regulations, and

(b)   gives notice in writing of that fact to the company,

this section has effect as if the reference in subsection (1)(b) to the date of the lodging of the transfer were a reference to the date of the notice.

(4)   Subsection (4A) applies in relation to a company—

(a)   of which shares or debentures are allotted to a financial institution,

(b)   of which debenture stock is allotted to a financial institution, or

(c)   with which a transfer for transferring shares, debentures or debenture stock to a financial institution is lodged.

(4A)   The company is not required, in consequence of that allotment or transfer, to comply with subsection (1).

(4B)   "Financial institution" means—

(a)   a recognised clearing house acting in relation to a recognised investment exchange; or

(b)   a nominee of—

(i)   a recognised clearing house acting in that way; or

(ii)   a recognised investment exchange.

(4C)   No person may be a nominee for the purposes of this section unless he is a person designated for those purposes in the rules of the recognised investment exchange in question.

(4D)   Expressions used in subsections (4B) and (4C) have the same meaning as in Part 18 of the Financial Services and Markets Act 2000.

(5)   If default is made in complying with subsection (1), the company and every officer of it who is in default is liable to a fine and, for continued contravention, to a daily default fine.

(6)   If a company on which a notice has been served requiring it to make good any default in complying with subsection (1) fails to make good the default within 10 days after service of the notice, the court may, on the application of the person entitled to have the certificates or the debentures delivered to him, exercise the power of the following subsection.

(7)   The court may make an order directing the company and any officer of it to make good the default within such time as may be specified in the order; and the order may provide that all costs of and incidental to the application shall be borne by the company or by an officer of it responsible for the default.

186.   Certificate to be evidence of title

(1)   A certificate under the common seal of the company ... specifying any shares held by a member is—

(a)   in England and Wales, prima facie evidence, and

(b)   in Scotland, sufficient evidence unless the contrary is shown,

of his title to the shares.

(2)   Without prejudice to subsection (1), as respects Scotland a certificate specifying any shares held by a member and subscribed by the company in accordance with the Requirements of Writing (Scotland) Act 1995 is, unless the contrary is shown, sufficient evidence of his title to the shares.

187.   Evidence of grant of probate or confirmation as executor

The production to a company of any document which is by law sufficient evidence of probate of the will, or letters of administration of the estate, or confirmation as executor, of a deceased person having been granted to some person shall be accepted by the company as sufficient evidence of the grant.

This has effect notwithstanding anything in the company's articles.

188.   Issue and effect of share warrant to bearer

(1)   A company limited by shares may, if so authorised by its articles, issue with respect to any fully paid shares a warrant (a "share warrant") stating that the bearer of the warrant is entitled to the shares specified in it.

(2)   A share warrant issued under the company's common seal (or, in the case of a company registered in Scotland, subscribed in accordance with the Requirements of Writing (Scotland) Act 1995) ... entitles the bearer to the shares specified in it; and the shares may be transferred by delivery of the warrant.

(3)   A company which issues a share warrant may, if so authorised by its articles, provide (by coupons or otherwise) for the payment of the future dividends on the shares included in the warrant.

189.   Offences in connection with share warrants (Scotland)

(1)   If in Scotland a person—

(a)   with intent to defraud, forges or alters, or offers, utters, disposes of, or puts off, knowing the same to be forged or altered, any share warrant or coupon, or any document purporting to be a share warrant or coupon, issued in pursuance of this Act; or

(b)   by means of any such forged or altered share warrant, coupon, or document, purporting as aforesaid, demands or endeavours to obtain or receive any share or interest in any company under this Act, or to receive any dividend or money payable in respect thereof, knowing the warrant, coupon, or document to be forged or altered;

he is on conviction thereof liable to imprisonment or a fine, or both.

(2)   If in Scotland a person without lawful authority or excuse (proof whereof lies on him)—

(a)   engraves or makes on any plate, wood, stone, or other material , any share warrant or coupon purporting to be—

(i)   a share warrant or coupon issued or made by any particular company in pursuance of this Act; or

(ii)   a blank share warrant or coupon so issued or made; or

(iii)   a part of such a share warrant or coupon; or

(b)   uses any such plate, wood, stone, or other material, for the making or printing of any such share warrant or coupon, or of any such blank share warrant or coupon, or any part thereof respectively; or

(c)   knowingly has in his custody or possession any such plate, wood, stone, or other material;

he is on conviction thereof liable to imprisonment or a fine, or both.

Debentures

190.   Register of debenture holders

(1)   A company registered in England and Wales shall not keep in Scotland any register of holders of debentures of the company or any duplicate of any such register or part of any such register which is kept outside Great Britain.

(2)   A company registered in Scotland shall not keep in England and Wales any such register or duplicate as above-mentioned.

(3)   Neither a register of holders of debentures of a company nor a duplicate of any such register or part of any such register which is kept outside Great Britain shall be kept in England and Wales (in the case of a company registered in England and Wales) or in Scotland (in the case of a company registered in Scotland) elsewhere than—

(a)   at the company's registered office; or

(b) at any office of the company at which the work of making it up is done; or

(c) if the company arranges with some other person for the making up of the register or duplicate to be undertaken on its behalf by that other person, at the office of that other person at which the work is done.

(4) Where a company keeps (in England and Wales or in Scotland, as the case may be) both such a register and such a duplicate, it shall keep them at the same place.

(5) Every company which keeps any such register or duplicate in England and Wales or Scotland shall send to the registrar of companies notice (in the prescribed form) of the place where the register or duplicate is kept and of any change in that place.

(6) But a company is not bound to send notice under subsection (5) where the register or duplicate has, at all times since it came into existence, been kept at the company's registered office.

191. Right to inspect register

(1) Every register of holders of debentures of a company shall, except when duly closed ..., be open to the inspection—

(a) of the registered holder of any such debentures or any holder of shares in the company without fee; and

(b) of any other person on payment of such fee as may be prescribed.

(2) Any such registered holder of debentures or holder of shares, or any other person, may require a copy of the register of the holders of debentures of the company or any part of it, on payment of such fee as may be prescribed.

(3) A copy of any trust deed for securing an issue of debentures shall be forwarded to every holder of any such debentures at his request on payment of such fee as may be prescribed
(a), (b)...

(4) If inspection is refused, or a copy is refused or not forwarded, the company and every officer of it who is in default is liable to a fine and, for continued contravention, to a daily default fine.

(5) Where a company is in default as above-mentioned, the court may by order compel an immediate inspection of the register or direct that the copies required be sent to the person requiring them.

(6) For purposes of this section, a register is deemed to be duly closed if closed in accordance with provisions contained in the articles or in the debentures or, in the case of debenture stock, in the stock certificates, or in the trust deed or other document securing the debentures or debenture stock, during such period or periods not exceeding in the whole 30 days in any year, as may be therein specified.

(7) Liability incurred by a company from the making or deletion of an entry in its register of debenture holders, or from a failure to make or delete any such entry, is not enforceable more than 20 years after the date on which the entry was made or deleted or, in the case of any such failure, the failure first occurred.

This is without prejudice to any lesser period of limitation.

192. Liability of trustees of debentures

(1) Subject to this section, any provision contained—

(a) in a trust deed for securing an issue of debentures, or

(b) in any contract with the holders of debentures secured by a trust deed,

is void in so far as it would have the effect of exempting a trustee of the deed from, or indemnifying him against, liability for breach of trust where he fails to show the degree of care and diligence required of him as trustee, having regard to the provisions of the trust deed conferring on him any powers, authorities or discretions.

(2) Subsection (1) does not invalidate—

(a) a release otherwise validly given in respect of anything done or omitted to be done by a trustee before the giving of the release; or

(b) any provision enabling such a release to be given—

(i)   on the agreement thereto of a majority of not less than three-fourths in value of the debenture holders present and voting in person or, where proxies are permitted, by proxy at a meeting summoned for the purpose, and

(ii)   either with respect to specific acts or omissions or on the trustee dying or ceasing to act.

(3)   Subsection (1) does not operate—

(a)   to invalidate any provision in force on 1st July 1948 so long as any person then entitled to the benefit of that provision or afterwards given the benefit of that provision under the following subsection remains a trustee of the deed in question; or

(b)   to deprive any person of any exemption or right to be indemnified in respect of anything done or omitted to be done by him while any such provision was in force.

(4)   While any trustee of a trust deed remains entitled to the benefit of a provision saved by subsection (3), the benefit of that provision may be given either—

(a)   to all trustees of the deed, present and future; or

(b)   to any named trustees or proposed trustees of it,

by a resolution passed by a majority of not less than three-fourths in value of the debenture holders present in person or, where proxies are permitted, by proxy at a meeting summoned for the purpose in accordance with the provisions of the deed or, if the deed makes no provision for summoning meetings, a meeting summoned for the purpose in any manner approved by the court.

193.   Perpetual debentures

A condition contained in debentures, or in a deed for securing debentures, is not invalid by reason only that the debentures are thereby made irredeemable or redeemable only on the happening of a contingency (however remote), or on the expiration of a period (however long), any rule of equity to the contrary notwithstanding.

This applies to debentures whenever issued, and to deeds whenever executed.

194.   Power to re-issue redeemed debentures

(1)   Where (at any time) a company has redeemed debentures previously issued, then—

(a)   unless provision to the contrary, whether express or implied, is contained in the articles or in any contract entered into by the company; or

(b)   unless the company has, by passing a resolution to that effect or by some other act, manifested its intention that the debentures shall be cancelled,

the company has, and is deemed always to have had, power to re-issue the debentures, either by re-issuing the same debentures or by issuing other debentures in their place.

(2)   On a re-issue of redeemed debentures, the person entitled to the debentures has, and is deemed always to have had, the same priorities as if the debentures had never been redeemed.

(3)   Where a company has (at any time) deposited any of its debentures to secure advances from time to time on current account or otherwise, the debentures are not deemed to have been redeemed by reason only of the company's account having ceased to be in debit while the debentures remained so deposited.

(4)   The re-issue of a debenture or the issue of another debenture in its place under the power which by this section is given to or deemed to be possessed by a company is to be treated as the issue of a new debenture for purposes of stamp duty; but it is not to be so treated for the purposes of any provision limiting the amount or number of debentures to be issued.

This applies whenever the issue or re-issue was made.

(5)   A person lending money on the security of a debenture re-issued under this section which appears to be duly stamped may give the debenture in evidence in any proceedings for enforcing his security without payment of the stamp duty or any penalty in respect of it, unless he had notice (or, but for his negligence, might have discovered) that the debenture was not duly stamped; but in that case the company is liable to pay the proper stamp duty and penalty.

195. **Contract to subscribe for debentures**

A contract with a company to take up and pay for debentures of the company may be enforced by an order for specific performance.

196. **Payment of debts out of assets subject to floating charge (England and Wales)**

(1)   The following applies in the case of a company registered in England and Wales, where debentures of the company are secured by a charge which, as created, was a floating charge.

(2)   If possession is taken, by or on behalf of the holders of any of the debentures, of any property comprised in or subject to the charge, and the company is not at that time in course of being wound up, the company's preferential debts shall be paid out of assets coming to the hands of the person taking possession in priority to any claims for principal or interest in respect of the debentures.

(3)   "Preferential debts" means the categories of debts listed in Schedule 6 to the Insolvency Act; and for the purposes of that Schedule "the relevant date" is the date of possession being taken as above mentioned.

(4)   Payments made under this section shall be recouped, as far as may be, out of the assets of the company available for payment of general creditors.

197. **Debentures to bearer (Scotland)**

Notwithstanding anything in the statute of the Scots Parliament of 1696, chapter 25, debentures to bearer issued in Scotland are valid and binding according to their terms.

PART VI

DISCLOSURE OF INTERESTS IN SHARES

Individual and group acquisitions

198. **Obligation of disclosure: the cases in which it may arise and "the relevant time"**

(1)   Where a person either—

(a)   to his knowledge acquires an interest in shares comprised in a public company's relevant share capital, or ceases to be interested in shares so comprised (whether or not retaining an interest in other shares so comprised), or

(b)   becomes aware that he has acquired an interest in shares so comprised or that he has ceased to be interested in shares so comprised in which he was previously interested,

then in certain circumstances he comes under an obligation ("the obligation of disclosure") to make notification to the company with respect to his interests (if any) in its shares.

(2)   In relation to a public company, "relevant share capital" means the company's issued share capital of a class carrying rights to vote in all circumstances at general meetings of the company (excluding any shares in the company held as treasury shares); and it is hereby declared for the avoidance of doubt that—

(a)   where a company's share capital is divided into different classes of shares, references in this Part to a percentage of the nominal value of its relevant share capital are to a percentage of the nominal value of the issued shares comprised in each of the classes taken separately (excluding any shares of each class held as treasury shares), and

(b)   the temporary suspension of voting rights in respect of shares comprised in issued share capital of a company of any such class does not affect the application of this Part in relation to interests in those or any other shares comprised in that class.

(3)   Where, otherwise than in circumstances within subsection (1), a person—

(a)   is aware at the time when it occurs of any change of circumstances affecting facts relevant to the application of the next following section to an existing interest of his in shares comprised in a company's share capital of any description, or

(b)   otherwise becomes aware of any such facts (whether or not arising from any such change of circumstances),

then in certain circumstances he comes under the obligation of disclosure.

(4)   The existence of the obligation in a particular case depends (in part) on circumstances obtaining
        before and after whatever is in that case the relevant time; and that is—
        (a)   in a case within subsection (1)(a) or (3)(a), the time of the event or change of circumstances
               there mentioned, and
        (b)   in a case within subsection (1)(b) or (3)(b), the time at which the person became aware of
               the facts in question.

199.   Interests to be disclosed

(1)   For the purposes of the obligation of disclosure, the interests to be taken into account are those in
        relevant share capital of the company concerned.

(2)   Where a person is interested in shares comprised in relevant share capital, then—
        (a)   if in some or all of those shares he has interests which are material interests, he has a
               notifiable interest at any time when the aggregate nominal value of the shares in which those
               material interests subsist is equal to or more than 3 per cent of the nominal value of that
               share capital; and
        (b)   he has a notifiable interest at any time when, not having such an interest by virtue of
               paragraph (a), the aggregate nominal value of the shares in which he has interests (whether
               or not including material interests) is equal to or more than 10 per cent of the nominal value
               of the relevant share capital.

(2A)   For the purposes of this Part, a material interest is any interest other than—
        (a)   an interest which a person who may lawfully manage investments belonging to another has
               by virtue of having the management of such investments under an agreement in or
               evidenced in writing;
        (b)   an interest which a person has by virtue of being the operator of—
               (i)   an authorised unit trust scheme;
               (ii)   a recognised scheme; or
               (iii) a UCITS (as defined in subsection (8));
        (bb)   an interest belonging to an open-ended investment company;
        (c)   an interest in shares in a listed company which, if that company were not listed, would fall
               to be disregarded by virtue of section 209(10); or
        (d)   an interest of another which a person is taken to have by virtue of the application of section
               203 or 205, where the interest of that other person falls within paragraph (a), (b), (bb) or (c).

(3)   All facts relevant to determining whether a person has a notifiable interest at any time (or the
        percentage level of his interest) are taken to be what he knows the facts to be at that time.

(4)   The obligation of disclosure arises under section 198(1) or (3) where the person has a notifiable
        interest immediately after the relevant time, but did not have such an interest immediately before
        that time.

(5)   The obligation also arises under section 198(1) or (3) where—
        (a)   the person had a notifiable interest immediately before the relevant time, but does not have
               such an interest immediately after it, or
        (b)   he had a notifiable interest immediately before that time, and has such an interest
               immediately after it, but the percentage levels of his interest immediately before and
               immediately after that time are not the same.

(6)   For the purposes of subsection (2A), a person ("A") may lawfully manage investments belonging
        to another if—
        (a)   A can manage those investments in accordance with a permission which A has under Part 4
               of the Financial Services and Markets Act 2000;
        (b)   A is an EEA firm of the kind mentioned in sub-paragraph (a) or (b) of paragraph 5 of
               Schedule 3 to that Act, and can manage those investments in accordance with its EEA
               authorisation;
        (c)   A can, in accordance with section 327 of that Act, manage those investments without
               contravening the prohibition contained in section 19 of that Act; or

(d)   A can lawfully manage those investments in another Member State and would, if he were to manage those investments in the United Kingdom, require permission under Part 4 of that Act.

(7)   References in this section to the management of investments must be read with—

(a)   section 22 of the Financial Services and Markets Act 2000;

(b)   any relevant order under that section; and

(c)   Schedule 2 to that Act.

(8)   In this Part "UCITS" means a collective investment scheme which—

(a)   is constituted in a member State other than the United Kingdom, and

(b)   is certified by the competent authority in that member State as complying with the conditions imposed by Council Directive 85/611/EEC on the co-ordination of laws, regulations and administrative provisions relating to undertakings for collective investment in transferable securities, as last amended by European Parliament and Council Directive 2001/108/EC;

and subsection (5) of section 264 of the Financial Services and Markets Act 2000 (meaning of "constituted in a member State") applies for the purposes of paragraph (a) of this subsection as it applies for the purposes of that section.

200.   "Percentage level" in relation to notifiable interests

(1)   Subject to the qualifications mentioned below, "percentage level", in section 199(5)(b), means the percentage figure found by expressing the aggregate nominal value of all the shares comprised in the share capital concerned in which the person has material interests immediately before or (as the case may be) immediately after the relevant time as a percentage of the nominal value of that share capital and rounding that figure down, if it is not a whole number, to the next whole number.

(2)   In relation to a notifiable interest which a person has when the aggregate nominal value of the shares in which he is interested is equal to or more than 10 per cent of the nominal value of that relevant share capital, subsection (1) shall have effect as if for the words "has material interests" there were substituted "is interested".

(3)   Where the nominal value of the share capital is greater immediately after the relevant time than it was immediately before, the percentage level of the person's interest immediately before (as well as immediately after) that time is determined by reference to the larger amount.

201.   ...

202.   Particulars to be contained in notification

(1)   Where notification is required by section 198 with respect to a person's interest (if any) in shares comprised in relevant share capital of a public company, the obligation to make the notification must ... be performed within the period of 2 days next following the day on which that obligation arises; and the notification must be in writing to the company.

(2)   The notification must specify the share capital to which it relates, and must also—

(a)   subject to subsections (2A) and (2B), state the number of shares comprised in that share capital in which the person making the notification knows he had material interests immediately after the time when the obligation arose, or

(b)   in a case where the person no longer has a notifiable interest in shares comprised in that share capital, state that he no longer has that interest.

(2A)   Where, immediately after the relevant time, the aggregate nominal value of the shares in which the person making the notification is interested is equal to or more than 10 per cent of the nominal value of that relevant share capital, subsection (2)(a) shall have effect as if for the words "had material interests" there were substituted "was interested".

(2B)   Nothing in subsection (2) or (2A) requires a notification to state, in relation to any shares, whether the interest of the person making the notification is (or is not) a material interest.

(3)   A notification (other than one stating that a person no longer has a notifiable interest) shall include the following particulars, so far as known to the person making the notification at the date when it is made—

(a)   the identity of each registered holder of shares to which the notification relates and the number of such shares held by each of them, and

(b)   the number of such shares in which the interest of the person giving the notification is such an interest as is mentioned in section 208(5).

(4)   A person who has an interest in shares comprised in a company's relevant share capital, that interest being notifiable, is under obligation to notify the company in writing—

(a)   of any particulars in relation to those shares which are specified in subsection (3), and

(b)   of any change in those particulars,

of which in either case he becomes aware at any time after any interest notification date and before the first occasion following that date on which he comes under any further obligation of disclosure with respect to his interest in shares comprised in that share capital.

An obligation arising under this section must be performed within the period of 2 days next following the day on which it arises.

(5)   The reference in subsection (4) to an interest notification date, in relation to a person's interest in shares comprised in a public company's relevant share capital, is to either of the following—

(a)   the date of any notification made by him with respect to his interest under this Part, and

(b)   where he has failed to make a notification, the date on which the period allowed for making it came to an end.

(6)   A person who at any time has an interest in shares which is notifiable is to be regarded under subsection (4) as continuing to have a notifiable interest in them unless and until he comes under obligation to make a notification stating that he no longer has such an interest in those shares.

203.   Notification of family and corporate interests

(1)   For purposes of sections 198 to 202, a person is taken to be interested in any shares in which his spouse *or civil partner* or any infant child or step-child of his is interested; and "infant" means, in relation to Scotland, person under the age of 18 years.

(2)   For those purposes, a person is taken to be interested in shares if a body corporate is interested in them and—

(a)   that body or its directors are accustomed to act in accordance with his directions or instructions, or

(b)   he is entitled to exercise or control the exercise of one-third or more of the voting power at general meetings of that body corporate.

(3)   Where a person is entitled to exercise or control the exercise of one-third or more of the voting power at general meetings of a body corporate and that body corporate is entitled to exercise or control the exercise of any of the voting power at general meetings of another body corporate ("the effective voting power") then, for purposes of subsection (2)(b), the effective voting power is taken as exercisable by that person.

(4)   For purposes of subsections (2) and (3), a person is entitled to exercise or control the exercise of voting power if—

(a)   he has a right (whether subject to conditions or not) the exercise of which would make him so entitled, or

(b)   he is under an obligation (whether or not so subject) the fulfilment of which would make him so entitled.

Note. The italicized words in subsection (1) are inserted by the Civil Partnership Act 2004, s. 261(1), Sch. 27, para. 99, as from a day to be appointed.

204.   Agreement to acquire interests in a particular company

(1)   In certain circumstances the obligation of disclosure may arise from an agreement between two or more persons which includes provision for the acquisition by any one or more of them of interests in shares of a particular public company ("the target company"), being shares comprised in the relevant share capital company.

(2)   This section applies to such an agreement if—

(a)   the agreement also includes provisions imposing obligations or restrictions on any one or more of the parties to it with respect to their use, retention or disposal of their interests in that company's shares acquired in pursuance of the agreement (whether or not together with any other interests of theirs in the company's shares to which the agreement relates), and

(b)   any interest in the company's shares is in fact acquired by any of the parties in pursuance of the agreement;

and in relation to such an agreement references below in this section, and in sections 205 and 206, to the target company are to the company which is the target company for that agreement in accordance with this and the previous subsection.

(3)   The reference in subsection (2)(a) to the use of interests in shares in the target company is to the exercise of any rights or of any control or influence arising from those interests (including the right to enter into any agreement for the exercise, or for control of the exercise, of any of those rights by another person).

(4)   Once any interest in shares in the target company has been acquired in pursuance of such an agreement as is mentioned above, this section continues to apply to that agreement irrespective of—

(a)   whether or not any further acquisitions of interests in the company's shares take place in pursuance of the agreement, and

(b)   any change in the persons who are for the time being parties to it, and

(c)   any variation of the agreement,

so long as the agreement continues to include provisions of any description mentioned in subsection (2)(a).

References in this subsection to the agreement include any agreement having effect (whether directly or indirectly) in substitution for the original agreement.

(5)   In this section, and also in references elsewhere in this Part to an agreement to which this section applies, "agreement" includes any agreement or arrangement; and references in this section to provisions of an agreement—

(a)   accordingly include undertakings, expectations or understandings operative under any arrangement, and

(b)   (without prejudice to the above) also include any provisions, whether express or implied and whether absolute or not.

(6)   However, this section does not apply to an agreement which is not legally binding unless it involves mutuality in the undertakings, expectations or understandings of the parties to it; nor does the section apply to an agreement to underwrite or sub-underwrite any offer of shares in a company, provided the agreement is confined to that purpose and any matters incidental to it.

205.   Obligation of disclosure arising under s 204

(1)   In the case of an agreement to which section 204 applies, each party to the agreement is taken (for purposes of the obligation of disclosure) to be interested in all shares in the target company in which any other party to it is interested apart from the agreement (whether or not the interest of the other party in question was acquired, or includes any interest which was acquired, in pursuance of the agreement).

(2)   For those purposes, and also for those of the next section, an interest of a party to such an agreement in shares in the target company is an interest apart from the agreement if he is interested in those shares otherwise than by virtue of the application of section 204 and this section in relation to the agreement.

(3)   Accordingly, any such interest of the person (apart from the agreement) includes for those purposes any interest treated as his under section 203 or by the application of section 204 and this section in relation to any other agreement with respect to shares in the target company to which he is a party.

(4)   A notification with respect to his interest in shares in the target company made to that company under this Part by a person who is for the time being a party to an agreement to which section 204 applies shall—

(a)   state that the person making the notification is a party to such an agreement,

(b)   include the names and (so far as known to him) the addresses of the other parties to the agreement, identifying them as such, and

(c)   state whether or not any of the shares to which the notification relates are shares in which he is interested by virtue of section 204 and this section and, if so, the number of those shares.

(5)   Where a person makes a notification to a company under this Part in consequence of ceasing to be interested in any shares of that company by virtue of the fact that he or any other person has ceased to be a party to an agreement to which section 204 applies, the notification shall include a statement that he or that other person has ceased to be a party to the agreement (as the case may require) and also (in the latter case) the name and (if known to him) the address of that other.

206.   Obligation of persons acting together to keep each other informed

(1)   A person who is a party to an agreement to which section 204 applies is subject to the requirements of this section at any time when—

(a)   the target company is a public company, and he knows it to be so, and

(b)   the shares in that company to which the agreement relates consist of or include shares comprised in relevant share capital of the company, and he knows that to be the case; and

(c)   he knows the facts which make the agreement one to which section 204 applies.

(2)   Such a person is under obligation to notify every other party to the agreement, in writing, of the relevant particulars of his interest (if any) apart from the agreement in shares comprised in relevant share capital of the target company—

(a)   on his first becoming subject to the requirements of this section, and

(b)   on each occurrence after that time while he is still subject to those requirements of any event or circumstances within section 198(1) (as it applies to his case otherwise than by reference to interests treated as his under section 205 as applying to that agreement).

(3)   The relevant particulars to be notified under subsection (2) are—

(a)   the number of shares (if any) comprised in the target company's relevant share capital in which the person giving the notice would be required to state his interest if he were under the wide obligation of disclosure with respect to that interest (apart from the agreement) immediately after the time when the obligation to give notice under subsection (2) arose, and

(b)   the relevant particulars with respect to the registered ownership of those shares, so far as known to him at the date of the notice and

(c)   except in the circumstance mentioned in subsection (3A), the number of shares (if any) out of the number given under paragraph (a) in which he knows that, immediately after the time when the obligation to give the notice arose, he had interests (apart from the agreement) which were not material interests.

(3A) The circumstance referred to in subsection (3)(c) is that the aggregate nominal value of the shares comprised in relevant share capital in which the person is interested (apart from the agreement) is equal to or more than 10 per cent of the nominal value of the relevant share capital.

(3B) For the purposes of subsection (3)(a) "the wide obligation of disclosure" means the obligation to disclose the number of shares in which the person concerned has any interest (material or otherwise).

(4)   A person who is for the time being subject to the requirements of this section is also under obligation to notify every other party to the agreement, in writing—

(a)   of any relevant particulars with respect to the registered ownership of any shares comprised in relevant share capital of the target company in which he is interested apart from the agreement, and

(b)   of any change in those particulars,

of which in either case he becomes aware at any time after any interest notification date and before the first occasion following that date on which he becomes subject to any further obligation to give notice under subsection (2) with respect to his interest in shares comprised in that share capital.

(5)   The reference in subsection (4) to an interest notification date, in relation to a person's interest in shares comprised in the target company's relevant share capital, is to either of the following—
    (a)   the date of any notice given by him with respect to his interest under subsection (2), and
    (b)   where he has failed to give that notice, the date on which the period allowed by this section for giving the notice came to an end.

(6)   A person who is a party to an agreement to which section 204 applies is under an obligation to notify each other party to the agreement, in writing, of his current address—
    (a)   on his first becoming subject to the requirements of this section, and
    (b)   on any change in his address occurring after that time and while he is still subject to those requirements.

(7)   A reference to the relevant particulars with respect to the registered ownership of shares is to such particulars in relation to those shares as are mentioned in section 202(3)(a) or (b).

(8)   A person's obligation to give any notice required by this section to any other person must be performed within the period of 2 days next following the day on which that obligation arose.

207.   Interests in shares by attribution

(1)   Where section 198 or 199 refers to a person acquiring an interest in shares or ceasing to be interested in shares, that reference in certain cases includes his becoming or ceasing to be interested in those shares by virtue of another person's interest.

(2)   Such is the case where he becomes or ceases to be interested by virtue of section 203 or (as the case may be) section 205 whether—
    (a)   by virtue of the fact that the person who is interested in the shares becomes or ceases to be a person whose interests (if any) fall by virtue of either section to be treated as his, or
    (b)   in consequence of the fact that such a person has become or ceased to be interested in the shares, or
    (c)   in consequence of the fact that he himself becomes or ceases to be a party to an agreement to which section 204 applies to which the person interested in the shares is for the time being a party, or
    (d)   in consequence of the fact that an agreement to which both he and that person are parties becomes or ceases to be one to which that section applies.

(3)   The person is then to be treated as knowing he has acquired an interest in the shares or (as the case may be) that he has ceased to be interested in them, if and when he knows both—
    (a)   the relevant facts with respect to the other person's interest in the shares, and
    (b)   the relevant facts by virtue of which he himself has become or ceased to be interested in them in accordance with section 203 or 205.

(4)   He has the knowledge referred to in subsection (3)(a) if he knows (whether contemporaneously or not) either of the subsistence of the other person's interest at any material time or of the fact that the other has become or ceased to be interested in the shares at any such time; and "material time" is any time at which the other's interests (if any) fall or fell to be treated as his under section 203 or 205.

(5)   A person is to be regarded as knowing of the subsistence of another's interest in shares or (as the case may be) that another has become or ceased to be interested in shares if he has been notified under section 206 of facts with respect to the other's interest which indicate that he is or has become or ceased to be interested in the shares (whether on his own account or by virtue of a third party's interest in them).

208.   Interests in shares which are to be notified

(1)   This section applies, subject to the section next following, in determining for purposes of sections 198 to 202 whether a person has a notifiable interest in shares.

(2)   A reference to an interest in shares is to be read as including an interest of any kind whatsoever in the shares; and accordingly there are to be disregarded any restraints or restrictions to which the exercise of any right attached to the interest is or may be subject.

(3)   Where property is held on trust and an interest in shares is comprised in the property, a beneficiary of the trust who apart from this subsection does not have an interest in the shares is to be taken as having such an interest.

(4)   A person is taken to have an interest in shares if—

   (a)   he enters into a contract for their purchase by him (whether for cash or other consideration), or

   (b)   not being the registered holder, he is entitled to exercise any right conferred by the holding of the shares or is entitled to control the exercise of any such right.

(5)   A person is taken to have an interest in shares if, otherwise than by virtue of having an interest under a trust—

   (a)   he has a right to call for delivery of the shares to himself or to his order, or

   (b)   he has a right to acquire an interest in shares or is under an obligation to take an interest in shares,

   whether in any case the right or obligation is conditional or absolute.

(6)   For purposes of subsection (4)(b), a person is entitled to exercise or control the exercise of any right conferred by the holding of shares if he—

   (a)   has a right (whether subject to conditions or not) the exercise of which would make him so entitled, or

   (b)   is under an obligation (whether so subject or not) the fulfilment of which would make him so entitled.

(7)   Persons having a joint interest are taken each of them to have that interest.

(8)   It is immaterial that shares in which a person has an interest are unidentifiable.

209. Interests to be disregarded

(1)   Subject to subsections (5) and (6), the following interests in shares are disregarded for the purposes of sections 198 to 202—

   (a)   where property is held on trust and an interest in shares is comprised in that property, an interest of a person, being a discretionary interest or an interest in reversion or remainder or an interest of a bare trustee;

   (b)   an interest which a person has by virtue of holding units in—

      (i)   an authorised unit trust scheme;

      (ii)   a recognised scheme; or

      (iii) a UCITS;

   (c)   an interest of a person which is an exempt security interest within the meaning of subsection (2);

   (d)   an interest which a person has by virtue of his being a beneficiary under a retirement benefits scheme as defined in section 611 of the Income and Corporation Taxes Act 1988;

   (e)   an interest which a person has in shares as a result of the acceptance of a takeover offer made by him (either alone or jointly with one or more other persons) for shares where—

      (i)   the offer is subject to a threshold acceptance condition; and

      (ii)   the threshold acceptance condition is not fulfilled;

   (f)   an interest of a person which is an exempt custodian interest within the meaning of subsection (4);

   (g)   an interest which a person has by virtue of his being a personal representative of any estate;

   (h)   an interest which a person has—

      (i)   by virtue of his being a trustee of an authorised unit trust scheme, …

      (ii)   in relation to a recognised scheme or a UCITS, by virtue of his being entrusted with the custody of the property in question (whether or not under a trust), or

      (iii) by virtue of his being a depositary, within the meaning of the Open-Ended Investment Companies Regulations 2001, of an open-ended investment company.

(2)   An interest in shares is an exempt security interest for the purposes of subsection (1)(c) if the condition mentioned in subsection (2A) is satisfied and it is held by—

    (a)   a person who has permission under Part 4 of the Financial Services and Markets Act 2000 to accept deposits;

    (b)   an EEA firm of the kind mentioned in paragraph 5(b) of Schedule 3 to that Act which falls within article 1(1)(a) of the banking consolidation directive (within the meaning of that Schedule);

    (c)   a person authorised under the law of a member State other than the United Kingdom to accept deposits who—

        (i)   would not qualify for authorisation under paragraph 12 of Schedule 3 to that Act; and

        (ii)   would require permission under another provision of that Act to accept such deposits in the United Kingdom;

    (d)   an authorised insurance undertaking;

    (e)   a person authorised under the law of a member State to deal in securities or derivatives, who deals in securities or derivatives on a relevant stock exchange or a relevant investment exchange, whether as a member or otherwise;

    (f)   a relevant stock exchange;

    (g)   a relevant investment exchange;

    (h)   a recognised clearing house;

    (i)   the Bank of England; or

    (j)   the central bank of a member State other than the United Kingdom.

(2A)   The condition is that the interest in the shares must be held by way of security only for the purposes of a transaction entered into in the ordinary course of his or its business as a person or other body falling within any of paragraphs (a) to (j) of subsection (2).

(2B)   Paragraphs (a) to (c) of subsection (2) must be read with—

    (a)   section 22 of the Financial Services and Markets Act 2000;

    (b)   any relevant order under that section; and

    (c)   Schedule 2 to that Act.

(2C)   But paragraph (a) of subsection (2) does not include—

    (a)   a building society incorporated, or deemed to be incorporated, under the Building Societies Act 1986; or

    (b)   a credit union, within the meaning of the Credit Unions Act 1979 or the Credit Unions (Northern Ireland) Order 1985.

(3)   For the purposes of subsection (1)(e)—

    (a)   "takeover offer" has the same meaning as in Part XIIIA; and

    (b)   "a threshold acceptance condition" means a condition that acceptances are received in respect of such proportion of the shares for which the takeover offer is made as is specified in or determined in accordance with the terms of the takeover offer.

(4)   For the purposes of subsection (1)(f) an interest of a person is an exempt custodian interest if it is held by him—

    (a)   as a custodian (whether under a trust or by a contract); or

    (b)   under an arrangement pursuant to which he has issued, or is to issue, depositary receipts in respect of the shares concerned.

(5)   An interest referred to in any paragraph of subsection (1) (except for paragraph (c)) is disregarded only if the person referred to in the relevant paragraph or in subsection (4) is not entitled to exercise or control the exercise of voting rights in respect of the shares concerned; and for this purpose he is not so entitled if he is bound (whether by contract or otherwise) not to exercise the voting rights, or not to exercise them otherwise than in accordance with the instructions of another.

(6)   In the case of an interest referred to in paragraph (c) of subsection (1), an interest of a person referred to in subsection (2) is disregarded only if that person—

    (a)   is not entitled (within the meaning of subsection (5)) to exercise or control the exercise of voting rights in respect of the shares concerned; or

(b)   is so entitled, but has not evidenced any intention to exercise them or control their exercise nor taken any step to do so.

(7)   For the purposes of subsections (5) and (6), voting rights which a person is entitled to exercise or of which he is entitled to control the exercise only in certain circumstances shall be taken into account only when the circumstances have arisen and for so long as they continue to obtain.

(8)   An interest in shares of a company is also disregarded for the purposes of sections 198 to 202—

(a)   if it is held by a market maker in securities or derivatives for the purposes of his business, but

(b)   only in so far as it is not used by him for the purpose of intervening in the management of the company.

(9)   For the purposes of subsection (8) a person is a market maker in securities or derivatives if—

(a)   he is authorised under the law of a member State to deal in securities or derivatives and so deals on a relevant stock exchange or on a relevant investment exchange (whether as a member or otherwise); and

(b)   he holds himself out at all normal times as willing to acquire and dispose of securities or derivatives at prices specified by him and in so doing is subject to the rules of that exchange; and he holds an interest for the purposes of his business if he holds it for the purposes of a business carried on by him as a market maker in a member State.

(9A) Where—

(a)   in pursuance of arrangements made with the operator of a relevant system—

(i)   securities of a particular aggregate value are on any day transferred by means of that system from a person ("A") to another person ("B");

(ii)   the securities are of kinds and amounts determined by the operator-system; and

(iii) the securities, or securities of the same kinds and amounts, are on the following day transferred by means of the relevant system from B to A; and

(b)   the securities comprise any shares of a company,

any interest of B in those shares is also disregarded for the purposes of sections 198 to 202.

(9B) For the purposes of subsection (9A)—

(a)   any day which, in England and Wales, is a non-business day for the purposes of the Bills of Exchange Act 1882 is disregarded; and

(b)   expressions which are used in the Uncertificated Securities Regulations 2001 have the same meanings as in those Regulations.

(10) The following interests in shares in a public company which is not listed are also disregarded for the purposes of sections 198 to 202—

(a)   an interest which subsists by virtue of—

(i)   a scheme made under section 24 or 25 of the Charities Act 1993, section 25 of the Charities Act (Northern Ireland) 1964, section 11 of the Trustee Investments Act 1961 or section 42 of the Administration of Justice Act 1982, or

(ii)   the scheme set out in the Schedule to the Church Funds Investment Measure 1958;

(b)   an interest of the Church of Scotland General Trustees or of the Church of Scotland Trust in shares held by them or of any other person in shares held by those Trustees or that Trust otherwise than as simple trustees;

(c)   an interest for the life of himself or another of a person under a settlement in the case of which the property comprised in the settlement consists of or includes shares, and the conditions mentioned in subsection (11) are satisfied;

(d)   ...

(e)   an interest of the Accountant General of the Supreme Court in shares held by him;

(f)   an interest of the Public Trustee;

(g)   an interest of the Probate Judge subsisting by virtue of section 3 of the Administration of Estates Act (Northern Ireland) 1955.

(11) The conditions referred to in subsection (10)(c) are, in relation to a settlement—

(a)   that it is irrevocable, and

(b)   that the settlor (within the meaning of section 670 of the Income and Corporation Taxes Act 1988) has no interest in any income arising under, or property comprised in, the settlement.

(12)   A person is not by virtue of section 208(4)(b) taken to be interested in shares by reason only that he has been appointed a proxy to vote at a specified meeting of a company or of any class of its members and at any adjournment of that meeting, or has been appointed by a corporation to act as its representative at any meeting of a company or of any class of its members.

(13)   In the application of subsection (1)(a) to property held on trust according to the law of Scotland, for the words "or remainder or an interest of a bare trustee" there shall be substituted "or in fee or an interest of a simple trustee".

210.   Other provisions about notification under this Part

(1)   Where a person authorises another ("the agent") to acquire or dispose of, on his behalf, interests in shares comprised in relevant share capital of a public company, he shall secure that the agent notifies him immediately of acquisitions or disposals effected by the agent which will or may give rise to any obligation of disclosure imposed on him by this Part with respect to his interest in that share capital.

(2)   An obligation of disclosure imposed on a person by any provision of sections 198 to 202 is treated as not being fulfilled unless the notice by means of which it purports to be fulfilled identifies him and gives his address and, in a case where he is a director of the company, is expressed to be given in fulfilment of that obligation.

(3)   A person who—
(a)   fails to fulfil, within the proper period, an obligation of disclosure imposed on him by this Part, or
(b)   in purported fulfilment of any such obligation makes to a company a statement which he knows to be false, or recklessly makes to a company a statement which is false, or
(c)   fails to fulfil, within the proper period, an obligation to give another person a notice required by section 206, or
(d)   fails without reasonable excuse to comply with subsection (1) of this section,
is guilty of an offence and liable to imprisonment or a fine, or both.

(4)   It is a defence for a person charged with an offence under subsection (3)(c) to prove that it was not possible for him to give the notice to the other person required by section 206 within the proper period, and either—
(a)   that it has not since become possible for him to give the notice so required, or
(b)   that he gave the notice as soon after the end of that period as it became possible for him to do so.

(5)   Where a person is convicted of an offence under this section (other than an offence relating to his ceasing to be interested in a company's shares), the Secretary of State may by order direct that the shares in relation to which the offence was committed shall, until further order, be subject to the restrictions of Part XV of this Act; and such an order may be made notwithstanding any power in the company's memorandum or articles enabling the company to impose similar restrictions on those shares.

(5A)   If the Secretary of State is satisfied that an order under subsection (5) may unfairly affect the rights of third parties in respect of shares then the Secretary of State, for the purpose of protecting such rights and subject to such terms as he thinks fit, may direct that such acts by such persons or descriptions of persons and for such purposes as may be set out in the order, shall not constitute a breach of the restrictions of Part XV of this Act.

(6)   Sections 732 (restriction on prosecutions) and 733(2) and (3) (liability of directors, etc) apply to offences under this section.

210A   Power to make further provision by regulations

(1)   The Secretary of State may by regulations amend—
(a)   the definition of "relevant share capital" (section 198(2)),
(b)   the percentage giving rise to a "notifiable interest" (section 199(2)),

     (c)   the periods within which an obligation of disclosure must be fulfilled or a notice must be given (sections 202(1) and (4) and 206(8)),

     (d)   the provisions as to what is taken to be an interest in shares (section 208) and what interests are to be disregarded (section 209), and

     (e)   the provisions as to company investigations (section 212);

and the regulations may amend, replace or repeal the provisions referred to above and make such other consequential amendments or repeals of provisions of this Part as appear to the Secretary of State to be appropriate.

(2)   The regulations may in any case make different provision for different descriptions of company; and regulations under subsection (1)(b), (c) or (d) may make different provision for different descriptions of person, interest or share capital.

(3)   The regulations may contain such transitional and other supplementary and incidental provisions as appear to the Secretary of State to be appropriate, and may in particular make provision as to the obligations of a person whose interest in a company's shares becomes or ceases to be notifiable by virtue of the regulations.

(4)   Regulations under this section shall be made by statutory instrument.

(5)   No regulations shall be made under this section unless a draft of the regulations has been laid before and approved by a resolution of each House of Parliament.

Registration and investigation of share acquisitions and disposals

211.   Register of interests in shares

(1)   Every public company shall keep a register for purposes of sections 198 to 202, and whenever the company receives information from a person in consequence of the fulfilment of an obligation imposed on him by any of those sections, it is under obligation to inscribe in the register, against that person's name, that information and the date of the inscription.

(2)   Without prejudice to subsection (1), where a company receives a notification under this Part which includes a statement that the person making the notification, or any other person, has ceased to be a party to an agreement to which section 204 applies, the company is under obligation to record that information against the name of that person in every place where his name appears in the register as a party to that agreement (including any entry relating to him made against another person's name).

(3)   An obligation imposed by subsection (1) or (2) must be fulfilled within the period of 3 days next following the day on which it arises.

(4)   The company is not, by virtue of anything done for the purposes of this section, affected with notice of, or put upon enquiry as to, the rights of any person in relation to any shares.

(5)   The register must be so made up that the entries against the several names entered in it appear in chronological order.

(6)   Unless the register is in such form as to constitute in itself an index, the company shall keep an index of the names entered in the register which shall in respect of each name contain a sufficient indication to enable the information entered against it to be readily found; and the company shall, within 10 days after the date on which a name is entered in the register, make any necessary alteration in the index.

(7)   If the company ceases to be a public company it shall continue to keep the register and any associated index until the end of the period of 6 years beginning with the day next following that on which it ceases to be such a company.

(8)   The register and any associated index—

     (a)   shall be kept at the place at which the register required to be kept by the company by section 325 (register of directors' interests) is kept, and

     (b)   subject to the next subsection, shall be available for inspection in accordance with section 219 below.

(9)   Neither the register nor any associated index shall be available for inspection in accordance with that section in so far as it contains information with respect to a company for the time being

entitled to avail itself of the benefit conferred by section 231(3) (disclosure of shareholdings not required if it would be harmful to company's business).

(10)   If default is made in complying with subsection (1) or (2), or with any of subsections (5) to (7), the company and every officer of it who is in default is liable to a fine and, for continued contravention, to a daily default fine.

(11)   Any register kept by a company immediately before 15th June 1982 under section 34 of the Companies Act 1967 shall continue to be kept by the company under and for the purposes of this section.

212.   Company investigations

(1)   A public company may by notice in writing require a person whom the company knows or has reasonable cause to believe to be or, at any time during the 3 years immediately preceding the date on which the notice is issued, to have been interested in shares comprised in the company's relevant share capital—

  (a)   to confirm that fact or (as the case may be) to indicate whether or not it is the case, and

  (b)   where he holds or has during that time held an interest in shares so comprised, to give such further information as may be required in accordance with the following subsection.

(2)   A notice under this section may require the person to whom it is addressed—

  (a)   to give particulars of his own past or present interest in shares comprised in relevant share capital of the company (held by him at any time during the 3-year period mentioned in subsection (1)),

  (b)   where the interest is a present interest and any other interest in the shares subsists or, in any case, where another interest in the shares subsisted during that 3-year period at any time when his own interest subsisted, to give (so far as lies within his knowledge) such particulars with respect to that other interest as may be required by the notice,

  (c)   where his interest is a past interest, to give (so far as lies within his knowledge) particulars of the identity of the person who held that interest immediately upon his ceasing to hold it.

(3)   The particulars referred to in subsection (2)(a) and (b) include particulars of the identity of persons interested in the shares in question and of whether persons interested in the same shares are or were parties to any agreement to which section 204 applies or to any agreement or arrangement relating to the exercise of any rights conferred by the holding of the shares.

(4)   A notice under this section shall require any information given in response to the notice to be given in writing within such reasonable time as may be specified in the notice.

(5)   Sections 203 to 205 and 208 apply for the purpose of construing references in this section to persons interested in shares and to interests in shares respectively, as they apply in relation to sections 198 to 201 (but with the omission of any reference to section 209).

(6)   This section applies in relation to a person who has or previously had, or is or was entitled to acquire, a right to subscribe for shares in a public company which would on issue be comprised in relevant share capital of that company as it applies in relation to a person who is or was interested in shares so comprised; and references above in this section to an interest in shares so comprised and to shares so comprised are to be read accordingly in any such case as including respectively any such right and shares which would on issue be so comprised.

213.   Registration of interests disclosed under s 212

(1)   Whenever in pursuance of a requirement imposed on a person under section 212 a company receives information to which this section applies relating to shares comprised in its relevant share capital, it is under obligation to enter against the name of the registered holder of those shares, in a separate part of its register of interests in shares—

  (a)   the fact that the requirement was imposed and the date on which it was imposed, and

  (b)   any information to which this section applies received in pursuance of the requirement.

(2)   This section applies to any information received in pursuance of a requirement imposed by section 212 which relates to the present interests held by any persons in shares comprised in relevant share capital of the company in question.

(3)   Subsections (3) to (10) of section 211 apply in relation to any part of the register maintained in accordance with subsection (1) of this section as they apply in relation to the remainder of the register, reading references to subsection (1) of that section to include subsection (1) of this.

(4)   In the case of a register kept by a company immediately before 15th June 1982 under section 34 of the Companies Act 1967, any part of the register so kept for the purposes of section 27 of the Companies Act 1976 shall continue to be kept by the company under and for the purposes of this section.

214.   Company investigation on requisition by members

(1)   A company may be required to exercise its powers under section 212 on the requisition of members of the company holding at the date of the deposit of the requisition not less than one-tenth of such of the paid-up capital of the company as carries at that date the right of voting at general meetings of the company (excluding any shares in the company held as treasury shares).

(2)   The requisition must—
   (a)   state that the requisitionists are requiring the company to exercise its powers under section 212,
   (b)   specify the manner in which they require those powers to be exercised, and
   (c)   give reasonable grounds for requiring the company to exercise those powers in the manner specified,
   and must be signed by the requisitionists and deposited at the company's registered office.

(3)   The requisition may consist of several documents in like form each signed by one or more requisitionists.

(4)   On the deposit of a requisition complying with this section it is the company's duty to exercise its powers under section 212 in the manner specified in the requisition.

(5)   If default is made in complying with subsection (4), the company and every officer of it who is in default is liable to a fine.

215.   Company report to members

(1)   On the conclusion of an investigation carried out by a company in pursuance of a requisition under section 214, it is the company's duty to cause a report of the information received in pursuance of that investigation to be prepared, and the report shall be made available at the company's registered office within a reasonable period after the conclusion of that investigation.

(2)   Where—
   (a)   a company undertakes an investigation in pursuance of a requisition under section 214, and
   (b)   the investigation is not concluded before the end of 3 months beginning with the date immediately following the date of the deposit of the requisition,
   it is the duty of the company to cause to be prepared, in respect of that period and each successive period of 3 months ending before the conclusion of the investigation, an interim report of the information received during that period in pursuance of the investigation. Each such report shall be made available at the company's registered office within a reasonable period after the end of the period to which it relates.

(3)   The period for making any report prepared under this section available as required by subsection (1) or (2) shall not exceed 15 days.

(4)   Such a report shall not include any information with respect to a company entitled to avail itself of the benefit conferred by section 231(3) (disclosure of shareholdings not required if it would be harmful to company's business); but where any such information is omitted, that fact shall be stated in the report.

(5)   The company shall, within 3 days of making any report prepared under this section available at its registered office, notify the requisitionists that the report is so available.

(6)   An investigation carried out by a company in pursuance of a requisition under section 214 is regarded for purposes of this section as concluded when the company has made all such inquiries as are necessary or expedient for the purposes of the requisition and in the case of each such

inquiry, either a response has been received by the company or the time allowed for a response has elapsed.

(7)   A report prepared under this section—

    (a)   shall be kept at the company's registered office from the day on which it is first available there in accordance with subsection (1) or (2) until the expiration of 6 years beginning with the day next following that day, and

    (b)   shall be available for inspection in accordance with section 219 below so long as it is so kept.

(8)   If default is made in complying with subsection (1), (2), (5) or (7)(a), the company and every officer of it who is in default is liable to a fine.

216.   Penalty for failure to provide information

(1)   Where notice is served by a company under section 212 on a person who is or was interested in shares of the company and that person fails to give the company any information required by the notice within the time specified in it, the company may apply to the court for an order directing that the shares in question be subject to the restrictions of Part XV of this Act.

(1A)   On an application made under subsection (1) the court may make an interim order and any such order may be made unconditionally or on such terms as the court thinks fit.

(1B)   If the court is satisfied that an order under subsection (1) may unfairly affect the rights of third parties in respect of shares then the court, for the purpose of protecting such rights and subject to such terms as it thinks fit, may direct that such acts by such persons or descriptions of persons and for such purposes as may be set out in the order, shall not constitute a breach of the restrictions of Part XV of this Act.

(2)   An order under this section may be made by the court notwithstanding any power contained in the applicant company's memorandum or articles enabling the company itself to impose similar restrictions on the shares in question.

(3)   Subject to the following subsections, a person who fails to comply with a notice under section 212 or who, in purported compliance with such a notice, makes any statement which he knows to be false in a material particular or recklessly makes any statement which is false in a material particular is guilty of an offence and liable to imprisonment or a fine, or both.

Section 733(2) and (3) of this Act (liability of individuals for corporate default) apply to offences under this subsection.

(4)   A person is not guilty of an offence by virtue of failing to comply with a notice under section 212 if he proves that the requirement to give the information was frivolous or vexatious.

(5)   A person is not obliged to comply with a notice under section 212 if he is for the time being exempted by the Secretary of State from the operation of that section; but the Secretary of State shall not grant any such exemption unless—

    (a)   he has consulted with the Governor of the Bank of England, and

    (b)   he (the Secretary of State) is satisfied that, having regard to any undertaking given by the person in question with respect to any interest held or to be held by him in any shares, there are special reasons why that person should not be subject to the obligations imposed by that section.

217.   Removal of entries from register

(1)   A company may remove an entry against a person's name from its register of interests in shares if more than 6 years have elapsed since the date of the entry being made, and either—

    (a)   that entry recorded the fact that the person in question had ceased to have an interest notifiable under this Part in relevant share capital of the company, or

    (b)   it has been superseded by a later entry made under section 211 against the same person's name;

and in a case within paragraph (a) the company may also remove that person's name from the register.

(2)   If a person in pursuance of an obligation imposed on him by any provision of this Part gives to a company the name and address of another person as being interested in shares in the company, the company shall, within 15 days of the date on which it was given that information, notify the other person that he has been so named and shall include in that notification—

(a)   particulars of any entry relating to him made, in consequence of its being given that information, by the company in its register of interests in shares, and

(b)   a statement informing him of his right to apply to have the entry removed in accordance with the following provisions of this section.

(3)   A person who has been notified by a company in pursuance of subsection (2) that an entry relating to him has been made in the company's register of interests in shares may apply in writing to the company for the removal of that entry from the register; and the company shall remove the entry if satisfied that the information in pursuance of which the entry was made was incorrect.

(4)   If a person who is identified in a company's register of interests in shares as being a party to an agreement to which section 204 applies (whether by an entry against his own name or by an entry relating to him made against another person's name as mentioned in subsection (2)(a)) ceases to be a party to that agreement, he may apply in writing to the company for the inclusion of that information in the register; and if the company is satisfied that he has ceased to be a party to the agreement, it shall record that information (if not already recorded) in every place where his name appears as a party to that agreement in the register.

(5)   If an application under subsection (3) or (4) is refused (in a case within subsection (4), otherwise than on the ground that the information has already been recorded) the applicant may apply to the court for an order directing the company to remove the entry in question from the register or (as the case may be) to include the information in question in the register; and the court may, if it thinks fit, make such an order.

(6)   Where a name is removed from a company's register of interests in shares in pursuance of subsection (1) or (3) or an order under subsection (5), the company shall within 14 days of the date of that removal make any necessary alteration in any associated index.

(7)   If default is made in complying with subsection (2) or (6), the company and every officer of it who is in default is liable to a fine and, for continued contravention, to a daily default fine.

218.   Otherwise, entries not to be removed

(1)   Entries in a company's register of interests in shares shall not be deleted except in accordance with section 217.

(2)   If an entry is deleted from a company's register of interests in shares in contravention of subsection (1), the company shall restore that entry to the register as soon as is reasonably practicable.

(3)   If default is made in complying with subsection (1) or (2), the company and every officer of it who is in default is liable to a fine and, for continued contravention of subsection (2), to a daily default fine.

219.   Inspection of register and reports

(1)   Any register of interests in shares and any report which is required by section 215(7) to be available for inspection in accordance with this section shall, ... be open to the inspection of any member of the company or of any other person without charge.

(2)   Any such member or other person may require a copy of any such register or report, or any part of it, on payment of such fee as may be prescribed; and the company shall cause any copy so required by a person to be sent to him before the expiration of the period of 10 days beginning with the day next following that on which the requirement is received by the company.

(3)   If an inspection required under this section is refused or a copy so required is not sent within the proper period, the company and every officer of it who is in default is liable to a fine and, for continued contravention, to a daily default fine.

(4)   In the case of a refusal of an inspection required under this section of any register or report, the court may by order compel an immediate inspection of it; and in the case of failure to send a copy required under this section, the court may by order direct that the copy required shall be sent to the person requiring it.

(5)   The Secretary of State may by regulations made by statutory instrument substitute a sum specified in the regulations for the sum for the time being mentioned in subsection (2).

Supplementary

220.   Definitions for Part VI

(1)   In this Part of this Act—

"associated index", in relation to a register, means the index kept in relation to that register in pursuance of section 211(6);

...

"authorised insurance undertaking" means an insurance undertaking which has been authorised in accordance with Article 6 or 23 of Council Directive 73/239/EEC or Article 4 or 51 of Directive 2002/83/EC of the European Parliament and of the Council of 5th November 2002 concerning life assurance, or is authorised under the law of a member State to carry on insurance business restricted to re-insurance;

"authorised unit trust scheme" has the same meaning as in Part 17 of the Financial Services and Markets Act 2000;

"depositary receipt" means a certificate or other record (whether or not in the form of a document)—

(a)   which is issued by or on behalf of a person who holds shares or who holds evidence of the right to receive shares, or has an interest in shares, in a particular company; and

(b)   which evidences or acknowledges that another person is entitled to rights in relation to those shares or shares of the same kind, which shall include the right to receive such shares (or evidence of the right to receive such shares) from the person mentioned in paragraph (a);

"derivatives" means options and futures in relation to shares;

"EEA authorisation" has the same meaning as in paragraph 6 of Schedule 3 to the Financial Services and Markets Act 2000;

...

...

"listed company" means a company any of the shares in which are officially listed on a relevant stock exchange and "listed" shall be construed accordingly;

"material interest" shall be construed in accordance with section 199(2A);

"open-ended investment company" has the same meaning as in the Open-Ended Investment Companies Regulations 2001;

"operator", in relation to a collective investment scheme, shall be construed in accordance with section 237(2) of the Financial Services and Markets Act 2000;

"recognised clearing house" has the same meaning as in the Financial Services and Markets Act 2000;

"recognised scheme" has the same meaning as in Part 17 of the Financial Services and Markets Act 2000;

"register of interests in shares" means the register kept in pursuance of section 211 including, except where the context otherwise requires, that part of the register kept in pursuance of section 213;

"relevant investment exchange" means an exchange situated or operating in a member State on which derivatives are traded;

"relevant share capital" has the meaning given by section 198(2);

"relevant stock exchange" means a stock exchange situated or operating in a member State;

"UCITS" has the meaning given by section 199(8);

"units" has the same meaning as in section 237(2) of the Financial Services and Markets Act 2000.

(1A) References in subsection (1) to contracts of insurance (of any description), options and futures must be read with—

(a) section 22 of the Financial Services and Markets Act 2000;

(b) any relevant order under that section; and

(c) Schedule 2 to that Act.

(2) Where the period allowed by any provision of this Part for fulfilling an obligation is expressed as a number of days, any day that is a Saturday or Sunday or a bank holiday in any part of Great Britain is to be disregarded in reckoning that period.

PART VII
ACCOUNTS AND AUDIT

CHAPTER I
PROVISIONS APPLYING TO COMPANIES GENERALLY

Accounting records

221.　Duty to keep accounting records

(1) Every company shall keep accounting records which are sufficient to show and explain the company's transactions and are such as to—

(a) disclose with reasonable accuracy, at any time, the financial position of the company at that time, and

(b) enable the directors to ensure that any accounts required to be prepared under this Part comply with the requirements of this Act (and, where applicable, of Article 4 of the IAS Regulation).

(2) The accounting records shall in particular contain—

(a) entries from day to day of all sums of money received and expended by the company, and the matters in respect of which the receipt and expenditure takes place, and

(b) a record of the assets and liabilities of the company.

(3) If the company's business involves dealing in goods, the accounting records shall contain—

(a) statements of stock held by the company at the end of each financial year of the company,

(b) all statements of stocktakings from which any such statement of stock as is mentioned in paragraph (a) has been or is to be prepared, and

(c) except in the case of goods sold by way of ordinary retail trade, statements of all goods sold and purchased, showing the goods and the buyers and sellers in sufficient detail to enable all these to be identified.

(4) A parent company which has a subsidiary undertaking in relation to which the above requirements do not apply shall take reasonable steps to secure that the undertaking keeps such accounting records as to enable the directors of the parent company to ensure that any accounts required to be prepared under this Part comply with the requirements of this Act (and, where applicable, of Article 4 of the IAS Regulation).

(5) If a company fails to comply with any provision of this section, every officer of the company who is in default is guilty of an offence unless he shows that he acted honestly and that in the circumstances in which the company's business was carried on the default was excusable.

(6) A person guilty of an offence under this section is liable to imprisonment or a fine, or both.

222.　Where and for how long records to be kept

(1) A company's accounting records shall be kept at its registered office or such other place as the directors think fit, and shall at all times be open to inspection by the company's officers.

(2) If accounting records are kept at a place outside Great Britain, accounts and returns with respect to the business dealt with in the accounting records so kept shall be sent to, and kept at, a place in Great Britain, and shall at all times be open to such inspection.

(3)   The accounts and returns to be sent to Great Britain shall be such as to—

    (a)   disclose with reasonable accuracy the financial position of the business in question at intervals of not more than six months, and

    (b)   enable the directors to ensure that the accounts required to be prepared under this Part comply with the requirements of this Act (and, where applicable, Article 4 of the IAS Regulation).

(4)   If a company fails to comply with any provision of subsections (1) to (3), every officer of the company who is in default is guilty of an offence, and liable to imprisonment or a fine or both, unless he shows that he acted honestly and that in the circumstances in which the company's business was carried on the default was excusable.

(5)   Accounting records which a company is required by section 221 to keep shall be preserved by it—

    (a)   in the case of a private company, for three years from the date on which they are made, and

    (b)   in the case of a public company, for six years from the date on which they are made.

This is subject to any provision contained in rules made under section 411 of the Insolvency Act 1986 (company insolvency rules).

(6)   An officer of a company is guilty of an offence, and liable to imprisonment or a fine or both, if he fails to take all reasonable steps for securing compliance by the company with subsection (5) or intentionally causes any default by the company under that subsection.

A company's financial year and accounting reference periods

223.   A company's financial year

(1)   A company's "financial year" is determined as follows.

(2)   Its first financial year begins with the first day of its first accounting reference period and ends with the last day of that period or such other date, not more than seven days before or after the end of that period, as the directors may determine.

(3)   Subsequent financial years begin with the day immediately following the end of the company's previous financial year and end with the last day of its next accounting reference period or such other date, not more than seven days before or after the end of that period, as the directors may determine.

(4)   In relation to an undertaking which is not a company, references in this Act to its financial year are to any period in respect of which a profit and loss account of the undertaking is required to be made up (by its constitution or by the law under which it is established), whether that period is a year or not.

(5)   The directors of a parent company shall secure that, except where in their opinion there are good reasons against it, the financial year of each of its subsidiary undertakings coincides with the company's own financial year.

224.   Accounting reference periods and accounting reference date

(1)   A company's accounting reference periods are determined according to its accounting reference date.

(2)   A company incorporated before 1st April 1996 may, at any time before the end of the period of nine months beginning with the date of its incorporation, by notice in the prescribed form given to the registrar specify its accounting reference date, that is, the date on which its accounting reference period ends in each calendar year.

(3)   Failing such notice, the accounting reference date of such a company is—

    (a)   in the case of a company incorporated before 1st April 1990, 31st March;

    (b)   in the case of a company incorporated after 1st April 1990, the last day of the month in which the anniversary of its incorporation falls.

(3A)   The accounting reference date of a company incorporated on or after 1st April 1996 is the last day of the month in which the anniversary of its incorporation falls.

(4)   A company's first accounting reference period is the period of more than six months, but not more than 18 months, beginning with the date of its incorporation and ending with its accounting reference date.

(5)   Its subsequent accounting reference periods are successive periods of twelve months beginning immediately after the end of the previous accounting reference period and ending with its accounting reference date.

(6)   This section has effect subject to the provisions of section 225 relating to the alteration of accounting reference dates and the consequences of such alteration.

225.   Alteration of accounting reference date

(1)   A company may by notice in the prescribed form given to the registrar specify a new accounting reference date having effect in relation to—
        (a)   the company's current accounting reference period and subsequent periods; or
        (b)   the company's previous accounting reference period and subsequent periods.
        A company's "previous accounting reference period" means that immediately preceding its current accounting reference period.

(2)   ...

(3)   The notice shall state whether the current or previous accounting reference period—
        (a)   is to be shortened, so as to come to an end on the first occasion on which the new accounting reference date falls or fell after the beginning of the period, or
        (b)   is to be extended, so as to come to an end on the second occasion on which that date falls or fell after the beginning of the period.

(4)   A notice under subsection (1) stating that the current or previous accounting reference period is to be extended is ineffective, except as mentioned below, if given less than five years after the end of an earlier accounting reference period of the company which was extended by virtue of this section.
        This subsection does not apply—
        (a)   to a notice given by a company which is a subsidiary undertaking or parent undertaking of another EEA undertaking if the new accounting reference date coincides with that of the other EEA undertaking or, where that undertaking is not a company, with the last day of its financial year, or
        (b)   where the company is in administration under Part II of the Insolvency Act 1986,
        or where the Secretary of State directs that it should not apply, which he may do with respect to a notice which has been given or which may be given.

(5)   A notice under subsection (1) may not be given in respect of a previous accounting reference period if the period allowed for laying and delivering accounts and reports in relation to that period has already expired.

(6)   A company's accounting reference period may not in any case, unless the company is in administration under Part II of the Insolvency Act 1986, be extended so as to exceed 18 months and a notice under this section is ineffective if the current or previous accounting reference period as extended in accordance with the notice would exceed that limit.

(7)   In this section "EEA undertaking" means an undertaking established under the law of any part of the United Kingdom or the law of any other EEA State.

Annual accounts

226.   Duty to prepare individual accounts

(1)   The directors of every company shall prepare accounts for the company for each of its financial years.
        Those accounts are referred to in this Part as the company's "individual accounts".

(2)   A company's individual accounts may be prepared—
        (a)   in accordance with section 226A ("Companies Act individual accounts"), or
        (b)   in accordance with international accounting standards ("IAS individual accounts").

This subsection is subject to the following provisions of this section and section 227C (consistency of accounts).

(3)   The individual accounts of a company that is a charity must be Companies Act individual accounts.

(4)   After the first financial year in which the directors of a company prepare IAS individual accounts ("the first IAS year"), all subsequent individual accounts of the company must be prepared in accordance with international accounting standards unless there is a relevant change of circumstance.

(5)   There is a relevant change of circumstance if, at any time during or after the first IAS year—

    (a)   the company becomes a subsidiary undertaking of another undertaking that does not prepare IAS individual accounts,

    (b)   the company ceases to be a company with securities admitted to trading on a regulated market, or

    (c)   a parent undertaking of the company ceases to be an undertaking with securities admitted to trading on a regulated market.

In this subsection "regulated market" has the same meaning as it has in Council Directive 93/22/EEC on investment services in the securities field.

(6)   If, having changed to preparing Companies Act individual accounts following a relevant change of circumstance, the directors again prepare IAS individual accounts for the company, subsections (4) and (5) apply again as if the first financial year for which such accounts are again prepared were the first IAS year.

226A. Companies Act individual accounts

(1)   Companies Act individual accounts must comprise—

    (a)   a balance sheet as at the last day of the financial year, and

    (b)   a profit and loss account.

(2)   The balance sheet must give a true and fair view of the state of affairs of the company as at the end of the financial year; and the profit and loss account must give a true and fair view of the profit or loss of the company for the financial year.

(3)   Companies Act individual accounts must comply with the provisions of Schedule 4 as to the form and content of the balance sheet and profit and loss account and additional information to be provided by way of notes to the accounts.

(4)   Where compliance with the provisions of that Schedule, and the other provisions of this Act as to the matters to be included in a company's individual accounts or in notes to those accounts, would not be sufficient to give a true and fair view, the necessary additional information must be given in the accounts or in a note to them.

(5)   If in special circumstances compliance with any of those provisions is inconsistent with the requirement to give a true and fair view, the directors must depart from that provision to the extent necessary to give a true and fair view.

(6)   Particulars of any such departure, the reasons for it and its effect must be given in a note to the accounts.

226B. IAS individual accounts

Where the directors of a company prepare IAS individual accounts, they must state in the notes to those accounts that the accounts have been prepared in accordance with international accounting standards.

227. Duty to prepare group accounts

(1)   If at the end of a financial year a company is a parent company the directors, as well as preparing individual accounts for the year, shall prepare consolidated accounts for the group for the year. Those accounts are referred to in this Part as the company's "group accounts".

(2)   The group accounts of certain parent companies are required by Article 4 of the IAS Regulation to be prepared in accordance with international accounting standards ("IAS group accounts").

(3)   The group accounts of other companies may be prepared—

(a)   in accordance with section 227A ("Companies Act group accounts"), or

(b)   in accordance with international accounting standards ("IAS group accounts").

This subsection is subject to the following provisions of this section.

(4)   The group accounts of a parent company that is a charity must be Companies Act group accounts.

(5)   After the first financial year in which the directors of a parent company prepare IAS group accounts ("the first IAS year"), all subsequent group accounts of the company must be prepared in accordance with international accounting standards unless there is a relevant change of circumstance.

(6)   There is a relevant change of circumstance if, at any time during or after the first IAS year—

   (a)   the company becomes a subsidiary undertaking of another undertaking that does not prepare IAS group accounts,

   (b)   the company ceases to be a company with securities admitted to trading on a regulated market, or

   (c)   a parent undertaking of the company ceases to be an undertaking with securities admitted to trading on a regulated market.

   In this subsection "regulated market" has the same meaning as it has in Council Directive 93/22/EEC on investment services in the securities field.

(7)   If, having changed to preparing Companies Act group accounts following a relevant change of circumstance, the directors again prepare IAS group accounts for the company, subsections (5) and (6) apply again as if the first financial year for which such accounts are again prepared were the first IAS year.

(8)   This section is subject to the exemptions provided by sections 228 (parent companies included in accounts of larger EEA group), 228A (parent companies included in non-EEA group accounts), 229(5) (all subsidiary undertakings excluded from consolidation) and 248 (small and medium-sized groups).

227A.   Companies Act group accounts

(1)   Companies Act group accounts must comprise—

   (a)   a consolidated balance sheet dealing with the state of affairs of the parent company and its subsidiary undertakings, and

   (b)   a consolidated profit and loss account dealing with the profit or loss of the parent company and its subsidiary undertakings.

(2)   The accounts must give a true and fair view of the state of affairs as at the end of the financial year, and the profit or loss for the financial year, of the undertakings included in the consolidation as a whole, so far as concerns members of the company.

(3)   Companies Act group accounts must comply with the provisions of Schedule 4A as to the form and content of the consolidated balance sheet and consolidated profit and loss account and additional information to be provided by way of notes to the accounts.

(4)   Where compliance with the provisions of that Schedule, and the other provisions of this Act as to the matters to be included in a company's group accounts or in notes to those accounts, would not be sufficient to give a true and fair view, the necessary additional information must be given in the accounts or in a note to them.

(5)   If in special circumstances compliance with any of those provisions is inconsistent with the requirement to give a true and fair view, the directors must depart from that provision to the extent necessary to give a true and fair view.

(6)   Particulars of any such departure, the reasons for it and its effect must be given in a note to the accounts.

227B.   IAS group accounts

Where the directors of a parent company prepare IAS group accounts, they must state in the notes to those accounts that the accounts have been prepared in accordance with international accounting standards.

227C. Consistency of accounts

(1) The directors of a parent company must secure that the individual accounts of—

    (a)   the parent company, and

    (b)   each of its subsidiary undertakings,

are all prepared using the same financial reporting framework, except to the extent that in their opinion there are good reasons for not doing so.

(2) Subsection (1) does not apply if the directors do not prepare group accounts for the parent company.

(3) Subsection (1) only applies to accounts of subsidiary undertakings that are required to be prepared under this Part.

(4) Subsection (1) does not require accounts of undertakings that are charities to be prepared using the same financial reporting framework as accounts of undertakings which are not charities.

(5) Subsection (1)(a) does not apply where the directors of a parent company prepare IAS group accounts and IAS individual accounts.

228. Exemption for parent companies included in accounts of larger group

(1) A company is exempt from the requirement to prepare group accounts if it is itself a subsidiary undertaking and its immediate parent undertaking is established under the law of an EEA State, in the following cases—

    (a)   where the company is a wholly-owned subsidiary of that parent undertaking;

    (b)   where that parent undertaking holds more than 50 per cent of the shares in the company and notice requesting the preparation of group accounts has not been served on the company by shareholders holding in aggregate—

        (i)   more than half of the remaining shares in the company, or

        (ii)   5 per cent of the total shares in the company.

Such notice must be served not later than six months after the end of the financial year before that to which it relates.

(2) Exemption is conditional upon compliance with all of the following conditions—

    (a)   that the company is included in consolidated accounts for a larger group drawn up to the same date, or to an earlier date in the same financial year, by a parent undertaking established under the law of an EEA State;

    (b)   that those accounts are drawn up and audited, and that parent undertaking's annual report is drawn up, according to that law, in accordance with the provisions of the Seventh Directive (83/349/EEC) (where applicable as modified by the provisions of the Bank Accounts Directive (86/635/EEC) or the Insurance Accounts Directive (91/674/EEC)) or in accordance with international accounting standards;

    (c)   that the company discloses in its individual accounts that it is exempt from the obligation to prepare and deliver group accounts;

    (d)   that the company states in its individual accounts the name of the parent undertaking which draws up the group accounts referred to above and—

        (i)   if it is incorporated outside Great Britain, the country in which it is incorporated,

        (ii)   ... and

        (iii)   if it is unincorporated, the address of its principal place of business;

    (e)   that the company delivers to the registrar, within the period allowed for delivering its individual accounts, copies of those group accounts and of the parent undertaking's annual report, together with the auditors' report on them; and

    (f)   (subject to section 710B(6) (delivery of certain Welsh documents without translation)) that if any document comprised in accounts and reports delivered in accordance with paragraph (e) is in a language other than English, there is annexed to the copy of that copy document delivered a translation of it into English, certified in the prescribed manner to be a correct translation.

(3)   The exemption does not apply to a company any of whose securities are admitted to trading on a regulated market of any EEA State within the meaning of Council Directive 93/22/EEC on investment services in the securities field.

(4)   Shares held by directors of a company for the purpose of complying with any share qualification requirement shall be disregarded in determining for the purposes of subsection (1)(a) whether the company is a wholly-owned subsidiary.

(5)   For the purposes of subsection (1)(b) shares held by a wholly-owned subsidiary of the parent undertaking, or held on behalf of the parent undertaking or a wholly-owned subsidiary, shall be attributed to the parent undertaking.

(6)   In subsection (3) "securities" includes—

    (a)   shares and stock,

    (b)   debentures, including debenture stock, loan stock, bonds, certificates of deposit and other instruments creating or acknowledging indebtedness,

    (c)   warrants or other instruments entitling the holder to subscribe for securities falling within paragraph (a) or (b), and

    (d)   certificates or other instruments which confer—

        (i)   property rights in respect of a security falling within paragraph (a), (b) or (c),

        (ii)   any right to acquire, dispose of, underwrite or convert a security, being a right to which the holder would be entitled if he held any such security to which the certificate or other instrument relates, or

        (iii) a contractual right (other than an option) to acquire any such security otherwise than by subscription.

228A.   Exemption for parent companies included in non-EEA group accounts

(1)   A company is exempt from the requirement to prepare group accounts if it is itself a subsidiary undertaking and its parent undertaking is not established under the law of an EEA State, in the following cases—

    (a)   where the company is a wholly-owned subsidiary of that parent undertaking;

    (b)   where that parent undertaking holds more than 50 per cent of the shares in the company and notice requesting the preparation of group accounts has not been served on the company by shareholders holding in aggregate—

        (i)   more than half of the remaining shares in the company, or

        (ii)   5 per cent of the total shares in the company.

Such notice must be served not later than six months after the end of the financial year before that to which it relates.

(2)   Exemption is conditional upon compliance with all of the following conditions—

    (a)   that the company and all of its subsidiary undertakings are included in consolidated accounts for a larger group drawn up to the same date, or to an earlier date in the same financial year, by a parent undertaking;

    (b)   that those accounts and, where appropriate, the group's annual report, are drawn up in accordance with the provisions of the Seventh Directive (83/349/EEC) (where applicable as modified by the provisions of the Bank Accounts Directive (86/635/EEC) or the Insurance Accounts Directive (91/674/EEC)), or in a manner equivalent to consolidated accounts and consolidated annual reports so drawn up;

    (c)   that the consolidated accounts are audited by one or more persons authorised to audit accounts under the law under which the parent undertaking which draws them up is established;

    (d)   that the company discloses in its individual accounts that it is exempt from the obligation to prepare and deliver group accounts;

    (e)   that the company states in its individual accounts the name of the parent undertaking which draws up the group accounts referred to above and—

        (i)   if it is incorporated outside Great Britain, the country in which it is incorporated, and

        (ii)   if it is unincorporated, the address of its principal place of business;

    (f)   that the company delivers to the registrar, within the period allowed for delivering its individual accounts, copies of the group accounts and, where appropriate, of the consolidated annual report, together with the auditors' report on them; and

    (g)   subject to section 710B(6) (delivery of certain Welsh documents without a translation) that if any document comprised in accounts and reports delivered in accordance with paragraph (f) is in a language other than English, there is annexed to the copy of that document delivered a translation of it into English, certified in the prescribed manner to be a correct translation.

(3)   The exemption does not apply to a company any of whose securities are admitted to trading on a regulated market of any EEA State within the meaning of Council Directive 93/22/EEC on investment services in the securities field.

(4)   Shares held by directors of a company for the purpose of complying with any share qualification requirement are disregarded in determining for the purposes of subsection (1)(a) whether the company is a wholly-owned subsidiary.

(5)   For the purposes of subsection (1)(b), shares held by a wholly-owned subsidiary of the parent undertaking, or held on behalf of the parent undertaking or a wholly-owned subsidiary, are attributed to the parent undertaking.

(6)   In subsection (3) "securities" includes—

    (a)   shares and stock,

    (b)   debentures, including debenture stock, loan stock, bonds, certificates of deposit and other instruments creating or acknowledging indebtedness,

    (c)   warrants or other instruments entitling the holder to subscribe for securities falling within paragraph (a) or (b), and

    (d)   certificates or other instruments which confer—

        (i)   property rights in respect of a security falling within paragraph (a), (b) or (c),

        (ii)   any right to acquire, dispose of, underwrite or convert a security, being a right to which the holder would be entitled if he held any such security to which the certificate or other instrument relates, or

        (iii)   a contractual right (other than an option) to acquire any such security otherwise than by subscription.

229.   Subsidiary undertakings included in the consolidation

(1)   In the case of Companies Act group accounts, subject to the exceptions authorised ... by this section, all the subsidiary undertakings of the parent company shall be included in the consolidation.

(2)   A subsidiary undertaking may be excluded from consolidation in Companies Act group accounts if its inclusion is not material for the purpose of giving a true and fair view; but two or more undertakings may be excluded only if they are not material taken together.

(3)   In addition, a subsidiary undertaking may be excluded from consolidation in Companies Act group accounts where—

    (a)   severe long-term restrictions substantially hinder the exercise of the rights of the parent company over the assets or management of that undertaking, or

    (b)   the information necessary for the preparation of group accounts cannot be obtained without disproportionate expense or undue delay, or

    (c)   the interest of the parent company is held exclusively with a view to subsequent resale ...

The reference in paragraph (a) to the rights of the parent company and the reference in paragraph (c) to the interest of the parent company are, respectively, to rights and interests held by or attributed to the company for the purposes of section 258 (definition of "parent undertaking") in the absence of which it would not be the parent company.

(4)   ...

(5)   A parent company is exempt from the requirement to prepare group accounts if under subsection (2) or (3) all of its subsidiary undertakings could be excluded from consolidation in Companies Act group accounts.

230.   Treatment of individual profit and loss account where group accounts prepared

(1)   The following provisions apply with respect to the individual profit and loss account of a parent company where—

    (a)   the company is required to prepare and does prepare group accounts in accordance with this Act, and

    (b)   the notes to the company's individual balance sheet show the company's profit or loss for the financial year determined in accordance with this Act.

(2)   Where the company prepares Companies Act individual accounts, the profit and loss account need not contain the information specified in paragraphs 52 to 57 of Schedule 4 (information supplementing the profit and loss account).

(3)   The profit and loss account must be approved in accordance with section 233(1) (approval by board of directors) but may be omitted from the company's annual accounts for the purposes of the other provisions below in this Chapter.

(4)   The exemption conferred by this section is conditional upon its being disclosed in the company's annual accounts that the exemption applies.

231.   Disclosure required in notes to accounts: related undertakings

(1)   The information specified in Schedule 5 shall be given in notes to a company's annual accounts.

(2)   Where the company is not required to prepare group accounts, the information specified in Part I of that Schedule shall be given; and where the company is required to prepare group accounts, the information specified in Part II of that Schedule shall be given.

(3)   The information required by Schedule 5 need not be disclosed with respect to an undertaking which—

    (a)   is established under the law of a country outside the United Kingdom, or

    (b)   carries on business outside the United Kingdom,

    if in the opinion of the directors of the company the disclosure would be seriously prejudicial to the business of that undertaking, or to the business of the company or any of its subsidiary undertakings, and the Secretary of State agrees that the information need not be disclosed.

    This subsection does not apply in relation to the information required under paragraph ... 6, 9A, 20 or 28A of that Schedule.

(4)   Where advantage is taken of subsection (3), that fact shall be stated in a note to the company's annual accounts.

(5)   If the directors of the company are of the opinion that the number of undertakings in respect of which the company is required to disclose information under any provision of Schedule 5 to this Act is such that compliance with that provision would result in information of excessive length being given, the information need only be given in respect of—

    (a)   the undertakings whose results or financial position, in the opinion of the directors, principally affected the figures shown in the company's annual accounts, and

    (b)   undertakings excluded from consolidation under section 229(3) ...

    ...

(6)   If advantage is taken of subsection (5)—

    (a)   there shall be included in the notes to the company's annual accounts a statement that the information is given only with respect to such undertakings as are mentioned in that subsection, and

    (b)   the full information (both that which is disclosed in the notes to the accounts and that which is not) shall be annexed to the company's next annual return.

    For this purpose the "next annual return" means that next delivered to the registrar after the accounts in question have been approved under section 233.

(7)   If a company fails to comply with subsection (6)(b), the company and every officer of it who is in default is liable to a fine and, for continued contravention, to a daily default fine.

231A.   Disclosure required in notes to annual accounts: particulars of staff

(1)   The following information with respect to the employees of the company must be given in notes
         to the company's annual accounts—
         (a)   the average number of persons employed by the company in the financial year, and
         (b)   the average number of persons so employed within each category of persons employed by
               the company.

(2)   The average number required by subsection (1)(a) or (b) is determined by dividing the relevant
         annual number by the number of months in the financial year.

(3)   The relevant annual number is determined by ascertaining for each month in the financial year—
         (a)   for the purposes of subsection (1)(a), the number of persons employed under contracts of
               service by the company in that month (whether throughout the month or not);
         (b)   for the purposes of subsection (1)(b), the number of persons in the category in question of
               persons so employed;
         and, in either case, adding together all the monthly numbers.

(4)   In respect of all persons employed by the company during the financial year who are taken into
         account in determining the relevant annual number for the purposes of subsection (1)(a) there
         must also be stated the aggregate amounts respectively of—
         (a)   wages and salaries paid or payable in respect of that year to those persons;
         (b)   social security costs incurred by the company on their behalf; and
         (c)   other pension costs so incurred.
         This does not apply in so far as those amounts, or any of them, are stated elsewhere in the
         company's accounts.

(5)   For the purposes of subsection (1)(b), the categories of person employed by the company are such
         as the directors may select, having regard to the manner in which the company's activities are
         organised.

(6)   This section applies in relation to group accounts as if the undertakings included in the
         consolidation were a single company.

(7)   In this section "social security costs" and "pension costs" have the same meaning as in Schedule
         4 (see paragraph 94(1) and (2) of that Schedule).

**232.   Disclosure required in notes to accounts: emoluments and other benefits of directors and
         others**

(1)   The information specified in Schedule 6 shall be given in notes to a company's annual accounts,
         save that the information specified in paragraphs 2–14 in Part I of Schedule 6 shall be given only
         in the case of a company which is not a quoted company.

(2)   In that Schedule—
         Part I relates to the emoluments of directors (including emoluments waived), pensions of
               directors and past directors, compensation for loss of office to directors and past directors
               and sums paid to third parties in respect of directors' services,
         Part II relates to loans, quasi-loans and other dealings in favour of directors and connected
               persons, and
         Part III relates to transactions, arrangements and agreements made by the company or a
               subsidiary undertaking for officers of the company other than directors.

(3)   It is the duty of any director of a company, and any person who is or has at any time in the
         preceding five years been an officer of the company, to give notice to the company of such
         matters relating to himself as may be necessary for the purposes of Part I Schedule 6.

(4)   A person who makes default in complying with subsection (3) commits an offence and is liable to
         a fine.

Approval and signing of accounts

233.   Approval and signing of accounts

(1)   A company's annual accounts shall be approved by the board of directors and signed on behalf of the board by a director of the company.

(2)   The signature shall be on the company's balance sheet.

(3)   Every copy of the balance sheet which is laid before the company in general meeting, or which is otherwise circulated, published or issued, shall state the name of the person who signed the balance sheet on behalf of the board.

(4)   The copy of the company's balance sheet which is delivered to the registrar shall be signed on behalf of the board by a director of the company.

(5)   If annual accounts are approved which do not comply with the requirements of this Act (or, where applicable, of Article 4 of the IAS Regulation), every director of the company who is party to their approval and who knows that they do not comply or is reckless as to whether they comply is guilty of an offence and liable to a fine.

For this purpose every director of the company at the time the accounts are approved shall be taken to be a party to their approval unless he shows that he took all reasonable steps to prevent their being approved.

(6)   If a copy of the balance sheet—

(a)   is laid before the company, or otherwise circulated, published or issued, without the balance sheet having been signed as required by this section or without the required statement of the signatory's name being included, or

(b)   is delivered to the registrar without being signed as required by this section,

the company and every officer of it who is in default is guilty of an offence and liable to a fine.

Directors' report

234.   Duty to prepare director's report

(1)   The directors of a company shall for each financial year prepare a report—

(a)   containing a fair review of the development of the business of the company and its subsidiary undertakings during the financial year and of their position at the end of it, and

(b)   stating the amount (if any) which they recommend should be paid as dividend …

(2)   The report shall state the names of the persons who, at any time during the financial year, were directors of the company, and the principal activities of the company and its subsidiary undertakings in the course of the year and any significant change in those activities in the year.

(2A)   If section 234ZA applies to the report, it shall contain the statement required by subsection (2) of that section.

(3)   The report shall also comply with Schedule 7 as regards the disclosure of the matters mentioned there.

(4)   In Schedule 7—

Part I relates to matters of a general nature, including changes in asset values, directors' shareholdings and other interests and contributions for political and charitable purposes,

Part II relates to the acquisition by a company of its own shares or a charge on them,

Part III relates to the employment, training and advancement of disabled persons,

…

Part V relates to the involvement of employees in the affairs, policy and performance of the company,

Part VI relates to the company's policy and practice on the payment of creditors.

(5)   In the case of any failure to comply with the provisions of this part as to the preparation of a directors' report and the contents of the report, every person who was a director of the company immediately before the end of the period for laying and delivering accounts and reports for the financial year in question is guilty of an offence and liable to a fine.

(6)   In proceedings against a person for an offence under this section it is a defence for him to prove that he took all reasonable steps for securing compliance with the requirements in question.

234ZA. Statement as to disclosure of information to auditors

(1)   This section applies to a directors' report unless the directors have taken advantage of the exemption conferred by section 249A(1) or 249AA(1).

(2)   The report must contain a statement to the effect that, in the case of each of the persons who are directors at the time when the report is approved under section 234A, the following applies—

(a)   so far as the director is aware, there is no relevant audit information of which the company's auditors are unaware, and

(b)   he has taken all the steps that he ought to have taken as a director in order to make himself aware of any relevant audit information and to establish that the company's auditors are aware of that information.

(3)   In subsection (2) "relevant audit information" means information needed by the company's auditors in connection with preparing their report.

(4)   For the purposes of subsection (2) a director has taken all the steps that he ought to have taken as a director in order to do the things mentioned in paragraph (b) of that subsection if he has—

(a)   made such enquiries of his fellow directors and of the company's auditors for that purpose, and

(b)   taken such other steps (if any) for that purpose,

as were required by his duty as a director of the company to exercise due care, skill and diligence.

(5)   In determining for the purposes of subsection (2) the extent of that duty in the case of a particular director, the following considerations (in particular) are relevant—

(a)   the knowledge, skill and experience that may reasonably be expected of a person carrying out the same functions as are carried out by the director in relation to the company, and

(b)   (so far as they exceed what may reasonably be so expected) the knowledge, skill and experience that the director in fact has.

(6)   Where a directors' report containing the statement required by subsection (2) is approved under section 234A but the statement is false, every director of the company who—

(a)   knew that the statement was false, or was reckless as to whether it was false, and

(b)   failed to take reasonable steps to prevent the report from being approved,

is guilty of an offence and liable to imprisonment or a fine, or both.

234A.   Approval and signing of directors' report

(1)   The directors' report shall be approved by the board of directors and signed on behalf of the board by a director or the secretary of the company.

(2)   Every copy of the directors' report which is laid before the company in general meeting, or which is otherwise circulated, published or issued, shall state the name of the person who signed it on behalf of the board.

(3)   The copy of the directors' report which is delivered to the registrar shall be signed on behalf of the board by a director or the secretary of the company.

(4)   If a copy of the directors' report—

(a)   is laid before the company, or otherwise circulated, published or issued, without the report having been signed as required by this section or without the required statement of the signatory's name being included, or

(b)   is delivered to the registrar without being signed as required by this section,

the company and every officer of it who is in default is guilty of an offence and liable to a fine.

Quoted companies: directors' remuneration report

234B.   Duty to prepare directors' remuneration report

(1)   The directors of a quoted company shall for each financial year prepare a directors' remuneration report which shall contain the information specified in Schedule 7A and comply with any requirement of that Schedule as to how information is to be set out in the report.

(2)   In Schedule 7A—

Part 1 is introductory,

Part 2 relates to information about remuneration committees, performance related remuneration and liabilities in respect of directors' contracts,

Part 3 relates to detailed information about directors' remuneration (information included under Part 3 is required to be reported on by the auditors, see section 235), and

Part 4 contains interpretative and supplementary provisions.

(3)   In the case of any failure to comply with the provisions of this Part as to the preparation of a directors' remuneration report and the contents of the report, every person who was a director of the quoted company immediately before the end of the period for laying and delivering accounts and reports for the financial year in question is guilty of an offence and liable to a fine.

(4)   In proceedings against a person for an offence under subsection (3) it is a defence for him to prove that he took all reasonable steps for securing compliance with the requirements in question.

(5)   It is the duty of any director of a company, and any person who has at any time in the preceding five years been a director of the company, to give notice to the company of such matters relating to himself as may be necessary for the purposes of Parts 2 and 3 of Schedule 7A.

(6)   A person who makes default in complying with subsection (5) commits an offence and is liable to a fine.

234C. Approval and signing of directors' remuneration report

(1)   The directors' remuneration report shall be approved by the board of directors and signed on behalf of the board by a director or the secretary of the company.

(2)   Every copy of the directors' remuneration report which is laid before the company in general meeting, or which is otherwise circulated, published or issued, shall state the name of the person who signed it on behalf of the board.

(3)   The copy of the directors' remuneration report which is delivered to the registrar shall be signed on behalf of the board by a director or the secretary of the company.

(4)   If a copy of the directors' remuneration report—

    (a)   is laid before the company, or otherwise circulated, published or issued, without the report having been signed as required by this section or without the required statement of the signatory's name being included, or

    (b)   is delivered to the registrar without being signed as required by this section,

the company and every officer of it who is in default is guilty of an offence and liable to a fine.

Auditors' report

235. Auditors' report

(1)   A company's auditors shall make a report to the company's members on all annual accounts of the company of which copies are to be laid before the company in general meeting during their tenure of office.

(1A)   The auditors' report must include—

    (a)   an introduction identifying the annual accounts that are the subject of the audit and the financial reporting framework that has been applied in their preparation;

    (b)   a description of the scope of the audit identifying the auditing standards in accordance with which the audit was conducted.

(1B)   The report must state clearly whether in the auditors' opinion the annual accounts have been properly prepared in accordance with the requirements of this Act (and, where applicable, Article 4 of the IAS Regulation).

(2)   The report must state in particular whether the annual accounts give a true and fair view, in accordance with the relevant financial reporting framework—

    (a)   in the case of an individual balance sheet, of the state of affairs of the company as at the end of the financial year,

    (b)   in the case of an individual profit and loss account, of the profit or loss of the company for the financial year,

(c)   in the case of group accounts, of the state of affairs as at the end of the financial year and of the profit or loss for the financial year, of the undertakings included in the consolidation as a whole, so far as concerns members of the company.

(2A)   The auditors' report—

(a)   must be either unqualified or qualified, and

(b)   must include a reference to any matters to which the auditors wish to draw attention by way of emphasis without qualifying the report.

(3)   The auditors shall consider whether the information given in the directors' report for the financial year for which the annual accounts are prepared is consistent with those accounts; and if they are of opinion that it is not they shall state that fact in their report.

(4)   If a directors' remuneration report is prepared for the financial year for which the annual accounts are prepared the auditors shall in their report

(a)   report to the company's members on the auditable part of the directors' remuneration report, and

(b)   state whether in their opinion that part of the directors' remuneration report has been properly prepared in accordance with this Act.

(5)   For the purposes of this Part, "the auditable part" of a directors' remuneration report is the part containing the information required by Part 3 of Schedule 7A.

236.   Signature of auditors' report

(1)   The auditors' report shall state the names of the auditors and be signed and dated by them.

(2)   Every copy of the auditors' report which is laid before the company in general meeting, or which is otherwise circulated, published or issued, shall state the names of the auditors.

(3)   The copy of the auditors' report which is delivered to the registrar shall state the names of the auditors and be signed by them.

(4)   If a copy of the auditors' report—

(a)   is laid before the company, or otherwise circulated, published or issued, without the required statement of the auditors' names, or

(b)   is delivered to the registrar without the required statement of the auditors' names or without being signed as required by this section,

the company and every officer of it who is in default is guilty of an offence and liable to a fine.

(5)   References in this section to signature by the auditors are, where the office of auditor is held by a body corporate or partnership, to signature in the name of the body corporate or partnership by a person authorised to sign on its behalf.

237.   Duties of auditors

(1)   A company's auditors shall, in preparing their report, carry out such investigations as will enable them to form an opinion as to—

(a)   whether proper accounting records have been kept by the company and proper returns adequate for their audit have been received from branches not visited by them, and

(b)   whether the company's individual accounts are in agreement with the accounting records and returns, and

(c)   (in the case of a quoted company) whether the auditable part of the company's directors' remuneration report is in agreement with the accounting records and returns.

(2)   If the auditors are of opinion that proper accounting records have not been kept, or that proper returns adequate for their audit have not been received from branches not visited by them, or if the company's individual accounts are not in agreement with the accounting records and returns, or if in the case of a quoted company the auditable part of its directors' remuneration report is not in agreement with the accounting records and returns, the auditors shall state that fact in their report.

(3)   If the auditors fail to obtain all the information and explanations which, to the best of their knowledge and belief, are necessary for the purposes of their audit, they shall state that fact in their report.

(4) If—
    (a)   the requirements of Schedule 6 (disclosure of information: emoluments and other benefits of directors and others) are not complied with in the annual accounts, or
    (b)   where a directors' remuneration report is required to be prepared, the requirements of Part 3 of Schedule 7A (directors' remuneration report) are not complied with in that report,
the auditors shall include in their report, so far as they are reasonably able to do so, a statement giving the required particulars.

(4A) If the directors of the company have taken advantage of the exemption conferred by section 248 (exemption for small and medium-sized groups from the need to prepare group accounts) and in the auditors' opinion they were not entitled so to do, the auditors shall state that fact in their report.

Publication of accounts and reports

238. **Persons entitled to receive copies of accounts and reports**

(1) A copy of each of the documents mentioned in subsection (1A) shall be sent to—
    (a)   every member of the company,
    (b)   every holder of the company's debentures, and
    (c)   every person who is entitled to receive notice of general meetings,
not less than 21 days before the date of the meeting at which copies of those documents are to be laid in accordance with section 241.

(1A) Those documents are—
    (a)   the company's annual accounts for the financial year,
    (b)   the directors' report for that financial year,
    (c)   (in the case of a quoted company) the directors' remuneration report for that financial year, and
    (d)   the auditors' report on those accounts or (in the case of a quoted company) on those accounts and the auditable part of the directors' remuneration report.

(2) Copies need not be sent—
    (a)   to a person who is not entitled to receive notices of general meetings and of whose address the company is unaware, or
    (b)   to more than one of the joint holders of shares or debentures none of whom is entitled to receive such notices, or
    (c)   in the case of joint holders of shares or debentures some of whom are, and some not, entitled to receive such notices, to those who are not so entitled.

(3) In the case of a company not having a share capital, copies need not be sent to anyone who is not entitled to receive notices of general meetings of the company.

(4) If copies are sent less than 21 days before the date of the meeting, they shall, notwithstanding that fact, be deemed to have been duly sent if it is so agreed by all the members entitled to attend and vote at the meeting.

(4A) References in this section to sending to any person copies of copies of the documents mentioned in subsection (1A) include references to using electronic communications for sending copies of those documents to such address as may for the time being be notified to the company by that person for that purpose.

(4B) For the purposes of this section copies of those documents are also to be treated as sent to a person where—
    (a)   the company and that person have agreed to his having access to the documents on a web site (instead of their being sent to him);
    (b)   the documents are documents to which that agreement applies; and
    (c)   that person is notified, in a manner for the time being agreed for the purpose between him and the company, of—
        (i)   the publication of the documents on a web site;
        (ii)   the address of that web site; and

(iii) the place on that web site where the documents may be accessed, and how they may be accessed.

(4C) For the purposes of this section documents treated in accordance with subsection (4B) as sent to any person are to be treated as sent to him not less than 21 days before the date of a meeting if, and only if—

    (a) the documents are published on the web site throughout a period beginning at least 21 days before the date of the meeting and ending with the conclusion of the meeting; and

    (b) the notification given for the purposes of paragraph (c) of that subsection is given not less than 21 days before the date of the meeting.

(4D) Nothing in subsection (4C) shall invalidate the proceedings of a meeting where—

    (a) any documents that are required to be published as mentioned in paragraph (a) of that subsection are published for a part, but not all, of the period mentioned in that paragraph; and

    (b) the failure to publish those documents throughout that period is wholly attributable to circumstances which it would not be reasonable to have expected the company to prevent or avoid.

(4E) A company may, notwithstanding any provision to the contrary in its articles, take advantage of any of subsections (4A) to (4D).

(5) If default is made in complying with this section, the company and every officer of it who is in default is guilty of an offence and liable to a fine.

(6) Where copies are sent out under this section over a period of days, references elsewhere in this Act to the day on which copies are sent out shall be construed as references to the last day of that period.

239. Right to demand copies of accounts and reports

(1) Any member of a company and any holder of a company's debentures is entitled to be furnished, on demand and without charge, with a copy of—

    (a) the company's last annual accounts,

    (b) the last directors' report,

    (c) (in the case of a quoted company) the last directors' remuneration report, and

    (d) the auditors' report on those accounts or (in the case of a quoted company) on those accounts and the auditable part of the directors' remuneration report for the financial year for which those accounts are prepared.

(2) The entitlement under this section is to a single copy of those documents, but that is in addition to any copy to which a person may be entitled under section 238.

(2A) Any obligation by virtue of subsection (1) to furnish a person with a document may be complied with by using electronic communications for sending that document to such address as may for the time being be notified to the company by that person for that purpose.

(2B) A company may, notwithstanding any provision to the contrary in its articles, take advantage of subsection (2A).

(3) If a demand under this section is not complied with within seven days, the company and every officer of it who is in default is guilty of an offence and liable to a fine and, for continued contravention, to a daily default fine.

(4) If in proceedings for such an offence the issue arises whether a person had already been furnished with a copy of the relevant document under this section, it is for the defendant to prove that he had.

240. Requirements in connection with publication of accounts

(1) If a company publishes any of its statutory accounts, they must be accompanied by the relevant auditors' report under section 235 or, as the case may be, the relevant report made for the purposes of section 249A(2).

(2)   A company which is required to prepare group accounts for a financial year shall not publish its statutory individual accounts for that year without also publishing with them its statutory group accounts.

(3)   If a company publishes non-statutory accounts, it shall publish with them a statement indicating—

    (a)   that they are not the company's statutory accounts,

    (b)   whether statutory accounts dealing with any financial year with which the non-statutory accounts purport to deal have been delivered to the registrar,

    (c)   whether the company's auditors have made a report under section 235 on the statutory accounts for any such financial year and, if no such report has been made, whether the company's reporting accountant has made a report for the purposes of section 249A(2) on the statutory accounts for any such financial year, ...

    (d)   whether any such auditors' report—

        (i)   was qualified or unqualified, or included a reference to any matters to which the auditors drew attention by way of emphasis without qualifying the report, or

        (ii)   contained a statement under section 237(2) or (3) (accounting records or returns inadequate, accounts not agreeing with records and returns or failure to obtain necessary information and explanations); and

    (e)   whether any report made for the purposes of section 249A(2) was qualified;

and it shall not publish with the non-statutory accounts any auditors' report under section 235 or any report made for the purposes of section 249A(2).

(4)   For the purposes of this section a company shall be regarded as publishing a document if it publishes, issues or circulates it or otherwise makes it available for public inspection in a manner calculated to invite members of the public generally, or any class of members of the public, to read it.

(5)   References in this section to a company's statutory accounts are to its individual or group accounts for a financial year as required to be delivered to the registrar under section 242; and references to the publication by a company of "non-statutory accounts" are to the publication of—

    (a)   any balance sheet or profit and loss account relating to, or purporting to deal with, a financial year of the company, or

    (b)   an account in any form purporting to be a balance sheet or profit and loss account for the group consisting of the company and its subsidiary undertakings relating to, or purporting to deal with, a financial year of the company,

otherwise than as part of the company's statutory accounts.

(6)   A company which contravenes any provision of this section, and any officer of it who is in default, is guilty of an offence and liable to a fine.

Laying and delivering of accounts and reports

241.   Accounts and reports to be laid before company in general meeting

(1)   The directors of a company shall in respect of each financial year lay before the company in general meeting copies of—

    (a)   the company's annual accounts,

    (b)   the directors' report,

    (c)   (in the case of a quoted company) the directors' remuneration report, and

    (d)   the auditors' report on those accounts or (in the case of a quoted company) on those accounts and the auditable part of the directors' remuneration report.

(2)   If the requirements of subsection (1) are not complied with before the end of the period allowed for laying and delivering accounts and reports, every person who immediately before the end of that period was a director of the company is guilty of an offence and liable to a fine and, for continued contravention, to a daily default fine.

(3)   It is a defence for a person charged with such an offence to prove that he took all reasonable steps for securing that those requirements would be complied with before the end of that period.

(4)   It is not a defence to prove that the documents in question were not in fact prepared as required by this Part.

241A. Members' approval of directors' remuneration report

(1)   This section applies to every company that is a quoted company immediately before the end of a financial year.

(2)   In this section "the meeting" means the general meeting of the company before which the company's annual accounts for the financial year are to be laid.

(3)   The company must, prior to the meeting, give to the members of the company entitled to be sent notice of the meeting notice of the intention to move at the meeting, as an ordinary resolution, a resolution approving the directors' remuneration report for the financial year.

(4)   Notice under subsection (3) shall be given to each such member in any manner permitted for the service on him of notice of the meeting.

(5)   The business that may be dealt with at the meeting includes the resolution.

(6)   The existing directors must ensure that the resolution is put to the vote of the meeting.

(7)   Subsection (5) has effect notwithstanding—

(a)   any default in complying with subsections (3) and (4);

(b)   anything in the company's articles.

(8)   No entitlement of a person to remuneration is made conditional on the resolution being passed by reason only of the provision made by this section.

(9)   In the event of default in complying with the requirements of subsections (3) and (4), every officer of the company who is in default is liable to a fine.

(10)   If the resolution is not put to the vote of the meeting, each existing director is guilty of an offence and liable to a fine.

(11)   If an existing director is charged with an offence under subsection (10), it is a defence for him to prove that he took all reasonable steps for securing that the resolution was put to the vote of the meeting.

(12)   In this section "existing director" means a person who, immediately before the meeting, is a director of the company.

242. Accounts and reports to be delivered to the registrar

(1)   The directors of a company shall in respect of each financial year deliver to the registrar a copy of—

(a)   the company's annual accounts,

(b)   the directors' report,

(c)   (in the case of a quoted company) the directors' remuneration report, and

(d)   the auditors' report on those accounts or (in the case of a quoted company) on those accounts and the auditable part of the directors' remuneration report.

... If any document comprised in those accounts or reports is in a language other than English then, subject to section 710B(6) (delivery of certain Welsh documents without a translation), the directors shall annex to the copy of that document delivered a translation of it into English, certified in the prescribed manner to be a correct translation.

(2)   If the requirements of subsection (1) are not complied with before the end of the period allowed for laying and delivering accounts and reports, every person who immediately before the end of that period was a director of the company is guilty of an offence and liable to a fine and, for continued contravention, to a daily default fine.

(3)   Further, if the directors of the company fail to make good the default within 14 days after the service of a notice on them requiring compliance, the court may on the application of any member or creditor of the company or of the registrar, make an order directing the directors (or any of them) to make good the default within such time as may be specified in the order.

The court's order may provide that all costs of and incidental to the application shall be borne by the directors.

(4)   It is a defence for a person charged with an offence under this section to prove that he took all reasonable steps for securing that the requirements of subsection (1) would be complied with before the end of the period allowed for laying and delivering accounts and reports.

(5)   It is not a defence in any proceedings under this section to prove that the documents in question were not in fact prepared as required by this Part.

242A.   Civil penalty for failure to deliver accounts

(1)   Where the requirements of section 242(1) are not complied with before the end of the period allowed for laying and delivering accounts and reports, the company is liable to a civil penalty. This is in addition to any liability of the directors under section 242.

(2)   The amount of the penalty is determined by reference to the length of the period between the end of the period allowed for laying and delivering accounts and reports and the day on which the requirements are complied with, and whether the company is a public or private company, as follows:—

Length of period	Public company	Private company
Not more than 3 months	£500	£100
More than 3 months but not more than 6 months	£1,000	£250
More than 6 months but not more than 12 months	£2,000	£500
More than 12 months	£5,000	£1,000

(3)   The penalty may be recovered by the registrar and shall be paid by him into the Consolidated Fund.

(4)   It is not a defence in proceedings under this section to prove that the documents in question were not in fact prepared as required by this Part.

242B.   Delivery and publication of accounts in ECUs

(1)   The amounts set out in the annual accounts of a company may also be shown in the same accounts translated into ECUs.

(2)   When complying with section 242, the directors of a company may deliver to the registrar an additional copy of the company's annual accounts in which the amounts have been translated into ECUs.

(3)   In both cases—
   (a)   the amounts must have been translated at the relevant exchange rate prevailing on the balance sheet date, and
   (b)   that rate must be disclosed in the notes to the accounts.

(4)   For the purposes of section 240 any additional copy of the company's annual accounts delivered to the registrar under subsection (2) shall be treated as statutory accounts of the company and, in the case of such a copy, references in section 240 to the auditors' report under section 235 shall be read as references to the auditors' report on the annual accounts of which it is a copy.

(5)   In this section—
   "ECU" means a unit with a value equal to the value of the unit of account known as the ecu used in the European Monetary System, and
   "relevant exchange rate" means the rate of exchange used for translating the value of the ecu for the purposes of that System.

243.   ...

244.   Period allowed for laying and delivering accounts and reports

(1)   The period allowed for laying and delivering accounts and reports is—
   (a)   for a private company, 10 months after the end of the relevant accounting reference period, and

(b)   for a public company, 7 months after the end of that period.
       This is subject to the following provisions of this section.

(2)   If the relevant accounting reference period is the company's first and is a period of more than 12 months, the period allowed is—

(a)   10 months or 7 months, as the case may be, from the first anniversary of the incorporation of the company, or

(b)   3 months from the end of the accounting reference period,

       whichever last expires.

(3)   ...

(4)   If the relevant accounting period is treated as shortened by virtue of a notice given by the company under section 225 (alteration of accounting reference date), the period allowed for laying and delivering accounts is that applicable in accordance with the above provisions or 3 months from the date of the notice under that section, whichever last expires.

(5)   If for any special reason the Secretary of State thinks fit he may, on an application made before the expiry of the period otherwise allowed, by notice in writing to a company extend that period by such further period as may be specified in the notice.

(6)   In this section "the relevant accounting reference period" means the accounting reference period by reference to which the financial year for the accounts in question was determined.

Revision of defective accounts and reports

245.   Voluntary revision of annual accounts or directors' report

(1)   If it appears to the directors of a company that any annual accounts or summary financial statement of the company, or any directors' report or directors' remuneration report, did not comply with the requirements of this Act (or, where applicable, of Article 4 of the IAS Regulation), they may prepare revised accounts or a revised statement or report.

(2)   Where copies of the previous accounts or report have been laid before the company in general meeting or delivered to the registrar, the revisions shall be confined to—

(a)   the correction of those respects in which the previous accounts or report did not comply with the requirements of this Act (or, where applicable, of Article 4 of the IAS Regulation), and

(b)   the making of any necessary consequential alterations.

(3)   The Secretary of State may make provision by regulations as to the application of the provisions of this Act in relation to revised annual accounts or a revised summary financial statement or a revised directors' report or a revised directors' remuneration report.

(4)   The regulations may, in particular—

(a)   make different provision according to whether the previous accounts, statement or report are replaced or are supplemented by a document indicating the corrections to be made;

(b)   make provision with respect to the functions of the company's auditors or reporting accountant in relation to the revised accounts, statement or report;

(c)   require the directors to take such steps as may be specified in the regulations where the previous accounts or report have been—

       (i)   sent out to members and others under section 238(1),

       (ii)   laid before the company in general meeting, or

       (iii) delivered to the registrar,

       or where a summary financial statement based on the previous accounts or report has been sent to members under section 251;

(d)   apply the provisions of this Act (including those creating criminal offences) subject to such additions, exceptions and modifications as are specified in the regulations.

(5)   Regulations under this section shall be made by statutory instrument which shall be subject to annulment in pursuance of a resolution of either House of Parliament.

245A.   Secretary of State's notice in respect of annual accounts

(1)   Where copies of a company's annual accounts have been sent out under section 238, or a copy of a company's annual accounts has been laid before the company in general meeting or delivered to the registrar, and it appears to the Secretary of State that there is, or may be, a question whether the accounts comply with the requirements of this Act (or, where applicable, of Article 4 of the IAS Regulation), he may give notice to the directors of the company indicating the respects in which it appears to him that such a question arises, or may arise.

(2)   The notice shall specify a period of not less than one month for the directors to give him an explanation of the accounts or prepare revised accounts.

(3)   If at the end of the specified period, or such longer period as he may allow, it appears to the Secretary of State that no satisfactory explanation of the accounts has been given and that the accounts have not been revised so as to comply with the requirements of this Act, he may if he thinks fit apply to the court.

(4)   The provisions of this section apply equally to revised annual accounts, in which case the references to revised accounts shall be read as references to further revised accounts.

245B.   Application to court in respect of defective accounts

(1)   An application may be made to the court—
    (a)   by the Secretary of State, after having complied with section 245A, or
    (b)   by a person authorised by the Secretary of State for the purposes of this section,
for a declaration or declarator that the annual accounts of a company do not comply with the requirements of this Act (or, where applicable, of Article 4 of the IAS Regulation) and for an order requiring the directors of the company to prepare revised accounts.

(2)   Notice of the application, together with a general statement of the matters at issue in the proceedings, shall be given by the applicant to the registrar for registration.

(3)   If the court orders the preparation of revised accounts, it may give directions with respect to—
    (a)   the auditing of the accounts,
    (b)   the revision of any directors' report, directors' remuneration report or summary financial statement, and
    (c)   the taking of steps by the directors to bring the making of the order to the notice of persons likely to rely on the previous accounts,
and such other matters as the court thinks fit.

(4)   If the court finds that the accounts did not comply with the requirements of this Act (or, where applicable, of Article 4 of the IAS Regulation) it may order that all or part of—
    (a)   the costs (or in Scotland expenses) of and incidental to the application, and
    (b)   any reasonable expenses incurred by the company in connection with or in consequence of the preparation of revised accounts,
shall be borne by such of the directors as were party to the approval of the defective accounts.
For this purpose every director of the company at the time the accounts were approved shall be taken to have been a party to their approval unless he shows that he took all reasonable steps to prevent their being approved.

(5)   Where the court makes an order under subsection (4) it shall have regard to whether the directors party to the approval of the defective accounts knew or ought to have known that the accounts did not comply with the requirements of this Act (or, where applicable, of Article 4 of the IAS Regulation), and it may exclude one or more directors from the order or order the payment of different amounts by different directors.

(6)   On the conclusion of proceedings on an application under this section, the applicant shall give to the registrar for registration an office copy of the court order or, as the case may be, notice that the application has failed or been withdrawn.

(7)   The provisions of this section apply equally to revised annual accounts, in which case the references to revised accounts shall be read as references to further revised accounts.

245C. Other persons authorised to apply to court

(1) The Secretary of State may authorise for the purposes of section 245B any person appearing to him—

    (a) to have an interest in, and to have satisfactory procedures directed to securing, compliance by companies with the accounting requirements of this Act (or, where applicable, of Article 4 of the IAS Regulation),

    (b) to have satisfactory procedures for receiving and investigating complaints about the annual accounts of companies, and

    (c) otherwise to be a fit and proper person to be authorised.

(1A) But where the order giving authorisation (see subsection (4)) is to contain any requirements or other provisions specified under subsection (4A), the Secretary of State may not authorise a person unless, in addition, it appears to him that the person would, if authorised, exercise his functions as an authorised person in accordance with any such requirements or provisions.

(2) A person may be authorised generally or in respect of particular classes of case, and different persons may be authorised in respect of different classes of case.

(3) The Secretary of State may refuse to authorise a person if he considers that his authorisation is unnecessary having regard to the fact that there are one or more other persons who have been or are likely to be authorised.

(4) Authorisation shall be by order made by statutory instrument which shall be subject to annulment in pursuance of a resolution of either House of Parliament.

(4A) An order under subsection (4) may contain such requirements or other provisions relating to the exercise of functions by the authorised person as appear to the Secretary of State to be appropriate.

(4B) If the authorised person is an unincorporated association, any relevant proceedings may be brought by or against that association in the name of any body corporate whose constitution provides for the establishment of the association.

For this purpose "relevant proceedings" means proceedings brought in, or in connection with, the exercise of any function by the association as an authorised person.

(5) Where authorisation is revoked, the revoking order may make such provision as the Secretary of State thinks fit with respect to pending proceedings.

(6) ...

245D. Disclosure of information held by Inland Revenue to persons authorised to apply to court

(1) Information which is held by or on behalf of the Commissioners of Inland Revenue may be disclosed to a person who is authorised under section 245C of this Act, or under Article 253C of the Companies (Northern Ireland) Order 1986 (S.I. 1986/1032 (N.I. 6)), if the disclosure—

    (a) is made for a permitted purpose, and

    (b) is made by the Commissioners or is authorised by them.

(2) Such information—

    (a) may be so disclosed despite any other restriction on the disclosure of information whether imposed by any statutory provision or otherwise, but

    (b) in the case of personal data (within the meaning of the Data Protection Act 1998), may not be disclosed in contravention of that Act.

(3) For the purposes of subsection (1), a disclosure is made for a permitted purpose if it is made for the purpose of facilitating—

    (a) the taking of steps by the authorised person to discover whether there are grounds for an application to the court under section 245B of this Act or Article 253B of the Companies (Northern Ireland) Order 1986; or

    (b) a determination by the authorised person as to whether or not to make such an application.

(4) The power of the Commissioners to authorise a disclosure under subsection (1)(b) may be delegated (either generally or for a specified purpose) to an officer of the Board of Inland Revenue.

245E.   Restrictions on use and further disclosure of information disclosed under section 245D

(1)   Information that is disclosed to an authorised person under section 245D may not be used except in or in connection with—

(a)   taking steps to discover whether there are grounds for an application to the court as mentioned in section 245D(3)(a);

(b)   determining whether or not to make such an application; or

(c)   proceedings on any such application.

(2)   Information that is disclosed to an authorised person under section 245D may not be further disclosed except—

(a)   to the person to whom the information relates; or

(b)   in or in connection with proceedings on any such application to the court.

(3)   A person who contravenes subsection (1) or (2) is guilty of an offence and liable to imprisonment or a fine, or both.

(4)   It is a defence for a person charged with an offence under subsection (3) to prove—

(a)   that he did not know, and had no reason to suspect, that the information had been disclosed under section 245D; or

(b)   that he took all reasonable steps and exercised all due diligence to avoid the commission of the offence.

(5)   Sections 732 (restriction on prosecutions), 733(2) and (3) (liability of individuals for corporate default) and 734 (criminal proceedings against unincorporated bodies) apply to offences under this section.

245F.   Power of authorised persons to require documents, information and explanations

(1)   This section applies where it appears to a person who is authorised under section 245C of this Act that there is, or may be, a question whether the annual accounts of a company comply with the requirements of this Act.

(2)   The authorised person may require any of the persons mentioned in subsection (3) to produce any document, or to provide him with any information or explanations, that he may reasonably require for the purpose of—

(a)   discovering whether there are grounds for an application to the court under section 245B; or

(b)   determining whether or not to make such an application.

(3)   Those persons are—

(a)   the company;

(b)   any officer, employee, or auditor of the company;

(c)   any persons who fell within paragraph (b) at a time to which the document or information required by the authorised person relates.

(4)   If a person fails to comply with a requirement under subsection (2), the authorised person may apply to the court for an order under subsection (5).

(5)   If on such an application the court decides that the person has failed to comply with the requirement under subsection (2), it may order the person to take such steps as it directs for securing that the documents are produced or the information or explanations are provided.

(6)   A statement made by a person in response to a requirement under subsection (2) or an order under subsection (5) may not be used in evidence against him in any criminal proceedings.

(7)   Nothing in this section compels any person to disclose documents or information in respect of which in an action in the High Court a claim to legal professional privilege, or in an action in the Court of Session a claim to confidentiality of communications, could be maintained.

(8)   In this section "document" includes information recorded in any form.

245G.   Restrictions on further disclosure of information obtained under section 245F

(1)   This section applies to information (in whatever form) which—

(a)   has been obtained in pursuance of a requirement or order under section 245F, and

(b)   relates to the private affairs of an individual or to any particular business.

(2)   No such information may, during the lifetime of that individual or so long as that business continues to be carried on, be disclosed without the consent of that individual or the person for the time being carrying on that business.

(3)   Subsection (2) does not apply to any disclosure of information which—

     (a)   is made for the purpose of facilitating the carrying out by a person authorised under section 245C of his functions under section 245B;

     (b)   is made to a person specified in Part 1 of Schedule 7B;

     (c)   is of a description specified in Part 2 of that Schedule; or

     (d)   is made in accordance with Part 3 of that Schedule.

(4)   The Secretary of State may by order amend Schedule 7B.

(5)   An order under subsection (4) must not—

     (a)   amend Part 1 of Schedule 7B by specifying a person unless the person exercises functions of a public nature (whether or not he exercises any other function);

     (b)   amend Part 2 of Schedule 7B by adding or modifying a description of disclosure unless the purpose for which the disclosure is permitted is likely to facilitate the exercise of a function of a public nature;

     (c)   amend Part 3 of Schedule 7B so as to have the effect of permitting disclosures to be made to a body other than one that exercises functions of a public nature in a country or territory outside the United Kingdom.

(6)   An order under subsection (4) shall be made by statutory instrument which shall be subject to annulment in pursuance of a resolution of either House of Parliament.

(7)   A person who discloses any information in contravention of this section—

     (a)   is guilty of an offence, and

     (b)   is liable on conviction to imprisonment or a fine, or both.

(8)   However, it is a defence for a person charged with an offence under subsection (7) to prove—

     (a)   that he did not know, and had no reason to suspect, that the information had been disclosed under section 245F; or

     (b)   that he took all reasonable steps and exercised all due diligence to avoid the commission of the offence.

(9)   Sections 732 (restriction on prosecutions), 733 (liability of individuals for corporate default) and 734 (criminal proceedings against unincorporated bodies) apply to offences under this section.

(10)   This section does not prohibit the disclosure of information if the information is or has been available to the public from any other source.

(11)   Nothing in this section authorises the making of a disclosure in contravention of the Data Protection Act 1998.

CHAPTER II
EXEMPTIONS, EXCEPTIONS AND SPECIAL PROVISIONS

Small and medium-sized companies and groups

246.   **Special provisions for small companies**

(1)   Subject to section 247A, this section applies where a company qualifies as a small company in relation to a financial year.

(2)   If the company's individual accounts for the year are Companies Act individual accounts and—

     (a)   comply with the provisions of Schedule 8, or

     (b)   fail to comply with those provisions only in so far as they comply instead with one or more corresponding provisions of Schedule 4,

     they need not comply with the provisions or, as the case may be, the remaining provisions of Schedule 4; and where advantage is taken of this subsection, references in section 226A to compliance with the provisions of Schedule 4 shall be construed accordingly.

(3)   The company's individual accounts for the year—

(a)   may give the total of the aggregates required by paragraphs (a), (c) and (d) of paragraph 1(1) of Schedule 6 (emoluments and other benefits etc of directors) instead of giving those aggregates individually; and

(b)   need not give the information required by—

   (i)   paragraph 4 of Schedule 5 (financial years of subsidiary undertakings);

   (ii)   paragraph 1(2)(b) of Schedule 6 (numbers of directors exercising share options and receiving shares under long term incentive schemes);

   (iii) paragraph 2 of Schedule 6 (details of highest paid director's emoluments etc); or

   (iv)   paragraph 7 of Schedule 6 (excess retirement benefits of directors and past directors).

(4)   The directors' report for the year need not give the information required by—

(a)   section 234(1)(a) and (b) (fair review of business and amount to be paid as dividend);

(b)   paragraph 1(2) of Schedule 7 (statement of market value of fixed assets where substantially different from balance sheet amount);

(ba) paragraph 5A of Schedule 7 (disclosures relating to the use of financial instruments);

(c)   paragraph 6 of Schedule 7 (miscellaneous disclosures); or

(d)   paragraph 11 of Schedule 7 (employee involvement).

(5)   Notwithstanding anything in section 242(1), the directors of the company need not deliver to the registrar any of the following, namely—

(a)   a copy of the company's profit and loss account for the year;

(b)   a copy of the directors' report for the year; and

(c)   if they prepare Companies Act individual accounts and they deliver a copy of a balance sheet drawn up as at the last day of the year which complies with the requirements of Schedule 8A, a copy of the company's balance sheet drawn up as at that day.

(6)   Neither a copy of the company's accounts for the year delivered to the registrar under section 242(1), nor a copy of a balance sheet delivered to the registrar under subsection (5)(c), need give the information required by—

(a)   paragraph 4 of Schedule 5 (financial years of subsidiary undertakings);

(b)   paragraph 6 of Schedule 5 (shares of company held by subsidiary undertakings);

(c)   Part I of Schedule 6 (directors' and chairman's emoluments, pensions and compensation for loss of office); or

(d)   section 390A(3) (amount of auditors' remuneration).

(7)   The provisions of section 233 as to the signing of the copy of the balance sheet delivered to the registrar apply to a copy of a balance sheet delivered under subsection (5)(c).

(8)   Subject to subsection (9), each of the following, namely—

(a)   accounts prepared in accordance with subsection (2) or (3),

(b)   a report prepared in accordance with subsection (4), and

(c)   a copy of accounts delivered to the registrar in accordance with subsection (5) or (6),

shall contain a statement in a prominent position on the balance sheet, in the report or, as the case may be, on the copy of the balance sheet, above the signature required by section 233, 234A or subsection (7), that they are prepared in accordance with the special provisions of this Part relating to small companies.

(9)   Subsection (8) does not apply where the directors of the company have taken advantage of the exemption from audit conferred by section 249AA (dormant companies).

246A. Special provisions for medium-sized companies

(1)   Subject to section 247A, this section applies where a company qualifies as a medium-sized company in relation to a financial year and its directors prepare Companies Act individual accounts for that year.

(2)   The company's individual accounts for the year need not comply with the requirements of paragraph 36A of Schedule 4 (disclosure with respect to compliance with accounting standards).

(3)   The company may deliver to the registrar a copy of the company's accounts for the year—

(a)   which includes a profit and loss account in which the following items listed in the profit and loss account formats set out in Part I of Schedule 4 are combined as one item under the heading "gross profit or loss"—

  Items 1, 2, 3 and 6 in Format 1;

  Items 1 to 5 in Format 2;

  Items A.1, B.1 and B.2 in Format 3;

  Items A.1, A.2 and B.1 to B.4 in Format 4;

(b)   which does not contain the information required by paragraph 55 of Schedule 4 (particulars of turnover).

(4)   A copy of accounts delivered to the registrar in accordance with subsection (3) shall contain a statement in a prominent position on the copy of the balance sheet, above the signature required by section 233, that the accounts are prepared in accordance with the special provisions of this Part relating to medium-sized companies.

247.   Qualification of company as small or medium-sized

(1)   A company qualifies as small or medium-sized in relation to a financial year if the qualifying conditions are met—

(a)   in the case of the company's first financial year, in that year, and

(b)   in the case of any subsequent financial year, in that year and the preceding year.

(2)   A company shall be treated as qualifying as small or medium-sized in relation to a financial year—

(a)   if it so qualified in relation to the previous financial year under subsection (1) above or was treated as so qualifying under paragraph (b) below; or

(b)   if it was treated as so qualifying in relation to the previous year by virtue of paragraph (a) and the qualifying conditions are met in the year in question.

(3)   The qualifying conditions are met by a company in a year in which it satisfies two or more of the following requirements—

Small company

1. Turnover	Not more than £5.6 million
2. Balance sheet total	Not more than £2.8 million
3. Number of employees	Not more than 50

Medium-sized company

1. Turnover	Not more than £22.8 million
2. Balance sheet total	Not more than £11.4 million
3. Number of employees	Not more than 250.

(4)   For a period which is a company's financial year but not in fact a year the maximum figures for turnover shall be proportionately adjusted.

(5)   The balance sheet total means—

(a)   in the case of Companies Act individual accounts—

  (i)   the aggregate of the amounts shown in the balance sheet under the headings corresponding to items A to D of Format 1 in Part 1 of Schedule 4 or Part 1 of Schedule 8, or

  (ii)   if Format 2 is adopted, the aggregate of the amounts shown under the general heading "ASSETS";

(b)   in the case of IAS individual accounts, the aggregate of the amounts shown as assets in the balance sheet.

(6)   The number of employees means the average number of persons employed by the company in the year (determined on a monthly basis).

That number shall be determined by applying the method of calculation prescribed by paragraph 56(2) and (3) of Schedule 4 for determining the corresponding number required to be stated in a note to the company's accounts.

247A. Cases in which special provisions do not apply

(1)   Nothing in section 246 or 246A shall apply where—

    (a)   the company is, or was at any time within the financial year to which the accounts relate—

        (i)   a public company,

        (ii) a person who has permission under Part 4 of the Financial Services and Markets Act 2000 to carry on one or more regulated activities, or

        (iii) a person who carries on insurance market activity; or

    (b)   the company is, or was at any time during that year, a member of an ineligible group.

(2)   A group is ineligible if any of its members is—

    (a)   a public company or a body corporate which (not being a company) has power under its constitution to offer its shares or debentures to the public and may lawfully exercise that power,

    (b)   a person who has permission under Part 4 of the Financial Services and Markets Act 2000 to carry on a regulated activity, or

    (c)   a person who carries on an insurance market activity.

(3)   A parent company shall not be treated as qualifying as a small company in relation to a financial year unless the group headed by it qualifies as a small group, and shall not be treated as qualifying as a medium-sized company in relation to a financial year unless that group qualifies as a medium-sized group (see section 249).

247B. Special auditors' report

(1)   This section applies where—

    (a)   the directors of a company propose to deliver to the registrar copies of accounts ("abbreviated accounts") prepared in accordance with section 246(5) or (6) or 246A(3) ("the relevant provision"),

    (b)   the directors have not taken advantage of the exemption from audit conferred by section 249A(1) or (2) or section 249AA, …

    (c)   …

(2)   If abbreviated accounts prepared in accordance with the relevant provision are delivered to the registrar, they shall be accompanied by a copy of a special report of the auditors stating that in their opinion—

    (a)   the company is entitled to deliver abbreviated accounts prepared in accordance with that provision, and

    (b)   the abbreviated accounts to be delivered are properly prepared in accordance with that provision.

(3)   In such a case a copy of the auditors' report under section 235 need not be delivered, but—

    (a)   if that report was qualified, the special report shall set out that report in full together with any further material necessary to understand the qualification; and

    (b)   if that report contained a statement under—

        (i)   section 237(2) (accounts, records or returns inadequate or accounts not agreeing with records and returns), or

        (ii) section 237(3) (failure to obtain necessary information and explanations),

    the special report shall set out that statement in full.

(4)   Section 236 (signature of auditors' report) applies to a special report under this section as it applies to a report under section 235.

(5)   If abbreviated accounts prepared in accordance with the relevant provision are delivered to the registrar, references in section 240 (requirements in connection with publication of accounts) to the auditors' report under section 235 shall be read as references to the special auditors' report under this section.

248.   **Exemption for small and medium-sized groups**

(1)   A parent company need not prepare group accounts for a financial year in relation to which the group headed by that company qualifies as a small or medium-sized group and is not an ineligible group.

(2)   A group is ineligible if any of its members is—

(a)   a public company or a body corporate which (not being a company) has power under its constitution to offer its shares or debentures to the public and may lawfully exercise that power,

(b)   a person who has permission under Part IV of the Financial Services and Markets Act 2000 to carry on a regulated activity, or

(c)   a person who carries on an insurance market activity.

(3), (4) ...

248A.   **Group accounts prepared by small company**

(1)   This section applies where a small company—

(a)   has prepared individual accounts for a financial year in accordance with section 246(2) or (3), and

(b)   is preparing Companies Act group accounts in respect of the same year.

(2)   If the group accounts—

(a)   comply with the provisions of Schedule 8, or

(b)   fail to comply with those provisions only in so far as they comply instead with one or more corresponding provisions of Schedule 4,

they need not comply with the provisions or, as the case may be, the remaining provisions of Schedule 4; and where advantage is taken of this subsection, references in Schedule 4A to compliance with the provisions of Schedule 4 shall be construed accordingly.

(3)   For the purposes of this section, Schedule 8 shall have effect as if, in each balance sheet format set out in that Schedule, for item B.III there were substituted the following item—

"B.III Investments

1 Shares in group undertakings

2 Interests in associated undertakings

3 Other participating interests

4 Loans to group undertakings and undertakings in which a participating interest is held

5 Other investments other than loans

6 Others."

(4)   The group accounts need not give the information required by the provisions specified in section 246(3).

(5)   Group accounts prepared in accordance with this section shall contain a statement in a prominent position on the balance sheet, above the signature required by section 233, that they are prepared in accordance with the special provisions of this Part relating to small companies.

249.   **Qualification of group as small or medium-sized**

(1)   A group qualifies as small or medium-sized in relation to a financial year if the qualifying conditions are met—

(a)   in the case of the parent company's first financial year, in that year, and

(b)   in the case of any subsequent financial year, in that year and the preceding year.

(2)   A group shall be treated as qualifying as small or medium-sized in relation to a financial year—

(a)   if it so qualified in relation to the previous financial year under subsection (1) above or was treated as so qualifying under paragraph (b) below; or

(b)   if it was treated as so qualifying in relation to the previous year by virtue of paragraph (a) and the qualifying conditions are met in the year in question.

(3)   The qualifying conditions are met by a group in a year in which it satisfies two or more of the following requirements—

Small group

1. Aggregate turnover	Not more than £5.6 million net (or £6.72 million gross)
2. Aggregate balance sheet total	Not more than £2.8 million net (or £3.36 million gross)
3. Aggregate number of employees	Not more than 50

Medium-sized group

1. Aggregate turnover	Not more than £22.8 million net (or £27.36 million gross)
2. Aggregate balance sheet total	Not more than £11.4 million net (or £13.68 million gross)
3. Aggregate number of employees	Not more than 250.

(4)   The aggregate figures shall be ascertained by aggregating the relevant figures determined in accordance with section 247 for each member of the group.

In relation to the aggregate figures for turnover and balance sheet total, "net" means with the set-offs and other adjustments required by Schedule 4A in the case of group accounts and "gross" means without those set-offs and other adjustments; and a company may satisfy the relevant requirement on the basis of either the net or the gross figure.

(5)   The figures for each subsidiary undertaking shall be those included in its accounts for the relevant financial year, that is—

(a)   if its financial year ends with that of the parent company, that financial year, and

(b)   if not, its financial year ending last before the end of the financial year of the parent company.

(6)   If those figures cannot be obtained without disproportionate expense or undue delay, the latest available figures shall be taken.

Exemptions from audit for certain categories of small companies

249A.   Exemptions from audit

(1)   Subject to section 249B, a company which meets the total exemption conditions set out below in respect of a financial year is exempt from the provisions of this Part relating to the audit of accounts in respect of that year.

(2)   Subject to section 249B, a company which is a charity and which meets the report conditions set out below in respect of a financial year is exempt from the provisions of this Part relating to the audit of accounts in respect of that year if the directors cause a report in respect of the company's individual accounts for that year to be prepared in accordance with section 249C and made to the company's members.

(3)   The total exemption conditions are met by a company in respect of a financial year if—

(a)   it qualifies as a small company in relation to that year for the purposes of section 246,

(b)   its turnover in that year is not more than £5.6 million, and

(c)   its balance sheet total for that year is not more than £2.8 million.

(3A)   In relation to any company which is a charity, subsection (3)(b) shall have effect with the substitution—

(a)   for the reference to turnover of a reference to gross income, and

(b)   for the reference to £5.6 million of a reference to £90,000.

(4)   The report conditions are met by a company which is a charity in respect of a financial year if—

(a)   it qualifies as a small company in relation to that year for the purposes of section 246,

(b)   its gross income in that year is more than £90,000 but not more than £250,000, and

(c)   its balance sheet total for that year is not more than £1.4 million.

(5)   ...

(6)   For a period which is a company's financial year but not in fact a year the maximum figures for turnover or gross income shall be proportionately adjusted.

(6A)   A company is entitled to the exemption conferred by subsection (1) or (2) notwithstanding that it falls within paragraph (a) or (b) of section 249AA(1).

(7)   In this section—

"balance sheet total" has the meaning given by section 247(5), and "gross income" means the company's income from all sources, as shown in the company's income and expenditure account.

249AA. Dormant companies

(1) Subject to section 249B(2) to (5), a company is exempt from the provisions of this Part relating to the audit of accounts in respect of a financial year if—

    (a) it has been dormant since its formation, or

    (b) it has been dormant since the end of the previous financial year and subsection (2) applies.

(2) This subsection applies if the company—

    (a) is entitled in respect of its individual accounts for the financial year in question to prepare accounts in accordance with section 246, or would be so entitled but for the application of section 247A(1)(a)(i) or (b), and

    (b) is not required to prepare group accounts for that year.

(3) Subsection (1) does not apply if at any time in the financial year in question the company was—

    (a) a person who has permission under Part 4 of the Financial Services and Markets Act 2000 to carry on one or more regulated activities; or

    (b) a person who carries on insurance market activity.

(4) A company is "dormant" during any period in which it has no significant accounting transaction.

(5) "Significant accounting transaction" means a transaction which—

    (a) is required by section 221 to be entered in the company's accounting records; but

    (b) is not a transaction to which subsection (6) or (7) applies.

(6) This subsection applies to a transaction arising from the taking of shares in the company by a subscriber to the memorandum as a result of an undertaking of his in the memorandum.

(7) This subsection applies to a transaction consisting of the payment of—

    (a) a fee to the registrar on a change of name under section 28 (change of name),

    (b) a fee to the registrar on the re-registration of a company under Part II (re-registration as a means of altering a company's status),

    (c) a penalty under section 242A (penalty for failure to deliver accounts), or

    (d) a fee to the registrar for the registration of an annual return under Chapter III of Part XI.

249B. Cases where exemptions not available

(1) Subject to subsection (1A) to (1C), a company is not entitled to the exemption conferred by subsection (1) or (2) of section 249A in respect of a financial year if at any time within that year—

    (a) it was a public company,

    (b) it was a person who had permission under Part 4 of the Financial Services and Markets Act 2000 to carry on a regulated activity,

    (bb) it carried on an insurance market activity,

    (c) ...

    (d) it was an appointed representative, within the meaning of section 39 of the Financial Services and Markets Act 2000,

    (e) it was a special register body as defined in section 117(1) of the Trade Union and Labour Relations (Consolidation) Act 1992 or an employers' association as defined in section 122 of that Act, or

    (f) it was a parent company or a subsidiary undertaking.

(1A) A company which, apart from this subsection, would fall within subsection (1)(f) by virtue of its being a subsidiary undertaking for any period within a financial year shall not be treated as so falling if it is dormant (within the meaning of section 249AA) throughout that period.

(1B) A company which, apart from this subsection, would fall within subsection (1)(f) by virtue of its being a parent company or a subsidiary undertaking for any period within a financial year, shall not be treated as so falling if throughout that period it was a member of a group meeting the conditions set out in subsection (1C).

(1C) The conditions referred to in subsection (1B) are—

    (a)   that the group qualifies as a small group, in relation to the financial year within which the period falls, for the purposes of section 249 (or if all bodies corporate in such group were companies, would so qualify) and is not, and was not at any time within that year, an ineligible group within the meaning of section 248(2),

    (b)   that the group's aggregate turnover in that year (calculated in accordance with section 249) is, where the company referred to in subsection (1B) is a charity, not more than £350,000 net (or £420,000 gross) or, where the company so referred to is not a charity, not more than £5.6 million net (or £6.72 million gross), and

    (c)   that the group's aggregate balance sheet total for that year (calculated in accordance with section 249) is not more than £2.8 million net (or £3.36 million gross).

(2)   Any member or members holding not less in the aggregate than 10 per cent in nominal value of the company's issued share capital or any class of it or, if the company does not have a share capital, not less than 10 per cent in number of the members of the company, may, by notice in writing deposited at the registered office of the company during a financial year but not later than one month before the end of that year, require the company to obtain an audit of its accounts for that year.

(3)   Where a notice has been deposited under subsection (2), the company is not entitled to the exemption conferred by subsection (1) or (2) of section 249A or by subsection (1) of section 249AA in respect of the financial year to which the notice relates.

(4)   A company is not entitled to the exemption conferred by subsection (1) or (2) of section 249A or by subsection (1) of section 249AA unless its balance sheet contains a statement by the directors—

    (a)   to the effect that for the year in question the company was entitled to exemption under subsection (1) or (2) ... of section 249A or subsection (1) of section 249AA,

    (b)   to the effect that members have not required the company to obtain an audit of its accounts for the year in question in accordance with subsection (2) of this section, and

    (c)   to the effect that the directors acknowledge their responsibilities for—

        (i)   ensuring that the company keeps accounting records which comply with section 221, and

        (ii)   preparing accounts which give a true and fair view of the state of affairs of the company as at the end of the financial year and of its profit or loss for the financial year in accordance with the requirements of section 226, and which otherwise comply with the requirements of this Act relating to accounts, so far as applicable to the company.

(5)   The statement required by subsection (4) shall appear in the balance sheet above the signature required by section 233.

249C.   The report required for the purposes of section 249A(2)

(1)   The report required for the purposes of section 249A(2) shall be prepared by a person (referred to in this Part as "the reporting accountant") who is eligible under section 249D.

(2)   The report shall state whether in the opinion of the reporting accountant making it—

    (a)   the accounts of the company for the financial year in question are in agreement with the accounting records kept by the company under section 221, and

    (b)   having regard only to, and on the basis of, the information contained in those accounting records, those accounts have been drawn up in a manner consistent with the provisions of this Act specified in subsection (6), so far as applicable to the company.

(3)   The report shall also state that in the opinion of the reporting accountant, having regard only to, and on the basis of, the information contained in the accounting records kept by the company under section 221, the company satisfied the requirements of subsection (4) of section 249A ... for the financial year in question, and did not fall within section 249B(1)(a) to (f) at any time within that financial year.

(4)   The report shall state the name of the reporting accountant and be signed by him.

(5) Where the reporting accountant is a body corporate or partnership, any reference to signature of the report, or any copy of the report, by the reporting accountant is a reference to signature in the name of the body corporate or partnership by a person authorised to sign on its behalf.

(6) The provisions referred to in subsection (2)(b) are—

 (a) section 226A(3) and Schedule 4,

 (b) section 231 and paragraphs 7 to 9A and 13(1), (3) and (4) of Schedule 5, and

 (c) section 232 and Schedule 6,

where appropriate as modified by section 246(2) and (3).

249D. The reporting accountant

(1) The reporting accountant shall be either—

 (a) any member of a body listed in subsection (3) who, under the rules of the body—

  (i) is entitled to engage in public practice, and

  (ii) is not ineligible for appointment as a reporting accountant, or

 (b) any person (whether or not a member of any such body) who—

  (i) is subject to the rules of any such body in seeking appointment or acting as auditor under Chapter V of Part XI, and

  (ii) under those rules, is eligible for appointment as auditor under that Chapter.

(1A) In subsection (1), references to the rules of a body listed in subsection (3) are to the rules (whether or not laid down by the body itself) which the body has power to enforce and which are relevant for the purposes of Part II of the Companies Act 1989 or this section.

This includes rules relating to the admission and expulsion of members of the body, so far as relevant for the purposes of that Part or this section.

(2) An individual, a body corporate or a partnership may be appointed as a reporting accountant, and section 26 of the Companies Act 1989 (effect of appointment of partnership) shall apply to the appointment as reporting accountant of a partnership constituted under the law of England and Wales or Northern Ireland, or under the law of any other country or territory in which a partnership is not a legal person.

(3) The bodies referred to in subsections (1) and (1A) are—

 (a) the Institute of Chartered Accountants in England and Wales,

 (b) the Institute of Chartered Accountants of Scotland,

 (c) the Institute of Chartered Accountants in Ireland,

 (d) the Association of Chartered Certified Accountants, ...

 (e) the Association of Authorised Public Accountants,

 (f) the Association of Accounting Technicians,

 (g) the Association of International Accountants, ...

 (h) the Chartered Institute of Management Accountants, and

 (i) the Institute of Chartered Secretaries and Administrators.

(4) A person is ineligible for appointment by a company as reporting accountant if he would be ineligible for appointment as an auditor of that company under section 27 of the Companies Act 1989 (ineligibility on ground of lack of independence).

249E. Effect of exemptions

(1) Where the directors of a company have taken advantage of the exemption conferred by section 249A(1) or 249AA(1)—

 (a) sections 238 and 239 (right to receive or demand copies of accounts and reports) shall have effect with the omission of references to the auditors' report;

 (b) no copy of an auditors' report need be delivered to the registrar or laid before the company in general meeting;

 (c) subsections (3) to (5) of section 271 (accounts by reference to which distribution to be justified) shall not apply.

(1A) Where the directors of a company have taken advantage of the exemption conferred by section 249AA, then for the purposes of that section the company shall be treated as a company entitled to prepare accounts in accordance with section 246 even though it is a member of an ineligible group.

(2)   Where the directors of a company have taken advantage of the exemption conferred by section 249A(2)—

    (a)   subsections (2) to (4) of section 236 (which require copies of the auditors' report to state the names of the auditors) shall have effect with the substitution for references to the auditors and the auditors' report of references to the reporting accountant and the report made for the purposes of section 249A(2) respectively;

    (b)   sections 238 and 239 (right to receive or demand copies of accounts and reports), section 241 (accounts and reports to be laid before company in general meeting) and section 242 (accounts and reports to be delivered to the registrar) shall have effect with the substitution for references to the auditors' report of references to the report made for the purposes of section 249A(2);

    (c)   subsections (3) to (5) of section 271 (accounts by reference to which distribution to be justified) shall not apply;

    (d)   sections 389A(1) and 389B(1) and (5) (rights to information) shall have effect with the substitution for references to an auditor of references to the reporting accountant.

250.   ...

Summary financial statement

251.   **Provision of summary financial statement to shareholders**

(1)   A company need not, in such cases as may be specified by regulations made by the Secretary of State, and provided any conditions so specified are complied with, send copies of the documents referred to in section 238(1) to entitled persons, but may instead send them a summary financial statement.

In this section—

    "entitled persons ", in relation to a company, means such of the persons specified in paragraphs (a) to (c) of subsection (1) of section 238 as are or would apart from this section be entitled to be sent copies of those documents relating to the company which are referred to in that subsection;

    ...

(2)   Copies of the documents referred to in section 238(1) shall, however, be sent to any entitled person who wishes to receive them; and the Secretary of State may by regulations make provision as to the manner in which it is to be ascertained (whether before or after he becomes an entitled person) whether an entitled person wishes to receive them.

(2A)   References in this section to sending a summary financial statement to an entitled person include references to using electronic communications for sending the statement to such address as may for the time being be notified to the company by that person for that purpose.

(2B)   For the purposes of this section a summary financial statement is also to be treated as sent to an entitled person where—

    (a)   the company and that person have agreed to his having access to summary financial statements on a web site (instead of their being sent to him);

    (b)   the statement is a statement to which that agreement applies; and

    (c)   that person is notified, in a manner for the time being agreed for the purpose between him and the company, of—

        (i)   the publication of the statement on a web site;

        (ii)   the address of that web site; and

        (iii)   the place on that web site where the statement may be accessed, and how it may be accessed.

(2C)   For the purposes of this section a statement treated in accordance with subsection (2B) as sent to an entitled person is to be treated as sent to him if, and only if—

(a)   the statement is published on the web site throughout a period beginning at least 21 days before the date of the meeting at which the accounts and directors' report from which the statement is derived are to be laid and ending with the conclusion of that meeting; and

(b)   the notification given for the purposes of paragraph (c) of that subsection is given not less than 21 days before the date of the meeting.

(2D)   Nothing in subsection (2C) shall invalidate the proceedings of a meeting where—

(a)   any statement that is required to be published as mentioned in paragraph (a) of that subsection is published for a part, but not all, of the period mentioned in that paragraph; and

(b)   the failure to publish that statement throughout that period is wholly attributable to circumstances which it would not be reasonable to have expected the company to prevent or avoid.

(2E)   A company may, notwithstanding any provision to the contrary in its articles, take advantage of any of subsections (2A) to (2D).

(3)   The summary financial statement—

(a)   shall be derived from the company's annual accounts, the directors' report and (in the case of a quoted company) the directors' remuneration report, and

(b)   shall be in such form and contain such information as may be specified by regulations made by the Secretary of State.

(4)   Every summary financial statement shall—

(a)   state that it is only a summary of information in the company's annual accounts, the directors' report and (in the case of a quoted company) the directors' remuneration report;

(b)   contain a statement by the company's auditors of their opinion as to whether the summary financial statement is consistent with those accounts and those reports and complies with the requirements of this section and regulations made under it;

(c)   state whether the auditors' report on the annual accounts, or on the annual accounts and the auditable part of the directors' remuneration report, was unqualified or qualified, and if it was qualified set out the report in full together with any further material needed to understand the qualification;

(d)   state whether that auditors' report contained a statement under—

(i)   section 237(2) (accounting records or returns inadequate or accounts or directors' remuneration report not agreeing with records and returns); or

(ii)   section 237(3) (failure to obtain necessary information and explanations),

and if so, set out the statement in full.

(5)   Regulations under this section shall be made by statutory instrument which shall be subject to annulment in pursuance of a resolution of either House of Parliament.

(6)   If default is made in complying with this section or regulations made under it, the company and every officer of it who is in default is guilty of an offence and liable to a fine.

(7)   Section 240 (requirements in connection with publication of accounts) does not apply in relation to the provision to entitled persons of a summary financial statement in accordance with this section.

Private companies

252.   Election to dispense with laying of accounts and reports before general meeting

(1)   A private company may elect (by elective resolution in accordance with section 379A) to dispense with the laying of accounts and reports before the company in general meeting.

(2)   An election has effect in relation to the accounts and reports in respect of the financial year in which the election is made and subsequent financial years.

(3)   Whilst an election is in force, the references in the following provisions of this Act to the laying of accounts before the company in general meeting shall be read as references to the sending of copies of the accounts to members and others under section 238(1)—

(a)   section 235(1) (accounts on which auditors are to report),

(b)   section 270(3) and (4) (accounts by reference to which distributions are justified), and

(c)   section 320(2) (accounts relevant for determining company's net assets for purposes of ascertaining whether approval required for certain transactions);

and the requirement in section 271(4) that the auditors' statement under that provision be laid before the company in general meeting shall be read as a requirement that it be sent to members and others along with the copies of the accounts sent to them under section 238(1).

(4)   If an election under this section ceases to have effect, section 241 applies in relation to the accounts and reports in respect of the financial year in which the election ceases to have effect and subsequent financial years.

253.   Right of shareholder to require laying of accounts

(1)   Where an election under section 252 is in force, the copies of the accounts and reports sent out in accordance with section 238(1)—

(a)   shall be sent not less than 28 days before the end of the period allowed for laying and delivering accounts and reports, and

(b)   shall be accompanied, in the case of a member of the company, by a notice informing him of his right to require the laying of the accounts and reports before a general meeting;

and section 238(5) (penalty for default) applies in relation to the above requirements as to the requirements contained in that section.

(2)   Before the end of the period of 28 days beginning with the day on which the accounts and reports are sent out in accordance with section 238(1), any member or auditor of the company may by notice in writing deposited at the registered office of the company require that a general meeting be held for the purpose of laying the accounts and reports before the company.

(2A)   The power of a member or auditor under subsection (2) to require the holding of a general meeting is exercisable not only by the deposit of a notice in writing but also by the transmission to the company at such address as may for the time being be specified for the purpose by or on behalf of the company of an electronic communication containing the requirement.

(3)   If the directors do not within 21 days from the date of—

(a)   the deposit of a notice containing a requirement under subsection (2), or

(b)   the receipt of such a requirement contained in an electronic communication, proceed duly to convene a meeting, the person who required the holding of the meeting may do so himself.

(4)   A meeting so convened shall not be held more than three months from that date and shall be convened in the same manner, as nearly as possible, as that in which meetings are to be convened by directors.

(5)   Where the directors do not duly convene a meeting, any reasonable expenses incurred by reason of that failure by the person who required the holding of the meeting shall be made good to him by the company, and shall be recouped by the company out of any fees, or other remuneration in respect of their services, due or to become due to such of the directors as were in default.

(6)   The directors shall be deemed not to have duly convened a meeting if they convene a meeting for a date more than 28 days after the date of the notice convening it.

Unlimited companies

254.   Exemption from requirement to deliver accounts and reports

(1)   The directors of an unlimited company are not required to deliver accounts and reports to the registrar in respect of a financial year if the following conditions are met.

(2)   The conditions are that at no time during the relevant accounting reference period—

(a)   has the company been, to its knowledge, a subsidiary undertaking of an undertaking which was then limited, or

(b)   have there been, to its knowledge, exercisable by or on behalf of two or more undertakings which were then limited, rights which if exercisable by one of them would have made the company a subsidiary undertaking of it, or

(c)   has the company been a parent company of an undertaking which was then limited.

The references above to an undertaking being limited at a particular time are to an undertaking (under whatever law established) the liability of whose members is at that time limited.

(3)   The exemption conferred by this section does not apply if—

    (a)   the company is a banking or insurance company or the parent company of a banking or insurance group, or

    (b)   the company is a qualifying company within the meaning of the Partnerships and Unlimited Companies (Accounts) Regulations 1993, or

    (c)   any time during the relevant accounting period the company carried on business as the promoter of a trading stamp scheme within the Trading Stamps Act 1964.

(4)   Where a company is exempt by virtue of this section from the obligation to deliver accounts, section 240 (requirements in connection with publication of accounts) has effect with the following modifications—

    (a)   in subsection (3)(b) for the words from "whether statutory accounts" to "have been delivered to the registrar" substitute "that the company is exempt from the requirement to deliver statutory accounts", and

    (b)   in subsection (5) for "as required to be delivered to the registrar under section 242" substitute "as prepared in accordance with this Part and approved by the board of directors".

Banking and insurance companies and groups

255.   Special provisions for banking and insurance companies

(1)   A banking company shall prepare its individual accounts in accordance with Part I of Schedule 9 rather than Schedule 4.

(2)   An insurance company shall prepare its individual accounts in accordance with Part I of Schedule 9A rather than Schedule 4.

(3)   Accounts so prepared shall contain a statement that they are prepared in accordance with the special provisions of this Part relating to banking companies or to insurance companies, as the case may be.

(4)   In relation to the preparation of individual accounts in accordance with the special provisions of this Part, the references to Schedule 4 in section 226(4) and (5) (relationship between specific requirements and duty to give true and fair view) shall be read as references to the provisions of Part I of Schedule 9, in the case of the accounts of banking companies, or to the provisions of Part I of Schedule 9A, in the case of the accounts of insurance companies.

(4A)   References to Companies Act individual accounts include accounts prepared in accordance with this section.

(4B)   This section does not apply to banking companies and insurance companies that prepare IAS individual accounts.

(5)   …

255A.   Special provisions for banking and insurance groups

(1)   The parent company of a banking group shall prepare group accounts in accordance with the provisions of this Part as modified by Part II of Schedule 9.

(2)   The parent company of an insurance group shall prepare group accounts in accordance with the provisions of this Part as modified by Part II of Schedule 9A.

(3)   Accounts so prepared shall contain a statement that they are prepared in accordance with the special provisions of this Part relating to banking groups or to insurance groups, as the case may be.

(4)   References in this Part to a banking group are to a group where the parent company is a banking company or where—

    (a)   the parent company's principal subsidiary undertakings are wholly or mainly credit institutions, and

    (b)   the parent company does not itself carry on any material business apart from the acquisition, management and disposal of interests in subsidiary undertakings.

(5)   References in this Part to an insurance group are to a group where the parent company is an insurance company or where—

    (a)   the parent company's principal subsidiary undertakings are wholly or mainly insurance companies, and

    (b)   the parent company does not itself carry on any material business apart from the acquisition, management and disposal of interests in subsidiary undertakings.

(5A)   For the purposes of subsections (4) and (5) above—

    (a)   a parent company's principal subsidiary undertakings are the subsidiary undertakings of the company whose results or financial position would principally affect the figures shown in the group accounts, and

    (b)   the management of interests in subsidiary undertakings includes the provision of services to such undertakings.

(6)   In relation to the preparation of group accounts in accordance with the special provisions of this Part:

    (a)   the references to the provisions of Schedule 4A in section 227A(4) and (5) (relationship between specific requirements and duty to give true and fair view) shall be read as references to those provisions as modified by Part II of Schedule 9, in the case of the group accounts of a banking group, or Part II of Schedule 9A, in the case of the group accounts of an insurance group; and

    (b)   the reference to paragraphs 52 to 57 of Schedule 4 in section 230(2) (relief from obligation to comply with those paragraphs where group accounts prepared) shall be read as a reference to paragraphs 75 to 77, 80 and 81 of Part I of Schedule 9, in the case of the group accounts of a banking group, and as a reference to paragraphs 73, 74, 79 and 80 of Part I of Schedule 9A, in the case of the group accounts of an insurance group.

(6A)   References to Companies Act group accounts include accounts prepared in accordance with subsections (1) to (3).

(6B)   Subsections (1) to (3) and (6) do not apply to parent companies of banking groups or insurance groups that prepare IAS group accounts.

(7)   ...

255B.   Modification of disclosure requirements in relation to banking company or group

(1)   In relation to a banking company, or the parent company of a banking group, the provisions of Schedule 5 (Disclosure of information: related undertakings) have effect subject to Part III of Schedule 9.

(2)   In relation to a banking company, or the holding company of a credit institution, the provisions of Schedule 6 (Disclosure of information: emoluments and other benefits of directors and others) have effect subject to Part IV of Schedule 9.

255C. ...

255D.   Power to apply provisions to banking

(1)   The Secretary of State may by regulations apply to banking partnerships, subject to such exceptions, adaptations and modifications as he considers appropriate, the provisions of this Part applying to banking companies.

(2)   A "banking partnership" means a partnership which has permission under Part 4 of the Financial Services and Markets Act 2000.

(2A)   But a partnership is not a banking partnership if it has permission to accept deposits only for the purpose of carrying on another regulated activity in accordance with that permission.

(3)   Regulations under this section shall be made by statutory instrument.

(4)   No regulations under this section shall be made unless a draft of the instrument containing the regulations has been laid before Parliament and approved by a resolution of each House.

(5)   Subsections (2) and (2A) must be read with—

    (a)   section 22 of the Financial Services and Markets Act 2000;

    (b)   any relevant order under that section; and

    (c)   Schedule 2 to that Act.

255E. ...

CHAPTER III
SUPPLEMENTARY PROVISIONS

Accounting standards

256. Accounting standards

(1)   In this Part "accounting standards" means statements of standard accounting practice issued by such body or bodies as may be prescribed by regulations.

(2)   References in this Part to accounting standards applicable to a company's annual accounts are to such standards as are, in accordance with their terms, relevant to the company's circumstances and to the accounts.

(3)   ...

(4)   Regulations under this section may contain such transitional and other supplementary and incidental provisions as appear to the Secretary of State to be appropriate.

Power to alter accounting requirements

257. Power of Secretary of State to alter accounting requirements

(1)   The Secretary of State may by regulations made by statutory instrument modify the provisions of this Part.

(2)   Regulations which—

(a)   add to the classes of documents required to be prepared, laid before the company in general meeting or delivered to the registrar,

(b)   restrict the classes of company which have the benefit of any exemption, exception or special provision,

(c)   require additional matter to be included in a document of any class, or

(d)   otherwise render the requirements of this Part more onerous,

shall not be made unless a draft of the instrument containing the regulations has been laid before Parliament and approved by a resolution of each House.

(3)   Otherwise, a statutory instrument containing regulations under this section shall be subject to annulment in pursuance of a resolution of either House of Parliament.

(4)   Regulations under this section may—

(a)   make different provision for different cases or classes of case,

(b)   repeal and re-enact provisions with modifications of form or arrangement, whether or not they are modified in substance,

(c)   make consequential amendments or repeals in other provisions of this Act, or in other enactments, and

(d)   contain such transitional and other incidental and supplementary provisions as the Secretary of State thinks fit.

(4A)   Regulations under this section may also make provision—

(a)   for the issuing, by such body or bodies as may be specified, of standards in relation to matters to be contained in reports which are required by this Part to be prepared by the directors of a company;

(b)   for directors of a company who have complied with any such standard, or any of its provisions, in relation to any such report, to be presumed (unless the contrary is proved) to have complied with any requirements of this Part relating to the contents of the report to which the standard or provision relates.

(4B)   In subsection (4A) "specified" means specified in an order made by the Secretary of State; and such an order—

(a)   shall be made by statutory instrument which shall be subject to annulment in pursuance of a resolution of either House of Parliament;

(b)   may contain such transitional provisions as the Secretary of State thinks fit.

(5)   Any modification by regulations under this section of section 258 or Schedule 10A (parent and subsidiary undertakings) does not apply for the purposes of enactments outside the Companies Acts unless the regulations so provide.

Parent and subsidiary undertakings

258.   Parent and subsidiary undertakings

(1)   The expressions "parent undertaking" and "subsidiary undertaking" in this Part shall be construed as follows; and a "parent company" means a parent undertaking which is a company.

(2)   An undertaking is a parent undertaking in relation to another undertaking, a subsidiary undertaking, if—

     (a)   it holds a majority of the voting rights in the undertaking, or

     (b)   it is a member of the undertaking and has the right to appoint or remove a majority of its board of directors, or

     (c)   it has the right to exercise a dominant influence over the undertaking—

         (i)   by virtue of provisions contained in the undertaking's memorandum or articles, or

         (ii)   by virtue of a control contract, or

     (d)   it is a member of the undertaking and controls alone, pursuant to an agreement with other shareholders or members, a majority of the voting rights in the undertaking.

(3)   For the purposes of subsection (2) an undertaking shall be treated as a member of another undertaking—

     (a)   if any of its subsidiary undertakings is a member of that undertaking, or

     (b)   if any shares in that other undertaking are held by a person acting on behalf of the undertaking or any of its subsidiary undertakings.

(4)   An undertaking is also a parent undertaking in relation to another undertaking, a subsidiary undertaking, if ...—

     (a)   it has the power to exercise, or actually exercises, dominant influence or control over it, or

     (b)   it and the subsidiary undertaking are managed on a unified basis.

(5)   A parent undertaking shall be treated as the parent undertaking of undertakings in relation to which any of its subsidiary undertakings are, or are to be treated as, parent undertakings; and references to its subsidiary undertakings shall be construed accordingly.

(6)   Schedule 10A contains provisions explaining expressions used in this section and otherwise supplementing this section.

Other interpretation provisions

259.   Meaning of "undertaking" and related expressions

(1)   In this Part "undertaking" means—

     (a)   a body corporate or partnership, or

     (b)   an unincorporated association carrying on a trade or business, with or without a view to profit.

(2)   In this Part references to shares—

     (a)   in relation to an undertaking with a share capital, are to allotted shares;

     (b)   in relation to an undertaking with capital but no share capital, are to rights to share in the capital of the undertaking; and

     (c)   in relation to an undertaking without capital, are to interests—

         (i)   conferring any right to share in the profits or liability to contribute to the losses of the undertaking, or

         (ii)   giving rise to an obligation to contribute to the debts or expenses of the undertaking in the event of a winding up.

(3)   Other expressions appropriate to companies shall be construed, in relation to an undertaking which is not a company, as references to the corresponding persons, officers, documents or organs, as the case may be, appropriate to undertakings of that description.

This is subject to provision in any specific context providing for the translation of such expressions.

(4) References in this Part to "fellow subsidiary undertakings" are to undertakings which are subsidiary undertakings of the same parent undertaking but are not parent undertakings or subsidiary undertakings of each other.

(5) In this Part "group undertaking", in relation to an undertaking, means an undertaking which is—
  (a) a parent undertaking or subsidiary undertaking of that undertaking, or
  (b) a subsidiary undertaking of any parent undertaking of that undertaking.

260. Participating interests

(1) In this Part a "participating interest" means an interest held by an undertaking in the shares of another undertaking which it holds on a long-term basis for the purpose of securing a contribution to its activities by the exercise of control or influence arising from or related to that interest.

(2) A holding of 20 per cent or more of the shares of an undertaking shall be presumed to be a participating interest unless the contrary is shown.

(3) The reference in subsection (1) to an interest in shares includes—
  (a) an interest which is convertible into an interest in shares, and
  (b) an option to acquire shares or any such interest;
  and an interest or option falls within paragraph (a) or (b) notwithstanding that the shares to which it relates are, until the conversion or the exercise of the option, unissued.

(4) For the purposes of this section an interest held on behalf of an undertaking shall be treated as held by it.

(5) ...

(6) In the balance sheet and profit and loss formats set out in Part I of Schedule 4, Part I of Schedule 8, Schedule 8A, Chapter I of Part I of Schedule 9 and Chapter I of Part I of Schedule 9A, "participating interest" does not include an interest in a group undertaking.

(7) For the purposes of this section as it applies in relation to the expression "participating interest"—
  (a) in those formats as they apply in relation to group accounts, and
  (b) in paragraph 20 of Schedule 4A (group accounts: undertakings to be accounted for as associated undertakings),
  the references in subsection (1) to (4) to the interest held by, and the purposes and activities of, the undertaking concerned shall be construed as references to the interest held by, and the purposes and activities of, the group (within the meaning of paragraph 1 of that Schedule).

261. Notes to the accounts

(1) Information required by this Part to be given in notes to a company's annual accounts may be contained in the accounts or in a separate document annexed to the accounts.

(2) References in this Part to a company's annual accounts, or to a balance sheet or profit and loss account, include notes to the accounts giving information which is required by any provision of this Act or international accounting standards, and required or allowed by any such provision to be given in a note to company accounts.

262. Minor definitions

(1) In this Part—
  "address", except in section 228, in relation to electronic communications, includes any number or address used for the purposes of such communications;
  "annual accounts" means—
  (a) the individual accounts required by section 226, and
  (b) any group accounts required by section 227,
  (but see also section 230 (treatment of individual profit and loss account where group accounts prepared));
  "annual report", in relation to a company, means the directors' report required by section 234;
  "balance sheet date" means the date as at which the balance sheet was made up;

"capitalisation", in relation to work or costs, means treating that work or those costs as a fixed asset;

"Companies Act accounts" means Companies Act individual accounts or Companies Act group accounts;

"credit institution" means a credit institution as defined in article 1(1)(a) of Directive 2000/12/EC of the European Parliament and of the Council of 20 March 2000 relating to the taking up and pursuit of the business of credit institutions, that is to say an undertaking whose business is to receive deposits or other repayable funds from the public and to grant credits for its own account;

...

"fixed assets" means assets of a company which are intended for use on a continuing basis in the company's activities, and "current assets" means assets not intended for such use;

"group" means a parent undertaking and its subsidiary undertakings;

"IAS accounts" means IAS individual accounts or IAS group accounts;

"IAS Regulation" means EC Regulation No. 1606/2002 of the European Parliament and of the Council of 19th July 2002 on the application of international accounting standards;

"included in the consolidation", in relation to group accounts, or "included in consolidated group accounts", means that the undertaking is included in the accounts by the method of full (and not proportional) consolidation, and references to an undertaking excluded from consolidation shall be construed accordingly;

"international accounting standards" means the international accounting standards, within the meaning of the IAS Regulation, adopted from time to time by the European Commission in accordance with that Regulation;

"profit and loss account", in relation to a company that prepares IAS accounts, includes an income statement or other equivalent financial statement required to be prepared by international accounting standards;

"purchase price", in relation to an asset of a company or any raw materials or consumables used in the production of such an asset, includes any consideration (whether in cash or otherwise) given by the company in respect of that asset or those materials or consumables, as the case may be;

"qualified", in relation to an auditors' report, means that the report does not state the auditors' unqualified opinion that the accounts have been properly prepared in accordance with this Act or, in the case of an undertaking not required to prepare accounts in accordance with this Act, under any corresponding legislation under which it is required to prepare accounts;

"quoted company" means a company whose equity share capital—

(a)   has been included in the official list in accordance with the provisions of Part VI of the Financial Services and Markets Act 2000; or

(b)   is officially listed in an EEA State; or

(c)   is admitted to dealing on either the New York Stock Exchange or the exchange known as Nasdaq;

and in paragraph (a) "the official list" shall have the meaning given it by section 103(1) of the Financial Services and Markets Act 2000;

...

"turnover", in relation to a company, means the amounts derived from the provision of goods and services falling within the company's ordinary activities, after deduction of—

(i)   trade discounts,

(ii)   value added tax, and

(iii) any other taxes based on the amounts so derived.

(2)   In the case of an undertaking not trading for profit, any reference in this Part to a profit and loss account is to an income and expenditure account; and references to profit and loss and, in relation to group accounts, to a consolidated profit and loss account shall be construed accordingly.

(2A)   References in this Part to accounts giving a "true and fair view" are references—
(a)   in the case of Companies Act individual accounts, to the requirement under section 226A that such accounts give a true and fair view;
(b)   in the case of Companies Act group accounts, to the requirement under section 227A that such accounts give a true and fair view; and
(c)   in the case of IAS accounts, to the requirement under international accounting standards that such accounts achieve a fair presentation.

(3)   References in this Part to "realised profits" and "realised losses", in relation to a company's accounts, are to such profits or losses of the company as fall to be treated as realised in accordance with principles generally accepted, at the time when the accounts are prepared, with respect to the determination for accounting purposes of realised profits or losses.
This is without prejudice to—
(a)   the construction of any other expression (where appropriate) by reference to accepted accounting principles or practice, or
(b)   any specific provision for the treatment of profits or losses of any description as realised.

262A. Index of defined expressions

The following Table shows the provisions of this Part defining or otherwise explaining expressions used in this Part (other than expressions used only in the same section or paragraph)—

"the 1982 Act" (in Schedule 9A)	paragraph 81 of Part 1 of that Schedule
accounting reference date and accounting reference period	section 224
accounting standards and applicable accounting standards	section 256
"address"	section 262(1)
annual accounts (generally)	section 262(1)
(includes notes to the accounts)	section 261(2)
annual report	section 262(1)
associated undertaking (in Schedule 4A)	paragraph 20 of that Schedule
auditable part (of a directors' remuneration report)	section 235(5)
balance sheet (includes notes)	section 261(2)
balance sheet date	section 262(1)
...	...
banking group	section 255A(4)
...	...
capitalisation (in relation to work or costs)	section 262(1)
Companies Act accounts	section 262(1)
Companies Act group accounts	sections 227(2) and 255A(6A)
Companies Act individual accounts	sections 226(2) and 255(4A)
credit institution	section 262(1)
current assets	section 262(1)
...	...
fellow subsidiary undertaking	section 259(4)
financial fixed assets (in Schedule 9)	Paragraph 82 of Part I of that Schedule
financial year	section 223
fixed assets	section 262(1)
"general business" (in Schedule 9A)	paragraph 81 of Part 1 of that Schedule
group	section 262(1)
group accounts	section 227(1)
group undertaking	section 259(5)
historical cost accounting rules	

—in Schedule 4	paragraph 29 of that Schedule
—in Schedule 8	paragraph 29 of that Schedule
—in Schedule 9	paragraph 39 of Part I of that Schedule
—in Schedule 9A	paragraph 20(1) of Part I of that Schedule
IAS accounts	section 262(1)
IAS group accounts	section 227(2) and (3)
IAS individual accounts	section 226(2)
IAS Regulation	section 262(1)
included in the consolidation and related expressions	section 262(1)
individual accounts	section 262(1)
insurance group	section 255A(5)
international accounting standards	section 262(1)
land of freehold tenure and land of leasehold tenure (in relation to Scotland)	
—in Schedule 4	paragraph 93 of that Schedule
—in Schedule 9	paragraph 86 of Part I of that Schedule
—in Schedule 9A	paragraph 85 of Part I of that Schedule
lease, long lease and short lease	
—in Schedule 4	paragraph 83 of that Schedule
—in Schedule 9	paragraph 82 of Part I of that Schedule
—in Schedule 9A	paragraph 81 of Part I of that Schedule
listed investment	
—in Schedule 4	paragraph 84 of that Schedule
—in Schedule 8	paragraph 54 of that Schedule
—in Schedule 9A	paragraph 81 of Part I of that Schedule
listed security (in Schedule 9)	paragraph 82 of Part I of that Schedule
"long term business" (in Schedule 9A)	paragraph 81 of Part I of that Schedule
"long term fund" (in Schedule 9A)	paragraph 81 of Part I of that Schedule
notes to the accounts	section 261(1)
parent undertaking (and parent company)	section 258 and Schedule 10A
participating interest	section 260
pension costs	
—in Schedule 4	paragraph 94(2) of that Schedule
—in Schedule 8	paragraph 59(2) of that Schedule
—in Schedule 9	paragraph 87(b) of Part I of that Schedule
—in Schedule 9A	paragraph 86(b) of Part I of that Schedule
period allowed for laying and delivering accounts and reports	section 244

"policy holder" (in Schedule 9A)	paragraph 81 of Part 1 of that Schedule
profit and loss account	
(includes notes)	section 261(2)
(in relation to IAS accounts)	section 262(1)
(in relation to a company not trading for profit)	section 262(2)
provision	
—in Schedule 4	paragraphs 88 and 89 of that Schedule
—in Schedule 8	paragraphs 57 and 58 of that Schedule
—in Schedule 9	paragraph 85 of Part I of that Schedule
—in Schedule 9A	paragraph 84 of Part I of that Schedule
"provision for unexpired risks" (in Schedule 9A)	paragraph 81 of Part 1 of that Schedule;
purchase price	section 262(1)
qualified	section 262(1)
quoted company	section 262(1)
realised losses and realised profits	section 262(3)
repayable on demand (in Schedule 9)	paragraph 82 of Part I of that Schedule
reporting accountant	section 249C(1)
reserve (in Schedule 9A)	paragraph 32 of that Schedule
sale and repurchase transaction (in Schedule 9)	paragraph 82 of Part I of that Schedule
sale and option to resell transaction (in Schedule 9)	paragraph 82 of Part I of that Schedule
shares	section 259(2)
social security costs	
—in Schedule 4	paragraph 94(1) and (3) of that Schedule
—in Schedule 8	paragraph 59(1) and (3) of that Schedule
—in Schedule 9	paragraph 87(a) and (c) of Part I of that Schedule
—in Schedule 9A	paragraph 86(a) and (c) of Part I of that Schedule
special provisions for banking and insurance companies and groups	sections 255 and 255A
subsidiary undertaking	section 258 and Schedule 10A
true and fair view	section 262(2A)
turnover	section 262(1)
undertaking and related expressions	section 259(1) to (3)

PART VIII
DISTRIBUTION OF PROFITS AND ASSETS

Limits of company's power of distribution

263. Certain distributions prohibited

(1) A company shall not make a distribution except out of profits available for the purpose.

(2)   In this Part, "distribution" means every description of distribution of a company's assets to its members, whether in cash or otherwise, except distribution by way of—

(a)   an issue of shares as fully or partly paid bonus shares,

(b)   the redemption or purchase of any of the company's own shares out of capital (including the proceeds of any fresh issue of shares) or out of unrealised profits in accordance with Chapter VII of Part V,

(c)   the reduction of share capital by extinguishing or reducing the liability of any of the members on any of the company's shares in respect of share capital not paid up, or by paying off paid up share capital, and

(d)   a distribution of assets to members of the company on its winding up.

(3)   For purposes of this Part, a company's profits available for distribution are its accumulated, realised profits, so far as not previously utilised by distribution or capitalisation, less its accumulated, realised losses, so far as not previously written off in a reduction or reorganisation of capital duly made.

This is subject to the provision made by sections 265 and 266 for investment and other companies.

(4)   A company shall not apply an unrealised profit in paying up debentures, or any amounts unpaid on its issued shares.

(5)   Where the directors of a company are, after making all reasonable enquiries, unable to determine whether a particular profit made before 22nd December 1980 is realised or unrealised, they may treat the profit as realised; and where after making such enquiries they are unable to determine whether a particular loss so made is realised or unrealised, they may treat the loss as unrealised.

264.   Restriction on distribution of assets

(1)   A public company may only make a distribution at any time—

(a)   if at that time the amount of its net assets is not less than the aggregate of its called-up share capital and undistributable reserves, and

(b)   if, and to the extent that, the distribution does not reduce the amount of those assets to less than that aggregate.

This is subject to the provision made by sections 265 and 266 for investment and other companies.

(2)   In subsection (1), "net assets" means the aggregate of the company's assets less the aggregate of its liabilities ("liabilities" to include any provision for liabilities within paragraph 89 of Schedule 4 that is made in Companies Act accounts and any provision that is made in IAS accounts).

(3)   A company's undistributable reserves are—

(a)   the share premium account,

(b)   the capital redemption reserve,

(c)   the amount by which the company's accumulated, unrealised profits, so far as not previously utilised by capitalisation of a description to which this paragraph applies, exceed its accumulated, unrealised losses (so far as not previously written off in a reduction or reorganisation of capital duly made), and

(d)   any other reserve which the company is prohibited from distributing by any enactment (other than one contained in this Part) or by its memorandum or articles;

and paragraph (c) applies to every description of capitalisation except a transfer of profits of the company to its capital redemption reserve on or after 22nd December 1980.

(4)   A public company shall not include any uncalled share capital as an asset in any accounts relevant for purposes of this section.

265.   Other distributions by investment companies

(1)   Subject to the following provisions of this section, an investment company (defined in section 266) may also make a distribution at any time out of its accumulated, realised revenue profits, so far as not previously utilised by a distribution or capitalisation, less its accumulated revenue

losses (whether realised or unrealised), so far as not previously written off in a reduction or reorganisation of capital duly made—

    (a)   if at that time the amount of its assets is at least equal to one and a half times the aggregate of its liabilities, and

    (b)   if, and to the extent that, the distribution does not reduce that amount to less than one and a half times that aggregate.

(2)   In subsection (1)(a), "liabilities" includes any provision for liabilities (within the meaning of paragraph 89 of Schedule 4) that is made in Companies Act accounts and any provision that is made in IAS accounts.

(3)   The company shall not include any uncalled share capital as an asset in any accounts relevant for purposes of this section.

(4)   An investment company may not make a distribution by virtue of subsection (1) unless—

    (a)   its shares are listed on a recognised investment exchange other than an overseas investment exchange ..., and

    (b)   during the relevant period it has not—

        (i)   distributed any of its capital profits otherwise than by way of the redemption or purchase of any of the company's own shares in accordance with section 160 or 162 in Chapter VII of Part V, or

        (ii)   applied any unrealised profits or any capital profits (realised or unrealised) in paying up debentures or amounts unpaid on its issued shares.

(4A)   In subsection (4)(a) "recognised investment exchange" and "overseas investment exchange" have the same meaning as in Part 18 of the Financial Services and Markets Act 2000.

(5)   The "relevant period" under subsection (4) is the period beginning with—

    (a)   the first day of the accounting reference period immediately preceding that in which the proposed distribution is to be made, or

    (b)   where the distribution is to be made in the company's first accounting reference period, the first day of that period,

and ending with the date of the distribution.

(6)   An investment company may not make a distribution by virtue of subsection (1) unless the company gave to the registrar of companies the requisite notice (that is, notice under section 266(1)) of the company's intention to carry on business as an investment company—

    (a)   before the beginning of the relevant period under subsection (4), or

    (b)   in the case of a company incorporated on or after 22nd December 1980, as soon as may have been reasonably practicable after the date of its incorporation.

266.   **Meaning of "investment company"**

(1)   In section 265 "investment company" means a public company which has given notice in the prescribed form (which has not been revoked) to the registrar of companies of its intention to carry on business as an investment company, and has since the date of that notice complied with the requirements specified below.

(2)   Those requirements are—

    (a)   that the business of the company consists of investing its funds mainly in securities, with the aim of spreading investment risk and giving members of the company the benefit of the results of the management of its funds,

    (b)   that none of the company's holdings in companies (other than those which are for the time being in investment companies) represents more than 15 per cent by value of the investing company's investments,

    (c)   that subject to subsection (2A), distribution of the company's capital profits is prohibited by its memorandum or articles of association,

    (d)   that the company has not retained, otherwise than in compliance with this Part, in respect of any accounting reference period more than 15 per cent of the income it derives from securities.

(2A)   An investment company need not be prohibited by its memorandum or articles from redeeming or purchasing its own shares in accordance with section 160 or 162 in Chapter VII of Part V out of its capital profits.

(3)   Notice to the registrar of companies under subsection (1) may be revoked at any time by the company on giving notice in the prescribed form to the registrar that it no longer wishes to be an investment company within the meaning of this section; and, on giving such notice, the company ceases to be such a company.

(4)   Subsections (1A) to (3) of section 842 of the Income and Corporation Taxes Act 1988 apply for the purposes of subsection (2)(b) above as for those of subsection (1)(b) of that section.

267.   Extension of ss 265, 266 to other companies

(1)   The Secretary of State may by regulations in a statutory instrument extend the provisions of sections 265 and 266 (with or without modifications) to companies whose principal business consists of investing their funds in securities, land or other assets with the aim of spreading investment risk and giving their members the benefit of the results of the management of the assets.

(2)   Regulations under this section—

    (a)   may make different provision for different classes of companies and may contain such transitional and supplemental provisions as the Secretary of State considers necessary, and

    (b)   shall not be made unless a draft of the statutory instrument containing them has been laid before Parliament and approved by a resolution of each House.

268.   Realised profits of insurance company with long term business

(1)   Where an authorised insurance company carries on long term business—

    (a)   any amount included in the relevant part of the balance sheet of the company which represents a surplus in the fund or funds maintained by it in respect of that business and which has not been allocated to policy holders or, as the case may be, carried forward unappropriated, in accordance with asset identification rules made under section 142(2) of the Financial Services and Markets Act 2000, and

    (b)   any deficit in that fund or those funds,

are to be (respectively) treated, for purposes of this Part, as a realised profit and a realised loss; and, subject to this, any profit or loss arising in that business is to be left out of account for those purposes.

(2)   In subsection (1)—

    (aa)   the reference to the relevant part of the balance sheet is

        (i)   in the case of Companies Act individual accounts, to that part of the balance sheet which represents Liabilities item A.V (profit and loss account) in the balance sheet format set out in section B of Chapter I of Part I of Schedule 9A, and

        (ii)   in the case of IAS individual accounts, to that part of the balance sheet which represents accumulated profit or loss,

    (a)   the reference to a surplus in any fund or funds of an insurance company is to an excess of the assets representing that fund or those funds over the liabilities of the company attributable to its long term business, as shown by an actuarial investigation, and

    (b)   the reference to a deficit in any such fund or funds is to the excess of those liabilities over those assets, as so shown.

(3)   In this section—

    (a)   "actuarial investigation" means—

        (i)   an investigation made into the financial condition of an authorised insurance company in respect of its long term business, carried out once in every period of twelve months in accordance with rules made under Part 10 of the Financial Services and Markets Act 2000 by an actuary appointed as actuary to that company; or

        (ii)   an investigation made into the financial condition of an authorised insurance company in respect of its long term business carried out in accordance with a requirement imposed under section 166 of that Act by an actuary appointed as actuary to that company; and

(b)   "long term business" means business which consists of effecting or carrying out contracts of long term insurance.

(4)   The definition of "long term business" in subsection (3) must be read with—

(a)   section 22 of the Financial Services and Markets Act 2000;

(b)   any relevant order under that section; and

(c)   Schedule 2 to that Act.

269.   Treatment of development costs

(1)   Subject as follows, where development costs are shown as an asset in a company's accounts, any amount shown in respect of those costs is to be treated—

(a)   under section 263, as a realised loss, and

(b)   under section 265, as a realised revenue loss.

(2)   This does not apply to any part of that amount representing an unrealised profit made on revaluation of those costs; nor does it apply if—

(a)   there are special circumstances in the company's case justifying the directors in deciding that the amount there mentioned is not to be treated as required by subsection (1), ...

(b)   it is stated—

(i)   in the case of Companies Act individual accounts, in the note to the accounts required by paragraph 20 of Schedule 4 paragraph 20 of Schedule 8 (reasons for showing development costs as an asset), or

(ii)   in the case of IAS individual accounts, in any note to the accounts, that the amount is not to be so treated, and

(c)   the note explains the circumstances relied upon to justify the decision of the directors to that effect.

Relevant accounts

270.   Distribution to be justified by reference to company's accounts

(1)   This section and sections 271 to 276 below are for determining the question whether a distribution may be made by a company without contravening sections 263, 264 or 265.

(2)   The amount of a distribution which may be made is determined by reference to the following items as stated in the company's accounts—

(a)   profits, losses, assets and liabilities,

(b)   the following provisions—

(i)   in the case of Companies Act individual accounts, provisions of any of the kinds mentioned in paragraphs 88 and 89 of Schedule 4 (depreciation, diminution in value of assets, retentions to meet liabilities, etc), and

(ii)   in the case of IAS individual accounts, provisions of any kind, and

(c)   share capital and reserves (including undistributable reserves).

(3)   Except in a case falling within the next subsection, the company's accounts which are relevant for this purpose are its last annual accounts, that is to say those prepared under Part VII which were laid in respect of the last preceding accounting reference period in respect of which accounts so prepared were laid; and for this purpose accounts are laid if section 241(1) has been complied with in relation to them.

(4)   In the following two cases—

(a)   where the distribution would be found to contravene the relevant section if reference were made only to the company's last annual accounts, or

(b)   where the distribution is proposed to be declared during the company's first accounting reference period, or before any accounts are laid in respect of that period,

the accounts relevant under this section (called "interim accounts" in the first case, and "initial accounts" in the second) are those necessary to enable a reasonable judgment to be made as to the amounts of the items mentioned in subsection (2) above.

(5)   The relevant section is treated as contravened in the case of a distribution unless the statutory requirements about the relevant accounts (that is, the requirements of this and the following three sections, as and where applicable) are complied with in relation to that distribution.

271.   Requirements for last annual accounts

(1)   If the company's last annual accounts constitute the only accounts relevant under section 270, the statutory requirements in respect of them are as follows.

(2)   The accounts must have been properly prepared in accordance with this Act, or have been so prepared subject only to matters which are not material for determining, by reference to items mentioned in section 270(2), whether the distribution would contravene the relevant section; and, without prejudice to the foregoing—

    (a)   so much of the accounts as consists of a balance sheet must give a true and fair view of the state of the company's affairs as at the balance sheet date, and

    (b)   so much of the accounts as consists of a profit and loss account must give a true and fair view of the company's profit or loss for the period in respect of which the accounts were prepared.

(3)   The auditors must have made their report on the accounts under section 235; and the following subsection applies if the report is a qualified report, that is to say, it is not a report without qualification to the effect that in the auditors' opinion the accounts have been properly prepared in accordance with this Act.

(4)   The auditors must in that case also have stated in writing (either at the time of their report or subsequently) whether, in their opinion, the matter in respect of which their report is qualified is material for determining, by reference to items mentioned in section 270(2), whether the distribution would contravene the relevant section; and a copy of the statement must have been laid before the company in general meeting.

(5)   A statement under subsection (4) suffices for purposes of a particular distribution not only if it relates to a distribution which has been proposed but also if it relates to distributions of any description which includes that particular distribution, notwithstanding that at the time of the statement it has not been proposed.

272.   Requirements for interim accounts

(1)   The following are the statutory requirements in respect of interim accounts prepared for a proposed distribution by a public company.

(2)   The accounts must have been properly prepared, or have been so prepared subject only to matters which are not material for determining, by reference to items mentioned in section 270(2), whether the proposed distribution would contravene the relevant section.

(3)   "Properly prepared" means that the accounts must comply with section 226 (applying that section and sections 226A and 226B and Schedule 4 with such modifications as are necessary because the accounts are prepared otherwise than in respect of an accounting reference period) and any balance sheet comprised in the accounts must have been signed in accordance with section 233; and, without prejudice to the foregoing—

    (a)   so much of the accounts as consists of a balance sheet must give a true and fair view of the state of the company's affairs as at the balance sheet date, and

    (b)   so much of the accounts as consists of a profit and loss account must give a true and fair view of the company's profit or loss for the period in respect of which the accounts were prepared.

(4)   A copy of the accounts must have been delivered to the registrar of companies.

(5)   If the accounts are in a language other than English and the second sentence of section 242(1) (translation) does not apply, then, subject to section 710B(6) (delivery of certain Welsh documents without a translation), a translation into English of the accounts, certified in the prescribed manner to be a correct translation, must also have been delivered to the registrar.

273. Requirements for initial accounts

(1)   The following are the statutory requirements in respect of initial accounts prepared for a proposed distribution by a public company.

(2)   The accounts must have been properly prepared, or they must have been so prepared subject only to matters which are not material for determining, by reference to items mentioned in section 270(2), whether the proposed distribution would contravene the relevant section.

(3)   Section 272(3) applies as respects the meaning of "properly prepared".

(4)   The company's auditors must have made a report stating whether, in their opinion, the accounts have been properly prepared; and the following subsection applies if their report is a qualified report, that is to say it is not a report without qualification to the effect that in the auditors' opinion the accounts have been so prepared.

(5)   The auditors must in that case also have stated in writing whether, in their opinion, the matter in respect of which their report is qualified is material for determining, by reference to items mentioned in section 270(2), whether the distribution would contravene the relevant section.

(6)   A copy of the accounts, of the auditors' report under subsection (4) and of the auditors' statement (if any) under subsection (5) must have been delivered to the registrar of companies.

(7)   If the accounts are, or the auditors' report under subsection (4) or their statement (if any) under subsection (5) is, in a language other than English and the second sentence of section 242(1) (translation) does not apply, then, subject to section 710B(6) (delivery of certain Welsh documents without a translation), a translation into English of the accounts, the report or the statement (as the case may be), certified in the prescribed manner to be a correct translation, must also have been delivered to the registrar.

274. Method of applying s 270 to successive distributions

(1)   For the purpose of determining by reference to particular accounts whether a proposed distribution may be made by a company, section 270 has effect, in a case where one or more distributions have already been made in pursuance of determinations made by reference to those same accounts, as if the amount of the proposed distribution was increased by the amount of the distributions so made.

(2)   Subsection (1) of this section applies (if it would not otherwise do so) to—

    (a)   financial assistance lawfully given by a public company out of its distributable profits in a case where the assistance is required to be so given by section 154,

    (b)   financial assistance lawfully given by a private company out of its distributable profits in a case where the assistance is required to be so given by section 155(2),

    (c)   financial assistance given by a company in contravention of section 151, in a case where the giving of that assistance reduces the company's net assets or increases its net liabilities,

    (d)   a payment made by a company in respect of the purchase by it of shares in the company (except a payment lawfully made otherwise than out of distributable profits), and

    (e)   a payment of any description specified in section 168 (company's purchase of right to acquire its own shares, etc),

being financial assistance given or payment made since the relevant accounts were prepared, as if any such financial assistance or payment were a distribution already made in pursuance of a determination made by reference to those accounts.

(3)   In this section the following definitions apply—

    "financial assistance" means the same as in Chapter VI of Part V;

    "net assets" has the meaning given by section 154(2)(a); and

    "net liabilities", in relation to the giving of financial assistance by a company, means the amount by which the aggregate amount of the company's liabilities (within the meaning of section 154(2)(b)) exceeds the aggregate amount of its assets, taking the amount of the assets and liabilities to be as stated in the company's accounting records immediately before the financial assistance is given.

(4)   Subsections (2) and (3) of this section are deemed to be included in Chapter VII of Part V for purposes of the Secretary of State's power to make regulations under section 179.

275.   Treatment of assets in the relevant accounts

(1)   For purposes of sections 263 and 264, the following are treated as realised losses—

    (a)   in the case of Companies Act individual accounts, provisions of any kind mentioned in paragraphs 88 and 89 of Schedule 4 (other than revaluation provisions), and

    (b)   in the case of IAS individual accounts, provisions of any kind (other than revaluation provisions).

(1A)   In subsection (1), a revaluation provision means a provision in respect of a diminution in value of a fixed asset appearing on a revaluation of all the fixed assets of the company, or of all of its fixed assets other than goodwill.

(2)   If, on the revaluation of a fixed asset, an unrealised profit is shown to have been made and, on or after the revaluation, a sum is written off or retained for depreciation of that asset over a period, then an amount equal to the amount by which that sum exceeds the sum which would have been so written off or retained for the depreciation of that asset over that period, if that profit had not been made, is treated for purposes of sections 263 and 264 as a realised profit made over that period.

(3)   Where there is no record of the original cost of an asset, or a record cannot be obtained without unreasonable expense or delay, then for the purpose of determining whether the company has made a profit or loss in respect of that asset, its cost is taken to be the value ascribed to it in the earliest available record of its value made on or after its acquisition by the company.

(4)   Subject to subsection (6), any consideration by the directors of the value at a particular time of a fixed asset is treated as a revaluation of the asset for the purposes of determining whether any such revaluation of the company's fixed asset as is required for purposes of the exception from subsection (1) has taken place at that time.

(5)   But where any such assets which have not actually been revalued are treated as revalued for those purposes under subsection (4), that exception applies only if the directors are satisfied that their aggregate value at the time in question is not less than the aggregate amount at which they are for the time being stated in the company's accounts.

(6)   Where section 271(2), 272(2) or 273(2) applies to the relevant accounts, subsections (4) and (5) above do not apply for the purpose of determining whether a revaluation of the company's fixed assets affecting the amount of the relevant items (that is, the items mentioned in section 270(2)) as stated in those accounts has taken place, unless it is stated in a note to the accounts—

    (a)   that the directors have considered the value at any time of any fixed assets of the company, without actually revaluing those assets,

    (b)   that they are satisfied that the aggregate value of those assets at the time in question is or was not less than the aggregate amount at which they are or were for the time being stated in the company's accounts, and

    (c)   that the relevant items in question are accordingly stated in the relevant accounts on the basis that a revaluation of the company's fixed assets which by virtue of subsections (4) and (5) included the assets in question took place at that time.

276.   Distributions in kind

Where a company makes a distribution of or including a non-cash asset, and any part of the amount at which that asset is stated in the accounts relevant for the purposes of the distribution in accordance with sections 270 to 275 represents an unrealised profit, that profit is to be treated as a realised profit—

    (a)   for the purpose of determining the lawfulness of the distribution in accordance with this Part (whether before or after the distribution takes place), and

    (b)   for the purpose of the application of paragraphs 12(a) and 34(3)(a) of Schedule 4 or paragraphs 12(a) and 34(3)(a) of Schedule 8 (only realised profits to be included in or transferred to the profit and loss account) in relation to anything done with a view to or in connection with the making of that distribution.

Supplementary

277. Consequences of unlawful distribution

(1)   Where a distribution, or part of one, made by a company to one of its members is made in contravention of this Part and, at the time of the distribution, he knows or has reasonable grounds for believing that it is so made, he is liable to repay it (or that part of it, as the case may be) to the company or (in the case of a distribution made otherwise than in cash) to pay the company a sum equal to the value of the distribution (or part) at that time.

(2)   The above is without prejudice to any obligation imposed apart from this section on a member of a company to repay a distribution unlawfully made to him; but this section does not apply in relation to—

(a)   financial assistance given by a company in contravention of section 151, or

(b)   any payment made by a company in respect of the redemption or purchase by the company of shares in itself.

(3)   Subsection (2) of this section is deemed included in Chapter VII of Part V for purposes of the Secretary of State's power to make regulations under section 179.

278. Saving for provision in articles operative before Act of 1980

Where immediately before 22nd December 1980 a company was authorised by a provision of its articles to apply its unrealised profits in paying up in full or in part unissued shares to be allotted to members of the company as fully or partly paid bonus shares, that provision continues (subject to any alteration of the articles) as authority for those profits to be so applied after that date.

279. Distributions by banking or insurance companies

Where a company's accounts relevant for the purposes of this Part are prepared in accordance with the special provisions of Part VII relating to banking or insurance companies, sections 264 to 275 apply with the modifications shown in Schedule 11.

280. Definitions for Part VIII

(1)   The following has effect for the interpretation of this Part.

(2)   "Capitalisation", in relation to a company's profits, means any of the following operations (whenever carried out)—

(a)   applying the profits in wholly or partly paying up unissued shares in the company to be allotted to members of the company as fully or partly paid bonus shares, or

(b)   transferring the profits to capital redemption reserve.

(3)   References to profits and losses of any description are (respectively) to profits and losses of that description made at any time and, except where the context otherwise requires, are (respectively) to revenue and capital profits and revenue and capital losses.

281. Saving for other restraints on distribution

The provisions of this Part are without prejudice to any enactment or rule of law, or any provision of a company's memorandum or articles, restricting the sums out of which, or the cases in which, a distribution may be made.

PART IX
A COMPANY'S MANAGEMENT; DIRECTORS AND SECRETARIES; THEIR QUALIFICATIONS, DUTIES AND RESPONSIBILITIES

Officers and registered office

282. Directors

(1)   Every company registered on or after 1st November 1929 (other than a private company) shall have at least two directors.

(2)   Every company registered before that date (other than a private company) shall have at least one director.

(3)   Every private company shall have at least one director.

283. Secretary

(1)   Every company shall have a secretary.

(2)   A sole director shall not also be secretary.

(3)   Anything required or authorised to be done by or to the secretary may, if the office is vacant or there is for any other reason no secretary capable of acting, be done by or to any assistant or deputy secretary or, if there is no assistant or deputy secretary capable of acting, by or to any officer of the company authorised generally or specially in that behalf by the directors.

(4)   No company shall—

  (a)   have as secretary to the company a corporation the sole director of which is a sole director of the company;

  (b)   have as sole director of the company a corporation the sole director of which is secretary to the company.

284. Acts done by person in dual capacity

A provision requiring or authorising a thing to be done by or to a director and the secretary is not satisfied by its being done by or to the same person acting both as director and as, or in place of, the secretary.

285. Validity of acts of directors

The acts of a director or manager are valid notwithstanding any defect that may afterwards be discovered in his appointment or qualification; and this provision is not excluded by section 292(2) (void resolution to appoint).

286. Qualifications of company secretaries

(1)   It is the duty of the directors of a public company to take all reasonable steps to secure that the secretary (or each joint secretary) of the company is a person who appears to them to have the requisite knowledge and experience to discharge the functions of secretary of the company and who—

  (a)   on 22nd December 1980 held the office of secretary or assistant or deputy secretary of the company; or

  (b)   for at least 3 of the 5 years immediately preceding his appointment as secretary held the office of secretary of a company other than a private company; or

  (c)   is a member of any of the bodies specified in the following subsection; or

  (d)   is a barrister, advocate or solicitor called or admitted in any part of the United Kingdom; or

  (e)   is a person who, by virtue of his holding or having held any other position or his being a member of any other body, appears to the directors to be capable of discharging those functions.

(2)   The bodies referred to in subsection (1)(c) are—

  (a)   the Institute of Chartered Accountants in England and Wales;

  (b)   the Institute of Chartered Accountants of Scotland;

  (c)   the Chartered Association of Certified Accountants;

  (d)   the Institute of Chartered Accountants in Ireland;

  (e)   the Institute of Chartered Secretaries and Administrators;

  (f)   the Institute of Cost and Management Accountants;

  (g)   the Chartered Institute of Public Finance and Accountancy.

287. Registered office

(1)   A company shall at all times have a registered office to which all communications and notices may be addressed.

(2)   On incorporation the situation of the company's registered office is that specified in the statement sent to the registrar under section 10.

(3)   The company may change the situation of its registered office from time to time by giving notice in the prescribed form to the registrar.

(4)   The change takes effect upon the notice being registered by the registrar, but until the end of the period of 14 days beginning with the date on which it is registered a person may validly serve any document on the company at its previous registered office.

(5)   For the purposes of any duty of a company—
        (a)   to keep at its registered office, or make available for public inspection there, any register, index or other document, or
        (b)   to mention the address of its registered office in any document,
        a company which has given notice to the registrar of a change in the situation of its registered office may act on the change as from such date, not more than 14 days after the notice is given, as it may determine.

(6)   Where a company unavoidably ceases to perform at its registered office any such duty as is mentioned in subsection (5)(a) in circumstances in which it was not practicable to give prior notice to the registrar of a change in the situation of its registered office, but—
        (a)   resumes performance of that duty at other premises as soon as practicable, and
        (b)   gives notice accordingly to the registrar of a change in the situation of its registered office within 14 days of doing so,
        it shall not be treated as having failed to comply with that duty.

(7)   In proceedings for an offence of failing to comply with any such duty as is mentioned in subsection (5), it is for the person charged to show that by reason of the matters referred to in that subsection or subsection (6) no offence was committed.

288.   Register of directors and secretaries

(1)   Every company shall keep at its registered office a register of its directors and secretaries; and the register shall, with respect to the particulars to be contained in it of those persons, comply with sections 289 and 290 below.

(2)   The company shall, within the period of 14 days from the occurrence of—
        (a)   any change among its directors or in its secretary, or
        (b)   any change in the particulars contained in the register,
        send to the registrar of companies a notification in the prescribed form of the change and of the date on which it occurred; and a notification of a person having become a director or secretary, or one of joint secretaries, of the company shall contain a consent, signed by that person, to act in the relevant capacity.

(3)   The register shall ... be open to the inspection of any member of the company without charge and of any other person on payment of such fee as may be prescribed.

(4)   If an inspection required under this section is refused, or if default is made in complying with subsection (1) or (2), the company and every officer of it who is in default is liable to a fine and, for continued contravention, to a daily default fine.

(5)   In the case of a refusal of inspection of the register, the court may by order compel an immediate inspection of it.

(5A)   Where a confidentiality order made under section 723B is in force in respect of a director or secretary of a company, subsections (3) and (5) shall not apply in relation to that part of the register of the company as contains particulars of the usual residential address of that individual.

(6)   For purposes of this and the next section, a shadow director of a company is deemed a director and officer of it.

(7)   ...

288A.

        If an individual in respect of whom a confidentiality order under section 723B as applied to limited liability partnerships becomes a member of a limited liability partnership—
        (a)   the notice to be delivered to the registrar under section 9(1) of the Limited Liability Partnerships Act 2000 shall contain the address for the time being notified by the member to

the limited liability partnership under the Limited Liability Partnerships (Particulars of Usual Residential Address) (Confidentiality Orders) Regulations 2002 but shall not contain his usual residential address; and

(b)   with that notice the limited liability partnership shall deliver to the registrar a notice in the prescribed form containing the usual residential address of that member.

289.   **Particulars of directors to be registered under s 288**

(1)   Subject to the provisions of this section, the register kept by a company under section 288 shall contain the following particulars with respect to each director—

    (a)   in the case of an individual—

        (i)   his present name,

        (ii)   any former name,

        (iii)   his usual residential address,

        (iv)   his nationality,

        (v)   his business occupation (if any),

        (vi)   particulars of any other directorships held by him or which have been held by him, and

        (vii)   the date of his birth;

    (b)   in the case of a corporation or Scottish firm, its corporate or firm name and registered or principal office.

(1A)   Where a confidentiality order made under section 723B is in force in respect of a director, the register shall contain, in addition to the particulars specified in subsection (1)(a), such address as is for the time being notified by the director to the company under regulations made under sections 723B to 723F.

(2)   In subsection (1)(a)—

    (a)   "name" means a person's Christian name (or other forenames) and surname, except that in the case of a peer, or an individual usually known by a title, the title may be stated instead of his Christian name (or other forename) and surname, or in addition to either or both of them; and

    (b)   the reference to a former name does not include—

        (i)   in the case of a peer, or an individual normally known by a British title, the name by which he was known previous to the adoption of or succession to the title, or

        (ii)   in the case of any person, a former name which was changed or disused before he attained the age of 18 years or which has been changed or disused for 20 years or more, or

        (iii)   in the case of a married woman, the name by which she was known previous to the marriage.

(3)   It is not necessary for the register to contain on any day particulars of a directorship—

    (a)   which has not been held by a director at any time during the 5 years preceding that day,

    (b)   which is held by a director in a company which—

        (i)   is dormant or grouped with the company keeping the register, and

        (ii)   if he also held that directorship for any period during those 5 years, was for the whole of that period either dormant or so grouped,

    (c)   which was held by a director for any period during those 5 years in a company which for the whole of that period was either dormant or grouped with the company keeping the register.

(4)   For purposes of subsection (3), "company" includes any body corporate incorporated in Great Britain; and—

    (a)   section 249AA(3) applies as regards whether and when a company is or has been dormant, and

    (b)   a company is to be regarded as being, or having been, grouped with another at any time if at that time it is or was a company of which the other is or was a wholly-owned subsidiary, or if it is or was a wholly-owned subsidiary of the other or of another company of which that other is or was a wholly-owned subsidiary.

290. Particulars of secretaries to be registered under s 288

(1) The register to be kept by a company under section 288 shall contain the following particulars with respect to the secretary or, where there are joint secretaries, with respect to each of them—

    (a) in the case of an individual, his present name, any former name and his usual residential address, and

    (b) in the case of a corporation or a Scottish firm, its corporate or firm name and registered or principal office.

(1A) Where a confidentiality order made under section 723B is in force in respect of a director, the register shall contain, in addition to the particulars specified in subsection (1)(a), such address as is for the time being notified by the director to the company under regulations made under sections 723B to 723F.

(2) Where all the partners in a firm are joint secretaries, the name and principal office of the firm may be stated instead of the particulars specified above.

(3) Section 289(2)(a) and (b) apply for the purposes of the obligation under subsection (1)(a) of this section to state the name or former name of an individual.

Provisions governing appointment of directors

291. Share qualification of directors

(1) It is the duty of every director who is by the company's articles required to hold a specified share qualification, and who is not already qualified, to obtain his qualification within 2 months after his appointment, or such shorter time as may be fixed by the articles.

(2) For the purpose of any provision of the articles requiring a director or manager to hold any specified share qualification, the bearer of a share warrant is not deemed the holder of the shares specified in the warrant.

(3) The office of director of a company is vacated if the director does not within 2 months from the date of his appointment (or within such shorter time as may be fixed by the articles) obtain his qualification, or if after the expiration of that period or shorter time he ceases at any time to hold his qualification.

(4) A person vacating office under this section is incapable of being reappointed to be a director of the company until he has obtained his qualification.

(5) If after the expiration of that period or shorter time any unqualified person acts as a director of the company, he is liable to a fine and, for continued contravention, to a daily default fine.

292. Appointment of directors to be voted on individually

(1) At a general meeting of a public company, a motion for the appointment of two or more persons as directors of the company by a single resolution shall not be made, unless a resolution that it shall be so made has first been agreed to by the meeting without any vote being given against it.

(2) A resolution moved in contravention of this section is void, whether or not its being so moved was objected to at the time; but where a resolution so moved is passed, no provision for the automatic reappointment of retiring directors in default of another appointment applies.

(3) For purposes of this section, a motion for approving a person's appointment, or for nominating a person for appointment, is to be treated as a motion for his appointment.

(4) Nothing in this section applies to a resolution altering the company's articles.

293. Age limit for directors

(1) A company is subject to this section if—

    (a) it is a public company, or

    (b) being a private company, it is a subsidiary of a public company or of a body corporate registered under the law relating to companies for the time being in force in Northern Ireland as a public company.

(2) No person is capable of being appointed a director of a company which is subject to this section if at the time of his appointment he has attained the age of 70.

(3)   A director of such a company shall vacate his office at the conclusion of the annual general meeting commencing next after he attains the age of 70; but acts done by a person as director are valid notwithstanding that it is afterwards discovered that his appointment had terminated under this subsection.

(4)   Where a person retires under subsection (3), no provision for the automatic reappointment of retiring directors in default of another appointment applies; and if at the meeting at which he retires the vacancy is not filled, it may be filled as a casual vacancy.

(5)   Nothing in subsections (2) to (4) prevents the appointment of a director at any age, or requires a director to retire at any time, if his appointment is or was made or approved by the company in general meeting; but special notice is required of a resolution appointing or approving the appointment of a director for it to have effect under this subsection, and the notice of the resolution given to the company, and by the company to its members, must state, or have stated, the age of the person to whom it relates.

(6)   A person reappointed director on retiring under subsection (3), or appointed in place of a director so retiring, is to be treated, for the purpose of determining the time at which he or any other director is to retire, as if he had become director on the day on which the retiring director was last appointed before his retirement.
        Subject to this, the retirement of a director out of turn under subsection (3) is to be disregarded in determining when any other directors are to retire.

(7)   In the case of a company first registered after the beginning of 1947, this section has effect subject to the provisions of the company's articles; and in the case of a company first registered before the beginning of that year—
        (a)   this section has effect subject to any alterations of the company's articles made after the beginning of that year; and
        (b)   if at the beginning of that year the company's articles contained provision for retirement of directors under an age limit, or for preventing or restricting appointments of directors over a given age, this section does not apply to directors to whom that provision applies.

294.   Duty of director to disclose his age

(1)   A person who is appointed or to his knowledge proposed to be appointed director of a company subject to section 293 at a time when he has attained any retiring age applicable to him under that section or under the company's articles shall give notice of his age to the company.

(2)   For purposes of this section, a company is deemed subject to section 293 notwithstanding that all or any of the section's provisions are excluded or modified by the company's articles.

(3)   Subsection (1) does not apply in relation to a person's reappointment on the termination of a previous appointment as director of the company.

(4)   A person who—
        (a)   fails to give notice of his age as required by this section; or
        (b)   acts as director under any appointment which is invalid or has terminated by reason of his age,
        is liable to a fine and, for continued contravention, to a daily default fine.

(5)   For purposes of subsection (4), a person who has acted as director under an appointment which is invalid or has terminated is deemed to have continued so to act throughout the period from the invalid appointment or the date on which the appointment terminated (as the case may be), until the last day on which he is shown to have acted thereunder.

295–302....

Removal of directors

303.   Resolution to remove director

(1)   A company may by ordinary resolution remove a director before the expiration of his period of office, notwithstanding anything in its articles or in any agreement between it and him.

(2)   Special notice is required of a resolution to remove a director under this section or to appoint somebody instead of a director so removed at the meeting at which he is removed.

(3)   A vacancy created by the removal of a director under this section, if not filled at the meeting at which he is removed, may be filled as a casual vacancy.

(4)   A person appointed director in place of a person removed under this section is treated, for the purpose of determining the time at which he or any other director is to retire, as if he had become director on the day on which the person in whose place he is appointed was last appointed a director.

(5)   This section is not to be taken as depriving a person removed under it of compensation or damages payable to him in respect of the termination of his appointment as director or of any appointment terminating with that as director, or as derogating from any power to remove a director which may exist apart from this section.

304.   Director's right to protest removal

(1)   On receipt of notice of an intended resolution to remove a director under section 303, the company shall forthwith send a copy of the notice to the director concerned; and he (whether or not a member of the company) is entitled to be heard on the resolution at the meeting.

(2)   Where notice is given of an intended resolution to remove a director under that section, and the director concerned makes with respect to it representations in writing to the company (not exceeding a reasonable length) and requests their notification to members of the company, the company shall, unless the representations are received by it too late for it to do so—

(a)   in any notice of the resolution given to members of the company state the fact of the representations having been made; and

(b)   send a copy of the representations to every member of the company to whom notice of the meeting is sent (whether before or after receipt of the representations by the company).

(3)   If a copy of the representations is not sent as required by subsection (2) because received too late or because of the company's default, the director may (without prejudice to his right to be heard orally) require that the representations shall be read out at the meeting.

(4)   But copies of the representations need not be sent out and the representations need not be read out at the meeting if, on the application either of the company or of any other person who claims to be aggrieved, the court is satisfied that the rights conferred by this section are being abused to secure needless publicity for defamatory matter.

(5)   The court may order the company's costs on an application under this section to be paid in whole or in part by the director, notwithstanding that he is not a party to the application.

Other provisions about directors and officers

305.   Directors' names on company correspondence, etc

(1)   A company to which this section applies shall not state, in any form, the name of any of its directors (otherwise than in the text or as a signatory) on any business letter on which the company's name appears unless it states on the letter in legible characters the name of every director in the company.

(2)   This section applies to—

(a)   every company registered under this Act or under the former Companies Acts (except a company registered before 23rd November 1916); and

(b)   every company incorporated outside Great Britain which has an established place of business within Great Britain, unless it had established such a place of business before that date.

(3)   If a company makes default in complying with this section, every officer of the company who is in default is liable for each offence to a fine; and for this purpose, where a corporation is an officer of the company, any officer of the corporation is deemed an officer of the company.

(4)   For the purposes of the obligation under subsection (1) to state the name of every director of the company, a person's "name" means—

(a)   in the case of an individual, his Christian name (or other forename) and surname; and

(b)   in the case of a corporation or Scottish firm, its corporate or firm name.

(5)   The initial or a recognised abbreviation of a person's Christian name or other forename may be stated instead of the full Christian name or other forename.

(6)   In the case of a peer, or an individual usually known by a title, the title may be stated instead of his Christian name (or other forename) and surname or in addition to either or both of them.

(7)   In this section "director" includes a shadow director and the reference in subsection (3) to an "officer" shall be construed accordingly.

306.   Limited company may have directors with unlimited liability

(1)   In the case of a limited company the liability of the directors or managers, or of the managing director, may, if so provided by the memorandum, be unlimited.

(2)   In the case of a limited company in which the liability of a director or manager is unlimited, the directors and any managers of the company and the member who proposes any person for election or appointment to the office of director or manager, shall add to that proposal a statement that the liability of the person holding that office will be unlimited.

(3)   Before the person accepts the office or acts in it, notice in writing that his liability will be unlimited shall be given to him by the following or one of the following persons, namely—
(a)   the promoters of the company,
(b)   the directors of the company,
(c)   any managers of the company,
(d)   the company secretary.

(4)   If a director, manager or proposer makes default in adding such a statement, or if a promoter, director, manager or secretary makes default in giving the notice required by subsection (3), then—
(a)   he is liable to a fine, and
(b)   he is also liable for any damage which the person so elected or appointed may sustain from the default;
but the liability of the person elected or appointed is not affected by the default.

307.   Special resolution making liability of directors unlimited

(1)   A limited company, if so authorised by its articles, may by special resolution alter its memorandum so as to render unlimited the liability of its directors or managers, or of any managing director.

(2)   When such a special resolution is passed, its provisions are as valid as if they had been originally contained in the memorandum.

308.   Assignment of office by directors

If provision is made by a company's articles, or by any agreement entered into between any person and the company, for empowering a director or manager of the company to assign his office as such to another person, any assignment of office made in pursuance of that provision is (notwithstanding anything to the contrary contained in the provision) of no effect unless and until it is approved by a special resolution of the company.

309.   Directors to have regard to interests of employees

(1)   The matters to which the directors of a company are to have regard in the performance of their functions include the interests of the company's employees in general, as well as the interests of its members.

(2)   Accordingly, the duty imposed by this section on the directors is owed by them to the company (and the company alone) and is enforceable in the same way as any other fiduciary duty owed to a company by its directors.

(3)   This section applies to shadow directors as it does to directors.

309A. Provisions protecting directors from liability

(1)   This section applies in relation to any liability attaching to a director of a company in connection with any negligence, default, breach of duty or breach of trust by him in relation to the company.

(2)   Any provision which purports to exempt (to any extent) a director of a company from any liability within subsection (1) is void.

(3)   Any provision by which a company directly or indirectly provides (to any extent) an indemnity for a director of—

    (a)   the company, or

    (b)   an associated company,

against any liability within subsection (1) is void

This is subject to subsections (4) and (5).

(4)   Subsection (3) does not apply to a qualifying third party indemnity provision (see section 309B(1)).

(5)   Subsection (3) does not prevent a company from purchasing and maintaining for a director of—

    (a)   the company, or

    (b)   an associated company,

insurance against any liability within subsection (1).

(6)   In this section—

    "associated company", in relation to a company ("C"), means a company which is C's subsidiary, or C's holding company or a subsidiary of C's holding company;

    "provision" means a provision of any nature, whether or not it is contained in a company's articles or in any contract with a company.

309B. Qualifying third party indemnity provisions

(1)   For the purposes of section 309A(4) a provision is a qualifying third party indemnity provision if it is a provision such as is mentioned in section 309A(3) in relation to which conditions A to C below are satisfied.

(2)   Condition A is that the provision does not provide any indemnity against any liability incurred by the director—

    (a)   to the company, or

    (b)   to any associated company.

(3)   Condition B is that the provision does not provide any indemnity against any liability incurred by the director to pay—

    (a)   a fine imposed in criminal proceedings, or

    (b)   a sum payable to a regulatory authority by way of a penalty in respect of non-compliance with any requirement of a regulatory nature (however arising).

(4)   Condition C is that the provision does not provide any indemnity against any liability incurred by the director—

    (a)   in defending any criminal proceedings in which he is convicted, or

    (b)   in defending any civil proceedings brought by the company, or an associated company, in which judgment is given against him, or

    (c)   in connection with any application under any of the following provisions in which the court refuses to grant him relief, namely—

        (i)   section 144(3) or (4) (acquisition of shares by innocent nominee), or

        (ii)   section 727 (general power to grant relief in case of honest and reasonable conduct).

(5)   In paragraph (a), (b) or (c) of subsection (4) the reference to any such conviction, judgment or refusal of relief is a reference to one that has become final.

(6)   For the purposes of subsection (5) a conviction, judgment or refusal of relief becomes final—

    (a)   if not appealed against, at the end of the period for bringing an appeal, or

    (b)   if appealed against, at the time when the appeal (or any further appeal) is disposed of.

(7)   An appeal is disposed of—

    (a)   if it is determined and the period for bringing any further appeal has ended, or

    (b)   if it is abandoned or otherwise ceases to have effect.

(8)   In this section "associated company" and "provision" have the same meaning as in section 309A.

309C. Disclosure of qualifying third party indemnity provisions

(1)   Subsections (2) and (3) impose disclosure requirements in relation to a directors' report under section 234 in respect of a financial year.

(2)   If—

    (a)   at the time when the report is approved under section 234A, any qualifying third party indemnity provision (whether made by the company or otherwise) is in force for the benefit of one or more directors of the company, or

    (b)   at any time during the financial year, any such provision was in force for the benefit of one or more persons who were then directors of the company,

the report must state that any such provision is or (as the case may be) was so in force.

(3)   If the company has made a qualifying third party indemnity provision and—

    (a)   at the time when the report is approved under section 234A, any qualifying third party indemnity provision made by the company is in force for the benefit of one or more directors of an associated company, or

    (b)   at any time during the financial year, any such provision was in force for the benefit of one or more persons who were then directors of an associated company,

the report must state that any such provision is or (as the case may be) was so in force.

(4)   Subsection (5) applies where a company has made a qualifying third party indemnity provision for the benefit of a director of the company or of an associated company.

(5)   Section 318 shall apply to—

    (a)   the company, and

    (b)   if the director is a director of an associated company, the associated company,

as if a copy of the provision, or (if it is not in writing) a memorandum setting out its terms, were included in the list of documents in section 318(1).

(6)   In this section—

    "associated company" and "provision" have the same meaning as in section 309A; and

    "qualifying third party indemnity provision" has the meaning given by section 309B(1).

310. Provisions protecting auditors from liability

(1)   This section applies to any provision, whether contained in a company's articles or in any contract with the company or otherwise, for exempting ... any person (whether an officer or not) employed by the company as auditor from, or indemnifying him against, any liability which by virtue of any rule of law would otherwise attach to him in respect of any negligence, default, breach of duty or breach of trust of which he may be guilty in relation to the company.

(2)   Except as provided by the following subsection, any such provision is void.

(3)   This section does not prevent a company—

    (a)   from purchasing and maintaining for any such ... auditor insurance against any such liability, or

    (b)   from indemnifying any such ... auditor against any liability incurred by him—

        (i)   in defending any proceedings (whether civil or criminal) in which judgment is given in his favour or he is acquitted, or

        (ii)   in connection with any application under ... section 727 (general power to grant relief in case of honest and reasonable conduct) in which relief is granted to him by the court.

PART X
ENFORCEMENT OF FAIR DEALING BY DIRECTORS

Restrictions on directors taking financial advantage

311. Prohibition on tax-free payments to directors

(1)   It is not lawful for a company to pay a director remuneration (whether as director or otherwise) free of income tax, or otherwise calculated by reference to or varying with the amount of his income tax, or to or with any rate of income tax.

(2)   Any provision contained in a company's articles, or in any contract, or in any resolution of a company or a company's directors, for payment to a director of remuneration as above mentioned has effect as if it provided for payment, as a gross sum subject to income tax, of the net sum for which it actually provides.

312. Payment to director for loss of office, etc

It is not lawful for a company to make to a director of the company any payment by way of compensation for loss of office, or as consideration for or in connection with his retirement from office, without particulars of the proposed payment (including its amount) being disclosed to members of the company and the proposal being approved by the company.

313. Company approval for property transfer

(1)   It is not lawful, in connection with the transfer of the whole or any part of the undertaking or property of a company, for any payment to be made to a director of the company by way of compensation for loss of office, or as consideration for or in connection with his retirement from office, unless particulars of the proposed payment (including its amount) have been disclosed to members of the company and the proposal approved by the company.

(2)   Where a payment unlawful under this section is made to a director, the amount received is deemed to be received by him in trust for the company.

314. Director's duty of disclosure on takeover, etc

(1)   This section applies where, in connection with the transfer to any persons of all or any of the shares in a company, being a transfer resulting from—
   (a)   an offer made to the general body of shareholders; or
   (b)   an offer made by or on behalf of some other body corporate with a view to the company becoming its subsidiary or a subsidiary of its holding company; or
   (c)   an offer made by or on behalf of an individual with a view to his obtaining the right to exercise or control the exercise of not less than one-third of the voting power at any general meeting of the company; or
   (d)   any other offer which is conditional on acceptance to a given extent,
   a payment is to be made to a director of the company by way of compensation for loss of office, or as consideration for or in connection with his retirement from office.

(2)   It is in those circumstances the director's duty to take all reasonable steps to secure that particulars of the proposed payment (including its amount) are included in or sent with any notice of the offer made for their shares which is given to any shareholders.

(3)   If—
   (a)   the director fails to take those steps, or
   (b)   any person who has been properly required by the director to include those particulars in or send them with the notice required by subsection (2) fails to do so,
   he is liable to a fine.

315. Consequences of non-compliance with s 314

(1)   If in the case of any such payment to a director as is mentioned in section 314(1)—
   (a)   his duty under that section is not complied with, or
   (b)   the making of the proposed payment is not, before the transfer of any shares in pursuance of the offer, approved by a meeting (summoned for the purpose) of the holders of the shares to

which the offer relates and of other holders of shares of the same class as any of those shares,

any sum received by the director on account of the payment is deemed to have been received by him in trust for persons who have sold their shares as a result of the offer made; and the expenses incurred by him in distributing that sum amongst those persons shall be borne by him and not retained out of that sum.

(2)   Where—

    (a)   the shareholders referred to in subsection (1)(b) are not all the members of the company, and

    (b)   no provision is made by the articles for summoning or regulating the meeting referred to in that paragraph,

the provisions of this Act and of the company's articles relating to general meetings of the company apply (for that purpose) to the meeting either without modification or with such modifications as the Secretary of State on the application of any person concerned may direct for the purpose of adapting them to the circumstances of the meeting.

(3)   If at a meeting summoned for the purpose of approving any payment as required by subsection (1)(b) a quorum is not present and, after the meeting has been adjourned to a later date, a quorum is again not present, the payment is deemed for the purposes of that subsection to have been approved.

316.   Provisions supplementing ss 312 to 315

(1)   Where in proceedings for the recovery of any payment as having, by virtue of section 313(2) or 315(1) been received by any person in trust, it is shown that—

    (a)   the payment was made in pursuance of any arrangement entered into as part of the agreement for the transfer in question, or within one year before or two years after that agreement or the offer leading to it; and

    (b)   the company or any person to whom the transfer was made was privy to that arrangement,

the payment is deemed, except in so far as the contrary is shown, to be one to which the provisions mentioned above in this subsection apply.

(2)   If in connection with any such transfer as is mentioned in any of sections 313 to 315—

    (a)   the price to be paid to a director of the company whose office is to be abolished or who is to retire from office for any shares in the company held by him is in excess of the price which could at the time have been obtained by other holders of the like shares; or

    (b)   any valuable consideration is given to any such director,

the excess or the money value of the consideration (as the case may be) is deemed for the purposes of that section to have been a payment made to him by way of compensation for loss of office or as consideration for or in connection with his retirement from office.

(3)   References in sections 312 to 315 to payments made to a director by way of compensation for loss of office or as consideration for or in connection with his retirement from office, do not include any bona fide payment by way of damages for breach of contract or by way of pension in respect of past services.

"Pension" here includes any superannuation allowance, superannuation gratuity or similar payment.

(4)   Nothing in sections 313 to 315 prejudices the operation of any rule of law requiring disclosure to be made with respect to such payments as are there mentioned, or with respect to any other like payments made or to be made to a company's directors.

317.   Directors to disclose interest in contracts

(1)   It is the duty of a director of a company who is in any way, whether directly or indirectly, interested in a contract or proposed contract with the company to declare the nature of his interest at a meeting of the directors of the company.

(2)   In the case of a proposed contract, the declaration shall be made—

    (a)   at the meeting of the directors at which the question of entering into the contract is first taken into consideration; or

      (b)   if the director was not at the date of that meeting interested in the proposed contract, at the next meeting of the directors held after he became so interested;

and, in a case where the director becomes interested in a contract after it is made, the declaration shall be made at the first meeting of the directors held after he becomes so interested.

(3)   For purposes of this section, a general notice given to the directors of a company by a director to the effect that—

      (a)   he is a member of a specified company or firm and is to be regarded as interested in any contract which may, after the date of the notice, be made with that company or firm; or

      (b)   he is to be regarded as interested in any contract which may after the date of the notice be made with a specified person who is connected with him (within the meaning of section 346 below),

is deemed a sufficient declaration of interest in relation to any such contract.

(4)   However, no such notice is of effect unless either it is given at a meeting of the directors or the director takes reasonable steps to secure that it is brought up and read at the next meeting of the directors after it is given.

(5)   A reference in this section to a contract includes any transaction or arrangement (whether or not constituting a contract) made or entered into on or after 22nd December 1980.

(6)   For purposes of this section, a transaction or arrangement of a kind described in section 330 (prohibition of loans, quasi-loans etc to directors) made by a company for a director of the company or a person connected with such a director is treated (if it would not otherwise be so treated, and whether or not it is prohibited by that section) as a transaction or arrangement in which that director is interested.

(7)   A director who fails to comply with this section is liable to a fine.

(8)   This section applies to a shadow director as it applies to a director, except that a shadow director shall declare his interest, not at a meeting of the directors, but by a notice in writing to the directors which is either—

      (a)   a specific notice given before the date of the meeting at which, if he had been a director, the declaration would be required by subsection (2) to be made; or

      (b)   a notice which under subsection (3) falls to be treated as a sufficient declaration of that interest (or would fall to be so treated apart from subsection (4)).

(9)   Nothing in this section prejudices the operation of any rule of law restricting directors of a company from having an interest in contracts with the company.

318.   **Directors' service contracts to be open to inspection**

(1)   Subject to the following provisions, every company shall keep at an appropriate place—

      (a)   in the case of each director whose contract of service with the company is in writing, a copy of that contract;

      (b)   in the case of each director whose contract of service with the company is not in writing, a written memorandum setting out its terms; and

      (c)   in the case of each director who is employed under a contract of service with a subsidiary of the company, a copy of that contract or, if it is not in writing, a written memorandum setting out its terms.

(2)   All copies and memoranda kept by a company in pursuance of subsection (1) shall be kept at the same place.

(3)   The following are appropriate places for the purposes of subsection (1)—

      (a)   the company's registered office;

      (b)   the place where its register of members is kept (if other than its registered office);

      (c)   its principal place of business, provided that is situated in that part of Great Britain in which the company is registered.

(4)   Every company shall send notice in the prescribed form to the registrar of companies of the place where copies and memoranda are kept in compliance with subsection (1), and of any change in that place, save in a case in which they have at all times been kept at the company's registered office.

(5)   Subsection (1) does not apply to a director's contract of service with the company or with a subsidiary of it if that contract required him to work wholly or mainly outside the United Kingdom; but the company shall keep a memorandum—

         (a)   in the case of a contract of service with the company, giving the director's name and setting out the provisions of the contract relating to its duration;

         (b)   in the case of a contract of service with a subsidiary, giving the director's name and the name and place of incorporation of the subsidiary, and setting out the provisions of the contract relating to its duration,

     at the same place as copies and memoranda are kept by the company in pursuance of subsection (1).

(6)   A shadow director is treated for purposes of this section as a director.

(7)   Every copy and memorandum required by subsection (1) or (5) to be kept shall ... be open to inspection of any member of the company without charge.

(8)   If—

         (a)   default is made in complying with subsection (1) or (5), or

         (b)   an inspection required under subsection (7) is refused, or

         (c)   default is made for 14 days in complying with subsection (4),

     the company and every officer of it who is in default is liable to a fine and, for continued contravention, to a daily default fine.

(9)   In the case of a refusal of an inspection required under subsection (7) of a copy or memorandum, the court may by order compel an immediate inspection of it.

(10)   Subsections (1) and (5) apply to a variation of a director's contract of service as they apply to the contract.

(11)   This section does not require that there be kept a copy of, or memorandum setting out the terms of, a contract (or its variation) at a time when the unexpired portion of the term for which the contract is to be in force is less than 12 months, or at a time at which the contract can, within the next ensuing 12 months, be terminated by the company without payment of compensation.

319.   Director's contract of employment for more than 5 years

(1)   This section applies in respect of any term of an agreement whereby a director's employment with the company of which he is a director or, where he is the director of a holding company, his employment within the group is to continue, or may be continued, otherwise than at the instance of the company (whether under the original agreement or under a new agreement entered into in pursuance of it), for a period of more than 5 years during which the employment—

         (a)   cannot be terminated by the company by notice; or

         (b)   can be so terminated only in specified circumstances.

(2)   In any case where—

         (a)   a person is or is to be employed with a company under an agreement which cannot be terminated by the company by notice or can be so terminated only in specified circumstances; and

         (b)   more than 6 months before the expiration of the period for which he is or is to be so employed, the company enters into a further agreement (otherwise than in pursuance of a right conferred by or under the original agreement on the other party to it) under which he is to be employed with the company or, where he is a director of a holding company, within the group,

     this section applies as if to the period for which he is to be employed under that further agreement there were added a further period equal to the unexpired period of the original agreement.

(3)   A company shall not incorporate in an agreement such a term as is mentioned in subsection (1), unless the term is first approved by a resolution of the company in general meeting and, in the case of a director of a holding company, by a resolution of that company in general meeting.

(4)   No approval is required to be given under this section by any body corporate unless it is a company within the meaning of this Act, or is registered under section 680, or if it is a wholly-owned subsidiary of any body corporate, wherever incorporated.

(5)   A resolution of a company approving such a term as is mentioned in subsection (1) shall not be passed at a general meeting of the company unless a written memorandum setting out the proposed agreement incorporating the term is available for inspection by members of the company both—

(a)   at the company's registered office for not less than 15 days ending with the date of the meeting; and

(b)   at the meeting itself.

(6)   A term incorporated in an agreement in contravention of this section is, to the extent that it contravenes the section, void; and that agreement and, in a case where subsection (2) applies, the original agreement are deemed to contain a term entitling the company to terminate it at any time by the giving of reasonable notice.

(7)   In this section—

(a)   "employment" includes employment under a contract for services; and

(b)   "group", in relation to a director of a holding company, means the group which consists of that company and its subsidiaries;

and for purposes of this section a shadow director is treated as a director.

320.   Substantial property transactions involving directors, etc

(1)   With the exceptions provided by the section next following, a company shall not enter into an arrangement—

(a)   whereby a director of the company or its holding company, or a person connected with such a director, acquires or is to acquire one or more non-cash assets of the requisite value from the company; or

(b)   whereby the company acquires or is to acquire one or more non-cash assets of the requisite value from such a director or a person so connected,

unless the arrangement is first approved by a resolution of the company in general meeting and, if the director or connected person is a director of its holding company or a person connected with such a director, by a resolution in general meeting of the holding company.

(2)   For this purpose a non-cash asset is of the requisite value if at the time the arrangement in question is entered into its value is not less than £2,000 but (subject to that) exceeds £100,000 or 10 per cent of the company's asset value, that is—

(a)   except in a case falling within paragraph (b) below, the value of the company's net assets determined by reference to the accounts prepared and laid under Part VII in respect of the last preceding financial year in respect of which such accounts were so laid; and

(b)   where no accounts have been so prepared and laid before that time, the amount of the company's called-up share capital.

(3)   For purposes of this section and sections 321 and 322, a shadow director is treated as a director.

321.   Exceptions from s 320

(1)   No approval is required to be given under section 320 by any body corporate unless it is a company within the meaning of this Act or registered under section 680 or, if it is a wholly-owned subsidiary of any body corporate, wherever incorporated.

(2)   Section 320(1) does not apply to an arrangement for the acquisition of a non-cash asset—

(a)   if the asset is to be acquired by a holding company from any of its wholly-owned subsidiaries or from a holding company by any of its wholly-owned subsidiaries, or by one wholly-owned subsidiary of a holding company from another wholly-owned subsidiary of that same holding company, or

(b)   if the arrangement is entered into by a company which is being wound up, unless the winding up is a members' voluntary winding up.

(3)   Section 320(1)(a) does not apply to an arrangement whereby a person is to acquire an asset from a company of which he is a member, if the arrangement is made with that person in his character as a member.

(4)   Section 320(1) does not apply to a transaction on a recognised investment exchange which is effected by a director, or a person connected with him, through the agency of a person who in relation to the transaction acts as an independent broker.
        For this purpose an "independent broker" means—

        (a)   in relation to a transaction on behalf of a director, a person who independently of the director selects the person with whom the transaction is to be effected, and

        (b)   in relation to a transaction on behalf of a person connected with a director, a person who independently of that person or the director selects the person with whom the transaction is to be effected;

        and "recognised", in relation to an investment exchange, means recognised under the Financial Services and Markets Act 2000.

322.   Liabilities arising from contravention of s 320

(1)   An arrangement entered into by a company in contravention of section 320, and any transaction entered into in pursuance of the arrangement (whether by the company or any other person) is voidable at the instance of the company unless one or more of the conditions specified in the next subsection is satisfied.

(2)   Those conditions are that—

        (a)   restitution of any money or other asset which is the subject-matter of the arrangement or transaction is no longer possible or the company has been indemnified in pursuance of this section by any other person for the loss or damage suffered by it; or

        (b)   any rights acquired bona fide for value and without actual notice of the contravention by any person who is not a party to the arrangement or transaction would be affected by its avoidance; or

        (c)   the arrangement is, within a reasonable period, affirmed by the company in general meeting and, if it is an arrangement for the transfer of an asset to or by a director of its holding company or a person who is connected with such a director, is so affirmed with the approval of the holding company given by a resolution in general meeting.

(3)   If an arrangement is entered into with a company by a director of the company or its holding company or a person connected with him in contravention of section 320, that director and the person so connected, and any other director of the company who authorised the arrangement or any transaction entered into in pursuance of such an arrangement, is liable—

        (a)   to account to the company for any gain which he has made directly or indirectly by the arrangement or transaction, and

        (b)   (jointly and severally with any other person liable under this subsection) to indemnify the company for any loss or damage resulting from the arrangement or transaction.

(4)   Subsection (3) is without prejudice to any liability imposed otherwise than by that subsection, and is subject to the following two subsections; and the liability under subsection (3) arises whether or not the arrangement or transaction entered into has been avoided in pursuance of subsection (1).

(5)   If an arrangement is entered into by a company and a person connected with a director of the company or its holding company in contravention of section 320, that director is not liable under subsection (3) if he shows that he took all reasonable steps to secure the company's compliance with that section.

(6)   In any case, a person so connected and any such other director as is mentioned in subsection (3) is not so liable if he shows that, at the time the arrangement was entered into, he did not know the relevant circumstances constituting the contravention.

322A.   Invalidity of certain transactions involving directors, etc

(1)   This section applies where a company enters into a transaction to which the parties include—

        (a)   a director of the company or of its holding company, or

        (b)   a person connected with such a director or a company with whom such a director is associated, and the board of directors, in connection with the transaction, exceed any limitation on their powers under the company's constitution.

(2)   The transaction is voidable at the instance of the company.

(3)   Whether or not it is avoided, any such party to the transaction as is mentioned in subsection (1)(a) or (b), and any director of the company who authorised the transaction, is liable—

(a)   to account to the company for any gain which he has made directly or indirectly by the transaction, and

(b)   to idemnify the company for any loss or damage resulting from the transaction.

(4)   Nothing in the above provisions shall be construed as excluding the operation of any other enactment or rule of law by virtue of which the transaction may be called in question or any liability to the company may arise.

(5)   The transaction ceases to be voidable if—

(a)   restitution of any money or other asset which was the subject-matter of the transaction is no longer possible, or

(b)   the company is indemnified for any loss or damage resulting from the transaction, or

(c)   rights acquired bona fide for value and without actual notice of the directors' exceeding their powers by a person who is not party to the transaction would be affected by the avoidance, or

(d)   the transaction is ratified by the company in general meeting, by ordinary or special resolution or otherwise as the case may require.

(6)   A person other than a director of the company is not liable under subsection (3) if he shows that at the time the transaction was entered into he did not know that the directors were exceeding their powers.

(7)   This section does not affect the operation of section 35A in relation to any party to the transaction not within subsection (1)(a) or (b).

But where a transaction is voidable by virtue of this section and valid by virtue of that section in favour of such a person, the court may, on the application of that person or of the company, make such order affirming, severing or setting aside the transaction, on such terms, as appear to the court to be just.

(8)   In this section "transaction" includes any act; and the reference in subsection (1) to limitations under the company's constitution includes limitations deriving—

(a)   from a resolution of the company in general meeting or a meeting of any class of shareholders, or

(b)   from any agreement between the members of the company or of any class of shareholders.

322B.   Contracts with sole members who are directors

(1)   Subject to subsection (2), where a private company limited by shares or by guarantee having only one member enters into a contract with the sole member of the company and the sole member is also a director of the company, the company shall, unless the contract is in writing, ensure that the terms of the contract are either set out in a written memorandum or are recorded in the minutes of the first meeting of the directors of the company following the making of the contract.

(2)   Subsection (1) shall not apply to contracts entered into in the ordinary course of the company's business.

(3)   For the purposes of this section a sole member who is a shadow director is treated as a director.

(4)   If a company fails to comply with subsection (1), the company and every officer of it who is in default is liable to a fine.

(5)   Subject to subsection (6), nothing in this section shall be construed as excluding the operation of any other enactment or rule of law applying to contracts between a company and a director of that company.

(6)   Failure to comply with subsection (1) with respect to a contract shall not affect the validity of that contract.

Share dealings by directors and their families

323.   Prohibition on directors dealing in share options

(1)   It is an offence for a director of a company to buy—

    (a)   a right to call for delivery at a specified price and within a specified time of a specified number of relevant shares or a specified amount of relevant debentures; or

    (b)   a right to make delivery at a specified price and within a specified time of a specified number of relevant shares or a specified amount of relevant debentures; or

    (c)   a right (as he may elect) to call for delivery at a specified price and within a specified time or to make delivery at a specified price and within a specified time of a specified number of relevant shares or a specified amount of relevant debentures.

(2)   A person guilty of an offence under subsection (1) is liable to imprisonment or a fine, or both.

(3)   In subsection (1)—

    (a)   "relevant shares", in relation to a director of a company, means shares in the company or in any other body corporate, being the company's subsidiary or holding company, or a subsidiary of the company's holding company, being shares as respects which there has been granted a listing on a stock exchange (whether in Great Britain or elsewhere);

    (b)   "relevant debentures", in relation to a director of a company, means debentures of the company or of any other body corporate, being the company's subsidiary or holding company or a subsidiary of the company's holding company, being debentures as respects which there has been granted such a listing; and

    (c)   "price" includes any consideration other than money.

(4)   This section applies to a shadow director as to a director.

(5)   This section is not to be taken as penalising a person who buys a right to subscribe for shares in, or debentures of, a body corporate or buys debentures of a body corporate that confer upon the holder of them a right to subscribe for, or to convert the debentures (in whole or in part) into, shares of that body.

(6)   This section is not to be taken as penalising a director of a company who buys a right to call for delivery at a specified price within a specified time of a specified number of shares held as treasury shares by the company or by a relevant company which is that company's subsidiary or holding company or a subsidiary of that company's holding company.

(7)   For the purposes of subsection (6)—

    (a)   "relevant company" means a company listed in Article 1 of Council Directive 77/91/EEC; and

    (b)   shares of a relevant company (other than a company within the meaning of section 735(1)) are held as treasury shares if—

        (i)   they fall within section 162(4)(a) to (d) (qualifying shares); and

        (ii)   they are held by the relevant company in accordance with provisions of the law of a member State implementing Articles 19 to 22 of that Directive.

324.   Duty of director to disclose shareholdings in own company

(1)   A person who becomes a director of a company and at the time when he does so is interested in shares in, or debentures of, the company or any other body corporate, being the company's subsidiary or holding company or a subsidiary of the company's holding company, is under obligation to notify the company in writing—

    (a)   of the subsistence of his interests at that time; and

    (b)   of the number of shares of each class in, and the amount of debentures of each class of, the company or other such body corporate in which each interest of his subsists at that time.

(2)   A director of a company is under obligation to notify the company in writing of the occurrence, while he is a director, of any of the following events—

    (a)   any event in consequence of whose occurrence he becomes, or ceases to be, interested in shares in, or debentures of, the company or any other body corporate, being the company's subsidiary or holding company or a subsidiary of the company's holding company;

       (b)   the entering into by him of a contract to sell any such shares or debentures;

       (c)   the assignment by him of a right granted to him by the company to subscribe for shares in, or debentures of, the company; and

       (d)   the grant to him by another body corporate, being the company's subsidiary or holding company or a subsidiary of the company's holding company, of a right to subscribe for shares in, or debentures of, that other body corporate, the exercise of such a right granted to him and the assignment by him of such a right so granted;

and notification to the company must state the number or amount, and class, of shares or debentures involved.

(3)   Schedule 13 has effect in connection with subsections (1) and (2) above; and of that Schedule—

       (a)   Part I contains rules for the interpretation of, and otherwise in relation to, those subsections and applies in determining, for purposes of those subsections, whether a person has an interest in shares or debentures;

       (b)   Part II applies with respect to the periods within which obligations imposed by the subsections must be fulfilled; and

       (c)   Part III specifies certain circumstances in which obligations arising from subsection (2) are to be treated as not discharged;

and subsections (1) and (2) are subject to any exceptions for which provision may be made by regulations made by the Secretary of State by statutory instrument.

(4)   Subsection (2) does not require the notification by a person of the occurrence of an event whose occurrence comes to his knowledge after he has ceased to be a director.

(5)   An obligation imposed by this section is treated as not discharged unless the notice by means of which it purports to be discharged is expressed to be given in fulfilment of that obligation.

(6)   This section applies to shadow directors as to directors; but nothing in it operates so as to impose an obligation with respect to shares in a body corporate which is the wholly-owned subsidiary of another body corporate.

(7)   A person who—

       (a)   fails to discharge, within the proper period, an obligation to which he is subject under subsection (1) or (2), or

       (b)   in purported discharge of an obligation to which he is so subject, makes to the company a statement which he knows to be false, or recklessly makes to it a statement which is false,

is guilty of an offence and liable to imprisonment or a fine, or both.

(8)   Section 732 (restriction on prosecutions) applies to an offence under this section.

325.   Register of directors' interests notified under s 324

(1)   Every company shall keep a register for the purposes of section 324.

(2)   Whenever a company receives information from a director given in fulfilment of an obligation imposed on him by that section, it is under obligation to enter in the register, against the director's name, the information received and the date of the entry.

(3)   The company is also under obligation, whenever it grants to a director a right to subscribe for shares in, or debentures of, the company to enter in the register against his name—

       (a)   the date on which the right is granted,

       (b)   the period during which, or time at which, it is exercisable,

       (c)   the consideration for the grant (or, if there is no consideration, that fact), and

       (d)   the description of shares or debentures involved and the number or amount of them, and the price to be paid for them (or the consideration, if otherwise than in money).

(4)   Whenever such a right as is mentioned above is exercised by a director, the company is under obligation to enter in the register against his name that fact (identifying the right), the number or amount of shares or debentures in respect of which it is exercised and, if they were registered in his name, that fact and, if not, the name or names of the person or persons in whose name or names they were registered, together (if they were registered in the names of two persons or more) with the number or amount of the shares or debentures registered in the name of each of them.

(5)   Part IV of Schedule 13 has effect with respect to the register to be kept under this section, to the way in which entries in it are to be made, to the right of inspection, and generally.

(6)   For purposes of this section, a shadow director is deemed a director.

326.   Sanctions for non-compliance

(1)   The following applies with respect to defaults in complying with, and to contraventions of, section 325 and Part IV of Schedule 13.

(2)   If default is made in complying with any of the following provisions—

(a)   section 325(1), (2), (3) or (4), or

(b)   Schedule 13, paragraph 21, 22 or 28,

the company and every officer of it who is in default is liable to a fine and, for continued contravention, to a daily default fine.

(3)   If an inspection of the register required under paragraph 25 of the Schedule is refused, or a copy required under paragraph 26 is not sent within the proper period, the company and every officer of it who is in default is liable to a fine and, for continued contravention, to a daily default fine.

(4)   If default is made for 14 days in complying with paragraph 27 of the Schedule (notice to registrar of where register is kept), the company and every officer of it who is in default is liable to a fine and, for continued contravention, to a daily default fine.

(5)   If default is made in complying with paragraph 29 of the Schedule (register to be produced at annual general meeting), the company and every officer of it who is in default is liable to a fine.

(6)   In the case of a refusal of an inspection of the register required under paragraph 25 of the Schedule, the court may by order compel an immediate inspection of it; and in the case of failure to send within the proper period a copy required under paragraph 26, the court may by order direct that the copy be sent to the person requiring it.

327.   Extension of s 323 to spouses, *civil partners* and children

(1)   Section 323 applies to—

(a)   the wife or husband *or civil partner* of a director of a company (not being herself or himself a director of it), and

(b)   an infant son or infant daughter of a director (not being himself or herself a director of the company),

as it applies to the director; but it is a defence for a person charged by virtue of this section with an offence under section 323 to prove that he (she) had no reason to believe that his (her) spouse or, as the case may be, *civil partner or* parent was a director of the company in question.

(2)   For purposes of this section—

(a)   "son" includes step-son, and "daughter" includes step-daughter ("parent" being construed accordingly),

(b)   "infant" means, in relation to Scotland, person under the age of 18 years, and

(c)   a shadow director of a company is deemed a director of it.

Note. The italicized words in this section are inserted by the Civil Partnership Act 2004, s. 261(1), Sch. 27, para. 100, as from a day to be appointed.

328.   Extension of s 324 to spouses, *civil partners* and children

(1)   For the purposes of section 324—

(a)   an interest of the wife or husband *or civil partner* of a director of a company (not being herself or himself a director of it) in shares or debentures is to be treated as the director's interest; and

(b)   the same applies to an interest of an infant son or infant daughter of a director of a company (not being himself or herself a director of it) in shares or debentures.

(2)   For those purposes—

(a)   a contract, assignment or right of subscription entered into, exercised or made by, or a grant made to, the wife or husband *or civil partner* of a director of a company (not being herself or himself a director of it) is to be treated as having been entered into, exercised or made by, or (as the case may be) as having been made to, the director; and

(b)   the same applies to a contract, assignment or right of subscription entered into, exercised or made by, or grant made to, an infant son or infant daughter of a director of a company (not being himself or herself a director of it).

(3)   A director of a company is under obligation to notify the company in writing of the occurrence while he or she is a director, of either of the following events, namely—

(a)   the grant by the company to his (her) spouse *or civil partner*, or to his or her infant son or infant daughter, of a right to subscribe for shares in, or debentures of, the company; and

(b)   the exercise by his (her) spouse *or civil partner* or by his or her infant son or infant daughter of such a right granted by the company to the wife, husband, *civil partner*, son or daughter.

(4)   In a notice given to the company under subsection (3) there shall be stated—

(a)   in the case of the grant of a right, the like information as is required by section 324 to be stated by the director on the grant to him by another body corporate of a right to subscribe for shares in, or debentures of, that other body corporate; and

(b)   in the case of the exercise of a right, the like information as is required by that section to be stated by the director on the exercise of a right granted to him by another body corporate to subscribe for shares in, or debentures of, that other body corporate.

(5)   An obligation imposed by subsection (3) on a director must be fulfilled by him before the end of 5 days beginning with the day following that on which the occurrence of the event giving rise to it comes to his knowledge; but in reckoning that period of days there is disregarded any Saturday or Sunday, and any day which is a bank holiday in any part of Great Britain.

(6)   A person who—

(a)   fails to fulfil, within the proper period, an obligation to which he is subject under subsection (3), or

(b)   in purported fulfilment of such an obligation, makes to a company a statement which he knows to be false, or recklessly makes to a company a statement which is false,

is guilty of an offence and liable to imprisonment or a fine, or both.

(7)   The rules set out in Part I of Schedule 13 have effect for the interpretation of, and otherwise in relation to, subsections (1) and (2); and subsections (5), (6) and (8) of section 324 apply with any requisite modification.

(8)   In this section, "son" includes step-son, "daughter" includes step-daughter, and "infant" means, in relation to Scotland, person under the age of 18 years.

(9)   For purposes of section 325, an obligation imposed on a director by this section is to be treated as if imposed by section 324.

Note. The italicized words in this section are inserted by the Civil Partnership Act 2004, s. 261(1), Sch. 27, para. 101, as from a day to be appointed.

329.   Duty to notify stock exchange of matters notified under preceding sections

(1)   Whenever a company whose shares or debentures are listed on a recognised investment exchange other than an overseas investment exchange … is notified of any matter by a director in consequence of the fulfilment of an obligation imposed by section 324 or 328, and that matter relates to shares or debentures so listed, the company is under obligation to notify that investment exchange of that matter; and the investment exchange may publish, in such manner as it may determine, any information received by it under this subsection.

(2)   An obligation imposed by subsection (1) must be fulfilled before the end of the day next following that on which it arises; but there is disregarded for this purpose a day which is a Saturday or a Sunday or a bank holiday in any part of Great Britain.

(3)   If default is made in complying with this section, the company and every officer of it who is in default is guilty of an offence and liable to a fine and, for continued contravention, to a daily default fine.

Section 732 (restriction on prosecutions) applies to an offence under this section.

(4)   In subsection (1) "recognised investment exchange" and "overseas investment exchange" have the same meaning as in Part XVIII of the Financial Services and Markets Act 2000.

Restrictions on a company's power to make loans, etc, to directors
and persons connected with them

330.   General restriction on loans, etc, to directors and persons connected with them

(1)   The prohibitions listed below in this section are subject to the exceptions in sections 332 to 338.

(2)   A company shall not—
   (a)   make a loan to a director of the company or of its holding company;
   (b)   enter into any guarantee or provide any security in connection with a loan made by any person to such a director.

(3)   A relevant company shall not—
   (a)   make a quasi-loan to a director of the company or of its holding company;
   (b)   make a loan or a quasi-loan to a person connected with such a director;
   (c)   enter into a guarantee or provide any security in connection with a loan or quasi-loan made by any other person for such a director or a person so connected.

(4)   A relevant company shall not—
   (a)   enter into a credit transaction as creditor for such a director or a person so connected;
   (b)   enter into any guarantee or provide any security in connection with a credit transaction made by any other person for such a director or a person so connected.

(5)   For purposes of sections 330 to 346, a shadow director is treated as a director.

(6)   A company shall not arrange for the assignment to it, or the assumption by it, of any rights, obligations or liabilities under a transaction which, if it had been entered into by the company, would have contravened subsection (2), (3) or (4); but for the purposes of sections 330 to 347 the transaction is to be treated as having been entered into on the date of the arrangement.

(7)   A company shall not take part in any arrangement whereby—
   (a)   another person enters into a transaction which, if it had been entered into by the company, would have contravened any of subsections (2), (3), (4) or (6); and
   (b)   that other person, in pursuance of the arrangement, has obtained or is to obtain any benefit from the company or its holding company or a subsidiary of the company or its holding company.

331.   Definitions for ss 330 ff

(1)   The following subsections apply for the interpretation of sections 330 to 346.

(2)   "Guarantee" includes indemnity, and cognate expressions are to be construed accordingly.

(3)   A quasi-loan is a transaction under which one party ("the creditor") agrees to pay, or pays otherwise than in pursuance of an agreement, a sum for another ("the borrower") or agrees to reimburse, or reimburses otherwise than in pursuance of an agreement, expenditure incurred by another party for another ("the borrower")—
   (a)   on terms that the borrower (or a person on his behalf) will reimburse the creditor; or
   (b)   in circumstances giving rise to a liability on the borrower to reimburse the creditor.

(4)   Any reference to the person to whom a quasi-loan is made is a reference to the borrower; and the liabilities of a borrower under a quasi-loan include the liabilities of any person who has agreed to reimburse the creditor on behalf of the borrower.

(5)   ...

(6)   "Relevant company" means a company which—
   (a)   is a public company, or
   (b)   is a subsidiary of a public company, or
   (c)   is a subsidiary of a company which has as another subsidiary a public company, or
   (d)   has a subsidiary which is a public company.

(7)   A credit transaction is a transaction under which one party ("the creditor")—
   (a)   supplies any goods or sells any land under a hire-purchase agreement or a conditional sale agreement;
   (b)   leases or hires any land or goods in return for periodical payments;

(c)   otherwise disposes of land or supplies goods or services on the understanding that payment (whether in a lump sum or instalments or by way of periodical payments or otherwise) is to be deferred.

(8)   "Services" means anything other than goods or land.

(9)   A transaction or arrangement is made "for" a person if—

(a)   in the case of a loan or quasi-loan, it is made to him;

(b)   in the case of a credit transaction, he is the person to whom goods or services are supplied, or land is sold or otherwise disposed of, under the transaction;

(c)   in the case of a guarantee or security, it is entered into or provided in connection with a loan or quasi-loan made to him or a credit transaction made for him;

(d)   in the case of an arrangement within subsection (6) or (7) of section 330, the transaction to which the arrangement relates was made for him; and

(e)   in the case of any other transaction or arrangement for the supply or transfer of, or of any interest in, goods, land or services, he is the person to whom the goods, land or services (or the interest) are supplied or transferred.

(10) "Conditional sale agreement" means the same as in the Consumer Credit Act 1974.

332.   Short-term quasi-loans

(1)   Subsection (3) of section 330 does not prohibit a company ("the creditor") from making a quasi-loan to one of its directors or to a director of its holding company if—

(a)   the quasi-loan contains a term requiring the director or a person on his behalf to reimburse the creditor his expenditure within 2 months of its being incurred; and

(b)   the aggregate of the amount of that quasi-loan and of the amount outstanding under each relevant quasi-loan does not exceed £5,000.

(2)   A quasi-loan is relevant for this purpose if it was made to the director by virtue of this section by the creditor or its subsidiary or, where the director is a director of the creditor's holding company, any other subsidiary of that company; and "the amount outstanding" is the amount of the outstanding liabilities of the person to whom the quasi-loan was made.

333.   Inter-company loans in same group

In the case of a relevant company which is a member of a group of companies (meaning a holding company and its subsidiaries), paragraphs (b) and (c) of section 330(3) do not prohibit the company from—

(a)   making a loan or quasi-loan to another member of that group; or

(b)   entering into a guarantee or providing any security in connection with a loan or quasi-loan made by any person to another member of the group,

by reason only that a director of one member of the group is associated with another.

334.   Loans of small amounts

Without prejudice to any other provision of sections 332 to 338, paragraph (a) of section 330(2) does not prohibit a company from making a loan to a director of the company or of its holding company if the aggregate of the relevant amounts does not exceed £5,000.

335.   Minor and business transactions

(1)   Section 330(4) does not prohibit a company from entering into a transaction for a person if the aggregate of the relevant amounts does not exceed £10,000.

(2)   Section 330(4) does not prohibit a company from entering into a transaction for a person if—

(a)   the transaction is entered into by the company in the ordinary course of its business; and

(b)   the value of the transaction is not greater, and the terms on which it is entered into are no more favourable, in respect of the person for whom the transaction is made, than that or those which it is reasonable to expect the company to have offered to or in respect of a person of the same financial standing but unconnected with the company.

336.   Transactions at behest of holding company

The following transactions are excepted from the prohibitions of section 330—

(a)   a loan or quasi-loan by a company to its holding company, or a company entering into a guarantee or providing any security in connection with a loan or quasi-loan made by any person to its holding company;

(b)   a company entering into a credit transaction as creditor for its holding company, or entering into a guarantee or providing any security in connection with a credit transaction made by any other person for its holding company.

337.   Funding of director's expenditure on duty to company

(1)   A company is not prohibited by section 330 from doing anything to provide a director with funds to meet expenditure incurred or to be incurred by him for the purposes of the company or for the purpose of enabling him properly to perform his duties as an officer of the company.

(2)   Nor does the section prohibit a company from doing any thing to enable a director to avoid incurring such expenditure.

(3)   Subsections (1) and (2) apply only if one of the following conditions is satisfied—

(a)   the thing in question is done with prior approval of the company given at a general meeting at which there are disclosed all the matters mentioned in the next subsection;

(b)   that thing is done on condition that, if the approval of the company is not so given at or before the next annual general meeting, the loan is to repaid, or any other liability arising under any such transaction discharged, within 6 months from the conclusion of that meeting;

but those subsections do not authorise a relevant company to enter into any transaction if the aggregate of the relevant amounts exceeds £20,000.

(4)   The matters to be disclosed under subsection (3)(a) are—

(a)   the purpose of the expenditure incurred or to be incurred, or which would otherwise be incurred, by the director,

(b)   the amount of the funds to be provided by the company, and

(c)   the extent of the company's liability under any transaction which is or is connected with the thing in question.

337A.   Funding of director's expenditure on defending proceedings

(1)   A company is not prohibited by section 330 from doing anything to provide a director with funds to meet expenditure incurred or to be incurred by him—

(a)   in defending any criminal or civil proceedings, or

(b)   in connection with any application under any of the provisions mentioned in subsection (2).

(2)   The provisions are—

section 144(3) and (4) (acquisition of shares by innocent nominee), and

section 727 (general power to grant relief in case of honest and reasonable conduct).

(3)   Nor does section 330 prohibit a company from doing anything to enable a director to avoid incurring such expenditure.

(4)   Subsections (1) and (3) only apply to a loan or other thing done as mentioned in those subsections if the terms on which it is made or done will result in the loan falling to be repaid, or any liability of the company under any transaction connected with the thing in question falling to be discharged, not later than—

(a)   in the event of the director being convicted in the proceedings, the date when the conviction becomes final,

(b)   in the event of judgment being given against him in the proceedings, the date when the judgment becomes final, or

(c)   in the event of the court refusing to grant him relief on the application, the date when the refusal of relief becomes final.

(5)   For the purposes of subsection (4) a conviction, judgment or refusal of relief becomes final—

(a)   if not appealed against, at the end of the period for bringing an appeal, or

(b)   if appealed against, at the time when the appeal (or any further appeal) is disposed of.

(6)   An appeal is disposed of—

    (a)   if it is determined and the period for bringing any further appeal has ended, or

    (b)   if it is abandoned or otherwise ceases to have effect.

338.   Loan or quasi-loan by money-lending company

(1)   There is excepted from the prohibitions in section 330—

    (a)   a loan or quasi-loan made by a money-lending company to any person; or

    (b)   a money-lending company entering into a guarantee in connection with any other loan or quasi-loan.

(2)   "Money-lending company" means a company whose ordinary business includes the making of loans or quasi-loans, or the giving of guarantees in connection with loans or quasi-loans.

(3)   Subsection (1) applies only if both the following conditions are satisfied—

    (a)   the loan or quasi-loan in question is made by the company, or it enters into the guarantee, in the ordinary course of the company's business; and

    (b)   the amount of the loan or quasi-loan, or the amount guaranteed, is not greater, and the terms of the loan, quasi-loan or guarantee are not more favourable, in the case of the person to whom the loan or quasi-loan is made or in respect of whom the guarantee is entered into, than that or those which it is reasonable to expect that company to have offered to or in respect of a person of the same financial standing but unconnected with the company.

(4)   But subsection (1) does not authorise a relevant company (unless it is a banking company) to enter into any transaction if the aggregate of the relevant amounts exceeds £100,000.

(5)   In determining that aggregate, a company which a director does not control is deemed not to be connected with him.

(6)   The condition specified in subsection (3)(b) does not of itself prevent a company from making a loan to one of its directors or a director of its holding company—

    (a)   for the purpose of facilitating the purchase, for use as that director's only or main residence, of the whole or part of any dwelling-house together with any land to be occupied and enjoyed with it;

    (b)   for the purpose of improving a dwelling-house or part of a dwelling-house so used or any land occupied and enjoyed with it;

    (c)   in substitution for any loan made by any person and falling within paragraph (a) or (b) of this subsection,

if loans of that description are ordinarily made by the company to its employees and on terms no less favourable than those on which the transaction in question is made, and the aggregate of the relevant amounts does not exceed £100,000.

339.   "Relevant amounts" for purposes of ss 334 ff

(1)   This section has effect for defining the "relevant amounts" to be aggregated under sections 334, 335(1), 337(3) and 338(4); and in relation to any proposed transaction or arrangement and the question whether it falls within one or other of the exceptions provided by those sections, "the relevant exception" is that exception; but where the relevant exception is the one provided by section 334 (loan of small amount), references in this section to a person connected with a director are to be disregarded.

(2)   Subject as follows, the relevant amounts in relation to a proposed transaction or arrangement are—

    (a)   the value of the proposed transaction or arrangement,

    (b)   the value of any existing arrangement which—

        (i)   falls within subsection (6) or (7) of section 330, and

        (ii)   also falls within subsection (3) of this section, and

        (iii) was entered into by virtue of the relevant exception by the company or by a subsidiary of the company or, where the proposed transaction or arrangement is to be made for a director of its holding company or a person connected with such a director, by that holding company or any of its subsidiaries;

(c) the amount outstanding under any other transaction—
   (i) falling within subsection (3) below, and
   (ii) made by virtue of the relevant exception, and
   (iii) made by the company or by a subsidiary of the company or, where the proposed transaction or arrangement is to be made for a director of its holding company or a person connected with such a director, by that holding company or any of its subsidiaries.

(3) A transaction falls within this subsection if it was made—
   (a) for the director for whom the proposed transaction or arrangement is to be made, or for any person connected with that director; or
   (b) where the proposed transaction or arrangement is to be made for a person connected with a director of a company, for that director or any person connected with him;
   and an arrangement also falls within this subsection if it relates to a transaction which does so.

(4) But where the proposed transaction falls within section 338 and is one which a banking company proposes to enter into under subsection (6) of that section (housing loans, etc), any other transaction or arrangement which apart from this subsection would fall within subsection (3) of this section does not do so unless it was entered into in pursuance of section 338(6).

(5) A transaction entered into by a company which is (at the time of that transaction being entered into) a subsidiary of the company which is to make the proposed transaction, or is a subsidiary of that company's holding company, does not fall within subsection (3) if at the time when the question arises (that is to say, the question whether the proposed transaction or arrangement falls within any relevant exception), it no longer is such a subsidiary.

(6) Values for purposes of subsection (2) of this section are to be determined in accordance with the section next following; and "the amount outstanding" for purposes of subsection (2)(c) above is the value of the transaction less any amount by which that value has been reduced.

340. "Value" of transactions and arrangements

(1) This section has effect for determining the value of a transaction or arrangement for purposes of sections 330 to 339.

(2) The value of a loan is the amount of its principal.

(3) The value of a quasi-loan is the amount, or maximum amount, which the person to whom the quasi-loan is made is liable to reimburse the creditor.

(4) The value of a guarantee or security is the amount guaranteed or secured.

(5) The value of an arrangement to which section 330(6) or (7) applies is the value of the transaction to which the arrangement relates less any amount by which the liabilities under the arrangement or transaction of the person for whom the transaction was made have been reduced.

(6) The value of a transaction or arrangement not falling within subsections (2) to (5) above is the price which it is reasonable to expect could be obtained for the goods, land or services to which the transaction or arrangement relates if they had been supplied (at the time the transaction or arrangement is entered into) in the ordinary course of business and on the same terms (apart from price) as they have been supplied, or are to be supplied, under the transaction or arrangement in question.

(7) For purposes of this section, the value of a transaction or arrangement which is not capable of being expressed as a specific sum of money (because the amount of any liability arising under the transaction or arrangement is unascertainable, or for any other reason), whether or not any liability under the transaction or arrangement has been reduced, is deemed to exceed £100,000.

341. Civil remedies for breach of s 330

(1) If a company enters into a transaction or arrangement in contravention of section 330, the transaction or arrangement is voidable at the instance of the company unless—

(a) restitution of any money or any other asset which is the subject matter of the arrangement or transaction is no longer possible, or the company has been indemnified in pursuance of subsection (2)(b) below for the loss or damage suffered by it, or

(b) any rights acquired bona fide for value and without actual notice of the contravention by a person other than the person for whom the transaction or arrangement was made would be affected by its avoidance.

(2) Where an arrangement or transaction is made by a company for a director of the company or its holding company or a person connected with such a director in contravention of section 330, that director and the person so connected and any other director of the company who authorised the transaction or arrangement (whether or not it has been avoided in pursuance of subsection (1)) is liable—

(a) to account to the company for any gain which he has made directly or indirectly by the arrangement or transaction; and

(b) (jointly and severally with any other person liable under this subsection) to indemnify the company for any loss or damage resulting from the arrangement or transaction.

(3) Subsection (2) is without prejudice to any liability imposed otherwise than by that subsection, but is subject to the next two subsections.

(4) Where an arrangement or transaction is entered into by a company and a person connected with a director of the company or its holding company in contravention of section 330, that director is not liable under subsection (2) of this section if he shows that he took all reasonable steps to secure the company's compliance with that section.

(5) In any case, a person so connected and any such other director as is mentioned in subsection (2) is not so liable if he shows that, at the time the arrangement or transaction was entered into, he did not know the relevant circumstances constituting the contravention.

342. Criminal penalties for breach of s 330

(1) A director of a relevant company who authorises or permits the company to enter into a transaction or arrangement knowing or having reasonable cause to believe that the company was thereby contravening section 330 is guilty of an offence.

(2) A relevant company which enters into a transaction or arrangement for one of its directors or for a director of its holding company in contravention of section 330 is guilty of an offence.

(3) A person who procures a relevant company to enter into a transaction or arrangement knowing or having reasonable cause to believe that the company was thereby contravening section 330 is guilty of an offence.

(4) A person guilty of an offence under this section is liable to imprisonment or a fine, or both.

(5) A relevant company is not guilty of an offence under subsection (2) if it shows that, at the time the transaction or arrangement was entered into, it did not know the relevant circumstances.

343. Record of transactions not disclosed in company accounts

(1) The following provisions of this section—

(a) apply in the case of a company which is a banking company, or is the holding company of a credit institution, and

(b) are subject to the exceptions provided by section 344.

(2) Where such a company takes advantage of the provisions of paragraph 2 of Part IV of Schedule 9 in relation to a financial year, that company shall keep a register containing a copy of every transaction, arrangement or agreement of which particulars would, but for that paragraph, be required to be disclosed in the company's accounts or group accounts for that financial year and for each financial year in the preceding 10 in relation to which the company has taken advantage of the provisions of that paragraph.

(3) In the case of a transaction, arrangement or agreement which is not in writing, there shall be contained in the register a written memorandum setting out its terms.

(4) Where such a company takes advantage of the provisions of paragraph 2 of Part IV of Schedule 9 in relation to the last complete financial year preceding its annual general meeting, that company

shall before that meeting make available at its registered office for not less than 15 days ending with the date of the meeting a statement containing the particulars of transactions, arrangements and agreements which the company would, but for that paragraph, be required to disclose in its accounts or group accounts for that financial year.

(5)   The statement shall be so made available for inspection by members of the company; and such a statement shall also be made available for their inspection at the annual general meeting.

(6)   It is the duty of the company's auditors to examine the statement before it is made available to members of the company and to make a report to the members on it; and the report shall be annexed to the statement before it is made so available.

(7)   The auditors' report shall state whether in their opinion the statement contains the particulars required by subsection (4); and, where their opinion is that it does not, they shall include in the report, so far as they are reasonably able to do so, a statement giving the required particulars.

(8)   If a company fails to comply with any provision of subsections (2) to (5), every person who at the time of the failure is a director of it is guilty of an offence and liable to a fine; but—

    (a)   it is a defence in proceedings against a person for this offence to prove that he took all reasonable steps for securing compliance with the subsection concerned, and

    (b)   a person is not guilty of the offence by virtue only of being a shadow director of the company.

(9)   For purposes of the application of this section to loans and quasi-loans made by a company to persons connected with a person who at any time is a director of the company or of its holding company, a company which a person does not control is not connected with him.

344.   Exceptions from s 343

(1)   Section 343 does not apply in relation to—

    (a)   transactions or arrangements made or subsisting during a financial year by a company or by a subsidiary of a company for a person who was at any time during that year a director of the company or of its holding company or was connected with such a director, or

    (b)   an agreement made or subsisting during that year to enter into such a transaction or arrangement,

if the aggregate of the values of each transaction or arrangement made for that person, and of each agreement for such a transaction or arrangement, less the amount (if any) by which the value of those transactions, arrangements and agreements has been reduced, did not exceed £2,000 at any time during the financial year.

For purposes of this subsection, values are to be determined as under section 340.

(2)   Section 343(4) and (5) do not apply to a banking company which is the wholly-owned subsidiary of a company incorporated in the United Kingdom.

Supplementary

345.   Power to increase financial limits

(1)   The Secretary of State may by order in a statutory instrument substitute for any sum of money specified in this Part a larger sum specified in the order.

(2)   An order under this section is subject to annulment in pursuance of a resolution of either House of Parliament.

(3)   Such an order does not have effect in relation to anything done or not done before its coming into force; and accordingly, proceedings in respect of any liability (whether civil or criminal) incurred before that time may be continued or instituted as if the order had not been made.

346.   "Connected persons", etc

(1)   This section has effect with respect to references in this Part to a person being "connected" with a director of a company, and to a director being "associated with" or "controlling" a body corporate.

(2)   A person is connected with a director of a company if, but only if, he (not being himself a director of it) is—

(a) that director's spouse, *civil partner*, child or step-child; or

(b) except where the context otherwise requires, a body corporate with which the director is associated; or

(c) a person acting in his capacity as trustee of any trust the beneficiaries of which include—

    (i) the director, his spouse *or civil partner* or any children or step-children of his, or

    (ii) a body corporate with which he is associated,

or of a trust whose terms confer a power on the trustees that may be exercised for the benefit of the director, his spouse, or any children or step-children of his, or any such body corporate; or

(d) a person acting in his capacity as partner of that director or of any person who, by virtue of paragraph (a), (b) or (c) of this subsection, is connected with that director; or

(e) a Scottish firm in which—

    (i) that director is a partner,

    (ii) a partner is a person who, by virtue of paragraph (a), (b) or (c) above, is connected with that director, or

    (iii) a partner is a Scottish firm in which that director is a partner or in which there is a partner who, by virtue of paragraph (a), (b) or (c) above, is connected with that director.

(3) In subsection (2)—

(a) a reference to the child or step-child of any person includes an illegitimate child of his, but does not include any person who has attained the age of 18; and

(b) paragraph (c) does not apply to a person acting in his capacity as trustee under an employees' share scheme or a pension scheme.

(4) A director of a company is associated with a body corporate if, but only if, he and the persons connected with him, together—

(a) are interested in shares comprised in the equity share capital of that body corporate of a nominal value equal to at least one-fifth of that share capital (excluding any shares in the company held as treasury shares); or

(b) are entitled to exercise or control the exercise of more than one-fifth of the voting power at any general meeting of that body (excluding any voting rights attached to any shares in the company held as treasury shares).

(5) A director of a company is deemed to control a body corporate if, but only if—

(a) he or any person connected with him is interested in any part of the equity share capital of that body or is entitled to exercise or control the exercise of any part of the voting power at any general meeting of that body; and

(b) that director, the persons connected with him and the other directors of that company, together, are interested in more than one-half of that share capital (excluding any shares in the company held as treasury shares) or are entitled to exercise or control the exercise of more than one-half of that voting power (excluding any voting rights attached to any shares in the company held as treasury shares).

(6) For purposes of subsections (4) and (5)—

(a) a body corporate with which a director is associated is not to be treated as connected with that director unless it is also connected with him by virtue of subsection (2)(c) or (d); and

(b) a trustee of a trust the beneficiaries of which include (or may include) a body corporate with which a director is associated is not to be treated as connected with a director by reason only of that fact.

(7) The rules set out in Part I of Schedule 13 apply for the purposes of subsections (4) and (5).

(8) References in those subsections to voting power the exercise of which is controlled by a director include voting power whose exercise is controlled by a body corporate controlled by him; but this is without prejudice to other provisions of subsections (4) and (5).

Note. The italicized words in this section are inserted by the Civil Partnership Act 2004, s. 261(1), Sch. 27, para. 102, as from a day to be appointed.

347. **Transactions under foreign law**

For purposes of sections 319 to 322 and 330 to 343, it is immaterial whether the law which (apart from this Act) governs any arrangement or transaction is the law of the United Kingdom, or of a part of it, or not.

PART XA
CONTROL OF POLITICAL DONATIONS

347A. **Introductory provisions**

(1) This Part has effect for controlling—

(a) contributions and other donations made by companies to registered parties and other EU political organisations; and

(b) EU political expenditure incurred by companies.

(2) The following provisions have effect for the purposes of this Part, but subsections (4) and (7) have effect subject to section 347B.

(3) "Director" includes shadow director.

(4) "Donation", in relation to an organisation, means anything that would constitute a donation for the purposes of Part IV of the Political Parties, Elections and Referendums Act 2000 in accordance with sections 50 to 52 of that Act (references in those sections to a registered party being read as applying equally to an organisation which is not such a party); and—

(a) subsections (3) to (8) of section 50 of that Act shall apply, with any necessary modifications, for the purpose of determining whether something is a donation to an organisation for the purposes of this Part as they apply for the purpose of determining whether something is a donation to a registered party for the purposes of Part IV of that Act; and

(b) section 53 of that Act shall similarly apply for the purpose of determining, for the purposes of this Part, the value of any donation.

(5) "EU political expenditure", in relation to a company, means any expenditure incurred by the company—

(a) in respect of the preparation, publication or dissemination of any advertising or any other promotional or publicity material—

(i) of whatever nature, and

(ii) however published or otherwise disseminated,

which, at the time of publication or dissemination, is capable of being reasonably regarded as intended to affect public support for any EU political organisation, or

(b) in respect of any activities on the part of the company such as are mentioned in subsection (7)(b) or (c).

(6) "EU political organisation" means—

(a) a registered party; or

(b) any other organisation to which subsection (7) applies.

(7) This subsection applies to an organisation if—

(a) it is a political party which carries on, or proposes to carry on, activities for the purpose of or in connection with the participation of the party in any election or elections to public office held in a member State other than the United Kingdom;

(b) it carries on, or proposes to carry on, activities which are capable of being reasonably regarded as intended to affect public support for—

(i) any registered party,

(ii) any other political party within paragraph (a), or

(iii) independent candidates at any election or elections of the kind mentioned in that paragraph; or

(c) it carries on, or proposes to carry on, activities which are capable of being reasonably regarded as intended to influence voters in relation to any national or regional referendum held under the law of any member State.

(8)   "Organisation" includes any body corporate and any combination of persons or other unincorporated association.

(9)   "Registered party" means a party registered under Part II of the Political Parties, Elections and Referendums Act 2000.

(10)   "The relevant time", in relation to any donation or expenditure made or incurred by a company or subsidiary undertaking, means—

    (a)   the time when the donation or expenditure is made or incurred; or

    (b)   if earlier, the time when any contract is entered into by the company or undertaking in pursuance of which the donation or expenditure is made or incurred.

(11)   "Subsidiary undertaking" has the same meaning as in Part VII.

347B.   Exemptions

(1)   Section 347A(4) does not extend to a subscription paid to an EU trade association for membership of the association, and accordingly such a payment is not a donation to the association for the purposes of this Part.

(2)   In subsection (1)—

    "EU trade association" means any organisation formed for the purpose of furthering the trade interests—

        (a)   of its members, or

        (b)   of persons represented by its members,

    which carries on its activities wholly or mainly in one or more of the member States;

    "subscription", in relation to a trade association, does not include any payment to the association to the extent that it is made for the purpose of financing any particular activity of the association.

(3)   Section 347A(7) does not apply to any all-party parliamentary group composed of members of one or both of the Houses of Parliament (or of such members and other persons), and accordingly any such group is not an EU political organisation for the purposes of this Part.

(4)   For the purposes of this Part—

    (a)   a company does not need to be authorised as mentioned in section 347C(1) or section 347D(2) or (3), and

    (b)   a subsidiary undertaking does not need to be authorised as mentioned in section 347E(2),

    in connection with any donation or donations to any EU political organisation or organisations made in a particular qualifying period, except to the extent (if any) that the amount or aggregate amount of any such donation or donations made in that period exceeds £5,000.

(5)   The restrictions imposed by sections 347C(1), 347D(2) and (3) and 347E(2) accordingly have effect subject to subsection (4); and, where a resolution is passed for the purposes of any of those provisions, any amount of donations in relation to which, by virtue of subsection (4), no authorisation is needed shall accordingly not count towards the sum specified in the resolution.

(6)   In subsection (4) "qualifying period" means—

    (a)   the period of 12 months beginning with the relevant date for the company or (in the case of a subsidiary undertaking) the parent company; and

    (b)   each succeeding period of twelve months.

(7)   For the purposes of subsection (6) the relevant date for a company is—

    (a)   if an annual general meeting of the company is held within the period of 12 months beginning with the date of the coming into force of this section, the date of that meeting; and

    (b)   otherwise, the date immediately following the end of that period.

(8)   For the purposes of this Part—

    (a)   a company does not need to be authorised as mentioned in section 347C(1) or section 347D(2) or (3), and

    (b)   a subsidiary undertaking does not need to be authorised as mentioned in section 347E(2),

    in connection with any EU political expenditure in relation to which an exemption is conferred on the company or (as the case may be) subsidiary undertaking by virtue of an order made by the Secretary of State by statutory instrument.

(9)   The restrictions imposed by sections 347C(1), 347D(2) and (3) and 347E(2) accordingly have effect subject to subsection (8); and, where a resolution is passed for the purposes of any of those provisions, any amount of EU political expenditure in relation to which, by virtue of subsection (8), no authorisation is needed shall accordingly not count towards the sum specified in the resolution.

(10)   An order under subsection (8) may confer an exemption for the purposes of that subsection in relation to—

    (a)   companies or subsidiary undertakings of any description or category specified in the order, or

    (b)   expenditure of any description or category so specified (whether framed by reference to goods, services or other matters in respect of which such expenditure is incurred or otherwise),

    or both.

(11)   An order shall not be made under subsection (8) unless a draft of the statutory instrument containing the order has been laid before and approved by each House of Parliament.

347C. Prohibition on donations and political expenditure by companies

(1)   A company must not—

    (a)   make any donation to any registered party or to any other EU political organisation, or

    (b)   incur any EU political expenditure,

    unless the donation or expenditure is authorised by virtue of an approval resolution passed by the company in general meeting before the relevant time.

    This subsection has effect subject to section 347D(3).

(2)   For the purposes of this section an approval resolution is a qualifying resolution which authorises the company to do either (or both) of the following, namely—

    (a)   make donations to EU political organisations not exceeding in total a sum specified in the resolution, or

    (b)   incur EU political expenditure not exceeding in total a sum so specified,

    during the requisite period beginning with the date of the resolution.

(3)   In subsection (2)—

    (a)   "qualifying resolution" means an ordinary resolution or, if the directors so determine or the articles so require—

        (i)   a special resolution, or

        (ii)   a resolution passed by any percentage of the members greater than that required for an ordinary resolution;

    (b)   "the requisite period" means four years or such shorter period as the directors may determine or the articles may require;

    and the directors may make a determination for the purposes of paragraph (a) or (b) above except where any provision of the articles operates to prevent them from doing so.

(4)   The resolution must be expressed in general terms conforming with subsection (2), and accordingly may not purport to authorise particular donations or expenditure.

(5)   Where a company makes any donation or incurs any expenditure in contravention of subsection (1), no ratification or other approval made or given by the company or its members after the relevant time is capable of operating to nullify that contravention.

(6)   Nothing in this section enables a company to be authorised to do anything that it could not lawfully do apart from this section.

347D. Special rules for subsidiaries

(1)   This section applies where a company is a subsidiary of another company ("the holding company").

(2)   Where the subsidiary is not a wholly-owned subsidiary of the holding company—

    (a)   it must not make any donation or incur any expenditure to which subsection (1) of section 347C applies unless the donation or expenditure is authorised by virtue of a subsidiary approval resolution passed by the holding company in general meeting before the relevant time; and

    (b)   this requirement applies in addition to that imposed by that subsection.

(3)   Where the subsidiary is a wholly-owned subsidiary of the holding company—

    (a)   it must not make any donation or incur any expenditure to which subsection (1) of section 347C applies unless the donation or expenditure is authorised by virtue of a subsidiary approval resolution passed by the holding company in general meeting before the relevant time; and

    (b)   this requirement applies in place of that imposed by that subsection.

(4)   For the purposes of this section a subsidiary approval resolution is a qualifying resolution of the holding company which authorises the subsidiary to do either (or both) of the following, namely—

    (a)   make donations to EU political organisations not exceeding in total a sum specified in the resolution, or

    (b)   incur EU political expenditure not exceeding in total a sum so specified,

during the requisite period beginning with the date of the resolution.

(5)   Subsection (3) of section 347C shall apply for the purposes of subsection (4) above as it applies for the purposes of subsection (2) of that section.

(6)   The resolution must be expressed in general terms conforming with subsection (4), and accordingly may not purport to authorise particular donations or expenditure.

(7)   The resolution may not relate to donations or expenditure by more than one subsidiary.

(8)   Where a subsidiary makes any donation or incurs any expenditure in contravention of subsection (2) or (3), no ratification or other approval made or given by the holding company or its members after the relevant time is capable of operating to nullify that contravention.

(9)   Nothing in this section enables a company to be authorised to do anything that it could not lawfully do apart from this section.

347E. Special rule for parent company of non-GB subsidiary undertaking

(1)   This section applies where a company ("the parent company") has a subsidiary undertaking which is incorporated or otherwise established outside Great Britain.

(2)   The parent company shall take all such steps as are reasonably open to it to secure that the subsidiary undertaking does not make any donation or incur any expenditure to which subsection (1) of section 347C applies except to the extent that the donation or expenditure is authorised by virtue of a subsidiary approval resolution passed by the parent company in general meeting before the relevant time.

(3)   For the purposes of this section a subsidiary approval resolution is a qualifying resolution of the parent company which authorises the subsidiary undertaking to do either (or both) of the following, namely—

    (a)   make donations to EU political organisations not exceeding in total a sum specified in the resolution, or

    (b)   incur EU political expenditure not exceeding in total a sum so specified,

during the requisite period beginning with the date of the resolution.

(4)   Subsection (3) of section 347C shall apply for the purposes of subsection (3) above as it applies for the purposes of subsection (2) of that section.

(5)   The resolution must be expressed in general terms conforming with subsection (3), and accordingly may not purport to authorise particular donations or expenditure.

(6)   The resolution may not relate to donations or expenditure by more than one subsidiary undertaking.

(7)   Where a subsidiary undertaking makes any donation or incurs any expenditure which (to any extent) is not authorised as mentioned in subsection (2), no ratification or other approval made or given by the parent company or its members after the relevant time is capable of operating to authorise that donation or expenditure.

347F.   Remedies for breach of prohibitions on company donations etc

(1)   This section applies where a company has made any donation or incurred any expenditure in contravention of any of the provisions of sections 347C and 347D.

(2)   Every person who was a director of the company at the relevant time is liable to pay the company—

(a)   the amount of the donation or expenditure made or incurred in contravention of the provisions in question; and

(b)   damages in respect of any loss or damage sustained by the company as a result of the donation or expenditure having been made or incurred in contravention of those provisions.

(3)   Every such person is also liable to pay the company interest on the amount mentioned in subsection (2)(a) in respect of the period—

(a)   beginning with the date when the donation or expenditure was made or incurred, and

(b)   ending with the date when that amount is paid to the company by any such person;

and such interest shall be payable at such rate as the Secretary of State may prescribe by regulations.

(4)   Where two or more persons are subject to a particular liability arising by virtue of any provision of this section, each of those persons is jointly and severally liable.

(5)   Where only part of any donation or expenditure was made or incurred in contravention of any of the provisions of sections 347C and 347D, this section applies only to so much of it as was so made or incurred.

(6)   Where—

(a)   this section applies as mentioned in subsection (1), and

(b)   the company in question is a subsidiary of another company ("the holding company"),

then (subject to subsection (7)) subsections (2) to (5) shall, in connection with the donation or expenditure made or incurred by the subsidiary, apply in relation to the holding company as they apply in relation to the subsidiary.

(7)   Those subsections do not apply in relation to the holding company if—

(a)   the subsidiary is not a wholly-owned subsidiary of the holding company; and

(b)   the donation or expenditure was authorised by such a resolution of the holding company as is mentioned in section 347D(2)(a).

(8)   Nothing in section 727 shall apply in relation to any liability of any person arising under this section.

347G.   Remedy for unauthorised donation or expenditure by non-GB subsidiary

(1)   This section applies where—

(a)   a company ("the parent company") has a subsidiary undertaking falling within subsection (1) of section 347E;

(b)   the subsidiary undertaking has made any donation or incurred any expenditure to which subsection (1) of section 347C applies; and

(c)   the parent company has, in relation to that donation or expenditure, failed to discharge its duty under subsection (2) of section 347E to take all such steps as are mentioned in that subsection.

(2)   Subsections (2) to (4) of section 347F shall, in connection with the donation or expenditure made or incurred by the subsidiary undertaking, apply in relation to the holding company as if—

(a)   it were a company falling within subsection (1) of that section, and

(b)   the donation or expenditure had been made or incurred by it in contravention of section 347C or 347D.

(3)   Where only part of the donation or expenditure was not authorised as mentioned in section 347E(2), those subsections shall so apply only to that part of it.

(4)   Section 347F(8) applies to any liability of any person arising under section 347F by virtue of this section.

347H. **Exemption of directors from liability in respect of unauthorised donation or expenditure**

(1) Where proceedings are brought against a director or former director of a company in respect of any liability arising under section 347F(2)(a) in connection with a donation or expenditure made or incurred by the company, it shall be a defence for that person to show that—

(a) the unauthorised amount has been repaid to the company, together with any interest on that amount due under section 347F(3);

(b) that repayment has been approved by the company in general meeting; and

(c) in the notice of the relevant resolution submitted to that meeting full disclosure was made—

(i) of the circumstances in which the donation or expenditure was made or incurred in contravention of section 347C or 347D, and

(ii) of the circumstances in which, and the person or persons by whom, the repayment was made.

(2) Where proceedings are brought against a director or former director of a holding company in respect of any liability arising under section 347F(2)(a) in connection with a donation or expenditure made or incurred by a subsidiary of the company, it shall be a defence for that person to show that—

(a) the unauthorised amount has been repaid either to the subsidiary or to the holding company, together with any interest on that amount due under section 347F(3);

(b) that repayment has been approved—

(i) (if made to the subsidiary) by both the subsidiary and the holding company in general meeting, or

(ii) (if made to the holding company) by the holding company in general meeting; and

(c) in the notice of the relevant resolution submitted to each of those meetings or (as the case may be) to that meeting, full disclosure was made—

(i) of the circumstances in which the donation or expenditure was made in contravention of section 347D, and

(ii) of the circumstances in which, and the person or persons by whom, the repayment was made.

(3) If the subsidiary is a wholly-owned subsidiary of the holding company, it is not necessary for the purposes of subsection (2) to show (where the repayment was made to the subsidiary) that the repayment has been approved by the subsidiary, and paragraphs (b) and (c) of that subsection shall apply accordingly.

(4) Where proceedings are brought against a director or former director of a holding company in respect of any liability arising under section 347F(2)(a) in connection with a donation or expenditure made or incurred by a subsidiary of the company which is not a wholly-owned subsidiary, then (subject to subsection (5)) it shall be a defence for that person to show that—

(a) proceedings have been instituted by the subsidiary against all or any of its directors in respect of the unauthorised amount; and

(b) those proceedings are being pursued with due diligence by the subsidiary.

(5) A person may not avail himself of the defence provided by subsection (4) except with the leave of the court; and on an application for leave under this subsection the court may make such order as it thinks fit, including an order adjourning, or sanctioning the continuation of, the proceedings against the applicant on such terms and conditions as it thinks fit.

(6) Where proceedings are brought against a director or former director of a company in respect of any liability arising under section 347F(2)(a) (as applied by virtue of section 347G) in connection with a donation or expenditure made or incurred by a subsidiary undertaking of the company, it shall be a defence for that person to show that—

(a) the unauthorised amount has been repaid to the subsidiary undertaking, together with any interest on that amount due under section 347F(3) (as so applied);

(b) that repayment has been approved by the company in general meeting; and

(c) in the notice of the relevant resolution submitted to that meeting full disclosure was made—

(i)   of the circumstances in which the donation or expenditure was made without having been authorised as mentioned in section 347E(2), and

(ii)   of the circumstances in which, and the person or persons by whom, the repayment was made.

(7)   In this section "the unauthorised amount", in relation to any donation or expenditure, means the amount of the donation or expenditure—

(a)   which was made or incurred in contravention of section 347C or 347D, or

(b)   which was not authorised as mentioned in section 347E(2),

as the case may be.

347I.   Enforcement of directors' liabilities by shareholder action

(1)   Any liability of any person under section 347F or 347G as a director or former director of a company is (in addition to being enforceable by proceedings brought by the company) enforceable by proceedings brought under this section in the name of the company by an authorised group of members of the company.

(2)   For the purposes of this section "authorised group", in relation to the members of a company, means any such combination of members as is specified in section 54(2)(a), (b) or (c).

(3)   An authorised group of members of a company may not bring proceedings under this section unless—

(a)   the group has given written notice to the company stating—

(i)   the cause of action and a summary of the facts on which the proceedings are to be based,

(ii)   the names and addresses of the members of the company comprising the group, and

(iii)   the grounds on which it is alleged that those members constitute an authorised group; and

(b)   not less than 28 days have elapsed between the date of the giving of the notice to the company and the institution of the proceedings.

(4)   Where such a notice is given to a company, any director may apply to the court within the period of 28 days beginning with the date of the giving of the notice for an order directing that the proposed proceedings are not to be instituted.

(5)   An application under subsection (4) may be made on one or more of the following grounds—

(a)   that the unauthorised amount within the meaning of section 347H has been repaid to the company or subsidiary undertaking as mentioned in subsection (1), (2), (4) or (6) of that section (as the case may be) and the other conditions mentioned in that subsection were satisfied with respect to that repayment;

(b)   that proceedings to enforce the liability have been instituted by the company and are being pursued with due diligence by the company;

(c)   that the members proposing to institute proceedings under this section do not constitute an authorised group.

(6)   Where such an application is made on the ground mentioned in subsection (5)(b), the court may make such order as it thinks fit; and such an order may, as an alternative to directing that the proposed proceedings under this section are not to be instituted, direct—

(a)   that those proceedings may be instituted on such terms and conditions as the court thinks fit;

(b)   that the proceedings instituted by the company are to be discontinued;

(c)   that the proceedings instituted by the company may be continued on such terms and conditions as the court thinks fit.

(7)   If proceedings are brought under this section by an authorised group of members of a company, the group shall owe the same duties to the company in relation to the bringing of those proceedings on behalf of the company as would be owed by the directors of the company if the proceedings were being brought by the company itself; but no proceedings to enforce any duty owed by virtue of this subsection shall be brought by the company except with the leave of the court.

(8)   Proceedings brought under this section may not be discontinued or settled by the group except with the leave of the court; and the court may grant leave under this subsection on such terms as it thinks fit.

347J.   Costs of shareholder action

(1)   This section applies in relation to proceedings brought under section 347I by an authorised group of members of a company ("the group").

(2)   The group may apply to the court for an order directing the company to indemnify the group in respect of costs incurred or to be incurred by the group in connection with the proceedings; and on such an application the court may make such an order on such terms as it thinks fit.

(3)   The group shall not be entitled to be paid any such costs out of the assets of the company except by virtue of such an order.

(4)   If—
   (a)   the company is awarded costs in connection with the proceedings or it is agreed that costs incurred by the company in connection with the proceedings should be paid by any defendant, and
   (b)   no order has been made with respect to the proceedings under subsection (2),
   the costs shall be paid to the group.

(5)   If—
   (a)   any defendant is awarded costs in connection with the proceedings or it is agreed that any defendant should be paid costs incurred by him in connection with the proceedings, and
   (b)   no order has been made with respect to the proceedings under subsection (2),
   the costs shall be paid by the group.

(6)   In the application of this section to Scotland references to costs are to expenses and references to any defendant are to any defender.

347K.   Information for purposes of shareholder action

(1)   Where any proceedings have been instituted under section 347I by an authorised group within the meaning of that section, the group is entitled to require the company to provide the group with all information relating to the subject matter of the proceedings which is in the company's possession or under its control or which is reasonably obtainable by it.

(2)   If the company, having been required by the group to provide the information referred to in subsection (1), refuses to provide the group with all or any of the information, the court may, on an application made by the group, make an order directing—
   (a)   the company, and
   (b)   any of its officers or employees specified in the application,
   to provide the group with the information in question in such form and by such means as the court may direct.

PART XI
COMPANY ADMINISTRATION AND PROCEDURE

CHAPTER I
COMPANY IDENTIFICATION

348.   Company name to appear outside place of business

(1)   Every company shall paint or affix, and keep painted or affixed, its name on the outside of every office or place in which its business is carried on, in a conspicuous position and in letters easily legible.

(2)   If a company does not paint or affix its name as required above, the company and every officer of it who is in default is liable to a fine; and if a company does not keep its name painted or affixed as so required, the company and every officer of it who is in default is liable to a fine and, for continued contravention, to a daily default fine.

349.   Company's name to appear in its correspondence, etc

(1)   Every company shall have its name mentioned in legible characters—

    (a)   in all business letters of the company,

    (b)   in all its notices and other official publications,

    (c)   in all bills of exchange, promissory notes, endorsements, cheques and orders for money or goods purporting to be signed by or on behalf of the company, and

    (d)   in all its bills of parcels, invoices, receipts and letters of credit.

(2)   If a company fails to comply with subsection (1) it is liable to a fine.

(3)   If an officer of a company or a person on its behalf—

    (a)   issues or authorises the issue of any business letter of the company, or any notice or other official publication of the company, in which the company's name is not mentioned as required by subsection (1), or

    (b)   issues or authorises the issue of any bill of parcels, invoice, receipt or letter of credit of the company in which its name is not so mentioned,

he is liable to a fine.

(4)   If an officer of a company or a person on its behalf signs or authorises to be signed on behalf of the company any bill of exchange, promissory note, endorsement, cheque or order for money or goods in which the company's name is not mentioned as required by subsection (1), he is liable to a fine; and he is further personally liable to the holder of the bill of exchange, promissory note, cheque or order for money or goods for the amount of it (unless it is duly paid by the company).

350.   Company seal

(1)   A company which has a common seal shall have its name engraved in legible characters on the seal; and if it fails to comply with this subsection it is liable to a fine.

(2)   If an officer of a company or a person on its behalf uses or authorises the use of any seal purporting to be a seal of the company on which its name is not engraved as required by subsection (1), he is liable to a fine.

351.   Particulars in correspondence etc

(1)   Every company shall have the following particulars mentioned in legible characters in all business letters and order forms of the company, that is to say—

    (a)   the company's place of registration and the number with which it is registered,

    (b)   the address of its registered office,

    (c)   in the case of an investment company (as defined in section 266), the fact that it is such a company, and

    (d)   in the case of a limited company exempt from the obligation to use the word "limited" as part of its name *under section 30 or a community interest company which is not a public company*, the fact that it is a limited company.

(2)   If in the case of a company having a share capital there is on the stationery used for any such letters, or on the company's order forms, a reference to the amount of share capital, the reference must be to paid-up share capital.

(3), (4)   ...

(5)   As to contraventions of this section, the following applies—

    (a)   if a company fails to comply with subsection (1) or (2), it is liable to a fine,

    (b)   if an officer of a company or a person on its behalf issues or authorises the issue of any business letter or order form not complying with those subsections, he is liable to a fine, ...

    (c)   ...

Note. The italicized words in subsection (1)(d) are inserted by the Companies (Audit, Investigations and Community Enterprise) Act 2004, s. 33(6), Sch. 6, paras. 1, 8, as from 1 July 2005.

CHAPTER II
REGISTER OF MEMBERS

352.   Obligation to keep and enter up register

(1)   Every company shall keep a register of its members and enter in it the particulars required by this section.

(2)   There shall be entered in the register—

(a)   the names and addresses of the members;

(b)   the date on which each person was registered as a member; and

(c)   the date at which any person ceased to be a member.

(3)   The following applies in the case of a company having a share capital—

(a)   with the names and addresses of the members there shall be entered a statement—

(i)   of the shares held by each member, distinguishing each share by its number (so long as the share has a number) and, where the company has more than one class of issued shares, by its class, and

(ii)   of the amount paid or agreed to be considered as paid on the shares of each member;

(b)   where the company has converted any of its shares into stock and given notice of the conversion to the registrar of companies, the register shall show the amount and class of stock held by each member, instead of the amount of shares and the particulars relating to shares specified in paragraph (a).

(3A)   Where a company purchases one or more of its own shares in circumstances in which section 162A applies—

(a)   the requirements of subsection (2) and (3) must be complied with unless the company cancels all of the shares forthwith after the purchase in accordance with section 162D(1), but

(b)   any share which is so cancelled must be disregarded for the purposes of subsection (3).

(4)   In the case of a company which does not have a share capital but has more than one class of members, there shall be entered in the register, with the names and addresses of the members, the class to which each member belongs.

(5)   If a company makes default in complying with this section, the company and every officer of it who is in default is liable to a fine and, for continued contravention, to a daily default fine.

(6)   An entry relating to a former member of the company may be removed from the register after the expiration of 20 years from the date on which he ceased to be a member.

(7)   Liability incurred by a company from the making or deletion of an entry in its register of members, or from a failure to make or delete any such entry, is not enforceable more than 20 years after the date on which the entry was made or deleted or, in the case of any such failure, the failure first occurred.

This is without prejudice to any lesser period of limitation.

352A.   Statement that company has only one member

(1)   If the number of members of a private company limited by shares or by guarantee falls to one there shall upon the occurrence of that event be entered in the company's register of members with the name and address of the sole member—

(i)   a statement that the company has only one member, and

(ii)   the date on which the company became a company having only one member.

(2)   If the membership of a private company limited by shares or by guarantee increases from one to two or more members there shall upon the occurrence of that event be entered in the company's register of members, with the name and address of the person who was formerly the sole member, a statement that the company has ceased to have only one member together with the date on which that event occurred.

(3)   If a company makes default in complying with this section, the company and every officer of it who is in default is liable to a fine and, for continued contravention, to a daily default fine.

353.   Location of register

(1)   A company's register of members shall be kept at its registered office, except that—

  (a)   if the work of making it up is done at another office of the company, it may be kept there; and

  (b)   if the company arranges with some other person for the making up of the register to be undertaken on its behalf by that other, it may be kept at the office of the other at which the work is done;

  but it must not be kept, in the case of a company registered in England and Wales, at any place elsewhere than in England and Wales or, in the case of a company registered in Scotland, at any place elsewhere than in Scotland.

(2)   Subject as follows, every company shall send notice in the prescribed form to the registrar of companies of the place where its register of members is kept, and of any change in that place.

(3)   The notice need not be sent if the register has, at all times since it came into existence (or, in the case of a register in existence on 1st July 1948, at all times since then) been kept at the company's registered office.

(4)   If a company makes default for 14 days in complying with subsection (2), the company and every officer of it who is in default is liable to a fine and, for continued contravention, to a daily default fine.

354.   Index of members

(1)   Every company having more than 50 members shall, unless the register of members is in such a form as to constitute in itself an index, keep an index of the names of the members of the company and shall, within 14 days after the date on which any alteration is made in the register of members, make any necessary alteration in the index.

(2)   The index shall in respect of each member contain a sufficient indication to enable the account of that member in the register to be readily found.

(3)   The index shall be at all times kept at the same place as the register of members.

(4)   If default is made in complying with this section, the company and every officer of it who is in default is liable to a fine and, for continued contravention, to a daily default fine.

355.   Entries in register in relation to share warrants

(1)   On the issue of a share warrant the company shall strike out of its register of members the name of the member then entered in it as holding the shares specified in the warrant as if he had ceased to be a member, and shall enter in the register the following particulars, namely—

  (a)   the fact of the issue of the warrant;

  (b)   a statement of the shares included in the warrant, distinguishing each share by its number so long as the share has a number; and

  (c)   the date of the issue of the warrant.

(2)   Subject to the company's articles, the bearer of a share warrant is entitled, on surrendering it for cancellation, to have his name entered as a member in the register of members.

(3)   The company is responsible for any loss incurred by any person by reason of the company entering in the register the name of a bearer of a share warrant in respect of the shares specified in it without the warrant being surrendered and cancelled.

(4)   Until the warrant is surrendered, the particulars specified in subsection (1) are deemed to be those required by this Act to be entered in the register of members; and, on the surrender, the date of the surrender must be entered.

(5)   Except as provided by section 291(2) (director's share qualification), the bearer of a share warrant may, if the articles of the company so provide, be deemed a member of the company within the meaning of this Act, either to the full extent or for any purposes defined in the articles.

356.   Inspection of register and index

(1)   Except when the register of members is closed under the provisions of this Act, the register and the index of members' names shall ... be open to the inspection of any member of the company without charge, and of any other person on payment of such fee as may be prescribed.

(2)   ...

(3)   Any member of the company or other person may require a copy of the register, or of any part of it, on payment of such fee as may be prescribed; and the company shall cause any copy so required by a person to be sent to him within 10 days beginning with the day next following that on which the requirement is received by the company.

(4)   ...

(5)   If an inspection required under this section is refused, or if a copy so required is not sent within the proper period, the company and every officer of it who is in default is liable in respect of each offence to a fine.

(6)   In the case of such refusal or default, the court may by order compel an immediate inspection of the register and index, or direct that the copies required be sent to the persons requiring them.

357.   Non-compliance with ss 353, 354, 356; agent's default

Where under section 353(1)(b), the register of members is kept at the office of some person other than the company, and by reason of any default of his the company fails to comply with—

          section 353(2) (notice to registrar),
          section 354(3) (index to be kept with register), or
          section 356 (inspection),

or with any requirement of this Act as to the production of the register, that other person is liable to the same penalties as if he were an officer of the company who was in default, and the power of the court under section 356(6) extends to the making of orders against that other and his officers and servants.

358.   Power to close register

A company may, on giving notice by advertisement in a newspaper circulating in the district in which the company's registered office is situated, close the register of members for any time or times not exceeding in the whole 30 days in each year.

359.   Power of court to rectify register

(1)   If—

          (a)   the name of any person is, without sufficient cause, entered in or omitted from a company's register of members, or

          (b)   default is made or unnecessary delay takes place in entering on the register the fact of any person having ceased to be a member,

          the person aggrieved, or any member of the company, or the company, may apply to the court for rectification of the register.

(2)   The court may either refuse the application or may order rectification of the register and payment by the company of any damages sustained by any party aggrieved.

(3)   On such an application the court may decide any question relating to the title of a person who is a party to the application to have his name entered in or omitted from the register, whether the question arises between members or alleged members, or between members or alleged members on the one hand and the company on the other hand, and generally may decide any question necessary or expedient to be decided for rectification of the register.

(4)   In the case of a company required by this Act to send a list of its members to the registrar of companies, the court, when making an order for rectification of the register, shall by its order direct notice of the rectification to be given to the registrar.

360.   Trusts not to be entered on register in England and Wales

No notice of any trust, expressed, implied or constructive, shall be entered on the register, or be receivable by the registrar, in the case of companies registered in England and Wales.

361.   Register to be evidence

The register of members is prima facie evidence of any matters which are by this Act directed or authorised to be inserted in it.

362.   Overseas branch registers

(1)   A company having a share capital whose objects comprise the transaction of business in any of the countries or territories specified in Part I of Schedule 14 to this Act may cause to be kept in any such country or territory in which it transacts business a branch register of members resident in that country or territory.

(2)   Such a branch register is to be known as an "overseas branch register"; and—

    (a)   any dominion register kept by a company under section 119 of the Companies Act 1948 is to become known as an overseas branch register of the company;

    (b)   where any Act or instrument (including in particular a company's articles) refers to a company's dominion register, that reference is to be read (unless the context otherwise requires) as being to an overseas branch register kept under this section; and

    (c)   references to a colonial register occurring in articles registered before 1st November 1929 are to be read as referring to an overseas branch register.

(3)   Part II of Schedule 14 has effect with respect to overseas branch registers kept under this section; and Part III of the Schedule enables corresponding facilities in Great Britain to be accorded to companies incorporated in other parts of the world.

(4)   The Foreign Jurisdiction Act 1890 has effect as if subsection (1) of this section, and Part II of Schedule 14, were included among the enactments which by virtue of section 5 of that Act may be applied by Order in Council to foreign countries in which for the time being Her Majesty has jurisdiction.

(5)   Her Majesty may by Order in Council direct that subsection (1) above and Part II of Schedule 14 shall extend, with such exceptions, modifications or adaptations (if any) as may be specified in the Order, to any territories under Her Majesty's protection to which those provisions cannot be extended under the Foreign Jurisdiction Act 1890.

CHAPTER III

ANNUAL RETURN

363.   Duty to deliver annual returns

(1)   Every company shall deliver to the registrar successive annual returns each of which is made up to a date not later than the date which is from time to time the company's "return date", that is—

    (a)   the anniversary of the company's incorporation, or

    (b)   if the company's last return delivered in accordance with this Chapter was made up to a different date, the anniversary of that date.

(2)   Each return shall—

    (a)   be in the prescribed form,

    (b)   contain the information required by or under the following provisions of this Chapter, and

    (c)   be signed by a director or the secretary of the company;

and it shall be delivered to the registrar within 28 days after the date to which it is made up.

(3)   If a company fails to deliver an annual return in accordance with this Chapter before the end of the period of 28 days after a return date, the company is guilty of an offence and liable to a fine and, in the case of continued contravention, to a daily default fine.

The contravention continues until such time as an annual return made up to that return date and complying with the requirements of subsection (2) (except as to date of delivery) is delivered by the company to the registrar.

(4)   Where a company is guilty of an offence under subsection (3), every director or secretary of the company is similarly liable unless he shows that he took all reasonable steps to avoid the commission or continuation of the offence.

(5)   The references in this section to a return being delivered "in accordance with this Chapter" are—
       (a)   in relation to a return made on or after 1st October 1990, to a return with respect to which all
              the requirements of subsection (2) are complied with;
       (b)   in relation to a return made before 1st October 1990, to a return with respect to which the
              formal and substantive requirements of this Chapter as it then had effect were complied
              with, whether or not the return was delivered in time.

364.   Contents of annual return: general

(1)   Every annual return shall state the date to which it is made up and shall contain the following
       information—
       (a)   the address of the company's registered office;
       (b)   the type of company it is and its principal business activities;
       (c)   the name and address of the company secretary;
       (d)   the name and address of every director of the company;
       (e)   in the case of each individual director—
              (i)   his nationality, date of birth and business occupation; ...
              (ii)   ...
       (f)   ...
       (g)   if the register of members is not kept at the company's registered office, the address of the
              place where it is kept;
       (h)   if any register of debenture holders (or a duplicate of any such register or a part of it) is not
              kept at the company's registered office, the address of the place where it is kept;
       (i)   ....

(2)   The information as to the company's type shall be given by reference to the classification scheme
       prescribed for the purposes of this section.

(3)   The information as to the company's principal business activities may be given by reference to
       one or more categories of any prescribed system of classifying business activities.

(4)   A person's "name" and "address" mean, respectively—
       (a)   in the case of an individual, his Christian name (or other forename) and surname and his
              usual residential address;
       (b)   in the case of a corporation or a Scottish firm, its corporate or firm name and its registered
              or principal office.

(5)   In the case of a peer, or an individual usually known by a title, the title may be stated instead of
       his Christian name (or other forename) and surname or in addition to either or both of them.

(6)   Where all the partners in a firm are joint secretaries, the name and principal office of the firm may
       be stated instead of the names and addresses of the partners.

364A.   Contents of annual return: particulars of share capital and shareholders

(1)   The annual return of a company having a share capital shall contain the following information
       with respect to its share capital and members.

(2)   The return shall state the total number of issued shares of the company at the date to which the
       return is made up and the aggregate nominal value of those shares.

(3)   The return shall state with respect to each class of shares in the company—
       (a)   the nature of the class, and
       (b)   the total number and aggregate nominal value of issued shares of that class at the date to
              which the return is made up.

(4)   The return shall contain a list of the names and addresses of every person who—
       (a)   is a member of the company on the date to which the return is made up, or
       (b)   has ceased to be a member of the company since the date to which the last return was made
              up (or, in the case of the first return, since the incorporation of the company);
       and if the names are not arranged in alphabetical order the return shall have annexed to it an index
       sufficient to enable the name of any person in the list to be easily found.

(5)   The return shall also state—

(a)   the number of shares of each class held by each member of the company at the date to which the return is made up, and

(b)   the number of shares of each class transferred since the date to which the last return was made up (or, in the case of the first return, since the incorporation of the company) by each member or person who has ceased to be a member, and the dates of registration of the transfers.

(6)   The return may, if either of the two immediately preceding returns has given the full particulars required by subsections (4) and (5), give only such particulars as relate to persons ceasing to be or becoming members since the date of the last return and to shares transferred since that date.

(7)   Subsections (4) and (5) do not require the inclusion of particulars entered in an overseas branch register if copies of those entries have not been received at the company's registered office by the date to which the return is made up.

Those particulars shall be included in the company's next annual return after they are received.

(8)   Where the company has converted any of its shares into stock, the return shall give the corresponding information in relation to that stock, stating the amount of stock instead of the number or nominal value of shares.

365.   Supplementary provisions: regulations and interpretation

(1)   The Secretary of State may by regulations make further provision as to the information to be given in a company's annual return, which may amend or repeal the provisions of sections 364 and 364A.

(2)   Regulations under this section shall be made by statutory instrument which shall be subject to annulment in pursuance of a resolution of either House of Parliament.

(3)   For the purposes of this Chapter, except section 363(2)(c) (signature of annual return), a shadow director shall be deemed to be a director.

CHAPTER IV
MEETINGS AND RESOLUTIONS

Meetings

366.   Annual general meeting

(1)   Every company shall in each year hold a general meeting as its annual general meeting in addition to any other meetings in that year, and shall specify the meeting as such in the notices calling it.

(2)   However, so long as a company holds its first annual general meeting within 18 months of its incorporation, it need not hold it in the year of its incorporation or in the following year.

(3)   Not more than 15 months shall elapse between the date of one annual general meeting of a company and that of the next.

(4)   If default is made in holding a meeting in accordance with this section, the company and every officer of it who is in default is liable to a fine.

366A.   Election by private company to dispense with annual general meetings

(1)   A private company may elect (by elective resolution in accordance with section 379A) to dispense with the holding of annual general meetings.

(2)   An election has effect for the year in which it is made and subsequent years, but does not affect any liability already incurred by reason of default in holding an annual general meeting.

(3)   In any year in which an annual general meeting would be required to be held but for the election, and in which no such meeting has been held, any member of the company may, by notice to the company not later than three months before the end of the year, require the holding of an annual general meeting in that year.

(3A)   The power of a member under subsection (3) to require the holding of an annual general meeting is exercisable not only by the giving of a notice but also by the transmission to the company at such address as may for the time being be specified for the purpose by or on behalf of the company of an electronic communication containing the requirement.

(4)   If such a notice is given or electronic communication is transmitted, the provisions of section 366(1) and (4) apply with respect to the calling of the meeting and the consequences of default.

(5)   If the election ceases to have effect, the company is not obliged under section 366 to hold an annual general meeting in that year if, when the election ceases to have effect, less than three months of the year remains.

This does not affect any obligation of the company to hold an annual general meeting in that year in pursuance of a notice given or electronic communication is transmitted under subsection (3).

(5A)   In this section, "address" includes any number or address used for the purposes of electronic communications.

367. Secretary of State's power to call meeting in default

(1)   If default is made in holding a meeting in accordance with section 366, the Secretary of State may, on the application of any member of the company, call, or direct the calling of, a general meeting of the company and give such ancillary or consequential directions as he thinks expedient, including directions modifying or supplementing, in relation to the calling, holding and conduct of the meeting, the operation of the company's articles.

(2)   The directions that may be given under subsection (1) include a direction that one member of the company present in person or by proxy shall be deemed to constitute a meeting.

(3)   If default is made in complying with directions of the Secretary of State under subsection (1), the company and every officer of it who is in default is liable to a fine.

(4)   A general meeting held under this section shall, subject to any directions of the Secretary of State, be deemed to be an annual general meeting of the company; but, where a meeting so held is not held in the year in which the default in holding the company's annual general meeting occurred, the meeting so held shall not be treated as the annual general meeting for the year in which it is held unless at that meeting the company resolves that it be so treated.

(5)   Where a company so resolves, a copy of the resolution shall, within 15 days after its passing, be forwarded to the registrar of companies and recorded by him; and if default is made in complying with this subsection, the company and every officer of it who is in default is liable to a fine and, for continued contravention, to a daily default fine.

368. Extraordinary general meeting on members' requisition

(1)   The directors of a company shall, on a members' requisition, forthwith proceed duly to convene an extraordinary general meeting of the company.

This applies notwithstanding anything in the company's articles.

(2)   A members' requisition is a requisition of—

(a)   members of the company holding at the date of the deposit of the requisition not less than one-tenth of such of the paid-up capital of the company as at that date carries the right of voting at general meetings of the company; or

(b)   in the case of a company not having a share capital, members of it representing not less than one-tenth of the total voting rights of all the members having at the date of deposit of the requisition a right to vote at general meetings.

(2A)   For the purposes of subsection (2)(a) any of the company's paid up capital held as treasury shares must be disregarded.

(3)   The requisition must state the objects of the meeting, and must be signed by the requisitionists and deposited at the registered office of the company, and may consist of several documents in like form each signed by one or more requisitionists.

(4)   If the directors do not within 21 days from the date of the deposit of the requisition proceed duly to convene a meeting, the requisitionists, or any of them representing more than one half of the total voting rights of all of them, may themselves convene a meeting, but any meeting so convened shall not be held after the expiration of 3 months from that date.

(5)   A meeting convened under this section by requisitionists shall be convened in the same manner, as nearly as possible, as that in which meetings are to be convened by directors.

(6)   Any reasonable expenses incurred by the requisitionists by reason of the failure of the directors duly to convene a meeting shall be repaid to the requisitionists by the company, and any sum so repaid shall be retained by the company out of any sums due or to become due from the company by way of fees or other remuneration in respect of their services to such of the directors as were in default.

(7)   In the case of a meeting at which a resolution is to be proposed as a special resolution, the directors are deemed not to have duly convened the meeting if they do not give the notice required for special resolutions by section 378(2).

(8)   The directors are deemed not to have duly convened a meeting if they convene a meeting for a date more than 28 days after the date of the notice convening the meeting.

369.   Length of notice for calling meetings

(1)   A provision of a company's articles is void in so far as it provides for the calling of a meeting of the company (other than an adjourned meeting) by a shorter notice than—

    (a)   in the case of the annual general meeting, 21 days' notice in writing; and

    (b)   in the case of a meeting other than an annual general meeting or a meeting for the passing of a special resolution—

        (i)   7 days' notice in writing in the case of an unlimited company, and

        (ii) otherwise, 14 days' notice in writing.

(2)   Save in so far as the articles of a company make other provision in that behalf (not being a provision avoided by subsection (1)), a meeting of the company (other than an adjourned meeting) may be called—

    (a)   in the case of the annual general meeting, by 21 days' notice in writing; and

    (b)   in the case of a meeting other than an annual general meeting or a meeting for the passing of a special resolution—

        (i)   by 7 days' notice in writing in the case of an unlimited company, and

        (ii) otherwise, 14 days' notice in writing.

(3)   Notwithstanding that a meeting is called by shorter notice than that specified in subsection (2) or in the company's articles (as the case may be), it is deemed to have been duly called if it is so agreed—

    (a)   in the case of a meeting called as the annual general meeting, by all the members entitled to attend and vote at it; and

    (b)   otherwise, by the requisite majority.

(4)   The requisite majority for this purpose is a majority in number of the members having a right to attend and vote at the meeting, being a majority—

    (a)   together holding not less than 95 per cent in nominal value of the shares giving a right to attend and vote at the meeting (excluding any shares in the company held as treasury shares); or

    (b)   in the case of a company not having a share capital, together representing not less than 95 per cent of the total voting rights at that meeting of all the members.

A private company may elect (by elective resolution in accordance with section 379A) that the above provisions shall have effect in relation to the company as if for the references to 95 per cent there were substituted references to such lesser percentage, but not less than 90 per cent, as may be specified in the resolution or subsequently determined by the company in general meeting.

(4A)   For the purposes of this section the cases in which notice in writing of a meeting is to be taken as given to a person include any case in which notice of the meeting is sent using electronic communications to such address as may for the time being be notified by that person to the company for that purpose.

(4B)   For the purposes of this section a notice in writing of a meeting is also to be treated as given to a person where—

(a) the company and that person have agreed that notices of meetings required to be given to that person may instead be accessed by him on a web site;

(b) the meeting is a meeting to which that agreement applies;

(c) that person is notified, in a manner for the time being agreed between him and the company for the purpose, of—

   (i) the publication of the notice on a web site;

   (ii) the address of that web site; and

   (iii) the place on that web site where the notice may be accessed, and how it may be accessed; and

(d) the notice continues to be published on that web site throughout the period beginning with the giving of that notification and ending with the conclusion of the meeting;

and for the purposes of this section a notice treated in accordance with this subsection as given to any person is to be treated as so given at the time of the notification mentioned in paragraph (c).

(4C) A notification given for the purposes of subsection (4B)(c) must—

(a) state that it concerns a notice of a company meeting served in accordance with this Act,

(b) specify the place, date and time of the meeting, and

(c) state whether the meeting is to be an annual or extraordinary general meeting.

(4D) Nothing in subsection (4B) shall invalidate the proceedings of a meeting where—

(a) any notice that is required to be published as mentioned in paragraph (d) of that subsection is published for a part, but not all, of the period mentioned in that paragraph; and

(b) the failure to publish that notice throughout that period is wholly attributable to circumstances which it would not be reasonable to have expected the company to prevent or avoid.

(4E) A company may, notwithstanding any provision to the contrary in a company's articles, take advantage of any of subsections (4A) to (4D).

(4F) In so far as the articles of the company do not provide for notices and notifications to be served using electronic communications, the provisions of Table A (as for the time being in force) as to such service shall apply.

(4G) In this section, "address" includes any number or address used for the purposes of electronic communications.

370. General provisions as to meetings and votes

(1) The following provisions have effect in so far as the articles of the company do not make other provision in that behalf.

(2) Notice of the meeting of a company shall be served on every member of it in the manner in which notices are required to be served by Table A (as for the time being in force).

(3) Two or more members holding not less than one-tenth of the issued share capital (excluding any shares in the company held as treasury shares) or, if the company does not have a share capital, not less than 5 per cent in number of the members of the company may call a meeting.

(4) Two members personally present are a quorum.

(5) Any member elected by the members present at a meeting may be chairman of it.

(6) In the case of a company originally having a share capital, every member has one vote in respect of each share or each £10 of stock held by him; and in any other case every member has one vote.

370A. Quorum at meetings of the sole member

Notwithstanding any provision to the contrary in the articles of a private company limited by shares or by guarantee having only one member, one member present in person or by proxy shall be a quorum.

371. Power of court to order meeting

(1) If for any reason it is impracticable to call a meeting of a company in any manner in which meetings of that company may be called, or to conduct the meeting in manner prescribed by the articles or this Act, the court may, either of its own motion or on the application—

(a) of any director of the company, or

(b)　of any member of the company who would be entitled to vote at the meeting,

order a meeting to be called, held and conducted in any manner the court thinks fit.

(2)　Where such an order is made, the court may give such ancillary or consequential directions as it thinks expedient; and these may include a direction that one member of the company present in person or by proxy be deemed to constitute a meeting.

(3)　A meeting called, held and conducted in accordance with an order under subsection (1) is deemed for all purposes a meeting of the company duly called, held and conducted.

372.　Proxies

(1)　Any member of a company entitled to attend and vote at a meeting of it is entitled to appoint another person (whether a member or not) as his proxy to attend and vote instead of him; and in the case of a private company a proxy appointed to attend and vote instead of a member has also the same right as the member to speak at the meeting.

(2)　But, unless the articles otherwise provide—

(a)　subsection (1) does not apply in the case of a company not having a share capital; and

(b)　a member of a private company is not entitled to appoint more than one proxy to attend on the same occasion; and

(c)　a proxy is not entitled to vote except on a poll.

(2A)　The appointment of a proxy may, notwithstanding any provision to the contrary in a company's articles, be contained in an electronic communication sent to such address as may be notified by or on behalf of the company for that purpose.

(2B)　In so far as the articles of the company do not make other provision in that behalf, the appointment of a proxy may be contained in an electronic communication in accordance with the provisions of Table A (as for the time being in force).

(3)　In the case of a company having a share capital, in every notice calling a meeting of the company there shall appear with reasonable prominence a statement that a member entitled to attend and vote is entitled to appoint a proxy or, where that is allowed, one or more proxies to attend and vote instead of him, and that a proxy need not also be a member.

(4)　If default is made in complying with subsection (3) as respects any meeting, every officer of the company who is in default is liable to a fine.

(5)　A provision contained in a company's articles is void in so far as it would have the effect of requiring the appointment of a proxy or any document necessary to show the validity of, or otherwise relating to, the appointment of a proxy, to be received by the company or any other person more than 48 hours before a meeting or adjourned meeting in order that the appointment may be effective.

(6)　If for the purpose of any meeting of a company invitations to appoint as proxy a person or one of a number of persons specified in the invitations are issued at the company's expense to some only of the members entitled to be sent a notice of the meeting and to vote at it by proxy, then every officer of the company who knowingly and wilfully authorises or permits their issue in that manner is liable to a fine.

However, an officer is not so liable by reason only of the issue to a member at his request ... of a form of appointment naming the proxy, or of a list of persons willing to act as proxy, if the form or list is available on request ... to every member entitled to vote at the meeting by proxy.

(6A)　In this section, "address" includes any number or address used for the purposes of electronic communications.

(7)　This section applies to meetings of any class of members of a company as it applies to general meetings of the company.

373.　Right to demand a poll

(1)　A provision contained in a company's articles is void in so far as it would have the effect either—

(a)　of excluding the right to demand a poll at a general meeting on any question other than the election of the chairman of the meeting or the adjournment of the meeting; or

(b)　of making ineffective a demand for a poll on any such question which is made either—

     (i)   by not less than 5 members having the right to vote at the meeting; or

    (ii) by a member or members representing not less than one-tenth of the total voting rights of all the members having the right to vote at the meeting (excluding any voting rights attached to any shares in the company held as treasury shares); or

   (iii) by a member or members holding shares in the company conferring a right to vote at the meeting, being shares on which an aggregate sum has been paid up equal to not less than one-tenth of the total sum paid up on all the shares conferring that right (excluding any shares in the company conferring a right to vote at the meeting which are held as treasury shares).

(2)   The appointment of a proxy to vote at a meeting of a company is deemed also to confer authority to demand or join in demanding a poll; and for the purposes of subsection (1) a demand by a person as proxy for a member is the same as a demand by the member.

374.   **Voting on a poll**

On a poll taken at a meeting of a company or a meeting of any class of members of a company, a member entitled to more than one vote need not, if he votes, use all his votes or cast all the votes he uses in the same way.

375.   **Representation of corporations at meetings**

(1)   A corporation, whether or not a company within the meaning of this Act, may—

    (a)   if it is a member of another corporation, being such a company, by resolution of its directors or other governing body authorise such person as it thinks fit to act as its representative at any meeting of the company or at any meeting of any class of members of the company;

    (b)   if it is a creditor (including a holder of debentures) of another corporation, being such a company, by resolution of its directors or other governing body authorise such person as it thinks fit to act as its representative at any meeting of creditors of the company held in pursuance of this Act or of rules made under it, or in pursuance of the provisions contained in any debenture or trust deed, as the case may be.

(2)   A person so authorised is entitled to exercise the same powers on behalf of the corporation which he represents as that corporation could exercise if it were an individual shareholder, creditor or debenture-holder of the other company.

Resolutions

376.   **Circulation of members' resolutions**

(1)   Subject to the section next following, it is the duty of a company, on the requisition in writing of such number of members as is specified below and (unless the company otherwise resolves) at the expense of the requisitionists—

    (a)   to give to members of the company entitled to receive notice of the next annual general meeting notice of any resolution which may properly be moved and is intended to be moved at that meeting;

    (b)   to circulate to members entitled to have notice of any general meeting sent to them any statement of not more than 1,000 words with respect to the matter referred to in any proposed resolution or the business to be dealt with at that meeting.

(2)   The number of members necessary for a requisition under subsection (1) is—

    (a)   any number representing not less than one-twentieth of the total voting rights of all the members having at the date of the requisition a right to vote at the meeting to which the requisition relates (excluding any voting rights attached to any shares in the company held as treasury shares); or

    (b)   not less than 100 members holding shares in the company on which there has been paid up an average sum, per member, of not less than £100.

(3)   Notice of any such resolution shall be given, and any such statement shall be circulated, to members of the company entitled to have notice of the meeting sent to them, by serving a copy of

the resolution or statement on each such member in any manner permitted for service of notice of the meeting.

(4)   Notice of any such resolution shall be given to any other member of the company by giving notice of the general effect of the resolution in any manner permitted for giving him notice of meetings of the company.

(5)   For compliance with subsections (3) and (4), the copy must be served, or notice of the effect of the resolution be given (as the case may be) in the same manner and (so far as practicable) at the same time as notice of the meeting; and, where it is not practicable for it to be served or given at the same time, it must be served or given as soon as practicable thereafter.

(6)   The business which may be dealt with at an annual general meeting includes any resolution of which notice is given in accordance with this section; and for purposes of this subsection notice is deemed to have been so given notwithstanding the accidental omission, in giving it, of one or more members. This has effect notwithstanding anything in the company's articles.

(7)   In the event of default in complying with this section, every officer of the company who is in default is liable to a fine.

377.   In certain cases, compliance with s 376 not required

(1)   A company is not bound under section 376 to give notice of a resolution or to circulate a statement unless—

(a)   a copy of the requisition signed by the requisitionists (or two or more copies which between them contain the signatures of all the requisitionists) is deposited at the registered office of the company—

(i)   in the case of a requisition requiring notice of a resolution, not less than 6 weeks before the meeting, and

(ii)   otherwise, not less than one week before the meeting; and

(b)   there is deposited or tendered with the requisition a sum reasonably sufficient to meet the company's expenses in giving effect to it.

(2)   But if, after a copy of a requisition requiring notice of a resolution has been deposited at the company's registered office, an annual general meeting is called for a date 6 weeks or less after the copy has been deposited, the copy (though not deposited within the time required by subsection (1)) is deemed properly deposited for the purposes of that subsection.

(3)   The company is also not bound under section 376 to circulate a statement if, on the application either of the company or of any other person who claims to be aggrieved, the court is satisfied that the rights conferred by that section are being abused to secure needless publicity for defamatory matter; and the court may order the company's costs on such an application to be paid in whole or in part by the requisitionists, notwithstanding that they are not parties to the application.

378.   Extraordinary and special resolutions

(1)   A resolution is an extraordinary resolution when it has been passed by a majority of not less than three-fourths of such members as (being entitled to do so) vote in person or, where proxies are allowed, by proxy, at a general meeting of which notice specifying the intention to propose the resolution as an extraordinary resolution has been duly given.

(2)   A resolution is a special resolution when it has been passed by such a majority as is required for the passing of an extraordinary resolution and at a general meeting of which not less than 21 days' notice, specifying the intention to propose the resolution as a special resolution, has been duly given.

(3)   If it is so agreed by a majority in number of the members having the right to attend and vote at such a meeting, being a majority—

(a)   together holding not less than 95 per cent in nominal value of the shares giving that right (excluding any shares in the company held as treasury shares); or

(b)   in the case of a company not having a share capital, together representing not less than 95 per cent of the total voting rights at that meeting of all the members, a resolution may be proposed and passed as a special resolution at a meeting of which less than 21 days' notice has been given.

A private company may elect (by elective resolution in accordance with section 379A) that the above provisions shall have effect in relation to the company as if for the references to 95 per cent there were substituted references to such lesser percentage, but not less than 90 per cent, as may be specified in the resolution or subsequently determined by the company in general meeting.

(4)   At any meeting at which an extraordinary resolution or a special resolution is submitted to be passed, a declaration by the chairman that the resolution is carried is, unless a poll is demanded, conclusive evidence of the fact without proof of the number or proportion of the votes recorded in favour of or against the resolution.

(5)   In computing the majority on a poll demanded on the question that an extraordinary resolution or a special resolution be passed, reference is to be had to the number of votes cast for and against the resolution.

(6)   For purposes of this section, notice of a meeting is deemed duly given, and the meeting duly held, when the notice is given and the meeting held in the manner provided by this Act or the company's articles.

379.   Resolution requiring special notice

(1)   Where by any provision of this Act special notice is required of a resolution, the resolution is not effective unless notice of the intention to move it has been given to the company at least 28 days before the meeting at which it is moved.

(2)   The company shall give its members notice of any such resolution at the same time and in the same manner as it gives notice of the meeting or, if that is not practicable, shall give them notice either by advertisement in a newspaper having an appropriate circulation or in any other mode allowed by the company's articles, at least 21 days before the meeting.

(3)   If, after notice of the intention to move such a resolution has been given to the company, a meeting is called for a date 28 days or less after the notice has been given, the notice is deemed properly given, though not given within the time required.

379A.   Elective resolution of private company

(1)   An election by a private company for the purposes of—
    (a)   section 80A (election as to duration of authority to allot shares),
    (b)   section 252 (election to dispense with laying of accounts and reports before general meeting),
    (c)   section 366A (election to dispense with holding of annual general meeting),
    (d)   section 369(4) or 378(3) (election as to majority required to authorise short notice of meeting), or
    (e)   section 386 (election to dispense with appointment of auditors annually),
shall be made by resolution of the company in general meeting in accordance with this section. Such a resolution is referred to in this Act as an "elective resolution".

(2)   An elective resolution is not effective unless—
    (a)   at least 21 days' notice in writing is given of the meeting, stating that an elective resolution is to be proposed and stating the terms of the resolution, and
    (b)   the resolution is agreed to at the meeting, in person or by proxy, by all the members entitled to attend and vote at the meeting.

(2A)   An elective resolution is effective notwithstanding the fact that less than 21 days' notice in writing of the meeting is given if all the members entitled to attend and vote at the meeting so agree.

(2B)   For the purposes of this section, notice in writing of the meeting is to be taken as given to a person where notice of the meeting is sent using electronic communications to such address as may for the time being be notified by that person to the company for that purpose.

(2C)   For the purposes of this section a notice in writing of the meeting is also to be treated as given to a person where—

(a) the company and that person have agreed that notices of meetings required to be given to that person may instead be accessed by him on a web site;

(b) the meeting is a meeting to which that agreement applies;

(c) that person is notified, in a manner for the time being agreed between him and the company for the purpose, of—

    (i)   the publication of the notice on a web site;

    (ii) the address of that web site; and

    (iii) the place on that web site where the notice may be accessed, and how it may be accessed; and

(d) the notice continues to be published on that web site throughout the period beginning with the giving of that notification and ending with the conclusion of the meeting;

and for the purposes of this section a notice treated in accordance with this subsection as given to any person is to be treated as so given at the time of the notification mentioned in paragraph (c).

(2D) A notification given for the purposes of subsection (2C)(c) must—

(a) state that it concerns a notice of a company meeting at which an elective resolution is to be proposed, and

(b) specify the place, date and time of the meeting.

(2E) Nothing in subsection (2C) shall invalidate the proceedings of a meeting where—

(a) any notice that is required to be published as mentioned in paragraph (d) of that subsection is published for a part, but not all, of the period mentioned in that paragraph; and

(b) the failure to publish that notice throughout that period is wholly attributable to circumstances which it would not be reasonable to have expected the company to prevent or avoid.

(2F) In so far as the articles of the company do not provide for notices and notifications to be served using electronic communications, the provisions of Table A (as for the time being in force) as to such service shall apply.

(3) The company may revoke an elective resolution by passing an ordinary resolution to that effect.

(4) An elective resolution shall cease to have effect if the company is re-registered as a public company.

(5) An elective resolution may be passed or revoked in accordance with this section, and the provisions referred to in subsections (1) and (2B) to (2E) have effect, notwithstanding any contrary provision in the company's articles of association.

(5A) In this section, "address" includes any number or address used for the purposes of electronic communications.

380. Registration, etc of resolutions and agreements

(1) A copy of every resolution or agreement to which this section applies shall, within 15 days after it is passed or made, be forwarded to the registrar of companies and recorded by him; and it must be either a printed copy or else a copy in some other form approved by the registrar.

(2) Where articles have been registered, a copy of every such resolution or agreement for the time being in force shall be embodied in or annexed to every copy of the articles issued after the passing of the resolution or the making of the agreement.

(3) Where articles have not been registered, a printed copy of every such resolution or agreement shall be forwarded to any member at his request on payment of 5 pence or such less sum as the company may direct.

(4) This section applies to—

(a) special resolutions;

(b) extraordinary resolutions;

(bb) an elective resolution or a resolution revoking such a resolution;

(c) resolutions or agreements which have been agreed to by all the members of a company but which, if not so agreed to, would not have been effective for their purpose unless (as the case may be) they had been passed as special resolutions or as extraordinary resolutions;

(d)   resolutions or agreements which have been agreed to by all the members of some class of shareholders but which, if not so agreed to, would not have been effective for their purpose unless they had been passed by some particular majority or otherwise in some particular manner, and all resolutions or agreements which effectively bind all the members of any class of shareholders though not agreed to by all those members;

(e)   a resolution passed by the directors of a company in compliance with a direction under section 31(2) (change of name on Secretary of State's direction);

(f)   a resolution of a company to give, vary, revoke or renew an authority to the directors for the purposes of section 80 (allotment of relevant securities);

(g)   a resolution of the directors passed under section 147(2) (alteration of memorandum on company ceasing to be a public company, following acquisition of its own shares);

(h)   a resolution conferring, varying, revoking or renewing authority under section 166 (market purchase of company's own shares);

(j)   a resolution for voluntary winding up, passed under section 84(1)(a) of the Insolvency Act;

(k)   a resolution passed by the directors of an old public company, under section 2(1) of the Consequential Provisions Act, that the company should be re-registered as a public company;

(l)   a resolution of the directors passed by virtue of regulation 16(2) of the Uncertificated Securities Regulations 2001 (which allows title to a company's shares to be evidenced and transferred without written instrument); and

(m)   a resolution of a company passed by virtue of regulation 16(6) of the Uncertificated Securities Regulations 2001 (which prevents or reverses a resolution of the directors under regulation 16(2) of those Regulations).

(4A)   For the purposes of this section, references to a member of a company do not include the company itself where it is such a member by virtue only of its holding shares as treasury shares, and accordingly, in such circumstances, the company is not, for those purposes, to be treated as a member of any class of the company's shareholders.

(5)   If a company fails to comply with subsection (1), the company and every officer of it who is in default is liable to a fine and, for continued contravention, to a daily default fine.

(6)   If a company fails to comply with subsection (2) or (3), the company and every officer of it who is in default is liable to a fine.

(7)   For purposes of subsections (5) and (6), a liquidator of a company is deemed an officer of it.

381.   Resolution passed at adjourned meeting

Where a resolution is passed at an adjourned meeting of—

(a)   a company;

(b)   the holders of any class of shares in a company;

(c)   the directors of a company;

the resolution is for all purposes to be treated as having been passed on the date on which it was in fact passed, and is not to be deemed passed on any earlier date.

Written resolutions of private companies

381A.   Written resolutions of private companies

(1)   Anything which in the case of a private company may be done—

(a)   by resolution of the company in general meeting, or

(b)   by resolution of a meeting of any class of members of the company,

may be done, without a meeting and without any previous notice being required, by resolution in writing signed by or on behalf of all the members of the company who at the date of the resolution would be entitled to attend and vote at such meeting.

(2)   The signatures need not be on a single document provided each is on a document which accurately states the terms of the resolution.

(3)   The date of the resolution means when the resolution is signed by or on behalf of the last member to sign.

(4)   A resolution agreed to in accordance with this section has effect as if passed—
          (a)   by the company in general meeting, or
          (b)   by a meeting of the relevant class of members of the company,
          as the case may be; and any reference in any enactment to a meeting at which a resolution is
          passed or to members voting in favour of a resolution shall be construed accordingly.

(5)   Any reference in any enactment to the date of passing of a resolution is, in relation to a resolution
          agreed to in accordance with this section, a reference to the date of the resolution, ...

(6)   A resolution may be agreed to in accordance with this section which would otherwise be required
          to be passed as a special, extraordinary or elective resolution; and any reference in any enactment
          to a special, extraordinary or elective resolution includes such a resolution.

(7)   This section has effect subject to the exceptions specified in Part I of Schedule 15A; and in
          relation to certain descriptions of resolution under this section the procedural requirements of this
          Act have effect with the adaptations specified in Part II of that Schedule.

381B.   Duty to notify auditors of proposed written resolution

(1)   If a director or secretary of a company—
          (a)   knows that it is proposed to seek agreement to a resolution in accordance with section 381A,
                and
          (b)   knows the terms of the resolution,
          he shall, if the company has auditors, secure that a copy of the resolution is sent to them, or that
          they are otherwise notified of its contents, at or before the time the resolution is supplied to a
          member for signature.

(2)   A person who fails to comply with subsection (1) is liable to a fine.

(3)   In any proceedings for an offence under this section it is a defence for the accused to prove—
          (a)   that the circumstances were such that it was not practicable for him to comply with
                subsection (1), or
          (b)   that he believed on reasonable grounds that a copy of the resolution had been sent to the
                company's auditors or that they had otherwise been informed of its contents.

(4)   Nothing in this section affects the validity of any resolution.

381C.   Written resolutions: supplementary provisions

(1)   Sections 381A and 381B have effect notwithstanding any provision of the company's
          memorandum or articles, but do not prejudice any power conferred by any such provision.

(2)   Nothing in those sections affects any enactment or rule of law as to—
          (a)   things done otherwise than by passing a resolution, or
          (b)   cases in which a resolution is treated as having been passed, or a person is precluded from
                alleging that a resolution has not been duly passed.

Records of proceedings

382.   Minutes of meetings

(1)   Every company shall cause minutes of all proceedings of general meetings, all proceedings at
          meetings of its directors and, where there are managers, all proceedings at meetings of its
          managers to be entered in books kept for that purpose.

(2)   Any such minute, if purporting to be signed by the chairman of the meeting at which the
          proceedings were had, or by the chairman of the next succeeding meeting, is evidence of the
          proceedings.

(3)   Where a shadow director by means of a notice required by section 317(8) declares an interest in a
          contract or proposed contract, this section applies—
          (a)   if it is a specific notice under paragraph (a) of that subsection, as if the declaration had been
                made at the meeting there referred to, and
          (b)   otherwise, as if it had been made at the meeting of the directors next following the giving of
                the notice;

and the making of the declaration is in either case deemed to form part of the proceedings at the meeting.

(4)   Where minutes have been made in accordance with this section of the proceedings at any general meeting of the company or meeting of directors or managers, then, until the contrary is proved, the meeting is deemed duly held and convened, and all proceedings had at the meeting to have been duly had; and all appointments of directors, managers or liquidators are deemed valid.

(5)   If a company fails to comply with subsection (1), the company and every officer of it who is in default is liable to a fine and, for continued contravention, to a daily default fine.

382A. Recording of written resolutions

(1)   Where a written resolution is agreed to in accordance with section 381A which has effect as if agreed by the company in general meeting, the company shall cause a record of the resolution (and of the signatures) to be entered in a book in the same way as minutes of proceedings of a general meeting of the company.

(2)   Any such record, if purporting to be signed by a director of the company or by the company secretary, is evidence of the proceedings in agreeing to the resolution; and where a record is made in accordance with this section, then, until the contrary is proved, the requirements of this Act with respect to those proceedings shall be deemed to be complied with.

(3)   Section 382(5) (penalties) applies in relation to a failure to comply with subsection (1) above as it applies in relation to a failure to comply with subsection (1) of that section; and section 383 (inspection of minute books) applies in relation to a record made in accordance with this section as it applies in relation to the minutes of a general meeting.

382B. Recording of decisions by the sole member

(1)   Where a private company limited by shares or by guarantee has only one member and he takes any decision which may be taken by the company in general meeting and which has effect as if agreed by the company in general meeting, he shall (unless that decision is taken by way of a written resolution) provide the company with a written record of that decision.

(2)   If the sole member fails to comply with subsection (1) he shall be liable to a fine.

(3)   Failure by the sole member to comply with subsection (1) shall not affect the validity of any decision referred to in that subsection.

383. Inspection of minute books

(1)   The books containing the minutes of proceedings of any general meeting of a company held on or after 1st November 1929 shall be kept at the company's registered office, and shall … be open to the inspection of any member without charge.

(2)   …

(3)   Any member shall be entitled on payment of such fee as may be prescribed to be furnished, within 7 days after he has made a request in that behalf to the company, with a copy of any such minutes as are referred to above, …

(4)   If an inspection required under this section is refused or if a copy required under this section is not sent within the proper time, the company and every officer of it who is in default is liable in respect of each offence to a fine.

(5)   In the case of any such refusal or default, the court may by order compel an immediate inspection of the books in respect of all proceedings of general meetings, or direct that the copies required be sent to the persons requiring them.

CHAPTER V

AUDITORS

Appointment of auditors

384. Duty to appoint auditors

(1)   Every company shall appoint an auditor or auditors in accordance with this Chapter.

This is subject to section 388A (certain companies exempt from obligation to appoint auditors).

(2)   Auditors shall be appointed in accordance with section 385 (appointment at general meeting at which accounts are laid), except in the case of a private company which has elected to dispense with the laying of accounts in which case the appointment shall be made in accordance with section 385A.

(3)   References in this Chapter to the end of the time for appointing auditors are to the end of the time within which an appointment must be made under section 385(2) or 385A(2), according to whichever of those sections applies.

(4)   Sections 385 and 385A have effect subject to section 386 under which a private company may elect to dispense with the obligation to appoint auditors annually.

385.   Appointment at general meeting at which accounts laid

(1)   This section applies to every public company and to a private company which has not elected to dispense with the laying of accounts.

(2)   The company shall, at each general meeting at which accounts are laid, appoint an auditor or auditors to hold office from the conclusion of that meeting until the conclusion of the next general meeting at which accounts are laid.

(3)   The first auditors of the company may be appointed by the directors at any time before the first general meeting of the company at which accounts are laid; and auditors so appointed shall hold office until the conclusion of that meeting.

(4)   If the directors fail to exercise their powers under subsection (3), the powers may be exercised by the company in general meeting.

385A.   Appointment by private company which is not obliged to lay accounts

(1)   This section applies to a private company which has elected in accordance with section 252 to dispense with the laying of accounts before the company in general meeting.

(2)   Auditors shall be appointed by the company in general meeting before the end of the period of 28 days beginning with the day on which copies of the company's annual accounts for the previous financial year are sent to members under section 238 or, if notice is given under section 253(2) requiring the laying of the accounts before the company in general meeting, the conclusion of that meeting.

        Auditors so appointed shall hold office from the end of that period or, as the case may be, the conclusion of that meeting until the end of the time for appointing auditors for the next financial year.

(3)   The first auditors of the company may be appointed by the directors at any time before—

        (a)   the end of the period of 28 days beginning with the day on which copies of the company's first annual accounts are sent to members under section 238, or

        (b)   if notice is given under section 253(2) requiring the laying of the accounts before the company in general meeting, the beginning of that meeting;

        and auditors so appointed shall hold office until the end of that period or, as the case may be, the conclusion of that meeting.

(4)   If the directors fail to exercise their powers under subsection (3), the powers may be exercised by the company in general meeting.

(5)   Auditors holding office when the election is made shall, unless the company in general meeting determines otherwise, continue to hold office until the end of the time for appointing auditors for the next financial year; and auditors holding office when an election ceases to have effect shall continue to hold office until the conclusion of the next general meeting of the company at which accounts are laid.

386.   Election by private company to dispense with annual appointment

(1)   A private company may elect (by elective resolution in accordance with section 379A) to dispense with the obligation to appoint auditors annually.

(2)   When such an election is in force the company's auditors shall be deemed to be re-appointed for each succeeding financial year on the expiry of the time for appointing auditors for that year, unless—

(a)   the directors of the company have taken advantage of the exemption conferred by section 249A or 249AA, or

(b)   a resolution has been passed under section 393 to the effect that their appointment should be brought to an end.

(3)   If the election ceases to be in force, the auditors then holding office shall continue to hold office—

(a)   where section 385 then applies, until the conclusion of the next general meeting of the company at which accounts are laid;

(b)   where section 385A then applies, until the end of the time for appointing auditors for the next financial year under that section.

(4)   No account shall be taken of any loss of the opportunity of further deemed re-appointment under this section in ascertaining the amount of any compensation or damages payable to an auditor on his ceasing to hold office for any reason.

387.   Appointment by Secretary of State in default of appointment by company

(1)   If in any case no auditors are appointed, re-appointed or deemed to be re-appointed before the end of the time for appointing auditors, the Secretary of State may appoint a person to fill the vacancy.

(2)   In such a case the company shall within one week of the end of the time for appointing auditors give notice to the Secretary of State of his power having become exercisable.

        If a company fails to give the notice required by this subsection, the company and every officer of it who is in default is guilty of an offence and liable to a fine and, for continued contravention, to a daily default fine.

388.   Filling of casual vacancies

(1)   The directors, or the company in general meeting, may fill a casual vacancy in the office of auditor.

(2)   While such a vacancy continues, any surviving or continuing auditor or auditors may continue to act.

(3)   Special notice is required for a resolution at a general meeting of a company—

(a)   filling a casual vacancy in the office of auditor, or

(b)   re-appointing as auditor a retiring auditor who was appointed by the directors to fill a casual vacancy.

(4)   On receipt of notice of such an intended resolution the company shall forthwith send a copy of it—

(a)   to the person proposed to be appointed, and

(b)   if the casual vacancy was caused by the resignation of an auditor, to the auditor who resigned.

388A.   Certain companies exempt from obligation to appoint auditors

(1)   A company which by virtue of section 249A (certain categories of small company) or section 249AA (dormant companies) is exempt from the provisions of Part VII relating to the audit of accounts is also exempt from the obligation to appoint auditors.

(2)   The following provisions apply if a company which has been exempt from those provisions ceases to be so exempt.

(3)   Where section 385 applies (appointment at general meeting at which accounts are laid), the directors may appoint auditors at any time before the next meeting of the company at which accounts are to be laid; and auditors so appointed shall hold office until the conclusion of that meeting.

(4)   Where section 385A applies (appointment by private company not obliged to lay accounts), the directors may appoint auditors at any time before—

(a)   the end of the period of 28 days beginning with the day on which copies of the company's annual accounts are next sent to members under section 238, or

(b)   if notice is given under section 253(2) requiring the laying of the accounts before the company in general meeting, the beginning of that meeting;

and auditors so appointed shall hold office until the end of that period or, as the case may be, the conclusion of that meeting.

(5)   If the directors fail to exercise their powers under subsection (3) or (4), the powers may be exercised by the company in general meeting.

389.   ...

Rights of auditors

389A. Rights to information

(1)   An auditor of a company—

(a)   has a right of access at all times to the company's books, accounts and vouchers (in whatever form they are held), and

(b)   may require any of the persons mentioned in subsection (2) to provide him with such information or explanations as he thinks necessary for the performance of his duties as auditor.

(2)   Those persons are—

(a)   any officer or employee of the company;

(b)   any person holding or accountable for any of the company's books, accounts or vouchers;

(c)   any subsidiary undertaking of the company which is a body corporate incorporated in Great Britain;

(d)   any officer, employee or auditor of any such subsidiary undertaking or any person holding or accountable for any books, accounts or vouchers of any such subsidiary undertaking;

(e)   any person who fell within any of paragraphs (a) to (d) at a time to which the information or explanations required by the auditor relates or relate.

(3)   Where a parent company has a subsidiary undertaking which is not a body corporate incorporated in Great Britain, the auditor of the parent company may require it to obtain from any of the persons mentioned in subsection (4) such information or explanations as he may reasonably require for the purposes of his duties as auditor.

(4)   Those persons are—

(a)   the undertaking;

(b)   any officer, employee or auditor of the undertaking;

(c)   any person holding or accountable for any of the undertaking's books, accounts or vouchers;

(d)   any person who fell within paragraph (b) or (c) at a time to which the information or explanations relates or relate.

(5)   If so required, the parent company must take all such steps as are reasonably open to it to obtain the information or explanations from the person within subsection (4) from whom the auditor has required the company to obtain the information or explanations.

(6)   A statement made by a person in response to a requirement under subsection (1)(b) or (3) may not be used in evidence against him in any criminal proceedings except proceedings for an offence under section 389B.

(7)   Nothing in this section or section 389B compels any person to disclose information in respect of which in an action in the High Court a claim to legal professional privilege, or in an action in the Court of Session a claim to confidentiality of communications, could be maintained.

389B. Offences relating to the provision of information to auditors

(1)   If a person knowingly or recklessly makes to an auditor of a company a statement (oral or written) that—

(a)   conveys or purports to convey any information or explanations which the auditor requires, or is entitled to require, under section 389A(1)(b), and

(b)   is misleading, false or deceptive in a material particular,
the person is guilty of an offence and liable to imprisonment or a fine, or both.

(2)   A person who fails to comply with a requirement under section 389A(1)(b) without delay is guilty of an offence and is liable to a fine.

(3)   However, it is a defence for a person charged with an offence under subsection (2) to prove that it was not reasonably practicable for him to provide the required information or explanations.

(4)   If a company fails to comply with section 389A(5), the company and every officer of it who is in default is guilty of an offence and liable to a fine.

(5)   Nothing in this section affects any right of an auditor to apply for an injunction to enforce any of his rights under section 389A.

390. Right to attend company meetings, &c

(1)   A company's auditors are entitled—
    (a)   to receive all notices of, and other communications relating to, any general meeting which a member of the company is entitled to receive;
    (b)   to attend any general meeting of the company; and
    (c)   to be heard at any general meeting which they attend on any part of the business of the meeting which concerns them as auditors.

(1A)   Subsections (4A) to (4G) of section 369 (electronic communication of notices of meetings) apply for the purpose of determining whether notice of a meeting is received by the company's auditors as they apply in determining whether such a notice is given to any person.

(2)   In relation to a written resolution proposed to be agreed to by a private company in accordance with section 381A, the company's auditors are entitled—
    (a)   to receive all such communications relating to the resolution as, by virtue of any provision of Schedule 15A, are required to be supplied to a member of the company,
    (b)–(d)...

(3)   The right to attend or be heard at a meeting is exercisable in the case of a body corporate or partnership by an individual authorised by it in writing to act as its representative at the meeting.

Remuneration of auditors

390A. Remuneration of auditors

(1)   The remuneration of auditors appointed by the company in general meeting shall be fixed by the company in general meeting or in such manner as the company in general meeting may determine.

(2)   The remuneration of auditors appointed by the directors of the Secretary of State shall be fixed by the directors of the Secretary of State, as the case may be.

(3)   There shall be stated in a note to the company's annual accounts the amount of the remuneration of the company's auditors in their capacity as such.

(4)   For the purposes of this section "remuneration" includes sums paid in respect of expenses.

(5)   This section applies in relation to benefits in kind as to *payments in cash, and in relation to any such benefit references to its amount are to its estimated money value [payments of money].*
The nature of any such benefit shall also be disclosed.

Note. Subsection (3) and the italicized words in subsection (5) are repealed, and the subsequent italicized words in square brackets in subsection (5) are substituted, by the Companies (Audit, Investigations and Community Enterprise) Act 2004, ss. 7(2), 64, Sch. 8, as from 1 October 2005.

390B. *Remuneration of auditors or their associates for non-audit work*

(1)   The Secretary of State may make provision by regulations for securing the disclosure of the amount of any remuneration received or receivable by a company's auditors or their associates in respect of services other than those of auditors in their capacity as such.

(2)   The regulations may—
    (a)   provide that "remuneration" includes sums paid in respect of expenses,

(b)   apply in relation to benefits in kind as to payments in cash, and in relation to any such
       benefit require disclosure of its nature and its estimated money value,

(c)   define "associate" in relation to an auditor,

(d)   require the disclosure of remuneration in respect of services rendered to associated
       undertakings of the company, and

(e)   define "associated undertaking" for that purpose.

(3)   The regulations may require the auditors to disclose the relevant information in their report or
       require the relevant information to be disclosed in a note to the company's accounts and require
       the auditors to supply the directors of the company with such information as is necessary to
       enable that disclosure to be made.

(4)   The regulations may make different provision for different cases.

(5)   Regulations under this section shall be made by statutory instrument which shall be subject to
       annulment in pursuance of a resolution of either House of Parliament.

       Note. This section is substituted by the following provision by the Companies (Audit, Investigations and
       Community Enterprise) Act 2004, s. 7(1), as from 1 October 2005.

390B.   Disclosure of services provided by auditors or associates and related remuneration

(1)   The Secretary of State may make provision by regulations for securing the disclosure of—

(a)   the nature of any services provided for a company by the company's auditors (whether in
       their capacity as such or otherwise) or by their associates;

(b)   the amount of any remuneration received or receivable by a company's auditors, or their
       associates, in respect of any services within paragraph (a).

(2)   The regulations may provide—

(a)   for disclosure of the nature of any services provided to be made by reference to any class or
       description of services specified in the regulations (or any combination of services, however
       described);

(b)   for the disclosure of amounts of remuneration received or receivable in respect of services
       of any class or description specified in the regulations (or any combination of services,
       however described);

(c)   for the disclosure of separate amounts so received or receivable by the company's auditors
       or any of their associates, or of aggregate amounts so received or receivable by all or any of
       those persons.

(3)   The regulations may—

(a)   provide that "remuneration" includes sums paid in respect of expenses;

(b)   apply to benefits in kind as well as to payments of money, and require the disclosure of the
       nature of any such benefits and their estimated money value;

(c)   apply to services provided for associates of a company as well as to those provided for a
       company;

(d)   define "associate" in relation to an auditor and a company respectively.

(4)   The regulations may provide that any disclosure required by the regulations is to be made—

(a)   in a note to the company's annual accounts (in the case of its individual accounts) or in such
       manner as is specified in the regulations (in the case of group accounts),

(b)   in the directors' report required by section 234, or

(c)   in the auditors' report under section 235.

(5)   If the regulations provide that any such disclosure is to be made as mentioned in subsection (4)(a)
       or (b), the regulations may—

(a)   require the auditors to supply the directors of the company with any information necessary
       to enable the disclosure to be made;

(b)   provide for any provision within subsection (6) to apply in relation to a failure to make the
       disclosure as it applies in relation to a failure to comply with a requirement of this Act or (as
       the case may be) a provision of Part 7.

(6)   The provisions are—

(a)   sections 233(5) and 234(5); and

(b)   any provision of sections 245 to 245C.

(7)   *The regulations may make different provision for different cases.*

(8)   *Nothing in subsections (2) to (7) affects the generality of subsection (1).*

(9)   *Regulations under this section shall be made by statutory instrument which shall be subject to annulment in pursuance of a resolution of either House of Parliament.*

Note. See the note to the original section 390B above.

Removal, resignation, &c of auditors

391.   Removal of auditors

(1)   A company may by ordinary resolution at any time remove an auditor from office, notwithstanding anything in any agreement between it and him.

(2)   Where a resolution removing an auditor is passed at a general meeting of a company, the company shall within 14 days give notice of that fact in the prescribed form to the registrar.

If a company fails to give the notice required by this subsection, the company and every officer of it who is in default is guilty of an offence and liable to a fine and, for continued contravention, to a daily default fine.

(3)   Nothing in this section shall be taken as depriving a person removed under it of compensation or damages payable to him in respect of the termination of his appointment as auditor or of any appointment terminating with that as auditor.

(4)   An auditor of a company who has been removed has, notwithstanding his removal, the rights conferred by section 390 in relation to any general meeting of the company—

(a)   at which his term of office would otherwise have expired, or

(b)   at which it is proposed to fill the vacancy caused by his removal.

In such a case the references in that section to matters concerning the auditors as auditors shall be construed as references to matters concerning him as a former auditor.

391A.   Rights of auditors who are removed or not re-appointed

(1)   Special notice is required for a resolution at a general meeting of a company—

(a)   removing an auditor before the expiration of his term of office, or

(b)   appointing as auditor a person other than a retiring auditor.

(2)   On receipt of notice of such an intended resolution the company shall forthwith send a copy of it to the person proposed to be removed or, as the case may be, to the person proposed to be appointed and to the retiring auditor.

(3)   The auditor proposed to be removed or (as the case may be) the retiring auditor may make with respect to the intended resolution representations in writing to the company (not exceeding a reasonable length) and request their notification to members of the company.

(4)   The company shall (unless the representations are received by it too late for it to do so)—

(a)   in any notice of the resolution given to members of the company, state the fact of the representations having been made, and

(b)   send a copy of the representations to every member of the company to whom notice of the meeting is or has been sent.

(5)   If a copy of any such representations is not sent out as required because received too late or because of the company's default, the auditor may (without prejudice to his right to be heard orally) require that the representations be read out at the meeting.

(6)   Copies of the representations need not be sent out and the representations need not be read at the meeting if, on the application either of the company or of any other person claiming to be aggrieved, the court is satisfied that the rights conferred by this section are being abused to secure needless publicity for defamatory matter; and the court may order the company's costs on the application to be paid in whole or in part by the auditor, notwithstanding that he is not a party to the application.

392.   Resignation of auditors

(1)   An auditor of a company may resign his office by depositing a notice in writing to that effect at the company's registered office.

The notice is not effective unless it is accompanied by the statement required by section 394.

(2)   An effective notice of resignation operates to bring the auditor's term of office to an end as of the date on which the notice is deposited or on such later date as may be specified in it.

(3)   The company shall within 14 days of the deposit of a notice of resignation send a copy of the notice to the registrar of companies.

If default is made in complying with this subsection, the company and every officer of it who is in default is guilty of an offence and liable to a fine and, for continued contravention, a daily default fine.

392A. Rights of resigning auditors

(1)   This section applies where an auditor's notice of resignation is accompanied by a statement of circumstances which he considers should be brought to the attention of members or creditors of the company.

(2)   He may deposit with the notice a signed requisition calling on the directors of the company forthwith duly to convene an extraordinary general meeting of the company for the purpose of receiving and considering such explanation of the circumstances connected with his resignation as he may wish to place before the meeting.

(3)   He may request the company to circulate to its members—

(a)   before the meeting convened on his requisition, or

(b)   before any general meeting at which his term of office would otherwise have expired or at which it is proposed to fill the vacancy caused by his resignation,

a statement in writing (not exceeding a reasonable length) of the circumstances connected with his resignation.

(4)   The company shall (unless the statement is received too late for it to comply)—

(a)   in any notice of the meeting given to members of the company, state the fact of the statement having been made, and

(b)   send a copy of the statement to every member of the company to whom notice of the meeting is or has been sent.

(5)   If the directors do not within 21 days from the date of the deposit of a requisition under this section proceed duly to convene a meeting for a day not more than 28 days after the date on which the notice convening the meeting is given, every director who failed to take all reasonable steps to secure that a meeting was convened as mentioned above is guilty of an offence and liable to a fine.

(6)   If a copy of the statement mentioned above is not sent out as required because received too late or because of the company's default, the auditor may (without prejudice to his right to be heard orally) require that the statement be read out at the meeting.

(7)   Copies of a statement need not be sent out and the statement need not be read out at the meeting if, on the application either of the company or of any other person who claims to be aggrieved, the court is satisfied that the rights conferred by this section are being abused to secure needless publicity for defamatory matter; and the court may order the company's costs on such an application to be paid in whole or in part by the auditor, notwithstanding that he is not a party to the application.

(8)   An auditor who has resigned has, notwithstanding his resignation, the rights conferred by section 390 in relation to any such general meeting of the company as is mentioned in subsection (3)(a) or (b).

In such a case the references in that section to matters concerning the auditors as auditors shall be construed as references to matters concerning him as a former auditor.

393.   Termination of appointment of auditors not appointed annually

(1)   When an election is in force under section 386 (election by private company to dispense with annual appointment), any member of the company may deposit notice in writing at the company's registered office proposing that the appointment of the company's auditors be brought to an end. No member may deposit more than one such notice in any financial year of the company.

(2)   If such a notice is deposited it is the duty of the directors—

   (a)   to convene a general meeting of the company for a date not more than 28 days after the date on which the notice was given, and

   (b)   to propose at the meeting a resolution in a form enabling the company to decide whether the appointment of the company's auditors should be brought to an end.

(3)   If the decision of the company at the meeting is that the appointment of the auditors should be brought to an end, the auditors shall not be deemed to be re-appointed when next they would be and, if the notice was deposited within the period immediately following the distribution of accounts, any deemed re-appointment for the financial year following that to which those accounts relate which has already occurred shall cease to have effect.

   The period immediately following the distribution of accounts means the period beginning with the day on which copies of the company's annual accounts are sent to members of the company under section 238 and ending 14 days after that day.

(4)   If the directors do not within 14 days from the date of the deposit of the notice proceed duly to convene a meeting, the member who deposited the notice (or, if there was more than one, any of them) may himself convene the meeting; but any meeting so convened shall not be held after the expiration of three months from that date.

(5)   A meeting convened under this section by a member shall be convened in the same manner, as nearly as possible, as that in which meetings are to be convened by directors.

(6)   Any reasonable expenses incurred by a member by reason of the failure of the directors duly to convene a meeting shall be made good to him by the company; and any such sums shall be recouped by the company from such of the directors as were in default out of any sums payable, or to become payable, by the company by way of fees or other remuneration in respect of their services.

(7)   This section has effect notwithstanding anything in any agreement between the company and its auditors; and no compensation or damages shall be payable by reason of the auditors' appointment being terminated under this section.

394.   Statement by person ceasing to hold office as auditors

(1)   Where an auditor ceases for any reason to hold office, he shall deposit at the company's registered office a statement of any circumstances connected with his ceasing to hold office which he considers should be brought to the attention of the members or creditors of the company or, if he considers that there are no such circumstances, a statement that there are none.

(2)   In the case of resignation, the statement shall be deposited along with the notice of resignation; in the case of failure to seek re-appointment, the statement shall be deposited not less than 14 days before the end of the time allowed for next appointing auditors; in any other case, the statement shall be deposited not later than the end of the period of 14 days beginning with the date on which he ceases to hold office.

(3)   If the statement is of circumstances which the auditor considers should be brought to the attention of the members or creditors of the company, the company shall within 14 days of the deposit of the statement either—

   (a)   send a copy of it to every person who under section 238 is entitled to be sent copies of the accounts, or

   (b)   apply to the court.

(4)   The company shall if it applies to the court notify the auditor of the application.

(5)   Unless the auditor receives notice of such an application before the end of the period of 21 days beginning with the day on which he deposited the statement, he shall within a further seven days send a copy of the statement to the registrar.

(6)   If the court is satisfied that the auditor is using the statement to secure needless publicity for
        defamatory matter—
        (a)   it shall direct that copies of the statement need not be sent out, and
        (b)   it may further order the company's costs on the application to be paid in whole or in part by
              the auditor, notwithstanding that he is not a party to the application;
        and the company shall within 14 days of the court's decision send to the persons mentioned in
        subsection (3)(a) a statement setting out the effect of the order.
(7)   If the court is not so satisfied, the company shall within 14 days of the court's decision—
        (a)   send copies of the statement to the persons mentioned in subsection (3)(a), and
        (b)   notify the auditor of the court's decision;
        and the auditor shall within seven days of receiving such notice send a copy of the statement to
        the registrar.

394A. Offences of failing to comply with s 394

(1)   If a person ceasing to hold office as auditor fails to comply with section 394 he is guilty of an
        offence and liable to a fine.
(2)   In proceedings for an offence under subsection (1) it is a defence for the person charged to show
        that he took all reasonable steps and exercised all due diligence to avoid the commission of the
        offence.
(3)   Sections 733 (liability of individuals for corporate default) and 734 (criminal proceedings against
        unincorporated bodies) apply to an offence under subsection (1).
(4)   If a company makes default in complying with section 394, the company and every officer of it
        who is in default is guilty of an offence and liable to a fine and, for continued contravention, to a
        daily default fine.

PART XII

REGISTRATION OF CHARGES

Note. It is widely believed that sections 395–420, inserted by Part IV of the Companies Act 1989, in place of
the original sections 395–424 reproduced below, as from a day to be appointed, will not now be brought into
force in their current form.

CHAPTER I

REGISTRATION OF CHARGES (ENGLAND AND WALES)

395.   Certain charges void if not registered

(1)   Subject to the provisions of this Chapter, a charge created by a company registered in England
        and Wales and being a charge to which this section applies is, so far as any security on the
        company's property or undertaking is conferred by the charge, void against the liquidator or
        administrator and any creditor of the company, unless the prescribed particulars of the charge
        together with the instrument (if any) by which the charge is created or evidenced, are delivered to
        or received by the registrar of companies for registration in the manner required by this Chapter
        within 21 days after the date of the charge's creation.
(2)   Subsection (1) is without prejudice to any contract or obligation for repayment of the money
        secured by the charge; and when a charge becomes void under this section, the money secured by
        it immediately becomes payable.

396.   Charges which have to be registered

(1)   Section 395 applies to the following charges—
        (a)   a charge for the purpose of securing any issue of debentures,
        (b)   a charge on uncalled share capital of the company,
        (c)   a charge created or evidenced by an instrument which, if executed by an individual, would
              require registration as a bill of sale,

    (d)   a charge on land (wherever situated) or any interest in it, but not including a charge for any rent or other periodical sum issuing out of the land,

    (e)   a charge on book debts of the company,

    (f)   a floating charge on the Company's undertaking or property,

    (g)   a charge on calls made but not paid,

    (h)   a charge on a ship or aircraft, or any share in a ship,

    (j)   a charge on goodwill, or on any intellectual property.

(2)   Where a negotiable instrument has been given to secure the payment of any book debts of a company, the deposit of the instrument for the purpose of securing an advance to the company is not, for purposes of sections 395, to be treated as a charge on those book debts.

(3)   The holding of debentures entitling the holder to a charge on land is not for purposes of this section deemed to be an interest in land.

(3A)   The following are "intellectual property" for the purposes of this section—

    (a)   any patent, trade mark, ... registered design, copyright or design right;

    (b)   any licence under or in respect of any such right.

(4)   In this Chapter, "charge" includes mortgage.

397.   Formalities of registration (debentures)

(1)   Where a series of debentures containing, or giving by reference to another instrument, any charge to the benefit of which the debenture holders of that series are entitled pari passu is created by a company, it is for purposes of section 395 sufficient if there are delivered to or received by the registrar, within 21 days after the execution of the deed containing the charge (or, if there is no such deed, after the execution of any debentures of the series), the following particulars in the prescribed form—

    (a)   the total amount secured by the whole series, and

    (b)   the dates of the resolutions authorising the issue of the series and the date of the covering deed (if any) by which the security is created or defined, and

    (c)   a general description of the property charged, and

    (d)   the names of the trustees (if any) for the debenture holders,

together with the deed containing the charge or, if there is no such deed, one of the debentures of the series:

Provided that there shall be sent to the registrar of companies, for entry in the register, particulars in the prescribed form of the date and amount of each issue of debentures of the series, but any omission to do this does not affect the validity of any of those debentures.

(2)   Where any commission, allowance or discount has been paid or made either directly or indirectly by a company to a person in consideration of his—

    (a)   subscribing or agreeing to subscribe, whether absolutely or conditionally, for debentures of the company, or

    (b)   procuring or agreeing to procure subscriptions, whether absolute or conditional, for such debentures,

the particulars required to be sent for registration under section 395 shall include particulars as to the amount or rate per cent of the commission, discount or allowance so paid or made, but omission to do this does not affect the validity of the debentures issued.

(3)   The deposit of debentures as security for a debt of the company is not, for the purposes of subsection (2), treated as the issue of the debentures at a discount.

398.   Verification of charge on property outside United Kingdom

(1)   In the case of a charge created out of the United Kingdom comprising property situated outside the United Kingdom, the delivery to and the receipt by the registrar of companies of a copy (verified in the prescribed manner) of the instrument by which the charge is created or evidenced has the same effect for purposes of sections 395 to 398 as the delivery and receipt of the instrument itself.

(2)   In that case, 21 days after the date on which the instrument or copy could, in due course of post (and if despatched with due diligence), have been received in the United Kingdom are substituted for the 21 days mentioned in section 395(2) (or as the case may be, section 397(1)) as the time within which the particulars and instrument or copy are to be delivered to the registrar.

(3)   Where a charge is created in the United Kingdom but comprises property outside the United Kingdom, the instrument creating or purporting to create the charge may be sent for registration under section 395 notwithstanding that further proceedings may be necessary to make the charge valid or effectual according to the law of the country in which the property is situated.

(4)   Where a charge comprises property situated in Scotland or Northern Ireland and registration in the country where the property is situated is necessary to make the charge valid or effectual according to the law of that country, the delivery to and receipt by the registrar of a copy (verified in the prescribed manner) of the instrument by which the charge is created or evidenced, together with a certificate in the prescribed form stating that the charge was presented for registration in Scotland or Northern Ireland (as the case may be) on the date on which it was so presented has, for purposes of sections 395 to 398, the same effect as the delivery and receipt of the instrument itself.

399.   Company's duty to register charges it creates

(1)   It is a company's duty to send to the registrar of companies for registration the particulars of every charge created by the company and of the issues of debentures of a series requiring registration under sections 395 to 398; but registration of any such charge may be effected on the application of any person interested in it.

(2)   Where registration is effected on the application of some person other than the company, that person is entitled to recover from the company the amount of any fees properly paid by him to the registrar on the registration.

(3)   If a company fails to comply with subsection (1), then, unless the registration has been effected on the application of some other person, the company and every officer of it who is in default is liable to a fine and, for continued contravention, to a daily default fine.

400.   Charges existing on property acquired

(1)   This section applies where a company registered in England and Wales acquires property which is subject to a charge of any such kind as would, if it had been created by the company after the acquisition of the property, have been required to be registered under this Chapter.

(2)   The company shall cause the prescribed particulars of the charge, together with a copy (certified in the prescribed manner to be a correct copy) of the instrument (if any) by which the charge was created or is evidenced, to be delivered to the registrar of companies for registration in manner required by this Chapter within 21 days after the date on which the acquisition is completed.

(3)   However, if the property is situated and the charge was created outside Great Britain, 21 days after the date on which the copy of the instrument could in due course of post, and if despatched with due diligence, have been received in the United Kingdom is substituted for the 21 days above-mentioned as the time within which the particulars and copy of the instrument are to be delivered to the registrar.

(4)   If default is made in complying with this section, the company and every officer of it who is in default is liable to a fine and, for continued contravention, to a daily default fine.

401.   Register of charges to be kept by registrar of companies

(1)   The registrar of companies shall keep, with respect to each company, a register in the prescribed form of all the charges requiring registration under this Chapter; and he shall enter in the register with respect to such charges the following particulars—

        (a)   in the case of a charge to the benefit of which the holders of a series of debentures are entitled, the particulars specified in section 397(1),

        (b)   in the case of any other charge—

            (i)   if it is a charge created by the company, the date of its creation, and if it is a charge which was existing on property acquired by the company, the date of the acquisition of the property, and

    (ii)   the amount secured by the charge, and

    (iii) short particulars of the property charged, and

    (iv) the persons entitled to the charge.

(2)   The registrar shall give a certificate of the registration of any charge registered in pursuance of this Chapter, stating the amount secured by the charge.

The certificate—

    (a)   shall be either signed by the registrar, or authenticated by his official seal, and

    (b)   is conclusive evidence that the requirements of this Chapter as to registration have been satisfied.

(3)   The register kept in pursuance of this section shall be open to inspection by any person.

402.   Endorsement of certificate on debentures

(1)   The company shall cause a copy of every certificate of registration given under section 401 to be endorsed on every debenture or certificate of debenture stock which is issued by the company, and the payment of which is secured by the charge so registered.

(2)   But this does not require a company to cause a certificate of registration of any charge so given to be endorsed on any debenture or certificate of debenture stock issued by the company before the charge was created.

(3)   If a person knowingly and wilfully authorises or permits the delivery of a debenture or certificate of debenture stock which under this section is required to have endorsed on it a copy of a certificate of registration, without the copy being so endorsed upon it, he is liable (without prejudice to any other liability) to a fine.

403.   Entries of satisfaction and release

(1)   Subject to subsection (1A), the registrar of companies, on receipt of a statutory declaration in the prescribed form verifying, with respect to a registered charge,—

    (a)   that the debt for which the charge was given has been paid or satisfied in whole or in part, or

    (b)   that part of the property or undertaking charged has been released from the charge or has ceased to form part of the company's property or undertaking,

may enter on the register a memorandum of satisfaction in whole or in part, or of the fact that part of the property or undertaking has been released from the charge or has ceased to form part of the company's property or undertaking (as the case may be).

(1A)   The registrar of companies may make any such entry as is mentioned in subsection (1) where, instead of receiving such a statutory declaration as is mentioned in that subsection, he receives a statement by a director, secretary, administrator or administrative receiver of the company which is contained in an electronic communication and that statement—

    (a)   verifies the matters set out in paragraph (a) or (b) of that subsection,

    (b)   contains a description of the charge,

    (c)   states the date of creation of the charge and the date of its registration under this Chapter,

    (d)   states the name and address of the chargee or, in the case of a debenture, trustee, and

    (e)   where paragraph (b) of subsection (1) applies, contains short particulars of the property or undertaking which has been released from the charge, or which has ceased to form part of the company's property or undertaking (as the case may be).

(2)   Where the registrar enters a memorandum of satisfaction in whole, he shall if required furnish the company with a copy of it.

(2A)   Any person who makes a false statement under subsection (1A) which he knows to be false or does not believe to be true is liable to imprisonment or a fine, or both.

404.   Rectification of register of charges

(1)   The following applies if the court is satisfied that the omission to register a charge within the time required by this Chapter or that the omission or mis-statement of any particular with respect to any such charge or in a memorandum of satisfaction was accidental, or due to inadvertence or to

some other sufficient cause, or is not of a nature to prejudice the position of creditors or shareholders of the company, or that on other grounds it is just and equitable to grant relief.

(2) The court may, on the application of the company or a person interested, and on such terms and conditions as seem to the court just and expedient, order that the time for registration shall be extended or, as the case may be, that the omission or mis-statement shall be rectified.

405.   Registration of enforcement of security

(1) If a person obtains an order for the appointment of a receiver or manager of a company's property, or appoints such a receiver or manager under powers contained in an instrument, he shall within 7 days of the order or of the appointment under those powers, give notice of the fact to the registrar of companies; and the registrar shall enter the fact in the register of charges.

(2) Where a person appointed receiver or manager of a company's property under powers contained in an instrument ceases to act as such receiver or manager, he shall, on so ceasing, give the registrar notice to that effect, and the registrar shall enter the fact in the register of charges.

(3) A notice under this section shall be in the prescribed form.

(4) If a person makes default in complying with the requirements of this section, he is liable to a fine and, for continued contravention, to a daily default fine.

406.   Companies to keep copies of instruments creating charges

(1) Every company shall cause a copy of every instrument creating a charge requiring registration under this Chapter to be kept at its registered office.

(2) In the case of a series of uniform debentures, a copy of one debenture of the series is sufficient.

407.   Company's register of charges

(1) Every limited company shall keep at its registered office a register of charges and enter in it all charges specifically affecting property of the company and all floating charges on the company's undertaking or any of its property.

(2) The entry shall in each case give a short description of the property charged, the amount of the charge and, except in the case of securities to bearer, the names of the persons entitled to it.

(3) If an officer of the company knowingly and wilfully authorises or permits the omission of an entry required to be made in pursuance of this section, he is liable to a fine.

408.   Right to inspect instruments which create charges, etc

(1) The copies of instruments creating any charge requiring registration under this Chapter with the registrar of companies, and the register of charges kept in pursuance of section 407, shall be open during business hours (but subject to such reasonable restrictions as the company in general meeting may impose, so that not less than 2 hours in each day be allowed for inspection) to the inspection of any creditor or member of the company without fee.

(2) The register of charges shall also be open to the inspection of any other person on payment of such fee, not exceeding 5 pence, for each inspection, as the company may prescribe.

(3) If inspection of the copies referred to, or of the register, is refused, every officer of the company who is in default is liable to a fine and, for continued contravention, to a daily default fine.

(4) If such a refusal occurs in relation to a company registered in England and Wales, the court may by order compel an immediate inspection of the copies or register.

409.   Charges on property in England and Wales created by oversea company

(1) This Chapter extends to charges on property in England and Wales which are created, and to charges on property in England and Wales which is acquired, by a company (whether a company within the meaning of this Act or not) incorporated outside Great Britain which has an established place of business in England and Wales.

(2) In relation to such a company, sections 406 and 407 apply with the substitution, for the reference to the company's registered office, of a reference to its principal place of business in England and Wales.

CHAPTER II
REGISTRATION OF CHARGES (SCOTLAND)

410. Charges void unless registered

(1)   The following provisions of this Chapter have effect for the purpose of securing the registration in Scotland of charges created by companies.

(2)   Every charge created by a company, being a charge to which this section applies, is, so far as any security on the company's property or any part of it is conferred by the charge, void against the liquidator or administrator and any creditor of the company unless the prescribed particulars of the charge, together with a copy (certified in the prescribed manner to be a correct copy) of the instrument (if any) by which the charge is created or evidenced, are delivered to or received by the registrar of companies for registration in the manner required by this Chapter within 21 days after the date of the creation of the charge.

(3)   Subsection (2) is without prejudice to any contract or obligation for repayment of the money secured by the charge; and when a charge becomes void under this section the money secured by it immediately becomes payable.

(4)   This section applies to the following charges—

   (a)   a charge on land wherever situated, or any interest in such land (not including a charge for any rent ... or other periodical sum payable in respect of the land, but including a charge created by a heritable security within the meaning of section 9(8) of the Conveyancing and Feudal Reform (Scotland) Act 1970),

   (b)   a security over the uncalled share capital of the company,

   (c)   a security over incorporeal moveable property of any of the following categories—

      (i)   the book debts of the company,

      (ii)   calls made but not paid,

      (iii)   goodwill,

      (iv)   a patent or a licence under a patent,

      (v)   a trade mark,

      (vi)   a copyright or a licence under a copyright,

      (vii)   a registered design or a licence in respect of such a design,

      (viii) a design right or a licence under a design right,

   (d)   a security over a ship or aircraft or any share in a ship, and

   (e)   a floating charge.

(5)   In this Chapter "company" (except in section 424) means an incorporated company registered in Scotland; "registrar of companies" means the registrar or other officer performing under this Act the duty of registration of companies in Scotland; and references to the date of creation of a charge are—

   (a)   in the case of a floating charge, the date on which the instrument creating the floating charge was executed by the company creating the charge, and

   (b)   in any other case, the date on which the right of the person entitled to the benefit of the charge was constituted as a real right.

411. Charges on property outside United Kingdom

(1)   In the case of a charge created out of the United Kingdom comprising property situated outside the United Kingdom, the period of 21 days after the date on which the copy of the instrument creating it could (in due course of post, and if despatched with due diligence) have been received in the United Kingdom is substituted for the period of 21 days after the date of the creation of the charge as the time within which, under section 410(2), the particulars and copy are to be delivered to the registrar.

(2)   Where a charge is created in the United Kingdom but comprises property outside the United Kingdom, the copy of the instrument creating or purporting to create the charge may be sent for registration under section 410 notwithstanding that further proceedings may be necessary to make the charge valid or effectual according to the law of the country in which the property is situated.

412.   Negotiable instrument to secure book debts

Where a negotiable instrument has been given to secure the payment of any book debts of a company, the deposit of the instrument for the purpose of securing an advance to the company is not, for purposes of section 410, to be treated as a charge on those book debts.

413.   Charges associated with debentures

(1)   The holding of debentures entitling the holder to a charge on land is not, for the purposes of section 410, deemed to be an interest in land.

(2)   Where a series of debentures containing, or giving by reference to any other instrument, any charge to the benefit of which the debenture-holders of that series are entitled pari passu, is created by a company, it is sufficient for purposes of section 410 if there are delivered to or received by the registrar of companies within 21 days after the execution of the deed containing the charge or if there is no such deed, after the execution of any debentures of the series, the following particulars in the prescribed form—

(a)   the total amount secured by the whole series,

(b)   the dates of the resolutions authorising the issue of the series and the date of the covering deed (if any) by which the security is created or defined,

(c)   a general description of the property charged,

(d)   the names of the trustees (if any) for the debenture holders, and

(e)   in the case of a floating charge, a statement of any provisions of the charge and of any instrument relating to it which prohibit or restrict or regulate the power of the company to grant further securities ranking in priority to, or pari passu with, the floating charge, or which vary or otherwise regulate the order of ranking of the floating charge in relation to subsisting securities,

together with a copy of the deed containing the charge or, if there is no such deed, of one of the debentures of the series:

Provided that where more than one issue is made of debentures in the series, there shall be sent to the registrar of companies for entry in the register particulars (in the prescribed form) of the date and amount of each issue of debentures of the series, but any omission to do this does not affect the validity of any of those debentures.

(3)   Where any commission, allowance or discount has been paid or made, either directly or indirectly, by a company to any person in consideration of his subscribing or agreeing to subscribe, whether absolutely or conditionally, for any debentures of the company, or procuring or agreeing to procure subscriptions (whether absolute or conditional) for any such debentures, the particulars required to be sent for registration under section 410 include particulars as to the amount or rate per cent of the commission, discount or allowance so paid or made; but any omission to do this does not affect the validity of the debentures issued.

The deposit of any debentures as security for any debt of the company is not, for purposes of this subsection, treated as the issue of the debentures at a discount.

414.   Charge by way of ex facie absolute disposition, etc

(1)   For the avoidance of doubt, it is hereby declared that, in the case of a charge created by way of an ex facie absolute disposition or assignation qualified by a back letter or other agreement, or by a standard security qualified by an agreement, compliance with section 410(2) does not of itself render the charge unavailable as security for indebtedness incurred after the date of compliance.

(2)   Where the amount secured by a charge so created is purported to be increased by a further back letter or agreement, a further charge is held to have been created by the ex facie absolute disposition or assignation or (as the case may be) by the standard security, as qualified by the further back letter or agreement; and the provisions of this Chapter apply to the further charge as if—

(a)   references in this Chapter (other than in this section) to the charge were references to the further charge, and

(b)   references to the date of the creation of the charge were references to the date on which the further back letter or agreement was executed.

415.   Company's duty to register charges created by it

(1)   It is a company's duty to send to the registrar of companies for registration the particulars of every charge created by the company and of the issues of debentures of a series requiring registration under sections 410 to 414; but registration of any such charge may be effected on the application of any person interested in it.

(2)   Where registration is effected on the application of some person other than the company, that person is entitled to recover from the company the amount of any fees properly paid by him to the registrar on the registration.

(3)   If a company makes default in sending to the registrar for registration the particulars of any charge created by the company or of the issues of debentures of a series requiring registration as above mentioned, then, unless the registration has been effected on the application of some other person, the company and every officer of it who is in default is liable to a fine and, for continued contravention, to a daily default fine.

416.   Duty to register charges existing on property acquired

(1)   Where a company acquires any property which is subject to a charge of any kind as would, if it had been created by the company after the acquisition of the property, have been required to be registered under this Chapter, the company shall cause the prescribed particulars of the charge, together with a copy (certified in the prescribed manner to be a correct copy) of the instrument (if any) by which the charge was created or is evidenced, to be delivered to the registrar of companies for registration in the manner required by this Chapter within 21 days after the date on which the transaction was settled.

(2)   If, however, the property is situated and the charge was created outside Great Britain, 21 days after the date on which the copy of the instrument could (in due course of post, and if despatched with due diligence) have been received in the United Kingdom are substituted for 21 days after the settlement of the transaction as the time within which the particulars and the copy of the instrument are to be delivered to the registrar.

(3)   If default is made in complying with this section, the company and every officer of it who is in default is liable to a fine and, for continued contravention, to a daily default fine.

417.   Register of charges to be kept by registrar of companies

(1)   The registrar of companies shall keep, with respect to each company, a register in the prescribed form of all the charges requiring registration under this Chapter, and shall enter in the register with respect to such charges the particulars specified below.

(2)   In the case of a charge to the benefit of which the holders of a series of debentures are entitled, there shall be entered in the register the particulars specified in section 413(2).

(3)   In the case of any other charge there shall be entered—
(a)   if it is a charge created by the company, the date of its creation, and if it was a charge existing on property acquired by the company, the date of the acquisition of the property,
(b)   the amount secured by the charge,
(c)   short particulars of the property charged,
(d)   the persons entitled to the charge, and
(e)   in the case of a floating charge, a statement of any of the provisions of the charge and of any instrument relating to it which prohibit or restrict or regulate the company's power to grant further securities ranking in priority to, or pari passu with, the floating charge, or which vary or otherwise regulate the order of ranking of the floating charge in relation to subsisting securities.

(4)   The register kept in pursuance of this section shall be open to inspection by any person.

418.   Certificate of registration to be issued

(1)   The registrar of companies shall give a certificate of the registration of any charge registered in pursuance of this Chapter.

(2)   The certificate—

   (a)   shall be either signed by the registrar, or authenticated by his official seal,

   (b)   shall state the name of the company and the person first-named in the charge among those entitled to the benefit of the charge (or, in the case of a series of debentures, the name of the holder of the first such debenture to be issued) and the amount secured by the charge, and

   (c)   is conclusive evidence that the requirements of this Chapter as to registration have been complied with.

419.   Entries of satisfaction and relief

(1)   Subject to subsections (1A) and (1B), the registrar of companies, on application being made to him in the prescribed form, and on receipt of a statutory declaration in the prescribed form verifying, with respect to any registered charge,—

   (a)   that the debt for which the charge was given has been paid or satisfied in whole or in part, or

   (b)   that part of the property charged has been released from the charge or has ceased to form part of the company's property,

   may enter on the register a memorandum of satisfaction (in whole or in part) regarding that fact.

(1A)   On an application being made to him in the prescribed form, the registrar of companies may make any such entry as is mentioned in subsection (1) where, instead of receiving such a statutory declaration as is mentioned in that subsection, he receives a statement by a director, secretary, liquidator, receiver or administrator of the company which is contained in an electronic communication and that statement—

   (a)   verifies the matters set out in paragraph (a) or (b) of that subsection,

   (b)   contains a description of the charge,

   (c)   states the date of creation of the charge and the date of its registration under this Chapter,

   (d)   states the name and address of the chargee or, in the case of a debenture, trustee, and

   (e)   where paragraph (b) of subsection (1) applies, contains short particulars of the property which has been released from the charge, or which has ceased to form part of the company's property (as the case may be).

(1B)   Where the statement under subsection (1A) concerns the satisfaction of a floating charge, then there shall be delivered to the registrar a further statement which—

   (a)   is made by the creditor entitled to the benefit of the floating charge or a person authorised to act on his behalf;

   (b)   is incorporated into, or logically associated with, the electronic communication containing the statement; and

   (c)   certifies that the particulars contained in the statement are correct.

(2)   Where the registrar enters a memorandum of satisfaction in whole, he shall, if required, furnish the company with a copy of the memorandum.

(3)   Without prejudice to the registrar's duty under this section to require to be satisfied as above mentioned, he shall not be so satisfied unless—

   (a)   the creditor entitled to the benefit of the floating charge, or a person authorised to do so on his behalf, certifies as correct the particulars submitted to the registrar with respect to the entry on the register of a memorandum under this section, or

   (b)   the court, on being satisfied that such certification cannot readily be obtained, directs him accordingly.

(4)   Nothing in this section requires the company to submit particulars with respect to the entry in the register of a memorandum of satisfaction where the company, having created a floating charge over all or any part of its property, disposes of part of the property subject to the floating charge.

(5)   A memorandum or certification required for the purposes of this section shall be in such form as may be prescribed.

(5A)   Any person who makes a false statement under subsection (1A) or (1B) which he knows to be false or does not believe to be true is liable to imprisonment or a fine, or both.

420.   Rectification of register

The court, on being satisfied that the omission to register a charge within the time required by this Act or that the omission or mis-statement of any particular with respect to any such charge or in a memorandum of satisfaction was accidental, or due to inadvertence or to some other sufficient cause, or is not of a nature to prejudice the position of creditors or shareholders of the company, or that it is on other grounds just and equitable to grant relief, may, on the application of the company or any person interested, and on such terms and conditions as seem to the court just and expedient, order that the time for registration shall be extended or (as the case may be) that the omission or mis-statement shall be rectified.

421.   Copies of instruments creating charges to be kept by company

(1)   Every company shall cause a copy of every instrument creating a charge requiring registration under this Chapter to be kept at the company's registered office.

(2)   In the case of a series of uniform debentures, a copy of one debenture of the series is sufficient.

422.   Company's register of charges

(1)   Every company shall keep at its registered office a register of charges and enter in it all charges specifically affecting property of the company, and all floating charges on any property of the company.

(2)   There shall be given in each case a short description of the property charged, the amount of the charge and, except in the case of securities to bearer, the names of the persons entitled to it.

(3)   If an officer of the company knowingly and wilfully authorises or permits the omission of an entry required to be made in pursuance of this section, he is liable to a fine.

423.   Right to inspect copies of instruments, and company's register

(1)   The copies of instruments creating charges requiring registration under this Chapter with the registrar of companies, and the register of charges kept in pursuance of section 422, shall be open during business hours (but subject to such reasonable restrictions as the company in general meeting may impose, so that not less than 2 hours in each day be allowed for inspection) to the inspection of any creditor or member of the company without fee.

(2)   The register of charges shall be open to the inspection of any other person on payment of such fee, not exceeding 5 pence for each inspection, as the company may prescribe.

(3)   If inspection of the copies or register is refused, every officer of the company who is in default is liable to a fine and, for continued contravention, to a daily default fine.

(4)   If such a refusal occurs in relation to a company, the court may by order compel an immediate inspection of the copies or register.

424.   Extension of Chapter II

(1)   This Chapter extends to charges on property in Scotland which are created, and to charges on property in Scotland which is acquired, by a company incorporated outside Great Britain which has a place of business in Scotland.

(2)   In relation to such a company, sections 421 and 422 apply with the substitution, for the reference to the company's registered office, of a reference to its principal place of business in Scotland.

PART XIII
ARRANGEMENTS AND RECONSTRUCTIONS

425.   Power of company to compromise with creditors and members

(1)   Where a compromise or arrangement is proposed between a company and its creditors, or any class of them, or between the company and its members, or any class of them, the court may on the application of the company or any creditor or member of it, or in the case of a company being wound up or in administration, of the liquidator or administrator, order a meeting of the creditors

or class of creditors, or of the members of the company or class of members (as the case may be), to be summoned in such manner as the court directs.

(2) If a majority in number representing three-fourths in value of the creditors or class of creditors or members or class of members (as the case may be), present and voting either in person or by proxy at the meeting, agree to any compromise or arrangement, the compromise or arrangement, if sanctioned by the court, is binding on all creditors or the class of creditors or on the members or class of members (as the case may be), and also on the company or, in the case of a company in the course of being wound up, on the liquidator and contributories of the company.

(3) The court's order under subsection (2) has no effect until an office copy of it has been delivered to the registrar of companies for registration; and a copy of every such order shall be annexed to every copy of the company's memorandum issued after the order has been made or, in the case of a company not having a memorandum, of every copy so issued of the instrument constituting the company or defining its constitution.

(4) If a company makes default in complying with subsection (3), the company and every officer of it who is in default is liable to a fine.

(5) An order under subsection (1) pronounced in Scotland by the judge acting as vacation judge in pursuance of section 4 of the Administration of Justice (Scotland) Act 1933 is not subject to review, reduction, suspension or stay of execution.

(6) In this section and the next—
(a) "company" means any company liable to be wound up under this Act, and
(b) "arrangement" includes a reorganisation of the company's share capital by the consolidation of shares of different classes or by the division of shares into shares of different classes, or by both of those methods.

426.   Information as to compromise to be circulated

(1) The following applies where a meeting of creditors or any class of creditors, or of members or any class of members, is summoned under section 425.

(2) With every notice summoning the meeting which is sent to a creditor or member there shall be sent also a statement explaining the effect of the compromise or arrangement and in particular stating any material interests of the directors of the company (whether as directors or as members or as creditors of the company or otherwise) and the effect on those interests of the compromise or arrangement, in so far as it is different from the effect on the like interests of other persons.

(3) In every notice summoning the meeting which is given by advertisement there shall be included either such a statement as above-mentioned or a notification of the place at which, and the manner in which, creditors or members entitled to attend the meeting may obtain copies of the statement.

(4) Where the compromise or arrangement affects the rights of debenture holders of the company, the statement shall give the like explanation as respects the trustees of any deed for securing the issue of the debentures as it is required to give as respects the company's directors.

(5) Where a notice given by advertisement includes a notification that copies of a statement explaining the effect of the compromise or arrangement proposed can be obtained by creditors or members entitled to attend the meeting, every such creditor or member shall, on making application in the manner indicated by the notice, be furnished by the company free of charge with a copy of the statement.

(6) If a company makes default in complying with any requirement of this section, the company and every officer of it who is in default is liable to a fine; and for this purpose a liquidator or administrator of the company and a trustee of a deed for securing the issue of debentures of the company is deemed an officer of it.
However, a person is not liable under this subsection if he shows that the default was due to the refusal of another person, being a director or trustee for debenture holders, to supply the necessary particulars of his interests.

(7) It is the duty of any director of the company, and of any trustee for its debenture holders, to give notice to the company of such matters relating to himself as may be necessary for purposes of this section; and any person who makes default in complying with this subsection is liable to a fine.

427. Provisions for facilitating company reconstruction or amalgamation

(1)   The following applies where application is made to the court under section 425 for the sanctioning of a compromise or arrangement proposed between a company and any such persons as are mentioned in that section.

(2)   If it is shown—

(a)   that the compromise or arrangement has been proposed for the purposes of, or in connection with, a scheme for the reconstruction of any company or companies, or the amalgamation of any two or more companies, and

(b)   that under the scheme the whole or any part of the undertaking or the property of any company concerned in the scheme ("a transferor company") is to be transferred to another company ("the transferee company"),

the court may, either by the order sanctioning the compromise or arrangement or by any subsequent order, make provision for all or any of the following matters.

(3)   The matters for which the court's order may make provision are—

(a)   the transfer to the transferee company of the whole or any part of the undertaking and of the property or liabilities of any transferor company,

(b)   the allotting or appropriation by the transferee company of any shares, debentures, policies or other like interests in that company which under the compromise or arrangement are to be allotted or appropriated by that company to or for any person,

(c)   the continuation by or against the transferee company of any legal proceedings pending by or against any transferor company,

(d)   the dissolution, without winding up, of any transferor company,

(e)   the provision to be made for any persons who, within such time and in such manner as the court directs, dissent from the compromise or arrangement,

(f)   such incidental, consequential and supplemental matters as are necessary to secure that the reconstruction or amalgamation is fully and effectively carried out.

(4)   If an order under this section provides for the transfer of property or liabilities, then—

(a)   that property is by virtue of the order transferred to, and vests in, the transferee company, and

(b)   those liabilities are, by virtue of the order, transferred to and become liabilities of that company;

and property (if the order so directs) vests freed from any charge which is by virtue of the compromise or arrangement to cease to have effect.

(5)   Where an order is made under this section, every company in relation to which the order is made shall cause an office copy of the order to be delivered to the registrar of companies for registration within 7 days after its making; and if default is made in complying with this subsection, the company and every officer of it who is in default is liable to a fine and, for continued contravention, to a daily default fine.

(6)   In this section the expression "property" includes property, rights and powers of every description; the expression "liabilities" includes duties and "company" includes only a company as defined in section 735(1).

427A. Application of ss 425–427 to mergers and divisions of public companies

(1)   Where—

(a)   a compromise or arrangement is proposed between a public company and any such persons as are mentioned in section 425(1) for the purposes of, or in connection with, a scheme for the reconstruction of any company or companies or the amalgamation of any two or more companies,

(b)   the circumstances are as specified in any of the Cases described in subsection (2), and

(c)   the consideration for the transfer or each of the transfers envisaged in the Case in question is to be shares in the transferee company or any of the transferee companies receivable by members of the transferor company or transferor companies, with or without any cash payment to members, sections 425 to 427 shall, as regards that compromise or arrangement, have effect subject to the provisions of this section and Schedule 15B.

(2)   The Cases referred to in subsection (1) are as follows—

Case 1

Where under the scheme the undertaking, property and liabilities of the company in respect of which the compromise or arrangement in question is proposed are to be transferred to another public company, other than one formed for the purpose of, or in connection with, the scheme.

Case 2

Where under the scheme the undertaking, property and liabilities of each of two or more public companies concerned in the scheme, including the company in respect of which the compromise or arrangement in question is proposed, are to be transferred to a company (whether or not a public company) formed for the purpose of, or in connection with, the scheme.

Case 3

Where under the scheme the undertaking, property and liabilities of the company in respect of which the compromise or arrangement in question is proposed are to be divided among and transferred to two or more companies each of which is either—

(a)   a public company, or

(b)   a company (whether or not a public company) formed for the purposes of, or in connection with, the scheme.

(3)   Before sanctioning any compromise or arrangement under section 425(2) the court may, on the application of any pre-existing transferee company or any member or creditor of it or, where the company is in administration, the administrator, order a meeting of the members of the company or any class of them or of the creditors of the company or any class of them to be summoned in such manner as the court directs.

(4)   This section does not apply where the company in respect of which the compromise or arrangement is proposed is being wound up.

(5)   This section does not apply to compromises or arrangements in respect of which an application has been made to the court for an order under section 425(1) before 1st January 1988.

(6)   Where section 427 would apply in the case of a scheme but for the fact that the transferee company or any of the transferee companies is a company within the meaning of Article 3 of the Companies (Northern Ireland) Order 1986 (and thus not within the definition of "company" in subsection (6) of section 427), section 427 shall apply notwithstanding that fact.

(7)   In the case of a scheme mentioned in subsection (1), for a company within the meaning of Article 3 of the Companies (Northern Ireland) Order 1986, the reference in section 427(5) to the registrar of companies shall have effect as a reference to the registrar as defined in Article 2 of that Order.

(8)   In this section and Schedule 15B—

"transferor company" means a company whose undertaking, property and liabilities are to be transferred by means of a transfer envisaged in any of the Cases specified in subsection (2);

"transferee company" means a company to which a transfer envisaged in any of those Cases is to be made;

"pre-existing transferee company" means a transferee company other than one formed for the purpose of, or in connection with, the scheme;

"compromise or arrangement" means a compromise or arrangement to which subsection (1) applies;

"the scheme" means the scheme mentioned in subsection (1)(a);

"company" includes only a company as defined in section 735(1) except that, in the case of a transferee company, it also includes a company as defined in Article 3 of the Companies (Northern Ireland) Order 1986 (referred to in these definitions as a "Northern Ireland company");

"public company" means, in relation to a transferee company which is a Northern Ireland company, a public company within the meaning of article 12 of the Companies (Northern Ireland) Order 1986;

"the registrar of companies" means, in relation to a transferee company which is a Northern Ireland company, the registrar as defined in Article 2 of the Companies (Northern Ireland) Order 1986;

"the Gazette" means, in relation to a transferee company which is a Northern Ireland company, the Belfast Gazette;

"Case 1 Scheme", "Case 2 Scheme" and "Case 3 Scheme" mean a scheme of the kind described in Cases 1, 2 and 3 of subsection (2) respectively;

"property" and "liabilities" have the same meaning as in section 427.

PART XIIIA
TAKEOVER OFFERS

428. **"Takeover offers"**

(1) In this Part of this Act "a takeover offer" means an offer to acquire all the shares, or all the shares of any class or classes, in a company (other than shares which at the date of the offer are already held by the offeror), being an offer on terms which are the same in relation to all the shares to which the offer relates or, where those shares include shares of different classes, in relation to all the shares of each class.

(2) In subsection (1) "shares" means shares (other than relevant treasury shares) which have been allotted on the date of the offer, but a takeover offer may include among the shares to which it relates—

   (a)   all or any shares that are allotted after the date of the offer but before a specified date;

   (b)   all or any relevant treasury shares that cease to be held as treasury shares before a specified date;

   (c)   all or any other relevant treasury shares.

(2A) In this section—

   "relevant treasury shares" means shares which—

   (a)   are held by the company as treasury shares on the date of the offer; or

   (b)   become shares held by the company as treasury shares after that date but before a specified date;

   "specified date" means a date specified in or determined in accordance with the terms of the offer.

(3) The terms offered in relation to any shares shall for the purposes of this section be treated as being the same in relation to all the shares or, as the case may be, all the shares of a class to which the offer relates notwithstanding any variation permitted by subsection (4).

(4) A variation is permitted by this subsection where—

   (a)   the law of a country or territory outside the United Kingdom precludes an offer of consideration in the form or any of the forms specified in the terms in question or precludes it except after compliance by the offeror with conditions with which he is unable to comply or which he regards as unduly onerous; and

   (b)   the variation is such that the persons to whom an offer of consideration in that form is precluded are able to receive consideration otherwise than in that form but of substantially equivalent value.

(5) The reference in subsection (1) to shares already held by the offeror includes a reference to shares which he has contracted to acquire but that shall not be construed as including shares which are the subject of a contract binding the holder to accept the offer when it is made, being a contract entered into by the holder either for no consideration and under seal or for no consideration other than a promise by the offeror to make the offer.

(6) In the application of subsection (5) to Scotland, the words "and under seal" shall be omitted.

(7)   Where the terms of an offer make provision for their revision and for acceptances on the previous terms to be treated as acceptances on the revised terms, the revision shall not be regarded for the purposes of this Part of this Act as the making of a fresh offer and references in this Part of this Act to the date of the offer shall accordingly be construed as references to the date on which the original offer was made.

(8)   In this Part of this Act "the offeror" means, subject to section 430D, the person making a takeover offer and "the company" means the company whose shares are the subject of the offer.

429.   Right of offeror to buy out minority shareholders

(1)   If, in a case in which a takeover offer does not relate to shares of different classes, the offeror has by virtue of acceptances of the offer acquired or contracted to acquire not less than nine-tenths in value of the shares to which the offer relates ... he may give notice to the holder of any shares to which the offer relates which the offeror has not acquired or contracted to acquire that he desires to acquire those shares.

(2)   If, in a case in which a takeover offer relates to shares of different classes, the offeror has by virtue of acceptances of the offer acquired or contracted to acquire not less than nine-tenths in value of the shares of any class to which the offer relates ..., he may give notice to the holder of any shares of that class which the offeror has not acquired or contracted to acquire that he desires to acquire those shares.

(3)   No notice shall be given under subsection (1) or (2) unless the offeror has acquired or contracted to acquire the shares necessary to satisfy the minimum specified in that subsection before the end of the period of four months beginning with the date of the offer; and no such notice shall be given after the end of the period of two months beginning with the date on which he has acquired or contracted to acquire shares which satisfy that minimum.

(4)   Any notice under this section shall be given in the prescribed manner; and when the offeror gives the first notice in relation to an offer he shall send a copy of it to the company together with a statutory declaration by him in the prescribed form stating that the conditions for the giving of the notice are satisfied.

(5)   Where the offeror is a company (whether or not a company within the meaning of this Act) the statutory declaration shall be signed by a director.

(6)   Any person who fails to send a copy of a notice or a statutory declaration as required by subsection (4) or makes such a declaration for the purposes of that subsection knowing it to be false or without having reasonable grounds for believing it to be true shall be liable to imprisonment or a fine, or both, and for continued failure to send the copy or declaration, to a daily default fine.

(7)   If any person is charged with an offence for failing to send a copy of a notice as required by subsection (4) it is a defence for him to prove that he took reasonable steps for securing compliance with that subsection.

(8)   Where during the period within which a takeover offer can be accepted the offeror acquires or contracts to acquire any of the shares to which the offer relates but otherwise than by virtue of acceptances of the offer, then, if—

(a)   the value of the consideration for which they are acquired or contracted to be acquired ("the acquisition consideration") does not at that time exceed the value of the consideration specified in the terms of the offer; or

(b)   those terms are subsequently revised so that when the revision is announced the value of the acquisition consideration, at the time mentioned in paragraph (a) above, no longer exceeds the value of the consideration specified in those terms,

the offeror shall be treated for the purposes of this section as having acquired or contracted to acquire those shares by virtue of acceptances of the offer; but in any other case those shares shall be treated as excluded from those to which the offer relates.

430. **Effect of notice under s 429**

(1)   The following provisions shall, subject to section 430C, have effect where a notice is given in respect of any shares under section 429.

(2)   The offeror shall be entitled and bound to acquire those shares on the terms of the offer.

(3)   Where the terms of an offer are such as to give the holder of any shares a choice of consideration the notice shall give particulars of the choice and state—

    (a)   that the holder of the shares may within six weeks from the date of the notice indicate his choice by a written communication sent to the offeror at an address specified in the notice; and

    (b)   which consideration specified in the offer is to be taken as applying in default of his indicating a choice as aforesaid;

and the terms of the offer mentioned in subsection (2) shall be determined accordingly.

(4)   Subsection (3) applies whether or not any time-limit or other conditions applicable to the choice under the terms of the offer can still be complied with; and if the consideration chosen by the holder of the shares—

    (a)   is not cash and the offeror is no longer able to provide it;

    (b)   was to have been provided by a third party who is no longer bound or able to provide it,

the consideration shall be taken to consist of an amount of cash payable by the offeror which at the date of the notice is equivalent to the chosen consideration.

(5)   At the end of six weeks from the date of the notice the offeror shall forthwith—

    (a)   send a copy of the notice to the company; and

    (b)   pay or transfer to the company the consideration for the shares to which the notice relates.

(6)   If the shares to which the notice relates are registered the copy of the notice sent to the company under subsection (5)(a) shall be accompanied by an instrument of transfer executed on behalf of the shareholder by a person appointed by the offeror; and on receipt of that instrument the company shall register the offeror as the holder of those shares.

(7)   If the shares to which the notice relates are transferable by the delivery of warrants or other instruments the copy of the notice sent to the company under subsection (5)(a) shall be accompanied by a statement to that effect; and the company shall on receipt of the statement issue the offeror with warrants or other instruments in respect of the shares and those already in issue in receipt of the shares shall become void.

(8)   Where the consideration referred to in paragraph (b) of subsection (5) consists of shares or securities to be allotted by the offeror the reference in that paragraph to the transfer of the consideration shall be construed as a reference to the allotment of the shares or securities to the company.

(9)   Any sum received by a company under paragraph (b) of subsection (5) and any other consideration received under that paragraph shall be held by the company on trust for the person entitled to the shares in respect of which the sum or other consideration was received.

(10)   Any sum received by a company under paragraph (e) of subsection (5), and any dividend or other sum accruing from any other consideration received by a company under that paragraph, shall be paid into a separate bank account, being an account the balance on which bears interest at an appropriate rate and can be withdrawn by such notice (if any) as is appropriate.

(11)   Where after reasonable enquiry made at such intervals as are reasonable the person entitled to any consideration held on trust by virtue of subsection (9) cannot be found and twelve years have elapsed since the consideration was received or the company is wound up the consideration (together with any interest, dividend or other benefit that has accrued from it) shall be paid into court.

(12)   In relation to a company registered in Scotland, subsections (13) and (14) shall apply in place of subsection (11).

(13)   Where after reasonable enquiry made at such intervals as are reasonable the person entitled to any consideration held on trust by virtue of subsection (9) cannot be found and twelve years have elapsed since the consideration was received or the company is wound up—

(a) the trust shall terminate;

(b) the company or, as the case may be, the liquidator shall sell any consideration other than cash and any benefit other than cash that has accrued from the consideration; and

(c) a sum representing—

    (i)   the consideration so far as it is cash;

    (ii) the proceeds of any sale under paragraph (b) above; and

    (iii) any interest, dividend or other benefit that has accrued from the consideration,

shall be deposited in the name of the Accountant of Court in a bank account such as is referred to in subsection (10) and the receipt for the deposit shall be transmitted to the Account of Court.

(14) Section 58 of the Bankruptcy (Scotland) Act 1985 (so far as consistent with this Act) shall apply with any necessary modifications to sums deposited under subsection (13) as that section applies to sums deposited under section 57(1)(a) of that Act.

(15) The expenses of any such enquiry as is mentioned in subsection (11) or (13) may be defrayed out of the money or other property held on trust for the person or persons to whom the enquiry relates.

430A. Right of minority shareholder to be bought out by offeror

(1) If a takeover offer relates to all the shares in a company and at any time before the end of the period within which the offer can be accepted—

(a) the offeror has by virtue of acceptances of the offer acquired or contracted to acquire some (but not all) of the shares to which the offer relates; and

(b) those shares, with or without any other shares in the company which he has acquired or contracted to acquire, amount to not less than nine-tenths in value of all the shares in the company ...,

the holder of any shares to which the offer relates who has not accepted the offer may by a written communication addressed to the offeror require him to acquire those shares.

(1A) For the purposes of subsection (1), a takeover offer relates to all the shares in a company if it is an offer to acquire all the shares in the company within the meaning of section 428.

(2) If a takeover offer relates to shares of any class or classes and at any time before the end of the period within which the offer can be accepted—

(a) the offeror has by virtue of acceptances of the offer required or contracted to acquire some (but not all) of the shares of any class to which the offer relates; and

(b) those shares, with or without any other shares of that class which he has acquired or contracted to acquire, amount to not less than nine-tenths in value of all the shares of that class ...,

the holder of any shares of that class who has not accepted the offer may by a written communication addressed to the offeror require him to acquire those shares.

(2A) For the purposes of subsections (1) and (2), in calculating nine-tenths of the value of all the shares in the company, or all the shares of any class or classes of shares of the company, any shares held by the company as treasury shares shall be treated as having been acquired by the offeror.

(3) Within one month of the time specified in subsection (1) or, as the case may be, subsection (2) the offeror shall give any shareholder who has not accepted the offer notice in the prescribed manner of the rights that are exercisable by him under that subsection; and if the notice is given before the end of the period mentioned in that subsection it shall state that the offer is still open for acceptance.

(4) A notice under subsection (3) may specify a period for the exercise of the rights conferred by this section and in that event the rights shall not be exercisable after the end of that period; but no such period shall end less than three months after the end of the period within which the offer can be accepted.

(5) Subsection (3) does not apply if the offeror has given the shareholder a notice in respect of the shares in question under section 429.

(6)   If the offeror fails to comply with subsection (3) he and, if the offeror is a company, every officer of the company who is in default or to whose neglect the failure is attributable, shall be liable to a fine and, for continued contravention, to a daily default fine.

(7)   If an offeror other than a company is charged with an offence for failing to comply with subsection (3) it is a defence for him to prove that he took all reasonable steps for securing compliance with that subsection.

430B. Effect of requirement under s 430A

(1)   The following provisions shall, subject to section 430C, have effect where a shareholder exercises his rights in respect of any shares under section 430A.

(2)   The offeror shall be entitled and bound to acquire those shares on the terms of the offer or on such other terms as may be agreed.

(3)   Where the terms of an offer are such as to give the holder of shares a choice of consideration the holder of the shares may indicate his choice when requiring the offeror to acquire them and the notice given to the holder under section 430A(3)—

    (a)   shall give particulars of the choice and of the rights conferred by this subsection; and

    (b)   may state which consideration specified in the offer is to be taken as applying in default of his indicating a choice;

    and the terms of the offer mentioned in subsection (2) shall be determined accordingly.

(4)   Subsection (3) applies whether or not any time-limit or other conditions applicable to the choice under the terms of the offer can still be complied with; and if the consideration chosen by the holder of the shares—

    (a)   is not cash and the offeror is no longer able to provide it; or

    (b)   was to have been provided by a third party who is no longer bound or able to provide it,

    the consideration shall be taken to consist of an amount of cash payable by the offeror which at the date when the holder of the shares requires the offeror to acquire them is equivalent to the chosen consideration.

430C. Applications to the court

(1)   Where a notice is given under section 429 to the holder of any shares the court may, on an application made by him within six weeks from the date on which the notice was given—

    (a)   order that the offeror shall not be entitled and bound to acquire the shares; or

    (b)   specify terms of acquisition different from those of the offer.

(2)   If an application to the court under subsection (1) is pending at the end of the period mentioned in subsection (5) of section 430 that subsection shall not have effect until the application has been disposed of.

(3)   Where the holder of any shares exercises his rights under section 430A the court may, on an application made by him or the offeror, order that the terms on which the offeror is entitled and bound to acquire the shares shall be such as the court thinks fit.

(4)   No order for costs or expenses shall be made against a shareholder making an application under subsection (1) or (3) unless the court considers—

    (a)   that the application was unnecessary, improper or vexatious; or

    (b)   that there has been unreasonable delay in making the application or unreasonable conduct on his part in conducting the proceedings on the application.

(5)   Where a takeover offer has not been accepted to the extent necessary for entitling the offeror to give notices under subsection (1) or (2) of section 429 the court may, on the application of the offeror, make an order authorising him to give notices under that subsection if satisfied—

    (a)   that the offeror has after reasonable enquiry been unable to trace one or more of the persons holding shares to which the offer relates;

    (b)   that the shares which the offeror has acquired or contracted to acquire by virtue of acceptances of the offer, together with the shares held by the person or persons mentioned in paragraph (a), amount to not less than the minimum specified in that subsection; and

    (c)   that the consideration offered is fair and reasonable;

but the court shall not make an order under this subsection unless it considers that it is just and equitable to do so having regard, in particular, to the number of shareholders who have been traced but who have not accepted the offer.

430D. Joint offers

(1)   A takeover offer may be made by two or more persons jointly and in that event this Part of this Act has effect with the following modifications.

(2)   The conditions for the exercise of the rights conferred by sections 429 and 430A shall be satisfied by the joint offerors acquiring or contracting to acquire the necessary shares jointly (as respects acquisitions by virtue of acceptances of the offer) and either jointly or separately (in other cases); and, subject to the following provisions, the rights and obligations of the offeror under those sections and sections 430 and 430B shall be respectively joint rights and joint and several obligations of the joint offerors.

(3)   It shall be a sufficient compliance with any provision of those sections requiring or authorising a notice or other document to be given or sent by or to the joint offerors that it is given or sent by or to any of them; but the statutory declaration required by section 429(4) shall be made by all of them and, in the case of a joint offeror being a company, signed by a director of that company.

(4)   In sections 428, 430(8) and 430E references to the offeror shall be construed as references to the joint offerors or any of them.

(5)   In section 430(6) and (7) references to the offeror shall be construed as references to the joint offerors or such of them as they may determine.

(6)   In sections 430(4)(a) and 430B(4)(a) references to the offeror being no longer able to provide the relevant consideration shall be construed as references to none of the joint offerors being able to do so.

(7)   In section 430C references to the offeror shall be construed as references to the joint offerors except that any application under subsection (3) or (5) may be made by any of them and the reference in subsection (5)(a) to the offeror having been unable to trace one or more of the persons holding shares shall be construed as a reference to none of the offerors having been able to do so.

430E. Associates

(1)   The requirement in section 428(1) that a takeover offer must extend to all the shares, or all the shares of any class or classes, in a company shall be regarded as satisfied notwithstanding that the offer does not extend to shares which associates of the offeror hold or have contracted to acquire; but, subject to subsection (2), shares which any such associate holds or has contracted to acquire, whether at the time when the offer is made or subsequently, shall be disregarded for the purposes of any reference in this Part of this Act to the shares to which a takeover offer relates.

(2)   Where during the period within which a takeover offer can be accepted any associate of the offeror acquires or contracts to acquire any of the shares to which the offer relates, then, if the condition specified in subsection (8)(a) or (b) of section 429 is satisfied as respects those shares they shall be treated for the purposes of that section as shares to which the offer relates.

(3)   In section 430A(1)(b) and (2)(b) the reference to shares which the offeror has acquired or contracted to acquire shall include a reference to shares which any associate of his has acquired or contracted to acquire.

(4)   In this section "associate", in relation to an offeror means—

(a)   a nominee of the offeror;

(b)   a holding company, subsidiary or fellow subsidiary of the offeror or a nominee of such a holding company, subsidiary or fellow subsidiary;

(c)   a body corporate in which the offeror is substantially interested; or

(d)   any person who is, or is a nominee of, a party to an agreement with the offeror for the acquisition of, or of an interest in, the shares which are the subject of the takeover offer, being an agreement which includes provisions imposing obligations or restrictions such as are mentioned in section 204(2)(a).

(5) For the purposes of subsection (4)(b) a company is a fellow subsidiary of another body corporate if both are subsidiaries of the same body corporate but neither is a subsidiary of the other.

(6) For the purposes of subsection (4)(c) an offeror has a substantial interest in a body corporate if—

(a) that body or its directors are accustomed to act in accordance with his directions or instructions; or

(b) he is entitled to exercise or control the exercise of one-third or more of the voting power at general meetings of that body.

(7) Subsections (5) and (6) of section 204 shall apply to subsection (4)(d) above as they apply to that section and subsections (3) and (4) of section 203 shall apply for the purposes of subsection (6) above as they apply for the purposes of subsection (2)(b) of that section.

(8) Where the offeror is an individual his associates shall also include his spouse *or civil partner* and any minor child or step-child of his.

Note. The italicized words in subsection (8) are inserted by the Civil Partnership Act 2004, s. 261(1), Sch. 27, para. 103, as from a day to be appointed.

430F. Convertible securities

(1) For the purposes of this Part of this Act securities of a company shall be treated as shares in the company if they are convertible into or entitle the holder to subscribe for such shares; and references to the holder of shares or a shareholder shall be construed accordingly.

(2) Subsection (1) shall not be construed as requiring any securities to be treated—

(a) as shares of the same class as those into which they are convertible or for which the holder is entitled to subscribe; or

(b) as shares of the same class as other securities by reason only that the shares into which they are convertible or for which the holder is entitled to subscribe are of the same class.

PART XIV

INVESTIGATION OF COMPANIES AND THEIR AFFAIRS; REQUISITION OF DOCUMENTS

Appointment and functions of inspectors

431. Investigation of a company on its own application or that of its members

(1) The Secretary of State may appoint one or more competent inspectors to investigate the affairs of a company and to report on them in such manner as he may direct.

(2) The appointment may be made—

(a) in the case of a company having a share capital, on the application either of not less than 200 members or of members holding not less than one tenth of the shares issued (excluding any shares held as treasury shares),

(b) in the case of a company not having a share capital, on the application of not less than one fifth in number of the persons on the company's register of members, and

(c) in any case, on application of the company.

(3) The application shall be supported by such evidence as the Secretary of State may require for the purpose of showing that the applicant or applicants have good reason for requiring the investigation.

(4) The Secretary of State may, before appointing inspectors, require the applicant or applicants to give security, to an amount not exceeding £5,000, or such other sum as he may by order specify, for payment of the costs of the investigation.

An order under this subsection shall be made by statutory instrument subject to annulment in pursuance of a resolution of either House of Parliament.

432. Other company investigations

(1) The Secretary of State shall appoint one or more competent inspectors to investigate the affairs of a company and report on them in such manner as he directs, if the court by order declares that its affairs ought to be so investigated.

(2)   The Secretary of State may make such an appointment if it appears to him that there are circumstances suggesting—

       (a)   that the company's affairs are being or have been conducted with intent to defraud its creditors or the creditors of any other person, or otherwise for a fraudulent or unlawful purpose, or in a manner which is unfairly prejudicial to some part of its members, or

       (b)   that any actual or proposed act or omission of the company (including an act or omission on its behalf) is or would be so prejudicial, or that the company was formed for any fraudulent or unlawful purpose, or

       (c)   that persons concerned with the company's formation or the management of its affairs have in connection therewith been guilty of fraud, misfeasance or other misconduct towards it or towards its members, or

       (d)   that the company's members have not been given all the information with respect to its affairs which they might reasonably expect.

(2A)   Inspectors may be appointed under subsection (2) on terms that any report they may make is not for publication; and in such a case, the provisions of section 437(3) (availability and publication of inspectors' reports) do not apply.

(3)   Subsections (1) and (2) are without prejudice to the powers of the Secretary of State under section 431; and the power conferred by subsection (2) is exercisable with respect to a body corporate notwithstanding that it is in course of being voluntarily wound up.

(4)   The reference in subsection (2)(a) to a company's members includes any person who is not a member but to whom shares in the company have been transferred or transmitted by operation of law.

433.   Inspectors' powers during investigation

(1)   If inspectors appointed under section 431 or 432 to investigate the affairs of a company think it necessary for the purposes of their investigation to investigate also the affairs of another body corporate which is or at any relevant time has been the company's subsidiary or holding company, or a subsidiary of its holding company or a holding company of its subsidiary, they have power to do so; and they shall report on the affairs of the other body corporate so far as they think that the results of their investigation of its affairs are relevant to the investigation of the affairs of the company first mentioned above.

(2)   ...

434.   Production of documents and evidence to inspectors

(1)   When inspectors are appointed under section 431 or 432, it is the duty of all officers and agents of the company, and of all officers and agents of any other body corporate whose affairs are investigated under section 433(1)—

       (a)   to produce to the inspectors all documents of or relating to the company or, as the case may be, the other body corporate which are in their custody or power,

       (b)   to attend before the inspectors when required to do so, and

       (c)   otherwise to give the inspectors all assistance in connection with the investigation which they are reasonably able to give.

(2)   If the inspectors consider that an officer or agent of the company or other body corporate, or any other person, is or may be in possession of information relating to a matter which they believe to be relevant to the investigation, they may require him—

       (a)   to produce to them any documents in his custody or power relating to that matter,

       (b)   to attend before them, and

       (c)   otherwise to give them all assistance in connection with the investigation which he is reasonably able to give;

    and it is that person's duty to comply with the requirement.

(3)   An inspector may for the purposes of the investigation examine any person on oath, and may administer an oath accordingly.

(4)   In this section a reference to officers or to agents includes past, as well as present, officers or agents (as the case may be); and "agents", in relation to a company or other body corporate, includes its bankers and solicitors and persons employed by it as auditors, whether these persons are or are not officers of the company or other body corporate.

(5)   An answer given by a person to a question put to him in exercise of powers conferred by this section (whether as it has effect in relation to an investigation under any of sections 431 to 433, or as applied by any other section in this Part) may be used in evidence against him.

(5A)   However, in criminal proceedings in which that person is charged with an offence to which this subsection applies—

      (a)   no evidence relating to the answer may be adduced, and

      (b)   no question relating to it may be asked,

      by or on behalf of the prosecution, unless evidence relating to it is adduced, or a question relating to it is asked, in the proceedings by or on behalf of that person.

(5B)   Subsection (5A) applies to any offence other than—

      (a)   an offence under section 2 or 5 of the Perjury Act 1911 (false statements made on oath otherwise than in judicial proceedings or made otherwise than on oath); or

      (b)   an offence under section 44(1) or (2) of the Criminal Law (Consolidation) (Scotland) Act 1995 (false statements made on oath or otherwise than on oath).

(6)   In this section "documents" includes information recorded in any form; and, in relation to information recorded otherwise than in legible form, the power to require its production includes power to require the production of a copy of the information in legible form, or in a form from which it can readily be produced in visible and legible form.

435.   ....

436.   **Obstruction of inspectors treated as contempt of court**

(1)   If any person—

      (a)   fails to comply with section 434(1)(a) or (c),

      (b)   refuses to comply with a requirement under section 434(1)(b) or (2), or

      (c)   refuses to answer any question put to him by the inspectors for the purposes of the investigation,

      the inspectors may certify that fact in writing to the court.

(2)   If that person—

      (a)   refuses to produce any book or document which it is his duty under section 434 or 435 to produce, or

      (b)   refuses to attend before the inspectors when required to do so, or

      (c)   refuses to answer any question put to him by the inspectors with respect to the affairs of the company or other body corporate (as the case may be),

      the inspectors may certify the refusal in writing to the court.

(3)   The court may thereupon enquire into the case; and, after hearing any witnesses who may be produced against or on behalf of the alleged offender and after hearing any statement which may be offered in defence, the court may punish the offender in like manner as if he had been guilty of contempt of the court.

437.   **Inspectors' reports**

(1)   The inspectors may, and if so directed by the Secretary of State shall, make interim reports to the Secretary of State, and on the conclusion of their investigation shall make a final report to him. Any such report shall be written or printed, as the Secretary of State directs.

(1A)   Any persons who have been appointed under section 431 or 432 may at any time and, if the Secretary of State directs them to do so, shall inform him of any matters coming to their knowledge as a result of their investigations.

(1B)   If it appears to the Secretary of State that matters have come to light in the course of the inspectors' investigation which suggest that a criminal offence has been committed, and those matters have been referred to the appropriate prosecuting authority, he may direct the inspectors to take no further steps in the investigation or to take only such further steps as are specified in the direction.

(1C)   Where an investigation is the subject of a direction under subsection (1B), the inspectors shall make a final report to the Secretary of State only where—

   (a)   they were appointed under section 432(1) (appointment in pursuance of an order of the court), or

   (b)   the Secretary of State directs them to do so.

(2)   If the inspectors were appointed under section 432 in pursuance of an order of the court, the Secretary of State shall furnish a copy of any report of theirs to the court.

(3)   In any case the Secretary of State may, if he thinks fit—

   (a)   forward a copy of any report made by the inspectors to the company's registered office,

   (b)   furnish a copy on request and on payment of the prescribed fee to—

      (i)   any member of the company or other body corporate which is the subject of the report,

      (ii)   any person whose conduct is referred to in the report,

      (iii)   the auditors of that company or body corporate,

      (iv)   the applicants for the investigation,

      (v)   any other person whose financial interests appear to the Secretary of State to be affected by the matters dealt with in the report, whether as a creditor of the company or body corporate, or otherwise, and

   (c)   cause any such report to be printed and published.

438.   Power to bring civil proceedings on company's behalf

(1)   If from any report made or information obtained under this Part it appears to the Secretary of State that any civil proceedings ought in the public interest to be brought by any body corporate, he may himself bring such proceedings in the name and on behalf of the body corporate.

(2)   The Secretary of State shall indemnify the body corporate against any costs or expenses incurred by it in or in connection with proceedings brought under this section.

439.   Expenses of investigating a company's affairs

(1)   The expenses of an investigation under any of the powers conferred by this Part shall be defrayed in the first instance by the Secretary of State, but he may recover those expenses from the persons liable in accordance with this section.

There shall be treated as expenses of the investigation, in particular, such reasonable sums as the Secretary of State may determine in respect of general staff costs and overheads.

(2)   A person who is convicted on a prosecution instituted as a result of the investigation, or is ordered to pay the whole or any part of the costs of proceedings brought under section 438, may in the same proceedings be ordered to pay those expenses to such extent as may be specified in the order.

(3)   A body corporate in whose name proceedings are brought under that section is liable to the amount or value of any sums or property recovered by it as a result of those proceedings; and any amount for which a body corporate is liable under this subsection is a first charge on the sums or property recovered.

(4)   A body corporate dealt with by an inspector's report, where the inspectors were appointed otherwise than of the Secretary of State's own motion, is liable except where it was the applicant for the investigation, and except so far as the Secretary of State otherwise directs.

(5)   Where inspectors were appointed—

   (a)   under section 431, or

   (b)   on an application under section 442(3),

the applicant or applicants for the investigation is or are liable to such extent (if any) as the Secretary of State may direct.

(6)   The report of inspectors appointed otherwise than of the Secretary of State's own motion may, if they think fit, and shall if the Secretary of State so directs, include a recommendation as to the

directions (if any) which they think appropriate, in the light of their investigation, to be given under subsection (4) or (5) of this section.

(7)   For purposes of this section, any costs or expenses incurred by the Secretary of State in or in connection with proceedings brought under section 438 (including expenses incurred under subsection (2) of it) are to be treated as expenses of the investigation giving rise to the proceedings.

(8)   Any liability to repay the Secretary of State imposed by subsections (2) and (3) above is (subject to satisfaction of his right to repayment) a liability also to indemnify all persons against liability under subsections (4) and (5); and any such liability imposed by subsection (2) is (subject as mentioned above) a liability also to indemnify all persons against liability under subsection (3).

(9)   A person liable under any one of those subsections is entitled to contribution from any other person liable under the same subsection, according to the amount of their respective liabilities under it.

(10)   Expenses to be defrayed by the Secretary of State under this section shall, so far as not recovered under it, be paid out of money provided by Parliament.

440.   ...

441. Inspectors' report to be evidence

(1)   A copy of any report of inspectors appointed under this Part, certified by the Secretary of State to be a true copy, is admissible in any legal proceedings as evidence of the opinion of the inspectors in relation to any matter contained in the report and, in proceedings on an application under section 8 of the Company Directors Disqualification Act 1986, as evidence of any fact stated therein.

(2)   A document purporting to be such a certificate as is mentioned above shall be received in evidence and be deemed to be such a certificate, unless the contrary is proved.

Other powers of investigation available to the Secretary of State

442. Power to investigate company ownership

(1)   Where it appears to the Secretary of State that there is good reason to do so, he may appoint one or more competent inspectors to investigate and report on the membership of any company, and otherwise with respect to the company, for the purpose of determining the true persons who are or have been financially interested in the success or failure (real or apparent) of the company or able to control or materially to influence its policy.

(2)   The appointment of inspectors under this section may define the scope of their investigation (whether as respects the matter or the period to which it is to extend or otherwise) and in particular may limit the investigation to matters connected with particular shares or debentures.

(3)   If an application for investigation under this section with respect to particular shares or debentures of a company is made to the Secretary of State by members of the company, and the number of applicants or the amount of shares held by them is not less than that required for an application for the appointment of inspectors under section 431(2)(a) or (b), then, subject to the following provisions, the Secretary of State shall appoint inspectors to conduct the investigation applied for.

(3A)   The Secretary of State shall not appoint inspectors if he is satisfied that the application is vexatious; and where inspectors are appointed their terms of appointment shall exclude any matter in so far as the Secretary of State is satisfied that it is unreasonable for it to be investigated.

(3B)   The Secretary of State may, before appointing inspectors, require the applicant or applicants to give security, to an amount not exceeding £5,000, or such other sum as he may by order specify, for payment of the costs of the investigation.

        An order under this subsection shall be made by statutory instrument which shall be subject to annulment in pursuance of a resolution of either House of Parliament.

(3C)   If on an application under subsection (3) it appears to the Secretary of State that the powers conferred by section 444 are sufficient for the purposes of investigating the matters which inspectors would be appointed to investigate, he may instead conduct the investigation under that section.

(4)   Subject to the terms of their appointment, the inspectors' powers extend to the investigation of any circumstances suggesting the existence of an arrangement or understanding which, though not legally binding, is or was observed or likely to be observed in practice and which is relevant to the purposes of the investigation.

443.   Provisions applicable on investigation under s 442

(1)   For purposes of an investigation under section 442, sections 433(1), 434, 436 and 437 apply with the necessary modifications of references to the affairs of the company or to those of any other body corporate, subject however to the following subsections.

(2)   Those sections apply to—

    (a)   all persons who are or have been, or whom the inspector has reasonable cause to believe to be or have been, financially interested in the success or failure or the apparent success or failure of the company or any other body corporate whose membership is investigated with that of the company, or able to control or materially influence its policy (including persons concerned only on behalf of others), and

    (b)   any other person whom the inspector has reasonable cause to believe possesses information relevant to the investigation,

as they apply in relation to officers and agents of the company or the other body corporate (as the case may be).

(3)   If the Secretary of State is of opinion that there is good reason for not divulging any part of a report made by virtue of section 442 and this section, he may under section 437 disclose the report with the omission of that part; and he may cause to be kept by the registrar of companies a copy of the report with that part omitted or, in the case of any other such report, a copy of the whole report.

(4)   ...

444.   Power to obtain information as to those interested in shares, etc

(1)   If it appears to the Secretary of State that there is good reason to investigate the ownership of any shares in or debentures of a company and that it is unnecessary to appoint inspectors for the purpose, he may require any person whom he has reasonable cause to believe to have or to be able to obtain any information as to the present and past interests in those shares or debentures and the names and addresses of the persons interested and of any persons who act or have acted on their behalf in relation to the shares or debentures to give any such information to the Secretary of State.

(2)   For this purpose a person is deemed to have an interest in shares or debentures if he has any right to acquire or dispose of them or of any interest in them, or to vote in respect of them, or if his consent is necessary for the exercise of any of the rights of other persons interested in them, or if other persons interested in them can be required, or are accustomed, to exercise their rights in accordance with his instructions.

(3)   A person who fails to give information required of him under this section, or who in giving such information makes any statement which he knows to be false in a material particular, or recklessly makes any statement which is false in a material particular, is liable to imprisonment or a fine, or both.

445.   Power to impose restrictions on shares and debentures

(1)   If in connection with an investigation under either section 442 or 444 it appears to the Secretary of State that there is difficulty in finding out the relevant facts about any shares (whether issued or to be issued), he may by order direct that the shares shall until further order be subject to the restrictions of Part XV of this Act.

(1A)   If the Secretary of State is satisfied that an order under subsection (1) may unfairly affect the rights of third parties in respect of shares then the Secretary of State, for the purpose of protecting such rights and subject to such terms as he thinks fit, may direct that such acts by such persons or descriptions of persons and for such purposes as may be set out in the order, shall not constitute a breach of the restrictions of Part XV of this Act.

(2)   This section, and Part XV in its application to orders under it, apply in relation to debentures as in relation to shares save that subsection (1A) shall not so apply.

446.   Investigation of share dealings

(1)   If it appears to the Secretary of State that there are circumstances suggesting that contraventions may have occurred, in relation to a company's shares or debentures, of section 323 or 324 (taken with Schedule 13), or of subsections (3) to (5) of section 328 (restrictions on share dealing by directors and their families; obligation of director to disclose shareholding in his own company), he may appoint one or more competent inspectors to carry out such investigations as are requisite to establish whether or not such contraventions have occurred and to report the result of their investigations to him.

(2)   The appointment of inspectors under this section may limit the period to which their investigation is to extend or confine it to shares or debentures of a particular class, or both.

(3)   For purposes of an investigation under this section, sections 434 to 437 apply—

    (a)   with the substitution, for references to any other body corporate whose affairs are investigated under section 433(1), of a reference to any other body corporate which is, or has at any relevant time been, the company's subsidiary or holding company, or a subsidiary of its holding company, ...

    (b)   ...

(4)   Sections 434 to 436 apply for the purposes of an investigation under this section to the following persons as they apply to officers of the company or of the other body corporate—

    (a)   an authorised person;

    (b)   a relevant professional;

    (c)   a person not falling within paragraph (a) or (b) who may carry on a regulated activity without contravening the prohibition imposed by section 19 of the Financial Services and Markets Act 2000; and

    (d)   in relation to an authorised person, to a relevant professional or to a person falling within paragraph (c)—

        (i)   if it is a body corporate, any person who is or has been an officer of it;

        (ii)   if it is a partnership, any person who is or has been a partner in it;

        (iii)   if it is an unincorporated association, any person who is or has been a member of its governing body or an officer of it.

(4A)   In subsection (4)—

    "authorised person" has the meaning given in section 31(2) of the Financial Services and Markets Act 2000;

    "relevant professional" means a member of a profession in relation to which a body has been designated under section 326(1) of that Act, and, in relation to such a profession, "member" has the meaning given in section 325(2) of that Act.

(5)–(7) ...

Requisition and seizure of books and papers

447.   Power to require documents and information

(1)   The Secretary of State may act under subsections (2) and (3) in relation to a company.

(2)   The Secretary of State may give directions to the company requiring it—

    (a)   to produce such documents (or documents of such description) as may be specified in the directions;

    (b)   to provide such information (or information of such description) as may be so specified.

(3)   The Secretary of State may authorise a person (an investigator) to require the company or any other person—

    (a)   to produce such documents (or documents of such description) as the investigator may specify;

(b)   to provide such information (or information of such description) as the investigator may specify.

(4)   A person on whom a requirement under subsection (3) is imposed may require the investigator to produce evidence of his authority.

(5)   A requirement under subsection (2) or (3) must be complied with at such time and place as may be specified in the directions or by the investigator (as the case may be).

(6)   The production of a document in pursuance of this section does not affect any lien which a person has on the document.

(7)   The Secretary of State or the investigator (as the case may be) may take copies of or extracts from a document produced in pursuance of this section.

(8)   A "document" includes information recorded in any form.

(9)   In relation to information recorded otherwise than in legible form, the power to require production of it includes power to require the production of a copy of it in legible form or in a form from which it can readily be produced in visible and legible form.

447A.   Information provided: evidence

(1)   A statement made by a person in compliance with a requirement under section 447 may be used in evidence against him.

(2)   But in criminal proceedings in which the person is charged with a relevant offence—

(a)   no evidence relating to the statement may be adduced by or on behalf of the prosecution, and

(b)   no question relating to it may be asked by or on behalf of the prosecution,

unless evidence relating to it is adduced or a question relating to it is asked in the proceedings by or on behalf of that person.

(3)   A relevant offence is any offence other than the following—

(a)   an offence under section 451,

(b)   an offence under section 5 of the Perjury Act 1911 (false statement made otherwise than on oath), or

(c)   an offence under section 44(2) of the Criminal Law (Consolidation) (Scotland) Act 1995 (false statement made otherwise than on oath).

448.   Entry and search of premises

(1)   A justice of the peace may issue a warrant under this section if satisfied on information on oath given by or on behalf of the Secretary of State, or by a person appointed or authorised to exercise powers under this Part, that there are reasonable grounds for believing that there are on any premises documents whose production has been required under this Part and which have not been produced in compliance with the requirement.

(2)   A justice of the peace may also issue a warrant under this section if satisfied on information on oath given by or on behalf of the Secretary of State, or by a person appointed or authorised to exercise powers under this Part—

(a)   that there are reasonable grounds for believing that an offence has been committed for which the penalty on conviction on indictment is imprisonment for a term of not less than two years and that there are on any premises documents relating to whether the offence has been committed,

(b)   that the Secretary of State, or the person so appointed or authorised, has power to require the production of the documents under this Part, and

(c)   that there are reasonable grounds for believing that if production was so required the documents would not be produced but would be removed from the premises, hidden, tampered with or destroyed.

(3)   A warrant under this section shall authorise a constable, together with any other person named in it and any other constables—

(a)   to enter the premises specified in the information, using such force as is reasonably necessary for the purpose;

(b)   to search the premises and take possession of any documents appearing to be such documents as are mentioned in subsection (1) or (2), as the case may be, or to take, in relation to any such documents, any other steps which may appear to be necessary for preserving them or preventing interference with them;

(c)   to take copies of any such documents; and

(d)   to require any person named in the warrant to provide an explanation of them or to state where they may be found.

(4)   If in the case of a warrant under subsection (2) the justice of the peace is satisfied on information on oath that there are reasonable grounds for believing that there are also on the premises other documents relevant to the investigation, the warrant shall also authorise the actions mentioned in subsection (3) to be taken in relation to such documents.

(5)   A warrant under this section shall continue in force until the end of the period of one month beginning with the day on which it is issued.

(6)   Any documents of which possession is taken under this section may be retained—

(a)   for a period of three months; or

(b)   if within that period proceedings to which the documents are relevant are commenced against any person for any criminal offence, until the conclusion of those proceedings.

(7)   Any person who intentionally obstructs the exercise of any rights conferred by a warrant issued under this section or fails without reasonable excuse to comply with any requirement imposed in accordance with subsection (3)(d) is guilty of an offence and liable to a fine.

Sections 732 (restrictions on prosecutions), 733 (liability of individuals for corporate default) and 734 (criminal proceedings against unincorporated bodies) apply to this offence.

(8)   For the purposes of sections 449 and 451A (provision for security of information) documents obtained under this section shall be treated as if they had been obtained under the provision of this Part under which their production was or, as the case may be, could have been required.

(9)   In the application of this section to Scotland for the references to a justice of the peace substitute references to a justice of the peace or a sheriff, and for the references to information on oath substitute references to evidence on oath.

(10)   In this section "document" includes information recorded in any form.

448A. Protection in relation to certain disclosures: information provided to Secretary of State

(1)   A person who makes a relevant disclosure is not liable by reason only of that disclosure in any proceedings relating to a breach of an obligation of confidence.

(2)   A relevant disclosure is a disclosure which satisfies each of the following conditions—

(a)   it is made to the Secretary of State otherwise than in compliance with a requirement under this Part;

(b)   it is of a kind that the person making the disclosure could be required to make in pursuance of this Part;

(c)   the person who makes the disclosure does so in good faith and in the reasonable belief that the disclosure is capable of assisting the Secretary of State for the purposes of the exercise of his functions under this Part;

(d)   the information disclosed is not more than is reasonably necessary for the purpose of assisting the Secretary of State for the purposes of the exercise of those functions;

(e)   the disclosure is not one falling within subsection (3) or (4).

(3)   A disclosure falls within this subsection if the disclosure is prohibited by virtue of any enactment.

(4)   A disclosure falls within this subsection if—

(a)   it is made by a person carrying on the business of banking or by a lawyer, and

(b)   it involves the disclosure of information in respect of which he owes an obligation of confidence in that capacity.

(5)   An enactment includes an enactment—

(a)   comprised in, or in an instrument made under, an Act of the Scottish Parliament;

(b)   comprised in subordinate legislation (within the meaning of the Interpretation Act 1978);

(c)   whenever passed or made.

449.   Provision for security of information obtained

(1)   This section applies to information (in whatever form) obtained—

    (a)   in pursuance of a requirement imposed under section 447;

    (b)   by means of a relevant disclosure within the meaning of section 448A(2);

    (c)   by an investigator in consequence of the exercise of his powers under section 453A.

(2)   Such information must not be disclosed unless the disclosure—

    (a)   is made to a person specified in Schedule 15C, or

    (b)   is of a description specified in Schedule 15D.

(3)   The Secretary of State may by order amend Schedules 15C and 15D.

(4)   An order under subsection (3) must not—

    (a)   amend Schedule 15C by specifying a person unless the person exercises functions of a public nature (whether or not he exercises any other function);

    (b)   amend Schedule 15D by adding or modifying a description of disclosure unless the purpose for which the disclosure is permitted is likely to facilitate the exercise of a function of a public nature.

(5)   An order under subsection (3) must be made by statutory instrument subject to annulment in pursuance of a resolution of either House of Parliament.

(6)   A person who discloses any information in contravention of this section—

    (a)   is guilty of an offence, and

    (b)   is liable on conviction to imprisonment or a fine or to both.

(7)   Sections 732 (restriction on prosecutions), 733 (liability of individuals for corporate default) and 734 (criminal proceedings against unincorporated bodies) apply to the offence under subsection (6).

(8)   Any information which may by virtue of this section be disclosed to a person specified in Schedule 15C may be disclosed to any officer or employee of the person.

(9)   This section does not prohibit the disclosure of information if the information is or has been available to the public from any other source.

(10)   For the purposes of this section, information obtained by an investigator in consequence of the exercise of his powers under section 453A includes information obtained by a person accompanying the investigator in pursuance of subsection (4) of that section in consequence of that person's accompanying the investigator.

(11)   Nothing in this section authorises the making of a disclosure in contravention of the Data Protection Act 1998.

450.   Punishment for destroying, mutilating etc company documents

(1)   An officer of a company ... ... who—

    (a)   destroys, mutilates or falsifies, or is privy to the destruction, mutilation or falsification of a document affecting or relating to the company's property or affairs, or

    (b)   makes, or is privy to the making of, a false entry in such a document,

    is guilty of an offence, unless he proves that he had no intention to conceal the state of affairs of the company or to defeat the law.

(1A)   Subsection (1) applies to an officer of an authorised insurance company which is not a body corporate as it applies to an officer of a company.

(2)   Such a person as above mentioned who fraudulently either parts with, alters or makes an omission in any such document or is privy to fraudulent parting with, fraudulent altering or fraudulent making of an omission in, any such document, is guilty of an offence.

(3)   A person guilty of an offence under this section is liable to imprisonment or a fine, or both.

(4)   Sections 732 (restriction on prosecutions), 733 (liability of individuals for corporate default) and 734 (criminal proceedings against unincorporated bodies) apply to an offence under this section.

(5)   In this section "document" includes information recorded in any form.

451. Punishment for furnishing false information

(1) A person commits an offence if in purported compliance with a requirement under section 447 to provide information—

    (a) he provides information which he knows to be false in a material particular;

    (b) he recklessly provides information which is false in a material particular.

(2) A person guilty of an offence under this section is liable on conviction to imprisonment or a fine or to both.

(3) Sections 732 (restriction on prosecutions), 733 (liability of individuals for corporate default) and 734 (criminal proceedings against unincorporated bodies) apply to an offence under this section.

451A. Disclosure of information by Secretary of State or inspector

(1) This section applies to information obtained—

    (a) under sections 434 to 446;

    (b) by an inspector in consequence of the exercise of his powers under section 453A.

(2) The Secretary of State may, if he thinks fit—

    (a) disclose any information to which this section applies to any person to whom, or for any purpose for which, disclosure is permitted under section 449, or

    (b) authorise or require an inspector appointed under this Part to disclose such information to any such person or for any such purpose.

(3) Information to which this section applies may also be disclosed by an inspector appointed under this Part to—

    (a) another inspector appointed under this Part;

    (b) a person appointed under—

        (i) section 167 of the Financial Services and Markets Act 2000 (general investigations),

        (ii) section 168 of that Act (investigations in particular cases),

        (iii) section 169(1)(b) of that Act (investigation in support of overseas regulator),

        (iv) section 284 of that Act (investigations into affairs of certain collective investment schemes), or

        (v) regulations made as a result of section 262(2)(k) of that Act (investigations into open-ended investment companies),

    to conduct an investigation; or

    (c) a person authorised to exercise powers under—

        (i) section 447 of this Act; or

        (ii) section 84 of the Companies Act 1989 (exercise of powers to assist overseas regulatory authority).

(4) Any information which may by virtue of subsection (3) be disclosed to any person may be disclosed to any officer or servant of that person.

(5) The Secretary of State may, if he thinks fit, disclose any information obtained under section 444 to—

    (a) the company whose ownership was the subject of the investigation,

    (b) any member of the company,

    (c) any person whose conduct was investigated in the course of the investigation,

    (d) the auditors of the company, or

    (e) any person whose financial interests appear to the Secretary of State to be affected by matters covered by the investigation.

(6) For the purposes of this section, information obtained by an inspector in consequence of the exercise of his powers under section 453A includes information obtained by a person accompanying the inspector in pursuance of subsection (4) of that section in consequence of that person's accompanying the inspector.

(7) The reference to an inspector in subsection (2)(b) above includes a reference to a person accompanying an inspector in pursuance of section 453A(4).

Supplementary

452.   **Privileged information**

(1)   Nothing in sections 431 to 446 compels the disclosure by any person to the Secretary of State or to an inspector appointed by him of information in respect of which in an action in the High Court a claim to legal professional privilege, or in an action in the Court of Session a claim to confidentiality of communications, could be maintained.

(1A)   Nothing in section 434, 443 or 446 requires a person (except as mentioned in subsection (1B) below) to disclose information or produce documents in respect of which he owes an obligation of confidence by virtue of carrying on the business of banking unless—

    (a)   the person to whom the obligation of confidence is owed is the company or other body corporate under investigation,

    (b)   the person to whom the obligation of confidence is owed consents to the disclosure or production, or

    (c)   the making of the requirement is authorised by the Secretary of State.

(1B)   Subsection (1A) does not apply where the person owing the obligation of confidence is the company or other body corporate under investigation under section 431, 432 or 433.

(2)   Nothing in sections 447 to 451—

    (a)   compels the production by any person of a document or the disclosure by any person of information in respect of which in an action in the High Court a claim to legal professional privilege, or in an action in the Court of Session a claim to confidentiality of communications, could be maintained;

    (b)   authorises the taking of possession of any such document which is in the person's possession.

(3)   The Secretary of State must not under section 447 require, or authorise a person to require—

    (a)   the production by a person carrying on the business of banking of a document relating to the affairs of a customer of his, or

    (b)   the disclosure by him of information relating to those affairs,

    unless one of the conditions in subsection (4) is met.

(4)   The conditions are—

    (a)   the Secretary of State thinks it is necessary to do so for the purpose of investigating the affairs of the person carrying on the business of banking;

    (b)   the customer is a person on whom a requirement has been imposed under section 447;

    (c)   the customer is a person on whom a requirement to produce information or documents has been imposed by an investigator appointed by the Secretary of State in pursuance of section 171 or 173 of the Financial Services and Markets Act 2000 (powers of persons appointed under section 167 or as a result of section 168(2) to conduct an investigation).

(5)   Despite subsections (1) and (2) a person who is a lawyer may be compelled to disclose the name and address of his client.

453.   **Investigation of oversea companies**

(1)   The provisions of this Part apply to bodies corporate incorporated outside Great Britain which are carrying on business in Great Britain, or have at any time carried on business there, as they apply to companies under this Act; but subject to the following exceptions, adaptations and modifications.

(1A)   The following provisions do not apply to such bodies—

    (a)   section 431 (investigation on application of company or its members),

    (b)   section 438 (power to bring civil proceedings on the company's behalf),

    (c)   sections 442 to 445 (investigation of company ownership and power to obtain information as to those interested in shares, &c), and

    (d)   section 446 (investigation of share dealings).

(1B)   The other provisions of this Part apply to such bodies subject to such adaptations and modifications as may be specified by regulations made by the Secretary of State.

(2)   Regulations under this section shall be made by statutory instrument subject to annulment in pursuance of a resolution of either House of Parliament.

453A. Power to enter and remain on premises

(1)   An inspector or investigator may act under subsection (2) in relation to a company if—
    (a)   he is authorised to do so by the Secretary of State, and
    (b)   he thinks that to do so will materially assist him in the exercise of his functions under this Part in relation to the company.

(2)   An inspector or investigator may at all reasonable times—
    (a)   require entry to relevant premises, and
    (b)   remain there for such period as he thinks necessary for the purpose mentioned in subsection (1)(b).

(3)   Relevant premises are premises which the inspector or investigator believes are used (wholly or partly) for the purposes of the company's business.

(4)   In exercising his powers under subsection (2), an inspector or investigator may be accompanied by such other persons as he thinks appropriate.

(5)   A person who intentionally obstructs a person lawfully acting under subsection (2) or (4)—
    (a)   is guilty of an offence, and
    (b)   is liable on conviction to a fine.

(6)   Sections 732 (restriction on prosecutions), 733 (liability of individuals for corporate default) and 734 (criminal proceedings against unincorporated bodies) apply to the offence under subsection (5).

(7)   An inspector is a person appointed under section 431, 432 or 442.

(8)   An investigator is a person authorised for the purposes of section 447.

453B. Power to enter and remain on premises: procedural

(1)   This section applies for the purposes of section 453A.

(2)   The requirements of subsection (3) must be complied with at the time an inspector or investigator seeks to enter relevant premises under section 453A(2)(a).

(3)   The requirements are—
    (a)   the inspector or investigator must produce evidence of his identity and evidence of his appointment or authorisation (as the case may be);
    (b)   any person accompanying the inspector or investigator must produce evidence of his identity.

(4)   The inspector or investigator must, as soon as practicable after obtaining entry, give to an appropriate recipient a written statement containing such information as to—
    (a)   the powers of the investigator or inspector (as the case may be) under section 453A;
    (b)   the rights and obligations of the company, occupier and the persons present on the premises, as may be prescribed by regulations.

(5)   If during the time the inspector or investigator is on the premises there is no person present who appears to him to be an appropriate recipient for the purposes of subsection (8), the inspector or investigator must as soon as reasonably practicable send to the company—
    (a)   a notice of the fact and time that the visit took place, and
    (b)   the statement mentioned in subsection (4).

(6)   As soon as reasonably practicable after exercising his powers under section 453A(2), the inspector or investigator must prepare a written record of the visit and—
    (a)   if requested to do so by the company he must give it a copy of the record;
    (b)   in a case where the company is not the sole occupier of the premises, if requested to do so by an occupier he must give the occupier a copy of the record.

(7)   The written record must contain such information as may be prescribed by regulations.

(8)   If the inspector or investigator thinks that the company is the sole occupier of the premises an appropriate recipient is a person who is present on the premises and who appears to the inspector or investigator to be—

(a)   an officer of the company, or

(b)   a person otherwise engaged in the business of the company if the inspector or investigator thinks that no officer of the company is present on the premises.

(9)   If the inspector or investigator thinks that the company is not the occupier or sole occupier of the premises an appropriate recipient is—

(a)   a person who is an appropriate recipient for the purposes of subsection (8), and (if different)

(b)   a person who is present on the premises and who appears to the inspector or investigator to be an occupier of the premises or otherwise in charge of them.

(10)   A statutory instrument containing regulations made under this section is subject to annulment in pursuance of a resolution of either House of Parliament.

453C.   Failure to comply with certain requirements

(1)   This section applies if a person fails to comply with a requirement imposed by an inspector, the Secretary of State or an investigator in pursuance of either of the following provisions—

(a)   section 447;

(b)   section 453A.

(2)   The inspector, Secretary of State or investigator (as the case may be) may certify the fact in writing to the court.

(3)   If, after hearing—

(a)   any witnesses who may be produced against or on behalf of the alleged offender;

(b)   any statement which may be offered in defence,

the court is satisfied that the offender failed without reasonable excuse to comply with the requirement, it may deal with him as if he had been guilty of contempt of the court.

PART XV
ORDERS IMPOSING RESTRICTIONS ON SHARES (SECTIONS 210, 216, 445)

454.   Consequence of order imposing restrictions

(1)   So long as any shares are directed to be subject to the restrictions of this Part then, subject to any directions made in relation to an order pursuant to sections 210(5A), 216(1B), 445(1A) or 456(1A) or subject in the case of an interim order pursuant to section 216(1A) to the terms of that order—

(a)   any transfer of those shares or, in the case of unissued shares, any transfer of the right to be issued with them, and any issue of them, is void;

(b)   no voting rights are exercisable in respect of the shares;

(c)   no further shares shall be issued in right of them or in pursuance of any offer made to their holder; and

(d)   except in a liquidation, no payment shall be made of any sums due from the company on the shares, whether in respect of capital or otherwise.

(2)   Where shares are subject to the restrictions of subsection (1)(a), any agreement to transfer the shares or, in the case of unissued shares, the right to be issued with them is void (except such agreement or right as may be made or exercised under the terms of directions made by the Secretary of State or the court under sections 210(5A), 216(1B), 445(1A), 456(1A) or of an interim order made under section 216(1A) or an agreement to transfer the shares on the making of an order under section 456(3)(b) below).

(3)   Where shares are subject to the restrictions of subsection (1)(c) or (d), an agreement to transfer any right to be issued with other shares in right of those shares, or to receive any payment on them (otherwise than in a liquidation) is void (except such agreement or right as may be made or exercised under the terms of directions made by the Secretary of State or the court under sections 210(5A), 216(1B), 445(1A), 456(1A) or of an interim order made under section 216(1A) or an agreement to transfer any such right on the transfer of the shares on the making of an order under section 456(3)(b) below).

455.   Punishment for attempted evasion of restrictions

(1)   Subject to the terms of any directions made under sections 210(5A), 216(1B) or 445(1A) or 456 or of an interim order made under section 216(1A) a person is liable to a fine if he—

(a)   exercises or purports to exercise any right to dispose of any shares which, to his knowledge, are for the time being subject to the restrictions of this Part or of any right to be issued with any such shares, or

(b)   votes in respect of any such shares (whether as holder or proxy), or appoints a proxy to vote in respect of them, or

(c)   being the holder of any such shares, fails to notify of their being subject to those restrictions any person whom he does not know to be aware of that fact but does know to be entitled (apart from the restrictions) to vote in respect of those shares whether as holder or as proxy, or

(d)   being the holder of any such shares, or being entitled to any right to be issued with other shares in right of them, or to receive any payment on them (otherwise than in a liquidation), enters into any agreement which is void under section 454(2) or (3).

(2)   Subject to the terms of any directions made under sections 210(5A), 216(1B), 445(1A) or 456 or of an interim order made under section 216(1A) if shares in a company are issued in contravention of the restrictions, the company and every officer of it who is in default is liable to a fine.

(3)   Section 732 (restriction on prosecutions) applies to an offence under this section.

456.   Relaxation and removal of restrictions

(1)   Where shares in a company are by order made subject to the restrictions of this Part, application may be made to the court for an order directing that the shares be no longer so subject.

(1A)   Where the court is satisfied that an order subjecting the shares to the restrictions of this Part unfairly affects the rights of third parties in respect of shares then the court, for the purpose of protecting such rights and subject to such terms as it thinks fit and in addition to any order it may make under subsection (1), may direct on an application made under that subsection that such acts by such persons or descriptions of persons and for such purposes, as may be set out in the order, shall not constitute a breach of the restrictions of Part XV of this Act.

Subsection (3) does not apply to an order made under this subsection.

(2)   If the order applying the restrictions was made by the Secretary of State, or he has refused to make an order disapplying them, the application may be made by any person aggrieved; and if the order was made by the court under section 216 (non-disclosure of share holding), it may be made by any such person or by the company.

(3)   Subject as follows, an order of the court or the Secretary of State directing that shares shall cease to be subject to the restrictions may be made only if—

(a)   the court or (as the case may be) the Secretary of State is satisfied that the relevant facts about the shares have been disclosed to the company and no unfair advantage has accrued to any person as a result of the earlier failure to make that disclosure, or

(b)   the shares are to be transferred for valuable consideration and the court (in any case) or the Secretary of State (if the order was made under section 210 or 445) approves the transfer.

(4)   Without prejudice to the power of the court to give directions under subsection (1A), where shares in a company are subject to the restrictions, the court may on application order the shares to be sold, subject to the court's approval as to the sale, and may also direct that the shares shall cease to be subject to the restrictions.

An application to the court under this subsection may be made by the Secretary of State (unless the restrictions were imposed by court order under section 216), or by the company.

(5)   Where an order has been made under subsection (4), the court may on application make such further order relating to the sale or transfer of the shares as it thinks fit.

An application to the court under this subsection may be made—

(a)   by the Secretary of State (unless the restrictions on the shares were imposed by court order under section 216), or

(b)   by the company, or

(c)   by the person appointed by or in pursuance of the order to effect the sale, or

(d)   by any person interested in the shares.

(6)   An order (whether of the Secretary of State or the court) directing that shares shall cease to be subject to the restrictions of this Part, if it is—

(a)   expressed to be made with a view to permitting a transfer of the shares, or

(b)   made under subsection (4) of this section,

may continue the restrictions mentioned in paragraphs (c) and (d) of section 454(1), either in whole or in part, so far as they relate to any right acquired or offer made before the transfer.

(7)   Subsection (3) does not apply to an order directing that shares shall cease to be subject to any restrictions which have been continued in force in relation to those shares under subsection (6).

457.   Further provisions on sale by court order of restricted shares

(1)   Where shares are sold in pursuance of an order of the court under section 456(4) the proceeds of sale, less the costs of the sale, shall be paid into court for the benefit of the persons who are beneficially interested in the shares; and any such person may apply to the court for the whole or part of those proceeds to be paid to him.

(2)   On application under subsection (1) the court shall (subject as provided below) order the payment to the applicant of the whole of the proceeds of sale together with any interest thereon or, if any other person had a beneficial interest in the shares at the time of their sale, such proportion of those proceeds and interest as is equal to the proportion which the value of the applicant's interest in the shares bears to the total value of the shares.

(3)   On granting an application for an order under section 456(4) or (5) the court may order that the applicant's costs be paid out of the proceeds of sale; and if that order is made, the applicant is entitled to payment of his costs out of those proceeds before any person interested in the shares in question receives any part of those proceeds.

PART XVI
FRAUDULENT TRADING BY A COMPANY

458.   Punishment for fraudulent trading

If any business of a company is carried on with intent to defraud creditors of the company or creditors of any other person, or for any fraudulent purpose, every person who was knowingly a party to the carrying on of the business in that manner is liable to imprisonment or a fine, or both.

This applies whether or not the company has been, or is in the course of being, wound up.

PART XVII
PROTECTION OF COMPANY'S MEMBERS AGAINST UNFAIR PREJUDICE

459.   Order on application of company member

(1)   A member of a company may apply to the court by petition for an order under this Part on the ground that the company's affairs are being or have been conducted in a manner which is unfairly prejudicial to the interests of its members generally or of some part of its members (including at least himself) or that any actual or proposed act or omission of the company (including an act or omission on its behalf) is or would be so prejudicial.

(2)   The provisions of this Part apply to a person who is not a member of a company but to whom shares in the company have been transferred or transmitted by operation of law, as those provisions apply to a member of the company; and references to a member or members are to be construed accordingly.

(3)   In this section (and so far as applicable for the purposes of this section, in section 461(2)) "company" means any company within the meaning of this Act or any company which is not such a company but is a statutory water company within the meaning of the Statutory Water Companies Act 1991.

460.   **Order on application of Secretary of State**

(1)   If it appears to the Secretary of State that—

    (a)   the affairs of a company to which this subsection applies are being or have been conducted in a manner which is unfairly prejudicial to the interests of its members generally or of some part of its members, or

    (b)   any actual or proposed act or omission of a company to which this subsection applies, including an act or omission on its behalf, is or would be so prejudicial,

    he may himself (in addition to or instead of presenting a petition for the winding up of the company) apply to the court by petition for an order under this Part.

(1A)   Subsection (1) applies to a company in respect of which—

    (a)   the Secretary of State has received a report under section 437 of this Act;

    (b)   the Secretary of State has exercised his powers under section 447 or 448 of this Act; or

    (c)   the Secretary of State or the Financial Services Authority has exercised his or its powers under Part 11 of the Financial Services and Markets Act 2000; or

    (d)   the Secretary of State has received a report from an investigator appointed by him or the Financial Services Authority under that Part.

(2)   In this section (and, so far as applicable for its purposes, in the section next following) "company" means any body corporate which is liable to be wound up under this Act.

461.   **Provisions as to petitions and orders under this Part**

(1)   If the court is satisfied that a petition under this Part is well founded, it may make such order as it thinks fit for giving relief in respect of the matters complained of.

(2)   Without prejudice to the generality of subsection (1), the court's order may—

    (a)   regulate the conduct of the company's affairs in the future,

    (b)   require the company to refrain from doing or continuing an act complained of by the petitioner or to do an act which the petitioner has complained it has omitted to do,

    (c)   authorise civil proceedings to be brought in the name and on behalf of the company by such person or persons and on such terms as the court may direct,

    (d)   provide for the purchase of the shares of any members of the company by other members or by the company itself and, in the case of a purchase by the company itself, the reduction of the company's capital accordingly.

(3)   If an order under this Part requires the company not to make any, or any specified, alteration in the memorandum or articles, the company does not then have power without leave of the court to make any such alteration in breach of that requirement.

(4)   Any alteration in the company's memorandum or articles made by virtue of an order under this Part is of the same effect as if duly made by resolution of the company, and the provisions of this Act apply to the memorandum or articles as so altered accordingly.

(5)   An office copy of an order under this Part altering, or giving leave to alter, a company's memorandum or articles shall, within 14 days from the making of the order or such longer period as the court may allow, be delivered by the company to the registrar of companies for registration; and if a company makes default in complying with this subsection, the company and every officer of it who is in default is liable to a fine and, for continued contravention, to a daily default fine.

(6)   The power under section 411 of the Insolvency Act to make rules shall, so far as it relates to a winding-up petition, apply for the purposes of a petition under this Part.

PART XVIII
FLOATING CHARGES AND RECEIVERS (SCOTLAND)

CHAPTER I
FLOATING CHARGES

462. Power of incorporated company to create floating charge

(1)   It is competent under the law of Scotland for an incorporated company (whether a company within the meaning of this Act or not), for the purpose of securing any debt or other obligation (including a cautionary obligation) incurred or to be incurred by, or binding upon, the company or any other person, to create in favour of the creditor in the debt or obligation a charge, in this Part referred to as a floating charge, over all or any part of the property (including uncalled capital) which may from time to time be comprised in its property and undertaking.

(2), (3)   ...

(4)   References in this Part to the instrument by which a floating charge was created are, in the case of a floating charge created by words in a bond or other written acknowledgment, references to the bond or, as the case may be, the other written acknowledgment.

(5)   Subject to this Act, a floating charge has effect in accordance with this Part and Part III of the Insolvency Act 1986 in relation to any heritable property in Scotland to which it relates, notwithstanding that the instrument creating it is not recorded in the Register of Sasines or, as appropriate, registered in accordance with the Land Registration (Scotland) Act 1979.

463. Effect of floating charge on winding up

(1)   Where a company goes into liquidation within the meaning of section 247(2) of the Insolvency Act 1986, a floating charge created by the company attaches to the property then comprised in the company's property and undertaking or, as the case may be, in part of that property and undertaking, but does so subject to the rights of any person who—

(a)   has effectually executed diligence on the property or any part of it; or

(b)   holds a fixed security over the property or any part of it ranking in priority to the floating charge; or

(c)   holds over the property or any part of it another floating charge so ranking.

(2)   The provisions of Part IV of the Insolvency Act (except section 185) have effect in relation to a floating charge, subject to subsection (1), as if the charge were a fixed security over the property to which it has attached in respect of the principal of the debt or obligation to which it relates and any interest due or to become due thereon.

(3)   Nothing in this section derogates from the provisions of sections 53(7) and 54(6) of the Insolvency Act (attachment of floating charge on appointment of receiver), or prejudices the operation of sections 175 and 176 of that Act (payment of preferential debts in winding up)

(4)   ... interest accrues, in respect of a floating charge which after 16th November 1972 attaches to the property of the company, until payment of the sum due under the charge is made.

464. Ranking of floating charges

(1)   Subject to subsection (2), the instrument creating a floating charge over all or any part of the company's property under section 462 may contain—

(a)   provisions prohibiting or restricting the creation of any fixed security or any other floating charge having priority over, or ranking pari passu with, the floating charge; or

(b)   with the consent of the holder of any subsisting floating charge or fixed security which would be adversely affected, provisions regulating the order in which the floating charge shall rank with any other subsisting or future floating charges or fixed securities over that property or any part of it.

(1A)   Where an instrument creating a floating charge contains any such provision as is mentioned in subsection (1)(a), that provision shall be effective to confer priority on the floating charge over any fixed security or floating charge created after the date of the instrument.

(2)   Where all or any part of the property of a company is subject both to a floating charge and to a fixed security arising by operation of law, the fixed security has priority over the floating charge.

(3)   The order of ranking of the floating charge with any other subsisting or future floating charges or fixed securities over all or any part of the company's property is determined in accordance with the provisions of subsections (4) and (5) except where it is determined in accordance with any provision such as is mentioned in paragraph (a) or (b) of subsection (1).

(4)   Subject to the provisions of this section—
   (a)   a fixed security, the right to which has been constituted as a real right before a floating charge has attached to all or any part of the property of the company, has priority of ranking over the floating charge;
   (b)   floating charges rank with one another according to the time of registration in accordance with Chapter II of Part XII;
   (c)   floating charges which have been received by the registrar for registration by the same postal delivery rank with one another equally.

(5)   Where the holder of a floating charge over all or any part of the company's property which has been registered in accordance with Chapter II of Part XII has received intimation in writing of the subsequent registration in accordance with that Chapter of another floating charge over the same property or any part thereof, the preference in ranking of the first-mentioned floating charge is restricted to security for—
   (a)   the holder's present advances;
   (b)   future advances which he may be required to make under the instrument creating the floating charge or under any ancillary document;
   (c)   interest due or to become due on all such advances; ...
   (d)   any expenses or outlays which may reasonably be incurred by the holder ; and
   (e)   (in the case of a floating charge to secure a contingent liability other than a liability arising under any further advances made from time to time) the maximum sum to which that contingent liability is capable of amounting whether or not it is contractually limited.

(6)   This section is subject to Part XII and to sections 175 and 176 of the Insolvency Act.

465.   Continued effect of certain charges validated by Act of 1972

(1)   Any floating charge which—
   (a)   purported to subsist as a floating charge on 17th November 1972, and
   (b)   if it had been created on or after that date, would have been validly created by virtue of the Companies (Floating Charges and Receivers) (Scotland) Act 1972,
is deemed to have subsisted as a valid floating charge as from the date of its creation.

(2)   Any provision which—
   (a)   is contained in an instrument creating a floating charge or in any ancillary document executed prior to, and still subsisting at, the commencement of that Act,
   (b)   relates to the ranking of charges, and
   (c)   if it had been made after the commencement of that Act, would have been a valid provision,
is deemed to have been a valid provision as from the date of its making.

466.   Alteration of floating charges

(1)   The instrument creating a floating charge under section 462 or any ancillary document may be altered by the execution of an instrument of alteration by the company, the holder of the charge and the holder of any other charge (including a fixed security) which would be adversely affected by the alteration.

(2)   Without prejudice to any enactment or rule of law regarding the execution of documents, such an instrument of alteration is validly executed if it is executed—
   (a)   ...
   (b)   where trustees for debenture-holders are acting under and in accordance with a trust deed, by those trustees; or
   (c)   where, in the case of a series of secured debentures, no such trustees are acting, by or on behalf of—

(i) a majority in nominal value of those present or represented by proxy and voting at a meeting of debenture-holders at which the holders of at least one-third in nominal value of the outstanding debentures of the series are present or so represented; or

(ii) where no such meeting is held, the holders of at least one-half in nominal value of the outstanding debentures of the series; ...

(d) ...

(3) Section 464 applies to an instrument of alteration under this section as it applies to an instrument creating a floating charge.

(4) *Subject to the next subsection, section 410(2) and (3) and section 420 apply to an instrument of alteration under this section which—*

(a) *prohibits or restricts the creation of any fixed security or any other floating charge having priority over, or ranking pari passu with, the floating charge; or*

(b) *varies, or otherwise regulates the order of, the ranking of the floating charge in relation to fixed securities or to other floating charges; or*

(c) *releases property from the floating charge; or*

(d) *increases the amount secured by the floating charge.*

(5) *Section 410(2) and (3) and section 420 apply to an instrument of alteration falling under subsection (4) of this section as if references in the said sections to a charge were references to an alteration to a floating charge, and as if in section 410(2) and (3)—*

(a) *references to the creation of a charge were references to the execution of such alteration; and*

(b) *for the words from the beginning of subsection (2) to the word "applies" there were substituted the words "Every alteration to a floating charge created by a company".*

(6) Any reference (however expressed) in any enactment, including this Act, to a floating charge is, for the purposes of this section and unless the context otherwise requires, to be construed as including a reference to the floating charge as altered by an instrument of alteration *falling under subsection (4) of this section.*

Note. Subsections (4) and (5) and the italicized words in subsection (6) are repealed by the Companies Act 1989, ss. 140(8), 212, Sch. 24, as from a day to be appointed.

467–85....

CHAPTER III
GENERAL

486.   Interpretation for Part XVIII generally

(1) In this Part, unless the context otherwise requires, the following expressions have the following meanings respectively assigned to them, that is to say—

"ancillary document" means—

(a) a document which relates to the floating charge and which was executed by the debtor or creditor in the charge before the registration of the charge in accordance with Chapter II of Part XII; or

(b) an instrument of alteration such as is mentioned in section 466 in this Part;

"company", ... means an incorporated company (whether a company within the meaning of this Act or not);

"fixed security", in relation to any property of a company, means any security, other than a floating charge or a charge having the nature of a floating charge, which on the winding up of the company in Scotland would be treated as an effective security over that property, and (without prejudice to that generality) includes a security over that property, being a heritable security within the meaning of section 9(8) of the Conveyancing and Feudal Reform (Scotland) Act 1970;

...

"Register of Sasines" means the appropriate division of the General Register of Sasines.

487.   Extent of Part XVIII

This Part extends to Scotland only.

488–650....

PART XX

WINDING UP OF COMPANIES REGISTERED UNDER THIS ACT OR THE
FORMER COMPANIES ACTS

CHAPTER VI
MATTERS ARISING SUBSEQUENT TO WINDING UP

651.   Power of court to declare dissolution of company void

(1)   Where a company has been dissolved, the court may ..., on an application made for the purpose by the liquidator of the company or by any other person appearing to the court to be interested, make an order, on such terms as the court thinks fit, declaring the dissolution to have been void.

(2)   Thereupon such proceedings may be taken as might have been taken if the company had not been dissolved.

(3)   It is the duty of the person on whose application the order was made, within 7 days after its making (or such further time as the court may allow), to deliver to the registrar of companies for registration an office copy of the order.

If the person fails to do so, he is liable to a fine and, for continued contravention, to a daily default fine.

(4)   Subject to the following provisions, an application under this section may not be made after the end of the period of two years from the date of the dissolution of the company.

(5)   An application for the purposes of bringing proceedings against the company—

(a)   for damages in respect of personal injuries (including any sum claimed by virtue of section 1(2)(c) of the Law Reform (Miscellaneous Provisions) Act 1934 (funeral expenses)), or

(b)   for damages under the Fatal Accidents Act 1976 or the Damages (Scotland) Act 1976,

may be made at any time; but no order shall be made on such an application if it appears to the court that the proceedings would fail by virtue of any enactment as to the time within which proceedings must be brought.

(6)   Nothing in subsection (5) affects the power of the court on making an order under this section to direct that the period between the dissolution of the company and the making of the order shall not count for the purposes of any such enactment.

(7)   In subsection (5)(a) "personal injuries" includes any disease and any impairment of a person's physical or mental condition.

652.   Registrar may strike defunct company off register

(1)   If the registrar of companies has reasonable cause to believe that a company is not carrying on business or in operation, he may send to the company by post a letter inquiring whether the company is carrying on business or in operation.

(2)   If the registrar does not within one month of sending the letter receive any answer to it, he shall within 14 days after the expiration of that month send to the company by post a registered letter referring to the first letter, and stating that no answer to it has been received, and that if an answer is not received to the second letter within one month from its date, a notice will be published in the Gazette with a view to striking the company's name off the register.

(3)   If the registrar either receives an answer to the effect that the company is not carrying on business or in operation, or does not within one month after sending the second letter receive any answer, he may publish in the Gazette, and send to the company by post, a notice that at the expiration of 3 months from the date of that notice the name of the company mentioned in it will, unless cause is shown to the contrary, be struck off the register and the company will be dissolved.

(4)   If, in a case where a company is being wound up, the registrar has reasonable cause to believe either that no liquidator is acting, or that the affairs of the company are fully wound up, and the returns required to be made by the liquidator have not been made for a period of 6 consecutive months, the registrar shall publish in the Gazette and send to the company or the liquidator (if any) a like notice as is provided in subsection (3).

(5)   At the expiration of the time mentioned in the notice the registrar may, unless cause to the contrary is previously shown by the company, strike its name off the register, and shall publish notice of this in the Gazette; and on the publication of that notice in the Gazette the company is dissolved.

(6)   However—

    (a)   the liability (if any) of every director, managing officer and member of the company continues and may be enforced as if the company had not been dissolved, and

    (b)   nothing in subsection (5) affects the power of the court to wind up a company the name of which has been struck off the register.

(7)   A notice to be sent to a liquidator under this section may be addressed to him at his last known place of business; and a letter or notice to be sent under this section to a company may be addressed to the company at its registered office or, if no office has been registered, to the care of some officer of the company.

If there is no officer of the company whose name and address are known to the registrar of companies, the letter or notice may be sent to each of the persons who subscribed the memorandum, addressed to him at the address mentioned in the memorandum.

652A.   Registrar may strike private company off register on application

(1)   On application by a private company, the registrar of companies may strike the company's name off the register.

(2)   An application by a company under this section shall—

    (a)   be made on its behalf by its directors or by a majority of them,

    (b)   be in the prescribed form, and

    (c)   contain the prescribed information.

(3)   The registrar shall not strike a company off under this section until after the expiration of 3 months from the publication by him in the Gazette of a notice—

    (a)   stating that he may exercise his power under this section in relation to the company, and

    (b)   inviting any person to show cause why he should not do so.

(4)   Where the registrar strikes a company off under this section, he shall publish notice of that fact in the Gazette.

(5)   On the publication in the Gazette of a notice under subsection (4), the company to which the notice relates is dissolved.

(6)   However, the liability (if any) of every director, managing officer and member of the company continues and may be enforced as if the company had not been dissolved.

(7)   Nothing in this section affects the power of the court to wind up a company the name of which has been struck off the register.

652B.   Duties in connection with making application under section 652A

(1)   A person shall not make an application under section 652A on behalf of a company if, at any time in the previous 3 months, the company has—

    (a)   changed its name,

    (b)   traded or otherwise carried on business,

    (c)   made a disposal for value of property or rights which, immediately before ceasing to trade or otherwise carry on business, it held for the purpose of disposal for gain in the normal course of trading or otherwise carrying on business, or

    (d)   engaged in any other activity, except one which is—

        (i)   necessary or expedient for the purpose of making an application under section 652A, or deciding whether to do so,

        (ii)   necessary or expedient for the purpose of concluding the affairs of the company,

(iii) necessary or expedient for the purpose of complying with any statutory requirement, or

(iv) specified by the Secretary of State by order for the purposes of this sub-paragraph.

(2)   For the purposes of subsection (1), a company shall not be treated as trading or otherwise carrying on business by virtue only of the fact that it makes a payment in respect of a liability incurred in the course of trading or otherwise carrying on business.

(3)   A person shall not make an application under section 652A on behalf of a company at a time when any of the following is the case—

(a)   an application has been made to the court under section 425 on behalf of the company for the sanctioning of a compromise or arrangement and the matter has not been finally concluded;

(b)   a voluntary arrangement in relation to the company has been proposed under Part I of the Insolvency Act 1986 and the matter has not been finally concluded;

(c)   the company is in administration under Part II of that Act;

(ca)   an application to the court for an administration order in respect of the company has been made and not finally dealt with or withdrawn;

(cb)   a copy of notice of intention to appoint an administrator of the company under paragraph 14 of Schedule B1 to that Act has been filed with the court and neither of the events mentioned in paragraph 44(2)(a) and (b) of that Schedule has occurred;

(cc)   a copy of notice of intention to appoint an administrator of the company under paragraph 22 of that Schedule has been filed with the court and neither of the events mentioned in paragraph 44(4)(a) and (b) of that Schedule has occurred;

(d)   the company is being wound up under Part IV of that Act, whether voluntarily or by the court, or a petition under that Part for the winding up of the company by the court has been presented and not finally dealt with or withdrawn;

(e)   there is a receiver or manager of the company's property;

(f)   the company's estate is being administered by a judicial factor.

(4)   For the purposes of subsection (3)(a), the matter is finally concluded if—

(a)   the application has been withdrawn,

(b)   the application has been finally dealt with without a compromise or arrangement being sanctioned by the court, or

(c)   a compromise or arrangement has been sanctioned by the court and has, together with anything required to be done under any provision made in relation to the matter by order of the court, been fully carried out.

(5)   For the purposes of subsection (3)(b), the matter is finally concluded if—

(a)   no meetings are to be summoned under section 3 of the Insolvency Act 1986,

(b)   meetings summoned under that section fail to approve the arrangement with no, or the same, modifications,

(c)   an arrangement approved by meetings summoned under that section, or in consequence of a direction under section 6(4)(b) of that Act, has been fully implemented, or

(d)   the court makes an order under subsection (5) of section 6 of that Act revoking approval given at previous meetings and, if the court gives any directions under subsection (6) of that section, the company has done whatever it is required to do under those directions.

(6)   A person who makes an application under section 652A on behalf of a company shall secure that a copy of the application is given, within 7 days from the day on which the application is made, to every person who, at any time on that day, is—

(a)   a member of the company,

(b)   an employee of the company,

(c)   a creditor of the company,

(d)   a director of the company,

(e)   a manager or trustee of any pension fund established for the benefit of employees of the company, or

(f)   a person of a description specified for the purposes of this paragraph by regulations made by the Secretary of State.

(7)   Subsection (6) shall not require a copy of the application to be given to a director who is a party to the application.

(8)   The duty imposed by subsection (6) shall cease to apply if the application is withdrawn before the end of the period for giving the copy application.

(9)   The Secretary of State may by order amend subsection (1) for the purpose of altering the period in relation to which the doing of the things mentioned in paragraphs (a) to (d) of that subsection is relevant.

652C.   Directors' duties following application under section 652A

(1)   Subsection (2) applies in relation to any time after the day on which a company makes an application under section 652A and before the day on which the application is finally dealt with or withdrawn.

(2)   A person who is a director of the company at the end of a day on which a person other than himself becomes—

    (a)   a member of the company,

    (b)   an employee of the company,

    (c)   a creditor of the company,

    (d)   a director of the company,

    (e)   a manager or trustee of any pension fund established for the benefit of employees of the company, or

    (f)   a person of a description specified for the purposes of this paragraph by regulations made by the Secretary of State,

shall secure that a copy of the application is given to that person within 7 days from that day.

(3)   The duty imposed by subsection (2) shall cease to apply if the application is finally dealt with or withdrawn before the end of the period for giving the copy application.

(4)   Subsection (5) applies where, at any time on or after the day on which a company makes an application under section 652A and before the day on which the application is finally dealt with or withdrawn—

    (a)   the company—

        (i)   changes its name,

        (ii)   trades or otherwise carries on business,

        (iii)   makes a disposal for value of any property or rights other than those which it was necessary or expedient for it to hold for the purpose of making, or proceeding with, an application under section 652A, or

        (iv)   engages in any other activity, except one to which subsection (6) applies;

    (b)   an application is made to the court under section 425 on behalf of the company for the sanctioning of a compromise or arrangement;

    (c)   a voluntary arrangement in relation to the company is proposed under of the Insolvency Act 1986;

    (d)   an application to the court for an administration order in respect of the company is made under paragraph 12 of Schedule B1 to that Act;

    (da)   an administrator is appointed in respect of the company under paragraph 14 or 22 of that Schedule;

    (db)   a copy of notice of intention to appoint an administrator of the company under paragraph 14 or 22 of that Schedule is filed with the court;

    (e)   there arise any of the circumstances in which, under section 84(1) of that Act, the company may be voluntarily wound up;

    (f)   a petition is presented for the winding up of the company by the court under Part IV of that Act;

    (g)   a receiver or manager of the company's property is appointed; or

    (h)   a judicial factor is appointed to administer the company's estate.

(5)   A person who, at the end of a day on which an event mentioned in any of paragraphs (a) to (h) of subsection (4) occurs, is a director of the company shall secure that the company's application is withdrawn forthwith.

(6)   This subsection applies to any activity which is—

(a)   necessary or expedient for the purpose of making, or proceeding with, an application under section 652A,

(b)   necessary or expedient for the purpose of concluding affairs of the company which are outstanding because of what has been necessary or expedient for the purpose of making, or proceeding with, such an application,

(c)   necessary or expedient for the purpose of complying with any statutory requirement, or

(d)   specified by the Secretary of State by order for the purposes of this subsection.

(7)   For the purposes of subsection (4)(a), a company shall not be treated as trading or otherwise carrying on business by virtue only of the fact that it makes a payment in respect of a liability incurred in the course of trading or otherwise carrying on business.

652D.   Sections 652B and 652C: supplementary provisions

(1)   For the purposes of sections 652B(6) and 652C(2), a document shall be treated as given to a person if it is delivered to him or left at his proper address or sent by post to him at that address.

(2)   For the purposes of subsection (1) and section 7 of the Interpretation Act 1978 (which relates to the service of documents by post) in its application to that subsection, the proper address of any person shall be his last known address, except that—

(a)   in the case of a body corporate, other than one to which subsection (3) applies, it shall be the address of its registered or principal office,

(b)   in the case of a partnership, other than one to which subsection (3) applies, it shall be the address of its principal office, and

(c)   in the case of a body corporate or partnership to which subsection (3) applies, it shall be the address of its principal office in the United Kingdom.

(3)   This subsection applies to a body corporate or partnership which—

(a)   is incorporated or formed under the law of a country or territory outside the United Kingdom, and

(b)   has a place of business in the United Kingdom.

(4)   Where a creditor of the company has more than one place of business, subsection (1) shall have effect, so far as concerns the giving of a document to him, as if for the words from "delivered" to the end there were substituted "left, or sent by post to him, at each place of business of his with which the company has had dealings in relation to a matter by virtue of which he is a creditor of the company."

(5)   Any power to make an order or regulations under section 652B or 652C shall—

(a)   include power to make different provision for different cases or classes of case,

(b)   include power to make such transitional provisions as the Secretary of State considers appropriate, and

(c)   be exercisable by statutory instrument subject to annulment in pursuance of a resolution of either House of Parliament.

(6)   For the purposes of sections 652B and 652C, an application under section 652A is withdrawn if notice of withdrawal in the prescribed form is given to the registrar of companies.

(7)   In sections 652B and 652C, "disposal" includes part disposal.

(8)   In sections 652B and 652C and this section, "creditor" includes a contingent or prospective creditor.

652E.   Sections 652B and 652C: enforcement

(1)   A person who breaches or fails to perform a duty imposed on him by section 652B or 652C is guilty of an offence and liable to a fine.

(2)   A person who fails to perform a duty imposed on him by section 652B(6) or 652C(2) with the intention of concealing the making of the application in question from the person concerned is guilty of an offence and liable to imprisonment or a fine, or both.

(3)   In any proceedings for an offence under subsection (1) consisting of breach of a duty imposed by section 652B(1) or (3), it shall be a defence for the accused to prove that he did not know, and could not reasonably have known, of the existence of the facts which led to the breach.

(4)   In any proceedings for an offence under subsection (1) consisting of failure to perform the duty imposed by section 652B(6), it shall be a defence for the accused to prove that he took all reasonable steps to perform the duty.

(5)   In any proceedings for an offence under subsection (1) consisting of failure to perform a duty imposed by section 652C(2) or (5), it shall be a defence for the accused to prove—

(a)   that at the time of the failure he was not aware of the fact that the company had made an application under section 652A, or

(b)   that he took all reasonable steps to perform the duty.

652F.   Other offences connected with section 652A

(1)   Where a company makes an application under section 652A, any person who, in connection with the application, knowingly or recklessly furnishes any information to the registrar of companies which is false or misleading in a material particular is guilty of an offence and liable to a fine.

(2)   Any person who knowingly or recklessly makes an application to the registrar of companies which purports to be an application under section 652A, but which is not, is guilty of an offence and liable to a fine.

653.   Objection to striking off by person aggrieved

(1)   Subsection (2) applies if a company or any member or creditor of it feels aggrieved by the company having been struck off the register under section 652.

(2)   The court, on an application by the company or the member or creditor made before the expiration of 20 years from publication in the Gazette of notice under section 652, may, if satisfied that the company was at the time of the striking off carrying on business or in operation, or otherwise that it is just that the company be restored to the register, order the company's name to be restored.

(2A)   Subsections (2B) and (2D) apply if a company has been struck off the register under section 652A.

(2B)   The court, on an application by a notifiable person made before the expiration of 20 years from publication in the Gazette of notice under section 652A(4), may, if satisfied—

(a)   that any duty under section 652B or 652C with respect to the giving to that person of a copy of the company's application under section 652A was not performed,

(b)   that the making of the company's application under section 652A involved a breach of duty under section 652B(1) or (3), or

(c)   that it is for some other reason just to do so,

order the company's name to be restored to the register.

(2C)   In subsection (2B), "notifiable person" means a person to whom a copy of the company's application under section 652A was required to be given under section 652B or 652C.

(2D)   The court, on an application by the Secretary of State made before the expiration of 20 years from publication in the Gazette of notice under section 652A(4), may, if satisfied that it is in the public interest to do so, order the company's name to be restored.

(3)   On an office copy of an order under subsection (2), (2B) or (2D) being delivered to the registrar of companies for registration the company to which the order relates is deemed to have continued in existence as if its name had not been struck off; and the court may by the order give such directions and make such provisions as seem just for placing the company and all other persons in the same position (as nearly as may be) as if the company's name had not been struck off.

654. **Property of dissolved company to be bona vacantia**

(1) When a company is dissolved, all property and rights whatsoever vested in or held on trust for the company immediately before its dissolution (including leasehold property, but not including property held by the company on trust for any other person) are deemed to be bona vacantia and—

    (a) accordingly belong to the Crown, or to the Duchy of Lancaster or to the Duke of Cornwall for the time being (as the case may be), and

    (b) vest and may be dealt with in the same manner as other bona vacantia accruing to the Crown, to the Duchy of Lancaster or to the Duke of Cornwall.

(2) Except as provided by the section next following, the above has effect subject and without prejudice to any order made by the court under section 651 or 653.

655. **Effect on s 654 of company's revival after dissolution**

(1) The person in whom any property or right is vested by section 654 may dispose of, or of an interest in, that property or right notwithstanding that an order may be made under section 651 or 653.

(2) Where such an order is made—

    (a) it does not affect the disposition (but without prejudice to the order so far as it relates to any other property or right previously vested in or held on trust for the company), and

    (b) the Crown or, as the case may be, the Duke of Cornwall shall pay to the company an amount equal to—

        (i) the amount of any consideration received for the property or right, or interest therein, or

        (ii) the value of any such consideration at the time of the disposition,

    or, if no consideration was received, an amount equal to the value of the property, right or interest disposed of, as at the date of the disposition.

(3) Where a liability accrues under subsection (2) in respect of any property or right which, before the order under section 651 or 653 was made, had accrued as bona vacantia to the Duchy of Lancaster, the Attorney General of the Duchy shall represent Her Majesty in any proceedings arising in connection with that liability.

(4) Where a liability accrues under subsection (2) in respect of any property or right which, before the order under section 651 or 653 was made, had accrued as bona vacantia to the Duchy of Cornwall, such persons as the Duke of Cornwall (or other possessor for the time being of the Duchy) may appoint shall represent the Duke (or other possessor) in any proceedings arising out of that liability.

(5) This section applies in relation to the disposition of any property, right or interest on or after 22nd December 1981, whether the company concerned was dissolved before, on or after that day.

656. **Crown disclaimer of property vesting as bona vacantia**

(1) Where property vests in the Crown under section 654, the Crown's title to it under that section may be disclaimed by a notice signed by the Crown representative, that is to say the Treasury Solicitor, or, in relation to property in Scotland, the Queen's and Lord Treasurer's Remembrancer.

(2) The right to execute a notice of disclaimer under this section may be waived by or on behalf of the Crown either expressly or by taking possession or other act evincing that intention.

(3) A notice of disclaimer under this section is of no effect unless it is executed—

    (a) within 12 months of the date on which the vesting of the property under section 654 came to the notice of the Crown representative, or

    (b) if an application in writing is made to the Crown representative by any person interested in the property requiring him to decide whether he will or will not disclaim, within a period of 3 months after the receipt of the application or such further period as may be allowed by the court which would have had jurisdiction to wind up the company if it had not been dissolved.

(4)   A statement in a notice of disclaimer of any property under this section that the vesting of it came to the notice of the Crown representative on a specified date, or that no such application as above mentioned was received by him with respect to the property before a specified date, is sufficient evidence of the fact stated, until the contrary is proved.

(5)   A notice of disclaimer under this section shall be delivered to the registrar of companies and retained and registered by him; and copies of it shall be published in the Gazette and sent to any persons who have given the Crown representative notice that they claim to be interested in the property.

(6)   This section applies to property vested in the Duchy of Lancaster or the Duke of Cornwall under section 654 as if for references to the Crown and the Crown representative there were respectively substituted references to the Duchy of Lancaster and to the Solicitor to that Duchy, or to the Duke of Cornwall and to the Solicitor to the Duchy of Cornwall, as the case may be.

657. Effect of Crown disclaimer under s 656

(1)   Where notice of disclaimer is executed under section 656 as respects any property, that property is deemed not to have vested in the Crown under section 654.

(2)   As regards property in England and Wales, section 178(4) and sections 179 to 182 of the Insolvency Act shall apply as if the property had been disclaimed by the liquidator under the said section 91 immediately before the dissolution of the company.

(3)   As regards property in Scotland, the following 4 subsections apply.

(4)   The Crown's disclaimer operates to determine, as from the date of the disclaimer, the rights, interests and liabilities of the company, and the property of the company, in or in respect of the property disclaimed; but it does not (except so far as is necessary for the purpose of releasing the company and its property from liability) affect the rights or liabilities of any other person.

(5)   The court may, on application by a person who either claims an interest in disclaimed property or is under a liability not discharged by this Act in respect of disclaimed property, and on hearing such persons as it thinks fit, make an order for the vesting of the property in or its delivery to any persons entitled to it, or to whom it may seem just that the property should be delivered by way of compensation for such liability, or a trustee for him, and on such terms as the court thinks just.

(6)   On such a vesting order being made, the property comprised in it vests accordingly in the person named in that behalf in the order, without conveyance or assignation for that purpose.

(7)   Part II of Schedule 20 has effect for the protection of third parties where the property disclaimed is held under a lease.

658. Liability for rentcharge on company's land after dissolution

(1)   Section 180 of the Insolvency Act shall apply to land in England and Wales which by operation of law vests subject to a rentcharge in the Crown or any other person on the dissolution of a company as it applies to land so vesting on a disclaimer under that section.

(2)   In this section "company" includes any body corporate.

659–74....

PART XXII
BODIES CORPORATE SUBJECT, OR BECOMING SUBJECT, TO THIS ACT (OTHERWISE THAN BY ORIGINAL FORMATION UNDER PART I)

CHAPTER I
COMPANIES FORMED OR REGISTERED UNDER FORMER COMPANIES ACTS

675. Companies formed and registered under former Companies Acts

(1)   In its application to existing companies, this Act applies in the same manner—

     (a)   in the case of a limited company (other than a company limited by guarantee) as if the company had been formed and registered under Part I of this Act as a company limited by shares,

(b)   in the case of a company limited by guarantee, as if the company had been formed and registered under that Part as a company limited by guarantee, and

(c)   in the case of a company other than a limited company, as if the company had been formed and registered under that Part as an unlimited company.

(2)   But reference, express or implied, to the date of registration is to be read as the date at which the company was registered under the Joint Stock Companies Acts, the Companies Act 1862, the Companies (Consolidation) Act 1908, the Companies Act 1929, or the Companies Act 1948.

676.   Companies registered but not formed under former Companies Acts

(1)   This Act applies to every company registered but not formed under the Joint Stock Companies Acts, the Companies Act 1862, the Companies (Consolidation) Act 1908, the Companies Act 1929, or the Companies Act 1948, in the same manner as it is in Chapter II of this Part declared to apply to companies registered but not formed under this Act.

(2)   But reference, express or implied, to the date of registration is to be read as referring to the date at which the company was registered under the Joint Stock Companies Acts, the Companies Act 1862, the Companies (Consolidation) Act 1908, the Companies Act 1929, or the Companies Act 1948.

677.   Companies re-registered with altered status under former Companies Acts

(1)   This Act applies to every unlimited company registered or re-registered as limited in pursuance of the Companies Act 1879, section 57 of the Companies (Consolidation) Act 1908, section 16 of the Companies Act 1929, section 16 of the Companies Act 1948 or section 44 of the Companies Act 1967 as it (this Act) applies to an unlimited company re-registered as limited in pursuance of Part II of this Act.

(2)   But reference, express or implied, to the date of registration or re-registration is to be read as referring to the date at which the company was registered or re-registered as a limited company under the relevant enactment.

678.   Companies registered under Joint Stock Companies Acts

(1)   A company registered under the Joint Stock Companies Acts may cause its shares to be transferred in manner hitherto in use, or in such other manner as the company may direct.

(2)   The power of altering articles under section 9 of this Act extends, in the case of an unlimited company formed and registered under the Joint Stock Companies Acts, to altering any regulations relating to the amount of capital or to its distribution into shares, notwithstanding that those regulations are contained in the memorandum.

679.   Northern Ireland and Irish companies

Nothing in sections 675 to 678 applies to companies registered in Northern Ireland or the Republic of Ireland.

CHAPTER II
COMPANIES NOT FORMED UNDER COMPANIES LEGISLATION,
BUT AUTHORISED TO REGISTER

680.   Companies capable of being registered under this Chapter

(1)   With the exceptions and subject to the provisions contained in this section and the next—

(a)   any company consisting of two or more members, which was in existence on 2nd November 1862, including any company registered under the Joint Stock Companies Acts, and

(b)   any company formed after that date (whether before or after the commencement of this Act), in pursuance of any Act of Parliament (other than this Act), or of letters patent, or being otherwise duly constituted according to law, and consisting of two or more members,

may at any time, on making application in the prescribed form, register under this Act as an unlimited company, or as a company limited by shares, or as a company limited by guarantee; and the registration is not invalid by reason that it has taken place with a view to the company's being wound up.

(1A)   A company shall not be prevented from registering under this Act as a private company limited by shares or by guarantee solely because it has only one member.

(2)   A company registered in any part of the United Kingdom under the Companies Act 1862, the Companies (Consolidation) Act 1908, the Companies Act 1929 or the Companies Act 1948 shall not register under this section.

(3)   A company having the liability of its members limited by Act of Parliament or letters patent, and not being a joint stock company, shall not register under this section.

(4)   A company having the liability of its members limited by Act of Parliament or letters patent shall not register in pursuance of this section as an unlimited company or as a company limited by guarantee.

(5)   A company that is not a joint stock company shall not register under this section as a company limited by shares.

681.   Procedural requirements for registration

(1)   A company shall not register under section 680 without the assent of a majority of such of its members as are present in person or by proxy (in cases where proxies are allowed) at a general meeting summoned for the purpose.

(2)   Where a company not having the liability of its members limited by Act of Parliament or letters patent is about to register as a limited company, the majority required to assent as required by subsection (1) shall consist of not less than three-fourths of the members present in person or by proxy at the meeting.

(3)   In computing any majority under this section when a poll is demanded, regard is to be had to the number of votes to which each member is entitled according to the company's regulations.

(4)   Where a company is about to register (under section 680) as a company limited by guarantee, the assent to its being so registered shall be accompanied by a resolution declaring that each member undertakes to contribute to the company's assets, in the event of its being wound up while he is a member, or within one year after he ceases to be a member, for payment of the company's debts and liabilities contracted before he ceased to be a member, and of the costs and expenses of winding up and for the adjustment of the rights of the contributories among themselves, such amount as may be required, not exceeding a specified amount.

(5)   Before a company is registered under section 680, it shall deliver to the registrar of companies—

    (a)   a statement that the registered office of the company is to be situated in England and Wales or in Wales, or in Scotland (as the case may be),

    (b)   a statement specifying the intended situation of the company's registered office after registration, and

    (c)   in an appropriate case, if the company wishes to be registered with the Welsh equivalent of "public limited company" or, as the case may be, "limited" as the last words or word of its name, a statement to that effect.

(6)   Any statement delivered to the registrar under subsection (5) shall be made in the prescribed form.

682.   Change of name on registration

(1)   Where the name of a company seeking registration under section 680 is a name by which it is precluded from registration by section 26 of this Act, either because it falls within subsection (1) of that section or, if it falls within subsection (2), because the Secretary of State would not approve the company's being registered with that name, the company may change its name with effect from the date on which it is registered under this Chapter.

(2)   A change of name under this section requires the like assent of the company's members as is required by section 681 for registration.

683. Definition of "joint stock company"

(1) For purposes of this Chapter, as far as relates to registration of companies as companies limited by shares, "joint stock company" means a company—

(a) having a permanent paid-up or nominal share capital of fixed amount divided into shares, also of fixed amount, or held and transferable as stock, or divided and held partly in one way and partly in the other, and

(b) formed on the principle of having for its members the holders of those shares or that stock, and no other persons.

(2) Such a company when registered with limited liability under this Act is deemed a company limited by shares.

684. Requirements for registration by joint stock companies

(1) Before the registration under section 680 of a joint stock company, there shall be delivered to the registrar of companies the following documents—

(a) a statement in the prescribed form specifying the name with which the company is proposed to be registered,

(b) a list in the prescribed form showing the names and addresses of all persons who on a day named in the list (not more than 28 clear days before the day of registration) were members of the company, with the addition of the shares or stock held by them respectively (distinguishing, in cases where the shares are numbered, each share by its number), and

(c) a copy of any Act of Parliament, royal charter, letters patent, deed of settlement, contract of copartnery or other instrument constituting or regulating the company.

(2) If the company is intended to be registered as a limited company, there shall also be delivered to the registrar of companies a statement in the prescribed form specifying the following particulars—

(a) the nominal share capital of the company and the number of shares into which it is divided, or the amount of stock of which it consists, and

(b) the number of shares taken and the amount paid on each share.

685. Registration of joint stock company as public company

(1) A joint stock company applying to be registered under section 680 as a company limited by shares may, subject to—

(a) satisfying the conditions set out in section 44(2)(a) and (b) (where applicable) and section 45(2) to (4) as applied by this section, and

(b) complying with subsection (4) below,

apply to be so registered as a public company.

(2) Sections 44 and 45 apply for this purpose as in the case of a private company applying to be re-registered under section 43, but as if a reference to the special resolution required by section 43 were to the joint stock company's resolution that it be a public company.

(3) The resolution may change the company's name by deleting the word "company" or the words "and company", or its or their equivalent in Welsh ("cwmni", "a'r cwmni"), including any abbreviation of them.

(4) The joint stock company's application shall be made in the form prescribed for the purpose, and shall be delivered to the registrar of companies together with the following documents (as well as those required by section 684), namely—

(a) a copy of the resolution that the company be a public company,

(b) a copy of a written statement by an accountant with the appropriate qualifications that in his opinion a relevant balance sheet shows that at the balance sheet date the amount of the company's net assets was not less than the aggregate of its called up share capital and undistributable reserves,

(c) a copy of the relevant balance sheet, together with a copy of an unqualified report (by an accountant with such qualifications) in relation to that balance sheet,

    (d)   a copy of any valuation report prepared under section 44(2)(b) as applied by this section, and

    (e)   subject to subsection (4A), a statutory declaration in the prescribed form by a director or secretary of the company—

        (i)   that the conditions set out in section 44(2)(a) and (b) (where applicable) and section 45(2) to (4) have been satisfied, and

       (ii)   that, between the balance sheet date referred to in paragraph (b) of this subsection and the joint stock company's application, there has been no change in the company's financial position that has resulted in the amount of its net assets becoming less than the aggregate of its called up share capital and undistributable reserves.

(4A)   In place of the statutory declaration referred to in paragraph (e) of subsection (4), there may be delivered to the registrar of companies using electronic communications a statement made by a director or secretary of the company as to the matters set out in sub-paragraphs (i) and (ii) of that paragraph.

(5)   The registrar may accept a declaration under subsection (4)(e) or statement under subsection (4A) as sufficient evidence that the conditions referred to in that paragraph have been satisfied.

(6)   In this section—

        "accountant with the appropriate qualifications" means a person who would be eligible for appointment as the company's auditor, if it were a company registered under this Act,

        "relevant balance sheet" means a balance sheet prepared as at a date not more than 7 months before the joint stock company's application to be registered as a public company limited by shares, and

        "undistributable reserves" has the meaning given by section 264(3);

    and section 46 applies (with necessary modifications) for the interpretation of the reference in subsection (4)(c) above to an unqualified report by the accountant.

(6A)   Any person who makes a false statement under subsection (4A) which he knows to be false or does not believe to be true is liable to imprisonment or a fine, or both.

686.   Other requirements for registration

(1)   Before the registration in pursuance of this Chapter of any company (not being a joint stock company), there shall be delivered to the registrar of companies—

    (a)   a statement in the prescribed form specifying the name with which the company is proposed to be registered,

    (b)   a list showing with respect to each director or manager of the company—

        (i)   in the case of an individual, his name, address, occupation and date of birth,

       (ii)   in the case of a corporation or Scottish firm, its corporate or firm name and registered or principal office,

    (c)   a copy of any Act of Parliament, letters patent, deed of settlement, contract of copartnery or other instrument constituting or regulating the company, and

    (d)   in the case of a company intended to be registered as a company limited by guarantee, a copy of the resolution declaring the amount of the guarantee.

(1A)   For the purposes of subsection (1)(b)(i) a person's "name" means his Christian name (or other forename) and surname, except that in the case of a peer, or an individual usually known by a title, the title may be stated instead of his Christian name (or other forename) and surname or in addition to either or both of them.

(2)   Subject to subsection (2A), the lists of members and directors and any other particulars relating to the company which are required by this Chapter to be delivered to the registrar shall be verified by a statutory declaration in the prescribed form made by any two or more directors or other principal officers of the company.

(2A)   In place of the statutory declaration referred to in subsection (2), there may be delivered to the registrar of companies using electronic communications a statement made by any two or more directors or other principal officers of the company verifying the matters set out in that subsection.

(3)   The registrar may require such evidence as he thinks necessary for the purpose of satisfying himself whether a company proposing to be registered is or is not a joint stock company as defined by section 683.

(3A)   Any person who makes a false statement under subsection (2A) which he knows to be false or does not believe to be true is liable to imprisonment or a fine, or both.

687.   Name of company registering

(1)   The following applies with respect to the name of a company registering under this Chapter (whether a joint stock company or not).

(2)   If the company is to be registered as a public company, its name must end with the words "public limited company" or, if it is stated that the company's registered office is to be situated in Wales, with those words or their equivalent in Welsh ("cwmni cyfyngedig chyoeddus"); and those words or that equivalent may not be preceded by the word "limited" or its equivalent in Welsh ("cyfyngedig").

(3)   In the case of a company limited by shares or by guarantee (not being a public company), the name must have "limited" as its last word (or, if the company's registered office is to be situated in Wales, "cyfyngedig"); but this is subject to section 30 (exempting a company, in certain circumstances, from having "limited" as part of the name).

(4)   If the company is registered with limited liability, then any additions to the company's name set out in the statements delivered under section 684(1)(a) or 686(1)(a) shall form and be registered as the last part of the company's name.

688.   Certificate of registration under this Chapter

(1)   On compliance with the requirements of this Chapter with respect to registration, the registrar of companies shall give a certificate (which may be signed by him, or authenticated by his official seal) that the company applying for registration is incorporated as a company under this Act and, in the case of a limited company, that it is limited.

(2)   On the issue of the certificate, the company shall be so incorporated; and a banking company in Scotland so incorporated is deemed a bank incorporated, constituted or established by or under Act of Parliament.

(3)   The certificate is conclusive evidence that the requirements of this Chapter in respect of registration, and of matters precedent and incidental to it, have been complied with.

(4)   Where on an application by a joint stock company to register as a public company limited by shares the registrar of companies is satisfied that the company may be registered as a public company so limited, the certificate of incorporation given under this section shall state that the company is a public company; and that statement is conclusive evidence that the requirements of section 685 have been complied with and that the company is a public company so limited.

689.   Effect of registration

Schedule 21 to this Act has effect with respect to the consequences of registration under this Chapter, the vesting of property, savings for existing liabilities, continuation of existing actions, status of the company following registration, and other connected matters.

690.   Power to substitute memorandum and articles for deed of settlement

(1)   Subject as follows, a company registered in pursuance of this Chapter may by special resolution alter the form of its constitution by substituting a memorandum and articles for a deed of settlement.

(2)   The provisions of sections 4 to 6 to this Act with respect to applications to the court for cancellation of alterations of the objects of a company and matters consequential on the passing of resolutions for such alterations (so far as applicable) apply, but with the following modifications—

        (a)   there is substituted for the printed copy of the altered memorandum required to be delivered to the registrar of companies a printed copy of the substituted memorandum and articles, and

(b)   on the delivery to the registrar of the substituted memorandum and articles or the date when
      the alteration is no longer liable to be cancelled by order of the court (whichever is the
      later)—
      (i)   the substituted memorandum and articles apply to the company in the same manner as
            if it were a company registered under Part I with that memorandum and those articles,
            and
      (ii) the company's deed of settlement ceases to apply to the company.

(3)   An alteration under this section may be made either with or without alteration of the company's
       objects.

(4)   In this section "deed of settlement" includes any contract of copartnery or other instrument
       constituting or regulating the company, not being an Act of Parliament, a royal charter or letters
       patent.

PART XXIII

OVERSEA COMPANIES

CHAPTER I

REGISTRATION, ETC

690A. Branch registration under the Eleventh Company Law Directive (89/666/EEC)

(1)   This section applies to any limited company which—
       (a)   is incorporated outside the United Kingdom and Gibraltar, and
       (b)   has a branch in Great Britain.

(2)   Schedule 21A to this Act (Branch registration under the Eleventh Company Law Directive (89/
       666/EEC)) shall have effect in relation to any company to which this section applies.

690B. Scope of sections 691 and 692

Sections 691 and 692 shall not apply to any limited company which—
(a)   is incorporated outside the United Kingdom and Gibraltar, and
(b)   has a branch in the United Kingdom.

691.   Documents to be delivered to registrar

(1)   When a company incorporated outside Great Britain establishes a place of business in Great
       Britain, it shall within one month of doing so deliver to the registrar of companies for
       registration—
       (a)   a certified copy of the charter, statutes or memorandum and articles of the company or other
             instrument constituting or defining the company's constitution, and, if the instrument is not
             written in the English language, a certified translation of it; and
       (b)   a return in the prescribed form containing—
             (i)   a list of the company's directors and secretary, containing (subject to subsection (5))
                   the particulars specified in the next subsection,
             (ii) a list of the names and addresses of some one or more persons resident in Great Britain
                   authorised to accept on the company's behalf service of process and any notices
                   required to be served on it,
             (iii) a list of the documents delivered in compliance with paragraph (a) of this subsection,
                   and
             (iv) subject to subsection (3A), a statutory declaration (made by a director or secretary of
                   the company or by any person whose name and address are given in the list required
                   by sub-paragraph (ii)), stating the date on which the company's place of business in
                   Great Britain was established.

(2)   The list referred to in subsection (1)(b)(i) shall contain the following particulars with respect to
       each director—
       (a)   in the case of an individual—

        (i)   his name,

        (ii)   any former name,

        (iii) his usual residential address,

        (iv) his nationality,

        (v)   his business occupation (if any),

        (vi) if he has no business occupation but holds other directorships, particulars of them, and

        (vii) his date of birth;

    (b)   in the case of a corporation or Scottish firm, its corporate firm name and registered or principal office.

(3)   The list referred to in subsection (1)(b)(i) shall contain the following particulars with respect to the secretary (or, where there are joint secretaries, with respect to each of them)—

    (a)   in the case of an individual, his name, any former name and his usual residential address;

    (b)   in the case of a corporation or Scottish firm, its corporate or firm name and registered or principal office.

Where all the partners in a firm are joint secretaries of the company, the name and principal office of the firm may be stated instead of the particulars required by paragraph (a).

(3A)   In place of the statutory declaration referred to in sub-paragraph (iv) of paragraph (b) of subsection (1), there may be delivered to the registrar of companies using electronic communications a statement made by any person by whom the declaration could have been made stating the date on which the company's place of business in Great Britain was established.

(4)   In subsections (2)(a) and (3)(a) above—

    (a)   "name" means a person's Christian name (or other forename) and surname, except that in the case of a peer, or an individual usually known by a title, the title may be stated instead of his Christian name (or other forename) and surname, or in addition to either or both of them; and

    (b)   the reference to a former name does not include—

        (i)   in the case of a peer, or an individual normally known by a British title, the name by which he was known previous to the adoption of or succession to the title, or

        (ii) in the case of any person, a former name which was changed or disused before he attained the age of 18 years or which has been changed or disused for 20 years or more, or

        (iii) in the case of a married woman, the name by which she was known previous to the marriage.

(4A)   Any person who makes a false statement under subsection (3A) which he knows to be false or does not believe to be true is liable to imprisonment or a fine, or both.

(5)   Where a confidentiality order made under section 723B is in force in respect of a director or secretary required to be specified in the list under subsection (1)(b)(i)—

    (a)   if the order is in respect of a director, subsection (2) has effect in respect of that director as if the reference in subsection (2)(a)(iii) to his usual residential address were a reference to the address for the time being notified by him to the company under regulations made under sections 723B to 723F;

    (b)   if the order is in respect of a secretary, subsection (3) has effect in respect of that secretary as if the reference in subsection (3)(a) to his usual residential address were a reference to the address for the time being notified by him to the company under such regulations; and

    (c)   in either case the company shall deliver to the registrar, in addition to the return required by subsection (1), a return in the prescribed form containing the usual residential address of the director or secretary to whom the confidentiality order relates, and any such return shall be delivered to the registrar within one month of the company establishing a place of business in Great Britain.

692.   Registration of altered particulars

(1)   If any alteration is made in—

(a)   the charter, statutes, or memorandum and articles of an oversea company or any such instrument as is mentioned above, or

(b)   the directors or secretary of an oversea company or the particulars contained in the list of the directors and secretary, or

(c)   the names or addresses of the persons authorised to accept service on behalf of an oversea company,

the company shall, within the time specified below, deliver to the registrar of companies for registration a return containing the prescribed particulars of the alteration.

(1A)   If an individual in respect of whom a confidentiality order under section 723B is in force becomes a director or secretary of an oversea company—

(a)   the return required to be delivered to the registrar under subsection (1) shall contain the address for the time being notified by the director or secretary to the company under regulations made under sections 723B to 723F, but shall not contain his usual residential address; and

(b)   with that return the company shall deliver to the registrar a return in the prescribed form containing the usual residential address of that director or secretary.

(1B)   If a confidentiality order under section 723B is made in respect of an existing director or secretary of an oversea company, the company shall within the time specified below deliver to the registrar of companies for registration a return in the prescribed form containing the address for the time being notified to it by the director or secretary under regulations made under sections 723B to 723F.

(1C)   If while a confidentiality order made under section 723B is in force in respect of a director or secretary of an oversea company there is an alteration in his usual residential address, the company shall within the time specified below deliver to the registrar of companies for registration a return in the prescribed form containing the new address.

(2)   If any change is made in the corporate name of an oversea company, the company shall, with the time specified below, deliver to the registrar of companies for registration a return containing the prescribed particulars of the change.

(3)   The time for delivery of the returns required by subsections (1), (1B), (1C) and (2) is—

(a)   in the case of an alteration to which subsection (1)(c) applies, 21 days after the making of the alteration, and

(b)   otherwise, 21 days after the date on which notice of the alteration or change in question could have been received in Great Britain in due course of post (if despatched with due diligence).

692A.   Change in registration regime

(1)   Where a company ceases to be a company to which section 690A applies and, immediately after ceasing to be such a company—

(a)   continues to have in Great Britain a place of business which it had immediately before ceasing to be such a company, and

(b)   does not have a branch in Northern Ireland,

it shall be treated for the purposes of section 691 as having established the place of business on the date when it ceased to be a company to which section 690A applies.

(2)   Where a limited company incorporated outside the United Kingdom and Gibraltar—

(a)   ceases to have a branch in Northern Ireland, and

(b)   both immediately before and immediately after ceasing to do so, has a place of business, but not a branch, in Great Britain,

it shall be treated for the purposes of section 691 as having established the place of business on the date when it ceased to have a branch in Northern Ireland.

(3)   Where a company—

(a)   becomes a company to which section 690A applies,

(b)   immediately after becoming such a company, has in a part of Great Britain an established place of business but no branch, and

(c)   immediately before becoming such a company, had an established place of business in that part,

sections 691 and 692 shall, in relation to that part, continue to apply to the company (notwith-standing section 690B) until such time as it gives notice to the registrar for that part that it is a company to which that section applies.

(4)   Schedule 21B to this Act (transitional provisions in relation to change in registration regime) shall have effect.

693.   Obligation to state name and other particulars

(1)   Every oversea company shall—

(a)   *in every prospectus inviting subscriptions for its shares or debentures in Great Britain, state the country in which the company is incorporated,*

(b)   conspicuously exhibit on every place where it carries on business in Great Britain the company's name and the country in which it is incorporated,

(c)   cause the company's name and the country in which it is incorporated to be stated in legible characters in all bill-heads and letter paper, and in all notices and other official publications of the company, and

(d)   if the liability of the members of the company is limited, cause notice of that fact to be stated in legible characters *in every such prospectus as above mentioned and* in all bill-heads, letter paper, notices and other official publications of the company in Great Britain, and to be affixed on every place where it carries on its business.

(2)   Every company to which section 690A applies shall, in the case of each branch of the company registered under paragraph 1 of Schedule 21A, cause the following particulars to be stated in legible characters in all letter paper and order forms used in carrying on the business of the branch—

(a)   the place of registration of the branch, and

(b)   the registered number of the branch.

(3)   Every company to which section 690A applies, which is not incorporated in a Member State and which is required by the law of the country in which it is incorporated to be registered shall, in the case of each branch of the company registered under paragraph 1 of Schedule 21A, cause the following particulars to be stated in legible characters in all letter paper and order forms used in carrying on the business of the branch—

(a)   the identity of the registry in which the company is registered in its country of incorporation, and

(b)   the number with which it is registered.

(4)   Every company to which section 690A applies and which is not incorporated in a Member State shall, in the case of each branch of the company registered under paragraph 1 of Schedule 21A, cause the following particulars to be stated in legible characters in all letter paper and order forms used in carrying on the business of the branch—

(a)   the legal form of the company,

(b)   the location of its head office, and

(c)   if applicable, the fact that it is being wound up.

Note. The italicized words in subsection (1) are repealed for certain purposes by the Financial Services Act 1986, s. 212(3), Sch. 17, Pt. I and for remaining purposes as from a day to be appointed.

694.   Regulation of oversea companies in respect of their names

(1)   If it appears to the Secretary of State that the corporate name of an oversea company is a name by which the company, had it been formed under this Act, would on the relevant date (determined in accordance with subsections (3A) and (3B)) have been precluded from being registered by section 26 either—

(a)   because it falls within subsection (1) of that section, or

(b)   if it falls within subsection (2) of that section, because the Secretary of State would not approve the company's being registered with that name, the Secretary of State may serve a notice on the company, stating why the name would not have been registered.

(2)   If the corporate name of an oversea company is in the Secretary of State's opinion too like a name appearing on the relevant date in the index of names kept by the registrar of companies under section 714 or which should have appeared in that index on that date, or is the same as a name which should have so appeared, the Secretary of State may serve a notice on the company specifying the name in the index which the company's name is too like or which is the same as the company's name.

(3)   No notice shall be served on a company under subsection (1) or (2) later than 12 months after the relevant date, …

(3A)   For the purposes of subsections (1) to (3), the relevant date, in relation to a company, is the date on which it has complied with paragraph 1 of Schedule 21A or section 691(1) or, if there is more than one such date, the first date on which it has complied with that paragraph or that subsection since becoming an oversea company.

(3B)   But where the company's corporate name has changed since the date ascertained in accordance with subsection (3A), the relevant date is the date on which the company has, in respect of the change or, if more than one, the latest change, complied with paragraph 7(1) of Schedule 21A or section 692(2), as the case may be.

(4)   An oversea company on which a notice is served under subsection (1) or (2)—

    (a)   may deliver to the registrar of companies for registration a statement in the prescribed form specifying a name approved by the Secretary of State other than its corporate name under which it proposes to carry on business in Great Britain, and

    (b)   may, after that name has been registered, at any time deliver to the registrar for registration a statement in the prescribed form specifying a name approved by the Secretary of State (other than its corporate name) in substitution for the name previously registered.

(5)   The name by which an oversea company is for the time being registered under subsection (4) is, for all purposes of the law applying in Great Britain (including this Act and the Business Names Act 1985), deemed to be the company's corporate name; but—

    (a)   this does not affect references to the corporate name in this section, or any rights or obligations of the company, or render defective any legal proceedings by or against the company, and

    (b)   any legal proceedings that might have been continued or commenced against the company by its corporate name or its name previously registered under this section may be continued or commenced against it by its name for the time being so registered.

(6)   An oversea company on which a notice is served under subsection (1) or (2) shall not at any time after the expiration of 2 months from the service of that notice (or such longer period as may be specified in that notice) carry on business in Great Britain under its corporate name.

        Nothing in this subsection, or in section 697(2) (which imposes penalties for its contravention) invalidates any transaction entered into by the company.

(7)   The Secretary of State may withdraw a notice served under subsection (1) or (2) at any time before the end of the period mentioned in subsection (6); and that subsection does not apply to a company served with a notice which has been withdrawn.

694A.   Service of documents: companies to which section 690A applies

(1)   This section applies to any company to which section 690A applies.

(2)   Any process or notice required to be served on a company to which this section applies in respect of the carrying on of the business of a branch registered by it under paragraph 1 of Schedule 21A is sufficiently served if—

    (a)   addressed to any person whose name has, in respect of the branch, been delivered to the registrar as a person falling within paragraph 3(e) of that Schedule, and

    (b)   left at or sent by post to the address for that person which has been so delivered.

(3)   Where—

(a) a company to which this section applies makes default, in respect of a branch, in delivering to the registrar the particulars mentioned in paragraph 3(e) of Schedule 21A, or

(b) all the persons whose names have, in respect of a branch, been delivered to the registrar as persons falling within paragraph 3(e) of that Schedule are dead or have ceased to reside in Great Britain, or refuse to accept service on the company's behalf, or for any reason cannot be served,

a document may be served on the company in respect of the carrying on of the business of the branch by leaving it at, or sending it by post to, any place of business established by the company in Great Britain.

(4) Where a company to which this section applies has more than one branch in Great Britain, any notice or process required to be served on the company which is not required to be served in respect of the carrying on of the business of one branch rather than another shall be treated for the purposes of this section as required to be served in respect of the carrying on of the business of each of its branches.

695. Service of documents on oversea company

(1) Any process or notice required to be served on an oversea company to which section 691 applies is sufficiently served if addressed to any person whose name has been delivered to the registrar under preceding sections in this Part and left at or sent by post to the address which has been so delivered.

(2) However—

(a) where such a company makes default in delivering to the registrar the name and address of a person resident in Great Britain who is authorised to accept on behalf of the company service of process or notices, or

(b) if at any time all the persons whose names and addresses have been so delivered are dead or have ceased so to reside, or refuse to accept service on the company's behalf, or for any reason cannot be served,

a document may be served on the company by leaving it at, or sending it by post to, any place of business established by the company in Great Britain.

695A. Registrar to whom documents to be delivered: companies to which section 690A applies

(1) References to the registrar, in relation to a company to which section 690A applies, (except references in Schedule 21C *or Chapter III of this Part*) shall be construed in accordance with the following provisions.

(2) The documents which a company is required to deliver to the registrar shall be delivered—

(a) to the registrar for England and Wales, if required to be delivered in respect of a branch in England and Wales, and

(b) to the registrar for Scotland, if required to be delivered in respect of a branch in Scotland.

(3) If a company closes a branch in a part of Great Britain, it shall forthwith give notice of that fact to the registrar for that part; and from the date on which notice is so given it is no longer obliged to deliver documents to that registrar in respect of that branch.

(4) In subsection (3) above, the reference to closing a branch in either part of Great Britain includes a reference to a branch ceasing to be situated in that part on becoming situated elsewhere.

Note. The italicized words in subsection (1) are inserted by the Companies Act 1989, s. 107, Sch. 16, para. 1A, as from a day to be appointed.

696. *Office where documents to be filed*

(1) Any document which an oversea company to which section 691 applies is required to deliver to the registrar of companies shall be delivered to the registrar at the registration office in England and Wales or Scotland, according to where the company has established a place of business.

(2) If the company has established a place of business both in England and Wales and in Scotland, the document shall be delivered at the registration office both in England and Wales and in Scotland.

(3)   References in this Part (except references in Schedule 21C) to the registrar of companies, in relation to a company to which section 691 applies, are to be construed in accordance with the above subsections.

(4)   If an oversea company to which section 691 applies ceases to have a place of business in either part of Great Britain, it shall forthwith give notice of that fact to the registrar of companies for that part; and as from the date on which notice is so given the obligation of the company to deliver any document to the registrar ceases.

Note. This section is substituted by the following provision by the Companies Act 1989, s. 145, Sch. 19, para. 13, as from a day to be appointed.

696.   Registrar to whom documents to be delivered

(1)   References to the registrar in relation to an oversea company to which section 691 applies (except references in Schedule 21C or Chapter III of this Part), shall be construed in accordance with the following provisions.

(2)   The documents which an oversea company is required to deliver to the registrar shall be delivered—

(a)   to the registrar for England and Wales if the company has established a place of business in England and Wales, and

(b)   to the registrar for Scotland if the company has established a place of business in Scotland; and if the company has an established place of business in both parts of Great Britain, the documents shall be delivered to both registrars.

(3)   If a company ceases to have a place of business in either part of Great Britain, it shall forthwith give notice of that fact to the registrar for that part; and from the date on which notice is so given it is no longer obliged to deliver documents to that registrar.

Note. See the note to the original section 696 above.

697.   Penalties for non-compliance

(1)   If an oversea company fails to comply with any of sections 691 to 693 and 696, the company, and every officer or agent of the company who knowingly and wilfully authorises or permits the default, is liable to a fine and, in the case of a continuing offence, to a daily default fine for continued contravention.

(2)   If an oversea company contravenes section 694(6), the company and every officer or agent of it who knowingly and wilfully authorises or permits the contravention is guilty of an offence and liable to a fine and, for continued contravention, to a daily default fine.

(3)   if an oversea company fails to comply with section 695A or Schedule 21A, the company, and every officer or agent of the company who knowingly and wilfully authorises or permits the default, is liable to a fine and, in the case of a continuing offence, to a daily default fine for continued contravention.

698.   Definitions ...

(1)   For purposes of this Chapter—

"certified" means certified in the prescribed manner to be a true copy or a correct translation;

"director", in relation to an oversea company, includes shadow director; and

"secretary" includes any person occupying the position of secretary by whatever name called.

(2)   For the purposes of this Part (except section 699A and Schedule 21C):

(a)   where a branch comprises places of business in more than one part of the United Kingdom, the branch shall be treated as being situated in that part of the United Kingdom where its principal place of business is situated; and

(b)   "branch" means a branch within the meaning of the Council Directive concerning disclosure requirements in respect of branches opened in a Member State by certain types of company governed by the law of another State (the Eleventh Company Law Directive, 89/666/EEC).

699.   Channel Islands and Isle of Man companies

(1)   With the exceptions specified in subsection (3) below, the provisions of this Act requiring documents to be forwarded or delivered to or filed with the registrar of companies and applying to companies formed and registered under Part I apply also (if they would not otherwise) to an oversea company to which section 691 applies incorporated in the Channel Islands or the Isle of Man.

(2)   Those provisions apply to such a company—

(a)   if it has established a place of business in England and Wales, as if it were registered in England and Wales,

(b)   if it has established a place of business in Scotland, as if it were registered in Scotland, and

(c)   if it has established a place of business both in England and Wales and in Scotland, as if it were registered in both England and Wales and Scotland,

with such modifications as may be necessary and, in particular, apply in a similar way to documents relating to things done outside Great Britain as if they had been done in Great Britain.

(3)   The exceptions are—

section 6(1) (resolution altering company's objects),

section 18 (alteration of memorandum or articles by statute or statutory instrument),

section 242(1) (directors' duty to file accounts),

section 288(2) (notice to registrar of change of directors or secretary), and

section 380 (copies of certain resolutions and agreements to be sent to registrar within 15 days), so far as applicable to a resolution altering a company's memorandum or articles.

CHAPTER II
DELIVERY OF ACCOUNTS AND REPORTS

699A.   Credit and financial institutions to which the Bank Branches Directive (89/117/EEC) applies

(1)   This section applies to any credit or financial institution—

(a)   which is incorporated or otherwise formed outside the United Kingdom and Gibraltar,

(b)   whose head office is outside the United Kingdom and Gibraltar, and

(c)   which has a branch in Great Britain.

(2)   Schedule 21C (delivery of accounts and reports) shall have effect in relation to any institution to which this section applies.

(3)   In this section—

"branch", in relation to a credit or financial institution, means a place of business which forms a legally dependent part of the institution and which conducts directly all or some of the operations inherent in its business;

"credit institution" means a credit institution as defined in article 1(1)(a) of Directive 2000/12/EC of the European Parliament and of the Council of 20 March 2000 relating to the taking up and pursuit of the business of credit institutions, that is to say an undertaking whose business is to receive deposits or other repayable funds from the public and to grant credits for its own account;

"financial institution" means a financial institution within the meaning of Article 1 of the Council Directive on the obligations of branches established in a Member State of credit and financial institutions having their head offices outside that Member State regarding the publication of annual accounting documents (the Bank Branches Directive, 89/117/EEC); and

"undertaking" has the same meaning as in Part VII.

699AA. Companies to which the Eleventh Company Law Directive applies

(1)   This section applies to any limited company which—

(a)   is incorporated outside the United Kingdom and Gibraltar,

(b)   has a branch in Great Britain, and

(c)   is not an institution to which section 699A applies.

(2)   Schedule 21D to this Act (delivery of accounts and reports) shall have effect in relation to any company to which this section applies.

699B.   Scope of sections 700 to 703

Sections 700 to 703 shall not apply to any institution to which section 699A applies or to any limited company which is incorporated outside the United Kingdom and Gibraltar and has a branch in the United Kingdom.

700.   Preparation of accounts and reports by oversea companies

(1)   Every oversea company shall in respect of each financial year of the company prepare the like accounts and directors' report, and cause to be prepared such an auditors' report, as would be required if the company were formed and registered under this Act.

(2)   The Secretary of State may by order—
        (a)   modify the requirements referred to in subsection (1) for the purpose of their application to oversea companies;
        (b)   exempt an oversea company from those requirements or from such of them as may be specified in the order.

(3)   An order may make different provision for different cases or classes of case and may contain such incidental and supplementary provisions as the Secretary of State thinks fit.

(4)   An order under this section shall be made by statutory instrument which shall be subject to annulment in pursuance of a resolution of either House of Parliament.

701.   Oversea company's financial year and accounting reference periods

(1)   Sections 223 to 225 (financial year and accounting reference periods) apply to an oversea company, subject to the following modifications.

(2)   For the references to the incorporation of the company substitute references to the company establishing a place of business in Great Britain.

(3)   Omit section 225(4) (restriction on frequency with which current accounting reference period may be extended).

702.   Delivery to registrar of accounts and reports of oversea company

(1)   An oversea company shall in respect of each financial year of the company deliver to the registrar copies of the accounts and reports prepared in accordance with section 700.
        If any document comprised in those accounts or reports is in a language other than English, the directors shall annex to the copy delivered a translation of it into English, certified in the prescribed manner to be a correct translation.

(2)   In relation to an oversea company the period allowed for delivering accounts and reports is 13 months after the end of the relevant accounting reference period.
        This is subject to the following provisions of this section.

(3)   If the relevant accounting reference period is the company's first and is a period of more than 12 months, the period allowed is 13 months from the first anniversary of the company's establishing a place of business in Great Britain.

(4)   If the relevant accounting period is treated as shortened by virtue of a notice given by the company under section 225 (alteration of accounting reference date), the period allowed is that applicable in accordance with the above provisions or three months from the date of the notice under that section, whichever last expires.

(5)   If for any special reason the Secretary of State thinks fit he may, on an application made before the expiry of the period otherwise allowed, by notice in writing to an oversea company extend that period by such further period as may be specified in the notice.

(6)   In this section "the relevant accounting reference period" means the accounting reference period by reference to which the financial year for the accounts in question was determined.

703. **Penalty for non-compliance**

(1)   If the requirements of section 702(1) are not complied with before the end of the period allowed for delivering accounts and reports, or if the accounts and reports delivered do not comply with the requirements of this Act, the company and every person who immediately before the end of that period was a director of the company is guilty of an offence and liable to a fine and, for continued contravention, to a daily default fine.

(2)   It is a defence for a person charged with such an offence to prove that he took all reasonable steps for securing that the requirements in question would be complied with.

(3)   It is not a defence in relation to a failure to deliver copies to the registrar to prove that the documents in question were not in fact prepared as required by this Act.

CHAPTER III
REGISTRATION OF CHARGES

Note. This Chapter (ss. 703A–703N) is inserted by the Companies Act 1989, s. 105, Sch. 15, as from a day to be appointed.

703A. *Introductory provisions*

(1)   *The provisions of this Chapter have effect for securing the registration in Great Britain of charges on the property of a registered oversea company.*

(2)   *Section 395(2) and (3) (meaning of "charge" and "property") have effect for the purposes of this Chapter.*

(3)   *A "registered oversea company", in relation to England and Wales or Scotland, means an oversea company which*

    (a)   *has duly delivered documents under paragraph 1 of Schedule 21A to the registrar for that part of Great Britain and has not subsequently given notice to him under section 695A(3) that it has closed the branch in respect of which the documents were registered, or*

    (b)   *has duly delivered documents to the registrar for that part of Great Britain under section 691 and has not subsequently given notice to him under section 696(4) that it has ceased to have an established place of business in that part.*

(4)   *References in this Chapter to the registrar shall be construed in accordance with section 703E below and references to registration, in relation to a charge, are to registration in the register kept by him under this Chapter.*

Note. See the note to Chapter III above.

703B. *Charges requiring registration*

(1)   *The charges requiring registration under this Chapter are those which if created by a company registered in Great Britain would require registration under Part XII of this Act.*

(2)   *Whether a charge is one requiring registration under this Chapter shall be determined—*

    (a)   *in the case of a charge over property of a company at the date when it becomes a registered oversea company, as at that date,*

    (b)   *in the case of a charge created by a registered oversea company, as at the date the charge is created, and*

    (c)   *in the case of a charge over property acquired by a registered oversea company, as at the date of the acquisition.*

(3)   *In the following provisions of this Chapter references to a charge are, unless the context otherwise requires, to a charge requiring registration under this Chapter.*

Where a charge not otherwise requiring registration relates to property by virtue of which it requires to be registered and to other property, the references are to the charge so far as it relates to property of the former description.

Note. See the note to Chapter III above.

703C. The register

(1)   *The registrar shall keep for each registered oversea company a register, in such form as he thinks fit, of charges on property of the company.*

(2)   *The register shall consist of a file containing with respect to each such charge the particulars and other information delivered to the registrar under or by virtue of the following provisions of this Chapter.*

(3)   *Section 397(3) to (5) (registrar's certificate as to date of delivery of particulars) applies in relation to the delivery of any particulars or other information under this Chapter.*

Note. See the note to Chapter III above.

703D. Company's duty to deliver particulars of charges for registration

(1)   *If when an oversea company*

  (a)   delivers documents for registration under paragraph 1 of Schedule 21A—

      (i)   in respect of a branch in England and Wales, or

      (ii)   in respect of a branch in Scotland,

  for the first time since becoming a company to which section 690A applies, or

  (b)   delivers documents for registration under section 691,

  any of its property is situated in Great Britain and subject to a charge, it is the company's duty at the same time to deliver the prescribed particulars of the charge, in the prescribed form, to the registrar for registration.

(1A)   *Subsection (1) above does not apply in relation to a charge if—*

  (a)   the particulars of it required to be delivered under that subsection have already been so delivered to the registrar to whom the documents mentioned in subsection (1) above are delivered, and

  (b)   the company has at all times since they were so delivered to him been a registered oversea company in relation to the part of Great Britain for which he is registrar.

(2)   *Where a registered oversea company—*

  (a)   creates a charge on property situated in Great Britain, or

  (b)   acquires property which is situated in Great Britain and subject to a charge,

  it is the company's duty to deliver the prescribed particulars of the charge, in the prescribed form, to the registrar for registration within 21 days after the date of the charge's creation or, as the case may be, the date of the acquisition.

  This subsection does not apply if the property subject to the charge is at the end of that period no longer situated in Great Britain.

(3)   *Where the preceding subsections do not apply and property of a registered oversea company is for a continuous period of four months situated in Great Britain and subject to a charge, it is the company's duty before the end of that period to deliver the prescribed particulars of the charge, in the prescribed form, to the registrar for registration.*

(4)   *Particulars of a charge required to be delivered under subsections (1), (2) or (3) may be delivered for registration by any person interested in the charge.*

(5)   *If a company fails to comply with subsection (1), (2) or (3), then, unless particulars of the charge have been delivered for registration by another person, the company and every officer of it who is in default is liable to a fine.*

(6)   *Section 398(2), (4) and (5) (recovery of fees paid in connection with registration, filing of particulars in register and sending of copy of particulars filed and note as to date) apply in relation to particulars delivered under this Chapter.*

Note. See the note to Chapter III above.

703E. Registrar to whom particulars, &c to be delivered

(1)   *The particulars required to be delivered by section 703D(1) (charges over property of oversea company becoming registered in a part of Great Britain) shall be delivered to the registrar to whom the documents are delivered under paragraph 1 of Schedule 21A or, as the case may be, section 691.*

(2)   *The particulars required to be delivered by section 703D(2) or (3) (charges over property of registered oversea company) shall be delivered—*

    (a)   *where the company is a company to which section 690A applies—*

        (i)   *if it has registered a branch in one part of Great Britain but has not registered a branch in the other, to the registrar for the part in which it has registered a branch,*

        (ii)   *if it has registered a branch in both parts of Great Britain but the property subject to the charge is situated in one part of Great Britain only, to the registrar for that part, and*

        (iii)   *in any other case, to the registrars for both parts of Great Britain; and*

    (b)   *where the company is a company to which section 691 applies—*

        (i)   *if it is registered in one part of Great Britain and not in the other, to the registrar for the part in which it is registered,*

        (ii)   *if it is registered in both parts of Great Britain but the property subject to the charge is situated in one part of Great Britain only, to the registrar for that part, and*

        (iii)   *in any other case, to the registrar for both parts of Great Britain.*

(3)   *Other documents required or authorised by virtue of this Chapter to be delivered to the registrar shall be delivered to the registrar or registrars to whom particulars of the charge to which they relate have been, or ought to have been, delivered.*

(4)   *If a company ceases to be a registered oversea company in relation to either part of Great Britain, charges over property of the company shall cease to be subject to the provisions of this Chapter, as regards registration in that part of Great Britain, as from the date on which the notice under section 695A(3) or, as the case may be, 696(3) is given.*

    This is without prejudice to rights arising by reason of events occurring before that date.

    Note. See the note to Chapter III above.

703F.   **Effect of failure to deliver particulars, late delivery and effect of errors and omissions**

(1)   *The following provisions of Part XII—*

    (a)   *section 399 (effect of failure to deliver particulars),*

    (b)   *section 400 (late delivery of particulars), and*

    (c)   *section 402 (effect of errors and omissions in particulars delivered),*

    apply, with the following modifications, in relation to a charge created by a registered oversea company of which particulars are required to be delivered under this Chapter.

(2)   *Those provisions do not apply to a charge of which particulars are required to be delivered under section 703D(1) (charges existing when company delivers documents under section 691).*

(3)   *In relation to a charge of which particulars are required to be delivered under section 703D(3) (charges registrable by virtue of property being within Great Britain for requisite period), the references to the period of 21 days after the charge's creation shall be construed as references to the period of four months referred to in that subsection.*

    Note. See the note to Chapter III above.

703G.   **Delivery of further particulars or memorandum**

    Sections 401 and 403 (delivery of further particulars and memorandum of charge ceasing to affect company's property) apply in relation to a charge of which particulars have been delivered under this Chapter.

    Note. This section is inserted by the Companies Act 1989, s. 105, Sch. 15, as from a day to be appointed.

703H.   **Further provisions with respect to voidness of charges**

(1)   *The following provisions of Part XII apply in relation to the voidness of a charge by virtue of this Chapter—*

    (a)   *section 404 (exclusion of voidness as against unregistered charges),*

    (b)   *section 405 (restrictions on cases in which charge is void),*

    (c)   *section 406 (effect of exercise of power of sale), and*

    (d)   *section 407 (effect of voidness on obligation secured).*

(2)   *In relation to a charge of which particulars are required to be delivered under section 703D(3) (charges registrable by virtue of property being within Great Britain for requisite period), the reference in section 404 to the period of 21 days after the charge's creation shall be construed as a reference to the period of four months referred to in that subsection.*

          Note. See the note to Chapter III above.

703I.   Additional information to be registered

(1)   *Section 408 (particulars of taking up of issue of debentures) applies in relation to a charge of which particulars have been delivered under this Chapter.*

(2)   *Section 409 (notice of appointment of receiver or manager) applies in relation to the appointment of a receiver or manager of property of a registered oversea company.*

(3)   *Regulations under section 410 (notice of crystallisation of floating charge, &c) may apply in relation to a charge of which particulars have been delivered under this Chapter; but subject to such exceptions, adaptations and modifications as may be specified in the regulations.*

          Note. See the note to Chapter III above.

703J.   Copies of instruments and register to be kept by company

(1)   *Sections 411 and 412 (copies of instruments and register to be kept by company) apply in relation to a registered oversea company and any charge over property of the company situated in Great Britain.*

(2)   *They apply to any charge, whether or not particulars are required to be delivered to the registrar.*

(3)   *In relation to such a company the references to the company's registered office shall be construed as references to its principal place of business in Great Britain.*

          Note. See the note to Chapter III above.

703K.   Power to make further provision by regulations

(1)   *The Secretary of State may by regulations make further provision as to the application of the provisions of this Chapter, or the provisions of Part XII applied by this Chapter, in relation to charges of any description specified in the regulations.*

(2)   *The regulations may apply any provisions of regulations made under section 413 (power to make further provision with respect to application of Part XII) or make any provision which may be made under that section with respect to the application of provisions of Part XII.*

          Note. See the note to Chapter III above.

703L.   Provisions as to situation of property

(1)   *The following provisions apply for determining for the purposes of this Chapter whether a vehicle which is the property of an oversea company is situated in Great Britain—*

  (a)   *a ship, aircraft or hovercraft shall be regarded as situated in Great Britain if, and only if, it is registered in Great Britain;*

  (b)   *any other description of vehicle shall be regarded as situated in Great Britain on a day if, and only if, at any time on that day the management of the vehicle is directed from a place of business of the company in Great Britain;*

          and for the purposes of this Chapter a vehicle shall not be regarded as situated in one part of Great Britain only.

(2)   *For the purposes of this Chapter as it applies to a charge on future property, the subject-matter of the charge shall be treated as situated in Great Britain unless it relates exclusively to property of a kind which cannot, after being acquired or coming into existence, be situated in Great Britain; and references to property situated in a part of Great Britain shall be similarly construed.*

          Note. See the note to Chapter III above.

703M. Other supplementary provisions

          The following provisions of Part XII apply for the purposes of this Chapter—

  (a)   *section 414 (construction of references to date of creation of charge),*

  (b)   *section 415 (prescribed particulars and related expressions),*

(c)   section 416 (notice of matters disclosed on the register),

(d)   section 417 (power of court to dispense with signature),

(e)   section 418 (regulations), and

(f)   section 419 (minor definitions).

Note. See the note to Chapter III above.

703N. *Index of defined expressions*

The following Table shows the provisions of this Chapter and Part XII defining or otherwise explaining expressions used in this Chapter (other than expressions used only in the same section)—

charge	sections 703A(2), 703B(3) and 395(2)
charge requiring registration	sections 703B(1) and 396
creation of charge	sections 703M(f) and 419(2)
date of acquisition (of property by a company)	sections 703M(f) and 419(3)
date of creation of charge	sections 703M(a) and 414
property	sections 703A(2) and 395(2)
registered oversea company	section 703A(3)
registrar and registration in relation to a charge situated in Great Britain	sections 703A(4) and 703E
in relation to vehicles	section 703L(1)
in relation to future property	section 703L(2)

Note. See the note to Chapter III above.

CHAPTER IV
WINDING UP ETC

703O. **Scope of Chapter**

This Chapter applies to any company to which section 690A applies.

703P. **Particulars to be delivered to the registrar: winding up**

(1)   Subject to subsection (8), where a company to which this Chapter applies is being wound up, it shall deliver to the registrar for registration a return in the prescribed form containing the following particulars—

(a)   the name of the company;

(b)   whether the company is being wound up by an order of a court and, if so, the name and address of the court and the date of the order;

(c)   if the company is not being so wound up, as a result of what action the winding up has commenced;

(d)   whether the winding up has been instigated by:

(i)   the company's members;

(ii)   the company's creditors; or

(iii) some other person or persons,

and, in the case of (iii) the identity of that person or those persons shall be given; and

(e)   the date on which the winding up became or will become effective.

(2)   The period allowed for delivery of a return under subsection (1) above is 14 days from the date on which the winding up begins.

(3)   Subject to subsection (8), a person appointed to be the liquidator of a company to which this Chapter applies shall deliver to the registrar for registration a return in the prescribed form containing the following particulars—

(a)   his name and address,

(b)   the date of his appointment, and

(c)   a description of such of his powers, if any, as are derived otherwise than from the general law or the company's constitution.

(4)   The period allowed for delivery of a return under subsection (3) above is 14 days from the date of the liquidator's appointment.

(5)   Subject to subsection (8), the liquidator of a company to which this Chapter applies shall deliver to the registrar for registration a return in the prescribed form upon the occurrence of the following events—

(a)   the termination of the winding up of the company, and

(b)   the company ceasing to be registered, in circumstances where ceasing to be registered is an event of legal significance.

The following particulars shall be given:

(i)   in the case of (a), the name of the company and the date on which the winding up terminated; and

(ii)   in the case of (b), the name of the company and the date on which the company ceased to be registered.

(6)   The period allowed for delivery of a return under subsection (5) is 14 days from the date of the event concerned.

(7)   The obligation to deliver a return under subsection (1), (3) or (5) above shall apply in respect of each branch which the company has in Great Britain (though where the company has more than one branch in a part of Great Britain a return which gives the branch numbers of two or more such branches is to be regarded as a return in respect of each branch whose number is given).

(8)   No return is required under subsection (1), (3), or (5) above in respect of a winding up under Part V of the Insolvency Act 1986.

703Q. Particulars to be delivered to the registrar: insolvency proceedings etc

(1)   Where a company to which this Chapter applies becomes subject to any of the following proceedings (other than proceedings for the winding up of the company), that is to say, insolvency proceedings or an arrangement or composition or any analogous proceedings, it shall deliver to the registrar for registration a return in the prescribed form containing the following particulars—

(a)   the name of the company;

(b)   whether the proceedings are by order of a court and, if so, the name and address of the court and the date of the order;

(c)   if the proceedings are not by order of a court, as a result of what action the proceedings have been commenced;

(d)   whether the proceedings have been instigated by:

(i)   the company's members;

(ii)   the company's creditors; or

(iii)   some other person or persons,

and, in the case of (iii) the identity of that person or those persons shall be given; and

(e)   the date on which the proceedings became or will become effective.

(2)   Where a company to which this Chapter applies ceases to be subject to any of the proceedings mentioned in subsection (1) it shall deliver to the registrar for registration a return in the prescribed form containing the following particulars:

(a)   the name of the company; and

(b)   the date on which it ceased to be subject to the proceedings.

(3)   The period allowed for delivery of a return under subsection (1) or (2) is 14 days from the date on which the company becomes subject, or (as the case may be) ceases to be subject to the proceedings concerned.

(4)   The obligation to deliver a return under subsection (1) or (2) shall apply in respect of each branch which the company has in Great Britain (though where the company has more than one branch in a part of Great Britain a return which gives the branch numbers of two or more such branches is to be regarded as a return in respect of each branch whose number is given).

703R.　Penalty for non-compliance

(1)　　If a company fails to comply with section 703P(1) or 703Q(1) or (2) within the period allowed for compliance, it, and every person who immediately before the end of that period was a director of it, is guilty of an offence and liable to a fine and, for continued contravention, to a daily default fine.

(2)　　If a liquidator fails to comply with section 703P(3) or (5) within the period allowed for compliance, he is guilty of an offence and liable to a fine and, for continued contravention, to a daily default fine.

(3)　　It is a defence for a person charged with an offence under this section to prove that he took all reasonable steps for securing compliance with the requirements concerned.

PART XXIV

THE REGISTRAR OF COMPANIES, HIS FUNCTIONS AND OFFICES

704.　Registration offices

(1)　　For the purposes of the registration of companies under the Companies Acts, there shall continue to be offices in England and Wales and in Scotland, at such places as the Secretary of State thinks fit.

(2)　　The Secretary of State may appoint such registrars, assistant registrars, clerks and servants as he thinks necessary for that purpose, and may make regulations with respect to their duties, and may remove any persons so appointed.

(3)　　The salaries of the persons so appointed continue to be fixed by the Secretary of State, with the concurrence of the Treasury, and shall be paid out of money provided by Parliament.

(4)　　The Secretary of State may direct a seal or seals to be prepared for the authentication of documents required for or in connection with the registration of companies; and any seal so prepared is referred to in this Act as the registrar's official seal.

(5)　　Wherever any act is by the Companies Acts directed to be done to or by the registrar of companies, it shall (until the Secretary of State otherwise directs) be done to or by the existing registrar of companies in England and Wales or in Scotland (as the case may be), or to or by such person as the Secretary of State may for the time being authorise.

(6)　　In the event of the Secretary of State altering the constitution of the existing registration offices or any of them, any such act shall be done to or by such officer and at such place with reference to the local situation of the registered offices of the companies to be registered as the Secretary of State may appoint.

(7)　　Subsection (8) below applies where by virtue of an order made under section 69 of the Deregulation and Contracting Out Act 1994 a person is authorised by the registrar of companies to accept delivery of any class of documents which are under any provision of the Companies Acts to be delivered to the registrar.

(8)　　If—

(a)　the registrar directs that documents of that class shall be delivered to a specified address of the authorised person; and

(b)　the direction is printed and made available to the public (with or without payment),

any document of that class which is delivered to an address other than the specified address shall be treated for the purposes of those Acts as not having been delivered.

705.　Companies' registered numbers

(1)　　The registrar shall allocate to every company a number, which shall be known as the company's registered number.

(2)　　Companies' registered numbers shall be in such form, consisting of one or more sequences of figures or letters, as the registrar may from time to time determine.

(3)　　The registrar may upon adopting a new form of registered number make such changes of existing registered numbers as appear to him necessary.

(4)   A change of a company's registered number has effect from the date on which the company is notified by the registrar of the change; but for a period of three years beginning with the date on which that notification is sent by the registrar the requirement of section 351(1)(a) as to the use of the company's registered number on business letters and order forms is satisfied by the use of either the old number or the new.

(5)   In this section "company" includes—

(za)   any oversea company which has complied with paragraph 1 of Schedule 21A other than a company which appears to the registrar not to have a branch in Great Britain;

(a)   any oversea company which has complied with section 691 (delivery of statutes to registrar, &c), other than a company which appears to the registrar not to have a place of business in Great Britain; and

(b)   any body to which any provision of this Act applies by virtue of section 718 (unregistered companies).

705A.   Registration of branches of oversea companies

(1)   For each company to which section 690A applies the registrar, shall keep, in such form as he thinks fit, a register of the branches registered by the company under paragraph 1 of Schedule 21A.

(2)   The registrar shall allocate to every branch registered by him under this section a number, which shall be known as the branch's registered number.

(3)   Branches' registered numbers shall be in such form, consisting of one or more sequences of figures or letters, as the registrar may from time to time determine.

(4)   The registrar may upon adopting a new form of registered number make such changes of existing registered numbers as appear to him necessary.

(5)   A change of a branch's registered number has effect from the date on which the company is notified by the registrar of the change; but for a period of three years beginning with the date on which that notification is sent by the registrar the requirement of section 693(2) as to the use of the branch's registered number on business letters and order forms is satisfied by the use of either the old number or the new.

(6)   Where an oversea company to which section 690A applies files particulars, in any circumstances permitted by this Act, by:

(i)   adopting particulars already filed in respect of another branch; or

(ii)   including in one document particulars which are to relate to two or more branches,

the registrar shall ensure that the particulars concerned become part of the registered particulars of each branch concerned.

706.   Delivery to the registrar of documents in legible form

(1)   This section applies to the delivery to the registrar under any provision of the Companies Acts of documents in legible form.

(2)   The document must—

(a)   state in a prominent position the registered number of the company to which it relates, and, if the document is delivered under sections 695A(3), 703P or 703Q or Schedules 21A or 21D the registered number of the branch to which it relates,

(b)   satisfy any requirements prescribed by regulations for the purposes of this section, and

(c)   conform to such requirements as the registrar may specify for the purpose of enabling him to copy the document.

(3)   If a document is delivered to the registrar which does not comply with the requirements of this section, he may serve on the person by whom the document was delivered (or, if there are two or more such persons, on any of them) a notice indicating the respect in which the document does not comply.

(4)   Where the registrar serves such a notice, then, unless a replacement document—

(a)   is delivered to him within 14 days after the service of the notice, and

(b)   complies with the requirements of this section (or section 707B) or is not rejected by him for failure to comply with those requirements,

the original document shall be deemed not to have been delivered to him.

But for the purposes of any enactment imposing a penalty for failure to deliver, so far as it imposes a penalty for continued contravention, no account shall be taken of the period between the delivery of the original document and the end of the period of 14 days after service of the registrar's notice.

(5)   Regulations made for the purposes of this section may make different provision with respect to different descriptions of document.

707.   ...

707A. The keeping of company records by the registrar

(1)   The information contained in a document delivered to the registrar under the Companies Acts may be recorded and kept by him in any form he thinks fit, provided it is possible to inspect the information and to produce a copy of it in legible form.

This is sufficient compliance with any duty of his to keep, file or register the document.

(2)   The originals of documents delivered to the registrar in legible form shall be kept by him for ten years, after which they may be destroyed.

(3)   Where a company has been dissolved, the registrar may, at any time after the expiration of two years from the date of the dissolution, direct that any records in his custody relating to the company may be removed to the Public Record Office; and records in respect of which such a direction is given shall be disposed of in accordance with the enactments relating to that Office and the rules made under them.

This subsection does not extend to Scotland.

(4)   In subsection (3) "company" includes a company provisionally or completely registered under the Joint Stock Companies Act 1844.

707B. Delivery to the registrar using electronic communications

(1)   Electronic communications may be used for the delivery of any document to the registrar under any provision of the Companies Acts (including delivery of a document in the prescribed form), provided that such delivery is in such form and manner as is directed by the registrar.

(2)   Where the document is required under any provision of the Companies Acts to be signed or sealed, it shall instead be authenticated in such manner as is directed by the registrar.

(3)   The document must contain in a prominent position—

(a)   the name and registered number of the company to which it relates, or

(b)   if the document is delivered under Part XXIII, the registered number of the branch or place of business of the company to which it relates.

(4)   If a document is delivered to the registrar which does not comply with the requirements imposed by or under this section, he may serve on the person by whom the document was delivered (or, if there are two or more such persons, on any of them) a notice indicating the respect in which the document does not comply.

(5)   Where the registrar serves such a notice, then unless a replacement document—

(a)   is delivered to him within 14 days after the service of the notice, and

(b)   complies with the requirements of this section (or section 706) or is not rejected by him for failure to comply with those requirements,

the original document shall be deemed not to have been delivered to him.

But for the purposes of any enactment imposing a penalty for failure to deliver, so far as it imposes a penalty for continued contravention, no account shall be taken of the period between the delivery of the original document and the end of the period of 14 days after service of the registrar's notice.

(6)   In this section references to the delivery of a document include references to the forwarding, lodging, registering, sending or submission of a document and to the giving of a notice, and cognate expressions are to be construed accordingly.

708.   Fees payable to registrar

(1)   The Secretary of State may by regulations made by statutory instrument require the payment to the registrar of companies of such fees as may be specified in the regulations in respect of—

      (a)   the performance by the registrar of such functions under the Companies Acts as may be so specified, including the receipt by him of any document which under those Acts is required to be delivered to him,

      (b)   the inspection of documents ... kept by him under those Acts.

(2)   A statutory instrument containing regulations under this section requiring the payment of a fee in respect of a matter for which no fee was previously payable, or increasing a fee, shall be laid before Parliament after being made and shall cease to have effect at the end of the period of 28 days beginning with the day on which the regulations were made (but without prejudice to anything previously done under the regulations or to the making of further regulations) unless in that period the regulations are approved by resolution of each House of Parliament.

      In reckoning that period of 28 days no account is to be taken of any time during which Parliament is dissolved or prorogued or during which both Houses are adjourned for more than 4 days.

(3)   A statutory instrument containing regulations under this section, where subsection (2) does not apply, is subject to annulment in pursuance of a resolution of either House of Parliament.

(4)   Fees paid to the registrar under the Companies Acts shall be paid into the Consolidated Fund.

(5)   It is hereby declared that the registrar may charge a fee for any services provided by him otherwise than in pursuance of an obligation imposed on him by law.

709.   Inspection, &c of records kept by the registrar

(1)   Subject to section 723B, any person may inspect any records kept by the registrar for the purposes of the Companies Acts and may require—

      (a)   a copy, in such form as the registrar considers appropriate, of any information contained in those records, or

      (b)   a certified copy of, or extract from, any such record.

(2)   The right of inspection extends to the originals of documents delivered to the registrar in legible form only where the record kept by the registrar of the contents of the document is illegible or unavailable.

(3)   A copy of or extract from a record kept at any of the offices for the registration of companies in England and Wales or Scotland, certified in writing by the registrar (whose official position it is unnecessary to prove) to be an accurate record of the contents of any document delivered to him under the Companies Acts, is in all legal proceedings admissible in evidence as of equal validity with the original document and as evidence of any fact stated therein of which direct oral evidence would be admissible.

(4)   Copies of or extracts from records furnished by the registrar may, instead of being certified by him in writing to be an accurate record, be sealed with his official seal.

(5)   No process for compelling the production of a record kept by the registrar shall issue from any court except with the leave of the court; and any such process shall bear on it a statement that it is issued with the leave of the court.

710.   Certificate of incorporation

Any person may require a certificate of the incorporation of a company, signed by the registrar or authenticated by his official seal.

710A.   Provision and authentication by registrar of documents in non-legible form

(1)   Any requirement of the Companies Acts as to the supply by the registrar of a document may, if the registrar thinks fit, be satisfied by the communication by the registrar of the requisite information in any non-legible form prescribed for the purposes of this section by regulations or approved by him.

(2) Where the document is required to be signed by him or sealed with his official seal, it shall instead be authenticated in such manner as may be prescribed by regulations or approved by the registrar.

710B. Documents relating to Welsh companies

(1) This section applies to any document which—
   (a) is delivered to the registrar under this Act or the Insolvency Act 1986, and
   (b) relates to a company (whether already registered or to be registered) whose memorandum states that its registered office is to be situated in Wales.

(2) A document to which this section applies may be in Welsh but, subject to subsection (3), shall on delivery to the registrar be accompanied by a certified translation into English.

(3) The requirement for a translation imposed by subsection (2) shall not apply—
   (a) to documents of such descriptions as may be prescribed for the purposes of this paragraph, or
   (b) to documents in a form prescribed in Welsh (or partly in Welsh and partly in English) by virtue of section 26 of the Welsh Language Act 1993.

(4) Where by virtue of subsection (3) the registrar receives a document in Welsh without a certified translation into English, he shall, if that document is to be available for inspection, himself obtain such a translation; and that translation shall be treated as delivered to him in accordance with the same provision as the original.

(5) A company whose memorandum states that its registered office is to be situated in Wales may deliver to the registrar a certified translation into Welsh of any document in English which relates to the company and which is or has been delivered to the registrar.

(6) The provisions within subsection (7) (which require certified translations into English of certain documents delivered to the registrar) shall not apply where a translation is required by subsection (2) or would be required but for subsection (3).

(7) The provisions within this subsection are section 228(2)(f), the second sentence of section 242(1), sections 243(4), 272(5) and 273(7) and paragraph 7(3) of Part II of Schedule 9.

(8) In this section "certified translation" means a translation certified in the prescribed manner to be a correct translation.

711. Public notice by registrar of receipt and issue of certain documents

(1) The registrar of companies shall cause to be published in the Gazette notice of the issue or receipt by him of documents of any of the following descriptions (stating in the notice the name of the company, the description of document and the date of issue or receipt)—
   (a) any certificate of incorporation of a company,
   (b) any document making or evidencing an alteration in a company's memorandum or articles,
   (c) any notification of a change among the directors of a company,
   (d) any copy of a resolution of a public company which gives, varies, revokes or renews an authority for the purposes of section 80 (allotment of relevant securities),
   (e) any copy of a special resolution of a public company passed under section 95(1), (2) or (3) (disapplication of pre-emption rights),
   (f) any report under section 103 or 104 as to the value of a non-cash asset,
   (g) any statutory declaration or statement delivered under section 117 (public company share capital requirements),
   (h) any notification (given under section 122) of the redemption of shares,
   (j) any statement or notice delivered by a public company under section 128 (registration of particulars of special rights),
   (k) any documents delivered by a company under section 242(1) (accounts and reports),
   (l) a copy of any resolution or agreement to which section 380 applies and which—
      (i) states the rights attached to any shares in a public company, other than shares which are in all respects uniform (for purposes of section 128) with shares previously allotted, or

(ii)   varies rights attached to any shares in a public company, or

(iii) assigns a name or other designation, or a new name or designation, to any class of shares in a public company,

(m) any return of allotments of a public company,

(n)   any notice of a change in the situation of a company's registered office,

(p)   any copy of a winding-up order in respect of a company,

(q)   any order for the dissolution of a company on a winding up,

(r)   any return by a liquidator of the final meeting of a company on a winding up,

(s)   any copy of a draft of the terms of a scheme delivered to the registrar of companies under paragraph 2(1) of Schedule 15A,

(t)   any copy of an order under section 425(2) or section 427 in respect of a compromise or arrangement to which section 427A(1) applies,

(u)   any return delivered under paragraph 1, 7 or 8 of Schedule 21A (branch registration),

(v)   any document delivered under paragraph 1 or 8 of that Schedule,

(w) any notice under section 695A(3) of the closure of a branch,

(x)   any document delivered under Schedule 21C (accounts and reports of foreign credit and financial institutions),

(y)   any document delivered under Schedule 21D (accounts and reports of oversea companies subject to branch registration, other than credit and financial institutions),

(z)   any return delivered under section 703P (particulars of winding up of oversea companies subject to branch registration).

(2)   In section 42 "official notification" means—

(a)   in relation to anything stated in a document of any of the above descriptions, the notification of that document in the Gazette under this section, and

(b)   in relation to the appointment of a liquidator in a voluntary winding up, the notification of it in the Gazette under section 109 of the Insolvency Act;

and "officially notified" is to be construed accordingly.

711A. *Exclusion of deemed notice*

(1)   A person shall not be taken to have notice of any matter merely because of its being disclosed in any document kept by the registrar of companies (and thus available for inspection) or made available by the company for inspection.

(2)   This does not affect the question whether a person is affected by notice of any matter by reason of a failure to make such inquiries as ought reasonably to be made.

(3)   In this section "document" includes any material which contains information.

(4)   Nothing in this section affects the operation of—

(a)   section 416 of this Act (under which a person taking a charge over a company's property is deemed to have notice of matters disclosed on the companies charges register), or

(b)   section 198 of the Law of Property Act 1925 as it applies by virtue of section 3(7) of the Land Charges Act 1972 (under which the registration of certain land charges under Part XII, or Chapter III of Part XXIII, of this Act is deemed to constitute actual notice for all purposes connected with the land affected).

Note. This section is inserted by the Companies Act 1989, s. 142(1), as from a day to be appointed.

712.   ...

713.   Enforcement of company's duty to make returns

(1)   If a company, having made default in complying with any provision of the Companies Acts which requires it to deliver a document to the registrar of companies, or to give notice to him of any matter, fails to make good the default within 14 days after the service of a notice on the company requiring it to do so, the court may, on an application made to it by any member or creditor of the company or by the registrar of companies, make an order directing the company and any officer of it to make good the default within such time as may be specified in the order.

(2)   The court's order may provide that all costs of and incidental to the application shall be borne by the company or by any officers of it responsible for the default.

(3)   Nothing in this section prejudices the operation of any enactment imposing penalties on a company or its officers in respect of any such default as is mentioned above.

714. Registrar's index of company and corporate names

(1)   The registrar of companies shall keep an index of the names of the following bodies—
   (a)   companies as defined by this Act,
   (aa)   companies incorporated outside the United Kingdom and Gibraltar which have complied with paragraph 1 of Schedule 21A and which do not appear to the registrar of companies not to have a branch in Great Britain,
   (b)   companies incorporated outside Great Britain which have complied with section 691 and which do not appear to the registrar of companies not to have a place of business in Great Britain,
   (c)   incorporated and unincorporated bodies to which any provision of this Act applies by virtue of section 718 (unregistered companies),
   (d)   limited partnerships registered under the Limited Partnerships Act 1907,
   (da)   limited liability partnerships incorporated under the Limited Liability Partnerships Act 2000,
   (e)   companies within the meaning of the Companies Act (Northern Ireland) 1960,
   (f)   companies incorporated outside Northern Ireland which have complied with section 356 of that Act (which corresponds with section 691 of this Act), and which do not appear to the registrar not to have a place of business in Northern Ireland, and
   (g)   societies registered under the Industrial and Provident Societies Act 1965 or the Industrial and Provident Societies Act (Northern Ireland) 1969.

(2)   The Secretary of State may by order in a statutory instrument vary subsection (1) by the addition or deletion of any class of body, except any within paragraph (a) or (b) of the subsection, whether incorporated or unincorporated; and any such statutory instrument is subject to annulment in pursuance of a resolution of either House of Parliament.

715. ...

715A. Interpretation

(1)   In this Part—
       "document" includes information recorded in any form; and
       "legible", in the context of documents in legible or non-legible form, means capable of being read with the naked eye.

(2)   References in this Part to delivering a document include sending, forwarding, producing or (in the case of a notice) giving it.

PART XXV
MISCELLANEOUS AND SUPPLEMENTARY PROVISIONS

716, 717....

718. Unregistered companies

(1)   The provisions of this Act specified in the first column of Schedule 22 (relating respectively to the matters specified in the second column of the Schedule) apply to all bodies corporate incorporated in and having a principal place of business in Great Britain, other than those mentioned in subsection (2) below, as if they were companies registered under this Act, but subject to any limitations mentioned in relation to those provisions respectively in the third column and to such adaptations and modifications (if any) as may be specified by regulations made by the Secretary of State.

(2)   Those provisions of this Act do not apply by virtue of this section to any of the following—
   (a)   any body incorporated by or registered under any public general Act of Parliament,

(b)   any body not formed for the purpose of carrying on a business which has for its object the acquisition of gain by the body or its individual members,

(c)   any body for the time being exempted by direction of the Secretary of State (or before him by the Board of Trade),

(d)   any open-ended investment company within the meaning of the Open-Ended Investment Companies Regulations 2001.

(3)   Where against any provision of this Act specified in the first column of Schedule 22 there appears in the third column the entry "Subject to section 718(3)", it means that the provision is to apply by virtue of this section so far only as may be specified by regulations made by the Secretary of State and to such bodies corporate as may be so specified.

(4)   ...

(5)   This section does not repeal or revoke in whole or in part any enactment, royal charter or other instrument constituting or regulating any body in relation to which those provisions are applied by virtue of this section, or restrict the power of Her Majesty to grant a charter in lieu or supplementary to any such charter as above mentioned; but, in relation to any such body, the operation of any such enactment, charter or instrument is suspended in so far as it is inconsistent with any of those provisions as they apply for the time being to that body.

(6)   The power to make regulations conferred by this section (whether regulations under subsection (1) or subsection (3)) is exercisable by statutory instrument subject to annulment in pursuance of a resolution of either House of Parliament.

719.   Power of company to provide for employees on cessation or transfer of business

(1)   The powers of a company include (if they would not otherwise do so apart from this section) power to make the following provision for the benefit of persons employed or formerly employed by the company or any of its subsidiaries, that is to say, provision in connection with the cessation or the transfer to any person of the whole or part of the undertaking of the company or that subsidiary.

(2)   The power conferred by subsection (1) is exercisable notwithstanding that its exercise is not in the best interests of the company.

(3)   The power which a company may exercise by virtue only of subsection (1) shall only be exercised by the company if sanctioned—

(a)   in a case not falling within paragraph (b) or (c) below, by an ordinary resolution of the company, or

(b)   if so authorised by the memorandum or articles, a resolution of the directors, or

(c)   if the memorandum or articles require the exercise of the power to be sanctioned by a resolution of the company of some other description for which more than a simple majority of the members voting is necessary, with the sanction of a resolution of that description;

and in any case after compliance with any other requirements of the memorandum or articles applicable to its exercise.

(4)   Any payment which may be made by a company under this section may, if made before the commencement of any winding up of the company, be made out of profits of the company which are available for dividend.

720.   Certain companies to publish periodical statement

(1)   Every company, being an insurer or a deposit, provident or benefit society, shall before it commences business, and also on the first Monday in February and the first Tuesday in August in every year during which it carries on business, make a statement in the form set out in Schedule 23, or as near to it as circumstances admit.

(2)   A copy of the statement shall be put up in a conspicuous place in the company's registered office, and in every branch office or place where the business of the company is carried on.

(3)   Every member and every creditor of the company is entitled to a copy of the statement, on payment of a sum not exceeding 2 1/2 pence.

(4)   If default is made in complying with this section, the company and every officer of it who is in default is liable to a fine and, for continued contravention, to a daily default fine.

(5)   For purposes of this Act, a company which carries on the business of insurance in common with any other business or businesses is deemed an insurer.

(6)   This section does not apply to an insurer which is—

    (a)   an insurance company which is subject to, and complies with, rules made by the Financial Services Authority under Part 10 of the Financial Services and Markets Act 2000 as to the accounts and balance sheet to be prepared annually and deposited; or

    (b)   an EEA firm of the kind mentioned in paragraph 5(d) of Schedule 3 to the Financial Services and Markets Act 2000, if the firm complies with the provisions of law of its home State as to the accounts and balance sheets to be prepared annually and deposited.

(7)   The Secretary of State may, by regulations in a statutory instrument (subject to annulment in pursuance of a resolution of either House of Parliament), alter the form in Schedule 23.

(8)   For the purposes of this section—

    (a)   "insurer" means a person who effects or carries out contracts of insurance in the United Kingdom; and

    (b)   "contract of insurance" includes a contract of insurance under which the benefits provided by the insurer are exclusively or primarily benefits in kind in the event of accident to or breakdown of a vehicle.

(9)   Subsection (8) must be read with—

    (a)   section 22 of the Financial Services and Markets Act 2000;

    (b)   any relevant order under that Schedule; and

    (c)   Schedule 2 to that Act.

721.   Production and inspection of books where offence suspected

(1)   The following applies if on an application made—

    (a)   in England and Wales, to a judge of the High Court by the Director of Public Prosecutions, the Secretary of State or a chief officer of police, or

    (b)   in Scotland, to one of the Lords Commissioners of Justiciary by the Lord Advocate,

there is shown to be reasonable cause to believe that any person has, while an officer of a company, committed an offence in connection with the management of the company's affairs and that evidence of the commission of the offence is to be found in any books or papers of or under the control of the company.

(2)   An order may be made—

    (a)   authorising any person named in it to inspect the books or papers in question, or any of them, for the purpose of investigating and obtaining evidence of the offence, or

    (b)   requiring the secretary of the company or such other officer of it as may be named in the order to produce the books or papers (or any of them) to a person named in the order at a place so named.

(3)   The above applies also in relation to any books or papers of a person carrying on the business of banking so far as they relate to the company's affairs, as it applies to any books or papers of or under the control of the company, except that no such order as is referred to in subsection (2)(b) shall be made by virtue of this subsection.

(4)   The decision of a judge of the High Court or of any of the Lords Commissioners of Justiciary on an application under this section is not appealable.

722.   Form of company registers, etc

(1)   Any register, index, minute book or accounting record, required by the Companies Acts to be kept by a company may be kept either by making entries in bound books or by recording the matters in question in any other manner.

(2)   Where any such register, index, minute book or accounting record is not kept by making entries in a bound book, but by some other means, adequate precautions shall be taken for guarding against falsification and facilitating its discovery.

(3)   If default is made in complying with subsection (2), the company and every officer of it who is in
default is liable to a fine and, for continued contravention, to a daily default fine.

723.   Use of computers for company records

(1)   The power conferred on a company by section 722(1) to keep a register or other record by
recording the matters in question otherwise than by making entries in bound books includes
power to keep the register or other record by recording those matters otherwise than in a legible
form, so long as the recording is capable of being reproduced in a legible form.

(2)   Any provision of an instrument made by a company before 12th February 1979 which requires a
register of holders of the company's debentures to be kept in a legible form is to be read as
requiring the register to be kept in a legible or non-legible form.

(3)   If any such register or other record of a company as is mentioned in section 722(1), or a register
of holders of a company's debentures, is kept by the company by recording the matters in
question otherwise than in a legible form, any duty imposed on the company by this Act to allow
inspection of, or to furnish a copy of, the register or other record or any part of it is to be treated as
a duty to allow inspection of, or to furnish, a reproduction of the recording or of the relevant part
of it in a legible form.

(4)   The Secretary of State may by regulations in a statutory instrument make such provision in
addition to subsection (3) as he considers appropriate in connection with such registers or other
records as are mentioned in that subsection, and are kept as so mentioned; and the regulations
may make modifications of provisions of this Act relating to such registers or other records.

(5)   A statutory instrument under subsection (4) is subject to annulment in pursuance of a resolution
of either House of Parliament.

723A.   Obligations of company as to inspection of registers, &c

(1)   The Secretary of State may make provision by regulations as to the obligations of a company
which is required by any provision of this Act—
  (a)   to make available for inspection any register, index or document, or
  (b)   to provide copies of any such register, index or document, or part of it;
  and a company which fails to comply with the regulations shall be deemed to have refused
  inspection or, as the case may be, to have failed to provide a copy.

(2)   The regulations may make provision as to the time, duration and manner of inspection, including
the circumstances in which and extent to which the copying of information is permitted in the
course of inspection.

(3)   The regulations may define what may be required of the company as regards the nature, extent
and manner of extracting or presenting any information for the purposes of inspection or the
provision of copies.

(4)   Where there is power to charge a fee, the regulations may make provision as to the amount of the
fee and the basis of its calculation.

(5)   Regulations under this section may make different provision for different classes of case.

(6)   Nothing in any provision of this Act or in the regulations shall be construed as preventing a
company from affording more extensive facilities than are required by the regulations or, where a
fee may be charged, from charging a lesser fee than that prescribed or no fee at all.

(7)   Regulations under this section shall be made by statutory instrument which shall be subject to
annulment in pursuance of a resolution of either House of Parliament.

723B.   Confidentiality orders

(1)   Subject to the provisions of this section, an individual may make an application under this section
to the Secretary of State where the condition in subsection (2) is satisfied.

(2)   That condition is that the individual—
  (a)   is or proposes to become a director, secretary or permanent representative of a relevant
        company; and
  (b)   considers that the availability for inspection by members of the public of particulars of his
        usual residential address creates, or (if an order is not made under this section) is likely to

create, a serious risk that he or a person who lives with him will be subjected to violence or intimidation.

(3)   Where, on an application made by an individual under this section, the Secretary of State is satisfied that the availability for inspection by members of the public of particulars of the individual's usual residential address creates, or (if an order is not made under this section) is likely to create, a serious risk that the individual, or a person who lives with him, will be subjected to violence or intimidation, he shall make an order under this section ("a confidentiality order") in relation to him.

(4)   Otherwise, he shall dismiss the application.

(5)   An application under this section shall specify, in relation to each company of which the individual is a director, secretary or permanent representative, an address satisfying such conditions as may be prescribed.

(6)   The Secretary of State shall give the applicant notice of his decision under subsection (3) or (4); and a notice under this subsection shall be given within the prescribed period after the making of the decision and contain such information as may be prescribed.

(7)   Regulations may make provision about applications for confidentiality orders; and the regulations may in particular—

(a)   require the payment, on the making of an application, of such fees as may be specified in the regulations;

(b)   make provision about the form and manner in which applications are to be made;

(c)   provide that applications shall contain such information, and be accompanied by such evidence, as the Secretary of State may from time to time direct.

(8)   Regulations may make provision—

(a)   about the manner in which determinations are to be made under subsection (3) or (4);

(b)   for questions to be referred to such persons as the Secretary of State thinks fit for the purposes of such determinations;

(c)   about the review of such determinations;

(d)   about the period for which confidentiality orders shall remain in force and the renewal of confidentiality orders.

(9)   The Secretary of State may at any time revoke a confidentiality order if he is satisfied that such conditions as may be prescribed are satisfied.

(10)   Regulations may make provision about the manner in which a determination under subsection (9) is to be made and notified to the individual concerned.

723C.   Effect of confidentiality orders

(1)   At any time when a confidentiality order is in force in relation to an individual—

(a)   section 709(1) shall not apply to so much of any record kept by the registrar as contains information which is recorded as particulars of the individual's usual residential address that were contained in a document delivered to the registrar after the order came into force;

(b)   section 364 shall have effect in relation to each affected company of which the individual is a director or secretary as if the reference in subsection (4)(a) of that section to the individual's usual residential address were a reference to the address for the time being specified by the individual in relation to that company under section 723B(5) or subsection (7) below.

(2)   Regulations may make provision about the inspection and copying of confidential records, and such provision may include—

(a)   provision as to the persons by whom, and the circumstances in which, confidential records may be inspected or copies taken of such records;

(b)   provision under which the registrar may be required to provide certified copies of, or of extracts from, such records.

(3)   Provision under subsection (2) may include provision—

(a)   for persons of a prescribed description to be entitled to apply to the court for authority to inspect or take copies of confidential records;

(b)   as to the criteria to be used by the court in determining whether an authorisation should be given.

(4)   Regulations may make provision for restricting the persons to whom, and the purposes for which, relevant information may be disclosed.

(5)   In subsection (4) 'relevant information' means information, relating to the usual residential address of an individual in relation to whom a confidentiality order is in force, which has been obtained in prescribed circumstances.

(6)   Regulations may—

(a)   provide that, where a confidentiality order is in force in relation to an individual who is a director or secretary of a company, subsections (3) and (5) of section 288 shall not apply in relation to so much of the register kept by the company under that section as contains particulars of the usual residential address of that individual ("the protected part of the register"); and

(b)   make provision as to the persons by whom the protected part of the register may be inspected and the conditions (which may include conditions as to the payment of a fee) on which they may inspect it.

(7)   Regulations may make provision—

(a)   requiring any individual in relation to whom a confidentiality order is in force to specify in the prescribed manner, in relation to each company of which he becomes a director, secretary or permanent representative at a time when the order is in force, an address satisfying such conditions as may be prescribed;

(b)   as to the manner in which the address specified in relation to a company under section 723B(5) or this subsection may be changed.

(8)   A company is an affected company for the purposes of subsection (1) if—

(a)   it is required to deliver annual returns in accordance with section 363; and

(b)   the individual has specified an address in relation to it under section 723B(5) or subsection (7) above.

723D.   Construction of sections 723B and 723C

(1)   In section 723B "relevant company" means—

(a)   a company formed and registered under this Act or an existing company; or

(b)   an overseas company.

(2)   For the purposes of sections 723B and 723C, an individual is a permanent representative of a company if—

(a)   the company is a company to which section 690A applies; and

(b)   he is authorised to represent the company as a permanent representative of the company for the business of one or more of its branches in Great Britain.

(3)   In section 723C "confidential records" means so much of any records kept by the registrar for the purposes of the Companies Acts as contains information—

(a)   which relates to an individual in relation to whom a confidentiality order is in force; and

(b)   is recorded as particulars of the individual's usual residential address that were contained in a document delivered to the registrar after the order came into force.

(4)   In sections 723B and 723C—

"confidentiality order" means an order under section 723B;

"the court" means such court as may be specified in regulations;

"director" and "secretary", in relation to an overseas company, have the same meanings as in Chapter 1 of Part 23 of this Act;

"document" has the same meaning as in Part 24 of this Act;

"prescribed" means prescribed by regulations.

(5)   Section 715A(2) applies in relation to sections 723B and 723C as it applies in relation to Part 24 of this Act.

(6)   Regulations may provide that in determining for the purposes of sections 723B and 723C whether a document has been delivered after the coming into force of a confidentiality order, any

document delivered to the registrar after the latest time permitted for the delivery of that document shall be deemed to have been delivered at that time.

(7)   For the purposes of section 723B(2)(a) and subsection (2) above it is immaterial whether or not the company in question has already been incorporated or become a relevant company or a company to which section 690A applies at the time of the application under section 723B.

(8)   For the purposes of section 723C(1) and subsection (3) above, it is immaterial whether the record in question consists in the original document concerned.

723E. Sections 723B and 723C: offences

(1)   Regulations may provide—
  (a)   that any person who in an application under section 723B makes a statement which he knows to be false in a material particular, or recklessly makes a statement which is false in a material particular, shall be guilty of an offence;
  (b)   that any person who discloses information in contravention of regulations under section 723C(4) shall be guilty of an offence.

(2)   Regulations may provide that a person guilty of an offence under subsection (1) shall be liable—
  (a)   on conviction on indictment, to imprisonment for a term not exceeding two years, or to a fine, or to both; and
  (b)   on summary conviction, to imprisonment for a term not exceeding six months, or to a fine not exceeding the statutory maximum, or to both.

723F. Regulations under sections 723B to 723E

(1)   In sections 723B to 723E "regulations" means regulations made by the Secretary of State.

(2)   Any power of the Secretary of State to make regulations under any of those sections shall be exercisable by statutory instrument.

(3)   Regulations under sections 723B to 723E—
  (a)   may make different provision for different cases;
  (b)   may contain such incidental, supplemental, consequential and transitional provision, as the Secretary of State thinks fit.

(4)   The provision that may be made by virtue of subsection (3)(b) includes provision repealing or modifying any enactment.

(5)   No regulations shall be made under any of sections 723B to 723E unless a draft of the instrument containing them has been laid before Parliament and approved by a resolution of each House.

724. ...

725. Service of documents

(1)   A document may be served on a company by leaving it at, or sending it by post to, the company's registered office.

(2)   Where a company registered in Scotland carries on business in England and Wales, the process of any court in England and Wales may be served on the company by leaving it at, or sending it by post to, the company's principal place of business in England and Wales, addressed to the manager or other head officer in England and Wales of the company.

(3)   Where process is served on a company under subsection (2), the person issuing out the process shall send a copy of it by post to the company's registered office.

726. Costs and expenses in actions by certain limited companies

(1)   Where in England and Wales a limited company is plaintiff in an action or other legal proceeding, the court having jurisdiction in the matter may, if it appears by credible testimony that there is reason to believe that the company will be unable to pay the defendant's costs if successful in his defence, require sufficient security to be given for those costs, and may stay all proceedings until the security is given.

(2)   Where in Scotland a limited company is pursuer in an action or other legal proceeding, the court having jurisdiction in the matter may, if it appears by credible testimony that there is reason to

believe that the company will be unable to pay the defender's expenses if successful in his defence, order the company to find caution and sist the proceedings until caution is found.

727.   Power of court to grant relief in certain cases

(1)   If in any proceedings for negligence, default, breach of duty or breach of trust against an officer of a company or a person employed by a company as auditor (whether he is or is not an officer of the company) it appears to the court hearing the case that that officer or person is or may be liable in respect of the negligence, default, breach of duty or breach of trust, but that he has acted honestly and reasonably, and that having regard to all the circumstances of the case (including those connected with his appointment) he ought fairly to be excused for the negligence, default, breach of duty or breach of trust, that court may relieve him, either wholly or partly, from his liability on such terms as it thinks fit.

(2)   If any such officer or person as above-mentioned has reason to apprehend that any claim will or might be made against him in respect of any negligence, default, breach of duty or breach of trust, he may apply to the court for relief; and the court on the application has the same power to relieve him as under this section it would have had if it had been a court before which proceedings against that person for negligence, default, breach of duty or breach of trust had been brought.

(3)   Where a case to which subsection (1) applies is being tried by a judge with a jury, the judge, after hearing the evidence, may, if he is satisfied that the defendant or defender ought in pursuance of that subsection to be relieved either in whole or in part from the liability sought to be enforced against him, withdraw the case in whole or in part from the jury and forthwith direct judgment to be entered for the defendant or defender on such terms as to costs or otherwise as the judge may think proper.

728.   Enforcement of High Court orders

Orders made by the High Court under this Act may be enforced in the same manner as orders made in an action pending in that court.

729.   Annual report by Secretary of State

The Secretary of State shall cause a general annual report of matters within the Companies Acts to be prepared and laid before both Houses of Parliament.

730.   Punishment of offences

(1)   Schedule 24 to this Act has effect with respect to the way in which offences under this Act are punishable on conviction.

(2)   In relation to an offence under a provision of this Act specified in the first column of the Schedule (the general nature of the offence being described in the second column), the third column shows whether the offence is punishable on conviction on indictment, or on summary conviction, or either in the one way or the other.

(3)   The fourth column of the Schedule shows, in relation to an offence, the maximum punishment by way of fine or imprisonment under this Act which may be imposed on a person convicted of the offence in the way specified in relation to it in the third column (that is to say, on indictment or summarily), a reference to a period of years or months being to a term of imprisonment of that duration.

(4)   The fifth column shows (in relation to an offence for which there is an entry in that column) that a person convicted of the offence after continued contravention is liable to a daily default fine; that is to say, he is liable on a second or subsequent summary conviction of the offence to the fine specified in that column for each day on which the contravention is continued (instead of the penalty specified for the offence in the fourth column of the Schedule).

(5)   For the purpose of any enactment in the Companies Acts which provides that an officer of a company or other body who is in default is liable to a fine or penalty, the expression "officer who is in default" means any officer of the company or other body who knowingly and wilfully authorises or permits the default, refusal or contravention mentioned in the enactment.

731.   Summary proceedings

(1)   Summary proceedings for any offence under the Companies Acts may (without prejudice to any jurisdiction exercisable apart from this subsection) be taken against a body corporate at any place at which the body has a place of business, and against any other person at any place at which he is for the time being.

(2)   Notwithstanding anything in section 127(1) of the Magistrates' Courts Act 1980, an information relating to an offence under the Companies Acts which is triable by a magistrates' court in England and Wales may be so tried if it is laid at any time within 3 years after the commission of the offence and within 12 months after the date on which evidence sufficient in the opinion of the Director of Public Prosecutions or the Secretary of State (as the case may be) to justify the proceedings comes to his knowledge.

(3)   Summary proceedings in Scotland for an offence under the Companies Acts shall not be commenced after the expiration of 3 years from the commission of the offence.
Subject to this (and notwithstanding anything in section 136 of the Criminal Procedure (Scotland) Act 1995), such proceedings may (in Scotland) be commenced at any time within 12 months after the date on which evidence sufficient in the Lord Advocate's opinion to justify the proceedings came to his knowledge or, where such evidence was reported to him by the Secretary of State, within 12 months after the date on which it came to the knowledge of the latter; and subsection (3) of that section applies for the purpose of this subsection as it applies for the purpose of that section.

(4)   For purposes of this section, a certificate of the Director of Public Prosecutions, the Lord Advocate or the Secretary of State (as the case may be) as to the date on which such evidence as is referred to above came to his knowledge is conclusive evidence.

732.   Prosecution by public authorities

(1)   In respect of an offence under any of sections 210, 245E, 245G, 324, 329, 448, 449 to 451, 453A and 455, proceedings shall not, in England and Wales, be instituted except by or with the consent of the appropriate authority.

(2)   That authority is—

(a)   for an offence under any of sections 210, 245E, 245G, 324 and 329, the Secretary of State or the Director of Public Prosecutions,

(b)   for an offence under any of sections 448, 449 to 451 and 453A, either one of those two persons or the Friendly Societies Commission, and

(c)   for an offence under section 455, the Secretary of State.

(3)   Where proceedings are instituted under the Companies Acts against any person by the Director of Public Prosecutions or by or on behalf of the Secretary of State or the Lord Advocate, nothing in those Acts is to be taken to require any person to disclose any information which he is entitled to refuse to disclose on grounds of legal professional privilege or, in Scotland, confidentiality of communications.

733.   Offences by bodies corporate

(1)   The following applies to offences under any of sections 210, 216(3), 245E(3), 245G(7) ... , 394A(1), 448, 449 to 451 and 453A.

(2)   Where a body corporate is guilty of such an offence and it is proved that the offence occurred with the consent or connivance of, or was attributable to any neglect on the part of any director, manager, secretary or other similar officer of the body, or any person who was purporting to act in any such capacity, he as well as the body corporate is guilty of that offence and is liable to be proceeded against and punished accordingly.

(3)   Where the affairs of a body corporate are managed by its members, ... subsection (2) above applies in relation to the acts and defaults of a member in connection with his functions of management as if he were a director of the body corporate.

(4)   In this section "director", in relation to an offence under any of sections 448, 449 to 451 and 453A, includes a shadow director.

734.   Criminal proceedings against unincorporated bodies

(1)   Proceedings for an offence alleged to have been committed under section 245E(3), section 245G(7), section 394A(1) or any of sections 448, 449 to 451 or section 453A by an unincorporated body shall be brought in the name of that body (and not in that of any of its members), and for the purposes of any such proceedings, any rules of court relating to the service of documents apply as if that body were a corporation.

(2)   A fine imposed on an unincorporated body on its conviction of such an offence shall be paid out of the funds of that body.

(3)   In a case in which an unincorporated body is charged in England and Wales with such an offence, section 33 of the Criminal Justice Act 1925 and Schedule 3 to the Magistrates' Courts Act 1980 (procedure on charge of an offence against a corporation) have effect in like manner as in the case of a corporation so charged.

(4)   In relation to proceedings on indictment in Scotland for such an offence alleged to have been committed by an unincorporated body, section 70 of the Criminal Procedure (Scotland) Act 1995 (proceedings on indictment against bodies corporate) has effect as if that body were a body corporate.

(5)   Where such an offence committed by a partnership is proved to have been committed with the consent or connivance of, or to be attributable to any neglect on the part of, a partner, he as well as the partnership is guilty of the offence and liable to be proceeded against and punished accordingly.

(6)   Where such an offence committed by an unincorporated body (other than a partnership) is proved to have been committed with the consent or connivance of, or to be attributable to any neglect on the part of, any officer of the body or any member of its governing body, he as well as the body is guilty of the offence and liable to be proceeded against and punished accordingly.

PART XXVI
INTERPRETATION

735.   "Company", etc

(1)   In this Act—

    (a)   "company" means a company formed and registered under this Act, or an existing company;

    (b)   "existing company" means a company formed and registered under the former Companies Acts, but does not include a company registered under the Joint Stock Companies Acts, the Companies Act 1862 or the Companies (Consolidation) Act 1908 in what was then Ireland;

    (c)   "the former Companies Acts" means the Joint Stock Companies Acts, the Companies Act 1862, the Companies (Consolidation) Act 1908, the Companies Act 1929 and the Companies Acts 1948 to 1983.

(2)   "Public company" and "private company" have the meanings given by section 1(3).

(3)   "The Joint Stock Companies Acts" means the Joint Stock Companies Act 1856, the Joint Stock Companies Acts 1856, 1857, the Joint Stock Banking Companies Act 1857 and the Act to enable Joint Stock Banking Companies to be formed on the principle of limited liability, or any one or more of those Acts (as the case may require), but does not include the Joint Stock Companies Act 1844.

(4)   The definitions in this section apply unless the contrary intention appears.

735A.   Relationship of this Act to Insolvency Act

(1)   In this Act "the Insolvency Act" means the Insolvency Act 1986; and in the following provisions of this Act, namely, sections 375(1)(b), 425(6)(a), ... 460(2), 675, 676, 677, 699(1), 728 and Schedule 21, paragraph 6(1), the words "this Act" are to be read as including Parts I to VII of that Act, sections 411, 413, 414, 416 and 417 in Part XV of that Act, and also the Company Directors Disqualifications Act 1986.

(2)   In sections 704(5), (7) and (8), 706(1), 707B(1), 707A(1), 708(1)(a) and (4), 709(1) and (3), 710A, 713(1), 729 and 732(3) references to the Companies Acts include Parts I to VII of the Insolvency Act, sections 411, 413, 414, 416 and 417 in Part XV of that Act, and also the Company Directors Disqualification Act 1986.

(3)   Subsections (1) and (2) apply unless the contrary intention appears.

735B.   Relationship of this Act to Part VI of the Financial Services and Markets Act 2000

In sections 704(5), (7) and (8), 706(1), 707(1), 707A(1), 708(1)(a) and (4), 709(1) and (3), 710A and 713(1) references to the Companies Acts include Part VI of the Financial Services and Markets Act 2000.

736.   "Subsidiary", "holding company" and "wholly owned subsidiary"

(1)   A company is a "subsidiary" of another company, its "holding company", if that other company—

(a)   holds a majority of the voting rights in it, or

(b)   is a member of it and has the right to appoint or remove a majority of its board of directors, or

(c)   is a member of it and controls alone, pursuant to an agreement with other shareholders or members, a majority of the voting rights in it,

or if it is a subsidiary of a company which is itself a subsidiary of that other company.

(2)   A company is a "wholly-owned subsidiary" of another company if it has no members except that other and that other's wholly-owned subsidiaries or persons acting on behalf of that other or its wholly-owned subsidiaries.

(3)   In this section "company" includes any body corporate.

736A.   Provisions supplementing s 736

(1)   The provisions of this section explain expressions used in section 736 and otherwise supplement that section.

(2)   In section 736(1)(a) and (c) the references to the voting rights in a company are to the rights conferred on shareholders in respect of their shares or, in the case of a company not having a share capital, on members, to vote at general meetings of the company on all, or substantially all, matters.

(3)   In section 736(1)(b) the reference to the right to appoint or remove a majority of the board of directors is to the right to appoint or remove directors holding a majority of the voting rights at meetings of the board on all, or substantially all, matters; and for the purposes of that provision—

(a)   a company shall be treated as having the right to appoint to a directorship if—

(i)   a person's appointment to it follows necessarily from his appointment as director of the company, or

(ii)   the directorship is held by the company itself; and

(b)   a right to appoint or remove which is exercisable only with the consent or concurrence of another person shall be left out of account unless no other person has a right to appoint or, as the case may be, remove in relation to that directorship.

(4)   Rights which are exercisable only in certain circumstances shall be taken into account only—

(a)   when the circumstances have arisen, and for so long as they continue to obtain, or

(b)   when the circumstances are within the control of the person having the rights;

and rights which are normally exercisable but are temporarily incapable of exercise shall continue to be taken into account.

(5)   Rights held by a person in a fiduciary capacity shall be treated as not held by him.

(6)   Rights held by a person as nominee for another shall be treated as held by the other; and rights shall be regarded as held as nominee for another if they are exercisable only on his instructions or with his consent or concurrence.

(7)   Rights attached to shares held by way of security shall be treated as held by the person providing the security—

(a)   where apart from the right to exercise them for the purpose of preserving the value of the security, or of realising it, the rights are exercisable only in accordance with his instructions;

(b)   where the shares are held in connection with the granting of loans as part of normal business activities and apart from the right to exercise them for the purpose of preserving the value of the security, or of realising it, the rights are exercisable only in his interests.

(8)   Rights shall be treated as held by a company if they are held by any of its subsidiaries; and nothing in subsection (6) or (7) shall be construed as requiring rights held by a company to be treated as held by any of its subsidiaries.

(9)   For the purposes of subsection (7) rights shall be treated as being exercisable in accordance with the instructions or in the interests of a company if they are exercisable in accordance with the instructions of or, as the case may be, in the interests of—

(a)   any subsidiary or holding company of that company, or

(b)   any subsidiary of a holding company of that company.

(10)   The voting rights in a company shall be reduced by any rights held by the company itself.

(11)   References in any provision of subsections (5) to (10) to rights held by a person include rights falling to be treated as held by him by virtue of any other provision of those subsections but not rights which by virtue of any such provision are to be treated as not held by him.

(12)   In this section "company" includes any body corporate.

736B.   Power to amend ss 736 and 736A

(1)   The Secretary of State may by regulations amend sections 736 and 736A so as to alter the meaning of the expressions "holding company", "subsidiary" or "wholly-owned subsidiary".

(2)   The regulations may make different provision for different cases or classes of case and may contain such incidental and supplementary provisions as the Secretary of State thinks fit.

(3)   Regulations under this section shall be made by statutory instrument which shall be subject to annulment in pursuance of a resolution of either House of Parliament.

(4)   Any amendment made by regulations under this section does not apply for the purposes of enactments outside the Companies Acts unless the regulations so provide.

(5)   So much of section 23(3) of the Interpretation Act 1978 as applies section 17(2)(a) of that Act (effect of repeal and re-enactment) to deeds, instruments and documents other than enactments shall not apply in relation to any repeal and re-enactment effected by regulations made under this section.

737.   "Called-up share capital"

(1)   In this Act, "called-up share capital", in relation to a company, means so much of its share capital as equals the aggregate amount of the calls made on its shares (whether or not those calls have been paid), together with any share capital paid up without being called and any share capital to be paid on a specified future date under the articles, the terms of allotment of the relevant shares or any other arrangements for payment of those shares.

(2)   "Uncalled share capital" is to be construed accordingly.

(3)   The definitions in this section apply unless the contrary intention appears.

738.   "Allotment" and "paid up"

(1)   In relation to an allotment of shares in a company, the shares are to be taken for the purposes of this Act to be allotted when a person acquires the unconditional right to be included in the company's register of members in respect of those shares.

(2)   For purposes of this Act, a share in a company is deemed paid up (as to its nominal value or any premium on it) in cash, or allotted for cash, if the consideration for the allotment or payment up is cash received by the company, or is a cheque received by it in good faith which the directors have no reason for suspecting will not be paid, or is a release of a liability of the company for a liquidated sum, or is an undertaking to pay cash to the company at a future date.

(3)   In relation to the allotment or payment up of any shares in a company, references in this Act (except sections 89 to 94) to consideration other than cash and to the payment up of shares and

premiums on shares otherwise than in cash include the payment of, or any undertaking to pay, cash to any person other than the company.

(4) For the purpose of determining whether a share is or is to be allotted for cash, or paid up in cash, "cash" includes foreign currency.

739. "Non-cash asset"

(1) In this Act "non-cash asset" means any property or interest in property other than cash; and for this purpose "cash" includes foreign currency.

(2) A reference to the transfer or acquisition of a non-cash asset includes the creation or extinction of an estate or interest in, or a right over, any property and also the discharge of any person's liability, other than a liability for a liquidated sum.

740. "Body corporate" and "corporation"

References in this Act to a body corporate or to a corporation do not include a corporation sole, but include a company incorporated elsewhere than in Great Britain.

Such references to a body corporate do not include a Scottish firm.

741. "Director" and "shadow director"

(1) In this Act, "director" includes any person occupying the position of director, by whatever name called.

(2) In relation to a company, "shadow director" means a person in accordance with whose directions or instructions the directors of the company are accustomed to act.

However, a person is not deemed a shadow director by reason only that the directors act on advice given by him in a professional capacity.

(3) For the purposes of the following provisions of this Act, namely—

   section 309 (directors' duty to have regard to interests of employees),

   section 319 (directors' long-term contracts of employment),

   sections 320 to 322 (substantial property transactions involving directors), ...

   section 322B (contracts with sole members who are directors), and

   sections 330 to 346 (general restrictions on power of companies to make loans, etc, to directors and others connected with them),

(being provisions under which shadow directors are treated as directors), a body corporate is not to be treated as a shadow director of any of its subsidiary companies by reason only that the directors of the subsidiary are accustomed to act in accordance with its directions or instructions.

742. Expressions used in connection with accounts

(1) In this Act, unless a contrary intention appears, the following expressions have the same meaning as in Part VII (accounts)—

   "annual accounts",

   "accounting reference date" and "accounting reference period",

   "balance sheet" and "balance sheet date",

   "Companies Act accounts"

   "Companies Act individual accounts"

   "current assets",

   "financial year", in relation to a company,

   "fixed assets",

   "IAS accounts"

   "IAS individual accounts"

   "parent company" and "parent undertaking",

   "profit and loss account", and

   "subsidiary undertaking".

(2) References in this Act to "realised profits" and "realised losses", in relation to a company's accounts, shall be construed in accordance with section 262(3).

(2A)   References in this Act to sending or sending out copies of any of the documents referred to in section 238(1) include sending or sending out such copies in accordance with section 238(4A) or (4B).

742A.   Meaning of "offer to the public"

(1)   Any reference in Part IV (allotment of shares and debentures), Part 7 (accounts) or section 744 (general interpretation) to offering shares or debentures to the public is to be read as including a reference to offering them to any section of the public, however selected.

(2)   This section does not require an offer to be treated as made to the public if it can properly be regarded, in all the circumstances—

   (a)   as not being calculated to result, directly or indirectly, in the shares or debentures becoming available for subscription or purchase by persons other than those receiving the offer; or

   (b)   as being a domestic concern of the persons receiving and making it.

(3)   An offer of shares in or debentures of a private company (other than an offer to which subsection (5) applies) is to be regarded (unless the contrary is proved) as being a domestic concern of the persons making and receiving it if—

   (a)   it is made to—

      (i)   an existing member of the company making the offer;

      (ii)   an existing employee of that company;

      (iii)   the widow or widower *or surviving civil partner* of a person who was a member or employee of that company;

      (iv)   a member of the family of a person who is or was a member of that company; or

      (v)   an existing debenture holder; or

   (b)   it is an offer to subscribe for shares or debentures to be held under an employee's share scheme.

(4)   Subsection (5) applies to an offer—

   (a)   which falls within paragraph (a) or (b) of subsection (3); but

   (b)   which is made on terms which permit the person to whom it is made to renounce his right to the allotment of shares or issue of debentures.

(5)   The offer is to be regarded (unless the contrary is proved) as being a domestic concern of the persons making and receiving it if the terms are such that the right may be renounced only in favour—

   (a)   of any person mentioned in subsection (3)(a), or

   (b)   in the case of an employee's share scheme, of a person entitled to hold shares or debentures under the scheme.

(6)   For the purposes of subsection (3)(a)(iv), the members of a person's family are—

   (a)   the person's spouse *or civil partner* and children (including step-children) and their descendants, and

   (b)   any trustee (acting in his capacity as such) of a trust the principal beneficiary of which is the person him or herself or of any of those relatives.

(7)   Where an application has been made to the competent authority in any EEA State for the admission of any securities to official listing, then an offer of those securities for subscription or sale to a person whose ordinary business it is to buy or sell shares or debentures (whether as principal or agent) is not to be regarded as an offer to the public for the purposes of this Part.

(8)   For the purposes of subsection (7)—

   (a)   "competent authority" means a competent authority appointed for the purposes of the Council Directive of 28 May 2001 on the admission of securities to official stock exchange listing and on information to be published on those securities; and

   (b)   "official listing" means official listing pursuant to that directive.

Note. The italicized words in subsections (3) and (6) are inserted by the Civil Partnership Act 2004, s. 261(1), Sch. 27, para. 104, as from a day to be appointed.

742B. Meaning of "banking company"

(1)   Subject to subsection (2), "banking company" means a person who has permission under Part 4 of the Financial Services and Markets Act 2000 to accept deposits.

(2)   A banking company does not include—

(a)   a person who is not a company, and

(b)   a person who has permission to accept deposits only for the purpose of carrying on another regulated activity in accordance with that permission.

(3)   This section must be read with—

(a)   section 22 of the Financial Services and Markets Act 2000;

(b)   any relevant order under that section; and

(c)   Schedule 2 to that Act.

742C. Meaning of "insurance company" and "authorised insurance company"

(1)   For the purposes of this Act, "insurance company" has the meaning given in subsection (2) and "authorised insurance company" has the meaning given in subsection (3).

(2)   Subject to subsection (3), "insurance company" means a person (whether incorporated or not)—

(a)   who has permission under Part 4 of the Financial Services and Markets Act 2000 to effect or carry out contracts of insurance; or

(b)   who carries on insurance market activity; or

(c)   who may effect or carry out contracts of insurance under which the benefits provided by that person are exclusively or primarily benefits in kind in the event of accident to or breakdown of a vehicle, and does not fall within paragraph (a).

(3)   An insurance company does not include a friendly society, within the meaning of section 116 of the Friendly Societies Act 1992.

(4)   An "authorised insurance company" means a person falling within paragraph (a) of subsection (2).

(5)   References in this section to contracts of insurance and the effecting or carrying out of such contracts must be read with—

(a)   section 22 of the Financial Services and Markets Act 2000;

(b)   any relevant order under that section; and

(c)   Schedule 2 to that Act.

743. "Employees' share scheme"

For purposes of this Act, an employees' share scheme is a scheme for encouraging or facilitating the holding of shares or debentures in a company by or for the benefit of—

(a)   the bona fide employees or former employees of the company, the company's subsidiary or holding company or a subsidiary of the company's holding company, or

(b)   the wives, husbands, widows, widowers or children or step-children under the age of 18 of such employees or former employees.

743A. Meaning of "office copy" in Scotland

References in this Act to an office copy of a court order shall be construed, as respects Scotland, as references to a certified copy interlocutor.

744. Expressions used generally in this Act

In this Act, unless the contrary intention appears, the following definitions apply—

"agent" does not include a person's counsel acting as such;

...

"articles" means, in relation to a company, its articles of association, as originally framed or as altered by resolution, including (so far as applicable to the company) regulations contained in or annexed to any enactment relating to companies passed before this Act, as altered by or under any such enactment;

...

"authorised minimum" has the meaning given by section 118;

"bank holiday" means a holiday under the Banking and Financial Dealings Act 1971;

...

"books and papers" and "books or papers" include accounts, deeds, writings and documents;

"communication" means the same as in the Electronic Communications Act 2000;

"the Companies Acts" means this Act, the insider dealing legislation and the Consequential Provisions Act;

"the Consequential Provisions Act" means the Companies Consolidation (Consequential Provisions) Act 1985;

"the court", in relation to a company, means the court having jurisdiction to wind up the company;

"debenture" includes debenture stock, bonds and any other securities of a company, whether constituting a charge on the assets of the company or not;

"document" includes summons, notice, order, and other legal process, and registers;

"EEA State" means a State which is a Contracting Party to the Agreement on the European Economic Area signed at Oporto on 2nd May 1992 as adjusted by the Protocol signed at Brussels on 17th March 1993;

"electronic communication" means the same as in the Electronic Communications Act 2000;

"equity share capital" means, in relation to a company, its issued share capital excluding any part of that capital which, neither as respects dividends nor as respects capital, carries any right to participate beyond a specified amount in a distribution;

"expert" has the meaning given by section 62;

"floating charge" includes a floating charge within the meaning given by section 462;

"the Gazette" means, as respects companies registered in England and Wales, the London Gazette and, as respects companies registered in Scotland, the Edinburgh Gazette;

...

"hire-purchase agreement" has the same meaning as in the Consumer Credit Act 1974;

"the insider dealing legislation" means Part V of the Criminal Justice Act 1993 (insider dealing).

"insurance market activity" has the meaning given in section 316(3) of the Financial Services and Markets Act 2000;

...

"joint stock company" has the meaning given by section 683;

"memorandum", in relation to a company, means its memorandum of association, as originally framed or as altered in pursuance of any enactment;

"number", in relation to shares, includes amount, where the context admits of the reference to shares being construed to include stock;

"officer", in relation to a body corporate, includes a director, manager or secretary;

"official seal", in relation to the registrar of companies, means a seal prepared under section 704(4) for the authentication of documents required for or in connection with the registration of companies;

"oversea company" means—

(a) a company incorporated elsewhere than in Great Britain which, after the commencement of this Act, establishes a place of business in Great Britain, and

(b) a company so incorporated which has, before that commencement, established a place of business and continues to have an established place of business in Great Britain at that commencement;

"place of business" includes a share transfer or share registration office;

"prescribed" means—

(a) as respects provisions of this Act relating to winding up, prescribed by general rules ..., and

(b)   otherwise, prescribed by statutory instrument made by the Secretary of State;

"prospectus" means any prospectus, notice, circular, advertisement, or other invitation, offering to the public for subscription or purchase any shares in or debentures of a company;

"prospectus issued generally" means a prospectus issued to persons who are not existing members of the company or holders of its debentures;

...

"regulated activity" has the meaning given in section 22 of the Financial Services and Markets Act 2000;

"the registrar of companies" and "the registrar" mean the registrar or other officer performing under this Act the duty of registration of companies in England and Wales or in Scotland, as the case may require;

"share" means share in the share capital of a company, and includes stock (except where a distinction between shares and stock is express or implied); and

"undistributable reserves" has the meaning given by section 264(3).

Note. The definitions "authorised minimum", "expert", "floating charge", "joint stock company" and "undistributable reserves" are repealed by the Companies Act 1989, s. 212, Sch. 24, as from a day to be appointed. The definition "prospectus issued generally" is repealed for certain purposes by the Financial Services Act 1986, s. 212(3), Sch. 17, Pt. I and for remaining purposes as from a day to be appointed.

744A.   Index of defined expressions

The following Table shows provisions defining or otherwise explaining expressions for the purposes of this Act generally—

accounting reference date, accounting reference period	sections 224 and 742(1)
acquisition (in relation to a non-cash asset)	section 739(2)
agent	section 744
allotment (and related expressions)	section 738
annual accounts	sections 261(2), 262(1) and 742(1)
annual general meeting	section 366
annual return	section 363
articles	section 744
authorised insurance company	section 742C
authorised minimum	section 118
balance sheet and balance sheet date	sections 261(2), 262(1) and 742(1)
bank holiday	section 744
banking company	section 742B
body corporate	section 740
books and papers, books or papers	section 744
called-up share capital	section 737(1)
capital redemption reserve	section 170(1)
communication	section 744
the Companies Acts	section 744
Companies Act accounts	sections 262(1) and 742(1)
Companies Act individual accounts	sections 226(2), 255(4A) and 742(1)
companies charges register	section 397
company	section 735(1)
the Consequential Provisions Act	section 744
corporation	section 740
the court (in relation to a company)	section 744
current assets	sections 262(1) and 742(1)
debenture	section 744
director	section 741(1)

document	section 744
EEA State	section 744
elective resolution	section 379A
electronic communication	section 744
employees' share scheme	section 743
equity share capital	section 744
existing company	section 735(1)
extraordinary general meeting	section 368
extraordinary resolution	section 378(1)
financial year (of a company)	sections 223 and 742(1)
fixed assets	sections 262(1) and 742(1)
floating charge (in Scotland)	section 462
the former Companies Acts	section 735(1)
the Gazette	section 744
hire-purchase agreement	section 744
holding company	section 736
IAS accounts	sections 262(1) and 742(1)
IAS individual accounts	sections 226(2) and 742(1)
the insider dealing legislation	section 744
the Insolvency Act	section 735A(1)
insurance company	section 742C
insurance market activity	section 744
the Joint Stock Companies Acts	section 735(3)
limited company	section 1(2)
member (of a company)	section 22
memorandum (in relation to a company)	section 744
non-cash asset	section 739(1)
number (in relation to shares)	section 744
office copy (in relation to a court order in Scotland)	section 743A
officer (in relation to a body corporate)	section 744
official seal (in relation to the registrar of companies)	section 744
oversea company	section 744
overseas branch register	section 362
paid up (and related expressions)	section 738
parent company and parent undertaking	sections 258 and 742(1)
place of business	section 744
prescribed	section 744
private company	section 1(3)
profit and loss account	sections 261(2), 262(1) and (2) and 742(1)
prospectus	section 744
public company	section 1(3)
realised profits or losses	sections 262(3) and 742(2)
registered number (of a company)	section 705(1)
registered office (of a company)	section 287
registrar and registrar of companies	section 744
regulated activity	section 744
resolution for reducing share capital	section 135(3)
shadow director	section 741(2) and (3)
share	section 744
share premium account	section 130(1)
share warrant	section 188

special notice (in relation to a resolution)	section 379
special resolution	section 378(2)
subsidiary	section 736
subsidiary undertaking	sections 258 and 742(1)
transfer (in relation to a non-cash asset)	section 739(2)
treasury shares	section 162A(3)
uncalled share capital	section 737(2)
undistributable reserves	section 264(3)
unlimited company	section 1(2)
unregistered company	section 718
wholly-owned subsidiary	section 736(2)

PART XXVII

FINAL PROVISIONS

745.   Northern Ireland

(1)   Except where otherwise expressly provided, nothing in this Act (except provisions relating expressly to companies registered or incorporated in Northern Ireland or outside Great Britain) applies to or in relation to companies so registered or incorporated.

(2)   Subject to any such provision, and to any express provision as to extent, this Act does not extend to Northern Ireland.

746.   Commencement

... this Act comes into force on 1st July 1985.

747.   Citation

This Act may be cited as the Companies Act 1985.

SCHEDULE 1

PARTICULARS OF DIRECTORS ETC TO BE CONTAINED IN STATEMENT
UNDER SECTION 10

Section 10

Directors

1.   Subject as provided below, the statement under section 10(2) shall contain the following particulars with respect to each person named as director—

   (a)   in the case of an individual, his present name, any former name, his usual residential address, his nationality, his business occupation (if any), particulars of any other directorships held by him, or which have been held by him and his date of birth;

   (b)   in the case of a corporation or Scottish firm, its corporate or firm name and registered or principal office.

2.—   (1)   It is not necessary for the statement to contain particulars of a directorship—

   (a)   which has not been held by a director at any time during the 5 years preceding the date on which the statement is delivered to the registrar,

   (b)   which is held by a director in a company which—

     (i)   is dormant or grouped with the company delivering the statement, and

     (ii)   if he also held that directorship for any period during those 5 years, was for the whole of that period either dormant or so grouped,

   (c)   which was held by a director for any period during those 5 years in a company which for the whole of that period was either dormant or grouped with the company delivering the statement.

(2)   For these purposes, "company" includes any body corporate incorporated in Great Britain; and—

     (a)   section 249AA(3) applies as regards whether and when a company is or has been "dormant", and

     (b)   a company is treated as being or having been at any time grouped with another company if at that time it is or was a company of which that other is or was a wholly-owned subsidiary, or if it is or was a wholly-owned subsidiary of the other or of another company of which that other is or was a wholly-owned subsidiary.

Secretaries

3.—   (1)   The statement shall contain the following particulars with respect to the person named as secretary or, where there are to be joint secretaries, with respect to each person named as one of them—

     (a)   in the case of an individual, his present name, any former name and his usual residential address,

     (b)   in the case of a corporation or a Scottish firm, its corporate or firm name and registered or principal office.

     (2)   However, if all the partners in a firm are joint secretaries, the name and principal office of the firm may be stated instead of the particulars otherwise required by this paragraph.

Interpretation

4.   In paragraphs 1(a) and 3(1)(a) above—

     (a)   "name" means a person's Christian name (or other forename) and surname, except that in the case of a peer, or an individual usually known by a title, the title may be stated instead of his Christian name (or other forename) and surname or in addition to either or both of them; and

     (b)   the reference to a former name does not include—

         (i)   in the case of a peer, or an individual normally known by a British title, the name by which he was known previous to the adoption of or succession to the title, or

         (ii)   in the case of any person, a former name which was changed or disused before he attained the age of 18 years or which has been changed or disused for 20 years or more, or

         (iii)   in the case of a married woman, the name by which she was known previous to the marriage.

5.   Where a confidentiality order made under section 723B is in force in respect of any individual named as a director or secretary, paragraphs 1(a) and 3(1)(a) have effect as if the references to the usual residential address of the individual were references to the address for the time being notified by him under regulations made under sections 723B to 723F to any companies or oversea companies of which he is a director, secretary or permanent representative, or, if he is not such a director, secretary or permanent representative either the address specified in his application for a confidentiality order under regulations made under section 723B or the address last notified by him under regulations made under sections 723B to 723F as the case may be.

SCHEDULE 2

INTERPRETATION OF REFERENCES TO "BENEFICIAL INTEREST"

Sections 23, 145, 146, 148

PART I
REFERENCES IN SECTIONS 23, 145, 146 AND 148

Residual interests under pension and employees' share schemes

1.— (1) Where shares in a company are held on trust for the purposes of a pension scheme or an employees' share scheme, there is to be disregarded any residual interest which has not vested in possession, being an interest of the company or, as this paragraph applies for the purposes of section 23(2), ... of any subsidiary of the company.

(2) In this paragraph, "a residual interest" means a right of the company or subsidiary in question ("the residual beneficiary") to receive any of the trust property in the event of—

(a) all the liabilities arising under the scheme having been satisfied or provided for, or

(b) the residual beneficiary ceasing to participate in the scheme, or

(c) the trust property at any time exceeding what is necessary for satisfying the liabilities arising or expected to arise under the scheme.

(3) In sub-paragraph (2), references to a right include a right dependent on the exercise of a discretion vested by the scheme in the trustee or any other person; and references to liabilities arising under a scheme include liabilities that have resulted or may result from the exercise of any such discretion.

(4) For purposes of this paragraph, a residual interest vests in possession—

(a) in a case within (a) of sub-paragraph (2), on the occurrence of the event there mentioned, whether or not the amount of the property receivable pursuant to the right mentioned in that sub-paragraph is then ascertained, and

(b) in a case within (b) or (c) of that sub-paragraph, when the residual beneficiary becomes entitled to require the trustee to transfer to that beneficiary any of the property receivable pursuant to that right.

(5) ...

2.— (1) The following has effect as regards the operation of sections ... 144, 145 and 146 to 149 in cases where a residual interest vests in possession.

(2) ...

(3) Where by virtue of paragraph 1 of this Schedule any shares are exempt from section 144 or 145 at the time when they are issued or acquired but the residual interest in question vests in possession before they are disposed of or fully paid up, those sections apply to the shares as if they had been issued or acquired on the date on which that interest vests in possession.

(4) Where by virtue of paragraph 1 any shares are exempt from sections 146 to 149 at the time when they are acquired but the residual interest in question vests in possession before they are disposed of, those sections apply to the shares as if they had been acquired on the date on which that interest vests in possession.

(5) The above sub-paragraphs apply irrespective of the date on which the residual interest vests or vested in possession; but where the date on which it vested was before 26th July 1983 (the passing of the Companies (Beneficial Interests) Act 1983), they have effect as if the vesting had occurred on that date.

Employer's charges and other rights of recovery

3.— (1) Where shares in a company are held on trust, there are to be disregarded—

(a) if the trust is for the purposes of a pension scheme, any such rights as are mentioned in the following sub-paragraph, and

      (b)   if the trust is for the purposes of an employees' share scheme, any such rights as are mentioned in (a) of the sub-paragraph,

being rights of the company or, as this paragraph applies for the purposes of section 23(2),, ... of any subsidiary of the company.

(2)   The rights referred to are—

      (a)   any charge or lien on, or set-off against, any benefit or other right or interest under the scheme for the purpose of enabling the employer or former employer of a member of the scheme to obtain the discharge of a monetary obligation due to him from the member, and

      (b)   any right to receive from the trustee of the scheme, or as trustee of the scheme to retain, an amount that can be recovered or retained under section 61 of the Pension Schemes Act 1993 (deduction of contributions equivalent premium from refund of scheme contributions) or otherwise as reimbursement or partial reimbursement for any ... contributions equivalent premium paid in connection with the scheme under Part III of that Act.

(3)   ...

Trustee's right to expenses, remuneration, indemnity, etc

4.—   (1)   Where a company is a trustee ..., there are to be disregarded any rights which the company has in its capacity as trustee including, in particular, any right to recover its expenses or be remunerated out of the trust property and any right to be indemnified out of that property for any liability incurred by reason of any act or omission of the company in the performance of its duties as trustee.

      (2)   As this paragraph applies for the purposes of section 23(2) ..., sub-paragraph (1) has effect as if references to a company included any body corporate which is a subsidiary of a company.

      (3)   As respects sections 145, 146 and 148, sub-paragraph (1) above applies where a company is a personal representative as it applies where a company is a trustee.

Supplementary

5.—   (1)   The following applies for the interpretation of this Part of this Schedule.

      (2)   "Pension scheme" means any scheme for the provision of benefits consisting of or including relevant benefits for or in respect of employees or former employees; and "relevant benefits" means any pension, lump sum, gratuity or other like benefit given or to be given on retirement or on death or in anticipation of retirement or, in connection with past service, after retirement or death.

      (3)   In sub-paragraph (2) of this paragraph, and in paragraph 3(2)(a), "employer" and "employee" are to be read as if a director of a company were employed by it.

PART II
REFERENCES IN SCHEDULE 5

Residual interests under pension and employees' share schemes

6.—   (1)   Where shares in an undertaking are held on trust for the purposes of a pension scheme or an employees' share scheme, there shall be disregarded any residual interest which has not vested in possession, being an interest of the undertaking or any of its subsidiary undertakings.

      (2)   In this paragraph a "residual interest" means a right of the undertaking in question (the "residual beneficiary") to receive any of the trust property in the event of—

      (a)   all the liabilities arising under the scheme having been satisfied or provided for, or

      (b)   the residual beneficiary ceasing to participate in the scheme, or

      (c)   the trust property at any time exceeding what is necessary for satisfying the liabilities arising or expected to arise under the scheme.

(3) In sub-paragraph (2) references to a right include a right dependent on the exercise of a discretion vested by the scheme in the trustee or any other person; and references to liabilities arising under a scheme include liabilities that have resulted or may result from the exercise of any such discretion.

(4) For the purposes of this paragraph a residual interest vests in possession—

    (a) in a case within sub-paragraph (2)(a), on the occurrence of the event there mentioned, whether or not the amount of the property receivable pursuant to the right mentioned in that sub-paragraph is then ascertained;

    (b) in a case within sub-paragraph (2)(b) or (c), when the residual beneficiary becomes entitled to require the trustee to transfer to that beneficiary any of the property receivable pursuant to that right.

Employer's charges and other rights of recovery

7.— (1) Where shares in an undertaking are held on trust, there shall be disregarded—

    (a) if the trust is for the purposes of a pension scheme, any such rights as are mentioned in sub-paragraph (2) below;

    (b) if the trust is for the purposes of an employees' share scheme, any such rights as are mentioned in paragraph (a) of that sub-paragraph,

being rights of the undertaking or any of its subsidiary undertakings.

(2) The rights referred to are—

    (a) any charge or lien on, or set-off against, any benefit or other right or interest under the scheme for the purpose of enabling the employer or former employer of a member of the scheme to obtain the discharge of a monetary obligation due to him from the member, and

    (b) any right to receive from the trustee of the scheme, or as trustee of the scheme to retain, an amount that can be recovered or retained under section 61 of the Pension Schemes Act 1993 (deduction of contributions equivalent premium from refund of scheme contributions) or otherwise as reimbursement or partial reimbursement for any contributions equivalent premium paid in connection with the scheme under Chapter III of Part III of that Act.

Trustee's right to expenses, remuneration, indemnity, &c

8. Where an undertaking is a trustee, there shall be disregarded any rights which the undertaking has in its capacity as trustee including, in particular, any right to recover its expenses or be remunerated out of the trust property and any right to be indemnified out of that property for any liability incurred by reason of any act or omission of the undertaking in the performance of its duties as trustee.

Supplementary

9.— (1) The following applies for the interpretation of this Part of this Schedule.

(2) "Undertaking", and "shares" in relation to an undertaking, have the same meaning as in Part VII.

(3) This Part of this Schedule applies in relation to debentures as it applies in relation to shares.

(4) "Pension scheme" means any scheme for the provision of benefits consisting of or including relevant benefits for or in respect of employees or former employees; and "relevant benefits" means any pension, lump sum, gratuity or other like benefit given or to be given on retirement or on death or in anticipation of retirement or, in connection with past service, after retirement or death.

(5) In sub-paragraph (4) of this paragraph and in paragraph 7(2) "employee" and "employer" shall be read as if a director of an undertaking were employed by it.

SCHEDULE 3

...

SCHEDULE 4

FORM AND CONTENT OF COMPANY ACCOUNTS

Section 226

PART I
GENERAL RULES AND FORMATS

SECTION A
GENERAL RULES

1.— (1) Subject to the following provisions of this Schedule—
    (a) every balance sheet of a company shall show the items listed in either of the balance sheet formats set out below in section B of this Part; and
    (b) every profit and loss account of a company shall show the items listed in any one of the profit and loss account formats so set out;
    in either case in the order and under the headings and sub-headings given in the format adopted.

(2) Sub-paragraph (1) above is not to be read as requiring the heading or sub-heading for any item to be distinguished by any letter or number assigned to that item in the format adopted.

2.— (1) Where in accordance with paragraph 1 a company's balance sheet or profit and loss account for any financial year has been prepared by reference to one of the formats set out in section B below, the directors of the company shall adopt the same format in preparing the accounts for subsequent financial years of the company unless in their opinion there are special reasons for a change.

(2) Particulars of any change in the format adopted in preparing a company's balance sheet or profit and loss account in accordance with paragraph 1 shall be disclosed, and the reasons for the change shall be explained, in a note to the accounts in which the new format is first adopted.

3.— (1) Any item required in accordance with paragraph 1 to be shown in a company's balance sheet or profit and loss account may be shown in greater detail than required by the format adopted.

(2) A company's balance sheet or profit and loss account may include an item representing or covering the amount of any asset or liability, income or expenditure not otherwise covered by any of the items listed in the format adopted, but the following shall not be treated as assets in any company's balance sheet—
    (a) preliminary expenses;
    (b) expenses of and commission on any issue of shares or debentures; and
    (c) costs of research.

(3) In preparing a company's balance sheet or profit and loss account the directors of the company shall adapt the arrangement and headings and sub-headings otherwise required by paragraph 1 in respect of items to which an Arabic number is assigned in the format adopted, in any case where the special nature of the company's business requires such adaptation.

(4) Items to which Arabic numbers are assigned in any of the formats set out in section B below may be combined in a company's accounts for any financial year if either—
    (a) their individual amounts are not material to assessing the state of affairs or profit or loss of the company for that year; or

(b) the combination facilitates that assessment;

but in a case within paragraph (b) the individual amounts of any items so combined shall be disclosed in a note to the accounts.

(5) Subject to paragraph 4(3) below, a heading or sub-heading corresponding to an item listed in the format adopted in preparing a company's balance sheet or profit and loss account shall not be included if there is no amount to be shown for that item in respect of the financial year to which the balance sheet or profit and loss account relates.

(6) Every profit and loss account of a company shall show the amount of the company's profit or loss on ordinary activities before taxation.

(7) ...

4.— (1) In respect of every item shown in a company's balance sheet or profit and loss account the corresponding amount for the financial year immediately preceding that to which the balance sheet or profit and loss account relates shall also be shown.

(2) Where that corresponding amount is not comparable with the amount to be shown for the item in question in respect of the financial year to which the balance sheet or profit and loss account relates, the former amount shall be adjusted and particulars of the adjustment and the reasons for it shall be disclosed in a note to the accounts.

(3) Paragraph 3(5) does not apply in any case where an amount can be shown for the item in question in respect of the financial year immediately preceding that to which the balance sheet or profit and loss account relates, and that amount shall be shown under the heading or sub-heading required by paragraph 1 for that item.

5. Amounts in respect of items representing assets or income may not be set off against amounts in respect of items representing liabilities or expenditure (as the case may be), or vice versa.

5A. The directors of a company must, in determining how amounts are presented within items in the profit and loss account and balance sheet, have regard to the substance of the reported transaction or arrangement, in accordance with generally accepted accounting principles or practice.

SECTION B
THE REQUIRED FORMATS FOR ACCOUNTS

Preliminary

6. References in this Part of this Schedule to the items listed in any of the formats set out below are to those items read together with any of the notes following the formats which apply to any of those items, and the requirement imposed by paragraph 1 to show the items listed in any such format in the order adopted in the format is subject to any provision in those notes for alternative positions for any particular items.

7. A number in brackets following any item in any of the formats set out below is a reference to the note of that number in the notes following the formats.

8. In the notes following the formats—

(a) the heading of each note gives the required heading or sub-heading for the item to which it applies and a reference to any letters and numbers assigned to that item in the formats set out below (taking a reference in the case of Format 2 of the balance sheet formats to the item listed under "Assets" or under "Liabilities" as the case may require); and

(b) references to a numbered format are to the balance sheet format or (as the case may require) to the profit and loss account format of that number set out below.

Balance Sheet Formats

Format 1

A. Called up share capital not paid *(1)*

B. Fixed assets

    I   Intangible assets

         1.   Development costs

      2.   Concessions, patents, licences, trade marks and similar rights and assets *(2)*

      3.   Goodwill *(3)*

      4.   Payments on account

  II   Tangible assets

      1.   Land and buildings

      2.   Plant and machinery

      3.   Fixtures, fittings, tools and equipment

      4.   Payments on account and assets in course of construction

  III   Investments

      1.   Shares in group undertakings

      2.   Loans to group undertakings

      3.   Participating interests

      4.   Loans to undertakings in which the company has a participating interest

      5.   Other investments other than loans

      6.   Other loans

      7.   Own shares *(4)*

C.   Current assets

  I   Stocks

      1.   Raw materials and consumables

      2.   Work in progress

      3.   Finished goods and goods for resale

      4.   Payments on account

  II   Debtors *(5)*

      1.   Trade debtors

      2.   Amounts owed by group undertakings

      3.   Amounts owed by undertakings in which the company has a participating interest

      4.   Other debtors

      5.   Called up share capital not paid *(1)*

      6.   Prepayments and accrued income *(6)*

  III   Investments

      1.   Shares in group undertakings

      2.   Own shares *(4)*

      3.   Other investments

  IV   Cash at bank and in hand

D.   Prepayments and accrued income *(6)*

E.   Creditors: amounts falling due within one year

      1.   Debenture loans *(7)*

      2.   Bank loans and overdrafts

      3.   Payments received on account *(8)*

      4.   Trade creditors

      5.   Bills of exchange payable

      6.   Amounts owed to group undertakings

      7.   Amounts owed to undertakings in which the company has a participating interest

      8.   Other creditors including taxation and social security *(9)*

      9.   Accruals and deferred income *(10)*

F.   Net current assets (liabilities) *(11)*

G.   Total assets less current liabilities

H.   Creditors: amounts falling due after more than one year

      1.   Debenture loans *(7)*

      2.   Bank loans and overdrafts

      3.   Payments received on account *(8)*

      4.   Trade creditors

     5.   Bills of exchange payable

     6.   Amounts owed to group undertakings

     7.   Amounts owed to undertakings in which the company has a participating interest

     8.   Other creditors including taxation and social security *(9)*

     9.   Accruals and deferred income *(10)*

I.   Provisions for liabilities

     1.   Pensions and similar obligations

     2.   Taxation, including deferred taxation

     3.   Other provisions

J.   Accruals and deferred income *(10)*

K.   Capital and reserves

     I   Called up share capital *(12)*

     II   Share premium account

     III Revaluation reserve

     IV Other reserves

         1.   Capital redemption reserve

         2.   Reserve for own shares

         3.   Reserves provided for by the articles of association

         4.   Other reserves

     V   Profit and loss account

Balance Sheet Formats

Format 2

ASSETS

A.   Called up share capital not paid *(1)*

B.   Fixed assets

     I   Intangible assets

         1.   Development costs

         2.   Concessions, patents, licences, trade marks and similar rights and assets *(2)*

         3.   Goodwill *(3)*

         4.   Payments on account

     II   Tangible assets

         1.   Land and buildings

         2.   Plant and machinery

         3.   Fixtures, fittings, tools and equipment

         4.   Payments on account and assets in course of construction

     III Investments

         1.   Shares in group undertakings

         2.   Loans to group undertakings

         3.   Participating interests

         4.   Loans to undertakings in which the company has a participating interest

         5.   Other investments other than loans

         6.   Other loans

         7.   Own shares *(4)*

C.   Current assets

     I   Stocks

         1.   Raw materials and consumables

         2.   Work in progress

         3.   Finished goods and goods for resale

         4.   Payments on account

     II   Debtors *(5)*

         1.   Trade debtors

          2.   Amounts owed by group undertakings

          3.   Amounts owed by undertakings in which the company has a participating interest

          4.   Other debtors

          5.   Called up share capital not paid *(1)*

          6.   Prepayments and accrued income *(6)*

    III   Investments

          1.   Shares in group undertakings

          2.   Own shares *(4)*

          3.   Other investments

    IV   Cash at bank and in hand

D.   Prepayments and accrued income *(6)*

LIABILITIES

A.   Capital and reserves

    I   Called up share capital *(12)*

    II   Share premium account

    III   Revaluation reserve

    IV   Other reserves

          1.   Capital redemption reserve

          2.   Reserve for own shares

          3.   Reserves provided for by the articles of association

          4.   Other reserves

    V   Profit and loss account

B.   Provisions for liabilities

          1.   Pensions and similar obligations

          2.   Taxation including deferred taxation

          3.   Other provisions

C.   Creditors *(13)*

          1.   Debenture loans *(7)*

          2.   Bank loans and overdrafts

          3.   Payments received on account *(8)*

          4.   Trade creditors

          5.   Bills of exchange payable

          6.   Amounts owed to group undertakings

          7.   Amounts owed to undertakings in which the company has a participating interest

          8.   Other creditors including taxation and social security *(9)*

          9.   Accruals and deferred income *(10)*

D.   Accruals and deferred income *(10)*

Notes on the balance sheet formats

(1)   *Called up share capital not paid*

      (Formats 1 and 2, items A and C.II.5.)

      This item may be shown in either of the two positions given in Formats 1 and 2.

(2)   *Concessions, patents, licences, trade marks and similar rights and assets*

      (Formats 1 and 2, item B.I.2.)

      Amounts in respect of assets shall only be included in a company's balance sheet under this item if either—

      (a)   the assets were acquired for valuable consideration and are not required to be shown under goodwill; or

      (b)   the assets in question were created by the company itself.

(3)   *Goodwill*

      (Formats 1 and 2, item B.I.3.)

      Amounts representing goodwill shall only be included to the extent that the goodwill was acquired for valuable consideration.

(4)   *Own shares*

(Formats 1 and 2, items B.III.7 and C.III.2.)

The nominal value of the shares held shall be shown separately.

(5)   *Debtors*

(Formats 1 and 2, items C.II.1 to 6.)

The amount falling due after more than one year shall be shown separately for each item included under debtors.

(6)   *Prepayments and accrued income*

(Formats 1 and 2, items C.II.6 and D.)

This item may be shown in either of the two positions given in Formats 1 and 2.

(7)   *Debenture loans*

(Format 1, items E.1 and H.1 and Format 2, item C.1.)

The amount of any convertible loans shall be shown separately.

(8)   *Payments received on account*

(Format 1, items E.3 and H.3 and Format 2, item C.3.)

Payments received on account of orders shall be shown for each of these items in so far as they are not shown as deductions from stocks.

(9)   *Other creditors including taxation and social security*

(Format 1, items E.8 and H.8 and Format 2, item C.8.)

The amount for creditors in respect of taxation and social security shall be shown separately from the amount for other creditors.

(10)   *Accruals and deferred income*

(Format 1, items E.9, H.9 and J and Format 2, items C.9 and D.)

The two positions given for this item in Format 1 at E.9 and H.9 are an alternative to the position at J, but if the item is not shown in a position corresponding to that at J it may be shown in either or both of the other two positions (as the case may require).

The two positions given for this item in Format 2 are alternatives.

(11)   *Net current assets (liabilities)*

(Format 1, item F.)

In determining the amount to be shown for this item any amount shown under "prepayments and accrued income" shall be taken into account wherever shown.

(12)   *Called up share capital*

(Format 1, item K.I and Format 2, item A.I.)

The amount of allotted share capital and the amount of called up share capital which has been paid up shall be shown separately.

(13)   *Creditors*

(Format 2, items C.1 to 9.)

Amounts falling due within one year and after one year shall be shown separately for each of these items and for the aggregate of all of these items.

Profit and loss account formats

Format 1
(see note *(17)* below)

1.   Turnover
2.   Cost of sales *(14)*
3.   Gross profit or loss
4.   Distribution costs *(14)*
5.   Administrative expenses *(14)*
6.   Other operating income
7.   Income from shares in group undertakings
8.   Income from participating interests
9.   Income from other fixed asset investments *(15)*

10.   Other interest receivable and similar income *(15)*
11.   Amounts written off investments
12.   Interest payable and similar charges *(16)*
13.   Tax on profit or loss on ordinary activities
14.   Profit or loss on ordinary activities after taxation
15.   Extraordinary income
16.   Extraordinary charges
17.   Extraordinary profit or loss
18.   Tax on extraordinary profit or loss
19.   Other taxes not shown under the above items
20.   Profit or loss for the financial year

Profit and loss account formats

Format 2

1.   Turnover
2.   Change in stocks of finished goods and in work in progress
3.   Own work capitalised
4.   Other operating income
5.   (a)   Raw materials and consumables
        (b)   Other external charges
6.   Staff costs:
        (a)   wages and salaries
        (b)   social security costs
        (c)   other pension costs
7.   (a)   Depreciation and other amounts written off tangible and intangible fixed assets
        (b)   Exceptional amounts written off current assets
8.   Other operating charges
9.   Income from shares in group undertakings
10.   Income from participating interests
11.   Income from other fixed asset investments *(15)*
12.   Other interest receivable and similar income *(15)*
13.   Amounts written off investments
14.   Interest payable and similar charges *(16)*
15.   Tax on profit or loss on ordinary activities
16.   Profit or loss on ordinary activities after taxation
17.   Extraordinary income
18.   Extraordinary charges
19.   Extraordinary profit or loss
20.   Tax on extraordinary profit or loss
21.   Other taxes not shown under the above items
22.   Profit or loss for the financial year

Profit and loss account formats

Format 3
(see note *(17)* below)

A.   Charges
        1.   Cost of sales *(14)*
        2.   Distribution costs *(14)*
        3.   Administrative expenses *(14)*
        4.   Amounts written off investments
        5.   Interest payable and similar charges *(16)*
        6.   Tax on profit or loss on ordinary activities

7. Profit or loss on ordinary activities after taxation
8. Extraordinary charges
9. Tax on extraordinary profit or loss
10. Other taxes not shown under the above items
11. Profit or loss for the financial year

B. Income
1. Turnover
2. Other operating income
3. Income from shares in group undertakings
4. Income from participating interests
5. Income from other fixed asset investments *(15)*
6. Other interest receivable and similar income *(15)*
7. Profit or loss on ordinary activities after taxation
8. Extraordinary income
9. Profit or loss for the financial year

Profit and loss account formats

Format 4

A. Charges
1. Reduction in stocks of finished goods and in work in progress
2. (a) Raw materials and consumables
    (b) Other external charges
3. Staff costs:
    (a) wages and salaries
    (b) social security costs
    (c) other pension costs
4. (a) Depreciation and other amounts written off tangible and intangible fixed assets
    (b) Exceptional amounts written off current assets
5. Other operating charges
6. Amounts written off investments
7. Interest payable and similar charges *(16)*
8. Tax on profit or loss on ordinary activities
9. Profit or loss on ordinary activities after taxation
10. Extraordinary charges
11. Tax on extraordinary profit or loss
12. Other taxes not shown under the above items
13. Profit or loss for the financial year

B. Income
1. Turnover
2. Increase in stocks of finished goods and in work in progress
3. Own work capitalised
4. Other operating income
5. Income from shares in group undertakings
6. Income from participating interests
7. Income from other fixed asset investments *(15)*
8. Other interest receivable and similar income *(15)*
9. Profit or loss on ordinary activities after taxation
10. Extraordinary income
11. Profit or loss for the financial year

Notes on the profit and loss account formats

(14)   *Cost of sales: distribution costs: administrative expenses*
          (Format 1, items 2, 4 and 5 and Format 3, items A.1, 2 and 3.)

These items shall be stated after taking into account any necessary provisions for depreciation or diminution in value of assets.

(15)   *Income from other fixed asset investments: other interest receivable and similar income*
(Format 1, items 9 and 10: Format 2, items 11 and 12: Format 3, items B.5 and 6: Format 4, items B.7 and 8.)
Income and interest derived from group undertakings shall be shown separately from income and interest derived from other sources.

(16)   *Interest payable and similar charges*
(Format 1, item 12: Format 2, item 14: Format 3, item A.5: Format 4, item A.7.)
The amount payable to group undertakings shall be shown separately.

(17)   *Formats 1 and 3*
The amount of any provisions for depreciation and diminution in value of tangible and intangible fixed assets falling to be shown under items 7(a) and A.4(a) respectively in Formats 2 and 4 shall be disclosed in a note to the accounts in any case where the profit and loss account is prepared by reference to Format 1 or Format 3.

PART II
ACCOUNTING PRINCIPLES AND RULES

SECTION A
ACCOUNTING PRINCIPLES

Preliminary

9.   Subject to paragraph 15 below, the amounts to be included in respect of all items shown in a company's accounts shall be determined in accordance with the principles set out in paragraphs 10 to 14.

Accounting principles

10.   The company shall be presumed to be carrying on business as a going concern.

11.   Accounting policies shall be applied consistently within the same accounts and from one financial year to the next.

12.   The amount of any item shall be determined on a prudent basis, and in particular—
   (a)   only profits realised at the balance sheet date shall be included in the profit and loss account; and
   (b)   all liabilities ... which have arisen ... in respect of the financial year to which the accounts relate or a previous financial year shall be taken into account, including those which only become apparent between the balance sheet date and the date on which it is signed on behalf of the board of directors in pursuance of section 233 of this Act.

13.   All income and charges relating to the financial year to which the accounts relate shall be taken into account, without regard to the date of receipt or payment.

14.   In determining the aggregate amount of any item the amount of each individual asset or liability that falls to be taken into account shall be determined separately.

Departure from the accounting principles

15.   If it appears to the directors of a company that there are special reasons for departing from any of the principles stated above in preparing the company's accounts in respect of any financial year they may do so, but particulars of the departure, the reasons for it and its effect shall be given in a note to the accounts.

SECTION B
HISTORICAL COST ACCOUNTING RULES

Preliminary

16.   Subject to sections C and D of this Part of this Schedule, the amounts to be included in respect of all items shown in a company's accounts shall be determined in accordance with the rules set out in paragraphs 17 to 28.

Fixed assets

General rules

17.   Subject to any provision for depreciation or diminution in value made in accordance with paragraph 18 or 19 the amount to be included in respect of any fixed asset shall be its purchase price or production cost.

18.   In the case of any fixed asset which has a limited useful economic life, the amount of—

(a)   its purchase price or production cost; or

(b)   where it is estimated that any such asset will have a residual value at the end of the period of its useful economic life, its purchase price or production cost less that estimated residual value;

shall be reduced by provisions for depreciation calculated to write off that amount systematically over the period of the asset's useful economic life.

19.—   (1)   Where a fixed asset investment of a description falling to be included under item B.III of either of the balance sheet formats set out in Part I of this Schedule has diminished in value provisions for diminution in value may be made in respect of it and the amount to be included in respect of it may be reduced accordingly; and any such provisions which are not shown in the profit and loss account shall be disclosed (either separately or in aggregate) in a note to the accounts.

        (2)   Provisions for diminution in value shall be made in respect of any fixed asset which has diminished in value if the reduction in its value is expected to be permanent (whether its useful economic life is limited or not), and the amount to be included in respect of it shall be reduced accordingly; and any such provisions which are not shown in the profit and loss account shall be disclosed (either separately or in aggregate) in a note to the accounts.

        (3)   Where the reasons for which any provision was made in accordance with sub-paragraph (1) or (2) have ceased to apply to any extent, that provision shall be written back to the extent that it is no longer necessary; and any amounts written back in accordance with this sub-paragraph which are not shown in the profit and loss account shall be disclosed (either separately or in aggregate) in a note to the accounts.

Rules for determining particular fixed asset items

20.—   (1)   Notwithstanding that an item in respect of "development costs" is included under "fixed assets" in the balance sheet formats set out in Part I of this Schedule, an amount may only be included in a company's balance sheet in respect of development costs in special circumstances.

        (2)   If any amount is included in a company's balance sheet in respect of development costs the following information shall be given in a note to the accounts—

           (a)   the period over which the amount of those costs originally capitalised is being or is to be written off; and

           (b)   the reasons for capitalising the development costs in question.

21.—   (1)   The application of paragraphs 17 to 19 in relation to goodwill (in any case where goodwill is treated as an asset) is subject to the following provisions of this paragraph.

        (2)   Subject to sub-paragraph (3) below, the amount of the consideration for any goodwill acquired by a company shall be reduced by provisions for depreciation calculated to write off that amount systematically over a period chosen by the directors of the company.

(3)   The period chosen shall not exceed the useful economic life of the goodwill in question.

(4)   In any case where any goodwill acquired by a company is shown or included as an asset in the company's balance sheet the period chosen for writing off the consideration for that goodwill and the reasons for choosing that period shall be disclosed in a note to the accounts.

Current assets

22.   Subject to paragraph 23, the amount to be included in respect of any current asset shall be its purchase price or production cost.

23.—   (1)   If the net realisable value of any current asset is lower than its purchase price or production cost the amount to be included in respect of that asset shall be the net realisable value.

(2)   Where the reasons for which any provision for diminution in value was made in accordance with sub-paragraph (1) have ceased to apply to any extent, that provision shall be written back to the extent that it is no longer necessary.

Miscellaneous and supplementary provisions

Excess of money owed over value received as an asset item

24.—   (1)   Where the amount repayable on any debt owed by a company is greater than the value of the consideration received in the transaction giving rise to the debt, the amount of the difference may be treated as an asset.

(2)   Where any such amount is so treated—

(a)   it shall be written off by reasonable amounts each year and must be completely written off before repayment of the debt; and

(b)   if the current amount is not shown as a separate item in the company's balance sheet it must be disclosed in a note to the accounts.

Assets included at a fixed amount

25.—   (1)   Subject to the following sub-paragraph, assets which fall to be included—

(a)   amongst the fixed assets of a company under the item "tangible assets"; or

(b)   amongst the current assets of a company under the item "raw materials and consumables";

may be included at a fixed quantity and value.

(2)   Sub-paragraph (1) applies to assets of a kind which are constantly being replaced, where—

(a)   their overall value is not material to assessing the company's state of affairs; and

(b)   their quantity, value and composition are not subject to material variation.

Determination of purchase price or production cost

26.—   (1)   The purchase price of an asset shall be determined by adding to the actual price paid any expenses incidental to its acquisition.

(2)   The production cost of an asset shall be determined by adding to the purchase price of the raw materials and consumables used the amount of the costs incurred by the company which are directly attributable to the production of that asset.

(3)   In addition, there may be included in the production cost of an asset—

(a)   a reasonable proportion of the costs incurred by the company which are only indirectly attributable to the production of that asset, but only to the extent that they relate to the period of production; and

(b)   interest on capital borrowed to finance the production of that asset, to the extent that it accrues in respect of the period of production;

provided, however, in a case within paragraph (b) above, that the inclusion of the interest in determining the cost of that asset and the amount of the interest so included is disclosed in a note to the accounts.

(4)   In the case of current assets distribution costs may not be included in production costs.

27.—   (1)   Subject to the qualification mentioned below, the purchase price or production cost of—

(a)   any assets which fall to be included under any item shown in a company's balance sheet under the general item "stocks"; and

(b)   any assets which are fungible assets (including investments);

may be determined by the application of any of the methods mentioned in sub-paragraph (2) below in relation to any such assets of the same class.

The method chosen must be one which appears to the directors to be appropriate in the circumstances of the company.

(2)   Those methods are—

(a)   the method known as "first in, first out" (FIFO);

(b)   the method known as "last in, first out" (LIFO);

(c)   a weighted average price; and

(d)   any other method similar to any of the methods mentioned above.

(3)   Where in the case of any company—

(a)   the purchase price or production cost of assets falling to be included under any item shown in the company's balance sheet has been determined by the application of any method permitted by this paragraph; and

(b)   the amount shown in respect of that item differs materially from the relevant alternative amount given below in this paragraph;

the amount of that difference shall be disclosed in a note to the accounts.

(4)   Subject to sub-paragraph (5) below, for the purposes of sub-paragraph (3)(b) above, the relevant alternative amount, in relation to any item shown in a company's balance sheet, is the amount which would have been shown in respect of that item if assets of any class included under that item at an amount determined by any method permitted by this paragraph had instead been included at their replacement cost as at the balance sheet date.

(5)   The relevant alternative amount may be determined by reference to the most recent actual purchase price or production cost before the balance sheet date of assets of any class included under the item in question instead of by reference to their replacement cost as at that date, but only if the former appears to the directors of the company to constitute the more appropriate standard of comparison in the case of assets of that class.

(6)   For the purposes of this paragraph, assets of any description shall be regarded as fungible if assets of that description are substantially indistinguishable one from another.

Substitution of original stated amount where price or cost unknown

28.   Where there is no record of the purchase price or production cost of any asset of a company or of any price, expenses or costs relevant for determining its purchase price or production cost in accordance with paragraph 26, or any such record cannot be obtained without unreasonable expense or delay, its purchase price or production cost shall be taken for the purposes of paragraphs 17 to 23 to be the value ascribed to it in the earliest available record of its value made on or after its acquisition or production by the company.

SECTION C
ALTERNATIVE ACCOUNTING RULES

Preliminary

29.— (1)   The rules set out in section B are referred to below in this Schedule as the historical cost accounting rules.

(2)   Those rules, with the omission of paragraphs 16, 21 and 25 to 28, are referred to below in this Part of this Schedule as the depreciation rules; and references below in this Schedule to the historical cost accounting rules do not include the depreciation rules as they apply by virtue of paragraph 32.

30.   Subject to paragraphs 32 to 34, the amounts to be included in respect of assets of any description mentioned in paragraph 31 may be determined on any basis so mentioned.

Alternative accounting rules

31.—   (1)   Intangible fixed assets, other than goodwill, may be included at their current cost.

         (2)   Tangible fixed assets may be included at a market value determined as at the date of their last valuation or at their current cost.

         (3)   Investments of any description falling to be included under item B.III of either of the balance sheet formats set out in Part I of this Schedule may be included either—

             (a)   at a market value determined as at the date of their last valuation; or

             (b)   at a value determined on any basis which appears to the directors to be appropriate in the circumstances of the company;

         but in the latter case particulars of the method of valuation adopted and of the reasons for adopting it shall be disclosed in a note to the accounts.

         (4)   Investments of any description falling to be included under item C.III of either of the balance sheet formats set out in Part I of this Schedule may be included at their current cost.

         (5)   Stocks may be included at their current cost.

Application of the depreciation rules

32.—   (1)   Where the value of any asset of a company is determined on any basis mentioned in paragraph 31, that value shall be, or (as the case may require) be the starting point for determining, the amount to be included in respect of that asset in the company's accounts, instead of its purchase price or production cost or any value previously so determined for that asset; and the depreciation rules shall apply accordingly in relation to any such asset with the substitution for any reference to its purchase price or production cost of a reference to the value most recently determined for that asset on any basis mentioned in paragraph 31.

         (2)   The amount of any provision for depreciation required in the case of any fixed asset by paragraph 18 or 19 as it applies by virtue of sub-paragraph (1) is referred to below in this paragraph as the adjusted amount, and the amount of any provision which would be required by that paragraph in the case of that asset according to the historical cost accounting rules is referred to as the historical cost amount.

         (3)   Where sub-paragraph (1) applies in the case of any fixed asset the amount of any provision for depreciation in respect of that asset—

             (a)   included in any item shown in the profit and loss account in respect of amounts written off assets of the description in question; or

             (b)   taken into account in stating any item so shown which is required by note (14) of the notes on the profit and loss account formats set out in Part I of this Schedule to be stated after taking into account any necessary provisions for depreciation or diminution in value of assets included under it;

         may be the historical cost amount instead of the adjusted amount, provided that the amount of any difference between the two is shown separately in the profit and loss account or in a note to the accounts.

Additional information to be provided in case of departure from historical cost accounting rules

33.—   (1)   This paragraph applies where the amounts to be included in respect of assets covered by any items shown in a company's accounts have been determined on any basis mentioned in paragraph 31.

         (2)   The items affected and the basis of valuation adopted in determining the amounts of the assets in question in the case of each such item shall be disclosed in a note to the accounts.

         (3)   In the case of each balance sheet item affected (except stocks) either—

             (a)   the comparable amounts determined according to the historical cost accounting rules; or

             (b)   the differences between those amounts and the corresponding amounts actually shown in the balance sheet in respect of that item;

         shall be shown separately in the balance sheet or in a note to the accounts.

(4) In sub-paragraph (3) above, references in relation to any item to the comparable amounts determined as there mentioned are references to—

    (a) the aggregate amount which would be required to be shown in respect of that item if the amounts to be included in respect of all the assets covered by that item were determined according to the historical cost accounting rules; and

    (b) the aggregate amount of the cumulative provisions for depreciation or diminution in value which would be permitted or required in determining those amounts according to those rules.

Revaluation reserve

34.— (1) With respect to any determination of the value of an asset of a company on any basis mentioned in paragraph 31, the amount of any profit or loss arising from that determination (after allowing, where appropriate, for any provisions for depreciation or diminution in value made otherwise than by reference to the value so determined and any adjustments of any such provisions made in the light of that determination) shall be credited or (as the case may be) debited to a separate reserve ("the revaluation reserve").

(2) The amount of the revaluation reserve shall be shown in the company's balance sheet under a separate sub-heading in the position given for the item "revaluation reserve" in Format 1 or 2 of the balance sheet formats set out in Part I of this Schedule, but need not be shown under that name.

(3) An amount may be transferred

    (a) from the revaluation reserve—

        (i) to the profit and loss account, if the amount was previously charged to that account or represents realised profit, or

        (ii) on capitalisation,

    (b) to or from the revaluation reserve in respect of the taxation relating to any profit or loss credited or debited to the reserve;

and the revaluation reserve shall be reduced to the extent that the amounts transferred to it are no longer necessary for the purposes of the valuation method used.

(3A) In sub-paragraph (3)(a)(ii) "capitalisation", in relation to an amount standing to the credit of the revaluation reserve, means applying it in wholly or partly paying up unissued shares in the company to be allotted to members of the company as fully or partly paid shares.

(3B) The revaluation reserve shall not be reduced except as mentioned in this paragraph.

(4) The treatment for taxation purposes of amounts credited or debited to the revaluation reserve shall be disclosed in a note to the accounts.

SECTION D
FAIR VALUE ACCOUNTING

Inclusion of financial instruments at fair value

34A.— (1) Subject to sub-paragraphs (2) to (4), financial instruments (including derivatives) may be included at fair value.

(2) Sub-paragraph (1) does not apply to financial instruments which constitute liabilities unless—

    (a) they are held as part of a trading portfolio, or

    (b) they are derivatives.

(3) Sub-paragraph (1) does not apply to—

    (a) financial instruments (other than derivatives) held to maturity;

    (b) loans and receivables originated by the company and not held for trading purposes;

    (c) interests in subsidiary undertakings, associated undertakings and joint ventures;

    (d) equity instruments issued by the company;

    (e) contracts for contingent consideration in a business combination;

      (f)   other financial instruments with such special characteristics that the instruments, according to generally accepted accounting principles or practice, should be accounted for differently from other financial instruments.

    (4)   If the fair value of a financial instrument cannot be determined reliably in accordance with paragraph 34B, sub-paragraph (1) does not apply to that financial instrument.

    (5)   In this paragraph—
        "associated undertaking" has the meaning given by paragraph 20 of Schedule 4A; and
        "joint venture" has the meaning given by paragraph 19 of that Schedule.

Determination of fair value

34B.— (1)   The fair value of a financial instrument is determined in accordance with this paragraph.

    (2)   If a reliable market can readily be identified for the financial instrument, its fair value is determined by reference to its market value.

    (3)   If a reliable market cannot readily be identified for the financial instrument but can be identified for its components or for a similar instrument, its fair value is determined by reference to the market value of its components or of the similar instrument.

    (4)   If neither sub-paragraph (2) nor (3) applies, the fair value of the financial instrument is a value resulting from generally accepted valuation models and techniques.

    (5)   Any valuation models and techniques used for the purposes of sub-paragraph (4) must ensure a reasonable approximation of the market value.

Inclusion of hedged items at fair value

34C.   A company may include any assets and liabilities that qualify as hedged items under a fair value hedge accounting system, or identified portions of such assets or liabilities, at the amount required under that system.

Other assets that may be included at fair value

34D.— (1)   This paragraph applies to—
      (a)   investment property, and
      (b)   living animals and plants,
      that, under international accounting standards, may be included in accounts at fair value.

    (2)   Such investment property and such living animals and plants may be included at fair value, provided that all such investment property or, as the case may be, all such living animals and plants are so included where their fair value can reliably be determined.

    (3)   In this paragraph, "fair value" means fair value determined in accordance with relevant international accounting standards.

Accounting for changes in value

34E.— (1)   This paragraph applies where a financial instrument is valued in accordance with paragraph 34A or 34C or an asset is valued in accordance with paragraph 34D.

    (2)   Notwithstanding paragraph 12 of this Schedule, and subject to sub-paragraphs (3) and (4) below, a change in the value of the financial instrument or of the investment property or living animal or plant must be included in the profit and loss account.

    (3)   Where—
      (a)   the financial instrument accounted for is a hedging instrument under a hedge accounting system that allows some or all of the change in value not to be shown in the profit and loss account, or
      (b)   the change in value relates to an exchange difference arising on a monetary item that forms part of a company's net investment in a foreign entity,
      the amount of the change in value must be credited to or (as the case may be) debited from a separate reserve ("the fair value reserve").

    (4)   Where the instrument accounted for—
      (a)   is an available for sale financial asset, and
      (b)   is not a derivative,

the change in value may be credited to or (as the case may be) debited from the fair value reserve.

The fair value reserve

34F.— (1) The fair value reserve must be adjusted to the extent that the amounts shown in it are no longer necessary for the purposes of paragraph 34E(3) or (4).

(2) The treatment for taxation purposes of amounts credited or debited to the fair value reserve must be disclosed in a note to the accounts.

PART III
NOTES TO THE ACCOUNTS

Preliminary

35. Any information required in the case of any company by the following provisions of this Part of this Schedule shall (if not given in the company's accounts) be given by way of a note to those accounts.

Reserves and dividends

35A. There must be stated—

(a) any amount set aside or proposed to be set aside to, or withdrawn or proposed to be withdrawn from, reserves,

(b) the aggregate amount of dividends paid in the financial year (other than those for which a liability existed at the immediately preceding balance sheet date),

(c) the aggregate amount of dividends that the company is liable to pay at the balance sheet date, and

(d) the aggregate amount of dividends that are proposed before the date of approval of the accounts, and not otherwise disclosed under paragraph (b) or (c).

Disclosure of accounting policies

36. The accounting policies adopted by the company in determining the amounts to be included in respect of items shown in the balance sheet and in determining the profit or loss of the company shall be stated (including such policies with respect to the depreciation and diminution in value of assets).

36A. It shall be stated whether the accounts have been prepared in accordance with applicable accounting standards and particulars of any material departure from those standards and the reasons for it shall be given.

Information supplementing the balance sheet

37. Paragraphs 38 to 51 require information which either supplements the information given with respect to any particular items shown in the balance sheet or is otherwise relevant to assessing the company's state of affairs in the light of the information so given.

Share capital and debentures

38.— (1) The following information shall be given with respect to the company's share capital—

(a) the authorised share capital; ...

(b) where shares of more than one class have been allotted, the number and aggregate nominal value of shares of each class allotted; and

(c) where shares are held as treasury shares, the number and aggregate nominal value of the treasury shares and, where shares of more than one class have been allotted, the number and aggregate nominal value of the shares of each class held as treasury shares.

(2) In the case of any part of the allotted share capital that consists of redeemable shares, the following information shall be given—

(a) the earliest and latest dates on which the company has power to redeem those shares;

(b) whether those shares must be redeemed in any event or are liable to be redeemed at the option of the company or of the shareholder; and

(c) whether any (and, if so, what) premium is payable on redemption.

39.   If the company has allotted any shares during the financial year, the following information shall be given—

(a) ...

(b) the classes of shares allotted; and

(c) as respects each class of shares, the number allotted, their aggregate nominal value, and the consideration received by the company for the allotment.

40.— (1) With respect to any contingent right to the allotment of shares in the company the following particulars shall be given—

(a) the number, description and amount of the shares in relation to which the right is exercisable;

(b) the period during which it is exercisable; and

(c) the price to be paid for the shares allotted.

(2) In sub-paragraph (1) above "contingent right to the allotment of shares" means any option to subscribe for shares and any other right to require the allotment of shares to any person whether arising on the conversion into shares of securities of any other description or otherwise.

41.— (1) If the company has issued any debentures during the financial year to which the accounts relate, the following information shall be given—

(a) ...

(b) the classes of debentures issued; and

(c) as respects each class of debentures, the amount issued and the consideration received by the company for the issue.

(2) ...

(3) Where any of the company's debentures are held by a nominee of or trustee for the company, the nominal amount of the debentures and the amount at which they are stated in the accounting records kept by the company in accordance with section 221 of this Act shall be stated.

Fixed assets

42.— (1) In respect of each item which is or would but for paragraph 3(4)(b) be shown under the general item "fixed assets" in the company's balance sheet the following information shall be given—

(a) the appropriate amounts in respect of that item as at the date of the beginning of the financial year and as at the balance sheet date respectively;

(b) the effect on any amount shown in the balance sheet in respect of that item of—

(i) any revision of the amount in respect of any assets included under that item made during that year on any basis mentioned in paragraph 31;

(ii) acquisitions during that year of any assets;

(iii) disposals during that year of any assets; and

(iv) any transfers of assets of the company to and from that item during that year.

(2) The reference in sub-paragraph (1)(a) to the appropriate amounts in respect of any item as at any date there mentioned is a reference to amounts representing the aggregate amounts determined, as at that date, in respect of assets falling to be included under that item on either of the following bases, that is to say—

(a) on the basis of purchase price or production cost (determined in accordance with paragraphs 26 and 27); or

(b) on any basis mentioned in paragraph 31,

(leaving out of account in either case any provisions for depreciation or diminution in value).

(3) In respect of each item within sub-paragraph (1)—

(a) the cumulative amount of provisions for depreciation or diminution in value of assets included under that item as at each date mentioned in sub-paragraph (1)(a);

(b) the amount of any such provisions made in respect of the financial year;

(c) the amount of any adjustments made in respect of any such provisions during that year in consequence of the disposal of any assets; and

(d) the amount of any other adjustments made in respect of any such provisions during that year;

shall also be stated.

43. Where any fixed assets of the company (other than listed investments) are included under any item shown in the company's balance sheet at an amount determined on any basis mentioned in paragraph 31, the following information shall be given—

(a) the years (so far as they are known to the directors) in which the assets were severally valued and the several values; and

(b) in the case of assets that have been valued during the financial year, the names of the persons who valued them or particulars of their qualifications for doing so and (whichever is stated) the bases of valuation used by them.

44. In relation to any amount which is or would but for paragraph 3(4)(b) be shown in respect of the item "land and buildings" in the company's balance sheet there shall be stated—

(a) how much of that amount is ascribable to land of freehold tenure and how much to land of leasehold tenure; and

(b) how much of the amount ascribable to land of leasehold tenure is ascribable to land held on long lease and how much to land held on short lease.

Investments

45.— (1) In respect of the amount of each item which is or would but for paragraph 3(4)(b) be shown in the company's balance sheet under the general item "investments" (whether as fixed assets or as current assets) there shall be stated—

(a) how much of that amount is ascribable to listed investments; ...

(b) ...

(2) Where the amount of any listed investments is stated for any item in accordance with sub-paragraph (1)(a), the following amounts shall also be stated—

(a) the aggregate market value of those investments where it differs from the amount so stated; and

(b) both the market value and the stock exchange value of any investments of which the former value is, for the purposes of the accounts, taken as being higher than the latter.

Information about fair value of assets and liabilities

45A.— (1) This paragraph applies where financial instruments have been valued in accordance with paragraph 34A or 34C.

(2) There must be stated—

(a) where the fair value of the instruments has been determined in accordance with paragraph 34B(4), the significant assumptions underlying the valuation models and techniques used,

(b) for each category of financial instrument, the fair value of the instruments in that category and the changes in value—

(i) included in the profit and loss account, or

(ii) credited to or (as the case may be) debited from the fair value reserve,

in respect of those instruments, and

(c) for each class of derivatives, the extent and nature of the instruments, including significant terms and conditions that may affect the amount, timing and certainty of future cash flows.

(3) Where any amount is transferred to or from the fair value reserve during the financial year, there must be stated in tabular form—

    (a)   the amount of the reserve as at the date of the beginning of the financial year and as at the balance sheet date respectively;

    (b)   the amount transferred to or from the reserve during that year; and

    (c)   the source and application respectively of the amounts so transferred.

45B.   Where the company has derivatives that it has not included at fair value, there must be stated for each class of such derivatives—

    (a)   the fair value of the derivatives in that class, if such a value can be determined in accordance with paragraph 34B, and

    (b)   the extent and nature of the derivatives.

45C.— (1)   Sub-paragraph (2) applies if—

    (a)   the company has financial fixed assets that could be included at fair value by virtue of paragraph 34A,

    (b)   the amount at which those assets are included under any item in the company's accounts is in excess of their fair value, and

    (c)   the company has not made provision for diminution in value of those assets in accordance with paragraph 19(1) of this Schedule.

    (2)   There must be stated—

    (a)   the amount at which either the individual assets or appropriate groupings of those individual assets are included in the company's accounts,

    (b)   the fair value of those assets or groupings, and

    (c)   the reasons for not making a provision for diminution in value of those assets, including the nature of the evidence that provides the basis for the belief that the amount at which they are stated in the accounts will be recovered.

Information where investment property and living animals and plants included at fair value

45D.— (1)   This paragraph applies where the amounts to be included in a company's accounts in respect of investment property or living animals and plants have been determined in accordance with paragraph 34D.

    (2)   The balance sheet items affected and the basis of valuation adopted in determining the amounts of the assets in question in the case of each such item must be disclosed in a note to the accounts.

    (3)   In the case of investment property, for each balance sheet item affected there must be shown, either separately in the balance sheet or in a note to the accounts—

    (a)   the comparable amounts determined according to the historical cost accounting rules; or

    (b)   the differences between those amounts and the corresponding amounts actually shown in the balance sheet in respect of that item.

    (4)   In sub-paragraph (3) above, references in relation to any item to the comparable amounts determined in accordance with that sub-paragraph are references to—

    (a)   the aggregate amount which would be required to be shown in respect of that item if the amounts to be included in respect of all the assets covered by that item were determined according to the historical cost accounting rules; and

    (b)   the aggregate amount of the cumulative provisions for depreciation or diminution in value which would be permitted or required in determining those amounts according to those rules.

Reserves and provisions

46.— (1)   Where any amount is transferred—

    (a)   to or from any reserves; or

    (b)   to any provisions for liabilities; or

    (c)   from any provision for liabilities otherwise than for the purpose for which the provision was established;

and the reserves or provisions are or would but for paragraph 3(4)(b) be shown as separate items in the company's balance sheet, the information mentioned in the following sub-paragraph shall be given in respect of the aggregate of reserves or provisions included in the same item.

(2)   That information is—

    (a)   the amount of the reserves or provisions as at the date of the beginning of the financial year and as at the balance sheet date respectively;

    (b)   any amounts transferred to or from the reserves or provisions during that year; and

    (c)   the source and application respectively of any amounts so transferred.

(3)   Particulars shall be given of each provision included in the item "other provisions" in the company's balance sheet in any case where the amount of that provision is material.

Provision for taxation

47.   The amount of any provision for deferred taxation shall be stated separately from the amount of any provision for other taxation.

Details of indebtedness

48.—   (1)   In respect of each item shown under "creditors" in the company's balance sheet there shall be stated the aggregate of the following amounts, that is to say—

    (a)   the amount of any debts included under that item which are payable or repayable otherwise than by instalments and fall due for payment or repayment after the end of the period of five years beginning with the day next following the end of the financial year; and

    (b)   in the case of any debts so included which are payable or repayable by instalments, the amount of any instalments which fall due for payment after the end of that period.

(2)   Subject to sub-paragraph (3), in relation to each debt falling to be taken into account under sub-paragraph (1), the terms of payment or repayment and the rate of any interest payable on the debt shall be stated.

(3)   If the number of debts is such that, in the opinion of the directors, compliance with sub-paragraph (2) would result in a statement of excessive length, it shall be sufficient to give a general indication of the terms of payment or repayment and the rates of any interest payable on the debts.

(4)   In respect of each item shown under "creditors" in the company's balance sheet there shall be stated—

    (a)   the aggregate amount of any debts included under that item in respect of which any security has been given by the company; and

    (b)   an indication of the nature of the securities so given.

(5)   References above in this paragraph to an item shown under "creditors" in the company's balance sheet include references, where amounts falling due to creditors within one year and after more than one year are distinguished in the balance sheet—

    (a)   in a case within sub-paragraph (1), to an item shown under the latter of those categories; and

    (b)   in a case within sub-paragraph (4), to an item shown under either of those categories; and references to items shown under "creditors" include references to items which would but for paragraph 3(4)(b) be shown under that heading.

49.   If any fixed cumulative dividends on the company's shares are in arrear, there shall be stated—

(a)   the amount of the arrears; and

(b)   the period for which the dividends or, if there is more than one class, each class of them are in arrear.

Guarantees and other financial commitments

50.—   (1)   Particulars shall be given of any charge on the assets of the company to secure the liabilities of any other person, including, where practicable, the amount secured.

(2)   The following information shall be given with respect to any other contingent liability not provided for—

    (a)   the amount or estimated amount of that liability;

    (b)   its legal nature; and

    (c)   whether any valuable security has been provided by the company in connection with that liability and if so, what.

(3)   There shall be stated, where practicable—

    (a)   the aggregate amount or estimated amount of contracts for capital expenditure, so far as not provided for;

    (b)   ...

(4)   Particulars shall be given of—

    (a)   any pension commitments included under any provision shown in the company's balance sheet; and

    (b)   any such commitments for which no provision has been made;

and where any such commitment relates wholly or partly to pensions payable to past directors of the company separate particulars shall be given of that commitment so far as it relates to such pensions.

(5)   Particulars shall also be given of any other financial commitments which—

    (a)   have not been provided for; and

    (b)   are relevant to assessing the company's state of affairs.

(6)   ...

Miscellaneous matters

51.— (1)   Particulars shall be given of any case where the purchase price or production cost of any asset is for the first time determined under paragraph 28.

(2)   Where any outstanding loans made under the authority of section 153(4)(b), (bb) or (c) or section 155 of this Act (various cases of financial assistance by a company for purchase of its own shares) are included under any item shown in the company's balance sheet, the aggregate amount of those loans shall be disclosed for each item in question.

(3)   ...

Information supplementing the profit and loss account

52.   Paragraphs 53 to 57 require information which either supplements the information given with respect to any particular items shown in the profit and loss account or otherwise provides particulars of income or expenditure of the company or of circumstances affecting the items shown in the profit and loss account.

Separate statement of certain items of income and expenditure

53.— (1)   Subject to the following provisions of this paragraph, each of the amounts mentioned below shall be stated.

(2)   The amount of the interest on or any similar charges in respect of—

    (a)   bank loans and overdrafts, ...; and

    (b)   loans of any other kind made to the company.

This sub-paragraph does not apply to interest or charges on loans to the company from group undertakings, but, with that exception, it applies to interest or charges on all loans, whether made on the security of debentures or not.

(3)–(6)   ...

(7)   ...

Particulars of tax

54.— (1)...

(2) Particulars shall be given of any special circumstances which affect liability in respect of taxation of profits, income or capital gains for the financial year or liability in respect of taxation of profits, income or capital gains for succeeding financial years.

(3) The following amounts shall be stated—

    (a) the amount of the charge for United Kingdom corporation tax;

    (b) if that amount would have been greater but for relief from double taxation, the amount which it would have been but for such relief;

    (c) the amount of the charge for United Kingdom income tax; and

    (d) the amount of the charge for taxation imposed outside the United Kingdom of profits, income and (so far as charged to revenue) capital gains.

These amounts shall be stated separately in respect of each of the amounts which is or would but for paragraph 3(4)(b) be shown under the following items in the profit and loss account, that is to say "tax on profit or loss on ordinary activities" and "tax on extraordinary profit or loss".

Particulars of turnover

55.— (1) If in the course of the financial year the company has carried on business of two or more classes that, in the opinion of the directors, differ substantially from each other, there shall be stated in respect of each class (describing it)—

    (a) the amount of the turnover attributable to that class;

    (b) ...

(2) If in the course of the financial year the company has supplied markets that, in the opinion of the directors, differ substantially from each other, the amount of the turnover attributable to each such market shall also be stated.

In this paragraph "market" means a market delimited by geographical bounds.

(3) In analysing for the purposes of this paragraph the source (in terms of business or in terms of market) of turnover ..., the directors of the company shall have regard to the manner in which the company's activities are organised.

(4) For the purposes of this paragraph—

    (a) classes of business which, in the opinion of the directors, do not differ substantially from each other shall be treated as one class; and

    (b) markets which, in the opinion of the directors, do not differ substantially from each other shall be treated as one market;

and any amounts properly attributable to one class of business or (as the case may be) to one market which are not material may be included in the amount stated in respect of another.

(5) Where in the opinion of the directors the disclosure of any information required by this paragraph would be seriously prejudicial to the interests of the company, that information need not be disclosed, but the fact that any such information has not been disclosed must be stated.

56. ...

Miscellaneous matters

57.— (1) Where any amount relating to any preceding financial year is included in any item in the profit and loss account, the effect shall be stated.

(2) Particulars shall be given of any extraordinary income or charges arising in the financial year.

(3) The effect shall be stated of any transactions that are exceptional by virtue of size or incidence though they fall within the ordinary activities of the company.

General

58.— (1) Where sums originally denominated in foreign currencies have been brought into account under any items shown in the balance sheet or profit and loss account, the basis on which those sums have been translated into sterling shall be stated.

(2)   Subject to the following sub-paragraph, in respect of every item stated in a note to the accounts the corresponding amount for the financial year immediately preceding that to which the accounts relate shall also be stated and where the corresponding amount is not comparable, it shall be adjusted and particulars of the adjustment and the reasons for it shall be given.

(3)   Sub-paragraph (2) does not apply in relation to any amounts stated by virtue of any of the following provisions of this Act—

   (a)   paragraph 13 of Schedule 4A (details of accounting treatment of acquisitions),

   (b)   paragraphs 2, 8(3), 16, 21(1)(d), 22(4) and (5), 24(3) and (4) and 27(3) and (4) of Schedule 5 (shareholdings in other undertakings),

   (c)   Parts II and III of Schedule 6 (loans and other dealings in favour of directors and others), and

   (d)   paragraphs 42 and 46 above (fixed assets and reserves and provisions).

Dormant Companies Acting as Agents

58A.   Where the directors of a company take advantage of the exemption conferred by section 249AA, and the company has during the financial year in question acted as an agent for any person, the fact that it has so acted must be stated.

PART IV
SPECIAL PROVISIONS WHERE COMPANY IS A PARENT COMPANY OR SUBSIDIARY UNDERTAKING

Company's own accounts

59.   ...

Guarantees and other financial commitments in favour of group undertakings

59A.   Commitments within any of sub-paragraphs (1) to (5) of paragraph 50 (guarantees and other financial commitments) which are undertaken on behalf of or for the benefit of—

   (a)   any parent undertaking or fellow subsidiary undertaking, or

   (b)   any subsidiary undertaking of the company,

shall be stated separately from the other commitments within that sub-paragraph, and commitments within paragraph (a) shall also be stated separately from those within paragraph (b).

60–70. ...

PART V
SPECIAL PROVISIONS WHERE THE COMPANY IS AN INVESTMENT COMPANY

71.—   (1)   Paragraph 34 does not apply to the amount of any profit or loss arising from a determination of the value of any investments of an investment company on any basis mentioned in paragraph 31(3).

   (2)   Any provisions made by virtue of paragraph 19(1) or (2) in the case of an investment company in respect of any fixed asset investments need not be charged to the company's profit and loss account provided they are either—

   (a)   charged against any reserve account to which any amount excluded by sub-paragraph (1) from the requirements of paragraph 34 has been credited; or

   (b)   shown as a separate item in the company's balance sheet under the sub-heading "other reserves".

   (3)   For the purposes of this paragraph, as it applies in relation to any company, "fixed asset investment" means any asset falling to be included under any item shown in the company's balance sheet under the subdivision "investments" under the general item "fixed assets".

72.— (1) Any distribution made by an investment company which reduces the amount of its net assets to less than the aggregate of its called-up share capital and undistributable reserves shall be disclosed in a note to the company's accounts.

(2) For purposes of this paragraph, a company's net assets are the aggregate of its assets less the aggregate of its liabilities (including any provision for liabilities within paragraph 89 that is made in Companies Act accounts and any provision that is made in IAS accounts); and "undistributable reserves" has the meaning given by section 264(3) of this Act.

73. A company shall be treated as an investment company for the purposes of this Part of this Schedule in relation to any financial year of the company if—

(a) during the whole of that year it was an investment company as defined by section 266 of this Act, and

(b) it was not at any time during that year prohibited under section 265(4) of this Act (no distribution where capital profits have been distributed, etc) from making a distribution by virtue of that section.

74. ...

PART VI

...

PART VII
INTERPRETATION OF SCHEDULE

76. The following paragraphs apply for the purposes of this Schedule and its interpretation.

Financial instruments

76A. References to "derivatives" include commodity-based contracts that give either contracting party the right to settle in cash or in some other financial instrument, except when such contracts—

(a) were entered into for the purpose of, and continue to meet, the company's expected purchase, sale or usage requirements,

(b) were designated for such purpose at their inception, and

(c) are expected to be settled by delivery of the commodity.

76B.— (1) The expressions listed in sub-paragraph (2) have the same meaning as they have in Council Directive 78/660/EEC on the annual accounts of certain types of companies, as amended.

(2) Those expressions are "available for sale financial asset", "business combination", "commodity-based contracts", "derivative", "equity instrument", "exchange difference", "fair value hedge accounting system", "financial fixed asset", "financial instrument", "foreign entity", "hedge accounting", "hedge accounting system", "hedged items", "hedging instrument", "held for trading purposes", "held to maturity", "monetary item", "receivables", "reliable market" and "trading portfolio".

Historical cost accounting rules

77–81. ...

82. References to the historical cost accounting rules shall be read in accordance with paragraph 29.

Investment property

82A. "Investment property" means land held to earn rent or for capital appreciation.

Leases

83.— (1) "Long lease" means a lease in the case of which the portion of the term for which it was granted remaining unexpired at the end of the financial year is not less than 50 years.

(2) "Short lease" means a lease which is not a long lease.

(3) "Lease" includes an agreement for a lease.

Listed investments

84.— (1) "Listed investment" means an investment as respects which there has been granted a listing on—

    (a) a recognised investment exchange other than an overseas investment exchange; or

    (b) a stock exchange of repute outside Great Britain.

(2) "Recognised investment exchange" and "overseas investment exchange" have the meaning given in Part 18 of the Financial Services and Markets Act 2000.

Loans

85. A loan is treated as falling due for repayment, and an instalment of a loan is treated as falling due for payment, on the earliest date on which the lender could require repayment or (as the case may be) payment, if he exercised all options and rights available to him.

Materiality

86. Amounts which in the particular context of any provision of this Schedule are not material may be disregarded for the purposes of that provision.

Notes to the accounts

87. ...

Provisions

88.— (1) References to provisions for depreciation or diminution in value of assets are to any amount written off by way of providing for depreciation or diminution in value of assets.

(2) Any reference in the profit and loss account formats set out in Part I of this Schedule to the depreciation of, or amounts written off, assets of any description is to any provision for depreciation or diminution in value of assets of that description.

89. References to provisions for liabilities are to any amount retained as reasonably necessary for the purpose of providing for any liability the nature of which is clearly defined and which is either likely to be incurred, or certain to be incurred but uncertain as to amount or as to the date on which it will arise.

90–2. ...

Scots land tenure

93. In the application of this Schedule to Scotland, "land of freehold tenure" means land in respect of which the company ... is the owner; "land of leasehold tenure" means land of which the company is the tenant under a lease ... .

Staff costs

94.— (1) "Social security costs" means any contributions by the company to any state social security or pension scheme, fund or arrangement.

(2) "Pension costs" includes any costs incurred by the company in respect of any pension scheme established for the purpose of providing pensions for persons currently or formerly employed by the company, any sums set aside for the future payment of pensions directly by the company to current or former employees and any pensions paid directly to such persons without having first been set aside.

(3) Any amount stated in respect of the item "social security costs" or in respect of the item "wages and salaries" in the company's profit and loss account shall be determined by reference to payments made or costs incurred in respect of all persons employed by the company during the financial year who are taken into account in determining the relevant annual number for the purposes of section 231A(1)(a).

Turnover

95. ...

SCHEDULE 4A

FORM AND CONTENT OF GROUP ACCOUNTS

Section 227

General rules

1.— (1) Group accounts shall comply so far as practicable with the provisions of *section 390A(3) (amount of auditors' remuneration) and* Schedule 4 (form and content of company accounts) as if the undertakings included in the consolidation ("the group") were a single company.

(2) ...

(3) Where the parent company is treated as an investment company for the purposes of Part V of that Schedule (special provisions for investment companies) the group shall be similarly treated.

2.— (1) The consolidated balance sheet and profit and loss account shall incorporate in full the information contained in the individual accounts of the undertakings included in the consolidation, subject to the adjustments authorised or required by the following provisions of this Schedule and to such other adjustments (if any) as may be appropriate in accordance with generally accepted accounting principles or practice.

(2) If the financial year of a subsidiary undertaking included in the consolidation does not end with that of the parent company, the group accounts shall be made up—

(a) from the accounts of the subsidiary undertaking for its financial year last ending before the end of the parent company's financial year, provided that year ended no more than three months before that of the parent company, or

(b) from interim accounts prepared by the subsidiary undertaking as at the end of that parent company's financial year.

3.— (1) Where assets and liabilities to be included in the group accounts have been valued or otherwise determined by undertakings according to accounting rules differing from those used for the group accounts, the values or amounts shall be adjusted so as to accord with the rules used for the group accounts.

(2) If it appears to the directors of the parent company that there are special reasons for departing from sub-paragraph (1) they may do so, but particulars of any such departure, the reasons for it and its effect shall be given in a note to the accounts.

(3) The adjustments referred to in this paragraph need not be made if they are not material for the purpose of giving a true and fair view.

4. Any differences of accounting rules as between a parent company's individual accounts for a financial year and its group accounts shall be disclosed in a note to the latter accounts and the reasons for the difference given.

5. Amounts which in the particular context of any provision of this Schedule are not material may be disregarded for the purposes of that provision.

Elimination of group transactions

6.— (1) Debts and claims between undertakings included in the consolidation, and income and expenditure relating to transactions between such undertakings, shall be eliminated in preparing the group accounts.

(2) Where profits and losses resulting from transactions between undertakings included in the consolidation are included in the book value of assets, they shall be eliminated in preparing the group accounts.

(3) The elimination required by sub-paragraph (2) may be effected in proportion to the group's interest in the shares of the undertakings.

(4) Sub-paragraphs (1) and (2) need not be complied with if the amounts concerned are not material for the purpose of giving a true and fair view.

Acquisition and merger accounting

7.— (1) The following provisions apply where an undertaking becomes a subsidiary undertaking of the parent company.

   (2) That event is referred to in those provisions as an "acquisition", and references to the "undertaking acquired" shall be construed accordingly.

8.   An acquisition shall be accounted for by the acquisition method of accounting unless the conditions for accounting for it as a merger are met and the merger method of accounting is adopted.

9.— (1) The acquisition method of accounting is as follows.

   (2) The identifiable assets and liabilities of the undertaking acquired shall be included in the consolidated balance sheet at their fair values as at the date of acquisition.

   In this paragraph the "identifiable" assets or liabilities of the undertaking acquired means the assets or liabilities which are capable of being disposed of or discharged separately, without disposing of a business of the undertaking.

   (3) The income and expenditure of the undertaking acquired shall be brought into the group accounts only as from the date of the acquisition.

   (4) There shall be set off against the acquisition cost of the interest in the shares of the undertaking held by the parent company and its subsidiary undertakings the interest of the parent company and its subsidiary undertakings in the adjusted capital and reserves of the undertaking acquired.

   For this purpose—

   "the acquisition cost" means the amount of any cash consideration and the fair value of any other consideration, together with such amount (if any) in respect of fees and other expenses of the acquisition as the company may determine, and

   "the adjusted capital and reserves" of the undertaking acquired means its capital and reserves at the date of the acquisition after adjusting the identifiable assets and liabilities of the undertaking to fair values as at that date.

   (5) The resulting amount if positive shall be treated as goodwill, and if negative as a negative consolidation difference.

10.— (1) The conditions for accounting for an acquisition as a merger are—

   (a) that at least 90 per cent of the nominal value of the relevant shares in the undertaking acquired (excluding any shares in the undertaking held as treasury shares) is held by or on behalf of the parent company and its subsidiary undertakings,

   (b) that the proportion referred to in paragraph (a) was attained pursuant to an arrangement providing for the issue of equity shares by the parent company or one or more of its subsidiary undertakings,

   (c) that the fair value of any consideration other than the issue of equity shares given pursuant to the arrangement by the parent company and its subsidiary undertakings did not exceed 10 per cent of the nominal value of the equity shares issued, and

   (d) that adoption of the merger method of accounting accords with generally accepted accounting principles or practice.

   (2) The reference in sub-paragraph (1)(a) to the "relevant shares" in an undertaking acquired is to those carrying unrestricted rights to participate both in distributions and in the assets of the undertaking upon liquidation.

11.— (1) The merger method of accounting is as follows.

   (2) The assets and liabilities of the undertaking acquired shall be brought into the group accounts at the figures at which they stand in the undertaking's accounts, subject to any adjustment authorised or required by this Schedule.

   (3) The income and expenditure of the undertaking acquired shall be included in the group accounts for the entire financial year, including the period before the acquisition.

    (4)   The group accounts shall show corresponding amounts relating to the previous financial year as if the undertaking acquired had been included in the consolidation throughout that year.

    (5)   There shall be set off against the aggregate of—

        (a)   the appropriate amount in respect of qualifying shares issued by the parent company or its subsidiary undertakings in consideration for the acquisition of shares in the undertaking acquired, and

        (b)   the fair value of any other consideration for the acquisition of shares in the undertaking acquired, determined as at the date when those shares were acquired,

the nominal value of the issued share capital of the undertaking acquired held by the parent company and its subsidiary undertakings.

    (6)   The resulting amount shall be shown as an adjustment to the consolidated reserves.

    (7)   In sub-paragraph (5)(a) "qualifying shares" means—

        (a)   shares in relation to which section 131 (merger relief) applies, in respect of which the appropriate amount is the nominal value; or

        (b)   shares in relation to which section 132 (relief in respect of group reconstructions) applies, in respect of which the appropriate amount is the nominal value together with any minimum premium value within the meaning of that section.

12.—   (1)   Where a group is acquired, paragraphs 9 to 11 apply with the following adaptations.

    (2)   References to shares of the undertaking acquired shall be construed as references to shares of the parent undertaking of the group.

    (3)   Other references to the undertaking acquired shall be construed as references to the group; and references to the assets and liabilities, income and expenditure and capital and reserves of the undertaking acquired shall be construed as references to the assets and liabilities, income and expenditure and capital and reserves of the group after making the set-offs and other adjustments required by this Schedule in the case of group accounts.

13.—   (1)   The following information with respect to acquisitions taking place in the financial year shall be given in a note to the accounts.

    (2)   There shall be stated—

        (a)   the name of the undertaking acquired or, where a group was acquired, the name of the parent undertaking of that group, and

        (b)   whether the acquisition has been accounted for by the acquisition or the merger method of accounting;

and in relation to an acquisition which significantly affects the figures shown in the group accounts, the following further information shall be given.

    (3)   The composition and fair value of the consideration for the acquisition given by the parent company and its subsidiary undertakings shall be stated.

    (4)   ...

    (5)   Where the acquisition method of accounting has been adopted, the book values immediately prior to the acquisition, and the fair values at the date of acquisition, of each class of assets and liabilities of the undertaking or group acquired shall be stated in tabular form, including a statement of the amount of any goodwill or negative consolidation difference arising on the acquisition, together with an explanation of any significant adjustments made.

    (6)   Where the merger method of accounting has been adopted, an explanation shall be given of any significant adjustments made in relation to the amounts of the assets and liabilities of the undertaking or group acquired, together with a statement of any resulting adjustment to the consolidated reserves (including the re-statement of opening consolidated reserves).

    (7)   In ascertaining for the purposes of sub-paragraph ..., (5) or (6) the profit or loss of a group, the book values and fair values of assets and liabilities of a group or the amount of the assets and liabilities of a group, the set-offs and other adjustments required by this Schedule in the case of group accounts shall be made.

14.— (1) There shall also be stated in a note to the accounts the cumulative amount of goodwill resulting from acquisitions in that and earlier financial years which has been written off otherwise than in the consolidated profit and loss account for that or any earlier financial year.

(2) That figure shall be shown net of any goodwill attributable to subsidiary undertakings or businesses disposed of prior to the balance sheet date.

15.   Where during the financial year there has been a disposal of an undertaking or group which significantly affects the figures shown in the group accounts, there shall be stated in a note to the accounts—

(a) the name of that undertaking or, as the case may be, of the parent undertaking of that group, and

(b) the extent to which the profit or loss shown in the group accounts is attributable to profit or loss of that undertaking or group.

16.— The information required by paragraph 13, 14 or 15 above need not be disclosed with respect to an undertaking which—

(a) is established under the law of a country outside the United Kingdom, or

(b) carries on business outside the United Kingdom,

if in the opinion of the directors of the parent company the disclosure would be seriously prejudicial to the business of that undertaking or to the business of the parent company or any of its subsidiary undertakings and the Secretary of State agrees that the information should not be disclosed.

Minority interests

17.— (1) The formats set out in Schedule 4 have effect in relation to group accounts with the following additions.

(2) In the Balance Sheet Formats a further item headed "Minority interests" shall be added—

(a) in Format 1, either after item J or at the end (after item K), and

(b) in Format 2, under the general heading "LIABILITIES", between items A and B;

and under that item shall be shown the amount of capital and reserves attributable to shares in subsidiary undertakings included in the consolidation held by or on behalf of persons other than the parent company and its subsidiary undertakings.

(3) In the Profit and Loss Account Formats a further item headed "Minority interests" shall be added—

(a) in Format 1, between items 14 and 15,

(b) in Format 2, between items 16 and 17,

(c) in Format 3, between items 7 and 8 in both sections A and B, and

(d) in Format 4, between items 9 and 10 in both sections A and B;

and under that item shall be shown the amount of any profit or loss on ordinary activities attributable to shares in subsidiary undertakings included in the consolidation held by or on behalf of persons other than the parent company and its subsidiary undertakings.

(4) In the Profit and Loss Account Formats a further item headed "Minority interests" shall be added—

(a) in Format 1, between items 18 and 19,

(b) in Format 2, between items 20 and 21,

(c) in Format 3, between items 9 and 10 in section A and between items 8 and 9 in section B, and

(d) in Format 4, between items 11 and 12 in section A and between items 10 and 11 in section B;

and under that item shall be shown the amount of any profit or loss on extraordinary activities attributable to shares in subsidiary undertakings included in the consolidation held by or on behalf of persons other than the parent company and its subsidiary undertakings.

(5) For the purposes of paragraph 3(3) and (4) of Schedule 4 (power to adapt or combine items)—

(a)   the additional item required by sub-paragraph (2) above shall be treated as one to which a letter is assigned, and

(b)   the additional items required by sub-paragraphs (3) and (4) above shall be treated as ones to which an Arabic number is assigned.

18.   ...

Joint ventures

19.— (1)   Where an undertaking included in the consolidation manages another undertaking jointly with one or more undertakings not included in the consolidation, that other undertaking ("the joint venture") may, if it is not—

(a)   a body corporate, or

(b)   a subsidiary undertaking of the parent company,

be dealt with in the group accounts by the method of proportional consolidation.

(2)   The provisions of this Schedule relating to the preparation of consolidated accounts apply, with any necessary modifications, to proportional consolidation under this paragraph.

Associated undertakings

20.— (1)   An "associated undertaking" means an undertaking in which an undertaking included in the consolidation has a participating interest and over whose operating and financial policy it exercises a significant influence, and which is not—

(a)   a subsidiary undertaking of the parent company, or

(b)   a joint venture dealt with in accordance with paragraph 19.

(2)   Where an undertaking holds 20 per cent or more of the voting rights in another undertaking, it shall be presumed to exercise such an influence over it unless the contrary is shown.

(3)   The voting rights in an undertaking means the rights conferred on shareholders in respect of their shares or, in the case of an undertaking not having a share capital, on members, to vote at general meetings of the undertaking on all, or substantially all, matters.

(4)   The provisions of paragraphs 5 to 11 of Schedule 10A (rights to be taken into account and attribution of rights) apply in determining for the purposes of this paragraph whether an undertaking holds 20 per cent or more of the voting rights in another undertaking.

21.— (1)   The formats set out in Schedule 4 have effect in relation to group accounts with the following modifications.

(2)   In the Balance Sheet Formats the items headed "Participating interests", that is—

(a)   in Format 1, item B.III.3, and

(b)   in Format 2, item B.III.3 under the heading "ASSETS",

shall be replaced by two items, "Interests in associated undertakings" and "Other participating interests".

(3)   In the Profit and Loss Account Formats, the items headed "Income from participating interests", that is—

(a)   in Format 1, item 8,

(b)   in Format 2, item 10,

(c)   in Format 3, item B.4, and

(d)   in Format 4, item B.6,

shall be replaced by two items, "Income from interests in associated undertakings" and "Income from other participating interests".

22.— (1)   The interest of an undertaking in an associated undertaking, and the amount of profit or loss attributable to such an interest, shall be shown by the equity method of accounting (including dealing with any goodwill arising in accordance with paragraphs 17 to 19 and 21 of Schedule 4).

(2)   Where the associated undertaking is itself a parent undertaking, the net assets and profits or losses to be taken into account are those of the parent and its subsidiary undertakings (after making any consolidation adjustments).

(3)   The equity method of accounting need not be applied if the amounts in question are not
      material for the purpose of giving a true and fair view.

Note. The italicized words in paragraph 1(1) are repealed by the Companies (Audit, Investigations and Community Enterprise) Act 2004, ss. 7(3), 64, Sch. 8, as from a 1 October 2005.

SCHEDULE 5

DISCLOSURE OF INFORMATION: RELATED UNDERTAKINGS

Section 231

PART I
COMPANIES NOT REQUIRED TO PREPARE GROUP ACCOUNTS

Subsidiary undertakings

1.—   (1)   The following information shall be given where at the end of the financial year the company
             has subsidiary undertakings.
       (2)   The name of each subsidiary undertaking shall be stated.
       (3)   There shall be stated with respect to each subsidiary undertaking—
             (a)   if it is incorporated outside Great Britain, the country in which it is incorporated;
             (b)   ...
             (c)   if it is unincorporated, the address of its principal place of business.
       (4)   The reason why the company is not required to prepare group accounts shall be stated.
       (5)   If the reason is that all the subsidiary undertakings of the company fall within the exclusions
             provided for in section 229, it shall be stated with respect to each subsidiary undertaking
             which of those exclusions applies.

Holdings in subsidiary undertakings

2.—   (1)   There shall be stated in relation to shares of each class held by the company in a subsidiary
             undertaking—
             (a)   the identity of the class, and
             (b)   the proportion of the nominal value of the shares of that class represented by those
                   shares.
       (2)   The shares held by or on behalf of the company itself shall be distinguished from those
             attributed to the company which are held by or on behalf of a subsidiary undertaking.

Financial information about subsidiary undertakings

3.—   (1)   There shall be disclosed with respect to each subsidiary undertaking—
             (a)   the aggregate amount of its capital and reserves as at the end of its relevant financial
                   year, and
             (b)   its profit or loss for that year.
       (2)   That information need not be given if the company is exempt by virtue of section 228 from
             the requirement to prepare group accounts (parent company included in accounts of larger
             group).
       (2A) That information need not be given if the company's investment in the subsidiary
             undertaking is included in the company's accounts by way of the equity method of
             valuation.
       (3)   That information need not be given if—
             (a)   the subsidiary undertaking is not required by any provision of this Act to deliver a
                   copy of its balance sheet for its relevant financial year and does not otherwise publish
                   that balance sheet in Great Britain or elsewhere, and
             (b)   the company's holding is less than 50 per cent of the nominal value of the shares in the
                   undertaking.

(4)   Information otherwise required by this paragraph need not be given if it is not material.

(5)   For the purposes of this paragraph the "relevant financial year" of a subsidiary undertaking is—

    (a)   if its financial year ends with that of the company, that year, and

    (b)   if not, its financial year ending last before the end of the company's financial year.

Financial years of subsidiary undertakings

4.   Where—

    (a)   disclosure is made under paragraph 3(1) with respect to a subsidiary undertaking, and

    (b)   that undertaking's financial year does not end with that of the company,

there shall be stated in relation to that undertaking the date on which its last financial year ended (last before the end of the company's financial year).

5.   ...

Shares and debentures of company held by subsidiary undertakings

6.—   (1)   The number, description and amount of the shares in ... the company held by or on behalf of its subsidiary undertakings shall be disclosed.

    (2)   Sub-paragraph (1) does not apply in relation to shares ... in the case of which the subsidiary undertaking is concerned as personal representative or, subject as follows, as trustee.

    (3)   The exception for shares ... in relation to which the subsidiary undertaking is concerned as trustee does not apply if the company, or any subsidiary undertaking of the company, is beneficially interested under the trust, otherwise than by way of security only for the purposes of a transaction entered into by it in the ordinary course of a business which includes the lending of money.

    (4)   Schedule 2 to this Act has effect for the interpretation of the reference in sub-paragraph (3) to a beneficial interest under a trust.

Significant holdings in undertakings other than subsidiary undertakings

7.—   (1)   The information required by paragraphs 8 and 9 shall be given where at the end of the financial year the company has a significant holding in an undertaking which is not a subsidiary undertaking of the company.

    (2)   A holding is significant for this purpose if—

      (a)   it amounts to 20 per cent or more of the nominal value of any class of shares in the undertaking, or

      (b)   the amount of the holding (as stated or included in the company's accounts) exceeds one-fifth of the amount (as so stated) of the company's assets.

8.—   (1)   The name of the undertaking shall be stated.

    (2)   There shall be stated—

      (a)   if the undertaking is incorporated outside Great Britain, the country in which it is incorporated;

      (b)   ...

      (c)   if it is unincorporated, the address of its principal place of business.

    (3)   There shall also be stated—

      (a)   the identity of each class of shares in the undertaking held by the company, and

      (b)   the proportion of the nominal value of the shares of that class represented by those shares.

9.—   (1)   ... there shall also be stated—

      (a)   the aggregate amount of the capital and reserves of the undertaking as at the end of its relevant financial year, and

      (b)   its profit or loss for that year.

    (2)   That information need not be given if—

      (a)   the company is exempt by virtue of section 228 from the requirement to prepare group accounts (parent company included in accounts of larger group), and

(b) the investment of the company in all undertakings in which it has such a holding as is mentioned in sub-paragraph (1) is shown, in aggregate, in the notes to the accounts by way of the equity method of valuation.

(3) That information need not be given in respect of an undertaking if—

(a) the undertaking is not required by any provision of this Act to deliver a copy of its balance sheet for its relevant financial year and does not otherwise publish that balance sheet in Great Britain or elsewhere, and

(b) the company's holding is less than 50 per cent. of the nominal value of the shares in the undertaking.

(4) Information otherwise required by this paragraph need not be given if it is not material.

(5) For the purposes of this paragraph the "relevant financial year" of an undertaking is—

(a) if its financial year ends with that of the company, that year, and

(b) if not, its financial year ending last before the end of the company's financial year.

Membership of certain undertakings

9A.— (1) The information required by this paragraph shall be given where at the end of the financial year the company is a member of a qualifying undertaking.

(2) There shall be stated—

(a) the name and legal form of the undertaking, and

(b) the address of the undertaking's registered office (whether in or outside Great Britain) or, if it does not have such an office, its head office (whether in or outside Great Britain).

(3) Where the undertaking is a qualifying partnership there shall also be stated either—

(a) that a copy of the latest accounts of the undertaking has been or is to be appended to the copy of the company's accounts sent to the registrar under section 242 of this Act, or

(b) the name of at least one body corporate (which may be the company) in whose group accounts the undertaking has been or is to be dealt with on a consolidated basis.

(4) Information otherwise required by sub-paragraph (2) above need not be given if it is not material.

(5) Information otherwise required by sub-paragraph (3)(b) above need not be given if the notes to the company's accounts disclose that advantage has been taken of the exemption conferred by regulation 7 of the Partnerships and Unlimited Companies (Accounts) Regulations 1993.

(6) In this paragraph—

"dealt with on a consolidated basis", "member", "qualifying company" and "qualifying partnership" have the same meanings as in the Partnerships and Unlimited Companies (Accounts) Regulations 1993;

"qualifying undertaking" means a qualifying partnership or a qualifying company.

10. ...

Parent undertaking drawing up accounts for larger group

11.— (1) Where the company is a subsidiary undertaking, the following information shall be given with respect to the parent undertaking of—

(a) the largest group of undertakings for which group accounts are drawn up and of which the company is a member, and

(b) the smallest such group of undertakings.

(2) The name of the parent undertaking shall be stated.

(3) There shall be stated—

(a) if the undertaking is incorporated outside Great Britain, the country in which it is incorporated;

(b) ...

(c) if it is unincorporated, the address of its principal place of business.

(4)   If copies of the group accounts referred to in sub-paragraph (1) are available to the public, there shall also be stated the addresses from which copies of the accounts can be obtained.

Identification of ultimate parent company

12.— (1)   Where the company is a subsidiary undertaking, the following information shall be given with respect to the company (if any) regarded by the directors as being the company's ultimate parent company.

(2)   The name of that company shall be stated.

(3)   If known to the directors, there shall be stated—

(a)   if that company is incorporated outside Great Britain, the country in which it is incorporated;

(b)   ...

(4)   In this paragraph "company" includes any body corporate.

Constructions of references to shares held by company

13.— (1)   References in this Part of this Schedule to shares held by a company shall be construed as follows.

(2)   For the purposes of paragraphs 2 to 4 (information about subsidiary undertakings)—

(a)   there shall be attributed to the company any shares held by a subsidiary undertaking, or by a person acting on behalf of the company or a subsidiary undertaking; but

(b)   there shall be treated as not held by the company any shares held on behalf of a person other than the company or a subsidiary undertaking.

(3)   For the purposes of paragraphs 7 to 9 (information about undertakings other than subsidiary undertakings)—

(a)   there shall be attributed to the company shares held on its behalf by any person; but

(b)   there shall be treated as not held by a company shares held on behalf of a person other than the company.

(4)   For the purposes of any of those provisions, shares held by way of security shall be treated as held by the person providing the security—

(a)   where apart from the right to exercise them for the purpose of preserving the value of the security, or of realising it, the rights attached to the shares are exercisable only in accordance with his instructions, and

(b)   where the shares are held in connection with the granting of loans as part of normal business activities and apart from the right to exercise them for the purpose of preserving the value of the security, or of realising it, the rights attached to the shares are exercisable only in his interests.

PART II
COMPANIES REQUIRED TO PREPARE GROUP ACCOUNTS

Introductory

14.   In this Part of this Schedule "the group" means the group consisting of the parent company and its subsidiary undertakings.

Subsidiary undertakings

15.— (1)   The following information shall be given with respect to the undertakings which are subsidiary undertakings of the parent company at the end of the financial year.

(2)   The name of each undertaking shall be stated.

(3)   There shall be stated—

(a)   if the undertaking is incorporated outside Great Britain, the country in which it is incorporated;

(b)   ...

(c)   if it is unincorporated, the address of its principal place of business.

(4)	It shall also be stated whether the subsidiary undertaking is included in the consolidation and, if it is not, the reasons for excluding it from consolidation shall be given.

(5)	It shall be stated with respect to each subsidiary undertaking by virtue of which of the conditions specified in section 258(2) or (4) it is a subsidiary undertaking of its immediate parent undertaking.

That information need not be given if the relevant condition is that specified in subsection (2)(a) of that section (holding of a majority of the voting rights) and the immediate parent undertaking holds the same proportion of the shares in the undertaking as it holds voting rights.

Holdings in subsidiary undertakings

16.—	(1)	The following information shall be given with respect to the shares of a subsidiary undertaking held—

(a)	by the parent company, and

(b)	by the group;

and the information under paragraphs (a) and (b) shall (if different) be shown separately.

(2)	There shall be stated—

(a)	the identity of each class of shares held, and

(b)	the proportion of the nominal value of the shares of that class represented by those shares.

Financial information about subsidiary undertakings
not included in the consolidation

17.—	(1)	There shall be shown with respect to each subsidiary undertaking not included in the consolidation—

(a)	the aggregate amount of its capital and reserves as at the end of its relevant financial year, and

(b)	its profit or loss for that year.

(2)	That information need not be given if the group's investment in the undertaking is included in the accounts by way of the equity method of valuation or if—

(a)	the undertaking is not required by any provision of this Act to deliver a copy of its balance sheet for its relevant financial year and does not otherwise publish that balance sheet in Great Britain or elsewhere, and

(b)	the holding of the group is less than 50 per cent of the nominal value of the shares in the undertaking.

(3)	Information otherwise required by this paragraph need not be given if it is not material.

(4)	For the purposes of this paragraph the "relevant financial year" of a subsidiary undertaking is—

(a)	if its financial year ends with that of the company, that year, and

(b)	if not, its financial year ending last before the end of the company's financial year.

18, 19.	...

Shares and debentures of company held by
subsidiary undertakings

20.—	(1)	The number, description and amount of the shares in ... the company held by or on behalf of its subsidiary undertakings shall be disclosed.

(2)	Sub-paragraph (1) does not apply in relation to shares ... in the case of which the subsidiary undertaking is concerned as personal representative or, subject as follows, as trustee.

(3)	The exception for shares ... in relation to which the subsidiary undertaking is concerned as trustee does not apply if the company or any of its subsidiary undertakings is beneficially interested under the trust, otherwise than by way of security only for the purposes of a transaction entered into by it in the ordinary course of a business which includes the lending of money.

(4)   Schedule 2 to this Act has effect for the interpretation of the reference in sub-paragraph (3) to a beneficial interest under a trust.

Joint ventures

21.— (1)   The following information shall be given where an undertaking is dealt with in the consolidated accounts by the method of proportional consolidation in accordance with paragraph 19 of Schedule 4A (joint ventures)—
  (a)   the name of the undertaking;
  (b)   the address of the principal place of business of the undertaking;
  (c)   the factors on which joint management of the undertaking is based; and
  (d)   the proportion of the capital of the undertaking held by undertakings included in the consolidation.
  (2)   Where the financial year of the undertaking did not end with that of the company, there shall be stated the date on which a financial year of the undertaking last ended before that date.

Associated undertakings

22.— (1)   The following information shall be given where an undertaking included in the consolidation has an interest in an associated undertaking.
  (2)   The name of the associated undertaking shall be stated.
  (3)   There shall be stated—
  (a)   if the undertaking is incorporated outside Great Britain, the country in which it is incorporated;
  (b)   ...
  (c)   if it is unincorporated, the address of its principal place of business.
  (4)   The following information shall be given with respect to the shares of the undertaking held—
  (a)   by the parent company, and
  (b)   by the group;
  and the information under paragraphs (a) and (b) shall be shown separately.
  (5)   There shall be stated—
  (a)   the identity of each class of shares held, and
  (b)   the proportion of the nominal value of the shares of that class represented by those shares.
  (6)   In this paragraph "associated undertaking" has the meaning given by paragraph 20 of Schedule 4A; and the information required by this paragraph shall be given notwithstanding that paragraph 22(3) of that Schedule (materiality) applies in relation to the accounts themselves.

Other significant holdings of parent company or group

23.— (1)   The information required by paragraphs 24 and 25 shall be given where at the end of the financial year the parent company has a significant holding in an undertaking which is not one of its subsidiary undertakings and does not fall within paragraph 21 (joint ventures) or paragraph 22 (associated undertakings).
  (2)   A holding is significant for this purpose if—
  (a)   it amounts to 20 per cent or more of the nominal value of any class of shares in the undertaking, or
  (b)   the amount of the holding (as stated or included in the company's individual accounts) exceeds one-fifth of the amount of its assets (as so stated).

24.— (1)   The name of the undertaking shall be stated.
  (2)   There shall be stated—
  (a)   if the undertaking is incorporated outside Great Britain, the country in which it is incorporated;
  (b)   ...

        (c)   if it is unincorporated, the address of its principal place of business.

(3)   The following information shall be given with respect to the shares of the undertaking held by the parent company.

(4)   There shall be stated—
        (a)   the identity of each class of shares held, and
        (b)   the proportion of the nominal value of the shares of that class represented by those shares.

25.— (1)   ... there shall also be stated—
        (a)   the aggregate amount of the capital and reserves of the undertaking as at the end of its relevant financial year, and
        (b)   its profit or loss for that year.

      (2)   That information need not be given in respect of an undertaking if—
        (a)   the undertaking is not required by any provision of this Act to deliver a copy of its balance sheet for its relevant financial year and does not otherwise publish that balance sheet in Great Britain or elsewhere, and
        (b)   the company's holding is less than 50 per cent of the nominal value of the shares in the undertaking.

      (3)   Information otherwise required by this paragraph need not be given if it is not material.

      (4)   For the purposes of this paragraph the "relevant financial year" of an undertaking is—
        (a)   if its financial year ends with that of the company, that year, and
        (b)   if not, its financial year ending last before the end of the company's financial year.

26.— (1)   The information required by paragraphs 27 and 28 shall be given where at the end of the financial year the group has a significant holding in an undertaking which is not a subsidiary undertaking of the parent company and does not fall within paragraph 21 (joint ventures) or paragraph 22 (associated undertakings).

      (2)   A holding is significant for this purpose if—
        (a)   it amounts to 20 per cent or more of the nominal value of any class of shares in the undertaking, or
        (b)   the amount of the holding (as stated or included in the group accounts) exceeds one-fifth of the amount of the group's assets (as so stated).

27.— (1)   The name of the undertaking shall be stated.

      (2)   There shall be stated—
        (a)   if the undertaking is incorporated outside Great Britain, the country in which it is incorporated;
        (b)   ...
        (c)   if it is unincorporated, the address of its principal place of business.

      (3)   The following information shall be given with respect to the shares of the undertaking held by the group.

      (4)   There shall be stated—
        (a)   the identity of each class of shares held, and
        (b)   the proportion of the nominal value of the shares of that class represented by those shares.

28.— (1)   ... there shall also be stated—
        (a)   the aggregate amount of the capital and reserves of the undertaking as at the end of its relevant financial year, and
        (b)   its profit or loss for that year.

      (2)   That information need not be given if—
        (a)   the undertaking is not required by any provision of this Act to deliver a copy of its balance sheet for its relevant financial year and does not otherwise publish that balance sheet in Great Britain or elsewhere, and
        (b)   the holding of the group is less than 50 per cent of the nominal value of the shares in the undertaking.

(3)   Information otherwise required by this paragraph need not be given if it is not material.

(4)   For the purposes of this paragraph the "relevant financial year" of an outside undertaking is—

    (a)   if its financial year ends with that of the parent company, that year, and

    (b)   if not, its financial year ending last before the end of the parent company's financial year.

Parent company's or group's membership of certain undertakings

28A.— (1)   The information required by this paragraph shall be given where at the end of the financial year the parent company or group is a member of a qualifying undertaking.

(2)   There shall be stated—

    (a)   the name and legal form of the undertaking, and

    (b)   the address of the undertaking's registered office (whether in or outside Great Britain) or, if it does not have such an office, its head office (whether in or outside Great Britain).

(3)   Where the undertaking is a qualifying partnership there shall also be stated either—

    (a)   that a copy of the latest accounts of the undertaking has been or is to be appended to the copy of the company's accounts sent to the registrar under section 242 of this Act, or

    (b)   the name of at least one body corporate (which may be the company) in whose group accounts the undertaking has been or is to be dealt with on a consolidated basis.

(4)   Information otherwise required by sub-paragraph (2) above need not be given if it is not material.

(5)   Information otherwise required by sub-paragraph (3)(b) above need not be given if the notes to the company's accounts disclose that advantage has been taken of the exemption conferred by regulation 7 of the Partnerships and Unlimited Companies (Accounts) Regulations 1993.

(6)   In this paragraph—

    "dealt with on a consolidated basis", "member", "qualifying company" and "qualifying partnership" have the same meanings as in the Partnerships and Unlimited Companies (Accounts) Regulations 1993;

    "qualifying undertaking" means a qualifying partnership or a qualifying company.

29.   ...

Parent undertaking drawing up accounts for larger group

30.— (1)   Where the parent company is itself a subsidiary undertaking, the following information shall be given with respect to that parent undertaking of the company which heads—

    (a)   the largest group of undertakings for which group accounts are drawn up and of which that company is a member, and

    (b)   the smallest such group of undertakings.

(2)   The name of the parent undertaking shall be stated.

(3)   There shall be stated—

    (a)   if the undertaking is incorporated outside Great Britain, the country in which it is incorporated;

    (b)   ...

    (c)   if it is unincorporated, the address of its principal place of business.

(4)   If copies of the group accounts referred to in sub-paragraph (1) are available to the public, there shall also be stated the addresses from which copies of the accounts can be obtained.

Identification of ultimate parent company

31.— (1) Where the parent company is itself a subsidiary undertaking, the following information shall be given with respect to the company (if any) regarded by the directors as being that company's ultimate parent company.

(2) The name of that company shall be stated.

(3) If known to the directors, there shall be stated—

    (a) if that company is incorporated outside Great Britain, the country in which it is incorporated;

    (b) ...

(4) In this paragraph "company" includes any body corporate.

Construction of references to shares held by
parent company or group

32.— (1) References in this Part of this Schedule to shares held by the parent company or group shall be construed as follows.

(2) For the purposes of paragraphs 16, 22(4) and (5) and 23 to 25 (information about holdings in subsidiary and other undertakings)—

    (a) there shall be attributed to the parent company shares held on its behalf by any person; but

    (b) there shall be treated as not held by the parent company shares held on behalf of a person other than the company.

(3) References to shares held by the group are to any shares held by or on behalf of the parent company or any of its subsidiary undertakings; but there shall be treated as not held by the group any shares held on behalf of a person other than the parent company or any of its subsidiary undertakings.

(4) Shares held by way of security shall be treated as held by the person providing the security—

    (a) where apart from the right to exercise them for the purpose of preserving the value of the security, or of realising it, the rights attached to the shares are exercisable only in accordance with his instructions, and

    (b) where the shares are held in connection with the granting of loans as part of normal business activities and apart from the right to exercise them for the purpose of preserving the value of the security, or of realising it, the rights attached to the shares are exercisable only in his interests.

SCHEDULE 6

DISCLOSURE OF INFORMATION: EMOLUMENTS AND OTHER BENEFITS OF DIRECTORS AND OTHERS

Section 232

PART I
CHAIRMAN'S AND DIRECTORS' EMOLUMENTS, PENSIONS AND COMPENSATION FOR LOSS OF OFFICE

CHAPTER 1
PROVISIONS APPLYING TO QUOTED AND UNQUOTED COMPANIES

Aggregate amount of directors' emoluments etc

1.— (1) Subject to sub-paragraph (2), the following shall be shown, namely—

    (a) the aggregate amount of emoluments paid to or receivable by directors in respect of qualifying services;

(b) the aggregate of the amount of gains made by directors on the exercise of share options;

(c) the aggregate of the following, namely—

(i) the amount of money paid to or receivable by directors under long term incentive schemes in respect of qualifying services; and

(ii) the net value of assets (other than money and share options) received or receivable by directors under such schemes in respect of such services;

(d) the aggregate value of any company contributions paid, or treated as paid, to a pension scheme in respect of directors' qualifying services, being contributions by reference to which the rate or amount of any money purchase benefits that may become payable will be calculated; and

(e) in the case of each of the following, namely—

(i) money purchase schemes; and

(ii) defined benefit schemes,

the number of directors (if any) to whom retirement benefits are accruing under such schemes in respect of qualifying services.

(2) In the case of a company which is not a quoted company and whose equity share capital is not listed on the market known as AIM—

(a) sub-paragraph (1) shall have effect as if paragraph (b) were omitted and, in paragraph (c)(ii), "assets" did not include shares; and

(b) the number of each of the following (if any) shall be shown, namely—

(i) the directors who exercised share options; and

(ii) the directors in respect of whose qualifying services shares were received or receivable under long term incentive schemes.

(3) In this paragraph "emoluments" of a director—

(a) includes salary, fees and bonuses, sums paid by way of expenses allowance (so far as they are chargeable to United Kingdom income tax) and, subject to paragraph (b), the estimated money value of any other benefits received by him otherwise than in cash; but

(b) does not include any of the following, namely—

(i) the value of any share options granted to him or the amount of any gains made on the exercise of any such options;

(ii) any company contributions paid, or treated as paid, in respect of him under any pension scheme or any benefits to which he is entitled under any such scheme; or

(iii) any money or other assets paid to or received or receivable by him under any long term incentive scheme.

(4) In this paragraph "long term incentive scheme" means any agreement or arrangement under which money or other assets may become receivable by a director and which includes one or more qualifying conditions with respect to service or performance which cannot be fulfilled within a single financial year; and for this purpose the following shall be disregarded, namely—

(a) bonuses the amount of which falls to be determined by reference to service or performance within a single financial year;

(b) compensation for loss of office, payments for breach of contract and other termination payments; and

(c) retirement benefits.

(5) In this paragraph—

"amount", in relation to a gain made on the exercise of a share option, means the difference between—

(a) the market price of the shares on the day on which the option was exercised; and

(b) the price actually paid for the shares;

"company contributions", in relation to a pension scheme and a director, means any payments (including insurance premiums) made, or treated as made, to the scheme in respect of the director by a person other than the director;

"defined benefits" means retirement benefits payable under a pension scheme which are not money purchase benefits;

"defined benefit scheme", in relation to a director, means a pension scheme which is not a money purchase scheme;

...

"money purchase benefits", in relation to a director, means retirement benefits payable under a pension scheme the rate or amount of which is calculated by reference to payments made, or treated as made, by the director or by any other person in respect of the director and which are not average salary benefits;

"money purchase scheme", in relation to a director, means a pension scheme under which all of the benefits that may become payable to or in respect of the director are money purchase benefits;

"net value", in relation to any assets received or receivable by a director, means value after deducting any money paid or other value given by the director in respect of those assets;

"the official list" has the meaning given in section 103(1) of the Financial Services and Markets Act 2000;

"qualifying services", in relation to any person, means his services as a director of the company, and his services while director of the company—

(a)   as director of any of its subsidiary undertakings; or

(b)   otherwise in connection with the management of the affairs of the company or any of its subsidiary undertakings;

"recognised investment exchange" has the same meaning as in the Financial Services and Markets Act 2000;

"shares" means shares (whether allotted or not) in the company, or any undertaking which is a group undertaking in relation to the company, and includes a share warrant as defined by section 188(1);

"share option" means a right to acquire shares;

"value", in relation to shares received or receivable by a director on any day, means the market price of the shares on that day.

(6)   For the purposes of this paragraph—

(a)   any information, other than the aggregate amount of gains made by directors on the exercise of share options, shall be treated as shown if it is capable of being readily ascertained from other information which is shown; and

(b)   emoluments paid or receivable or share options granted in respect of a person's accepting office as a director shall be treated as emoluments paid or receivable or share options granted in respect of his services as a director.

(7)   Where a pension scheme provides for any benefits that may become payable to or in respect of any director to be whichever are the greater of—

(a)   money purchase benefits as determined by or under the scheme; and

(b)   defined benefits as so determined,

the company may assume for the purposes of this paragraph that those benefits will be money purchase benefits, or defined benefits, according to whichever appears more likely at the end of the financial year.

(8)   For the purpose of determining whether a pension scheme is a money purchase or defined benefit scheme, any death in service benefits provided for by the scheme shall be disregarded.

CHAPTER 2
PROVISIONS APPLYING ONLY TO UNQUOTED COMPANIES

Details of highest paid director's emoluments etc

2.— (1) Where the aggregates shown under paragraph 1(1)(a), (b) and (c) total £200,000 or more, the following shall be shown, namely—

(a) so much of the total of those aggregates as is attributable to the highest paid director; and

(b) so much of the aggregate mentioned in paragraph 1(1)(d) as is so attributable.

(2) Where sub-paragraph (1) applies and the highest paid director has performed qualifying services during the financial year by reference to which the rate or amount of any defined benefits that may become payable will be calculated, there shall also be shown—

(a) the amount at the end of the year of his accrued pension; and

(b) where applicable, the amount at the end of the year of his accrued lump sum.

(3) Subject to sub-paragraph (4), where sub-paragraph (1) applies in the case of a company which is not a listed company, there shall also be shown—

(a) whether the highest paid director exercised any share options; and

(b) whether any shares were received or receivable by that director in respect of qualifying services under a long term incentive scheme.

(4) Where the highest paid director has not been involved in any of the transactions specified in sub-paragraph (3), that fact need not be stated.

(5) In this paragraph—

"accrued pension" and "accrued lump sum", in relation to any pension scheme and any director, mean respectively the amount of the annual pension, and the amount of the lump sum, which would be payable under the scheme on his attaining normal pension age if—

(a) he had left the company's service at the end of the financial year;

(b) there were no increase in the general level of prices in Great Britain during the period beginning with the end of that year and ending with his attaining that age;

(c) no question arose of any commutation of the pension or inverse commutation of the lump sum; and

(d) any amounts attributable to voluntary contributions paid by the director to the scheme, and any money purchase benefits which would be payable under the scheme, were disregarded;

"the highest paid director" means the director to whom is attributable the greatest part of the total of the aggregates shown under paragraph 1(1)(a), (b) and (c);

"normal pension age", in relation to any pension scheme and any director, means the age at which the director will first become entitled to receive a full pension on retirement of an amount determined without reduction to take account of its payment before a later age (but disregarding any entitlement to pension upon retirement in the event of illness, incapacity or redundancy).

(6) Sub-paragraphs (4) to (8) of paragraph 1 apply for the purposes of this paragraph as they apply for the purposes of that paragraph.

...

Excess retirement benefits of directors and past directors

7.— (1) Subject to sub-paragraph (2), there shall be shown the aggregate amount of—

(a) so much of retirement benefits paid to or receivable by directors under pension schemes; and

(b) so much of retirement benefits paid to or receivable by past directors under such schemes, as (in each case) is in excess of the retirement benefits to which they were respectively entitled on the date on which the benefits first became payable or 31st March 1997, whichever is the later.

(2)   Amounts paid or receivable under a pension scheme need not be included in the aggregate amount if—

(a)   the funding of the scheme was such that the amounts were or, as the case may be, could have been paid without recourse to additional contributions; and

(b)   amounts were paid to or receivable by all pensioner members of the scheme on the same basis;

and in this sub-paragraph "pensioner member", in relation to a pension scheme, means any person who is entitled to the present payment of retirement benefits under the scheme.

(3)   In this paragraph—

(a)   references to retirement benefits include benefits otherwise than in cash; and

(b)   in relation to so much of retirement benefits as consists of a benefit otherwise than in cash, references to their amount are to the estimated money value of the benefit;

and the nature of any such benefit shall also be disclosed.

Compensation to directors for loss of office

8.—   (1)   There shall be shown the aggregate amount of any compensation to directors or past directors in respect of loss of office.

(2)   This amount includes compensation received or receivable by a director or past director for—

(a)   loss of office as director of the company, or

(b)   loss, while director of the company or on or in connection with his ceasing to be a director of it, of—

(i)   any other office in connection with the management of the company's affairs, or

(ii)   any office as director or otherwise in connection with the management of the affairs of any subsidiary undertaking of the company; ...

(3)   References to compensation include benefits otherwise than in cash; and in relation to such compensation references to its amount are to the estimated money value of the benefit.

The nature of any such compensation shall be disclosed.

(4)   In this paragraph, references to compensation for loss of office include the following, namely—

(a)   compensation in consideration for, or in connection with, a person's retirement from office; and

(b)   where such a retirement is occasioned by a breach of the person's contract with the company or with a subsidiary undertaking of the company—

(i)   payments made by way of damages for the breach; or

(ii)   payments made by way of settlement or compromise of any claim in respect of the breach.

(5)   Sub-paragraph (6)(a) of paragraph 1 applies for the purposes of this paragraph as it applies for the purposes of that paragraph.

Sums paid to third parties in respect of directors' services

9.—   (1)   There shall be shown the aggregate amount of any consideration paid to or receivable by third parties for making available the services of any person—

(a)   as a director of the company, or

(b)   while director of the company—

(i)   as director of any of its subsidiary undertakings, or

(ii)   otherwise in connection with the management of the affairs of the company or any of its subsidiary undertakings.

(2) The reference to consideration includes benefits otherwise than in cash; and in relation to such consideration the reference to its amount is to the estimated money value of the benefit.

The nature of any such consideration shall be disclosed.

(3) The reference to third parties is to persons other than—

  (a) the director himself or a person connected with him or body corporate controlled by him, and

  (b) the company or any of its subsidiary undertakings.

Supplementary

10.— (1) The following applies with respect to the amounts to be shown under this Part of this schedule.

  (2) The amount in each case includes all relevant sums paid by or receivable from—

    (a) the company; and

    (b) the company's subsidiary undertakings; and

    (c) any other person,

  except sums to be accounted for to the company or any of its subsidiary undertakings or, by virtue of sections 314 and 315 of this Act (duty of directors to make disclosure on company takeover; consequence of non-compliance), to past or present members of the company or any of its subsidiaries or any class of those members.

  (3) ...

  (4) References to amounts paid to or receivable by a person include amounts paid to or receivable by a person connected with him or a body corporate controlled by him (but not so as to require an amount to be counted twice).

11.— (1) The amounts to be shown for any financial year under this Part of this Schedule are the sums receivable in respect of that year (whenever paid) or, in the case of sums not receivable in respect of a period, the sums paid during that year.

  (2) But where—

    (a) any sums are not shown in a note to the accounts for the relevant financial year on the ground that the person receiving them is liable to account for them as mentioned in paragraph 10(2), but the liability is thereafter wholly or partly released or is not enforced within a period of 2 years; or

    (b) any sums paid by way of expenses allowance are charged to United Kingdom income tax after the end of the relevant financial year,

  those sums shall, to the extent to which the liability is released or not enforced or they are charged as mentioned above (as the case may be), be shown in a note to the first accounts in which it is practicable to show them and shall be distinguished from the amounts to be shown apart from this provision.

12. Where it is necessary to do so for the purpose of making any distinction required by the preceding paragraphs in an amount to be shown in compliance with this Part of this Schedule, the directors may apportion any payments between the matters in respect of which these have been paid or are receivable in such manner as they think appropriate.

Interpretation

13.— (1) The following applies for the interpretation of this Part of this Schedule.

  (2) A reference to a subsidiary undertaking of the company—

    (a) in relation to a person who is or was, while a director of the company, a director also, by virtue of the company's nomination (direct or indirect) of any other undertaking, includes (subject to the following sub-paragraph) that undertaking, whether or not it is or was in fact a subsidiary undertaking of the company, and

    (b) for the purposes of paragraphs 1 to 7 ... is to an undertaking which is a subsidiary undertaking at the time the services were rendered, and for the purposes of paragraph 8 to a subsidiary undertaking immediately before the loss of office as director.

(3)   The following definitions apply—

       (a)   "pension scheme" has the meaning assigned to "retirement benefits scheme" by section 611 of the Income and Corporation Taxes Act 1988;

       (b)   "retirement benefits" has the meaning assigned to relevant benefits by section 612(1) of that Act.

(4)   References in this Part of this Schedule to a person being "connected" with a director, and to a director "controlling" a body corporate, shall be construed in accordance with section 346.

Supplementary

14.   This Part of this Schedule requires information to be given only so far as it is contained in the company's books and papers or the company has the right to obtain it from the persons concerned.

PART II
LOANS, QUASI-LOANS AND OTHER DEALINGS IN FAVOUR OF DIRECTORS

15.   The group accounts of a holding company, or if it is not required to prepare group accounts its individual accounts, shall contain the particulars required by this Schedule of—

       (a)   any transaction or arrangement of a kind described in section 330 entered into by the company or by a subsidiary of the company for a person who at any time during the financial year was a director of the company or its holding company, or was connected with such a director;

       (b)   an agreement by the company or by a subsidiary of the company to enter into any such transaction or arrangement for a person who was at any time during the financial year a director of the company or its holding company, or was connected with such a director; and

       (c)   any other transaction or arrangement with the company or a subsidiary of it in which a person who at any time during the financial year was a director of the company or its holding company had, directly or indirectly, a material interest.

16.   The accounts prepared by a company other than a holding company shall contain the particulars required by this Schedule of—

       (a)   any transaction or arrangement of a kind described in section 330 entered into by the company for a person who at any time during the financial year was a director of it or of its holding company or was connected with such a director;

       (b)   an agreement by the company to enter into any such transaction or arrangement for a person who at any time during the financial year was a director of the company or its holding company or was connected with such a director; and

       (c)   any other transaction or arrangement with the company in which a person who at any time during the financial year was a director of the company or of its holding company had, directly or indirectly, a material interest.

17.— (1)   For purposes of paragraphs 15(c) and 16(c), a transaction or arrangement between a company and a director of it or of its holding company, or a person connected with such a director, is to be treated (if it would not otherwise be so) as a transaction, arrangement or agreement in which that director is interested.

     (2)   An interest in such a transaction or arrangement is not "material" for purposes of those sub-paragraphs if in the board's opinion it is not so; but this is without prejudice to the question whether or not such an interest is material in a case where the board have not considered the matter.

"The board" here means the directors of the company preparing the accounts, or a majority of those directors, but excluding in either case the director whose interest it is.

18.   Paragraphs 15 and 16 do not apply in relation to the following transactions, arrangements and agreements—

(a)   a transaction, arrangement or agreement between one company and another in which a director of the former or of its subsidiary or holding company is interested only by virtue of his being a director of the latter;

(b)   a contract of service between a company and one of its directors or a director of its holding company, or between a director of a company and any of that company's subsidiaries;

(c)   a transaction, arrangement or agreement which was not entered into during the financial year and which did not subsist at any time during that year.

19.   Paragraphs 15 and 16 apply whether or not—

(a)   the transaction or arrangement was prohibited by section 330;

(b)   the person for whom it was made was a director of the company or was connected with a director of it at the time it was made;

(c)   in the case of a transaction or arrangement made by a company which at any time during a financial year is a subsidiary of another company, it was a subsidiary of that other company at the time the transaction or arrangement was made.

20.   Neither paragraph 15(c) nor paragraph 16(c) applies in relation to any transaction or arrangement if—

(a)   each party to the transaction or arrangement which is a member of the same group of companies (meaning a holding company and its subsidiaries) as the company entered into the transaction or arrangement in the ordinary course of business, and

(b)   the terms of the transaction or arrangement are not less favourable to any such party than it would be reasonable to expect if the interest mentioned in that sub-paragraph had not been an interest of a person who was a director of the company or of its holding company.

21.   Neither paragraph 15(c) nor paragraph 16(c) applies in relation to any transaction or arrangement if—

(a)   the company is a member of a group of companies (meaning a holding company and its subsidiaries), and

(b)   either the company is a wholly-owned subsidiary or no body corporate (other than the company or a subsidiary of the company) which is a member of the group of companies which includes the company's ultimate holding company was a party to the transaction or arrangement, and

(c)   the director in question was at some time during the relevant period associated with the company, and

(d)   the material interest of the director in question in the transaction or arrangement would not have arisen if he had not been associated with the company at any time during the relevant period.

The particulars required by this Part

22.— (1)   Subject to the next paragraph, the particulars required by this Part are those of the principal terms of the transaction, arrangement or agreement.

(2)   Without prejudice to the generality of sub-paragraph (1), the following particulars are required—

(a)   a statement of the fact either that the transaction, arrangement or agreement was made or subsisted (as the case may be) during the financial year;

(b)   the name of the person for whom it was made and, where that person is or was connected with a director of the company or of its holding company, the name of that director;

(c)   in a case where paragraph 15(c) or 16(c) applies, the name of the director with the material interest and the nature of that interest;

(d)   in the case of a loan or an agreement for a loan or an arrangement within section 330(6) or (7) of this Act relating to a loan—

(i)   the amount of the liability of the person to whom the loan was or was agreed to be made, in respect of principal and interest, at the beginning and at the end of the financial year;

(ii)   the maximum amount of that liability during that year;

(iii) the amount of any interest which, having fallen due, has not been paid; and

(iv)   the amount of any provision (within the meaning of Schedule 4 to this Act) made in respect of any failure or anticipated failure by the borrower to repay the whole or part of the loan or to pay the whole or part of any interest on it;

(e)   in the case of a guarantee or security or an arrangement within section 330(6) relating to a guarantee or security—

(i)   the amount for which the company (or its subsidiary) was liable under the guarantee or in respect of the security both at the beginning and at the end of the financial year;

(ii)   the maximum amount for which the company (or its subsidiary) may become so liable; and

(iii) any amount paid and any liability incurred by the company (or its subsidiary) for the purpose of fulfilling the guarantee or discharging the security (including any loss incurred by reason of the enforcement of the guarantee or security); and

(f)   in the case of any transaction, arrangement or agreement other than those mentioned in sub-paragraphs (d) and (e), the value of the transaction or arrangement or (as the case may be) the value of the transaction or arrangement to which the agreement relates.

23.   In paragraph 22(2) above, sub-paragraphs (c) to (f) do not apply in the case of a loan or quasi-loan made or agreed to be made by a company to or for a body corporate which is either—

(a)   a body corporate of which that company is a wholly-owned subsidiary, or

(b)   a wholly-owned subsidiary of a body corporate of which that company is a wholly-owned subsidiary, or

(c)   a wholly-owned subsidiary of that company,

if particulars of that loan, quasi-loan or agreement for it would not have been required to be included in that company's annual accounts if the first-mentioned body corporate had not been associated with a director of that company at any time during the relevant period.

Excluded transactions

24.—   (1)   In relation to a company's accounts for a financial year, compliance with this Part is not required in the case of transactions of a kind mentioned in the following sub-paragraph which are made by the company or a subsidiary of it for a person who at any time during that financial year was a director of the company or of its holding company, or was connected with such a director, if the aggregate of the values of each transaction, arrangement or agreement so made for that director or any person connected with him, less the amount (if any) by which the liabilities of the person for whom the transaction or arrangement was made has been reduced, did not at any time during the financial year exceed £5,000.

(2)   The transactions in question are—

(a)   credit transactions,

(b)   guarantees provided or securities entered into in connection with credit transactions,

(c)   arrangements within subsection (6) or (7) of section 330 relating to credit transactions,

(d)   agreements to enter into credit transactions.

25.   In relation to a company's accounts for a financial year, compliance with this Part is not required by virtue of paragraph 15(c) or 16(c) in the case of any transaction or arrangement with a company or any of its subsidiaries in which a director of the company or its holding company had, directly or indirectly, a material interest if—

(a)   the value of each transaction or arrangement within paragraph 15(c) or 16(c) (as the case may be) in which that director had (directly or indirectly) a material interest and which was made after the commencement of the financial year with the company or any of its subsidiaries, and

(b)   the value of each such transaction or arrangement which was made before the commencement of the financial year less the amount (if any) by which the liabilities of the person for whom the transaction or arrangement was made have been reduced,

did not at any time during the financial year exceed in the aggregate £1,000 or, if more, did not exceed £5,000 or 1 per cent of the value of the net assets of the company preparing the accounts in question as at the end of the financial year, whichever is the less.

For this purpose a company's net assets are the aggregate of its assets, less the aggregate of its liabilities ("liabilities" to include any provisions for liabilities within paragraph 89 of Schedule 4 that is made in Companies Act accounts and any provision that is made in IAS accounts).

26.   Section 345 of this Act (power of Secretary of State to alter sums by statutory instrument subject to negative resolution in Parliament) applies as if the money sums specified in paragraph 24 or 25 above were specified in Part X.

Interpretation

27.—   (1) The following provisions of this Act apply for purposes of this Part of this Schedule—

(a)   section 331(2), ... and (7), as regards the meaning of "guarantee", ... and "credit transaction";

(b)   section 331(9), as to the interpretation of references to a transaction or arrangement being made "for" a person;

(c)   section 340, in assigning values to transactions and arrangements; and

(d)   section 346, as to the interpretation of references to a person being "connected with" a director of a company.

(2)   In this Part of this Schedule "director" includes a shadow director.

PART III
OTHER TRANSACTIONS, ARRANGEMENTS AND AGREEMENTS

28.   This Part of this Schedule applies in relation to the following classes of transactions, arrangements and agreements—

(a)   loans, guarantees and securities relating to loans, arrangements of a kind described in subsection (6) or (7) of section 330 of this Act relating to loans and agreements to enter into any of the foregoing transactions and arrangements;

(b)   quasi-loans, guarantees and securities relating to quasi-loans arrangements of a kind described in either of those subsections relating to quasi-loans and agreements to enter into any of the foregoing transactions and arrangements;

(c)   credit transactions, guarantees and securities relating to credit transactions, arrangements of a kind described in either of those subsections relating to credit transactions and agreements to enter into any of the foregoing transactions and arrangements.

29.—   (1)   To comply with this Part of this Schedule, the accounts must contain a statement, in relation to transactions, arrangements and agreements made by the company or a subsidiary of it for persons who at any time during the financial year were officers of the company (but not directors or shadow directors), of—

(a)   the aggregate amounts outstanding at the end of the financial year under transactions, arrangements and agreements within sub-paragraphs (a), (b) and (c) respectively of paragraph 28 above, and

(b)   the numbers of officers for whom the transactions, arrangements and agreements falling within each of those sub-paragraphs were made.

(2)   This paragraph does not apply to transactions, arrangements and agreements made by the company or any of its subsidiaries for an officer of the company if the aggregate amount outstanding at the end of the financial year under the transactions, arrangements and agreements so made for that officer does not exceed £2,500.

(3)   Section 345 of this Act (power of Secretary of State to alter money sums by statutory instrument subject to negative resolution in Parliament) applies as if the money sum specified above in this paragraph were specified in Part X.

30.   The following provisions of this Act apply for purposes of this Part—

    (a)   section 331(2), (3), ... and (7), as regards the meaning of "guarantee", "quasi-loan", ... and "credit transaction", and

    (b)   section 331(9), as to the interpretation of references to a transaction or arrangement being made "for" a person;

and "amount outstanding" means the amount of the outstanding liabilities of the person for whom the transaction, arrangement or agreement was made or, in the case of a guarantee or security, the amount guaranteed or secured.

SCHEDULE 7

MATTERS TO BE DEALT WITH IN DIRECTORS' REPORT

Section 234

PART I
MATTERS OF A GENERAL NATURE

Asset values

1.—   (1)   ...

    (2)   If, in the case of such of the fixed assets of the company or of any of its subsidiary undertakings as consist in interests in land, their market value (as at the end of the financial year) differs substantially from the amount at which they are included in the balance sheet, and the difference is, in the directors' opinion, of such significance as to require that the attention of members of the company or of holders of its debentures should be drawn to it, the report shall indicate the difference with such degree of precision as is practicable.

Directors' interests

2.—   (1)   The information required by paragraphs 2A and 2B shall be given in the directors' report, or by way of notes to the company's annual accounts, with respect to each person who at the end of the financial year was a director of the company.

    (2)   In those paragraphs—

        (a)   "the register" means the register of directors' interests kept by the company under section 325; and

        (b)   references to a body corporate being in the same group as the company are to its being a subsidiary or holding company, or another subsidiary of a holding company, of the company.

2A.—   (1)   It shall be stated with respect to each director whether, according to the register, he was at the end of the financial year interested in shares in or debentures of the company or any other body corporate in the same group.

    (2)   If he was so interested, there shall be stated the number of shares in and amount of debentures of each body (specifying it) in which, according to the register, he was then interested.

    (3)   If a director was interested at the end of the financial year in shares in or debentures of the company or any other body corporate in the same group—

        (a)   it shall also be stated whether, according to the register, he was at the beginning of the financial year (or, if he was not then a director, when he became one) interested in shares in or debentures of the company or any other body corporate in the same group, and

(b) if he was so interested, there shall be stated the number of shares in and amount of debentures of each body (specifying it) in which, according to the register, he was then interested.

(4) In this paragraph references to an interest in shares or debentures have the same meaning as in section 324; and references to the interest of a director include any interest falling to be treated as his for the purposes of that section.

(5) The reference above to the time when a person became a director is, in the case of a person who became a director on more than one occasion, to the time when he first became a director.

2B.— (1) It shall be stated with respect to each director whether, according to the register, any right to subscribe for shares in or debentures of the company or another body corporate in the same group was during the financial year granted to, or exercised by, the director or a member of his immediate family.

(2) If any such right was granted to, or exercised by, any such person during the financial year, there shall be stated the number of shares in and amount of debentures of each body (specifying it) in respect of which, according to the register, the right was granted or exercised.

(3) A director's "immediate family" means his or her spouse *or civil partner* and infant children; and for this purpose "children" includes step-children, and "infant", in relation to Scotland, means pupil or minor.

(4) The reference above to a member of the director's immediate family does not include a person who is himself or herself a director of the company.

Political donations and expenditure

3.— (1) If—

(a) the company (not being the wholly-owned subsidiary of a company incorporated in Great Britain) has in the financial year—

(i) made any donation to any registered party or to any other EU political organisation, or

(ii) incurred any EU political expenditure, and

(b) the amount of the donation or expenditure, or (as the case may be) the aggregate amount of all donations and expenditure falling within paragraph (a), exceeded £200,

the directors' report for the year shall contain the particulars specified in sub-paragraph (2).

(2) Those particulars are—

(a) as respects donations falling within sub-paragraph (1)(a)(i)—

(i) the name of each registered party or other organisation to whom any such donation has been made, and

(ii) the total amount given to that party or organisation by way of such donations in the financial year; and

(b) as respects expenditure falling within sub-paragraph (1)(a)(ii), the total amount incurred by way of such expenditure in the financial year.

(3) If—

(a) at the end of the financial year the company has subsidiaries which have, in that year, made any donations or incurred any such expenditure as is mentioned in sub-paragraph (1)(a), and

(b) it is not itself the wholly-owned subsidiary of a company incorporated in Great Britain,

the directors' report for the year is not, by virtue of sub-paragraph (1), required to contain the particulars specified in sub-paragraph (2); but, if the total amount of any such donations or expenditure (or both) made or incurred in that year by the company and the subsidiaries between them exceeds £200, the directors' report for the year shall contain those particulars in relation to each body by whom any such donation or expenditure has been made or incurred.

(4)   Any expression used in this paragraph which is also used in Part XA of this Act has the same meaning as in that Part.

4.—   (1)   If the company (not being the wholly-owned subsidiary of a company incorporated in Great Britain) has in the financial year made any contribution to a non-EU political party, the directors' report for the year shall contain—

    (a)   a statement of the amount of the contribution, or

    (b)   (if it has made two or more such contributions in the year) a statement of the total amount of the contributions.

(2)   If—

    (a)   at the end of the financial year the company has subsidiaries which have, in that year, made any such contributions as are mentioned in sub-paragraph (1), and

    (b)   it is not itself the wholly-owned subsidiary of a company incorporated in Great Britain,

the directors' report for the year is not, by virtue of sub-paragraph (1), required to contain any such statement as is there mentioned, but it shall instead contain a statement of the total amount of the contributions made in the year by the company and the subsidiaries between them.

(3)   In this paragraph "contribution", in relation to an organisation, means—

    (a)   any gift of money to the organisation (whether made directly or indirectly);

    (b)   any subscription or other fee paid for affiliation to, or membership of, the organisation; or

    (c)   any money spent (otherwise than by the organisation or a person acting on its behalf) in paying any expenses incurred directly or indirectly by the organisation.

(4)   In this paragraph "non-EU political party" means any political party which carries on, or proposes to carry on, its activities wholly outside the member States.

Charitable donations

5.—   (1)   If—

    (a)   the company (not being the wholly-owned subsidiary of a company incorporated in Great Britain) has in the financial year given money for charitable purposes, and

    (b)   the money given exceeded £200 in amount,

the directors' report for the year shall contain, in the case of each of the purposes for which money has been given, a statement of the amount of money given for that purpose.

(2)   If—

    (a)   at the end of the financial year the company has subsidiaries which have, in that year, given money for charitable purposes, and

    (b)   it is not itself the wholly-owned subsidiary of a company incorporated in Great Britain,

sub-paragraph (1) does not apply to the company; but, if the amount given in that year for charitable purposes by the company and the subsidiaries between them exceeds £200, the directors' report for the year shall contain, in the case of each of the purposes for which money has been given by the company and the subsidiaries between them, a statement of the amount of money given for that purpose.

(3)   Money given for charitable purposes to a person who, when it was given, was ordinarily resident outside the United Kingdom is to be left out of account for the purposes of this paragraph.

(4)   For the purposes of this paragraph "charitable purposes" means purposes which are exclusively charitable, and as respects Scotland "charitable" is to be construed as if it were contained in the Income Tax Acts.

5A.   ...

Financial instruments

5A.— (1) In relation to the use of financial instruments by a company and by its subsidiary undertakings, the directors' report must contain an indication of—

    (a) the financial risk management objectives and policies of the company and its subsidiary undertakings included in the consolidation, including the policy for hedging each major type of forecasted transaction for which hedge accounting is used, and

    (b) the exposure of the company and its subsidiary undertakings included in the consolidation to price risk, credit risk, liquidity risk and cash flow risk,

    unless such information is not material for the assessment of the assets, liabilities, financial position and profit or loss of the company and its subsidiary undertakings included in the consolidation.

(2) In sub-paragraph (1) the expressions "hedge accounting", "price risk", "credit risk", "liquidity risk" and "cash flow risk" have the same meaning as they have in Council Directive 78/660/EEC on the annual accounts of certain types of companies, and in Council Directive 83/349/EEC on consolidated accounts, as amended.

Miscellaneous

6. The directors' report shall contain—

    (a) particulars of any important events affecting the company or any of its subsidiary undertakings which have occurred since the end of the financial year,

    (b) an indication of likely future developments in the business of the company and of its subsidiary undertakings, ...

    (c) an indication of the activities (if any) of the company and its subsidiary undertakings in the field of research and development, and

    (d) (unless the company is an unlimited company) an indication of the existence of branches (as defined in section 698(2)) of the company outside the United Kingdom.

PART II
DISCLOSURE REQUIRED BY COMPANY ACQUIRING ITS OWN SHARES, ETC

7. This Part of this Schedule applies where shares in a company—

    (a) are purchased by the company or are acquired by it by forfeiture or surrender in lieu of forfeiture, or in pursuance of section 143(3) of this Act (acquisition of own shares by company limited by shares), or

    (b) are acquired by another person in circumstances where paragraph (c) or (d) of section 146(1) applies (acquisition by company's nominee, or by another with company financial assistance, the company having a beneficial interest), or

    (c) are made subject to a lien or other charge taken (whether expressly or otherwise) by the company and permitted by section 150(2) or (4), or section 6(3) of the Consequential Provisions Act (exceptions from general rule against a company having a lien or charge on its own shares).

8. The directors' report with respect to a financial year shall state—

    (a) the number and nominal value of the shares so purchased, the aggregate amount of the consideration paid by the company for such shares and the reasons for their purchase;

    (b) the number and nominal value of the shares so acquired by the company, acquired by another person in such circumstances and so charged respectively during the financial year;

    (c) the maximum number and nominal value of shares which, having been so acquired by the company, acquired by another person in such circumstances or so charged (whether or not during that year) are held at any time by the company or that other person during that year;

    (d) the number and nominal value of the shares so acquired by the company, acquired by another person in such circumstances or so charged (whether or not during that year) which are disposed of by the company or that other person or cancelled by the company during that year;

    (e)   where the number and nominal value of the shares of any particular description are stated in pursuance of any of the preceding sub-paragraphs, the percentage of the called-up share capital which shares of that description represent;

    (f)   where any of the shares have been so charged the amount of the charge in each case; and

    (g)   where any of the shares have been disposed of by the company or the person who acquired them in such circumstances for money or money's worth the amount or value of the consideration in each case.

PART III
DISCLOSURE CONCERNING EMPLOYMENT, ETC, OF DISABLED PERSONS

9.—   (1)   This Part of this Schedule applies to the directors' report where the average number of persons employed by the company in each week during the financial year exceeded 250.

     (2)   That average number is the quotient derived by dividing, by the number of weeks in the financial year, the number derived by ascertaining, in relation to each of those weeks, the number of persons who, under contracts of service, were employed in the week (whether throughout it or not) by the company, and adding up the numbers ascertained.

     (3)   The directors' report shall in that case contain a statement describing such policy as the company has applied during the financial year—

        (a)   for giving full and fair consideration to applications for employment by the company made by disabled persons, having regard to their particular aptitudes and abilities,

        (b)   for continuing the employment of, and for arranging appropriate training for, employees of the company who have become disabled persons during the period when they were employed by the company, and

        (c)   otherwise for the training, career development and promotion of disabled persons employed by the company.

     (4)   In this Part—

        (a)   "employment" means employment other than employment to work wholly or mainly outside the United Kingdom, and "employed" and "employee" shall be construed accordingly; and

        (b)   "disabled person" means the same as in the Disability Discrimination Act 1995.

PART IV

...

PART V
EMPLOYEE INVOLVEMENT

11.—   (1)   This Part of this Schedule applies to the directors' report where the average number of persons employed by the company in each week during the financial year exceeded 250.

     (2)   That average number is the quotient derived by dividing by the number of weeks in the financial year the number derived by ascertaining, in relation to each of those weeks, the number of persons who, under contracts of service, were employed in the week (whether throughout it or not) by the company, and adding up the numbers ascertained.

     (3)   The directors' report shall in that case contain a statement describing the action that has been taken during the financial year to introduce, maintain or develop arrangements aimed at—

        (a)   providing employees systematically with information on matters of concern to them as employees,

     (b)   consulting employees or their representatives on a regular basis so that the views of employees can be taken into account in making decisions which are likely to affect their interests,

     (c)   encouraging the involvement of employees in the company's performance through an employees' share scheme or by some other means,

     (d)   achieving a common awareness on the part of all employees of the financial and economic factors affecting the performance of the company.

  (4)   In sub-paragraph (3) "employee" does not include a person employed to work wholly or mainly outside the United Kingdom; and for the purposes of sub-paragraph (2) no regard is to be had to such a person.

PART VI
POLICY AND PRACTICE ON PAYMENT OF CREDITORS

12.— (1)   This Part of this Schedule applies to the directors' report for a financial year if—

     (a)   the company was at any time within the year a public company, or

     (b)   the company did not quality as small or medium-sized in relation to the year by virtue of section 247 and was at any time within the year a member of a group of which the parent company was a public company.

  (2)   The report shall state, with respect to the next following financial year—

     (a)   whether in respect of some or all of its suppliers it is the company's policy to follow any code or standard on payment practice and, if so, the name of the code or standard and the place where information about, and copies of, the code or standard can be obtained,

     (b)   whether in respect of some or all of its suppliers it is the company's policy—

        (i)   to settle the terms of payment with those suppliers when agreeing the terms of each transaction,

        (ii)   to ensure that those suppliers are made aware of the terms of payment, and

        (iii) to abide by the terms of payment,

     (c)   where the company's policy is not as mentioned in paragraph (a) or (b) in respect of some or all of its suppliers, what its policy is with respect to the payment of those suppliers;

and if the company's policy is different for different suppliers or classes of suppliers, the report shall identify the suppliers to which the different policies apply.

In this sub-paragraph references to the company's suppliers are references to persons who are or may become its suppliers.

  (3)   The report shall also state the number of days which bears to the number of days in the financial year the same proportion as X bears to Y where—

$X =$ the aggregate of the amounts which were owed to trade creditors at the end of the year; and

$Y =$ the aggregate of the amounts in which the company was invoiced by suppliers during the year.

  (4)   For the purposes of sub-paragraphs (2) and (3) a person is a supplier of the company at any time if—

     (a)   at that time, he is owed an amount in respect of goods or services supplied, and

     (b)   that amount would be included under the heading corresponding to item E.4 (trade creditors) in Format 1 if—

        (i)   the company's accounts fell to be prepared as at that time,

        (ii)   those accounts were prepared in accordance with Schedule 4, and

        (iii) that Format were adopted.

  (5)   For the purpose of sub-paragraph (3), the aggregate of the amounts which at the end of the financial year were owed to trade creditors shall be taken to be—

    (a)   where in the company's accounts Format 1 of the balance sheet formats set out in Part
          I of Schedule 4 is adopted, the amount shown under the heading corresponding to item
          E.4 (trade creditors) in that Format,
    (b)   where Format 2 is adopted, the amount which, under the heading corresponding to
          item C.4 (trade creditors) in that Format, is shown as falling due within one year, and
    (c)   where the company's accounts are prepared in accordance with Schedule 9 or 9A or
          the company's accounts are IAS accounts, the amount which would be shown under
          the heading corresponding to item E.4 (trade creditors) in Format 1 if the company's
          accounts were prepared in accordance with Schedule 4 and that Format were adopted.

Note. The italicized words in paragraph 2B(3) are inserted by the Civil Partnership Act 2004, s. 261(1), Sch.
27, para. 105, as from a day to be appointed.

SCHEDULE 7A

DIRECTORS' REMUNERATION REPORT

Section 234B

PART 1
INTRODUCTORY

1.—   (1)   In the directors' remuneration report for a financial year ("the relevant financial year") there
         shall be shown the information specified in Parts 2 and 3 below.
    (2)   Information required to be shown in the report for or in respect of a particular person shall
         be shown in the report in a manner that links the information to that person identified by
         name.

PART 2
INFORMATION NOT SUBJECT TO AUDIT

*Consideration by the directors of matters
relating to directors' remuneration*

2.—   (1)   If a committee of the company's directors has considered matters relating to the directors'
         remuneration for the relevant financial year, the directors' remuneration report shall—
    (a)   name each director who was a member of the committee at any time when the commit-
         tee was considering any such matter;
    (b)   name any person who provided to the committee advice, or services, that materially
         assisted the committee in their consideration of any such matter;
    (c)   in the case of any person named under paragraph (b), who is not a director of the com-
         pany, state—
        (i)   the nature of any other services that that person has provided to the company
           during the relevant financial year; and
        (ii)   whether that person was appointed by the committee.
    (2)   In sub-paragraph (1)(b) "person" includes (in particular) any director of the company who
         does not fall within sub-paragraph (1)(a).

Statement of company's policy on directors' remuneration

3.—   (1)   The directors' remuneration report shall contain a statement of the company's policy on
         directors' remuneration for the following financial year and for financial years subsequent
         to that.
    (2)   The policy statement shall include—
    (a)   for each director, a detailed summary of any performance conditions to which any
         entitlement of the director—

> > (i)   to share options, or
> >
> > (ii)   under a long-term incentive scheme,
>
> is subject;
>
> (b)   an explanation as to why any such performance conditions were chosen;
>
> (c)   a summary of the methods to be used in assessing whether any such performance conditions are met and an explanation as to why those methods were chosen;
>
> (d)   if any such performance condition involves any comparison with factors external to the company—
>
> > (i)   a summary of the factors to be used in making each such comparison, and
> >
> > (ii)   if any of the factors relates to the performance of another company, of two or more other companies or of an index on which the securities of a company or companies are listed, the identity of that company, of each of those companies or of the index;
>
> (e)   a description of, and an explanation for, any significant amendment proposed to be made to the terms and conditions of any entitlement of a director to share options or under a long term incentive scheme; and
>
> (f)   if any entitlement of a director to share options, or under a long-term incentive scheme, is not subject to performance conditions, an explanation as to why that is the case.

(3)   The policy statement shall, in respect of each director's terms and conditions relating to remuneration, explain the relative importance of those elements which are, and those which are not, related to performance.

(4)   The policy statement shall summarise, and explain, the company's policy on—

> (a)   the duration of contracts with directors, and
>
> (b)   notice periods, and termination payments, under such contracts.

(5)   In sub-paragraphs (2) and (3), references to a director are to any person who serves as a director of the company at any time in the period beginning with the end of the relevant financial year and ending with date on which the directors' remuneration report is laid before the company in general meeting.

Performance graph

4.— (1)   The directors' remuneration report shall—

> (a)   contain a line graph that shows for each of—
>
> > (i)   a holding of shares of that class of the company's equity share capital whose listing, or admission to dealing, has resulted in the company falling within the definition of "quoted company", and
> >
> > (ii)   a hypothetical holding of shares made up of shares of the same kinds and number as those by reference to which a broad equity market index is calculated,
> >
> > a line drawn by joining up points plotted to represent, for each of the financial years in the relevant period, the total shareholder return on that holding; and
>
> (b)   state the name of the index selected for the purposes of the graph and set out the reasons for selecting that index.

(2)   For the purposes of sub-paragraphs (1) and (4), "relevant period" means the five financial years of which the last is the relevant financial year.

(3)   Where the relevant financial year

> (a)   is the company's second, third or fourth financial year, sub-paragraph (2) has effect with the substitution of "two", "three" or "four" (as the case may be) for "five"; and
>
> (b)   is the company's first financial year, "relevant period", for the purposes of sub-paragraphs (1) and (4), means the relevant financial year.

(4)   For the purposes of sub-paragraph (1), the "total shareholder return" for a relevant period on a holding of shares must be calculated using a fair method that—

> (a)   takes as its starting point the percentage change over the period in the market price of the holding;

(b)   involves making—
    (i)   the assumptions specified in sub-paragraph (5) as to reinvestment of income, and
    (ii) the assumption specified in sub-paragraph (7) as to the funding of liabilities; and
(c)   makes provision for any replacement of shares in the holding by shares of a different description;
and the same method must be used for each of the holdings mentioned in sub-paragraph (1).

(5)   The assumptions as to reinvestment of income are—
    (a)   that any benefit in the form of shares of the same kind as those in the holding is added to the holding at the time the benefit becomes receivable; and
    (b)   that any benefit in cash, and an amount equal to the value of any benefit not in cash and not falling within paragraph (a), is applied at the time the benefit becomes receivable in the purchase at their market price of shares of the same kind as those in the holding and that the shares purchased are added to the holding at that time.

(6)   In sub-paragraph (5) "benefit" means any benefit (including, in particular, any dividend) receivable in respect of any shares in the holding by the holder from the company of whose share capital the shares form part.

(7)   The assumption as to the funding of liabilities is that, where the holder has a liability to the company of whose capital the shares in the holding form part, shares are sold from the holding—
    (a)   immediately before the time by which the liability is due to be satisfied, and
    (b)   in such numbers that, at the time of the sale, the market price of the shares sold equals the amount of the liability in respect of the shares in the holding that are not being sold.

(8)   In sub-paragraph (7) "liability" means a liability arising in respect of any shares in the holding or from the exercise of a right attached to any of those shares.

Service contracts

5.— (1)   The directors' remuneration report shall contain, in respect of the contract of service or contract for services of each person who has served as a director of the company at any time during the relevant financial year, the following information:
    (a)   the date of the contract, the unexpired term and the details of any notice periods;
    (b)   any provision for compensation payable upon early termination of the contract; and
    (c)   such details of other provisions in the contract as are necessary to enable members of the company to estimate the liability of the company in the event of early termination of the contract.

(2)   The directors' remuneration report shall contain an explanation for any significant award made to a person in the circumstances described in paragraph 14.

PART 3

INFORMATION SUBJECT TO AUDIT

Amount of each director's emoluments and compensation in the relevant financial year

6.— (1)   The directors' remuneration report shall for the relevant financial year show, for each person who has served as a director of the company at any time during that year, each of the following—
    (a)   the total amount of salary and fees paid to or receivable by the person in respect of qualifying services;
    (b)   the total amount of bonuses so paid or receivable;
    (c)   the total amount of sums paid by way of expenses allowance that are—
        (i)   chargeable to United Kingdom income tax (or would be if the person were an individual); and
        (ii) paid to or receivable by the person in respect of qualifying services;

(d)   the total amount of—
  (i)   any compensation for loss of office paid to or receivable by the person, and
  (ii)   any other payments paid to or receivable by the person in connection with the termination of qualifying services;

(e)   the total estimated value of any benefits received by the person otherwise than in cash that—
  (i)   do not fall within any of sub-paragraphs (a)—(d) or paragraphs 7–11 below,
  (ii)   are emoluments of the person, and
  (iii)   are received by the person in respect of qualifying services; and

(f)   the amount that is the total of the sums mentioned in paragraphs (a) to (e).

(2)   The directors' remuneration report shall show, for each person who has served as a director of the company at any time during the relevant financial year, the amount that for the financial year preceding the relevant financial year is the total of the sums mentioned in paragraphs (a) to (e) of sub-paragraph (1).

(3)   The directors' remuneration report shall also state the nature of any element of a remuneration package which is not cash.

(4)   The information required by sub-paragraphs (1) and (2) shall be presented in tabular form.

Share options

7.—   (1)   The directors' remuneration report shall contain, in respect of each person who has served as a director of the company at any time in the relevant financial year, the information specified in paragraph 8.

(2)   Sub-paragraph (1) is subject to paragraph 9 (aggregation of information to avoid excessively lengthy reports).

(3)   The information specified in paragraphs (a) to (c) of paragraph 8 shall be presented in tabular form in the report.

(4)   In paragraph 8 "share option", in relation to a person, means a share option granted in respect of qualifying services of the person.

8.   The information required by sub-paragraph (1) of paragraph 7 in respect of such a person as is mentioned in that sub-paragraph is—

(a)   the number of shares that are subject to a share option—
  (i)   at the beginning of the relevant financial year or, if later, on the date of the appointment of the person as a director of the company, and
  (ii)   at the end of the relevant financial year or, if earlier, on the cessation of the person's appointment as a director of the company,
  in each case differentiating between share options having different terms and conditions;

(b)   information identifying those share options that have been awarded in the relevant financial year, those that have been exercised in that year, those that in that year have expired unexercised and those whose terms and conditions have been varied in that year;

(c)   for each share option that is unexpired at any time in the relevant financial year—
  (i)   the price paid, if any, for its award,
  (ii)   the exercise price,
  (iii)   the date from which the option may be exercised, and
  (iv)   the date on which the option expires;

(d)   a description of any variation made in the relevant financial year in the terms and conditions of a share option;

(e)   a summary of any performance criteria upon which the award or exercise of a share option is conditional, including a description of any variation made in such performance criteria during the relevant financial year;

(f)   for each share option that has been exercised during the relevant financial year, the market price of the shares, in relation to which it is exercised, at the time of exercise; and

(g)   for each share option that is unexpired at the end of the relevant financial year—
  (i)   the market price at the end of that year, and

      (ii)   the highest and lowest market prices during that year,
of each share that is subject to the option.

9.—   (1)   If, in the opinion of the directors of the company, disclosure in accordance with paragraphs 7 and 8 would result in a disclosure of excessive length then, (subject to sub-paragraphs (2) and (3))—

      (a)   information disclosed for a person under paragraph 8(a) need not differentiate between share options having different terms and conditions;

      (b)   for the purposes of disclosure in respect of a person under paragraph 8(c)(i) and (ii) and (g), share options may be aggregated and (instead of disclosing prices for each share option) disclosure may be made of weighted average prices of aggregations of share options;

      (c)   for the purposes of disclosure in respect of a person under paragraph 8(c)(iii) and (iv), share options may be aggregated and (instead of disclosing dates for each share option) disclosure may be made of ranges of dates for aggregation of share options.

    (2)   Sub-paragraph (1)(b) and (c) does not permit the aggregation of—

      (a)   share options in respect of shares whose market price at the end of the relevant financial year is below the option exercise price, with

      (b)   share options in respect of shares whose market price at the end of the relevant financial year is equal to, or exceeds, the option exercise price.

    (3)   Subparagraph (1) does not apply (and accordingly, full disclosure must be made in accordance with paragraphs 7 and 8) in respect of share options that during the relevant financial year have been awarded or exercised or had their terms and conditions varied.

Long term incentive schemes

10.— (1)   The directors' remuneration report shall contain, in respect of each person who has served as a director of the company at any time in the relevant financial year, the information specified in paragraph 11.

    (2)   Sub-paragraph (1) does not require the report to contain share option details that are contained in the report in compliance with paragraphs 7 to 9.

    (3)   The information specified in paragraph 11 shall be presented in tabular form in the report.

    (4)   For the purposes of paragraph 11—

      (a)   "scheme interest", in relation to a person, means an interest under a long term incentive scheme that is an interest in respect of which assets may become receivable under the scheme in respect of qualifying services of the person; and

      (b)   such an interest "vests" at the earliest time when—

         (i)   it has been ascertained that the qualifying conditions have been fulfilled, and

        (ii)   the nature and quantity of the assets receivable under the scheme in respect of the interest have been ascertained.

    (5)   In this Schedule "long term incentive scheme" means any agreement or arrangement under which money or other assets may become receivable by a person and which includes one or more qualifying conditions with respect to service or performance that cannot be fulfilled within a single financial year, and for this purpose the following shall be disregarded, namely—

      (a)   any bonus the amount of which falls to be determined by reference to service or performance within a single financial year;

      (b)   compensation in respect of loss of office, payments for breach of contract and other termination payments; and

      (c)   retirement benefits.

11.— (1)   The information required by sub-paragraph (1) of paragraph 10 in respect of such a person as is mentioned in that sub-paragraph is—

      (a)   details of the scheme interests that the person has at the beginning of the relevant financial year or if later on the date of the appointment of the person as a director of the company;

    (b)   details of the scheme interests awarded to the person during the relevant financial year;

    (c)   details of the scheme interests that the person has at the end of the relevant financial year or if earlier on the cessation of the person's appointment as a director of the company;

    (d)   for each scheme interest within paragraphs (a) to (c)—

        (i)   the end of the period over which the qualifying conditions for that interest have to be fulfilled (or if there are different periods for different conditions, the end of whichever of those periods ends last); and

        (ii)   a description of any variation made in the terms and conditions of the scheme interests during the relevant financial year; and

    (e)   for each scheme interest that has vested in the relevant financial year—

        (i)   the relevant details (see sub-paragraph (3)) of any shares,

        (ii)   the amount of any money, and

        (iii) the value of any other assets,

        that have become receivable in respect of the interest.

(2)   The details that sub-paragraph (1)(b) requires of a scheme interest awarded during the relevant financial year include, if shares may become receivable in respect of the interest, the following—

    (a)   the number of those shares;

    (b)   the market price of each of those shares when the scheme interest was awarded; and

    (c)   details of qualifying conditions that are conditions with respect to performance.

(3)   In sub-paragraph (1)(e)(i) "the relevant details", in relation to any shares that have become receivable in respect of a scheme interest, means—

    (a)   the number of those shares;

    (b)   the date on which the scheme interest was awarded;

    (c)   the market price of each of those shares when the scheme interest was awarded;

    (d)   the market price of each of those shares when the scheme interest vested; and

    (e)   details of qualifying conditions that were conditions with respect to performance.

Pensions

12.— (1)   The directors' remuneration report shall, for each person who has served as a director of the company at any time during the relevant financial year, contain the information in respect of pensions that is specified in sub-paragraphs (2) and (3).

     (2)   Where the person has rights under a pension scheme that is a defined benefit scheme in relation to the person and any of those rights are rights to which he has become entitled in respect of qualifying services of his—

    (a)   details—

        (i)   of any changes during the relevant financial year in the person's accrued benefits under the scheme, and

        (ii)   of the person's accrued benefits under the scheme as at the end of that year;

    (b)   the transfer value, calculated in a manner consistent with "Retirement Benefit Schemes—Transfer Values (GN 11)" published by the Institute of Actuaries and the Faculty of Actuaries and dated 6th April 2001, of the person's accrued benefits under the scheme at the end of the relevant financial year;

    (c)   the transfer value of the person's accrued benefits under the scheme that in compliance with paragraph (b) was contained in the director's remuneration report for the previous financial year or, if there was no such report or no such value was contained in that report, the transfer value, calculated in such a manner as is mentioned in paragraph (b), of the person's accrued benefits under the scheme at the beginning of the relevant financial year;

    (d)   the amount obtained by subtracting—

        (i)   the transfer value of the person's accrued benefits under the scheme that is required to be contained in the report by paragraph (c), from

    (ii)   the transfer value of those benefits that is required to be contained in the report by paragraph (b),

and then subtracting from the result of that calculation the amount of any contributions made to the scheme by the person in the relevant financial year.

    (3)   Where—

        (a)   the person has rights under a pension scheme that is a money purchase scheme in relation to the person, and

        (b)   any of those rights are rights to which he has become entitled in respect of qualifying services of his,

details of any contribution to the scheme in respect of the person that is paid or payable by the company for the relevant financial year or paid by the company in that year for another financial year.

Excess retirement benefits of directors and past directors

13.—   (1)   Subject to sub-paragraph (3), the directors' remuneration report shall show in respect of each person who has served as a director of the company—

        (a)   at any time during the relevant financial year, or

        (b)   at any time before the beginning of that year,

the amount of so much of retirement benefits paid to or receivable by the person under pension schemes as is in excess of the retirement benefits to which he was entitled on the date on which the benefits first became payable or 31st March 1997, whichever is the later.

    (2)   In subsection (1) "retirement benefits" means retirement benefits to which the person became entitled in respect of qualifying services of his.

    (3)   Amounts paid or receivable under a pension scheme need not be included in an amount required to be shown under sub-paragraph (1) if—

        (a)   the funding of the scheme was such that the amounts were or, as the case may be, could have been paid without recourse to additional contributions; and

        (b)   amounts were paid to or receivable by all pensioner members of the scheme on the same basis;

and in this sub-paragraph "pensioner member", in relation to a pension scheme, means any person who is entitled to the present payment of retirement benefits under the scheme.

    (4)   In this paragraph—

        (a)   references to retirement benefits include benefits otherwise than in cash; and

        (b)   in relation to so much of retirement benefits as consists of a benefit otherwise than in cash, references to their amount are to the estimated money value of the benefit;

and the nature of any such benefit shall also be shown in the report.

Compensation for past directors

14.   The directors' remuneration report shall contain details of any significant award made in the relevant financial year to any person who was not a director of the company at the time the award was made but had previously been a director of the company, including (in particular) compensation in respect of loss of office and pensions but excluding any sums which have already been shown in the report under paragraph 6(1)(d).

Sums paid to third parties in respect of a director's services

15.—   (1)   The directors' remuneration report shall show, in respect of each person who served as a director of the company at any time during the relevant financial year, the aggregate amount of any consideration paid to or receivable by third parties for making available the services of the person—

        (a)   as a director of the company, or

        (b)   while director of the company—

            (i)   as director of any of its subsidiary undertakings, or

   (ii) as director of any other undertaking of which he was (while director of the company) a director by virtue of the company's nomination (direct or indirect), or

   (iii) otherwise in connection with the management of the affairs of the company or any such other undertaking.

 (2) The reference to consideration includes benefits otherwise than in cash; and in relation to such consideration the reference to its amount is to the estimated money value of the benefit.

The nature of any such consideration shall be shown in the report.

 (3) The reference to third parties is to persons other than—

  (a) the person himself or a person connected with him or a body corporate controlled by him, and

  (b) the company or any such other undertaking as is mentioned in sub-paragraph (1)(b)(ii).

PART 4
INTERPRETATION AND SUPPLEMENTARY

16.— (1) In this Schedule—

"amount", in relation to a gain made on the exercise of a share option, means the difference between—

  (a) the market price of the shares on the day on which the option was exercised; and

  (b) the price actually paid for the shares;

"company contributions", in relation to a pension scheme and a person, means any payments (including insurance premiums) made, or treated as made, to the scheme in respect of the person by anyone other than the person;

"defined benefit scheme", in relation to a person, means a pension scheme which is not a money purchase scheme in relation to the person;

"emoluments" of a person—

  (a) includes salary, fees and bonuses, sums paid by way of expenses allowance (so far as they are chargeable to United Kingdom income tax or would be if the person were an individual) but,

  (b) does not include any of the following, namely—

   (i) the value of any share options granted to him or the amount of any gains made on the exercise of any such options;

   (ii) any company contributions paid, or treated as paid, in respect of him under any pension scheme or any benefits to which he is entitled under any such scheme; or

   (iii) any money or other assets paid to or received or receivable by him under any long term incentive scheme;

"long term incentive scheme" has the meaning given by paragraph 10(5);

"money purchase benefits", in relation to a person, means retirement benefits the rate or amount of which is calculated by reference to payments made, or treated as made, by the person or by any other person in respect of that person and which are not average salary benefits;

"money purchase scheme", in relation to a person, means a pension scheme under which all of the benefits that may become payable to or in respect of the person are money purchase benefits in relation to the person;

"pension scheme" means a retirement benefits scheme within the meaning given by section 611 of the Income and Corporation Taxes Act 1988;

"qualifying services", in relation to any person, means his services as a director of the company, and his services at any time while he is a director of the company—

  (a) as a director of an undertaking that is a subsidiary undertaking of the company at that time;

(b)   as a director of any other undertaking of which he is a director by virtue of the company's nomination (direct or indirect); or

(c)   otherwise in connection with the management of the affairs of the company or any such subsidiary undertaking or any such other undertaking;

"retirement benefits" means relevant benefits within the meaning given by section 612(1) of the Income and Corporation Taxes Act 1988;

"shares" means shares (whether allotted or not) in the company, or any undertaking which is a group undertaking in relation to the company, and includes a share warrant as defined by section 188(1);

"share option" means a right to acquire shares;

"value" , in relation to shares received or receivable on any day by a person who is or has been a director of the company, means the market price of the shares on that day.

(2)   In this Schedule "compensation in respect of loss of office" includes compensation received or receivable by a person for—

(a)   loss of office as director of the company, or

(b)   loss, while director of the company or on or in connection with his ceasing to be a director of it, of—

(i)   any other office in connection with the management of the company's affairs, or

(ii)   any office as director or otherwise in connection with the management of the affairs of any undertaking that, immediately before the loss, is a subsidiary undertaking of the company or an undertaking of which he is a director by virtue of the company's nomination (direct or indirect);

(c)   compensation in consideration for, or in connection with, a person's retirement from office; and

(d)   where such a retirement is occasioned by a breach of the person's contract with the company or with an undertaking that, immediately before the breach, is a subsidiary undertaking of the company or an undertaking of which he is a director by virtue of the company' s nomination (direct or indirect)—

(i)   payments made by way of damages for the breach; or

(ii)   payments made by way of settlement or compromise of any claim in respect of the breach.

(3)   References in this Schedule to compensation include benefits otherwise than in cash; and in relation to such compensation references in this Schedule to its amount are to the estimated money value of the benefit.

(4)   References in this Schedule to a person being "connected" with a director, and to a director "controlling" a body corporate, shall be construed in accordance with section 346.

17.— (1)   For the purposes of this Schedule emoluments paid or receivable or share options granted in respect of a person's accepting office as a director shall be treated as emoluments paid or receivable or share options granted in respect of his services as a director.

(2)   Where a pension scheme provides for any benefits that may become payable to or in respect of a person to be whichever are the greater of—

(a)   such benefits determined by or under the scheme as are money purchase benefits in relation to the person; and

(b)   such retirement benefits determined by or under the scheme to be payable to or in respect of the person as are not money purchase benefits in relation to the person,

the company may assume for the purposes of this Schedule that those benefits will be money purchase benefits in relation to the person, or not, according to whichever appears more likely at the end of the relevant financial year.

(3)   In determining for the purposes of this Schedule whether a pension scheme is a money purchase scheme in relation to a person or a defined benefit scheme in relation to a person, any death in service benefits provided for by the scheme shall be disregarded.

18.— (1)   The following applies with respect to the amounts to be shown under this Schedule.

(2)   The amount in each case includes all relevant sums paid by or receivable from—

    (a)   the company; and

    (b)   the company's subsidiary undertakings; and

    (c)   any other person,

except sums to be accounted for to the company or any of its subsidiary undertakings or any other undertaking of which any person has been a director while director of the company, by virtue of sections 314 and 315 of this Act (duty of directors to make disclosure on company takeover; consequence of non-compliance), to past or present members of the company or any of its subsidiaries or any class of those members.

(3)   References to amounts paid to or receivable by a person include amounts paid to or receivable by a person connected with him or a body corporate controlled by him (but not so as to require an amount to be counted twice).

19.—   (1)   The amounts to be shown for any financial year under Part 3 of this Schedule are the sums receivable in respect of that year (whenever paid) or, in the case of sums not receivable in respect of a period, the sums paid during that year.

    (2)   But where—

    (a)   any sums are not shown in the directors' remuneration report for the relevant financial year on the ground that the person receiving them is liable to account for them as mentioned in paragraph 18(2), but the liability is thereafter wholly or partly released or is not enforced within a period of 2 years; or

    (b)   any sums paid by way of expenses allowance are charged to United Kingdom income tax after the end of the relevant financial year or, in the case of any such sums paid otherwise than to an individual, it does not become clear until the end of the relevant financial year that those sums would be charged to such tax were the person an individual,

those sums shall, to the extent to which the liability is released or not enforced or they are charged as mentioned above (as the case may be), be shown in the first directors' remuneration report in which it is practicable to show them and shall be distinguished from the amounts to be shown apart from this provision.

20.   Where it is necessary to do so for the purpose of making any distinction required by the preceding paragraphs in an amount to be shown in compliance with this Part of this Schedule, the directors may apportion any payments between the matters in respect of which these have been paid or are receivable in such manner as they think appropriate.

21.   This Schedule requires information to be given only so far as it is contained in the company's books and papers, available to members of the public or the company has the right to obtain it.

SCHEDULE 7B

Section 245G(3)

SPECIFIED PERSONS, DESCRIPTIONS OF DISCLOSURES ETC.
FOR THE PURPOSES OF SECTION 245G

PART 1
SPECIFIED PERSONS

1.   The Secretary of State.
2.   The Department of Enterprise, Trade and Investment for Northern Ireland.
3.   The Treasury.
4.   The Bank of England.
5.   The Financial Services Authority.
6.   The Commissioners of Inland Revenue.

PART 2
SPECIFIED DESCRIPTIONS OF DISCLOSURES

7.   A disclosure for the purpose of assisting a body designated by an order under section 46 of the Companies Act 1989 (delegation of functions of Secretary of State) to exercise its functions under Part 2 of that Act.

8.   A disclosure with a view to the institution of, or otherwise for the purposes of, disciplinary proceedings relating to the performance by an accountant or auditor of his professional duties.

9.   A disclosure for the purpose of enabling or assisting the Secretary of State or the Treasury to exercise any of their functions under any of the following—

   (a)   this Act;
   (b)   the insider dealing legislation;
   (c)   the Insolvency Act 1986;
   (d)   the Company Directors Disqualification Act 1986;
   (e)   the Financial Services and Markets Act 2000.

10.   A disclosure for the purpose of enabling or assisting the Department of Enterprise, Trade and Investment for Northern Ireland to exercise any powers conferred on it by the enactments relating to companies or insolvency.

11.   A disclosure for the purpose of enabling or assisting the Bank of England to exercise its functions.

12.   A disclosure for the purpose of enabling or assisting the Commissioners of Inland Revenue to exercise their functions.

13.   A disclosure for the purpose of enabling or assisting the Financial Services Authority to exercise its functions under any of the following—

   (a)   the legislation relating to friendly societies or to industrial and provident societies;
   (b)   the Building Societies Act 1986;
   (c)   Part 7 of the Companies Act 1989;
   (d)   the Financial Services and Markets Act 2000.

14.   A disclosure in pursuance of any Community obligation.

PART 3
OVERSEAS REGULATORY BODIES

15.   A disclosure is made in accordance with this Part of this Schedule if—

   (a)   it is made to a body within paragraph 16, and
   (b)   it is made for the purpose of enabling or assisting that body to exercise the functions mentioned in that paragraph.

16.   A body is within this paragraph if it exercises functions of a public nature under legislation in any country or territory outside the United Kingdom which appear to the authorised person to be similar to his functions under section 245B of this Act.

17.   In determining whether to disclose information to a body in accordance with this Part of this Schedule, the authorised person must have regard to the following considerations—

   (a)   whether the use which the body is likely to make of the information is sufficiently important to justify making the disclosure; and
   (b)   whether the body has adequate arrangements to prevent the information from being used or further disclosed other than for the purposes of carrying out the functions mentioned in paragraph 16 or any other purposes substantially similar to those for which information disclosed to the authorised person could be used or further disclosed.

SCHEDULE 8

FORM AND CONTENT OF ACCOUNTS PREPARED BY SMALL COMPANIES

Sections 247, 249, 250, 253, 254

PART I
GENERAL RULES AND FORMATS

SECTION A
GENERAL RULES

1.— (1) Subject to the following provisions of this Schedule—

    (a) every balance sheet of a small company shall show the items listed in either of the balance sheet formats set out below in section B of this Part; and

    (b) every profit and loss account of a small company shall show the items listed in any one of the profit and loss account formats so set out;

in either case in the order and under the headings and sub-headings given in the format adopted.

  (2) Sub-paragraph (1) above is not to be read as requiring the heading or sub-heading for any item to be distinguished by any letter or number assigned to that item in the format adopted.

2.— (1) Where in accordance with paragraph 1 a small company's balance sheet or profit and loss account for any financial year has been prepared by reference to one of the formats set out in section B below, the directors of the company shall adopt the same format in preparing the accounts for subsequent financial years of the company unless in their opinion there are special reasons for a change.

  (2) Particulars of any change in the format adopted in preparing a small company's balance sheet or profit and loss account in accordance with paragraph 1 shall be disclosed, and the reasons for the change shall be explained, in a note to the accounts in which the new format is first adopted.

3.— (1) Any item required in accordance with paragraph 1 to be shown in a small company's balance sheet or profit and loss account may be shown in greater detail than required by the format adopted.

  (2) A small company's balance sheet or profit and loss account may include an item representing or covering the amount of any asset or liability, income or expenditure not otherwise covered by any of the items listed in the format adopted, but the following shall not be treated as assets in any small company's balance sheet—

    (a) preliminary expenses;

    (b) expenses of and commission on any issue of shares or debentures; and

    (c) costs of research.

  (3) In preparing a small company's balance sheet or profit and loss account the directors of the company shall adapt the arrangement and headings and sub-headings otherwise required by paragraph 1 in respect of items to which an Arabic number is assigned in the format adopted, in any case where the special nature of the company's business requires such adaptation.

  (4) Items to which Arabic numbers are assigned in any of the formats set out in section B below may be combined in a small company's accounts for any financial year if either—

    (a) their individual amounts are not material to assessing the state of affairs or profit or loss of the company for that year; or

    (b) the combination facilitates that assessment;

but in a case within paragraph (b) the individual amounts of any items so combined shall be disclosed in a note to the accounts.

(5)   Subject to paragraph 4(3) below, a heading or sub-heading corresponding to an item listed in the format adopted in preparing a small company's balance sheet or profit and loss account shall not be included if there is no amount to be shown for that item in respect of the financial year to which the balance sheet or profit and loss account relates.

(6)   Every profit and loss account of a small company shall show the amount of the company's profit or loss on ordinary activities before taxation.

(7)   ...

4.— (1)   In respect of every item shown in a small company's balance sheet or profit and loss account the corresponding amount for the financial year immediately preceding that to which the balance sheet or profit and loss account relates shall also be shown.

(2)   Where that corresponding amount is not comparable with the amount to be shown for the item in question in respect of the financial year to which the balance sheet or profit and loss account relates, the former amount shall be adjusted and particulars of the adjustment and the reasons for it shall be disclosed in a note to the accounts.

(3)   Paragraph 3(5) does not apply in any case where an amount can be shown for the item in question in respect of the financial year immediately preceding that to which the balance sheet or profit and loss account relates, and that amount shall be shown under the heading or sub-heading required by paragraph 1 for that item.

5.   Amounts in respect of items representing assets or income may not be set off against amounts in respect of items representing liabilities or expenditure (as the case may be), or vice versa.

5A.   The directors of a company must, in determining how amounts are presented within items in the profit and loss account and balance sheet, have regard to the substance of the reported transaction or arrangement, in accordance with generally accepted accounting principles or practice.

SECTION B
THE REQUIRED FORMATS FOR ACCOUNTS

Preliminary

6.   References in this Part of this Schedule to the items listed in any of the formats set out below are to those items read together with any of the notes following the formats which apply to any of those items, and the requirement imposed by paragraph 1 to show the items listed in any such format in the order adopted in the format is subject to any provision in those notes for alternative positions for any particular items.

7.   A number in brackets following any item in any of the formats set out below is a reference to the note of that number in the notes following the formats.

8.   In the notes following the formats—

(a)   the heading of each note gives the required heading or sub-heading for the item to which it applies and a reference to any letters and numbers assigned to that item in the formats set out below (taking a reference in the case of Format 2 of the balance sheet formats to the item listed under "Assets" or under "Liabilities" as the case may require); and

(b)   references to a numbered format are to the balance sheet format or (as the case may require) to the profit and loss account format of that number set out below.

Balance Sheet Formats

Format 1

A.   Called up share capital not paid *(1)*
B.   Fixed assets
    I   Intangible assets
        1.   Goodwill *(2)*
        2.   Other intangible assets *(3)*
    II   Tangible assets
        1.   Land and buildings

        2.   Plant and machinery etc

   III   Investments

        1.   Shares in group undertakings and participating interests

        2.   Loans to group undertakings and undertakings in which the company has a participating interest

        3.   Other investments other than loans

        4.   Other investments *(4)*

C.   Current assets

   I   Stocks

        1.   Stocks

        2.   Payments on account

   II   Debtors *(5)*

        1.   Trade debtors

        2.   Amounts owed by group undertakings and undertakings in which the company has a participating interest

        3.   Other debtors

   III   Investments

        1.   Shares in group undertakings

        2.   Other investments

   IV   Cash at bank and in hand

D.   Prepayments and accrued income *(6)*

E.   Creditors: amounts falling due within one year

    1.   Bank loans and overdrafts

    2.   Trade creditors

    3.   Amounts owed to group undertakings and undertakings in which the company has a participating interest

    4.   Other creditors *(7)*

F.   Net current assets (liabilities) *(8)*

G.   Total assets less current liabilities

H.   Creditors: amounts falling due after more than one year

    1.   Bank loans and overdrafts

    2.   Trade creditors

    3.   Amounts owed to group undertakings and undertakings in which the company has a participating interest

    4.   Other creditors *(7)*

I.   Provisions for liabilities

J.   Accruals and deferred income *(7)*

K.   Capital and reserves

   I   Called up share capital *(9)*

   II   Share premium account

   III   Revaluation reserve

   IV   Other reserves

   V   Profit and loss account

Balance Sheet Formats

Format 2

ASSETS

A.   Called up share capital not paid *(1)*

B.   Fixed assets

   I   Intangible assets

        1.   Goodwill *(2)*

        2.   Other intangible assets *(3)*

       II   Tangible assets
           1.   Land and buildings
           2.   Plant and machinery etc
       III   Investments
           1.   Shares in group undertakings and participating interests
           2.   Loans to group undertakings and undertakings in which the company has a participating interest
           3.   Other investments other than loans
           4.   Other investments *(4)*

C.   Current assets
       I   Stocks
           1.   Stocks
           2.   Payments on account
       II   Debtors *(5)*
           1.   Trade debtors
           2.   Amounts owed by group undertakings and undertakings in which the company has a participating interest
           3.   Other debtors
       III   Investments
           1.   Shares in group undertakings
           2.   Other investments
       IV   Cash at bank and in hand
D.   Prepayments and accrued income *(6)*

LIABILITIES

A.   Capital and reserves
       I   Called up share capital *(9)*
       II   Share premium account
       III   Revaluation reserve
       IV   Other reserves
       V   Profit and loss account
B.   Provisions for liabilities
C.   Creditors *(10)*
       1.   Bank loans and overdrafts
       2.   Trade creditors
       3.   Amounts owed to group undertakings and undertakings in which the company has a participating interest
       4.   Other creditors *(7)*
D.   Accruals and deferred income *(7)*

Notes on the balance sheet formats

(1)   *Called up share capital not paid*
       (Formats 1 and 2, items A and C.II.3.)
       This item may either be shown at item A or included under item C.II.3 in Format 1 or 2.

(2)   *Goodwill*
       (Formats 1 and 2, item B.I.1.)
       Amounts representing goodwill shall only be included to the extent that the goodwill was acquired for valuable consideration.

(3)   *Other intangible assets*
       (Formats 1 and 2, item B.I.2.)
       Amounts in respect of concessions, patents, licences, trade marks and similar rights and assets shall only be included in a company's balance sheet under this item if either—
       (a)   the assets were acquired for valuable consideration and are not required to be shown under goodwill; or

(b)   the assets in question were created by the company itself.

(4)   *Others: Other investments*

(Formats 1 and 2, items B.III.4 and C.III.2.)

Where amounts in respect of own shares held are included under either of these items, the nominal value of such shares shall be shown separately.

(5)   *Debtors*

(Formats 1 and 2, items C.II 1 to 3.)

The amount falling due after more than one year shall be shown separately for each item included under debtors unless the aggregate amount of debtors falling due after more than one year is disclosed in the notes to the accounts.

(6)   *Prepayments and accrued income*

(Formats 1 and 2, item D.)

This item may alternatively be included under item C.II.3 in Format 1 or 2.

(7)   *Other creditors*

(Format 1, items E.4, H.4 and J and Format 2, items C.4 and D.)

There shall be shown separately—

(a)   the amount of any convertible loans, and

(b)   the amount for creditors in respect of taxation and social security.

Payments received on account of orders shall be included in so far as they are not shown as deductions from stocks.

In Format 1, accruals and deferred income may be shown under item J or included under item E.4 or H.4, or both (as the case may require). In Format 2, accruals and deferred income may be shown under item D or within item C.4 under Liabilities.

(8)   *Net current assets (liabilities)*

(Format 1, item F.)

In determining the amount to be shown under this item any prepayments and accrued income shall be taken into account wherever shown.

(9)   *Called up share capital*

(Format 1, item K.I and Format 2, item A.I.)

The amount of allotted share capital and the amount of called up share capital which has been paid up shall be shown separately.

(10)   *Creditors*

(Format 2, items C.I to 4.)

Amounts falling due within one year and after one year shall be shown separately for each of these items and for the aggregate of all of these items unless the aggregate amount of creditors falling due within one year and the aggregate amount of creditors falling due after more than one year is disclosed in the notes to the accounts.

Profit and loss account formats

Format 1
(see note (14) below)

1.   Turnover

2.   Cost of sales *(11)*

3.   Gross profit or loss

4.   Distribution costs *(11)*

5.   Administrative expenses *(11)*

6.   Other operating income

7.   Income from shares in group undertakings

8.   Income from participating interests

9.   Income from other fixed asset investments *(12)*

10.   Other interest receivable and similar income *(12)*

11.   Amounts written off investments

12.   Interest payable and similar charges *(13)*
13.   Tax on profit or loss on ordinary activities
14.   Profit or loss on ordinary activities after taxation
15.   Extraordinary income
16.   Extraordinary charges
17.   Extraordinary profit or loss
18.   Tax on extraordinary profit or loss
19.   Other taxes not shown under the above items
20.   Profit or loss for the financial year

Profit and loss account formats

Format 2

1.   Turnover
2.   Change in stocks of finished goods and in work in progress
3.   Own work capitalised
4.   Other operating income
5.   (a)   Raw materials and consumables
       (b)   Other external charges
6.   Staff costs:
       (a)   wages and salaries
       (b)   social security costs
       (c)   other pension costs
7.   (a)   Depreciation and other amounts written off tangible and intangible fixed assets
       (b)   Exceptional amounts written off current assets
8.   Other operating charges
9.   Income from shares in group undertakings
10.   Income from participating interests
11.   Income from other fixed asset investments *(12)*
12.   Other interest receivable and similar income *(12)*
13.   Amounts written off investments
14.   Interest payable and similar charges *(13)*
15.   Tax on profit or loss on ordinary activities
16.   Profit or loss on ordinary activities after taxation
17.   Extraordinary income
18.   Extraordinary charges
19.   Extraordinary profit or loss
20.   Tax on extraordinary profit or loss
21.   Other taxes not shown under the above items
22.   Profit or loss for the financial year

Profit and loss account formats

Format 3
(see note (14) below)

A.   Charges
       1.   Cost of sales *(11)*
       2.   Distribution costs *(11)*
       3.   Administrative expenses *(11)*
       4.   Amounts written off investments
       5.   Interest payable and similar charges *(13)*
       6.   Tax on profit or loss on ordinary activities
       7.   Profit or loss on ordinary activities after taxation
       8.   Extraordinary charges

9. Tax on extraordinary profit or loss
10. Other taxes not shown under the above items
11. Profit or loss for the financial year
B. Income
1. Turnover
2. Other operating income
3. Income from shares in group undertakings
4. Income from participating interests
5. Income from other fixed asset investments *(12)*
6. Other interest receivable and similar income *(12)*
7. Profit or loss on ordinary activities after taxation
8. Extraordinary income
9. Profit or loss for the financial year

Profit and loss account formats

Format 4

A. Charges
1. Reduction in stocks of finished goods and in work in progress
2. (a) Raw materials and consumables
   (b) Other external charges
3. Staff costs:
   (a) wages and salaries
   (b) social security costs
   (c) other pension costs
4. (a) Depreciation and other amounts written off tangible and intangible fixed assets
   (b) Exceptional amounts written off current assets
5. Other operating charges
6. Amounts written off investments
7. Interest payable and similar charges *(13)*
8. Tax on profit or loss on ordinary activities
9. Profit or loss on ordinary activities after taxation
10. Extraordinary charges
11. Tax on extraordinary profit or loss
12. Other taxes not shown under the above items
13. Profit or loss for the financial year
B. Income
1. Turnover
2. Increase in stocks of finished goods and in work in progress
3. Own work capitalised
4. Other operating income
5. Income from shares in group undertakings
6. Income from participating interests
7. Income from other fixed asset investments *(12)*
8. Other interest receivable and similar income *(12)*
9. Profit or loss on ordinary activities after taxation
10. Extraordinary income
11. Profit or loss for the financial year

Notes on the profit and loss account formats

(11) *Cost of sales: distribution costs: administrative expenses*
(Format 1, items 2, 4 and 5 and Format 3, items A.1, 2 and 3.)
These items shall be stated after taking into account any necessary provisions for depreciation or diminution in value of assets.

(12)   *Income from other fixed asset investments: other interest receivable and similar income*
        (Format 1, items 9 and 10: Format 2, items 11 and 12: Format 3, items B.5 and 6: Format 4, items
        B.7 and 8.)
        Income and interest derived from group undertakings shall be shown separately from income and
        interest derived from other sources.

(13)   *Interest payable and similar charges*
        (Format 1, item 12: Format 2, item 14: Format 3, item A.5: Format 4, item A.7.)
        The amount payable to group undertakings shall be shown separately.

(14)   *Formats 1 and 3*
        The amount of any provisions for depreciation and diminution in value of tangible and intangible
        fixed assets falling to be shown under items 7(a) and A.4(a) respectively in Formats 2 and 4 shall
        be disclosed in a note to the accounts in any case where the profit and loss account is prepared by
        reference to Format 1 or Format 3.

PART II
ACCOUNTING PRINCIPLES AND RULES

SECTION A
ACCOUNTING PRINCIPLES

Preliminary

9.   Subject to paragraph 15 below, the amounts to be included in respect of all items shown in a small
        company's accounts shall be determined in accordance with the principles set out in paragraphs
        10 to 14.

Accounting principles

10.   The company shall be presumed to be carrying on business as a going concern.

11.   Accounting policies shall be applied consistently within the same accounts and from one financial
        year to the next.

12.   The amount of any item shall be determined on a prudent basis, and in particular—
        (a)   only profits realised at the balance sheet date shall be included in the profit and loss account;
              and
        (b)   all liabilities ... which have arisen ... in respect of the financial year to which the accounts
              relate or a previous financial year shall be taken into account, including those which only
              become apparent between the balance sheet date and the date on which it is signed on behalf
              of the board of directors in pursuance of section 233 of this Act.

13.   All income and charges relating to the financial year to which the accounts relate shall be taken
        into account, without regard to the date of receipt or payment.

14.   In determining the aggregate amount of any item the amount of each individual asset or liability
        that falls to be taken into account shall be determined separately.

Departure from the accounting principles

15.   If it appears to the directors of a small company that there are special reasons for departing from
        any of the principles stated above in preparing the company's accounts in respect of any financial
        year they may do so, but particulars of the departure, the reasons for it and its effect shall be given
        in a note to the accounts.

SECTION B
HISTORICAL COST ACCOUNTING RULES

Preliminary

16.   Subject to sections C and D of this Part of this Schedule, the amounts to be included in respect of all items shown in a small company's accounts shall be determined in accordance with the rules set out in paragraphs 17 to 28.

Fixed assets

General rules

17.   Subject to any provision for depreciation or diminution in value made in accordance with paragraph 18 or 19 the amount to be included in respect of any fixed asset shall be its purchase price or production cost.

18.   In the case of any fixed asset which has a limited useful economic life, the amount of—

    (a)   its purchase price or production cost; or

    (b)   where it is estimated that any such asset will have a residual value at the end of the period of its useful economic life, its purchase price or production cost less that estimated residual value;

shall be reduced by provisions for depreciation calculated to write off that amount systematically over the period of the asset's useful economic life.

19.—   (1)   Where a fixed asset investment of a description falling to be included under item B III of either of the balance sheet formats set out in Part I of this Schedule has diminished in value provisions for diminution in value may be made in respect of it and the amount to be included in respect of it may be reduced accordingly; and any such provisions which are not shown in the profit and loss account shall be disclosed (either separately or in aggregate) in a note to the accounts.

    (2)   Provisions for diminution in value shall be made in respect of any fixed asset which has diminished in value if the reduction in its value is expected to be permanent (whether its useful economic life is limited or not), and the amount to be included in respect of it shall be reduced accordingly; and any such provisions which are not shown in the profit and loss account shall be disclosed (either separately or in aggregate) in a note to the accounts.

    (3)   Where the reasons for which any provision was made in accordance with sub-paragraph (1) or (2) have ceased to apply to any extent, that provision shall be written back to the extent that it is no longer necessary; and any amounts written back in accordance with this sub-paragraph which are not shown in the profit and loss account shall be disclosed (either separately or in aggregate) in a note to the accounts.

Rules for determining particular fixed asset items

20.—   (1)   Notwithstanding that an item in respect of "development costs" is included under "fixed assets" in the balance sheet formats set out in Part I of this Schedule, an amount may only be included in a small company's balance sheet in respect of development costs in special circumstances.

    (2)   If any amount is included in a small company's balance sheet in respect of development costs the following information shall be given in a note to the accounts—

        (a)   the period over which the amount of those costs originally capitalised is being or is to be written off; and

        (b)   the reasons for capitalising the development costs in question.

21.—   (1)   The application of paragraphs 17 to 19 in relation to goodwill (in any case where goodwill is treated as an asset) is subject to the following provisions of this paragraph.

    (2)   Subject to sub-paragraph (3) below, the amount of the consideration for any goodwill acquired by a small company shall be reduced by provisions for depreciation calculated to write off that amount systematically over a period chosen by the directors of the company.

(3)   The period chosen shall not exceed the useful economic life of the goodwill in question.

(4)   In any case where any goodwill acquired by a small company is shown or included as an asset in the company's balance sheet the period chosen for writing off the consideration for that goodwill and the reasons for choosing that period shall be disclosed in a note to the accounts.

Current assets

22.   Subject to paragraph 23, the amount to be included in respect of any current asset shall be its purchase price or production cost.

23.—   (1)   If the net realisable value of any current asset is lower than its purchase price or production cost the amount to be included in respect of that asset shall be the net realisable value.

        (2)   Where the reasons for which any provision for diminution in value was made in accordance with sub-paragraph (1) have ceased to apply to any extent, that provision shall be written back to the extent that it is no longer necessary.

Miscellaneous and supplementary provisions

Excess of money owed over value received as an asset item

24.—   (1)   Where the amount repayable on any debt owed by a small company is greater than the value of the consideration received in the transaction giving rise to the debt, the amount of the difference may be treated as an asset.

        (2)   Where any such amount is so treated—
              (a)   it shall be written off by reasonable amounts each year and must be completely written off before repayment of the debt; and
              (b)   if the current amount is not shown as a separate item in the company's balance sheet it must be disclosed in a note to the accounts.

Assets included at a fixed amount

25.—   (1)   Subject to the following sub-paragraph, assets which fall to be included—
              (a)   amongst the fixed assets of a small company under the item "tangible assets"; or
              (b)   amongst the current assets of a small company under the item "raw materials and con-sumables";
              may be included at a fixed quantity and value.

        (2)   Sub-paragraph (1) applies to assets of a kind which are constantly being replaced, where—
              (a)   their overall value is not material to assessing the company's state of affairs; and
              (b)   their quantity, value and composition are not subject to material variation.

Determination of purchase price or production cost

26.—   (1)   The purchase price of an asset shall be determined by adding to the actual price paid any expenses incidental to its acquisition.

        (2)   The production cost of an asset shall be determined by adding to the purchase price of the raw materials and consumables used the amount of the costs incurred by the company which are directly attributable to the production of that asset.

        (3)   In addition, there may be included in the production cost of an asset—
              (a)   a reasonable proportion of the costs incurred by the company which are only indirectly attributable to the production of that asset, but only to the extent that they relate to the period of production; and
              (b)   interest on capital borrowed to finance the production of that asset, to the extent that it accrues in respect of the period of production;
              provided, however, in a case within paragraph (b) above, that the inclusion of the interest in determining the cost of that asset and the amount of the interest so included is disclosed in a note to the accounts.

        (4)   In the case of current assets distribution costs may not be included in production costs.

27.—   (1)   Subject to the qualification mentioned below, the purchase price or production cost of—

(a)   any assets which fall to be included under any item shown in a small company's balance sheet under the general item "stocks"; and

(b)   any assets which are fungible assets (including investments);

may be determined by the application of any of the methods mentioned in sub-paragraph (2) below in relation to any such assets of the same class.

The method chosen must be one which appears to the directors to be appropriate in the circumstances of the company.

(2)   Those methods are—

(a)   the method known as "first in, first out" (FIFO);

(b)   the method known as "last in, first out" (LIFO);

(c)   a weighted average price; and

(d)   any other method similar to any of the methods mentioned above.

(3)   For the purposes of this paragraph, assets of any description shall be regarded as fungible if assets of that description are substantially indistinguishable one from another.

Substitution of original stated amount where price or cost unknown

28.   Where there is no record of the purchase price or production cost of any asset of a small company or of any price, expenses or costs relevant for determining its purchase price or production cost in accordance with paragraph 26, or any such record cannot be obtained without unreasonable expense or delay, its purchase price or production cost shall be taken for the purposes of paragraphs 17 to 23 to be the value ascribed to it in the earliest available record of its value made on or after its acquisition or production by the company.

SECTION C
ALTERNATIVE ACCOUNTING RULES

Preliminary

29.—   (1)   The rules set out in section B are referred to below in this Schedule as the historical cost accounting rules.

(2)   Those rules, with the omission of paragraphs 16, 21 and 25 to 28, are referred to below in this Part of this Schedule as the depreciation rules; and references below in this Schedule to the historical cost accounting rules do not include the depreciation rules as they apply by virtue of paragraph 32.

30.   Subject to paragraphs 32 to 34, the amounts to be included in respect of assets of any description mentioned in paragraph 31 may be determined on any basis so mentioned.

Alternative accounting rules

31.—   (1)   Intangible fixed assets, other than goodwill, may be included at their current cost.

(2)   Tangible fixed assets may be included at a market value determined as at the date of their last valuation or at their current cost.

(3)   Investments of any description falling to be included under item B III of either of the balance sheet formats set out in Part I of this Schedule may be included either—

(a)   at a market value determined as at the date of their last valuation; or

(b)   at a value determined on any basis which appears to the directors to be appropriate in the circumstances of the company;

but in the latter case particulars of the method of valuation adopted and of the reasons for adopting it shall be disclosed in a note to the accounts.

(4)   Investments of any description falling to be included under item C III of either of the balance sheet formats set out in Part I of this Schedule may be included at their current cost.

(5)   Stocks may be included at their current cost.

Application of the depreciation rules

32.— (1)   Where the value of any asset of a small company is determined on any basis mentioned in paragraph 31, that value shall be, or (as the case may require) be the starting point for determining, the amount to be included in respect of that asset in the company's accounts, instead of its purchase price or production cost or any value previously so determined for that asset; and the depreciation rules shall apply accordingly in relation to any such asset with the substitution for any reference to its purchase price or production cost of a reference to the value most recently determined for that asset on any basis mentioned in paragraph 31.

(2)   The amount of any provision for depreciation required in the case of any fixed asset by paragraph 18 or 19 as it applies by virtue of sub-paragraph (1) is referred to below in this paragraph as the adjusted amount, and the amount of any provision which would be required by that paragraph in the case of that asset according to the historical cost accounting rules is referred to as the historical cost amount.

(3)   Where sub-paragraph (1) applies in the case of any fixed asset the amount of any provision for depreciation in respect of that asset—

(a)   included in any item shown in the profit and loss account in respect of amounts written off assets of the description in question; or

(b)   taken into account in stating any item so shown which is required by note (11) of the notes on the profit and loss account formats set out in Part I of this Schedule to be stated after taking into account any necessary provision for depreciation or diminution in value of assets included under it;

may be the historical cost amount instead of the adjusted amount, provided that the amount of any difference between the two is shown separately in the profit and loss account or in a note to the accounts.

Additional information to be provided in case of departure
from historical cost accounting rules

33.— (1)   This paragraph applies where the amounts to be included in respect of assets covered by any items shown in a small company's accounts have been determined on any basis mentioned in paragraph 31.

(2)   The items affected and the basis of valuation adopted in determining the amounts of the assets in question in the case of each such item shall be disclosed in a note to the accounts.

(3)   In the case of each balance sheet item affected (except stocks) either—

(a)   the comparable amounts determined according to the historical cost accounting rules; or

(b)   the differences between those amounts and the corresponding amounts actually shown in the balance sheet in respect of that item;

shall be shown separately in the balance sheet or in a note to the accounts.

(4)   In sub-paragraph (3) above, references in relation to any item to the comparable amounts determined as there mentioned are references to—

(a)   the aggregate amount which would be required to be shown in respect of that item if the amounts to be included in respect of all the assets covered by that item were determined according to the historical cost accounting rules; and

(b)   the aggregate amount of the cumulative provisions for depreciation or diminution in value which would be permitted or required in determining those amounts according to those rules.

Revaluation reserve

34.— (1)   With respect to any determination of the value of an asset of a small company on any basis mentioned in paragraph 31, the amount of any profit or loss arising from that determination (after allowing, where appropriate, for any provisions for depreciation or diminution in value made otherwise than by reference to the value so determined and any adjustments of any such provisions made in the light of that determination) shall be credited or (as the case may be) debited to a separate reserve ("the revaluation reserve").

(2) The amount of the revaluation reserve shall be shown in the company's balance sheet under a separate sub-heading in the position given for the item "revaluation reserve" in Format 1 or 2 of the balance sheet formats set out in Part I of this Schedule, but need not be shown under that name.

(3) An amount may be transferred—
  (a) from the revaluation reserve—
    (i) to the profit and loss account, if the amount was previously charged to that account or represents realised profit, or
    (ii) on capitalisation,
  (b) to or from the revaluation reserve in respect of the taxation relating to any profit or loss credited or debited to the reserve;

and the revaluation reserve shall be reduced to the extent that the amounts transferred to it are no longer necessary for the purposes of the valuation method used.

(4) In sub-paragraph (3)(a)(ii) "capitalisation", in relation to an amount standing to the credit of the revaluation reserve, means applying it in wholly or partly paying up unissued shares in the company to be allotted to members of the company as fully or partly paid shares.

(5) The revaluation reserve shall not be reduced except as mentioned in this paragraph.

(6) The treatment for taxation purposes of amounts credited or debited to the revaluation reserve shall be disclosed in a note to the accounts.

SECTION D
FAIR VALUE ACCOUNTING

Inclusion of financial instruments at fair value

34A.— (1) Subject to sub-paragraphs (2) to (4), financial instruments (including derivatives) may be included at fair value.

(2) Sub-paragraph (1) does not apply to financial instruments which constitute liabilities unless—
  (a) they are held as part of a trading portfolio, or
  (b) they are derivatives.

(3) Sub-paragraph (1) does not apply to—
  (a) financial instruments (other than derivatives) held to maturity;
  (b) loans and receivables originated by the company and not held for trading purposes;
  (c) interests in subsidiary undertakings, associated undertakings and joint ventures;
  (d) equity instruments issued by the company;
  (e) contracts for contingent consideration in a business combination;
  (f) other financial instruments with such special characteristics that the instruments, according to generally accepted accounting principles or practice, should be accounted for differently from other financial instruments.

(4) If the fair value of a financial instrument cannot be determined reliably in accordance with paragraph 34B, sub-paragraph (1) does not apply to that financial instrument.

(5) In this paragraph—
  "associated undertaking" has the meaning given by paragraph 20 of Schedule 4A; and
  "joint venture" has the meaning given by paragraph 19 of that Schedule.

Determination of fair value

34B.— (1) The fair value of a financial instrument is determined in accordance with this paragraph.

(2) If a reliable market can readily be identified for the financial instrument, its fair value is determined by reference to its market value.

(3)   If a reliable market cannot readily be identified for the financial instrument but can be identified for its components or for a similar instrument, its fair value is determined by reference to the market value of its components or of the similar instrument.

(4)   If neither sub-paragraph (2) nor (3) applies, the fair value of the financial instrument is a value resulting from generally accepted valuation models and techniques.

(5)   Any valuation models and techniques used for the purposes of sub-paragraph (4) must ensure a reasonable approximation of the market value.

Inclusion of hedged items at fair value

34C.   A company may include any assets and liabilities that qualify as hedged items under a fair value hedge accounting system, or identified portions of such assets or liabilities, at the amount required under that system.

Other assets that may be included at fair value

34D.— (1)   This paragraph applies to—
    (a)   investment property, and
    (b)   living animals and plants,
that, under international accounting standards, may be included in accounts at fair value.

(2)   Such investment property and such living animals and plants may be included at fair value, provided that all such investment property or, as the case may be, all such living animals and plants are so included where their fair value can reliably be determined.

(3)   In this paragraph, "fair value" means fair value determined in accordance with relevant international accounting standards.

Accounting for changes in value

34E.— (1)   This paragraph applies where a financial instrument is valued in accordance with paragraph 34A or 34C or an asset is valued in accordance with paragraph 34D.

(2)   Notwithstanding paragraph 12 of this Schedule, and subject to sub-paragraphs (3) and (4) below, a change in the value of the financial instrument or of the investment property or living animal or plant must be included in the profit and loss account.

(3)   Where—
    (a)   the financial instrument accounted for is a hedging instrument under a hedge accounting system that allows some or all of the change in value not to be shown in the profit and loss account, or
    (b)   the change in value relates to an exchange difference arising on a monetary item that forms part of a company's net investment in a foreign entity,
the amount of the change in value must be credited to or (as the case may be) debited from a separate reserve ("the fair value reserve").

(4)   Where the instrument accounted for—
    (a)   is an available for sale financial asset, and
    (b)   is not a derivative,
the change in value may be credited to or (as the case may be) debited from the fair value reserve.

The fair value reserve

34F.— (1)   The fair value reserve must be adjusted to the extent that the amounts shown in it are no longer necessary for the purposes of paragraph 34E(3) or (4).

(2)   The treatment for taxation purposes of amounts credited or debited to the fair value reserve must be disclosed in a note to the accounts.

PART III
NOTES TO THE ACCOUNTS

Preliminary

35.   Any information required in the case of any small company by the following provisions of this Part of this Schedule shall (if not given in the company's accounts) be given by way of a note to those accounts.

Reserves and dividends

35A.   There must be stated—

    (a)   any amount set aside or proposed to be set aside to, or withdrawn or proposed to be withdrawn from, reserves,

    (b)   the aggregate amount of dividends paid in the financial year (other than those for which a liability existed at the immediately preceding balance sheet date),

    (c)   the aggregate amount of dividends that the company is liable to pay at the balance sheet date, and

    (d)   the aggregate amount of dividends that are proposed before the date of approval of the accounts, and not otherwise disclosed under paragraph (b) or (c).

Disclosure of accounting policies

36.   The accounting policies adopted by the company in determining the amounts to be included in respect of items shown in the balance sheet and in determining the profit or loss of the company shall be stated (including such policies with respect to the depreciation and diminution in value of assets).

Information supplementing the balance sheet

37.   Paragraphs 38 to 47 require information which either supplements the information given with respect to any particular items shown in the balance sheet or is otherwise relevant to assessing the company's state of affairs in the light of the information so given.

Share capital and debentures

38.—   (1)   The following information shall be given with respect to the company's share capital—

        (a)   the authorised share capital; and

        (b)   where shares of more than one class have been allotted, the number and aggregate nominal value of shares of each class allotted.

    (2)   In the case of any part of the allotted share capital that consists of redeemable shares, the following information shall be given—

        (a)   the earliest and latest dates on which the company has power to redeem those shares;

        (b)   whether those shares must be redeemed in any event or are liable to be redeemed at the option of the company or of the shareholder; and

        (c)   whether any (and, if so, what) premium is payable on redemption.

39.   If the company has allotted any shares during the financial year, the following information shall be given—

    (a)   the classes of shares allotted; and

    (b)   as respects each class of shares, the number allotted, their aggregate nominal value, and the consideration received by the company for the allotment.

Fixed assets

40.—   (1)   In respect of each item which is or would but for paragraph 3(4)(b) be shown under the general item "fixed assets" in the company's balance sheet the following information shall be given—

        (a)   the appropriate amounts in respect of that item as at the date of the beginning of the financial year and as at the balance sheet date respectively;

        (b)   the effect on any amount shown in the balance sheet in respect of that item of—

(i)　　any revision of the amount in respect of any assets included under that item made during that year on any basis mentioned in paragraph 31;

(ii)　　acquisitions during that year of any assets;

(iii)　　disposals during that year of any assets; and

(iv)　　any transfers of assets of the company to and from that item during that year.

(2)　　The reference in sub-paragraph (1)(a) to the appropriate amounts in respect of any item as at any date there mentioned is a reference to amounts representing the aggregate amounts determined, as at that date, in respect of assets falling to be included under that item on either of the following bases, that is to say—

(a)　　on the basis of purchase price or production cost (determined in accordance with paragraphs 26 and 27); or

(b)　　on any basis mentioned in paragraph 31,

(leaving out of account in either case any provisions for depreciation or diminution in value).

(3)　　In respect of each item within sub-paragraph (1)—

(a)　　the cumulative amount of provisions for depreciation or diminution in value of assets included under that item as at each date mentioned in sub-paragraph (1)(a);

(b)　　the amount of any such provisions made in respect of the financial year;

(c)　　the amount of any adjustments made in respect of any such provisions during that year in consequence of the disposal of any assets; and

(d)　　the amount of any other adjustments made in respect of any such provisions during that year;

shall also be stated.

41.　　Where any fixed assets of the company (other than listed investments) are included under any item shown in the company's balance sheet at an amount determined on any basis mentioned in paragraph 31, the following information shall be given—

(a)　　the years (so far as they are known to the directors) in which the assets were severally valued and the several values; and

(b)　　in the case of assets that have been valued during the financial year, the names of the persons who valued them or particulars of their qualifications for doing so and (whichever is stated) the bases of valuation used by them.

Investments

42.—　(1)　　In respect of the amount of each item which is or would but for paragraph 3(4)(b) be shown in the company's balance sheet under the general item "investments" (whether as fixed assets or as current assets) there shall be stated how much of that amount is ascribable to listed investments.

(2)　　Where the amount of any listed investments is stated for any item in accordance with sub-paragraph (1), the following amounts shall also be stated—

(a)　　the aggregate market value of those investments where it differs from the amount so stated; and

(b)　　both the market value and the stock exchange value of any investments of which the former value is, for the purposes of the accounts, taken as being higher than the latter.

Information about fair value of assets and liabilities

42A.—　(1)　　This paragraph applies where financial instruments have been valued in accordance with paragraph 34A or 34C.

(2)　　There must be stated—

(a)　　where the fair value of the instruments has been determined in accordance with paragraph 34B(4), the significant assumptions underlying the valuation models and techniques used,

(b)　　for each category of financial instrument, the fair value of the instruments in that category and the changes in value—

        (i)   included in the profit and loss account, and

        (ii)   credited to or (as the case may be) debited from the fair value reserve,

in respect of those instruments, and

   (c)   for each class of derivatives, the extent and nature of the instruments, including significant terms and conditions that may affect the amount, timing and certainty of future cash flows.

(3)   Where any amount is transferred to or from the fair value reserve during the financial year, there must be stated in tabular form—

   (a)   the amount of the reserve as at the date of the beginning of the financial year and as at the balance sheet date respectively;

   (b)   the amount transferred to or from the reserve during that year; and

   (c)   the source and application respectively of the amounts so transferred.

42B.— (1)   Sub-paragraph (2) applies if—

   (a)   the company has financial fixed assets that could be included at fair value by virtue of paragraph 34A,

   (b)   the amount at which those assets are included under any item in the company's accounts is in excess of their fair value, and

   (c)   the company has not made provision for diminution in value of those assets in accordance with paragraph 19(1) of this Schedule.

(2)   There must be stated—

   (a)   the amount at which either the individual assets or appropriate groupings of those individual assets are included in the company's accounts,

   (b)   the fair value of those assets or groupings, and

   (c)   the reasons for not making a provision for diminution in value of those assets, including the nature of the evidence that provides the basis for the belief that the amount at which they are stated in the accounts will be recovered.

Information where investment property and living animals and plants included at fair value

42C.— (1)   This paragraph applies where the amounts to be included in a company's accounts in respect of investment property or living animals and plants have been determined in accordance with paragraph 34D.

(2)   The balance sheet items affected and the basis of valuation adopted in determining the amounts of the assets in question in the case of each such item must be disclosed in a note to the accounts.

(3)   In the case of investment property, for each balance sheet item affected there must be shown, either separately in the balance sheet or in a note to the accounts—

   (a)   the comparable amounts determined according to the historical cost accounting rules; or

   (b)   the differences between those amounts and the corresponding amounts actually shown in the balance sheet in respect of that item.

(4)   In sub-paragraph (3) above, references in relation to any item to the comparable amounts determined in accordance with that sub-paragraph are references to—

   (a)   the aggregate amount which would be required to be shown in respect of that item if the amounts to be included in respect of all the assets covered by that item were determined according to the historical cost accounting rules; and

   (b)   the aggregate amount of the cumulative provisions for depreciation or diminution in value which would be permitted or required in determining those amounts according to those rules.

Reserves and provisions

43.— (1)   Where any amount is transferred—

   (a)   to or from any reserves; or

   (b)   to any provisions for liabilities; or

(c)   from any provision for liabilities otherwise than for the purpose for which the provision was established;

and the reserves or provisions are or would but for paragraph 3(4)(b) be shown as separate items in the company's balance sheet, the information mentioned in the following sub-paragraph shall be given in respect of the aggregate of reserves or provisions included in the same item.

(2)   That information is—

   (a)   the amount of the reserves or provisions as at the date of the beginning of the financial year and as at the balance sheet date respectively;

   (b)   any amounts transferred to or from the reserves or provisions during that year; and

   (c)   the source and application respectively of any amounts so transferred.

(3)   Particulars shall be given of each provision included in the item "other provisions" in the company's balance sheet in any case where the amount of that provision is material.

Details of indebtedness

44.— (1)   For the aggregate of all items shown under "creditors" in the company's balance sheet there shall be stated the aggregate of the following amounts, that is to say—

   (a)   the amount of any debts included under "creditors" which are payable or repayable otherwise than by instalments and fall due for payment or repayment after the end of the period of five years beginning with the day next following the end of the financial year; and

   (b)   in the case of any debts so included which are payable or repayable by instalments, the amount of any instalments which fall due for payment after the end of that period.

(2)   In respect of each item shown under "creditors" in the company's balance sheet there shall be stated the aggregate amount of any debts included under that item in respect of which any security has been given by the company.

(3)   References above in this paragraph to an item shown under "creditors" in the company's balance sheet include references, where amounts falling due to creditors within one year and after more than one year are distinguished in the balance sheet—

   (a)   in a case within sub-paragraph (1), to an item shown under the latter of those categories; and

   (b)   in a case within sub-paragraph (2), to an item shown under either of those categories;

and references to items shown under "creditors" include references to items which would but for paragraph 3(4)(b) be shown under that heading.

45.   If any fixed cumulative dividends on the company's shares are in arrear, there shall be stated—

   (a)   the amount of the arrears; and

   (b)   the period for which the dividends or, if there is more than one class, each class of them are in arrear.

Guarantees and other financial commitments

46.— (1)   Particulars shall be given of any charge on the assets of the company to secure the liabilities of any other person, including, where practicable, the amount secured.

(2)   The following information shall be given with respect to any other contingent liability not provided for—

   (a)   the amount or estimated amount of that liability;

   (b)   its legal nature; and

   (c)   whether any valuable security has been provided by the company in connection with that liability and if so, what.

(3)   There shall be stated, where practicable, the aggregate amount or estimated amount of contracts for capital expenditure, so far as not provided for.

(4)   Particulars shall be given of—

   (a)   any pension commitments included under any provision shown in the company's balance sheet; and

(b)   any such commitments for which no provision has been made;

and where any such commitment relates wholly or partly to pensions payable to past directors of the company separate particulars shall be given of that commitment so far as it relates to such pensions.

(5)   Particulars shall also be given of any other financial commitments which—

(a)   have not been provided for; and

(b)   are relevant to assessing the company's state of affairs.

(6)   Commitments within any of sub-paragraphs (1) to (5) which are undertaken on behalf of or for the benefit of—

(a)   any parent undertaking or fellow subsidiary undertaking, or

(b)   any subsidiary undertaking of the company,

shall be stated separately from the other commitments within that sub-paragraph, and commitments within paragraph (a) shall also be stated separately from those within paragraph (b).

Miscellaneous matters

47.   Particulars shall be given of any case where the purchase price or production cost of any asset is for the first time determined under paragraph 28.

Information supplementing the profit and loss account

48.   Paragraphs 49 and 50 require information which either supplements the information given with respect to any particular items shown in the profit and loss account or otherwise provides particulars of income or expenditure of the company or of circumstances affecting the items shown in the profit and loss account.

Particulars of turnover

49.— (1)   If the company has supplied geographical markets outside the United Kingdom during the financial year in question, there shall be stated the percentage of its turnover that, in the opinion of the directors, is attributable to those markets.

(2)   In analysing for the purposes of this paragraph the source of turnover, the directors of the company shall have regard to the manner in which the company's activities are organised.

Miscellaneous matters

50.— (1)   Where any amount relating to any preceding financial year is included in any item in the profit and loss account, the effect shall be stated.

(2)   Particulars shall be given of any extraordinary income or charges arising in the financial year.

(3)   The effect shall be stated of any transactions that are exceptional by virtue of size or incidence though they fall within the ordinary activities of the company.

General

51.— (1)   Where sums originally denominated in foreign currencies have been brought into account under any items shown in the balance sheet or profit and loss account, the basis on which those sums have been translated into sterling shall be stated.

(2)   Subject to the following sub-paragraph, in respect of every item stated in a note to the accounts the corresponding amount for the financial year immediately preceding that to which the accounts relate shall also be stated and where the corresponding amount is not comparable, it shall be adjusted and particulars of the adjustment and the reasons for it shall be given.

(3)   Sub-paragraph (2) does not apply in relation to any amounts stated by virtue of any of the following provisions of this Act—

(a)   paragraph 13 of Schedule 4A (details of accounting treatment of acquisitions),

(b)   paragraphs 2, 8(3), 16, 21(1)(d), 22(4) and (5), 24(3) and (4) and 27(3) and (4) of Schedule 5 (shareholdings in other undertakings),

(c)   Parts II and III of Schedule 6 (loans and other dealings in favour of directors and others), and

(d)   paragraphs 40 and 43 above (fixed assets and reserves and provisions).

Dormant Companies Acting as Agents

51A.   Where the directors of a company take advantage of the exemption conferred by section 249AA, and the company has during the financial year in question acted as an agent for any person, the fact that it has so acted must be stated.

PART IV
INTERPRETATION OF SCHEDULE

52.   The following paragraphs apply for the purposes of this Schedule and its interpretation.

Financial instruments

52A.   References to "derivatives" include commodity-based contracts that give either contracting party the right to settle in cash or in some other financial instrument, except when such contracts—

(a)   were entered into for the purpose of, and continue to meet, the company's expected purchase, sale or usage requirements,

(b)   were designated for such purpose at their inception, and

(c)   are expected to be settled by delivery of the commodity.

52B.— (1)   The expressions listed in sub-paragraph (2) have the same meaning as they have in Council Directive 78/660/EEC on the annual accounts of certain types of companies, as amended.

(2)   Those expressions are "available for sale financial asset", "business combination", "commodity-based contracts", "derivative", "equity instrument", "exchange difference", "fair value hedge accounting system", "financial fixed asset", "financial instrument", "foreign entity", "hedge accounting", "hedge accounting system", "hedged items", "hedging instrument", "held for trading purposes", "held to maturity", "monetary item", "receivables", "reliable market" and "trading portfolio".

Historical cost accounting rules

53.   References to the historical cost accounting rules shall be read in accordance with paragraph 29.

Investment property

53A.   "Investment property" means land held to earn rent or for capital appreciation.

Listed investments

54.— (1)   "Listed investment" means an investment as respects which there has been granted a listing on—

(a)   a recognised investment exchange other than an overseas investment exchange; or

(b)   a stock exchange of repute outside Great Britain.

(2)   "Recognised investment exchange" and "overseas investment exchange" have the meaning given in Part 18 of the Financial Services and Markets Act 2000.

Loans

55.   A loan is treated as falling due for repayment, and an instalment of a loan is treated as falling due for payment, on the earliest date on which the lender could require repayment or (as the case may be) payment, if he exercised all options and rights available to him.

Materiality

56.   Amounts which in the particular context of any provision of this Schedule are not material may be disregarded for the purposes of that provision.

Provisions

57.— (1) References to provisions for depreciation or diminution in value of assets are to any amount written off by way of providing for depreciation or diminution in value of assets.

(2) Any reference in the profit and loss account formats set out in Part I of this Schedule to the depreciation of, or amounts written off, assets of any description is to any provision for depreciation or diminution in value of assets of that description.

58. References to provisions for liabilities are to any amount retained as reasonably necessary for the purpose of providing for any liability the nature of which is clearly defined and which is either likely to be incurred, or certain to be incurred but uncertain as to amount or as to the date on which it will arise.

Staff costs

59.— (1) "Social security costs" means any contributions by the company to any state social security or pension scheme, fund or arrangement.

(2) "Pension costs" includes any costs incurred by the company in respect of any pension scheme established for the purpose of providing pensions for persons currently or formerly employed by the company, any sums set aside for the future payment of pensions directly by the company to current or former employees and any pensions paid directly to such persons without having first been set aside.

(3) Any amount stated in respect of the item "social security costs" or in respect of the item "wages and salaries" in the company's profit and loss account shall be determined by reference to payments made or costs incurred in respect of all persons employed by the company during the financial year under contracts of service.

SCHEDULE 8A

FORM AND CONTENT OF ABBREVIATED ACCOUNTS OF SMALL COMPANIES DELIVERED TO REGISTRAR

Section 246

PART I
BALANCE SHEET FORMATS

1. A small company may deliver to the registrar a copy of the balance sheet showing the items listed in either of the balance sheet formats set out in paragraph 2 below in the order and under the headings and sub-headings given in the format adopted, but in other respects corresponding to the full balance sheet.

2. The formats referred to in paragraph 1 are as follows—

Balance Sheet Formats

Format 1

A. Called up share capital not paid
B. Fixed assets
    I   Intangible assets
    II   Tangible assets
    III Investments
C. Current assets
    I   Stocks
    II   Debtors *(1)*
    III Investments
    IV   Cash at bank and in hand
D. Prepayments and accrued income

E.   Creditors: amounts falling due within one year
F.   Net current assets (liabilities)
G.   Total assets less current liabilities
H.   Creditors: amounts falling due after more than one year
I.   Provisions for liabilities
J.   Accruals and deferred income
K.   Capital and reserves
        I   Called up share capital
        II   Share premium account
        III   Revaluation reserve
        IV   Other reserves
        V   Profit and loss account

Balance Sheet Formats

Format 2

ASSETS
A.   Called up share capital not paid
B.   Fixed assets
        I   Intangible assets
        II   Tangible assets
        III   Investments
C.   Current assets
        I   Stocks
        II   Debtors *(1)*
        III   Investments
        IV   Cash at bank and in hand
D.   Prepayments and accrued income

LIABILITIES
A.   Capital and reserves
        I   Called up share capital
        II   Share premium account
        III   Revaluation reserve
        IV   Other reserves
        V   Profit and loss account
B.   Provisions for liabilities
C.   Creditors *(2)*
D.   Accruals and deferred income

Notes on the balance sheet formats

(1)   *Debtors*
        (Formats 1 and 2, item C.II.)
        The aggregate amount of debtors falling due after more than one year shall be shown separately,
        unless it is disclosed in the notes to the accounts.

(2)   *Creditors*
        (Format 2, Liabilities item C.)
        The aggregate amount of creditors falling due within one year and of creditors falling due after
        more than one year shall be shown separately, unless it is disclosed in the notes to the accounts.

PART II
NOTES TO THE ACCOUNTS

Preliminary

3.   Any information required in the case of any small company by the following provisions of this Part of this Schedule shall (if not given in the company's accounts) be given by way of a note to those accounts.

Disclosure of accounting policies

4.   The accounting policies adopted by the company in determining the amounts to be included in respect of items shown in the balance sheet and in determining the profit or loss of the company shall be stated (including such policies with respect to the depreciation and diminution in value of assets).

Information supplementing the balance sheet

Share capital and debentures

5.— (1) The following information shall be given with respect to the company's share capital—
       (a)   the authorised share capital; and
       (b)   where shares of more than one class have been allotted, the number and aggregate nominal value of shares of each class allotted.
      (2) In the case of any part of the allotted share capital that consists of redeemable shares, the following information shall be given—
       (a)   the earliest and latest dates on which the company has power to redeem those shares;
       (b)   whether those shares must be redeemed in any event or are liable to be redeemed at the option of the company or of the shareholder; and
       (c)   whether any (and, if so, what) premium is payable on redemption.

6.   If the company has allotted any shares during the financial year, the following information shall be given—
      (a)   the classes of shares allotted; and
      (b)   as respects each class of shares, the number allotted, their aggregate nominal value, and the consideration received by the company for the allotment.

Fixed assets

7.— (1) In respect of each item to which a letter or Roman number is assigned under the general item "fixed assets" in the company's balance sheet the following information shall be given—
       (a)   the appropriate amounts in respect of that item as at the date of the beginning of the financial year and as at the balance sheet date respectively;
       (b)   the effect on any amount shown in the balance sheet in respect of that item of—
             (i)   any revision of the amount in respect of any assets included under that item made during that year on any basis mentioned in paragraph 31 of Schedule 8;
             (ii)   acquisitions during that year of any assets;
             (iii) disposals during that year of any assets; and
             (iv)   any transfers of assets of the company to and from that item during that year.
      (2) The reference in sub-paragraph (1)(a) to the appropriate amounts in respect of any item as at any date there mentioned is a reference to amounts representing the aggregate amounts determined, as at that date, in respect of assets falling to be included under that item on either of the following bases, that is to say—
       (a)   on the basis of purchase price or production cost (determined in accordance with paragraphs 26 and 27 of Schedule 8); or
       (b)   on any basis mentioned in paragraph 31 of that Schedule,
      (leaving out of account in either case any provisions for depreciation or diminution in value).

    (3)   In respect of each item within sub-paragraph (1)—

        (a)   the cumulative amount of provisions for depreciation or diminution in value of assets included under that item as at each date mentioned in sub-paragraph (1)(a);

        (b)   the amount of any such provisions made in respect of the financial year;

        (c)   the amount of any adjustments made in respect of any such provisions during that year in consequence of the disposal of any assets; and

        (d)   the amount of any other adjustments made in respect of any such provisions during that year;

shall also be stated.

Financial fixed assets

7A.— (1) Sub-paragraph (2) applies if—

        (a)   the company has financial fixed assets that could be included at fair value by virtue of paragraph 34A of Schedule 8,

        (b)   the amount at which those assets are included under any item in the company's accounts is in excess of their fair value, and

        (c)   the company has not made provision for diminution in value of those assets in accordance with paragraph 19(1) of that Schedule.

    (2)   There must be stated—

        (a)   the amount at which either the individual assets or appropriate groupings of those individual assets are included in the company's accounts,

        (b)   the fair value of those assets or groupings, and

        (c)   the reasons for not making a provision for diminution in value of those assets, including the nature of the evidence that provides the basis for the belief that the amount at which they are stated in the accounts will be recovered.

Details of indebtedness

8.— (1) For the aggregate of all items shown under "creditors" in the company's balance sheet there shall be stated the aggregate of the following amounts, that is to say—

        (a)   the amount of any debts included under "creditors" which are payable or repayable otherwise than by instalments and fall due for payment or repayment after the end of the period of five years beginning with the day next following the end of the financial year; and

        (b)   in the case of any debts so included which are payable or repayable by instalments, the amount of any instalments which fall due for payment after the end of that period.

    (2)   In respect of each item shown under "creditors" in the company's balance sheet there shall be stated the aggregate amount of any debts included under that item, in respect of which any security has been given by the company.

General

9.— (1) Where sums originally denominated in foreign currencies have been brought into account under any items shown in the balance sheet or profit and loss account, the basis on which those sums have been translated into sterling shall be stated.

    (2)   Subject to the following sub-paragraph, in respect of every item required to be stated in a note to the accounts by or under any provision of this Act, the corresponding amount for the financial year immediately preceding that to which the accounts relate shall also be stated and where the corresponding amount is not comparable, it shall be adjusted and particulars of the adjustment and the reasons for it shall be given.

    (3)   Sub-paragraph (2) does not apply in relation to any amounts stated by virtue of any of the following provisions of this Act—

        (a)   paragraph 13 of Schedule 4A (details of accounting treatment of acquisitions),

        (b)   paragraphs 2, 8(3), 16, 21(1)(d), 22(4) and (5), 24(3) and (4) and 27(3) and (4) of Schedule 5 (shareholdings in other undertakings),

(c)   Parts II and III of Schedule 6 (loans and other dealings in favour of directors and others), and

(d)   paragraph 7 above (fixed assets).

Dormant Companies Acting as Agents

9A.   Where the directors of a company take advantage of the exemption conferred by section 249AA, and the company has during the financial year in question acted as an agent for any person, the fact that it has so acted must be stated.

SCHEDULE 9

SPECIAL PROVISIONS FOR BANKING COMPANIES AND GROUPS

Sections 255, 255A, 255B

PART I
INDIVIDUAL ACCOUNTS

CHAPTER 1
GENERAL RULES AND FORMATS

SECTION A
GENERAL RULES

1.—   (1)   Subject to the following provisions of this Part of this Schedule:
          (a)   every balance sheet of a company shall show the items listed in the balance sheet format set out below in section B of this Chapter of this Schedule; and
          (b)   every profit and loss account of a company shall show the items listed in either of the profit and loss account formats so set out;
       in either case in the order and under the headings and sub-headings given in the format adopted.

      (2)   Sub-paragraph (1) above is not to be read as requiring the heading or sub-heading for any item to be distinguished by any number or letter assigned to that item in the format adopted.

      (3)   Where the heading of an item in the format adopted contains any wording in square brackets, that wording may be omitted if not applicable to the company.

2.—   (1)   Where in accordance with paragraph 1 a company's profit and loss account for any financial year has been prepared by reference to one of the formats set out in section B below, the directors of the company shall adopt the same format in preparing the profit and loss account for subsequent financial years of the company unless in their opinion there are special reasons for a change.

      (2)   Particulars of any change in the format adopted in preparing a company's profit and loss account in accordance with paragraph 1 shall be disclosed, and the reasons for the change shall be explained, in a note to the accounts in which the new format is first adopted.

3.—   (1)   Any item required in accordance with paragraph 1 to be shown in a company's balance sheet or profit and loss account may be shown in greater detail than so required.

      (2)   A company's balance sheet or profit and loss account may include an item representing or covering the amount of any asset or liability, income or expenditure not specifically covered by any of the items listed in the balance sheet format provided or the profit and loss account format adopted, but the following shall not be treated as assets in any company's balance sheet:
          (i)   preliminary expenses;
          (ii)   expenses of and commission on any issue of shares or debentures; and
          (iii) costs of research.

      (3)   Items to which lower case letters are assigned in any of the formats set out in section B below may be combined in a company's accounts for any financial year if either:

(a) their individual amounts are not material for the purpose of giving a true and fair view; or

(b) the combination facilitates the assessment of the state of affairs or profit or loss of the company for that year;

but in a case within paragraph (b) the individual amounts of any items so combined shall be disclosed in a note to the accounts and any notes required by this Schedule to the items so combined shall, notwithstanding the combination, be given.

(4) Subject to paragraph 4(3) below, a heading or sub-heading corresponding to an item listed in the balance sheet format or the profit and loss account format adopted in preparing a company's balance sheet or profit and loss account shall not be included if there is no amount to be shown for that item in respect of the financial year to which the balance sheet or profit and loss account relates.

4.— (1) In respect of every item shown in the balance sheet or profit and loss account, there shall be shown or stated the corresponding amount for the financial year immediately preceding that to which the accounts relate.

(2) Where the corresponding amount is not comparable with the amount to be shown for the item in question in respect of the financial year to which the balance sheet or profit and loss account relates, the former amount shall be adjusted and particulars of the adjustment and the reasons for it shall be given in a note to the accounts.

(3) Paragraph 3(4) does not apply in any case where an amount can be shown for the item in question in respect of the financial year immediately preceding that to which the balance sheet or profit and loss account relates, and that amount shall be shown under the heading or sub-heading required by paragraph 1 for that item.

5.— (1) Subject to the following provisions of this paragraph and without prejudice to note (6) to the balance sheet format, amounts in respect of items representing assets or income may not be set off against amounts in respect of items representing liabilities or expenditure (as the case may be), or vice versa.

(2) Charges required to be included in profit and loss account format 1, items 11(a) and 11(b) or format 2, items A7(a) and A7(b) may however be set off against income required to be included in format 1, items 12(a) and 12(b) or format 2, items B5(a) and B5(b) and the resulting figure shown as a single item (in format 2 at position A7 if negative and at position B5 if positive).

(3) Charges required to be included in profit and loss account format 1, item 13 or format 2, item A8 may also be set off against income required to be included in format 1, item 14 or format 2, item B6 and the resulting figure shown as a single item (in format 2 at position A8 if negative and at position B6 if positive).

6.— (1) Assets shall be shown under the relevant balance sheet headings even where the company has pledged them as security for its own liabilities or for those of third parties or has otherwise assigned them as security to third parties.

(2) A company shall not include in its balance sheet assets pledged or otherwise assigned to it as security unless such assets are in the form of cash in the hands of the company.

7. Assets acquired in the name of and on behalf of third parties shall not be shown in the balance sheet.

8. ...

8A. The directors of a company must, in determining how amounts are presented within items in the profit and loss account and balance sheet, have regard to the substance of the reported transaction or arrangement, in accordance with generally accepted accounting principles or practice.

SECTION B
THE REQUIRED FORMATS FOR ACCOUNTS

Preliminary

9.—   (1)   References in this Part of this Schedule to the balance sheet format or to profit and loss
               account formats are to the balance sheet format or profit and loss account formats set out
               below and references to the items listed in any of the formats are to those items read
               together with any of the notes following the formats which apply to any of those items.

        (2)   The requirement imposed by paragraph 1 of this Part of this Schedule to show the items
               listed in any such format in the order adopted in the format is subject to any provision in the
               notes following the formats for alternative positions for any particular items.

10.   A number in brackets following any item in any of the formats set out below is a reference to the
               note of that number in the notes following the formats.

Balance Sheet Format

ASSETS

1.   Cash and balances at central (or post office) banks *(1)*
2.   Treasury bills and other eligible bills *(20)*
        (a)   Treasury bills and similar securities *(2)*
        (b)   Other eligible bills *(3)*
3.   Loans and advances to banks *(4)*, *(20)*
        (a)   Repayable on demand
        (b)   Other loans and advances
4.   Loans and advances to customers *(5)*, *(20)*
5.   Debt securities (and other fixed income securities) *(6)*, *(20)*
        (a)   Issued by public bodies
        (b)   Issued by other issuers
6.   Equity shares (and other variable-yield securities)
7.   Participating interests
8.   Shares in group undertakings
9.   Intangible fixed assets *(7)*
10.   Tangible fixed assets *(8)*
11.   Called up capital not paid *(9)*
12.   Own shares *(10)*
13.   Other assets
14.   Called up capital not paid *(9)*
15.   Prepayments and accrued income
Total assets

LIABILITIES

1.   Deposits by banks *(11)*, *(20)*
        (a)   Repayable on demand
        (b)   With agreed maturity dates or periods of notice
2.   Customer accounts *(12)*, *(20)*
        (a)   Repayable on demand
        (b)   With agreed maturity dates or periods of notice
3.   Debt securities in issue *(13)*, *(20)*
        (a)   Bonds and medium term notes
        (b)   Others
4.   Other liabilities
5.   Accruals and deferred income
6.   Provisions for liabilities
        (a)   Provisions for pensions and similar obligations
        (b)   Provisions for tax

      (c)   Other provisions
7.   Subordinated liabilities *(14), (20)*
8.   Called up share capital *(15)*
9.   Share premium account
10.   Reserves
      (a)   Capital redemption reserve
      (b)   Reserve for own shares
      (c)   Reserves provided for by the articles of association
      (d)   Other reserves
11.   Revaluation reserve
12.   Profit and loss account
Total liabilities

MEMORANDUM ITEMS
1.   Contingent liabilities *(16)*
      (1)   Acceptances and endorsements
      (2)   Guarantees and assets pledged as collateral security *(17)*
      (3)   Other contingent liabilities
2.   Commitments *(18)*
      (1)   Commitments arising out of sale and option to resell transactions *(19)*
      (2)   Other commitments

Notes on the balance sheet format and memorandum items

(1)   *Cash and balances at central (or post office) banks*
       (Assets item 1)
       Cash shall comprise all currency including foreign notes and coins.
       Only those balances which may be withdrawn without notice and which are deposited with central or post office banks of the country or countries in which the company is established shall be included in this item. All other claims on central or post office banks must be shown under Assets items 3 or 4.

(2)   *Treasury bills and other eligible bills: Treasury bills and similar securities*
       (Assets item 2(a))
       Treasury bills and similar securities shall comprise treasury bills and similar debt instruments issued by public bodies which are eligible for refinancing with central banks of the country or countries in which the company is established. Any treasury bills or similar debt instruments not so eligible shall be included under Assets item 5, sub-item (a).

(3)   *Treasury bills and other eligible bills: Other eligible bills*
       (Assets item 2(b))
       Other eligible bills shall comprise all bills purchased to the extent that they are eligible, under national law, for refinancing with the central banks of the country or countries in which the company is established.

(4)   *Loans and advances to banks*
       (Assets item 3)
       Loans and advances to banks shall comprise all loans and advances to domestic or foreign credit institutions made by the company arising out of banking transactions. However loans and advances to credit institutions represented by debt securities or other fixed income securities shall be included under Assets item 5 and not this item.

(5)   *Loans and advances to customers*
       (Assets item 4)
       Loans and advances to customers shall comprise all types of assets in the form of claims on domestic and foreign customers other than credit institutions. However loans and advances represented by debt securities or other fixed income securities shall be included under Assets item 5 and not this item.

(6)   *Debt securities (and other fixed income securities)*
        (Assets item 5)
        This item shall comprise transferable debt securities and any other transferable fixed income securities issued by credit institutions, other undertakings or public bodies. Debt securities and other fixed income securities issued by public bodies shall however only be included in this item if they may not be shown under Assets item 2.
        Where a company holds its own debt securities these shall not be included under this item but shall be deducted from Liabilities item 3(a) or (b), as appropriate.
        Securities bearing interest rates that vary in accordance with specific factors, for example the interest rate on the inter-bank market or on the Euromarket, shall also be regarded as fixed income securities to be included under this item.

(7)   *Intangible fixed assets*
        (Assets item 9)
        This item shall comprise:
        (a)   development costs;
        (b)   concessions, patents, licences, trade marks and similar rights and assets;
        (c)   goodwill; and
        (d)   payments on account.
        Amounts shall, however, be included in respect of (b) only if the assets were acquired for valuable consideration or the assets in question were created by the company itself.
        Amounts representing goodwill shall only be included to the extent that the goodwill was acquired for valuable consideration.
        There shall be disclosed, in a note to the accounts, the amount of any goodwill included in this item.

(8)   *Tangible fixed assets*
        (Assets item 10)
        This item shall comprise:
          –land and buildings;
          –plant and machinery;
          –fixtures and fittings, tools and equipment; and
          –payments on account and assets in the course of construction.
        There shall be disclosed in a note to the accounts the amount included in this item with respect to land and buildings occupied by the company for its own activities.

(9)   *Called up capital not paid*
        (Assets items 11 and 14)
        The two positions shown for this item are alternatives.

(10)   *Own shares*
        (Assets item 12)
        The nominal value of the shares held shall be shown separately under this item.

(11)   *Deposits by banks;*
        (Liabilities item 1)
        Deposits by banks shall comprise all amounts arising out of banking transactions owed to other domestic or foreign credit institutions by the company. However liabilities in the form of debt securities and any liabilities for which transferable certificates have been issued shall be included under Liabilities item 3 and not this item.

(12)   *Customer accounts*
        (Liabilities item 2)
        This item shall comprise all amounts owed to creditors that are not credit institutions. However liabilities in the form of debt securities and any liabilities for which transferable certificates have been issued shall be shown under Liabilities item 3 and not this item.

(13)   Debt securities in issue
(Liabilities item 3)
This item shall include both debt securities and debts for which transferable certificates have been issued, including liabilities arising out of own acceptances and promissory notes. (Only acceptances which a company has issued for its own refinancing and in respect of which it is the first party liable shall be treated as own acceptances.)

(14)   Subordinated liabilities
(Liabilities item 7)
This item shall comprise all liabilities in respect of which there is a contractual obligation that, in the event of winding up or bankruptcy, they are to be repaid only after the claims of other creditors have been met.
This item shall include all subordinated liabilities, whether or not a ranking has been agreed between the subordinated creditors concerned.

(15)   Called up share capital
(Liabilities item 8)
The amount of allotted share capital and the amount of called up share capital which has been paid up shall be shown separately.

(16)   Contingent liabilities
(Memorandum item 1)
This item shall include all transactions whereby the company has underwritten the obligations of a third party.
Liabilities arising out of the endorsement of rediscounted bills shall be included in this item. Acceptances other than own acceptances shall also be included.

(17)   Contingent liabilities: Guarantees and assets pledged as collateral security
(Memorandum item 1(2))
This item shall include all guarantee obligations incurred and assets pledged as collateral security on behalf of third parties, particularly in respect of sureties and irrevocable letters of credit.

(18)   Commitments
(Memorandum item 2)
This item shall include every irrevocable commitment which could give rise to a credit risk.

(19)   Commitments: Commitments arising out of sale and option to resell transactions
(Memorandum item 2(1))
This sub-item shall comprise commitments entered into by the company in the context of sale and option to resell transactions.

(20)   Claims on, and liabilities to, undertakings in which a participating interest is held or group undertakings
(Assets items 2 to 5, Liabilities items 1 to 3 and 7)
The following information must be given either by way of subdivision of the relevant items or by way of notes to the accounts.
The amount of the following must be shown for each of Assets items 2 to 5:
(a)   claims on group undertakings included therein; and
(b)   claims on undertakings in which the company has a participating interest included therein.
The amount of the following must be shown for each of Liabilities items 1, 2, 3 and 7:
    (i)   liabilities to group undertakings included therein; and
    (ii)   liabilities to undertakings in which the company has a participating interest included therein.

Special rules

Subordinated assets

11.—   (1)   The amount of any assets that are subordinated must be shown either as a subdivision of any relevant asset item or in the notes to the accounts; in the latter case disclosure shall be by reference to the relevant asset item or items in which the assets are included.

(2) In the case of Assets items 2 to 5 in the balance sheet format, the amounts required to be shown by note (20) to the format as sub-items of those items shall be further subdivided so as to show the amount of any claims included therein that are subordinated.

(3) For this purpose, assets are subordinated if there is a contractual obligation to the effect that, in the event of winding up or bankruptcy, they are to be repaid only after the claims of other creditors have been met, whether or not a ranking has been agreed between the subordinated creditors concerned.

Syndicated loans

12.— (1) Where a company is a party to a syndicated loan transaction the company shall include only that part of the total loan which it itself has funded.

(2) Where a company is a party to a syndicated loan transaction and has agreed to reimburse (in whole or in part) any other party to the syndicate any funds advanced by that party or any interest thereon upon the occurrence of any event, including the default of the borrower, any additional liability by reason of such a guarantee shall be included as a contingent liability in Memorandum item 1, sub-item (2).

Sale and repurchase transactions

13. (1) The following rules apply where a company is a party to a sale and repurchase transaction.

(2) Where the company is the transferor of the assets under the transaction:

    (a) the assets transferred shall, notwithstanding the transfer, be included in its balance sheet;

    (b) the purchase price received by it shall be included in its balance sheet as an amount owed to the transferee; and

    (c) the value of the assets transferred shall be disclosed in a note to its accounts.

(3) Where the company is the transferee of the assets under the transaction it shall not include the assets transferred in its balance sheet but the purchase price paid by it to the transferor shall be so included as an amount owed by the transferor.

Sale and option to resell transactions

14.— (1) The following rules apply where a company is a party to a sale and option to resell transaction.

(2) Where the company is the transferor of the assets under the transaction it shall not include in its balance sheet the assets transferred but it shall enter under Memorandum item 2 an amount equal to the price agreed in the event of repurchase.

(3) Where the company is the transferee of the assets under the transaction it shall include those assets in its balance sheet.

Managed funds

15.— (1) For the purposes of this paragraph "managed funds" are funds which the company administers in its own name but on behalf of others and to which it has legal title.

(2) The company shall, in any case where claims and obligations arising in respect of managed funds fall to be treated as claims and obligations of the company, adopt the following accounting treatment: claims and obligations representing managed funds are to be included in the company's balance sheet, with the notes to the accounts disclosing the total amount included with respect to such assets and liabilities in the balance sheet and showing the amount included under each relevant balance sheet item in respect of such assets or (as the case may be) liabilities.

Profit and Loss Account Formats

FORMAT 1
Vertical layout

1. Interest receivable *(1)*

(1) Interest receivable and similar income arising from debt securities (and other fixed income securities)

(2) Other interest receivable and similar income

2. Interest payable *(2)*

3. Dividend income

(a) Income from equity shares (and other variable-yield securities)

(b) Income from participating interests

(c) Income from shares in group undertakings

4. Fees and commissions receivable *(3)*

5. Fees and commissions payable *(4)*

6. Dealing (profits) (losses) *(5)*

7. Other operating income

8. Administrative expenses

(a) Staff costs

(i) Wages and salaries

(ii) Social security costs

(iii) Other pension costs

(b) Other administrative expenses

9. Depreciation and amortisation *(6)*

10. Other operating charges

11. Provisions

(a) Provisions for bad and doubtful debts *(7)*

(b) Provisions for contingent liabilities and commitments *(8)*

12. Adjustments to provisions

(a) Adjustments to provisions for bad and doubtful debts *(9)*

(b) Adjustments to provisions for contingent liabilities and commitments *(10)*

13. Amounts written off fixed asset investments *(11)*

14. Adjustments to amounts written off fixed asset investments *(12)*

15. (Profit) (loss) on ordinary activities before tax

16. Tax on (profit) (loss) on ordinary activities

17. (Profit) (loss) on ordinary activities after tax

18. Extraordinary income

19. Extraordinary charges

20. Extraordinary (profit) (loss)

21. Tax on extraordinary (profit) (loss)

22. Extraordinary (profit) (loss) after tax

23. Other taxes not shown under the preceding items

24. (Profit) (loss) for the financial year

FORMAT 2
Horizontal layout

A. Charges

1. Interest payable *(2)*

2. Fees and commissions payable *(4)*

3. Dealing losses *(5)*

4. Administrative expenses

(a) Staff costs

(i) Wages and salaries

(ii) Social security costs

(iii) Other pension costs

(b) Other administrative expenses

5. Depreciation and amortisation *(6)*

6. Other operating charges

    7.   Provisions
        (a)   Provisions for bad and doubtful debts *(7)*
        (b)   Provisions for contingent liabilities and commitments *(8)*
    8.   Amounts written off fixed asset investments *(11)*
    9.   Profit on ordinary activities before tax
   10. Tax on (profit) (loss) on ordinary activities
   11. Profit on ordinary activities after tax
   12. Extraordinary charges
   13. Tax on extraordinary (profit) (loss)
   14. Extraordinary loss after tax
   15. Other taxes not shown under the preceding items
   16. Profit for the financial year

B.   Income
    1.   Interest receivable *(1)*
        (1)   Interest receivable and similar income arising from debt securities (and other fixed income securities)
        (2)   Other interest receivable and similar income
    2.   Dividend income
        (a)   Income from equity shares (and other variable-yield securities)
        (b)   Income from participating interests
        (c)   Income from shares in group undertakings
    3.   Fees and commissions receivable *(3)*
    4.   Dealing profits *(5)*
    5.   Adjustments to provisions
        (a)   Adjustments to provisions for bad and doubtful debts *(9)*
        (b)   Adjustments to provisions for contingent liabilities and commitments *(10)*
    6.   Adjustments to amounts written off fixed asset investments *(12)*
    7.   Other operating income
    8.   Loss on ordinary activities before tax
    9.   Loss on ordinary activities after tax
   10. Extraordinary income
   11. Extraordinary profit after tax
   12. Loss for the financial year

Notes on the profit and loss account formats

(1)   *Interest receivable*
     (Format 1, item 1; Format 2, item B.1)
     This item shall include all income arising out of banking activities, including:
     (a)   income from assets included in Assets items 1 to 5 in the balance sheet format, however calculated;
     (b)   income resulting from covered forward contracts spread over the actual duration of the contract and similar in nature to interest; and
     (c)   fees and commissions receivable similar in nature to interest and calculated on a time basis or by reference to the amount of the claim (but not other fees and commissions receivable).

(2)   *Interest payable*
     (Format 1, item 2; Format 2, item A.1)
     This item shall include all expenditure arising out of banking activities, including:
     (a)   charges arising out of liabilities included in Liabilities items 1, 2, 3 and 7 in the balance sheet format, however calculated;
     (b)   charges resulting from covered forward contracts, spread over the actual duration of the contract and similar in nature to interest; and
     (c)   fees and commissions payable similar in nature to interest and calculated on a time basis or by reference to the amount of the liability (but not other fees and commissions payable).

(3)   *Fees and commissions receivable*
       (Format 1, item 4; Format 2, item B.3)
       Fees and commissions receivable shall comprise income in respect of all services supplied by the company to third parties, but not fees or commissions required to be included under interest receivable (Format 1, item 1; Format 2, item B.1).
       In particular the following fees and commissions receivable must be included (unless required to be included under interest receivable):
       –fees and commissions for guarantees, loan administration on behalf of other lenders and securities transactions;
       –fees, commissions and other income in respect of payment transactions, account administration charges and commissions for the safe custody and administration of securities;
       –fees and commissions for foreign currency transactions and for the sale and purchase of coin and precious metals; and
       –fees and commissions charged for brokerage services in connection with savings and insurance contracts and loans.

(4)   *Fees and commissions payable*
       (Format 1, item 5; Format 2, item A.2)
       Fees and commissions payable shall comprise charges for all services rendered to the company by third parties but not fees or commissions required to be included under interest payable (Format 1, item 2; Format 2, item A.1).
       In particular the following fees and commissions payable must be included (unless required to be included under interest payable):
       –fees and commissions for guarantees, loan administration and securities transactions;
       –fees, commissions and other charges in respect of payment transactions, account administration charges and commissions for the safe custody and administration of securities;
       –fees and commissions for foreign currency transactions and for the sale and purchase of coin and precious metals; and
       –fees and commissions for brokerage services in connection with savings and insurance contracts and loans.

(5)   *Dealing (profits) (losses)*
       (Format 1, item 6; Format 2, items B.4 and A.3)
       This item shall comprise:
       (a)   the net profit or net loss on transactions in securities which are not held as financial fixed assets together with amounts written off or written back with respect to such securities, including amounts written off or written back as a result of the application of paragraph 34(1) below;
       (b)   the net profit or loss on exchange activities, save in so far as the profit or loss is included in interest receivable or interest payable (Format 1, items 1 or 2; Format 2, items B1 or A1); and
       (c)   the net profits and losses on other dealing operations involving financial instruments, including precious metals.

(6)   *Depreciation and amortisation*
       (Format 1, item 9; Format 2, item A.5)
       This item shall comprise depreciation and other amounts written off in respect of balance sheet Assets items 9 and 10.

(7)   *Provisions: Provisions for bad and doubtful debts*
       (Format 1, item 11(a); Format 2, item A.7(a))
       Provisions for bad and doubtful debts shall comprise charges for amounts written off and for provisions made in respect of loans and advances shown under balance sheet Assets items 3 and 4.

(8)   *Provisions: Provisions for contingent liabilities and commitments*
       (Format 1, item 11(b); Format 2, item A.7(b))

This item shall comprise charges for provisions for contingent liabilities and commitments of a type which would, if not provided for, be shown under Memorandum items 1 and 2.

(9) *Adjustments to provisions: Adjustments to provisions for bad and doubtful debts*
(Format 1, item 12(a); Format 2, item B.5(a))
This item shall include credits from the recovery of loans that have been written off, from other advances written back following earlier write offs and from the reduction of provisions previously made with respect to loans and advances.

(10) *Adjustments to provisions: Adjustments to provisions for contingent liabilities and commitments*
(Format 1, item 12(b); Format 2, item B.5(b))
This item comprises credits from the reduction of provisions previously made with respect to contingent liabilities and commitments.

(11) *Amounts written off fixed asset investments*
(Format 1, item 13; Format 2, item A.8)
Amounts written off fixed asset investments shall comprise amounts written off in respect of assets which are transferable securities held as financial fixed assets, participating interests and shares in group undertakings and which are included in Assets items 5 to 8 in the balance sheet format.

(12) *Adjustments to amounts written off fixed asset investments*
(Format 1, item 14; Format 2, item B.6)
Adjustments to amounts written off fixed asset investments shall include amounts written back following earlier write offs and provisions in respect of assets which are transferable securities held as financial fixed assets, participating interests and group undertakings and which are included in Assets items 5 to 8 in the balance sheet format.

CHAPTER II
ACCOUNTING PRINCIPLES AND RULES

SECTION A
ACCOUNTING PRINCIPLES

16. Subject to paragraph 22 below, the amounts to be included in respect of all items shown in a company's accounts shall be determined in accordance with the principles set out in paragraphs 17 to 21.

Accounting principles

17. The company shall be presumed to be carrying on business as a going concern.

18. Accounting policies shall be applied consistently within the same accounts and from one financial year to the next.

19. The amount of any item shall be determined on a prudent basis, and in particular:
   (a) only profits realised at the balance sheet date shall be included in the profit and loss account; and
   (b) all liabilities ... which have arisen ... in respect of the financial year to which the accounts relate or a previous financial year shall be taken into account, including those which only become apparent between the balance sheet date and the date on which it is signed on behalf of the board of directors in pursuance of section 233 of this Act.

20. All income and charges relating to the financial year to which the accounts relate shall be taken into account, without regard to the date of receipt or payment.

21. In determining the aggregate amount of any item the amount of each individual asset or liability that falls to be taken into account shall be determined separately.

Departure from the accounting principles

22. If it appears to the directors of a company that there are special reasons for departing from any of the principles stated above in preparing the company's accounts in respect of any financial year

they may do so, but particulars of the departure, the reasons for it and its effect shall be given in a note to the accounts.

SECTION B
VALUATION RULES

HISTORICAL COST ACCOUNTING RULES

Preliminary

23.   Subject to paragraphs 39 to 44F of this Part of this Schedule, the amounts to be included in respect of all items shown in a company's accounts shall be determined in accordance with the rules set out in paragraphs 24 to 38 of this Part of this Schedule.

Fixed assets

General rules

24.   Subject to any provision for depreciation or diminution in value made in accordance with paragraph 25 or 26 the amount to be included in respect of any fixed asset shall be its cost.

25.   In the case of any fixed asset which has a limited useful economic life, the amount of:
   (a)   its cost; or
   (b)   where it is estimated that any such asset will have a residual value at the end of the period of its useful economic life, its cost less that estimated residual value;
   shall be reduced by provisions for depreciation calculated to write off that amount systematically over the period of the asset's useful economic life.

26.   (1)   Where a fixed asset investment of a description falling to be included under Assets items 7 (Participating interests) or 8 (Shares in group undertakings) in the balance sheet format, or any other holding of securities held as a financial fixed asset, has diminished in value, provisions for diminution in value may be made in respect of it and the amount to be included in respect of it may be reduced accordingly; and any such provisions which are not shown in the profit and loss account shall be disclosed (either separately or in aggregate) in a note to the accounts.

   (2)   Provisions for diminution in value shall be made in respect of any fixed asset which has diminished in value if the reduction in its value is expected to be permanent (whether its useful economic life is limited or not), and the amount to be included in respect of it shall be reduced accordingly; and any such provisions which are not shown in the profit and loss account shall be disclosed (either separately or in aggregate) in a note to the accounts.

   (3)   Where the reasons for which any provision was made in accordance with sub-paragraph (1) or (2) have ceased to apply to any extent, that provision shall be written back to the extent that it is no longer necessary; and any amounts written back in accordance with this sub-paragraph which are not shown in the profit and loss account shall be disclosed (either separately or in aggregate) in a note to the accounts.

Development costs

27.   (1)   Notwithstanding that amounts representing "development costs" may be included under Assets item 9 in the balance sheet format, an amount may only be included in a company's balance sheet in respect of development costs in special circumstances.

   (2)   If any amount is included in a company's balance sheet in respect of development costs the following information shall be given in a note to the accounts:
   (a)   the period over which the amount of those costs originally capitalised is being or is to be written off; and
   (b)   the reasons for capitalising the development costs in question.

Goodwill

28.— (1) The application of paragraphs 24 to 26 in relation to goodwill (in any case where goodwill is treated as an asset) is subject to the following provisions of this paragraph.

(2) Subject to sub-paragraph (3) below the amount of the consideration for any goodwill acquired by a company shall be reduced by provisions for depreciation calculated to write off that amount systematically over a period chosen by the directors of the company.

(3) The period chosen shall not exceed the useful economic life of the goodwill in question.

(4) In any case where any goodwill acquired by a company is included as an asset in the company's balance sheet the period chosen for writing off the consideration for that goodwill and the reasons for choosing that period shall be disclosed in a note to the accounts.

Intangible and tangible fixed assets

29. Assets included in Assets items 9 (Intangible fixed assets) and 10 (Tangible fixed assets) in the balance sheet format shall be valued as fixed assets.

Other fixed assets

30. Other assets falling to be included in the balance sheet shall be valued as fixed assets where they are intended for use on a continuing basis in the company's activities.

Financial fixed assets

31.— (1) Debt securities, including fixed income securities, held as financial fixed assets shall be included in the balance sheet at an amount equal to their maturity value plus any premium, or less any discount, on their purchase, subject to the following provisions of this paragraph.

(2) The amount included in the balance sheet with respect to such securities purchased at a premium shall be reduced each financial year on a systematic basis so as to write the premium off over the period to the maturity date of the security and the amounts so written off shall be charged to the profit and loss account for the relevant financial years.

(3) The amount included in the balance sheet with respect to such securities purchased at a discount shall be increased each financial year on a systematic basis so as to extinguish the discount over the period to the maturity date of the security and the amounts by which the amount is increased shall be credited to the profit and loss account for the relevant years.

(4) The notes to the accounts shall disclose the amount of any unamortised premium or discount not extinguished which is included in the balance sheet by virtue of sub-paragraph (1).

(5) For the purposes of this paragraph "premium" means any excess of the amount paid for a security over its maturity value and "discount" means any deficit of the amount paid for a security over its maturity value.

Current assets

32. The amount to be included in respect of loans and advances, debt or other fixed income securities and equity shares or other variable yield securities not held as financial fixed assets shall be their cost, subject to paragraphs 33 and 34 below.

33.— (1) If the net realisable value of any asset referred to in paragraph 32 is lower than its cost the amount to be included in respect of that asset shall be the net realisable value.

(2) Where the reasons for which any provision for diminution in value was made in accordance with sub-paragraph (1) have ceased to apply to any extent, that provision shall be written back to the extent that it is no longer necessary.

34.— (1) Subject to paragraph 33 above, the amount to be included in the balance sheet in respect of transferable securities not held as financial fixed assets may be the higher of their cost or their market value at the balance sheet date.

(2) The difference between the cost of any securities included in the balance sheet at a valuation under sub-paragraph (1) and their market value shall be shown (in aggregate) in the notes to the accounts.

Miscellaneous and supplementary provisions

Excess of money owed over value received as an asset item

35.— (1) Where the amount repayable on any debt owed by a company is greater than the value of the consideration received in the transaction giving rise to the debt, the amount of the difference may be treated as an asset.

(2) Where any such amount is so treated:

(a) it shall be written off by reasonable amounts each year and must be completely written off before repayment of the debt; and

(b) if the current amount is not shown as a separate item in the company's balance sheet it must be disclosed in a note to the accounts.

Determination of cost

36.— (1) The cost of an asset that has been acquired by the company shall be determined by adding to the actual price paid any expenses incidental to its acquisition.

(2) The cost of an asset constructed by the company shall be determined by adding to the purchase price of the raw materials and consumables used the amount of the costs incurred by the company which are directly attributable to the construction of that asset.

(3) In addition, there may be included in the cost of an asset constructed by the company:

(a) a reasonable proportion of the costs incurred by the company which are only indirectly attributable to the construction of that asset, but only to the extent that they relate to the period of construction; and

(b) interest on capital borrowed to finance the construction of that asset, to the extent that it accrues in respect of the period of construction;

provided, however, in a case within sub-paragraph (b) above, that the inclusion of the interest in determining the cost of that asset and the amount of the interest so included is disclosed in a note to the accounts.

37.— (1) Subject to the qualification mentioned below, the cost of any assets which are fungible assets (including investments) may be determined by the application of any of the methods mentioned in sub-paragraph (2) below in relation to any such assets of the same class.

The method chosen must be one which appears to the directors to be appropriate in the circumstances of the company.

(2) Those methods are:

(a) the method known as "first in, first out" (FIFO);

(b) the method known as "last in, first out" (LIFO);

(c) a weighted average price; and

(d) any other method similar to any of the methods mentioned above.

(3) Where in the case of any company:

(a) the cost of assets falling to be included under any item shown in the company's balance sheet has been determined by the application of any method permitted by this paragraph; and

(b) the amount shown in respect of that item differs materially from the relevant alternative amount given below in this paragraph;

the amount of that difference shall be disclosed in a note to the accounts.

(4) Subject to sub-paragraph (5) below, for the purposes of sub-paragraph (3)(b) above, the relevant alternative amount, in relation to any item shown in a company's balance sheet, is the amount which would have been shown in respect of that item if assets of any class included under that item at an amount determined by any method permitted by this paragraph had instead been included at their replacement cost as at the balance sheet date.

(5) The relevant alternative amount may be determined by reference to the most recent actual purchase price before the balance sheet date of assets of any class included under the item in question instead of by reference to their replacement cost as at that date, but only if the

former appears to the directors of the company to constitute the more appropriate standard of comparison in the case of assets of that class.

Substitution of original amount where price or cost unknown

38. Where there is no record of the purchase price of any asset acquired by a company or of any price, expenses or costs relevant for determining its cost in accordance with paragraph 36, or any such record cannot be obtained without unreasonable expense or delay, its cost shall be taken for the purposes of paragraphs 24 to 34 to be the value ascribed to it in the earliest available record of its value made on or after its acquisition by the company.

ALTERNATIVE ACCOUNTING RULES

Preliminary

39.— (1) The rules set out in paragraphs 24 to 38 are referred to below in this Schedule as the historical cost accounting rules.

(2) Paragraphs 24 to 27 and 31 to 35 are referred to below in this section of this Part of this Schedule as the depreciation rules; and references below in this Schedule to the historical cost accounting rules do not include the depreciation rules as they apply by virtue of paragraph 42.

40. Subject to paragraphs 42 to 44, the amounts to be included in respect of assets of any description mentioned in paragraph 41 may be determined on any basis so mentioned.

Alternative accounting rules

41.— (1) Intangible fixed assets, other than goodwill, may be included at their current cost.

(2) Tangible fixed assets may be included at a market value determined as at the date of their last valuation or at their current cost.

(3) Investments of any description falling to be included under Assets items 7 (Participating interests) or 8 (Shares in group undertakings) of the balance sheet format and any other securities held as financial fixed assets may be included either:

(a) at a market value determined as at the date of their last valuation; or

(b) at a value determined on any basis which appears to the directors to be appropriate in the circumstances of the company;

but in the latter case particulars of the method of valuation adopted and of the reasons for adopting it shall be disclosed in a note to the accounts.

(4) Securities of any description not held as financial fixed assets (if not valued in accordance with paragraph 34 above) may be included at their current cost.

Application of the depreciation rules

42.— (1) Where the value of any asset of a company is determined in accordance with paragraph 41, that value shall be, or (as the case may require) be the starting point for determining, the amount to be included in respect of that asset in the company's accounts, instead of its cost or any value previously so determined for that asset; and the depreciation rules shall apply accordingly in relation to any such asset with the substitution for any reference to its cost of a reference to the value most recently determined for that asset in accordance with paragraph 41.

(2) The amount of any provision for depreciation required in the case of any fixed asset by paragraph 25 or 26 as it applies by virtue of sub-paragraph (1) is referred to below in this paragraph as the "adjusted amount", and the amount of any provision which would be required by that paragraph in the case of that asset according to the historical cost accounting rules is referred to as the "historical cost amount".

(3) Where sub-paragraph (1) applies in the case of any fixed asset the amount of any provision for depreciation in respect of that asset included in any item shown in the profit and loss account in respect of amounts written off assets of the description in question may be the

historical cost amount instead of the adjusted amount, provided that the amount of any difference between the two is shown separately in the profit and loss account or in a note to the accounts.

Additional information to be provided in case of departure
from historical cost accounting rules

43.— (1)   This paragraph applies where the amounts to be included in respect of assets covered by any items shown in a company's accounts have been determined in accordance with paragraph 41.

(2)   The items affected and the basis of valuation adopted in determining the amounts of the assets in question in the case of each such item shall be disclosed in a note to the accounts.

(3)   In the case of each balance sheet item affected either:

(a)   the comparable amounts determined according to the historical cost accounting rules; or

(b)   the differences between those amounts and the corresponding amounts actually shown in the balance sheet in respect of that item;

shall be shown separately in the balance sheet or in a note to the accounts.

(4)   In sub-paragraph (3) above, references in relation to any item to the comparable amounts determined as there mentioned are references to:

(a)   the aggregate amount which would be required to be shown in respect of that item if the amounts to be included in respect of all the assets covered by that item were determined according to the historical cost accounting rules; and

(b)   the aggregate amount of the cumulative provisions for depreciation or diminution in value which would be permitted or required in determining those amounts according to those rules.

Revaluation reserve

44.— (1)   With respect to any determination of the value of an asset of a company in accordance with paragraph 41, the amount of any profit or loss arising from that determination (after allowing, where appropriate, for any provisions for depreciation or diminution in value made otherwise than by reference to the value so determined and any adjustments of any such provisions made in the light of that determination) shall be credited or (as the case may be) debited to a separate reserve ("the revaluation reserve").

(2)   The amount of the revaluation reserve shall be shown in the company's balance sheet under Liabilities item 11 in the balance sheet format, but need not be shown under that name.

(3)   An amount may be transferred

(a)   from the revaluation reserve—

(i)   to the profit and loss account, if the amount was previously charged to that account or represents realised profit, or

(ii)   on capitalisation,

(b)   to or from the revaluation reserve in respect of the taxation relating to any profit or loss credited or debited to the reserve;

and the revaluation reserve shall be reduced to the extent that the amounts transferred to it are no longer necessary for the purposes of the valuation method used.

(4)   In sub-paragraph (3)(a)(ii) "capitalisation", in relation to an amount standing to the credit of the revaluation reserve, means applying it in wholly or partly paying up unissued shares in the company to be allotted to members of the company as fully or partly paid shares.

(5)   The revaluation reserve shall not be reduced except as mentioned in this paragraph.

(6)   The treatment for taxation purposes of amounts credited or debited to the revaluation reserve shall be disclosed in a note to the accounts.

FAIR VALUE ACCOUNTING

Inclusion of financial instruments at fair value

44A.— (1) Subject to sub-paragraphs (2) to (4), financial instruments (including derivatives) may be included at fair value.

(2) Sub-paragraph (1) does not apply to financial instruments which constitute liabilities unless—

(a) they are held as part of a trading portfolio, or

(b) they are derivatives.

(3) Sub-paragraph (1) does not apply to—

(a) financial instruments (other than derivatives) held to maturity;

(b) loans and receivables originated by the company and not held for trading purposes;

(c) interests in subsidiary undertakings, associated undertakings and joint ventures;

(d) equity instruments issued by the company;

(e) contracts for contingent consideration in a business combination;

(f) other financial instruments with such special characteristics that the instruments, according to generally accepted accounting principles or practice, should be accounted for differently from other financial instruments.

(4) If the fair value of a financial instrument cannot be determined reliably in accordance with paragraph 44B, sub-paragraph (1) does not apply to that financial instrument.

(5) In this paragraph—

"associated undertaking" has the meaning given by paragraph 20 of Schedule 4A; and "joint venture" has the meaning given by paragraph 19 of that Schedule.

Determination of fair value

44B.— (1) The fair value of a financial instrument is determined in accordance with this paragraph.

(2) If a reliable market can readily be identified for the financial instrument, its fair value is determined by reference to its market value.

(3) If a reliable market cannot readily be identified for the financial instrument but can be identified for its components or for a similar instrument, its fair value is determined by reference to the market value of its components or of the similar instrument.

(4) If neither sub-paragraph (2) nor (3) applies, the fair value of the financial instrument is a value resulting from generally accepted valuation models and techniques.

(5) Any valuation models and techniques used for the purposes of sub-paragraph (4) must ensure a reasonable approximation of the market value.

Inclusion of hedged items at fair value

44C. A company may include any assets and liabilities that qualify as hedged items under a fair value hedge accounting system, or identified portions of such assets or liabilities, at the amount required under that system.

Other assets that may be included at fair value

44D.— (1) This paragraph applies to—

(a) investment property, and

(b) living animals and plants,

that, under international accounting standards, may be included in accounts at fair value.

(2) Such investment property and such living animals and plants may be included at fair value, provided that all such investment property or, as the case may be, all such living animals and plants are so included where their fair value can reliably be determined.

(3) In this paragraph, "fair value" means fair value determined in accordance with relevant international accounting standards.

Accounting for changes in value

44E.— (1)   This paragraph applies where a financial instrument is valued in accordance with paragraph 44A or 44C or an asset is valued in accordance with paragraph 44D.

(2)   Notwithstanding paragraph 19 of this Schedule, and subject to sub-paragraphs (3) and (4) below, a change in the value of the financial instrument or of the investment property or living animal or plant must be included in the profit and loss account.

(3)   Where—

(a)   the financial instrument accounted for is a hedging instrument under a hedge accounting system that allows some or all of the change in value not to be shown in the profit and loss account, or

(b)   the change in value relates to an exchange difference arising on a monetary item that forms part of a company's net investment in a foreign entity,

the amount of the change in value must be credited to or (as the case may be) debited from a separate reserve ("the fair value reserve").

(4)   Where the instrument accounted for—

(a)   is an available for sale financial asset, and

(b)   is not a derivative,

the change in value may be credited to or (as the case may be) debited from the fair value reserve.

The fair value reserve

44F.— (1)   The fair value reserve must be adjusted to the extent that the amounts shown in it are no longer necessary for the purposes of paragraph 44E(3) or (4).

(2)   The treatment for taxation purposes of amounts credited or debited to the fair value reserve shall be disclosed in a note to the accounts.

ASSETS AND LIABILITIES DENOMINATED IN FOREIGN CURRENCIES

45.— (1)   Subject to the following sub-paragraphs, amounts to be included in respect of assets and liabilities denominated in foreign currencies shall be in sterling (or the currency in which the accounts are drawn up) after translation at an appropriate spot rate of exchange prevailing at the balance sheet date.

(2)   An appropriate rate of exchange prevailing on the date of purchase may however be used for assets held as financial fixed assets and assets to be included under Assets items 9 (Intangible fixed assets) and 10 (Tangible fixed assets) in the balance sheet format, if they are not covered or not specifically covered in either the spot or forward currency markets.

(3)   An appropriate spot rate of exchange prevailing at the balance sheet date shall be used for translating uncompleted spot exchange transactions.

(4)   An appropriate forward rate of exchange prevailing at the balance sheet date shall be used for translating uncompleted forward exchange transactions.

(5)   This paragraph does not apply to any assets or liabilities held, or any transactions entered into, for hedging purposes or to any assets or liabilities which are themselves hedged.

46.— (1)   Subject to sub-paragraph (2), any difference between the amount to be included in respect of an asset or liability under paragraph 45 and the book value, after translation into sterling (or the currency in which the accounts are drawn up) at an appropriate rate, of that asset or liability shall be credited or, as the case may be, debited to the profit and loss account.

(2)   In the case, however, of assets held as financial fixed assets, of assets to be included under Assets items 9 (Intangible fixed assets) and 10 (Tangible fixed assets) in the balance sheet format and of transactions undertaken to cover such assets, any such difference may be deducted from or credited to any non-distributable reserve available for the purpose.

CHAPTER III
NOTES TO THE ACCOUNTS

Preliminary

47.— (1) Any information required in the case of a company by the following provisions of this Part of this Schedule shall (if not given in the company's accounts) be given by way of a note to the accounts ...

(2) Subject to the next sub-paragraph, in respect of every item stated in a note to the accounts the corresponding amount for the financial year immediately preceding that to which the accounts relate shall also be stated and where the corresponding amount is not comparable, it shall be adjusted and particulars of the adjustment and the reasons for it shall be given.

(3) The last sub-paragraph does not apply to:

(a) paragraphs 55 and 59 of this Part of this Schedule;

(b) paragraph 13 of Schedule 4A;

(c) paragraphs 2, 8(3), 16, 21(1)(d), 22(4) and (5), 24(3) and (4) and 27(3) and (4) of Schedule 5; and

(d) Parts II and III of Schedule 6 as modified by Part IV of this Schedule (loans and other dealings in favour of directors).

General

Disclosure of accounting policies

48. The accounting policies adopted by the company in determining the amounts to be included in respect of items shown in the balance sheet and in determining the profit or loss of the company shall be stated (including such policies with respect to the depreciation and diminution in value of assets).

49. It shall be stated whether the accounts have been prepared in accordance with applicable accounting standards and particulars of any material departure from those standards and the reasons for it shall be given.

Sums denominated in foreign currencies

50. Where any sums originally denominated in foreign currencies have been brought into account under any items shown in the balance sheet format or the profit and loss account formats, the basis on which those sums have been translated into sterling (or the currency in which the accounts are drawn up) shall be stated.

Reserves and dividends

50A. There must be stated—

(a) any amount set aside or proposed to be set aside to, or withdrawn or proposed to be withdrawn from, reserves,

(b) the aggregate amount of dividends paid in the financial year (other than those for which a liability existed at the immediately preceding balance sheet date),

(c) the aggregate amount of dividends that the company is liable to pay at the balance sheet date, and

(d) the aggregate amount of dividends that are proposed before the date of approval of the accounts, and not otherwise disclosed under paragraph (b) or (c).

Information supplementing the balance sheet

Share capital and debentures

51.— (1) The following information shall be given with respect to the company's share capital:

(a) the authorised share capital; and

(b) where shares of more than one class have been allotted, the number and aggregate nominal value of shares of each class allotted.

(2)   In the case of any part of the allotted share capital that consists of redeemable shares, the following information shall be given:

(a)   the earliest and latest dates on which the company has power to redeem those shares;

(b)   whether those shares must be redeemed in any event or are liable to be redeemed at the option of the company or of the shareholder; and

(c)   whether any (and, if so, what) premium is payable on redemption.

52.   If the company has allotted any shares during the financial year, the following information shall be given:

(a)   ...

(b)   the classes of shares allotted; and

(c)   as respects each class of shares, the number allotted, their aggregate nominal value and the consideration received by the company for the allotment.

53.—   (1)   With respect to any contingent right to the allotment of shares in the company the following particulars shall be given:

(a)   the number, description and amount of the shares in relation to which the right is exercisable;

(b)   the period during which it is exercisable; and

(c)   the price to be paid for the shares allotted.

(2)   In sub-paragraph (1) above "contingent right to the allotment of shares" means any option to subscribe for shares and any other right to require the allotment of shares to any person whether arising on the conversion into shares of securities of any other description or otherwise.

54.—   (1)   If the company has issued any debentures during the financial year to which the accounts relate, the following information shall be given:

(a)   ...

(b)   the classes of debentures issued; and

(c)   as respects each class of debentures, the amount issued and the consideration received by the company for the issue.

(2)   ...

(3)   Where any of the company's debentures are held by a nominee of or trustee for the company, the nominal amount of the debentures and the amount at which they are stated in the accounting records kept by the company in accordance with section 221 of this Act shall be stated.

Fixed assets

55.—   (1)   In respect of any fixed assets of the company included in any assets item in the company's balance sheet the following information shall be given by reference to each such item:

(a)   the appropriate amounts in respect of those assets included in the item as at the date of the beginning of the financial year and as at the balance sheet date respectively;

(b)   the effect on any amount included in the item in respect of those assets of:

(i)   any determination during that year of the value to be ascribed to any of those assets in accordance with paragraph 41 above;

(ii)   acquisitions during that year of any fixed assets;

(iii)   disposals during that year of any fixed assets; and

(iv)   any transfers of fixed assets of the company to and from the item during that year.

(2)   The reference in sub-paragraph (1)(a) to the appropriate amounts in respect of any fixed assets (included in an assets item) as at any date there mentioned is a reference to amounts representing the aggregate amounts determined, as at that date, in respect of fixed assets falling to be included under the item on either of the following bases, that is to say:

(a)   on the basis of cost (determined in accordance with paragraphs 36 and 37); or

(b)   on any basis permitted by paragraph 41;

(leaving out of account in either case any provisions for depreciation or diminution in value).

(3) In addition, in respect of any fixed assets of the company included in any assets item in the company's balance sheet, there shall be stated (by reference to each such item):

   (a) the cumulative amount of provisions for depreciation or diminution in value of those assets included under the item as at each date mentioned in sub-paragraph (1)(a);

   (b) the amount of any such provisions made in respect of the financial year;

   (c) the amount of any adjustments made in respect of any such provisions during that year in consequence of the disposal of any of those assets; and

   (d) the amount of any other adjustments made in respect of any such provisions during that year.

(4) The requirements of this paragraph need not be complied with to the extent that a company takes advantage of the option of setting off charges and income afforded by paragraph 5(3) of this Part of this Schedule.

56. Where any fixed assets of the company (other than listed investments) are included under any item shown in the company's balance sheet at an amount determined in accordance with paragraph 41, the following information shall be given:

   (a) the years (so far as they are known to the directors) in which the assets were severally valued and the several values; and

   (b) in the case of assets that have been valued during the financial year, the names of the persons who valued them or particulars of their qualifications for doing so and (whichever is stated) the bases of valuation used by them.

57. In relation to any amount which is included under Assets item 10 in the balance sheet format (Tangible fixed assets) with respect to land and buildings there shall be stated:

   (a) how much of that amount is ascribable to land of freehold tenure and how much to land of leasehold tenure; and

   (b) how much of the amount ascribable to land of leasehold tenure is ascribable to land held on long lease and how much to land held on short lease.

58. There shall be disclosed separately the amount of:

   (a) any participating interests; and

   (b) any shares in group undertakings that are held in credit institutions.

Information about fair value of assets and liabilities

58A.— (1) This paragraph applies where financial instruments have been valued in accordance with paragraph 44A or 44C.

   (2) There must be stated—

   (a) where the fair value of the instruments has been determined in accordance with paragraph 44B(4), the significant assumptions underlying the valuation models and techniques used,

   (b) for each category of financial instrument, the fair value of the instruments in that category and the changes in value—

      (i) included in the profit and loss account, and

      (ii) credited to or (as the case may be) debited from the fair value reserve,

   in respect of those instruments, and

   (c) for each class of derivatives, the extent and nature of the instruments, including significant terms and conditions that may affect the amount, timing and certainty of future cash flows.

   (3) Where any amount is transferred to or from the fair value reserve during the financial year, there must be stated in tabular form—

   (a) the amount of the reserve as at the date of the beginning of the financial year and as at the balance sheet date respectively;

   (b) the amount transferred to or from the reserve during that year; and

   (c) the source and application respectively of the amounts so transferred.

58B.   Where the company has derivatives that it has not included at fair value, there must be stated for
        each class of such derivatives—
        (a)   the fair value of the derivatives in that class, if such a value can be determined in accordance
               with paragraph 44B, and
        (b)   the extent and nature of the derivatives.

58C.— (1)   Sub-paragraph (2) applies if—
        (a)   the company has financial fixed assets that could be included at fair value by virtue of
               paragraph 44A,
        (b)   the amount at which those assets are included under any item in the company's
               accounts is in excess of their fair value, and
        (c)   the company has not made provision for diminution in value of those assets in accor-
               dance with paragraph 26(1) of this Part of this Schedule.
      (2)   There must be stated—
        (a)   the amount at which either the individual assets or appropriate groupings of those indi-
               vidual assets are included in the company's accounts,
        (b)   the fair value of those assets or groupings, and
        (c)   the reasons for not making a provision for diminution in value of those assets, includ-
               ing the nature of the evidence that provides the basis for the belief that the amount at
               which they are stated in the accounts will be recovered.

Information where investment property and living animals and plants included at fair value

58D.— (1)   This paragraph applies where the amounts to be included in a company's accounts in respect
             of investment property or living animals and plants have been determined in accordance
             with paragraph 44D.
      (2)   The balance sheet items affected and the basis of valuation adopted in determining the
             amounts of the assets in question in the case of each such item must be disclosed in a note to
             the accounts.
      (3)   In the case of investment property, for each balance sheet item affected there must be
             shown, either separately in the balance sheet or in a note to the accounts—
        (a)   the comparable amounts determined according to the historical cost accounting rules;
               or
        (b)   the differences between those amounts and the corresponding amounts actually shown
               in the balance sheet in respect of that item.
      (4)   In sub-paragraph (3) above, references in relation to any item to the comparable amounts
             determined in accordance with that sub-paragraph are references to—
        (a)   the aggregate amount which would be required to be shown in respect of that item if
               the amounts to be included in respect of all the assets covered by that item were deter-
               mined according to the historical cost accounting rules; and
        (b)   the aggregate amount of the cumulative provisions for depreciation or diminution in
               value which would be permitted or required in determining those amounts according
               to those rules.

Reserves and provisions

59.   (1)   Where any amount is transferred:
        (a)   to or from any reserves;
        (b)   to any provisions for liabilities; or
        (c)   from any provision for liabilities otherwise than for the purpose for which the provi-
               sion was established;
             and the reserves or provisions are or would but for paragraph 3(3) of this Part of this
             Schedule be shown as separate items in the company's balance sheet, the information
             mentioned in the following sub-paragraph shall be given in respect of the aggregate of
             reserves or provisions included in the same item.
      (2)   That information is:

      (a)   the amount of the reserves or provisions as at the date of the beginning of the financial year and as at the balance sheet date respectively;

      (b)   any amounts transferred to or from the reserve or provisions during that year; and

      (c)   the source and application respectively of any amounts so transferred.

(3) Particulars shall be given of each provision included in Liabilities item 6(c) (Other provisions) in the company's balance sheet in any case where the amount of that provision is material.

Provision for taxation

60. The amount of any provision for deferred taxation shall be stated separately from the amount of any provision for other taxation.

Maturity analysis

61.— (1) A company shall disclose separately for each of Assets items 3(b) and 4 and Liabilities items 1(b), 2(b) and 3(b) the aggregate amount of the loans and advances and liabilities included in those items broken down into the following categories:

      (a)   those repayable in not more than three months

      (b)   those repayable in more than three months but not more than one year

      (c)   those repayable in more than one year but not more than five years

      (d)   those repayable in more than five years

from the balance sheet date.

(2) A company shall also disclose the aggregate amounts of all loans and advances falling within Assets item 4 (Loans and advances to customers) which are:

      (a)   repayable on demand; or

      (b)   are for an indeterminate period, being repayable upon short notice.

(3) For the purposes of sub-paragraph (1), where a loan or advance or liability is repayable by instalments, each such instalment is to be treated as a separate loan or advance or liability.

Debt and other fixed income securities

62. A company shall disclose the amount of debt and fixed income securities included in Assets item 5 (Debt securities (and other fixed income securities)) and the amount of such securities included in Liabilities item 3(a) (Bonds and medium term notes) that (in each case) will become due within one year of the balance sheet date.

Subordinated liabilities

63.— (1) The following information must be disclosed in relation to any borrowing included in Liabilities item 7 (Subordinated liabilities) that exceeds 10 per cent. of the total for that item:

      (a)   its amount;

      (b)   the currency in which it is denominated;

      (c)   the rate of interest and the maturity date (or the fact that it is perpetual);

      (d)   the circumstances in which early repayment may be demanded;

      (e)   the terms of the subordination; and

      (f)   the existence of any provisions whereby it may be converted into capital or some other form of liability and the terms of any such provisions.

(2) The general terms of any other borrowings included in Liabilities item 7 shall also be stated.

Fixed cumulative dividends

64. If any fixed cumulative dividends on the company's shares are in arrear, there shall be stated:

      (a)   the amount of the arrears; and

      (b)   the period for which the dividends or, if there is more than one class, each class of them are in arrear.

Details of assets charged

65.— (1) There shall be disclosed, in relation to each liabilities and memorandum item of the balance sheet format, the aggregate amount of any assets of the company which have been charged to secure any liability or potential liability included thereunder, the aggregate amount of the liabilities or potential liabilities so secured and an indication of the nature of the security given.

(2) Particulars shall also be given of any other charge on the assets of the company to secure the liabilities of any other person, including, where practicable, the amount secured.

Guarantees and other financial commitments

66.— (1) There shall be stated, where practicable:

(a)   the aggregate amount or estimated amount of contracts for capital expenditure, so far as not provided for; …

(b)   …

(2) Particulars shall be given of:

(a)   any pension commitments included under any provision shown in the company's balance sheet; and

(b)   any such commitments for which no provision has been made;

and where any such commitment relates wholly or partly to pensions payable to past directors of the company separate particulars shall be given of that commitment so far as it relates to such pensions.

(3) Particulars shall also be given of any other financial commitments, including any contingent liabilities, which:

(a)   have not been provided for;

(b)   have not been included in the memorandum items in the balance sheet format; and

(c)   are relevant to assessing the company's state of affairs.

(4) Commitments within any of the preceding sub-paragraphs undertaken on behalf of or for the benefit of:

(a)   any parent company or fellow subsidiary undertaking of the company; or

(b)   any subsidiary undertaking of the company;

shall be stated separately from the other commitments within that sub-paragraph (and commitments within paragraph (a) shall be stated separately from those within paragraph (b)).

(5) There shall be disclosed the nature and amount of any contingent liabilities and commitments included in Memorandum items 1 and 2 which are material in relation to the company's activities.

Memorandum items: Group undertakings

67.— (1) With respect to contingent liabilities required to be included under Memorandum item 1 in the balance sheet format, there shall be stated in a note to the accounts the amount of such contingent liabilities incurred on behalf of or for the benefit of:

(a)   any parent undertaking or fellow subsidiary undertaking; or

(b)   any subsidiary undertaking

of the company; in addition the amount incurred in respect of the undertakings referred to in paragraph (a) shall be stated separately from the amount incurred in respect of the undertakings referred to in paragraph (b).

(2) With respect to commitments required to be included under Memorandum item 2 in the balance sheet format, there shall be stated in a note to the accounts the amount of such commitments undertaken on behalf of or for the benefit of:

(a)   any parent undertaking or fellow subsidiary undertaking; or

(b)   any subsidiary undertaking

of the company; in addition the amount incurred in respect of the undertakings referred to in paragraph (a) shall be stated separately from the amount incurred in respect of the undertakings referred to in paragraph (b).

Transferable securities

68.— (1) There shall be disclosed for each of Assets items 5 to 8 in the balance sheet format the amount of transferable securities included under those items:
(a)   that are listed and the amount of those that are unlisted; ...
(b)   ...

(2) In the case of each amount shown in respect of listed securities under sub-paragraph (1)(a) above, there shall also be disclosed the aggregate market value of those securities, if different from the amount shown.

(3) There shall also be disclosed for each of Assets items 5 and 6 the amount of transferable securities included under those items that are held as financial fixed assets and the amount of those that are not so held, together with the criterion used by the directors to distinguish those held as financial fixed assets.

Leasing transactions

69. The aggregate amount of all property (other than land) leased by the company to other persons shall be disclosed, broken down so as to show the aggregate amount included in each relevant balance sheet item.

Assets and liabilities denominated in a currency other than sterling
(or the currency in which the accounts are drawn up)

70.— (1) The aggregate amount, in sterling (or the currency in which the accounts are drawn up), of all assets denominated in a currency other than sterling (or the currency used), together with the aggregate amount, in sterling (or the currency used), of all liabilities so denominated, is to be disclosed.

(2) For the purposes of this paragraph an appropriate rate of exchange prevailing at the balance sheet date shall be used to determine the amounts concerned.

Sundry assets and liabilities

71. Where any amount shown under either of the following items is material, particulars shall be given of each type of asset or liability included therein, including an explanation of the nature of the asset or liability and the amount included with respect to assets or liabilities of that type:
(a)   Assets item 13 (Other assets);
(b)   Liabilities item 4 (Other liabilities).

Unmatured forward transactions

72.— (1) The following shall be disclosed with respect to unmatured forward transactions outstanding at the balance sheet date:
(a)   the categories of such transactions, by reference to an appropriate system of classification;
(b)   whether, in the case of each such category, they have been made, to any material extent, for the purpose of hedging the effects of fluctuations in interest rates, exchange rates and market prices or whether they have been made, to any material extent, for dealing purposes.

(2) Transactions falling within sub-paragraph (1) shall include all those in relation to which income or expenditure is to be included in:
(a)   format 1, item 6 or format 2, items B4 or A3 (Dealing (profits) (losses)),
(b)   format 1, items 1 or 2, or format 2, items B1 or A1, by virtue of notes (1)(b) and (2)(b) to the profit and loss account formats (forward contracts, spread over the actual duration of the contract and similar in nature to interest).

Miscellaneous matters

73.— (1) Particulars shall be given of any case where the cost of any asset is for the first time determined under paragraph 38 of this Part of this Schedule.

(2) Where any outstanding loans made under the authority of section 153(4)(b), (bb) or (c) or section 155 of this Act (various cases of financial assistance by a company for purchase of its own shares) are included under any item shown in the company's balance sheet, the aggregate amount of those loans shall be disclosed for each item in question.

(3) ...

Information supplementing the profit and loss account

74. ...

Particulars of tax

75.— (1) ...

(2) Particulars shall be given of any special circumstances which affect liability in respect of taxation of profits, income or capital gains for the financial year or liability in respect of taxation of profits, income or capital gains for succeeding financial years.

(3) The following amounts shall be stated:

(a) the amount of the charge for United Kingdom corporation tax;

(b) if that amount would have been greater but for relief from double taxation, the amount which it would have been but for such relief;

(c) the amount of the charge for United Kingdom income tax; and

(d) the amount of the charge for taxation imposed outside the United Kingdom of profits, income and (so far as charged to revenue) capital gains.

These amounts shall be stated separately in respect of each of the amounts which is shown under the following items in the profit and loss account, that is to say format 1 item 16, format 2 item A10 (Tax on (profit) (loss) on ordinary activities) and format 1 item 21, format 2 item A13 (Tax on extraordinary (profit) (loss)).

Particulars of income

76.— (1) A company shall disclose, with respect to income included in the following items in the profit and loss account formats, the amount of that income attributable to each of the geographical markets in which the company has operated during the financial year:

(a) format 1 item 1, format 2 item B1 (Interest receivable);

(b) format 1 item 3, format 2 item B2 (Dividend income);

(c) format 1 item 4, format 2 item B3 (Fees and commissions receivable);

(d) format 1 item 6, format 2 item B4 (Dealing profits); and

(e) format 1 item 7, format 2 item B7 (Other operating income).

(2) In analysing for the purposes of this paragraph the source of any income, the directors shall have regard to the manner in which the company's activities are organised.

(3) For the purposes of this paragraph, markets which do not differ substantially from each other shall be treated as one market.

(4) Where in the opinion of the directors the disclosure of any information required by this paragraph would be seriously prejudicial to the interests of the company, that information need not be disclosed, but the fact that any such information has not been disclosed must be stated.

77. ...

Management and agency services

78. A company providing any management and agency services to customers shall disclose that fact, if the scale of such services provided is material in the context of its business as a whole.

Subordinated liabilities

79.   Any amounts charged to the profit and loss account representing charges incurred during the year with respect to subordinated liabilities shall be disclosed.

Sundry income and charges

80.   Where any amount to be included in any of the following items is material, particulars shall be given of each individual component of the figure, including an explanation of their nature and amount:

(a)   In format 1:

      (i)   Items 7 and 10 (Other operating income and charges);

      (ii)   Items 18 and 19 (Extraordinary income and charges);

(b)   In format 2:

      (i)   Items A6 and B7 (Other operating charges and income);

      (ii)   Items A12 and B10 (Extraordinary charges and income).

Miscellaneous matters

81.— (1)   Where any amount relating to any preceding financial year is included in any item in the profit and loss account, the effect shall be stated.

(2)   The effect shall be stated of any transactions that are exceptional by virtue of size or incidence though they fall within the ordinary activities of the company.

CHAPTER IV
INTERPRETATION OF PART I

General

82.   The following definitions apply for the purposes of this Part of this Schedule and its interpretation:

    …

    …

"Financial fixed assets" means loans and advances and securities held as fixed assets; participating interests and shareholdings in group undertakings shall be regarded as financial fixed assets;

"Fungible assets" means assets of any description which are substantially indistinguishable one from another;

"Investment property" means land held to earn rent or for capital appreciation.

"Lease" includes an agreement for a lease;

"Listed security" means a security listed on a recognised stock exchange, or on any stock exchange of repute outside Great Britain and the expression "unlisted security" shall be construed accordingly;

"Long lease" means a lease in the case of which the portion of the term for which it was granted remaining unexpired at the end of the financial year is not less than 50 years;

"Repayable on demand", in connection with deposits, loans or advances, means those amounts which can at any time be withdrawn or demanded without notice or for which a maturity or period of notice of not more than 24 hours or one working day has been agreed;

"Sale and repurchase transaction" means a transaction which involves the transfer by a credit institution or customer ("the transferor") to another credit institution or customer ("the transferee") of assets subject to an agreement that the same assets, or (in the case of fungible assets) equivalent assets, will subsequently be transferred back to the transferor at a specified price on a date specified or to be specified by the transferor; but the following shall not be regarded as sale and repurchase transactions: forward exchange transactions, options, transactions involving the issue of debt securities with a commitment to repurchase all or part of the issue before maturity or any similar transactions;

"Sale and option to resell transaction" means a transaction which involves the transfer by a credit institution or customer ("the transferor") to another credit institution or customer ("the transferee") of assets subject to an agreement that the transferee is entitled to require the subsequent transfer of the same assets, or (in the case of fungible assets) equivalent assets, back to the transferor at the purchase price or another price agreed in advance on a date specified or to be specified; and

"Short lease" means a lease which is not a long lease.

Financial instruments

82A.   For the purposes of this Part of this Schedule, references to "derivatives" include commodity-based contracts that give either contracting party the right to settle in cash or in some other financial instrument, except when such contracts—

    (a)   were entered into for the purpose of, and continue to meet, the company's expected purchase, sale or usage requirements,

    (b)   were designated for such purpose at their inception, and

    (c)   are expected to be settled by delivery of the commodity.

82B.— (1)   The expressions listed in sub-paragraph (2) have the same meaning in paragraphs 44A to 44F, 58A to 58C and 82A of this Part of this Schedule as they have in Council Directives 78/660/EEC on the annual accounts of certain types of companies and 86/635/EEC on the annual accounts and consolidated accounts of banks and other financial institutions, as amended.

    (2)   Those expressions are "available for sale financial asset", "business combination", "commodity-based contracts", "derivative", "equity instrument", "exchange difference", "fair value hedge accounting system", "financial fixed asset", "financial instrument", "foreign entity", "hedge accounting", "hedge accounting system", "hedged items", "hedging instrument", "held for trading purposes", "held to maturity", "monetary item", "receivables", "reliable market" and "trading portfolio".

Loans

83.   For the purposes of this Part of this Schedule a loan or advance (including a liability comprising a loan or advance) is treated as falling due for repayment, and an instalment of a loan or advance is treated as falling due for payment, on the earliest date on which the lender could require repayment or (as the case may be) payment, if he exercised all options and rights available to him.

Materiality

84.   For the purposes of this Part of this Schedule amounts which in the particular context of any provision of this Part are not material may be disregarded for the purposes of that provision.

Provisions

85.   For the purposes of this Part of this Schedule and its interpretation:

    (a)   references in this Part to provisions for depreciation or diminution in value of assets are to any amount written off by way of providing for depreciation or diminution in value of assets;

    (b)   any reference in the profit and loss account formats or the notes thereto set out in Section B of this Part to the depreciation of, or amounts written off, assets of any description is to any provision for depreciation or diminution in value of assets of that description; and

    (c)   references in this Part to provisions for liabilities are to any amount retained as reasonably necessary for the purpose of providing for any liability the nature of which is clearly defined and which is either likely to be incurred, or certain to be incurred but uncertain as to amount or as to the date on which it will arise.

Scots land tenure

86. In the application of this Part of this Schedule to Scotland, "land of freehold tenure" means land in respect of which the company ... is the owner; "land of leasehold tenure" means land of which the company is the tenant under a lease ...

Staff costs

87. For the purposes of this Part of this Schedule and its interpretation:
   (a) "Social security costs" means any contributions by the company to any state social security or pension scheme, fund or arrangement;
   (b) "Pension costs" includes any costs incurred by the company in respect of any pension scheme established for the purpose of providing pensions for persons currently or formerly employed by the company, any sums set aside for the future payment of pensions directly by the company to current or former employees and any pensions paid directly to such persons without having first been set aside; and
   (c) any amount stated in respect of the item "social security costs" or in respect of the item "wages and salaries" in the company's profit and loss account shall be determined by reference to payments made or costs incurred in respect of all persons employed by the company during the financial year who are taken into account in determining the relevant annual number for the purposes of section 231A(1)(a).

PART II
CONSOLIDATED ACCOUNTS

1. ...

General application of provisions applicable to individual accounts

2.— (1) In paragraph 1 of Schedule 4A (application to group accounts of provisions applicable to individual accounts), the reference in sub-paragraph (1) to the provisions of Schedule 4 shall be construed as a reference to the provisions of Part I of this Schedule; and accordingly:
   (a) ...
   (b) sub-paragraph (3) shall be omitted.
   (2) The general application of the provisions of Part I of this Schedule in place of those of Schedule 4 is subject to the following provisions.

Minority interests and associated undertakings

3.— (1) The provisions of this paragraph shall have effect so as to adapt paragraphs 17 and 21 of Schedule 4A (which require items in respect of "Minority interests" and associated undertakings to be added to the formats set out in Schedule 4) to the formats prescribed by Part I of this Schedule.
   (2) The item required to be added to the balance sheet format by paragraph 17(2) shall be added either between Liabilities items 7 and 8 or after Liabilities item 12.
   (3) The item required to be added to the profit and loss account format by paragraph 17(3) shall be added:
   (a) in the case of format 1, between items 17 and 18; or
   (b) in the case of format 2, between items A11 and A12 or between items B9 and B10.
   (4) The item required to be added to the profit and loss account format by paragraph 17(4) shall be added:
   (a) in the case of format 1, between items 22 and 23; or
   (b) in the case of format 2, between items A14 and A15 or between items B11 and B12.
   (5) Paragraph 17(5) shall not apply but for the purposes of paragraph 3(3) of Part I of this Schedule (power to combine items) the additional items required by the foregoing provisions of this paragraph shall be treated as items to which a letter is assigned.

(6) Paragraph 21(2) shall apply with respect to a balance sheet prepared under this Schedule as if it required Assets item 7 (Participating interests) in the balance sheet format to be replaced by the two replacement items referred to in that paragraph.

(7) Paragraph 21(3) shall not apply, but the following items in the profit and loss account formats, namely:

(a) format 1 item 3(b) (Income from participating interests),

(b) format 2 item B2(b) (Income from participating interests),

shall be replaced by the following two replacement items:

(i) "Income from participating interests other than associated undertakings", which shall be shown at position 3(b) in format 1 and position B2(b) in format 2; and

(ii) "Income from associated undertakings", which shall be shown at an appropriate position.

4. Paragraphs 18 and 22(1) of Schedule 4A shall apply as if, in substitution for the references therein to paragraphs 17 to 19 and 21 of Schedule 4, they referred to paragraphs 24 to 26 and 28 of Part I of this Schedule.

Foreign currency translation

5. Any difference between:

(a) the amount included in the consolidated accounts for the previous financial year with respect to any undertaking included in the consolidation or the group's interest in any associated undertaking, together with the amount of any transactions undertaken to cover any such interest; and

(b) the opening amount for the financial year in respect of those undertakings and in respect of any such transactions

arising as a result of the application of paragraph 45 of Part I of this Schedule may be credited to (where (a) is less than (b)), or deducted from (where (a) is greater than (b)), (as the case may be) consolidated reserves.

6. Any income and expenditure of undertakings included in the consolidation and associated undertakings in a foreign currency may be translated for the purposes of the consolidated accounts at the average rates of exchange prevailing during the financial year.

Information as to undertaking in which shares held
as a result of financial assistance operation

7.— (1) The following provisions apply where the parent company of a banking group has a subsidiary undertaking which:

(a) is a credit institution of which shares are held as a result of a financial assistance operation with a view to its reorganisation or rescue; and

(b) is excluded from consolidation under section 229(3)(c) (interest held with a view to resale).

(2) Information as to the nature and terms of the operations shall be given in a note to the group accounts and there shall be appended to the copy of the group accounts delivered to the registrar in accordance with section 242 a copy of the undertaking's latest individual accounts and, if it is a parent undertaking, its latest group accounts.

If the accounts appended are required by law to be audited, a copy of the auditors' report shall also be appended.

(3) ... If any document required to be appended is in a language other than English then, subject to section 710B(6) (delivery of certain Welsh documents without a translation), the directors shall annex a translation of it into English, certified in the prescribed manner to be a correct translation.

(4) The above requirements are subject to the following qualifications:

(a) an undertaking is not required to prepare for the purposes of this paragraph accounts which would not otherwise be prepared, and if no accounts satisfying the above requirements are prepared none need be appended;

(b)　the accounts of an undertaking need not be appended if they would not otherwise be required to be published, or made available for public inspection, anywhere in the world, but in that case the reason for not appending the accounts shall be stated in a note to the consolidated accounts.

(5)　Where a copy of an undertaking's accounts is required to be appended to the copy of the group accounts delivered to the registrar, that fact shall be stated in a note to the group accounts.

(6)　Sub-sections (2) to (4) of section 242 (penalties, &c in case of default) apply in relation to the requirements of this paragraph as regards the delivery of documents to the registrar as they apply in relation to the requirements of sub-section (1) of that section.

PART III
ADDITIONAL DISCLOSURE: RELATED UNDERTAKINGS

1.—　(1)　Where accounts are prepared in accordance with the special provisions of this Schedule relating to banking companies or groups:

(a)　the information required by paragraphs 8 and 24 of Schedule 5 (information about significant holdings of the company in undertakings other than subsidiary undertakings) need only be given in respect of undertakings (otherwise falling within the class of undertakings in respect of which disclosure is required) in which the company has a significant holding amounting to 20 per cent or more of the nominal value of the shares in the undertaking; and

(b)　the information required by paragraph 27 of Schedule 5 (information about significant holdings of the group in undertakings other than subsidiary undertakings) need only be given in respect of undertakings (otherwise falling within the class of undertakings in respect of which disclosure is required) in which the group has a significant holding amounting to 20 per cent or more of the nominal value of the shares in the undertaking.

In addition any information required by those paragraphs may be omitted if it is not material.

(2)　Paragraph 13(3) and (4) of Schedule 5 shall apply *mutatis mutandis* for the purposes of sub-paragraph (1)(a) above and paragraph 32(3) and (4) of that Schedule shall apply *mutatis mutandis* for the purposes of sub-paragraph (1)(b) above.

PART IV
ADDITIONAL DISCLOSURE: EMOLUMENTS AND OTHER
BENEFITS OF DIRECTORS AND OTHERS

1.　The provisions of this Part of this Schedule have effect with respect to the application of Schedule 6 (additional disclosure: emoluments and other benefits of directors and others) to a banking company or the holding company of a credit institution.

Loans, quasi-loans and other dealings

2.　Where a banking company, or a company which is the holding company of a credit institution, prepares annual accounts for a financial year, it need not comply with the provisions of Part II of Schedule 6 (loans, quasi-loans and other dealings) in relation to a transaction or arrangement of a kind mentioned in section 330, or an agreement to enter into such a transaction or arrangement, to which that banking company or (as the case may be) credit institution is a party.

Other transactions, arrangements and agreements

3.—　(1)　Where a banking company, or a company which is the holding company of a credit institution, takes advantage of the provisions of paragraph 2 of this Part of this Schedule for the purposes of its annual accounts for a financial year, then, in preparing those accounts, it shall comply with the provisions of Part III of Schedule 6 (other transactions, arrangements and agreements) only in relation to a transaction, arrangement or agreement made by that banking company or (as the case may be) credit institution for—

    (a)   a person who was a director of the company preparing the accounts, or who was connected with such a director, or

    (b)   a person who was a chief executive or manager ... of that company or its holding company.

   (2) References in that Part to officers of the company shall be construed accordingly as including references to such persons.

   (3) In this paragraph—

    (a)   "director" includes a shadow director;

    (b)   "chief executive" has the meaning given in section 417 of the Financial Services and Markets Act 2000; and

    (c)   "manager" has the meaning given in section 423(3) of that Act.

   (4) For the purposes of that Part as it applies by virtue of this paragraph, a body corporate which a person does not control shall not be treated as connected with him.

   (5) Section 346 of this Act applies for the purposes of this paragraph as regards the interpretation of references to a person being connected with a director or controlling a body corporate.

SCHEDULE 9A

FORM AND CONTENT OF ACCOUNTS OF INSURANCE COMPANIES AND GROUPS

Sections 255, 255A, 255B

PART I
INDIVIDUAL ACCOUNTS

CHAPTER I
GENERAL RULES AND FORMATS

SECTION A
GENERAL RULES

1.— (1) Subject to the following provisions of this Part of this Schedule—

    (a)   every balance sheet of a company shall show the items listed in the balance sheet format set out below in section B of this Chapter; and

    (b)   every profit and loss account of a company shall show the items listed in the profit and loss account format so set out,

in either case in the order and under the headings and sub-headings given in the format.

   (2) Sub-paragraph (1) above is not to be read as requiring the heading or sub-heading for any item to be distinguished by any letter or number assigned to that item in the format.

2.— (1) Any item required in accordance with paragraph 1 above to be shown in a company's balance sheet or profit and loss account may be shown in greater detail than so required.

   (2) A company's balance sheet or profit and loss account may include an item representing or covering the amount of any asset or liability, income or expenditure not specifically covered by any of the items listed in the balance sheet or profit and loss account format set out in section B below, but the following shall not be treated as assets in any company's balance sheet—

    (a)   preliminary expenses;

    (b)   expenses of and commission on any issue of shares or debentures; and

    (c)   costs of research.

(3)   Items to which Arabic numbers are assigned in the balance sheet format set out in section B below (except for items concerning technical provisions and the reinsurers' share of technical provisions), and items to which lower case letters in parentheses are assigned in the profit and loss account format so set out (except for items within items I.1 and 4 and II.1, 5 and 6) may be combined in a company's accounts for any financial year if either—

    (a)   their individual amounts are not material for the purpose of giving a true and fair view; or

    (b)   the combination facilitates the assessment of the state of affairs or profit or loss of the company for that year;

but in a case within paragraph (b) above the individual amounts of any items so combined shall be disclosed in a note to the accounts and any notes required by this Schedule to the items so combined under that paragraph shall, notwithstanding the combination, be given.

(4)   Subject to paragraph 3(3) below, a heading or sub-heading corresponding to an item listed in the format adopted in preparing a company's balance sheet or profit and loss account shall not be included if there is no amount to be shown for that item in respect of the financial year to which the balance sheet or profit and loss account relates.

3.—   (1)   In respect of every item shown in the balance sheet or profit and loss account, there shall be shown or stated the corresponding amount for the financial year immediately preceding that to which the accounts relate.

(2)   Where the corresponding amount is not comparable with the amount to be shown for the item in question in respect of the financial year to which the balance sheet or profit and loss account relates, the former amount shall be adjusted and particulars of the adjustment and the reasons for it shall be given in a note to the accounts.

(3)   Paragraph 2(4) above does not apply in any case where an amount can be shown for the item in question in respect of the financial year immediately preceding that to which the balance sheet or profit and loss account relates, and that amount shall be shown under the heading or sub-heading required by paragraph 1 above for that item.

4.   Subject to the provisions of this Schedule, amounts in respect of items representing assets or income may not be set off against amounts in respect of items representing liabilities or expenditure (as the case may be), or vice versa.

5.   ...

6.—   (1) The provisions of this Schedule which relate to long term business shall apply, with necessary modifications, to business which consists of effecting or carrying out relevant contracts of general insurance which—

    (a)   is transacted exclusively or principally according to the technical principles of long term business, and

    (b)   is a significant amount of the business of the company.

(2)   For the purposes of paragraph (1), a contract of general insurance is a relevant contract if the risk insured against relates to—

    (a)   accident; or

    (b)   sickness.

(3)   Sub-paragraph (2) must be read with—

    (a)   section 22 of the Financial Services and Markets Act 2000;

    (b)   any relevant order under that section; and

    (c)   Schedule 2 to that Act.

6A.   The directors of a company must, in determining how amounts are presented within items in the profit and loss account and balance sheet, have regard to the substance of the reported transaction or arrangement, in accordance with generally accepted accounting principles or practice.

SECTION B
THE REQUIRED FORMATS FOR ACCOUNTS

Preliminary

7.—   (1)   References in this Part of this Schedule to the balance sheet format or profit and loss
account format are to the balance sheet format or profit and loss account format set out
below, and references to the items listed in either of the formats are to those items read
together with any of the notes following the formats which apply to any of those items.

(2)   The requirement imposed by paragraph 1 to show the items listed in either format in the
order adopted in the format is subject to any provision in the notes following the format for
alternative positions for any particular items.

(3)   Where in respect of any item to which an Arabic number is assigned in either format, the
gross amount and reinsurance amount or reinsurers' share are required to be shown, a sub-
total of those amounts shall also be given.

(4)   Where in respect of any item to which an Arabic number is assigned in the profit and loss
account format, separate items are required to be shown, then a separate sub-total of those
items shall also be given in addition to any sub-total required by sub-paragraph (3) above.

8.   A number in brackets following any item in either of the formats set out below is a reference to
the note of that number in the notes following the format.

9.—   (1) In the profit and loss account format set out below—

(a)   the heading "Technical account—General business" is for business which consists of
effecting or carrying out contracts of general insurance; and

(b)   the heading "Technical account—Long term business" is for business which consists
of effecting or carrying out contracts of long term insurance.

(2)   In sub-paragraph (1), references to—

(a)   contracts of general or long term insurance; and

(b)   the effecting or carrying out of such contracts,

must be read with section 22 of the Financial Services and Markets Act 2000, any relevant
order under that section, and Schedule 2 to that Act.

Balance Sheet Format

ASSETS

A.   *Called up share capital not paid (1)*

B.   *Intangible assets*

1.   Development costs

2.   Concessions, patents, licences, trade marks and similar rights and assets *(2)*

3.   Goodwill *(3)*

4.   Payments on account

C.   *Investments*

I   Land and buildings *(4)*

II   Investments in group undertakings and participating interests

1.   Shares in group undertakings

2.   Debt securities issued by, and loans to, group undertakings

3.   Participating interests

4.   Debt securities issued by, and loans to, undertakings in which the company has a participating interest

III   Other financial investments

1.   Shares and other variable-yield securities and units in unit trusts

2.   Debt securities and other fixed income securities *(5)*

3.   Participation in investment pools *(6)*

4.   Loans secured by mortgages *(7)*

5.   Other loans *(7)*

6.   Deposits with credit institutions *(8)*

7.   Other *(9)*
   IV   Deposits with ceding undertakings *(10)*
D.   *Assets held to cover linked liabilities (11)*
Da.   *Reinsurers' share of technical provisions (12)*
   1.   Provision for unearned premiums
   2.   Long term business provision
   3.   Claims outstanding
   4.   Provisions for bonuses and rebates
   5.   Other technical provisions
   6.   Technical provisions for unit-linked liabilities
E.   *Debtors (13)*
   I   Debtors arising out of direct insurance operations
      1.   Policy holders
      2.   Intermediaries
   II   Debtors arising out of reinsurance operations
   III   Other debtors
   IV   Called up share capital not paid *(1)*
F.   *Other assets*
   I   Tangible assets
      1.   Plant and machinery
      2.   Fixtures, fittings, tools and equipment
      3.   Payments on account (other than deposits paid on land and buildings) and assets (other than buildings) in course of construction
   II   Stocks
      1.   Raw materials and consumables
      2.   Work in progress
      3.   Finished goods and goods for resale
      4.   Payments on account
   III   Cash at bank and in hand
   IV   Own shares *(14)*
   V   Other *(15)*
G.   *Prepayments and accrued income*
   I   Accrued interest and rent *(16)*
   II   Deferred acquisition costs *(17)*
   III   Other prepayments and accrued income

LIABILITIES

A.   Capital and reserves
   I   Called up share capital or equivalent funds
   II   Share premium account
   III   Revaluation reserve
   IV   Reserves
      1.   Capital redemption reserve
      2.   Reserve for own shares
      3.   Reserves provided for by the articles of association
      4.   Other reserves
   V   Profit and loss account
B.   *Subordinated liabilities (18)*
Ba.   *Fund for future appropriations (19)*
C.   *Technical provisions*
   1.   Provision for unearned premiums *(20)*
      (a)   gross amount
      (b)   reinsurance amount *(12)*

      2.   Long term business provision *(20) (21) (26)*
          (a)   gross amount
          (b)   reinsurance amount *(12)*
      3.   Claims outstanding *(22)*
          (a)   gross amount
          (b)   reinsurance amount *(12)*
      4.   Provision for bonuses and rebates *(23)*
          (a)   gross amount
          (b)   reinsurance amount *(12)*
      5.   Equalisation provision *(24)*
      6.   Other technical provisions *(25)*
          (a)   gross amount
          (b)   reinsurance amount *(12)*

D.   *Technical provisions for linked liabilities (26)*
          (a)   gross amount
          (b)   reinsurance amount *(12)*

E.   *Provisions for other risks*
      1.   Provisions for pensions and similar obligations
      2.   Provisions for taxation
      3.   Other provisions

F.   *Deposits received from reinsurers (27)*

G.   *Creditors (28)*
      I   Creditors arising out of direct insurance operations
      II   Creditors arising out of reinsurance operations
      III   Debenture loans *(29)*
      IV   Amounts owed to credit institutions
      V   Other creditors including taxation and social security

H.   *Accruals and deferred income*

Notes on the balance sheet format

(1)   *Called up share capital not paid*
       (Assets items A and E.IV)
       This item may be shown in either of the positions given in the format.

(2)   *Concessions, patents, licences, trade marks and similar rights and assets*
       (Assets item B.2)
       Amounts in respect of assets shall only be included in a company's balance sheet under this item
       if either—
       (a)   the assets were acquired for valuable consideration and are not required to be shown under
            goodwill; or
       (b)   the assets in question were created by the company itself.

(3)   *Goodwill*
       (Assets item B.3)
       Amounts representing goodwill shall only be included to the extent that the goodwill was
       acquired for valuable consideration.

(4)   *Land and buildings*
       (Assets item C.I.)
       The amount of any land and buildings occupied by the company for its own activities shall be
       shown separately in the notes to the accounts.

(5)   *Debt securities and other fixed income securities*
       (Assets item C.III.2)
       This item shall comprise transferable debt securities and any other transferable fixed income
       securities issued by credit institutions, other undertakings or public bodies, in so far as they are
       not covered by Assets item C.II.2 or C.II.4.

Securities bearing interest rates that vary in accordance with specific factors, for example the interest rate on the inter-bank market or on the Euromarket, shall also be regarded as debt securities and other fixed income securities and so be included under this item.

(6)   *Participation in investment pools*
        (Assets item C.III.3)
        This item shall comprise shares held by the company in joint investments constituted by several undertakings or pension funds, the management of which has been entrusted to one of those undertakings or to one of those pension funds.

(7)   *Loans secured by mortgages and other loans*
        (Assets items C.III.4 and C.III.5)
        Loans to policy holders for which the policy is the main security shall be included under "Other loans" and their amount shall be disclosed in the notes to the accounts. Loans secured by mortgage shall be shown as such even where they are also secured by insurance policies. Where the amount of "Other loans" not secured by policies is material, an appropriate breakdown shall be given in the notes to the accounts.

(8)   *Deposits with credit institutions*
        (Assets item C.III.6)
        This item shall comprise sums the withdrawal of which is subject to a time restriction. Sums deposited with no such restriction shall be shown under Assets item F.III even if they bear interest.

(9)   *Other*
        (Assets item C.III.7)
        This item shall comprise those investments which are not covered by Assets items C.III.1 to 6. Where the amount of such investments is significant, they must be disclosed in the notes to the accounts.

(10)   *Deposits with ceding undertakings*
        (Assets item C.IV)
        Where the company accepts reinsurance this item shall comprise amounts, owed by the ceding undertakings and corresponding to guarantees, which are deposited with those ceding undertakings or with third parties or which are retained by those undertakings.
        These amounts may not be combined with other amounts owed by the ceding insurer to the reinsurer or set off against amounts owed by the reinsurer to the ceding insurer.
        Securities deposited with ceding undertakings or third parties which remain the property of the company shall be entered in the company's accounts as an investment, under the appropriate item.

(11)   *Assets held to cover linked liabilities*
        (Assets item D)
        In respect of long term business, this item shall comprise investments made pursuant to long term policies under which the benefits payable to the policy holder are wholly or partly to be determined by reference to the value of, or the income from, property of any description (whether or not specified in the contract) or by reference to fluctuations in, or in an index of, the value of property of any description (whether or not so specified).
        This item shall also comprise investments which are held on behalf of the members of a tontine and are intended for distribution among them.

(12)   *Reinsurance amounts*
        (Assets item Da: Liabilities items C.1(b), 2(b), 3(b), 4(b) and 6(b) and D(b))
        The reinsurance amounts may be shown either under Assets item Da or under Liabilities items C.1(b), 2(b), 3(b), 4(b) and 6(b) and D(b).
        The reinsurance amounts shall comprise the actual or estimated amounts which, under contractual reinsurance arrangements, are deducted from the gross amounts of technical provisions.
        As regards the provision for unearned premiums, the reinsurance amounts shall be calculated according to the methods referred to in paragraph 44 above or in accordance with the terms of the reinsurance policy.

(13)   *Debtors*
        (Assets item E)
        Amounts owed by group undertakings and undertakings in which the company has a participating
        interest shall be shown separately as sub-items of Assets items E.I, II and III.

(14)   *Own shares*
        (Assets item F.IV)
        The nominal value of the shares shall be shown separately under this item.

(15)   *Other*
        (Assets item F.V)
        This item shall comprise those assets which are not covered by Assets items F.I to IV. Where such
        assets are material they must be disclosed in the notes to the accounts.

(16)   *Accrued interest and rent*
        (Assets item G.I)
        This item shall comprise those items that represent interest and rent that have been earned up to
        the balance-sheet date but have not yet become receivable.

(17)   *Deferred acquisition costs*
        (Assets item G.II)
        This item shall comprise the costs of acquiring insurance policies which are incurred during a
        financial year but relate to a subsequent financial year ("deferred acquisition costs"), except in so
        far as—
        (a)   allowance has been made in the computation of the long term business provision made
               under paragraph 46 below and shown under Liabilities item C2 or D in the balance sheet,
               for—
               (i)   the explicit recognition of such costs, or
               (ii)   the implicit recognition of such costs by virtue of the anticipation of future income
                      from which such costs may prudently be expected to be recovered, or
        (b)   allowance has been made for such costs in respect of general business policies by a
               deduction from the provision for unearned premiums made under paragraph 44 below and
               shown under Liabilities item C.I in the balance sheet.
        Deferred acquisition costs arising in general business shall be distinguished from those arising in
        long term business.
        In the case of general business, the amount of any deferred acquisition costs shall be established
        on a basis compatible with that used for unearned premiums.
        There shall be disclosed in the notes to the accounts—
        (a)   how the deferral of acquisition costs has been treated (unless otherwise expressly stated in
               the accounts), and
        (b)   where such costs are included as a deduction from the provisions at Liabilities item C.I, the
               amount of such deduction, or
        (c)   where the actuarial method used in the calculation of the provisions at Liabilities item C.2
               or D has made allowance for the explicit recognition of such costs, the amount of the costs
               so recognised.

(18)   *Subordinated liabilities*
        (Liabilities item B)
        This item shall comprise all liabilities in respect of which there is a contractual obligation that, in
        the event of winding up or of bankruptcy, they are to be repaid only after the claims of all other
        creditors have been met (whether or not they are represented by certificates).

(19)   *Fund for future appropriations*
        (Liabilities item Ba)
        This item shall comprise all funds the allocation of which either to policy holders or to
        shareholders has not been determined by the end of the financial year.
        Transfers to and from this item shall be shown in item II.12a in the profit and loss account.

(20)   *Provision for unearned premiums*
(Liabilities item C.1)
In the case of long term business the provision for unearned premiums may be included in Liabilities item C.2 rather than in this item.
The provision for unearned premiums shall comprise the amount representing that part of gross premiums written which is estimated to be earned in the following financial year or to subsequent financial years.

(21)   *Long term business provision*
(Liabilities item C.2)
This item shall comprise the actuarially estimated value of the company's liabilities (excluding technical provisions included in Liabilities item D), including bonuses already declared and after deducting the actuarial value of future premiums.
This item shall also comprise claims incurred but not reported, plus the estimated costs of settling such claims.

(22)   *Claims outstanding*
(Liabilities item C.3)
This item shall comprise the total estimated ultimate cost to the company of settling all claims arising from events which have occurred up to the end of the financial year (including, in the case of general business, claims incurred but not reported) less amounts already paid in respect of such claims.

(23)   *Provision for bonuses and rebates*
(Liabilities item C.4)
This item shall comprise amounts intended for policy holders or contract beneficiaries by way of bonuses and rebates as defined in Note (5) on the profit and loss account format to the extent that such amounts have not been credited to policy holders or contract beneficiaries or included in Liabilities item Ba or in Liabilities item C.2.

(24)   *Equalisation provision*
(Liabilities item C.5)
This item shall comprise the amount of any equalisation reserve maintained in respect of general business by the company, in accordance with rules made by the Financial Services Authority under Part X of the Financial Services and Markets Act 2000.
This item shall also comprise any amounts which, in accordance with Council Directive 87/343/EEC, are required to be set aside by a company to equalise fluctuations in loss ratios in future years or to provide for special risks.
A company which otherwise constitutes reserves to equalise fluctuations in loss ratios in future years or to provide for special risks shall disclose that fact in the notes to the accounts.

(25)   *Other technical provisions*
(Liabilities item C.6)
This item shall comprise, inter alia, the provision for unexpired risks as defined in paragraph 81 below. Where the amount of the provision for unexpired risks is significant, it shall be disclosed separately either in the balance sheet or in the notes to the accounts.

(26)   *Technical provisions for linked liabilities*
(Liabilities item D)
This item shall comprise technical provisions constituted to cover liabilities relating to investment in the context of long term policies under which the benefits payable to policy holders are wholly or partly to be determined by reference to the value of, or the income from, property of any description (whether or not specified in the contract) or by reference to fluctuations in, or in an index of, the value of property of any description (whether or not so specified).
Any additional technical provisions constituted to cover death risks, operating expenses or other risks (such as benefits payable at the maturity date or guaranteed surrender values) shall be included under Liabilities item C.2.

This item shall also comprise technical provisions representing the obligations of a tontine's organiser in relation to its members.

(27)   *Deposits received from reinsurers*
        (Liabilities item F)
        Where the company cedes reinsurance, this item shall comprise amounts deposited by or withheld from other insurance undertakings under reinsurance contracts. These amounts may not be merged with other amounts owed to or by those other undertakings.

        Where the company cedes reinsurance and has received as a deposit securities which have been transferred to its ownership, this item shall comprise the amount owed by the company by virtue of the deposit.

(28)   *Creditors*
        (Liabilities item G)
        Amounts owed to group undertakings and undertakings in which the company has a participating interest shall be shown separately as sub-items.

(29)   *Debenture loans*
        (Liabilities item G.III)
        The amount of any convertible loans shall be shown separately.

Special rules for balance sheet format

Additional items

10.—   (1)   Every balance sheet of a company which carries on long term business shall show separately as an additional item the aggregate of any amounts included in Liabilities item A (capital and reserves) which are required not to be treated as realised profits under section 268 of this Act.

        (2)   A company which carries on long term business shall show separately, in the balance sheet or in the notes to the accounts, the total amount of assets representing the long term fund valued in accordance with the provisions of this Schedule.

Managed funds

11.—   (1)   For the purposes of this paragraph "managed funds" are funds of a group pension fund—
               (a)   the management of which constitutes long term insurance business, and
               (b)   which the company administers in its own name but on behalf of others, and
               (c)   to which it has legal title.

        (2)   The company shall, in any case where assets and liabilities arising in respect of managed funds fall to be treated as assets and liabilities of the company, adopt the following accounting treatment: assets and liabilities representing managed funds are to be included in the company's balance sheet, with the notes to the accounts disclosing the total amount included with respect to such assets and liabilities in the balance sheet and showing the amount included under each relevant balance sheet item in respect of such assets or (as the case may be) liabilities.

Deferred acquisition costs

12.   The costs of acquiring insurance policies which are incurred during a financial year but which relate to a subsequent financial year shall be deferred in a manner specified in Note *(17)* on the balance sheet format.

Profit and loss account format

I   Technical account—General business

1.   Earned premiums, net of reinsurance
        (a)   gross premiums written *(1)*
        (b)   outward reinsurance premiums *(2)*
        (c)   change in the gross provision for unearned premiums
        (d)   change in the provision for unearned premiums, reinsurers' share

2.   Allocated investment return transferred from the non-technical account (item III.6) *(10)*
2a.   Investment income *(8) (10)*
        (a)   income from participating interests, with a separate indication of that derived from group undertakings
        (b)   income from other investments, with a separate indication of that derived from group undertakings
              (aa) income from land and buildings
              (bb) income from other investments
        (c)   value re-adjustments on investments
        (d)   gains on the realisation of investments
3.   Other technical income, net of reinsurance
4.   Claims incurred, net of reinsurance *(4)*
        (a)   claims paid
              (aa) gross amount
              (bb) reinsurers' share
        (b)   change in the provision for claims
              (aa) gross amount
              (bb) reinsurers' share
5.   Changes in other technical provisions, net of reinsurance, not shown under other headings
6.   Bonuses and rebates, net of reinsurance *(5)*
7.   Net operating expenses
        (a)   acquisition costs *(6)*
        (b)   change in deferred acquisition costs
        (c)   administrative expenses *(7)*
        (d)   reinsurance commissions and profit participation
8.   Other technical charges, net of reinsurance
8a.   Investment expenses and charges *(8)*
        (a)   investment management expenses, including interest
        (b)   value adjustments on investments
        (c)   losses on the realisation of investments
9.   Change in the equalisation provision
10.   Sub-total (balance on the technical account for general business) (item III.1)
II   Technical account—Long term business
1.   Earned premiums, net of reinsurance
        (a)   gross premiums written *(1)*
        (b)   outward reinsurance premiums *(2)*
        (c)   change in the provision for unearned premiums, net of reinsurance *(3)*
2.   Investment income *(8) (10)*
        (a)   income from participating interests, with a separate indication of that derived from group undertakings
        (b)   income from other investments, with a separate indication of that derived from group undertakings
              (aa) income from land and buildings
              (bb) income from other investments
        (c)   value re-adjustments on investments
        (d)   gains on the realisation of investments
3.   Unrealised gains on investments *(9)*
4.   Other technical income, net of reinsurance
5.   Claims incurred, net of reinsurance *(4)*
        (a)   claims paid
              (aa) gross amount
              (bb) reinsurers' share

      (b)   change in the provision for claims
          (aa) gross amount
          (bb) reinsurers' share

6.   Change in other technical provisions, net of reinsurance, not shown under other headings
      (a)   long term business provision, net of reinsurance *(3)*
          (aa) gross amount
          (bb) reinsurers' share
      (b)   other technical provisions, net of reinsurance

7.   Bonuses and rebates, net of reinsurance *(5)*

8.   Net operating expenses
      (a)   acquisition costs *(6)*
      (b)   change in deferred acquisition costs
      (c)   administrative expenses *(7)*
      (d)   reinsurance commissions and profit participation

9.   Investment expenses and charges *(8)*
      (a)   investment management expenses, including interest
      (b)   value adjustments on investments
      (c)   losses on the realisation of investments

10.   Unrealised losses on investments *(9)*

11.   Other technical charges, net of reinsurance

11a.   Tax attributable to the long term business

12.   Allocated investment return transferred to the non-technical account (item III.4)

12a.   Transfers to or from the fund for future appropriations

13.   Sub-total (balance on the technical account—long term business) (item III.2)

III   Non-technical account

1.   Balance on the general business technical account—(item I.10)

2.   Balance on the long term business technical account—(item II.13)

2a.   Tax credit attributable to balance on the long term business technical account

3.   Investment income *(8)*
      (a)   income from participating interests, with a separate indication of that derived from group undertakings
      (b)   income from other investments, with a separate indication of that derived from group undertakings
          (aa) income from land and buildings
          (bb) income from other investments
      (c)   value re-adjustments on investments
      (d)   gains on the realisation of investments

3a.   Unrealised gains on investments *(9)*

4.   Allocated investment return transferred from the long term business technical account (item II.12) *(10)*

5.   Investment expenses and charges *(8)*
      (a)   investment management expenses, including interest
      (b)   value adjustments on investments
      (c)   losses on the realisation of investments

5a.   Unrealised losses on investments *(9)*

6.   Allocated investment return transferred to the general business technical account (item I.2) *(10)*

7.   Other income

8.   Other charges, including value adjustments

8a.   Profit or loss on ordinary activities before tax

9.   Tax on profit or loss on ordinary activities

10.   Profit or loss on ordinary activities after tax

11.   Extraordinary income

12.   Extraordinary charges
13.   Extraordinary profit or loss
14.   Tax on extraordinary profit or loss
15.   Other taxes not shown under the preceding items
16.   Profit or loss for the financial year

Notes on the profit and loss account format

(1)   *Gross premiums written*
         (General business technical account: item I.1.(a)
         Long term business technical account: item II.1.(a))
         This item shall comprise all amounts due during the financial year in respect of insurance
         contracts entered into regardless of the fact that such amounts may relate in whole or in part to a
         later financial year, and shall include inter alia—
         (i)   premiums yet to be determined, where the premium calculation can be done only at the end
                 of the year;
         (ii)   single premiums, including annuity premiums, and, in long term business, single premiums
                 resulting from bonus and rebate provisions in so far as they must be considered as premiums
                 under the terms of the contract;
         (iii)   additional premiums in the case of half-yearly, quarterly or monthly payments and
                 additional payments from policy holders for expenses borne by the company;
         (iv)   in the case of co-insurance, the company's portion of total premiums;
         (v)   reinsurance premiums due from ceding and retroceding insurance undertakings, including
                 portfolio entries,
         after deduction of cancellations and portfolio withdrawals credited to ceding and retroceding
         insurance undertakings.
         The above amounts shall not include the amounts of taxes or duties levied with premiums.

(2)   *Outward reinsurance premiums*
         (General business technical account: item I.1.(b)
         Long term business technical account: item II.1.(b))
         This item shall comprise all premiums paid or payable in respect of outward reinsurance contracts
         entered into by the company. Portfolio entries payable on the conclusion or amendment of
         outward reinsurance contracts shall be added; portfolio withdrawals receivable must be deducted.

(3)   *Change in the provision for unearned premiums, net of reinsurance*
         (Long term business technical account: items II.1.(c) and II.6.(a))
         In the case of long term business, the change in unearned premiums may be included either in
         item II.1.(c) or in item II.6.(a) of the long term business technical account.

(4)   *Claims incurred, net of reinsurance*
         (General business technical account: item I.4
         Long term business technical account: item II.5)
         This item shall comprise all payments made in respect of the financial year with the addition of
         the provision for claims (but after deducting the provision for claims for the preceding financial
         year).
         These amounts shall include annuities, surrenders, entries and withdrawals of loss provisions to
         and from ceding insurance undertakings and reinsurers and external and internal claims
         management costs and charges for claims incurred but not reported such as are referred to in
         paragraphs 47(2) and 49 below.
         Sums recoverable on the basis of subrogation and salvage (within the meaning of paragraph 47
         below) shall be deducted.
         Where the difference between—
         (a)   the loss provision made at the beginning of the year for outstanding claims incurred in
                 previous years, and
         (b)   the payments made during the year on account of claims incurred in previous years and the
                 loss provision shown at the end of the year for such outstanding claims,

is material, it shall be shown in the notes to the accounts, broken down by category and amount.

(5)   *Bonuses and rebates, net of reinsurance*
       (General business technical account: item I.6
       Long term business technical account: item II.7)
       Bonuses shall comprise all amounts chargeable for the financial year which are paid or payable to policy holders and other insured parties or provided for their benefit, including amounts used to increase technical provisions or applied to the reduction of future premiums, to the extent that such amounts represent an allocation of surplus or profit arising on business as a whole or a section of business, after deduction of amounts provided in previous years which are no longer required.
       Rebates shall comprise such amounts to the extent that they represent a partial refund of premiums resulting from the experience of individual contracts.
       Where material, the amount charged for bonuses and that charged for rebates shall be disclosed separately in the notes to the accounts.

(6)   *Acquisition costs*
       (General business technical account: item I.7.(a)
       Long term business technical account: item II.8.(a))
       This item shall comprise the costs arising from the conclusion of insurance contracts. They shall cover both direct costs, such as acquisition commissions or the cost of drawing up the insurance document or including the insurance contract in the portfolio, and indirect costs, such as advertising costs or the administrative expenses connected with the processing of proposals and the issuing of policies.
       In the case of long term business, policy renewal commissions shall be included under item II.8.(c) in the long term business technical account.

(7)   *Administrative expenses*
       (General business technical account: item I.7.(c)
       Long term business technical account: item II.8.(c))
       This item shall include the costs arising from premium collection, portfolio administration, handling of bonuses and rebates, and inward and outward reinsurance. They shall in particular include staff costs and depreciation provisions in respect of office furniture and equipment in so far as these need not be shown under acquisition costs, claims incurred or investment charges.
       Item II.8.(c) shall also include policy renewal commissions.

(8)   *Investment income, expenses and charges*
       (General business technical account: items I.2a and 8a
       Long term business technical account: items II.2 and 9
       Non-technical account: items III.3 and 5)
       Investment income, expenses and charges shall, to the extent that they arise in the long term fund, be disclosed in the long term business technical account. Other investment income, expenses and charges shall either be disclosed in the non-technical account or attributed between the appropriate technical and non-technical accounts. Where the company makes such an attribution it shall disclose the basis for it in the notes to the accounts.

(9)   *Unrealised gains and losses on investments*
       (Long term business technical account: items II.3 and 10
       Non-technical account: items III.3a and 5a)
       In the case of investments attributed to the long term fund, the difference between the valuation of the investments and their purchase price or, if they have previously been valued, their valuation as at the last balance sheet date, may be disclosed (in whole or in part) in item II.3 or II.10 (as the case may be) of the long term business technical account, and in the case of investments shown as assets under Assets item D (assets held to cover linked liabilities) shall be so disclosed.
       In the case of other investments, the difference between the valuation of the investments and their purchase price or, if they have previously been valued, their valuation as at the last balance sheet

date, may be disclosed (in whole or in part) in item III.3a or III.5a (as the case may require) of the non-technical account.

(10)   *Allocated investment return*
(General business technical account: item I.2
Long term business technical account: item II.12
Non-technical account: items III.4 and 6)
The allocated return may be transferred from one part of the profit and loss account to another.
Where part of the investment return is transferred to the general business technical account, the transfer from the non-technical account shall be deducted from item III.6 and added to item I.2.
Where part of the investment return disclosed in the long term business technical account is transferred to the non-technical account, the transfer to the non-technical account shall be deducted from item II.12 and added to item III.4.
The reasons for such transfers (which may consist of a reference to any relevant statutory requirement) and the bases on which they are made shall be disclosed in the notes to the accounts.

CHAPTER II
ACCOUNTING PRINCIPLES AND RULES

SECTION A
ACCOUNTING PRINCIPLES

Preliminary

13.   Subject to paragraph 19 below, the amounts to be included in respect of all items shown in a company's accounts shall be determined in accordance with the principles set out in paragraphs 14 to 18 below.

Accounting principles

14.   The company shall be presumed to be carrying on business as a going concern.

15.   Accounting policies shall be applied consistently within the same accounts and from one financial year to the next.

16.   The amount of any item shall be determined on a prudent basis, and in particular—
    (a)   subject to note *(9)* on the profit and loss account format, only profits realised at the balance sheet date shall be included in the profit and loss account; and
    (b)   all liabilities ... which have arisen ... in respect of the financial year to which the accounts relate or a previous financial year shall be taken into account, including those which only become apparent between the balance sheet date and the date on which it is signed on behalf of the board of directors in pursuance of section 233 of this Act.

17.   All income and charges relating to the financial year to which the accounts relate shall be taken into account, without regard to the date of receipt or payment.

18.   In determining the aggregate amount of any item the amount of each individual asset or liability that falls to be taken into account shall be determined separately.

Departure from accounting principles

19.   If it appears to the directors of a company that there are special reasons for departing from any of the principles stated above in preparing the company's accounts in respect of any financial year they may do so, but particulars of the departure, the reasons for it and its effect shall be given in a note to the accounts.

Valuation

19A.— (1)   The amounts to be included in respect of assets of any description mentioned in paragraph 22 (valuation of assets: general) are determined either—
        (a)   in accordance with that paragraph and paragraph 24 (but subject to paragraphs 27 to 29); or

       (b)   so far as applicable to an asset of that description, in accordance with section BA (valuation at fair value).

(2)   The amounts to be included in respect of assets of any description mentioned in paragraph 23 (alternative valuation of fixed-income securities) may be determined—

       (a)   in accordance with that paragraph (but subject to paragraphs 27 to 29); or

       (b)   so far as applicable to an asset of that description, in accordance with section BA.

(3)   The amounts to be included in respect of assets which—

       (a)   are not assets of a description mentioned in paragraph 22 or 23, but

       (b)   are assets of a description to which section BA is applicable,

       may be determined in accordance with that section.

(4)   Subject to sub-paragraphs (1) to (3), the amounts to be included in respect of all items shown in a company's accounts are determined in accordance with section C.

SECTION B

CURRENT VALUE ACCOUNTING RULES

20, 21. ...

Valuation of assets: general

22.— (1)   Subject to paragraph 24 below, investments falling to be included under Assets item C (investments) shall be included at their current value calculated in accordance with paragraphs 25 and 26 below.

     (2)   Investments falling to be included under Assets item D (assets held to cover linked liabilities) shall be shown at their current value calculated in accordance with paragraphs 25 and 26 below.

23.— (1)   Intangible assets other than goodwill may be shown at their current cost.

     (2)   Assets falling to be included under Assets items F.I (tangible assets) and F.IV (own shares) in the balance sheet format may be shown at their current value calculated in accordance with paragraphs 25 and 26 below or at their current cost.

     (3)   Assets falling to be included under Assets item F.II (stocks) may be shown at current cost.

Alternative valuation of fixed-income securities

24.— (1)   This paragraph applies to debt securities and other fixed-income securities shown as assets under Assets items C.II (investments in group undertakings and participating interests) and C.III (other financial investments).

     (2)   Securities to which this paragraph applies may either be valued in accordance with paragraph 22 above or their amortised value may be shown in the balance sheet, in which case the provisions of this paragraph apply.

     (3)   Subject to sub-paragraph (4) below, where the purchase price of securities to which this paragraph applies exceeds the amount repayable at maturity, the amount of the difference—

       (a)   shall be charged to the profit and loss account, and

       (b)   shall be shown separately in the balance sheet or in the notes to the accounts.

     (4)   The amount of the difference referred to in sub-paragraph (3) above may be written off in instalments so that it is completely written off when the securities are repaid, in which case there shall be shown separately in the balance sheet or in the notes to the accounts the difference between the purchase price (less the aggregate amount written off) and the amount repayable at maturity.

     (5)   Where the purchase price of securities to which this paragraph applies is less than the amount repayable at maturity, the amount of the difference shall be released to income in instalments over the period remaining until repayment, in which case there shall be shown separately in the balance sheet or in the notes to the accounts the difference between the purchase price (plus the aggregate amount released to income) and the amount repayable at maturity.

(6)   Both the purchase price and the current value of securities valued in accordance with this paragraph shall be disclosed in the notes to the accounts.

(7)   Where securities to which this paragraph applies which are not valued in accordance with paragraph 22 above are sold before maturity, and the proceeds are used to purchase other securities to which this paragraph applies, the difference between the proceeds of sale and their book value may be spread uniformly over the period remaining until the maturity of the original investment.

Meaning of "current value"

25.—   (1)   Subject to sub-paragraph (5) below, in the case of investments other than land and buildings, current value shall mean market value determined in accordance with this paragraph.

        (2)   In the case of listed investments, market value shall mean the value on the balance sheet date or, when the balance sheet date is not a stock exchange trading day, on the last stock exchange trading day before that date.

        (3)   Where a market exists for unlisted investments, market value shall mean the average price at which such investments were traded on the balance sheet date or, when the balance sheet date is not a trading day, on the last trading day before that date.

        (4)   Where, on the date on which the accounts are drawn up, listed or unlisted investments have been sold or are to be sold within the short term, the market value shall be reduced by the actual or estimated realisation costs.

        (5)   Except where the equity method of accounting is applied, all investments other than those referred to in sub-paragraphs (2) and (3) above shall be valued on a basis which has prudent regard to the likely realisable value.

26.—   (1)   In the case of land and buildings, current value shall mean the market value on the date of valuation, where relevant reduced as provided in sub-paragraphs (4) and (5) below.

        (2)   Market value shall mean the price at which land and buildings could be sold under private contract between a willing seller and an arm's length buyer on the date of valuation, it being assumed that the property is publicly exposed to the market, that market conditions permit orderly disposal and that a normal period, having regard to the nature of the property, is available for the negotiation of the sale.

        (3)   The market value shall be determined through the separate valuation of each land and buildings item, carried out at least every five years in accordance with generally recognised methods of valuation.

        (4)   Where the value of any land and buildings item has diminished since the preceding valuation under sub-paragraph (3), an appropriate value adjustment shall be made.

        (5)   The lower value arrived at under sub-paragraph (4) shall not be increased in subsequent balance sheets unless such increase results from a new determination of market value arrived at in accordance with sub-paragraphs (2) and (3).

        (6)   Where, on the date on which the accounts are drawn up, land and buildings have been sold or are to be sold within the short term, the value arrived at in accordance with sub-paragraphs (2) and (4) shall be reduced by the actual or estimated realisation costs.

        (7)   Where it is impossible to determine the market value of a land and buildings item, the value arrived at on the basis of the principle of purchase price or production cost shall be deemed to be its current value.

Application of the depreciation rules

27.—   (1)   Where—

           (a)   the value of any asset of a company is determined in accordance with paragraph 22 or 23 above, and

           (b)   in the case of a determination under paragraph 22 above, the asset falls to be included under Assets item C.I,

        that value shall be, or (as the case may require) be the starting point for determining, the amount to be included in respect of that asset in the company's accounts, instead of its cost or any value previously so determined for that asset; and paragraphs 31 to 35 and 37 below shall apply accordingly in relation to any such asset with the substitution for any reference to its cost of a reference to the value most recently determined for that asset in accordance with paragraph 22 or 23 above (as the case may be).

(2) The amount of any provision for depreciation required in the case of any asset by paragraph 32 or 33 below as it applies by virtue of sub-paragraph (1) is referred to below in this paragraph as the "adjusted amount", and the amount of any provision which would be required by that paragraph in the case of that asset according to the historical cost accounting rules is referred to as the "historical cost amount".

(3) Where sub-paragraph (1) applies in the case of any asset the amount of any provision for depreciation in respect of that asset included in any item shown in the profit and loss account in respect of amounts written off assets of the description in question may be the historical cost amount instead of the adjusted amount, provided that the amount of any difference between the two is shown separately in the profit and loss account or in a note to the accounts.

Additional information to be provided

28.—   (1) This paragraph applies where the amounts to be included in respect of assets covered by any items shown in a company's accounts have been determined in accordance with paragraph 22 or 23 above.

(2) The items affected and the basis of valuation adopted in determining the amounts of the assets in question in the case of each such item shall be disclosed in a note to the accounts.

(3) The purchase price of investments valued in accordance with paragraph 22 above shall be disclosed in the notes to the accounts.

(4) In the case of each balance sheet item valued in accordance with paragraph 23 above either—
  (a) the comparable amounts determined according to the historical cost accounting rules (without any provision for depreciation or diminution in value); or
  (b) the differences between those amounts and the corresponding amounts actually shown in the balance sheet in respect of that item,
  shall be shown separately in the balance sheet or in a note to the accounts.

(5) In sub-paragraph (4) above, references in relation to any item to the comparable amounts determined as there mentioned are references to—
  (a) the aggregate amount which would be required to be shown in respect of that item if the amounts to be included in respect of all the assets covered by that item were determined according to the historical cost accounting rules; and
  (b) the aggregate amount of the cumulative provisions for depreciation or diminution in value which would be permitted or required in determining those amounts according to those rules.

Revaluation reserve

29.—   (1) Subject to sub-paragraph (7) below, with respect to any determination of the value of an asset of a company in accordance with paragraph 22 or 23 above, the amount of any profit or loss arising from that determination (after allowing, where appropriate, for any provisions for depreciation or diminution in value made otherwise than by reference to the value so determined and any adjustments of any such provisions made in the light of that determination) shall be credited or (as the case may be) debited to a separate reserve ("the revaluation reserve").

(2) The amount of the revaluation reserve shall be shown in the company's balance sheet under Liabilities item A.III, but need not be shown under the name "revaluation reserve".

(3) An amount may be transferred ...
  (a) from the revaluation reserve—
      (i)   to the profit and loss account, if the amount was previously charged to that

account or represents realised profit, or

(ii)   on capitalisation,

(b)   to or from the revaluation reserve in respect of the taxation relating to any profit or loss credited or debited to the reserve;

and the revaluation reserve shall be reduced to the extent that the amounts transferred to it are no longer necessary for the purposes of the valuation method used.

(4)   In sub-paragraph (3)(a)(ii) "capitalisation", in relation to an amount standing to the credit of the revaluation reserve, means applying it in wholly or partly paying up unissued shares in the company to be allotted to members of the company as fully or partly paid shares.

(5)   The revaluation reserve shall not be reduced except as mentioned in this paragraph.

(6)   The treatment for taxation purposes of amounts credited or debited to the revaluation reserve shall be disclosed in a note to the accounts.

(7)   This paragraph does not apply to the difference between the valuation of investments and their purchase price or previous valuation shown in the long term business technical account or the non-technical account in accordance with note (9) on the profit and loss account format.

SECTION BA
VALUATION AT FAIR VALUE

Inclusion of financial instruments at fair value

29A.— (1)   Subject to sub-paragraphs (2) to (4), financial instruments (including derivatives) may be included at fair value.

(2)   Sub-paragraph (1) does not apply to financial instruments which constitute liabilities unless—

(a)   they are held as part of a trading portfolio, or

(b)   they are derivatives.

(3)   Except where they fall to be included under Assets item D (assets held to cover linked liabilities), sub-paragraph (1) does not apply to—

(a)   financial instruments (other than derivatives) held to maturity;

(b)   loans and receivables originated by the company and not held for trading purposes;

(c)   interests in subsidiary undertakings, associated undertakings and joint ventures;

(d)   equity instruments issued by the company;

(e)   contracts for contingent consideration in a business combination;

(f)   other financial instruments with such special characteristics that the instruments, according to generally accepted accounting principles or practice, should be accounted for differently from other financial instruments.

(4)   If the fair value of a financial instrument cannot be determined reliably in accordance with paragraph 29B, sub-paragraph (1) does not apply to that financial instrument.

(5)   In this paragraph—

"associated undertaking" has the meaning given by paragraph 20 of Schedule 4A; and "joint venture" has the meaning given by paragraph 19 of that Schedule.

Determination of fair value

29B.— (1)   The fair value of a financial instrument is determined in accordance with this paragraph.

(2)   If a reliable market can readily be identified for the financial instrument, its fair value is determined by reference to its market value.

(3)   If a reliable market cannot readily be identified for the financial instrument but can be identified for its components or for a similar instrument, its fair value is determined by reference to the market value of its components or of the similar instrument.

(4)   If neither sub-paragraph (2) nor (3) applies, the fair value of the financial instrument is a value resulting from generally accepted valuation models and techniques.

(5)   Any valuation models and techniques used for the purposes of sub-paragraph (4) must ensure a reasonable approximation of the market value.

Inclusion of hedged items at fair value

29C.   A company may include any assets and liabilities that qualify as hedged items under a fair value hedge accounting system, or identified portions of such assets or liabilities, at the amount required under that system.

Other assets that may be included at fair value

29D.— (1)   This paragraph applies to—
    (a)   investment property, and
    (b)   living animals and plants,
that, under international accounting standards, may be included in accounts at fair value.

(2)   Such investment property and such living animals and plants may be included at fair value, provided that all such investment property or, as the case may be, all such living animals and plants are so included where their fair value can reliably be determined.

(3)   In this paragraph, "fair value" means fair value determined in accordance with relevant international accounting standards.

Accounting for changes in value

29E.— (1)   This paragraph applies where a financial instrument is valued in accordance with paragraph 29A or 29C or an asset is valued in accordance with paragraph 29D.

(2)   Notwithstanding paragraph 16 in this Part of this Schedule, and subject to sub-paragraphs (3) and (4) below, a change in the value of the financial instrument or of the investment property or living animal or plant must be included in the profit and loss account.

(3)   Where—
    (a)   the financial instrument accounted for is a hedging instrument under a hedge accounting system that allows some or all of the change in value not to be shown in the profit and loss account, or
    (b)   the change in value relates to an exchange difference arising on a monetary item that forms part of a company's net investment in a foreign entity,
the amount of the change in value must be credited to or (as the case may be) debited from a separate reserve ("the fair value reserve").

(4)   Where the instrument accounted for—
    (a)   is an available for sale financial asset, and
    (b)   is not a derivative,
the change in value may be credited to or (as the case may be) debited from the fair value reserve.

The fair value reserve

29F.— (1)   The fair value reserve must be adjusted to the extent that the amounts shown in it are no longer necessary for the purposes of paragraph 29E(3) or (4).

(2)   The treatment for taxation purposes of amounts credited or debited to the fair value reserve shall be disclosed in a note to the accounts.

SECTION C
HISTORICAL COST ACCOUNTING RULES

30.   ....

Valuation of assets

General rules

31.   Subject to any provision for depreciation or diminution in value made in accordance with paragraph 32 or 33 below, the amount to be included in respect of any asset in the balance sheet format shall be its cost.

32.   In the case of any asset included under Assets item B (intangible assets), C.I (land and buildings), F.I. (tangible assets) or F.II (stocks) which has a limited useful economic life, the amount of—

(a)   its cost; or

(b)   where it is estimated that any such asset will have a residual value at the end of the period of its useful economic life, its cost less that estimated residual value,

shall be reduced by provisions for depreciation calculated to write off that amount systematically over the period of the asset's useful economic life.

33.—   (1)   This paragraph applies to any asset included under Assets item B (tangible assets), C (investments), F.I (tangible assets) or F.IV (own shares).

(2)   Where an asset to which this paragraph applies has diminished in value, provisions for diminution in value may be made in respect of it and the amount to be included in respect of it may be reduced accordingly; and any such provisions which are not shown in the profit and loss account shall be disclosed (either separately or in aggregate) in a note to the accounts.

(3)   Provisions for diminution in value shall be made in respect of any asset to which this paragraph applies if the reduction in its value is expected to be permanent (whether its useful economic life is limited or not), and the amount to be included in respect of it shall be reduced accordingly; and any such provisions which are not shown in the profit and loss account shall be disclosed (either separately or in aggregate) in a note to the accounts.

(4)   Where the reasons for which any provision was made in accordance with sub-paragraph (1) or (2) have ceased to apply to any extent, that provision shall be written back to the extent that it is no longer necessary; and any amounts written back in accordance with this sub-paragraph which are not shown in the profit and loss account shall be disclosed (either separately or in aggregate) in a note to the accounts.

34.—   (1)   This paragraph applies to assets included under Assets items E.I, II and III (debtors) and F.III (cash at bank and in hand) in the balance sheet.

(2)   If the net realisable value of an asset to which this paragraph applies is lower than its cost the amount to be included in respect of that asset shall be the net realisable value.

(3)   Where the reasons for which any provision for diminution in value was made in accordance with sub-paragraph (2) have ceased to apply to any extent, that provision shall be written back to the extent that it is no longer necessary.

Development costs

35.—   (1)   Notwithstanding that amounts representing "development costs" may be included under Assets item B (intangible assets) in the balance sheet format, an amount may only be included in a company's balance sheet in respect of development costs in special circumstances.

(2)   If any amount is included in a company's balance sheet in respect of development costs the following information shall be given in a note to the accounts—

(a)   the period over which the amount of those costs originally capitalised is being or is to be written off; and

(b)   the reasons for capitalising the development costs in question.

Goodwill

36.—   (1)   The application of paragraphs 31 to 33 above in relation to goodwill (in any case where goodwill is treated as an asset) is subject to the following provisions of this paragraph.

(2)   Subject to sub-paragraph (3) below, the amount of the consideration for any goodwill acquired by a company shall be reduced by provisions for depreciation calculated to write off that amount systematically over a period chosen by the directors of the company.

(3)   The period chosen shall not exceed the useful economic life of the goodwill in question.

(4)   In any case where any goodwill acquired by a company is included as an asset in the company's balance sheet the period chosen for writing off the consideration for that goodwill and the reasons for choosing that period shall be disclosed in a note to the accounts.

Miscellaneous and supplemental

Excess of money owed over value received as an asset item

37.— (1)   Where the amount repayable on any debt owed by a company is greater than the value of the consideration received in the transaction giving rise to the debt, the amount of the difference may be treated as an asset.

(2)   Where any such amount is so treated—

(a)   it shall be written off by reasonable amounts each year and must be completely written off before repayment of the debt; and

(b)   if the current amount is not shown as a separate item in the company's balance sheet it must be disclosed in a note to the accounts.

Assets included at a fixed amount

38.— (1)   Subject to the following sub-paragraph, assets which fall to be included under Assets item F.I (tangible assets) in the balance sheet format may be included at a fixed quantity and value.

(2)   Sub-paragraph (1) applies to assets of a kind which are constantly being replaced, where—

(a)   their overall value is not material to assessing the company's state of affairs; and

(b)   their quantity, value and composition are not subject to material variation.

Determination of cost

39.— (1)   The cost of an asset that has been acquired by the company shall be determined by adding to the actual price paid any expenses incidental to its acquisition.

(2)   The cost of an asset constructed by the company shall be determined by adding to the purchase price of the raw materials and consumables used the amount of the costs incurred by the company which are directly attributable to the construction of that asset.

(3)   In addition, there may be included in the cost of an asset constructed by the company—

(a)   a reasonable proportion of the costs incurred by the company which are only indirectly attributable to the construction of that asset, but only to the extent that they relate to the period of construction; and

(b)   interest on capital borrowed to finance the construction of that asset, to the extent that it accrues in respect of the period of construction;

provided, however, in a case within sub-paragraph (b) above, that the inclusion of the interest in determining the cost of that asset and the amount of the interest so included is disclosed in a note to the accounts.

40.— (1)   Subject to the qualification mentioned below, the cost of any assets which are fungible assets may be determined by the application of any of the methods mentioned in sub-paragraph (2) below in relation to any such assets of the same class.

The method chosen must be one which appears to the directors to be appropriate in the circumstances of the company.

(2)   Those methods are—

(a)   the method known as "first in, first out" (FIFO);

(b)   the method known as "last in, first out" (LIFO);

(c)   a weighted average price; and

(d)   any other method similar to any of the methods mentioned above.

(3) Where in the case of any company—

    (a) the cost of assets falling to be included under any item shown in the company's balance sheet has been determined by the application of any method permitted by this paragraph; and

    (b) the amount shown in respect of that item differs materially from the relevant alternative amount given below in this paragraph;

the amount of that difference shall be disclosed in a note to the accounts.

(4) Subject to sub-paragraph (5) below, for the purposes of sub-paragraph (3)(b) above, the relevant alternative amount, in relation to any item shown in a company's balance sheet, is the amount which would have been shown in respect of that item if assets of any class included under that item at an amount determined by any method permitted by this paragraph had instead been included at their replacement cost as at the balance sheet date.

(5) The relevant alternative amount may be determined by reference to the most recent actual purchase price before the balance sheet date of assets of any class included under the item in question instead of by reference to their replacement cost as at that date, but only if the former appears to the directors of the company to constitute the more appropriate standard of comparison in the case of assets of that class.

Substitution of original amount where price or cost unknown

41. Where there is no record of the purchase price of any asset acquired by a company or of any price, expenses or costs relevant for determining its cost in accordance with paragraph 39 above, or any such record cannot be obtained without unreasonable expense or delay, its cost shall be taken for the purposes of paragraphs 31 to 36 above to be the value ascribed to it in the earliest available record of its value made on or after its acquisition by the company.

SECTION D
RULES FOR DETERMINING PROVISIONS

Preliminary

42. Provisions which are to be shown in a company's accounts shall be determined in accordance with paragraphs 43 to 53 below.

Technical provisions

43. The amount of technical provisions must at all times be sufficient to cover any liabilities arising out of insurance contracts as far as can reasonably be foreseen.

Provision for unearned premiums

44.— (1) The provision for unearned premiums shall in principle be computed separately for each insurance contract, save that statistical methods (and in particular proportional and flat rate methods) may be used where they may be expected to give approximately the same results as individual calculations.

    (2) Where the pattern of risk varies over the life of a contract, this shall be taken into account in the calculation methods.

Provision for unexpired risks

45. The provision for unexpired risks (as defined in paragraph 81 below) shall be computed on the basis of claims and administrative expenses likely to arise after the end of the financial year from contracts concluded before that date, in so far as their estimated value exceeds the provision for unearned premiums and any premiums receivable under those contracts.

Long term business provision

46.— (1) The long term business provision shall in principle be computed separately for each long term contract, save that statistical or mathematical methods may be used where they may be expected to give approximately the same results as individual calculations.

(2) A summary of the principal assumptions in making the provision under sub-paragraph (1) shall be given in the notes to the accounts.

(3) The computation shall be made annually by a Fellow of the Institute or Faculty of Actuaries on the basis of recognised actuarial methods, with due regard to the actuarial principles laid down in Directive 2002/83/EC of the European Parliament and of the Council of 5th November 2002 concerning life assurance.

Provisions for claims outstanding

General business

47.— (1) A provision shall in principle be computed separately for each claim on the basis of the costs still expected to arise, save that statistical methods may be used if they result in an adequate provision having regard to the nature of the risks.

(2) This provision shall also allow for claims incurred but not reported by the balance sheet date, the amount of the allowance being determined having regard to past experience as to the number and magnitude of claims reported after previous balance sheet dates.

(3) All claims settlement costs (whether direct or indirect) shall be included in the calculation of the provision.

(4) Recoverable amounts arising out of subrogation or salvage shall be estimated on a prudent basis and either deducted from the provision for claims outstanding (in which case if the amounts are material they shall be shown in the notes to the accounts) or shown as assets.

(5) In sub-paragraph (4) above, "subrogation" means the acquisition of the rights of policy holders with respect to third parties, and "salvage" means the acquisition of the legal ownership of insured property.

(6) Where benefits resulting from a claim must be paid in the form of annuity, the amounts to be set aside for that purpose shall be calculated by recognised actuarial methods, and paragraph 48 below shall not apply to such calculations.

(7) Implicit discounting or deductions, whether resulting from the placing of a current value on a provision for an outstanding claim which is expected to be settled later at a higher figure or otherwise effected, is prohibited.

48.— (1) Explicit discounting or deductions to take account of investment income is permitted, subject to the following conditions:

     (a) the expected average interval between the date for the settlement of claims being discounted and the accounting date shall be at least four years;

     (b) the discounting or deductions shall be effected on a recognised prudential basis;

     (c) when calculating the total cost of settling claims, the company shall take account of all factors that could cause increases in that cost;

     (d) the company shall have adequate data at its disposal to construct a reliable model of the rate of claims settlements;

     (e) the rate of interest used for the calculation of present values shall not exceed a rate prudently estimated to be earned by assets of the company which are appropriate in magnitude and nature to cover the provisions for claims being discounted during the period necessary for the payment of such claims, and shall not exceed either—

         (i) a rate justified by the performance of such assets over the preceding five years, or

         (ii) a rate justified by the performance of such assets during the year preceding the balance sheet date.

(2) When discounting or effecting deductions, the company shall, in the notes to the accounts, disclose—

      (a)   the total amount of provisions before discounting or deductions,

      (b)   the categories of claims which are discounted or from which deductions have been made,

      (c)   for each category of claims, the methods used, in particular the rates used for the estimates referred to in sub-paragraph (1)(d) and (e), and the criteria adopted for estimating the period that will elapse before the claims are settled.

Long term business

49.   The amount of the provision for claims shall be equal to the sums due to beneficiaries, plus the costs of settling claims.

Equalisation reserves

50.   The amount of any equalisation reserve maintained in respect of general business, in accordance with rules made by the Financial Services Authority under Part X of the Financial Services and Markets Act 2000, shall be determined in accordance with such rules.

Accounting on a non-annual basis

51.— (1)   Either of the methods described in paragraphs 52 and 53 below may be applied where, because of the nature of the class or type of insurance in question, information about premiums receivable or claims payable (or both) for the underwriting years is insufficient when the accounts are drawn up for reliable estimates to be made.

      (2)   The use of either of the methods referred to in sub-paragraph (1) shall be disclosed in the notes to the accounts together with the reasons for adopting it.

      (3)   Where one of the methods referred to in sub-paragraph (1) above is adopted, it shall be applied systematically in successive years unless circumstances justify a change.

      (4)   In the event of a change in the method applied, the effect on the assets, liabilities, financial position and profit or loss shall be stated in the notes to the accounts.

      (5)   For the purposes of this paragraph and paragraph 52 below, "underwriting year" means the financial year in which the insurance contracts in the class or type of insurance in question commenced.

52.— (1)   The excess of the premiums written over the claims and expenses paid in respect of contracts commencing in the underwriting year shall form a technical provision included in the technical provision for claims outstanding shown in the balance sheet under Liabilities item C.3.

      (2)   The provision may also be computed on the basis of a given percentage of the premiums written where such a method is appropriate for the type of risk insured.

      (3)   If necessary, the amount of this technical provision shall be increased to make it sufficient to meet present and future obligations.

      (4)   The technical provision constituted under this paragraph shall be replaced by a provision for claims outstanding estimated in accordance with paragraph 47 above as soon as sufficient information has been gathered and not later than the end of the third year following the underwriting year.

      (5)   The length of time that elapses before a provision for claims outstanding is constituted in accordance with sub-paragraph (4) above shall be disclosed in the notes to the accounts.

53.— (1)   The figures shown in the technical account or in certain items within it shall relate to a year which wholly or partly precedes the financial year (but by no more than 12 months).

      (2)   The amounts of the technical provisions shown in the accounts shall if necessary be increased to make them sufficient to meet present and future obligations.

      (3)   The length of time by which the earlier year to which the figures relate precedes the financial year and the magnitude of the transactions concerned shall be disclosed in the notes to the accounts.

CHAPTER III
NOTES TO THE ACCOUNTS

Preliminary

54.— (1) Any information required in the case of any company by the following provisions of this Part of this Schedule shall (if not given in the company's accounts) be given by way of a note to those accounts.

(2) Subject to sub-paragraph (3) below, in respect of every item stated in a note to the accounts—

(a) the corresponding amount for the financial year immediately preceding that to which the accounts relate shall also be stated, and

(b) where the corresponding amount is not comparable, that amount shall be adjusted and particulars of the adjustment and the reasons for it shall be given.

(3) Sub-paragraph (2) above does not apply to—

(a) paragraphs 62 and 66 of this Part of this Schedule (assets and reserves and provisions),

(b) paragraph 13 of Schedule 4A (details of accounting treatment of acquisitions),

(c) paragraphs 2, 8(3), 16, 21(1)(d), 22(4) and (5), 24(3) and (4) and 27(3) and (4) of Schedule 5 (shareholdings in other undertakings), and

(d) Parts II and III of Schedule 6 (loans and other dealings in favour of directors and others).

General

Disclosure of accounting policies

55. The accounting policies adopted by the company in determining the amounts to be included in respect of items shown in the balance sheet and in determining the profit or loss of the company shall be stated (including such accounting policies with respect to the depreciation and diminution in value of assets).

56. It shall be stated whether the accounts have been prepared in accordance with applicable accounting standards and particulars of any material departure from those standards and the reasons for it shall be given.

Sums denominated in foreign currencies

57. Where any sums originally denominated in foreign currencies have been brought into account under any items shown in the balance sheet or profit and loss account format, the basis on which those sums have been translated into sterling (or the currency in which the accounts are drawn up) shall be stated.

Reserves and dividends

57A. There must be stated—

(a) any amount set aside or proposed to be set aside to, or withdrawn or proposed to be withdrawn from, reserves,

(b) the aggregate amount of dividends paid in the financial year (other than those for which a liability existed at the immediately preceding balance sheet date),

(c) the aggregate amount of dividends that the company is liable to pay at the balance sheet date, and

(d) the aggregate amount of dividends that are proposed before the date of approval of the accounts, and not otherwise disclosed under paragraph (b) or (c).

Information supplementing the balance sheet

Share capital and debentures

58.— (1) The following information shall be given with respect to the company's share capital—

(a) the authorised share capital; and

    (b)   where shares of more than one class have been allotted, the number and aggregate nominal value of shares of each class allotted.

  (2) In the case of any part of the allotted share capital that consists of redeemable shares, the following information shall be given—

    (a)   the earliest and latest dates on which the company has power to redeem those shares;

    (b)   whether those shares must be redeemed in any event or are liable to be redeemed at the option of the company or of the shareholder; and

    (c)   whether any (and, if so, what) premium is payable on redemption.

59.   If the company has allotted any shares during the financial year, the following information shall be given—

    (a)   ...

    (b)   the classes of shares allotted; and

    (c)   as respects each class of shares, the number allotted, their aggregate nominal value and the consideration received by the company for the allotment.

60.— (1) With respect to any contingent right to the allotment of shares in the company the following particulars shall be given—

    (a)   the number, description and amount of the shares in relation to which the right is exercisable;

    (b)   the period during which it is exercisable; and

    (c)   the price to be paid for the shares allotted.

  (2) In sub-paragraph (1) above "contingent right to the allotment of shares" means any option to subscribe for shares and any other right to require the allotment of shares to any person whether arising on the conversion into shares of securities of any other description or otherwise.

61.— (1) If the company has issued any debentures during the financial year to which the accounts relate, the following information shall be given—

    (a)   ...

    (b)   the classes of debentures issued; and

    (c)   as respects each class of debentures, the amount issued and the consideration received by the company for the issue.

  (2) ...

  (3) Where any of the company's debentures are held by a nominee of or trustee for the company, the nominal amount of the debentures and the amount at which they are stated in the accounting records kept by the company in accordance with section 221 of this Act shall be stated.

Assets

62.— (1) In respect of any assets of the company included in Assets items B (intangible assets), C.I (land and buildings) and C.II (investments in group undertakings and participating interests) in the company's balance sheet the following information shall be given by reference to each such item—

    (a)   the appropriate amounts in respect of those assets included in the item as at the date of the beginning of the financial year and as at the balance sheet date respectively;

    (b)   the effect on any amount included in Assets item B in respect of those assets of—

        (i)   any determination during that year of the value to be ascribed to any of those assets in accordance with paragraph 23 above;

        (ii)   acquisitions during that year of any assets;

        (iii)   disposals during that year of any assets; and

        (iv)   any transfers of assets of the company to and from the item during that year.

  (2) The reference in sub-paragraph (1)(a) to the appropriate amounts in respect of any assets (included in an assets item) as at any date there mentioned is a reference to amounts representing the aggregate amounts determined, as at that date, in respect of assets falling to be included under the item on either of the following bases, that is to say—

      (a)   on the basis of cost (determined in accordance with paragraphs 39 and 40 above); or

      (b)   on any basis permitted by paragraph 22 or 23 above,

      (leaving out of account in either case any provisions for depreciation or diminution in value).

  (3)   In addition, in respect of any assets of the company included in any assets item in the company's balance sheet, there shall be stated (by reference to each such item)—

      (a)   the cumulative amount of provisions for depreciation or diminution in value of those assets included under the item as at each date mentioned in sub-paragraph (1)(a);

      (b)   the amount of any such provisions made in respect of the financial year;

      (c)   the amount of any adjustments made in respect of any such provisions during that year in consequence of the disposal of any of those assets; and

      (d)   the amount of any other adjustments made in respect of any such provisions during that year.

63.   Where any assets of the company (other than listed investments) are included under any item shown in the company's balance sheet at an amount determined on any basis mentioned in paragraph 22 or 23 above, the following information shall be given—

      (a)   the years (so far as they are known to the directors) in which the assets were severally valued and the several values; and

      (b)   in the case of assets that have been valued during the financial year, the names of the persons who valued them or particulars of their qualifications for doing so and (whichever is stated) the bases of valuation used by them.

64.   In relation to any amount which is included under Assets item C.I (land and buildings) there shall be stated—

      (a)   how much of that amount is ascribable to land of freehold tenure and how much to land of leasehold tenure; and

      (b)   how much of the amount ascribable to land of leasehold tenure is ascribable to land held on long lease and how much to land held on short lease.

Investments

65.   In respect of the amount of each item which is shown in the company's balance sheet under Assets item C (investments) there shall be stated—

      (a)   how much of that amount is ascribable to listed investments; ...

      (b)   ...

Information about fair value of assets and liabilities

65A.— (1)   This paragraph applies where financial instruments have been valued in accordance with paragraph 29A or 29C.

  (2)   The items affected and the basis of valuation adopted in determining the amounts of the financial instruments must be disclosed.

  (3)   The purchase price of the financial instruments must be disclosed.

  (4)   There must be stated—

      (a)   where the fair value of the instruments has been determined in accordance with paragraph 29B(4), the significant assumptions underlying the valuation models and techniques used,

      (b)   for each category of financial instrument, the fair value of the instruments in that category and the changes in value—

          (i)   included in the profit and loss account, or

          (ii)   credited to or (as the case may be) debited from the fair value reserve,

      in respect of those instruments, and

      (c)   for each class of derivatives, the extent and nature of the instruments, including significant terms and conditions that may affect the amount, timing and certainty of future cash flows.

(5)   Where any amount is transferred to or from the fair value reserve during the financial year, there must be stated in tabular form—

    (a)   the amount of the reserve as at the date of the beginning of the financial year and as at the balance sheet date respectively;

    (b)   the amount transferred to or from the reserve during that year; and

    (c)   the source and application respectively of the amounts so transferred.

65B.   Where the company has derivatives that it has not included at fair value, there must be stated for each class of such derivatives—

    (a)   the fair value of the derivatives in that class, if such a value can be determined in accordance with paragraph 29B, and

    (b)   the extent and nature of the derivatives.

65C.— (1)   Sub-paragraph (2) applies if—

    (a)   the company has financial fixed assets that could be included at fair value by virtue of paragraph 29A,

    (b)   the amount at which those assets are included under any item in the company's accounts is in excess of their fair value, and

    (c)   the company has not made provision for diminution in value of those assets in accordance with paragraph 33(2) of this Part of this Schedule.

(2)   There must be stated—

    (a)   the amount at which either the individual assets or appropriate groupings of those individual assets are included in the company's accounts,

    (b)   the fair value of those assets or groupings, and

    (c)   the reasons for not making a provision for diminution in value of those assets, including the nature of the evidence that provides the basis for the belief that the amount at which they are stated in the accounts will be recovered.

Information where investment property and living animals and plants included at fair value

65D.— (1)   This paragraph applies where the amounts to be included in a company's accounts in respect of investment property or living animals and plants have been determined in accordance with paragraph 29D.

(2)   The balance sheet items affected and the basis of valuation adopted in determining the amounts of the assets in question in the case of each such item must be disclosed in a note to the accounts.

(3)   In the case of investment property, for each balance sheet item affected there must be shown, either separately in the balance sheet or in a note to the accounts—

    (a)   the comparable amounts determined according to the historical cost accounting rules; or

    (b)   the differences between those amounts and the corresponding amounts actually shown in the balance sheet in respect of that item.

(4)   In sub-paragraph (3) above, references in relation to any item to the comparable amounts determined in accordance with that sub-paragraph are references to—

    (a)   the aggregate amount which would be required to be shown in respect of that item if the amounts to be included in respect of all the assets covered by that item were determined according to the historical cost accounting rules; and

    (b)   the aggregate amount of the cumulative provisions for depreciation or diminution in value which would be permitted or required in determining those amounts according to those rules.

Reserves and provisions

66.—   (1)   Where any amount is transferred—

    (a)   to or from any reserves;

    (b)   to any provisions for other risks; or

(c)   from any provisions for other risks otherwise than for the purpose for which the provision was established;

and the reserves or provisions are or would but for paragraph 2(3) above be shown as separate items in the company's balance sheet, the information mentioned in the following sub-paragraph shall be given in respect of the aggregate of reserves or provisions included in the same item.

(2)   That information is—

(a)   the amount of the reserves or provisions as at the date of the beginning of the financial year and as at the balance sheet date respectively;

(b)   any amounts transferred to or from the reserves or provisions during that year; and

(c)   the source and application respectively of any amounts so transferred.

(3)   Particulars shall be given of each provision included in Liabilities item E.3 (other provisions) in the company's balance sheet in any case where the amount of that provision is material.

Provision for taxation

67.   The amount of any provision for deferred taxation shall be stated separately from the amount of any provision for other taxation.

Details of indebtedness

68.—   (1)   In respect of each item shown under "creditors" in the company's balance sheet there shall be stated the aggregate of the following amounts, that is to say—

(a)   the amount of any debts included under that item which are payable or repayable otherwise than by instalments and fall due for payment or repayment after the end of the period of five years beginning with the day next following the end of the financial year; and

(b)   in the case of any debts so included which are payable or repayable by instalments, the amount of any instalments which fall due for payment after the end of that period.

(2)   Subject to sub-paragraph (3), in relation to each debt falling to be taken into account under sub-paragraph (1), the terms of payment or repayment and the rate of any interest payable on the debt shall be stated.

(3)   If the number of debts is such that, in the opinion of the directors, compliance with sub-paragraph (2) would result in a statement of excessive length, it shall be sufficient to give a general indication of the terms of payment or repayment and the rates of any interest payable on the debts.

(4)   In respect of each item shown under "creditors" in the company's balance sheet there shall be stated—

(a)   the aggregate amount of any debts included under that item in respect of which any security has been given by the company; and

(b)   an indication of the nature of the securities so given.

(5)   References above in this paragraph to an item shown under "creditors" in the company's balance sheet include references, where amounts falling due to creditors within one year and after more than one year are distinguished in the balance sheet—

(a)   in a case within sub-paragraph (1), to an item shown under the latter of those categories; and

(b)   in a case within sub-paragraph (4), to an item shown under either of those categories; and references to items shown under "creditors" include references to items which would but for paragraph 2(3)(b) above be shown under that heading.

69.   If any fixed cumulative dividends on the company's shares are in arrear, there shall be stated—

(a)   the amount of the arrears; and

(b)   the period for which the dividends or, if there is more than one class, each class of them are in arrear.

Guarantees and other financial commitments

70.— (1) Particulars shall be given of any charge on the assets of the company to secure the liabilities of any other person, including, where practicable, the amount secured.

(2) The following information shall be given with respect to any other contingent liability not provided for (other than a contingent liability arising out of an insurance contract)—
 (a) the amount or estimated amount of that liability;
 (b) its legal nature;
 (c) whether any valuable security has been provided by the company in connection with that liability and if so, what.

(3) There shall be stated, where practicable—
 (a) the aggregate amount or estimated amount of contracts for capital expenditure, so far as not provided for;
 (b) ...

(4) Particulars shall be given of—
 (a) any pension commitments included under any provision shown in the company's balance sheet; and
 (b) any such commitments for which no provision has been made;
 and where any such commitment relates wholly or partly to pensions payable to past directors of the company separate particulars shall be given of that commitment so far as it relates to such pensions.

(5) Particulars shall also be given of any other financial commitments, other than commitments arising out of insurance contracts, which—
 (a) have not been provided for; and
 (b) are relevant to assessing the company's state of affairs.

(6) Commitments within any of the preceding sub-paragraphs undertaken on behalf of or for the benefit of—
 (a) any parent undertaking or fellow subsidiary undertaking, or
 (b) any subsidiary undertaking of the company,
 shall be stated separately from the other commitments within that sub-paragraph, and commitments within paragraph (a) shall also be stated separately from those within paragraph (b).

Dealings with or interests in group undertakings

71.   ...

Miscellaneous matters

72.— (1) Particulars shall be given of any case where the cost of any asset is for the first time determined under paragraph 41 above.

(2) Where any outstanding loans made under the authority of section 153(4)(b), (bb) or (c) or section 155 of this Act (various cases of financial assistance by a company for purchase of its own shares) are included under any item shown in the company's balance sheet, the aggregate amount of those loans shall be disclosed for each item in question.

(3) ...

Information supplementing the profit and loss account

Separate statement of certain items of income and expenditure

73.— (1) Subject to the following provisions of this paragraph, each of the amounts mentioned below shall be stated.

(2) The amount of the interest on or any similar charges in respect of—
 (a) bank loans and overdrafts, ...; and
 (b) loans of any other kind made to the company.

This sub-paragraph does not apply to interest or charges on loans to the company from group undertakings, but, with that exception, it applies to interest or charges on all loans, whether made on the security of debentures or not.

(3)–(5)

Particulars of tax

74.— (1) ...

(2) Particulars shall be given of any special circumstances which affect liability in respect of taxation of profits, income or capital gains for the financial year or liability in respect of taxation of profits, income or capital gains for succeeding financial years.

(3) The following amounts shall be stated—

  (a) the amount of the charge for United Kingdom corporation tax;

  (b) if that amount would have been greater but for relief from double taxation, the amount which it would have been but for such relief;

  (c) the amount of the charge for United Kingdom income tax; and

  (d) the amount of the charge for taxation imposed outside the United Kingdom of profits, income and (so far as charged to revenue) capital gains.

Those amounts shall be stated separately in respect of each of the amounts which is shown under the following items in the profit and loss account, that is to say item III.9 (tax on profit or loss on ordinary activities) and item III.14 (tax on extraordinary profit or loss).

Particulars of business

75.— (1) As regards general business a company shall disclose—

  (a) gross premiums written,

  (b) gross premiums earned,

  (c) gross claims incurred,

  (d) gross operating expenses, and

  (e) the reinsurance balance.

(2) The amounts required to be disclosed by sub-paragraph (1) shall be broken down between direct insurance and reinsurance acceptances, if reinsurance acceptances amount to 10 per cent or more of gross premiums written.

(3) Subject to sub-paragraph (4) below, the amounts required to be disclosed by sub-paragraphs (1) and (2) above with respect to direct insurance shall be further broken down into the following groups of classes—

  (a) accident and health,

  (b) motor (third party liability),

  (c) motor (other classes),

  (d) marine, aviation and transport,

  (e) fire and other damage to property,

  (f) third-party liability,

  (g) credit and suretyship,

  (h) legal expenses,

  (i) assistance, and

  (j) miscellaneous,

where the amount of the gross premiums written in direct insurance for each such group exceeds 10 million ECUs.

(4) The company shall in any event disclose the amounts relating to the three largest groups of classes in its business.

76.— (1) As regards long term business, the company shall disclose—

  (a) gross premiums written, and

  (b) the reinsurance balance.

(2) Subject to sub-paragraph (3) below—

(a)   gross premiums written shall be broken down between those written by way of direct insurance and those written by way of reinsurance; and

(b)   gross premiums written by way of direct insurance shall be broken down—

   (i)   between individual premiums and premiums under group contracts;

   (ii) between periodic premiums and single premiums; and

   (iii) between premiums from non-participating contracts, premiums from participating contracts and premiums from contracts where the investment risk is borne by policy holders.

(3)   Disclosure of any amount referred to in sub-paragraph (2)(a) or (2)(b)(i), (ii) or (iii) above shall not be required if it does not exceed 10 per cent of the gross premiums written or (as the case may be) of the gross premiums written by way of direct insurance.

77.— (1)   Subject to sub-paragraph (2) below, there shall be disclosed as regards both general and long term business the total gross direct insurance premiums resulting from contracts concluded by the company—

   (a)   in the member State of its head office,

   (b)   in the other member States, and

   (c)   in other countries.

(2)   Disclosure of any amount referred to in sub-paragraph (1) above shall not be required if it does not exceed 5 per cent of total gross premiums.

Commissions

78.   There shall be disclosed the total amount of commissions for direct insurance business accounted for in the financial year, including acquisition, renewal, collection and portfolio management commissions.

79.   ...

Miscellaneous matters

80.— (1)   Where any amount relating to any preceding financial year is included in any item in the profit and loss account, the effect shall be stated.

(2)   Particulars shall be given of any extraordinary income or charges arising in the financial year.

(3)   The effect shall be stated of any transactions that are exceptional by virtue of sire or incidence though they fall within the ordinary activities of the company.

CHAPTER IV
INTERPRETATIONS OF PART I

General

81.— (1)   The following definitions apply for the purposes of this Part of this Schedule and its interpretation—

   ...

"fungible assets" means assets of any description which are substantially indistinguishable one from another;

"general business" means business which consists of effecting or carrying out contracts of general insurance;

"investment property" means land held to earn rent or for capital appreciation.

"lease" includes an agreement for a lease;

"listed investment" means an investment listed on a recognised stock exchange, or on any stock exchange of repute outside Great Britain and the expression "unlisted investment" shall be construed accordingly;

"long lease" means a lease in the case of which the portion of the term for which it was granted remaining unexpired at the end of the financial year is not less than 50 years;

"long term business" means business which consists of effecting or carrying out contracts of long term insurance;

"long term fund" means the fund or funds maintained by a company in respect of its long term business in accordance with rules made by the Financial Services Authority under Part X of the Financial Services and Markets Act 2000;

"policy holder" has the meaning given in any relevant order under section 424(2) of the Financial Services and Markets Act 2000;

"provision for unexpired risks" means the amount set aside in addition to unearned premiums in respect of risks to be borne by the company after the end of the financial year, in order to provide for all claims and expenses in connection with insurance contracts in force in excess of the related unearned premiums and any premiums receivable on those contracts;

"short lease" means a lease which is not a long lease.

(2) In this Part of this Schedule the "ECU" means the unit of account of that name defined in Council Regulation (EEC) No 3180/78 as amended.

The exchange rates as between the ECU and the currencies of the member States to be applied for each financial year shall be the rates applicable on the last day of the preceding October for which rates for the currencies of all the member States were published in the Official Journal of the Communities.

Financial instruments

81A. For the purposes of this Part of this Schedule, references to "derivatives" include commodity-based contracts that give either contracting party the right to settle in cash or some other financial instrument, except when such contracts—

(a) were entered into for the purpose of, and continue to meet, the company's expected purchase, sale or usage requirements,

(b) were designated for such purpose at their inception, and

(c) are expected to be settled by delivery of the commodity.

81B.— (1) The expressions listed in sub-paragraph (2) have the same meaning in Section BA of Chapter 2 and paragraphs 65A to 65C and 81A of this Part of this Schedule as they have in Council Directives 78/660/EEC on the annual accounts of certain types of companies and 91/674/EEC on the annual accounts and consolidated accounts of insurance undertakings, as amended.

(2) Those expressions are "available for sale financial asset", "business combination", "commodity-based contracts", "derivative", "equity instrument", "exchange difference", "fair value hedge accounting system", "financial fixed asset", "financial instrument", "foreign entity", "hedge accounting", "hedge accounting system", "hedged items", "hedging instrument", "held for trading purposes", "held to maturity", "monetary item", "receivables", "reliable market" and "trading portfolio".

Loans

82. For the purposes of this Part of this Schedule a loan or advance (including a liability comprising a loan or advance) is treated as falling due for repayment, and an instalment of a loan or advance is treated as falling due for payment, on the earliest date on which the lender could require repayment or (as the case may be) payment, if he exercised all options and rights available to him.

Materiality

83. For the purposes of this Part of this Schedule amounts which in the particular context of any provision of this Part are not material may be disregarded for the purposes of that provision.

Provisions

84. For the purposes of this Part of this Schedule and its interpretation—

    (a)   references in this Part to provisions for depreciation or diminution in value of assets are to any amount written off by way of providing for depreciation or diminution in value of assets;

    (b)   any reference in the profit and loss account format or the notes thereto set out in Section B of this Part to the depreciation of, or amounts written off, assets of any description is to any provision for depreciation or diminution in value of assets of that description; and

    (c)   references in this Part to provisions for other risks ... are to any amount retained as reasonably necessary for the purpose of providing for any liability the nature of which is clearly defined and which is either likely to be incurred, or certain to be incurred but uncertain as to amount or as to the date on which it will arise.

Scots land tenure

85.   In the application of this Part of this Schedule to Scotland—

    "land of freehold tenure" means land in respect of which the company is the proprietor of the *dominium utile* or, in the case of land not held on feudal tenure, is the owner;

    "land of leasehold tenure" means land of which the company is the tenant under a lease;

and the reference to ground-rents, rates and other outgoings includes feu-duty and ground annual.

Staff costs

86.   For the purposes of this Part of this Schedule and its interpretation—

    (a)   "Social security costs" means any contributions by the company to any state social security or pension scheme, fund or arrangement;

    (b)   "Pension costs" includes any costs incurred by the company in respect of any pension scheme established for the purpose of providing pensions for persons currently or formerly employed by the company, any sums set aside for the future payment of pensions directly by the company to current or former employees and any pensions paid directly to such persons without having first been set aside; and

    (c)   any amount stated in respect of the item "social security costs" or in respect of the item "wages and salaries" in the company's profit and loss account shall be determined by reference to payments made or costs incurred in respect of all persons employed by the company during the financial year who are taken into account in determining the relevant annual number for the purposes of section 231A(1)(a).

PART II
CONSOLIDATED ACCOUNTS

Schedule 4A to apply Part I of this Schedule with modifications

1.—   (1)   In its application to insurance groups, Schedule 4A shall have effect with the following modifications.

    (2)   In paragraph 1—

    (a)   for the reference in sub-paragraph (1) to the provisions of Schedule 4 there shall be substituted a reference to the provisions of Part I of this Schedule modified as mentioned in paragraph 2 below;

    (b)   ... and

    (c)   sub-paragraph (3) shall be omitted.

    (3)   In paragraph 2(2)(a), for the words "three months" there shall be substituted the words "six months".

    (4)   In paragraph 3, after sub-paragraph (1) there shall be inserted the following sub-paragraphs—

    "(1A)Sub-paragraph (1) shall not apply to those liabilities items the valuation of which by the undertakings included in a consolidation is based on the application of provisions applying only to insurance undertakings, nor to those assets items changes in the values of which also affect or establish policy holders' rights.

(1B) Where sub-paragraph (1A) applies, that fact shall be disclosed in the notes on the consolidated accounts."

(5) For sub-paragraph (4) of paragraph 6 there shall be substituted the following sub-paragraphs—

"(4) Sub-paragraphs (1) and (2) need not be complied with—

(a) where a transaction has been concluded according to normal market conditions and a policy holder has rights in respect of that transaction, or

(b) if the amounts concerned are not material for the purpose of giving a true and fair view.

(5) Where advantage is taken of-sub-paragraph (4)(a) above that fact shall be disclosed in the notes to the accounts, and where the transaction in question has a material effect on the assets, liabilities, financial position and profit or loss of all the undertakings included in the consolidation that fact shall also be so disclosed."

(6) In paragraph 17—

(a) in sub-paragraph (1), for the reference to Schedule 4 there shall be substituted a reference to Part I of this Schedule;

(b) in sub-paragraph (2), paragraph (a) and, in paragraph (b), the words "in Format 2" shall be omitted;

(c) in sub-paragraph (3), for paragraphs (a) to (d) there shall be substituted the words "between items 10 and 11 in section III";

(d) in sub-paragraph (4), for paragraphs (a) to (d) there shall be substituted the words "between items 14 and 15 in section III"; and

(e) for sub-paragraph (5) there shall be substituted the following sub-paragraph—

"(5) Paragraph 2(3) of Part I of Schedule 9A (power to combine items) shall not apply in relation to the additional items required by the foregoing provisions of this paragraph."

(7) In paragraph 18, for the reference to paragraphs 17 to 19 and 21 of Schedule 4 there shall be substituted a reference to paragraphs 31 to 33 and 36 of Part I of this Schedule.

(8) In paragraph 21—

(a) in sub-paragraph (1), for the reference to Schedule 4 there shall be substituted a reference to Part I of this Schedule; and

(b) for sub-paragraphs (2) and (3) there shall be substituted the following sub-paragraphs—

"(2) In the Balance Sheet Format, Asset item C.II.3 (participating interests) shall be replaced by two items, "Interests in associated undertakings" and "Other participating interests".

(3) In the Profit and Loss Account Format, items II.2(a) and III.3(a) (income from participating interests, with a separate indication of that derived from group undertakings) shall each be replaced by the following items—

(a) "Income from participating interests other than associated undertakings, with a separate indication of that derived from group undertakings", which shall be shown as items II.2(a) and III.3(a), and

(b) "Income from associated undertakings", which shall be shown as items II.2(aa) and III.3(aa)."

(9) In paragraph 22(1), for the reference to paragraphs 17 to 19 and 21 of Schedule 4 there shall be substituted a reference to paragraphs 31 to 33 and 36 of Part I of this Schedule.

Modifications of Part I of this Schedule
for purposes of paragraph 1

2.— (1) For the purposes of paragraph 1 above, Part I of this Schedule shall be modified as follows.

(2) The information required by paragraph 10 need not be given.

(3) In the case of general business, investment income, expenses and charges may be disclosed in the non-technical account rather than in the technical account.

(4) In the case of subsidiary undertakings which are not authorised to carry on long term business in Great Britain, notes (8) and (9) to the profit and loss account format shall have effect as if references to investment income, expenses and charges arising in the long term fund or to investments attributed to the long term fund were references to investment income, expenses and charges or (as the case may be) investments relating to long term business.

(5) In the case of subsidiary undertakings which do not have a head office in Great Britain, the computation required by paragraph 46 shall be made annually by an actuary or other specialist in the field on the basis of recognised actuarial methods.

(6) The information required by paragraphs 75 to 78 need not be shown.

...

SCHEDULE 10A

PARENT AND SUBSIDIARY UNDERTAKINGS: SUPPLEMENTARY PROVISIONS

Section 258(6)

Introduction

1. The provisions of this Schedule explain expressions used in section 258 (parent and subsidiary undertakings) and otherwise supplement that section.

Voting rights in an undertaking

2.— (1) In section 258(2)(a) and (d) the references to the voting rights in an undertaking are to the rights conferred on shareholders in respect of their shares or, in the case of an undertaking not having a share capital, on members, to vote at general meetings of the undertaking on all, or substantially all, matters.

(2) In relation to an undertaking which does not have general meetings at which matters are decided by the exercise of voting rights, the references to holding a majority of the voting rights in the undertaking shall be construed as references to having the right under the constitution of the undertaking to direct the overall policy of the undertaking or to alter the terms of its constitution.

Right to appoint or remove a majority of the directors

3.— (1) In section 258(2)(b) the reference to the right to appoint or remove a majority of the board of directors is to the right to appoint or remove directors holding a majority of the voting rights at meetings of the board on all, or substantially all, matters.

(2) An undertaking shall be treated as having the right to appoint to a directorship if—

(a) a person's appointment to it follows necessarily from his appointment as director of the undertaking, or

(b) the directorship is held by the undertaking itself.

(3) A right to appoint or remove which is exercisable only with the consent or concurrence of another person shall be left out of account unless no other person has a right to appoint or, as the case may be, remove in relation to that directorship.

Right to exercise dominant influence

4.— (1) For the purposes of section 258(2)(c) an undertaking shall not be regarded as having the right to exercise a dominant influence over another undertaking unless it has a right to give directions with respect to the operating and financial policies of that other undertaking which its directors are obliged to comply with whether or not they are for the benefit of that other undertaking.

(2) A "control contract" means a contract in writing conferring such a right which—

      (a)   is of a kind authorised by the memorandum or articles of the undertaking in relation to which the right is exercisable, and

      (b)   is permitted by the law under which that undertaking is established.

    (3)   This paragraph shall not be read as affecting the construction of the expression "actually exercises a dominant influence" in section 258(4)(a).

Rights exercisable only in certain circumstances or temporarily incapable of exercise

5.—— (1)   Rights which are exercisable only in certain circumstances shall be taken into account only—

      (a)   when the circumstances have arisen, and for so long as they continue to obtain, or

      (b)   when the circumstances are within the control of the person having the rights.

    (2)   Rights which are normally exercisable but are temporarily incapable of exercise shall continue to be taken into account.

Rights held by one person on behalf of another

6.   Rights held by a person in a fiduciary capacity shall be treated as not held by him.

7.—— (1)   Rights held by a person as nominee for another shall be treated as held by the other.

    (2)   Rights shall be regarded as held as nominee for another if they are exercisable only on his instructions or with his consent or concurrence.

Rights attached to shares held by way of security

8.   Rights attached to shares held by way of security shall be treated as held by the person providing the security—

      (a)   where apart from the right to exercise them for the purpose of preserving the value of the security, or of realising it, the rights are exercisable only in accordance with his instructions, and

      (b)   where the shares are held in connection with the granting of loans as part of normal business activities and apart from the right to exercise them for the purpose of preserving the value of the security, or of realising it, the rights are exercisable only in his interests.

Rights attributed to parent undertaking

9.—— (1)   Rights shall be treated as held by a parent undertaking if they are held by any of its subsidiary undertakings.

    (2)   Nothing in paragraph 7 or 8 shall be construed as requiring rights held by a parent undertaking to be treated as held by any of its subsidiary undertakings.

    (3)   For the purposes of paragraph 8 rights shall be treated as being exercisable in accordance with the instructions or in the interests of an undertaking if they are exercisable in accordance with the instructions of or, as the case may be, in the interests of any group undertaking.

Disregard of certain rights

10.   The voting rights in an undertaking shall be reduced by any rights held by the undertaking itself.

Supplementary

11.   References in any provision of paragraphs 6 to 10 to rights held by a person include rights falling to be treated as held by him by virtue of any other provision of those paragraphs but not rights which by virtue of any such provision are to be treated as not held by him.

SCHEDULE 11

MODIFICATIONS OF PART VIII WHERE COMPANY'S ACCOUNTS PREPARED IN ACCORDANCE WITH SPECIAL PROVISIONS FOR BANKING OR INSURANCE COMPANIES

Section 279

1.   Paragraphs 2 to 6 below apply where a company has prepared accounts in accordance with the special provisions of Part VII relating to banking companies and paragraphs 7 to 13 below apply where a company has prepared accounts in accordance with the special provisions of Part VII relating to insurance companies.

*Modifications where accounts prepared in accordance with
special provisions for banking companies*

2.   Section 264(2) shall apply as if the reference to paragraph 89 of Schedule 4 therein was a reference to paragraph 85(c) of Part I of Schedule 9.

3.   Section 269 shall apply as if:

(a)   there were substituted for the words "are shown as an asset" in sub-section (1) the words "are included as an asset"; and

(b)   the reference to paragraph 20 of Schedule 4 in sub-section (2)(b) was to paragraph 27 of Part I of Schedule 9.

4.   Sections 270(2) and 275 shall apply as if the references therein to paragraphs 88 and 89 of Schedule 4 were to paragraph 85 of Part I of Schedule 9.

5.   Sections 272 and 273 shall apply as if in section 272(3) there were substituted, for the references to sections 226, 226A and 226B and Schedule 4, references to section 255 and Part I of Schedule 9.

6.   Section 276 shall apply as if the references to paragraphs 12(a) and 34(3)(a)(d) of Schedule 4 were to paragraphs 19(a) and 44(3)(a) of Schedule 9.

*Modifications where accounts prepared in accordance with
special provisions for insurance companies*

7.   Section 264(2) shall apply as if for the words in parentheses there were substituted "("liabilities" to include any provision for other risks and charges within paragraph 84(c) of Part I of Schedule 9A and any amount included under Liabilities items Ba (fund for future appropriations), C (technical provisions) and D (technical provisions for linked liabilities) in a balance sheet drawn up in accordance with the balance sheet format set out in section B of Part I of Schedule 9A).

8.   Section 269 shall apply as if the reference to paragraph 20 of Schedule 4 in subsection (2)(b) were a reference to paragraph 35 of Part I of Schedule 9A.

9.   In the case of Companies Act accounts, sections 270(2) and 275 shall apply as if the reference to provisions of any of the kinds mentioned in paragraphs 88 and 89 of Schedule 4 were a reference to provisions of any of the kinds mentioned in paragraph 84 of Part I of Schedule 9A and to any amount included under Liabilities items Ba (fund for future appropriations), C (technical provisions) and D (technical provisions for linked liabilities) in a balance sheet drawn up in accordance with the balance sheet format set out in section B of Part I of Schedule 9A.

10.   Sections 272 and 273 shall apply as if the references in section 272(3) to sections 226, 226A and 226B and Schedule 4 were references to section 255 and Part I of Schedule 9A.

11.   Section 276 shall apply as if the references to paragraphs 12(a) and 34(3)(a) of Schedule 4 were references to paragraphs 16(a) and 29(3)(a) of Part I of Schedule 9A.

SCHEDULE 12

...

SCHEDULE 13

PROVISIONS SUPPLEMENTING AND INTERPRETING SECTIONS 324 TO 328

Sections 324, 325, 326, 328 and 346

PART I
RULES FOR INTERPRETATION OF THE SECTIONS AND ALSO SECTION 346(4) AND (5)

1.— (1) A reference to an interest in shares or debentures is to be read as including any interest of any kind whatsoever in shares or debentures.

(2) Accordingly, there are to be disregarded any restraints or restrictions to which the exercise of any right attached to the interest is or may be subject.

2. Where property is held on trust and any interest in shares or debentures is comprised in the property, any beneficiary of the trust who (apart from this paragraph) does not have an interest in the shares or debentures is to be taken as having such an interest; but this paragraph is without prejudice to the following provisions of this Part of this Schedule.

3.— (1) A person is taken to have an interest in shares or debentures if—

(a) he enters into a contract for their purchase by him (whether for cash or other consideration), or

(b) not being the registered holder, he is entitled to exercise any right conferred by the holding of the shares or debentures, or is entitled to control the exercise of any such right.

(2) For purposes of sub-paragraph (1)(b), a person is taken to be entitled to exercise or control the exercise of a right conferred by the holding of shares or debentures if he—

(a) has a right (whether subject to conditions or not) the exercise of which would make him so entitled, or

(b) is under an obligation (whether or not so subject) the fulfilment of which would make him so entitled.

(3) A person is not by virtue of sub-paragraph (1)(b) taken to be interested in shares or debentures by reason only that he—

(a) has been appointed a proxy to vote at a specified meeting of a company or of any class of its members and at any adjournment of that meeting, or

(b) has been appointed by a corporation to act as its representative at any meeting of a company or of any class of its members.

4. A person is taken to be interested in shares or debentures if a body corporate is interested in them and—

(a) that body corporate or its directors are accustomed to act in accordance with his directions or instructions, or

(b) he is entitled to exercise or control the exercise of one-third or more of the voting power at general meetings of that body corporate.

As this paragraph applies for the purposes of section 346(4) and (5), "more than one-half" is substituted for "one-third or more".

5. Where a person is entitled to exercise or control the exercise of one-third or more of the voting power at general meetings of a body corporate, and that body corporate is entitled to exercise or control the exercise of any of the voting power at general meetings of another body corporate ("the effective voting power"), then, for purposes of paragraph 4(b), the effective voting power is taken to be exercisable by that person.

As this paragraph applies for the purposes of section 346(4) and (5), "more than one-half" is substituted for "one-third or more".

6.— (1) A person is taken to have an interest in shares or debentures if, otherwise than by virtue of having an interest under a trust—

       (a)   he has a right to call for delivery of the shares or debentures to himself or to his order, or

       (b)   he has a right to acquire an interest in shares or debentures or is under an obligation to take an interest in shares or debentures;

       whether in any case the right or obligation is conditional or absolute.

    (2)   Rights or obligations to subscribe for shares or debentures are not to be taken, for purposes of sub-paragraph (1), to be rights to acquire, or obligations to take, an interest in shares or debentures.

       This is without prejudice to paragraph 1.

7.   Persons having a joint interest are deemed each of them to have that interest.

8.   It is immaterial that shares or debentures in which a person has an interest are unidentifiable.

9.   So long as a person is entitled to receive, during the lifetime of himself or another, income from trust property comprising shares or debentures, an interest in the shares or debentures in reversion or remainder or (as regards Scotland) in fee, are to be disregarded.

10.   A person is to be treated as uninterested in shares or debentures if, and so long as, he holds them under the law in force in England and Wales as a bare trustee or as a custodian trustee, or under the law in force in Scotland, as a simple trustee.

11.— (1) There is to be disregarded an interest of a person subsisting by virtue of—

       (a)   any unit trust scheme which is an authorised unit trust scheme ...

       (b)   a scheme made under section 22 or 22A of the Charities Act 1960 or section 24 or 25 of the Charities Act 1993, section 11 of the Trustee Investments Act 1961 or section 1 of the Administration of Justice Act 1965; or

       (c)   the scheme set out in the Schedule to the Church Funds Investment Measure 1958.

    (2)   "Unit trust scheme" and "authorised unit trust scheme" have the meaning given in section 237 of the Financial Services and Markets Act 2000.

12.   There is to be disregarded any interest—

    (a)   of the Church of Scotland General Trustees or of the Church of Scotland Trust in shares or debentures held by them;

    (b)   of any other person in shares or debentures held by those Trustees or that Trust otherwise than as simple trustees.

"The Church of Scotland General Trustees" are the body incorporated by the order confirmed by the Church of Scotland (General Trustees) Order Confirmation Act 1921; and "the Church of Scotland Trust" is the body incorporated by the order confirmed by the Church of Scotland Trust Order Confirmation Act 1932.

13.   Delivery to a person's order of shares or debentures in fulfilment of a contract for the purchase of them by him or in satisfaction of a right of his to call for their delivery, or failure to deliver shares or debentures in accordance with the terms of such a contract or on which such a right falls to be satisfied, is deemed to constitute an event in consequence of the occurrence of which he ceases to be interested in them, and so is the lapse of a person's right to call for delivery of shares or debentures.

PART II
PERIODS WITHIN WHICH OBLIGATIONS IMPOSED BY SECTION 324
MUST BE FULFILLED

14.— (1)   An obligation imposed on a person by section 324(1) to notify an interest must, if he knows of the existence of the interest on the day on which he becomes a director, be fulfilled before the expiration of the period of 5 days beginning with the day following that day.

    (2)   Otherwise, the obligation must be fulfilled before the expiration of the period of 5 days beginning with the day following that on which the existence of the interest comes to his knowledge.

15.— (1)   An obligation imposed on a person by section 324(2) to notify the occurrence of an event must, if at the time at which the event occurs he knows of its occurrence and of the fact that its occurrence gives rise to the obligation, be fulfilled before the expiration of the period of 5 days beginning with the day following that on which the event occurs.

(2) Otherwise, the obligation must be fulfilled before the expiration of a period of 5 days beginning with the day following that on which the fact that the occurrence of the event gives rise to the obligation comes to his knowledge.

16. In reckoning, for purposes of paragraphs 14 and 15, any period of days, a day that is a Saturday or Sunday, or a bank holiday in any part of Great Britain, is to be disregarded.

PART III
CIRCUMSTANCES IN WHICH OBLIGATION IMPOSED BY SECTION 324 IS NOT DISCHARGED

17.— (1) Where an event of whose occurrence a director is, by virtue of section 324(2)(a), under obligation to notify a company consists of his entering into a contract for the purchase by him of shares or debentures, the obligation is not discharged in the absence of inclusion in the notice of a statement of the price to be paid by him under the contract.

(2) An obligation imposed on a director by section 324(2)(b) is not discharged in the absence of inclusion in the notice of the price to be received by him under the contract.

18.— (1) An obligation imposed on a director by virtue of section 324(2)(c) to notify a company is not discharged in the absence of inclusion in the notice of a statement of the consideration for the assignment (or, if it be the case that there is no consideration, that fact).

(2) Where an event of whose occurrence a director is, by virtue of section 324(2)(d), under obligation to notify a company consists in his assigning a right, the obligation is not discharged in the absence of inclusion in the notice of a similar statement.

19.— (1) Where an event of whose occurrence a director is, by virtue of section 324(2)(d), under obligation to notify a company consists in the grant to him of a right to subscribe for shares or debentures, the obligation is not discharged in the absence of inclusion in the notice of a statement of—

(a) the date on which the right was granted,

(b) the period during which or the time at which the right is exercisable,

(c) the consideration for the grant (or, if it be the case that there is no consideration, that fact), and

(d) the price to be paid for the shares or debentures.

(2) Where an event of whose occurrence a director is, by section 324(2)(d), under obligation to notify a company consists in the exercise of a right granted to him to subscribe for shares or debentures, the obligation is not discharged in the absence of inclusion in the notice of a statement of—

(a) the number of shares or amount of debentures in respect of which the right was exercised, and

(b) if it be the case that they were registered in his name, that fact, and, if not, the name or names of the person or persons in whose name or names they were registered, together (if they were registered in the names of 2 persons or more) with the number or amount registered in the name of each of them.

20. In this Part, a reference to price paid or received includes any consideration other than money.

PART IV
PROVISIONS WITH RESPECT TO REGISTER OF DIRECTORS' INTERESTS TO BE KEPT UNDER SECTION 325

21. The register must be so made up that the entries in it against the several names appear in chronological order.

22. An obligation imposed by section 325(2) to (4) must be fulfilled before the expiration of the period of 3 days beginning with the day after that on which the obligation arises; but in reckoning

that period, a day which is a Saturday or Sunday or a bank holiday in any part of Great Britain is to be disregarded.

23. The nature and extent of an interest recorded in the register of a director in any shares or debentures shall, if he so requires, be recorded in the register.

24. The company is not, by virtue of anything done for the purposes of section 325 or this Part of this Schedule, affected with notice of, or put upon enquiry as to, the rights of any person in relation to any shares or debentures.

25. The register shall—

    (a) if the company's register of members is kept at its registered office, be kept there;

    (b) if the company's register of members is not so kept, be kept at the company's registered office or at the place where its register of members is kept;

    and shall ... be open to the inspection of any member of the company without charge and of any other person on payment of such fee as may be prescribed.

26.— (1) Any member of the company or other person may require a copy of the register, or of any part of it, on payment of such fee as may be prescribed.

    (2) The company shall cause any copy so required by a person to be sent to him within the period of 10 days beginning with the day after that on which the requirement is received by the company.

27. The company shall send notice in the prescribed form to the registrar of companies of the place where the register is kept and of any change in that place, save in a case in which it has at all times been kept at its registered office.

28. Unless the register is in such a form as to constitute in itself an index, the company shall keep an index of the names inscribed in it, which shall—

    (a) in respect of each name, contain a sufficient indication to enable the information entered against it to be readily found; and

    (b) be kept at the same place as the register;

    and the company shall, within 14 days after the date on which a name is entered in the register, make any necessary alteration in the index.

29. The register shall be produced at the commencement of the company's annual general meeting and remain open and accessible during the continuance of the meeting to any person attending the meeting.

SCHEDULE 14

OVERSEAS BRANCH REGISTERS

Section 362

PART I
COUNTRIES AND TERRITORIES IN WHICH OVERSEAS BRANCH REGISTER MAY BE KEPT

Northern Ireland

Any part of Her Majesty's dominions outside the United Kingdom, the Channel Islands or the Isle of Man

Bangladesh	Malaysia
Cyprus	Malta
Dominica	Nigeria
The Gambia	Pakistan
Ghana	Republic of Ireland
Guyana	Seychelles
The Hong Kong Special Administrative	Sierra Leone
Region of the People's Republic of	Singapore
China	South Africa

India	Sri Lanka
Kenya	Swaziland
Kiribati	Trinidad and Tobago
Lesotho	Uganda
Malawi	Zimbabwe

PART II
GENERAL PROVISIONS WITH RESPECT TO OVERSEAS BRANCH REGISTERS

1.— (1) A company keeping an overseas branch register shall give to the registrar of companies notice in the prescribed form of the situation of the office where any overseas branch register is kept and of any change in its situation, and, if it is discontinued, of its discontinuance.

   (2) Any such notice shall be given within 14 days of the opening of the office or of the change or discontinuance, as the case may be.

   (3) If default is made in complying with this paragraph, the company and every officer of it who is in default is liable to a fine and, for continued contravention, to a daily default fine.

2.— (1) An overseas branch register is deemed to be part of the company's register of members ("the principal register").

   (2) It shall be kept in the same manner in which the principal register is by this Act required to be kept, except that the advertisement before closing the register shall be inserted in a newspaper circulating in the district where the overseas branch register is kept.

3.— (1) A competent court in a country or territory where an overseas branch register is kept may exercise the same jurisdiction of rectifying the register as is under this Act exercisable by the court in Great Britain; and the offences of refusing inspection or copies of the register, and of authorising or permitting the refusal, may be prosecuted summarily before any tribunal having summary criminal jurisdiction.

   (2) This paragraph extends only to those countries and territories where, immediately before the coming into force of this Act, provision to the same effect made by section 120(2) of the Companies Act 1948 had effect as part of the local law.

4.— (1) The company shall—

   (a) transmit to its registered office a copy of every entry in its overseas branch register as soon as may be after the entry is made, and

   (b) cause to be kept at the place where the company's principal register is kept a duplicate of its overseas branch register duly entered up from time to time.

   Every such duplicate is deemed for all purposes of this Act to be part of the principal register.

   (2) If default is made in complying with sub-paragraph (1), the company and every officer of it who is in default is liable to a fine and, for continued contravention, to a daily default fine.

   (3) Where, by virtue of section 353(1)(b), the principal register is kept at the office of some person other than the company, and by reason of any default of his the company fails to comply with sub-paragraph (1)(b) above he is liable to the same penalty as if he were an officer of the company who was in default.

5. Subject to the above provisions with respect to the duplicate register, the shares registered in an overseas branch register shall be distinguished from those registered in the principal register; and no transaction with respect to any shares registered in an overseas branch register shall, during the continuance of that registration, be registered in any other register.

6. A company may discontinue to keep an overseas branch register, and thereupon all entries in that register shall be transferred to some other overseas branch register kept by the company in the same country or territory, or to the principal register.

7. Subject to the provisions of this Act, any company may, by its articles, make such provisions as it thinks fit respecting the keeping of overseas branch registers.

8.   An instrument of transfer of a share registered in an overseas branch register (other than such a register kept in Northern Ireland) is deemed a transfer of property situated outside the United Kingdom *and, unless executed in a part of the United Kingdom, is exempt from stamp duty chargeable in Great Britain.*

Note. The italicized words in paragraph 8 are prospectively repealed by the Finance Act 1990, s. 132, Sch. 19, Pt. VI.

PART III
PROVISIONS FOR BRANCH REGISTERS OF OVERSEA COMPANIES TO BE KEPT IN GREAT BRITAIN

9.——   (1)   If by virtue of the law in force in any country or territory to which this paragraph applies companies incorporated under that law have power to keep in Great Britain branch registers of their members resident in Great Britain, Her Majesty may by Order in Council direct that—

        (a)   so much of section 353 as requires a company's register of members to be kept at its registered office,

        (b)   section 356 (register to be open to inspection by members), and

        (c)   section 359 (power of court to rectify),

       shall, subject to any modifications and adaptations specified in the Order, apply to and in relation to any such branch registers kept in Great Britain as they apply to and in relation to the registers of companies subject to those sections.

     (2)   The countries and territories to which this paragraph applies are—

        (a)   all those specified in Part I of this Schedule, plus the Channel Islands and the Isle of Man,

        (b)   Botswana, Zambia and Tonga, and

        (c)   any territory for the time being under Her Majesty's protection or administered by the Government of the United Kingdom under the Trusteeship System of the United Nations.

SCHEDULE 15

...

SCHEDULE 15A

WRITTEN RESOLUTIONS OF PRIVATE COMPANIES

Section 381A(7)

PART I
EXCEPTIONS

1.   Section 381A does not apply to—

        (a)   a resolution under section 303 removing a director before the expiration of his period of office, or

        (b)   a resolution under section 391 removing an auditor before the expiration of his term of office.

PART II
ADAPTATION OF PROCEDURAL REQUIREMENTS

Introductory

2.— (1) In this Part of this Schedule (which adapts certain requirements of this Act in relation to proceedings under section 381A)—

    (a) a "written resolution" means a resolution agreed to, or proposed to be agreed to, in accordance with that section, and

    (b) a "relevant member" means a member by whom, or on whose behalf, the resolution is required to be signed in accordance with that section.

  (2) A written resolution is not effective if any of the requirements of this Part of this Schedule is not complied with.

Section 95 (disapplication of pre-emption rights)

3.— (1) The following adaptations have effect in relation to a written resolution under section 95(2) (disapplication of pre-emption rights), or renewing a resolution under that provision.

  (2) So much of section 95(5) as requires the circulation of a written statement by the directors with a notice of meeting does not apply, but such a statement must be supplied to each relevant member at or before the time at which the resolution is supplied to him for signature.

  (3) Section 95(6) (offences) applies in relation to the inclusion in any such statement of matter which is misleading, false or deceptive in a material particular.

Section 155 (financial assistance for purchase of company's
own shares or those of holding company)

4.   In relation to a written resolution giving approval under section 155(4) or (5) (financial assistance for purchase of company's own shares or those of holding company), section 157(4)(a) (documents to be available at meeting) does not apply, but the documents referred to in that provision must be supplied to each relevant member at or before the time at which the resolution is supplied to him for signature.

Sections 164, 165 and 167 (authority for off-market purchase
or contingent purchase contract of company's own shares)

5.— (1) The following adaptations have effect in relation to a written resolution—

    (a) conferring authority to make an off-market purchase of the company's own shares under section 164(2),

    (b) conferring authority to vary a contract for an off-market purchase of the company's own shares under section 164(7), or

    (c) varying, revoking or renewing any such authority under section 164(3).

  (2) Section 164(5) (resolution ineffective if passed by exercise of voting rights by member holding shares to which the resolution relates) does not apply; but for the purposes of section 381A(1) a member holding shares to which the resolution relates shall not be regarded as a member who would be entitled to attend and vote.

  (3) Section 164(6) (documents to be available at company's registered office and at meeting) does not apply, but the documents referred to in that provision and, where that provision applies by virtue of section 164(7), the further documents referred to in that provision must be supplied to each relevant member at or before the time at which the resolution is supplied to him for signature.

  (4) The above adaptations also have effect in relation to a written resolution in relation to which the provisions of section 164(3) to (7) apply by virtue of—

    (a) section 165(2) (authority for contingent purchase contract), or

    (b) section 167(2) (approval of release of rights under contract approved under section 164 or 165).

Section 173 (approval for payment out of capital)

6.— (1) The following adaptations have effect in relation to a written resolution giving approval under section 173(2) (redemption or purchase of company's own shares out of capital).

(2) Section 174(2) (resolution ineffective if passed by exercise of voting rights by member holding shares to which the resolution relates) does not apply; but for the purposes of section 381A(1) a member holding shares to which the resolution relates shall not be regarded as a member who would be entitled to attend and vote.

(3) Section 174(4) (documents to be available at meeting) does not apply, but the documents referred to in that provision must be supplied to each relevant member at or before the time at which the resolution is supplied to him for signature.

Section 319 (approval of director's service contract)

7. In relation to a written resolution approving any such term as is mentioned in section 319(1) (director's contract of employment for more than five years), section 319(5) (documents to be available at company's registered office and at meeting) does not apply, but the documents referred to in that provision must be supplied to each relevant member at or before the time at which the resolution supplied to him for signature.

Section 337 (funding of director's expenditure in performing his duties)

8.In relation to a written resolution giving approval under section 337(3)(a) (funding a director's expenditure in performing his duties), the requirement of that provision that certain matters be disclosed at the meeting at which the resolution is passed does not apply, but those matters must be disclosed to each relevant member at or before the time at which the resolution is supplied to him for signature.

SCHEDULE 15B

PROVISIONS SUBJECT TO WHICH SS 425–427 HAVE EFFECT IN THEIR APPLICATION TO MERGERS AND DIVISIONS OF PUBLIC COMPANIES

Section 427A

Meetings of transferee company

1. Subject to paragraphs 10(1), 12(4) and 14(2), the court shall not sanction a compromise or arrangement under section 425(2) unless a majority in number representing three-fourths in value of each class of members of every pre-existing transferee company concerned in the scheme, present and voting either in person or by proxy at a meeting, agree to the scheme.

Draft terms of merger

2.— (1) The court shall not sanction the compromise or arrangement under section 425(2) unless—

(a) a draft of the proposed terms of the scheme (from here on referred to as the "draft terms") has been drawn up and adopted by the directors of all the transferor and pre-existing transferee companies concerned in the scheme,

(b) subject to paragraph 11(3), in the case of each of those companies the directors have delivered a copy of the draft terms to the registrar of companies and the registrar has published in the Gazette notice of receipt by him of a copy of the draft terms from that company, and

(c) subject to paragraphs 10 to 14, that notice was so published at least one month before the date of any meeting of that company summoned under section 425(1) or for the purposes of paragraph 1.

(2) Subject to paragraph 12(2), the draft terms shall give particulars of at least the following matters—

(a)   in respect of each transferor company and transferee company concerned in the scheme, its name, the address of its registered office and whether it is a company limited by shares or a company limited by guarantee and having a share capital;

(b)   the number of shares in any transferee company to be allotted to members of any transferor company for a given number of their shares (from here on referred to as the "share exchange ratio") and the amount of any cash payment;

(c)   the terms relating to the allotment of shares in any transferee company;

(d)   the date from which the holding of shares in a transferee company will entitle the holders to participate in profits, and any special conditions affecting that entitlement;

(e)   the date from which the transactions of any transferor company are to be treated for accounting purposes as being those of any transferee company;

(f)   any rights or restrictions attaching to shares or other securities in any transferee company to be allotted under the scheme to the holders of shares to which any special rights or restrictions attach, or of other securities, in any transferor company, or the measures proposed concerning them;

(g)   any amount or benefit paid or given or intended to be paid or given to any of the experts referred to in paragraph 5 or to any director of a transferor company or pre-existing transferee company, and the consideration for the payment of benefit.

(3)   Where the scheme is a Case 3 Scheme the draft terms shall also—

(a)   give particulars of the property and liabilities to be transferred (to the extent these are known to the transferor company) and their allocation among the transferee companies;

(b)   make provision for the allocation among and transfer to the transferee companies of any other property and liabilities which the transferor company has or may subsequently acquire; and

(c)   specify the allocation to members of the transferor company of shares in the transferee companies and the criteria upon which that allocation is based.

Documents and information to be made available

3.   Subject to paragraphs 10 to 14, the court shall not sanction the compromise or arrangement under section 425(2) unless—

(a)   in the case of each transferor company and each pre-existing transferee company the directors have drawn up and adopted a report complying with paragraph 4 (from here on referred to as a "directors' report");

(b)   where the scheme is a Case 3 Scheme, the directors of the transferor company have reported to every meeting of the members or any class of members of that company summoned under section 425(1), and to the directors of each transferee company, any material changes in the property and liabilities of the transferor company between the date when the draft terms were adopted and the date of the meeting in question;

(c)   where the directors of a transferor company have reported to the directors of a transferee company such a change as is mentioned in sub-paragraph (b) above, the latter have reported that change to every meeting of the members or any class of members of that transferee company summoned for the purposes of paragraph 1, or have sent a report of that change to every member who would have been entitled to receive a notice of such a meeting;

(d)   a report complying with paragraph 5 has been drawn up on behalf of each transferor company and pre-existing transferee company (from here on referred to as an "expert's report");

(e)   the members of any transferor company or transferee company were able to inspect at the registered office of that company copies of the documents listed in paragraph 6(1) in relation to every transferor company and pre-existing transferee company concerned in the scheme during a period beginning one month before, and ending on, the date of the first meeting of the members or any class of members of the first-mentioned transferor or transferee company summoned either under section 425(1) or for the purposes of paragraph

1 and those members were able to obtain copies of those documents or any part of them on request during that period free of charge; and

(f) the memorandum and articles of association of any transferee company which is not a pre-existing transferee company, or a draft thereof, has been approved by ordinary resolution of every transferor company concerned in the scheme.

Directors' report

4.— (1) The directors' report shall consist of—

(a) the statement required by section 426, and

(b) insofar as that statement does not contain the following matters, a further statement—

(i) setting out the legal and economic grounds for the draft terms, and in particular for the share exchange ratio, and, where the scheme is a Case 3 Scheme, for the criteria upon which the allocation to the members of the transferor company of shares in the transferee companies was based, and

(ii) specifying any special valuation difficulties.

(2) Where the scheme is a Case 3 Scheme the directors' report shall also state whether a report has been made to the transferee company under section 103 (non-cash consideration to be valued before allotment) and, if so, whether that report has been delivered to the registrar of companies.

Expert's report

5.— (1) Except where a joint expert is appointed under sub-paragraph (2) below, an expert's report shall consist of a separate written report on the draft terms to the members of one transferor company or pre-existing transferee company concerned in the scheme drawn up by a separate expert appointed on behalf of that company.

(2) The court may, on the joint application of all the transferor companies and pre-existing transferee companies concerned in the scheme, approve the appointment of a joint expert to draw up a single report on behalf of all those companies.

(3) An expert shall be independent of any of the companies concerned in the scheme, that is to say a person qualified at the time of the report to be appointed, or to continue to be, an auditor of those companies.

(4) However, where it appears to an expert that a valuation is reasonably necessary to enable him to draw up the report, and it appears to him to be reasonable for that valuation, or part of it, to be made (or for him to accept such a valuation) by another person who—

(a) appears to him to have the requisite knowledge and experience to make the valuation or that part of it; and

(b) is not an officer or servant of any of the companies concerned in the scheme or any other body corporate which is one of those companies' subsidiary or holding company or a subsidiary of one of those companies' holding company or a partner or employee of such an officer or servant,

he may arrange for or accept such a valuation, together with a report which will enable him to make his own report under this paragraph.

(5) The reference in sub-paragraph (4) above to an officer or servant does not include an auditor.

(6) Where any valuation is made by a person other than the expert himself, the latter's report shall state that fact and shall also—

(a) state the former's name and what knowledge and experience he has to carry out the valuation, and

(b) describe so much of the undertaking, property and liabilities as were valued by the other person, and the method used to value them, and specify the date of the valuation.

(7) An expert's report shall—

(a) indicate the method or methods used to arrive at the share exchange ratio proposed;

(b) give an opinion as to whether the method or methods used are reasonable in all the circumstances of the case, indicate the values arrived at using each such method and (if there is more than one method) give an opinion on the relative importance attributed to such methods in arriving at the value decided on;

(c) describe any special valuation difficulties which have arisen;

(d) state whether in the expert's opinion the share exchange ratio is reasonable; and

(e) in the case of a valuation made by a person other than himself, state that it appeared to himself reasonable to arrange for it to be so made or to accept a valuation so made.

(8) Each expert has the right of access to all such documents of all the transferor companies and pre-existing transferee companies concerned in the scheme, and the right to require from the companies' officers all such information, as he thinks necessary for the purpose of making his report.

Inspection of documents

6.— (1) The documents referred to in paragraph 3(e) are, in relation to any company,—

(a) the draft terms;

(b) the directors' report referred to in paragraph 4 above;

(c) the expert's report;

(d) the company's annual accounts, together with the relevant directors' report and auditors' report, for the last three financial years ending on or before the relevant date; and

(e) if the last of those financial years ended more than six months before the relevant date, an accounting statement in the form described in the following provisions.

In paragraphs (d) and (e) "the relevant date" means one month before the first meeting of the company summoned under section 425(1) or for the purposes of paragraph 1.

(2) The accounting statement shall consist of—

(a) a balance sheet dealing with the state of the affairs of the company as at a date not more than three months before the draft terms were adopted by the directors, and

(b) where the company would be required to prepare group accounts if that date were the last day of a financial year, a consolidated balance sheet dealing with the state of affairs of the company and its subsidiary undertakings as at that date.

(3) The requirements of this Act as to balance sheets forming part of a company's annual accounts, and the matters to be included in notes thereto, apply to any balance sheet required for the accounting statement, with such modifications as are necessary by reason of its being prepared otherwise than as at the last day of a financial year.

(4) Any balance sheet required for the accounting statement shall be approved by the board of directors and signed on behalf of the board by a director of the company.

(5) In relation to a company within the meaning of Article 3 of the Companies (Northern Ireland) Order 1986, the references in this paragraph to the requirements of this Act shall be construed as reference to the corresponding requirements of that Order.

Transferor company holding its own shares

7. The court shall not sanction under section 425(2) a compromise or arrangement under which any shares in a transferee company are to be allotted to a transferor company or its nominee in respect of shares in that transferor company held by it or its nominee.

Securities other than shares to which special rights are attached

8.— (1) Where any security of a transferor company to which special rights are attached is held by a person other than as a member or creditor of the company, the court shall not sanction a compromise or arrangement under section 425(2) unless under the scheme that person is to receive rights in a transferee company of equivalent value.

(2) Sub-paragraph (1) above shall not apply in the case of any such security where—

(a) the holder has agreed otherwise; or

(b)   the holder is, or under the scheme is to be, entitled to have the security purchased by a transferee company involved in the scheme on terms which the court considers reasonable.

Date and consequences of the compromise or arrangement

9.—   (1)   The following provisions of this paragraph shall apply where the court sanctions a compromise or arrangement.

(2)   The court shall in the order sanctioning the compromise or arrangement or in a subsequent order under section 427 fix a date on which the transfer or transfers to the transferee company or transferee companies of the undertaking, property and liabilities of the transferor company shall take place; and any such order which provide for the dissolution of the transferor company shall fix the same date for the dissolution.

(3)   If it is necessary for the transferor company to take any steps to ensure that the undertaking, property and liabilities are fully transferred, the court shall fix a date, not later than six months after the date fixed under sub-paragraph (2) above, by which such steps must be taken and for that purpose may postpone the dissolution of the transferor company until that date.

(4)   The court may postpone or further postpone the date fixed under sub-paragraph (3) above if it is satisfied that the steps there mentioned cannot be completed by the date (or latest date) fixed under that sub-paragraph.

Exceptions

10.—   (1)   The court may sanction a compromise or arrangement under section 425(2) notwithstanding that—

(a)   any meeting otherwise required by paragraph 1 has not been summoned by a pre-existing transferee company ("the relevant company"), and

(b)   paragraphs 2(1)(c) and 3(e) have not been complied with in respect of that company,

if the court is satisfied that the conditions specified in sub-paragraph (2) below have been complied with.

(2)   Subject to paragraphs 11(3) and 12(3), the conditions mentioned in sub-paragraph (1) above are—

(a)   that the publication of notice of receipt of the draft terms by the registrar of companies referred to in paragraph 2(1)(b) took place in respect of the relevant company at least one month before the date of any meeting of members of any transferor company concerned in the scheme summoned under section 425(1);

(b)   that the members of the relevant company were able to inspect at the registered office of that company the documents listed in paragraph 6(1) in relation to every transferor company and transferee company concerned in the scheme during a period ("the relevant period") beginning one month before, and ending on, the date of any such meeting, and that they were able to obtain copies of those documents or any part of them on request during that period free of charge; and

(c)   that one or more members of the relevant company, who together held not less than five per cent. of the paid-up capital of that company which carried the right to vote at general meetings of the company (excluding any shares in the company held as treasury shares), would have been able during the relevant period to require that a meeting of each class of members be called for the purpose of deciding whether or not to agree to the scheme but that no such requisition had been made.

11.—   (1)   The following sub-paragraphs apply where the scheme is a Case 3 Scheme.

(2)   Sub-paragraphs (a) to (d) of paragraph 3 shall not apply and sub-paragraph (e) of that paragraph shall not apply as regards the documents listed in paragraph 6(1)(b), (c) and (e), if all members holding shares in, and all persons holding other securities of, any of the transferor companies and pre-existing transferee companies concerned in the scheme on the

date of the application to the court under section 425(1), being shares or securities which as at that date carry the right to vote in general meetings of the company, so agree.

(3) The court may by order direct in respect of any transferor company or pre-existing transferee company that the requirements relating to—

    (a) delivering copies of the draft terms and publication of notice of receipt of the draft terms under paragraph 2(1)(b) and (c), or

    (b) inspection under paragraph 3(e),

shall not apply, and may by order direct that paragraph 10 shall apply to any pre-existing transferee company with the omission of sub-paragraph (2)(a) and (b) of that paragraph.

(4) The court shall not make any order under sub-paragraph (3) above unless it is satisfied that the following conditions will be fulfilled—

    (a) that the members of the company will have received or will have been able to obtain free of charge copies of the documents listed in paragraph 6(1) in time to examine them before the date of the first meeting of the members or any class of members of the company summoned under section 425(1) or for the purposes of paragraph 1;

    (b) in the case of a pre-existing transferee company, where in the circumstances described in paragraph 10 no meeting is held, that the members of that company will have received or will have been able to obtain free of charge copies of those documents in time to require a meeting under paragraph 10(2)(c);

    (c) that the creditors of the company will have received or will have been able to obtain free of charge copies of the draft terms in time to examine them before the date of the meeting of the members or any class of members of the company, or, in the circumstances referred to in paragraph (b) above, at the same time as the members of the company; and

    (d) that no prejudice would be caused to the members or creditors of any transferor company or transferee company concerned in the scheme by making the order in question.

Transferee company or companies holding shares in the transferor company

12.— (1) Where the scheme is a Case 1 Scheme and in the case of every transferor company concerned—

    (a) the shares in that company, and

    (b) such securities of that company (other than shares) as carry the right to vote at general meetings of that company,

are all held by or on behalf of the transferee company, section 427A and this Schedule shall apply subject to the following sub-paragraphs.

(2) The draft terms need not give particulars of the matters mentioned in paragraph 2(2)(b), (c) or (d).

(3) Section 426 and sub-paragraphs (a) and (d) of paragraph 3 shall not apply, and sub-paragraph (e) of that paragraph shall not apply as regards the documents listed in paragraph 6(1)(b) and (c).

(4) The court may sanction the compromise or arrangement under section 425(2) notwithstanding that—

    (a) any meeting otherwise required by section 425 or paragraph 1 has not been summoned by any company concerned in the scheme, and

    (b) paragraphs 2(1)(c) and 3(e) have not been complied with in respect of that company,

if it is satisfied that the conditions specified in the following sub-paragraphs have been complied with.

(5) The conditions mentioned in the previous sub-paragraph are—

    (a) that the publication of notice of receipt of the draft terms by the registrar of companies referred to in paragraph 2(1)(b) took place in respect of every transferor company and transferee company concerned in the scheme at least one month before the date of the order under section 425(2) ("the relevant date");

(b)   that the members of the transferee company were able to inspect at the registered office of that company copies of the documents listed in paragraphs 6(1)(a), (d) and (e) in relation to every transferor company or transferee company concerned in the scheme during a period ("the relevant period") beginning one month before, and ending on, the relevant date and that they were able to obtain copies of those documents or any part of them on request during that period free of charge; and

(c)   that one or more members of the transferee company who together held not less than five per cent. of the paid-up capital of the company which carried the right to vote at general meetings of the company (excluding any shares in the company held as treasury shares) would have been able during the relevant period to require that a meeting of each class of members be called for the purpose of deciding whether or not to agree to the scheme but that no such requisition has been made.

13.—   (1)   Where the scheme is a Case 3 Scheme and—

(a)   the shares in the transferor company, and

(b)   such securities of that company (other than shares) as carry the right to vote at general meetings of that company,

are all held by or on behalf of one or more transferee companies, section 427A and this Schedule shall apply subject to the following sub-paragraphs.

(2)   The court may sanction a compromise or arrangement under section 425(2) notwithstanding that—

(a)   any meeting otherwise required by section 425 has not been summoned by the transferor company, and

(b)   paragraphs 2(1)(c) and 3(b) and (e) have not been complied with in respect of that company,

if it is satisfied that the conditions specified in the following sub-paragraph have been complied with.

(3)   The conditions referred to in the previous sub-paragraph are—

(a)   the conditions set out in paragraph 12(5)(a) and (c);

(b)   that the members of the transferor company and every transferee company concerned in the scheme were able to inspect at the registered office of the company of which they were members copies of the documents listed in paragraph 6(1) in relation to every such company during a period beginning one month before, and ending on, the date of the order under section 425(2) ("the relevant date"), and that they were able to obtain copies of those documents or any part of them on request during that period free of charge; and

(c)   that the directors of the transferor company have sent to every member who would have been entitled to receive a notice of the meeting (had it been called), and to the directors of each transferee company, a report of any material changes in the property and liabilities of the transferor company between the date when the draft terms were adopted and a date one month before the relevant date.

14.—   (1)   Where the scheme is a Case 1 Scheme and in the case of every transferor company concerned ninety per cent or more (but not all) of—

(a)   the shares in that company, and

(b)   such securities of that company (other than shares) as carry the right to vote at general meetings of that company,

are held by or on behalf of the transferee company, section 427A and this Schedule shall apply subject to the following sub-paragraphs.

(2)   The court may sanction a compromise or arrangement under section 425(2) notwithstanding that—

(a)   any meeting otherwise required by paragraph 1 has not been summoned by the transferee company, and

(b)   paragraphs 2(1)(c) and 3(e) have not been complied with in respect of that company, if the court is satisfied that the conditions specified in the following sub-paragraph have been complied with.

(3) The conditions referred to in the previous sub-paragraph are the same conditions as those specified in paragraph 10(2), save that for this purpose the condition contained in paragraph 10(2)(b) shall be treated as referring only to the documents listed in paragraph 6(1)(a), (d) and (e).

Liability of transferee companies for the default of another

15.— (1) Where the scheme is a Case 3 Scheme, each transferee company shall be jointly and severally liable, subject to sub-paragraph (2) below, for any liability transferred to any other transferee company under the scheme to the extent that that other company has made default in satisfying that liability, but so that no transferee company shall be so liable for an amount greater than the amount arrived at by calculating the value at the time of the transfer of the property transferred to it under the scheme less the amount at that date of the liabilities so transferred.

(2) If a majority in number representing three-fourths in value of the creditors or any class of creditors of the transferor company present and voting either in person or by proxy at a meeting summoned under section 425(1) so agree, sub-paragraph (1) above shall not apply in respect of the liabilities of the creditors or that class of creditors.

SCHEDULE 15C

Section 449

SPECIFIED PERSONS

1. The Secretary of State.
2. The Department of Enterprise, Trade and Investment for Northern Ireland.
3. The Treasury.
4. The Lord Advocate.
5. The Director of Public Prosecutions.
6. The Director of Public Prosecutions for Northern Ireland.
7. The Financial Services Authority.
8. A constable.
9. A procurator fiscal.
10. The Scottish Ministers.

SCHEDULE 15D

Section 449

DISCLOSURES

1. *A disclosure for the purpose of enabling or assisting a person authorised under section 245C to exercise his functions.*

2. *A disclosure for the purpose of enabling or assisting an inspector appointed under Part 14 to exercise his functions.*

3. *A disclosure for the purpose of enabling or assisting a person authorised under section 447 of this Act or section 84 of the Companies Act 1989 to exercise his functions.*

4. *A disclosure for the purpose of enabling or assisting a person appointed under section 167 of the Financial Services and Markets Act 2000 (general investigations) to conduct an investigation to exercise his functions.*

5. *A disclosure for the purpose of enabling or assisting a person appointed under section 168 of the Financial Services and Markets Act 2000 (investigations in particular cases) to conduct an investigation to exercise his functions.*

6.   *A disclosure for the purpose of enabling or assisting a person appointed under section 169(1)(b) of the Financial Services and Markets Act 2000 (investigation in support of overseas regulator) to conduct an investigation to exercise his functions.*

7.   *A disclosure for the purpose of enabling or assisting a person appointed under section 284 of the Financial Services and Markets Act 2000 (investigations into affairs of certain collective investment schemes) to conduct an investigation to exercise his functions.*

8.   *A disclosure for the purpose of enabling or assisting a person appointed under regulations made under sections 262(1) and (2)(k) of the Financial Services and Markets Act 2000 (investigations into open-ended investment companies) to conduct an investigation to exercise his functions.*

9.   *A disclosure for the purpose of enabling or assisting the Secretary of State or the Treasury to exercise any of their functions under any of the following—*
    (a)   this Act;
    (b)   the insider dealing legislation;
    (c)   the Insolvency Act 1986;
    (d)   the Company Directors Disqualification Act 1986;
    (e)   Part 2, 3 or 7 of the Companies Act 1989;
    (f)   the Financial Services and Markets Act 2000.

10.   *A disclosure for the purpose of enabling or assisting the Scottish Ministers to exercise their functions under the enactments relating to insolvency.*

11.   *A disclosure for the purpose of enabling or assisting the Department of Enterprise, Trade and Investment for Northern Ireland to exercise any powers conferred on it by the enactments relating to companies or insolvency.*

12.   *A disclosure for the purpose of enabling or assisting a person appointed or authorised by the Department of Enterprise, Trade and Investment for Northern Ireland under the enactments relating to companies or insolvency to exercise his functions.*

13.   *A disclosure for the purpose of enabling or assisting the Occupational Pensions Regulatory Authority to exercise their functions under any of the following—*
    (a)   the Pension Schemes Act 1993;
    (b)   the Pensions Act 1995;
    (c)   any enactment in force in Northern Ireland corresponding to either of the above.

[13.   *A disclosure for the purpose of enabling or assisting the Pensions Regulator to exercise the functions conferred on it by or by virtue of any of the following—*
    (a)   the Pension Schemes Act 1993;
    (b)   the Pensions Act 1995;
    (c)   the Welfare Reform and Pensions Act 1999;
    (d)   the Pensions Act 2004;
    (e)   any enactment in force in Northern Ireland corresponding to any of those enactments.]

13A.   *A disclosure for the purpose of enabling or assisting the Board of the Pension Protection Fund to exercise the functions conferred on it by or by virtue of Part 2 of the Pensions Act 2004 or any enactment in force in Northern Ireland corresponding to that Part.*

14.   *A disclosure for the purpose of enabling or assisting the Bank of England to exercise its functions.*

15.   *A disclosure for the purpose of enabling or assisting the body known as the Panel on Takeovers and Mergers to exercise its functions.*

16.   *A disclosure for the purpose of enabling or assisting organs of the Society of Lloyd's (being organs constituted by or under the Lloyd's Act 1982) to exercise their functions under or by virtue of the Lloyd's Acts 1871 to 1982.*

17.   *A disclosure for the purpose of enabling or assisting the Office of Fair Trading to exercise its functions under any of the following—*
    (a)   the Fair Trading Act 1973;
    (b)   the Consumer Credit Act 1974;
    (c)   the Estate Agents Act 1979;
    (d)   the Competition Act 1980;

     (e)   *the Competition Act 1998;*
     (f)   *the Financial Services and Markets Act 2000;*
     (g)   *the Enterprise Act 2002;*
     (h)   *the Control of Misleading Advertisements Regulations 1988 (S.I. 1988/915);*
     (i)   *the Unfair Terms in Consumer Contracts Regulations 1999 (S.I. 1999/2083).*

18.   *A disclosure for the purpose of enabling or assisting the Competition Commission to exercise its functions under any of the following—*
     (a)   *the Fair Trading Act 1973;*
     (b)   *the Competition Act 1980;*
     (c)   *the Competition Act 1998;*
     (d)   *the Enterprise Act 2002.*

19.   *A disclosure with a view to the institution of, or otherwise for the purposes of, proceedings before the Competition Appeal Tribunal.*

20.   *A disclosure for the purpose of enabling or assisting an enforcer under Part 8 of the Enterprise Act 2002 to exercise its functions under that Part.*

21.   *A disclosure for the purpose of enabling or assisting the Charity Commissioners to exercise their functions.*

22.   *A disclosure for the purpose of enabling or assisting the Attorney General to exercise his functions in connection with charities.*

23.   *A disclosure for the purpose of enabling or assisting the National Lottery Commission to exercise its functions under sections 5 to 10 and 15 of the National Lottery etc. Act 1993.*

24.   *A disclosure by the National Lottery Commission to the National Audit Office for the purpose of enabling or assisting the Comptroller and Auditor General to carry out an examination under Part 2 of the National Audit Act 1983 into the economy, effectiveness and efficiency with which the National Lottery Commission has used its resources in discharging its functions under sections 5 to 10 of the National Lottery etc. Act 1993.*

25.   *A disclosure for the purpose of enabling or assisting a qualifying body under the Unfair Terms in Consumer Contracts Regulations 1999 (S.I. 1999/2083) to exercise its functions under those Regulations.*

26.   *A disclosure for the purpose of enabling or assisting an enforcement authority under the Consumer Protection (Distance Selling) Regulations 2000 (S.I. 2000/2334) to exercise its functions under those Regulations.*

27.   *A disclosure for the purpose of enabling or assisting a local weights and measures authority in England and Wales to exercise its functions under section 230(2) of the Enterprise Act 2002.*

28.   *A disclosure for the purpose of enabling or assisting the Financial Services Authority to exercise its functions under any of the following—*
     (a)   *the legislation relating to friendly societies or to industrial and provident societies;*
     (b)   *the Building Societies Act 1986;*
     (c)   *Part 7 of the Companies Act 1989;*
     (d)   *the Financial Services and Markets Act 2000.*

29.   *A disclosure for the purpose of enabling or assisting the competent authority for the purposes of Part 6 of the Financial Services and Markets Act 2000 to exercise its functions under that Part.*

30.   *A disclosure for the purpose of enabling or assisting a body corporate established in accordance with section 212(1) of the Financial Services and Markets Act 2000 (compensation scheme manager) to exercise its functions.*

31.— (1) *A disclosure for the purpose of enabling or assisting a recognised investment exchange or a recognised clearing house to exercise its functions as such.*
     (2)   *Recognised investment exchange and recognised clearing house have the same meaning as in section 285 of the Financial Services and Markets Act 2000.*

32.   *A disclosure for the purpose of enabling or assisting a body designated under section 326(1) of the Financial Services and Markets Act 2000 (designated professional bodies) to exercise its functions in its capacity as a body designated under that section.*

33.   A disclosure with a view to the institution of, or otherwise for the purposes of, civil proceedings arising under or by virtue of the Financial Services and Markets Act 2000.

34.   A disclosure for the purpose of enabling or assisting a body designated by order under section 46 of the Companies Act 1989 (delegation of functions of Secretary of State) to exercise its functions under Part 2 of that Act.

35.   A disclosure for the purpose of enabling or assisting a recognised supervisory or qualifying body (within the meaning of Part 2 of the Companies Act 1989) to exercise its functions as such.

36.   A disclosure for the purpose of enabling or assisting an official receiver (including the Accountant in Bankruptcy in Scotland and the Official Assignee in Northern Ireland) to exercise his functions under the enactments relating to insolvency.

37.   A disclosure for the purpose of enabling or assisting the Insolvency Practitioners Tribunal to exercise its functions under the Insolvency Act 1986.

38.   A disclosure for the purpose of enabling or assisting a body which is for the time being a recognised professional body for the purposes of section 391 of the Insolvency Act 1986 (recognised professional bodies) to exercise its functions as such.

39.—   (1) A disclosure for the purpose of enabling or assisting an overseas regulatory authority to exercise its regulatory functions.

       (2) Overseas regulatory authority and regulatory functions have the same meaning as in section 82 of the Companies Act 1989.

40.   A disclosure for the purpose of enabling or assisting the Regulator of Community Interest Companies to exercise functions under the Companies (Audit, Investigations and Community Enterprise) Act 2004.

41.   A disclosure with a view to the institution of, or otherwise for the purposes of, criminal proceedings.

42.   A disclosure with a view to the institution of, or otherwise for the purposes of, proceedings on an application under section 6, 7 or 8 of the Company Directors Disqualification Act 1986.

43.   A disclosure with a view to the institution of, or otherwise for the purposes of, proceedings before the Financial Services and Markets Tribunal.

44.   A disclosure for the purposes of proceedings before the Financial Services Tribunal by virtue of the Financial Services and Markets Act 2000 (Transitional Provisions) (Partly Completed Procedures) Order 2001 (S.I. 2001/3592).

44A.   A disclosure for the purposes of proceedings before the Pensions Regulator Tribunal.

45.   A disclosure for the purpose of enabling or assisting a body appointed under section 14 of the Companies (Audit, Investigations and Community Enterprise) Act 2004 (supervision of periodic accounts and reports of issuers of listed securities) to exercise functions mentioned in subsection (2) of that section.

46.   A disclosure with a view to the institution of, or otherwise for the purposes of, disciplinary proceedings relating to the performance by a solicitor, barrister, auditor, accountant, valuer or actuary of his professional duties.

47.—   (1) A disclosure with a view to the institution of, or otherwise for the purposes of, disciplinary proceedings relating to the performance by a public servant of his duties.

       (2) Public servant means an officer or employee of the Crown or of any public or other authority for the time being designated for the purposes of this paragraph by the Secretary of State by order.

       (3) An order under sub-paragraph (2) must be made by statutory instrument subject to annulment in pursuance of a resolution of either House of Parliament.

48.   A disclosure for the purpose of the provision of a summary or collection of information framed in such a way as not to enable the identity of any person to whom the information relates to be ascertained.

49.   A disclosure in pursuance of any Community obligation.

Note. Schedule 15D is inserted by the Companies (Audit, Investigations and Community Enterprise) Act 2004, s. 25(1), Sch. 2, Pt. 3, paras. 16, 25, as from 6 April 2005 (for certain purposes) and from 1 July 2005 (for remaining purposes). Paragraph 13 is substituted, and paragraphs 13A and 44A are inserted, by the Pensions Act 2004, ss. 102(4), 319(1), Sch. 4, Pt. 4, para. 19, Sch. 12, para. 5(1), (3), as from a day to be appointed.

SCHEDULES 16–19

...

SCHEDULE 20

VESTING OF DISCLAIMED PROPERTY; PROTECTION OF THIRD PARTIES

Section 619

PART I

...

PART II
CROWN DISCLAIMER UNDER SECTION 656

5.   The court shall not under section 657 make a vesting order, where the property disclaimed is held under a lease, in favour of a person claiming under the company (whether as sub-lessee or as creditor in a duly registered or, as appropriate, recorded heritable security over a lease), except on the following terms.

6.   The person must by the order be made subject—
   (a)   to the same liabilities and obligations as those to which the company was subject under the lease in respect of the property at the commencement of the winding up, or
   (b)   (if the court thinks fit) only to the same liabilities and obligations as if the lease had been assigned to him at that date;
   and in either event (if the case so requires) the liabilities and obligations must be as if the lease had comprised only the property comprised in the vesting order.

7.   A creditor or sub-lessee declining to accept a vesting order on such terms is excluded from all interest in and security over the property.

8.   If there is no person claiming under the company who is willing to accept an order on such terms, the court has power to vest the company's estate and interest in the property in any person liable (either personally or in a representative character, and either alone or jointly with the company) to perform the lessee's obligations under the lease, freed and discharged from all interests, rights and obligations created by the company in the lease or in relation to the lease.

9.   For the purposes of paragraph 5 above, a heritable security is duly recorded if it is recorded in the Register of Sasines and is duly registered if registered in accordance with the Land Registration (Scotland) Act 1979.

SCHEDULE 21

EFFECT OF REGISTRATION UNDER SECTION 680

Section 689

Interpretation

1.   In this Schedule—
        "registration" means registration in pursuance of section 680 in Chapter II of Part XXII of this Act, and "registered" has the corresponding meaning, and
        "instrument" includes deed of settlement, contract of copartnery and letters patent.

Vesting of property

2.   All property belonging to or vested in the company at the date of its registration passes to and vests in the company on registration for all the estate and interest of the company in the property.

Existing liabilities

3.   Registration does not affect the company's rights or liabilities in respect of any debt or obligation incurred, or contract entered into, by, to, with or on behalf of the company before registration.

Pending actions at law

4.— (1)   All actions and other legal proceedings which at the time of the company's registration are pending by or against the company, or the public officer or any member of it, may be continued in the same manner as if the registration had not taken place.

(2)   However, execution shall not issue against the effects of any individual member of the company on any judgment, decree or order obtained in such an action or proceeding; but in the event of the company's property and effects being insufficient to satisfy the judgment, decree or order, an order may be obtained for winding up the company.

The company's constitution

5.— (1)   All provisions contained in any Act of Parliament or other instrument constituting or regulating the company are deemed to be conditions and regulations of the company, in the same manner and with the same incidents as if so much of them as would, if the company had been formed under this Act, have been required to be inserted in the memorandum, were contained in a registered memorandum, and the residue were contained in registered articles.

(2)   The provisions brought in under this paragraph include, in the case of a company registered as a company limited by guarantee, those of the resolution declaring the amount of the guarantee; and they include also the statement under section 681(5)(a), and any statement under section 684(2).

6.— (1)   All the provisions of this Act apply to the company, and to its members, contributories and creditors, in the same manner in all respects as if it had been formed under this Act, subject as follows.

(2)   Table A does not apply unless adopted by special resolution.

(3)   Provisions relating to the numbering of shares do not apply to any joint stock company whose shares are not numbered.

(4)   Subject to the provisions of this Schedule, the company does not have power—

(a)   to alter any provision contained in an Act of Parliament relating to the company,

(b)   without the sanction of the Secretary of State, to alter any provision contained in letters patent relating to the company.

(5)   The company does not have power to alter any provision contained in a royal charter or letters patent with respect to the company's objects.

(6)   Where by virtue of sub-paragraph (4) or (5) a company does not have power to alter a provision, it does not have power to ratify acts of the directors in contravention of the provision.

Capital structure

7.   Provisions of this Act with respect to—

(a)   the registration of an unlimited company as limited,

(b)   the powers of an unlimited company on registration as a limited company to increase the nominal amount of its share capital and to provide that a portion of its share capital shall not be capable of being called up except in the event of winding up, and

(c)   the power of a limited company to determine that a portion of its share capital shall not be capable of being called up except in that event, apply, notwithstanding any provisions contained in an Act of Parliament, royal charter or other instrument constituting or regulating the company.

Supplementary

8.   Nothing in paragraphs 5 to 7 authorises a company to alter any such provisions contained in an instrument constituting or regulating the company as would, if the company had originally been formed under this Act, have been required to be contained in the memorandum and are not authorised to be altered by this Act.

9.   None of the provisions of this Act (except section 461(3)) derogate from any power of altering the company's constitution or regulations which may, by virtue of any Act of Parliament or other instrument constituting or regulating it, be vested in the company.

SCHEDULE 21A

BRANCH REGISTRATION UNDER THE ELEVENTH COMPANY LAW DIRECTIVE (89/666/EEC)

Section 690A

Duty to register

1.—   (1)   A company shall, within one month of having opened a branch in a part of Great Britain, deliver to the registrar for registration a return in the prescribed form containing—

       (a)   such particulars about the company as are specified in paragraph 2,

       (b)   such particulars about the branch as are specified in paragraph 3, and

       (c)   if the company is one to which section 699AA applies, such particulars in relation to the registration of documents under Schedule 21D as are specified in paragraph 4.

     (2)   The return shall, except where sub-paragraph (3) below applies, be accompanied by the documents specified in paragraph 5 and, if the company is one to which Part I of Schedule 21D applies, the documents specified in paragraph 6.

     (3)   This sub-paragraph applies where—

       (a)   at the time the return is delivered, the company has another branch in the United Kingdom,

       (b)   the return contains a statement to the effect that the documents specified in paragraph 5, and, if the company is one to which Part I of Schedule 21D applies, paragraph 6, are included in the material registered in respect of the other branch, and

       (c)   the return states where the other branch is registered and what is its registered number.

     (4)   In sub-paragraph (1) above, the reference to having opened a branch in a part of Great Britain includes a reference to a branch having become situated there on ceasing to be situated elsewhere.

     (5)   If at the date on which the company opens the branch in Great Britain the company is subject to any proceedings referred to in section 703P(1) (winding up) or 703Q(1) (insolvency proceedings etc), the company shall deliver a return under section 703P(1) or (as the case may be) 703Q(1) within one month of that date.

If on or before that date a person has been appointed to be liquidator of the company and continues in that office at that date, section 703P(3) and (4) (liquidator to make return within 14 days of appointment) shall have effect as if it required a return to be made under that section within one month of the date of the branch being opened.

Particulars required

2.—   (1)   The particulars referred to in paragraph 1(1)(a) are—

       (a)   the corporate name of the company,

       (b)   its legal form,

(c) if it is registered in the country of its incorporation, the identity of the register in which it is registered and the number with which it is so registered,

(d) a list of its directors and secretary, containing (subject to paragraph 4A)—

    (i) with respect to each director, the particulars specified in sub-paragraph (3) below, and

    (ii) with respect to the secretary (or where there are joint secretaries, with respect to each of them) the particulars specified in sub-paragraph (4) below,

(e) the extent of the powers of the directors to represent the company in dealings with third parties and in legal proceedings, together with a statement as to whether they may act alone or must act jointly and, if jointly, the name of any other person concerned, and

(f) whether the company is an institution to which section 699A (or the equivalent provision in Northern Ireland) applies.

(2) In the case of a company which is not incorporated in a Member State, those particulars also include—

(a) the law under which the company is incorporated,

(b) in the case of a company to which either paragraphs 2 and 3 of Part I of Schedule 21C or Schedule 21D applies) the period for which the company is required by the law under which it is incorporated to prepare accounts, together with the period allowed for the preparation and public disclosure of accounts for such a period, and

(c) unless disclosed by the documents specified in paragraph 5—

    (i) the address of its principal place of business in its country of incorporation,

    (ii) its objects, and

    (iii) the amount of its issued share capital.

(3) The particulars referred to in sub-paragraph (1)(d)(i) above are—

(a) in the case of an individual—

    (i) his name,

    (ii) any former name,

    (iii) his usual residential address,

    (iv) his nationality,

    (v) his business occupation (if any),

    (vi) particulars of any other directorships held by him, and

    (vii) his date of birth;

(b) in the case of a corporation or Scottish firm, its corporate or firm name and registered or principal office.

(4) The particulars referred to in sub-paragraph (1)(d)(ii) above are—

(a) in the case of an individual, his name, any former name and his usual residential address;

(b) in the case of a corporation or Scottish firm, its corporate or firm name and registered or principal office.

Where all the partners in a firm are joint secretaries of the company, the name and principal office of the firm may be stated instead of the particulars required by paragraph (a) above.

(5) In sub-paragraphs (3)(a) and (4)(a) above—

(a) "name" means a person's forename and surname, except that in the case of a peer, or an individual usually known by a title, the title may be stated instead of his forename and surname, or in addition to either or both of them; and

(b) the reference to a former name does not include—

    (i) in the case of a peer, or an individual normally known by a title, the name by which he was known previous to the adoption of or succession to the title;

    (ii) in the case of any person, a former name which was changed or disused before he attained the age of 18 years or which has been changed or disused for 20 years or more;

              (iii)   in the case of a married woman, the name by which she was known previous to the marriage.

      (6)   Where—

           (a)   at the time a return is delivered under paragraph 1(1) the company has another branch in the same part of Great Britain as the branch covered by the return; and

           (b)   the company has delivered the particulars required by sub-paragraphs (1)(b) to (f) and (2) to (5) to the registrar with respect to that branch (or to the extent it is required to do so by virtue of Schedule 21B to this Act) and has no outstanding obligation to make a return to the registrar in respect of that branch under paragraph 7 in relation to any alteration to those particulars,

the company may adopt the particulars so delivered as particulars which the registrar is to treat as having been filed by the return by referring in the return to the fact that the particulars have been filed in respect of that other branch and giving the number with which the other branch is registered.

3.   The particulars referred to in paragraph 1(1)(b) are—

      (a)   the address of the branch,

      (b)   the date on which it was opened,

      (c)   the business carried on at it,

      (d)   if different from the name of the company, the name in which that business is carried on,

      (e)   a list of the names and addresses of all persons resident in Great Britain authorised to accept on the company's behalf service of process in respect of the business of the branch and of any notices required to be served on the company in respect of the business of the branch,

      (f)   a list of the names and (subject to paragraph 4A) usual residential addresses of all persons authorised to represent the company as permanent representatives of the company for the business of the branch,

      (g)   the extent of the authority of any person falling within paragraph (f) above, including whether that person is authorised to act alone or jointly, and

      (h)   if a person falling within paragraph (f) above is not authorised to act alone, the name of any person with whom he is authorised to act.

4.   The particulars referred to in paragraph 1(1)(c) are—

      (a)   whether it is intended to register documents under paragraph 2(2) or, as the case may be, 10(1) of Schedule 21D in respect of the branch or in respect of some other branch in the United Kingdom, and

      (b)   if it is, where that other branch is registered and what is its registered number.

4A.   Where a confidentiality order made under section 723B is in force in respect of a director or secretary required to be specified in the list under paragraph 2(1)(d) or a permanent representative required to be specified in the list under paragraph 3(f)—

      (a)   if the order is in respect of a director, paragraph 2(1)(d) has effect in respect of that director as if the reference in paragraph 2(3)(a)(iii) to his usual residential address were a reference to the address for the time being notified by him to the company under regulations made under sections 723B to 723F;

      (b)   if the order is in respect of a secretary, paragraph 2(1)(d) has effect in respect of that secretary as if the reference in paragraph 2(4)(a) to his usual residential address were a reference to the address for the time being notified by him to the company under such regulations;

      (c)   if the order is in respect of a permanent representative, paragraph 3(f) has effect in respect of that representative as if the reference to his usual residential address were a reference to the address for the time being notified by him to the company under such regulations; and

      (d)   in any case the company shall deliver to the registrar, in addition to the return required by paragraph 1(1) a return in the prescribed form containing particulars of the usual residential address of the director, secretary or permanent representative to whom the confidentiality order relates, and any such return shall be delivered to the registrar within one month of having opened a branch in a part of Great Britain.

Documents required

5.   The first documents referred to in paragraph 1(2) are—

    (a)   a certified copy of the charter, statutes or memorandum and articles of the company (or other instrument constituting or defining the company's constitution), and

    (b)   if any of the documents mentioned in paragraph (a) above is not written in the English language, a translation of it into English certified in the prescribed manner to be a correct translation.

6.—   (1)   The second documents referred to in paragraph 1(2) are—

    (a)   copies of the latest accounting documents prepared in relation to a financial period of the company to have been publicly disclosed in accordance with the law of the country in which it is incorporated before the end of the period allowed for compliance with paragraph 1 in respect of the branch or, if earlier, the date on which the company complies with paragraph 1 in respect of the branch, and

    (b)   if any of the documents mentioned in paragraph (a) above is not written in the English language, a translation of it into English certified in the prescribed manner to be a correct translation.

    (2)   In sub-paragraph (1)(a) above, "financial period" and "accounting documents" shall be construed in accordance with paragraph 6 of Schedule 21D.

Alterations

7.—   (1)   If, after a company has delivered a return under paragraph 1(1) above, any alteration is made in—

    (a)   its charter, statutes or memorandum and articles (or other instrument constituting or defining its constitution), or

    (b)   any of the particulars referred to in paragraph 1(1),

the company shall, within the time specified below, deliver to the registrar for registration a return in the prescribed form containing the prescribed particulars of the alteration.

In the case of an alteration in any of the documents referred to in paragraph (a), the return shall be accompanied by a certified copy of the document as altered, together with, if the document is not written in the English language, a translation of it into English certified in the prescribed manner to be a correct translation.

    (2)   The time for the delivery of the return required by sub-paragraph (1) above is—

    (a)   in the case of an alteration in any of the particulars specified in paragraph 3, 21 days after the alteration is made; or

    (b)   in the case of any other alteration, 21 days after the date on which notice of the alteration in question could have been received in Great Britain in due course of post (if despatched with due diligence).

    (3)   Where—

    (a)   a company has more than one branch in Great Britain, and

    (b)   an alteration relates to more than one of those branches,

sub-paragraph (1) above shall have effect to require the company to deliver a return in respect of each of the branches to which the alteration relates.

    (4)   For the purposes of sub-paragraph (3) above—

    (a)   an alteration in any of the particulars specified in paragraph 2 shall be treated as relating to every branch of the company (though where the company has more than one branch in a part of Great Britain a return in respect of an alteration in any of those particulars which gives the branch numbers of two or more such branches shall be treated as a return in respect of each branch whose number is given), but

        (b)   an alteration in the company's charter, statutes or memorandum and articles (or other instrument constituting or defining its constitution) shall only be treated as relating to a branch if the document altered is included in the material registered in respect of it.

8.—   (1)   Sub-paragraph (2) below applies where—

        (a)   a company's return under paragraph 1(1) includes a statement to the effect mentioned in paragraph 1(3)(b), and

        (b)   the statement ceases to be true so far as concerns the documents specified in paragraph 5.

    (2)   The company shall, within the time specified below, deliver to the registrar of companies for registration in respect of the branch to which the return relates—

        (a)   the documents specified in paragraph 5, or

        (b)   a return in the prescribed form—

            (i)   containing a statement to the effect that those documents are included in the material which is registered in respect of another branch of the company in the United Kingdom, and

            (ii)   stating where the other branch is registered and what is its registered number.

    (3)   The time for complying with sub-paragraph (2) above is 21 days after the date on which notice of the fact that the statement in the earlier return has ceased to be true could have been received in Great Britain in due course of post (if despatched with due diligence).

    (4)   Sub-paragraph (2) above shall also apply where, after a company has made a return under sub-paragraph (2)(b) above, the statement to the effect mentioned in sub-paragraph (2)(b)(i) ceases to be true.

    (5)   For the purposes of sub-paragraph (2)(b), where the company has more than one branch in a part of Great Britain a return which gives the branch numbers of two or more such branches shall be treated as a return in respect of each branch whose number is given.

9.—   (1)   If an individual in respect of whom a confidentiality order under section 723B is in force becomes a director, secretary or permanent representative of a company that has delivered a return under paragraph 1(1)—

        (a)   the return required to be delivered to the registrar under paragraph 7(1) shall contain the address for the time being notified to the company by the director, secretary or permanent representative under regulations made under sections 723B to 723F, but shall not contain his usual residential address; and

        (b)   with the return under paragraph 7(1) the company shall deliver to the registrar a return in the prescribed form containing the usual residential address of that director, secretary or permanent representative.

    (2)   If after a company has delivered a return under paragraph 1(1) a confidentiality order under section 723B is made in respect of an existing director, secretary or permanent representative of the company, the company shall within the time specified below deliver to the registrar of companies for registration a return in the prescribed form containing the address for the time being notified to it by the director, secretary or permanent representative under regulations made under sections 723B to 723F.

    (3)   Sub-paragraph (4) applies if, at any time after a company has delivered a return under paragraph 1(1), there is an alteration in the usual residential address of a director, secretary or permanent representative of the company in respect of whom a confidentiality order under section 723B is in force.

    (4)   The company shall within the time specified below deliver to the registrar of companies for registration a return in the prescribed form containing the new address.

    (5)   The time for the delivery of a return required by sub-paragraph (2) or (4) is 21 days after the date on which notice of the alteration in question could have been received in Great Britain in due course of post (if despatched with due diligence).

    (6)   Where a company has more than one branch in Great Britain and any provision of this paragraph requires a return to be made to the registrar, that provision requires the company

to deliver a return in respect of each of the branches; but a return which gives the branch numbers of two or more such branches shall be treated as a return in respect of each branch whose number is given.

SCHEDULE 21B

CHANGE IN REGISTRATION REGIME: TRANSITIONAL PROVISIONS

Section 692A

1.— (1) This paragraph applies where a company which becomes a company to which section 690A applies was, immediately before becoming such a company (referred to in this paragraph as the relevant time), a company to which section 691 applies.

(2) The company need not include the particulars specified in paragraph 2(1)(d) of Schedule 21A in the first return to be delivered under paragraph 1(1) of that Schedule to the registrar for a part of Great Britain if at the relevant time—

(a) it had an established place of business in that part,

(b) it had complied with its obligations under section 691(1)(b)(i), and

(c) it had no outstanding obligation to make a return to the registrar for that part under subsection (1) of section 692, so far as concerns any alteration of the kind mentioned in subsection (1)(b) of that section,

and if it states in the return that the particulars have been previously filed in respect of a place of business of the company in that part, giving the company's registered number.

(3) The company shall not be required to deliver the documents mentioned in paragraph 5 of Schedule 21A with the first return to be delivered under paragraph 1(1) of that Schedule to the registrar for a part of Great Britain if at the relevant time—

(a) it had an established place of business in that part,

(b) it had delivered the documents mentioned in section 691(1)(a) to the registrar for that part, and

(c) it had no outstanding obligation to make a return to that registrar under subsection (1) of section 692, so far as concerns any alteration in any of the documents mentioned in paragraph (a) of that subsection,

and if it states in the return that the documents have been previously filed in respect of a place of business of the company in that part, giving the company's registered number.

2.— (1) This paragraph applies where a company which becomes a company to which section 691 applies was, immediately before becoming such a company (referred to in this paragraph as the relevant time), a company to which section 690A applies.

(2) The company shall not be required to deliver the documents mentioned in section 691(1)(a) to the registrar for a part of Great Britain if at the relevant time—

(a) it had a branch in that part,

(b) the documents mentioned in paragraph 5 of Schedule 21A were included in the material registered in respect of the branch, and

(c) it had no outstanding obligation to make a return to the registrar for that part under paragraph 7 of that Schedule, so far as concerns any alteration in any of the documents mentioned in sub-paragraph (1)(a) of that paragraph,

and if it states in the return that the documents have been previously filed in respect of a branch of the company, giving the branch's registered number.

(3) The company need not include the particulars mentioned in section 691(1)(b)(i) in the return to be delivered under section 691(1)(b) to the registrar for a part of Great Britain if at the relevant time—

(a) it had a branch in that part,

        (b)   it had complied with its obligations under paragraph 1(1)(a) of Schedule 21A in respect of the branch so far as the particulars required by paragraph 2(1)(d) of that Schedule are concerned, and

        (c)   it had no outstanding obligation to make a return to the registrar for that part under paragraph 7 of that Schedule, so far as concerns any alteration in any of the particulars required by paragraph 2(1)(d) of that Schedule,

and if it states in the return that the particulars have been previously filed in respect of a branch of the company, giving the branch's registered number.

(4)   Where sub-paragraph (3) above applies, the reference in section 692(1)(b) to the list of the directors and secretary shall be construed as a reference to the list contained in the return under paragraph 1(1) of Schedule 21A with any alterations in respect of which a return under paragraph 7(1) of that Schedule has been made.

SCHEDULE 21C

DELIVERY OF REPORTS AND ACCOUNTS: CREDIT AND FINANCIAL INSTITUTIONS TO WHICH THE BANK BRANCHES DIRECTIVE (89/117/EEC) APPLIES

Section 699A

PART I

INSTITUTIONS REQUIRED TO PREPARE ACCOUNTS UNDER PARENT LAW

Scope of Part and Interpretation

1.—   (1)   This Part of this Schedule applies to any institution to which section 699A applies which is required by its parent law to prepare and have audited accounts for its financial periods and whose only or principal branch within the United Kingdom is in Great Britain.

       (2)   In this Part of this Schedule, "branch" has the meaning given by section 699A.

Duty to deliver copies in Great Britain

2.—   (1)   An institution to which this Part of this Schedule applies shall, within one month of becoming such an institution, deliver to the registrar for registration—

        (a)   copies of the latest accounting documents of the institution prepared in accordance with its parent law to have been disclosed before the end of the period allowed for compliance with this sub-paragraph or, if earlier, the date of compliance with it, and

        (b)   if any of the documents mentioned in paragraph (a) above is not written in the English language, a translation of it into English certified in the prescribed manner to be a correct translation.

Where an institution to which this Part of this Schedule applies had, immediately prior to becoming such an institution, a branch in Northern Ireland which was its only or principal branch within the United Kingdom it may, instead of delivering the documents mentioned in sub-paragraph (1)(a) under that paragraph, deliver thereunder a notice that it has become an institution to which this Part of this Schedule applies, provided that those documents have been delivered to the registrar for Northern Ireland pursuant to the Companies (Northern Ireland) Order 1986.

3.—   (1)   An institution to which this Part of this Schedule applies shall deliver to the registrar for registration—

        (a)   copies of all the accounting documents of the institution prepared in accordance with its parent law which are disclosed on or after the end of the period allowed for compliance with paragraph 2(1) or, if earlier, the date on which it complies with that paragraph, and

        (b)   if any of the documents mentioned in paragraph (a) above is not written in the English language, a translation of it into English, certified in the prescribed manner to be a correct translation.

(2)   The period allowed for delivery, in relation to a document required to be delivered under this paragraph, is 3 months from the date on which the document is first disclosed.

4.   Where an institution's parent law permits it to discharge an obligation with respect to the disclosure of accounting documents by disclosing documents in a modified form, it may discharge its obligation under paragraph 2 or 3 by delivering copies of documents modified as permitted by that law.

5.—   (1)   Neither paragraph 2 nor paragraph 3 shall require an institution to deliver documents to the registrar if at the end of the period allowed for compliance with that paragraph—

        (a)   it is not required by its parent law to register them,

        (b)   they are made available for inspection at each branch of the institution in Great Britain, and

        (c)   copies of them are available on request at a cost not exceeding the cost of supplying them.

(2)   Where by virtue of sub-paragraph (1) above an institution is not required to deliver documents under paragraph 2 or 3 and any of the conditions specified in that sub-paragraph ceases to be met, the institution shall deliver the documents to the registrar for registration within 7 days of the condition ceasing to be met.

Registrar to whom documents to be delivered

6.   The documents which an institution is required to deliver to the registrar under this Part of this Schedule shall be delivered—

        (a)   to the registrar for England and Wales if the institution's only branch, or (if it has more than one) its principal branch within the United Kingdom, is in England and Wales; or

        (b)   to the registrar for Scotland if the institution's only branch, or (if it has more than one) its principal branch within the United Kingdom, is in Scotland.

Penalty for non-compliance

7.—   (1)   If an institution fails to comply with paragraph 2, 3 or 5(2) before the end of the period allowed for compliance, the institution and every person who immediately before the end of that period was a director of the institution, or, in the case of an institution which does not have directors, a person occupying an equivalent office, is guilty of an offence and liable to a fine and, for continued contravention, to a daily default fine.

(2)   It is a defence for a person charged with an offence under this paragraph to prove that he took all reasonable steps for securing compliance with paragraph 2, 3 or 5(2), as the case may be.

Interpretation

8.—   (1)   In this Part of this Schedule—

           "financial period" in relation to an institution, means a period for which the institution is required or permitted by its parent law to prepare accounts;

           "parent law", in relation to an institution, means the law of the country in which the institution has its head office;

      and references to disclosure are to public disclosure, except where an institution is not required under its parent law, any enactment (including any subordinate legislation within the meaning of section 21 of the Interpretation Act 1978) having effect for Great Britain or its constitution to publicly disclose its accounts, in which case such references are to the disclosure of the accounts to the persons for whose information they have been prepared.

(2)   For the purposes of this Part of this Schedule, the following are accounting documents in relation to a financial period of an institution—

(a) the accounts of the institution for the period, including, if it has one or more subsidiaries, any consolidated accounts of the group,

(b) any annual report of the directors (or, in the case of an institution which does not have directors, the persons occupying equivalent offices) for the period,

(c) the report of the auditors on the accounts mentioned in paragraph (a) above, and

(d) any report of the auditors on the report mentioned in paragraph (b) above.

PART II
INSTITUTIONS NOT REQUIRED TO PREPARE ACCOUNTS UNDER PARENT LAW

Scope of Part and Interpretation

9.— (1) This Part of this Schedule applies to any institution to which section 699A applies which—

(a) is incorporated, and

(b) is not required by the law of the country in which it has its head office to prepare and have audited accounts.

(2) In this Part of this Schedule, "branch" has the meaning given by section 699A.

Preparation of accounts and reports

10. An institution to which this Part of this Schedule applies shall in respect of each financial year of the institution prepare the like accounts and directors' report, and cause to be prepared such an auditors' report, as would be required if the institution were a company to which section 700 applied.

11. Sections 223 to 225 apply to an institution to which this Part of this Schedule applies subject to the following modifications—

(a) for the references to the incorporation of the company there shall be substituted references to the institution becoming an institution to which this Part of this Schedule applies; and

(b) section 225(4) shall be omitted.

Duty to deliver accounts and reports

12.— (1) An institution to which this Part of this Schedule applies shall in respect of each financial year of the institution deliver to the registrar copies of the accounts and reports prepared in accordance with paragraph 10.

(2) If any document comprised in those accounts or reports is in a language other than English, the institution shall annex to the copy delivered a translation of it into English, certified in the prescribed manner to be a correct translation.

Time for delivery

13.— (1) The period allowed for delivering accounts and reports under paragraph 12 above is 13 months after the end of the relevant accounting reference period, subject to the following provisions of this paragraph.

(2) If the relevant accounting reference period is the institution's first and is a period of more than 12 months, the period allowed is 13 months from the first anniversary of the institution's becoming an institution to which this Part of this Schedule applies.

(3) If the relevant accounting reference period is treated as shortened by virtue of a notice given by the institution under section 225, the period allowed is that applicable in accordance with the above provisions or 3 months from the date of the notice under that section, whichever last expires.

(4) If for any special reason the Secretary of State thinks fit he may, on an application made before the expiry of the period otherwise allowed, by notice in writing to an institution to which this Part of this Schedule applies, extend that period by such further period as may be specified in the notice.

(5) In this paragraph "the relevant accounting reference period" means the accounting reference period by reference to which the financial year for the accounts in question was determined.

Registrar to whom documents to be delivered

14. The documents which an institution is required to deliver to the registrar under this Part of the Schedule shall be delivered—

(a) to the registrar for England and Wales if the institution's only branch, or (if it has more than one) its principal branch within Great Britain, is in England and Wales; or

(b) to the registrar for Scotland if the institution's only branch, or (if it has more than one) its principal branch within Great Britain, is in Scotland.

Penalty for non-compliance

15.— (1) If the requirements of paragraph 12 are not complied with before the end of the period allowed for delivering accounts and reports, or if the accounts and reports delivered do not comply with the requirements of this Act, the institution and every person who immediately before the end of that period was a director of the institution, or, in the case of an institution which does not have directors, a person occupying an equivalent office, is guilty of an offence and liable to a fine and, for continued contravention, to a daily default fine.

(2) It is a defence for a person charged with such an offence to prove that he took all reasonable steps for securing that the requirements in question would be complied with.

(3) It is not a defence in relation to a failure to deliver copies to the registrar to prove that the documents in question were not in fact prepared as required by this Schedule.

SCHEDULE 21D

DELIVERY OF REPORTS AND ACCOUNTS:
COMPANIES TO WHICH THE ELEVENTH COMPANY LAW DIRECTIVE APPLIES

Section 699AA

PART I
COMPANIES REQUIRED TO MAKE DISCLOSURE UNDER PARENT LAW

Scope of Part

1. This Part of this Schedule applies to any company to which section 699AA applies which is required by its parent law to prepare, have audited and disclose accounts.

Duty to deliver copies in Great Britain

2.— (1) This paragraph applies in respect of each branch which a company to which this Part of this Schedule applies has in Great Britain.

(2) The company shall deliver to the registrar for registration in respect of the branch copies of all the accounting documents prepared in relation to a financial period of the company which are disclosed in accordance with its parent law on or after the end of the period allowed for compliance in respect of the branch with paragraph 1 of Schedule 21A or, if earlier, the date on which the company complies with that paragraph in respect of the branch.

(3) Where the company's parent law permits it to discharge its obligation with respect to the disclosure of accounting documents by disclosing documents in a modified form, it may discharge its obligation under sub-paragraph (2) above by delivering copies of documents modified as permitted by that law.

(4) If any document, a copy of which is delivered under sub-paragraph (2) above, is in a language other than English, the company shall annex to the copy delivered a translation of it into English, certified in the prescribed manner to be a correct translation.

3. Paragraph 2 above shall not require documents to be delivered in respect of a branch if—

(a) before the end of the period allowed for compliance with that paragraph, they are delivered in respect of another branch in the United Kingdom, and

(b)   the particulars registered under Schedule 21A in respect of the branch indicate an intention that they are to be registered in respect of that other branch and include the details of that other branch mentioned in paragraph 4(b) of that Schedule.

Time for delivery

4.   The period allowed for delivery, in relation to a document required to be delivered under paragraph 2, is 3 months from the date on which the document is first disclosed in accordance with the company's parent law.

Penalty for non-compliance

5.—   (1)   If a company fails to comply with paragraph 2 before the end of the period allowed for compliance, it, and every person who immediately before the end of that period was a director of it, is guilty of an offence and liable to a fine and, for continued contravention, to a daily default fine.

(2)   It is a defence for a person charged with an offence under this paragraph to prove that he took all reasonable steps for securing compliance with paragraph 2.

Interpretation

6.—   (1)   In this Part of this Schedule—

"financial period", in relation to a company, means a period for which the company is required or permitted by its parent law to prepare accounts;

"parent law", in relation to a company, means the law of the country in which the company is incorporated;

and references to disclosure are to public disclosure.

(2)   For the purposes of this Part of this Schedule, the following are accounting documents in relation to a financial period of a company—

(a)   the accounts of the company for the period, including, if it has one or more subsidiaries, any consolidated accounts of the group,

(b)   any annual report of the directors for the period,

(c)   the report of the auditors on the accounts mentioned in paragraph (a) above, and

(d)   any report of the auditors on the report mentioned in paragraph (b) above.

PART II
COMPANIES NOT REQUIRED TO MAKE DISCLOSURE UNDER PARENT LAW

Scope of Part

7.   This Part of this Schedule applies to any company to which section 699AA applies which is not required by the law of the country in which it is incorporated to prepare, have audited and publicly disclose accounts.

Preparation of accounts and reports

8.   A company to which this Part of this Schedule applies shall in respect of each financial year of the company prepare the like accounts and directors' report, and cause to be prepared such an auditors' report, as would be required if the company were a company to which section 700 applied.

9.   Sections 223 to 225 apply to a company to which this Part of this Schedule applies subject to the following modifications—

(a)   for the references to the incorporation of the company there shall be substituted references to the company becoming a company to which this Part of this Schedule applies, and

(b)   section 225(4) shall be omitted.

Duty to deliver accounts and reports

10.— (1) A company to which this Part of this Schedule applies shall in respect of each financial year of the company deliver to the registrar copies of the accounts and reports prepared in accordance with paragraph 8.

(2) If any document comprised in those accounts or reports is in a language other than English, the company shall annex to the copy delivered a translation of it into English, certified in the prescribed manner to be a correct translation.

(3) A company required to deliver documents under this paragraph in respect of a financial year shall deliver them in respect of each branch which it has in Great Britain at the end of that year.

(4) Sub-paragraph (3) above is without prejudice to section 695A(3).

11. Paragraph 10 shall not require documents to be delivered in respect of a branch if—

(a) before the end of the period allowed for compliance with that paragraph, they are delivered in respect of another branch in the United Kingdom, and

(b) the particulars registered under paragraph 1 of Schedule 21A in respect of the branch indicate an intention that they are to be registered in respect of that other branch and include the details of that other branch mentioned in paragraph 4(b) of that Schedule.

Time for delivery

12.— (1) The period allowed for delivering accounts and reports under paragraph 10 is 13 months after the end of the relevant accounting reference period, subject to the following provisions of this paragraph.

(2) If the relevant accounting reference period is the company's first and is a period of more than 12 months, the period allowed is 13 months from the first anniversary of the company's becoming a company to which this Part of this Schedule applies.

(3) If the relevant accounting reference period is treated as shortened by virtue of a notice given by the company under section 225, the period allowed is that applicable in accordance with the above provisions or 3 months from the date of the notice under that section, whichever last expires.

(4) If for any special reason the Secretary of State thinks fit he may, on an application made before the expiry of the period otherwise allowed, by notice in writing to a company to which this Part of this Schedule applies extend that period by such further period as may be specified in the notice.

(5) In this paragraph "the relevant accounting reference period" means the accounting reference period by reference to which the financial year for the accounts in question was determined.

Penalty for non-compliance

13.— (1) If the requirements of paragraph 10 are not complied with before the end of the period allowed for delivering accounts and reports, or if the accounts and reports delivered do not comply with the requirements of this Act, the company and every person who immediately before the end of that period was a director of the company is guilty of an offence and liable to a fine and, for continued contravention, to a daily default fine.

(2) It is a defence for a person charged with such an offence to prove that he took all reasonable steps for securing that the requirements in question would be complied with.

(3) It is not a defence in relation to a failure to deliver copies to the registrar to prove that the documents in question were not in fact prepared as required by this Act.

SCHEDULE 22

PROVISIONS OF THIS ACT APPLYING TO UNREGISTERED COMPANIES

Section 718

Provisions of this Act applied	Subject matter	Limitations and exceptions (if any)
In Part I—		
section 18	Statutory and other amendments of memorandum and articles to be registered	Subject to section 718(3).
sections 35 to 35B	Company's capacity; power of directors to bind it	Subject to section 718(3).
section 36	Company contracts	Subject to section 718(3).
sections 36A and 36B	Execution of documents	Subject to section 718(3).
section 36C	Pre-incorporation contracts, deeds and obligations	Subject to section 718(3).
	…	
section 40	Official seal for share certificates, etc	Subject to section 718(3).
section 42	Events affecting a company's status to be officially notified	Subject to section 718(3).
	…	
In Part IV, sections 82, 86 and 87	*Allotments*	*Subject to section 718(3).*
In Part V—		
section 185(4)	Exemption from duty to prepare certificates where shares etc issued to clearing house or nominee	Subject to section 718(3).
section 186	Certificate as evidence of title	Subject to section 718(3).
Part VII, with—		
Schedules 4 to 9		
Schedule 9A	Accounts and audit	
… , and		
Schedules 10 and 10A		
In Part IX—		
section 287	Registered office	Subject to section 718(3).
sections 288 to 290	Register of directors and secretaries	—
In Part X—		
section 322A	Invalidity of certain transactions involving directors, etc	Subject to section 718(3).
sections 343 to 347	Register to be kept of certain transactions not disclosed in accounts; other related matters	Subject to section 718(3).
Part XA	Control of political donations by companies	Subject to section 718(3)
In Part XI—		
section 351(1), (2), and (5)(a)	Particulars of company to be given in correspondence	Subject to section 718(3).

Provisions of this Act applied	Subject matter	Limitations and exceptions (if any)
sections 363 ... to 365	Annual return	Subject to section 718(3).
sections 384 to 394A	Appointment, ... etc, of auditors	Subject to section 718(3).
Part XII	*Registration of company charges; copies of instruments and register to be kept by company*	*Subject to section 718(3).*
Part XIV (except section 446)	Investigation of companies and their affairs; requisition of documents.	—
Part XV	Effect of order imposing restrictions on shares	To apply so far only as relates to orders under section 445.
Part XVI	Fraudulent trading by a company	—
In Part XXIV—		
sections 706 to 710A, 713 and 715A	Miscellaneous provisions about registration	—
section 711	Public notice by registrar of companies with respect to certain documents	Subject to section 718(3).
section 711A	*Abolition of doctrine of deemed notice*	*Subject to section 718(3).*
In Part XXV—		
section 720	Companies to publish periodical statement	Subject to section 718(3).
section 721	Production and inspection of company's books	To apply so far only as these provisions applying by virtue of the foregoing provisions of this Schedule.
section 722	Form of company registers, etc	
section 723	Use of computers for company records	
section 723A	Rights of inspection and related matters	
section 725	Service of documents	
section 730, with Schedule 24	Punishment of offences; meaning of "officer in default"	
section 731	Summary proceedings	
section 732	Prosecution by public authorities	
Part XXVI	Interpretation	To apply so far as requisite for the interpretation of other provisions applied by section 718 and this Schedule.

Note. The entry relating to Part IV is repealed for certain purposes by the Financial Services Act 1986, s. 212(3), Sch. 17, Pt. I and for remaining purposes as from a day to be appointed. The entries relating to Part XII and section 711A are inserted by the Companies Act 1989, ss. 106, 142(2), as from a day to be appointed.

SCHEDULE 23

FORM OF STATEMENT TO BE PUBLISHED BY
CERTAIN COMPANIES UNDER SECTION 720

Section 720

* The share capital of the company is .. .., divided into .. .. .. shares of .. .. .. each.

The number of shares issued is .. .. ..

Calls to the amount of .. .. .. pounds per share have been made, under which the sum of .. .. .. pounds has been received.

The liabilities of the company on the first day of January (*or* July) were—

Debts owing to sundry persons by the company.

On judgment (in Scotland, in respect of which decree has been granted), £ .. ..

On specialty, £ .. ..

On notes or bills, £ .. ..

On simple contracts, £ .. ..

On estimated liabilities, £ .. ..

The assets of the company on that day were—

Government securities (*stating them*)

Bills of exchange and promissory notes, £ .. ..

Cash at the bankers, £ .. ..

Other securities, £ .. ..

* If the company has no share capital the portion of the statement relating to capital and shares must be omitted.

SCHEDULE 24

PUNISHMENT OF OFFENCES UNDER THIS ACT

Section 730

Section of Act creating offence	General nature of offence	Mode of prosecution	Punishment	Daily default fine (where applicable)
6(3)	Company failing to deliver to registrar notice or other document, following alteration of its objects	Summary	One-fifth of the statutory maximum	One-fiftieth of the statutory maximum.
12(3B)	Person making false statement under section 12(3A) which he knows to be false or does not believe to be true	1. On indictment 2. Summary	2 years or a fine; or both 6 months or the statutory maximum; or both	
18(3)	Company failing to register change in memorandum or articles	Summary	One-fifth of the statutory maximum	One-fiftieth of the statutory maximum.

Section of Act creating offence	General nature of offence	Mode of prosecution	Punishment	Daily default fine (where applicable)
19(2)	Company failing to send to one of its members a copy of the memorandum or articles, when so required by the member	Summary	One-fifth of the statutory maximum	
20(2)	Where company's memorandum altered, company issuing copy of the memorandum without the alteration	Summary	One-fifth of the statutory maximum for each occasion on which copies are so issued after the date of the alteration	
28(5)	Company failing to change name on direction of Secretary of State	Summary	One-fifth of the statutory maximum	One-fiftieth of the statutory maximum.
30(5C)	Person making false statement under section 30(5A) which he knows to be false or does not believe to be true	1. On indictment 2. Summary	2 years or a fine; or both 6 months or the statutory maximum; or both	
31(5)	Company altering its memorandum or articles, so ceasing to be exempt from having "limited" as part of its name	Summary	The statutory maximum	One-tenth of the statutory maximum.
31(6)	Company failing to change name, on Secretary of State's direction, so as to have "limited" (or Welsh equivalent) at the end	Summary	One-fifth of the statutory maximum	One-fiftieth of the statutory maximum.
32(4)	Company failing to comply with Secretary of State's direction to change its name, on grounds that the name is misleading	Summary	One-fifth of the statutory maximum	One-fiftieth of the statutory maximum.
33	Trading under misleading name (use of "public limited company" or Welsh equivalent etc. when not so entitled); purporting to be a private company	Summary	One-fifth of the statutory maximum	One-fiftieth of the statutory maximum.

Section of Act creating offence	General nature of offence	Mode of prosecution	Punishment	Daily default fine (where applicable)
34	Trading or carrying on business with improper use of "limited" or "cyfyngedig"	Summary	One-fifth of the statutory maximum	One-fiftieth of the statutory maximum.
34A	*Trading with improper use of "community interest company" etc.*	*Summary*	*Level 3 on the standard scale*	*One-tenth of level 3 on the standard scale.*
43(3B)	Person making false statement under section 43(3A) which he knows to be false or does not believe to be true	1. On indictment 2. Summary	2 years or a fine; or both 6 months or the statutory maximum; or both	
49(8B)	Person making false statement under section 49(8A) which he knows to be false or does not believe to be true	1. On indictment 2. Summary	2 years or a fine; or both 6 months or the statutory maximum; or both	
54(10)	Public company failing to give notice, or copy of court order, to registrar, concerning application to re-register as private company	Summary	One-fifth of the statutory maximum	One fiftieth of the statutory maximum.
		...		
80(9)	Directors exercising company's power of allotment without the authority required by section 80(1)	1. On indictment 2. Summary	A fine The statutory maximum	
81(2)	*Private limited company offering shares to the public, or allotting shares with a view to their being so offered*	*1. On indictment 2. Summary*	*A fine The statutory maximum*	
82(5)	*Allotting shares or debentures before third day after issue of prospectus*	*1. On indictment 2. Summary*	*A fine The statutory maximum*	

Section of Act creating offence	General nature of offence	Mode of prosecution	Punishment	Daily default fine (where applicable)
86(6)	Company failing to keep money in separate bank account, where received in pursuance of prospectus stating that stock exchange listing is to be applied for	1. On indictment 2. Summary	A fine The statutory maximum	
87(4)	Offeror of shares for sale failing to keep proceeds in separate bank account	1. On indictment 2. Summary	A fine The statutory maximum	
88(5)	Officer of company failing to deliver return of allotments, etc, to registrar	1. On indictment 2. Summary	A fine The statutory maximum	One-tenth of the statutory maximum.
95(6)	Knowingly or recklessly authorising or permitting misleading, false or deceptive material in statement by directors under section 95(5)	1. On indictment 2. Summary	2 years or a fine; or both 6 months, or the statutory maximum; or both	
97(4)	Company failing to deliver to registrar the prescribed form disclosing amount or rate of share commission	Summary	One-fiftieth of the statutory maximum	
110(2)	Making misleading, false or deceptive statement in connection with valuation under section 103 or 104	1. On indictment 2. Summary	2 years or a fine; or both 6 months or the statutory maximum; or both	
111(3)	Officer of company failing to deliver copy of asset valuation report to registrar	1. On indictment 2. Summary	A fine The statutory maximum	One-tenth of the statutory maximum.
111(4)	Company failing to deliver to registrar copy of resolution under section 104(4), with respect to transfer of an asset as consideration for allotment	Summary	One-fifth of the statutory maximum	One-fiftieth of the statutory maximum.
114	Contravention of any of the provisions of sections 99 to 104, 106	1. On indictment 2. Summary	A fine The statutory maximum	

Section of Act creating offence	General nature of offence	Mode of prosecution	Punishment	Daily default fine (where applicable)
117(7)	Company doing business or exercising borrowing powers contrary to section 117	1. On indictment 2. Summary	A fine The statutory maximum	
117(7A)	Person making false statement under section 117(3A) which he knows to be false or does not believe to be true	1. On indictment 2. Summary	2 years or a fine; or both 6 months or the statutory maximum; or both	
122(2)	Company failing to give notice to registrar of re-organisation of share capital	Summary	One-fifth of the statutory maximum	One-fiftieth of the statutory maximum.
123(4)	Company failing to give notice to registrar of increase of share capital	Summary	One-fifth of the statutory maximum	One-fiftieth of the statutory maximum.
127(5)	Company failing to forward to registrar copy of court order, when application made to cancel resolution varying shareholder's rights	Summary	One-fifth of the statutory maximum	One-fiftieth of the statutory maximum.
128(5)	Company failing to send to registrar statement or notice required by section 128 (particulars of shares carrying special rights)	Summary	One-fifth of the statutory maximum	One-fiftieth of the statutory maximum.
129(4)	Company failing to deliver to registrar statement or notice required by section 129 (registration of newly created class rights)	Summary	One-fifth of the statutory maximum	One-fiftieth of the statutory maximum.
141	Officer of company concealing name of creditor entitled to object to reduction of capital, or wilfully misrepresenting nature or amount of debt or claim, etc	1. On indictment 2. Summary	A fine The statutory maximum	

Section of Act creating offence	General nature of offence	Mode of prosecution	Punishment	Daily default fine (where applicable)
142(2)	Director authorising or permitting non-compliance with section 142 (requirement to convene company meeting to consider serious loss of capital)	1. On indictment 2. Summary	A fine The statutory maximum	
143(2)	Company acquiring its own shares in breach of section 143	1. On indictment	In the case of the company, a fine In the case of an officer of the company who is in default, 2 years or a fine; or both	
		2. Summary	In the case of the company, the statutory maximum In the case of an officer of the company who is in default, 6 months or the statutory maximum; or both	
149(2)	Company failing to cancel its own shares, acquired by itself, as required by section 146(2); or failing to apply for re-registration as private company as so required in the case there mentioned	Summary	One-fifth of the statutory maximum	One-fiftieth of the statutory maximum.
151(3)	Company giving financial assistance towards acquisition of its own shares	1. On indictment	Where the company is convicted, a fine	

Section of Act creating offence	General nature of offence	Mode of prosecution	Punishment	Daily default fine (where applicable)
			Where an officer of the company is convicted, 2 years or a fine; or both	
		2. Summary	Where the company is convicted, the statutory maximum Where an officer of the company is convicted, 6 months or the statutory maximum; or both	
156(6)	Company failing to register statutory declaration or statement under section 155	Summary	The statutory maximum	One-fiftieth of the statutory maximum.
156(7)	Director making statutory declaration or statement under section 155, without having reasonable grounds for opinion expressed in it	1. On indictment 2. Summary	2 years, or a fine; or both 6 months or the statutory maximum; or both	
162G	Contravention of any provision of sections 162A–162F (dealings by company in treasury shares, etc)	1. On indictment 2. Summary	A fine The statutory maximum	
169(6)	Default by company's officer in delivering to registrar the return required by section 169 (disclosure by company of purchase of own shares)	1. On indictment 2. Summary	A fine The statutory maximum	One-tenth of the statutory maximum.

Section of Act creating offence	General nature of offence	Mode of prosecution	Punishment	Daily default fine (where applicable)
169(7)	Company failing to keep copy of contract, etc, at registered office; refusal of inspection to person demanding it	Summary	One-fifth of the statutory maximum	One-fiftieth of the statutory maximum.
169A(4)	Default by company's officer in delivering to registrar the return required by section 169A (disclosure by company of cancellation or disposal of treasury shares)	1. On indictment 2. Summary	A fine The statutory maximum	One-tenth of the statutory maximum.
173(6)	Director making statutory declaration under section 173 without having reasonable grounds for the opinion expressed in the declaration	1. On indictment 2. Summary	2 years or a fine; or both 6 months or the statutory maximum; or both	
175(7)	Refusal of inspection of statutory declaration and auditors' report under section 173, etc	Summary	One-fifth of the statutory maximum	One-fiftieth of the statutory maximum.
176(4)	Company failing to give notice to registrar of application to court under section 176, or to register court order	Summary	One-fifth of the statutory maximum	One-fiftieth of the statutory maximum.
183(6)	Company failing to send notice of refusal to register a transfer of shares or debentures	Summary	One-fifth of the statutory maximum	One-fiftieth of the statutory maximum.
185(5)	Company default in compliance with section 185(1) (certificates to be made ready following allotment or transfer of shares, etc)	Summary	One-fifth of the statutory maximum	One-fiftieth of the statutory maximum.
189(1)	Offences of fraud and forgery in connection with share warrants in Scotland	1. On indictment 2. Summary	7 years or a fine; or both 6 months or the statutory maximum; or both	

Section of Act creating offence	General nature of offence	Mode of prosecution	Punishment	Daily default fine (where applicable)
189(2)	Unauthorised making of, or using or possessing apparatus for making, share warrants in Scotland	1. On indictment 2. Summary	7 years or a fine; or both 6 months or the statutory maximum; or both	
191(4)	Refusal of inspection or copy of register of debenture-holders, etc	Summary	One-fifth of the statutory maximum	One-fiftieth of the statutory maximum.
210(3)	Failure to discharge obligation of disclosure under Part VI; other forms of non-compliance with that Part	1. On indictment 2. Summary	2 years or a fine; or both 6 months or the statutory maximum; or both	
211(10)	Company failing to keep register of interests disclosed under Part VI; other contraventions of section 211	Summary	One-fifth of the statutory maximum	One-fiftieth of the statutory maximum.
214(5)	Company failing to exercise powers under section 212, when so required by the members	1. On indictment 2. Summary	A fine The statutory maximum	
215(8)	Company default in compliance with section 215 (company report of investigation of shareholdings on members' requisition)	1. On indictment 2. Summary	A fine The statutory maximum	
216(3)	Failure to comply with company notice under section 212; making false statement in response, etc	1. On indictment 2. Summary	2 years or a fine; or both 6 months or the statutory maximum; or both	
217(7)	Company failing to notify a person that he has been named as a shareholder; on removal of name from register, failing to alter associated index	Summary	One-fifth of the statutory maximum	One-fiftieth of the statutory maximum.

Section of Act creating offence	General nature of offence	Mode of prosecution	Punishment	Daily default fine (where applicable)
218(3)	Improper removal of entry from register of interests disclosed; company failing to restore entry improperly removed	Summary	One-fifth of the statutory maximum	For continued contravention of section 218(2) one-fiftieth of the statutory maximum.
219(3)	Refusal of inspection of register or report under Part VI; failure to send copy when required	Summary	One-fifth of the statutory maximum	One-fiftieth of the statutory maximum.
221(5) or 222(4)	Company failing to keep accounting records (liability of officers)	1. On indictment 2. Summary	2 years or a fine; or both 6 months or the statutory maximum; or both	
222(6)	Officer of company failing to secure compliance with, or intentionally causing default under section 222(5) (preservation of accounting records for requisite number of years)	1. On indictment 2. Summary	2 years or a fine; or both 6 months or the statutory maximum; or both	
231(6)	Company failing to annex to its annual return certain particulars required by Schedule 5 and not included in annual accounts	Summary	One-fifth of the statutory maximum	One-fiftieth of the statutory maximum.
232(4)	Default by director or officer of a company in giving notice of matters relating to himself for purposes of Schedule 6, Part I	Summary	One-fifth of the statutory maximum	
233(5)	Approving defective accounts	1. On indictment 2. Summary	A fine The statutory maximum	

Section of Act creating offence	General nature of offence	Mode of prosecution	Punishment	Daily default fine (where applicable)
233(6)	Laying or delivery of unsigned balance sheet; circulating copies of balance sheet without signature	Summary	One-fifth of the statutory maximum	
234(5)	Non-compliance with Part VII, as to directors' report and its content; directors individually liable	1. On indictment 2. Summary	A fine The statutory maximum	
234ZA(6)	Making a statement in a directors' report as mentioned in section 234ZA(2) which is false	1. On indictment 2. Summary	2 years or a fine; or both 12 months or the statutory maximum; or both	
234A(4)	Laying, circulating or delivering directors' report without required signature	Summary	One-fifth of the statutory maximum	
234B(3)	Non-compliance with requirements as to preparation and content of directors' remuneration report	Summary	One-fifth of the statutory maximum	
234B(6)	Default in complying with section 234B(5)	Summary	One-fifth of the statutory maximum	
236(4)	Laying, circulating or delivering auditors' report without required signature	Summary	One-fifth of the statutory maximum	
238(5)	Failing to send company's annual accounts, directors' report and auditors' report to those entitled to receive them	1. On indictment 2. Summary	A fine The statutory maximum	
239(3)	Company failing to supply copy of accounts and reports to shareholder on demand	Summary	One-fifth of the statutory maximum	One-fiftieth of the statutory maximum.
240(6)	Failure to comply with requirements in connection with publication of accounts	Summary	One-fifth of the statutory maximum	

Section of Act creating offence	General nature of offence	Mode of prosecution	Punishment	Daily default fine (where applicable)
241(2) or 242(2)	Director in default as regards duty to lay and deliver company's annual accounts, directors' report and auditors' report	Summary	The statutory maximum	One-tenth of the statutory maximum.
241A(9)	Default in complying with the requirements of section 241A(3) and (4)	Summary	One fifth of the statutory maximum.	
241A(10)	Failure to put resolution to vote of meeting	Summary	One fifth of the statutory maximum.	
		...		
245E(3)	Using or disclosing tax information in contravention of section 245E(1) or (2)	1. On indictment 2. Summary	2 years or a fine; or both 12 months or the statutory maximum; or both	
245G(7)	Disclosing information in contravention of section 245F(2) and (3)	1. On indictment 2. Summary	2 years or a fine; or both 12 months or the statutory maximum; or both	
251(6)	Failure to comply with requirements in relation to summary financial statements	Summary	One-fifth of the statutory maximum	
		...		
288(4)	Default in complying with section 288 (keeping register of directors and secretaries, refusal of inspection).	Summary	The statutory maximum	One-tenth of the statutory maximum.
291(5)	Acting as director of a company without having the requisite share qualification	Summary	One-fifth of the statutory maximum	One-fiftieth of the statutory maximum.
294(3)	Director failing to give notice of his attaining retirement age; acting as director under appointment invalid due to his attaining it	Summary	One-fifth of the statutory maximum	One-fiftieth of the statutory maximum.
		...		

Section of Act creating offence	General nature of offence	Mode of prosecution	Punishment	Daily default fine (where applicable)
305(3)	Company default in complying with section 305 (directors' names to appear on company correspondence, etc)	Summary	One-fifth of the statutory maximum	
306(4)	Failure to state that liability of proposed director or manager is unlimited; failure to give notice of that fact to person accepting office	1. On indictment 2. Summary	A fine The statutory maximum	
314(3)	Director failing to comply with section 314 (duty to disclose compensation payable on takeover, etc); a person's failure to include required particulars in a notice he has to give of such matters	Summary	One-fifth of the statutory maximum	
317(7)	Director failing to disclose interest in contract	1. On indictment 2. Summary	A fine The statutory maximum	
318(8)	Company default in complying with section 318(1) or (5) (directors' service contracts to be open to inspection); 14 days' default in complying with section 318(4) (notice to registrar as to where copies of contracts and memoranda are kept); refusal of inspection required under section 318(7)	Summary	One-fifth of the statutory maximum	One-fiftieth of the statutory maximum.

Section of Act creating offence	General nature of offence	Mode of prosecution	Punishment	Daily default fine (where applicable)
322B(4)	Terms of unwritten contract between sole member of a private company limited by shares or by guarantee and the company not set out in a written memorandum or recorded in minutes of a directors' meeting	Summary	Level 5 on the standard scale.	
323(2)	Director dealing in options to buy or sell company's listed shares or debentures	1. On indictment 2. Summary	2 years or a fine; or both 6 months or the statutory maximum; or both	
324(7)	Director failing to notify interest in company's shares; making false statement in purported notification	1. On indictment 2. Summary	2 years or a fine; or both 6 months or the statutory maximum; or both	
326(2), (3), (4), (5).	Various defaults in connection with company register of directors' interests	Summary	One-fifth of the statutory maximum	Except in the case of section 326(5), one-fiftieth of the statutory maximum.
328(6)	Director failing to notify company that members of his family have, or have exercised, options to buy shares or debentures; making false statement in purported notification	1. On indictment 2. Summary	2 years or a fine; or both 6 months or the statutory maximum; or both	
329(3)	Company failing to notify investment exchange of acquisition of its securities by a director	Summary	One-fifth of the statutory maximum	One-fiftieth of the statutory maximum.

Section of Act creating offence	General nature of offence	Mode of prosecution	Punishment	Daily default fine (where applicable)
342(1)	Director of relevant company authorising or permitting company to enter into transaction or arrangement, knowing or suspecting it to contravene section 330	1. On indictment 2. Summary	2 years or a fine; or both 6 months or the statutory maximum; or both	
342(2)	Relevant company entering into transaction or arrangement for a director in contravention of section 330	1. On indictment 2. Summary	2 years or a fine; or both 6 months or the statutory maximum; or both	
342(3)	Procuring a relevant company to enter into transaction or arrangement known to be contrary to section 330	1. On indictment 2. Summary	2 years or a fine; or both 6 months or the statutory maximum; or both	
343(8)	Company failing to maintain register of transactions, etc, made with and for directors and not disclosed in company accounts; failing to make register available at registered office or at company meeting	1. On indictment 2. Summary	A fine The statutory maximum	
348(2)	Company failing to paint or affix name; failing to keep it painted or affixed	Summary	One-fifth of the statutory maximum	In the case of failure to keep the name painted or affixed, one-fiftieth of the statutory maximum.
349(2)	Company failing to have name on business correspondence, invoices, etc	Summary	One-fifth of the statutory maximum	
349(3)	Officer of company issuing business letter or document not bearing company's name	Summary	One-fifth of the statutory maximum	

Section of Act creating offence	General nature of offence	Mode of prosecution	Punishment	Daily default fine (where applicable)
349(4)	Officer of company signing cheque, bill of exchange, etc on which company's name not mentioned	Summary	One-fifth of the statutory maximum	
350(1)	Company failing to have its name engraved on company seal	Summary	One-fifth of the statutory maximum	
350(2)	Officer of company, etc, using company seal without name engraved on it	Summary	One-fifth of the statutory maximum	
351(5)(a)	Company failing to comply with section 351(1) or (2) (matters to be stated on business correspondence, etc)	Summary	One-fifth of the statutory maximum	
351(5)(b)	Officer or agent of company issuing or authorising issue of, business document not complying with those subsections	Summary	One-fifth of the statutory maximum	
351(5)(c)	Contravention of section 351(3) or (4) (information in English to be stated on Welsh company's business correspondence, etc)	Summary	One-fifth of the statutory maximum	For contravention of section 351(3), one-fiftieth of the statutory maximum.
352(5)	Company default in complying with section 352 (requirement to keep register of members and their particulars)	Summary	One-fifth of the statutory maximum	One-fiftieth of the statutory maximum.
352A(3)	Company default in complying with section 352A (statement that company has only one member)	Summary	Level 2 on the standard scale.	One-tenth of level 2 on the standard scale.
353(4)	Company failing to send notice to registrar as to place where register of members is kept	Summary	One-fifth of the statutory maximum	One-fiftieth of the statutory maximum.

Section of Act creating offence	General nature of offence	Mode of prosecution	Punishment	Daily default fine (where applicable)
354(4)	Company failing to keep index of members	Summary	One-fifth of the statutory maximum	One-fiftieth of the statutory maximum.
356(5)	Refusal of inspection of members' register; failure to send copy on requisition	Summary	One-fifth of the statutory maximum	
363(3)	Company with share capital failing to make annual return	Summary	The statutory maximum	One-tenth of the statutory maximum.
364(4)	Company without share capital failing to complete and register annual return in due time	Summary	The statutory maximum	One-tenth of the statutory maximum.
		...		
366(4)	Company default in holding annual general meeting	1. On indictment 2. Summary	A fine The statutory maximum	
367(3)	Company default in complying with Secretary of State's direction to hold company meeting	1. On indictment 2. Summary	A fine The statutory maximum	
367(5)	Company failing to register resolution that meeting held under section 367 is to be its annual general meeting	Summary	One-fifth of the statutory maximum	One-fiftieth of the statutory maximum.
372(4)	Failure to give notice, to member entitled to vote at company meeting, that he may do so by proxy	Summary	One-fifth of the statutory maximum	
372(6)	Officer of company authorising or permitting issue of irregular invitations to appoint proxies	Summary	One-fifth of the statutory maximum	
376(7)	Officer of company in default as to circulation of members' resolutions for company meeting	1. On indictment 2. Summary	A fine The statutory maximum	

Section of Act creating offence	General nature of offence	Mode of prosecution	Punishment	Daily default fine (where applicable)
380(5)	Company failing to comply with section 380 (copies of certain resolutions etc to be sent to registrar of companies)	Summary	One-fifth of the statutory maximum	One-fiftieth of the statutory maximum.
380(6)	Company failing to include copy of resolution to which section 380 applies in articles; failing to forward copy to member on request	Summary	One-fifth of the statutory maximum for each occasion on which copies are issued or, as the case may be, requested.	
381B(2)	Director or secretary of company failing to notify auditors of proposed written resolution	Summary	Level 3 on the standard scale.	
382(5)	Company failing to keep minutes of proceedings at company and board meetings, etc	Summary	One-fifth of the statutory maximum	One-fiftieth of the statutory maximum.
382B(2)	Failure of sole member to provide the company with a written record of decision	Summary	Level 2 on the standard scale.	
383(4)	Refusal of inspection of minutes of general meeting; failure to send copy of minutes on member's request	Summary	One-fifth of the statutory maximum	
		...		
387(2)	Company failing to give Secretary of State notice of non-appointment of auditors	Summary	One-fifth of the statutory maximum	One-fiftieth of the statutory maximum.
389(10)	Person acting as company auditor knowing himself to be disqualified; failing to give notice vacating office when he becomes disqualified	1. On indictment 2. Summary	A fine The statutory maximum	One-tenth of the statutory maximum.

Section of Act creating offence	General nature of offence	Mode of prosecution	Punishment	Daily default fine (where applicable)
389B(1)	Person making false, misleading or deceptive statement to auditor	1. On indictment 2. Summary	2 years or a fine; or both 6 months or the statutory maximum; or both	
389B(2)	Failure to provide information or explanations to auditor	Summary	Level 3 on the standard scale	
389B(4)	Parent company failing to obtain from subsidiary undertaking information for purposes of audit	Summary	Level 3 on the standard scale	
		...		
391(2)	Failing to give notice to registrar of removal of auditor	Summary	One-fifth of the statutory maximum	One-fiftieth of the statutory maximum.
		...		
392(3)	Company failing to forward notice of auditor's resignation to registrar	1. On indictment 2. Summary	A fine The statutory maximum	One-tenth of the statutory maximum.
392A(5)	Directors failing to convene meeting requisitioned by resigning auditor	1. On indictment 2. Summary	A fine The statutory maximum	
		...		
394A(1)	Person ceasing to hold office as auditor failing to deposit statement as to circumstances	1. On indictment 2. Summary	A fine The statutory maximum	
394A(4)	Company failing to comply with requirements as to statement of person ceasing to hold office as auditor	1. On indictment 2. Summary	A fine The statutory maximum	One-tenth of the statutory maximum.
399(3)	Company failing to send to registrar particulars of charge created by it, or of issue of debentures which requires registration	1. On indictment 2. Summary	A fine The statutory maximum	One-tenth of the statutory maximum.
400(4)	Company failing to send to registrar particulars of charge on property acquired	1. On indictment 2. Summary	A fine The statutory maximum	One-tenth of the statutory maximum.

Section of Act creating offence	General nature of offence	Mode of prosecution	Punishment	Daily default fine (where applicable)
402(3)	Authorising or permitting delivery of debenture or certificate of debenture stock, without endorsement on it of certificate of registration of charge	Summary	One-fifth of the statutory maximum	
403(2A)	Person making false statement under section 403(1A) which he knows to be false or does not believe to be true	1. On indictment 2. Summary	2 years or a fine; or both 6 months or the statutory maximum; or both	
405(4)	Failure to give notice to registrar of appointment of receiver or manager, or of his ceasing to act	Summary	One-fifth of the statutory maximum	One-fiftieth of the statutory maximum.
407(3)	Authorising or permitting omission from company register of charges	1. On indictment 2. Summary	A fine The statutory maximum	
408(3)	Officer of company refusing inspection of charging instrument, or of register of charges	Summary	One-fifth of the statutory maximum	One-fiftieth of the statutory maximum.
415(3)	Scottish company failing to send to registrar particulars of charge created by it, or of issue of debentures which requires registration	1. On indictment 2. Summary	A fine The statutory maximum	One-tenth of the statutory maximum.
416(3)	Scottish company failing to send to registrar particulars of charge on property acquired by it	1. On indictment 2. Summary	A fine The statutory maximum	One-tenth of the statutory maximum.
419(5A)	Person making false statement under section 419(1A) or (1B) which he knows to be false or does not believe to be true	1. On indictment 2. Summary	2 years or a fine; or both 6 months or the statutory maximum; or both	
422(3)	Scottish company authorising or permitting omission from its register of charges	1. On indictment 2. Summary	A fine The statutory maximum	

Section of Act creating offence	General nature of offence	Mode of prosecution	Punishment	Daily default fine (where applicable)
423(3)	Officer of Scottish company refusing inspection of charging instrument, or of a register of charges	Summary	One-fifth of the statutory maximum	One-fiftieth of the statutory maximum.
425(4)	Company failing to annex to memorandum court order sanctioning compromise or arrangement with creditors	Summary	One-fifth of the statutory maximum	
426(6)	Company failing to comply with requirements of section 426 (information to members and creditors about compromise or arrangement)	1. On indictment 2. Summary	A fine The statutory maximum	
426(7)	Director or trustee for debenture holders failing to give notice to company of matters necessary for purposes of section 426	Summary	One-fifth of the statutory maximum	
427(5)	Failure to deliver to registrar office copy of court order under section 427 (company reconstruction or amalgamation)	Summary	One-fifth of the statutory maximum	One-fiftieth of the statutory maximum.
429(6)	Offeror failing to send copy of notice or making statutory declaration knowing it to be false, etc	1. On indictment 2. Summary	2 years or a fine; or both 6 months or the statutory maximum; or both	One-fiftieth of the statutory maximum.
430A(6)	Offeror failing to give notice of rights to minority shareholder	1. On indictment 2. Summary	A fine The statutory maximum	One-fiftieth of the statutory maximum.
444(3)	Failing to give Secretary of State, when required to do so, information about interests in shares, etc; giving false information	1. On indictment 2. Summary	2 years, or a fine; or both 6 months or the statutory maximum; or both	

Section of Act creating offence	General nature of offence	Mode of prosecution	Punishment	Daily default fine (where applicable)
...				
448(7)	Obstructing the exercise of any rights conferred by a warrant or failing to comply with a requirement imposed under subsection (3)(d)	1. On indictment 2. Summary	A fine The statutory maximum	
449(6)	Wrongful disclosure of information to which section 449 applies	1. On indictment 2. Summary	2 years, or a fine; or both 12 months, or the statutory maximum; or both	
450	Destroying or mutilating company documents; falsifying such documents or making false entries; parting with such documents or altering them or making omissions	1. On indictment 2. Summary	7 years, or a fine; or both 6 months, or the statutory maximum; or both	
451	Providing false information in purported compliance with section 447	1. On indictment 2. Summary	2 years, or a fine; or both 12 months, or the statutory maximum; or both	
453A(5)	Intentionally obstructing a person lawfully acting under section 453A(2) or (4).	1. On indictment 2. Summary	A fine The statutory maximum	
455(1)	Exercising a right to dispose of, or vote in respect of, shares which are subject to restrictions under Part XV; failing to give notice in respect of shares so subject; entering into agreement void under section 454(2), (3)	1. On indictment 2. Summary	A fine The statutory maximum	
455(2)	Issuing shares in contravention of restrictions of Part XV	1. On indictment 2. Summary	A fine The statutory maximum	

Section of Act creating offence	General nature of offence	Mode of prosecution	Punishment	Daily default fine (where applicable)
458	Being a party to carrying on company's business with intent to defraud creditors, or for any fraudulent purpose	1. On indictment 2. Summary	7 years or a fine; or both 6 months or the statutory maximum; or both	
461(5)	Failure to register office copy of court order under Part XVII altering, or giving leave to alter, company's memorandum	Summary	One-fifth of the statutory maximum	One-fiftieth of the statutory maximum.
		...		
651(3)	Person obtaining court order to declare company's dissolution void, then failing to register the order	Summary	One-fifth of the statutory maximum	One-fiftieth of the statutory maximum.
652E(1)	Person breaching or failing to perform duty imposed by section 652B or 652C	1. On indictment 2. Summary	A fine The statutory maximum	
652E(2)	Person failing to perform duty imposed by section 652B(6) or 652C(2) with intent to conceal the making of application under section 652A	1. On indictment 2. Summary	7 years or a fine; or both 6 months or the statutory maximum; or both	
652F(1)	Person furnishing false or misleading information in connection with application under section 652A	1. On indictment 2. Summary	A fine The statutory maximum	
652F(2)	Person making false application under section 652A	1. On indictment 2. Summary	A fine The statutory maximum	
685(6A)	Person making false statement under section 685(4A) which he knows to be false or does not believe to be true	1. On indictment 2. Summary	2 years or a fine; or both 6 months or the statutory maximum; or both	

Section of Act creating offence	General nature of offence	Mode of prosecution	Punishment	Daily default fine (where applicable)
686(3A)	Person making false statement under section 686(2A) which he knows to be false or does not believe to be true	1. On indictment 2. Summary	2 years or a fine; or both 6 months or the statutory maximum; or both	
691(4A)	Person making false statement under section 691(3A) which he knows to be false or does not believe to be true	1. On indictment 2. Summary	2 years or a fine; or both 6 months or the statutory maximum; or both	
697(1)	Oversea company failing to comply with any of sections 691 to 693 or 696	Summary	For an offence which is not a continuing offence, one-fifth of the statutory maximum	
			For an offence which is a continuing offence, one-fifth of the statutory maximum	One-fiftieth of the statutory maximum.
697(2)	Oversea company contravening section 694(6) (carrying on business under its corporate name after Secretary of State's direction)	1. On indictment 2. Summary	A fine The statutory maximum	One-tenth of the statutory maximum.
697(3)	Oversea Company failing to comply with Section 695A or Schedule 21A	Summary	For an offence which is a continuing offence one fifth of level 5 of the standard scale.	

Section of Act creating offence	General nature of offence	Mode of prosecution	Punishment	Daily default fine (where applicable)
			For an offence which is a continuing offence one fifth of level 5 of the standard scale.	£100
703(1)	Oversea company failing to comply with requirements as to accounts and reports	1. On indictment 2. Summary	A fine The statutory maximum	One-tenth of the statutory maximum.
703D(5)	Oversea company failing to deliver particulars of charge to registrar	1. On indictment 2. Summary	A fine The statutory maximum	
703R(1)	Company failing to register winding up or commencement of insolvency proceedings etc	1. On indictment 2. Summary	A fine The statutory maximum	£100
703R(2)	Liquidator failing to register appointment, termination of winding up or striking-off of company	1. On indictment 2. Summary	A fine The statutory maximum	£100
		...		
720(4)	Insurance company etc failing to send twice yearly statement in form of Schedule 23	Summary	One-fifth of the statutory maximum	One fiftieth of the statutory maximum.
722(3)	Company failing to comply with section 722(2), as regards the manner of keeping registers, minute books and accounting records	Summary	One-fifth of the statutory maximum	One fiftieth of the statutory maximum.
Sch 14, Pt II, para 1(3)	Company failing to give notice of location of overseas branch register, etc	Summary	One-fifth of the statutory maximum	One-fiftieth of the statutory maximum.

Section of Act creating offence	General nature of offence	Mode of prosecution	Punishment	Daily default fine (where applicable)
Sch 14, Pt II, para 4(2)	Company failing to transmit to its registered office in Great Britain copies of entries in overseas branch register, or to keep a duplicate of overseas branch register	Summary	One-fifth of the statutory maximum	One-fiftieth of the statutory maximum.
Sch 21C, Pt I, para 7	Credit or financial institution failing to deliver accounting documents	1. On indictment 2. Summary	A fine The statutory maximum	£100
Sch 21C, Pt II, para 15	Credit or financial institution failing to deliver accounts and reports	1. On indictment 2. Summary	A fine The statutory maximum	£100
Sch 21D, Pt I, para 5	Company failing to deliver accounting documents	1. On indictment 2. Summary	A fine The statutory maximum	£100
Sch 21D, Pt I, para 13	Company failing to deliver accounts and reports	1. On indictment 2. Summary	A fine The statutory maximum	£100

Note. The word "etc." in the entry relating to section 33 and the entry relating to section 34A are inserted by the Companies (Audit, Investigations and Community Enterprise) Act 2004, s. 33(6), Sch. 6, paras. 1, 9, as from 1 July 2005.

The entries relating to sections 81(2), 82(5), 86(6), 87(4) and 97(4) are repealed for certain purposes by the Financial Services Act 1986, s. 212(3), Sch. 17, Pt. I and for remaining purposes as from a day to be appointed.

The entry relating to section 389(10) is repealed by the Companies Act 1989, s. 212, Sch. 24, as from a day to be appointed.

The entries relating to sections 399(3), 400(4), 402(3), 405(4), 407(3), 408(3), 415(3), 416(3), 422(3), 423(3) are substituted by the following entries relating to ss 398(3), 408(3), 409(4), 410(4), 411(4), 412(4) by the Companies Act 1989, s. 107, Sch. 16, para. 2(1), (2), as from a day to be appointed:

Section of Act creating offence	General nature of offence	Mode of prosecution	Punishment
408(3)	Company failing to deliver particulars of taking up of issue of debentures	Summary	One-fifth of the statutory maximum.
409(4)	Failure to give notice to registrar of appointment of receiver or manager, of his ceasing to act	Summary	One-fifth of the statutory maximum.
410(4)	Failure to comply with requirements of regulations under s 410	Summary	One-fifth of the statutory maximum.
411(4)	Failure to keep copies of charging instruments or register at registered office	1. On indictment 2. Summary	A fine The statutory maximum.

Section of Act creating offence	General nature of offence	Mode of prosecution	Punishment
412(4)	Refusing inspection of charging instrument or register or failing to supply copies	Summary	A fine The statutory maximum.

SCHEDULE 25

COMPANIES ACT 1981, SECTION 38, AS ORIGINALLY ENACTED

Section 132(7)

38.   Relief from section 56 in respect of group reconstructions.

(1)   This section applies where the issuing company—

    (a)   is a wholly-owned subsidiary of another company ("the holding company"); and

    (b)   allots shares to the holding company or to another wholly-owned subsidiary of the holding company in consideration for the transfer to it of shares in another subsidiary (whether wholly-owned or not) of the holding company.

(2)   Where the shares in the issuing company allotted in consideration for the transfer are issued at a premium, the issuing company shall not be required by section 56 of the 1948 Act to transfer any amount in excess of the minimum premium value to the share premium amount.

(3)   In subsection (2) above "the minimum premium value" means the amount (if any) by which the base value of the shares transferred exceeds the aggregate nominal value of the shares allotted in consideration for the transfer.

(4)   For the purposes of subsection (3) above, the base value of the shares transferred shall be taken as—

    (a)   the cost of those shares to the company transferring them; or

    (b)   the amount at which those shares are stated in that company's accounting records immediately before the transfer;

    whichever is the less.

(5)   Section 37 of this Act shall not apply in a case to which this section applies.

Company Directors Disqualification Act 1986

1986 c. 46

An Act to consolidate certain enactments relating to the disqualification of persons from being directors of companies, and from being otherwise concerned with a company's affairs

[25th July 1986]

Preliminary

1. Disqualification orders: general

(1) In the circumstances specified below in this Act a court may, and under sections 6 and 9A shall, make against a person a disqualification order, that is to say an order that for a period specified in the order—

    (a) he shall not be a director of a company, act as receiver of a company's property or in any way, whether directly or indirectly, be concerned or take part in the promotion, formation or management of a company unless (in each case) he has the leave of the court, and

    (b) he shall not act as an insolvency practitioner.

(2) In each section of this Act which gives to a court power or, as the case may be, imposes on it the duty to make a disqualification order there is specified the maximum (and, in section 6, the minimum) period of disqualification which may or (as the case may be) must be imposed by means of the order and, unless the court otherwise orders, the period of disqualification so imposed shall begin at the end of the period of 21 days beginning with the date of the order.

(3) Where a disqualification order is made against a person who is already subject to such an order or to a disqualification undertaking, the periods specified in those orders or, as the case may be, in the order and the undertaking shall run concurrently.

(4) A disqualification order may be made on grounds which are or include matters other than criminal convictions, notwithstanding that the person in respect of whom it is to be made may be criminally liable in respect of those matters.

1A. Disqualification undertakings: general

(1) In the circumstances specified in sections 7 and 8 the Secretary of State may accept a disqualification undertaking, that is to say an undertaking by any person that, for a period specified in the undertaking, the person—

    (a) will not be a director of a company, act as receiver of a company's property or in any way, whether directly or indirectly, be concerned or take part in the promotion, formation or management of a company unless (in each case) he has the leave of a court, and

    (b) will not act as an insolvency practitioner.

(2) The maximum period which may be specified in a disqualification undertaking is 15 years; and the minimum period which may be specified in a disqualification undertaking under section 7 is two years.

(3) Where a disqualification undertaking by a person who is already subject to such an undertaking or to a disqualification order is accepted, the periods specified in those undertakings or (as the case may be) the undertaking and the order shall run concurrently.

(4) In determining whether to accept a disqualification undertaking by any person, the Secretary of State may take account of matters other than criminal convictions, notwithstanding that the person may be criminally liable in respect of those matters.

Disqualification for general misconduct in connection with companies

2. Disqualification on conviction of indictable offence

(1) The court may make a disqualification order against a person where he is convicted of an indictable offence (whether on indictment or summarily) in connection with the promotion,

formation, management, liquidation or striking off of a company, with the receivership of a company's property or with his being an administrative receiver of a company.

(2) "The court" for this purpose means—

(a) any court having jurisdiction to wind up the company in relation to which the offence was committed, or

(b) the court by or before which the person is convicted of the offence, or

(c) in the case of a summary conviction in England and Wales, any other magistrates' court acting *for the same petty sessions [in the same local justice]* area;

and for the purposes of this section the definition of "indictable offence" in Schedule 1 to the Interpretation Act 1978 applies for Scotland as it does for England and Wales.

(3) The maximum period of disqualification under this section is—

(a) where the disqualification order is made by a court of summary jurisdiction, 5 years, and

(b) in any other case, 15 years.

Note. The italicized words in subsection (2) are substituted by the subsequent words in square brackets by the Courts Act 2003, s. 109(1), Sch. 8, para. 300, as from a day to be appointed.

3. Disqualification for persistent breaches of companies legislation

(1) The court may make a disqualification order against a person where it appears to it that he has been persistently in default in relation to provisions of the companies legislation requiring any return, account or other document to be filed with, delivered or sent, or notice of any matter to be given, to the registrar of companies.

(2) On an application to the court for an order to be made under this section, the fact that a person has been persistently in default in relation to such provisions as are mentioned above may (without prejudice to its proof in any other manner) be conclusively proved by showing that in the 5 years ending with the date of the application he has been adjudged guilty (whether or not on the same occasion) of three or more defaults in relation to those provisions.

(3) A person is to be treated under subsection (2) as being adjudged guilty of a default in relation to any provision of that legislation if—

(a) he is convicted (whether on indictment or summarily) of an offence consisting in a contravention of or failure to comply with that provision (whether on his own part or on the part of any company), or

(b) a default order is made against him, that is to say an order under any of the following provisions—

(i) section 242(4) of the Companies Act (order requiring delivery of company accounts),

(ia) section 245B of that Act (order requiring preparation of revised accounts),

(ii) section 713 of that Act (enforcement of company's duty to make returns),

(iii) section 41 of the Insolvency Act (enforcement of receiver's or manager's duty to make returns), or

(iv) section 170 of that Act (corresponding provision for liquidator in winding up),

in respect of any such contravention of or failure to comply with that provision (whether on his own part or on the part of any company).

(4) In this section "the court" means any court having jurisdiction to wind up any of the companies in relation to which the offence or other default has been or is alleged to have been committed.

(5) The maximum period of disqualification under this section is 5 years.

4. Disqualification for fraud, etc, in winding up

(1) The court may make a disqualification order against a person if, in the course of the winding up of a company, it appears that he—

(a) has been guilty of an offence for which he is liable (whether he has been convicted or not) under section 458 of the Companies Act (fraudulent trading), or

(b) has otherwise been guilty, while an officer or liquidator of the company receiver of the company's property or administrative receiver of the company, of any fraud in relation to the company or of any breach of his duty as such officer, liquidator, receiver or administrative receiver.

(2) In this section "the court" means any court having jurisdiction to wind up any of the companies in relation to which the offence or other default has been or is alleged to have been committed; and "officer" includes a shadow director.

(3) The maximum period of disqualification under this section is 15 years.

5. Disqualification on summary conviction

(1) An offence counting for the purposes of this section is one of which a person is convicted (either on indictment or summarily) in consequence of a contravention of, or failure to comply with, any provision of the companies legislation requiring a return, account or other document to be filed with, delivered or sent, or notice of any matter to be given, to the registrar of companies (whether the contravention or failure is on the person's own part or on the part of any company).

(2) Where a person is convicted of a summary offence counting for those purposes, the court by which he is convicted (or, in England and Wales, any other magistrates' court acting *for the same petty sessions [in the same local justice]* area) may make a disqualification order against him if the circumstances specified in the next subsection are present.

(3) Those circumstances are that, during the 5 years ending with the date of the conviction, the person has had made against him, or has been convicted of, in total not less than 3 default orders and offences counting for the purposes of this section; and those offences may include that of which he is convicted as mentioned in subsection (2) and any other offence of which he is convicted on the same occasion.

(4) For the purposes of this section—
  (a) the definition of "summary offence" in Schedule 1 to the Interpretation Act 1978 applies for Scotland as for England and Wales, and
  (b) "default order" means the same as in section 3(3)(b).

(5) The maximum period of disqualification under this section is 5 years.

Note. The italicized words in subsection (2) are substituted by the subsequent words in square brackets by the Courts Act 2003, s. 109(1), Sch. 8, para. 300, as from a day to be appointed.

Disqualification for unfitness

6. Duty of court to disqualify unfit directors of insolvent companies

(1) The court shall make a disqualification order against a person in any case where, on an application under this section, it is satisfied—
  (a) that he is or has been a director of a company which has at any time become insolvent (whether while he was a director or subsequently), and
  (b) that his conduct as a director of that company (either taken alone or taken together with his conduct as a director of any other company or companies) makes him unfit to be concerned in the management of a company.

(2) For the purposes of this section and the next, a company becomes insolvent if—
  (a) the company goes into liquidation at a time when its assets are insufficient for the payment of its debts and other liabilities and the expenses of the winding up,
  (b) the company enters administration, or
  (c) an administrative receiver of the company is appointed;
and references to a person's conduct as a director of any company or companies include, where that company or any of those companies has become insolvent, that person's conduct in relation to any matter connected with or arising out of the insolvency of that company.

(3) In this section and section 7(2), "the court" means—
  (a) where the company in question is being or has been wound up by the court, that court,
  (b) where the company in question is being or has been wound up voluntarily, any court which has or (as the case may be) had jurisdiction to wind it up,

(c)   where neither paragraph (a) nor (b) applies but an administrator or administrative receiver has at any time been appointed in respect of the company in question, any court which has jurisdiction to wind it up.

(3A)   Sections 117 and 120 of the Insolvency Act 1986 (jurisdiction) shall apply for the purposes of subsection (3) as if the references in the definitions of "registered office" to the presentation of the petition for winding up were references—

(a)   in a case within paragraph (b) of that subsection, to the passing of the resolution for voluntary winding up,

(b)   in a case within paragraph (c) of that subsection, to the appointment of the administrator or (as the case may be) administrative receiver.

(3B)   Nothing in subsection (3) invalidates any proceedings by reason of their being taken in the wrong court; and proceedings—

(a)   for or in connection with a disqualification order under this section, or

(b)   in connection with a disqualification undertaking accepted under section 7,

may be retained in the court in which the proceedings were commenced, although it may not be the court in which they ought to have been commenced.

(3C)   In this section and section 7, "director" includes a shadow director.

(4)   Under this section the minimum period of disqualification is 2 years, and the maximum period is 15 years.

7.   Disqualification order or undertaking; and reporting provisions

(1)   If it appears to the Secretary of State that it is expedient in the public interest that a disqualification order under section 6 should be made against any person, an application for the making of such an order against that person may be made—

(a)   by the Secretary of State, or

(b)   if the Secretary of State so directs in the case of a person who is or has been a director of a company which is being or has been wound up by the court in England and Wales, by the official receiver.

(2)   Except with the leave of the court, an application for the making under that section of a disqualification order against any person shall not be made after the end of the period of 2 years beginning with the day on which the company of which that person is or has been a director became insolvent.

(2A)   If it appears to the Secretary of State that the conditions mentioned in section 6(1) are satisfied as respects any person who has offered to give him a disqualification undertaking, he may accept the undertaking if it appears to him that it is expedient in the public interest that he should do so (instead of applying, or proceeding with an application, for a disqualification order).

(3)   If it appears to the office-holder responsible under this section, that is to say—

(a)   in the case of a company which is being wound up by the court in England and Wales, the official receiver,

(b)   in the case of a company which is being wound up otherwise, the liquidator,

(c)   in the case of a company which is in administration, the administrator, or

(d)   in the case of a company of which there is an administrative receiver, that receiver,

that the conditions mentioned in section 6(1) are satisfied as respects a person who is or has been a director of that company, the office-holder shall forthwith report the matter to the Secretary of State.

(4)   The Secretary of State or the official receiver may require the liquidator, administrator or administrative receiver of a company, or the former liquidator, administrator or administrative receiver of a company—

(a)   to furnish him with such information with respect to any person's conduct as a director of the company, and

(b)   to produce and permit inspection of such books, papers and other records relevant to that person's conduct as such a director, as the Secretary of State or the official receiver may reasonably require for the purpose of determining whether to exercise, or of exercising, any function of his under this section.

8.   Disqualification after investigation of company

(1)   If it appears to the Secretary of State from investigative material that it is expedient in the public interest that a disqualification order should be made against a person who is, or has been, a director or shadow director of a company, he may apply to the court for such an order.

(1A)   "Investigative material" means—

    (a)   a report made by inspectors under—

        (i)   section 437 of the Companies Act 1985;

        (ii)   section 167, 168, 169 or 284 of the Financial Services and Markets Act 2000; or

        (iii)   where the company is an open-ended investment company (within the meaning of that Act) regulations made as a result of section 262(2)(k) of that Act; and

    (b)   information or documents obtained under—

        (i)   section 447, 448 or 453A of the Companies Act 1985;

        (ii)   section 2 of the Criminal Justice Act 1987;

        (iii)   section 28 of the Criminal Law (Consolidation) (Scotland) Act 1995;

        (iv)   section 83 of the Companies Act 1989; or

        (v)   section 165, 171, 172, 173 or 175 of the Financial Services and Markets Act 2000.

(2)   The court may make a disqualification order against a person where, on an application under this section, it is satisfied that his conduct in relation to the company makes him unfit to be concerned in the management of a company.

(2A)   Where it appears to the Secretary of State from such report, information or documents that, in the case of a person who has offered to give him a disqualification undertaking—

    (a)   the conduct of the person in relation to a company of which the person is or has been a director or shadow director makes him unfit to be concerned in the management of a company, and

    (b)   it is expedient in the public interest that he should accept the undertaking (instead of applying, or proceeding with an application, for a disqualification order),

he may accept the undertaking.

(3)   In this section "the court" means the High Court or, in Scotland, the Court of Session.

(4)   The maximum period of disqualification under this section is 15 years.

8A.   Variation etc of disqualification undertaking

(1)   The court may, on the application of a person who is subject to a disqualification undertaking—

    (a)   reduce the period for which the undertaking is to be in force, or

    (b)   provide for it to cease to be in force.

(2)   On the hearing of an application under subsection (1), the Secretary of State shall appear and call the attention of the court to any matters which seem to him to be relevant, and may himself give evidence or call witnesses.

(2A)   Subsection (2) does not apply to an application in the case of an undertaking given under section 9B, and in such a case on the hearing of the application whichever of the OFT or a specified regulator (within the meaning of section 9E) accepted the undertaking—

    (a)   must appear and call the attention of the court to any matters which appear to it or him (as the case may be) to be relevant;

    (b)   may give evidence or call witnesses.

(3)   In this section "the court"—

    (a)   in the case of an undertaking given under section 9B means the High Court or (in Scotland) the Court of Session;

    (b)   in any other case has the same meaning as in section 7(2) or 8 (as the case may be).

9.   Matters for determining unfitness of directors

(1)   Where it falls to a court to determine whether a person's conduct as a director ... of any particular company or companies makes him unfit to be concerned in the management of a company, the

court shall, as respects his conduct as a director of that company or, as the case may be, each of those companies, have regard in particular—

    (a)   to the matters mentioned in Part I of Schedule 1 to this Act, and

    (b)   where the company has become insolvent, to the matters mentioned in Part II of that Schedule;

and references in that Schedule to the director and the company are to be read accordingly.

(1A)   In determining whether he may accept a disqualification undertaking from any person the Secretary of State shall, as respects the person's conduct as a director of any company concerned, have regard in particular—

    (a)   to the matters mentioned in Part I of Schedule 1 to this Act, and

    (b)   where the company has become insolvent, to the matters mentioned in Part II of that Schedule;

and references in that Schedule to the director and the company are to be read accordingly.

(2)   Section 6(2) applies for the purposes of this section and Schedule 1 as it applies for the purposes of sections 6 and 7 and in this section and that Schedule "director" includes a shadow director.

(3)   Subject to the next subsection, any reference in Schedule 1 to an enactment contained in the Companies Act or the Insolvency Act includes, in relation to any time before the coming into force of that enactment, the corresponding enactment in force at that time.

(4)   The Secretary of State may by order modify any of the provisions of Schedule 1; and such an order may contain such transitional provisions as may appear to the Secretary of State necessary or expedient.

(5)   The power to make orders under this section is exercisable by statutory instrument subject to annulment in pursuance of a resolution of either House of Parliament.

Disqualification for competition infringements

9A.   Competition disqualification order

(1)   The court must make a disqualification order against a person if the following two conditions are satisfied in relation to him.

(2)   The first condition is that an undertaking which is a company of which he is a director commits a breach of competition law.

(3)   The second condition is that the court considers that his conduct as a director makes him unfit to be concerned in the management of a company.

(4)   An undertaking commits a breach of competition law if it engages in conduct which infringes any of the following—

    (a)   the Chapter 1 prohibition (within the meaning of the Competition Act 1998) (prohibition on agreements, etc preventing, restricting or distorting competition);

    (b)   the Chapter 2 prohibition (within the meaning of that Act) (prohibition on abuse of a dominant position);

    (c)   Article 81 of the Treaty establishing the European Community (prohibition on agreements, etc preventing, restricting or distorting competition);

    (d)   Article 82 of that Treaty (prohibition on abuse of a dominant position).

(5)   For the purpose of deciding under subsection (3) whether a person is unfit to be concerned in the management of a company the court—

    (a)   must have regard to whether subsection (6) applies to him;

    (b)   may have regard to his conduct as a director of a company in connection with any other breach of competition law;

    (c)   must not have regard to the matters mentioned in Schedule 1.

(6)   This subsection applies to a person if as a director of the company—

    (a)   his conduct contributed to the breach of competition law mentioned in subsection (2);

    (b)   his conduct did not contribute to the breach but he had reasonable grounds to suspect that the conduct of the undertaking constituted the breach and he took no steps to prevent it;

(c)   he did not know but ought to have known that the conduct of the undertaking constituted the breach.

(7)   For the purposes of subsection (6)(a) it is immaterial whether the person knew that the conduct of the undertaking constituted the breach.

(8)   For the purposes of subsection (4)(a) or (c) references to the conduct of an undertaking are references to its conduct taken with the conduct of one or more other undertakings.

(9)   The maximum period of disqualification under this section is 15 years.

(10)   An application under this section for a disqualification order may be made by the OFT or by a specified regulator.

(11)   Section 60 of the Competition Act 1998 (c 41) (consistent treatment of questions arising under United Kingdom and Community law) applies in relation to any question arising by virtue of subsection (4)(a) or (b) above as it applies in relation to any question arising under Part 1 of that Act.

9B.   Competition undertakings

(1)   This section applies if—

    (a)   the OFT or a specified regulator thinks that in relation to any person an undertaking which is a company of which he is a director has committed or is committing a breach of competition law,

    (b)   the OFT or the specified regulator thinks that the conduct of the person as a director makes him unfit to be concerned in the management of a company, and

    (c)   the person offers to give the OFT or the specified regulator (as the case may be) a disqualification undertaking.

(2)   The OFT or the specified regulator (as the case may be) may accept a disqualification undertaking from the person instead of applying for or proceeding with an application for a disqualification order.

(3)   A disqualification undertaking is an undertaking by a person that for the period specified in the undertaking he will not—

    (a)   be a director of a company;

    (b)   act as receiver of a company's property;

    (c)   in any way, whether directly or indirectly, be concerned or take part in the promotion, formation or management of a company;

    (d)   act as an insolvency practitioner.

(4)   But a disqualification undertaking may provide that a prohibition falling within subsection (3)(a) to (c) does not apply if the person obtains the leave of the court.

(5)   The maximum period which may be specified in a disqualification undertaking is 15 years.

(6)   If a disqualification undertaking is accepted from a person who is already subject to a disqualification undertaking under this Act or to a disqualification order the periods specified in those undertakings or the undertaking and the order (as the case may be) run concurrently.

(7)   Subsections (4) to (8) of section 9A apply for the purposes of this section as they apply for the purposes of that section but in the application of subsection (5) of that section the reference to the court must be construed as a reference to the OFT or a specified regulator (as the case may be).

9C.   Competition investigations

(1)   If the OFT or a specified regulator has reasonable grounds for suspecting that a breach of competition law has occurred it or he (as the case may be) may carry out an investigation for the purpose of deciding whether to make an application under section 9A for a disqualification order.

(2)   For the purposes of such an investigation sections 26 to 30 of the Competition Act 1998 (c 41) apply to the OFT and the specified regulators as they apply to the OFT for the purposes of an investigation under section 25 of that Act.

(3)   Subsection (4) applies if as a result of an investigation under this section the OFT or a specified regulator proposes to apply under section 9A for a disqualification order.

(4)   Before making the application the OFT or regulator (as the case may be) must—

(a)   give notice to the person likely to be affected by the application, and

(b)   give that person an opportunity to make representations.

9D.   Co-ordination

(1)   The Secretary of State may make regulations for the purpose of co-ordinating the performance of functions under sections 9A to 9C (relevant functions) which are exercisable concurrently by two or more persons.

(2)   Section 54(5) to (7) of the Competition Act 1998 (c. 41) applies to regulations made under this section as it applies to regulations made under that section and for that purpose in that section—

(a)   references to Part 1 functions must be read as references to relevant functions;

(b)   references to a regulator must be read as references to a specified regulator;

(c)   a competent person also includes any of the specified regulators.

(3)   The power to make regulations under this section must be exercised by statutory instrument subject to annulment in pursuance of a resolution of either House of Parliament.

(4)   Such a statutory instrument may—

(a)   contain such incidental, supplemental, consequential and transitional provision as the Secretary of State thinks appropriate;

(b)   make different provision for different cases.

9E.   Interpretation

(1)   This section applies for the purposes of sections 9A to 9D.

(2)   Each of the following is a specified regulator for the purposes of a breach of competition law in relation to a matter in respect of which he or it has a function—

(a)   the Office of Communications;

(b)   the Gas and Electricity Markets Authority;

(c)   *the Director General of Water Services;*

[*(c)   the Water Services Regulation Authority;*]

(d)   the Office of Rail Regulation;

(e)   the Civil Aviation Authority.

(3)   The court is the High Court or (in Scotland) the Court of Session.

(4)   Conduct includes omission.

(5)   Director includes shadow director.

Note. Subsection (2)(c) prospectively substituted by the Water Act 2003, s. 101(1), Sch. 7, Pt. 2, para. 25, as from a day to be appointed.

Other cases of disqualification

10.   Participation in wrongful trading

(1)   Where the court makes a declaration under section 213 or 214 of the Insolvency Act that a person is liable to make a contribution to a company's assets, then, whether or not an application for such an order is made by any person, the court may, if it thinks fit, also make a disqualification order against the person to whom the declaration relates.

(2)   The maximum period of disqualification under this section is 15 years.

11.   Undischarged bankrupts

(1)   It is an offence for a person to act as director of a company or directly or indirectly to take part in or be concerned in the promotion, formation or management of a company, without the leave of the court, at a time when—

(a)   he is an undischarged bankrupt, or

(b)   a bankruptcy restrictions order is in force in respect of him.

(2)   "The court" for this purpose is the court by which the person was adjudged bankrupt or, in Scotland, sequestration of his estates was awarded.

(3)   In England and Wales, the leave of the court shall not be given unless notice of intention to apply for it has been served on the official receiver; and it is the latter's duty, if he is of opinion that it is

contrary to the public interest that the application should be granted, to attend on the hearing of the application and oppose it.

12.   Failure to pay under county court administration order

(1)   The following has effect where a court under section 429 of the Insolvency Act revokes an administration order under Part VI of the County Courts Act 1984.

(2)   A person to whom that section applies by virtue of the order under section 429(2)(b) shall not, except with the leave of the court which made the order, act as director or liquidator of, or directly or indirectly take part or be concerned in the promotion, formation or management of, a company.

12A.   Northern Irish disqualification orders

A person subject to a disqualification order under Part II of the Companies (Northern Ireland) Order 1989—

(a)   shall not be a director of a company, act as receiver of a company's property or in any way, whether directly or indirectly, be concerned or take part in the promotion, formation or management of a company unless (in each case) he has the leave of the High Court of Northern Ireland, and

(b)   shall not act as an insolvency practitioner.

12B.   Northern Irish disqualification undertakings

A person subject to a disqualification undertaking under the Company Directors Disqualification (Northern Ireland) Order 2002—

(a)   shall not be a director of a company, act as receiver of a company's property or in any way, whether directly or indirectly, be concerned or take part in the promotion, formation or management of a company unless (in each case) he has the leave of the High Court of Northern Ireland, and

(b)   shall not act as an insolvency practitioner.

Consequences of contravention

13.   Criminal penalties

(1)   If a person acts in contravention of a disqualification order or disqualification undertaking or in contravention of section 12(2), 12A or 12B, or is guilty of an offence under section 11, he is liable—

(a)   on conviction on indictment, to imprisonment for not more than 2 years or a fine, or both; and

(b)   on summary conviction, to imprisonment for not more than 6 months or a fine not exceeding the statutory maximum, or both.

14.   Offences by body corporate

(1)   Where a body corporate is guilty of an offence of acting in contravention of a disqualification order or disqualification undertaking or in contravention of section 12A or 12B, and it is proved that the offence occurred with the consent or connivance of, or was attributable to any neglect on the part of any director, manager, secretary or other similar officer of the body corporate, or any person who was purporting to act in any such capacity he, as well as the body corporate, is guilty of the offence and liable to be proceeded against and punished accordingly.

(2)   Where the affairs of a body corporate are managed by its members, subsection (1) applies in relation to the acts and defaults of a member in connection with his functions of management as if he were a director of the body corporate.

15.   Personal liability for company's debts where person acts while disqualified

(1)   A person is personally responsible for all the relevant debts of a company if at any time—

(a)   in contravention of a disqualification order or disqualification undertaking or in contravention of section 11, 12A or 12B of this Act he is involved in the management of the company, or

(b)   as a person who is involved in the management of the company, he acts or is willing to act
       on instructions given without the leave of the court by a person whom he knows at that time
       to be the subject of a disqualification order or disqualification undertaking or a
       disqualification order under Part II of the Companies (Northern Ireland) Order 1989 or
       disqualification undertaking under the Company Directors Disqualification (Northern
       Ireland) Order 2002 or to be an undischarged bankrupt.

(2)   Where a person is personally responsible under this section for the relevant debts of a company,
       he is jointly and severally liable in respect of those debts with the company and any other person
       who, whether under this section or otherwise, is so liable.

(3)   For the purposes of this section the relevant debts of a company are—
       (a)   in relation to a person who is personally responsible under paragraph (a) of subsection (1),
              such debts and other liabilities of the company as are incurred at a time when that person
              was involved in the management of the company, and
       (b)   in relation to a person who is personally responsible under paragraph (b) of that subsection,
              such debts and other liabilities of the company as are incurred at a time when that person
              was acting or was willing to act on instructions given as mentioned in that paragraph.

(4)   For the purposes of this section, a person is involved in the management of a company if he is a
       director of the company or if he is concerned, whether directly or indirectly, or takes part, in the
       management of the company.

(5)   For the purposes of this section a person who, as a person involved in the management of a
       company, has at any time acted on instructions given without the leave of the court by a person
       whom he knew at that time to be the subject of a disqualification order or disqualification
       undertaking or a disqualification order under Part II of the Companies (Northern Ireland) Order
       1989 or disqualification undertaking under the Company Directors Disqualification (Northern
       Ireland) Order 2002 or to be an undischarged bankrupt is presumed, unless the contrary is shown,
       to have been willing at any time thereafter to act on any instructions given by that person.

Supplementary provisions

16.   Application for disqualification order

(1)   A person intending to apply for the making of a disqualification order by the court having
       jurisdiction to wind up a company shall give not less than 10 days' notice of his intention to the
       person against whom the order is sought; and on the hearing of the application the last-mentioned
       person may appear and himself give evidence or call witnesses.

(2)   An application to a court with jurisdiction to wind up companies for the making against any
       person of a disqualification order under any of sections 2 to 4 may be made by the Secretary of
       State or the official receiver, or by the liquidator or any past or present member or creditor of any
       company in relation to which that person has committed or is alleged to have committed an
       offence or other default.

(3)   On the hearing of any application under this Act made by a person falling within subsection (4),
       the applicant shall appear and call the attention of the court to any matters which seem to him to
       be relevant, and may himself give evidence or call witnesses.

(4)   The following fall within this subsection—
       (a)   the Secretary of State;
       (b)   the official receiver;
       (c)   the OFT;
       (d)   the liquidator;
       (e)   a specified regulator (within the meaning of section 9E).

17.   Application for leave under an order or undertaking

(1)   Where a person is subject to a disqualification order made by a court having jurisdiction to wind
       up companies, any application for leave for the purposes of section 1(1)(a) shall be made to that
       court.

(2)   Where—

(a)   a person is subject to a disqualification order made under section 2 by a court other than a court having jurisdiction to wind up companies, or

(b)   a person is subject to a disqualification order made under section 5,

any application for leave for the purposes of section 1(1)(a) shall be made to any court which, when the order was made, had jurisdiction to wind up the company (or, if there is more than one such company, any of the companies) to which the offence (or any of the offences) in question related.

(3)   Where a person is subject to a disqualification undertaking accepted at any time under section 7 or 8, any application for leave for the purposes of section 1A(1)(a) shall be made to any court to which, if the Secretary of State had applied for a disqualification order under the section in question at that time, his application could have been made.

(3A)   Where a person is subject to a disqualification undertaking accepted at any time under section 9B any application for leave for the purposes of section 9B(4) must be made to the High Court or (in Scotland) the Court of Session.

(4)   But where a person is subject to two or more disqualification orders or undertakings (or to one or more disqualification orders and to one or more disqualification undertakings), any application for leave for the purposes of section 1(1)(a), 1A(1)(a) or 9B(4) shall be made to any court to which any such application relating to the latest order to be made, or undertaking to be accepted, could be made.

(5)   On the hearing of an application for leave for the purposes of section 1(1)(a) or 1A(1)(a), the Secretary of State shall appear and call the attention of the court to any matters which seem to him to be relevant, and may himself give evidence or call witnesses.

(6)   Subsection (5) does not apply to an application for leave for the purposes of section 1(1)(a) if the application for the disqualification order was made under section 9A.

(7)   In such a case and in the case of an application for leave for the purposes of section 9B(4) on the hearing of the application whichever of the OFT or a specified regulator (within the meaning of section 9E) applied for the order or accepted the undertaking (as the case may be)—

(a)   must appear and draw the attention of the court to any matters which appear to it or him (as the case may be) to be relevant;

(b)   may give evidence or call witnesses.

18.   Register of disqualification orders and undertakings

(1)   The Secretary of State may make regulations requiring officers of courts to furnish him with such particulars as the regulations may specify of cases in which—

(a)   a disqualification order is made, or

(b)   any action is taken by a court in consequence of which such an order or a disqualification undertaking is varied or ceases to be in force, or

(c)   leave is granted by a court for a person subject to such an order to do any thing which otherwise the order prohibits him from doing, or

(d)   leave is granted by a court for a person subject to such an undertaking to do anything which otherwise the undertaking prohibits him from doing;

and the regulations may specify the time within which, and the form and manner in which, such particulars are to be furnished.

(2)   The Secretary of State shall, from the particulars so furnished, continue to maintain the register of orders, and of cases in which leave has been granted as mentioned in subsection (1)(c), which was set up by him under section 29 of the Companies Act 1976 and continued under section 301 of the Companies Act 1985.

(2A)   The Secretary of State must include in the register such particulars as he considers appropriate of—

(a)   disqualification undertakings accepted by him under section 7 or 8;

(b)   disqualification undertakings accepted by the OFT or a specified regulator under section 9B;

(c)   cases in which leave has been granted as mentioned in subsection (1)(d).

(3)   When an order or undertaking of which entry is made in the register ceases to be in force, the Secretary of State shall delete the entry from the register and all particulars relating to it which have been furnished to him under this section or any previous corresponding provision and, in the case of a disqualification undertaking, any other particulars he has included in the register.

(4)   The register shall be open to inspection on payment of such fee as may be specified by the Secretary of State in regulations.

(4A)   Regulations under this section may extend the preceding provisions of this section, to such extent and with such modifications as may be specified in the regulations, to disqualification orders made under Part II of the Companies (Northern Ireland) Order 1989 or disqualification undertakings made under the Company Directors Disqualification (Northern Ireland) Order 2002.

(5)   Regulations under this section shall be made by statutory instrument subject to annulment in pursuance of a resolution of either House of Parliament.

19.   Special savings from repealed enactments

        Schedule 2 to this Act has effect—

        (a)   in connection with certain transitional cases arising under sections 93 and 94 of the Companies Act 1981, so as to limit the power to make a disqualification order, or to restrict the duration of an order, by reference to events occurring or things done before the sections came into force,

        (b)   to preserve orders made under section 28 of the Companies Act 1976 (repealed by the Act of 1981), and

        (c)   to preclude any applications for a disqualification order under section 6 or 8, where the relevant company went into liquidation before 28th April 1986.

Miscellaneous and general

20.   Admissibility in evidence of statements

(1)   In any proceedings (whether or not under this Act), any statement made in pursuance of a requirement imposed by or under sections 6 to 10, 15 or 19(c) of, or Schedule 1 to, this Act, or by or under rules made for the purposes of this Act under the Insolvency Act, may be used in evidence against any person making or concurring in making the statement.

(2)   However, in criminal proceedings in which any such person is charged with an offence to which this subsection applies—

        (a)   no evidence relating to the statement may be adduced, and

        (b)   no question relating to it may be asked,

        by or on behalf of the prosecution, unless evidence relating to it is adduced, or a question relating to it is asked, in the proceedings by or on behalf of that person.

(3)   Subsection (2) applies to any offence other than—

        (a)   an offence which is—

                (i)   created by rules made for the purposes of this Act under the Insolvency Act, and

                (ii)   designated for the purposes of this subsection by such rules or by regulations made by the Secretary of State;

        (b)   an offence which is—

                (i)   created by regulations made under any such rules, and

                (ii)   designated for the purposes of this subsection by such regulations;

        (c)   an offence under section 5 of the Perjury Act 1911 (false statements made otherwise than on oath); or

        (d)   an offence under section 44(2) of the Criminal Law (Consolidation) (Scotland) Act 1995 (false statements made otherwise than on oath).

(4)   Regulations under subsection (3)(a)(ii) shall be made by statutory instrument and, after being made, shall be laid before each House of Parliament.

21. **Interaction with Insolvency Act**

(1) References in this Act to the official receiver, in relation to the winding up of a company or the bankruptcy of an individual, are to any person who, by virtue of section 399 of the Insolvency Act, is authorised to act as the official receiver in relation to that winding up or bankruptcy; and, in accordance with section 401(2) of that Act, references in this Act to an official receiver includes a person appointed as his deputy.

(2) Sections 1A, 6 to 10, 13, 14, 15, 19(c) and 20 of, and Schedule 1 to, this Act and sections 1 and 17 of this Act as they apply for the purposes of those provisions are deemed included in Parts I to VII of the Insolvency Act for the purposes of the following sections of that Act—

section 411 (power to make insolvency rules);

section 414 (fees orders);

section 420 (orders extending provisions about insolvent companies to insolvent partnerships);

section 422 (modification of such provisions in their application to recognised banks); ...

(3) Section 434 of that Act (Crown application) applies to sections 1A, 6 to 10, 13, 14, 15, 19(c) and 20 of, and Schedule 1 to, this Act and sections 1 and 17 of this Act as they apply for the purposes of those provisions as it does to the provisions of that Act which are there mentioned.

(4) For the purposes of summary proceedings in Scotland, section 431 of that Act applies to summary proceedings for an offence under section 11 or 13 of this Act as it applies to summary proceedings for an offence under Parts I to VII of that Act.

22. **Interpretation**

(1) This section has effect with respect to the meaning of expressions used in this Act, and applies unless the context otherwise requires.

(2) The expression "company"—

    (a) in section 11, includes an unregistered company and a company incorporated outside Great Britain which has an established place of business in Great Britain, and

    (b) elsewhere, includes any company which may be wound up under Part V of the Insolvency Act.

(3) Section 247 in Part VII of the Insolvency Act (interpretation for the first Group of Parts to that Act) applies as regards references to a company's insolvency and to its going into liquidation; and "administrative receiver" has the meaning given by section 251 of that Act and references to acting as an insolvency practitioner are to be read in accordance with section 388 of that Act.

(4) "Director" includes any person occupying the position of director, by whatever name called ... .

(5) "Shadow director", in relation to a company, means a person in accordance with whose directions or instructions the directors of the company are accustomed to act (but so that a person is not deemed a shadow director by reason only that the directors act on advice given by him in a professional capacity).

(6) Section 740 of the Companies Act applies as regards the meaning of "body corporate"; and "officer" has the meaning given by section 744 of that Act.

(7) In references to legislation other than this Act—

"the Companies Act" means the Companies Act 1985;

"the Companies Acts" has the meaning given by section 744 of that Act; and

"the Insolvency Act" means the Insolvency Act 1986;

and in sections 3(1) and 5(1) of this Act "the companies legislation" means the Companies Acts (except the Insider Dealing Act), Parts I to VII of the Insolvency Act and, in Part XV of that Act, sections 411, 413, 414, 416 and 417.

(8) Any reference to provisions, or a particular provision, of the Companies Acts or the Insolvency Act includes the corresponding provisions or provision of the former Companies Acts (as defined by section 735(1)(c) of the Companies Act, but including also that Act itself) or, as the case may be, the Insolvency Act 1985.

(9) Any expression for whose interpretation provision is made by Part XXVI of the Companies Act (and not by subsections (3) to (8) above) is to be construed in accordance with that provision.

(10) Any reference to acting as receiver—

(a)   includes acting as manager or as both receiver and manager, but

(b)   does not include acting as administrative receiver;

and "receivership" is to be read accordingly.

22A.   Application of Act to building societies

(1)   This Act applies to building societies as it applies to companies.

(2)   References in this Act to a company, or to a director or an officer of a company include, respectively, references to a building society within the meaning of the Building Societies Act 1986 or to a director or officer, within the meaning of that Act, of a building society.

(3)   In relation to a building society the definition of "shadow director" in section 22(5) applies with the substitution of "building society" for "company".

(4)   In the application of Schedule 1 to the directors of a building society, references to provisions of the Insolvency Act or the Companies Act include references to the corresponding provisions of the Building Societies Act 1986.

22B.   Application of Act to incorporated friendly societies

(1)   This Act applies to incorporated friendly societies as it applies to companies.

(2)   References in this Act to a company, or to a director or an officer of a company include, respectively, references to an incorporated friendly society within the meaning of the Friendly Societies Act 1992 or to a member of the committee of management or officer, within the meaning of the Act, of an incorporated friendly society.

(3)   In relation to an incorporated friendly society every reference to a shadow director shall be omitted.

(4)   In the application of Schedule 1 to the members of the committee of management of an incorporated friendly society, references to provisions of the Insolvency Act or the Companies Act include references to the corresponding provisions of the Friendly Societies Act 1992.

22C.   Application of Act to NHS foundation trusts

(1)   This Act applies to NHS foundation trusts as it applies to companies within the meaning of this Act.

(2)   References in this Act to a company, or to a director or officer of a company, include, _____ an NHS foundation trust or to a director or officer of the trust; but _____ tors are omitted.

_____ dule 1 to the directors of an NHS foundation trust, references to the _____ cy Act or the Companies Act include references to the corresponding _____ Health and Social Care (Community Health and Standards) Act 2003.

_____ avings, repeals

_____ s and savings in Schedule 3 to this Act have effect, and are without _____ e Interpretation Act 1978 with regard to the effect of repeals.

_____ in the second column of Schedule 4 to this Act are repealed to the _____ l column of that Schedule.

24.   Extent

(1)   This Act extends to England and Wales and to Scotland.

(2)   Nothing in this Act extends to Northern Ireland.

25.   Commencement

This Act comes into force simultaneously with the Insolvency Act 1986.

26.   Citation

This Act may be cited as the Company Directors Disqualification Act 1986.

SCHEDULE 1

MATTERS FOR DETERMINING UNFITNESS OF DIRECTORS

Section 9

PART I
MATTERS APPLICABLE IN ALL CASES

1.   Any misfeasance or breach of any fiduciary or other duty by the director in relation to the company.

2.   Any misapplication or retention by the director of, or any conduct by the director giving rise to an obligation to account for, any money or other property of the company.

3.   The extent of the director's responsibility for the company entering into any transaction liable to be set aside under Part XVI of the Insolvency Act (provisions against debt avoidance).

4.   The extent of the director's responsibility for any failure by the company to comply with any of the following provisions of the Companies Act, namely—

    (a)   section 221 (companies to keep accounting records);

    (b)   section 222 (where and for how long records to be kept);

    (c)   section 288 (register of directors and secretaries);

    (d)   section 352 (obligation to keep and enter up register of members);

    (e)   section 353 (location of register of members);

    (f)   section 363 (duty of company to make annual returns);

    (h)   sections 399 and 415 (company's duty to register charges it creates).

    [(h)   sections 398 and 703D (duty of company to deliver particulars of charges on its property).]

5.   The extent of the director's responsibility for any failure by the directors of the company to comply with—

    (a)   section 226 or 227 of the Companies Act (duty to prepare annual accounts), or

    (b)   section 233 of that Act (approval and signature of accounts).

5A.   In the application of this Part of this Schedule in relation to any person who is a director of an open-ended investment company, any reference to a provision of the Companies Act is to be taken to be a reference to the corresponding provision of the Open-Ended Investment Companies Regulations 2001 or of any rules made under regulation 6 of those Regulations (Financial Services Authority rules).

Note. Paragraph 4(h) prospectively substituted by the Companies Act 1989, s. 107, Sch. 16, para. 4, as from a day to be appointed.

PART II
MATTERS APPLICABLE WHERE COMPANY HAS BECOME INSOLVENT

6.   The extent of the director's responsibility for the causes of the company becoming insolvent.

7.   The extent of the director's responsibility for any failure by the company to supply any goods or services which have been paid for (in whole or in part).

8.   The extent of the director's responsibility for the company entering into any transaction or giving any preference, being a transaction or preference—

    (a)   liable to be set aside under section 127 or sections 238 to 240 of the Insolvency Act, or

    (b)   challengeable under section 242 or 243 of that Act or under any rule of law in Scotland.

9.   The extent of the director's responsibility for any failure by the directors of the company to comply with section 98 of the Insolvency Act (duty to call creditors' meeting in creditors' voluntary winding up).

10.   Any failure by the director to comply with any obligation imposed on him by or under any of the following provisions of the Insolvency Act—

    (a)   paragraph 47 of Schedule B1 (company's statement of affairs in administration);

(b)   section 47 (statement of affairs to administrative receiver);

(c)   section 66 (statement of affairs in Scottish receivership);

(d)   section 99 (directors' duty to attend meeting; statement of affairs in creditors' voluntary winding up);

(e)   section 131 (statement of affairs in winding up by the court);

(f)   section 234 (duty of any one with company property to deliver it up);

(g)   section 235 (duty to co-operate with liquidator, etc).

SCHEDULE 2

SAVINGS FROM COMPANIES ACT 1981 SS 93, 94, AND INSOLVENCY ACT 1985 SCHEDULE 9

Section 19

1.   Sections 2 and 4(1)(b) do not apply in relation to anything done before 15th June 1982 by a person in his capacity as liquidator of a company or as receiver or manager of a company's property.

2.   Subject to paragraph 1—

(a)   section 2 applies in a case where a person is convicted on indictment of an offence which he committed (and, in the case of a continuing offence, has ceased to commit) before 15th June 1982; but in such a case a disqualification order under that section shall not be made for a period in excess of 5 years;

(b)   that section does not apply in a case where a person is convicted summarily—

(i)   in England and Wales, if he had consented so to be tried before that date, or

(ii)   in Scotland, if the summary proceedings commenced before that date.

3.   Subject to paragraph 1, section 4 applies in relation to an offence committed or other thing done before 15th June 1982; but a disqualification order made on the grounds of such an offence or other thing done shall not be made for a period in excess of 5 years.

4.   The powers of a court under section 5 are not exercisable in a case where a person is convicted of an offence which he committed (and, in the case of a continuing offence, had ceased to commit) before 15th June 1982.

5.   For purposes of section 3(1) and section 5, no account is to be taken of any offence which was committed, or any default order which was made, before 1st June 1977.

6.   An order made under section 28 of the Companies Act 1976 has effect as if made under section 3 of this Act; and an application made before 15th June 1982 for such an order is to be treated as an application for an order under the section last mentioned.

7.   Where—

(a)   an application is made for a disqualification order under section 6 of this Act by virtue of paragraph (a) of subsection (2) of that section, and

(b)   the company in question went into liquidation before 28th April 1986 (the coming into force of the provision replaced by section 6),

the court shall not make an order under that section unless it could have made a disqualification order under section 300 of the Companies Act as it had effect immediately before the date specified in sub-paragraph (b) above.

8.   An application shall not be made under section 8 of this Act in relation to a report made or information or documents obtained before 28th April 1986.

SCHEDULE 3

TRANSITIONAL PROVISIONS AND SAVINGS

Section 23(1)

1.   In this Schedule, "the former enactments" means so much of the Companies Act, and so much of the Insolvency Act, as is repealed and replaced by this Act; and "the appointed day" means the day on which this Act comes into force.

2.   So far as anything done or treated as done under or for the purposes of any provision of the former enactments could have been done under or for the purposes of the corresponding provision of this Act, it is not invalidated by the repeal of that provision but has effect as if done under or for the purposes of the corresponding provision; and any order, regulation, rule or other instrument made or having effect under any provision of the former enactments shall, insofar as its effect is preserved by this paragraph, be treated for all purposes as made and having effect under the corresponding provision.

3.   Where any period of time specified in a provision of the former enactments is current immediately before the appointed day, this Act has effect as if the corresponding provision had been in force when the period began to run; and (without prejudice to the foregoing) any period of time so specified and current is deemed for the purposes of this Act—

    (a)   to run from the date or event from which it was running immediately before the appointed day, and

    (b)   to expire (subject to any provision of this Act for its extension) whenever it would have expired if this Act had not been passed;

and any rights, priorities, liabilities, reliefs, obligations, requirements, powers, duties or exemptions dependent on the beginning, duration or end of such a period as above mentioned shall be under this Act as they were or would have been under the former enactments.

4.   Where in any provision of this Act there is a reference to another such provision, and the first-mentioned provision operates, or is capable of operating, in relation to things done or omitted, or events occurring or not occurring, in the past (including in particular past acts of compliance with any enactment, failures of compliance, contraventions, offences and convictions of offences) the reference to the other provision is to be read as including a reference to the corresponding provision of the former enactments.

5.   Offences committed before the appointed day under any provision of the former enactments may, notwithstanding any repeal by this Act, be prosecuted and punished after that day as if this Act had not passed.

6.   A reference in any enactment, instrument or document (whether express or implied, and in whatever phraseology) to a provision of the former enactments (including the corresponding provision of any yet earlier enactment) is to be read, where necessary to retain for the enactment, instrument or document the same force and effect as it would have had but for the passing of this Act, as, or as including, a reference to the corresponding provision by which it is replaced in this Act.

SCHEDULE 4

REPEALS

Section 23(2)

Chapter	Short title	Extent of repeal
1985 c 6	The Companies Act 1985	Sections 295 to 299. Section 301. Section 302. Schedule 12. In Schedule 24, the entries relating to sections 295(7) and 302(1).
1985 c 65	The Insolvency Act 1985	Sections 12 to 14. Section 16. Section 18. Section 108(2). Schedule 2. In Schedule 6, paragraphs 1, 2, 7, and 14. In Schedule 9, paragraphs 2 and 3.

Criminal Justice Act 1993

1996 c. 36

An Act to make provision about the jurisdiction of courts in England and Wales in relation to certain offences of dishonesty and blackmail; to amend the law about drug trafficking offences and to implement provisions of the Community Council Directive No 91/308/EEC; to amend Part VI of the Criminal Justice Act 1988; to make provision with respect to the financing of terrorism, the proceeds of terrorist-related activities and the investigation of terrorist activities; to amend Part I of the Criminal Justice Act 1991; to implement provisions of the Community Council Directive No 89/592/EEC and to amend and restate the law about insider dealing in securities; to provide for certain offences created by the Banking Coordination (Second Council Directive) Regulations 1992 to be punishable in the same way as offences under sections 39, 40 and 41 of the Banking Act 1987 and to enable regulations implementing Article 15 of the Community Council Directive No 89/646/EEC and Articles 3, 6 and 7 of the Community Council Directive No 92/30/EEC to create offences punishable in that way; to make provision with respect to the penalty for causing death by dangerous driving or causing death by careless driving while under the influence of drink or drugs; to make it an offence to assist in or induce certain conduct which for the purposes of, or in connection with, the provisions of Community law is unlawful in another member State; to provide for the introduction of safeguards in connection with the return of persons under backing of warrants arrangements; to amend the Criminal Procedure (Scotland) Act 1975 and Part I of the Prisoners and Criminal Proceedings (Scotland) Act 1993; and for connected purposes

[27th July 1993]

PART V
INSIDER DEALING

The offence of insider dealing

52. **The offence**

(1) An individual who has information as an insider is guilty of insider dealing if, in the circumstances mentioned in subsection (3), he deals in securities that are price-affected securities in relation to the information.

(2) An individual who has information as an insider is also guilty of insider dealing if—

    (a) he encourages another person to deal in securities that are (whether or not that other knows it) price-affected securities in relation to the information, knowing or having reasonable cause to believe that the dealing would take place in the circumstances mentioned in subsection (3); or

    (b) he discloses the information, otherwise than in the proper performance of the functions of his employment, office or profession, to another person.

(3) The circumstances referred to above are that the acquisition or disposal in question occurs on a regulated market, or that the person dealing relies on a professional intermediary or is himself acting as a professional intermediary.

(4) This section has effect subject to section 53.

53. **Defences**

(1) An individual is not guilty of insider dealing by virtue of dealing in securities if he shows—

    (a) that he did not at the time expect the dealing to result in a profit attributable to the fact that the information in question was price-sensitive information in relation to the securities, or

    (b) that at the time he believed on reasonable grounds that the information had been disclosed widely enough to ensure that none of those taking part in the dealing would be prejudiced by not having the information, or

    (c) that he would have done what he did even if he had not had the information.

(2)   An individual is not guilty of insider dealing by virtue of encouraging another person to deal in
        securities if he shows—
        (a)   that he did not at the time expect the dealing to result in a profit attributable to the fact that
              the information in question was price-sensitive information in relation to the securities, or
        (b)   that at the time he believed on reasonable grounds that the information had been or would be
              disclosed widely enough to ensure that none of those taking part in the dealing would be
              prejudiced by not having the information, or
        (c)   that he would have done what he did even if he had not had the information.
(3)   An individual is not guilty of insider dealing by virtue of a disclosure of information if he
        shows—
        (a)   that he did not at the time expect any person, because of the disclosure, to deal in securities
              in the circumstances mentioned in subsection (3) of section 52; or
        (b)   that, although he had such an expectation at the time, he did not expect the dealing to result
              in a profit attributable to the fact that the information was price-sensitive information in
              relation to the securities.
(4)   Schedule 1 (special defences) shall have effect.
(5)   The Treasury may by order amend Schedule 1.
(6)   In this section references to a profit include references to the avoidance of a loss.

Interpretation

54.   Securities to which Part V applies
(1)   This Part applies to any security which—
        (a)   falls within any paragraph of Schedule 2; and
        (b)   satisfies any conditions applying to it under an order made by the Treasury for the purposes
              of this subsection;
        and in the provisions of this Part (other than that Schedule) any reference to a security is a refer-
        ence to a security to which this Part applies.
(2)   The Treasury may by order amend Schedule 2.

55.   "Dealing" in securities
(1)   For the purposes of this Part, a person deals in securities if—
        (a)   he acquires or disposes of the securities (whether as principal or agent); or
        (b)   he procures, directly or indirectly, an acquisition or disposal of the securities by any other
              person.
(2)   For the purposes of this Part, "acquire", in relation to a security, includes—
        (a)   agreeing to acquire the security; and
        (b)   entering into a contract which creates the security.
(3)   For the purposes of this Part, "dispose", in relation to a security, includes—
        (a)   agreeing to dispose of the security; and
        (b)   bringing to an end a contract which created the security.
(4)   For the purposes of subsection (1), a person procures an acquisition or disposal of a security if the
        security is acquired or disposed of by a person who is—
        (a)   his agent,
        (b)   his nominee, or
        (c)   a person who is acting at his direction,
        in relation to the acquisition or disposal.
(5)   Subsection (4) is not exhaustive as to the circumstances in which one person may be regarded as
        procuring an acquisition or disposal of securities by another.

56.   "Inside information", etc
(1)   For the purposes of this section and section 57, "inside information" means information which—
        (a)   relates to particular securities or to a particular issuer of securities or to particular issuers of
              securities and not to securities generally or to issuers of securities generally;

(b)   is specific or precise;

(c)   has not been made public; and

(d)   if it were made public would be likely to have a significant effect on the price of any securities.

(2)   For the purposes of this Part, securities are "price-affected securities" in relation to inside information, and inside information is "price-sensitive information" in relation to securities, if and only if the information would, if made public, be likely to have a significant effect on the price of the securities.

(3)   For the purposes of this section "price" includes value.

57. "Insiders"

(1)   For the purposes of this Part, a person has information as an insider if and only if—

(a)   it is, and he knows that it is, inside information, and

(b)   he has it, and knows that he has it, from an inside source.

(2)   For the purposes of subsection (1), a person has information from an inside source if and only if—

(a)   he has it through—

    (i)   being a director, employee or shareholder of an issuer of securities; or

    (ii)   having access to the information by virtue of his employment, office or profession; or

(b)   the direct or indirect source of his information is a person within paragraph (a).

58. Information "made public"

(1)   For the purposes of section 56, "made public", in relation to information, shall be construed in accordance with the following provisions of this section; but those provisions are not exhaustive as to the meaning of that expression.

(2)   Information is made public if—

(a)   it is published in accordance with the rules of a regulated market for the purpose of informing investors and their professional advisers;

(b)   it is contained in records which by virtue of any enactment are open to inspection by the public;

(c)   it can be readily acquired by those likely to deal in any securities—

    (i)   to which the information relates, or

    (ii)   of an issuer to which the information relates; or

(d)   it is derived from information which has been made public.

(3)   Information may be treated as made public even though—

(a)   it can be acquired only by persons exercising diligence or expertise;

(b)   it is communicated to a section of the public and not to the public at large;

(c)   it can be acquired only by observation;

(d)   it is communicated only on payment of a fee; or

(e)   it is published only outside the United Kingdom.

59. "Professional intermediary"

(1)   For the purposes of this Part, a "professional intermediary" is a person—

(a)   who carries on a business consisting of an activity mentioned in subsection (2) and who holds himself out to the public or any section of the public (including a section of the public constituted by persons such as himself) as willing to engage in any such business; or

(b)   who is employed by a person falling within paragraph (a) to carry out any such activity.

(2)   The activities referred to in subsection (1) are—

(a)   acquiring or disposing of securities (whether as principal or agent); or

(b)   acting as an intermediary between persons taking part in any dealing in securities.

(3)   A person is not to be treated as carrying on a business consisting of an activity mentioned in subsection (2)—

(a)   if the activity in question is merely incidental to some other activity not falling within subsection (2); or

(b)   merely because he occasionally conducts one of those activities.

(4)   For the purposes of section 52, a person dealing in securities relies on a professional intermediary if and only if a person who is acting as a professional intermediary carries out an activity mentioned in subsection (2) in relation to that dealing.

60.   Other interpretation provisions

(1)   For the purposes of this Part, "regulated market" means any market, however operated, which, by an order made by the Treasury, is identified (whether by name or by reference to criteria prescribed by the order) as a regulated market for the purposes of this Part.

(2)   For the purposes of this Part an "issuer", in relation to any securities, means any company, public sector body or individual by which or by whom the securities have been or are to be issued.

(3)   For the purposes of this Part—

(a)   "company" means any body (whether or not incorporated and wherever incorporated or constituted) which is not a public sector body; and

(b)   "public sector body" means—

(i)   the government of the United Kingdom, of Northern Ireland or of any country or territory outside the United Kingdom;

(ii)   a local authority in the United Kingdom or elsewhere;

(iii)   any international organisation the members of which include the United Kingdom or another member State;

(iv)   the Bank of England; or

(v)   the central bank of any sovereign State.

(4)   For the purposes of this Part, information shall be treated as relating to an issuer of securities which is a company not only where it is about the company but also where it may affect the company's business prospects.

Miscellaneous

61.   Penalties and prosecution

(1)   An individual guilty of insider dealing shall be liable—

(a)   on summary conviction, to a fine not exceeding the statutory maximum or imprisonment for a term not exceeding six months or to both; or

(b)   on conviction on indictment, to a fine or imprisonment for a term not exceeding seven years or to both.

(2)   Proceedings for offences under this Part shall not be instituted in England and Wales except by or with the consent of—

(a)   the Secretary of State; or

(b)   the Director of Public Prosecutions.

(3)   In relation to proceedings in Northern Ireland for offences under this Part, subsection (2) shall have effect as if the reference to the Director of Public Prosecutions were a reference to the Director of Public Prosecutions for Northern Ireland.

62.   Territorial scope of offence of insider dealing

(1)   An individual is not guilty of an offence falling within subsection (1) of section 52 unless—

(a)   he was within the United Kingdom at the time when he is alleged to have done any act constituting or forming part of the alleged dealing;

(b)   the regulated market on which the dealing is alleged to have occurred is one which, by an order made by the Treasury, is identified (whether by name or by reference to criteria prescribed by the order) as being, for the purposes of this Part, regulated in the United Kingdom; or

(c)   the professional intermediary was within the United Kingdom at the time when he is alleged to have done anything by means of which the offence is alleged to have been committed.

(2)   An individual is not guilty of an offence falling within subsection (2) of section 52 unless—

(a) he was within the United Kingdom at the time when he is alleged to have disclosed the information or encouraged the dealing; or

(b) the alleged recipient of the information or encouragement was within the United Kingdom at the time when he is alleged to have received the information or encouragement.

63. Limits on section 52

(1) Section 52 does not apply to anything done by an individual acting on behalf of a public sector body in pursuit of monetary policies or policies with respect to exchange rates or the management of public debt or foreign exchange reserves.

(2) No contract shall be void or unenforceable by reason only of section 52.

64. Orders

(1) Any power under this Part to make an order shall be exercisable by statutory instrument.

(2) No order shall be made under this Part unless a draft of it has been laid before and approved by a resolution of each House of Parliament.

(3) An order under this Part—

(a) may make different provision for different cases; and

(b) may contain such incidental, supplemental and transitional provisions as the Treasury consider expedient.

...

SCHEDULE 1

SPECIAL DEFENCES

Section 53(4)

Market makers

1.— (1) An individual is not guilty of insider dealing by virtue of dealing in securities or encouraging another person to deal if he shows that he acted in good faith in the course of—

(a) his business as a market maker, or

(b) his employment in the business of a market maker.

(2) A market maker is a person who—

(a) holds himself out at all normal times in compliance with the rules of a regulated market or an approved organisation as willing to acquire or dispose of securities; and

(b) is recognised as doing so under those rules.

(3) In this paragraph "approved organisation" means an international securities self-regulating organisation approved by the Treasury under any relevant order under section 22 of the Financial Services and Markets Act 2000.

Market information

2.— (1) An individual is not guilty of insider dealing by virtue of dealing in securities or encouraging another person to deal if he shows that—

(a) the information which he had as an insider was market information; and

(b) it was reasonable for an individual in his position to have acted as he did despite having that information as an insider at the time.

(2) In determining whether it is reasonable for an individual to do any act despite having market information at the time, there shall, in particular, be taken into account—

(a) the content of the information;

(b) the circumstances in which he first had the information and in what capacity; and

(c) the capacity in which he now acts.

3. An individual is not guilty of insider dealing by virtue of dealing in securities or encouraging another person to deal if he shows—

    (a)   that he acted—

        (i)   in connection with an acquisition or disposal which was under consideration or the subject of negotiation, or in the course of a series of such acquisitions or disposals; and

        (ii)   with a view to facilitating the accomplishment of the acquisition or disposal or the series of acquisitions or disposals; and

    (b)   that the information which he had as an insider was market information arising directly out of his involvement in the acquisition or disposal or series of acquisitions or disposals.

4.   For the purposes of paragraphs 2 and 3 market information is information consisting of one or more of the following facts—

    (a)   that securities of a particular kind have been or are to be acquired or disposed of, or that their acquisition or disposal is under consideration or the subject of negotiation;

    (b)   that securities of a particular kind have not been or are not to be acquired or disposed of;

    (c)   the number of securities acquired or disposed of or to be acquired or disposed of or whose acquisition or disposal is under consideration or the subject of negotiation;

    (d)   the price (or range of prices) at which securities have been or are to be acquired or disposed of or the price (or range of prices) at which securities whose acquisition or disposal is under consideration or the subject of negotiation may be acquired or disposed of;

    (e)   the identity of the persons involved or likely to be involved in any capacity in an acquisition or disposal.

Price stabilisation

5.—   (1)   An individual is not guilty of insider dealing by virtue of dealing in securities or encouraging another person to deal if he shows that he acted in conformity with the price stabilisation rules.

        (2)   "Price stabilisation rules" means rules made under section 144(1) of the Financial Services and Markets Act 2000.

SCHEDULE 2

SECURITIES

Section 54

Shares

1.   Shares and stock in the share capital of a company ("shares").

Debt securities

2.   Any instrument creating or acknowledging indebtedness which is issued by a company or public sector body, including, in particular, debentures, debenture stock, loan stock, bonds and certificates of deposit ("debt securities").

Warrants

3.   Any right (whether conferred by warrant or otherwise) to subscribe for shares or debt securities ("warrants").

Depositary receipts

4.—   (1)   The rights under any depositary receipt.

        (2)   For the purposes of sub-paragraph (1) a "depositary receipt" means a certificate or other record (whether or not in the form of a document)—

        (a)   which is issued by or on behalf of a person who holds any relevant securities of a particular issuer; and

        (b)   which acknowledges that another person is entitled to rights in relation to the relevant securities or relevant securities of the same kind.

        (3)   In sub-paragraph (2) "relevant securities" means shares, debt securities and warrants.

Options

5. Any option to acquire or dispose of any security falling within any other paragraph of this Schedule.

Futures

6.— (1) Rights under a contract for the acquisition or disposal of relevant securities under which delivery is to be made at a future date and at a price agreed when the contract is made.

(2) In sub-paragraph (1)—

(a) the references to a future date and to a price agreed when the contract is made include references to a date and a price determined in accordance with terms of the contract; and

(b) "relevant securities" means any security falling within any other paragraph of this Schedule.

Contracts for differences

7.— (1) Rights under a contract which does not provide for the delivery of securities but whose purpose or pretended purpose is to secure a profit or avoid a loss by reference to fluctuations in—

(a) a share index or other similar factor connected with relevant securities;

(b) the price of particular relevant securities; or

(c) the interest rate offered on money placed on deposit.

(2) In sub-paragraph (1) "relevant securities" means any security falling within any other paragraph of this Schedule.

Companies (Tables A to F) Regulations 1985

S.I. 1985/805

1. These Regulations may be cited as the Companies (Tables A to F) Regulations 1985 and shall come into operation on 1st July 1985.
2. The regulations in Table A and the forms in Tables B, C, D, E and F in the Schedule to these Regulations shall be the regulations and forms of memorandum and articles of association for the purposes of sections 3 and 8 of the Companies Act 1985.
3. ...

SCHEDULE

Regulation 2

TABLE A
REGULATIONS FOR MANAGEMENT OF A COMPANY LIMITED BY SHARES

INTERPRETATION

1. In these regulations—

"the Act" means the Companies Act 1985 including any statutory modification or re-enactment thereof for the time being in force.

"the articles" means the articles of the company.

"clear days" in relation to the period of a notice means that period excluding the day when the notice is given or deemed to be given and the day for which it is given or on which it is to take effect.

"communication" means the same as in the Electronic Communications Act 2000.

"electronic communication" means the same as in the Electronic Communications Act 2000.

"executed" includes any mode of execution.

"office" means the registered office of the company.

"the holder" in relation to shares means the member whose name is entered in the register of members as the holder of the shares.

"the seal" means the common seal of the company.

"secretary" means the secretary of the company or any other person appointed to perform the duties of the secretary of the company, including a joint, assistant or deputy secretary.

"the United Kingdom" means Great Britain and Northern Ireland.

Unless the context otherwise requires, words or expressions contained in these regulations bear the same meaning as in the Act but excluding any statutory modification thereof not in force when these regulations become binding on the company.

SHARE CAPITAL

2. Subject to the provisions of the Act and without prejudice to any rights attached to any existing shares, any share may be issued with such rights or restrictions as the company may by ordinary resolution determine.
3. Subject to the provisions of the Act, shares may be issued which are to be redeemed or are to be liable to be redeemed at the option of the company or the holder on such terms and in such manner as may be provided by the articles.

4. The company may exercise the powers of paying commissions conferred by the Act. Subject to the provisions of the Act, any such commission may be satisfied by the payment of cash or by the allotment of fully or partly paid shares or partly in one way and partly in the other.

5. Except as required by law, no person shall be recognised by the company as holding any share upon any trust and (except as otherwise provided by the articles or by law) the company shall not be bound by or recognise any interest in any share except an absolute right to the entirety thereof in the holder.

SHARE CERTIFICATES

6. Every member, upon becoming the holder of any shares, shall be entitled without payment to one certificate for all the shares of each class held by him (and, upon transferring a part of his holding of shares of any class, to a certificate for the balance of such holding) or several certificates each for one or more of his shares of any class, to a certificate for the balance of such holding) or several certificates each for one or more of his shares upon payment for every certificate after the first of such reasonable sum as the directors may determine. Every certificate shall be sealed with the seal and shall specify the number, class and distinguishing numbers (if any) of the shares to which it relates and the amount or respective amounts paid up thereon. The company shall not be bound to issue more than one certificate for shares held jointly by several persons and delivery of a certificate to one joint holder shall be a sufficient delivery to all of them.

7. If a share certificate is defaced, worn-out, lost or destroyed, it may be renewed on such terms (if any) as to evidence and indemnity and payment of the expenses reasonably incurred by the company in investigating evidence as the directors may determine but otherwise free of charge, and (in the case of defacement or wearing-out) on delivery up of the old certificate.

LIEN

8. The company shall have a first and paramount lien on every share (not being a fully paid share) for all moneys (whether presently payable or not) payable at a fixed time or called in respect of that share. The directors may at any time declare any share to be wholly or in part exempt from the provisions of this regulation. The company's lien on a share shall extend to any amount payable in respect of it.

9. The company may sell in such manner as the directors determine any shares on which the company has a lien if a sum in respect of which the lien exists is presently payable and is not paid within fourteen clear days after notice has been given to the holder of the share or to the person entitled to it in consequence of the death or bankruptcy of the holder, demanding payment and stating that if the notice is not complied with the shares may be sold.

10. To give effect to a sale the directors may authorise some person to execute an instrument of transfer of the shares sold to, or in accordance with the directions of, the purchaser. The title of the transferee to the shares shall not be affected by any irregularity in or invalidity of the proceedings in reference to the sale.

11. The net proceeds of the sale, after payment of the costs, shall be applied in payment of so much of the sum for which the lien exists as is presently payable, and any residue shall (upon surrender to the company for cancellation of the certificate for the shares sold and subject to a like lien for any moneys not presently payable as existed upon the shares before the sale) be paid to the person entitled to the shares at the date of the sale.

CALLS ON SHARES AND FORFEITURE

12. Subject to the terms of allotment, the directors may make calls upon the members in respect of any moneys unpaid on their shares (whether in respect of nominal value or premium) and each member shall (subject to receiving at least fourteen clear days' notice specifying when and where payment is to be made) pay to the company as required by the notice the amount called on his

shares. A call may be required to be paid by instalments. A call may, before receipt by the company of any sum due thereunder, be revoked in whole or part and payment of a call may be postponed in whole or part. A person upon whom a call is made shall remain liable for calls made upon him notwithstanding the subsequent transfer of the shares in respect whereof the call was made.

13. A call shall be deemed to have been made at the time when the resolution of the directors authorising the call was passed.

14. The joint holders of a share shall be jointly and severally liable to pay all calls in respect thereof.

15. If a call remains unpaid after it has become due and payable the person from whom it is due and payable shall pay interest on the amount unpaid from the day it became due and payable until it is paid at the rate fixed by the terms of allotment of the share or in the notice of the call or, if no rate is fixed, at the appropriate rate (as defined by the Act) but the directors may waive payment of the interest wholly or in part.

16. An amount payable in respect of a share on allotment or at any fixed date, whether in respect of nominal value or premium or as an instalment of a call, shall be deemed to be a call and if it is not paid the provisions of the articles shall apply as if that amount had become due and payable by virtue of a call.

17. Subject to the terms of allotment, the directors may make arrangements on the issue of shares for a difference between the holders in the amounts and times of payment of calls on their shares.

18. If a call remains unpaid after it has become due and payable the directors may give to the person from whom it is due not less than fourteen clear days' notice requiring payment of the amount unpaid together with any interest which may have accrued. The notice shall name the place where payment is to be made and shall state that if the notice is not complied with the shares in respect of which the call was made will be liable to be forfeited.

19. If the notice is not complied with any share in respect of which it was given may, before the payment required by the notice has been made, be forfeited by a resolution of the directors and the forfeiture shall include all dividends or other moneys payable in respect of the forfeited shares and not paid before the forfeiture.

20. Subject to the provisions of the Act, a forfeited share may be sold, re-alloted or otherwise disposed of on such terms and in such manner as the directors determine either to the person who was before the forfeiture the holder or to any other person and at any time before sale, re-allotment or other disposition, the forfeiture may be cancelled on such terms as the directors think fit. Where for the purposes of its disposal a forfeited share is to be transferred to any person the directors may authorise some person to execute an instrument of transfer of the share to that person.

21. A person any of whose shares have been forfeited shall cease to be a member in respect of them and shall surrender to the company for cancellation the certificate for the shares forfeited but shall remain liable to the company for all moneys which at the date of forfeiture were presently payable by him to the company in respect of those shares with interest at the rate at which interest was payable on those moneys before the forfeiture or, if no interest was so payable, at the appropriate rate (as defined in the Act) from the date of forfeiture until payment but the directors may waive payment wholly or in part or enforce payment without any allowance for the value of the shares at the time of forfeiture or for any consideration received on their disposal.

22. A statutory declaration by a director or the secretary that a share has been forfeited on a specified date shall be conclusive evidence of the facts stated in it as against all persons claiming to be entitled to the share and the declaration shall (subject to the execution of an instrument of transfer if necessary) constitute a good title to the share and the person to whom the share is disposed of shall not be bound to see to the application of the consideration, if any, nor shall his title to the share be affected by any irregularity in or invalidity of the proceedings in reference to the forfeiture or disposal of the share.

TRANSFER OF SHARES

23. The instrument of transfer of a share may be in any usual form or in any other form which the directors may approve and shall be executed by or on behalf of the transferor and, unless the share is fully paid, by or on behalf of the transferee.

24. The directors may refuse to register the transfer of a share which is not fully paid to a person of whom they do not approve and they may refuse to register the transfer of a share on which the company has a lien. They may also refuse to register a transfer unless—

    (a) it is lodged at the office or at such other place as the directors may appoint and is accompanied by the certificate for the shares to which it relates and such other evidence as the directors may reasonably require to show the right of the transferor to make the transfer;

    (b) it is in respect of only one class of shares; and

    (c) it is in favour of not more than four transferees.

25. If the directors refuse to register a transfer of a share, they shall within two months after the date on which the transfer was lodged with the company send to the transferee notice of the refusal.

26. The registration of transfers of shares or of transfers of any class of shares may be suspended at such times and for such periods (not exceeding thirty days in any year) as the directors may determine.

27. No fee shall be charged for the registration of any instrument of transfer or other document relating to or affecting the title to any share.

28. The company shall be entitled to retain any instrument of transfer which is registered, but any instrument of transfer which the directors refuse to register shall be returned to the person lodging it when notice of the refusal is given.

TRANSMISSION OF SHARES

29. If a member dies the survivor or survivors where he was a joint holder, and his personal representatives where he was a sole holder or the only survivor of joint holders, shall be the only persons recognised by the company as having any title to his interest; but nothing herein contained shall release the estate of a deceased member from any liability in respect of any share which had been jointly held by him.

30. A person becoming entitled to a share in consequence of the death or bankruptcy of a member may, upon such evidence being produced as the directors may properly require, elect either to become the holder of the share or to have some person nominated by him registered as the transferee. If he elects to become the holder he shall give notice to the company to that effect. If he elects to have another person registered he shall execute an instrument of transfer of the share to that person. All the articles relating to the transfer of shares shall apply to the notice or instrument of transfer as if it were an instrument of transfer executed by the member and the death or bankruptcy of the member had not occurred.

31. A person becoming entitled to a share in consequence of the death or bankruptcy of a member shall have the rights to which he would be entitled if he were the holder of the share, except that he shall not, before being registered as the holder of the share, be entitled in respect of it to attend or vote at any meeting of the company or at any separate meeting of the holders of any class of shares in the company.

ALTERATION OF SHARE CAPITAL

32. The company may by ordinary resolution—

    (a) increase its share capital by new shares of such amount as the resolution prescribes;

    (b) consolidate and divide all or any of its share capital into shares of larger amount than its existing shares;

    (c) subject to the provisions of the Act, sub-divide its shares, or any of them, into shares of smaller amount and the resolution may determine that, as between the shares resulting from the sub-division, any of them may have any preference or advantage as compared with the others; and

(d)   cancel shares which, at the date of the passing of the resolution, have not been taken or agreed to be taken by any person and diminish the amount of its share capital by the amount of the shares so cancelled.

33.   Whenever as a result of a consolidation of shares any members would become entitled to fractions of a share, the directors may, on behalf of those members, sell the shares representing the fractions for the best price reasonably obtainable to any person (including, subject to the provisions of the Act, the company) and distribute the net proceeds of sale in due proportion among those members, and the directors may authorise some person to execute an instrument of transfer of the shares to, or in accordance with the directions of, the purchaser. The transferee shall not be bound to see to the application of the purchase money nor shall his title to the shares be affected by any irregularity in or invalidity of the proceedings in reference to the sale.

34.   Subject to the provisions of the Act, the company may by special resolution reduce its share capital, any capital redemption reserve and any share premium account in any way.

PURCHASE OF OWN SHARES

35.   Subject to the provisions of the Act, the company may purchase its own shares (including any redeemable shares) and, if it is a private company, make a payment in respect of the redemption or purchase of its own shares otherwise than out of distributable profits of the company or the proceeds of a fresh issue of shares.

GENERAL MEETINGS

36.   All general meetings other than annual general meetings shall be called extraordinary general meetings.

37.   The directors may call general meetings and, on the requisition of members pursuant to the provisions of the Act, shall forthwith proceed to convene an extraordinary general meeting for a date not later than eight weeks after receipt of the requisition. If there are not within the United Kingdom sufficient directors to call a general meeting, any director or any member of the company may call a general meeting.

NOTICE OF GENERAL MEETINGS

38.   An annual general meeting and an extraordinary general meeting called for the passing of a special resolution or a resolution appointing a person as a director shall be called by at least twenty-one clear days' notice. All other extraordinary general meetings shall be called by at least fourteen clear days' notice but a general meeting may be called by shorter notice if is so agreed—

(a)   in the case of an annual general meeting, by all the members entitled to attend and vote thereat; and

(b)   in the case of any other meeting by a majority in number of the members having a right to attend and vote being a majority together holding not less than ninety-five per cent in nominal value of the shares giving that right.

The notice shall specify the time and place of the meeting and the general nature of the business to be transacted and, in the case of an annual general meeting, shall specify the meeting as such. Subject to the provisions of the articles and to any restrictions imposed on any shares, the notice shall be given to all the members, to all persons entitled to a share in consequence of the death or bankruptcy of a member and to the directors and auditors.

39.   The accidental omission to give notice of a meeting to, or the non-receipt of notice of a meeting by, any person entitled to receive notice shall not invalidate the proceedings at that meeting.

PROCEEDINGS AT GENERAL MEETINGS

40. No business shall be transacted at any meeting unless a quorum is present. Two persons entitled to vote upon the business to be transacted, each being a member or a proxy for a member or a duly authorised representative of a corporation, shall be a quorum.

41. If such a quorum is not present within half an hour from the time appointed for the meeting, or if during a meeting such a quorum ceases to be present, the meeting shall stand adjourned to the same day in the next week at the same time and place or to such time and place as the directors may determine.

42. The chairman, if any, of the board of directors or in his absence some other director nominated by the directors shall preside as chairman of the meeting, but if neither the chairman nor such other director (if any) be present within fifteen minutes after the time appointed for holding the meeting and willing to act, the directors present shall elect one of their number to be chairman and, if there is only one director present and willing to act, he shall be chairman.

43. If no director is willing to act as chairman, or if no director is present within fifteen minutes after the time appointed for holding the meeting, the members present and entitled to vote shall choose one of their number to be chairman.

44. A director shall, notwithstanding that he is not a member, be entitled to attend and speak at any general meeting and at any separate meeting of the holders of any class of shares in the company.

45. The chairman may, with the consent of a meeting at which a quorum is present (and shall if so directed by the meeting), adjourn the meeting from time to time and from place to place, but no business shall be transacted at an adjourned meeting other than business which might properly have been transacted at the meeting had the adjournment not taken place. When a meeting is adjourned for fourteen days or more, at least seven clear days' notice shall be given specifying the time and place of the adjourned meeting and the general nature of the business to be transacted. Otherwise it shall not be necessary to give any such notice.

46. A resolution put to the vote of a meeting shall be decided on a show of hands unless before, or on the declaration of the result of, the show of hands a poll is duly demanded. Subject to the provisions of the Act, a poll may be demanded—
    (a) by the chairman; or
    (b) by at least two members having the right to vote at the meeting; or
    (c) by a member or members representing not less than one-tenth of the total voting rights of all the members having the right to vote at the meeting; or
    (d) by a member or members holding shares conferring a right to vote at the meeting being shares on which an aggregate sum has been paid up equal to not less than one-tenth of the total sum paid up on all the shares conferring that right;
    and a demand by a person as proxy for a member shall be the same as a demand by the member.

47. Unless a poll is duly demanded a declaration by the chairman that a resolution has been carried or carried unanimously, or by a particular majority, or lost, or not carried by a particular majority and an entry to that effect in the minutes of the meeting shall be conclusive evidence of the fact without proof of the number or proportion of the votes recorded in favour of or against the resolution.

48. The demand for a poll may, before the poll is taken, be withdrawn but only with the consent of the chairman and a demand so withdrawn shall not be taken to have invalidated the result of a show of hands declared before the demand was made.

49. A poll shall be taken as the chairman directs and he may appoint scrutineers (who need not be members) and fix a time and place for declaring the result of the poll. The result of the poll shall be deemed to be the resolution of the meeting at which the poll was demanded.

50. In the case of an equality of votes, whether on a show of hands or on a poll, the chairman shall be entitled to a casting vote in addition to any other vote he may have.

51. A poll demanded on the election of a chairman or on a question of adjournment shall be taken forthwith. A poll demanded on any other question shall be taken either forthwith or at such time and place as the chairman directs not being more than thirty days after the poll is demanded. The

demand for a poll shall not prevent the continuance of a meeting for the transaction of any business other than the question on which the poll was demanded. If a poll is demanded before the declaration of the result of a show of hands and the demand is duly withdrawn, the meeting shall continue as if the demand had not been made.

52. No notice need be given of a poll not taken forthwith if the time and place at which it is to be taken are announced at the meeting at which it is demanded. In any other case at least seven clear days' notice shall be given specifying the time and place at which the poll is to be taken.

53. A resolution in writing executed by or on behalf of each member who would have been entitled to vote upon it if it had been proposed at a general meeting at which he was present shall be as effectual as if it had been passed at a general meeting duly convened and held and may consist of several instruments in the like form each executed by or on behalf of one or more members.

VOTES OF MEMBERS

54. Subject to any rights or restrictions attached to any shares, on a show of hands every member who (being an individual) is present in person or (being a corporation) is present by a duly authorised representative, not being himself a member entitled to vote, shall have one vote and on a poll every member shall have one vote for every share of which he is the holder.

55. In the case of joint holders the vote of the senior who tenders a vote, whether in person or by proxy, shall be accepted to the exclusion of the votes of the other joint holders; and seniority shall be determined by the order in which the names of the holders stand in the register of members.

56. A member in respect of whom an order has been made by any court having jurisdiction (whether in the United Kingdom or elsewhere) in matters concerning mental disorder may vote, whether on a show of hands or on a poll, by his receiver, curator bonis or other person authorised in that behalf appointed by that court, and any such receiver, curator bonis or other person may, on a poll, vote by proxy. Evidence to the satisfaction of the directors of the authority of the person claiming to exercise the right to vote shall be deposited at the office, or at such other place as is specified in accordance with the articles for the deposit of instruments of proxy, not less than 48 hours before the time appointed for holding the meeting or adjourned meeting at which the right to vote is to be exercised and in default the right to vote shall not be exercisable.

57. No member shall vote at any general meeting or at any separate meeting of the holders of any class of shares in the company, either in person or by proxy, in respect of any share held by him unless all moneys presently payable by him in respect of that share have been paid.

58. No objection shall be raised to the qualification of any voter except at the meeting or adjourned meeting at which the vote objected to is tendered, and every vote not disallowed at the meeting shall be valid. Any objection made in due time shall be referred to the chairman whose decision shall be final and conclusive.

59. On a poll votes may be given either personally or by proxy. A member may appoint more than one proxy to attend on the same occasion.

60. The appointment of a proxy shall be ..., executed by or on behalf of the appointor and shall be in the following form (or in a form as near thereto as circumstances allow or in any other form which is usual or which the directors may approve)—

" .. .. PLC/Limited .. .. I/We, ..., of .. .., being a member/members of the above-named company, hereby appoint .. .. of .. .., or failing him, ... of .. .., as my/our proxy to vote in my/our names and on my/our behalf at the annual/ extraordinary general meeting of the company to be held on .. .. 19 .. .., and at any adjournment thereof.

Signed on .. .. 19 .. .."

61. Where it is desired to afford members an opportunity of instructing the proxy how he shall act the appointment of a proxy shall be in the following form (or in a form as near thereto as circumstances allow or in any other form which is usual or which the directors may approve)—

".. .. .. PLC/Limited .. .. I/We, ..., of .. .., being a member/members of the above-named company, hereby appoint .. .. of .. .., or failing him .. .. of

.. .., as my/our proxy to vote in my/our names and on my/our behalf at the annual/extraor-
dinary general meeting of the company, to be held on .. .. 19 , ..., and at any
adjournment thereof.

This form is to be used in respect of the resolutions mentioned below as follows:

Resolution No. 1 *for *against

Resolution No. 2 *for *against.

*Strike out whichever is not desired.

Unless otherwise instructed, the proxy may vote as he thinks fit or abstain from voting.

Signed this .. .. day of .. .. 19 .. .."

62.   The appointment of a proxy and any authority under which it is executed or a copy of such
        authority certified notarially or in some other way approved by the directors may—

        (a)   in the case of an instrument in writing be deposited at the office or at such other place within
               the United kingdom as is specified in the notice convening the meeting or in any instrument
               of proxy sent out by the company in relation to the meeting not less than 48 hours before the
               time for holding the meeting or adjourned meeting at which the person named in the
               instrument proposes to vote; or

        (aa)   in the case of an appointment contained in an electronic communication, where an address
               has been specified for the purpose of receiving electronic communications—

               (i)   in the notice convening the meeting, or

               (ii)   in any instrument of proxy sent out by the company in relation to the meeting, or

               (iii) in any invitation contained in an electronic communication to appoint a proxy issued
                      by the company in relation to the meeting,

               be received at such address not less than 48 hours before the time for holding the meeting or
               adjourned meeting at which the person named in the appointment proposes to vote;

        (b)   in the case of a poll taken more than 48 hours after it is demanded, be deposited or received
               as aforesaid after the poll has been demanded and not less than 24 hours before the time
               appointed for the taking of the poll; or

        (c)   where the poll is not taken forthwith but is taken not more than 48 hours after it was
               demanded, be delivered at the meeting at which the poll was demanded to the chairman or
               to the secretary or to any director;

        and an appointment of proxy which is not deposited, delivered or received in a manner so
        permitted shall be invalid.

        In this regulation and the next, "address", in relation to electronic communications, includes any
        number or address used for the purposes of such communications.

63.   A vote given or poll demanded by proxy or by the duly authorised representative of a corporation
        shall be valid notwithstanding the previous determination of the authority of the person voting or
        demanding a poll unless notice of the determination was received by the company at the office or
        at such other place at which the instrument of proxy was duly deposited or, where the
        appointment of the proxy was contained in an electronic communication, at the address at which
        such appointment was duly received before the commencement of the meeting or adjourned
        meeting at which the vote is given or the poll demanded or (in the case of a poll taken otherwise
        than on the same day as the meeting or adjourned meeting) the time appointed for taking the poll.

NUMBER OF DIRECTORS

64.   Unless otherwise determined by ordinary resolution, the number of directors (other than alternate
        directors) shall not be subject to any maximum but shall be not less than two.

ALTERNATE DIRECTORS

65.   Any director (other than an alternate director) may appoint any other director, or any other person
        approved by resolution of the directors and willing to act, to be an alternate director and may
        remove from office an alternate director so appointed by him.

66.   An alternate director shall be entitled to receive notice of all meetings of directors and of all meetings of committees of directors of which his appointor is a member, to attend and vote at any such meeting at which the director appointing him is not personally present and generally to perform all the functions of his appointor as a director in his absence but shall not be entitled to receive any remuneration from the company for his services as an alternate director. But it shall not be necessary to give notice of such a meeting to an alternate director who is absent from the United Kingdom.

67.   An alternate director shall cease to be an alternate director if his appointor ceases to be a director; but, if a director retires by rotation or otherwise but is reappointed or deemed to have been reappointed at the meeting at which he retires, any appointment of an alternate director made by him which was in force immediately prior to his retirement shall continue after his reappointment.

68.   Any appointment or removal of an alternate director shall be by notice to the company signed by the director making or revoking the appointment or in any other manner approved by the directors.

69.   Save as otherwise provided in the articles, an alternate director shall be deemed for all purposes to be a director and shall alone be responsible for his own acts and defaults and he shall not be deemed to be the agent of the director appointing him.

POWERS OF DIRECTORS

70.   Subject to the provisions of the Act, the memorandum and the articles and to any directions given by special resolution, the business of the company shall be managed by the directors who may exercise all the powers of the company. No alteration of the memorandum or articles and no such direction shall invalidate any prior act of the directors which would have been valid if that alteration had not been made or that direction had not been given. The powers given by this regulation shall not be limited by any special power given to the directors by the articles and a meeting of directors at which a quorum is present may exercise all powers exercisable by the directors.

71.   The directors may, by power of attorney or otherwise, appoint any person to be the agent of the company for such purposes and on such conditions as they determine, including authority for the agent to delegate all or any of his powers.

DELEGATION OF DIRECTORS' POWERS

72.   The directors may delegate any of their powers to any committee consisting of one or more directors. They may also delegate to any managing director or any director holding any other executive office such of their powers as they consider desirable to be exercised by him. Any such delegation may be made subject to any conditions the directors may impose, and either collaterally with or to the exclusion of their own powers and may be revoked or altered. Subject to any such conditions, the proceedings of a committee with two or more members shall be governed by the articles regulating the proceedings of directors so far as they are capable of applying.

APPOINTMENT AND RETIREMENT OF DIRECTORS

73.   At the first annual general meeting all the directors shall retire from office, and at every subsequent annual general meeting one-third of the directors who are subject to retirement by rotation or, if their number is not three or a multiple of three, the number nearest to one-third shall retire from office; but, if there is only one director who is subject to retirement by rotation, he shall retire.

74.   Subject to the provisions of the Act, the directors to retire by rotation shall be those who have been longest in office since their last appointment or reappointment, but as between persons who

became or were last reappointed directors on the same day those to retire shall (unless they otherwise agree among themselves) be determined by lot.

75. If the company, at the meeting at which a director retires by rotation, does not fill the vacancy the retiring director shall, if willing to act, be deemed to have been reappointed unless at the meeting it is resolved not to fill the vacancy or unless a resolution for the reappointment of the director is put to the meeting and lost.

76. No person other than a director retiring by rotation shall be appointed or reappointed a director at any general meeting unless—

   (a)   he is recommended by the directors; or

   (b)   not less than fourteen nor more than thirty-five clear days before the date appointed for the meeting, notice executed by a member qualified to vote at the meeting has been given to the company of the intention to propose that person for appointment or reappointment stating the particulars which would, if he were so appointed or reappointed, be required to be included in the company's register of directors together with notice executed by that person of his willingness to be appointed or reappointed.

77. Not less than seven nor more than twenty-eight clear days before the date appointed for holding a general meeting notice shall be given to all who are entitled to receive notice of the meeting of any person (other than a director retiring by rotation at the meeting) who is recommended by the directors for appointment or reappointment as a director at the meeting or in respect of whom notice has been duly given to the company of the intention to propose him at the meeting for appointment or reappointment as a director. The notice shall give the particulars of that person which would, if he were so appointed or reappointed, be required to be included in the company's register of directors.

78. Subject as aforesaid, the company may by ordinary resolution appoint a person who is willing to act to be a director either to fill a vacancy or as an additional director and may also determine the rotation in which any additional directors are to retire.

79. The directors may appoint a person who is willing to act to be a director, either to fill a vacancy or as an additional director, provided that the appointment does not cause the number of directors to exceed any number fixed by or in accordance with the articles as the maximum number of directors. A director so appointed shall hold office only until the next following annual general meeting and shall not be taken into account in determining the directors who are to retire by rotation at the meeting. If not reappointed at such annual general meeting, he shall vacate office at the conclusion thereof.

80. Subject as aforesaid, a director who retires at an annual general meeting may, if willing to act, be reappointed. If he is not reappointed, he shall retain office until the meeting appoints someone in his place, or if it does not do so, until the end of the meeting.

DISQUALIFICATION AND REMOVAL OF DIRECTORS

81. The office of a director shall be vacated if—

   (a)   he ceases to be a director by virtue of any provision of the Act or he becomes prohibited by law from being a director; or

   (b)   he becomes bankrupt or makes any arrangement or composition with his creditors generally; or

   (c)   he is, or may be, suffering from mental disorder and either—

      (i)   he is admitted to hospital in pursuance of an application for admission for treatment under the Mental Health Act 1983 or, in Scotland, an application for admission under the Mental Health (Scotland) Act 1960, or

      (ii)   an order is made by a court having jurisdiction (whether in the United Kingdom or elsewhere) in matters concerning mental disorder for his detention or for the appointment of a receiver, curator bonis or other person to exercise powers with respect to his property or affairs; or

   (d)   he resigns his office by notice to the company; or

(e)   he shall for more than six consecutive months have been absent without permission of the directors from meetings of directors held during that period and the directors resolve that his office be vacated.

REMUNERATION OF DIRECTORS

82.   The directors shall be entitled to such remuneration as the company may by ordinary resolution determine and, unless the resolution provides otherwise, the remuneration shall be deemed to accrue from day to day.

DIRECTORS' EXPENSES

83.   The directors may be paid all travelling, hotel, and other expenses properly incurred by them in connection with their attendance at meetings of directors or committees of directors or general meetings or separate meetings of the holders of any class of shares or of debentures of the company or otherwise in connection with the discharge of their duties.

DIRECTORS' APPOINTMENTS AND INTERESTS

84.   Subject to the provisions of the Act, the directors may appoint one or more of their number to the office of managing director or to any other executive office under the company and may enter into an agreement or arrangement with any director for his employment by the company or for the provision by him of any services outside the scope of the ordinary duties of a director. Any such appointment, agreement or arrangement may be made upon such terms as the directors determine and they may remunerate any such director for his services as they think fit. Any appointment of a director to an executive office shall terminate if he ceases to be a director but without prejudice to any claim to damages for breach of the contract of service between the director and the company. A managing director and a director holding any other executive office shall not be subject to retirement by rotation.

85.   Subject to the provisions of the Act, and provided that he has disclosed to the directors the nature and extent of any material interest of his, a director notwithstanding his office—

     (a)   may be a party to, or otherwise interested in, any transaction or arrangement with the company or in which the company or in which the company is otherwise interested;

     (b)   may be a director or other officer of, or employed by, or a party to any transaction or arrangement with, or otherwise interested in, any body corporate promoted by the company or in which the company is otherwise interested; and

     (c)   shall not, by reason of his office, be accountable to the company for any benefit which he derives from any such office or employment or from any such transaction or arrangement or from any interest in any such body corporate and no such transaction or arrangement shall be liable to be avoided on the ground of any such interest or benefit.

86.   For the purposes of regulation 85—

     (a)   a general notice given to the directors that a director is to be regarded as having an interest of the nature and extent specified in the notice in any transaction or arrangement in which a specified person or class of persons is interested shall be deemed to be a disclosure that the director has an interest in any such transaction of the nature and extent so specified; and

     (b)   an interest of which a director has no knowledge and of which it is unreasonable to expect him to have knowledge shall not be treated as an interest of his.

DIRECTORS' GRATUITIES AND PENSIONS

87.   The directors may provide benefits, whether by the payment of gratuities or pensions or by insurance or otherwise, for any director who has held but no longer holds any executive office or employment with the company or with any body corporate which is or has been a subsidiary of

the company or a predecessor in business of the company or of any such subsidiary, and for any member of his family (including a spouse and a former spouse) or any person who is or was dependent on him, and may (as well before as after he ceases to hold such office or employment) contribute to any fund and pay premiums for the purchase or provision of any such benefit.

PROCEEDINGS OF DIRECTORS

88. Subject to the provisions of the articles, the directors may regulate their proceedings as they think fit. A director may, and the secretary at the request of a director shall, call a meeting of the directors. It shall not be necessary to give notice of a meeting to a director who is absent from the United Kingdom. Questions arising at a meeting shall be decided by a majority of votes. In the case of an equality of votes, the chairman shall have a second or casting vote. A director who is also an alternate director shall be entitled in the absence of his appointor to a separate vote on behalf of his appointor in addition to his own vote.

89. The quorum for the transaction of the business of the directors may be fixed by the directors and unless so fixed at any other number shall be two. A person who holds office only as an alternate director shall, if his appointor is not present, be counted in the quorum.

90. The continuing directors or a sole continuing director may act notwithstanding any vacancies in their number, but, if the number of directors is less than the number fixed as the quorum, the continuing directors or director may act only for the purpose of filling vacancies or of calling a general meeting.

91. The directors may appoint one of their number to be the chairman of the board of directors and may at any time remove him from that office. Unless he is unwilling to do so, the director so appointed shall preside at every meeting of directors at which he is present. But if there is no director holding that office, or if the director holding it is unwilling to preside or is not present within five minutes after the time appointed for the meeting, the directors present may appoint one of their number to be chairman of the meeting.

92. All acts done by a meeting of directors, or of a committee of directors, or by a person acting as a director shall, notwithstanding that it be afterwards discovered that there was a defect in the appointment of any director or that any of them were disqualified from holding office, or had vacated office, or were not entitled to vote, be as valid as if every such person had been duly appointed and was qualified and had continued to be a director and had been entitled to vote.

93. A resolution in writing signed by all the directors entitled to receive notice of a meeting of directors or of a committee of directors shall be as valid and effectual as it if had been passed at a meeting of directors or (as the case may be) a committee of directors duly convened and held and may consist of several documents in the like form each signed by one or more directors; but a resolution signed by an alternate director need not also be signed by his appointor and, if it is signed by a director who has appointed an alternate director, it need not be signed by the alternate director in that capacity.

94. Save as otherwise provided by the articles, a director shall not vote at a meeting of directors or of a committee of directors on any resolution concerning a matter in which he has, directly or indirectly, an interest or duty which is material and which conflicts or may conflict with the interests of the company unless his interest or duty arises only because the case falls within one or more of the following paragraphs—

(a) the resolution relates to the giving to him of a guarantee, security, or indemnity in respect of money lent to, or an obligation incurred by him for the benefit of, the company or any of its subsidiaries;

(b) the resolution relates to the giving to a third party of a guarantee, security, or indemnity in respect of an obligation of the company or any of its subsidiaries for which the director has assumed responsibility in whole or part and whether alone or jointly with others under a guarantee or indemnity or by the giving of security;

(c) his interest arises by virtue of his subscribing or agreeing to subscribe for any shares, debentures, or other securities of the company or any of its subsidiaries, or by virtue of his being, or intending to become, a participant in the underwriting or sub-underwriting of an offer of any such shares, debentures, or other securities by the company or any of its subsidiaries for subscription, purchase or exchange;

(d) the resolution relates in any way to a retirement benefits scheme which has been approved, or is conditional upon approval, by the Board of Inland Revenue for taxation purposes.

For the purposes of this regulation, an interest of a person who is, for any purpose of the Act (excluding any statutory modification thereof not in force when this regulation becomes binding on the company), connected with a director shall be treated as an interest of the director and, in relation to an alternate director, an interest of his appointor shall be treated as an interest of the alternate director without prejudice to any interest which the alternate director has otherwise.

95. A director shall not be counted in the quorum present at a meeting in relation to a resolution on which he is not entitled to vote.

96. The company may by ordinary resolution suspend or relax to any extent, either generally or in respect of any particular matter, any provision of the articles prohibiting a director from voting at a meeting of directors or of a committee of directors.

97. Where proposals are under consideration concerning the appointment of two or more directors to offices or employments with the company or any body corporate in which the company is interested the proposals may be divided and considered in relation to each director separately and (provided he is not for another reason precluded from voting) each of the directors concerned shall be entitled to vote and be counted in the quorum in respect of each resolution except that concerning his own appointment.

98. If a question arises at a meeting of directors or of a committee of directors as to the right of a director to vote, the question may, before the conclusion of the meeting, be referred to the chairman of the meeting and his ruling in relation to any director other than himself shall be final and conclusive.

SECRETARY

99. Subject to the provisions of the Act, the secretary shall be appointed by the directors for such term, at such remuneration and upon such conditions as they may think fit; and any secretary so appointed may be removed by them.

MINUTES

100. The directors shall cause minutes to be made in books kept for the purpose—
(a) of all appointments of officers made by the directors; and
(b) of all proceedings at meetings of the company, of the holders of any class of shares in the company, and of the directors, and of committees of directors, including the names of the directors present at each such meeting.

THE SEAL

101. The seal shall only be used by the authority of the directors or of a committee of directors authorised by the directors. The directors may determine who shall sign any instrument to which the seal is affixed and unless otherwise so determined it shall be signed by a director and by the secretary or by a second director.

DIVIDENDS

102. Subject to the provisions of the Act, the company may by ordinary resolution declare dividends in accordance with the respective rights of the members, but no dividend shall exceed the amount recommended by the directors.

103.   Subject to the provisions of the Act, the directors may pay interim dividends if it appears to them
        that they are justified by the profits of the company available for distribution. If the share capital
        is divided into different classes, the directors may pay interim dividends on shares which confer
        deferred or non-preferred rights with regard to dividend as well as on shares which confer
        preferential rights with regard to dividend, but no interim dividend shall be paid on shares
        carrying deferred or non-preferred rights if, at the time of payment, any preferential dividend is in
        arrear. The directors may also pay at intervals settled by them any dividend payable at a fixed rate
        if it appears to them that the profits available for distribution justify the payment. Provided the
        directors act in good faith they shall not incur any liability to the holders of shares conferring
        preferred rights for any loss they may suffer by the lawful payment of an interim dividend on any
        shares having deferred or non-preferred rights.

104.   Except as otherwise provided by the rights attached to shares, all dividends shall be declared and
        paid according to the amounts paid up on the shares on which the dividend is paid. All dividends
        shall be apportioned and paid proportionately to the amounts paid up on the shares during any
        portion or portions of the period in respect of which the dividend is paid; but, if any share is
        issued on terms providing that it shall rank for dividend as from a particular date, that share shall
        rank for dividend accordingly.

105.   A general meeting declaring a dividend may, upon the recommendation of the directors, direct
        that it shall be satisfied wholly or partly by the distribution of assets and, where any difficulty
        arises in regard to the distribution, the directors may settle the same and in particular may issue
        fractional certificates and fix the value for distribution of any assets and may determine that cash
        shall be paid to any member upon the footing of the value so fixed in order to adjust the rights of
        members and may vest any assets in trustees.

106.   Any dividend or other moneys payable in respect of a share may be paid by cheque sent by post to
        the registered address of the person entitled or, if two or more persons are the holders of the share
        or are jointly entitled to it by reason of the death or bankruptcy of the holder, to the registered
        address of that one of those persons who is first named in the register of members or to such
        person and to such address as the person or persons entitled may in writing direct. Every cheque
        shall be made payable to the order of the person or persons entitled or to such other person as the
        person or persons entitled may in writing direct and payment of the cheque shall be a good
        discharge to the company. Any joint holder or other person jointly entitled to a share as aforesaid
        may give receipts for any dividend or other moneys payable in respect of the share.

107.   No dividend or other moneys payable in respect of a share shall bear interest against the company
        unless otherwise provided by the rights attached to the share.

108.   Any dividend which has remained unclaimed for twelve years from the date when it became due
        for payment shall, if the directors so resolve, be forfeited and cease to remain owing by the
        company.

ACCOUNTS

109.   No member shall (as such) have any right of inspecting any accounting records or other book or
        document of the company except as conferred by statute or authorised by the directors or by
        ordinary resolution of the company.

CAPITALISATION OF PROFITS

110.   The directors may with the authority of an ordinary resolution of the company—

        (a)   subject as hereinafter provided, resolve to capitalise any undivided profits of the company
               not required for paying any preferential dividend (whether or not they are available for
               distribution) or any sum standing to the credit of the company's share premium account or
               capital redemption reserve;

        (b)   appropriate the sum resolved to be capitalised to the members who would have been entitled
               to it if it were distributed by way of dividend and in the same proportions and apply such

sum on their behalf either in or towards paying up the amounts, if any, for the time being unpaid on any shares held by them respectively, or in paying up in full unissued shares or debentures of the company of a nominal amount equal to that sum, and allot the shares or debentures credited as fully paid to those members, or as they may direct, in those proportions, or partly in one way and partly in the other: but the share premium account, the capital redemption reserve, and any profits which are not available for distribution may, for the purposes of this regulation, only be applied in paying up unissued shares to be allotted to members credited as fully paid;

(c)   make such provision by the issue of fractional certificates or by payment in cash or otherwise as they determine in the case of shares or debentures becoming distributable under this regulation in fractions; and

(d)   authorise any person to enter on behalf of all the members concerned into an agreement with the company providing for the allotment to them respectively, credited as fully paid, of any shares or debentures to which they are entitled upon such capitalisation, any agreement made under such authority being binding on all such members.

NOTICES

111.   Any notice to be given to or by any person pursuant to the articles (other than a notice calling a meeting of the directors) shall be in writing or shall be given using electronic communications to an address for the time being notified for that purpose to the person giving the notice.
In this regulation, "address", in relation to electronic communications, includes any number or address used for the purposes of such communications.

112.   The company may give any notice to a member either personally or by sending it by post in a prepaid envelope addressed to the member at his registered address or by leaving it at that address or by giving it using electronic communications to an address for the time being notified to the company by the member. In the case of joint holders of a share, all notices shall be given to the joint holder whose name stands first in the register of members in respect of the joint holding and notice so given shall be sufficient notice to all the joint holders. A member whose registered address is not within the United Kingdom and who gives to the company an address within the United Kingdom at which notices may be given to him, or an address to which notices may be sent using electronic communications, shall be entitled to have notices given to him at that address, but otherwise no such member shall be entitled to receive any notice from the company.
In this regulation and the next, "address", in relation to electronic communications, includes any number or address used for the purposes of such communications.

113.   A member present, either in person or by proxy, at any meeting of the company or of the holders of any class of shares in the company shall be deemed to have received notice of the meeting and, where requisite, of the purposes for which it was called.

114.   Every person who becomes entitled to a share shall be bound by any notice in respect of that share which, before his name is entered in the register of members, has been duly given to a person from whom he derives his title.

115.   Proof that an envelope containing a notice was properly addressed, prepaid and posted shall be conclusive evidence that that the notice was given. Proof that a notice contained in an electronic communication was sent in accordance with guidance issued by the Institute of Chartered Secretaries and Administrators shall be conclusive evidence that the notice was given. A notice shall, ... be deemed to be given at the expiration of 48 hours after the envelope containing it was posted or, in the case of a notice contained in an electronic communication, at the expiration of 48 hours after the time it was sent.

116.   A notice may be given by the company to the persons entitled to a share in consequence of the death or bankruptcy of a member by sending or delivering it, in any manner authorised by the articles for the giving of notice to a member, addressed to them by name, or by the title of representatives of the deceased, or trustee of the bankrupt or by any like description at the address, if any, within the United Kingdom supplied for that purpose by the persons claiming to

be so entitled. Until such an address has been supplied, a notice may be given in any manner in which it might have been given if the death or bankruptcy had not occurred.

WINDING UP

117.   If the company is wound up, the liquidator may, with the sanction of an extraordinary resolution of the company and any other sanction required by the Act, divide among the members in specie the whole or any part of the assets of the company and may, for that purpose, value any assets and determine how the division shall be carried out as between the members or different classes of members. The liquidator may, with the like sanction, vest the whole or any part of the assets in trustees upon such trusts for the benefit of the members as he with the like sanction determines, but no member shall be compelled to accept any assets upon which there is a liability.

INDEMNITY

118.   Subject to the provisions of the Act but without prejudice to any indemnity to which a director may otherwise be entitled, every director or other officer or auditor of the company shall be indemnified out of the assets of the company against any liability incurred by him in defending any proceedings, whether civil or criminal, in which judgment is given in his favour or in which he is acquitted or in connection with any application in which relief is granted to him by the court from liability for negligence, default, breach of duty or breach of trust in relation to the affairs of the company.

TABLE B
A PRIVATE COMPANY LIMITED BY SHARES

MEMORANDUM OF ASSOCIATION

1.   The company's name is "The South Wales Motor Transport Company cyfyngedig".
2.   The company's registered office is to be situated in Wales.
3.   The company's objects are the carriage of passengers and goods in motor vehicles between such places as the company may from time to time determine and the doing of all such other things as are incidental or conducive to the attainment of that object.
4.   The liability of the members is limited.
5.   The company's share capital is £50,000 divided into 50,000 shares of £1 each.

We, the subscribers to this memorandum of association, wish to be formed into a company pursuant to this memorandum; and we agree to take the number of shares shown opposite our respective names.

Names and Addresses of Subscribers	Number of shares taken by each Subsciber
1. Thomas Jones, 138 Mountfield Street, Tredegar.	1
2. Mary Evans, 19 Merthyr Road, Aberystwyth.	1
	Total shares taken 2

Dated .. .. 19 .. ..
Witness to the above signatures,
Anne Brown, "Woodlands", Fieldside Road, Bryn Mawr.

TABLE C
A COMPANY LIMITED BY GUARANTEE AND NOT HAVING A SHARE CAPITAL

MEMORANDUM OF ASSOCIATION

1. The company's name is "The Dundee School Association Limited".
2. The company's registered office is to be situated in Scotland.
3. The company's objects are the carrying on of a school for boys and girls in Dundee and the doing of all such other things as are incidental or conducive to the attainment of that object.
4. The liability of the members is limited.
5. Every member of the company undertakes to contribute such amount as may be required (not exceeding £100) to the company's assets if it should be wound up while he is member or within one year after he ceases to be a member, for payment of the company's debts and liabilities contracted before he ceases to be a member, and of the costs, charges and expenses of winding up, and for the adjustment of the rights of the contributories among themselves.

We, the subscribers to this memorandum of association, wish to be formed into a company pursuant to this memorandum.

Names and Addresses of Subscribers.

1. Kenneth Brodie, 14 Bute Street, Dundee.
2. Ian Davis, 2 Burns Avenue, Dundee.

Dated .. .. 19 .. ..

Witness to the above signatures.

Anne Brown, 149 Princes Street, Edinburgh.

ARTICLES OF ASSOCIATION

PRELIMINARY

1. Regulations 2 to 35 inclusive, 54, 55, 57, 59, 102 to 108 inclusive, 110, 114, 116 and 117 of Table A, shall not apply to the company but the articles hereinafter contained and, subject to the modifications hereinafter expressed, the remaining regulations of Table A shall constitute the articles of association of the company.

INTERPRETATION

2. In regulation 1 of Table A, the definition of "the holder" shall be omitted.

MEMBERS

3. The subscribers to the memorandum of association of the company and such other persons as are admitted to membership in accordance with the articles shall be members of the company. No person shall be admitted a member of the company unless he is approved by the directors. Every person who wishes to become a member shall deliver to the company an application for membership in such form as the directors require executed by him.
4. A member may at any time withdraw from the company by giving at least seven clear days' notice to the company. Membership shall not be transferable and shall cease on death.

NOTICE OF GENERAL MEETINGS

5. In regulation 38 of Table A—
   (a) in paragraph (b) the words "of the total voting rights at the meeting of all the members" shall be substituted for "in nominal value of the shares giving that right"; and

(b)   the words "The notice shall be given to all the members and to the directors and auditors" shall be substituted for the last sentence.

PROCEEDINGS AT GENERAL MEETINGS

6.   The words "and at any separate meeting of the holders of any class of shares in the company" shall be omitted from regulation 44 of Table A.
7.   Paragraph (d) of regulation 46 of Table A shall be omitted.

VOTES OF MEMBERS

8.   On a show of hands every member present in person shall have one vote. On a poll every member present in person or by proxy shall have one vote.

DIRECTORS' EXPENSES

9.   The words "of any class of shares or" shall be omitted from regulation 83 of Table A.

PROCEEDINGS OF DIRECTORS

10.   In paragraph (c) of regulation 94 of Table A the word "debentures" shall be substituted for the words "shares, debentures or other securities" in both places where they occur.

MINUTES

11.   The words "of the holders of any class of shares in the company" shall be omitted from regulation 100 of Table A.

NOTICES

12.   The second sentence of regulation 112 of Table A shall be omitted.
13.   The words "or of the holders of any class of shares in the company" shall be omitted from regulation 113 of Table A.

TABLE D

PART I
A PUBLIC COMPANY LIMITED BY GUARANTEE AND HAVING A SHARE CAPITAL

MEMORANDUM OF ASSOCIATION

1.   The company's name is "Gwestai Glyndwr, cwmni cyfyngedig cyhoeddus".
2.   The company is to be a public company.
3.   The company's registered office is to be situated in Wales.
4.   The company's objects are facilitating travelling in Wales by providing hotels and conveyances by sea and by land for the accommodation of travellers and the doing of all such other things as are incidental or conducive to the attainment of those objects.
5.   The liability of the members is limited.
6.   Every member of the company undertakes to contribute such amount as may be required (not exceeding £100) to the company's assets if it should be wound up while he is a member or within one year after he ceases to be a member, for payment of the company's debts and liabilities contracted before he ceases to be a member, and of the costs, charges and expenses of winding up, and for the adjustment of the rights of the contributories among themselves.

7.   The company's share capital is £50,000 divided into 50,000 shares of £1 each.

We, the subscribers to this memorandum of association, wish to be formed into a company pursuant to this memorandum; and we agree to take the number of shares shown opposite our respective names..

Names and Addresses of Subscribers	Number of shares taken by each Subsciber
1. Thomas Jones, 138 Mountfield Street,Tredegar.	1
2. Mary Evans, 19 Merthyr Road, Aberystwyth.	<u>1</u>
	Total shares taken <u>2</u>

Dated .. .. 19 .. ..

Witness to the above signatures,

Anne Brown, "Woodlands", Fieldside Road, Bryn Mawr.

PART II
A PRIVATE COMPANY LIMITED BY GUARANTEE AND HAVING A SHARE CAPITAL

MEMORANDUM OF ASSOCIATION

1.   The company's name is "The Highland Hotel Company Limited".
2.   The company's registered office is to be situated in Scotland.
3.   The company's objects are facilitating travelling in the Highlands of Scotland by providing hotels and conveyances by sea and by land for the accommodation of travellers and the doing of all such other things as are incidental or conducive to the attainment of those objects.
4.   The liability of the members is limited.
5.   Every member of the company undertakes to contribute such amount as may be required (not exceeding £100) to the company's assets if it should be wound up while he is a member or within one year after he ceases to be a member, for payment of the company's debts and liabilities contracted before he ceases to be a member, and of the costs, charges and expenses of winding up, and for the adjustment of the rights of the contributories among themselves.
6.   The company's share capital is £50,000 divided into 50,000 shares of £1 each.

We, the subscribers to this memorandum of association, wish to be formed into a company pursuant to this memorandum; and we agree to take the number of shares shown opposite our respective names..

Names and Addresses of Subscribers	Number of shares taken by each Subsciber
Kenneth Brodie, 14 Bute Street, Dundee.	1
Ian Davis, 2 Burns Avenue, Dundee.	<u>1</u>
	Total shares taken <u>2</u>

Dated .. .. 19 .. ..

Witness to the above signatures.

Anne Brown, 149 Princes Street, Edinburgh.

PART III
A COMPANY (PUBLIC OR PRIVATE) LIMITED BY GUARANTEE AND HAVING A SHARE CAPITAL

ARTICLES OF ASSOCIATION

The regulations of Table A shall constitute the articles of association of the company.

TABLE E
AN UNLIMITED COMPANY HAVING A SHARE CAPITAL

MEMORANDUM OF ASSOCIATION

1. The company's name is "The Woodford Engineering Company".
2. The company's registered office is to be situated in England and Wales.
3. The company's objects are the working of certain patented inventions relating to the application of microchip technology to the improvement of food processing, and the doing of all such other things as are incidental or conducive to the attainment of that object.

   We, the subscribers to this memorandum of association, wish to be formed into a company pursuant to this memorandum; and we agree to take the number of shares shown opposite our respective names.

Names and Addresses of Subscribers	Number of shares taken by each Subsciber
1. Brian Smith, 24 Nibley Road, Wotton-under-Edge, Gloucestershire.	3
2. William Green, 278 High Street, Chipping Sodbury, Avon.	<u>5</u>
	Total shares taken <u>8</u>

Dated .. .. 19 .. ..
Witness to the above signatures,
Anne Brown, 108 Park Way, Bristol 8.

ARTICLES OF ASSOCIATION

1. Regulations 3, 32, 34 and 35 of Table A shall not apply to the company, but the articles hereinafter contained and, subject to the modification hereinafter expressed, the remaining regulations of Table A shall constitute the articles of association of the company.
2. The words "at least seven clear days' notice" shall be substituted for the words "at least fourteen days' notice" in regulation 38 of Table A.
3. The share capital of the company is £20,000 divided into 20,000 shares of £1 each.
4. The company may by special resolution—
   (a) increase the share capital by such sum to be divided into shares of such amount as the resolution may prescribe;
   (b) consolidate and divide all or any of its share capital into shares of a larger amount than its existing shares;
   (c) subdivide its shares, or any of them, into shares of a smaller amount than its existing shares;
   (d) cancel any shares which at the date of the passing of the resolution have not been taken or agreed to be taken by any person;
   (e) reduce its share capital and any share premium account in any way.

TABLE F
A PUBLIC COMPANY LIMITED BY SHARES

MEMORANDUM OF ASSOCIATION

1. The company's name is "Western Electronics Public Limited Company".
2. The company is to be a public company.
3. The company's registered office is to be situated in England and Wales.
4. The company's objects are the manufacture and development of such descriptions of electronic equipment, instruments and appliances as the company may from time to time determine, and the doing of all such other things as are incidental or conducive to the attainment of that object.

5.   The liability of the members is limited.

6.   The company's share capital is £5,000,000 divided into 5,000,000 shares of £1 each.

We, the subscribers to this memorandum of association, wish to be formed into a company pursuant to this memorandum; and we agree to take the number of shares shown opposite our respective names.

Names and Addresses of Subscribers	Number of shares taken by each Subsciber
1. James White, 12 Broadmead, Birmingham.	1
2. Patrick Smith, 145A Huntley House, London Wall, London, EC2.	<u>1</u>
	Total shares taken <u>2</u>

Dated .. .. 19 .. ..

Witness to the above signatures,

Anne Brown, 13 Hute Street, London WC2.

The City Code on Takeovers and Mergers

INTRODUCTION

I THE CODE

(a) Nature and purpose of the Code

The City Code on Takeovers and Mergers is issued on behalf of the Panel on Takeovers and Mergers. The Code is kept under review by the Code Committee of the Panel.

The Code is designed principally to ensure fair and equal treatment of all shareholders in relation to takeovers. The Code also provides an orderly framework within which takeovers are conducted. The Panel operates in accordance with the requirements of the Human Rights Act 1998.

The Code is not concerned with the financial or commercial advantages or disadvantages of a takeover. These are matters for the company and its shareholders. Nor is the Code concerned with those issues, such as competition policy, which are the responsibility of government.

The Code represents the collective opinion of those professionally involved in the field of takeovers as to business standards and as to how fairness to shareholders can be achieved.

(b) Code responsibilities

The responsibilities described in the Code apply most directly to those who are actively engaged in the securities markets. They are also regarded by the Panel as applying to directors of companies which are subject to the Code and to persons or groups of persons who seek to gain or consolidate effective control of such companies or who otherwise participate in, or are connected with, transactions to which the Code applies. They also apply to all professional advisers, in so far as they advise on the transactions in question. These responsibilities apply irrespective of whether those involved are directly affiliated to any of the bodies who nominate members of the Panel. The Panel also expects any other persons who issue circulars to shareholders in connection with takeovers to observe the highest standards of care and accuracy.

(c) Enforcement of the Code

The Code has not, and does not seek to have, the force of law. It has, however, been acknowledged by both government and other regulatory authorities that those who seek to take advantage of the facilities of the securities markets in the United Kingdom should conduct themselves in matters relating to takeovers in accordance with high business standards and so according to the Code.

In particular, the Code has been endorsed by the Financial Services Authority ("FSA") under the Financial Services and Markets Act 2000 ("the FSMA"). The effect of endorsement of the Code is that the FSA may, at the request of the Panel, take enforcement action against a person authorised under the FSMA who contravenes the Code or a Panel ruling. Such action can include public censure, fines, the removal of authorisation, the imposition of injunctions and orders for restitution. In addition, the FSA may, again at the request of the Panel, take enforcement action against an individual who is an "approved person" (eg a director of an authorised firm).

Therefore, those who do not conduct themselves in accordance with high business standards and so according to the Code may find that, by way of sanction, the facilities of the securities markets of the United Kingdom are withheld. In particular, the FSA's rules require a person authorised under the FSMA not to act, or continue to act, for any person in connection with a transaction to which the Code applies if the firm has reasonable grounds for believing that the person in question, or his principal, is not complying or is not likely to comply with the Code. Where a person has been named in a notice published by the Panel as someone who in the Panel's opinion is not likely to comply with the Code, the FSA expects an authorised person not to act (or continue to act) for that person. In addition, certain professional bodies have similar requirements.

2 THE PANEL AND THE EXECUTIVE

(a) Membership of the Panel

The Chairman, Deputy Chairmen and certain further members of the Panel are appointed by the Governor of the Bank of England. In addition, its membership comprises individuals nominated by the following bodies, all of which are committed to support its activities:—

The Association of British Insurers
The Association of Investment Trust Companies
The Association of Private Client Investment Managers and Stockbrokers
The British Bankers' Association
The Confederation of British Industry
The Institute of Chartered Accountants in England and Wales
Investment Management Association
The London Investment Banking Association (with separate representation for its Corporate Finance
    Committee and Securities Trading Committee)
The National Association of Pension Funds

Each of the bodies listed above may also nominate designated alternates.

(b) The Panel Executive

The Panel works on a day-to-day basis through its Executive, headed by the Director General. The Executive is responsible for the general administration of the Code. This includes, either on its own initiative or at the instigation of third parties, the conduct of investigations, and the monitoring of relevant dealings, in connection with the Code. The Executive is available both for consultation and to give rulings on points of interpretation before or during takeover or merger transactions.

(c) Co-operation with other authorities

The Panel co-operates with other regulatory authorities, such as the Department of Trade and Industry, London Stock Exchange plc ("the Stock Exchange"), other recognised investment exchanges, the FSA, professional bodies, the Bank of England and OFEX. This co-operation extends to the mutual exchange of information and, where appropriate, reporting breaches of the Code to the relevant authority. The Panel works closely with the Stock Exchange in monitoring dealings. The FSA and certain professional bodies will require investment businesses to co-operate with the Panel in enquiries and investigations and the Panel is designated under the Companies Act 1985 and the FSMA to receive regulatory information, the disclosure of which is restricted by statute.

3 THE CODE IN PRACTICE

(a) General Principles and Rules

The Code is based upon a number of General Principles, which are essentially statements of standards of commercial behaviour. These General Principles apply to all transactions with which the Code is concerned. They are, however, expressed in broad general terms and the Code does not define the precise extent of, or the limitations on, their application. They are applied by the Panel in accordance with their spirit to achieve their underlying purpose; the Panel may modify or relax the effect of their precise wording accordingly.

In addition to the General Principles, the Code contains a series of Rules, of which some are effectively expansions of the General Principles and examples of their application and others are provisions governing specific aspects of takeover procedure. Although most of the Rules are expressed in more detailed language than the General Principles, they are not framed in technical language and, like the General Principles, are to be interpreted to achieve their underlying purpose. Therefore, their spirit must be observed as well as their letter and the Panel may modify or relax the application of a Rule if it considers that, in the particular circumstances of the case, it would operate unduly harshly or in an unnecessarily restrictive or burdensome, or otherwise inappropriate, manner.

The Panel may delegate the rule-making function concerning amendments to the Code to a Code Committee, whose members would not normally participate in Panel hearings. Normally, the Code Committee consults publicly on proposed Code amendments.

(b) Consulting the Executive

The Executive gives general guidance on the interpretation of the Code. In addition, it gives rulings which are based on the particular facts of the case.

When there is any doubt whatsoever as to whether a proposed course of conduct is in accordance with the General Principles or the Rules, parties or their advisers should consult the Executive in advance. In this way, the parties can obtain a conditional ruling (on an ex parte basis) or an unconditional ruling as to the basis on which they can properly proceed and thus minimise the risk of taking action which might, in the event, be a breach of the Code.

Both principals and their advisers are encouraged to make full use of this service. To take legal, or other professional, advice on the interpretation or application of the Code is not an appropriate alternative to obtaining a ruling (either on a conditional (ex parte) or an unconditional basis) from the Executive.

The nature of the Executive's rulings will depend on whether or not the Executive is able to hear the views of other parties involved. If the Executive is not able to hear the views of other parties involved, it may give a conditional ruling (on an ex parte basis), which may be varied or set aside when any views of the other parties have been heard; if the Executive is able to hear the views of other parties involved, it may give an unconditional ruling.

The Executive may refer a matter to the Panel for decision without itself giving a ruling when it considers that there is a particularly unusual, important or difficult point at issue.

If a complaint is to be made that the Code has been breached, it must be made promptly. Delay may result in the Executive declining to investigate the complaint.

It is the Panel's practice to focus on the specific consequences for shareholders of breaches of the Code with the aim of providing appropriate redress in a timely manner. Furthermore, disciplinary action may be appropriate.

The Panel expects prompt co-operation from those to whom enquiries are directed so that decisions may be both properly informed and given as speedily as possible.

(c) Appeals to the Panel

If a party or his adviser wishes to contest a ruling of the Executive, he is entitled to request that the matter be reconsidered by the Panel, which can be convened at short notice. The Panel may also reconsider a matter at the request of an aggrieved shareholder. The Panel (or its Chairman) retains a discretion to deal summarily with frivolous or vexatious appeals. When the Executive considers that it is necessary to resolve an issue urgently, it may stipulate a reasonable time within which an appeal must be notified; in any other case, the Panel must be notified as soon as possible and, in any event, within one month of the event giving rise to the appeal.

(d) Disciplinary proceedings

The Executive may institute disciplinary proceedings before the Panel when it considers that there has been a breach of the Code. A disciplinary case is one the main purpose of which is to propose that disciplinary action should be taken following an alleged breach of the Code. In any such case, the Executive invites the person concerned to appear before the Panel. He is informed in writing of the alleged breach and of the matters which the Executive will present. If, subsequently, any additional matter of a material nature becomes relevant, he may request an adjournment.

If the Panel finds that there has been a breach of the Code, it may have recourse to one or more of the following:—
(i)   private reprimand;
(ii) public censure;
(iii) reporting the offender's conduct to another regulatory authority (eg the Department of Trade and Industry, the Stock Exchange, the FSA or the relevant professional body);

(iv) taking action for the purpose of the requirements of the FSA and certain professional bodies
      which oblige their members, in certain circumstances, not to act for the offender in a transaction
      to which the Code applies.

The Executive may itself deal with a disciplinary matter where the party which is to be subject to
disciplinary action agrees the facts and the action proposed by the Executive.

(e) Procedure before the Panel

At hearings before the Panel, the case is normally presented in person by the parties, which include the
Executive, or their advisers. Although not usual, parties may, if they so wish, be represented by legal
advisers. Normally, the parties should set out their case briefly in writing beforehand. The parties are
permitted to call such witnesses as they may feel necessary.

Proceedings before the Panel are usually in private, unless the Chairman, at his discretion, directs
otherwise. Parties may request that the hearing be held in public. Any such request will be considered and
ruled upon by the Chairman (or, at the discretion of the Chairman, by the Panel itself). In the event of a
public hearing, the Chairman may, at his discretion, direct that the Panel hears part or parts of the hearing
in private.

In general, all parties are entitled to be present throughout the hearing and to see all papers submitted to
the Panel. Occasionally, however, a party may wish to present evidence to the Panel which is of a
confidential commercial nature. In such exceptional cases, the Panel or the Chairman may, if satisfied that
such course is justified, direct that the evidence in question be heard in the absence of some, or all, of the
other parties involved. Parties are absent during the Panel's consideration of the case. Representations by
shareholders may be presented in writing and are usually heard by the Panel in their absence.

The Panel recognises that its authority can only be sustained if its impartiality is beyond doubt.
Accordingly, where a matter may create a conflict of interest for any Panel member, he will not attend and
one of his designated alternates may be appointed for the purposes of the hearing. The parties will be
given the opportunity to raise with the Chairman issues concerning possible conflicts of interest of
members of the Panel and any other objections, such issues to be resolved by decision of the Chairman.

The quorum for a Panel hearing is five, including a Chairman.

Proceedings before the Panel are informal. There are no rules of evidence. A tape recording will be
taken for the administrative assistance of the Panel, but it will not normally be retained once the
proceedings are at an end. In addition, a transcript of the hearing is normally made. A party to the hearing
may request a copy of the transcript, which may be provided subject to conditions, including conditions as
to its confidentiality and use.

It is the Panel's policy normally to publish its decisions and the reasons for them so that its activities
may be explained to the public.

The Panel will provide its reasoned decision to the parties in writing as soon as practicable following a
hearing. A public statement will normally be issued as promptly as possible, having regard to all the
circumstances of the case, after the reasoned decision has been provided in writing to the parties. In
certain circumstances, the Panel may make a separate public statement of its decision (without providing
reasons at this stage) in advance of the publication of its reasoned decision in writing.

(f) The Appeal Committee

There is a right of appeal to the Appeal Committee in each of the following cases:—
   (i)   where the Panel finds a breach of the Code and proposes to take disciplinary action;
   (ii) where it is alleged that the Panel has acted outside its jurisdiction; or
   (iii) in respect of any refusal by the Panel to recognise, or any decision of the Panel to cease to
         recognise, a market-maker or fund manager as an exempt market-maker or exempt fund manager
         as the case may be.

An appeal may in other cases be made to the Appeal Committee, but only with leave of the Panel.
Applications for leave to appeal may be made to the Panel by any party within a reasonable time to be
stipulated by the Chairman (or, at the discretion of the Chairman, by the Panel itself) or, in the absence of
such stipulation, within two business days of the receipt in writing of the reasoned decision in question.
The application will be determined by the Chairman (or, at the discretion of the Chairman, by the Panel

itself). The Panel would not normally expect to grant leave to appeal against a finding of fact or against a decision of the Panel on the interpretation of the Code. However, leave to appeal (including the terms, if any, of such leave) may be granted if the Chairman (or the Panel, where it is hearing any such application) considers that the case is one of general importance or one which for some other special reason should be considered by the Appeal Committee.

In all cases, notice of appeal must be given within such time as is stipulated on the grant of leave to appeal or, in the absence of such stipulation, within two business days of the grant of leave (where leave is required) or (in other cases) within two business days of the receipt in writing of the reasoned decision in question. The Panel may suspend publication in full of its findings during this time, although an appropriate interim announcement may be made. If there is an appeal, publication may, at the discretion of the Chairman, be suspended until after the decision of the Appeal Committee.

The Chairman and/or Deputy Chairman of the Appeal Committee (or, if unavailable, their alternates), who will normally have held high judicial office, sits with members of the Panel who have not been involved in the decision of the Panel under appeal. The quorum for the Appeal Committee is three.

The Appeal Committee may, although it does not normally, hear new evidence.

If an appeal is upheld, the appellant is consulted on the form of statement, if any, which is to be published. If an appeal is dismissed, the findings of the Panel are published and any steps decided upon by way of action implemented. In either case, the Appeal Committee may make any further comment it thinks fit.

(g) Procedure before the Appeal Committee

Proceedings before the Appeal Committee are generally conducted in a similar way to those before the Panel.

(h) Procedural directions

On the application of any party, the Chairman or one of the Deputy Chairmen of the Panel (or, in the case of an appeal to the Appeal Committee, the Chairman or the Deputy Chairman of the Appeal Committee) may give such procedural directions as he considers appropriate for the determination of a case. An appeal may be made to the Chairman or the Deputy Chairman of the Appeal Committee, against any directions given by the Chairman or one of the Deputy Chairmen of the Panel. For the efficient conduct of a case, the Chairman or one of the Deputy Chairmen of the Panel may direct when any such appeal may be made.

4 COMPANIES AND TRANSACTIONS TO WHICH THE CODE APPLIES

(a) Companies

In determining whether or not the Code applies, it is the nature of the company which is the offeree or potential offeree company, or in which control (as defined) may change or be consolidated, that is relevant.

The Code applies to offers for all listed and unlisted public companies (and, where appropriate, statutory and chartered companies) considered by the Panel to be resident in the United Kingdom, the Channel Islands or the Isle of Man. The Code does not, however, apply to Open-Ended Investment Companies. It also applies to offers for private companies considered to be so resident but only when:—

- (i) their equity share capital has been admitted to the Official List ("Official List") of the UK Listing Authority ("UKLA") at any time during the 10 years prior to the relevant date; or
- (ii) dealings and/or prices at which persons were willing to deal in their equity share capital have been published on a regular basis for a continuous period of at least six months in the 10 years prior to the relevant date, whether via a newspaper, electronic price quotation system or otherwise; or
- (iii) their equity share capital has been subject to a marketing arrangement as described in Section 1 63(2)(b) of the Companies Act 1985 at any time during the 10 years prior to the relevant date (eg their shares were dealt in on the Unlisted Securities Market); or
- (iv) they have tiled a prospectus for the issue of equity share capital with the registrar of companies at any time during the 10 years prior to the relevant date.

In each case, the relevant date is the date on which an announcement is made of a proposed or possible offer for the company or the date on which some other event occurs in relation to the company which has significance under the Code.

The Panel appreciates that the provisions of the Code may not be appropriate to all statutory and chartered companies or to all private companies falling within the categories listed above and will, therefore, apply the Code with a degree of flexibility in suitable cases.

Any public company having more than one beneficial owner that proposes to re-register as a private company to which the Code will not apply should consult the Executive.

The Panel will normally consider a company to be resident only if it is incorporated in the United Kingdom, the Channel Islands or the Isle of Man and has its place of central management in one of those jurisdictions.

(b) Transactions

The Code is concerned with takeover and merger transactions, however effected, of all relevant companies; these include partial offers, offers by a parent company for shares in its subsidiary and certain other transactions where control of a company (as defined) is to be obtained or consolidated. References in the Code to "takeovers" and "offers" include, where appropriate, all such transactions. The Code does not apply to offers for non-voting, non-equity capital unless they are offers required by Rule 15.

(c) Dual jurisdiction

Code transactions may from time to time be subject to the dual jurisdiction of the Panel and an overseas takeover regulator. In such cases, early consultation with the Executive is required so that guidance can be given on how any conflicts between the relevant regulations may be resolved.

GENERAL PRINCIPLES

Introduction

It is impracticable to devise rules in sufficient detail to cover all circumstances which can arise in offers. Accordingly, persons engaged in offers should be aware that the spirit as well as the precise wording of the General Principles and the ensuing Rules must be observed. Moreover, the General Principles and the spirit of the Code will apply in areas or circumstances not explicitly covered by any Rule.

While the boards of an offeror and the offeree company and their respective advisers have a duty to act in the best interests of their respective shareholders, these General Principles and the ensuing Rules will, inevitably, impinge on the freedom of action of boards and persons involved in offers; they must, therefore, accept that there are limitations in connection with offers on the manner in which the pursuit of those interests can be carried out.

Each director of an offeror and of the offeree company has a responsibility to ensure, so far as he is reasonably able, that the Code is complied with in the conduct of an offer (see Appendix 3 for Guidance Note). Financial advisers have a particular responsibility to comply with the Code and to ensure, so far as they are reasonably able, that an offeror and the offeree company, and their respective directors, are aware of their responsibilities under the Code and will comply with them. Financial advisers should ensure that the Panel is consulted whenever relevant and should co-operate fully with any enquiries made by the Panel. Financial advisers must also be mindful of conflicts of interest (see Appendix 3 for Guidance Note).

General Principles

1.   *All shareholders of the same class of an offeree company must be treated similarly by an offeror.*
2.   *During the course of an offer, or when an offer is in contemplation, neither an offeror, nor the offeree company, nor any of their respective advisers may furnish information to some shareholders which is not made available to all shareholders. This principle does not apply to the furnishing of information in confidence by the offeree company to a bona tide potential offeror or vice versa.*

3.   *An offeror should only announce an otter after the most careful and responsible consideration. Such an announcement should be made only when the offeror has every reason to believe that it can and will continue to be able to implement the offer: responsibility in this connection also rests on the financial adviser to the offeror.*

4.   *Shareholders must be given sufficient information and advice to enable them to reach a properly informed decision and must have sufficient time to do so. No relevant information should be withheld from them.*

5.   *Any document or advertisement addressed to shareholders containing information or advice from an offeror or the board of the offeree company or their respective advisers must, as is the case with a prospectus, be prepared with the highest standards of care and accuracy.*

6.   *All parties to an offer must use every endeavour to prevent the creation of a false market in the securities of an otferor or the offeree company. Parties involved in offers must take care that statements are not made which may mislead shareholders or the market.*

7.   *At no time after a bona fide offer has been communicated to the board of the offeree company, or after the board of the offeree company has reason to believe that a bona tide offer might be imminent, may any action be taken by the board of the offeree company in relation to the affairs of the company, without the approval of the shareholders in general meeting, which could effectively result in any bona tide offer being frustrated or in the shareholders being denied an opportunity to decide on its merits.*

8.   *Rights of control must be exercised in good faith and the oppression of a minority is wholly unacceptable.*

9.   *Directors of an offeror and the offeree company must always, in advising their shareholders, act only in their capacity as directors and not have regard to their personal or family shareholdings or to their personal relationships with the companies. It is the shareholders' interests taken as a whole, together with those of employees and creditors, which should be considered when the directors are giving advice to shareholders. Directors of the offeree company should give careful consideration before they enter into any commitment with an offeror (or anyone else) which would restrict their freedom to advise their shareholders in the future. Such commitments may give rise to conflicts of interest or result in a breach of the directors' fiduciary duties.*

10.   *Where control of a company is acquired by a person, or persons acting in concert, a general offer to all other shareholders is normally required; a similar obligation may arise if control is consolidated. Where an acquisition is contemplated as a result of which a person may incur such an obligation, he must, before making the acquisition, ensure that he can and will continue to be able to implement such an offer.*

Business Names Act 1985

1985 c. 7

An Act to consolidate certain enactments relating to the names under which persons may carry on business in Great Britain

[11th March 1985]

1.   **Persons subject to this Act**

(1)   This Act applies to any person who has a place of business in Great Britain and who carries on business in Great Britain under a name which—

    (a)   in the case of a partnership, does not consist of the surnames of all partners who are individuals and the corporate names of all partners who are bodies corporate without any addition other than an addition permitted by this Act;

    (b)   in the case of an individual, does not consist of his surname without any addition other than one so permitted;

    (c)   in the case of a company, being a company which is capable of being wound up under the Companies Act 1985, does not consist of its corporate name without any addition other than one so permitted;

    (d)   in the case of a limited liability partnership, does not consist of its corporate name without any addition other than one so permitted.

(2)   The following are permitted additions for the purposes of subsection (1)—

    (a)   in the case of a partnership, the forenames of individual partners or the initials of those forenames or, where two or more individual partners have the same surname, the addition of "s" at the end of that surname; or

    (b)   in the case of an individual, his forename or its initial;

    (c)   in any case, any addition merely indicating that the business is carried on in succession to a former owner of the business.

2.   **Prohibition of use of certain business names**

(1)   Subject to the following subsections, a person to whom this Act applies shall not, without the written approval of the Secretary of State, carry on business in Great Britain under a name which—

    (a)   would be likely to give the impression that the business is connected with Her Majesty's Government, with any part of the Scottish Administration, or with any local authority; or

    (b)   includes any word or expression for the time being specified in regulations made under this Act.

(2)   Subsection (1) does not apply to the carrying on of a business by a person—

    (a)   to whom the business has been transferred on or after 26th February 1982; and

    (b)   who carries on the business under the name which was its lawful business name immediately before that transfer,

during the period of 12 months beginning with the date of that transfer.

(3)   Subsection (1) does not apply to the carrying on of a business by a person who—

    (a)   carried on that business immediately before 26th February 1982; and

    (b)   continues to carry it on under the name which immediately before that date was its lawful business name.

(4)   A person who contravenes subsection (1) is guilty of an offence.

3.   **Words and expressions requiring Secretary of State's approval**

(1)   The Secretary of State may by regulations—

    (a)   specify words or expressions for the use of which as or as part of a business name his approval is required by section 2(1)(b); and

(b)   in relation to any such word or expression, specify a Government department or other body as the relevant body for purposes of the following subsection.

(2)   Where a person to whom this Act applies proposes to carry on a business under a name which is or includes any such word or expression, and a Government department or other body is specified under subsection (1)(b) in relation to that word or expression, that person shall—

(a)   request (in writing) the relevant body to indicate whether (and if so why) it has any objections to the proposal; and

(b)   submit to the Secretary of State a statement that such a request has been made and a copy of any response received from the relevant body.

4.   Disclosure required of persons using business names

(1)   A person to whom this Act applies shall—

(a)   subject to subsections (3) and (3A), state in legible characters on all business letters, written orders for goods or services to be supplied to the business, invoices and receipts issued in the course of the business and written demands for payment of debts arising in the course of the business—

    (i)   in the case of a partnership, the name of each partner,

    (ii)   in the case of an individual, his name,

    (iii)   in the case of a company, its corporate name, ...

    (iiia)   In the case of a limited liability partnership, its corporate name and the name of each member, and

    (iv)   in relation to each person so named, an address in Great Britain at which service of any document relating in any way to the business will be effective; and

(b)   in any premises where the business is carried on and to which the customers of the business or suppliers of any goods or services to the business have access, display in a prominent position so that it may easily be read by such customers or suppliers a notice containing such names and addresses.

(2)   A person to whom this Act applies shall secure that the names and addresses required by subsection (1)(a) to be stated on his business letters, or which would have been so required but for subsection (3) or (3A), are immediately given, by written notice to any person with whom anything is done or discussed in the course of the business and who asks for such names and addresses.

(3)   Subsection (1)(a) does not apply in relation to any document issued by a partnership of more than 20 persons which maintains at its principal place of business a list of the names of all the partners if—

(a)   none of the names of the partners appears in the document otherwise than in the text or as a signatory; and

(b)   the document states in legible characters the address of the partnership's principal place of business and that the list of the partners' names is open to inspection at that place.

(3A)   Subsection (1)(a) does not apply in relation to any document issued by a limited liability partnership with more than 20 members which maintains at its principal place of business a list of the names of all the members if—

(a)   none of the names of the members appears in the document otherwise than in the text or as a signatory; and

(b)   the document states in legible characters the address of the principal place of business of the limited liability partnership and that the list of the members' names is open to inspection at that place.

(4)   Where a partnership maintains a list of the partners' names for purposes of subsection (3), any person may inspect the list during office hours.

(4A)   Where a limited liability partnership maintains a list of the members' names for the purposes of subsection (3A), any person may inspect the list during office hours.

(5)   The Secretary of State may by regulations require notices under subsection (1)(b) or (2) to be displayed or given in a specified form.

(6) A person who without reasonable excuse contravenes subsection (1) or (2), or any regulations made under subsection (5), is guilty of an offence.

(7) Where an inspection required by a person in accordance with subsection (4) or (4A) is refused, any partner of the partnership concerned, or any member of the limited liability partnership concerned, who without reasonable excuse refused that inspection, or permitted it to be refused, is guilty of an offence.

5. Civil remedies for breach of s 4

(1) Any legal proceedings brought by a person to whom this Act applies to enforce a right arising out of a contract made in the course of a business in respect of which he was, at the time the contract was made, in breach of subsection (1) or (2) of section 4 shall be dismissed if the defendant (or, in Scotland, the defender) to the proceedings shows—

    (a) that he has a claim against the plaintiff (pursuer) arising out of that contract which he has been unable to pursue by reason of the latter's breach of section 4(1) or (2), or

    (b) that he has suffered some financial loss in connection with the contract by reason of the plaintiff's (pursuer's) breach of section 4(1) or (2),

unless the court before which the proceedings are brought is satisfied that it is just and equitable to permit the proceedings to continue.

(2) This section is without prejudice to the right of any person to enforce such rights as he may have against another person in any proceedings brought by that person.

6. Regulations

(1) Regulations under this Act shall be made by statutory instrument and may contain such transitional provisions and savings as the Secretary of State thinks appropriate, and may make different provision for different cases or classes of case.

(2) In the case of regulations made under section 3, the statutory instrument containing them shall be laid before Parliament after the regulations are made and shall cease to have effect at the end of the period of 28 days beginning with the day on which they were made (but without prejudice to anything previously done by virtue of them or to the making of new regulations) unless during that period they are approved by a resolution of each House of Parliament.

In reckoning this period of 28 days, no account is to be taken of any time during which Parliament is dissolved or prorogued, or during which both Houses are adjourned for more than 4 days.

(3) In the case of regulations made under section 4, the statutory instrument containing them is subject to annulment in pursuance of a resolution of either House of Parliament.

7. Offences

(1) Offences under this Act are punishable on summary conviction.

(2) A person guilty of an offence under this Act is liable to a fine not exceeding one-fifth of the statutory maximum.

(3) If after a person has been convicted summarily of an offence under section 2 or 4(6) the original contravention is continued, he is liable on a second or subsequent summary conviction of the offence to a fine not exceeding one-fiftieth of the statutory maximum for each day on which the contravention is continued (instead of to the penalty which may be imposed on the first conviction of the offence).

(4) Where an offence under section 2 or 4(6) or (7) committed by a body corporate is proved to have been committed with the consent or connivance of, or to be attributable to any neglect on the part of, any director, manager, secretary or other similar officer of the body corporate, or any person who was purporting to act in any such capacity, he as well as the body corporate is guilty of the offence and liable to be proceeded against and punished accordingly.

(5) Where the affairs of a body corporate are managed by its members, subsection (4) applies in relation to the acts and defaults of a member in connection with his functions of management as if he were a director of the body corporate.

(6) For purposes of the following provisions of the Companies Act 1985—

    (a) section 731 (summary proceedings under the Companies Acts), and

(b)   section 732(3) (legal professional privilege),

this Act is to be treated as included in those Acts.

8.   Interpretation

(1)   The following definitions apply for purposes of this Act—

"business" includes a profession;

"initial" includes any recognised abbreviation of a name;

"lawful business name", in relation to a business, means a name under which the business was carried on without contravening section 2(1) of this Act or section 2 of the Registration of Business Names Act 1916;

"local authority" means any local authority within the meaning of the Local Government Act 1972 or the Local Government (Scotland) Act 1973, the Common Council of the City of London or the Council of the Isles of Scilly;

"partnership" includes a foreign partnership;

...

and "surname", in relation to a peer or person usually known by a British title different from his surname, means the title by which he is known.

(2)   Any expression used in this Act and also in the Companies Act 1985 has the same meaning in this Act as in that.

9.   Northern Ireland

This Act does not extend to Northern Ireland.

10.   Commencement

This Act comes into force on 1st July 1985.

11.   Citation

This Act may be cited as the Business Names Act 1985.

Company and Business Names Regulations 1981

S.I. 1981/1685

1. These Regulations may be cited as the Company and Business Names Regulations 1981 and shall come into operation on 26th February 1982.

2. In these Regulations, unless the context otherwise requires, "the Act" means the Companies Act 1981.

3. The words and expressions stated in column (1) of the Schedule hereto (together with the plural and the possessive forms of those words and expressions) are hereby specified as words and expressions for the registration of which as or as part of a company's corporate name the approval of the Secretary of State is required by section 22(2)(b) of the Act or for the use of which as or as part of a business name his approval is required by section 28(2)(b) of the Act.

4. Subject to Regulation 5, each Government department or other body stated in column (2) of the Schedule hereto is hereby specified as the relevant body for the purposes of section 31(2) and (3) of the Act in relation to the word or expression (and the plural and the possessive forms of that word or expression) opposite to it in column (1).

5. Where two Government departments or other bodies are specified in the alternative in Column (2) of the Schedule hereto the second alternative is to be treated as specified,
    (a) in the case of the corporate name of a company,
        (i) if the company has not yet been registered and its principal or only place of business in Great Britain is to be in Scotland or, if it will have no place of business in Great Britain, its proposed registered office is in Scotland, and
        (ii) if the company is already registered and its principal or only place of business in Great Britain is in Scotland or, if it has no place of business in Great Britain, its registered office is in Scotland, and
    (b) in the case of a business name, if the principal or only place of the business carried on or to be carried on in Great Britain is or is to be in Scotland,
    and the first alternative is to be treated as specified in any other case.

SCHEDULE

SPECIFICATION OF WORDS, EXPRESSIONS AND RELEVANT BODIES

Regulations 3, 5

Column (1)	Column (2)
Word or expression	Relevant body
Abortion	Department of Health and Social Security
Apothecary	Worshipful Society of Apothecaries of London or Pharmaceutical Society of Great Britain
Association	
Assurance	
Assurer	
Authority	
Benevolent	
Board	
...	...
British	
...	

Column (1)	Column (2)
Word or expression	Relevant body
Chamber (or Chambers) of Business (or their Welsh equivalents, Siambr Fusnes; Siambrau Busnes)	
Chamber (or Chambers) of Commerce (or their Welsh equivalents, Siambr Fasnach; Siambrau Masnach)	
Chamber (or Chambers) of Commerce and Industry (or their Welsh equivalents, Siambr Masnach a Diwydiant; Siambrau Masnach a Diwydiant)	
Chamber (or Chambers) of Commerce, Training and Enterprise (or their Welsh equivalents, Siambr Masnach, Hyfforddiant a Menter; Siambrau Masnach, Hyfforddiant a Menter)	
Chamber (or Chambers) of Enterprise (or their Welsh equivalents, Siambr Fenter; Siambrau Menter)	
Chamber (or Chambers) of Industry (or their Welsh equivalents, Siambr Ddiwydiant; Siambrau Diwydiant)	
Chamber (or Chambers) of Trade (or their Welsh equivalents, Siambr Fasnach; Siambrau Masnach)	
Chamber (or Chambers) of Trade and Industry (or their Welsh equivalents, Siambr Masnach a Diwydiant; Siambrau Masnach a Diwydiant)	
Chamber (or Chambers) of Training (or their Welsh equivalents, Siambr Hyfforddiant; Siambrau Hyfforddiant)	
Chamber (or Chambers) of Training and Enterprise (or their Welsh equivalents, Siambr Hyfforddiant a Menter; Siambrau Hyfforddiant a Menter)	
Charitable	Charity Commission or the Scottish Ministers
Charity	Charity Commission or the Scottish Ministers
Charter	
Chartered	
Chemist	
Chemistry	
Contact Lens	General Optical Council
Co-operative	
Council	
Dental	General Dental Council
Dentistry	General Dental Council
District Nurse	Nursing and Midwifery Council
Duke	Home Office or the Scottish Ministers

Column (1)	Column (2)
Word or expression	Relevant body
England	
English	
European	
Federation	
Friendly Society	
Foundation	
Fund	
Giro	
Great Britain	
Group	
Health Centre	Department of Health and Social Security
Health Service	Department of Health and Social Security
Health Visitor	Nursing and Midwifery Council
Her Majesty	Home Office or the Scottish Ministers
His Majesty	Home Office or the Scottish Ministers
Holding	
Industrial and Provident Society	
Institute	
Institution	
Insurance	
Insurer	
International	
Ireland	
Irish	
King	Home Office or the Scottish Ministers
Midwife	Nursing and Midwifery Council
Midwifery	Nursing and Midwifery Council
National	
Nurse	Nursing and Midwifery Council
Nursing	Nursing and Midwifery Council
…	…
Patent	
Patentee	
Police	Home Office or the Scottish Ministers
Polytechnic	Department for Education and Skills
Post Office	
Pregnancy Termination	Department of Health and Social Security
Prince	Home Office or the Scottish Ministers
Princess	Home Office or the Scottish Ministers
Queen	Home Office or the Scottish Ministers
Reassurance	
Reassurer	
Register	
Registered	
Reinsurance	

Column (1)	Column (2)
Word or expression	Relevant body
Reinsurer	
Royal	Home Office or the Scottish Ministers
Royale	Home Office or the Scottish Ministers
Royalty	Home Office or the Scottish Ministers
Scotland	
Scottish	
Sheffield	
Society	
Special School	Department for Education and Skills
Stock Exchange	
Trade Union	
Trust	
United Kingdom	
University	The Privy Council
Wales	
Welsh	
Windsor	Home Office or the Scottish Ministers

Note: The reference in Column (2) to the Home Office shall be treated as a reference to the Lord Chancellor's Department in relation to the following entries in Column (1)—

(a)   Duke,
(b)   Her Majesty,
(c)   His Majesty,
(d)   King,
(e)   Prince,
(f)   Princess,
(g)   Queen,
(h)   Royal,
(i)   - Royale,
(j)   Royalty, and
(k)   Windsor.

Partnership Act 1890

1890 c. 39

An Act to declare and amend the Law of Partnership

[14th August 1890]

Nature of Partnership

1.   Definition of Partnership

(1)   Partnership is the relation which subsists between persons carrying on a business in common with a view of profit.

(2)   But the relation between members of any company or association which is—

    (a)   Registered as a Company under the Companies Act 1862 or any other Act of Parliament for the time being in force and relating to the registration of joint stock companies; or

    (b)   Formed or incorporated by or in pursuance of any other Act of Parliament or letters patent, or Royal Charter …

    (c)   …

is not a partnership within the meaning of this Act.

2.   Rules for determining existence of partnership

In determining whether a partnership does or does not exist, regard shall be had to the following rules:

(1)   Joint tenancy, tenancy in common, joint property, common property, or part ownership does not of itself create a partnership as to anything so held or owned, whether the tenants or owners do or do not share any profits made by the use thereof.

(2)   The sharing of gross returns does not of itself create a partnership, whether the persons sharing such returns have or have not a joint or common right or interest in any property from which or from the use of which the returns are derived.

(3)   The receipt by a person of a share of the profits of a business is *prima facie* evidence that he is a partner in the business, but receipt of such a share, or of a payment contingent on or varying with the profits of a business, does not of itself make him a partner in the business; and in particular—

    (a)   The receipt by a person of a debt or other liquidated amount by instalments or otherwise out of the accruing profits of a business does not of itself make him a partner in the business or liable as such:

    (b)   A contract for the remuneration of a servant or agent of a person engaged in a business by a share of the profits of the business does not of itself make the servant or agent a partner in the business or liable as such:

    (c)   A person being the *widow, widower, surviving civil partner* or child of a deceased partner, and receiving by way of annuity a portion of the profits made in the business in which the deceased person was a partner, is not by reason only of such receipt a partner in the business or liable as such:

    (d)   The advance of money by way of loan to a person engaged or about to engage in any business on a contract with that person that the lender shall receive a rate of interest varying with the profits, or shall receive a share of the profits arising from carrying on the business, does not of itself make the lender a partner with the person or persons carrying on the business or liable as such. Provided that the contract is in writing, and signed by or on behalf of all the parties thereto:

    (e)   A person receiving by way of annuity or otherwise a portion of the profits of a business in consideration of the sale by him of the goodwill of the business is not by reason only of such receipt a partner in the business or liable as such.

Note. The italicized words in subsection (3)(c) are inserted by the Civil Partnership Act 2004, s. 261(1), Sch. 27, para. 2, as from a day to be appointed.

3.   **Postponement of rights of person lending or selling in consideration of share of profits in case of insolvency**

In the event of any person to whom money has been advanced by way of loan upon such a contract as is mentioned in the last foregoing section, or of any buyer of a goodwill in consideration of a share of the profits of the business, being adjudged a bankrupt, entering into an arrangement to pay his creditors less than 100p in the pound, or dying in insolvent circumstances, the lender of the loan shall not be entitled to recover anything in respect of his loan, and the seller of the goodwill shall not be entitled to recover anything in respect of the share of profits contracted for, until the claims of the other creditors of the borrower or buyer for valuable consideration in money or money's worth have been satisfied.

4.   **Meaning of firm**

(1)   Persons who have entered into partnership with one another are for the purposes of this Act called collectively a firm, and the name under which their business is carried on is called the firm-name.

(2)   In Scotland a firm is a legal person distinct from the partners of whom it is composed, but an individual partner may be charged on a decree or diligence directed against the firm, and on payment of the debts is entitled to relief pro rata from the firm and its other members.

Relations of Partners to persons dealing with them

5.   **Power of partner to bind the firm**

Every partner is an agent of the firm and his other partners for the purpose of the business of the partnership; and the acts of every partner who does any act for carrying on in the usual way business of the kind carried on by the firm of which he is a member bind the firm and his partners, unless the partner so acting has in fact no authority to act for the firm in the particular matter, and the person with whom he is dealing either knows that he has no authority, or does not know or believe him to be a partner.

6.   **Partners bound by acts on behalf of firm**

An act or instrument relating to the business of the firm done or executed in the firm-name, or in any other manner showing an intention to bind the firm, by any person thereto authorised, whether a partner or not, is binding on the firm and all the partners.

Provided that this section shall not affect any general rule of law relating to the execution of deeds or negotiable instruments.

7.   **Partner using credit of firm for private purposes**

Where one partner pledges the credit of the firm for a purpose apparently not connected with the firm's ordinary course of business, the firm is not bound, unless he is in fact specially authorised by the other partners; but this section does not affect any personal liability incurred by an individual partner.

8.   **Effect of notice that firm will not be bound by acts of partner**

If it has been agreed between the partners that any restriction shall be placed on the power of any one or more of them to bind the firm, no act done in contravention of the agreement is binding on the firm with respect to persons having notice of the agreement.

9.   **Liability of partners**

Every partner in a firm is liable jointly with the other partners, and in Scotland severally also, for all debts and obligations of the firm incurred while he is a partner; and after his death his estate is also severally liable in a due course of administration for such debts and obligations, so far as they remain unsatisfied, but subject in England or Ireland to the prior payment of his separate debts.

10.   Liability of the firm for wrongs

Where, by any wrongful act or omission of any partner acting in the ordinary course of the business of the firm, or with the authority of his co-partners, loss or injury is caused to any person not being a partner in the firm, or any penalty is incurred, the firm is liable therefor to the same extent as the partner so acting or omitting to act.

11.   Misapplication of money or property received for or in custody of the firm

In the following cases; namely—

(a)   Where one partner acting within the scope of his apparent authority receives the money or property of a third person and misapplies it; and

(b)   Where a firm in the course of its business receives money or property of a third person, and the money or property so received is misapplied by one or more of the partners while it is in the custody of the firm;

the firm is liable to make good the loss.

12.   Liability for wrongs joint and several

Every partner is liable jointly with his co-partners and also severally for everything for which the firm while he is a partner therein becomes liable under either of the two last preceding sections.

13.   Improper employment of trust-property for partnership purposes

If a partner, being a trustee, improperly employs trust-property in the business or on the account of the partnership, no other partner is liable for the trust property to the persons beneficially interested therein:

Provided as follows:—

(1)   This section shall not affect any liability incurred by any partner by reason of his having notice of a breach of trust; and

(2)   Nothing in this section shall prevent trust money from being followed and recovered from the firm if still in its possession or under its control.

14.   Persons liable by "holding out"

(1)   Every one who by words spoken or written or by conduct represents himself, or who knowingly suffers himself to be represented, as a partner in a particular firm, is liable as a partner to any one who has on the faith of any such representation given credit to the firm, whether the representation has or has not been made or communicated to the person so giving credit by or with the knowledge of the apparent partner making the representation or suffering it to be made.

(2)   Provided that where after a partner's death the partnership business is continued in the old firm's name, the continued use of that name or of the deceased partner's name as part thereof shall not of itself make his executors or administrators estate or effects liable for any partnership debts contracted after his death.

15.   Admissions and representation of partners

An admission or representation made by any partner concerning the partnership affairs, and in the ordinary course of its business, is evidence against the firm.

16.   Notice to acting partner to be notice to the firm

Notice to any partner who habitually acts in the partnership business of any matter relating to partnership affairs operates as notice to the firm, except in the case of a fraud on the firm committed by or with the consent of that partner.

17.   Liabilities of incoming and outgoing partners

(1)   A person who is admitted as a partner into an existing firm does not thereby become liable to the creditors of the firm for anything done before he became a partner.

(2)   A partner who retires from a firm does not thereby cease to be liable for partnership debts or obligations incurred before his retirement.

(3)   A retiring partner may be discharged from any existing liabilities, by an agreement to that effect between himself and the members of the firm as newly constituted and the creditors, and this agreement may be either expressed or inferred as a fact from the course of dealing between the creditors and the firm as newly constituted.

18.   **Revocation of continuing guaranty by change in firm**

A continuing guaranty or cautionary obligation given either to a firm or to a third person in respect of the transactions of a firm is, in the absence of agreement to the contrary, revoked as to future transactions by any change in the constitution of the firm to which, or of the firm in respect of the transactions of which, the guaranty or obligation was given.

Relations of Partners to one another

19.   **Variation by consent of terms of partnership**

The mutual rights and duties of partners, whether ascertained by agreement or defined by this Act, may be varied by the consent of all the partners, and such consent may be either express or inferred from a course of dealing.

20.   **Partnership property**

(1)   All property and rights and interests in property originally brought into the partnership stock or acquired, whether by purchase or otherwise, on account of the firm, or for the purposes and in the course of the partnership business, are called in this Act partnership property, and must be held and applied by the partners exclusively for the purposes of the partnership and in accordance with the partnership agreement.

(2)   Provided that the legal estate or interest in any land, or in Scotland the title to and interest in any heritable estate, which belongs to the partnership shall devolve according to the nature and tenure thereof, and the general rules of law thereto applicable, but in trust, so far as necessary, for the persons beneficially interested in the land under this section.

(3)   Where co-owners of an estate or interest in any land, or in Scotland of any heritable estate, not being itself partnership property, are partners as to profits made by the use of that land or estate, and purchase other land or estate out of the profits to be used in like manner, the land or estate so purchased belongs to them, in the absence of an agreement to the contrary, not as partners, but as co-owners for the same respective estates and interests as are held by them in the land or estate first mentioned at the date of the purchase.

21.   **Property bought with partnership money**

Unless the contrary intention appears, property bought with money belonging to the firm is deemed to have been bought on account of the firm.

22.   ...

23.   **Procedure against partnership property for a partner's separate judgement debt**

(1)   ... A writ of execution shall not issue against any partnership property except on a judgment against the firm.

(2)   The High Court, or a judge thereof, ..., or a county court, may, on the application by summons of any judgment creditor of a partner, make an order charging that partner's interest in the partnership property and profits with payment of the amount of the judgment debt and interest thereon, and may by the same or a subsequent order appoint a receiver of that partner's share of profits (whether already declared or accruing), and of any other money which may be coming to him in respect of the partnership, and direct all accounts and inquiries, and give all other orders and directions which might have been directed or given if the charge had been made in favour of the judgment creditor by the partner, or which the circumstances of the case may require.

(3)   The other partner or partners shall be at liberty at any time to redeem the interest charged, or in case of a sale being directed, to purchase the same.

(4)   ...

(5)   This section shall not apply to Scotland.

24.   Rules as to interests and duties of partners subject to special agreement ∧ Should know

The interests of partners in the partnership property and their rights and duties in relation to the partnership shall be determined, subject to any agreement express or implied between the partners, by the following rules:

(1)   All the partners are entitled to share equally in the capital and profits of the business, and must contribute equally towards the losses whether of capital or otherwise sustained by the firm.

(2)   The firm must indemnify every partner in respect of payments made and personal liabilities incurred by him—

(a)   In the ordinary and proper conduct of the business of the firm; or,

(b)   In or about anything necessarily done for the preservation of the business or property of the firm.

(3)   A partner making, for the purpose of the partnership, any actual payment or advance beyond the amount of capital which he has agreed to subscribe, is entitled to interest at the rate of five per cent. per annum from the date of the payment or advance.

(4)   A partner is not entitled, before the ascertainment of profits, to interest on the capital subscribed by him.

(5)   Every partner may take part in the management of the partnership business.

(6)   No partner shall be entitled to remuneration for acting in the partnership business.

(7)   No person may be introduced as a partner without the consent of all existing partners.

(8)   Any difference arising as to ordinary matters connected with the partnership business may be decided by a majority of the partners, but no change may be made in the nature of the partnership business without the consent of all existing partners.

(9)   The partnership books are to be kept at the place of business of the partnership (or the principal place, if there is more than one), and every partner may, when he thinks fit, have access to and inspect and copy any of them.

25.   Expulsion of partner

No majority of the partners can expel any partner unless a power to do so has been conferred by express agreement between the partners.

26.   Retirement from partnership at will

(1)   Where no fixed term has been agreed upon for the duration of the partnership, any partner may determine the partnership at any time on giving notice of his intention so to do to all the other partners.

(2)   Where the partnership has originally been constituted by deed, a notice in writing, signed by the partner giving it, shall be sufficient for this purpose.

27.   Where partnership for term is continued over, continuance on old terms presumed

(1)   Where a partnership entered into for a fixed term is continued after the term has expired, and without any express new agreement, the rights and duties of the partners remain the same as they were at the expiration of the term, so far as is consistent with the incidents of a partnership at will.

(2)   A continuance of the business by the partners or such of them as habitually acted therein during the term, without any settlement or liquidation of the partnership affairs, is presumed to be a continuance of the partnership.

28.   Duty of partners to render accounts, etc

Partners are bound to render true accounts and full information of all things affecting the partnership to any partner or his legal representatives.

29.   Accountability of partners for private profits

(1)   Every partner must account to the firm for any benefit derived by him without the consent of the other partners from any transaction concerning the partnership, or from any use by him of the partnership property name or business connexion.

(2)   This section applies also to transactions undertaken after a partnership has been dissolved by the death of a partner, and before the affairs thereof have been completely wound up, either by any surviving partner or by the representatives of the deceased partner.

30.   Duty of partner not to compete with firm

If a partner, without the consent of the other partners, carries on any business of the same nature as and competing with that of the firm, he must account for and pay over to the firm all profits made by him in that business.

31.   Rights of assignee of share in partnership

(1)   An assignment by any partner of his share in the partnership, either absolute or by way of mortgage or redeemable charge, does not, as against the other partners, entitle the assignee, during the continuance of the partnership, to interfere in the management or administration of the partnership business or affairs, or to require any accounts of the partnership transactions, or to inspect the partnership books, but entitles the assignee only to receive the share of profits to which the assigning partner would otherwise be entitled, and the assignee must accept the account of profits agreed to by the partners.

(2)   In case of a dissolution of the partnership, whether as respects all the partners or as respects the assigning partner, the assignee is entitled to receive the share of the partnership assets to which the assigning partner is entitled as between himself and the other partners, and, for the purpose of ascertaining that share, to an account as from the date of the dissolution.

Dissolution of Partnership, and its consequences

32.   Dissolution by expiration or notice

Subject to any agreement between the partners, a partnership is dissolved—
(a)   If entered into for a fixed term, by the expiration of that term:
(b)   If entered into for a single adventure or undertaking, by the termination of that adventure or undertaking:
(c)   If entered into for an undefined time, by any partner giving notice to the other or others of his intention to dissolve the partnership.

In the last-mentioned case the partnership is dissolved as from the date mentioned in the notice as the date of dissolution, or, if no date is so mentioned, as from the date of the communication of the notice.

33.   Dissolution by bankruptcy, death or charge

(1)   Subject to any agreement between the partners, every partnership is dissolved as regards all the partners by the death or bankruptcy of any partner.

(2)   A partnership may, at the option of the other partners, be dissolved if any partner suffers his share of the partnership property to be charged under this Act for his separate debt.

34.   Dissolution by illegality of partnership

A partnership is in every case dissolved by the happening of any event which makes it unlawful for the business of the firm to be carried on or for the members of the firm to carry it on in partnership.

35.   Dissolution by the Court

On application by a partner the Court may decree a dissolution of the partnership in any of the following cases:
(a)   ...
(b)   When a partner, other than the partner suing, becomes in any other way permanently incapable of performing his part of the partnership contract:
(c)   When a partner, other than the partner suing, has been guilty of such conduct as, in the opinion of the Court, regard being had to the nature of the business, is calculated to prejudicially affect the carrying on of the business:

    (d)   When a partner, other than the partner suing, wilfully or persistently commits a breach of the partnership agreement, or otherwise so conducts himself in matters relating to the partnership business that it is not reasonably practicable for the other partner or partners to carry on the business in partnership with him:

    (e)   When the business of the partnership can only be carried on at a loss:

    (f)   Whenever in any case circumstances have arisen which, in the opinion of the Court, render it just and equitable that the partnership be dissolved.

36.   Rights of persons dealing with firm against apparent members of firm

(1)   Where a person deals with a firm after a change in its constitution he is entitled to treat all apparent members of the old firm as still being members of the firm until he has notice of the change.

(2)   An advertisement in the London Gazette as to a firm whose principal place of business is in England or Wales, in the Edinburgh Gazette as to a firm whose principal place of business is in Scotland, and in the Belfast Gazette as to a firm whose principal place of business is in Ireland, shall be notice as to persons who had not dealings with the firm before the date of the dissolution or change so advertised.

(3)   The estate of a partner who dies, or who becomes bankrupt, or of a partner who, not having been known to the person dealing with the firm to be a partner, retires from the firm, is not liable for partnership debts contracted after the date of the death, bankruptcy, or retirement respectively.

37.   Right of partners to notify dissolution

On the dissolution of a partnership or retirement of a partner any partner may publicly notify the same, and may require the other partner or partners to concur for that purpose in all necessary or proper acts, if any, which cannot be done without his or their concurrence.

38.   Continuing authority of partners for purposes of winding up

After the dissolution of a partnership the authority of each partner to bind the firm, and the other rights and obligations of the partners, continue notwithstanding the dissolution so far as may be necessary to wind up the affairs of the partnership, and to complete transactions begun but unfinished at the time of the dissolution, but not otherwise.

Provided that the firm is in no case bound by the acts of a partner who has become bankrupt; but this proviso does not affect the liability of any person who has after the bankruptcy represented himself or knowingly suffered himself to be represented as a partner of the bankrupt.

39.   Rights of partners as to application of partnership property

On the dissolution of a partnership every partner is entitled, as against the other partners in the firm, and all persons claiming through them in respect of their interests as partners, to have the property of the partnership applied in payment of the debts and liabilities of the firm, and to have the surplus assets after such payment applied in payment of what may be due to the partners respectively after deducting what may be due from them as partners to the firm; and for that purpose any partner or his representatives may on the termination of the partnership apply to the Court to wind up the business and affairs of the firm.

40.   Apportionment of premium where partnership prematurely dissolved

Where one partner has paid a premium to another on entering into a partnership for a fixed term, and the partnership is dissolved before the expiration of that term otherwise than by the death of a partner, the Court may order the repayment of the premium, or of such part thereof as it thinks just, having regard to the terms of the partnership contract and to the length of time during which the partnership has continued; unless

    (a)   the dissolution is, in the judgment of the Court, wholly or chiefly due to the misconduct of the partner who paid the premium; or

    (b)   the partnership has been dissolved by an agreement containing no provision for a return of any part of the premium.

41. **Rights where partnership dissolved for fraud or misrepresentation**

Where a partnership contract is rescinded on the ground of the fraud or misrepresentation of one of the parties thereto, the party entitled to rescind is, without prejudice to any other right, entitled—

(a) to a lien on, or right of retention of, the surplus of the partnership assets, after satisfying the partnership liabilities, for any sum of money paid by him for the purchase of a share in the partnership and for any capital contributed by him, and is

(b) to stand in the place of the creditors of the firm for any payments made by him in respect of the partnership liabilities, and

(c) to be indemnified by the person guilty of the fraud or making the representation against all the debts and liabilities of the firm.

42. **Right of outgoing partner in certain cases to share profits made after dissolution**

(1) Where any member of a firm has died or otherwise ceased to be a partner, and the surviving or continuing partners carry on the business of the firm with its capital or assets without any final settlement of accounts as between the firm and the outgoing partner or his estate, then, in the absence of any agreement to the contrary, the outgoing partner or his estate is entitled at the option of himself or his representatives to such share of the profits made since the dissolution as the Court may find to be attributable to the use of his share of the partnership assets, or to interest at the rate of five per cent. per annum on the amount of his share of the partnership assets.

(2) Provided that where by the partnership contract an option is given to surviving or continuing partners to purchase the interest of a deceased or outgoing partner, and that option is duly exercised, the estate of the deceased partner, or the outgoing partner or his estate, as the case may be, is not entitled to any further or other share of profits; but if any partner assuming to act in exercise of the option does not in all material respects comply with the terms thereof, he is liable to account under the foregoing provisions of this section.

43. **Retiring or deceased partner's share to be a debt**

Subject to any agreement between the partners, the amount due from surviving or continuing partners to an outgoing partner or the representatives of a deceased partner in respect of the out-going or deceased partner's share is a debt accruing at the date of the dissolution or death.

44. **Rule for distribution of assets on final settlement of accounts**

In settling accounts between the partners after a dissolution of partnership, the following rules shall, subject to any agreement, be observed:

(a) Losses, including losses and deficiencies of capital, shall be paid first out of profits, next out of capital, and lastly, if necessary, by the partners individually in the proportion in which they were entitled to share profits:

(b) The assets of the firm including the sums, if any, contributed by the partners to make up losses or deficiencies of capital, shall be applied in the following manner and order:

   1. In paying the debts and liabilities of the firm to persons who are not partners therein:
   2. In paying to each partner rateably what is due from the firm to him for advances as distinguished from capital:
   3. In paying to each partner rateably what is due from the firm to him in respect of capital:
   4. The ultimate residue, if any, shall be divided among the partners in the proportion in which profits are divisible.

Supplemental

45. **Definitions of "court" and "business"**

In this Act, unless the contrary intention appears,—

The expression "court" includes every court and judge having jurisdiction in the case:

The expression "business" includes every trade, occupation, or profession.

46.   **Saving for rules of equity and common law**

The rules of equity and of common law applicable to partnership shall continue in force except so far as they are inconsistent with the express provisions of this Act.

47.   **Provision as to bankruptcy in Scotland**

(1)   In the application of this Act to Scotland the bankruptcy of a firm or of an individual shall mean sequestration under the Bankruptcy (Scotland) Acts, and also in the case of an individual the issue against him of a decree of cessio bonorum.

(2)   Nothing in this Act shall alter the rules of the law of Scotland relating to the bankruptcy of a firm or of the individual partners thereof.

48, 49. ...

50.   **Short title**

This Act may be cited as the Partnership Act 1890.

SCHEDULE

...

Limited Liability Partnerships Act 2000

2000 c. 12

An Act to make provision for limited liability partnerships

[20th July 2000]

Introductory

1.   Limited liability partnerships

(1)   There shall be a new form of legal entity to be known as a limited liability partnership.

(2)   A limited liability partnership is a body corporate (with legal personality separate from that of its members) which is formed by being incorporated under this Act; and—

    (a)   in the following provisions of this Act (except in the phrase "oversea limited liability partnership"), and

    (b)   in any other enactment (except where provision is made to the contrary or the context otherwise requires),

references to a limited liability partnership are to such a body corporate.

(3)   A limited liability partnership has unlimited capacity.

(4)   The members of a limited liability partnership have such liability to contribute to its assets in the event of its being wound up as is provided for by virtue of this Act.

(5)   Accordingly, except as far as otherwise provided by this Act or any other enactment, the law relating to partnerships does not apply to a limited liability partnership.

(6)   The Schedule (which makes provision about the names and registered offices of limited liability partnerships) has effect.

Incorporation

2.   Incorporation document etc

(1)   For a limited liability partnership to be incorporated—

    (a)   two or more persons associated for carrying on a lawful business with a view to profit must have subscribed their names to an incorporation document,

    (b)   there must have been delivered to the registrar either the incorporation document or a copy authenticated in a manner approved by him, and

    (c)   there must have been so delivered a statement in a form approved by the registrar, made by either a solicitor engaged in the formation of the limited liability partnership or anyone who subscribed his name to the incorporation document, that the requirement imposed by paragraph (a) has been complied with.

(2)   The incorporation document must—

    (a)   be in a form approved by the registrar (or as near to such a form as circumstances allow),

    (b)   state the name of the limited liability partnership,

    (c)   state whether the registered office of the limited liability partnership is to be situated in England and Wales, in Wales or in Scotland,

    (d)   state the address of that registered office,

    (e)   state the name and address of each of the persons who are to be members of the limited liability partnership on incorporation, and

    (f)   either specify which of those persons are to be designated members or state that every person who from time to time is a member of the limited liability partnership is a designated member.

(2A)   Where a confidentiality order, made under section 723B of the Companies Act 1985 as applied to limited liability partnerships, is in force in respect of any individual named as a member of a limited liability partnership under subsection (2) that subsection shall have effect as if the reference to the address of the individual were a reference to the address for the time being notified by him under the Limited Liability Partnerships (Particulars of Usual Residential Address) (Confidentiality Orders) Regulations 2002 to any limited liability partnership of which he is a member or if he is not such a member either the address specified in his application for a confidentiality order or the address last notified by him under such a confidentiality order as the case may be.

(2B)   Where the incorporation document or a copy of such delivered under this section includes an address specified in reliance on subsection (2A) there shall be delivered with it or the copy of it a statement in a form approved by the registrar containing particulars of the usual residential address of the member whose address is so specified.

(3)   If a person makes a false statement under subsection (1)(c) which he—
    (a)   knows to be false, or
    (b)   does not believe to be true,
    he commits an offence.

(4)   A person guilty of an offence under subsection (3) is liable—
    (a)   on summary conviction, to imprisonment for a period not exceeding six months or a fine not exceeding the statutory maximum, or to both, or
    (b)   on conviction on indictment, to imprisonment for a period not exceeding two years or a fine, or to both.

3.   Incorporation by registration

(1)   When the requirements imposed by paragraphs (b) and (c) of subsection (1) of section 2 have been complied with, the registrar shall retain the incorporation document or copy delivered to him and, unless the requirement imposed by paragraph (a) of that subsection has not been complied with, he shall—
    (a)   register the incorporation document or copy, and
    (b)   give a certificate that the limited liability partnership is incorporated by the name specified in the incorporation document.

(2)   The registrar may accept the statement delivered under paragraph (c) of subsection (1) of section 2 as sufficient evidence that the requirement imposed by paragraph (a) of that subsection has been complied with.

(3)   The certificate shall either be signed by the registrar or be authenticated by his official seal.

(4)   The certificate is conclusive evidence that the requirements of section 2 are complied with and that the limited liability partnership is incorporated by the name specified in the incorporation document.

Membership

4.   Members

(1)   On the incorporation of a limited liability partnership its members are the persons who subscribed their names to the incorporation document (other than any who have died or been dissolved).

(2)   Any other person may become a member of a limited liability partnership by and in accordance with an agreement with the existing members.

(3)   A person may cease to be a member of a limited liability partnership (as well as by death or dissolution) in accordance with an agreement with the other members or, in the absence of agreement with the other members as to cessation of membership, by giving reasonable notice to the other members.

(4)   A member of a limited liability partnership shall not be regarded for any purpose as employed by the limited liability partnership unless, if he and the other members were partners in a partnership, he would be regarded for that purpose as employed by the partnership.

5.   Relationship of members etc

(1)   Except as far as otherwise provided by this Act or any other enactment, the mutual rights and duties of the members of a limited liability partnership, and the mutual rights and duties of a limited liability partnership and its members, shall be governed—

(a) by agreement between the members, or between the limited liability partnership and its members, or

(b) in the absence of agreement as to any matter, by any provision made in relation to that matter by regulations under section 15(c).

(2) An agreement made before the incorporation of a limited liability partnership between the persons who subscribe their names to the incorporation document may impose obligations on the limited liability partnership (to take effect at any time after its incorporation).

6. Members as agents

(1) Every member of a limited liability partnership is the agent of the limited liability partnership.

(2) But a limited liability partnership is not bound by anything done by a member in dealing with a person if—

(a) the member in fact has no authority to act for the limited liability partnership by doing that thing, and

(b) the person knows that he has no authority or does not know or believe him to be a member of the limited liability partnership.

(3) Where a person has ceased to be a member of a limited liability partnership, the former member is to be regarded (in relation to any person dealing with the limited liability partnership) as still being a member of the limited liability partnership unless—

(a) the person has notice that the former member has ceased to be a member of the limited liability partnership, or

(b) notice that the former member has ceased to be a member of the limited liability partnership has been delivered to the registrar.

(4) Where a member of a limited liability partnership is liable to any person (other than another member of the limited liability partnership) as a result of a wrongful act or omission of his in the course of the business of the limited liability partnership or with its authority, the limited liability partnership is liable to the same extent as the member.

7. Ex-members

(1) This section applies where a member of a limited liability partnership has either ceased to be a member or—

(a) has died,

(b) has become bankrupt or had his estate sequestrated or has been wound up,

(c) has granted a trust deed for the benefit of his creditors, or

(d) has assigned the whole or any part of his share in the limited liability partnership (absolutely or by way of charge or security).

(2) In such an event the former member or—

(a) his personal representative,

(b) his trustee in bankruptcy or permanent or interim trustee (within the meaning of the Bankruptcy (Scotland) Act 1985) or liquidator,

(c) his trustee under the trust deed for the benefit of his creditors, or

(d) his assignee,

may not interfere in the management or administration of any business or affairs of the limited liability partnership.

(3) But subsection (2) does not affect any right to receive an amount from the limited liability partnership in that event.

8. Designated members

(1) If the incorporation document specifies who are to be designated members—

(a) they are designated members on incorporation, and

(b) any member may become a designated member by and in accordance with an agreement with the other members,

and a member may cease to be a designated member in accordance with an agreement with the other members.

(2)   But if there would otherwise be no designated members, or only one, every member is a designated member.

(3)   If the incorporation document states that every person who from time to time is a member of the limited liability partnership is a designated member, every member is a designated member.

(4)   A limited liability partnership may at any time deliver to the registrar—

    (a)   notice that specified members are to be designated members, or

    (b)   notice that every person who from time to time is a member of the limited liability partnership is a designated member,

and, once it is delivered, subsection (1) (apart from paragraph (a)) and subsection (2), or subsection (3), shall have effect as if that were stated in the incorporation document.

(5)   A notice delivered under subsection (4)—

    (a)   shall be in a form approved by the registrar, and

    (b)   shall be signed by a designated member of the limited liability partnership or authenticated in a manner approved by the registrar.

(6)   A person ceases to be a designated member if he ceases to be a member.

9.   Registration of membership changes

(1)   A limited liability partnership must ensure that—

    (a)   where a person becomes or ceases to be a member or designated member, notice is delivered to the registrar within fourteen days, and

    (b)   where there is any change in the name or address of a member, notice is delivered to the registrar within 28 days.

(2)   Where all the members from time to time of a limited liability partnership are designated members, subsection (1)(a) does not require notice that a person has become or ceased to be a designated member as well as a member.

(3)   A notice delivered under subsection (1)—

    (a)   shall be in a form approved by the registrar, and

    (b)   shall be signed by a designated member of the limited liability partnership or authenticated in a manner approved by the registrar,

and, if it relates to a person becoming a member or designated member, shall contain a statement that he consents to becoming a member or designated member signed by him or authenticated in a manner approved by the registrar.

(3A)   Where a confidentiality order under section 723B of the Companies Act 1985 as applied to limited liability partnerships is made in respect of an existing member, the limited liability partnership must ensure that there is delivered within 28 days to the registrar notice in a form approved by the registrar containing the address for the time being notified to it by the member under the Limited Liability Partnerships (Particulars of Usual Residential Address) (Confidentiality Orders) Regulations 2002.

(3B)   Where such a confidentiality order is in force in respect of a member the requirement in subsection (1)(b) to notify a change in the address of a member shall be read in relation to that member as a requirement to deliver to the registrar, within 28 days, notice of—

    (a)   any change in the usual residential address of that member; and

    (b)   any change in the address for the time being notified to the limited liability partnership by the member under the Limited Liability Partnerships (Particulars of Usual Residential Address) (Confidentiality Orders) Regulations 2002,

and the registrar may approve different forms for the notification of each kind of address.

(4)   If a limited liability partnership fails to comply with subsection (1), the partnership and every designated member commits an offence.

(5)   But it is a defence for a designated member charged with an offence under subsection (4) to prove that he took all reasonable steps for securing that subsection (1) was complied with.

(6)   A person guilty of an offence under subsection (4) is liable on summary conviction to a fine not exceeding level 5 on the standard scale.

Taxation

10, 11. ...

12.   **Stamp duty**

(1)   Stamp duty shall not be chargeable on an instrument by which property is conveyed or transferred by a person to a limited liability partnership in connection with its incorporation within the period of one year beginning with the date of incorporation if the following two conditions are satisfied.

(2)   The first condition is that at the relevant time the person—

   (a)   is a partner in a partnership comprised of all the persons who are or are to be members of the limited liability partnership (and no-one else), or

   (b)   holds the property conveyed or transferred as nominee or bare trustee for one or more of the partners in such a partnership.

(3)   The second condition is that—

   (a)   the proportions of the property conveyed or transferred to which the persons mentioned in subsection (2)(a) are entitled immediately after the conveyance or transfer are the same as those to which they were entitled at the relevant time, or

   (b)   none of the differences in those proportions has arisen as part of a scheme or arrangement of which the main purpose, or one of the main purposes, is avoidance of liability to any duty or tax.

(4)   For the purposes of subsection (2) a person holds property as bare trustee for a partner if the partner has the exclusive right (subject only to satisfying any outstanding charge, lien or other right of the trustee to resort to the property for payment of duty, taxes, costs or other outgoings) to direct how the property shall be dealt with.

(5)   In this section "the relevant time" means—

   (a)   if the person who conveyed or transferred the property to the limited liability partnership acquired the property after its incorporation, immediately after he acquired the property, and

   (b)   in any other case, immediately before its incorporation.

(6)   An instrument in respect of which stamp duty is not chargeable by virtue of subsection (1) shall not be taken to be duly stamped unless—

   (a)   it has, in accordance with section 12 of the Stamp Act 1891, been stamped with a particular stamp denoting that it is not chargeable with any duty or that it is duly stamped, or

   (b)   it is stamped with the duty to which it would be liable apart from that subsection.

13.   ...

Regulations

14.   **Insolvency and winding up**

(1)   Regulations shall make provision about the insolvency and winding up of limited liability partnerships by applying or incorporating, with such modifications as appear appropriate, Parts I to IV, VI and VII of the Insolvency Act 1986.

(2)   Regulations may make other provision about the insolvency and winding up of limited liability partnerships, and provision about the insolvency and winding up of oversea limited liability partnerships, by—

   (a)   applying or incorporating, with such modifications as appear appropriate, any law relating to the insolvency or winding up of companies or other corporations which would not otherwise have effect in relation to them, or

   (b)   providing for any law relating to the insolvency or winding up of companies or other corporations which would otherwise have effect in relation to them not to apply to them or to apply to them with such modifications as appear appropriate.

(3)   In this Act "oversea limited liability partnership" means a body incorporated or otherwise established outside Great Britain and having such connection with Great Britain, and such other features, as regulations may prescribe.

15.   Application of company law etc

Regulations may make provision about limited liability partnerships and oversea limited liability partnerships (not being provision about insolvency or winding up) by—

(a)   applying or incorporating, with such modifications as appear appropriate, any law relating to companies or other corporations which would not otherwise have effect in relation to them,

(b)   providing for any law relating to companies or other corporations which would otherwise have effect in relation to them not to apply to them or to apply to them with such modifications as appear appropriate, or

(c)   applying or incorporating, with such modifications as appear appropriate, any law relating to partnerships.

16.   Consequential amendments

(1)   Regulations may make in any enactment such amendments or repeals as appear appropriate in consequence of this Act or regulations made under it.

(2)   The regulations may, in particular, make amendments and repeals affecting companies or other corporations or partnerships

17.   General

(1)   In this Act "regulations" means regulations made by the Secretary of State by statutory instrument.

(2)   Regulations under this Act may in particular—

(a)   make provisions for dealing with non-compliance with any of the regulations (including the creation of criminal offences),

(b)   impose fees (which shall be paid into the Consolidated Fund), and

(c)   provide for the exercise of functions by persons prescribed by the regulations.

(3)   Regulations under this Act may—

(a)   contain any appropriate consequential, incidental, supplementary or transitional provisions or savings, and

(b)   make different provision for different purposes.

(4)   No regulations to which this subsection applies shall be made unless a draft of the statutory instrument containing the regulations (whether or not together with other provisions) has been laid before, and approved by a resolution of, each House of Parliament.

(5)   Subsection (4) applies to—

(a)   regulations under section 14(2) not consisting entirely of the application or incorporation (with or without modifications) of provisions contained in or made under the Insolvency Act 1986,

(b)   regulations under section 15 not consisting entirely of the application or incorporation (with or without modifications) of provisions contained in or made under Part I, Chapter VIII of Part V, Part VII, Parts XI to XIII, Parts XVI to XVIII, Part XX or Parts XXIV to XXVI of the Companies Act 1985,

(c)   regulations under section 14 or 15 making provision about oversea limited liability partnerships, and

(d)   regulations under section 16.

(6)   A statutory instrument containing regulations under this Act shall (unless a draft of it has been approved by a resolution of each House of Parliament) be subject to annulment in pursuance of a resolution of either House of Parliament.

Supplementary

18.   Interpretation

In this Act—

"address", in relation to a member of a limited liability partnership, means—

(a)   if an individual, his usual residential address, and

(b)   if a corporation or Scottish firm, its registered or principal office,

"business" includes every trade, profession and occupation,

"designated member" shall be construed in accordance with section 8,

"enactment" includes subordinate legislation (within the meaning of the Interpretation Act 1978),

"incorporation document" shall be construed in accordance with section 2,

"limited liability partnership" has the meaning given by section 1(2),

"member" shall be construed in accordance with section 4,

"modifications" includes additions and omissions,

"name", in relation to a member of a limited liability partnership, means—

(a)   if an individual, his forename and surname (or, in the case of a peer or other person usually known by a title, his title instead of or in addition to either or both his forename and surname), and

(b)   if a corporation or Scottish firm, its corporate or firm name,

"oversea limited liability partnership" has the meaning given by section 14(3),

"the registrar" means—

(a)   if the registered office of the limited liability partnership is, or is to be, situated in England and Wales or in Wales, the registrar or other officer performing under the Companies Act 1985 the duty of registration of companies in England and Wales, and

(b)   if its registered office is, or is to be, situated in Scotland, the registrar or other officer performing under that Act the duty of registration of companies in Scotland, and

"regulations" has the meaning given by section 17(1).

19.   Commencement, extent and short title

(1)   The preceding provisions of this Act shall come into force on such day as the Secretary of State may by order made by statutory instrument appoint; and different days may be appointed for different purposes.

(2)   The Secretary of State may by order made by statutory instrument make any transitional provisions and savings which appear appropriate in connection with the coming into force of any provision of this Act.

(3)   For the purposes of the Scotland Act 1998 this Act shall be taken to be a pre-commencement enactment within the meaning of that Act.

(4)   Apart from sections 10 to 13 (and this section), this Act does not extend to Northern Ireland.

(5)   This Act may be cited as the Limited Liability Partnerships Act 2000.

SCHEDULE

NAMES AND REGISTERED OFFICES

Section 1

PART I

NAMES

1.   ...

Name to indicate status

2.—   (1)   The name of a limited liability partnership must end with—
            (a)   the expression "limited liability partnership", or
            (b)   the abbreviation "llp" or "LLP".
        (2)   But if the incorporation document for a limited liability partnership states that the registered office is to be situated in Wales, its name must end with—

     (a)   one of the expressions "limited liability partnership" and "partneriaeth atebolrwydd cyfyngedig", or

     (b)   one of the abbreviations "llp", "LLP", "pac" and "PAC".

Registration of names

3.—   (1)   A limited liability partnership shall not be registered by a name—

     (a)   which includes, otherwise than at the end of the name, either of the expressions "limited liability partnership" and "partneriaeth atebolrwydd cyfyngedig" or any of the abbreviations "llp", "LLP", "pac" and "PAC",

     (b)   which is the same as a name appearing in the index kept under section 714(1) of the Companies Act 1985,

     (c)   the use of which by the limited liability partnership would in the opinion of the Secretary of State constitute a criminal offence, or

     (d)   which in the opinion of the Secretary of State is offensive.

   (2)   Except with the approval of the Secretary of State, a limited liability partnership shall not be registered by a name which—

     (a)   in the opinion of the Secretary of State would be likely to give the impression that it is connected in any way with Her Majesty's Government or with any local authority, or

     (b)   includes any word or expression for the time being specified in regulations under section 29 of the Companies Act 1985 (names needing approval),

and in paragraph (a) "local authority" means any local authority within the meaning of the Local Government Act 1972 or the Local Government etc (Scotland) Act 1994, the Common Council of the City of London or the Council of the Isles of Scilly.

Change of name

4.—   (1)   A limited liability partnership may change its name at any time.

   (2)   Where a limited liability partnership has been registered by a name which—

     (a)   is the same as or, in the opinion of the Secretary of State, too like a name appearing at the time of registration in the index kept under section 714(1) of the Companies Act 1985, or

     (b)   is the same as or, in the opinion of the Secretary of State, too like a name which should have appeared in the index at that time,

the Secretary of State may within twelve months of that time in writing direct the limited liability partnership to change its name within such period as he may specify.

   (3)   If it appears to the Secretary of State—

     (a)   that misleading information has been given for the purpose of the registration of a limited liability partnership by a particular name, or

     (b)   that undertakings or assurances have been given for that purpose and have not been fulfilled,

he may, within five years of the date of its registration by that name, in writing direct the limited liability partnership to change its name within such period as he may specify.

   (4)   If in the Secretary of State's opinion the name by which a limited liability partnership is registered gives so misleading an indication of the nature of its activities as to be likely to cause harm to the public, he may in writing direct the limited liability partnership to change its name within such period as he may specify.

   (5)   But the limited liability partnership may, within three weeks from the date of the direction apply to the court to set it aside and the court may set the direction aside or confirm it and, if it confirms it, shall specify the period within which it must be complied with.

   (6)   In sub-paragraph (5) "the court" means—

     (a)   if the registered office of the limited liability partnership is situated in England and Wales or in Wales, the High Court, and

     (b)   if it is situated in Scotland, the Court of Session.

(7)   Where a direction has been given under sub-paragraph (2), (3) or (4) specifying a period within which a limited liability partnership is to change its name, the Secretary of State may at any time before that period ends extend it by a further direction in writing.

(8)   If a limited liability partnership fails to comply with a direction under this paragraph—
    (a)   the limited liability partnership, and
    (b)   any designated member in default,
    commits an offence.

(9)   A person guilty of an offence under sub-paragraph (8) is liable on summary conviction to a fine not exceeding level 3 on the standard scale.

Notification of change of name

5.—   (1)   Where a limited liability partnership changes its name it shall deliver notice of the change to the registrar.

(2)   A notice delivered under sub-paragraph (1)—
    (a)   shall be in a form approved by the registrar, and
    (b)   shall be signed by a designated member of the limited liability partnership or authenticated in a manner approved by the registrar.

(3)   Where the registrar receives a notice under sub-paragraph (2) he shall (unless the new name is one by which a limited liability partnership may not be registered)—
    (a)   enter the new name in the index kept under section 714(1) of the Companies Act 1985, and
    (b)   issue a certificate of the change of name.

(4)   The change of name has effect from the date on which the certificate is issued.

Effect of change of name

6.   A change of name by a limited liability partnership does not—
    (a)   affect any of its rights or duties,
    (b)   render defective any legal proceedings by or against it,
    and any legal proceedings that might have been commenced or continued against it by its former name may be commenced or continued against it by its new name.

Improper use of "limited liability partnership" etc

7.—   (1)   If any person carries on a business under a name or title which includes as the last words—
    (a)   the expression "limited liability partnership" or "partneriaeth atebolrwydd cyfyngedig", or
    (b)   any contraction or imitation of either of those expressions,
    that person, unless a limited liability partnership or oversea limited liability partnership, commits an offence.

(2)   A person guilty of an offence under sub-paragraph (1) is liable on summary conviction to a fine not exceeding level 3 on the standard scale.

Similarity of names

8.   In determining for the purposes of this Part whether one name is the same as another there are to be disregarded—
    (1)   the definite article as the first word of the name,
    (2)   any of the following (or their Welsh equivalents or abbreviations of them or their Welsh equivalents) at the end of the name—
        "limited liability partnership",
        "company",
        "and company",
        "company limited",
        "and company limited",
        "limited",

"unlimited",

"public limited company", ...

"community interest company",

"community interest public limited company",

"investment company with variable capital", and

"open-ended investment company", and

(3)   type and case of letters, accents, spaces between letters and punctuation marks,

and "and" and "&" are to be taken as the same.

PART II
REGISTERED OFFICES

Situation of registered office

9.—   (1)   A limited liability partnership shall—

   (a)   at all times have a registered office situated in England and Wales or in Wales, or

   (b)   at all times have a registered office situated in Scotland,

to which communications and notices may be addressed.

(2)   On the incorporation of a limited liability partnership the situation of its registered office shall be that stated in the incorporation document.

(3)   Where the registered office of a limited liability partnership is situated in Wales, but the incorporation document does not state that it is to be situated in Wales (as opposed to England and Wales), the limited liability partnership may deliver notice to the registrar stating that its registered office is to be situated in Wales.

(4)   A notice delivered under sub-paragraph (3)—

   (a)   shall be in a form approved by the registrar, and

   (b)   shall be signed by a designated member of the limited liability partnership or authenticated in a manner approved by the registrar.

Change of registered office

10.—   (1)   A limited liability partnership may change its registered office by delivering notice of the change to the registrar.

(2)   A notice delivered under sub-paragraph (1)—

   (a)   shall be in a form approved by the registrar, and

   (b)   shall be signed by a designated member of the limited liability partnership or authenticated in a manner approved by the registrar.

Note. The italicized entries in paragraph 8(2) are inserted by the Companies (Audit, Investigations and Community Enterprise) Act 2004, s. 33(6), Sch. 6, para. 10, as from 1 July 2005.

Limited Liability Partnerships Regulations 2001

S.I. 2001/1090

PART I

CITATION, COMMENCEMENT AND INTERPRETATION

1.   **Citation and commencement**

These Regulations may be cited as the Limited Liability Partnerships Regulations 2001 and shall come into force on 6th April 2001.

2.   **Interpretation**

In these Regulations—

"the 1985 Act" means the Companies Act 1985;

"the 1986 Act" means the Insolvency Act 1986;

"the 2000 Act" means the Financial Services and Markets Act 2000;

"devolved", in relation to the provisions of the 1986 Act, means the provisions of the 1986 Act which are listed in Schedule 4 and, in their application to Scotland, concern wholly or partly, matters which are set out in Section C 2 of Schedule 5 to the Scotland Act 1998 as being exceptions to the reservations made in that Act in the field of insolvency;

"limited liability partnership agreement", in relation to a limited liability partnership, means any agreement express or implied between the members of the limited liability partnership or between the limited liability partnership and the members of the limited liability partnership which determines the mutual rights and duties of the members, and their rights and duties in relation to the limited liability partnership;

"the principal Act" means the Limited Liability Partnerships Act 2000; and

"shadow member", in relation to limited liability partnerships, means a person in accordance with whose directions or instructions the members of the limited liability partnership are accustomed to act (but so that a person is not deemed a shadow member by reason only that the members of the limited partnership act on advice given by him in a professional capacity).

PART II

ACCOUNTS AND AUDIT

3.   **Application of the accounts and audit provisions of the 1985 Act to limited liability partnerships**

(1)   Subject to paragraph (2), the provisions of Part VII of the 1985 Act (Accounts and Audit) shall apply to limited liability partnerships.

(2)   The enactments referred to in paragraph (1) shall apply to limited liability partnerships, except where the context otherwise requires, with the following modifications—

(a)   references to a company shall include references to a limited liability partnership;

(b)   references to a director or to an officer of a company shall include references to a member of a limited liability partnership;

(c)   references to other provisions of the 1985 Act and to provisions of the Insolvency Act 1986 shall include references to those provisions as they apply to limited liability partnerships in accordance with Parts III and IV of these Regulations;

(d)   the modifications set out in Schedule 1 to these Regulations; and

(e)   such further modifications as the context requires for the purpose of giving effect to those provisions as applied by this Part of these Regulations.

PART III

COMPANIES ACT 1985 AND COMPANY DIRECTORS DISQUALIFICATION ACT 1986

4.   Application of the remainder of the provisions of the 1985 Act and of the provisions of the Company Directors Disqualification Act 1986 to limited liability partnerships

(1)   The provisions of the 1985 Act specified in the first column of Part I of Schedule 2 to these Regulations shall apply to limited liability partnerships, except where the context otherwise requires, with the following modifications—
(a)   references to a company shall include references to a limited liability partnership;
(b)   references to the Companies Acts shall include references to the principal Act and regulations made thereunder;
(c)   references to the Insolvency Act 1986 shall include references to that Act as it applies to limited liability partnerships by virtue of Part IV of these Regulations;
(d)   references in a provision of the 1985 Act to other provisions of that Act shall include references to those other provisions as they apply to limited liability partnerships by virtue of these Regulations;
(e)   references to the memorandum of association of a company shall include references to the incorporation document of a limited liability partnership;
(f)   references to a shadow director shall include references to a shadow member;
(g)   references to a director of a company or to an officer of a company shall include references to a member of a limited liability partnership;
(h)   the modifications, if any, specified in the second column of Part I of Schedule 2 opposite the provision specified in the first column; and
(i)   such further modifications as the context requires for the purpose of giving effect to that legislation as applied by these Regulations.

(2)   The provisions of the Company Director Disqualification Act 1986 shall apply to limited liability partnerships, except where the context otherwise requires, with the following modifications—
(a)   references to a company shall include references to a limited liability partnership;
(b)   references to the Companies Acts shall include references to the principal Act and regulations made thereunder;
(c)   references to the Insolvency Act 1986 shall include references to that Act as it applies to limited liability partnerships by virtue of Part IV of these Regulations;
(d)   references in a provision of the 1985 Act to other provisions of that Act shall include references to those other provisions as they apply to limited liability partnerships by virtue of these Regulations;
(e)   references to the memorandum of association of a company shall include references to the incorporation document of a limited liability partnership;
(f)   references to a shadow director shall include references to a shadow member;
(g)   references to a director of a company or to an officer of a company shall include references to a member of a limited liability partnership;
(h)   the modifications, if any, specified in the second column of Part II of Schedule 2 opposite the provision specified in the first column; and
(i)   such further modifications as the context requires for the purpose of giving effect to that legislation as applied by these Regulations.

PART IV

WINDING UP AND INSOLVENCY

5.   Application of the 1986 Act to limited liability partnerships

(1)   Subject to paragraphs (2) and (3), the following provisions of the 1986 Act, shall apply to limited liability partnerships—

    (a)   Parts I, II, III, IV, VI and VII of the First Group of Parts (company insolvency; companies winding up),

    (b)   the Third Group of Parts (miscellaneous matters bearing on both company and individual insolvency; general interpretation; final provisions).

(2)   The provisions of the 1986 Act referred to in paragraph (1) shall apply to limited liability partnerships, except where the context otherwise requires, with the following modifications—

    (a)   references to a company shall include references to a limited liability partnership;

    (b)   references to a director or to an officer of a company shall include references to a member of a limited liability partnership;

    (c)   references to a shadow director shall include references to a shadow member;

    (d)   references to the 1985 Act, the Company Directors Disqualification Act 1986, the Companies Act 1989 or to any provisions of those Acts or to any provisions of the 1986 Act shall include references to those Acts or provisions as they apply to limited liability partnerships by virtue of the principal Act;

    (e)   references to the memorandum of association of a company and to the articles of association of a company shall include references to the limited liability partnership agreement of a limited liability partnership;

    (f)   the modifications set out in Schedule 3 to these Regulations; and

    (g)   such further modifications as the context requires for the purpose of giving effect to that legislation as applied by these Regulations.

(3)   In the application of this regulation to Scotland, the provisions of the 1986 Act referred to in paragraph (1) shall not include the provisions listed in Schedule 4 to the extent specified in that Schedule.

PART V

FINANCIAL SERVICES AND MARKETS

6.   Application of provisions contained in Parts XV and XXIV of the 2000 Act to limited liability partnerships

(1)   Subject to paragraph (2), sections 215(3),(4) and (6), 356, 359(1) to (4), 361 to 365, 367, 370 and 371 of the 2000 Act shall apply to limited liability partnerships.

(2)   The provisions of the 2000 Act referred to in paragraph (1) shall apply to limited liability partnerships, except where the context otherwise requires, with the following modifications—

    (a)   references to a company shall include references to a limited liability partnership;

    (b)   references to body shall include references to a limited liability partnership; and

    (c)   references to the 1985 Act, the 1986 Act or to any of the provisions of those Acts shall include references to those Acts or provisions as they apply to limited liability partnerships by virtue of the principal Act.

PART VI

DEFAULT PROVISION

7.   Default provision for limited liability partnerships

The mutual rights and duties of the members and the mutual rights and duties of the limited liability partnership and the members shall be determined, subject to the provisions of the general law and to the terms of any limited liability partnership agreement, by the following rules:

(1)   All the members of a limited liability partnership are entitled to share equally in the capital and profits of the limited liability partnership.

(2)   The limited liability partnership must indemnify each member in respect of payments made and personal liabilities incurred by him—

    (a)   in the ordinary and proper conduct of the business of the limited liability partnership; or

    (b)   in or about anything necessarily done for the preservation of the business or property of the limited liability partnership.

(3)   Every member may take part in the management of the limited liability partnership.

(4)   No member shall be entitled to remuneration for acting in the business or management of the limited liability partnership.

(5)   No person may be introduced as a member or voluntarily assign an interest in a limited liability partnership without the consent of all existing members.

(6)   Any difference arising as to ordinary matters connected with the business of the limited liability partnership may be decided by a majority of the members, but no change may be made in the nature of the business of the limited liability partnership without the consent of all the members.

(7)   The books and records of the limited liability partnership are to be made available for inspection at the registered office of the limited liability partnership or at such other place as the members think fit and every member of the limited liability partnership may when he thinks fit have access to and inspect and copy any of them.

(8)   Each member shall render true accounts and full information of all things affecting the limited liability partnership to any member or his legal representatives.

(9)   If a member, without the consent of the limited liability partnership, carries on any business of the same nature as and competing with the limited liability partnership, he must account for and pay over to the limited liability partnership all profits made by him in that business.

(10)   Every member must account to the limited liability partnership for any benefit derived by him without the consent of the limited liability partnership from any transaction concerning the limited liability partnership, or from any use by him of the property of the limited liability partnership, name or business connection.

8.   Expulsion

No majority of the members can expel any member unless a power to do so has been conferred by express agreement between the members.

PART VII

MISCELLANEOUS

9.   General and consequential amendments

(1)   Subject to paragraph (2), the enactments mentioned in Schedule 5 shall have effect subject to the amendments specified in that Schedule.

(2)   In the application of this regulation to Scotland—

    (a)   paragraph 15 of Schedule 5 which amends section 110 of the 1986 Act shall not extend to Scotland; and

(b)   paragraph 22 of Schedule 5 which applies to limited liability partnerships the culpable officer provisions in existing primary legislation shall not extend to Scotland insofar as it relates to matters which have not been reserved by Schedule 5 to the Scotland Act 1998.

10.   Application of subordinate legislation

(1)   The subordinate legislation specified in Schedule 6 shall apply as from time to time in force to limited liability partnerships and—

(a)   in the case of the subordinate legislation listed in Part I of that Schedule with such modifications as the context requires for the purpose of giving effect to the provisions of the Companies Act 1985 which are applied by these Regulations;

(b)   in the case of the subordinate legislation listed in Part II of that Schedule with such modifications as the context requires for the purpose of giving effect to the provisions of the Insolvency Act 1986 which are applied by these Regulations; and

(c)   in the case of the subordinate legislation listed in Part III of that Schedule with such modifications as the context requires for the purpose of giving effect to the provisions of the Business Names Act 1985 and the Company Directors Disqualification Act 1986 which are applied by these Regulations.

(2)   In the case of any conflict between any provision of the subordinate legislation applied by paragraph (1) and any provision of these Regulations, the latter shall prevail.

SCHEDULES

SCHEDULE 1

MODIFICATIONS TO PROVISIONS OF PART VII OF THE 1985 ACT APPLIED BY THESE REGULATIONS

Regulation 3

Provision of Part VII	Modification
Section 222 (Where and for how long accounting records to be kept)	
subsection (5)	In paragraph (a), omit the words "in the case of a private company," and the word "and" Omit paragraph (b).
Section 224 (accounting reference periods and accounting reference date)	
subsections (2) and (3)	Omit subsections (2) and (3).
subsection (3A)	Omit the words "incorporated on or after 1st April 1996".
Section 225 (alteration of accounting reference date)	
subsection (5)	For the words "laying and delivering accounts and reports" substitute "delivering the accounts and the auditors' report".
Section 228 (exemption for parent companies included in accounts of larger group)	Omit subsection (4).
Section 231 (disclosure required in notes to accounts: related undertakings)	
subsection (3)	Omit the words from "This subsection" to the end.
Section 232 (disclosure in notes to accounts: emoluments etc of directors and others)	Omit section 232, save that Schedule 6 shall apply for the purpose of paragraph 56A of Schedule 4, as inserted by this Schedule.

Provision of Part VII	Modification
Section 233 (approval and signing of accounts)	
subsection (1)	For subsection (1) substitute— "(1) A limited liability partnership's annual accounts shall be approved by the members, and shall be signed on behalf of all the members by a designated member.".
subsection (3)	Omit the words from "laid before" to "otherwise", and for the words "the board" substitute "the members of the limited liability partnership".
subsection (4)	For the words "the board by a director of the company" substitute "the members by a designated member".
subsection (6)	In paragraph (a), omit the words "laid before the company, or otherwise".
Sections 234 (duty to prepare directors' report) and 234A (approval and signing of directors' report)	Omit sections 234 and 234A.
Section 235 (auditors' report)	
subsection (1)	For subsection (1) substitute— "(1) The limited liability partnership's annual accounts shall be submitted to its auditors, who shall make a report on them to the members of the limited liability partnership.".
subsection (3)	Omit subsection (3).
Section 236 (signature of auditors' report)	
subsection (2)	For subsection (2) substitute— "(2) Every copy of the auditors' report which is circulated, published or issued shall state the names of the auditors.".
subsection (4)	In paragraph (a) omit the words "laid before the company, or otherwise".
Section 237 (duties of auditors)	
subsection (4)	Omit subsection (4).
Section 238 (persons entitled to receive copies of accounts and report)	
subsection (1)	For subsection (1) substitute— "(1) A copy of the limited liability partnership's annual accounts, together with a copy of the auditors' report on those accounts, shall be sent to every member of the limited liability partnership and to every holder of the limited liability partnership's debentures, within one month of their being signed in accordance with section 233(1) and in any event not later than 10 months after the end of the relevant accounting reference period."
subsection (2)	(a) In paragraph (a), omit the words from "who is" to "meetings and", and (b) in paragraph (b) and (c), omit the words "shares or" in both places where they occur.
subsections (3) and (4)	Omit subsections (3) and (4).
subsection (4A)	Omit the words ", of the directors' report".
subsections (4C) to (4E)	Omit subsections (4C) to (4E).

Provision of Part VII	Modification
Section 239 (right to demand copies of accounts and report)	
subsection (1)	Omit the words "and directors' report".
subsection (2B)	Omit subsection (2B).
Section 240 (requirements in connection with publication of accounts)	
subsection (1)	Omit the words from "or, as the case may be," to the end.
subsection (3)	(a) In paragraph (c) omit the words from "and, if no such report has been made", to "any financial year", (b) in paragraph (d), omit the words "or whether any report made for the purposes of section 249A(2) was qualified", and (c) omit the words "or any report made for the purposes of section 249A(2)".
Section 241 (accounts and report to be laid before general meeting)	Omit section 241.
Section 242 (accounts and report to be delivered to registrar)	
subsection (1)	(a) For the words "The directors of a company" substitute "The designated members of a limited liability partnership", (b) omit the words "a copy of the directors' report for that year and", (c) for the words "or reports" substitute "or that report", and (d) for the words "the directors shall annex" substitute "the designated members shall annex".
subsection (2)	(a) For the words "laying and delivering accounts and reports", substitute "delivering the accounts and the auditors' report", and (b) for the word "director" substitute the words "designated member".
subsection (3)	For the words "the directors" in each place where they occur substitute the words "the designated members".
subsection (4)	For the words "laying and delivering accounts and reports", substitute "delivering the accounts and the auditors' report".
Section 242A (civil penalty for failure to deliver accounts)	
subsection (1)	(a) For the words "laying and delivering accounts and reports" substitute "delivering the accounts and the auditors' report", and (b) for the words "the directors" substitute "the designated members".
subsection (2)	(a) For the words "laying and delivering accounts and reports" substitute "delivering the accounts and the auditors' report",

Provision of Part VII	**Modification**
	(b) omit the words ,"and whether the company is a public or private company,",
	(c) omit the heading "*Public company*" and all entries under it, and
	(d) for the heading "*Private company*" substitute "*Amount of penalty*".
Section 242B (delivery and publications of accounts in euros)	
subsection (2)	For the words "the directors of a company" substitute "the designated members of a limited liability partnership".
Section 243 (accounts of subsidiary undertakings to be appended in certain cases)	
subsection (4)	For the words "the directors" substitute "the designated members".
Section 244 (period allowed for delivering accounts and report)	
subsection (1)	For subsection (1), substitute the following— "(1) The period allowed for delivering the accounts and the auditors' report is 10 months after the end of the relevant accounting reference period. This is subject to the following provisions of this section."
subsection (2)	In paragraph (a), omit the words "or 7 months, as the case may be,".
subsection (3)	(a) For the words "the directors" substitute "the designated members", and (b) in paragraph (b), for the words "laying and delivering accounts and reports" substitute "delivering the accounts and the auditors' report".
subsection (4)	For the words "laying and delivering accounts" substitute "delivering the accounts and the auditors' report".
Section 245 (voluntary revision of accounts)	
subsection (1)	Omit the words ,"or any directors' report," and the words "or a revised report".
subsection (2)	(a) Omit the words "or report" in both places where they occur, and (b) omit the words "laid before the company in general meeting or".
subsection (3)	Omit the words "or a revised directors' report".
subsection (4)	(a) In paragraph (a), omit the words "or report", (b) in paragraph (b), omit the words "or reporting accountant" and the words "or report", and (c) in paragraph (c)— (i) for the words "previous accounts or report" substitute "previous accounts", (ii) omit sub-paragraph (ii), and (iii) omit the words from ", or where a summary financial statement" to the end.

Provision of Part VII	Modification
Section 245A (Secretary of State's notice in respect of annual accounts)	
subsection (1)	For the words from "copies of" to "general meeting or" substitute "a copy of a limited liability partnership's annual accounts has been".
Section 245B (application to court in respect of defective accounts)	
subsection (3)	Omit paragraph (b).
Section 246 special provisions for small companies)	
subsection (3)	Omit paragraph (a), and paragraph (b) (ii), (iii) and (iv).
subsection (4)	Omit subsection (4).
subsection (5)	(a) For the words "the directors of the company" substitute "the designated members of the limited liability partnership", and
	(b) omit paragraph (b).
subsection (6)	Omit paragraphs (b) and (c).
subsection (8)	Omit paragraph (b) and the words ", in the report" and ", 234A".
Section 246A (special provisions for medium-sized companies)	
subsection (3)	(a) For the words "The company" substitute "The designated members", and
	(b) for paragraph (a), substitute the following— "(a) which includes a profit and loss account in which the following items listed in the profit and loss account formats set out in Part I of Schedule 4 are combined as one item under the heading gross profit or loss"— Items 1 to 3 and 6 in Format 1 Items 1 to 5 in Format 2.".
Section 247 (qualification of company as small or medium sized)	
subsection (5)	In paragraph (a), for the words "items A to D" substitute "items B to D".
Section 247A (cases in which special provisions do not apply)	
subsection (1)	For paragraph (a) of subsection (1) substitute the following— "(a) the limited liability partnership is, or was at any time within the financial year to which the accounts relate, a person (other than a banking limited liability partnership) who has permission under Part 4 of the Financial Services and Markets Act 2000 to carry on one or more regulated activities;".
Section 247B (special auditors' report)	
subsection (1)	(a) In paragraph (a), for the words "the directors of a company" substitute "the designated members of a limited liability partnership", and

Provision of Part VII	Modification
	(b) in paragraph (b) omit the words "or (2)".
Section 249A (exemptions from audit)	
subsection (2)	Omit subsection (2).
subsection (3A)	Omit subsection (3A).
subsection (4)	Omit subsection (4).
subsection (6)	Omit the words "or gross income".
subsection (6A)	Omit the words "or (2)".
subsection (7)	Omit the words from ", and 'gross income'" to the end.
Section 249AA (dormant companies)	
subsection (1)	For the words section 249B(2) to (5) substitute "section 249B (4) and (5)".
subsection (2)	In paragraph (a), for the words "section 247A(1)(a)(i) or (b)" substitute "section 247A(1)(b)".
subsection (3)	For subsection (3) substitute the following— "(3) Subsection (1) does not apply if at any time in the financial year in question the limited liability partnership was a person (other than a banking limited liability partnership) who has permission under Part 4 of the Financial Services and Markets Act 2000 to carry on one or more regulated activities.".
subsection (5)	In paragraph (b), omit the words "(6) or".
subsection (6)	Omit subsection (6).
subsection (7)	In paragraph (a), for the words "section 28 (change of name)" substitute "paragraph 5 of the Schedule to the Limited Liability Partnerships Act 2000". Omit paragraph (b).
Section 249B (cases where audit exemption not available)	
subsection (1)	(a) omit the words "or (2)" and paragraphs (a) and (bb), and (b) in paragraph (b), after "it was a person" insert "(other than a banking limited liability partnership)".
subsection (1C)	For paragraph (b), substitute "that the group's aggregate turnover in that year (calculated in accordance with section 249) is not more than £1 million net (or £1.2 million gross),".
subsections (2) and (3)	Omit subsections (2) and (3).
subsection (4)	(a) Omit the words "or (2)" in both places where they occur, and (b) omit paragraph (b).
Sections 249C (the report required for the purposes of section 249A(2)) and 249D (the reporting accountant)	Omit sections 249C and 249D.
Section 249E (effect of exemption from audit)	
subsection (1)	(a) In paragraph (b) omit the words from "or laid" to the end, and (b) omit paragraph (c).
subsection (2)	Omit subsection (2).
Section 251 (provision of summary financial statement by listed public companies)	Omit section 251.

Provision of Part VII	Modification
Sections 252 and 253 (private company election to dispense with laying of accounts and reports)	Omit section 252 and 253.
Section 254 (exemption for unlimited companies from requirement to deliver accounts and reports)	Omit section 254.
Section 255 (special provisions for banking and insurance companies)	Omit section 255.
Section 255A (special provisions for banking and insurance groups)	Omit section 255A.
Section 255B (modification of disclosure requirements in relation to banking company or group)	Omit section 255B.
Section 255D (power to apply provisions to banking partnerships)	Omit section 255D.
Section 257 (power of Secretary of State to alter accounting requirements)	Omit section 257.
Section 260 (participating interests) subsection (6)	For the words from ", Schedule 8A," to "Schedule 9A" substitute the words "and Schedule 8A".
Section 262 (minor definitions) subsection (1)	(a) Omit the definitions of "annual report", and "credit institution", and (b) insert the following definitions at the appropriate place— "banking limited liability partnership" means a limited liability partnership which has permission under Part 4 of the Financial Services and Markets Act 2000 to accept deposits (but does not include such a partnership which has permission to accept deposits only for the purpose of carrying on another regulated activity in accordance with that permission); "limited liability partnership" means a limited liability partnership formed and registered under the Limited Liability Partnerships Act 2000;".
subsection (2)	Omit subsection (2).
subsection (3)	Insert the following subsection after subsection (3)— "(3A) The definition of banking limited liability partnership in subsection (1) must be read with— (a) section 22 of the Financial Services and Markets Act 2000, (b) any relevant order under that section, and (c) Schedule 2 to that Act.".
Section 262A (index of defined expressions)	In the index of defined expressions— (a) the entries relating to "annual report" "credit institution" and "reporting accountant", and all entries relating to sections 255 and 255A and to Schedules 9 and 9A, shall be omitted, and

Provision of Part VII	Modification
	(b) the following entries shall be inserted at the appropriate place— "banking limited liability partnership" section 262 "limited liability partnership" section 262 .
Schedule 4 (form and content of company accounts)	
Paragraph 1	In sub-paragraph (1)(b), for the words "any one of" substitute "either of".
Paragraph 3	In sub-paragraph (2)(b), omit the words "shares or". Omit sub-paragraph (7)(b) and (c).
Balance Sheet Format 1	Omit the following items and the notes on the balance sheet formats which relate to them— (a) item A (called up share capital not paid), (b) item B.III.7 (own shares), (c) item C.II.5 (called up share capital not paid), and (d) item C.III.2 (own shares). For item K (capital and reserves) substitute— "K. Loans and other debts due to members *(12)* L. Members' other interests I Members' capital II Revaluation reserve III Other reserves."
Balance Sheet Format 2	Omit the following items and the notes on the balance sheet format which relate to them— (a) Assets item A (called up share capital not paid), (b) Assets item B.III.7 (own shares), (c) Assets item C.II.5 (called up share capital not paid), and (d) Assets item C.III.2 (own shares). For Liabilities item A (capital and reserves) substitute— "A. Loans and other debts due to members *(12)* AA. Members' other interests I Members' capital II Revaluation reserve III Other reserves."
Notes on the balance sheet formats	
Note (12)	Substitute the following as Note *(12)*— "*(12) Loans and other debts due to members* (Format 1, item K and Format 2, item A)

Provision of Part VII	Modification
	The following amounts shall be shown separately under this item—
	(a) the aggregate amount of money advanced to the limited liability partnership by the members by way of loan,
	(b) the aggregate amount of money owed to members by the limited liability partnership in respect of profits,
	(c) any other amounts."
Profit and Loss Account Formats	In Format 1, for item 20 (profit or loss for the financial year) substitute "20. Profit or loss for the financial year before members' remuneration and profit shares"
	In Format 2, for item 22 (profit or loss for the financial year) substitute "22. Profit or loss for the financial year before members' remuneration and profit shares"
	Omit Profit and Loss Account Formats 3 and 4 and the notes on the profit and loss account formats which relate to them.
Notes on the profit and loss account Formats	
Note *(15)* (income from other fixed asset investments: other interest receivable and similar income)	At the end of Note *(15)* insert the words "Interest receivable from members shall not be included under this item."
Note *(16)* (interest payable and similar charges)	At the end of Note *(16)* insert "Interest payable to members shall not be included under this item."
Accounting principles and rules	
Paragraph 12	In sub-paragraph (b) omit the words "on behalf of the board of directors".
Paragraph 34	Omit sub-paragraph (3), (3A) and (3B).
Notes to the accounts	
Paragraph 37	For the words "38 to 51" substitute the words "41 to 51(1)".
Insertion of new paragraph after paragraph 37	Insert the following new paragraph after paragraph 37—
	"Loans and other debts due to members
	37A. The following information shall be given—
	(a) the aggregate amounts of loans and other debts due to members as at the date of the beginning of the financial year,
	(b) the aggregate amounts contributed by members during the financial year,
	(c) the aggregate amounts transferred to or from the profit and loss account during that year,
	(d) the aggregate amounts withdrawn by members or applied on behalf of members during that year,
	(e) the aggregate amount of loans and other debts due to members as at the balance sheet date, and
	(f) the aggregate amount of loans and other debts due to members that fall due after one year.
Paragraphs 38 to 40	Omit paragraphs 38 to 40.

Provision of Part VII	**Modification**
Paragraphs 49 and 51(2)	Omit paragraphs 49 and 51(2).
Paragraph 56	Insert the following paragraph after paragraph 56—

"Particulars of members

56A.—(1) Particulars shall be given of the average number of members of the limited liability partnership in the financial year, which number shall be determined by dividing the relevant annual number by the number of months in the financial year.

(2) The relevant annual number shall be determined by ascertaining for each month in the financial year the number of members of the limited liability partnership for all or part of that month, and adding together all the monthly numbers.

(3) Where the amount of the profit of the limited liability partnership for the financial year before members' remuneration and profit shares exceeds £200,000, there shall be disclosed the amount of profit (including remuneration) which is attributable to the member with the largest entitlement to profit (including remuneration). For the purpose of determining the amount to be disclosed, "remuneration" includes any emoluments specified in paragraph 1(1)(a), (c) or (d) of Schedule 6 to this Act which are paid by or receivable from—

(i) the limited liability partnership; and

(ii) the limited liability partnership's subsidiary undertakings; and

(iii) any other person.".

| Paragraph 58 | Omit sub-paragraph (3)(c). |

Special provisions where the company is an investment company

| Paragraphs 71 to 73 | Omit paragraphs 71 to 73. |

Schedule 4A (form and content of group accounts)

Paragraph 1	Omit sub-paragraph (3).
Paragraph 10	Omit sub-paragraph (1)(a) to (c). Omit sub-paragraph (2).
Paragraph 11	For sub-paragraph (1), substitute—

"(1) Where a limited liability partnership adopts the merger method of accounting, it must comply with this paragraph, and with generally accepted accounting principles or practice."

Omit sub-paragraphs (5) to (7).

| Paragraph 17 | (a) In sub-paragraph (2)(a), for the words "item K" substitute "item L", |

(b) in sub-paragraph (2)(b), for the words "item A" substitute "item AA", and

Provision of Part VII	Modification
	(c) In sub-paragraphs (3) and (4), omit paragraphs (c) and (d).
Paragraph 21	In sub-paragraph (3), omit paragraphs (c) and (d).
Schedule 5 (disclosure of information: related undertakings)	
Paragraph 6	Omit paragraph 6.
Paragraph 9A	Omit paragraph 9A.
Paragraph 20	Omit paragraph 20.
Paragraph 28A	Omit paragraph 28A.
Schedule 8 (form and content of accounts prepared by small companies)	
Paragraph 1	In sub-paragraph (1)(b), for the words "any one of" substitute "either of".
Paragraph 3	In sub-paragraph (2)(b), omit the words "shares or".
	Omit sub-paragraph (7)(b).
Balance Sheet Format 1	Omit item A (called up share capital not paid) and note (1) on the balance sheet format.
	For item K (capital and reserves) substitute—
	"K Loans and other debts due to members *(9)*
	L Members' other interests
	I Members' capital
	II Revaluation reserve
	III Other reserves ."
Balance Sheet Format 2	Omit Assets item A (called up share capital not paid) and note (1) on the balance sheet format.
	For Liabilities item A (capital and reserves) substitute—
	A. Loans and other debts due to members *(9)*
	AA. Members' other interests
	I Members' capital
	II Revaluation reserve
	III Other reserves ."
Notes on the balance sheet formats	
Note *(4)* (Others: Other investments)	Omit Note *(4)*.
Note *(9)*	Substitute the following as Note (9)—
	"(9) Loans and other debts due to members
	(Format 1, item K and Format 2, item A)
	The following amounts shall be shown separately under this item—
	(a) the aggregate amount of money advanced to the limited liability partnership by the members by way of loan,
	(b) the aggregate amount of money owed to members by the limited liability partnership in respect of profits,
	(c) any other amounts.".

Provision of Part VII Profit and Loss Account Formats	Modification
	In Format 1, for item 20 (profit or loss for the financial year) substitute "20. Profit or loss for the financial year before members' remuneration and profit shares" In Format 2, for item 22 (profit or loss for the financial year) substitute "22. Profit or loss for the financial year before members' remuneration and profit shares" Omit Profit and Loss Account Formats 3 and 4 and the notes on the profit and loss account formats which relate to them.
Notes on the profit and loss account formats Note *(12)* (income from other fixed asset investments: other interest receivable and similar income) Note *(13)* (interest payable and similar charges)	At the end of Note *(12)* insert the words "Interest receivable from members shall not be included under this item." At the end of Note *(13)* insert "Interest payable to members shall not be included under this item.".
Accounting principles and rules Paragraph 12	In sub-paragraph (b), omit the words "on behalf of the board of directors".
Paragraph 34 **Notes to the accounts** Paragraph 37	Omit sub-paragraphs (3), (4) and (5). For the words "Paragraphs 38 to 47" substitute "Paragraphs 40 to 47".
Insertion of new paragraph after paragraph 37	Insert the following new paragraph after paragraph 37— "*Loans and other debts due to members* 37A. The following information shall be given— (a) the aggregate amount of loans and other debts due to members as at the date of the beginning of the financial year, (b) the aggregate amounts contributed by members during the financial year, (c) the aggregate amounts transferred to or from the profit and loss account during that year, (d) the aggregate amounts withdrawn by members or applied on behalf of members during that year, (e) the aggregate amount of loans and other debts due to members as at the balance sheet date, and (f) the aggregate amount of loans and other debts due to members that fall due after one year."
Paragraphs 38 and 39 Paragraph 45 Paragraph 51 Schedule 8A (form and content of abbreviated accounts of small companies delivered to registrar)	Omit paragraphs 38 and 39. Omit paragraph 45. Omit sub-paragraph (3)(c).

Provision of Part VII	**Modification**
Balance Sheet Format 1	Omit item A (called up share capital not paid). For item K (capital and reserves) substitute—
	K Loans and other debts due to members
	L Members' other interests
	I Members' capital
	II Revaluation reserve
	III Other reserves".
Balance Sheet Format 2	Omit Assets item A (called up share capital not paid).
	For Liabilities item A (capital and reserves) substitute—
	"A Loans and other debts due to members
	AA Members' other interests
	I Members' capital
	II Revaluation reserve
	III Other reserves".
Notes to the accounts	
Paragraphs 5 and 6	Omit paragraphs 5 and 6.
Paragraph 9	Omit sub-paragraph (3)(c).

SCHEDULE 2

Regulation 4

PART I

MODIFICATIONS TO PROVISIONS OF THE 1985 ACT APPLIED TO LIMITED LIABILITY PARTNERSHIPS

Provisions	**Modifications**
Formalities of Carrying on Business	
24 (minimum membership for carrying on business)	In the first paragraph omit the words ", other than a private company limited by shares or by guarantee,".
36 (company contracts England and Wales)	
36A (execution of documents England and Wales)	In subsection (4) for "a director and the secretary of a company, or by two directors of a company," substitute "two members of a limited liability partnership".
	In subsection (6) for "a director and the secretary of a company, or by two directors of the company" substitute "two members of a limited liability partnership".
36C (pre-incorporation contracts, deeds and obligations)	
37 (bills of exchange and promissory notes)	
38 (execution of deeds abroad)	

Provisions	Modifications
39 (power of company to have official seal for use abroad)	In subsection (1), omit the words "whose objects require or comprise the transaction of business in foreign countries may, if authorised by its articles" and before the word "have" insert the word "may".
41 (authentication of documents)	For "director, secretary or other authorised officer" substitute "member".
42 (events affecting a company's status)	
subsection (1)	In subsection (1), for "other persons" substitute "persons other than members of the limited liability partnership".
subsection (1)(b)	In subsection (1)(b) omit the words "or articles".
subsection (1)(c)	Omit subsection (1)(c).

Miscellaneous provisions about shares and debentures

183 (transfer and registration)	
subsection (1)	Subsection (1), omit the words "shares in or". For the words "company's articles" substitute "limited liability partnership agreement.".
subsection (2)	Subsection (2), omit the words "shareholder or" together with the words "shares in or".
subsection (3)	Omit subsection (3).
subsection (4)	Omit subsection (4).
subsection (5)	Omit the words "shares or".
184 (certification of transfers)	
subsection (1)	Subsection (1), omit the words "shares in or" together with the words "shares or".
185 (duty of company as to issue of certificates)	
subsection (1)	Subsection (1), omit the words "shares," in each of the four places that it occurs.
subsection (3)	Omit subsection (3).
subsection (4)	Omit the words "shares or" together with the words "shares,".

Debentures

190 (register of debenture holders)	
191 (right to inspect register)	
subsection (1)	In subsection (1), paragraph (a), for the words "or any holder of shares in the company" substitute "or any member of the limited liability partnership".
subsection (2)	In subsection (2), delete "or holder of shares".
subsection (6)	In subsection (6), delete the words "in the articles or".
192 (liability of trustees of debentures)	
193 (perpetual debentures)	
194 (power to re-issue redeemed debentures)	
subsection (1)(a)	In subsection (1)(a), omit the words "in the articles or".
subsection (1)(b)	In subsection (1)(b), for "passing a resolution" substitute "making a determination".

Provisions	Modifications
195 (contract to subscribe for debentures)	
196 (payment of debts out of assets subject to floating charge (England and Wales))	

Officers and registered office

287 (registered office)	For section 287 there shall be substituted: "(1) The change of registered office takes effect upon the notice of change of registered office (delivered to the registrar in accordance with paragraph 10 of the Schedule to the Limited Liability Partnerships Act 2000), being registered by the registrar, but until the end of the period of 14 days beginning with the date on which it is registered a person may validly serve any document on the limited liability partnership at its previous registered office. (2) Where a limited liability partnership unavoidably ceases to perform at its registered office any duty to keep at its registered office any register, index or other document or to mention the address of its registered office in any document in circumstances in which it was not practicable to give prior notice to the registrar of a change in the situation of the registered office, but— (a) resumes performance of that duty at other premises as soon as practicable, and (b) gives notice accordingly to the registrar of a change in the situation of its registered office within 14 days of doing so it shall not be treated as having failed to comply with that duty".
288 (register of directors and secretaries)	For section 288 there shall be substituted:

Provisions	Modifications
	"Where a person becomes a member or designated member of a limited liability partnership the notice to be delivered to the registrar under section 9(1)(a) of the Limited Liability Partnerships Act 2000 shall contain the following particulars with respect to that person:
	(1) name, which
	(a) in the case of an individual means his forename and surname (or, in the case of a peer or other person usually known by a title, his title instead of or in addition to either or both his forename and surname), and
	(b) if a corporation or a Scottish firm, its corporate or firm name; and
	(2) address, which
	(a) in the case of an individual means his usual residential address; and
	(b) if a corporation or a Scottish firm, its registered or principal office; and
	(3) in the case of an individual, the date of his birth."

Company Identification

Provisions	Modifications
348 (company name to appear outside place of business)	
349 (company's name to appear in its correspondence)	
350 (company seal)	
351 (particulars in correspondence etc)	In subsection (1) for paragraph (c) substitute the words "in the case of a limited liability partnership, whose name ends with the abbreviation "llp", "LLP", "pac" or "PAC", the fact that it is a limited liability partnership or a partneriaeth atebolrwydd cyfyngedig."
	Also in subsection (1) delete paragraph (d) and delete subsection (2).

Annual Return

Provisions

363 (duty to deliver annual returns)

Modifications

Section 363 of the 1985 Act shall apply to a limited liability partnership being modified so as to read as follows:

"(1) Every limited liability partnership shall deliver to the registrar successive annual returns each of which is made up to a date not later than the date which is from time to time the "return date" of the limited liability partnership, that is—

(a) the anniversary of the incorporation of the limited liability partnership, or

(b) if the last return delivered by the limited liability partnership in accordance with this section was made up to a different date, the anniversary of that date.

(2) Each return shall—

(a) be in a form approved by the registrar,

(b) contain the information required by section 364, and

(c) be signed by a designated member of the limited liability partnership

(3) If a limited liability partnership fails to deliver an annual return in accordance with this section before the end of the period of 28 days after the return date, the limited liability partnership is guilty of an offence and liable on summary conviction to a fine not exceeding level 5 on the standard scale. The contravention continues until such time as an annual return made up to that return date and complying with the requirements of subsection (2) (except as to date of delivery) is delivered by the limited liability partnership to the registrar.

(4) Where a limited liability partnership is guilty of an offence under subsection (3) every designated member of the limited liability partnership is similarly liable unless he shows that he took all reasonable steps to avoid the commission of or the continuance of the offence."

Provisions	Modifications
364 (contents of annual return: general)	For section 364 substitute the following— "Every annual return shall state the date to which it is made up and shall contain the following information— (a) the address of the registered office of the limited liability partnership, (b) the names and usual residential addresses of the members of the limited liability partnership and, if some only of them are designated members, which of them are designated members, and (c) if any register of debenture holders (or a duplicate of any such register or a part of it) is not kept at the registered office of the limited liability partnership, the address of the place where it is kept."

Auditors

384 (duty to appoint auditors) subsection (2)	In subsection (2), for the words from "(appointment at general meeting at which accounts are laid)" to the end substitute the words "(appointment of auditors)".
subsection (3)	In subsection (3), omit the words from "or 385A(2)" to the end.
subsection (4)	For subsection (4) substitute the following subsection: "(4) A person is eligible for appointment by a limited liability partnership as auditor only if, were the limited liability partnership a company, he would be eligible under Part II of the Companies Act 1989 for appointment as a "company auditor"."
subsection (5)	Insert a new subsection (5): "(5) Part II of the Companies Act 1989 shall apply in respect of auditors of limited liability partnerships as if the limited liability partnerships were companies formed and registered under this Act, and references in Part II to an officer of a company shall include reference to a member of a limited liability partnership."
385 (appointment at general meeting at which accounts laid) title to the section	In the title to the section for the existing wording substitute "Appointment of auditors".
subsection (1)	Omit subsection (1).
subsection (2)	For subsection (2) substitute:

Provisions	Modifications
	"(2) The designated members of a limited liability partnership shall appoint the auditors for the first financial year in respect of which auditors are appointed before the end of that financial year and thereafter before the expiration of not more than two months following the approval of the accounts for the preceding financial year in accordance with section 233.".
subsection (3)	For subsection (3) substitute: "(3) The auditor of a limited liability partnership shall hold office until not later than the expiration of two months following the approval in accordance with section 233 of the accounts for the financial year in respect of which the auditor was appointed."
subsection (4)	For subsection (4) substitute: "(4) If the designated members fail to exercise their powers under subsection (2), the powers may be exercised by the members of the limited liability partnership in a meeting convened for the purpose".
387 (appointment by Secretary of State in default of appointment by company)	
subsection (1)	In subsection (1), omit the words "re-appointed or deemed to be re-appointed".
subsection (2)	In subsection (2), for the word "officer"substitute the words "designated member".
388 (filling of casual vacancies)	
subsection (1)	In subsection (1), for "directors, or the company in general meeting,"substitute "designated members".
subsection (3)	Omit subsection (3).
subsection (4)	Omit subsection (4).
388A (certain companies exempt from obligation to appoint auditors)	
subsection (3)	For subsection (3) substitute: "(3) The designated members may appoint auditors and the auditors so appointed shall hold office until the expiration of two months following the approval in accordance with section 233 of the accounts for the financial year in respect of which the auditor was appointed."
subsection (4)	Omit subsection (4).
subsection (5)	For subsection (5) substitute: "(5) If the designated members fail to exercise their powers under subsection (3), the powers may be exercised by the members of the limited liability partnership in a meeting convened for the purpose."
389A (rights to information)	
390 (right to attend company meetings)	

Provisions	Modifications
subsection (1)	In paragraph (a), (b) and (c) of subsection (1) omit the word "general"in each place where it occurs. At the end of paragraph (a) add the words "and where any part of the business of the meeting concerns them as auditors." At the end of paragraph (b) add the words "where any part of the business of the meeting concerns them as auditors."
subsection (1A)	Omit subsection (1A).
subsection (2)	Omit subsection (2).
390A (remuneration of auditors)	
subsection (1)	For subsection (1) substitute: "The remuneration of auditors appointed by the limited liability partnership shall be fixed by the designated members or in such manner as the members of the limited liability partnership may determine".
subsection (2)	In subsection (2), omit the words "directors or the", in both places where they occur, and omit the words "as the case may be".
390B (remuneration of auditors or their associates for non-audit work)	
391 (removal of auditors)	
subsection (1)	In subsection (1), for the words "A company may by ordinary resolution"substitute "The designated members of a limited liability partnership may"and for the words "between it and"substitute "with".
subsection (2)	(a) In subsection (2), for the words "a resolution removing an auditor is passed at a general meeting of a company, the company"substitute the words "the designated members of the limited liability partnership have made a determination to remove an auditor, the designated members". (b) For the words "every officer of it who is in default"substitute "every designated member of it who is in default".
subsection (4)	In subsection (4), omit the word "general".
391A (rights of auditors who are removed or not re-appointed)	
subsection (1)	For subsection (1) substitute "The designated members shall give seven days' prior written notice to (a) any auditor whom it is proposed to remove before the expiration of his term of office; or (b) a retiring auditor where it is proposed to appoint as auditor a person other than the retiring auditor."
subsection (2)	Omit subsection (2).
subsection (3)	In subsection (3), for the words "intended resolution"substitute the word "proposal"and omit the words "of the company".

Provisions	Modifications
subsection (4)	Omit the words "(unless the representations are received by it too late for it to do so)". Omit subsection (4)(a). In subsection (4)(b), for the words "of the company to whom notice in writing of the meeting is or has been sent."Substitute "within twenty one days' of receipt.".
subsection (5)	For subsection (5) substitute: "If a copy of the representations is not sent out as required by subsection (4), then unless subsection (6) applies, the limited liability partnership and any designated member in default commits an offence. A person guilty of an offence under this section is liable on summary conviction to a fine not exceeding level 3 on the standard scale."
subsection (6)	In subsection (6), the words "and the representations need not be read at the meeting"shall be omitted.
392 (resignation of auditors) subsection (3)	In the second paragraph of subsection (3) for "and every officer of it who is in default"substitute "and every designated member of it who is in default".
392A (rights of resigning auditors) subsection (2)	In subsection (2), for "directors"substitute "designated members"and for "an extraordinary general meeting of the company"substitute "a meeting of the members of the limited liability partnership".
subsection (3)	In subsection (3), omit ",or"from paragraph (a) and omit paragraph (b).
subsection (5)	In subsection (5), for "directors"substitute "designated members"and for "director"substitute "designated member".
subsection (8)	In subsection (8), omit the word "general"and the phrase "(a) or (b)".
394 (statement by person ceasing to hold office as auditor) 394A (offences of failing to comply with section 394)	

Registration of charges

The following references are to sections of the 1985 Act which were replaced by section 92 of the Companies Act 1989. They will apply to limited liability partnerships until the said section 92 is commenced.

395 (certain charges void if not registered)	
396 (charges which have to be registered)	In subsection (1) delete paragraphs (b) and (g).
397 (formalities of registration (debentures))	In subsection (1), paragraph (b) for the word "resolutions"substitute "determinations of the limited liability partnership".

Provisions	Modifications
398 (verification of charge on property outside United Kingdom)	
399 (company's duty to register charges it creates)	
400 (charges existing on property acquired)	
401 (register of charges to be kept by registrar of companies)	
402 (endorsement of certificate on debentures)	
403 (entries of satisfaction and release)	In subsection (1A), after "of the company"insert "or designated member, administrator or administrative receiver of the limited liability partnership".
404 (rectification of register of charges)	In subsection (1), omit the words "or shareholders".
405 (registration of enforcement of security)	
406 (companies to keep copies of instruments creating charges)	
407 (company's register of charges)	In subsection (1), for "limited company"substitute "company (including limited liability partnership)".
408 (right to inspect instruments which create charges etc)	In subsection (1) delete "in general meeting".
410 (charges void unless registered)	In subsection (4) delete paragraph (b) and sub-paragraph (ii) of paragraph (c). In subsection (5) for "an incorporated company"substitute "a limited liability partnership".
411 (charges on property outside the United Kingdom)	
412 (negotiable instrument to secure book debts)	
413 (charges associated with debentures)	In subsection (2)(b), for the word "resolutions"substitute "determinations of the limited liability partnership".
414 (charge by way of ex facie absolute disposition, etc)	
415 (company's duty to register charges created by it)	
416 (duty to register charges existing on property acquired)	
417 (register of charges to be kept by registrar of companies)	
418 (certificate of registration to be issued)	
419 (entries of satisfaction and relief)	In subsection (1A), after the words "of the company"insert "or a designated member, liquidator, receiver or administrative receiver of the limited liability partnership".
420 (rectification of the register)	Omit the words "or shareholders".
421 (copies of instruments creating charges to be kept by the company)	
422 (company's register of charges)	
423 (right to inspect copies of instruments, and the company's register)	In subsection (1) delete "in general meeting".

Provisions	**Modifications**

Arrangements and Reconstructions

Provisions	Modifications
425 (power of company to compromise with creditors and members)	
subsection (3)	Omit the words "and a copy of every such order shall be annexed to every copy of the company's memorandum issued after the order has been made or, in the case of a company not having a memorandum, of every copy so issued of the instrument constituting the company or defining its constitution."For the semi-colon after the word "registration"substitute a full stop.
subsection (6)	Omit subsection (6).
426 (information as to compromise to be circulated)	
subsection (2)	Omit the words "as directors or".
427 (provisions for facilitating company reconstruction or amalgamation)	
subsection (3)	In paragraph (b) for the words "policies or other like interests"substitute "policies, other like interests or, in the case of a limited liability partnership, property or interests in the limited liability partnership".
subsection (6)	For the words ""company"includes only a company as defined in section 735(1)"substitute ""company"includes only a company as defined in section 735(1) or a limited liability partnership".

Investigation of companies and their affairs: Requisition of documents

Provisions	Modifications
431 (investigation of a company on its own application or that of its members)	For subsection (2) substitute the following: "(2)—The appointment may be made on the application of the limited liability partnership or on the application of not less than one-fifth in number of those who appear from notifications made to the registrar of companies to be currently members of the limited liability partnership."
432 (other company investigations)	
subsection (4)	For the words "but to whom shares in the company have been transferred or transmitted by operation of law"substitute "but to whom a member's share in the limited liability partnership has been transferred or transmitted by operation of law."
433 (inspectors' powers during investigation)	
434 (production of documents and evidence to inspectors)	
436 (obstruction of inspectors treated as contempt of court)	
437 (inspectors' reports)	

Provisions	Modifications
438 (power to bring civil proceedings on company's behalf)	
439 (expenses of investigating a company's affairs) subsection (5)	Omit paragraph (b) together with the word "or"at the end of paragraph (a).
441 (inspectors' report to be evidence)	
447 (Secretary of State's power to require production of documents)	
448 (entry and search of premises)	
449 (provision for security of information obtained)	
450 (punishment for destroying, mutilating etc company documents)	Omit subsection (1A).
451 (punishment for furnishing false information)	
451A (disclosure of information by Secretary of State or inspector)	In subsection (1), for the words "sections 434 to 446"substitute "sections 434 to 441". Omit subsection (5).
452 (privileged information)	In subsection (1), for the words "sections 431 to 446"substitute "sections 431 to 441". In subsection (1A), for the words "sections 434, 443 or 446"substitute "section 434".

Fraudulent Trading

458 (punishment for fraudulent trading)	

Protection of company's members against unfair prejudice

459 (order on application of company member)	At the beginning of subsection (1), insert the words "Subject to subsection (1A),". After subsection (1) insert as subsection (1A): "The members of a limited liability partnership may by unanimous agreement exclude the right contained in subsection 459(1) for such period as shall be agreed. The agreement referred to in this subsection shall be recorded in writing." Omit subsections (2) and (3).
460 (order on application of Secretary of State)	. . . Omit subsection (2).
461 (provisions as to orders and petitions under this Part)	In subsection (2)(d) for the words "the shares of any members of the company by other members or by the company itself and, in the case of a purchase by the company itself, the reduction of the company's capital accordingly"substitute the words "the shares of any members in the limited liability partnership by other members or by the limited liability partnership itself.".

Provisions	Modifications
	In subsection (3) for the words "memorandum or articles"substitute the words "limited liability partnership agreement".
	For the existing words of subsection (4) substitute the words "Any alteration in the limited liability partnership agreement made by virtue of an order under this Part is of the same effect as if duly agreed by the members of the limited liability partnership and the provisions of this Act apply to the limited liability partnership agreement as so altered accordingly.".
	Omit subsection (5).

Floating charges and Receivers (Scotland)

Provisions	Modifications
464 (ranking of floating charges)	In subsection (1), for the words "section 462"substitute "the law of Scotland".
466 (alteration of floating charges)	Omit subsections (1), (2), (3) and (6).
486 (interpretation for Part XVIII generally)	For the current definition of "company"substitute""company"means a limited liability partnership;"
	Omit the definition of "Register of Sasines".
487 (extent of Part XVIII)	

Matters arising subsequent to winding up

Provisions	Modifications
651 (power of court to declare dissolution of company void)	
652 (registrar may strike defunct company off the register)	In subsection (6) paragraph (a) omit the word "director".
652A (registrar may strike private company off the register on application)	In this section the references to "a private company"shall include a reference to "a limited liability partnership".
subsection (1)	In subsection (1) the following shall be substituted for the existing wording "On application by two or more designated members of a limited liability partnership, the registrar of companies may strike the limited liability partnership's name off the register".
	Omit subsection 2(a) and in subsection 2(b) after the word "be"insert the word "made".
	In subsection (6), omit the word "director".
652B (duties in connection with making an application under section 652A)	In paragraph (a) of subsection (5) for "no meetings are"substitute "no meeting is".
	In paragraph (b) of subsection (5) for "meetings summoned under that section fail"substitute "the meeting summoned under that section fails".
	In paragraph (c) of subsection (5) for "meetings"substitute "a meeting".
	In paragraph (d) of subsection (5) for "at previous meetings"substitute "at a previous meeting".

Provisions	Modifications
652C (directors' duties following application under section 652A)	In subsection (2), for the words "is a director of the company"substitute "is a designated member of the limited liability partnership".
	In subsection (2) omit paragraph (d).
	In subsection (5) for the words "is a director of the company"substitute "is a designated member of the limited liability partnership".
	In subsection (6), omit paragraph (d).
652D (sections 652B and 652C: supplementary provisions)	
652E (sections 652B and 652C: enforcement)	
652F (other offences connected with section 652A)	
653 (objection to striking off by person aggrieved)	
654 (property of dissolved company to be bona vacantia)	
655 (effect on section 654 of company's revival after dissolution)	
656 (crown disclaimer of property vesting as bona vacantia)	
657 (effect of crown disclaimer under section 656)	
658 (liability for rentcharge on company's land after dissolution)	

Oversea Limited Liability Partnerships

693 (obligation to state name and other particulars)	For the wording of subsection (1) there shall be substituted the following words: "Every oversea limited liability partnership shall— (a) in every prospectus inviting subscriptions for its debentures in Great Britain, state the country in which the limited liability partnership is incorporated, (b) conspicuously exhibit on every place where it carries on business in Great Britain the name of the limited liability partnership and the country in which it is incorporated, (c) cause the name of the limited liability partnership and the country in which it is incorporated to be stated in legible characters in all bill heads, letter paper, and in all notices and other official publications and communications of the limited liability partnership." For subsection (2) there shall be substituted the following words "For the purposes of this section "oversea limited liability partnership"means a body incorporated or otherwise established outside Great Britain whose name under its law of incorporation or establishment includes the words "limited liability partnership."". Subsections (3) and (4) shall be omitted.

Provisions	**Modifications**

The Registrar of Companies: His functions and offices

704 (registration offices)	
705 (companies' registered numbers)	Omit subsection (5).
706 (delivery to the registrar of documents in legible form)	In subsection (2)(a), omit the words from "and, if the document is delivered"to the end of that paragraph.
707A (the keeping of company records by the registrar)	Omit subsection (4).
707B (delivery to the registrar using electronic communications)	In subsection (3), omit the "or"at the end of paragraph (a) and omit paragraph (b).
708 (fees payable to the registrar)	
709 (inspection of records kept by the registrar)	
710 (certificate of incorporation)	
710A (provision and authentication by registrar of documents in non-legible form)	
710B (documents relating to Welsh companies)	In subsection (7), omit the words "272(5) and 273(7) and paragraph 7(3) of Part II of Schedule 9".
711 (public notice by registrar of receipt and issue of certain documents)	In subsection (1) delete "or articles"in paragraph (b) and delete paragraphs (d) to (j), (l), (m) and (s) to (z).
713 (enforcement of company's duty to make returns)	In subsection (1), in the penultimate line for "any officer"substitute "any designated member". In subsections (2) and (3) for "officers"substitute "designated members".
714 (registrar's index of company and corporate names)	
715A (interpretation)	

Miscellaneous and supplementary provisions

721 (production and inspection of books where offence suspected)	In subsection (2)(b), for the words "the secretary of the company or such other"substitute "such".
722 (form of company registers, etc)	
723 (use of computers for company records)	Omit subsection (2).
723A (obligations of company as to inspections of registers, & etc)	
725 (service of documents)	In subsection (2), for the words "other head officer"substitute "a designated member".
726 (costs and expenses in actions by certain limited companies)	References to a "limited company"shall include references to a "limited liability partnership".
727 (power of court to grant relief in certain cases)	In subsection (1) delete the words "an officer of a company or"and "officer or". In subsection (2), delete the words "officer or".
728 (enforcement of High Court orders)	
729 (annual report by Secretary of State)	
730 (punishment of offences)	
731 (summary proceedings)	

Provisions	Modifications
732 (prosecution by public authorities)	Delete the references to sections 210, 324, 329 and 455. Omit subsection (2) paragraphs (a) and (c). In subsection (2)(b), for the words "either one of those two persons"substitute "either the Secretary of State, the Director of Public Prosecutions". Omit subsection (3).
733 (offences by bodies corporate) subsection (1)	In subsection (1), delete the references to section 210 and 216(3).
subsection (2)	In subsection (2), omit the word "secretary".
subsection (3)	Omit subsection (3).
734 (criminal proceedings against unincorporated bodies)	

Interpretation

735A (relationship of this Act to the Insolvency Act)	In subsection (1), delete all the references to provisions of the 1985 Act other than the references to sections 425(6)(a), 460(2) and 728.
736 ("subsidiary", "holding company", and "wholly-owned subsidiary") subsection (1)	For subsection (1) there shall be substituted the following words: "(1) Subject to subsection (1A), a company is a subsidiary of a limited liability partnership, its "holding company", if that limited liability partnership— (a) holds a majority of the voting rights in it, or (b) is a member of it and has the right to appoint or remove a majority of its board of directors, or (c) is a member of it and controls alone, pursuant to an agreement with other shareholders or members, a majority of the voting rights in it, or if it is a subsidiary of a company or limited liability partnership which is itself a subsidiary of that other company."

Provisions	**Modifications**
subsection (1A)	Insert as subsection (1A)—
	"(1A) A limited liability partnership is a subsidiary of a company or a subsidiary of another limited liability partnership, (such company or limited liability partnership being referred to in this section as its "holding company") if that company or limited liability partnership—
	(a) holds a majority of the voting rights in it;
	(b) is a member of it and has the right to appoint or remove a majority of other members; or
	(c) is a member of it and controls, alone or pursuant to an agreement with other members, a majority of voting rights in it,
	or if it is a subsidiary of a company or limited liability partnership which is itself a subsidiary of that holding company".
subsection (2)	For subsection (2) substitute "A company or a limited liability partnership is a "wholly-owned subsidiary"of another company or limited liability partnership if it has no members except that other and that other's wholly-owned subsidiaries or persons acting on behalf of that other or its wholly-owned subsidiaries."
736A (provisions supplementing section 736)	After subsection (1) insert a new subsection (1A) in the following form—
	"(1A) In section 736(1A)(a) and (c) the references to the voting rights in a limited liability partnership are to the rights conferred on members in respect of their interest in the limited liability partnership to vote on those matters which are to be decided upon by a vote of the members of the limited liability partnership."
	After subsection (2) insert the new subsection (2A) in the following form—
	"(2A) In section 736(1A)(b) the reference to the right to appoint or remove a majority of the members of the limited liability partnership is to the right to appoint or remove members holding a majority of the voting rights referred to in subsection (1A) and for this purpose—
	(a) a person shall be treated as having the right to appoint a member if
	(i) a person's appointment as member results directly from his appointment as a director or member of the holding company, or
	(ii) the member of the limited liability partnership is the company or limited liability partnership which is the holding company; and
	(b) a right to appoint or remove which is exercisable only with the consent or concurrence of another person shall be left out of account."

Provisions	Modifications
	In subsection (7) after the words "Rights attached to shares"insert the words "or to a member's interest in a limited liability partnership".
	In subsection (8) after the words "held by a company", in both places where they occur, insert "or a limited liability partnership".
	In subsection (9) after the words "in the interest of company"insert "or a limited liability partnership"and after the words "that company"in both places where they occur insert "or limited liability partnership".
	In subsection (10) after the words "a company"insert the words "or a limited liability partnership"and after the words "by the company"insert the words "or the limited liability partnership".
	In subsection (12) for the existing words substitute "In this section "company"includes a body corporate other than a limited liability partnership."
739 ("non-cash asset")	
740 ("body corporate"and "corporation")	
741 ("director"and "shadow director")	Omit subsection (3).
742 (expressions used in connection with accounts)	
743A (meaning of "office copy"in Scotland)	
744 (expressions used generally in this Act)	Delete the definitions of expressions not used in provisions which apply to limited liability partnerships and insert the following definitions— ""limited liability partnership"has the meaning given it in section 1(2) of the Limited Liability Partnerships Act 2000.". "shadow member"has the same meaning as it has in the Limited Liability Partnerships Regulations 2000.
744A (index of defined expressions)	Delete the references to expressions not used in provisions which apply to limited liability partnerships including, in particular, the following expressions: Allotment (and related expressions) Section 738 Annual general meeting Section 366 Authorised minimum Section 118 Called up share capital Section 737(1) Capital redemption reserve Section 170(1) Elective resolution Section 379A Employees' share scheme

Provisions	Modifications
	Section 743
	Existing company
	Section 735(1)
	Extraordinary general meeting
	Section 368
	Extraordinary resolution
	Section 378(1)
	The former Companies Acts
	Section 735(1)
	The Joint Stock Companies Acts
	Section 735(3)
	Overseas branch register
	Section 362
	Paid up (and related expressions)
	Section 738
	Registered office (of a company)
	Section 287
	Resolution for reducing share capital
	Section 135(3)
	Share premium account
	Section 130(1)
	Share warrant
	Section 188
	Special notice (in relation to a resolution)
	Section 379
	Special resolution
	Section 378(2)
	Uncalled share capital
	Section 737 (2)
	Undistributable reserves
	Section 264(3)
	Unlimited company
	Section 1(2)
	Unregistered company
	Section 718
SCHEDULE 24 (PUNISHMENT OF OFFENCES UNDER THIS ACT)	Delete the references to those sections which are not applied to limited liability partnerships including, in particular, the following sections: Section 6(3) company failing to deliver to the registrar notice or other document, following alteration of its objects; Section 18(3) company failing to register change in memorandum or articles; Section 19(2) company failing to send to one of its members a copy of the memorandum or articles, when so required by the member; Section 20(2) where company's memorandum altered, company issuing copy of the memorandum without the alteration; Section 28(5) company failing to change name on direction of Secretary of State;

Provisions	Modifications
	Section 31(5) company altering its memorandum or articles, so ceasing to be exempt from having "limited"after its name;
	Section 31(6) company failing to change name, on Secretary of State's direction, so as to have "limited"(or Welsh equivalent) at the end;
	Section 32(4) company failing to comply with the Secretary of State's direction to change its name, on grounds that the name is misleading;
	Section 33 trading under misleading name (use of "public limited company"or Welsh equivalent when not so entitled); purporting to be a private company;
	Section 34 trading or carrying on business with improper use of "limited"or "cyfyngedig";
	Section 54(10) public company failing to give notice, or copy of court order, to registrar, concerning application to re-register as private company;
	Section 80(9) directors exercising company's power of allotment without the authority required by section 80(1);
	Section 81(2) private company offering shares to the public, or allotting shares with a view to their being so offered;
	Section 82(5) allotting shares or debentures before third day after issue of prospectus;
	Section 86(6) company failing to keep money in separate bank account, where received in pursuance of prospectus stating that stock exchange listing is to be applied for;
	Section 87(4) offeror of shares for sale failing to keep proceeds in separate bank account;
	Section 88(5) officer of company failing to deliver return of allotments, etc to the registrar;
	Section 95(6) knowingly or recklessly authorising or permitting misleading, false or deceptive material in statement by directors under section 95(5);
	Section 97(4) company failing to deliver to registrar the prescribed form disclosing amount or rate of share commission;
	Section 110(2) making misleading, false or deceptive statement in connection with valuation under section 103 or 104;
	Section 111(3) officer of company failing to deliver copy of asset valuation report to registrar;
	Section 111(4) company failing to deliver to registrar copy of resolution under Section 104(4), with respect to transfer of an asset as consideration for allotment;

Provisions	Modifications
	Section 114 contravention of any of the provisions of sections 99 to 104, 106;
	Section 117(7) company doing business or exercising borrowing powers contrary to section 117;
	Section 122(2) company failing to give notice to registrar of reorganisation of share capital;
	Section 123(4) company failing to give notice to registrar of increase of share capital;
	Section 127(5) company failing to forward to registrar copy of court order, when application made to cancel resolution varying shareholders' rights;
	Section 128(5) company failing to send to registrar statement or notice required by section 128 (particulars of shares carrying special rights);
	Section 129(4) company failing to deliver to registrar statement or notice required by section 129 (registration of newly created class rights);
	Section 141 officer of company concealing name of creditor entitled to object to reduction of capital, or wilfully misrepresenting the nature or amount of debt or claim, etc;
	Section 142(2) director authorising or permitting non-compliance with section 142 (requirement to convene company meeting to consider serious loss of capital);
	Section 143(2) company acquiring its own shares in breach of section 143;
	Section 149(2) company failing to cancel its own shares acquired by itself, as required by section 146(2); or failing to apply for re-registration as private company as so required in the case there mentioned;
	Section 151(3) company giving financial assistance towards acquisition of its own shares;
	Section 156(6) company failing to register statutory declaration under section 155;
	Section 156(7) director making statutory declaration under section 155, without having reasonable grounds for opinion expressed in it;
	Section 169(6) default by company's officer in delivering to registrar the return required by section 169 (disclosure by company of purchase of its own shares);
	Section 169(7) company failing to keep copy of contract, etc, at registered office; refusal of inspection to person demanding it;

Provisions	Modifications
	Section 173(6) director making statutory declaration under section 173 without having reasonable grounds for the opinion expressed in the declaration; Section 175(7) refusal of inspection of statutory declaration and auditor's report under section 173, etc; Section 176(4) company failing to give notice to registrar of application to court under section 176, or to register court order; Section 183(6) company failing to send notice of refusal to register a transfer of shares or debentures; Section 185(5) company default in compliance with section 185(1) (certificates to be made ready following allotment or transfer of shares, etc); Section 189(1) offences of fraud and forgery in connection with share warrants in Scotland; Section 189(2) unauthorised making of, or using or possessing apparatus for making share warrants in Scotland; Section 210(3) failure to discharge obligation of disclosure under Part VI; other forms of non-compliance with that Part; Section 211(10) company failing to keep register of interests disclosed under Part IV; other contraventions of section 211; Section 214(5) company failing to exercise powers under section 212, when so required by the members; Section 215(8) company default in compliance with section 215 (company report of investigation of shareholdings on members' requisition); Section 216(3) failure to comply with company notice under section 212; Making false statement in response etc; Section 217(7) company failing to notify a person that he has been named as a shareholder; on removal of name from register, failing to alter associated index; Section 218(3) improper removal of entry from register of interests disclosed; company failing to restore entry improperly removed; Section 219(3) refusal of inspection of register or report under Part VI; failure to send copy when required; Section 232(4) default by director or officer of a company in giving notice of matters relating to himself for purposes of Schedule 6 Part I;

Provisions

Modifications

Section 234(5) non-compliance with Part VII as to directors' report and its content;
directors individually liable;
Section 234A(4) laying, circulating or delivering directors' report without required signature;
Section 241(2) failure to lay accounts and reports before the company in general meeting before the end of the period allowed for doing this;
Section 251(6) failure to comply with requirements in relation to summary financial statements;
Section 288(4) default in complying with section 288 (keeping register of directors and secretaries, refusal of inspection);
Section 291(5) acting as director of a company without having the requisite share qualification;
Section 294(3) director failing to give notice of his attaining retirement age;
acting as director under appointment invalid due to his attaining it;
Section 305(3) company default in complying with section 305 (directors' name to appear on company correspondence, etc);
Section 306(4) failure to state that liability of proposed director or manager is unlimited; failure to give notice of that fact to person accepting office;
Section 314(3) director failing to comply with section 314;
Section 317(7) director failing to disclose interest in contract;
Section 318(8) company in default in complying with section 318(1) or (5);
Section 322B(4) terms of unwritten contract between sole member of a private company limited by shares or by guarantee and the company not set out in a written memorandum or recorded in minutes of a directors' meeting;
Section 323(2) director dealing in options to buy or sell company's listed shares or debentures;
Section 324(7) director failing to notify interest in company's shares; making false statement in purported notification;
Section 326(2), (3), (4) and (5) various defaults in connection with company register of directors' interests;
Section 328(6) director failing to notify company that members of his family etc have or have exercised options to buy shares or debentures; making false statement in purported notification;

Provisions	**Modifications**
	Section 329(3) company failing to notify investment exchange of acquisition of its securities by a director;
	Section 342(1) director or relevant company authorising or permitting company to enter into transaction or arrangement, knowing or suspecting it to contravene section 330;
	Section 342(2) relevant company entering into transaction or arrangement for a director in contravention of section 330;
	Section 342(3) procuring a relevant company to enter into transaction or arrangement known to be contrary to section 330;
	Section 343(8) company failing to maintain register of transactions etc made with and for directors and not disclosed in company accounts; failing to make register available at registered office or at company meeting;
	Section 352(5) company default in complying with section 352 (requirement to keep register of members and their particulars);
	Section 352A(3) company default in complying with section 352A (statement that company has only one member);
	Section 353(4) company failing to send notice to registrar as to place where register of members is kept;
	Section 354(4) company failing to keep index of members;
	Section 356(5) refusal of inspection of members' register; failure to send copy on requisition;
	Section 364(4) company without share capital failing to complete and register annual return in due time;
	Section 366(4) company default in holding annual general meeting;
	Section 367(3) company default in complying with Secretary of State's direction to hold a company meeting;
	Section 367(5) company failing to register resolution that meeting held under section 367 is to be its annual general meeting;
	Section 372(4) failure to give notice, to member entitled to vote at company meeting, that he may do so by proxy;
	Section 372(6) officer of company authorising or permitting issue of irregular invitations to appoint proxies;
	Section 376(7) officer of company in default as to circulation of members' resolutions for company meeting;

Provisions	Modifications
	Section 380(5) company failing to comply with section 380 (copies of certain resolutions etc to be sent to registrar of companies); Section 380(6) company failing to include copy of resolution to which section 380 applies in articles; failing to forward copy to member on request; Section 381B(2) director or secretary of company failing to notify auditors of proposed written resolution; Section 382(5) company failing to keep minutes of proceedings at company and board meetings, etc; Section 382B(2) failure of sole member to provide the company with a written record of a decision; Section 383(4) refusal of inspection of minutes of general meeting; failure to send copy of minutes on member's request; Section 389(10) person acting as a company auditor knowing himself to be disqualified: failing to give notice vacating office when he becomes disqualified; Section 429(6) offeror failing to send copy of notice or making statutory declaration knowing it to be false etc; Section 430A(6) offeror failing to give rights to minority shareholder; Section 444(3) failing to give Secretary of State, when required to do so, information about interests in shares etc; giving false information; Section 455(1) exercising a right to dispose of, or vote in respect of, shares which are subject to restrictions under Part XV; failing to give notice in respect of shares so subject; entering into agreement void under section 454(2), (3); Section 455(2) issuing shares in contravention of restrictions under Part XV; Section 461(5) failure to register office copy of court order under Part XVII altering, or giving leave to alter, company's memorandum; Section 697(1) oversea company failing to comply with any of sections 691 to 693 or 696; Section 697(2) oversea company contravening section 694(6) (carrying on business under its corporate name after Secretary of State's direction); Section 697(3) oversea company failing to comply with section 695A or Schedule 21A; Section 703(1) oversea company failing to comply with requirements as to accounts and reports; Section 703D(5) oversea company failing to deliver particulars of charge to registrar;

Provisions	Modifications
	Section 703R(1) company failing to register winding up or commencement of insolvency proceedings etc;
	Section 703R(2) liquidator failing to register appointment, termination of winding up or striking off of company;
	Section 720(4) insurance company etc failing to send twice yearly statement in form of Schedule 23;
	Schedule 14, Pt II, paragraph 1(3) company failing to give notice of location of overseas branch register, etc;
	Schedule 14, Pt II, paragraph 4(2) company failing to transmit to its registered office in Great Britain copies of entries in overseas branch register or to keep duplicate of overseas branch register;
	Schedule 21C, Pt I, paragraph 7 credit or financial institution failing to deliver accounting documents;
	Schedule 21C, Pt II, paragraph 15 credit or financial institution failing to deliver accounts and reports;
	Schedule 21D, Pt I, paragraph 5 company failing to deliver accounting documents;
	Schedule 21D, Pt I, Paragraph 13 company failing to deliver accounts and reports.

PART II

MODIFICATIONS TO THECOMPANY DIRECTORS DISQUALIFICATION ACT 1986

Part II of Schedule I	After paragraph 8 insert— "8A The extent of the member's and shadow members' responsibility for events leading to a member or shadow member, whether himself or some other member or shadow member, being declared by the court to be liable to make a contribution to the assets of the limited liability partnership under section 214A of the Insolvency Act 1986."

SCHEDULE 3

MODIFICATIONS TO THE 1986 ACT

Regulation 5

Provisions	Modifications
Section 1 (those who may propose an arrangement) subsection (1)	For "The directors of a company" substitute "A limited liability partnership" and delete "to the company and".

Provisions	Modifications
subsection (3)	At the end add "but where a proposal is so made it must also be made to the limited liability partnership".

The following modifications to sections 2 to 7 apply where a proposal under section 1 has been made by the limited liability partnership.

Section 2 (procedure where the nominee is not the liquidator or administrator)	
subsection (2)	In paragraph (a) for "meetings of the company and of it creditors" substitute "a meeting of the creditors of the limited liability partnership"; In paragraph (b) for the first "meetings" substitute "a meeting" and for the second "meetings" substitute "meeting".
subsection (3)	For "the person intending to make the proposal" substitute "the designated members of the limited liability partnership".
subsection (4)	For "the person intending to make the proposal" substitute "the designated members of the limited liability partnership".
Section 3 (summoning of meetings)	
subsection (1)	For "such meetings as are mentioned in section 2(2)" substitute "a meeting of creditors" and for "those meetings" substitute "that meeting".
subsection (2)	Delete subsection (2).
Section 4 (decisions of meetings)	
subsection (1)	For "meetings" substitute "meeting".
subsection (5)	For "each of the meetings" substitute "the meeting".
new subsection (5A)	Insert a new subsection (5A) as follows— "(5A) If modifications to the proposal are proposed at the meeting the chairman of the meeting shall, before the conclusion of the meeting, ascertain from the limited liability partnership whether or not it accepts the proposed modifications; and if at that conclusion the limited liability partnership has failed to respond to a proposed modification it shall be presumed not to have agreed to it."
subsection (6)	For "either" substitute "the"; after "the result of the meeting", in the first place where it occurs, insert "(including, where modifications to the proposal were proposed at the meeting, the response to those proposed modifications made by the limited liability partnership)"; and at the end add "and to the limited liability partnership".
Section 5 (effect of approval)	
subsection (1)	For "each of the meetings" substitute "the meeting" and for "with the same modifications" substitute "with modifications agreed to by the limited liability partnership".

Provisions	Modifications
subsection (4)	For "each of the reports" substitute "the report".
Section 6 (challenge of decisions)	
subsection (1)	For "meetings" substitute "meeting" and for "either of the meetings" substitute "the meeting".
subsection (2)	For "either of the meetings" substitute "the meeting" and after paragraph (a) add a new paragraph (aa) as follows— "(aa) any member of the limited liability partnership; and". Omit the word "and" at the end of paragraph (b) and omit paragraph (c).
subsection (3)	For "each of the reports" substitute "the report".
subsection (4)	For subsection (4) substitute the following— "(4) Where on such an application the court is satisfied as to either of the grounds mentioned in subsection (1), it may do one or both of the following, namely— (a) revoke or suspend the approval given by the meeting; (b) give a direction to any person for the summoning of a further meeting to consider any revised proposal the limited liability partnership may make or, in a case falling within subsection (1)(b), a further meeting to consider the original proposal.".
subsection (5)	For the first "meetings" substitute "a meeting", for the second "meetings" substitute "meeting" and for "person who made the original proposal" substitute "limited liability partnership".
Section 7 (implementation of proposal)	
subsection (1)	For "meetings" substitute "meeting".

The following modifications to sections 2 and 3 apply where a proposal under section 1 has been made, where an administration order is in force in relation to the limited liability partnership, by the administrator or, where the limited liability partnership is being wound up, by the liquidator.

Section 2 (procedure where the nominee is not the liquidator or administrator)	
subsection (2)	In paragraph (a) for "meetings of the company" substitute "meetings of the members of the limited liability partnership".
Section 3 (summoning of meetings)	
subsection (2)	For "meetings of the company" substitute "a meeting of the members of the limited liability partnership".
Section 8 (power of court to make order)	
. . .	. . .
subsection (4)	Omit subsection (4).
subsection (5)	Omit subsection (5).
subsection (6)	Omit subsection (6).
Section 9 (application for order)	

Provisions	Modifications
subsection (1)	Delete ", or the directors".
Section 10 (effect of application)	
subsection (1)	In paragraph (a) for "no resolution may be passed" to the end of the subsection substitute "no determination may be made or order made for the winding up of the limited liability partnership.".
Section 11 (effect of order)	
subsection (3)	In paragraph (a) for "no resolution may be passed" to the end of the subsection substitute "no determination may be made or order made for the winding up of the limited liability partnership.".
Section 13 (appointment of administrator)	
subsection (3)	In paragraph (c) delete "or the directors".
Section 14 (general powers)	
subsection (2)	For paragraph (a) substitute— "(a) to prevent any person from taking part in the management of the business of the limited liability partnership and to appoint any person to be a manager of that business, and"; and at the end add the following— "Subsections (3) and (4) of section 92 shall apply for the purposes of this subsection as they apply for the purposes of that section."
Section 73 (alternative modes of winding up)	
subsection (1)	Delete ", within the meaning given to that expression by section 735 of the Companies Act,".
Section 74 (liability as contributories of present and past members)	For section 74 there shall be substituted the following— "74. When a limited liability partnership is wound up every present and past member of the limited liability partnership who has agreed with the other members or with the limited liability partnership that he will, in circumstances which have arisen, be liable to contribute to the assets of the limited liability partnership in the event that the limited liability partnership goes into liquidation is liable, to the extent that he has so agreed, to contribute to its assets to any amount sufficient for payment of its debts and liabilities, and the expenses of the winding up, and for the adjustment of the rights of the contributories among themselves. However, a past member shall only be liable if the obligation arising from such agreement survived his ceasing to be a member of the limited liability partnership."
Section 75 to 78	Delete sections 75 to 78.
Section 79 (meaning of "contributory")	
subsection (1)	In subsection (1) for "every person" substitute "(a) every present member of the limited liability partnership and (b) every past member of the limited liability partnership".

Provisions	Modifications
subsection (2)	After "section 214 (wrongful trading)" insert "or 214A (adjustment of withdrawals)".
subsection (3)	Delete subsection (3).
Section 83 (companies registered under Companies Act, Part XXII, Chapter II)	Delete section 83.
Section 84 (circumstances in which company may be wound up voluntarily)	
subsection (1)	For subsection (1) substitute the following— "(1) A limited liability partnership may be wound up voluntarily when it determines that it is to be wound up voluntarily."
subsection (2)	Omit subsection (2).
subsection (3)	For subsection (3) substitute the following— "(3) Within 15 days after a limited liability partnership has determined that it be wound up there shall be forwarded to the registrar of companies either a printed copy or else a copy in some other form approved by the registrar of the determination."
subsection (4)	After subsection (3) insert a new subsection (4)— "(4) If a limited liability partnership fails to comply with this regulation the limited liability partnership and every designated member of it who is in default is liable on summary conviction to a fine not exceeding level 3 on the standard scale."
Section 85 (notice of resolution to wind up)	
subsection (1)	For subsection (1) substitute the following— "(1) When a limited liability partnership has determined that it shall be wound up voluntarily, it shall within 14 days after the making of the determination give notice of the determination by advertisement in the Gazette."
Section 86 (commencement of winding up)	Substitute the following new section— "86. A voluntary winding up is deemed to commence at the time when the limited liability partnership determines that it be wound up voluntarily.".
Section 87 (effect on business and status of company)	
subsection (2)	In subsection (2), for "articles" substitute "limited liability partnership agreement".
Section 88 (avoidance of share transfers, etc after winding-up resolution)	For "shares" substitute "the interest of any member in the property of the limited liability partnership".
Section 89 (statutory declaration of solvency)	For "director(s)" wherever it appears in section 89 substitute "designated member(s)";
subsection (2)	For paragraph (a) substitute the following— "(a) it is made within the 5 weeks immediately preceding the date when the limited liability partnership determined that it be wound up voluntarily or on that date but before the making of the determination, and".

Provisions	Modifications
subsection (3)	For "the resolution for winding up is passed" substitute "the limited liability partnership determined that it be wound up voluntarily".
subsection (5)	For "in pursuance of a resolution passed" substitute "voluntarily".
Section 90 (distinction between "members" and "creditors" voluntary winding up)	For "directors'" substitute "designated members'".
Section 91 (appointment of liquidator)	
subsection (1)	Delete "in general meeting".
subsection (2)	For the existing wording substitute "(2) On the appointment of a liquidator the powers of the members of the limited liability partnership shall cease except to the extent that a meeting of the members of the limited liability partnership summoned for the purpose or the liquidator sanctions their continuance." After subsection (2) insert— "(3) Subsections (3) and (4) of section 92 shall apply for the purposes of this section as they apply for the purposes of that section."
Section 92 (power to fill vacancy in office of liquidator)	
subsection (1)	For "the company in general meeting" substitute "a meeting of the members of the limited liability partnership summoned for the purpose".
subsection (2)	For "a general meeting" substitute "a meeting of the members of the limited liability partnership".
subsection (3)	In subsection (3), for "articles" substitute "limited liability partnership agreement".
new subsection (4)	Add a new subsection (4) as follows— "(4) The quorum required for a meeting of the members of the limited liability partnership shall be any quorum required by the limited liability partnership agreement for meetings of the members of the limited liability partnership and if no requirement for a quorum has been agreed upon the quorum shall be 2 members."
Section 93 (general company meeting at each year's end)	
subsection (1)	For "a general meeting of the company" substitute "a meeting of the members of the limited liability partnership".
new subsection (4)	Add a new subsection (4) as follows— "(4) subsections (3) and (4) of section 92 shall apply for the purposes of this section as they apply for the purposes of that section."
Section 94 (final meeting prior to dissolution)	
subsection (1)	For "a general meeting of the company" substitute "a meeting of the members of the limited liability partnership".
new subsection (5A)	Add a new subsection (5A) as follows—

Provisions	Modifications
	"(5A) Subsections (3) and (4) of section 92 shall apply for the purposes of this section as they apply for the purposes of that section."
subsection (6)	For "a general meeting of the company" substitute "a meeting of the members of the limited liability partnership".
Section 95 (effect of company's insolvency)	
subsection (1)	For "directors'" substitute "designated members'".
subsection (7)	For subsection (7) substitute the following— "(7) In this section "the relevant period" means the period of 6 months immediately preceding the date on which the limited liability partnership determined that it be wound up voluntarily."
Section 96 (conversion to creditors' voluntary winding up)	
paragraph (a)	For "directors'" substitute "designated members'".
paragraph (b)	Substitute a new paragraph (b) as follows— "(b) the creditors' meeting was the meeting mentioned in section 98 in the next Chapter;".
Section 98 (meeting of creditors)	
subsection (1)	For paragraph (a) substitute the following— "(a) cause a meeting of its creditors to be summoned for a day not later than the 14th day after the day on which the limited liability partnership determines that it be wound up voluntarily;".
subsection (5)	For "were sent the notices summoning the company meeting at which it was resolved that the company be wound up voluntarily" substitute "the limited liability partnership determined that it be wound up voluntarily".
Section 99 (directors to lay statement of affairs before creditors)	
subsection (1)	For "the directors of the company" substitute "the designated members" and for "the director so appointed" substitute "the designated member so appointed".
subsection (2)	For "directors" substitute "designated members".
subsection (3)	For "directors" substitute "designated members" and for "director" substitute "designated member".
Section 100 (appointment of liquidator)	
subsection (1)	For "The creditors and the company at their respective meetings mentioned in section 98" substitute "The creditors at their meeting mentioned in section 98 and the limited liability partnership".
subsection (3)	Delete "director,".
Section 101 (appointment of liquidation committee)	
subsection (2)	For subsection (2) substitute the following—

Provisions	Modifications
	"(2) If such a committee is appointed, the limited liability partnership may, when it determines that it be wound up voluntarily or at any time thereafter, appoint such number of persons as they think fit to act as members of the committee, not exceeding 5."
Section 105 (meetings of company and creditors at each year's end)	
subsection (1)	For "a general meeting of the company" substitute "a meeting of the members of the limited liability partnership".
new subsection (5)	Add a new subsection (5) as follows— "(5) Subsections (3) and (4) of section 92 shall apply for the purposes of this section as they apply for the purposes of that section."
Section 106 (final meeting prior to dissolution)	
subsection (1)	For "a general meeting of the company" substitute "a meeting of the members of the limited liability partnership".
new subsection (5A)	After subsection (5) insert a new subsection (5A) as follows— "5A) Subsections (3) and (4) of section 92 shall apply for the purposes of this section as they apply for the purposes of that section."
subsection (6)	For "a general meeting of the company" substitute "a meeting of the members of the limited liability partnership".
Section 110 (acceptance of shares, etc, as consideration for sale of company property)	For the existing section substitute the following: "(1) This section applies, in the case of a limited liability partnership proposed to be, or being, wound up voluntarily, where the whole or part of the limited liability partnership's business or property is proposed to be transferred or sold to another company whether or not it is a company within the meaning of the Companies Act ("the transferee company") or to a limited liability partnership ("the transferee limited liability partnership"). (2) With the requisite sanction, the liquidator of the limited liability partnership being, or proposed to be, wound up ("the transferor limited liability partnership") may receive, in compensation or part compensation for the transfer or sale, shares, policies or other like interests in the transferee company or the transferee limited liability partnership for distribution among the members of the transferor limited liability partnership.

Provisions

Section 111 (dissent from arrangement under section 110)

subsections (1)–(3)

Modifications

(3) The sanction required under subsection (2) is—

(a) in the case of a members' voluntary winding up, that of a determination of the limited liability partnership at a meeting of the members of the limited liability partnership conferring either a general authority on the liquidator or an authority in respect of any particular arrangement, (subsections (3) and (4) of section 92 to apply for this purpose as they apply for the purposes of that section), and

(b) in the case of a creditor's voluntary winding up, that of either court or the liquidation committee.

(4) Alternatively to subsection (2), the liquidator may (with the sanction) enter into any other arrangement whereby the members of the transferor limited liability partnership may, in lieu of receiving cash, shares, policies or other like interests (or in addition thereto), participate in the profits, or receive any other benefit from the transferee company or the transferee limited liability partnership.

(5) A sale or arrangement in pursuance of this section is binding on members of the transferor limited liability partnership.

(6) A determination by the limited liability partnership is not invalid for the purposes of this section by reason that it is made before or concurrently with a determination by the limited liability partnership that it be wound up voluntarily or for appointing liquidators; but, if an order is made within a year for winding up the limited liability partnership by the court, the determination by the limited liability partnership is not valid unless sanctioned by the court."

For subsections (1)–(3) substitute the following—

"(1) This section applies in the case of a voluntary winding up where, for the purposes of section 110(2) or (4), a determination of the limited liability partnership has provided the sanction requisite for the liquidator under that section.

Provisions	Modifications
	(2) If a member of the transferor limited liability partnership who did not vote in favour of providing the sanction required for the liquidator under section 110 expresses his dissent from it in writing addressed to the liquidator and left at the registered office of the limited liability partnership within 7 days after the date on which that sanction was given, he may require the liquidator either to abstain from carrying the arrangement so sanctioned into effect or to purchase his interest at a price to be determined by agreement or arbitration under this section. (3) If the liquidator elects to purchase the member's interest, the purchase money must be paid before the limited liability partnership is dissolved and be raised by the liquidator in such manner as may be determined by the limited liability partnership."
subsection (4)	Omit subsection (4).
Section 117 (high court and county court jurisdiction)	
subsection (2)	Delete "Where the amount of a company's share capital paid up or credited as paid up does not exceed £120,000, then (subject to this section)".
subsection (3)	Delete subsection (3).
Section 120 (court of session and sheriff court jurisdiction)	
subsection (3)	Delete "Where the amount of a company's share capital paid up or credited as paid up does not exceed £120,000,".
subsection (5)	Delete subsection (5).
Section 122 (circumstances in which company may be wound up by the court)	
subsection (1)	For subsection (1) substitute the following— "(1) A limited liability partnership may be wound up by the court if— (a) the limited liability partnership has determined that the limited liability partnership be wound up by the court, (b) the limited liability partnership does not commence its business within a year from its incorporation or suspends its business for a whole year, (c) the number of members is reduced below two, (d) the limited liability partnership is unable to pay its debts, or (e) the court is of the opinion that it is just and equitable that the limited liability partnership should be wound up."
Section 124 (application for winding up)	
subsections (2), (3)and (4)(a)	Delete these subsections.

Provisions	Modifications
Section 124A (petition for winding-up on grounds of public interest)	
subsection (1)	Omit paragraphs (b) and (bb).
Section 126 (power to stay or restrain proceedings against company)	
subsection (2)	Delete subsection (2).
Section 127 (avoidance of property dispositions, etc)	For "any transfer of shares" substitute "any transfer by a member of the limited liability partnership of his interest in the property of the limited liability partnership".
Section 129 (commencement of winding up by the court)	
subsection (1)	For "a resolution has been passed by the company" substitute "a determination has been made" and for "at the time of the passing of the resolution" substitute "at the time of that determination".
Section 130 (consequences of winding-up order)	
subsection (3)	Delete subsection (3).
Section 148 (settlement of list of contributories and application of assets)	
subsection (1)	Delete ", with power to rectify the register of members in all cases where rectification is required in pursuance of the Companies Act or this Act,".
Section 149 (debts due from contributory to company)	
subsection (1)	Delete "the Companies Act or".
subsection (2)	Delete subsection (2).
subsection (3)	Delete ", whether limited or unlimited,".
Section 160 (delegation of powers to liquidator (England and Wales))	
subsection (1)	In subsection (1)(b) delete "and the rectifying of the register of members".
subsection (2)	For subsection (2) substitute the following— "(2) But the liquidator shall not make any call without the special leave of the court or the sanction of the liquidation committee."
Section 165 (voluntary winding up)	
subsection (2)	In paragraph (a) for "an extraordinary resolution of the company" substitute "a determination by a meeting of the members of the limited liability partnership".
subsection (4)	For paragraph (c) substitute the following— "(c) summon meetings of the members of the limited liability partnership for the purpose of obtaining their sanction or for any other purpose he may think fit."
new subsection (4A)	Insert a new subsection (4A) as follows— "(4A) Subsections (3) and (4) of section 92 shall apply for the purposes of this section as they apply for the purposes of that section."
Section 166 (creditors' voluntary winding up)	

Provisions	Modifications
subsection (5)	In paragraph (b) for "directors" substitute "designated members".
Section 171 (removal, etc (voluntary winding up))	
subsection (2)	For paragraph (a) substitute the following— "(a) in the case of a members' voluntary winding up, by a meeting of the members of the limited liability partnership summoned specially for that purpose, or".
subsection (6)	In paragraph (a) for "final meeting of the company" substitute "final meeting of the members of the limited liability partnership" and in paragraph (b) for "final meetings of the company" substitute "final meetings of the members of the limited liability partnership".
new subsection (7)	Insert a new subsection (7) as follows— "(7) Subsections (3) and (4) of section 92 are to apply for the purposes of this section as they apply for the purposes of that section."
Section 173 (release (voluntary winding up))	
subsection (2)	In paragraph (a) for "a general meeting of the company" substitute "a meeting of the members of the limited liability partnership".
Section 183 (effect of execution or attachment (England and Wales))	
subsection (2)	Delete paragraph (a).
Section 184 (duties of sheriff (England and Wales))	
subsection (1)	For "a resolution for voluntary winding up has been passed" substitute "the limited liability partnership has determined that it be wound up voluntarily".
subsection (4)	Delete "or of a meeting having been called at which there is to be proposed a resolution for voluntary winding up," and "or a resolution is passed (as the case may be)".
Section 187 (power to make over assets to employees)	Delete section 187.
Section 194 (resolutions passed at adjourned meetings)	After "contributories" insert "or of the members of a limited liability partnership".
Section 195 (meetings to ascertain wishes of creditors or contributories)	
subsection (3)	Delete "the Companies Act or".
Section 206 (fraud, etc in anticipation of winding up)	
subsection (1)	For "passes a resolution for voluntary winding up" substitute "makes a determination that it be wound up voluntarily".
Section 207 (transactions in fraud of creditors)	
subsection (1)	For "passes a resolution for voluntary winding up" substitute "makes a determination that it be wound up voluntarily".

Provisions	Modifications
Section 210 (material omissions from statement relating to company's affairs) subsection (2)	For "passed a resolution for voluntary winding up" substitute "made a determination that it be wound up voluntarily".
Section 214 (wrongful trading) subsection (2)	Delete from "but the court shall not" to the end of the subsection.
After section 214	Insert the following new section 214A

"214A. Adjustment of withdrawals

(1) This section has effect in relation to a person who is or has been a member of a limited liability partnership where, in the course of the winding up of that limited liability partnership, it appears that subsection (2) of this section applies in relation to that person.

(2) This subsection applies in relation to a person if—

(a) within the period of two years ending with the commencement of the winding up, he was a member of the limited liability partnership who withdrew property of the limited liability partnership, whether in the form of a share of profits, salary, repayment of or payment of interest on a loan to the limited liability partnership or any other withdrawal of property, and

(b) it is proved by the liquidator to the satisfaction of the court that at the time of the withdrawal he knew or had reasonable ground for believing that the limited liability partnership—

(i) was at the time of the withdrawal unable to pay its debts within the meaning of section 123, or

(ii) would become so unable to pay its debts after the assets of the limited liability partnership had been depleted by that withdrawal taken together with all other withdrawals (if any) made by any members contemporaneously with that withdrawal or in contemplation when that withdrawal was made.

(3) Where this section has effect in relation to any person the court, on the application of the liquidator, may declare that that person is to be liable to make such contribution (if any) to the limited liability partnership's assets as the court thinks proper.

(4) The court shall not make a declaration in relation to any person the amount of which exceeds the aggregate of the amounts or values of all the withdrawals referred to in subsection (2) made by that person within the period of two years referred to in that subsection.

Provisions	Modifications
	(5) The court shall not make a declaration under this section with respect to any person unless that person knew or ought to have concluded that after each withdrawal referred to in subsection (2) there was no reasonable prospect that the limited liability partnership would avoid going into insolvent liquidation.
	(6) For the purposes of subsection (5) the facts which a member ought to know or ascertain and the conclusions which he ought to reach are those which would be known, ascertained, or reached by a reasonably diligent person having both:
	(a) the general knowledge, skill and experience that may reasonably be expected of a person carrying out the same functions as are carried out by that member in relation to the limited liability partnership, and
	(b) the general knowledge, skill and experience that that member has.
	(7) For the purposes of this section a limited liability partnership goes into insolvent liquidation if it goes into liquidation at a time when its assets are insufficient for the payment of its debts and other liabilities and the expenses of the winding up.
	(8) In this section "member" includes a shadow member.
	(9) This section is without prejudice to section 214."
Section 215 (proceedings under ss 213, 214)	
subsection (1)	Omit the word "or" between the words "213" and "214" and insert after "214" "or 214A".
subsection (2)	For "either section" substitute "any of those sections".
subsection (4)	For "either section" substitute "any of those sections".
subsection (5)	For "Sections 213 and 214" substitute "Sections 213, 214 or 214A".
Section 218 (prosecution of delinquent officers and members of company)	
subsection (1)	For "officer, or any member, of the company" substitute "member of the limited liability partnership".
subsections (3), (4) and (6)	For "officer of the company, or any member of it," substitute "officer or member of the limited liability partnership".
Section 233 (supplies of gas, water, electricity etc)	
subsection (1)	For paragraph (c) substitute the following— "(c) a voluntary arrangement under Part I has taken effect in accordance with section 5".

Provisions	Modifications
subsection (4)	For paragraph (c) substitute the following— "(c) the date on which the voluntary arrangement took effect in accordance with section 5".
Section 247 ("insolvency" and "go into liquidation")	
subsection (2)	For "passes a resolution for voluntary winding up" substitute "makes a determination that it be wound up voluntarily" and for "passing such a resolution" substitute "making such a determination".
Section 249 ("connected with a company")	For the existing words substitute "For the purposes of any provision in this Group of Parts, a person is connected with a company (including a limited liability partnership) if— (a) he is a director or shadow director of a company or an associate of such a director or shadow director (including a member or a shadow member of a limited liability partnership or an associate of such a member or shadow member); or (b) he is an associate of the company or of the limited liability partnership."
Section 250 ("member" of a company)	Delete section 250.
Section 251 (expressions used generally)	Delete the word "and" appearing after the definition of "the rules" and insert the word "and" after the definition of "shadow director". After the definition of "shadow director" insert the following— ""shadow member", in relation to a limited liability partnership, means a person in accordance with whose directions or instructions the members of the limited liability partnership are accustomed to act (but so that a person is not deemed a shadow member by reason only that the members of the limited liability partnership act on advice given by him in a professional capacity);".
Section 386 (categories of preferential debts)	
subsection (1)	In subsection (1), omit the words "or an individual".
subsection (2)	In subsection (2), omit the words "or the individual".
Section 387 ("the relevant date")	
subsection (3)	In paragraph (c) for "passing of the resolution for the winding up of the company" substitute "making of the determination by the limited liability partnership that it be wound up voluntarily".
subsection (5)	Omit subsection (5).
subsection (6)	Omit subsection (6).
Section 388 (meaning of "act as insolvency practitioner")	
subsection (2)	Omit subsection (2).
subsection (3)	Omit subsection (3).

Provisions	Modifications
subsection (4)	Delete ""company" means a company within the meaning given by section 735(1) of the Companies Act or a company which may be wound up under Part V of this Act (unregistered companies);" and delete ""interim trustee" and "permanent trustee" mean the same as the Bankruptcy (Scotland) Act 1985".
Section 389 (acting without qualification an offence)	
subsection (1)	Omit the words "or an individual".
Section 402 (official petitioner)	Delete section 402.
Section 412 (individual insolvency rules (England and Wales))	Delete section 412.
Section 415 (Fees orders (individual insolvency proceedings in England and Wales))	Delete section 415.
Section 416 (monetary limits (companies winding up))	
subsection (1)	In subsection (1), omit the words "section 117(2) (amount of company's share capital determining whether county court has jurisdiction to wind it up);" and the words "section 120(3) (the equivalent as respects sheriff court jurisdiction in Scotland);".
subsection (3)	In subsection (3), omit the words "117(2), 120(3) or".
Section 418 (monetary limits (bankruptcy))	Delete section 418.
Section 420 (insolvent partnerships)	Delete section 420.
Section 421 (insolvent estates of deceased persons)	Delete section 421.
Section 422 (recognised banks, etc)	Delete section 422.
Section 427 (parliamentary disqualification)	Delete section 427.
Section 429 (disabilities on revocation or administration order against an individual)	Delete section 429.
Section 432 (offences by bodies corporate)	
subsection (2)	Delete "secretary or".
Section 435 (meaning of "associate")	
new subsection (3A)	Insert a new subsection (3A) as follows—"(3A) A member of a limited liability partnership is an associate of that limited liability partnership and of every other member of that limited liability partnership and of the husband or wife or relative of every other member of that limited liability partnership.".
subsection (11)	For subsection (11) there shall be substituted "(11) In this section "company" includes any body corporate (whether incorporated in Great Britain or elsewhere); and references to directors and other officers of a company and to voting power at any general meeting of a company have effect with any necessary modifications."

Provisions	Modifications
Section 436 (expressions used generally)	The following expressions and definitions shall be added to the section— "designated member" has the same meaning as it has in the Limited Liability Partnerships Act 2000; "limited liability partnership" means a limited liability partnership formed and registered under the Limited Liability Partnerships Act 2000; "limited liability partnership agreement", in relation to a limited liability partnership, means any agreement, express or implied, made between the members of the limited liability partnership or between the limited liability partnership and the members of the limited liability partnership which determines the mutual rights and duties of the members, and their rights and duties in relation to the limited liability partnership.
Section 437 (transitional provisions, and savings)	Delete section 437.
Section 440 (extent (Scotland)) subsection (2)	In subsection (2), omit paragraph (b).
Section 441 (extent (Northern Ireland))	Delete section 441.
Section 442 (extent (other territories))	Delete section 442.
Schedule 1 Paragraph 19	For paragraph 19 substitute the following— "19. Power to enforce any rights the limited liability partnership has against the members under the terms of the limited liability partnership agreement."
Schedule 10 Section 85(2)	In the entry relating to section 85(2) for "resolution for voluntary winding up" substitute "making of determination for voluntary winding up".
Section 89(4)	In the entry relating to section 89(4) for "Director" substitute "Designated member".
Section 93(3)	In the entry relating to section 93(3) for "general meeting of the company" substitute "meeting of members of the limited liability partnership".
Section 99(3)	In the entries relating to section 99(3) for "director" and "directors" where they appear substitute "designated member" or "designated members" as appropriate.
Section 105(3)	In the entry relating to section 105(3) for "company general meeting" substitute "meeting of the members of the limited liability partnership".
Section 106(6)	In the entry relating to section 106(6) for "final meeting of the company" substitute "final meeting of the members of the limited liability partnership".
Sections 353(1) to 362	Delete the entries relating to sections 353(1) to 362 inclusive.
Section 429(5)	Delete the entry relating to section 429(5).

SCHEDULE 4

Regulation 5(3)

The provisions listed in this Schedule are not applied to Scotland to the extent specified below:

Sections 50 to 52;

Section 53(1) and (2), to the extent that those subsections do not relate to the requirement for a copy of the instrument and notice being forwarded to the registrar of companies;

Section 53(4) (6) and (7);

Section 54(1), (2), (3) (to the extent that that subsection does not relate to the requirement for a copy of the interlocutor to be sent to the registrar of companies), and subsections (5), (6) and (7);

Sections 55 to 58;

Section 60, other than subsection (1);

Section 61, including subsections (6) and (7) to the extent that those subsections do not relate to anything to be done or which may be done to or by the registrar of companies;

Section 62, including subsection (5) to the extent that that subsection does not relate to anything to be done or which may be done to or by the registrar of companies;

Sections 63 to 66;

Section 67, including subsections (1) and (8) to the extent that those subsections do not relate to anything to be done or which may be done to the registrar of companies;

Section 68;

Section 69, including subsections (1) and (2) to the extent that those subsections do not relate to anything to be done or which may be done by the registrar of companies;

Sections 70 and 71;

Subsection 84(3), to the extent that it does not concern the copy of the resolution being forwarded to the registrar of companies within 15 days;

Sections 91 to 93;

Section 94, including subsections (3) and (4) to the extent that those subsections do not relate to the liquidator being required to send to the registrar of companies a copy of the account and a return of the final meeting;

Section 95;

Section 97;

Sections 100 to 102;

Sections 104 to 105;

Section 106, including subsections (3), (4) and (5) to the extent that those subsections do not relate to the liquidator being required to send to the registrar of companies a copy of the account of winding up and a return of the final meeting/quorum;

Sections 109 to 111;

Section 112, including subsection (3) to the extent that that subsection does not relate to the liquidator being required to send to the registrar a copy of the order made by the court;

Sections 113 to 115;

Sections 126 to 128;

Section 130(1) to the extent that that subsection does not relate to a copy of the order being forwarded by the court to the registrar;

Section 131;

Sections 133 to 135;

Sections 138 to 140;

Sections 142 to 146;

Section 147, including subsection (3) to the extent that that subsection does not relate to a copy of the order being forwarded by the company to the registrar;

Section 162 to the extent that that section concerns the matters set out in Section C.2 of Schedule 5 to the Scotland Act 1998 as being exceptions to the insolvency reservation;

Sections 163 to 167;

Section 169;

Section 170, including subsection (2) to the extent that that subsection does not relate to an application being made by the registrar to make good the default;

Section 171;

Section 172, including subsection (8) to the extent that that subsection does not relate to the liquidator being required to give notice to the registrar;

Sections 173 and 174;

Section 177;

Sections 185 to 189;

Sections 191 to 194;

Section 196 to the extent that that section applies to the specified devolved functions of Part IV of the Insolvency Act 1986;

Section 199;

Section 200 to the extent that it applies to the specified devolved functions of Part IV of the First Group of Parts of the 1986 Act;

Sections 206 to 215;

Section 218 subsections (1), (2), (4) and (6);

Section 231 to 232 to the extent that the sections apply to administrative receivers, liquidators and provisional liquidators;

Section 233, to the extent that that section applies in the case of the appointment of an administrative receiver, of a voluntary arrangement taking effect, of a company going into liquidation or where a provisional liquidator is appointed;

Section 234 to the extent that that section applies to situations other than those where an administration order applies;

Section 235 to the extent that that section applies to situations other than those where an administration order applies;

Sections 236 to 237 to the extent that those sections apply to situations other than administration orders and winding up;

Sections 242 to 243;

Section 244 to the extent that that section applies in circumstances other than a company which is subject to an administration order;

Section 245;

Section 251, to the extent that that section contains definitions which apply only to devolved matters;

Section 416(1) and (4), to the extent that those subsections apply to section 206(1)(a) and (b) in connection with the offence provision relating to the winding up of a limited liability partnership;

Schedule 2;

Schedule 3;

Schedule 4;

Schedule 8, to the extent that that Schedule does not apply to voluntary arrangements or administrations within the meaning of Parts I and II of the 1986 Act.

In addition, Schedule 10, which concerns punishment of offences under the Insolvency Act 1986, lists various sections of the Insolvency Act 1986 which create an offence. The following sections, which are listed in Schedule 10, are devolved in their application to Scotland:

Section 51(4);

Section 51(5);

Sections 53(2) to 62(5) to the extent that those subsections relate to matters other than delivery to the registrar of companies;

Section 64(2);

Section 65(4);

Section 66(6);

Section 67(8) to the extent that that subsection relates to matters other than delivery to the registrar of companies;

Section 93(3);

Section 94(4) to the extent that that subsection relates to matters other than delivery to the registrar of companies;

Section 94(6);

Section 95(8);

Section 105(3);

Section 106(4) to the extent that that subsection relates to matters other than delivery to the registrar of companies;

Section 106(6);

Section 109(2);

Section 114(4);

Section 131(7);

Section 164;

Section 166(7);

Section 188(2);

Section 192(2);

Sections 206 to 211; and

Section 235(5) to the extent that it relates to matters other than administration orders.

SCHEDULE 5

GENERAL AND CONSEQUENTIAL AMENDMENTS IN OTHER LEGISLATION

Regulation 9

...

SCHEDULE 6

APPLICATION OF SUBORDINATE LEGISLATION

Regulation 10

PART I

REGULATIONS MADE UNDER THE 1985 ACT

1.   The Companies (Revision of Defective Accounts and Report) Regulations 1990
2.   The Companies (Defective Accounts) (Authorised Person) Order 1991
3.   The Accounting Standards (Prescribed Body) Regulations 1990
4.   The Companies (Inspection and Copying of Registers, Indices and Documents) Regulations 1991
5.   The Companies (Registers and other Records) Regulations 1985
6.   Companies Act 1985 (Disclosure of Remuneration for Non-Audit Work) Regulations 1991

PART II

REGULATIONS MADE UNDER THE 1986 ACT

1.   Insolvency Practitioners Regulations 1990
2.   The Insolvency Practitioners (Recognised Professional Bodies) Order 1986
3.   The Insolvency Rules 1986 and the Insolvency (Scotland) Rules 1986 (except in so far as they relate to the exceptions to the reserved matters specified in section C 2 of Part II of Schedule 5 to the Scotland Act 1998)
4.   The Insolvency Fees Order 1986

PART III

REGULATIONS MADE UNDER OTHER LEGISLATION

Sale of Goods Act 1979

1979 c. 54

An Act to consolidate the law relating to the sale of goods

[6th December 1979]

PART I
CONTRACTS TO WHICH ACT APPLIES

1.   Contracts to which Act applies

(1)   This Act applies to contracts of sale of goods made on or after (but not to those made before) 1 January 1894.

(2)   In relation to contracts made on certain dates, this Act applies subject to the modification of certain of its sections as mentioned in Schedule 1 below.

(3)   Any such modification is indicated in the section concerned by a reference to Schedule 1 below.

(4)   Accordingly, where a section does not contain such a reference, this Act applies in relation to the contract concerned without such modification of the section.

PART II
FORMATION OF THE CONTRACT

Contract of sale

2.   Contract of sale

(1)   A contract of sale of goods is a contract by which the seller transfers or agrees to transfer the property in goods to the buyer for a money consideration, called the price.

(2)   There may be a contract of sale between one part owner and another.

(3)   A contract of sale may be absolute or conditional.

(4)   Where under a contract of sale the property in the goods is transferred from the seller to the buyer the contract is called a sale.

(5)   Where under a contract of sale the transfer of the property in the goods is to take place at a future time or subject to some condition later to be fulfilled the contract is called an agreement to sell.

(6)   An agreement to sell becomes a sale when the time elapses or the conditions are fulfilled subject to which the property in the goods is to be transferred.

3.   Capacity to buy and sell

(1)   Capacity to buy and sell is regulated by the general law concerning capacity to contract and to transfer and acquire property.

(2)   Where necessaries are sold and delivered to a minor or to a person who by reason of mental incapacity or drunkenness is incompetent to contract, he must pay a reasonable price for them.

(3)   In subsection (2) above "necessaries" means goods suitable to the condition in life of the minor or other person concerned and to his actual requirements at the time of the sale and delivery.

Formalities of contract

4.   How contract of sale is made

(1)   Subject to this and any other Act, a contract of sale may be made in writing (either with or without seal), or by word of mouth, or partly in writing and partly by word of mouth, or may be implied from the conduct of the parties.

(2)   Nothing in this section affects the law relating to corporations.

Subject matter of contract

5.   Existing or future goods

(1)   The goods which form the subject of a contract of sale may be either existing goods, owned or possessed by the seller, or goods to be manufactured or acquired by him after the making of the contract of sale, in this Act called future goods.

(2)   There may be a contract for the sale of goods the acquisition of which by the seller depends on a contingency which may or may not happen.

(3)   Where by a contract of sale the seller purports to effect a present sale of future goods, the contract operates as an agreement to sell the goods.

6.   Goods which have perished

Where there is a contract for the sale of specific goods, and the goods without the knowledge of the seller have perished at the time when the contract is made, the contract is void.

7.   Goods perishing before sale but after agreement to sell

Where there is an agreement to sell specific goods and subsequently the goods, without any fault on the part of the seller or buyer, perish before the risk passes to the buyer, the agreement is avoided.

The price

8.   Ascertainment of price

(1)   The price in a contract of sale may be fixed by the contract, or may be left to be fixed in a manner agreed by the contract, or may be determined by the course of dealing between the parties.

(2)   Where the price is not determined as mentioned in subsection (1) above the buyer must pay a reasonable price.

(3)   What is a reasonable price is a question of fact dependent on the circumstances of each particular case.

9.   Agreement to sell at valuation

(1)   Where there is an agreement to sell goods on the terms that the price is to be fixed by the valuation of a third party, and he cannot or does not make the valuation, the agreement is avoided; but if the goods or any part of them have been delivered to and appropriated by the buyer he must pay a reasonable price for them.

(2)   Where the third party is prevented from making the valuation by the fault of the seller or buyer, the party not at fault may maintain an action for damages against the party at fault.

Implied terms etc

10.   Stipulations about time

(1)   Unless a different intention appears from the terms of the contract, stipulations as to time of payment are not of the essence of a contract of sale.

(2)   Whether any other stipulation as to time is or is not of the essence of the contract depends on the terms of the contract.

(3)   In a contract of sale "month" prima facie means calendar month.

11.   When condition to be treated as warranty

(1)   This section does not apply to Scotland.

(2)   Where a contract of sale is subject to a condition to be fulfilled by the seller, the buyer may waive the condition, or may elect to treat the breach of the condition as a breach of warranty and not as a ground for treating the contract as repudiated.

(3)   Whether a stipulation in a contract of sale is a condition, the breach of which may give rise to a right to treat the contract as repudiated, or a warranty, the breach of which may give rise to a claim for damages but not to a right to reject the goods and treat the contract as repudiated,

depends in each case on the construction of the contract; and a stipulation may be a condition, though called a warranty in the contract.

(4) Subject to section 35A below where a contract of sale is not severable and the buyer has accepted the goods or part of them, the breach of a condition to be fulfilled by the seller can only be treated as a breach of warranty, and not as a ground for rejecting the goods and treating the contract as repudiated, unless there is an express or implied term of the contract to that effect.

(5) ...

(6) Nothing in this section affects a condition or warranty whose fulfilment is excused by law by reason of impossibility or otherwise.

(7) Paragraph 2 of Schedule 1 below applies in relation to a contract made before 22 April 1967 or (in the application of this Act to Northern Ireland) 28 July 1967.

12. Implied terms about title, etc

(1) In a contract of sale, other than one to which subsection (3) below applies, there is an implied term on the part of the seller that in the case of a sale he has a right to sell the goods, and in the case of an agreement to sell he will have such a right at the time when the property is to pass.

(2) In a contract of sale, other than one to which subsection (3) below applies, there is also an implied term that—

    (a) the goods are free, and will remain free until the time when the property is to pass, from any charge or encumbrance not disclosed or known to the buyer before the contract is made, and

    (b) the buyer will enjoy quiet possession of the goods except so far as it may be disturbed by the owner or other person entitled to the benefit of any charge or encumbrance so disclosed or known.

(3) This subsection applies to a contract of sale in the case of which there appears from the contract or is to be inferred from its circumstances an intention that the seller should transfer only such title as he or a third person may have.

(4) In a contract to which subsection (3) above applies there is an implied term that all charges or encumbrances known to the seller and not known to the buyer have been disclosed to the buyer before the contract is made.

(5) In a contract to which subsection (3) above applies there is also an implied term that none of the following will disturb the buyer's quiet possession of the goods, namely—

    (a) the seller;

    (b) in a case where the parties to the contract intend that the seller should transfer only such title as a third person may have, that person;

    (c) anyone claiming through or under the seller or that third person otherwise than under a charge or encumbrance disclosed or known to the buyer before the contract is made.

(5A) As regards England and Wales and Northern Ireland, the term implied by subsection (1) above is a condition and the terms implied by subsections (2), (4) and (5) above are warranties.

(6) Paragraph 3 of Schedule 1 below applies in relation to a contract made before 18 May 1973.

13. Sale by description

(1) Where there is a contract for the sale of goods by description, there is an implied term that the goods will correspond with the description.

(1A) As regards England and Wales and Northern Ireland, the term implied by subsection (1) above is a condition.

(2) If the sale is by sample as well as by description it is not sufficient that the bulk of the goods corresponds with the sample if the goods do not also correspond with the description.

(3) A sale of goods is not prevented from being a sale by description by reason only that, being exposed for sale or hire, they are selected by the buyer.

(4) Paragraph 4 of Schedule 1 below applies in relation to a contract made before 18 May 1973.

14.   **Implied terms about quality or fitness**

(1)   Except as provided by this section and section 15 below and subject to any other enactment, there is no implied term about the quality or fitness for any particular purpose of goods supplied under a contract of sale.

(2)   Where the seller sells goods in the course of a business, there is an implied term that the goods supplied under the contract are of satisfactory quality.

(2A)   For the purposes of this Act, goods are of satisfactory quality if they meet the standard that a reasonable person would regard as satisfactory, taking account of any description of the goods, the price (if relevant) and all the other relevant circumstances.

(2B)   For the purposes of this Act, the quality of goods includes their state and condition and the following (among others) are in appropriate cases aspects of the quality of goods—

    (a)   fitness for all the purposes for which goods of the kind in question are commonly supplied,

    (b)   appearance and finish,

    (c)   freedom from minor defects,

    (d)   safety, and

    (e)   durability.

(2C)   The term implied by subsection (2) above does not extend to any matter making the quality of goods unsatisfactory—

    (a)   which is specifically drawn to the buyer's attention before the contract is made,

    (b)   where the buyer examines the goods before the contract is made, which that examination ought to reveal, or

    (c)   in the case of a contract for sale by sample, which would have been apparent on a reasonable examination of the sample.

(2D)   If the buyer deals as consumer or, in Scotland, if a contract of sale is a consumer contract, the relevant circumstances mentioned in subsection (2A) above include any public statements on the specific characteristics of the goods made about them by the seller, the producer or his representative, particularly in advertising or on labelling.

(2E)   A public statement is not by virtue of subsection (2D) above a relevant circumstance for the purposes of subsection (2A) above in the case of a contract of sale, if the seller shows that—

    (a)   at the time the contract was made, he was not, and could not reasonably have been, aware of the statement,

    (b)   before the contract was made, the statement had been withdrawn in public or, to the extent that it contained anything which was incorrect or misleading, it had been corrected in public, or

    (c)   the decision to buy the goods could not have been influenced by the statement.

(2F)   Subsections (2D) and (2E) above do not prevent any public statement from being a relevant circumstance for the purposes of subsection (2A) above (whether or not the buyer deals as consumer or, in Scotland, whether or not the contract of sale is a consumer contract) if the statement would have been such a circumstance apart from those subsections.

(3)   Where the seller sells goods in the course of a business and the buyer, expressly or by implication, makes known—

    (a)   to the seller, or

    (b)   where the purchase price or part of it is payable by instalments and the goods were previously sold by a credit-broker to the seller, to that credit-broker,

any particular purpose for which the goods are being bought, there is an implied term that the goods supplied under the contract are reasonably fit for that purpose, whether or not that is a purpose for which such goods are commonly supplied, except where the circumstances show that the buyer does not rely, or that it is unreasonable for him to rely, on the skill or judgment of the seller or credit-broker.

(4)   An implied term about quality or fitness for a particular purpose may be annexed to a contract of sale by usage.

(5)   The preceding provisions of this section apply to a sale by a person who in the course of a business is acting as agent for another as they apply to a sale by a principal in the course of a business, except where that other is not selling in the course of a business and either the buyer knows that fact or reasonable steps are taken to bring it to the notice of the buyer before the contract is made.

(6)   As regards England and Wales and Northern Ireland, the terms implied by subsections (2) and (3) above are conditions.

(7)   Paragraph 5 of Schedule 1 below applies in relation to a contract made on or after 18 May 1973 and before the appointed day, and paragraph 6 in relation to one made before 18 May 1973.

(8)   In subsection (7) above and paragraph 5 of Schedule 1 below references to the appointed day are to the day appointed for the purposes of those provisions by an order of the Secretary of State made by statutory instrument.

Sale by sample

15.   Sale by sample

(1)   A contract of sale is a contract for sale by sample where there is an express or implied term to that effect in the contract.

(2)   In the case of a contract for sale by sample there is an implied term—
        (a)   that the bulk will correspond with the sample in quality;
        (b)   ...
        (c)   that the goods will be free from any defect, making their quality unsatisfactory, which would not be apparent on reasonable examination of the sample.

(3)   As regards England and Wales and Northern Ireland, the term implied by subsection (2) above is a condition.

(4)   Paragraph 7 of Schedule 1 below applies in relation to a contract made before 18 May 1973.

Miscellaneous

15A.   Modification of remedies for breach of condition in non-consumer cases

(1)   Where in the case of a contract of sale—
        (a)   the buyer would, apart from this subsection, have the right to reject goods by reason of a breach on the part of the seller of a term implied by section 13, 14 or 15 above, but
        (b)   the breach is so slight that it would be unreasonable for him to reject them,
        then, if the buyer does not deal as consumer, the breach is not to be treated as a breach of condition but may be treated as a breach of warranty.

(2)   This section applies unless a contrary intention appears in, or is to be implied from, the contract.

(3)   It is for the seller to show that a breach fell within subsection (1)(b) above.

(4)   This section does not apply to Scotland.

15B.   Remedies for breach of contract as respects Scotland

(1)   Where in a contract of sale the seller is in breach of any term of the contract (express or implied), the buyer shall be entitled—
        (a)   to claim damages, and
        (b)   if the breach is material, to reject any goods delivered under the contract and treat it as repudiated.

(2)   Where a contract of sale is a consumer contract, then, for the purposes of subsection (1)(b) above, breach by the seller of any term (express or implied)—
        (a)   as to the quality of the goods or their fitness for a purpose,
        (b)   if the goods are, or are to be, sold by description, that the goods will correspond with the description,
        (c)   if the goods are, or are to be, sold by reference to a sample, that the bulk will correspond with the sample in quality,
        shall be deemed to be a material breach.

(3)   This section applies to Scotland only.

PART III
EFFECTS OF THE CONTRACT

Transfer of property as between seller and buyer

16.   **Goods must be ascertained**

Subject to section 20A below where there is a contract for the sale of unascertained goods no property in the goods is transferred to the buyer unless and until the goods are ascertained.

17.   **Property passes when intended to pass**

(1)   Where there is a contract for the sale of specific or ascertained goods the property in them is transferred to the buyer at such time as the parties to the contract intend it to be transferred.

(2)   For the purpose of ascertaining the intention of the parties regard shall be had to the terms of the contract, the conduct of the parties and the circumstances of the case.

18.   **Rules for ascertaining intention**

Unless a different intention appears, the following are rules for ascertaining the intention of the parties as to the time at which the property in the goods is to pass to the buyer.

Rule 1—

Where there is an unconditional contract for the sale of specific goods in a deliverable state the property in the goods passes to the buyer when the contract is made, and it is immaterial whether the time of payment or the time of delivery, or both, be postponed.

Rule 2—

Where there is a contract for the sale of specific goods and the seller is bound to do something to the goods for the purpose of putting them into a deliverable state, the property does not pass until the thing is done and the buyer has notice that it has been done.

Rule 3—

Where there is a contract for the sale of specific goods in a deliverable state but the seller is bound to weigh, measure, test, or do some other act or thing with reference to the goods for the purpose of ascertaining the price, the property does not pass until the act or thing is done and the buyer has notice that it has been done.

Rule 4—

When goods are delivered to the buyer on approval or on sale or return or other similar terms the property in the goods passes to the buyer:—

     (a)   when he signifies his approval or acceptance to the seller or does any other act adopting the transaction;

     (b)   if he does not signify his approval or acceptance to the seller but retains the goods without giving notice of rejection, then, if a time has been fixed for the return of the goods, on the expiration of that time, and, if no time has been fixed, on the expiration of a reasonable time.

Rule 5—

(1)   Where there is a contract for the sale of unascertained or future goods by description, and goods of that description and in a deliverable state are unconditionally appropriated to the contract, either by the seller with the assent of the buyer or by the buyer with the assent of the seller, the property in the goods then passes to the buyer; and the assent may be express or implied, and may be given either before or after the appropriation is made.

(2)   Where, in pursuance of the contract, the seller delivers the goods to the buyer or to a carrier or other bailee or custodier (whether named by the buyer or not) for the purpose of transmission to the buyer, and does not reserve the right of disposal, he is to be taken to have unconditionally appropriated the goods to the contract.

(3)   Where there is a contract for the sale of a specified quantity of unascertained goods in a deliverable state forming part of a bulk which is identified either in the contract or by

subsequent agreement between the parties and the bulk is reduced to (or to less than) that quantity, then, if the buyer under that contract is the only buyer to whom goods are then due out of the bulk—

(a) the remaining goods are to be taken as appropriated to that contract at the time when the bulk is so reduced; and

(b) the property in those goods then passes to that buyer.

(4) Paragraph (3) above applies also (with the necessary modifications) where a bulk is reduced to (or to less than) the aggregate of the quantities due to a single buyer under separate contracts relating to that bulk and he is the only buyer to whom goods are then due out of that bulk.

19. Reservation of right of disposal

(1) Where there is a contract for the sale of specific goods or where goods are subsequently appropriated to the contract, the seller may, by the terms of the contract or appropriation, reserve the right of disposal of the goods until certain conditions are fulfilled; and in such a case, notwithstanding the delivery of the goods to the buyer, or to a carrier or other bailee or custodier for the purpose of transmission to the buyer, the property in the goods does not pass to the buyer until the conditions imposed by the seller are fulfilled.

(2) Where goods are shipped, and by the bill of lading the goods are deliverable to the order of the seller or his agent, the seller is prima facie to be taken to reserve the right of disposal.

(3) Where the seller of goods draws on the buyer for the price, and transmits the bill of exchange and bill of lading to the buyer together to secure acceptance or payment of the bill of exchange, the buyer is bound to return the bill of lading if he does not honour the bill of exchange, and if he wrongfully retains the bill of lading the property in the goods does not pass to him.

20. Passing of risk

(1) Unless otherwise agreed, the goods remain at the seller's risk until the property in them is transferred to the buyer, but when the property in them is transferred to the buyer the goods are at the buyer's risk whether delivery has been made or not.

(2) But where delivery has been delayed through the fault of either buyer or seller the goods are at the risk of the party at fault as regards any loss which might not have occurred but for such fault.

(3) Nothing in this section affects the duties or liabilities of either seller or buyer as a bailee or custodier of the goods of the other party.

(4) In a case where the buyer deals as consumer or, in Scotland, where there is a consumer contract in which the buyer is a consumer, subsections (1) to (3) above must be ignored and the goods remain at the seller's risk until they are delivered to the consumer.

20A. Undivided shares in goods forming part of a bulk

(1) This section applies to a contract for the sale of a specified quantity of unascertained goods if the following conditions are met—

(a) the goods or some of them form part of a bulk which is identified either in the contract or by subsequent agreement between the parties; and

(b) the buyer has paid the price for some or all of the goods which are the subject of the contract and which form part of the bulk.

(2) Where this section applies, then (unless the parties agree otherwise), as soon as the conditions specified in paragraphs (a) and (b) of subsection (1) above are met or at such later time as the parties may agree—

(a) property in an undivided share in the bulk is transferred to the buyer, and

(b) the buyer becomes an owner in common of the bulk.

(3) Subject to subsection (4) below, for the purposes of this section, the undivided share of a buyer in a bulk at any time shall be such share as the quantity of goods paid for and due to the buyer out of the bulk bears to the quantity of goods in the bulk at that time.

(4) Where the aggregate of the undivided shares of buyers in a bulk determined under subsection (3) above would at any time exceed the whole of the bulk at that time, the undivided share in the bulk

of each buyer shall be reduced proportionately so that the aggregate of the undivided shares is equal to the whole bulk.

(5)   Where a buyer has paid the price for only some of the goods due to him out of a bulk, any delivery to the buyer out of the bulk shall, for the purposes of this section, be ascribed in the first place to the goods in respect of which payment has been made.

(6)   For the purposes of this section payment of part of the price for any goods shall be treated as payment for a corresponding part of the goods.

20B.   Deemed consent by co-owner to dealings in bulk goods

(1)   A person who has become an owner in common of a bulk by virtue of section 20A above shall be deemed to have consented to—

   (a)   any delivery of goods out of the bulk to any other owner in common of the bulk, being goods which are due to him under his contract;

   (b)   any dealing with or removal, delivery or disposal of goods in the bulk by any other person who is an owner in common of the bulk in so far as the goods fall within that co-owner's undivided share in the bulk at the time of the dealing, removal, delivery or disposal.

(2)   No cause of action shall accrue to anyone against a person by reason of that person having acted in accordance with paragraph (a) or (b) of subsection (1) above in reliance on any consent deemed to have been given under that subsection.

(3)   Nothing in this section or section 20A above shall—

   (a)   impose an obligation on a buyer of goods out of a bulk to compensate any other buyer of goods out of that bulk for any shortfall in the goods received by that other buyer;

   (b)   affect any contractual arrangement between buyers of goods out of a bulk for adjustments between themselves; or

   (c)   affect the rights of any buyer under his contract.

Transfer of title

21.   Sale by person not the owner

(1)   Subject to this Act, where goods are sold by a person who is not their owner, and who does not sell them under the authority or with the consent of the owner, the buyer acquires no better title to the goods than the seller had, unless the owner of the goods is by his conduct precluded from denying the seller's authority to sell.

(2)   Nothing in this Act affects—

   (a)   the provisions of the Factors Acts or any enactment enabling the apparent owner of goods to dispose of them as if he were their true owner;

   (b)   the validity of any contract of sale under any special common law or statutory power of sale or under the order of a court of competent jurisdiction.

22.   Market overt

(1)   …

(2)   This section does not apply to Scotland.

(3)   Paragraph 8 of Schedule 1 below applies in relation to a contract under which goods were sold before 1st January 1968 or (in the application of this Act to Northern Ireland) 29th August 1967.

23.   Sale under voidable title

When the seller of goods has a voidable title to them, but his title has not been avoided at the time of the sale, the buyer acquires a good title to the goods, provided he buys them in good faith and without notice of the seller's defect of title.

24.   Seller in possession after sale

Where a person having sold goods continues or is in possession of the goods, or of the documents of title to the goods, the delivery or transfer by that person, or by a mercantile agent acting for him, of the goods or documents of title under any sale, pledge, or other disposition thereof, to any person receiving the same in good faith and without notice of the previous sale, has the same effect as if the person making the delivery or transfer were expressly authorised by the owner of the goods to make the same.

25.   Buyer in possession after sale

(1)   Where a person having bought or agreed to buy goods obtains, with the consent of the seller, possession of the goods or the documents of title to the goods, the delivery or transfer by that person, or by a mercantile agent acting for him, of the goods or documents of title, under any sale, pledge, or other disposition thereof, to any person receiving the same in good faith and without notice of any lien or other right of the original seller in respect of the goods, has the same effect as if the person making the delivery or transfer were a mercantile agent in possession of the goods or documents of title with the consent of the owner.

(2)   For the purposes of subsection (1) above—

(a)   the buyer under a conditional sale agreement is to be taken not to be a person who has bought or agreed to buy goods, and

(b)   "conditional sale agreement" means an agreement for the sale of goods which is a consumer credit agreement within the meaning of the Consumer Credit Act 1974 under which the purchase price or part of it is payable by instalments, and the property in the goods is to remain in the seller (notwithstanding that the buyer is to be in possession of the goods) until such conditions as to the payment of instalments or otherwise as may be specified in the agreement are fulfilled.

(3)   Paragraph 9 of Schedule 1 below applies in relation to a contract under which a person buys or agrees to buy goods and which is made before the appointed day.

(4)   In subsection (3) above and paragraph 9 of Schedule 1 below references to the appointed day are to the day appointed for the purposes of those provisions by an order of the Secretary of State made by statutory instrument.

26.   Supplementary to sections 24 and 25

In sections 24 and 25 above "mercantile agent" means a mercantile agent having in the customary course of his business as such agent authority either—

(a)   to sell goods, or

(b)   to consign goods for the purpose of sale, or

(c)   to buy goods, or

(d)   to raise money on the security of goods.

PART IV
PERFORMANCE OF THE CONTRACT

27.   Duties of seller and buyer

It is the duty of the seller to deliver the goods, and of the buyer to accept and pay for them, in accordance with the terms of the contract of sale.

28.   Payment and delivery are concurrent conditions

Unless otherwise agreed, delivery of the goods and payment of the price are concurrent conditions, that is to say, the seller must be ready and willing to give possession of the goods to the buyer in exchange for the price and the buyer must be ready and willing to pay the price in exchange for possession of the goods.

29.   Rules about delivery

(1)   Whether it is for the buyer to take possession of the goods or for the seller to send them to the buyer is a question depending in each case on the contract, express or implied, between the parties.

(2)   Apart from any such contract, express or implied, the place of delivery is the seller's place of business if he has one, and if not, his residence; except that, if the contract is for the sale of

specific goods, which to the knowledge of the parties when the contract is made are in some other place, then that place is the place of delivery.

(3)   Where under the contract of sale the seller is bound to send the goods to the buyer, but no time for sending them is fixed, the seller is bound to send them within a reasonable time.

(4)   Where the goods at the time of sale are in the possession of a third person, there is no delivery by seller to buyer unless and until the third person acknowledges to the buyer that he holds the goods on his behalf; but nothing in this section affects the operation of the issue or transfer of any document of title to goods.

(5)   Demand or tender of delivery may be treated as ineffectual unless made at a reasonable hour; and what is a reasonable hour is a question of fact.

(6)   Unless otherwise agreed, the expenses of and incidental to putting the goods into a deliverable state must be borne by the seller.

30.   Delivery of wrong quantity

(1)   Where the seller delivers to the buyer a quantity of goods less than he contracted to sell, the buyer may reject them, but if the buyer accepts the goods so delivered he must pay for them at the contract rate.

(2)   Where the seller delivers to the buyer a quantity of goods larger than he contracted to sell, the buyer may accept the goods included in the contract and reject the rest, or he may reject the whole.

(2A)   A buyer who does not deal as consumer may not—

      (a)   where the seller delivers a quantity of goods less than he contracted to sell, reject the goods under subsection (1) above, or

      (b)   where the seller delivers a quantity of goods larger than he contracted to sell, reject the whole under subsection (2) above,

if the shortfall or, as the case may be, excess is so slight that it would be unreasonable for him to do so.

(2B)   It is for the seller to show that a shortfall or excess fell within subsection (2A) above.

(2C)   Subsections (2A) and (2B) above do not apply to Scotland.

(2D), (2E) ...

(3)   Where the seller delivers to the buyer a quantity of goods larger than he contracted to sell and the buyer accepts the whole of the goods so delivered he must pay for them at the contract rate.

(4)   ...

(5)   This section is subject to any usage of trade, special agreement, or course of dealing between the parties.

31.   Instalment deliveries

(1)   Unless otherwise agreed, the buyer of goods is not bound to accept delivery of them by instalments.

(2)   Where there is a contract for the sale of goods to be delivered by stated instalments, which are to be separately paid for, and the seller makes defective deliveries in respect of one or more instalments, or the buyer neglects or refuses to take delivery of or pay for one or more instalments, it is a question in each case depending on the terms of the contract and the circumstances of the case whether the breach of contract is a repudiation of the whole contract or whether it is a severable breach giving rise to a claim for compensation but not to a right to treat the whole contract as repudiated.

32.   Delivery to carrier

(1)   Where, in pursuance of a contract of sale, the seller is authorised or required to send the goods to the buyer, delivery of the goods to a carrier (whether named by the buyer or not) for the purpose of transmission to the buyer is prima facie deemed to be a delivery of the goods to the buyer.

(2)   Unless otherwise authorised by the buyer, the seller must make such contract with the carrier on behalf of the buyer as may be reasonable having regard to the nature of the goods and the other circumstances of the case; and if the seller omits to do so, and the goods are lost or damaged in

course of transit, the buyer may decline to treat the delivery to the carrier as a delivery to himself or may hold the seller responsible in damages.

(3) Unless otherwise agreed, where goods are sent by the seller to the buyer by a route involving sea transit, under circumstances in which it is usual to insure, the seller must give such notice to the buyer as may enable him to insure them during their sea transit; and if the seller fails to do so, the goods are at his risk during such sea transit.

(4) In a case where the buyer deals as consumer or, in Scotland, where there is a consumer contract in which the buyer is a consumer, subsections (1) to (3) above must be ignored, but if in pursuance of a contract of sale the seller is authorised or required to send the goods to the buyer, delivery of the goods to the carrier is not delivery of the goods to the buyer.

33.   Risk where goods are delivered at distant place

Where the seller of goods agrees to deliver them at his own risk at a place other than that where they are when sold, the buyer must nevertheless (unless otherwise agreed) take any risk of deterioration in the goods necessarily incident to the course of transit.

34.   Buyer's right of examining the goods

... Unless otherwise agreed, when the seller tenders delivery of goods to the buyer, he is bound on request to afford the buyer a reasonable opportunity of examining the goods for the purpose of ascertaining whether they are in conformity with the contract and, in the case of a contract for sale by sample, of comparing the bulk with the sample.

35.   Acceptance

(1) The buyer is deemed to have accepted the goods subject to subsection (2) below—
   (a)   when he intimates to the seller that he has accepted them, or
   (b)   when the goods have been delivered to him and he does any act in relation to them which is inconsistent with the ownership of the seller.

(2) Where goods are delivered to the buyer, and he has not previously examined them, he is not deemed to have accepted them under subsection (1) above until he has had a reasonable opportunity of examining them for the purpose—
   (a)   of ascertaining whether they are in conformity with the contract, and
   (b)   in the case of a contract for sale by sample, of comparing the bulk with the sample.

(3) Where the buyer deals as consumer or (in Scotland) the contract of sale is a consumer contract, the buyer cannot lose his right to rely on subsection (2) above by agreement, waiver or otherwise.

(4) The buyer is also deemed to have accepted the goods when after the lapse of a reasonable time he retains the goods without intimating to the seller that he has rejected them.

(5) The questions that are material in determining for the purposes of subsection (4) above whether a reasonable time has elapsed include whether the buyer has had a reasonable opportunity of examining the goods for the purpose mentioned in subsection (2) above.

(6) The buyer is not by virtue of this section deemed to have accepted the goods merely because—
   (a)   he asks for, or agrees to, their repair by or under an arrangement with the seller, or
   (b)   the goods are delivered to another under a sub-sale or other disposition.

(7) Where the contract is for the sale of goods making one or more commercial units, a buyer accepting any goods included in a unit is deemed to have accepted all the goods making the unit; and in this subsection "commercial unit" means a unit division of which would materially impair the value of the goods or the character of the unit.

(8) Paragraph 10 of Schedule 1 below applies in relation to a contract made before 22 April 1967 or (in the application of this Act to Northern Ireland) 28 July 1967.

35A.   Right of partial rejection

(1) If the buyer—
   (a)   has the right to reject the goods by reason of a breach on the part of the seller that affects some or all of them, but

(b)   accepts some of the goods, including, where there are any goods unaffected by the breach,
       all such goods,

he does not by accepting them lose his right to reject the rest.

(2)   In the case of a buyer having the right to reject an instalment of goods, subsection (1) above
        applies as if references to the goods were references to the goods comprised in the instalment.

(3)   For the purposes of subsection (1) above, goods are affected by a breach if by reason of the breach
        they are not in conformity with the contract.

(4)   This section applies unless a contrary intention appears in, or is to be implied from, the contract.

36.   Buyer not bound to return rejected goods

Unless otherwise agreed, where goods are delivered to the buyer, and he refuses to accept them,
having the right to do so, he is not bound to return them to the seller, but it is sufficient if he intimates to the seller that he refuses to accept them.

37.   Buyer's liability for not taking delivery of goods

(1)   When the seller is ready and willing to deliver the goods, and requests the buyer to take delivery,
        and the buyer does not within a reasonable time after such request take delivery of the goods, he
        is liable to the seller for any loss occasioned by his neglect or refusal to take delivery, and also for
        a reasonable charge for the care and custody of the goods.

(2)   Nothing in this section affects the rights of the seller where the neglect or refusal of the buyer to
        take delivery amounts to a repudiation of the contract.

PART V

RIGHTS OF UNPAID SELLER AGAINST THE GOODS

Preliminary

38.   Unpaid seller defined

(1)   The seller of goods is an unpaid seller within the meaning of this Act—
        (a)   when the whole of the price has not been paid or tendered;
        (b)   when a bill of exchange or other negotiable instrument has been received as conditional
               payment, and the condition on which it was received has not been fulfilled by reason of the
               dishonour of the instrument or otherwise.

(2)   In this Part of this Act "seller" includes any person who is in the position of a seller, as, for
        instance, an agent of the seller to whom the bill of lading has been indorsed, or a consignor or
        agent who has himself paid (or is directly responsible for) the price.

39.   Unpaid seller's rights

(1)   Subject to this and any other Act, notwithstanding that the property in the goods may have passed
        to the buyer, the unpaid seller of goods, as such, has by implication of law—
        (a)   a lien on the goods or right to retain them for the price while he is in possession of them;
        (b)   in case of the insolvency of the buyer, a right of stopping the goods in transit after he has
               parted with the possession of them;
        (c)   a right of re-sale as limited by this Act.

(2)   Where the property in goods has not passed to the buyer, the unpaid seller has (in addition to his
        other remedies) a right of withholding delivery similar to and co-extensive with his rights of lien
        or retention and stoppage in transit where the property has passed to the buyer.

40.   …

Unpaid seller's lien

41.   Seller's lien

(1)   Subject to this Act, the unpaid seller of goods who is in possession of them is entitled to retain
        possession of them until payment or tender of the price in the following cases:—
        (a)   where the goods have been sold without any stipulation as to credit;

(b)   where the goods have been sold on credit but the term of credit has expired;

(c)   where the buyer becomes insolvent.

(2)   The seller may exercise his lien or right of retention notwithstanding that he is in possession of the goods as agent or bailee or custodier for the buyer.

42.   Part delivery

Where an unpaid seller has made part delivery of the goods, he may exercise his lien or right of retention on the remainder, unless such part delivery has been made under such circumstances as to show an agreement to waive the lien or right of retention.

43.   Termination of lien

(1)   The unpaid seller of goods loses his lien or right of retention in respect of them—

(a)   when he delivers the goods to a carrier or other bailee or custodier for the purpose of transmission to the buyer without reserving the right of disposal of the goods;

(b)   when the buyer or his agent lawfully obtains possession of the goods;

(c)   by waiver of the lien or right of retention.

(2)   An unpaid seller of goods who has a lien or right of retention in respect of them does not lose his lien or right of retention by reason only that he has obtained judgment or decree for the price of the goods.

Stoppage in transit

44.   Right of stoppage in transit

Subject to this Act, when the buyer of goods becomes insolvent the unpaid seller who has parted with the possession of the goods has the right of stopping them in transit, that is to say, he may resume possession of the goods as long as they are in course of transit, and may retain them until payment or tender of the price.

45.   Duration of transit

(1)   Goods are deemed to be in course of transit from the time when they are delivered to a carrier or other bailee or custodier for the purpose of transmission to the buyer, until the buyer or his agent in that behalf takes delivery of them from the carrier or other bailee or custodier.

(2)   If the buyer or his agent in that behalf obtains delivery of the goods before their arrival at the appointed destination, the transit is at an end.

(3)   If, after the arrival of the goods at the appointed destination, the carrier or other bailee or custodier acknowledges to the buyer or his agent that he holds the goods on his behalf and continues in possession of them as bailee or custodier for the buyer or his agent, the transit is at an end, and it is immaterial that a further destination for the goods may have been indicated by the buyer.

(4)   If the goods are rejected by the buyer, and the carrier or other bailee or custodier continues in possession of them, the transit is not deemed to be at an end, even if the seller has refused to receive them back.

(5)   When goods are delivered to a ship chartered by the buyer it is a question depending on the circumstances of the particular case whether they are in the possession of the master as a carrier or as agent to the buyer.

(6)   Where the carrier or other bailee or custodier wrongfully refuses to deliver the goods to the buyer or his agent in that behalf, the transit is deemed to be at an end.

(7)   Where part delivery of the goods has been made to the buyer or his agent in that behalf, the remainder of the goods may be stopped in transit, unless such part delivery has been made under such circumstances as to show an agreement to give up possession of the whole of the goods.

46.   How stoppage in transit is effected

(1)   The unpaid seller may exercise his right of stoppage in transit either by taking actual possession of the goods or by giving notice of his claim to the carrier or other bailee or custodier in whose possession the goods are.

(2)   The notice may be given either to the person in actual possession of the goods or to his principal.

(3)   If given to the principal, the notice is ineffective unless given at such time and under such circumstances that the principal, by the exercise of reasonable diligence, may communicate it to his servant or agent in time to prevent a delivery to the buyer.

(4)   When notice of stoppage in transit is given by the seller to the carrier or other bailee or custodier in possession of the goods, he must re-deliver the goods to, or according to the directions of, the seller; and the expenses of the re-delivery must be borne by the seller.

Re-sale etc by buyer

47.   Effect of sub-sale etc by buyer

(1)   Subject to this Act, the unpaid seller's right of lien or retention or stoppage in transit is not affected by any sale or other disposition of the goods which the buyer may have made, unless the seller has assented to it.

(2)   Where a document of title to goods has been lawfully transferred to any person as buyer or owner of the goods, and that person transfers the document to a person who takes it in good faith and for valuable consideration, then—

     (a)   if the last-mentioned transfer was by way of sale the unpaid seller's right of lien or retention or stoppage in transit is defeated; and

     (b)   if the last-mentioned transfer was made by way of pledge or other disposition for value, the unpaid seller's right of lien or retention or stoppage in transit can only be exercised subject to the rights of the transferee.

Rescission: and re-sale by seller

48.   Rescission: and re-sale by seller

(1)   Subject to this section, a contract of sale is not rescinded by the mere exercise by an unpaid seller of his right of lien or retention or stoppage in transit.

(2)   Where an unpaid seller who has exercised his right of lien or retention or stoppage in transit re-sells the goods, the buyer acquires a good title to them as against the original buyer.

(3)   Where the goods are of a perishable nature, or where the unpaid seller gives notice to the buyer of his intention to re-sell, and the buyer does not within a reasonable time pay or tender the price, the unpaid seller may re-sell the goods and recover from the original buyer damages for any loss occasioned by his breach of contract.

(4)   Where the seller expressly reserves the right of re-sale in case the buyer should make default, and on the buyer making default re-sells the goods, the original contract of sale is rescinded but without prejudice to any claim the seller may have for damages.

PART 5A
ADDITIONAL RIGHTS OF BUYER IN CONSUMER CASES

48A.   Introductory

(1)   This section applies if—

     (a)   the buyer deals as consumer or, in Scotland, there is a consumer contract in which the buyer is a consumer, and

     (b)   the goods do not conform to the contract of sale at the time of delivery.

(2)   If this section applies, the buyer has the right—

     (a)   under and in accordance with section 48B below, to require the seller to repair or replace the goods, or

     (b)   under and in accordance with section 48C below—

         (i)   to require the seller to reduce the purchase price of the goods to the buyer by an appropriate amount, or

         (ii)   to rescind the contract with regard to the goods in question.

(3)   For the purposes of subsection (1)(b) above goods which do not conform to the contract of sale at any time within the period of six months starting with the date on which the goods were delivered to the buyer must be taken not to have so conformed at that date.

(4)   Subsection (3) above does not apply if—
        (a)   it is established that the goods did so conform at that date;
        (b)   its application is incompatible with the nature of the goods or the nature of the lack of conformity.

48B.   Repair or replacement of the goods

(1)   If section 48A above applies, the buyer may require the seller—
        (a)   to repair the goods, or
        (b)   to replace the goods.

(2)   If the buyer requires the seller to repair or replace the goods, the seller must—
        (a)   repair or, as the case may be, replace the goods within a reasonable time but without causing significant inconvenience to the buyer;
        (b)   bear any necessary costs incurred in doing so (including in particular the cost of any labour, materials or postage).

(3)   The buyer must not require the seller to repair or, as the case may be, replace the goods if that remedy is—
        (a)   impossible, or
        (b)   disproportionate in comparison to the other of those remedies, or
        (c)   disproportionate in comparison to an appropriate reduction in the purchase price under paragraph (a), or rescission under paragraph (b), of section 48C(1) below.

(4)   One remedy is disproportionate in comparison to the other if the one imposes costs on the seller which, in comparison to those imposed on him by the other, are unreasonable, taking into account—
        (a)   the value which the goods would have if they conformed to the contract of sale,
        (b)   the significance of the lack of conformity, and
        (c)   whether the other remedy could be effected without significant inconvenience to the buyer.

(5)   Any question as to what is a reasonable time or significant inconvenience is to be determined by reference to—
        (a)   the nature of the goods, and
        (b)   the purpose for which the goods were acquired.

48C.   Reduction of purchase price or rescission of contract

(1)   If section 48A above applies, the buyer may—
        (a)   require the seller to reduce the purchase price of the goods in question to the buyer by an appropriate amount, or
        (b)   rescind the contract with regard to those goods,
        if the condition in subsection (2) below is satisfied.

(2)   The condition is that—
        (a)   by virtue of section 48B(3) above the buyer may require neither repair nor replacement of the goods; or
        (b)   the buyer has required the seller to repair or replace the goods, but the seller is in breach of the requirement of section 48B(2)(a) above to do so within a reasonable time and without significant inconvenience to the buyer.

(3)   For the purposes of this Part, if the buyer rescinds the contract, any reimbursement to the buyer may be reduced to take account of the use he has had of the goods since they were delivered to him.

48D.   Relation to other remedies etc

(1)   If the buyer requires the seller to repair or replace the goods the buyer must not act under subsection (2) until he has given the seller a reasonable time in which to repair or replace (as the case may be) the goods.

(2)　　　The buyer acts under this subsection if—

　　　(a)　in England and Wales or Northern Ireland he rejects the goods and terminates the contract for breach of condition;

　　　(b)　in Scotland he rejects any goods delivered under the contract and treats it as repudiated;

　　　(c)　he requires the goods to be replaced or repaired (as the case may be).

48E.　Powers of the court

(1)　　　In any proceedings in which a remedy is sought by virtue of this Part the court, in addition to any other power it has, may act under this section.

(2)　　　On the application of the buyer the court may make an order requiring specific performance or, in Scotland, specific implement by the seller of any obligation imposed on him by virtue of section 48B above.

(3)　　　Subsection (4) applies if—

　　　(a)　the buyer requires the seller to give effect to a remedy under section 48B or 48C above or has claims to rescind under section 48C, but

　　　(b)　the court decides that another remedy under section 48B or 48C is appropriate.

(4)　　　The court may proceed—

　　　(a)　as if the buyer had required the seller to give effect to the other remedy, or if the other remedy is rescission under section 48C;

　　　(b)　as if the buyer had claimed to rescind the contract under that section.

(5)　　　If the buyer has claimed to rescind the contract the court may order that any reimbursement to the buyer is reduced to take account of the use he has had of the goods since they were delivered to him.

(6)　　　The court may make an order under this section unconditionally or on such terms and conditions as to damages, payment of the price and otherwise as it thinks just.

48F.　Conformity with the contract

For the purposes of this Part, goods do not conform to a contract of sale if there is, in relation to the goods, a breach of an express term of the contract or a term implied by section 13, 14 or 15 above.

PART VI

ACTIONS FOR BREACH OF THE CONTRACT

Seller's remedies

49.　Action for price

(1)　　　Where, under a contract of sale, the property in the goods has passed to the buyer and he wrongfully neglects or refuses to pay for the goods according to the terms of the contract, the seller may maintain an action against him for the price of the goods.

(2)　　　Where, under a contract of sale, the price is payable on a day certain irrespective of delivery and the buyer wrongfully neglects or refuses to pay such price, the seller may maintain an action for the price, although the property in the goods has not passed and the goods have not been appropriated to the contract.

(3)　　　Nothing in this section prejudices the right of the seller in Scotland to recover interest on the price from the date of tender of the goods, or from the date on which the price was payable, as the case may be.

50.　Damages for non-acceptance

(1)　　　Where the buyer wrongfully neglects or refuses to accept and pay for the goods, the seller may maintain an action against him for damages for non-acceptance.

(2)　　　The measure of damages is the estimated loss directly and naturally resulting, in the ordinary course of events, from the buyer's breach of contract.

(3)   Where there is an available market for the goods in question the measure of damages is prima facie to be ascertained by the difference between the contract price and the market or current price at the time or times when the goods ought to have been accepted or (if no time was fixed for acceptance) at the time of the refusal to accept.

Buyer's remedies

51.   Damages for non-delivery

(1)   Where the seller wrongfully neglects or refuses to deliver the goods to the buyer, the buyer may maintain an action against the seller for damages for non-delivery.

(2)   The measure of damages is the estimated loss directly and naturally resulting, in the ordinary course of events, from the seller's breach of contract.

(3)   Where there is an available market for the goods in question the measure of damages is prima facie to be ascertained by the difference between the contract price and the market or current price of the goods at the time or times when they ought to have been delivered or (if no time was fixed) at the time of the refusal to deliver.

52.   Specific performance

(1)   In any action for breach of contract to deliver specific or ascertained goods the court may, if it thinks fit, on the plaintiff's application, by its judgment or decree direct that the contract shall be performed specifically, without giving the defendant the option of retaining the goods on payment of damages.

(2)   The plaintiff's application may be made at any time before judgment or decree.

(3)   The judgment or decree may be unconditional, or on such terms and conditions as to damages, payment of the price and otherwise as seem just to the court.

(4)   The provisions of this section shall be deemed to be supplementary to, and not in derogation of, the right of specific implement in Scotland.

53.   Remedy for breach of warranty

(1)   Where there is a breach of warranty by the seller, or where the buyer elects (or is compelled) to treat any breach of a condition on the part of the seller as a breach of warranty, the buyer is not by reason only of such breach of warranty entitled to reject the goods; but he may—

   (a)   set up against the seller the breach of warranty in diminution or extinction of the price, or

   (b)   maintain an action against the seller for damages for the breach of warranty.

(2)   The measure of damages for breach of warranty is the estimated loss directly and naturally resulting, in the ordinary course of events, from the breach of warranty.

(3)   In the case of breach of warranty of quality such loss is prima facie the difference between the value of the goods at the time of delivery to the buyer and the value they would have had if they had fulfilled the warranty.

(4)   The fact that the buyer has set up the breach of warranty in diminution or extinction of the price does not prevent him from maintaining an action for the same breach of warranty if he has suffered further damage.

(5)   This section does not apply to Scotland.

53A.   Measure of damages as respects Scotland

(1)   The measure of damages for the seller's breach of contract is the estimated loss directly and naturally resulting, in the ordinary course of events, from the breach.

(2)   Where the seller's breach consists of the delivery of goods which are not of the quality required by the contract and the buyer retains the goods, such loss as aforesaid is prima facie the difference between the value of the goods at the time of the delivery to the buyer and the value they would have had if they had fulfilled the contract.

(3)   This section applies to Scotland only.

Interest, etc

54.   Interest

Nothing in this Act affects the right of the buyer or the seller to recover interest or special damages in any case where by law interest or special damages may be recoverable, or to recover money paid where the consideration for the payment of it has failed.

PART VII
SUPPLEMENTARY

55.   Exclusion of implied terms

(1)   Where a right, duty or liability would arise under a contract of sale of goods by implication of law, it may (subject to the Unfair Contract Terms Act 1977) be negatived or varied by express agreement, or by the course of dealing between the parties, or by such usage as binds both parties to the contract.

(2)   An express term does not negative a term implied by this Act unless inconsistent with it.

(3)   Paragraph 11 of Schedule 1 below applies in relation to a contract made on or after 18 May 1973 and before 1 February 1978, and paragraph 12 in relation to one made before 18 May 1973.

56.   Conflict of laws

Paragraph 13 of Schedule 1 below applies in relation to a contract made on or after 18 May 1973 and before 1 February 1978, so as to make provision about conflict of laws in relation to such a contract.

57.   Auction sales

(1)   Where goods are put up for sale by auction in lots, each lot is prima facie deemed to be the subject of a separate contract of sale.

(2)   A sale by auction is complete when the auctioneer announces its completion by the fall of the hammer, or in other customary manner; and until the announcement is made any bidder may retract his bid.

(3)   A sale by auction may be notified to be subject to a reserve or upset price, and a right to bid may also be reserved expressly by or on behalf of the seller.

(4)   Where a sale by auction is not notified to be subject to a right to bid by or on behalf of the seller, it is not lawful for the seller to bid himself or to employ any person to bid at the sale, or for the auctioneer knowingly to take any bid from the seller or any such person.

(5)   A sale contravening subsection (4) above may be treated as fraudulent by the buyer.

(6)   Where, in respect of a sale by auction, a right to bid is expressly reserved (but not otherwise) the seller or any one person on his behalf may bid at the auction.

58.   Payment into court in Scotland

In Scotland where a buyer has elected to accept goods which he might have rejected, and to treat a breach of contract as only giving rise to a claim for damages, he may, in an action by the seller for the price, be required, in the discretion of the court before which the action depends, to consign or pay into court the price of the goods, or part of the price, or to give other reasonable security for its due payment.

59.   Reasonable time a question of fact

Where a reference is made in this Act to a reasonable time the question what is a reasonable time is a question of fact.

60.   Rights etc enforceable by action

Where a right, duty or liability is declared by this Act, it may (unless otherwise provided by this Act) be enforced by action.

61.   Interpretation

(1)   In this Act, unless the context or subject matter otherwise requires—

"action" includes counterclaim and set-off, and in Scotland condescendence and claim and compensation;

"bulk" means a mass or collection of goods of the same kind which—

(a)   is contained in a defined space or area; and

(b)   is such that any goods in the bulk are interchangeable with any other goods therein of the same number or quantity;

"business" includes a profession and the activities of any government department (including a Northern Ireland department) or local or public authority;

"buyer" means a person who buys or agrees to buy goods;

"consumer contract" has the same meaning as in section 25(1) of the Unfair Contract Terms Act 1977; and for the purposes of this Act the onus of proving that a contract is not to be regarded as a consumer contract shall lie on the seller;

"contract of sale" includes an agreement to sell as well as a sale;

"credit-broker" means a person acting in the course of a business of credit brokerage carried on by him, that is a business of effecting introductions of individuals desiring to obtain credit—

(a)   to persons carrying on any business so far as it relates to the provision of credit, or

(b)   to other persons engaged in credit brokerage;

"defendant" includes in Scotland defender, respondent, and claimant in a multiple poinding;

"delivery" means voluntary transfer of possession from one person to another except that in relation to sections 20A and 20B above it includes such appropriation of goods to the contract as results in property in the goods being transferred to the buyer;

"document of title to goods" has the same meaning as it has in the Factors Acts;

"Factors Acts" means the Factors Act 1889, the Factors (Scotland) Act 1890, and any enactment amending or substituted for the same;

"fault" means wrongful act or default;

"future goods" means goods to be manufactured or acquired by the seller after the making of the contract of sale;

"goods" includes all personal chattels other than things in action and money, and in Scotland all corporeal moveables except money; and in particular "goods" includes emblements, industrial growing crops, and things attached to or forming part of the land which are agreed to be severed before sale or under the contract of sale and includes an undivided share in goods;

"plaintiff" includes pursuer, complainer, claimant in a multiplepoinding and defendant or defender counter-claiming;

"producer" means the manufacturer of goods, the importer of goods into the European Economic Area or any person purporting to be a producer by placing his name, trade mark or other distinctive sign on the goods;

"property" means the general property in goods, and not merely a special property;

...

"repair" means, in cases where there is a lack of conformity in goods for the purposes of section 48F of this Act, to bring the goods into conformity with the contract;

"sale" includes a bargain and sale as well as a sale and delivery;

"seller" means a person who sells or agrees to sell goods;

"specific goods" means goods identified and agreed on at the time a contract of sale is made and includes an undivided share, specified as a fraction or percentage, of goods identified and agreed on as aforesaid;

"warranty" (as regards England and Wales and Northern Ireland) means an agreement with reference to goods which are the subject of a contract of sale, but collateral to the main purpose of such contract, the breach of which gives rise to a claim for damages, but not to a right to reject the goods and treat the contract as repudiated.

(2)   ...

(3)   A thing is deemed to be done in good faith within the meaning of this Act when it is in fact done honestly, whether it is done negligently or not.

(4)   A person is deemed to be insolvent within the meaning of this Act if he has either ceased to pay his debts in the ordinary course of business or he cannot pay his debts as they become due, ...

(5)   Goods are in a deliverable state within the meaning of this Act when they are in such a state that the buyer would under the contract be bound to take delivery of them.

(5A)   References in this Act to dealing as consumer are to be construed in accordance with Part I of the Unfair Contract Terms Act 1977; and, for the purposes of this Act, it is for a seller claiming that the buyer does not deal as consumer to show that he does not.

(6)   As regards the definition of "business" in subsection (1) above, paragraph 14 of Schedule 1 below applies in relation to a contract made on or after 18 May 1973 and before 1 February 1978, and paragraph 15 in relation to one made before 18 May 1973.

62.   Savings: rules of law etc

(1)   The rules in bankruptcy relating to contracts of sale apply to those contracts, notwithstanding anything in this Act.

(2)   The rules of the common law, including the law merchant, except in so far as they are inconsistent with the provisions of this Act, and in particular the rules relating to the law of principal and agent and the effect of fraud, misrepresentation, duress or coercion, mistake, or other invalidating cause, apply to contracts for the sale of goods.

(3)   Nothing in this Act or the Sale of Goods Act 1893 affects the enactments relating to bills of sale, or any enactment relating to the sale of goods which is not expressly repealed or amended by this Act or that.

(4)   The provisions of this Act about contracts of sale do not apply to a transaction in the form of a contract of sale which is intended to operate by way of mortgage, pledge, charge, or other security.

(5)   Nothing in this Act prejudices or affects the landlord's right of hypothec or sequestration for rent in Scotland.

63.   Consequential amendments, repeals and savings

(1)   Without prejudice to section 17 of the Interpretation Act 1978 (repeal and re-enactment), the enactments mentioned in Schedule 2 below have effect subject to the amendments there specified (being amendments consequential on this Act).

(2)   The enactments mentioned in Schedule 3 below are repealed to the extent specified in column 3, but subject to the savings in Schedule 4 below.

(3)   The savings in Schedule 4 below have effect.

64.   Short title and commencement

(1)   This Act may be cited as the Sale of Goods Act 1979.

(2)   This Act comes into force on 1 January 1980.

SCHEDULE 1

MODIFICATION OF ACT FOR CERTAIN CONTRACTS

Section 1

Preliminary

1.—   (1)   This Schedule modifies this Act as it applies to contracts of sale of goods made on certain dates.

         (2)   In this Schedule references to sections are to those of this Act and references to contracts are to contracts of sale of goods.

(3)   Nothing in this Schedule affects a contract made before 1 January 1894.

Section 11: condition treated as warranty

2.   In relation to a contract made before 22 April 1967 or (in the application of this Act to Northern Ireland) 28 July 1967, in section 11(4) after "or part of them," insert "or where the contract is for specific goods, the property in which has passed to the buyer,".

Section 12: implied terms about title, etc

3.   In relation to a contract made before 18 May 1973 substitute the following for section 12:—

12.   Implied terms about title, etc

In a contract of sale, unless the circumstances of the contract are such as to show a different intention, there is—

(a)   an implied condition on the part of the seller that in the case of a sale he has a right to sell the goods, and in the case of an agreement to sell he will have such a right at the time when the property is to pass;

(b)   an implied warranty that the buyer will have and enjoy quiet possession of the goods;

(c)   an implied warranty that the goods will be free from any charge or encumbrance in favour of any third party, not declared or known to the buyer before or at the time when the contract is made.

Section 13: sale by description

4.   In relation to a contract made before 18 May 1973, omit section 13(3).

Section 14: quality or fitness (i)

5.   In relation to a contract made on or after 18 May 1973 and before the appointed day, substitute the following for section 14:—

14.   Implied terms about quality or fitness

(1)   Except as provided by this section and section 15 below and subject to any other enactment, there is no implied condition or warranty about the quality or fitness for any particular purpose of goods supplied under a contract of sale.

(2)   Where the seller sells goods in the course of a business, there is an implied condition that the goods supplied under the contract are of merchantable quality, except that there is no such condition—

(a)   as regards defects, specifically drawn to the buyer's attention before the contract is made; or

(b)   if the buyer examines the goods before the contract is made, as regards defects which that examination ought to reveal.

(3)   Where the seller sells goods in the course of a business and the buyer, expressly or by implication, makes known to the seller any particular purpose for which the goods are being bought, there is an implied condition that the goods supplied under the contract are reasonably fit for that purpose, whether or not that is a purpose for which such goods are commonly supplied, except where the circumstances show that the buyer does not rely, or that it is unreasonable for him to rely, on the seller's skill or judgment.

(4)   An implied condition or warranty about quality or fitness for a particular purpose may be annexed to a contract of sale by usage.

(5)   The preceding provisions of this section apply to a sale by a person who in the course of a business is acting as agent for another as they apply to a sale by a principal in the course of a business, except where that other is not selling in the course of a business and either the buyer knows that fact or reasonable steps are taken to bring it to the notice of the buyer before the contract is made.

(6)   Goods of any kind are of merchantable quality within the meaning of subsection (2) above if they are as fit for the purpose or purposes for which goods of that kind are

commonly bought as it is reasonable to expect having regard to any description applied to them, the price (if relevant) and all the other relevant circumstances.

(7) In the application of subsection (3) above to an agreement for the sale of goods under which the purchase price or part of it is payable by instalments any reference to the seller includes a reference to the person by whom any antecedent negotiations are conducted; and section 58(3) and (5) of the Hire-Purchase Act 1965, section 54(3) and (5) of the Hire-Purchase (Scotland) Act 1965 and section 65(3) and (5) of the Hire-Purchase Act (Northern Ireland) 1966 (meaning of antecedent negotiations and related expressions) apply in relation to this subsection as in relation to each of those Acts, but as if a reference to any such agreement were included in the references in subsection (3) of each of those sections to the agreements there mentioned.

Section 14: quality or fitness (ii)

6.   In relation to a contract made before 18 May 1973 substitute the following for section 14:—

14. Implied terms about quality or fitness

(1) Subject to this and any other Act, there is no implied condition or warranty about the quality or fitness for any particular purpose of goods supplied under a contract of sale.

(2) Where the buyer, expressly or by implication, makes known to the seller the particular purpose for which the goods are required, so as to show that the buyer relies on the seller's skill or judgment, and the goods are of a description which it is in the course of the seller's business to supply (whether he is the manufacturer or not), there is an implied condition that the goods will be reasonably fit for such purpose, except that in the case of a contract for the sale of a specified article under its patent or other trade name there is no implied condition as to its fitness for any particular purpose.

(3) Where goods are bought by description from a seller who deals in goods of that description (whether he is the manufacturer or not), there is an implied condition that the goods will be of merchantable quality; but if the buyer has examined the goods, there is no implied condition as regards defects which such examination ought to have revealed.

(4) An implied condition or warranty about quality or fitness for a particular purpose may be annexed by the usage of trade.

(5) An express condition or warranty does not negative a condition or warranty implied by this Act unless inconsistent with it.

Section 15: sale by sample

7.   In relation to a contract made before 18 May 1973, omit section 15(3).

Section 22: market overt

8.   In relation to a contract under which goods were sold before 1 January 1968 or (in the application of this Act to Northern Ireland) 29 August 1967, add the following paragraph at the end of section 22(1):—

"Nothing in this subsection affects the law relating to the sale of horses."

Section 25: buyer in possession

9.   In relation to a contract under which a person buys or agrees to buy goods and which is made before the appointed day, omit section 25(2).

Section 35: acceptance

10.   In relation to a contract made before 22 April 1967 or (in the application of this Act to Northern Ireland) 28 July 1967, in section 35(1) omit "(except where section 34 above otherwise provides)".

Section 55: exclusion of implied terms (i)

11. In relation to a contract made on or after 18 May 1973 and before 1 February 1978 substitute the following for section 55:—

55. Exclusion of implied terms

(1) Where a right, duty or liability would arise under a contract of sale of goods by implication of law, it may be negatived or varied by express agreement, or by the course of dealing between the parties, or by such usage as binds both parties to the contract, but the preceding provision has effect subject to the following provisions of this section.

(2) An express condition or warranty does not negative a condition or warranty implied by this Act unless inconsistent with it.

(3) In the case of a contract of sale of goods, any term of that or any other contract exempting from all or any of the provisions of section 12 above is void.

(4) In the case of a contract of sale of goods, any term of that or any other contract exempting from all or any of the provisions of section 13, 14 or 15 above is void in the case of a consumer sale and is, in any other case, not enforceable to the extent that it is shown that it would not be fair or reasonable to allow reliance on the term.

(5) In determining for the purposes of subsection (4) above whether or not reliance on any such term would be fair or reasonable regard shall be had to all the circumstances of the case and in particular to the following matters—

    (a) the strength of the bargaining positions of the seller and buyer relative to each other, taking into account, among other things, the availability of suitable alternative products and sources of supply;

    (b) whether the buyer received an inducement to agree to the term or in accepting it had an opportunity of buying the goods or suitable alternatives without it from any source of supply;

    (c) whether the buyer knew or ought reasonably to have known of the existence and extent of the term (having regard, among other things, to any custom of the trade and any previous course of dealing between the parties);

    (d) where the term exempts from all or any of the provisions of section 13, 14 or 15 above if some condition is not complied with, whether it was reasonable at the time of the contract to expect that compliance with that condition would be practicable;

    (e) whether the goods were manufactured, processed, or adapted to the special order of the buyer.

(6) Subsection (5) above does not prevent the court from holding, in accordance with any rule of law, that a term which purports to exclude or restrict any of the provisions of section 13, 14 or 15 above is not a term of the contract.

(7) In this section "consumer sale" means a sale of goods (other than a sale by auction or by competitive tender) by a seller in the course of a business where the goods—

    (a) are of a type ordinarily bought for private use or consumption; and

    (b) are sold to a person who does not buy or hold himself out as buying them in the course of a business.

(8) The onus of proving that a sale falls to be treated for the purposes of this section as not being a consumer sale lies on the party so contending.

(9) Any reference in this section to a term exempting from all or any of the provisions of any section of this Act is a reference to a term which purports to exclude or restrict, or has the effect of excluding or restricting, the operation of all or any of the provisions of that section, or the exercise of a right conferred by any provision of that section, or any liability of the seller for breach of a condition or warranty implied by any provision of that section.

(10) It is hereby declared that any reference in this section to a term of a contract includes a reference to a term which although not contained in a contract is incorporated in the contract by another term of the contract.

(11) Nothing in this section prevents the parties to a contract for the international sale of goods from negativing or varying any right, duty or liability which would otherwise arise by implication of law under sections 12 to 15 above.

(12) In subsection (11) above "contract for the international sale of goods" means a contract of sale of goods made by parties whose places of business (or, if they have none, habitual residences) are in the territories of different States (the Channel Islands and the Isle of Man being treated for this purpose as different States from the United Kingdom) and in the case of which one of the following conditions is satisfied:—

    (a)   the contract involves the sale of goods which are at the time of the conclusion of the contract in the course of carriage or will be carried from the territory of one State to the territory of another; or

    (b)   the acts constituting the offer and acceptance have been effected in the territories of different States; or

    (c)   delivery of the goods is to be made in the territory of a State other than that within whose territory the acts constituting the offer and the acceptance have been effected.

Section 55: exclusion of implied terms (ii)

12.   In relation to a contract made before 18 May 1973 substitute the following for section 55:—

55. Exclusion of implied terms

Where a right, duty or liability would arise under a contract of sale by implication of law, it may be negatived or varied by express agreement, or by the course of dealing between the parties, or by such usage as binds both parties to the contract.

Section 56: conflict of laws

13.— (1) In relation to a contract on or after 18 May 1973 and before 1 February 1978 substitute for section 56 the section set out in sub-paragraph (3) below.

    (2) In relation to a contract made otherwise than as mentioned in sub-paragraph (1) above, ignore section 56 and this paragraph.

    (3) The section mentioned in sub-paragraph (1) above is as follows:—

56. Conflict of laws

    (1) Where the proper law of a contract for the sale of goods would, apart from a term that it should be the law of some other country or a term to the like effect, be the law of any part of the United Kingdom, or where any such contract contains a term which purports to substitute, or has the effect of substituting, provisions of the law of some other country for all or any of the provisions of sections 12 to 15 and 55 above, those sections shall, notwithstanding that term but subject to subsection (2) below, apply to the contract.

    (2) Nothing in subsection (1) above prevents the parties to a contract for the international sale of goods from negativing or varying any right, duty or liability which would otherwise arise by implication of law under sections 12 to 15 above.

    (3) In subsection (2) above "contract for the international sale of goods" means a contract of sale of goods made by parties whose places of business (or, if they have none, habitual residences) are in the territories of different States (the Channel Islands and the Isle of Man being treated for this purpose as different States from the United Kingdom) and in the case of which one of the following conditions is satisfied:—

(a)   the contract involves the sale of goods which are at the time of the conclusion of the contract in the course of carriage or will be carried from the territory of one State to the territory of another; or

(b)   the acts constituting the offer and acceptance have been effected in the territories of different States; or

(c)   delivery of the goods is to be made in the territory of a State other than that within whose territory the acts constituting the offer and the acceptance have been effected.

Section 61(1): definition of "business" (i)

14.   In relation to a contract made on or after 18 May 1973 and before 1 February 1978, in the definition of "business" in section 61(1) for "or local or public authority" substitute "local authority or statutory undertaker".

Section 61(1): definition of "business" (ii)

15.   In relation to a contract made before 18 May 1973 omit the definition of "business" in section 61(1).

SCHEDULE 2

CONSEQUENTIAL AMENDMENTS

Section 63

...

SCHEDULE 4

SAVINGS

Section 63

Preliminary

1.   In this Schedule references to the 1893 Act are to the Sale of Goods Act 1893.

Orders

2.   An order under section 14 (8) or 25 (4) above may make provision that it is to have effect only as provided by the order (being provision corresponding to that which could, apart from this Act, have been made by an order under section 192 (4) of the Consumer Credit Act 1974 bringing into operation an amendment or repeal making a change corresponding to that made by the order under section 14 (8) or 25 (4) above).

Offences

3.   Where an offence was committed in relation to goods before 1st January 1969 or (in the application of this Act to Northern Ireland) 1st August 1969, the effect of a conviction in respect of the offence is not affected by the repeal by this Act of section 24 of the 1893 Act.

1893 Act, section 26

4.   The repeal by this Act of provisions of the 1893 Act does not extend to the following provisions of that Act in so far as they are needed to give effect to or interpret section 26 of that Act, namely, the definitions of "goods" and "property" in section 62 (1), section 62 (2) and section 63 (which was repealed subject to savings by the Statute Law Revision Act 1908).

Things done before 1st January 1894

5.   The repeal by this Act of section 60 of and the Schedule to the 1893 Act (which effected repeals and which were themselves repealed subject to savings by the Statute Law Revision Act 1908) does not affect those savings, and accordingly does not affect things done or acquired before 1st January 1894.

6.   In so far as the 1893 Act applied (immediately before the operation of the repeals made by this Act) to contracts made before 1st January 1894 (when the 1893 Act came into operation), the 1893 Act shall continue so to apply notwithstanding this Act.

Unfair Contract Terms Act 1977

1977 c. 50

An Act to impose further limits on the extent to which under the law of England and Wales and Northern Ireland civil liability for breach of contract, or for negligence or other breach of duty, can be avoided by means of contract terms and otherwise, and under the law of Scotland civil liability can be avoided by means of contract terms

[26th October 1977]

PART I
AMENDMENT OF LAW FOR ENGLAND AND WALES AND NORTHERN IRELAND

Introductory

1.   Scope of Part I

(1)   For the purposes of this Part of this Act, "negligence" means the breach—

    (a)   of any obligation, arising from the express or implied terms of a contract, to take reasonable care or exercise reasonable skill in the performance of the contract;

    (b)   of any common law duty to take reasonable care or exercise reasonable skill (but not any stricter duty);

    (c)   of the common duty of care imposed by the Occupiers' Liability Act 1957 or the Occupiers' Liability Act (Northern Ireland) 1957.

(2)   This Part of this Act is subject to Part III; and in relation to contracts, the operation of sections 2 to 4 and 7 is subject to the exceptions made by Schedule 1.

(3)   In the case of both contract and tort, sections 2 to 7 apply (except where the contrary is stated in section 6(4)) only to business liability, that is liability for breach of obligations or duties arising—

    (a)   from things done or to be done by a person in the course of a business (whether his own business or another's); or

    (b)   from the occupation of premises used for business purposes of the occupier;

and references to liability are to be read accordingly but liability of an occupier of premises for breach of an obligation or duty towards a person obtaining access to the premises for recreational or educational purposes, being liability for loss or damage suffered by reason of the dangerous state of the premises, is not a business liability of the occupier unless granting that person such access for the purposes concerned falls within the business purposes of the occupier.

(4)   In relation to any breach of duty or obligation, it is immaterial for any purpose of this Part of this Act whether the breach was inadvertent or intentional, or whether liability for it arises directly or vicariously.

Avoidance of liability for negligence, breach of contract, etc

2.   Negligence liability

(1)   A person cannot by reference to any contract term or to a notice given to persons generally or to particular persons exclude or restrict his liability for death or personal injury resulting from negligence.

(2)   In the case of other loss or damage, a person cannot so exclude or restrict his liability for negligence except in so far as the term or notice satisfies the requirement of reasonableness.

(3)   Where a contract term or notice purports to exclude or restrict liability for negligence a person's agreement to or awareness of it is not of itself to be taken as indicating his voluntary acceptance of any risk.

3.   Liability arising in contract

(1)   This section applies as between contracting parties where one of them deals as consumer or on the other's written standard terms of business.

(2)   As against that party, the other cannot by reference to any contract term—

  (a)   when himself in breach of contract, exclude or restrict any liability of his in respect of the breach; or

  (b)   claim to be entitled—

      (i)   to render a contractual performance substantially different from that which was reasonably expected of him, or

      (ii)   in respect of the whole or any part of his contractual obligation, to render no performance at all,

except in so far as (in any of the cases mentioned above in this subsection) the contract term satisfies the requirement of reasonableness.

4.   Unreasonable indemnity clauses

(1)   A person dealing as consumer cannot by reference to any contract term be made to indemnify another person (whether a party to the contract or not) in respect of liability that may be incurred by the other for negligence or breach of contract, except in so far as the contract term satisfies the requirement of reasonableness.

(2)   This section applies whether the liability in question—

  (a)   is directly that of the person to be indemnified or is incurred by him vicariously;

  (b)   is to the person dealing as consumer or to someone else.

Liability arising from sale or supply of goods

5.   "Guarantee" of consumer goods

(1)   In the case of goods of a type ordinarily supplied for private use or consumption, where loss or damage—

  (a)   arises from the goods proving defective while in consumer use; and

  (b)   results from the negligence of a person concerned in the manufacture or distribution of the goods,

liability for the loss or damage cannot be excluded or restricted by reference to any contract term or notice contained in or operating by reference to a guarantee of the goods.

(2)   For these purposes—

  (a)   goods are to be regarded as "in consumer use" when a person is using them, or has them in his possession for use, otherwise than exclusively for the purposes of a business; and

  (b)   anything in writing is a guarantee if it contains or purports to contain some promise or assurance (however worded or presented) that defects will be made good by complete or partial replacement, or by repair, monetary compensation or otherwise.

(3)   This section does not apply as between the parties to a contract under or in pursuance of which possession or ownership of the goods passed.

6.   Sale and hire-purchase

(1)   Liability for breach of the obligations arising from—

  (a)   section 12 of the Sale of Goods Act 1979 (seller's implied undertakings as to title, etc);

  (b)   section 8 of the Supply of Goods (Implied Terms) Act 1973 (the corresponding thing in relation to hire-purchase),

cannot be excluded or restricted by reference to any contract term.

(2)   As against a person dealing as consumer, liability for breach of the obligations arising from—

  (a)   section 13, 14 or 15 of the 1979 Act (seller's implied undertakings as to conformity of goods with description or sample, or as to their quality or fitness for a particular purpose);

  (b)   section 9, 10 or 11 of the 1973 Act (the corresponding things in relation to hire-purchase),

cannot be excluded or restricted by reference to any contract term.

(3) As against a person dealing otherwise than as consumer, the liability specified in subsection (2) above can be excluded or restricted by reference to a contract term, but only in so far as the term satisfies the requirement of reasonableness.

(4) The liabilities referred to in this section are not only the business liabilities defined by section 1(3), but include those arising under any contract of sale of goods or hire-purchase agreement.

7.   Miscellaneous contracts under which goods pass

(1) Where the possession or ownership of goods passes under or in pursuance of a contract not governed by the law of sale of goods or hire-purchase, subsections (2) to (4) below apply as regards the effect (if any) to be given to contract terms excluding or restricting liability for breach of obligation arising by implication of law from the nature of the contract.

(2) As against a person dealing as consumer, liability in respect of the goods' correspondence with description or sample, or their quality or fitness for any particular purpose, cannot be excluded or restricted by reference to any such term.

(3) As against a person dealing otherwise than as consumer, that liability can be excluded or restricted by reference to such a term, but only in so far as the term satisfies the requirement of reasonableness.

(3A) Liability for breach of the obligations arising under section 2 of the Supply of Goods and Services Act 1982 (implied terms about title etc in certain contracts for the transfer of the property in goods) cannot be excluded or restricted by references to any such term.

(4) Liability in respect of—
     (a) the right to transfer ownership of the goods, or give possession; or
     (b) the assurance of quiet possession to a person taking goods in pursuance of the contract,
     cannot (in a case to which subsection (3A) above does not apply) be excluded or restricted by reference to any such term except in so far as the term satisfies the requirement of reasonableness.

(5) This section does not apply in the case of goods passing on a redemption of trading stamps within the Trading Stamps Act 1964 or the Trading Stamps Act (Northern Ireland) 1965.

Other provisions about contracts

8.   Misrepresentation

...

9.   Effect of breach

(1) Where for reliance upon it a contract term has to satisfy the requirement of reasonableness, it may be found to do so and be given effect accordingly notwithstanding that the contract has been terminated either by breach or by a party electing to treat it as repudiated.

(2) Where on a breach the contract is nevertheless affirmed by a party entitled to treat it as repudiated, this does not of itself exclude the requirement of reasonableness in relation to any contract term.

10.   Evasion by means of secondary contract

A person is not bound by any contract term prejudicing or taking away rights of his which arise under, or in connection with the performance of, another contract, so far as those rights extend to the enforcement of another's liability which this Part of this Act prevents that other from excluding or restricting.

Explanatory provisions

11.   The "reasonableness" test

(1) In relation to a contract term, the requirement of reasonableness for the purposes of this Part of this Act, section 3 of the Misrepresentation Act 1967 and section 3 of the Misrepresentation Act (Northern Ireland) 1967 is that the term shall have been a fair and reasonable one to be included having regard to the circumstances which were, or ought reasonably to have been, known to or in the contemplation of the parties when the contract was made.

(2)   In determining for the purposes of section 6 or 7 above whether a contract term satisfies the requirement of reasonableness, regard shall be had in particular to the matters specified in Schedule 2 to this Act; but this subsection does not prevent the court or arbitrator from holding, in accordance with any rule of law, that a term which purports to exclude or restrict any relevant liability is not a term of the contract.

(3)   In relation to a notice (not being a notice having contractual effect), the requirement of reasonableness under this Act is that it should be fair and reasonable to allow reliance on it, having regard to all the circumstances obtaining when the liability arose or (but for the notice) would have arisen.

(4)   Where by reference to a contract term or notice a person seeks to restrict liability to a specified sum of money, and the question arises (under this or any other Act) whether the term or notice satisfies the requirement of reasonableness, regard shall be had in particular (but without prejudice to subsection (2) above in the case of contract terms) to—

   (a)   the resources which he could expect to be available to him for the purpose of meeting the liability should it arise; and

   (b)   how far it was open to him to cover himself by insurance.

(5)   It is for those claiming that a contract term or notice satisfies the requirement of reasonableness to show that it does.

12.   "Dealing as consumer"

(1)   A party to a contract "deals as consumer" in relation to another party if—

   (a)   he neither makes the contract in the course of a business nor holds himself out as doing so; and

   (b)   the other party does make the contract in the course of a business; and

   (c)   in the case of a contract governed by the law of sale of goods or hire-purchase, or by section 7 of this Act, the goods passing under or in pursuance of the contract are of a type ordinarily supplied for private use or consumption.

(1A)   But if the first party mentioned in subsection (1) is an individual paragraph (c) of that subsection must be ignored.

(2)   But the buyer is not in any circumstances to be regarded as dealing as consumer—

   (a)   if he is an individual and the goods are second hand goods sold at public auction at which individuals have the opportunity of attending the sale in person;

   (b)   if he is not an individual and the goods are sold by auction or by competitive tender.

(3)   Subject to this, it is for those claiming that a party does not deal as consumer to show that he does not.

13.   Varieties of exemption clause

(1)   To the extent that this Part of this Act prevents the exclusion or restriction of any liability it also prevents—

   (a)   making the liability or its enforcement subject to restrictive or onerous conditions;

   (b)   excluding or restricting any right or remedy in respect of the liability, or subjecting a person to any prejudice in consequence of his pursuing any such right or remedy;

   (c)   excluding or restricting rules of evidence or procedure;

and (to that extent) sections 2 and 5 to 7 also prevent excluding or restricting liability by reference to terms and notices which exclude or restrict the relevant obligation or duty.

(2)   But an agreement in writing to submit present or future differences to arbitration is not to be treated under this Part of this Act as excluding or restricting any liability.

14.   Interpretation of Part I

In this Part of this Act—

   "business" includes a profession and the activities of any government department or local or public authority;

   "goods" has the same meaning as in the Sale of Goods Act 1979:

   "hire-purchase agreement" has the same meaning as in the Consumer Credit Act 1974;

"negligence" has the meaning given by section 1(1);

"notice" includes an announcement, whether or not in writing, and any other communication or pretended communication; and

"personal injury" includes any disease and any impairment of physical or mental condition.

PART II
AMENDMENT OF LAW FOR SCOTLAND

15. Scope of Part II

(1) This Part of this Act ..., is subject to Part III of this Act and does not affect the validity of any discharge or indemnity given by a person in consideration of the receipt by him of compensation in settlement of any claim which he has.

(2) Subject to subsection (3) below, sections 16 to 18 of this Act apply to any contract only to the extent that the contract—

  (a) relates to the transfer of the ownership or possession of goods from one person to another (with or without work having been done on them);

  (b) constitutes a contract of service or apprenticeship;

  (c) relates to services of whatever kind, including (without prejudice to the foregoing generality) carriage, deposit and pledge, care and custody, mandate, agency, loan and services relating to the use of land;

  (d) relates to the liability of an occupier of land to persons entering upon or using that land;

  (e) relates to a grant of any right or permission to enter upon or use land not amounting to an estate or interest in the land.

(3) Notwithstanding anything in subsection (2) above, section 16 to 18—

  (a) do not apply to any contract to the extent that the contract—

   (i) is a contract of insurance (including a contract to pay an annuity on human life);

   (ii) relates to the formation, constitution or dissolution of any body corporate or unincorporated association or partnership;

  (b) apply to—

    a contract of marine salvage or towage;

    a charter party of a ship or hovercraft;

    a contract for the carriage of goods by ship or hovercraft; or,

    a contract to which subsection (4) below relates,

    only to the extent that—

   (i) both parties deal or hold themselves out as dealing in the course of a business (and then only in so far as the contract purports to exclude or restrict liability for breach of duty in respect of death or personal injury); or

   (ii) the contract is a consumer contract (and then only in favour of the consumer).

(4) This subsection relates to a contract in pursuance of which goods are carried by ship or hovercraft and which either—

  (a) specifies ship or hovercraft as the means of carriage over part of the journey to be covered; or

  (b) makes no provision as to the means of carriage and does not exclude ship or hovercraft as that means,

in so far as the contract operates for and in relation to the carriage of the goods by that means.

16. Liability for breach of duty

(1) Subject to subsection (1A) below, where a term of a contract , or a provision of a notice given to persons generally or to particular persons, purports to exclude or restrict liability for breach of duty arising in the course of any business or from the occupation of any premises used for business purposes of the occupier, that term or provision—

  (a) shall be void in any case where such exclusion or restriction is in respect of death or personal injury;

(b)   shall, in any other case, have no effect if it was not fair and reasonable to incorporate the term in the contract or, as the case may be, if it is not fair and reasonable to allow reliance on the provision.

(1A)   Nothing in paragraph (b) of subsection (1) above shall be taken as implying that a provision of a notice has effect in circumstances where, apart from that paragraph, it would not have effect.

(2)   Subsection (1)(a) above does not affect the validity of any discharge and indemnity given by a person, on or in connection with an award to him of compensation for pneumoconiosis attributable to employment in the coal industry, in respect of any further claim arising from his contracting that disease.

(3)   Where under subsection (1) above a term of a contract or a provision of a notice is void or has no effect, the fact that a person agreed to, or was aware of, the term or provision shall not of itself be sufficient evidence that he knowingly and voluntarily assumed any risk.

17.   Control of unreasonable exemptions in consumer or standard form contracts

(1)   Any term of a contract which is a consumer contract or a standard form contract shall have no effect for the purpose of enabling a party to the contract—

(a)   who is in breach of a contractual obligation, to exclude or restrict any liability of his to the consumer or customer in respect of the breach;

(b)   in respect of a contractual obligation, to render no performance, or to render a performance substantially different from that which the consumer or customer reasonably expected from the contract;

if it was not fair and reasonable to incorporate the term in the contract.

(2)   In this section "customer" means a party to a standard form contract who deals on the basis of written standard terms of business of the other party to the contract who himself deals in the course of a business.

18.   Unreasonable indemnity clauses in consumer contracts

(1)   Any term of a contract which is a consumer contract shall have no effect for the purpose of making the consumer indemnify another person (whether a party to the contract or not) in respect of liability which that other person may incur as a result of breach of duty or breach of contract, if it was not fair and reasonable to incorporate the term in the contract.

(2)   In this section "liability" means liability arising in the course of any business or from the occupation of any premises used for business purposes of the occupier.

19.   "Guarantee of consumer goods"

(1)   This section applies to a guarantee—

(a)   in relation to goods which are of a type ordinarily supplied for private use or consumption; and

(b)   which is not a guarantee given by one party to the other party to a contract under or in pursuance of which the ownership or possession of the goods to which the guarantee relates is transferred.

(2)   A term of a guarantee to which this section applies shall be void in so far as it purports to exclude or restrict liability for loss or damage (including death or personal injury)—

(a)   arising from the goods proving defective while—

(i)   in use otherwise than exclusively for the purposes of a business; or

(ii)   in the possession of a person for such use; and

(b)   resulting from the breach of duty of a person concerned in the manufacture or distribution of the goods.

(3)   For the purposes of this section, any document is a guarantee if it contains or purports to contain some promise or assurance (however worded or presented) that defects will be made good by complete or partial replacement, or by repair, monetary compensation otherwise.

20.   Obligations implied by law in sale and hire-purchase contracts

(1)   Any term of a contract which purports to exclude or restrict liability for breach of the obligations arising from—

(a)   section 12 of the Sale of Goods Act 1979 (seller's implied undertakings as to title etc.);

(b)   section 8 of the Supply of Goods (Implied Terms) Act 1973 (implied terms as to title in hire-purchase agreements),

shall be void.

(2)   Any term of a contract which purports to exclude or restrict liability for breach of the obligations arising from—

(a)   section 13, 14 or 15 of the said Act of 1979 (seller's implied undertakings as to conformity of goods with description or sample, or as to their quality or fitness for a particular purpose);

(b)   section 9, 10 or 11 of the said Act of 1973 (the corresponding provisions in relation to hire-purchase),

shall—

(i)   in the case of a consumer contract, be void against the consumer;

(ii)   in any other case, have no effect if it was not fair and reasonable to incorporate the term in the contract.

21.   Obligations implied by law in other contracts for the supply of goods

(1)   Any term of a contract to which this section applies purporting to exclude or restrict liability for breach of an obligation—

(a)   such as is referred to in subsection (3)(a) below—

(i)   in the case of a consumer contract, shall be void against the consumer, and

(ii)   in any other case, shall have no effect if it was not fair and reasonable to incorporate the term in the contract;

(b)   such as is referred to in subsection (3)(b) below, shall have no effect if it was not fair and reasonable to incorporate the term in the contract.

(2)   This section applies to any contract to the extent that it relates to any such matter as is referred to in section 15(2)(a) of this Act, but does not apply to—

(a)   a contract of sale of goods or a hire-purchase agreement; or

(b)   a charter party of a ship or hovercraft unless it is a consumer contract (and then only in favour of the consumer).

(3)   An obligation referred to in this subsection is an obligation incurred under a contract in the course of a business and arising by implication of law from the nature of the contract which relates—

(a)   to the correspondence of goods with description or sample, or to the quality or fitness of goods for any particular purpose; or

(b)   to any right to transfer ownership or possession of goods, or to the enjoyment of quiet possession of goods.

(4)   Nothing in this section applies to the supply of goods on a redemption of trading stamps within the Trading Stamps Act 1964.

22.   Consequence of breach

For the avoidance of doubt, where any provision of this Part of this Act requires that the incorporation of a term in a contract must be fair and reasonable for that term to have effect—

(a)   if that requirement is satisfied, the term may be given effect to notwithstanding that the contract has been terminated in consequence of breach of that contract;

(b)   for the term to be given effect to, that requirement must be satisfied even where a party who is entitled to rescind the contract elects not to rescind it.

23.   Evasion by means of secondary contract

Any term of any contract shall be void which purports to exclude or restrict, or has the effect of excluding or restricting—

    (a)   the exercise, by a party to any other contract, of any right or remedy which arises in respect of that other contract in consequence of breach of duty, or of obligation, liability for which could not by virtue of the provisions of this Part of this Act be excluded or restricted by a term of that other contract;

    (b)   the application of the provisions of this Part of this Act in respect of that or any other contract.

24.   The "reasonableness" test

(1)   In determining for the purposes of this Part of this Act whether it was fair and reasonable to incorporate a term in a contract, regard shall be had only to the circumstances which were, or ought reasonably to have been, known to or in the contemplation of the parties to the contract at the time the contract was made.

(2)   In determining for the purposes of section 20 or 21 of this Act whether it was fair and reasonable to incorporate a term in a contract, regard shall be had in particular to the matters specified in Schedule 2 to this Act; but this subsection shall not prevent a court or arbiter from holding, in accordance with any rule of law, that a term which purports to exclude or restrict any relevant liability is not a term of the contract.

(2A)   In determining for the purposes of this Part of this Act whether it is fair and reasonable to allow reliance on a provision of a notice (not being a notice having contractual effect), regard shall be had to all the circumstances obtaining when the liability arose of (but for the provision) would have arisen.

(3)   Where a term in a contract or a provision of a notice purports to restrict liability to a specified sum of money, and the question arises for the purposes of this Part of this Act whether it was fair and reasonable to incorporate the term in the contract or whether it is fair and reasonable to allow reliance on the provision, then, without prejudice to subsection (2) above in the case of a term in a contract, regard shall be had in particular to—

    (a)   the resources which the party seeking to rely on that term or provision could expect to be available to him for the purpose of meeting the liability should it arise;

    (b)   how far it was open to that party to cover himself by insurance.

(4)   The onus of proving that it was fair and reasonable to incorporate a term in a contract or that it is fair and reasonable to allow reliance on a provision of a notice shall lie on the party so contending.

25.   Interpretation of Part II

(1)   In this Part of this Act—

"breach of duty" means the breach—

    (a)   of any obligation, arising from the express or implied terms of a contract, to take reasonable care or exercise reasonable skill in the performance of the contract;

    (b)   of any common law duty to take reasonable care or exercise reasonable skill;

    (c)   of the duty of reasonable care imposed by section 2(1) of the Occupiers' Liability (Scotland) Act 1960;

"business" includes a profession and the activities of any government department or local or public authority;

"consumer" has the meaning assigned to that expression in the definition in this section of "consumer contract";

"consumer contract" means subject to subsections (1A) and (1B) below a contract ... in which—

    (a)   one party to the contract deals, and the other party to the contract ("the consumer") does not deal or hold himself out as dealing, in the course of a business, and

    (b)   in the case of a contract such as is mentioned in section 15(2)(a) of this Act, the goods are of a type ordinarily supplied for private use or consumption;

and for the purposes of this Part of this Act the onus of proving that a contract is not to be regarded as a consumer contract shall lie on the party so contending;

"goods" has the same meaning as in the Sale of Goods Act 1979;

"hire-purchase agreement" has the same meaning as in section 189(1) of the Consumer Credit Act 1974;

"notice" includes an announcement, whether or not in writing, and any other communication or pretended communication;

"personal injury" includes any disease and any impairment of physical or mental condition.

(1A)   Where the consumer is an individual, paragraph (b) in the definition of "consumer contract" in subsection (1) must be disregarded.

(1B)   The expression of "consumer contract" does not include a contract in which—

(a)   the buyer is an individual and the goods are second hand goods sold by public auction at which individuals have the opportunity of attending in person; or

(b)   the buyer is not an individual and the goods are sold by auction or competitive tender.

(2)   In relation to any breach of duty or obligation, it is immaterial for any purpose of this Part of this Act whether the act or omission giving rise to that breach was inadvertent or intentional, or whether liability for it arises directly or vicariously.

(3)   In this Part of this Act, any reference to excluding or restricting any liability includes—

(a)   making the liability or its enforcement subject to any restrictive or onerous conditions;

(b)   excluding or restricting any right or remedy in respect of the liability, or subjecting a person to any prejudice in consequence of his pursuing any such right or remedy;

(c)   excluding or restricting any rule of evidence or procedure;

(d)   ...

but does not include an agreement to submit any question to arbitration.

(4)   ...

(5)   In sections 15 and 16 and 19 to 21 of this Act, any reference to excluding or restricting liability for breach of an obligation or duty shall include a reference to excluding or restricting the obligation or duty itself.

PART III
PROVISIONS APPLYING TO WHOLE OF UNITED KINGDOM

Miscellaneous

26.   International supply contracts

(1)   The limits imposed by this Act on the extent to which a person may exclude or restrict liability by reference to a contract term do not apply to liability arising under such a contract as is described in subsection (3) below.

(2)   The terms of such a contract are not subject to any requirement of reasonableness under section 3 or 4: and nothing in Part II of this Act shall require the incorporation of the terms of such a contract to be fair and reasonable for them to have effect.

(3)   Subject to subsection (4), that description of contract is one whose characteristics are the following—

(a)   either it is a contract of sale of goods or it is one under or in pursuance of which the possession or ownership of goods passes; and

(b)   it is made by parties whose places of business (or, if they have none, habitual residences) are in the territories of different States (the Channel Islands and the Isle of Man being treated for this purpose as different States from the United Kingdom).

(4)   A contract falls within subsection (3) above only if either—

(a)   the goods in question are, at the time of the conclusion of the contract, in the course of carriage, or will be carried, from the territory of one State to the territory of another; or

(b)   the acts constituting the offer and acceptance have been done in the territories of different States; or

(c)   the contract provides for the goods to be delivered to the territory of a State other than that within whose territory those acts were done.

27.   Choice of law clauses

(1)   Where the law applicable to a contract is the law of any part of the United Kingdom only by choice of the parties (and apart from that choice would be the law of some country outside the United Kingdom) sections 2 to 7 and 16 to 21 of this Act do not operate as part of the law applicable to the contract.

(2)   This Act has effect notwithstanding any contract term which applies or purports to apply the law of some country outside the United Kingdom, where (either or both)—

    (a)   the term appears to the court, or arbitrator or arbiter to have been imposed wholly or mainly for the purpose of enabling the party imposing it to evade the operation of this Act; or

    (b)   in the making of the contract one of the parties dealt as consumer, and he was then habitually resident in the United Kingdom, and the essential steps necessary for the making of the contract were taken there, whether by him or by others on his behalf.

(3)   In the application of subsection (2) above to Scotland, for paragraph (b) there shall be substituted—

    "(b)   the contract is a consumer contract as defined in Part II of this Act, and the consumer at the date when the contract was made was habitually resident in the United Kingdom, and the essential steps necessary for the making of the contract were taken there, whether by him or by others on his behalf.".

28.   Temporary provision for sea carriage of passengers

(1)   This section applies to a contract for carriage by sea of a passenger or of a passenger and his luggage where the provisions of the Athens Convention (with or without modification) do not have, in relation to the contract, the force of law in the United Kingdom.

(2)   In a case where—

    (a)   the contract is not made in the United Kingdom, and

    (b)   neither the place of departure nor the place of destination under it is in the United Kingdom, a person is not precluded by this Act from excluding or restricting liability for loss or damage, being loss or damage for which the provisions of the Convention would, if they had the force of law in relation to the contract, impose liability on him.

(3)   In any other case, a person is not precluded by this Act from excluding or restricting liability for that loss or damage—

    (a)   in so far as the exclusion or restriction would have been effective in that case had the provisions of the Convention had the force of law in relation to the contract; or

    (b)   in such circumstances and to such extent as may be prescribed, by reference to a prescribed term of the contract.

(4)   For the purposes of subsection (3) (*a*), the values which shall be taken to be the official values in the United Kingdom of the amounts (expressed in gold francs) by reference to which liability under the provisions of the Convention is limited shall be such amounts in sterling as the Secretary of State may from time to time by order made by statutory instrument specify.

(5)   In this section,—

    (a)   the references to excluding or restricting liability include doing any of those things in relation to the liability which are mentioned in section 13 or section 25 (3) and (5); and

    (b)   "the Athens Convention" means the Athens Convention relating to the Carriage of Passengers and their Luggage by Sea, 1974; and

    (c)   "prescribed" means prescribed by the Secretary of State by regulations made by statutory instrument;

and a statutory instrument containing the regulations shall be subject to annulment in pursuance of a resolution of either House of Parliament.

29.   Saving for other relevant legislation

(1)   Nothing in this Act removes or restricts the effect of, or prevents reliance upon, any contractual provision which—

    (a)   is authorised or required by the express terms or necessary implication of an enactment; or

(b)   being made with a view to compliance with an international agreement to which the United Kingdom is a party, does not operate more restrictively than is contemplated by the agreement.

(2)   A contract term is to be taken—

(a)   for the purposes of Part I of this Act, as satisfying the requirement of reasonableness; and

(b)   for those of Part II, to have been fair and reasonable to incorporate,

if it is incorporated or approved by, or incorporated pursuant to a decision or ruling of, a competent authority acting in the exercise of any statutory jurisdiction or function and is not a term in a contract to which the competent authority is itself a party.

(3)   In this section—

"competent authority" means any court, arbitrator or arbiter, government department or public authority;

"enactment" means any legislation (including subordinate legislation) of the United Kingdom or Northern Ireland and any instrument having effect by virtue of such legislation;

"statutory" means conferred by an enactment.

30.   ...

General

31.   Commencement; amendments; repeals

(1)   This Act comes into force on 1st February 1978.

(2)   Nothing in this Act applies to contracts made before the date on which it comes into force; but subject to this, it applies to liability for any loss or damage which is suffered on or after that date.

(3)   The enactments specified in Schedule 3 to this Act are amended as there shown.

(4)   The enactments specified in Schedule 4 to this Act are repealed to the extent specified in column 3 of that Schedule.

32.   Citation and extent

(1)   This Act may be cited as the Unfair Contract Terms Act 1977.

(2)   Part I of this Act extends to England and Wales and to Northern Ireland; but it does not extend to Scotland.

(3)   Part II of this Act extends to Scotland only.

(4)   This Part of this Act extends to the whole of the United Kingdom.

SCHEDULE 1

SCOPE OF SECTIONS 2 TO 4 AND 7

Section 1(2)

1.   Sections 2 to 4 of this Act do not extend to—

(a)   any contract of insurance (including a contract to pay an annuity on human life);

(b)   any contract so far as it relates to the creation or transfer of an interest in land, or to the termination of such an interest, whether by extinction, merger, surrender, forfeiture or otherwise;

(c)   any contract so far as it relates to the creation or transfer of a right or interest in any patent, trade mark, copyright or design right, registered design, technical or commercial information or other intellectual property, or relates to the termination of any such right or interest;

(d)   any contract so far as it relates—

(i)   to the formation or dissolution of a company (which means any body corporate or unincorporated association and includes a partnership), or

(ii)   to its constitution or the rights or obligations of its corporators or members;

(e) any contract so far as it relates to the creation or transfer of securities or of any right or interest in securities.

2. Section 2(1) extends to—
    (a) any contract of marine salvage or towage;
    (b) any charterparty of a ship or hovercraft; and
    (c) any contract for the carriage of goods by ship or hovercraft;
    but subject to this sections 2 to 4 and 7 do not extend to any such contract except in favour of a person dealing as consumer.

3. Where goods are carried by ship or hovercraft in pursuance of a contract which either—
    (a) specifies that as the means of carriage over part of the journey to be covered, or
    (b) makes no provision as to the means of carriage and does not exclude that means,
    then sections 2(2), 3 and 4 do not, except in favour of a person dealing as consumer, extend to the contract as it operates for and in relation to the carriage of the goods by that means.

4. Section 2(1) and (2) do not extend to a contract of employment, except in favour of the employee.

5. Section 2(1) does not affect the validity of any discharge and indemnity given by a person, on or in connection with an award to him of compensation for pneumoconiosis attributable to employment in the coal industry, in respect of any further claim arising from his contracting that disease.

SCHEDULE 2

"GUIDELINES" FOR APPLICATION OF REASONABLENESS TEST

Sections 11(2), 24(2)

The matters to which regard is to be had in particular for the purposes of sections 6(3), 7(3) and (4), 20 and 21 are any of the following which appear to be relevant—

(a) the strength of the bargaining positions of the parties relative to each other, taking into account (among other things) alternative means by which the customer's requirements could have been met;

(b) whether the customer received an inducement to agree to the term, or in accepting it had an opportunity of entering into a similar contract with other persons, but without having to accept a similar term;

(c) whether the customer knew or ought reasonably to have known of the existence and extent of the term (having regard, among other things, to any custom of the trade and any previous course of dealing between the parties);

(d) where the term excludes or restricts any relevant liability if some condition is not complied with, whether it was reasonable at the time of the contract to expect that compliance with that condition would be practicable;

(e) whether the goods were manufactured, processed or adapted to the special order of the customer.

SCHEDULE 3

AMENDMENT OF ENACTMENTS

Section 31(3)

...

SCHEDULE 4

REPEALS

Section 31(4)

...

Insolvency Act 1986

1986 c. 45

An Act to consolidate the enactments relating to company insolvency and winding up (including the winding up of companies that are not insolvent, and of unregistered companies); enactments relating to the insolvency and bankruptcy of individuals; and other enactments bearing on those two subject matters, including the functions and qualification of insolvency practitioners, the public administration of insolvency, the penalisation and redress of malpractice and wrongdoing, and the avoidance of certain transactions at an undervalue

[25th July 1986]

THE FIRST GROUP OF PARTS
COMPANY INSOLVENCY; COMPANIES WINDING UP

PART I
COMPANY VOLUNTARY ARRANGEMENTS

The proposal

1. **Those who may propose an arrangement**

(1) The directors of a company (other than one which is in administration or being wound up) may make a proposal under this Part to the company and to its creditors for a composition in satisfaction of its debts or a scheme of arrangement of its affairs (from here on referred to, in either case, as a "voluntary arrangement").

(2) A proposal under this Part is one which provides for some person ("the nominee") to act in relation to the voluntary arrangement either as trustee or otherwise for the purpose of supervising its implementation; and the nominee must be a person who is qualified to act as an insolvency practitioner or authorised to act as nominee, in relation to the voluntary arrangement.

(3) Such a proposal may also be made—
(a) where the company is in administration, by the administrator, and
(b) where the company is being wound up, by the liquidator.

(4) In this Part a reference to a company includes a reference to a company in relation to which a proposal for a voluntary arrangement may be made by virtue of Article 3 of the EC Regulation.

1A. **Moratorium**

(1) Where the directors of an eligible company intend to make a proposal for a voluntary arrangement, they may take steps to obtain a moratorium for the company.

(2) The provisions of Schedule A1 to this Act have effect with respect to—
(a) companies eligible for a moratorium under this section,
(b) the procedure for obtaining such a moratorium,
(c) the effects of such a moratorium, and
(d) the procedure applicable (in place of sections 2 to 6 and 7) in relation to the approval and implementation of a voluntary arrangement where such a moratorium is or has been in force.

2. **Procedure where nominee is not the liquidator or administrator**

(1) This section applies where the nominee under section 1 is not the liquidator or administrator of the company and the directors do not propose to take steps to obtain a moratorium under section 1A for the company.

(2) The nominee shall, within 28 days (or such longer period as the court may allow) after he is given notice of the proposal for a voluntary arrangement, submit a report to the court stating—

(a) whether, in his opinion, the proposed voluntary arrangement has a reasonable prospect of being approved and implemented,

(aa) whether, in his opinion, meetings of the company and of its creditors should be summoned to consider the proposal, and

(b) if in his opinion such meetings should be summoned, the date on which, and time and place at which, he proposes the meetings should be held.

(3) For the purposes of enabling the nominee to prepare his report, the person intending to make the proposal shall submit to the nominee—

(a) a document setting out the terms of the proposed voluntary arrangement, and

(b) a statement of the company's affairs containing—

(i) such particulars of its creditors and of its debts and other liabilities and of its assets as may be prescribed, and

(ii) such other information as may be prescribed.

(4) The court may—

(a) on an application made by the person intending to make the proposal, in a case where the nominee has failed to submit the report required by this section or has died, or

(b) on an application made by that person or the nominee, in a case where it is impracticable or inappropriate for the nominee to continue to act as such,

direct that the nominee be replaced as such by another person qualified to act as an insolvency practitioner, or authorised to act as nominee, in relation to the voluntary arrangement.

3. Summoning of meetings

(1) Where the nominee under section 1 is not the liquidator or administrator, and it has been reported to the court that such meetings as are mentioned in section 2(2) should be summoned, the person making the report shall (unless the court otherwise directs) summon those meetings for the time, date and place proposed in the report.

(2) Where the nominee is the liquidator or administrator, he shall summon meetings of the company and of its creditors to consider the proposal for such a time, date and place as he thinks fit.

(3) The persons to be summoned to a creditors' meeting under this section are every creditor of the company of whose claim and address the person summoning the meeting is aware.

Consideration and implementation of proposal

4. Decisions of meetings

(1) The meetings summoned under section 3 shall decide whether to approve the proposed voluntary arrangement (with or without modifications).

(2) The modifications may include one conferring the functions proposed to be conferred on the nominee on another person qualified to act as an insolvency practitioner or authorised to act as nominee, in relation to the voluntary arrangement.

But they shall not include any modification by virtue of which the proposal ceases to be a proposal such as is mentioned in section 1.

(3) A meeting so summoned shall not approve any proposal or modification which affects the right of a secured creditor of the company to enforce his security, except with the concurrence of the creditor concerned.

(4) Subject as follows, a meeting so summoned shall not approve any proposal or modification under which—

(a) any preferential debt of the company is to be paid otherwise than in priority to such of its debts as are not preferential debts, or

(b) a preferential creditor of the company is to be paid an amount in respect of a preferential debt that bears to that debt a smaller proportion than is borne to another preferential debt by the amount that is to be paid in respect of that other debt.

However, the meeting may approve such a proposal or modification with the concurrence of the preferential creditor concerned.

(5) Subject as above, each of the meetings shall be conducted in accordance with the rules.

(6) After the conclusion of either meeting in accordance with the rules, the chairman of the meeting shall report the result of the meeting to the court, and, immediately after reporting to the court, shall give notice of the result of the meeting to such persons as may be prescribed.

(7) References in this section to preferential debts and preferential creditors are to be read in accordance with section 386 in Part XII of this Act.

4A. Approval of arrangement

(1) This section applies to a decision, under section 4, with respect to the approval of a proposed voluntary arrangement.

(2) The decision has effect if, in accordance with the rules—
 (a) it has been taken by both meetings summoned under section 3, or
 (b) (subject to any order made under subsection (4)) it has been taken by the creditors' meeting summoned under that section.

(3) If the decision taken by the creditors' meeting differs from that taken by the company meeting, a member of the company may apply to the court.

(4) An application under subsection (3) shall not be made after the end of the period of 28 days beginning with—
 (a) the day on which the decision was taken by the creditors' meeting, or
 (b) where the decision of the company meeting was taken on a later day, that day.

(5) Where a member of a regulated company, within the meaning given by paragraph 44 of Schedule A1, applies to the court under subsection (3), the Financial Services Authority is entitled to be heard on the application.

(6) On an application under subsection (3), the court may—
 (a) order the decision of the company meeting to have effect instead of the decision of the creditors' meeting, or
 (b) make such other order as it thinks fit.

5. Effect of approval

(1) This section applies where a decision approving a voluntary arrangement has effect under section 4A.

(2) The ... voluntary arrangement—
 (a) takes effect as if made by the company at the creditors' meeting, and
 (b) binds every person who in accordance with the rules—
  (i) was entitled to vote at that meeting (whether or not he was present or represented at it), or
  (ii) would have been so entitled if he had had notice of it,
  as if he were a party to the voluntary arrangement.

(2A) If—
 (a) when the arrangement ceases to have effect any amount payable under the arrangement to a person bound by virtue of subsection (2)(b)(ii) has not been paid, and
 (b) the arrangement did not come to an end prematurely,
the company shall at that time become liable to pay to that person the amount payable under the arrangement.

(3) Subject as follows, if the company is being wound up or is in administration, the court may do one or both of the following, namely—
 (a) by order stay or sist all proceedings in the winding up or provide for the appointment of the administrator to cease to have effect;
 (b) give such directions with respect to the conduct of the winding up or the administration as it thinks appropriate for facilitating the implementation of the ... voluntary arrangement.

(4) The court shall not make an order under subsection (3)(a)—
 (a) at any time before the end of the period of 28 days beginning with the first day on which each of the reports required by section 4(6) has been made to the court, or

(b)   at any time when an application under the next section or an appeal in respect of such an application is pending, or at any time in the period within which such an appeal may be brought.

(5)   Where the company is in energy administration, the court shall not make an order or give a direction under subsection (3) unless—

(a)   the court has given the Secretary of State or the Gas and Electricity Markets Authority a reasonable opportunity of making representations to it about the proposed order or direction; and

(b)   the order or direction is consistent with the objective of the energy administration.

(6)   In subsection (5) "in energy administration" and "objective of the energy administration" are to be construed in accordance with Schedule B1 to this Act, as applied by Part 1 of Schedule 20 to the Energy Act 2004.

6.   Challenge of decisions

(1)   Subject to this section, an application to the court may be made, by any of the persons specified below, on one or both of the following grounds, namely—

(a)   that a voluntary arrangement which has effect under section 4A unfairly prejudices the interests of a creditor, member or contributory of the company;

(b)   that there has been some material irregularity at or in relation to either of the meetings.

(2)   The persons who may apply under subsection (1) are—

(a)   a person entitled, in accordance with the rules, to vote at either of the meetings;

(aa) a person who would have been entitled, in accordance with the rules, to vote at the creditors' meeting if he had had notice of it;

(b)   the nominee or any person who has replaced him under section 2(4) or 4(2); and

(c)   if the company is being wound up or is in administration, the liquidator or administrator.

(2A) Subject to this section, where a voluntary arrangement in relation to a company in energy administration is approved at the meetings summoned under section 3, an application to the court may be made—

(a)   by the Secretary of State, or

(b)   with the consent of the Secretary of State, by the Gas and Electricity Markets Authority,

on the ground that the voluntary arrangement is not consistent with the achievement of the objective of the energy administration.

(3)   An application under this section shall not be made—

(a)   after the end of the period of 28 days beginning with the first day on which each of the reports required by section 4(6) has been made to the court, or

(b)   in the case of a person who was not given notice of the creditors' meeting, after the end of the period of 28 days beginning with the day on which he became aware that the meeting had taken place,

but (subject to that) an application made by a person within subsection (2)(aa) on the ground that the voluntary arrangement prejudices his interests may be made after the arrangement has ceased to have effect, unless it came to an end prematurely.

(4)   Where on such an application the court is satisfied as to either of the grounds mentioned in subsection (1) or, in the case of an application under subsection (2A), as to the ground mentioned in that subsection, it may do one or both of the following, namely—

(a)   revoke or suspend any decision approving the voluntary arrangement which has effect under section 4A or, in a case falling within subsection (1)(b), any decision taken by the meeting in question which has effect under that section;

(b)   give a direction to any person for the summoning of further meetings to consider any revised proposal the person who made the original proposal may make or, in a case falling within subsection (1)(b), a further company or (as the case may be) creditors' meeting to reconsider the original proposal.

(5)   Where at any time after giving a direction under subsection (4)(b) for the summoning of meetings to consider a revised proposal the court is satisfied that the person who made the original proposal

does not intend to submit a revised proposal, the court shall revoke the direction and revoke or suspend any decision approving the voluntary arrangement which has effect under section 4A.

(6) In a case where the court, on an application under this section with respect to any meeting—
   (a) gives a direction under subsection (4)(b), or
   (b) revokes or suspends an approval under subsection (4)(a) or (5),
   the court may give such supplemental directions as it thinks fit and, in particular, directions with respect to things done under the voluntary arrangement since it took effect.

(7) Except in pursuance of the preceding provisions of this section, a decision taken at a meeting summoned under section 3 is not invalidated by any irregularity at or in relation to the meeting.

(8) In this section "in energy administration" and "objective of the energy administration" are to be construed in accordance with Schedule B1 to this Act, as applied by Part 1 of Schedule 20 to the Energy Act 2004.

6A. False representations, etc

(1) If, for the purpose of obtaining the approval of the members or creditors of a company to a proposal for a voluntary arrangement, a person who is an officer of the company—
   (a) makes any false representation, or
   (b) fraudulently does, or omits to do, anything,
   he commits an offence.

(2) Subsection (1) applies even if the proposal is not approved.

(3) For purposes of this section "officer" includes a shadow director.

(4) A person guilty of an offence under this section is liable to imprisonment or a fine, or both.

7. Implementation of proposal

(1) This section applies where a voluntary arrangement has effect under section 4A.

(2) The person who is for the time being carrying out in relation to the voluntary arrangement the functions conferred—
   (a) on the nominee by virtue of the approval given at one or both of the meetings summoned under section 3,
   (b) by virtue of section 2(4) or 4(2) on a person other than the nominee,
   shall be known as the supervisor of the voluntary arrangement.

(3) If any of the company's creditors or any other person is dissatisfied by any act, omission or decision of the supervisor, he may apply to the court; and on the application the court may—
   (a) confirm, reverse or modify any act or decision of the supervisor,
   (b) give him directions, or
   (c) make such other order as it thinks fit.

(4) The supervisor—
   (a) may apply to the court for directions in relation to any particular matter arising under the voluntary arrangement, and
   (b) is included among the persons who may apply to the court for the winding up of the company or for an administration order to be made in relation to it.

(5) The court may, whenever—
   (a) it is expedient to appoint a person to carry out the functions of the supervisor, and
   (b) it is inexpedient, difficult or impracticable for an appointment to be made without the assistance of the court,
   make an order appointing a person who is qualified to act as an insolvency practitioner or authorised to act as supervisor, in relation to the voluntary arrangement, either in substitution for the existing supervisor or to fill a vacancy.

(6) The power conferred by subsection (5) is exercisable so as to increase the number of persons exercising the functions of supervisor or, where there is more than one person exercising those functions, so as to replace one or more of those persons.

7A.   Prosecution of delinquent officers of company

(1)   This section applies where a moratorium under section 1A has been obtained for a company or the approval of a voluntary arrangement in relation to a company has taken effect under section 4A or paragraph 36 of Schedule A1.

(2)   If it appears to the nominee or supervisor that any past or present officer of the company has been guilty of any offence in connection with the moratorium or, as the case may be, voluntary arrangement for which he is criminally liable, the nominee or supervisor shall forthwith—

(a)   report the matter to the appropriate authority, and

(b)   provide the appropriate authority with such information and give the authority such access to and facilities for inspecting and taking copies of documents (being information or documents in the possession or under the control of the nominee or supervisor and relating to the matter in question) as the authority requires.

In this subsection, "the appropriate authority" means—

(i)   in the case of a company registered in England and Wales, the Secretary of State, and

(ii)   in the case of a company registered in Scotland, the Lord Advocate.

(3)   Where a report is made to the Secretary of State under subsection (2), he may, for the purpose of investigating the matter reported to him and such other matters relating to the affairs of the company as appear to him to require investigation, exercise any of the powers which are exercisable by inspectors appointed under section 431 or 432 of the Companies Act to investigate a company's affairs.

(4)   For the purpose of such an investigation any obligation imposed on a person by any provision of the Companies Act to produce documents or give information to, or otherwise to assist, inspectors so appointed is to be regarded as an obligation similarly to assist the Secretary of State in his investigation.

(5)   An answer given by a person to a question put to him in exercise of the powers conferred by subsection (3) may be used in evidence against him.

(6)   However, in criminal proceedings in which that person is charged with an offence to which this subsection applies—

(a)   no evidence relating to the answer may be adduced, and

(b)   no question relating to it may be asked,

by or on behalf of the prosecution, unless evidence relating to it is adduced, or a question relating to it is asked, in the proceedings by or on behalf of that person.

(7)   Subsection (6) applies to any offence other than—

(a)   an offence under section 2 or 5 of the Perjury Act 1911 (false statements made on oath otherwise than in judicial proceedings or made otherwise than on oath), or

(b)   an offence under section 44(1) or (2) of the Criminal Law (Consolidation) (Scotland) Act 1995 (false statements made on oath or otherwise than on oath).

(8)   Where a prosecuting authority institutes criminal proceedings following any report under subsection (2), the nominee or supervisor, and every officer and agent of the company past and present (other than the defendant or defender), shall give the authority all assistance in connection with the prosecution which he is reasonably able to give.

For this purpose—

"agent" includes any banker or solicitor of the company and any person employed by the company as auditor, whether that person is or is not an officer of the company,

"prosecuting authority" means the Director of Public Prosecutions, the Lord Advocate or the Secretary of State.

(9)   The court may, on the application of the prosecuting authority, direct any person referred to in subsection (8) to comply with that subsection if he has failed to do so.

7B.   Arrangements coming to an end prematurely

For the purposes of this Part, a voluntary arrangement the approval of which has taken effect under section 4A or paragraph 36 of Schedule A1 comes to an end prematurely if, when it ceases to have effect, it has not been fully implemented in respect of all persons bound by the arrangement by virtue of section 5(2)(b)(i) or, as the case may be, paragraph 37(2)(b)(i) of Schedule A1.

PART II
ADMINISTRATION

8. Administration

Schedule B1 to this Act (which makes provision about the administration of companies) shall have effect.

9–27. ...

PART III
RECEIVERSHIP

CHAPTER I
RECEIVERS AND MANAGERS (ENGLAND AND WALES)

Preliminary and general provisions

28. Extent of this Chapter

This Chapter does not apply to receivers appointed under Chapter II of this Part (Scotland).

29. Definitions

(1) It is hereby declared that, except where the context otherwise requires—

(a) any reference in the Companies Act or this Act to a receiver or manager of the property of a company, or to a receiver of it, includes a receiver or manager, or (as the case may be) a receiver of part only of that property and a receiver only of the income arising from the property or from part of it; and

(b) any reference in the Companies Act or this Act to the appointment of a receiver or manager under powers contained in an instrument includes an appointment made under powers which, by virtue of any enactment, are implied in and have effect as if contained in an instrument.

(2) In this Chapter "administrative receiver" means—

(a) a receiver or manager of the whole (or substantially the whole) of a company's property appointed by or on behalf of the holders of any debentures of the company secured by a charge which, as created, was a floating charge, or by such a charge and one or more other securities; or

(b) a person who would be such a receiver or manager but for the appointment of some other person as the receiver of part of the company's property.

30. Disqualification of body corporate from acting as receiver

A body corporate is not qualified for appointment as receiver of the property of a company, and any body corporate which acts as such a receiver is liable to a fine.

31. Disqualification of bankrupt

(1) A person commits an offence if he acts as receiver or manager of the property of a company on behalf of debenture holders while—

(a) he is an undischarged bankrupt, or

(b) a bankruptcy restrictions order is in force in respect of him.

(2) A person guilty of an offence under subsection (1) shall be liable to imprisonment, a fine or both.

(3) This section does not apply to a receiver or manager acting under an appointment made by the court.

32.   Power for court to appoint official receiver

Where application is made to the court to appoint a receiver on behalf of the debenture holders or other creditors of a company which is being wound up by the court, the official receiver may be appointed.

Receivers and managers appointed out of court

33.   Time for which appointment is effective

(1)   The appointment of a person as a receiver or manager of a company's property under powers contained in an instrument—

(a)   is of no effect unless it is accepted by that person before the end of the business day next following that on which the instrument of appointment is received by him or on his behalf, and

(b)   subject to this, is deemed to be made at the time at which the instrument of appointment is so received.

(2)   This section applies to the appointment of two or more persons as joint receivers or managers of a company's property under powers contained in an instrument, subject to such modifications as may be prescribed by the rules.

34.   Liability for invalid appointment

Where the appointment of a person as the receiver or manager of a company's property under powers contained in an instrument is discovered to be invalid (whether by virtue of the invalidity of the instrument or otherwise), the court may order the person by whom or on whose behalf the appointment was made to indemnify the person appointed against any liability which arises solely by reason of the invalidity of the appointment.

35.   Application to court for directions

(1)   A receiver or manager of the property of a company appointed under powers contained in an instrument, or the persons by whom or on whose behalf a receiver or manager has been so appointed, may apply to the court for directions in relation to any particular matter arising in connection with the performance of the functions of the receiver or manager.

(2)   On such an application, the court may give such directions, or may make such order declaring the rights of persons before the court or otherwise, as it thinks just.

36.   Court's power to fix remuneration

(1)   The court may, on an application made by the liquidator of a company, by order fix the amount to be paid by way of remuneration to a person who, under powers contained in an instrument, has been appointed receiver or manager of the company's property.

(2)   The court's power under subsection (1), where no previous order has been made with respect thereto under the subsection—

(a)   extends to fixing the remuneration for any period before the making of the order or the application for it,

(b)   is exercisable notwithstanding that the receiver or manager has died or ceased to act before the making of the order or the application, and

(c)   where the receiver or manager has been paid or has retained for his remuneration for any period before the making of the order any amount in excess of that so fixed for that period, extends to requiring him or his personal representatives to account for the excess or such part of it as may be specified in the order.

But the power conferred by paragraph (c) shall not be exercised as respects any period before the making of the application for the order under this section, unless in the court's opinion there are special circumstances making it proper for the power to be exercised.

(3)   The court may from time to time on an application made either by the liquidator or by the receiver or manager, vary or amend an order made under subsection (1).

37.   Liability for contracts, etc

(1)   A receiver or manager appointed under powers conferred in an instrument (other than an administrative receiver) is, to the same extent as if he had been appointed by order of the court—

    (a)   personally liable on any contract entered into by him in the performance of his functions (except in so far as the contract otherwise provides) and on any contract of employment adopted by him in the performance of those functions, and

    (b)   entitled in respect of that liability to indemnity out of the assets.

(2)   For the purposes of subsection (1)(a), the receiver or manager is not to be taken to have adopted a contract of employment by reason of anything done or omitted to be done within 14 days after his appointment.

(3)   Subsection (1) does not limit any right to indemnity which the receiver or manager would have apart from it, nor limit his liability on contracts entered into without authority, nor confer any right to indemnity in respect of that liability.

(4)   Where at any time the receiver or manager so appointed vacates office—

    (a)   his remuneration and any expenses properly incurred by him, and

    (b)   any indemnity to which he is entitled out of the assets of the company,

shall be charged on and paid out of any property of the company which is in his custody or under his control at that time in priority to any charge or other security held by the person by or on whose behalf he was appointed.

38.   Receivership accounts to be delivered to registrar

(1)   Except in the case of an administrative receiver, every receiver or manager of a company's property who has been appointed under powers contained in an instrument shall deliver to the registrar of companies for registration the requisite accounts of his receipts and payments.

(2)   The accounts shall be delivered within one month (or such longer period as the registrar may allow) after the expiration of 12 months from the date of his appointment and of every subsequent period of 6 months, and also within one month after he ceases to act as receiver or manager.

(3)   The requisite accounts shall be an abstract in the prescribed form showing—

    (a)   receipts and payments during the relevant period of 12 or 6 months, or

    (b)   where the receiver or manager ceases to act, receipts and payments during the period from the end of the period of 12 or 6 months to which the last preceding abstract related (or, if no preceding abstract has been delivered under this section, from the date of his appointment) up to the date of his so ceasing, and the aggregate amount of receipts and payments during all preceding periods since his appointment.

(4)   In this section "prescribed" means prescribed by regulations made by statutory instrument by the Secretary of State.

(5)   A receiver or manager who makes default in complying with this section is liable to a fine and, for continued contravention, to a daily default fine.

Provisions applicable to every receivership

39.   Notification that receiver or manager appointed

(1)   When a receiver or manager of the property of a company has been appointed, every invoice, order for goods or business letter issued by or on behalf of the company or the receiver or manager or the liquidator of the company, being a document on or in which the company's name appears, shall contain a statement that a receiver or manager has been appointed.

(2)   If default is made in complying with this section, the company and any of the following persons, who knowingly and wilfully authorises or permits the default, namely, any officer of the company, any liquidator of the company and any receiver or manager, is liable to a fine.

40.   Payment of debts out of assets subject to floating charge

(1)   The following applies, in the case of a company, where a receiver is appointed on behalf of the holders of any debentures of the company secured by a charge which, as created, was a floating charge.

(2)　　　If the company is not at the time in course of being wound up, its preferential debts (within the meaning given to that expression by section 386 in Part XII) shall be paid out of the assets coming to the hands of the receiver in priority to any claims for principal or interest in respect of the debentures.

(3)　　　Payments made under this section shall be recouped, as far as may be, out of the assets of the company available for payment of general creditors.

41.　Enforcement of duty to make returns

(1)　　　If a receiver or manager of a company's property—

　　　(a)　having made default in filing, delivering or making any return, account or other document, or in giving any notice, which a receiver or manager is by law required to file, deliver, make or give, fails to make good the default within 14 days after the service on him of a notice requiring him to do so, or

　　　(b)　having been appointed under powers contained in an instrument, has, after being required at any time by the liquidator of the company to do so, failed to render proper accounts of his receipts and payments and to vouch them and pay over to the liquidator the amount properly payable to him,

the court may, on an application made for the purpose, make an order directing the receiver or manager (as the case may be) to make good the default within such time as may be specified in the order.

(2)　　　In the case of the default mentioned in subsection (1)(a), application to the court may be made by any member or creditor of the company or by the registrar of companies; and in the case of the default mentioned in subsection (1)(b), the application shall be made by the liquidator.

In either case the court's order may provide that all costs of and incidental to the application shall be borne by the receiver or manager, as the case may be.

(3)　　　Nothing in this section prejudices the operation of any enactment imposing penalties on receivers in respect of any such default as is mentioned in subsection (1).

Administrative receivers: general

42.　General powers

(1)　　　The powers conferred on the administrative receiver of a company by the debentures by virtue of which he was appointed are deemed to include (except in so far as they are inconsistent with any of the provisions of those debentures) the powers specified in Schedule 1 to this Act.

(2)　　　In the application of Schedule 1 to the administrative receiver of a company—

　　　(a)　the words "he" and "him" refer to the administrative receiver, and

　　　(b)　references to the property of the company are to the property of which he is or, but for the appointment of some other person as the receiver of part of the company's property, would be the receiver or manager.

(3)　　　A person dealing with the administrative receiver in good faith and for value is not concerned to inquire whether the receiver is acting within his powers.

43.　Power to dispose of charged property, etc

(1)　　　Where, on an application by the administrative receiver, the court is satisfied that the disposal (with or without other assets) of any relevant property which is subject to a security would be likely to promote a more advantageous realisation of the company's assets than would otherwise be effected, the court may by order authorise the administrative receiver to dispose of the property as if it were not subject to the security.

(2)　　　Subsection (1) does not apply in the case of any security held by the person by or on whose behalf the administrative receiver was appointed, or of any security to which a security so held has priority.

(3)　　　It shall be a condition of an order under this section that—

　　　(a)　the net proceeds of the disposal, and

     (b)   where those proceeds are less than such amount as may be determined by the court to be the net amount which would be realised on a sale of the property in the open market by a willing vendor, such sums as may be required to make good the deficiency,

shall be applied towards discharging the sums secured by the security.

(4)   Where a condition imposed in pursuance of subsection (3) relates to two or more securities, that condition shall require the net proceeds of the disposal and, where paragraph (b) of that subsection applies, the sums mentioned in that paragraph to be applied towards discharging the sums secured by those securities in the order of their priorities.

(5)   An office copy of an order under this section shall, within 14 days of the making of the order, be sent by the administrative receiver to the registrar of companies.

(6)   If the administrative receiver without reasonable excuse fails to comply with subsection (5), he is liable to a fine and, for continued contravention, to a daily default fine.

(7)   In this section "relevant property", in relation to the administrative receiver, means the property of which he is or, but for the appointment of some other person as the receiver of part of the company's property, would be the receiver or manager.

44.   Agency and liability for contracts

(1)   The administrative receiver of a company—

     (a)   is deemed to be the company's agent, unless and until the company goes into liquidation;

     (b)   is personally liable on any contract entered into by him in the carrying out of his functions (except in so far as the contract otherwise provides) and, to the extent of any qualifying liability, on any contract of employment adopted by him in the carrying out of those functions; and

     (c)   is entitled in respect of that liability to an indemnity out of the assets of the company.

(2)   For the purposes of subsection (1)(b) the administrative receiver is not to be taken to have adopted a contract of employment by reason of anything done or omitted to be done within 14 days after his appointment.

(2A)   For the purposes of subsection (1)(b), a liability under a contract of employment is a qualifying liability if—

     (a)   it is a liability to pay a sum by way of wages or salary or contribution to an occupational pension scheme,

     (b)   it is incurred while the administrative receiver is in office, and

     (c)   it is in respect of services rendered wholly or partly after the adoption of the contract.

(2B)   Where a sum payable in respect of a liability which is a qualifying liability for the purposes of subsection (1)(b) is payable in respect of services rendered partly before and partly after the adoption of the contract, liability under subsection (1)(b) shall only extend to so much of the sum as is payable in respect of services rendered after the adoption of the contract.

(2C)   For the purposes of subsections (2A) and (2B)—

     (a)   wages or salary payable in respect of a period of holiday or absence from work through sickness or other good cause are deemed to be wages or (as the case may be) salary in respect of services rendered in that period, and

     (b)   a sum payable in lieu of holiday is deemed to be wages or (as the case may be) salary in respect of services rendered in the period by reference to which the holiday entitlement arose.

(2D)   In subsection (2C)(a), the reference to wages or salary payable in respect of a period of holiday includes any sums which, if they had been paid, would have been treated for the purposes of the enactments relating to social security as earnings in respect of that period.

(3)   This section does not limit any right to indemnity which the administrative receiver would have apart from it, nor limit his liability on contracts entered into or adopted without authority, nor confer any right to indemnity in respect of that liability.

45.   Vacation of office

(1)   An administrative receiver of a company may at any time be removed from office by order of the court (but not otherwise) and may resign his office by giving notice of his resignation in the prescribed manner to such persons as may be prescribed.

(2)   An administrative receiver shall vacate office if he ceases to be qualified to act as an insolvency practitioner in relation to the company.

(3)   Where at any time an administrative receiver vacates office—

        (a)   his remuneration and any expenses properly incurred by him, and

        (b)   any indemnity to which he is entitled out of the assets of the company,

        shall be charged on and paid out of any property of the company which is in his custody or under his control at that time in priority to any security held by the person by or on whose behalf he was appointed.

(4)   Where an administrative receiver vacates office otherwise than by death, he shall, within 14 days after his vacation of office, send a notice to that effect to the registrar of companies.

(5)   If an administrative receiver without reasonable excuse fails to comply with subsection (4), he is liable to a fine *and, for continued contravention, to a daily default fine.*

        Note. The italicized words in subsection (5) are repealed by the Companies Act 1989, ss. 107, 212, Sch. 16, para. 3(3), Sch. 24, as from a day to be appointed.

Administrative receivers:
ascertainment and investigation of company's affairs

46.   Information to be given by administrative receiver

(1)   Where an administrative receiver is appointed, he shall—

        (a)   forthwith send to the company and publish in the prescribed manner a notice of his appointment, and

        (b)   within 28 days after his appointment, unless the court otherwise directs, send such a notice to all the creditors of the company (so far as he is aware of their addresses).

(2)   This section and the next do not apply in relation to the appointment of an administrative receiver to act—

        (a)   with an existing administrative receiver, or

        (b)   in place of an administrative receiver dying or ceasing to act,

        except that, where they apply to an administrative receiver who dies or ceases to act before they have been fully complied with, the references in this section and the next to the administrative receiver include (subject to the next subsection) his successor and any continuing administrative receiver.

(3)   If the company is being wound up, this section and the next apply notwithstanding that the administrative receiver and the liquidator are the same person, but with any necessary modifications arising from that fact.

(4)   If the administrative receiver without reasonable excuse fails to comply with this section, he is liable to a fine and, for continued contravention, to a daily default fine.

47.   Statement of affairs to be submitted

(1)   Where an administrative receiver is appointed, he shall forthwith require some or all of the persons mentioned below to make out and submit to him a statement in the prescribed form as to the affairs of the company.

(2)   A statement submitted under this section shall be verified by affidavit by the persons required to submit it and shall show—

        (a)   particulars of the company's assets, debts and liabilities;

        (b)   the names and addresses of its creditors;

        (c)   the securities held by them respectively;

        (d)   the dates when the securities were respectively given; and

        (e)   such further or other information as may be prescribed.

(3)   The persons referred to in subsection (1) are—
         (a)   those who are or have been officers of the company;
         (b)   those who have taken part in the company's formation at any time within one year before
                the date of the appointment of the administrative receiver;
         (c)   those who are in the company's employment, or have been in its employment within that
                year, and are in the administrative receiver's opinion capable of giving the information
                required;
         (d)   those who are or have been within that year officers of or in the employment of a company
                which is, or within that year was, an officer of the company.
         In this subsection "employment" includes employment under a contract for services.
(4)   Where any persons are required under this section to submit a statement of affairs to the
         administrative receiver, they shall do so (subject to the next subsection) before the end of the
         period of 21 days beginning with the day after that on which the prescribed notice of the
         requirement is given to them by the administrative receiver.
(5)   The administrative receiver, if he thinks fit, may—
         (a)   at any time release a person from an obligation imposed on him under subsection (1) or (2),
                or
         (b)   either when giving notice under subsection (4) or subsequently, extend the period so
                mentioned;
         and where the administrative receiver has refused to exercise a power conferred by this subsec-
         tion, the court, if it thinks fit, may exercise it.
(6)   If a person without reasonable excuse fails to comply with any obligation imposed under this
         section, he is liable to a fine and, for continued contravention, to a daily default fine.

48.   **Report by administrative receiver**
(1)   Where an administrative receiver is appointed, he shall, within 3 months (or such longer period as
         the court may allow) after his appointment, send to the registrar of companies, to any trustees for
         secured creditors of the company and (so far as he is aware of their addresses) to all such creditors
         a report as to the following matters, namely—
         (a)   the events leading up to his appointment, so far as he is aware of them;
         (b)   the disposal or proposed disposal by him of any property of the company and the carrying
                on or proposed carrying on by him of any business of the company;
         (c)   the amounts of principal and interest payable to the debenture holders by whom or on whose
                behalf he was appointed and the amounts payable to preferential creditors; and
         (d)   the amount (if any) likely to be available for the payment of other creditors.
(2)   The administrative receiver shall also, within 3 months (or such longer period as the court may
         allow) after his appointment, either—
         (a)   send a copy of the report (so far as he is aware of their addresses) to all unsecured creditors
                of the company; or
         (b)   publish in the prescribed manner a notice stating an address to which unsecured creditors of
                the company should write for copies of the report to be sent to them free of charge,
         and (in either case), unless the court otherwise directs, lay a copy of the report before a meeting of
         the company's unsecured creditors summoned for the purpose on not less than 14 days' notice.
(3)   The court shall not give a direction under subsection (2) unless—
         (a)   the report states the intention of the administrative receiver to apply for the direction, and
         (b)   a copy of the report is sent to the persons mentioned in paragraph (a) of that subsection, or a
                notice is published as mentioned in paragraph (b) of that subsection, not less than 14 days
                before the hearing of the application.
(4)   Where the company has gone or goes into liquidation, the administrative receiver—
         (a)   shall, within 7 days after his compliance with subsection (1) or, if later, the nomination or
                appointment of the liquidator, send a copy of the report to the liquidator, and
         (b)   where he does so within the time limited for compliance with subsection (2), is not required
                to comply with that subsection.

(5)   A report under this section shall include a summary of the statement of affairs made out and submitted to the administrative receiver under section 47 and of his comments (if any) upon it.

(6)   Nothing in this section is to be taken as requiring any such report to include any information the disclosure of which would seriously prejudice the carrying out by the administrative receiver of his functions.

(7)   Section 46(2) applies for the purposes of this section also.

(8)   If the administrative receiver without reasonable excuse fails to comply with this section, he is liable to a fine and, for continued contravention, to a default fine.

49.   Committee of creditors

(1)   Where a meeting of creditors is summoned under section 48, the meeting may, if it thinks fit, establish a committee ("the creditors' committee") to exercise the functions conferred on it by or under this Act.

(2)   If such a committee is established, the committee may, on giving not less than 7 days' notice, require the administrative receiver to attend before it at any reasonable time and furnish it with such information relating to the carrying out by him of his functions as it may reasonably require.

CHAPTER II
RECEIVERS (SCOTLAND)

50.   Extent of this Chapter

This Chapter extends to Scotland only.

51.   Power to appoint receiver

(1)   It is competent under the law of Scotland for the holder of a floating charge over all or any part of the property (including uncalled capital), which may from time to time be comprised in the property and undertaking of an incorporated company (whether a company within the meaning of the Companies Act or not) which the Court of Session has jurisdiction to wind up, to appoint a receiver of such part of the property of the company as is subject to the charge.

(2)   It is competent under the law of Scotland for the court, on the application of the holder of such a floating charge, to appoint a receiver of such part of the property of the company as is subject to the charge.

(2A)   Subsections (1) and (2) are subject to section 72A.

(3)   The following are disqualified from being appointed as receiver—

   (a)   a body corporate;

   (b)   an undischarged bankrupt; and

   (c)   a firm according to the law of Scotland.

(4)   A body corporate or a firm according to the law of Scotland which acts as a receiver is liable to a fine.

(5)   An undischarged bankrupt who so acts is liable to imprisonment or a fine, or both.

(6)   In this section, "receiver" includes joint receivers.

52.   Circumstances justifying appointment

(1)   A receiver may be appointed under section 51(1) by the holder of the floating charge on the occurrence of any event which, by the provisions of the instrument creating the charge, entitles the holder of the charge to make that appointment and, in so far as not otherwise provided for by the instrument, on the occurrence of any of the following events, namely—

   (a)   the expiry of a period of 21 days after the making of a demand for payment of the whole or any part of the principal sum secured by the charge, without payment having been made;

   (b)   the expiry of a period of 2 months during the whole of which interest due and payable under the charge has been in arrears;

   (c)   the making of an order or the passing of a resolution to wind up the company;

   (d)   the appointment of a receiver by virtue of any other floating charge created by the company.

(2)   A receiver may be appointed by the court under section 51(2) on the occurrence of any event which, by the provisions of the instrument creating the floating charge, entitles the holder of the charge to make that appointment and, in so far as not otherwise provided for by the instrument, on the occurrence of any of the following events, namely—

    (a)   where the court, on the application of the holder of the charge, pronounces itself satisfied that the position of the holder of the charge is likely to be prejudiced if no such appointment is made;

    (b)   any of the events referred to in paragraphs (a) to (c) of subsection (1).

53. Mode of appointment by holder of charge

(1)   The appointment of a receiver by the holder of the floating charge under section 51(1) shall be by means of an instrument subscribed in accordance with the Requirements of Writing (Scotland) Act 1995 ("the instrument of appointment"), a copy (certified in the prescribed manner to be a correct copy) whereof shall be delivered by or on behalf of the person making the appointment to the registrar of companies for registration within 7 days of its execution and shall be accompanied by a notice in the prescribed form.

(2)   If any person without reasonable excuse makes default in complying with the requirements of subsection (1), he is liable to a fine *and, for continued contravention, to a daily default fine*.

(3)   ...

(4)   If the receiver is to be appointed by the holders of a series of secured debentures, the instrument of appointment may be executed on behalf of the holders of the floating charge by any person authorised by resolution of the debenture-holders to execute the instrument.

(5)   On receipt of the certified copy of the instrument of appointment in accordance with subsection (1), the registrar shall, on payment of the prescribed fee, enter the particulars of the appointment in the register of charges.

(6)   The appointment of a person as a receiver by an instrument of appointment in accordance with subsection (1)—

    (a)   is of no effect unless it is accepted by that person before the end of the business day next following that on which the instrument of appointment is received by him or on his behalf, and

    (b)   subject to paragraph (a), is deemed to be made on the day on and at the time at which the instrument of appointment is so received, as evidenced by a written docquet by that person or on his behalf;

and this subsection applies to the appointment of joint receivers subject to such modifications as may be prescribed.

(7)   On the appointment of a receiver under this section, the floating charge by virtue of which he was appointed attaches to the property then subject to the charge; and such attachment has effect as if the charge was a fixed security over the property to which it has attached.

Note. The italicized words in subsection (2) are repealed by the Companies Act 1989, ss. 107, 212, Sch. 16, para. 3(3), Sch. 24, as from a day to be appointed.

54. Appointment by court

(1)   Application for the appointment of a receiver by the court under section 51(2) shall be by petition to the court, which shall be served on the company.

(2)   On such an application, the court shall, if it thinks fit, issue an interlocutor making the appointment of the receiver.

(3)   A copy (certified by the clerk of the court to be a correct copy) of the court's interlocutor making the appointment shall be delivered by or on behalf of the petitioner to the registrar of companies for registration, accompanied by a notice in the prescribed form, within 7 days of the date of the interlocutor or such longer period as the court may allow.

If any person without reasonable excuse makes default in complying with the requirements of this subsection, he is liable to a fine *and, for continued contravention, to a daily default fine*.

(4)   On receipt of the certified copy interlocutor in accordance with subsection (3), the registrar shall, on payment of the prescribed fee, enter the particulars of the appointment in the register of charges.

(5)   The receiver is to be regarded as having been appointed on the date of his being appointed by the court.

(6)   On the appointment of a receiver under this section, the floating charge by virtue of which he was appointed attaches to the property then subject to the charge; and such attachment has effect as if the charge were a fixed security over the property to which it has attached.

(7)   In making rules of court for the purposes of this section, the Court of Session shall have regard to the need for special provision for cases which appear to the court to require to be dealt with as a matter of urgency.

> **Note.** The italicized words in subsection (3) are repealed by the Companies Act 1989, ss. 107, 212, Sch. 16, para. 3(3), Sch. 24, as from a day to be appointed.

55.   Powers of receiver

(1)   Subject to the next subsection, a receiver has in relation to such part of the property of the company as is attached by the floating charge by virtue of which he was appointed, the powers, if any, given to him by the instrument creating that charge.

(2)   In addition, the receiver has under this Chapter the powers as respects that property (in so far as these are not inconsistent with any provision contained in that instrument) which are specified in Schedule 2 to this Act.

(3)   Subsections (1) and (2) apply—

     (a)   subject to the rights of any person who has effectually executed diligence on all or any part of the property of the company prior to the appointment of the receiver, and

     (b)   subject to the rights of any person who holds over all or any part of the property of the company a fixed security or floating charge having priority over, or ranking pari passu with, the floating charge by virtue of which the receiver was appointed.

(4)   A person dealing with a receiver in good faith and for value is not concerned to enquire whether the receiver is acting within his powers.

56.   Precedence among receivers

(1)   Where there are two or more floating charges subsisting over all or any part of the property of the company, a receiver may be appointed under this Chapter by virtue of each such charge; but a receiver appointed by, or on the application of, the holder of a floating charge having priority of ranking over any other floating charge by virtue of which a receiver has been appointed has the powers given to a receiver by section 55 and Schedule 2 to the exclusion of any other receiver.

(2)   Where two or more floating charges rank with one another equally, and two or more receivers have been appointed by virtue of such charges, the receivers so appointed are deemed to have been appointed as joint receivers.

(3)   Receivers appointed, or deemed to have been appointed, as joint receivers shall act jointly unless the instrument of appointment or respective instruments of appointment otherwise provide.

(4)   Subject to subsection (5) below, the powers of a receiver appointed by, or on the application of, the holder of a floating charge are suspended by, and as from the date of, the appointment of a receiver by, or on the application of, the holder of a floating charge having priority of ranking over that charge to such extent as may be necessary to enable the receiver second mentioned to exercise his powers under section 55 and Schedule 2; and any powers so suspended take effect again when the floating charge having priority of ranking ceases to attach to the property then subject to the charge, whether such cessation is by virtue of section 62(6) or otherwise.

(5)   The suspension of the powers of a receiver under subsection (4) does not have the effect of requiring him to release any part of the property (including any letters or documents) of the company from his control until he receives from the receiver superseding him a valid indemnity (subject to the limit of the value of such part of the property of the company as is subject to the

charge by virtue of which he was appointed) in respect of any expenses, charges and liabilities he may have incurred in the performance of his functions as receiver.

(6) The suspension of the powers of a receiver under subsection (4) does not cause the floating charge by virtue of which he was appointed to cease to attach to the property to which it attached by virtue of section 53(7) or 54(6).

(7) Nothing in this section prevents the same receiver being appointed by virtue of two or more floating charges.

57. Agency and liability of receiver for contracts

(1) A receiver is deemed to be the agent of the company in relation to such property of the company as is attached by the floating charge by virtue of which he was appointed.

(1A) Without prejudice to subsection (1), a receiver is deemed to be the agent of the company in relation to any contract of employment adopted by him in the carrying out of his functions.

(2) A receiver (including a receiver whose powers are subsequently suspended under section 56) is personally liable on any contract entered into by him in the performance of his functions, except in so far as the contract otherwise provides, and, to the extent of any qualifying liability, on any contract of employment adopted by him in the carrying out of those functions.

(2A) For the purposes of subsection (2), a liability under a contract of employment is a qualifying liability if—

(a) it is a liability to pay a sum by way of wages or salary or contribution to an occupational pension scheme,

(b) it is incurred while the receiver is in office, and

(c) it is in respect of services rendered wholly or partly after the adoption of the contract.

(2B) Where a sum payable in respect of a liability which is a qualifying liability for the purposes of subsection (2) is payable in respect of services rendered partly before and partly after the adoption of the contract, liability under that subsection shall only extend to so much of the sum as is payable in respect of services rendered after the adoption of the contract.

(2C) For the purposes of subsections (2A) and (2B)—

(a) wages or salary payable in respect of a period of holiday or absence from work through sickness or other good cause are deemed to be wages or (as the case may be) salary in respect of services rendered in that period, and

(b) a sum payable in lieu of holiday is deemed to be wages or (as the case may be) salary in respect of services rendered in the period by reference to which the holiday entitlement arose.

(2D) In subsection (2C)(a), the reference to wages or salary payable in respect of a period of holiday includes any sums which, if they had been paid, would have been treated for the purposes of the enactments relating to social security as earnings in respect of that period.

(3) A receiver who is personally liable by virtue of subsection (2) is entitled to be indemnified out of the property in respect of which he was appointed.

(4) Any contract entered into by or on behalf of the company prior to the appointment of a receiver continues in force (subject to its terms) notwithstanding that appointment, but the receiver does not by virtue only of his appointment incur any personal liability on any such contract.

(5) For the purposes of subsection (2), a receiver is not to be taken to have adopted a contract of employment by reason of anything done or omitted to be done within 14 days after his appointment.

(6) This section does not limit any right to indemnity which the receiver would have apart from it, nor limit his liability on contracts entered into or adopted without authority, nor confer any right to indemnity in respect of that liability.

(7) Any contract entered into by a receiver in the performance of his functions continues in force (subject to its terms) although the powers of the receiver are subsequently suspended under section 56.

58.   Remuneration of receiver

(1)   The remuneration to be paid to a receiver is to be determined by agreement between the receiver and the holder of the floating charge by virtue of which he was appointed.

(2)   Where the remuneration to be paid to the receiver has not been determined under subsection (1), or where it has been so determined but is disputed by any of the persons mentioned in paragraphs (a) to (d) below, it may be fixed instead by the Auditor of the Court of Session on application made to him by—

    (a)   the receiver;

    (b)   the holder of any floating charge or fixed security over all or any part of the property of the company;

    (c)   the company; or

    (d)   the liquidator of the company.

(3)   Where the receiver has been paid or has retained for his remuneration for any period before the remuneration has been fixed by the Auditor of the Court of Session under subsection (2) any amount in excess of the remuneration so fixed for that period, the receiver or his personal representatives shall account for the excess.

59.   Priority of debts

(1)   Where a receiver is appointed and the company is not at the time of the appointment in course of being wound up, the debts which fall under subsection (2) of this section shall be paid out of any assets coming to the hands of the receiver in priority to any claim for principal or interest by the holder of the floating charge by virtue of which the receiver was appointed.

(2)   Debts falling under this subsection are preferential debts (within the meaning given by section 386 in Part XII) which, by the end of a period of 6 months after advertisement by the receiver for claims in the Edinburgh Gazette and in a newspaper circulating in the district where the company carries on business either—

    (i)   have been intimated to him, or

    (ii)   have become known to him.

(3)   Any payments made under this section shall be recouped as far as may be out of the assets of the company available for payment of ordinary creditors.

60.   Distribution of moneys

(1)   Subject to the next section, and to the rights of any of the following categories of persons (which rights shall, except to the extent otherwise provided in any instrument, have the following order of priority), namely—

    (a)   the holder of any fixed security which is over property subject to the floating charge and which ranks prior to, or pari passu with, the floating charge;

    (b)   all persons who have effectually executed diligence on any part of the property of the company which is subject to the charge by virtue of which the receiver was appointed;

    (c)   creditors in respect of all liabilities, charges and expenses incurred by or on behalf of the receiver;

    (d)   the receiver in respect of his liabilities, expenses and remuneration, and any indemnity to which he is entitled out of the property of the company; and

    (e)   the preferential creditors entitled to payment under section 59,

the receiver shall pay moneys received by him to the holder of the floating charge by virtue of which the receiver was appointed in or towards satisfaction of the debt secured by the floating charge.

(2)   Any balance of moneys remaining after the provisions of subsection (1) and section 61 below have been satisfied shall be paid in accordance with their respective rights and interests to the following persons, as the case may require—

    (a)   any other receiver;

    (b)   the holder of a fixed security which is over property subject to the floating charge;

    (c)   the company or its liquidator, as the case may be.

(3)   Where any question arises as to the person entitled to a payment under this section, or where a receipt or a discharge of a security cannot be obtained in respect of any such payment, the receiver shall consign the amount of such payment in any joint stock bank of issue in Scotland in name of the Accountant of Court for behoof of the person or persons entitled thereto.

61.   Disposal of interest in property

(1)   Where the receiver sells or disposes, or is desirous of selling or disposing, of any property or interest in property of the company which is subject to the floating charge by virtue of which the receiver was appointed and which is—

(a)   subject to any security or interest of, or burden or encumbrance in favour of, a creditor the ranking of which is prior to, or pari passu with, or postponed to the floating charge, or

(b)   property or an interest in property affected or attached by effectual diligence executed by any person,

and the receiver is unable to obtain the consent of such creditor or, as the case may be, such person to such a sale or disposal, the receiver may apply to the court for authority to sell or dispose of the property or interest in property free of such security, interest, burden, encumbrance or diligence.

(2)   Subject to the next subsection, on such an application the court may, if it thinks fit, authorise the sale or disposal of the property or interest in question free of such security, interest, burden, encumbrance or diligence, and such authorisation may be on such terms or conditions as the court thinks fit.

(3)   In the case of an application where a fixed security over the property or interest in question which ranks prior to the floating charge has not been met or provided for in full, the court shall not authorise the sale or disposal of the property or interest in question unless it is satisfied that the sale or disposal would be likely to provide a more advantageous realisation of the company's assets than would otherwise be effected.

(4)   It shall be a condition of an authorisation to which subsection (3) applies that—

(a)   the net proceeds of the disposal, and

(b)   where those proceeds are less than such amount as may be determined by the court to be the net amount which would be realised on a sale of the property or interest in the open market by a willing seller, such sums as may be required to make good the deficiency,

shall be applied towards discharging the sums secured by the fixed security.

(5)   Where a condition imposed in pursuance of subsection (4) relates to two or more such fixed securities, that condition shall require the net proceeds of the disposal and, where paragraph (b) of that subsection applies, the sums mentioned in that paragraph to be applied towards discharging the sums secured by those fixed securities in the order of their priorities.

(6)   A copy of an authorisation under subsection (2) certified by the clerk of court shall, within 14 days of the granting of the authorisation, be sent by the receiver to the registrar of companies.

(7)   If the receiver without reasonable excuse fails to comply with subsection (6), he is liable to a fine and, for continued contravention, to a daily default fine.

(8)   Where any sale or disposal is effected in accordance with the authorisation of the court under subsection (2), the receiver shall grant to the purchaser or disponee an appropriate document of transfer or conveyance of the property or interest in question, and that document has the effect, or, where recording, intimation or registration of that document is a legal requirement for completion of title to the property or interest, then that recording, intimation or registration (as the case may be) has the effect, of—

(a)   disencumbering the property or interest of the security, interest, burden or encumbrance affecting it, and

(b)   freeing the property or interest from the diligence executed upon it.

(9)   Nothing in this section prejudices the right of any creditor of the company to rank for his debt in the winding up of the company.

62.   Cessation of appointment of receiver

(1)   A receiver may be removed from office by the court under subsection (3) below and may resign his office by giving notice of his resignation in the prescribed manner to such persons as may be prescribed.

(2)   A receiver shall vacate office if he ceases to be qualified to act as an insolvency practitioner in relation to the company.

(3)   Subject to the next subsection, a receiver may, on application to the court by the holder of the floating charge by virtue of which he was appointed, be removed by the court on cause shown.

(4)   Where at any time a receiver vacates office—

(a)   his remuneration and any expenses properly incurred by him, and

(b)   any indemnity to which he is entitled out of the property of the company,

shall be paid out of the property of the company which is subject to the floating charge and shall have priority as provided for in section 60(1).

(5)   When a receiver ceases to act as such otherwise than by death he shall, and, when a receiver is removed by the court, the holder of the floating charge by virtue of which he was appointed shall, within 14 days of the cessation or removal (as the case may be) give the registrar of companies notice to that effect, and the registrar shall enter the notice in the register of charges.

If the receiver or the holder of the floating charge (as the case may require) makes default in complying with the requirements of this subsection, he is liable to a fine *and, for continued contravention, to a daily default fine.*

(6)   If by the expiry of a period of one month following upon the removal of the receiver or his ceasing to act as such no other receiver has been appointed, the floating charge by virtue of which the receiver was appointed—

(a)   thereupon ceases to attach to the property then subject to the charge, and

(b)   again subsists as a floating charge;

and for the purposes of calculating the period of one month under this subsection no account shall be taken of any period during which the company is in administration, under Part II of this Act ...

Note. The italicized words in subsection (5) are repealed by the Companies Act 1989, ss. 107, 212, Sch. 16, para. 3(3), Sch. 24, as from a day to be appointed.

63.   Powers of court

(1)   The court on the application of—

(a)   the holder of a floating charge by virtue of which a receiver was appointed, or

(b)   a receiver appointed under section 51,

may give directions to the receiver in respect of any matter arising in connection with the performance by him of his functions.

(2)   Where the appointment of a person as a receiver by the holder of a floating charge is discovered to be invalid (whether by virtue of the invalidity of the instrument or otherwise), the court may order the holder of the floating charge to indemnify the person appointed against any liability which arises solely by reason of the invalidity of the appointment.

64.   Notification that receiver appointed

(1)   Where a receiver has been appointed, every invoice, order for goods or business letter issued by or on behalf of the company or the receiver or the liquidator of the company, being a document on or in which the name of the company appears, shall contain a statement that a receiver has been appointed.

(2)   If default is made in complying with the requirements of this section, the company and any of the following persons who knowingly and wilfully authorises or permits the default, namely any officer of the company, any liquidator of the company and any receiver, is liable to a fine.

65.   Information to be given by receiver

(1)   Where a receiver is appointed, he shall—

(a)   forthwith send to the company and publish notice of his appointment, and

(b) within 28 days after his appointment, unless the court otherwise directs, send such notice to all the creditors of the company (so far as he is aware of their addresses).

(2) This section and the next do not apply in relation to the appointment of a receiver to act—

(a) with an existing receiver, or

(b) in place of a receiver who has died or ceased to act,

except that, where they apply to a receiver who dies or ceases to act before they have been fully complied with, the references in this section and the next to the receiver include (subject to subsection (3) of this section) his successor and any continuing receiver.

(3) If the company is being wound up, this section and the next apply notwithstanding that the receiver and the liquidator are the same person, but with any necessary modifications arising from that fact.

(4) If a person without reasonable excuse fails to comply with this section, he is liable to a fine and, for continued contravention, to a daily default fine.

66. Company's statement of affairs

(1) Where a receiver of a company is appointed, the receiver shall forthwith require some or all of the persons mentioned in subsection (3) below to make out and submit to him a statement in the prescribed form as to the affairs of the company.

(2) A statement submitted under this section shall be verified by affidavit by the persons required to submit it and shall show—

(a) particulars of the company's assets, debts and liabilities;

(b) the names and addresses of its creditors;

(c) the securities held by them respectively;

(d) the dates when the securities were respectively given; and

(e) such further or other information as may be prescribed.

(3) The persons referred to in subsection (1) are—

(a) those who are or have been officers of the company;

(b) those who have taken part in the company's formation at any time within one year before the date of the appointment of the receiver;

(c) those who are in the company's employment or have been in its employment within that year, and are in the receiver's opinion capable of giving the information required;

(d) those who are or have been within that year officers of or in the employment of a company which is, or within that year was, an officer of the company.

In this subsection "employment" includes employment under a contract for services.

(4) Where any persons are required under this section to submit a statement of affairs to the receiver they shall do so (subject to the next subsection) before the end of the period of 21 days beginning with the day after that on which the prescribed notice of the requirement is given to them by the receiver.

(5) The receiver, if he thinks fit, may—

(a) at any time release a person from an obligation imposed on him under subsection (1) or (2), or

(b) either when giving the notice mentioned in subsection (4) or subsequently extend the period so mentioned,

and where the receiver has refused to exercise a power conferred by this subsection, the court, if it thinks fit, may exercise it.

(6) If a person without reasonable excuse fails to comply with any obligation imposed under this section, he is liable to a fine and, for continued contravention, to a daily default fine.

67. Report by receiver

(1) Where a receiver is appointed under section 51, he shall within 3 months (or such longer period as the court may allow) after his appointment, send to the registrar of companies, to the holder of the floating charge by virtue of which he was appointed and to any trustees for secured creditors of

the company and (so far as he is aware of their addresses) to all such creditors a report as to the following matters, namely—

(a)   the events leading up to his appointment, so far as he is aware of them;

(b)   the disposal or proposed disposal by him of any property of the company and the carrying on or proposed carrying on by him of any business of the company;

(c)   the amounts of principal and interest payable to the holder of the floating charge by virtue of which he was appointed and the amounts payable to preferential creditors; and

(d)   the amount (if any) likely to be available for the payment of other creditors.

(2)   The receiver shall also, within 3 months (or such longer period as the court may allow) after his appointment, either—

(a)   send a copy of the report (so far as he is aware of their addresses) to all unsecured creditors of the company, or

(b)   publish in the prescribed manner a notice stating an address to which unsecured creditors of the company should write for copies of the report to be sent to them free of charge,

and (in either case), unless the court otherwise directs, lay a copy of the report before a meeting of the company's unsecured creditors summoned for the purpose on not less than 14 days' notice.

(3)   The court shall not give a direction under subsection (2) unless—

(a)   the report states the intention of the receiver to apply for the direction; and

(b)   a copy of the report is sent to the persons mentioned in paragraph (a) of that subsection, or a notice is published as mentioned in paragraph (b) of that subsection, not less than 14 days before the hearing of the application.

(4)   Where the company has gone or goes into liquidation, the receiver—

(a)   shall, within 7 days after his compliance with subsection (1) or, if later, the nomination or appointment of the liquidator, send a copy of the report to the liquidator, and

(b)   where he does so within the time limited for compliance with subsection (2), is not required to comply with that subsection.

(5)   A report under this section shall include a summary of the statement of affairs made out and submitted under section 66 and of his comments (if any) on it.

(6)   Nothing in this section shall be taken as requiring any such report to include any information the disclosure of which would seriously prejudice the carrying out by the receiver of his functions.

(7)   Section 65(2) applies for the purposes of this section also.

(8)   If a person without reasonable excuse fails to comply with this section, he is liable to a fine and, for continued contravention, to a daily default fine.

(9)   In this section "secured creditor", in relation to a company, means a creditor of the company who holds in respect of his debt a security over property of the company, and "unsecured creditor" shall be construed accordingly.

68.   Committee of creditors

(1)   Where a meeting of creditors is summoned under section 67, the meeting may, if it thinks fit, establish a committee ("the creditors' committee") to exercise the functions conferred on it by or under this Act.

(2)   If such a committee is established, the committee may on giving not less than 7 days' notice require the receiver to attend before it at any reasonable time and furnish it with such information relating to the carrying out by him of his functions as it may reasonably require.

69.   Enforcement of receiver's duty to make returns, etc

(1)   If any receiver—

(a)   having made default in filing, delivering or making any return, account or other document, or in giving any notice, which a receiver is by law required to file, deliver, make or give, fails to make good the default within 14 days after the service on him of a notice requiring him to do so; or

(b) has, after being required at any time by the liquidator of the company so to do, failed to render proper accounts of his receipts and payments and to vouch the same and to pay over to the liquidator the amount properly payable to him,

the court may, on an application made for the purpose, make an order directing the receiver to make good the default within such time as may be specified in the order.

(2) In the case of any such default as is mentioned in subsection (1)(a), an application for the purposes of this section may be made by any member or creditor of the company or by the registrar of companies; and, in the case of any such default as is mentioned in subsection (1)(b), the application shall be made by the liquidator; and, in either case, the order may provide that all expenses of and incidental to the application shall be borne by the receiver.

(3) Nothing in this section prejudices the operation of any enactments imposing penalties on receivers in respect of any such default as is mentioned in subsection (1).

70. Interpretation for Chapter II

(1) In this Chapter, unless the contrary intention appears, the following expressions have the following meanings respectively assigned to them—

"company" means an incorporated company (whether or not a company within the meaning of the Companies Act) which the Court of Session has jurisdiction to wind up;

"fixed security", in relation to any property of a company, means any security, other than a floating charge or a charge having the nature of a floating charge, which on the winding up of the company in Scotland would be treated as an effective security over that property, and (without prejudice to that generality) includes a security over that property, being a heritable security within the meaning of the Conveyancing and Feudal Reform (Scotland) Act 1970;

"instrument of appointment" has the meaning given by section 53(1);

"prescribed" means prescribed by regulations made under this Chapter by the Secretary of State;

"receiver" means a receiver of such part of the property of the company as is subject to the floating charge by virtue of which he has been appointed under section 51;

"register of charges" means the register kept by the registrar of companies for the purposes of Chapter II of Part XII of the Companies Act;

"secured debenture" means a bond, debenture, debenture stock or other security which, either itself or by reference to any other instrument, creates a floating charge over all or any part of the property of the company, but does not include a security which creates no charge other than a fixed security; and

"series of secured debentures" means two or more secured debentures created as a series by the company in such a manner that the holders thereof are entitled pari passu to the benefit of the floating charge.

(2) Where a floating charge, secured debenture or series of secured debentures has been created by the company, then, except where the context otherwise requires, any reference in this Chapter to the holder of the floating charge shall—

(a) where the floating charge, secured debenture or series of secured debentures provides for a receiver to be appointed by any person or body, be construed as a reference to that person or body;

(b) where, in the case of a series of secured debentures, no such provision has been made therein but—

(i) there are trustees acting for the debenture-holders under and in accordance with a trust deed, be construed as a reference to those trustees, and

(ii) where no such trustees are acting, be construed as a reference to—

(aa) a majority in nominal value of those present or represented by proxy and voting at a meeting of debenture-holders at which the holders of at least one-third in nominal value of the outstanding debentures of the series are present or so represented, or (bb) where no such meeting is held, the holders of at least one-half in nominal value of the outstanding debentures of the series.

(3)   Any reference in this Chapter to a floating charge, secured debenture, series of secured debentures or instrument creating a charge includes, except where the context otherwise requires, a reference to that floating charge, debenture, series of debentures or instrument as varied by any instrument.

(4)   References in this Chapter to the instrument by which a floating charge was created are, in the case of a floating charge created by words in a bond or other written acknowledgement, references to the bond or, as the case may be, the other written acknowledgement.

71.   **Prescription of forms etc; regulations**

(1)   The notice referred to in section 62(5), and the notice referred to in section 65(1)(a) shall be in such form as may be prescribed.

(2)   Any power conferred by this Chapter on the Secretary of State to make regulations is exercisable by statutory instrument; and a statutory instrument made in the exercise of the power so conferred to prescribe a fee is subject to annulment in pursuance of a resolution of either House of Parliament.

CHAPTER III

RECEIVERS' POWERS IN GREAT BRITAIN AS A WHOLE

72.   **Cross-border operation of receivership provisions**

(1)   A receiver appointed under the law of either part of Great Britain in respect of the whole or any part of any property or undertaking of a company and in consequence of the company having created a charge which, as created, was a floating charge may exercise his powers in the other part of Great Britain so far as their exercise is not inconsistent with the law applicable there.

(2)   In subsection (1) "receiver" includes a manager and a person who is appointed both receiver and manager.

CHAPTER IV

PROHIBITION OF APPOINTMENT OF
ADMINISTRATIVE RECEIVER

72A.   **Floating charge holder not to appoint administrative receiver**

(1)   The holder of a qualifying floating charge in respect of a company's property may not appoint an administrative receiver of the company.

(2)   In Scotland, the holder of a qualifying floating charge in respect of a company's property may not appoint or apply to the court for the appointment of a receiver who on appointment would be an administrative receiver of property of the company.

(3)   In subsections (1) and (2)—

        "holder of a qualifying floating charge in respect of a company's property" has the same meaning as in paragraph 14 of Schedule B1 to this Act, and

        "administrative receiver" has the meaning given by section 251.

(4)   This section applies—

     (a)   to a floating charge created on or after a date appointed by the Secretary of State by order made by statutory instrument, and

     (b)   in spite of any provision of an agreement or instrument which purports to empower a person to appoint an administrative receiver (by whatever name).

(5)   An order under subsection (4)(a) may—

     (a)   make provision which applies generally or only for a specified purpose;

     (b)   make different provision for different purposes;

     (c)   make transitional provision.

(6)   This section is subject to the exceptions specified in sections 72B to 72GA.

72B. First exception: capital market

(1) Section 72A does not prevent the appointment of an administrative receiver in pursuance of an agreement which is or forms part of a capital market arrangement if—

    (a) a party incurs or, when the agreement was entered into was expected to incur, a debt of at least £50 million under the arrangement, and

    (b) the arrangement involves the issue of a capital market investment.

(2) In subsection (1)—

    "capital market arrangement" means an arrangement of a kind described in paragraph 1 of Schedule 2A, and

    "capital market investment" means an investment of a kind described in paragraph 2 or 3 of that Schedule.

72C. Second exception: public-private partnership

(1) Section 72A does not prevent the appointment of an administrative receiver of a project company of a project which—

    (a) is a public-private partnership project, and

    (b) includes step-in rights.

(2) In this section "public-private partnership project" means a project—

    (a) the resources for which are provided partly by one or more public bodies and partly by one or more private persons, or

    (b) which is designed wholly or mainly for the purpose of assisting a public body to discharge a function.

(3) In this section—

    "step-in rights" has the meaning given by paragraph 6 of Schedule 2A, and

    "project company" has the meaning given by paragraph 7 of that Schedule.

72D. Third exception: utilities

(1) Section 72A does not prevent the appointment of an administrative receiver of a project company of a project which—

    (a) is a utility project, and

    (b) includes step-in rights.

(2) In this section—

    (a) "utility project" means a project designed wholly or mainly for the purpose of a regulated business,

    (b) "regulated business" means a business of a kind listed in paragraph 10 of Schedule 2A,

    (c) "step-in rights" has the meaning given by paragraph 6 of that Schedule, and

    (d) "project company" has the meaning given by paragraph 7 of that Schedule.

72DA. Exception in respect of urban regeneration projects

(1) Section 72A does not prevent the appointment of an administrative receiver of a project company of a project which—

    (a) is designed wholly or mainly to develop land which at the commencement of the project is wholly or partly in a designated disadvantaged area outside Northern Ireland, and

    (b) includes step-in rights.

(2) In subsection (1) "develop" means to carry out—

    (a) building operations,

    (b) any operation for the removal of substances or waste from land and the levelling of the surface of the land, or

    (c) engineering operations in connection with the activities mentioned in paragraph (a) or (b).

(3) In this section—

    "building" includes any structure or erection, and any part of a building as so defined, but does not include plant and machinery comprised in a building,

    "building operations" includes—

(a)   demolition of buildings,

(b)   filling in of trenches,

(c)   rebuilding,

(d)   structural alterations of, or additions to, buildings, and

(e)   other operations normally undertaken by a person carrying on business as a builder,
       "designated disadvantaged area" means an area designated as a disadvantaged area under
       section 92 of the Finance Act 2001,
       "engineering operations" includes the formation and laying out of means of access to
       highways,
       "project company" has the meaning given by paragraph 7 of Schedule 2A,
       "step-in rights" has the meaning given by paragraph 6 of that Schedule,
       "substance" means any natural or artificial substance whether in solid or liquid form or in
       the form of a gas or vapour, and
       "waste" includes any waste materials, spoil, refuse or other matter deposited on land.

72E.   Fourth exception: project finance

(1)   Section 72A does not prevent the appointment of an administrative receiver of a project company
       of a project which—

(a)   is a financed project, and

(b)   includes step-in rights.

(2)   In this section—

(a)   a project is "financed" if under an agreement relating to the project a project company
       incurs, or when the agreement is entered into is expected to incur, a debt of at least £50
       million for the purposes of carrying out the project,

(b)   "project company" has the meaning given by paragraph 7 of Schedule 2A, and

(c)   "step-in rights" has the meaning given by paragraph 6 of that Schedule.

72F.   Fifth exception: financial market

Section 72A does not prevent the appointment of an administrative receiver of a company by virtue of—

(a)   a market charge within the meaning of section 173 of the Companies Act 1989 (c 40),

(b)   a system-charge within the meaning of the Financial Markets and Insolvency Regulations
       1996 (SI 1996/1469),

(c)   a collateral security charge within the meaning of the Financial Markets and Insolvency
       (Settlement Finality) Regulations 1999 (SI 1999/2979).

72G.   Sixth exception: registered social landlord

Section 72A does not prevent the appointment of an administrative receiver of a company which
is registered as a social landlord under Part I of the Housing Act 1996 (c 52) or under Part 3 of the
Housing (Scotland) Act 2001 (asp 10).

72GA.   Exception in relation to protected railway companies etc

Section 72A does not prevent the appointment of an administrative receiver of—

(a)   a company holding an appointment under Chapter I of Part II of the Water Industry Act
       1991,

(b)   a protected railway company within the meaning of section 59 of the Railways Act 1993
       (including that section as it has effect by virtue of section 19 of the Channel Tunnel Rail
       Link Act 1996), or

(c)   a licence company within the meaning of section 26 of the Transport Act 2000.

72H.   Sections 72A to 72G: supplementary

(1)   Schedule 2A (which supplements sections 72B to 72G) shall have effect.

(2)   The Secretary of State may by order—

(a)   insert into this Act provision creating an additional exception to section 72A(1) or (2);

(b)   provide for a provision of this Act which creates an exception to section 72A(1) or (2) to cease to have effect;

(c)   amend section 72A in consequence of provision made under paragraph (a) or (b);

(d)   amend any of sections 72B to 72G;

(e)   amend Schedule 2A.

(3)   An order under subsection (2) must be made by statutory instrument.

(4)   An order under subsection (2) may make—

(a)   provision which applies generally or only for a specified purpose;

(b)   different provision for different purposes;

(c)   consequential or supplementary provision;

(d)   transitional provision.

(5)   An order under subsection (2)—

(a)   in the case of an order under subsection (2)(e), shall be subject to annulment in pursuance of a resolution of either House of Parliament,

(b)   in the case of an order under subsection (2)(d) varying the sum specified in section 72B(1)(a) or 72E(2)(a) (whether or not the order also makes consequential or transitional provision), shall be subject to annulment in pursuance of a resolution of either House of Parliament, and

(c)   in the case of any other order under subsection (2)(a) to (d), may not be made unless a draft has been laid before and approved by resolution of each House of Parliament.

PART IV
WINDING UP OF COMPANIES REGISTERED UNDER THE COMPANIES ACTS

CHAPTER I
PRELIMINARY

Modes of winding up

73.   Alternative modes of winding up

(1)   The winding up of a company, within the meaning given to that expression by section 735 of the Companies Act, may be either voluntary (Chapters II, III, IV and V in this Part) or by the court (Chapter VI).

(2)   This Chapter, and Chapters VII to X, relate to winding up generally, except where otherwise stated.

Contributories

74.   Liability as contributories of present and past members

(1)   When a company is wound up, every present and past member is liable to contribute to its assets to any amount sufficient for payment of its debts and liabilities, and the expenses of the winding up, and for the adjustment of the rights of the contributories among themselves.

(2)   This is subject as follows—

(a)   a past member is not liable to contribute if he has ceased to be a member for one year or more before the commencement of the winding up;

(b)   a past member is not liable to contribute in respect of any debt or liability of the company contracted after he ceased to be a member;

(c)   a past member is not liable to contribute, unless it appears to the court that the existing members are unable to satisfy the contributions required to be made by them in pursuance of the Companies Act and this Act;

(d)   in the case of a company limited by shares, no contribution is required from any member exceeding the amount (if any) unpaid on the shares in respect of which he is liable as a present or past member;

(e) nothing in the Companies Act or this Act invalidates any provision contained in a policy of insurance or other contract whereby the liability of individual members on the policy or contract is restricted, or whereby the funds of the company are alone made liable in respect of the policy or contract;

(f) a sum due to any member of the company (in his character of a member) by way of dividends, profits or otherwise is not deemed to be a debt of the company, payable to that member in a case of competition between himself and any other creditor not a member of the company, but any such sum may be taken into account for the purpose of the final adjustment of the rights of the contributories among themselves.

(3) In the case of a company limited by guarantee, no contribution is required from any member exceeding the amount undertaken to be contributed by him to the company's assets in the event of its being wound up; but if it is a company with a share capital, every member of it is liable (in addition to the amount so undertaken to be contributed to the assets), to contribute to the extent of any sums unpaid on shares held by him.

75.   Directors, etc with unlimited liability

(1) In the winding up of a limited company, any director or manager (whether past or present) whose liability is under the Companies Act unlimited is liable, in addition to his liability (if any) to contribute as an ordinary member, to make a further contribution as if he were at the commencement of the winding up a member of an unlimited company.

(2) However—

(a) a past director or manager is not liable to make such further contribution if he has ceased to hold office for a year or more before the commencement of the winding up;

(b) a past director or manager is not liable to make such further contribution in respect of any debt or liability of the company contracted after he ceased to hold office;

(c) subject to the company's articles, a director or manager is not liable to make such further contribution unless the court deems it necessary to require that contribution in order to satisfy the company's debts and liabilities, and the expenses of the winding up.

76.   Liability of past directors and shareholders

(1) This section applies where a company is being wound up and—

(a) it has under Chapter VII of Part V of the Companies Act (redeemable shares; purchase by a company of its own shares) made a payment out of capital in respect of the redemption or purchase of any of its own shares (the payment being referred to below as "the relevant payment"), and

(b) the aggregate amount of the company's assets and the amounts paid by way of contribution to its assets (apart from this section) is not sufficient for payment of its debts and liabilities, and the expenses of the winding up.

(2) If the winding up commenced within one year of the date on which the relevant payment was made, then—

(a) the person from whom the shares were redeemed or purchased, and

(b) the directors who signed the statutory declaration made in accordance with section 173(3) of the Companies Act for purposes of the redemption or purchase (except a director who shows that he had reasonable grounds for forming the opinion set out in the declaration),

are, so as to enable that insufficiency to be met, liable to contribute to the following extent to the company's assets.

(3) A person from whom any of the shares were redeemed or purchased is liable to contribute an amount not exceeding so much of the relevant payment as was made by the company in respect of his shares; and the directors are jointly and severally liable with that person to contribute that amount.

(4) A person who has contributed any amount to the assets in pursuance of this section may apply to the court for an order directing any other person jointly and severally liable in respect of that amount to pay him such amount as the court thinks just and equitable.

(5)   Sections 74 and 75 do not apply in relation to liability accruing by virtue of this section.

(6)   This section is deemed included in Chapter VII of Part V of the Companies Act for the purposes of the Secretary of State's power to make regulations under section 179 of that Act.

77.   **Limited company formerly unlimited**

(1)   This section applies in the case of a company being wound up which was at some former time registered as unlimited but has re-registered—

     (a)   as a public company under section 43 of the Companies Act (or the former corresponding provision, section 5 of the Companies Act 1980), or

     (b)   as a limited company under section 51 of the Companies Act (or the former corresponding provision, section 44 of the Companies Act 1967).

(2)   Notwithstanding section 74(2)(a) above, a past member of the company who was a member of it at the time of re-registration, if the winding up commences within the period of 3 years beginning with the day on which the company was re-registered, is liable to contribute to the assets of the company in respect of debts and liabilities contracted before that time.

(3)   If no persons who were members of the company at that time are existing members of it, a person who at that time was a present or past member is liable to contribute as above notwithstanding that the existing members have satisfied the contributions required to be made by them under the Companies Act and this Act.

     This applies subject to section 74(2)(a) above and to subsection (2) of this section, but notwithstanding section 74(2)(c).

(4)   Notwithstanding section 74(2)(d) and (3), there is no limit on the amount which a person who, at that time, was a past or present member of the company is liable to contribute as above.

78.   **Unlimited company formerly limited**

(1)   This section applies in the case of a company being wound up which was at some former time registered as limited but has been re-registered as unlimited under section 49 of the Companies Act (or the former corresponding provision, section 43 of the Companies Act 1967).

(2)   A person who, at the time when the application for the company to be re-registered was lodged, was a past member of the company and did not after that again become a member of it is not liable to contribute to the assets of the company more than he would have been liable to contribute had the company not been re-registered.

79.   **Meaning of "contributory"**

(1)   In this Act and the Companies Act the expression "contributory" means every person liable to contribute to the assets of a company in the event of its being wound up, and for the purposes of all proceedings for determining, and all proceedings prior to the final determination of, the persons who are to be deemed contributories, includes any person alleged to be a contributory.

(2)   The reference in subsection (1) to persons liable to contribute to the assets does not include a person so liable by virtue of a declaration by the court under section 213 (imputed responsibility for company's fraudulent trading) or section 214 (wrongful trading) in Chapter X of this Part.

(3)   A reference in a company's articles to a contributory does not (unless the context requires) include a person who is a contributory only by virtue of section 76.

     This subsection is deemed included in Chapter VII of Part V of the Companies Act for the purposes of the Secretary of State's power to make regulations under section 179 of that Act.

80.   **Nature of contributory's liability**

     The liability of a contributory creates a debt (in England and Wales in the nature of a specialty) accruing due from him at the time when his liability commenced, but payable at the times when calls are made for enforcing the liability.

81.   **Contributories in case of death of a member**

(1)   If a contributory dies either before or after he has been placed on the list of contributories, his personal representatives, and the heirs and legatees of heritage of his heritable estate in Scotland,

are liable in a due course of administration to contribute to the assets of the company in discharge of his liability and are contributories accordingly.

(2)   Where the personal representatives are placed on the list of contributories, the heirs or legatees of heritage need not be added, but they may be added as and when the court thinks fit.

(3)   If in England and Wales the personal representatives make default in paying any money ordered to be paid by them, proceedings may be taken for administering the estate of the deceased contributory and for compelling payment out of it of the money due.

82.   Effect of contributory's bankruptcy

(1)   The following applies if a contributory becomes bankrupt, either before or after he has been placed on the list of contributories.

(2)   His trustee in bankruptcy represents him for all purposes of the winding up, and is a contributory accordingly.

(3)   The trustee may be called on to admit to proof against the bankrupt's estate, or otherwise allow to be paid out of the bankrupt's assets in due course of law, any money due from the bankrupt in respect of his liability to contribute to the company's assets.

(4)   There may be proved against the bankrupt's estate the estimated value of his liability to future calls as well as calls already made.

83.   Companies registered under Companies Act, Part XXII, Chapter II

(1)   The following applies in the event of a company being wound up which has been registered under section 680 of the Companies Act (or previous corresponding provisions in the Companies Act 1948 or earlier Acts).

(2)   Every person is a contributory, in respect of the company's debts and liabilities contracted before registration, who is liable—

     (a)   to pay, or contribute to the payment of, any debt or liability so contracted, or

     (b)   to pay, or contribute to the payment of, any sum for the adjustment of the rights of the members among themselves in respect of any such debt or liability, or

     (c)   to pay, or contribute to the amount of, the expenses of winding up the company, so far as relates to the debts or liabilities above-mentioned.

(3)   Every contributory is liable to contribute to the assets of the company, in the course of the winding up, all sums due from him in respect of any such liability.

(4)   In the event of the death, bankruptcy or insolvency of any contributory, provisions of this Act, with respect to the personal representatives, to the heirs and legatees of heritage of the heritable estate in Scotland of deceased contributories and to the trustees of bankrupt or insolvent contributories respectively, apply.

CHAPTER II
VOLUNTARY WINDING UP
(INTRODUCTORY AND GENERAL)

Resolutions for, and commencement of, voluntary winding up

84.   Circumstances in which company may be wound up voluntarily

(1)   A company may be wound up voluntarily—

     (a)   when the period (if any) fixed for the duration of the company by the articles expires, or the event (if any) occurs, on the occurrence of which the articles provide that the company is to be dissolved, and the company in general meeting has passed a resolution requiring it to be wound up voluntarily;

     (b)   if the company resolves by special resolution that it be wound up voluntarily;

     (c)   if the company resolves by extraordinary resolution to the effect that it cannot by reason of its liabilities continue its business, and that it is advisable to wind up.

(2)   In this Act the expression "a resolution for voluntary winding up" means a resolution passed under any of the paragraphs of subsection (1).

(2A)   Before a company passes a resolution for voluntary winding up it must give written notice of the resolution to the holder of any qualifying floating charge to which section 72A applies.

(2B)   Where notice is given under subsection (2A) a resolution for voluntary winding up may be passed only—

(a)   after the end of the period of five business days beginning with the day on which the notice was given, or

(b)   if the person to whom the notice was given has consented in writing to the passing of the resolution.

(3)   A resolution passed under paragraph (a) of subsection (1), as well as a special resolution under paragraph (b) and an extraordinary resolution under paragraph (c), is subject to section 380 of the Companies Act (copy of resolution to be forwarded to registrar of companies within 15 days).

(4)   This section has effect subject to section 43 of the Commonhold and Leasehold Reform Act 2002.

85.   Notice of resolution to wind up

(1)   When a company has passed a resolution for voluntary winding up, it shall, within 14 days after the passing of the resolution, give notice of the resolution by advertisement in the Gazette.

(2)   If default is made in complying with this section, the company and every officer of it who is in default is liable to a fine and, for continued contravention, to a daily default fine.

For the purposes of this subsection the liquidator is deemed an officer of the company.

86.   Commencement of winding up

A voluntary winding up is deemed to commence at the time of the passing of the resolution for voluntary winding up.

Consequences of resolution to wind up

87.   Effect on business and status of company

(1)   In case of a voluntary winding up, the company shall from the commencement of the winding up cease to carry on its business, except so far as may be required for its beneficial winding up.

(2)   However, the corporate state and corporate powers of the company, notwithstanding anything to the contrary in its articles, continue until the company is dissolved.

88.   Avoidance of share transfers, etc after winding-up resolution

Any transfer of shares, not being a transfer made to or with the sanction of the liquidator, and any alteration in the status of the company's members, made after the commencement of a voluntary winding up, is void.

Declaration of solvency

89.   Statutory declaration of solvency

(1)   Where it is proposed to wind up a company voluntarily, the directors (or, in the case of a company having more than two directors, the majority of them) may at a directors' meeting make a statutory declaration to the effect that they have made a full inquiry into the company's affairs and that, having done so, they have formed the opinion that the company will be able to pay its debts in full, together with interest at the official rate (as defined in section 251), within such period, not exceeding 12 months from the commencement of the winding up, as may be specified in the declaration.

(2)   Such a declaration by the directors has no effect for purposes of this Act unless—

(a)   it is made within the 5 weeks immediately preceding the date of the passing of the resolution for winding up, or on that date but before the passing of the resolution, and

(b)   it embodies a statement of the company's assets and liabilities as at the latest practicable date before the making of the declaration.

(3)   The declaration shall be delivered to the registrar of companies before the expiration of 15 days immediately following the date on which the resolution for winding up is passed.

(4)   A director making a declaration under this section without having reasonable grounds for the opinion that the company will be able to pay its debts in full, together with interest at the official rate, within the period specified is liable to imprisonment or a fine, or both.

(5)   If the company is wound up in pursuance of a resolution passed within 5 weeks after the making of the declaration, and its debts (together with interest at the official rate) are not paid or provided for in full within the period specified, it is to be presumed (unless the contrary is shown) that the director did not have reasonable grounds for his opinion.

(6)   If a declaration required by subsection (3) to be delivered to the registrar is not so delivered within the time prescribed by that subsection, the company and every officer in default is liable to a fine and, for continued contravention, to a daily default fine.

90.   Distinction between "members'" and "creditors'" voluntary winding up

A winding up in the case of which a directors' statutory declaration under section 89 has been made is a "members' voluntary winding up"; and a winding up in the case of which such a declaration has not been made is a "creditors' voluntary winding up".

CHAPTER III
MEMBERS' VOLUNTARY WINDING UP

91.   Appointment of liquidator

(1)   In a members' voluntary winding up, the company in general meeting shall appoint one or more liquidators for the purpose of winding up the company's affairs and distributing its assets.

(2)   On the appointment of a liquidator all the powers of the directors cease, except so far as the company in general meeting or the liquidator sanctions their continuance.

92.   Power to fill vacancy in office of liquidator

(1)   If a vacancy occurs by death, resignation or otherwise in the office of liquidator appointed by the company, the company in general meeting may, subject to any arrangement with its creditors, fill the vacancy.

(2)   For that purpose a general meeting may be convened by any contributory or, if there were more liquidators than one, by the continuing liquidators.

(3)   The meeting shall be held in manner provided by this Act or by the articles, or in such manner as may, on application by any contributory or by the continuing liquidators, be determined by the court.

93.   General company meeting at each year's end

(1)   Subject to sections 96 and 102, in the event of the winding up continuing for more than one year, the liquidator shall summon a general meeting of the company at the end of the first year from the commencement of the winding up, and of each succeeding year, or at the first convenient date within 3 months from the end of the year or such longer period as the Secretary of State may allow.

(2)   The liquidator shall lay before the meeting an account of his acts and dealings, and of the conduct of the winding up, during the preceding year.

(3)   If the liquidator fails to comply with this section, he is liable to a fine.

94.   Final meeting prior to dissolution

(1)   As soon as the company's affairs are fully wound up, the liquidator shall make up an account of the winding up, showing how it has been conducted and the company's property has been disposed of, and thereupon shall call a general meeting of the company for the purpose of laying before it the account, and giving an explanation of it.

(2)   The meeting shall be called by advertisement in the Gazette, specifying its time, place and object and published at least one month before the meeting.

(3)   Within one week after the meeting, the liquidator shall send to the registrar of companies a copy of the account, and shall make a return to him of the holding of the meeting and of its date.

(4)   If the copy is not sent or the return is not made in accordance with subsection (3), the liquidator is liable to a fine and, for continued contravention, to a daily default fine.

(5)   If a quorum is not present at the meeting, the liquidator shall, in lieu of the return mentioned above, make a return that the meeting was duly summoned and that no quorum was present; and upon such a return being made, the provisions of subsection (3) as to the making of the return are deemed complied with.

(6)   If the liquidator fails to call a general meeting of the company as required by subsection (1), he is liable to a fine.

95.   Effect of company's insolvency

(1)   This section applies where the liquidator is of the opinion that the company will be unable to pay its debts in full (together with interest at the official rate) within the period stated in the directors' declaration under section 89.

(2)   The liquidator shall—
(a)   summon a meeting of creditors for a day not later than the 28th day after the day on which he formed that opinion;
(b)   send notices of the creditors' meeting to the creditors by post not less than 7 days before the day on which that meeting is to be held;
(c)   cause notice of the creditors' meeting to be advertised once in the Gazette and once at least in 2 newspapers circulating in the relevant locality (that is to say the locality in which the company's principal place of business in Great Britain was situated during the relevant period); and
(d)   during the period before the day on which the creditors' meeting is to be held, furnish creditors free of charge with such information concerning the affairs of the company as they may reasonably require;
and the notice of the creditors' meeting shall state the duty imposed by paragraph (d) above.

(3)   The liquidator shall also—
(a)   make out a statement in the prescribed form as to the affairs of the company;
(b)   lay that statement before the creditors' meeting; and
(c)   attend and preside at that meeting.

(4)   The statement as to the affairs of the company shall be verified by affidavit by the liquidator and shall show—
(a)   particulars of the company's assets, debts and liabilities;
(b)   the names and addresses of the company's creditors;
(c)   the securities held by them respectively;
(d)   the dates when the securities were respectively given; and
(e)   such further or other information as may be prescribed.

(5)   Where the company's principal place of business in Great Britain was situated in different localities at different times during the relevant period, the duty imposed by subsection (2)(c) applies separately in relation to each of those localities.

(6)   Where the company had no place of business in Great Britain during the relevant period, references in subsections (2)(c) and (5) to the company's principal place of business in Great Britain are replaced by references to its registered office.

(7)   In this section "the relevant period" means the period of 6 months immediately preceding the day on which were sent the notices summoning the company meeting at which it was resolved that the company be wound up voluntarily.

(8)   If the liquidator without reasonable excuse fails to comply with this section, he is liable to a fine.

96.   Conversion to creditors' voluntary winding up

As from the day on which the creditors' meeting is held under section 95, this Act has effect as if—
(a)   the directors' declaration under section 89 had not been made; and

(b)   the creditors' meeting and the company meeting at which it was resolved that the company be wound up voluntarily were the meetings mentioned in section 98 in the next Chapter;

and accordingly the winding up becomes a creditors' voluntary winding up.

CHAPTER IV
CREDITORS' VOLUNTARY WINDING UP

97.   **Application of this Chapter**

(1)   Subject as follows, this Chapter applies in relation to a creditors' voluntary winding up.

(2)   Sections 98 and 99 do not apply where, under section 96 in Chapter III, a members' voluntary winding up has become a creditors' voluntary winding up.

98.   **Meeting of creditors**

(1)   The company shall—

      (a)   cause a meeting of its creditors to be summoned for a day not later than the 14th day after the day on which there is to be held the company meeting at which the resolution for voluntary winding up is to be proposed;

      (b)   cause the notices of the creditors' meeting to be sent by post to the creditors not less than 7 days before the day on which that meeting is to be held; and

      (c)   cause notice of the creditors' meeting to be advertised once in the Gazette and once at least in two newspapers circulating in the relevant locality (that is to say the locality in which the company's principal place of business in Great Britain was situated during the relevant period).

(2)   The notice of the creditors' meeting shall state either—

      (a)   the name and address of a person qualified to act as an insolvency practitioner in relation to the company who, during the period before the day on which that meeting is to be held, will furnish creditors free of charge with such information concerning the company's affairs as they may reasonably require; or

      (b)   a place in the relevant locality where, on the two business days falling next before the day on which that meeting is to be held, a list of the names and addresses of the company's creditors will be available for inspection free of charge.

(3)   Where the company's principal place of business in Great Britain was situated in different localities at different times during the relevant period, the duties imposed by subsections (1)(c) and (2)(b) above apply separately in relation to each of those localities.

(4)   Where the company had no place of business in Great Britain during the relevant period, references in subsections (1)(c) and (3) to the company's principal place of business in Great Britain are replaced by references to its registered office.

(5)   In this section "the relevant period" means the period of 6 months immediately preceding the day on which were sent the notices summoning the company meeting at which it was resolved that the company be wound up voluntarily.

(6)   If the company without reasonable excuse fails to comply with subsection (1) or (2), it is guilty of an offence and liable to a fine.

99.   **Directors to lay statement of affairs before creditors**

(1)   The directors of the company shall—

      (a)   make out a statement in the prescribed form as to the affairs of the company;

      (b)   cause that statement to be laid before the creditors' meeting under section 98; and

      (c)   appoint one of their number to preside at that meeting;

and it is the duty of the director so appointed to attend the meeting and preside over it.

(2)   The statement as to the affairs of the company shall be verified by affidavit by some or all of the directors and shall show—

      (a)   particulars of the company's assets, debts and liabilities;

      (b)   the names and addresses of the company's creditors;

(c)   the securities held by them respectively;

(d)   the dates when the securities were respectively given; and

(e)   such further or other information as may be prescribed.

(3)   If—

(a)   the directors without reasonable excuse fail to comply with subsection (1) or (2); or

(b)   any director without reasonable excuse fails to comply with subsection (1), so far as requiring him to attend and preside at the creditors' meeting,

the directors are or (as the case may be) the director is guilty of an offence and liable to a fine.

100.   Appointment of liquidator

(1)   The creditors and the company at their respective meetings mentioned in section 98 may nominate a person to be liquidator for the purpose of winding up the company's affairs and distributing its assets.

(2)   The liquidator shall be the person nominated by the creditors or, where no person has been so nominated, the person (if any) nominated by the company.

(3)   In the case of different persons being nominated, any director, member or creditor of the company may, within 7 days after the date on which the nomination was made by the creditors, apply to the court for an order either—

(a)   directing that the person nominated as liquidator by the company shall be liquidator instead of or jointly with the person nominated by the creditors, or

(b)   appointing some other person to be liquidator instead of the person nominated by the creditors.

(4)   *The court shall grant an application under subsection (3) made by the holder of a qualifying floating charge in respect of the company's property (within the meaning of paragraph 14 of Schedule B1) unless the court thinks it right to refuse the application because of the particular circumstances of the case.*

Note. Subsection (4) is inserted by the Enterprise Act 2002, s. 248(3), Sch. 17, paras. 9, 14, as from a day to be appointed.

101.   Appointment of liquidation committee

(1)   The creditors at the meeting to be held under section 98 or at any subsequent meeting may, if they think fit, appoint a committee ("the liquidation committee") of not more than 5 persons to exercise the functions conferred on it by or under this Act.

(2)   If such a committee is appointed, the company may, either at the meeting at which the resolution for voluntary winding up is passed or at any time subsequently in general meeting, appoint such number of persons as they think fit to act as members of the committee, not exceeding 5.

(3)   However, the creditors may, if they think fit, resolve that all or any of the persons so appointed by the company ought not to be members of the liquidation committee; and if the creditors so resolve—

(a)   the persons mentioned in the resolution are not then, unless the court otherwise directs, qualified to act as members of the committee; and

(b)   on any application to the court under this provision the court may, if it thinks fit, appoint other persons to act as such members in place of the persons mentioned in the resolution.

(4)   In Scotland, the liquidation committee has, in addition to the powers and duties conferred and imposed on it by this Act, such of the powers and duties of commissioners on a bankrupt estate as may be conferred and imposed on liquidation committees by the rules.

102.   Creditors' meeting where winding up converted under s 96

Where, in the case of a winding up which was, under section 96 in Chapter III, converted to a creditors' voluntary winding up, a creditors' meeting is held in accordance with section 95, any appointment made or committee established by that meeting is deemed to have been made or established by a meeting held in accordance with section 98 in this Chapter.

103. Cesser of directors' powers

On the appointment of a liquidator, all the powers of the directors cease, except so far as the liquidation committee (or, if there is no such committee, the creditors) sanction their continuance.

104. Vacancy in office of liquidator

If a vacancy occurs, by death, resignation or otherwise, in the office of a liquidator (other than a liquidator appointed by, or by the direction of, the court) the creditors may fill the vacancy.

105. Meetings of company and creditors at each year's end

(1) If the winding up continues for more than one year, the liquidator shall summon a general meeting of the company and a meeting of the creditors at the end of the first year from the commencement of the winding up, and of each succeeding year, or at the first convenient date within 3 months from the end of the year or such longer period as the Secretary of State may allow.

(2) The liquidator shall lay before each of the meetings an account of his acts and dealings and of the conduct of the winding up during the preceding year.

(3) If the liquidator fails to comply with this section, he is liable to a fine.

(4) Where under section 96 a members' voluntary winding up has become a creditors' voluntary winding up, and the creditors' meeting under section 95 is held 3 months or less before the end of the first year from the commencement of the winding up, the liquidator is not required by this section to summon a meeting of creditors at the end of that year.

106. Final meeting prior to dissolution

(1) As soon as the company's affairs are fully wound up, the liquidator shall make up an account of the winding up, showing how it has been conducted and the company's property has been disposed of, and thereupon shall call a general meeting of the company and a meeting of the creditors for the purpose of laying the account before the meetings and giving an explanation of it.

(2) Each such meeting shall be called by advertisement in the Gazette specifying the time, place and object of the meeting, and published at least one month before it.

(3) Within one week after the date of the meetings (or, if they are not held on the same date, after the date of the later one) the liquidator shall send to the registrar of companies a copy of the account, and shall make a return to him of the holding of the meetings and of their dates.

(4) If the copy is not sent or the return is not made in accordance with subsection (3), the liquidator is liable to a fine and, for continued contravention, to a daily default fine.

(5) However, if a quorum is not present at either such meeting, the liquidator shall, in lieu of the return required by subsection (3), make a return that the meeting was duly summoned and that no quorum was present; and upon such return being made the provisions of that subsection as to the making of the return are, in respect of that meeting, deemed complied with.

(6) If the liquidator fails to call a general meeting of the company or a meeting of the creditors as required by this section, he is liable to a fine.

CHAPTER V
PROVISIONS APPLYING TO BOTH KINDS OF VOLUNTARY WINDING UP

107. Distribution of company's property

Subject to the provisions of this Act as to preferential payments, the company's property in a voluntary winding up shall on the winding up be applied in satisfaction of the company's liabilities pari passu and, subject to that application, shall (unless the articles otherwise provide) be distributed among the members according to their rights and interests in the company.

108. Appointment or removal of liquidator by the court

(1) If from any cause whatever there is no liquidator acting, the court may appoint a liquidator.

(2) The court may, on cause shown, remove a liquidator and appoint another.

109.   Notice by liquidator of his appointment

(1)   The liquidator shall, within 14 days after his appointment, publish in the Gazette and deliver to the registrar of companies for registration a notice of his appointment in the form prescribed by statutory instrument made by the Secretary of State.

(2)   If the liquidator fails to comply with this section, he is liable to a fine and, for continued contravention, to a daily default fine.

110.   Acceptance of shares, etc, as consideration for sale of company property

(1)   This section applies, in the case of a company proposed to be, or being, wound up voluntarily, where the whole or part of the company's business or property is proposed to be transferred or sold—

(a)   to another company ("the transferee company"), whether or not the latter is a company within the meaning of the Companies Act, or

(b)   to a limited liability partnership (the "transferee limited liability partnership").

(2)   With the requisite sanction, the liquidator of the company being, or proposed to be, wound up ("the transferor company") may receive, in compensation or part compensation for the transfer or sale—

(a)   in the case of the transferee company, shares, policies or other like interests in the transferee company for distribution among the members of the transferor company, or

(b)   in the case of the transferee limited liability partnership, membership in the transferee limited liability partnership for distribution among the members of the transferor company.

(3)   The sanction requisite under subsection (2) is—

(a)   in the case of a members' voluntary winding up, that of a special resolution of the company, conferring either a general authority on the liquidator or an authority in respect of any particular arrangement, and

(b)   in the case of a creditors' voluntary winding up, that of either the court or the liquidation committee.

(4)   Alternatively to subsection (2), the liquidator may (with that sanction) enter into any other arrangement whereby the members of the transferor company may—

(a)   in the case of the transferee company, in lieu of receiving cash, shares, policies or other like interests (or in addition thereto) participate in the profits of, or receive any other benefit from, the transferee company, or

(b)   in the case of the transferee limited liability partnership, in lieu of receiving cash or membership (or in addition thereto), participate in some other way in the profits of, or receive any other benefit from, the transferee limited liability partnership.

(5)   A sale or arrangement in pursuance of this section is binding on members of the transferor company.

(6)   A special resolution is not invalid for purposes of this section by reason that it is passed before or concurrently with a resolution for voluntary winding up or for appointing liquidators; but, if an order is made within a year for winding up the company by the court, the special resolution is not valid unless sanctioned by the court.

111.   Dissent from arrangement under s 110

(1)   This section applies in the case of a voluntary winding up where, for the purposes of section 110(2) or (4), there has been passed a special resolution of the transferor company providing the sanction requisite for the liquidator under that section.

(2)   If a member of the transferor company who did not vote in favour of the special resolution expresses his dissent from it in writing, addressed to the liquidator and left at the company's registered office within 7 days after the passing of the resolution, he may require the liquidator either to abstain from carrying the resolution into effect or to purchase his interest at a price to be determined by agreement or by arbitration under this section.

(3)   If the liquidator elects to purchase the member's interest, the purchase money must be paid before
        the company is dissolved and be raised by the liquidator in such manner as may be determined by
        special resolution.

(4)   For purposes of an arbitration under this section, the provisions of the Companies Clauses
        Consolidation Act 1845 or, in the case of a winding up in Scotland, the Companies Clauses
        Consolidation (Scotland) Act 1845 with respect to the settlement of disputes by arbitration are
        incorporated with this Act, and—

        (a)   in the construction of those provisions this Act is deemed the special Act and "the
               company" means the transferor company, and

        (b)   any appointment by the incorporated provisions directed to be made under the hand of the
               secretary or any two of the directors may be made in writing by the liquidator (or, if there is
               more than one liquidator, then any two or more of them).

112.   Reference of questions to court

(1)   The liquidator or any contributory or creditor may apply to the court to determine any question
        arising in the winding up of a company, or to exercise, as respects the enforcing of calls or any
        other matter, all or any of the powers which the court might exercise if the company were being
        wound up by the court.

(2)   The court, if satisfied that the determination of the question or the required exercise of power will
        be just and beneficial, may accede wholly or partially to the application on such terms and
        conditions as it thinks fit, or may make such other order on the application as it thinks just.

(3)   A copy of an order made by virtue of this section staying the proceedings in the winding up shall
        forthwith be forwarded by the company, or otherwise as may be prescribed, to the registrar of
        companies, who shall enter it in his records relating to the company.

113.   Court's power to control proceedings (Scotland)

If the court, on the application of the liquidator in the winding up of a company registered in Scotland, so directs, no action or proceeding shall be proceeded with or commenced against the company except by leave of the court and subject to such terms as the court may impose.

114.   No liquidator appointed or nominated by company

(1)   This section applies where, in the case of a voluntary winding up, no liquidator has been
        appointed or nominated by the company.

(2)   The powers of the directors shall not be exercised, except with the sanction of the court or (in the
        case of a creditors' voluntary winding up) so far as may be necessary to secure compliance with
        sections 98 (creditors' meeting) and 99 (statement of affairs), during the period before the
        appointment or nomination of a liquidator of the company.

(3)   Subsection (2) does not apply in relation to the powers of the directors—

        (a)   to dispose of perishable goods and other goods the value of which is likely to diminish if
               they are not immediately disposed of, and

        (b)   to do all such other things as may be necessary for the protection of the company's assets.

(4)   If the directors of the company without reasonable excuse fail to comply with this section, they
        are liable to a fine.

115.   Expenses of voluntary winding up

All expenses properly incurred in the winding up, including the remuneration of the liquidator,
are payable out of the company's assets in priority to all other claims.

116.   Saving for certain rights

The voluntary winding up of a company does not bar the right of any creditor or contributory to
have it wound up by the court; but in the case of an application by a contributory the court must
be satisfied that the rights of the contributories will be prejudiced by a voluntary winding up.

CHAPTER VI
WINDING UP BY THE COURT

Jurisdiction (England and Wales)

117. High Court and county court jurisdiction

(1) The High Court has jurisdiction to wind up any company registered in England and Wales.

(2) Where the amount of a company's share capital paid up or credited as paid up does not exceed £120,000, then (subject to this section) the county court of the district in which the company's registered office is situated has concurrent jurisdiction with the High Court to wind up the company.

(3) The money sum for the time being specified in subsection (2) is subject to increase or reduction by order under section 416 in Part XV.

(4) The Lord Chancellor may by order in a statutory instrument exclude a county court from having winding-up jurisdiction, and for the purposes of that jurisdiction may attach its district, or any part thereof, to any other county court, and may by statutory instrument revoke or vary any such order.

In exercising the powers of this section, the Lord Chancellor shall provide that a county court is not to have winding-up jurisdiction unless it has for the time being jurisdiction for the purposes of Parts VIII to XI of this Act (individual insolvency).

(5) Every court in England and Wales having winding-up jurisdiction has for the purposes of that jurisdiction all the powers of the High Court; and every prescribed officer of the court shall perform any duties which an officer of the High Court may discharge by order of a judge of that court or otherwise in relation to winding up.

(6) For the purposes of this section, a company's "registered office" is the place which has longest been its registered office during the 6 months immediately preceding the presentation of the petition for winding up.

(7) This section is subject to Article 3 of the EC Regulation (jurisdiction under EC Regulation).

118. Proceedings taken in wrong court

(1) Nothing in section 117 invalidates a proceeding by reason of its being taken in the wrong court.

(2) The winding up of a company by the court in England and Wales, or any proceedings in the winding up, may be retained in the court in which the proceedings were commenced, although it may not be the court in which they ought to have been commenced.

119. Proceedings in county court; case stated for High Court

(1) If any question arises in any winding-up proceedings in a county court which all the parties to the proceedings, or which one of them and the judge of the court, desire to have determined in the first instance in the High Court, the judge shall state the facts in the form of a special case for the opinion of the High Court.

(2) Thereupon the special case and the proceedings (or such of them as may be required) shall be transmitted to the High Court for the purposes of the determination.

Jurisdiction (Scotland)

120. Court of Session and sheriff court jurisdiction

(1) The Court of Session has jurisdiction to wind up any company registered in Scotland.

(2) When the Court of Session is in vacation, the jurisdiction conferred on that court by this section may (subject to the provisions of this Part) be exercised by the judge acting as vacation judge …

(3) Where the amount of a company's share capital paid up or credited as paid up does not exceed £120,000, the sheriff court of the sheriffdom in which the company's registered office is situated has concurrent jurisdiction with the Court of Session to wind up the company; but—

    (a) the Court of Session may, if it thinks expedient having regard to the amount of the company's assets to do so—

        (i)   remit to sheriff court any petition presented to the Court of Session for winding up such a company, or

        (ii)   require such a petition presented to a sheriff court to be remitted to the Court of Session; and

  (b)   the Court of Session may require any such petition as above-mentioned presented to one sheriff court to be remitted to another sheriff court; and

  (c)   in a winding up in the sheriff court the sheriff may submit a stated case for the opinion of the Court of Session on any question of law arising in that winding up.

(4)   For purposes of this section, the expression "registered office" means the place which has longest been the company's registered office during the 6 months immediately preceding the presentation of the petition for winding up.

(5)   The money sum for the time being specified in subsection (3) is subject to increase or reduction by order under section 416 in Part XV.

(6)   This section is subject to Article 3 of the EC Regulation (jurisdiction under EC Regulation).

121.   **Power to remit winding up to Lord Ordinary**

(1)   The Court of Session may, by Act of Sederunt, make provision for the taking of proceedings in a winding up before one of the Lords Ordinary; and, where provision is so made, the Lord Ordinary has, for the purposes of the winding up, all the powers and jurisdiction of the court.

(2)   However, the Lord Ordinary may report to the Inner House any matter which may arise in the course of a winding up.

Grounds and effect of winding-up petition

122.   **Circumstances in which company may be wound up by the court**

(1)   A company may be wound up by the court if—

  (a)   the company has by special resolution resolved that the company be wound up by the court,

  (b)   being a public company which was registered as such on its original incorporation, the company has not been issued with a certificate under section 117 of the Companies Act (public company share capital requirements) and more than a year has expired since it was so registered,

  (c)   it is an old public company, within the meaning of the Consequential Provisions Act,

  (d)   the company does not commence its business within a year from its incorporation or suspends its business for a whole year,

  (e)   except in the case of a private company limited by shares or by guarantee, the number of members is reduced below 2,

  (f)   the company is unable to pay its debts,

  (fa) at the time at which a moratorium for the company under section 1A comes to an end, no voluntary arrangement approved under Part I has effect in relation to the company,

  (g)   the court is of the opinion that it is just and equitable that the company should be wound up.

(2)   In Scotland, a company which the Court of Session has jurisdiction to wind up may be wound up by the Court if there is subsisting a floating charge over property comprised in the company's property and undertaking, and the court is satisfied that the security of the creditor entitled to the benefit of the floating charge is in jeopardy.

For this purpose a creditor's security is deemed to be in jeopardy if the Court is satisfied that events have occurred or are about to occur which render it unreasonable in the creditor's interests that the company should retain power to dispose of the property which is subject to the floating charge.

123.   **Definition of inability to pay debts**

(1)   A company is deemed unable to pay its debts—

  (a)   if a creditor (by assignment or otherwise) to whom the company is indebted in a sum exceeding £750 then due has served on the company, by leaving it at the company's registered office, a written demand (in the prescribed form) requiring the company to pay the sum so due and the company has for 3 weeks thereafter neglected to pay the sum or to secure or compound for it to the reasonable satisfaction of the creditor, or

(b)   if, in England and Wales, execution or other process issued on a judgment, decree or order of any court in favour of a creditor of the company is returned unsatisfied in whole or in part, or

(c)   if, in Scotland, the induciae of a charge for payment on an extract decree, or an extract registered bond, or an extract registered protest, have expired without payment being made, or

(d)   if, in Northern Ireland, a certificate of unenforceability has been granted in respect of a judgment against the company, or

(e)   if it is proved to the satisfaction of the court that the company is unable to pay its debts as they fall due.

(2)   A company is also deemed unable to pay its debts if it is proved to the satisfaction of the court that the value of the company's assets is less than the amount of its liabilities, taking into account its contingent and prospective liabilities.

(3)   The money sum for the time being specified in subsection (1)(a) is subject to increase or reduction by order under section 416 in Part XV.

124.   Application for winding up

(1)   Subject to the provisions of this section, an application to the court for the winding up of a company shall be by petition presented either by the company, or the directors, or by any creditor or creditors (including any contingent or prospective creditor or creditors), contributory or contributories, or by a liquidator (within the meaning of Article 2(b) of the EC Regulation) appointed in proceedings by virtue of Article 3(1) of the EC Regulation or a temporary administrator (within the meaning of Article 38 of the EC Regulation) or by *a justices' chief executive [the designated officer for a magistrates' court]* in the exercise of the power conferred by section 87A of the Magistrates' Courts Act 1980 (enforcement of fines imposed on companies), or by all or any of those parties, together or separately.

(2)   Except as mentioned below, a contributory is not entitled to present a winding-up petition unless either—

(a)   the number of members is reduced below 2, or

(b)   the shares in respect of which he is a contributory, or some of them, either were originally allotted to him, or have been held by him, and registered in his name, for at least 6 months during the 18 months before the commencement of the winding up, or have devolved on him through the death of a former holder.

(3)   A person who is liable under section 76 to contribute to a company's assets in the event of its being wound up may petition on either of the grounds set out in section 122(1)(f) and (g), and subsection (2) above does not then apply; but unless the person is a contributory otherwise than under section 76, he may not in his character as contributory petition on any other ground.

This subsection is deemed included in Chapter VII of Part V of the Companies Act (redeemable shares; purchase by a company of its own shares) for the purposes of the Secretary of State's power to make regulations under section 179 of that Act.

(3A)   A winding-up petition on the ground set out in section 122(1)(fa) may only be presented by one or more creditors.

(4)   A winding-up petition may be presented by the Secretary of State—

(a)   if the ground of the petition is that in section 122(1)(b) or (c), or

(b)   in a case falling within section 124A or 124B below.

(4A)   *A winding-up petition may be presented by the Regulator of Community Interest Companies in a case falling within section 50 of the Companies (Audit, Investigations and Community Enterprise) Act 2004.*

(5)   Where a company is being wound up voluntarily in England and Wales, a winding-up petition may be presented by the official receiver attached to the court as well as by any other person authorised in that behalf under the other provisions of this section; but the court shall not make a

winding-up order on the petition unless it is satisfied that the voluntary winding up cannot be continued with due regard to the interests of the creditors or contributories.

Note. The italicized words in subsection (1) are substituted by the subsequent words in square brackets by the Courts Act 2003, s. 109(1), Sch. 8, para. 294, as from a day to be appointed. Subsection (4A) is inserted by the Companies (Audit, Investigations and Community Enterprise) Act 2004, s. 50(3), as from 1 July 2005.

124A. Petition for winding up on grounds of public interest

(1)   Where it appears to the Secretary of State from—

    (a)   any report made or information obtained under Part XIV (except section 448A) of the Companies Act 1985 (company investigations, &c.),

    (b)   any report made by inspectors under—

        (i)   section 167, 168, 169 or 284 of the Financial Services and Markets Act 2000, or

        (ii)   where the company is an open-ended investment company (within the meaning of that Act), regulations made as a result of section 262(2)(k) of that Act,

    (bb)   any information or documents obtained under section 165, 171, 172, 173 or 175 of that Act,

    (c)   any information obtained under section 2 of the Criminal Justice Act 1987 or section 52 of the Criminal Justice (Scotland) Act 1987 (fraud investigations), or

    (d)   any information obtained under section 83 of the Companies Act 1989 (powers exercisable for purpose of assisting overseas regulatory authorities),

that it is expedient in the public interest that a company should be wound up, he may present a petition for it to be wound up if the court thinks it just and equitable for it to be so.

(2)   This section does not apply if the company is already being wound up by the court.

124B. Petition for winding up of SE

(1)   Where—

    (a)   an SE whose registered office is in Great Britain is not in compliance with Article 7 of Council Regulation (EC) No 2157/2001 on the Statute for a European company (the "EC Regulation") (location of head office and registered office), and

    (b)   it appears to the Secretary of State that the SE should be wound up, he may present a petition for it to be wound up if the court thinks it is just and equitable for it to be so.

(2)   This section does not apply if the SE is already being wound up by the court.

(3)   In this section "SE" has the same meaning as in the EC Regulation.

125. Powers of court on hearing of petition

(1)   On hearing a winding-up petition the court may dismiss it, or adjourn the hearing conditionally or unconditionally, or make an interim order, or any other order that it thinks fit; but the court shall not refuse to make a winding-up order on the ground only that the company's assets have been mortgaged to an amount equal to or in excess of those assets, or that the company has no assets.

(2)   If the petition is presented by members of the company as contributories on the ground that it is just and equitable that the company should be wound up, the court, if it is of opinion—

    (a)   that the petitioners are entitled to relief either by winding up the company or by some other means, and

    (b)   that in the absence of any other remedy it would be just and equitable that the company should be wound up,

shall make a winding-up order; but this does not apply if the court is also of the opinion both that some other remedy is available to the petitioners and that they are acting unreasonably in seeking to have the company wound up instead of pursuing that other remedy.

126. Power to stay or restrain proceedings against company

(1)   At any time after the presentation of a winding-up petition, and before a winding-up order has been made, the company, or any creditor or contributory, may—

    (a)   where any action or proceeding against the company is pending in the High Court or Court of Appeal in England and Wales or Northern Ireland, apply to the court in which the action or proceeding is pending for a stay of proceedings therein, and

(b) where any other action or proceeding is pending against the company, apply to the court having jurisdiction to wind up the company to restrain further proceedings in the action or proceeding;

and the court to which application is so made may (as the case may be) stay, sist or restrain the proceedings accordingly on such terms as it thinks fit.

(2) In the case of a company registered under section 680 of the Companies Act (pre-1862 companies; companies formed under legislation other than the Companies Acts) or the previous corresponding legislation, where the application to stay, sist or restrain is by a creditor, this section extends to actions and proceedings against any contributory of the company.

127. Avoidance of property dispositions, etc

(1) In a winding up by the court, any disposition of the company's property, and any transfer of shares, or alteration in the status of the company's members, made after the commencement of the winding up is, unless the court otherwise orders, void.

(2) This section has no effect in respect of anything done by an administrator of a company while a winding-up petition is suspended under paragraph 40 of Schedule B1.

128. Avoidance of attachments, etc

(1) Where a company registered in England and Wales is being wound up by the court, any attachment, sequestration, distress or execution put in force against the estate or effects of the company after the commencement of the winding up is void.

(2) This section, so far as relates to any estate or effects of the company situated in England and Wales, applies in the case of a company registered in Scotland as it applies in the case of a company registered in England and Wales.

Commencement of winding up

129. Commencement of winding up by the court

(1) If, before the presentation of a petition for the winding up of a company by the court, a resolution has been passed by the company for voluntary winding up, the winding up of the company is deemed to have commenced at the time of the passing of the resolution; and unless the court, on proof of fraud or mistake, directs otherwise, all proceedings taken in the voluntary winding up are deemed to have been validly taken.

(1A) Where the court makes a winding-up order by virtue of paragraph 13(1)(e) of Schedule B1, the winding up is deemed to commence on the making of the order.

(2) In any other case, the winding up of a company by the court is deemed to commence at the time of the presentation of the petition for winding up.

130. Consequences of winding-up order

(1) On the making of a winding-up order, a copy of the order must forthwith be forwarded by the company (or otherwise as may be prescribed) to the registrar of companies, who shall enter it in his records relating to the company.

(2) When a winding-up order has been made or a provisional liquidator has been appointed, no action or proceeding shall be proceeded with or commenced against the company or its property, except by leave of the court and subject to such terms as the court may impose.

(3) When an order has been made for winding up a company registered under section 680 of the Companies Act, no action or proceeding shall be commenced or proceeded with against the company or its property or any contributory of the company, in respect of any debt of the company, except by leave of the court, and subject to such terms as the court may impose.

(4) An order for winding up a company operates in favour of all the creditors and of all contributories of the company as if made on the joint petition of a creditor and of a contributory.

Investigation procedures

131. Company's statement of affairs

(1)   Where the court has made a winding-up order or appointed a provisional liquidator, the official receiver may require some or all of the persons mentioned in subsection (3) below to make out and submit to him a statement in the prescribed form as to the affairs of the company.

(2)   The statement shall be verified by affidavit by the persons required to submit it and shall show—
  (a)   particulars of the company's assets, debts and liabilities;
  (b)   the names and addresses of the company's creditors;
  (c)   the securities held by them respectively;
  (d)   the dates when the securities were respectively given; and
  (e)   such further or other information as may be prescribed or as the official receiver may require.

(3)   The persons referred to in subsection (1) are—
  (a)   those who are or have been officers of the company;
  (b)   those who have taken part in the formation of the company at any time within one year before the relevant date;
  (c)   those who are in the company's employment, or have been in its employment within that year, and are in the official receiver's opinion capable of giving the information required;
  (d)   those who are or have been within that year officers of, or in the employment of, a company which is, or within that year was, an officer of the company.

(4)   Where any persons are required under this section to submit a statement of affairs to the official receiver, they shall do so (subject to the next subsection) before the end of the period of 21 days beginning with the day after that on which the prescribed notice of the requirement is given to them by the official receiver.

(5)   The official receiver, if he thinks fit, may—
  (a)   at any time release a person from an obligation imposed on him under subsection (1) or (2) above; or
  (b)   either when giving the notice mentioned in subsection (4) or subsequently, extend the period so mentioned;
  and where the official receiver has refused to exercise a power conferred by this subsection, the court, if it thinks fit, may exercise it.

(6)   In this section—
    "employment" includes employment under a contract for services; and
    "the relevant date" means—
    (a)   in a case where a provisional liquidator is appointed, the date of his appointment; and
    (b)   in a case where no such appointment is made, the date of the winding-up order.

(7)   If a person without reasonable excuse fails to comply with any obligation imposed under this section, he is liable to a fine and, for continued contravention, to a daily default fine.

(8)   In the application of this section to Scotland references to the official receiver are to the liquidator or, in a case where a provisional liquidator is appointed, the provisional liquidator.

132. Investigation by official receiver

(1)   Where a winding-up order is made by the court in England and Wales, it is the duty of the official receiver to investigate—
  (a)   if the company has failed, the causes of the failure; and
  (b)   generally, the promotion, formation, business, dealings and affairs of the company,
  and to make such report (if any) to the court as he thinks fit.

(2)   The report is, in any proceedings, prima facie evidence of the facts stated in it.

133. Public examination of officers

(1)   Where a company is being wound up by the court, the official receiver or, in Scotland, the liquidator may at any time before the dissolution of the company apply to the court for the public examination of any person who—

    (a)   is or has been an officer of the company; or

    (b)   has acted as liquidator or administrator of the company or as receiver or manager or, in Scotland, receiver of its property; or

    (c)   not being a person falling within paragraph (a) or (b), is or has been concerned, or has taken part, in the promotion, formation or management of the company.

(2)   Unless the court otherwise orders, the official receiver or, in Scotland, the liquidator shall make an application under subsection (1) if he is requested in accordance with the rules to do so by—

    (a)   one-half, in value, of the company's creditors; or

    (b)   three-quarters, in value, of the company's contributories.

(3)   On an application under subsection (1), the court shall direct that a public examination of the person to whom the application relates shall be held on a day appointed by the court; and that person shall attend on that day and be publicly examined as to the promotion, formation or management of the company or as to the conduct of its business and affairs, or his conduct or dealings in relation to the company.

(4)   The following may take part in the public examination of a person under this section and may question that person concerning the matters mentioned in subsection (3), namely—

    (a)   the official receiver;

    (b)   the liquidator of the company;

    (c)   any person who has been appointed as special manager of the company's property or business;

    (d)   any creditor of the company who has tendered a proof or, in Scotland, submitted a claim in the winding up;

    (e)   any contributory of the company.

134.   Enforcement of s 133

(1)   If a person without reasonable excuse fails at any time to attend his public examination under section 133, he is guilty of a contempt of court and liable to be punished accordingly.

(2)   In a case where a person without reasonable excuse fails at any time to attend his examination under section 133 or there are reasonable grounds for believing that a person has absconded, or is about to abscond, with a view to avoiding or delaying his examination under that section, the court may cause a warrant to be issued to a constable or prescribed officer of the court—

    (a)   for the arrest of that person; and

    (b)   for the seizure of any books, papers, records, money or goods in that person's possession.

(3)   In such a case the court may authorise the person arrested under the warrant to be kept in custody, and anything seized under such a warrant to be held, in accordance with the rules, until such time as the court may order.

Appointment of liquidator

135.   Appointment and powers of provisional liquidator

(1)   Subject to the provisions of this section, the court may, at any time after the presentation of a winding-up petition, appoint a liquidator provisionally.

(2)   In England and Wales, the appointment of a provisional liquidator may be made at any time before the making of a winding-up order; and either the official receiver or any other fit person may be appointed.

(3)   In Scotland, such an appointment may be made at any time before the first appointment of liquidators.

(4)   The provisional liquidator shall carry out such functions as the court may confer on him.

(5)   When a liquidator is provisionally appointed by the court, his powers may be limited by the order appointing him.

136.   Functions of official receiver in relation to office of liquidator

(1)   The following provisions of this section have effect, subject to section 140 below, on a winding-up order being made by the court in England and Wales.

(2)   The official receiver, by virtue of his office, becomes the liquidator of the company and continues in office until another person becomes liquidator under the provisions of this Part.

(3)   The official receiver is, by virtue of his office, the liquidator during any vacancy.

(4)   At any time when he is the liquidator of the company, the official receiver may summon separate meetings of the company's creditors and contributories for the purpose of choosing a person to be liquidator of the company in place of the official receiver.

(5)   It is the duty of the official receiver—

    (a)   as soon as practicable in the period of 12 weeks beginning with the day on which the winding-up order was made, to decide whether to exercise his power under subsection (4) to summon meetings, and

    (b)   if in pursuance of paragraph (a) he decides not to exercise that power, to give notice of his decision, before the end of that period, to the court and to the company's creditors and contributories, and

    (c)   (whether or not he has decided to exercise that power) to exercise his power to summon meetings under subsection (4) if he is at any time requested, in accordance with the rules, to do so by one-quarter, in value, of the company's creditors;

and accordingly, where the duty imposed by paragraph (c) arises before the official receiver has performed a duty imposed by paragraph (a) or (b), he is not required to perform the latter duty.

(6)   A notice given under subsection (5)(b) to the company's creditors shall contain an explanation of the creditors' power under subsection (5)(c) to require the official receiver to summon meetings of the company's creditors and contributories.

137.   Appointment by Secretary of State

(1)   In a winding up by the court in England and Wales the official receiver may, at any time when he is the liquidator of the company, apply to the Secretary of State for the appointment of a person as liquidator in his place.

(2)   If meetings are held in pursuance of a decision under section 136(5)(a), but no person is chosen to be liquidator as a result of those meetings, it is the duty of the official receiver to decide whether to refer the need for an appointment to the Secretary of State.

(3)   On an application under subsection (1), or a reference made in pursuance of a decision under subsection (2), the Secretary of State shall either make an appointment or decline to make one.

(4)   Where a liquidator has been appointed by the Secretary of State under subsection (3), the liquidator shall give notice of his appointment to the company's creditors or, if the court so allows, shall advertise his appointment in accordance with the directions of the court.

(5)   In that notice or advertisement the liquidator shall—

    (a)   state whether he proposes to summon a general meeting of the company's creditors under section 141 below for the purpose of determining (together with any meeting of contributories) whether a liquidation committee should be established under that section, and

    (b)   if he does not propose to summon such a meeting, set out the power of the company's creditors under that section to require him to summon one.

138.   Appointment of liquidator in Scotland

(1)   Where a winding-up order is made by the court in Scotland, a liquidator shall be appointed by the court at the time when the order is made.

(2)   The liquidator so appointed (here referred to as "the interim liquidator") continues in office until another person becomes liquidator in his place under this section or the next.

(3)   The interim liquidator shall (subject to the next subsection) as soon as practicable in the period of 28 days beginning with the day on which the winding-up order was made or such longer period as the court may allow, summon separate meetings of the company's creditors and contributories for the purpose of choosing a person (who may be the person who is the interim liquidator) to be liquidator of the company in place of the interim liquidator.

(4)   If it appears to the interim liquidator, in any case where a company is being wound up on grounds including its inability to pay its debts, that it would be inappropriate to summon under subsection (3) a meeting of the company's contributories, he may summon only a meeting of the company's creditors for the purpose mentioned in that subsection.

(5)   If one or more meetings are held in pursuance of this section but no person is appointed or nominated by the meeting or meetings, the interim liquidator shall make a report to the court which shall appoint either the interim liquidator or some other person to be liquidator of the company.

(6)   A person who becomes liquidator of the company in place of the interim liquidator shall, unless he is appointed by the court, forthwith notify the court of that fact.

139.   Choice of liquidator at meetings of creditors and contributories

(1)   This section applies where a company is being wound up by the court and separate meetings of the company's creditors and contributories are summoned for the purpose of choosing a person to be liquidator of the company.

(2)   The creditors and the contributories at their respective meetings may nominate a person to be liquidator.

(3)   The liquidator shall be the person nominated by the creditors or, where no person has been so nominated, the person (if any) nominated by the contributories.

(4)   In the case of different persons being nominated, any contributory or creditor may, within 7 days after the date on which the nomination was made by the creditors, apply to the court for an order either—

(a)   appointing the person nominated as liquidator by the contributories to be a liquidator instead of, or jointly with, the person nominated by the creditors; or

(b)   appointing some other person to be liquidator instead of the person nominated by the creditors.

140.   Appointment by the court following administration or voluntary arrangement

(1)   Where a winding-up order is made immediately upon the appointment of an administrator ceasing to have effect, the court may appoint as liquidator of the company the person whose appointment as administrator has ceased to have effect.

(2)   Where a winding-up order is made at a time when there is a supervisor of a voluntary arrangement approved in relation to the company under Part I, the court may appoint as liquidator of the company the person who is the supervisor at the time when the winding-up order is made.

(3)   Where the court makes an appointment under this section, the official receiver does not become the liquidator as otherwise provided by section 136(2), and he has no duty under section 136(5)(a) or (b) in respect of the summoning of creditors' or contributories' meetings.

Liquidation committees

141.   Liquidation committee (England and Wales)

(1)   Where a winding-up order has been made by the court in England and Wales and separate meetings of creditors and contributories have been summoned for the purpose of choosing a person to be liquidator, those meetings may establish a committee ("the liquidation committee") to exercise the functions conferred on it by or under this Act.

(2)   The liquidator (not being the official receiver) may at any time, if he thinks fit, summon separate general meetings of the company's creditors and contributories for the purpose of determining whether such a committee should be established and, if it is so determined, of establishing it.

        The liquidator (not being the official receiver) shall summon such a meeting if he is requested, in accordance with the rules, to do so by one-tenth, in value, of the company's creditors.

(3)   Where meetings are summoned under this section, or for the purpose of choosing a person to be liquidator, and either the meeting of creditors or the meeting of contributories decides that a liquidation committee should be established, but the other meeting does not so decide or decides

that a committee should not be established, the committee shall be established in accordance with the rules, unless the court otherwise orders.

(4)   The liquidation committee is not to be able or required to carry out its functions at any time when the official receiver is liquidator; but at any such time its functions are vested in the Secretary of State except to the extent that the rules otherwise provide.

(5)   Where there is for the time being no liquidation committee, and the liquidator is a person other than the official receiver, the functions of such a committee are vested in the Secretary of State except to the extent that the rules otherwise provide.

142.   Liquidation committee (Scotland)

(1)   Where a winding-up order has been made by the court in Scotland and separate meetings of creditors and contributories have been summoned for the purpose of choosing a person to be liquidator or, under section 138(4), only a meeting of creditors has been summoned for that purpose, those meetings or (as the case may be) that meeting may establish a committee ("the liquidation committee") to exercise the functions conferred on it by or under this Act.

(2)   The liquidator may at any time, if he thinks fit, summon separate general meetings of the company's creditors and contributories for the purpose of determining whether such a committee should be established and, if it is so determined, of establishing it.

(3)   The liquidator, if appointed by the court otherwise than under section 139(4)(a), is required to summon meetings under subsection (2) if he is requested, in accordance with the rules, to do so by one-tenth, in value, of the company's creditors.

(4)   Where meetings are summoned under this section, or for the purpose of choosing a person to be liquidator, and either the meeting of creditors or the meeting of contributories decides that a liquidation committee should be established, but the other meeting does not so decide or decides that a committee should not be established, the committee shall be established in accordance with the rules, unless the court otherwise orders.

(5)   Where in the case of any winding up there is for the time being no liquidation committee, the functions of such a committee are vested in the court except to the extent that the rules otherwise provide.

(6)   In addition to the powers and duties conferred and imposed on it by this Act, a liquidation committee has such of the powers and duties of commissioners in a sequestration as may be conferred and imposed on such committees by the rules.

The liquidator's functions

143.   General functions in winding up by the court

(1)   The functions of the liquidator of a company which is being wound up by the court are to secure that the assets of the company are got in, realised and distributed to the company's creditors and, if there is a surplus, to the persons entitled to it.

(2)   It is the duty of the liquidator of a company which is being wound up by the court in England and Wales, if he is not the official receiver—

(a)   to furnish the official receiver with such information,

(b)   to produce to the official receiver, and permit inspection by the official receiver of, such books, papers and other records, and

(c)   to give the official receiver such other assistance,

as the official receiver may reasonably require for the purposes of carrying out his functions in relation to the winding up.

144.   Custody of company's property

(1)   When a winding-up order has been made, or where a provisional liquidator has been appointed, the liquidator or the provisional liquidator (as the case may be) shall take into his custody or under his control all the property and things in action to which the company is or appears to be entitled.

(2)   In a winding up by the court in Scotland, if and so long as there is no liquidator, all the property of the company is deemed to be in the custody of the court.

145.   Vesting of company property in liquidator

(1)   When a company is being wound up by the court, the court may on the application of the liquidator by order direct that all or any part of the property of whatsoever description belonging to the company or held by trustees on its behalf shall vest in the liquidator by his official name; and thereupon the property to which the order relates vests accordingly.

(2)   The liquidator may, after giving such indemnity (if any) as the court may direct, bring or defend in his official name any action or other legal proceeding which relates to that property or which it is necessary to bring or defend for the purpose of effectually winding up the company and recovering its property.

146.   Duty to summon final meeting

(1)   Subject to the next subsection, if it appears to the liquidator of a company which is being wound by the court that the winding up of the company is for practical purposes complete and the liquidator is not the official receiver, the liquidator shall summon a final general meeting of the company's creditors which—

(a)   shall receive the liquidator's report of the winding up, and

(b)   shall determine whether the liquidator should have his release under section 174 in Chapter VII of this Part.

(2)   The liquidator may, if he thinks fit, give the notice summoning the final general meeting at the same time as giving notice of any final distribution of the company's property but, if summoned for an earlier date, that meeting shall be adjourned (and, if necessary, further adjourned) until a date on which the liquidator is able to report to the meeting that the winding up of the company is for practical purposes complete.

(3)   In the carrying out of his functions in the winding up it is the duty of the liquidator to retain sufficient sums from the company's property to cover the expenses of summoning and holding the meeting required by this section.

General powers of court

147.   Power to stay or sist winding up

(1)   The court may at any time after an order for winding up, on the application either of the liquidator or the official receiver or any creditor or contributory, and on proof to the satisfaction of the court that all proceedings in the winding up ought to be stayed or sisted, make an order staying or sisting the proceedings, either altogether or for a limited time, on such terms and conditions as the court thinks fit.

(2)   The court may, before making an order, require the official receiver to furnish to it a report with respect to any facts or matters which are in his opinion relevant to the application.

(3)   A copy of every order made under this section shall forthwith be forwarded by the company, or otherwise as may be prescribed, to the registrar of companies, who shall enter it in his records relating to the company.

148.   Settlement of list of contributories and application of assets

(1)   As soon as may be after making a winding-up order, the court shall settle a list of contributories, with power to rectify the register of members in all cases where rectification is required in pursuance of the Companies Act or this Act, and shall cause the company's assets to be collected, and applied in discharge of its liabilities.

(2)   If it appears to the court that it will not be necessary to make calls on or adjust the rights of contributories, the court may dispense with the settlement of a list of contributories.

(3)   In settling the list, the court shall distinguish between persons who are contributories in their own right and persons who are contributories as being representatives of or liable for the debts of others.

149.   **Debts due from contributory to company**

(1)   The court may, at any time after making a winding-up order, make an order on any contributory for the time being on the list of contributories to pay, in manner directed by the order, any money due from him (or from the estate of the person who he represents) to the company, exclusive of any money payable by him or the estate by virtue of any call in pursuance of the Companies Act or this Act.

(2)   The court in making such an order may—

     (a)   in the case of an unlimited company, allow to the contributory by way of set-off any money due to him or the estate which he represents from the company on any independent dealing or contract with the company, but not any money due to him as a member of the company in respect of any dividend or profit, and

     (b)   in the case of a limited company, make to any director or manager whose liability is unlimited or to his estate the like allowance.

(3)   In the case of any company, whether limited or unlimited, when all the creditors are paid in full (together with interest at the official rate), any money due on any account whatever to a contributory from the company may be allowed to him by way of set-off against any subsequent call.

150.   **Power to make calls**

(1)   The court may, at any time after making a winding-up order, and either before or after it has ascertained the sufficiency of the company's assets, make calls on all or any of the contributories for the time being settled on the list of the contributories to the extent of their liability, for payment of any money which the court considers necessary to satisfy the company's debts and liabilities, and the expenses of winding up, and for the adjustment of the rights of the contributories among themselves, and make an order for payment of any calls so made.

(2)   In making a call the court may take into consideration the probability that some of the contributories may partly or wholly fail to pay it.

151.   **Payment into bank of money due to company**

(1)   The court may order any contributory, purchaser or other person from whom money is due to the company to pay the amount due into the Bank of England (or any branch of it) to the account of the liquidator instead of to the liquidator, and such an order may be enforced in the same manner as if it had directed payment to the liquidator.

(2)   All money and securities paid or delivered into the Bank of England (or branch) in the event of a winding up by the court are subject in all respects to the orders of the court.

152.   **Order on contributory to be conclusive evidence**

(1)   An order made by the court on a contributory is conclusive evidence that the money (if any) thereby appearing to be due or ordered to be paid is due, but subject to any right of appeal.

(2)   All other pertinent matters stated in the order are to be taken as truly stated as against all persons and in all proceedings except proceedings in Scotland against the heritable estate of a deceased contributory; and in that case the order is only prima facie evidence for the purpose of charging his heritable estate, unless his heirs or legatees of heritage were on the list of contributories at the time of the order being made.

153.   **Power to exclude creditors not proving in time**

The court may fix a time or times within which creditors are to prove their debts or claims or to be excluded from the benefit of any distribution made before those debts are proved.

154.   **Adjustment of rights of contributories**

The court shall adjust the rights of the contributories among themselves and distribute any surplus among the persons entitled to it.

155.   Inspection of books by creditors, etc

(1)   The court may, at any time after making a winding-up order, make such order for inspection of the company's books and papers by creditors and contributories as the court thinks just; and any books and papers in the company's possession may be inspected by creditors and contributories accordingly, but not further or otherwise.

(2)   Nothing in this section excludes or restricts any statutory rights of a government department or person acting under the authority of a government department.

(3)   For the purposes of subsection (2) above, references to a government department shall be construed as including references to any part of the Scottish Administration.

156.   Payment of expenses of winding up

The court may, in the event of the assets being insufficient to satisfy the liabilities, make an order as to the payment out of the assets of the expenses incurred in the winding up in such order of priority as the court thinks just.

157.   Attendance at company meetings (Scotland)

In the winding up by the court of a company registered in Scotland, the court has power to require the attendance of any officer of the company at any meeting of creditors or of contributories, or of a liquidation committee, for the purpose of giving information as to the trade, dealings, affairs or property of the company.

158.   Power to arrest absconding contributory

The court, at any time either before or after making a winding-up order, on proof of probable cause for believing that a contributory is about to quit the United Kingdom or otherwise to abscond or to remove or conceal any of his property for the purpose of evading payment of calls, may cause the contributory to be arrested and his books and papers and movable personal property to be seized and him and them to be kept safely until such time as the court may order.

159.   Powers of court to be cumulative

Powers conferred by this Act and the Companies Act on the court are in addition to, and not in restriction of, any existing powers of instituting proceedings against a contributory or debtor of the company, or the estate of any contributory or debtor, for the recovery of any call or other sums.

160.   Delegation of powers to liquidator (England and Wales)

(1)   Provision may be made by rules for enabling or requiring all or any of the powers and duties conferred and imposed on the court in England and Wales by the Companies Act and this Act in respect of the following matters—

(a)   the holding and conducting of meetings to ascertain the wishes of creditors and contributories,

(b)   the settling of lists of contributories and the rectifying of the register of members where required, and the collection and application of the assets,

(c)   the payment, delivery, conveyance, surrender or transfer of money, property, books or papers to the liquidator,

(d)   the making of calls,

(e)   the fixing of a time within which debts and claims must be proved,

to be exercised or performed by the liquidator as an officer of the court, and subject to the court's control.

(2)   But the liquidator shall not, without the special leave of the court, rectify the register of members, and shall not make any call without either that special leave or the sanction of the liquidation committee.

Enforcement of, and appeal from, orders

161.   **Orders for calls on contributories (Scotland)**

(1)   In Scotland, where an order, interlocutor or decree has been made for winding up a company by the court, it is competent to the court, on production by the liquidators of a list certified by them of the names of the contributories liable in payment of any calls, and of the amount due by each contributory, and of the date when that amount became due, to pronounce forthwith a decree against those contributories for payment of the sums so certified to be due, with interest from that date until payment (at 5 per cent. per annum) in the same way and to the same effect as if they had severally consented to registration for execution, on a charge of 6 days, of a legal obligation to pay those calls and interest.

(2)   The decree may be extracted immediately, and no suspension of it is competent, except on caution or consignation, unless with special leave of the court.

162.   **Appeals from orders in Scotland**

(1)   Subject to the provisions of this section and to rules of court, an appeal from any order or decision made or given in the winding up of a company by the court in Scotland under this Act lies in the same manner and subject to the same conditions as an appeal from an order or decision of the court in cases within its ordinary jurisdiction.

(2)   In regard to orders or judgments pronounced by the judge acting as vacation judge ... —

     (a)   none of the orders specified in Part I of Schedule 3 to this Act are subject to review, reduction, suspension or stay of execution, and

     (b)   every other order or judgment (except as mentioned below) may be submitted to review by the Inner House by reclaiming motion enrolled within 14 days from the date of the order or judgment.

(3)   However, an order being one of those specified in Part II of that Schedule shall, from the date of the order and notwithstanding that it has been submitted to review as above, be carried out and receive effect until the Inner House have disposed of the matter.

(4)   In regard to orders or judgments pronounced in Scotland by a Lord Ordinary before whom proceedings in a winding up are being taken, any such order or judgment may be submitted to review by the Inner House by reclaiming motion enrolled within 14 days from its date; but should it not be so submitted to review during session, the provisions of this section in regard to orders or judgments pronounced by the judge acting as vacation judge apply.

(5)   Nothing in this section affects provisions of the Companies Act or this Act in reference to decrees in Scotland for payment of calls in the winding up of companies, whether voluntary or by the court.

CHAPTER VII
LIQUIDATORS

Preliminary

163.   **Style and title of liquidators**

The liquidator of a company shall be described—

     (a)   where a person other than the official receiver is liquidator, by the style of "the liquidator" of the particular company, or

     (b)   where the official receiver is liquidator, by the style of "the official receiver and liquidator" of the particular company;

and in neither case shall he be described by an individual name.

164.   **Corrupt inducement affecting appointment**

A person who gives, or agrees or offers to give, to any member or creditor of a company any valuable consideration with a view to securing his own appointment or nomination, or to securing or preventing the appointment or nomination of some person other than himself, as the company's liquidator is liable to a fine.

Liquidator's powers and duties

165.   Voluntary winding up

(1)   This section has effect where a company is being wound up voluntarily, but subject to section 166 below in the case of a creditors' voluntary winding up.

(2)   The liquidator may—

    (a)   in the case of a member's voluntary winding up, with the sanction of an extraordinary resolution of the company, and

    (b)   in the case of a creditors' voluntary winding up, with the sanction of the court or the liquidation committee (or, if there is no such committee, a meeting of the company's creditors),

exercise any of the powers specified in Part I of Schedule 4 to this Act (payment of debts, compromise of claims, etc).

(3)   The liquidator may, without sanction, exercise either of the powers specified in Part II of that Schedule (institution and defence of proceedings; carrying on the business of the company) and any of the general powers specified in Part III of that Schedule.

(4)   The liquidator may—

    (a)   exercise the court's power of settling a list of contributories (which list is prima facie evidence of the liability of the persons named in it to be contributories),

    (b)   exercise the court's power of making calls,

    (c)   summon general meetings of the company for the purpose of obtaining its sanction by special or extraordinary resolution or for any other purpose he may think fit.

(5)   The liquidator shall pay the company's debts and adjust the rights of the contributories among themselves.

(6)   Where the liquidator in exercise of the powers conferred on him by this Act disposes of any property of the company to a person who is connected with the company (within the meaning of section 249 in Part VII), he shall, if there is for the time being a liquidation committee, give notice to the committee of that exercise of his powers.

166.   Creditors' voluntary winding up

(1)   This section applies where, in the case of a creditors' voluntary winding up, a liquidator has been nominated by the company.

(2)   The powers conferred on the liquidator by section 165 shall not be exercised, except with the sanction of the court, during the period before the holding of the creditors' meeting under section 98 in Chapter IV.

(3)   Subsection (2) does not apply in relation to the power of the liquidator—

    (a)   to take into his custody or under his control all the property to which the company is or appears to be entitled;

    (b)   to dispose of perishable goods and other goods the value of which is likely to diminish if they are not immediately disposed of; and

    (c)   to do all such other things as may be necessary for the protection of the company's assets.

(4)   The liquidator shall attend the creditors' meeting held under section 98 and shall report to the meeting on any exercise by him of his powers (whether or not under this section or under section 112 or 165).

(5)   If default is made—

    (a)   by the company in complying with subsection (1) or (2) of section 98, or

    (b)   by the directors in complying with subsection (1) or (2) of section 99,

the liquidator shall, within 7 days of the relevant day, apply to the court for directions as to the manner in which that default is to be remedied.

(6)   "The relevant day" means the day on which the liquidator was nominated by the company or the day on which he first became aware of the default, whichever is the later.

(7)   If the liquidator without reasonable excuse fails to comply with this section, he is liable to a fine.

167.   Winding up by the court

(1)   Where a company is being wound up by the court, the liquidator may—

    (a)   with the sanction of the court or the liquidation committee, exercise any of the powers specified in Parts I and II of Schedule 4 to this Act (payment of debts; compromise of claims, etc; institution and defence of proceedings; carrying on of the business of the company), and

    (b)   with or without that sanction, exercise any of the general powers specified in Part III of that Schedule.

(2)   Where the liquidator (not being the official receiver), in exercise of the powers conferred on him by this Act—

    (a)   disposes of any property of the company to a person who is connected with the company (within the meaning of section 249 in Part VII), or

    (b)   employs a solicitor to assist him in the carrying out of his functions,

he shall, if there is for the time being a liquidation committee, give notice to the committee of that exercise of his powers.

(3)   The exercise by the liquidator in a winding up by the court of the powers conferred by this section is subject to the control of the court, and any creditor or contributory may apply to the court with respect to any exercise or proposed exercise of any of those powers.

168.   Supplementary powers (England and Wales)

(1)   This section applies in the case of a company which is being wound up by the court in England and Wales.

(2)   The liquidator may summon general meetings of the creditors or contributories for the purpose of ascertaining their wishes; and it is his duty to summon meetings at such times as the creditors or contributories by resolution (either at the meeting appointing the liquidator or otherwise) may direct, or whenever requested in writing to do so by one-tenth in value of the creditors or contributories (as the case may be).

(3)   The liquidator may apply to the court (in the prescribed manner) for directions in relation to any particular matter arising in the winding up.

(4)   Subject to the provisions of this Act, the liquidator shall use his own discretion in the management of the assets and their distribution among the creditors.

(5)   If any person is aggrieved by an act or decision of the liquidator, that person may apply to the court; and the court may confirm, reverse or modify the act or decision complained of, and make such order in the case as it thinks just.

(5A)   Where at any time after a winding-up petition has been presented to the court against any person (including an insolvent partnership or other body which may be wound up under Part V of the Act as an unregistered company), whether by virtue of the provisions of the Insolvent Partnerships Order 1994 or not, the attention of the court is drawn to the fact that the person in question is a member of an insolvent partnership, the court may make an order as to the future conduct of the insolvency proceedings and any such order may apply any provisions of that Order with any necessary modifications.

(5B)   Any order or directions under subsection (5A) may be made or given on the application of the official receiver, any responsible insolvency practitioner, the trustee of the partnership or any other interested person and may include provisions as to the administration of the joint estate of the partnership, and in particular how it and the separate estate of any member are to be administered.

(5C)   Where the court makes an order for the winding up of an insolvent partnership under—

    (a)   section 72(1)(a) of the Financial Services Act 1986;

    (b)   section 92(1)(a) of the Banking Act 1987; or

    (c)   section 367(3)(a) of the Financial Services and Markets Act 2000, the court may make an order as to the future conduct of the winding up proceedings, and any such order may apply any provisions of the Insolvent Partnerships Order 1994 with any necessary modifications.

169. Supplementary powers (Scotland)

(1)   In the case of a winding up in Scotland, the court may provide by order that the liquidator may, where there is no liquidation committee, exercise any of the following powers, namely—

    (a)   to bring or defend any action or other legal proceeding in the name and on behalf of the company, or

    (b)   to carry on the business of the company so far as may be necessary for its beneficial winding up,

without the sanction or intervention of the court.

(2)   In a winding up by the court in Scotland, the liquidator has (subject to the rules) the same powers as a trustee on a bankrupt estate.

170. Enforcement of liquidator's duty to make returns, etc

(1)   If a liquidator who has made any default—

    (a)   in filing, delivering or making any return, account or other document, or

    (b)   in giving any notice which he is by law required to file, deliver, make or give,

fails to make good the default within 14 days after the service on him of a notice requiring him to do so, the court has the following powers.

(2)   On an application made by any creditor or contributory of the company, or by the registrar of companies, the court may make an order directing the liquidator to make good the default within such time as may be specified in the order.

(3)   The court's order may provide that all costs of and incidental to the application shall be borne by the liquidator.

(4)   Nothing in this section prejudices the operation of any enactment imposing penalties on a liquidator in respect of any such default as is mentioned above.

Removal; vacation of office

171. Removal, etc (voluntary winding up)

(1)   This section applies with respect to the removal from office and vacation of office of the liquidator of a company which is being wound up voluntarily.

(2)   Subject to the next subsection, the liquidator may be removed from office only by an order of the court or—

    (a)   in the case of a members' voluntary winding up, by a general meeting of the company summoned specially for that purpose, or

    (b)   in the case of a creditors' voluntary winding up, by a general meeting of the company's creditors summoned specially for that purpose in accordance with the rules.

(3)   Where the liquidator was appointed by the court under section 108 in Chapter V, a meeting such as is mentioned in subsection (2) above shall be summoned for the purpose of replacing him only if he thinks fit or the court so directs or the meeting is requested, in accordance with the rules—

    (a)   in the case of a members' voluntary winding up, by members representing not less than one-half of the total voting rights of all the members having at the date of the request a right to vote at the meeting, or

    (b)   in the case of a creditors' voluntary winding up, by not less than one-half, in value, of the company's creditors.

(4)   A liquidator shall vacate office if he ceases to be a person who is qualified to act as an insolvency practitioner in relation to the company.

(5)   A liquidator may, in the prescribed circumstances, resign his office by giving notice of his resignation to the registrar of companies.

(6)   Where—

(a)   in the case of a members' voluntary winding up, a final meeting of the company has been held under section 94 in Chapter III, or

(b)   in the case of a creditors' voluntary winding up, final meetings of the company and of the creditors have been held under section 106 in ChapterIV,

the liquidator whose report was considered at the meeting or meetings shall vacate office as soon as he has complied with subsection (3) of that section and has given notice to the registrar of companies that the meeting or meetings have been held and of the decisions (if any) of the meeting or meetings.

172.   Removal, etc (winding up by the court)

(1)   This section applies with respect to the removal from office and vacation of office of the liquidator of a company which is being wound up by the court, or of a provisional liquidator.

(2)   Subject as follows, the liquidator may be removed from office only by an order of the court or by a general meeting of the company's creditors summoned specially for that purpose in accordance with the rules; and a provisional liquidator may be removed from office only by an order of the court.

(3)   Where—

(a)   the official receiver is liquidator otherwise than in succession under section 136(3) to a person who held office as a result of a nomination by a meeting of the company's creditors or contributories, or

(b)   the liquidator was appointed by the court otherwise than under section 139(4)(a) or 140(1), or was appointed by the Secretary of State,

a general meeting of the company's creditors shall be summoned for the purpose of replacing him only if he thinks fit, or the court so directs, or the meeting is requested, in accordance with the rules, by not less that one-quarter, in value, of the creditors.

(4)   If appointed by the Secretary of State, the liquidator may be removed from office by a direction of the Secretary of State.

(5)   A liquidator or provisional liquidator, not being the official receiver, shall vacate office if he ceases to be a person who is qualified to act as an insolvency practitioner in relation to the company.

(6)   A liquidator may, in the prescribed circumstances, resign his office by giving notice of his resignation to the court.

(7)   Where an order is made under section 204 (early dissolution in Scotland) for the dissolution of the company, the liquidator shall vacate office when the dissolution of the company takes effect in accordance with that section.

(8)   Where a final meeting has been held under section 146 (liquidator's report on completion of winding up), the liquidator whose report was considered at the meeting shall vacate office as soon as he has given notice to the court and the registrar of companies that the meeting has been held and of the decisions (if any) of the meeting.

Release of liquidator

173.   Release (voluntary winding up)

(1)   This section applies with respect to the release of the liquidator of a company which is being wound up voluntarily.

(2)   A person who has ceased to be a liquidator shall have his release with effect from the following time, that is to say—

(a)   in the case of a person who has been removed from office by a general meeting of the company or by a general meeting of the company's creditors that has not resolved against his release or who has died, the time at which notice is given to the registrar of companies in accordance with the rules that that person has ceased to hold office;

(b)   in the case of a person who has been removed from office by a general meeting of the company's creditors that has resolved against his release, or by the court, or who has vacated office under section 171(4) above, such time as the Secretary of State may, on the application of that person, determine;

(c) in the case of a person who has resigned, such time as may be prescribed;

(d) in the case of a person who has vacated office under subsection (6)(a) of section 171, the time at which he vacated office;

(e) in the case of a person who has vacated office under subsection (6)(b) of that section—

  (i) if the final meeting of the creditors referred to in that subsection has resolved against that person's release, such time as the Secretary of State may, on an application by that person, determine, and

  (ii) if that meeting has not resolved against that person's release, the time at which he vacated office.

(3) In the application of subsection (2) to the winding up of a company registered in Scotland, the references to a determination by the Secretary of State as to the time from which a person who has ceased to be liquidator shall have his release are to be read as references to such a determination by the Accountant of Court.

(4) Where a liquidator has his release under subsection (2), he is, with effect from the time specified in that subsection, discharged from all liability both in respect of acts or omissions of his in the winding up and otherwise in relation to his conduct as liquidator.

But nothing in this section prevents the exercise, in relation to a person who has had his release under subsection (2), of the court's powers under section 212 of this Act (summary remedy against delinquent directors, liquidators, etc).

174. Release (winding up by the court)

(1) This section applies with respect to the release of the liquidator of a company which is being wound up by the court, or of a provisional liquidator.

(2) Where the official receiver has ceased to be liquidator and a person becomes liquidator in his stead, the official receiver has his release with effect from the following time, that is to say—

(a) in a case where that person was nominated by a general meeting of creditors or contributories, or was appointed by the Secretary of State, the time at which the official receiver gives notice to the court that he has been replaced;

(b) in a case where that person is appointed by the court, such time as the court may determine.

(3) If the official receiver while he is a liquidator gives notice to the Secretary of State that the winding up is for practical purposes complete, he has his release with effect from such time as the Secretary of State may determine.

(4) A person other than the official receiver who has ceased to be a liquidator has his release with effect from the following time, that is to say—

(a) in the case of a person who has been removed from office by a general meeting of creditors that has not resolved against his release or who has died, the time at which notice is given to the court in accordance with the rules that that person has ceased to hold office;

(b) in the case of a person who has been removed from office by a general meeting of creditors that has resolved against his release, or by the court or the Secretary of State, or who has vacated office under section 172(5) or (7), such time as the Secretary of State may, on an application by that person, determine;

(c) in the case of a person who has resigned, such time as may be prescribed;

(d) in the case of a person who has vacated office under section 172(8)—

  (i) if the final meeting referred to in that subsection has resolved against that person's release, such time as the Secretary of State may, on an application by that person, determine, and

  (ii) if that meeting has not so resolved, the time at which that person vacated office.

(5) A person who has ceased to hold office as a provisional liquidator has his release with effect from such time as the court may, on an application by him, determine.

(6) Where the official receiver or a liquidator or provisional liquidator has his release under this section, he is, with effect from the time specified in the preceding provisions of this section,

discharged from all liability both in respect of acts or omissions of his in the winding up and otherwise in relation to his conduct as liquidator or provisional liquidator.

But nothing in this section prevents the exercise, in relation to a person who has had his release under this section, of the court's powers under section 212 (summary remedy against delinquent directors, liquidators, etc).

(7) In the application of this section to a case where the order for winding up has been made by the court in Scotland, the references to a determination by the Secretary of State as to the time from which a person who has ceased to be liquidator has his release are to such a determination by the Accountant of Court.

CHAPTER VIII
PROVISIONS OF GENERAL APPLICATION IN WINDING UP

Preferential debts

175. Preferential debts (general provision)

(1) In a winding up the company's preferential debts (within the meaning given by section 386 in Part XII) shall be paid in priority to all other debts.

(2) Preferential debts—
    (a) rank equally among themselves after the expenses of the winding up and shall be paid in full, unless the assets are insufficient to meet them, in which case they abate in equal proportions; and
    (b) so far as the assets of the company available for payment of general creditors are insufficient to meet them, have priority over the claims of holders of debentures secured by, or holders of, any floating charge created by the company, and shall be paid accordingly out of any property comprised in or subject to that charge.

176. Preferential charge on goods distrained

(1) This section applies where a company is being wound up by the court in England and Wales, and is without prejudice to section 128 (avoidance of attachments, etc).

(2) Where any person (whether or not a landlord or person entitled to rent) has distrained upon the goods or effects of the company in the period of 3 months ending with the date of the winding-up order, those goods or effects, or the proceeds of their sale, shall be charged for the benefit of the company with the preferential debts of the company to the extent that the company's property is for the time being insufficient for meeting them.

(3) Where by virtue of a charge under subsection (2) any person surrenders any goods or effects to a company or makes a payment to a company, that person ranks, in respect of the amount of the proceeds of sale of those goods or effects by the liquidator or (as the case may be) the amount of the payment, as a preferential creditor of the company, except as against so much of the company's property as is available for the payment of preferential creditors by virtue of the surrender or payment.

Property subject to floating charge

176A. Share of assets for unsecured creditors

(1) This section applies where a floating charge relates to property of a company—
    (a) which has gone into liquidation,
    (b) which is in administration,
    (c) of which there is a provisional liquidator, or
    (d) of which there is a receiver.

(2) The liquidator, administrator or receiver—
    (a) shall make a prescribed part of the company's net property available for the satisfaction of unsecured debts, and

(b)   shall not distribute that part to the proprietor of a floating charge except in so far as it exceeds the amount required for the satisfaction of unsecured debts.

(3)   Subsection (2) shall not apply to a company if—

(a)   the company's net property is less than the prescribed minimum, and

(b)   the liquidator, administrator or receiver thinks that the cost of making a distribution to unsecured creditors would be disproportionate to the benefits.

(4)   Subsection (2) shall also not apply to a company if or in so far as it is disapplied by—

(a)   a voluntary arrangement in respect of the company, or

(b)   a compromise or arrangement agreed under section 425 of the Companies Act (compromise with creditors and members).

(5)   Subsection (2) shall also not apply to a company if—

(a)   the liquidator, administrator or receiver applies to the court for an order under this subsection on the ground that the cost of making a distribution to unsecured creditors would be disproportionate to the benefits, and

(b)   the court orders that subsection (2) shall not apply.

(6)   In subsections (2) and (3) a company's net property is the amount of its property which would, but for this section, be available for satisfaction of claims of holders of debentures secured by, or holders of, any floating charge created by the company.

(7)   An order under subsection (2) prescribing part of a company's net property may, in particular, provide for its calculation—

(a)   as a percentage of the company's net property, or

(b)   as an aggregate of different percentages of different parts of the company's net property.

(8)   An order under this section—

(a)   must be made by statutory instrument, and

(b)   shall be subject to annulment pursuant to a resolution of either House of Parliament.

(9)   In this section—

"floating charge" means a charge which is a floating charge on its creation and which is created after the first order under subsection (2)(a) comes into force, and

"prescribed" means prescribed by order by the Secretary of State.

(10)   An order under this section may include transitional or incidental provision.

Special managers

177.   Power to appoint special manager

(1)   Where a company has gone into liquidation or a provisional liquidator has been appointed, the court may, on an application under this section, appoint any person to be the special manager of the business or property of the company.

(2)   The application may be made by the liquidator or provisional liquidator in any case where it appears to him that the nature of the business or property of the company, or the interests of the company's creditors or contributories or members generally, require the appointment of another person to manage the company's business or property.

(3)   The special manager has such powers as may be entrusted to him by the court.

(4)   The court's power to entrust powers to the special manager includes power to direct that any provision of this Act that has effect in relation to the provisional liquidator or liquidator of a company shall have the like effect in relation to the special manager for the purposes of the carrying out by him of any of the functions of the provisional liquidator or liquidator.

(5)   The special manager shall—

(a)   give such security or, in Scotland, caution as may be prescribed;

(b)   prepare and keep such accounts as may be prescribed; and

(c)   produce those accounts in accordance with the rules to the Secretary of State or to such other persons as may be prescribed.

Disclaimer (England and Wales only)

178.   Power to disclaim onerous property

(1)   This and the next two sections apply to a company that is being wound up in England and Wales.

(2)   Subject as follows, the liquidator may, by the giving of the prescribed notice, disclaim any onerous property and may do so notwithstanding that he has taken possession of it, endeavoured to sell it, or otherwise exercised rights of ownership in relation to it.

(3)   The following is onerous property for the purposes of this section—

       (a)   any unprofitable contract, and

       (b)   any other property of the company which is unsaleable or not readily saleable or is such that it may give rise to a liability to pay money or perform any other onerous act.

(4)   A disclaimer under this section—

       (a)   operates so as to determine, as from the date of the disclaimer, the rights, interests and liabilities of the company in or in respect of the property disclaimed; but

       (b)   does not, except so far as is necessary for the purpose of releasing the company from any liability, affect the rights or liabilities of any other person.

(5)   A notice of disclaimer shall not be given under this section in respect of any property if—

       (a)   a person interested in the property has applied in writing to the liquidator or one of his predecessors as liquidator requiring the liquidator or that predecessor to decide whether he will disclaim or not, and

       (b)   the period of 28 days beginning with the day on which that application was made, or such longer period as the court may allow, has expired without a notice of disclaimer having been given under this section in respect of that property.

(6)   Any person sustaining loss or damage in consequence of the operation of a disclaimer under this section is deemed a creditor of the company to the extent of the loss or damage and accordingly may prove for the loss or damage in the winding up.

179.   Disclaimer of leaseholds

(1)   The disclaimer under section 178 of any property of a leasehold nature does not take effect unless a copy of the disclaimer has been served (so far as the liquidator is aware of their addresses) on every person claiming under the company as underlessee or mortgagee and either—

       (a)   no application under section 181 below is made with respect to that property before the end of the period of 14 days beginning with the day on which the last notice served under this subsection was served; or

       (b)   where such an application has been made, the court directs that the disclaimer shall take effect.

(2)   Where the court gives a direction under subsection (1)(b) it may also, instead of or in addition to any order it makes under section 181, make such orders with respect to fixtures, tenant's improvements and other matters arising out of the lease as it thinks fit.

180.   Land subject to rentcharge

(1)   The following applies where, in consequence of the disclaimer under section 178 of any land subject to a rentcharge, that land vests by operation of law in the Crown or any other person (referred to in the next subsection as "the proprietor").

(2)   The proprietor and the successors in title of the proprietor are not subject to any personal liability in respect of any sums becoming due under the rentcharge except sums becoming due after the proprietor, or some person claiming under or through the proprietor, has taken possession or control of the land or has entered into occupation of it.

181.   Powers of court (general)

(1)   This section and the next apply where the liquidator has disclaimed property under section 178.

(2)   An application under this section may be made to the court by—

       (a)   any person who claims an interest in the disclaimed property, or

(b)   any person who is under any liability in respect of the disclaimed property, not being a liability discharged by the disclaimer.

(3)   Subject as follows, the court may on the application make an order, on such terms as it thinks fit, for the vesting of the disclaimed property in, or for its delivery to—

(a)   a person entitled to it or a trustee for such a person, or

(b)   a person subject to such a liability as is mentioned in subsection (2)(b) or a trustee for such a person.

(4)   The court shall not make an order under subsection (3)(b) except where it appears to the court that it would be just to do so for the purpose of compensating the person subject to the liability in respect of the disclaimer.

(5)   The effect of any order under this section shall be taken into account in assessing for the purpose of section 178(6) the extent of any loss or damage sustained by any person in consequence of the disclaimer.

(6)   An order under this section vesting property in any person need not be completed by conveyance, assignment or transfer.

182.   Powers of court (leaseholds)

(1)   The court shall not make an order under section 181 vesting property of a leasehold nature in any person claiming under the company as underlessee or mortgagee except on terms making that person—

(a)   subject to the same liabilities and obligations as the company was subject to under the lease at the commencement of the winding up, or

(b)   if the court thinks fit, subject to the same liabilities and obligations as that person would be subject to if the lease had been assigned to him at the commencement of the winding up.

(2)   For the purposes of an order under section 181 relating to only part of any property comprised in a lease, the requirements of subsection (1) apply as if the lease comprised only the property to which the order relates.

(3)   Where subsection (1) applies and no person claiming under the company as underlessee or mortgagee is willing to accept an order under section 181 on the terms required by virtue of that subsection, the court may, by order under that section, vest the company's estate or interest in the property in any person who is liable (whether personally or in a representative capacity, and whether alone or jointly with the company) to perform the lessee's covenants in the lease.

The court may vest that estate and interest in such a person freed and discharged from all estates, incumbrances and interests created by the company.

(4)   Where subsection (1) applies and a person claiming under the company as underlessee or mortgagee declines to accept an order under section 181, that person is excluded from all interest in the property.

Execution, attachment and the Scottish equivalents

183.   Effect of execution or attachment (England and Wales)

(1)   Where a creditor has issued execution against the goods or land of a company or has attached any debt due to it, and the company is subsequently wound up, he is not entitled to retain the benefit of the execution or attachment against the liquidator unless he has completed the execution or attachment before the commencement of the winding up.

(2)   However—

(a)   if a creditor has had notice of a meeting having been called at which a resolution for voluntary winding up is to be proposed, the date on which he had notice is substituted, for the purpose of subsection (1), for the date of commencement of the winding up;

(b)   a person who purchases in good faith under a sale by the enforcement officer or other officer charged with the execution of the writ any goods of a company on which execution has been levied in all cases acquires a good title to them against the liquidator; and

(c)   the rights conferred by subsection (1) on the liquidator may be set aside by the court in favour of the creditor to such extent and subject to such terms as the court thinks fit.

(3)   For the purposes of this Act—

   (a)   an execution against goods is completed by seizure and sale, or by the making of a charging order under section 1 of the Charging Orders Act 1979;

   (b)   an attachment of a debt is completed by receipt of the debt; and

   (c)   an execution against land is completed by seizure, by the appointment of a receiver, or by the making of a charging order under section 1 of the Act above-mentioned.

(4)   In this section "goods" includes all chattels personal; and "enforcement officer" means an individual who is authorised to act as an enforcement officer under the Courts Act 2003

(5)   This section does not apply in the case of a winding up in Scotland.

184.   Duties of officers charged with execution of writs and other processes (England and Wales)

(1)   The following applies where a company's goods are taken in execution and, before their sale or the completion of the execution (by the receipt or recovery of the full amount of the levy), notice is served on the enforcement officer, or other officer, charged with execution of the writ or other process, that a provisional liquidator has been appointed or that a winding-up order has been made, or that a resolution for voluntary winding up has been passed.

(2)   The enforcement officer or other officer shall, on being so required, deliver the goods and any money seized or received in part satisfaction of the execution to the liquidator; but the costs of execution are a first charge on the goods or money so delivered, and the liquidator may sell the goods, or a sufficient part of them, for the purpose of satisfying the charge.

(3)   If under an execution in respect of a judgment for a sum exceeding £500 a company's goods are sold or money is paid in order to avoid sale, the enforcement officer or other officer shall deduct the costs of the execution from the proceeds of sale or the money paid and retain the balance for 14 days.

(4)   If within that time notice is served on the enforcement officer or other officer of a petition for the winding up of the company having been presented, or of a meeting having been called at which there is to be proposed a resolution for voluntary winding up, and an order is made or a resolution passed (as the case may be), the enforcement officer or other officer shall pay the balance to the liquidator, who is entitled to retain it as against the execution creditor.

(5)   The rights conferred by this section on the liquidator may be set aside by the court in favour of the creditor to such extent and subject to such terms as the court thinks fit.

(6)   In this section, "goods" includes all chattels personal; and "enforcement officer" means an individual who is authorised to act as an enforcement officer under the Courts Act 2003.

(7)   The money sum for the time being specified in subsection (3) is subject to increase or reduction by order under section 416 in Part XV.

(8)   This section does not apply in the case of a winding up in Scotland.

185.   Effect of diligence (Scotland)

(1)   In the winding up of a company registered in Scotland, the following provisions of the Bankruptcy (Scotland) Act 1985—

   (a)   subsections (1) to (6) of section 37 (effect of sequestration on diligence); and

   (b)   subsections (3), (4), (7) and (8) of section 39 (realisation of estate),

   apply, so far as consistent with this Act, in like manner as they apply in the sequestration of a debtor's estate, with the substitutions specified below and with any other necessary modifications.

(2)   The substitutions to be made in those sections of the Act of 1985 are as follows—

   (a)   for references to the debtor, substitute references to the company;

   (b)   for references to the sequestration, substitute references to the winding up;

   (c)   for references to the date of sequestration, substitute references to the commencement of the winding up of the company; and

   (d)   for references to the permanent trustee, substitute references to the liquidator.

(3)   In this section, "the commencement of the winding up of the company" means, where it is being wound up by the court, the day on which the winding-up order is made.

(4)　　This section, so far as relating to any estate or effects of the company situated in Scotland, applies in the case of a company registered in England and Wales as in the case of one registered in Scotland.

Miscellaneous matters

186.　Rescission of contracts by the court

(1)　　The court may, on the application of a person who is, as against the liquidator, entitled to the benefit or subject to the burden of a contract made with the company, make an order rescinding the contract on such terms as to payment by or to either party of damages for the non-performance of the contract, or otherwise as the court thinks just.

(2)　　Any damages payable under the order to such a person may be proved by him as a debt in the winding up.

187.　Power to make over assets to employees

(1)　　On the winding up of a company (whether by the court or voluntarily), the liquidator may, subject to the following provisions of this section, make any payment which the company has, before the commencement of the winding up, decided to make under section 719 of the Companies Act (power to provide for employees or former employees on cessation or transfer of business).

(2)　　The power which a company may exercise by virtue only of that section may be exercised by the liquidator after the winding up has commenced if, after the company's liabilities have been fully satisfied and provision has been made for the expenses of the winding up, the exercise of that power has been sanctioned by such a resolution of the company as would be required of the company itself by section 719(3) before that commencement, if paragraph (b) of that subsection were omitted and any other requirement applicable to its exercise by the company had been met.

(3)　　Any payment which may be made by a company under this section (that is, a payment after the commencement of its winding up) may be made out of the company's assets which are available to the members on the winding up.

(4)　　On a winding up by the court, the exercise by the liquidator of his powers under this section is subject to the court's control, and any creditor or contributory may apply to the court with respect to any exercise or proposed exercise of the power.

(5)　　Subsections (1) and (2) above have effect notwithstanding anything in any rule of law or in section 107 of this Act (property of company after satisfaction of liabilities to be distributed among members).

188.　Notification that company is in liquidation

(1)　　When a company is being wound up, whether by the court or voluntarily, every invoice, order for goods or business letter issued by or on behalf of the company, or a liquidator of the company, or a receiver or manager of the company's property, being a document on or in which the name of the company appears, shall contain a statement that the company is being wound up.

(2)　　If default is made in complying with this section, the company and any of the following persons who knowingly and wilfully authorises or permits the default, namely, any officer of the company, any liquidator of the company and any receiver or manager, is liable to a fine.

189.　Interest on debts

(1)　　In a winding up interest is payable in accordance with this section on any debt proved in the winding up, including so much of any such debt as represents interest on the remainder.

(2)　　Any surplus remaining after the payment of the debts proved in a winding up shall, before being applied for any other purpose, be applied in paying interest on those debts in respect of the periods during which they have been outstanding since the company went into liquidation.

(3)　　All interest under this section ranks equally, whether or not the debts on which it is payable rank equally.

(4)   The rate of interest payable under this section in respect of any debt ("the official rate" for the purposes of any provision of this Act in which that expression is used) is whichever is the greater of—

(a)   the rate specified in section 17 of the Judgments Act 1838 on the day on which the company went into liquidation, and

(b)   the rate applicable to that debt apart from the winding up.

(5)   In the application of this section to Scotland—

(a)   references to a debt proved in a winding up have effect as references to a claim accepted in a winding up, and

(b)   the reference to section 17 of the Judgments Act 1838 has effect as a reference to the rules.

190.   Documents exempt from stamp duty

(1)   In the case of a winding up by the court, or of a creditors' voluntary winding up, the following has effect as regards exemption from duties chargeable under the enactments relating to stamp duties.

(2)   If the company is registered in England and Wales, the following documents are exempt from stamp duty—

(a)   every assurance relating solely to freehold or leasehold property, or to any estate, right or interest in, any real or personal property, which forms part of the company's assets and which, after the execution of the assurance, either at law or in equity, is or remains part of those assets, and

(b)   every writ, order, certificate, or other instrument or writing relating solely to the property of any company which is being wound up as mentioned in subsection (1), or to any proceeding under such a winding up.

"Assurance" here includes deed, conveyance, assignment and surrender.

(3)   If the company is registered in Scotland, the following documents are exempt from stamp duty—

(a)   every conveyance relating solely to property which forms part of the company's assets and which, after the execution of the conveyance, is or remains the company's property for the benefit of its creditors,

(b)   any articles of roup or sale, submission and every other instrument and writing whatsoever relating solely to the company's property, and

(c)   every deed or writing forming part of the proceedings in the winding up.

"Conveyance" here includes assignation, instrument, discharge, writing and deed.

191.   Company's books to be evidence

Where a company is being wound up, all books and papers of the company and of the liquidators are, as between the contributories of the company, prima facie evidence of the truth of all matters purporting to be recorded in them.

192.   Information as to pending liquidations

(1)   If the winding up of a company is not concluded within one year after its commencement, the liquidator shall, at such intervals as may be prescribed, until the winding up is concluded, send to the registrar of companies a statement in the prescribed form and containing the prescribed particulars with respect to the proceedings in, and position of, the liquidation.

(2)   If a liquidator fails to comply with this section, he is liable to a fine and, for continued contravention, to a daily default fine.

193.   Unclaimed dividends (Scotland)

(1)   The following applies where a company registered in Scotland has been wound up, and is about to be dissolved.

(2)   The liquidator shall lodge in an appropriate bank or institution as defined in section 73(1) of the Bankruptcy (Scotland) Act 1985 (not being a bank or institution in or of which the liquidator is acting partner, manager, agent or cashier) in the name of the Accountant of Court the whole unclaimed dividends and unapplied or undistributable balances, and the deposit receipts shall be transmitted to the Accountant of Court.

(3) The provisions of section 58 of the Bankruptcy (Scotland) Act 1985 (so far as consistent with this Act and the Companies Act) apply with any necessary modifications to sums lodged in a bank or institution under this section as they apply to sums deposited under section 57 of the Act first mentioned.

194. Resolutions passed at adjourned meetings

Where a resolution is passed at an adjourned meeting of a company's creditors or contributories, the resolution is treated for all purposes as having been passed on the date on which it was in fact passed, and not as having been passed on any earlier date.

195. Meetings to ascertain wishes of creditors or contributories

(1) The court may—
   (a) as to all matters relating to the winding up of a company, have regard to the wishes of the creditors or contributories (as proved to it by any sufficient evidence), and
   (b) if it thinks fit, for the purpose of ascertaining those wishes, direct meetings of the creditors or contributories to be called, held and conducted in such manner as the court directs, and appoint a person to act as chairman of any such meeting and report the result of it to the court.

(2) In the case of creditors, regard shall be had to the value of each creditor's debt.

(3) In the case of contributories, regard shall be had to the number of votes conferred on each contributory by the Companies Act or the articles.

196. Judicial notice of court documents

In all proceedings under this Part, all courts, judges and persons judicially acting, and all officers, judicial or ministerial, of any court, or employed in enforcing the process of any court shall take judicial notice—
   (a) of the signature of any officer of the High Court or of a county court in England and Wales, or of the Court of Session or a sheriff court in Scotland, or of the High Court in Northern Ireland, and also
   (b) of the official seal or stamp of the several offices of the High Court in England and Wales or Northern Ireland, or of the Court of Session, appended to or impressed on any document made, issued or signed under the provisions of this Act or the Companies Act, or any official copy of such a document.

197. Commission for receiving evidence

(1) When a company is wound up in England and Wales or in Scotland, the court may refer the whole or any part of the examination of witnesses—
   (a) to a specified county court in England and Wales, or
   (b) to the sheriff principal for a special sheriffdom in Scotland, or
   (c) to the High Court in Northern Ireland or a specified Northern Ireland County Court,
("specified" meaning specified in the order of the winding-up court).

(2) Any person exercising jurisdiction as a judge of the court to which the reference is made (or, in Scotland, the sheriff principal to whom it is made) shall then, by virtue of this section, be a commissioner for the purpose of taking the evidence of those witnesses.

(3) The judge or sheriff principal has in the matter referred the same power of summoning and examining witnesses, of requiring the production and delivery of documents, of punishing defaults by witnesses, and of allowing costs and expenses to witnesses, as the court which made the winding-up order.

These powers are in addition to any which the judge or sheriff principal might lawfully exercise apart from this section.

(4) The examination so taken shall be returned or reported to the court which made the order in such manner as that court requests.

(5) This section extends to Northern Ireland.

198.   Court order for examination of persons in Scotland

(1)   The court may direct the examination in Scotland of any person for the time being in Scotland (whether a contributory of the company or not), in regard to the trade, dealings, affairs or property of any company in course of being wound up, or of any person being a contributory of the company, so far as the company may be interested by reason of his being a contributory.

(2)   The order or commission to take the examination shall be directed to the sheriff principal of the sheriffdom in which the person to be examined is residing or happens to be for the time; and the sheriff principal shall summon the person to appear before him at a time and place to be specified in the summons for examination on oath as a witness or as a haver, and to produce any books or papers called for which are in his possession or power.

(3)   The sheriff principal may take the examination either orally or on written interrogatories, and shall report the same in writing in the usual form to the court, and shall transmit with the report the books and papers produced, if the originals are required and specified by the order or commission, or otherwise copies or extracts authenticated by the sheriff.

(4)   If a person so summoned fails to appear at the time and place specified, or refuses to be examined or to make the production required, the sheriff principal shall proceed against him as a witness or haver duly cited; and failing to appear or refusing to give evidence or make production may be proceeded against by the law of Scotland.

(5)   The sheriff principal is entitled to such fees, and the witness is entitled to such allowances, as sheriffs principal when acting as commissioners under appointment from the Court or Session and as witnesses and havers are entitled to in the like cases according to the law and practice of Scotland.

(6)   If any objection is stated to the sheriff principal by the witness, either on the ground of his incompetency as a witness, or as to the production required, or on any other ground, the sheriff principal may, if he thinks fit, report the objection to the court, and suspend the examination of the witness until it has been disposed of by the court.

199.   Costs of application for leave to proceed (Scottish companies)

Where a petition or application for leave to proceed with an action or proceeding against a company which is being wound up in Scotland is unopposed and is granted by the court, the costs of the petition or application shall, unless the court otherwise directs, be added to the amount of the petitioner's or applicant's claim against the company.

200.   Affidavits etc in United Kingdom and overseas

(1)   An affidavit required to be sworn under or for the purposes of this Part may be sworn in the United Kingdom, or elsewhere in Her Majesty's dominions, before any court, judge or person lawfully authorised to take and receive affidavits, or before any of Her Majesty's consuls or vice-consuls in any place outside Her dominions.

(2)   All courts, judges, justices, commissioners and persons acting judicially shall take judicial notice of the seal or stamp or signature (as the case may be) of any such court, judge, person, consul or vice-consul attached, appended or subscribed to any such affidavit, or to any other document to be used for the purposes of this Part.

CHAPTER IX
DISSOLUTION OF COMPANIES AFTER WINDING UP

201.   Dissolution (voluntary winding up)

(1)   This section applies, in the case of a company wound up voluntarily, where the liquidator has sent to the registrar of companies his final account and return under section 94 (members' voluntary) or section 106 (creditors' voluntary).

(2)   The registrar on receiving the account and return shall forthwith register them; and on the expiration of 3 months from the registration of the return the company is deemed to be dissolved.

(3)   However, the court may, on the application of the liquidator or any other person who appears to the court to be interested, make an order deferring the date at which the dissolution of the company is to take effect for such time as the court thinks fit.

(4)   It is the duty of the person on whose application an order of the court under this section is made within 7 days after the making of the order to deliver to the registrar an office copy of the order for registration; and if that person fails to do so he is liable to a fine and, for continued contravention, to a daily default fine.

202.   Early dissolution (England and Wales)

(1)   This section applies where an order for the winding up of a company has been made by the court in England and Wales.

(2)   The official receiver, if—

     (a)   he is the liquidator of the company, and

     (b)   it appears to him—

         (i)   that the realisable assets of the company are insufficient to cover the expenses of the winding up, and

         (ii) that the affairs of the company do not require any further investigation,

     may at any time apply to the registrar of companies for the early dissolution of the company.

(3)   Before making that application, the official receiver shall give not less than 28 days' notice of his intention to do so to the company's creditors and contributories and, if there is an administrative receiver of the company, to that receiver.

(4)   With the giving of that notice the official receiver ceases (subject to any directions under the next section) to be required to perform any duties imposed on him in relation to the company, its creditors or contributories by virtue of any provision of this Act, apart from a duty to make an application under subsection (2) of this section.

(5)   On the receipt of the official receiver's application under subsection (2) the registrar shall forthwith register it and, at the end of the period of 3 months beginning with the day of the registration of the application, the company shall be dissolved.

     However, the Secretary of State may, on the application of the official receiver or any other person who appears to the Secretary of State to be interested, give directions under section 203 at any time before the end of that period.

203.   Consequence of notice under s 202

(1)   Where a notice has been given under section 202(3), the official receiver or any creditor or contributory of the company, or the administrative receiver of the company (if there is one) may apply to the Secretary of State for directions under this section.

(2)   The grounds on which that application may be made are—

     (a)   that the realisable assets of the company are sufficient to cover the expenses of the winding up;

     (b)   that the affairs of the company do require further investigation; or

     (c)   that for any other reason the early dissolution of the company is inappropriate.

(3)   Directions under this section—

     (a)   are directions making such provision as the Secretary of State thinks fit for enabling the winding up of the company to proceed as if no notice had been given under section 202(3), and

     (b)   may, in the case of an application under section 202(5), include a direction deferring the date at which the dissolution of the company is to take effect for such period as the Secretary of State thinks fit.

(4)   An appeal to the court lies from any decision of the Secretary of State on an application for directions under this section.

(5)   It is the duty of the person on whose application any directions are given under this section, or in whose favour an appeal with respect to an application for such directions is determined, within 7

days after the giving of the directions or the determination of the appeal, to deliver to the registrar of companies for registration such a copy of the directions or determination as is prescribed.

(6)   If a person without reasonable excuse fails to deliver a copy as required by subsection (5), he is liable to a fine and, for continued contravention, to a daily default fine.

204.   Early dissolution (Scotland)

(1)   This section applies where a winding-up order has been made by the court in Scotland.

(2)   If after a meeting or meetings under section 138 (appointment of liquidator in Scotland) it appears to the liquidator that the realisable assets of the company are insufficient to cover the expenses of the winding up, he may apply to the court for an order that the company be dissolved.

(3)   Where the liquidator makes that application, if the court is satisfied that the realisable assets of the company are insufficient to cover the expenses of the winding up and it appears to the court appropriate to do so, the court shall make an order that the company be dissolved in accordance with this section.

(4)   A copy of the order shall within 14 days from its date be forwarded by the liquidator to the registrar of companies, who shall forthwith register it; and, at the end of the period of 3 months beginning with the day of the registration of the order, the company shall be dissolved.

(5)   The court may, on an application by any person who appears to the court to have an interest, order that the date at which the dissolution of the company is to take effect shall be deferred for such period as the court thinks fit.

(6)   It is the duty of the person on whose application an order is made under subsection (5), within 7 days after the making of the order, to deliver to the registrar of companies such a copy of the order as is prescribed.

(7)   If the liquidator without reasonable excuse fails to comply with the requirements of subsection (4), he is liable to a fine and, for continued contravention, to a daily default fine.

(8)   If a person without reasonable excuse fails to deliver a copy as required by subsection (6), he is liable to a fine and, for continued contravention, to a daily default fine.

205.   Dissolution otherwise than under ss 202–204

(1)   This section applies where the registrar of companies receives—

(a)   a notice served for the purposes of section 172(8) (final meeting of creditors and vacation of office by liquidator), or

(b)   a notice from the official receiver that the winding up of a company by the court is complete.

(2)   The registrar shall, on receipt of the notice, forthwith register it; and, subject as follows, at the end of the period of 3 months beginning with the day of the registration of the notice, the company shall be dissolved.

(3)   The Secretary of State may, on the application of the official receiver or any other person who appears to the Secretary of State to be interested, give a direction deferring the date at which the dissolution of the company is to take effect for such period as the Secretary of State thinks fit.

(4)   An appeal to the court lies from any decision of the Secretary of State on an application for a direction under subsection (3).

(5)   Subsection (3) does not apply in a case where the winding-up order was made by the court in Scotland, but in such a case the court may, on an application by any person appearing to the court to have an interest, order that the date at which the dissolution of the company is to take effect shall be deferred for such period as the court thinks fit.

(6)   It is the duty of the person—

(a)   on whose application a direction is given under subsection (3);

(b)   in whose favour an appeal with respect to an application for such a direction is determined; or

(c)   on whose application an order is made under subsection (5), within 7 days after the giving of the direction, the determination of the appeal or the making of the order, to deliver to the registrar for registration such a copy of the direction, determination or order as is prescribed.

(7) If a person without reasonable excuse fails to deliver a copy as required by subsection (6), he is liable to a fine and, for continued contravention to a daily default fine.

CHAPTER X
MALPRACTICE BEFORE AND DURING LIQUIDATION; PENALISATION OF COMPANIES AND COMPANY OFFICERS; INVESTIGATIONS AND PROSECUTIONS

Offences of fraud, deception, etc

206. **Fraud, etc in anticipation of winding up**

(1) When a company is ordered to be wound up by the court, or passes a resolution for voluntary winding up, any person, being a past or present officer of the company, is deemed to have committed an offence if, within the 12 months immediately preceding the commencement of the winding up, he has—

    (a) concealed any part of the company's property to the value of £500 or more, or concealed any debt due to or from the company, or

    (b) fraudulently removed any part of the company's property to the value of £500 or more, or

    (c) concealed, destroyed, mutilated or falsified any book or paper affecting or relating to the company's property or affairs, or

    (d) made any false entry in any book or paper affecting or relating to the company's property or affairs, or

    (e) fraudulently parted with, altered or made any omission in any document affecting or relating to the company's property or affairs, or

    (f) pawned, pledged or disposed of any property of the company which has been obtained on credit and has not been paid for (unless the pawning, pledging or disposal was in the ordinary way of the company's business).

(2) Such a person is deemed to have committed an offence if within the period above mentioned he has been privy to the doing by others of any of the things mentioned in paragraphs (c), (d) and (e) of subsection (1); and he commits an offence if, at any time after the commencement of the winding up, he does any of the things mentioned in paragraphs (a) to (f) of that subsection, or is privy to the doing by others of any of the things mentioned in paragraphs (c) to (e) of it.

(3) For purposes of this section, "officer" includes a shadow director.

(4) It is a defence—

    (a) for a person charged under paragraph (a) or (f) of subsection (1) (or under subsection (2) in respect of the things mentioned in either of those two paragraphs) to prove that he had no intent to defraud, and

    (b) for a person charged under paragraph (c) or (d) of subsection (1) (or under subsection (2) in respect of the things mentioned in either of those two paragraphs) to prove that he had no intent to conceal the state of affairs of the company or to defeat the law.

(5) Where a person pawns, pledges or disposes of any property in circumstances which amount to an offence under subsection (1)(f), every person who takes in pawn or pledge, or otherwise receives, the property knowing it to be pawned, pledged or disposed of in such circumstances, is guilty of an offence.

(6) A person guilty of an offence under this section is liable to imprisonment or a fine, or both.

(7) The money sums specified in paragraphs (a) and (b) of subsection (1) are subject to increase or reduction by order under section 416 in Part XV.

207.   **Transactions in fraud of creditors**

(1)   When a company is ordered to be wound up by the court or passes a resolution for voluntary winding up, a person is deemed to have committed an offence if he, being at the time an officer of the company—

     (a)   has made or caused to be made any gift or transfer of, or charge on, or has caused or connived at the levying of any execution against, the company's property, or

     (b)   has concealed or removed any part of the company's property since, or within 2 months before, the date of any unsatisfied judgment or order for the payment of money obtained against the company.

(2)   A person is not guilty of an offence under this section—

     (a)   by reason of conduct constituting an offence under subsection (1)(a) which occurred more than 5 years before the commencement of the winding up, or

     (b)   if he proves that, at the time of the conduct constituting the offence, he had no intent to defraud the company's creditors.

(3)   A person guilty of an offence under this section is liable to imprisonment or a fine, or both.

208.   **Misconduct in course of winding up**

(1)   When a company is being wound up, whether by the court or voluntarily, any person, being a past or present officer of the company, commits an offence if he—

     (a)   does not to the best of his knowledge and belief fully and truly discover to the liquidator all the company's property, and how and to whom and for what consideration and when the company disposed of any part of that property (except such part as has been disposed of in the ordinary way of the company's business), or

     (b)   does not deliver up to the liquidator (or as he directs) all such part of the company's property as is in his custody or under his control, and which he is required by law to deliver up, or

     (c)   does not deliver up to the liquidator (or as he directs) all books and papers in his custody or under his control belonging to the company and which he is required by law to deliver up, or

     (d)   knowing or believing that a false debt has been proved by any person in the winding up, fails to inform the liquidator as soon as practicable, or

     (e)   after the commencement of the winding up, prevents the production of any book or paper affecting or relating to the company's property or affairs.

(2)   Such a person commits an offence if after the commencement of the winding up he attempts to account for any part of the company's property by fictitious losses or expenses; and he is deemed to have committed that offence if he has so attempted at any meeting of the company's creditors within the 12 months immediately preceding the commencement of the winding up.

(3)   For purposes of this section, "officer" includes a shadow director.

(4)   It is a defence—

     (a)   for a person charged under paragraph (a), (b) or (c) of subsection (1) to prove that he had no intent to defraud, and

     (b)   for a person charged under paragraph (e) of that subsection to prove that he had no intent to conceal the state of affairs of the company or to defeat the law.

(5)   A person guilty of an offence under this section is liable to imprisonment or a fine, or both.

209.   **Falsification of company's books**

(1)   When a company is being wound up, an officer or contributory of the company commits an offence if he destroys, mutilates, alters or falsifies any books, papers or securities, or makes or is privy to the making of any false or fraudulent entry in any register, book of account or document belonging to the company with intent to defraud or deceive any person.

(2)   A person guilty of an offence under this section is liable to imprisonment or a fine, or both.

210. **Material omissions from statement relating to company's affairs**

(1)   When a company is being wound up, whether by the court or voluntarily, any person, being a past or present officer of the company, commits an offence if he makes any material omission in any statement relating to the company's affairs.

(2)   When a company has been ordered to be wound up by the court, or has passed a resolution for voluntary winding up, any such person is deemed to have committed that offence if, prior to the winding up, he has made any material omission in any such statement.

(3)   For purposes of this section, "officer" includes a shadow director.

(4)   It is a defence for a person charged under this section to prove that he had no intent to defraud.

(5)   A person guilty of an offence under this section is liable to imprisonment or a fine, or both.

211. **False representations to creditors**

(1)   When a company is being wound up, whether by the court or voluntarily, any person, being a past or present officer of the company—

    (a)   commits an offence if he makes any false representation or commits any other fraud for the purpose of obtaining the consent of the company's creditors or any of them to an agreement with reference to the company's affairs or to the winding up, and

    (b)   is deemed to have committed that offence if, prior to the winding up, he has made any false representation, or committed any other fraud, for that purpose.

(2)   For purposes of this section, "officer" includes a shadow director.

(3)   A person guilty of an offence under this section is liable to imprisonment or a fine, or both.

Penalisation of directors and officers

212. **Summary remedy against delinquent directors, liquidators, etc**

(1)   This section applies if in the course of the winding up of a company it appears that a person who—

    (a)   is or has been an officer of the company,

    (b)   has acted as liquidator... or administrative receiver of the company, or

    (c)   not being a person falling within paragraph (a) or (b), is or has been concerned, or has taken part, in the promotion, formation or management of the company,

has misapplied or retained, or become accountable for, any money or other property of the company, or been guilty of any misfeasance or breach of any fiduciary or other duty in relation to the company.

(2)   The reference in subsection (1) to any misfeasance or breach of any fiduciary or other duty in relation to the company includes, in the case of a person who has acted as liquidator ... of the company, any misfeasance or breach of any fiduciary or other duty in connection with the carrying out of his functions as liquidator ... of the company.

(3)   The court may, on the application of the official receiver or the liquidator, or of any creditor or contributory, examine into the conduct of the person falling within subsection (1) and compel him—

    (a)   to repay, restore or account for the money or property or any part of it, with interest at such rate as the court thinks just, or

    (b)   to contribute such sum to the company's assets by way of compensation in respect of the misfeasance or breach of fiduciary or other duty as the court thinks just.

(4)   The power to make an application under subsection (3) in relation to a person who has acted as liquidator ... of the company is not exercisable, except with the leave of the court, after he has had his release.

(5)   The power of a contributory to make an application under subsection (3) is not exercisable except with the leave of the court, but is exercisable notwithstanding that he will not benefit from any order the court may make on the application.

213.   Fraudulent trading

(1)   If in the course of the winding up of a company it appears that any business of the company has been carried on with intent to defraud creditors of the company or creditors of any other person, or for any fraudulent purpose, the following has effect.

(2)   The court, on the application of the liquidator may declare that any persons who were knowingly parties to the carrying on of the business in the manner above-mentioned are to be liable to make such contributions (if any) to the company's assets as the court thinks proper.

214.   Wrongful trading

(1)   Subject to subsection (3) below, if in the course of the winding up of a company it appears that subsection (2) of this section applies in relation to a person who is or has been a director of the company, the court, on the application of the liquidator, may declare that that person is to be liable to make such contribution (if any) to the company's assets as the court thinks proper.

(2)   This subsection applies in relation to a person if—
    (a)   the company has gone into insolvent liquidation,
    (b)   at some time before the commencement of the winding up of the company, that person knew or ought to have concluded that there was no reasonable prospect that the company would avoid going into insolvent liquidation, and
    (c)   that person was a director of the company at that time;
    but the court shall not make a declaration under this section in any case where the time mentioned in paragraph (b) above was before 28th April 1986.

(3)   The court shall not make a declaration under this section with respect to any person if it is satisfied that after the condition specified in subsection (2)(b) was first satisfied in relation to him that person took every step with a view to minimising the potential loss to the company's creditors as (assuming him to have known that there was no reasonable prospect that the company would avoid going into insolvent liquidation) he ought to have taken.

(4)   For the purposes of subsections (2) and (3), the facts which a director of a company ought to know or ascertain, the conclusions which he ought to reach and the steps which he ought to take are those which would be known or ascertained, or reached or taken, by a reasonably diligent person having both—
    (a)   the general knowledge, skill and experience that may reasonably be expected of a person carrying out the same functions as are carried out by that director in relation to the company, and
    (b)   the general knowledge, skill and experience that that director has.

(5)   The reference in subsection (4) to the functions carried out in relation to a company by a director of the company includes any functions which he does not carry out but which have been entrusted to him.

(6)   For the purposes of this section a company goes into insolvent liquidation if it goes into liquidation at a time when its assets are insufficient for the payment of its debts and other liabilities and the expenses of the winding up.

(7)   In this section "director" includes a shadow director.

(8)   This section is without prejudice to section 213.

215.   Proceedings under ss 213, 214

(1)   On the hearing of an application under section 213 or 214, the liquidator may himself give evidence or call witnesses.

(2)   Where under either section the court makes a declaration, it may give such further directions as it thinks proper for giving effect to the declaration; and in particular, the court may—
    (a)   provide for the liability of any person under the declaration to be a charge on any debt or obligation due from the company to him, or on any mortgage or charge or any interest in a mortgage or charge on assets of the company held by or vested in him, or any person on his behalf, or any person claiming as assignee from or through the person liable or any person acting on his behalf, and

(b)   from time to time make such further order as may be necessary for enforcing any charge imposed under this subsection.

(3)   For the purposes of subsection (2), "assignee"—

(a)   includes a person to whom or in whose favour, by the directions of the person made liable, the debt, obligation, mortgage or charge was created, issued or transferred or the interest created, but

(b)   does not include an assignee for valuable consideration (not including consideration by way of marriage *or the formation of a civil partnership*) given in good faith and without notice of any of the matters on the ground of which the declaration is made.

(4)   Where the court makes a declaration under either section in relation to a person who is a creditor of the company, it may direct that the whole or any part of any debt owed by the company to that person and any interest thereon shall rank in priority after all other debts owed by the company and after any interest on those debts.

(5)   Sections 213 and 214 have effect notwithstanding that the person concerned may be criminally liable in respect of matters on the ground of which the declaration under the section is to be made.

Note. The italicized words in subsection (3)(b) are inserted by the Civil Partnership Act 2004, s. 261(1), Sch. 27, para. 112, as from a day to be appointed.

216.   Restriction on re-use of company names

(1)   This section applies to a person where a company ("the liquidating company") has gone into insolvent liquidation on or after the appointed day and he was a director or shadow director of the company at any time in the period of 12 months ending with the day before it went into liquidation.

(2)   For the purposes of this section, a name is a prohibited name in relation to such a person if—

(a)   it is a name by which the liquidating company was known at any time in that period of 12 months, or

(b)   it is a name which is so similar to a name falling within paragraph (a) as to suggest an association with that company.

(3)   Except with leave of the court or in such circumstances as may be prescribed, a person to whom this section applies shall not at any time in the period of 5 years beginning with the day on which the liquidating company went into liquidation—

(a)   be a director of any other company that is known by a prohibited name, or

(b)   in any way, whether directly or indirectly, be concerned or take part in the promotion, formation or management of any such company, or

(c)   in any way, whether directly or indirectly, be concerned or take part in the carrying on of a business carried on (otherwise than by a company) under a prohibited name.

(4)   If a person acts in contravention of this section, he is liable to imprisonment or a fine, or both.

(5)   In subsection (3) "the court" means any court having jurisdiction to wind up companies; and on an application for leave under that subsection, the Secretary of State or the official receiver may appear and call the attention of the court to any matters which seem to him to be relevant.

(6)   References in this section, in relation to any time, to a name by which a company is known are to the name of the company at that time or to any name under which the company carries on business at that time.

(7)   For the purposes of this section a company goes into insolvent liquidation if it goes into liquidation at a time when its assets are insufficient for the payment of its debts and other liabilities and the expenses of the winding up.

(8)   In this section "company" includes a company which may be wound up under Part V of this Act.

217.   Personal liability for debts, following contravention of s 216

(1)   A person is personally responsible for all the relevant debts of a company if at any time—

(a)   in contravention of section 216, he is involved in the management of the company, or

(b) as a person who is involved in the management of the company, he acts or is willing to act on instructions given (without the leave of the court) by a person whom he knows at that time to be in contravention in relation to the company of section 216.

(2) Where a person is personally responsible under this section for the relevant debts of a company, he is jointly and severally liable in respect of those debts with the company and any other person who, whether under this section or otherwise, is so liable.

(3) For the purposes of this section the relevant debts of a company are—
(a) in relation to a person who is personally responsible under paragraph (a) of subsection (1), such debts and other liabilities of the company as are incurred at a time when that person was involved in the management of the company, and
(b) in relation to a person who is personally responsible under paragraph (b) of that subsection, such debts and other liabilities of the company as are incurred at a time when that person was acting or was willing to act on instructions given as mentioned in that paragraph.

(4) For the purposes of this section, a person is involved in the management of a company if he is a director of the company or if he is concerned, whether directly or indirectly, or takes part, in the management of the company.

(5) For the purposes of this section a person who, as a person involved in the management of a company, has at any time acted on instructions given (without the leave of the court) by a person whom he knew at that time to be in contravention in relation to the company of section 216 is presumed, unless the contrary is shown, to have been willing at any time thereafter to act on any instructions given by that person.

(6) In this section "company" includes a company which may be wound up under PartV.

Investigation and prosecution of malpractice

218.   Prosecution of delinquent officers and members of company

(1) If it appears to the court in the course of a winding up by the court that any past or present officer, or any member, of the company has been guilty of any offence in relation to the company for which he is criminally liable, the court may (either on the application of a person interested in the winding up or of its own motion) direct the liquidator to refer the matter
(a) in the case of a winding up in England and Wales, to the Secretary of State, and
(b) in the case of a winding up in Scotland, to the Lord Advocate.

(2) …

(3) If in the case of a winding up by the court in England and Wales it appears to the liquidator, not being the official receiver, that any past or present officer of the company, or any member of it, has been guilty of an offence in relation to the company for which he is criminally liable, the liquidator shall report the matter to the official receiver.

(4) If it appears to the liquidator in the course of a voluntary winding up that any past or present officer of the company, or any member of it, has been guilty of an offence in relation to the company for which he is criminally liable, he shall forthwith report the matter—
(a) in the case of a winding up in England and Wales, to the Secretary of State, and
(b) in the case of a winding up in Scotland, to the Lord Advocate,
and shall furnish to the Secretary of State or (as the case may be) the Lord Advocate such information and give to him such access to and facilities for inspecting and taking copies of documents (being information or documents in the possession or under the control of the liquidator and relating to the matter in question) as the Secretary of State or (as the case may be) the Lord Advocate requires.

(5) Where a report is made to the Secretary of State under subsection (4) he may, for the purpose of investigating the matter reported to him and such other matters relating to the affairs of the company as appear to him to require investigation, exercise any of the powers which are exercisable by inspectors appointed under section 431 or 432 of the Companies Act to investigate a company's affairs.

(6) If it appears to the court in the course of a voluntary winding up that—

(a)   any past or present officer of the company, or any member of it, has been guilty as above-mentioned, and

(b)   no report with respect to the matter has been made by the liquidator … under subsection (4),

the court may (on the application of any person interested in the winding up or of its own motion) direct the liquidator to make such a report.

On a report being made accordingly, this section has effect as though the report had been made in pursuance of subsection (4).

219.   Obligations arising under s 218

(1)   For the purpose of an investigation by the Secretary of State in consequence of a report made to him under section 218(4), any obligation imposed on a person by any provision of the Companies Act to produce documents or give information to, or otherwise to assist, inspectors appointed as mentioned in section 218(5) is to be regarded as an obligation similarly to assist the Secretary of State in his investigation.

(2)   An answer given by a person to a question put to him in exercise of the powers conferred by section 218(5) may be used in evidence against him.

(2A)   However, in criminal proceedings in which that person is charged with an offence to which this subsection applies—

(a)   no evidence relating to the answer may be adduced, and

(b)   no question relating to it may be asked,

by or on behalf of the prosecution, unless evidence relating to it is adduced, or a question relating to it is asked, in the proceedings by or on behalf of that person.

(2B)   Subsection (2A) applies to any offence other than—

(a)   an offence under section 2 or 5 of the Perjury Act 1911 (false statements made on oath otherwise than in judicial proceedings or made otherwise than on oath), or

(b)   an offence under section 44(1) or (2) of the Criminal Law (Consolidation) (Scotland) Act 1995 (false statements made on oath or otherwise than on oath).

(3)   Where criminal proceedings are instituted by the Director of Public Prosecutions, the Lord Advocate or the Secretary of State following any report or reference under section 218, it is the duty of the liquidator and every officer and agent of the company past and present (other than the defendant or defender) to give to the Director of Public Prosecutions, the Lord Advocate or the Secretary of State (as the case may be) all assistance in connection with the prosecution which he is reasonably able to give.

For this purpose "agent" includes any banker or solicitor of the company and any person employed by the company as auditor, whether that person is or is not an officer of the company.

(4)   If a person fails or neglects to give assistance in the manner required by subsection (3), the court may, on the application of the Director of Public Prosecutions, the Lord Advocate or the Secretary of State (as the case may be) direct the person to comply with that subsection; and if the application is made with respect to a liquidator, the court may (unless it appears that the failure or neglect to comply was due to the liquidator not having in his hands sufficient assets of the company to enable him to do so) direct that the costs shall be borne by the liquidator personally.

PART V

WINDING UP OF UNREGISTERED COMPANIES

220.   Meaning of "unregistered company"

(1)   For the purposes of this Part, the expression "unregistered company" includes … any association and any company, with the following exceptions—

(a)   …

(b)   a company registered in any part of the United Kingdom under the Joint Stock Companies Acts or under the legislation (past or present) relating to companies in Great Britain.

(2)   On such day as the Treasury appoints by order under section 4(3) of the Trustee Savings Banks Act 1985, the words in subsection (1) from "any trustee" to "banks" cease to have effect and are hereby repealed.

221.   Winding up of unregistered companies

(1)   Subject to the provisions of this Part, any unregistered company may be wound up under this Act; and all the provisions of this Act and the Companies Act about winding up apply to an unregistered company with the exceptions and additions mentioned in the following subsections.

(2)   If an unregistered company has a principal place of business situated in Northern Ireland, it shall not be wound up under this Part unless it has a principal place of business situated in England and Wales or Scotland, or in both England and Wales and Scotland.

(3)   For the purpose of determining a court's winding-up jurisdiction, an unregistered company is deemed—

    (a)   to be registered in England and Wales or Scotland, according as its principal place of business is situated in England and Wales or Scotland, or

    (b)   if it has a principal place of business situated in both countries, to be registered in both countries;

and the principal place of business situated in that part of Great Britain in which proceedings are being instituted is, for all purposes of the winding up, deemed to be the registered office of the company.

(4)   No unregistered company shall be wound up under this Act voluntarily, except in accordance with the EC Regulation.

(5)   The circumstances in which an unregistered company may be wound up are as follows—

    (a)   if the company is dissolved, or has ceased to carry on business, or is carrying on business only for the purpose of winding up its affairs;

    (b)   if the company is unable to pay its debts;

    (c)   if the court is of opinion that it is just and equitable that the company should be wound up.

(6)   …

(7)   In Scotland, an unregistered company which the Court of Session has jurisdiction to wind up may be wound up by the court if there is subsisting a floating charge over property comprised in the company's property and undertaking, and the court is satisfied that the security of the creditor entitled to the benefit of the floating charge is in jeopardy.

For this purpose a creditor's security is deemed to be in jeopardy if the court is satisfied that events have occurred or are about to occur which render it unreasonable in the creditor's interests that the company should retain power to dispose of the property which is subject to the floating charge.

222.   Inability to pay debts: unpaid creditor for £750 or more

(1)   An unregistered company is deemed (for the purposes of section 221) unable to pay its debts if there is a creditor, by assignment or otherwise, to whom the company is indebted in a sum exceeding £750 then due and—

    (a)   the creditor has served on the company, by leaving at its principal place of business, or by delivering to the secretary or some director, manager or principal officer of the company, or by otherwise serving in such manner as the court may approve or direct, a written demand in the prescribed form requiring the company to pay the sum due, and

    (b)   the company has for 3 weeks after the service of the demand neglected to pay the sum or to secure or compound for it to the creditor's satisfaction.

(2)   The money sum for the time being specified in subsection (1) is subject to increase or reduction by regulations under section 417 in Part XV; but no increase in the sum so specified affects any case in which the winding-up petition was presented before the coming into force of the increase.

223. Inability to pay debts: debt remaining unsatisfied after action brought

An unregistered company is deemed (for the purposes of section 221) unable to pay its debts if an action or other proceeding has been instituted against any member for any debt or demand due, or claimed to be due, from the company, or from him in his character of member, and—

(a) notice in writing of the institution of the action or proceeding has been served on the company by leaving it at the company's principal place of business (or by delivering it to the secretary, or some director, manager or principal officer of the company, or by otherwise serving it in such manner as the court may approve or direct), and

(b) the company has not within 3 weeks after service of the notice paid, secured or compounded for the debt or demand, or procured the action or proceeding to be stayed or sisted, or indemnified the defendant or defender to his reasonable satisfaction against the action or proceeding, and against all costs, damages and expenses to be incurred by him because of it.

224. Inability to pay debts: other cases

(1) An unregistered company is deemed (for purposes of section 221) unable to pay its debts—

(a) if in England and Wales execution or other process issued on a judgment, decree or order obtained in any court in favour of a creditor against the company, or any member of it as such, or any person authorised to be sued as nominal defendant on behalf of the company, is returned unsatisfied;

(b) if in Scotland the induciae of a charge for payment on an extract decree, or an extract registered bond, or an extract registered protest, have expired without payment being made;

(c) if in Northern Ireland a certificate of unenforceability has been granted in respect of any judgment, decree or order obtained as mentioned in paragraph (a);

(d) if it is otherwise proved to the satisfaction of the court that the company is unable to pay its debts as they fall due.

(2) An unregistered company is also deemed unable to pay its debts if it is proved to the satisfaction of the court that the value of the company's assets is less than the amount of its liabilities, taking into account its contingent and prospective liabilities.

225. Oversea company may be wound up though dissolved

(1) Where a company incorporated outside Great Britain which has been carrying on business in Great Britain ceases to carry on business in Great Britain, it may be wound up as an unregistered company under this Act, notwithstanding that it has been dissolved or otherwise ceased to exist as a company under or by virtue of the laws of the country under which it was incorporated.

(2) This section is subject to the EC Regulation.

226. Contributories in winding up of unregistered company

(1) In the event of an unregistered company being wound up, every person is deemed a contributory who is liable to pay or contribute to the payment of any debt or liability of the company, or to pay or contribute to the payment of any sum for the adjustment of the rights of members among themselves, or to pay or contribute to the payment of the expenses of winding up the company.

(2) Every contributory is liable to contribute to the company's assets all sums due from him in respect of any such liability as is mentioned above.

(3) In the case of an unregistered company engaged in or formed for working mines within the stannaries, a past member is not liable to contribute to the assets if he has ceased to be a member for 2 years or more either before the mine ceased to be worked or before the date of the winding-up order.

(4) In the event of the death, bankruptcy or insolvency of any contributory, the provisions of this Act with respect to the personal representatives, to the heirs and legatees of heritage of the heritable estate in Scotland of deceased contributories, and to the trustees of bankrupt or insolvent contributories, respectively apply.

227.   Power of court to stay, sist or restrain proceedings

The provisions of this Part with respect to staying, sisting or restraining actions and proceedings against a company at any time after the presentation of a petition for winding up and before the making of a winding-up order extend, in the case of an unregistered company, where the application to stay, sist or restrain is presented by a creditor, to actions and proceedings against any contributory of the company.

228.   Actions stayed on winding-up order

Where an order has been made for winding up an unregistered company, no action or proceeding shall be proceeded with or commenced against any contributory of the company in respect of any debt of the company, except by leave of the court, and subject to such terms as the court may impose.

229.   Provisions of this Part to be cumulative

(1)   The provisions of this Part with respect to unregistered companies are in addition to and not in restriction of any provisions in Part IV with respect to winding up companies by the court; and the court or liquidator may exercise any powers or do any act in the case of unregistered companies which might be exercised or done by it or him in winding up companies formed and registered under the Companies Act.

(2)   However, an unregistered company is not, except in the event of its being wound up, deemed to be a company under the Companies Act, and then only to the extent provided by this Part of this Act.

PART VI
MISCELLANEOUS PROVISIONS APPLYING TO COMPANIES
WHICH ARE INSOLVENT OR IN LIQUIDATION

Office-holders

230.   Holders of office to be qualified insolvency practitioners

(1)   …

(2)   Where an administrative receiver of a company is appointed, he must be a person who is so qualified.

(3)   Where a company goes into liquidation, the liquidator must be a person who is so qualified.

(4)   Where a provisional liquidator is appointed, he must be a person who is so qualified.

(5)   Subsections (3) and (4) are without prejudice to any enactment under which the official receiver is to be, or may be, liquidator or provisional liquidator.

231.   Appointment to office of two or more persons

(1)   This section applies if an appointment or nomination of any person to the office of … administrative receiver, liquidator or provisional liquidator—
(a)   relates to more than one person, or
(b)   has the effect that the office is to be held by more than one person.

(2)   The appointment or nomination shall declare whether any act required or authorised under any enactment to be done by the … administrative receiver, liquidator or provisional liquidator is to be done by all or any one or more of the persons for the time being holding the office in question.

232.   Validity of office-holder's acts

The acts of an individual as … administrative receiver, liquidator or provisional liquidator of a company are valid notwithstanding any defect in his appointment, nomination or qualifications.

Management by administrators, liquidators, etc

233.   Supplies of gas, water, electricity, etc

(1)   This section applies in the case of a company where—

(a) the company enters administration, or

(b) an administrative receiver is appointed, or

(ba) a moratorium under section 1A is in force, or

(c) a voluntary arrangement approved under Part I, has taken effect, or

(d) the company goes into liquidation, or

(e) a provisional liquidator is appointed;

and "the office-holder" means the administrator, the administrative receiver, the nominee, the supervisor of the voluntary arrangement, the liquidator or the provisional liquidator, as the case may be.

(2) If a request is made by or with the concurrence of the office-holder for the giving, after the effective date, of any of the supplies mentioned in the next subsection, the supplier—

(a) may make it a condition of the giving of the supply that the office-holder personally guarantees the payment of any charges in respect of the supply, but

(b) shall not make it a condition of the giving of the supply, or do anything which has the effect of making it a condition of the giving of the supply, that any outstanding charges in respect of a supply given to the company before the effective date are paid.

(3) The supplies referred to in subsection (2) are—

(a) a supply of gas by a gas supplier within the meaning of Part I of the Gas Act 1986;

(b) a supply of electricity by an electricity supplier within the meaning of Part I of the Electricity Act 1989;

(c) a supply of water by a water undertaker or, in Scotland, Scottish Water,

(d) a supply of communications services by a provider of a public electronic communications service.

(4) "The effective date" for the purposes of this section is whichever is applicable of the following dates—

(a) the date on which the company entered administration,

(b) the date on which the administrative receiver was appointed (or, if he was appointed in succession to another administrative receiver, the date on which the first of his predecessors was appointed),

(ba) the date on which the moratorium came into force,

(c) the date on which the voluntary arrangement took effect,

(d) the date on which the company went into liquidation,

(e) the date on which the provisional liquidator was appointed.

(5) The following applies to expressions used in subsection (3)—

(a)–(c)...

(d) "communications services" do not include electronic communications services to the extent that they are used to broadcast or otherwise transmit programme services (within the meaning of the Communications Act 2003).

234. Getting in the company's property

(1) This section applies in the case of a company where—

(a) the company enters administration, or

(b) an administrative receiver is appointed, or

(c) the company goes into liquidation, or

(d) a provisional liquidator is appointed;

and "the office-holder" means the administrator, the administrative receiver, the liquidator or the provisional liquidator, as the case may be.

(2) Where any person has in his possession or control any property, books, papers or records to which the company appears to be entitled, the court may require that person forthwith (or within such period as the court may direct) to pay, deliver, convey, surrender or transfer the property, books, papers or records to the office-holder.

(3) Where the office-holder—

(a) seizes or disposes of any property which is not property of the company, and

(b)   at the time of seizure or disposal believes, and has reasonable grounds for believing, that he is entitled (whether in pursuance of an order of the court or otherwise) to seize or dispose of that property,

the next subsection has effect.

(4)   In that case the office-holder—

(a)   is not liable to any person in respect of any loss or damage resulting from the seizure or disposal except in so far as that loss or damage is caused by the office-holder's own negligence, and

(b)   has a lien on the property, or the proceeds of its sale, for such expenses as were incurred in connection with the seizure or disposal.

235.   Duty to co-operate with office-holder

(1)   This section applies as does section 234; and it also applies, in the case of a company in respect of which a winding-up order has been made by the court in England and Wales, as if references to the office-holder included the official receiver, whether or not he is the liquidator.

(2)   Each of the persons mentioned in the next subsection shall—

(a)   give to the office-holder such information concerning the company and its promotion, formation, business, dealings, affairs or property as the office-holder may at any time after the effective date reasonably require, and

(b)   attend on the office-holder at such times as the latter may reasonably require.

(3)   The persons referred to above are—

(a)   those who are or have at any time been officers of the company,

(b)   those who have taken part in the formation of the company at any time within one year before the effective date,

(c)   those who are in the employment of the company, or have been in its employment (including employment under a contract for services) within that year, and are in the office-holder's opinion capable of giving information which he requires,

(d)   those who are, or have within that year been, officers of, or in the employment (including employment under a contract for services) of, another company which is, or within that year was, an officer of the company in question, and

(e)   in the case of a company being wound up by the court, any person who has acted as administrator, administrative receiver or liquidator of the company.

(4)   For the purposes of subsections (2) and (3), "the effective date" is whichever is applicable of the following dates—

(a)   the date on which the company entered administration,

(b)   the date on which the administrative receiver was appointed or, if he was appointed in succession to another administrative receiver, the date on which the first of his predecessors was appointed,

(c)   the date on which the provisional liquidator was appointed, and

(d)   the date on which the company went into liquidation.

(5)   If a person without reasonable excuse fails to comply with any obligation imposed by this section, he is liable to a fine and, for contravention, to a daily default fine.

236.   Inquiry into company's dealings, etc

(1)   This section applies as does section 234; and it also applies in the case of a company in respect of which a winding-up order has been made by the court in England and Wales as if references to the office-holder included the official receiver, whether or not he is the liquidator.

(2)   The court may, on the application of the office-holder, summon to appear before it—

(a)   any officer of the company,

(b)   any person known or suspected to have in his possession any property of the company or supposed to be indebted to the company, or

(c)   any person whom the court thinks capable of giving information concerning the promotion, formation, business, dealings, affairs or property of the company.

(3)   The court may require any such person as is mentioned in subsection (2)(a) to (c) to submit an affidavit to the court containing an account of his dealings with the company or to produce any books, papers or other records in his possession or under his control relating to the company or the matters mentioned in paragraph (c) of the subsection.

(4)   The following applies in a case where—

    (a)   a person without reasonable excuse fails to appear before the court when he is summoned to do so under this section, or

    (b)   there are reasonable grounds for believing that a person has absconded, or is about to abscond, with a view to avoiding his appearance before the court under this section.

(5)   The court may, for the purpose of bringing that person and anything in his possession before the court, cause a warrant to be issued to a constable or prescribed officer of the court—

    (a)   for the arrest of that person, and

    (b)   for the seizure of any books, papers, records, money or goods in that person's possession.

(6)   The court may authorise a person arrested under such a warrant to be kept in custody, and anything seized under such a warrant to be held, in accordance with the rules, until that person is brought before the court under the warrant or until such other time as the court may order.

237.   **Court's enforcement powers under s 236**

(1)   If it appears to the court, on consideration of any evidence obtained under section 236 or this section, that any person has in his possession any property of the company, the court may, on the application of the office-holder, order that person to deliver the whole or any part of the property to the office-holder at such time, in such manner and on such terms as the court thinks fit.

(2)   If it appears to the court, on consideration of any evidence so obtained, that any person is indebted to the company, the court may, on the application of the office-holder, order that person to pay to the office-holder, at such time and in such manner as the court may direct, the whole or any part of the amount due, whether in full discharge of the debt or otherwise, as the court thinks fit.

(3)   The court may, if it thinks fit, order that any person who if within the jurisdiction of the court would be liable to be summoned to appear before it under section 236 or this section shall be examined in any part of the United Kingdom where he may for the time being be, or in a place outside the United Kingdom.

(4)   Any person who appears or is brought before the court under section 236 or this section may be examined on oath, either orally or (except in Scotland) by interrogatories, concerning the company or the matters mentioned in section 236(2)(c).

Adjustment of prior transactions (administration and liquidation)

238.   **Transactions at an undervalue (England and Wales)**

(1)   This section applies in the case of a company where—

    (a)   the company enters administration, or

    (b)   the company goes into liquidation;

    and "the office-holder" means the administrator or the liquidator, as the case may be.

(2)   Where the company has at a relevant time (defined in section 240) entered into a transaction with any person at an undervalue, the office-holder may apply to the court for an order under this section.

(3)   Subject as follows, the court shall, on such an application, make such order as it thinks fit for restoring the position to what it would have been if the company had not entered into that transaction.

(4)   For the purposes of this section and section 241, a company enters into a transaction with a person at an undervalue if—

    (a)   the company makes a gift to that person or otherwise enters into a transaction with that person on terms that provide for the company to receive no consideration, or

    (b)   the company enters into a transaction with that person for a consideration the value of which, in money or money's worth, is significantly less than the value, in money or money's worth, of the consideration provided by the company.

(5) The court shall not make an order under this section in respect of a transaction at an undervalue if it is satisfied—

(a) that the company which entered into the transaction did so in good faith and for the purpose of carrying on its business, and

(b) that at the time it did so there were reasonable grounds for believing that the transaction would benefit the company.

239. Preferences (England and Wales)

(1) This section applies as does section 238.

(2) Where the company has at a relevant time (defined in the next section) given a preference to any person, the office-holder may apply to the court for an order under this section.

(3) Subject as follows, the court shall, on such an application, make such order as it thinks fit for restoring the position to what it would have been if the company had not given that preference.

(4) For the purposes of this section and section 241, a company gives a preference to a person if—

(a) that person is one of the company's creditors or a surety or guarantor for any of the company's debts or other liabilities, and

(b) the company does anything or suffers anything to be done which (in either case) has the effect of putting that person into a position which, in the event of the company going into insolvent liquidation, will be better than the position he would have been in if that thing had not been done.

(5) The court shall not make an order under this section in respect of a preference given to any person unless the company which gave the preference was influenced in deciding to give it by a desire to produce in relation to that person the effect mentioned in subsection (4)(b).

(6) A company which has given a preference to a person connected with the company (otherwise than by reason only of being its employee) at the time the preference was given is presumed, unless the contrary is shown, to have been influenced in deciding to give it by such a desire as is mentioned in subsection (5).

(7) The fact that something has been done in pursuance of the order of a court does not, without more, prevent the doing or suffering of that thing from constituting the giving of a preference.

240. "Relevant time" under ss 238, 239

(1) Subject to the next subsection, the time at which a company enters into a transaction at an undervalue or gives a preference is a relevant time if the transaction is entered into, or the preference given—

(a) in the case of a transaction at an undervalue or of a preference which is given to a person who is connected with the company (otherwise than by reason only of being its employee), at a time in the period of 2 years ending with the onset of insolvency (which expression is defined below),

(b) in the case of a preference which is not such a transaction and is not so given, at a time in the period of 6 months ending with the onset of insolvency, ...

(c) in either case, at a time between the making of an administration application in respect of the company and the making of an administration order on that application, and

(d) in either case, at a time between the filing with the court of a copy of notice of intention to appoint an administrator under paragraph 14 or 22 of Schedule B1 and the making of an appointment under that paragraph.

(2) Where a company enters into a transaction at an undervalue or gives a preference at a time mentioned in subsection (1)(a) or (b), that time is not a relevant time for the purposes of section 238 or 239 unless the company—

(a) is at that time unable to pay its debts within the meaning of section 123 in Chapter VI of Part IV, or

(b) becomes unable to pay its debts within the meaning of that section in consequence of the transaction or preference;

but the requirements of this subsection are presumed to be satisfied, unless the contrary is shown, in relation to any transaction at an undervalue which is entered into by a company with a person who is connected with the company.

(3)   For the purposes of subsection (1), the onset of insolvency is—

    (a)   in a case where section 238 or 239 applies by reason of an administrator of a company being appointed by administration order, the date on which the administration application is made,

    (b)   in a case where section 238 or 239 applies by reason of an administrator of a company being appointed under paragraph 14 or 22 of Schedule B1 following filing with the court of a copy of a notice of intention to appoint under that paragraph, the date on which the copy of the notice is filed,

    (c)   in a case where section 238 or 239 applies by reason of an administrator of a company being appointed otherwise than as mentioned in paragraph (a) or (b), the date on which the appointment takes effect,

    (d)   in a case where section 238 or 239 applies by reason of a company going into liquidation either following conversion of administration into winding up by virtue of Article 37 of the EC Regulation or at the time when the appointment of an administrator ceases to have effect, the date on which the company entered administration (or, if relevant, the date on which the application for the administration order was made or a copy of the notice of intention to appoint was filed), and

    (e)   in a case where section 238 or 239 applies by reason of a company going into liquidation at any other time, the date of the commencement of the winding up.

241.   Orders under ss 238, 239

(1)   Without prejudice to the generality of sections 238(3) and 239(3), an order under either of those sections with respect to a transaction or preference entered into or given by a company may (subject to the next subsection)—

    (a)   require any property transferred as part of the transaction, or in connection with the giving of the preference, to be vested in the company,

    (b)   require any property to be so vested if it represents in any person's hands the application either of the proceeds of sale of property so transferred or of money so transferred,

    (c)   release or discharge (in whole or in part) any security given by the company,

    (d)   require any person to pay, in respect of benefits received by him from the company, such sums to the office-holder as the court may direct,

    (e)   provide for any surety or guarantor whose obligations to any person were released or discharged (in whole or in part) under the transaction, or by the giving of the preference, to be under such new or revived obligations to that person as the court thinks appropriate,

    (f)   provide for security to be provided for the discharge of any obligation imposed by or arising under the order, for such an obligation to be charged on any property and for the security or charge to have the same priority as a security or charge released or discharged (in whole or in part) under the transaction or by the giving of the preference, and

    (g)   provide for the extent to which any person whose property is vested by the order in the company, or on whom obligations are imposed by the order, is to be able to prove in the winding up of the company for debts or other liabilities which arose from, or were released or discharged (in whole or in part) under or by, the transaction or the giving of the preference.

(2)   An order under section 238 or 239 may affect the property of, or impose any obligation on, any person whether or not he is the person with whom the company in question entered into the transaction or (as the case may be) the person to whom the preference was given; but such an order—

    (a)   shall not prejudice any interest in property which was acquired from a person other than the company and was acquired in good faith and for value, or prejudice any interest deriving from such an interest, and

(b)   shall not require a person who received a benefit from the transaction or preference in good faith and for value to pay a sum to the office-holder, except where that person was a party to the transaction or the payment is to be in respect of a preference given to that person at a time when he was a creditor of the company.

(2A)   Where a person has acquired an interest in property from a person other than the company in question, or has received a benefit from the transaction or preference, and at the time of that acquisition or receipt—

(a)   he had notice of the relevant surrounding circumstances and of the relevant proceedings, or

(b)   he was connected with, or was an associate of, either the company in question or the person with whom that company entered into the transaction or to whom that company gave the preference,

then, unless the contrary is shown, it shall be presumed for the purposes of paragraph (a) or (as the case may be) paragraph (b) of subsection (2) that the interest was acquired or the benefit was received otherwise than in good faith.

(3)   For the purposes of subsection (2A)(a), the relevant surrounding circumstances are (as the case may require)—

(a)   the fact that the company in question entered into the transaction at an undervalue; or

(b)   the circumstances which amounted to the giving of the preference by the company in question;

and subsections (3A) to (3C) have effect to determine whether, for those purposes, a person has notice of the relevant proceedings.

(3A)   Where section 238 or 239 applies by reason of a company's entering administration, a person has notice of the relevant proceedings if he has notice that—

(a)   an administration application has been made,

(b)   an administration order has been made,

(c)   a copy of a notice of intention to appoint an administrator under paragraph 14 or 22 of Schedule B1 has been filed, or

(d)   notice of the appointment of an administrator has been filed under paragraph 18 or 29 of that Schedule.

(3B)   Where section 238 or 239 applies by reason of a company's going into liquidation at the time when the appointment of an administrator of the company ceases to have effect, a person has notice of the relevant proceedings if he has notice that—

(a)   an administration application has been made,

(b)   an administration order has been made,

(c)   a copy of a notice of intention to appoint an administrator under paragraph 14 or 22 of Schedule B1 has been filed,

(d)   notice of the appointment of an administrator has been filed under paragraph 18 or 29 of that Schedule, or

(e)   the company has gone into liquidation.

(3C)   In a case where section 238 or 239 applies by reason of the company in question going into liquidation at any other time, a person has notice of the relevant proceedings if he has notice—

(a)   where the company goes into liquidation on the making of a winding-up order, of the fact that the petition on which the winding-up order is made has been presented or of the fact that the company has gone into liquidation;

(b)   in any other case, of the fact that the company has gone into liquidation.

(4)   The provisions of sections 238 to 241 apply without prejudice to the availability of any other remedy, even in relation to a transaction or preference which the company had no power to enter into or give.

242.   Gratuitous alienations (Scotland)

(1)   Where this subsection applies and—

(a)   the winding up of a company has commenced, an alienation by the company is challengeable by—

    (i)   any creditor who is a creditor by virtue of a debt incurred on or before the date of such commencement, or

    (ii) the liquidator;

(b) a company enters administration, an alienation by the company is challengeable by the administrator.

(2) Subsection (1) applies where—

    (a) by the alienation, whether before or after 1st April 1986 (the coming into force of section 75 of the Bankruptcy (Scotland) Act 1985), any part of the company's property is transferred or any claim or right of the company is discharged or renounced, and

    (b) the alienation takes place on a relevant day.

(3) For the purposes of subsection (2)(b), the day on which an alienation takes place is the day on which it becomes completely effectual; and in that subsection "relevant day" means, if the alienation has the effect of favouring—

    (a) a person who is an associate (within the meaning of the Bankruptcy (Scotland) Act 1985) of the company, a day not earlier than 5 years before the date on which—

      (i)   the winding up of the company commences, or

      (ii) as the case may be, the company enters administration; or

    (b) any other person, a day not earlier than 2 years before that date.

(4) On a challenge being brought under subsection (1), the court shall grant decree of reduction or for such restoration of property to the company's assets or other redress as may be appropriate; but the court shall not grant such a decree if the person seeking to uphold the alienation establishes—

    (a) that immediately, or at any other time, after the alienation the company's assets were greater than its liabilities, or

    (b) that the alienation was made for adequate consideration, or

    (c) that the alienation—

      (i)   was a birthday, Christmas or other conventional gift, or

      (ii) was a gift made, for a charitable purpose, to a person who is not an associate of the company,

which, having regard to all the circumstances, it was reasonable for the company to make.

Provided that this subsection is without prejudice to any right or interest acquired in good faith and for value from or through the transferee in the alienation.

(5) In subsection (4) above, "charitable purpose" means any charitable, benevolent or philanthropic purpose, whether or not it is charitable within the meaning of any rule of law.

(6) For the purposes of the foregoing provisions of this section, an alienation in implementation of a prior obligation is deemed to be one for which there was no consideration or no adequate consideration to the extent that the prior obligation was undertaken for no consideration or no adequate consideration.

(7) A liquidator and an administrator have the same right as a creditor has under any rule of law to challenge an alienation of a company made for no consideration or no adequate consideration.

(8) This section applies to Scotland only.

243. Unfair preferences (Scotland)

(1) Subject to subsection (2) below, subsection (4) below applies to a transaction entered into by a company, whether before or after 1st April 1986, which has the effect of creating a preference in favour of a creditor to the prejudice of the general body of creditors, being a preference created not earlier than 6 months before the commencement of the winding up of the company or the company enters administration.

(2) Subsection (4) below does not apply to any of the following transactions—

    (a) a transaction in the ordinary course of trade or business;

    (b) a payment in cash for a debt which when it was paid had become payable, unless the transaction was collusive with the purpose of prejudicing the general body of creditors;

(c)   a transaction whereby the parties to it undertake reciprocal obligations (whether the performance by the parties of their respective obligations occurs at the same time or at different times) unless the transaction was collusive as aforesaid;

(d)   the granting of a mandate by a company authorising an arrestee to pay over the arrested funds or part thereof to the arrester where—

    (i)   there has been a decree for payment or a warrant for summary diligence, and

    (ii) the decree or warrant has been preceded by an arrestment on the dependence of the action or followed by an arrestment in execution.

(3)   For the purposes of subsection (1) above, the day on which a preference was created is the day on which the preference became completely effectual.

(4)   A transaction to which this subsection applies is challengeable by—

    (a)   in the case of a winding up—

       (i)   any creditor who is a creditor by virtue of a debt incurred on or before the date of commencement of the winding up, or

       (ii) the liquidator; and

    (b)   where the company has entered administration, the administrator.

(5)   On a challenge being brought under subsection (4) above, the court, if satisfied that the transaction challenged is a transaction to which this section applies, shall grant decree of reduction or for such restoration of property to the company's assets or other redress as may be appropriate:

Provided that this subsection is without prejudice to any right or interest acquired in good faith and for value from or through the creditor in whose favour the preference was created.

(6)   A liquidator and an administrator have the same right as a creditor has under any rule of law to challenge a preference created by a debtor.

(7)   This section applies to Scotland only.

244.   Extortionate credit transactions

(1)   This section applies as does section 238, and where the company is, or has been, a party to a transaction for, or involving, the provision of credit to the company.

(2)   The court may, on the application of the office-holder, make an order with respect to the transaction if the transaction is or was extortionate and was entered into in the period of 3 years ending with the day on which the company entered administration or went into liquidation.

(3)   For the purposes of this section a transaction is extortionate if, having regard to the risk accepted by the person providing the credit—

    (a)   the terms of it are or were such as to require grossly exorbitant payments to be made (whether unconditionally or in certain contingencies) in respect of the provision of the credit, or

    (b)   it otherwise grossly contravened ordinary principles of fair dealing;

and it shall be presumed, unless the contrary is proved, that a transaction with respect to which an application is made under this section is or, as the case may be, was extortionate.

(4)   An order under this section with respect to any transaction may contain such one or more of the following as the court thinks fit, that is to say—

    (a)   provision setting aside the whole or part of any obligation created by the transaction,

    (b)   provision otherwise varying the terms of the transaction or varying the terms on which any security for the purposes of the transaction is held,

    (c)   provision requiring any person who is or was a party to the transaction to pay to the office-holder any sums paid to that person, by virtue of the transaction, by the company,

    (d)   provision requiring any person to surrender to the office-holder any property held by him as security for the purposes of the transaction,

    (e)   provision directing accounts to be taken between any persons.

(5)   The powers conferred by this section are exercisable in relation to any transaction concurrently with any powers exercisable in relation to that transaction as a transaction at an undervalue or under section 242 (gratuitous alienations in Scotland).

245.   Avoidance of certain floating charges

(1)   This section applies as does section 238, but applies to Scotland as well as to England and Wales.

(2)   Subject as follows, a floating charge on the company's undertaking or property created at a relevant time is invalid except to the extent of the aggregate of—

    (a)   the value of so much of the consideration for the creation of the charge as consists of money paid, or goods or services supplied, to the company at the same time as, or after, the creation of the charge,

    (b)   the value of so much of that consideration as consists of the discharge or reduction, at the same time as, or after the creation of the charge, of any debt of the company, and

    (c)   the amount of such interest (if any) as is payable on the amount falling within paragraph (a) or (b) in pursuance of any agreement under which the money was so paid, the goods or services were so supplied or the debt was so discharged or reduced.

(3)   Subject to the next subsection, the time at which a floating charge is created by a company is a relevant time for the purposes of this section if the charge is created—

    (a)   in the case of a charge which is created in favour of a person who is connected with the company, at a time in the period of 2 years ending with the onset of insolvency,

    (b)   in the case of a charge which is created in favour of any other person, at a time in the period of 12 months ending with the onset of insolvency, …

    (c)   in either case, at a time between the making of an administration application in respect of the company and the making of an administration order on that application, or

    (d)   in either case, at a time between the filing with the court of a copy of notice of intention to appoint an administrator under paragraph 14 or 22 of Schedule B1 and the making of an appointment under that paragraph.

(4)   Where a company creates a floating charge at a time mentioned in subsection (3)(b) and the person in favour of whom the charge is created is not connected with the company, that time is not a relevant time for the purposes of this section unless the company—

    (a)   is at that time unable to pay its debts within the meaning of section 123 in Chapter VI of Part IV, or

    (b)   becomes unable to pay its debts within the meaning of that section in consequence of the transaction under which the charge is created.

(5)   For the purposes of subsection (3), the onset of insolvency is—

    (a)   in a case where this section applies by reason of an administrator of a company being appointed by administration order, the date on which the administration application is made,

    (b)   in a case where this section applies by reason of an administrator of a company being appointed under paragraph 14 or 22 of Schedule B1 following filing with the court of a copy of notice of intention to appoint under that paragraph, the date on which the copy of the notice is filed,

    (c)   in a case where this section applies by reason of an administrator of a company being appointed otherwise than as mentioned in paragraph (a) or (b), the date on which the appointment takes effect, and

    (d)   in a case where this section applies by reason of a company going into liquidation, the date of the commencement of the winding up.

(6)   For the purposes of subsection (2)(a) the value of any goods or services supplied by way of consideration for a floating charge is the amount in money which at the time they were supplied could reasonably have been expected to be obtained for supplying the goods or services in the ordinary course of business and on the same terms (apart from the consideration) as those on which they were supplied to the company.

246.   Unenforceability of liens on books, etc

(1)   This section applies in the case of a company where—

    (a)   the company enters administration, or

    (b)   the company goes into liquidation, or

    (c)   a provisional liquidator is appointed;

and "the office-holder" means the administrator, the liquidator or the provisional liquidator, as the case may be.

(2)   Subject as follows, a lien or other right to retain possession of any of the books, papers or other records of the company is unenforceable to the extent that its enforcement would deny possession of any books, papers or other records to the office-holder.

(3)   This does not apply to a lien on documents which give a title to property and are held as such.

PART VII
INTERPRETATION FOR FIRST GROUP OF PARTS

247.   "Insolvency" and "go into liquidation"

(1)   In this Group of Parts, except in so far as the context otherwise requires, "insolvency", in relation to a company, includes the approval of a voluntary arrangement under Part I, or the appointment of an administrator or administrative receiver.

(2)   For the purposes of any provision in this Group of Parts, a company goes into liquidation if it passes a resolution for voluntary winding up or an order for its winding up is made by the court at a time when it has not already gone into liquidation by passing such a resolution.

(3)   The reference to a resolution for voluntary winding up in subsection (2) includes a reference to a resolution which is deemed to occur by virtue of—

     (a)   paragraph 83(6)(b) of Schedule B1, or

     (b)   an order made following conversion of administration or a voluntary arrangement into winding up by virtue of Article 37 of the EC Regulation.

248.   "Secured creditor", etc

In this Group of Parts, except in so far as the context otherwise requires—

     (a)   "secured creditor", in relation to a company, means a creditor of the company who holds in respect of his debt a security over property of the company, and "unsecured creditor" is to be read accordingly; and

     (b)   "security" means—

         (i)   in relation to England and Wales, any mortgage, charge, lien or other security, and

         (ii)   in relation to Scotland, any security (whether heritable or moveable), any floating charge and any right of lien or preference and any right of retention (other than a right of compensation or set off).

249.   "Connected" with a company

For the purposes of any provision in this Group of Parts, a person is connected with a company if—

     (a)   he is a director or shadow director of the company or an associate of such a director or shadow director, or

     (b)   he is an associate of the company;

and "associate" has the meaning given by section 435 in Part XVIII of this Act.

250.   "Member" of a company

For the purposes of any provision in this Group of Parts, a person who is not a member of a company but to whom shares in the company have been transferred, or transmitted by operation of law, is to be regarded as a member of the company, and references to a member or members are to be read accordingly.

251.   Expressions used generally

In this Group of Parts, except in so far as the context otherwise requires—

        "administrative receiver" means—

     (a)   an administrative receiver as defined by section 29(2) in Chapter I of Part III, or

(b) a receiver appointed under section 51 in Chapter II of that Part in a case where the whole (or substantially the whole) of the company's property is attached by the floating charge;

"business day" means any day other than a Saturday, a Sunday, Christmas Day, Good Friday or a day which is a bank holiday in any part of Great Britain;

"chattel leasing agreement" means an agreement for the bailment or, in Scotland, the hiring of goods which is capable of subsisting for more than 3 months;

"contributory" has the meaning given by section 79;

"director" includes any person occupying the position of director, by whatever name called;

"floating charge" means a charge which, as created, was a floating charge and includes a floating charge within section 462 of the Companies Act (Scottish floating charges);

"office copy", in relation to Scotland, means a copy certified by the clerk of court;

"the official rate", in relation to interest, means the rate payable under section 189(4);

"prescribed" means prescribed by the rules;

"receiver", in the expression "receiver or manager", does not include a receiver appointed under section 51 in Chapter II of Part III;

"retention of title agreement" means an agreement for the sale of goods to a company, being an agreement—

(a) which does not constitute a charge on the goods, but

(b) under which, if the seller is not paid and the company is wound up, the seller will have priority over all other creditors of the company as respects the goods or any property representing the goods;

"the rules" means rules under section 411 in Part XV; and

"shadow director", in relation to a company, means a person in accordance with whose directions or instructions the directors of the company are accustomed to act (but so that a person is not deemed a shadow director by reason only that the directors act on advice given by him in a professional capacity);

and any expression for whose interpretation provision is made by Part XXVI of the Companies Act, other than an expression defined above in this section, is to be construed in accordance with that provision.

THE SECOND GROUP OF PARTS
INSOLVENCY OF INDIVIDUALS; BANKRUPTCY

PART VIII
INDIVIDUAL VOLUNTARY ARRANGEMENTS

Moratorium for insolvent debtor

252. **Interim order of court**

(1) In the circumstances specified below, the court may in the case of a debtor (being an individual) make an interim order under this section.

(2) An interim order has the effect that, during the period for which it is in force—

(a) no bankruptcy petition relating to the debtor may be presented or proceeded with,

(aa) no landlord or other person to whom rent is payable may exercise any right of forfeiture by peaceable re-entry in relation to premises let to the debtor in respect of a failure by the debtor to comply with any term or condition of his tenancy of such premises, except with the leave of the court, and

(b) no other proceedings, and no execution or other legal process, may be commenced or continued and no distress may be levied against the debtor or his property except with the leave of the court.

253.   Application for interim order

(1)   Application to the court for an interim order may be made where the debtor intends to make a proposal under this Part, that is, a proposal to his creditors for a composition in satisfaction of his debts or a scheme of arrangement of his affairs (from here on referred to, in either case, as a "voluntary arrangement").

(2)   The proposal must provide for some person ("the nominee") to act in relation to the voluntary arrangement either as trustee or otherwise for the purpose of supervising its implementation and the nominee must be a person who is qualified to act as an insolvency practitioner, or authorised to act as nominee, in relation to the voluntary arrangement.

(3)   Subject as follows, the application may be made—

(a)   if the debtor is an undischarged bankrupt, by the debtor, the trustee of his estate, or the official receiver, and

(b)   in any other case, by the debtor.

(4)   An application shall not be made under subsection (3)(a) unless the debtor has given notice of the proposal to the official receiver and, if there is one, the trustee of his estate.

(5)   An application shall not be made while a bankruptcy petition presented by the debtor is pending, if the court has, under section 273 below, appointed an insolvency practitioner to inquire into the debtor's affairs and report.

254.   Effect of application

(1)   At any time when an application under section 253 for an interim order is pending,

(a)   no landlord or other person to whom rent is payable may exercise any right of forfeiture by peaceable re-entry in relation to premises let to the debtor in respect of a failure by the debtor to comply with any term or condition of his tenancy of such premises, except with the leave of the court, and

(b)   the court may forbid the levying of any distress on the debtor's property or its subsequent sale, or both, and stay any action, execution or other legal process against the property or person of the debtor.

(2)   Any court in which proceedings are pending against an individual may, on proof that an application under that section has been made in respect of that individual, either stay the proceedings or allow them to continue on such terms as it thinks fit.

255.   Cases in which interim order can be made

(1)   The court shall not make an interim order on an application under section 253 unless it is satisfied—

(a)   that the debtor intends to make a proposal under this Part;

(b)   that on the day of the making of the application the debtor was an undischarged bankrupt or was able to petition for his own bankruptcy;

(c)   that no previous application has been made by the debtor for an interim order in the period of 12 months ending with that day; and

(d)   that the nominee under the debtor's proposal … is willing to act in relation to the proposal.

(2)   The court may make an order if it thinks that it would be appropriate to do so for the purpose of facilitating the consideration and implementation of the debtor's proposal.

(3)   Where the debtor is an undischarged bankrupt, the interim order may contain provision as to the conduct of the bankruptcy, and the administration of the bankrupt's estate, during the period for which the order is in force.

(4)   Subject as follows, the provision contained in an interim order by virtue of subsection (3) may include provision staying proceedings in the bankruptcy or modifying any provision in this Group of Parts, and any provision of the rules in their application to the debtor's bankruptcy.

(5)   An interim order shall not, in relation to a bankrupt, make provision relaxing or removing any of the requirements of provisions in this Group of Parts, or of the rules, unless the court is satisfied that that provision is unlikely to result in any significant diminution in, or in the value of, the debtor's estate for the purposes of the bankruptcy.

(6)   Subject to the following provisions of this Part, and interim order made on an application under section 253 ceases to have effect at the end of the period of 14 days beginning with the day after the making of the order.

256. Nominee's report on debtor's proposal

(1)   Where an interim order has been made on an application under section 253, the nominee shall, before the order ceases to have effect, submit a report to the court stating—

  (a)   whether, in his opinion, the voluntary arrangement which the debtor is proposing has a reasonable prospect of being approved and implemented,

  (aa) whether, in his opinion, a meeting of the debtor's creditors should be summoned to consider the debtor's proposal, and

  (b)   if in his opinion such a meeting should be summoned, the date on which, and time and place at which, he proposes the meeting should be held.

(2)   For the purpose of enabling the nominee to prepare his report the debtor shall submit to the nominee—

  (a)   a document setting out the terms of the voluntary arrangement which the debtor is proposing, and

  (b)   a statement of his affairs containing—

    (i)   such particulars of his creditors and of his debts and other liabilities and of his assets as may be prescribed, and

    (ii) such other information as may be prescribed.

(3)   The court may—

  (a)   on an application made by the debtor in a case where the nominee has failed to submit the report required by this section or has died, or

  (b)   on an application made by the debtor or the nominee in a case where it is impracticable or inappropriate for the nominee to continue to act as such,

direct that the nominee shall be replaced as such by another person qualified to act as an insolvency practitioner, or authorised to act as nominee, in relation to the voluntary arrangement.

(3A)   The court may, on an application made by the debtor in a case where the nominee has failed to submit the report required by this section, direct that the interim order shall continue, or (if it has ceased to have effect) be renewed, for such further period as the court may specify in the direction.

(4)   The court may, on the application of the nominee, extend the period for which the interim order has effect so as to enable the nominee to have more time to prepare his report.

(5)   If the court is satisfied on receiving the nominee's report that a meeting of the debtor's creditors should be summoned to consider the debtor's proposal, the court shall direct that the period for which the interim order has effect shall be extended, for such further period as it may specify in the direction, for the purpose of enabling the debtor's proposal to be considered by his creditors in accordance with the following provisions of this Part.

(6)   The court may discharge the interim order if it is satisfied, on the application of the nominee—

  (a)   that the debtor has failed to comply with his obligations under subsection (2), or

  (b)   that for any other reason it would be inappropriate for a meeting of the debtor's creditors to be summoned to consider the debtor's proposal.

Procedure where no interim order made

256A. Debtor's proposal and nominee's report

(1)   This section applies where a debtor (being an individual)—

  (a)   intends to make a proposal under this Part (but an interim order has not been made in relation to the proposal and no application for such an order is pending), and

  (b)   if he is an undischarged bankrupt, has given notice of the proposal to the official receiver and, if there is one, the trustee of his estate,

unless a bankruptcy petition presented by the debtor is pending and the court has, under section 273, appointed an insolvency practitioner to inquire into the debtor's affairs and report.

(2)   For the purpose of enabling the nominee to prepare a report to the court, the debtor shall submit to the nominee—

    (a)   a document setting out the terms of the voluntary arrangement which the debtor is proposing, and

    (b)   a statement of his affairs containing—

        (i)   such particulars of his creditors and of his debts and other liabilities and of his assets as may be prescribed, and

        (ii) such other information as may be prescribed.

(3)   If the nominee is of the opinion that the debtor is an undischarged bankrupt, or is able to petition for his own bankruptcy, the nominee shall, within 14 days (or such longer period as the court may allow) after receiving the document and statement mentioned in subsection (2), submit a report to the court stating—

    (a)   whether, in his opinion, the voluntary arrangement which the debtor is proposing has a reasonable prospect of being approved and implemented,

    (b)   whether, in his opinion, a meeting of the debtor's creditors should be summoned to consider the debtor's proposal, and

    (c)   if in his opinion such a meeting should be summoned, the date on which, and time and place at which, he proposes the meeting should be held.

(4)   The court may—

    (a)   on an application made by the debtor in a case where the nominee has failed to submit the report required by this section or has died, or

    (b)   on an application made by the debtor or the nominee in a case where it is impracticable or inappropriate for the nominee to continue to act as such,

    direct that the nominee shall be replaced as such by another person qualified to act as an insolvency practitioner, or authorised to act as nominee, in relation to the voluntary arrangement.

(5)   The court may, on an application made by the nominee, extend the period within which the nominee is to submit his report.

Creditors' meeting

257.   Summoning of creditors' meeting

(1)   Where it has been reported to the court under section 256 or 256A that a meeting of the debtor's creditors should be summoned, the nominee (or his replacement under section 256(3) or 256A(4)) shall, unless the court otherwise directs, summon that meeting for the time, date and place proposed in his report.

(2)   The persons to be summoned to the meeting are every creditor of the debtor of whose claim and address the person summoning the meeting is aware.

(3)   For this purpose the creditors of a debtor who is an undischarged bankrupt include—

    (a)   every person who is a creditor of the bankrupt in respect of a bankruptcy debt, and

    (b)   every person who would be such a creditor if the bankruptcy had commenced on the day on which notice of the meeting is given.

Consideration and implementation of debtor's proposal

258.   Decisions of creditors' meeting

(1)   A creditors' meeting summoned under section 257 shall decide whether to approve the proposed voluntary arrangement.

(2)   The meeting may approve the proposed voluntary arrangement with modifications, but shall not do so unless the debtor consents to each modification.

(3)   The modifications subject to which the proposed voluntary arrangement may be approved may include one conferring the functions proposed to be conferred on the nominee on another person qualified to act as an insolvency practitioner or authorised to act as nominee, in relation to the voluntary arrangement.

But they shall not include any modification by virtue of which the proposal ceases to be a proposal under this Part.

(4)   The meeting shall not approve any proposal or modification which affects the right of a secured creditor of the debtor to enforce his security, except with the concurrence of the creditor concerned.

(5)   Subject as follows, the meeting shall not approve any proposal or modification under which—
:   (a)   any preferential debt of the debtor is to be paid otherwise than in priority to such of his debts as are not preferential debts, or
:   (b)   a preferential creditor of the debtor is to be paid an amount in respect of a preferential debt that bears to that debt a smaller proportion than is borne to another preferential debt by the amount that is to be paid in respect of that other debt.

However, the meeting may approve such a proposal or modification with the concurrence of the preferential creditor concerned.

(6)   Subject as above, the meeting shall be conducted in accordance with the rules.

(7)   In this section "preferential debt" has the meaning given by section 386 in Part XII; and "preferential creditor" is to be construed accordingly.

259. Report of decisions to court

(1)   After the conclusion in accordance with the rules of the meeting summoned under section 257, the chairman of the meeting shall report the result of it to the court and, immediately after so reporting, shall give notice of the result of the meeting to such persons as may be prescribed.

(2)   If the report is that the meeting has declined (with or without modifications) to approve the debtor's proposal, the court may discharge any interim order which is in force in relation to the debtor.

260. Effect of approval

(1)   This section has effect where the meeting summoned under section 257 approves the proposed voluntary arrangement (with or without modifications).

(2)   The approved arrangement—
:   (a)   takes effect as if made by the debtor at the meeting, and
:   (b)   binds every person who in accordance with the rules—
:   :   (i)   was entitled to vote at the meeting (whether or not he was present or represented at it), or
:   :   (ii)   would have been so entitled if he had had notice of it,
as if he were a party to the arrangement.

(2A)   If—
:   (a)   when the arrangement ceases to have effect any amount payable under the arrangement to a person bound by virtue of subsection (2)(b)(ii) has not been paid, and
:   (b)   the arrangement did not come to an end prematurely,
the debtor shall at that time become liable to pay to that person the amount payable under the arrangement.

(3)   The Deeds of Arrangement Act 1914 does not apply to the approved voluntary arrangement.

(4)   Any interim order in force in relation to the debtor immediately before the end of the period of 28 days beginning with the day on which the report with respect to the creditors' meeting was made to the court under section 259 ceases to have effect at the end of that period.

This subsection applies except to such extent as the court may direct for the purposes of any application under section 262 below.

(5)   Where proceedings on a bankruptcy petition have been stayed by an interim order which ceases to have effect under subsection (4), the petition is deemed, unless the court otherwise orders, to have been dismissed.

261. Additional effect on undischarged bankrupt

(1)   This section applies where—

(a)   the creditors' meeting summoned under section 257 approves the proposed voluntary arrangement (with or without modifications), and

(b)   the debtor is an undischarged bankrupt.

(2)   Where this section applies the court shall annul the bankruptcy order on an application made—

(a)   by the bankrupt, or

(b)   where the bankrupt has not made an application within the prescribed period, by the official receiver.

(3)   An application under subsection (2) may not be made—

(a)   during the period specified in section 262(3)(a) during which the decision of the creditors' meeting can be challenged by application under section 262,

(b)   while an application under that section is pending, or

(c)   while an appeal in respect of an application under that section is pending or may be brought.

(4)   Where this section applies the court may give such directions about the conduct of the bankruptcy and the administration of the bankrupt's estate as it thinks appropriate for facilitating the implementation of the approved voluntary arrangement.

262.   Challenge of meeting's decision

(1)   Subject to this section, an application to the court may be made, by any of the persons specified below, on one or both of the following grounds, namely—

(a)   that a voluntary arrangement approved by a creditors' meeting summoned under section 257 unfairly prejudices the interests of a creditor of the debtor;

(b)   that there has been some material irregularity at or in relation to such a meeting.

(2)   The persons who may apply under this section are—

(a)   the debtor;

(b)   a person who—

(i)   was entitled, in accordance with the rules, to vote at the creditors' meeting, or

(ii)   would have been so entitled if he had had notice of it;

(c)   the nominee (or his replacement under section 256(3), 256A(4) or 258(3)); and

(d)   if the debtor is an undischarged bankrupt, the trustee of his estate or the official receiver.

(3)   An application under this section shall not be made—

(a)   after the end of the period of 28 days beginning with the day on which the report of the creditors' meeting was made to the court under section 259, or

(b)   in the case of a person who was not given notice of the creditors' meeting, after the end of the period of 28 days beginning with the day on which he became aware that the meeting had taken place,

but (subject to that) an application made by a person within subsection (2)(b)(ii) on the ground that the arrangement prejudices his interests may be made after the arrangement has ceased to have effect, unless it has come to an end prematurely.

(4)   Where on an application under this section the court is satisfied as to either of the grounds mentioned in subsection (1), it may do one or both of the following, namely—

(a)   revoke or suspend any approval given by the meeting;

(b)   give a direction to any person for the summoning of a further meeting of the debtor's creditors to consider any revised proposal he may make or, in a case falling within subsection (1)(b), to reconsider his original proposal.

(5)   Where at any time after giving a direction under subsection (4)(b) for the summoning of a meeting to consider a revised proposal the court is satisfied that the debtor does not intend to submit such a proposal, the court shall revoke the direction and revoke or suspend any approval given at the previous meeting.

(6)   Where the court gives a direction under subsection (4)(b), it may also give a direction continuing or, as the case may require, renewing, for such period as may be specified in the direction, the effect in relation to the debtor of any interim order.

(7)   In any case where the court, on an application made under this section with respect to a creditors' meeting, gives a direction under subsection (4)(b) or revokes or suspends an approval under

subsection (4)(a) or (5), the court may give such supplemental directions as it thinks fit and, in particular, directions with respect to—

(a) things done since the meeting under any voluntary arrangement approved by the meeting, and

(b) such things done since the meeting as could not have been done if an interim order had been in force in relation to the debtor when they were done.

(8) Except in pursuance of the preceding provisions of this section, an approval given at a creditors' meeting summoned under section 257 is not invalidated by any irregularity at or in relation to the meeting.

262A. False representations etc

(1) If for the purpose of obtaining the approval of his creditors to a proposal for a voluntary arrangement, the debtor—

(a) makes any false representation, or

(b) fraudulently does, or omits to do, anything,

he commits an offence.

(2) Subsection (1) applies even if the proposal is not approved.

(3) A person guilty of an offence under this section is liable to imprisonment or a fine, or both.

262B. Prosecution of delinquent debtors

(1) This section applies where a voluntary arrangement approved by a creditors' meeting summoned under section 257 has taken effect.

(2) If it appears to the nominee or supervisor that the debtor has been guilty of any offence in connection with the arrangement for which he is criminally liable, he shall forthwith—

(a) report the matter to the Secretary of State, and

(b) provide the Secretary of State with such information and give the Secretary of State such access to and facilities for inspecting and taking copies of documents (being information or documents in his possession or under his control and relating to the matter in question) as the Secretary of State requires.

(3) Where a prosecuting authority institutes criminal proceedings following any report under subsection (2), the nominee or, as the case may be, supervisor shall give the authority all assistance in connection with the prosecution which he is reasonably able to give.

For this purpose, "prosecuting authority" means the Director of Public Prosecutions or the Secretary of State.

(4) The court may, on the application of the prosecuting authority, direct a nominee or supervisor to comply with subsection (3) if he has failed to do so.

262C. Arrangements coming to an end prematurely

For the purposes of this Part, a voluntary arrangement approved by a creditors' meeting summoned under section 257 comes to an end prematurely if, when it ceases to have effect, it has not been fully implemented in respect of all persons bound by the arrangement by virtue of section 260(2)(b)(i).

263. Implementation and supervision of approved voluntary arrangement

(1) This section applies where a voluntary arrangement approved by a creditors' meeting summoned under section 257 has taken effect.

(2) The person who is for the time being carrying out, in relation to the voluntary arrangement, the functions conferred by virtue of the approval on the nominee (or his replacement under section 256(3), 256A(4) or 258(3)) shall be known as the supervisor of the voluntary arrangement.

(3) If the debtor, any of his creditors or any other person is dissatisfied by any act, omission or decision of the supervisor, he may apply to the court; and on such an application the court may—

(a) confirm, reverse or modify any act or decision of the supervisor,

(b) give him directions, or

(c) make such other order as it thinks fit.

(4)   The supervisor may apply to the court for directions in relation to any particular matter arising under the voluntary arrangement.

(5)   The court may, whenever—

    (a)   it is expedient to appoint a person to carry out the functions of the supervisor, and

    (b)   it is inexpedient, difficult or impracticable for an appointment to be made without the assistance of the court,

make an order appointing a person who is qualified to act as an insolvency practitioner or authorised to act as supervisor, in relation to the voluntary arrangement, either in substitution for the existing supervisor or to fill a vacancy.

This is without prejudice to section 41(2) of the Trustee Act 1925 (power of court to appoint trustees of deeds of arrangement).

(6)   The power conferred by subsection (5) is exercisable so as to increase the number of persons exercising the functions of the supervisor or, where there is more than one person exercising those functions, so as to replace one or more of those persons.

Fast-track voluntary arrangement

263A. Availability

Section 263B applies where an individual debtor intends to make a proposal to his creditors for a voluntary arrangement and—

    (a)   the debtor is an undischarged bankrupt,

    (b)   the official receiver is specified in the proposal as the nominee in relation to the voluntary arrangement, and

    (c)   no interim order is applied for under section 253.

263B. Decision

(1)   The debtor may submit to the official receiver—

    (a)   a document setting out the terms of the voluntary arrangement which the debtor is proposing, and

    (b)   a statement of his affairs containing such particulars as may be prescribed of his creditors, debts, other liabilities and assets and such other information as may be prescribed.

(2)   If the official receiver thinks that the voluntary arrangement proposed has a reasonable prospect of being approved and implemented, he may make arrangements for inviting creditors to decide whether to approve it.

(3)   For the purposes of subsection (2) a person is a "creditor" only if—

    (a)   he is a creditor of the debtor in respect of a bankruptcy debt, and

    (b)   the official receiver is aware of his claim and his address.

(4)   Arrangements made under subsection (2)—

    (a)   must include the provision to each creditor of a copy of the proposed voluntary arrangement,

    (b)   must include the provision to each creditor of information about the criteria by reference to which the official receiver will determine whether the creditors approve or reject the proposed voluntary arrangement, and

    (c)   may not include an opportunity for modifications to the proposed voluntary arrangement to be suggested or made.

(5)   Where a debtor submits documents to the official receiver under subsection (1) no application under section 253 for an interim order may be made in respect of the debtor until the official receiver has—

    (a)   made arrangements as described in subsection (2), or

    (b)   informed the debtor that he does not intend to make arrangements (whether because he does not think the voluntary arrangement has a reasonable prospect of being approved and implemented or because he declines to act).

263C. Result

As soon as is reasonably practicable after the implementation of arrangements under section 263B(2) the official receiver shall report to the court whether the proposed voluntary arrangement has been approved or rejected.

263D. Approval of voluntary arrangement

(1) This section applies where the official receiver reports to the court under section 263C that a proposed voluntary arrangement has been approved.

(2) The voluntary arrangement—
   (a) takes effect,
   (b) binds the debtor, and
   (c) binds every person who was entitled to participate in the arrangements made under section 263B(2).

(3) The court shall annul the bankruptcy order in respect of the debtor on an application made by the official receiver.

(4) An application under subsection (3) may not be made—
   (a) during the period specified in section 263F(3) during which the voluntary arrangement can be challenged by application under section 263F(2),
   (b) while an application under that section is pending, or
   (c) while an appeal in respect of an application under that section is pending or may be brought.

(5) The court may give such directions about the conduct of the bankruptcy and the administration of the bankrupt's estate as it thinks appropriate for facilitating the implementation of the approved voluntary arrangement.

(6) The Deeds of Arrangement Act 1914 (c 47) does not apply to the voluntary arrangement.

(7) A reference in this Act or another enactment to a voluntary arrangement approved under this Part includes a reference to a voluntary arrangement which has effect by virtue of this section.

263E. Implementation

Section 263 shall apply to a voluntary arrangement which has effect by virtue of section 263D(2) as it applies to a voluntary arrangement approved by a creditors' meeting.

263F. Revocation

(1) The court may make an order revoking a voluntary arrangement which has effect by virtue of section 263D(2) on the ground—
   (a) that it unfairly prejudices the interests of a creditor of the debtor, or
   (b) that a material irregularity occurred in relation to the arrangements made under section 263B(2).

(2) An order under subsection (1) may be made only on the application of—
   (a) the debtor,
   (b) a person who was entitled to participate in the arrangements made under section 263B(2),
   (c) the trustee of the bankrupt's estate, or
   (d) the official receiver.

(3) An application under subsection (2) may not be made after the end of the period of 28 days beginning with the date on which the official receiver makes his report to the court under section 263C.

(4) But a creditor who was not made aware of the arrangements under section 263B(2) at the time when they were made may make an application under subsection (2) during the period of 28 days beginning with the date on which he becomes aware of the voluntary arrangement.

263G. Offences

(1) Section 262A shall have effect in relation to obtaining approval to a proposal for a voluntary arrangement under section 263D.

(2)   Section 262B shall have effect in relation to a voluntary arrangement which has effect by virtue of section 263D(2) (for which purposes the words "by a creditors' meeting summoned under section 257" shall be disregarded).

PART IX
BANKRUPTCY

CHAPTER I
BANKRUPTCY PETITIONS; BANKRUPTCY ORDERS

Preliminary

264.   Who may present a bankruptcy petition

(1)   A petition for a bankruptcy order to be made against an individual may be presented to the court in accordance with the following provisions of this Part—
   (a)   by one of the individual's creditors or jointly by more than one of them,
   (b)   by the individual himself,
   (ba) by a temporary administrator (within the meaning of Article 38 of the EC Regulation),
   (bb) by a liquidator (within the meaning of Article 2(b) of the EC Regulation) appointed in proceedings by virtue of Article 3(1) of the EC Regulation,
   (c)   by the supervisor of, or any person (other than the individual) who is for the time being bound by, a voluntary arrangement proposed by the individual and approved under Part VIII, *or*
   (d)   *where a criminal bankruptcy order has been made against the individual, by the Official Petitioner or by any person specified in the order in pursuance of section 39(3)(b) of the Powers of Criminal Courts Act 1973.*

(2)   Subject to those provisions, the court may make a bankruptcy order on any such petition.

Note. Subsection (1)(d) and the italicized word preceding it are repealed by the Criminal Justice Act 1988, s. 170(2), Sch. 16, as from a day to be appointed.

265.   Conditions to be satisfied in respect of debtor

(1)   A bankruptcy petition shall not be presented to the court under section 264(1)(a) or (b) unless the debtor—
   (a)   is domiciled in England and Wales,
   (b)   is personally present in England and Wales on the day on which the petition is presented, or
   (c)   at any time in the period of 3 years ending with that day—
         (i)   has been ordinarily resident, or has had a place of residence, in England and Wales, or
         (ii)   has carried on business in England and Wales.

(2)   The reference in subsection (1)(c) to an individual carrying on business includes—
   (a)   the carrying on of business by a firm or partnership of which the individual is a member, and
   (b)   the carrying on of business by an agent or manager for the individual or for such a firm or partnership.

(3)   This section is subject to Article 3 of the EC Regulation.

266.   Other preliminary conditions

(1)   Where a bankruptcy petition relating to an individual is presented by a person who is entitled to present a petition under two or more paragraphs of section 264(1), the petition is to be treated for the purposes of this Part as a petition under such one of those paragraphs as may be specified in the petition.

(2)   A bankruptcy petition shall not be withdrawn without the leave of the court.

(3)   The court has a general power, if it appears to it appropriate to do so on the grounds that there has been a contravention of the rules or for any other reason, to dismiss a bankruptcy petition or to stay proceedings on such a petition; and, where it stays proceedings on a petition, it may do so on such terms and conditions as it thinks fit.

(4)   Without prejudice to subsection (3), where a petition under section 264(1)(a), (b) or (c) in respect of an individual is pending at a time when a criminal bankruptcy order is made against him, or is presented after such an order has been so made, the court may on the application of the Official Petitioner dismiss the petition if it appears to it appropriate to do so.

Note. Subsection (4) is repealed by the Criminal Justice Act 1988, s. 170(2), Sch. 16, as from a day to be appointed.

Creditor's petition

267.   Grounds of creditor's petition

(1)   A creditor's petition must be in respect of one or more debts owed by the debtor, and the petitioning creditor or each of the petitioning creditors must be a person to whom the debt or (as the case may be) at least one of the debts is owed.

(2)   Subject to the next three sections, a creditor's petition may be presented to the court in respect of a debt or debts only if, at the time the petition is presented—

(a)   the amount of the debt, or the aggregate amount of the debts, is equal to or exceeds the bankruptcy level,

(b)   the debt, or each of the debts, is for a liquidated sum payable to the petitioning creditor, or one or more of the petitioning creditors, either immediately or at some certain, future time, and is unsecured,

(c)   the debt, or each of the debts, is a debt which the debtor appears either to be unable to pay or to have no reasonable prospect of being able to pay, and

(d)   there is no outstanding application to set aside a statutory demand served (under section 268 below) in respect of the debt or any of the debts.

(3)   A debt is not to be regarded for the purposes of subsection (2) as a debt for a liquidated sum by reason only that the amount of the debt is specified in a criminal bankruptcy order.

(4)   "The bankruptcy level" is £750; but the Secretary of State may by order in a statutory instrument substitute any amount specified in the order for that amount or (as the case may be) for the amount which by virtue of such an order is for the time being the amount of the bankruptcy level.

(5)   An order shall not be made under subsection (4) unless a draft of it has been laid before, and approved by a resolution of, each House of Parliament.

Note. Subsection (3) is repealed by the Criminal Justice Act 1988, s. 170(2), Sch. 16, as from a day to be appointed.

268.   Definition of "inability to pay", etc; the statutory demand

(1)   For the purposes of section 267(2)(c), the debtor appears to be unable to pay a debt if, but only if, the debt is payable immediately and either—

(a)   the petitioning creditor to whom the debt is owed has served on the debtor a demand (known as "the statutory demand") in the prescribed form requiring him to pay the debt or to secure or compound for it to the satisfaction of the creditor, at least 3 weeks have elapsed since the demand was served and the demand has been neither complied with nor set aside in accordance with the rules, or

(b)   execution or other process issued in respect of the debt on a judgment or order of any court in favour of the petitioning creditor, or one or more of the petitioning creditors to whom the debt is owed, has been returned unsatisfied in whole or in part.

(2)   For the purposes of section 267(2)(c) the debtor appears to have no reasonable prospect of being able to pay a debt if, but only if, the debt is not immediately payable and—

(a)   the petitioning creditor to whom it is owed has served on the debtor a demand (also known as "the statutory demand") in the prescribed form requiring him to establish to the satisfaction of the creditor that there is a reasonable prospect that the debtor will be able to pay the debt when it falls due,

(b)   at least 3 weeks have elapsed since the demand was served, and

(c)   the demand has been neither complied with nor set aside in accordance with the rules.

269.   Creditor with security

(1)   A debt which is the debt, or one of the debts, in respect of which a creditor's petition is presented need not be unsecured if either—

    (a)   the petition contains a statement by the person having the right to enforce the security that he is willing, in the event of a bankruptcy order being made, to give up his security for the benefit of all the bankrupt's creditors, or

    (b)   the petition is expressed not to be made in respect of the secured part of the debt and contains a statement by that person of the estimated value at the date of the petition of the security for the secured part of the debt.

(2)   In a case falling within subsection (1)(b) the secured and unsecured parts of the debt are to be treated for the purposes of sections 267 and 270 as separate debts.

270.   Expedited petition

In the case of a creditor's petition presented wholly or partly in respect of a debt which is the subject of a statutory demand under section 268, the petition may be presented before the end of the 3-week period there mentioned if there is a serious possibility that the debtor's property or the value of any of his property will be significantly diminished during that period and the petition contains a statement to that effect.

271.   Proceedings on creditor's petition

(1)   The court shall not make a bankruptcy order on a creditor's petition unless it is satisfied that the debt, or one of the debts, in respect of which the petition was presented is either—

    (a)   a debt which, having been payable at the date of the petition or having since become payable, has been neither paid nor secured or compounded for, or

    (b)   a debt which the debtor has no reasonable prospect of being able to pay when it falls due.

(2)   In a case in which the petition contains such a statement as is required by section 270, the court shall not make a bankruptcy order until at least 3 weeks have elapsed since the service of any statutory demand under section 268.

(3)   The court may dismiss the petition if it is satisfied that the debtor is able to pay all his debts or is satisfied—

    (a)   that the debtor has made an offer to secure or compound for a debt in respect of which the petition is presented,

    (b)   that the acceptance of that offer would have required the dismissal of the petition, and

    (c)   that the offer has been unreasonably refused;

and, in determining for the purposes of this subsection whether the debtor is able to pay all his debts, the court shall take into account his contingent and prospective liabilities.

(4)   In determining for the purposes of this section what constitutes a reasonable prospect that a debtor will be able to pay a debt when it falls due, it is to be assumed that the prospect given by the facts and other matters known to the creditor at the time he entered into the transaction resulting in the debt was a reasonable prospect.

(5)   Nothing in sections 267 to 271 prejudices the power of the court, in accordance with the rules, to authorise a creditor's petition to be amended by the omission of any creditor or debt and to be proceeded with as if things done for the purposes of those sections had been done only by or in relation to the remaining creditors or debts.

Debtor's petition

272.   Grounds of debtor's petition

(1)   A debtor's petition may be presented to the court only on the grounds that the debtor is unable to pay his debts.

(2)   The petition shall be accompanied by a statement of the debtor's affairs containing—

    (a)   such particulars of the debtor's creditors and of his debts and other liabilities and of his assets as may be prescribed, and

    (b)   such other information as may be prescribed.

273. Appointment of insolvency practitioner by the court

(1)   Subject to the next section, on the hearing of a debtor's petition the court shall not make a bankruptcy order if it appears to the court—

    (a)   that if a bankruptcy order were made the aggregate amount of the bankruptcy debts, so far as unsecured, would be less than the small bankruptcies level,

    (b)   that if a bankruptcy order were made, the value of the bankrupt's estate would be equal to or more than the minimum amount,

    (c)   that within the period of 5 years ending with the presentation of the petition the debtor has neither been adjudged bankrupt nor made a composition with his creditors in satisfaction of his debts or a scheme of arrangement of his affairs, and

    (d)   that it would be appropriate to appoint a person to prepare a report under section 274.

"The minimum amount" and "the small bankruptcies level" mean such amounts as may for the time being be prescribed for the purposes of this section.

(2)   Where on the hearing of the petition, it appears to the court as mentioned in subsection (1), the court shall appoint a person who is qualified to act as an insolvency practitioner in relation to the debtor—

    (a)   to prepare a report under the next section, and

    (b)   subject to section 258(3) in Part VIII, to act in relation to any voluntary arrangement to which the report relates either as trustee or otherwise for the purpose of supervising its implementation.

274. Action on report of insolvency practitioner

(1)   A person appointed under section 273 shall inquire into the debtor's affairs and, within such period as the court may direct, shall submit a report to the court stating whether the debtor is willing, for the purposes of Part VIII, to make a proposal for a voluntary arrangement.

(2)   A report which states that the debtor is willing as above mentioned shall also state—

    (a)   whether, in the opinion of the person making the report, a meeting of the debtor's creditors should be summoned to consider the proposal, and

    (b)   if in that person's opinion such a meeting should be summoned, the date on which, and time and place at which, he proposes the meeting should be held.

(3)   On considering a report under this section the court may—

    (a)   without any application, make an interim order under section 252, if it thinks that it is appropriate to do so for the purpose of facilitating the consideration and implementation of the debtor's proposal, or

    (b)   if it thinks it would be inappropriate to make such an order, make a bankruptcy order.

(4)   An interim order made by virtue of this section ceases to have effect at the end of such period as the court may specify for the purpose of enabling the debtor's proposal to be considered by his creditors in accordance with the applicable provisions of Part VIII.

(5)   Where it has been reported to the court under this section that a meeting of the debtor's creditors should be summoned, the person making the report shall, unless the court otherwise directs, summon that meeting for the time, date and place proposed in his report.

The meeting is then deemed to have been summoned under section 257 in Part VIII, and subsections (2) and (3) of that section, and sections 258 to 263 apply accordingly.

275.   ...

Other cases for special consideration

276. Default in connection with voluntary arrangement

(1)   The court shall not make a bankruptcy order on a petition under section 264(1)(c) (supervisor of, or person bound by, voluntary arrangement proposed and approved) unless it is satisfied—

    (a)   that the debtor has failed to comply with his obligations under the voluntary arrangement, or

    (b)   that information which was false or misleading in any material particular or which contained material omissions—

      (i)   was contained in any statement of affairs or other document supplied by the debtor under Part VIII to any person, or

      (ii)   was otherwise made available by the debtor to his creditors at or in connection with a meeting summoned under that Part, or

  (c)   that the debtor has failed to do all such things as may for the purposes of the voluntary arrangement have been reasonably required of him by the supervisor of the arrangement.

(2)   Where a bankruptcy order is made on a petition under section 264(1)(c), any expenses properly incurred as expenses of the administration of the voluntary arrangement in question shall be a first charge on the bankrupt's estate.

277.   Petition based on criminal bankruptcy order

(1)   Subject to section 266(3), the court shall make a bankruptcy order on a petition under section 264(1)(d) on production of a copy of the criminal bankruptcy order on which the petition is based. This does not apply if it appears to the court that the criminal bankruptcy order has been rescinded on appeal.

(2)   Subject to the provisions of this Part, the fact that an appeal is pending against any conviction by virtue of which a criminal bankruptcy order was made does not affect any proceedings on a petition under section 264(1)(d) based on that order.

(3)   For the purposes of this section, an appeal against a conviction is pending—

  (a)   in any case, until the expiration of the period of 28 days beginning with the date of conviction;

  (b)   if notice of appeal to the Court of Appeal is given during that period and during that period the appellant notifies the official receiver of it, until the determination of the appeal and thereafter for so long as an appeal to the House of Lords is pending within the meaning of section 40(5) of the Powers of Criminal Courts Act 1973.

Note. This section is repealed by the Criminal Justice Act 1988, s. 170(2), Sch. 16, as from a day to be appointed.

Commencement and duration of bankruptcy; discharge

278.   Commencement and continuance

The bankruptcy of an individual against whom a bankruptcy order has been made—

  (a)   commences with the day on which the order is made, and

  (b)   continues until the individual is discharged under the following provisions of this Chapter.

279.   Duration

(1)   A bankrupt is discharged from bankruptcy at the end of the period of one year beginning with the date on which the bankruptcy commences.

(2)   If before the end of that period the official receiver files with the court a notice stating that investigation of the conduct and affairs of the bankrupt under section 289 is unnecessary or concluded, the bankrupt is discharged when the notice is filed.

(3)   On the application of the official receiver or the trustee of a bankrupt's estate, the court may order that the period specified in subsection (1) shall cease to run until—

  (a)   the end of a specified period, or

  (b)   the fulfilment of a specified condition.

(4)   The court may make an order under subsection (3) only if satisfied that the bankrupt has failed or is failing to comply with an obligation under this Part.

(5)   In subsection (3)(b) "condition" includes a condition requiring that the court be satisfied of something.

(6)   In the case of an individual who is adjudged bankrupt on a petition under section 264(1)(d)—

  (a)   subsections (1) to (5) shall not apply, and

  (b)   the bankrupt is discharged from bankruptcy by an order of the court under section 280.

(7)   This section is without prejudice to any power of the court to annul a bankruptcy order.

280.   **Discharge by order of the court**

(1)   An application for an order of the court discharging an individual from bankruptcy in a case falling within section 279(6) may be made by the bankrupt at any time after the end of the period of 5 years beginning with the date on which the bankruptcy commences.

(2)   On an application under this section the court may—

     (a)   refuse to discharge the bankrupt from bankruptcy,

     (b)   make an order discharging him absolutely, or

     (c)   make an order discharging him subject to such conditions with respect to any income which may subsequently become due to him, or with respect to property devolving upon him, or acquired by him, after his discharge, as may be specified in the order.

(3)   The court may provide for an order falling within subsection (2)(b) or (c) to have immediate effect or to have its effect suspended for such period, or until the fulfilment of such conditions (including a condition requiring the court to be satisfied as to any matter), as may be specified in the order.

281.   **Effect of discharge**

(1)   Subject as follows, where a bankrupt is discharged, the discharge releases him from all the bankruptcy debts, but has no effect—

     (a)   on the functions (so far as they remain to be carried out) of the trustee of his estate, or

     (b)   on the operation, for the purposes of the carrying out of those functions, of the provisions of this Part;

and, in particular, discharge does not affect the right of any creditor of the bankrupt to prove in the bankruptcy for any debt from which the bankrupt is released.

(2)   Discharge does not affect the right of any secured creditor of the bankrupt to enforce his security for the payment of a debt from which the bankrupt is released.

(3)   Discharge does not release the bankrupt from any bankruptcy debt which he incurred in respect of, or forbearance in respect of which was secured by means of, any fraud or fraudulent breach of trust to which he was a party.

(4)   Discharge does not release the bankrupt from any liability in respect of a fine imposed for an offence or from any liability under a recognisance except, in the case of a penalty imposed for an offence under an enactment relating to the public revenue or of a recognisance, with the consent of the Treasury.

(4A)   In subsection (4) the reference to a fine includes a reference to a confiscation order under Part 2, 3 or 4 of the Proceeds of Crime Act 2002.

(5)   Discharge does not, except to such extent and on such conditions as the court may direct, release the bankrupt from any bankruptcy debt which—

     (a)   consists in a liability to pay damages for negligence, nuisance or breach of a statutory, contractual or other duty, or to pay damages by virtue of Part I of the Consumer Protection Act 1987, being in either case damages in respect of personal injuries to any person, or

     (b)   arises under any order made in family proceedings or under a *maintenance assessment [maintenance calculation]* made under the Child Support Act 1991 ... .

(6)   Discharge does not release the bankrupt from such other bankruptcy debts, not being debts provable in his bankruptcy, as are prescribed.

(7)   Discharge does not release any person other than the bankrupt from any liability (whether as partner or co-trustee of the bankrupt or otherwise) from which the bankrupt is released by the discharge, or from any liability as surety for the bankrupt or as a person in the nature of such a surety.

(8)   In this section—

     "family proceedings" means—

       (a)   family proceedings within the meaning of the Magistrates' Courts Act 1980 and any proceedings which would be such proceedings but for section 65(1)(ii) of that Act (proceedings for variation of order for periodical payments); and

(b)   family proceedings within the meaning of Part V of the Matrimonial and Family Proceedings Act 1984;

"fine" means the same as in the Magistrates' Courts Act 1980; and

"personal injuries" includes death and any disease or other impairment of a person's physical or mental condition.

Note. The words "maintenance assessment" in subsection (5)(b) are repealed and the subsequent italicized words in square brackets are substituted by the Child Support, Pensions and Social Security Act 2000, s. 26, Sch. 3, para. 6, from 3 March 2003 in relation to certain cases (see S.I. 2003/192) and as from a day to be appointed otherwise.

281A.   Post-discharge restrictions

Schedule 4A to this Act (bankruptcy restrictions order and bankruptcy restrictions undertaking) shall have effect.

282.   Court's power to annul bankruptcy order

(1)   The court may annul a bankruptcy order if it at any time appears to the court—

(a)   that, on the grounds existing at the time the order was made, the order ought not to have been made, or

(b)   that, to the extent required by the rules, the bankruptcy debts and the expenses of the bankruptcy have all, since the making of the order, been either paid or secured for to the satisfaction of the court.

(2)   *The court may annual a bankruptcy order made against an individual on a petition under paragraph (a), (b) or (c) of section 264(1) if it at any time appears to the court, on an application by the Official Petitioner—*

(a)   *that the petition was pending at a time when a criminal bankruptcy order was made against the individual or was presented after such an order was so made, and*

(b)   *no appeal is pending (within the meaning of section 277) against the individual's conviction of any offence by virtue of which the criminal bankruptcy order was made;*

and the court shall annul a bankruptcy order made on a petition under section 264(1)(d) if it at any time appears to the court that the criminal bankruptcy order on which the petition was based has been rescinded in consequence of an appeal.

(3)   The court may annul a bankruptcy order whether or not the bankrupt has been discharged from the bankruptcy.

(4)   Where the court annuls a bankruptcy order (whether under this section or under section 261 or 263D in Part VIII)—

(a)   any sale or other disposition of property, payment made or other thing duly done, under any provision in this Group of Parts, by or under the authority of the official receiver or a trustee of the bankrupt's estate or by the court is valid, but

(b)   if any of the bankrupt's estate is then vested, under any such provision, in such a trustee, it shall vest in such person as the court may appoint or, in default of any such appointment, revert to the bankrupt on such terms (if any) as the court may direct;

and the court may include in its order such supplemental provisions as may be authorised by the rules.

(5)   ...

Note. Subsection (2) is repealed by the Criminal Justice Act 1988, s. 170(2), Sch. 16, as from a day to be appointed.

CHAPTER II
PROTECTION OF BANKRUPT'S ESTATE AND
INVESTIGATION OF HIS AFFAIRS

283.   Definition of bankrupt's estate

(1)   Subject as follows, a bankrupt's estate for the purposes of any of this Group of Parts comprises—

(a)   all property belonging to or vested in the bankrupt at the commencement of the bankruptcy, and

(b)   any property which by virtue of any of the following provisions of this Part is comprised in that estate or is treated as falling within the preceding paragraph.

(2)   Subsection (1) does not apply to—

(a)   such tools, books, vehicles and other items of equipment as are necessary to the bankrupt for use personally by him in his employment, business or vocation;

(b)   such clothing, bedding, furniture, household equipment and provisions as are necessary for satisfying the basic domestic needs of the bankrupt and his family.

This subsection is subject to section 308 in Chapter IV (certain excluded property reclaimable by trustee).

(3)   Subsection (1) does not apply to—

(a)   property held by the bankrupt on trust for any other person, or

(b)   the right of nomination to a vacant ecclesiastical benefice.

(3A)   Subject to section 308A in Chapter IV, subsection (1) does not apply to—

(a)   a tenancy which is an assured tenancy or an assured agricultural occupancy, within the meaning of Part I of the Housing Act 1988, and the terms of which inhibit an assignment as mentioned in section 127(5) of the Rent Act 1977, or

(b)   a protected tenancy, within the meaning of the Rent Act 1977, in respect of which, by virtue of any provision of Part IX of that Act, no premium can lawfully be required as a condition of assignment, or

(c)   a tenancy of a dwelling-house by virtue of which the bankrupt is, within the meaning of the Rent (Agriculture) Act 1976, a protected occupier of the dwelling-house, and the terms of which inhibit an assignment as mentioned in section 127(5) of the Rent Act 1977, or

(d)   a secure tenancy, within the meaning of Part IV of the Housing Act 1985, which is not capable of being assigned, except in the cases mentioned in section 91(3) of that Act.

(4)   References in any of this Group of Parts to property, in relation to a bankrupt, include references to any power exercisable by him over or in respect of property except in so far as the power is exercisable over or in respect of property not for the time being comprised in the bankrupt's estate and—

(a)   is so exercisable at a time after either the official receiver has had his release in respect of that estate under section 299(2) in Chapter III or a meeting summoned by the trustee of that estate under section 331 in Chapter IV has been held, or

(b)   cannot be so exercised for the benefit of the bankrupt;

and a power exercisable over or in respect of property is deemed for the purposes of any of this Group of Parts to vest in the person entitled to exercise it at the time of the transaction or event by virtue of which it is exercisable by that person (whether or not it becomes so exercisable at that time).

(5)   For the purposes of any such provision in this Group of Parts, property comprised in a bankrupt's estate is so comprised subject to the rights of any person other than the bankrupt (whether as a secured creditor of the bankrupt or otherwise) in relation thereto, but disregarding—

(a)   any rights in relation to which a statement such as is required by section 269(1)(a) was made in the petition on which the bankrupt was adjudged bankrupt, and

(b)   any rights which have been otherwise given up in accordance with the rules.

(6)   This section has effect subject to the provisions of any enactment not contained in this Act under which any property is to be excluded from a bankrupt's estate.

283A.   Bankrupt's home ceasing to form part of estate

(1)   This section applies where property comprised in the bankrupt's estate consists of an interest in a dwelling-house which at the date of the bankruptcy was the sole or principal residence of—

(a)   the bankrupt,

(b)   the bankrupt's spouse *or civil partner*, or

(c)   a former spouse *or former civil partner* of the bankrupt.

(2)   At the end of the period of three years beginning with the date of the bankruptcy the interest mentioned in subsection (1) shall—

         (a)   cease to be comprised in the bankrupt's estate, and

         (b)   vest in the bankrupt (without conveyance, assignment or transfer).

(3)   Subsection (2) shall not apply if during the period mentioned in that subsection—

         (a)   the trustee realises the interest mentioned in subsection (1),

         (b)   the trustee applies for an order for sale in respect of the dwelling-house,

         (c)   the trustee applies for an order for possession of the dwelling-house,

         (d)   the trustee applies for an order under section 313 in Chapter IV in respect of that interest, or

         (e)   the trustee and the bankrupt agree that the bankrupt shall incur a specified liability to his estate (with or without the addition of interest from the date of the agreement) in consideration of which the interest mentioned in subsection (1) shall cease to form part of the estate.

(4)   Where an application of a kind described in subsection (3)(b) to (d) is made during the period mentioned in subsection (2) and is dismissed, unless the court orders otherwise the interest to which the application relates shall on the dismissal of the application—

         (a)   cease to be comprised in the bankrupt's estate, and

         (b)   vest in the bankrupt (without conveyance, assignment or transfer).

(5)   If the bankrupt does not inform the trustee or the official receiver of his interest in a property before the end of the period of three months beginning with the date of the bankruptcy, the period of three years mentioned in subsection (2)—

         (a)   shall not begin with the date of the bankruptcy, but

         (b)   shall begin with the date on which the trustee or official receiver becomes aware of the bankrupt's interest.

(6)   The court may substitute for the period of three years mentioned in subsection (2) a longer period—

         (a)   in prescribed circumstances, and

         (b)   in such other circumstances as the court thinks appropriate.

(7)   The rules may make provision for this section to have effect with the substitution of a shorter period for the period of three years mentioned in subsection (2) in specified circumstances (which may be described by reference to action to be taken by a trustee in bankruptcy).

(8)   The rules may also, in particular, make provision—

         (a)   requiring or enabling the trustee of a bankrupt's estate to give notice that this section applies or does not apply;

         (b)   about the effect of a notice under paragraph (a);

         (c)   requiring the trustee of a bankrupt's estate to make an application to the Chief Land Registrar.

(9)   Rules under subsection (8)(b) may, in particular—

         (a)   disapply this section;

         (b)   enable a court to disapply this section;

         (c)   make provision in consequence of a disapplication of this section;

         (d)   enable a court to make provision in consequence of a disapplication of this section;

         (e)   make provision (which may include provision conferring jurisdiction on a court or tribunal) about compensation.

Note. The italicized words in subsection (1) are inserted by the Civil Partnership Act 2004, s. 261(1), Sch. 27, para. 113, as from a day to be appointed.

284.   Restrictions on dispositions of property

(1)   Where a person is adjudged bankrupt, any disposition of property made by that person in the period to which this section applies is void except to the extent that it is or was made with the consent of the court, or is or was subsequently ratified by the court.

(2)   Subsection (1) applies to a payment (whether in cash or otherwise) as it applies to a disposition of property and, accordingly, where any payment is void by virtue of that subsection, the person paid shall hold the sum paid for the bankrupt as part of his estate.

(3)   This section applies to the period beginning with the day of the presentation of the petition for the bankruptcy order and ending with the vesting, under Chapter IV of this Part, of the bankrupt's estate in a trustee.

(4)   The preceding provisions of this section do not give a remedy against any person—

    (a)   in respect of any property or payment which he received before the commencement of the bankruptcy in good faith, for value and without notice that the petition had been presented, or

    (b)   in respect of any interest in property which derives from an interest in respect of which there is, by virtue of this subsection, no remedy.

(5)   Where after the commencement of his bankruptcy the bankrupt has incurred a debt to a banker or other person by reason of the making of a payment which is void under this section, that debt is deemed for the purposes of any of this Group of Parts to have been incurred before the commencement of the bankruptcy unless—

    (a)   that banker or person had notice of the bankruptcy before the debt was incurred, or

    (b)   it is not reasonably practicable for the amount of the payment to be recovered from the person to whom it was made.

(6)   A disposition of property is void under this section notwithstanding that the property is not or, as the case may be, would not be comprised in the bankrupt's estate; but nothing in this section affects any disposition made by a person of property held by him on trust for any other person.

285. Restriction on proceedings and remedies

(1)   At any time when proceedings on a bankruptcy petition are pending or an individual has been adjudged bankrupt the court may stay any action, execution or other legal process against the property or person of the debtor or, as the case may be, of the bankrupt.

(2)   Any court in which proceedings are pending against any individual may, on proof that a bankruptcy petition has been presented in respect of that individual or that he is an undischarged bankrupt, either stay the proceedings or allow them to continue on such terms as it thinks fit.

(3)   After the making of a bankruptcy order no person who is a creditor of the bankrupt in respect of a debt provable in the bankruptcy shall—

    (a)   have any remedy against the property or person of the bankrupt in respect of that debt, or

    (b)   before the discharge of the bankrupt, commence any action or other legal proceedings against the bankrupt except with the leave of the court and on such terms as the court may impose.

    This is subject to sections 346 (enforcement procedures) and 347 (limited right to distress).

(4)   Subject as follows, subsection (3) does not affect the right of a secured creditor of the bankrupt to enforce his security.

(5)   Where any goods of an undischarged bankrupt are held by any person by way of pledge, pawn or other security, the official receiver may, after giving notice in writing of his intention to do so, inspect the goods.

    Where such a notice has been given to any person, that person is not entitled, without leave of the court, to realise his security unless he has given the trustee of the bankrupt's estate a reasonable opportunity of inspecting the goods and of exercising the bankrupt's right of redemption.

(6)   References in this section to the property or goods of the bankrupt are to any of his property or goods, whether or not comprised in his estate.

286. Power to appoint interim receiver

(1)   The court may, if it is shown to be necessary for the protection of the debtor's property, at any time after the presentation of a bankruptcy petition and before making a bankruptcy order, appoint the official receiver to be interim receiver of the debtor's property.

(2)   Where the court has, on a debtor's petition, appointed an insolvency practitioner under section 273 and it is shown to the court as mentioned in subsection (1) of this section, the court may, without making a bankruptcy order, appoint that practitioner, instead of the official receiver, to be interim receiver of the debtor's property.

(3)   The court may by an order appointing any person to be an interim receiver direct that his powers shall be limited or restricted in any respect; but, save as so directed, an interim receiver has, in relation to the debtor's property, all the rights, powers, duties and immunities of a receiver and manager under the next section.

(4)   An order of the court appointing any person to be an interim receiver shall require that person to take immediate possession of the debtor's property or, as the case may be, the part of it to which his powers as interim receiver are limited.

(5)   Where an interim receiver has been appointed, the debtor shall give him such inventory of his property and such other information, and shall attend on the interim receiver at such times, as the latter may for the purpose of carrying out his functions under this section reasonably require.

(6)   Where an interim receiver is appointed, section 285(3) applies for the period between the appointment and the making of a bankruptcy order on the petition, or the dismissal of the petition, as if the appointment were the making of such an order.

(7)   A person ceases to be interim receiver of a debtor's property if the bankruptcy petition relating to the debtor is dismissed, if a bankruptcy order is made on the petition or if the court by order otherwise terminates the appointment.

(8)   References in this section to the debtor's property are to all his property, whether or not it would be comprised in his estate if he were adjudged bankrupt.

287.   Receivership pending appointment of trustee

(1)   Between the making of a bankruptcy order and the time at which the bankrupt's estate vests in a trustee under Chapter IV of this Part, the official receiver is the receiver and (subject to section 370 (special manager)) the manager of the bankrupt's estate and is under a duty to act as such.

(2)   The function of the official receiver while acting as receiver or manager of the bankrupt's estate under this section is to protect the estate; and for this purpose—

(a)   he has the same powers as if he were a receiver or manager appointed by the High Court, and

(b)   he is entitled to sell or otherwise dispose of any perishable goods comprised in the estate and any other goods so comprised the value of which is likely to diminish if they are not disposed of.

(3)   The official receiver while acting as receiver or manager of the estate under this section—

(a)   shall take all such steps as he thinks fit for protecting any property which may be claimed for the estate by the trustee of that estate,

(b)   is not, except in pursuance of directions given by the Secretary of State, required to do anything that involves his incurring expenditure,

(c)   may, if he thinks fit (and shall, if so directed by the court) at any time summon a general meeting of the bankrupt's creditors.

(4)   Where—

(a)   the official receiver acting as receiver or manager of the estate under this section seizes or disposes of any property which is not comprised in the estate, and

(b)   at the time of the seizure or disposal the official receiver believes, and has reasonable grounds for believing, that he is entitled (whether in pursuance of an order of the court or otherwise) to seize or dispose of that property,

the official receiver is not to be liable to any person in respect of any loss or damage resulting from the seizure or disposal except in so far as that loss or damage is caused by his negligence; and he has a lien on the property, or the proceeds of its sale, for such of the expenses of the bankruptcy as were incurred in connection with the seizure or disposal.

(5)   This section does not apply where by virtue of section 297 (appointment of trustee; special cases) the bankrupt's estate vests in a trustee immediately on the making of the bankruptcy order.

288. Statement of affairs

(1) Where a bankruptcy order has been made otherwise than on a debtor's petition, the bankrupt shall submit a statement of his affairs to the official receiver before the end of the period of 21 days beginning with the commencement of the bankruptcy.

(2) The statement of affairs shall contain—

(a) such particulars of the bankrupt's creditors and of his debts and other liabilities and of his assets as may be prescribed, and

(b) such other information as may be prescribed.

(3) The official receiver may, if he thinks fit—

(a) release the bankrupt from his duty under subsection (1), or

(b) extend the period specified in that subsection;

and where the official receiver has refused to exercise a power conferred by this section, the court, if it thinks fit, may exercise it.

(4) A bankrupt who—

(a) without reasonable excuse fails to comply with the obligation imposed by this section, or

(b) without reasonable excuse submits a statement of affairs that does not comply with the prescribed requirements,

is guilty of a contempt of court and liable to be punished accordingly (in addition to any other punishment to which he may be subject).

289. Investigatory duties of official receiver

(1) The official receiver shall—

(a) investigate the conduct and affairs of each bankrupt (including his conduct and affairs before the making of the bankruptcy order), and

(b) make such report (if any) to the court as the official receiver thinks fit.

(2) Subsection (1) shall not apply to a case in which the official receiver thinks an investigation under that subsection unnecessary.

(3) Where a bankrupt makes an application for discharge under section 280—

(a) the official receiver shall make a report to the court about such matters as may be prescribed, and

(b) the court shall consider the report before determining the application.

(4) A report by the official receiver under this section shall in any proceedings be prima facie evidence of the facts stated in it.

290. Public examination of bankrupt

(1) Where a bankruptcy order has been made, the official receiver may at any time before the discharge of the bankrupt apply to the court for the public examination of the bankrupt.

(2) Unless the court otherwise orders, the official receiver shall make an application under subsection (1) if notice requiring him to do so is given to him, in accordance with the rules, by one of the bankrupt's creditors with the concurrence of not less than one-half, in value, of those creditors (including the creditor giving notice).

(3) On an application under subsection (1), the court shall direct that a public examination of the bankrupt shall be held on a day appointed by the court; and the bankrupt shall attend on that day and be publicly examined as to his affairs, dealings and property.

(4) The following may take part in the public examination of the bankrupt and may question him concerning his affairs, dealings and property and the causes of his failure, namely—

(a) the official receiver and, in the case of an individual adjudged bankrupt on a petition under section 264(1)(d), the Official Petitioner,

(b) the trustee of the bankrupt's estate, if his appointment has taken effect,

(c) any person who has been appointed as special manager of the bankrupt's estate or business,

(d) any creditor of the bankrupt who has tendered a proof in the bankruptcy.

(5)   If a bankrupt without reasonable excuse fails at any time to attend his public examination under this section he is guilty of a contempt of court and liable to be punished accordingly (in addition to any other punishment to which he may be subject).

291.   **Duties of bankrupt in relation to official receiver**

(1)   Where a bankruptcy order has been made, the bankrupt is under a duty—

     (a)   to deliver possession of his estate to the official receiver, and

     (b)   to deliver up to the official receiver all books, papers and other records of which he has possession or control and which relate to his estate and affairs (including any which would be privileged from disclosure in any proceedings).

(2)   In the case of any part of the bankrupt's estate which consists of things possession of which cannot be delivered to the official receiver, and in the case of any property that may be claimed for the bankrupt's estate by the trustee, it is the bankrupt's duty to do all such things as may reasonably be required by the official receiver for the protection of those things or that property.

(3)   Subsections (1) and (2) do not apply where by virtue of section 297 below the bankrupt's estate vests in a trustee immediately on the making of the bankruptcy order.

(4)   The bankrupt shall give the official receiver such inventory of his estate and such other information, and shall attend on the official receiver at such times, as the official receiver may reasonably require—

     (a)   for a purpose of this Chapter, or

     (b)   in connection with the making of a bankruptcy restrictions order.

(5)   Subsection (4) applies to a bankrupt after his discharge.

(6)   If the bankrupt without reasonable excuse fails to comply with any obligation imposed by this section, he is guilty of a contempt of court and liable to be punished accordingly (in addition to any other punishment to which he may be subject).

CHAPTER III

TRUSTEES IN BANKRUPTCY

Tenure of office as trustee

292.   **Power to make appointments**

(1)   The power to appoint a person as trustee of a bankrupt's estate (whether the first such trustee or a trustee appointed to fill any vacancy) is exercisable—

     (a)   … by a general meeting of the bankrupt's creditors;

     (b)   under section 295(2), 296(2) or 300(6) below in this Chapter, by the Secretary of State; or

     (c)   under section 297, by the court.

(2)   No person may be appointed as trustee of a bankrupt's estate unless he is, at the time of the appointment, qualified to act as an insolvency practitioner in relation to the bankrupt.

(3)   Any power to appoint a person as trustee of a bankrupt's estate includes power to appoint two or more persons as joint trustees; but such an appointment must make provision as to the circumstances in which the trustees must act together and the circumstances in which one or more of them may act for the others.

(4)   The appointment of any person as trustee takes effect only if that person accepts the appointment in accordance with the rules. Subject to this, the appointment of any person as trustee takes effect at the time specified in his certificate of appointment.

(5)   This section is without prejudice to the provisions of this Chapter under which the official receiver is, in certain circumstances, to be trustee of the estate.

293.   **Summoning of meeting to appoint first trustee**

(1)   Where a bankruptcy order has been made … it is the duty of the official receiver, as soon as practicable in the period of 12 weeks beginning with the day on which the order was made, to decide whether to summon a general meeting of the bankrupt's creditors for the purpose of appointing a trustee of the bankrupt's estate.

This section does not apply where the bankruptcy order was made on a petition under section 264(1)(d) (criminal bankruptcy); and it is subject to the provision made in sections 294(3) and 297(6) below.

(2) Subject to the next section, if the official receiver decides not to summon such a meeting, he shall, before the end of the period of 12 weeks above mentioned, give notice of his decision to the court and to every creditor of the bankrupt who is known to the official receiver or is identified in the bankrupt's statement of affairs.

(3) As from the giving to the court of a notice under subsection (2), the official receiver is the trustee of the bankrupt's estate.

Note. The italicized words in subsection (1) are repealed by the Criminal Justice Act 1988, s. 170(2), Sch. 16, as from a day to be appointed.

294. Power of creditors to requisition meeting

(1) Where in the case of any bankruptcy—

(a) the official receiver has not yet summoned, or has decided not to summon, a general meeting of the bankrupt's creditors for the purpose of appointing the trustee, ...

any creditor of the bankrupt may request the official receiver to summon such a meeting for that purpose.

(2) If such a request appears to the official receiver to be made with the concurrence of not less than one-quarter, in value, of the bankrupt's creditors (including the creditor making the request), it is the duty of the official receiver to summon the requested meeting.

(3) Accordingly, where the duty imposed by subsection (2) has arisen, the official receiver is required neither to reach a decision for the purposes of section 293(1) nor (if he has reached one) to serve any notice under section 293(2).

295. Failure of meeting to appoint trustee

(1) If a meeting summoned under section 293 or 294 is held but no appointment of a person as trustee is made, it is the duty of the official receiver to decide whether to refer the need for an appointment to the Secretary of State.

(2) On a reference made in pursuance of that decision, the Secretary of State shall either make an appointment or decline to make one.

(3) If—

(a) the official receiver decides not to refer the need for an appointment to the Secretary of State, or

(b) on such a reference the Secretary of State declines to make an appointment,

the official receiver shall give notice of his decision or, as the case may be, of the Secretary of State's decision to the court.

(4) As from the giving of notice under subsection (3) in a case in which no notice has been given under section 293(2), the official receiver shall be trustee of the bankrupt's estate.

296. Appointment of trustee by Secretary of State

(1) At any time when the official receiver is the trustee of a bankrupt's estate by virtue of any provision of this Chapter (other than section 297(1) below) he may apply to the Secretary of State for the appointment of a person as trustee instead of the official receiver.

(2) On an application under subsection (1) the Secretary of State shall either make an appointment or decline to make one.

(3) Such an application may be made notwithstanding that the Secretary of State has declined to make an appointment either on a previous application under subsection (1) or on a reference under section 295 or under section 300(4) below.

(4) Where the trustee of a bankrupt's estate has been appointed by the Secretary of State (whether under this section or otherwise), the trustee shall give notice to the bankrupt's creditors of his appointment or, if the court so allows, shall advertise his appointment in accordance with the court's directions.

(5) In that notice or advertisement the trustee shall—

(a) state whether he proposes to summon a general meeting of the bankrupt's creditors for the purposes of establishing a creditor's committee under section 301, and

(b) if he does not propose to summon such a meeting, set out the power of the creditors under this Part to require him to summon one.

297. Special cases

(1) Where a bankruptcy order is made on a petition under section 264(1)(d) (criminal bankruptcy), the official receiver shall be trustee of the bankrupt's estate.

(2), (3) …

(4) Where a bankruptcy order is made in a case in which an insolvency practitioner's report has been submitted to the court under section 274 …, the court, if it thinks fit, may on making the order appoint the person who made the report as trustee.

(5) Where a bankruptcy order is made (whether or not on a petition under section 264(1)(c)) at a time when there is a supervisor of a voluntary arrangement approved in relation to the bankrupt under Part VIII, the court, if it thinks fit, may on making the order appoint the supervisor of the arrangement as trustee.

(6) Where an appointment is made under subsection (4) or (5) of this section, the official receiver is not under the duty imposed by section 293(1) (to decide whether or not to summon a meeting of creditors).

(7) Where the trustee of a bankrupt's estate has been appointed by the court, the trustee shall give notice to the bankrupt's creditors of his appointment or, if the court so allows, shall advertise his appointment in accordance with the directions of the court.

(8) In that notice or advertisement he shall—

(a) state whether he proposes to summon a general meeting of the bankrupt's creditors for the purpose of establishing a creditor's committee under section 301 below, and

(b) if he does not propose to summon such a meeting, set out the power of the creditors under this Part to require him to summon one.

Note. Subsection (1) is repealed by the Criminal Justice Act 1988, s. 170(2), Sch. 16, as from a day to be appointed.

298. Removal of trustee; vacation of office

(1) Subject as follows, the trustee of a bankrupt's estate may be removed from office only by an order of the court or by a general meeting of the bankrupt's creditors summoned specially for that purpose in accordance with the rules.

(2) Where the official receiver is trustee by virtue of section 297(1), he shall not be removed from office under this section.

(3) …

(4) Where the official receiver is trustee by virtue of section 293(3) or 295(4) or a trustee is appointed by the Secretary of State or (otherwise than under section 297(5)) by the court, a general meeting of the bankrupt's creditors shall be summoned for the purpose of replacing the trustee only if—

(a) the trustee thinks fit, or

(b) the court so directs, or

(c) the meeting is requested by one of the bankrupt's creditors with the concurrence of not less than one-quarter, in value, of the creditors (including the creditor making the request).

(5) If the trustee was appointed by the Secretary of State, he may be removed by a direction of the Secretary of State.

(6) The trustee (not being the official receiver) shall vacate office if he ceases to be a person who is for the time being qualified to act as an insolvency practitioner in relation to the bankrupt.

(7) The trustee may, in the prescribed circumstances, resign his office by giving notice of his resignation to the court.

(8) The trustee shall vacate office on giving notice to the court that a final meeting has been held under section 331 in Chapter IV and of the decision (if any) of that meeting.

(9) The trustee shall vacate office if the bankruptcy order is annulled.

299.   Release of trustee

(1)   Where the official receiver has ceased to be the trustee of a bankrupt's estate and a person is appointed in his stead, the official receiver shall have his release with effect from the following time, that is to say—

(a)   where that person is appointed by a general meeting of the bankrupt's creditors or by the Secretary of State, the time at which the official receiver gives notice to the court that he has been replaced, and

(b)   where that person is appointed by the court, such time as the court may determine.

(2)   If the official receiver while he is the trustee gives notice to the Secretary of State that the administration of the bankrupt's estate in accordance with Chapter IV of this Part is for practical purposes complete, he shall have his release with effect from such time as the Secretary of State may determine.

(3)   A person other than the official receiver who has ceased to be the trustee shall have his release with effect from the following time, that is to say—

(a)   in the case of a person who has been removed from office by a general meeting of the bankrupt's creditors that has not resolved against his release or who has died, the time at which notice is given to the court in accordance with the rules that that person has ceased to hold office;

(b)   in the case of a person who has been removed from office by a general meeting of the bankrupt's creditors that has resolved against his release, or by the court, or by the Secretary of State, or who has vacated office under section 298(6), such time as the Secretary of State may, on an application by that person, determine;

(c)   in the case of a person who has resigned, such time as may be prescribed;

(d)   in the case of a person who has vacated office under section 298(8)—

(i)   if the final meeting referred to in that subsection has resolved against that person's release, such time as the Secretary of State may, on an application by that person, determine; and

(ii)   if that meeting has not so resolved, the time at which the person vacated office.

(4)   Where a bankruptcy order is annulled, the trustee at the time of the annulment has his release with effect from such time as the court may determine.

(5)   Where the official receiver or the trustee has his release under this section, he shall, with effect from the time specified in the preceding provisions of this section, be discharged from all liability both in respect of acts or omissions of his in the administration of the estate and otherwise in relation to his conduct as trustee.

But nothing in this section prevents the exercise, in relation to a person who has had his release under this section, of the court's powers under section 304.

300.   Vacancy in office of trustee

(1)   This section applies where the appointment of any person as trustee of a bankrupt's estate fails to take effect or, such an appointment having taken effect, there is otherwise a vacancy in the office of trustee.

(2)   The official receiver shall be trustee until the vacancy is filled.

(3)   The official receiver may summon a general meeting of the bankrupt's creditors for the purpose of filling the vacancy and shall summon such a meeting if required to do so in pursuance of section 314(7) (creditors' requisition).

(4)   If at the end of the period of 28 days beginning with the day on which the vacancy first came to the official receiver's attention he has not summoned, and is not proposing to summon, a general meeting of creditors for the purpose of filling the vacancy, he shall refer the need for an appointment to the Secretary of State.

(5)   ...

(6)   On a reference to the Secretary of State under subsection (4) ... the Secretary of State shall either make an appointment or decline to make one.

(7)   If on a reference under subsection (4) … no appointment is made, the official receiver shall continue to be trustee of the bankrupt's estate, but without prejudice to his power to make a further reference.

(8)   References in this section to a vacancy include a case where it is necessary, in relation to any property which is or may be comprised in a bankrupt's estate, to revive the trusteeship of that estate after the holding of a final meeting summoned under section 331 or the giving by the official receiver of notice under section 299(2).

Control of trustee

301.   Creditors' committee

(1)   Subject as follows, a general meeting of a bankrupt's creditors (whether summoned under the preceding provisions of this Chapter or otherwise) may, in accordance with the rules, establish a committee (known as "the creditors' committee") to exercise the functions conferred on it by or under this Act.

(2)   A general meeting of the bankrupt's creditors shall not establish such a committee, or confer any functions on such a committee, at any time when the official receiver is the trustee of the bankrupt's estate, except in connection with an appointment made by that meeting of a person to be trustee instead of the official receiver.

302.   Exercise by Secretary of State of functions of creditors' committee

(1)   The creditors' committee is not to be able or required to carry out its functions at any time when the official receiver is trustee of the bankrupt's estate; but at any such time the functions of the committee under this Act shall be vested in the Secretary of State, except to the extent that the rules otherwise provide.

(2)   Where in the case of any bankruptcy there is for the time being no creditors' committee and the trustee of the bankrupt's estate is a person other than the official receiver, the functions of such a committee shall be vested in the Secretary of State, except to the extent that the rules otherwise provide.

303.   General control of trustee by the court

(1)   If a bankrupt or any of his creditors or any other person is dissatisfied by any act, omission or decision of a trustee of the bankrupt's estate, he may apply to the court; and on such an application the court may confirm, reverse or modify any act or decision of the trustee, may give him directions or may make such other order as it thinks fit.

(2)   The trustee of a bankrupt's estate may apply to the court for directions in relation to any particular matter arising under the bankruptcy.

(2A)   Where at any time after a bankruptcy petition has been presented to the court against any person, whether under the provisions of the Insolvent Partnerships Order 1994 or not, the attention of the court is drawn to the fact that the person in question is a member of an insolvent partnership, the court may make an order as to the future conduct of the insolvency proceedings and any such order may apply any provisions of that Order with any necessary modifications.

(2B)   Where a bankruptcy petition has been presented against more than one individual in the circumstances mentioned in subsection (2A) above, the court may give such directions for consolidating the proceedings, or any of them, as it thinks just.

(2C)   Any order or directions under subsection (2A) or (2B) may be made or given on the application of the official receiver, any responsible insolvency practitioner, the trustee of the partnership or any other interested person and may include provisions as to the administration of the joint estate of the partnership, and in particular how it and the separate estate of any member are to be administered.

304.   Liability of trustee

(1)   Where on an application under this section the court is satisfied—

(a)   that the trustee of a bankrupt's estate has misapplied or retained, or become accountable for, any money or other property comprised in the bankrupt's estate, or

(b)   that a bankrupt's estate has suffered any loss in consequence of any misfeasance or breach of fiduciary or other duty by a trustee of the estate in the carrying out of his functions,

the court may order the trustee, for the benefit of the estate, to repay, restore or account for money or other property (together with interest at such rate as the court thinks just) or, as the case may require, to pay such sum by way of compensation in respect of the misfeasance or breach of fiduciary or other duty as the court thinks just.

This is without prejudice to any liability arising apart from this section.

(2)   An application under this section may be made by the official receiver, the Secretary of State, a creditor of the bankrupt or (whether or not there is, or is likely to be, a surplus for the purposes of section 330(5) (final distribution)) the bankrupt himself.

But the leave of the court is required for the making of an application if it is to be made by the bankrupt or if it is to be made after the trustee has had his release under section 299.

(3)   Where—

(a)   the trustee seizes or disposes of any property which is not comprised in the bankrupt's estate, and

(b)   at the time of the seizure or disposal the trustee believes, and has reasonable grounds for believing, that he is entitled (whether in pursuance of an order of the court or otherwise) to seize or dispose of that property,

the trustee is not liable to any person (whether under this section or otherwise) in respect of any loss or damage resulting from the seizure or disposal except in so far as that loss or damage is caused by the negligence of the trustee; and he has a lien on the property, or the proceeds of its sale, for such of the expenses of the bankruptcy as were incurred in connection with the seizure or disposal.

CHAPTER IV

ADMINISTRATION BY TRUSTEE

Preliminary

305.   General functions of trustee

(1)   This Chapter applies in relation to any bankruptcy where either—

(a)   the appointment of a person as trustee of a bankrupt's estate takes effect, or

(b)   the official receiver becomes trustee of a bankrupt's estate.

(2)   The function of the trustee is to get in, realise and distribute the bankrupt's estate in accordance with the following provisions of this Chapter; and in the carrying out of that function and in the management of the bankrupt's estate the trustee is entitled, subject to those provisions, to use his own discretion.

(3)   It is the duty of the trustee, if he is not the official receiver—

(a)   to furnish the official receiver with such information,

(b)   to produce to the official receiver, and permit inspection by the official receiver of, such books, papers and other records, and

(c)   to give the official receiver such other assistance,

as the official receiver may reasonably require for the purpose of enabling him to carry out his functions in relation to the bankruptcy.

(4)   The official name of the trustee shall be "the trustee of the estate of .. .., a bankrupt" (inserting the name of the bankrupt); be he may be referred to as "the trustee in bankruptcy" of the particular bankrupt.

Acquisition, control and realisation of bankrupt's estate

306. Vesting of bankrupt's estate in trustee

(1)   The bankrupt's estate shall vest in the trustee immediately on his appointment taking effect or, in the case of the official receiver, on his becoming trustee.

(2)   Where any property which is, or is to be, comprised in the bankrupt's estate vests in the trustee (whether under this section or under any other provision of this Part), it shall so vest without any conveyance, assignment or transfer.

306A. Property subject to restraint order

(1)   This section applies where—

    (a)   property is excluded from the bankrupt's estate by virtue of section 417(2)(a) of the Proceeds of Crime Act 2002 (property subject to a restraint order),

    (b)   an order under section 50, 52, 128, 198 or 200 of that Act has not been made in respect of the property, and

    (c)   the restraint order is discharged.

(2)   On the discharge of the restraint order the property vests in the trustee as part of the bankrupt's estate.

(3)   But subsection (2) does not apply to the proceeds of property realised by a management receiver under section 49(2)(d) or 197(2)(d) of that Act (realisation of property to meet receiver's remuneration and expenses).

306B. Property in respect of which receivership or administration order made

(1)   This section applies where—

    (a)   property is excluded from the bankrupt's estate by virtue of section 417(2)(b), (c) or (d) of the Proceeds of Crime Act 2002 (property in respect of which an order for the appointment of a receiver or administrator under certain provisions of that Act is in force),

    (b)   a confiscation order is made under section 6, 92 or 156 of that Act,

    (c)   the amount payable under the confiscation order is fully paid, and

    (d)   any of the property remains in the hands of the receiver or administrator (as the case may be).

(2)   The property vests in the trustee as part of the bankrupt's estate.

306C. Property subject to certain orders where confiscation order discharged or quashed

(1)   This section applies where—

    (a)   property is excluded from the bankrupt's estate by virtue of section 417(2)(a), (b), (c) or (d) of the Proceeds of Crime Act 2002 (property in respect of which a restraint order or an order for the appointment of a receiver or administrator under that Act is in force),

    (b)   a confiscation order is made under section 6, 92 or 156 of that Act, and

    (c)   the confiscation order is discharged under section 30, 114 or 180 of that Act (as the case may be) or quashed under that Act or in pursuance of any enactment relating to appeals against conviction or sentence.

(2)   Any such property in the hands of a receiver appointed under Part 2 or 4 of that Act or an administrator appointed under Part 3 of that Act vests in the trustee as part of the bankrupt's estate.

(3)   But subsection (2) does not apply to the proceeds of property realised by a management receiver under section 49(2)(d) or 197(2)(d) of that Act (realisation of property to meet receiver's remuneration and expenses).

307. After-acquired property

(1)   Subject to this section and section 309, the trustee may by notice in writing claim for the bankrupt's estate any property which has been acquired by, or has devolved upon, the bankrupt since the commencement of the bankruptcy.

(2)   A notice under this section shall not served in respect of—

(a) any property falling within subsection (2) or (3) of section 283 in Chapter II,

(aa) any property vesting in the bankrupt by virtue of section 283A in Chapter II,

(b) any property which by virtue of any other enactment is excluded from the bankrupt's estate, or

(c) without prejudice to section 280(2)(c) (order of court on application for discharge), any property which is acquired by or, devolves upon, the bankrupt after his discharge.

(3) Subject to the next subsection, upon the service on the bankrupt of a notice under this section the property to which the notice relates shall vest in the trustee as part of the bankrupt's estate; and the trustee's title to that property has relation back to the time at which the property was acquired by, or devolved upon, the bankrupt.

(4) Where, whether before or after service of a notice under this section—

(a) a person acquires property in good faith, for value and without notice of the bankruptcy, or

(b) a banker enters into a transaction in good faith and without such notice,

the trustee is not in respect of that property or transaction entitled by virtue of this section to any remedy against that person or banker, or any person whose title to any property derives from that person or banker.

(5) References in this section to property do not include any property which, as part of the bankrupt's income, may be the subject of an income payments order under section 310.

308. Vesting in trustee of certain items of excess value

(1) Subject to section 309, where—

(a) property is excluded by virtue of section 283(2) (tools of trade, household effects, etc) from the bankrupt's estate, and

(b) it appears to the trustee that the realisable value of the whole or any part of that property exceeds the cost of a reasonable replacement for that property or that part of it,

the trustee may by notice in writing claim that property or, as the case may be, that part of it for the bankrupt's estate.

(2) Upon the service on the bankrupt of a notice under this section, the property to which the notice relates vests in the trustee as part of the bankrupt's estate; and, except against a purchaser in good faith, for value and without notice of the bankruptcy, the trustee's title to that property has relation back to the commencement of the bankruptcy.

(3) The trustee shall apply funds comprised in the estate to the purchase by or on behalf of the bankrupt of a reasonable replacement for any property vested in the trustee under this section; and the duty imposed by this subsection has priority over the obligation of the trustee to distribute the estate.

(4) For the purposes of this section property is a reasonable replacement for other property if it is reasonably adequate for meeting the needs met by the other property.

308A. Vesting in trustee of certain tenancies

Upon the service on the bankrupt by the trustee of a notice in writing under this section, any tenancy—

(a) which is excluded by virtue of section 283(3A) from the bankrupt's estate, and

(b) to which the notice relates,

vests in the trustee as part of the bankrupt's estate; and, except against a purchaser in good faith, for value and without notice of the bankruptcy, the trustee's title to that tenancy has relation back to the commencement of the bankruptcy.

309. Time-limit for notice under s 307 or 308

(1) Except with the leave of the court, a notice shall not be served—

(a) under section 307, after the end of the period of 42 days beginning with the day on which it first came to the knowledge of the trustee that the property in question had been acquired by, or had devolved upon, the bankrupt;

(b) under section 308 or section 308A, after the end of the period of 42 days beginning with the day on which the property or tenancy in question first came to the knowledge of the trustee.

(2)   For the purposes of this section—

      (a)   anything which comes to the knowledge of the trustee is deemed in relation to any successor of his as trustee to have come to the knowledge of the successor at the same time; and

      (b)   anything which comes (otherwise than under paragraph (a)) to the knowledge of a person before he is the trustee is deemed to come to his knowledge on his appointment taking effect or, in the case of the official receiver, on his becoming trustee.

310.   Income payments orders

(1)   The court may, ... make an order ("an income payments order") claiming for the bankrupt's estate so much of the income of the bankrupt during the period for which the order is in force as may be specified in the order.

(1A)   An income payments order may be made only on an application instituted—

      (a)   by the trustee, and

      (b)   before the discharge of the bankrupt.

(2)   The court shall not make an income payments order the effect of which would be to reduce the income of the bankrupt when taken together with any payments to which subsection (8) applies below what appears to the court to be necessary for meeting the reasonable domestic needs of the bankrupt and his family.

(3)   An income payments order shall, in respect of any payment of income to which it is to apply, either—

      (a)   require the bankrupt to pay the trustee an amount equal to so much of that payment as is claimed by the order, or

      (b)   require the person making the payment to pay so much of it as is so claimed to the trustee, instead of to the bankrupt.

(4)   Where the court makes an income payments order it may, if it thinks fit, discharge or vary any attachment of earnings order that is for the time being in force to secure payments by the bankrupt.

(5)   Sums received by the trustee under an income payments order form part of the bankrupt's estate.

(6)   An income payments order must specify the period during which it is to have effect; and that period—

      (a)   may end after the discharge of the bankrupt, but

      (b)   may not end after the period of three years beginning with the date on which the order is made.

(6A)   An income payments order may (subject to subsection (6)(b)) be varied on the application of the trustee or the bankrupt (whether before or after discharge).

(7)   For the purposes of this section the income of the bankrupt comprises every payment in the nature of income which is from time to time made to him or to which he from time to time becomes entitled, including any payment in respect of the carrying on of any business or in respect of any office or employment and (despite anything in section 11 or 12 of the Welfare Reform and Pensions Act 1999) any payment under a pension scheme but excluding any payment to which subsection (8) applies.

(8)   This subsection applies to—

      (a)   payments by way of guaranteed minimum pension; and

      (b)   payments giving effect to the bankrupt's protected rights as a member of a pension scheme.

(9)   In this section, "guaranteed minimum pension" and "protected rights" have the same meaning as in the Pension Schemes Act 1993.

310A.   Income payments agreement

(1)   In this section "income payments agreement" means a written agreement between a bankrupt and his trustee or between a bankrupt and the official receiver which provides—

      (a)   that the bankrupt is to pay to the trustee or the official receiver an amount equal to a specified part or proportion of the bankrupt's income for a specified period, or

(b)   that a third person is to pay to the trustee or the official receiver a specified proportion of money due to the bankrupt by way of income for a specified period.

(2)   A provision of an income payments agreement of a kind specified in subsection (1)(a) or (b) may be enforced as if it were a provision of an income payments order.

(3)   While an income payments agreement is in force the court may, on the application of the bankrupt, his trustee or the official receiver, discharge or vary an attachment of earnings order that is for the time being in force to secure payments by the bankrupt.

(4)   The following provisions of section 310 shall apply to an income payments agreement as they apply to an income payments order—

(a)   subsection (5) (receipts to form part of estate), and

(b)   subsections (7) to (9) (meaning of income).

(5)   An income payments agreement must specify the period during which it is to have effect; and that period—

(a)   may end after the discharge of the bankrupt, but

(b)   may not end after the period of three years beginning with the date on which the agreement is made.

(6)   An income payments agreement may (subject to subsection (5)(b)) be varied—

(a)   by written agreement between the parties, or

(b)   by the court on an application made by the bankrupt, the trustee or the official receiver.

(7)   The court—

(a)   may not vary an income payments agreement so as to include provision of a kind which could not be included in an income payments order, and

(b)   shall grant an application to vary an income payments agreement if and to the extent that the court thinks variation necessary to avoid the effect mentioned in section 310(2).

311.   Acquisition by trustee of control

(1)   The trustee shall take possession of all books, papers and other records which relate to the bankrupt's estate or affairs and which belong to him or are in his possession or under his control (including any which would be privileged from disclosure in any proceedings).

(2).   In relation to, and for the purpose of acquiring or retaining possession of, the bankrupt's estate, the trustee is in the same position as if he were a receiver of property appointed by the High Court; and the court may, on his application, enforce such acquisition or retention accordingly.

(3)   Where any part of the bankrupt's estate consists of stock or shares in a company, shares in a ship or any other property transferable in the books of a company, office or person, the trustee may exercise the right to transfer the property to the same extent as the bankrupt might have exercised it if he had not become bankrupt.

(4)   Where any part of the estate consists of things in action, they are deemed to have been assigned to the trustee; but notice of the deemed assignment need not be given except in so far as it is necessary, in a case where the deemed assignment is from the bankrupt himself, for protecting the priority of the trustee.

(5)   Where any goods comprised in the estate are held by any person by way of pledge, pawn or other security and no notice has been served in respect of those goods by the official receiver under subsection (5) of section 285 (restriction on realising security), the trustee may serve such a notice in respect of the goods; and whether or not a notice has been served under this subsection or that subsection, the trustee may, if he thinks fit, exercise the bankrupt's right of redemption in respect of any such goods.

(6)   A notice served by the trustee under subsection (5) has the same effect as a notice served by the official receiver under section 285(5).

312.   Obligation to surrender control to trustee

(1)   The bankrupt shall deliver up to the trustee possession of any property, books, papers or other records of which he has possession or control and of which the trustee is required to take possession.

This is without prejudice to the general duties of the bankrupt under section 333 in this Chapter.

(2) If any of the following is in possession of any property, books, papers or other records of which the trustee is required to take possession, namely—

    (a)   the official receiver,

    (b)   a person who has ceased to be trustee of the bankrupt's estate, or

    (c)   a person who has been the supervisor of a voluntary arrangement approved in relation to the bankrupt under Part VIII,

    the official receiver or, as the case may be, that person shall deliver up possession of the property, books, papers or records to the trustee.

(3) Any banker or agent of the bankrupt or any other person who holds any property to the account of, or for, the bankrupt shall pay or deliver to the trustee all property in his possession or under his control which forms part of the bankrupt's estate and which he is not by law entitled to retain as against the bankrupt or trustee.

(4) If any person without reasonable excuse fails to comply with any obligation imposed by this section, he is guilty of a contempt of court and liable to be punished accordingly (in addition to any other punishment to which he may be subject).

313. Charge on bankrupt's home

(1) Where any property consisting of an interest in a dwelling house which is occupied by the bankrupt or by his spouse or former spouse *or by his civil partner or former civil partner* is comprised in the bankrupt's estate and the trustee is, for any reason, unable for the time being to realise that property, the trustee may apply to the court for an order imposing a charge on the property for the benefit of the bankrupt's estate.

(2) If on an application under this section the court imposes a charge on any property, the benefit of that charge shall be comprised in the bankrupt's estate and is enforceable, up to the charged value from time to time, for the payment of any amount which is payable otherwise than to the bankrupt out of the estate and of interest on that amount at the prescribed rate.

(2A) In subsection (2) the charged value means—

    (a)   the amount specified in the charging order as the value of the bankrupt's interest in the property at the date of the order, plus

    (b)   interest on that amount from the date of the charging order at the prescribed rate.

(2B) In determining the value of an interest for the purposes of this section the court shall disregard any matter which it is required to disregard by the rules.

(3) An order under this section made in respect of property vested in the trustee shall provide, in accordance with the rules, for the property to cease to be comprised in the bankrupt's estate and, subject to the charge (and any prior charge), to vest in the bankrupt.

(4) Subsections (1) and (2) and (4) to (6) of section 3 of the Charging Orders Act 1979 (supplemental provisions with respect to charging orders) have effect in relation to orders under this section as in relation to charging orders under that Act.

(5) But an order under section 3(5) of that Act may not vary a charged value.

Note. The italicized words in subsection (1) are inserted by the Civil Partnership Act 2004, s. 261(1), Sch. 27, para. 114, as from a day to be appointed.

313A. Low value home: application for sale, possession or charge

(1) This section applies where—

    (a)   property comprised in the bankrupt's estate consists of an interest in a dwelling-house which at the date of the bankruptcy was the sole or principal residence of—

        (i)   the bankrupt,

        (ii)   the bankrupt's spouse *or civil partner*, or

        (iii) a former spouse *or former civil partner* of the bankrupt, and

    (b)   the trustee applies for an order for the sale of the property, for an order for possession of the property or for an order under section 313 in respect of the property.

(2)   The court shall dismiss the application if the value of the interest is below the amount prescribed for the purposes of this subsection.

(3)   In determining the value of an interest for the purposes of this section the court shall disregard any matter which it is required to disregard by the order which prescribes the amount for the purposes of subsection (2).

Note. The italicized words in subsection (1)(a)(ii), (iii) are inserted by the Civil Partnership Act 2004, s. 261(1), Sch. 27, para. 115, as from a day to be appointed.

314.   Powers of trustee

(1)   The trustee may—
> (a)   with the permission of the creditors' committee or the court, exercise any of the powers specified in Part I of Schedule 5 to this Act, and
> (b)   without that permission, exercise any of the general powers specified in Part II of that Schedule.

(2)   With the permission of the creditors' committee or the court, the trustee may appoint the bankrupt—
> (a)   to superintend the management of his estate or any part of it,
> (b)   to carry on his business (if any) for the benefit of his creditors, or
> (c)   in any other respect to assist in administering the estate in such manner and on such terms as the trustee may direct.

(3)   A permission given for the purposes of subsection (1)(a) or (2) shall not be a general permission but shall relate to a particular proposed exercise of the power in question; and a person dealing with the trustee in good faith and for value is not to be concerned to enquire whether any permission required in either case has been given.

(4)   Where the trustee has done anything without the permission required by subsection (1)(a) or (2), the court or the creditors' committee may, for the purpose of enabling him to meet his expenses out of the bankrupt's estate, ratify what the trustee has done.

But the committee shall not do so unless it is satisfied that the trustee has acted in a case of urgency and has sought its ratification without undue delay.

(5)   Part III of Schedule 5 to this Act has effect with respect to the things which the trustee is able to do for the purposes of, or in connection with, the exercise of any of his powers under any of this Group of Parts.

(6)   Where the trustee (not being the official receiver) in exercise of the powers conferred on him by any provision in this Group of Parts—
> (a)   disposes of any property comprised in the bankrupt's estate to an associate of the bankrupt, or
> (b)   employs a solicitor,

he shall, if there is for the time being a creditors' committee, give notice to the committee of that exercise of his powers.

(7)   Without prejudice to the generality of subsection (5) and Part III of Schedule 5, the trustee may, if he thinks fit, at any time summon a general meeting of the bankrupt's creditors.

Subject to the preceding provisions in this Group of Parts, he shall summon such a meeting if he is requested to do so by a creditor of the bankrupt and the request is made with the concurrence of not less than one-tenth, in value, of the bankrupt's creditors (including the creditor making the request).

(8)   Nothing in this Act is to be construed as restricting the capacity of the trustee to exercise any of his powers outside England and Wales.

Disclaimer of onerous property

315.   Disclaimer (general power)

(1)   Subject as follows, the trustee may, by the giving of the prescribed notice, disclaim any onerous property and may do so notwithstanding that he has taken possession of it, endeavoured to sell it or otherwise exercised rights of ownership in relation to it.

(2)   The following is onerous property for the purposes of this section, that is to say—
(a)   any unprofitable contract, and
(b)   any other property comprised in the bankrupt's estate which is unsaleable or not readily saleable, or is such that it may give rise to a liability to pay money or perform any other onerous act.

(3)   A disclaimer under this section—
(a)   operates so as to determine, as from the date of the disclaimer, the rights, interests and liabilities of the bankrupt and his estate in or in respect of the property disclaimed, and
(b)   discharges the trustee from all personal liability in respect of that property as from the commencement of his trusteeship,
but does not, except so far as is necessary for the purpose of releasing the bankrupt, the bankrupt's estate and the trustee from any liability, affect the rights or liabilities of any other person.

(4)   A notice of disclaimer shall not be given under this section in respect of any property that has been claimed for the estate under section 307 (after-acquired property) or 308 (personal property of bankrupt exceeding reasonable replacement value) or 308A, except with the leave of the court.

(5)   Any person sustaining loss or damage in consequence of the operation of a disclaimer under this section is deemed to be a creditor of the bankrupt to the extent of the loss or damage and accordingly may prove for the loss or damage as a bankruptcy debt.

316.   Notice requiring trustee's decision

(1)   Notice of disclaimer shall not be given under section 315 in respect of any property if—
(a)   a person interested in the property has applied in writing to the trustee or one of his predecessors as trustee requiring the trustee or that predecessor to decide whether he will disclaim or not, and
(b)   the period of 28 days beginning with the day on which that application was made has expired without a notice of disclaimer having been given under section 315 in respect of that property.

(2)   The trustee is deemed to have adopted any contract which by virtue of this section he is not entitled to disclaim.

317.   Disclaimer of leaseholds

(1)   The disclaimer of any property of a leasehold nature does not take effect unless a copy of the disclaimer has been served (so far as the trustee is aware of their addresses) on every person claiming under the bankrupt as underlessee or mortgagee and either—
(a)   no application under section 320 below is made with respect to the property before the end of the period of 14 days beginning with the day on which the last notice served under this subsection was served, or
(b)   where such an application has been made, the court directs that the disclaimer is to take effect.

(2)   Where the court gives a direction under subsection (1)(b) it may also, instead of or in addition to any order it makes under section 320, make such orders with respect to fixtures, tenant's improvements and other matters arising out of the lease as it thinks fit.

318.   Disclaimer of dwelling house

Without prejudice to section 317, the disclaimer of any property in a dwelling house does not take effect unless a copy of the disclaimer has been served (so far as the trustee is aware of their addresses) on every person in occupation of or claiming a right to occupy the dwelling house and either—
(a)   no application under section 320 is made with respect to the property before the end of the period of 14 days beginning with the day on which the last notice served under this section was served, or
(b)   where such an application has been made, the court directs that the disclaimer is to take effect.

319.   **Disclaimer of land subject to rentcharge**

(1)   The following applies where, in consequence of the disclaimer under section 315 of any land subject to a rentcharge, that land vests by operation of law in the Crown or any other person (referred to in the next subsection as "the proprietor").

(2)   The proprietor, and the successors in title of the proprietor, are not subject to any personal liability in respect of any sums becoming due under the rentcharge, except sums becoming due after the proprietor, or some person claiming under or through the proprietor, has taken possession or control of the land or has entered into occupation of it.

320.   **Court order vesting disclaimed property**

(1)   This section and the next apply where the trustee has disclaimed property under section 315.

(2)   An application may be made to the court under this section by—

    (a)   any person who claims an interest in the disclaimed property,

    (b)   any person who is under any liability in respect of the disclaimed property, not being a liability discharged by the disclaimer, or

    (c)   where the disclaimed property is property in a dwelling-house, any person who at the time when the bankruptcy petition was presented was in occupation of or entitled to occupy the dwelling house.

(3)   Subject as follows in this section and the next, the court may, on an application under this section, make an order on such terms as it thinks fit for the vesting of the disclaimed property in, or for its delivery to—

    (a)   a person entitled to it or a trustee for such a person,

    (b)   a person subject to such a liability as is mentioned in subsection (2)(b) or a trustee for such a person, or

    (c)   where the disclaimed property is property in a dwelling-house, any person who at the time when the bankruptcy petition was presented was in occupation of or entitled to occupy the dwelling house.

(4)   The court shall not make an order by virtue of subsection (3)(b) except where it appears to the court that it would be just to do so for the purpose of compensating the person subject to the liability in respect of the disclaimer.

(5)   The effect of any order under this section shall be taken into account in assessing for the purposes of section 315(5) the extent of any loss or damage sustained by any person in consequence of the disclaimer.

(6)   An order under this section vesting property in any person need not be completed by any conveyance, assignment or transfer.

321.   **Order under s 320 in respect of leaseholds**

(1)   The court shall not make an order under section 320 vesting property of a leasehold nature in any person, except on terms making that person—

    (a)   subject to the same liabilities and obligations as the bankrupt was subject to under the lease on the day the bankruptcy petition was presented, or

    (b)   if the court thinks fit, subject to the same liabilities and obligations as that person would be subject to if the lease had been assigned to him on that day.

(2)   For the purposes of an order under section 320 relating to only part of any property comprised in a lease, the requirements of subsection (1) apply as if the lease comprised only the property to which the order relates.

(3)   Where subsection (1) applies and no person is willing to accept an order under section 320 on the terms required by that subsection, the court may (by order under section 320) vest the estate or interest of the bankrupt in the property in any person who is liable (whether personally or in a representative capacity and whether alone or jointly with the bankrupt) to perform the lessee's covenants in the lease.

The court may by virtue of this subsection vest that estate and interest in such a person freed and discharged from all estates, incumbrances and interests created by the bankrupt.

(4)   Where subsection (1) applies and a person declines to accept any order under section 320, that person shall be excluded from all interest in the property.

Distribution of bankrupt's estate

322.   Proof of debts

(1)   Subject to this section and the next, the proof of any bankruptcy debt by a secured or unsecured creditor of the bankrupt and the admission or rejection of any proof shall take place in accordance with the rules.

(2)   Where a bankruptcy debt bears interest, that interest is provable as part of the debt except in so far as it is payable in respect of any period after the commencement of the bankruptcy.

(3)   The trustee shall estimate the value of any bankruptcy debt which, by reason of its being subject to any contingency or contingencies or for any other reason, does not bear a certain value.

(4)   Where the value of a bankruptcy debt is estimated by the trustee under subsection (3) or, by virtue of section 303 in Chapter III, by the court, the amount provable in the bankruptcy in respect of the debt is the amount of the estimate.

323.   Mutual credit and set-off

(1)   This section applies where before the commencement of the bankruptcy there have been mutual credits, mutual debts or other mutual dealings between the bankrupt and any creditor of the bankrupt proving or claiming to prove for a bankruptcy debt.

(2)   An account shall be taken of what is due from each party to the other in respect of the mutual dealings and the sums due from one party shall be set off against the sums due from the other.

(3)   Sums due from the bankrupt to another party shall not be included in the account taken under subsection (2) if that other party had notice at the time they became due that a bankruptcy petition relating to the bankrupt was pending.

(4)   Only the balance (if any) of the account taken under subsection (2) is provable as a bankruptcy debt or, as the case may be, to be paid to the trustee as part of the bankrupt's estate.

324.   Distribution by means of dividend

(1)   Whenever the trustee has sufficient funds in hand for the purpose he shall, subject to the retention of such sums as may be necessary for the expenses of the bankruptcy, declare and distribute dividends among the creditors in respect of the bankruptcy debts which they have respectively proved.

(2)   The trustee shall give notice of his intention to declare and distribute a dividend.

(3)   Where the trustee has declared a dividend, he shall give notice of the dividend and of how it is proposed to distribute it; and a notice given under this subsection shall contain the prescribed particulars of the bankrupt's estate.

(4)   In the calculation and distribution of a dividend the trustee shall make provision—

(a)   for any bankruptcy debts which appear to him to be due to persons who, by reason of the distance of their place of residence, may not have had sufficient time to tender and establish their proofs,

(b)   for any bankruptcy debts which are the subject of claims which have not yet been determined, and

(c)   for disputed proofs and claims.

325.   Claims by unsatisfied creditors

(1)   A creditor who has not proved his debt before the declaration of any dividend is not entitled to disturb, by reason that he has not participated in it, the distribution of that dividend or any other dividend declared before his debt was proved, but—

(a)   when he has proved that debt he is entitled to be paid, out of any money for the time being available for the payment of any further dividend, any dividend or dividends which he has failed to receive; and

(b) any dividend or dividends payable under paragraph (a) shall be paid before that money is applied to the payment of any such further dividend.

(2) No action lies against the trustee for a dividend, but if the trustee refuses to pay a dividend the court may, if it thinks fit, order him to pay it and also to pay, out of his own money—

(a) interest on the dividend, at the rate for the time being specified in section 17 of the Judgments Act 1838, from the time it was withheld, and

(b) the costs of the proceedings in which the order to pay is made.

326. Distribution of property in specie

(1) Without prejudice to sections 315 to 319 (disclaimer), the trustee may, with the permission of the creditors' committee, divide in its existing form amongst the bankrupt's creditors, according to its estimated value, any property which from its peculiar nature or other special circumstances cannot be readily or advantageously sold.

(2) A permission given for the purposes of subsection (1) shall not be a general permission but shall relate to a particular proposed exercise of the power in question; and a person dealing with the trustee in good faith and for value is not to be concerned to enquire whether any permission required by subsection (1) has been given.

(3) Where the trustee has done anything without the permission required by subsection (1), the court or the creditors' committee may, for the purpose of enabling him to meet his expenses out of the bankrupt's estate, ratify what the trustee has done.

But the committee shall not do so unless it is satisfied that the trustee acted in a case of urgency and has sought its ratification without undue delay.

327. *Distribution in criminal bankruptcy*

Where the bankruptcy order was made on a petition under section 264(1)(d) (criminal bankruptcy), no distribution shall be made under sections 324 to 326 so long as an appeal is pending (within the meaning of section 277) against the bankrupt's conviction of any offence by virtue of which the criminal bankruptcy order on which the petition was based was made.

Note. This section is repealed by the Criminal Justice Act 1988, s. 170(2), Sch. 16, as from a day to be appointed.

328. Priority of debts

(1) In the distribution of the bankrupt's estate, his preferential debts (within the meaning given by section 386 in Part XII) shall be paid in priority to other debts.

(2) Preferential debts rank equally between themselves after the expenses of the bankruptcy and shall be paid in full unless the bankrupt's estate is insufficient for meeting them, in which case they abate in equal proportions between themselves.

(3) Debts which are neither preferential debts nor debts to which the next section applies also rank equally between themselves and, after the preferential debts, shall be paid in full unless the bankrupt's estate is insufficient for meeting them, in which case they abate in equal proportions between themselves.

(4) Any surplus remaining after the payment of the debts that are preferential or rank equally under subsection (3) shall be applied in paying interest on those debts in respect of the periods during which they have been outstanding since the commencement of the bankruptcy; and interest on preferential debts ranks equally with interest on debts other than preferential debts.

(5) The rate of interest payable under subsection (4) in respect of any debt is whichever is the greater of the following—

(a) the rate specified in section 17 of the Judgments Act 1838 at the commencement of the bankruptcy, and

(b) the rate applicable to that debt apart from the bankruptcy.

(6) This section and the next are without prejudice to any provision of this Act or any other Act under which the payment of any debt or the making of any other payment is, in the event of bankruptcy, to have a particular priority or to be postponed.

329.   Debts to spouse *or civil partner*

(1)   This section applies to bankruptcy debts owed in respect of credit provided by a person who (whether or not the bankrupt's spouse *or civil partner* at the time the credit was provided) was the bankrupt's spouse *or civil partner* at the commencement of the bankruptcy.

(2)   Such debts—

(a)   rank in priority after the debts and interest required to be paid in pursuance of section 328(3) and (4), and

(b)   are payable with interest at the rate specified in section 328(5) in respect of the period during which they have been outstanding since the commencement of the bankruptcy;

and the interest payable under paragraph (b) has the same priority as the debts on which it is payable.

Note. The italicized words in the section heading and in subsections (1) and (2) are inserted by the Civil Partnership Act 2004, s. 261(1), Sch. 27, para. 116, as from a day to be appointed.

330.   Final distribution

(1)   When the trustee has realised all the bankrupt's estate or so much of it as can, in the trustee's opinion, be realised without needlessly protracting the trusteeship, he shall give notice in the prescribed manner either—

(a)   of his intention to declare a final dividend, or

(b)   that no dividend, or further dividend, will be declared.

(2)   The notice under subsection (1) shall contain the prescribed particulars and shall require claims against the bankrupt's estate to be established by a date ("the final date") specified in the notice.

(3)   The court may, on the application of any person, postpone the final date.

(4)   After the final date, the trustee shall—

(a)   defray any outstanding expenses of the bankruptcy out of the bankrupt's estate, and

(b)   if he intends to declare a final dividend, declare and distribute that dividend without regard to the claim of any person in respect of a debt not already proved in the bankruptcy.

(5)   If a surplus remains after payment in full and with interest of all the bankrupt's creditors and the payment of the expenses of the bankruptcy, the bankrupt is entitled to the surplus.

(6)   Subsection (5) is subject to Article 35 of the EC Regulation (surplus in secondary proceedings to be transferred to main proceedings).

331.   Final meeting

(1)   Subject as follows in this section and the next, this section applies where—

(a)   it appears to the trustee that the administration of the bankrupt's estate in accordance with this Chapter is for practical purposes complete, and

(b)   the trustee is not the official receiver.

(2)   The trustee shall summon a final general meeting of the bankrupt's creditors which—

(a)   shall receive the trustee's report of his administration of the bankrupt's estate, and

(b)   shall determine whether the trustee should have his release under section 299 in Chapter III.

(3)   The trustee may, if he thinks fit, give the notice summoning the final general meeting at the same time as giving notice under section 330(1); but, if summoned for an earlier date, that meeting shall be adjourned (and, if necessary, further adjourned) until a date on which the trustee is able to report to the meeting that the administration of the bankrupt's estate is for practical purposes complete.

(4)   In the administration of the estate it is the trustee's duty to retain sufficient sums from the estate to cover the expenses of summoning and holding the meeting required by this section.

332.   Saving for bankrupt's home

(1)   This section applies where—

(a)   there is comprised in the bankrupt's estate property consisting of an interest in a dwelling house which is occupied by the bankrupt or by his spouse or former spouse *or by his civil partner or former civil partner*, and

(b)   the trustee has been unable for any reason to realise that property.

(2)   The trustee shall not summon a meeting under section 331 unless either—

(a)   the court has made an order under section 313 imposing a charge on that property for the benefit of the bankrupt's estate, or

(b)   the court has declined, on an application under that section, to make such an order, or

(c)   the Secretary of State has issued a certificate to the trustee stating that it would be inappropriate or inexpedient for such an application to be made in the case in question.

Note. The italicized words in subsection (1) are inserted by the Civil Partnership Act 2004, s. 261(1), Sch. 27, para. 117, as from a day to be appointed.

Supplemental

333.   Duties of bankrupt in relation to trustee

(1)   The bankrupt shall—

(a)   give to the trustee such information as to his affairs,

(b)   attend on the trustee at such times, and

(c)   do all such other things,

as the trustee may for the purposes of carrying out his functions under any of this Group of Parts reasonably require.

(2)   Where at any time after the commencement of the bankruptcy any property is acquired by, or devolves upon, the bankrupt or there is an increase of the bankrupt's income, the bankrupt shall, within the prescribed period, give the trustee notice of the property or, as the case may be, of the increase.

(3)   Subsection (1) applies to a bankrupt after his discharge.

(4)   If the bankrupt without reasonable excuse fails to comply with any obligation imposed by this section, he is guilty of a contempt of court and liable to be punished accordingly (in addition to any other punishment to which he may be subject).

334.   Stay of distribution in case of second bankruptcy

(1)   This section and the next apply where a bankruptcy order is made against an undischarged bankrupt; and in both sections—

(a)   "the later bankruptcy" means the bankruptcy arising from that order,

(b)   "the earlier bankruptcy" means the bankruptcy (or, as the case may be, most recent bankruptcy) from which the bankrupt has not been discharged at the commencement of the later bankruptcy, and

(c)   "the existing trustee" means the trustee (if any) of the bankrupt's estate for the purposes of the earlier bankruptcy.

(2)   Where the existing trustee has been given the prescribed notice of the presentation of the petition for the later bankruptcy, any distribution or other disposition by him of anything to which the next subsection applies, if made after the giving of the notice, is void except to the extent that it was made with the consent of the court or is or was subsequently ratified by the court.

This is without prejudice to section 284 (restrictions on dispositions of property following bankruptcy order).

(3)   This subsection applies to—

(a)   any property which is vested in the existing trustee under section 307(3) (after-acquired property);

(b)   any money paid to the existing trustee in pursuance of an income payments order under section 310; and

(c)   any property or money which is, or in the hands of the existing trustee represents, the proceeds of sale or application of property or money falling within paragraph (a) or (b) of this subsection.

335.   Adjustment between earlier and later bankruptcy estates

(1)   With effect from the commencement of the later bankruptcy anything to which section 334(3) applies which, immediately before the commencement of that bankruptcy, is comprised in the bankrupt's estate for the purposes of the earlier bankruptcy is to be treated as comprised in the bankrupt's estate for the purposes of the later bankruptcy and, until there is a trustee of that estate, is to be dealt with by the existing trustee in accordance with the rules.

(2)   Any sums which in pursuance of an income payments order under section 310 are payable after the commencement of the later bankruptcy to the existing trustee shall form part of the bankrupt's estate for the purposes of the later bankruptcy; and the court may give such consequential directions for the modification of the order as it thinks fit.

(3)   Anything comprised in a bankrupt's estate by virtue of subsection (1) or (2) is so comprised subject to a first charge in favour of the existing trustee for any bankruptcy expenses incurred by him in relation thereto.

(4)   Except as provided above and in section 334, property which is, or by virtue of section 308 (personal property of bankrupt exceeding reasonable replacement value) or section 308A (vesting in trustee of certain tenancies) is capable of being, comprised in the bankrupt's estate for the purposes of the earlier bankruptcy, or of any bankruptcy prior to it, shall not be comprised in his estate for the purposes of the later bankruptcy.

(5)   The creditors of the bankrupt in the earlier bankruptcy and the creditors of the bankrupt in any bankruptcy prior to the earlier one, are not to be creditors of his in the later bankruptcy in respect of the same debts; but the existing trustee may prove in the later bankruptcy for—

  (a)   the unsatisfied balance of the debts (including any debt under this subsection) provable against the bankrupt's estate in the earlier bankruptcy;

  (b)   any interest payable on that balance; and

  (c)   any unpaid expenses of the earlier bankruptcy.

(6)   Any amount provable under subsection (5) ranks in priority after all the other debts provable in the later bankruptcy and after interest on those debts and, accordingly, shall not be paid unless those debts and that interest have first been paid in full.

CHAPTER V
EFFECT OF BANKRUPTCY ON CERTAIN RIGHTS, TRANSACTIONS, ETC

Rights under trusts of land

335A. Rights under trusts of land

(1)   Any application by a trustee of a bankrupt's estate under section 14 of the Trusts of Land and Appointment of Trustees Act 1996 (powers of court in relation to trusts of land) for an order under that section for the sale of land shall be made to the court having jurisdiction in relation to the bankruptcy.

(2)   On such an application the court shall make such order as it thinks just and reasonable having regard to—

  (a)   the interests of the bankrupt's creditors;

  (b)   where the application is made in respect of land which includes a dwelling house which is or has been the home of the bankrupt or the *bankrupt's spouse or former spouse [bankrupt's spouse or civil partner or former spouse or former civil partner]*—

    (i)   the conduct of the *spouse or former spouse [spouse, civil partner, former spouse or former civil partner]*, so far as contributing to the bankruptcy,

    (ii) the needs and financial resources of the *spouse or former spouse [spouse, civil partner, former spouse or former civil partner]*, and

    (iii) the needs of any children; and

  (c)   all the circumstances of the case other than the needs of the bankrupt.

(3)   Where such an application is made after the end of the period of one year beginning with the first vesting under Chapter IV of this Part of the bankrupt's estate in a trustee, the court shall assume,

unless the circumstances of the case are exceptional, that the interests of the bankrupt's creditors outweigh all other considerations.

(4)   The powers conferred on the court by this section are exercisable on an application whether it is made before or after the commencement of this section.

Note. The italicized words in subsection (2)(b) are substituted by the subsequent words in square brackets by the Civil Partnership Act 2004, s. 261(1), Sch. 27, para. 118, as from a day to be appointed.

Rights of occupation

336.   Rights of occupation etc of bankrupt's spouse *or civil partner*

(1)   Nothing occurring in the initial period of the bankruptcy (that is to say, the period beginning with the day of the presentation of the petition for the bankruptcy order and ending with the vesting of the bankrupt's estate in a trustee) is to be taken as having given rise to any *matrimonial home rights [home rights]* under Part IV of the Family Law Act 1996 in relation to a dwelling house comprised in the bankrupt's estate.

(2)   Where *a spouse's matrimonial home rights [a spouse's or civil partner's home rights]* under the Act of 1996 are a charge on the estate or interest of the other spouse *or civil partner*, or of trustees for the other spouse *or civil partner*, and the other spouse *or civil partner* is adjudged bankrupt—

(a)   the charge continues to subsist notwithstanding the bankruptcy and, subject to the provisions of that Act, binds the trustee of the bankrupt's estate and persons deriving title under that trustee, and

(b)   any application for an order under section 33 of that Act shall be made to the court having jurisdiction in relation to the bankruptcy.

(3)   ...

(4)   On such an application as is mentioned in subsection (2) ... the court shall make such order under section 33 of the Act of 1996 ... as it thinks just and reasonable having regard to—

(a)   the interests of the bankrupt's creditors,

(b)   the conduct of the spouse or former spouse *or civil partner or former civil partner*, so far as contributing to the bankruptcy,

(c)   the needs and financial resources of the spouse or former spouse *or civil partner or former civil partner*,

(d)   the needs of any children, and

(e)   all the circumstances of the case other than the needs of the bankrupt.

(5)   Where such an application is made after the end of the period of one year beginning with the first vesting under Chapter IV of this Part of the bankrupt's estate in a trustee, the court shall assume, unless the circumstances of the case are exceptional, that the interests of the bankrupt's creditors outweigh all other considerations.

Note. The italicized words "or civil partner" in the section heading and in subsection (2), and the italicized words "or civil partner or former civil partner" in subsection (4)(b), (c), are inserted, and the italicized words "matrimonial home rights" in subsection (1) and the italicized words "a spouse's matrimonial home rights" in subsection (2), are substituted by the subsequent italicized words in square brackets, by the Civil Partnership Act 2004, s. 82, Sch. 9, Pt. 2, paras. 21, 22, as from a day to be appointed.

337.   Rights of occupation of bankrupt

(1)   This section applies where—

(a)   a person who is entitled to occupy a dwelling house by virtue of a beneficial estate or interest is adjudged bankrupt, and

(b)   any persons under the age of 18 with whom that person had at some time occupied that dwelling house had their home with that person at the time when the bankruptcy petition was presented and at the commencement of the bankruptcy.

(2)   Whether or not the bankrupt's *spouse (if any) has matrimonial home rights [spouse or civil partner (if any) has home rights]* under Part IV of the Family Law Act 1996—

(a)   the bankrupt has the following rights as against the trustee of his estate—

> (i)   if in occupation, a right not to be evicted or excluded from the dwelling house or any part of it, except with the leave of the court,
>
> (ii)   if not in occupation, a right with the leave of the court to enter into and occupy the dwelling house, and

(b)   the bankrupt's rights are a charge, having the like priority as an equitable interest created immediately before the commencement of the bankruptcy, on so much of his estate or interest in the dwelling house as vests in the trustee.

(3)   The Act of 1996 has effect, with the necessary modifications, as if—

     (a)   the rights conferred by paragraph (a) of subsection (2) were *matrimonial home rights [home rights]* under that Act,

     (b)   any application for such leave as is mentioned in that paragraph were an application for an order under section 33 of that Act, and

     (c)   any charge under paragraph (b) of that subsection on the estate or interest of the trustee were a charge under that Act on the estate or interest of a spouse *or civil partner*.

(4)   Any application for leave such as is mentioned in subsection (2)(a) or otherwise by virtue of this section for an order under section 33 of the Act of 1996 shall be made to the court having jurisdiction in relation to the bankruptcy.

(5)   On such an application the court shall make such order under section 33 of the Act of 1996 as it thinks just and reasonable having regard to the interests of the creditors, to the bankrupt's financial resources, to the needs of the children and to all the circumstances of the case other than the needs of the bankrupt.

(6)   Where such an application is made after the end of the period of one year beginning with the vesting (under Chapter IV of this Part) of the bankrupt's estate in a trustee, the court shall assume, unless the circumstances of the case are exceptional, that the interests of the bankrupt's creditors outweigh all other considerations.

Note. The italicized words in subsections (2), (3)(a) are substituted by the subsequent italicized words in square brackets, and the words in subsection (3)(c) are inserted, by the Civil Partnership Act 2004, s. 82, Sch. 9, Pt. 2, para. 22, as from a day to be appointed.

338.   Payments in respect of premises occupied by bankrupt

Where any premises comprised in a bankrupt's estate are occupied by him (whether by virtue of the preceding section or otherwise) on condition that he makes payments towards satisfying any liability arising under a mortgage of the premises or otherwise towards the outgoings of the premises, the bankrupt does not, by virtue of those payments, acquire any interest in the premises.

Adjustment of prior transactions, etc

339.   Transactions at an undervalue

(1)   Subject as follows in this section and sections 341 and 342, where an individual is adjudged bankrupt and he has at a relevant time (defined in section 341) entered into a transaction with any person at an undervalue, the trustee of the bankrupt's estate may apply to the court for an order under this section.

(2)   The court shall, on such an application, make such order as it thinks fit for restoring the position to what it would have been if that individual had not entered into that transaction.

(3)   For the purposes of this section and sections 341 and 342, an individual enters into a transaction with a person at an undervalue if—

     (a)   he makes a gift to that person or he otherwise enters into a transaction with that person on terms that provide for him to receive no consideration,

     (b)   he enters into a transaction with that person in consideration of marriage *or the formation of a civil partnership*, or

     (c)   he enters into a transaction with that person for a consideration the value of which, in money or money's worth, is significantly less than the value, in money or money's worth, of the consideration provided by the individual.

Note. The italicized words in subsection (3)(b) are inserted by the Civil Partnership Act 2004, s. 261(1), Sch. 27, para. 119, as from a day to be appointed.

340. Preferences

(1) Subject as follows in this and the next two sections, where an individual is adjudged bankrupt and he has at a relevant time (defined in section 341) given a preference to any person, the trustee of the bankrupt's estate may apply to the court for an order under this section.

(2) The court shall, on such an application, make such order as it thinks fit for restoring the position to what it would have been if that individual had not given that preference.

(3) For the purposes of this and the next two sections, an individual gives a preference to a person if—

    (a) that person is one of the individual's creditors or a surety or guarantor for any of his debts or other liabilities, and

    (b) the individual does anything or suffers anything to be done which (in either case) has the effect of putting that person into a position which, in the event of the individual's bankruptcy, will be better than the position he would have been in if that thing had not been done.

(4) The court shall not make an order under this section in respect of a preference given to any person unless the individual who gave the preference was influenced in deciding to give it by a desire to produce in relation to that person the effect mentioned in subsection (3)(b) above.

(5) An individual who has given a preference to a person who, at the time the preference was given, was an associate of his (otherwise than by reason only of being his employee) is presumed, unless the contrary is shown, to have been influenced in deciding to give it by such a desire as is mentioned in subsection (4).

(6) The fact that something has been done in pursuance of the order of a court does not, without more, prevent the doing or suffering of that thing from constituting the giving of a preference.

341. "Relevant time" under ss 339, 340

(1) Subject as follows, the time at which an individual enters into a transaction at an undervalue or gives a preference is a relevant time if the transaction is entered into or the preference given—

    (a) in the case of a transaction at an undervalue, at a time in the period of 5 years ending with the day of the presentation of the bankruptcy petition on which the individual is adjudged bankrupt,

    (b) in the case of a preference which is not a transaction at an undervalue and is given to a person who is an associate of the individual (otherwise than by reason only of being his employee), at a time in the period of 2 years ending with that day, and

    (c) in any other case of a preference which is not a transaction at an undervalue, at a time in the period of 6 months ending with that day.

(2) Where an individual enters into a transaction at an undervalue or gives a preference at a time mentioned in paragraph (a), (b) or (c) of subsection (1) (not being, in the case of a transaction at an undervalue, a time less than 2 years before the end of the period mentioned in paragraph (a)), that time is not a relevant time for the purposes of sections 339 and 340 unless the individual—

    (a) is insolvent at that time, or

    (b) becomes insolvent in consequence of the transaction or preference;

but the requirements of this subsection are presumed to be satisfied, unless the contrary is shown, in relation to any transaction at an undervalue which is entered into by an individual with a person who is an associate of his (otherwise than by reason only of being his employee).

(3) For the purposes of subsection (2), an individual is insolvent if—

    (a) he is unable to pay his debts as they fall due, or

    (b) the value of his assets is less than the amount of his liabilities, taking into account his contingent and prospective liabilities.

(4) *A transaction entered into or preference given by a person who is subsequently adjudged bankrupt on a petition under section 264(1)(d) (criminal bankruptcy) is to be treated as having*

been entered into or given at a relevant time for the purposes of sections 339 and 340 if it was entered into or given at any time on or after the date specified for the purposes of this subsection in the criminal bankruptcy order on which the petition was based.

(5)   *No order shall be made under section 339 or 340 by virtue of subsection (4) of this section where an appeal is pending (within the meaning of section 277) against the individual's conviction of any offence by virtue of which the criminal bankruptcy order was made.*

Note. Subsections (4) and (5) are repealed by the Criminal Justice Act 1988, s. 170(2), Sch. 16, as from a day to be appointed.

342.   Orders under ss 339, 340

(1)   Without prejudice to the generality of section 339(2) or 340(2), an order under either of those sections with respect to a transaction or preference entered into or given by an individual who is subsequently adjudged bankrupt may (subject as follows)—

(a)   require any property transferred as part of the transaction, or in connection with the giving of the preference, to be vested in the trustee of the bankrupt's estate as part of that estate;

(b)   require any property to be so vested if it represents in any person's hands the application either of the proceeds of sale of property so transferred or of money so transferred;

(c)   release or discharge (in whole or in part) any security given by the individual;

(d)   require any person to pay, in respect of benefits received by him from the individual, such sums to the trustee of his estate as the court may direct;

(e)   provide for any surety or guarantor whose obligations to any person were released or discharged (in whole or in part) under the transaction or by the giving of the preference to be under such new or revived obligations to that person as the court thinks appropriate;

(f)   provide for security to be provided for the discharge of any obligation imposed by or arising under the order, for such an obligation to be charged on any property and for the security or charge to have the same priority as a security or charge released or discharged (in whole or in part) under the transaction or by the giving of the preference; and

(g)   provide for the extent to which any person whose property is vested by the order in the trustee of the bankrupt's estate, or on whom obligations are imposed by the order, is to be able to prove in the bankruptcy for debts or other liabilities which arose from, or were released or discharged (in whole or in part) under or by, the transaction or the giving of the preference.

(2)   An order under section 339 or 340 may affect the property of, or impose any obligation on, any person whether or not he is the person with whom the individual in question entered into the transaction or, as the case may be, the person to whom the preference was given; but such an order—

(a)   shall not prejudice any interest in property which was acquired from a person other than that individual and was acquired in good faith and for value, or prejudice any interest deriving from such an interest, and

(b)   shall not require a person who received a benefit from the transaction or preference in good faith and for value to pay a sum to the trustee of the bankrupt's estate, except where he was a party to the transaction or the payment is to be in respect of a preference given to that person at a time when he was a creditor of that individual.

(2A)   Where a person has acquired an interest in property from a person other than the individual in question, or has received a benefit from the transaction or preference, and at the time of that acquisition or receipt—

(a)   he had notice of the relevant surrounding circumstances and of the relevant proceedings, or

(b)   he was an associate of, or was connected with, either the individual in question or the person with whom that individual entered into the transaction or to whom that individual gave the preference,

then, unless the contrary is shown, it shall be presumed for the purposes of paragraph (a) or (as the case may be) paragraph (b) of subsection (2) that the interest was acquired or the benefit was received otherwise than in good faith.

(3) Any sums required to be paid to the trustee in accordance with an order under section 339 or 340 shall be comprised in the bankrupt's estate.

(4) For the purposes of subsection (2A)(a), the relevant surrounding circumstances are (as the case may require)—

(a) the fact that the individual in question entered into the transaction at an undervalue; or

(b) the circumstances which amounted to the giving of the preference by the individual in question.

(5) For the purposes of subsection (2A)(a), a person has notice of the relevant proceedings if he has notice—

(a) of the fact that the petition on which the individual in question is adjudged bankrupt has been presented; or

(b) of the fact that the individual in question has been adjudged bankrupt.

(6) Section 249 in Part VII of this Act shall apply for the purposes of subsection (2A)(b) as it applies for the purposes of the first Group of Parts.

342A. Recovery of excessive pension contributions

(1) Where an individual who is adjudged bankrupt—

(a) has rights under an approved pension arrangement, or

(b) has excluded rights under an unapproved pension arrangement,

the trustee of the bankrupt's estate may apply to the court for an order under this section.

(2) If the court is satisfied—

(a) that the rights under the arrangement are to any extent, and whether directly or indirectly, the fruits of relevant contributions, and

(b) that the making of any of the relevant contributions ("the excessive contributions") has unfairly prejudiced the individual's creditors,

the court may make such order as it thinks fit for restoring the position to what it would have been had the excessive contributions not been made.

(3) Subsection (4) applies where the court is satisfied that the value of the rights under the arrangement is, as a result of rights of the individual under the arrangement or any other pension arrangement having at any time become subject to a debit under section 29(1)(a) of the Welfare Reform and Pensions Act 1999 (debits giving effect to pension-sharing), less than it would otherwise have been.

(4) Where this subsection applies—

(a) any relevant contributions which were represented by the rights which became subject to the debit shall, for the purposes of subsection (2), be taken to be contributions of which the rights under the arrangement are the fruits, and

(b) where the relevant contributions represented by the rights under the arrangement (including those so represented by virtue of paragraph (a)) are not all excessive contributions, relevant contributions which are represented by the rights under the arrangement otherwise than by virtue of paragraph (a) shall be treated as excessive contributions before any which are so represented by virtue of that paragraph.

(5) In subsections (2) to (4) "relevant contributions" means contributions to the arrangement or any other pension arrangement—

(a) which the individual has at any time made on his own behalf, or

(b) which have at any time been made on his behalf.

(6) The court shall, in determining whether it is satisfied under subsection (2)(b), consider in particular—

(a) whether any of the contributions were made for the purpose of putting assets beyond the reach of the individual's creditors or any of them, and

(b) whether the total amount of any contributions—

(i) made by or on behalf of the individual to pension arrangements, and

(ii) represented (whether directly or indirectly) by rights under approved pension arrangements or excluded rights under unapproved pension arrangements, is an amount which is excessive in view of the individual's circumstances when those contributions were made.

(7)   For the purposes of this section and sections 342B and 342C ("the recovery provisions"), rights of an individual under an unapproved pension arrangement are excluded rights if they are rights which are excluded from his estate by virtue of regulations under section 12 of the Welfare Reform and Pensions Act 1999.

(8)   In the recovery provisions—

"approved pension arrangement" has the same meaning as in section 11 of the Welfare Reform and Pensions Act 1999;

"unapproved pension arrangement" has the same meaning as in section 12 of that Act.

342B.   Orders under section 342A

(1)   Without prejudice to the generality of section 342A(2), an order under section 342A may include provision—

(a)   requiring the person responsible for the arrangement to pay an amount to the individual's trustee in bankruptcy,

(b)   adjusting the liabilities of the arrangement in respect of the individual,

(c)   adjusting any liabilities of the arrangement in respect of any other person that derive, directly or indirectly, from rights of the individual under the arrangement,

(d)   for the recovery by the person responsible for the arrangement (whether by deduction from any amount which that person is ordered to pay or otherwise) of costs incurred by that person in complying in the bankrupt's case with any requirement under section 342C(1) or in giving effect to the order.

(2)   In subsection (1), references to adjusting the liabilities of the arrangement in respect of a person include (in particular) reducing the amount of any benefit or future benefit to which that person is entitled under the arrangement.

(3)   In subsection (1)(c), the reference to liabilities of the arrangement does not include liabilities in respect of a person which result from giving effect to an order or provision falling within section 28(1) of the Welfare Reform and Pensions Act 1999 (pension sharing orders and agreements).

(4)   The maximum amount which the person responsible for an arrangement may be required to pay by an order under section 342A is the lesser of—

(a)   the amount of the excessive contributions, and

(b)   the value of the individual's rights under the arrangement (if the arrangement is an approved pension arrangement) or of his excluded rights under the arrangement (if the arrangement is an unapproved pension arrangement).

(5)   An order under section 342A which requires the person responsible for an arrangement to pay an amount ("the restoration amount") to the individual's trustee in bankruptcy must provide for the liabilities of the arrangement to be correspondingly reduced.

(6)   For the purposes of subsection (5), liabilities are correspondingly reduced if the difference between—

(a)   the amount of the liabilities immediately before the reduction, and

(b)   the amount of the liabilities immediately after the reduction,

is equal to the restoration amount.

(7)   An order under section 342A in respect of an arrangement—

(a)   shall be binding on the person responsible for the arrangement, and

(b)   overrides provisions of the arrangement to the extent that they conflict with the provisions of the order.

342C.   Orders under section 342A: supplementary

(1)   The person responsible for—

(a)   an approved pension arrangement under which a bankrupt has rights,

(b)   an unapproved pension arrangement under which a bankrupt has excluded rights, or

(c)   a pension arrangement under which a bankrupt has at any time had rights, shall, on the bankrupt's trustee in bankruptcy making a written request, provide the trustee with such information about the arrangement and rights as the trustee may reasonably require for, or in connection with, the making of applications under section 342A.

(2) Nothing in—

(a) any provision of section 159 of the Pension Schemes Act 1993 or section 91 of the Pensions Act 1995 (which prevent assignment and the making of orders that restrain a person from receiving anything which he is prevented from assigning),

(b) any provision of any enactment (whether passed or made before or after the passing of the Welfare Reform and Pensions Act 1999) corresponding to any of the provisions mentioned in paragraph (a), or

(c) any provision of the arrangement in question corresponding to any of those provisions,

applies to a court exercising its powers under section 342A.

(3) Where any sum is required by an order under section 342A to be paid to the trustee in bankruptcy, that sum shall be comprised in the bankrupt's estate.

(4) Regulations may, for the purposes of the recovery provisions, make provision about the calculation and verification of—

(a) any such value as is mentioned in section 342B(4)(b);

(b) any such amounts as are mentioned in section 342B(6)(a) and (b).

(5) The power conferred by subsection (4) includes power to provide for calculation or verification—

(a) in such manner as may, in the particular case, be approved by a prescribed person; or

(b) in accordance with guidance—

(i) from time to time prepared by a prescribed person, and

(ii) approved by the Secretary of State.

(6) References in the recovery provisions to the person responsible for a pension arrangement are to—

(a) the trustees, managers or provider of the arrangement, or

(b) the person having functions in relation to the arrangement corresponding to those of a trustee, manager or provider.

(7) In this section and sections 342A and 342B—

"prescribed" means prescribed by regulations;

"the recovery provisions" means this section and sections 342A and 342B;

"regulations" means regulations made by the Secretary of State.

(8) Regulations under the recovery provisions may—

(a) make different provision for different cases;

(b) contain such incidental, supplemental and transitional provisions as appear to the Secretary of State necessary or expedient.

(9) Regulations under the recovery provisions shall be made by statutory instrument subject to annulment in pursuance of a resolution of either House of Parliament.

342D. Recovery of excessive contributions in pension-sharing cases

(1) For the purposes of sections 339, 341 and 342, a pension-sharing transaction shall be taken—

(a) to be a transaction, entered into by the transferor with the transferee, by which the appropriate amount is transferred by the transferor to the transferee; and

(b) to be capable of being a transaction entered into at an undervalue only so far as it is a transfer of so much of the appropriate amount as is recoverable.

(2) For the purposes of sections 340 to 342, a pension-sharing transaction shall be taken—

(a) to be something (namely a transfer of the appropriate amount to the transferee) done by the transferor; and

(b) to be capable of being a preference given to the transferee only so far as it is a transfer of so much of the appropriate amount as is recoverable.

(3) If on an application under section 339 or 340 any question arises as to whether, or the extent to which, the appropriate amount in the case of a pension-sharing transaction is recoverable, the question shall be determined in accordance with subsections (4) to (8).

(4)   The court shall first determine the extent (if any) to which the transferor's rights under the shared arrangement at the time of the transaction appear to have been (whether directly or indirectly) the fruits of contributions ("personal contributions")—

(a)   which the transferor has at any time made on his own behalf, or

(b)   which have at any time been made on the transferor's behalf,

to the shared arrangement or any other pension arrangement.

(5)   Where it appears that those rights were to any extent the fruits of personal contributions, the court shall then determine the extent (if any) to which those rights appear to have been the fruits of personal contributions whose making has unfairly prejudiced the transferor's creditors ("the unfair contributions").

(6)   If it appears to the court that the extent to which those rights were the fruits of the unfair contributions is such that the transfer of the appropriate amount could have been made out of rights under the shared arrangement which were not the fruits of the unfair contributions, then the appropriate amount is not recoverable.

(7)   If it appears to the court that the transfer could not have been wholly so made, then the appropriate amount is recoverable to the extent to which it appears to the court that the transfer could not have been so made.

(8)   In making the determination mentioned in subsection (5) the court shall consider in particular—

(a)   whether any of the personal contributions were made for the purpose of putting assets beyond the reach of the transferor's creditors or any of them, and

(b)   whether the total amount of any personal contributions represented, at the time the pension-sharing transaction was made, by rights under pension arrangements is an amount which is excessive in view of the transferor's circumstances when those contributions were made.

(9)   In this section and sections 342E and 342F—

"appropriate amount", in relation to a pension-sharing transaction, means the appropriate amount in relation to that transaction for the purposes of section 29(1) of the Welfare Reform and Pensions Act 1999 (creation of pension credits and debits);

"pension-sharing transaction" means an order or provision falling within section 28(1) of the Welfare Reform and Pensions Act 1999 (orders and agreements which activate pension-sharing);

"shared arrangement", in relation to a pension-sharing transaction, means the pension arrangement to which the transaction relates;

"transferee", in relation to a pension-sharing transaction, means the person for whose benefit the transaction is made;

"transferor", in relation to a pension-sharing transaction, means the person to whose rights the transaction relates.

342E.   Orders under section 339 or 340 in respect of pension-sharing transactions

(1)   This section and section 342F apply if the court is making an order under section 339 or 340 in a case where—

(a)   the transaction or preference is, or is any part of, a pension-sharing transaction, and

(b)   the transferee has rights under a pension arrangement ("the destination arrangement", which may be the shared arrangement or any other pension arrangement) that are derived, directly or indirectly, from the pension-sharing transaction.

(2)   Without prejudice to the generality of section 339(2) or 340(2), or of section 342, the order may include provision—

(a)   requiring the person responsible for the destination arrangement to pay an amount to the transferor's trustee in bankruptcy,

(b)   adjusting the liabilities of the destination arrangement in respect of the transferee,

(c)   adjusting any liabilities of the destination arrangement in respect of any other person that derive, directly or indirectly, from rights of the transferee under the destination arrangement,

(d)   for the recovery by the person responsible for the destination arrangement (whether by deduction from any amount which that person is ordered to pay or otherwise) of costs incurred by that person in complying in the transferor's case with any requirement under section 342F(1) or in giving effect to the order,

(e)   for the recovery, from the transferor's trustee in bankruptcy, by the person responsible for a pension arrangement, of costs incurred by that person in complying in the transferor's case with any requirement under section 342F(2) or (3).

(3)   In subsection (2), references to adjusting the liabilities of the destination arrangement in respect of a person include (in particular) reducing the amount of any benefit or future benefit to which that person is entitled under the arrangement.

(4)   The maximum amount which the person responsible for the destination arrangement may be required to pay by the order is the smallest of—

(a)   so much of the appropriate amount as, in accordance with section 342D, is recoverable,

(b)   so much (if any) of the amount of the unfair contributions (within the meaning given by section 342D(5)) as is not recoverable by way of an order under section 342A containing provision such as is mentioned in section 342B(1)(a), and

(c)   the value of the transferee's rights under the destination arrangement so far as they are derived, directly or indirectly, from the pension-sharing transaction.

(5)   If the order requires the person responsible for the destination arrangement to pay an amount ("the restoration amount") to the transferor's trustee in bankruptcy it must provide for the liabilities of the arrangement to be correspondingly reduced.

(6)   For the purposes of subsection (5), liabilities are correspondingly reduced if the difference between—

(a)   the amount of the liabilities immediately before the reduction, and

(b)   the amount of the liabilities immediately after the reduction,

is equal to the restoration amount.

(7)   The order—

(a)   shall be binding on the person responsible for the destination arrangement, and

(b)   overrides provisions of the destination arrangement to the extent that they conflict with the provisions of the order.

342F.   Orders under section 339 or 340 in pension-sharing cases: supplementary

(1)   On the transferor's trustee in bankruptcy making a written request to the person responsible for the destination arrangement, that person shall provide the trustee with such information about—

(a)   the arrangement,

(b)   the transferee's rights under it, and

(c)   where the destination arrangement is the shared arrangement, the transferor's rights under it,

as the trustee may reasonably require for, or in connection with, the making of applications under sections 339 and 340.

(2)   Where the shared arrangement is not the destination arrangement, the person responsible for the shared arrangement shall, on the transferor's trustee in bankruptcy making a written request to that person, provide the trustee with such information about—

(a)   the arrangement, and

(b)   the transferor's rights under it,

as the trustee may reasonably require for, or in connection with, the making of applications under sections 339 and 340.

(3)   On the transferor's trustee in bankruptcy making a written request to the person responsible for any intermediate arrangement, that person shall provide the trustee with such information about—

(a)   the arrangement, and

(b)   the transferee's rights under it,

as the trustee may reasonably require for, or in connection with, the making of applications under sections 339 and 340.

(4)   In subsection (3) "intermediate arrangement" means a pension arrangement, other than the shared arrangement or the destination arrangement, in relation to which the following conditions are fulfilled—

(a)   there was a time when the transferee had rights under the arrangement that were derived (directly or indirectly) from the pension-sharing transaction, and

(b)   the transferee's rights under the destination arrangement (so far as derived from the pension-sharing transaction) are to any extent derived (directly or indirectly) from the rights mentioned in paragraph (a).

(5)   Nothing in—

(a)   any provision of section 159 of the Pension Schemes Act 1993 or section 91 of the Pensions Act 1995 (which prevent assignment and the making of orders which restrain a person from receiving anything which he is prevented from assigning),

(b)   any provision of any enactment (whether passed or made before or after the passing of the Welfare Reform and Pensions Act 1999) corresponding to any of the provisions mentioned in paragraph (a), or

(c)   any provision of the destination arrangement corresponding to any of those provisions,

applies to a court exercising its powers under section 339 or 340.

(6)   Regulations may, for the purposes of sections 339 to 342, sections 342D and 342E and this section, make provision about the calculation and verification of—

(a)   any such value as is mentioned in section 342E(4)(c);

(b)   any such amounts as are mentioned in section 342E(6)(a) and (b).

(7)   The power conferred by subsection (6) includes power to provide for calculation or verification—

(a)   in such manner as may, in the particular case, be approved by a prescribed person; or

(b)   in accordance with guidance—

(i)   from time to time prepared by a prescribed person, and

(ii)   approved by the Secretary of State.

(8)   In section 342E and this section, references to the person responsible for a pension arrangement are to—

(a)   the trustees, managers or provider of the arrangement, or

(b)   the person having functions in relation to the arrangement corresponding to those of a trustee, manager or provider.

(9)   In this section—

"prescribed" means prescribed by regulations;

"regulations" means regulations made by the Secretary of State.

(10)   Regulations under this section may—

(a)   make different provision for different cases;

(b)   contain such incidental, supplemental and transitional provisions as appear to the Secretary of State necessary or expedient.

(11)   Regulations under this section shall be made by statutory instrument subject to annulment in pursuance of a resolution of either House of Parliament.

343.   Extortionate credit transactions

(1)   This section applies where a person is adjudged bankrupt who is or has been a party to a transaction for, or involving, the provision to him of credit.

(2)   The court may, on the application of the trustee of the bankrupt's estate, make an order with respect to the transaction if the transaction is or was extortionate and was not entered into more than 3 years before the commencement of the bankruptcy.

(3)   For the purposes of this section a transaction is extortionate if, having regard to the risk accepted by the person providing the credit—

(a)   the terms of it are or were such as to require grossly exorbitant payments to be made (whether unconditionally or in certain contingencies) in respect of the provision of the credit, or

(b)   it otherwise grossly contravened ordinary principles of fair dealing;

and it shall be presumed, unless the contrary is proved, that a transaction with respect to which an application is made under this section is or, as the case may be, was extortionate.

(4) An order under this section with respect to any transaction may contain such one or more of the following as the court thinks fit, that is to say—

(a) provision setting aside the whole or part of any obligation created by the transaction;

(b) provision otherwise varying the terms of the transaction or varying the terms on which any security for the purposes of the transaction is held;

(c) provision requiring any person who is or was party to the transaction to pay to the trustee any sums paid to that person, by virtue of the transaction, by the bankrupt;

(d) provision requiring any person to surrender to the trustee any property held by him as security for the purposes of the transaction;

(e) provision directing accounts to be taken between any persons.

(5) Any sums or property required to be paid or surrendered to the trustee in accordance with an order under this section shall be comprised in the bankrupt's estate.

(6) Neither the trustee of a bankrupt's estate nor an undischarged bankrupt is entitled to make an application under section 139(1)(a) of the Consumer Credit Act 1974 (re-opening of extortionate credit agreements) for any agreement by which credit is or has been provided to the bankrupt to be re-opened.

But the powers conferred by this section are exercisable in relation to any transaction concurrently with any powers exercisable under this Act in relation to that transaction as a transaction at an undervalue.

344. Avoidance of general assignment of book debts

(1) The following applies where a person engaged in any business makes a general assignment to another person of his existing or future book debts, or any class of them, and is subsequently adjudged bankrupt.

(2) The assignment is void against the trustee of the bankrupt's estate as regards book debts which were not paid before the presentation of the bankruptcy petition, unless the assignment has been registered under the Bills of Sale Act 1878.

(3) For the purposes of subsections (1) and (2)—

(a) "assignment" includes an assignment by way of security or charge on book debts, and

(b) "general assignment" does not include—

(i) an assignment of book debts due at the date of the assignment from specified debtors or of debts becoming due under specified contracts, or

(ii) an assignment of book debts included either in a transfer of a business made in good faith and for value or in an assignment of assets for the benefit of creditors generally.

(4) For the purposes of registration under the Act of 1878 an assignment of book debts is to be treated as if it were a bill of sale given otherwise than by way of security for the payment of a sum of money; and the provisions of that Act with respect to the registration of bills of sale apply accordingly with such necessary modifications as may be made by rules under that Act.

345. Contracts to which bankrupt is a party

(1) The following applies where a contract has been made with a person who is subsequently adjudged bankrupt.

(2) The court may, on the application of any other party to the contract, make an order discharging obligations under the contract on such terms as to payment by the applicant or the bankrupt of damages for non-performance or otherwise as appear to the court to be equitable.

(3) Any damages payable by the bankrupt by virtue of an order of the court under this section are provable as a bankruptcy debt.

(4) Where an undischarged bankrupt is a contractor in respect of any contract jointly with any person, that person may sue or be sued in respect of the contract without the joinder of the bankrupt.

346.   Enforcement procedures

(1)   Subject to section 285 in Chapter II (restrictions on proceedings and remedies) and to the following provisions of this section, where the creditor of any person who is adjudged bankrupt has, before the commencement of the bankruptcy—

(a)   issued execution against the goods or land of that person, or

(b)   attached a debt due to that person from another person,

that creditor is not entitled, as against the official receiver or trustee of the bankrupt's estate, to retain the benefit of the execution or attachment, or any sums paid to avoid it, unless the execution or attachment was completed, or the sums were paid, before the commencement of the bankruptcy.

(2)   Subject as follows, where any goods of a person have been taken in execution, then, if before the completion of the execution notice is given to the enforcement officer or other officer charged with the execution that that person has been adjudged bankrupt—

(a)   the enforcement officer or other officer shall on request deliver to the official receiver or trustee of the bankrupt's estate the goods and any money seized or recovered in part satisfaction of the execution, but

(b)   the costs of the execution are a first charge on the goods or money so delivered and the official receiver or trustee may sell the goods or a sufficient part of them for the purpose of satisfying the charge.

(3)   Subject to subsection (6) below, where—

(a)   under an execution in respect of a judgment for a sum exceeding such sum as may be prescribed for the purposes of this subsection, the goods of any person are sold or money is paid in order to avoid a sale, and

(b)   before the end of the period of 14 days beginning with the day of the sale or payment the enforcement officer or other officer charged with the execution is given notice that a bankruptcy petition has been presented in relation to that person, and

(c)   a bankruptcy order is or has been made on that petition,

the balance of the proceeds of sale or money paid, after deducting the costs of execution, shall (in priority to the claim of the execution creditor) be comprised in the bankrupt's estate.

(4)   Accordingly, in the case of an execution in respect of a judgment for a sum exceeding the sum prescribed for the purposes of subsection (3), the enforcement officer or other officer charged with the execution—

(a)   shall not dispose of the balance mentioned in subsection (3) at any time within the period of 14 days so mentioned or while there is pending a bankruptcy petition of which he has been given notice under that subsection, and

(b)   shall pay that balance, where by virtue of that subsection it is comprised in the bankrupt's estate, to the official receiver or (if there is one) to the trustee of that estate.

(5)   For the purposes of this section—

(a)   an execution against goods is completed by seizure and sale or by the making of a charging order under section 1 of the Charging Orders Act 1979;

(b)   an execution against land is completed by seizure, by the appointment of a receiver or by the making of a charging order under that section;

(c)   an attachment of a debt is completed by the receipt of the debt.

(6)   The rights conferred by subsections (1) to (3) on the official receiver or the trustee may, to such extent and on such terms as it thinks fit, be set aside by the court in favour of the creditor who has issued the execution or attached the debt.

(7)   Nothing in this section entitles the trustee of a bankrupt's estate to claim goods from a person who has acquired them in good faith under a sale by an enforcement officer or other officer charged with an execution.

(8)   Neither subsection (2) nor subsection (3) applies in relation to any execution against property which has been acquired by or has devolved upon the bankrupt since the commencement of the bankruptcy, unless, at the time the execution is issued or before it is completed—

(a)   the property has been or is claimed for the bankrupt's estate under section 307 (after-acquired property), and

(b)   a copy of the notice given under that section has been or is served on the enforcement officer or other officer charged with the execution.

(9)   In this section "enforcement officer" means an individual who is authorised to act as an enforcement officer under the Courts Act 2003.

347.   Distress, etc

(1)   The right of any landlord or other person to whom rent is payable to distrain upon the goods and effects of an undischarged bankrupt for rent due to him from the bankrupt is available (subject to sections 252(2)(b) and 254(1) above and subsection (5) below) against goods and effects comprised in the bankrupt's estate, but only for 6 months' rent accrued due before the commencement of the bankruptcy.

(2)   Where a landlord or other person to whom rent is payable has distrained for rent upon the goods and effects of an individual to whom a bankruptcy petition relates and a bankruptcy order is subsequently made on that petition, any amount recovered by way of that distress which—

(a)   is in excess of the amount which by virtue of subsection (1) would have been recoverable after the commencement of the bankruptcy, or

(b)   is in respect of rent for a period or part of a period after the distress was levied,

shall be held for the bankrupt as part of his estate.

(3)   Where any person (whether or not a landlord or person entitled to rent) has distrained upon the goods or effects of an individual who is adjudged bankrupt before the end of the period of 3 months beginning with the distraint, so much of those goods or effects, or of the proceeds of their sale, as is not held for the bankrupt under subsection (2) shall be charged for the benefit of the bankrupt's estate with the preferential debts of the bankrupt to the extent that the bankrupt's estate is for the time being insufficient for meeting those debts.

(4)   Where by virtue of any charge under subsection (3) any person surrenders any goods or effects to the trustee of a bankrupt's estate or makes a payment to such a trustee, that person ranks, in respect of the amount of the proceeds of the sale of those goods or effects by the trustee or, as the case may be, the amount of the payment, as a preferential creditor of the bankrupt, except as against so much of the bankrupt's estate as is available for the payment of preferential creditors by virtue of the surrender or payment.

(5)   A landlord or other person to whom rent is payable is not at any time after the discharge of a bankrupt entitled to distrain upon any goods or effects comprised in the bankrupt's estate.

(6)   Where in the case of any execution—

(a)   a landlord is (apart from this section) entitled under section 1 of the Landlord and Tenant Act 1709 or section 102 of the County Courts Act 1984 (claims for rent where goods seized in execution) to claim for an amount not exceeding one year's rent, and

(b)   the person against whom the execution is levied is adjudged bankrupt before the notice of claim is served on the enforcement officer, or other officer charged with the execution,

the right of the landlord to claim under that section is restricted to a right to claim for an amount not exceeding 6 months' rent and does not extend to any rent payable in respect of a period after the notice of claim is so served.

(7)   Nothing in subsection (6) imposes any liability on an enforcement officer or other officer charged with an execution to account to the official receiver or the trustee of a bankrupt's estate for any sums paid by him to a landlord at any time before the enforcement officer or other officer was served with notice of the bankruptcy order in question.

But this subsection is without prejudice to the liability of the landlord.

(8)   Subject to sections 252(2)(b) and 254(1) above nothing in this Group of Parts affects any right to distrain otherwise than for rent; and any such right is at any time exercisable without restriction against property comprised in a bankrupt's estate, even if that right is expressed by any enactment to be exercisable in like manner as a right to distrain for rent.

(9)   Any right to distrain against property comprised in a bankrupt's estate is exercisable notwithstanding that the property has vested in the trustee.

(10)   The provisions of this section are without prejudice to a landlord's right in a bankruptcy to prove for any bankruptcy debt in respect of rent.

(11)   In this section "enforcement officer" means an individual who is authorised to act as an enforcement officer under the Courts Act 2003.

348.   Apprenticeships, etc

(1)   This section applies where—

    (a)   a bankruptcy order is made in respect of an individual to whom another individual was an apprentice or articled clerk at the time when the petition on which the order was made was presented, and

    (b)   the bankrupt or the apprentice or clerk gives notice to the trustee terminating the apprenticeship or articles.

(2)   Subject to subsection (6) below, the indenture of apprenticeship or, as the case may be, the articles of agreement shall be discharged with effect from the commencement of the bankruptcy.

(3)   If any money has been paid by or on behalf of the apprentice or clerk to the bankrupt as a fee, the trustee may, on an application made by or on behalf of the apprentice or clerk, pay such sum to the apprentice or clerk as the trustee thinks reasonable, having regard to—

    (a)   the amount of the fee,

    (b)   the proportion of the period in respect of which the fee was paid that has been served by the apprentice or clerk before the commencement of the bankruptcy, and

    (c)   the other circumstances of the case.

(4)   The power of the trustee to make a payment under subsection (3) has priority over his obligation to distribute the bankrupt's estate.

(5)   Instead of making a payment under subsection (3), the trustee may, if it appears to him expedient to do so on an application made by or on behalf of the apprentice or clerk, transfer the indenture or articles to a person other than the bankrupt.

(6)   Where a transfer is made under subsection (5), subsection (2) has effect only as between the apprentice or clerk and the bankrupt.

349.   Unenforceability of liens on books, etc

(1)   Subject as follows, a lien or other right to retain possession of any of the books, papers or other records of a bankrupt is unenforceable to the extent that its enforcement would deny possession of any books, papers or other records to the official receiver or the trustee of the bankrupt's estate.

(2)   Subsection (1) does not apply to a lien on documents which give a title to property and are held as such.

349A.   Arbitration agreements to which bankrupt is party

(1)   This section applies where a bankrupt had become party to a contract containing an arbitration agreement before the commencement of his bankruptcy.

(2)   If the trustee in bankruptcy adopts the contract, the arbitration agreement is enforceable by or against the trustee in relation to matters arising from or connected with the contract.

(3)   If the trustee in bankruptcy does not adopt the contract and a matter to which the arbitration agreement applies requires to be determined in connection with or for the purposes of the bankruptcy proceedings—

    (a)   the trustee with the consent of the creditors' committee, or

    (b)   any other party to the agreement,

may apply to the court which may, if it thinks fit in all the circumstances of the case, order that the matter be referred to arbitration in accordance with the arbitration agreement.

(4)   In this section—

    "arbitration agreement" has the same meaning as in Part I of the Arbitration Act 1996; and

    "the court" means the court which has jurisdiction in the bankruptcy proceedings.

CHAPTER VI
BANKRUPTCY OFFENCES

Preliminary

350. Scheme of this Chapter

(1) Subject to section 360(3) below, this Chapter applies where the court has made a bankruptcy order on a bankruptcy petition.

(2) This Chapter applies whether or not the bankruptcy order is annulled, but proceedings for an offence under this Chapter shall not be instituted after the annulment.

(3) Without prejudice to his liability in respect of a subsequent bankruptcy, the bankrupt is not guilty of an offence under this Chapter in respect of anything done after his discharge; but nothing in this Group of Parts prevents the institution of proceedings against a discharged bankrupt for an offence committed before his discharge.

(3A) Subsection (3) is without prejudice to any provision of this Chapter which applies to a person in respect of whom a bankruptcy restrictions order is in force.

(4) It is not a defence in proceedings for an offence under this Chapter that anything relied on, in whole or in part, as constituting that offence was done outside England and Wales.

(5) Proceedings for an offence under this Chapter or under the rules shall not be instituted except by the Secretary of State or by or with the consent of the Director of Public Prosecutions.

(6) A person guilty of an offence under this Chapter is liable to imprisonment or a fine, or both.

351. Definitions

In the following provisions of this Chapter—

(a) references to property comprised in the bankrupt's estate or to property possession of which is required to be delivered up to the official receiver or the trustee of the bankrupt's estate include any property which would be such property if a notice in respect of it were given under section 307 (after-acquired property), section 308 (personal property and effects of bankrupt having more than replacement value) or section 308A (vesting in trustee of certain tenancies);

(b) "the initial period" means the period between the presentation of the bankruptcy petition and the commencement of the bankruptcy; and

(c) a reference to a number of months or years before petition is to that period ending with the presentation of the bankruptcy petition.

352. Defence of innocent intention

Where in the case of an offence under any provision of this Chapter it is stated that this section applies, a person is not guilty of the offence if he proves that, at the time of the conduct constituting the offence, he had no intent to defraud or to conceal the state of his affairs.

Wrongdoing by the bankrupt before and after bankruptcy

353. Non-disclosure

(1) The bankrupt is guilty of an offence if—

(a) he does not to the best of his knowledge and belief disclose all the property comprised in his estate to the official receiver or the trustee, or

(b) he does not inform the official receiver or the trustee of any disposal of any property which but for the disposal would be so comprised, stating how, when, to whom and for what consideration the property was disposed of.

(2) Subsection (1)(b) does not apply to any disposal in the ordinary course of a business carried on by the bankrupt or to any payment of the ordinary expenses of the bankrupt or his family.

(3) Section 352 applies to this offence.

354. Concealment of property

(1) The bankrupt is guilty of an offence if—

    (a)   he does not deliver up possession to the official receiver or trustee, or as the official receiver or trustee may direct, of such part of the property comprised in his estate as is in his possession or under his control and possession of which he is required by law so to deliver up,

    (b)   he conceals any debt due to or from him or conceals any property the value of which is not less than the prescribed amount and possession of which he is required to deliver up to the official receiver or trustee, or

    (c)   in the 12 months before petition, or in the initial period, he did anything which would have been an offence under paragraph (b) above if the bankruptcy order had been made immediately before he did it.

Section 352 applies to this offence.

(2)   The bankrupt is guilty of an offence if he removes, or in the initial period removed, any property the value of which was not less than the prescribed amount and possession of which he has or would have been required to deliver up to the official receiver or the trustee.

Section 352 applies to this offence.

(3)   The bankrupt is guilty of an offence if he without reasonable excuse fails, on being required to do so by the official receiver, the trustee or the court—

    (a)   to account for the loss of any substantial part of his property incurred in the 12 months before petition or in the initial period, or

    (b)   to give a satisfactory explanation of the manner in which such a loss was incurred.

355.   Concealment of books and papers; falsification

(1)   The bankrupt is guilty of an offence if he does not deliver up possession to the official receiver or the trustee, or as the official receiver or trustee may direct, of all books, papers and other records of which he has possession or control and which relate to his estate or his affairs.

Section 352 applies to this offence.

(2)   The bankrupt is guilty of an offence if—

    (a)   he prevents, or in the initial period prevented, the production of any books, papers or records relating to his estate or affairs;

    (b)   he conceals, destroys, mutilates or falsifies, or causes or permits the concealment, destruction, mutilation or falsification of, any books, papers or other records relating to his estate or affairs;

    (c)   he makes, or causes or permits the making of, any false entries in any book, document or record relating to his estate or affairs; or

    (d)   in the 12 months before petition, or in the initial period, he did anything which would have been an offence under paragraph (b) or (c) above if the bankruptcy order had been made before he did it.

Section 352 applies to this offence.

(3)   The bankrupt is guilty of an offence if—

    (a)   he disposes of, or alters or makes any omission in, or causes or permits the disposal, altering or making of any omission in, any book, document or record relating to his estate or affairs, or

    (b)   in the 12 months before petition, or in the initial period, he did anything which would have been an offence under paragraph (a) if the bankruptcy order had been made before he did it.

Section 352 applies to this offence.

(4)   In their application to a trading record subsections (2)(d) and (3)(b) shall have effect as if the reference to 12 months were a reference to two years.

(5)   In subsection (4) "trading record" means a book, document or record which shows or explains the transactions or financial position of a person's business, including—

    (a)   a periodic record of cash paid and received,

    (b)   a statement of periodic stock-taking, and

    (c)   except in the case of goods sold by way of retail trade, a record of goods sold and purchased which identifies the buyer and seller or enables them to be identified.

356. False statements

(1) The bankrupt is guilty of an offence if he makes or has made any material omission in any statement made under any provision in this Group of Parts and relating to his affairs.
Section 352 applies to this offence.

(2) The bankrupt is guilty of an offence if—

(a) knowing or believing that a false debt has been proved by any person under the bankruptcy, he fails to inform the trustee as soon as practicable; or

(b) he attempts to account for any part of his property by fictitious losses or expenses; or

(c) at any meeting of his creditors in the 12 months before petition or (whether or not at such a meeting) at any time in the initial period, he did anything which would have been an offence under paragraph (b) if the bankruptcy order had been made before he did it; or

(d) he is, or at any time has been, guilty of any false representation or other fraud for the purpose of obtaining the consent of his creditors, or any of them, to an agreement with reference to his affairs or to his bankruptcy.

357. Fraudulent disposal of property

(1) The bankrupt is guilty of an offence if he makes or causes to be made, or has in the period of 5 years ending with the commencement of the bankruptcy made or caused to be made, any gift or transfer of, or any charge on, his property.
Section 352 applies to this offence.

(2) The reference to making a transfer of or charge on any property includes causing or conniving at the levying of any execution against that property.

(3) The bankrupt is guilty of an offence if he conceals or removes, or has at any time before the commencement of the bankruptcy concealed or removed, any part of his property after, or within 2 months before, the date on which a judgment or order for the payment of money has been obtained against him, being a judgment or order which was not satisfied before the commencement of the bankruptcy.
Section 352 applies to this offence.

358. Absconding

The bankrupt is guilty of an offence if—

(a) he leaves, or attempts or makes preparations to leave, England and Wales with any property the value of which is not less than the prescribed amount and possession of which he is required to deliver up to the official receiver or the trustee, or

(b) in the 6 months before petition, or in the initial period, he did anything which would have been an offence under paragraph (a) if the bankruptcy order had been made immediately before he did it.

Section 352 applies to this offence.

359. Fraudulent dealing with property obtained on credit

(1) The bankrupt is guilty of an offence if, in the 12 months before petition, or in the initial period, he disposed of any property which he had obtained on credit and, at the time he disposed of it, had not paid for.
Section 352 applies to this offence.

(2) A person is guilty of an offence if, in the 12 months before petition or in the initial period, he acquired or received property from the bankrupt knowing or believing—

(a) that the bankrupt owed money in respect of the property, and

(b) that the bankrupt did not intend, or was unlikely to be able, to pay the money he so owed.

(3) A person is not guilty of an offence under subsection (1) or (2) if the disposal, acquisition or receipt of the property was in the ordinary course of a business carried on by the bankrupt at the time of the disposal, acquisition or receipt.

(4)   In determining for the purposes of this section whether any property is disposed of, acquired or received in the ordinary course of a business carried on by the bankrupt, regard may be had, in particular, to the price paid for the property.

(5)   In this section references to disposing of property include pawning or pledging it; and references to acquiring or receiving property shall be read accordingly.

360.   Obtaining credit; engaging in business

(1)   The bankrupt is guilty of an offence if—

    (a)   either alone or jointly with any other person, he obtains credit to the extent of the prescribed amount or more without giving the person from whom he obtains it the relevant information about his status; or

    (b)   he engages (whether directly or indirectly) in any business under a name other than that in which he was adjudged bankrupt without disclosing to all persons with whom he enters into any business transaction the name in which he was so adjudged.

(2)   The reference to the bankrupt obtaining credit includes the following cases—

    (a)   where goods are bailed to him under a hire-purchase agreement, or agreed to be sold to him under a conditional sale agreement, and

    (b)   where he is paid in advance (whether in money or otherwise) for the supply of goods or services.

(3)   A person whose estate has been sequestrated in Scotland, or who has been adjudged bankrupt in Northern Ireland, is guilty of an offence if, before his discharge, he does anything in England and Wales which would be an offence under subsection (1) if he were an undischarged bankrupt and the sequestration of his estate or the adjudication in Northern Ireland were an adjudication under this Part.

(4)   For the purposes of subsection (1)(a), the relevant information about the status of the person in question is the information that he is an undischarged bankrupt or, as the case may be, that his estate has been sequestrated in Scotland and that he has not been discharged.

(5)   This section applies to the bankrupt after discharge while a bankruptcy restrictions order is in force in respect of him.

(6)   For the purposes of subsection (1)(a) as it applies by virtue of subsection (5), the relevant information about the status of the person in question is the information that a bankruptcy restrictions order is in force in respect of him.

361, 362. ....

CHAPTER VII
POWERS OF COURT IN BANKRUPTCY

363.   General control of court

(1)   Every bankruptcy is under the general control of the court and, subject to the provisions in this Group of Parts, the court has full power to decide all questions of priorities and all other questions, whether of law or fact, arising in any bankruptcy.

(2)   Without prejudice to any other provision in this Group of Parts, an undischarged bankrupt or a discharged bankrupt whose estate is still being administered under Chapter IV of this Part shall do all such things as he may be directed to do by the court for the purposes of his bankruptcy or, as the case may be, the administration of that estate.

(3)   The official receiver or the trustee of a bankrupt's estate may at any time apply to the court for a direction under subsection (2).

(4)   If any person without reasonable excuse fails to comply with any obligation imposed on him by subsection (2), he is guilty of a contempt of court and liable to be punished accordingly (in addition to any other punishment to which he may be subject).

364. Power of arrest

(1)   In the cases specified in the next subsection the court may cause a warrant to be issued to a constable or prescribed officer of the court—

(a)   for the arrest of a debtor to whom a bankruptcy petition relates or of an undischarged bankrupt, or of a discharged bankrupt whose estate is still being administered under Chapter IV of this Part, and

(b)   for the seizure of any books, papers, records, money or goods in the possession of a person arrested under the warrant,

and may authorise a person arrested under such a warrant to be kept in custody, and anything seized under such a warrant to be held, in accordance with the rules, until such time as the court may order.

(2)   The powers conferred by subsection (1) are exercisable in relation to a debtor or undischarged or discharged bankrupt if, at any time after the presentation of the bankruptcy petition relating to him or the making of the bankruptcy order against him, it appears to the court—

(a)   that there are reasonable grounds for believing that he has absconded, or is about to abscond, with a view to avoiding or delaying the payment of any of his debts or his appearance to a bankruptcy petition or to avoiding, delaying or disrupting any proceedings in bankruptcy against him or any examination of his affairs, or

(b)   that he is about to remove his goods with a view to preventing or delaying possession being taken of them by the official receiver or the trustee of his estate, or

(c)   that there are reasonable grounds for believing that he has concealed or destroyed, or is about to conceal or destroy, any of his goods or any books, papers or records which might be of use to his creditors in the course of his bankruptcy or in connection with the administration of his estate, or

(d)   that he has, without the leave of the official receiver or the trustee of his estate, removed any goods in his possession which exceed in value such sum as may be prescribed for the purposes of this paragraph, or

(e)   that he has failed, without reasonable excuse, to attend any examination ordered by the court.

365. Seizure of bankrupt's property

(1)   At any time after a bankruptcy order has been made, the court may, on the application of the official receiver or the trustee of the bankrupt's estate, issue a warrant authorising the person to whom it is directed to seize any property comprised in the bankrupt's estate which is, or any books, papers or records relating to the bankrupt's estate or affairs which are, in the possession or under the control of the bankrupt or any other person who is required to deliver the property, books, papers or records to the official receiver or trustee.

(2)   Any person executing a warrant under this section may, for the purpose of seizing any property comprised in the bankrupt's estate or any books, papers or records relating to the bankrupt's estate or affairs, break open any premises where the bankrupt or anything that may be seized under the warrant is or is believed to be and any receptacle of the bankrupt which contains or is believed to contain anything that may be so seized.

(3)   If, after a bankruptcy order has been made, the court is satisfied that any property comprised in the bankrupt's estate is, or any books, papers or records relating to the bankrupt's estate or affairs are, concealed in any premises not belonging to him, it may issue a warrant authorising any constable or prescribed officer of the court to search those premises for the property, books, papers or records.

(4)   A warrant under subsection (3) shall not be executed except in the prescribed manner and in accordance with its terms.

366. Inquiry into bankrupt's dealings and property

(1)   At any time after a bankruptcy order has been made the court may, on the application of the official receiver or the trustee of the bankrupt's estate, summon to appear before it—

(a)   the bankrupt or the bankrupt's spouse or former spouse *or civil partner or former civil partner,*

(b)   any person known or believed to have any property comprised in the bankrupt's estate in his possession or to be indebted to the bankrupt,

(c)   any person appearing to the court to be able to give information concerning the bankrupt or the bankrupt's dealings, affairs or property.

The court may require any such person as is mentioned in paragraph (b) or (c) to submit an affidavit to the court containing an account of his dealings with the bankrupt or to produce any documents in his possession or under his control relating to the bankrupt or the bankrupt's dealings, affairs or property.

(2)   Without prejudice to section 364, the following applies in a case where—

(a)   a person without reasonable excuse fails to appear before the court when he is summoned to do so under this section, or

(b)   there are reasonable grounds for believing that a person has absconded, or is about to abscond, with a view to avoiding his appearance before the court under this section.

(3)   The court may, for the purpose of bringing that person and anything in his possession before the court, cause a warrant to be issued to a constable or prescribed officer of the court—

(a)   for the arrest of that person, and

(b)   for the seizure of any books, papers, records, money or goods in that person's possession.

(4)   The court may authorise a person arrested under such a warrant to be kept in custody, and anything seized under such a warrant to be held, in accordance with the rules, until that person is brought before the court under the warrant or until such other time as the court may order.

Note. The italicized words in subsection (1)(a) are inserted by the Civil Partnership Act 2004, s. 261(1), Sch. 27, para. 120, as from a day to be appointed.

367.   Court's enforcement powers under s 366

(1)   If it appears to the court, on consideration of any evidence obtained under section 366 or this section, that any person has in his possession any property comprised in the bankrupt's estate, the court may, on the application of the official receiver or the trustee of the bankrupt's estate, order that person to deliver the whole or any part of the property to the official receiver or the trustee at such time, in such manner and on such terms as the court thinks fit.

(2)   If it appears to the court, on consideration of any evidence obtained under section 366 or this section, that any person is indebted to the bankrupt, the court may, on the application of the official receiver or the trustee of the bankrupt's estate, order that person to pay to the official receiver or trustee, at such time and in such manner as the court may direct, the whole or part of the amount due, whether in full discharge of the debt or otherwise as the court thinks fit.

(3)   The court may, if it thinks fit, order that any person who if within the jurisdiction of the court would be liable to be summoned to appear before it under section 366 shall be examined in any part of the United Kingdom where he may be for the time being, or in any place outside the United Kingdom.

(4)   Any person who appears or is brought before the court under section 366 or this section may be examined on oath, either orally or by interrogatories, concerning the bankrupt or the bankrupt's dealings, affairs and property.

368.   Provision corresponding to s 366, where interim receiver appointed

Sections 366 and 367 apply where an interim receiver has been appointed under section 286 as they apply where a bankruptcy order has been made, as if—

(a)   references to the official receiver or the trustee were to the interim receiver, and

(b)   references to the bankrupt and to his estate were (respectively) to the debtor and his property.

369.   **Order for production of documents by inland revenue**

(1)   For the purposes of an examination under section 290 (public examination of bankrupt) or proceedings under sections 366 to 368, the court may, on the application of the official receiver or the trustee of the bankrupt's estate, order an inland revenue official to produce to the court—

     (a)   any return, account or accounts submitted (whether before or after the commencement of the bankruptcy) by the bankrupt to any inland revenue official,

     (b)   any assessment or determination made (whether before or after the commencement of the bankruptcy) in relation to the bankrupt by any inland revenue official, or

     (c)   any correspondence (whether before or after the commencement of the bankruptcy) between the bankrupt and any inland revenue official.

(2)   Where the court has made an order under subsection (1) for the purposes of any examination or proceedings, the court may, at any time after the document to which the order relates is produced to it, by order authorise the disclosure of the document, or of any part of its contents, to the official receiver, the trustee of the bankrupt's estate or the bankrupt's creditors.

(3)   The court shall not address an order under subsection (1) to an inland revenue official unless it is satisfied that that official is dealing, or has dealt, with the affairs of the bankrupt.

(4)   Where any document to which an order under subsection (1) relates is not in the possession of the official to whom the order is addressed, it is the duty of that official to take all reasonable steps to secure possession of it and, if he fails to do so, to report the reasons for his failure to the court.

(5)   Where any document to which an order under subsection (1) relates is in the possession of an inland revenue official other than the one to whom the order is addressed, it is the duty of the official in possession of the document, at the request of the official to whom the order is addressed, to deliver it to the official making the request.

(6)   In this section "inland revenue official" means any inspector or collector of taxes appointed by the Commissioners of Inland Revenue or any person appointed by the Commissioners to serve in any other capacity.

(7)   This section does not apply for the purposes of an examination under sections 366 and 367 which takes place by virtue of section 368 (interim receiver).

370.   **Power to appoint special manager**

(1)   The court may, on an application under this section, appoint any person to be the special manager—

     (a)   of a bankrupt's estate, or

     (b)   of the business of an undischarged bankrupt, or

     (c)   of the property or business of a debtor in whose case the official receiver has been appointed interim receiver under section 286.

(2)   An application under this section may be made by the official receiver or the trustee of the bankrupt's estate in any case where it appears to the official receiver or trustee that the nature of the estate, property or business, or the interests of the creditors generally, require the appointment of another person to manage the estate, property or business.

(3)   A special manager appointed under this section has such powers as may be entrusted to him by the court.

(4)   The power of the court under subsection (3) to entrust powers to a special manager includes power to direct that any provision in this Group of Parts that has effect in relation to the official receiver, interim receiver or trustee shall have the like effect in relation to the special manager for the purposes of the carrying out by the special manager of any of the functions of the official receiver, interim receiver or trustee.

(5)   A special manager appointed under this section shall—

     (a)   give such security as may be prescribed,

     (b)   prepare and keep such accounts as may be prescribed, and

     (c)   produce those accounts in accordance with the rules to the Secretary of State or to such other persons as may be prescribed.

371. Re-direction of bankrupt's letters, etc

(1)   Where a bankruptcy order has been made, the court may from time to time, on the application of the official receiver or the trustee of the bankrupt's estate, order a postal operator (within the meaning of the Postal Services Act 2000) to re-direct and send or deliver to the official receiver or trustee or otherwise any postal packet (within the meaning of that Act) which would otherwise be sent or delivered by the operator concerned to the bankrupt at such place or places as may be specified in the order.

(2)   An order under this section has effect for such period, not exceeding 3 months, as may be specified in the order.

PART X
INDIVIDUAL INSOLVENCY: GENERAL PROVISIONS

372. Supplies of gas, water, electricity, etc

(1)   This section applies where on any day ("the relevant day")—
(a)   a bankruptcy order is made against an individual or an interim receiver of an individual's property is appointed, or
(b)   a voluntary arrangement proposed by an individual is approved under Part VIII, or
(c)   a deed of arrangement is made for the benefit of an individual's creditors;
and in this section "the office-holder" means the official receiver, the trustee in bankruptcy, the interim receiver, the supervisor of the voluntary arrangement or the trustee under the deed of arrangement, as the case may be.

(2)   If a request falling within the next subsection is made for the giving after the relevant day of any of the supplies mentioned in subsection (4), the supplier—
(a)   may make it a condition of the giving of the supply that the office-holder personally guarantees the payment of any charges in respect of the supply, but
(b)   shall not make it a condition of the giving of the supply, or do anything which has the effect of making it a condition of the giving of the supply, that any outstanding charges in respect of a supply given to the individual before the relevant day are paid.

(3)   A request falls within this subsection if it is made—
(a)   by or with the concurrence of the office-holder, and
(b)   for the purposes of any business which is or has been carried on by the individual, by a firm or partnership of which the individual is or was a member, or by an agent or manager for the individual or for such a firm or partnership.

(4)   The supplies referred to in subsection (2) are—
(a)   a supply of gas by a gas supplier within the meaning of Part I of the Gas Act 1986;
(b)   a supply of electricity by an electricity supplier within the meaning of Part I of the Electricity Act 1989;
(c)   a supply of water by a water undertaker,
(d)   a supply of communications services by a provider of a public electronic communications service.

(5)   The following applies to expressions used in subsection (4)—
(a)   ...
(b)   ... and
(c)   "communications services" do not include electronic communications services to the extent that they are used to broadcast or otherwise transmit programme services (within the meaning of the Communications Act 2003).

373. Jurisdiction in relation to insolvent individuals

(1)   The High Court and the county courts have jurisdiction throughout England and Wales for the purposes of the Parts in this Group.

(2)   For the purposes of those Parts, a county court has, in addition to its ordinary jurisdiction, all the powers and jurisdiction of the High Court; and the orders of the court may be enforced accordingly in the prescribed manner.

(3)   Jurisdiction for the purposes of those Parts is exercised—

(a)   by the High Court in relation to the proceedings which, in accordance with the rules, are allocated to the London insolvency district, and

(b)   by each county court in relation to the proceedings which are so allocated to the insolvency district of that court.

(4)   Subsection (3) is without prejudice to the transfer of proceedings from one court to another in the manner prescribed by the rules; and nothing in that subsection invalidates any proceedings on the grounds that they were initiated or continued in the wrong court.

374.   Insolvency districts

(1)   The Lord Chancellor may by order designate the areas which are for the time being to be comprised, for the purposes of the Parts in this Group, in the London Insolvency district and the insolvency district of each county court; and an order under this section may—

(a)   exclude any county court from having jurisdiction for the purposes of those Parts, or

(b)   confer jurisdiction for those purposes on any county court which has not previously had that jurisdiction.

(2)   An order under this section may contain such incidental, supplemental and transitional provisions as may appear to the Lord Chancellor necessary or expedient.

(3)   An order under this section shall be made by statutory instrument and, after being made, shall be laid before each House of Parliament.

(4)   Subject to any order under this section—

(a)   the district which, immediately before the appointed day, is the London bankruptcy district becomes, on that day, the London insolvency district;

(b)   any district which immediately before that day is the bankruptcy district of a county court becomes, on that day, the insolvency district of that court, and

(c)   any county court which immediately before that day is excluded from having jurisdiction in bankruptcy is excluded, on and after that day, from having jurisdiction for the purposes of the Parts in this Group.

375.   Appeals etc from courts exercising insolvency jurisdiction

(1)   Every court having jurisdiction for the purposes of the Parts in this Group may review, rescind or vary any order made by it in the exercise of that jurisdiction.

(2)   An appeal from a decision made in the exercise of jurisdiction for the purposes of those Parts by a county court or by a registrar in bankruptcy of the High Court lies to a single judge of the High Court; and an appeal from a decision of that judge on such an appeal lies... to the Court of Appeal.

(3)   A county court is not, in the exercise of its jurisdiction for the purposes of those Parts, to be subject to be restrained by the order of any other court, and no appeal lies from its decision in the exercise of that jurisdiction except as provided by this section.

376.   Time-limits

Where by any provision in this Group of Parts or by the rules the time for doing anything is limited, the court may extend the time, either before or after it has expired, on such terms, if any, as it thinks fit.

377.   Formal defects

The acts of a person as the trustee of a bankrupt's estate or as a special manager, and the acts of the creditors' committee established for any bankruptcy, are valid notwithstanding any defect in the appointment, election or qualifications of the trustee or manager or, as the case may be, of any member of the committee.

378. Exemption from stamp duty

Stamp duty shall not be charged on—

(a) any document, being a deed, conveyance, assignment, surrender, admission or other assurance relating solely to property which is comprised in a bankrupt's estate and which, after the execution of that document, is or remains at law or in equity the property of the bankrupt or of the trustee of that estate,

(b) any writ, order, certificate or other instrument relating solely to the property of a bankrupt or to any bankruptcy proceedings.

379. Annual report

As soon as practicable after the end of 1986 and each subsequent calendar year, the Secretary of State shall prepare and lay before each House of Parliament a report about the operation during that year of so much of this Act as is comprised in this Group of Parts, and about proceedings in the course of that year under the Deeds of Arrangement Act 1914.

PART XI
INTERPRETATION FOR SECOND GROUP OF PARTS

380. Introductory

The next five sections have effect for the interpretation of the provisions of this Act which are comprised in this Group of Parts; and where a definition is provided for a particular expression, it applies except so far as the context otherwise requires.

381. "Bankrupt" and associated terminology

(1) "Bankrupt" means an individual who has been adjudged bankrupt and, in relation to a bankruptcy order, it means the individual adjudged bankrupt by that order.

(2) "Bankruptcy order" means an order adjudging an individual bankrupt.

(3) "Bankruptcy petition" means a petition to the court for a bankruptcy order.

382. "Bankruptcy debt", etc

(1) "Bankruptcy debt", in relation to a bankrupt, means (subject to the next subsection) any of the following—

(a) any debt or liability to which he is subject at the commencement of the bankruptcy,

(b) any debt or liability to which he may become subject after the commencement of the bankruptcy (including after his discharge from bankruptcy) by reason of any obligation incurred before the commencement of the bankruptcy,

(c) *any amount specified in pursuance of section 39(3)(c) of the Powers of Criminal Courts Act 1973 in any criminal bankruptcy order made against him before the commencement of the bankruptcy, and*

(d) any interest provable as mentioned in section 322(2) in Chapter IV of Part IX.

(2) In determining for the purposes of any provision in this Group of Parts whether any liability in tort is a bankruptcy debt, the bankrupt is deemed to become subject to that liability by reason of an obligation incurred at the time when the cause of action accrued.

(3) For the purposes of references in this Group of Parts to a debt or liability, it is immaterial whether the debt or liability is present or future, whether it is certain or contingent or whether its amount is fixed or liquidated, or is capable of being ascertained by fixed rules or as a matter of opinion; and references in this Group of Parts to owing a debt are to be read accordingly.

(4) In this Group of Parts, except in so far as the context otherwise requires, "liability" means (subject to subsection (3) above) a liability to pay money or money's worth, including any liability under an enactment, any liability for breach of trust, any liability in contract, tort or bailment and any liability arising out of an obligation to make restitution.

Note. Subsection (1)(c) is repealed by the Criminal Justice Act 1988, s. 170(2), Sch. 16, as from a day to be appointed.

383.   "Creditor", "security", etc

(1)   "Creditor"—

 (a) in relation to a bankrupt, means a person to whom any of the bankruptcy debts is owed *(being, in the case of an amount falling within paragraph (c) of the definition in section 382(1) of "bankruptcy debt", the person in respect of whom that amount is specified in the criminal bankruptcy order in question)*, and

 (b) in relation to an individual to whom a bankruptcy petition relates, means a person who would be a creditor in the bankruptcy if a bankruptcy order were made on that petition.

(2)   Subject to the next two subsections and any provision of the rules requiring a creditor to give up his security for the purposes of proving a debt, a debt is secured for the purposes of this Group of Parts to the extent that the person to whom the debt is owed holds any security for the debt (whether a mortgage, charge, lien or other security) over any property of the person by whom the debt is owed.

(3)   Where a statement such as is mentioned in section 269(1)(a) in Chapter I of Part IX has been made by a secured creditor for the purposes of any bankruptcy petition and a bankruptcy order is subsequently made on that petition, the creditor is deemed for the purposes of the Parts in this Group to have given up the security specified in the statement.

(4)   In subsection (2) the reference to a security does not include a lien on books, papers or other records, except to the extent that they consist of documents which give a title to property and are held as such.

Note. The italicized words in subsection (1)(a) are repealed by the Criminal Justice Act 1988, s. 170(2), Sch. 16, as from a day to be appointed.

384.   "Prescribed" and "the rules"

(1)   Subject to the next subsection and sections 342C(7) and 342F(9) in Chapter V of Part IX, "prescribed" means prescribed by the rules; and "the rules" means rules made under section 412 in Part XV.

(2)   References in this Group of Parts to the amount prescribed for the purposes of any of the following provisions—

section 273;

section 313A;

section 346(3);

section 354(1) and (2);

section 358;

section 360(1);

section 361(2); and

section 364(2)(d),

and references in those provisions to the prescribed amount are to be read in accordance with section 418 in Part XV and orders made under that section.

385.   Miscellaneous definitions

(1)   The following definitions have effect—

 "the court", in relation to any matter, means the court to which, in accordance with section 373 in Part X and the rules, proceedings with respect to that matter are allocated or transferred;

 "creditor's petition" means a bankruptcy petition under section 264(1)(a);

 "criminal bankruptcy order" means an order under section 39(1) of the Powers of Criminal Courts Act 1973;

 "debt" is to be construed in accordance with section 382(3);

 "the debtor"—

 (a) in relation to a proposal for the purposes of Part VIII, means the individual making or intending to make that proposal, and

 (b) in relation to a bankruptcy petition, means the individual to whom the petition relates;

"debtor's petition" means a bankruptcy petition presented by the debtor himself under section 264(1)(b);

"dwelling house" includes any building or part of a building which is occupied as a dwelling and any yard, garden, garage or outhouse belonging to the dwelling house and occupied with it;

"estate", in relation to a bankrupt is to be construed in accordance with section 283 in Chapter II of Part IX;

"family", in relation to a bankrupt, means the persons (if any) who are living with him and are dependent on him;

"insolvency administration order" means an order for the administration in bankruptcy of the insolvent estate of a deceased debtor (being an individual at the date of his death);

"insolvency administration petition" means a petition for an insolvency administration order;

"the Rules" means the Insolvency Rules 1986;

"secured" and related expressions are to be construed in accordance with section 383; and

"the trustee", in relation to a bankruptcy and the bankrupt, means the trustee of the bankrupt's estate.

(2)   References in this Group of Parts to a person's affairs include his business, if any.

Note. The italicized definition of "criminal bankruptcy order" in subsection (1) is repealed by the Criminal Justice Act 1988, s. 170(2), Sch. 16, as from a day to be appointed.

THE THIRD GROUP OF PARTS
MISCELLANEOUS MATTERS BEARING ON BOTH COMPANY
AND INDIVIDUAL INSOLVENCY;
GENERAL INTERPRETATION; FINAL PROVISIONS

PART XII
PREFERENTIAL DEBTS IN COMPANY AND INDIVIDUAL INSOLVENCY

386.   Categories of preferential debts

(1)   A reference in this Act to the preferential debts of a company or an individual is to the debts listed in Schedule 6 to this Act (contributions to occupational pension schemes; remuneration, &c of employees; levies on coal and steel production); and references to preferential creditors are to be read accordingly.

(2)   In that Schedule "the debtor" means the company or the individual concerned.

(3)   Schedule 6 is to be read with Schedule 4 to the Pension Schemes Act 1993 (occupational pension scheme contributions).

387.   "The relevant date"

(1)   This section explains references in Schedule 6 to the relevant date (being the date which determines the existence and amount of a preferential debt).

(2)   For the purposes of section 4 in Part I (meetings to consider company voluntary arrangement), the relevant date in relation to a company which is not being wound up is—

(a)   if the company is in administration, the date on which it entered administration, and

(b)   if the company is not in administration, the date on which the voluntary arrangement takes effect.

(2A) For the purposes of paragraph 31 of Schedule A1 (meetings to consider company voluntary arrangement where a moratorium under section 1A is in force), the relevant date in relation to a company is the date of filing.

(3)   In relation to a company which is being wound up, the following applies—

(a)   if the winding up is by the court, and the winding-up order was made immediately upon the discharge of an administration order, the relevant date is the date on which the company entered administration;

(aa) if the winding up is by the court and the winding-up order was made following conversion of administration into winding up by virtue of Article 37 of the EC Regulation, the relevant date is the date on which the company entered administration;

(ab) if the company is deemed to have passed a resolution for voluntary winding up by virtue of an order following conversion of administration into winding up under Article 37 of the EC Regulation, the relevant date is the date on which the company entered administration;

(b) if the case does not fall within paragraph (a), (aa) or (ab) and the company—

(i) is being wound up by the court, and

(ii) had not commenced to be wound up voluntarily before the date of the making of the winding-up order,

the relevant date is the date of the appointment (or first appointment) of a provisional liquidator or, if no such appointment has been made, the date of the winding-up order;

(ba) if the case does not fall within paragraph (a), (aa), (ab) or (b) and the company is being wound up following administration pursuant to paragraph 83 of Schedule B1, the relevant date is the date on which the company entered administration;

(c) if the case does not fall within paragraph (a), (aa), (ab), (b) or (ba), the relevant date is the date of the passing of the resolution for the winding up of the company.

(3A) In relation to a company which is in administration (and to which no other provision of this section applies) the relevant date is the date on which the company enters administration.

(4) In relation to a company in receivership (where section 40 or, as the case may be, section 59 applies), the relevant date is—

(a) in England and Wales, the date of the appointment of the receiver by debenture-holders, and

(b) in Scotland, the date of the appointment of the receiver under section 53(6) or (as the case may be) 54(5).

(5) For the purposes of section 258 in Part VIII (individual voluntary arrangements), the relevant date is, in relation to a debtor who is not an undischarged bankrupt—

(a) where an interim order has been made under section 252 with respect to his proposal, the date of that order, and

(b) in any other case, the date on which the voluntary arrangement takes effect.

(6) In relation to a bankrupt, the following applies—

(a) where at the time the bankruptcy order was made there was an interim receiver appointed under section 286, the relevant date is the date on which the interim receiver was first appointed after the presentation of the bankruptcy petition;

(b) otherwise, the relevant date is the date of the making of the bankruptcy order.

PART XIII
INSOLVENCY PRACTITIONERS AND THEIR QUALIFICATION

*Restrictions on unqualified persons acting as
liquidator, trustee in bankruptcy, etc*

388. Meaning of "act as insolvency practitioner"

(1) A person acts as an insolvency practitioner in relation to a company by acting—

(a) as its liquidator, provisional liquidator, administrator or administrative receiver, or

(b) where a voluntary arrangement in relation to the company is proposed or approved under Part I, as nominee or supervisor.

(2) A person acts as an insolvency practitioner in relation to an individual by acting—

(a) as his trustee in bankruptcy or interim receiver of his property or as permanent or interim trustee in the sequestration of his estate; or

(b) as trustee under a deed which is a deed of arrangement made for the benefit of his creditors or, in Scotland, a trust deed for his creditors; or

(c) where a voluntary arrangement in relation to the individual is proposed or approved under Part VIII, as nominee or supervisor; or

(d)   in the case of a deceased individual to the administration of whose estate this section applies by virtue of an order under section 421 (application of provisions of this Act to insolvent estates of deceased persons), as administrator of that estate.

(2A)   A person acts as an insolvency practitioner in relation to an insolvent partnership by acting—

(a)   as its liquidator, provisional liquidator or administrator, or

(b)   as trustee of the partnership under article 11 of the Insolvent Partnerships Order 1994, or

(c)   where a voluntary arrangement in relation to the insolvent partnership is proposed or approved under Part I of the Act, as nominee or supervisor.

(2B)   In relation to a voluntary arrangement proposed under Part I or VIII, a person acts as nominee if he performs any of the functions conferred on nominees under the Part in question.

(3)   References in this section to an individual include, except in so far as the context otherwise requires, references ... to any debtor within the meaning of the Bankruptcy (Scotland) Act 1985.

(4)   In this section—

"administrative receiver" has the meaning given by section 251 in Part VII;

"company" means a company within the meaning given by section 735(1) of the Companies Act or a company which may be wound up under Part V of this Act (unregistered companies); and

"interim trustee" and "permanent trustee" mean the same as in the Bankruptcy (Scotland) Act 1985.

(5)   Nothing in this section applies to anything done by—

(a)   the official receiver; or

(b)   the Accountant in Bankruptcy (within the meaning of the Bankruptcy (Scotland) Act 1985).

(6)   Nothing in this section applies to anything done (whether in the United Kingdom or elsewhere) in relation to insolvency proceedings under the EC Regulation in a member State other than the United Kingdom.

389.   Acting without qualification an offence

(1)   A person who acts as an insolvency practitioner in relation to a company or an individual at a time when he is not qualified to do so is liable to imprisonment or a fine, or to both.

(1A)   This section is subject to section 389A.

(2)   This section does not apply to the official receiver or the Accountant in Bankruptcy (within the meaning of the Bankruptcy (Scotland) Act 1985.

389A.   Authorisation of nominees and supervisors

(1)   Section 389 does not apply to a person acting, in relation to a voluntary arrangement proposed or approved under Part I or Part VIII, as nominee or supervisor if he is authorised so to act.

(2)   For the purposes of subsection (1) and those Parts, an individual to whom subsection (3) does not apply is authorised to act as nominee or supervisor in relation to such an arrangement if—

(a)   he is a member of a body recognised for the purpose by the Secretary of State, and

(b)   there is in force security (in Scotland, caution) for the proper performance of his functions and that security or caution meets the prescribed requirements with respect to his so acting in relation to the arrangement.

(3)   This subsection applies to a person if—

(a)   he has been adjudged bankrupt or sequestration of his estate has been awarded and (in either case) he has not been discharged,

(b)   he is subject to a disqualification order made or a disqualification undertaking accepted under the Company Directors Disqualification Act 1986 or to a disqualification order made under Part II of the Companies (Northern Ireland) Order 1989 or a disqualification undertaking accepted under the Company Directors Disqualification (Northern Ireland) Order 2002, or

(c)   he is a patient within the meaning of Part VII of the Mental Health Act 1983 or section 125(1) of the Mental Health (Scotland) Act 1984.

(4)   The Secretary of State may by order declare a body which appears to him to fall within subsection (5) to be a recognised body for the purposes of subsection (2)(a).

(5)   A body may be recognised if it maintains and enforces rules for securing that its members—
    (a)   are fit and proper persons to act as nominees or supervisors, and
    (b)   meet acceptable requirements as to education and practical training and experience.

(6)   For the purposes of this section, a person is a member of a body only if he is subject to its rules when acting as nominee or supervisor (whether or not he is in fact a member of the body).

(7)   An order made under subsection (4) in relation to a body may be revoked by a further order if it appears to the Secretary of State that the body no longer falls within subsection (5).

(8)   An order of the Secretary of State under this section has effect from such date as is specified in the order; and any such order revoking a previous order may make provision for members of the body in question to continue to be treated as members of a recognised body for a specified period after the revocation takes effect.

389B.   Official receiver as nominee or supervisor

(1)   The official receiver is authorised to act as nominee or supervisor in relation to a voluntary arrangement approved under Part VIII provided that the debtor is an undischarged bankrupt when the arrangement is proposed.

(2)   The Secretary of State may by order repeal the proviso in subsection (1).

(3)   An order under subsection (2)—
    (a)   must be made by statutory instrument, and
    (b)   shall be subject to annulment in pursuance of a resolution of either House of Parliament.

The requisite qualification, and the means of obtaining it

390.   Persons not qualified to act as insolvency practitioners

(1)   A person who is not an individual is not qualified to act as an insolvency practitioner.

(2)   A person is not qualified to act as an insolvency practitioner at any time unless at that time—
    (a)   he is authorised so to act by virtue of membership of a professional body recognised under section 391 below, being permitted so to act by or under the rules of that body, or
    (b)   he holds an authorisation granted by a competent authority under section 393.

(3)   A person is not qualified to act as an insolvency practitioner in relation to another person at any time unless—
    (a)   there is in force at that time security or, in Scotland, caution for the proper performance of his functions, and
    (b)   that security or caution meets the prescribed requirements with respect to his so acting in relation to that other person.

(4)   A person is not qualified to act as an insolvency practitioner at any time if at that time—
    (a)   he has been adjudged bankrupt or sequestration of his estate has been awarded and (in either case) he has not been discharged,
    (b)   he is subject to a disqualification order made or a disqualification undertaking accepted under the Company Directors Disqualification Act 1986 or to a disqualification order made under Part II of the Companies (Northern Ireland) Order 1989 or to a disqualification undertaking accepted under the Company Directors Disqualification (Northern Ireland) Order 2002, or
    (c)   he is a patient within the meaning of Part VII of the Mental Health Act 1983 or section 125(1) of the Mental Health (Scotland) Act 1984 or has had a guardian appointed to him under the Adults with Incapacity (Scotland) Act 2000 (asp 4).

(5)   A person is not qualified to act as an insolvency practitioner while a bankruptcy restrictions order is in force in respect of him.

391.   Recognised professional bodies

(1)   The Secretary of State may by order declare a body which appears to him to fall within subsection (2) below to be a recognised professional body for the purposes of this section.

(2)   A body may be recognised if it regulates the practice of a profession and maintains and enforces rules for securing that such of its members as are permitted by or under the rules to act as insolvency practitioners—

    (a)   are fit and proper persons so to act, and

    (b)   meet acceptable requirements as to education and practical training and experience.

(3)   References to members of a recognised professional body are to persons who, whether members of that body or not, are subject to its rules in the practice of the profession in question.

    The reference in section 390(2) above to membership of a professional body recognised under this section is to be read accordingly.

(4)   An order made under subsection (1) in relation to a professional body may be revoked by a further order if it appears to the Secretary of State that the body no longer falls within subsection (2).

(5)   An order of the Secretary of State under this section has effect from such date as is specified in the order; and any such order revoking a previous order may make provision whereby members of the body in question continue to be treated as authorised to act as insolvency practitioners for a specified period after the revocation takes effect.

392.   Authorisation by competent authority

(1)   Application may be made to a competent authority for authorisation to act as an insolvency practitioner.

(2)   The competent authorities for this purpose are—

    (a)   in relation to a case of any description specified in directions given by the Secretary of State, the body or person so specified in relation to cases of that description, and

    (b)   in relation to a case not falling within paragraph (a), the Secretary of State.

(3)   The application—

    (a)   shall be made in such manner as the competent authority may direct,

    (b)   shall contain or be accompanied by such information as that authority may reasonably require for the purpose of determining the application, and

    (c)   shall be accompanied by the prescribed fee;

    and the authority may direct that notice of the making of the application shall be published in such manner as may be specified in the direction.

(4)   At any time after receiving the application and before determining it the authority may require the applicant to furnish additional information.

(5)   Directions and requirements given or imposed under subsection (3) or (4) may differ as between different applications.

(6)   Any information to be furnished to the competent authority under this section shall, if it so requires, be in such form or verified in such manner as it may specify.

(7)   An application may be withdrawn before it is granted or refused.

(8)   Any sums received under this section by a competent authority other than the Secretary of State may be retained by the authority; and any sums so received by the Secretary of State shall be paid into the Consolidated Fund.

(9)   Subsection (3)(c) shall not have effect in respect of an application made to the Secretary of State (but this subsection is without prejudice to section 415A).

393.   Grant, refusal and withdrawal of authorisation

(1)   The competent authority may, on an application duly made in accordance with section 392 and after being furnished with all such information as it may require under that section, grant or refuse the application.

(2)   The authority shall grant the application if it appears to it from the information furnished by the applicant and having regard to such other information, if any, as it may have—

    (a)   that the applicant is a fit and proper person to act as an insolvency practitioner, and

    (b)   that the applicant meets the prescribed requirements with respect to education and practical training and experience.

(3)   An authorisation granted under this section, if not previously withdrawn, continues in force for such period not exceeding the prescribed maximum as may be specified in the authorisation.

(4)   An authorisation so granted may be withdrawn by the competent authority if it appears to it—

     (a)   that the holder of the authorisation is no longer a fit and proper person to act as an insolvency practitioner, or

     (b)   without prejudice to paragraph (a), that the holder—

          (i)   has failed to comply with any provision of this Part or of any regulations made under this Part or Part XV, or

          (ii)   in purported compliance with any such provision, has furnished the competent authority with false, inaccurate or misleading information.

(5)   An authorisation granted under this section may be withdrawn by the competent authority at the request or with the consent of the holder of the authorisation.

394.   Notices

(1)   Where a competent authority grants an authorisation under section 393, it shall give written notice of that fact to the applicant, specifying the date on which the authorisation takes effect.

(2)   Where the authority proposes to refuse an application, or to withdraw an authorisation under section 393(4), it shall give the applicant or holder of the authorisation written notice of its intention to do so, setting out particulars of the grounds on which it proposes to act.

(3)   In the case of a proposed withdrawal the notice shall state the date on which it is proposed that the withdrawal should take effect.

(4)   A notice under subsection (2) shall give particulars of the rights exercisable under the next two sections by a person on whom the notice is served.

395.   Right to make representations

(1)   A person on whom a notice is served under section 394(2) may within 14 days after the date of service make written representations to the competent authority.

(2)   The competent authority shall have regard to any representations so made in determining whether to refuse the application or withdraw the authorisation, as the case may be.

396.   Reference to Tribunal

(1)   The Insolvency Practitioners Tribunal ("the Tribunal") continues in being; and the provisions of Schedule 7 apply to it.

(2)   Where a person is served with a notice under section 394(2), he may—

     (a)   at any time within 28 days after the date of service of the notice, or

     (b)   at any time after the making by him of representations under section 395 and before the end of the period of 28 days after the date of the service on him of a notice by the competent authority that the authority does not propose to alter its decision in consequence of the representations,

give written notice to the authority requiring the case to be referred to the Tribunal.

(3)   Where a requirement is made under subsection (2), then, unless the competent authority—

     (a)   has decided or decides to grant the application or, as the case may be, not to withdraw the authorisation, and

     (b)   within 7 days after the date of the making of the requirement, gives written notice of that decision to the person by whom the requirement was made,

it shall refer the case to the Tribunal.

397.   Action of Tribunal on reference

(1)   On a reference under section 396 the Tribunal shall—

     (a)   investigate the case, and

     (b)   make a report to the competent authority stating what would in their opinion be the appropriate decision in the matter and the reasons for that opinion,

and it is the duty of the competent authority to decide the matter accordingly.

(2)   The Tribunal shall send a copy of the report to the applicant or, as the case may be, the holder of the authorisation; and the competent authority shall serve him with a written notice of the decision made by it in accordance with the report.

(3)   The competent authority may, if he thinks fit, publish the report of the Tribunal.

398. Refusal or withdrawal without reference to Tribunal

Where in the case of any proposed refusal or withdrawal of an authorisation either—

(a)   the period mentioned in section 396(2)(a) has expired without the making of any requirement under that subsection or of any representations under section 395, or

(b)   the competent authority has given a notice such as is mentioned in section 396(2)(b) and the period so mentioned has expired without the making of any such requirement,

the competent authority may give written notice of the refusal or withdrawal to the person concerned in accordance with the proposal in the notice given under section 394(2).

PART XIV
PUBLIC ADMINISTRATION (ENGLAND AND WALES)

Official receivers

399. Appointment, etc of official receivers

(1)   For the purposes of this Act the official receiver, in relation to any bankruptcy, winding up or individual voluntary arrangement, is any person who by virtue of the following provisions of this section or section 401 below is authorised to act as the official receiver in relation to that bankruptcy, winding up or individual voluntary arrangement.

(2)   The Secretary of State may (subject to the approval of the Treasury as to numbers) appoint persons to the office of official receiver, and a person appointed to that office (whether under this section or section 70 of the Bankruptcy Act 1914)—

(a)   shall be paid out of money provided by Parliament such salary as the Secretary of State may with the concurrence of the Treasury direct,

(b)   shall hold office on such other terms and conditions as the Secretary of State may with the concurrence of the Treasury direct, and

(c)   may be removed from office by a direction of the Secretary of State.

(3)   Where a person holds the office of official receiver, the Secretary of State shall from time to time attach him either to the High Court or to a county court having jurisdiction for the purposes of the second Group of Parts of this Act.

(4)   Subject to any directions under subsection (6) below, an official receiver attached to a particular court is the person authorised to act as the official receiver in relation to every bankruptcy, winding up or individual voluntary arrangement falling within the jurisdiction of that court.

(5)   The Secretary of State shall ensure that there is, at all times, at least one official receiver attached to the High Court and at least one attached to each county court having jurisdiction for the purposes of the second Group of Parts; but he may attach the same official receiver to two or more different courts.

(6)   The Secretary of State may give directions with respect to the disposal of the business of official receivers, and such directions may, in particular—

(a)   authorise an official receiver attached to one court to act as the official receiver in relation to any case or description of cases falling within the jurisdiction of another court;

(b)   provide, where there is more than one official receiver authorised to act as the official receiver in relation to cases falling within the jurisdiction of any court, for the distribution of their business between or among themselves.

(7)   A person who at the coming into force of section 222 of the Insolvency Act 1985 (replaced by this section) is an official receiver attached to a court shall continue in office after the coming into force of that section as an official receiver attached to that court under this section.

400.   Functions and status of official receivers

(1)   In addition to any functions conferred on him by this Act, a person holding the office of official receiver shall carry out such other functions as may from time to time be conferred on him by the Secretary of State.

(2)   In the exercise of the functions of his office a person holding the office of official receiver shall act under the general directions of the Secretary of State and shall also be an officer of the court in relation to which he exercises those functions.

(3)   Any property vested in his official capacity in a person holding the office of official receiver shall, on his dying, ceasing to hold office or being otherwise succeeded in relation to the bankruptcy or winding up in question by another official receiver, vest in his successor without any conveyance, assignment or transfer.

401.   Deputy official receivers and staff

(1)   The Secretary of State may, if he thinks it expedient to do so in order to facilitate the disposal of the business of the official receiver attached to any court, appoint an officer of his department to act as deputy to that official receiver.

(2)   Subject to any directions given by the Secretary of State under section 399 or 400, a person appointed to act as deputy to an official receiver has, on such conditions and for such period as may be specified in the terms of his appointment, the same status and functions as the official receiver to whom he is appointed deputy.

Accordingly, references in this Act (except section 399(1) to (5)) to an official receiver include a person appointed to act as his deputy.

(3)   An appointment made under subsection (1) may be terminated at any time by the Secretary of State.

(4)   The Secretary of State may, subject to the approval of the Treasury as to numbers and remuneration and as to the other terms and conditions of the appointments, appoint officers of his department to assist official receivers in the carrying out of their functions.

The Official Petitioner

402.   Official Petitioner

(1)   There continues to be an officer known as the Official Petitioner for the purpose of discharging, in relation to cases in which a criminal bankruptcy order is made, the functions assigned to him by or under this Act; and the Director of Public Prosecutions continues, by virtue of his office, to be the Official Petitioner.

(2)   The functions of the Official Petitioner include the following—

(a)   to consider whether, in a case in which a criminal bankruptcy order is made, it is in the public interest that he should himself present a petition under section 264(1)(d) of this Act;

(b)   to present such a petition in any case where he determines that it is in the public interest for him to do so;

(c)   to make payments, in such cases as he may determine, towards expenses incurred by other persons in connection with proceedings in pursuance of such a petition; and

(d)   to exercise, so far as he considers it in the public interest to do so, any of the powers conferred on him by or under this Act.

(3)   Any functions of the Official Petitioner may be discharged on his behalf by any person acting with his authority.

(4)   Neither the Official Petitioner nor any person acting with his authority is liable to any action or proceeding in respect of anything done or omitted to be done in the discharge, or purported discharge, of the functions of the Official Petitioner.

(5)   In this section "criminal bankruptcy order" means an order under section 39(1) of the Powers of Criminal Courts Act 1973.

Note. This section is repealed by the Criminal Justice Act 1988, s. 170(2), Sch. 16, as from a day to be appointed.

Insolvency Service finance, accounting and investment

403.   Insolvency Services Account

(1)   All money received by the Secretary of State in respect of proceedings under this Act as it applies to England and Wales shall be paid into the Insolvency Services Account kept by the Secretary of State with the Bank of England; and all payments out of money standing to the credit of the Secretary of State in that account shall be made by the Bank of England in such manner as he may direct.

(2)   Whenever the cash balance standing to the credit of the Insolvency Services Account is in excess of the amount which in the opinion of the Secretary of State is required for the time being to answer demands in respect of bankrupts' estates or companies' estates, the Secretary of State shall—

(a)   notify the excess to the National Debt Commissioners, and

(b)   pay into the Insolvency Services Investment Account ("the Investment Account") kept by the Commissioners with the Bank of England the whole or any part of the excess as the Commissioners may require for investment in accordance with the following provisions of this Part.

(3)   Whenever any part of the money so invested is, in the opinion of the Secretary of State, required to answer any demand in respect of bankrupt's estates or companies' estates, he shall notify to the National Debt Commissioners the amount so required and the Commissioners—

(a)   shall thereupon repay to the Secretary of State such sum as may be required to the credit of the Insolvency Services Account, and

(b)   for that purpose may direct the sale of such part of the securities in which the money has been invested as may be necessary.

404.   Investment Account

Any money standing to the credit of the Investment Account (including any money received by the National Debt Commissioners by way of interest on or proceeds of any investment under this section) may be invested by the Commissioners, in accordance with such directions as may be given by the Treasury, in any manner for the time being specified in Part II of Schedule 1 to the Trustee Investments Act 1961.

405.   ...

406.   Interest on money received by liquidators or trustees in bankruptcy and invested

Where under rules made by virtue of paragraph 16 of Schedule 8 to this Act (investment of money received by company liquidators) or paragraph 21 of Schedule 9 to this Act (investment of money received by trustee in bankruptcy) a company or a bankrupt's estate has become entitled to any sum by way of interest, the Secretary of State shall certify that sum and the amount of tax payable on it to the National Debt Commissioners; and the Commissioners shall pay, out of the Investment Account—

(a)   into the Insolvency Services Account, the sum so certified less the amount of tax so certified, and

(b)   to the Commissioners of Inland Revenue, the amount of tax so certified.

407.   Unclaimed dividends and undistributed balances

(1)   The Secretary of State shall from time to time pay into the Consolidated Fund out of the Insolvency Services Account so much of the sums standing to the credit of that Account as represents—

(a)   dividends which were declared before such date as the Treasury may from time to time determine and have not been claimed, and

(b)   balances ascertained before that date which are too small to be divided among the persons entitled to them.

(2)   For the purposes of this section the sums standing to the credit of the Insolvency Services Account are deemed to include any sums paid out of that Account and represented by any sums or securities standing to the credit of the Investment Account.

(3)   The Secretary of State may require the National Debt Commissioners to pay out of the Investment Account into the Insolvency Services Account the whole or part of any sum which he is required to pay out of that account under subsection (1); and the Commissioners may direct the sale of such securities standing to the credit of the Investment Account as may be necessary for that purpose.

408.   Adjustment of balances

(1)   The Treasury may direct the payment out of the Consolidated Fund of sums into—
    (a)   the Insolvency Services Account;
    (b)   the Investment Account.

(2)   The Treasury shall certify to the House of Commons the reason for any payment under subsection (1).

(3)   The Secretary of State may pay sums out of the Insolvency Services Account into the Consolidated Fund.

(4)   The National Debt Commissioners may pay sums out of the Investment Account into the Consolidated Fund.

409.   Annual financial statement and audit

(1)   The National Debt Commissioners shall for each year ending on 31st March prepare a statement of the sums credited and debited to the Investment Account in such form and manner as the Treasury may direct and shall transmit it to the Comptroller and Auditor General before the end of November next following the year.

(2)   The Secretary of State shall for each year ending 31st March prepare a statement of the sums received or paid by him under section 403 above in such form and manner as the Treasury may direct and shall transmit each statement to the Comptroller and Auditor General before the end of November next following the year.

(3)   Every such statement shall include such additional information as the Treasury may direct.

(4)   The Comptroller and Auditor General shall examine, certify and report on every such statement and shall lay copies of it, and of his report, before Parliament.

Supplementary

410.   Extent of this Part

This Part of this Act extends to England and Wales only.

PART XV

SUBORDINATE LEGISLATION

General insolvency rules

411.   Company insolvency rules

(1)   Rules may be made—
    (a)   in relation to England and Wales, by the Lord Chancellor with the concurrence of the Secretary of State, or
    (b)   in relation to Scotland, by the Secretary of State,
    for the purpose of giving effect to Parts I to VII of this Act or the EC Regulation.

(2)   Without prejudice to the generality of subsection (1), or to any provision of those Parts by virtue of which rules under this section may be made with respect to any matter, rules under this section may contain—
    (a)   any such provision as is specified in Schedule 8 to this Act or corresponds to provision contained immediately before the coming into force of section 106 of the Insolvency Act

1985 in rules made, or having effect as if made, under section 663(1) or (2) of the Companies Act (old winding-up rules), and

(b)   such incidental, supplemental and transitional provisions as may appear to the Lord Chancellor or, as the case may be, the Secretary of State necessary or expedient.

(2A)   For the purposes of subsection (2), a reference in Schedule 8 to this Act to doing anything under or for the purposes of a provision of this Act includes a reference to doing anything under or for the purposes of the EC Regulation (in so far as the provision of this Act relates to a matter to which the EC Regulation applies).

(2B)   Rules under this section for the purpose of giving effect to the EC Regulation may not create an offence of a kind referred to in paragraph 1(1)(d) of Schedule 2 to the European Communities Act 1972.

(3)   In Schedule 8 to this Act "liquidator" includes a provisional liquidator; and references above in this section to Parts I to VII of this Act are to be read as including the Companies Act so far as relating to, and to matters connected with or arising out of, the insolvency or winding up of companies.

(4)   Rules under this section shall be made by statutory instrument subject to annulment in pursuance of a resolution of either House of Parliament.

(5)   Regulations made by the Secretary of State under a power conferred by rules under this section shall be made by statutory instrument and, after being made, shall be laid before each House of Parliament.

(6)   Nothing in this section prejudices any power to make rules of court.

412.   Individual insolvency rules (England and Wales)

(1)   The Lord Chancellor may, with the concurrence of the Secretary of State, make rules for the purpose of giving effect to Parts VIII to XI of this Act or the EC Regulation.

(2)   Without prejudice to the generality of subsection (1), or to any provision of those Parts by virtue of which rules under this section may be made with respect to any matter, rules under this section may contain—

(a)   any such provision as is specified in Schedule 9 to this Act or corresponds to provision contained immediately before the appointed day in rules made under section 132 of the Bankruptcy Act 1914; and

(b)   such incidental, supplemental and transitional provisions as may appear to the Lord Chancellor necessary or expedient.

(2A)   For the purposes of subsection (2), a reference in Schedule 9 to this Act to doing anything under or for the purposes of a provision of this Act includes a reference to doing anything under or for the purposes of the EC Regulation (in so far as the provision of this Act relates to a matter to which the EC Regulation applies).

(2B)   Rules under this section for the purpose of giving effect to the EC Regulation may not create an offence of a kind referred to in paragraph 1(1)(d) of Schedule 2 to the European Communities Act 1972.

(3)   Rules under this section shall be made by statutory instrument subject to annulment in pursuance of a resolution of either House of Parliament.

(4)   Regulations made by the Secretary of State under a power conferred by rules under this section shall be made by statutory instrument and, after being made, shall be laid before each House of Parliament.

(5)   Nothing in this section prejudices any power to make rules of court.

413.   Insolvency Rules Committee

(1)   The committee established under section 10 of the Insolvency Act 1976 (advisory committee on bankruptcy and winding-up rules) continues to exist for the purpose of being consulted under this section.

(2)   The Lord Chancellor shall consult the committee before making any rules under section 411 or 412 other than rules which contain a statement that the only provision made by the rules is

provision applying rules made under section 411, with or without modifications, for the purposes of provision made by any of sections 23 to 26 of the Water Industry Act 1991 or Schedule 3 to that Act or by any of sections 59 to 65 of, or Schedule 6 or 7 to, the Railways Act 1993.

(3) Subject to the next subsection, the committee shall consist of—

    (a) a judge of the High Court attached to the Chancery Division;

    (b) a circuit judge;

    (c) a registrar in bankruptcy of the High Court;

    (d) the registrar of a county court;

    (e) a practising barrister;

    (f) a practising solicitor; and

    (g) a practising accountant;

and the appointment of any person as a member of the committee shall be made by the Lord Chancellor.

(4) The Lord Chancellor may appoint as additional members of the committee any persons appearing to him to have qualifications or experience that would be of value to the committee in considering any matter with which it is concerned.

Fees orders

414. Fees orders (company insolvency proceedings)

(1) There shall be paid in respect of—

    (a) proceedings under any of Parts I to VII of this Act, and

    (b) the performance by the official receiver or the Secretary of State of functions under those Parts,

such fees as the competent authority may with the sanction of the Treasury by order direct.

(2) That authority is—

    (a) in relation to England and Wales, the Lord Chancellor, and

    (b) in relation to Scotland, the Secretary of State.

(3) The Treasury may by order direct by whom and in what manner the fees are to be collected and accounted for.

(4) The Lord Chancellor may, with the sanction of the Treasury, by order provide for sums to be deposited, by such persons, in such manner and in such circumstances as may be specified in the order, by way of security for fees payable by virtue of this section.

(5) An order under this section may contain such incidental, supplemental and transitional provisions as may appear to the Lord Chancellor, the Secretary of State or (as the case may be) the Treasury necessary or expedient.

(6) An order under this section shall be made by statutory instrument and, after being made, shall be laid before each House of Parliament.

(7) Fees payable by virtue of this section shall be paid into the Consolidated Fund.

(8) References in subsection (1) to Parts I to VII of this Act are to be read as including the Companies Act so far as relating to, and to matters connected with or arising out of, the insolvency or winding up of companies.

(9) Nothing in this section prejudices any power to make rules of court; and the application of this section to Scotland is without prejudice to section 2 of the Courts of Law Fees (Scotland) Act 1895.

415. Fees orders (individual insolvency proceedings in England and Wales)

(1) There shall be paid in respect of—

    (a) proceedings under Parts VIII to XI of this Act, and

    (b) the performance by the official receiver or the Secretary of State of functions under those Parts,

such fees as the Lord Chancellor may with the sanction of the Treasury by order direct.

(2) The Treasury may by order direct by whom and in what manner the fees are to be collected and accounted for.

(3)   The Lord Chancellor may, with the sanction of the Treasury, by order provide for sums to be deposited, by such persons, in such manner and in such circumstances as may be specified in the order, by way of security for—

        (a)   fees payable by virtue of this section, and

        (b)   fees payable to any person who has prepared an insolvency practitioner's report under section 274 in Chapter I of Part IX.

(4)   An order under this section may contain such incidental, supplemental and transitional provisions as may appear to the Lord Chancellor or, as the case may be, the Treasury, necessary or expedient.

(5)   An order under this section shall be made by statutory instrument and, after being made, shall be laid before each House of Parliament.

(6)   Fees payable by virtue of this section shall be paid into the Consolidated Fund.

(7)   Nothing in this section prejudices any power to make rules of court.

415A. Fees orders (general)

(1)   The Secretary of State—

        (a)   may by order require a body to pay a fee in connection with the grant or maintenance of recognition of the body under section 391, and

        (b)   may refuse recognition, or revoke an order of recognition under section 391(1) by a further order, where a fee is not paid.

(2)   The Secretary of State—

        (a)   may by order require a person to pay a fee in connection with the grant or maintenance of authorisation of the person under section 393, and

        (b)   may disregard an application or withdraw an authorisation where a fee is not paid.

(3)   The Secretary of State may by order require the payment of fees in respect of—

        (a)   the operation of the Insolvency Services Account;

        (b)   payments into and out of that Account.

(4)   The following provisions of section 414 apply to fees under this section as they apply to fees under that section—

        (a)   subsection (3) (manner of payment),

        (b)   subsection (5) (additional provision),

        (c)   subsection (6) (statutory instrument),

        (d)   subsection (7) (payment into Consolidated Fund), and

        (e)   subsection (9) (saving for rules of court).

Specification, increase and reduction of money sums
relevant in the operation of this Act

416. Monetary limits (companies winding up)

(1)   The Secretary of State may by order in a statutory instrument increase or reduce any of the money sums for the time being specified in the following provisions in the first Group of Parts—

        section 117(2) (amount of company's share capital determining whether county court has jurisdiction to wind it up);

        section 120(3) (the equivalent as respects sheriff court jurisdiction in Scotland);

        section 123(1)(a) (minimum debt for service of demand on company by unpaid creditor);

        section 184(3) (minimum value of judgment, affecting sheriff's duties on levying execution);

        section 206(1)(a) and (b) (minimum value of company property concealed or fraudulently removed, affecting criminal liability of company's officer).

(2)   An order under this section may contain such transitional provisions as may appear to the Secretary of State necessary or expedient.

(3)   No order under this section increasing or reducing any of the money sums for the time being specified in section 117(2), 120(3), or 123(1)(a) shall be made unless a draft of the order has been laid before and approved by a resolution of each House of Parliament.

(4)   A statutory instrument containing an order under this section, other than an order to which subsection (3) applies, is subject to annulment in pursuance of a resolution of either House of Parliament.

417.   Money sum in s 222

The Secretary of State may by regulations in a statutory instrument increase or reduce the money sum for the time being specified in section 222(1) (minimum debt for service of demand on unregistered company by unpaid creditor); but such regulations shall not be made unless a draft of the statutory instrument containing them has been approved by resolution of each House of Parliament.

417A.   Money sums (company moratorium)

(1)   The Secretary of State may by order increase or reduce any of the money sums for the time being specified in the following provisions of Schedule A1 to this Act—

> paragraph 17(1) (maximum amount of credit which company may obtain without disclosure of moratorium);
>
> paragraph 41(4) (minimum value of company property concealed or fraudulently removed, affecting criminal liability of company's officer).

(2)   An order under this section may contain such transitional provisions as may appear to the Secretary of State necessary or expedient.

(3)   An order under this section shall be made by statutory instrument subject to annulment in pursuance of a resolution of either House of Parliament.

418.   Monetary limits (bankruptcy)

(1)   The Secretary of State may by order prescribe amounts for the purposes of the following provisions in the second Group of Parts—

> section 273 (minimum value of debtor's estate determining whether immediate bankruptcy order should be made; small bankruptcies level);
>
> section 313A (value of property below which application for sale, possession or charge to be dismissed);
>
> section 346(3) (minimum amount of judgment, determining whether amount recovered on sale of debtor's goods is to be treated as part of his estate in bankruptcy);
>
> section 354(1) and (2) (minimum amount of concealed debt, or value of property concealed or removed, determining criminal liability under the section);
>
> section 358 (minimum value of property taken by a bankrupt out of England and Wales, determining his criminal liability);
>
> section 360(1) (maximum amount of credit which bankrupt may obtain without disclosure of his status);
>
> section 361(2) (exemption of bankrupt from criminal liability for failure to keep proper accounts, if unsecured debts not more than the prescribed minimum);
>
> section 364(2)(d) (minimum value of goods removed by the bankrupt, determining his liability to arrest);

and references in the second Group of Parts to the amount prescribed for the purposes of any of those provisions, and references in those provisions to the prescribed amount, are to be construed accordingly.

(2)   An order under this section may contain such transitional provisions as may appear to the Secretary of State necessary or expedient.

(3)   An order under this section shall be made by statutory instrument subject to annulment in pursuance of a resolution of either House of Parliament.

Insolvency practice

419. Regulations for purposes of Part XIII

(1)   The Secretary of State may make regulations for the purpose of giving effect to Part XIII of this Act; and "prescribed" in that Part means prescribed by regulations made by the Secretary of State.

(2)   Without prejudice to the generality of subsection (1) or to any provision of that Part by virtue of which regulations may be made with respect to any matter, regulations under this section may contain—

     (a)   provision as to the matters to be taken into account in determining whether a person is a fit and proper person to act as an insolvency practitioner;

     (b)   provision prohibiting a person from so acting in prescribed cases, being cases in which a conflict of interest will or may arise;

     (c)   provision imposing requirements with respect to—

         (i)   the preparation and keeping by a person who acts as an insolvency practitioner of prescribed books, accounts and other records, and

         (ii)   the production of those books, accounts and records to prescribed persons;

     (d)   provision conferring power on prescribed persons—

         (i)   to require any person who acts or has acted as an insolvency practitioner to answer any inquiry in relation to a case in which he is so acting or has so acted, and

         (ii)   to apply to a court to examine such a person or any other person on oath concerning such a case;

     (e)   provision making non-compliance with any of the regulations a criminal offence; and

     (f)   such incidental, supplemental and transitional provisions as may appear to the Secretary of State necessary or expedient.

(3)   Any power conferred by Part XIII or this Part to make regulations, rules or orders is exercisable by statutory instrument subject to annulment by resolution of either House of Parliament.

(4)   Any rule or regulation under Part XIII or this Part may make different provision with respect to different cases or descriptions of cases, including different provision for different areas.

Other order-making powers

420. Insolvent partnerships

(1)   The Lord Chancellor may, by order made with the concurrence of the Secretary of State, provide that such provisions of this Act as may be specified in the order shall apply in relation to insolvent partnerships with such modifications as may be so specified.

(1A)   An order under this section may make provision in relation to the EC Regulation.

(1B)   But provision made by virtue of this section in relation to the EC Regulation may not create an offence of a kind referred to in paragraph 1(1)(d) of Schedule 2 to the European Communities Act 1972.

(2)   An order under this section may make different provision for different cases and may contain such incidental, supplemental and transitional provisions as may appear to the Lord Chancellor necessary or expedient.

(3)   An order under this section shall be made by statutory instrument subject to annulment in pursuance of a resolution of either House of Parliament.

421. Insolvent estates of deceased persons

(1)   The Lord Chancellor may, by order made with the concurrence of the Secretary of State, provide that such provisions of this Act as may be specified in the order shall apply in relation to the administration of the insolvent estates of deceased persons with such modifications as may be so specified.

(1A)   An order under this section may make provision in relation to the EC Regulation.

(1B)   But provision made by virtue of this section in relation to the EC Regulation may not create an offence of a kind referred to in paragraph 1(1)(d) of Schedule 2 to the European Communities Act 1972.

(2)   An order under this section may make different provision for different cases and may contain such incidental, supplemental and transitional provisions as may appear to the Lord Chancellor necessary or expedient.

(3)   An order under this section shall be made by statutory instrument subject to annulment in pursuance of a resolution of either House of Parliament.

(4)   For the purposes of this section the estate of a deceased person is insolvent if, when realised, it will be insufficient to meet in full all the debts and other liabilities to which it is subject.

421A.   Insolvent estates: joint tenancies

(1)   This section applies where—

   (a)   an insolvency administration order has been made in respect of the insolvent estate of a deceased person,

   (b)   the petition for the order was presented after the commencement of this section and within the period of five years beginning with the day on which he died, and

   (c)   immediately before his death he was beneficially entitled to an interest in any property as joint tenant.

(2)   For the purpose of securing that debts and other liabilities to which the estate is subject are met, the court may, on an application by the trustee appointed pursuant to the insolvency administration order, make an order under this section requiring the survivor to pay to the trustee an amount not exceeding the value lost to the estate.

(3)   In determining whether to make an order under this section, and the terms of such an order, the court must have regard to all the circumstances of the case, including the interests of the deceased's creditors and of the survivor; but, unless the circumstances are exceptional, the court must assume that the interests of the deceased's creditors outweigh all other considerations.

(4)   The order may be made on such terms and conditions as the court thinks fit.

(5)   Any sums required to be paid to the trustee in accordance with an order under this section shall be comprised in the estate.

(6)   The modifications of this Act which may be made by an order under section 421 include any modifications which are necessary or expedient in consequence of this section.

(7)   In this section, "survivor" means the person who, immediately before the death, was beneficially entitled as joint tenant with the deceased or, if the person who was so entitled dies after the making of the insolvency administration order, his personal representatives.

(8)   If there is more than one survivor—

   (a)   an order under this section may be made against all or any of them, but

   (b)   no survivor shall be required to pay more than so much of the value lost to the estate as is properly attributable to him.

(9)   In this section—

   "insolvency administration order" has the same meaning as in any order under section 421 having effect for the time being,

   "value lost to the estate" means the amount which, if paid to the trustee, would in the court's opinion restore the position to what it would have been if the deceased had been adjudged bankrupt immediately before his death.

422.   Formerly authorised banks

(1)   The Secretary of State may by order made with the concurrence of the Treasury and after consultation with the Financial Services Authority provide that specified provisions in the first Group of Parts shall apply with specified modifications in relation to any person who—

   (a)   has a liability in respect of a deposit which he accepted in accordance with the Banking Act 1979 (c 37) or 1987 (c 22), but

   (b)   does not have permission under Part IV of the Financial Services and Markets Act 2000 (c 8) (regulated activities) to accept deposits.

(1A)   Subsection (1)(b) shall be construed in accordance with—

(a)   section 22 of the Financial Services and Markets Act 2000 (classes of regulated activity and categories of investment),

(b)   any relevant order under that section, and

(c)   Schedule 2 to that Act (regulated activities).

(2)   An order under this section may make different provision for different cases and may contain such incidental, supplemental and transitional provisions as may appear to the Secretary of State necessary or expedient.

(3)   An order under this section shall be made by statutory instrument subject to annulment in pursuance of a resolution of either House of Parliament.

PART XVI
PROVISIONS AGAINST DEBT AVOIDANCE
(ENGLAND AND WALES ONLY)

423.   Transactions defrauding creditors

(1)   This section relates to transactions entered into at an undervalue; and a person enters into such a transaction with another person if—

(a)   he makes a gift to the other person or he otherwise enters into a transaction with the other on terms that provide for him to receive no consideration;

(b)   he enters into a transaction with the other in consideration of marriage *or the formation of a civil partnership*; or

(c)   he enters into a transaction with the other for a consideration the value of which, in money or money's worth, is significantly less than the value, in money or money's worth, of the consideration provided by himself.

(2)   Where a person has entered into such a transaction, the court may, if satisfied under the next subsection, make such order as it thinks fit for—

(a)   restoring the position to what it would have been if the transaction had not been entered into, and

(b)   protecting the interests of persons who are victims of the transaction.

(3)   In the case of a person entering into such a transaction, an order shall only be made if the court is satisfied that it was entered into by him for the purpose—

(a)   of putting assets beyond the reach of a person who is making, or may at some time make, a claim against him, or

(b)   of otherwise prejudicing the interests of such a person in relation to the claim which he is making or may make.

(4)   In this section "the court" means the High Court or—

(a)   if the person entering into the transaction is an individual, any other court which would have jurisdiction in relation to a bankruptcy petition relating to him;

(b)   if that person is a body capable of being wound up under Part IV or V of this Act, any other court having jurisdiction to wind it up.

(5)   In relation to a transaction at an undervalue, references here and below to a victim of the transaction are to a person who is, or is capable of being, prejudiced by it; and in the following two sections the person entering into the transaction is referred to as "the debtor".

Note. The italicized words in subsection (1)(b) are inserted by the Civil Partnership Act 2004, s. 261(1), Sch. 27, para. 121, as from a day to be appointed.

424.   Those who may apply for an order under s 423

(1)   An application for an order under section 423 shall not be made in relation to a transaction except—

(a)   in a case where the debtor has been adjudged bankrupt or is a body corporate which is being wound up or is in administration, by the official receiver, by the trustee of the bankrupt's estate or the liquidator or administrator of the body corporate or (with the leave of the court) by a victim of the transaction;

(b) in a case where a victim of the transaction is bound by a voluntary arrangement approved under Part I or Part VIII of this Act, by the supervisor of the voluntary arrangement or by any person who (whether or not so bound) is such a victim; or

(c) in any other case, by a victim of the transaction.

(2) An application made under any of the paragraphs of subsection (1) is to be treated as made on behalf of every victim of the transaction.

425. Provision which may be made by order under s 423

(1) Without prejudice to the generality of section 423, an order made under that section with respect to a transaction may (subject as follows)—

(a) require any property transferred as part of the transaction to be vested in any person, either absolutely or for the benefit of all the persons on whose behalf the application for the order is treated as made;

(b) require any property to be so vested if it represents, in any person's hands, the application either of the proceeds of sale of property so transferred or of money so transferred;

(c) release or discharge (in whole or in part) any security given by the debtor;

(d) require any person to pay to any other person in respect of benefits received from the debtor such sums as the court may direct;

(e) provide for any surety or guarantor whose obligations to any person were released or discharged (in whole or in part) under the transaction to be under such new or revived obligations as the court thinks appropriate;

(f) provide for security to be provided for the discharge of any obligation imposed by or arising under the order, for such an obligation to be charged on any property and for such security or charge to have the same priority as a security or charge released or discharged (in whole or in part) under the transaction.

(2) An order under section 423 may affect the property of, or impose any obligation on, any person whether or not he is the person with whom the debtor entered into the transaction; but such an order—

(a) shall not prejudice any interest in property which was acquired from a person other than the debtor and was acquired in good faith, for value and without notice of the relevant circumstances, or prejudice any interest deriving from such an interest, and

(b) shall not require a person who received a benefit from the transaction in good faith, for value and without notice of the relevant circumstances to pay any sum unless he was a party to the transaction.

(3) For the purposes of this section the relevant circumstances in relation to a transaction are the circumstances by virtue of which an order under section 423 may be made in respect of the transaction.

(4) In this section "security" means any mortgage, charge, lien or other security.

PART XVII
MISCELLANEOUS AND GENERAL

426. Co-operation between courts exercising jurisdiction in relation to insolvency

(1) An order made by a court in any part of the United Kingdom in the exercise of jurisdiction in relation to insolvency law shall be enforced in any other part of the United Kingdom as if it were made by a court exercising the corresponding jurisdiction in that other part.

(2) However, without prejudice to the following provisions of this section, nothing in subsection (1) requires a court in any part of the United Kingdom to enforce, in relation to property situated in that part, any order made by a court in any other part of the United Kingdom.

(3) The Secretary of State, with the concurrence in relation to property situated in England and Wales of the Lord Chancellor, may by order make provision for securing that a trustee or assignee under the insolvency law of any part of the United Kingdom has, with such modifications as may be specified in the order, the same rights in relation to any property situated in another part of the

United Kingdom as he would have in the corresponding circumstances if he were a trustee or assignee under the insolvency law of that other part.

(4)   The courts having jurisdiction in relation to insolvency law in any part of the United Kingdom shall assist the courts having the corresponding jurisdiction in any other part of the United Kingdom or any relevant country or territory.

(5)   For the purposes of subsection (4) a request made to a court in any part of the United Kingdom by a court in any other part of the United Kingdom or in a relevant country or territory is authority for the court to which the request is made to apply, in relation to any matters specified in the request, the insolvency law which is applicable by either court in relation to comparable matters falling within its jurisdiction.

In exercising its discretion under this subsection, a court shall have regard in particular to the rules of private international law.

(6)   Where a person who is a trustee or assignee under the insolvency law of any part of the United Kingdom claims property situated in any other part of the United Kingdom (whether by virtue of an order under subsection (3) or otherwise), the submission of that claim to the court exercising jurisdiction in relation to insolvency law in that other part shall be treated in the same manner as a request made by a court for the purpose of subsection (4).

(7)   Section 38 of the Criminal Law Act 1977 (execution of warrant of arrest throughout the United Kingdom) applies to a warrant which, in exercise of any jurisdiction in relation to insolvency law, is issued in any part of the United Kingdom for the arrest of a person as it applies to a warrant issued in that part of the United Kingdom for the arrest of a person charged with an offence.

(8)   Without prejudice to any power to make rules of court, any power to make provision by subordinate legislation for the purpose of giving effect in relation to companies or individuals to the insolvency law of any part of the United Kingdom includes power to make provision for the purpose of giving effect in that part to any provision made by or under the preceding provisions of this section.

(9)   An order under subsection (3) shall be made by statutory instrument subject to annulment in pursuance of a resolution of either House of Parliament.

(10)   In this section "insolvency law" means—

(a)   in relation to England and Wales, provision extending to England and Wales and made by or under this Act or sections 1A, 6 to 10, 12 to 15, 19(c) and 20 (with Schedule 1) of the Company Directors Disqualification Act 1986 and sections 1 to 17 of that Act as they apply for the purposes of those provisions of that Act;

(b)   in relation to Scotland, provision extending to Scotland and made by or under this Act, sections 1A, 6 to 10, 12 to 15, 19(c) and 20 (with Schedule 1) of the Company Directors Disqualification Act 1986 and sections 1 to 17 of that Act as they apply for the purposes of those provisions of that Act, Part XVIII of the Companies Act or the Bankruptcy (Scotland) Act 1985;

(c)   in relation to Northern Ireland, provision made by or under the Insolvency (Northern Ireland) Order 1989 *or Part II of the Companies (Northern Ireland) Order 1989* [*or the Company Directors Disqualification (Northern Ireland) Order 2002*];

(d)   in relation to any relevant country or territory, so much of the law of that country or territory as corresponds to provisions falling within any of the foregoing paragraphs;

and references in this subsection to any enactment include, in relation to any time before the coming into force of that enactment the corresponding enactment in force at that time.

(11)   In this section "relevant country or territory" means—

(a)   any of the Channel Islands or the Isle of Man, or

(b)   any country or territory designated for the purposes of this section by the Secretary of State by order made by statutory instrument.

(12)   In the application of this section to Northern Ireland—

(a)   for any reference to the Secretary of State there is substituted a reference to the Department of Economic Development in Northern Ireland;

(b)   in subsection (3) for the words "another part of the United Kingdom" and the words "that other part" there are substituted the words "Northern Ireland";

(c)   for subsection (9) there is substituted the following subsection—

"(9) An order made under subsection (3) by the Department of Economic Development in Northern Ireland shall be a statutory rule for the purposes of the Statutory Rules (Northern Ireland) Order 1979 and shall be subject to negative resolution within the meaning of section 41(6) of the Interpretation Act (Northern Ireland) 1954.".

Note. The italicized words "or Part II of the Companies (Northern Ireland) Order 1989" in subsection (10)(c) are repealed and the subsequent italicized words in square brackets are substituted by S.I. 2002/3150, art. 26(2), Sch. 3, para. 2, as from a day to be appointed.

426A. Disqualification from Parliament (England and Wales)

(1)   A person in respect of whom a bankruptcy restrictions order has effect shall be disqualified—

(a)   from membership of the House of Commons,

(b)   from sitting or voting in the House of Lords, and

(c)   from sitting or voting in a committee of the House of Lords or a joint committee of both Houses.

(2)   If a member of the House of Commons becomes disqualified under this section, his seat shall be vacated.

(3)   If a person who is disqualified under this section is returned as a member of the House of Commons, his return shall be void.

(4)   No writ of summons shall be issued to a member of the House of Lords who is disqualified under this section.

(5)   If a court makes a bankruptcy restrictions order or interim order in respect of a member of the House of Commons or the House of Lords the court shall notify the Speaker of that House.

(6)   If the Secretary of State accepts a bankruptcy restrictions undertaking made by a member of the House of Commons or the House of Lords, the Secretary of State shall notify the Speaker of that House.

426B. Devolution

(1)   If a court makes a bankruptcy restrictions order or interim order in respect of a member of the Scottish Parliament, the Northern Ireland Assembly or the National Assembly for Wales, the court shall notify the presiding officer of that body.

(2)   If the Secretary of State accepts a bankruptcy restrictions undertaking made by a member of the Scottish Parliament, the Northern Ireland Assembly or the National Assembly for Wales, the Secretary of State shall notify the presiding officer of that body.

426C. Irrelevance of privilege

(1)   An enactment about insolvency applies in relation to a member of the House of Commons or the House of Lords irrespective of any Parliamentary privilege.

(2)   In this section "enactment" includes a provision made by or under—

(a)   an Act of the Scottish Parliament, or

(b)   Northern Ireland legislation.

427. Disqualification from Parliament (Scotland and Northern Ireland)

(1)   Where a court in … Northern Ireland adjudges an individual bankrupt or a court in Scotland awards sequestration of an individual's estate, the individual is disqualified—

(a)   for sitting or voting in the House of Lords,

(b)   for being elected to, or sitting or voting in, the House of Commons, and

(c)   for sitting or voting in a committee of either House.

(2)   Where an individual is disqualified under this section, the disqualification ceases—

(a)   except where the adjudication is annulled or the award recalled or reduced without the individual having been first discharged, on the discharge of the individual, and

(b)   in the excepted case, on the annulment, recall or reduction, as the case may be.

(3)   No writ of summons shall be issued to any lord of Parliament who is for the time being disqualified under this section for sitting and voting in the House of Lords.

(4)   Where a member of the House of Commons who is disqualified under this section continues to be so disqualified until the end of the period of 6 months beginning with the day of the adjudication or award, his seat shall be vacated at the end of that period.

(5)   A court which makes an adjudication or award such as is mentioned in subsection (1) in relation to any lord of Parliament or member of the House of Commons shall forthwith certify the adjudication or award to the Speaker of the House of Lords or, as the case may be, to the Speaker of the House of Commons.

(6)   Where a court has certified an adjudication or award to the Speaker of the House of Commons under subsection (5), then immediately after it becomes apparent which of the following certificates is applicable, the court shall certify to the Speaker of the House of Commons—

    (a)   that the period of 6 months beginning with the day of the adjudication or award has expired without the adjudication or award having been annulled, recalled or reduced, or

    (b)   that the adjudication or award has been annulled, recalled or reduced before the end of that period.

(6A)   Subsections (4) to (6) have effect in relation to a member of the Scottish Parliament but as if—

    (a)   references to the House of Commons were to the Parliament and references to the Speaker were to the Presiding Officer, and

    (b)   in subsection (4), for "under this section" there were substituted "under section 15(1)(b) of the Scotland Act 1998 by virtue of this section".

(6B)   Subsections (4) to (6) have effect in relation to a member of the National Assembly for Wales but as if—

    (a)   references to the House of Commons were to the Assembly and references to the Speaker were to the presiding officer, and

    (b)   in subsection (4), for "under this section" there were substituted "under section 12(2) of the Government of Wales Act 1998 by virtue of this section".

(6C)   Subsection (1), as applied to a member of the Northern Ireland Assembly by virtue of section 36(4) of the Northern Ireland Act 1998, has effect as if "or Northern Ireland" were omitted; and subsections (4) to (6) have effect in relation to such a member as if—

    (a)   references to the House of Commons were to the Assembly and references to the Speaker were to the Presiding Officer; and

    (b)   in subsection (4), for "under this section" there were substituted "under section 36(4) of the Northern Ireland Act 1998 by virtue of this section".

(7)   …

428.   Exemptions from Restrictive Trade Practices Act

(1), (2)   …

(3)   In this section "insolvency services" means the services of persons acting as insolvency practitioners or carrying out under the law of Northern Ireland functions corresponding to those mentioned in section 388(1) or (2) in Part XIII, in their capacity as such….

429.   Disabilities on revocation of administration order against an individual

(1)   The following applies where a person fails to make any payment which he is required to make by virtue of an administration order under Part VI of the County Courts Act 1984.

(2)   The court which is administering that person's estate under the order may, if it thinks fit—

    (a)   revoke the administration order, and

    (b)   make an order directing that this section and section 12 of the Company Directors Disqualification Act 1986 shall apply to the person for such period, not exceeding one year, as may be specified in the order.

(3)   A person to whom this section so applies shall not—

    (a)   either alone or jointly with another person, obtain credit to the extent of the amount prescribed for the purposes of section 360(1)(a) or more, or

(b)   enter into any transaction in the course of or for the purposes of any business in which he is directly or indirectly engaged,

without disclosing to the person from whom he obtains the credit, or (as the case may be) with whom the transaction is entered into, the fact that this section applies to him.

(4)   The reference in subsection (3) to a person obtaining credit includes—

(a)   a case where goods are bailed or hired to him under a hire-purchase agreement or agreed to be sold to him under a conditional sale agreement, and

(b)   a case where he is paid in advance (whether in money or otherwise) for the supply of goods or services.

(5)   A person who contravenes this section is guilty of an offence and liable to imprisonment or a fine, or both.

430.   Provision introducing Schedule of punishments

(1)   Schedule 10 to this Act has effect with respect to the way in which offences under this Act are punishable on conviction.

(2)   In relation to an offence under a provision of this Act specified in the first column of the Schedule (the general nature of the offence being described in the second column), the third column shows whether the offence is punishable on conviction on indictment, or on summary conviction, or either in the one way or the other.

(3)   The fourth column of the Schedule shows, in relation to an offence, the maximum punishment by way of fine or imprisonment under this Act which may be imposed on a person convicted of the offence in the way specified in relation to it in the third column (that is to say, on indictment or summarily) a reference to a period of years or months being to a term of imprisonment of that duration.

(4)   The fifth column shows, (in relation to an offence for which there is an entry in that column) that a person convicted of the offence after continued contravention is liable to a daily default fine; that is to say, he is liable on a second or subsequent conviction of the offence to the fine specified in that column for each day on which the contravention is continued (instead of the penalty specified for the offence in the fourth column of the Schedule).

(5)   For the purpose of any enactment in this Act whereby an officer of a company who is in default is liable to a fine or penalty, the expression "officer who is in default" means any officer of the company who knowingly and wilfully authorises or permits the default, refusal or contravention mentioned in the enactment.

431.   Summary proceedings

(1)   Summary proceedings for any offence under any of Parts I to VII of this Act may (without prejudice to any jurisdiction exercisable apart from this subsection) be taken against a body corporate at any place at which the body has a place of business, and against any other person at any place at which he is for the time being.

(2)   Notwithstanding anything in section 127(1) of the Magistrates' Courts Act 1980, an information relating to such an offence which is triable by a magistrates' court in England and Wales may be so tried if it is laid at any time within 3 years after the commission of the offence and within 12 months after the date on which evidence sufficient in the opinion of the Director of Public Prosecutions or the Secretary of State (as the case may be) to justify the proceedings comes to his knowledge.

(3)   Summary proceedings in Scotland for such an offence shall not be commenced after the expiration of 3 years from the commission of the offence.

Subject to this (and notwithstanding anything in section 136 of the Criminal Procedure (Scotland) Act 1995), such proceedings may (in Scotland) be commenced at any time within 12 months after the date on which evidence sufficient in the Lord Advocate's opinion to justify the proceedings came to his knowledge or, where such evidence was reported to him by the Secretary of State, within 12 months after the date on which it came to the knowledge of the latter; and subsection (3) of that section applies for the purpose of this subsection as it applies for the purpose of that section.

(4)   For purposes of this section, a certificate of the Director of Public Prosecutions, the Lord Advocate or the Secretary of State (as the case may be) as to the date on which such evidence as is referred to above came to his knowledge is conclusive evidence.

432.   Offences by bodies corporate

(1)   This section applies to offences under this Act other than those excepted by subsection (4).

(2)   Where a body corporate is guilty of an offence to which this section applies and the offence is proved to have been committed with the consent or connivance of, or to be attributable to any neglect on the part of, any director, manager, secretary or other similar officer of the body corporate or any person who was purporting to act in any such capacity he, as well as the body corporate, is guilty of the offence and liable to be proceeded against and punished accordingly.

(3)   Where the affairs of a body corporate are managed by its members, subsection (2) applies in relation to the acts and defaults of a member in connection with his functions of management as if he were a director of the body corporate.

(4)   The offences excepted from this section are those under sections 30, 39, 51, 53, 54, 62, 64, 66, 85, 89, 164, 188, 201, 206, 207, 208, 209, 210 and 211 and those under paragraphs 16(2), 17(3)(a), 18(3)(a), 19(3)(a), 22(1) and 23(1)(a) of Schedule A1.

433.   Admissibility in evidence of statements of affairs, etc

(1)   In any proceedings (whether or not under this Act)—

      (a)   a statement of affairs prepared for the purposes of any provision of this Act which is derived from the Insolvency Act 1985, and

      (b)   any other statement made in pursuance of a requirement imposed by or under any such provision or by or under rules made under this Act,

    may be used in evidence against any person making or concurring in making the statement.

(2)   However, in criminal proceedings in which any such person is charged with an offence to which this subsection applies—

      (a)   no evidence relating to the statement may be adduced, and

      (b)   no question relating to it may be asked,

    by or on behalf of the prosecution, unless evidence relating to it is adduced, or a question relating to it is asked, in the proceedings by or on behalf of that person.

(3)   Subsection (2) applies to any offence other than—

      (a)   an offence under section 22(6), 47(6), 48(8), 66(6), 67(8), 95(8), 98(6), 99(3)(a), 131(7), 192(2), 208(1)(a) or (d) or (2), 210, 235(5), 353(1), 354(1)(b) or (3) or 356(1) or (2)(a) or (b) or paragraph 4(3)(a) of Schedule 7;

      (b)   an offence which is—

          (i)   created by rules made under this Act, and

          (ii)   designated for the purposes of this subsection by such rules or by regulations made by the Secretary of State;

      (c)   an offence which is—

          (i)   created by regulations made under any such rules, and

          (ii)   designated for the purposes of this subsection by such regulations;

      (d)   an offence under section 1, 2 or 5 of the Perjury Act 1911 (false statements made on oath or made otherwise than on oath); or

      (e)   an offence under section 44(1) or (2) of the Criminal Law (Consolidation) (Scotland) Act 1995 (false statements made on oath or otherwise than on oath).

(4)   Regulations under subsection (3)(b)(ii) shall be made by statutory instrument and, after being made, shall be laid before each House of Parliament.

434.   Crown application

    For the avoidance of doubt it is hereby declared that provisions of this Act which derive from the Insolvency Act 1985 bind the Crown so far as affecting or relating to the following matters, namely—

      (a)   remedies against, or against the property of, companies or individuals;

      (b)   priorities of debts;

(c)   transactions at an undervalue or preferences;

(d)   voluntary arrangements approved under Part I or Part VIII, and

(e)   discharge from bankruptcy.

PART XVIII
INTERPRETATION

435.   Meaning of "associate"

(1)   For the purposes of this Act any question whether a person is an associate of another person is to be determined in accordance with the following provisions of this section (any provision that a person is an associate of another person being taken to mean that they are associates of each other).

(2)   *A person is an associate of an individual if that person is the individual's husband or wife, or is a relative, or the husband or wife of a relative, of the individual or of the individual's husband or wife.*

[(2)   *A person is an associate of an individual if that person is—*

(a)   *the individual's husband or wife or civil partner,*

(b)   *a relative of—*

(i)   *the individual, or*

(ii)   *the individual's husband or wife or civil partner, or*

(c)   *the husband or wife or civil partner of a relative of—*

(i)   *the individual, or*

(ii)   *the individual's husband or wife or civil partner.]*

(3)   A person is an associate of any person with whom he is in partnership, and of the husband or wife *or civil partner* or a relative of any individual with whom he is in partnership; and a Scottish firm is an associate of any person who is a member of the firm.

(4)   A person is an associate of any person whom he employs or by whom he is employed.

(5)   A person in his capacity as trustee of a trust other than—

(a)   a trust arising under any of the second Group of Parts or the Bankruptcy (Scotland) Act 1985, or

(b)   a pension scheme or an employees' share scheme (within the meaning of the Companies Act),

is an associate of another person if the beneficiaries of the trust include, or the terms of the trust confer a power that may be exercised for the benefit of, that other person or an associate of that other person.

(6)   A company is an associate of another company—

(a)   if the same person has control of both, or a person has control of one and persons who are his associates, or he and persons who are his associates, have control of the other, or

(b)   if a group of two or more persons has control of each company, and the groups either consist of the same persons or could be regarded as consisting of the same persons by treating (in one or more cases) a member of either group as replaced by a person of whom he is an associate.

(7)   A company is an associate of another person if that person has control of it or if that person and persons who are his associates together have control of it.

(8)   For the purposes of this section a person is a relative of an individual if he is that individual's brother, sister, uncle, aunt, nephew, niece, lineal ancestor or lineal descendant, treating—

(a)   any relationship of the half blood as a relationship of the whole blood and the stepchild or adopted child of any person as his child, and

(b)   an illegitimate child as the legitimate child of his mother and reputed father;

and references in this section to a husband or wife include a former husband or wife and a reputed husband or wife *and references to a civil partner include a former civil partner.*

(9)   For the purposes of this section any director or other officer of a company is to be treated as employed by that company.

(10)   For the purposes of this section a person is to be taken as having control of a company if—

       (a)   the directors of the company or of another company which has control of it (or any of them) are accustomed to act in accordance with his directions or instructions, or

       (b)   he is entitled to exercise, or control the exercise of, one third or more of the voting power at any general meeting of the company or of another company which has control of it;

    and where two or more persons together satisfy either of the above conditions, they are to be taken as having control of the company.

(11)   In this section "company" includes any body corporate (whether incorporated in Great Britain or elsewhere); and references to directors and other officers of a company and to voting power at any general meeting of a company have effect with any necessary modifications.

    Note. Subsection (2) is substituted, and the italicized words in subsections (3) and (8) are inserted, by the Civil Partnership Act 2004, s. 261(1), Sch. 27, para. 122, as from a day to be appointed.

436.   Expressions used generally

In this Act, except in so far as the context otherwise requires (and subject to Parts VII and XI)—

    ...

    "the appointed day" means the day on which this Act comes into force under section 443;

    "associate" has the meaning given by section 435;

    "business" includes a trade or profession;

    "the Companies Act" means the Companies Act 1985;

    "conditional sale agreement" and "hire-purchase agreement" have the same meanings as in the Consumer Credit Act 1974;

    ...

    "the EC Regulation" means Council Regulation (EC) No 1346/2000;

    "modifications" includes additions, alterations and omissions and cognate expressions shall be construed accordingly;

    ...

    "property" includes money, goods, things in action, land and every description of property wherever situated and also obligations and every description of interest, whether present or future or vested or contingent, arising out of, or incidental to, property;

    "records" includes computer records and other non-documentary records;

    ...

    "subordinate legislation" has the same meaning as in the Interpretation Act 1978; and

    "transaction" includes a gift, agreement or arrangement, and references to entering into a transaction shall be construed accordingly.

    ...

436A.   Proceedings under EC Regulation: modified definition of property

In the application of this Act to proceedings by virtue of Article 3 of the EC Regulation, a reference to property is a reference to property which may be dealt with in the proceedings.

PART XIX

FINAL PROVISIONS

437.   Transitional provisions, and savings

The transitional provisions and savings set out in Schedule 11 to this Act shall have effect, the Schedule comprising the following Parts—

    Part I: company insolvency and winding up (matters arising before appointed day, and continuance of proceedings in certain cases as before that day);

    Part II: individual insolvency (matters so arising, and continuance of bankruptcy proceedings in certain cases as before that day);

    Part III: transactions entered into before the appointed day and capable of being affected by orders of the court under Part XVI of this Act;

    Part IV: insolvency practitioners acting as such before the appointed day; and

Part V: general transitional provisions and savings required consequentially on, and in connection with, the repeal and replacement by this Act and the Company Directors Disqualification Act 1986 of provisions of the Companies Act, the greater part of the Insolvency Act 1985 and other enactments.

438.   Repeals

The enactments specified in the second column of Schedule 12 to this Act are repealed to the extent specified in the third column of that Schedule.

439.   Amendment of enactments

(1)   The Companies Act is amended as shown in Parts I and II of Schedule 13 to this Act, being amendments consequential on this Act and the Company Directors Disqualification Act 1986.

(2)   The enactments specified in the first column of Schedule 14 to this Act (being enactments which refer, or otherwise relate, to those which are repealed and replaced by this Act or the Company Directors Disqualification Act 1986) are amended as shown in the second column of that Schedule.

(3)   The Lord Chancellor may by order make such consequential modifications of any provision contained in any subordinate legislation made before the appointed day and such transitional provisions in connection with those modifications as appear to him necessary or expedient in respect of—

(a)   any reference in that subordinate legislation to the Bankruptcy Act 1914;

(b)   any reference in that subordinate legislation to any enactment repealed by Part III or IV of Schedule 10 to the Insolvency Act 1985; or

(c)   any reference in that subordinate legislation to any matter provided for under the Act of 1914 or under any enactment so repealed.

(4)   An order under this section shall be made by statutory instrument subject to annulment in pursuance of a resolution of either House of Parliament.

440.   Extent (Scotland)

(1)   Subject to the next subsection, provisions of this Act contained in the first Group of Parts extend to Scotland except where otherwise stated.

(2)   The following provisions of this Act do not extend to Scotland—

(a)   in the first Group of Parts—
section 43;
sections 238 to 241; and
section 246;

(b)   the second Group of Parts;

(c)   in the third Group of Parts—
sections 399 to 402,
sections 412, 413, 415, 415A(3), 418, 420 and 421,
sections 423 to 425, and
section 429(1) and (2); and

(d)   in the Schedules—
Parts II and III of Schedule 11; and
Schedules 12 and 14 so far as they repeal or amend enactments which extend to England and Wales only.

441.   Extent (Northern Ireland)

(1)   The following provisions of this Act extend to Northern Ireland—

(a)   sections 197, 426, 427 and 428; and

(b)   so much of section 439 and Schedule 14 as relates to enactments which extend to Northern Ireland.

(2)   Subject as above, and to any provision expressly relating to companies incorporated elsewhere than in Great Britain, nothing in this Act extends to Northern Ireland or applies to or in relation to companies registered or incorporated in Northern Ireland.

442.   Extent (other territories)

Her Majesty may, by Order in Council, direct that such of the provisions of this Act as are specified in the Order, being provisions formerly contained in the Insolvency Act 1985, shall extend to any of the Channel Islands or any colony with such modifications as may be so specified.

443.   Commencement

This Act comes into force on the day appointed under section 236(2) of the Insolvency Act 1985 for the coming into force of Part III of that Act (individual insolvency and bankruptcy), immediately after that Part of that Act comes into force for England and Wales.

444.   Citation

This Act may be cited as the Insolvency Act 1986.

SCHEDULE A1

MORATORIUM WHERE DIRECTORS PROPOSE VOLUNTARY ARRANGEMENT

PART I
INTRODUCTORY

Interpretation

1.   In this Schedule—

"the beginning of the moratorium" has the meaning given by paragraph 8(1),

"the date of filing" means the date on which the documents for the time being referred to in paragraph 7(1) are filed or lodged with the court,

"hire-purchase agreement" includes a conditional sale agreement, a chattel leasing agreement and a retention of title agreement,

"market contract" and "market charge" have the meanings given by Part VII of the Companies Act 1989,

…

"moratorium" means a moratorium under section 1A,

"the nominee" includes any person for the time being carrying out the functions of a nominee under this Schedule,

…

"the settlement finality regulations" means the Financial Markets and Insolvency (Settlement Finality) Regulations 1999,

"system-charge" has the meaning given by the Financial Markets and Insolvency Regulations 1996.

Eligible companies

2.—   (1)   A company is eligible for a moratorium if it meets the requirements of paragraph 3, unless—

(a)   it is excluded from being eligible by virtue of paragraph 4, or

(b)   it falls within sub-paragraph (2).

(2)   A company falls within this sub-paragraph if—

(a)   it effects or carries out contracts of insurance, but is not exempt from the general prohibition, within the meaning of section 19 of the Financial Services and Markets Act 2000, in relation to that activity,

(b)   it has permission under Part IV of that Act to accept deposits,

(bb)   it has a liability in respect of a deposit which it accepted in accordance with the Banking Act 1979 (c 37) or 1987 (c 22),

(c)   it is a party to a market contract … or any of its property is subject to a market charge … or a system-charge, or

(d)   it is a participant (within the meaning of the settlement finality regulations) or any of its property is subject to a collateral security charge (within the meaning of those regulations).

(3)   Paragraphs (a), (b) and (bb) of sub-paragraph (2) must be read with—

    (a)   section 22 of the Financial Services and Markets Act 2000;

    (b)   any relevant order under that section; and

    (c)   Schedule 2 to that Act.

3.—   (1)   A company meets the requirements of this paragraph if the qualifying conditions are met—

    (a)   in the year ending with the date of filing, or

    (b)   in the financial year of the company which ended last before that date.

(2)   For the purposes of sub-paragraph (1)—

    (a)   the qualifying conditions are met by a company in a period if, in that period, it satisfies two or more of the requirements for being a small company specified for the time being in section 247(3) of the Companies Act 1985, and

    (b)   a company's financial year is to be determined in accordance with that Act.

(3)   Subsections (4), (5) and (6) of section 247 of that Act apply for the purposes of this paragraph as they apply for the purposes of that section.

(4)   A company does not meet the requirements of this paragraph if it is a holding company of a group of companies which does not qualify as a small group or a medium-sized group in respect of the financial year of the company which ended last before the date of filing.

(5)   For the purposes of sub-paragraph (4) "group" has the meaning given by section 262 of the Companies Act 1985 (c 6) (definitions for Part VII) and a group qualifies as small or medium-sized if it qualifies as such under section 249 of the Companies Act 1985 (qualification of group as small or medium-sized).

4.—   (1)   A company is excluded from being eligible for a moratorium if, on the date of filing—

    (a)   the company is in administration,

    (b)   the company is being wound up,

    (c)   there is an administrative receiver of the company,

    (d)   a voluntary arrangement has effect in relation to the company,

    (e)   there is a provisional liquidator of the company,

    (f)   a moratorium has been in force for the company at any time during the period of 12 months ending with the date of filing and—

        (i)   no voluntary arrangement had effect at the time at which the moratorium came to an end, or

        (ii)   a voluntary arrangement which had effect at any time in that period has come to an end prematurely,

    (fa)   an administrator appointed under paragraph 22 of Schedule B1 has held office in the period of 12 months ending with the date of filing, or

    (g)   a voluntary arrangement in relation to the company which had effect in pursuance of a proposal under section 1(3) has come to an end prematurely and, during the period of 12 months ending with the date of filing, an order under section 5(3)(a) has been made.

(2)   Sub-paragraph (1)(b) does not apply to a company which, by reason of a winding-up order made after the date of filing, is treated as being wound up on that date.

Capital market arrangement

4A.   A company is also excluded from being eligible for a moratorium if, on the date of filing, it is a party to an agreement which is or forms part of a capital market arrangement under which—

    (i)   a party has incurred, or when the agreement was entered into was expected to incur, a debt of at least £10 million under the arrangement, and

    (ii)   the arrangement involves the issue of a capital market investment.

Public private partnership

4B.   A company is also excluded from being eligible for a moratorium if, on the date of filing, it is a project company of a project which—

    (i)   is a public-private partnership project, and

    (ii) includes step-in rights.

Liability under an arrangement

4C.— (1) A company is also excluded from being eligible for a moratorium if, on the date of filing, it has incurred a liability under an agreement of £10 million or more.

    (2) Where the liability in sub-paragraph (1) is a contingent liability under or by virtue of a guarantee or an indemnity or security provided on behalf of another person, the amount of that liability is the full amount of the liability in relation to which the guarantee, indemnity or security is provided.

    (3) In this paragraph—

        (a) the reference to "liability" includes a present or future liability whether, in either case, it is certain or contingent,

        (b) the reference to "liability" includes a reference to a liability to be paid wholly or partly in foreign currency (in which case the sterling equivalent shall be calculated as at the time when the liability is incurred).

Interpretation of capital market arrangement

4D.— (1) For the purposes of paragraph 4A an arrangement is a capital market arrangement if—

        (a) it involves a grant of security to a person holding it as trustee for a person who holds a capital market investment issued by a party to the arrangement, or

        (b) at least one party guarantees the performance of obligations of another party, or

        (c) at least one party provides security in respect of the performance of obligations of another party, or

        (d) the arrangement involves an investment of a kind described in articles 83 to 85 of the Financial Services and Markets Act 2000 (Regulated Activities) Order 2001 (SI 2001/544) (options, futures and contracts for differences).

    (2) For the purposes of sub-paragraph (1)—

        (a) a reference to holding as trustee includes a reference to holding as nominee or agent,

        (b) a reference to holding for a person who holds a capital market investment includes a reference to holding for a number of persons at least one of whom holds a capital market investment, and

        (c) a person holds a capital market investment if he has a legal or beneficial interest in it.

    (3) In paragraph 4A, 4C, 4J and this paragraph—

        "agreement" includes an agreement or undertaking effected by—

        (a) contract,

        (b) deed, or

        (c) any other instrument intended to have effect in accordance with the law of England and Wales, Scotland or another jurisdiction, and

        "party" to an arrangement includes a party to an agreement which—

        (a) forms part of the arrangement,

        (b) provides for the raising of finance as part of the arrangement, or

        (c) is necessary for the purposes of implementing the arrangement.

Capital market investment

4E.— (1) For the purposes of paragraphs 4A and 4D, an investment is a capital market investment if—

        (a) it is within article 77 of the Financial Services and Markets Act 2000 (Regulated Activities) Order 2001 (SI 2001/544) (debt instruments) and

        (b) it is rated, listed or traded or designed to be rated, listed or traded.

(2)   In sub-paragraph (1)—

"listed" means admitted to the official list within the meaning given by section 103(1) of the Financial Services and Markets Act 2000 (c 8) (interpretation),

"rated" means rated for the purposes of investment by an internationally recognised rating agency,

"traded" means admitted to trading on a market established under the rules of a recognised investment exchange or on a foreign market.

(3)   In sub-paragraph (2)—

"foreign market" has the same meaning as "relevant market" in article 67(2) of the Financial Services and Markets Act 2000 (Financial Promotion) Order 2001 (SI 2001/1335) (foreign markets),

"recognised investment exchange" has the meaning given by section 285 of the Financial Services and Markets Act 2000 (recognised investment exchange).

4F.—   (1)   For the purposes of paragraphs 4A and 4D an investment is also a capital market investment if it consists of a bond or commercial paper issued to one or more of the following—

(a)   an investment professional within the meaning of article 19(5) of the Financial Services and Markets Act 2000 (Financial Promotion) Order 2001,

(b)   a person who is, when the agreement mentioned in paragraph 4A is entered into, a certified high net worth individual in relation to a communication within the meaning of article 48(2) of that order,

(c)   a person to whom article 49(2) of that order applies (high net worth company, &c.),

(d)   a person who is, when the agreement mentioned in paragraph 4A is entered into, a certified sophisticated investor in relation to a communication within the meaning of article 50(1) of that order, and

(e)   a person in a State other than the United Kingdom who under the law of that State is not prohibited from investing in bonds or commercial paper.

(2)   For the purposes of sub-paragraph (1)—

(a)   in applying article 19(5) of the Financial Services and Markets Act 2000 (Financial Promotion) Order 2001 for the purposes of sub-paragraph (1)(a)—

(i)   in article 19(5)(b), ignore the words after "exempt person",

(ii)   in article 19(5)(c)(i), for the words from "the controlled activity" to the end substitute "a controlled activity", and

(iii)   in article 19(5)(e) ignore the words from "where the communication" to the end, and

(b)   in applying article 49(2) of that order for the purposes of sub-paragraph (1)(c), ignore article 49(2)(e).

(3)   In sub-paragraph (1)—

"bond" shall be construed in accordance with article 77 of the Financial Services and Markets Act 2000 (Regulated Activities) Order 2001 (SI 2001/544), and

"commercial paper" has the meaning given by article 9(3) of that order.

Debt

4G.   The debt of at least £10 million referred to in paragraph 4A—

(a)   may be incurred at any time during the life of the capital market arrangement, and

(b)   may be expressed wholly or partly in a foreign currency (in which case the sterling equivalent shall be calculated as at the time when the arrangement is entered into).

Interpretation of project company

4H.—   (1)   For the purposes of paragraph 4B a company is a "project company" of a project if—

(a)   it holds property for the purpose of the project,

(b)   it has sole or principal responsibility under an agreement for carrying out all or part of the project,

(c)   it is one of a number of companies which together carry out the project,

    (d)   it has the purpose of supplying finance to enable the project to be carried out, or

    (e)   it is the holding company of a company within any of paragraphs (a) to (d).

  (2)   But a company is not a "project company" of a project if—

    (a)   it performs a function within sub-paragraph (1)(a) to (d) or is within sub-paragraph (1)(e), but

    (b)   it also performs a function which is not—

        (i)   within sub-paragraph (1)(a) to (d),

        (ii)   related to a function within sub-paragraph (1)(a) to (d), or

        (iii)   related to the project.

  (3)   For the purposes of this paragraph a company carries out all or part of a project whether or not it acts wholly or partly through agents.

Public-private partnership project

4I.— (1)   In paragraph 4B "public-private partnership project" means a project—

    (a)   the resources for which are provided partly by one or more public bodies and partly by one or more private persons, or

    (b)   which is designed wholly or mainly for the purpose of assisting a public body to discharge a function.

  (2)   In sub-paragraph (1) "resources" includes—

    (a)   funds (including payment for the provision of services or facilities),

    (b)   assets,

    (c)   professional skill,

    (d)   the grant of a concession or franchise, and

    (e)   any other commercial resource.

  (3)   In sub-paragraph (1) "public body" means—

    (a)   a body which exercises public functions,

    (b)   a body specified for the purposes of this paragraph by the Secretary of State, and

    (c)   a body within a class specified for the purposes of this paragraph by the Secretary of State.

  (4)   A specification under sub-paragraph (3) may be—

    (a)   general, or

    (b)   for the purpose of the application of paragraph 4B to a specified case.

Step-in rights

4J.— (1)   For the purposes of paragraph 4B a project has "step-in rights" if a person who provides finance in connection with the project has a conditional entitlement under an agreement to—

    (i)   assume sole or principal responsibility under an agreement for carrying out all or part of the project, or

    (ii)   make arrangements for carrying out all or part of the project.

  (2)   In sub-paragraph (1) a reference to the provision of finance includes a reference to the provision of an indemnity.

"Person"

4K.   For the purposes of paragraphs 4A to 4J, a reference to a person includes a reference to a partnership or another unincorporated group of persons.

5.   The Secretary of State may by regulations modify the qualifications for eligibility of a company for a moratorium.

PART II
OBTAINING A MORATORIUM

Nominee's statement

6.— (1) Where the directors of a company wish to obtain a moratorium, they shall submit to the nominee—

    (a) a document setting out the terms of the proposed voluntary arrangement,

    (b) a statement of the company's affairs containing—

        (i) such particulars of its creditors and of its debts and other liabilities and of its assets as may be prescribed, and

        (ii) such other information as may be prescribed, and

    (c) any other information necessary to enable the nominee to comply with sub-paragraph (2) which he requests from them.

(2) The nominee shall submit to the directors a statement in the prescribed form indicating whether or not, in his opinion—

    (a) the proposed voluntary arrangement has a reasonable prospect of being approved and implemented,

    (b) the company is likely to have sufficient funds available to it during the proposed moratorium to enable it to carry on its business, and

    (c) meetings of the company and its creditors should be summoned to consider the proposed voluntary arrangement.

(3) In forming his opinion on the matters mentioned in sub-paragraph (2), the nominee is entitled to rely on the information submitted to him under sub-paragraph (1) unless he has reason to doubt its accuracy.

(4) The reference in sub-paragraph (2)(b) to the company's business is to that business as the company proposes to carry it on during the moratorium.

Documents to be submitted to court

7.— (1) To obtain a moratorium the directors of a company must file (in Scotland, lodge) with the court—

    (a) a document setting out the terms of the proposed voluntary arrangement,

    (b) a statement of the company's affairs containing—

        (i) such particulars of its creditors and of its debts and other liabilities and of its assets as may be prescribed, and

        (ii) such other information as may be prescribed,

    (c) a statement that the company is eligible for a moratorium,

    (d) a statement from the nominee that he has given his consent to act, and

    (e) a statement from the nominee that, in his opinion—

        (i) the proposed voluntary arrangement has a reasonable prospect of being approved and implemented,

        (ii) the company is likely to have sufficient funds available to it during the proposed moratorium to enable it to carry on its business, and

        (iii) meetings of the company and its creditors should be summoned to consider the proposed voluntary arrangement.

(2) Each of the statements mentioned in sub-paragraph (1)(b) to (e), except so far as it contains the particulars referred to in paragraph (b)(i), must be in the prescribed form.

(3) The reference in sub-paragraph (1)(e)(ii) to the company's business is to that business as the company proposes to carry it on during the moratorium.

(4) The Secretary of State may by regulations modify the requirements of this paragraph as to the documents required to be filed (in Scotland, lodged) with the court in order to obtain a moratorium.

Duration of moratorium

8.— (1) A moratorium comes into force when the documents for the time being referred to in paragraph 7(1) are filed or lodged with the court and references in this Schedule to "the beginning of the moratorium" shall be construed accordingly.

   (2) A moratorium ends at the end of the day on which the meetings summoned under paragraph 29(1) are first held (or, if the meetings are held on different days, the later of those days), unless it is extended under paragraph 32.

   (3) If either of those meetings has not first met before the end of the period of 28 days beginning with the day on which the moratorium comes into force, the moratorium ends at the end of the day on which those meetings were to be held (or, if those meetings were summoned to be held on different days, the later of those days), unless it is extended under paragraph 32.

   (4) If the nominee fails to summon either meeting within the period required by paragraph 29(1), the moratorium ends at the end of the last day of that period.

   (5) If the moratorium is extended (or further extended) under paragraph 32, it ends at the end of the day to which it is extended (or further extended).

   (6) Sub-paragraphs (2) to (5) do not apply if the moratorium comes to an end before the time concerned by virtue of—

      (a) paragraph 25(4) (effect of withdrawal by nominee of consent to act),

      (b) an order under paragraph 26(3), 27(3) or 40 (challenge of actions of nominee or directors), or

      (c) a decision of one or both of the meetings summoned under paragraph 29.

   (7) If the moratorium has not previously come to an end in accordance with sub-paragraphs (2) to (6), it ends at the end of the day on which a decision under paragraph 31 to approve a voluntary arrangement takes effect under paragraph 36.

   (8) The Secretary of State may by order increase or reduce the period for the time being specified in sub-paragraph (3).

Notification of beginning of moratorium

9.— (1) When a moratorium comes into force, the directors shall notify the nominee of that fact forthwith.

   (2) If the directors without reasonable excuse fail to comply with sub-paragraph (1), each of them is liable to imprisonment or a fine, or both.

10.— (1) When a moratorium comes into force, the nominee shall, in accordance with the rules—

      (a) advertise that fact forthwith, and

      (b) notify the registrar of companies, the company and any petitioning creditor of the company of whose claim he is aware of that fact.

   (2) In sub-paragraph (1)(b), "petitioning creditor" means a creditor by whom a winding-up petition has been presented before the beginning of the moratorium, as long as the petition has not been dismissed or withdrawn.

   (3) If the nominee without reasonable excuse fails to comply with sub-paragraph (1)(a) or (b), he is liable to a fine.

Notification of end of moratorium

11.— (1) When a moratorium comes to an end, the nominee shall, in accordance with the rules—

      (a) advertise that fact forthwith, and

      (b) notify the court, the registrar of companies, the company and any creditor of the company of whose claim he is aware of that fact.

   (2) If the nominee without reasonable excuse fails to comply with sub-paragraph (1)(a) or (b), he is liable to a fine.

PART III
EFFECTS OF MORATORIUM

Effect on creditors, etc

12.— (1) During the period for which a moratorium is in force for a company—

    (a)   no petition may be presented for the winding up of the company,

    (b)   no meeting of the company may be called or requisitioned except with the consent of the nominee or the leave of the court and subject (where the court gives leave) to such terms as the court may impose,

    (c)   no resolution may be passed or order made for the winding up of the company,

    (d)   no administration application may be made in respect of the company,

    (da) no administrator of the company may be appointed under paragraph 14 or 22 of Schedule B1,

    (e)   no administrative receiver of the company may be appointed,

    (f)   no landlord or other person to whom rent is payable may exercise any right of forfeiture by peaceable re-entry in relation to premises let to the company in respect of a failure by the company to comply with any term or condition of its tenancy of such premises, except with the leave of the court and subject to such terms as the court may impose,

    (g)   no other steps may be taken to enforce any security over the company's property, or to repossess goods in the company's possession under any hire-purchase agreement, except with the leave of the court and subject to such terms as the court may impose, and

    (h)   no other proceedings and no execution or other legal process may be commenced or continued, and no distress may be levied, against the company or its property except with the leave of the court and subject to such terms as the court may impose.

    (2) Where a petition, other than an excepted petition, for the winding up of the company has been presented before the beginning of the moratorium, section 127 shall not apply in relation to any disposition of property, transfer of shares or alteration in status made during the moratorium or at a time mentioned in paragraph 37(5)(a).

    (3) In the application of sub-paragraph (1)(h) to Scotland, the reference to execution being commenced or continued includes a reference to diligence being carried out or continued, and the reference to distress being levied is omitted.

    (4) Paragraph (a) of sub-paragraph (1) does not apply to an excepted petition and, where such a petition has been presented before the beginning of the moratorium or is presented during the moratorium, paragraphs (b) and (c) of that sub-paragraph do not apply in relation to proceedings on the petition.

    (5) For the purposes of this paragraph, "excepted petition" means a petition under—

    (a)   section 124A or 124B of this Act,

    (b)   section 72 of the Financial Services Act 1986 on the ground mentioned in subsection (1)(b) of that section, or

    (c)   section 92 of the Banking Act 1987 on the ground mentioned in subsection (1)(b) of that section,

    (d)   section 367 of the Financial Services and Markets Act 2000 on the ground mentioned in subsection (3)(b) of that section.

13.— (1) This paragraph applies where there is an uncrystallised floating charge on the property of a company for which a moratorium is in force.

    (2) If the conditions for the holder of the charge to give a notice having the effect mentioned in sub-paragraph (4) are met at any time, the notice may not be given at that time but may instead be given as soon as practicable after the moratorium has come to an end.

    (3) If any other event occurs at any time which (apart from this sub-paragraph) would have the effect mentioned in sub-paragraph (4), then—

    (a)   the event shall not have the effect in question at that time, but

       (b)   if notice of the event is given to the company by the holder of the charge as soon as is practicable after the moratorium has come to an end, the event is to be treated as if it had occurred when the notice was given.

   (4)   The effect referred to in sub-paragraphs (2) and (3) is—

       (a)   causing the crystallisation of the floating charge, or

       (b)   causing the imposition, by virtue of provision in the instrument creating the charge, of any restriction on the disposal of any property of the company.

   (5)   Application may not be made for leave under paragraph 12(1)(g) or (h) with a view to obtaining—

       (a)   the crystallisation of the floating charge, or

       (b)   the imposition, by virtue of provision in the instrument creating the charge, of any restriction on the disposal of any property of the company.

14.   Security granted by a company at a time when a moratorium is in force in relation to the company may only be enforced if, at that time, there were reasonable grounds for believing that it would benefit the company.

Effect on company

15.—   (1)   Paragraphs 16 to 23 apply in relation to a company for which a moratorium is in force.

   (2)   The fact that a company enters into a transaction in contravention of any of paragraphs 16 to 22 does not—

       (a)   make the transaction void, or

       (b)   make it to any extent unenforceable against the company.

Company invoices, etc

16.—   (1)   Every invoice, order for goods or business letter which—

       (a)   is issued by or on behalf of the company, and

       (b)   on or in which the company's name appears,

shall also contain the nominee's name and a statement that the moratorium is in force for the company.

   (2)   If default is made in complying with sub-paragraph (1), the company and (subject to sub-paragraph (3)) any officer of the company is liable to a fine.

   (3)   An officer of the company is only liable under sub-paragraph (2) if, without reasonable excuse, he authorises or permits the default.

Obtaining credit during moratorium

17.—   (1)   The company may not obtain credit to the extent of £250 or more from a person who has not been informed that a moratorium is in force in relation to the company.

   (2)   The reference to the company obtaining credit includes the following cases—

       (a)   where goods are bailed (in Scotland, hired) to the company under a hire-purchase agreement, or agreed to be sold to the company under a conditional sale agreement, and

       (b)   where the company is paid in advance (whether in money or otherwise) for the supply of goods or services.

   (3)   Where the company obtains credit in contravention of sub-paragraph (1)—

       (a)   the company is liable to a fine, and

       (b)   if any officer of the company knowingly and wilfully authorised or permitted the contravention, he is liable to imprisonment or a fine, or both.

   (4)   The money sum specified in sub-paragraph (1) is subject to increase or reduction by order under section 417A in Part XV.

Disposals and payments

18.—   (1)   Subject to sub-paragraph (2), the company may only dispose of any of its property if—

    (a)   there are reasonable grounds for believing that the disposal will benefit the company, and

    (b)   the disposal is approved by the committee established under paragraph 35(1) or, where there is no such committee, by the nominee.

  (2) Sub-paragraph (1) does not apply to a disposal made in the ordinary way of the company's business.

  (3) If the company makes a disposal in contravention of sub-paragraph (1) otherwise than in pursuance of an order of the court—

    (a)   the company is liable to a fine, and

    (b)   if any officer of the company authorised or permitted the contravention, without reasonable excuse, he is liable to imprisonment or a fine, or both.

19.— (1) Subject to sub-paragraph (2), the company may only make any payment in respect of any debt or other liability of the company in existence before the beginning of the moratorium if—

    (a)   there are reasonable grounds for believing that the payment will benefit the company, and

    (b)   the payment is approved by the committee established under paragraph 35(1) or, where there is no such committee, by the nominee.

  (2) Sub-paragraph (1) does not apply to a payment required by paragraph 20(6).

  (3) If the company makes a payment in contravention of sub-paragraph (1) otherwise than in pursuance of an order of the court—

    (a)   the company is liable to a fine, and

    (b)   if any officer of the company authorised or permitted the contravention, without reasonable excuse, he is liable to imprisonment or a fine, or both.

Disposal of charged property, etc

20.— (1) This paragraph applies where—

    (a)   any property of the company is subject to a security, or

    (b)   any goods are in the possession of the company under a hire-purchase agreement.

  (2) If the holder of the security consents, or the court gives leave, the company may dispose of the property as if it were not subject to the security.

  (3) If the owner of the goods consents, or the court gives leave, the company may dispose of the goods as if all rights of the owner under the hire-purchase agreement were vested in the company.

  (4) Where property subject to a security which, as created, was a floating charge is disposed of under sub-paragraph (2), the holder of the security has the same priority in respect of any property of the company directly or indirectly representing the property disposed of as he would have had in respect of the property subject to the security.

  (5) Sub-paragraph (6) applies to the disposal under sub-paragraph (2) or (as the case may be) sub-paragraph (3) of—

    (a)   any property subject to a security other than a security which, as created, was a floating charge, or

    (b)   any goods in the possession of the company under a hire-purchase agreement.

  (6) It shall be a condition of any consent or leave under sub-paragraph (2) or (as the case may be) sub-paragraph (3) that—

    (a)   the net proceeds of the disposal, and

    (b)   where those proceeds are less than such amount as may be agreed, or determined by the court, to be the net amount which would be realised on a sale of the property or goods in the open market by a willing vendor, such sums as may be required to make good the deficiency,

shall be applied towards discharging the sums secured by the security or payable under the hire-purchase agreement.

(7) Where a condition imposed in pursuance of sub-paragraph (6) relates to two or more securities, that condition requires—

   (a)   the net proceeds of the disposal, and

   (b)   where paragraph (b) of sub-paragraph (6) applies, the sums mentioned in that paragraph,

   to be applied towards discharging the sums secured by those securities in the order of their priorities.

(8) Where the court gives leave for a disposal under sub-paragraph (2) or (3), the directors shall, within 14 days after leave is given, send an office copy of the order giving leave to the registrar of companies.

(9) If the directors without reasonable excuse fail to comply with sub-paragraph (8), they are liable to a fine.

21.— (1) Where property is disposed of under paragraph 20 in its application to Scotland, the company shall grant to the disponee an appropriate document of transfer or conveyance of the property, and

   (a)   that document, or

   (b)   where any recording, intimation or registration of the document is a legal requirement for completion of title to the property, that recording, intimation or registration,

   has the effect of disencumbering the property of, or (as the case may be) freeing the property from, the security.

(2) Where goods in the possession of the company under a hire-purchase agreement are disposed of under paragraph 20 in its application to Scotland, the disposal has the effect of extinguishing, as against the disponee, all rights of the owner of the goods under the agreement.

22.— (1) If the company—

   (a)   without any consent or leave under paragraph 20, disposes of any of its property which is subject to a security otherwise than in accordance with the terms of the security,

   (b)   without any consent or leave under paragraph 20, disposes of any goods in the possession of the company under a hire-purchase agreement otherwise than in accordance with the terms of the agreement, or

   (c)   fails to comply with any requirement imposed by paragraph 20 or 21,

   it is liable to a fine.

(2) If any officer of the company, without reasonable excuse, authorises or permits any such disposal or failure to comply, he is liable to imprisonment or a fine, or both.

Market contracts, etc

23.— (1) If the company enters into any transaction to which this paragraph applies—

   (a)   the company is liable to a fine, and

   (b)   if any officer of the company, without reasonable excuse, authorised or permitted the company to enter into the transaction, he is liable to imprisonment or a fine, or both.

(2) A company enters into a transaction to which this paragraph applies if it—

   (a)   enters into a market contract, …

   (b)   gives a transfer order,

   (c)   grants a market charge … or a system-charge, or

   (d)   provides any collateral security.

(3) The fact that a company enters into a transaction in contravention of this paragraph does not—

   (a)   make the transaction void, or

   (b)   make it to any extent unenforceable by or against the company.

(4) Where during the moratorium a company enters into a transaction to which this paragraph applies, nothing done by or in pursuance of the transaction is to be treated as done in contravention of paragraphs 12(1)(g), 14 or 16 to 22.

(5) Paragraph 20 does not apply in relation to any property which is subject to a market charge, … a system-charge or a collateral security charge.

(6) In this paragraph, "transfer order", "collateral security" and "collateral security charge" have the same meanings as in the settlement finality regulations.

PART IV
NOMINEES

Monitoring of company's activities

24.— (1) During a moratorium, the nominee shall monitor the company's affairs for the purpose of forming an opinion as to whether—

(a) the proposed voluntary arrangement or, if he has received notice of proposed modifications under paragraph 31(7), the proposed arrangement with those modifications has a reasonable prospect of being approved and implemented, and

(b) the company is likely to have sufficient funds available to it during the remainder of the moratorium to enable it to continue to carry on its business.

(2) The directors shall submit to the nominee any information necessary to enable him to comply with sub-paragraph (1) which he requests from them.

(3) In forming his opinion on the matters mentioned in sub-paragraph (1), the nominee is entitled to rely on the information submitted to him under sub-paragraph (2) unless he has reason to doubt its accuracy.

(4) The reference in sub-paragraph (1)(b) to the company's business is to that business as the company proposes to carry it on during the remainder of the moratorium.

Withdrawal of consent to act

25.— (1) The nominee may only withdraw his consent to act in the circumstances mentioned in this paragraph.

(2) The nominee must withdraw his consent to act if, at any time during a moratorium—

(a) he forms the opinion that—

(i) the proposed voluntary arrangement or, if he has received notice of proposed modifications under paragraph 31(7), the proposed arrangement with those modifications no longer has a reasonable prospect of being approved or implemented, or

(ii) the company will not have sufficient funds available to it during the remainder of the moratorium to enable it to continue to carry on its business,

(b) he becomes aware that, on the date of filing, the company was not eligible for a moratorium, or

(c) the directors fail to comply with their duty under paragraph 24(2).

(3) The reference in sub-paragraph (2)(a)(ii) to the company's business is to that business as the company proposes to carry it on during the remainder of the moratorium.

(4) If the nominee withdraws his consent to act, the moratorium comes to an end.

(5) If the nominee withdraws his consent to act he must, in accordance with the rules, notify the court, the registrar of companies, the company and any creditor of the company of whose claim he is aware of his withdrawal and the reason for it.

(6) If the nominee without reasonable excuse fails to comply with sub-paragraph (5), he is liable to a fine.

Challenge of nominee's actions, etc

26.— (1) If any creditor, director or member of the company, or any other person affected by a moratorium, is dissatisfied by any act, omission or decision of the nominee during the moratorium, he may apply to the court.

(2) An application under sub-paragraph (1) may be made during the moratorium or after it has ended.

(3)   On an application under sub-paragraph (1) the court may—
   (a)   confirm, reverse or modify any act or decision of the nominee,
   (b)   give him directions, or
   (c)   make such other order as it thinks fit.

(4)   An order under sub-paragraph (3) may (among other things) bring the moratorium to an end and make such consequential provision as the court thinks fit.

27.— (1)   Where there are reasonable grounds for believing that—
   (a)   as a result of any act, omission or decision of the nominee during the moratorium, the company has suffered loss, but
   (b)   the company does not intend to pursue any claim it may have against the nominee,
   any creditor of the company may apply to the court.

(2)   An application under sub-paragraph (1) may be made during the moratorium or after it has ended.

(3)   On an application under sub-paragraph (1) the court may—
   (a)   order the company to pursue any claim against the nominee,
   (b)   authorise any creditor to pursue such a claim in the name of the company, or
   (c)   make such other order with respect to such a claim as it thinks fit,
   unless the court is satisfied that the act, omission or decision of the nominee was in all the circumstances reasonable.

(4)   An order under sub-paragraph (3) may (among other things)—
   (a)   impose conditions on any authority given to pursue a claim,
   (b)   direct the company to assist in the pursuit of a claim,
   (c)   make directions with respect to the distribution of anything received as a result of the pursuit of a claim,
   (d)   bring the moratorium to an end and make such consequential provision as the court thinks fit.

(5)   On an application under sub-paragraph (1) the court shall have regard to the interests of the members and creditors of the company generally.

Replacement of nominee by court

28.— (1)   The court may—
   (a)   on an application made by the directors in a case where the nominee has failed to comply with any duty imposed on him under this Schedule or has died, or
   (b)   on an application made by the directors or the nominee in a case where it is impracticable or inappropriate for the nominee to continue to act as such,
   direct that the nominee be replaced as such by another person qualified to act as an insolvency practitioner, or authorised to act as nominee, in relation to the voluntary arrangement.

(2)   A person may only be appointed as a replacement nominee under this paragraph if he submits to the court a statement indicating his consent to act.

PART V
CONSIDERATION AND IMPLEMENTATION OF VOLUNTARY ARRANGEMENT

Summoning of meetings

29.— (1)   Where a moratorium is in force, the nominee shall summon meetings of the company and its creditors for such a time, date (within the period for the time being specified in paragraph 8(3)) and place as he thinks fit.

(2)   The persons to be summoned to a creditors' meeting under this paragraph are every creditor of the company of whose claim the nominee is aware.

Conduct of meetings

30.— (1) Subject to the provisions of paragraphs 31 to 35, the meetings summoned under paragraph 29 shall be conducted in accordance with the rules.

(2) A meeting so summoned may resolve that it be adjourned (or further adjourned).

(3) After the conclusion of either meeting in accordance with the rules, the chairman of the meeting shall report the result of the meeting to the court, and, immediately after reporting to the court, shall give notice of the result of the meeting to such persons as may be prescribed.

Approval of voluntary arrangement

31.— (1) The meetings summoned under paragraph 29 shall decide whether to approve the proposed voluntary arrangement (with or without modifications).

(2) The modifications may include one conferring the functions proposed to be conferred on the nominee on another person qualified to act as an insolvency practitioner, or authorised to act as nominee, in relation to the voluntary arrangement.

(3) The modifications shall not include one by virtue of which the proposal ceases to be a proposal such as is mentioned in section 1.

(4) A meeting summoned under paragraph 29 shall not approve any proposal or modification which affects the right of a secured creditor of the company to enforce his security, except with the concurrence of the creditor concerned.

(5) Subject to sub-paragraph (6), a meeting so summoned shall not approve any proposal or modification under which—

(a) any preferential debt of the company is to be paid otherwise than in priority to such of its debts as are not preferential debts, or

(b) a preferential creditor of the company is to be paid an amount in respect of a preferential debt that bears to that debt a smaller proportion than is borne to another preferential debt by the amount that is to be paid in respect of that other debt.

(6) The meeting may approve such a proposal or modification with the concurrence of the preferential creditor concerned.

(7) The directors of the company may, before the beginning of the period of seven days which ends with the meetings (or either of them) summoned under paragraph 29 being held, give notice to the nominee of any modifications of the proposal for which the directors intend to seek the approval of those meetings.

(8) References in this paragraph to preferential debts and preferential creditors are to be read in accordance with section 386 in Part XII of this Act.

Extension of moratorium

32.— (1) Subject to sub-paragraph (2), a meeting summoned under paragraph 29 which resolves that it be adjourned (or further adjourned) may resolve that the moratorium be extended (or further extended), with or without conditions.

(2) The moratorium may not be extended (or further extended) to a day later than the end of the period of two months which begins—

(a) where both meetings summoned under paragraph 29 are first held on the same day, with that day,

(b) in any other case, with the day on which the later of those meetings is first held.

(3) At any meeting where it is proposed to extend (or further extend) the moratorium, before a decision is taken with respect to that proposal, the nominee shall inform the meeting—

(a) of what he has done in order to comply with his duty under paragraph 24 and the cost of his actions for the company, and

(b) of what he intends to do to continue to comply with that duty if the moratorium is extended (or further extended) and the expected cost of his actions for the company.

      (4)   Where, in accordance with sub-paragraph (3)(b), the nominee informs a meeting of the expected cost of his intended actions, the meeting shall resolve whether or not to approve that expected cost.

      (5)   If a decision not to approve the expected cost of the nominee's intended actions has effect under paragraph 36, the moratorium comes to an end.

      (6)   A meeting may resolve that a moratorium which has been extended (or further extended) be brought to an end before the end of the period of the extension (or further extension).

      (7)   The Secretary of State may by order increase or reduce the period for the time being specified in sub-paragraph (2).

33.— (1)   The conditions which may be imposed when a moratorium is extended (or further extended) include a requirement that the nominee be replaced as such by another person qualified to act as an insolvency practitioner, or authorised to act as nominee, in relation to the voluntary arrangement.

      (2)   A person may only be appointed as a replacement nominee by virtue of sub-paragraph (1) if he submits to the court a statement indicating his consent to act.

      (3)   At any meeting where it is proposed to appoint a replacement nominee as a condition of extending (or further extending) the moratorium—

           (a)   the duty imposed by paragraph 32(3)(b) on the nominee shall instead be imposed on the person proposed as the replacement nominee, and

           (b)   paragraphs 32(4) and (5) and 36(1)(e) apply as if the references to the nominee were to that person.

34.— (1)   If a decision to extend, or further extend, the moratorium takes effect under paragraph 36, the nominee shall, in accordance with the rules, notify the registrar of companies and the court.

      (2)   If the moratorium is extended, or further extended, by virtue of an order under paragraph 36(5), the nominee shall, in accordance with the rules, send an office copy of the order to the registrar of companies.

      (3)   If the nominee without reasonable excuse fails to comply with this paragraph, he is liable to a fine.

Moratorium committee

35.— (1)   A meeting summoned under paragraph 29 which resolves that the moratorium be extended (or further extended) may, with the consent of the nominee, resolve that a committee be established to exercise the functions conferred on it by the meeting.

      (2)   The meeting may not so resolve unless it has approved an estimate of the expenses to be incurred by the committee in the exercise of the proposed functions.

      (3)   Any expenses, not exceeding the amount of the estimate, incurred by the committee in the exercise of its functions shall be reimbursed by the nominee.

      (4)   The committee shall cease to exist when the moratorium comes to an end.

Effectiveness of decisions

36.— (1)   Sub-paragraph (2) applies to references to one of the following decisions having effect, that is, a decision, under paragraph 31, 32 or 35, with respect to—

           (a)   the approval of a proposed voluntary arrangement,

           (b)   the extension (or further extension) of a moratorium,

           (c)   the bringing of a moratorium to an end,

           (d)   the establishment of a committee, or

           (e)   the approval of the expected cost of a nominee's intended actions.

      (2)   The decision has effect if, in accordance with the rules—

           (a)   it has been taken by both meetings summoned under paragraph 29, or

           (b)   (subject to any order made under sub-paragraph (5)) it has been taken by the creditors' meeting summoned under that paragraph.

(3)   If a decision taken by the creditors' meeting under any of paragraphs 31, 32 or 35 with respect to any of the matters mentioned in sub-paragraph (1) differs from one so taken by the company meeting with respect to that matter, a member of the company may apply to the court.

(4)   An application under sub-paragraph (3) shall not be made after the end of the period of 28 days beginning with—

    (a)   the day on which the decision was taken by the creditors' meeting, or

    (b)   where the decision of the company meeting was taken on a later day, that day.

(5)   On an application under sub-paragraph (3), the court may—

    (a)   order the decision of the company meeting to have effect instead of the decision of the creditors' meeting, or

    (b)   make such other order as it thinks fit.

Effect of approval of voluntary arrangement

37.—   (1)   This paragraph applies where a decision approving a voluntary arrangement has effect under paragraph 36.

    (2)   The approved voluntary arrangement—

    (a)   takes effect as if made by the company at the creditors' meeting, and

    (b)   binds every person who in accordance with the rules—

       (i)   was entitled to vote at that meeting (whether or not he was present or represented at it), or

       (ii)   would have been so entitled if he had had notice of it,

    as if he were a party to the voluntary arrangement.

    (3)   If—

    (a)   when the arrangement ceases to have effect any amount payable under the arrangement to a person bound by virtue of sub-paragraph (2)(b)(ii) has not been paid, and

    (b)   the arrangement did not come to an end prematurely,

    the company shall at that time become liable to pay to that person the amount payable under the arrangement.

    (4)   Where a petition for the winding up of the company, other than an excepted petition within the meaning of paragraph 12, was presented before the beginning of the moratorium, the court shall dismiss the petition.

    (5)   The court shall not dismiss a petition under sub-paragraph (4)—

    (a)   at any time before the end of the period of 28 days beginning with the first day on which each of the reports of the meetings required by paragraph 30(3) has been made to the court, or

    (b)   at any time when an application under paragraph 38 or an appeal in respect of such an application is pending, or at any time in the period within which such an appeal may be brought.

Challenge of decisions

38.—   (1)   Subject to the following provisions of this paragraph, any of the persons mentioned in sub-paragraph (2) may apply to the court on one or both of the following grounds—

    (a)   that a voluntary arrangement approved at one or both of the meetings summoned under paragraph 29 and which has taken effect unfairly prejudices the interests of a creditor, member or contributory of the company,

    (b)   that there has been some material irregularity at or in relation to either of those meetings.

    (2)   The persons who may apply under this paragraph are—

    (a)   a person entitled, in accordance with the rules, to vote at either of the meetings,

    (b)   a person who would have been entitled, in accordance with the rules, to vote at the creditors' meeting if he had had notice of it, and

    (c)   the nominee.

(3)   An application under this paragraph shall not be made—

    (a)   after the end of the period of 28 days beginning with the first day on which each of the reports required by paragraph 30(3) has been made to the court, or

    (b)   in the case of a person who was not given notice of the creditors' meeting, after the end of the period of 28 days beginning with the day on which he became aware that the meeting had taken place,

but (subject to that) an application made by a person within sub-paragraph (2)(b) on the ground that the arrangement prejudices his interests may be made after the arrangement has ceased to have effect, unless it came to an end prematurely.

(4)   Where on an application under this paragraph the court is satisfied as to either of the grounds mentioned in sub-paragraph (1), it may do any of the following—

    (a)   revoke or suspend—

        (i)   any decision approving the voluntary arrangement which has effect under paragraph 36, or

        (ii)   in a case falling within sub-paragraph (1)(b), any decision taken by the meeting in question which has effect under that paragraph,

    (b)   give a direction to any person—

        (i)   for the summoning of further meetings to consider any revised proposal for a voluntary arrangement which the directors may make, or

        (ii)   in a case falling within sub-paragraph (1)(b), for the summoning of a further company or (as the case may be) creditors' meeting to reconsider the original proposal.

(5)   Where at any time after giving a direction under sub-paragraph (4)(b)(i) the court is satisfied that the directors do not intend to submit a revised proposal, the court shall revoke the direction and revoke or suspend any decision approving the voluntary arrangement which has effect under paragraph 36.

(6)   Where the court gives a direction under sub-paragraph (4)(b), it may also give a direction continuing or, as the case may require, renewing, for such period as may be specified in the direction, the effect of the moratorium.

(7)   Sub-paragraph (8) applies in a case where the court, on an application under this paragraph—

    (a)   gives a direction under sub-paragraph (4)(b), or

    (b)   revokes or suspends a decision under sub-paragraph (4)(a) or (5).

(8)   In such a case, the court may give such supplemental directions as it thinks fit and, in particular, directions with respect to—

    (a)   things done under the voluntary arrangement since it took effect, and

    (b)   such things done since that time as could not have been done if a moratorium had been in force in relation to the company when they were done.

(9)   Except in pursuance of the preceding provisions of this paragraph, a decision taken at a meeting summoned under paragraph 29 is not invalidated by any irregularity at or in relation to the meeting.

Implementation of voluntary arrangement

39.—   (1)   This paragraph applies where a voluntary arrangement approved by one or both of the meetings summoned under paragraph 29 has taken effect.

    (2)   The person who is for the time being carrying out in relation to the voluntary arrangement the functions conferred—

        (a)   by virtue of the approval of the arrangement, on the nominee, or

        (b)   by virtue of paragraph 31(2), on a person other than the nominee,

shall be known as the supervisor of the voluntary arrangement.

    (3)   If any of the company's creditors or any other person is dissatisfied by any act, omission or decision of the supervisor, he may apply to the court.

    (4)   On an application under sub-paragraph (3) the court may—

       (a)   confirm, reverse or modify any act or decision of the supervisor,

       (b)   give him directions, or

       (c)   make such other order as it thinks fit.

  (5)   The supervisor—

       (a)   may apply to the court for directions in relation to any particular matter arising under the voluntary arrangement, and

       (b)   is included among the persons who may apply to the court for the winding up of the company or for an administration order to be made in relation to it.

  (6)   The court may, whenever—

       (a)   it is expedient to appoint a person to carry out the functions of the supervisor, and

       (b)   it is inexpedient, difficult or impracticable for an appointment to be made without the assistance of the court,

make an order appointing a person who is qualified to act as an insolvency practitioner, or authorised to act as supervisor, in relation to the voluntary arrangement, either in substitution for the existing supervisor or to fill a vacancy.

  (7)   The power conferred by sub-paragraph (6) is exercisable so as to increase the number of persons exercising the functions of supervisor or, where there is more than one person exercising those functions, so as to replace one or more of those persons.

PART VI
MISCELLANEOUS

Challenge of directors' actions

40.— (1)   This paragraph applies in relation to acts or omissions of the directors of a company during a moratorium.

  (2)   A creditor or member of the company may apply to the court for an order under this paragraph on the ground—

       (a)   that the company's affairs, business and property are being or have been managed by the directors in a manner which is unfairly prejudicial to the interests of its creditors or members generally, or of some part of its creditors or members (including at least the petitioner), or

       (b)   that any actual or proposed act or omission of the directors is or would be so prejudicial.

  (3)   An application for an order under this paragraph may be made during or after the moratorium.

  (4)   On an application for an order under this paragraph the court may—

       (a)   make such order as it thinks fit for giving relief in respect of the matters complained of,

       (b)   adjourn the hearing conditionally or unconditionally, or

       (c)   make an interim order or any other order that it thinks fit.

  (5)   An order under this paragraph may in particular—

       (a)   regulate the management by the directors of the company's affairs, business and property during the remainder of the moratorium,

       (b)   require the directors to refrain from doing or continuing an act complained of by the petitioner, or to do an act which the petitioner has complained they have omitted to do,

       (c)   require the summoning of a meeting of creditors or members for the purpose of considering such matters as the court may direct,

       (d)   bring the moratorium to an end and make such consequential provision as the court thinks fit.

  (6)   In making an order under this paragraph the court shall have regard to the need to safeguard the interests of persons who have dealt with the company in good faith and for value.

  (7)   Sub-paragraph (8) applies where—

      (a)   the appointment of an administrator has effect in relation to the company and that appointment was in pursuance of—

          (i)   an administration application made, or

          (ii) a notice of intention to appoint filed,

          before the moratorium came into force, or

      (b)   the company is being wound up in pursuance of a petition presented before the moratorium came into force.

(8)   No application for an order under this paragraph may be made by a creditor or member of the company; but such an application may be made instead by the administrator or (as the case may be) the liquidator.

Offences

41.— (1) This paragraph applies where a moratorium has been obtained for a company.

      (2) If, within the period of 12 months ending with the day on which the moratorium came into force, a person who was at the time an officer of the company—

      (a)   did any of the things mentioned in paragraphs (a) to (f) of sub-paragraph (4), or

      (b)   was privy to the doing by others of any of the things mentioned in paragraphs (c), (d) and (e) of that sub-paragraph,

      he is to be treated as having committed an offence at that time.

      (3) If, at any time during the moratorium, a person who is an officer of the company—

      (a)   does any of the things mentioned in paragraphs (a) to (f) of sub-paragraph (4), or

      (b)   is privy to the doing by others of any of the things mentioned in paragraphs (c), (d) and (e) of that sub-paragraph,

      he commits an offence.

      (4) Those things are—

      (a)   concealing any part of the company's property to the value of £500 or more, or concealing any debt due to or from the company, or

      (b)   fraudulently removing any part of the company's property to the value of £500 or more, or

      (c)   concealing, destroying, mutilating or falsifying any book or paper affecting or relating to the company's property or affairs, or

      (d)   making any false entry in any book or paper affecting or relating to the company's property or affairs, or

      (e)   fraudulently parting with, altering or making any omission in any document affecting or relating to the company's property or affairs, or

      (f)   pawning, pledging or disposing of any property of the company which has been obtained on credit and has not been paid for (unless the pawning, pledging or disposal was in the ordinary way of the company's business).

      (5) For the purposes of this paragraph, "officer" includes a shadow director.

      (6) It is a defence—

      (a)   for a person charged under sub-paragraph (2) or (3) in respect of the things mentioned in paragraph (a) or (f) of sub-paragraph (4) to prove that he had no intent to defraud, and

      (b)   for a person charged under sub-paragraph (2) or (3) in respect of the things mentioned in paragraph (c) or (d) of sub-paragraph (4) to prove that he had no intent to conceal the state of affairs of the company or to defeat the law.

      (7) Where a person pawns, pledges or disposes of any property of a company in circumstances which amount to an offence under sub-paragraph (2) or (3), every person who takes in pawn or pledge, or otherwise receives, the property knowing it to be pawned, pledged or disposed of in circumstances which—

      (a)   would, if a moratorium were obtained for the company within the period of 12 months beginning with the day on which the pawning, pledging or disposal took place, amount to an offence under sub-paragraph (2), or

(b)   amount to an offence under sub-paragraph (3),

commits an offence.

(8)   A person guilty of an offence under this paragraph is liable to imprisonment or a fine, or both.

(9)   The money sums specified in paragraphs (a) and (b) of sub-paragraph (4) are subject to increase or reduction by order under section 417A in Part XV.

42.— (1)   If, for the purpose of obtaining a moratorium, or an extension of a moratorium, for a company, a person who is an officer of the company—

(a)   makes any false representation, or

(b)   fraudulently does, or omits to do, anything,

he commits an offence.

(2)   Sub-paragraph (1) applies even if no moratorium or extension is obtained.

(3)   For the purposes of this paragraph, "officer" includes a shadow director.

(4)   A person guilty of an offence under this paragraph is liable to imprisonment or a fine, or both.

Void provisions in floating charge documents

43.— (1)   A provision in an instrument creating a floating charge is void if it provides for—

(a)   obtaining a moratorium, or

(b)   anything done with a view to obtaining a moratorium (including any preliminary decision or investigation),

to be an event causing the floating charge to crystallise or causing restrictions which would not otherwise apply to be imposed on the disposal of property by the company or a ground for the appointment of a receiver.

(2)   In sub-paragraph (1), "receiver" includes a manager and a person who is appointed both receiver and manager.

Functions of the Financial Services Authority

44.— (1)   This Schedule has effect in relation to a moratorium for a regulated company with the modifications in sub-paragraphs (2) to (16) below.

(2)   Any notice or other document required by virtue of this Schedule to be sent to a creditor of a regulated company must also be sent to the Authority.

(3)   The Authority is entitled to be heard on any application to the court for leave under paragraph 20(2) or 20(3) (disposal of charged property, etc).

(4)   Where paragraph 26(1) (challenge of nominee's actions, etc) applies, the persons who may apply to the court include the Authority.

(5)   If a person other than the Authority applies to the court under that paragraph, the Authority is entitled to be heard on the application.

(6)   Where paragraph 27(1) (challenge of nominee's actions, etc) applies, the persons who may apply to the court include the Authority.

(7)   If a person other than the Authority applies to the court under that paragraph, the Authority is entitled to be heard on the application.

(8)   The persons to be summoned to a creditors' meeting under paragraph 29 include the Authority.

(9)   A person appointed for the purpose by the Authority is entitled to attend and participate in (but not to vote at)—

(a)   any creditors' meeting summoned under that paragraph,

(b)   any meeting of a committee established under paragraph 35 (moratorium committee).

(10)   The Authority is entitled to be heard on any application under paragraph 36(3) (effectiveness of decisions).

(11)   Where paragraph 38(1) (challenge of decisions) applies, the persons who may apply to the court include the Authority.

(12) If a person other than the Authority applies to the court under that paragraph, the Authority is entitled to be heard on the application.

(13) Where paragraph 39(3) (implementation of voluntary arrangement) applies, the persons who may apply to the court include the Authority.

(14) If a person other than the Authority applies to the court under that paragraph, the Authority is entitled to be heard on the application.

(15) Where paragraph 40(2) (challenge of directors' actions) applies, the persons who may apply to the court include the Authority.

(16) If a person other than the Authority applies to the court under that paragraph, the Authority is entitled to be heard on the application.

(17) This paragraph does not prejudice any right the Authority has (apart from this paragraph) as a creditor of a regulated company.

(18) In this paragraph—

"the Authority" means the Financial Services Authority, and

"regulated company" means a company which—

(a) is, or has been, an authorised person within the meaning given by section 31 of the Financial Services and Markets Act 2000,

(b) is, or has been, an appointed representative within the meaning given by section 39 of that Act, or

(c) is carrying on, or has carried on, a regulated activity, within the meaning given by section 22 of that Act, in contravention of the general prohibition within the meaning given by section 19 of that Act.

Subordinate legislation

45.— (1) Regulations or an order made by the Secretary of State under this Schedule may make different provision for different cases.

(2) Regulations so made may make such consequential, incidental, supplemental and transitional provision as may appear to the Secretary of State necessary or expedient.

(3) Any power of the Secretary of State to make regulations under this Schedule may be exercised by amending or repealing any enactment contained in this Act (including one contained in this Schedule) or contained in the Company Directors Disqualification Act 1986.

(4) Regulations (except regulations under paragraph 5) or an order made by the Secretary of State under this Schedule shall be made by statutory instrument subject to annulment in pursuance of a resolution of either House of Parliament.

(5) Regulations under paragraph 5 of this Schedule are to be made by statutory instrument and shall only be made if a draft containing the regulations has been laid before and approved by resolution of each House of Parliament.

SCHEDULE B1

ADMINISTRATION

Section 8

ARRANGEMENT OF SCHEDULE

NATURE OF ADMINISTRATION

Administration

1.— (1) For the purposes of this Act "administrator" of a company means a person appointed under this Schedule to manage the company's affairs, business and property.

(2) For the purposes of this Act—

(a) a company is "in administration" while the appointment of an administrator of the company has effect,

(b) a company "enters administration" when the appointment of an administrator takes effect,

(c) a company ceases to be in administration when the appointment of an administrator of the company ceases to have effect in accordance with this Schedule, and

(d) a company does not cease to be in administration merely because an administrator vacates office (by reason of resignation, death or otherwise) or is removed from office.

2. A person may be appointed as administrator of a company—

(a) by administration order of the court under paragraph 10,

(b) by the holder of a floating charge under paragraph 14, or

(c) by the company or its directors under paragraph 22.

Purpose of administration

3.— (1) The administrator of a company must perform his functions with the objective of—

(a) rescuing the company as a going concern, or

(b) achieving a better result for the company's creditors as a whole than would be likely if the company were wound up (without first being in administration), or

(c) realising property in order to make a distribution to one or more secured or preferential creditors.

(2) Subject to sub-paragraph (4), the administrator of a company must perform his functions in the interests of the company's creditors as a whole.

(3) The administrator must perform his functions with the objective specified in sub-paragraph (1)(a) unless he thinks either—

(a) that it is not reasonably practicable to achieve that objective, or

(b) that the objective specified in sub-paragraph (1)(b) would achieve a better result for the company's creditors as a whole.

(4) The administrator may perform his functions with the objective specified in sub-paragraph (1)(c) only if—

(a) he thinks that it is not reasonably practicable to achieve either of the objectives specified in sub-paragraph (1)(a) and (b), and

(b) he does not unnecessarily harm the interests of the creditors of the company as a whole.

4.   The administrator of a company must perform his functions as quickly and efficiently as is reasonably practicable.

Status of administrator

5.   An administrator is an officer of the court (whether or not he is appointed by the court).

General restrictions

6.   A person may be appointed as administrator of a company only if he is qualified to act as an insolvency practitioner in relation to the company.

7.   A person may not be appointed as administrator of a company which is in administration (subject to the provisions of paragraphs 90 to 97 and 100 to 103 about replacement and additional administrators).

8.—   (1)   A person may not be appointed as administrator of a company which is in liquidation by virtue of—
        (a)   a resolution for voluntary winding up, or
        (b)   a winding-up order.
        (2)   Sub-paragraph (1)(a) is subject to paragraph 38.
        (3)   Sub-paragraph (1)(b) is subject to paragraphs 37 and 38.

9.—   (1)   A person may not be appointed as administrator of a company which—
        (a)   has a liability in respect of a deposit which it accepted in accordance with the Banking Act 1979 (c 37) or 1987 (c 22), but
        (b)   is not an authorised deposit taker.
        (2)   A person may not be appointed as administrator of a company which effects or carries out contracts of insurance.
        (3)   But sub-paragraph (2) does not apply to a company which—
        (a)   is exempt from the general prohibition in relation to effecting or carrying out contracts of insurance, or
        (b)   is an authorised deposit taker effecting or carrying out contracts of insurance in the course of a banking business.
        (4)   In this paragraph—
        "authorised deposit taker" means a person with permission under Part IV of the Financial Services and Markets Act 2000 (c 8) to accept deposits, and
        "the general prohibition" has the meaning given by section 19 of that Act.
        (5)   This paragraph shall be construed in accordance with—
        (a)   section 22 of the Financial Services and Markets Act 2000 (classes of regulated activity and categories of investment),
        (b)   any relevant order under that section, and
        (c)   Schedule 2 to that Act (regulated activities).

APPOINTMENT OF ADMINISTRATOR BY COURT

Administration order

10.   An administration order is an order appointing a person as the administrator of a company.

Conditions for making order

11.   The court may make an administration order in relation to a company only if satisfied—
        (a)   that the company is or is likely to become unable to pay its debts, and
        (b)   that the administration order is reasonably likely to achieve the purpose of administration.

Administration application

12.—   (1)   An application to the court for an administration order in respect of a company (an "administration application") may be made only by—
        (a)   the company,

    (b)   the directors of the company,

    (c)   one or more creditors of the company,

    (d)   *the justices' chief executive [designated officer]* for a magistrates' court in the exercise of the power conferred by section 87A of the Magistrates' Courts Act 1980 (c 43) (fine imposed on company), or

    (e)   a combination of persons listed in paragraphs (a) to (d).

  (2) As soon as is reasonably practicable after the making of an administration application the applicant shall notify—

    (a)   any person who has appointed an administrative receiver of the company,

    (b)   any person who is or may be entitled to appoint an administrative receiver of the company,

    (c)   any person who is or may be entitled to appoint an administrator of the company under paragraph 14, and

    (d)   such other persons as may be prescribed.

  (3) An administration application may not be withdrawn without the permission of the court.

  (4) In sub-paragraph (1) "creditor" includes a contingent creditor and a prospective creditor.

  (5) Sub-paragraph (1) is without prejudice to section 7(4)(b).

Powers of court

13.— (1) On hearing an administration application the court may—

    (a)   make the administration order sought;

    (b)   dismiss the application;

    (c)   adjourn the hearing conditionally or unconditionally;

    (d)   make an interim order;

    (e)   treat the application as a winding-up petition and make any order which the court could make under section 125;

    (f)   make any other order which the court thinks appropriate.

  (2) An appointment of an administrator by administration order takes effect—

    (a)   at a time appointed by the order, or

    (b)   where no time is appointed by the order, when the order is made.

  (3) An interim order under sub-paragraph (1)(d) may, in particular—

    (a)   restrict the exercise of a power of the directors or the company;

    (b)   make provision conferring a discretion on the court or on a person qualified to act as an insolvency practitioner in relation to the company.

  (4) This paragraph is subject to paragraph 39.

APPOINTMENT OF ADMINISTRATOR BY HOLDER OF FLOATING CHARGE

Power to appoint

14.— (1) The holder of a qualifying floating charge in respect of a company's property may appoint an administrator of the company.

  (2) For the purposes of sub-paragraph (1) a floating charge qualifies if created by an instrument which—

    (a)   states that this paragraph applies to the floating charge,

    (b)   purports to empower the holder of the floating charge to appoint an administrator of the company,

    (c)   purports to empower the holder of the floating charge to make an appointment which would be the appointment of an administrative receiver within the meaning given by section 29(2), or

    (d)   purports to empower the holder of a floating charge in Scotland to appoint a receiver who on appointment would be an administrative receiver.

(3)   For the purposes of sub-paragraph (1) a person is the holder of a qualifying floating charge in respect of a company's property if he holds one or more debentures of the company secured—

    (a)   by a qualifying floating charge which relates to the whole or substantially the whole of the company's property,

    (b)   by a number of qualifying floating charges which together relate to the whole or substantially the whole of the company's property, or

    (c)   by charges and other forms of security which together relate to the whole or substantially the whole of the company's property and at least one of which is a qualifying floating charge.

Restrictions on power to appoint

15.—   (1)   A person may not appoint an administrator under paragraph 14 unless—

    (a)   he has given at least two business days' written notice to the holder of any prior floating charge which satisfies paragraph 14(2), or

    (b)   the holder of any prior floating charge which satisfies paragraph 14(2) has consented in writing to the making of the appointment.

   (2)   One floating charge is prior to another for the purposes of this paragraph if—

    (a)   it was created first, or

    (b)   it is to be treated as having priority in accordance with an agreement to which the holder of each floating charge was party.

   (3)   Sub-paragraph (2) shall have effect in relation to Scotland as if the following were substituted for paragraph (a)—

    "(a) it has priority of ranking in accordance with section 464(4)(b) of the Companies Act 1985 (c 6),".

16.   An administrator may not be appointed under paragraph 14 while a floating charge on which the appointment relies is not enforceable.

17.   An administrator of a company may not be appointed under paragraph 14 if—

   (a)   a provisional liquidator of the company has been appointed under section 135, or

   (b)   an administrative receiver of the company is in office.

Notice of appointment

18.—   (1)   A person who appoints an administrator of a company under paragraph 14 shall file with the court—

    (a)   a notice of appointment, and

    (b)   such other documents as may be prescribed.

   (2)   The notice of appointment must include a statutory declaration by or on behalf of the person who makes the appointment—

    (a)   that the person is the holder of a qualifying floating charge in respect of the company's property,

    (b)   that each floating charge relied on in making the appointment is (or was) enforceable on the date of the appointment, and

    (c)   that the appointment is in accordance with this Schedule.

   (3)   The notice of appointment must identify the administrator and must be accompanied by a statement by the administrator—

    (a)   that he consents to the appointment,

    (b)   that in his opinion the purpose of administration is reasonably likely to be achieved, and

    (c)   giving such other information and opinions as may be prescribed.

   (4)   For the purpose of a statement under sub-paragraph (3) an administrator may rely on information supplied by directors of the company (unless he has reason to doubt its accuracy).

(5)   The notice of appointment and any document accompanying it must be in the prescribed form.

(6)   A statutory declaration under sub-paragraph (2) must be made during the prescribed period.

(7)   A person commits an offence if in a statutory declaration under sub-paragraph (2) he makes a statement—

    (a)   which is false, and

    (b)   which he does not reasonably believe to be true.

Commencement of appointment

19.   The appointment of an administrator under paragraph 14 takes effect when the requirements of paragraph 18 are satisfied.

20.   A person who appoints an administrator under paragraph 14—

    (a)   shall notify the administrator and such other persons as may be prescribed as soon as is reasonably practicable after the requirements of paragraph 18 are satisfied, and

    (b)   commits an offence if he fails without reasonable excuse to comply with paragraph (a).

Invalid appointment: indemnity

21.—   (1)   This paragraph applies where—

    (a)   a person purports to appoint an administrator under paragraph 14, and

    (b)   the appointment is discovered to be invalid.

    (2)   The court may order the person who purported to make the appointment to indemnify the person appointed against liability which arises solely by reason of the appointment's invalidity.

APPOINTMENT OF ADMINISTRATOR BY COMPANY OR DIRECTORS

Power to appoint

22.—   (1)   A company may appoint an administrator.

    (2)   The directors of a company may appoint an administrator.

Restrictions on power to appoint

23.—   (1)   This paragraph applies where an administrator of a company is appointed—

    (a)   under paragraph 22, or

    (b)   on an administration application made by the company or its directors.

    (2)   An administrator of the company may not be appointed under paragraph 22 during the period of 12 months beginning with the date on which the appointment referred to in sub-paragraph (1) ceases to have effect.

24.—   (1)   If a moratorium for a company under Schedule A1 ends on a date when no voluntary arrangement is in force in respect of the company, this paragraph applies for the period of 12 months beginning with that date.

    (2)   This paragraph also applies for the period of 12 months beginning with the date on which a voluntary arrangement in respect of a company ends if—

    (a)   the arrangement was made during a moratorium for the company under Schedule A1, and

    (b)   the arrangement ends prematurely (within the meaning of section 7B).

    (3)   While this paragraph applies, an administrator of the company may not be appointed under paragraph 22.

25.   An administrator of a company may not be appointed under paragraph 22 if—

    (a)   a petition for the winding up of the company has been presented and is not yet disposed of,

    (b)   an administration application has been made and is not yet disposed of, or

    (c)   an administrative receiver of the company is in office.

Notice of intention to appoint

26.— (1)   A person who proposes to make an appointment under paragraph 22 shall give at least five business days' written notice to—

       (a)   any person who is or may be entitled to appoint an administrative receiver of the company, and

       (b)   any person who is or may be entitled to appoint an administrator of the company under paragraph 14.

    (2)   A person who proposes to make an appointment under paragraph 22 shall also give such notice as may be prescribed to such other persons as may be prescribed.

    (3)   A notice under this paragraph must—

       (a)   identify the proposed administrator, and

       (b)   be in the prescribed form.

27.— (1)   A person who gives notice of intention to appoint under paragraph 26 shall file with the court as soon as is reasonably practicable a copy of—

       (a)   the notice, and

       (b)   any document accompanying it.

    (2)   The copy filed under sub-paragraph (1) must be accompanied by a statutory declaration made by or on behalf of the person who proposes to make the appointment—

       (a)   that the company is or is likely to become unable to pay its debts,

       (b)   that the company is not in liquidation, and

       (c)   that, so far as the person making the statement is able to ascertain, the appointment is not prevented by paragraphs 23 to 25, and

       (d)   to such additional effect, and giving such information, as may be prescribed.

    (3)   A statutory declaration under sub-paragraph (2) must—

       (a)   be in the prescribed form, and

       (b)   be made during the prescribed period.

    (4)   A person commits an offence if in a statutory declaration under sub-paragraph (2) he makes a statement—

       (a)   which is false, and

       (b)   which he does not reasonably believe to be true.

28.— (1)   An appointment may not be made under paragraph 22 unless the person who makes the appointment has complied with any requirement of paragraphs 26 and 27 and—

       (a)   the period of notice specified in paragraph 26(1) has expired, or

       (b)   each person to whom notice has been given under paragraph 26(1) has consented in writing to the making of the appointment.

    (2)   An appointment may not be made under paragraph 22 after the period of ten business days beginning with the date on which the notice of intention to appoint is filed under paragraph 27(1).

Notice of appointment

29.— (1)   A person who appoints an administrator of a company under paragraph 22 shall file with the court—

       (a)   a notice of appointment, and

       (b)   such other documents as may be prescribed.

    (2)   The notice of appointment must include a statutory declaration by or on behalf of the person who makes the appointment—

       (a)   that the person is entitled to make an appointment under paragraph 22,

       (b)   that the appointment is in accordance with this Schedule, and

       (c)   that, so far as the person making the statement is able to ascertain, the statements made and information given in the statutory declaration filed with the notice of intention to appoint remain accurate.

(3) The notice of appointment must identify the administrator and must be accompanied by a statement by the administrator—

    (a) that he consents to the appointment,

    (b) that in his opinion the purpose of administration is reasonably likely to be achieved, and

    (c) giving such other information and opinions as may be prescribed.

(4) For the purpose of a statement under sub-paragraph (3) an administrator may rely on information supplied by directors of the company (unless he has reason to doubt its accuracy).

(5) The notice of appointment and any document accompanying it must be in the prescribed form.

(6) A statutory declaration under sub-paragraph (2) must be made during the prescribed period.

(7) A person commits an offence if in a statutory declaration under sub-paragraph (2) he makes a statement—

    (a) which is false, and

    (b) which he does not reasonably believe to be true.

30. In a case in which no person is entitled to notice of intention to appoint under paragraph 26(1) (and paragraph 28 therefore does not apply)—

    (a) the statutory declaration accompanying the notice of appointment must include the statements and information required under paragraph 27(2), and

    (b) paragraph 29(2)(c) shall not apply.

Commencement of appointment

31. The appointment of an administrator under paragraph 22 takes effect when the requirements of paragraph 29 are satisfied.

32. A person who appoints an administrator under paragraph 22—

    (a) shall notify the administrator and such other persons as may be prescribed as soon as is reasonably practicable after the requirements of paragraph 29 are satisfied, and

    (b) commits an offence if he fails without reasonable excuse to comply with paragraph (a).

33. If before the requirements of paragraph 29 are satisfied the company enters administration by virtue of an administration order or an appointment under paragraph 14—

    (a) the appointment under paragraph 22 shall not take effect, and

    (b) paragraph 32 shall not apply.

Invalid appointment: indemnity

34.— (1) This paragraph applies where—

    (a) a person purports to appoint an administrator under paragraph 22, and

    (b) the appointment is discovered to be invalid.

(2) The court may order the person who purported to make the appointment to indemnify the person appointed against liability which arises solely by reason of the appointment's invalidity.

ADMINISTRATION APPLICATION—SPECIAL CASES

Application by holder of floating charge

35.— (1) This paragraph applies where an administration application in respect of a company—

    (a) is made by the holder of a qualifying floating charge in respect of the company's property, and

    (b) includes a statement that the application is made in reliance on this paragraph.

(2) The court may make an administration order—

    (a) whether or not satisfied that the company is or is likely to become unable to pay its debts, but

    (b) only if satisfied that the applicant could appoint an administrator under paragraph 14.

Intervention by holder of floating charge

36.— (1)　This paragraph applies where—

(a)　an administration application in respect of a company is made by a person who is not the holder of a qualifying floating charge in respect of the company's property, and

(b)　the holder of a qualifying floating charge in respect of the company's property applies to the court to have a specified person appointed as administrator (and not the person specified by the administration applicant).

(2)　The court shall grant an application under sub-paragraph (1)(b) unless the court thinks it right to refuse the application because of the particular circumstances of the case.

Application where company in liquidation

37.— (1)　This paragraph applies where the holder of a qualifying floating charge in respect of a company's property could appoint an administrator under paragraph 14 but for paragraph 8(1)(b).

(2)　The holder of the qualifying floating charge may make an administration application.

(3)　If the court makes an administration order on hearing an application made by virtue of sub-paragraph (2)—

(a)　the court shall discharge the winding-up order,

(b)　the court shall make provision for such matters as may be prescribed,

(c)　the court may make other consequential provision,

(d)　the court shall specify which of the powers under this Schedule are to be exercisable by the administrator, and

(e)　this Schedule shall have effect with such modifications as the court may specify.

38.— (1)　The liquidator of a company may make an administration application.

(2)　If the court makes an administration order on hearing an application made by virtue of sub-paragraph (1)—

(a)　the court shall discharge any winding-up order in respect of the company,

(b)　the court shall make provision for such matters as may be prescribed,

(c)　the court may make other consequential provision,

(d)　the court shall specify which of the powers under this Schedule are to be exercisable by the administrator, and

(e)　this Schedule shall have effect with such modifications as the court may specify.

Effect of administrative receivership

39.— (1)　Where there is an administrative receiver of a company the court must dismiss an administration application in respect of the company unless—

(a)　the person by or on behalf of whom the receiver was appointed consents to the making of the administration order,

(b)　the court thinks that the security by virtue of which the receiver was appointed would be liable to be released or discharged under sections 238 to 240 (transaction at under-value and preference) if an administration order were made,

(c)　the court thinks that the security by virtue of which the receiver was appointed would be avoided under section 245 (avoidance of floating charge) if an administration order were made, or

(d)　the court thinks that the security by virtue of which the receiver was appointed would be challengeable under section 242 (gratuitous alienations) or 243 (unfair preferences) or under any rule of law in Scotland.

(2)　Sub-paragraph (1) applies whether the administrative receiver is appointed before or after the making of the administration application.

EFFECT OF ADMINISTRATION

Dismissal of pending winding-up petition

40.— (1) A petition for the winding up of a company—

    (a) shall be dismissed on the making of an administration order in respect of the company, and

    (b) shall be suspended while the company is in administration following an appointment under paragraph 14.

  (2) Sub-paragraph (1)(b) does not apply to a petition presented under—

    (a) section 124A (public interest), or

    (aa) section 124B (SEs),

    (b) section 367 of the Financial Services and Markets Act 2000 (c 8) (petition by Financial Services Authority).

  (3) Where an administrator becomes aware that a petition was presented under a provision referred to in sub-paragraph (2) before his appointment, he shall apply to the court for directions under paragraph 63.

Dismissal of administrative or other receiver

41.— (1) When an administration order takes effect in respect of a company any administrative receiver of the company shall vacate office.

  (2) Where a company is in administration, any receiver of part of the company's property shall vacate office if the administrator requires him to.

  (3) Where an administrative receiver or receiver vacates office under sub-paragraph (1) or (2)—

    (a) his remuneration shall be charged on and paid out of any property of the company which was in his custody or under his control immediately before he vacated office, and

    (b) he need not take any further steps under section 40 or 59.

  (4) In the application of sub-paragraph (3)(a)—

    (a) "remuneration" includes expenses properly incurred and any indemnity to which the administrative receiver or receiver is entitled out of the assets of the company,

    (b) the charge imposed takes priority over security held by the person by whom or on whose behalf the administrative receiver or receiver was appointed, and

    (c) the provision for payment is subject to paragraph 43.

Moratorium on insolvency proceedings

42.— (1) This paragraph applies to a company in administration.

  (2) No resolution may be passed for the winding up of the company.

  (3) No order may be made for the winding up of the company.

  (4) Sub-paragraph (3) does not apply to an order made on a petition presented under—

    (a) section 124A (public interest), or

    (aa) section 124B (SEs),

    (b) section 367 of the Financial Services and Markets Act 2000 (c 8) (petition by Financial Services Authority).

  (5) If a petition presented under a provision referred to in sub-paragraph (4) comes to the attention of the administrator, he shall apply to the court for directions under paragraph 63.

Moratorium on other legal process

43.— (1) This paragraph applies to a company in administration.

  (2) No step may be taken to enforce security over the company's property except—

    (a) with the consent of the administrator, or

    (b) with the permission of the court.

(3) No step may be taken to repossess goods in the company's possession under a hire-purchase agreement except—
    (a) with the consent of the administrator, or
    (b) with the permission of the court.

(4) A landlord may not exercise a right of forfeiture by peaceable re-entry in relation to premises let to the company except—
    (a) with the consent of the administrator, or
    (b) with the permission of the court.

(5) In Scotland, a landlord may not exercise a right of irritancy in relation to premises let to the company except—
    (a) with the consent of the administrator, or
    (b) with the permission of the court.

(6) No legal process (including legal proceedings, execution, distress and diligence) may be instituted or continued against the company or property of the company except—
    (a) with the consent of the administrator, or
    (b) with the permission of the court.

(6A) An administrative receiver of the company may not be appointed.

(7) Where the court gives permission for a transaction under this paragraph it may impose a condition on or a requirement in connection with the transaction.

(8) In this paragraph "landlord" includes a person to whom rent is payable.

Interim moratorium

44.— (1) This paragraph applies where an administration application in respect of a company has been made and—
    (a) the application has not yet been granted or dismissed, or
    (b) the application has been granted but the administration order has not yet taken effect.

(2) This paragraph also applies from the time when a copy of notice of intention to appoint an administrator under paragraph 14 is filed with the court until—
    (a) the appointment of the administrator takes effect, or
    (b) the period of five business days beginning with the date of filing expires without an administrator having been appointed.

(3) Sub-paragraph (2) has effect in relation to a notice of intention to appoint only if it is in the prescribed form.

(4) This paragraph also applies from the time when a copy of notice of intention to appoint an administrator is filed with the court under paragraph 27(1) until—
    (a) the appointment of the administrator takes effect, or
    (b) the period specified in paragraph 28(2) expires without an administrator having been appointed.

(5) The provisions of paragraphs 42 and 43 shall apply (ignoring any reference to the consent of the administrator).

(6) If there is an administrative receiver of the company when the administration application is made, the provisions of paragraphs 42 and 43 shall not begin to apply by virtue of this paragraph until the person by or on behalf of whom the receiver was appointed consents to the making of the administration order.

(7) This paragraph does not prevent or require the permission of the court for—
    (a) the presentation of a petition for the winding up of the company under a provision mentioned in paragraph 42(4),
    (b) the appointment of an administrator under paragraph 14,
    (c) the appointment of an administrative receiver of the company, or
    (d) the carrying out by an administrative receiver (whenever appointed) of his functions.

Publicity

45.— (1) While a company is in administration every business document issued by or on behalf of the company or the administrator must state—

(a) the name of the administrator, and

(b) that the affairs, business and property of the company are being managed by him.

(2) Any of the following commits an offence if without reasonable excuse he authorises or permits a contravention of sub-paragraph (1)—

(a) the administrator,

(b) an officer of the company, and

(c) the company.

(3) In sub-paragraph (1) "business document" means—

(a) an invoice,

(b) an order for goods or services, and

(c) a business letter.

PROCESS OF ADMINISTRATION

Announcement of administrator's appointment

46.— (1) This paragraph applies where a person becomes the administrator of a company.

(2) As soon as is reasonably practicable the administrator shall—

(a) send a notice of his appointment to the company, and

(b) publish a notice of his appointment in the prescribed manner.

(3) As soon as is reasonably practicable the administrator shall—

(a) obtain a list of the company's creditors, and

(b) send a notice of his appointment to each creditor of whose claim and address he is aware.

(4) The administrator shall send a notice of his appointment to the registrar of companies before the end of the period of 7 days beginning with the date specified in sub-paragraph (6).

(5) The administrator shall send a notice of his appointment to such persons as may be prescribed before the end of the prescribed period beginning with the date specified in sub-paragraph (6).

(6) The date for the purpose of sub-paragraphs (4) and (5) is—

(a) in the case of an administrator appointed by administration order, the date of the order,

(b) in the case of an administrator appointed under paragraph 14, the date on which he receives notice under paragraph 20, and

(c) in the case of an administrator appointed under paragraph 22, the date on which he receives notice under paragraph 32.

(7) The court may direct that sub-paragraph (3)(b) or (5)—

(a) shall not apply, or

(b) shall apply with the substitution of a different period.

(8) A notice under this paragraph must—

(a) contain the prescribed information, and

(b) be in the prescribed form.

(9) An administrator commits an offence if he fails without reasonable excuse to comply with a requirement of this paragraph.

Statement of company's affairs

47.— (1) As soon as is reasonably practicable after appointment the administrator of a company shall by notice in the prescribed form require one or more relevant persons to provide the administrator with a statement of the affairs of the company.

(2) The statement must—

(a) be verified by a statement of truth in accordance with Civil Procedure Rules,

    (b)   be in the prescribed form,

    (c)   give particulars of the company's property, debts and liabilities,

    (d)   give the names and addresses of the company's creditors,

    (e)   specify the security held by each creditor,

    (f)   give the date on which each security was granted, and

    (g)   contain such other information as may be prescribed.

(3)   In sub-paragraph (1) "relevant person" means—

    (a)   a person who is or has been an officer of the company,

    (b)   a person who took part in the formation of the company during the period of one year ending with the date on which the company enters administration,

    (c)   a person employed by the company during that period, and

    (d)   a person who is or has been during that period an officer or employee of a company which is or has been during that year an officer of the company.

(4)   For the purpose of sub-paragraph (3) a reference to employment is a reference to employment through a contract of employment or a contract for services.

(5)   In Scotland, a statement of affairs under sub-paragraph (1) must be a statutory declaration made in accordance with the Statutory Declarations Act 1835 (c 62) (and sub-paragraph (2)(a) shall not apply).

48.— (1)   A person required to submit a statement of affairs must do so before the end of the period of 11 days beginning with the day on which he receives notice of the requirement.

(2)   The administrator may—

    (a)   revoke a requirement under paragraph 47(1), or

    (b)   extend the period specified in sub-paragraph (1) (whether before or after expiry).

(3)   If the administrator refuses a request to act under sub-paragraph (2)—

    (a)   the person whose request is refused may apply to the court, and

    (b)   the court may take action of a kind specified in sub-paragraph (2).

(4)   A person commits an offence if he fails without reasonable excuse to comply with a requirement under paragraph 47(1).

Administrator's proposals

49.— (1)   The administrator of a company shall make a statement setting out proposals for achieving the purpose of administration.

(2)   A statement under sub-paragraph (1) must, in particular—

    (a)   deal with such matters as may be prescribed, and

    (b)   where applicable, explain why the administrator thinks that the objective mentioned in paragraph 3(1)(a) or (b) cannot be achieved.

(3)   Proposals under this paragraph may include—

    (a)   a proposal for a voluntary arrangement under Part I of this Act (although this paragraph is without prejudice to section 4(3));

    (b)   a proposal for a compromise or arrangement to be sanctioned under section 425 of the Companies Act (compromise with creditors or members).

(4)   The administrator shall send a copy of the statement of his proposals—

    (a)   to the registrar of companies,

    (b)   to every creditor of the company of whose claim and address he is aware, and

    (c)   to every member of the company of whose address he is aware.

(5)   The administrator shall comply with sub-paragraph (4)—

    (a)   as soon as is reasonably practicable after the company enters administration, and

    (b)   in any event, before the end of the period of eight weeks beginning with the day on which the company enters administration.

(6)   The administrator shall be taken to comply with sub-paragraph (4)(c) if he publishes in the prescribed manner a notice undertaking to provide a copy of the statement of proposals free of charge to any member of the company who applies in writing to a specified address.

(7) An administrator commits an offence if he fails without reasonable excuse to comply with sub-paragraph (5).

(8) A period specified in this paragraph may be varied in accordance with paragraph 107.

Creditors' meeting

50.— (1) In this Schedule "creditors' meeting" means a meeting of creditors of a company summoned by the administrator—

(a) in the prescribed manner, and

(b) giving the prescribed period of notice to every creditor of the company of whose claim and address he is aware.

(2) A period prescribed under sub-paragraph (1)(b) may be varied in accordance with paragraph 107.

(3) A creditors' meeting shall be conducted in accordance with the rules.

Requirement for initial creditors' meeting

51.— (1) Each copy of an administrator's statement of proposals sent to a creditor under paragraph 49(4)(b) must be accompanied by an invitation to a creditors' meeting (an "initial creditors' meeting").

(2) The date set for an initial creditors' meeting must be—

(a) as soon as is reasonably practicable after the company enters administration, and

(b) in any event, within the period of ten weeks beginning with the date on which the company enters administration.

(3) An administrator shall present a copy of his statement of proposals to an initial creditors' meeting.

(4) A period specified in this paragraph may be varied in accordance with paragraph 107.

(5) An administrator commits an offence if he fails without reasonable excuse to comply with a requirement of this paragraph.

52.— (1) Paragraph 51(1) shall not apply where the statement of proposals states that the administrator thinks—

(a) that the company has sufficient property to enable each creditor of the company to be paid in full,

(b) that the company has insufficient property to enable a distribution to be made to unsecured creditors other than by virtue of section 176A(2)(a), or

(c) that neither of the objectives specified in paragraph 3(1)(a) and (b) can be achieved.

(2) But the administrator shall summon an initial creditors' meeting if it is requested—

(a) by creditors of the company whose debts amount to at least 10% of the total debts of the company,

(b) in the prescribed manner, and

(c) in the prescribed period.

(3) A meeting requested under sub-paragraph (2) must be summoned for a date in the prescribed period.

(4) The period prescribed under sub-paragraph (3) may be varied in accordance with paragraph 107.

Business and result of initial creditors' meeting

53.— (1) An initial creditors' meeting to which an administrator's proposals are presented shall consider them and may—

(a) approve them without modification, or

(b) approve them with modification to which the administrator consents.

(2) After the conclusion of an initial creditors' meeting the administrator shall as soon as is reasonably practicable report any decision taken to—

(a) the court,

(b) the registrar of companies, and

(c)   such other persons as may be prescribed.

(3)   An administrator commits an offence if he fails without reasonable excuse to comply with sub-paragraph (2).

Revision of administrator's proposals

54.— (1)   This paragraph applies where—
(a)   an administrator's proposals have been approved (with or without modification) at an initial creditors' meeting,
(b)   the administrator proposes a revision to the proposals, and
(c)   the administrator thinks that the proposed revision is substantial.

(2)   The administrator shall—
(a)   summon a creditors' meeting,
(b)   send a statement in the prescribed form of the proposed revision with the notice of the meeting sent to each creditor,
(c)   send a copy of the statement, within the prescribed period, to each member of the company of whose address he is aware, and
(d)   present a copy of the statement to the meeting.

(3)   The administrator shall be taken to have complied with sub-paragraph (2)(c) if he publishes a notice undertaking to provide a copy of the statement free of charge to any member of the company who applies in writing to a specified address.

(4)   A notice under sub-paragraph (3) must be published—
(a)   in the prescribed manner, and
(b)   within the prescribed period.

(5)   A creditors' meeting to which a proposed revision is presented shall consider it and may—
(a)   approve it without modification, or
(b)   approve it with modification to which the administrator consents.

(6)   After the conclusion of a creditors' meeting the administrator shall as soon as is reasonably practicable report any decision taken to—
(a)   the court,
(b)   the registrar of companies, and
(c)   such other persons as may be prescribed.

(7)   An administrator commits an offence if he fails without reasonable excuse to comply with sub-paragraph (6).

Failure to obtain approval of administrator's proposals

55.— (1)   This paragraph applies where an administrator reports to the court that—
(a)   an initial creditors' meeting has failed to approve the administrator's proposals presented to it, or
(b)   a creditors' meeting has failed to approve a revision of the administrator's proposals presented to it.

(2)   The court may—
(a)   provide that the appointment of an administrator shall cease to have effect from a specified time;
(b)   adjourn the hearing conditionally or unconditionally;
(c)   make an interim order;
(d)   make an order on a petition for winding up suspended by virtue of paragraph 40(1)(b);
(e)   make any other order (including an order making consequential provision) that the court thinks appropriate.

Further creditors' meetings

56.— (1)   The administrator of a company shall summon a creditors' meeting if—
(a)   it is requested in the prescribed manner by creditors of the company whose debts amount to at least 10% of the total debts of the company, or

(b) he is directed by the court to summon a creditors' meeting.

(2) An administrator commits an offence if he fails without reasonable excuse to summon a creditors' meeting as required by this paragraph.

Creditors' committee

57.— (1) A creditors' meeting may establish a creditors' committee.

(2) A creditors' committee shall carry out functions conferred on it by or under this Act.

(3) A creditors' committee may require the administrator—

(a) to attend on the committee at any reasonable time of which he is given at least seven days' notice, and

(b) to provide the committee with information about the exercise of his functions.

Correspondence instead of creditors' meeting

58.— (1) Anything which is required or permitted by or under this Schedule to be done at a creditors' meeting may be done by correspondence between the administrator and creditors—

(a) in accordance with the rules, and

(b) subject to any prescribed condition.

(2) A reference in this Schedule to anything done at a creditors' meeting includes a reference to anything done in the course of correspondence in reliance on sub-paragraph (1).

(3) A requirement to hold a creditors' meeting is satisfied by conducting correspondence in accordance with this paragraph.

FUNCTIONS OF ADMINISTRATOR

General powers

59.— (1) The administrator of a company may do anything necessary or expedient for the management of the affairs, business and property of the company.

(2) A provision of this Schedule which expressly permits the administrator to do a specified thing is without prejudice to the generality of sub-paragraph (1).

(3) A person who deals with the administrator of a company in good faith and for value need not inquire whether the administrator is acting within his powers.

60. The administrator of a company has the powers specified in Schedule 1 to this Act.

61. The administrator of a company—

(a) may remove a director of the company, and

(b) may appoint a director of the company (whether or not to fill a vacancy).

62. The administrator of a company may call a meeting of members or creditors of the company.

63. The administrator of a company may apply to the court for directions in connection with his functions.

64.— (1) A company in administration or an officer of a company in administration may not exercise a management power without the consent of the administrator.

(2) For the purpose of sub-paragraph (1)—

(a) "management power" means a power which could be exercised so as to interfere with the exercise of the administrator's powers,

(b) it is immaterial whether the power is conferred by an enactment or an instrument, and

(c) consent may be general or specific.

Distribution

65.— (1) The administrator of a company may make a distribution to a creditor of the company.

(2) Section 175 shall apply in relation to a distribution under this paragraph as it applies in relation to a winding up.

(3) A payment may not be made by way of distribution under this paragraph to a creditor of the company who is neither secured nor preferential unless the court gives permission.

66.   The administrator of a company may make a payment otherwise than in accordance with
          paragraph 65 or paragraph 13 of Schedule 1 if he thinks it likely to assist achievement of the
          purpose of administration.

General duties

67.   The administrator of a company shall on his appointment take custody or control of all the
          property to which he thinks the company is entitled.

68.—   (1)   Subject to sub-paragraph (2), the administrator of a company shall manage its affairs,
                business and property in accordance with—
                (a)   any proposals approved under paragraph 53,
                (b)   any revision of those proposals which is made by him and which he does not consider
                       substantial, and
                (c)   any revision of those proposals approved under paragraph 54.
          (2)   If the court gives directions to the administrator of a company in connection with any aspect
                 of his management of the company's affairs, business or property, the administrator shall
                 comply with the directions.
          (3)   The court may give directions under sub-paragraph (2) only if—
                 (a)   no proposals have been approved under paragraph 53,
                 (b)   the directions are consistent with any proposals or revision approved under paragraph
                        53 or 54,
                 (c)   the court thinks the directions are required in order to reflect a change in circum-
                        stances since the approval of proposals or a revision under paragraph 53 or 54, or
                 (d)   the court thinks the directions are desirable because of a misunderstanding about pro-
                        posals or a revision approved under paragraph 53 or 54.

Administrator as agent of company

69.   In exercising his functions under this Schedule the administrator of a company acts as its agent.

Charged property: floating charge

70.—   (1)   The administrator of a company may dispose of or take action relating to property which is
                subject to a floating charge as if it were not subject to the charge.
          (2)   Where property is disposed of in reliance on sub-paragraph (1) the holder of the floating
                 charge shall have the same priority in respect of acquired property as he had in respect of the
                 property disposed of.
          (3)   In sub-paragraph (2) "acquired property" means property of the company which directly or
                 indirectly represents the property disposed of.

Charged property: non-floating charge

71.—   (1)   The court may by order enable the administrator of a company to dispose of property which
                is subject to a security (other than a floating charge) as if it were not subject to the security.
          (2)   An order under sub-paragraph (1) may be made only—
                 (a)   on the application of the administrator, and
                 (b)   where the court thinks that disposal of the property would be likely to promote the pur-
                        pose of administration in respect of the company.
          (3)   An order under this paragraph is subject to the condition that there be applied towards
                 discharging the sums secured by the security—
                 (a)   the net proceeds of disposal of the property, and
                 (b)   any additional money required to be added to the net proceeds so as to produce the
                        amount determined by the court as the net amount which would be realised on a sale of
                        the property at market value.
          (4)   If an order under this paragraph relates to more than one security, application of money
                 under sub-paragraph (3) shall be in the order of the priorities of the securities.

(5) An administrator who makes a successful application for an order under this paragraph shall send a copy of the order to the registrar of companies before the end of the period of 14 days starting with the date of the order.

(6) An administrator commits an offence if he fails to comply with sub-paragraph (5) without reasonable excuse.

Hire-purchase property

72.— (1) The court may by order enable the administrator of a company to dispose of goods which are in the possession of the company under a hire-purchase agreement as if all the rights of the owner under the agreement were vested in the company.

(2) An order under sub-paragraph (1) may be made only—

(a) on the application of the administrator, and

(b) where the court thinks that disposal of the goods would be likely to promote the purpose of administration in respect of the company.

(3) An order under this paragraph is subject to the condition that there be applied towards discharging the sums payable under the hire-purchase agreement—

(a) the net proceeds of disposal of the goods, and

(b) any additional money required to be added to the net proceeds so as to produce the amount determined by the court as the net amount which would be realised on a sale of the goods at market value.

(4) An administrator who makes a successful application for an order under this paragraph shall send a copy of the order to the registrar of companies before the end of the period of 14 days starting with the date of the order.

(5) An administrator commits an offence if he fails without reasonable excuse to comply with sub-paragraph (4).

Protection for secured or preferential creditor

73.— (1) An administrator's statement of proposals under paragraph 49 may not include any action which—

(a) affects the right of a secured creditor of the company to enforce his security,

(b) would result in a preferential debt of the company being paid otherwise than in priority to its non-preferential debts, or

(c) would result in one preferential creditor of the company being paid a smaller proportion of his debt than another.

(2) Sub-paragraph (1) does not apply to—

(a) action to which the relevant creditor consents,

(b) a proposal for a voluntary arrangement under Part I of this Act (although this sub-paragraph is without prejudice to section 4(3)), or

(c) a proposal for a compromise or arrangement to be sanctioned under section 425 of the Companies Act (compromise with creditors or members).

(3) The reference to a statement of proposals in sub-paragraph (1) includes a reference to a statement as revised or modified.

Challenge to administrator's conduct of company

74.— (1) A creditor or member of a company in administration may apply to the court claiming that—

(a) the administrator is acting or has acted so as unfairly to harm the interests of the applicant (whether alone or in common with some or all other members or creditors), or

(b) the administrator proposes to act in a way which would unfairly harm the interests of the applicant (whether alone or in common with some or all other members or creditors).

(2)   A creditor or member of a company in administration may apply to the court claiming that the administrator is not performing his functions as quickly or as efficiently as is reasonably practicable.

(3)   The court may—

     (a)   grant relief;

     (b)   dismiss the application;

     (c)   adjourn the hearing conditionally or unconditionally;

     (d)   make an interim order;

     (e)   make any other order it thinks appropriate.

(4)   In particular, an order under this paragraph may—

     (a)   regulate the administrator's exercise of his functions;

     (b)   require the administrator to do or not do a specified thing;

     (c)   require a creditors' meeting to be held for a specified purpose;

     (d)   provide for the appointment of an administrator to cease to have effect;

     (e)   make consequential provision.

(5)   An order may be made on a claim under sub-paragraph (1) whether or not the action complained of—

     (a)   is within the administrator's powers under this Schedule;

     (b)   was taken in reliance on an order under paragraph 71 or 72.

(6)   An order may not be made under this paragraph if it would impede or prevent the implementation of—

     (a)   a voluntary arrangement approved under Part I,

     (b)   a compromise or arrangement sanctioned under section 425 of the Companies Act (compromise with creditors and members), or

     (c)   proposals or a revision approved under paragraph 53 or 54 more than 28 days before the day on which the application for the order under this paragraph is made.

Misfeasance

75.—   (1)   The court may examine the conduct of a person who—

     (a)   is or purports to be the administrator of a company, or

     (b)   has been or has purported to be the administrator of a company.

   (2)   An examination under this paragraph may be held only on the application of—

     (a)   the official receiver,

     (b)   the administrator of the company,

     (c)   the liquidator of the company,

     (d)   a creditor of the company, or

     (e)   a contributory of the company.

   (3)   An application under sub-paragraph (2) must allege that the administrator—

     (a)   has misapplied or retained money or other property of the company,

     (b)   has become accountable for money or other property of the company,

     (c)   has breached a fiduciary or other duty in relation to the company, or

     (d)   has been guilty of misfeasance.

   (4)   On an examination under this paragraph into a person's conduct the court may order him—

     (a)   to repay, restore or account for money or property;

     (b)   to pay interest;

     (c)   to contribute a sum to the company's property by way of compensation for breach of duty or misfeasance.

   (5)   In sub-paragraph (3) "administrator" includes a person who purports or has purported to be a company's administrator.

   (6)   An application under sub-paragraph (2) may be made in respect of an administrator who has been discharged under paragraph 98 only with the permission of the court.

ENDING ADMINISTRATION

Automatic end of administration

76.— (1) The appointment of an administrator shall cease to have effect at the end of the period of one year beginning with the date on which it takes effect.

(2) But—

(a) on the application of an administrator the court may by order extend his term of office for a specified period, and

(b) an administrator's term of office may be extended for a specified period not exceeding six months by consent.

77.— (1) An order of the court under paragraph 76—

(a) may be made in respect of an administrator whose term of office has already been extended by order or by consent, but

(b) may not be made after the expiry of the administrator's term of office.

(2) Where an order is made under paragraph 76 the administrator shall as soon as is reasonably practicable notify the registrar of companies.

(3) An administrator who fails without reasonable excuse to comply with sub-paragraph (2) commits an offence.

78.— (1) In paragraph 76(2)(b) "consent" means consent of—

(a) each secured creditor of the company, and

(b) if the company has unsecured debts, creditors whose debts amount to more than 50% of the company's unsecured debts, disregarding debts of any creditor who does not respond to an invitation to give or withhold consent.

(2) But where the administrator has made a statement under paragraph 52(1)(b) "consent" means—

(a) consent of each secured creditor of the company, or

(b) if the administrator thinks that a distribution may be made to preferential creditors, consent of—

(i) each secured creditor of the company, and

(ii) preferential creditors whose debts amount to more than 50% of the preferential debts of the company, disregarding debts of any creditor who does not respond to an invitation to give or withhold consent.

(3) Consent for the purposes of paragraph 76(2)(b) may be—

(a) written, or

(b) signified at a creditors' meeting.

(4) An administrator's term of office—

(a) may be extended by consent only once,

(b) may not be extended by consent after extension by order of the court, and

(c) may not be extended by consent after expiry.

(5) Where an administrator's term of office is extended by consent he shall as soon as is reasonably practicable—

(a) file notice of the extension with the court, and

(b) notify the registrar of companies.

(6) An administrator who fails without reasonable excuse to comply with sub-paragraph (5) commits an offence.

Court ending administration on application of administrator

79.— (1) On the application of the administrator of a company the court may provide for the appointment of an administrator of the company to cease to have effect from a specified time.

(2) The administrator of a company shall make an application under this paragraph if—

(a) he thinks the purpose of administration cannot be achieved in relation to the company,

(b)   he thinks the company should not have entered administration, or

(c)   a creditors' meeting requires him to make an application under this paragraph.

(3)   The administrator of a company shall make an application under this paragraph if—

(a)   the administration is pursuant to an administration order, and

(b)   the administrator thinks that the purpose of administration has been sufficiently achieved in relation to the company.

(4)   On an application under this paragraph the court may—

(a)   adjourn the hearing conditionally or unconditionally;

(b)   dismiss the application;

(c)   make an interim order;

(d)   make any order it thinks appropriate (whether in addition to, in consequence of or instead of the order applied for).

Termination of administration where objective achieved

80.—   (1)   This paragraph applies where an administrator of a company is appointed under paragraph 14 or 22.

(2)   If the administrator thinks that the purpose of administration has been sufficiently achieved in relation to the company he may file a notice in the prescribed form—

(a)   with the court, and

(b)   with the registrar of companies.

(3)   The administrator's appointment shall cease to have effect when the requirements of sub-paragraph (2) are satisfied.

(4)   Where the administrator files a notice he shall within the prescribed period send a copy to every creditor of the company of whose claim and address he is aware.

(5)   The rules may provide that the administrator is taken to have complied with sub-paragraph (4) if before the end of the prescribed period he publishes in the prescribed manner a notice undertaking to provide a copy of the notice under sub-paragraph (2) to any creditor of the company who applies in writing to a specified address.

(6)   An administrator who fails without reasonable excuse to comply with sub-paragraph (4) commits an offence.

Court ending administration on application of creditor

81.—   (1)   On the application of a creditor of a company the court may provide for the appointment of an administrator of the company to cease to have effect at a specified time.

(2)   An application under this paragraph must allege an improper motive—

(a)   in the case of an administrator appointed by administration order, on the part of the applicant for the order, or

(b)   in any other case, on the part of the person who appointed the administrator.

(3)   On an application under this paragraph the court may—

(a)   adjourn the hearing conditionally or unconditionally;

(b)   dismiss the application;

(c)   make an interim order;

(d)   make any order it thinks appropriate (whether in addition to, in consequence of or instead of the order applied for).

Public interest winding-up

82.—   (1)   This paragraph applies where a winding-up order is made for the winding up of a company in administration on a petition presented under—

(a)   section 124A (public interest), or

(aa) section 124B (SEs),

(b)   section 367 of the Financial Services and Markets Act 2000 (c 8) (petition by Financial Services Authority).

(2) This paragraph also applies where a provisional liquidator of a company in administration is appointed following the presentation of a petition under any of the provisions listed in sub-paragraph (1).

(3) The court shall order—

(a) that the appointment of the administrator shall cease to have effect, or

(b) that the appointment of the administrator shall continue to have effect.

(4) If the court makes an order under sub-paragraph (3)(b) it may also—

(a) specify which of the powers under this Schedule are to be exercisable by the administrator, and

(b) order that this Schedule shall have effect in relation to the administrator with specified modifications.

Moving from administration to creditors' voluntary liquidation

83.— (1) This paragraph applies in England and Wales where the administrator of a company thinks—

(a) that the total amount which each secured creditor of the company is likely to receive has been paid to him or set aside for him, and

(b) that a distribution will be made to unsecured creditors of the company (if there are any).

(2) This paragraph applies in Scotland where the administrator of a company thinks—

(a) that each secured creditor of the company will receive payment in respect of his debt, and

(b) that a distribution will be made to unsecured creditors (if there are any).

(3) The administrator may send to the registrar of companies a notice that this paragraph applies.

(4) On receipt of a notice under sub-paragraph (3) the registrar shall register it.

(5) If an administrator sends a notice under sub-paragraph (3) he shall as soon as is reasonably practicable—

(a) file a copy of the notice with the court, and

(b) send a copy of the notice to each creditor of whose claim and address he is aware.

(6) On the registration of a notice under sub-paragraph (3)—

(a) the appointment of an administrator in respect of the company shall cease to have effect, and

(b) the company shall be wound up as if a resolution for voluntary winding up under section 84 were passed on the day on which the notice is registered.

(7) The liquidator for the purposes of the winding up shall be—

(a) a person nominated by the creditors of the company in the prescribed manner and within the prescribed period, or

(b) if no person is nominated under paragraph (a), the administrator.

(8) In the application of Part IV to a winding up by virtue of this paragraph—

(a) section 85 shall not apply,

(b) section 86 shall apply as if the reference to the time of the passing of the resolution for voluntary winding up were a reference to the beginning of the date of registration of the notice under sub-paragraph (3),

(c) section 89 does not apply,

(d) sections 98, 99 and 100 shall not apply,

(e) section 129 shall apply as if the reference to the time of the passing of the resolution for voluntary winding up were a reference to the beginning of the date of registration of the notice under sub-paragraph (3), and

(f) any creditors' committee which is in existence immediately before the company ceases to be in administration shall continue in existence after that time as if appointed as a liquidation committee under section 101.

Moving from administration to dissolution

84.— (1) If the administrator of a company thinks that the company has no property which might permit a distribution to its creditors, he shall send a notice to that effect to the registrar of companies.

(2) The court may on the application of the administrator of a company disapply sub-paragraph (1) in respect of the company.

(3) On receipt of a notice under sub-paragraph (1) the registrar shall register it.

(4) On the registration of a notice in respect of a company under sub-paragraph (1) the appointment of an administrator of the company shall cease to have effect.

(5) If an administrator sends a notice under sub-paragraph (1) he shall as soon as is reasonably practicable—

(a) file a copy of the notice with the court, and

(b) send a copy of the notice to each creditor of whose claim and address he is aware.

(6) At the end of the period of three months beginning with the date of registration of a notice in respect of a company under sub-paragraph (1) the company is deemed to be dissolved.

(7) On an application in respect of a company by the administrator or another interested person the court may—

(a) extend the period specified in sub-paragraph (6),

(b) suspend that period, or

(c) disapply sub-paragraph (6).

(8) Where an order is made under sub-paragraph (7) in respect of a company the administrator shall as soon as is reasonably practicable notify the registrar of companies.

(9) An administrator commits an offence if he fails without reasonable excuse to comply with sub-paragraph (5).

Discharge of administration order where administration ends

85.— (1) This paragraph applies where—

(a) the court makes an order under this Schedule providing for the appointment of an administrator of a company to cease to have effect, and

(b) the administrator was appointed by administration order.

(2) The court shall discharge the administration order.

Notice to Companies Registrar where administration ends

86.— (1) This paragraph applies where the court makes an order under this Schedule providing for the appointment of an administrator to cease to have effect.

(2) The administrator shall send a copy of the order to the registrar of companies within the period of 14 days beginning with the date of the order.

(3) An administrator who fails without reasonable excuse to comply with sub-paragraph (2) commits an offence.

REPLACING ADMINISTRATOR

Resignation of administrator

87.— (1) An administrator may resign only in prescribed circumstances.

(2) Where an administrator may resign he may do so only—

(a) in the case of an administrator appointed by administration order, by notice in writing to the court,

(b) in the case of an administrator appointed under paragraph 14, by notice in writing to the holder of the floating charge by virtue of which the appointment was made,

(c) in the case of an administrator appointed under paragraph 22(1), by notice in writing to the company, or

      (d)   in the case of an administrator appointed under paragraph 22(2), by notice in writing to the directors of the company.

Removal of administrator from office

88.   The court may by order remove an administrator from office.

Administrator ceasing to be qualified

89.— (1)   The administrator of a company shall vacate office if he ceases to be qualified to act as an insolvency practitioner in relation to the company.

      (2)   Where an administrator vacates office by virtue of sub-paragraph (1) he shall give notice in writing—

          (a)   in the case of an administrator appointed by administration order, to the court,

          (b)   in the case of an administrator appointed under paragraph 14, to the holder of the floating charge by virtue of which the appointment was made,

          (c)   in the case of an administrator appointed under paragraph 22(1), to the company, or

          (d)   in the case of an administrator appointed under paragraph 22(2), to the directors of the company.

      (3)   An administrator who fails without reasonable excuse to comply with sub-paragraph (2) commits an offence.

Supplying vacancy in office of administrator

90.   Paragraphs 91 to 95 apply where an administrator—

      (a)   dies,

      (b)   resigns,

      (c)   is removed from office under paragraph 88, or

      (d)   vacates office under paragraph 89.

91.— (1)   Where the administrator was appointed by administration order, the court may replace the administrator on an application under this sub-paragraph made by—

          (a)   a creditors' committee of the company,

          (b)   the company,

          (c)   the directors of the company,

          (d)   one or more creditors of the company, or

          (e)   where more than one person was appointed to act jointly or concurrently as the administrator, any of those persons who remains in office.

      (2)   But an application may be made in reliance on sub-paragraph (1)(b) to (d) only where—

          (a)   there is no creditors' committee of the company,

          (b)   the court is satisfied that the creditors' committee or a remaining administrator is not taking reasonable steps to make a replacement, or

          (c)   the court is satisfied that for another reason it is right for the application to be made.

92.   Where the administrator was appointed under paragraph 14 the holder of the floating charge by virtue of which the appointment was made may replace the administrator.

93.— (1)   Where the administrator was appointed under paragraph 22(1) by the company it may replace the administrator.

      (2)   A replacement under this paragraph may be made only—

          (a)   with the consent of each person who is the holder of a qualifying floating charge in respect of the company's property, or

          (b)   where consent is withheld, with the permission of the court.

94.— (1)   Where the administrator was appointed under paragraph 22(2) the directors of the company may replace the administrator.

      (2)   A replacement under this paragraph may be made only—

          (a)   with the consent of each person who is the holder of a qualifying floating charge in respect of the company's property, or

          (b)   where consent is withheld, with the permission of the court.

95. The court may replace an administrator on the application of a person listed in paragraph 91(1) if the court—

(a) is satisfied that a person who is entitled to replace the administrator under any of paragraphs 92 to 94 is not taking reasonable steps to make a replacement, or

(b) that for another reason it is right for the court to make the replacement.

Substitution of administrator: competing floating charge-holder

96.— (1) This paragraph applies where an administrator of a company is appointed under paragraph 14 by the holder of a qualifying floating charge in respect of the company's property.

(2) The holder of a prior qualifying floating charge in respect of the company's property may apply to the court for the administrator to be replaced by an administrator nominated by the holder of the prior floating charge.

(3) One floating charge is prior to another for the purposes of this paragraph if—

(a) it was created first, or

(b) it is to be treated as having priority in accordance with an agreement to which the holder of each floating charge was party.

(4) Sub-paragraph (3) shall have effect in relation to Scotland as if the following were substituted for paragraph (a)—

"(a) it has priority of ranking in accordance with section 464(4)(b) of the Companies Act 1985 (c 6),".

Substitution of administrator appointed by company or directors: creditors' meeting

97.— (1) This paragraph applies where—

(a) an administrator of a company is appointed by a company or directors under paragraph 22, and

(b) there is no holder of a qualifying floating charge in respect of the company's property.

(2) A creditors' meeting may replace the administrator.

(3) A creditors' meeting may act under sub-paragraph (2) only if the new administrator's written consent to act is presented to the meeting before the replacement is made.

Vacation of office: discharge from liability

98.— (1) Where a person ceases to be the administrator of a company (whether because he vacates office by reason of resignation, death or otherwise, because he is removed from office or because his appointment ceases to have effect) he is discharged from liability in respect of any action of his as administrator.

(2) The discharge provided by sub-paragraph (1) takes effect—

(a) in the case of an administrator who dies, on the filing with the court of notice of his death,

(b) in the case of an administrator appointed under paragraph 14 or 22, at a time appointed by resolution of the creditors' committee or, if there is no committee, by resolution of the creditors, or

(c) in any case, at a time specified by the court.

(3) For the purpose of the application of sub-paragraph (2)(b) in a case where the administrator has made a statement under paragraph 52(1)(b), a resolution shall be taken as passed if (and only if) passed with the approval of—

(a) each secured creditor of the company, or

(b) if the administrator has made a distribution to preferential creditors or thinks that a distribution may be made to preferential creditors—

(i) each secured creditor of the company, and

(ii) preferential creditors whose debts amount to more than 50% of the preferential debts of the company, disregarding debts of any creditor who does not respond to an invitation to give or withhold approval.

(4) Discharge—

(a)   applies to liability accrued before the discharge takes effect, and

(b)   does not prevent the exercise of the court's powers under paragraph 75.

Vacation of office: charges and liabilities

99.— (1)   This paragraph applies where a person ceases to be the administrator of a company (whether because he vacates office by reason of resignation, death or otherwise, because he is removed from office or because his appointment ceases to have effect).

(2)   In this paragraph—

"the former administrator" means the person referred to in sub-paragraph (1), and

"cessation" means the time when he ceases to be the company's administrator.

(3)   The former administrator's remuneration and expenses shall be—

(a)   charged on and payable out of property of which he had custody or control immediately before cessation, and

(b)   payable in priority to any security to which paragraph 70 applies.

(4)   A sum payable in respect of a debt or liability arising out of a contract entered into by the former administrator or a predecessor before cessation shall be—

(a)   charged on and payable out of property of which the former administrator had custody or control immediately before cessation, and

(b)   payable in priority to any charge arising under sub-paragraph (3).

(5)   Sub-paragraph (4) shall apply to a liability arising under a contract of employment which was adopted by the former administrator or a predecessor before cessation; and for that purpose—

(a)   action taken within the period of 14 days after an administrator's appointment shall not be taken to amount or contribute to the adoption of a contract,

(b)   no account shall be taken of a liability which arises, or in so far as it arises, by reference to anything which is done or which occurs before the adoption of the contract of employment, and

(c)   no account shall be taken of a liability to make a payment other than wages or salary.

(6)   In sub-paragraph (5)(c) "wages or salary" includes—

(a)   a sum payable in respect of a period of holiday (for which purpose the sum shall be treated as relating to the period by reference to which the entitlement to holiday accrued),

(b)   a sum payable in respect of a period of absence through illness or other good cause,

(c)   a sum payable in lieu of holiday,

(d)   in respect of a period, a sum which would be treated as earnings for that period for the purposes of an enactment about social security, and

(e)   a contribution to an occupational pension scheme.

GENERAL

Joint and concurrent administrators

100.— (1)   In this Schedule—

(a)   a reference to the appointment of an administrator of a company includes a reference to the appointment of a number of persons to act jointly or concurrently as the administrator of a company, and

(b)   a reference to the appointment of a person as administrator of a company includes a reference to the appointment of a person as one of a number of persons to act jointly or concurrently as the administrator of a company.

(2)   The appointment of a number of persons to act as administrator of a company must specify—

(a)   which functions (if any) are to be exercised by the persons appointed acting jointly, and

        (b)   which functions (if any) are to be exercised by any or all of the persons appointed.

101.— (1)   This paragraph applies where two or more persons are appointed to act jointly as the administrator of a company.

      (2)   A reference to the administrator of the company is a reference to those persons acting jointly.

      (3)   But a reference to the administrator of a company in paragraphs 87 to 99 of this Schedule is a reference to any or all of the persons appointed to act jointly.

      (4)   Where an offence of omission is committed by the administrator, each of the persons appointed to act jointly—

         (a)   commits the offence, and

         (b)   may be proceeded against and punished individually.

      (5)   The reference in paragraph 45(1)(a) to the name of the administrator is a reference to the name of each of the persons appointed to act jointly.

      (6)   Where persons are appointed to act jointly in respect of only some of the functions of the administrator of a company, this paragraph applies only in relation to those functions.

102.— (1)   This paragraph applies where two or more persons are appointed to act concurrently as the administrator of a company.

      (2)   A reference to the administrator of a company in this Schedule is a reference to any of the persons appointed (or any combination of them).

103.— (1)   Where a company is in administration, a person may be appointed to act as administrator jointly or concurrently with the person or persons acting as the administrator of the company.

      (2)   Where a company entered administration by administration order, an appointment under sub-paragraph (1) must be made by the court on the application of—

         (a)   a person or group listed in paragraph 12(1)(a) to (e), or

         (b)   the person or persons acting as the administrator of the company.

      (3)   Where a company entered administration by virtue of an appointment under paragraph 14, an appointment under sub-paragraph (1) must be made by—

         (a)   the holder of the floating charge by virtue of which the appointment was made, or

         (b)   the court on the application of the person or persons acting as the administrator of the company.

      (4)   Where a company entered administration by virtue of an appointment under paragraph 22(1), an appointment under sub-paragraph (1) above must be made either by the court on the application of the person or persons acting as the administrator of the company or—

         (a)   by the company, and

         (b)   with the consent of each person who is the holder of a qualifying floating charge in respect of the company's property or, where consent is withheld, with the permission of the court.

      (5)   Where a company entered administration by virtue of an appointment under paragraph 22(2), an appointment under sub-paragraph (1) must be made either by the court on the application of the person or persons acting as the administrator of the company or—

         (a)   by the directors of the company, and

         (b)   with the consent of each person who is the holder of a qualifying floating charge in respect of the company's property or, where consent is withheld, with the permission of the court.

      (6)   An appointment under sub-paragraph (1) may be made only with the consent of the person or persons acting as the administrator of the company.

Presumption of validity

104.   An act of the administrator of a company is valid in spite of a defect in his appointment or qualification.

Majority decision of directors

105.   A reference in this Schedule to something done by the directors of a company includes a reference to the same thing done by a majority of the directors of a company.

Penalties

106.— (1)   A person who is guilty of an offence under this Schedule is liable to a fine (in accordance with section 430 and Schedule 10).

(2)   A person who is guilty of an offence under any of the following paragraphs of this Schedule is liable to a daily default fine (in accordance with section 430 and Schedule 10)—

(a)   paragraph 20,

(b)   paragraph 32,

(c)   paragraph 46,

(d)   paragraph 48,

(e)   paragraph 49,

(f)   paragraph 51,

(g)   paragraph 53,

(h)   paragraph 54,

(i)   paragraph 56,

(j)   paragraph 71,

(k)   paragraph 72,

(l)   paragraph 77,

(m)   paragraph 78,

(n)   paragraph 80,

(o)   paragraph 84,

(p)   paragraph 86, and

(q)   paragraph 89.

Extension of time limit

107.— (1)   Where a provision of this Schedule provides that a period may be varied in accordance with this paragraph, the period may be varied in respect of a company—

(a)   by the court, and

(b)   on the application of the administrator.

(2)   A time period may be extended in respect of a company under this paragraph—

(a)   more than once, and

(b)   after expiry.

108.— (1)   A period specified in paragraph 49(5), 50(1)(b) or 51(2) may be varied in respect of a company by the administrator with consent.

(2)   In sub-paragraph (1) "consent" means consent of—

(a)   each secured creditor of the company, and

(b)   if the company has unsecured debts, creditors whose debts amount to more than 50% of the company's unsecured debts, disregarding debts of any creditor who does not respond to an invitation to give or withhold consent.

(3)   But where the administrator has made a statement under paragraph 52(1)(b) "consent" means—

(a)   consent of each secured creditor of the company, or

(b)   if the administrator thinks that a distribution may be made to preferential creditors, consent of—

(i)   each secured creditor of the company, and

(ii)   preferential creditors whose debts amount to more than 50% of the total preferential debts of the company, disregarding debts of any creditor who does not respond to an invitation to give or withhold consent.

(4)   Consent for the purposes of sub-paragraph (1) may be—

(a)   written, or

(b)   signified at a creditors' meeting.

(5)   The power to extend under sub-paragraph (1)—

    (a)   may be exercised in respect of a period only once,

    (b)   may not be used to extend a period by more than 28 days,

    (c)   may not be used to extend a period which has been extended by the court, and

    (d)   may not be used to extend a period after expiry.

109.   Where a period is extended under paragraph 107 or 108, a reference to the period shall be taken as a reference to the period as extended.

Amendment of provision about time

110.— (1)   The Secretary of State may by order amend a provision of this Schedule which—

    (a)   requires anything to be done within a specified period of time,

    (b)   prevents anything from being done after a specified time, or

    (c)   requires a specified minimum period of notice to be given.

(2)   An order under this paragraph—

    (a)   must be made by statutory instrument, and

    (b)   shall be subject to annulment in pursuance of a resolution of either House of Parliament.

Interpretation

111.— (1)   In this Schedule—

"administrative receiver" has the meaning given by section 251,

"administrator" has the meaning given by paragraph 1 and, where the context requires, includes a reference to a former administrator,

"company" includes a company which may enter administration by virtue of Article 3 of the EC Regulation,

"correspondence" includes correspondence by telephonic or other electronic means,

"creditors' meeting" has the meaning given by paragraph 50,

"enters administration" has the meaning given by paragraph 1,

"floating charge" means a charge which is a floating charge on its creation,

"in administration" has the meaning given by paragraph 1,

"hire-purchase agreement" includes a conditional sale agreement, a chattel leasing agreement and a retention of title agreement,

"holder of a qualifying floating charge" in respect of a company's property has the meaning given by paragraph 14,

"market value" means the amount which would be realised on a sale of property in the open market by a willing vendor,

"the purpose of administration" means an objective specified in paragraph 3, and

"unable to pay its debts" has the meaning given by section 123.

(2)   A reference in this Schedule to a thing in writing includes a reference to a thing in electronic form.

(3)   In this Schedule a reference to action includes a reference to inaction.

Scotland

112.   In the application of this Schedule to Scotland—

    (a)   a reference to filing with the court is a reference to lodging in court, and

    (b)   a reference to a charge is a reference to a right in security.

113.   Where property in Scotland is disposed of under paragraph 70 or 71, the administrator shall grant to the disponee an appropriate document of transfer or conveyance of the property, and—

    (a)   that document, or

    (b)   recording, intimation or registration of that document (where recording, intimation or registration of the document is a legal requirement for completion of title to the property), has the effect of disencumbering the property of or, as the case may be, freeing the property from, the security.

114. In Scotland, where goods in the possession of a company under a hire-purchase agreement are disposed of under paragraph 72, the disposal has the effect of extinguishing as against the disponee all rights of the owner of the goods under the agreement.

115.— (1) In Scotland, the administrator of a company may make, in or towards the satisfaction of the debt secured by the floating charge, a payment to the holder of a floating charge which has attached to the property subject to the charge.

(2) In Scotland, where the administrator thinks that the company has insufficient property to enable a distribution to be made to unsecured creditors other than by virtue of section 176A(2)(a), he may file a notice to that effect with the registrar of companies.

(3) On delivery of the notice to the registrar of companies, any floating charge granted by the company shall, unless it has already so attached, attach to the property which is subject to the charge and that attachment shall have effect as if each floating charge is a fixed security over the property to which it has attached.

116. In Scotland, the administrator in making any payment in accordance with paragraph 115 shall make such payment subject to the rights of any of the following categories of persons (which rights shall, except to the extent provided in any instrument, have the following order of priority)—

(a) the holder of any fixed security which is over property subject to the floating charge and which ranks prior to, or pari passu with, the floating charge,

(b) creditors in respect of all liabilities and expenses incurred by or on behalf of the administrator,

(c) the administrator in respect of his liabilities, expenses and remuneration and any indemnity to which he is entitled out of the property of the company,

(d) the preferential creditors entitled to payment in accordance with paragraph 65,

(e) the holder of the floating charge in accordance with the priority of that charge in relation to any other floating charge which has attached, and

(f) the holder of a fixed security, other than one referred to in paragraph (a), which is over property subject to the floating charge.

Note. The italicized words in paragraph 12(1)(d) are substituted by the subsequent words in square brackets by the Courts Act 2003, s. 109(1), Sch. 8, para. 299, as from a day to be appointed.

SCHEDULE 1

POWERS OF ADMINISTRATOR OR ADMINISTRATIVE RECEIVER

Sections 14, 42

1. Power to take possession of, collect and get in the property of the company and, for that purpose, to take such proceedings as may seem to him expedient.

2. Power to sell or otherwise dispose of the property of the company by public auction or private contract or, in Scotland, to sell, ... hire out or otherwise dispose of the property of the company by public roup or private bargain.

3. Power to raise or borrow money and grant security therefor over the property of the company.

4. Power to appoint a solicitor or accountant or other professionally qualified person to assist him in the performance of his functions.

5. Power to bring or defend any action or other legal proceedings in the name and on behalf of the company.

6. Power to refer to arbitration any question affecting the company.

7. Power to effect and maintain insurances in respect of the business and property of the company.

8. Power to use the company's seal.

9.   Power to do all acts and to execute in the name and on behalf of the company any deed, receipt or other document.

10.   Power to draw, accept, make and endorse any bill of exchange or promissory note in the name and on behalf of the company.

11.   Power to appoint any agent to do any business which he is unable to do himself or which can more conveniently be done by an agent and power to employ and dismiss employees.

12.   Power to do all such things (including the carrying out of works) as may be necessary for the realisation of the property of the company.

13.   Power to make any payment which is necessary or incidental to the performance of his functions.

14.   Power to carry on the business of the company.

15.   Power to establish subsidiaries of the company.

16.   Power to transfer to subsidiaries of the company the whole or any part of the business and property of the company.

17.   Power to grant or accept a surrender of a lease or tenancy of any of the property of the company, and to take a lease or tenancy of any property required or convenient for the business of the company.

18.   Power to make any arrangement or compromise on behalf of the company.

19.   Power to call up any uncalled capital of the company.

20.   Power to rank and claim in the bankruptcy, insolvency, sequestration or liquidation of any person indebted to the company and to receive dividends, and to accede to trust deeds for the creditors of any such person.

21.   Power to present or defend a petition for the winding up of the company.

22.   Power to change the situation of the company's registered office.

23.   Power to do all other things incidental to the exercise of the foregoing powers.

SCHEDULE 2

POWERS OF A SCOTTISH RECEIVER (ADDITIONAL TO THOSE CONFERRED ON HIM BY THE INSTRUMENT OF CHARGE)

Section 55

1.   Power to take possession of, collect and get in the property from the company or a liquidator thereof or any other person, and for that purpose, to take such proceedings as may seem to him expedient.

2.   Power to sell, . . . hire out or otherwise dispose of the property by public roup or private bargain and with or without advertisement.

3.   Power to raise or borrow money and grant security therefor over the property.

4.   Power to appoint a solicitor or accountant or other professionally qualified person to assist him in the performance of his functions.

5.   Power to bring or defend any action or other legal proceedings in the name and on behalf of the company.

6.   Power to refer to arbitration all questions affecting the company.

7.   Power to effect and maintain insurances in respect of the business and property of the company.

8.   Power to use the company's seal.

9.   Power to do all acts and to execute in the name and on behalf of the company any deed, receipt or other document.

10.   Power to draw, accept, make and endorse any bill of exchange or promissory note in the name and on behalf of the company.

11.   Power to appoint any agent to do any business which he is unable to do himself or which can more conveniently be done by an agent, and power to employ and dismiss employees.

12.   Power to do all such things (including the carrying out of works), as may be necessary for the realisation of the property.

13. Power to make any payment which is necessary or incidental to the performance of his functions.

14. Power to carry on the business of the company or any part of it.

15. Power to grant or accept a surrender of a lease or tenancy of any of the property, and to take a lease or tenancy of any property required or convenient for the business of the company.

16. Power to make any arrangement or compromise on behalf of the company.

17. Power to call up any uncalled capital of the company.

18. Power to establish subsidiaries of the company.

19. Power to transfer to subsidiaries of the company the business of the company or any part of it and any of the property.

20. Power to rank and claim in the bankruptcy, insolvency, sequestration or liquidation of any person or company indebted to the company and to receive dividends, and to accede to trust deeds for creditors of any such person.

21. Power to present or defend a petition for the winding up of the company.

22. Power to change the situation of the company's registered office.

23. Power to do all other things incidental to the exercise of the powers mentioned in section 55(1) of this Act or above in this Schedule.

SCHEDULE 2A

EXCEPTIONS TO PROHIBITION ON APPOINTMENT OF ADMINISTRATIVE RECEIVER: SUPPLEMENTARY PROVISIONS

Section 72H(1)

Capital market arrangement

1.— (1) For the purposes of section 72B an arrangement is a capital market arrangement if—

    (a) it involves a grant of security to a person holding it as trustee for a person who holds a capital market investment issued by a party to the arrangement, or

    (aa) it involves a grant of security to—

        (i) a party to the arrangement who issues a capital market investment, or

        (ii) a person who holds the security as trustee for a party to the arrangement in connection with the issue of a capital market investment, or

    (ab) it involves a grant of security to a person who holds the security as trustee for a party to the arrangement who agrees to provide finance to another party, or

    (b) at least one party guarantees the performance of obligations of another party, or

    (c) at least one party provides security in respect of the performance of obligations of another party, or

    (d) the arrangement involves an investment of a kind described in articles 83 to 85 of the Financial Services and Markets Act 2000 (Regulated Activities) Order 2001 (SI 2001/544) (options, futures and contracts for differences).

  (2) For the purposes of sub-paragraph (1)—

    (a) a reference to holding as trustee includes a reference to holding as nominee or agent,

    (b) a reference to holding for a person who holds a capital market investment includes a reference to holding for a number of persons at least one of whom holds a capital market investment, and

    (c) a person holds a capital market investment if he has a legal or beneficial interest in it, and

    (d) the reference to the provision of finance includes the provision of an indemnity.

  (3) In section 72B(1) and this paragraph "party" to an arrangement includes a party to an agreement which—

    (a) forms part of the arrangement,

    (b) provides for the raising of finance as part of the arrangement, or

    (c) is necessary for the purposes of implementing the arrangement.

Capital market investment

2.—   (1)   For the purposes of section 72B an investment is a capital market investment if it—
            (a)   is within article 77 of the Financial Services and Markets Act 2000 (Regulated Activities) Order 2001 (SI 2001/544) (debt instruments), and
            (b)   is rated, listed or traded or designed to be rated, listed or traded.

         (2)   In sub-paragraph (1)—
            "rated" means rated for the purposes of investment by an internationally recognised rating agency,
            "listed" means admitted to the official list within the meaning given by section 103(1) of the Financial Services and Markets Act 2000 (c 8) (interpretation), and
            "traded" means admitted to trading on a market established under the rules of a recognised investment exchange or on a foreign market.

         (3)   In sub-paragraph (2)—
            "recognised investment exchange" has the meaning given by section 285 of the Financial Services and Markets Act 2000 (recognised investment exchange), and
            "foreign market" has the same meaning as "relevant market" in article 67(2) of the Financial Services and Markets Act 2000 (Financial Promotion) Order 2001 (SI 2001/1335) (foreign markets).

3.—   (1)   An investment is also a capital market investment for the purposes of section 72B if it consists of a bond or commercial paper issued to one or more of the following—
            (a)   an investment professional within the meaning of article 19(5) of the Financial Services and Markets Act 2000 (Financial Promotion) Order 2001,
            (b)   a person who is, when the agreement mentioned in section 72B(1) is entered into, a certified high net worth individual in relation to a communication within the meaning of article 48(2) of that order,
            (c)   a person to whom article 49(2) of that order applies (high net worth company, &c),
            (d)   a person who is, when the agreement mentioned in section 72B(1) is entered into, a certified sophisticated investor in relation to a communication within the meaning of article 50(1) of that order, and
            (e)   a person in a State other than the United Kingdom who under the law of that State is not prohibited from investing in bonds or commercial paper.

         (2)   In sub-paragraph (1)—
            "bond" shall be construed in accordance with article 77 of the Financial Services and Markets Act 2000 (Regulated Activities) Order 2001 (SI 2001/544), and
            "commercial paper" has the meaning given by article 9(3) of that order.

         (3)   For the purposes of sub-paragraph (1)—
            (a)   in applying article 19(5) of the Financial Promotion Order for the purposes of sub-paragraph (1)(a)—
                (i)   in article 19(5)(b), ignore the words after "exempt person",
                (ii)   in article 19(5)(c)(i), for the words from "the controlled activity" to the end substitute "a controlled activity", and
                (iii)   in article 19(5)(e) ignore the words from "where the communication" to the end, and
            (b)   in applying article 49(2) of that order for the purposes of sub-paragraph (1)(c), ignore article 49(2)(e).

"Agreement"

4.   For the purposes of sections 72B and 72E and this Schedule "agreement" includes an agreement or undertaking effected by—
            (a)   contract,
            (b)   deed, or

(c) any other instrument intended to have effect in accordance with the law of England and Wales, Scotland or another jurisdiction.

Debt

5. The debt of at least £50 million referred to in section 72B(1)(a) or 72E(2)(a)—

    (a) may be incurred at any time during the life of the capital market arrangement or financed project, and

    (b) may be expressed wholly or partly in foreign currency (in which case the sterling equivalent shall be calculated as at the time when the arrangement is entered into or the project begins).

Step-in rights

6.— (1) For the purposes of sections 72C to 72E a project has "step-in rights" if a person who provides finance in connection with the project has a conditional entitlement under an agreement to—

    (a) assume sole or principal responsibility under an agreement for carrying out all or part of the project, or

    (b) make arrangements for carrying out all or part of the project.

(2) In sub-paragraph (1) a reference to the provision of finance includes a reference to the provision of an indemnity.

Project company

7.— (1) For the purposes of sections 72C to 72E a company is a "project company" of a project if—

    (a) it holds property for the purpose of the project,

    (b) it has sole or principal responsibility under an agreement for carrying out all or part of the project,

    (c) it is one of a number of companies which together carry out the project,

    (d) it has the purpose of supplying finance to enable the project to be carried out, or

    (e) it is the holding company of a company within any of paragraphs (a) to (d).

(2) But a company is not a "project company" of a project if—

    (a) it performs a function within sub-paragraph (1)(a) to (d) or is within sub-paragraph (1)(e), but

    (b) it also performs a function which is not—

        (i) within sub-paragraph (1)(a) to (d),

        (ii) related to a function within sub-paragraph (1)(a) to (d), or

        (iii) related to the project.

(3) For the purposes of this paragraph a company carries out all or part of a project whether or not it acts wholly or partly through agents.

"Resources"

8. In section 72C "resources" includes—

    (a) funds (including payment for the provision of services or facilities),

    (b) assets,

    (c) professional skill,

    (d) the grant of a concession or franchise, and

    (e) any other commercial resource.

"Public body"

9.— (1) In section 72C "public body" means—

    (a) a body which exercises public functions,

    (b) a body specified for the purposes of this paragraph by the Secretary of State, and

    (c) a body within a class specified for the purposes of this paragraph by the Secretary of State.

(2) A specification under sub-paragraph (1) may be—

(a)   general, or

(b)   for the purpose of the application of section 72C to a specified case.

Regulated business

10.—   (1)   For the purposes of section 72D a business is regulated if it is carried on—

(a)   *in reliance on a licence granted to a person under section 7 of the Telecommunications Act 1984 (c 12) (telecommunications service),*

(b)   in reliance on a licence under section 7 or 7A of the Gas Act 1986 (c 44) (transport and supply of gas),

(c)   in reliance on a licence granted by virtue of section 41C of that Act (power to prescribe additional licensable activity),

(d)   in reliance on a licence under section 6 of the Electricity Act 1989 (c 29) (supply of electricity),

(e)   by a water undertaker,

(f)   by a sewerage undertaker,

(g)   by a universal service provider within the meaning given by section 4(3) and (4) of the Postal Services Act 2000 (c 26),

(h)   by the Post Office company within the meaning given by section 62 of that Act (transfer of property),

(i)   by a relevant subsidiary of the Post Office Company within the meaning given by section 63 of that Act (government holding),

(j)   in reliance on a licence under section 8 of the Railways Act 1993 (c 43) (railway services),

(k)   in reliance on a licence exemption under section 7 of that Act (subject to sub-paragraph (2) below),

(l)   by the operator of a system of transport which is deemed to be a railway for a purpose of Part I of that Act by virtue of section 81(2) of that Act (tramways, &c), or

(m)   by the operator of a vehicle carried on flanged wheels along a system within paragraph (l).

(2)   Sub-paragraph (1)(k) does not apply to the operator of a railway asset on a railway unless on some part of the railway there is a permitted line speed exceeding 40 kilometres per hour.

(2A)   *For the purposes of section 72D a business is also regulated to the extent that it consists in the provision of a public electronic communications network or a public electronic communications service.*

"Person"

11.   A reference to a person in this Schedule includes a reference to a partnership or another unincorporated group of persons.

Note. Paragraph 10(1)(a) is repealed and paragraph 10(2A) is inserted by the Communications Act 2003, s. 406(1), (7), Sch. 17, para. 82(1), (4), Sch. 19(1), as from a day to be appointed.

SCHEDULE 3

ORDERS IN COURSE OF WINDING UP PRONOUNCED INVACATION (SCOTLAND)

Section 162

PART I
ORDERS WHICH ARE TO BE FINAL

Orders under section 153, as to the time for proving debts and claims.

Orders under section 195 as to meetings for ascertaining wishes of creditors or contributories.

Orders under section 198, as to the examination of witnesses in regard to the property or affairs of a company.

PART II
ORDERS WHICH ARE TO TAKE EFFECT UNTIL MATTER
DISPOSED OF BY INNER HOUSE

Orders under section 126(1), 130(2) or (3), 147, 227 or 228, restraining or permitting the commencement or the continuance of legal proceedings.

Orders under section 135(5), limiting the powers of provisional liquidators.

Orders under section 108, appointing a liquidator to fill a vacancy.

Orders under section 167 or 169, sanctioning the exercise of any powers by a liquidator, other than the powers specified in paragraphs 1, 2 and 3 of Schedule 4 to this Act.

Orders under section 158, as to the arrest and detention of an absconding contributory and his property.

SCHEDULE 4

POWERS OF LIQUIDATOR IN A WINDING UP

Sections 165, 167

PART I
POWERS EXERCISABLE WITH SANCTION

1. Power to pay any class of creditors in full.

2. Power to make any compromise or arrangement with creditors or persons claiming to be creditors, or having or alleging themselves to have any claim (present or future, certain or contingent, ascertained or sounding only in damages) against the company, or whereby the company may be rendered liable.

3. Power to compromise, on such terms as may be agreed—

    (a) all calls and liabilities to calls, all debts and liabilities capable of resulting in debts, and all claims (present or future, certain or contingent, ascertained or sounding only in damages) subsisting or supposed to subsist between the company and a contributory or alleged contributory or other debtor or person apprehending liability to the company, and

    (b) all questions in any way relating to or affecting the assets or the winding up of the company, and take any security for the discharge of any such call, debt, liability or claim and give a complete discharge in respect of it.

3A. Power to bring legal proceedings under section 213, 214, 238, 239, 242, 243 or 423.

PART II
POWERS EXERCISABLE WITHOUT SANCTION IN VOLUNTARY WINDING UP, WITH
SANCTION IN WINDING UP BY THE COURT

4. Power to bring or defend any action or other legal proceeding in the name and on behalf of the company.

5. Power to carry on the business of the company so far as may be necessary for its beneficial winding up.

PART III
POWERS EXERCISABLE WITHOUT
SANCTION IN ANY WINDING UP

6. Power to sell any of the company's property by public auction or private contract with power to transfer the whole of it to any person or to sell the same in parcels.

7. Power to do all acts and execute, in the name and on behalf of the company, all deeds, receipts and other documents and for that purpose to use, when necessary, the company's seal.

8.   Power to prove, rank and claim in the bankruptcy, insolvency or sequestration of any contributory for any balance against his estate, and to receive dividends in the bankruptcy, insolvency or sequestration in respect of that balance, as a separate debt due from the bankrupt or insolvent, and rateably with the other separate creditors.

9.   Power to draw, accept, make and indorse any bill of exchange or promissory note in the name and on behalf of the company, with the same effect with respect to the company's liability as if the bill or note had been drawn, accepted, made or indorsed by or on behalf of the company in the course of its business.

10.   Power to raise on the security of the assets of the company any money requisite.

11.   Power to take out in his official name letters of administration to any deceased contributory, and to do in his official name any other act necessary for obtaining payment of any money due from a contributory or his estate which cannot conveniently be done in the name of the company.

        In all such cases the money due is deemed, for the purpose of enabling the liquidator to take out the letters of administration or recover the money, to be due to the liquidator himself.

12.   Power to appoint an agent to do any business which the liquidator is unable to do himself.

13.   Power to do all such other things as may be necessary for winding up the company's affairs and distributing its assets.

SCHEDULE 4A

BANKRUPTCY RESTRICTIONS ORDER AND UNDERTAKING

Section 281A

Bankruptcy restrictions order

1.—   (1)   A bankruptcy restrictions order may be made by the court.

        (2)   An order may be made only on the application of—

              (a)   the Secretary of State, or

              (b)   the official receiver acting on a direction of the Secretary of State.

Grounds for making order

2.—   (1)   The court shall grant an application for a bankruptcy restrictions order if it thinks it appropriate having regard to the conduct of the bankrupt (whether before or after the making of the bankruptcy order).

        (2)   The court shall, in particular, take into account any of the following kinds of behaviour on the part of the bankrupt—

              (a)   failing to keep records which account for a loss of property by the bankrupt, or by a business carried on by him, where the loss occurred in the period beginning 2 years before petition and ending with the date of the application;

              (b)   failing to produce records of that kind on demand by the official receiver or the trustee;

              (c)   entering into a transaction at an undervalue;

              (d)   giving a preference;

              (e)   making an excessive pension contribution;

              (f)   a failure to supply goods or services which were wholly or partly paid for which gave rise to a claim provable in the bankruptcy;

              (g)   trading at a time before commencement of the bankruptcy when the bankrupt knew or ought to have known that he was himself to be unable to pay his debts;

              (h)   incurring, before commencement of the bankruptcy, a debt which the bankrupt had no reasonable expectation of being able to pay;

              (i)   failing to account satisfactorily to the court, the official receiver or the trustee for a loss of property or for an insufficiency of property to meet bankruptcy debts;

        (j)   carrying on any gambling, rash and hazardous speculation or unreasonable extrava-
gance which may have materially contributed to or increased the extent of the bankruptcy or which took place between presentation of the petition and commencement of
the bankruptcy;

        (k)   neglect of business affairs of a kind which may have materially contributed to or
increased the extent of the bankruptcy;

        (l)   fraud or fraudulent breach of trust;

        (m) failing to cooperate with the official receiver or the trustee.

  (3)   The court shall also, in particular, consider whether the bankrupt was an undischarged
bankrupt at some time during the period of six years ending with the date of the bankruptcy
to which the application relates.

  (4)   For the purpose of sub-paragraph (2)—

        "before petition" shall be construed in accordance with section 351(c),

        "excessive pension contribution" shall be construed in accordance with section 342A,

        "preference" shall be construed in accordance with section 340, and

        "undervalue" shall be construed in accordance with section 339.

Timing of application for order

3.— (1)   An application for a bankruptcy restrictions order in respect of a bankrupt must be made—

        (a)   before the end of the period of one year beginning with the date on which the bank-
ruptcy commences, or

        (b)   with the permission of the court.

  (2)   The period specified in sub-paragraph (1)(a) shall cease to run in respect of a bankrupt while
the period set for his discharge is suspended under section 279(3).

Duration of order

4.— (1)   A bankruptcy restrictions order—

        (a)   shall come into force when it is made, and

        (b)   shall cease to have effect at the end of a date specified in the order.

  (2)   The date specified in a bankruptcy restrictions order under sub-paragraph (1)(b) must not
be—

        (a)   before the end of the period of two years beginning with the date on which the order is
made, or

        (b)   after the end of the period of 15 years beginning with that date.

Interim bankruptcy restrictions order

5.— (1)   This paragraph applies at any time between—

        (a)   the institution of an application for a bankruptcy restrictions order, and

        (b)   the determination of the application.

  (2)   The court may make an interim bankruptcy restrictions order if the court thinks that—

        (a)   there are prima facie grounds to suggest that the application for the bankruptcy restric-
tions order will be successful, and

        (b)   it is in the public interest to make an interim order.

  (3)   An interim order may be made only on the application of—

        (a)   the Secretary of State, or

        (b)   the official receiver acting on a direction of the Secretary of State.

  (4)   An interim order—

        (a)   shall have the same effect as a bankruptcy restrictions order, and

        (b)   shall come into force when it is made.

  (5)   An interim order shall cease to have effect—

        (a)   on the determination of the application for the bankruptcy restrictions order,

        (b)   on the acceptance of a bankruptcy restrictions undertaking made by the bankrupt, or

(c)   if the court discharges the interim order on the application of the person who applied for it or of the bankrupt.

6.—   (1)   This paragraph applies to a case in which both an interim bankruptcy restrictions order and a bankruptcy restrictions order are made.

     (2)   Paragraph 4(2) shall have effect in relation to the bankruptcy restrictions order as if a reference to the date of that order were a reference to the date of the interim order.

Bankruptcy restrictions undertaking

7.—   (1)   A bankrupt may offer a bankruptcy restrictions undertaking to the Secretary of State.

     (2)   In determining whether to accept a bankruptcy restrictions undertaking the Secretary of State shall have regard to the matters specified in paragraph 2(2) and (3).

8.   A reference in an enactment to a person in respect of whom a bankruptcy restrictions order has effect (or who is "the subject of" a bankruptcy restrictions order) includes a reference to a person in respect of whom a bankruptcy restrictions undertaking has effect.

9.—   (1)   A bankruptcy restrictions undertaking—

        (a)   shall come into force on being accepted by the Secretary of State, and

        (b)   shall cease to have effect at the end of a date specified in the undertaking.

     (2)   The date specified under sub-paragraph (1)(b) must not be—

        (a)   before the end of the period of two years beginning with the date on which the under-taking is accepted, or

        (b)   after the end of the period of 15 years beginning with that date.

     (3)   On an application by the bankrupt the court may—

        (a)   annul a bankruptcy restrictions undertaking;

        (b)   provide for a bankruptcy restrictions undertaking to cease to have effect before the date specified under sub-paragraph (1)(b).

Effect of annulment of bankruptcy order

10.   Where a bankruptcy order is annulled under section 282(1)(a) or (2)—

        (a)   any bankruptcy restrictions order, interim order or undertaking which is in force in respect of the bankrupt shall be annulled,

        (b)   no new bankruptcy restrictions order or interim order may be made in respect of the bankrupt, and

        (c)   no new bankruptcy restrictions undertaking by the bankrupt may be accepted.

11.   Where a bankruptcy order is annulled under section 261, 263D or 282(1)(b)—

        (a)   the annulment shall not affect any bankruptcy restrictions order, interim order or undertaking in respect of the bankrupt,

        (b)   the court may make a bankruptcy restrictions order in relation to the bankrupt on an application instituted before the annulment,

        (c)   the Secretary of State may accept a bankruptcy restrictions undertaking offered before the annulment, and

        (d)   an application for a bankruptcy restrictions order or interim order in respect of the bankrupt may not be instituted after the annulment.

Registration

12.   The Secretary of State shall maintain a register of—

        (a)   bankruptcy restrictions orders,

        (b)   interim bankruptcy restrictions orders, and

        (c)   bankruptcy restrictions undertakings.

SCHEDULE 5

POWERS OF TRUSTEE IN BANKRUPTCY

Section 314

PART I
POWERS EXERCISABLE WITH SANCTION

1. Power to carry on any business of the bankrupt so far as may be necessary for winding it up beneficially and so far as the trustee is able to do so without contravening any requirement imposed by or under any enactment.

2. Power to bring, institute or defend any action or legal proceedings relating to the property comprised in the bankrupt's estate.

2A. Power to bring legal proceedings under section 339, 340 or 423.

3. Power to accept as the consideration for the sale of any property comprised in the bankrupt's estate a sum of money payable at a future time subject to such stipulations as to security or otherwise as the creditors' committee or the court thinks fit.

4. Power to mortgage or pledge any part of the property comprised in the bankrupt's estate for the purpose of raising money for the payment of his debts.

5. Power, where any right, option or other power forms part of the bankrupt's estate, to make payments or incur liabilities with a view to obtaining, for the benefit of the creditors, any property which is the subject of the right, option or power.

6. Power to refer to arbitration, or compromise on such terms as may be agreed on, any debts, claims or liabilities subsisting or supposed to subsist between the bankrupt and any person who may have incurred any liability to the bankrupt.

7. Power to make such compromise or other arrangement as may be thought expedient with creditors, or persons claiming to be creditors, in respect of bankruptcy debts.

8. Power to make such compromise or other arrangement as may be thought expedient with respect to any claim arising out of or incidental to the bankrupt's estate made or capable of being made on the trustee by any person or by the trustee on any person.

PART II
GENERAL POWERS

9. Power to sell any part of the property for the time being comprised in the bankrupt's estate, including the goodwill and book debts of any business.

10. Power to give receipts for any money received by him, being receipts which effectually discharge the person paying the money from all responsibility in respect of its application.

11. Power to prove, rank, claim and draw a dividend in respect of such debts due to the bankrupt as are comprised in his estate.

12. Power to exercise in relation to any property comprised in the bankrupt's estate any powers the capacity to exercise which is vested in him under Parts VIII to XI of this Act.

13. Power to deal with any property comprised in the estate to which the bankrupt is beneficially entitled as tenant in tail in the same manner as the bankrupt might have dealt with it.

PART III
ANCILLARY POWERS

14. For the purposes of, or in connection with, the exercise of any of his powers under Parts VIII to XI of this Act, the trustee may, by his official name—
    (a) hold property of every description,
    (b) make contracts,
    (c) sue and be sued,
    (d) enter into engagements binding on himself and, in respect of the bankrupt's estate, on his successors in office,
    (e) employ an agent,
    (f) execute any power of attorney, deed or other instrument;

and he may do any other act which is necessary or expedient for the purposes of or in connection with the exercise of those powers.

SCHEDULE 6

THE CATEGORIES OF PREFERENTIAL DEBTS

Section 386

1–7. ....

Category 4:
Contributions to occupational pension schemes, etc

8.   Any sum which is owed by the debtor and is a sum to which Schedule 4 to the Pension Schemes Act 1993 applies (contributions to occupational pension schemes and state scheme premiums).

Category 5:
Remuneration, etc, of employees

9.   So much of any amount which—
    (a)   is owed by the debtor to a person who is or has been an employee of the debtor, and
    (b)   is payable by way of remuneration in respect of the whole or any part of the period of 4 months next before the relevant date,
as does not exceed so much as may be prescribed by order made by the Secretary of State.

10.   An amount owed by way of accrued holiday remuneration, in respect of any period of employment before the relevant date, to a person whose employment by the debtor has been terminated, whether before, on or after that date.

11.   So much of any sum owed in respect of money advanced for the purpose as has been applied for the payment of a debt which, if it had not been paid, would have been a debt falling within paragraph 9 or 10.

12.   So much of any amount which—
    (a)   is ordered (whether before or after the relevant date) to be paid by the debtor under the Reserve Forces (Safeguard of Employment) Act 1985, and
    (b)   is so ordered in respect of a default made by the debtor before that date in the discharge of his obligations under that Act,
as does no exceed such amount as may be prescribed by order made by the Secretary of State.

Interpretation for Category 5

13.—   (1)   For the purposes of paragraphs 9 to 12, a sum is payable by the debtor to a person by way of remuneration in respect of any period if—
    (a)   it is paid as wages or salary (whether payable for time or for piece work or earned wholly or partly by way of commission) in respect of services rendered to the debtor in that period, or
    (b)   it is an amount falling within the following sub-paragraph and is payable by the debtor in respect of that period.

    (2)   An amount falls within this sub-paragraph if it is—
    (a)   a guarantee payment under Part III of the Employment Rights Act 1996 (employee without work to do);
    (b)   any payment for time off under section 53 (time off to look for work or arrange training) or section 56 (time off for ante-natal care) of that Act or under section 169 of the Trade Union and Labour Relations (Consolidation) Act 1992 (time off for carrying out trade union duties etc);
    (c)   remuneration on suspension on medical grounds, or on maternity grounds, under Part VII of the Employment Rights Act 1996; or

      (d)   remuneration under a protective award under section 189 of the Trade Union and Labour Relations (Consolidation) Act 1992 (redundancy dismissal with compensation).

14.— (1)   This paragraph relates to a case in which a person's employment has been terminated by or in consequence of his employer going into liquidation or being adjudged bankrupt or (his employer being a company not in liquidation) by or in consequence of—

      (a)   a receiver being appointed as mentioned in section 40 of this Act (debenture-holders secured by floating charge), or

      (b)   the appointment of a receiver under section 53(6) or 54(5) of this Act (Scottish company with property subject to floating charge), or

      (c)   the taking of possession by debenture-holders (so secured), as mentioned in section 196 of the Companies Act.

     (2)   For the purposes of paragraphs 9 to 12, holiday remuneration is deemed to have accrued to that person in respect of any period of employment if, by virtue of his contract of employment or of any enactment that remuneration would have accrued in respect of that period if his employment had continued until he became entitled to be allowed the holiday.

     (3)   The reference in sub-paragraph (2) to any enactment includes an order or direction made under an enactment.

15.   Without prejudice to paragraphs 13 and 14—

      (a)   any remuneration payable by the debtor to a person in respect of a period of holiday or of absence from work through sickness or other good cause is deemed to be wages or (as the case may be) salary in respect of services rendered to the debtor in that period, and

      (b)   references here and in those paragraphs to remuneration in respect of a period of holiday include any sums which, if they had been paid, would have been treated for the purposes of the enactments to social security as earnings in respect of that period.

Category 6:
Levies on coal and steel production

15A.   Any sums due at the relevant date from the debtor in respect of—

      (a)   the levies on the production of coal and steel referred to in Articles 49 and 50 of the E.C.S.C. Treaty, or

      (b)   any surcharge for delay provided for in Article 50(3) of that Treaty and Article 6 of Decision 3/52 of the High Authority of the Coal and Steel Community.

Orders

16.   An order under paragraph 9 or 12—

      (a)   may contain such transitional provisions as may appear to the Secretary of State necessary or expedient;

      (b)   shall be made by statutory instrument subject to annulment in pursuance of a resolution of either House of Parliament.

SCHEDULE 7

INSOLVENCY PRACTITIONERS TRIBUNAL

Section 396

Panels of members

1.— (1)   The Secretary of State shall draw up and from time to time revise—

      (a)   a panel of persons who

         (i)   have a 7 year general qualification, within the meaning of section 71 of the Courts and Legal Services Act 1990;

        (ii)   are advocates or solicitors in Scotland of at least 7 years' standing, and are nominated for the purpose by the Lord Chancellor or the Lord President of the Court of Session, and

    (b)   a panel of persons who are experienced in insolvency matters;

and the members of the Tribunal shall be selected from those panels in accordance with this Schedule.

  (2)   The power to revise the panels includes power to terminate a person's membership of either of them, and is accordingly to that extent subject to section 7 of the Tribunals and Inquiries Act 1992 (which makes it necessary to obtain the concurrence of the Lord Chancellor and the Lord President of the Court of Session to dismissals in certain cases).

Remuneration of members

2.   The Secretary of State may out of money provided by Parliament pay to members of the Tribunal such remuneration as he may with the approval of the Treasury determine; and such expenses of the Tribunal as the Secretary of State and the Treasury may approve shall be defrayed by the Secretary of State out of money so provided.

Sittings of Tribunal

3.— (1)   For the purposes of carrying out their functions in relation to any cases referred to them, the Tribunal may sit either as a single tribunal or in two or more divisions.

  (2)   The functions of the Tribunal in relation to any case referred to them shall be exercised by three members consisting of—

    (a)   a chairman selected by the Secretary of State from the panel drawn up under paragraph 1(1)(a) above, and

    (b)   two other members selected by the Secretary of State from the panel drawn up under paragraph 1(1)(b).

Procedure of Tribunal

4.— (1)   Any investigation by the Tribunal shall be so conducted as to afford a reasonable opportunity for representations to be made to the Tribunal by or on behalf of the person whose case is the subject of the investigation.

  (2)   For the purposes of any such investigation, the Tribunal—

    (a)   may by summons require any person to attend, at such time and place as is specified in the summons, to give evidence or to produce any books, papers and other records in his possession or under his control which the Tribunal consider it necessary for the purposes of the investigation to examine, and

    (b)   may take evidence on oath, and for the purpose administer oaths, or may, instead of administering an oath, require the person examined to make and subscribe a declaration of the truth of the matter respecting which he is examined;

but no person shall be required, in obedience to such a summons, to go more than ten miles from his place of residence, unless the necessary expenses of his attendance are paid or tendered to him.

  (3)   Every person who—

    (a)   without reasonable excuse fails to attend in obedience to a summons issued under this paragraph, or refuses to give evidence, or

    (b)   intentionally alters, suppresses, conceals or destroys or refuses to produce any document which he may be required to produce for the purpose of an investigation by the Tribunal,

is liable to a fine.

  (4)   Subject to the provisions of this paragraph, the Secretary of State may make rules for regulating the procedure on any investigation by the Tribunal.

  (5)   In their application to Scotland, sub-paragraphs (2) and (3) above have effect as if for any reference to a summons there were substituted a reference to a notice in writing.

SCHEDULE 8

PROVISIONS CAPABLE OF INCLUSION IN COMPANY INSOLVENCY RULES

Section 411

Courts

1. Provision for supplementing, in relation to the insolvency or winding up of companies, any provision made by or under section 117 of this Act (jurisdiction in relation to winding up).

2.— (1) Provision for regulating the practice and procedure of any court exercising jurisdiction for the purposes of Parts I to VII of this Act or the Companies Act so far as relating to, and to matters connected with or arising out of, the insolvency or winding up of companies, being any provision that could be made by rules of court.

   (2) Rules made by virtue of this paragraph about the consequence of failure to comply with practice or procedure may, in particular, include provision about the termination of administration.

Notices, etc

3. Provision requiring notice of any proceedings in connection with or arising out of the insolvency or winding up of a company to be given or published in the manner prescribed by the rules.

4. Provision with respect to the form, manner of serving, contents and proof of any petition, application, order, notice, statement or other document required to be presented, made, given, published or prepared under any enactment or subordinate legislation relating to, or to matters connected with or arising out of, the insolvency or winding up of companies.

5. Provisions specifying the persons to whom any notice is to be given.

Registration of voluntary arrangements

6. Provision for the registration of voluntary arrangements approved under Part I of this Act, including provision for the keeping and inspection of a register.

Provisional liquidator

7. Provision as to the manner in which a provisional liquidator appointed under section 135 is to carry out his functions.

Conduct of insolvency

8. Provision with respect to the certification of any person as, and as to the proof that a person is, the liquidator, administrator or administrative receiver of a company.

9. The following provision with respect to meetings of a company's creditors, contributories or members—

   (a) provision as to the manner of summoning a meeting (including provision as to how any power to require a meeting is to be exercised, provision as to the manner of determining the value of any debt or contribution for the purposes of any such power and provision making the exercise of any such power subject to the deposit of a sum sufficient to cover the expenses likely to be incurred in summoning and holding a meeting);

   (b) provision specifying the time and place at which a meeting may be held and the period of notice required for a meeting;

   (c) provision as to the procedure to be followed at a meeting (including the manner in which decisions may be reached by a meeting and the manner in which the value of any vote at a meeting is to be determined);

   (d) provision for requiring a person who is or has been an officer of the company to attend a meeting;

   (e) provision creating, in the prescribed circumstances, a presumption that a meeting has been duly summoned and held;

   (f) provision as to the manner of proving the decisions of a meeting.

10.   (1)   Provision as to the functions, membership and proceedings of a committee established under section 49, 68, 101, 141 or 142 of, or paragraph 57 of Schedule B1 to, this Act.

      (2)   The following provision with respect to the establishment of a committee under section 101, 141 or 142 of this Act, that is to say—

         (a)   provision for resolving differences between a meeting of the company's creditors and a meeting of its contributories or members;

         (b)   provision authorising the establishment of the committee without a meeting of contributories in a case where a company is being wound up on grounds including its inability to pay its debts; and

         (c)   provision modifying the requirements of this Act with respect to the establishment of the committee in a case where a winding-up order has been made immediately upon the discharge of an administration order.

11.   Provision as to the manner in which any requirement that may be imposed on a person under any of Parts I to VII of this Act by the official receiver, the liquidator, administrator or administrative receiver of a company or a special manager appointed under section 177 is to be so imposed.

12.   Provision as to the debts that may be proved in a winding up, as to the manner and conditions of proving a debt and as to the manner and expenses of establishing the value of any debt or security.

13.   Provision with respect to the manner of the distribution of the property of a company that is being wound up, including provision with respect to unclaimed funds and dividends.

14.   Provision which, with or without modifications, applies in relation to the winding up of companies any enactment contained in Parts VIII to XI of this Act or in the Bankruptcy (Scotland) Act 1985.

14A.   Provision about the application of section 176A of this Act which may include, in particular—

      (a)   provision enabling a receiver to institute winding up proceedings;

      (b)   provision requiring a receiver to institute winding up proceedings.

Administration

14B.   Provision which—

      (a)   applies in relation to administration, with or without modifications, a provision of Parts IV to VII of this Act, or

      (b)   serves a purpose in relation to administration similar to a purpose that may be served by the rules in relation to winding up by virtue of a provision of this Schedule.

Financial provisions

15.   Provision as to the amount, or manner of determining the amount, payable to the liquidator, administrator or administrative receiver of a company or a special manager appointed under section 177, by way of remuneration for the carrying out of functions in connection with or arising out of the insolvency or winding up of a company.

16.   Provision with respect to the manner in which moneys received by the liquidator of a company in the course of carrying out his functions as such are to be invested or otherwise handled and with respect to the payment of interest on sums which, in pursuance of rules made by virtue of this paragraph, have been paid into the Insolvency Services Account.

16A.   Provision enabling the Secretary of State to set the rate of interest paid on sums which have been paid into the Insolvency Services Account.

17.   Provision as to the fees, costs, charges and other expenses that may be treated as the expenses of a winding up.

18.   Provision as to the fees, costs, charges and other expenses that may be treated as properly incurred by the administrator or administrative receiver of a company.

19.   Provision as to the fees, costs, charges and other expenses that may be incurred for any of the purposes of Part I of this Act or in the administration of any voluntary arrangement approved under that Part.

Information and records

20.   Provision requiring registrars and other officers of courts having jurisdiction in England and Wales in relation to, or to matters connected with or arising out of, the insolvency or winding up of companies—

    (a)   to keep books and other records with respect to the exercise of that jurisdiction, and

    (b)   to make returns to the Secretary of State of the business of those courts.

21.   Provision requiring a creditor, member or contributory, or such a committee as is mentioned in paragraph 10 above, to be supplied (on payment in prescribed cases of the prescribed fee) with such information and with copies of such documents as may be prescribed.

22.   Provision as to the manner in which public examinations under sections 133 and 134 of this Act and proceedings under sections 236 and 237 are to be conducted, as to the circumstances in which records of such examinations or proceedings are to be made available to prescribed persons and as to the costs of such examinations and proceedings.

23.   Provision imposing requirements with respect to—

    (a)   the preparation and keeping by the liquidator, administrator or administrative receiver of a company, or by the supervisor of a voluntary arrangement approved under Part I of this Act, of prescribed books, accounts and other records;

    (b)   the production of those books, accounts and records for inspection by prescribed persons;

    (c)   the auditing of accounts kept by the liquidator, administrator or administrative receiver of a company, or the supervisor of such a voluntary arrangement; and

    (d)   the issue by the administrator or administrative receiver of a company of such a certificate as is mentioned in section 22(3)(b) of the Value Added Tax Act 1983 (refund of tax in cases of bad debts) and the supply of copies of the certificate to creditors of the company.

24.   Provision requiring the person who is the supervisor of a voluntary arrangement approved under Part I, when it appears to him that the voluntary arrangement has been fully implemented and that nothing remains to be done by him under the arrangement—

    (a)   to give notice of that fact to persons bound by the voluntary arrangement, and

    (b)   to report to those persons on the carrying out of the functions conferred on the supervisor of the arrangement.

25.   Provision as to the manner in which the liquidator of a company is to act in relation to the books, papers and other records of the company, including provision authorising their disposal.

26.   Provision imposing requirements in connection with the carrying out of functions under section 7(3) of the Company Directors Disqualification Act 1986 (including, in particular, requirements with respect to the making of periodic returns).

General

27.   Provision conferring power on the Secretary of State to make regulations with respect to so much of any matter that may be provided for in the rules as relates to the carrying out of the functions of the liquidator, administrator or administrative receiver of a company.

28.   Provision conferring a discretion on the court.

29.   Provision conferring power on the court to make orders for the purpose of securing compliance with obligations imposed by or under section 47, 66, 131, 143(2) or 235 of, or paragraph 47 of Schedule B1 to, this Act or section 7(4) of the Company Directors Disqualification Act 1986.

30.   Provision making non-compliance with any of the rules a criminal offence.

31.   Provision making different provision for different cases or descriptions of cases, including different provisions for different areas.

SCHEDULE 9

PROVISIONS CAPABLE OF INCLUSION IN INDIVIDUAL INSOLVENCY RULES

Section 412

Courts

1. Provision with respect to the arrangement and disposition of the business under Parts VIII to XI of this Act of courts having jurisdiction for the purpose of those Parts, including provision for the allocation of proceedings under those Parts to particular courts and for the transfer of such proceedings from one court to another.

2. Provision for enabling a registrar in bankruptcy of the High Court or a registrar of a county court having jurisdiction for the purposes of those Parts to exercise such of the jurisdiction conferred for those purposes on the High Court or, as the case may be, that county court as may be prescribed.

3. Provision for regulating the practice and procedure of any court exercising jurisdiction for the purposes of those Parts, being any provision that could be made by rules of court.

4. Provision conferring rights of audience, in courts exercising jurisdiction for the purposes of those Parts, on the official receiver and on solicitors.

Notices, etc

5. Provision requiring notice of any proceedings under Parts VIII to XI of this Act or of any matter relating to or arising out of a proposal under Part VIII or a bankruptcy to be given or published in the prescribed manner.

6. Provision with respect to the form, manner of serving, contents and proof of any petition, application, order, notice, statement or other document required to be presented, made, given, published or prepared under any enactment contained in Parts VIII to XI or subordinate legislation under those Parts or Part XV (including provision requiring prescribed matters to be verified by affidavit).

7. Provision specifying the persons to whom any notice under Parts VIII to XI is to be given.

Registration of voluntary arrangements

8. Provision for the registration of voluntary arrangements approved under Part VIII of this Act, including provision for the keeping and inspection of a register.

Official receiver acting on voluntary arrangement

8A. Provision about the official receiver acting as nominee or supervisor in relation to a voluntary arrangement under Part VIII of this Act, including—
    (a) provision requiring the official receiver to act in specified circumstances;
    (b) provision about remuneration;
    (c) provision prescribing terms or conditions to be treated as forming part of a voluntary arrangement in relation to which the official receiver acts as nominee or supervisor;
    (d) provision enabling those terms or conditions to be varied or excluded, in specified circumstances or subject to specified conditions, by express provision in an arrangement.

Interim receiver

9. Provision as to the manner in which an interim receiver appointed under section 286 is to carry out his functions, including any such provision as is specified in relation to the trustee of a bankrupt's estate in paragraph 21 or 27 below.

Receiver or manager

10. Provision as to the manner in which the official receiver is to carry out his functions as receiver or manager of a bankrupt's estate under section 287, including any such provision as is specified in relation to the trustee of a bankrupt's estate in paragraph 21 or 27 below.

Administration of individual insolvency

11. Provision with respect to the certification of the appointment of any person as trustee of a bankrupt's estate and as to the proof of that appointment.

12. The following provision with respect to meetings of creditors—

(a) provision as to the manner of summoning a meeting (including provision as to how any power to require a meeting is to be exercised, provision as to the manner of determining the value of any debt for the purposes of any such power and provision making the exercise of any such power subject to the deposit of a sum sufficient to cover the expenses likely to be incurred in summoning and holding a meeting);

(b) provision specifying the time and place at which a meeting may be held and the period of notice required for a meeting;

(c) provision as to the procedure to be followed at such a meeting (including the manner in which decisions may be reached by a meeting and the manner in which the value of any vote at a meeting is to be determined);

(d) provision for requiring a bankrupt or debtor to attend a meeting;

(e) provision creating, in the prescribed circumstances, a presumption that a meeting has been duly summoned and held; and

(f) provision as to the manner of proving the decisions of a meeting.

13. Provision as to the functions, membership and proceedings of a creditors' committee established under section 301.

14. Provision as to the manner in which any requirement that may be imposed on a person under Parts VIII to XI of this Act by the official receiver, the trustee of a bankrupt's estate or a special manager appointed under section 370 is to be so imposed and, in the case of any requirement imposed under section 305(3) (information etc to be given by the trustee to the official receiver), provision conferring power on the court to make orders for the purpose of securing compliance with that requirement.

15. Provision as to the manner in which any requirement imposed by virtue of section 310(3) (compliance with income payments order) is to take effect.

16. Provision as to the terms and conditions that may be included in a charge under section 313 (dwelling house forming part of bankrupt's estate).

17. Provision as to the debts that may be proved in any bankruptcy, as to the manner and conditions of proving a debt and as to the manner and expenses of establishing the value of any debt or security.

18. Provision with respect to the manner of the distribution of a bankrupt's estate, including provision with respect to unclaimed funds and dividends.

19. Provision modifying the application of Parts VIII to XI of this Act in relation to a debtor or bankrupt who has died.

Financial provisions

20. Provision as to the amount, or manner of determining the amount, payable to an interim receiver, the trustee of a bankrupt's estate or a special manager appointed under section 370 by way of remuneration for the performance of functions in connection with or arising out of the bankruptcy of any person.

21. Provision with respect to the manner in which moneys received by the trustee of a bankrupt's estate in the course of carrying out his functions as such are to be invested or otherwise handled and with respect to the payment of interest on sums which, in pursuance of rules made by virtue of this paragraph, have been paid into the Insolvency Services Account.

21A. Provision enabling the Secretary of State to set the rate of interest paid on sums which have been paid into the Insolvency Services Account.

22. Provision as to the fees, costs, charges and other expenses that may be treated as the expenses of a bankruptcy.

23. Provision as to the fees, costs, charges and other expenses that may be incurred for any of the purposes of Part VIII of this Act or in the administration of any voluntary arrangement approved under that Part.

Information and records

24.   Provision requiring registrars and other officers of courts having jurisdiction for the purposes of Parts VIII to XI—

    (a)   to keep books and other records with respect to the exercise of that jurisdiction and of jurisdiction under the Deeds of Arrangement Act 1914, and

    (b)   to make returns to the Secretary of State of the business of those courts.

25.   Provision requiring a creditor or a committee established under section 301 to be supplied (on payment in prescribed cases of the prescribed fee) with such information and with copies of such documents as may be prescribed.

26.   Provision as to the manner in which public examinations under section 290 and proceedings under sections 366 to 368 are to be conducted, as to the circumstances in which records of such examinations and proceedings are to be made available to prescribed persons and as to the costs of such examinations and proceedings.

27.   Provision imposing requirements with respect to—

    (a)   the preparation and keeping by the trustee of a bankrupt's estate, or the supervisor of a voluntary arrangement approved under Part VIII, of prescribed books, accounts and other records;

    (b)   the production of those books, accounts and records for inspection by prescribed persons; and

    (c)   the auditing of accounts kept by the trustee of a bankrupt's estate or the supervisor of such a voluntary arrangement.

28.   Provision requiring the person who is the supervisor of a voluntary arrangement approved under Part VIII, when it appears to him that the voluntary arrangement has been fully implemented and that nothing remains to be done by him under it—

    (a)   to give notice of that fact to persons bound by the voluntary arrangement, and

    (b)   to report to those persons on the carrying out of the functions conferred on the supervisor of it.

29.   Provision as to the manner in which the trustee of a bankrupt's estate is to act in relation to the books, papers and other records of the bankrupt, including provision authorising their disposal.

Bankruptcy restrictions orders and undertakings

29A. Provision about bankruptcy restrictions orders, interim orders and undertakings, including—

    (a)   provision about evidence;

    (b)   provision enabling the amalgamation of the register mentioned in paragraph 12 of Schedule 4A with another register;

    (c)   provision enabling inspection of that register by the public.

General

30.   Provision conferring power on the Secretary of State to make regulations with respect to so much of any matter that may be provided for in the rules as relates to the carrying out of the functions of an interim receiver appointed under section 286, of the official receiver while acting as a receiver or manager under section 287 or of a trustee of a bankrupt's estate.

31.   Provision conferring a discretion on the court.

32.   Provision making non-compliance with any of the rules a criminal offence.

33.   Provision making different provision for different cases, including different provision for different areas.

SCHEDULE 10

PUNISHMENT OF OFFENCES UNDER THIS ACT

Section 430

Section of Act creating offence	General nature of offence	Mode of prosecution	Punishment	Daily default fine (where applicable)
6A(1)	False representation or fraud for purpose of obtaining members' or creditors' approval of proposed voluntary arrangement.	1. On indictment	7 years or a fine, or both.	
		2. Summary	6 months or the statutory maximum, or both.	
		...		
30	Body corporate acting as receiver.	1. On indictment	A fine.	
		2. Summary	The statutory maximum.	
31	... bankrupt acting as receiver or manager.	1. On indictment	2 years or a fine, or both.	
		2. Summary	6 months or the statutory maximum, or both.	
38(5)	Receiver failing to deliver accounts to registrar.	Summary	One-fifth of the statutory maximum.	One-fiftieth of the statutory maximum.
39(2)	Company and others failing to state in correspondence that receiver appointed.	Summary	One-fifth of the statutory maximum.	
43(6)	Administrative receiver failing to file office copy of order permitting disposal of charged property.	Summary	One-fifth of the statutory maximum.	One-fiftieth of the statutory maximum.
45(5)	Administrative receiver failing to file notice of vacation of office.	Summary	One-fifth of the statutory maximum.	*One-fiftieth of the statutory maximum.*
46(4)	Administrative receiver failing to give notice of his appointment.	Summary	One-fifth of the statutory maximum.	One-fiftieth of the statutory maximum.

Section of Act creating offence	General nature of offence	Mode of prosecution	Punishment	Daily default fine (where applicable)
47(6)	Failure to comply with provisions relating to statement of affairs, where administrative receiver appointed.	1. On indictment	A fine.	
		2. Summary	The statutory maximum.	One-tenth of the statutory maximum.
48(8)	Administrative receiver failing to comply with requirements as to his report.	Summary	One-fifth of the statutory maximum.	One-fiftieth of the statutory maximum.
51(4)	Body corporate or Scottish firm acting as receiver.	1. On indictment	A fine.	
		2. Summary	The statutory maximum.	
51(5)	Undischarged bankrupt acting as receiver (Scotland).	1. On indictment	2 years or a fine, or both.	
		2. Summary	6 months or the statutory maximum, or both.	
53(2)	Failing to deliver to registrar copy of instrument of appointment of receiver.	Summary	One-fifth of the statutory maximum.	*One-fiftieth of the statutory maximum.*
54(3)	Failing to deliver to registrar the court's interlocutor appointing receiver.	Summary	One-fifth of the statutory maximum.	*One-fiftieth of the statutory maximum.*
61(7)	Receiver failing to send to registrar certified copy of court order authorising disposal of charged property.	Summary	One-fifth of the statutory maximum.	One-fiftieth of the statutory maximum.
62(5)	Failing to give notice to registrar of cessation or removal of receiver.	Summary	One-fifth of the statutory maximum.	*One-fiftieth of the statutory maximum.*
64(2)	Company and others failing to state on correspondence etc that receiver appointed.	Summary	One-fifth of the statutory maximum.	

Section of Act creating offence	General nature of offence	Mode of prosecution	Punishment	Daily default fine (where applicable)
65(4)	Receiver failing to send or publish notice of his appointment.	Summary	One-fifth of the statutory maximum.	One-fiftieth of the statutory maximum.
66(6)	Failing to comply with provisions concerning statement of affairs, where receiver appointed.	1. On indictment	A fine.	
		2. Summary	The statutory maximum.	One-tenth of the statutory maximum.
67(8)	Receiver failing to comply with requirements as to his report.	Summary	One-fifth of the statutory maximum.	One-fiftieth of the statutory maximum.
85(2)	Company failing to give notice in Gazette of resolution for voluntary winding up.	Summary	One-fifth of the statutory maximum.	One-fiftieth of the statutory maximum.
89(4)	Director making statutory declaration of company's solvency without reasonable grounds for his opinion.	1. On indictment	2 years or a fine, or both.	
		2. Summary	6 months or the statutory maximum, or both.	
89(6)	Declaration under section 89 not delivered to registrar within prescribed time.	Summary	One-fifth of the statutory maximum.	One-fiftieth of the statutory maximum.
93(3)	Liquidator failing to summon general meeting of company at each year's end.	Summary	One-fifth of the statutory maximum.	
94(4)	Liquidator failing to send to registrar a copy of account of winding up and return of final meeting.	Summary	One-fifth of the statutory maximum.	One-fiftieth of the statutory maximum.
94(6)	Liquidator failing to call final meeting.	Summary	One-fifth of the statutory maximum.	

Section of Act creating offence	General nature of offence	Mode of prosecution	Punishment	Daily default fine (where applicable)
95(8)	Liquidator failing to comply with s 95, where company insolvent.	Summary	The statutory maximum.	
98(6)	Company failing to comply with s. 98 in respect of summoning and giving notice of creditors' meeting.	1. On indictment	A fine.	
		2. Summary	The statutory maximum.	
99(3)	Directors failing to attend and lay statement in prescribed form before creditors' meeting.	1. On indictment	A fine.	
		2. Summary	The statutory maximum.	
105(3)	Liquidator failing to summon company general meeting and creditors' meeting at each year's end.	Summary	One-fifth of the statutory maximum.	
106(4)	Liquidator failing to send to registrar account of winding up and return of final meetings.	Summary	One-fifth of the statutory maximum.	One-fiftieth of the statutory maximum.
106(6)	Liquidator failing to call final meeting of company or creditors.	Summary	One-fifth of the statutory maximum.	
109(2)	Liquidator failing to publish notice of his appointment.	Summary	One-fifth of the statutory maximum.	One-fiftieth of the statutory maximum.
114(4)	Directors exercising powers in breach of s 114, where no liquidator.	Summary	The statutory maximum.	
131(7)	Failing to comply with requirements as to statement of affairs, where liquidator appointed.	1. On indictment	A fine.	
		2. Summary	The statutory maximum.	One-tenth of the statutory maximum.

Section of Act creating offence	General nature of offence	Mode of prosecution	Punishment	Daily default fine (where applicable)
164	Giving, offering etc corrupt inducement affecting appointment of liquidator.	1. On indictment	A fine.	
		2. Summary	The statutory maximum.	
166(7)	Liquidator failing to comply with requirements of s 166 in creditors' voluntary winding up.	Summary	The statutory maximum.	
188(2)	Default in compliance with s 188 as to notification that company being wound up.	Summary	One-fifth of the statutory maximum.	
192(2)	Liquidator failing to notify registrar as to progress of winding up.	Summary	One-fifth of the statutory maximum.	One-fiftieth of the statutory maximum.
201(4)	Failing to deliver to registrar office copy of court order deferring dissolution.	Summary	One-fifth of the statutory maximum.	One-fiftieth of the statutory maximum.
203(6)	Failing to deliver to registrar copy of directions or result of appeal under s 203.	Summary	One-fifth of the statutory maximum.	One-fiftieth of the statutory maximum.
204(7)	Liquidator failing to deliver to registrar copy of court order for early dissolution.	Summary	One-fifth of the statutory maximum.	One-fiftieth of the statutory maximum.
204(8)	Failing to deliver to registrar copy of court order deferring early dissolution.	Summary	One-fifth of the statutory maximum.	One-fiftieth of the statutory maximum.
205(7)	Failing to deliver to registrar copy of Secretary of State's directions or court order deferring dissolution.	Summary	One-fifth of the statutory maximum.	One-fiftieth of the statutory maximum.
206(1)	Fraud etc in anticipation of winding up.	1. On indictment	7 years or a fine, or both.	
		2. Summary	6 months or the statutory maximum, or both.	

Section of Act creating offence	General nature of offence	Mode of prosecution	Punishment	Daily default fine (where applicable)
206(2)	Privity to fraud in anticipation of winding up; fraud, or privity to fraud, after commencement of winding up.	1. On indictment	7 years or a fine, or both.	
		2. Summary	6 months or the statutory maximum, or both.	
206(5)	Knowingly taking in pawn or pledge, or otherwise receiving, company property.	1. On indictment	7 years or a fine, or both.	
		2. Summary	6 months or the statutory maximum, or both.	
207	Officer of company entering into transaction in fraud of company's creditors.	1. On indictment	2 years or a fine, or both.	
		2. Summary	6 months or the statutory maximum, or both.	
208	Officer of company misconducting himself in course of winding up.	1. On indictment	7 years or a fine, or both.	
		2. Summary	6 months or the statutory maximum, or both.	
209	Officer or contributory destroying, falsifying, etc company's books.	1. On indictment	7 years or a fine, or both.	
		2. Summary	6 months or the statutory maximum, or both.	
210	Officer of company making material omission from statement relating to company's affairs.	1. On indictment	7 years or a fine, or both.	

Section of Act creating offence	General nature of offence	Mode of prosecution	Punishment	Daily default fine (where applicable)
		2. Summary	6 months or the statutory maximum, or both.	
211	False representation or fraud for purpose of obtaining creditors' consent to an agreement in connection with winding up.	1. On indictment	7 years or a fine, or both.	
		2. Summary	6 months or the statutory maximum, or both.	
216(4)	Contravening restrictions on re-use of name of company in insolvent liquidation.	1. On indictment	2 years or a fine, or both.	
		2. Summary	6 months or the statutory maximum, or both.	
235(5)	Failing to co-operate with office-holder.	1. On indictment.	A fine.	
		2. Summary	The statutory maximum.	One-tenth of the statutory maximum.
262A(1)	False representation or fraud for purpose of obtaining creditors' approval of proposed voluntary arrangement.	1. On indictment	7 years or a fine, or both.	
		2. Summary	6 months or the statutory maximum, or both.	
353(1)	Bankrupt failing to disclose property or disposals to official receiver or trustee.	1. On indictment	7 years or a fine, or both.	
		2. Summary	6 months or the statutory maximum, or both.	

Section of Act creating offence	General nature of offence	Mode of prosecution	Punishment	Daily default fine (where applicable)
354(1)	Bankrupt failing to deliver property to, or concealing property from, official receiver or trustee.	1. On indictment	7 years or a fine, or both.	
		2. Summary	6 months or the statutory maximum, or both.	
354(2)	Bankrupt removing property which he is required to deliver to official receiver or trustee.	1. On indictment	7 years or a fine, or both.	
		2. Summary	6 months or the statutory maximum, or both.	
354(3)	Bankrupt failing to account for loss of substantial part of property.	1. On indictment	2 years or a fine, or both.	
		2. Summary	6 months or the statutory maximum, or both.	
355(1)	Bankrupt failing to deliver books, papers and records to official receiver or trustee.	1. On indictment	7 years or a fine, or both.	
		2. Summary	6 months or the statutory maximum, or both.	
355(2)	Bankrupt concealing, destroying etc books, papers or records, or making false entries in them.	1. On indictment	7 years or a fine, or both.	
		2. Summary	6 months or the statutory maximum, or both.	
355(3)	Bankrupt disposing of, or altering, books, papers or records relating to his estate or affairs.	1. On indictment	7 years or a fine, or both.	

Section of Act creating offence	General nature of offence	Mode of prosecution	Punishment	Daily default fine (where applicable)
		2. Summary	6 months or the statutory maximum, or both.	
356(1)	Bankrupt making material omission in statement relating to his affairs.	1. On indictment	7 years or a fine, or both.	
		2. Summary	6 months or the statutory maximum, or both.	
356(2)	Bankrupt making false statement, or failing to inform trustee, where false debt proved.	1. On indictment	7 years or a fine, or both.	
		2. Summary	6 months or the statutory maximum, or both.	
357	Bankrupt fraudulently disposing of property.	1. On indictment	2 years or a fine, or both.	
		2. Summary	6 months or the statutory maximum, or both.	
358	Bankrupt absconding with property he is required to deliver to official receiver or trustee.	1. On indictment	2 years or a fine, or both.	
		2. Summary	6 months or the statutory maximum, or both.	
359(1)	Bankrupt disposing of property obtained on credit and not paid for.	1. On indictment	7 years or a fine, or both.	
		2. Summary	6 months or the statutory maximum, or both.	
359(2)	Obtaining property in respect of which money is owed by a bankrupt.	1. On indictment	7 years or a fine, or both.	

Section of Act creating offence	General nature of offence	Mode of prosecution	Punishment	Daily default fine (where applicable)
		2. Summary	6 months or the statutory maximum, or both.	
360(1)	Bankrupt obtaining credit or engaging in business without disclosing his status or name in which he was made bankrupt.	1. On indictment	2 years or a fine, or both.	
		2. Summary	6 months or the statutory maximum, or both.	
360(3)	Person made bankrupt in Scotland or Northern Ireland obtaining credit, etc in England and Wales.	1. On indictment	2 years or a fine, or both.	
		2. Summary	6 months or the statutory maximum, or both.	
		…		
389	Acting as insolvency practitioner when not qualified.	1. On indictment	2 years or a fine, or both.	
		2. Summary	6 months or the statutory maximum or both.	
429(5)	Contravening s 429 in respect of disabilities imposed by county court on revocation of administration order.	1. On indictment	2 years or a fine, or both.	
		2. Summary	6 months or the statutory maximum, or both.	
Sch A1, para 9(2)	Directors failing to notify nominee of beginning of moratorium.	1. On indictment	2 years or a fine, or both.	

Section of Act creating offence	General nature of offence	Mode of prosecution	Punishment	Daily default fine (where applicable)
		2. Summary	6 months or the statutory maximum, or both.	
Sch A1, para 10(3)	Nominee failing to advertise or notify beginning of moratorium.	Summary	One-fifth of the statutory maximum.	
Sch A1, para 11(2)	Nominee failing to advertise or notify end of moratorium.	Summary	One-fifth of the statutory maximum.	
Sch A1, para 16(2)	Company and officers failing to state in correspondence etc that moratorium in force.	Summary	One-fifth of the statutory maximum.	
Sch A1, para 17(3)(a)	Company obtaining credit without disclosing existence of moratorium.	1. On indictment	A fine.	
		2. Summary	The statutory maximum.	
Sch A1, para 17(3)(b)	Obtaining credit for company without disclosing existence of moratorium.	1. On indictment	2 years or a fine, or both.	
		2. Summary	6 months or the statutory maximum, or both.	
Sch A1, para 18(3)(a)	Company disposing of property otherwise than in ordinary way of business.	1. On indictment	A fine.	
		2. Summary	The statutory maximum.	
Sch A1, para 18(3)(b)	Authorising or permitting disposal of company property.	1. On indictment	2 years or a fine, or both.	
		2. Summary	6 months or the statutory maximum, or both.	
Sch A1, para 19(3)(a)	Company making payments in respect of liabilities existing before beginning of moratorium.	1. On indictment	A fine.	

Section of Act creating offence	General nature of offence	Mode of prosecution	Punishment	Daily default fine (where applicable)
Sch A1, para 19(3)(b)	Authorising or permitting such a payment.	2. Summary	The statutory maximum.	
		1. On indictment	2 years or a fine, or both.	
		2. Summary	6 months or the statutory maximum, or both.	
Sch A1, para. 20(9)	Directors failing to send to registrar office copy of court order permitting disposal of charged property.	Summary	One-fifth of the statutory maximum.	
Sch A1, para 22(1)	Company disposing of charged property.	1. On indictment	A fine.	
		2. Summary	The statutory maximum.	
Sch A1, para 22(2)	Authorising or permitting such a disposal.	1. On indictment	2 years or a fine, or both.	
		2. Summary	6 months or the statutory maximum, or both.	
Sch A1, para 23(1)(a)	Company entering into market contract, etc.	1. On indictment	A fine.	
		2. Summary	The statutory maximum.	
Sch A1, para 23(1)(b)	Authorising or permitting company to do so.	1. On indictment	2 years or a fine, or both.	
		2. Summary	6 months or the statutory maximum, or both.	
Sch A1, para 25(6)	Nominee failing to give notice of withdrawal of consent to act.	Summary	One-fifth of the statutory maximum.	
Sch A1, para 34(3)	Nominee failing to give notice of extension of moratorium.	Summary	One-fifth of the statutory maximum.	

Section of Act creating offence	General nature of offence	Mode of prosecution	Punishment	Daily default fine (where applicable)
Sch A1, para 41(2)	Fraud or privity to fraud in anticipation of moratorium.	1. On indictment	7 years or a fine, or both.	
		2. Summary	6 months or the statutory maximum, or both.	
Sch A1, para 41(3)	Fraud or privity to fraud during moratorium.	1. On indictment	7 years or a fine, or both.	
		2. Summary	6 months or the statutory maximum, or both.	
Sch A1, para 41(7)	Knowingly taking in pawn or pledge, or otherwise receiving, company property.	1. On indictment	7 years or a fine, or both.	
		2. Summary	6 months or the statutory maximum, or both.	
Sch A1, para 42(1)	False representation or fraud for purpose of obtaining or extending moratorium.	1. On indictment	7 years or a fine, or both.	
		2. Summary	6 months or the statutory maximum, or both.	
Sch B1, para 18(7)	Making false statement in statutory declaration where administrator appointed by holder of floating charge.	1. On indictment	2 years, or a fine or both.	
		2. Summary	6 months, or the statutory maximum or both.	
Sch B1, para 20	Holder of floating charge failing to notify administrator or others of commencement of appointment.	1. On indictment	2 years, or a fine or both.	
		2. Summary	6 months, or the statutory maximum or both.	One-tenth of the statutory maximum.

Section of Act creating offence	General nature of offence	Mode of prosecution	Punishment	Daily default fine (where applicable)
Sch B1, para 27(4)	Making false statement in statutory declaration where appointment of administrator proposed by company or directors.	1. On indictment	2 years, or a fine or both.	
		2. Summary	6 months, or the statutory maximum or both.	
Sch B1, para 29(7)	Making false statement in statutory declaration where administrator appointed by company or directors.	1. On indictment	2 years, or a fine or both.	
		2. Summary	6 months, or the statutory maximum or both.	
Sch B1, para 32	Company or directors failing to notify administrator or others of commencement of appointment.	1. On indictment	2 years, or a fine or both.	One-tenth of the statutory maximum.
		2. Summary	6 months, or the statutory maximum or both.	
Sch B1, para 45(2)	Administrator, company or officer failing to state in business document that administrator appointed.	Summary	One-fifth of the statutory maximum.	
Sch B1, para 46(9)	Administrator failing to give notice of his appointment.	Summary	One-fifth of the statutory maximum.	One-fiftieth of the statutory maximum.
Sch B1, para 48(4)	Failing to comply with provisions about statement of affairs where administrator appointed.	1. On indictment	A fine.	
		2. Summary	The statutory maximum.	One-tenth of the statutory maximum.
Sch B1, para 49(7)	Administrator failing to send out statement of his proposals.	Summary	One-fifth of the statutory maximum.	One-fiftieth of the statutory maximum.
Sch B1, para 51(5)	Administrator failing to arrange initial creditors' meeting.	Summary	One-fifth of the statutory maximum.	One-fiftieth of the statutory maximum.

Section of Act creating offence	General nature of offence	Mode of prosecution	Punishment	Daily default fine (where applicable)
Sch B1, para 53(3)	Administrator failing to report decision taken at initial creditors' meeting.	Summary	One-fifth of the statutory maximum.	One-fiftieth of the statutory maximum.
Sch B1, para 54(7)	Administrator failing to report decision taken at creditors' meeting summoned to consider revised proposal.	Summary	One-fifth of the statutory maximum.	One-fiftieth of the statutory maximum.
Sch B1, para 56(2)	Administrator failing to summon creditors' meeting.	Summary	One-fifth of the statutory maximum.	One-fiftieth of the statutory maximum.
Sch B1, para 71(6)	Administrator failing to file court order enabling disposal of charged property.	Summary	One-fifth of the statutory maximum.	One-fiftieth of the statutory maximum.
Sch B1, para 72(5)	Administrator failing to file court order enabling disposal of hire-purchase property.	Summary	One-fifth of the statutory maximum.	One-fiftieth of the statutory maximum.
Sch B1, para 77(3)	Administrator failing to notify Registrar of Companies of automatic end of administration.	Summary	One-fifth of the statutory maximum.	One-fiftieth of the statutory maximum.
Sch B1, para 78(6)	Administrator failing to give notice of extension by consent of term of office.	Summary	One-fifth of the statutory maximum.	One-fiftieth of the statutory maximum.
Sch B1, para 80(6)	Administrator failing to give notice of termination of administration where objective achieved.	Summary	One-fifth of the statutory maximum.	One-fiftieth of the statutory maximum.
Sch B1, para 84(9)	Administrator failing to comply with provisions where company moves to dissolution.	Summary	One-fifth of the statutory maximum.	One-fiftieth of the statutory maximum.
Sch B1, para 86(3)	Administrator failing to notify Registrar of Companies where court terminates administration.	Summary	One-fifth of the statutory maximum.	One-fiftieth of the statutory maximum.
Sch B1, para 89(3)	Administrator failing to give notice on ceasing to be qualified.	Summary	One-fifth of the statutory maximum.	One-fiftieth of the statutory maximum.

Section of Act creating offence	General nature of offence	Mode of prosecution	Punishment	Daily default fine (where applicable)
Sch 7, para 4(3)	Failure to attend and give evidence to Insolvency Practitioners Tribunal; suppressing, concealing, etc relevant documents.	Summary	Level 3 on the standard scale within the meaning given by section 75 of the Criminal Justice Act 1982.	

Note. The italicized words in the entries for "45(5)", "53(2)", "54(3)" and "62(5)" are repealed by the Companies Act 1989, s. 212, Sch. 24, as from a day to be appointed.

SCHEDULE 11

TRANSITIONAL PROVISIONS AND SAVINGS

Section 437

PART I
COMPANY INSOLVENCY AND WINDING UP

Administration orders

1.— (1) Where any right to appoint an administrative receiver of a company is conferred by any debentures or floating charge created before the appointed day, the conditions precedent to the exercise of that right are deemed to include the presentation of a petition applying for an administration order to be made in relation to the company.

(2) "Administrative receiver" here has the meaning assigned by section 251.

Receivers and managers (England and Wales)

2.— (1) In relation to any receiver or manager of a company's property who was appointed before the appointed day, the new law does not apply; and the relevant provisions of the former law continue to have effect.

(2) "The new law" here means Chapter I of Part III, and Part VI, of this Act; and "the former law" means the Companies Act and so much of this Act as replaces provisions of that Act (without the amendments in paragraphs 15 to 17 of Schedule 6 to the Insolvency Act 1985, or the associated repeals made by that Act), and any provision of the Insolvency Act 1985 which was in force before the appointed day.

(3) This paragraph is without prejudice to the power conferred by this Act under which rules under section 411 may make transitional provision in connection with the coming into force of those rules; and such provision may apply those rules in relation to the receiver or manager of a company's property notwithstanding that he was appointed before the coming into force of the rules or section 411.

Receivers (Scotland)

3.— (1) In relation to any receiver appointed under section 467 of the Companies Act before the appointed day, the new law does not apply and the relevant provisions of the former law continue to have effect.

(2) "The new law" here means Chapter II of Part III, and Part VI, of this Act; and "the former law" means the Companies Act and so much of this Act as replaces provisions of that Act (without the amendments in paragraphs 18 to 22 of Schedule 6 to the Insolvency Act 1985

or the associated repeals made by that Act), and any provision of the Insolvency Act 1985 which was in force before the appointed day.

(3) This paragraph is without prejudice to the power conferred by this Act under which rules under section 411 may make transitional provision in connection with the coming into force of those rules; and such provision may apply those rules in relation to a receiver appointed under section 467 notwithstanding that he was appointed before the coming into force of the rules or section 411.

Winding up already in progress

4.— (1) In relation to any winding up which has commenced, or is treated as having commenced, before the appointed day, the new law does not apply, and the former law continues to have effect, subject to the following paragraphs.

(2) "The new law" here means any provisions in the first Group of Parts of this Act which replace sections 66 to 87 and 89 to 105 of the Insolvency Act 1985; and "the former law" means Parts XX and XXI of the Companies Act (without the amendments in paragraphs 23 to 52 of Schedule 6 to the Insolvency Act 1985, or the associated repeals made by that Act).

Statement of affairs

5.— (1) Where a winding up by the court in England and Wales has commenced, or is treated as having commenced, before the appointed day, the official receiver or (on appeal from a refusal by him) the court may, at any time on or after that day—

  (a) release a person from an obligation imposed on him by or under section 528 of the Companies Act (statement of affairs), or

  (b) extend the period specified in subsection (6) of that section.

(2) Accordingly, on and after the appointed day, section 528(6) has effect in relation to a winding up to which this paragraph applies with the omission of the words from "or within" onwards.

Provisions relating to liquidator

6.— (1) This paragraph applies as regards the liquidator in the case of a winding up by the court in England and Wales commenced, or treated as having commenced, before the appointed day.

(2) The official receiver may, at any time when he is liquidator of the company, apply to the Secretary of State for the appointment of a liquidator in his (the official receiver's) place; and on any such application the Secretary of State shall either make an appointment or decline to make one.

(3) Where immediately before the appointed day the liquidator of the company has not made an application under section 545 of the Companies Act (release of liquidators), then—

  (a) except where the Secretary of State otherwise directs, sections 146(1) and (2) and 172(8) of this Act apply, and section 545 does not apply, in relation to any liquidator of that company who holds office on or at any time after the appointed day and is not the official receiver;

  (b) section 146(3) applies in relation to the carrying out at any time after that day by any liquidator of the company of any of his functions; and

  (c) a liquidator in relation to whom section 172(8) has effect by virtue of this paragraph has his release with effect from the time specified in section 174(4)(d) of this Act.

(4) Subsection (6) of section 174 of this Act has effect for the purposes of sub-paragraph (3)(c) above as it has for the purposes of that section, but as if the reference to section 212 were to section 631 of the Companies Act.

(5) The liquidator may employ a solicitor to assist him in the carrying out of his functions without the permission of the committee of inspection; but if he does so employ a solicitor he shall inform the committee of inspection that he has done so.

Winding up under supervision of the court

7.   The repeals in Part II of Schedule 10 to the Insolvency Act 1985 of references (in the Companies Act and elsewhere) to a winding up under the supervision of the court do not affect the operation of the enactments in which the references are contained in relation to any case in which an order under section 606 of the Companies Act (power to order winding up under supervision) was made before the appointed day.

Saving for power to make rules

8.—   (1)   Paragraphs 4 to 7 are without prejudice to the power conferred by this Act under which rules made under section 411 may make transitional provision in connection with the coming into force of those rules.

        (2)   Such provision may apply those rules in relation to a winding up notwithstanding that the winding up commenced, or is treated as having commenced, before the coming into force of the rules or section 411.

Setting aside of preferences and other transactions

9.—   (1)   Where a provision in Part VI of this Act applies in relation to a winding up or in relation to a case in which an administration order has been made, a preference given, floating charge created or other transaction entered into before the appointed day shall not be set aside under that provision except to the extent that it could have been set aside under the law in force immediately before that day, assuming for this purpose that any relevant administration order had been a winding-up order.

        (2)   The references above to setting aside a preference, floating charge or other transaction include the making of an order which varies or reverses any effect of a preference, floating charge or other transaction.

PART II
INDIVIDUAL INSOLVENCY

Bankruptcy (general)

10.—   (1)   Subject to the following provisions of this Part of this Schedule, so much of this Act as replaces Part III of the Insolvency Act 1985 does not apply in relation to any case in which a petition in bankruptcy was presented, or a receiving order or adjudication in bankruptcy was made, before the appointed day.

        (2)   In relation to any such case as is mentioned above, the enactments specified in Schedule 8 to that Act, so far as they relate to bankruptcy, and those specified in Parts III and IV of Schedule 10 to that Act, so far as they so relate, have effect without the amendments and repeals specified in those Schedules.

        (3)   Where any subordinate legislation made under an enactment referred to in sub-paragraph (2) is in force immediately before the appointed day, that subordinate legislation continues to have effect on and after that day in relation to any such case as is mentioned in sub-paragraph (1).

11.—   (1)   In relation to any such case as is mentioned in paragraph 10(1) the references in any enactment or subordinate legislation to a petition, order or other matter which is provided for under the Bankruptcy Act 1914 and corresponds to a petition, order or other matter provided for under provisions of this Act replacing Part III of the Insolvency Act 1985 continue on and after the appointed day to have effect as references to the petition, order or matter provided for by the Act of 1914; but otherwise those references have effect on and after that day as references to the petition, order or matter provided for by those provisions of this Act.

        (2)   Without prejudice to sub-paragraph (1), in determining for the purposes of section 279 of this Act (period of bankruptcy) or paragraph 13 below whether any person was an

undischarged bankrupt at a time before the appointed day, an adjudication in bankruptcy and an annulment of a bankruptcy under the Act of 1914 are to be taken into account in the same way, respectively, as a bankruptcy order under the provisions of this Act replacing Part III of the Insolvency Act 1985 and the annulment under section 282 of this Act of such an order.

12. Transactions entered into before the appointed day have effect on and after that day as if references to acts of bankruptcy in the provisions for giving effect to those transactions continued to be references to acts of bankruptcy within the meaning of the Bankruptcy Act 1914, but as if such acts included failure to comply with a statutory demand served under section 268 of this Act.

Discharge from old bankruptcy

13.— (1) Where a person—

   (a) was adjudged bankrupt before the appointed day or is adjudged bankrupt on or after that day on a petition presented before that day, and

   (b) that person was not an undischarged bankrupt at any time in the period of 15 years ending with the adjudication,

   that person is deemed (if not previously discharged) to be discharged from his bankruptcy for the purposes of the Bankruptcy Act 1914 at the end of the discharge period.

   (2) Subject to sub-paragraph (3) below, the discharge period for the purposes of this paragraph is—

   (a) in the case of a person adjudged bankrupt before the appointed day, the period of 3 years beginning with that day, and

   (b) in the case of a person who is adjudged bankrupt on or after that day on a petition presented before that day, the period of 3 years beginning with the date of the adjudication.

   (3) Where the court exercising jurisdiction in relation to a bankruptcy to which this paragraph applies is satisfied, on the application of the official receiver, that the bankrupt has failed, or is failing, to comply with any of his obligations under the Bankruptcy Act 1914, any rules made under that Act or any such rules as are mentioned in paragraph 19(1) below, the court may order that the discharge period shall cease to run for such period, or until the fulfilment of such conditions (including a condition requiring the court to be satisfied as to any matter) as may be specified in the order.

Provisions relating to trustee

14.— (1) This paragraph applies as regards the trustee in the case of a person adjudged bankrupt before the appointed day, or adjudged bankrupt on or after that day on a petition presented before that day.

   (2) The official receiver may at any time when he is the trustee of the bankrupt's estate apply to the Secretary of State for the appointment of a person as trustee instead of the official receiver; and on any such application the Secretary of State shall either make an appointment or decline to make one.

   (3) Where on the appointed day the trustee of a bankrupt's estate has not made an application under section 93 of the Bankruptcy Act 1914 (release of trustee), then—

   (a) except where the Secretary of State otherwise directs, sections 298(8), 304 and 331(1) to (3) of this Act apply, and section 93 of the Act of 1914 does not apply, in relation to any trustee of the bankrupt's estate who holds office on or at any time after the appointed day and is not the official receiver;

   (b) section 331(4) of this Act applies in relation to the carrying out at any time on or after the appointed day by the trustee of the bankrupt's estate of any of his functions; and

   (c) a trustee in relation to whom section 298(8) of this Act has effect by virtue of this paragraph has his release with effect from the time specified in section 299(3)(d).

   (4) Subsection (5) of section 299 has effect for the purposes of sub-paragraph (3)(c) as it has for the purposes of that section.

(5)   In the application of subsection (3) of section 331 in relation to a case by virtue of this
      paragraph, the reference in that subsection to section 330(1) has effect as a reference to
      section 67 of the Bankruptcy Act 1914.

(6)   The trustee of the bankrupt's estate may employ a solicitor to assist him in the carrying out
      of his functions without the permission of the committee of inspection; but if he does so
      employ a solicitor, he shall inform the committee of inspection that he has done so.

Copyright

15.   Where a person who is adjudged bankrupt on a petition presented on or after the appointed day is
      liable, by virtue of a transaction entered into before that day, to pay royalties or a share of the
      profits to any person in respect of any copyright or interest in copyright comprised in the
      bankrupt's estate, section 60 of the Bankruptcy Act 1914 (limitation on trustee's powers in
      relation to copyright) applies in relation to the trustee of that estate as it applies in relation to a
      trustee in bankruptcy under the Act of 1914.

Second bankruptcy

16.— (1)   Sections 334 and 335 of this Act apply with the following modifications where the earlier
            bankruptcy (within the meaning of section 334) is a bankruptcy in relation to which the Act
            of 1914 applies instead of the second Group of Parts in this Act, that is to say—
            (a)   references to property vested in the existing trustee under section 307(3) of this Act
                  have effect as references to such property vested in that trustee as was acquired by or
                  devolved on the bankrupt after the commencement (within the meaning of the Act of
                  1914) of the earlier bankruptcy; and
            (b)   references to an order under section 310 of this Act have effect as references to an
                  order under section 51 of the Act of 1914.

       (2)   Section 39 of the Act of 1914 (second bankruptcy) does not apply where a person who is an
             undischarged bankrupt under that Act is adjudged bankrupt under this Act.

Setting aside of preferences and other transactions

17.— (1)   A preference given, assignment made or other transaction entered into before the appointed
            day shall not be set aside under any of sections 339 to 344 of this Act except to the extent
            that it could have been set aside under the law in force immediately before that day.

       (2)   References in sub-paragraph (1) to setting aside a preference, assignment or other
             transaction include the making of any order which varies or reverses any effect of a
             preference, assignment or other transaction.

Bankruptcy offences

18.— (1)   Where a bankruptcy order is made under this Act on or after the appointed day, a person is
            not guilty of an offence under Chapter VI of Part IX in respect of anything done before that
            day; but, notwithstanding the repeal by the Insolvency Act 1985 of the Bankruptcy Act
            1914, is guilty of an offence under the Act of 1914 in respect of anything done before the
            appointed day which would have been an offence under that Act if the making of the
            bankruptcy order had been the making of a receiving order under that Act.

       (2)   Subsection (5) of section 350 of this Act applies (instead of sections 157(2), 158(2), 161 and
             165 of the Act of 1914) in relation to proceedings for an offence under that Act which are
             instituted (whether by virtue of sub-paragraph (1) or otherwise) after the appointed day.

Power to make rules

19.— (1)   The preceding provisions of this Part of this Schedule are without prejudice to the power
            conferred by this Act under which rules under section 412 may make transitional provision
            in connection with the coming into force of those rules; and such provision may apply those
            rules in relation to a bankruptcy notwithstanding that it arose from a petition presented
            before either the coming into force of the rules or the appointed day.

(2) Rules under section 412 may provide for such notices served before the appointed day as may be prescribed to be treated for the purposes of this Act as statutory demands served under section 268.

PART III
TRANSITIONAL EFFECT OF PART XVI

20.— (1) A transaction entered into before the appointed day shall not be set aside under Part XVI of this Act except to the extent that it could have been set aside under the law in force immediately before that day.

(2) References above to setting aside a transaction include the making of any order which varies or reverses any effect of a transaction.

PART IV
INSOLVENCY PRACTITIONERS

21. Where an individual began to act as an insolvency practitioner in relation to any person before the appointed day, nothing in section 390(2) or (3) prevents that individual from being qualified to act as an insolvency practitioner in relation to that person.

PART V
GENERAL TRANSITIONAL PROVISIONS AND SAVINGS

Interpretation for this Part

22. In this Part of this Schedule, "the former enactments" means so much of the Companies Act as is repealed and replaced by this Act, the Insolvency Act 1985 and the other enactments repealed by this Act.

General saving for past acts and events

23. So far as anything done or treated as done under or for the purposes of any provision of the former enactments could have been done under or for the purposes of the corresponding provision of this Act, it is not invalidated by the repeal of that provision but has effect as if done under or for the purposes of the corresponding provision; and any order, regulation, rule or other instrument made or having effect under any provision of the former enactments shall, insofar as its effect is preserved by this paragraph, be treated for all purposes as made and having effect under the corresponding provision.

Periods of time

24. Where any period of time specified in a provision of the former enactments is current immediately before the appointed day, this Act has effect as if the corresponding provision had been in force when the period began to run; and (without prejudice to the foregoing) any period of time so specified and current is deemed for the purposes of this Act—

(a) to run from the date or event from which it was running immediately before the appointed day, and

(b) to expire (subject to any provision of this Act for its extension) whenever it would have expired if this Act had not been passed;

and any rights, priorities, liabilities, reliefs, obligations, requirements, powers, duties or exemptions dependent on the beginning, duration or end of such a period as above mentioned shall be under this Act as they were or would have been under the former enactments.

Internal cross-references in this Act

25. Where in any provision of this Act there is a reference to another such provision, and the first-mentioned provision operates, or is capable of operating, in relation to things done or omitted, or events occurring or not occurring, in the past (including in particular past acts of compliance with

any enactment, failures of compliance, contraventions, offences and convictions of offences), the reference to the other provision is to be read as including a reference to the corresponding provision of the former enactments.

Punishment of offences

26.— (1) Offences committed before the appointed day under any provision of the former enactments may, notwithstanding any repeal by this Act, be prosecuted and punished after that day as if this Act had not passed.

(2) A contravention of any provision of the former enactments committed before the appointed day shall not be visited with any severer punishment under or by virtue of this Act than would have been applicable under that provision at the time of the contravention; but where an offence for the continuance of which a penalty was provided has been committed under any provision of the former enactments, proceedings may be taken under this Act in respect of the continuance of the offence on and after the appointed day in the like manner as if the offence had been committed under the corresponding provision of this Act.

References elsewhere to the former enactments

27.— (1) A reference in any enactment, instrument or document (whether express or implied, and in whatever phraseology) to a provision of the former enactments (including the corresponding provision of any yet earlier enactment) is to be read, where necessary to retain for the enactment, instrument or document the same force and effect as it would have had but for the passing of this Act, as, or as including, a reference to the corresponding provision by which it is replaced in this Act.

(2) The generality of the preceding sub-paragraph is not affected by any specific conversion of references made by this Act, nor by the inclusion in any provision of this Act of a reference (whether express or implied, and in whatever phraseology) to the provision of the former enactments corresponding to that provision, or to a provision of the former enactments which is replaced by a corresponding provision of this Act.

Saving for power to repeal provisions in section 51

28. The Secretary of State may by order in a statutory instrument repeal subsections (3) to (5) of section 51 of this Act and the entries in Schedule 10 relating to subsections (4) and (5) of that section.

Saving for Interpretation Act 1978 ss 16, 17

29. Nothing in this Schedule is to be taken as prejudicing sections 16 and 17 of the Interpretation Act 1978 (savings from, and effect of, repeals); and for the purposes of section 17(2) of that Act (construction of references to enactments repealed and replaced, etc), so much of section 18 of the Insolvency Act 1985 as is replaced by a provision of this Act is deemed to have been replaced by this Act and not by the Company Directors Disqualification Act 1986.

SCHEDULES 12–14

...

Stock Transfer Act 1963

1963 c. 18

An Act to amend the law with respect to the transfer of securities

[10th July 1963]

1.   Simplified transfer of securities

(1)   Registered securities to which this section applies may be transferred by means of an instrument under hand in the form set out in Schedule 1 to this Act (in this Act referred to as a stock transfer), executed by the transferor only and specifying (in addition to the particulars of the consideration, of the description and number or amount of the securities, and of the person by whom the transfer is made) the full name and address of the transferee.

(2)   The execution of a stock transfer need not be attested; and where such a transfer has been executed for the purpose of a stock exchange transaction, the particulars of the consideration and of the transferee may either be inserted in that transfer or, as the case may require, supplied by means of separate instruments in the form set out in Schedule 2 to this Act (in this Act referred to as brokers transfers), identifying the stock transfer and specifying the securities to which each such instrument relates and the consideration paid for those securities.

(3)   Nothing in this section shall be construed as affecting the validity of any instrument which would be effective to transfer securities apart from this section; and any instrument purporting to be made in any form which was common or usual before the commencement of this Act, or in any other form authorised or required for that purpose apart from this section, shall be sufficient, whether or not it is completed in accordance with the form, if it complies with the requirements as to execution and contents which apply to a stock transfer.

(4)   This section applies to fully paid up registered securities of any description, being—

(a)   securities issued by any company within the meaning of the Companies Act 1985 except a company limited by guarantee or an unlimited company;

(b)   securities issued by any body (other than a company within the meaning of the said Act) incorporated in Great Britain by or under any enactment or by Royal Charter except a building society within the meaning of the Building Societies Act 1986 or a society registered under the Industrial and Provident Societies Act 1893;

(c)   securities issued by the Government of the United Kingdom, except stock or bonds in the National Savings Stock Register …, and except national savings certificates;

(d)   securities issued by any local authority;

(e)   units of an authorised unit trust scheme or a recognised scheme within the meaning of Part 17 of the Financial Services and Markets Act 2000;

(f)   shares issued by an open-ended investment company within the meaning of the Open-Ended Investment Companies Regulations 2001.

2.   Supplementary provisions as to simplified transfer

(1)   Section 1 of this Act shall have effect in relation to the transfer of any securities to which that section applies notwithstanding anything to the contrary in any enactment or instrument relating to the transfer of those securities; but nothing in that section affects—

(a)   any right to refuse to register a person as the holder of any securities on any ground other than the form in which those securities purport to be transferred to him: or

(b)   any enactment or rule of law regulating the execution of documents by companies or other bodies corporate, or any articles of association or other instrument regulating the execution of documents by any particular company or body corporate.

(2)   Subject to the provisions of this section, any enactment or instrument relating to the transfer of securities to which section 1 of this Act applies shall, with any necessary modifications, apply in relation to an instrument of transfer authorised by that section as it applies in relation to an

instrument of transfer to which it applies apart from this subsection; and without prejudice to the generality of the foregoing provision, the reference in section 184 of the Companies Act 1985 (certification of transfers) to any instrument of transfer shall be construed as including a reference to a brokers transfer.

(3)   In relation to the transfer of securities by means of a stock transfer and a brokers transfer—

     (a)   any reference in any enactment or instrument (including in particular section 183(1) and (2) of the Companies Act 1985 …) to the delivery or lodging of an instrument (or proper instrument) of transfer shall be construed as a reference to the delivery or lodging of the stock transfer and the brokers transfer;

     (b)   any such reference to the date on which an instrument of transfer is delivered or lodged shall be construed as a reference to the data by which the later of those transfers to be delivered or lodged has been delivered or lodged; and

     (c)   subject to the foregoing provisions of this subsection, the brokers transfer (and not the stock transfer) shall be deemed to be the conveyance or transfer for the purposes of the enactments relating to stamp duty.

(4)   …

3.   Additional provisions as to transfer forms

(1)   References in this Act to the forms set out in Schedule 1 and Schedule 2 include references to forms substantially corresponding to those forms respectively.

(2)   The Treasury may by order amend the said Schedules either by altering the forms set out therein or by substituting different forms for those forms or by the addition of forms for use as alternatives to those forms; and references in this Act to the forms set out in those Schedules (including references in this section) shall be construed accordingly.

(3)   Any order under subsection (2) of this section which substitutes a different form for a form set out in Schedule 1 to this Act may direct that subsection (3) of section 1 of this Act shall apply, with any necessary modifications, in relation to the form for which that form is substituted as it applies to any form which was common or usual before the commencement of this Act.

(4)   Any order of the Treasury under this section shall be made by statutory instrument, and may be varied or revoked by a subsequent order; and any statutory instrument made by virtue of this section shall be subject to annulment in pursuance of a resolution of either House of Parliament.

(5)   An order under subsection (2) of this section may—

     (a)   provide for forms on which some of the particulars mentioned in subsection (1) of section 1 of this Act are not required to be specified;

     (b)   provide for that section to have effect, in relation to such forms as are mentioned in the preceding paragraph or other forms specified in the order, subject to such amendments as are so specified (which may include an amendment of the reference in subsection (1) of that section to an instrument under hand);

     (c)   provide for all or any of the provisions of the order to have effect in such cases only as are specified in the order.

4.   Interpretation

(1)   In this Act the following expressions have the meanings hereby respectively assigned to them, that is to say—

     "local authority" means, in relation to England and Wales,

     (a)   a billing authority or a precepting authority, as defined in section 69 of the Local Government Finance Act 1992;

     (aa)   a fire and rescue authority in Wales constituted by a scheme under section 2 of the Fire and Rescue Services Act 2004 or a scheme to which section 4 of that Act applies;

     (b)   a levying body within the meaning of section 74 of the Local Government Finance Act 1988; and

     (c)   a body as regards which section 75 of that Act applies, and, in relation to Scotland, a county council, a town council and any statutory authority, commissioners or trustees to whom section 270 of the Local Government (Scotland) Act 1947 applies;

"registered securities" means transferable securities the holders of which are entered in a register (whether maintained in Great Britain or not); "securities" means shares, stock, debentures, debenture stock, loan stock, bonds, units of a collective investment scheme within the meaning of the Financial Services and Markets Act 2000, and other securities of any description;

"stock exchange transaction" means a sale and purchase of securities in which each of the parties is a member of a stock exchange acting in the ordinary course of his business as such or is acting through the agency of such a member;

"stock exchange" means the Stock Exchange, London, and any other stock exchange (whether in Great Britain or not) which is declared by order of the Treasury to be a recognised stock exchange for the purposes of this Act.

(2) Any order of the Treasury under this section shall be made by statutory instrument, and may be varied or revoked by a subsequent order.

5. Application to Northern Ireland

(1) This Act, so far as it applies to things done outside Great Britain, extends to Northern Ireland.

(2) Without prejudice to subsection (1) of this section, the provisions of this Act affecting securities issued by the Government of the United Kingdom shall apply to any such securities entered in a register maintained in Northern Ireland.

(3) ...

(4) Except as provided by this section, this Act shall not extend to Northern Ireland.

6. Short title and commencement

(1) This Act may be cited as the Stock Transfer Act 1963.

(2) Subsection (3) of section 5 of this Act shall come into force on the passing of this Act, and the remaining provisions of this Act shall come into force on such date as the Treasury may by order made by statutory instrument direct.

SCHEDULES

SCHEDULE 1

STOCK TRANSFER FORM	**Certificate lodged with the Registrar**
Consideration Money £.............................	(For completion by the Registrar/Stock Exchange)

Name of Undertaking.		
Description of Security.		
Number or amount of Shares, Stock or other security and, in figures column only, number and denomination of units, if any.	Words	Figures
		(units of)
Name(s) of registered holder(s) should be given in full: the address should be given where there is only one holder. If the transfer is not made by the registered holder(s) insert also the name(s) and capacity (eg, Executor(s)), of the person(s) making the transfer.	in the name(s) of	

Delete words in italics except for stock exchange transactions.	I/We hereby transfer the above security out of the name(s) aforesaid to the person(s) named below *or to the several persons named in Parts 2 of Brokers Transfer Forms relating to the above security*: Signature(s) of transferor(s) 1 .... 3 .... 2 .... 4 .... A body corporate should execute this transfer under its common seal or otherwise in accordance with applicable statutory requirements.	Stamp of Selling Broker(s) or, for transactions which are not stock exchange transactions, of Agent(s), if any, acting for the Transferor(s). Date

Full name(s), full postal address(es) (including County or, if applicable, Postal District number) of the person(s) to whom the security is transferred. Please state title, if any, or whether Mr, Mrs or Miss. Please complete in type or in Block Capitals.	

I/We request that such entries be made in the register as are necessary to give effect to this transfer.	
Stamp of Buying Broker(s) (if any).	Stamp or name and address of person lodging this form (if other than the Buying Broker(s)).

Reference to the Registrar in this form means the registrar or registration agent of the undertaking, <u>not</u> the Registrar of Companies at Companies House.

(Endorsement for use only in stock exchange transactions)

The security represented by the transfer overleaf has been sold as follows:−

....*Shares/Stock*   ....*Shares/Stock*
....*Shares/Stock*   ....*Shares/Stock*
....*Shares/Stock*   ....*Shares/Stock*
....*Shares/Stock*   ....*Shares/Stock*
....*Shares/Stock*   ....*Shares/Stock*
....*Shares/Stock*   ....*Shares/Stock*

Balance (if any) due to Selling Broker(s)

Amount of Certificate(s)

Brokers Transfer Forms for above amount certified

Stamp of certifying Stock Exchange   *Stamp of Selling Broker(s)*

TALISMAN SOLD TRANSFER

This transfer is exempt from Transfer Stamp Duty

Above this line for Registrar's use only	
	Bargain Reference No:
Name of Undertaking	Certificate lodged with Registrar
Description of Security	(for completion by the Registrars/ Stock Exchange)
Amount of Stock or number of Stock units or shares or other security in words	Figures

In the name(s) of

Account Designation (if any)

Name(s) of registered holder(s) should be given in full; the address should be given where there is only one holder.

If the transfer is not made by the registered holder(s) insert also the name(s) and capacity (e.g. Executor(s)) of the person(s) making the transfer.

I/We hereby transfer the above security out of the name(s) aforesaid into the name of ___ and request the necessary entries to be made in the register.

Bodies corporate should affix their common seal and each signatory should state his/her representative capacity (e.g 'Company Secretary' 'Director') agaist his/her signature

PLEASE SIGN HERE

1 _____

2 _____

3 _____

4 _____

Balance Certificate Required for (amount or number in figures)

Stamp of Lodging Agent

Date

INSP Code (if applicable)

___ is lodging this transfer at the direction and on behalf of the Lodging Agent whose stamp appears herein ("the Original Lodging Agent") and does not in any manner or to any extent warrant or represent the validity, genuineness or correctness of the transfer instructions contained herein or the genuineness of the signature(s) of the transferor(s) The Original Lodging Agent be delivering this transfer to ___ authorises ___ to lodge this transfer for registration and agrees to be deemed for all purposes to be the person(s) actually lodging this transfer for registration

Transfer Number

TALISMAN BOUGHT TRANSFER

Above this line for Registrar's use only

Name of Undertaking

Rate   Description of Security

Stamp Duty	Bargain Date	Settlement	Price		Transfer Consideration	Figures

Amount of Stock or Number of Stock Units or Shares or Other Security in Words

Hundred Millions	Ten Millions	Millions	Hundred Thousands	Ten Thousands	Thousands	Hundreds	Tens	Units

Transferee Details

Account Designation

Apportionment Date

Registrar	Batch	Company	Security	Bargain Reference	Firm	Transfer Number	Quantity

hereby transfers the above security to the person(s) named under "Transferee Details" and requests the necessary entries to be made in the register. It confirms that the price and transfer consideration have been derived from information supplied by Member Firms

is lodging this transfer at the direction and on behalf of the Member Firm whose code number appears herein ('the Original Lodging Agent') and does not in any manner or to any extent warrant or represent the validity or correctness of the transfer instructions contained herein The Original Lodging Agent by instructing   to deliver this transfer for registration agrees to be deemed for all purposes to be the person(s) actually lodging this transfer for registration

Dated

It is hereby certified on behalf of The Stock Exchange that the Stamp Duty indicated hereon has been or will be accounted for to the Commissioners of Inland Revenue pursuant to an agreement under Section 33 of the Finance Act 1970 as amended.

TRANSFER

Counter Location Stamp	Barcode or reference

RN

Above this line for completion by the depositing system-user only.

Consideration Money	Certificate(s) lodged with Registrar (To be completed by Registrar)

Name of Undertaking.

Description of Security.

Please complete form in type or in block capitals.

Amount of shares or other security in words	Figures

Name(s) of registered holder(s) should be given in full; the address should be given where there is only one holder.

If the transfer is not made by the registered holder(s) insert also the name(s) and capacity (e.g. executor(s)) of the person(s) making the transfer.

In the name(s) of	Designation (if any)
	Balance certificate(s) required

Please Sign Here →

I/We hereby transfer the above security out of the name(s) aforesaid into the name(s) of the system-member set out below and request that the necessary entries be made in the undertaking's own register of members.

Signature(s) of transferor(s)

1.

2.

3.

4.

A body corporate should execute this transfer under its common seal or otherwise in accordance with applicable statutory requirements.

Stamp of depositing system-user

Date

Full name(s) of the person(s) to whom the security is transferred.

Such person(s) must be a system-member.

Participant ID

Member Account ID

.... is delivering this transfer at the direction and on behalf of the depositing system-user whose stamp appears herein and does not in any manner or to any extent warrant or represent the validity, genuineness or correctness of the transfer instructions contained herein or the genuineness of the signature(s) of the transferor(s). The depositing system-user by delivering this transfer to .... authorises .... to deliver this transfer for registration and agrees to be deemed for all purposes to be the person(s) actually so delivering this transfer for registration.

Reference to the Registrar in this form means the registrar or registration agent of the undertaking, not the Registrar of Companies at Companies House.

Financial Services and Markets Act 2000

2000 c. 8

An Act to make provision about the regulation of financial services and markets; to provide for the transfer of certain statutory functions relating to building societies, friendly societies, industrial and provident societies and certain other mutual societies; and for connected purposes

[14th June 2000]

PART I
THE REGULATOR

1. The Financial Services Authority

(1) The body corporate known as the Financial Services Authority ("the Authority") is to have the functions conferred on it by or under this Act.

(2) The Authority must comply with the requirements as to its constitution set out in Schedule 1.

(3) Schedule 1 also makes provision about the status of the Authority and the exercise of certain of its functions.

The Authority's general duties

2. The Authority's general duties

(1) In discharging its general functions the Authority must, so far as is reasonably possible, act in a way—
  (a) which is compatible with the regulatory objectives; and
  (b) which the Authority considers most appropriate for the purpose of meeting those objectives.

(2) The regulatory objectives are—
  (a) market confidence;
  (b) public awareness;
  (c) the protection of consumers; and
  (d) the reduction of financial crime.

(3) In discharging its general functions the Authority must have regard to—
  (a) the need to use its resources in the most efficient and economic way;
  (b) the responsibilities of those who manage the affairs of authorised persons;
  (c) the principle that a burden or restriction which is imposed on a person, or on the carrying on of an activity, should be proportionate to the benefits, considered in general terms, which are expected to result from the imposition of that burden or restriction;
  (d) the desirability of facilitating innovation in connection with regulated activities;
  (e) the international character of financial services and markets and the desirability of maintaining the competitive position of the United Kingdom;
  (f) the need to minimise the adverse effects on competition that may arise from anything done in the discharge of those functions;
  (g) the desirability of facilitating competition between those who are subject to any form of regulation by the Authority.

(4) The Authority's general functions are—
  (a) its function of making rules under this Act (considered as a whole);
  (b) its function of preparing and issuing codes under this Act (considered as a whole);
  (c) its functions in relation to the giving of general guidance (considered as a whole); and
  (d) its function of determining the general policy and principles by reference to which it performs particular functions.

(5) "General guidance" has the meaning given in section 158(5).

The regulatory objectives

3.   Market confidence

(1)   The market confidence objective is: maintaining confidence in the financial system.

(2)   "The financial system" means the financial system operating in the United Kingdom and includes—

(a)   financial markets and exchanges;

(b)   regulated activities; and

(c)   other activities connected with financial markets and exchanges.

4.   Public awareness

(1)   The public awareness objective is: promoting public understanding of the financial system.

(2)   It includes, in particular—

(a)   promoting awareness of the benefits and risks associated with different kinds of investment or other financial dealing; and

(b)   the provision of appropriate information and advice.

(3)   "The financial system" has the same meaning as in section 3.

5.   The protection of consumers

(1)   The protection of consumers objective is: securing the appropriate degree of protection for consumers.

(2)   In considering what degree of protection may be appropriate, the Authority must have regard to—

(a)   the differing degrees of risk involved in different kinds of investment or other transaction;

(b)   the differing degrees of experience and expertise that different consumers may have in relation to different kinds of regulated activity;

(c)   the needs that consumers may have for advice and accurate information; and

(d)   the general principle that consumers should take responsibility for their decisions.

(3)   "Consumers" means persons—

(a)   who are consumers for the purposes of section 138; or

(b)   who, in relation to regulated activities carried on otherwise than by authorised persons, would be consumers for those purposes if the activities were carried on by authorised persons.

6.   The reduction of financial crime

(1)   The reduction of financial crime objective is: reducing the extent to which it is possible for a business carried on—

(a)   by a regulated person, or

(b)   in contravention of the general prohibition,

to be used for a purpose connected with financial crime.

(2)   In considering that objective the Authority must, in particular, have regard to the desirability of—

(a)   regulated persons being aware of the risk of their businesses being used in connection with the commission of financial crime;

(b)   regulated persons taking appropriate measures (in relation to their administration and employment practices, the conduct of transactions by them and otherwise) to prevent financial crime, facilitate its detection and monitor its incidence;

(c)   regulated persons devoting adequate resources to the matters mentioned in paragraph (b).

(3)   "Financial crime" includes any offence involving—

(a)   fraud or dishonesty;

(b)   misconduct in, or misuse of information relating to, a financial market; or

(c)   handling the proceeds of crime.

(4)   "Offence" includes an act or omission which would be an offence if it had taken place in the United Kingdom.

(5)   "Regulated person" means an authorised person, a recognised investment exchange or a recognised clearing house.

Corporate governance

7. Duty of Authority to follow principles of good governance

In managing its affairs, the Authority must have regard to such generally accepted principles of good corporate governance as it is reasonable to regard as applicable to it.

Arrangements for consulting practitioners and consumers

8. The Authority's general duty to consult

The Authority must make and maintain effective arrangements for consulting practitioners and consumers on the extent to which its general policies and practices are consistent with its general duties under section 2.

9. The Practitioner Panel

(1) Arrangements under section 8 must include the establishment and maintenance of a panel of persons (to be known as "the Practitioner Panel") to represent the interests of practitioners.

(2) The Authority must appoint one of the members of the Practitioner Panel to be its chairman.

(3) The Treasury's approval is required for the appointment or dismissal of the chairman.

(4) The Authority must have regard to any representations made to it by the Practitioner Panel.

(5) The Authority must appoint to the Practitioner Panel such—
    (a) individuals who are authorised persons,
    (b) persons representing authorised persons,
    (c) persons representing recognised investment exchanges, and
    (d) persons representing recognised clearing houses,
as it considers appropriate.

10. The Consumer Panel

(1) Arrangements under section 8 must include the establishment and maintenance of a panel of persons (to be known as "the Consumer Panel") to represent the interests of consumers.

(2) The Authority must appoint one of the members of the Consumer Panel to be its chairman.

(3) The Treasury's approval is required for the appointment or dismissal of the chairman.

(4) The Authority must have regard to any representations made to it by the Consumer Panel.

(5) The Authority must appoint to the Consumer Panel such consumers, or persons representing the interests of consumers, as it considers appropriate.

(6) The Authority must secure that the membership of the Consumer Panel is such as to give a fair degree of representation to those who are using, or are or may be contemplating using, services otherwise than in connection with businesses carried on by them.

(7) "Consumers" means persons, other than authorised persons—
    (a) who are consumers for the purposes of section 138; or
    (b) who, in relation to regulated activities carried on otherwise than by authorised persons, would be consumers for those purposes if the activities were carried on by authorised persons.

11. Duty to consider representations by the Panels

(1) This section applies to a representation made, in accordance with arrangements made under section 8, by the Practitioner Panel or by the Consumer Panel.

(2) The Authority must consider the representation.

(3) If the Authority disagrees with a view expressed, or proposal made, in the representation, it must give the Panel a statement in writing of its reasons for disagreeing.

Reviews

12. Reviews

(1) The Treasury may appoint an independent person to conduct a review of the economy, efficiency and effectiveness with which the Authority has used its resources in discharging its functions.

(2)   A review may be limited by the Treasury to such functions of the Authority (however described) as the Treasury may specify in appointing the person to conduct it.

(3)   A review is not to be concerned with the merits of the Authority's general policy or principles in pursuing regulatory objectives or in exercising functions under Part VI.

(4)   On completion of a review, the person conducting it must make a written report to the Treasury—

         (a)   setting out the result of the review; and

         (b)   making such recommendations (if any) as he considers appropriate.

(5)   A copy of the report must be—

         (a)   laid before each House of Parliament; and

         (b)   published in such manner as the Treasury consider appropriate.

(6)   Any expenses reasonably incurred in the conduct of a review are to be met by the Treasury out of money provided by Parliament.

(7)   "Independent" means appearing to the Treasury to be independent of the Authority.

13.   Right to obtain documents and information

(1)   A person conducting a review under section 12—

         (a)   has a right of access at any reasonable time to all such documents as he may reasonably require for purposes of the review; and

         (b)   may require any person holding or accountable for any such document to provide such information and explanation as are reasonably necessary for that purpose.

(2)   Subsection (1) applies only to documents in the custody or under the control of the Authority.

(3)   An obligation imposed on a person as a result of the exercise of powers conferred by subsection (1) is enforceable by injunction or, in Scotland, by an order for specific performance under section 45 of the Court of Session Act 1988.

Inquiries

14.   Cases in which the Treasury may arrange independent inquiries

(1)   This section applies in two cases.

(2)   The first is where it appears to the Treasury that—

         (a)   events have occurred in relation to—

             (i)   a collective investment scheme, or

             (ii)   a person who is, or was at the time of the events, carrying on a regulated activity (whether or not as an authorised person),

     which posed or could have posed a grave risk to the financial system or caused or risked causing significant damage to the interests of consumers; and

         (b)   those events might not have occurred, or the risk or damage might have been reduced, but for a serious failure in—

             (i)   the system established by this Act for the regulation of such schemes or of such persons and their activities; or

             (ii)   the operation of that system.

(3)   The second is where it appears to the Treasury that—

         (a)   events have occurred in relation to listed securities or an issuer of listed securities which caused or could have caused significant damage to holders of listed securities; and

         (b)   those events might not have occurred but for a serious failure in the regulatory system established by Part VI or in its operation.

(4)   If the Treasury consider that it is in the public interest that there should be an independent inquiry into the events and the circumstances surrounding them, they may arrange for an inquiry to be held under section 15.

(5)   "Consumers" means persons—

         (a)   who are consumers for the purposes of section 138; or

         (b)   who, in relation to regulated activities carried on otherwise than by authorised persons, would be consumers for those purposes if the activities were carried on by authorised persons.

(6) "The financial system" has the same meaning as in section 3.

(7) "Listed securities" means anything which has been admitted to the official list under Part VI.

15. Power to appoint person to hold an inquiry

(1) If the Treasury decide to arrange for an inquiry to be held under this section, they may appoint such person as they consider appropriate to hold the inquiry.

(2) The Treasury may, by a direction to the appointed person, control—
   (a) the scope of the inquiry;
   (b) the period during which the inquiry is to be held;
   (c) the conduct of the inquiry; and
   (d) the making of reports.

(3) A direction may, in particular—
   (a) confine the inquiry to particular matters;
   (b) extend the inquiry to additional matters;
   (c) require the appointed person to discontinue the inquiry or to take only such steps as are specified in the direction;
   (d) require the appointed person to make such interim reports as are so specified.

16. Powers of appointed person and procedure

(1) The person appointed to hold an inquiry under section 15 may—
   (a) obtain such information from such persons and in such manner as he thinks fit;
   (b) make such inquiries as he thinks fit; and
   (c) determine the procedure to be followed in connection with the inquiry.

(2) The appointed person may require any person who, in his opinion, is able to provide any information, or produce any document, which is relevant to the inquiry to provide any such information or produce any such document.

(3) For the purposes of an inquiry, the appointed person has the same powers as the court in respect of the attendance and examination of witnesses (including the examination of witnesses abroad) and in respect of the production of documents.

(4) "Court" means—
   (a) the High Court; or
   (b) in Scotland, the Court of Session.

17. Conclusion of inquiry

(1) On completion of an inquiry under section 15, the person holding the inquiry must make a written report to the Treasury—
   (a) setting out the result of the inquiry; and
   (b) making such recommendations (if any) as he considers appropriate.

(2) The Treasury may publish the whole, or any part, of the report and may do so in such manner as they consider appropriate.

(3) Subsection (4) applies if the Treasury propose to publish a report but consider that it contains material—
   (a) which relates to the affairs of a particular person whose interests would, in the opinion of the Treasury, be seriously prejudiced by publication of the material; or
   (b) the disclosure of which would be incompatible with an international obligation of the United Kingdom.

(4) The Treasury must ensure that the material is removed before publication.

(5) The Treasury must lay before each House of Parliament a copy of any report or part of a report published under subsection (2).

(6) Any expenses reasonably incurred in holding an inquiry are to be met by the Treasury out of money provided by Parliament.

18. Obstruction and contempt

(1) If a person ("A")—

(a) fails to comply with a requirement imposed on him by a person holding an inquiry under section 15, or

(b) otherwise obstructs such an inquiry,

the person holding the inquiry may certify the matter to the High Court (or, in Scotland, the Court of Session).

(2) The court may enquire into the matter.

(3) If, after hearing—

(a) any witnesses who may be produced against or on behalf of A, and

(b) any statement made by or on behalf of A,

the court is satisfied that A would have been in contempt of court if the inquiry had been proceedings before the court, it may deal with him as if he were in contempt.

PART II
REGULATED AND PROHIBITED ACTIVITIES

The general prohibition

19.   The general prohibition

(1) No person may carry on a regulated activity in the United Kingdom, or purport to do so, unless he is—

(a) an authorised person; or

(b) an exempt person.

(2) The prohibition is referred to in this Act as the general prohibition.

Requirement for permission

20.   Authorised persons acting without permission

(1) If an authorised person carries on a regulated activity in the United Kingdom, or purports to do so, otherwise than in accordance with permission—

(a) given to him by the Authority under Part IV, or

(b) resulting from any other provision of this Act,

he is to be taken to have contravened a requirement imposed on him by the Authority under this Act.

(2) The contravention does not—

(a) make a person guilty of an offence;

(b) make any transaction void or unenforceable; or

(c) (subject to subsection (3)) give rise to any right of action for breach of statutory duty.

(3) In prescribed cases the contravention is actionable at the suit of a person who suffers loss as a result of the contravention, subject to the defences and other incidents applying to actions for breach of statutory duty.

Financial promotion

21.   Restrictions on financial promotion

(1) A person ("A") must not, in the course of business, communicate an invitation or inducement to engage in investment activity.

(2) But subsection (1) does not apply if—

(a) A is an authorised person; or

(b) the content of the communication is approved for the purposes of this section by an authorised person.

(3) In the case of a communication originating outside the United Kingdom, subsection (1) applies only if the communication is capable of having an effect in the United Kingdom.

(4) The Treasury may by order specify circumstances in which a person is to be regarded for the purposes of subsection (1) as—

(a) acting in the course of business;

    (b)   not acting in the course of business.

(5)   The Treasury may by order specify circumstances (which may include compliance with financial promotion rules) in which subsection (1) does not apply.

(6)   An order under subsection (5) may, in particular, provide that subsection (1) does not apply in relation to communications—
    (a)   of a specified description;
    (b)   originating in a specified country or territory outside the United Kingdom;
    (c)   originating in a country or territory which falls within a specified description of country or territory outside the United Kingdom; or
    (d)   originating outside the United Kingdom.

(7)   The Treasury may by order repeal subsection (3).

(8)   "Engaging in investment activity" means—
    (a)   entering or offering to enter into an agreement the making or performance of which by either party constitutes a controlled activity; or
    (b)   exercising any rights conferred by a controlled investment to acquire, dispose of, underwrite or convert a controlled investment.

(9)   An activity is a controlled activity if—
    (a)   it is an activity of a specified kind or one which falls within a specified class of activity; and
    (b)   it relates to an investment of a specified kind, or to one which falls within a specified class of investment.

(10)   An investment is a controlled investment if it is an investment of a specified kind or one which falls within a specified class of investment.

(11)   Schedule 2 (except paragraph 26) applies for the purposes of subsections (9) and (10) with references to section 22 being read as references to each of those subsections.

(12)   Nothing in Schedule 2, as applied by subsection (11), limits the powers conferred by subsection (9) or (10).

(13)   "Communicate" includes causing a communication to be made.

(14)   "Investment" includes any asset, right or interest.

(15)   "Specified" means specified in an order made by the Treasury.

Regulated activities

22.   **The classes of activity and categories of investment**

(1)   An activity is a regulated activity for the purposes of this Act if it is an activity of a specified kind which is carried on by way of business and—
    (a)   relates to an investment of a specified kind; or
    (b)   in the case of an activity of a kind which is also specified for the purposes of this paragraph, is carried on in relation to property of any kind.

(2)   Schedule 2 makes provision supplementing this section.

(3)   Nothing in Schedule 2 limits the powers conferred by subsection (1).

(4)   "Investment" includes any asset, right or interest.

(5)   "Specified" means specified in an order made by the Treasury.

Offences

23.   **Contravention of the general prohibition**

(1)   A person who contravenes the general prohibition is guilty of an offence and liable—
    (a)   on summary conviction, to imprisonment for a term not exceeding six months or a fine not exceeding the statutory maximum, or both;
    (b)   on conviction on indictment, to imprisonment for a term not exceeding two years or a fine, or both.

(2)   In this Act "an authorisation offence" means an offence under this section.

(3)   In proceedings for an authorisation offence it is a defence for the accused to show that he took all reasonable precautions and exercised all due diligence to avoid committing the offence.

24.   False claims to be authorised or exempt

(1)   A person who is neither an authorised person nor, in relation to the regulated activity in question, an exempt person is guilty of an offence if he—

    (a)   describes himself (in whatever terms) as an authorised person;

    (b)   describes himself (in whatever terms) as an exempt person in relation to the regulated activity; or

    (c)   behaves, or otherwise holds himself out, in a manner which indicates (or which is reasonably likely to be understood as indicating) that he is—

       (i)   an authorised person; or

       (ii)   an exempt person in relation to the regulated activity.

(2)   In proceedings for an offence under this section it is a defence for the accused to show that he took all reasonable precautions and exercised all due diligence to avoid committing the offence.

(3)   A person guilty of an offence under this section is liable on summary conviction to imprisonment for a term not exceeding six months or a fine not exceeding level 5 on the standard scale, or both.

(4)   But where the conduct constituting the offence involved or included the public display of any material, the maximum fine for the offence is level 5 on the standard scale multiplied by the number of days for which the display continued.

25.   Contravention of section 21

(1)   A person who contravenes section 21(1) is guilty of an offence and liable—

    (a)   on summary conviction, to imprisonment for a term not exceeding six months or a fine not exceeding the statutory maximum, or both;

    (b)   on conviction on indictment, to imprisonment for a term not exceeding two years or a fine, or both.

(2)   In proceedings for an offence under this section it is a defence for the accused to show—

    (a)   that he believed on reasonable grounds that the content of the communication was prepared, or approved for the purposes of section 21, by an authorised person; or

    (b)   that he took all reasonable precautions and exercised all due diligence to avoid committing the offence.

Enforceability of agreements

26.   Agreements made by unauthorised persons

(1)   An agreement made by a person in the course of carrying on a regulated activity in contravention of the general prohibition is unenforceable against the other party.

(2)   The other party is entitled to recover—

    (a)   any money or other property paid or transferred by him under the agreement; and

    (b)   compensation for any loss sustained by him as a result of having parted with it.

(3)   "Agreement" means an agreement—

    (a)   made after this section comes into force; and

    (b)   the making or performance of which constitutes, or is part of, the regulated activity in question.

(4)   This section does not apply if the regulated activity is accepting deposits.

27.   Agreements made through unauthorised persons

(1)   An agreement made by an authorised person ("the provider")—

    (a)   in the course of carrying on a regulated activity (not in contravention of the general prohibition), but

    (b)   in consequence of something said or done by another person ("the third party") in the course of a regulated activity carried on by the third party in contravention of the general prohibition,

is unenforceable against the other party.

(2)   The other party is entitled to recover—

    (a)   any money or other property paid or transferred by him under the agreement; and

(b) compensation for any loss sustained by him as a result of having parted with it.

(3) "Agreement" means an agreement—

    (a) made after this section comes into force; and

    (b) the making or performance of which constitutes, or is part of, the regulated activity in question carried on by the provider.

(4) This section does not apply if the regulated activity is accepting deposits.

28. Agreements made unenforceable by section 26 or 27

(1) This section applies to an agreement which is unenforceable because of section 26 or 27.

(2) The amount of compensation recoverable as a result of that section is—

    (a) the amount agreed by the parties; or

    (b) on the application of either party, the amount determined by the court.

(3) If the court is satisfied that it is just and equitable in the circumstances of the case, it may allow—

    (a) the agreement to be enforced; or

    (b) money and property paid or transferred under the agreement to be retained.

(4) In considering whether to allow the agreement to be enforced or (as the case may be) the money or property paid or transferred under the agreement to be retained the court must—

    (a) if the case arises as a result of section 26, have regard to the issue mentioned in subsection (5); or

    (b) if the case arises as a result of section 27, have regard to the issue mentioned in subsection (6).

(5) The issue is whether the person carrying on the regulated activity concerned reasonably believed that he was not contravening the general prohibition by making the agreement.

(6) The issue is whether the provider knew that the third party was (in carrying on the regulated activity) contravening the general prohibition.

(7) If the person against whom the agreement is unenforceable—

    (a) elects not to perform the agreement, or

    (b) as a result of this section, recovers money paid or other property transferred by him under the agreement,

he must repay any money and return any other property received by him under the agreement.

(8) If property transferred under the agreement has passed to a third party, a reference in section 26 or 27 or this section to that property is to be read as a reference to its value at the time of its transfer under the agreement.

(9) The commission of an authorisation offence does not make the agreement concerned illegal or invalid to any greater extent than is provided by section 26 or 27.

29. Accepting deposits in breach of general prohibition

(1) This section applies to an agreement between a person ("the depositor") and another person ("the deposit-taker") made in the course of the carrying on by the deposit-taker of accepting deposits in contravention of the general prohibition.

(2) If the depositor is not entitled under the agreement to recover without delay any money deposited by him, he may apply to the court for an order directing the deposit-taker to return the money to him.

(3) The court need not make such an order if it is satisfied that it would not be just and equitable for the money deposited to be returned, having regard to the issue mentioned in subsection (4).

(4) The issue is whether the deposit-taker reasonably believed that he was not contravening the general prohibition by making the agreement.

(5) "Agreement" means an agreement—

    (a) made after this section comes into force; and

    (b) the making or performance of which constitutes, or is part of, accepting deposits.

30. Enforceability of agreements resulting from unlawful communications

(1) In this section—

"unlawful communication" means a communication in relation to which there has been a contravention of section 21(1);

"controlled agreement" means an agreement the making or performance of which by either party constitutes a controlled activity for the purposes of that section; and

"controlled investment" has the same meaning as in section 21.

(2) If in consequence of an unlawful communication a person enters as a customer into a controlled agreement, it is unenforceable against him and he is entitled to recover—

    (a)   any money or other property paid or transferred by him under the agreement; and

    (b)   compensation for any loss sustained by him as a result of having parted with it.

(3) If in consequence of an unlawful communication a person exercises any rights conferred by a controlled investment, no obligation to which he is subject as a result of exercising them is enforceable against him and he is entitled to recover—

    (a)   any money or other property paid or transferred by him under the obligation; and

    (b)   compensation for any loss sustained by him as a result of having parted with it.

(4) But the court may allow—

    (a)   the agreement or obligation to be enforced, or

    (b)   money or property paid or transferred under the agreement or obligation to be retained,

if it is satisfied that it is just and equitable in the circumstances of the case.

(5) In considering whether to allow the agreement or obligation to be enforced or (as the case may be) the money or property paid or transferred under the agreement to be retained the court must have regard to the issues mentioned in subsections (6) and (7).

(6) If the applicant made the unlawful communication, the issue is whether he reasonably believed that he was not making such a communication.

(7) If the applicant did not make the unlawful communication, the issue is whether he knew that the agreement was entered into in consequence of such a communication.

(8) "Applicant" means the person seeking to enforce the agreement or obligation or retain the money or property paid or transferred.

(9) Any reference to making a communication includes causing a communication to be made.

(10) The amount of compensation recoverable as a result of subsection (2) or (3) is—

    (a)   the amount agreed between the parties; or

    (b)   on the application of either party, the amount determined by the court.

(11) If a person elects not to perform an agreement or an obligation which (by virtue of subsection (2) or (3)) is unenforceable against him, he must repay any money and return any other property received by him under the agreement.

(12) If (by virtue of subsection (2) or (3)) a person recovers money paid or property transferred by him under an agreement or obligation, he must repay any money and return any other property received by him as a result of exercising the rights in question.

(13) If any property required to be returned under this section has passed to a third party, references to that property are to be read as references to its value at the time of its receipt by the person required to return it.

...

PART VI
OFFICIAL LISTING

The competent authority

72.   **The competent authority**

(1) On the coming into force of this section, the functions conferred on the competent authority by this Part are to be exercised by the Authority.

(2) Schedule 7 modifies this Act in its application to the Authority when it acts as the competent authority.

(3)   But provision is made by Schedule 8 allowing some or all of those functions to be transferred by the Treasury so as to be exercisable by another person.

73.   General duty of the competent authority

(1)   In discharging its general functions the competent authority must have regard to—
  (a)   the need to use its resources in the most efficient and economic way;
  (b)   the principle that a burden or restriction which is imposed on a person should be proportionate to the benefits, considered in general terms, which are expected to arise from the imposition of that burden or restriction;
  (c)   the desirability of facilitating innovation in respect of listed securities;
  (d)   the international character of capital markets and the desirability of maintaining the competitive position of the United Kingdom;
  (e)   the need to minimise the adverse effects on competition of anything done in the discharge of those functions;
  (f)   the desirability of facilitating competition in relation to listed securities.
(2)   The competent authority's general functions are—
  (a)   its function of making rules under this Part (considered as a whole);
  (b)   its functions in relation to the giving of general guidance in relation to this Part (considered as a whole);
  (c)   its function of determining the general policy and principles by reference to which it performs particular functions under this Part.

The official list

74.   The official list

(1)   The competent authority must maintain the official list.
(2)   The competent authority may admit to the official list such securities and other things as it considers appropriate.
(3)   But—
  (a)   nothing may be admitted to the official list except in accordance with this Part; and
  (b)   the Treasury may by order provide that anything which falls within a description or category specified in the order may not be admitted to the official list.
(4)   The competent authority may make rules ("listing rules") for the purposes of this Part.
(5)   In the following provisions of this Part—
  "security" means anything which has been, or may be, admitted to the official list; and
  "listing" means being included in the official list in accordance with this Part.

Listing

75.   Applications for listing

(1)   Admission to the official list may be granted only on an application made to the competent authority in such manner as may be required by listing rules.
(2)   No application for listing may be entertained by the competent authority unless it is made by, or with the consent of, the issuer of the securities concerned.
(3)   No application for listing may be entertained by the competent authority in respect of securities which are to be issued by a body of a prescribed kind.
(4)   The competent authority may not grant an application for listing unless it is satisfied that—
  (a)   the requirements of listing rules (so far as they apply to the application), and
  (b)   any other requirements imposed by the authority in relation to the application,
  are complied with.
(5)   An application for listing may be refused if, for a reason relating to the issuer, the competent authority considers that granting it would be detrimental to the interests of investors.

(6)   An application for listing securities which are already officially listed in another EEA State may
         be refused if the issuer has failed to comply with any obligations to which he is subject as a result
         of that listing.

76.   Decision on application

(1)   The competent authority must notify the applicant of its decision on an application for listing—
         (a)   before the end of the period of six months beginning with the date on which the application
                is received; or
         (b)   if within that period the authority has required the applicant to provide further information
                in connection with the application, before the end of the period of six months beginning
                with the date on which that information is provided.
(2)   If the competent authority fails to comply with subsection (1), it is to be taken to have decided to
         refuse the application.
(3)   If the competent authority decides to grant an application for listing, it must give the applicant
         written notice.
(4)   If the competent authority proposes to refuse an application for listing, it must give the applicant
         a warning notice.
(5)   If the competent authority decides to refuse an application for listing, it must give the applicant a
         decision notice.
(6)   If the competent authority decides to refuse an application for listing, the applicant may refer the
         matter to the Tribunal.
(7)   If securities are admitted to the official list, their admission may not be called in question on the
         ground that any requirement or condition for their admission has not been complied with.

77.   Discontinuance and suspension of listing

(1)   The competent authority may, in accordance with listing rules, discontinue the listing of any
         securities if satisfied that there are special circumstances which preclude normal regular dealings
         in them.
(2)   The competent authority may, in accordance with listing rules, suspend the listing of any
         securities.
(3)   If securities are suspended under subsection (2) they are to be treated, for the purposes of sections
         96 and 99, as still being listed.
(4)   This section applies to securities whenever they were admitted to the official list.
(5)   If the competent authority discontinues or suspends the listing of any securities, the issuer may
         refer the matter to the Tribunal.

78.   Discontinuance or suspension: procedure

(1)   A discontinuance or suspension takes effect—
         (a)   immediately, if the notice under subsection (2) states that that is the case;
         (b)   in any other case, on such date as may be specified in that notice.
(2)   If the competent authority—
         (a)   proposes to discontinue or suspend the listing of securities, or
         (b)   discontinues or suspends the listing of securities with immediate effect,
         it must give the issuer of the securities written notice.
(3)   The notice must—
         (a)   give details of the discontinuance or suspension;
         (b)   state the competent authority's reasons for the discontinuance or suspension and for
                choosing the date on which it took effect or takes effect;
         (c)   inform the issuer of the securities that he may make representations to the competent
                authority within such period as may be specified in the notice (whether or not he has
                referred the matter to the Tribunal);
         (d)   inform him of the date on which the discontinuance or suspension took effect or will take
                effect; and
         (e)   inform him of his right to refer the matter to the Tribunal.

(4) The competent authority may extend the period within which representations may be made to it.

(5) If, having considered any representations made by the issuer of the securities, the competent authority decides—

(a) to discontinue or suspend the listing of the securities, or

(b) if the discontinuance or suspension has taken effect, not to cancel it,

the competent authority must give the issuer of the securities written notice.

(6) A notice given under subsection (5) must inform the issuer of the securities of his right to refer the matter to the Tribunal.

(7) If a notice informs a person of his right to refer a matter to the Tribunal, it must give an indication of the procedure on such a reference.

(8) If the competent authority decides—

(a) not to discontinue or suspend the listing of the securities, or

(b) if the discontinuance or suspension has taken effect, to cancel it,

the competent authority must give the issuer of the securities written notice.

(9) The effect of cancelling a discontinuance is that the securities concerned are to be readmitted, without more, to the official list.

(10) If the competent authority has suspended the listing of securities and proposes to refuse an application by the issuer of the securities for the cancellation of the suspension, it must give him a warning notice.

(11) The competent authority must, having considered any representations made in response to the warning notice—

(a) if it decides to refuse the application, give the issuer of the securities a decision notice;

(b) if it grants the application, give him written notice of its decision.

(12) If the competent authority decides to refuse an application for the cancellation of the suspension of listed securities, the applicant may refer the matter to the Tribunal.

(13) "Discontinuance" means a discontinuance of listing under section 77(1).

(14) "Suspension" means a suspension of listing under section 77(2).

Listing particulars

79. Listing particulars and other documents

(1) Listing rules may provide that securities (other than new securities) of a kind specified in the rules may not be admitted to the official list unless—

(a) listing particulars have been submitted to, and approved by, the competent authority and published; or

(b) in such cases as may be specified by listing rules, such document (other than listing particulars or a prospectus of a kind required by listing rules) as may be so specified has been published.

(2) "Listing particulars" means a document in such form and containing such information as may be specified in listing rules.

(3) For the purposes of this Part, the persons responsible for listing particulars are to be determined in accordance with regulations made by the Treasury.

(4) Nothing in this section affects the competent authority's general power to make listing rules.

80. General duty of disclosure in listing particulars

(1) Listing particulars submitted to the competent authority under section 79 must contain all such information as investors and their professional advisers would reasonably require, and reasonably expect to find there, for the purpose of making an informed assessment of—

(a) the assets and liabilities, financial position, profits and losses, and prospects of the issuer of the securities; and

(b) the rights attaching to the securities.

(2) That information is required in addition to any information required by—

(a) listing rules, or

(b) the competent authority,

as a condition of the admission of the securities to the official list.

(3)   Subsection (1) applies only to information—

    (a)   within the knowledge of any person responsible for the listing particulars; or

    (b)   which it would be reasonable for him to obtain by making enquiries.

(4)   In determining what information subsection (1) requires to be included in listing particulars, regard must be had (in particular) to—

    (a)   the nature of the securities and their issuer;

    (b)   the nature of the persons likely to consider acquiring them;

    (c)   the fact that certain matters may reasonably be expected to be within the knowledge of professional advisers of a kind which persons likely to acquire the securities may reasonably be expected to consult; and

    (d)   any information available to investors or their professional advisers as a result of requirements imposed on the issuer of the securities by a recognised investment exchange, by listing rules or by or under any other enactment.

81.   Supplementary listing particulars

(1)   If at any time after the preparation of listing particulars which have been submitted to the competent authority under section 79 and before the commencement of dealings in the securities concerned following their admission to the official list—

    (a)   there is a significant change affecting any matter contained in those particulars the inclusion of which was required by—

        (i)   section 80,

        (ii)   listing rules, or

        (iii)   the competent authority, or

    (b)   a significant new matter arises, the inclusion of information in respect of which would have been so required if it had arisen when the particulars were prepared,

the issuer must, in accordance with listing rules, submit supplementary listing particulars of the change or new matter to the competent authority, for its approval and, if they are approved, publish them.

(2)   "Significant" means significant for the purpose of making an informed assessment of the kind mentioned in section 80(1).

(3)   If the issuer of the securities is not aware of the change or new matter in question, he is not under a duty to comply with subsection (1) unless he is notified of the change or new matter by a person responsible for the listing particulars.

(4)   But it is the duty of any person responsible for those particulars who is aware of such a change or new matter to give notice of it to the issuer.

(5)   Subsection (1) applies also as respects matters contained in any supplementary listing particulars previously published under this section in respect of the securities in question.

82.   Exemptions from disclosure

(1)   The competent authority may authorise the omission from listing particulars of any information, the inclusion of which would otherwise be required by section 80 or 81, on the ground—

    (a)   that its disclosure would be contrary to the public interest;

    (b)   that its disclosure would be seriously detrimental to the issuer; or

    (c)   in the case of securities of a kind specified in listing rules, that its disclosure is unnecessary for persons of the kind who may be expected normally to buy or deal in securities of that kind.

(2)   But—

    (a)   no authority may be granted under subsection (1)(b) in respect of essential information; and

    (b)   no authority granted under subsection (1)(b) extends to any such information.

(3)   The Secretary of State or the Treasury may issue a certificate to the effect that the disclosure of any information (including information that would otherwise have to be included in listing particulars for which they are themselves responsible) would be contrary to the public interest.

(4)   The competent authority is entitled to act on any such certificate in exercising its powers under subsection (1)(a).

(5)   This section does not affect any powers of the competent authority under listing rules made as a result of section 101(2).

(6)   "Essential information" means information which a person considering acquiring securities of the kind in question would be likely to need in order not to be misled about any facts which it is essential for him to know in order to make an informed assessment.

(7)   "Listing particulars" includes supplementary listing particulars.

83.   Registration of listing particulars

(1)   On or before the date on which listing particulars are published as required by listing rules, a copy of the particulars must be delivered for registration to the registrar of companies.

(2)   A statement that a copy has been delivered to the registrar must be included in the listing particulars when they are published.

(3)   If there has been a failure to comply with subsection (1) in relation to listing particulars which have been published—

     (a)   the issuer of the securities in question, and

     (b)   any person who is a party to the publication and aware of the failure,

is guilty of an offence.

(4)   A person guilty of an offence under subsection (3) is liable—

     (a)   on summary conviction, to a fine not exceeding the statutory maximum;

     (b)   on conviction on indictment, to a fine.

(5)   "Listing particulars" includes supplementary listing particulars.

(6)   "The registrar of companies" means—

     (a)   if the securities are, or are to be, issued by a company incorporated in Great Britain whose registered office is in England and Wales, the registrar of companies in England and Wales;

     (b)   if the securities are, or are to be, issued by a company incorporated in Great Britain whose registered office is in Scotland, the registrar of companies in Scotland;

     (c)   if the securities are, or are to be, issued by a company incorporated in Northern Ireland, the registrar of companies for Northern Ireland; and

     (d)   in any other case, any of those registrars.

Prospectuses

84.   Prospectuses

(1)   Listing rules must provide that no new securities for which an application for listing has been made may be admitted to the official list unless a prospectus has been submitted to, and approved by, the competent authority and published.

(2)   "New securities" means securities which are to be offered to the public in the United Kingdom for the first time before admission to the official list.

(3)   "Prospectus" means a prospectus in such form and containing such information as may be specified in listing rules.

(4)   Nothing in this section affects the competent authority's general power to make listing rules.

85.   Publication of prospectus

(1)   If listing rules made under section 84 require a prospectus to be published before particular new securities are admitted to the official list, it is unlawful for any of those securities to be offered to the public in the United Kingdom before the required prospectus is published.

(2)   A person who contravenes subsection (1) is guilty of an offence and liable—

     (a)   on summary conviction, to imprisonment for a term not exceeding three months or a fine not exceeding level 5 on the standard scale;

     (b)   on conviction on indictment, to imprisonment for a term not exceeding two years or a fine, or both.

(3)   A person is not to be regarded as contravening subsection (1) merely because a prospectus does not fully comply with the requirements of listing rules as to its form or content.

(4)   But subsection (3) does not affect the question whether any person is liable to pay compensation under section 90.

(5)   Any contravention of subsection (1) is actionable, at the suit of a person who suffers loss as a result of the contravention, subject to the defences and other incidents applying to actions for breach of statutory duty.

86.   Application of this Part to prospectuses

(1)   The provisions of this Part apply in relation to a prospectus required by listing rules as they apply in relation to listing particulars.

(2)   In this Part—

(a)   any reference to listing particulars is to be read as including a reference to a prospectus; and

(b)   any reference to supplementary listing particulars is to be read as including a reference to a supplementary prospectus.

87.   Approval of prospectus where no application for listing

(1)   Listing rules may provide for a prospectus to be submitted to and approved by the competent authority if—

(a)   securities are to be offered to the public in the United Kingdom for the first time;

(b)   no application for listing of the securities has been made under this Part; and

(c)   the prospectus is submitted by, or with the consent of, the issuer of the securities.

(2)   "Non-listing prospectus" means a prospectus submitted to the competent authority as a result of any listing rules made under subsection (1).

(3)   Listing rules made under subsection (1) may make provision—

(a)   as to the information to be contained in, and the form of, a non-listing prospectus; and

(b)   as to the timing and manner of publication of a non-listing prospectus.

(4)   The power conferred by subsection (3)(b) is subject to such provision made by or under any other enactment as the Treasury may by order specify.

(5)   Schedule 9 modifies provisions of this Part as they apply in relation to non-listing prospectuses.

Sponsors

88.   Sponsors

(1)   Listing rules may require a person to make arrangements with a sponsor for the performance by the sponsor of such services in relation to him as may be specified in the rules.

(2)   "Sponsor" means a person approved by the competent authority for the purposes of the rules.

(3)   Listing rules made by virtue of subsection (1) may—

(a)   provide for the competent authority to maintain a list of sponsors;

(b)   specify services which must be performed by a sponsor;

(c)   impose requirements on a sponsor in relation to the provision of services or specified services;

(d)   specify the circumstances in which a person is qualified for being approved as a sponsor.

(4)   If the competent authority proposes—

(a)   to refuse a person's application for approval as a sponsor, or

(b)   to cancel a person's approval as a sponsor,

it must give him a warning notice.

(5)   If, after considering any representations made in response to the warning notice, the competent authority decides—

(a)   to grant the application for approval, or

(b)   not to cancel the approval,

it must give the person concerned, and any person to whom a copy of the warning notice was given, written notice of its decision.

(6) If, after considering any representations made in response to the warning notice, the competent authority decides—

(a) to refuse to grant the application for approval, or

(b) to cancel the approval,

it must give the person concerned a decision notice.

(7) A person to whom a decision notice is given under this section may refer the matter to the Tribunal.

89. Public censure of sponsor

(1) Listing rules may make provision for the competent authority, if it considers that a sponsor has contravened a requirement imposed on him by rules made as a result of section 88(3)(c), to publish a statement to that effect.

(2) If the competent authority proposes to publish a statement it must give the sponsor a warning notice setting out the terms of the proposed statement.

(3) If, after considering any representations made in response to the warning notice, the competent authority decides to make the proposed statement, it must give the sponsor a decision notice setting out the terms of the statement.

(4) A sponsor to whom a decision notice is given under this section may refer the matter to the Tribunal.

Compensation

90. Compensation for false or misleading particulars

(1) Any person responsible for listing particulars is liable to pay compensation to a person who has—

(a) acquired securities to which the particulars apply; and

(b) suffered loss in respect of them as a result of—

(i) any untrue or misleading statement in the particulars; or

(ii) the omission from the particulars of any matter required to be included by section 80 or 81.

(2) Subsection (1) is subject to exemptions provided by Schedule 10.

(3) If listing particulars are required to include information about the absence of a particular matter, the omission from the particulars of that information is to be treated as a statement in the listing particulars that there is no such matter.

(4) Any person who fails to comply with section 81 is liable to pay compensation to any person who has—

(a) acquired securities of the kind in question; and

(b) suffered loss in respect of them as a result of the failure.

(5) Subsection (4) is subject to exemptions provided by Schedule 10.

(6) This section does not affect any liability which may be incurred apart from this section.

(7) References in this section to the acquisition by a person of securities include references to his contracting to acquire them or any interest in them.

(8) No person shall, by reason of being a promoter of a company or otherwise, incur any liability for failing to disclose information which he would not be required to disclose in listing particulars in respect of a company's securities—

(a) if he were responsible for those particulars; or

(b) if he is responsible for them, which he is entitled to omit by virtue of section 82.

(9) The reference in subsection (8) to a person incurring liability includes a reference to any other person being entitled as against that person to be granted any civil remedy or to rescind or repudiate an agreement.

(10) "Listing particulars", in subsection (1) and Schedule 10, includes supplementary listing particulars.

Penalties

91.   Penalties for breach of listing rules

(1)   If the competent authority considers that—

(a)   an issuer of listed securities, or

(b)   an applicant for listing,

has contravened any provision of listing rules, it may impose on him a penalty of such amount as it considers appropriate.

(2)   If, in such a case, the competent authority considers that a person who was at the material time a director of the issuer or applicant was knowingly concerned in the contravention, it may impose on him a penalty of such amount as it considers appropriate.

(3)   If the competent authority is entitled to impose a penalty on a person under this section in respect of a particular matter it may, instead of imposing a penalty on him in respect of that matter, publish a statement censuring him.

(4)   Nothing in this section prevents the competent authority from taking any other steps which it has power to take under this Part.

(5)   A penalty under this section is payable to the competent authority.

(6)   The competent authority may not take action against a person under this section after the end of the period of two years beginning with the first day on which it knew of the contravention unless proceedings against that person, in respect of the contravention, were begun before the end of that period.

(7)   For the purposes of subsection (6)—

(a)   the competent authority is to be treated as knowing of a contravention if it has information from which the contravention can reasonably be inferred; and

(b)   proceedings against a person in respect of a contravention are to be treated as begun when a warning notice is given to him under section 92.

92.   Warning notices

(1)   If the competent authority proposes to take action against a person under section 91, it must give him a warning notice.

(2)   A warning notice about a proposal to impose a penalty must state the amount of the proposed penalty.

(3)   A warning notice about a proposal to publish a statement must set out the terms of the proposed statement.

(4)   If the competent authority decides to take action against a person under section 91, it must give him a decision notice.

(5)   A decision notice about the imposition of a penalty must state the amount of the penalty.

(6)   A decision notice about the publication of a statement must set out the terms of the statement.

(7)   If the competent authority decides to take action against a person under section 91, he may refer the matter to the Tribunal.

93.   Statement of policy

(1)   The competent authority must prepare and issue a statement ("its policy statement") of its policy with respect to—

(a)   the imposition of penalties under section 91; and

(b)   the amount of penalties under that section.

(2)   The competent authority's policy in determining what the amount of a penalty should be must include having regard to—

(a)   the seriousness of the contravention in question in relation to the nature of the requirement contravened;

(b)   the extent to which that contravention was deliberate or reckless; and

(c)   whether the person on whom the penalty is to be imposed is an individual.

(3)   The competent authority may at any time alter or replace its policy statement.

(4)   If its policy statement is altered or replaced, the competent authority must issue the altered or replacement statement.

(5)   In exercising, or deciding whether to exercise, its power under section 91 in the case of any particular contravention, the competent authority must have regard to any policy statement published under this section and in force at the time when the contravention in question occurred.

(6)   The competent authority must publish a statement issued under this section in the way appearing to the competent authority to be best calculated to bring it to the attention of the public.

(7)   The competent authority may charge a reasonable fee for providing a person with a copy of the statement.

(8)   The competent authority must, without delay, give the Treasury a copy of any policy statement which it publishes under this section.

94.   Statements of policy: procedure

(1)   Before issuing a statement under section 93, the competent authority must publish a draft of the proposed statement in the way appearing to the competent authority to be best calculated to bring it to the attention of the public.

(2)   The draft must be accompanied by notice that representations about the proposal may be made to the competent authority within a specified time.

(3)   Before issuing the proposed statement, the competent authority must have regard to any representations made to it in accordance with subsection (2).

(4)   If the competent authority issues the proposed statement it must publish an account, in general terms, of—

        (a)   the representations made to it in accordance with subsection (2); and

        (b)   its response to them.

(5)   If the statement differs from the draft published under subsection (1) in a way which is, in the opinion of the competent authority, significant, the competent authority must (in addition to complying with subsection (4)) publish details of the difference.

(6)   The competent authority may charge a reasonable fee for providing a person with a copy of a draft published under subsection (1).

(7)   This section also applies to a proposal to alter or replace a statement.

Competition

95.   Competition scrutiny

(1)   The Treasury may by order provide for—

        (a)   regulating provisions, and

        (b)   the practices of the competent authority in exercising its functions under this Part ("practices"),

        to be kept under review.

(2)   Provision made as a result of subsection (1) must require the person responsible for keeping regulating provisions and practices under review to consider—

        (a)   whether any regulating provision or practice has a significantly adverse effect on competition; or

        (b)   whether two or more regulating provisions or practices taken together have, or a particular combination of regulating provisions and practices has, such an effect.

(3)   An order under this section may include provision corresponding to that made by any provision of Chapter III of Part X.

(4)   Subsection (3) is not to be read as in any way restricting the power conferred by subsection (1).

(5)   Subsections (6) to (8) apply for the purposes of provision made by or under this section.

(6)   Regulating provisions or practices have a significantly adverse effect on competition if—

        (a)   they have, or are intended or likely to have, that effect; or

        (b)   the effect that they have, or are intended or likely to have, is to require or encourage behaviour which has, or is intended or likely to have, a significantly adverse effect on competition.

(7)   If regulating provisions or practices have, or are intended or likely to have, the effect of requiring or encouraging exploitation of the strength of a market position they are to be taken to have, or be intended or be likely to have, an adverse effect on competition.

(8)   In determining whether any of the regulating provisions or practices have, or are intended or likely to have, a particular effect, it may be assumed that the persons to whom the provisions concerned are addressed will act in accordance with them.

(9)   "Regulating provisions" means—
   (a)   listing rules,
   (b)   general guidance given by the competent authority in connection with its functions under this Part.

Miscellaneous

96.   Obligations of issuers of listed securities

(1)   Listing rules may—
   (a)   specify requirements to be complied with by issuers of listed securities; and
   (b)   make provision with respect to the action that may be taken by the competent authority in the event of non-compliance.

(2)   If the rules require an issuer to publish information, they may include provision authorising the competent authority to publish it in the event of his failure to do so.

(3)   This section applies whenever the listed securities were admitted to the official list.

97.   Appointment by competent authority of persons to carry out investigations

(1)   Subsection (2) applies if it appears to the competent authority that there are circumstances suggesting that—
   (a)   there may have been a breach of listing rules;
   (b)   a person who was at the material time a director of an issuer of listed securities has been knowingly concerned in a breach of listing rules by that issuer;
   (c)   a person who was at the material time a director of a person applying for the admission of securities to the official list has been knowingly concerned in a breach of listing rules by that applicant;
   (d)   there may have been a contravention of section 83, 85 or 98.

(2)   The competent authority may appoint one or more competent persons to conduct an investigation on its behalf.

(3)   Part XI applies to an investigation under subsection (2) as if—
   (a)   the investigator were appointed under section 167(1);
   (b)   references to the investigating authority in relation to him were to the competent authority;
   (c)   references to the offences mentioned in section 168 were to those mentioned in subsection (1)(d);
   (d)   references to an authorised person were references to the person under investigation.

98.   Advertisements etc in connection with listing applications

(1)   If listing particulars are, or are to be, published in connection with an application for listing, no advertisement or other information of a kind specified by listing rules may be issued in the United Kingdom unless the contents of the advertisement or other information have been submitted to the competent authority and that authority has—
   (a)   approved those contents; or
   (b)   authorised the issue of the advertisement or information without such approval.

(2)   A person who contravenes subsection (1) is guilty of an offence and liable—
   (a)   on summary conviction, to a fine not exceeding the statutory maximum;
   (b)   on conviction on indictment, to imprisonment for a term not exceeding two years or a fine, or both.

(3)   A person who issues an advertisement or other information to the order of another person is not guilty of an offence under subsection (2) if he shows that he believed on reasonable grounds that

the advertisement or information had been approved, or its issue authorised, by the competent authority.

(4)   If information has been approved, or its issue has been authorised, under this section, neither the person issuing it nor any person responsible for, or for any part of, the listing particulars incurs any civil liability by reason of any statement in or omission from the information if that information and the listing particulars, taken together, would not be likely to mislead persons of the kind likely to consider acquiring the securities in question.

(5)   The reference in subsection (4) to a person incurring civil liability includes a reference to any other person being entitled as against that person to be granted any civil remedy or to rescind or repudiate an agreement.

99.   Fees

(1)   Listing rules may require the payment of fees to the competent authority in respect of—
        (a)   applications for listing;
        (b)   the continued inclusion of securities in the official list;
        (c)   applications under section 88 for approval as a sponsor; and
        (d)   continued inclusion of sponsors in the list of sponsors.

(2)   In exercising its powers under subsection (1), the competent authority may set such fees as it considers will (taking account of the income it expects as the competent authority) enable it—
        (a)   to meet expenses incurred in carrying out its functions under this Part or for any incidental purpose;
        (b)   to maintain adequate reserves; and
        (c)   in the case of the Authority, to repay the principal of, and pay any interest on, any money which it has borrowed and which has been used for the purpose of meeting expenses incurred in relation to—
                (i)   its assumption of functions from the London Stock Exchange Limited in relation to the official list; and
                (ii)   its assumption of functions under this Part.

(3)   In fixing the amount of any fee which is to be payable to the competent authority, no account is to be taken of any sums which it receives, or expects to receive, by way of penalties imposed by it under this Part.

(4)   Subsection (2)(c) applies whether expenses were incurred before or after the coming into force of this Part.

(5)   Any fee which is owed to the competent authority under any provision made by or under this Part may be recovered as a debt due to it.

100.   Penalties

(1)   In determining its policy with respect to the amount of penalties to be imposed by it under this Part, the competent authority must take no account of the expenses which it incurs, or expects to incur, in discharging its functions under this Part.

(2)   The competent authority must prepare and operate a scheme for ensuring that the amounts paid to it by way of penalties imposed under this Part are applied for the benefit of issuers of securities admitted to the official list.

(3)   The scheme may, in particular, make different provision with respect to different classes of issuer.

(4)   Up to date details of the scheme must be set out in a document ("the scheme details").

(5)   The scheme details must be published by the competent authority in the way appearing to it to be best calculated to bring them to the attention of the public.

(6)   Before making the scheme, the competent authority must publish a draft of the proposed scheme in the way appearing to it to be best calculated to bring it to the attention of the public.

(7)   The draft must be accompanied by notice that representations about the proposals may be made to the competent authority within a specified time.

(8)   Before making the scheme, the competent authority must have regard to any representations made to it under subsection (7).

(9)   If the competent authority makes the proposed scheme, it must publish an account, in general terms, of—

    (a)   the representations made to it in accordance with subsection (7); and

    (b)   its response to them.

(10)   If the scheme differs from the draft published under subsection (6) in a way which is, in the opinion of the competent authority, significant the competent authority must (in addition to complying with subsection (9)) publish details of the difference.

(11)   The competent authority must, without delay, give the Treasury a copy of any scheme details published by it.

(12)   The competent authority may charge a reasonable fee for providing a person with a copy of—

    (a)   a draft published under subsection (6);

    (b)   scheme details.

(13)   Subsections (6) to (10) and (12) apply also to a proposal to alter or replace the scheme.

101.   Listing rules: general provisions

(1)   Listing rules may make different provision for different cases.

(2)   Listing rules may authorise the competent authority to dispense with or modify the application of the rules in particular cases and by reference to any circumstances.

(3)   Listing rules must be made by an instrument in writing.

(4)   Immediately after an instrument containing listing rules is made, it must be printed and made available to the public with or without payment.

(5)   A person is not to be taken to have contravened any listing rule if he shows that at the time of the alleged contravention the instrument containing the rule had not been made available as required by subsection (4).

(6)   The production of a printed copy of an instrument purporting to be made by the competent authority on which is endorsed a certificate signed by an officer of the authority authorised by it for that purpose and stating—

    (a)   that the instrument was made by the authority,

    (b)   that the copy is a true copy of the instrument, and

    (c)   that on a specified date the instrument was made available to the public as required by subsection (4),

is evidence (or in Scotland sufficient evidence) of the facts stated in the certificate.

(7)   A certificate purporting to be signed as mentioned in subsection (6) is to be treated as having been properly signed unless the contrary is shown.

(8)   A person who wishes in any legal proceedings to rely on a rule-making instrument may require the Authority to endorse a copy of the instrument with a certificate of the kind mentioned in subsection (6).

102.   Exemption from liability in damages

(1)   Neither the competent authority nor any person who is, or is acting as, a member, officer or member of staff of the competent authority is to be liable in damages for anything done or omitted in the discharge, or purported discharge, of the authority's functions.

(2)   Subsection (1) does not apply—

    (a)   if the act or omission is shown to have been in bad faith; or

    (b)   so as to prevent an award of damages made in respect of an act or omission on the ground that the act or omission was unlawful as a result of section 6(1) of the Human Rights Act 1998.

103.   Interpretation of this Part

(1)   In this Part—

    "application" means an application made under section 75;

    "issuer", in relation to anything which is or may be admitted to the official list, has such meaning as may be prescribed by the Treasury;

    "listing" has the meaning given in section 74(5);

"listing particulars" has the meaning given in section 79(2);

"listing rules" has the meaning given in section 74(4);

"new securities" has the meaning given in section 84(2);

"the official list" means the list maintained as the official list by the Authority immediately before the coming into force of section 74, as that list has effect for the time being;

"security" (except in section 74(2)) has the meaning given in section 74(5).

(2) In relation to any function conferred on the competent authority by this Part, any reference in this Part to the competent authority is to be read as a reference to the person by whom that function is for the time being exercisable.

(3) If, as a result of an order under Schedule 8, different functions conferred on the competent authority by this Part are exercisable by different persons, the powers conferred by section 91 are exercisable by such person as may be determined in accordance with the provisions of the order.

(4) For the purposes of this Part, a person offers securities if, and only if, as principal—

(a) he makes an offer which, if accepted, would give rise to a contract for their issue or sale by him or by another person with whom he has made arrangements for their issue or sale; or

(b) he invites a person to make such an offer.

(5) "Offer" and "offeror" are to be read accordingly.

(6) For the purposes of this Part, the question whether a person offers securities to the public in the United Kingdom is to be determined in accordance with Schedule 11.

(7) For the purposes of subsection (4) "sale" includes any disposal for valuable consideration.

...

PART VIII
PENALTIES FOR MARKET ABUSE

Market abuse

118. Market abuse

(1) For the purposes of this Act, market abuse is behaviour (whether by one person alone or by two or more persons jointly or in concert)—

(a) which occurs in relation to qualifying investments traded on a market to which this section applies;

(b) which satisfies any one or more of the conditions set out in subsection (2); and

(c) which is likely to be regarded by a regular user of that market who is aware of the behaviour as a failure on the part of the person or persons concerned to observe the standard of behaviour reasonably expected of a person in his or their position in relation to the market.

(2) The conditions are that—

(a) the behaviour is based on information which is not generally available to those using the market but which, if available to a regular user of the market, would or would be likely to be regarded by him as relevant when deciding the terms on which transactions in investments of the kind in question should be effected;

(b) the behaviour is likely to give a regular user of the market a false or misleading impression as to the supply of, or demand for, or as to the price or value of, investments of the kind in question;

(c) a regular user of the market would, or would be likely to, regard the behaviour as behaviour which would, or would be likely to, distort the market in investments of the kind in question.

(3) The Treasury may by order prescribe (whether by name or by description)—

(a) the markets to which this section applies; and

(b) the investments which are qualifying investments in relation to those markets.

(4) The order may prescribe different investments or descriptions of investment in relation to different markets or descriptions of market.

(5) Behaviour is to be disregarded for the purposes of subsection (1) unless it occurs—

(a)   in the United Kingdom; or
(b)   in relation to qualifying investments traded on a market to which this section applies which is situated in the United Kingdom or which is accessible electronically in the United Kingdom.

(6)   For the purposes of this section, the behaviour which is to be regarded as occurring in relation to qualifying investments includes behaviour which—

(a)   occurs in relation to anything which is the subject matter, or whose price or value is expressed by reference to the price or value, of those qualifying investments; or
(b)   occurs in relation to investments (whether qualifying or not) whose subject matter is those qualifying investments.

(7)   Information which can be obtained by research or analysis conducted by, or on behalf of, users of a market is to be regarded for the purposes of this section as being generally available to them.

(8)   Behaviour does not amount to market abuse if it conforms with a rule which includes a provision to the effect that behaviour conforming with the rule does not amount to market abuse.

(9)   Any reference in this Act to a person engaged in market abuse is a reference to a person engaged in market abuse whether alone or with one or more other persons.

(10) In this section—

"behaviour" includes action or inaction;
"investment" is to be read with section 22 and Schedule 2;
"regular user", in relation to a particular market, means a reasonable person who regularly deals on that market in investments of the kind in question.

The code

119.   The code

(1)   The Authority must prepare and issue a code containing such provisions as the Authority considers will give appropriate guidance to those determining whether or not behaviour amounts to market abuse.

(2)   The code may among other things specify—

(a)   descriptions of behaviour that, in the opinion of the Authority, amount to market abuse;
(b)   descriptions of behaviour that, in the opinion of the Authority, do not amount to market abuse;
(c)   factors that, in the opinion of the Authority, are to be taken into account in determining whether or not behaviour amounts to market abuse.

(3)   The code may make different provision in relation to persons, cases or circumstances of different descriptions.

(4)   The Authority may at any time alter or replace the code.

(5)   If the code is altered or replaced, the altered or replacement code must be issued by the Authority.

(6)   A code issued under this section must be published by the Authority in the way appearing to the Authority to be best calculated to bring it to the attention of the public.

(7)   The Authority must, without delay, give the Treasury a copy of any code published under this section.

(8)   The Authority may charge a reasonable fee for providing a person with a copy of the code.

120.   Provisions included in the Authority's code by reference to the City Code

(1)   The Authority may include in a code issued by it under section 119 ("the Authority's code") provision to the effect that in its opinion behaviour conforming with the City Code—

(a)   does not amount to market abuse;
(b)   does not amount to market abuse in specified circumstances; or
(c)   does not amount to market abuse if engaged in by a specified description of person.

(2)   But the Treasury's approval is required before any such provision may be included in the Authority's code.

(3)   If the Authority's code includes provision of a kind authorised by subsection (1), the Authority must keep itself informed of the way in which the Panel on Takeovers and Mergers interprets and administers the relevant provisions of the City Code.

(4)   "City Code" means the City Code on Takeovers and Mergers issued by the Panel as it has effect at the time when the behaviour occurs.

(5)   "Specified" means specified in the Authority's code.

121.   Codes: procedure

(1)   Before issuing a code under section 119, the Authority must publish a draft of the proposed code in the way appearing to the Authority to be best calculated to bring it to the attention of the public.

(2)   The draft must be accompanied by—
   (a)   a cost benefit analysis; and
   (b)   notice that representations about the proposal may be made to the Authority within a specified time.

(3)   Before issuing the proposed code, the Authority must have regard to any representations made to it in accordance with subsection (2)(b).

(4)   If the Authority issues the proposed code it must publish an account, in general terms, of—
   (a)   the representations made to it in accordance with subsection (2)(b); and
   (b)   its response to them.

(5)   If the code differs from the draft published under subsection (1) in a way which is, in the opinion of the Authority, significant—
   (a)   the Authority must (in addition to complying with subsection (4)) publish details of the difference; and
   (b)   those details must be accompanied by a cost benefit analysis.

(6)   Subsections (1) to (5) do not apply if the Authority considers that there is an urgent need to publish the code.

(7)   Neither subsection (2)(a) nor subsection (5)(b) applies if the Authority considers—
   (a)   that, making the appropriate comparison, there will be no increase in costs; or
   (b)   that, making that comparison, there will be an increase in costs but the increase will be of minimal significance.

(8)   The Authority may charge a reasonable fee for providing a person with a copy of a draft published under subsection (1).

(9)   This section also applies to a proposal to alter or replace a code.

(10)   "Cost benefit analysis" means an estimate of the costs together with an analysis of the benefits that will arise—
   (a)   if the proposed code is issued; or
   (b)   if subsection (5)(b) applies, from the code that has been issued.

(11)   "The appropriate comparison" means—
   (a)   in relation to subsection (2)(a), a comparison between the overall position if the code is issued and the overall position if it is not issued;
   (b)   in relation to subsection (5)(b), a comparison between the overall position after the issuing of the code and the overall position before it was issued.

122.   Effect of the code

(1)   If a person behaves in a way which is described (in the code in force under section 119 at the time of the behaviour) as behaviour that, in the Authority's opinion, does not amount to market abuse that behaviour of his is to be taken, for the purposes of this Act, as not amounting to market abuse.

(2)   Otherwise, the code in force under section 119 at the time when particular behaviour occurs may be relied on so far as it indicates whether or not that behaviour should be taken to amount to market abuse.

123.   Power to impose penalties in cases of market abuse

(1)   If the Authority is satisfied that a person ("A")—

    (a)   is or has engaged in market abuse, or

    (b)   by taking or refraining from taking any action has required or encouraged another person or persons to engage in behaviour which, if engaged in by A, would amount to market abuse,

    it may impose on him a penalty of such amount as it considers appropriate.

(2)   But the Authority may not impose a penalty on a person if, having considered any representations made to it in response to a warning notice, there are reasonable grounds for it to be satisfied that—

    (a)   he believed, on reasonable grounds, that his behaviour did not fall within paragraph (a) or (b) of subsection (1), or

    (b)   he took all reasonable precautions and exercised all due diligence to avoid behaving in a way which fell within paragraph (a) or (b) of that subsection.

(3)   If the Authority is entitled to impose a penalty on a person under this section it may, instead of imposing a penalty on him, publish a statement to the effect that he has engaged in market abuse.

124.   Statement of policy

(1)   The Authority must prepare and issue a statement of its policy with respect to—

    (a)   the imposition of penalties under section 123; and

    (b)   the amount of penalties under that section.

(2)   The Authority's policy in determining what the amount of a penalty should be must include having regard to—

    (a)   whether the behaviour in respect of which the penalty is to be imposed had an adverse effect on the market in question and, if it did, how serious that effect was;

    (b)   the extent to which that behaviour was deliberate or reckless; and

    (c)   whether the person on whom the penalty is to be imposed is an individual.

(3)   A statement issued under this section must include an indication of the circumstances in which the Authority is to be expected to regard a person as—

    (a)   having a reasonable belief that his behaviour did not amount to market abuse; or

    (b)   having taken reasonable precautions and exercised due diligence to avoid engaging in market abuse.

(4)   The Authority may at any time alter or replace a statement issued under this section.

(5)   If a statement issued under this section is altered or replaced, the Authority must issue the altered or replacement statement.

(6)   In exercising, or deciding whether to exercise, its power under section 123 in the case of any particular behaviour, the Authority must have regard to any statement published under this section and in force at the time when the behaviour concerned occurred.

(7)   A statement issued under this section must be published by the Authority in the way appearing to the Authority to be best calculated to bring it to the attention of the public.

(8)   The Authority may charge a reasonable fee for providing a person with a copy of a statement published under this section.

(9)   The Authority must, without delay, give the Treasury a copy of any statement which it publishes under this section.

125.   Statement of policy: procedure

(1)   Before issuing a statement of policy under section 124, the Authority must publish a draft of the proposed statement in the way appearing to the Authority to be best calculated to bring it to the attention of the public.

(2)   The draft must be accompanied by notice that representations about the proposal may be made to the Authority within a specified time.

(3)   Before issuing the proposed statement, the Authority must have regard to any representations made to it in accordance with subsection (2).

(4)   If the Authority issues the proposed statement it must publish an account, in general terms, of—
        (a)   the representations made to it in accordance with subsection (2); and
        (b)   its response to them.

(5)   If the statement differs from the draft published under subsection (1) in a way which is, in the opinion of the Authority, significant, the Authority must (in addition to complying with subsection (4)) publish details of the difference.

(6)   The Authority may charge a reasonable fee for providing a person with a copy of a draft published under subsection (1).

(7)   This section also applies to a proposal to alter or replace a statement.

Procedure

126.   Warning notices

(1)   If the Authority proposes to take action against a person under section 123, it must give him a warning notice.

(2)   A warning notice about a proposal to impose a penalty must state the amount of the proposed penalty.

(3)   A warning notice about a proposal to publish a statement must set out the terms of the proposed statement.

127.   Decision notices and right to refer to Tribunal

(1)   If the Authority decides to take action against a person under section 123, it must give him a decision notice.

(2)   A decision notice about the imposition of a penalty must state the amount of the penalty.

(3)   A decision notice about the publication of a statement must set out the terms of the statement.

(4)   If the Authority decides to take action against a person under section 123, that person may refer the matter to the Tribunal.

Miscellaneous

128.   Suspension of investigations

(1)   If the Authority considers it desirable or expedient because of the exercise or possible exercise of a power relating to market abuse, it may direct a recognised investment exchange or recognised clearing house—
        (a)   to terminate, suspend or limit the scope of any inquiry which the exchange or clearing house is conducting under its rules; or
        (b)   not to conduct an inquiry which the exchange or clearing house proposes to conduct under its rules.

(2)   A direction under this section—
        (a)   must be given to the exchange or clearing house concerned by notice in writing; and
        (b)   is enforceable, on the application of the Authority, by injunction or, in Scotland, by an order under section 45 of the Court of Session Act 1988.

(3)   The Authority's powers relating to market abuse are its powers—
        (a)   to impose penalties under section 123; or
        (b)   to appoint a person to conduct an investigation under section 168 in a case falling within subsection (2)(d) of that section.

129.   Power of court to impose penalty in cases of market abuse

(1)   The Authority may on an application to the court under section 381 or 383 request the court to consider whether the circumstances are such that a penalty should be imposed on the person to whom the application relates.

(2)   The court may, if it considers it appropriate, make an order requiring the person concerned to pay to the Authority a penalty of such amount as it considers appropriate.

130.   **Guidance**

(1)   The Treasury may from time to time issue written guidance for the purpose of helping relevant authorities to determine the action to be taken in cases where behaviour occurs which is behaviour—

     (a)   with respect to which the power in section 123 appears to be exercisable; and

     (b)   which appears to involve the commission of an offence under section 397 of this Act or Part V of the Criminal Justice Act 1993 (insider dealing).

(2)   The Treasury must obtain the consent of the Attorney General and the Secretary of State before issuing any guidance under this section.

(3)   In this section "relevant authorities"—

     (a)   in relation to England and Wales, means the Secretary of State, the Authority, the Director of the Serious Fraud Office and the Director of Public Prosecutions;

     (b)   in relation to Northern Ireland, means the Secretary of State, the Authority, the Director of the Serious Fraud Office and the Director of Public Prosecutions for Northern Ireland.

(4)   Subsections (1) to (3) do not apply to Scotland.

(5)   In relation to Scotland, the Lord Advocate may from time to time, after consultation with the Treasury, issue written guidance for the purpose of helping the Authority to determine the action to be taken in cases where behaviour mentioned in subsection (1) occurs.

131.   **Effect on transactions**

     The imposition of a penalty under this Part does not make any transaction void or unenforceable.

        ....

PART XX
PROVISION OF FINANCIAL SERVICES BY MEMBERS OF THE PROFESSIONS

325.   **Authority's general duty**

(1)   The Authority must keep itself informed about—

     (a)   the way in which designated professional bodies supervise and regulate the carrying on of exempt regulated activities by members of the professions in relation to which they are established;

     (b)   the way in which such members are carrying on exempt regulated activities.

(2)   In this Part—

     "exempt regulated activities" means regulated activities which may, as a result of this Part, be carried on by members of a profession which is supervised and regulated by a designated professional body without breaching the general prohibition; and

     "members", in relation to a profession, means persons who are entitled to practise the profession in question and, in practising it, are subject to the rules of the body designated in relation to that profession, whether or not they are members of that body.

(3)   The Authority must keep under review the desirability of exercising any of its powers under this Part.

(4)   Each designated professional body must co-operate with the Authority, by the sharing of information and in other ways, in order to enable the Authority to perform its functions under this Part.

326.   **Designation of professional bodies**

(1)   The Treasury may by order designate bodies for the purposes of this Part.

(2)   A body designated under subsection (1) is referred to in this Part as a designated professional body.

(3)   The Treasury may designate a body under subsection (1) only if they are satisfied that—

     (a)   the basic condition, and

     (b)   one or more of the additional conditions,

     are met in relation to it.

(4)   The basic condition is that the body has rules applicable to the carrying on by members of the profession in relation to which it is established of regulated activities which, if the body were to be designated, would be exempt regulated activities.

(5)   The additional conditions are that—

(a)   the body has power under any enactment to regulate the practice of the profession;

(b)   being a member of the profession is a requirement under any enactment for the exercise of particular functions or the holding of a particular office;

(c)   the body has been recognised for the purpose of any enactment other than this Act and the recognition has not been withdrawn;

(d)   the body is established in an EEA State other than the United Kingdom and in that State—

(i)   the body has power corresponding to that mentioned in paragraph (a);

(ii)   there is a requirement in relation to the body corresponding to that mentioned in paragraph (b); or

(iii)   the body is recognised in a manner corresponding to that mentioned in paragraph (c).

(6)   "Enactment" includes an Act of the Scottish Parliament, Northern Ireland legislation and subordinate legislation (whether made under an Act, an Act of the Scottish Parliament or Northern Ireland legislation).

(7)   "Recognised" means recognised by—

(a)   a Minister of the Crown;

(b)   the Scottish Ministers;

(c)   a Northern Ireland Minister;

(d)   a Northern Ireland department or its head.

327.   Exemption from the general prohibition

(1)   The general prohibition does not apply to the carrying on of a regulated activity by a person ("P") if—

(a)   the conditions set out in subsections (2) to (7) are satisfied; and

(b)   there is not in force—

(i)   a direction under section 328, or

(ii)   an order under section 329,

which prevents this subsection from applying to the carrying on of that activity by him.

(2)   P must be—

(a)   a member of a profession; or

(b)   controlled or managed by one or more such members.

(3)   P must not receive from a person other than his client any pecuniary reward or other advantage, for which he does not account to his client, arising out of his carrying on of any of the activities.

(4)   The manner of the provision by P of any service in the course of carrying on the activities must be incidental to the provision by him of professional services.

(5)   P must not carry on, or hold himself out as carrying on, a regulated activity other than—

(a)   one which rules made as a result of section 332(3) allow him to carry on; or

(b)   one in relation to which he is an exempt person.

(6)   The activities must not be of a description, or relate to an investment of a description, specified in an order made by the Treasury for the purposes of this subsection.

(7)   The activities must be the only regulated activities carried on by P (other than regulated activities in relation to which he is an exempt person).

(8)   "Professional services" means services—

(a)   which do not constitute carrying on a regulated activity, and

(b)   the provision of which is supervised and regulated by a designated professional body.

328.   Directions in relation to the general prohibition

(1)   The Authority may direct that section 327(1) is not to apply to the extent specified in the direction.

(2)   A direction under subsection (1)—

      (a)   must be in writing;

      (b)   may be given in relation to different classes of person or different descriptions of regulated activity.

(3)   A direction under subsection (1) must be published in the way appearing to the Authority to be best calculated to bring it to the attention of the public.

(4)   The Authority may charge a reasonable fee for providing a person with a copy of the direction.

(5)   The Authority must, without delay, give the Treasury a copy of any direction which it gives under this section.

(6)   The Authority may exercise the power conferred by subsection (1) only if it is satisfied either—

      (a)   that it is desirable to do so in order to protect the interests of clients; or

      (b)   that it is necessary to do so in order to comply with a Community obligation imposed by the insurance mediation directive.

(7)   In considering whether it is satisfied of the matter specified in subsection (6)(a), the Authority must have regard amongst other things to the effectiveness of any arrangements made by any designated professional body—

      (a)   for securing compliance with rules made under section 332(1);

      (b)   for dealing with complaints against its members in relation to the carrying on by them of exempt regulated activities;

      (c)   in order to offer redress to clients who suffer, or claim to have suffered, loss as a result of misconduct by its members in their carrying on of exempt regulated activities;

      (d)   for co-operating with the Authority under section 325(4).

(8)   In this Part "clients" means—

      (a)   persons who use, have used or are or may be contemplating using, any of the services provided by a member of a profession in the course of carrying on exempt regulated activities;

      (b)   persons who have rights or interests which are derived from, or otherwise attributable to, the use of any such services by other persons; or

      (c)   persons who have rights or interests which may be adversely affected by the use of any such services by persons acting on their behalf or in a fiduciary capacity in relation to them.

(9)   If a member of a profession is carrying on an exempt regulated activity in his capacity as a trustee, the persons who are, have been or may be beneficiaries of the trust are to be treated as persons who use, have used or are or may be contemplating using services provided by that person in his carrying on of that activity.

329.   Orders in relation to the general prohibition

(1)   Subsection (2) applies if it appears to the Authority that a person to whom, as a result of section 327(1), the general prohibition does not apply is not a fit and proper person to carry on regulated activities in accordance with that section.

(2)   The Authority may make an order disapplying section 327(1) in relation to that person to the extent specified in the order.

(3)   The Authority may, on the application of the person named in an order under subsection (1), vary or revoke it.

(4)   "Specified" means specified in the order.

(5)   If a partnership is named in an order under this section, the order is not affected by any change in its membership.

(6)   If a partnership named in an order under this section is dissolved, the order continues to have effect in relation to any partnership which succeeds to the business of the dissolved partnership.

(7)   For the purposes of subsection (6), a partnership is to be regarded as succeeding to the business of another partnership only if—

      (a)   the members of the resulting partnership are substantially the same as those of the former partnership; and

      (b)   succession is to the whole or substantially the whole of the business of the former partnership.

330. Consultation

(1) Before giving a direction under section 328(1), the Authority must publish a draft of the proposed direction.

(2) The draft must be accompanied by—

    (a) a cost benefit analysis; and

    (b) notice that representations about the proposed direction may be made to the Authority within a specified time.

(3) Before giving the proposed direction, the Authority must have regard to any representations made to it in accordance with subsection (2)(b).

(4) If the Authority gives the proposed direction it must publish an account, in general terms, of—

    (a) the representations made to it in accordance with subsection (2)(b); and

    (b) its response to them.

(5) If the direction differs from the draft published under subsection (1) in a way which is, in the opinion of the Authority, significant—

    (a) the Authority must (in addition to complying with subsection (4)) publish details of the difference; and

    (b) those details must be accompanied by a cost benefit analysis.

(6) Subsections (1) to (5) do not apply if the Authority considers that the delay involved in complying with them would prejudice the interests of consumers.

(7) Neither subsection (2)(a) nor subsection (5)(b) applies if the Authority considers—

    (a) that, making the appropriate comparison, there will be no increase in costs; or

    (b) that, making that comparison, there will be an increase in costs but the increase will be of minimal significance.

(8) The Authority may charge a reasonable fee for providing a person with a copy of a draft published under subsection (1).

(9) When the Authority is required to publish a document under this section it must do so in the way appearing to it to be best calculated to bring it to the attention of the public.

(10) "Cost benefit analysis" means an estimate of the costs together with an analysis of the benefits that will arise—

    (a) if the proposed direction is given; or

    (b) if subsection (5)(b) applies, from the direction that has been given.

(11) "The appropriate comparison" means—

    (a) in relation to subsection (2)(a), a comparison between the overall position if the direction is given and the overall position if it is not given;

    (b) in relation to subsection (5)(b), a comparison between the overall position after the giving of the direction and the overall position before it was given.

331. Procedure on making or varying orders under section 329

(1) If the Authority proposes to make an order under section 329, it must give the person concerned a warning notice.

(2) The warning notice must set out the terms of the proposed order.

(3) If the Authority decides to make an order under section 329, it must give the person concerned a decision notice.

(4) The decision notice must—

    (a) name the person to whom the order applies;

    (b) set out the terms of the order; and

    (c) be given to the person named in the order.

(5) Subsections (6) to (8) apply to an application for the variation or revocation of an order under section 329.

(6) If the Authority decides to grant the application, it must give the applicant written notice of its decision.

(7) If the Authority proposes to refuse the application, it must give the applicant a warning notice.

(8) If the Authority decides to refuse the application, it must give the applicant a decision notice.

(9)   A person—

    (a)   against whom the Authority have decided to make an order under section 329, or

    (b)   whose application for the variation or revocation of such an order the Authority had decided to refuse,

    may refer the matter to the Tribunal.

(10)   The Authority may not make an order under section 329 unless—

    (a)   the period within which the decision to make to the order may be referred to the Tribunal has expired and no such reference has been made; or

    (b)   if such a reference has been made, the reference has been determined.

332.   Rules in relation to persons to whom the general prohibition does not apply

(1)   The Authority may make rules applicable to persons to whom, as a result of section 327(1), the general prohibition does not apply.

(2)   The power conferred by subsection (1) is to be exercised for the purpose of ensuring that clients are aware that such persons are not authorised persons.

(3)   A designated professional body must make rules—

    (a)   applicable to members of the profession in relation to which it is established who are not authorised persons; and

    (b)   governing the carrying on by those members of regulated activities (other than regulated activities in relation to which they are exempt persons).

(4)   Rules made in compliance with subsection (3) must be designed to secure that, in providing a particular professional service to a particular client, the member carries on only regulated activities which arise out of, or are complementary to, the provision by him of that service to that client.

(5)   Rules made by a designated professional body under subsection (3) require the approval of the Authority.

333.   False claims to be a person to whom the general prohibition does not apply

(1)   A person who—

    (a)   describes himself (in whatever terms) as a person to whom the general prohibition does not apply, in relation to a particular regulated activity, as a result of this Part, or

    (b)   behaves, or otherwise holds himself out, in a manner which indicates (or which is reasonably likely to be understood as indicating) that he is such a person,

    is guilty of an offence if he is not such a person.

(2)   In proceedings for an offence under this section it is a defence for the accused to show that he took all reasonable precautions and exercised all due diligence to avoid committing the offence.

(3)   A person guilty of an offence under this section is liable on summary conviction to imprisonment for a term not exceeding six months or a fine not exceeding level 5 on the standard scale, or both.

(4)   But where the conduct constituting the offence involved or included the public display of any material, the maximum fine for the offence is level 5 on the standard scale multiplied by the number of days for which the display continued.

...

PART XXVII
OFFENCES

Miscellaneous offences

397.   Misleading statements and practices

(1)   This subsection applies to a person who—

    (a)   makes a statement, promise or forecast which he knows to be misleading, false or deceptive in a material particular;

(b)   dishonestly conceals any material facts whether in connection with a statement, promise or forecast made by him or otherwise; or

(c)   recklessly makes (dishonestly or otherwise) a statement, promise or forecast which is misleading, false or deceptive in a material particular.

(2)   A person to whom subsection (1) applies is guilty of an offence if he makes the statement, promise or forecast or conceals the facts for the purpose of inducing, or is reckless as to whether it may induce, another person (whether or not the person to whom the statement, promise or forecast is made)—

(a)   to enter or offer to enter into, or to refrain from entering or offering to enter into, a relevant agreement; or

(b)   to exercise, or refrain from exercising, any rights conferred by a relevant investment.

(3)   Any person who does any act or engages in any course of conduct which creates a false or misleading impression as to the market in or the price or value of any relevant investments is guilty of an offence if he does so for the purpose of creating that impression and of thereby inducing another person to acquire, dispose of, subscribe for or underwrite those investments or to refrain from doing so or to exercise, or refrain from exercising, any rights conferred by those investments.

(4)   In proceedings for an offence under subsection (2) brought against a person to whom subsection (1) applies as a result of paragraph (a) of that subsection, it is a defence for him to show that the statement, promise or forecast was made in conformity with price stabilising rules or control of information rules.

(5)   In proceedings brought against any person for an offence under subsection (3) it is a defence for him to show—

(a)   that he reasonably believed that his act or conduct would not create an impression that was false or misleading as to the matters mentioned in that subsection;

(b)   that he acted or engaged in the conduct—

(i)   for the purpose of stabilising the price of investments; and

(ii)   in conformity with price stabilising rules; or

(c)   that he acted or engaged in the conduct in conformity with control of information rules.

(6)   Subsections (1) and (2) do not apply unless—

(a)   the statement, promise or forecast is made in or from, or the facts are concealed in or from, the United Kingdom or arrangements are made in or from the United Kingdom for the statement, promise or forecast to be made or the facts to be concealed;

(b)   the person on whom the inducement is intended to or may have effect is in the United Kingdom; or

(c)   the agreement is or would be entered into or the rights are or would be exercised in the United Kingdom.

(7)   Subsection (3) does not apply unless—

(a)   the act is done, or the course of conduct is engaged in, in the United Kingdom; or

(b)   the false or misleading impression is created there.

(8)   A person guilty of an offence under this section is liable—

(a)   on summary conviction, to imprisonment for a term not exceeding six months or a fine not exceeding the statutory maximum, or both;

(b)   on conviction on indictment, to imprisonment for a term not exceeding seven years or a fine, or both.

(9)   "Relevant agreement" means an agreement—

(a)   the entering into or performance of which by either party constitutes an activity of a specified kind or one which falls within a specified class of activity; and

(b)   which relates to a relevant investment.

(10)   "Relevant investment" means an investment of a specified kind or one which falls within a prescribed class of investment.

(11)   Schedule 2 (except paragraphs 25 and 26) applies for the purposes of subsections (9) and (10) with references to section 22 being read as references to each of those subsections.

(12)   Nothing in Schedule 2, as applied by subsection (11), limits the power conferred by subsection (9) or (10).

(13)   "Investment" includes any asset, right or interest.

(14)   "Specified" means specified in an order made by the Treasury.

398.   Misleading the Authority: residual cases

(1)   A person who, in purported compliance with any requirement imposed by or under this Act, knowingly or recklessly gives the Authority information which is false or misleading in a material particular is guilty of an offence.

(2)   Subsection (1) applies only to a requirement in relation to which no other provision of this Act creates an offence in connection with the giving of information.

(3)   A person guilty of an offence under this section is liable—

     (a)   on summary conviction, to a fine not exceeding the statutory maximum;

     (b)   on conviction on indictment, to a fine.

399.   Misleading the OFT

Section 44 of the Competition Act 1998 (offences connected with the provision of false or misleading information) applies in relation to any function of the Office of Fair Trading under this Act as if it were a function under Part I of that Act.

Bodies corporate and partnerships

400.   Offences by bodies corporate etc

(1)   If an offence under this Act committed by a body corporate is shown—

     (a)   to have been committed with the consent or connivance of an officer, or

     (b)   to be attributable to any neglect on his part,

the officer as well as the body corporate is guilty of the offence and liable to be proceeded against and punished accordingly.

(2)   If the affairs of a body corporate are managed by its members, subsection (1) applies in relation to the acts and defaults of a member in connection with his functions of management as if he were a director of the body.

(3)   If an offence under this Act committed by a partnership is shown—

     (a)   to have been committed with the consent or connivance of a partner, or

     (b)   to be attributable to any neglect on his part,

the partner as well as the partnership is guilty of the offence and liable to be proceeded against and punished accordingly.

(4)   In subsection (3) "partner" includes a person purporting to act as a partner.

(5)   "Officer", in relation to a body corporate, means—

     (a)   a director, member of the committee of management, chief executive, manager, secretary or other similar officer of the body, or a person purporting to act in any such capacity; and

     (b)   an individual who is a controller of the body.

(6)   If an offence under this Act committed by an unincorporated association (other than a partnership) is shown—

     (a)   to have been committed with the consent or connivance of an officer of the association or a member of its governing body, or

     (b)   to be attributable to any neglect on the part of such an officer or member,

that officer or member as well as the association is guilty of the offence and liable to be proceeded against and punished accordingly.

(7)   Regulations may provide for the application of any provision of this section, with such modifications as the Treasury consider appropriate, to a body corporate or unincorporated association formed or recognised under the law of a territory outside the United Kingdom.

Institution of proceedings

401. Proceedings for offences

(1) In this section "offence" means an offence under this Act or subordinate legislation made under this Act.

(2) Proceedings for an offence may be instituted in England and Wales only—

(a) by the Authority or the Secretary of State; or

(b) by or with the consent of the Director of Public Prosecutions.

(3) Proceedings for an offence may be instituted in Northern Ireland only—

(a) by the Authority or the Secretary of State; or

(b) by or with the consent of the Director of Public Prosecutions for Northern Ireland.

(4) Except in Scotland, proceedings for an offence under section 203 may also be instituted by the Office of Fair Trading.

(5) In exercising its power to institute proceedings for an offence, the Authority must comply with any conditions or restrictions imposed in writing by the Treasury.

(6) Conditions or restrictions may be imposed under subsection (5) in relation to—

(a) proceedings generally; or

(b) such proceedings, or categories of proceedings, as the Treasury may direct.

402. Power of the Authority to institute proceedings for certain other offences

(1) Except in Scotland, the Authority may institute proceedings for an offence under—

(a) Part V of the Criminal Justice Act 1993 (insider dealing); or

(b) prescribed regulations relating to money laundering.

(2) In exercising its power to institute proceedings for any such offence, the Authority must comply with any conditions or restrictions imposed in writing by the Treasury.

(3) Conditions or restrictions may be imposed under subsection (2) in relation to—

(a) proceedings generally; or

(b) such proceedings, or categories of proceedings, as the Treasury may direct.

403. Jurisdiction and procedure in respect of offences

(1) A fine imposed on an unincorporated association on its conviction of an offence is to be paid out of the funds of the association.

(2) Proceedings for an offence alleged to have been committed by an unincorporated association must be brought in the name of the association (and not in that of any of its members).

(3) Rules of court relating to the service of documents are to have effect as if the association were a body corporate.

(4) In proceedings for an offence brought against an unincorporated association—

(a) section 33 of the Criminal Justice Act 1925 and Schedule 3 to the Magistrates' Courts Act 1980 (procedure) apply as they do in relation to a body corporate;

(b) section 70 of the Criminal Procedure (Scotland) Act 1995 (procedure) applies as if the association were a body corporate;

(c) section 18 of the Criminal Justice (Northern Ireland) Act 1945 and Schedule 4 to the Magistrates' Courts (Northern Ireland) Order 1981 (procedure) apply as they do in relation to a body corporate.

(5) Summary proceedings for an offence may be taken—

(a) against a body corporate or unincorporated association at any place at which it has a place of business;

(b) against an individual at any place where he is for the time being.

(6) Subsection (5) does not affect any jurisdiction exercisable apart from this section.

(7) "Offence" means an offence under this Act.

...

PART XXX

SUPPLEMENTAL

426. Consequential and supplementary provision

(1)   A Minister of the Crown may by order make such incidental, consequential, transitional or supplemental provision as he considers necessary or expedient for the general purposes, or any particular purpose, of this Act or in consequence of any provision made by or under this Act or for giving full effect to this Act or any such provision.

(2)   An order under subsection (1) may, in particular, make provision—

    (a)   for enabling any person by whom any powers will become exercisable, on a date set by or under this Act, by virtue of any provision made by or under this Act to take before that date any steps which are necessary as a preliminary to the exercise of those powers;

    (b)   for applying (with or without modifications) or amending, repealing or revoking any provision of or made under an Act passed before this Act or in the same Session;

    (c)   dissolving any body corporate established by any Act passed, or instrument made, before the passing of this Act;

    (d)   for making savings, or additional savings, from the effect of any repeal or revocation made by or under this Act.

(3)   Amendments made under this section are additional, and without prejudice, to those made by or under any other provision of this Act.

(4)   No other provision of this Act restricts the powers conferred by this section.

427. Transitional provisions

(1)   Subsections (2) and (3) apply to an order under section 426 which makes transitional provisions or savings.

(2)   The order may, in particular—

    (a)   if it makes provision about the authorisation and permission of persons who before commencement were entitled to carry on any activities, also include provision for such persons not to be treated as having any authorisation or permission (whether on an application to the Authority or otherwise);

    (b)   make provision enabling the Authority to require persons of such descriptions as it may direct to re-apply for permissions having effect by virtue of the order;

    (c)   make provision for the continuation as rules of such provisions (including primary and subordinate legislation) as may be designated in accordance with the order by the Authority, including provision for the modification by the Authority of provisions designated;

    (d)   make provision about the effect of requirements imposed, liabilities incurred and any other things done before commencement, including provision for and about investigations, penalties and the taking or continuing of any other action in respect of contraventions;

    (e)   make provision for the continuation of disciplinary and other proceedings begun before commencement, including provision about the decisions available to bodies before which such proceedings take place and the effect of their decisions;

    (f)   make provision as regards the Authority's obligation to maintain a record under section 347 as respects persons in relation to whom provision is made by the order.

(3)   The order may—

    (a)   confer functions on the Treasury, the Secretary of State, the Authority, the scheme manager, the scheme operator, members of the panel established under paragraph 4 of Schedule 17, the Competition Commission or the Office of Fair Trading;

    (b)   confer jurisdiction on the Tribunal;

    (c)   provide for fees to be charged in connection with the carrying out of functions conferred under the order;

    (d)   modify, exclude or apply (with or without modifications) any primary or subordinate legislation (including any provision of, or made under, this Act).

(4)   In subsection (2) "commencement" means the commencement of such provisions of this Act as may be specified by the order.

428. Regulations and orders

(1)   Any power to make an order which is conferred on a Minister of the Crown by this Act and any power to make regulations which is conferred by this Act is exercisable by statutory instrument.

(2)   The Lord Chancellor's power to make rules under section 132 is exercisable by statutory instrument.

(3)   Any statutory instrument made under this Act may—

    (a)   contain such incidental, supplemental, consequential and transitional provision as the person making it considers appropriate; and

    (b)   make different provision for different cases.

429. Parliamentary control of statutory instruments

(1)   No order is to be made under—

    (a)   section 144(4), 192(b) or (e), 236(5), 404 or 419, or

    (b)   paragraph 1 of Schedule 8,

unless a draft of the order has been laid before Parliament and approved by a resolution of each House.

(2)   No regulations are to be made under section 262 unless a draft of the regulations has been laid before Parliament and approved by a resolution of each House.

(3)   An order to which, if it is made, subsection (4) or (5) will apply is not to be made unless a draft of the order has been laid before Parliament and approved by a resolution of each House.

(4)   This subsection applies to an order under section 21 if—

    (a)   it is the first order to be made, or to contain provisions made, under section 21(4);

    (b)   it varies an order made under section 21(4) so as to make section 21(1) apply in circumstances in which it did not previously apply;

    (c)   it is the first order to be made, or to contain provision made, under section 21(5);

    (d)   it varies a previous order made under section 21(5) so as to make section 21(1) apply in circumstances in which it did not, as a result of that previous order, apply;

    (e)   it is the first order to be made, or to contain provisions made, under section 21(9) or (10);

    (f)   it adds one or more activities to those that are controlled activities for the purposes of section 21; or

    (g)   it adds one or more investments to those which are controlled investments for the purposes of section 21.

(5)   This subsection applies to an order under section 38 if—

    (a)   it is the first order to be made, or to contain provisions made, under that section; or

    (b)   it contains provisions restricting or removing an exemption provided by an earlier order made under that section.

(6)   An order containing a provision to which, if the order is made, subsection (7) will apply is not to be made unless a draft of the order has been laid before Parliament and approved by a resolution of each House.

(7)   This subsection applies to a provision contained in an order if—

    (a)   it is the first to be made in the exercise of the power conferred by subsection (1) of section 326 or it removes a body from those for the time being designated under that subsection; or

    (b)   it is the first to be made in the exercise of the power conferred by subsection (6) of section 327 or it adds a description of regulated activity or investment to those for the time being specified for the purposes of that subsection.

(8)   Any other statutory instrument made under this Act, apart from one made under section 431(2) or to which paragraph 26 of Schedule 2 applies, shall be subject to annulment in pursuance of a resolution of either House of Parliament.

430.   Extent

(1)   This Act, except Chapter IV of Part XVII, extends to Northern Ireland.

(2)   Except where Her Majesty by Order in Council provides otherwise, the extent of any amendment or repeal made by or under this Act is the same as the extent of the provision amended or repealed.

(3)   Her Majesty may by Order in Council provide for any provision of or made under this Act relating to a matter which is the subject of other legislation which extends to any of the Channel Islands or the Isle of Man to extend there with such modifications (if any) as may be specified in the Order.

431.   Commencement

(1)   The following provisions come into force on the passing of this Act—

(a)   this section;

(b)   sections 428, 430 and 433;

(c)   paragraphs 1 and 2 of Schedule 21.

(2)   The other provisions of this Act come into force on such day as the Treasury may by order appoint; and different days may be appointed for different purposes.

432.   Minor and consequential amendments, transitional provisions and repeals

(1)   Schedule 20 makes minor and consequential amendments.

(2)   Schedule 21 makes transitional provisions.

(3)   The enactments set out in Schedule 22 are repealed.

433.   Short title

This Act may be cited as the Financial Services and Markets Act 2000.

SCHEDULE 1

THE FINANCIAL SERVICES AUTHORITY

Section 1

PART I
GENERAL

Interpretation

1.—   (1)   In this Schedule—

"the 1985 Act" means the Companies Act 1985;

"non-executive committee" means the committee maintained under paragraph 3;

"functions", in relation to the Authority, means functions conferred on the Authority by or under any provision of this Act.

(2)   For the purposes of this Schedule, the following are the Authority's legislative functions—

(a)   making rules;

(b)   issuing codes under section 64 or 119;

(c)   issuing statements under section 64, 69, 124 or 210;

(d)   giving directions under section 316, 318 or 328;

(e)   issuing general guidance (as defined by section 158(5)).

Constitution

2.—   (1)   The constitution of the Authority must continue to provide for the Authority to have—

(a)   a chairman; and

(b)   a governing body.

(2)   The governing body must include the chairman.

(3) The chairman and other members of the governing body must be appointed, and be liable to removal from office, by the Treasury.

(4) The validity of any act of the Authority is not affected—

(a) by a vacancy in the office of chairman; or

(b) by a defect in the appointment of a person as a member of the governing body or as chairman.

Non-executive members of the governing body

3.— (1) The Authority must secure—

(a) that the majority of the members of its governing body are non-executive members; and

(b) that a committee of its governing body, consisting solely of the non-executive members, is set up and maintained for the purposes of discharging the functions conferred on the committee by this Schedule.

(2) The members of the non-executive committee are to be appointed by the Authority.

(3) The non-executive committee is to have a chairman appointed by the Treasury from among its members.

Functions of the non-executive committee

4.— (1) In this paragraph "the committee" means the non-executive committee.

(2) The non-executive functions are functions of the Authority but must be discharged by the committee.

(3) The non-executive functions are—

(a) keeping under review the question whether the Authority is, in discharging its functions in accordance with decisions of its governing body, using its resources in the most efficient and economic way;

(b) keeping under review the question whether the Authority's internal financial controls secure the proper conduct of its financial affairs; and

(c) determining the remuneration of—

(i) the chairman of the Authority's governing body; and

(ii) the executive members of that body.

(4) The function mentioned in sub-paragraph (3)(b) and those mentioned in sub-paragraph (3)(c) may be discharged on behalf of the committee by a sub-committee.

(5) Any sub-committee of the committee—

(a) must have as its chairman the chairman of the committee; but

(b) may include persons other than members of the committee.

(6) The committee must prepare a report on the discharge of its functions for inclusion in the Authority's annual report to the Treasury under paragraph 10.

(7) The committee's report must relate to the same period as that covered by the Authority's report.

Arrangements for discharging functions

5.— (1) The Authority may make arrangements for any of its functions to be discharged by a committee, sub-committee, officer or member of staff of the Authority.

(2) But in exercising its legislative functions, the Authority must act through its governing body.

(3) Sub-paragraph (1) does not apply to the non-executive functions.

Monitoring and enforcement

6.— (1) The Authority must maintain arrangements designed to enable it to determine whether persons on whom requirements are imposed by or under this Act are complying with them.

(2) Those arrangements may provide for functions to be performed on behalf of the Authority by any body or person who, in its opinion, is competent to perform them.

(3)   The Authority must also maintain arrangements for enforcing the provisions of, or made under, this Act.

(4)   Sub-paragraph (2) does not affect the Authority's duty under sub-paragraph (1).

Arrangements for the investigation of complaints

7.—   (1)   The Authority must—

        (a)   make arrangements ("the complaints scheme") for the investigation of complaints arising in connection with the exercise of, or failure to exercise, any of its functions (other than its legislative functions); and

        (b)   appoint an independent person ("the investigator") to be responsible for the conduct of investigations in accordance with the complaints scheme.

(2)   The complaints scheme must be designed so that, as far as reasonably practicable, complaints are investigated quickly.

(3)   The Treasury's approval is required for the appointment or dismissal of the investigator.

(4)   The terms and conditions on which the investigator is appointed must be such as, in the opinion of the Authority, are reasonably designed to secure—

        (a)   that he will be free at all times to act independently of the Authority; and

        (b)   that complaints will be investigated under the complaints scheme without favouring the Authority.

(5)   Before making the complaints scheme, the Authority must publish a draft of the proposed scheme in the way appearing to the Authority best calculated to bring it to the attention of the public.

(6)   The draft must be accompanied by notice that representations about it may be made to the Authority within a specified time.

(7)   Before making the proposed complaints scheme, the Authority must have regard to any representations made to it in accordance with sub-paragraph (6).

(8)   If the Authority makes the proposed complaints scheme, it must publish an account, in general terms, of—

        (a)   the representations made to it in accordance with sub-paragraph (6); and

        (b)   its response to them.

(9)   If the complaints scheme differs from the draft published under sub-paragraph (5) in a way which is, in the opinion of the Authority, significant the Authority must (in addition to complying with sub-paragraph (8)) publish details of the difference.

(10)   The Authority must publish up-to-date details of the complaints scheme including, in particular, details of—

        (a)   the provision made under paragraph 8(5); and

        (b)   the powers which the investigator has to investigate a complaint.

(11)   Those details must be published in the way appearing to the Authority to be best calculated to bring them to the attention of the public.

(12)   The Authority must, without delay, give the Treasury a copy of any details published by it under this paragraph.

(13)   The Authority may charge a reasonable fee for providing a person with a copy of—

        (a)   a draft published under sub-paragraph (5);

        (b)   details published under sub-paragraph (10).

(14)   Sub-paragraphs (5) to (9) and (13)(a) also apply to a proposal to alter or replace the complaints scheme.

Investigation of complaints

8.—   (1)   The Authority is not obliged to investigate a complaint in accordance with the complaints scheme which it reasonably considers would be more appropriately dealt with in another way (for example by referring the matter to the Tribunal or by the institution of other legal proceedings).

(2)   The complaints scheme must provide—

    (a)   for reference to the investigator of any complaint which the Authority is investigating; and

    (b)   for him—

        (i)   to have the means to conduct a full investigation of the complaint;

        (ii) to report on the result of his investigation to the Authority and the complainant; and

        (iii) to be able to publish his report (or any part of it) if he considers that it (or the part) ought to be brought to the attention of the public.

(3)   If the Authority has decided not to investigate a complaint, it must notify the investigator.

(4)   If the investigator considers that a complaint of which he has been notified under sub-paragraph (3) ought to be investigated, he may proceed as if the complaint had been referred to him under the complaints scheme.

(5)   The complaints scheme must confer on the investigator the power to recommend, if he thinks it appropriate, that the Authority—

    (a)   makes a compensatory payment to the complainant,

    (b)   remedies the matter complained of,

    or takes both of those steps.

(6)   The complaints scheme must require the Authority, in a case where the investigator—

    (a)   has reported that a complaint is well-founded, or

    (b)   has criticised the Authority in his report,

    to inform the investigator and the complainant of the steps which it proposes to take in response to the report.

(7)   The investigator may require the Authority to publish the whole or a specified part of the response.

(8)   The investigator may appoint a person to conduct the investigation on his behalf but subject to his direction.

(9)   Neither an officer nor an employee of the Authority may be appointed under sub-paragraph (8).

(10) Sub-paragraph (2) is not to be taken as preventing the Authority from making arrangements for the initial investigation of a complaint to be conducted by the Authority.

Records

9.   The Authority must maintain satisfactory arrangements for—

    (a)   recording decisions made in the exercise of its functions; and

    (b)   the safe-keeping of those records which it considers ought to be preserved.

Annual report

10.— (1)   At least once a year the Authority must make a report to the Treasury on—

    (a)   the discharge of its functions;

    (b)   the extent to which, in its opinion, the regulatory objectives have been met;

    (c)   its consideration of the matters mentioned in section 2(3); and

    (d)   such other matters as the Treasury may from time to time direct.

(2)   The report must be accompanied by—

    (a)   the report prepared by the non-executive committee under paragraph 4(6); and

    (b)   such other reports or information, prepared by such persons, as the Treasury may from time to time direct.

(3)   The Treasury must lay before Parliament a copy of each report received by them under this paragraph.

(4)   The Treasury may—

    (a)   require the Authority to comply with any provisions of the 1985 Act about accounts and their audit which would not otherwise apply to it; or

    (b)   direct that any such provision of that Act is to apply to the Authority with such modifications as are specified in the direction.

(5)   Compliance with any requirement imposed under sub-paragraph (4)(a) or (b) is enforceable by injunction or, in Scotland, an order under section 45(b) of the Court of Session Act 1988.

(6)   Proceedings under sub-paragraph (5) may be brought only by the Treasury.

Annual public meeting

11.— (1)   Not later than three months after making a report under paragraph 10, the Authority must hold a public meeting ("the annual meeting") for the purposes of enabling that report to be considered.

(2)   The Authority must organise the annual meeting so as to allow—
(a)   a general discussion of the contents of the report which is being considered; and
(b)   a reasonable opportunity for those attending the meeting to put questions to the Authority about the way in which it discharged, or failed to discharge, its functions during the period to which the report relates.

(3)   But otherwise the annual meeting is to be organised and conducted in such a way as the Authority considers appropriate.

(4)   The Authority must give reasonable notice of its annual meeting.

(5)   That notice must—
(a)   give details of the time and place at which the meeting is to be held;
(b)   set out the proposed agenda for the meeting;
(c)   indicate the proposed duration of the meeting;
(d)   give details of the Authority's arrangements for enabling persons to attend; and
(e)   be published by the Authority in the way appearing to it to be most suitable for bringing the notice to the attention of the public.

(6)   If the Authority proposes to alter any of the arrangements which have been included in the notice given under sub-paragraph (4) it must—
(a)   give reasonable notice of the alteration; and
(b)   publish that notice in the way appearing to the Authority to be best calculated to bring it to the attention of the public.

Report of annual meeting

12.   Not later than one month after its annual meeting, the Authority must publish a report of the proceedings of the meeting.

PART II
STATUS

13.   In relation to any of its functions—
(a)   the Authority is not to be regarded as acting on behalf of the Crown; and
(b)   its members, officers and staff are not to be regarded as Crown servants.

Exemption from requirement of "limited" in Authority's name

14.   The Authority is to continue to be exempt from the requirements of the 1985 Act relating to the use of "limited" as part of its name.

15.   If the Secretary of State is satisfied that any action taken by the Authority makes it inappropriate for the exemption given by paragraph 14 to continue he may, after consulting the Treasury, give a direction removing it.

PART III
PENALTIES AND FEES

Penalties

16.— (1) In determining its policy with respect to the amounts of penalties to be imposed by it under this Act, the Authority must take no account of the expenses which it incurs, or expects to incur, in discharging its functions.

(2) The Authority must prepare and operate a scheme for ensuring that the amounts paid to the Authority by way of penalties imposed under this Act are applied for the benefit of authorised persons.

(3) The scheme may, in particular, make different provision with respect to different classes of authorised person.

(4) Up to date details of the scheme must be set out in a document ("the scheme details").

(5) The scheme details must be published by the Authority in the way appearing to it to be best calculated to bring them to the attention of the public.

(6) Before making the scheme, the Authority must publish a draft of the proposed scheme in the way appearing to the Authority to be best calculated to bring it to the attention of the public.

(7) The draft must be accompanied by notice that representations about the proposals may be made to the Authority within a specified time.

(8) Before making the scheme, the Authority must have regard to any representations made to it in accordance with sub-paragraph (7).

(9) If the Authority makes the proposed scheme, it must publish an account, in general terms, of—

(a) the representations made to it in accordance with sub-paragraph (7); and

(b) its response to them.

(10) If the scheme differs from the draft published under sub-paragraph (6) in a way which is, in the opinion of the Authority, significant the Authority must (in addition to complying with sub-paragraph (9)) publish details of the difference.

(11) The Authority must, without delay, give the Treasury a copy of any scheme details published by it.

(12) The Authority may charge a reasonable fee for providing a person with a copy of—

(a) a draft published under sub-paragraph (6);

(b) scheme details.

(13) Sub-paragraphs (6) to (10) and (12)(a) also apply to a proposal to alter or replace the complaints scheme.

Fees

17.— (1) The Authority may make rules providing for the payment to it of such fees, in connection with the discharge of any of its functions under or as a result of this Act, as it considers will (taking account of its expected income from fees and charges provided for by any other provision of this Act) enable it—

(a) to meet expenses incurred in carrying out its functions or for any incidental purpose;

(b) to repay the principal of, and pay any interest on, any money which it has borrowed and which has been used for the purpose of meeting expenses incurred in relation to its assumption of functions under this Act or the Bank of England Act 1998; and

(c) to maintain adequate reserves.

(2) In fixing the amount of any fee which is to be payable to the Authority, no account is to be taken of any sums which the Authority receives, or expects to receive, by way of penalties imposed by it under this Act.

(3) Sub-paragraph (1)(b) applies whether expenses were incurred before or after the coming into force of this Act or the Bank of England Act 1998.

(4)   Any fee which is owed to the Authority under any provision made by or under this Act may be recovered as a debt due to the Authority.

Services for which fees may not be charged

18.   The power conferred by paragraph 17 may not be used to require—

(a)   a fee to be paid in respect of the discharge of any of the Authority's functions under paragraphs 13, 14, 19 or 20 of Schedule 3; or

(b)   a fee to be paid by any person whose application for approval under section 59 has been granted.

PART IV
MISCELLANEOUS

Exemption from liability in damages

19.—   (1)   Neither the Authority nor any person who is, or is acting as, a member, officer or member of staff of the Authority is to be liable in damages for anything done or omitted in the discharge, or purported discharge, of the Authority's functions.

(2)   Neither the investigator appointed under paragraph 7 nor a person appointed to conduct an investigation on his behalf under paragraph 8(8) is to be liable in damages for anything done or omitted in the discharge, or purported discharge, of his functions in relation to the investigation of a complaint.

(3)   Neither sub-paragraph (1) nor sub-paragraph (2) applies—

(a)   if the act or omission is shown to have been in bad faith; or

(b)   so as to prevent an award of damages made in respect of an act or omission on the ground that the act or omission was unlawful as a result of section 6(1) of the Human Rights Act 1998.

19A.   For the purposes of this Act anything done by an accredited financial investigator within the meaning of the Proceeds of Crime Act 2002 who is—

(a)   a member of the staff of the Authority, or

(b)   a person appointed by the Authority under section 97, 167 or 168 to conduct an investigation,

must be treated as done in the exercise or discharge of a function of the Authority.

Disqualification for membership of House of Commons

20.   In Part III of Schedule 1 to the House of Commons Disqualification Act 1975 (disqualifying offices), insert at the appropriate place—

"Member of the governing body of the Financial Services Authority".

Disqualification for membership of Northern Ireland Assembly

21.   In Part III of Schedule 1 to the Northern Ireland Assembly Disqualification Act 1975 (disqualifying offices), insert at the appropriate place—

"Member of the governing body of the Financial Services Authority".

SCHEDULE 2

REGULATED ACTIVITIES

Section 22(2)

PART I
REGULATED ACTIVITIES

General

1.   The matters with respect to which provision may be made under section 22(1) in respect of activities include, in particular, those described in general terms in this Part of this Schedule.

Dealing in investments

2.— (1) Buying, selling, subscribing for or underwriting investments or offering or agreeing to do so, either as a principal or as an agent.

(2) In the case of an investment which is a contract of insurance, that includes carrying out the contract.

Arranging deals in investments

3.   Making, or offering or agreeing to make—

(a) arrangements with a view to another person buying, selling, subscribing for or underwriting a particular investment;

(b) arrangements with a view to a person who participates in the arrangements buying, selling, subscribing for or underwriting investments.

Deposit taking

4.   Accepting deposits.

Safekeeping and administration of assets

5.— (1) Safeguarding and administering assets belonging to another which consist of or include investments or offering or agreeing to do so.

(2) Arranging for the safeguarding and administration of assets belonging to another, or offering or agreeing to do so.

Managing investments

6.   Managing, or offering or agreeing to manage, assets belonging to another person where—

(a) the assets consist of or include investments; or

(b) the arrangements for their management are such that the assets may consist of or include investments at the discretion of the person managing or offering or agreeing to manage them.

Investment advice

7.   Giving or offering or agreeing to give advice to persons on—

(a) buying, selling, subscribing for or underwriting an investment; or

(b) exercising any right conferred by an investment to acquire, dispose of, underwrite or convert an investment.

Establishing collective investment schemes

8.   Establishing, operating or winding up a collective investment scheme, including acting as—

(a) trustee of a unit trust scheme;

(b) depositary of a collective investment scheme other than a unit trust scheme; or

(c) sole director of a body incorporated by virtue of regulations under section 262.

Using computer-based systems for giving investment instructions

9.— (1) Sending on behalf of another person instructions relating to an investment by means of a computer-based system which enables investments to be transferred without a written instrument.

(2) Offering or agreeing to send such instructions by such means on behalf of another person.

(3) Causing such instructions to be sent by such means on behalf of another person.

(4)   Offering or agreeing to cause such instructions to be sent by such means on behalf of another person.

PART II
INVESTMENTS

General

10.   The matters with respect to which provision may be made under section 22(1) in respect of investments include, in particular, those described in general terms in this Part of this Schedule.

Securities

11.— (1)   Shares or stock in the share capital of a company.

(2)   "Company" includes—

(a)   any body corporate (wherever incorporated), and

(b)   any unincorporated body constituted under the law of a country or territory outside the United Kingdom,

other than an open-ended investment company.

Instruments creating or acknowledging indebtedness

12.   Any of the following—

(a)   debentures;

(b)   debenture stock;

(c)   loan stock;

(d)   bonds;

(e)   certificates of deposit;

(f)   any other instruments creating or acknowledging a present or future indebtedness.

Government and public securities

13.— (1)   Loan stock, bonds and other instruments—

(a)   creating or acknowledging indebtedness; and

(b)   issued by or on behalf of a government, local authority or public authority.

(2)   "Government, local authority or public authority" means—

(a)   the government of the United Kingdom, of Northern Ireland, or of any country or territory outside the United Kingdom;

(b)   a local authority in the United Kingdom or elsewhere;

(c)   any international organisation the members of which include the United Kingdom or another member State.

Instruments giving entitlement to investments

14.— (1)   Warrants or other instruments entitling the holder to subscribe for any investment.

(2)   It is immaterial whether the investment is in existence or identifiable.

Certificates representing securities

15.   Certificates or other instruments which confer contractual or property rights—

(a)   in respect of any investment held by someone other than the person on whom the rights are conferred by the certificate or other instrument; and

(b)   the transfer of which may be effected without requiring the consent of that person.

Units in collective investment schemes

16.— (1)   Shares in or securities of an open-ended investment company.

(2)   Any right to participate in a collective investment scheme.

Options

17.   Options to acquire or dispose of property.

Futures

18. Rights under a contract for the sale of a commodity or property of any other description under which delivery is to be made at a future date.

Contracts for differences

19. Rights under—
    (a) a contract for differences; or
    (b) any other contract the purpose or pretended purpose of which is to secure a profit or avoid a loss by reference to fluctuations in—
        (i) the value or price of property of any description; or
        (ii) an index or other factor designated for that purpose in the contract.

Contracts of insurance

20. Rights under a contract of insurance, including rights under contracts falling within head C of Schedule 2 to the Friendly Societies Act 1992.

Participation in Lloyd's syndicates

21.— (1) The underwriting capacity of a Lloyd's syndicate.
    (2) A person's membership (or prospective membership) of a Lloyd's syndicate.

Deposits

22. Rights under any contract under which a sum of money (whether or not denominated in a currency) is paid on terms under which it will be repaid, with or without interest or a premium, and either on demand or at a time or in circumstances agreed by or on behalf of the person making the payment and the person receiving it.

Loans secured on land

23.— (1) Rights under any contract under which—
    (a) one person provides another with credit; and
    (b) the obligation of the borrower to repay is secured on land.
    (2) "Credit" includes any cash loan or other financial accommodation.
    (3) "Cash" includes money in any form.

Rights in investments

24. Any right or interest in anything which is an investment as a result of any other provision made under section 22(1).

PART III
SUPPLEMENTAL PROVISIONS

The order-making power

25.— (1) An order under section 22(1) may—
    (a) provide for exemptions;
    (b) confer powers on the Treasury or the Authority;
    (c) authorise the making of regulations or other instruments by the Treasury for purposes of, or connected with, any relevant provision;
    (d) authorise the making of rules or other instruments by the Authority for purposes of, or connected with, any relevant provision;
    (e) make provision in respect of any information or document which, in the opinion of the Treasury or the Authority, is relevant for purposes of, or connected with, any relevant provision;
    (f) make such consequential, transitional or supplemental provision as the Treasury consider appropriate for purposes of, or connected with, any relevant provision.

(2)   Provision made as a result of sub-paragraph (1)(f) may amend any primary or subordinate legislation, including any provision of, or made under, this Act.

(3)   "Relevant provision" means any provision—

   (a)   of section 22 or this Schedule; or

   (b)   made under that section or this Schedule.

Parliamentary control

26.—   (1)   This paragraph applies to the first order made under section 22(1).

(2)   This paragraph also applies to any subsequent order made under section 22(1) which contains a statement by the Treasury that, in their opinion, the effect (or one of the effects) of the proposed order would be that an activity which is not a regulated activity would become a regulated activity.

(3)   An order to which this paragraph applies—

   (a)   must be laid before Parliament after being made; and

   (b)   ceases to have effect at the end of the relevant period unless before the end of that period the order is approved by a resolution of each House of Parliament (but without that affecting anything done under the order or the power to make a new order).

(4)   "Relevant period" means a period of twenty-eight days beginning with the day on which the order is made.

(5)   In calculating the relevant period no account is to be taken of any time during which Parliament is dissolved or prorogued or during which both Houses are adjourned for more than four days.

Interpretation

27.—   (1)   In this Schedule—

   "buying" includes acquiring for valuable consideration;

   "offering" includes inviting to treat;

   "property" includes currency of the United Kingdom or any other country or territory; and

   "selling" includes disposing for valuable consideration.

(2)   In sub-paragraph (1) "disposing" includes—

   (a)   in the case of an investment consisting of rights under a contract—

      (i)   surrendering, assigning or converting those rights; or

      (ii)   assuming the corresponding liabilities under the contract;

   (b)   in the case of an investment consisting of rights under other arrangements, assuming the corresponding liabilities under the contract or arrangements;

   (c)   in the case of any other investment, issuing or creating the investment or granting the rights or interests of which it consists.

(3)   In this Schedule references to an instrument include references to any record (whether or not in the form of a document).

...

SCHEDULE 7

THE AUTHORITY AS COMPETENT AUTHORITY FOR PART VI

Section 72(2)

General

1.   This Act applies in relation to the Authority when it is exercising functions under Part VI as the competent authority subject to the following modifications.

The Authority's general functions

2. In section 2—
   (a) subsection (4)(a) does not apply to listing rules;
   (b) subsection (4)(c) does not apply to general guidance given in relation to Part VI; and
   (c) subsection (4)(d) does not apply to functions under Part VI.

Duty to consult

3. Section 8 does not apply.

Rules

4.— (1) Sections 149, 153, 154 and 156 do not apply.
   (2) Section 155 has effect as if—
   (a) the reference in subsection (2)(c) to the general duties of the Authority under section 2 were a reference to its duty under section 73; and
   (b) section 99 were included in the provisions referred to in subsection (9).

Statements of policy

5.— (1) Paragraph 5 of Schedule 1 has effect as if the requirement to act through the Authority's governing body applied also to the exercise of its functions of publishing statements under section 93.
   (2) Paragraph 1 of Schedule 1 has effect as if section 93 were included in the provisions referred to in sub-paragraph (2)(d).

Penalties

6. Paragraph 16 of Schedule 1 does not apply in relation to penalties under Part VI (for which separate provision is made by section 100).

Fees

7. Paragraph 17 of Schedule 1 does not apply in relation to fees payable under Part VI (for which separate provision is made by section 99).

Exemption from liability in damages

8. Schedule 1 has effect as if—
   (a) sub-paragraph (1) of paragraph 19 were omitted (similar provision being made in relation to the competent authority by section 102); and
   (b) for the words from the beginning to "(a)" in sub-paragraph (3) of that paragraph, there were substituted "Sub-paragraph (2) does not apply".

SCHEDULE 8

TRANSFER OF FUNCTIONS UNDER PART VI

Section 72(3)

The power to transfer

1.— (1) The Treasury may by order provide for any function conferred on the competent authority which is exercisable for the time being by a particular person to be transferred so as to be exercisable by another person.
   (2) An order may be made under this paragraph only if—
   (a) the person from whom the relevant functions are to be transferred has agreed in writing that the order should be made;
   (b) the Treasury are satisfied that the manner in which, or efficiency with which, the functions are discharged would be significantly improved if they were transferred to the transferee; or

    (c)   the Treasury are satisfied that it is otherwise in the public interest that the order should be made.

Supplemental

2.—   (1) An order under this Schedule does not affect anything previously done by any person ("the previous authority") in the exercise of functions which are transferred by the order to another person ("the new authority").

    (2) Such an order may, in particular, include provision—

      (a) modifying or excluding any provision of Part VI, IX or XXVI in its application to any such functions;

      (b) for reviews similar to that made, in relation to the Authority, by section 12;

      (c) imposing on the new authority requirements similar to those imposed, in relation to the Authority, by sections 152, 155 and 354;

      (d) as to the giving of guidance by the new authority;

      (e) for the delegation by the new authority of the exercise of functions under Part VI and as to the consequences of delegation;

      (f) for the transfer of any property, rights or liabilities relating to any such functions from the previous authority to the new authority;

      (g) for the carrying on and completion by the new authority of anything in the process of being done by the previous authority when the order takes effect;

      (h) for the substitution of the new authority for the previous authority in any instrument, contract or legal proceedings;

      (i) for the transfer of persons employed by the previous authority to the new authority and as to the terms on which they are to transfer;

      (j) making such amendments to any primary or subordinate legislation (including any provision of, or made under, this Act) as the Treasury consider appropriate in consequence of the transfer of functions effected by the order.

    (3) Nothing in this paragraph is to be taken as restricting the powers conferred by section 428.

3.   If the Treasury have made an order under paragraph 1 ("the transfer order") they may, by a separate order made under this paragraph, make any provision of a kind that could have been included in the transfer order.

SCHEDULE 9

NON-LISTING PROSPECTUSES

Section 87(5)

General application of Part VI

1.   The provisions of Part VI apply in relation to a non-listing prospectus as they apply in relation to listing particulars but with the modifications made by this Schedule.

References to listing particulars

2.—   (1) Any reference to listing particulars is to be read as a reference to a prospectus.

    (2) Any reference to supplementary listing particulars is to be read as a reference to a supplementary prospectus.

General duty of disclosure

3.—   (1) In section 80(1), for "section 79" substitute "section 87".

    (2) In section 80(2), omit "as a condition of the admission of the securities to the official list".

Supplementary prospectuses

4.   In section 81(1), for "section 79 and before the commencement of dealings in the securities concerned following their admission to the official list" substitute "section 87 and before the end of the period during which the offer to which the prospectus relates remains open".

Exemption from liability for compensation

5.— (1) In paragraphs 1(3) and 2(3) of Schedule 10, for paragraph (d) substitute—
            "(d) the securities were acquired after such a lapse of time that he ought in the circumstances to be reasonably excused and, if the securities are dealt in on an approved exchange, he continued in that belief until after the commencement of dealings in the securities on that exchange."

       (2) After paragraph 8 of that Schedule, insert—

"Meaning of "approved exchange"

9.   "Approved exchange" has such meaning as may be prescribed."

Advertisements

6.   In section 98(1), for "If listing particulars are, or are to be, published in connection with an application for listing," substitute "If a prospectus is, or is to be, published in connection with an application for approval, then, until the end of the period during which the offer to which the prospectus relates remains open,".

Fees

7.   Listing rules made under section 99 may require the payment of fees to the competent authority in respect of a prospectus submitted for approval under section 87.

SCHEDULE 10

COMPENSATION: EXEMPTIONS

Section 90(2) and (5)

Statements believed to be true

1.— (1) In this paragraph "statement" means—
            (a) any untrue or misleading statement in listing particulars; or
            (b) the omission from listing particulars of any matter required to be included by section 80 or 81.

       (2) A person does not incur any liability under section 90(1) for loss caused by a statement if he satisfies the court that, at the time when the listing particulars were submitted to the competent authority, he reasonably believed (having made such enquiries, if any, as were reasonable) that—
            (a) the statement was true and not misleading, or
            (b) the matter whose omission caused the loss was properly omitted,
            and that one or more of the conditions set out in sub-paragraph (3) are satisfied.

       (3) The conditions are that—
            (a) he continued in his belief until the time when the securities in question were acquired;
            (b) they were acquired before it was reasonably practicable to bring a correction to the attention of persons likely to acquire them;
            (c) before the securities were acquired, he had taken all such steps as it was reasonable for him to have taken to secure that a correction was brought to the attention of those persons;

   (d) he continued in his belief until after the commencement of dealings in the securities
        following their admission to the official list and they were acquired after such a lapse
        of time that he ought in the circumstances to be reasonably excused.

Statements by experts

2.— (1) In this paragraph "statement" means a statement included in listing particulars which—
     (a) purports to be made by, or on the authority of, another person as an expert; and
     (b) is stated to be included in the listing particulars with that other person's consent.
     (2) A person does not incur any liability under section 90(1) for loss in respect of any securities
          caused by a statement if he satisfies the court that, at the time when the listing particulars
          were submitted to the competent authority, he reasonably believed that the other person—
     (a) was competent to make or authorise the statement, and
     (b) had consented to its inclusion in the form and context in which it was included,
     and that one or more of the conditions set out in sub-paragraph (3) are satisfied.
     (3) The conditions are that—
     (a) he continued in his belief until the time when the securities were acquired;
     (b) they were acquired before it was reasonably practicable to bring the fact that the expert
          was not competent, or had not consented, to the attention of persons likely to acquire
          the securities in question;
     (c) before the securities were acquired he had taken all such steps as it was reasonable for
          him to have taken to secure that that fact was brought to the attention of those persons;
     (d) he continued in his belief until after the commencement of dealings in the securities
          following their admission to the official list and they were acquired after such a lapse
          of time that he ought in the circumstances to be reasonably excused.

Corrections of statements

3.— (1) In this paragraph "statement" has the same meaning as in paragraph 1.
     (2) A person does not incur liability under section 90(1) for loss caused by a statement if he
          satisfies the court—
     (a) that before the securities in question were acquired, a correction had been published in
          a manner calculated to bring it to the attention of persons likely to acquire the securi-
          ties; or
     (b) that he took all such steps as it was reasonable for him to take to secure such publica-
          tion and reasonably believed that it had taken place before the securities were
          acquired.
     (3) Nothing in this paragraph is to be taken as affecting paragraph 1.

Corrections of statements by experts

4.— (1) In this paragraph "statement" has the same meaning as in paragraph 2.
     (2) A person does not incur liability under section 90(1) for loss caused by a statement if he
          satisfies the court—
     (a) that before the securities in question were acquired, the fact that the expert was not
          competent or had not consented had been published in a manner calculated to bring it
          to the attention of persons likely to acquire the securities; or
     (b) that he took all such steps as it was reasonable for him to take to secure such publica-
          tion and reasonably believed that it had taken place before the securities were
          acquired.
     (3) Nothing in this paragraph is to be taken as affecting paragraph 2.

Official statements

5.   A person does not incur any liability under section 90(1) for loss resulting from—
     (a) a statement made by an official person which is included in the listing particulars, or

(b)   a statement contained in a public official document which is included in the listing particulars,

if he satisfies the court that the statement is accurately and fairly reproduced.

False or misleading information known about

6.   A person does not incur any liability under section 90(1) or (4) if he satisfies the court that the person suffering the loss acquired the securities in question with knowledge—

(a)   that the statement was false or misleading,

(b)   of the omitted matter, or

(c)   of the change or new matter,

as the case may be.

Belief that supplementary listing particulars not called for

7.   A person does not incur any liability under section 90(4) if he satisfies the court that he reasonably believed that the change or new matter in question was not such as to call for supplementary listing particulars.

Meaning of "expert"

8.   "Expert" includes any engineer, valuer, accountant or other person whose profession, qualifications or experience give authority to a statement made by him.

SCHEDULE 11

OFFERS OF SECURITIES

Section 103(6)

The general rule

1.—   (1)   A person offers securities to the public in the United Kingdom if—

(a)   to the extent that the offer is made to persons in the United Kingdom, it is made to the public; and

(b)   the offer is not an exempt offer.

(2)   For this purpose, an offer which is made to any section of the public, whether selected—

(a)   as members or debenture holders of a body corporate,

(b)   as clients of the person making the offer, or

(c)   in any other manner,

is to be regarded as made to the public.

Exempt offers

2.—   (1)   For the purposes of this Schedule, an offer of securities is an "exempt offer" if, to the extent that the offer is made to persons in the United Kingdom—

(a)   the condition specified in any of paragraphs 3 to 24A is satisfied in relation to the offer; or

(b)   the condition specified in one relevant paragraph is satisfied in relation to part, but not the whole, of the offer and, in relation to each other part of the offer, the condition specified in a different relevant paragraph is satisfied.

(2)   The relevant paragraphs are 3 to 8, 12 to 18 and 21.

Offers for business purposes

3.   The securities are offered to persons—

(a)   whose ordinary activities involve them in acquiring, holding, managing or disposing of investments (as principal or agent) for the purposes of their businesses, or

(b)   who it is reasonable to expect will acquire, hold, manage or dispose of investments (as principal or agent) for the purposes of their businesses, or are otherwise offered to persons in the context of their trades, professions or occupations.

Offers to limited numbers

4.— (1) The securities are offered to no more than fifty persons.

     (2) In determining whether this condition is satisfied, the offer is to be taken together with any other offer of the same securities which was—

        (a) made by the same person;

        (b) open at any time within the period of 12 months ending with the date on which the offer is first made; and

        (c) not an offer to the public in the United Kingdom by virtue of this condition being satisfied.

     (3) For the purposes of this paragraph—

        (a) the making of an offer of securities to trustees or members of a partnership in their capacity as such, or

        (b) the making of such an offer to any other two or more persons jointly,

     is to be treated as the making of an offer to a single person.

Clubs and associations

5. The securities are offered to the members of a club or association (whether or not incorporated) and the members can reasonably be regarded as having a common interest with each other and with the club or association in the affairs of the club or association and in what is to be done with the proceeds of the offer.

Restricted circles

6.— (1) The securities are offered to a restricted circle of persons whom the offeror reasonably believes to be sufficiently knowledgeable to understand the risks involved in accepting the offer.

     (2) In determining whether a person is sufficiently knowledgeable to understand the risks involved in accepting an offer of securities, any information supplied by the person making the offer is to be disregarded, apart from information about—

        (a) the issuer of the securities; or

        (b) if the securities confer the right to acquire other securities, the issuer of those other securities.

Underwriting agreements

7. The securities are offered in connection with a genuine invitation to enter into an underwriting agreement with respect to them.

Offers to public authorities

8.— (1) The securities are offered to a public authority.

     (2) "Public authority" means—

        (a) the government of the United Kingdom;

        (b) the government of any country or territory outside the United Kingdom;

        (c) a local authority in the United Kingdom or elsewhere;

        (d) any international organisation the members of which include the United Kingdom or another EEA State; and

        (e) such other bodies, if any, as may be specified.

Maximum consideration

9.— (1) The total consideration payable for the securities cannot exceed 40,000 euros (or an equivalent amount).

     (2) In determining whether this condition is satisfied, the offer is to be taken together with any other offer of the same securities which was—

        (a) made by the same person;

      (b)   open at any time within the period of 12 months ending with the date on which the offer is first made; and

      (c)   not an offer to the public in the United Kingdom by virtue of this condition being satisfied.

  (3)   An amount (in relation to an amount denominated in euros) is an "equivalent amount" if it is an amount of equal value, calculated at the latest practicable date before (but in any event not more than 3 days before) the date on which the offer is first made, denominated wholly or partly in another currency or unit of account.

Minimum consideration

10.— (1)   The minimum consideration which may be paid by any person for securities acquired by him pursuant to the offer is at least 40,000 euros (or an equivalent amount).

  (2)   Paragraph 9(3) also applies for the purposes of this paragraph.

Securities denominated in euros

11.— (1)   The securities are denominated in amounts of at least 40,000 euros (or an equivalent amount).

  (2)   Paragraph 9(3) also applies for the purposes of this paragraph.

Takeovers

12.— (1)   The securities are offered in connection with a takeover offer.

  (2)   "Takeover offer" means—

      (a)   an offer to acquire shares in a body incorporated in the United Kingdom which is a takeover offer within the meaning of the takeover provisions (or would be such an offer if those provisions applied in relation to any body corporate);

      (b)   an offer to acquire all or substantially all of the shares, or of the shares of a particular class, in a body incorporated outside the United Kingdom; or

      (c)   an offer made to all the holders of shares, or of shares of a particular class, in a body corporate to acquire a specified proportion of those shares.

  (3)   "The takeover provisions" means—

      (a)   Part XIIIA of the Companies Act 1985; or

      (b)   in relation to Northern Ireland, Part XIVA of the Companies (Northern Ireland) Order 1986.

  (4)   For the purposes of sub-paragraph (2)(b), any shares which the offeror or any associate of his holds or has contracted to acquire are to be disregarded.

  (5)   For the purposes of sub-paragraph (2)(c), the following are not to be regarded as holders of the shares in question—

      (a)   the offeror;

      (b)   any associate of the offeror; and

      (c)   any person whose shares the offeror or any associate of the offeror has contracted to acquire.

  (6)   "Associate" has the same meaning as in—

      (a)   section 430E of the Companies Act 1985; or

      (b)   in relation to Northern Ireland, Article 423E of the Companies (Northern Ireland) Order 1986.

Mergers

13.   The securities are offered in connection with a merger (within the meaning of Council Directive No 78/855/EEC).

Free shares

14.— (1)   The securities are shares and are offered free of charge to any or all of the holders of shares in the issuer.

(2)   "Holders of shares" means the persons who at the close of business on a date—
    (a)   specified in the offer, and
    (b)   falling within the period of 60 days ending with the date on which the offer is first made,
were holders of such shares.

Exchange of shares

15.   The securities—
    (a)   are shares, or investments of a specified kind relating to shares, in a body corporate, and
    (b)   are offered in exchange for shares in the same body corporate,
and the offer cannot result in any increase in the issued share capital of the body corporate.

Qualifying persons

16.—   (1)   The securities are issued by a body corporate and are offered—
    (a)   by the issuer, by a body corporate connected with the issuer or by a relevant trustee;
    (b)   only to qualifying persons; and
    (c)   on terms that a contract to acquire any such securities may be entered into only by the qualifying person to whom they were offered or, if the terms of the offer so permit, any qualifying person.

    (2)   A person is a "qualifying person", in relation to an issuer, if he is a genuine employee or former employee of the issuer or of another body corporate in the same group or the wife, husband, widow, widower *, civil partner, surviving civil partner,* or child or stepchild under the age of eighteen of such an employee or former employee.

    (3)   In relation to an issuer of securities, "connected with" has such meaning as may be prescribed.

    (4)   "Group" and "relevant trustee" have such meaning as may be prescribed.

Convertible securities

17.—   (1)   The securities result from the conversion of convertible securities and listing particulars (or a prospectus) relating to the convertible securities were (or was) published in the United Kingdom under or by virtue of Part VI or such other provisions applying in the United Kingdom as may be specified.

    (2)   "Convertible securities" means securities of a specified kind which can be converted into, or exchanged for, or which confer rights to acquire, other securities.

    (3)   "Conversion" means conversion into or exchange for, or the exercise of rights conferred by the securities to acquire, other securities.

Charities

18.   The securities are issued by—
    (a)   a charity within the meaning of—
        (i)   section 96(1) of the Charities Act 1993, or
        (ii)   section 35 of the Charities Act (Northern Ireland) 1964,
    (b)   a recognised body within the meaning of section 1(7) of the Law Reform (Miscellaneous Provisions) (Scotland) Act 1990,
    (c)   a housing association within the meaning of—
        (i)   section 5(1) of the Housing Act 1985,
        (ii)   section 1 of the Housing Associations Act 1985, or
        (iii) Article 3 of the Housing (Northern Ireland) Order 1992,
    (d)   an industrial or provident society registered in accordance with—
        (i)   section 1(2)(b) of the Industrial and Provident Societies Act 1965, or
        (ii)   section 1(2)(b) of the Industrial and Provident Societies Act 1969, or

(e) a non-profit making association or body, recognised by the country or territory in which it is established, with objectives similar to those of a body falling within any of paragraphs (a) to (c),

and the proceeds of the offer will be used for the purposes of the issuer's objectives.

Building societies etc

19. The securities offered are shares which are issued by, or ownership of which entitles the holder to membership of or to obtain the benefit of services provided by—
  (a) a building society incorporated under the law of, or of any part of, the United Kingdom;
  (b) any body incorporated under the law of, or of any part of, the United Kingdom relating to industrial and provident societies or credit unions; or
  (c) a body of a similar nature established in another EEA State.

Euro-securities

20.— (1) The securities offered are Euro-securities and no advertisement relating to the offer is issued in the United Kingdom, or is caused to be so issued—
  (a) by the issuer of the Euro-securities;
  (b) by any credit institution or other financial institution through which the Euro-securities may be acquired pursuant to the offer; or
  (c) by any body corporate which is a member of the same group as the issuer or any of those institutions.
  (2) But sub-paragraph (1) does not apply to an advertisement of a prescribed kind.
  (3) "Euro-securities" means investments which—
  (a) are to be underwritten and distributed by a syndicate at least two of the members of which have their registered offices in different countries or territories;
  (b) are to be offered on a significant scale in one or more countries or territories, other than the country or territory in which the issuer has its registered office; and
  (c) may be acquired pursuant to the offer only through a credit institution or other financial institution.
  (4) "Credit institution" means a credit institution as defined in Article 1(1)(a) of the banking consolidation directive.
  (5) "Financial institution" means a financial institution as defined in Article 1 of the banking consolidation directive.
  (6) "Underwritten" means underwritten by whatever means, including by acquisition or subscription, with a view to resale.

Same class securities

21. The securities are of the same class, and were issued at the same time, as securities in respect of which a prospectus has been published under or by virtue of—
  (a) Part VI;
  (b) Part III of the Companies Act 1985; or
  (c) such other provisions applying in the United Kingdom as may be specified.

Short date securities

22. The securities are investments of a specified kind with a maturity of less than one year from their date of issue.

Government and public securities

23.— (1) The securities are investments of a specified kind creating or acknowledging indebtedness issued by or on behalf of a public authority.
  (2) "Public authority" means—
  (a) the government of the United Kingdom;
  (b) the government of any country or territory outside the United Kingdom;

(c)   a local authority in the United Kingdom or elsewhere;

(d)   any international organisation the members of which include the United Kingdom or another EEA State; and

(e)   such other bodies, if any, as may be specified.

Non-transferable securities

24.   The securities are not transferable.

Units in a collective investment scheme

24A.   The securities are units (as defined by section 237(2)) in a collective investment scheme.

General definitions

25.   For the purposes of this Schedule—

    "shares" has such meaning as may be specified; and

    "specified" means specified in an order made by the Treasury.

Note. The italicized words in paragraph 16(2) are inserted by the Civil Partnership Act 2004, s. 261(1), Sch. 27, para. 166, as from a day to be appointed.

Public Offers of Securities Regulations 1995

S.I. 1995/1537

PART I
GENERAL

1.   **Citation, commencement and extent**

(1)   These Regulations may be cited as the Public Offers of Securities Regulations 1995 and shall come into force on 19th June 1995.

(2)   These Regulations extend to Northern Ireland.

2.   **Interpretation**

(1)   In these Regulations, except where the context otherwise requires—

"the Act" means the Financial Services and Markets Act 2000;

"approved exchange" means, in relation to dealings in securities, a recognised investment exchange approved by the Treasury for the purposes of these Regulations either generally or in relation to such dealings, and the Treasury shall give notice in such manner as they think appropriate of the exchanges which are for the time being approved;

"body corporate" shall be construed in accordance with section 417(1) of the Act;

"convertible securities" means—

(i)   instruments creating or acknowledging indebtedness of a kind which can be converted into or exchanged for, or which confer rights to acquire, securities;

(ii)   instruments giving entitlements to securities; or

(iii)   certificates representing securities;

and "conversion" in relation to convertible securities means their conversion into or exchange for, or the exercise of rights conferred by them to acquire, other securities ("underlying securities");

"credit institution" means a credit institution as defined in Article 1(1)(a) of Directive 2000/12/EC of the European Parliament and of the Council;

"director" shall be construed in accordance with section 417(1) of the Act;

…

"Euro-securities" means securities which—

(a)   are to be underwritten (by whatever means, including acquisition or subscription, with a view to resale) and distributed by a syndicate at least two of the members of which have their registered offices in different countries or territories;

(b)   are to be offered on a significant scale in one or more countries or territories other than the country or territory in which the issuer has its registered office; and

(c)   may be acquired pursuant to the offer only through a credit institution or other financial institution;

"financial institution" means a financial institution as defined in Article 1 of the Directive 2000/12/EC of the European Parliament and of the Council;

"group", in relation to a body corporate ("A") means A and any other body corporate which is—

(i)   a subsidiary of A,

(ii)   a holding company of A, or

(iii)   a subsidiary of such a holding company;

…

"issuer", in relation to any securities, means the person by whom they have been or are to be issued;

"member State" means a State which is a Contracting Party to the Agreement on the European Economic Area signed at Oporto on 2nd May 1992 as adjusted by the Protocol signed at Brussels on 17th March 1993;

"private company" has the meaning given in section 1(3) of the Companies Act 1985;

"the registrar of companies", in relation to a prospectus relating to any securities, means—

    (a)   if the securities are or are to be issued by a company incorporated in Great Britain, the registrar of companies in England and Wales or the registrar of companies in Scotland according to whether the company's registered office is in England and Wales or in Scotland;

    (b)   if the securities are or are to be issued by a company incorporated in Northern Ireland, the registrar of companies for Northern Ireland;

    (c)   in any other case, any of those registrars;

"recognised investment exchange" has the meaning given in section 285 of the Act;

"securities" means investments to which Part II of these Regulations applies; and

"sale" includes any disposal for valuable consideration.

(1A)   Paragraphs (i), (ii) and (iii) of the definition of "convertible securities" in paragraph (1) above, together with regulations 3(2) and (5), 7(2)(f),(n), 8(4) and (5), and 9(4) must be read with—

    (a)   section 22 of the Financial Services and Markets Act 2000;

    (b)   any relevant order under that section; and

    (c)   Schedule 2 to that Act.

(2)   In the application of these Regulations to Scotland, references to a matter being actionable at the suit of a person shall be construed as references to the matter being actionable at the instance of that person.

(3)   References to the Companies Act 1985 include references to the corresponding Northern Ireland provision.

PART II
PUBLIC OFFERS OF UNLISTED SECURITIES

3.   **Investments to which this Part applies**

(1)   This Part of these Regulations applies to any investment which—

    (a)   is not admitted to official listing, nor is the subject of an application for listing, in accordance with Part VI of the Act; and

    (b)   is of a kind specified in paragraph (2).

(2)   Subject to paragraphs (3) to (5) below, the kinds of investments specified for the purposes of paragraph (1)(b) are—

    (a)   shares, including for those purposes deferred shares of a building society, within the meaning of section 119 of the Building Societies Act 1986;

    (b)   instruments creating or acknowledging indebtedness;

    (c)   instruments giving entitlements to securities, including warrants and other instruments entitling the holder to acquire any share or instrument creating or acknowledging indebtedness; and

    (d)   certificates representing securities.

(3)   For the purposes of paragraph (1)(b), investments of the kind specified in paragraph (2)(a) (shares) do not include transferable shares in a body incorporated under the law relating to industrial and provident societies.

(4)   For the purposes of paragraph (1)(b), investments of the kind specified in paragraph (2)(b) (instruments creating or acknowledging indebtedness) do not include—

    (a)   debentures having a maturity of less than one year from their date of issue, and

    (b)   bills of exchange accepted by a banker.

(5)   For the purposes of paragraph (1)(b)—

    (a)   investments of the kind specified in sub-paragraph (c) of paragraph (2) do not include instruments giving entitlements in connection with government and public securities; and

    (b)   investments of the kind specified in sub-paragraph (d) of paragraph (2) do not include investments and certificates representing government or public securities.

4.   Registration and publication of prospectus

(1)   When securities are offered to the public in the United Kingdom for the first time the offeror shall publish a prospectus by making it available to the public, free of charge, at an address in the United Kingdom, from the time he first offers the securities until the end of the period during which the offer remains open.

(2)   The offeror shall, before the time of publication of the prospectus, deliver a copy of it to the registrar of companies for registration.

(3)   Paragraph (2) and regulations 5, 6 and 8 to 15 shall not apply to a prospectus submitted for approval in accordance with listing rules made under section 87 of the Act.

5.   Offers of securities

A person is to be regarded as offering securities if, as principal—

(a)   he makes an offer which, if accepted, would give rise to a contract for the issue or sale of the securities by him or by another person with whom he has made arrangements for the issue or sale of the securities; or

(b)   he invites a person to make such an offer;

but not otherwise; and, except where the context otherwise requires, in this Part of these Regulations "offer" and "offeror" shall be construed accordingly.

6.   Offers to the public in the United Kingdom

A person offers securities to the public in the United Kingdom if, to the extent that the offer is made to persons in the United Kingdom, it is made to the public; and, for this purpose, an offer which is made to any section of the public, whether selected as members or debenture holders of a body corporate, or as clients of the person making the offer, or in any other manner, is to be regarded as made to the public.

7.   Exemptions

(1)   For the purposes of these Regulations, an offer of securities shall be deemed not to be an offer to the public in the United Kingdom if, to the extent that the offer is made to persons in the United Kingdom—

(a)   the condition specified in any one of the sub-paragraphs of paragraph (2) is satisfied in relation to the offer; or

(b)   paragraph (3) applies in relation to the offer.

(2)   The following are the conditions specified in this paragraph—

(a)   the securities are offered to persons—

(i)   whose ordinary activities involve them in acquiring, holding, managing or disposing of investments (as principal or agent) for the purposes of their businesses; or

(ii)   who it is reasonable to expect will acquire, hold, manage or dispose of investments (as principal or agent) for the purposes of their businesses;

or are otherwise offered to persons in the context of their trades, professions or occupations;

(b)   the securities are offered to no more than fifty persons;

(c)   the securities are offered to the members of a club or association (whether or not incorporated) and the members can reasonably be regarded as having a common interest with each other and with the club or association in the affairs of the club or association and in what is to be done with the proceeds of the offer;

(d)   the securities are offered to a restricted circle of persons whom the offeror reasonably believes to be sufficiently knowledgeable to understand the risks involved in accepting the offer;

(e)   the securities are offered in connection with a bona fide invitation to enter into an underwriting agreement with respect to them;

(f)   the securities are the securities of a private company and are offered by that company to—

(i)   members or employees of the company;

(ii)   members of the families of any such members or employees; or

        (iii)   persons holding instruments creating or acknowledging indebtedness issued by the company;

(ff)   the securities are the securities of a private company and are offered to holders of other securities in that company (whether or not of the same class) in pursuance of a requirement imposed by a provision in its articles of association or in an agreement between all the holders of securities, or all the holders of one or more classes of security, of that company;

(g)   the securities are offered to a government, local authority or public authority, ...;

(h)   the total consideration payable for the securities cannot exceed ecu 40,000 (or an equivalent amount);

(i)   the minimum consideration which may be paid by any person for securities acquired by him pursuant to the offer is at least ecu 40,000 (or an equivalent amount);

(j)   the securities are denominated in amounts of at least ecu 40,000 (or an equivalent amount);

(k)   the securities are offered in connection with a takeover offer;

(l)   the securities are offered in connection with a merger within the meaning of Council Directive No 78/855/EEC;

(m)   the securities are shares and are offered free of charge to any or all of the holders of shares in the issuer;

(n)   the securities are—
        (i)   shares,
        (ii)   instruments giving entitlements to subscribe for shares, or
        (iii)   certificates representing shares,

in a body corporate and are offered in exchange for shares in the same body corporate, and the offer cannot result in any increase in the issued share capital of the body corporate;

(o)   the securities are issued by a body corporate and offered—
        (i)   by the issuer, by a body corporate connected with the issuer a member of the same group as the issuer or by a relevant trustee;
        (ii)   only to qualifying persons; and
        (iii)   on terms that a contract to acquire any such securities may be entered into only by the qualifying person to whom they were offered or, if the terms of the offer so permit, any qualifying person;

(p)   the securities result from the conversion of convertible securities and listing particulars or a prospectus relating to the convertible securities were or was published in the United Kingdom under or by virtue of Part VI of the Act, Part III of the Companies Act 1985 or these Regulations;

(q)   the securities are issued by—
        (i)   a charity within the meaning of section 96(1) of the Charities Act 1993;
        (ii)   a housing association within the meaning of section 5(1) of the Housing Act 1985;
        (iii)   an industrial or provident society registered in accordance with section 1(2)(b) of the Industrial and Provident Societies Act 1965; or
        (iv)   a non-profit making association or body, recognised by the country or territory in which it is established, with objectives similar to those of a body falling within any of paragraphs (i) to (iii);

and the proceeds of the offer will be used for the purposes of the issuer's objectives;

(r)   the securities offered are shares and ownership of the securities entitles the holder—
        (i)   to obtain the benefit of services provided by a building society within the meaning of section 119(1) of the Building Societies Act, an industrial or provident society registered in accordance with section 1(2) of the Industrial and Provident Societies Act 1965 or a body of a like nature established in a member State; or
        (ii)   to membership of such a body;

(s)   the securities offered are Euro-securities, and no advertisement relating to the offer is issued in, or directed at persons in, the United Kingdom (or is caused to be so issued or so directed), by the issuer of the Euro-securities or by any credit institution or other financial institution through which the Euro-securities may be acquired pursuant to the offer, or by any body corporate which is a member of the same group as that issuer or any of those institutions, other than—

    (i)   an advertisement which is an exempt communication falling within article 19 of the Financial Services and Markets Act 2000 (Financial Promotion) Order 2001 (Investment professionals); or

    (ii)   an advertisement which would be an exempt communication falling within article 19 of that Order if the meaning of "investment professionals" in paragraph (5) of that article included a person with or for whom any credit institution or other financial institution through which the Euro-securities may be acquired pursuant to the offer has effected or arranged for the effecting of a transaction within the period of twelve months ending with the date on which the offer is first made;

    (t)   the securities are of the same class, and were issued at the same time, as securities in respect of which a prospectus has been published under or by virtue of Part VI of the Act, Part III of the Companies Act 1985 or these Regulations;

    (u)   the securities are not transferable.

(3)   This paragraph applies in relation to an offer where the condition specified in one relevant sub-paragraph is satisfied in relation to part, but not the whole, of the offer and, in relation to each other part of the offer, the condition specified in a different relevant sub-paragraph is satisfied.

(4)   For the purposes of paragraph (3), "relevant sub-paragraph" means any of sub-paragraphs (a) to (f), (g), (k) to (q) and (t) of paragraph (2).

(5)   For the purposes of this regulation, "shares", except in relation to a takeover offer, must be read with—

    (a)   section 22 to the Financial Services and Markets Act 2000,

    (b)   any relevant order under that section; and

    (c)   Schedule 2 to that Act.

(6)   For the purposes of determining whether the condition specified in sub-paragraph (b) or (h) of paragraph (2) is satisfied in relation to an offer, the offer shall be taken together with any other offer of securities of the same class which was—

    (a)   made by the same person;

    (b)   open at any time within the period of 12 months ending with the date on which the offer is first made; and

    (c)   deemed not to be an offer to the public in the United Kingdom by virtue of that condition being satisfied.

(6A)   For the purposes of paragraph (2)(b), the making of an offer of securities to trustees of a trust or members of a partnership in their capacity as such, or the making of such an offer to any other two or more persons jointly, shall be treated as the making of an offer to a single person.

(7)   In determining for the purposes of paragraph (2)(d) whether a person is sufficiently knowledgeable to understand the risks involved in accepting an offer of securities, any information supplied by the offeror shall be disregarded, apart from information about—

    (a)   the issuer of the securities, or

    (b)   if the securities confer the right to acquire other securities, the issuer of those other securities.

(8)   For the purposes of paragraph (2)(f)—

    (a)   the members of a person's family are the person's husband or wife, widow or widower and children (including stepchildren) and their descendants, and any trustee (acting in his capacity as such) of a trust the principal beneficiary of which is the person himself or herself, or any of those relatives; and

    (b)   regulation 3(2)(a) shall not apply.

(8A)   For the purposes of paragraph (2)(g), a government, local authority or public authority means—

    (a)   the government of the United Kingdom;

    (b)   the Scottish Administration;

(c)   the Executive Committee of the Northern Ireland Assembly;

(d)   the National Assembly for Wales;

(e)   the government of any country or territory outside the United Kingdom;

(f)   a local authority in the United Kingdom or elsewhere; or

(g)   a body the members of which comprise—

     (i)   states including the United Kingdom or another EEA State, or

     (ii)   bodies whose members comprise states including the United Kingdom or another EEA State.

(9)   For the purposes of determining whether the condition mentioned in sub-paragraph (h), (i) or (j) of paragraph (2) is satisfied in relation to an offer, an amount, in relation to an amount denominated in ecu, is an "equivalent amount" if it is an amount of equal value, calculated at the latest practicable date before (but in any event not more than 3 days before) the date on which the offer is first made, denominated wholly or partly in another currency or unit of account.

(10)   For the purposes of paragraph (2)(k), "takeover offer" means—

(a)   an offer to acquire shares in a body corporate incorporated in the United Kingdom which is a takeover offer within the meaning of Part XIIIA of the Companies Act 1985 (or would be such an offer if that Part of that Act applied in relation to any body corporate);

(b)   an offer to acquire all or substantially all the shares, or the shares of a particular class, in a body corporate incorporated outside the United Kingdom; or

(c)   an offer made to all the holders of shares, or of shares of a particular class, in a body corporate to acquire a specified proportion of those shares;

but in determining whether an offer falls within sub-paragraph (b) there shall be disregarded any shares which the offeror or any associate of his holds or has contracted to acquire; and in determining whether an offer falls within sub-paragraph (c) the offeror, any associate of his and any person whose shares the offeror or any such associate has contracted to acquire shall not be regarded as holders of the shares.

(10A)   In paragraph (10)—

"associate" has the same meaning as in section 430E of the Companies Act 1985; and

"share" has the same meaning as in section 428(1) of that Act.

(11)   For the purposes of paragraph (2)(m), "holders of shares" means the persons who, at the close of business on a date specified in the offer and falling within the period of 60 days ending with the date on which the offer is first made, were holders of such shares.

(12)   For the purposes of paragraph (2)(o), a person is a "qualifying person", in relation to an issuer, if he is a bona fide employee or former employee of the issuer or of another body corporate in the same group (within the meaning of section 421 of the Act) or the wife, husband, widow, widower or child or stepchild under the age of eighteen of such an employee or former employee.

(13)   In paragraph (2)(o)—

...

a body corporate is "connected with" another body corporate if—

(a)   they are in the same group, within the meaning of section 421 of the Act, or

(b)   one is entitled, either alone or with any other body corporate in the same group, to exercise or control the exercise of a majority of the voting rights attributable to the share capital which are exercisable in all circumstances at any general meeting of the other body corporate or its holding company; and

"a relevant trustee" has the same meaning as in article 71(6)(b) of the Financial Services and Markets Act 2000 (Regulated Activities) Order 2001 (Activities carried on in connection with employee share schemes).

8.   Form and content of prospectus

(1)   Subject to regulation 11 and to paragraphs (2), (4), (5) and (6), a prospectus shall contain the information specified in Parts II to X of Schedule 1 to these Regulations (which shall be construed in accordance with Part I of that Schedule).

(2)   Where the requirement to include in a prospectus any information (the "required information") is inappropriate to the issuer's sphere of activity or to the legal form of the issuer or the offeror or to the securities to which the prospectus relates, the requirement—

     (a)   shall have effect as a requirement that the prospectus contain information equivalent to the required information; but

     (b)   if there is no such equivalent information, shall not apply.

(3)   The information in a prospectus shall be presented in as easily analysable and comprehensible a form as possible.

(4)   Where, on the occasion of their admission to dealings on an approved exchange, shares are offered on a pre-emptive basis to some or all of the existing holders of such shares, a body or person designated for the purposes of this paragraph by the Treasury shall have power to authorise the omission from a prospectus subject to this regulation of specified information provided that up-to-date information equivalent to that which would otherwise be required by this regulation is available as a result of the requirements of that approved exchange.

In this paragraph, "specified information" means information specified in paragraphs 41 to 47 of Schedule 1 to these Regulations.

(4A)   In determining for the purposes of paragraph (4) whether information is equivalent to that specified in paragraph 45 of Schedule 1, there shall be disregarded—

     (a)   the requirements of sub-paragraphs (1)(a)(i), (1)(a)(iv), (1)(b)(iii), (2)(a)(ii), (2)(a)(iv) and (8)(b) of that paragraph; and

     (b)   any requirement of sub-paragraph (10)(a), (10)(b) or (11)(c) to include a statement by the person responsible for the interim accounts or report.

(5)   Where a class of shares has been admitted to dealings on an approved exchange, a body or person designated for the purposes of this paragraph by the Treasury shall have power to authorise the making of an offer without a prospectus, provided that—

     (a)   the number or estimated market value or the nominal value or, in the absence of a nominal value, the accounting par value of the shares offered amounts to less than ten per cent of the number or of the corresponding value of shares of the same class already admitted to dealings; and

     (b)   up-to-date information equivalent to that required by this regulation is available as a result of the requirements of that approved exchange.

(6)   Where a person—

     (a)   makes an offer to the public in the United Kingdom of securities which he proposes to issue; and

     (b)   has, within the 12 months preceding the date on which the offer is first made, published a full prospectus relating to a different class of securities which he has issued, or to an earlier issue of the same class of securities,

he may publish, instead of a full prospectus, a prospectus which contains only the differences which have arisen since the publication of the full prospectus mentioned in sub-paragraph (b) and any supplementary prospectus and which are likely to influence the value of the securities, provided that the prospectus is accompanied by that full prospectus and any supplementary prospectus or contains a reference to it or them; and, for this purpose, a full prospectus is one which contains the information specified in Parts II to X of Schedule 1 (other than any information whose omission is authorised by or under paragraph (2) or (4) or regulation 11).

9.   General duty of disclosure in prospectus

(1)   In addition to the information required to be included in a prospectus by virtue of regulation 8 a prospectus shall (subject to these Regulations) contain all such information as investors would reasonably require, and reasonably expect to find there, for the purpose of making an informed assessment of—

     (a)   the assets and liabilities, financial position, profits and losses, and prospects of the issuer of the securities; and

     (b)   the rights attaching to those securities.

(2)   The information to be included by virtue of this regulation shall be such information as is mentioned in paragraph (1) which is within the knowledge of any person responsible for the prospectus or which it would be reasonable for him to obtain by making enquiries.

(3)   In determining what information is required to be included in a prospectus by virtue of this regulation regard shall be had to the nature of the securities and of the issuer of the securities.

(4)   For the purposes of this regulation "issuer", in relation to a certificate or other instrument representing securities, means the person who issued or is to issue the securities to which the certificate or instrument relates.

10.   Supplementary prospectus

(1)   Where a prospectus has been registered under this Part of these Regulations in respect of an offer of securities and at any time while an agreement in respect of those securities can be entered into in pursuance of that offer—

    (a)   there is a significant change affecting any matter contained in the prospectus whose inclusion was required by regulation 8 or 9; or

    (b)   a significant new matter arises the inclusion of information in respect of which would have been so required if it had arisen when the prospectus was prepared; or

    (c)   there is a significant inaccuracy in the prospectus,

the offeror shall deliver to the registrar of companies for registration, and publish in accordance with paragraph (3), a supplementary prospectus containing particulars of the change or new matter or, in the case of an inaccuracy, correcting it.

(2)   In paragraph (1) "significant" means significant for the purpose of making an informed assessment of the matters mentioned in regulation 9(1)(a) and (b).

(3)   Regulation 4(1) shall apply to a supplementary prospectus delivered for registration to the registrar of companies in the same way as it applies to a prospectus except that the obligation to publish the supplementary prospectus shall begin with the time it is delivered for registration to the registrar of companies.

(4)   Where the offeror is not aware of the change, new matter or inaccuracy in question he shall not be under any duty to comply with paragraphs (1) and (3) unless he is notified of it by a person responsible for the prospectus; but any person responsible for the prospectus who is aware of such a matter shall be under a duty to give him notice of it.

(5)   Where a supplementary prospectus has been registered under this regulation in respect of an offer, the preceding paragraphs of this regulation have effect as if any reference to a prospectus were a reference to the prospectus originally registered and that supplementary prospectus, taken together.

11.   Exceptions

(1)   The Treasury or the Secretary of State may authorise the omission from a prospectus or supplementary prospectus of information whose inclusion would otherwise be required by these Regulations if they or he consider that disclosure of that information would be contrary to the public interest.

(2)   An offeror may omit from a prospectus or supplementary prospectus information with respect to an issuer whose inclusion would otherwise be required by these Regulations if—

    (a)   he is not that issuer, nor acting in pursuance of an agreement with that issuer;

    (b)   the information is not available to him because he is not that issuer; and

    (c)   he has been unable, despite making such efforts (if any) as are reasonable, to obtain the information.

(3)   The competent authority for the purposes of Part VI of the Act ("the competent authority") may authorise the omission from a prospectus or supplementary prospectus of information whose inclusion would otherwise be required by these Regulations, if—

    (a)   the information is of minor importance only, and is not likely to influence assessment of the issuer's assets and liabilities, financial position, profits and losses and prospects; or

(b)   disclosure of that information would be seriously detrimental to the issuer and its omission would not be likely to mislead investors with regard to facts and circumstances necessary for an informed assessment of the securities.

(4)   Paragraph (4) of regulation 9 applies for the purposes of paragraph (3) as it applies for the purposes of that regulation.

(5)   The competent authority may make rules providing for the payment of fees to it for the discharge of its functions under paragraph (3).

(6)   Section 101 of the Act shall apply to rules made under paragraph (5) as it applies to listing rules.

12.   Advertisements etc in connection with offer of securities

An advertisement, notice, poster or document (other than a prospectus) announcing a public offer of securities for which a prospectus is or will be required under this Part of these Regulations shall not be issued to or caused to be issued to the public in the United Kingdom by the person proposing to make the offer unless it states that a prospectus is or will be published, as the case may be, and gives an address in the United Kingdom from which it can be obtained or will be obtainable.

13.   Persons responsible for prospectus

(1)   For the purpose of this Part of these Regulations the persons responsible for a prospectus or supplementary prospectus are—

    (a)   the issuer of the securities to which the prospectus or supplementary prospectus relates;

    (b)   where the issuer is a body corporate, each person who is a director of that body corporate at the time when the prospectus or supplementary prospectus is published;

    (c)   where the issuer is a body corporate, each person who has authorised himself to be named, and is named, in the prospectus or supplementary prospectus as a director or as having agreed to become a director of that body either immediately or at a future time;

    (d)   each person who accepts, and is stated in the prospectus or supplementary prospectus as accepting, responsibility for, or for any part of, the prospectus or supplementary prospectus;

    (e)   the offeror of the securities, where he is not the issuer;

    (f)   where the offeror is a body corporate, but is not the issuer and is not making the offer in association with the issuer, each person who is a director of that body corporate at the time when the prospectus or supplementary prospectus is published; and

    (g)   each person not falling within any of the foregoing paragraphs who has authorised the contents of, or of any part of, the prospectus or supplementary prospectus.

(2)   A person is not responsible under paragraph (1)(a), (b) or (c) unless the issuer has made or authorised the offer in relation to which the prospectus or supplementary prospectus was published; and a person is not responsible for a prospectus or supplementary prospectus by virtue of paragraph (1)(b) if it is published without his knowledge or consent and on becoming aware of its publication he forthwith gives reasonable public notice that it was published without his knowledge or consent.

(2A)   A person is not responsible under paragraph (1)(e) as the offeror of the securities if—

    (a)   the issuer is responsible for the prospectus or supplementary prospectus in accordance with this regulation;

    (b)   the prospectus or supplementary prospectus was drawn up primarily by the issuer, or by one or more persons acting on behalf of the issuer; and

    (c)   the offeror is making the offer in association with the issuer.

(3)   Where a person has accepted responsibility for, or authorised, only part of the contents of any prospectus or supplementary prospectus, he is responsible under paragraph (1)(d) or (g) only for that part and only if it is included in (or substantially in) the form and context to which he has agreed.

(4)   Nothing in this regulation shall be construed as making a person responsible for any prospectus or supplementary prospectus by reason only of giving advice as to its contents in a professional capacity.

(5) Where by virtue of this regulation the issuer of any shares pays or is liable to pay compensation under regulation 14 for loss suffered in respect of shares for which a person has subscribed no account shall be taken of that liability or payment in determining any question as to the amount paid on subscription for those shares or as to the amount paid up or deemed to be paid up on them.

14. Compensation for false or misleading prospectus

(1) Subject to regulation 15 the person or persons responsible for a prospectus or supplementary prospectus shall be liable to pay compensation to any person who has acquired the securities to which the prospectus relates and suffered loss in respect of them as a result of any untrue or misleading statement in the prospectus or supplementary prospectus or the omission from it of any matter required to be included by regulation 9 or 10.

(2) Where regulation 8 requires a prospectus to include information as to any particular matter on the basis that the prospectus must include a statement either as to that matter or, if such is the case, that there is no such matter, the omission from the prospectus of the information shall be treated for the purposes of paragraph (1) as a statement that there is no such matter.

(3) Subject to regulation 15, a person who fails to comply with regulation 10 shall be liable to pay compensation to any person who has acquired any of the securities in question and suffered loss in respect of them as a result of the failure.

(4) This regulation does not affect any liability which any person may incur apart from this regulation.

(5) References in this regulation to the acquisition by any person of securities include references to his contracting to acquire them or an interest in them.

15. Exemption from liability to pay compensation

(1) A person shall not incur any liability under regulation 14(1) for any loss in respect of securities caused by any such statement or omission as is there mentioned if he satisfies the court that at the time when the prospectus or supplementary prospectus was delivered for registration he reasonably believed, having made such enquiries (if any) as were reasonable, that the statement was true and not misleading or that the matter whose omission caused the loss was properly omitted and—

(a) that he continued in that belief until the time when the securities were acquired; or

(b) that they were acquired before it was reasonably practicable to bring a correction to the attention of persons likely to acquire the securities in question; or

(c) that before the securities were acquired he had taken all such steps as it was reasonable for him to have taken to secure that a correction was forthwith brought to the attention of those persons; or

(d) that the securities were acquired after such a lapse of time that he ought in the circumstances to be reasonably excused, and, if the securities are dealt in on an approved exchange, that he continued in that belief until after the commencement of dealings in the securities on that exchange.

(2) A person shall not incur any liability under regulation 14(1) for any loss in respect of securities caused by a statement purporting to be made by or on the authority of another person as an expert which is, and is stated to be, included in the prospectus or supplementary prospectus with that other person's consent if he satisfies the court that at the time when the prospectus or supplementary prospectus was delivered for registration he believed on reasonable grounds that the other person was competent to make or authorise the statement and had consented to its inclusion in the form and context in which it was included and—

(a) that he continued in that belief until the time when the securities were acquired; or

(b) that they were acquired before it was reasonably practicable to bring the fact that the expert was not competent or had not consented to the attention of persons likely to acquire the securities in question; or

(c) that before the securities were acquired he had taken all such steps as it was reasonable for him to have taken to secure that that fact was forthwith brought to the attention of those persons; or

(d) that the securities were acquired after such a lapse of time that he ought in the circumstances to be reasonably excused and, if the securities are dealt in on an approved exchange, that he continued in that belief until after the commencement of dealings in the securities on that exchange.

(3) Without prejudice to paragraphs (1) and (2), a person shall not incur any liability under regulation 14(1) for any loss in respect of any securities caused by any such statement or omission as is there mentioned if he satisfies the court—

(a) that before the securities were acquired a correction or, where the statement was such as is mentioned in paragraph (2), the fact that the expert was not competent or had not consented had been published in a manner calculated to bring it to the attention of persons likely to acquire the securities in question; or

(b) that he took all such steps as it was reasonable for him to take to secure such publication and reasonably believed that it had taken place before the securities were acquired.

(4) A person shall not incur any liability under regulation 14(1) for any loss resulting from a statement made by an official person or contained in a public official document which is included in the prospectus or supplementary prospectus if he satisfies the court that the statement is accurately and fairly reproduced.

(5) A person shall not incur any liability under regulation 14(1) or (3) if he satisfies the court that the person suffering the loss acquired the securities in question with knowledge that the statement was false or misleading, of the omitted matter or of the change, new matter or inaccuracy, as the case may be.

(6) A person shall not incur any liability under regulation 14(3) if he satisfies the court that he reasonably believed that the change, new matter or inaccuracy in question was not such as to call for a supplementary prospectus.

(7) In this regulation "expert" includes any engineer, valuer, accountant or other person whose profession, qualifications or experience give authority to a statement made by him; and references to the acquisition of securities include references to contracting to acquire them or an interest in them.

16.   Contraventions

(1) An authorised person who contravenes regulation 4(1) or, where it applies, regulation 4(2), or who contravenes regulation 12, or who assists another person to contravene any of those provisions, shall be treated as having contravened rules under Part X of the Act.

(2) A person other than an authorised person who contravenes regulation 4(1) or, where it applies, regulation 4(2), or who contravenes regulation 12, or who assists another person to contravene any of those provisions, shall be guilty of an offence and liable—

(a) on conviction on indictment, to imprisonment for a term not exceeding two years or to a fine or to both;

(b) on summary conviction, to imprisonment for a term not exceeding three months or to a fine not exceeding level 5 on the standard scale.

(3) Without prejudice to any liability under regulation 14, a person shall not be regarded as having contravened regulation 4 by reason only of a prospectus not having fully complied with the requirements of these Regulations as to its form or content.

(4) Any contravention to which this regulation applies shall be actionable at the suit of a person who suffers loss as a result of the contravention subject to the defences and other incidents applying to actions for breach of statutory duty.

(5) In this regulation—

"authorised person" means a person who is authorised for the purposes of the Act; and

"exempt regulated activity" has the same meaning as in section 325(2) of the Act.

(6)   ...

PART III
AMENDMENTS TO PART IV OF THE ACT ETC

17.   ...

18.   **Penalties**

Where these Regulations amend, extend the application of, or modify the effect of, a provision contained in Part VI of the Act and thereby create a new criminal offence which, but for this regulation, would be punishable to a greater extent than is permitted under paragraph 1(1)(d) of Schedule 2 to the European Communities Act 1972, the maximum punishment for the offence shall be the maximum permitted under that paragraph at the time the offence was committed, on conviction on indictment or on summary conviction, as the case may be.

PART IV
MISCELLANEOUS

19.   **Designations**

For the purposes of Articles 11, 12, 13, 14, 18, 19, 20, 21 and 22 of Council Directive No 89/298/ EEC the Treasury may designate such bodies as they think fit and they shall give notice in such manner as they think appropriate of the designations they have made.

20.   **Mutual recognition**

Schedule 4 to these Regulations shall have effect to make provision for the recognition of prospectuses and listing particulars approved in other member States.

21.   ...

22.   **Registration of documents by the registrar of companies**

For the purposes of the provisions mentioned in section 735B of the Companies Act 1985, regulations 4(2) and 10(1) shall be regarded as provisions of the Companies Acts.

23.   **Miscellaneous and Supplementary**

(1)   Paragraph 19(1) of Schedule 1 to the Act shall apply to the competent authority in the discharge or purported discharge of its functions under these Regulations as it applies to it in the discharge or purported discharge of its functions under Part VI of the Act.

(2)   Section 415 of the Act shall apply to proceedings arising out of any act or omission (or proposed act or omission) of the competent authority in the discharge or purported discharge of any function under regulation 11 as it applies to the proceedings mentioned in that section.

(3)   Section 410 of the Act shall apply to a person designated under regulation 19 in respect of any action which he proposes to take or has power to take by virtue of being so designated.

(4)   Section 176 of the Act shall have effect, in relation to these Regulations, as if for the purposes of subsection (4) of section 176 the offences mentioned in section 168 of the Act included an offence under these Regulations.

(5)   Subsections (1) and (3) of section 398 of the Act shall apply in relation to information given to the competent authority—
(a)   for the purposes of or in connection with an application under these Regulations, or
(b)   in purported compliance with requirements imposed by or under these Regulations,
as they apply in relation to information given in purported compliance with any requirement imposed by or under the Act.

(6)   Sections 400, 401 and 403 of the Act shall apply to offences under these Regulations as they apply to offences under the Act.

24.   ...

SCHEDULE 1

FORM AND CONTENT OF PROSPECTUS

Regulation 8

PART I
INTERPRETATION

1.   In this Schedule, except where the context otherwise requires—

"annual accounts" has the same meaning as in Part VII of the Companies Act 1985;

"control" means the ability, in practice, to determine the actions of the issuer; and "joint control" means control exercised by two or more persons who have an agreement or understanding (whether formal or informal) which may lead to their adopting a common policy in respect of the issuer;

"debentures" means instruments creating or acknowledging indebtedness;

"financial year" has the same meaning as in Part VII of the Companies Act 1985;

"group accounts" has the same meaning as in Part VII of the Companies Act 1985;

"the last three years", in relation to an undertaking whose accounts are required to be dealt with in a prospectus, means three completed financial years which immediately precede the date on which the offer is first made and which cover a continuous period of at least 35 months, disregarding a financial year which ends less than three months before the date on which the offer is first made and for which accounts have not been prepared by that date;

"parent undertaking" and "subsidiary undertaking" have the same meaning as in Part VII of the Companies Act 1985;

"state of affairs" means the state of affairs of an undertaking, in relation to its balance sheet, at the end of a financial year;

"subsidiary" and "holding company" have the same meanings as in sections 736 and 736A of the Companies Act 1985; and

"undertaking" has the same meaning as in Part VII of the Companies Act 1985.

1A.   The definition of "debentures" in paragraph 1 must be read with—

(a)   section 22 of the Financial Services and Markets Act 2000;

(b)   any relevant order under that section; and

(c)   Schedule 2 to that Act.

PART II
GENERAL REQUIREMENTS

2.   The name of the issuer and the address of its registered office.

3.   If different, the name and address of the person offering the securities.

4.   The names and functions of the directors of the issuer.

5.   The date of publication of the prospectus.

6.   A statement that a copy of the prospectus has been delivered for registration to the registrar of companies in accordance with regulation 4(2), indicating to which registrar of companies it has been delivered.

7.   A statement that the prospectus has been drawn up in accordance with these Regulations.

8.   The following words, "If you are in any doubt about the contents of this document you should consult a person authorised for the purposes of the Financial Services and Markets Act 2000 who specialises in advising on the acquisition of shares and other securities", or words to the like effect.

PART III
THE PERSONS RESPONSIBLE FOR
THE PROSPECTUS AND ADVISERS

9.   The names, addresses (home or business) and functions of those persons responsible (which in this Part of this Schedule has the same meaning as in regulation 13) for the prospectus or any part of the prospectus, specifying such part.

10.—   (1)   A declaration by the directors of the issuer (where it is responsible for the prospectus) or (in any other case) by the directors of the offeror, that to the best of their knowledge the information contained in the prospectus is in accordance with the facts and that the prospectus makes no omission likely to affect the import of such information.

         (2)   Without prejudice to paragraph 45 of this Schedule, a statement by any person who accepts responsibility for the prospectus, or any part of it, that he does so.

PART IV
THE SECURITIES TO WHICH THE PROSPECTUS
RELATES AND THE OFFER

11.   A description of the securities being offered, including the class to which they belong and a description of the rights attaching to them including (where applicable)—

         (a)   if the securities are shares, rights as regards—

               (i)   voting;

               (ii)   dividends;

               (iii)   return of capital on the winding up of the issuer;

               (iv)   redemption;

            and a summary of the consents necessary for the variation of any of those rights;

         (b)   if the securities are debentures, rights as regards—

               (i)   interest payable;

               (ii)   repayment of principal;

         (c)   if the securities are convertible securities—

               (i)   the terms and dates on which the holder of the convertible securities is entitled to acquire the related underlying securities;

               (ii)   the procedures for exercising the entitlement to the underlying securities; and

               (iii)   such information relating to the underlying securities as would have been required under paragraphs (a) or (b) if the securities being offered had been the underlying securities.

12.   The date(s) (if any) on which entitlement to dividends or interest arises.

13.   Particulars of tax on income from the securities withheld at source, including tax credits.

14.   The procedure for the exercise of any right of preemption attaching to the securities.

15.   Any restrictions on the free transferability of the securities being offered.

16.—   (1)   A statement as to whether—

         (a)   the securities being offered have been admitted to dealings on a recognised investment exchange; or

         (b)   an application for such admission has been made.

         (2)   Where no such application for dealings has been made, or such an application has been made and refused, a statement as to whether or not there are, or are intended to be, any other arrangements for there to be dealings in the securities and, if there are, a brief description of such arrangements.

17.   The purpose for which the securities are being issued.

18.   The number of securities being issued.

19.   The number of securities being offered.

20.   The total proceeds which it is expected will be raised by the offer and the expected net proceeds, after deduction of the expenses, of the offer.

21. Where the prospectus relates to shares which are offered for subscription, particulars as to—

    (a) the minimum amount which, in the opinion of the directors of the issuer, must be raised by the issue of those shares in order to provide the sums (or, if any part of them is to be defrayed in any other manner, the balance of the sums) required to be provided in respect of each of the following—

        (i) the purchase price of any property purchased, or to be purchased, which is to be defrayed in whole or in part out of the proceeds of the issue;

        (ii) any preliminary expenses payable by the issuer and any commission so payable to any person in consideration of his agreeing to subscribe for, or of his procuring or agreeing to procure subscriptions for, any shares in the issuer;

        (iii) the repayment of any money borrowed by the issuer in respect of any of the foregoing matters;

        (iv) working capital; and

    (b) the amounts to be provided in respect of the matters mentioned otherwise than out of the proceeds of the issue and the sources out of which those amounts are to be provided.

22. The names of any persons underwriting or guaranteeing the offer.

23. The amount or the estimated amount of the expenses of the offer and by whom they are payable, including (except in so far as information is required to be included in the prospectus by section 97(3) of the Companies Act 1985) a statement as to any commission payable by the issuer to any person in consideration of his agreeing to subscribe for securities to which the prospectus relates or of his procuring or agreeing to procure subscriptions for such securities.

24. The names and addresses of the paying agents (if any).

25. The period during which the offer of the securities is open.

26. The price at which the securities are offered or, if appropriate, the procedure, method and timetable for fixing the price.

27. The arrangements for payment for the securities being offered and the arrangements and timetable for their delivery.

28. The arrangements during the period prior to the delivery of the securities being offered relating to the moneys received from applicants including the arrangements for the return of moneys to applicants where their applications are not accepted in whole or in part and the timetable for the return of such moneys.

PART V
GENERAL INFORMATION ABOUT THE ISSUER AND ITS CAPITAL

29. The date and place of incorporation of the issuer. In the case of an issuer not incorporated in the United Kingdom, the address of its principal place of business in the United Kingdom (if any).

30. The place of registration of the issuer and the number with which it is registered.

31. The legal form of the issuer, the legislation under which it was formed and (if different) the legislation now applicable to it.

32. A summary of the provisions in the issuer's memorandum of association determining its objects.

33. If the liability of the members of the issuer is limited, a statement of that fact.

34. The amount of the issuer's authorised share capital and any limit on the duration of the authorisation to issue such share capital.

35. The amount of the issuer's issued share capital.

36. The number and particulars of any listed and unlisted securities issued by the issuer not representing share capital.

37. The number of shares of each class making up each of the authorised and issued share capital, the nominal value of such shares and, in the case of the issued share capital, the amount paid up on the shares.

38. The amount of any outstanding listed and unlisted convertible securities issued by the issuer, the conditions and procedures for their conversion and the number of shares which would be issued as a result of their conversion.

39.   If the issuer is a member of a group, a brief description of the group and of the issuer's position in it, stating, where the issuer is a subsidiary, the name of its holding company.

40.   Insofar the offeror has the information, an indication of the persons, who, directly or indirectly, jointly or severally, exercise or could exercise control over the issuer and particulars of the proportion of the issuer's voting capital held by such persons.

PART VI
THE ISSUER'S PRINCIPAL ACTIVITIES

41.   A description of the issuer's principal activities and of any exceptional factors which have influenced its activities.

42.   A statement of any dependence of the issuer on patents or other intellectual property rights, licences or particular contracts, where any of these are of fundamental importance to the issuer's business.

43.   Information regarding investments in progress where they are significant.

44.   Information on any legal or arbitration proceedings, active, pending or threatened against, or being brought by, the issuer or any member of its group which are having or may have a significant effect on the issuer's financial position.

PART VII
THE ISSUER'S ASSETS AND LIABILITIES,
FINANCIAL POSITION AND PROFITS AND LOSSES

45.—   (1)   If the issuer is a company to which Part VII of the Companies Act 1985 applies otherwise than by virtue of section 700 of that Act—

      (a)   the issuer's annual accounts for the last three years together with—

          (i)   a statement by the directors of the issuer that the accounts have been prepared in accordance with the law, and that they accept responsibility for them, or a statement why they are unable to make such a statement;

          (ii)   the names and addresses of the auditors of the accounts;

          (iii) a copy of the auditors' reports on the accounts, within the meaning of section 235 of the Companies Act 1985; and

          (iv)   a statement by the auditors that they consent to the inclusion of their reports in the prospectus and accept responsibility for them, and have not become aware, since the date of any report, of any matter affecting the validity of that report at that date; or a statement why they are unable to make such a statement; or

      (b)   a report by a person qualified to act as an auditor with respect to the state of affairs and profit or loss shown by the issuer's annual accounts for the last three years together with—

          (i)   the name and address of the person responsible for the report;

          (ii)   if different, the name and address of the person who audited the accounts on which the report is based; and

          (iii) a statement by the person responsible for the report that in his opinion the report gives a true and fair view of the state of affairs and profit or loss of the issuer and its subsidiary undertakings, and that he consents to the inclusion of his report in the prospectus and accepts responsibility for it; or a statement why he is unable to make such a statement.

    (2)   If the issuer is not a company to which Part VII of the Companies Act 1985 applies (or is a company to which that Part of that Act applies by virtue of section 700 of that Act)—

      (a)   the issuer's accounts (and, if it is a parent undertaking, its subsidiary undertakings' accounts) for the last three years, prepared in accordance with the applicable law, together with—

          (i)   the name and address of the person responsible for the accounts;

(ii) a statement by the person responsible for the accounts that they have been properly prepared in accordance with the applicable law, and that he accepts responsibility for them, or statement why he is unable to make such a statement;

(iii) the names and addresses of the auditors of the accounts and their reports; and

(iv) a statement by the auditors that they consent to the inclusion of their reports in the prospectus and accept responsibility for them, and have not become aware, since the date of any report, of any matter affecting the validity of that report at that date; or a statement why they are unable to make such a statement; or

(b) a report by a person qualified to act as an auditor with respect to the state of affairs and profit or loss shown by the issuer's accounts (and, if the issuer is a parent undertaking, by its subsidiary undertakings' accounts) for the last three years, such report to be drawn up in accordance with the applicable law, or as if the provisions of the Companies Act 1985 relating to annual accounts applied to the issuer, together with—

(i) the name and address of the person responsible for the report;

(ii) if different, the name and address of the person who audited the accounts on which the report is based; and

(iii) a statement by the person responsible for the report that in his opinion the report gives a true and fair view of the state of affairs and profit or loss of the issuer and its subsidiary undertakings and that he consents to the inclusion of his report in the prospectus and accepts responsibility for it; or a statement why he is unable to make such a statement.

(3) If, in accordance with the law applicable to it, the accounts of an issuer falling within sub-paragraph (2) consist only of consolidated accounts with respect to itself and its subsidiary undertakings, the prospectus is not required by virtue of sub-paragraph (2) to include separate accounts for each undertaking, or to include a report which deals with the accounts of each undertaking separately.

(4) If, in the case of an issuer falling within sub-paragraph (1) or (2), the prospectus would, but for this sub-paragraph, include both separate accounts for the issuer and its subsidiary undertakings and consolidated accounts, either the separate accounts or the consolidated accounts may be omitted from the prospectus if their inclusion would not provide any significant additional information.

(5) If an issuer falling within sub-paragraph (2) is not required by the law applicable to it to have its accounts audited—

(a) if the accounts have not been audited—

(i) the prospectus shall contain a statement to that effect; and

(ii) paragraph (a)(iii) and (iv) or, as the case may be, paragraph (b)(ii) of sub-paragraph (2) shall not apply to the issuer; and

(b) if the accounts have nonetheless been audited, the prospectus shall contain a statement to that effect.

(6) Sub-paragraphs (7) and (8) shall apply in so far as the issuer has not been in existence for the whole of the last three years.

(7) Subject to sub-paragraph (8)—

(a) the requirement in sub-paragraphs (1)(a) and (2)(a) that the prospectus contain accounts for the last three years shall be construed as a requirement that the prospectus contain the accounts which the undertaking concerned was required (by its constitution or by the law under which it is established) to prepare for financial years during its existence, disregarding a financial year which ends less than three months before the date on which the offer is first made and for which accounts have not been prepared by that date; and

(b) the requirement in sub-paragraphs (1)(b) and (2)(b) that the prospectus contain a report with respect to the state of affairs and profit or loss for the last three years shall be construed as a requirement that the prospectus contain a report with respect to the accounts which the undertaking concerned was required (by its constitution or by the law under which it is established) to prepare for financial years during its existence, disregarding a financial year which ends less than three months before the date on which the offer is first made and for which accounts have not been prepared by that date.

(8) If an undertaking has not been required (by its constitution or by the law under which it is established) to prepare any accounts for financial years, the requirement in sub-paragraphs (1) and (2) that the prospectus contain accounts for, or a report with respect to, the last three years shall be construed as a requirement that the prospectus contain a report by a person qualified to act as an auditor which includes—

    (a) details of the profit or loss of the undertaking in respect of the period beginning with the date of its formation and ending on the latest practicable date before (but not in any event more than three months before) the date on which the offer is first made, and of its state of affairs at that latest practicable date; and

    (b) a statement by the person responsible for the report that in his opinion it gives a true and fair view of the state of affairs and profit or loss of the undertaking and that he consents to the inclusion of his report in the prospectus and accepts responsibility for it; or a statement why he is unable to make such a statement.

(9) If the issuer is a parent undertaking, the requirements of sub-paragraph (1) or, as the case may be, sub-paragraph (2), shall apply to each subsidiary undertaking in respect of any part of the last three years for which information is not otherwise required by those sub-paragraphs, and for this purpose any reference in sub-paragraphs (3) to (8) to the issuer shall have effect as a reference to the subsidiary undertaking.

(9A) Neither sub-paragraph (2) nor sub-paragraph (9) requires the inclusion in the prospectus of the accounts of a subsidiary undertaking, a report dealing with those accounts, or any other information relating to a subsidiary undertaking, if the accounts are not, or the report or the information is not, reasonably necessary for the purpose of making an informed assessment of the issuer's assets and liabilities, financial position, profits and losses and prospects, or of the securities being offered.

(10) Where more than nine months have elapsed at the date on which the offer is first made since the end of the last financial year in respect of which accounts or a report are required to be included in the prospectus by this paragraph, there shall also be included in the prospectus—

    (a) interim accounts of the undertaking concerned (which need not be audited but which must otherwise be prepared to the standard applicable to accounts required for each financial year) covering the period beginning at the end of the last financial year in respect of which accounts or a report are required to be included in the prospectus by this paragraph, and ending not less than six months after the end of that financial year, together with the name and address of the person responsible for the interim accounts and a statement by him that the interim accounts have been properly prepared in accordance with the law applicable to the undertaking, and that he consents to the inclusion of the accounts and statement in the prospectus and accepts responsibility for them; or a statement why he is unable to make such a statement; or

    (b) a report by a person qualified to act as an auditor covering the same period with respect to the state of affairs and profit or loss of the undertaking concerned, prepared in accordance with the law applicable to the undertaking, together with the name and address of the person responsible for preparing the report, and a statement by him that he consents to the inclusion of the report in the prospectus and accepts responsibility for it; or a statement why he is unable to make such a statement.

(11) If any interim accounts of the issuer have been published since the end of the last financial year of the issuer in respect of which accounts or a report are required to be included in the prospectus by this paragraph, other than interim accounts included in a prospectus in

accordance with sub-paragraph (10), they shall be included in the prospectus, together with—

(a) an explanation of the purpose for which the accounts were prepared;

(b) a reference to the legislation in accordance with which they were prepared; and

(c) the name and address of the person responsible for them, and a statement from him that he consents to the inclusion of the accounts in the prospectus and accepts responsibility for them.

PART VIII
THE ISSUER'S ADMINISTRATION, MANAGEMENT AND SUPERVISION

46. A concise description of the directors' existing or proposed service contracts with the issuer or any subsidiary of the issuer, excluding contracts expiring, or determinable by the employing company without payment of compensation within one year, or an appropriate negative statement.

47.— (1) The aggregate remuneration paid and benefits in kind granted to the directors of the issuer during the last completed financial year of the issuer, together with an estimate of the aggregate amount payable and benefits in kind to be granted to the directors, and proposed directors, for the current financial year under the arrangements in force at the date on which the offer is first made.

(2) The interests of each director of the issuer in the share capital of the issuer, distinguishing between beneficial and non-beneficial interests, or an appropriate negative statement.

PART IX
RECENT DEVELOPMENTS IN THE ISSUER'S BUSINESS AND PROSPECTS

48. The significant recent trends concerning the development of the issuer's business since the end of the last completed financial year of the issuer.

49. Information on the issuer's prospects for at least the current financial year of the issuer.

PART X
CONVERTIBLE SECURITIES AND GUARANTEED DEBENTURES

50. Where the prospectus relates to convertible securities, and the issuer of the related underlying securities is not the same as the issuer of the convertible securities, the information specified in this Schedule must be given in respect of the issuer of the convertible securities, and the information specified in paragraph 2 and Parts V, VI, VII, VIII and IX of this Schedule must be given in respect of the issuer of the underlying securities.

51. Where the prospectus relates to debentures which are guaranteed by one or more persons, the name and address and the information specified in Parts V, VI, VII, VIII and IX of this Schedule must also be given in respect of any guarantor who is not an individual.

...

SCHEDULE 4

MUTUAL RECOGNITION OF PROSPECTUSES AND LISTING PARTICULARS

Regulation 20

PART I
RECOGNITION FOR THE PURPOSES OF PART VI OF THE FINANCIAL SERVICES AND MARKETS ACT 2000 OF PROSPECTUSES AND LISTING PARTICULARS APPROVED IN OTHER MEMBER STATES

1.   In this Part of this Schedule—
   (a)   the term "competent authority" includes a body designated by a member State pursuant to Article 12 of Council Directive No 89/298/EEC;
   (b)   "the UK authority" means the competent authority for the purposes of Part 6 of the Act;
   (c)   "European document" means—
      (i)   listing particulars which have been approved by the competent authority in another member State and which Article 24a of Council Directive No 80/390/EEC requires or paragraph 5 of that article permits to be recognised as listing particulars;
      (ii)   a prospectus which has been approved by the competent authority in another member State and which Article 24b of Council Directive No 80/390/EEC requires or which paragraph 2 of that article, in referring to paragraph 5 of article 24a of that Directive, permits to be recognised as listing particulars; or
      (iii)   a prospectus which has been approved by the competent authority in another member State, which Article 21 of Council Directive No 89/298/EEC requires or which paragraph 4 of that article permits to be recognised and which relates to securities which are the subject of an application for listing in the United Kingdom and which are to be offered in the United Kingdom prior to admission to listing in the United Kingdom by means of the prospectus;
      including in each case any supplement to listing particulars or a prospectus which, before the completion of the preparation of the recognised document for submission to the UK authority pursuant to an application for listing, has been approved pursuant to Article 23 of Council Directive No 80/390/EEC or Article 18 of Council Directive No 89/298/EEC by the competent authorities which approved the listing particulars or prospectus.
      Where the European document submitted to the UK authority is a translation into English of the document approved by the competent authorities in another member State then, unless the context otherwise requires, the document as translated shall be regarded as the European document rather than the document as approved.

2.   In this Part of this Schedule, "recognised European document" means a document consisting of a European document submitted to the UK authority pursuant to an application for listing under section 75 of the Act and, if information is required to be added to it in accordance with listing rules, including that information.

3.   Subject to paragraph 4, Part VI of the Act shall apply to a recognised European document as it applies—
   (a)   in relation to listing particulars, within the meaning of section 79(2) of the Act (in a case where the securities to which it relates will not be offered in the United Kingdom prior to admission to listing in the United Kingdom); or
   (b)   in relation to a prospectus required by listing rules made under section 84 of the Act (in a case where the recognised European document is a prospectus and the securities to which it relates are to be offered in the United Kingdom prior to admission to listing in the United Kingdom).

4.   Part VI of the Act shall apply to a recognised European document subject to the following modifications—
   (a)   nothing in Part VI shall require the approval by the UK authority of a recognised European document which has been approved as described in paragraph 1(c);
   (b)   in sections 80, 81(1)(a) and 90(3) of the Act, any reference to information specified or required by listing rules or required by the competent authority or to matter whose inclusion was required by listing rules or by the competent authority shall apply as if it were a reference to information required by or to matter whose inclusion was required by the

legislation relating to the contents of prospectuses and listing particulars, or by the competent authorities, of the member State where the European document forming part of that recognised European document was approved;

   (c) nothing in section 81 of the Act shall require the approval by the UK authority of supplementary listing particulars or a supplementary prospectus which is, or is a translation into English of, a supplement which has been approved pursuant to Article 23 of Council Directive No 80/390/EEC or Article 18 of Council Directive No 89/298/EEC by the competent authority which approved the listing particulars or prospectus to which the supplement relates.

5.   Subject to paragraphs 1 and 3, references in Part VI of the Act to supplementary listing particulars shall be taken to include references to supplementary prospectuses.

6.   This Part of this Schedule shall not apply to listing particulars or a prospectus approved in another member State prior to the coming into force of these Regulations.

PART II
RECOGNITION FOR THE PURPOSES OF PART II OF THESE REGULATIONS OF PROSPECTUSES APPROVED IN OTHER MEMBER STATES

7.   In this Part of this Schedule "recognised prospectus" means a prospectus which has been approved in accordance with Article 20 of Council Directive No 89/298/EEC in another member State and satisfies the requirements of paragraphs (a) to (c) of paragraph 8(1); and where the prospectus has been translated into English, the English version shall be the recognised prospectus.

8.— (1) Where a prospectus has been approved in accordance with Article 20 of Council Directive No 89/298/EEC in another member State it shall, subject to sub-paragraph (2), be deemed for the purposes of regulation 4(1) to comply with regulations 8 and 9 of these Regulations provided that—

    (a) ...

    (b) the offer of securities to which the prospectus relates is made in the United Kingdom simultaneously with the making of the offer in the member State where the prospectus was approved or within 3 months after the making of that offer;

    (c) there is added to the information contained in the prospectus as approved in the other member State such of the following information as is not included in the prospectus as so approved—

      (i) ...

      (ii) the names and addresses of the paying agents for the securities in the United Kingdom (if any);

      (iii) a statement of how notice of meetings and other notices from the issuer of the securities will be given to United Kingdom resident holders of the securities; and

    (d) where a partial exemption or partial derogation has been granted in the other member State pursuant to Council Directive No 89/298/EEC—

      (i) the partial exemption or partial derogation in question is of a type for which a corresponding partial exemption or partial derogation is made in these Regulations; and

      (ii) the circumstances that justify the partial exemption or partial derogation also exist in the United Kingdom.

  (2) Where, prior to the delivery for registration to the registrar of companies of a prospectus which has been approved in another member State, a supplement to the prospectus has been approved pursuant to Article 23 of Council Directive No 80/390/EEC or Article 18 of Council Directive No 89/298/EEC in the member State where the prospectus was approved, the references in sub-paragraph (1) and in paragraph 7 to a prospectus shall be taken to be references to the prospectus taken together with the supplement.

9.   Subject to paragraph 8(2), Part II of these Regulations shall apply in relation to a recognised prospectus as it applies in relation to a prospectus to which the said Part II would apply apart from this paragraph except that in regulations 9(1), 10(1)(a) and 14(2) of these Regulations the references to information or any matter required to be included in a prospectus by these Regulations shall be taken to be references to information or any matter required to be included by virtue of the legislation relating to the contents of prospectuses of the member State where the recognised prospectus was approved and by virtue of paragraph 8(1)(c).

PART III
RECOGNITION FOR THE PURPOSES OF THE COMPANIES ACT 1985 OF PROSPECTUSES APPROVED IN OTHER MEMBER STATES

10.   In this Part of this Schedule, "recognised prospectus" has the same meaning as in Part II of this Schedule.

11.   …

12.   A recognised prospectus shall be deemed to comply with sections 97(3) and 693(1)(a) and (d) of the Companies Act 1985.

Financial Services and Markets Act 2000 (Regulated Activities) Order 2001

S.I. 2001/544

PART I
GENERAL

1. **Citation**

This Order may be cited as the Financial Services and Markets Act 2000 (Regulated Activities) Order 2001.

2. **Commencement**

(1) Except as provided by paragraph (2), this Order comes into force on the day on which section 19 of the Act comes into force.

(2) This Order comes into force—

    (a) for the purposes of articles 59, 60 and 87 (funeral plan contracts) on 1st January 2002; and

    (b) for the purposes of articles 61 to 63, 88, 90 and 91 (regulated mortgage contracts) on such a day as the Treasury may specify.

(3) Any day specified under paragraph (2)(b) must be caused to be notified in the London, Edinburgh and Belfast Gazettes published not later than one week before that day.

3. **Interpretation**

(1) In this Order—

"the Act" means the Financial Services and Markets Act 2000;

"annuities on human life" does not include superannuation allowances and annuities payable out of any fund applicable solely to the relief and maintenance of persons engaged, or who have been engaged, in any particular profession, trade or employment, or of the dependants of such persons;

"buying" includes acquiring for valuable consideration;

"close relative" in relation to a person means—

    (a) his spouse;

    (b) his children and step children, his parents and step-parents, his brothers and sisters and his step-brothers and step-sisters; and

    (c) the spouse of any person within sub-paragraph (b);

"contract of general insurance" means any contract falling within Part I of Schedule 1;

"contract of insurance" means any contract of insurance which is a contract of long-term insurance or a contract of general insurance, and includes—

    (a) fidelity bonds, performance bonds, administration bonds, bail bonds, customs bonds or similar contracts of guarantee, where these are—

        (i) effected or carried out by a person not carrying on a banking business;

        (ii) not effected merely incidentally to some other business carried on by the person effecting them; and

        (iii) effected in return for the payment of one or more premiums;

    (b) tontines;

    (c) capital redemption contracts or pension fund management contracts, where these are effected or carried out by a person who—

        (i) does not carry on a banking business; and

        (ii) otherwise carries on a regulated activity of the kind specified by article 10(1) or (2);

    (d) contracts to pay annuities on human life;

(e)   contracts of a kind referred to in article 1(2)(e) of the first life insurance directive (collective insurance etc); and

(f)   contracts of a kind referred to in article 1(3) of the first life insurance directive (social insurance);

but does not include a funeral plan contract (or a contract which would be a funeral plan contract but for the exclusion in article 60);

"contract of long-term insurance" means any contract falling within Part II of Schedule 1;

"contractually based investment" means—

(a)   rights under a qualifying contract of insurance;

(b)   any investment of the kind specified by any of articles 83, 84, 85 and 87; or

(c)   any investment of the kind specified by article 89 so far as relevant to an investment falling within (a) or (b);

"deposit" has the meaning given by article 5;

"electronic money" means monetary value, as represented by a claim on the issuer, which is—

(a)   stored on an electronic device;

(b)   issued on receipt of funds; and

(c)   accepted as a means of payment by persons other than the issuer;

"funeral plan contract" has the meaning given by article 59;

"instrument" includes any record whether or not in the form of a document;

"joint enterprise" means an enterprise into which two or more persons ("the participators") enter for commercial purposes related to a business or businesses (other than the business of engaging in a regulated activity) carried on by them; and, where a participator is a member of a group, each other member of the group is also to be regarded as a participator in the enterprise;

"local authority" means—

(a)   in England and Wales, a local authority within the meaning of the Local Government Act 1972, the Greater London Authority, the Common Council of the City of London or the Council of the Isles of Scilly;

(b)   in Scotland, a local authority within the meaning of the Local Government (Scotland) Act 1973;

(c)   in Northern Ireland, a district council within the meaning of the Local Government Act (Northern Ireland) 1972;

"managing agent" means a person who is permitted by the Council of Lloyd's in the conduct of his business as an underwriting agent to perform for a member of Lloyd's one or more of the following functions—

(a)   underwriting contracts of insurance at Lloyd's;

(b)   reinsuring such contracts in whole or in part;

(c)   paying claims on such contracts;

"occupational pension scheme" means any scheme or arrangement which is comprised in one or more instruments or agreements and which has, or is capable of having, effect in relation to one or more descriptions or categories of employment so as to provide benefits, in the form of pensions or otherwise, payable on termination of service, or on death or retirement, to or in respect of earners with qualifying service in an employment of any such description or category;

"overseas person" means a person who—

(a)   carries on activities of the kind specified by any of articles 14, 21, 25, 25A, 37, 39A, 40, 45, 51, 52, 53, 53A and 61 or, so far as relevant to any of those articles, article 64 (or activities of a kind which would be so specified but for the exclusion in article 72); but

(b)   does not carry on any such activities, or offer to do so, from a permanent place of business maintained by him in the United Kingdom;

"pension fund management contract" means a contract to manage the investments of pension funds (other than funds solely for the benefit of the officers or employees of the person effecting or carrying out the contract and their dependants or, in the case of a company, partly for the benefit of officers and employees and their dependants of its subsidiary or holding company or a subsidiary of its holding company); and for the purposes of this definition, "subsidiary" and "holding company" are to be construed in accordance with section 736 of the Companies Act 1985 or article 4 of the Companies (Northern Ireland) Order 1986;

"property" includes currency of the United Kingdom or any other country or territory;

"qualifying contract of insurance" means a contract of long-term insurance which is not—

(a)   a reinsurance contract; nor

(b)   a contract in respect of which the following conditions are met—

    (i)   the benefits under the contract are payable only on death or in respect of incapacity due to injury, sickness or infirmity;

    (ii)   the contract provides that benefits are payable on death (other than death due to an accident) only where the death occurs within ten years of the date on which the life of the person in question was first insured under the contract, or where the death occurs before that person attains a specified age not exceeding seventy years;

    (iii)   the contract has no surrender value, or the consideration consists of a single premium and the surrender value does not exceed that premium; and

    (iv)   the contract makes no provision for its conversion or extension in a manner which would result in it ceasing to comply with any of the above conditions;

"regulated mortgage contract" has the meaning given by article 61(3);

"relevant investment" means—

(a)   rights under a qualifying contract of insurance;

(b)   rights under any other contract of insurance;

(c)   any investment of the kind specified by any of articles 83, 84, 85 and 87; or

(d)   any investment of the kind specified by article 89 so far as relevant to an investment falling within (a) or (c);

"security" means (except where the context otherwise requires) any investment of the kind specified by any of articles 76 to 82 or, so far as relevant to any such investment, article 89;

"selling", in relation to any investment, includes disposing of the investment for valuable consideration, and for these purposes "disposing" includes—

(a)   in the case of an investment consisting of rights under a contract—

    (i)   surrendering, assigning or converting those rights; or

    (ii)   assuming the corresponding liabilities under the contract;

(b)   in the case of an investment consisting of rights under other arrangements, assuming the corresponding liabilities under the arrangements; and

(c)   in the case of any other investment, issuing or creating the investment or granting the rights or interests of which it consists;

"stakeholder pension scheme" has the meaning given by section 1 of the Welfare Reform and Pensions Act 1999;

"syndicate" means one or more persons, to whom a particular syndicate number has been assigned by or under the authority of the Council of Lloyd's, carrying out or effecting contracts of insurance written at Lloyd's;

"voting shares", in relation to a body corporate, means shares carrying voting rights attributable to share capital which are exercisable in all circumstances at any general meeting of that body corporate.

(2)   For the purposes of this Order, a transaction is entered into through a person if he enters into it as agent or arranges, in a manner constituting the carrying on of an activity of the kind specified by article 25(1), for it to be entered into by another person as agent or principal.

(3)   For the purposes of this Order, a contract of insurance is to be treated as falling within Part II of Schedule 1, notwithstanding the fact that it contains related and subsidiary provisions such that it might also be regarded as falling within Part I of that Schedule, if its principal object is that of a contract falling within Part II and it is effected or carried out by an authorised person who has permission to effect or carry out contracts falling within paragraph I of Part II of Schedule 1.

PART II
SPECIFIED ACTIVITIES

CHAPTER I
GENERAL

4.   Specified activities: general

(1)   The following provisions of this Part specify kinds of activity for the purposes of section 22 of the Act (and accordingly any activity of one of those kinds, which is carried on by way of business, and relates to an investment of a kind specified by any provision of Part III and applicable to that activity, is a regulated activity for the purposes of the Act).

(2)   The kinds of activity specified by articles 51 and 52 are also specified for the purposes of section 22(1)(b) of the Act (and accordingly any activity of one of those kinds, when carried on by way of business, is a regulated activity when carried on in relation to property of any kind).

(3)   Subject to paragraph (4), each provision specifying a kind of activity is subject to the exclusions applicable to that provision (and accordingly any reference in this Order to an activity of the kind specified by a particular provision is to be read subject to any such exclusions).

(4)   Where an investment firm—

     (a)   provides core investment services to third parties on a professional basis, and

     (b)   in doing so would be treated as carrying on an activity of a kind specified by a provision of this Part but for an exclusion in any of articles 15, 16, 19, 22, 23, 29, 38, 68, 69 and 70,

     that exclusion is to be disregarded (and accordingly the investment firm is to be treated as carrying on an activity of the kind specified by the provision in question).

(4A)   Where a person, other than a person specified by Article 1.2 of the insurance mediation directive (the text of which is set out in Part 1 of Schedule 4)—

     (a)   for remuneration, takes up or pursues insurance mediation or reinsurance mediation in relation to a risk or commitment located in an EEA State, and

     (b)   in doing so would be treated as carrying on an activity of a kind specified by a provision of this Part but for an exclusion in any of articles 30, 66 and 67,

     that exclusion is to be disregarded (and accordingly that person is to be treated as carrying on an activity of the kind specified by the provision in question).

(5)   In this article—

     "core investment service" means any service listed in section A of the Annex to the investment services directive, the text of which is set out in Schedule 2; ...

     "insurance mediation" has the meaning given by Article 2.3 of the insurance mediation directive, the text of which is set out in Part II of Schedule 4;

     "investment firm" means a person whose regular occupation or business is the provision of core investment services to third parties on a professional basis, other than—

     (a)   a person to whom the investment services directive does not apply by virtue of Article 2.2 of that directive (the text of which is set out in Schedule 3); or

     (b)   a person to whom (if he were incorporated in or formed under the law of an EEA State or, being an individual, had his head office in an EEA State) that directive would not apply by virtue of Article 2.2 of that directive.

     "reinsurance mediation" has the meaning given by Article 2.4 of the insurance mediation directive, the text of which is set out in Part III of Schedule 4.

CHAPTER II
ACCEPTING DEPOSITS

The activity

5.   Accepting deposits

(1)   Accepting deposits is a specified kind of activity if—

(a)   money received by way of deposit is lent to others; or

(b)   any other activity of the person accepting the deposit is financed wholly, or to a material extent, out of the capital of or interest on money received by way of deposit.

(2)   In paragraph (1), "deposit" means a sum of money, other than one excluded by any of articles 6 to 9A, paid on terms—

(a)   under which it will be repaid, with or without interest or premium, and either on demand or at a time or in circumstances agreed by or on behalf of the person making the payment and the person receiving it; and

(b)   which are not referable to the provision of property (other than currency) or services or the giving of security.

(3)   For the purposes of paragraph (2), money is paid on terms which are referable to the provision of property or services or the giving of security if, and only if—

(a)   it is paid by way of advance or part payment under a contract for the sale, hire or other provision of property or services, and is repayable only in the event that the property or services is or are not in fact sold, hired or otherwise provided;

(b)   it is paid by way of security for the performance of a contract or by way of security in respect of loss which may result from the non-performance of a contract; or

(c)   without prejudice to sub-paragraph (b), it is paid by way of security for the delivery up or return of any property, whether in a particular state of repair or otherwise.

Exclusions

6.   Sums paid by certain persons

(1)   A sum is not a deposit for the purposes of article 5 if it is—

(a)   paid by any of the following persons—

(i)   the Bank of England, the central bank of an EEA State other than the United Kingdom, or the European Central Bank;

(ii)   an authorised person who has permission to accept deposits, or to effect or carry out contracts of insurance;

(iii) an EEA firm falling within paragraph 5(b), (c) or (d) of Schedule 3 to the Act (other than one falling within paragraph (ii) above);

(iv)   the National Savings Bank;

(v)   a municipal bank, that is to say a company which was, immediately before the coming into force of this article, exempt from the prohibition in section 3 of the Banking Act 1987 by virtue of section 4(1) of, and paragraph 4 of Schedule 2 to, that Act;

(vi)   Keesler Federal Credit Union;

(vii) a body of persons certified as a school bank by the National Savings Bank or by an authorised person who has permission to accept deposits;

(viii) a local authority;

(xi)   any body which by virtue of any enactment has power to issue a precept to a local authority in England and Wales or a requisition to a local authority in Scotland, or to the expenses of which, by virtue of any enactment, a local authority in the United Kingdom is or can be required to contribute (and in this paragraph, "enactment" includes an enactment comprised in, or in an instrument made under, an Act of the Scottish Parliament);

(x)   the European Community, the European Atomic Energy Community or the European Coal and Steel Community;

   (xi) the European Investment Bank;

   (xii) the International Bank for Reconstruction and Development;

   (xiii) the International Finance Corporation;

   (xiv) the International Monetary Fund;

   (xv) the African Development Bank;

   (xvi) the Asian Development Bank;

   (xvii)the Caribbean Development Bank;

   (xviii)the Inter-American Development Bank;

   (xix) the European Bank for Reconstruction and Development;

   (xx) the Council of Europe Development Bank;

  (b) paid by a person other than one mentioned in sub-paragraph (a) in the course of carrying on a business consisting wholly or to a significant extent of lending money;

  (c) paid by one company to another at a time when both are members of the same group or when the same individual is a majority shareholder controller of both of them; or

  (d) paid by a person who, at the time when it is paid, is a close relative of the person receiving it or who is, or is a close relative of, a director or manager of that person or who is, or is a close relative of, a controller of that person.

(2) For the purposes of paragraph (1)(c), an individual is a majority shareholder controller of a company if he is a controller of the company by virtue of paragraph (a), (c), (e) or (g) of section 422(2) of the Act, and if in his case the greatest percentage of those referred to in those paragraphs is 50 or more.

(3) In the application of sub-paragraph (d) of paragraph (1) to a sum paid by a partnership, that sub-paragraph is to have effect as if, for the reference to the person paying the sum, there were substituted a reference to each of the partners.

7. Sums received by solicitors etc

(1) A sum is not a deposit for the purposes of article 5 if it is received by a practising solicitor acting in the course of his profession.

(2) In paragraph (1), "practising solicitor" means—

  (a) a solicitor who is qualified to act as such under section 1 of the Solicitors Act 1974, article 4 of the Solicitors (Northern Ireland) Order 1976 or section 4 of the Solicitors (Scotland) Act 1980;

  (b) a recognised body;

  (c) a registered foreign lawyer in the course of providing professional services as a member of a multi-national partnership;

  (d) a registered European lawyer; or

  (e) a partner of a registered European lawyer who is providing professional services in accordance with—

   (i) rules made under section 31 of the Solicitors Act 1974;

   (ii) regulations made under article 26 of the Solicitors (Northern Ireland) Order 1976; or

   (iii) rules made under section 34 of the Solicitors (Scotland) Act 1980.

(3) In this article—

  (a) "a recognised body" means a body corporate recognised by—

   (i) the Council of the Law Society under section 9 of the Administration of Justice Act 1985;

   (ii) the Incorporated Law Society of Northern Ireland under article 26A of the Solicitors (Northern Ireland) Order 1976; or

   (iii) the Council of the Law Society of Scotland under section 34 of the Solicitors (Scotland) Act 1980;

  (b) "registered foreign lawyer" has the meaning given by section 89 of the Courts and Legal Services Act 1990 or, in Scotland, section 65 of the Solicitors (Scotland) Act 1980;

    (c)   "multi-national partnership" has the meaning given by section 89 of the Courts and Legal Services Act 1990 but, in Scotland, is a reference to a "multi-national practice" within the meaning of section 60A of the Solicitors (Scotland) Act 1980; and

    (d)   "registered European lawyer" has the meaning given by regulation 2(1) of the European Communities (Lawyer's Practice) Regulations 2000 or regulation 2(1) of the European Communities (Lawyer's Practice) (Scotland) Regulation 2000.

8.   **Sums received by persons authorised to deal etc**

A sum is not a deposit for the purposes of article 5 if it is received by a person who is—

    (a)   an authorised person with permission to carry on an activity of the kind specified by any of articles 14, 21, 25, 37, 51 and 52, or

    (b)   an exempt person in relation to any such activity,

in the course of, or for the purpose of, carrying on any such activity (or any activity which would be such an activity but for any exclusion made by this Part) with or on behalf of the person by or on behalf of whom the sum is paid.

9.   **Sums received in consideration for the issue of debt securities**

(1)   Subject to paragraph (2), a sum is not a deposit for the purposes of article 5 if it is received by a person as consideration for the issue by him of any investment of the kind specified by article 77 or 78.

(2)   The exclusion in paragraph (1) does not apply to the receipt by a person of a sum as consideration for the issue by him of commercial paper unless—

    (a)   the commercial paper is issued to persons—

        (i)   whose ordinary activities involve them in acquiring, holding, managing or disposing of investments (as principal or agent) for the purposes of their businesses; or

        (ii)   who it is reasonable to expect will acquire, hold, manage or dispose of investments (as principal or agent) for the purposes of their businesses; and

    (b)   the redemption value of the commercial paper is not less than £100,000 (or an amount of equivalent value denominated wholly or partly in a currency other than sterling), and no part of the commercial paper may be transferred unless the redemption value of that part is not less than £100,000 (or such an equivalent amount).

(3)   In paragraph (2), "commercial paper" means an investment of the kind specified by article 77 or 78 having a maturity of less than one year from the date of issue.

9A.   **Sums received in exchange for electronic money**

A sum is not a deposit for the purposes of article 5 if it is immediately exchanged for electronic money.

9AA.   **Information society services**

Article 5 is subject to the exclusion in article 72A (information society services).

CHAPTER IIA
ELECTRONIC MONEY

The activity

9B.   **Issuing electronic money**

Issuing electronic money is a specified kind of activity.

Exclusions

9C.   **Persons certified as small issuers etc**

(1)   There is excluded from article 9B the issuing of electronic money by a person to whom the Authority has given a certificate under this article (provided the certificate has not been revoked).

(2)   An application for a certificate may be made by—

(a) a body corporate, or

(b) a partnership,

(other than a credit institution as defined in Article 1(1)(a) of the banking consolidation directive) which has its head office in the United Kingdom.

(3) The authority must, on the application of such a person ("A"), give A a certificate if it appears to the Authority that paragraph (4), (5) or (6) applies.

(4) This paragraph applies if—

(a) A does not issue electronic money except on terms that the electronic device on which the monetary value is stored is subject to a maximum storage amount of not more than 150 euro; and

(b) A's total liabilities with respect to the issuing of electronic money do not (or will not) usually exceed 5 million euro and do not (or will not) ever exceed 6 million euro.

(5) This paragraph applies if—

(a) the condition in paragraph (4)(a) is met;

(b) A's total liabilities with respect to the issuing of electronic money do not (or will not) exceed 10 million euro; and

(c) electronic money issued by A is accepted as a means of payment only by—

(i) subsidiaries of A which perform operational or other ancillary functions related to electronic money issued or distributed by A; or

(ii) other members of the same group as A (other than subsidiaries of A).

(6) This paragraph applies if—

(a) the conditions in paragraphs (4)(a) and (5)(b) are met; and

(b) electronic money issued by A is accepted as a means of payment, in the course of business, by not more than one hundred persons where—

(i) those persons accept such electronic money only at locations within the same premises or limited local area; or

(ii) those persons have a close financial or business relationship with A, such as a common marketing or distribution scheme.

(7) For the purposes of paragraph (6)(b)(i), locations are to be treated as situated within the same premises or limited local area if they are situated within—

(a) a shopping centre, airport, railway station, bus station, or campus of a university, polytechnic, college, school or similar educational establishment; or

(b) an area which does not exceed four square kilometres;

but sub-paragraphs (a) and (b) are illustrative only and are not to be treated as limiting the scope of paragraph (6)(b)(i).

(8) For the purposes of paragraph (6)(b)(ii), persons are not to be treated as having a close financial or business relationship with A merely because they participate in arrangements for the acceptance of electronic money issued by A.

(9) In this article, references to amounts in euro include references to equivalent amounts in sterling.

(10) A person to whom a certificate has been given under this article (and whose certificate has not been revoked) is referred to in this Chapter as a "certified person".

9D.   Applications for certificates

The following provisions of the Act apply to applications to the Authority for certificates under 9C (and the determination of such applications) as they apply to applications for Part IV permissions (and the determination of such applications)—

(a) section 51(1)(b) and (3) to (6);

(b) section 52, except subsections (6), (8) and (9)(a) and (b); and

(c) section 55(1).

9E.   Revocation of certificate on Authority's own initiative

(1) The Authority may revoke a certificate given to a person ("A") under article 9C if—

(a) it appears to it that A does not meet the relevant conditions, or has failed to meet the relevant conditions at any time since the certificate was given; or

(b) the person to whom the certificate was given has contravened any rule or requirement to which he is subject as a result of article 9G.

(2) For the purposes of paragraph (1), A meets the relevant conditions at any time if, at that time, paragraph (4), (5) or (6) of article 9C applies.

(3) Sections 54 and 55(2) of the Act apply to the revocation of a certificate under paragraph (1) as they apply to the cancellation of a Part IV permission on the Authority's own initiative, as if references in those sections to an authorised person were references to a certified person.

9F. Revocation of certificate on request

(1) A certified person ("B") may apply to the Authority for his certificate to be revoked, and the Authority must then revoke the certificate and give B written notice that it has done so.

(2) An application under paragraph (1) must be made in such manner as the Authority may direct.

(3) If—

(a) B has made an application under Part IV of the Act for permission to carry on a regulated activity of the kind specified by article 9B (or for variation of an existing permission so as to add a regulated activity of that kind), and

(b) on making an application for revocation of his certificate under paragraph (1), he requests that the revocation be conditional on the granting of his application under Part IV of the Act,

the revocation of B's certificate is to be conditional on the granting of his application under Part IV of the Act.

9G. Obtaining information from certified persons etc

(1) The Authority may make rules requiring certified persons to provide information to the Authority about their activities so far as relating to the issuing of electronic money, including the amount of their liabilities with respect to the issuing of electronic money.

(2) Section 148 of the Act (modification or waiver of rules) applies in relation to rules made under paragraph (1) as if references in that section to an authorised person were references to a certified person.

(3) Section 150 of the Act (actions for damages) applies in relation to a rule made under paragraph (1) as if the reference in subsection (1) of that section to an authorised person were a reference to a certified person.

(4) The Authority may, by notice in writing given to a certified person, require him—

(a) to provide specified information or information of a specified description; or

(b) to produce specified documents or documents of a specified description.

(5) Paragraph (4) applies only to information or documents reasonably required for the purposes of determining whether the certified person meets, or has met, the relevant conditions.

(6) Subsections (2), (5) and (6) of section 165 of the Act (Authority's power to require information) apply to a requirement imposed under paragraph (4) as they apply to a requirement imposed under that section.

(7) Section 166 of the Act (reports by skilled persons) has effect as if—

(a) the reference in subsection (1) of that section to section 165 included a reference to paragraph (4) above; and

(b) the reference in section 166(2)(a) of the Act to an authorised person included a reference to a certified person.

(8) Subsection (4) of section 168 of the Act (appointment of persons to carry out investigations in particular cases) has effect as if it provided for subsection (5) of that section to apply if it appears to the Authority that there are circumstances suggesting that a certified person may not meet, or may not have met, the relevant conditions.

(9) Sections 175 (information and documents: supplemental provisions), 176 (entry of premises under warrant) and 177 (offences) of the Act apply to a requirement imposed under paragraph (4)

as they apply to a requirement imposed under section 165 of the Act (the reference in section 176(3)(a) to an authorised person being read as a reference to a certified person).

(10)   In this article—

    (a)   "specified", in paragraph (4), means specified in the notice mentioned in that paragraph;

    (b)   a certified person ("A") meets the relevant conditions at any time if, at that time, paragraph (4), (5) or (6) of article 9C applies.

Supplemental

9H.   Rules prohibiting the issue of electronic money at a discount

(1)   The Authority may make rules applying to authorised persons with permission to carry on an activity of the kind specified by article 9B, prohibiting the issue of electronic money having a monetary value greater than the funds received.

(2)   Section 148 of the Act (modification or waiver of rules) applies in relation to rules made under paragraph (1).

9I.   False claims to be a certified person

A person who is not a certified person is to be treated as guilty of an offence under section 24 of the Act (false claims to be authorised or exempt) if he—

    (a)   describes himself (in whatever terms) as a certified person;

    (b)   behaves, or otherwise holds himself out, in a manner which indicates (or which is reasonably likely to be understood as indicating) that he is a certified person.

9J.   Exclusion of electronic money from the compensation scheme

The compensation scheme established under Part XV of the Act is not to provide for the compensation of persons in respect of claims made in connection with any activity of the kind specified by article 9B.

9K.   Record of certified persons

The record maintained by the Authority under section 347 of the Act (public record of authorised persons etc) must include every certified person.

CHAPTER III
INSURANCE

The activities

10.   Effecting and carrying out contracts of insurance

(1)   Effecting a contract of insurance as principal is a specified kind of activity.

(2)   Carrying out a contract of insurance as principal is a specified kind of activity.

Exclusions

11.   Community co-insurers

(1)   There is excluded from article 10(1) or (2) the effecting or carrying out of a contract of insurance by an EEA firm falling within paragraph 5(d) of Schedule 3 to the Act—

    (a)   other than through a branch in the United Kingdom; and

    (b)   pursuant to a Community co-insurance operation in which the firm is participating otherwise than as the leading insurer.

(2)   In paragraph (1), "Community co-insurance operation" and "leading insurer" have the same meaning as in the Council Directive of 30 May 1978 on the co-ordination of laws, regulations and administrative provisions relating to Community co-insurance (No 78/473/EEC).

12.   **Breakdown insurance**

(1)   There is excluded from article 10(1) or (2) the effecting or carrying out, by a person who does not otherwise carry on an activity of the kind specified by that article, of a contract of insurance which—

   (a)   is a contract under which the benefits provided by that person ("the provider") are exclusively or primarily benefits in kind in the event of accident to or breakdown of a vehicle; and

   (b)   contains the terms mentioned in paragraph (2).

(2)   Those terms are that—

   (a)   the assistance takes either or both of the forms mentioned in paragraph (3)(a) and (b);

   (b)   the assistance is not available outside the United Kingdom and the Republic of Ireland except where it is provided without the payment of additional premium by a person in the country concerned with whom the provider has entered into a reciprocal agreement; and

   (c)   assistance provided in the case of an accident or breakdown occurring in the United Kingdom or the Republic of Ireland is, in most circumstances, provided by the provider's servants.

(3)   The forms of assistance are—

   (a)   repairs to the relevant vehicle at the place where the accident or breakdown has occurred; this assistance may also include the delivery of parts, fuel, oil, water or keys to the relevant vehicle;

   (b)   removal of the relevant vehicle to the nearest or most appropriate place at which repairs may be carried out, or to—

      (i)   the home, point of departure or original destination within the United Kingdom of the driver and passengers, provided the accident or breakdown occurred within the United Kingdom;

      (ii)   the home, point of departure or original destination within the Republic of Ireland of the driver and passengers, provided the accident or breakdown occurred within the Republic of Ireland or within Northern Ireland;

      (iii)   the home, point of departure or original destination within Northern Ireland of the driver and passengers, provided the accident or breakdown occurred within the Republic of Ireland;

   and this form of assistance may include the conveyance of the driver or passengers of the relevant vehicle, with the vehicle, or (where the vehicle is to be conveyed only to the nearest or most appropriate place at which repairs may be carried out) separately, to the nearest location from which they may continue their journey by other means.

(4)   A contract does not fail to meet the condition in paragraph (1)(a) solely because the provider may reimburse the person entitled to the assistance for all or part of any sums paid by him in respect of assistance either because he failed to identify himself as a person entitled to the assistance or because he was unable to get in touch with the provider in order to claim the assistance.

(5)   In this article—

   "the assistance" means the benefits to be provided under a contract of the kind mentioned in paragraph (1);

   "breakdown" means an event—

   (a)   which causes the driver of the relevant vehicle to be unable to start a journey in the vehicle or involuntarily to bring the vehicle to a halt on a journey because of some malfunction of the vehicle or failure of it to function, and

   (b)   after which the journey cannot reasonably be commenced or continued in the relevant vehicle;

   "the relevant vehicle" means the vehicle (including a trailer or caravan) in respect of which the assistance is required.

12A.   Information society services

Article 10 is subject to the exclusion in article 72A (information society services), as qualified by paragraph (2) of that article.

Supplemental

13.   Application of sections 327 and 332 of the Act to insurance market activities

(1)   In sections 327(5) and (7) and 332(3)(b) of the Act (exemption from the general prohibition for members of the professions, and rules in relation to such persons), the references to "a regulated activity" and "regulated activities" do not include—

   (a)   any activity of the kind specified by article 10(1) or (2), where—

       (i)   P is a member of the Society; and

       (ii)   by virtue of section 316 of the Act (application of the Act to Lloyd's underwriting), the general prohibition does not apply to the carrying on by P of that activity; or

   (b)   any activity of the kind specified by article 10(2), where—

       (i)   P is a former underwriting member; and

       (ii)   the contract of insurance in question is one underwritten by P at Lloyd's.

(2)   In paragraph (1)—

   "member of the Society" has the same meaning as in Lloyd's Act 1982; and

   "former underwriting member" has the meaning given by section 324(1) of the Act.

CHAPTER IV
DEALING IN INVESTMENTS AS PRINCIPAL

The activity

14.   Dealing in investments as principal

Buying, selling, subscribing for or underwriting securities or contractually based investments (other than investments of the kind specified by article 87, or article 89 so far as relevant to that article) as principal is a specified kind of activity.

Exclusions

15.   Absence of holding out etc

(1)   Subject to paragraph (3), a person ("A") does not carry on an activity of the kind specified by article 14 by entering into a transaction which relates to a security or is the assignment (or, in Scotland, the assignation) of a qualifying contract of insurance (or an investment of the kind specified by article 89, so far as relevant to such a contract), unless—

   (a)   A holds himself out as willing, as principal, to buy, sell or subscribe for investments of the kind to which the transaction relates at prices determined by him generally and continuously rather than in respect of each particular transaction;

   (b)   A holds himself out as engaging in the business of buying investments of the kind to which the transaction relates, with a view to selling them;

   (c)   A holds himself out as engaging in the business of underwriting investments of the kind to which the transaction relates; or

   (d)   A regularly solicits members of the public with the purpose of inducing them, as principals or agents, to enter into transactions constituting activities of the kind specified by article 14, and the transaction is entered into as a result of his having solicited members of the public in that manner.

(2)   In paragraph (1)(d), "members of the public" means any persons other than—

   (a)   authorised persons or persons who are exempt persons in relation to activities of the kind specified by article 14;

   (b)   members of the same group as A;

   (c)   persons who are or who propose to become participators with A in a joint enterprise;

(d)   any person who is solicited by A with a view to the acquisition by A of 20 per cent or more of the voting shares in a body corporate;

(e)   if A (either alone or with members of the same group as himself) holds more than 20 per cent of the voting shares in a body corporate, any person who is solicited by A with a view to—

    (i)   the acquisition by A of further shares in the body corporate; or

    (ii)   the disposal by A of shares in the body corporate to the person solicited or to a member of the same group as the person solicited;

(f)   any person who—

    (i)   is solicited by A with a view to the disposal by A of shares in a body corporate to the person solicited or to a member of the same group as that person; and

    (ii)   either alone or with members of the same group holds 20 per cent or more of the voting shares in the body corporate;

(g)   any person whose head office is outside the United Kingdom, who is solicited by an approach made or directed to him at a place outside the United Kingdom and whose ordinary business involves him in carrying on activities of the kind specified by any of articles 14, 21, 25, 37, 40, 45, 51, 52 and 53 or (so far as relevant to any of those articles) article 64, or would do so apart from any exclusion from any of those articles made by this Order.

(3)   This article does not apply where A enters into the transaction as bare trustee or, in Scotland, as nominee for another person and is acting on that other person's instructions (but the exclusion in article 66(1) applies if the conditions set out there are met).

16.   Dealing in contractually based investments

A person who is not an authorised person does not carry on an activity of the kind specified by article 14 by entering into a transaction relating to a contractually based investment—

(a)   with or through an authorised person, or an exempt person acting in the course of a business comprising a regulated activity in relation to which he is exempt; or

(b)   through an office outside the United Kingdom maintained by a party to the transaction, and with or through a person whose head office is situated outside the United Kingdom and whose ordinary business involves him in carrying on activities of the kind specified by any of articles 14, 21, 25, 37, 40, 45, 51, 52 and 53 or, so far as relevant to any of those articles, article 64 (or would do so apart from any exclusion from any of those articles made by this Order).

17.   Acceptance of instruments creating or acknowledging indebtedness

(1)   A person does not carry on an activity of the kind specified by article 14 by accepting an instrument creating or acknowledging indebtedness in respect of any loan, credit, guarantee or other similar financial accommodation or assurance which he has made, granted or provided.

(2)   The reference in paragraph (1) to a person accepting an instrument includes a reference to a person becoming a party to an instrument otherwise than as a debtor or a surety.

18.   Issue by a company of its own shares etc

(1)   There is excluded from article 14 the issue by a company of its own shares or share warrants, and the issue by any person of his own debentures or debenture warrants.

(2)   In this article—

(a)   "company" means any body corporate other than an open-ended investment company;

(b)   "shares" and "debentures" include any investment of the kind specified by article 76 or 77;

(c)   "share warrants" and "debenture warrants" mean any investment of the kind specified by article 79 which relates to shares in the company concerned or, as the case may be, debentures issued by the person concerned.

18A. Dealing by a company in its own shares

(1) A company does not carry on an activity of the kind specified by article 14 by purchasing its own shares where section 162A of the Companies Act 1985 (Treasury shares) applies to the shares purchased.

(2) A company does not carry on an activity of the kind specified by article 14 by dealing in its own shares held as treasury shares, in accordance with section 162D of that Act (Treasury shares: disposal and cancellation).

(3) In this article "shares held as treasury shares" has the same meaning as in that Act.

19. Risk management

(1) A person ("B") does not carry on an activity of the kind specified by article 14 by entering as principal into a transaction with another person ("C") if—

(a) the transaction relates to investments of the kind specified by any of articles 83 to 85 (or article 89 so far as relevant to any of those articles);

(b) neither B nor C is an individual;

(c) the sole or main purpose for which B enters into the transaction (either by itself or in combination with other such transactions) is that of limiting the extent to which a relevant business will be affected by any identifiable risk arising otherwise than as a result of the carrying on of a regulated activity; and

(d) the relevant business consists mainly of activities other than—

(i) regulated activities; or

(ii) activities which would be regulated activities but for any exclusion made by this Part.

(2) In paragraph (1), "relevant business" means a business carried on by—

(a) B;

(b) a member of the same group as B; or

(c) where B and another person are, or propose to become, participators in a joint enterprise, that other person.

20. Other exclusions

Article 14 is also subject to the exclusions in articles 66 (trustees etc), 68 (sale of goods and supply of services), 69 (groups and joint enterprises), 70 (sale of body corporate), 71 (employee share schemes), 72 (overseas persons) and 72A (information society services).

CHAPTER V
DEALING IN INVESTMENTS AS AGENT

The activity

21. Dealing in investments as agent

Buying, selling, subscribing for or underwriting securities or relevant investments (other than investments of the kind specified by article 87, or article 89 so far as relevant to that article) as agent is a specified kind of activity.

Exclusions

22. Deals with or through authorised persons

(1) A person who is not an authorised person does not carry on an activity of the kind specified by article 21 by entering into a transaction as agent for another person ("the client") with or through an authorised person if—

(a) the transaction is entered into on advice given to the client by an authorised person; or

(b) it is clear, in all the circumstances, that the client, in his capacity as an investor, is not seeking and has not sought advice from the agent as to the merits of the client's entering into the transaction (or, if the client has sought such advice, the agent has declined to give it but has recommended that the client seek such advice from an authorised person).

(2)   But the exclusion in paragraph (1) does not apply if—
         (a)   the transaction relates to a contract of insurance; or
         (b)   the agent receives from any person other than the client any pecuniary reward or other advantage, for which he does not account to the client, arising out of his entering into the transaction.

23.   Risk management

(1)   A person ("B") does not carry on an activity of the kind specified by article 21 by entering as agent for a relevant person into a transaction with another person ("C") if—
         (a)   the transaction relates to investments of the kind specified by any of articles 83 to 85 (or article 89 so far as relevant to any of those articles);
         (b)   neither B nor C is an individual;
         (c)   the sole or main purpose for which B enters into the transaction (either by itself or in combination with other such transactions) is that of limiting the extent to which a relevant business will be affected by any identifiable risk arising otherwise than as a result of the carrying on of a regulated activity; and
         (d)   the relevant business consists mainly of activities other than—
                (i)   regulated activities; or
                (ii)   activities which would be regulated activities but for any exclusion made by this Part.

(2)   In paragraph (1), "relevant person" means—
         (a)   a member of the same group as B; or
         (b)   where B and another person are, or propose to become, participators in a joint enterprise, that other person;
         and "relevant business" means a business carried on by a relevant person.

24.   Other exclusions

         Article 21 is also subject to the exclusions in articles 67 (profession or non-investment business), 68 (sale of goods and supply of services), 69 (groups and joint enterprises), 70 (sale of body corporate), 71 (employee share schemes), 72 (overseas persons), 72A (information society services), 72B (activities carried on by a provider of relevant goods or services) and 72D (large risks contracts where risk situated outside the EEA).

CHAPTER VI
ARRANGING DEALS IN INVESTMENTS

The activities

25.   Arranging deals in investments

(1)   Making arrangements for another person (whether as principal or agent) to buy, sell, subscribe for or underwrite a particular investment which is—
         (a)   a security,
         (b)   a relevant investment, or
         (c)   an investment of the kind specified by article 86, or article 89 so far as relevant to that article,
         is a specified kind of activity.

(2)   Making arrangements with a view to a person who participates in the arrangements buying, selling, subscribing for or underwriting investments falling within paragraph (1)(a), (b) or (c) (whether as principal or agent) is also a specified kind of activity.

25A.   Arranging regulated mortgage contracts

(1)   Making arrangements—
         (a)   for another person to enter into a regulated mortgage contract as borrower; or

(b)   for another person to vary the terms of a regulated mortgage contract entered into by him as
borrower after the coming into force of article 61, in such a way as to vary his obligations
under that contract,

is a specified kind of activity.

(2)   Making arrangements with a view to a person who participates in the arrangements entering into
a regulated mortgage contract as borrower is also a specified kind of activity.

(3)   In this article "borrower" has the meaning given by article 61(3)(a)(i).

Exclusions

26.   Arrangements not causing a deal

There are excluded from article 25(1) and article 25A(1) arrangements which do not or would not
bring about the transaction to which the arrangements relate.

27.   Enabling parties to communicate

A person does not carry on an activity of the kind specified by article 25(2) and article 25A(2)
merely by providing means by which one party to a transaction (or potential transaction) is able to
communicate with other such parties.

28.   Arranging transactions to which the arranger is a party

(1)   There are excluded from article 25(1) any arrangements for a transaction into which the person
making the arrangements enters or is to enter as principal or as agent for some other person.

(2)   There are excluded from article 25(2) any arrangements which a person makes with a view to
transactions into which he enters or is to enter as principal or as agent for some other person.

(3)   But the exclusions in paragraphs (1) and (2) do not apply to arrangements made for or with a view
to a transaction which relates to a contract of insurance, unless the person making the
arrangements either—
(a)   is the only policyholder; or
(b)   as a result of the transaction, would become the only policyholder.

28A.   Arranging contracts to which the arranger is a party

(1)   There are excluded from article 25A(1) any arrangements—
(a)   for a contract into which the person making the arrangements enters or is to enter; or
(b)   for a variation of a contract to which that person is (or is to become) a party.

(2)   There are excluded from article 25A(2) any arrangements which a person makes with a view to
contracts into which he enters or is to enter.

29.   Arranging deals with or through authorised persons

(1)   There are excluded from article 25(1) and (2) and article 25A(1) and (2) arrangements made by a
person ("A") who is not an authorised person for or with a view to a transaction which is or is to
be entered into by a person ("the client") with or though an authorised person if—
(a)   the transaction is or is to be entered into on advice to the client by an authorised person; or
(b)   it is clear, in all the circumstances, that the client, in his capacity as an investor or (as the
case may be) a borrower under a regulated mortgage contract, is not seeking and has not
sought advice from A as to the merits of the client's entering into the transaction (or, if the
client has sought such advice, A has declined to give it but has recommended that the client
seek such advice from an authorised person).

(2)   But the exclusion in paragraph (1) does not apply if—
(a)   the transaction relates, or would relate, to a contract of insurance; or
(b)   A receives from any person other than the client any pecuniary reward or other advantage,
for which he does not account to the client, arising out of his making the arrangements.

29A.   Arrangements made in the course of administration by authorised person

A person who is not an authorised person ("A") does not carry on an activity of the kind specified
by article 25A(1)(b) as a result of—

(a)   anything done by an authorised person ("B") in relation to a regulated mortgage contract which B is administering pursuant to an arrangement of the kind mentioned in article 62(a); or

(b)   anything A does in connection with the administration of a regulated mortgage contract in circumstances falling within article 62(b).

30.   Arranging transactions in connection with lending on the security of insurance policies

(1)   There are excluded from article 25(1) and (2) arrangements made by a money-lender under which either—

(a)   a relevant authorised person or a person acting on his behalf will introduce to the money-lender persons with whom the relevant authorised person has entered, or proposes to enter, into a relevant transaction, or will advise such persons to approach the money-lender, with a view to the money-lender lending money on the security of any contract effected pursuant to a relevant transaction;

(b)   a relevant authorised person gives an assurance to the money-lender as to the amount which, on the security of any contract effected pursuant to a relevant transaction, will or may be received by the money-lender should the money-lender lend money to a person introduced to him pursuant to the arrangements.

(2)   In paragraph (1)—

"money-lender" means a person who is—

(a)   a money-lending company within the meaning of section 338 of the Companies Act 1985;

(b)   a body corporate incorporated under the law of, or of any part of, the United Kingdom relating to building societies; or

(c)   a person whose ordinary business includes the making of loans or the giving of guarantees in connection with loans;

"relevant authorised person" means an authorised person who has permission to effect contracts of insurance or to sell investments of the kind specified by article 89, so far as relevant to such contracts;

"relevant transaction" means the effecting of a contract of insurance or the sale of an investment of the kind specified by article 89, so far as relevant to such contracts.

31.   Arranging the acceptance of debentures in connection with loans

(1)   There are excluded from article 25(1) and (2) arrangements under which a person accepts or is to accept, whether as principal or agent, an instrument creating or acknowledging indebtedness in respect of any loan, credit, guarantee or other similar financial accommodation or assurance which is, or is to be, made, granted or provided by that person or his principal.

(2)   The reference in paragraph (1) to a person accepting an instrument includes a reference to a person becoming a party to an instrument otherwise than as a debtor or a surety.

32.   Provision of finance

There are excluded from article 25(2) arrangements having as their sole purpose the provision of finance to enable a person to buy, sell, subscribe for or underwrite investments.

33.   Introducing

There are excluded from article 25(2) and article 25A(2) arrangements where—

(a)   they are arrangements under which persons ("clients") will be introduced to another person;

(b)   the person to whom introductions are to be made is—

(i)   an authorised person;

(ii)   an exempt person acting in the course of a business comprising a regulated activity in relation to which he is exempt; or

(iii) a person who is not unlawfully carrying on regulated activities in the United Kingdom and whose ordinary business involves him in engaging in an activity of the kind specified by any of articles 14, 21, 25, 25A, 37, 39A, 40, 45, 51, 52, 53 and 53A (or, so far as relevant to any of those articles, article 64), or would do so apart from any exclusion from any of those articles made by this Order; ...

(c)   the introduction is made with a view to the provision of independent advice or the independent exercise of discretion in relation to investments generally or in relation to any class of investments to which the arrangements relate; and

(d)   the arrangements are made with a view to a person entering into a transaction which does not relate to a contract of insurance.

33A.   Introducing to authorised persons etc.

(1)   There are excluded from article 25A(2) arrangements where—

   (a)   they are arrangements under which a client is introduced to a person ("N") who is—

      (i)   an authorised person who has permission to carry on a regulated activity of the kind specified by any of articles 25A, 53A, and 61(1),

      (ii)   an appointed representative who may carry on a regulated activity of the kind specified by either of articles 25A and 53A without contravening the general prohibition, or

      (iii)   an overseas person who carries on activities specified by any of articles 25A, 53A and 61(1); and

   (b)   the conditions mentioned in paragraph (2) are satisfied.

(2)   Those conditions are—

   (a)   that the person making the introduction ("P") does not receive any money, other than money payable to P on his own account, paid by the client for or in connection with any transaction which the client enters into with or through N as a result of the introduction; and

   (b)   that before making the introduction P discloses to the client such of the information mentioned in paragraph (3) as applies to P.

(3)   That information is—

   (a)   that P is a member of the same group as N;

   (b)   details of any payment which P will receive from N, by way of fee or commission, for introducing the client to N;

   (c)   an indication of any other reward or advantage received or to be received by P that arises out of his introducing clients to N.

(4)   In this article, "client" means a borrower, within the meaning given by article 61(3)(a)(i), or a person who is or may be contemplating entering into a regulated mortgage contract as such a borrower (as the case may be).

34.   Arrangements for the issue of shares etc

(1)   There are excluded from article 25(1) and (2)—

   (a)   arrangements made by a company for the purposes of issuing its own shares or share warrants; and

   (b)   arrangements made by any person for the purposes of issuing his own debentures or debenture warrants;

and for the purposes of article 25(1) and (2), a company is not, by reason of issuing its own shares or share warrants, and a person is not, by reason of issuing his own debentures or debenture warrants, to be treated as selling them.

(2)   In paragraph (1), "company", "shares", "debentures", "share warrants" and "debenture warrants" have the meanings given by article 18(2).

35.   International securities self-regulating organisations

(1)   There are excluded from article 25(1) and (2) any arrangements made for the purposes of carrying out the functions of a body or association which is approved under this article as an international securities self-regulating organisation, whether the arrangements are made by the organisation itself or by a person acting on its behalf.

(2)   The Treasury may approve as an international securities self-regulating organisation any body corporate or unincorporated association with respect to which the conditions mentioned in

paragraph (3) appear to them to be met if, having regard to such matters affecting international trade, overseas earnings and the balance of payments or otherwise as they consider relevant, it appears to them that to do so would be desirable and not result in any undue risk to investors.

(3)   The conditions are that—

    (a)   the body or association does not have its head office in the United Kingdom;

    (b)   the body or association is not eligible for recognition under section 287 or 288 of the Act (applications by investment exchanges and clearing houses) on the ground that (whether or not it has applied, and whether or not it would be eligible on other grounds) it is unable to satisfy the requirements of one or both of paragraphs (a) and (b) of section 292(3) of the Act (requirements for overseas investment exchanges and overseas clearing houses);

    (c)   the body or association is able and willing to co-operate with the Authority by the sharing of information and in other ways;

    (d)   adequate arrangements exist for co-operation between the Authority and those responsible for the supervision of the body or association in the country or territory in which its head office is situated;

    (e)   the body or association has a membership composed of persons falling within any of the following categories, that is to say, authorised persons, exempt persons, and persons whose head offices are outside the United Kingdom and whose ordinary business involves them in engaging in activities which are activities of a kind specified by this Order (or would be apart from any exclusion made by this Part); and

    (f)   the body or association facilitates and regulates the activity of its members in the conduct of international securities business.

(4)   In paragraph (3)(f), "international securities business" means the business of buying, selling, subscribing for or underwriting investments (or agreeing to do so), either as principal or agent, where—

    (a)   the investments are securities or relevant investments and are of a kind which, by their nature, and the manner in which the business is conducted, may be expected normally to be bought or dealt in by persons sufficiently expert to understand the risks involved; and

    (b)   either the transaction is international or each of the parties may be expected to be indifferent to the location of the other;

and, for the purposes of this definition, it is irrelevant that the investments may ultimately be bought otherwise than in the course of such business by persons not so expert.

(5)   Any approval under this article is to be given by notice in writing; and the Treasury may by a further notice in writing withdraw any such approval if for any reason it appears to them that it is not appropriate to it to continue in force.

36.   Other exclusions

(1)   Article 25 is also subject to the exclusions in articles 66 (trustees etc), 67 (profession or non-investment business), 68 (sale of goods and supply of services), 69 (groups and joint enterprises), 70 (sale of body corporate), 71 (employee share schemes), 72 (overseas persons), 72A (information society services), 72B (activities carried on by a provider of relevant goods or services), 72C (provision of information about contracts of insurance on an incidental basis) and 72D (large risks contracts where risk situated outside the EEA).

(2)   Article 25A is also subject to the exclusions in articles 66 (trustees etc.), 67 (profession or non-investment business), 72 (overseas persons) and 72A (information society services).

CHAPTER VII
MANAGING INVESTMENTS

The activity

37.   Managing investments

Managing assets belonging to another person, in circumstances involving the exercise of discretion, is a specified kind of activity if—

(a)   the assets consist of or include any investment which is a security or a contractually based investment; or

(b)   the arrangements for their management are such that the assets may consist of or include such investments, and either the assets have at any time since 29th April 1988 done so, or the arrangements have at any time (whether before or after that date) been held out as arrangements under which the assets would do so.

Exclusions

38.   Attorneys

A person does not carry on an activity of the kind specified by article 37 if—

(a)   he is a person appointed to manage the assets in question under a power of attorney; and

(b)   all routine or day-to-day decisions, so far as relating to investments of a kind mentioned in article 37(a), are taken on behalf of that person by—

(i)   an authorised person with permission to carry on activities of the kind specified by article 37; ...

(ii)   a person who is an exempt person in relation to activities of that kind; or

(iii)   an overseas person.

39.   Other exclusions

Article 37 is also subject to the exclusions in articles 66 (trustees etc), 68 (sale of goods and supply of services), 69 (groups and joint enterprises), 72A (information society services) and 72C (provision of information about contracts of insurance on an incidental basis).

CHAPTER VIIA

ASSISTING IN THE ADMINISTRATION AND PERFORMANCE OF A CONTRACT OF INSURANCE

The activity

39A.   Assisting in the administration and performance of a contract of insurance

Assisting in the administration and performance of a contract of insurance is a specified kind of activity.

Exclusions

39B.   Claims management on behalf of an insurer etc.

(1)   A person does not carry on an activity of the kind specified by article 39A if he acts in the course of carrying on the activity of—

(a)   expert appraisal;

(b)   loss adjusting on behalf of a relevant insurer; or

(c)   managing claims on behalf of a relevant insurer,

and that activity is carried on in the course of carrying on any profession or business.

(2)   In this article—

(a)   "relevant insurer" means—

(i)   a person who has Part IV permission to carry on an activity of the kind specified by article 10;

(ii)   a person to whom the general prohibition does not apply by virtue of section 316(1)(a) of the Act (members of the Society of Lloyd's);

(iii)   an EEA firm falling within paragraph 5(d) of Schedule 3 to the Act (insurance undertaking); or

(iv)   a relevant reinsurer;

(b)   "relevant reinsurer" means a person whose main business consists of accepting risks ceded by—

(i)   a person falling within sub-paragraph (i), (ii) or (iii) of the definition of "relevant insurer"; or

(ii)   a person who is established outside the United Kingdom who carries on an activity of the kind specified by article 10 by way of business.

39C. Other exclusions

Article 39A is also subject to the exclusions in articles 66 (trustees etc.), 67 (profession or non-investment business), 72A (information society services), 72B (activities carried on by a provider of relevant goods or services), 72C (provision of information about contracts of insurance on an incidental basis) and 72D (large risks contracts where risk situated outside the EEA).

CHAPTER VIII
SAFEGUARDING AND ADMINISTERING INVESTMENTS

The activity

40. Safeguarding and administering investments

(1)   The activity consisting of both—

(a)   the safeguarding of assets belonging to another, and

(b)   the administration of those assets,

or arranging for one or more other persons to carry on that activity, is a specified kind of activity if the condition in sub-paragraph (a) or (b) of paragraph (2) is met.

(2)   The condition is that—

(a)   the assets consist of or include any investment which is a security or a contractually based investment; or

(b)   the arrangements for their safeguarding and administration are such that the assets may consist of or include such investments, and either the assets have at any time since 1st June 1997 done so, or the arrangements have at any time (whether before or after that date) been held out as ones under which such investments would be safeguarded and administered.

(3)   For the purposes of this article—

(a)   it is immaterial that title to the assets safeguarded and administered is held in uncertificated form;

(b)   it is immaterial that the assets safeguarded and administered may be transferred to another person, subject to a commitment by the person safeguarding and administering them, or arranging for their safeguarding and administration, that they will be replaced by equivalent assets at some future date or when so requested by the person to whom they belong.

Exclusions

41. Acceptance of responsibility by third party

(1)   There are excluded from article 40 any activities which a person carries on pursuant to arrangements which—

(a)   are ones under which a qualifying custodian undertakes to the person to whom the assets belong a responsibility in respect of the assets which is no less onerous than the qualifying custodian would have if the qualifying custodian were safeguarding and administering the assets; and

    (b)   are operated by the qualifying custodian in the course of carrying on in the United Kingdom an activity of the kind specified by article 40.

(2)   In paragraph (1), "qualifying custodian" means a person who is—

    (a)   an authorised person who has permission to carry on an activity of the kind specified by article 40, or

    (b)   an exempt person acting in the course of a business comprising a regulated activity in relation to which he is exempt.

42.   Introduction to qualifying custodians

(1)   There are excluded from article 40 any arrangements pursuant to which introductions are made by a person ("P") to a qualifying custodian with a view to the qualifying custodian providing in the United Kingdom a service comprising an activity of the kind specified by article 40, where the qualifying person (or other person who is to safeguard and administer the assets in question) is not connected with P.

(2)   For the purposes of paragraph (1)—

    (a)   "qualifying custodian" has the meaning given by article 41(2); and

    (b)   a person is connected with P if either he is a member of the same group as P, or P is remunerated by him.

43.   Activities not constituting administration

The following activities do not constitute the administration of assets for the purposes of article 40—

    (a)   providing information as to the number of units or the value of any assets safeguarded;

    (b)   converting currency;

    (c)   receiving documents relating to an investment solely for the purpose of onward transmission to, from or at the direction of the person to whom the investment belongs.

44.   Other exclusions

Article 40 is also subject to the exclusions in articles 66 (trustees etc), 67 (profession or non-investment business), 68 (sale of goods and supply of services), 69 (groups and joint enterprises), 71 (employee share schemes), 72A (information society services) and 72C (provision of information about contracts of insurance on an incidental basis).

CHAPTER IX
SENDING DEMATERIALISED INSTRUCTIONS

The activities

45.   Sending dematerialised instructions

(1)   Sending, on behalf of another person, dematerialised instructions relating to a security or a contractually based investment is a specified kind of activity, where those instructions are sent by means of a relevant system in respect of which an Operator is approved under the 2001 Regulations.

(2)   Causing dematerialised instructions relating to a security or a contractually based investment to be sent on behalf of another person by means of such a system is also a specified kind of activity where the person causing them to be sent is a system-participant.

(3)   In this Chapter—

    (a)   "the 2001 Regulations" means the Uncertificated Securities Regulations 2001; and

    (b)   "dematerialised instruction", "Operator", "settlement bank" and "system-participant" have the meaning given by regulation 3 of the 2001 Regulations.

46.   Instructions on behalf of participating issuers

There is excluded from article 45 the act of sending, or causing to be sent, a dematerialised instruction where the person on whose behalf the instruction is sent or caused to be sent is a participating issuer within the meaning of the 2001 Regulations.

47.   Instructions on behalf of settlement banks

There is excluded from article 45 the act of sending, or causing to be sent, a dematerialised instruction where the person on whose behalf the instruction is sent or caused to be sent is a settlement bank in its capacity as such.

48.   Instructions in connection with takeover offers

(1)   There is excluded from article 45 of the act of sending, or causing to be sent, a dematerialised instruction where the person on whose behalf the instruction is sent or caused to be sent is an offeror making a takeover offer.

(2)   In this article—

    (a)   "offeror" means, in the case of a takeover offer made by two or more persons jointly, the joint offers or any of them;

    (b)   "takeover offer" means—

        (i)   an offer to acquire shares (which in this sub-paragraph has the same meaning as in section 428(1) of the Companies Act 1985) in a body corporate incorporated in the United Kingdom which is a takeover offer within the meaning of Part XIIIA of that Act (or would be such an offer if that Part of that Act applied in relation to any body corporate);

        (ii)   an offer to acquire all or substantially all the shares, or all the shares of a particular class, in a body corporate incorporated outside the United Kingdom; or

        (iii)   an offer made to all the holders of shares, or shares of a particular class, in a body corporate to acquire a specified proportion of those shares;

but in determining whether an offer falls within paragraph (ii) there are to be disregarded any shares which the offeror or any associate of his (within the meaning of section 430E of the Companies Act 1985) holds or has contracted to acquire; and in determining whether an offer falls within paragraph (iii) the offeror, any such associate and any person whose shares the offeror or any such associate has contracted to acquire is not to be regarded as a holder of shares.

49.   Instructions in the course of providing a network

There is excluded from article 45 the act of sending, or causing to be sent, a dematerialised instruction as a necessary part of providing a network, the purpose of which is to carry dematerialised instructions which are at all time properly authenticated (within the meaning of the 2001 Regulations).

50.   Other exclusions

Article 45 is also subject to the exclusions in articles 66 (trustees etc), 69 (groups and joint enterprises) and 72A (information society services).

CHAPTER X
COLLECTIVE INVESTMENT SCHEMES

The activities

51.   Establishing etc a collective investment scheme

(1)   The following are specified kinds of activity—

    (a)   establishing, operating or winding up a collective investment scheme;

    (b)   acting as trustee of an authorised unit trust scheme;

    (c)   acting as the depositary or sole director of an open-ended investment company.

(2)   In this article, "trustee", "authorised unit trust scheme" and "depositary" have the meaning given by section 237 of the Act.

Exclusion

51A.   Information society services

Article 51 is subject to the exclusion in article 72A (information society services).

CHAPTER XI
STAKEHOLDER PENSION SCHEMES

The activities

52.   Establishing etc a stakeholder pension scheme

Establishing, operating or winding up a stakeholder pension scheme is a specified kind of activity.

Exclusion

52A.   Information society services

Article 52 is subject to the exclusion in article 72A (information society services).

CHAPTER XIA
PROVIDING BASIC ADVICE ON STAKEHOLDER PRODUCTS

The activity

52B.   Providing basic advice on stakeholder products

(1)   Providing basic advice to a retail consumer on a stakeholder product is a specified kind of activity.

(2)   For the purposes of paragraph (1), a person ("P") provides basic advice when—

(a)   he asks a retail consumer questions to enable him to assess whether a stakeholder product is appropriate for that consumer; and

(b)   relying on the information provided by the retail consumer P assesses that a stakeholder product is appropriate for the retail consumer and—

(i)   describes that product to that consumer;

(ii)   gives a recommendation of that product to that consumer; and

(c)   the retail consumer has indicated to P that he has understood the description and the recommendation in sub-paragraph (b).

(3)   In this article—

"retail consumer" means any person who is advised by P on the merits of opening or buying a stakeholder product in the course of a business carried on by P and who does not receive the advice in the course of a business carried on by him;

"stakeholder product" means—

(a)   an account which qualifies as a stakeholder child trust fund within the meaning given by the Child Trust Funds Regulations 2004;

(b)   rights under a relevant stakeholder pension scheme, and for these purposes—

"relevant stakeholder pension scheme" means a stakeholder pension scheme within the meaning given by section 1 of the Welfare Reform and Pensions Act 1999 and which is subject to lifestyling, and

"lifestyling" means the process, applied from a date at least five years before the member's retirement date, or, in the case of a member who joins the scheme less than five years before his retirement date, immediately after he becomes a member, and continuing until the member's retirement date, by which an investment strategy is adopted by the trustees or manager which aims progressively to minimise the variation or potential variation in the value of the member's rights caused by market conditions from time to time, and the words "member" and "scheme" have the same meaning as they have in the Welfare Reform and Pensions Act 1999;

(c)   an investment of a kind specified in regulations made by the Treasury.

CHAPTER XII
ADVISING ON INVESTMENTS

The activity

53.   Advising on investments

Advising a person is a specified kind of activity if the advice is—

(a)   given to the person in his capacity as an investor or potential investor, or in his capacity as agent for an investor or a potential investor; and

(b)   advice on the merits of his doing any of the following (whether as principal or agent)—

(i)   buying, selling, subscribing for or underwriting a particular investment which is a security or a relevant investment, or

(ii)   exercising any right conferred by such an investment to buy, sell, subscribe for or underwrite such an investment.

53A.   Advising on regulated mortgage contracts

(1)   Advising a person is a specified kind of activity if the advice—

(a)   is given to the person in his capacity as a borrower or potential borrower; and

(b)   is advice on the merits of his doing any of the following—

(i)   entering into a particular regulated mortgage contract, or

(ii)   varying the terms of a regulated mortgage contract entered into by him after the coming into force of article 61 in such a way as to vary his obligations under that contract.

(2)   In this article, "borrower" has the meaning given by article 61(3)(a)(i).

Exclusions

54.   Advice given in newspapers etc

(1)   There is excluded from article 53 and article 53A the giving of advice in writing or other legible form if the advice is contained in a newspaper, journal, magazine, or other periodical publication, or is given by way of a service comprising regularly updated news or information, if the principal purpose of the publication or service, taken as a whole and including any advertisements or other promotional material contained in it, is neither—

(a)   that of giving advice of a kind mentioned in article 53 or (as the case may be) article 53A; nor

(b)   that of leading or enabling persons—

(i)   to buy, sell, subscribe for or underwrite securities or contractually based investments, or (as the case may be),

(ii)   to enter as borrower into regulated mortgage contracts, or vary the terms of regulated mortgage contracts entered into by them as borrower.

(2)   There is also excluded from article 53 and article 53A the giving of advice in any service consisting of the broadcast or transmission of television or radio programmes, if the principal purpose of the service, taken as a whole and including any advertisements or other promotional material contained in it, is neither of those mentioned in paragraph (1)(a) and (b).

(3)   The Authority may, on the application of the proprietor of any such publication or service as is mentioned in paragraph (1) or (2), certify that it is of the nature described in that paragraph, and may revoke any such certificate if it considers that it is no longer justified.

(4)   A certificate given under paragraph (3) and not revoked is conclusive evidence of the matters certified.

54A.   Advice given in the course of administration by authorised person

A person who is not an authorised person ("A") does not carry on an activity of the kind specified by article 53A by reason of—

(a)   anything done by an authorised person ("B") in relation to a regulated mortgage contract which B is administering pursuant to arrangements of the kind mentioned in article 62(a); or

(b)   anything A does in connection with the administration of a regulated mortgage contract in circumstances falling within article 62(b).

55.   Other exclusions

(1)   Article 53 is also subject to the exclusions in articles 66 (trustees etc), 67, (profession or non-investment business), 68 (sale of goods and supply of services), 69 (groups and joint enterprises), 70 (sale of body corporate), 72 (overseas persons), 72A (information society services), 72B (activities carried on by a provider of relevant goods or services) and 72D (large risks contracts where risk situated outside the EEA).

(2)   Article 53A is also subject to the exclusions in articles 66 (trustees etc.), 67 (profession or non-investment business) and 72A (information society services).

CHAPTER XIII

LLOYD'S

The activities

56.   Advice on syndicate participation at Lloyd's

Advising a person to become, or continue or cease to be, a member of a particular Lloyd's syndicate is a specified kind of activity.

57.   Managing the underwriting capacity of a Lloyd's syndicate

Managing the underwriting capacity of a Lloyd's syndicate as a managing agent at Lloyd's is a specified kind of activity.

58.   Arranging deals in contracts of insurance written at Lloyd's

The arranging, by the society incorporated by Lloyd's Act 1871 by the name of Lloyd's, of deals in contracts of insurance written at Lloyd's, is a specified kind of activity.

Exclusion

58A.   Information society services

Articles 56 to 58 are subject to the exclusion in article 72A (information society services).

CHAPTER XIV

FUNERAL PLAN CONTRACTS

The activity

59.   Funeral plan contracts

(1)   Entering as provider into a funeral plan contract is a specified kind of activity.

(2)   A "funeral plan contract" is a contract (other than one excluded by article 60) under which—

(a)   a person ("the customer") makes one or more payments to another person ("the provider"); and

(b)   the provider undertakes to provide, or secure that another person provides, a funeral in the United Kingdom for the customer (or some other person who is living at the date when the contract is entered into) on his death;

unless, at the time of entering into the contract, the customer and the provider intend or expect the funeral to occur within one month.

Exclusions

60.   Plans covered by insurance or trust arrangements

(1)   There is excluded from article 59 any contract under which—

(a)   the provider undertakes to secure that sums paid by the customer under the contract will be applied towards a contract of whole life insurance on the life of the customer (or other person for whom the funeral is to be provided), effected and carried out by an authorised person who has permission to effect and carry out such contracts of insurance, for the purpose of providing the funeral; or

(b)   the provider undertakes to secure that sums paid by the customer under the contract will be held on trust for the purpose of providing the funeral, and that the following requirements are or will be met with respect to the trust—

(i)   the trust must be established by a written instrument;

(ii)   more than half of the trustees must be unconnected with the provider;

(iii)   the trustees must appoint, or have appointed, an independent fund manager who is an authorised person who has permission to carry on an activity of the kind specified by article 37, and who is a person who is unconnected with the provider, to manage the assets of the trust;

(iv)   annual accounts must be prepared, and audited by a person who is eligible for appointment as a company auditor under section 25 of the Companies Act 1989 , with respect to the assets and liabilities of the trust; and

(v)   the assets and liabilities of the trust must, at least once every three years, be determined, calculated and verified by an actuary who is a Fellow of the Institute of Actuaries or of the Faculty of Actuaries.

(2)   For the purposes of paragraph (1)(b)(ii) and (iii), a person is unconnected with the provider if he is a person other than—

(a)   the provider;

(b)   a member of the same group as the provider;

(c)   a director, other officer or employee of the provider, or of any member of the same group as the provider;

(d)   a partner of the provider;

(e)   a close relative of a person falling within sub-paragraph (a), (c) or (d); or

(f)   an agent of any person falling within sub-paragraphs (a) to (e).

60A.   Information society services

Article 59 is subject to the exclusion in article 72A (information society services).

CHAPTER XV
REGULATED MORTGAGE CONTRACTS

The activities

61.   Regulated mortgage contracts

(1)   Entering into a regulated mortgage contract as lender is a specified kind of activity.

(2)   Administering a regulated mortgage contract is also a specified kind of activity, where the contract was entered into *by way of business* after the coming into force of this article.

(3)   In this Chapter—

(a)   a "regulated mortgage contract" means a contract under which—

(i)   a person ("the lender") provides credit to an individual or to trustees ("the borrower"); and

(ii)   the obligation of the borrower to repay is secured by a first legal mortgage on land (other than timeshare accommodation) in the United Kingdom, at least 40% of which is used, or is intended to be used, as or in connection with a dwelling by the borrower or (in the case of credit provided to trustees) by an individual who is a beneficiary of the trust, or by a related person;

(b)   "administering" a regulated mortgage contract means either or both of—

      (i)   notifying the borrower of changes in interest rates or payments due under the contract, or of other matters of which the contract requires him to be notified; and

      (ii)   taking any necessary steps for the purposes of collecting or recovering payments due under the contract from the borrower;

but a person is not to be treated as administering a regulated mortgage contract merely because he has, or exercises, a right to take action for the purposes of enforcing the contract (or to require that such action is or is not taken);

(c)   "credit" includes a cash loan, and any other form of financial accommodation.

(4)   For the purposes of paragraph (3)(a)(ii)—

(a)   a "first legal mortgage" means a legal mortgage ranking in priority ahead of all other mortgages (if any) affecting the land in question, where "mortgage" includes charge and (in Scotland) a heritable security;

(b)   the area of any land which comprises a building or other structure containing two or more storeys is to be taken to be the aggregate of the floor areas of each of those storeys;

(c)   "related person", in relation to the borrower or (in the case of credit provided to trustees) a beneficiary of the trust, means—

      (i)   that person's spouse;

      (ii)   a person (whether or not of the opposite sex) whose relationship with that person has the characteristics of the relationship between husband and wife; or

      (iii)   that person's parent, brother, sister, child, grandparent or grandchild; and

(d)   "timeshare accommodation" has the meaning given by section 1 of the Timeshare Act 1992.

Note. The italicized words in paragraph (2) are inserted by S.I. 2001/3544, arts. 2, 8, as from a date to be notified in the London, Edinburgh and Belfast Gazettes.

Exclusions

62.   **Arranging administration by authorised person**

A person who is not an authorised person does not carry on an activity of the kind specified by article 61(2) in relation to a regulated mortgage contract where he—

(a)   arranges for another person, being an authorised person with permission to carry on an activity of that kind, to administer the contract; or

(b)   administers the contract himself during a period of not more than one month beginning with the day on which any such arrangement comes to an end.

63.   **Administration pursuant to agreement with authorised person**

A person who is not an authorised person does not carry on an activity of the kind specified by article 61(2) in relation to a regulated mortgage contract where he administers the contract pursuant to an agreement with an authorised person who has permission to carry on an activity of that kind.

63A.   **Other exclusions**

Article 61 is also subject to the exclusions in articles 66 (trustees etc), 72 (overseas persons) and 72A (information society services).

CHAPTER XVI
AGREEING TO CARRY ON ACTIVITIES

The activity

64. Agreeing to carry on specified kinds of activity

Agreeing to carry on an activity of the kind specified by any other provision of this Part (other than article 5, 9B, 10, 51 or 52) is a specified kind of activity.

Exclusions

65. Overseas persons etc

Article 64 is subject to the exclusions in articles 72 (overseas persons) and 72A (information society services).

CHAPTER XVII
EXCLUSIONS APPLYING TO
SEVERAL SPECIFIED KINDS OF ACTIVITY

66. Trustees, nominees and personal representatives

(1) A person ("X") does not carry on an activity of the kind specified by article 14 where he enters into a transaction as bare trustee or, in Scotland, as nominee for another person ("Y") and—

(a)   X is acting on Y's instructions; and

(b)   X does not hold himself out as providing a service of buying and selling securities or contractually based investments.

(2) Subject to paragraph (7), there are excluded from articles 25(1) and (2) and 25A(1) and (2) arrangements made by a person acting as trustee or personal representative for or with a view to a transaction which is or is to be entered into—

(a)   by that person and a fellow trustee or personal representative (acting in their capacity as such); or

(b)   by a beneficiary under the trust, will or intestacy.

(3) Subject to paragraph (7), there is excluded from article 37 any activity carried on by a person acting as trustee or personal representative, unless—

(a)   he holds himself out as providing a service comprising an activity of the kind specified by article 37; or

(b)   the assets in question are held for the purposes of an occupational pension scheme, and, by virtue of article 4 of the Financial Services and Markets Act 2000 (Carrying on Regulated Activities by Way of Business) Order 2001, he is to be treated as carrying on that activity by way of business.

(3A) Subject to paragraph (7), there is excluded from article 39A any activity carried on by a person acting as trustee or personal representative, unless he holds himself out as providing a service comprising an activity of the kind specified by article 39A.

(4) Subject to paragraph (7), there is excluded from article 40 any activity carried on by a person acting as trustee or personal representative, unless he holds himself out as providing a service comprising an activity of the kind specified by article 40.

(5) A person does not, by sending or causing to be sent a dematerialised instruction (within the meaning of article 45), carry on an activity of the kind specified by that article if the instruction relates to an investment which that person holds as trustee or personal representative.

(6) Subject to paragraph (7), there is excluded from articles 53 and 53A the giving of advice by a person acting as trustee or personal representative where he gives the advice to—

(a)   a fellow trustee or personal representative for the purposes of the trust or the estate; or

(b)   a beneficiary under the trust, will or intestacy concerning his interest in the trust fund or estate.

(6A) Subject to paragraph (7), a person acting as trustee or personal representative does not carry on an activity of the kind specified by article 61(1) or (2) where the borrower under the regulated mortgage contract in question is a beneficiary under the trust, will or intestacy.

(7) Paragraphs (2), (3), (3A), (4), (6) and (6A) do not apply if the person carrying on the activity is remunerated for what he does in addition to any remuneration he receives as trustee or personal representative, and for these purposes a person is not to be regarded as receiving additional remuneration merely because his remuneration is calculated by reference to time spent.

67. Activities carried on in the course of a profession or non-investment business

(1) There is excluded from articles 21, 25(1) and (2), 25A, 39A, 40, 53 and 53A any activity which—

    (a) is carried on in the course of carrying on any profession or business which does not otherwise consist of the carrying on of regulated activities in the United Kingdom; and

    (b) may reasonably be regarded as a necessary part of other services provided in the course of that profession or business.

(2) But the exclusion in paragraph (1) does not apply if the activity in question is remunerated separately from the other services.

68. Activities carried on in connection with the sale of goods or supply of services

(1) Subject to paragraphs (9), (10) and (11), this article concerns certain activities carried on for the purposes of or in connection with the sale of goods or supply of services by a supplier to a customer, where—

    "supplier" means a person whose main business is to sell goods or supply services and not to carry on any activities of the kind specified by any of articles 14, 21, 25, 37, 39A, 40, 45, 51, 52 and 53 and, where the supplier is a member of a group, also means any other member of that group; and

    "customer" means a person, other than an individual, to whom a supplier sells goods or supplies services, or agrees to do so, and, where the customer is a member of a group, also means any other member of that group;

and in this article "related sale or supply" means a sale of goods or supply of services to the customer otherwise than by the supplier, but for or in connection with the same purpose as the sale or supply mentioned above.

(2) There is excluded from article 14 any transaction entered into by a supplier with a customer, if the transaction is entered into for the purposes of or in connection with the sale of goods or supply of services, or a related sale or supply.

(3) There is excluded from article 21 any transaction entered into by a supplier as agent for a customer, if the transaction is entered into for the purposes of or in connection with the sale of goods or supply of services, or a related sale or supply, and provided that—

    (a) where the investment to which the transaction relates is a security, the supplier does not hold himself out (other than to the customer) as engaging in the business of buying securities of the kind to which the transaction relates with a view to selling them, and does not regularly solicit members of the public for the purpose of inducing them (as principals or agents) to buy, sell, subscribe for or underwrite securities;

    (b) where the investment to which the transaction relates is a contractually based investment, the supplier enters into the transaction—

        (i) with or through an authorised person, or an exempt person acting in the course of a business comprising a regulated activity in relation to which he is exempt; or

        (ii) through an office outside the United Kingdom maintained by a party to the transaction, and with or through a person whose head office is situated outside the United Kingdom and whose ordinary business involves him in carrying on activities of the kind specified by any of articles 14, 21, 25, 37, 40, 45, 51, 52 and 53 or, so far as relevant to any of those articles, article 64, or would do so apart from any exclusion from any of those articles made by this Order.

(4)   In paragraph (3)(a), "members of the public" has the meaning given by article 15(2), references to "A" being read as references to the supplier.

(5)   There are excluded from article 25(1) and (2) arrangements made by a supplier for, or with a view to, a transaction which is or is to be entered into by a customer for the purposes of or in connection with the sale of goods or supply of services, or a related sale or supply.

(6)   There is excluded from article 37 any activity carried on by a supplier where the assets in question—
       (a)   are those of a customer; and
       (b)   are managed for the purposes of or in connection with the sale of goods or supply of services, or a related sale or supply.

(7)   There is excluded from article 40 any activity carried on by a supplier where the assets in question are or are to be safeguarded and administered for the purposes of or in connection with the sale of goods or supply of services, or a related sale or supply.

(8)   There is excluded from article 53 the giving of advice by a supplier to a customer for the purposes of or in connection with the sale of goods or supply of services, or a related sale or supply, or to a person with whom the customer proposes to enter into a transaction for the purposes of or in connection with such a sale or supply or related sale or supply.

(9)   Paragraphs (2), (3) and (5) do not apply in the case of a transaction for the sale or purchase of a contract of insurance, an investment of the kind specified by article 81, or an investment of the kind specified by article 89 so far as relevant to such a contract or such an investment.

(10)   Paragraph (6) does not apply where the assets managed consist of qualifying contracts of insurance, investments of the kind specified by article 81, or investments of the kind specified by article 89 so far as relevant to such contracts or such investments.

(11)   Paragraph (8) does not apply in the case of advice in relation to an investment which is a contract of insurance, is of the kind specified by article 81, or is of the kind specified by article 89 so far as relevant to such a contract or such an investment.

69.   Groups and joint enterprises

(1)   There is excluded from article 14 any transaction into which a person enters as principal with another person if that other person is also acting as principal and—
       (a)   they are members of the same group; or
       (b)   they are, or propose to become, participators in a joint enterprise and the transaction is entered into for the purposes of or in connection with that enterprise.

(2)   There is excluded from article 21 any transaction into which a person enters as agent for another person if that other person is acting as principal, and the condition in paragraph (1)(a) or (b) is met, provided that—
       (a)   where the investment to which the transaction relates is a security, the agent does not hold himself out (other than to members of the same group or persons who are or propose to become participators with him in a joint enterprise) as engaging in the business of buying securities of the kind to which the transaction relates with a view to selling them, and does not regularly solicit members of the public for the purpose of inducing them (as principals or agents) to buy, sell, subscribe for or underwrite securities;
       (b)   where the investment to which the transaction relates is a contractually based investment, the agent enters into the transaction—
              (i)   with or through an authorised person, or an exempt person acting in the course of a business comprising a regulated activity in relation to which he is exempt; or
              (ii)   through an office outside the United Kingdom maintained by a party to the transaction, and with or through a person whose head office is situated outside the United Kingdom and whose ordinary business involves him in carrying on activities of the kind specified by any of articles 14, 21, 25, 37, 40, 45, 51, 52 and 53 or, so far as relevant to any of those articles, article 64, or would do so apart from any exclusion from any of those articles made by this Order.

(3)   In paragraph (2)(a), "members of the public" has the meaning given by article 15(2), references to "A" being read as references to the agent.

(4)   There are excluded from article 25(1) and (2) arrangements made by a person if—

    (a)   he is a member of a group and the arrangements in question are for, or with a view to, a transaction which is or is to be entered into, as principal, by another member of the same group; or

    (b)   he is or proposes to become a participator in a joint enterprise, and the arrangements in question are for, or with a view to, a transaction which is or is to be entered into, as principal, by another person who is or proposes to become a participator in that enterprise, for the purposes of or in connection with that enterprise.

(5)   There is excluded from article 37 any activity carried on by a person if—

    (a)   he is a member of a group and the assets in question belong to another member of the same group; or

    (b)   he is or proposes to become a participator in a joint enterprise with the person to whom the assets belong, and the assets are managed for the purposes of or in connection with that enterprise.

(6)   There is excluded from article 40 any activity carried on by a person if—

    (a)   he is a member of a group and the assets in question belong to another member of the same group; or

    (b)   he is or proposes to become a participator in a joint enterprise, and the assets in question—

        (i)   belong to another person who is or proposes to become a participator in that joint enterprise; and

        (ii)   are or are to be safeguarded and administered for the purposes of or in connection with that enterprise.

(7)   A person who is a member of a group does not carry on an activity of the kind specified by article 45 where he sends a dematerialised instruction, or causes one to be sent, on behalf of another member of the same group, if the investment to which the instruction relates is one in respect of which a member of the same group is registered as holder in the appropriate register of securities, or will be so registered as a result of the instruction.

(8)   In paragraph (7), "dematerialised instruction" and "register of securities" have the meaning given by regulation 3 of the Uncertificated Securities Regulations 2001.

(9)   There is excluded from article 53 the giving of advice by a person if—

    (a)   he is a member of a group and gives the advice in question to another member of the same group; or

    (b)   he is, or proposes to become, a participator in a joint enterprise and the advice in question is given to another person who is, or proposes to become, a participator in that enterprise for the purposes of or in connection with that enterprise.

(10)   Paragraph (2) does not apply to a transaction for the sale or purchase of a contract of insurance.

(11)   Paragraph (4) does not apply to arrangements for, or with a view to, a transaction for the sale or purchase of a contract of insurance.

(12)   Paragraph (9) does not apply where the advice relates to a transaction for the sale or purchase of a contract of insurance.

70.   Activities carried on in connection with the sale of a body corporate

(1)   A person does not carry on an activity of the kind specified by article 14 by entering as principal into a transaction if—

    (a)   the transaction is one to acquire or dispose of shares in a body corporate other than an open-ended investment company, or is entered into for the purposes of such an acquisition or disposal; and

    (b)   either—

        (i)   the conditions set out in paragraph (2) are met; or

(ii) those conditions are not met, but the object of the transaction may nevertheless reasonably be regarded as being the acquisition of day to day control of the affairs of the body corporate.

(2) The conditions mentioned in paragraph (1)(b) are that—

  (a) the shares consist of or include 50 per cent or more of the voting shares in the body corporate; or

  (b) the shares, together with any already held by the person acquiring them, consist of or include at least that percentage of such shares; and

  (c) in either case, the acquisition or disposal is between parties each of whom is a body corporate, a partnership, a single individual or a group of connected individuals.

(3) In paragraph (2)(c), "a group of connected individuals" means—

  (a) in relation to a party disposing of shares in a body corporate, a single group of persons each of whom is—

    (i) a director or manager of the body corporate;

    (ii) a close relative of any such director or manager;

    (iii) a person acting as trustee for any person falling within paragraph (i) or (ii); and

  (b) in relation to a party acquiring shares in a body corporate, a single group of persons each of whom is—

    (i) a person who is or is to be a director or manager of the body corporate;

    (ii) a close relative of any such person; or

    (iii) a person acting as trustee for any person falling within paragraph (i) or (ii).

(4) A person does not carry on an activity of the kind specified by article 21 by entering as agent into a transaction of the kind described in paragraph (1).

(5) There are excluded from article 25(1) and (2) arrangements made for, or with a view to, a transaction of the kind described in paragraph (1).

(6) There is excluded from article 53 the giving of advice in connection with a transaction (or proposed transaction) of the kind described in paragraph (1).

(7) Paragraphs (4), (5) and (6) do not apply in the case of a transaction for the sale or purchase of a contract of insurance.

71.   Activities carried on in connection with employee share schemes

(1) A person ("C"), a member of the same group as C or a relevant trustee does not carry on an activity of the kind specified by article 14 by entering as principal into a transaction the purpose of which is to enable or facilitate—

  (a) transactions in shares in, or debentures issued by, C between, or for the benefit of, any of the persons mentioned in paragraph (2); or

  (b) the holding of such shares or debentures by, or for the benefit of, such persons.

(2) The persons referred to in paragraph (1) are—

  (a) the bona fide employees or former employees of C or of another member of the same group as C;

  (b) the wives, husbands, widows, widowers, or children or step-children under the age of eighteen of such employees or former employees.

(3) C, a member of the same group as C or a relevant trustee does not carry on an activity of the kind specified by article 21 by entering as agent into a transaction of the kind described in paragraph (1).

(4) There are excluded from article 25(1) or (2) arrangements made by C, a member of the same group as C or a relevant trustee if the arrangements in question are for, or with a view to, a transaction of the kind described in paragraph (1).

(5) There is excluded from article 40 any activity if the assets in question are, or are to be, safeguarded and administered by C, a member of the same group as C or a relevant trustee for the purpose of enabling or facilitating transactions of the kind described in paragraph (1).

(6) In this article—

  (a) "shares" and "debentures" include—

　　　　　　　(i)　any investment of the kind specified by article 76 or 77;

　　　　　　　(ii)　any investment of the kind specified by article 79 or 80 so far as relevant to articles 76 and 77; and

　　　　　　　(iii)　any investment of the kind specified by article 89 so far as relevant to investments of the kind mentioned in paragraph (i) or (ii);

　　　(b)　"relevant trustee" means a person who, in pursuance of the arrangements made for the purpose mentioned in paragraph (1), holds, as trustee, shares in or debentures issued by C.

72.　Overseas persons

(1)　An overseas person does not carry on an activity of the kind specified by article 14 by—

　　　(a)　entering into a transaction as principal with or though an authorised person, or an exempt person acting in the course of a business comprising a regulated activity in relation to which he is exempt; or

　　　(b)　entering into a transaction as principal with a person in the United Kingdom, if the transaction is the result of a legitimate approach.

(2)　An overseas person does not carry on an activity of the kind specified by article 21 by—

　　　(a)　entering into a transaction as agent for any person with or through an authorised person or an exempt person acting in the course of a business comprising a regulated activity in relation to which he is exempt; or

　　　(b)　entering into a transaction with another party ("X") as agent for any person ("Y"), other than with or through an authorised person or such an exempt person, unless—

　　　　　　　(i)　either X or Y is in the United Kingdom; and

　　　　　　　(ii)　the transaction is the result of an approach (other than a legitimate approach) made by or on behalf of, or to, whichever of X or Y is in the United Kingdom.

(3)　There are excluded from article 25(1) arrangements made by an overseas person with an authorised person, or an exempt person acting in the course of a business comprising a regulated activity in relation to which he is exempt.

(4)　There are excluded from article 25(2) arrangements made by an overseas person with a view to transactions which are, as respects transactions in the United Kingdom, confined to—

　　　(a)　transactions entered into by authorised persons as principal or agent; and

　　　(b)　transactions entered into by exempt persons, as principal or agent, in the course of business comprising regulated activities in relation to which they are exempt.

(5)　There is excluded from article 53 the giving of advice by an overseas person as a result of a legitimate approach.

(5A)　An overseas person does not carry on an activity of the kind specified by article 25A(1)(a) where each person who may be contemplating entering into a regulated mortgage contract as borrower is a non-resident individual.

(5B)　There are excluded from article 25A(1)(b) arrangements made by an overseas person to vary the terms of a qualifying contract.

(5C)　There are excluded from article 25A(2) arrangements made by an overseas person which are made solely with a view to non-resident individuals who participate in those arrangements entering as borrower into regulated mortgage contracts.

(5D)　An overseas person does not carry on an activity of the kind specified by article 61(1) by entering into a qualifying contract.

(5E)　An overseas person does not carry on an activity of the kind specified by article 61(2) where he administers a qualifying contract.

(5F)　In paragraphs (5A) to (5E)—

　　　(a)　"non-resident individual" means an individual who is not normally resident in the United Kingdom; and

　　　(b)　"qualifying contract" means a regulated mortgage contract within the meaning of article 61(3)(a), the borrower or, as the case may be, each borrower under which is (or was) a non-resident individual at the time when he enters (or entered) into the contract.

(6)   There is excluded from article 64 any agreement made by an overseas person to carry on an activity of the kind specified by article 25(1) or (2), 37, 39A, 40 or 45 if the agreement is the result of a legitimate approach.

(7)   In this article, "legitimate approach" means—

(a)   an approach made to the overseas person which has not been solicited by him in any way, or has been solicited by him in a way which does not contravene section 21 of the Act; or

(b)   an approach made by or on behalf of the overseas person in a way which does not contravene that section.

72A. Information society services

(1)   There is excluded from this Part any activity consisting of the provision of an information society service from an EEA State other than the United Kingdom.

(2)   The exclusion in paragraph (1) does not apply to the activity of effecting or carrying out a contract of insurance as principal, where—

(a)   the activity is carried on by an undertaking which has received official authorisation in accordance with Article 4 of the life assurance consolidation directive or the first non-life insurance directive, and

(b)   the insurance falls within the scope of any of the insurance directives.

72B. Activities carried on by a provider of relevant goods or services

(1)   In this article—

"connected contract of insurance" means a contract of insurance which—

(a)   is not a contract of long-term insurance;

(b)   has a total duration (or would have a total duration were any right to renew conferred by the contract exercised) of five years or less;

(c)   has an annual premium (or, where the premium is paid otherwise than by way of annual premium, the equivalent of an annual premium) of 500 euro or less, or the equivalent amount in sterling or other currency;

(d)   covers the risk of—

(i)   breakdown, loss of, or damage to, non-motor goods supplied by the provider; or

(ii)   damage to, or loss of, baggage and other risks linked to the travel booked with the provider ("travel risks");

(e)   does not cover any liability risks (except, in the case of a contract which covers travel risks, where that cover is ancillary to the main cover provided by the contract);

(f)   is complementary to the non-motor goods being supplied or service being provided by the provider; and

(g)   is of such a nature that the only information that a person requires in order to carry on an activity of the kind specified by article 21, 25, 39A or 53 in relation to it is the cover provided by the contract;

"non-motor goods" means goods which are not mechanically propelled road vehicles;

"provider" means a person who supplies non-motor goods or provides services related to travel in the course of carrying on a profession or business which does not otherwise consist of the carrying on of regulated activities.

(2)   There is excluded from article 21 any transaction for the sale or purchase of a connected contract of insurance into which a provider enters as agent.

(3)   There are excluded from article 25(1) and (2) any arrangements made by a provider for, or with a view to, a transaction for the sale or purchase of a connected contract of insurance.

(4)   There is excluded from article 39A any activity carried on by a provider where the contract of insurance in question is a connected contract of insurance.

(5)   There is excluded from article 53 the giving of advice by a provider in relation to a transaction for the sale or purchase of a connected contract of insurance.

(6)   For the purposes of this article, a contract of insurance which covers travel risks is not to be treated as a contract of long-term insurance, notwithstanding the fact that it contains related and

subsidiary provisions such that it might be regarded as a contract of long-term insurance, if the cover to which those provisions relate is ancillary to the main cover provided by the contract.

72C.   Provision of information on an incidental basis

(1)   There is excluded from articles 25(1) and (2) the making of arrangements for, or with a view to, a transaction for the sale or purchase of a contract of insurance or an investment of the kind specified by article 89, so far as relevant to such a contract, where that activity meets the conditions specified in paragraph (4).

(2)   There is excluded from articles 37 and 40 any activity—

(a)   where the assets in question are rights under a contract of insurance or an investment of the kind specified by article 89, so far as relevant to such a contract; and

(b)   which meets the conditions specified in paragraph (4).

(3)   There is excluded from article 39A any activity which meets the conditions specified in paragraph (4).

(4)   The conditions specified in this paragraph are that the activity—

(a)   consists of the provision of information to the policyholder or potential policyholder;

(b)   is carried on by a person in the course of carrying on a profession or business which does not otherwise consist of the carrying on of regulated activities; and

(c)   may reasonably be regarded as being incidental to that profession or business.

72D.   Large risks contracts where risk situated outside the EEA

(1)   There is excluded from articles 21, 25(1) and (2), 39A and 53 any activity which is carried on in relation to a large risks contract of insurance, to the extent that the risk or commitment covered by the contract is not situated in an EEA State.

(2)   In this article, a "large risks contract of insurance" is a contract of insurance the principal object of which is to cover—

(a)   risks falling within paragraph 4 (railway rolling stock), 5 (aircraft), 6 (ships), 7 (goods in transit), 11 (aircraft liability) or 12 (liability of ships) of Part 1 of Schedule 1;

(b)   risks falling within paragraph 14 (credit) or 15 (suretyship) of that Part provided that the risks relate to a business carried on by the policyholder; or

(c)   risks falling within paragraph 3 (land vehicles), 8 (fire and natural forces), 9 (damage to property), 10 (motor vehicle liability), 13 (general liability) or 16 (miscellaneous financial loss) of that Part provided that the risks relate to a business carried on by the policyholder and that the condition specified in paragraph (3) is met in relation to that business.

(3)   The condition specified in this paragraph is that at least two of the three following criteria were met in the most recent financial year for which information is available—

(a)   the balance sheet total of the business (within the meaning of section 247(5) of the Companies Act 1985 or article 255(5) of the Companies (Northern Ireland) Order 1986) exceeded 6.2 million euro,

(b)   the net turnover (within the meaning given to "turnover" by section 262(1) of that Act or article 270(1) of that Order) exceeded 12.8 million euro,

(c)   the number of employees (within the meaning given by section 247(6) of that Act or article 255(6) of that Order) exceeded 250,

and for a financial year which is a company's financial year but not in fact a year, the net turnover of the policyholder shall be proportionately adjusted.

(4)   For the purposes of paragraph (3), where the policyholder is a member of a group for which consolidated accounts (within the meaning of the Seventh Company Law Directive) are drawn up, the question whether the condition specified by that paragraph is met is to be determined by reference to those accounts.

PART III
SPECIFIED INVESTMENTS

73. Investments: general

The following kinds of investment are specified for the purposes of section 22 of the Act.

74. Deposits

A deposit.

74A. Electronic money

Electronic money.

75. Contracts of insurance

Rights under a contract of insurance.

76. Shares etc

(1) Shares or stock in the share capital of—

    (a) any body corporate (wherever incorporated), and

    (b) any unincorporated body constituted under the law of a country or territory outside the United Kingdom.

(2) Paragraph (1) includes—

    (a) any shares of a class defined as deferred shares for the purposes of section 119 of the Building Societies Act 1986; and

    (b) any transferable shares in a body incorporated under the law of, or any part of, the United Kingdom relating to industrial and provident societies or credit unions, or in a body constituted under the law of another EEA State for purposes equivalent to those of such a body.

(3) But subject to paragraph (2) there are excluded from paragraph (1) shares or stock in the share capital of—

    (a) an open-ended investment company;

    (b) a building society incorporated under the law of, or any part of, the United Kingdom;

    (c) a body incorporated under the law of, or any part of, the United Kingdom relating to industrial and provident societies or credit unions;

    (d) any body constituted under the law of an EEA State for purposes equivalent to those of a body falling within sub-paragraph (b) or (c).

77. Instruments creating or acknowledging indebtedness

(1) Subject to paragraph (2), such of the following as do not fall within article 78—

    (a) debentures;

    (b) debenture stock;

    (c) loan stock;

    (d) bonds;

    (e) certificates of deposit;

    (f) any other instrument creating or acknowledging indebtedness.

(2) If and to the extent that they would otherwise fall within paragraph (1), there are excluded from that paragraph—

    (a) an instrument acknowledging or creating indebtedness for, or for money borrowed to defray, the consideration payable under a contract for the supply of goods or services;

    (b) a cheque or other bill of exchange, a banker's draft or a letter of credit (but not a bill of exchange accepted by a banker);

    (c) a banknote, a statement showing a balance on a current, deposit or savings account, a lease or other disposition of property, or a heritable security; and

    (d) a contract of insurance.

(3)   An instrument excluded from paragraph (1) of article 78 by paragraph (2)(b) of that article is not thereby to be taken to fall within paragraph (1) of this article.

78.   Government and public securities

(1)   Subject to paragraph (2), loan stock, bonds and other instruments creating or acknowledging indebtedness, issued by or on behalf of any of the following—

        (a)   the government of the United Kingdom;

        (b)   the Scottish Administration;

        (c)   the Executive Committee of the Northern Ireland Assembly;

        (d)   the National Assembly for Wales;

        (e)   the government of any country or territory outside the United Kingdom;

        (f)   a local authority in the United Kingdom or elsewhere; or

        (g)   a body the members of which comprise—

              (i)   states including the United Kingdom or another EEA State; or

              (ii)   bodies whose members comprise states including the United Kingdom or another EEA State.

(2)   There are excluded from paragraph (1)—

        (a)   so far as applicable, the instruments mentioned in article 77(2)(a) to (d);

        (b)   any instrument creating or acknowledging indebtedness in respect of—

              (i)   money received by the Director of Savings as deposits or otherwise in connection with the business of the National Savings Bank;

              (ii)   money raised under the National Loans Act 1968 under the auspices of the Director of Savings or treated as so raised by virtue of section 11(3) of the National Debt Act 1972.

79.   Instruments giving entitlements to investments

(1)   Warrants and other instruments entitling the holder to subscribe for any investment of the kind specified by article 76, 77 or 78.

(2)   It is immaterial whether the investment to which the entitlement relates is in existence or identifiable.

(3)   An investment of the kind specified by this article is not to be regarded as falling within article 83, 84 or 85.

80.   Certificates representing certain securities

(1)   Subject to paragraph (2), certificates or other instruments which confer contractual or property rights (other than rights consisting of an investment of the kind specified by article 83)—

        (a)   in respect of any investment of the kind specified by any of articles 76 to 79, being an investment held by a person other than the person on whom the rights are conferred by the certificate or instrument; and

        (b)   the transfer of which may be effected without the consent of that person.

(2)   There is excluded from paragraph (1) any certificate or other instrument which confers rights in respect of two or more investments issued by different persons, or in respect of two or more different investments of the kind specified by article 78 and issued by the same person.

81.   Units in a collective investment scheme

Units in a collective investment scheme (within the meaning of Part XVII of the Act).

82.   Rights under a stakeholder pension scheme

Rights under a stakeholder pension scheme.

83.   Options

Options to acquire or dispose of—

        (a)   a security or contractually based investment (other than one of a kind specified by this article);

        (b)   currency of the United Kingdom or any other country or territory;

(c)   palladium, platinum, gold or silver; or

(d)   an option to acquire or dispose of an investment of the kind specified by this article by virtue of paragraph (a), (b) or (c).

84.   Futures

(1)   Subject to paragraph (2), rights under a contract for the sale of a commodity or property of any other description under which delivery is to be made at a future date and at a price agreed on when the contract is made.

(2)   There are excluded from paragraph (1) rights under any contract which is made for commercial and not investment purposes.

(3)   A contract is to be regarded as made for investment purposes if it is made or traded on a recognised investment exchange, or is made otherwise than on a recognised investment exchange but is expressed to be as traded on such an exchange or on the same terms as those on which an equivalent contract would be made on such an exchange.

(4)   A contract not falling within paragraph (3) is to be regarded as made for commercial purposes if under the terms of the contract delivery is to be made within seven days, unless it can be shown that there existed an understanding that (notwithstanding the express terms of the contract) delivery would not be made within seven days.

(5)   The following are indications that a contract not falling within paragraph (3) or (4) is made for commercial purposes and the absence of them is an indication that it is made for investment purposes—

(a)   one or more of the parties is a producer of the commodity or other property, or uses it in his business;

(b)   the seller delivers or intends to deliver the property or the purchaser takes or intends to take delivery of it.

(6)   It is an indication that a contract is made for commercial purposes that the prices, the lot, the delivery date or other terms are determined by the parties for the purposes of the particular contract and not by reference (or not solely by reference) to regularly published prices, to standard lots or delivery dates or to standard terms.

(7)   The following are indications that a contract is made for investment purposes—

(a)   it is expressed to be as traded on an investment exchange;

(b)   performance of the contract is ensured by an investment exchange or a clearing house;

(c)   there are arrangements for the payment or provision of margin.

(8)   For the purposes of paragraph (1), a price is to be taken to be agreed on when a contract is made—

(a)   notwithstanding that it is left to be determined by reference to the price at which a contract is to be entered into on a market or exchange or could be entered into at a time and place specified in the contract; or

(b)   in a case where the contract is expressed to be by reference to a standard lot and quality, notwithstanding that provision is made for a variation in the price to take account of any variation in quantity or quality on delivery.

85.   Contracts for differences etc

(1)   Subject to paragraph (2), rights under—

(a)   a contract for differences; or

(b)   any other contract the purpose or pretended purpose of which is to secure a profit or avoid a loss by reference to fluctuations in—

(i)   the value or price of property of any description; or

(ii)   an index or other factor designated for that purpose in the contract.

(2)   There are excluded from paragraph (1)—

(a)   rights under a contract if the parties intend that the profit is to be secured or the loss is to be avoided by one or more of the parties taking delivery of any property to which the contract relates;

(b)   rights under a contract under which money is received by way of deposit on terms that any interest or other return to be paid on the sum deposited will be calculated by reference to fluctuations in an index or other factor;

(c)   rights under any contract under which—

    (i)   money is received by the Director of Savings as deposits or otherwise in connection with the business of the National Savings Bank; or

    (ii)   money is raised under the National Loans Act 1968 under the auspices of the Director of Savings or treated as so raised by virtue of section 11(3) of the National Debt Act 1972;

(d)   rights under a qualifying contract of insurance.

86.   Lloyd's syndicate capacity and syndicate membership

(1)   The underwriting capacity of a Lloyd's syndicate.

(2)   A person's membership (or prospective membership) of a Lloyd's syndicate.

87.   Funeral plan contracts

Rights under a funeral plan contract.

88.   Regulated mortgage contracts

Rights under a regulated mortgage contract.

89.   Rights to or interests in investments

(1)   Subject to paragraphs (2) to (4), any right to or interest in anything which is specified by any other provision of this Part (other than article 88).

(2)   Paragraph (1) does not include interests under the trusts of an occupational pension scheme.

(3)   Paragraph (1) does not include—

(a)   rights to or interests in a contract of insurance of the kind referred to in paragraph (1)(a) of article 60; or

(b)   interests under a trust of the kind referred to in paragraph (1)(b) of that article.

(4)   Paragraph (1) does not include anything which is specified by any other provision of this Part.

PART IV
CONSEQUENTIAL PROVISIONS

Regulated mortgage contracts: consequential provisions

90, 91. ...

PART V
UNATHORISED PERSONS CARRYING ON INSURANCE MEDIATION ACTIVITIES

92.   Interpretation

In this Part—

"designated professional body" means a body which is for the time being designated by the Treasury under section 326 of the Act (designation of professional bodies);

"insurance mediation activity" means any regulated activity of the kind specified by article 21, 25(1) or (2), 39A or 53, or, so far as relevant to any of those articles, article 64, which is carried on in relation to a contract of insurance;

"the record" means the record maintained by the Authority under section 347 of the Act (public record of authorised persons etc.);

"recorded insurance intermediary" has the meaning given by article 93(4);

"a relevant member", in relation to a designated professional body, means a member (within the meaning of section 325(2) of the Act) of the profession in relation to which that designated professional body is established, or a person who is controlled or managed by one or more such members.

93.   Duty to maintain a record of unauthorised persons carrying on insurance mediation activities

(1)   Subject to articles 95 and 96, the Authority must include in the record every person who—

    (a)   as a result of information obtained by virtue of its rules or by virtue of a direction given, or requirement imposed, under section 51(3) of the Act (procedure for applications under Part IV), appears to the Authority to fall within paragraph (2); or

    (b)   as a result of information obtained by virtue of article 94, appears to the Authority to fall within paragraph (3).

(2)   A person falls within this paragraph if he is, or has entered into a contract by virtue of which he will be, an appointed representative who carries on any insurance mediation activity.

(3)   A person falls within this paragraph if—

    (a)   he is a relevant member of a designated professional body who carries on, or is proposing to carry on, any insurance mediation activity; and

    (b)   the general prohibition does not (or will not) apply to the carrying on of those activities by virtue of section 327 of the Act (exemption from the general prohibition).

(4)   In this Part, "recorded insurance intermediary" means a person who is included in the record by virtue of paragraph (1).

(5)   The record must include—

    (a)   in the case of any recorded insurance intermediary, its address; and

    (b)   in the case of a recorded insurance intermediary which is not an individual, the name of the individuals who are responsible for the management of the business carried on by the intermediary, so far as it relates to insurance mediation activities.

94.   Members of designated professional bodies

(1)   A designated professional body must, by notice in writing, inform the Authority of—

    (a)   the name,

    (b)   the address, and

    (c)   in the case of a relevant member which is not an individual, the name of the individuals who are responsible for the management of the business carried on by the member, so far as it relates to insurance mediation activities,

    of any relevant member who falls within paragraph (2).

(2)   A relevant member of a designated professional body falls within this paragraph if, in accordance with the rules of that body, he carries on, or proposes to carry on any insurance mediation activity but does not have, and does not propose to apply for, Part IV permission on the basis that the general prohibition does not (or will not) apply to the carrying on of that activity by virtue of section 327 of the Act.

(3)   A designated professional body must also, by notice in writing, inform the Authority of any change in relation to the matters specified in sub-paragraphs (a) to (c) of paragraph (1).

(4)   A designated professional body must inform the Authority when a relevant member to whom paragraph (2) applies ceases, for whatever reason, to carry on insurance mediation activities.

(5)   The Authority may give directions to a designated professional body as to the manner in which the information referred to in paragraphs (1), (3) and (4) must be provided.

95.   Exclusion from record where not fit and proper to carry on insurance mediation activities

(1)   If it appears to the Authority that a person who falls within article 93(2) (appointed representatives) ("AR") is not a fit and proper person to carry on insurance mediation activities, it may decide not to include him in the record or, if that person is already included in the record, to remove him from the record.

(2)   Where the Authority proposes to make a determination under paragraph (1), it must give AR a warning notice.

(3)   If the Authority makes a determination under paragraph (1), it must give AR a decision notice.

(4)   If the Authority gives AR a decision notice under paragraph (3), AR may refer the matter to the Tribunal.

(5)   The Authority may, on the application of AR, revoke a determination under paragraph (1).

(6)   If the Authority decides to grant the application, it must give AR written notice of its decision.

(7)   If the Authority proposes to refuse the application, it must give AR a warning notice.

(8)   If the Authority decides to refuse the application, it must give AR a decision notice.

(9)   If the Authority gives AR a decision notice under paragraph (8), AR may refer the matter to the Tribunal.

(10)   Sections 393 and 394 of the Act (third party rights and access to Authority material) apply to a warning notice given in accordance with paragraph (2) or (7) and to a decision notice given in accordance with paragraph (3) or (8).

96.   Exclusion from the record where Authority has exercised its powers under Part XX of the Act

(1)   If a person who appears to the Authority to fall within article 93(3) (member of a designated professional body) falls within paragraph (2) or (3), the Authority must not include him in the record or, if that person is already included in the record, must remove him from the record.

(2)   A person falls within this paragraph if, by virtue of a direction given by the Authority under section 328(1) of the Act (directions in relation to the general prohibition), section 327(1) of the Act does not apply in relation to the carrying on by him of any insurance mediation activity.

(3)   A person falls within this paragraph if the Authority has made an order under section 329(2) of the Act (orders in relation to the general prohibition) disapplying section 327(1) of the Act in relation to the carrying on by him of any insurance mediation activity.

PART 6
MISCELLANEOUS

97.   Disapplication of section 49(2) of the Act

In section 49 of the Act (persons connected with an applicant for Part 4 permission), after subsection (2) insert—

"(2A)   But subsection (2) does not apply to the extent that the permission relates to—

(a)   an insurance mediation activity (within the meaning given by paragraph 2(5) of Schedule 6); or

(b)   a regulated activity involving a regulated mortgage contract.".

SCHEDULE 1

CONTRACTS OF INSURANCE

Article 3(1)

PART I
CONTRACTS OF GENERAL INSURANCE

1.   Accident

Contracts of insurance providing fixed pecuniary benefits or benefits in the nature of indemnity (or a combination of both) against risks of the person insured or, in the case of a contract made by virtue of section 140, 140A or 140B of the Local Government Act 1972 (or, in Scotland, section 86(1) of the Local Government (Scotland) Act 1973), a person for whose benefit the contract is made—

(a)   sustaining injury as the result of an accident or of an accident of a specified class; or

(b)   dying as a result of an accident or of an accident of a specified class; or

(c)   becoming incapacitated in consequence of disease or of disease of a specified class,

including contracts relating to industrial injury and occupational disease but excluding contracts falling within paragraph 2 of Part I of, or paragraph IV of Part II of, this Schedule.

2.   **Sickness**

Contracts of insurance providing fixed pecuniary benefits or benefits in the nature of indemnity (or a combination of both) against risks of loss to the persons insured attributable to sickness or infirmity but excluding contracts falling within paragraph IV of Part II of this Schedule.

3.   **Land vehicles**

Contracts of insurance against loss of or damage to vehicles used on land, including motor vehicles but excluding railway rolling stock.

4.   **Railway rolling stock**

Contract of insurance against loss of or damage to railway rolling stock.

5.   **Aircraft**

Contracts of insurance upon aircraft or upon the machinery, tackle, furniture or equipment of aircraft.

6.   **Ships**

Contracts of insurance upon vessels used on the sea or on inland water, or upon the machinery, tackle, furniture or equipment of such vessels.

7.   **Goods in transit**

Contracts of insurance against loss of or damage to merchandise, baggage and all other goods in transit, irrespective of the form of transport.

8.   **Fire and natural forces**

Contracts of insurance against loss of or damage to property (other than property to which paragraphs 3 to 7 relate) due to fire, explosion, storm, natural forces other than storm, nuclear energy or land subsidence.

9.   **Damage to property**

Contracts of insurance against loss of or damage to property (other than property to which paragraphs 3 to 7 relate) due to hail or frost or any other event (such as theft) other than those mentioned in paragraph 8.

10.   **Motor vehicle liability**

Contracts of insurance against damage arising out of or in connection with the use of motor vehicles on land, including third-party risks and carrier's liability.

11.   **Aircraft liability**

Contracts of insurance against damage arising out of or in connection with the use of aircraft, including third-party risks and carrier's liability.

12.   **Liability of ships**

Contracts of insurance against damage arising out of or in connection with the use of vessels on the sea or on inland water, including third party risks and carrier's liability.

13.   **General liability**

Contracts of insurance against risks of the persons insured incurring liabilities to third parties, the risks in question not being risks to which paragraph 10, 11 or 12 relates.

14.   **Credit**

Contracts of insurance against risks of loss to the persons insured arising from the insolvency of debtors of theirs or from the failure (otherwise than through insolvency) of debtors of theirs to pay their debts when due.

15.   Suretyship

(1)   Contracts of insurance against the risks of loss to the persons insured arising from their having to perform contracts of guarantee entered into by them.

(2)   Fidelity bonds, performance bonds, administration bonds, bail bonds or customs bonds or similar contracts of guarantee, where these are—

(a)   effected or carried out by a person not carrying on a banking business;

(b)   not effected merely incidentally to some other business carried on by the person effecting them; and

(c)   effected in return for the payment of one or more premiums.

16.   Miscellaneous financial loss

Contracts of insurance against any of the following risks, namely—

(a)   risks of loss to the persons insured attributable to interruptions of the carrying on of business carried on by them or to reduction of the scope of business so carried on;

(b)   risks of loss to the persons insured attributable to their incurring unforeseen expense (other than loss such as is covered by contracts falling within paragraph 18);

(c)   risks which do not fall within sub-paragraph (a) or (b) and which are not of a kind such that contracts of insurance against them fall within any other provision of this Schedule.

17.   Legal expenses

Contracts of insurance against risks of loss to the persons insured attributable to their incurring legal expenses (including costs of litigation).

18.   Assistance

Contracts of insurance providing either or both of the following benefits, namely—

(a)   assistance (whether in cash or in kind) for persons who get into difficulties while travelling, while away from home or while away from their permanent residence; or

(b)   assistance (whether in cash or in kind) for persons who get into difficulties otherwise than as mentioned in sub-paragraph (a).

PART II

CONTRACTS OF LONG-TERM INSURANCE

I.   Life and annuity

Contracts of insurance on human life or contracts to pay annuities on human life, but excluding (in each case) contracts within paragraph III.

II.   Marriage and birth

Contract of insurance to provide a sum on marriage or on the birth of a child, being contracts expressed to be in effect for a period of more than one year.

III.   Linked long term

Contracts of insurance on human life or contracts to pay annuities on human life where the benefits are wholly or party to be determined by references to the value of, or the income from, property of any description (whether or not specified in the contracts) or by reference to fluctuations in, or in an index of, the value of property of any description (whether or not so specified).

IV.   Permanent health

Contracts of insurance providing specified benefits against risks of persons becoming incapacitated in consequence of sustaining injury as a result of an accident or of an accident of a specified class or of sickness or infirmity, being contracts that—

(a)   are expressed to be in effect for a period of not less than five years, or until the normal retirement age for the persons concerned, or without limit of time; and

(b)   either are not expressed to be terminable by the insurer, or are expressed to be so terminable only in special circumstances mentioned in the contract.

V.   Tontines

Tontines.

VI.   Capital redemption contracts

Capital redemption contracts, where effected or carried out by a person who does not carry on a banking business, and otherwise carries on a regulated activity of the kind specified by article 10(1) or (2).

VII.   Pension fund management

(a)   Pension fund management contracts, and

(b)   pension fund management contracts which are combined with contracts of insurance covering either conservation of capital or payment of a minimum interest,

where effected or carried out by a person who does not carry on a banking business, and otherwise carries on a regulated activity of the kind specified by article 10(1) or (2).

VIII.   Collective insurance etc

Contracts of a kind referred to in article 1(2)(e) of the first life insurance directive.

IX.   Social insurance

Contracts of a kind referred to in article 1(3) of the first life insurance directive.

SCHEDULE 2

ANNEX TO THE INVESTMENT SERVICES DIRECTIVE

Article 4

"ANNEX

SECTION A

Services

1.—   (a)   Reception and transmission, on behalf of investors, of orders in relation to one or more instruments listed in Section B.

(b)   Execution of such orders other than for own account.

2.   Dealing in any of the instruments listed in Section B for own account.

3.   Managing portfolios of investments in accordance with mandates given by investors on a discretionary, client-by-client basis where such portfolios include one or more of the instruments listed in Section B.

4.   Underwriting in respect of issues of any of the instruments listed in Section B and/or the placing of such issues.

SECTION B

Investments

1.—   (a)   Transferable securities.

(b)   Units in collective investment undertakings.

2.   Money-market instruments.

3.   Financial-futures contracts, including equivalent cash-settled instruments.

4.   Forward interest-rate agreements (FRAs).

5.   Interest-rate, currency and equity swaps.

6.   Options to acquire or dispose of any instruments falling within this section of the Annex, including equivalent cash-settled instruments. This category includes in particular options on currency and on interest rates.

SECTION C

Non-core services

1. Safekeeping and administration in relation to one or more of the instruments listed in Section B.
2. Safe custody services.
3. Granting credits or loans to an investor to allow him to carry out a transaction in one or more of the instruments listed in Section B, where the firm granting the credit or loan is involved in the transaction.
4. Advice to undertakings on capital structure, industrial strategy and related matters and advice and service relating to mergers and the purchase of undertakings.
5. Services related to underwriting.
6. Investment advice concerning one or more of the instruments listed in Section B.
7. Foreign-exchange services where these are connected with the provision of investment services."

SCHEDULE 3

ARTICLE 2.2 OF THE INVESTMENT SERVICES DIRECTIVE

Article 4

"This Directive shall not apply to:

(a)   insurance undertakings as defined in Article 1 of Directive 73/239/EEC or Article 1 of Directive 79/267/EEC or undertakings carrying on the reinsurance and retrocession activities referred to in Directive 64/225/EEC;

(b)   firms which provide investment services exclusively for their parent undertakings, for their subsidiaries or for other subsidiaries of their parent undertakings;

(c)   persons providing an investment service where that service is provided in an incidental manner in the course of a professional activity and that activity is regulated by legal or regulatory provisions or a code of ethics governing the profession which do not exclude the provision of that service;

(d)   firms that provide investment services consisting exclusively in the administration of employee participation schemes;

(e)   firms that provide investment services that consist in providing both the services referred to in (b) and those referred to in (d);

(f)   the central banks of Member States and other national bodies performing similar functions and other public bodies charged with or intervening in the management of the public debt;

(g)   firms

— which may not hold clients' funds or securities and which for that reason may not at any time place themselves in debit with their clients, and

— which may not provide any investment service except the reception and transmission of orders in transferable securities and units in collective investment undertakings, and

— which in the course of providing that service may transmit orders only to

(i)   investment firms authorised in accordance with this Directive;

(ii)   credit institutions authorised in accordance with Directives 77/80/EEC and 89/646/EEC;

(iii)   branches of investment firms or of credit institutions which are authorised in a third country and which are subject to and comply with prudential rules considered by the competent authorities as at least as stringent as those laid down in this Directive, in Directive 89/646/EEC or in Directive 93/6/EEC;

(iv)   collective investment undertakings authorised under the law of a Member State to market units to the public and to the managers of such undertakings;

(v)   investment companies with fixed capital, as defined in Article 15(4) of Directive 79/91/EEC, the securities of which are listed or dealt in on a regulated market in a Member State;

—   the activities of which are governed at national level by rules or by a code of ethics;

(h)   collective investment undertakings whether coordinated at Community level or not and the depositaries and managers of such undertakings;

(i)   person whose main business is trading in commodities amongst themselves or with producers or professional users of such products and who provide investment services only for such producers and professional users to the extent necessary for their main business;

(j)   firms that provide investment services consisting exclusively in dealing for their own account on financial-futures or options markets or which deal for the accounts of other members of those markets or make prices for them and which are guaranteed by clearing members of the same markets. Responsibility for ensuring the performance of contracts entered into by such firms must be assumed by clearing members of the same markets;

(k)   associations set up by Danish pension funds with the sole aim of managing the assets of pension funds that are members of those associations;

(l)   "agenti di cambio" whose activities and functions are governed by Italian Royal Decree No 222 of 7 March 1925 and subsequent provisions amending it, and who are authorised to carry on their activities under Article 19 of Italian Law No 1 of 2 January 1991."

SCHEDULE 4

Article 4

RELEVANT TEXT OF THE INSURANCE MEDIATION DIRECTIVE

PART 1
ARTICLE 1.2

"This Directive shall not apply to persons providing mediation services for insurance contracts if all the following conditions are met:

(a)   the insurance contract only requires knowledge of the insurance cover that is provided;

(b)   the insurance contract is not a life assurance contract;

(c)   the insurance contract does not cover any liability risks;

(d)   the principal professional activity of the person is other than insurance mediation;

(e)   the insurance is complementary to the product or service supplied by any provider, where such insurance covers:

    (i)   the risk of breakdown, loss of or damage to goods supplied by that provider; or

    (ii)   damage to or loss of baggage and other risks linked to the travel booked with that provider, even if the insurance covers life assurance or liability risks, provided that the cover is ancillary to the main cover for the risks linked to that travel;

(f)   the amount of the annual premium does not exceed EUR 500 and the total duration of the insurance contract, including any renewals, does not exceed five years."

PART II
ARTICLE 2.3

""Insurance mediation" means the activities of introducing, proposing or carrying out other work preparatory to the conclusion of contracts of insurance, or of concluding such contracts, or of assisting in the administration and performance of such contracts, in particular in the event of a claim.

These activities when undertaken by an insurance undertaking or an employee of an insurance undertaking who is acting under the responsibility of the insurance undertaking shall not be considered as insurance mediation.

The provision of information on an incidental basis in the context of another professional activity provided that the purpose of that activity is not to assist the customer in concluding or performing an insurance contract, the management of claims of an insurance undertaking on a professional basis, and loss adjusting and expert appraisal of claims shall also not be considered as insurance mediation."

PART III

ARTICLE 2.4

""Reinsurance mediation" means the activities of introducing, proposing or carrying out other work preparatory to the conclusion of contracts of reinsurance, or of concluding such contracts, or of assisting in the administration and performance of such contracts, in particular in the event of a claim.

These activities when undertaken by a reinsurance undertaking or an employee of a reinsurance undertaking who is acting under the responsibility of the reinsurance undertaking are not considered as reinsurance mediation.

The provision of information on an incidental basis in the context of another professional activity provided that the purpose of that activity is not to assist the customer in concluding or performing a reinsurance contract, the management of claims of a reinsurance undertaking on a professional basis, and loss adjusting and expert appraisal of claims shall also not be considered as reinsurance mediation."

Financial Services and Markets Act 2000 (Financial Promotion) Order 2001

S.I. 2001/1335

1. Citation and commencement

(1) This Order may be cited as the Financial Services and Markets Act 2000 (Financial Promotion) Order 2001.

(2) Except as provided by paragraph (3), this Order comes into force on the day on which section 19 of the Act comes into force.

(3) This Order comes into force—

    (a) for the purposes of paragraphs 9 and 25 of Schedule 1 (qualifying funeral plan contracts) on 1st January 2002; and

    (b) for the purposes of paragraphs 10 and 26 of Schedule 1 (qualifying credit) on such a day as the Treasury may specify.

(4) Any day specified under paragraph (3)(b) must be caused to be notified in the London, Edinburgh and Belfast Gazettes published not later than one week before that day.

2. Interpretation: general

(1) In this Order, except where the context otherwise requires—

    "the 1985 Act" means the Companies Act 1985;

    "the 1986 Order" means the Companies (Northern Ireland) Order 1986;

    "the Act" means the Financial Services and Markets Act 2000;

    "close relative" in relation to a person means—

        (a) his spouse;

        (b) his children and step-children, his parents and step-parents, his brothers and sisters and his step-brothers and step-sisters; and

        (c) the spouse of any person within sub-paragraph (b);

    "controlled activity" has the meaning given by article 4 and Schedule 1;

    "controlled investment" has the meaning given by article 4 and Schedule 1;

    "deposit" means a sum of money which is a deposit for the purposes of article 5 of the Regulated Activities Order;

    "equity share capital" has the meaning given in the 1985 Act or in the 1986 Order;

    "financial promotion restriction" has the meaning given by article 5;

    "government" means the government of the United Kingdom, the Scottish Administration, the Executive Committee of the Northern Ireland Assembly, the National Assembly for Wales and any government of any country or territory outside the United Kingdom;

    "instrument" includes any record whether or not in the form of a document;

    "international organisation" means any body the members of which comprise—

        (a) states including the United Kingdom or another EEA State; or

        (b) bodies whose members comprise states including the United Kingdom or another EEA State;

    "overseas communicator" has the meaning given by article 30;

    "previously overseas customer" has the meaning given by article 31;

    "publication" means—

        (a) a newspaper, journal, magazine or other periodical publication;

        (b) a web site or similar system for the electronic display of information;

(c) any programme forming part of a service consisting of the broadcast or transmission of television or radio programmes;

(d) any teletext service, that is to say a service consisting of television transmissions consisting of a succession of visual displays (with or without accompanying sound) capable of being selected and held for separate viewing or other use;

"qualifying contract of insurance" has the meaning given in the Regulated Activities Order;

"qualifying credit" has the meaning given by paragraph 10 of Schedule 1;

"the Regulated Activities Order" means the Financial Services and Markets Act 2000 (Regulated Activities) Order 2001;

"relevant insurance activity" has the meaning given by article 21;

"relevant investment activities" has the meaning given by article 30;

"solicited real time communication" has the meaning given by article 8;

"units", in a collective investment scheme, has the meaning given by Part XVII of the Act;

"unsolicited real time communication" has the meaning given by article 8.

(2) References to a person engaging in investment activity are to be construed in accordance with subsection (8) of section 21 of the Act; and for these purposes, "controlled activity" and "controlled investment" in that subsection have the meaning given in this Order.

3. Interpretation: unlisted companies

(1) In this Order, an "unlisted company" means a body corporate the shares in which are not—

(a) listed or quoted on an investment exchange whether in the United Kingdom or elsewhere;

(b) shares in respect of which information is, with the agreement or approval of any officer of the company, published for the purpose of facilitating deals in the shares indicating prices at which persons have dealt or are willing to deal in them other than persons who, at the time the information is published, are existing members of a relevant class;

(c) subject to a marketing arrangement which accords to the company the facilities referred to in section 163(2)(b) of the 1985 Act or article 173(2)(b) of the 1986 Order; or

(d) the subject of an offer (whether in the United Kingdom or elsewhere) in relation to which a copy of the prospectus must be delivered to the relevant registrar of companies in accordance with section 64 of the 1985 Act or article 74 of the 1986 Order or Part II of the Public Offers of Securities Regulations 1995.

(2) For the purpose of paragraph (1)(b), a person is to be regarded as a member of a relevant class if he was, at the relevant time—

(a) an existing member or debenture holder of the company;

(b) an existing employee of the company;

(c) a close relative of such a member or employee; or

(d) a trustee (acting in his capacity as such) of a trust, the principal beneficiary of which is a person within any of sub-paragraphs (a), (b) and (c).

(3) In this Order references to shares in and debentures of an unlisted company are references to—

(a) in the case of a body corporate which is a company within the meaning of the 1985 Act, shares and debentures within the meaning of that Act;

(b) in the case of a body corporate which is a company within the meaning of the 1986 Order, shares and debentures within the meaning of that Order;

(c) in the case of any other body corporate, investments falling within paragraph 14 or 15 of Schedule 1 to this Order.

PART II
CONTROLLED ACTIVITIES AND CONTROLLED INVESTMENTS

4. Definition of controlled activities and controlled investments

(1) For the purposes of section 21(9) of the Act, a controlled activity is an activity which falls within any of paragraphs 1 to 11 of Schedule 1.

(2)   For the purposes of section 21(10) of the Act, a controlled investment is an investment which falls within any of paragraphs 12 to 27 of Schedule 1.

PART III
EXEMPTIONS: INTERPRETATION AND APPLICATION

5.   **Interpretation: financial promotion restriction**

In this Order, any reference to the financial promotion restriction is a reference to the restriction in section 21(1) of the Act.

6.   **Interpretation: communications**

In this Order—

(a)   any reference to a communication is a reference to the communication, in the course of business, of an invitation or inducement to engage in investment activity;

(b)   any reference to a communication being made to another person is a reference to a communication being addressed, whether verbally or in legible form, to a particular person or persons (for example where it is contained in a telephone call or letter);

(c)   any reference to a communication being directed at persons is a reference to a communication being addressed to persons generally (for example where it is contained in a television broadcast or web site);

(d)   "communicate" includes causing a communication to be made or directed;

(e)   a "recipient" of a communication is the person to whom the communication is made or, in the case of a non-real time communication which is directed at persons generally, any person who reads or hears the communication;

(f)   "electronic commerce communication" means a communication, the making of which constitutes the provision of an information society service;

(g)   "incoming electronic commerce communication" means an electronic commerce communication made from an establishment in an EEA State other than the United Kingdom;

(h)   "outgoing electronic commerce communication" means an electronic commerce communication made from an establishment in the United Kingdom to a person in an EEA State other than the United Kingdom.

7.   **Interpretation: real time communications**

(1)   In this Order, references to a real time communication are references to any communication made in the course of a personal visit, telephone conversation or other interactive dialogue.

(2)   A non-real time communication is a communication not falling within paragraph (1).

(3)   For the purposes of this Order, non-real time communications include communications made by letter or e-mail or contained in a publication.

(4)   For the purposes of this Order, the factors in paragraph (5) are to be treated as indications that a communication is a non-real time communication.

(5)   The factors are that—

(a)   the communication is made to or directed at more than one recipient in identical terms (save for details of the recipient's identity);

(b)   the communication is made or directed by way of a system which in the normal course constitutes or creates a record of the communication which is available to the recipient to refer to at a later time;

(c)   the communication is made or directed by way of a system which in the normal course does not enable or require the recipient to respond immediately to it.

8.   **Interpretation: solicited and unsolicited real time communications**

(1)   A real time communication is solicited where it is made in the course of a personal visit, telephone call or other interactive dialogue if that call, visit or dialogue—

(a)   was initiated by the recipient of the communication; or

(b)   takes place in response to an express request from the recipient of the communication.

(2)   A real time communication is unsolicited where it is made otherwise than as described in paragraph (1).

(3)   For the purposes of paragraph (1)—
  (a)   a person is not to be treated as expressly requesting a call, visit or dialogue—
    (i)   because he omits to indicate that he does not wish to receive any or any further visits or calls or to engage in any or any further dialogue;
    (ii)   because he agrees to standard terms that state that such visits, calls or dialogue will take place, unless he has signified clearly that, in addition to agreeing to the terms, he is willing for them to take place;
  (b)   a communication is solicited only if it is clear from all the circumstance when the call, visit or dialogue is initiated or requested that during the course of the visit, call or dialogue communications will be made concerning the kind of controlled activities or investments to which the communications in fact made relate;
  (c)   it is immaterial whether the express request was made before or after this article comes into force.

(4)   Where a real time communication is solicited by a recipient ("R"), it is treated as having also been solicited by any other person to whom it is made at the same time as it is made to R if that other recipient is—
  (a)   a close relative of R; or
  (b)   expected to engage in any investment activity jointly with R.

8A.   Interpretation: outgoing electronic commerce communications

(1)   For the purposes of the application of those articles to outgoing electronic commerce communications—
  (a)   any reference in article 48(4)(e), 50(1)(a) or (3)(c) or 52(3)(c) to an authorised person includes a reference to a person who is entitled, under the law of an EEA State other than the United Kingdom, to carry on regulated activities in that State;
  (b)   any reference in article 68, 72 or 73(2)(b) to Part II of the Public Offers of Securities Regulations 1995 includes a reference to provisions corresponding to that Part in the law of an EEA State other than the United Kingdom;
  (c)   any reference in article 48 or 49 to an amount in pounds sterling includes a reference to an equivalent amount in another currency.

(2)   For the purposes of the application of article 49 to outgoing electronic commerce communications, any reference in section 737 or 264(2) of the 1985 Act (or the equivalent provision in the 1986 Order) to a body corporate or company includes a reference to a body corporate or company registered under the law of an EEA State other than the United Kingdom.

(3)   For the purposes of the application of articles 63 to 66 to outgoing electronic commerce communications, any reference in article 3 to Part II of the Public Offers of Securities Regulations 1995 includes a reference to provisions corresponding to that Part in the law of an EEA State other than the United Kingdom.

(4)   For the purposes of the application of article 3 in respect of outgoing electronic commerce communications—
  (a)   any reference in section 163(2)(b) of the 1985 Act (or the equivalent provision in the 1986 Order) to a company includes a reference to a company registered under the law of an EEA State other than the United Kingdom;
  (b)   any reference in that section to an investment exchange includes a reference to an investment exchange which is recognised as an investment exchange under the law of an EEA State other than the United Kingdom.

9.   Degree of prominence to be given to required indications

Where a communication must, if it is to fall within any provision of this Order, be accompanied by an indication of any matter, the indication must be presented to the recipient—

(a)   in a way that can be easily understood; and

(b)   in such manner as, depending on the means by which the communication is made or directed, is best calculated to bring the matter in question to the attention of the recipient and to allow him to consider it.

10.   Application to qualifying contracts of insurance

(1)   Nothing in this Order exempts from the application of the financial promotion restriction a communication which invites or induces a person to enter into a qualifying contract of insurance with a person who is not—

(a)   an authorised person;

(b)   an exempt person who is exempt in relation to effecting or carrying out contracts of insurance of the class to which the communication relates;

(c)   a company which has its head office in an EEA State other than the United Kingdom and which is entitled under the law of that State to carry on there insurance business of the class to which the communication relates;

(d)   a company which has a branch or agency in an EEA State other than the United Kingdom and is entitled under the law of that State to carry on there insurance business of the class to which the communication relates;

(e)   a company authorised to carry on insurance business of the class to which the communication relates in any country or territory which is listed in Schedule 2.

(2)   In this article, references to a class of insurance are references to the class of insurance contract described in Schedule 1 to the Regulated Activities Order into which the effecting and carrying out of the contract to which the communication relates would fall.

11.   Combination of different exemptions

(1)   In respect of a communication relating to—

(a)   a controlled activity falling within paragraph 2 of Schedule 1 carried on in relation to a qualifying contract of insurance; or

(b)   a controlled activity falling within any of paragraphs 3 to 11 of Schedule 1,

a person may rely on the application of one or more of the exemptions in Parts IV and VI.

(2)   A person may rely, in respect of a communication relating to an activity falling within paragraph 1 of Schedule 1, on the application of one or more of the exemptions in Parts IV and V.

(3)   A person may rely, in respect of a communication relating to a relevant insurance activity, on the application of one or more of the exemptions in Parts IV and V.

PART IV
EXEMPT COMMUNICATIONS: ALL CONTROLLED ACTIVITIES

12.   Communications to overseas recipients

(1)   Subject to paragraphs (2) and (7), the financial promotion restriction does not apply to any communication—

(a)   which is made (whether from inside or outside the United Kingdom) to a person who receives the communication outside the United Kingdom; or

(b)   which is directed (whether from inside or outside the United Kingdom) only at persons outside the United Kingdom.

(2)   Paragraph (1) does not apply to an unsolicited real time communication unless—

(a)   it is made from a place outside the United Kingdom; and

(b)   it is made for the purposes of a business which is carried on outside the United Kingdom and which is not carried on in the United Kingdom.

(3)   For the purposes of paragraph (1)(b)—

(a)   if the conditions set out in paragraph (4)(a), (b), (c) and (d) are met, a communication directed from a place inside the United Kingdom is to be regarded as directed only at persons outside the United Kingdom;

(b)   if the conditions set out in paragraph (4)(c) and (d) are met, a communication directed from a place outside the United Kingdom is to be regarded as directed only at persons outside the United Kingdom;

(c)   in any other case where one or more of the conditions in paragraph (4)(a) to (e) are met, that fact is to be taken into account in determining whether or not a communication is to be regarded as directed only at persons outside the United Kingdom (but a communication may still be regarded as directed only at persons outside the United Kingdom even if none of the conditions in paragraph (4) is met).

(4)   The conditions are that—

(a)   the communication is accompanied by an indication that it is directed only at persons outside the United Kingdom;

(b)   the communication is accompanied by an indication that it must not be acted upon by persons in the United Kingdom;

(c)   the communication is not referred to in, or directly accessible from, any other communication which is made to a person or directed at persons in the United Kingdom by or on behalf of the same person;

(d)   there are in place proper systems and procedures to prevent recipients in the United Kingdom (other than those to whom the communication might otherwise lawfully have been made) engaging in the investment activity to which the communication relates with the person directing the communication, a close relative of his or a member of the same group;

(e)   the communication is included in—

      (i)   a web site, newspaper, journal, magazine or periodical publication which is principally accessed in or intended for a market outside the United Kingdom;

      (ii)   a radio or television broadcast or teletext service transmitted principally for reception outside the United Kingdom.

(5)   For the purpose of paragraph (1)(b), a communication may be treated as directed only at persons outside the United Kingdom even if—

(a)   it is also directed, for the purposes of article 19(1)(b), at investment professionals falling within article 19(5) (but disregarding paragraph (6) of that article for this purpose);

(b)   it is also directed, for the purposes of article 49(1)(b), at high net worth persons to whom article 49 applies (but disregarding paragraph (2)(e) of that article for this purpose) and it relates to a controlled activity to which article 49 applies.

(6)   Where a communication falls within paragraph (5)—

(a)   the condition in paragraph (4)(a) is to be construed as requiring an indication that the communication is directed only at persons outside the United Kingdom or persons having professional experience in matters relating to investments or high net worth persons (as the case may be);

(b)   the condition in paragraph (4)(b) is to be construed as requiring an indication that the communication must not be acted upon by persons in the United Kingdom or by persons who do not have professional experience in matters relating to investments or who are not high net worth persons (as the case may be).

(7)   Paragraph (1) does not apply to an outgoing electronic commerce communication.

13.   Communications from customers and potential customers

(1)   The financial promotion restriction does not apply to any communication made by or on behalf of a person ("customer") to one other person ("supplier")—

(a)   in order to obtain information about a controlled investment available from or a controlled service provided by the supplier; or

(b)   in order that the customer can acquire a controlled investment from that supplier or be supplied with a controlled service by that supplier.

(2)   For the purposes of paragraph (1), a controlled service is a service the provision of which constitutes engaging in a controlled activity by the supplier.

14.   Follow up non-real time communications and solicited real time communications

(1)   Where a person makes or directs a communication ("the first communication") which is exempt from the financial promotion restriction because, in compliance with the requirements of another provision of this Order, it is accompanied by certain indications or contains certain information, then the financial promotion restriction does not apply to any subsequent communication which complies with the requirements of paragraph (2).

(2)   The requirements of this paragraph are that the subsequent communication—

   (a)   is a non-real time communication or a solicited real time communication;

   (b)   is made by the same person who made the first communication;

   (c)   is made to a recipient of the first communication;

   (d)   relates to the same controlled activity and the same controlled investment as the first communication; and

   (e)   is made within 12 months of the recipient receiving the first communication.

(3)   A communication made or directed before this article comes into force is to be treated as a first communication falling within paragraph (1) if it would have fallen within that paragraph had it been made or directed after this article comes into force.

15.   Introductions

(1)   If the requirements of paragraph (2) are met, the financial promotion restriction does not apply to any real time communication which is made with a view to or for the purposes of introducing the recipient to—

   (a)   an authorised person who carries on the controlled activity to which the communication relates; or

   (b)   an exempt person where the communication relates to a controlled activity which is also a regulated activity in relation to which he is an exempt person.

(2)   The requirements of this paragraph are that—

   (a)   the maker of the communication ("A") is not a close relative of, nor a member of the same group as, the person to whom the introduction is, or is to be, made;

   (b)   A does not receive from any person other than the recipient any pecuniary reward or other advantage arising out of his making the introduction; and

   (c)   it is clear in all the circumstances that the recipient, in his capacity as an investor, is not seeking and has not sought advice from A as to the merits of the recipient engaging in investment activity (or, if the client has sought such advice, A has declined to give it, but has recommended that the recipient seek such advice from an authorised person).

16.   Exempt persons

(1)   The financial promotion restriction does not apply to any communication which—

   (a)   is a non-real time communication or a solicited real time communication;

   (b)   is made or directed by an exempt person; and

   (c)   is for the purposes of that exempt person's business of carrying on a controlled activity which is also a regulated activity in relation to which he is an exempt person.

(2)   The financial promotion restriction does not apply to any unsolicited real time communication made by a person ("AR") who is an appointed representative (within the meaning of section 39(2) of the Act) where—

   (a)   the communication is made by AR in carrying on the business—

      (i)   for which his principal ("P") has accepted responsibility for the purposes of section 39 of the Act; and

      (ii)   in relation to which AR is exempt from the general prohibition by virtue of that section; and

   (b)   the communication is one which, if it were made by P, would comply with any rules made by the Authority under section 145 of the Act (financial promotion rules) which are relevant to a communication of that kind.

17.   **Generic promotions**

The financial promotion restriction does not apply to any communication which—

(a)   does not identify (directly or indirectly) a person who provides the controlled investment to which the communication relates; and

(b)   does not identify (directly or indirectly) any person as a person who carries on a controlled activity in relation to that investment.

18.   **Mere conduits**

(1)   Subject to paragraph (4), the financial promotion restriction does not apply to any communication which is made or directed by a person who acts as a mere conduit for it.

(2)   A person acts as a mere conduit for a communication if—

(a)   he communicates it in the course of a business carried on by him, the principal purpose of which is transmitting or receiving material provided to him by others;

(b)   the content of the communication is wholly devised by another person; and

(c)   the nature of the service provided by him in relation to the communication is such that he does not select, modify or otherwise exercise control over its content prior to its transmission or receipt.

(3)   For the purposes of paragraph (2)(c) a person does not select, modify or otherwise exercise control over the content of a communication merely by removing or having the power to remove material—

(a)   which is, or is alleged to be, illegal, defamatory or in breach of copyright;

(b)   in response to a request to a body which is empowered by or under any enactment to make such a request; or

(c)   when otherwise required to do so by law.

(4)   This article does not apply to an electronic commerce communication.

18A.   **Electronic commerce communications: mere conduits, caching and hosting**

The financial promotion restriction does not apply to an electronic commerce communication in circumstances where—

(a)   the making of the communication constitutes the provision of an information society service of a kind falling within paragraph 1 of Article 12, 13 or 14 of the electronic commerce directive ("mere conduit", "caching" and "hosting"); and

(b)   the conditions mentioned in the paragraph in question, to the extent that they are applicable at the time of, or prior to, the making of the communication, are or have been met at that time.

19.   **Investment professionals**

(1)   The financial promotion restriction does not apply to any communication which—

(a)   is made only to recipients whom the person making the communication believes on reasonable grounds to be investment professionals; or

(b)   may reasonably be regarded as directed only at such recipients.

(2)   For the purposes of paragraph (1)(b), if all the conditions set out in paragraph (4)(a) to (c) are met in relation to the communication, it is to be regarded as directed only at investment professionals.

(3)   In any other case in which one or more of the conditions set out in paragraph (4)(a) to (c) are met, that fact is to be taken into account in determining whether the communication is directed only at investment professionals (but a communication may still be regarded as so directed even if none of the conditions in paragraph (4) is met).

(4)   The conditions are that—

(a)   the communication is accompanied by an indication that it is directed at persons having professional experience in matters relating to investments and that any investment or investment activity to which it relates is available only to such persons or will be engaged in only with such persons;

    (b)   the communication is accompanied by an indication that persons who do not have professional experience in matters relating to investments should not rely on it;

    (c)   there are in place proper systems and procedures to prevent recipients other than investment professionals engaging in the investment activity to which the communication relates with the person directing the communication, a close relative of his or a member of the same group.

(5)   "Investment professionals" means—

    (a)   an authorised person;

    (b)   an exempt person where the communication relates to a controlled activity which is a regulated activity in relation to which the person is exempt;

    (c)   any other person—

        (i)   whose ordinary activities involve him in carrying on the controlled activity to which the communication relates for the purpose of a business carried on by him; or

        (ii)   who it is reasonable to expect will carry on such activity for the purposes of a business carried on by him;

    (d)   a government, local authority (whether in the United Kingdom or elsewhere) or an international organisation;

    (e)   a person ("A") who is a director, officer or employee of a person ("B") falling within any of sub-paragraphs (a) to (d) where the communication is made to A in that capacity and where A's responsibilities when acting in that capacity involve him in the carrying on by B of controlled activities.

(6)   For the purposes of paragraph (1), a communication may be treated as made only to or directed only at investment professionals even if it is also made to or directed at other persons to whom it may lawfully be communicated.

20. Communications by journalists

(1)   Subject to paragraph (2), the financial promotion restriction does not apply to any non-real time communication if—

    (a)   the content of the communication is devised by a person acting in the capacity of a journalist;

    (b)   the communication is contained in a qualifying publication; and

    (c)   in the case of a communication requiring disclosure, one of the conditions in paragraph (2) is met.

(2)   The conditions in this paragraph are that—

    (a)   the communication is accompanied by an indication explaining the nature of the author's financial interest or that of a member of his family (as the case may be);

    (b)   the authors are subject to proper systems and procedures which prevent the publication of communications requiring disclosure without the explanation referred to in sub-paragraph (a); or

    (c)   the qualifying publication in which the communication appears falls within the remit of—

        (i)   the Code of Practice issued by the Press Complaints Commission;

        (ii)   the Programme Code of the Radio Authority; ...

        (iii)   the Producers' Guidelines issued by the British Broadcasting Corporation; or

        (iv)   the Programme Code of the Independent Television Commission.

(3)   For the purposes of this article, a communication requires disclosure if—

    (a)   an author of the communication or a member of his family is likely to obtain a financial benefit or avoid a financial loss if people act in accordance with the invitation or inducement contained in the communication;

    (b)   the communication relates to a controlled investment of a kind falling within paragraph (4); and

    (c)   the communication identifies directly a person who issues or provides the controlled investment to which the communication relates.

(4)   A controlled investment falls within this paragraph if it is—

    (a)   an investment falling within paragraph 14 of Schedule 1 to this Order (shares or stock in share capital);

    (b)   an investment falling within paragraph 21 of that Schedule (options) to acquire or dispose of an investment falling within sub-paragraph (a);

    (c)   an investment falling within paragraph 22 of that Schedule (futures) being rights under a contract for the sale of an investment falling within sub-paragraph (a); or

    (d)   an investment falling within paragraph 23 of that Schedule (contracts for differences) being rights under a contract relating to, or to fluctuations in, the value or price of an investment falling within sub-paragraph (a).

(5)   For the purposes of this article—

    (a)   the authors of the communication are the person who devises the content of the communication and the person who is responsible for deciding to include the communication in the qualifying publication;

    (b)   a "qualifying publication" is a publication or service of the kind mentioned in paragraph (1) or (2) of article 54 of the Regulated Activities Order and which is of the nature described in that article, and for the purposes of this article, a certificate given under article 54(3) of the Regulated Activities Order and not revoked is conclusive evidence of the matters certified;

    (c)   the members of a person's family are his spouse and any children of his under the age of 18 years.

20A. Promotion broadcast by company director etc

(1)   The financial promotion restriction does not apply to a communication which is communicated as part of a qualifying service by a person ("D") who is a director or employee of an undertaking ("U") where—

    (a)   the communication invites or induces the recipient to acquire—

        (i)   a controlled investment of a kind falling within article 20(4) which is issued by U (or by an undertaking in the same group as U); or

        (ii)   a controlled investment issued or provided by an authorised person in the same group as U;

    (b)   the communication—

        (i)   comprises words which are spoken by D and not broadcast, transmitted or displayed in writing; or

        (ii)   is displayed in writing only because it forms part of an interactive dialogue to which D is a party and in the course of which D is expected to respond immediately to questions put by a recipient of the communication;

    (c)   the communication is not part of an organised marketing campaign; and

    (d)   the communication is accompanied by an indication that D is a director or employee (as the case may be) of U.

(2)   For the purposes of this article, a "qualifying service" is a service—

    (a)   which is broadcast or transmitted in the form of television or radio programmes; or

    (b)   displayed on a web site (or similar system for the electronic display of information) comprising regularly updated news and information,

provided that the principal purpose of the service, taken as a whole and including any advertisements and other promotional material contained in it, is neither of the purposes described in article 54(1)(a) or (b) of the Regulated Activities Order.

(3)   For the purposes of paragraph (2), a certificate given under article 54(3) of the Regulated Activities Order and not revoked is conclusive evidence of the matters certified.

20B. Incoming electronic commerce communications

(1)   The financial promotion restriction does not apply to an incoming electronic commerce communication.

(2)   Paragraph (1) does not apply to—

    (a)   a communication which constitutes an advertisement by the operator of a UCITS Directive scheme of units in that scheme;

    (b)   a communication consisting of an invitation or inducement to enter into a contract of insurance, where—

        (i)   the communication is made by an undertaking which has received official authorisation in accordance with Article 6 of the first life insurance directive or the first non-life insurance directive, and

        (ii)   the insurance falls within the scope of any of the insurance directives; or

    (c)   an unsolicited communication made by electronic mail.

(3)   In this article, "UCITS Directive scheme" means an undertaking for collective investment in transferable securities which is subject to the UCITS directive, and has been authorised in accordance with Article 4 of that Directive.

(4)   For the purposes of this article, a communication by electronic mail is to be regarded as unsolicited, unless it is made in response to an express request from the recipient of the communication.

PART V
EXEMPT COMMUNICATIONS: DEPOSITS AND INSURANCE

21.   **Interpretation: relevant insurance activity**

In this Part, a "relevant insurance activity" means a controlled activity falling within paragraph 2 of Schedule 1 carried on in relation to an investment falling within paragraph 13 of that Schedule where that investment is not a qualifying contract of insurance.

22.   **Deposits: non-real time communications**

(1)   If the requirements of paragraph (2) are met, the financial promotion restriction does not apply to any non-real time communication which relates to a controlled activity falling within paragraph 1 of Schedule 1.

(2)   The requirements of this paragraph are that the communication is accompanied by an indication—

    (a)   of the full name of the person with whom the investment which is the subject of the communication is to be made ("deposit-taker");

    (b)   of the country or territory in which a deposit-taker that is a body corporate is incorporated (described as such);

    (c)   if different, of the country or territory in which the deposit-taker's principal place of business is situated (described as such);

    (d)   whether or not the deposit-taker is regulated in respect of his deposit-taking business;

    (e)   if the deposit-taker is so regulated, of the name of the regulator in the deposit-taker's principal place of business, or if there is more than one such regulator, the prudential regulator;

    (f)   whether any transaction to which the communication relates would, if entered into by the recipient and the deposit-taker, fall within the jurisdiction of any dispute resolution scheme or deposit guarantee scheme and if so, identifying each such scheme;

    (g)   the necessary capital information.

(3)   In this article—

"full name", in relation to a person, means the name under which that person carries on business and, if different, that person's corporate name;

"liabilities" includes provisions where such provisions have not been deducted from the value of the assets;

"necessary capital information" means—

    (a)   in relation to a deposit-taker which is a body corporate, either the amount of its paid up capital and reserves, described as such, or a statement that the amount of its paid up capital and reserves exceeds a particular amount (stating it);

(b)   in relation to a deposit-taker which is not a body corporate, either the amount of the total assets less liabilities (described as such) or a statement that the amount of its total assets exceeds a particular amount (stating it) and that its total liabilities do not exceed a particular amount (stating it).

23.   Deposits: real time communications

The financial promotion restriction does not apply to any real time communication (whether solicited or unsolicited) which relates to an activity falling within paragraph 1 of Schedule 1.

24.   Relevant insurance activity: non-real time communications

(1)   If the requirements of paragraph (2) are met, the financial promotion restriction does not apply to any non-real time communication which relates to a relevant insurance activity.

(2)   The requirements of this paragraph are that the communication is accompanied by an indication—

(a)   of the full name of the person with whom the investment which is the subject of the communication is to be made ("the insurer");

(b)   of the country or territory in which the insurer is incorporated (described as such);

(c)   if different, of the country or territory in which the insurer's principal place of business is situated (described as such);

(d)   whether or not the insurer is regulated in respect of its insurance business;

(e)   if the insurer is so regulated, of the name of the regulator of the insurer in its principal place of business or, if there is more than one such regulator, the name of the prudential regulator;

(f)   whether any transaction to which the communication relates would, if entered into by the recipient and the insurer, fall within the jurisdiction of any dispute resolution scheme or compensation scheme and if so, identifying each such scheme.

(3)   In this article "full name", in relation to a person, means the name under which that person carries on business and, if different, that person's corporate name.

25.   Relevant insurance activity: non-real time communications: reinsurance and large risks

(1)   The financial promotion restriction does not apply to any non-real time communication which relates to a relevant insurance activity and concerns only—

(a)   a contract of reinsurance; or

(b)   a contract that covers large risks.

(2)   "Large risks" means—

(a)   risks falling within paragraph 4 (railway rolling stock), 5 (aircraft), 6 (ships), 7 (goods in transit), 11 (aircraft liability) or 12 (liability of ships) of Schedule 1 to the Regulated Activities Order;

(b)   risks falling within paragraph 14 (credit) or 15 (suretyship) of that Schedule provided that the risks relate to a business carried on by the recipient;

(c)   risks falling within paragraph 3 (land vehicles), 8 (fire and natural forces), 9 (damage to property), 10 (motor vehicle liability), 13 (general liability) or 16 (miscellaneous financial loss) of that Schedule provided that the risks relate to a business carried on by the recipient and that the condition specified in paragraph (3) is met in relation to that business.

(3)   The condition specified in this paragraph is that at least two of the three following criteria were exceeded in the most recent financial year for which information is available prior to the making of the communication—

(a)   the balance sheet total of the business (with the meaning of section 247(5) of the 1985 Act or article 255(5) of the 1986 Order) was 6.2 million euros;

(b)   the net turnover (within the meaning given to "turnover" by section 262(1) of the 1985 Act or article 270(1) of the 1986 Order) was 12.8 million euros;

(c)   the number of employees (within the meaning given by section 247(6) of the 1985 Act or article 255(6) of the 1996 Order) was 250;

and for a financial year which is a company's financial year but not in fact a year, the net turnover of the recipient shall be proportionately adjusted.

(4)   For the purposes of paragraph (3), where the recipient is a member of a group for which consolidated accounts (within the meaning of the Seventh Company Law Directive) are drawn up, the question whether the condition met in that paragraph is met is to be determined by reference to those accounts.

26.   Relevant insurance activity: real time communication

The financial promotion restriction does not apply to any real time communication (whether solicited or unsolicited) which relates to a relevant insurance activity.

PART VI
EXEMPT COMMUNICATIONS:
CERTAIN CONTROLLED ACTIVITIES

27.   Application of exemptions in this Part

Except where otherwise stated, the exemptions in this Part apply to communications which relate to—

(a)   a controlled activity falling within paragraph 2 of Schedule 1 carried on in relation to a qualifying contract of insurance;

(b)   controlled activities falling within any of paragraphs 3 to 11 of Schedule 1.

28.   One off non-real time communications and solicited real time communications

(1)   The financial promotion restriction does not apply to a one off communication which is either a non-real time communication or a solicited real time communication.

(2)   If all the conditions set out in paragraph (3) are met in relation to a communication it is to be regarded as a one off communication. In any other case in which one or more of those conditions are met, that fact is to be taken into account in determining whether the communication is a one off communication (but a communication may still be regarded as a one off communication even if none of the conditions in paragraph (3) is met).

(3)   The conditions are that—

(a)   the communication is made only to one recipient or only to one group of recipients in the expectation that they would engage in any investment activity jointly;

(b)   the identity of the product or service to which the communication relates has been determined having regard to the particular circumstances of the recipient;

(c)   the communication is not part of an organised marketing campaign.

(4)   Notwithstanding article 11, the financial promotion restriction does not apply to a one off solicited real time communication relating to the controlled activity falling within paragraph 10 of Schedule 1 (or within paragraph 11 in so far as it relates to that activity) even if the communication also relates to the controlled activity falling within paragraph 1 of that Schedule.

28A.   One off unsolicited real time communications

(1)   The financial promotion restriction does not apply to an unsolicited real time communication if the conditions in paragraph (2) are met.

(2)   The conditions in this paragraph are that—

(a)   the communication is a one off communication;

(b)   the communicator believes on reasonable grounds that the recipient understands the risks associated with engaging in the investment activity to which the communication relates;

(c)   at the time that the communication is made, the communicator believes on reasonable grounds that the recipient would expect to be contacted by him in relation to the investment activity to which the communication relates.

(3)   Paragraphs (2) and (3) of article 28 apply in determining whether a communication is a one off communication for the purposes of this article as they apply for the purposes of article 28.

28B. **Real time communications: introductions in connection with qualifying credit**

(1)   If the requirements of paragraph (2) are met, the financial promotion restriction does not apply to any real time communication which—

(a)   relates to a controlled activity falling within paragraph 10, 10A or 10B of Schedule 1; and

(b)   is made for the purpose of, or with a view to, introducing the recipient to a person ('N') who is—

(i)   an authorised person who carries on the controlled activity to which the communication relates,

(ii)   an appointed representative, where the controlled activity to which the communication relates is also a regulated activity in respect of which he is exempt from the general prohibition, or

(iii)   an overseas person who carries on the controlled activity to which the communication relates.

(2)   The requirements of this paragraph are that the maker of the communication ('M')—

(a)   does not receive any money, other than money payable to M on his own account, paid by the recipient for or in connection with any transaction which the recipient enters into with or through N as a result of the introduction; and

(b)   before making the introduction, discloses to the recipient such of the information mentioned in paragraph (3) as applies to M.

(3)   That information is—

(a)   that M is a member of the same group as N;

(b)   details of any payment which M will receive from N, by way of fee or commission, for introducing the recipient to N;

(c)   an indication of any other reward or advantage received or to be received by M that arises out of his making introductions to N.

(4)   In this article, "overseas person" means a person who carries on controlled activities which fall within paragraph 10, 10A or 10B of Schedule 1, but who does not carry on any such activity, or offer to do so, from a permanent place of business maintained by him in the United Kingdom.

29. **Communications required or authorised by enactments**

(1)   Subject to paragraph (2), the financial promotion restriction does not apply to any communication which is required or authorised by or under any enactment other than the Act.

(2)   This article does not apply to a communication which relates to a controlled activity falling within paragraph 10, 10A or 10B of Schedule 1 or within paragraph 11 in so far as it relates to that activity.

30. **Overseas communicators: solicited real time communications**

(1)   The financial promotion restriction does not apply to any solicited real time communication which is made by an overseas communicator from outside the United Kingdom in the course of or for the purposes of his carrying on the business of engaging in relevant investment activities outside the United Kingdom.

(2)   In this article—

"overseas communicator" means a person who carries on relevant investment activities outside the United Kingdom but who does not carry on any such activity from a permanent place of business maintained by him in the United Kingdom;

"relevant investment activities" means controlled activities which fall within paragraphs 3 to 7 or 10 to 10B of Schedule 1 or, so far as relevant to any of those paragraphs, paragraph 11 of that Schedule.

31. **Overseas communicators: non-real time communications to previously overseas customers**

(1)   The financial promotion restriction does not apply to any non-real time communication which is communicated by an overseas communicator from outside the United Kingdom to a previously overseas customer of his.

(2)   In this article a "previously overseas customer" means a person with whom the overseas communicator has done business within the period of twelve months ending with the day on which the communication was received ("the earlier business") and where—

(a)   at the time that the earlier business was done, the customer was neither resident in the United Kingdom nor had a place of business there; or

(b)   at the time the earlier business was done, the overseas communicator had on a former occasion done business with the customer, being business of the same description as the business to which the communication relates, and on that former occasion the customer was neither resident in the United Kingdom nor had a place of business there.

(3)   For the purposes of this article, an overseas communicator has done business with a customer if, in the course of carrying on his relevant investment activities outside the United Kingdom, he has—

(a)   effected a transaction, or arranged for a transaction to be effected, with the customer;

(b)   provided, outside the United Kingdom, a service to the customer as described in paragraph 6 of Schedule 1 (whether or not that paragraph was in force at the time the business was done); or

(c)   given, outside the United Kingdom, any advice to the customer as described in paragraph 7 of that Schedule (whether or not that paragraph was in force at the time the business was done).

32.   Overseas communicators: unsolicited real time communications to previously overseas customers

(1)   If the requirements of paragraphs (2) and (3) are met, the financial promotion restriction does not apply to an unsolicited real time communication which is made by an overseas communicator from outside the United Kingdom to a previously overseas customer of his.

(2)   The requirements of this paragraph are that the terms on which previous transactions and services had been effected or provided by the overseas communicator to the previously overseas customer were such that the customer would reasonably expect, at the time that the unsolicited real time communication is made, to be contacted by the overseas communicator in relation to the investment activity to which the communication relates.

(3)   The requirements of this paragraph are that the previously overseas customer has been informed by the overseas communicator on an earlier occasion—

(a)   that the protections conferred by or under the Act will not apply to any unsolicited real time communication which is made by the overseas communicator and which relates to that investment activity;

(b)   that the protections conferred by or under the Act may not apply to any investment activity that may be engaged in as a result of the communication; and

(c)   whether any transaction between them resulting from the communication would fall within the jurisdiction of any dispute resolution scheme or compensation scheme or, if there is no such scheme, of that fact.

(4)   Where the earlier occasion referred to in paragraph (3) occurs before this article comes into force, the references in that paragraph to the protections conferred by or under the Act are to be construed as references to the protections to be conferred by or under the Act.

33.   Overseas communicators: unsolicited real time communications to knowledgeable customers

(1)   If the requirements of paragraphs (2), (3) and (4) are met, the financial promotion restriction does not apply to an unsolicited real time communication which is made by an overseas communicator from outside the United Kingdom in the course of his carrying on relevant investment activities outside the United Kingdom.

(2)   The requirements of this paragraph are that the overseas communicator believes on reasonable grounds that the recipient is sufficiently knowledgeable to understand the risks associated with engaging in the investment activity to which the communication relates.

(3)   The requirements of this paragraph are that, in relation to any particular investment activity, the recipient has been informed by the overseas communicator on an earlier occasion—

(a)   that the protections conferred by or under the Act will not apply to any unsolicited real time communication which is made by him and which relates to that activity;

(b)   that the protections conferred by or under the Act may not apply to any investment activity that may be engaged in as a result of the communication; and

(c)   whether any transaction between them resulting from the communication would fall within the jurisdiction of any dispute resolution scheme or compensation scheme or, if there is no such scheme, of that fact.

(4)   The requirements of this paragraph are that the recipient, after being given a proper opportunity to consider the information given to him in accordance with paragraph (3), has clearly signified that he understands the warnings referred to in paragraph (3)(a) and (b) and that he accepts that he will not benefit from the protections referred to.

(5)   Where the earlier occasion referred to in paragraph (3) occurs before this article comes into force, the references in that paragraph to the protection conferred by or under the Act are to be construed as references to the protections to be conferred by or under the Act.

34.   Governments, central banks etc

The financial promotion restriction does not apply to any communication which—

(a)   is a non-real time communication or a solicited real time communication;

(b)   is communicated by and relates only to controlled investments issued by—

    (i)   any government;

    (ii)   any local authority (in the United Kingdom or elsewhere);

    (iii)   any international organisation;

    (iv)   the Bank of England;

    (v)   the European Central Bank;

    (vi)   the central bank of any country or territory outside the United Kingdom.

35.   Industrial and provident societies

The financial promotion restriction does not apply to any communication which—

(a)   is a non-real time communication or a solicited real time communication;

(b)   is communicated by an industrial and provident society; and

(c)   relates only to an investment falling within paragraph 15 of Schedule 1 which is issued by the society in question.

36.   Nationals of EEA States other than United Kingdom

The financial promotion restriction does not apply to any communication which—

(a)   is a non-real time communication or a solicited real time communication;

(b)   is communicated by a national of an EEA State other than the United Kingdom in the course of any controlled activity lawfully carried on by him in that State; and

(c)   conforms with any rules made by the Authority under section 145 of the Act (financial promotion rules) which are relevant to a communication of that kind.

37.   Financial markets

(1)   The financial promotion restriction does not apply to any communication—

(a)   which is a non-real time communication or a solicited real time communication;

(b)   which is communicated by a relevant market; and

(c)   to which paragraph (2) or (3) applies.

(2)   This paragraph applies to a communication if—

(a)   it relates only to facilities provided by the market; and

(b)   it does not identify (directly or indirectly)—

    (i)   any particular investment issued by or available from an identified person as one that may be traded or dealt in on the market; or

(ii)   any particular person as a person through whom transactions on the market may be effected.

(3)   This paragraph applies to a communication if—

(a)   it relates only to a particular investment falling within paragraph 21, 22 or 23 of Schedule 1; and

(b)   it identifies the investment as one that may be traded or dealt in on the market.

(4)   "Relevant market" means a market which—

(a)   meets the criteria specified in Part I of Schedule 3; or

(b)   is specified in, or is established under the rules of an exchange specified in, Part II, III or IV of that Schedule.

38.   Persons in the business of placing promotional material

The financial promotion restriction does not apply to any communication which is made to a person whose business it is to place, or arrange for the placing of, promotional material provided that it is communicated so that he can place or arrange for placing it.

39.   Joint enterprises

(1)   The financial promotion restriction does not apply to any communication which is communicated by a participator in a joint enterprise to another participator in the same joint enterprise in connection with or for the purposes of that enterprise.

(2)   "Joint enterprise" means an enterprise into which two or more persons ("the participators") enter for commercial purposes related to a business or businesses (other than the business of engaging in a controlled activity) carried on by them; and, where a participator is a member of a group, each other member of the group is also to be regarded as a participator in the enterprise.

(3)   "Participator" includes potential participator.

40.   Participants in certain recognised collective investment schemes

The financial promotion restriction does not apply to any non-real time communication or solicited real time communication which is made—

(a)   by a person who is the operator of a scheme recognised under section 270 or 272 of the Act; and

(b)   to persons in the United Kingdom who are participants in any such recognised scheme operated by the person making the communication,

and which relates only to such recognised schemes as are operated by that person or to units in such schemes.

41.   Bearer instruments: promotions required or permitted by market rules

(1)   The financial promotion restriction does not apply to any communication which—

(a)   is a non-real time communication or a solicited real time communication;

(b)   is communicated by a body corporate ("A") that is not an open-ended investment company;

(c)   is made to or may reasonably be regarded as directed at persons entitled to bearer instruments issued by A, a parent undertaking of A or a subsidiary undertaking of A; and

(d)   is required or permitted by the rules of a relevant market to be communicated to holders of instruments of a class which consists of or includes the bearer instruments in question.

(2)   "Bearer instrument" means any of the following investments title to which is capable of being transferred by delivery—

(a)   any investment falling within paragraph 14 or 15 of Schedule 1;

(b)   any investment falling within paragraph 17 or 18 of that Schedule which confers rights in respect of an investment falling within paragraph 14 or 15.

(3)   For the purpose of this article, a bearer instrument falling within paragraph 17 or 18 of Schedule 1 is treated as issued by the person ("P") who issued the investment in respect of which the bearer instrument confers rights if it is issued by—

(a)   an undertaking in the same group as P; or

(b)   a person acting on behalf of, or pursuant to arrangements made with, P.

(4)　　"Relevant market", in relation to instruments of any particular class, means any market on which instruments of that class can be traded or dealt in and which—

　　　(a)　meets the criteria specified in Part I of Schedule 3; or

　　　(b)　is specified in, or established under the rules of an exchange specified in, Part II or III of that Schedule.

42.　Bearer instruments: promotions to existing holders

(1)　　The financial promotion restriction does not apply to any communication which—

　　　(a)　is a non-real time communication or a solicited real time communication;

　　　(b)　is communicated by a body corporate ("A") that is not an open-ended investment company;

　　　(c)　is made to or may reasonably be regarded as directed at persons entitled to bearer instruments issued by A, a parent undertaking of A or a subsidiary undertaking of A;

　　　(d)　relates only to instruments of a class which consists of or includes either the bearer instruments to which the communication relates or instruments in respect of which those bearer instruments confer rights; and

　　　(e)　is capable of being accepted or acted on only by persons who are entitled to instruments (whether or not bearer instruments) issued by A, a parent undertaking of A or a subsidiary undertaking of A.

(2)　　"Bearer instruments" has the meaning given by article 41.

(3)　　For the purposes of this article, an instrument falling within paragraph 17 or 18 of Schedule 1 is treated as issued by the person ("P") who issued the investment in respect of which the bearer instrument confers rights if it is issued by—

　　　(a)　an undertaking in the same group as P; or

　　　(b)　a person acting on behalf of, or pursuant to arrangements made with, P.

43.　Members and creditors of certain bodies corporate

(1)　　The financial promotion restriction does not apply to any non-real time communication or solicited real time communication which is communicated—

　　　(a)　by a body corporate ("A") that is not an open-ended investment company; and

　　　(b)　to persons whom the person making the communication believes on reasonable grounds to be persons to whom paragraph (2) applies,

and which relates only to a relevant investment which is issued or to be issued by A, or by an undertaking ("U") in the same group as A that is not an open-ended investment company.

(2)　　This paragraph applies to—

　　　(a)　a creditor or member of A or of U;

　　　(b)　a person who is entitled to a relevant investment which is issued by A or by U;

　　　(c)　a person who is entitled, whether conditionally or unconditionally, to become a member of A or U but who has not yet done so;

　　　(d)　a person who is entitled, whether conditionally or unconditionally, to have transferred to him title to a relevant investment which is issued by A or U but has not yet acquired title to the investment.

(3)　　"Relevant investment" means—

　　　(a)　an investment falling within paragraph 14 or 15 of Schedule 1;

　　　(b)　an investment falling within paragraph 17 or 18 of that Schedule so far as relating to any investments within sub-paragraph (a).

(4)　　For the purposes of this article, an investment falling within paragraph 17 or 18 of Schedule 1 is treated as issued by the person ("P") who issued the investment in respect of which the instrument confers rights if it is issued by—

　　　(a)　an undertaking in the same group as P; or

　　　(b)　a person acting on behalf of, or pursuant to arrangements made with, P.

44.　Members and creditors of open-ended investment companies

(1)　　The financial promotion restriction does not apply to any communication which—

　　　(a)　is a non-real time communication or a solicited real time communication;

(b)   is communicated by an open-ended investment company;

(c)   is communicated to persons whom the person making or directing the communication believes on reasonable grounds to be persons to whom paragraph (2) applies; and

(d)   relates only to an investment falling within paragraph 15, 17 or 19 of Schedule 1 which is issued or to be issued by the open-ended investment company.

(2)   This paragraph applies to—

(a)   a creditor or member of the open-ended investment company;

(b)   a person who is entitled to an investment falling within paragraph 15, 17 or 19 of Schedule 1 which is issued by the open-ended investment company;

(c)   a person who is entitled, whether conditionally or unconditionally, to become a member of the open-ended investment company but who has not yet done so;

(d)   a person who is entitled, whether conditionally or unconditionally, to have transferred to him title to an investment falling within paragraph 15, 17 or 19 of Schedule 1 which is issued by the open-ended investment company but has not yet acquired title to the investment.

(3)   For the purposes of this article, an investment falling within paragraph 17 of Schedule 1 is treated as issued by the person ("P") who issued the investment in respect of which the instrument confers rights if it is issued by—

(a)   an undertaking in the same group as P; or

(b)   a person acting on behalf of, or pursuant to arrangements made with, P.

45.   Group companies

The financial promotion restriction does not apply to any communication made by one body corporate in a group to another body corporate in the same group.

46.   Qualifying credit to bodies corporate

The financial promotion restriction does not apply to any communication which relates to a controlled activity falling within paragraph 10, 10A or 10B of Schedule 1 (or within paragraph 11 so far as it relates to that activity) if the communication is—

(a)   made to or directed at bodies corporate only; or

(b)   accompanied by an indication that the qualifying credit to which it relates is only available to bodies corporate.

47.   Persons in the business of disseminating information

(1)   The financial promotion restriction does not apply to any communication which is made only to recipients whom the person making the communication believes on reasonable grounds to be persons to whom paragraph (2) applies.

(2)   This paragraph applies to—

(a)   a person who receives the communication in the course of a business which involves the dissemination through a publication of information concerning controlled activities;

(b)   a person whilst acting in the capacity of director, officer or employee of a person falling within sub-paragraph (a) being a person whose responsibilities when acting in that capacity involve him in the business referred to in that sub-paragraph;

(c)   any person to whom the communication may otherwise lawfully be made.

48.   Certified high net worth individuals

(1)   If the requirements of paragraphs (4) and (7) are met, the financial promotion restriction does not apply to any communication which—

(a)   is a non-real time communication or a solicited real time communication;

(b)   is made to an individual whom the person making the communication believes on reasonable grounds to be a certified high net worth individual; and

(c)   relates only to one or more investments falling within paragraph (8).

(2)   "Certified high net worth individual" means an individual who has signed, within the period of twelve months ending with the day on which the communication is made, a statement complying with Part I of Schedule 5.

(3)   The validity of a statement signed for the purposes of paragraph (2) is not affected by a defect in the form or wording of the statement, provided that the defect does not alter the statement's meaning and that the words shown in bold type in Part I of Schedule 5 are so shown in the statement.

(4)   The requirements of this paragraph are that either the communication is accompanied by the giving of a warning in accordance with paragraphs (5) and (6) or, where because of the nature of the communication this is not reasonably practicable,—

    (a)   a warning in accordance with paragraph (5) is given to the recipient orally at the beginning of the communication together with an indication that he will receive the warning in legible form and that, before receipt of that warning, he should consider carefully any decision to engage in investment activity to which the communication relates; and

    (b)   a warning in accordance with paragraphs (5) and (6) (d) to (h) is sent to the recipient of the communication within two business days of the day on which the communication is made.

(5)   The warning must be in the following terms—

    "The content of this promotion has not been approved by an authorised person within the meaning of the Financial Services and Markets Act 2000. Reliance on this promotion for the purpose of engaging in any investment activity may expose an individual to a significant risk of losing all of the property or other assets invested.".

But, where a warning is sent pursuant to paragraph (4)(b), for the words "this promotion" in both places where they occur there must be substituted wording which clearly identifies the promotion which is the subject of the warning.

(6)   The warning must—

    (a)   be given at the beginning of the communication;

    (b)   precede any other written or pictorial matter;

    (c)   be in a font size consistent with the text forming the remainder of the communication;

    (d)   be indelible;

    (e)   be legible;

    (f)   be printed in black, bold type;

    (g)   be surrounded by a black border which does not interfere with the text of the warning; and

    (h)   not be hidden, obscured or interrupted by any other written or pictorial matter.

(7)   The requirements of this paragraph are that the communication is accompanied by an indication—

    (a)   that it is exempt from the general restriction (in section 21 of the Act) on the communication of invitations or inducements to engage in investment activity on the grounds that it is made to a certified high net worth individual;

    (b)   of the requirements that must be met for an individual to qualify as a certified high net worth individual; and

    (c)   that any individual who is in any doubt about the investment to which the communication relates should consult an authorised person specialising in advising on investments of the kind in question.

(8)   An investment falls within this paragraph if—

    (a)   it is an investment falling within paragraph 14 of Schedule 1 being stock or shares in an unlisted company;

    (b)   it is an investment falling within paragraph 15 of Schedule 1 being an investment acknowledging the indebtedness of an unlisted company;

    (c)   it is an investment falling within paragraph 17 or 18 of Schedule 1 conferring entitlement or rights with respect to investments falling within sub-paragraph (a) or (b);

    (d)   it comprises units in a collective investment scheme being a scheme which invests wholly or predominantly in investments falling within sub-paragraph (a) or (b);

(e)   it is an investment falling within paragraph 21 of Schedule 1 being an option to acquire or dispose of an investment falling within sub-paragraph (a), (b) or (c);

(f)   it is an investment falling within paragraph 22 of Schedule 1 being rights under a contract for the sale of an investment falling within sub-paragraph (a), (b) or (c);

(g)   it is an investment falling within paragraph 23 of Schedule 1 being a contract relating to, or to fluctuations in value or price of, an investment falling within sub-paragraph (a), (b) or (c),

provided in each case that it is an investment under the terms of which the investor cannot incur a liability or obligation to pay or contribute more than he commits by way of investment.

(9)   "Business day" means any day except a Saturday, a Sunday, Christmas Day, Good Friday or a day which is a bank holiday under the Banking and Financial Dealings Act 1971 in any part of the United Kingdom.

49.   High net worth companies, unincorporated associations etc

(1)   The financial promotion restriction does not apply to any communication which—
(a)   is made only to recipients whom the person making the communication believes on reasonable grounds to be persons to whom paragraph (2) applies; or
(b)   may reasonably be regarded as directed only at persons to whom paragraph (2) applies.

(2)   This paragraph applies to—
(a)   any body corporate which has, or which is a member of the same group as an undertaking which has, a called-up share capital or net assets of not less than—
(i)   if the body corporate has more than 20 members or is a subsidiary undertaking of an undertaking which has more than 20 members, £500,000;
(ii)   otherwise, £5 million;
(b)   any unincorporated association or partnership which has net assets of not less than £5 million;
(c)   the trustee of a high value trust;
(d)   any person ("A") whilst acting in the capacity of director, officer of employee of a person ("B") falling within any of sub-paragraphs (a) to (c) where A's responsibilities when acting in that capacity, involve him in B's engaging in investment activity;
(e)   any person to whom the communication may otherwise lawfully be made.

(3)   For the purposes of paragraph (1)(b)—
(a)   if all the conditions set out in paragraph (4)(a) to (c) are met, the communication is to be regarded as directed at persons to whom paragraph (2) applies;
(b)   in any other case in which one or more of those conditions are met, that fact is to be taken into account in determining whether the communication is directed at persons to whom paragraph (2) applies (but a communication may still be regarded as so directed even if none of the conditions in paragraph (4) is met).

(4)   The conditions are that—
(a)   the communication includes an indication of the description of persons to whom it is directed and an indication of the fact that the controlled investment or controlled activity to which it relates is available only to such persons;
(b)   the communication includes an indication that persons of any other description should not act upon it;
(c)   there are in place proper systems and procedures to prevent recipients other than persons to whom paragraph (2) applies engaging in the investment activity to which the communication relates with the person directing the communication, a close relative of his or a member of the same group.

(5)   "Called-up share capital" has the meaning give in the 1985 Act or in the 1986 Order.

(6)   "High value trust" means a trust where the aggregate value of the cash and investments which form part of the trust's assets (before deducting the amount of its liabilities)—
(a)   is £10 million or more; or
(b)   has been £10 million or more at any time during the year immediately preceding the date on which the communication in question was first made or directed.

(7)   "Net assets" has the meaning give by section 264 of the 1985 Act or the equivalent provision of the 1986 Order.

50.   Sophisticated investors

(1)   "Certified sophisticated investor", in relation to any description of investment, means a person—

    (a)   who has a current certificate in writing or other legible form signed by an authorised person to the effect that he is sufficiently knowledgeable to understand the risks associated with that description of investment; and

    (b)   who has signed, within the period of twelve months ending with the day on which the communication is made, a statement in the following terms:

> "I make this statement so that I am able to receive promotions which are exempt from the restrictions on financial promotion in the Financial Services and Markets Act 2000. The exemption relates to certified sophisticated investors and I declare that I qualify as such in relation to investments of the following kind list them. I accept that the contents of promotions and other material that I receive may not have been approved by an authorised person and that their content may not therefore be subject to controls which would apply if the promotion were made or approved by an authorised person. I am aware that it is open to me to seek advice from someone who specialises in advising on this kind of investment".

(1A)   The validity of a statement signed in accordance with paragraph (1)(b) is not affected by a defect in the wording of the statement, provided that the defect does not alter the statement's meaning.

(2)   If the requirements of paragraph (3) are met, the financial promotion restriction does not apply to any communication which—

    (a)   is made to a certified sophisticated investor;

    (b)   does not invite or induce the recipient to engage in investment activity with the person who has signed the certificate referred to in paragraph (1)(a); and

    (c)   relates only to a description of investment in respect of which that investor is certified.

(3)   The requirements of this paragraph are that the communication is accompanied by an indication—

    (a)   that it is exempt from the general restriction (in section 21 of the Financial Services and Markets Act 2000) on the communication of invitations or inducements to engage in investment activity on the ground that it is made to a certified sophisticated investor;

    (b)   of the requirements that must be met for a person to qualify as a certified sophisticated investor;

    (c)   that the content of the communication has not been approved by an authorised person and that such approval is, unless this exemption or any other exemption applies, required by section 21 of the Act;

    (d)   that reliance on the communication for the purpose of engaging in any investment activity may expose the individual to a significant risk of losing all of the property invested or of incurring additional liability;

    (e)   that any person who is in any doubt about the investment to which the communication relates should consult an authorised person specialising in advising on investments of the kind in question.

(4)   For the purposes of paragraph (1)(a), a certificate is current if it is signed and dated not more than three years before the date on which the communication is made.

50A.   Self-certified sophisticated investors

(1)   "Self-certified sophisticated investor" means an individual who has signed, within the period of twelve months ending with the day on which the communication is made, a statement complying with Part II of Schedule 5.

(2)   The validity of a statement signed for the purposes of paragraph (1) is not affected by a defect in the form or wording of the statement, provided that the defect does not alter the statement's

meaning and that the words shown in bold type in Part II of Schedule 5 are so shown in the statement.

(3)   If the requirements of paragraphs (4) and (7) are met, the financial promotion restriction does not apply to any communication which—

  (a)   is made to an individual whom the person making the communication believes on reasonable grounds to be a self-certified sophisticated investor; and

  (b)   relates only to one or more investments falling within paragraph (8).

(4)   The requirements of this paragraph are that either the communication is accompanied by the giving of a warning in accordance with paragraphs (5) and (6) or, where because of the nature of the communication this is not reasonably practicable,—

  (a)   a warning in accordance with paragraph (5) is given to the recipient orally at the beginning of the communication together with an indication that he will receive the warning in legible form and that, before receipt of that warning, he should consider carefully any decision to engage in investment activity to which the communication relates; and

  (b)   a warning in accordance with paragraphs (5) and (6) (d) to (h) is sent to the recipient of the communication within two business days of the day on which the communication is made.

(5)   The warning must be in the following terms—

  "The content of this promotion has not been approved by an authorised person within the meaning of the Financial Services and Markets Act 2000. Reliance on this promotion for the purpose of engaging in any investment activity may expose an individual to a significant risk of losing all of the property or other assets invested.".

  But, where a warning is sent pursuant to paragraph (4)(b), for the words "this promotion" in both places where they occur there must be substituted wording which clearly identifies the promotion which is the subject of the warning.

(6)   The warning must—

  (a)   be given at the beginning of the communication;

  (b)   precede any other written or pictorial matter;

  (c)   be in a font size consistent with the text forming the remainder of the communication;

  (d)   be indelible;

  (e)   be legible;

  (f)   be printed in black, bold type;

  (g)   be surrounded by a black border which does not interfere with the text of the warning; and

  (h)   not be hidden, obscured or interrupted by any other written or pictorial matter.

(7)   The requirements of this paragraph are that the communication is accompanied by an indication—

  (a)   that it is exempt from the general restriction (in section 21 of the Act) on the communication of invitations or inducements to engage in investment activity on the ground that it is made to a self-certified sophisticated investor;

  (b)   of the requirements that must be met for an individual to qualify as a self-certified sophisticated investor;

  (c)   that any individual who is in any doubt about the investment to which the communication relates should consult an authorised person specialising in advising on investments of the kind in question.

(8)   An investment falls within this paragraph if—

  (a)   it is an investment falling within paragraph 14 of Schedule 1 being stock or shares in an unlisted company;

  (b)   it is an investment falling within paragraph 15 of Schedule 1 being an investment acknowledging the indebtedness of an unlisted company;

  (c)   it is an investment falling within paragraph 17 or 18 of Schedule 1 conferring entitlement or rights with respect to investments falling within sub-paragraph (a) or (b);

  (d)   it comprises units in a collective investment scheme being a scheme which invests wholly or predominantly in investments falling within sub-paragraph (a) or (b);

(e)   it is an investment falling within paragraph 21 of Schedule 1 being an option to acquire or dispose of an investment falling within sub-paragraph (a), (b) or (c);

(f)   it is an investment falling within paragraph 22 of Schedule 1 being rights under a contract for the sale of an investment falling within sub-paragraph (a), (b) or (c);

(g)   it is an investment falling within paragraph 23 of Schedule 1 being a contract relating to, or to fluctuations in value or price of, an investment falling within sub-paragraph (a), (b) or (c),

provided in each case that it is an investment under the terms of which the investor cannot incur a liability or obligation to pay or contribute more than he commits by way of investment.

(9)   "Business day" means any day except a Saturday, a Sunday, Christmas Day, Good Friday or a day which is a bank holiday under the Banking and Financial Dealings Act 1971 in any part of the United Kingdom.

51.   Associations of high net worth or sophisticated investors

The financial promotion restriction does not apply to any non-real time communication or solicited real time communication which—

(a)   is made to an association the membership of which the person making the communication believes on reasonable grounds comprises wholly or predominantly persons who are—
   (i)   certified high net worth individuals within the meaning of article 48;
   (ii) high net worth persons falling within article 49(2)(a) to (d);
   (iii) certified sophisticated investors within the meaning of article 50; and

(b)   relates only to an investment under the terms of which a person cannot incur a liability or obligation to pay or contribute more than he commits by way of investment.

52.   Common interest group of a company

(1)   "Common interest group", in relation to a company, means an identified group of persons who at the time the communication is made might reasonably be regarded as having an existing and common interest with each other and that company in—

(a)   the affairs of the company; and

(b)   what is done with the proceeds arising from any investment to which the communication relates.

(2)   If the requirements of paragraphs (3) and either (4) or (5) are met, the financial promotion restriction does not apply to any communication which—

(a)   is a non-real time communication or a solicited real time communication;

(b)   is made only to persons who are members of a common interest group of a company, or may reasonably be regarded as directed only at such persons; and

(c)   relates to investments falling within paragraph 14 or 15 of Schedule 1 which are issued by that company.

(3)   The requirements of this paragraph are that the communication is accompanied by an indication—

(a)   that the directors of the company (or its promoters named in the communication) have taken all reasonable care to ensure that every statement of fact or opinion included in the communication is true and not misleading given the form and context in which it appears;

(b)   that the directors of the company (or its promoters named in the communication) have not limited their liability with respect to the communication; and

(c)   that any person who is in any doubt about the investment to which the communication relates should consult an authorised person specialising in advising on investments of the kind in question.

(4)   The requirements of this paragraph are that the communication is accompanied by an indication—

(a)   that the directors of the company (or its promoters named in the communication) have taken all reasonable care to ensure that any person belonging to the common interest group (and his professional advisers) can have access, at all reasonable times, to all the information that he or they would reasonably require, and reasonably expect to find, for the purpose of making an informed assessment of the assets and liabilities, financial position, profits and losses and prospects of the company and of the rights attaching to the investments in question; and

(b)   describing the means by which such information can be accessed.

(5)   The requirements of this paragraph are that the communication is accompanied by an indication that any person considering subscribing for the investments in question should regard any subscription as made primarily to assist the furtherance of the company's objectives (other than any purely financial objectives) and only secondarily, if at all, as an investment.

(6)   For the purposes of paragraph (2)(b)—

(a)   if all the conditions set out in paragraph (7)(a) to (c) are met, the communication is to be regarded as directed at persons who are members of the common interest group;

(b)   in any other case in which one or more of those conditions are met, that fact shall be taken into account in determining whether the communication is directed at persons who are members of the common interest group (but a communication may still be regarded as directed only at such persons even if none of the conditions in paragraph (7) is met).

(7)   The conditions are that—

(a)   the communication is accompanied by an indication that it is directed at persons who are members of the common interest group and that any investment or activity to which it relates is available only to such persons;

(b)   the communication is accompanied by an indication that it must not be acted upon by persons who are not members of the common interest group;

(c)   there are in place proper systems and procedures to prevent recipients other than members of the common interest group engaging in the investment activity to which the communication relates with the person directing the communication, a close relative of his or a member of the same group.

(8)   Person are not to be regarded as having an interest of the kind described in paragraph (1) if the only reason why they would be so regarded is that—

(a)   they will have such an interest if they become members or creditors of the company;

(b)   they all carry on a particular trade or profession; or

(c)   they are persons with whom the company has an existing business relationship, whether by being its clients, customers, contractors, suppliers or otherwise.

53.   Settlors, trustees and personal representatives

The financial promotion restriction does not apply to any communication which is made between—

(a)   a person when acting as a settlor or grantor of a trust, a trustee or a personal representative; and

(b)   a trustee of the trust, a fellow trustee or a fellow personal representative (as the case may be),

if the communication is made for the purposes of the trust or estate.

54.   Beneficiaries of trust, will or intestacy

The financial promotion restriction does not apply to any communication which is made—

(a)   between a person when acting as a settlor or grantor of a trust, trustee or personal representative and a beneficiary under the trust, will or intestacy; or

(b)   between a beneficiary under a trust, will or intestacy and another beneficiary under the same trust, will or intestacy,

if the communication relates to the management or distribution of that trust fund or estate.

55.   Communications by members of professions

(1)   The financial promotion restriction does not apply to a real time communication (whether solicited or unsolicited) which—

(a)   is made by a person ("P") who carries on a regulated activity to which the general prohibition does not apply by virtue of section 327 of the Act; and

(b)   is made to a recipient who has, prior to the communication being made, engaged P to
       provide professional services,

where the controlled activity to which the communication relates is an excluded activity which
would be undertaken by P for the purposes of, and incidental to, the provision by him of professional services to or at the request of the recipient.

(2)   "Professional services" has the meaning given in section 327 of the Act.

(3)   An "excluded activity" is an activity to which the general prohibition would apply but for the
       application of—
       (a)   section 327 of the Act; or
       (b)   article 67 of the Regulated Activities Order.

55A.   Non-real time communication by members of professions

(1)   The financial promotion restriction does not apply to a non-real time communication which is—
       (a)   made by a person ("P") who carries on Part XX activities; and
       (b)   limited to what is required or permitted by paragraphs (2) and (3).

(2)   The communication must be in the following terms—

       "This firm/company is not authorised under the Financial Services and Markets Act 2000
       but we are able in certain circumstances to offer a limited range of investment services to
       clients because we are members of relevant designated professional body. We can provide
       these investment services if they are an incidental part of the professional services we have
       been engaged to provide.".

(3)   The communication may in addition set out the Part XX activities which P is able to offer to his
       clients, provided it is clear that these are the investment services to which the statement in
       paragraph (2) relates.

(4)   "Part XX activities" means the regulated activities to which the general prohibition does not
       apply when they are carried on by P by virtue of section 327 of the Act.

56.   Remedy following report by Parliamentary Commissioner for Administration

The financial promotion restriction does not apply to any communication made or directed by a
person for the purpose of enabling any injustice, stated by the Parliamentary Commissioner for
Administration in a report under section 10 of the Parliamentary Commissioner Act 1967 to have
occurred, to be remedied with respect to the recipient.

57.   Persons placing promotional material in particular publications

The financial promotion restriction does not apply to any communication received by a person
who receives the publication in which the communication is contained because he has himself
placed an advertisement in that publication.

58.   Acquisition of interest in premises run by management companies

(1)   "Management company" means a company established for the purpose of—
       (a)   managing the common parts or fabric of premises used for residential or business purposes;
              or
       (b)   supplying services to such premises.

(2)   The financial promotion restriction does not apply to any non-real time communication or
       solicited real time communication if it relates to an investment falling within paragraph 14 of
       Schedule 1 which—
       (a)   is issued, or to be issued, by a management company; and
       (b)   is to be acquired by any person in connection with the acquisition of an interest in the
              premises in question.

59.   Annual accounts and directors' report

(1)   If the requirements in paragraphs (2) to (5) are met, the financial promotion restriction does not
       apply to any communication by a body corporate (other than an open-ended investment company)
       which—

(a)   consists of, or is accompanied by, the whole or any part of the annual accounts of a body corporate (other than an open-ended investment company); or

(b)   is accompanied by any report which is prepared and approved by the directors of such a body corporate under—

(i)   sections 234 and 234A of the 1985 Act;

(ii)   the corresponding Northern Ireland enactment; or

(iii) the law of an EEA State other than the United Kingdom which corresponds to the provisions mentioned in paragraph (i) or (ii).

(2)   The requirements of this paragraph are that the communication—

(a)   does not contain any invitation to persons to underwrite, subscribe for, or otherwise acquire or dispose of, a controlled investment; and

(b)   does not advise persons to engage in any of the activities within sub-paragraph (a).

(3)   The requirements of this paragraph are that the communication does not contain any invitation to persons to—

(a)   effect any transaction with the body corporate (or with any named person) in the course of that body's (or person's) carrying on of any activity falling within any of paragraphs 3 to 11 of Schedule 1; or

(b)   make use of any services provided by that body corporate (or by any named person) in the course of carrying on such activity.

(4)   The requirements of this paragraph are that the communication does not contain any inducement relating to an investment other than one issued by the body corporate (or another body corporate in the same group) which falls within—

(a)   paragraph 14 or 15 of Schedule 1; or

(b)   paragraph 17 or 18 of that Schedule, so far as relating to any investments within sub-paragraph (a).

(5)   The requirements of this paragraph are that the communication does not contain any reference to—

(a)   the price at which investments issued by the body corporate have in the past been bought or sold; or

(b)   the yield on such investments,

unless it is also accompanied by an indication that past performance cannot be relied on as a guide to future performance.

(6)   For the purposes of paragraph (5)(b), a reference, in relation to an investment, to earnings, dividend or nominal rate of interest payable shall not be taken to be a reference to the yield on the investment.

(7)   "Annual accounts" means—

(a)   accounts produced by virtue of Part VII of the 1985 Act (or of that Part as applied by virtue of any other enactment);

(b)   accounts produced by virtue of the corresponding Northern Ireland enactment (or of that enactment as applied by virtue of any other enactment);

(c)   a summary financial statement prepared under section 251 of the 1985 Act;

(d)   accounts delivered to the registrar under Chapter II of Part XXIII of the 1985 Act;

(e)   accounts which are produced or published by virtue of the law of an EEA State other than the United Kingdom and which correspond to accounts within any of sub-paragraphs (a) to (d).

60.   Participation in employee share schemes

(1)   The financial promotion restriction does not apply to any communication by a person ("C"), a member of the same group as C or a relevant trustee where the communication is for the purposes of an employee share scheme and relates to any of the following investments issued by C—

(a)   investments falling within paragraph 14 or 15 of Schedule 1;

(b)   investments falling within paragraph 17 or 18 of that Schedule so far as relating to any investments within sub-paragraph (a); or

(c)   investments falling within paragraph 27 so far as relating to any investments within sub-paragraph (a) or (b).

(2)   "Employee share scheme", in relation to any investments issued by C, means arrangements made or to be made by C or by a person in the same group as C to enable or facilitate—

     (a)   transactions in those investments between or for the benefit of—

         (i)   the bona fide employees or former employees of C or of another member of the same group as C;

         (ii)   the wives, husbands, widows, widowers, or children or step children under the age of eighteen of such employees or former employees; or

     (b)   the holding of those investments by, or for the benefit of, such persons.

(3)   "Relevant trustee" means a person who, in pursuance of an actual or proposed employee share scheme, holds as trustee or will hold as trustee investments issued by C.

61.   Sale of goods and supply of services

(1)   In this article—

     "supplier" means a person whose main business is to sell goods or supply services and not to carry on controlled activities falling within any of paragraphs 3 to 7 of Schedule 1 and, where the supplier is a member of a group, also means any other member of that group;

     "customer" means a person, other than an individual, to whom a supplier sells goods or supplies services, or agrees to do so, and, where the customer is a member of a group, also means any other member of that group;

     "a related sale or supply" means a sale of goods or supply of services to the customer otherwise than by the supplier, but for or in connection with the same purpose as the sale or supply mentioned above.

(2)   The financial promotion restriction does not apply to any non-real time communication or any solicited real time communication made by a supplier to a customer of his for the purposes of, or in connection with, the sale of goods or supply of services or a related sale or supply.

(3)   But the exemption in paragraph (2) does not apply if the communication relates to—

     (a)   a qualifying contract of insurance or units in a collective investment scheme; or

     (b)   investments falling within paragraph 27 of Schedule 1 so far as relating to investments within paragraph (a).

62.   Sale of body corporate

(1)   The financial promotion restriction does not apply to any communication by, or on behalf of, a body corporate, a partnership, a single individual or a group of connected individuals which relates to a transaction falling within paragraph (2).

(2)   A transaction falls within this paragraph if—

     (a)   it is one to acquire or dispose of shares in a body corporate other than an open-ended investment company, or is entered into for the purposes of such an acquisition or disposal; and

     (b)   either—

         (i)   the conditions set out in paragraph (3) are met; or

         (ii)   those conditions are not met, but the object of the transaction may nevertheless reasonably be regarded as being the acquisition of day to day control of the affairs of the body corporate.

(3)   The conditions mentioned in paragraph (2)(b) are that—

     (a)   the shares consist of or include 50 per cent or more of the voting shares in the body corporate; or

     (b)   the shares, together with any already held by the person acquiring them, consist of or include at least that percentage of such shares; and

     (c)   in either case, the acquisition or disposal is, or is to be, between parties each of whom is a body corporate, a partnership, a single individual or a group of connected individuals.

(4)   "A group of connected individuals" means—

    (a)   in relation to a party disposing of shares in a body corporate, a single group of persons each of whom is—

        (i)   a director or manager of the body corporate;

        (ii) a close relative of any such director or manager; or

        (iii) a person acting as trustee for any person falling within paragraph (i) or (ii); and

    (b)   in relation to a party acquiring shares in a body corporate, a single group of persons each of whom is—

        (i)   a person who is or is to be a director or manager of the body corporate;

        (ii) a close relative of any such person; or

        (iii) a person acting as trustee for any person falling within paragraph (i) or (ii).

(5)   "Voting shares", in relation to a body corporate, means shares carrying voting rights attributable to share capital which are exercisable in all circumstances at any general meeting of that body corporate.

63. Takeovers of relevant unlisted companies: interpretation

(1)   In this article and in articles 64, 65 and 66, a "relevant unlisted company", in relation to a takeover offer, means a company which is an unlisted company at the time that the offer is made and which has been an unlisted company throughout the period of ten years immediately preceding the date of the offer.

(2)   In this article and in articles 64, 65 and 66, references to a takeover offer for a relevant unlisted company are references to an offer which meets the requirements of Part I of Schedule 4 and which is an offer—

    (a)   for all the shares in, or all the shares comprised in the equity or non-equity share capital of, a relevant unlisted company (other than any shares already held by or on behalf of the person making the offer); or

    (b)   for all the debentures of such a company (other than any debentures already held by or on behalf of the person making the offer).

(3)   Shares in or debentures of an unlisted company are to be regarded as being held by or on behalf of the person making the offer if the person who holds them, or on whose behalf they are held, has agreed that an offer should not be made in respect of them.

64. Takeovers of relevant unlisted companies

(1)   If the requirements of paragraphs (2) and (3) are met, the financial promotion restriction does not apply to any communication which is communicated in connection with a takeover offer for a relevant unlisted company.

(2)   The requirements of this paragraph are that the communication is accompanied by the material listed in Part II of Schedule 4.

(3)   The requirements of this paragraph are that the material listed in Part III of Schedule 4 is available at a place in the United Kingdom at all times during normal office hours for inspection free of charge.

65. Takeovers of relevant unlisted companies: warrants etc

The financial promotion restriction does not apply to any communication which—

    (a)   is communicated at the same time as, or after, a takeover offer for a relevant unlisted company is made; and

    (b)   relates to investments falling within paragraph 17 or 18 of Schedule 1 so far as relating to the shares in or debentures of the unlisted company which are the subject of the offer.

66. Takeovers of relevant unlisted companies: application forms

The financial promotion restriction does not apply to any communication made in connection with a takeover offer for a relevant unlisted company which is a form of application for—

    (a)   shares in or debentures of the unlisted company; or

    (b)   investments falling within paragraph 17 or 18 of Schedule 1 so far as relating to the shares in or debentures of the company which are the subject of the offer.

67.   **Promotions required or permitted by market rules**

(1)   The financial promotion restriction does not apply to any communication which—

      (a)   is a non-real time communication or a solicited real time communication;

      (b)   relates to an investment which falls within any of paragraphs 14 to 18 of Schedule 1 and which is permitted to be traded or dealt in on a relevant market; and

      (c)   is required or permitted to be communicated by—

           (i)   the rules of the relevant market;

           (ii)   a body which regulates the market; or

           (iii)   a body which regulates offers or issues of investments to be traded on such a market.

(2)   "Relevant market" means a market which—

      (a)   meets the criteria specified in Part I of Schedule 3; or

      (b)   is specified in, or established under the rules of an exchange specified in, Part II or III of that Schedule.

68.   **Promotions in connection with admission to certain EEA markets**

(1)   The financial promotion restriction does not apply to any communication—

      (a)   which is a non-real time communication or a solicited real time communication;

      (b)   which a relevant EEA market requires to be communicated before an investment can be admitted to trading on that market;

      (c)   which, if it were included in a prospectus issued in accordance with Part II of the Public Offers of Securities Regulations 1995, would be required to be communicated by those Regulations; and

      (d)   which is not accompanied by any information other than information which is required or permitted to be published by the rules of that market.

(2)   In this article "relevant EEA market" means any market on which investments can be traded or dealt in and which—

      (a)   meets the criteria specified in Part I of Schedule 3; or

      (b)   is specified in, or established under the rules of an exchange specified in, Part II of that Schedule.

69.   **Promotions of securities already admitted to certain markets**

(1)   In this article—

      "relevant investment" means any investment falling within—

      (a)   paragraph 14 or 15 of Schedule 1; or

      (b)   paragraph 17 or 18 of that Schedule so far as relating to any investment mentioned in sub-paragraph (a);

      "relevant market" means any market on which investments can be traded or dealt in and which—

      (a)   meets the criteria specified in Part I of Schedule 3; or

      (b)   is specified in, or established under the rules of an exchange specified in, Part II or III of that Schedule.

(2)   If the requirements of paragraphs (3) to (6) are met, the financial promotion restriction does not apply to any communication which is—

      (a)   a non-real time communication or a solicited real time communication;

      (b)   communicated by a body corporate ("A"), other than an open-ended investment company; and

      (c)   relates only to investments issued by A or by another body corporate in the same group,

      if relevant investments issued by A or by any parent undertaking of A are permitted to be traded, or dealt in, on a relevant market.

(3)   The requirements of this paragraph are that the communication—

      (a)   is not, and is not accompanied by, an invitation to underwrite, subscribe for, or otherwise acquire or dispose of, a controlled investment; and

      (b)   does not advise persons to engage in one of the activities within sub-paragraph (a).

(4)   The requirements of this paragraph are that the communication is not, and is not accompanied by, an invitation to—

(a)   effect any transaction with A (or with any named person) in the course of the carrying on by A (or the named person) of any activity falling within any of paragraphs 3 to 11 of Schedule 1; or

(b)   make use of any services provided by A (or by any named person) in the course of carrying on such activity.

(5)   The requirements of this paragraph are that the communication is not, and is not accompanied by, an inducement relating to a relevant investment other than one issued by A (or another body corporate in the same group).

(6)   The requirements of this paragraph are that the communication does not refer, and is not accompanied by a reference, to—

(a)   the price at which the investments have been bought or sold in the past; or

(b)   the yield on such investments,

unless it is also accompanied by an indication that past performance cannot be relied on as a guide to future performance.

(7)   For the purposes of paragraph (6)(b), a reference, in relation to an investment, to earnings, dividend or nominal rate of interest payable shall not be taken to be a reference to the yield on the investment.

70.   Promotions in connection with listing applications

The financial promotion restriction does not apply to any non-real time communication or any solicited real time communication to which listing rules made under section 98(1) of the Act apply.

71.   Promotions included in listing particulars etc

(1)   The financial promotion restriction does not apply to any non-real time communication which is included in—

(a)   listing particulars;

(b)   supplementary listing particulars;

(c)   a prospectus approved in accordance with listing rules made under section 84 or 87 of the Act;

(d)   a supplementary prospectus approved in accordance with listing rules made for the purposes of section 81 of the Act as applied by section 86 or 87; or

(e)   any other document required or permitted to be published by listing rules under Part VI of the Act.

(2)   In this article "listing particulars" and "listing rules" have the meaning given by Part VI of the Act.

72.   Promotions included in prospectus for public offer of unlisted securities

The financial promotion restriction does not apply to any non-real time communication which is included in a prospectus or supplementary prospectus that is issued in accordance with Part II of the Public Offers of Securities Regulations 1995.

73.   Material relating to prospectus for public offer of unlisted securities

(1)   The financial promotion restriction does not apply to any non-real time communication relating to a prospectus or supplementary prospectus where the only reason for considering it to be an invitation or inducement is that it does one or more of the following—

(a)   it states the name and address of the person by whom the securities to which the prospectus or supplementary prospectus relates are to be offered;

(b)   it gives other details for contacting that person;

(c)   it states the nature and the nominal value of the securities to which the prospectus or supplementary prospectus relates, the number offered and the price at which they are offered;

(d)   it states that a prospectus or supplementary prospectus is or will be available (and, if it is not yet available, when it is expected to be);

(e)   it gives instructions for obtaining a copy of the prospectus or supplementary prospectus.

(2)   In this article—

   (a)   "securities" and "offer" have the same meaning as in Part II of the Public Offers of Securities Regulations 1995;

   (b)   references to a prospectus or supplementary prospectus are references to a prospectus or supplementary prospectus which is published in accordance with Part II of the Public Offers of Securities Regulations 1995.

PART VII
TRANSITIONAL PROVISION

74.   Approval of communication prior to Order coming into force

(1)   The financial promotion restriction does not apply to a communication which falls within paragraph (2) or (3).

(2)   A communication falls within this paragraph if—

   (a)   before this article comes into force, the content of the communication has been approved for the purposes of section 57 of the Financial Services Act 1986 by a person authorised under Chapter III of Part I of that Act; and

   (b)   the communication is made or directed within one month starting with the date on which this article comes into force.

(3)   A communication falls within this paragraph if—

   (a)   before this article comes into force, the content of the communication had been approved by a person who is an authorised person (within the meaning of the Act) immediately after this article comes into force;

   (b)   the approval if it had been given immediately after this article comes into force would have complied with any relevant rules made by the Authority under section 145; and

   (c)   the communication is made or directed within the period of one month starting with the date on which this article comes into force.

(4)   For the purpose of paragraph (2)(b) and (3)(c) a communication contained in a web site is directed on the date when it is posted on the site.

SCHEDULE 1

Article 4

PART I
CONTROLLED ACTIVITIES

1.   Accepting deposits

Accepting deposits is a controlled activity if—

(a)   money received by way of deposit is lent to others; or

(b)   any other activity of the person accepting the deposit is financed wholly, or to a material extent, out of the capital of or interest on money received by way of deposit,

and the person accepting the deposit holds himself out as accepting deposits on a day to day basis.

2.   Effecting and carrying out contracts of insurance

(1)   Effecting a contract of insurance as principal is a controlled activity.

(2)   Carrying out a contract of insurance as principal is a controlled activity.

(3)   There is excluded from sub-paragraph (1) or (2) the effecting or carrying out of a contract of insurance of the kind described in article 12 of the Regulated Activities Order by a person who does not otherwise carry on an activity falling within those sub-paragraphs.

3.   Dealing in securities and contractually based investments

(1)   Buying, selling, subscribing for or underwriting securities or contractually based investments (other than investments of the kind specified by paragraph 25, or paragraph 27 so far as relevant to that paragraph) as principal or agent is a controlled activity.

(2)   A person does not carry on the activity in sub-paragraph (1) by accepting an instrument creating or acknowledging indebtedness in respect of any loan, credit, guarantee or other similar financial accommodation or assurance which he has made, granted or provided.

(3)   The reference in sub-paragraph (2) to a person accepting an instrument includes a reference to a person becoming a party to an instrument otherwise than as a debtor or a surety.

4.   Arranging deals in investments

(1)   Making arrangements for another person (whether as principal or agent) to buy, sell, subscribe for or underwrite a particular investment which is—

(a)   a security;

(b)   a contractually based investment; or

(c)   an investment of the kind specified by paragraph 24, or paragraph 27 so far as relevant to that paragraph,

is a controlled activity.

(2)   Making arrangements with a view to a person who participates in the arrangements buying, selling, subscribing for or underwriting investments falling within sub-paragraph (1)(a), (b) or (c) (whether as principal or agent) is also a controlled activity.

(3)   A person does not carry on an activity falling within paragraph (2) merely by providing means by which one party to a transaction (or potential transaction) is able to communicate with other such parties.

5.   Managing investments

Managing assets belonging to another person, in circumstances involving the exercise of discretion, is a controlled activity if—

(a)   the assets consist of or include any investment which is a security or a contractually based investment; or

(b)   the arrangements for their management are such that the assets may consist of or include such investments, and either the assets have at any time since 29th April 1988 done so, or the arrangements have at any time (whether before or after that date) been held out as arrangements under which the assets would do so.

6.   Safeguarding and administering investments

(1)   The activity consisting of both—

(a)   the safeguarding of assets belonging to another; and

(b)   the administration of those assets,

or arranging for one or more other persons to carry on that activity, is a controlled activity if either the condition in paragraph (a) or (b) of sub-paragraph (2) is met.

(2)   The condition is that—

(a)   the assets consist of or include any investment which is a security or a contractually based investment; or

(b)   the arrangements for their safeguarding and administration are such that the assets may consist of or include investments of the kind mentioned in sub-paragraph (a) and either the assets have at any time since 1st June 1997 done so, or the arrangements have at any time (whether before or after that date) been held out as ones under which such investments would be safeguarded and administered.

(3)   For the purposes of this article—

(a)   it is immaterial that title to the assets safeguarded and administered is held in uncertificated form;

(b)   it is immaterial that the assets safeguarded and administered may be transferred to another person, subject to a commitment by the person safeguarding and administering them, or arranging for their safeguarding and administration, that they will be replaced by equivalent assets at some future date or when so requested by the person to whom they belong.

(4)   For the purposes of this article, the following activities do not constitute the administration of assets—

(a)   providing information as to the number of units or the value of any assets safeguarded;

(b)   converting currency;

(c)   receiving documents relating to an investment solely for the purpose of onward transmission to, from or at the direction of the person to whom the investment belongs.

7.   Advising on investments

Advising a person is a controlled activity if the advice is—

(a)   given to the person in his capacity as an investor or potential investor, or in his capacity as agent for an investor or a potential investor; and

(b)   advice on the merits of his doing any of the following (whether as principal or agent)—

(i)   buying, selling, subscribing for or underwriting a particular investment which is a security or a contractually based investment; or

(ii)   exercising any right conferred by such an investment to buy, sell, subscribe for or underwrite such an investment.

8.   Advising on syndicate participation at Lloyd's

Advising a person to become, or continue or cease to be, a member of a particular Lloyd's syndicate is a controlled activity.

9.   Providing funeral plan contracts

(1)   Entering as provider into a qualifying funeral plan contract is a controlled activity.

(2)   A "qualifying funeral plan contract" is a contract under which—

(a)   a person ("the customer") makes one or more payments to another person ("the provider");

(b)   the provider undertakes to provide, or to secure that another person provides, a funeral in the United Kingdom for the customer (or some other person who is living at the date when the contract is entered into) on his death; and

(c)   the provider is a person who carries on the regulated activity specified in article 59 of the Regulated Activities Order.

10.   Providing qualifying credit

(1)   Providing qualifying credit is a controlled activity.

(2)   "Qualifying credit" is a credit provided pursuant to an agreement under which—

(a)   the lender is a person who carries on the regulated activity specified in article 61 of the Regulated Activities Order; and

(b)   the obligation of the borrower to repay is secured (in whole or in part) on land.

(3)   "Credit" includes a cash loan and any other form of financial accommodation.

10A.   Arranging qualifying credit etc.

Making arrangements—

(a)   for another person to enter as borrower into an agreement for the provision of qualifying credit; or

(b)   for a borrower under a regulated mortgage contract, within the meaning of article 61(3) of the Regulated Activities Order entered into after the coming into force of that article, to vary the terms of that contract in such a way as to vary his obligations under that contract,

is a controlled activity.

10B.   Advising on qualifying credit etc.

(1)   Advising a person is a controlled activity if the advice is—

(a)   given to the person in his capacity as a borrower or potential borrower; and

(b)   advice on the merits of his doing any of the following—

(i)   entering into an agreement for the provision of qualifying credit, or

(ii)   varying the terms of a regulated mortgage contract entered into by him after the coming into force of article 61 of the Regulated Activities Order in such a way as to vary his obligations under that contract.

(2)   In this paragraph, "borrower" and "regulated mortgage contract" have the meaning given by article 61(3) of the Regulated Activities Order.

11.   Agreeing to carry on specified kinds of activity

Agreeing to carry on any controlled activity falling within any of paragraphs 3 to 10B above is a controlled activity.

PART II
CONTROLLED INVESTMENTS

12.

A deposit.

13.

Rights under a contract of insurance.

14.

(1)   Shares or stock in the share capital of—

(a)   any body corporate (wherever incorporated);

(b)   any unincorporated body constituted under the law of a country or territory outside the United Kingdom.

(2)   Sub-paragraph (1) includes—

(a)   any shares of a class defined as deferred shares for the purposes of section 119 of the Building Societies Act 1986;

(b)   any transferable shares in a body incorporated under the law of, or any part of, the United Kingdom relating to industrial and provident societies or credit unions or in a body constituted under the law of another EEA State for purposes equivalent to those of such a body.

(3)   But subject to sub-paragraph (2) there are excluded from sub-paragraph (1) shares or stock in the share capital of—

(a)   an open-ended investment company;

(b)   a building society incorporated under the law of, or any part of, the United Kingdom;

(c)   any body incorporated under the law of, or any part of, the United Kingdom relating to industrial and provident societies or credit unions;

(d)   any body constituted under the law of an EEA State for purposes equivalent to those of a body falling within paragraph (b) or (c).

15.   Instruments creating or acknowledging indebtedness

(1)   Subject to sub-paragraph (2), such of the following as do not fall within paragraph 16—

(a)   debentures;

(b)   debenture stock;

(c)   loan stock;

(d)   bonds;

(e)   certificates of deposit;

(f)   any other instrument creating or acknowledging indebtedness.

(2)   If and to the extent that they would otherwise fall within sub-paragraph (1), there are excluded from that sub-paragraph—

(a)   any instrument acknowledging or creating indebtedness for, or for money borrowed to defray, the consideration payable under a contract for the supply of goods or services;

(b)   a cheque or other bill of exchange, a banker's draft or a letter of credit (but not a bill of exchange accepted by a banker);

(c)   a banknote, a statement showing a balance on a current, deposit or saving account, a lease or other disposition of property, a heritable security; and

(d)   a contract of insurance.

(3)   An instrument excluded from sub-paragraph (1) of paragraph 16 by paragraph 16(2)(b) is not thereby to be taken to fall within sub-paragraph (1) of this paragraph.

16.   Government and public securities

(1)   Subject to sub-paragraph (2), loan stock, bonds and other instruments—

(a)   creating or acknowledging indebtedness; and

(b)   issued by or on behalf of a government, local authority (whether in the United Kingdom or elsewhere) or international organisation.

(2)   There are excluded from sub-paragraph (1)—

(a)   so far as applicable, the instruments mentioned in paragraph 15(2)(a) to (d);

(b)   any instrument creating or acknowledging indebtedness in respect of—

(i)   money received by the Director of Savings as deposits or otherwise in connection with the business of the National Savings Bank;

(ii)   money raised under the National Loans Act 1968 under the auspices of the Director of Savings or treated as so raised by virtue of section 11(3) of the National Debt Act 1972.

17.   Instruments giving entitlements to investments

(1)   Warrants and other instruments entitling the holder to subscribe for any investment falling within paragraph 14, 15 or 16.

(2)   It is immaterial whether the investment to which the entitlement relates is in existence or identifiable.

(3)   An investment falling within this paragraph shall not be regarded as falling within paragraph 21, 22 or 23.

18.   Certificates representing certain securities

(1)   Subject to sub-paragraph (2), certificates or other instruments which confer contractual or property rights (other than rights consisting of an investment of the kind specified by paragraph 21)—

(a)   in respect of any investment of the kind specified by any of paragraphs 14 to 17 being an investment held by a person other than the person on whom the rights are conferred by the certificate or instrument; and

(b)   the transfer of which may be effected without the consent of that person.

(2)   There is excluded from sub-paragraph (1) any instrument which confers rights in respect of two or more investments issued by different persons, or in respect of two or more different investments of the kind specified by paragraph 16 and issued by the same person.

19.   Units in a collective investment scheme

Units in a collective investment scheme.

20.   Rights under a stakeholder pension scheme

(1)   Rights under a stakeholder pension scheme.

(2)   "Stakeholder pension scheme" has the meaning given by section 1 of the Welfare Reform and Pensions Act 1999 .

21.   Options

Options to acquire or dispose of—

(a)   a security or contractually based investment (other than one of a kind specified in this paragraph);

(b)   currency of the United Kingdom or of any other country or territory;

(c)   palladium, platinum, gold or silver; or

(d)   an option to acquire or dispose of an investment falling within this paragraph by virtue of sub-paragraph (a), (b) or (c).

22.   Futures

(1)   Subject to sub-paragraph (2), rights under a contract for the sale of a commodity or property of any other description under which delivery is to be made at a future date and at a price agreed on when the contract is made.

(2)   There are excluded from sub-paragraph (1) rights under any contract which is made for commercial and not investment purposes.

(3)   For the purposes of sub-paragraph (2), in considering whether a contract is to be regarded as made for investment purposes or for commercial purposes, the indicators set out in article 84 of the Regulated Activities Order shall be applied in the same way as they are applied for the purposes of that article.

23.   Contracts for differences etc

(1)   Subject to sub-paragraph (2), rights under—

(a)   a contract for differences; or

(b)   any other contract the purpose or pretended purpose of which is to secure a profit or avoid a loss by reference to fluctuations in—

(i)   the value or price of property of any description;

(ii)   an index or other factor designated for that purpose in the contract.

(2)   There are excluded from sub-paragraph (1)—

(a)   rights under a contract if the parties intend that the profit is to be secured or the loss is to be avoided by one or more of the parties taking delivery of any property to which the contract relates;

(b)   rights under a contract under which money is received by way of deposit on terms that any interest or other return to be paid on the sum deposited will be calculated by reference to fluctuations in an index or other factor;

(c)   rights under any contract under which—

(i)   money is received by the Director of Savings as deposits or otherwise in connection with the business of the National Savings Bank; or

(ii)   money is raised under the National Loans Act 1968 under the auspices of the Director of Savings or treated as so raised by virtue of section 11(3) of the National Debt Act 1972;

(d)   rights under a qualifying contract of insurance.

24.   Lloyd's syndicate capacity and syndicate membership

(1)   The underwriting capacity of a Lloyd's syndicate.

(2)   A person's membership (or prospective membership) of a Lloyd's syndicate.

25.   Funeral plan contracts

Rights under a qualifying funeral plan contract.

26.   Agreements for qualifying credit

Rights under an agreement for qualifying credit.

27.   Rights to or interests in investments

(1)   Subject to sub-paragraphs (2) and (3), any right to or interest in anything which is specified by any other provision of this Part of this Schedule (other than paragraph 26).

(2)   Sub-paragraph (1) does not apply to interests under the trusts of an occupational pension scheme.

(2A)   Sub-paragraph (1) does not apply to any right or interest acquired as a result of entering into a funeral plan contract (and for this purpose a "funeral plan contract" is a contract of a kind described in paragraph 9(2)(a) and (b)).

(3)   Sub-paragraph (1) does not apply to anything which falls within any other provision of this Part of this Schedule.

28.   Interpretation

In this Schedule unless the context otherwise requires—

"buying" includes acquiring for valuable consideration;

"contract of insurance" has the meaning given in the Regulated Activities Order;

"contractually based investment" means—

(a)   rights under a qualifying contract of insurance;

(b)   any investment of the kind specified by any of paragraphs 21, 22, 23 and 25;

(c)   any investment of the kind specified by paragraph 27 so far as relevant to an investment falling within (a) or (b);

"occupational pension scheme" means any scheme or arrangement which is comprised in one or more instruments or agreements and which has, or is capable of having, effect in relation to one or more descriptions or categories of employment so as to provide benefits, in the form of pensions or otherwise, payable on termination of service, or on death or retirement, to or in respect of earners with qualifying service in an employment of any such description or category;

"property" includes currency of the United Kingdom or any other country or territory;

"qualifying funeral plan contract" has the meaning given by paragraph 9;

"security" means a controlled investment falling within any of paragraphs 14 to 20 or, so far as relevant to any such investment, paragraph 27;

"selling", in relation to any investment, includes disposing of the investment for valuable consideration, and for these purposes "disposing" includes—

(a)   in the case of an investment consisting of rights under a contract—

(i)   surrendering, assigning or converting those rights; or

(ii)   assuming the corresponding liabilities under the contract;

(b)   in the case of an investment consisting of rights under other arrangements, assuming the corresponding liabilities under the arrangements; and

(c)   in the case of any other investment, issuing or creating the investment or granting the rights or interests of which it consists;

"syndicate" has the meaning given in the Regulated Activities Order.

SCHEDULE 2

COUNTRIES AND TERRITORIES

Article 10

1.   The Bailiwick of Guernsey.
2.   The Isle of Man.
3.   The Commonwealth of Pennsylvania.
4.   The State of Iowa.
5.   The Bailiwick of Jersey.

SCHEDULE 3

MARKETS AND EXCHANGES

Articles 37, 41, 67, 68 and 69

PART I
CRITERIA FOR RELEVANT EEA MARKETS

The criteria are—
(a)   the head office of the market must be situated in an EEA State; and
(b)   the market must be subject to requirements in the EEA State in which its head office is situated as to—
    (i)   the manner in which it operates;
    (ii)   the means by which access may be had to the facilities it provides;
    (iii)   the conditions to be satisfied before an investment may be traded or dealt in by means of its facilities;
    (iv)   the reporting and publication of transactions effected by means of its facilities.

PART II
CERTAIN INVESTMENT EXCHANGES OPERATING RELEVANT EEA MARKETS
AND CERTAIN RELEVANT EEA MARKETS

Aktietorget I Norden (Sweden).
Amsterdam Stock Exchange (Netherlands).
Amsterdam Options Exchange (Netherlands).
Amsterdam Financial Futures Market (Netherlands).
Amsterdam New Market (Netherlands).
Athens Stock Exchange (Greece).
Athens Derivative Exchange (Greece).
Barcelona Stock Exchange (Spain).
Bavarian Stock Exchange (Germany).
Belfox Futures and Options Exchange (Belgium).
Belgian Secondary Market for Treasury Certificates (Belgium).
Berlin Stock Exchange (Germany).
Bilbao Stock Exchange (Spain).
Bremen Stock Exchange (Germany).
Brussels Stock Exchange (including Primary, Secondary and New Markets) (Belgium).
Copenhagen Stock Exchange (Denmark).
COREDEAL (UK).
Danish Authorised Market Place (Denmark).
Dusseldorf Stock Market (Germany).
EASDAQ (Belgium).
Eurex Deutschland (Germany).
Frankfurt Stock Exchange (including Neuer Markt) (Germany).
Hamburg Stock Exchange (Germany).
Hanover Stock Exchange (Germany).
Hex Ltd (including Helsinki Stock Exchange and Securities and Derivatives Exchange) (Finland).
IDEM—Derivatives Market (Italy).
IM Marketplace—(Sweden).
Irish Stock Exchange (Ireland).
Italian/Milan Stock Exchange (Italy).
Italian and Foreign Government Bonds Market (Italy).
Jiway (UK)
Le MATIF (France).
Le Monep (France).
Le Noveau Marche (France).
Lisbon Stock Exchange (including Exchanges for the Officially Quoted, Secondary and Unquoted Markets) (Portugal).

London International Financial Futures and Options Exchange (UK).
London Stock Exchange (UK).
Luxembourg Stock Exchange (Luxembourg).
Madrid Stock Exchange (Spain).
Market for Public Debt (Spain).
MEFF Renta Variable Futures & Options Exchange (Spain).
MEFF Renta fija Equity Futures Exchange (Spain).
MIF Derivatives Market (Italy).
Nuovo Mercato (Italy).
OFEX (UK).
OMLX (UK).
OM Stockholm (Sweden).
Paris Stock Exchange (France).
Porto Derivatives Exchange (Portugal).
Stockholm Stock Exchange (Sweden).
Stuttgart Stock Exchange (Germany).
Swedish Bond & Money Market Exchange (Sweden).
Unlisted Securities Market (Italy).
Valencia Stock Exchange (Spain).
Vienna Stock Exchange (Austria).
Virt-x (UK)

PART III
CERTAIN NON-EEA INVESTMENT EXCHANGES OPERATING RELEVANT MARKETS

...

America Stock Exchange.
Australian Stock Exchange.
Basler Effektenbourse.
Boston Stock Exchange.
Bourse de Geneve.
Buenos Aires Stock Exchange.
Canadian Venture Exchange.
Chicago Board Options Exchange.
Cincinnati Stock Exchange.
Effektenborsenverein Zurich.
Fukuoka Stock Exchange.
Hiroshima Stock Exchange.
Iceland Stock Exchange.
Johannesburg Stock Exchange.
Korean Stock Exchange.
Kuala Lumpur Stock Exchange.
Kyoto Stock Exchange.
Midwest Stock Exchange.
Montreal Stock Exchange.
Nagoya Stock Exchange.
NASDAQ
New York Stock Exchange.
New Zealand Stock Exchange.
Niigita Stock Exchange.
Osaka Stock Exchange.
Oslo Stock Exchange.
Pacific Stock Exchange.

Philadelphia Stock Exchange.
Sapporo Stock Exchange
Securities Exchange of Thailand.
Singapore Stock Exchange.
Stock Exchange of Hong Kong Limited.
Tokyo Stock Exchange.
Toronto Stock Exchange.
…

PART IV
OTHER RELEVANT MARKETS

American Commodity Exchange.
Amex Commodity Corporation.
Australian Financial Futures Market.
Cantor Financial Futures Exchange.
Chicago Board of Trade.
Chicago Mercantile Exchange.
Chicago Rice and Cotton Exchange.
Commodity Exchange Inc.
Eurex Zurich
International Securities Market Association.
International Petroleum Exchange.
Kansas City Board of Trade.
London Metal Exchange.
Mid-America Commodity Exchange.
Minneapolis Grain Exchange.
New York Board of Trade.
New York Futures Exchange.
New York Mercantile Exchange.
New Zealand Futures Exchange.
Pacific Commodity Exchange.
Pacific Futures Exchange.
Philadelphia Board of Trade.
Singapore International Monetary Exchange.
Sydney Futures Exchange.
Toronto Futures Exchange.
Twin Cities Board of Trade.

SCHEDULE 4

TAKEOVERS OF RELEVANT UNLISTED COMPANIES

Articles 63 and 64

PART I
REQUIREMENTS RELATING TO THE OFFER

1.   The terms of the offer must be recommended by all the directors of the company other than any director who is—
   (a)   the person by whom, or on whose behalf, an offer is made ("offeror"); or
   (b)   a director of the offeror.
2.—   (1)   This paragraph applies to an offer for debentures or for non-equity share capital.

(2)   Where, at the date of the offer, shares carrying 50 per cent or less of the voting rights attributable to the equity share capital are held by or on behalf of the offeror, the offer must include or be accompanied by an offer made by the offeror for the rest of the shares comprised in the equity share capital.

3.—   (1)   This paragraph applies to an offer for shares comprised in the equity share capital.

(2)   Where, at the date of the offer, shares which carry 50 per cent or less of the categories of voting rights described in sub-paragraph (3) are held by or on behalf of the offeror, it must be a condition of the offer that sufficient shares will be acquired or agreed to be acquired by the offeror pursuant to or during the offer so as to result in shares carrying more than 50 per cent of one or both categories of relevant voting rights being held by him or on his behalf.

(3)   The categories of voting rights mentioned in sub-paragraph (2) are—

(a)   voting rights exercisable in general meetings of the company;

(b)   voting rights attributable to the equity share capital.

4.—   (1)   Subject to sub-paragraph (2), the offer must be open for acceptance by every recipient for the period of at least 21 days beginning with the day after the day on which the invitation or inducement in question was first communicated to recipients of the offer.

(2)   Sub-paragraph (1) does not apply if the offer is totally withdrawn and all persons released from any obligation incurred under it.

5.   The acquisition of the shares or debentures to which the offer relates must not be conditional upon the recipients approving, or consenting, to any payment or other benefit being made or given to any director or former director of the company in connection with, or as compensation or consideration for,—

(a)   his ceasing to be a director;

(b)   his ceasing to hold any office held in conjunction with any directorship; or

(c)   in the case of a former director, his ceasing to hold any office which he held in conjunction with his former directorship and which he continued to hold after ceasing to be a director.

6.   The consideration for the shares or debentures must be—

(a)   cash; or

(b)   in the case of an offeror which is a body corporate other than an open-ended investment company, either cash or shares in, or debentures of, the body corporate or any combination of such cash, shares or debentures.

PART II
ACCOMPANYING MATERIAL

7.   An indication of the identity of the offeror and, if the offer is being made on behalf of another person, the identity of that person.

8.   An indication of the fact that the terms of the offer are recommended by all directors of the company other than (if that is the case) any director who is the offeror or a director of the offeror.

9.   An indication to the effect that any person who is in any doubt about the invitation or inducement should consult a person authorised under the Act.

10.   An indication that, except insofar as the offer may be totally withdrawn and all persons released from any obligation incurred under it, the offer is open for acceptance by every recipient for the period of at least 21 days beginning with the day after the day on which the invitation or inducement in question was first communicated to recipients of the offer.

11.   An indication of the date on which the invitation or inducement was first communicated to the recipients of the offer.

12.   An indication that the acquisition of the shares or debentures to which the offer relates is not conditional upon the recipients approving, or consenting, to any payment or other benefit being made or given to any director or former director of the company in connection with, or as compensation or consideration for,—

(a)   his ceasing to be a director;

(b)   his ceasing to hold any office held in conjunction with any directorship; or

(c)   in the case of a former director, his ceasing to hold any office which he held in conjunction with his former directorship and which he continued to hold after ceasing to be a director.

13.   An indication of the place where additional material listed in Part III may be inspected.

14.   The audited accounts of the company in respect of the latest accounting reference period for which the period for laying and delivering accounts under the 1985 Act or the 1986 Order has passed or, if accounts in respect of a later accounting reference period have been delivered under the relevant legislation, as shown in those accounts and not the earlier accounts.

15.   Advice to the directors of the company on the financial implications of the offer which is given by a competent person who is independent of and who has no substantial financial interest in the company or the offeror, being advice which gives the opinion of that person in relation to the offer.

16.   An indication by the directors of the company, acting as a board, of the following matters—

(a)   whether or not there has been any material change in the financial position or prospects of the company since the end of the latest accounting reference period in respect of which audited accounts have been delivered to the relevant registrar of companies under the relevant legislation;

(b)   if there has been any such change, the particulars of it;

(c)   any interests, in percentage terms, which any of them have in the shares in or debentures of the company and which are required to be entered in the register kept by the company under section 325 of the 1985 Act or article 333 of the 1986 Order;

(d)   any interests, in percentage terms, which any of them have in the shares in or debentures of any offeror which is a body corporate and which, if the director were a director of the offeror, would—

(i)   in the case of a company within the meaning of the 1985 Act or the 1986 Order, be required to be entered in the register kept by the offeror under section 325 of the 1985 Act or article 333 of the 1986 Order; and

(ii)   in any other case, be required to be so entered if the offeror were such a company.

17.   An indication of any material interest which any director has in any contract entered into by the offeror and in any contract entered into by any member of any group of which the offeror is a member.

18.   An indication as to whether or not each director intends to accept the offer in respect of his own beneficial holdings in the company.

19.   In the case of an offeror which is a body corporate and the shares in or debentures of which are to be the consideration or any part of the consideration for the offer, an indication by the directors of the offeror that the information concerning the offeror and those shares or debentures contained in the document is correct.

20.   If the offeror is making the offer on behalf of another person—

(a)   an indication by the offeror as to whether or not he has taken any steps to ascertain whether that person will be in a position to implement the offer;

(b)   if he has taken any such steps, an indication by him as to what those steps are; and

(c)   the offeror's opinion as to whether that person will be in a position to implement the offer.

21.   An indication that each of the following—

(a)   each of the directors of the company;

(b)   the offeror; and

(c)   if the offeror is a body corporate, each of the directors of the offeror;

is responsible for the information required by Part I and this Part of this Schedule insofar as it relates to themselves or their respective bodies corporate and that, to the best of their knowledge and belief (having taken all reasonable care to ensure that such is the case) the information is in accordance with the facts and that no material fact has been omitted.

22.   The particulars of—

(a)   all shares in or debentures of the company; and

(b)   all investments falling within paragraph 17, 18 or 21 of Schedule 1 so far as relating to shares in or debentures of the company;

which are held by or on behalf of the offeror or each offeror, if there is more than one, or if none are so held an appropriate negative statement.

23.   An indication as to whether or not the offer is conditional upon acceptance in respect of a minimum number of shares or debentures being received and, if the offer is so conditional, what the minimum number is.

24.   Where the offer is conditional upon acceptances, an indication of the date which is the latest date on which it can become unconditional.

25.   If the offer is, or has become, unconditional an indication of the fact that it will remain open until further notice and that at least 14 days notice will be given before it is closed.

26.   An indication as to whether or not, if circumstances arise in which an offeror is able compulsorily to acquire shares of any dissenting minority under Part XIIIA of the 1985 Act or articles 421 or 423 of the 1986 Order, that offeror intends to so acquire those shares.

27.   If shares or debentures are to be acquired for cash, an indication of the period within which the payment will be made.

28.— (1)   Subject to sub-paragraph (2), if the consideration or any part of the consideration for the shares or debentures to be acquired is shares in or debentures of an offeror—

(a)   an indication of the nature and particulars of the offeror's business, its financial and trading prospects and its place of incorporation;

(b)   the following information, in respect of any offeror which is a body corporate and in respect of the company, for the period of five years immediately preceding the date on which the invitation or inducement in question was first communicated to recipients of the offer—

(i)   turnover,

(ii)   profit on ordinary activities before and after tax,

(iii) extraordinary items,

(iv)   profits and loss, and

(v)   the rate per cent of any dividends paid, adjusted as appropriate to take account of relevant changes over the period and the total amount absorbed thereby.

(2)   In the case of a body corporate—

(a)   which was incorporated during the period of five years immediately preceding the date on which the invitation or inducement in question was first communicated to recipients of the offer; or

(b)   which has, at any time during that period, been exempt from the provisions of Part VII of the 1985 Act relating to the audit of accounts by virtue of section 249A or 249AA of that Act or been exempt from the provisions of Part VIII of the 1986 Order relating to the audit of accounts by virtue of article 257A or 257AA of the 1986 Order;

the information described in sub-paragraph (1) with respect to that body corporate need be included only in relation to the period since its incorporation or since it last ceased to be exempt from those provisions of Part VII of the 1985 Act or Part VIII of the 1986 Order, as the case may be.

29.   Particulars of the first dividend in which any such shares or debentures will participate and of the rights attaching to them (including in the case of debentures, rights as to interest) and of any restrictions on their transfer.

30.   An indication of the effect of the acceptance on the capital and income position of the holder of the shares in or debentures of the company.

31.   Particulars of all material contracts (not being contracts which were entered into in the ordinary course of business) which were entered into by each of the company and the offeror during the period of two years immediately preceding the date on which the invitation or inducement in question was first communicated to recipients of the offer.

32.   Particulars of the terms on which shares in or debentures of the company acquired in pursuance of the offer will be transferred and any restrictions on their transfer.

33.   An indication as to whether or not it is proposed, in connection with the offer, that any payment or other benefit be made or given to any director or former director of the company in connection with, or as compensation or consideration for—

    (a)   his ceasing to be a director;

    (b)   his ceasing to hold any office held in conjunction with any directorship; or

    (c)   in the case of a former director, his ceasing to hold any office which he held in conjunction with his former directorship and which he continued to hold after ceasing to be a director;

    and, if such payments or benefits are proposed, details of each one.

34.   An indication as to whether or not there exists any agreement or arrangement between—

    (a)   the offeror or any person with whom the offeror has an agreement of the kind described in section 204 of the 1985 Act or article 216 of the 1986 Order; and

    (b)   any director or shareholder of the company or any person who has been such a director or shareholder;

    at any time during the period of twelve months immediately preceding the date on which the invitation or inducement in question was first communicated to recipients of the offer, being an agreement or arrangement which is connected with or dependent on the offer and, if there is any such agreement or arrangement particulars of it.

35.   An indication whether or not the offeror has reason to believe that there has been any material change in the financial position or prospects of the company since the end of the accounting reference period to which the accounts referred to in paragraph 14 relate, and if the offeror has reason to believe that there has been such a change, the particulars of it.

36.   An indication as to whether or not there is any agreement or arrangement whereby any shares or debentures acquired by the offeror in pursuance of the offer will or may be transferred to any other person, together with the names of the parties to any such agreement or arrangement and particulars of all shares and debentures in the company held by such persons.

37.   Particulars of any dealings—

    (a)   in the shares in or debentures of the company; and

    (b)   if the offeror is a body corporate, in the shares in or debentures of the offeror;

    which took place during the period of twelve months immediately preceding the date on which the invitation or inducement in question was first communicated to recipients of the offer and which were entered into by every person who was a director of either the company or the offeror during that period; and, if there have been no such dealings, an indication to that effect.

38.   In a case in which the offeror is a body corporate which is required to deliver accounts under the 1985 Act or the 1986 Order, particulars of the assets and liabilities as shown in its audited accounts in respect of the latest accounting reference period for which the period for laying and delivering accounts under the relevant legislation has passed or, if accounts in respect of a later accounting reference period have been delivered under the relevant legislation, as shown in those accounts and not the earlier accounts.

39.   Where valuations of assets are given in connection with the offer, the basis on which the valuation was made and the names and addresses of the persons who valued them and particulars of any relevant qualifications.

40.   If any profit forecast is given in connection with the offer, an indication of the assumptions on which the forecast is based.

PART III
ADDITIONAL MATERIAL AVAILABLE FOR INSPECTION

41.   The memorandum and articles of association of the company.

42.   If the offeror is a body corporate, the memorandum and articles of association of the offeror or, if there is no such memorandum and articles, any instrument constituting or defining the

constitution of the offeror and, in either case, if the relevant document is not written in English, a certified translation in English.

43. In the case of a company that does not fall within paragraph 45—

    (a)   the audited accounts of the company in respect of the last two accounting reference periods for which the laying and delivering of accounts under the 1985 Act or the 1986 Order has passed; and

    (b)   if accounts have been delivered to the relevant registrar of companies, in respect of a later accounting reference period, a copy of those accounts;

44. In the case of an offeror which is required to deliver accounts to the registrar of companies and which does not fall within paragraph 45—

    (a)   the audited accounts of the offeror in respect of the last two accounting reference periods for which the laying and delivering of accounts under the 1985 Act or the 1986 Order has passed; and

    (b)   if accounts have been delivered to the relevant registrar of companies in respect of a later accounting reference period, a copy of those accounts.

45. In the case of a company or an offeror—

    (a)   which was incorporated during the period of three years immediately preceding the date on which the invitation or inducement in question was first communicated to recipients of the offer; or

    (b)   which has, at any time during that period, been exempt from the provisions of Part VII of the 1985 Act relating to the audit of accounts by virtue of section 249A or 249AA of that Act or been exempt from the provisions of Part VIII of the 1986 Order relating to the audit of accounts by virtue of article 257A or 257AA of the 1986 Order;

the information described in whichever is relevant of paragraph 43 or 44 with respect to that body corporate need be included only in relation to the period since its incorporation or since it last ceased to be exempt from those provisions of Part VII of the 1985 Act or Part VIII of the 1986 Order, as the case may be.

46. All existing contracts of service entered into for a period of more than one year between the company and any of its directors and, if the offeror is a body corporate, between the offeror and any of its directors.

47. Any report, letter, valuation or other document any part of which is exhibited or referred to in the information required to be made available by Part II and this Part of this Schedule.

48. If the offer document contains any statement purporting to have been made by an expert, that expert's written consent to the inclusion of that statement.

49. All material contracts (if any) of the company and of the offeror (not, in either case, being contracts which were entered into in the ordinary course of business) which were entered into during the period of two years immediately preceding the date on which the invitation or inducement in question was first communicated to recipients of the offer.

SCHEDULE 5

Articles 48 and 50A

STATEMENTS FOR CERTIFIED HIGH NET WORTH INDIVIDUALS AND SELF-CERTIFIED SOPHISTICATED INVESTORS

PART 1
STATEMENT FOR CERTIFIED HIGH NET WORTH INDIVIDUALS

1. The statement to be signed for the purposes of article 48(2) (definition of high net worth individual) must be in the following form and contain the following content—

    "Statement for Certified High Net Worth Individual

    I declare that I am a certified high net worth individual for the purposes of the Financial Services and Markets Act 2000 (Financial Promotion) Order 2001.

I understand that this means:

(a)   I can receive financial promotions that may not have been approved by a person authorised by the Financial Services Authority;

(b)   the content of such financial promotions may not conform to rules issued by the Financial Services Authority;

(c)   by signing this statement I may lose significant rights;

(d)   I may have no right to complain to either of the following—

    (i)   the Financial Services Authority; or

    (ii)   the Financial Ombudsman Scheme;

(e)   I may have no right to seek compensation from the Financial Services Compensation Scheme.

I am a certified high net worth individual because at least one of the following applies—

(a)   I had, during the financial year immediately preceding the date below, an annual income to the value of £100,000 or more;

(b)   I held, throughout the financial year immediately preceding the date below, net assets to the value of £250,000 or more. Net assets for these purposes do not include—

    (i)   the property which is my primary residence or any loan secured on that residence;

    (ii)   any rights of mine under a qualifying contract of insurance within the meaning of the Financial Services and Markets Act 2000 (Regulated Activities) Order 2001; or

    (iii)   any benefits (in the form of pensions or otherwise) which are payable on the termination of my service or on my death or retirement and to which I am (or my dependants are), or may be, entitled.

I accept that I can lose my property and other assets from making investment decisions based on financial promotions.

I am aware that it is open to me to seek advice from someone who specialises in advising on investments.

Signature   Date".

PART II
STATEMENT FOR SELF-CERTIFIED SOPHISTICATED INVESTORS

2.   The statement to be signed for the purposes of article 50A(1) (definition of self-certified sophisticated investor) must be in the following form and contain the following content—

"Statement for Self-Certified Sophisticated Investor

I declare that I am a self-certified sophisticated investor for the purposes of the Financial Services and Markets Act (Financial Promotion) Order 2001.

I understand that this means:

(a)   I can receive financial promotions that may not have been approved by a person authorised by the Financial Services Authority;

(b)   the content of such financial promotions may not conform to rules issued by the Financial Services Authority;

(c)   by signing this statement I may lose significant rights;

(d)   I may have no right to complain to either of the following—

    (i)   the Financial Services Authority; or

    (ii)   the Financial Ombudsman Scheme;

(e)   I may have no right to seek compensation from the Financial Services Compensation Scheme.

I am a self-certified sophisticated investor because at least one of the following applies—

(a)   I am a member of a network or syndicate of business angels and have been so for at least the last six months prior to the date below;

(b)   I have made more than one investment in an unlisted company in the two years prior to the date below;

(c)   I am working, or have worked in the two years prior to the date below, in a professional capacity in the private equity sector, or in the provision of finance for small and medium enterprises;

(d)   I am currently, or have been in the two years prior to the date below, a director of a company with an annual turnover of at least £1 million.

I accept that I can lose my property and other assets from making investment decisions based on financial promotions.

I am aware that it is open to me to seek advice from someone who specialises in advising on investments.

Signature   Date".

Financial Services and Markets Act 2000 (Official Listing of Securities) Regulations 2001

S.I. 2001/2956

PART 1
GENERAL

1. Citation and commencement

These Regulations may be cited as the Financial Services and Markets Act 2000 (Official Listing of Securities) Regulations 2001 and come into force on the day on which section 74(1) comes into force.

2. Interpretation

(1) In these Regulations—

"the Act" means the Financial Services and Markets Act 2000;

"competent authority" is to be construed in accordance with section 72;

"the Financial Promotion Order" means the Financial Services and Markets Act 2000 (Financial Promotion) Order 2001;

"issuer" has the same meaning as is given, for the purposes of section 103(1), in regulation 4 below;

"non-listing prospectus" has the meaning given in section 87(2); and

"the Regulated Activities Order" means the Financial Services and Markets Act 2000 (Regulated Activities) Order 2001.

(2) Any reference in these Regulations to a section or Schedule is, unless otherwise stated or unless the context otherwise requires, a reference to that section of or Schedule to the Act.

PART 2
MISCELLANEOUS MATTERS PRESCRIBED
FOR THE PURPOSES OF PART VI OF THE ACT

3. Bodies whose securities may not be listed

For the purposes of section 75(3) (which provides that no application for listing may be entertained in respect of securities issued by a body of a prescribed kind) there are prescribed the following kinds of body—

(a) where the securities are securities within the meaning of the Regulated Activities Order, a private company within the meaning of section 1(3) of the Companies Act 1985 or article 12(3) of the Companies (Northern Ireland) Order 1986;

(b) an old public company within the meaning of section 1 of the Companies Consolidation (Consequential Provisions) Act 1985 or article 3 of the Companies Consolidation (Consequential Provisions) (Northern Ireland) Order 1986.

4. Meaning of "issuer"

(1) For the purposes of section 103(1), "issuer" has the meaning given in this regulation.

(2) In relation to certificates or other instruments falling within article 80 of the Regulated Activities Order (certificates representing certain securities), "issuer" means—

(a) for the purposes of paragraph 16 of Schedule 11 (exemption from prospectus requirement for securities issued by a body corporate and offered to qualifying persons), the person by whom the certificates or instruments have been or are to be issued;

(b) for all other purposes, the person who issued or is to issue the securities to which the certificates or instruments relate.

(3)   In relation to any other securities, "issuer" means the person by whom the securities have been or are to be issued.

5.   Meaning of "approved exchange"

For the purposes of paragraph 9 of Schedule 10, "approved exchange" means a recognised investment exchange approved by the Treasury for the purposes of the Public Offers of Securities Regulations 1995 (either generally or in relation to dealings in securities).

PART 3

PERSONS RESPONSIBLE FOR LISTING PARTICULARS, PROSPECTUSES AND NON-LISTING PROSPECTUSES

6.   Responsibility for listing particulars

(1)   Subject to the following provisions of this Part, for the purposes of Part VI of the Act the persons responsible for listing particulars (including supplementary listing particulars) are—

(a)   the issuer of the securities to which the particulars relate;

(b)   where the issuer is a body corporate, each person who is a director of that body at the time when the particulars are submitted to the competent authority;

(c)   where the issuer is a body corporate, each person who has authorised himself to be named, and is named, in the particulars as a director or as having agreed to become a director of that body either immediately or at a future time;

(d)   each person who accepts, and is stated in the particulars as accepting, responsibility for the particulars;

(e)   each person not falling within any of the foregoing sub-paragraphs who has authorised the contents of the particulars.

(2)   A person is not to be treated as responsible for any particulars by virtue of paragraph (1)(b) above if they are published without his knowledge or consent and on becoming aware of their publication he forthwith gives reasonable public notice that they were published without his knowledge or consent.

(3)   When accepting responsibility for particulars under paragraph (1)(d) above or authorising their contents under paragraph (1)(e) above, a person may state that he does so only in relation to certain specified parts of the particulars, or only in certain specified respects, and in such a case he is responsible under paragraph (1)(d) or (e) above—

(a)   only to the extent specified; and

(b)   only if the material in question is included in (or substantially in) the form and context to which he has agreed.

(4)   Nothing in this regulation is to be construed as making a person responsible for any particulars by reason of giving advice as to their contents in a professional capacity.

(5)   Where by virtue of this regulation the issuer of any shares pays or is liable to pay compensation under section 90 for loss suffered in respect of shares for which a person has subscribed no account is to be taken of that liability or payment in determining any question as to the amount paid on subscription for those shares or as to the amount paid up or deemed to be paid up on them.

7.   Securities issued in connection with takeovers and mergers

(1)   This regulation applies where—

(a)   listing particulars relate to securities which are to be issued in connection with—

(i)   an offer by the issuer (or by a wholly-owned subsidiary of the issuer) for securities issued by another person ("A");

(ii)   an agreement for the acquisition by the issuer (or by a wholly-owned subsidiary of the issuer) of securities issued by another person ("A"); or

(iii)   any arrangement whereby the whole of the undertaking of another person ("A") is to become the undertaking of the issuer (or of a wholly-owned subsidiary of the issuer, or of a body corporate which will become such a subsidiary by virtue of the arrangement); and

(b) each of the specified persons is responsible by virtue of regulation 6(1)(d) above for any part ("the relevant part") of the particulars relating to A or to the securities or undertaking to which the offer, agreement or arrangement relates.

(2)   In paragraph (1)(b) above the "specified persons" are—

(a)   A; and

(b)   where A is a body corporate—

(i)   each person who is a director of A at the time when the particulars are submitted to the competent authority; and

(ii)   each other person who has authorised himself to be named, and is named, in the particulars as a director of A.

(3)   Where this regulation applies, no person is to be treated as responsible for the relevant part of the particulars under regulation 6(1)(a), (b) or (c) above but without prejudice to his being responsible under regulation 6(1)(d).

(4)   In this regulation—

(a)   "listing particulars" includes supplementary listing particulars; and

(b)   "wholly-owned subsidiary" is to be construed in accordance with section 736 of the Companies Act 1985 (and, in relation to an issuer which is not a body corporate, means a body corporate which would be a wholly-owned subsidiary of the issuer within the meaning of that section if the issuer were a body corporate).

8.   Successor companies under legislation relating to electricity

(1)   Where—

(a)   the same document contains listing particulars relating to the securities of—

(i)   two or more successor companies within the meaning of Part II of the Electricity Act 1989, or

(ii)   two or more successor companies within the meaning of Part III of the Electricity (Northern Ireland) Order 1992; and

(b)   the responsibility of any person for any information included in the document ("the relevant information") is stated in the document to be confined to its inclusion as part of the particulars relating to the securities of any one of those companies,

that person is not to be treated as responsible, by virtue of regulation 6 above, for the relevant information in so far as it is stated in the document to form part of the particulars relating to the securities of any other of those companies.

(2)   "Listing particulars" includes supplementary listing particulars.

9.   Specialist securities

(1)   This regulation applies where listing particulars relate to securities of a kind specified by listing rules for the purposes of section 82(1)(c), other than securities which are to be issued in the circumstances mentioned in regulation 7(1)(a) above.

(2)   No person is to be treated as responsible for the particulars under regulation 6(1)(a), (b) or (c) above but without prejudice to his being responsible under regulation 6(1)(d).

(3)   "Listing particulars" includes supplementary listing particulars.

10.   Responsibility for prospectuses and non-listing prospectuses

(1)   This part of these Regulations applies in relation to a prospectus required by listing rules in accordance with section 84(1), or to a non-listing prospectus, as it applies in relation to listing particulars, but as if—

(a)   any reference to listing particulars were a reference to a prospectus and any reference to supplementary listing particulars were a reference to a supplementary prospectus; and

(b)   notwithstanding the definition of "issuer" given in regulation 2(1) above, any reference in this Part (other than in regulation 6(1)(b) or (c) or in paragraph (2) below) to the issuer of securities included a reference to the person offering or proposing to offer them.

(2)   In the application of regulation 6 above to a prospectus or non-listing prospectus in accordance with this regulation, a person is not responsible under regulation 6(1)(a) where—

(a)   he is not the issuer, but is making the offer in association with the issuer; and

(b)   the prospectus or supplementary prospectus was drawn up primarily by the issuer, or by one or more persons acting on behalf of the issuer.

PART 4
MATTERS PRESCRIBED FOR THE PURPOSES OF SCHEDULE 11 (OFFERS NOT TO BE TREATED AS PUBLIC OFFERS OF SECURITIES)

11.   Offers of securities to "qualifying persons": definitions

(1)   For the purposes of paragraph 16(3) of Schedule 11 (offers of securities to "qualifying persons") and for the purposes of paragraph (2) below, a body corporate is "connected with" another body corporate if—

(a)   they are in the same group; or

(b)   one is entitled, either alone or with any other body corporate in the same group, to exercise or control the exercise of a majority of the voting rights attributable to the share capital which are exercisable in all circumstances at any general meeting of the other body corporate or its holding company.

(2)   For the purposes of paragraph 16(4) of Schedule 11, "relevant trustee" means a person holding shares in or debentures of a body corporate as trustee, in pursuance of arrangements made by that body corporate (or by another body corporate connected with it) for the purpose of enabling or facilitating the holding of such shares or debentures by or for the benefit of qualifying persons (within the meaning of paragraph 16(2) of Schedule 11), or enabling or facilitating transactions in such shares or debentures between or for the benefit of such persons.

(3)   In paragraph (2) above, "shares" and "debentures" include—

(a)   any investment of the kind specified by article 76 of the Regulated Activities Order (shares) or article 77 of that Order (instruments creating or acknowledging indebtedness);

(b)   any investment of the kind specified by article 79 or 80 of that Order (instruments giving entitlements to investments, and certificates representing certain securities) so far as relevant to articles 76 and 77; and

(c)   any investment of the kind specified by article 89 of that Order (rights to or interests in investments) so far as relevant to investments of the kind mentioned in sub-paragraph (a) or (b) above.

(4)   For the purposes of paragraph 16(4) of Schedule 11 and for the purposes of paragraph (1) above, "group", in relation to a body corporate, means that body corporate, any other body corporate which is its holding company or subsidiary, and any other body corporate which is a subsidiary of that holding company, together with any body corporate in which a member of the group holds a qualifying capital interest.

(5)   In this regulation—

(a)   "equity share capital" is to be construed in accordance with section 744 of the Companies Act 1985 (or, in relation to a company registered in Northern Ireland, in accordance with article 2(3) of the Companies (Northern Ireland) Order 1986);

(b)   "holding company" and "subsidiary" are to be construed in accordance with section 736 of the Companies Act 1985 (or, in relation to a company registered in Northern Ireland, in accordance with article 4 of the Companies (Northern Ireland) Order 1986);

(c)   "qualifying capital interest", in relation to a body corporate, means an interest, in relevant shares of the body corporate, which is held on a long-term basis for the purpose of securing a contribution to the holder's own activities by the exercise of control or influence arising from that interest, and a holding of 20 per cent or more of the nominal value of the relevant shares of a body corporate is to be presumed to be a qualifying capital interest unless the contrary is shown; and

(d)   "relevant shares", in relation to a body corporate, means shares, comprised in the equity share capital of the body corporate, of a class carrying rights to vote in all circumstances at general meetings of the body.

12.   Euro-securities: permitted advertisements

(1)   For the purposes of paragraph 20(2) of Schedule 11 (advertisements which may be issued in relation to offers of Euro-securities), there is prescribed any advertisement which is issued only to persons who are on reasonable grounds believed, by the person issuing the advertisement or causing it to be issued, to be permitted recipients.

(2)   A person is a permitted recipient for the purposes of paragraph (1) above if he is—

   (a)   an investment professional within the meaning of article 19 of the Financial Promotion Order;

   (b)   a person to whom paragraph (2) of article 47 of that Order (communications to persons in the business of disseminating information) applies by virtue of sub-paragraph (a) or (b) of that paragraph;

   (c)   a person to whom paragraph (2) of article 49 of that Order (communications to high net worth companies, unincorporated associations etc) applies by virtue of any of sub-paragraphs (a) to (d) of that paragraph (read with paragraphs (5) to (7) of that article); or

   (d)   a person who is a certified sophisticated investor within the meaning of article 50 of that Order in relation to investments of a description which includes the securities which are the subject of the offer.

(3)   For the purposes of paragraph (2)(a) above, article 19(5) of the Financial Promotion Order is to be read as if—

   (a)   in sub-paragraph (b) for the words from "where" to the end there were substituted "who is exempt in relation to regulated activities of a kind which are capable of being carried on in relation to the investments of the kind to which the offer relates";

   (b)   in sub-paragraph (c)(i) for the words "the controlled activity to which the communication relates" there were substituted "a controlled activity, in relation to investments of that kind,";

   (c)   in sub-paragraph (e) for the words "communication is made" there were substituted "advertisement is issued"; and

   (d)   after sub-paragraph (e) there were added—

      "(f) a person with or for whom any credit institution or other financial institution through which the Euro-securities may be acquired pursuant to the offer has effected or arranged for the effecting of a transaction within the period of twelve months ending with the date on which the offer is first made.".

Financial Services and Markets Act 2000 (Prescribed Markets and Qualifying Investments) Order 2001

S.I. 2001/996

1.   Citation

This Order may be cited as the Financial Services and Markets Act 2000 (Prescribed Markets and Qualifying Investments) Order 2001.

2.   Commencement

This Order comes into force on the day on which section 123 of the Act (power to impose penalties in cases of market abuse) comes into force.

3.   Interpretation

In this Order—

"the Act" means the Financial Services and Markets Act 2000; and

"UK recognised investment exchange" means a body corporate or unincorporated association in respect of which there is in effect a recognition order made under section 290(1)(a) of the Act (recognition orders in respect of investment exchanges other than overseas investment exchanges).

4.   Prescribed markets

There are prescribed, as markets to which section 118 of the Act applies, all markets which are established under the rules of a UK recognised investment exchange.

4A.

There is prescribed, as a market to which section 118 of the Act applies, the market known as OFEX.

5.   Qualifying investments

There are prescribed, as qualifying investments in relation to the markets prescribed by article 4, all investments of a kind specified for the purposes of section 22 of the Act.

Financial Services and Markets Act 2000 (Professions) (Non-Exempt Activities) Order 2001

S.I. 2001/1227

1.   **Citation and Commencement**

(1)   This Order may be cited as the Financial Services and Markets Act 2000 (Professions) (Non-Exempt Activities) Order 2001.

(2)   Subject to paragraph (3), this Order comes into force on the day on which section 19 of the Act comes into force.

(3)   This Order comes into force—

      (a)   for the purposes of article 4(g), on 1st January 2002; and

      (b)   for the purposes of article 6A, on such a day as the Treasury may specify.

(4)   Any day specified under paragraph (3)(b) must be caused to be notified in the London, Edinburgh and Belfast Gazettes published not later than one week before that day.

2.   **Interpretation**

(1)   In this Order—

      "the Act" means the Financial Services and Markets Act 2000;

      "contract of insurance" has the meaning given by article 3(1) of the Regulated Activities Order;

      "contractually based investment" has the meaning given by article 3(1) of the Regulated Activities Order;

      "occupational pension scheme" and "personal pension scheme" have the meaning given by section 1 of the Pension Schemes Act 1993;

      "record of insurance intermediaries" means the record maintained by the Authority under section 347 of the Act (the public record) by virtue of article 93 of the Regulated Activities Order (recorded insurance intermediaries);

      "the Regulated Activities Order" means the Financial Services and Markets Act 2000 (Regulated Activities) Order 2001;

      "relevant investment" has the meaning given by article 3(1) of the Regulated Activities Order;

      "security" has the meaning given by article 3(1) of the Regulated Activities Order;

      "syndicate" has the meaning given by article 3(1) of the Regulated Activities Order.

(2)   For the purposes of this Order, a person is a member of a personal pension scheme if he is a person to or in respect of whom benefits are or may become payable under the scheme.

3.   **Activities to which exemption from the general prohibition does not apply**

The activities in articles 4 to 8 are specified for the purposes of section 327(6) of the Act.

4.

An activity of the kind specified by any of the following provisions of the Regulated Activities Order—

      (a)   article 5 (accepting deposits);

      (aa)   article 9B (issuing electronic money);

      (b)   article 10 (effecting and carrying out contracts of insurance);

      (c)   article 14 (dealing in investments as principal);

      (d)   article 51 (establishing etc. a collective investment scheme);

      (e)   article 52 (establishing etc. a stakeholder pension scheme);

      (ea)   article 52B (providing basic advice on stakeholder products);

      (f)   article 57 (managing the underwriting capacity of a Lloyd's syndicate);

    (g)   article 59 (funeral plan contracts);

    (h)   ...

4A.

An activity of the kind specified by article 21 or 25 of the Regulated Activities Order (dealing in investments as agent or arranging deals in investments) in so far as it—

    (a)   relates to a transaction for the sale or purchase of rights under a contract of insurance; and

    (b)   is carried on by a person who is not included in the record of insurance intermediaries.

5.

(1)   An activity of the kind specified by article 37 of the Regulated Activities Order (managing investments) in so far as it consists of buying or subscribing for a security or contractually based investment.

(2)   Paragraph (1) does not apply—

    (a)   if all routine or day to day decisions, so far as relating to that activity, are taken by an authorised person with permission to carry on that activity or by a person who is an exempt person in relation to such an activity; or

    (b)   to an activity undertaken in accordance with the advice of an authorised person with permission to give advice in relation to such an activity or a person who is an exempt person in relation to the giving of such advice.

5A.

An activity of the kind specified by article 39A of the Regulated Activities Order (assisting in the administration and performance of a contract of insurance) if it is carried on by a person who is not included in the record of insurance intermediaries.

6.

(1)   An activity of the kind specified by article 53 of the Regulated Activities Order (advising on investments) where the advice in question falls within paragraph (2), (3) or (5).

(2)   Subject to paragraph (4), advice falls within this paragraph in so far as—

    (a)   it is given to an individual (or his agent) other than where the individual acts—

        (i)   in connection with the carrying on of a business of any kind by himself or by an undertaking of which he is, or would become as a result of the transaction to which the advice relates, a controller; or

        (ii)   in his capacity as a trustee of an occupational pension scheme;

    (b)   it consists of a recommendation to buy or subscribe for a particular security or contractually based investment; and

    (c)   the transaction to which the advice relates would be made—

        (i)   with a person acting in the course of carrying on the business of buying, selling, subscribing for or underwriting the security or contractually based investment, whether as principal or agent;

        (ii)   on an investment exchange or any other market to which that investment is admitted for dealing; or

        (iii)   in response to an invitation to subscribe for such an investment which is, or is to be, admitted for dealing on an investment exchange or any other market.

(3)   Subject to paragraph (4), advice falls within this paragraph in so far as it consists of a recommendation to a member of a personal pension scheme (or his agent) to dispose of any rights or interests which the member has in or under the scheme.

(4)   Advice does not fall within paragraph (2) or (3) if it endorses a corresponding recommendation given to the individual (or, as the case may be, the member) by an authorised person with permission to give advice in relation to the proposed transaction or a person who is an exempt person in relation to the giving of such advice.

(5)   Advice falls within this paragraph in so far as—

    (a)   it relates to a transaction for the sale or purchase of rights under a contract of insurance; and

    (b)   it is given by a person who is not included in the record of insurance intermediaries.

6A.

(1)   An activity of the kind specified by article 53A of the Regulated Activities Order (advising on regulated mortgage contracts) where the advice in question falls within paragraph (2).

(2)   Subject to paragraph (3), advice falls within this paragraph in so far as—

    (a)   it consists of a recommendation, given to an individual, to enter as borrower into a regulated mortgage contract with a particular person; and

    (b)   in entering into a regulated mortgage contract that person would be carrying on an activity of the kind specified by article 61(1) of the Regulated Activities Order (regulated mortgage contracts).

(3)   Advice does not fall within paragraph (2) if it endorses a corresponding recommendation given to the individual by an authorised person with permission to carry on an activity of the kind specified by article 53A of the Regulated Activities Order or a person who is an exempt person in relation to an activity of that kind.

6B.

(1)   An activity of the kind specified by article 61(1) or (2) of the Regulated Activities Order (regulated mortgage contracts).

(2)   Paragraph (1) does not apply to an activity carried on by a person in his capacity as a trustee or personal representative where the borrower under the regulated mortgage contract in question is a beneficiary under the trust, will or intestacy.

7.

(1)   Advising a person to become a member of a particular Lloyd's syndicate.

(2)   Paragraph (1) does not apply to advice which endorses that of an authorised person with permission to give such advice or a person who is an exempt person in relation to the giving of such advice.

8.

Agreeing to carry on any of the activities mentioned in articles 4 to 7 other than the activities mentioned in article 4(a), (aa), (b), (d) and (e).

Enterprise Act 2002

2002 c. 40

An Act to establish and provide for the functions of the Office of Fair Trading, the Competition Appeal Tribunal and the Competition Service; to make provision about mergers and market structures and conduct; to amend the constitution and functions of the Competition Commission; to create an offence for those entering into certain anti-competitive agreements; to provide for the disqualification of directors of companies engaging in certain anti-competitive practices; to make other provision about competition law; to amend the law relating to the protection of the collective interests of consumers; to make further provision about the disclosure of information obtained under competition and consumer legislation; to amend the Insolvency Act 1986 and make other provision about insolvency; and for connected purposes.

[7th November 2002]

PART 1
THE OFFICE OF FAIR TRADING

Establishment of OFT

1. The Office of Fair Trading

(1) There shall be a body corporate to be known as the Office of Fair Trading (in this Act referred to as "the OFT").

(2) The functions of the OFT are carried out on behalf of the Crown.

(3) Schedule 1 (which makes further provision about the OFT) has effect.

(4) In managing its affairs the OFT shall have regard, in addition to any relevant general guidance as to the governance of public bodies, to such generally accepted principles of good corporate governance as it is reasonable to regard as applicable to the OFT.

2. The Director General of Fair Trading

(1) The functions of the Director General of Fair Trading (in this Act referred to as "the Director"), and his property, rights and liabilities, are transferred to the OFT.

(2) The office of the Director is abolished.

(3) Any enactment, instrument or other document passed or made before the commencement of subsection (1) which refers to the Director shall have effect, so far as necessary for the purposes of or in consequence of anything being transferred, as if any reference to the Director were a reference to the OFT.

3. Annual plan

(1) The OFT shall, before each financial year, publish a document (the "annual plan") containing a statement of its main objectives and priorities for the year.

(2) The OFT shall for the purposes of public consultation publish a document containing proposals for its annual plan at least two months before publishing the annual plan for any year.

(3) The OFT shall lay before Parliament a copy of each document published under subsection (2) and each annual plan.

4. Annual and other reports

(1) The OFT shall, as soon as practicable after the end of each financial year, make to the Secretary of State a report (the "annual report") on its activities and performance during that year.

(2) The annual report for each year shall include—

    (a) a general survey of developments in respect of matters relating to the OFT's functions;

    (b) an assessment of the extent to which the OFT's main objectives and priorities for the year (as set out in the annual plan) have been met;

(c)   a summary of the significant decisions, investigations or other activities made or carried out by the OFT during the year;

(d)   a summary of the allocation of the OFT's financial resources to its various activities during the year; and

(e)   an assessment of the OFT's performance and practices in relation to its enforcement functions.

(3)   The OFT shall lay a copy of each annual report before Parliament and arrange for the report to be published.

(4)   The OFT may—

(a)   prepare other reports in respect of matters relating to any of its functions; and

(b)   arrange for any such report to be published.

General functions of OFT

5.   Acquisition of information etc.

(1)   The OFT has the function of obtaining, compiling and keeping under review information about matters relating to the carrying out of its functions.

(2)   That function is to be carried out with a view to (among other things) ensuring that the OFT has sufficient information to take informed decisions and to carry out its other functions effectively.

(3)   In carrying out that function the OFT may carry out, commission or support (financially or otherwise) research.

6.   Provision of information etc. to the public

(1)   The OFT has the function of—

(a)   making the public aware of the ways in which competition may benefit consumers in, and the economy of, the United Kingdom; and

(b)   giving information or advice in respect of matters relating to any of its functions to the public.

(2)   In carrying out those functions the OFT may—

(a)   publish educational materials or carry out other educational activities; or

(b)   support (financially or otherwise) the carrying out by others of such activities or the provision by others of information or advice.

7.   Provision of information and advice to Ministers etc.

(1)   The OFT has the function of—

(a)   making proposals, or

(b)   giving other information or advice,

on matters relating to any of its functions to any Minister of the Crown or other public authority (including proposals, information or advice as to any aspect of the law or a proposed change in the law).

(2)   A Minister of the Crown may request the OFT to make proposals or give other information or advice on any matter relating to any of its functions; and the OFT shall, so far as is reasonably practicable and consistent with its other functions, comply with the request.

8.   Promoting good consumer practice

(1)   The OFT has the function of promoting good practice in the carrying out of activities which may affect the economic interests of consumers in the United Kingdom.

(2)   In carrying out that function the OFT may (without prejudice to the generality of subsection (1)) make arrangements for approving consumer codes and may, in accordance with the arrangements, give its approval to or withdraw its approval from any consumer code.

(3)   Any such arrangements must specify the criteria to be applied by the OFT in determining whether to give approval to or withdraw approval from a consumer code.

(4)   Any such arrangements may in particular—

(a)   specify descriptions of consumer code which may be the subject of an application to the OFT for approval (and any such description may be framed by reference to any feature of a consumer code, including the persons who are, or are to be, subject to the code, the manner in which it is, or is to be, operated and the persons responsible for its operation); and

(b)   provide for the use in accordance with the arrangements of an official symbol intended to signify that a consumer code is approved by the OFT.

(5)   The OFT shall publish any arrangements under subsection (2) in such manner it considers appropriate.

(6)   In this section "consumer code" means a code of practice or other document (however described) intended, with a view to safeguarding or promoting the interests of consumers, to regulate by any means the conduct of persons engaged in the supply of goods or services to consumers (or the conduct of their employees or representatives).

Miscellaneous

9.   Repeal of certain powers of direction

Section 12 of the Fair Trading Act 1973 (c. 41) (in this Act referred to as "the 1973 Act") and section 13 of the Competition Act 1980 (c. 21) (powers of Secretary of State to give directions) shall cease to have effect.

10.   Part 2 of the 1973 Act

(1)   The following provisions of the 1973 Act shall cease to have effect—

(a)   section 3 and Schedule 2 (which establish, and make provision with respect to, the Consumer Protection Advisory Committee);

(b)   sections 13 to 21 (which relate to references made to, and reports of, that Committee); and

(c)   section 22 (power of Secretary of State to make orders in pursuance of a report of that Committee).

(2)   But subsection (1)(c) does not affect—

(a)   any order under section 22 of the 1973 Act which is in force immediately before the commencement of this section;

(b)   the continued operation of that section so far as applying to the revocation of any such order.

(3)   If the orders saved by subsection (2)(a) have been revoked, the Secretary of State may by order—

(a)   repeal any unrepealed provision of Part 2 of the 1973 Act and subsection (2) above; and

(b)   make such other consequential modifications of any Act or subordinate legislation (whenever passed or made) as he thinks fit.

(4)   An order under subsection (3)—

(a)   may make transitional or saving provision in connection with any modification made by the order; and

(b)   shall be made by statutory instrument subject to annulment in pursuance of a resolution of either House of Parliament.

11.   Super-complaints to OFT

(1)   This section applies where a designated consumer body makes a complaint to the OFT that any feature, or combination of features, of a market in the United Kingdom for goods or services is or appears to be significantly harming the interests of consumers.

(2)   The OFT must, within 90 days after the day on which it receives the complaint, publish a response stating how it proposes to deal with the complaint, and in particular—

(a)   whether it has decided to take any action, or to take no action, in response to the complaint, and

(b)   if it has decided to take action, what action it proposes to take.

(3)   The response must state the OFT's reasons for its proposals.

(4)   The Secretary of State may by order amend subsection (2) by substituting any period for the period for the time being specified there.

(5)   "Designated consumer body" means a body designated by the Secretary of State by order.

(6)   The Secretary of State—
        (a)   may designate a body only if it appears to him to represent the interests of consumers of any
               description, and
        (b)   must publish (and may from time to time vary) other criteria to be applied by him in
               determining whether to make or revoke a designation.
(7)   The OFT—
        (a)   must issue guidance as to the presentation by the complainant of a reasoned case for the
               complaint, and
        (b)   may issue such other guidance as appears to it to be appropriate for the purposes of this
               section.
(8)   An order under this section—
        (a)   shall be made by statutory instrument, and
        (b)   shall be subject to annulment in pursuance of a resolution of either House of Parliament.
(9)   In this section—
        (a)   references to a feature of a market in the United Kingdom for goods or services have the
               same meaning as if contained in Part 4, and
        (b)   "consumer" means an individual who is a consumer within the meaning of that Part.

PART 2
THE COMPETITION APPEAL TRIBUNAL

The Competition Appeal Tribunal

12.   The Competition Appeal Tribunal
(1)   There shall be a tribunal, to be called the Competition Appeal Tribunal (in this Part referred to as
        "the Tribunal").
(2)   The Tribunal shall consist of—
        (a)   a person appointed by the Lord Chancellor to preside over the Tribunal (in this Part referred
               to as "the President");
        (b)   members appointed by the Lord Chancellor to form a panel of chairmen; and
        (c)   members appointed by the Secretary of State to form a panel of ordinary members.
(3)   The Tribunal shall have a Registrar appointed by the Secretary of State.
(4)   The expenses of the Tribunal shall be paid by the Competition Service.
(5)   Schedule 2 (which makes further provision about the Tribunal) has effect.

13.   The Competition Service
(1)   There shall be a body corporate called the Competition Service (in this Part referred to as "the
        Service").
(2)   The purpose of the Service is to fund, and provide support services to, the Competition Appeal
        Tribunal.
(3)   In subsection (2) "support services" includes the provision of staff, accommodation and
        equipment and any other services which facilitate the carrying out by the Tribunal of its functions.
(4)   The activities of the Service are not carried out on behalf of the Crown (and its property is not to
        be regarded as held on behalf of the Crown).
(5)   The Secretary of State shall pay to the Service such sums as he considers appropriate to enable it
        to fund the activities of the Tribunal and to carry out its other activities.
(6)   Schedule 3 (which makes further provision about the Service) has effect.

14.   Constitution of Tribunal for particular proceedings and its decisions
(1)   For the purposes of any proceedings before it the Tribunal shall consist of a chairman and two
        other members.
(2)   The chairman must be the President or a member of the panel of chairmen.
(3)   The other members may be chosen from either the panel of chairmen or the panel of ordinary
        members.

(4)   If the members of the Tribunal as constituted in accordance with this section are unable to agree on any decision, the decision is to be taken by majority vote.

(5)   This section has effect subject to paragraph 18 of Schedule 4 (consequences of a member of the Tribunal being unable to continue after the proceedings have begun to be heard).

(6)   Part 1 of Schedule 4 (which makes further provision about the decisions of the Tribunal and their enforcement) has effect.

15. Tribunal rules

(1)   The Secretary of State may, after consulting the President and such other persons as he considers appropriate, make rules (in this Part referred to as "Tribunal rules") with respect to proceedings before the Tribunal.

(2)   Tribunal rules may make provision with respect to matters incidental to or consequential upon appeals provided for by or under any Act to the Court of Appeal or the Court of Session in relation to a decision of the Tribunal.

(3)   Tribunal rules may—

        (a)   specify qualifications for appointment as Registrar;

        (b)   confer functions on the President or the Registrar in relation to proceedings before the Tribunal; and

        (c)   contain incidental, supplemental, consequential or transitional provision.

(4)   The power to make Tribunal rules is exercisable by statutory instrument subject to annulment in pursuance of a resolution of either House of Parliament.

(5)   Part 2 of Schedule 4 (which makes further provision about the rules) has effect, but without prejudice to the generality of subsection (1).

16. Transfers of certain proceedings to and from Tribunal

(1)   The Lord Chancellor may by regulations—

        (a)   make provision enabling the court—

            (i)   to transfer to the Tribunal for its determination so much of any proceedings before the court as relates to an infringement issue; and

            (ii)   to give effect to the determination of that issue by the Tribunal; and

        (b)   make such incidental, supplementary, consequential, transitional or saving provision as the Lord Chancellor may consider appropriate.

(2)   The power to make regulations under subsection (1) is exercisable by statutory instrument subject to annulment in pursuance of a resolution of either House of Parliament.

(3)   Rules of court may prescribe the procedure to be followed in connection with a transfer mentioned in subsection (1).

(4)   The court may transfer to the Tribunal, in accordance with rules of court, so much of any proceedings before it as relates to a claim to which section 47A of the 1998 Act applies.

(5)   Rules of court may make provision in connection with the transfer from the Tribunal to the High Court or the Court of Session of a claim made in proceedings under section 47A of the 1998 Act.

(6)   In this section—

        "the court" means—

        (a)   the High Court or a county court; or

        (b)   the Court of Session or a sheriff court; and

        "infringement issue" means any question relating to whether or not an infringement of —

        (a)   the Chapter I prohibition or the Chapter II prohibition; or

        (b)   Article 81 or 82 of the Treaty,

        has been or is being committed;

but otherwise any terms used in this section and Part 1 of the 1998 Act have the same meaning as they have in that Part.

17–21. ....

PART 3

MERGERS

CHAPTER 1

DUTY TO MAKE REFERENCES

Duty to make references: completed mergers

22. **Duty to make references in relation to completed mergers**

(1)   The OFT shall, subject to subsections (2) and (3), make a reference to the Commission if the OFT believes that it is or may be the case that—

(a)   a relevant merger situation has been created; and

(b)   the creation of that situation has resulted, or may be expected to result, in a substantial lessening of competition within any market or markets in the United Kingdom for goods or services.

(2)   The OFT may decide not to make a reference under this section if it believes that—

(a)   the market concerned is not, or the markets concerned are not, of sufficient importance to justify the making of a reference to the Commission; or

(b)   any relevant customer benefits in relation to the creation of the relevant merger situation concerned outweigh the substantial lessening of competition concerned and any adverse effects of the substantial lessening of competition concerned.

(3)   No reference shall be made under this section if—

(a)   the making of the reference is prevented by section ... 74(1) or 96(3) or paragraph 4 of Schedule 7;

(b)   the OFT is considering whether to accept undertakings under section 73 instead of making such a reference;

(c)   the relevant merger situation concerned is being, or has been, dealt with in connection with a reference made under section 33;

(d)   a notice under section 42(2) is in force in relation to the matter or the matter to which such a notice relates has been finally determined under Chapter 2 otherwise than in circumstances in which a notice is then given to the OFT under section 56(1); ...

(e)   the European Commission is considering a request made, in relation to the matter concerned, by the United Kingdom (whether alone or with others) under article 22(1) of the EC Merger Regulation, is proceeding with the matter in pursuance of such a request or has dealt with the matter in pursuance of such a request; or

(f)   subject to subsection (3A), a reasoned submission requesting referral to the European Commission has been submitted to the European Commission under article 4(5) of the EC Merger Regulation.

(3A)   Subsection (3)(f) shall cease to apply if the OFT is informed that a Member State competent to examine the concentration under its national competition law has, within the time permitted by Article 4(5) of the EC Merger Regulation, expressed its disagreement as regards the request to refer the case to the European Commission; and this subsection shall be construed in accordance with that Regulation.

(4)   A reference under this section shall, in particular, specify—

(a)   the enactment under which it is made; and

(b)   the date on which it is made.

(5)   The references in this section to the creation of a relevant merger situation shall be construed in accordance with section 23, the reference in subsection (2) of this section to relevant customer benefits shall be construed in accordance with section 30 and the reference in subsection (3) of this section to a matter to which a notice under section 42(2) relates being finally determined under Chapter 2 shall be construed in accordance with section 43(4) and (5).

(6)   In this Part "market in the United Kingdom" includes—

   (a)   so far as it operates in the United Kingdom or a part of the United Kingdom, any market which operates there and in another country or territory or in a part of another country or territory; and

   (b)   any market which operates only in a part of the United Kingdom;

   and references to a market for goods or services include references to a market for goods and services.

(7)   In this Part "the decision-making authority" means—

   (a)   in the case of a reference or possible reference under this section or section 33, the OFT or (as the case may be) the Commission; and

   (b)   in the case of a notice or possible notice under section 42(2) or 59(2) or a reference or possible reference under section 45 or 62, the OFT, the Commission or (as the case may be) the Secretary of State.

23.   Relevant merger situations

(1)   For the purposes of this Part, a relevant merger situation has been created if—

   (a)   two or more enterprises have ceased to be distinct enterprises at a time or in circumstances falling within section 24; and

   (b)   the value of the turnover in the United Kingdom of the enterprise being taken over exceeds £70 million.

(2)   For the purposes of this Part, a relevant merger situation has also been created if—

   (a)   two or more enterprises have ceased to be distinct enterprises at a time or in circumstances falling within section 24; and

   (b)   as a result, one or both of the conditions mentioned in subsections (3) and (4) below prevails or prevails to a greater extent.

(3)   The condition mentioned in this subsection is that, in relation to the supply of goods of any description, at least one-quarter of all the goods of that description which are supplied in the United Kingdom, or in a substantial part of the United Kingdom—

   (a)   are supplied by one and the same person or are supplied to one and the same person; or

   (b)   are supplied by the persons by whom the enterprises concerned are carried on, or are supplied to those persons.

(4)   The condition mentioned in this subsection is that, in relation to the supply of services of any description, the supply of services of that description in the United Kingdom, or in a substantial part of the United Kingdom, is to the extent of at least one-quarter—

   (a)   supply by one and the same person, or supply for one and the same person; or

   (b)   supply by the persons by whom the enterprises concerned are carried on, or supply for those persons.

(5)   For the purpose of deciding whether the proportion of one-quarter mentioned in subsection (3) or (4) is fulfilled with respect to goods or (as the case may be) services of any description, the decision-making authority shall apply such criterion (whether value, cost, price, quantity, capacity, number of workers employed or some other criterion, of whatever nature), or such combination of criteria, as the decision-making authority considers appropriate.

(6)   References in subsections (3) and (4) to the supply of goods or (as the case may be) services shall, in relation to goods or services of any description which are the subject of different forms of supply, be construed in whichever of the following ways the decision-making authority considers appropriate—

   (a)   as references to any of those forms of supply taken separately;

   (b)   as references to all those forms of supply taken together; or

   (c)   as references to any of those forms of supply taken in groups.

(7)   For the purposes of subsection (6) the decision-making authority may treat goods or services as being the subject of different forms of supply whenever—

   (a)   the transactions concerned differ as to their nature, their parties, their terms or their surrounding circumstances; and

(b)   the difference is one which, in the opinion of the decision-making authority, ought for the purposes of that subsection to be treated as a material difference.

(8)   The criteria for deciding when goods or services can be treated, for the purposes of this section, as goods or services of a separate description shall be such as in any particular case the decision-making authority considers appropriate in the circumstances of that case.

(9)   For the purposes of this Chapter, the question whether a relevant merger situation has been created shall be determined as at—

(a)   in the case of a reference which is treated as having been made under section 22 by virtue of section 37(2), such time as the Commission may determine; and

(b)   in any other case, immediately before the time when the reference has been, or is to be, made.

24.   Time-limits and prior notice

(1)   For the purposes of section 23 two or more enterprises have ceased to be distinct enterprises at a time or in circumstances falling within this section if—

(a)   the two or more enterprises ceased to be distinct enterprises before the day on which the reference relating to them is to be made and did so not more than four months before that day; or

(b)   notice of material facts about the arrangements or transactions under or in consequence of which the enterprises have ceased to be distinct enterprises has not been given in accordance with subsection (2).

(2)   Notice of material facts is given in accordance with this subsection if—

(a)   it is given to the OFT prior to the entering into of the arrangements or transactions concerned or the facts are made public prior to the entering into of those arrangements or transactions; or

(b)   it is given to the OFT, or the facts are made public, more than four months before the day on which the reference is to be made.

(3)   In this section—

"made public" means so publicised as to be generally known or readily ascertainable; and

"notice" includes notice which is not in writing.

25.   Extension of time-limits

(1)   The OFT and the persons carrying on the enterprises which have or may have ceased to be distinct enterprises may agree to extend by no more than 20 days the four month period mentioned in section 24(1)(a) or (2)(b).

(2)   The OFT may by notice to the persons carrying on the enterprises which have or may have ceased to be distinct enterprises extend the four month period mentioned in section 24(1)(a) or (2)(b) if it considers that any of those persons has failed to provide, within the period stated in a notice under section 31 and in the manner authorised or required, information requested of him in that notice.

(3)   An extension under subsection (2) shall be for the period beginning with the end of the period within which the information is to be provided and which is stated in the notice under section 31 and ending with—

(a)   the provision of the information to the satisfaction of the OFT; or

(b)   if earlier, the cancellation by the OFT of the extension.

(4)   The OFT may by notice to the persons carrying on the enterprises which have or may have ceased to be distinct enterprises extend the four month period mentioned in section 24(1)(a) or (2)(b) if it is seeking undertakings from any of those persons under section 73.

(5)   An extension under subsection (4) shall be for the period beginning with the receipt of the notice under that subsection and ending with the earliest of the following events—

(a)   the giving of the undertakings concerned;

(b)   the expiry of the period of 10 days beginning with the first day after the receipt by the OFT of a notice from the person who has been given a notice under subsection (4) and from whom the undertakings are being sought stating that he does not intend to give the undertakings; or

    (c)   the cancellation by the OFT of the extension.

(6)   The OFT may by notice to the persons carrying on the enterprises which have or may have ceased to be distinct enterprises extend the four month period mentioned in section 24(1)(a) or (2)(b) if the European Commission is considering a request made, in relation to the matter concerned, by the United Kingdom (whether alone or with others) under article 22(1) of the EC Merger Regulation (but is not yet proceeding with the matter in pursuance of such a request).

(7)   An extension under subsection (6) shall be for the period beginning with the receipt of the notice under that subsection and ending with the receipt of a notice under subsection (8).

(8)   The OFT shall, in connection with any notice given by it under subsection (6), by notice inform the persons carrying on the enterprises which have or may have ceased to be distinct enterprises of the completion by the European Commission of its consideration of the request of the United Kingdom.

(9)   Subject to subsections (10) and (11), where the four month period mentioned in section 24(1)(a) or (2)(b) is extended or further extended by virtue of this section in relation to a particular case, any reference to that period in section 24 or the preceding provisions of this section shall have effect in relation to that case as if it were a reference to a period equivalent to the aggregate of the period being extended and the period of the extension (whether or not those periods overlap in time).

(10)   Subsection (11) applies where—

    (a)   the four month period mentioned in section 24(1)(a) or (2)(b) is further extended;

    (b)   the further extension and at least one previous extension is made under one or more of subsections (2), (4) and (6); and

    (c)   the same days or fractions of days are included in or comprise the further extension and are included in or comprise at least one such previous extension.

(11)   In calculating the period of the further extension, any days or fractions of days of the kind mentioned in subsection (10)(c) shall be disregarded.

(12)   No more than one extension is possible under subsection (1).

26.   Enterprises ceasing to be distinct enterprises

(1)   For the purposes of this Part any two enterprises cease to be distinct enterprises if they are brought under common ownership or common control (whether or not the business to which either of them formerly belonged continues to be carried on under the same or different ownership or control).

(2)   Enterprises shall, in particular, be treated as being under common control if they are—

    (a)   enterprises of interconnected bodies corporate;

    (b)   enterprises carried on by two or more bodies corporate of which one and the same person or group of persons has control; or

    (c)   an enterprise carried on by a body corporate and an enterprise carried on by a person or group of persons having control of that body corporate.

(3)   A person or group of persons able, directly or indirectly, to control or materially to influence the policy of a body corporate, or the policy of any person in carrying on an enterprise but without having a controlling interest in that body corporate or in that enterprise, may, for the purposes of subsections (1) and (2), be treated as having control of it.

(4)   For the purposes of subsection (1), in so far as it relates to bringing two or more enterprises under common control, a person or group of persons may be treated as bringing an enterprise under his or their control if—

    (a)   being already able to control or materially to influence the policy of the person carrying on the enterprise, that person or group of persons acquires a controlling interest in the enterprise or, in the case of an enterprise carried on by a body corporate, acquires a controlling interest in that body corporate; or

(b)   being already able materially to influence the policy of the person carrying on the enterprise, that person or group of persons becomes able to control that policy.

27.   **Time when enterprises cease to be distinct**

(1)   Subsection (2) applies in relation to any arrangements or transaction—
      (a)   not having immediate effect or having immediate effect only in part; but
      (b)   under or in consequence of which any two enterprises cease to be distinct enterprises.

(2)   The time when the parties to any such arrangements or transaction become bound to such extent as will result, on effect being given to their obligations, in the enterprises ceasing to be distinct enterprises shall be taken to be the time at which the two enterprises cease to be distinct enterprises.

(3)   In accordance with subsections (1) and (2) (but without prejudice to the generality of those subsections) for the purpose of determining the time at which any two enterprises cease to be distinct enterprises no account shall be taken of any option or other conditional right until the option is exercised or the condition is satisfied.

(4)   Subsections (1) to (3) are subject to subsections (5) to (8) and section 29.

(5)   The decision-making authority may, for the purposes of a reference, treat successive events to which this subsection applies as having occurred simultaneously on the date on which the latest of them occurred.

(6)   Subsection (5) applies to successive events—
      (a)   which occur within a period of two years under or in consequence of the same arrangements or transaction, or successive arrangements or transactions between the same parties or interests; and
      (b)   by virtue of each of which, under or in consequence of the arrangements or the transaction or transactions concerned, any enterprises cease as between themselves to be distinct enterprises.

(7)   The decision-making authority may, for the purposes of subsections (5) and (6), treat such arrangements or transactions as the decision-making authority considers appropriate as arrangements or transactions between the same interests.

(8)   In deciding whether it is appropriate to treat arrangements or transactions as arrangements or transactions between the same interests the decision-making authority shall, in particular, have regard to the persons substantially concerned in the arrangements or transactions concerned.

28.   **Turnover test**

(1)   For the purposes of section 23 the value of the turnover in the United Kingdom of the enterprise being taken over shall be determined by taking the total value of the turnover in the United Kingdom of the enterprises which cease to be distinct enterprises and deducting—
      (a)   the turnover in the United Kingdom of any enterprise which continues to be carried on under the same ownership and control; or
      (b)   if no enterprise continues to be carried on under the same ownership and control, the turnover in the United Kingdom which, of all the turnovers concerned, is the turnover of the highest value.

(2)   For the purposes of this Part (other than section 121(4)(c)(ii)) the turnover in the United Kingdom of an enterprise shall be determined in accordance with such provisions as may be specified in an order made by the Secretary of State.

(3)   An order under subsection (2) may, in particular, make provision as to—
      (a)   the amounts which are, or which are not, to be treated as comprising an enterprise's turnover;
      (b)   the date or dates by reference to which an enterprise's turnover is to be determined;
      (c)   the connection with the United Kingdom by virtue of which an enterprise's turnover is turnover in the United Kingdom.

(4) An order under subsection (2) may, in particular, make provision enabling the decision-making authority to determine matters of a description specified in the order (including any of the matters mentioned in paragraphs (a) to (c) of subsection (3)).

(5) The OFT shall—
   (a) keep under review the sum for the time being mentioned in section 23(1)(b); and
   (b) from time to time advise the Secretary of State as to whether the sum is still appropriate.

(6) The Secretary of State may by order amend section 23(1)(b) so as to alter the sum for the time being mentioned there.

29. Obtaining control by stages

(1) Where an enterprise is brought under the control of a person or group of persons in the course of two or more transactions (in this section a "series of transactions") to which subsection (2) applies, those transactions may, if the decision-making authority considers it appropriate, be treated for the purposes of a reference as having occurred simultaneously on the date on which the latest of them occurred.

(2) This subsection applies to—
   (a) any transaction which—
       (i) enables that person or group of persons directly or indirectly to control or materially to influence the policy of any person carrying on the enterprise;
       (ii) enables that person or group of persons to do so to a greater degree; or
       (iii) is a step (whether direct or indirect) towards enabling that person or group of persons to do so; and
   (b) any transaction by virtue of which that person or group of persons acquires a controlling interest in the enterprise or, where the enterprise is carried on by a body corporate, in that body corporate.

(3) Where a series of transactions includes a transaction falling within subsection (2)(b), any transaction occurring after the occurrence of that transaction is to be disregarded for the purposes of subsection (1).

(4) Where the period within which a series of transactions occurs exceeds two years, the transactions that may be treated as mentioned in subsection (1) are any of those transactions that occur within a period of two years.

(5) Sections 26(2) to (4) and 127(1), (2) and (4) to (6) shall apply for the purposes of this section to determine—
   (a) whether an enterprise is brought under the control of a person or group of persons; and
   (b) whether a transaction is one to which subsection (2) applies;
   as they apply for the purposes of section 26 to determine whether enterprises are brought under common control.

(6) In determining for the purposes of this section the time at which any transaction occurs, no account shall be taken of any option or other conditional right until the option is exercised or the condition is satisfied.

30. Relevant customer benefits

(1) For the purposes of this Part a benefit is a relevant customer benefit if—
   (a) it is a benefit to relevant customers in the form of—
       (i) lower prices, higher quality or greater choice of goods or services in any market in the United Kingdom (whether or not the market or markets in which the substantial lessening of competition concerned has, or may have, occurred or (as the case may be) may occur); or
       (ii) greater innovation in relation to such goods or services; and
   (b) the decision-making authority believes—
       (i) in the case of a reference or possible reference under section 22 or 45(2), as mentioned in subsection (2); and

      (ii)   in the case of a reference or possible reference under section 33 or 45(4), as mentioned
           in subsection (3).

(2)   The belief, in the case of a reference or possible reference under section 22 or section 45(2), is
       that—

     (a)   the benefit has accrued as a result of the creation of the relevant merger situation concerned
         or may be expected to accrue within a reasonable period as a result of the creation of that
         situation; and

     (b)   the benefit was, or is, unlikely to accrue without the creation of that situation or a similar
         lessening of competition.

(3)   The belief, in the case of a reference or possible reference under section 33 or 45(4), is that—

     (a)   the benefit may be expected to accrue within a reasonable period as a result of the creation
         of the relevant merger situation concerned; and

     (b)   the benefit is unlikely to accrue without the creation of that situation or a similar lessening
         of competition.

(4)   In subsection (1) "relevant customers" means—

     (a)   customers of any person carrying on an enterprise which, in the creation of the relevant
         merger situation concerned, has ceased to be, or (as the case may be) will cease to be, a
         distinct enterprise;

     (b)   customers of such customers; and

     (c)   any other customers in a chain of customers beginning with the customers mentioned in
         paragraph (a);

    and in this subsection "customers" includes future customers.

31.   Information powers in relation to completed mergers

(1)   The OFT may by notice to any of the persons carrying on the enterprises which have or may have
    ceased to be distinct enterprises request him to provide the OFT with such information as the OFT
    may require for the purpose of deciding whether to make a reference under section 22.

(2)   The notice shall state—

     (a)   the information required;

     (b)   the period within which the information is to be provided; and

     (c)   the possible consequences of not providing the information within the stated period and in
         the authorised or required manner.

32.   Supplementary provision for purposes of sections 25 and 31

(1)   The Secretary of State may make regulations for the purposes of sections 25 and 31.

(2)   The regulations may, in particular—

     (a)   provide for the manner in which any information requested by the OFT under section 31 is
         authorised or required to be provided, and the time at which such information is to be
         treated as provided (including the time at which it is to be treated as provided to the
         satisfaction of the OFT for the purposes of section 25(3));

     (b)   provide for the persons carrying on the enterprises which have or may have ceased to be
         distinct enterprises to be informed, in circumstances in which section 25(3) applies—

       (i)   of the fact that the OFT is satisfied as to the provision of the information requested by
           it or (as the case may be) of the OFT's decision to cancel the extension; and

      (ii)   of the time at which the OFT is to be treated as so satisfied or (as the case may be) of
           the time at which the cancellation is to be treated as having effect;

     (c)   provide for the persons carrying on the enterprises which have or may have ceased to be
         distinct enterprises to be informed, in circumstances in which section 25(5) applies—

       (i)   of the OFT's decision to cancel the extension; and

      (ii)   of the time at which the cancellation is to be treated as having effect;

     (d)   provide for the time at which any notice under section 25(4), (5)(b), (6) or (8) is to be treated
         as received;

(e)   provide that a person is, or is not, to be treated, in such circumstances as may be specified in the regulations, as acting on behalf of a person carrying on an enterprise which has or may have ceased to be a distinct enterprise.

(3)   A notice under section 25(2)—

(a)   shall be given within 5 days of the end of the period within which the information is to be provided and which is stated in the notice under section 31; and

(b)   shall inform the person to whom it is addressed of—

(i)   the OFT's opinion as mentioned in section 25(2); and

(ii)   the OFT's intention to extend the period for considering whether to make a reference.

(4)   In determining for the purposes of section 25(1) or (5)(b) or subsection (3)(a) above any period which is expressed in the enactment concerned as a period of days or number of days no account shall be taken of—

(a)   Saturday, Sunday, Good Friday and Christmas Day; and

(b)   any day which is a bank holiday in England and Wales.

Duty to make references: anticipated mergers

33.   Duty to make references in relation to anticipated mergers

(1)   The OFT shall, subject to subsections (2) and (3), make a reference to the Commission if the OFT believes that it is or may be the case that—

(a)   arrangements are in progress or in contemplation which, if carried into effect, will result in the creation of a relevant merger situation; and

(b)   the creation of that situation may be expected to result in a substantial lessening of competition within any market or markets in the United Kingdom for goods or services.

(2)   The OFT may decide not to make a reference under this section if it believes that—

(a)   the market concerned is not, or the markets concerned are not, of sufficient importance to justify the making of a reference to the Commission;

(b)   the arrangements concerned are not sufficiently far advanced, or are not sufficiently likely to proceed, to justify the making of a reference to the Commission; or

(c)   any relevant customer benefits in relation to the creation of the relevant merger situation concerned outweigh the substantial lessening of competition concerned and any adverse effects of the substantial lessening of competition concerned.

(3)   No reference shall be made under this section if—

(a)   the making of the reference is prevented by section ... 74(1) or 96(3) or paragraph 4 of Schedule 7;

(b)   the OFT is considering whether to accept undertakings under section 73 instead of making such a reference;

(c)   the arrangements concerned are being, or have been, dealt with in connection with a reference made under section 22;

(d)   a notice under section 42(2) is in force in relation to the matter or the matter to which such a notice relates has been finally determined under Chapter 2 otherwise than in circumstances in which a notice is then given to the OFT under section 56(1); ...

(e)   the European Commission is considering a request made, in relation to the matter concerned, by the United Kingdom (whether alone or with others) under article 22(1) of the EC Merger Regulation, is proceeding with the matter in pursuance of such a request or has dealt with the matter in pursuance of such a request; or

(f)   subject to subsection (3A), a reasoned submission requesting referral to the European Commission has been submitted to the European Commission under article 4(5) of the EC Merger Regulation.

(3A)   Section 33(3)(f) shall cease to apply if the OFT is informed that a Member State competent to examine the concentration under its national competition law has, within the time permitted by Article 4(5) of the EC Merger Regulation, expressed its disagreement as regards the request to refer the case to the European Commission; and this subsection shall be construed in accordance with that Regulation.

(4)   A reference under this section shall, in particular, specify—
        (a)   the enactment under which it is made; and
        (b)   the date on which it is made.

34.   Supplementary provision in relation to anticipated mergers

(1)   The Secretary of State may by order make such provision as he considers appropriate about the operation of sections 27 and 29 in relation to—
        (a)   references under this Part which relate to arrangements which are in progress or in contemplation; or
        (b)   notices under section 42(2), 59(2) or 67(2) which relate to such arrangements.

(2)   An order under subsection (1) may, in particular—
        (a)   provide for sections 27(5) to (8) and 29 to apply with modifications in relation to such references or notices or in relation to particular descriptions of such references or notices;
        (b)   enable particular descriptions of events, arrangements or transactions which have already occurred—
               (i)   to be taken into account for the purposes of deciding whether to make such references or such references of a particular description or whether to give such notices or such notices of a particular description;
               (ii)   to be dealt with under such references or such references of a particular description or under such notices or such notices of a particular description.

Cases referred by European Commission under EC Merger Regulation

34A.   Duty of OFT where case referred by the European Commission

(1)   Subsection (2) applies if the European Commission has by a decision referred the whole or part of a case to the OFT under Article 4(4) or 9 of the EC Merger Regulation, or is deemed to have taken such a decision, unless an intervention notice is in force in relation to that case.

(2)   Before the end of the preliminary assessment period, the OFT shall—
        (a)   decide whether to make a reference to the Commission under section 22 or 33; and
        (b)   inform the persons carrying on the enterprises concerned by notice of that decision and of the reasons for it.

(3)   The OFT may, for the purposes of subsection (2), decide not to make a reference on the basis that it is considering whether to seek or accept undertakings under section 73 instead of making a reference; but a decision taken on that basis does not prevent the OFT from making a reference under section 22 or 33 in the event of no such undertakings being offered or accepted.

(4)   In this section—
        "the preliminary assessment period" means, subject to subsection (5), the period of 45 working days beginning with the day after the day on which the decision of the European Commission to refer the case is taken (or is deemed to have been taken); and
        "working day" means any day which is not—
        (a)   a Saturday;
        (b)   a Sunday; or
        (c)   a day which is a European Commission holiday (as published in the Official Journal of the European Communities before the beginning of the year in which it occurs).

(5)   If the OFT has imposed a requirement under section 34B and it considers that the person on whom that requirement was imposed has failed to comply with it, the OFT may, by notice to the persons carrying on the enterprises concerned, extend the preliminary assessment period.

(6)   The period of an extension under subsection (5) shall—
        (a)   begin with the end of the period within which the requirement under section 34B could be complied with; and
        (b)   end with the earlier of either compliance with the requirement to the satisfaction of the OFT or cancellation by the OFT of the extension.

(7) A notice under subsection (6) shall—
    (a) be given within 5 working days of the end of the period mentioned in paragraph (a) of that subsection; and
    (b) inform the person to whom it is addressed that the OFT is of the opinion mentioned in subsection (5) and that it intends to extend the preliminary assessment period.

34B. Power to request information in referred cases

(1) In a case mentioned in section 34A(1), the OFT may by notice to any of the persons carrying on the enterprises concerned request him to provide the OFT with such information as the OFT may require for the purpose of making a decision for the purposes of section 34A(2).

(2) The notice shall state—
    (a) the information required;
    (b) the period within which the information is to be provided;
    (c) the manner (if any) in which the information is required to be provided; and
    (d) the possible consequences—
        (i) of not providing the information within the stated period; and
        (ii) if a manner for its provision is stated in the notice, of not providing it in that manner.

Determination of references

35. Questions to be decided in relation to completed mergers

(1) Subject to subsections (6) and (7) and section 127(3), the Commission shall, on a reference under section 22, decide the following questions—
    (a) whether a relevant merger situation has been created; and
    (b) if so, whether the creation of that situation has resulted, or may be expected to result, in a substantial lessening of competition within any market or markets in the United Kingdom for goods or services.

(2) For the purposes of this Part there is an anti-competitive outcome if—
    (a) a relevant merger situation has been created and the creation of that situation has resulted, or may be expected to result, in a substantial lessening of competition within any market or markets in the United Kingdom for goods or services; or
    (b) arrangements are in progress or in contemplation which, if carried into effect, will result in the creation of a relevant merger situation and the creation of that situation may be expected to result in a substantial lessening of competition within any market or markets in the United Kingdom for goods or services.

(3) The Commission shall, if it has decided on a reference under section 22 that there is an anti-competitive outcome (within the meaning given by subsection (2)(a)), decide the following additional questions—
    (a) whether action should be taken by it under section 41(2) for the purpose of remedying, mitigating or preventing the substantial lessening of competition concerned or any adverse effect which has resulted from, or may be expected to result from, the substantial lessening of competition;
    (b) whether it should recommend the taking of action by others for the purpose of remedying, mitigating or preventing the substantial lessening of competition concerned or any adverse effect which has resulted from, or may be expected to result from, the substantial lessening of competition; and
    (c) in either case, if action should be taken, what action should be taken and what is to be remedied, mitigated or prevented.

(4) In deciding the questions mentioned in subsection (3) the Commission shall, in particular, have regard to the need to achieve as comprehensive a solution as is reasonable and practicable to the substantial lessening of competition and any adverse effects resulting from it.

(5) In deciding the questions mentioned in subsection (3) the Commission may, in particular, have regard to the effect of any action on any relevant customer benefits in relation to the creation of the relevant merger situation concerned.

(6)   In relation to the question whether a relevant merger situation has been created, a reference under section 22 may be framed so as to require the Commission to exclude from consideration—

             (a)   subsection (1) of section 23;

             (b)   subsection (2) of that section; or

             (c)   one of those subsections if the Commission finds that the other is satisfied.

(7)   In relation to the question whether any such result as is mentioned in section 23(2)(b) has arisen, a reference under section 22 may be framed so as to require the Commission to confine its investigation to the supply of goods or services in a part of the United Kingdom specified in the reference.

36.   **Questions to be decided in relation to anticipated mergers**

(1)   Subject to subsections (5) and (6) and section 127(3), the Commission shall, on a reference under section 33, decide the following questions—

             (a)   whether arrangements are in progress or in contemplation which, if carried into effect, will result in the creation of a relevant merger situation; and

             (b)   if so, whether the creation of that situation may be expected to result in a substantial lessening of competition within any market or markets in the United Kingdom for goods or services.

(2)   The Commission shall, if it has decided on a reference under section 33 that there is an anti-competitive outcome (within the meaning given by section 35(2)(b)), decide the following additional questions—

             (a)   whether action should be taken by it under section 41(2) for the purpose of remedying, mitigating or preventing the substantial lessening of competition concerned or any adverse effect which may be expected to result from the substantial lessening of competition;

             (b)   whether it should recommend the taking of action by others for the purpose of remedying, mitigating or preventing the substantial lessening of competition concerned or any adverse effect which may be expected to result from the substantial lessening of competition; and

             (c)   in either case, if action should be taken, what action should be taken and what is to be remedied, mitigated or prevented.

(3)   In deciding the questions mentioned in subsection (2) the Commission shall, in particular, have regard to the need to achieve as comprehensive a solution as is reasonable and practicable to the substantial lessening of competition and any adverse effects resulting from it.

(4)   In deciding the questions mentioned in subsection (2) the Commission may, in particular, have regard to the effect of any action on any relevant customer benefits in relation to the creation of the relevant merger situation concerned.

(5)   In relation to the question whether a relevant merger situation will be created, a reference under section 33 may be framed so as to require the Commission to exclude from consideration—

             (a)   subsection (1) of section 23;

             (b)   subsection (2) of that section; or

             (c)   one of those subsections if the Commission finds that the other is satisfied.

(6)   In relation to the question whether any such result as is mentioned in section 23(2)(b) will arise, a reference under section 33 may be framed so as to require the Commission to confine its investigation to the supply of goods or services in a part of the United Kingdom specified in the reference.

37.   **Cancellation and variation of references under section 22 or 33**

(1)   The Commission shall cancel a reference under section 33 if it considers that the proposal to make arrangements of the kind mentioned in the reference has been abandoned.

(2)   The Commission may, if it considers that doing so is justified by the facts (including events occurring on or after the making of the reference concerned), treat a reference made under section 22 or 33 as if it had been made under section 33 or (as the case may be) 22; and, in such cases, references in this Part to references under those sections shall, so far as may be necessary, be construed accordingly.

(3)   Where, by virtue of subsection (2), the Commission treats a reference made under section 22 or
        33 as if it had been made under section 33 or (as the case may be) 22, sections 77 to 81 shall, in
        particular, apply as if the reference had been made under section 33 or (as the case may be) 22
        instead of under section 22 or 33.

(4)   Subsection (5) applies in relation to any undertaking accepted under section 80, or any order
        made under section 81, which is in force immediately before the Commission, by virtue of
        subsection (2), treats a reference made under section 22 or 33 as if it had been made under section
        33 or (as the case may be) 22.

(5)   The undertaking or order shall, so far as applicable, continue in force as if—
        (a)   in the case of an undertaking or order which relates to a reference made under section 22,
                accepted or made in relation to a reference made under section 33; and
        (b)   in the case of an undertaking or order which relates to a reference made under section 33,
                accepted or made in relation to a reference made under section 22;
        and the undertaking or order concerned may be varied, superseded, released or revoked
        accordingly.

(6)   The OFT may at any time vary a reference under section 22 or 33.

(7)   The OFT shall consult the Commission before varying any such reference.

(8)   Subsection (7) shall not apply if the Commission has requested the variation concerned.

(9)   No variation by the OFT under this section shall be capable of altering the period permitted by
        section 39 within which the report of the Commission under section 38 is to be prepared and
        published.

38.   Investigations and reports on references under section 22 or 33

(1)   The Commission shall prepare and publish a report on a reference under section 22 or 33 within
        the period permitted by section 39.

(2)   The report shall, in particular, contain—
        (a)   the decisions of the Commission on the questions which it is required to answer by virtue of
                section 35 or (as the case may be) 36;
        (b)   its reasons for its decisions; and
        (c)   such information as the Commission considers appropriate for facilitating a proper
                understanding of those questions and of its reasons for its decisions.

(3)   The Commission shall carry out such investigations as it considers appropriate for the purposes of
        preparing a report under this section.

(4)   The Commission shall, at the same time as a report prepared under this section is published, give
        it to the OFT.

39.   Time-limits for investigations and reports

(1)   The Commission shall prepare and publish its report under section 38 within the period of 24
        weeks beginning with the date of the reference concerned.

(2)   ...

(3)   The Commission may extend, by no more than 8 weeks, the period within which a report under
        section 38 is to be prepared and published if it considers that there are special reasons why the
        report cannot be prepared and published within that period.

(4)   The Commission may extend the period within which a report under section 38 is to be prepared
        and published if it considers that a relevant person has failed (whether with or without a
        reasonable excuse) to comply with any requirement of a notice under section 109.

(5)   In subsection (4) "relevant person" means—
        (a)   any person carrying on any of the enterprises concerned;
        (b)   any person who (whether alone or as a member of a group) owns or has control of any such
                person; or
        (c)   any officer, employee or agent of any person mentioned in paragraph (a) or (b).

(6)   For the purposes of subsection (5) a person or group of persons able, directly or indirectly, to
        control or materially to influence the policy of a body of persons corporate or unincorporate, but

without having a controlling interest in that body of persons, may be treated as having control of it.

(7)   An extension under subsection (3) or (4) shall come into force when published under section 107.

(8)   An extension under subsection (4) shall continue in force until—

    (a)   the person concerned provides the information or documents to the satisfaction of the Commission or (as the case may be) appears as a witness in accordance with the requirements of the Commission; or

    (b)   the Commission publishes its decision to cancel the extension.

(9)   References in this Part to the date of a reference shall be construed as references to the date specified in the reference as the date on which it is made.

(10)   This section is subject to section 40.

40.   Section 39: supplementary

(1), (2) ...

(3)   A period extended under subsection (3) of section 39 may also be extended under subsection (4) of that section and a period extended under subsection (4) of that section may also be extended under subsection (3) of that section.

(4)   No more than one extension is possible under section 39(3).

(5)   Where a period within which a report under section 38 is to be prepared and published is extended or further extended under section 39(3) or (4), the period as extended or (as the case may be) further extended shall, subject to subsections (6) and (7), be calculated by taking the period being extended and adding to it the period of the extension (whether or not those periods overlap in time).

(6)   Subsection (7) applies where—

    (a)   the period within which the report under section 38 is to be prepared and published is further extended;

    (b)   the further extension and at least one previous extension is made under section 39(4); and

    (c)   the same days or fractions of days are included in or comprise the further extension and are included in or comprise at least one such previous extension.

(7)   In calculating the period of the further extension, any days or fractions of days of the kind mentioned in subsection (6)(c) shall be disregarded.

(8)   The Secretary of State may by order amend section 39 so as to alter any one or more of the following periods—

    (a)   the period of 24 weeks mentioned in subsection (1) of that section or any period for the time being mentioned in that subsection in substitution for that period;

    (b)   ...

    (c)   the period of 8 weeks mentioned in subsection (3) of that section or any period for the time being mentioned in that subsection in substitution for that period.

(9)   No alteration shall be made by virtue of subsection (8) which results in the period for the time being mentioned in subsection (1) ... of section 39 exceeding 24 weeks or the period for the time being mentioned in subsection (3) of that section exceeding 8 weeks.

(10)   An order under subsection (8) shall not affect any period of time within which the Commission is under a duty to prepare and publish its report under section 38 in relation to a reference under section 22 or 33 if the Commission is already under that duty in relation to that reference when the order is made.

(11)   Before making an order under subsection (8) the Secretary of State shall consult the Commission and such other persons as he considers appropriate.

(12)   The Secretary of State may make regulations for the purposes of section 39(8).

(13)   The regulations may, in particular—

    (a)   provide for the time at which information or documents are to be treated as provided (including the time at which they are to be treated as provided to the satisfaction of the Commission for the purposes of section 39(8));

(b) provide for the time at which a person is to be treated as appearing as a witness (including the time at which he is to be treated as appearing as a witness in accordance with the requirements of the Commission for the purposes of section 39(8));

(c) provide for the persons carrying on the enterprises which have or may have ceased to be, or may cease to be, distinct enterprises to be informed, in circumstances in which section 39(8) applies, of the fact that—

    (i) the Commission is satisfied as to the provision of the information or documents required by it; or

    (ii) the person concerned has appeared as a witness in accordance with the requirements of the Commission;

(d) provide for the persons carrying on the enterprises which have or may have ceased to be, or may cease to be, distinct enterprises to be informed, in circumstances in which section 39(8) applies, of the time at which the Commission is to be treated as satisfied as mentioned in paragraph (c)(i) above or the person concerned is to be treated as having appeared as mentioned in paragraph (c)(ii) above.

41. Duty to remedy effects of completed or anticipated mergers

(1) Subsection (2) applies where a report of the Commission has been prepared and published under section 38 within the period permitted by section 39 and contains the decision that there is an anti-competitive outcome.

(2) The Commission shall take such action under section 82 or 84 as it considers to be reasonable and practicable—

(a) to remedy, mitigate or prevent the substantial lessening of competition concerned; and

(b) to remedy, mitigate or prevent any adverse effects which have resulted from, or may be expected to result from, the substantial lessening of competition.

(3) The decision of the Commission under subsection (2) shall be consistent with its decisions as included in its report by virtue of section 35(3) or (as the case may be) 36(2) unless there has been a material change of circumstances since the preparation of the report or the Commission otherwise has a special reason for deciding differently.

(4) In making a decision under subsection (2), the Commission shall, in particular, have regard to the need to achieve as comprehensive a solution as is reasonable and practicable to the substantial lessening of competition and any adverse effects resulting from it.

(5) In making a decision under subsection (2), the Commission may, in particular, have regard to the effect of any action on any relevant customer benefits in relation to the creation of the relevant merger situation concerned.

CHAPTER 2
PUBLIC INTEREST CASES

Power to make references

42. Intervention by Secretary of State in certain public interest cases

(1) Subsection (2) applies where—

(a) the Secretary of State has reasonable grounds for suspecting that it is or may be the case that a relevant merger situation has been created or that arrangements are in progress or in contemplation which, if carried into effect, will result in the creation of a relevant merger situation;

(b) no reference under section 22 or 33 has been made in relation to the relevant merger situation concerned;

(c) no decision has been made not to make such a reference (other than a decision made by virtue of subsection (2)(b) of section 33 or a decision to accept undertakings under section 73 instead of making such a reference); and

(d) no reference is prevented from being made under section 22 or 33 by virtue of—

	(i)	section 22(3)(a) or (e) or (as the case may be) 33(3)(a) or (e); or

      (ii)   Community law or anything done under or in accordance with it.

(2)   The Secretary of State may give a notice to the OFT (in this Part "an intervention notice") if he believes that it is or may be the case that one or more than one public interest consideration is relevant to a consideration of the relevant merger situation concerned.

(3)   For the purposes of this Part a public interest consideration is a consideration which, at the time of the giving of the intervention notice concerned, is specified in section 58 or is not so specified but, in the opinion of the Secretary of State, ought to be so specified.

(4)   No more than one intervention notice shall be given under subsection (2) in relation to the same relevant merger situation.

(5)   For the purposes of deciding whether a relevant merger situation has been created or whether arrangements are in progress or in contemplation which, if carried into effect, will result in the creation of a relevant merger situation, sections 23 to 32 (read together with section 34) shall apply for the purposes of this Chapter as they do for the purposes of Chapter 1 but subject to subsection (6).

(6)   In their application by virtue of subsection (5) sections 23 to 32 shall have effect as if—

    (a)   for paragraph (a) of section 23(9) there were substituted—

       "(a) in relation to the giving of an intervention notice, the time when the notice is given;

    (aa) in relation to the making of a report by the OFT under section 44, the time of the making of the report;

    (ab) in the case of a reference which is treated as having been made under section 45(2) or (3) by virtue of section 49(1), such time as the Commission may determine; and";

    (b)   the references to the OFT in sections 25(1) to (3), (6) and (8) and 31 included references to the Secretary of State;

    (c)   the references to the OFT in section 25(4) and (5) were references to the Secretary of State;

    (d)   the reference in section 25(4) to section 73 were a reference to paragraph 3 of Schedule 7;

    (e)   after section 25(5) there were inserted—

       "(5A) The Secretary of State may by notice to the persons carrying on the enterprises which have or may have ceased to be distinct enterprises extend the four month period mentioned in section 24(1)(a) or (2)(b) if, by virtue of section 46(5) or paragraph 3(6) of Schedule 7, he decides to delay a decision as to whether to make a reference under section 45.

       (5B)   An extension under subsection (5A) shall be for the period of the delay.";

    (f)   in section 25(10)(b) after the word "(4)" there were inserted ", (5A)";

    (g)   the reference in section 25(12) to one extension were a reference to one extension by the OFT and one extension by the Secretary of State;

    (h)   the powers to extend time-limits under section 25 as applied by subsection (5) above, and the power to request information under section 31(1) as so applied, were not exercisable by the OFT or the Secretary of State before the giving of an intervention notice but the existing time-limits in relation to possible references under section 22 or 33 were applicable for the purposes of the giving of that notice;

    (i)   the existing time-limits in relation to possible references under section 22 or 33 (except for extensions under section 25(4)) remained applicable on and after the giving of an intervention notice as if any extensions were made under section 25 as applied by subsection (5) above but subject to further alteration by the OFT or the Secretary of State under section 25 as so applied;

    (j)   in subsection (1) of section 31 for the words "section 22" there were substituted "section 45(2) or (3)" and, in the application of that subsection to the OFT, for the word "deciding" there were substituted "enabling the Secretary of State to decide";

    (k)   in the case of the giving of intervention notices, the references in sections 23 to 32 to the making of a reference or a reference were, so far as necessary, references to the giving of an intervention notice or an intervention notice; and

(l) the references to the OFT in section 32(2)(a) to (c) and (3) were construed in accordance with the above modifications.

(7) Where the Secretary of State has given an intervention notice mentioning a public interest consideration which, at that time, is not finalised, he shall, as soon as practicable, take such action as is within his power to ensure that it is finalised.

(8) For the purposes of this Part a public interest consideration is finalised if—

(a) it is specified in section 58 otherwise than by virtue of an order under subsection (3) of that section; or

(b) it is specified in that section by virtue of an order under subsection (3) of that section and the order providing for it to be so specified has been laid before, and approved by, Parliament in accordance with subsection (7) of section 124 and within the period mentioned in that subsection.

43. Intervention notices under section 42

(1) An intervention notice shall state—

(a) the relevant merger situation concerned;

(b) the public interest consideration or considerations which are, or may be, relevant to a consideration of the relevant merger situation concerned; and

(c) where any public interest consideration concerned is not finalised, the proposed timetable for finalising it.

(2) Where the Secretary of State believes that it is or may be the case that two or more public interest considerations are relevant to a consideration of the relevant merger situation concerned, he may decide not to mention in the intervention notice such of those considerations as he considers appropriate.

(3) An intervention notice shall come into force when it is given and shall cease to be in force when the matter to which it relates is finally determined under this Chapter.

(4) For the purposes of this Part, a matter to which an intervention notice relates is finally determined under this Chapter if—

(a) the time within which the OFT or (if relevant) OFCOM is to report to the Secretary of State under section 44 or (as the case may be) 44A has expired and no such report has been made;

(b) the Secretary of State decides to accept an undertaking or group of undertakings under paragraph 3 of Schedule 7 instead of making a reference under section 45;

(c) the Secretary of State otherwise decides not to make a reference under that section;

(d) the Commission cancels such a reference under section 48(1) or 53(1);

(e) the time within which the Commission is to prepare a report under section 50 and give it to the Secretary of State has expired and no such report has been prepared and given to the Secretary of State;

(f) the time within which the Secretary of State is to make and publish a decision under section 54(2) has expired and no such decision has been made and published;

(g) the Secretary of State decides under section 54(2) to make no finding at all in the matter;

(h) the Secretary of State otherwise decides under section 54(2) not to make an adverse public interest finding;

(i) the Secretary of State decides under section 54(2) to make an adverse public interest finding but decides neither to accept an undertaking under paragraph 9 of Schedule 7 nor to make an order under paragraph 11 of that Schedule; or

(j) the Secretary of State decides under section 54(2) to make an adverse public interest finding and accepts an undertaking under paragraph 9 of Schedule 7 or makes an order under paragraph 11 of that Schedule.

(5) For the purposes of this Part the time when a matter to which an intervention notice relates is finally determined under this Chapter is—

(a) in a case falling within subsection (4)(a), (e) or (f), the expiry of the time concerned;

(b) in a case falling within subsection (4)(b), the acceptance of the undertaking or group of undertakings concerned;

(c)   in a case falling within subsection (4)(c), (d), (g) or (h), the making of the decision concerned;

(d)   in a case falling within subsection (4)(i), the making of the decision neither to accept an undertaking under paragraph 9 of Schedule 7 nor to make an order under paragraph 11 of that Schedule; and

(e)   in a case falling within subsection (4)(j), the acceptance of the undertaking concerned or (as the case may be) the making of the order concerned.

(6)   In this Part "OFCOM" means the Office of Communications.

44.   Investigation and report by OFT

(1)   Subsection (2) applies where the Secretary of State has given an intervention notice in relation to a relevant merger situation.

(2)   The OFT shall, within such period as the Secretary of State may require, give a report to the Secretary of State in relation to the case.

(3)   The report shall contain—

(a)   advice from the OFT on the considerations relevant to the making of a reference under section 22 or 33 which are also relevant to the Secretary of State's decision as to whether to make a reference under section 45; and

(b)   a summary of any representations about the case which have been received by the OFT and which relate to any public interest consideration mentioned in the intervention notice concerned (other than a media public interest consideration) and which is or may be relevant to the Secretary of State's decision as to whether to make a reference under section 45.

(4)   The report shall, in particular, include decisions as to whether the OFT believes that it is, or may be, the case that—

(a)   a relevant merger situation has been created or arrangements are in progress or in contemplation which, if carried into effect, will result in the creation of a relevant merger situation;

(b)   the creation of that situation has resulted, or may be expected to result, in a substantial lessening of competition within any market or markets in the United Kingdom for goods or services;

(c)   the market or markets concerned would not be of sufficient importance to justify the making of a reference to the Commission under section 22 or 33;

(d)   in the case of arrangements which are in progress or in contemplation, the arrangements are not sufficiently far advanced, or not sufficiently likely to proceed, to justify the making of such a reference;

(e)   any relevant customer benefits in relation to the creation of the relevant merger situation concerned outweigh the substantial lessening of competition and any adverse effects of the substantial lessening of competition; or

(f)   it would be appropriate to deal with the matter (disregarding any public interest considerations mentioned in the intervention notice concerned) by way of undertakings under paragraph 3 of Schedule 7.

(5)   If the OFT believes that it is or may be the case that it would be appropriate to deal with the matter (disregarding any public interest considerations mentioned in the intervention notice concerned) by way of undertakings under paragraph 3 of Schedule 7, the report shall contain descriptions of the undertakings which the OFT believes are, or may be, appropriate.

(5A)   The report may, in particular, contain a summary of any representations about the case which have been received by the OFT and which relate to any media public interest consideration mentioned in the intervention notice concerned and which is or may be relevant to the Secretary of State's decision as to whether to make a reference under section 45.

(6)   The report may, in particular, include advice and recommendations on any public interest consideration mentioned in the intervention notice concerned and which is or may be relevant to the Secretary of State's decision as to whether to make a reference under section 45.

(7) The OFT shall carry out such investigations as it considers appropriate for the purposes of producing a report under this section.

(8) In this Part "media public interest consideration" means any consideration which, at the time of the giving of the intervention notice concerned—

(a) is specified in section 58(2A) to (2C); or

(b) in the opinion of the Secretary of State, is concerned with broadcasting or newspapers and ought to be specified in section 58.

(9) In this Part 'broadcasting' means the provision of services the provision of which—

(a) is required to be licensed under Part 1 or 3 of the Broadcasting Act 1990 or Part 1 or 2 of the Broadcasting Act 1996; or

(b) would be required to be so licensed if provided by a person subject to licensing under the Part in question.

(10) In this Part 'newspaper' means a daily, Sunday or local (other than daily or Sunday) newspaper circulating wholly or mainly in the United Kingdom or in a part of the United Kingdom.

(11) The Secretary of State may by order amend subsections (9) and (10).

44A. Additional investigation and report by OFCOM: media mergers

(1) Subsection (2) applies where—

(a) the Secretary of State has given an intervention notice in relation to a relevant merger situation; and

(b) the intervention notice mentions any media public interest consideration.

(2) OFCOM shall, within such period as the Secretary of State may require, give a report to the Secretary of State on the effect of the consideration or considerations concerned on the case.

(3) The report shall contain—

(a) advice and recommendations on any media public interest consideration mentioned in the intervention notice concerned and which is or may be relevant to the Secretary of State's decision as to whether to make a reference under section 45; and

(b) a summary of any representations about the case which have been received by OFCOM and which relate to any such consideration.

(4) OFCOM shall carry out such investigations as they consider appropriate for the purposes of producing a report under this section.

45. Power of Secretary of State to refer matter to Commission

(1) Subsections (2) to (5) apply where the Secretary of State—

(a) has given an intervention notice in relation to a relevant merger situation; and

(b) has received a report of the OFT under section 44, and any report of OFCOM which is required by virtue of section 44A, in relation to the matter.

(2) The Secretary of State may make a reference to the Commission if he believes that it is or may be the case that—

(a) a relevant merger situation has been created;

(b) the creation of that situation has resulted, or may be expected to result, in a substantial lessening of competition within any market or markets in the United Kingdom for goods or services;

(c) one or more than one public interest consideration mentioned in the intervention notice is relevant to a consideration of the relevant merger situation concerned; and

(d) taking account only of the substantial lessening of competition and the relevant public interest consideration or considerations concerned, the creation of that situation operates or may be expected to operate against the public interest.

(3) The Secretary of State may make a reference to the Commission if he believes that it is or may be the case that—

(a) a relevant merger situation has been created;

(b) the creation of that situation has not resulted, and may be expected not to result, in a substantial lessening of competition within any market or markets in the United Kingdom for goods or services;

(c) one or more than one public interest consideration mentioned in the intervention notice is relevant to a consideration of the relevant merger situation concerned; and

(d) taking account only of the relevant public interest consideration or considerations concerned, the creation of that situation operates or may be expected to operate against the public interest.

(4) The Secretary of State may make a reference to the Commission if he believes that it is or may be the case that—

(a) arrangements are in progress or in contemplation which, if carried into effect, will result in the creation of a relevant merger situation;

(b) the creation of that situation may be expected to result in a substantial lessening of competition within any market or markets in the United Kingdom for goods or services;

(c) one or more than one public interest consideration mentioned in the intervention notice is relevant to a consideration of the relevant merger situation concerned; and

(d) taking account only of the substantial lessening of competition and the relevant public interest consideration or considerations concerned, the creation of the relevant merger situation may be expected to operate against the public interest.

(5) The Secretary of State may make a reference to the Commission if he believes that it is or may be the case that—

(a) arrangements are in progress or in contemplation which, if carried into effect, will result in the creation of a relevant merger situation;

(b) the creation of that situation may be expected not to result in a substantial lessening of competition within any market or markets in the United Kingdom for goods or services;

(c) one or more than one public interest consideration mentioned in the intervention notice is relevant to a consideration of the relevant merger situation concerned; and

(d) taking account only of the relevant public interest consideration or considerations concerned, the creation of the relevant merger situation may be expected to operate against the public interest.

(6) For the purposes of this Chapter any anti-competitive outcome shall be treated as being adverse to the public interest unless it is justified by one or more than one public interest consideration which is relevant.

(7) This section is subject to section 46.

46. References under section 45: supplementary

(1) No reference shall be made under section 45 if—

(a) the making of the reference is prevented by section … 74(1) or 96(3) or paragraph 4 of Schedule 7; …

(b) the European Commission is considering a request made, in relation to the matter concerned, by the United Kingdom (whether alone or with others) under article 22(1) of the EC Merger Regulation, is proceeding with the matter in pursuance of such a request or has dealt with the matter in pursuance of such a request; or

(c) subject to subsection (1A), a reasoned submission requesting referral to the European Commission has been submitted to the European Commission under article 4(5) of the EC Merger Regulation.

(1A) Subsection (1)(c) shall cease to apply if the Secretary of State is informed that a Member State competent to examine the concentration under its national competition law has, within the time permitted by Article 4(5) of the EC Merger Regulation, expressed its disagreement as regards the request to refer the case to the European Commission; and this subsection shall be construed in accordance with that Regulation.

(2)   The Secretary of State, in deciding whether to make a reference under section 45, shall accept the decisions of the OFT included in its report by virtue of subsection (4) of section 44 and any descriptions of undertakings as mentioned in subsection (5) of that section.

(3)   Where the decision to make a reference under section 45 is made at any time on or after the end of the period of 24 weeks beginning with the giving of the intervention notice concerned, the Secretary of State shall, in deciding whether to make such a reference, disregard any public interest consideration which is mentioned in the intervention notice but which has not been finalised before the end of that period.

(4)   Subject to subsection (5), where the decision to make a reference under section 45(2) or (4) is made at any time before the end of the period of 24 weeks beginning with the giving of the intervention notice concerned, the Secretary of State shall, in deciding whether to make such a reference, disregard any public interest consideration which is mentioned in the intervention notice but which has not been finalised if its effect would be to prevent, or to help to prevent, an anti-competitive outcome from being adverse to the public interest.

(5)   The Secretary of State may, if he believes that there is a realistic prospect of the public interest consideration mentioned in subsection (4) being finalised within the period of 24 weeks beginning with the giving of the intervention notice concerned, delay deciding whether to make the reference concerned until the public interest consideration is finalised or, if earlier, the period expires.

(6)   A reference under section 45 shall, in particular, specify—
        (a)   the subsection of that section under which it is made;
        (b)   the date on which it is made; and
        (c)   the public interest consideration or considerations mentioned in the intervention notice concerned which the Secretary of State is not under a duty to disregard by virtue of subsection (3) above and which he believes are or may be relevant to a consideration of the relevant merger situation concerned.

Cases referred by European Commission under the EC Merger Regulation

46A.   Cases referred by the European Commission where intervention notice is in force

(1)   Subsection (2) applies if the European Commission has by a decision referred the whole or part of a case to the OFT under Article 4(4) or 9 of the EC Merger Regulation, or is deemed to have taken such a decision, and an intervention notice is in force in relation to that case.

(2)   Before the end of the preliminary assessment period, the Secretary of State shall—
        (a)   decide whether to make a reference to the Commission under section 45; and
        (b)   inform the persons carrying on the enterprises concerned by notice of that decision and of the reasons for it.

(3)   The Secretary of State may, for the purposes of subsection (2), decide not to make a reference on the basis that he is considering whether to seek or accept undertakings under paragraph 3 of Schedule 7 instead of making a reference; but a decision taken on that basis does not prevent the Secretary of State from making a reference under section 45 in the event of no such undertakings being offered or accepted.

(4)   In this section—
        "the preliminary assessment period" means, subject to section 46B, the period of 45 working days beginning with the day after the day on which the decision of the European Commission to refer the case is taken (or is deemed to have been taken); and
        "working day" means any day which is not—
        (a)   a Saturday;
        (b)   a Sunday; or
        (c)   a day which is a European Commission holiday (as published in the Official Journal of the European Communities before the beginning of the year in which it occurs).

46B.   Extension of preliminary assessment period

(1)   If the OFT has imposed a requirement under section 46C and it considers that the person on whom that requirement was imposed has failed to comply with it, the OFT may, by notice to the persons carrying on the enterprises concerned, extend the preliminary assessment period.

(2)   If the Secretary of State has imposed a requirement under section 46C and he considers that the person on whom that requirement was imposed has failed to comply with it, he may, by notice to the persons carrying on the enterprises concerned, extend the preliminary assessment period.

(3)   The period of an extension under this section shall—

    (a)   begin with the end of the period within which the requirement under section 46C could be complied with; and

    (b)   end with—

        (i)   in the case of a notice under subsection (1), the earlier of either compliance with the requirement to the satisfaction of the OFT or cancellation by the OFT of the extension.

        (ii)   in the case of a notice under subsection (2), the earlier of either compliance with the requirement to the satisfaction of the Secretary of State or cancellation by him of the extension.

(4)   A notice under this section shall—

    (a)   be given within 5 working days of the end of the period mentioned in subsection (3)(a); and

    (b)   inform the person to whom it is addressed—

        (i)   in the case of a notice under subsection (1), that the OFT is of the opinion mentioned in that subsection and that it intends to extend the preliminary assessment period.

        (ii)   in the case of a notice under subsection (2), that the Secretary of State is of the opinion mentioned in that subsection and that he intends to extend the preliminary assessment period.

46C.   Power to request information in referred cases

(1)   In a case mentioned in section 46A(1), the OFT may by notice to any of the persons carrying on the enterprises concerned request him to provide the OFT with such information as the OFT may require for the purpose of enabling the Secretary of State to make a decision for the purposes of section 46A(2).

(2)   In such a case, the Secretary of State may by notice to any of the persons carrying on the enterprises concerned request him to provide the Secretary of State with such information as he may require for the purpose of enabling him to make a decision for the purposes of section 46A(2).

(3)   A notice under subsection (1) or (2) shall state—

    (a)   the information required;

    (b)   the period within which the information is to be provided; and

    (c)   the manner (if any) in which the information is required to be provided; and

    (d)   the possible consequences—

        (i)   of not providing the information within the stated period; and

        (ii)   if a manner for its provision is stated in the notice, of not providing it in that manner.

Reports on references

47.   Questions to be decided on references under section 45

(1)   The Commission shall, on a reference under section 45(2) or (3), decide whether a relevant merger situation has been created.

(2)   If the Commission decides that such a situation has been created, it shall, on a reference under section 45(2), decide the following additional questions—

    (a)   whether the creation of that situation has resulted, or may be expected to result, in a substantial lessening of competition within any market or markets in the United Kingdom for goods or services; and

(b) whether, taking account only of any substantial lessening of competition and the admissible public interest consideration or considerations concerned, the creation of that situation operates or may be expected to operate against the public interest.

(3) If the Commission decides that a relevant merger situation has been created, it shall, on a reference under section 45(3), decide whether, taking account only of the admissible public interest consideration or considerations concerned, the creation of that situation operates or may be expected to operate against the public interest.

(4) The Commission shall, on a reference under section 45(4) or (5), decide whether arrangements are in progress or in contemplation which, if carried into effect, will result in the creation of a relevant merger situation.

(5) If the Commission decides that such arrangements are in progress or in contemplation, it shall, on a reference under section 45(4), decide the following additional questions—

(a) whether the creation of that situation may be expected to result in a substantial lessening of competition within any market or markets in the United Kingdom for goods or services; and

(b) whether, taking account only of any substantial lessening of competition and the admissible public interest consideration or considerations concerned, the creation of that situation may be expected to operate against the public interest.

(6) If the Commission decides that arrangements are in progress or in contemplation which, if carried into effect, will result in the creation of a relevant merger situation, it shall, on a reference under section 45(5), decide whether, taking account only of the admissible public interest consideration or considerations concerned, the creation of that situation may be expected to operate against the public interest.

(7) The Commission shall, if it has decided on a reference under section 45 that the creation of a relevant merger situation operates or may be expected to operate against the public interest, decide the following additional questions—

(a) whether action should be taken by the Secretary of State under section 55 for the purpose of remedying, mitigating or preventing any of the effects adverse to the public interest which have resulted from, or may be expected to result from, the creation of the relevant merger situation;

(b) whether the Commission should recommend the taking of other action by the Secretary of State or action by persons other than itself and the Secretary of State for the purpose of remedying, mitigating or preventing any of the effects adverse to the public interest which have resulted from, or may be expected to result from, the creation of the relevant merger situation; and

(c) in either case, if action should be taken, what action should be taken and what is to be remedied, mitigated or prevented.

(8) Where the Commission has decided by virtue of subsection (2)(a) or (5)(a) that there is or will be a substantial lessening of competition within any market or markets in the United Kingdom for goods or services, it shall also decide separately the following questions (on the assumption that it is proceeding as mentioned in section 56(6))—

(a) whether action should be taken by it under section 41 for the purpose of remedying, mitigating or preventing the substantial lessening of competition concerned or any adverse effect which has resulted from, or may be expected to result from, the substantial lessening of competition;

(b) whether the Commission should recommend the taking of action by other persons for the purpose of remedying, mitigating or preventing the substantial lessening of competition concerned or any adverse effect which has resulted from, or may be expected to result from, the substantial lessening of competition; and

(c) in either case, if action should be taken, what action should be taken and what is to be remedied, mitigated or prevented.

(9) In deciding the questions mentioned in subsections (7) and (8) the Commission shall, in particular, have regard to the need to achieve as comprehensive a solution as is reasonable and practicable to—

 (a) the adverse effects to the public interest; or

 (b) (as the case may be) the substantial lessening of competition and any adverse effects resulting from it.

(10) In deciding the questions mentioned in subsections (7) and (8) in a case where it has decided by virtue of subsection (2)(a) or (5)(a) that there is or will be a substantial lessening of competition, the Commission may, in particular, have regard to the effect of any action on any relevant customer benefits in relation to the creation of the relevant merger situation concerned.

(11) In this section "admissible public interest consideration" means any public interest consideration which is specified in the reference under section 45 and which the Commission is not under a duty to disregard.

48. Cases where references or certain questions need not be decided

(1) The Commission shall cancel a reference under section 45(4) or (5) if it considers that the proposal to make arrangements of the kind mentioned in that reference has been abandoned.

(2) In relation to the question whether a relevant merger situation has been created or the question whether a relevant merger situation will be created, a reference under section 45 may be framed so as to require the Commission to exclude from consideration—

 (a) subsection (1) of section 23;

 (b) subsection (2) of that section; or

 (c) one of those subsections if the Commission finds that the other is satisfied.

(3) In relation to the question whether any such result as is mentioned in section 23(2)(b) has arisen or the question whether any such result will arise, a reference under section 45 may be framed so as to require the Commission to confine its investigation to the supply of goods or services in a part of the United Kingdom specified in the reference.

49. Variation of references under section 45

(1) The Commission may, if it considers that doing so is justified by the facts (including events occurring on or after the making of the reference concerned), treat—

 (a) a reference made under subsection (2) or (3) of section 45 as if it had been made under subsection (4) or (as the case may be) (5) of that section; or

 (b) a reference made under subsection (4) or (5) of section 45 as if it had been made under subsection (2) or (as the case may be) (3) of that section;

and, in such cases, references in this Part to references under those enactments shall, so far as may be necessary, be construed accordingly.

(2) Where, by virtue of subsection (1), the Commission treats a reference made under subsection (2) or (3) of section 45 as if it had been made under subsection (4) or (as the case may be) (5) of that section, paragraphs 1, 2, 7 and 8 of Schedule 7 shall, in particular, apply as if the reference had been made under subsection (4) or (as the case may be) (5) of that section instead of under subsection (2) or (3) of that section.

(3) Where, by virtue of subsection (1), the Commission treats a reference made under subsection (4) or (5) of section 45 as if it had been made under subsection (2) or (as the case may be) (3) of that section, paragraphs 1, 2, 7 and 8 of Schedule 7 shall, in particular, apply as if the reference had been made under subsection (2) or (as the case may be) (3) of that section instead of under subsection (4) or (5) of that section.

(4) Subsection (5) applies in relation to any undertaking accepted under paragraph 1 of Schedule 7, or any order made under paragraph 2 of that Schedule, which is in force immediately before the Commission, by virtue of subsection (1), treats a reference as mentioned in subsection (1).

(5) The undertaking or order shall, so far as applicable, continue in force as if—

    (a)   in the case of an undertaking or order which relates to a reference under subsection (2) or (3) of section 45, accepted or made in relation to a reference made under subsection (4) or (as the case may be) (5) of that section; and

    (b)   in the case of an undertaking or order which relates to a reference made under subsection (4) or (5) of that section, accepted or made in relation to a reference made under subsection (2) or (as the case may be) (3) of that section;

and the undertaking or order concerned may be varied, superseded, released or revoked accordingly.

(6)   The Secretary of State may at any time vary a reference under section 45.

(7)   The Secretary of State shall consult the Commission before varying any such reference.

(8)   Subsection (7) shall not apply if the Commission has requested the variation concerned.

(9)   No variation by the Secretary of State under this section shall be capable of altering the public interest consideration or considerations specified in the reference or the period permitted by section 51 within which the report of the Commission under section 50 is to be prepared and given to the Secretary of State.

50.   **Investigations and reports on references under section 45**

(1)   The Commission shall prepare a report on a reference under section 45 and give it to the Secretary of State within the period permitted by section 51.

(2)   The report shall, in particular, contain—

    (a)   the decisions of the Commission on the questions which it is required to answer by virtue of section 47;

    (b)   its reasons for its decisions; and

    (c)   such information as the Commission considers appropriate for facilitating a proper understanding of those questions and of its reasons for its decisions.

(2A)   Where the report relates to a reference under section 45 which has been made after a report of OFCOM under section 44A, the Commission shall give a copy of its report (whether or not published) to OFCOM.

(3)   The Commission shall carry out such investigations as it considers appropriate for the purpose of producing a report under this section.

51.   **Time-limits for investigations and reports by Commission**

(1)   The Commission shall prepare its report under section 50 and give it to the Secretary of State under that section within the period of 24 weeks beginning with the date of the reference concerned.

(2)   ...

(3)   The Commission may extend, by no more than 8 weeks, the period within which a report under section 50 is to be prepared and given to the Secretary of State if it considers that there are special reasons why the report cannot be prepared and given to the Secretary of State within that period.

(4)   The Commission may extend the period within which a report under section 50 is to be prepared and given to the Secretary of State if it considers that a relevant person has failed (whether with or without a reasonable excuse) to comply with any requirement of a notice under section 109.

(5)   In subsection (4) "relevant person" means—

    (a)   any person carrying on any of the enterprises concerned;

    (b)   any person who (whether alone or as a member of a group) owns or has control of any such person; or

    (c)   any officer, employee or agent of any person mentioned in paragraph (a) or (b).

(6)   For the purposes of subsection (5) a person or group of persons able, directly or indirectly, to control or materially to influence the policy of a body of persons corporate or unincorporate, but without having a controlling interest in that body of persons, may be treated as having control of it.

(7)   An extension under subsection (3) or (4) shall come into force when published under section 107.

(8)   An extension under subsection (4) shall continue in force until—

(a)   the person concerned provides the information or documents to the satisfaction of the Commission or (as the case may be) appears as a witness in accordance with the requirements of the Commission; or

(b)   the Commission publishes its decision to cancel the extension.

(9)   This section is subject to sections 52 and 53.

52.   Section 51: supplementary

(1), (2)   ...

(3)   A period extended under subsection (3) of section 51 may also be extended under subsection (4) of that section and a period extended under subsection (4) of that section may also be extended under subsection (3) of that section.

(4)   No more than one extension is possible under section 51(3).

(5)   Where a period within which a report under section 50 is to be prepared and given to the Secretary of State is extended or further extended under section 51(3) or (4), the period as extended or (as the case may be) further extended shall, subject to subsections (6) and (7), be calculated by taking the period being extended and adding to it the period of the extension (whether or not those periods overlap in time).

(6)   Subsection (7) applies where—

(a)   the period within which the report under section 50 is to be prepared and given to the Secretary of State is further extended;

(b)   the further extension and at least one previous extension is made under section 51(4); and

(c)   the same days or fractions of days are included in or comprise the further extension and are included in or comprise at least one such previous extension.

(7)   In calculating the period of the further extension, any days or fractions of days of the kind mentioned in subsection (6)(c) shall be disregarded.

(8)   The Secretary of State may by order amend section 51 so as to alter any one or more of the following periods—

(a)   the period of 24 weeks mentioned in subsection (1) of that section or any period for the time being mentioned in that subsection in substitution for that period;

(b)   ...

(c)   the period of 8 weeks mentioned in subsection (3) of that section or any period for the time being mentioned in that subsection in substitution for that period.

(9)   No alteration shall be made by virtue of subsection (8) which results in the period for the time being mentioned in subsection (1) ... of section 51 exceeding 24 weeks or the period for the time being mentioned in subsection (3) of that section exceeding 8 weeks.

(10)   An order under subsection (8) shall not affect any period of time within which the Commission is under a duty to prepare and give to the Secretary of State its report under section 50 in relation to a reference under section 45 if the Commission is already under that duty in relation to that reference when the order is made.

(11)   Before making an order under subsection (8) the Secretary of State shall consult the Commission and such other persons as he considers appropriate.

(12)   The Secretary of State may make regulations for the purposes of section 51(8).

(13)   The regulations may, in particular—

(a)   provide for the time at which information or documents are to be treated as provided (including the time at which they are to be treated as provided to the satisfaction of the Commission for the purposes of section 51(8));

(b)   provide for the time at which a person is to be treated as appearing as a witness (including the time at which he is to be treated as appearing as a witness in accordance with the requirements of the Commission for the purposes of section 51(8));

(c)   provide for the persons carrying on the enterprises which have or may have ceased to be, or may cease to be, distinct enterprises to be informed, in circumstances in which section 51(8) applies, of the fact that—

(i)   the Commission is satisfied as to the provision of the information or documents required by it; or

(ii) the person concerned has appeared as a witness in accordance with the requirements of the Commission;

(d) provide for the persons carrying on the enterprises which have or may have ceased to be, or may cease to be, distinct enterprises to be informed, in circumstances in which section 51(8) applies, of the time at which the Commission is to be treated as satisfied as mentioned in paragraph (c)(i) above or the person concerned is to be treated as having appeared as mentioned in paragraph (c)(ii) above.

53.   Restrictions on action where public interest considerations not finalised

(1)   The Commission shall cancel a reference under section 45 if—

(a) the intervention notice concerned mentions a public interest consideration which was not finalised on the giving of that notice or public interest considerations which, at that time, were not finalised;

(b) no other public interest consideration is mentioned in the notice;

(c) at least 24 weeks has elapsed since the giving of the notice; and

(d) the public interest consideration mentioned in the notice has not been finalised within that period of 24 weeks or (as the case may be) none of the public interest considerations mentioned in the notice has been finalised within that period of 24 weeks.

(2)   Where a reference to the Commission under section 45 specifies a public interest consideration which has not been finalised before the making of the reference, the Commission shall not give its report to the Secretary of State under section 50 in relation to that reference unless—

(a) the period of 24 weeks beginning with the giving of the intervention notice concerned has expired; or

(b) the public interest consideration concerned has been finalised; ...

(c) ...

(3)   The Commission shall, in reporting on any of the questions mentioned in section 47(2)(b), (3), (5)(b), (6) and (7), disregard any public interest consideration which has not been finalised before the giving of the report.

(4)   The Commission shall, in reporting on any of the questions mentioned in section 47(2)(b), (3), (5)(b), (6) and (7), disregard any public interest consideration which was not finalised on the giving of the intervention notice concerned and has not been finalised within the period of 24 weeks beginning with the giving of the notice concerned.

(5)   Subsections (1) to (4) are without prejudice to the power of the Commission to carry out investigations in relation to any public interest consideration to which it might be able to have regard in its report.

Decisions of the Secretary of State

54.   Decision of Secretary of State in public interest cases

(1)   Subsection (2) applies where the Secretary of State has received a report of the Commission under section 50 in relation to a relevant merger situation.

(2)   The Secretary of State shall decide whether to make an adverse public interest finding in relation to the relevant merger situation and whether to make no finding at all in the matter.

(3)   For the purposes of this Part the Secretary of State makes an adverse public interest finding in relation to a relevant merger situation if, in relation to that situation, he decides—

(a) in connection with a reference to the Commission under subsection (2) of section 45, that it is the case as mentioned in paragraphs (a) to (d) of that subsection or subsection (3) of that section;

(b) in connection with a reference to the Commission under subsection (3) of that section, that it is the case as mentioned in paragraphs (a) to (d) of that subsection;

      (c)   in connection with a reference to the Commission under subsection (4) of that section, that it is the case as mentioned in paragraphs (a) to (d) of that subsection or subsection (5) of that section; and

      (d)   in connection with a reference to the Commission under subsection (5) of that section, that it is the case as mentioned in paragraphs (a) to (d) of that subsection.

(4)   The Secretary of State may make no finding at all in the matter only if he decides that there is no public interest consideration which is relevant to a consideration of the relevant merger situation concerned.

(5)   The Secretary of State shall make and publish his decision under subsection (2) within the period of 30 days beginning with the receipt of the report of the Commission under section 50.

(6)   In making a decision under subsections (2) to (4), the Secretary of State shall disregard any public interest consideration not specified in the reference under section 45 and any public interest consideration disregarded by the Commission for the purposes of its report.

(7)   In deciding whether to make an adverse public interest finding under subsection (2), the Secretary of State shall accept—

      (a)   in connection with a reference to the Commission under section 45(2) or (4), the decision of the report of the Commission under section 50 as to whether there is an anti-competitive outcome; and

      (b)   in connection with a reference to the Commission under section 45(3) or (5)—

         (i)   the decision of the report of the Commission under section 50 as to whether a relevant merger situation has been created or (as the case may be) arrangements are in progress or in contemplation which, if carried into effect, will result in the creation of a relevant merger situation; and

         (ii)   the decision of the report of the OFT under section 44 as to the absence of a substantial lessening of competition.

(8)   In determining for the purposes of subsection (5) the period of 30 days no account shall be taken of—

      (a)   Saturday, Sunday, Good Friday and Christmas Day; and

      (b)   any day which is a bank holiday in England and Wales.

55.   Enforcement action by Secretary of State

(1)   Subsection (2) applies where the Secretary of State has decided under subsection (2) of section 54 within the period required by subsection (5) of that section to make an adverse public interest finding in relation to a relevant merger situation and has published his decision within the period so required.

(2)   The Secretary of State may take such action under paragraph 9 or 11 of Schedule 7 as he considers to be reasonable and practicable to remedy, mitigate or prevent any of the effects adverse to the public interest which have resulted from, or may be expected to result from, the creation of the relevant merger situation concerned.

(3)   In making a decision under subsection (2) the Secretary of State shall, in particular, have regard to the report of the Commission under section 50.

(4)   In making a decision under subsection (2) in any case of a substantial lessening of competition, the Secretary of State may, in particular, have regard to the effect of any action on any relevant customer benefits in relation to the creation of the relevant merger situation concerned.

Other

56.   Competition cases where intervention on public interest grounds ceases

(1)   Where the Secretary of State decides not to make a reference under section 45 on the ground that no public interest consideration to which he is able to have regard is relevant to a consideration of the relevant merger situation concerned, he shall by notice require the OFT to deal with the matter otherwise than under this Chapter.

(2)   Where a notice is given to the OFT in the circumstances mentioned in subsection (1), the OFT shall decide whether to make a reference under section 22 or 33; and any time-limits in relation to

the Secretary of State's decision whether to make a reference under section 45 (including any remaining powers of extension) shall apply in relation to the decision of the OFT whether to make a reference under section 22 or 33.

(3) Where the Commission cancels under section 53(1) a reference under section 45 and the report of the OFT under section 44 contains the decision that it is or may be the case that there is an anti-competitive outcome in relation to the relevant merger situation concerned, the Commission shall proceed under this Part as if a reference under section 22 or (as the case may be) 33 had been made to it by the OFT.

(4) In proceeding by virtue of subsection (3) to prepare and publish a report under section 38, the Commission shall proceed as if—

(a) the reference under section 22 or 33 had been made at the same time as the reference under section 45;

(b) the timetable for preparing and giving its report under section 50 (including any remaining powers of extension and as extended by an additional period of 20 days) were the timetable for preparing and publishing its report under section 38; and

(c) in relation to the question whether a relevant merger situation has been created or the question whether arrangements are in progress or in contemplation which, if carried into effect, will result in the creation of a relevant merger situation, the Commission were confined to the questions on the subject to be investigated by it under section 47.

(5) In determining the period of 20 days mentioned in subsection (4) no account shall be taken of—

(a) Saturday, Sunday, Good Friday and Christmas Day; and

(b) any day which is a bank holiday in England and Wales.

(6) Where the Secretary of State decides under section 54(2) to make no finding at all in the matter in connection with a reference under section 45(2) or (4), the Commission shall proceed under this Part as if a reference under section 22 or (as the case may be) 33 had been made to it instead of a reference under section 45 and as if its report to the Secretary of State under section 50 had been prepared and published by it under section 38 within the period permitted by section 39.

(7) In relation to proceedings by virtue of subsection (6), the reference in section 41(3) to decisions of the Commission as included in its report by virtue of section 35(3) or 36(2) shall be construed as a reference to decisions which were included in the report of the Commission by virtue of section 47(8).

(8) Where the Commission becomes under a duty to proceed as mentioned in subsection (3) or (6), references in this Part to references under sections 22 and 33 shall, so far as may be necessary, be construed accordingly; and, in particular, sections 77 to 81 shall apply as if a reference has been made to the Commission by the OFT under section 22 or (as the case may be) 33.

57. Duties of OFT and Commission to inform Secretary of State

(1) The OFT shall, in considering whether to make a reference under section 22 or 33, bring to the attention of the Secretary of State any case which it believes raises any consideration specified in section 58 unless it believes that the Secretary of State would consider any such consideration immaterial in the context of the particular case.

(2) The OFT, OFCOM and the Commission shall bring to the attention of the Secretary of State any representations about exercising his powers under section 58(3) which have been made to the OFT, OFCOM or (as the case may be) the Commission.

58. Specified considerations

(1) The interests of national security are specified in this section.

(2) In subsection (1) "national security" includes public security; and in this subsection "public security" has the same meaning as in article 21(4) of the EC Merger Regulation.

(2A) The need for—

(a) accurate presentation of news; and

(b) free expression of opinion;

in newspapers is specified in this section.

(2B) The need for, to the extent that it is reasonable and practicable, a sufficient plurality of views in newspapers in each market for newspapers in the United Kingdom or a part of the United Kingdom is specified in this section.

(2C) The following are specified in this section—

    (a) the need, in relation to every different audience in the United Kingdom or in a particular area or locality of the United Kingdom, for there to be a sufficient plurality of persons with control of the media enterprises serving that audience;

    (b) the need for the availability throughout the United Kingdom of a wide range of broadcasting which (taken as a whole) is both of high quality and calculated to appeal to a wide variety of tastes and interests; and

    (c) the need for persons carrying on media enterprises, and for those with control of such enterprises, to have a genuine commitment to the attainment in relation to broadcasting of the standards objectives set out in section 319 of the Communications Act 2003.

(3) The Secretary of State may by order modify this section for the purpose of specifying in this section a new consideration or removing or amending any consideration which is for the time being specified in this section.

(4) An order under this section may, in particular—

    (a) provide for a consideration to be specified in this section for a particular purpose or purposes or for all purposes;

    (b) apply in relation to cases under consideration by the OFT, OFCOM, the Commission or the Secretary of State before the making of the order as well as cases under consideration on or after the making of the order.

58A.   Construction of consideration specified in section 58(2C)

(1) For the purposes of section 58 and this section an enterprise is a media enterprise if it consists in or involves broadcasting.

(2) In the case of a merger situation in which at least one of the enterprises ceasing to be distinct consists in or involves broadcasting, the references in section 58(2C)(a) or this section to media enterprises include references to newspaper enterprises.

(3) In this Part "newspaper enterprise" means an enterprise consisting in or involving the supply of newspapers.

(4) Wherever in a merger situation two media enterprises serving the same audience cease to be distinct, the number of such enterprises serving that audience shall be assumed to be more immediately before they cease to be distinct than it is afterwards.

(5) For the purposes of section 58, where two or more media enterprises—

    (a) would fall to be treated as under common ownership or common control for the purposes of section 26, or

    (b) are otherwise in the same ownership or under the same control,

they shall be treated (subject to subsection (4)) as all under the control of only one person.

(6) A reference in section 58 or this section to an audience shall be construed in relation to a media enterprise in whichever of the following ways the decision-making authority considers appropriate—

    (a) as a reference to any one of the audiences served by that enterprise, taking them separately;

    (b) as a reference to all the audiences served by that enterprise, taking them together;

    (c) as a reference to a number of those audiences taken together in such group as the decision-making authority considers appropriate; or

    (d) as a reference to a part of anything that could be taken to be an audience under any of paragraphs (a) to (c) above.

(7) The criteria for deciding who can be treated for the purposes of this section as comprised in an audience, or as comprised in an audience served by a particular service—

    (a) shall be such as the decision-making authority considers appropriate in the circumstances of the case; and

(b)   may allow for persons to be treated as members of an audience if they are only potentially members of it.

(8)   In this section 'audience' includes readership.

(9)   The power under subsection (3) of section 58 to modify that section includes power to modify this section.

CHAPTER 3
OTHER SPECIAL CASES

Special public interest cases

59.   Intervention by Secretary of State in special public interest cases

(1)   Subsection (2) applies where the Secretary of State has reasonable grounds for suspecting that it is or may be the case that a special merger situation has been created or arrangements are in progress or in contemplation which, if carried into effect, will result in the creation of a special merger situation.

(2)   The Secretary of State may give a notice to the OFT (in this Part "a special intervention notice") if he believes that it is or may be the case that one or more than one consideration specified in section 58 is relevant to a consideration of the special merger situation concerned.

(3)   For the purposes of this Part a special merger situation has been created if—
    (a)   the condition mentioned in subsection (3A) is satisfied; and
    (b)   immediately before the enterprises concerned ceased to be distinct—
        (i)   the conditions mentioned in subsection (3B) were satisfied;
        (ii)   the condition mentioned in subsection (3C) was satisfied; or
        (iii)   the condition mentioned in subsection (3D) was satisfied.

(3A)   The condition mentioned in this subsection is that—
    (a)   no relevant merger situation has been created because of section 23(1)(b) and (2)(b); but
    (b)   a relevant merger situation would have been created if those enactments were disregarded.

(3B)   The conditions mentioned in this subsection are that—
    (a)   at least one of the enterprises concerned was carried on in the United Kingdom or by or under the control of a body corporate incorporated in the United Kingdom; and
    (b)   a person carrying on one or more of the enterprises concerned was a relevant government contractor.

(3C)   The condition mentioned in this subsection is that, in relation to the supply of newspapers of any description, at least one-quarter of all the newspapers of that description which were supplied in the United Kingdom, or in a substantial part of the United Kingdom, were supplied by the person or persons by whom one of the enterprises concerned was carried on.

(3D)   The condition mentioned in this subsection is that, in relation to the provision of broadcasting of any description, at least one-quarter of all broadcasting of that description provided in the United Kingdom, or in a substantial part of the United Kingdom, was provided by the person or persons by whom one of the enterprises concerned was carried on.

(4)   The conditions mentioned in this subsection are that, immediately before the enterprises concerned ceased to be distinct—
    (a)   at least one of the enterprises concerned was carried on in the United Kingdom or by or under the control of a body corporate incorporated in the United Kingdom; and
    (b)   a person carrying on one or more of the enterprises concerned was a relevant government contractor.

(5)   For the purposes of deciding whether a relevant merger situation has been created or whether arrangements are in progress or in contemplation which, if carried into effect, will result in the creation of a relevant merger situation, sections 23 to 32 (read together with section 34) shall apply for the purposes of this Chapter as they do for the purposes of Chapter 1 but subject to subsection (6).

(6)   In their application by virtue of subsection (5) sections 23 to 32 shall have effect as if—

    (a)   for paragraph (a) of section 23(9) there were substituted—

        "(a)   in relation to the giving of a special intervention notice, the time when the notice is given;

        (aa) in relation to the making of a report by the OFT under section 61, the time of the making of the report;

        (ab) in the case of a reference which is treated as having been made under section 62(2) by virtue of section 64(2), such time as the Commission may determine; and";

    (b)   the references to the OFT in section 24(2)(a) and (b) included references to the Secretary of State;

    (c)   the references to the OFT in sections 25(1) to (3), (6) and (8) and 31 included references to the Secretary of State;

    (d)   the references to the OFT in section 25(4) and (5) were references to the Secretary of State;

    (e)   the reference in section 25(4) to section 73 were a reference to paragraph 3 of Schedule 7;

    (f)   the reference in section 25(12) to one extension were a reference to one extension by the OFT and one extension by the Secretary of State;

    (g)   the powers to extend time-limits under section 25 as applied by subsection (5) above, and the power to request information under section 31(1) as so applied, were not exercisable by the OFT or the Secretary of State before the giving of a special intervention notice;

    (h)   in subsection (1) of section 31 for the words "section 22" there were substituted "section 62(2)" and, in the application of that subsection to the OFT, for the word "deciding" there were substituted "enabling the Secretary of State to decide";

    (i)   in the case of the giving of special intervention notices, the references in sections 23 to 32 to the making of a reference or a reference were, so far as necessary, references to the giving of a special intervention notice or a special intervention notice; and

    (j)   the references to the OFT in section 32(2)(a) to (c) and (3) were construed in accordance with the above modifications.

(6A)   The Secretary of State may by order amend the conditions mentioned in subsection (3)(b)(ii) and (iii).

(7)   No more than one special intervention notice shall be given under subsection (2) in relation to the same special merger situation.

(8)   In this section "relevant government contractor" means—

    (a)   a government contractor—

        (i)   who has been notified by or on behalf of the Secretary of State of information, documents or other articles relating to defence and of a confidential nature which the government contractor or an employee of his may hold or receive in connection with being such a contractor; and

        (ii) whose notification has not been revoked by or on behalf of the Secretary of State; or

    (b)   a former government contractor who was so notified when he was a government contractor and whose notification has not been revoked by or on behalf of the Secretary of State.

(9)   In this section—

        "defence" has the same meaning as in section 2 of the Official Secrets Act 1989 (c. 6); and

        "government contractor" has the same meaning as in the Act of 1989 and includes any sub-contractor of a government contractor, any sub-contractor of that sub-contractor and any other sub-contractor in a chain of sub-contractors which begins with the sub-contractor of the government contractor.

59A.   Construction of conditions in section 59(3C) and (3D)

(1)   For the purpose of deciding whether the proportion of one-quarter mentioned in section 59(3C) or (3D) is fulfilled with respect to—

    (a)   newspapers of any description, or

    (b)   broadcasting of any description,

the decision-making authority shall apply such criterion (whether value, cost, price, quantity, capacity, number of workers employed or some other criterion, of whatever nature), or such combination of criteria, as the decision-making authority considers appropriate.

(2) References in section 59(3C) to the supply of newspapers shall, in relation to newspapers of any description which are the subject of different forms of supply, be construed in whichever of the following ways the decision-making authority considers appropriate—

    (a)   as references to any of those forms of supply taken separately;

    (b)   as references to all those forms of supply taken together; or

    (c)   as references to any of those forms of supply taken in groups.

(3) For the purposes of subsection (2) the decision-making authority may treat newspapers as being the subject of different forms of supply whenever—

    (a)   the transactions concerned differ as to their nature, their parties, their terms or their surrounding circumstances; and

    (b)   the difference is one which, in the opinion of the decision-making authority, ought for the purposes of that subsection to be treated as a material difference.

(4) References in section 59(3D) to the provision of broadcasting shall, in relation to broadcasting of any description which is the subject of different forms of provision, be construed in whichever of the following ways the decision-making authority considers appropriate—

    (a)   as references to any of those forms of provision taken separately;

    (b)   as references to all those forms of provision taken together; or

    (c)   as references to any of those forms of provision taken in groups.

(5) For the purposes of subsection (4) the decision-making authority may treat broadcasting as being the subject of different forms of provision whenever—

    (a)   the transactions concerned differ as to their nature, their parties, their terms or their surrounding circumstances; and

    (b)   the difference is one which, in the opinion of the decision-making authority, ought for the purposes of that subsection to be treated as a material difference.

(6) The criteria for deciding when newspapers or broadcasting can be treated, for the purposes of section 59, as newspapers or broadcasting of a separate description shall be such as in any particular case the decision-making authority considers appropriate in the circumstances of that case.

(7) In section 59 and this section 'provision' and cognate expressions have the same meaning in relation to broadcasting as in Part 3 of the Communications Act 2003; but this subsection is subject to subsections (4) and (5) of this section.

60. **Special intervention notices under section 59**

(1) A special intervention notice shall state—

    (a)   the special merger situation concerned; and

    (b)   the consideration specified in section 58 or considerations so specified which are, or may be, relevant to the special merger situation concerned.

(2) Where the Secretary of State believes that it is or may be the case that two or more considerations specified in section 58 are relevant to a consideration of the special merger situation concerned, he may decide not to mention in the special intervention notice such of those considerations as he considers appropriate.

(3) A special intervention notice shall come into force when it is given and shall cease to be in force when the matter to which it relates is finally determined under this Chapter.

(4) For the purposes of this Part, a matter to which a special intervention notice relates is finally determined under this Chapter if—

    (a)   the time within which the OFT or (if relevant) OFCOM is to report to the Secretary of State under section 61 or (as the case may be) 61A has expired and no such report has been made;

    (b)   the Secretary of State decides to accept an undertaking or group of undertakings under paragraph 3 of Schedule 7 instead of making a reference under section 62;

    (c)   the Secretary of State otherwise decides not to make a reference under that section;

(d)   the Commission cancels such a reference under section 64(1);

(e)   the time within which the Commission is to prepare a report under section 65 and give it to the Secretary of State has expired and no such report has been prepared and given to the Secretary of State;

(f)   the time within which the Secretary of State is to make and publish a decision under section 66(2) has expired and no such decision has been made and published;

(g)   the Secretary of State decides under subsection (2) of section 66 otherwise than as mentioned in subsection (5) of that section;

(h)   the Secretary of State decides under subsection (2) of section 66 as mentioned in subsection (5) of that section but decides neither to accept an undertaking under paragraph 9 of Schedule 7 nor to make an order under paragraph 11 of that Schedule; or

(i)   the Secretary of State decides under subsection (2) of section 66 as mentioned in subsection (5) of that section and accepts an undertaking under paragraph 9 of Schedule 7 or makes an order under paragraph 11 of that Schedule.

(5)   For the purposes of this Part the time when a matter to which a special intervention notice relates is finally determined under this Chapter is—

(a)   in a case falling within subsection (4)(a), (e) or (f), the expiry of the time concerned;

(b)   in a case falling within subsection (4)(b), the acceptance of the undertaking or group of undertakings concerned;

(c)   in a case falling within subsection (4)(c), (d) or (g), the making of the decision concerned;

(d)   in a case falling within subsection (4)(h), the making of the decision neither to accept an undertaking under paragraph 9 of Schedule 7 nor to make an order under paragraph 11 of that Schedule; and

(e)   in a case falling within subsection (4)(i), the acceptance of the undertaking concerned or (as the case may be) the making of the order concerned.

61.   **Initial investigation and report by OFT**

(1)   Subsection (2) applies where the Secretary of State has given a special intervention notice in relation to a special merger situation.

(2)   The OFT shall, within such period as the Secretary of State may require, give a report to the Secretary of State in relation to the case.

(3)   The report shall contain—

(a)   advice from the OFT on the considerations relevant to the making of a reference under section 22 or 33 which are also relevant to the Secretary of State's decision as to whether to make a reference under section 62; and

(b)   a summary of any representations about the case which have been received by the OFT and which relate to any consideration mentioned in the special intervention notice concerned (other than a consideration which, at the time of the giving of the notice, was specified in section 58(2A) to (2C)) and which is or may be relevant to the Secretary of State's decision as to whether to make a reference under section 62.

(4)   The report shall include a decision as to whether the OFT believes (disregarding section 59(3B)(b)) that it is, or may be, the case that a special merger situation has been created or (as the case may be) arrangements are in progress or in contemplation which, if carried into effect, will result in the creation of a special merger situation.

(4A)   The report may, in particular, contain a summary of any representations about the case which have been received by the OFT and which relate to any consideration which—

(a)   is mentioned in the special intervention notice concerned and, at the time of the giving of that notice, was specified in section 58(2A) to (2C); and

(b)   is or may be relevant to the Secretary of State's decision as to whether to make a reference under section 62.

(5)   The report may, in particular, include advice and recommendations on any consideration mentioned in the special intervention notice concerned and which is or may be relevant to the Secretary of State's decision as to whether to make a reference under section 62.

(6)   The OFT shall carry out such investigations as it considers appropriate for the purposes of producing a report under this section.

61A.   Additional investigation and report by OFCOM: certain media mergers

(1)   Subsection (2) applies where—
        (a)   the Secretary of State has given a special intervention notice in relation to a special merger situation; and
        (b)   the special intervention notice mentions any consideration which, at the time of the giving of the notice, was specified in section 58(2A) to (2C).

(2)   OFCOM shall, within such period as the Secretary of State may require, give a report to the Secretary of State on the effect of the consideration or considerations concerned on the case.

(3)   The report shall contain—
        (a)   advice and recommendations on any consideration which—
               (i)   is mentioned in the special intervention notice concerned and, at the time of the giving of that notice, was specified in section 58(2A) to (2C); and
               (ii)   is or may be relevant to the Secretary of State's decision as to whether to make a reference under section 62; and
        (b)   a summary of any representations about the case which have been received by OFCOM and which relate to any such consideration.

(4)   OFCOM shall carry out such investigations as they consider appropriate for the purposes of producing a report under this section.

62.   Power of Secretary of State to refer the matter

(1)   Subsection (2) applies where the Secretary of State—
        (a)   has given a special intervention notice in relation to a special merger situation; and
        (b)   has received a report of the OFT under section 61, and any report of OFCOM which is required by virtue of section 61A, in relation to the matter.

(2)   The Secretary of State may make a reference to the Commission if he believes that it is or may be the case that—
        (a)   a special merger situation has been created;
        (b)   one or more than one consideration mentioned in the special intervention notice is relevant to a consideration of the special merger situation concerned; and
        (c)   taking account only of the relevant consideration or considerations concerned, the creation of that situation operates or may be expected to operate against the public interest.

(3)   The Secretary of State may make a reference to the Commission if he believes that it is or may be the case that—
        (a)   arrangements are in progress or in contemplation which, if carried into effect, will result in the creation of a special merger situation;
        (b)   one or more than one consideration mentioned in the special intervention notice is relevant to a consideration of the special merger situation concerned; and
        (c)   taking account only of the relevant consideration or considerations concerned, the creation of that situation may be expected to operate against the public interest.

(4)   No reference shall be made under this section if the making of the reference is prevented by … paragraph 4 of Schedule 7.

(5)   The Secretary of State, in deciding whether to make a reference under this section, shall accept the decision of the OFT included in its report under section 61 by virtue of subsection (4) of that section.

(6)   A reference under this section shall, in particular, specify—
        (a)   the subsection of this section under which it is made;
        (b)   the date on which it is made; and
        (c)   the consideration or considerations mentioned in the special intervention notice which the Secretary of State believes are, or may be, relevant to a consideration of the special merger situation concerned.

63.   **Questions to be decided on references under section 62**

(1)   The Commission shall, on a reference under section 62(2), decide whether a special merger situation has been created.

(2)   The Commission shall, on a reference under section 62(3), decide whether arrangements are in progress or in contemplation which, if carried into effect, will result in the creation of a special merger situation.

(3)   If the Commission decides that a special merger situation has been created or that arrangements are in progress or in contemplation which, if carried into effect, will result in the creation of a special merger situation, it shall, on a reference under section 62, decide whether, taking account only of the consideration or considerations mentioned in the reference, the creation of that situation operates or may be expected to operate against the public interest.

(4)   The Commission shall, if it has decided on a reference under section 62 that the creation of a special merger situation operates or may be expected to operate against the public interest, decide the following additional questions—

     (a)   whether action should be taken by the Secretary of State under section 66 for the purpose of remedying, mitigating or preventing any of the effects adverse to the public interest which have resulted from, or may be expected to result from, the creation of the special merger situation concerned;

     (b)   whether the Commission should recommend the taking of other action by the Secretary of State or action by persons other than itself and the Secretary of State for the purpose of remedying, mitigating or preventing any of the effects adverse to the public interest which have resulted from, or may be expected to result from, the creation of the special merger situation concerned; and

     (c)   in either case, if action should be taken, what action should be taken and what is to be remedied, mitigated or prevented.

64.   **Cancellation and variation of references under section 62**

(1)   The Commission shall cancel a reference under section 62(3) if it considers that the proposal to make arrangements of the kind mentioned in that reference has been abandoned.

(2)   The Commission may, if it considers that doing so is justified by the facts (including events occurring on or after the making of the reference concerned), treat a reference made under subsection (2) or (3) of section 62 as if it had been made under subsection (3) or (as the case may be) (2) of that section; and, in such cases, references in this Part to references under those enactments shall, so far as may be necessary, be construed accordingly.

(3)   Where, by virtue of subsection (2), the Commission treats a reference made under subsection (2) or (3) of section 62 as if it had been made under subsection (3) or (as the case may be) (2) of that section, paragraphs 1, 2, 7 and 8 of Schedule 7 shall, in particular, apply as if the reference had been made under subsection (3) or (as the case may be) (2) of that section instead of under subsection (2) or (3) of that section.

(4)   Subsection (5) applies in relation to any undertaking accepted under paragraph 1 of Schedule 7, or any order made under paragraph 2 of that Schedule, which is in force immediately before the Commission, by virtue of subsection (2), treats a reference made under subsection (2) or (3) of section 62 as if it had been made under subsection (3) or (as the case may be) (2) of that section.

(5)   The undertaking or order shall, so far as applicable, continue in force as if—

     (a)   in the case of an undertaking or order which relates to a reference under subsection (2) of section 62, accepted or made in relation to a reference made under subsection (3) of that section; and

     (b)   in the case of an undertaking or order which relates to a reference made under subsection (3) of that section, accepted or made in relation to a reference made under subsection (2) of that section;

and the undertaking or order concerned may be varied, superseded, released or revoked accordingly.

(6)   The Secretary of State may at any time vary a reference under section 62.

(7)   The Secretary of State shall consult the Commission before varying any such reference.

(8)   Subsection (7) shall not apply if the Commission has requested the variation concerned.

(9)   No variation by the Secretary of State under this section shall be capable of altering the consideration or considerations specified in the reference or the period permitted by virtue of section 65 within which the report of the Commission under that section is to be prepared and given to the Secretary of State.

65.   Investigations and reports on references under section 62

(1)   The Commission shall prepare a report on a reference under section 62 and give it to the Secretary of State within the period permitted by virtue of this section.

(2)   The report shall, in particular, contain—

    (a)   the decisions of the Commission on the questions which it is required to answer by virtue of section 63;

    (b)   its reasons for its decisions; and

    (c)   such information as the Commission considers appropriate for facilitating a proper understanding of those questions and of its reasons for its decisions.

(2A)   Where the report relates to a reference under section 62 which has been made after a report of OFCOM under section 61A, the Commission shall give a copy of its report (whether or not published) to OFCOM.

(3)   Sections 51 and 52 (but not section 53) shall apply for the purposes of a report under this section as they apply for the purposes of a report under section 50.

(4)   The Commission shall carry out such investigations as it considers appropriate for the purpose of producing a report under this section.

66.   Decision and enforcement action by Secretary of State

(1)   Subsection (2) applies where the Secretary of State has received a report of the Commission under section 65 in relation to a special merger situation.

(2)   The Secretary of State shall, in connection with a reference under section 62(2) or (3), decide the questions which the Commission is required to decide by virtue of section 63(1) to (3).

(3)   The Secretary of State shall make and publish his decision under subsection (2) within the period of 30 days beginning with the receipt of the report of the Commission under section 65; and subsection (8) of section 54 shall apply for the purposes of this subsection as it applies for the purposes of subsection (5) of that section.

(4)   In making his decisions under subsection (2), the Secretary of State shall accept the decisions of the report of the Commission under section 65 as to whether a special merger situation has been created or whether arrangements are in progress or in contemplation which, if carried into effect, will result in the creation of a special merger situation.

(5)   Subsection (6) applies where the Secretary of State has decided under subsection (2) that—

    (a)   a special merger situation has been created or arrangements are in progress or in contemplation which, if carried into effect, will result in the creation of a special merger situation;

    (b)   at least one consideration which is mentioned in the special intervention notice concerned is relevant to a consideration of the special merger situation concerned; and

    (c)   taking account only of the relevant consideration or considerations concerned, the creation of that situation operates or may be expected to operate against the public interest;

    and has so decided, and published his decision, within the period required by subsection (3).

(6)   The Secretary of State may take such action under paragraph 9 or 11 of Schedule 7 as he considers to be reasonable and practicable to remedy, mitigate or prevent any of the effects adverse to the public interest which have resulted from, or may be expected to result from, the creation of the special merger situation concerned.

(7)   In making a decision under subsection (6), the Secretary of State shall, in particular, have regard to the report of the Commission under section 65.

European mergers

67.   **Intervention to protect legitimate interests**

(1)   Subsection (2) applies where—

   (a)   the Secretary of State has reasonable grounds for suspecting that it is or may be the case that—

      (i)   a relevant merger situation has been created or that arrangements are in progress or in contemplation which, if carried into effect, will result in the creation of a relevant merger situation; and

      (ii)   a concentration with a Community dimension (within the meaning of the EC Merger Regulation), or a part of such a concentration, has thereby arisen or will thereby arise;

   (b)   a reference … is prevented from being made under section 22 or 33 in relation to the relevant merger situation concerned (whether or not there would otherwise have been a duty to make such a reference) by virtue of Community law or anything done under or in accordance with it; and

   (c)   the Secretary of State is considering whether to take appropriate measures to protect legitimate interests as permitted by article 21(4) of the EC Merger Regulation.

(2)   The Secretary of State may give a notice to the OFT (in this section "a European intervention notice") if he believes that it is or may be the case that one or more than one public interest consideration is relevant to a consideration of the relevant merger situation concerned.

(3)   A European intervention notice shall state—

   (a)   the relevant merger situation concerned;

   (b)   the public interest consideration or considerations which are, or may be, relevant to a consideration of the relevant merger situation concerned; and

   (c)   where any public interest consideration concerned is not finalised, the proposed timetable for finalising it.

(4)   Where the Secretary of State believes that it is or may be the case that two or more public interest considerations are relevant to a consideration of the relevant merger situation concerned, he may decide not to mention in the intervention notice such of those considerations as he considers appropriate.

(5)   No more than one European intervention notice shall be given under subsection (2) in relation to the same relevant merger situation.

(6)   Where the Secretary of State has given a European intervention notice mentioning a public interest consideration which, at that time, is not finalised, he shall, as soon as practicable, take such action as is within his power to ensure that it is finalised.

(7)   For the purposes of deciding whether a relevant merger situation has been created or whether arrangements are in progress or in contemplation which, if carried into effect, will result in the creation of a relevant merger situation, sections 23 to 32 (read together with section 34) shall apply for the purposes of this section as they do for the purposes of Chapter 1 but subject to subsection (8).

(8)   In their application by virtue of subsection (7) sections 23 to 32 shall have effect as if—

   (a)   references in those sections to the decision-making authority were references to the Secretary of State;

   (b)   for paragraphs (a) and (b) of section 23(9) there were substituted ", in relation to the giving of a European intervention notice, the time when the notice is given";

   (c)   the references to the OFT in section 24(2)(a) and (b) included references to the Secretary of State;

   (d)   sections 25, 31 and 32 were omitted; and

   (e)   the references in sections 23 to 29 to the making of a reference or a reference were, so far as necessary, references to the giving of a European intervention notice or a European intervention notice.

(9)   Section 42(3) shall, in its application to this section and section 68, have effect as if for the words "intervention notice" there were substituted "European intervention notice".

68. **Scheme for protecting legitimate interests**

(1) The Secretary of State may by order provide for the taking of action, where a European intervention notice has been given, to remedy, mitigate or prevent effects adverse to the public interest which have resulted from, or may be expected to result from, the creation of a European relevant merger situation.

(2) In subsection (1) "European relevant merger situation" means a relevant merger situation—

 (a) which has been created or will be created if arrangements which are in progress or in contemplation are carried into effect;

 (b) by virtue of which a concentration with a Community dimension (within the meaning of the EC Merger Regulation), or a part of such a concentration, has arisen or will arise; and

 (c) in relation to which a reference … was prevented from being made under section 22 or 33 (whether or not there would otherwise have been a duty to make such a reference) by virtue of Community law or anything done under or in accordance with it.

(3) Provision made under subsection (1) shall include provision ensuring that considerations which are not public interest considerations mentioned in the European intervention notice concerned may not be taken into account in determining whether anything operates, or may be expected to operate, against the public interest.

(4) Provision made under subsection (1) shall include provision—

 (a) applying with modifications sections 23 to 32 for the purposes of deciding for the purposes of this section whether a relevant merger situation has been created or whether arrangements are in progress or in contemplation which, if carried into effect, will result in the creation of a relevant merger situation;

 (b) requiring the OFT to make a report to the Secretary of State before a reference is made;

 (c) enabling the Secretary of State to make a reference to the Commission;

 (d) requiring the Commission to investigate and report to the Secretary of State on such a reference;

 (e) enabling the taking of interim and final enforcement action.

(5) An order under this section may include provision (including provision for the creation of offences and penalties, the payment of fees and the delegation of functions) corresponding to any provision made in, or in connection with, this Part in relation to intervention notices or special intervention notices and the cases to which they relate.

(6) In this section "European intervention notice" has the same meaning as in section 67.

69, 70. …

CHAPTER 4

ENFORCEMENT

Powers exercisable before references under section 22 or 33

71. **Initial undertakings: completed mergers**

(1) Subsection (2) applies where the OFT is considering whether to make a reference under section 22.

(2) The OFT may, for the purpose of preventing pre-emptive action, accept from such of the parties concerned as it considers appropriate undertakings to take such action as it considers appropriate.

(3) No undertaking shall be accepted under subsection (2) unless the OFT has reasonable grounds for suspecting that it is or may be the case that a relevant merger situation has been created.

(4) An undertaking under this section—

 (a) shall come into force when accepted;

 (b) may be varied or superseded by another undertaking; and

 (c) may be released by the OFT.

(5) An undertaking which—

(a)   is in force under this section in relation to a possible reference or reference under section 22; and

(b)   has not been adopted under section 80 or paragraph 1 of Schedule 7;

shall cease to be in force if an order under section 72 or 81 comes into force in relation to that reference or an order under paragraph 2 of that Schedule comes into force in relation to the matter.

(6)   An undertaking under this section shall, if it has not previously ceased to be in force and if it has not been adopted under section 80 or paragraph 1 of Schedule 7, cease to be in force—

(a)   where the OFT has decided to make the reference concerned under section 22, at the end of the period of 7 days beginning with the making of the reference;

(b)   where the OFT has decided to accept an undertaking under section 73 instead of making that reference, on the acceptance of that undertaking;

(c)   where an intervention notice is in force, at the end of the period of 7 days beginning with the giving of that notice; and

(d)   where the OFT has otherwise decided not to make the reference concerned under section 22, on the making of that decision.

(7)   The OFT shall, as soon as reasonably practicable, consider any representations received by it in relation to varying or releasing an undertaking under this section.

(8)   In this section and section 72 "pre-emptive action" means action which might prejudice the reference concerned or impede the taking of any action under this Part which may be justified by the Commission's decisions on the reference.

72.   Initial enforcement orders: completed mergers

(1)   Subsection (2) applies where the OFT is considering whether to make a reference under section 22.

(2)   The OFT may by order, for the purpose of preventing pre-emptive action—

(a)   prohibit or restrict the doing of things which the OFT considers would constitute pre-emptive action;

(b)   impose on any person concerned obligations as to the carrying on of any activities or the safeguarding of any assets;

(c)   provide for the carrying on of any activities or the safeguarding of any assets either by the appointment of a person to conduct or supervise the conduct of any activities (on such terms and with such powers as may be specified or described in the order) or in any other manner;

(d)   do anything which may be done by virtue of paragraph 19 of Schedule 8.

(3)   No order shall be made under subsection (2) unless the OFT has reasonable grounds for suspecting that it is or may be the case that—

(a)   a relevant merger situation has been created; and

(b)   pre-emptive action is in progress or in contemplation.

(4)   An order under this section—

(a)   shall come into force at such time as is determined by or under the order; and

(b)   may be varied or revoked by another order.

(5)   An order which—

(a)   is in force under this section in relation to a possible reference or a reference under section 22; and

(b)   has not been adopted under section 81 or paragraph 2 of Schedule 7;

shall cease to be in force if an undertaking under section 71 or 80 comes into force in relation to that reference or an undertaking under paragraph 1 of that Schedule comes into force in relation to the matter.

(6)   An order under this section shall, if it has not previously ceased to be in force and if it is not adopted under section 81 or paragraph 2 of Schedule 7, cease to be in force—

(a)   where the OFT has decided to make the reference concerned under section 22, at the end of the period of 7 days beginning with the making of the reference;

(b) where the OFT has decided to accept an undertaking under section 73 instead of making that reference, on the acceptance of that undertaking;

(c) where an intervention notice is in force, at the end of the period of 7 days beginning with the giving of that notice; and

(d) where the OFT has otherwise decided not to make the reference concerned under section 22, on the making of that decision.

(7) The OFT shall, as soon as reasonably practicable, consider any representations received by it in relation to varying or revoking an order under this section.

73. Undertakings in lieu of references under section 22 or 33

(1) Subsection (2) applies if the OFT considers that it is under a duty to make a reference under section 22 or 33 (disregarding the operation of section 22(3)(b) or (as the case may be) 33(3)(b) but taking account of the power of the OFT under section 22(2) or (as the case may be) 33(2) to decide not to make such a reference).

(2) The OFT may, instead of making such a reference and for the purpose of remedying, mitigating or preventing the substantial lessening of competition concerned or any adverse effect which has or may have resulted from it or may be expected to result from it, accept from such of the parties concerned as it considers appropriate undertakings to take such action as it considers appropriate.

(3) In proceeding under subsection (2), the OFT shall, in particular, have regard to the need to achieve as comprehensive a solution as is reasonable and practicable to the substantial lessening of competition and any adverse effects resulting from it.

(4) In proceeding under subsection (2), the OFT may, in particular, have regard to the effect of any action on any relevant customer benefits in relation to the creation of the relevant merger situation concerned.

(5) An undertaking under this section—

(a) shall come into force when accepted;

(b) may be varied or superseded by another undertaking; and

(c) may be released by the OFT.

(6) An undertaking under this section which is in force in relation to a relevant merger situation shall cease to be in force if an order comes into force under section 75 or 76 in relation to that undertaking.

(7) The OFT shall, as soon as reasonably practicable, consider any representations received by it in relation to varying or releasing an undertaking under this section.

74. Effect of undertakings under section 73

(1) The relevant authority shall not make a reference under section 22, 33 or 45 in relation to the creation of a relevant merger situation if—

(a) the OFT has accepted an undertaking or group of undertakings under section 73; and

(b) the relevant merger situation is the situation by reference to which the undertaking or group of undertakings was accepted.

(2) Subsection (1) does not prevent the making of a reference if material facts about relevant arrangements or transactions, or relevant proposed arrangements or transactions, were not notified (whether in writing or otherwise) to the OFT or made public before any undertaking concerned was accepted.

(3) For the purposes of subsection (2) arrangements or transactions, or proposed arrangements or transactions, are relevant if they are the ones in consequence of which the enterprises concerned ceased or may have ceased, or may cease, to be distinct enterprises.

(4) In subsection (2) "made public" means so publicised as to be generally known or readily ascertainable.

(5) In this section "relevant authority" means—

(a) in relation to a possible reference under section 22 or 33, the OFT; and

(b) in relation to a possible reference under section 45, the Secretary of State.

75.   Order-making power where undertakings under section 73 not fulfilled etc.

(1)   Subsection (2) applies where the OFT considers that—

      (a)   an undertaking accepted by it under section 73 has not been, is not being or will not be fulfilled; or

      (b)   in relation to an undertaking accepted by it under that section, information which was false or misleading in a material respect was given to the OFT by the person giving the undertaking before the OFT decided to accept the undertaking.

(2)   The OFT may, for any of the purposes mentioned in section 73(2), make an order under this section.

(3)   Subsections (3) and (4) of section 73 shall apply for the purposes of subsection (2) above as they apply for the purposes of subsection (2) of that section.

(4)   An order under this section may contain—

      (a)   anything permitted by Schedule 8; and

      (b)   such supplementary, consequential or incidental provision as the OFT considers appropriate.

(5)   An order under this section—

      (a)   shall come into force at such time as is determined by or under the order;

      (b)   may contain provision which is different from the provision contained in the undertaking concerned; and

      (c)   may be varied or revoked by another order.

(6)   The OFT shall, as soon as reasonably practicable, consider any representations received by it in relation to varying or revoking an order under this section.

76.   Supplementary interim order-making power

(1)   Subsection (2) applies where—

      (a)   the OFT has the power to make an order under section 75 in relation to a particular undertaking and intends to make such an order; or

      (b)   the Commission has the power to make an order under section 83 in relation to a particular undertaking and intends to make such an order.

(2)   The OFT or (as the case may be) the Commission may, for the purpose of preventing any action which might prejudice the making of that order, make an order under this section.

(3)   No order shall be made under subsection (2) unless the OFT or (as the case may be) the Commission has reasonable grounds for suspecting that it is or may be the case that action which might prejudice the making of the order under section 75 or (as the case may be) 83 is in progress or in contemplation.

(4)   An order under subsection (2) may—

      (a)   prohibit or restrict the doing of things which the OFT or (as the case may be) the Commission considers would prejudice the making of the order under section 75 or (as the case may be) 83;

      (b)   impose on any person concerned obligations as to the carrying on of any activities or the safeguarding of any assets;

      (c)   provide for the carrying on of any activities or the safeguarding of any assets either by the appointment of a person to conduct or supervise the conduct of any activities (on such terms and with such powers as may be specified or described in the order) or in any other manner;

      (d)   do anything which may be done by virtue of paragraph 19 of Schedule 8.

(5)   An order under this section—

      (a)   shall come into force at such time as is determined by or under the order; and

      (b)   may be varied or revoked by another order.

(6)   An order under this section shall, if it has not previously ceased to be in force, cease to be in force on—

      (a)   the coming into force of an order under section 75 or (as the case may be) 83 in relation to the undertaking concerned; or

      (b)   the making of the decision not to proceed with such an order.

(7)   The OFT or (as the case may be) the Commission shall, as soon as reasonably practicable, consider any representations received by it in relation to varying or revoking an order under this section.

Interim restrictions and powers

77.   Restrictions on certain dealings: completed mergers

(1)   Subsections (2) and (3) apply where—

    (a)   a reference has been made under section 22 but not finally determined; and

    (b)   no undertakings under section 71 or 80 are in force in relation to the relevant merger situation concerned and no orders under section 72 or 81 are in force in relation to that situation.

(2)   No relevant person shall, without the consent of the Commission—

    (a)   complete any outstanding matters in connection with any arrangements which have resulted in the enterprises concerned ceasing to be distinct enterprises;

    (b)   make any further arrangements in consequence of that result (other than arrangements which reverse that result); or

    (c)   transfer the ownership or control of any enterprises to which the reference relates.

(3)   No relevant person shall, without the consent of the Commission, assist in any of the activities mentioned in paragraphs (a) to (c) of subsection (2).

(4)   The prohibitions in subsections (2) and (3) do not apply in relation to anything which the person concerned is required to do by virtue of any enactment.

(5)   The consent of the Commission under subsection (2) or (3)—

    (a)   may be general or special;

    (b)   may be revoked by the Commission; and

    (c)   shall be published in such manner as the Commission considers appropriate for the purpose of bringing it to the attention of any person entitled to the benefit of it.

(6)   Paragraph (c) of subsection (5) shall not apply if the Commission considers that publication is not necessary for the purpose mentioned in that paragraph.

(7)   Subsections (2) and (3) shall apply to a person's conduct outside the United Kingdom if (and only if) he is—

    (a)   a United Kingdom national;

    (b)   a body incorporated under the law of the United Kingdom or of any part of the United Kingdom; or

    (c)   a person carrying on business in the United Kingdom.

(8)   In this section "relevant person" means—

    (a)   any person who carries on any enterprise to which the reference relates or who has control of any such enterprise;

    (b)   any subsidiary of any person falling within paragraph (a); or

    (c)   any person associated with any person falling within paragraph (a) or any subsidiary of any person so associated.

78.   Restrictions on certain share dealings: anticipated mergers

(1)   Subsection (2) applies where—

    (a)   a reference has been made under section 33; and

    (b)   no undertakings under section 80 are in force in relation to the relevant merger situation concerned and no orders under section 81 are in force in relation to that situation.

(2)   No relevant person shall, without the consent of the Commission, directly or indirectly acquire during the relevant period an interest in shares in a company if any enterprise to which the reference relates is carried on by or under the control of that company.

(3)   The consent of the Commission under subsection (2)—

    (a)   may be general or special;

    (b)   may be revoked by the Commission; and

(c)   shall be published in such manner as the Commission considers appropriate for bringing it to the attention of any person entitled to the benefit of it.

(4)   Paragraph (c) of subsection (3) shall not apply if the Commission considers that publication is not necessary for the purpose mentioned in that paragraph.

(5)   Subsection (2) shall apply to a person's conduct outside the United Kingdom if (and only if) he is—

(a)   a United Kingdom national;

(b)   a body incorporated under the law of the United Kingdom or of any part of the United Kingdom; or

(c)   a person carrying on business in the United Kingdom.

(6)   In this section and section 79—

"company" includes any body corporate;

"relevant period" means the period beginning with the making of the reference concerned and ending when the reference is finally determined;

"relevant person" means—

(a)   any person who carries on any enterprise to which the reference relates or who has control of any such enterprise;

(b)   any subsidiary of any person falling within paragraph (a); or

(c)   any person associated with any person falling within paragraph (a) or any subsidiary of any person so associated; and

"share" means share in the capital of a company, and includes stock.

79.   Sections 77 and 78: further interpretation provisions

(1)   For the purposes of this Part a reference under section 22 or 33 is finally determined if—

(a)   the reference is cancelled under section 37(1);

(b)   the time within which the Commission is to prepare and publish a report under section 38 in relation to the reference has expired and no such report has been prepared and published;

(c)   the report of the Commission under section 38 contains the decision that there is not an anti-competitive outcome;

(d)   the report of the Commission under section 38 contains the decision that there is an anti-competitive outcome and the Commission has decided under section 41(2) neither to accept an undertaking under section 82 nor to make an order under section 84; or

(e)   the report of the Commission under section 38 contains the decision that there is an anti-competitive outcome and the Commission has decided under section 41(2) to accept an undertaking under section 82 or to make an order under section 84.

(2)   For the purposes of this Part the time when a reference under section 22 or 33 is finally determined is—

(a)   in a case falling within subsection (1)(a), the making of the decision concerned;

(b)   in a case falling within subsection (1)(b), the expiry of the time concerned;

(c)   in a case falling within subsection (1)(c), the publication of the report;

(d)   in a case falling within subsection (1)(d), the making of the decision under section 41(2); and

(e)   in a case falling within subsection (1)(e), the acceptance of the undertaking concerned or (as the case may be) the making of the order concerned.

(3)   For the purposes of section 78 and subject to subsection (4) below, the circumstances in which a person acquires an interest in shares include those where—

(a)   he enters into a contract to acquire the shares (whether or not for cash);

(b)   he is not the registered holder but acquires the right to exercise, or to control the exercise of, any right conferred by the holding of the shares; or

(c)   he—

(i)   acquires a right to call for delivery of the shares to himself or to his order or to acquire an interest in the shares; or

(ii)   assumes an obligation to acquire such an interest.

(4)   The circumstances in which a person acquires an interest in shares for the purposes of section 78 do not include those where he acquires an interest in pursuance of an obligation assumed before the publication by the OFT of the reference concerned.

(5)   The circumstances in which a person acquires a right mentioned in subsection (3)—

   (a)   include those where he acquires a right, or assumes an obligation, whose exercise or fulfilment would give him that right; but

   (b)   do not include those where he is appointed as proxy to vote at a specified meeting of a company or of any class of its members or at any adjournment of the meeting or he is appointed by a corporation to act as its representative at any meeting of the company or of any class of its members.

(6)   References to rights and obligations in subsections (3) to (5) include conditional rights and conditional obligations.

(7)   References in sections 77 and 78 to a person carrying on or having control of any enterprise includes a group of persons carrying on or having control of an enterprise and any member of such a group.

(8)   Sections 26(2) to (4) and 127(1), (2) and (4) to (6) shall apply for the purposes of sections 77 and 78 to determine whether any person or group of persons has control of any enterprise and whether persons are associated as they apply for the purposes of section 26 to determine whether enterprises are brought under common control.

(9)   Sections 736 and 736A of the Companies Act 1985 (c. 6) shall apply for the purposes of sections 77 and 78 to determine whether a company is a subsidiary of an individual or of a group of persons as they apply to determine whether it is a subsidiary of a company; and references to a subsidiary in subsections (8) and (9) of section 736A as so applied shall be construed accordingly.

80.   Interim undertakings

(1)   Subsections (2) and (3) apply where a reference under section 22 or 33 has been made but is not finally determined.

(2)   The Commission may, for the purpose of preventing pre-emptive action, accept from such of the parties concerned as it considers appropriate undertakings to take such action as it considers appropriate.

(3)   The Commission may, for the purpose of preventing pre-emptive action, adopt an undertaking accepted by the OFT under section 71 if the undertaking is still in force when the Commission adopts it.

(4)   An undertaking adopted under subsection (3)—

   (a)   shall continue in force, in accordance with its terms, when adopted;

   (b)   may be varied or superseded by an undertaking under this section; and

   (c)   may be released by the Commission.

(5)   Any other undertaking under this section—

   (a)   shall come into force when accepted;

   (b)   may be varied or superseded by another undertaking; and

   (c)   may be released by the Commission.

(6)   References in this Part to undertakings under this section shall, unless the context otherwise requires, include references to undertakings adopted under this section; and references to the acceptance or giving of undertakings under this section shall be construed accordingly.

(7)   An undertaking which is in force under this section in relation to a reference under section 22 or 33 shall cease to be in force if an order under section 81 comes into force in relation to that reference.

(8)   An undertaking under this section shall, if it has not previously ceased to be in force, cease to be in force when the reference under section 22 or 33 is finally determined.

(9)   The Commission shall, as soon as reasonably practicable, consider any representations received by it in relation to varying or releasing an undertaking under this section.

(10)   In this section and section 81 "pre-emptive action" means action which might prejudice the reference concerned or impede the taking of any action under this Part which may be justified by the Commission's decisions on the reference.

81.   Interim orders

(1)   Subsections (2) and (3) apply where a reference has been made under section 22 or 33 but is not finally determined.

(2)   The Commission may by order, for the purpose of preventing pre-emptive action—

     (a)   prohibit or restrict the doing of things which the Commission considers would constitute pre-emptive action;

     (b)   impose on any person concerned obligations as to the carrying on of any activities or the safeguarding of any assets;

     (c)   provide for the carrying on of any activities or the safeguarding of any assets either by the appointment of a person to conduct or supervise the conduct of any activities (on such terms and with such powers as may be specified or described in the order) or in any other manner;

     (d)   do anything which may be done by virtue of paragraph 19 of Schedule 8.

(3)   The Commission may, for the purpose of preventing pre-emptive action, adopt an order made by the OFT under section 72 if the order is still in force when the Commission adopts it.

(4)   An order adopted under subsection (3)—

     (a)   shall continue in force, in accordance with its terms, when adopted; and

     (b)   may be varied or revoked by an order under this section.

(5)   Any other order under this section—

     (a)   shall come into force at such time as is determined by or under the order; and

     (b)   may be varied or revoked by another order.

(6)   References in this Part to orders under this section shall, unless the context otherwise requires, include references to orders adopted under this section; and references to the making of orders under this section shall be construed accordingly.

(7)   An order which is in force under this section in relation to a reference under section 22 or 33 shall cease to be in force if an undertaking under section 80 comes into force in relation to that reference.

(8)   An order under this section shall, if it has not previously ceased to be in force, cease to be in force when the reference under section 22 or 33 is finally determined.

(9)   The Commission shall, as soon as reasonably practicable, consider any representations received by it in relation to varying or revoking an order under this section.

Final powers

82.   Final undertakings

(1)   The Commission may, in accordance with section 41, accept, from such persons as it considers appropriate, undertakings to take action specified or described in the undertakings.

(2)   An undertaking under this section—

     (a)   shall come into force when accepted;

     (b)   may be varied or superseded by another undertaking; and

     (c)   may be released by the Commission.

(3)   An undertaking which is in force under this section in relation to a reference under section 22 or 33 shall cease to be in force if an order under section 76(1)(b) or 83 comes into force in relation to the subject-matter of the undertaking.

(4)   No undertaking shall be accepted under this section in relation to a reference under section 22 or 33 if an order has been made under—

     (a)   section 76(1)(b) or 83 in relation to the subject-matter of the undertaking; or

     (b)   section 84 in relation to that reference.

(5)   The Commission shall, as soon as reasonably practicable, consider any representations received by it in relation to varying or releasing an undertaking under this section.

83. **Order-making power where final undertakings not fulfilled**

(1) Subsection (2) applies where the Commission considers that—

    (a) an undertaking accepted by it under section 82 has not been, is not being or will not be fulfilled; or

    (b) in relation to an undertaking accepted by it under that section, information which was false or misleading in a material respect was given to the Commission or the OFT by the person giving the undertaking before the Commission decided to accept the undertaking.

(2) The Commission may, for any of the purposes mentioned in section 41(2), make an order under this section.

(3) Subsections (3) to (5) of section 41 shall apply for the purposes of subsection (2) above as they apply for the purposes of subsection (2) of that section.

(4) An order under this section may contain—

    (a) anything permitted by Schedule 8; and

    (b) such supplementary, consequential or incidental provision as the Commission considers appropriate.

(5) An order under this section—

    (a) shall come into force at such time as is determined by or under the order;

    (b) may contain provision which is different from the provision contained in the undertaking concerned; and

    (c) may be varied or revoked by another order.

(6) No order shall be varied or revoked under this section unless the OFT advises that such a variation or revocation is appropriate by reason of a change of circumstances.

84. **Final orders**

(1) The Commission may, in accordance with section 41, make an order under this section.

(2) An order under this section may contain—

    (a) anything permitted by Schedule 8; and

    (b) such supplementary, consequential or incidental provision as the Commission considers appropriate.

(3) An order under this section—

    (a) shall come into force at such time as is determined by or under the order; and

    (b) may be varied or revoked by another order.

(4) No order shall be varied or revoked under this section unless the OFT advises that such a variation or revocation is appropriate by reason of a change of circumstances.

(5) No order shall be made under this section in relation to a reference under section 22 or 33 if an undertaking has been accepted under section 82 in relation to that reference.

Public interest and special public interest cases

85. **Enforcement regime for public interest and special public interest cases**

(1) Schedule 7 (which provides for the enforcement regime in public interest and special public interest cases) shall have effect.

(2) The OFT may advise the Secretary of State in relation to the taking by him of enforcement action under Schedule 7.

Undertakings and orders: general provisions

86. **Enforcement orders: general provisions**

(1) An enforcement order may extend to a person's conduct outside the United Kingdom if (and only if) he is—

    (a) a United Kingdom national;

    (b) a body incorporated under the law of the United Kingdom or of any part of the United Kingdom; or

    (c) a person carrying on business in the United Kingdom.

(2)   Nothing in an enforcement order shall have effect so as to—
         (a)   cancel or modify conditions in licences granted—
               (i)   under a patent granted under the Patents Act 1977 (c. 37) or a European patent (UK)
                      (within the meaning of the Act of 1977); or
               (ii)   in respect of a design registered under the Registered Designs Act 1949 (c. 88);

               by the proprietor of the patent or design; or

         (b)   require an entry to be made in the register of patents or the register of designs to the effect
               that licences under such a patent or such a design are to be available as of right.
(3)   An enforcement order may prohibit the performance of an agreement already in existence when
         the order is made.
(4)   Schedule 8 (which provides for the contents of certain enforcement orders) shall have effect.
(5)   Part 1 of Schedule 9 (which enables certain enforcement orders to modify licence conditions etc.
         in regulated markets) shall have effect.
(6)   In this Part "enforcement order" means an order made under section 72, 75, 76, 81, 83 or 84 or
         under paragraph 2, 5, 6, 10 or 11 of Schedule 7.

87.   Delegated power of directions

(1)   An enforcement order may authorise the person making the order to give directions falling within
         subsection (2) to—
         (a)   a person specified in the directions; or
         (b)   the holder for the time being of an office so specified in any body of persons corporate or
               unincorporate.
(2)   Directions fall within this subsection if they are directions—
         (a)   to take such action as may be specified or described in the directions for the purpose of
               carrying out, or ensuring compliance with, the enforcement order concerned; or
         (b)   to do, or refrain from doing, anything so specified or described which the person might be
               required by that order to do or refrain from doing.
(3)   An enforcement order may authorise the person making the order to vary or revoke any directions
         so given.
(4)   The court may by order require any person who has failed to comply with directions given by
         virtue of this section to comply with them, or otherwise remedy his failure, within such time as
         may be specified in the order.
(5)   Where the directions related to anything done in the management or administration of a body of
         persons corporate or unincorporate, the court may by order require the body of persons concerned
         or any officer of it to comply with the directions, or otherwise remedy the failure to comply with
         them, within such time as may be specified in the order.
(6)   An order under subsection (4) or (5) shall be made on the application of the person authorised by
         virtue of this section to give the directions concerned.
(7)   An order under subsection (4) or (5) may provide for all the costs or expenses of, or incidental to,
         the application for the order to be met by any person in default or by any officers of a body of
         persons corporate or unincorporate who are responsible for its default.
(8)   In this section "the court" means—
         (a)   in relation to England and Wales or Northern Ireland, the High Court; and
         (b)   in relation to Scotland, the Court of Session.

88.   Contents of certain enforcement orders

(1)   This section applies in relation to any order under section 75, 83 or 84 or under paragraph 5, 10 or
         11 of Schedule 7.
(2)   The order or any explanatory material accompanying the order shall state—
         (a)   the actions that the persons or description of persons to whom the order is addressed must
               do or (as the case may be) refrain from doing;
         (b)   the date on which the order comes into force;

(c) the possible consequences of not complying with the order; and

(d) the section of this Part under which a review can be sought in relation to the order.

89. Subject-matter of undertakings

(1) The provision which may be contained in an enforcement undertaking is not limited to the provision which is permitted by Schedule 8.

(2) In this Part "enforcement undertaking" means an undertaking under section 71, 73, 80 or 82 or under paragraph 1, 3 or 9 of Schedule 7.

90. Procedural requirements for certain undertakings and orders

Schedule 10 (which provides for the procedure for accepting certain enforcement undertakings and making certain enforcement orders and for their termination) shall have effect.

91. Register of undertakings and orders

(1) The OFT shall compile and maintain a register for the purposes of this Part.

(2) The register shall be kept in such form as the OFT considers appropriate.

(3) The OFT shall ensure that the following matters are entered in the register—

(a) the provisions of any enforcement undertaking accepted under this Part;

(b) the provisions of any enforcement order made under this Part;

(c) the details of any variation, release or revocation of such an undertaking or order; and

(d) the details of any consent given by the Commission under section 77(2) or (3) or 78(2) or by the Secretary of State under paragraph 7(2) or (3) or 8(2) of Schedule 7.

(4) The duty in subsection (3) does not extend to anything of which the OFT is unaware.

(5) The Commission and the Secretary of State shall inform the OFT of any matters which are to be included in the register by virtue of subsection (3) and which relate to enforcement undertakings accepted by them, enforcement orders made by them or consents given by them.

(6) The OFT shall ensure that the contents of the register are available to the public—

(a) during (as a minimum) such hours as may be specified in an order made by the Secretary of State; and

(b) subject to such reasonable fees (if any) as the OFT may determine.

(7) If requested by any person to do so and subject to such reasonable fees (if any) as the OFT may determine, the OFT shall supply the person concerned with a copy (certified to be true) of the register or of an extract from it.

Enforcement functions of OFT

92. Duty of OFT to monitor undertakings and orders

(1) The OFT shall keep under review—

(a) the carrying out of any enforcement undertaking or any enforcement order; and

(b) compliance with the prohibitions in sections 77(2) and (3) and 78(2) and in paragraphs 7(2) and (3) and 8(2) of Schedule 7.

(2) The OFT shall, in particular, from time to time consider—

(a) whether an enforcement undertaking or enforcement order has been or is being complied with;

(b) whether, by reason of any change of circumstances, an enforcement undertaking is no longer appropriate and—

(i) one or more of the parties to it can be released from it; or

(ii) it needs to be varied or to be superseded by a new enforcement undertaking; and

(c) whether, by reason of any change of circumstances, an enforcement order is no longer appropriate and needs to be varied or revoked.

(3) The OFT shall give the Commission or (as the case may be) the Secretary of State such advice as it considers appropriate in relation to—

(a) any possible variation or release by the Commission or (as the case may be) the Secretary of State of an enforcement undertaking accepted by it or (as the case may be) him;

(b)   any possible new enforcement undertaking to be accepted by the Commission or (as the case may be) the Secretary of State so as to supersede another enforcement undertaking given to the Commission or (as the case may be) the Secretary of State;

(c)   any possible variation or revocation by the Commission or (as the case may be) the Secretary of State of an enforcement order made by the Commission or (as the case may be) the Secretary of State;

(d)   any possible enforcement undertaking to be accepted by the Commission or (as the case may be) the Secretary of State instead of an enforcement order or any possible enforcement order to be made by the Commission or (as the case may be) the Secretary of State instead of an enforcement undertaking;

(e)   the enforcement by virtue of section 94(6) to (8) of any enforcement undertaking or enforcement order; or

(f)   the enforcement by virtue of section 95(4) and (5) of the prohibitions in sections 77(2) and (3) and 78(2) and in paragraphs 7(2) and (3) and 8(2) of Schedule 7.

(4)   The OFT shall take such action as it considers appropriate in relation to—

(a)   any possible variation or release by it of an enforcement undertaking accepted by it;

(b)   any possible new enforcement undertaking to be accepted by it so as to supersede another enforcement undertaking given to it;

(c)   any possible variation or revocation by it of an enforcement order made by it;

(d)   any possible enforcement undertaking to be accepted by it instead of an enforcement order or any possible enforcement order to be made by it instead of an enforcement undertaking;

(e)   the enforcement by it by virtue of section 94(6) of any enforcement undertaking or enforcement order; or

(f)   the enforcement by it by virtue of section 95(4) and (5) of the prohibitions in sections 77(2) and (3) and 78(2) and in paragraphs 7(2) and (3) and 8(2) of Schedule 7.

(5)   The OFT shall keep under review the effectiveness of enforcement undertakings accepted under this Part and enforcement orders made under this Part.

(6)   The OFT shall, whenever requested to do so by the Secretary of State and otherwise from time to time, prepare a report of its findings under subsection (5).

(7)   The OFT shall—

(a)   give any report prepared by it under subsection (6) to the Commission;

(b)   give a copy of the report to the Secretary of State; and

(c)   publish the report.

93.   **Further role of OFT in relation to undertakings and orders**

(1)   Subsections (2) and (3) apply where—

(a)   the Commission is considering whether to accept undertakings under section 80 or 82; or

(b)   the Secretary of State is considering whether to accept undertakings under paragraph 1, 3 or 9 of Schedule 7.

(2)   The Commission or (as the case may be) the Secretary of State (in this section "the relevant authority") may require the OFT to consult with such persons as the relevant authority considers appropriate with a view to discovering whether they will offer undertakings which the relevant authority would be prepared to accept under section 80 or 82 or (as the case may be) paragraph 1, 3 or 9 of Schedule 7.

(3)   The relevant authority may require the OFT to report to the relevant authority on the outcome of the OFT's consultations within such period as the relevant authority may require.

(4)   A report under subsection (3) shall, in particular, contain advice from the OFT as to whether any undertakings offered should be accepted by the relevant authority under section 80 or 82 or (as the case may be) paragraph 1, 3 or 9 of Schedule 7.

(5)   The powers conferred on the relevant authority by subsections (1) to (4) are without prejudice to the power of the relevant authority to consult the persons concerned itself.

(6)   If asked by the relevant authority for advice in relation to the taking of enforcement action (whether or not by way of undertaking) in a particular case, the OFT shall give such advice as it considers appropriate.

Other

94.   Rights to enforce undertakings and orders

(1)   This section applies to any enforcement undertaking or enforcement order.

(2)   Any person to whom such an undertaking or order relates shall have a duty to comply with it.

(3)   The duty shall be owed to any person who may be affected by a contravention of the undertaking or (as the case may be) order.

(4)   Any breach of the duty which causes such a person to sustain loss or damage shall be actionable by him.

(5)   In any proceedings brought under subsection (4) against a person to whom an enforcement undertaking or an enforcement order relates it shall be a defence for that person to show that he took all reasonable steps and exercised all due diligence to avoid contravening the undertaking or (as the case may be) order.

(6)   Compliance with an enforcement undertaking or an enforcement order shall also be enforceable by civil proceedings brought by the OFT for an injunction or for interdict or for any other appropriate relief or remedy.

(7)   Compliance with an undertaking under section 80 or 82, an order made by the Commission under section 76 or an order under section 81, 83 or 84, shall also be enforceable by civil proceedings brought by the Commission for an injunction or for interdict or for any other appropriate relief or remedy.

(8)   Compliance with an undertaking under paragraph 1, 3 or 9 of Schedule 7, an order made by the Secretary of State under paragraph 2 of that Schedule or an order under paragraph 5, 6, 10 or 11 of that Schedule, shall also be enforceable by civil proceedings brought by the Secretary of State for an injunction or for interdict or for any other appropriate relief or remedy.

(9)   Subsections (6) to (8) shall not prejudice any right that a person may have by virtue of subsection (4) to bring civil proceedings for contravention or apprehended contravention of an enforcement undertaking or an enforcement order.

95.   Rights to enforce statutory restrictions

(1)   The obligation to comply with section 77(2) or (3) or 78(2) or paragraph 7(2) or (3) or 8(2) of Schedule 7 shall be a duty owed to any person who may be affected by a contravention of the enactment concerned.

(2)   Any breach of the duty which causes such a person to sustain loss or damage shall be actionable by him.

(3)   In any proceedings brought under subsection (2) against a person who has an obligation to comply with section 77(2) or (3) or 78(2) or paragraph 7(2) or (3) or 8(2) of Schedule 7 it shall be a defence for that person to show that he took all reasonable steps and exercised all due diligence to avoid contravening the enactment concerned.

(4)   Compliance with section 77(2) or (3) or 78(2) shall also be enforceable by civil proceedings brought by the OFT or the Commission for an injunction or for interdict or for any other appropriate relief or remedy.

(5)   Compliance with paragraph 7(2) or (3) or 8(2) of Schedule 7 shall also be enforceable by civil proceedings brought by the OFT or the Secretary of State for an injunction or for interdict or for any other appropriate relief or remedy.

(6)   Subsections (4) and (5) shall not prejudice any right that a person may have by virtue of subsection (2) to bring civil proceedings for contravention or apprehended contravention of section 77(2) or (3) or 78(2) or paragraph 7(2) or (3) or 8(2) of Schedule 7.

CHAPTER 5

SUPPLEMENTARY

Merger notices

96.　　Merger notices

(1)　　A person authorised to do so by regulations under section 101 may give notice to the OFT of proposed arrangements which might result in the creation of a relevant merger situation.

(2)　　Any such notice (in this Part a "merger notice")—

　　(a)　　shall be in the prescribed form; and

　　(b)　　shall state that the existence of the proposal has been made public.

(3)　　No reference shall be made under section 22, 33 or 45 in relation to—

　　(a)　　arrangements of which notice is given under subsection (1) above or arrangements which do not differ from them in any material respect; or

　　(b)　　the creation of any relevant merger situation which is, or may be, created in consequence of carrying such arrangements into effect;

　　if the period for considering the merger notice has expired without a reference being made under that section in relation to those arrangements.

(4)　　Subsection (3) is subject to section 100.

(5)　　In this section and sections 99(5)(c) and 100(1)(c) "prescribed" means prescribed by the OFT by notice having effect for the time being and published in the London, Edinburgh and Belfast Gazettes.

(6)　　In this Part "notified arrangements" means arrangements of which notice is given under subsection (1) above or arrangements not differing from them in any material respect.

97.　　Period for considering merger notices

(1)　　The period for considering a merger notice is, subject as follows, the period of 20 days beginning with the first day after—

　　(a)　　the notice has been received by the OFT; and

　　(b)　　any fee payable by virtue of section 121 to the OFT in respect of the notice has been paid.

(2)　　Where no intervention notice is in force in relation to the matter concerned, the OFT may by notice to the person who gave the merger notice extend by a further 10 days the period for considering the merger notice.

(3)　　Where an intervention notice is in force in relation to the matter concerned and there has been no extension under subsection (2), the OFT may by notice to the person who gave the merger notice extend by a further 20 days the period for considering the merger notice.

(4)　　Where an intervention notice is in force in relation to the matter concerned and there has been an extension under subsection (2), the OFT may by notice to the person who gave the merger notice extend the period for considering the merger notice by a further number of days which, including any extension already made under subsection (2), does not exceed 20 days.

(5)　　The OFT may by notice to the person who gave the merger notice extend the period for considering a merger notice if the OFT considers that the person has failed to provide, within the period stated in a notice under section 99(2) and in the authorised or required manner, information requested of him in that notice.

(6)　　An extension under subsection (5) shall be for the period until the person concerned provides the information to the satisfaction of the OFT or, if earlier, the cancellation by the OFT of the extension.

(7)　　The OFT may by notice to the person who gave the merger notice extend the period for considering a merger notice if the OFT is seeking undertakings under section 73 or (as the case may be) the Secretary of State is seeking undertakings under paragraph 3 of Schedule 7.

(8)　　An extension under subsection (7) shall be for the period beginning with the receipt of the notice under that subsection and ending with the earliest of the following events—

　　(a)　　the giving of the undertakings concerned;

(b)   the expiry of the period of 10 days beginning with the first day after the receipt by the OFT of a notice from the person from whom the undertakings are being sought stating that he does not intend to give the undertakings; or

(c)   the cancellation by the OFT of the extension.

(9)   The Secretary of State may by notice to the person who gave the merger notice extend the period for considering a merger notice if, by virtue of paragraph 3(6) of Schedule 7, he decides to delay a decision as to whether to make a reference under section 45.

(10)   An extension under subsection (9) shall be for the period of the delay.

(11)   The OFT may by notice to the person who gave the merger notice extend the period for considering a merger notice if the European Commission is considering a request made, in relation to the matter concerned, by the United Kingdom (whether alone or with others) under article 22(1) of the EC Merger Regulation (but is not yet proceeding with the matter in pursuance of such a request).

(12)   An extension under subsection (11) shall be for the period beginning with the receipt of the notice under that subsection and ending with the receipt of a notice under subsection (13).

(13)   The OFT shall, in connection with any notice given by it under subsection (11), by notice inform the person who gave the merger notice of the completion by the European Commission of its consideration of the request of the United Kingdom.

98.   Section 97: supplementary

(1)   A notice under section 97(2), (3), (4), (5), (7), (9) or (11) shall be given, before the end of the period for considering the merger notice, to the person who gave the merger notice.

(2)   A notice under section 97(5)—

(a)   shall also be given within 5 days of the end of the period within which the information is to be provided and which is stated in the notice under section 99(2); and

(b)   shall also inform the person who gave the merger notice of—

(i)   the OFT's opinion as mentioned in section 97(5); and

(ii)   the OFT's intention to extend the period for considering a merger notice.

(3)   In determining for the purposes of section 97(1), (2), (3), (4) or (8)(b) or subsection (2)(a) above any period which is expressed in the enactment concerned as a period of days or number of days no account shall be taken of—

(a)   Saturday, Sunday, Good Friday and Christmas Day; and

(b)   any day which is a bank holiday in England and Wales.

(4)   Any reference in this Part (apart from in section 97(1) and section 99(1)) to the period for considering a merger notice shall, if that period is extended by virtue of any one or more of subsections (2), (3), (4) (5), (7), (9) and (11) of section 97 in relation to a particular case, be construed in relation to that case as a reference to that period as so extended; but only one extension is possible under section 97(2), (3) or (4).

(5)   Where the period for considering a merger notice is extended or further extended by virtue of section 97, the period as extended or (as the case may be) further extended shall, subject to subsections (6) and (7), be calculated by taking the period being extended and adding to it the period of the extension (whether or not those periods overlap in time).

(6)   Subsection (7) applies where—

(a)   the period for considering a merger notice is further extended;

(b)   the further extension and at least one previous extension is made under one or more of subsections (5), (7), (9) and (11) of section 97; and

(c)   the same days or fractions of days are included in or comprise the further extension and are included in or comprise at least one such previous extension.

(7)   In calculating the period of the further extension, any days or fractions of days of the kind mentioned in subsection (6)(c) shall be disregarded.

99.   Certain functions of OFT and Secretary of State in relation to merger notices

(1)   The OFT shall, so far as practicable and when the period for considering any merger notice begins, take such action as the OFT considers appropriate to bring—

    (a)   the existence of the proposal;

    (b)   the fact that the merger notice has been given; and

    (c)   the date on which the period for considering the notice may expire;

to the attention of those whom the OFT considers would be affected if the arrangements were carried into effect.

(2)   The OFT may by notice to the person who gave the merger notice request him to provide the OFT with such information as the OFT or (as the case may be) the Secretary of State may require for the purpose of carrying out its or (as the case may be) his functions in relation to the merger notice.

(3)   A notice under subsection (2) shall state—

    (a)   the information required;

    (b)   the period within which the information is to be provided; and

    (c)   the possible consequences of not providing the information within the stated period and in the authorised or required manner.

(4)   A notice by the OFT under subsection (2) shall be given, before the end of the period for considering the merger notice, to the person who gave the merger notice.

(5)   The OFT may, at any time before the end of the period for considering any merger notice, reject the notice if—

    (a)   the OFT suspects that any information given in respect of the notified arrangements (whether in the merger notice or otherwise) by the person who gave the notice or any connected person is in any material respect false or misleading;

    (b)   the OFT suspects that it is not proposed to carry the notified arrangements into effect;

    (c)   any prescribed information is not given in the merger notice or any information requested by notice under subsection (2) is not provided as required; or

    (d)   the OFT considers that the notified arrangements are, or if carried into effect would result in, a concentration with a Community dimension within the meaning of the EC Merger Regulation.

(6)   In this section and section 100 "connected person", in relation to the person who gave a merger notice, means—

    (a)   any person who, for the purposes of section 127, is associated with him; or

    (b)   any subsidiary of the person who gave the merger notice or of any person so associated with him.

100.   Exceptions to protection given by merger notices

(1)   Section 96(3) does not prevent any reference being made to the Commission if—

    (a)   before the end of the period for considering the merger notice, the OFT rejects the notice under section 99(5);

    (b)   before the end of that period, any of the enterprises to which the notified arrangements relate cease to be distinct from each other;

    (c)   any information (whether prescribed information or not) that—

        (i)   is, or ought to be, known to the person who gave the merger notice or any connected person; and

        (ii)   is material to the notified arrangements;

    is not disclosed to the OFT by such time before the end of that period as may be specified in regulations under section 101;

    (d)   at any time after the merger notice is given but before the enterprises to which the notified arrangements relate cease to be distinct from each other, any of those enterprises ceases to be distinct from any enterprise other than an enterprise to which those arrangements relate;

(e) the six months beginning with the end of the period for considering the merger notice expires without the enterprises to which the notified arrangements relate ceasing to be distinct from each other;

(f) the merger notice is withdrawn; or

(g) any information given in respect of the notified arrangements (whether in the merger notice or otherwise) by the person who gave the notice or any connected person is in any material respect false or misleading.

(2) Subsection (3) applies where—

(a) two or more transactions which have occurred, or, if any arrangements are carried into effect, will occur, may be treated for the purposes of a reference under section 22, 33 or 45 as having occurred simultaneously on a particular date; and

(b) section 96(3) does not prevent such a reference in relation to the last of those transactions.

(3) Section 96(3) does not prevent such a reference in relation to any of those transactions which actually occurred less than six months before—

(a) that date; or

(b) the actual occurrence of another of those transactions in relation to which such a reference may be made (whether or not by virtue of this subsection).

(4) In determining for the purposes of subsections (2) and (3) the time at which any transaction actually occurred, no account shall be taken of any option or other conditional right until the option is exercised or the condition is satisfied.

(5) In this section references to the enterprises to which the notified arrangements relate are references to those enterprises that would have ceased to be distinct from one another if the arrangements mentioned in the merger notice concerned had been carried into effect at the time when the notice was given.

101. Merger notices: regulations

(1) The Secretary of State may make regulations for the purposes of sections 96 to 100.

(2) The regulations may, in particular—

(a) provide for section 97(1), (2), (3) or (4) or section 100(1)(e) to apply as if any reference to a period of days or months were a reference to a period specified in the regulations for the purposes of the enactment concerned;

(b) provide for the manner in which any merger notice is authorised or required to be rejected or withdrawn, and the time at which any merger notice is to be treated as received or rejected;

(c) provide for the time at which any notice under section 97(7), (8)(b), (11) or (13) is to be treated as received;

(d) provide for the manner in which any information requested by the OFT or any other material information is authorised or required to be provided or disclosed, and the time at which such information is to be treated as provided or disclosed (including the time at which it is to be treated as provided to the satisfaction of the OFT for the purposes of section 97(6));

(e) provide for the person who gave the merger notice to be informed, in circumstances in which section 97(6) applies—

(i) of the fact that the OFT is satisfied as to the provision of the information requested by the OFT or (as the case may be) of the OFT's decision to cancel the extension; and

(ii) of the time at which the OFT is to be treated as so satisfied or (as the case may be) of the time at which the cancellation is to be treated as having effect;

(f) provide for the person who gave the merger notice to be informed, in circumstances in which section 97(8) applies—

(i) of any decision by the OFT to cancel the extension; and

(ii) of the time at which such a cancellation is to be treated as having effect;

(g) provide for the time at which any fee is to be treated as paid;

(h)   provide that a person is, or is not, to be treated, in such circumstances as may be specified in the regulations, as acting on behalf of a person authorised by regulations under this section to give a merger notice or a person who has given such a notice.

102.   Power to modify sections 97 to 101

The Secretary of State may, for the purposes of determining the effect of giving a merger notice and the action which may be or is to be taken by any person in connection with such a notice, by order modify sections 97 to 101.

General duties in relation to references

103.   Duty of expedition in relation to references

(1)   In deciding whether to make a reference under section 22 or 33 the OFT shall have regard, with a view to the prevention or removal of uncertainty, to the need for making a decision as soon as reasonably practicable.

(2)   In deciding whether to make a reference under section 45 or 62 the Secretary of State shall have regard, with a view to the prevention or removal of uncertainty, to the need for making a decision as soon as reasonably practicable.

104.   Certain duties of relevant authorities to consult

(1)   Subsection (2) applies where the relevant authority is proposing to make a relevant decision in a way which the relevant authority considers is likely to be adverse to the interests of a relevant party.

(2)   The relevant authority shall, so far as practicable, consult that party about what is proposed before making that decision.

(3)   In consulting the party concerned, the relevant authority shall, so far as practicable, give the reasons of the relevant authority for the proposed decision.

(4)   In considering what is practicable for the purposes of this section the relevant authority shall, in particular, have regard to—

(a)   any restrictions imposed by any timetable for making the decision; and

(b)   any need to keep what is proposed, or the reasons for it, confidential.

(5)   The duty under this section shall not apply in relation to the making of any decision so far as particular provision is made elsewhere by virtue of this Part for consultation before the making of that decision.

(6)   In this section—

"the relevant authority" means the OFT, the Commission or the Secretary of State;

"relevant decision" means—

(a)   in the case of the OFT, any decision by the OFT—

(i)   as to whether to make a reference under section 22 or 33 or accept undertakings under section 73 instead of making such a reference; or

(ii)   to vary under section 37 such a reference;

(b)   in the case of the Commission, any decision on the questions mentioned in section 35(1) or (3), 36(1) or (2), 47 or 63; and

(c)   in the case of the Secretary of State, any decision by the Secretary of State—

(i)   as to whether to make a reference under section 45 or 62; or

(ii)   to vary under section 49 or (as the case may be) 64 such a reference; and

"relevant party" means any person who appears to the relevant authority to control enterprises which are the subject of the reference or possible reference concerned.

104A.   Public consultation in relation to media mergers

(1)   Subsection (2) applies where the Commission—

(a)   is preparing—

(i)   a report under section 50 on a reference which specifies a media public interest consideration; or

      (ii) a report under section 65 on a reference which specifies a consideration specified in section 58(2A) to (2C); and

  (b) is not under a duty to disregard the consideration concerned.

(2)   The Commission shall have regard (among other things) to the need to consult the public so far as they might be affected by the creation of the relevant merger situation or special merger situation concerned and so far as such consultation is practicable.

(3)   Any consultation of the kind mentioned in subsection (2) may be undertaken by the Commission by consulting such representative sample of the public or section of the public concerned as the Commission considers appropriate.

Information and publicity requirements

105. General information duties of OFT and Commission

(1)   Where the OFT decides to investigate a matter so as to enable it to decide whether to make a reference under section 22 or 33, or so as to make a report under section 44 or 61, it shall, so far as practicable, take such action as it considers appropriate to bring information about the investigation to the attention of those whom it considers might be affected by the creation of the relevant merger situation concerned or (as the case may be) the special merger situation concerned.

(1A)   Where OFCOM decide to investigate a matter so as to make a report under section 44A or 61A, they shall, so far as practicable, take such action as they consider appropriate to bring information about the investigation to the attention of those who they consider might be affected by the creation of the relevant merger situation concerned or (as the case may be) the special merger situation concerned.

(2)   Subsections (1) and (1A) do not apply in relation to arrangements which might result in the creation of a relevant merger situation if a merger notice has been given in relation to those arrangements under section 96.

(3)   The OFT shall give the Commission or OFCOM—

  (a) such information in its possession as the Commission or (as the case may be) OFCOM may reasonably require to enable the Commission (as the case may be) OFCOM to carry out its functions under this Part; and

  (b) any other assistance which the Commission (as the case may be) OFCOM may reasonably require for the purpose of assisting it in carrying out its functions under this Part and which it is within the power of the OFT to give.

(3A)   OFCOM shall give the Commission or the OFT—

  (a) such information in their possession as the Commission or (as the case may be) the OFT may reasonably require to enable the Commission or (as the case may be) the OFT to carry out its functions under this Part; and

  (b) any other assistance which the Commission or (as the case may be) the OFT may reasonably require for the purpose of assisting it in carrying out its functions under this Part and which it is within the power of OFCOM to give.

(4)   The OFT shall give the Commission or OFCOM any information in its possession which has not been requested by the Commission or (as the case may be) OFCOM but which, in the opinion of the OFT, would be appropriate to give to the Commission or (as the case may be) OFCOM for the purpose of assisting it in carrying out its functions under this Part.

(4A)   OFCOM shall give the Commission or the OFT any information in their possession which has not been requested by the Commission or (as the case may be) the OFT but which, in the opinion of OFCOM, would be appropriate to give to the Commission or (as the case may be) the OFT for the purpose of assisting it in carrying out its functions under this Part.

(5)   The OFT, OFCOM and the Commission shall give the Secretary of State—

  (a) such information in their possession as the Secretary of State may by direction reasonably require to enable him to carry out his functions under this Part; and

(b)   any other assistance which the Secretary of State may by direction reasonably require for the purpose of assisting him in carrying out his functions under this Part and which it is within the power of the OFT, OFCOM or (as the case may be) the Commission to give.

(6)   The OFT and OFCOM shall give the Secretary of State any information in their possession which has not been requested by the Secretary of State but which, in the opinion of the OFT or (as the case may be) OFCOM, would be appropriate to give to the Secretary of State for the purpose of assisting him in carrying out his functions under this Part.

(7)   The Commission shall have regard to any information given to it under subsection (3), (3A), (4) or (4A); and the Secretary of State shall have regard to any information given to him under subsection (5) or (6).

(7A)   OFCOM shall have regard to any information given to them under subsection (3) or (4); and the OFT shall have regard to any information given to it under subsection (3A) or (4A).

(8)   Any direction given under subsection (5)—
         (a)   shall be in writing; and
         (b)   may be varied or revoked by a subsequent direction.

106.   Advice and information about references under sections 22 and 33

(1)   As soon as reasonably practicable after the passing of this Act, the OFT shall prepare and publish general advice and information about the making of references by it under section 22 or 33.

(2)   The OFT may at any time publish revised, or new, advice or information.

(3)   As soon as reasonably practicable after the passing of this Act, the Commission shall prepare and publish general advice and information about the consideration by it of references under section 22 or 33 and the way in which relevant customer benefits may affect the taking of enforcement action in relation to such references.

(4)   The Commission may at any time publish revised, or new, advice or information.

(5)   Advice and information published under this section shall be prepared with a view to—
         (a)   explaining relevant provisions of this Part to persons who are likely to be affected by them; and
         (b)   indicating how the OFT or (as the case may be) the Commission expects such provisions to operate.

(6)   Advice (or information) published by virtue of subsection (1) or (3) may include advice (or information) about the factors which the OFT or (as the case may be) the Commission may take into account in considering whether, and if so how, to exercise a function conferred by this Part.

(7)   Any advice or information published by the OFT or the Commission under this section shall be published in such manner as the OFT or (as the case may be) the Commission considers appropriate.

(8)   In preparing any advice or information under this section, the OFT shall consult the Commission and such other persons as it considers appropriate.

(9)   In preparing any advice or information under this section, the Commission shall consult the OFT and such other persons as it considers appropriate.

106A.   Advice and information in relation to media mergers

(1)   The Secretary of State may prepare and publish general advice and information about the considerations specified in section 58(2A) to (2C).

(2)   The Secretary of State may at any time publish revised, or new, advice or information.

(3)   Advice or information published under this section shall be prepared with a view to—
         (a)   explaining the considerations specified in section 58(2A) to (2C) to persons who are likely to be affected by them; and
         (b)   indicating how the Secretary of State expects this Part to operate in relation to such considerations.

(4)   Any advice or information published by the Secretary of State under this section shall be published in such manner as the Secretary of State considers appropriate.

(5)   In preparing any advice or information under this section, the Secretary of State shall consult the OFT, OFCOM, the Commission and such other persons as he considers appropriate.

106B.   General advisory functions of OFCOM

(1)   OFCOM may, in connection with any case on which they are required to give a report by virtue of section 44A or 61A, give such advice as they consider appropriate to the Secretary of State in relation to—

(a)   any report made in such a case by the Commission under section 50 or 65; and

(b)   the taking by the Secretary of State of enforcement action under Schedule 7.

(2)   OFCOM may, if requested to do so by the Secretary of State, give such other advice as they consider appropriate to the Secretary of State in connection with any case on which they are required to give a report by virtue of section 44A or 61A.

(3)   OFCOM shall publish any advice given by them under this section but advice given by them in relation to a report of the Commission under section 50 or 65 or related enforcement action shall not be published before the report itself is published.

107.   Further publicity requirements

(1)   The OFT shall publish—

(a)   any reference made by it under section 22 or 33 or any decision made by it not to make such a reference (other than a decision made by virtue of subsection (2)(b) of section 33);

(b)   any variation made by it under section 37 of a reference under section 22 or 33;

(c)   such information as it considers appropriate about any decision made by it under section 57(1) to bring a case to the attention of the Secretary of State;

(d)   any enforcement undertaking accepted by it under section 71;

(e)   any enforcement order made by it under section 72 or 76 or paragraph 2 of Schedule 7;

(f)   any variation, release or revocation of such an undertaking or order;

(g)   any decision made by it as mentioned in section 76(6)(b); and

(h)   any decision made by it to dispense with the requirements of Schedule 10.

(2)   The Commission shall publish—

(a)   any cancellation by it under section 37(1) of a reference under section 33;

(b)   any decision made by it under section 37(2) to treat a reference made under section 22 or 33 as if it had been made under section 33 or (as the case may be) 22;

(c)   any extension by it under section 39 of the period within which a report under section 38 is to be prepared and published;

(d)   any decision made by it to cancel an extension as mentioned in section 39(8)(b);

(e)   any decision made by it under section 41(2) neither to accept an undertaking under section 82 nor to make an order under section 84;

(f)   any decision made by it that there has been a material change of circumstances as mentioned in subsection (3) of section 41 or there is another special reason as mentioned in that subsection of that section;

(g)   any cancellation by it under section 48(1) or 53(1) of a reference under section 45 or any cancellation by it under section 64(1) of a reference under section 62;

(h)   any decision made by it under section 49(1) to treat—

(i)   a reference made under subsection (2) or (3) of section 45 as if it had been made under subsection (4) or (as the case may be) (5) of that section; or

(ii)   a reference made under subsection (4) or (5) of section 45 as if it had been made under subsection (2) or (as the case may be) (3) of that section;

(i)   any extension by it under section 51 of the period within which a report under section 50 is to be prepared and published;

(j)   any decision made by it under section 51(8)(b) to cancel such an extension;

(k)   any extension by it under section 51 as applied by section 65(3) of the period within which a report under section 65 is to be prepared and published;

      (l)   any decision made by it under section 51(8)(b) as applied by section 65(3) to cancel such an extension;

      (m)   any decision made by it under section 64(2) to treat a reference made under subsection (2) or (3) of section 62 as if it had been made under subsection (3) or (as the case may be) (2) of that section;

      (n)   any decision made by it as mentioned in section 76(6)(b);

      (o)   any enforcement order made by it under section 76 or 81;

      (p)   any enforcement undertaking accepted by it under section 80;

      (q)   any variation, release or revocation of such an order or undertaking; and

      (r)   any decision made by it to dispense with the requirements of Schedule 10.

(3)   The Secretary of State shall publish—

      (a)   any intervention notice or special intervention notice given by him;

      (b)   any report of the OFT under section 44 or 61 which has been received by him;

      (ba) any report of OFCOM under section 44A or 61A which has been received by him;

      (c)   any reference made by him under section 45 or 62 or any decision made by him not to make such a reference;

      (d)   any variation made by him under section 49 of a reference under section 45 or under section 64 of a reference under section 62;

      (e)   any report of the Commission under section 50 or 65 which has been received by him;

      (f)   any decision made by him neither to accept an undertaking under paragraph 9 of Schedule 7 nor to make an order under paragraph 11 of that Schedule;

      (g)   any notice given by him under section 56(1);

      (h)   any enforcement undertaking accepted by him under paragraph 1 of Schedule 7;

      (i)   any variation or release of such an undertaking;

      (j)   any decision made by him as mentioned in paragraph 6(6)(b) of Schedule 7; and

      (k)   any decision made by him to dispense with the requirements of Schedule 10.

(4)   Where any person is under a duty by virtue of subsection (1), (2) or (3) to publish the result of any action taken by that person or any decision made by that person, the person concerned shall, subject to subsections (5) and (6), also publish that person's reasons for the action concerned or (as the case may be) the decision concerned.

(5)   Such reasons need not, if it is not reasonably practicable to do so, be published at the same time as the result of the action concerned or (as the case may be) as the decision concerned.

(6)   Subsections (4) and (5) shall not apply in relation to any information published under subsection (1)(c).

(7)   The Secretary of State shall publish his reasons for—

      (a)   any decision made by him under section 54(2) or 66(2); or

      (b)   any decision to make an order under section 58(3) or vary or revoke such an order.

(8)   Such reasons may be published after—

      (a)   in the case of subsection (7)(a), the publication of the decision concerned; and

      (b)   in the case of subsection (7)(b), the making of the order or of the variation or revocation;

     if it is not reasonably practicable to publish them at the same time as the publication of the decision or (as the case may be) the making of the order or variation or revocation.

(9)   The Secretary of State shall publish—

      (a)   the report of the OFT under section 44, and any report of OFCOM under section 44A, in relation to a matter no later than publication of his decision as to whether to make a reference under section 45 in relation to that matter; and

      (b)   the report of the Commission under section 50 in relation to a matter no later than publication of his decision under section 54(2) in relation to that matter.

(10)   The Secretary of State shall publish—

      (a)   the report of the OFT under section 61, and any report of OFCOM under section 61A, in relation to a matter no later than publication of his decision as to whether to make a reference under section 62 in relation to that matter; and

(b)   the report of the Commission under section 65 in relation to a matter no later than publication of his decision under section 66(2) in relation to that matter.

(11)   Where the Secretary of State has decided under section 55(2) or 66(6) to accept an undertaking under paragraph 9 of Schedule 7 or to make an order under paragraph 11 of that Schedule, he shall (after the acceptance of the undertaking or (as the case may be) the making of the order) lay details of his decision and his reasons for it, and the Commission's report under section 50 or (as the case may be) 65, before each House of Parliament.

108.   Defamation

For the purposes of the law relating to defamation, absolute privilege attaches to any advice, guidance, notice or direction given, or decision or report made, by the OFT, OFCOM, the Commission or the Secretary of State in the exercise of any of their functions under this Part.

Investigation powers

109.   Attendance of witnesses and production of documents etc.

(1)   The Commission may, for the purpose of any investigation on a reference made to it under this Part, give notice to any person requiring him—
(a)   to attend at a time and place specified in the notice; and
(b)   to give evidence to the Commission or a person nominated by the Commission for the purpose.

(2)   The Commission may, for the purpose of any investigation on a reference made to it under this Part, give notice to any person requiring him—
(a)   to produce any documents which—
(i)   are specified or described in the notice, or fall within a category of document which is specified or described in the notice; and
(ii)   are in that person's custody or under his control; and
(b)   to produce them at a time and place so specified and to a person so specified.

(3)   The Commission may, for the purpose of any investigation on a reference made to it under this Part, give notice to any person who carries on any business requiring him—
(a)   to supply to the Commission such estimates, forecasts, returns or other information as may be specified or described in the notice; and
(b)   to supply it at a time and place, and in a form and manner, so specified and to a person so specified.

(4)   A notice under this section shall include information about the possible consequences of not complying with the notice.

(5)   The Commission or any person nominated by it for the purpose may, for the purpose of any investigation on a reference made to it under this Part, take evidence on oath, and for that purpose may administer oaths.

(6)   The person to whom any document is produced in accordance with a notice under this section may, for the purpose of any investigation on a reference made to the Commission under this Part, copy the document so produced.

(7)   No person shall be required under this section—
(a)   to give any evidence or produce any documents which he could not be compelled to give or produce in civil proceedings before the court; or
(b)   to supply any information which he could not be compelled to supply in evidence in such proceedings.

(8)   No person shall be required, in compliance with a notice under this section, to go more than 10 miles from his place of residence unless his necessary travelling expenses are paid or offered to him.

(9)   Any reference in this section to the production of a document includes a reference to the production of a legible and intelligible copy of information recorded otherwise than in legible form.

(10)   In this section "the court" means—

(a)   in relation to England and Wales or Northern Ireland, the High Court; and

(b)   in relation to Scotland, the Court of Session.

110.   Enforcement of powers under section 109: general

(1)   Where the Commission considers that a person has, without reasonable excuse, failed to comply with any requirement of a notice under section 109, it may impose a penalty in accordance with section 111.

(2)   The Commission may proceed (whether at the same time or at different times) under subsection (1) and section 39(4) or (as the case may be) 51(4) (including that enactment as applied by section 65(3)) in relation to the same failure.

(3)   Where the Commission considers that a person has intentionally obstructed or delayed another person in the exercise of his powers under section 109(6), it may impose a penalty in accordance with section 111.

(4)   No penalty shall be imposed by virtue of subsection (1) or (3) if more than 4 weeks have passed since the publication of the report of the Commission on the reference concerned; but this subsection shall not apply in relation to any variation or substitution of the penalty which is permitted by virtue of this Part.

(5)   A person, subject to subsection (6), commits an offence if he intentionally alters, suppresses or destroys any document which he has been required to produce by a notice under section 109.

(6)   A person does not commit an offence under subsection (5) in relation to any act which constitutes a failure to comply with a notice under section 109 if the Commission has proceeded against that person under subsection (1) above in relation to that failure.

(7)   A person who commits an offence under subsection (5) shall be liable—

(a)   on summary conviction, to a fine not exceeding the statutory maximum;

(b)   on conviction on indictment, to imprisonment for a term not exceeding two years or to a fine or to both.

(8)   The Commission shall not proceed against a person under subsection (1) in relation to an act which constitutes an offence under subsection (5) if that person has been found guilty of that offence.

(9)   In deciding whether and, if so, how to proceed under subsection (1) or (3) or section 39(4) or 51(4) (including that enactment as applied by section 65(3)), the Commission shall have regard to the statement of policy which was most recently published under section 116 at the time when the failure concerned or (as the case may be) the obstruction or delay concerned occurred.

(10)   The reference in this section to the production of a document includes a reference to the production of a legible and intelligible copy of information recorded otherwise than in legible form; and the reference to suppressing a document includes a reference to destroying the means of reproducing information recorded otherwise than in legible form.

111.   Penalties

(1)   A penalty imposed under section 110(1) or (3) shall be of such amount as the Commission considers appropriate.

(2)   The amount may, in the case of a penalty imposed under section 110(1), be a fixed amount, an amount calculated by reference to a daily rate or a combination of a fixed amount and an amount calculated by reference to a daily rate.

(3)   The amount shall, in the case of a penalty imposed under section 110(3), be a fixed amount.

(4)   No penalty imposed under section 110(1) shall—

(a)   in the case of a fixed amount, exceed such amount as the Secretary of State may by order specify;

(b)   in the case of an amount calculated by reference to a daily rate, exceed such amount per day as the Secretary of State may so specify; and

(c)   in the case of a fixed amount and an amount calculated by reference to a daily rate, exceed such fixed amount and such amount per day as the Secretary of State may so specify.

(5)   In imposing a penalty by reference to a daily rate—

     (a)   no account shall be taken of any days before the service of the notice under section 112 on the person concerned; and

     (b)   unless the Commission determines an earlier date (whether before or after the penalty is imposed), the amount payable shall cease to accumulate at the beginning of—

         (i)   the day on which the requirement of the notice concerned under section 109 is satisfied or (as the case may be) the obstruction or delay is removed; or

         (ii)   if earlier, the day on which the report of the Commission on the reference concerned is published (or, in the case of a report under section 50 or 65, given) or, if no such report is published (or given) within the period permitted for that purpose by this Part, the latest day on which the report may be published (or given) within the permitted period.

(6)   No penalty imposed under section 110(3) shall exceed such amount as the Secretary of State may by order specify.

(7)   An order under subsection (4) or (6) shall not specify—

     (a)   in the case of a fixed amount, an amount exceeding £30,000;

     (b)   in the case of an amount calculated by reference to a daily rate, an amount per day exceeding £15,000; and

     (c)   in the case of a fixed amount and an amount calculated by reference to a daily rate, a fixed amount exceeding £30,000 and an amount per day exceeding £15,000.

(8)   Before making an order under subsection (4) or (6) the Secretary of State shall consult the Commission and such other persons as he considers appropriate.

112. Penalties: main procedural requirements

(1)   As soon as practicable after imposing a penalty under section 110(1) or (3), the Commission shall give notice of the penalty.

(2)   The notice shall state—

     (a)   that the Commission has imposed a penalty on the person concerned;

     (b)   whether the penalty is of a fixed amount, of an amount calculated by reference to a daily rate or of both a fixed amount and an amount calculated by reference to a daily rate;

     (c)   the amount or amounts concerned and, in the case of an amount calculated by reference to a daily rate, the day on which the amount first starts to accumulate and the day or days on which it might cease to accumulate;

     (d)   the failure or (as the case may be) the obstruction or delay which the Commission considers gave it the power to impose the penalty;

     (e)   any other facts which the Commission considers justify the imposition of a penalty and the amount or amounts of the penalty;

     (f)   the manner in which, and place at which, the penalty is required to be paid to the Commission;

     (g)   the date or dates, no earlier than the end of the relevant period beginning with the date of service of the notice on the person concerned, by which the penalty or (as the case may be) different portions of it are required to be paid;

     (h)   that the penalty or (as the case may be) different portions of it may be paid earlier than the date or dates by which it or they are required to be paid; and

     (i)   that the person concerned has the right to apply under subsection (3) below or to appeal under section 114 and the main details of those rights.

(3)   The person against whom the penalty was imposed may, within 14 days of the date of service on him of a notice under subsection (1), apply to the Commission for it to specify a different date or (as the case may be) different dates by which the penalty or (as the case may be) different portions of it are to be paid.

(4)   A notice under this section shall be given by—

     (a)   serving a copy of the notice on the person on whom the penalty was imposed; and

     (b)   publishing the notice.

(5)   In this section "relevant period" means the period of 28 days mentioned in subsection (3) of section 114 or, if another period is specified by the Secretary of State under that subsection, that period.

113.   Payments and interest by instalments

(1)   If the whole or any portion of a penalty is not paid by the date by which it is required to be paid, the unpaid balance from time to time shall carry interest at the rate for the time being specified in section 17 of the Judgments Act 1838 (c. 110).

(2)   Where an application has been made under section 112(3), the penalty shall not be required to be paid until the application has been determined, withdrawn or otherwise dealt with.

(3)   If a portion of a penalty has not been paid by the date required for it, the Commission may, where it considers it appropriate to do so, require so much of the penalty as has not already been paid (and is capable of being paid immediately) to be paid immediately.

(4)   Any sums received by the Commission in or towards the payment of a penalty, or interest on a penalty, shall be paid into the Consolidated Fund.

114.   Appeals in relation to penalties

(1)   This section applies if a person on whom a penalty is imposed under section 110(1) or (3) is aggrieved by—

    (a)   the imposition or nature of the penalty;

    (b)   the amount or amounts of the penalty; or

    (c)   the date by which the penalty is required to be paid or (as the case may be) the different dates by which portions of the penalty are required to be paid.

(2)   The person aggrieved may apply to the Competition Appeal Tribunal.

(3)   If a copy of the notice under section 112(1) was served on the person on whom the penalty was imposed, the application to the Competition Appeal Tribunal shall, subject to subsection (4), be made within—

    (a)   the period of 28 days starting with the day on which the copy was served on the person concerned; or

    (b)   such other period as the Secretary of State may by order specify.

(4)   If the application relates to a decision of the Commission on an application by the person on whom the penalty was imposed under section 112(3), the application to the Competition Appeal Tribunal shall be made within—

    (a)   the period of 28 days starting with the day on which the person concerned is notified of the decision; or

    (b)   such other period as the Secretary of State may by order specify.

(5)   On an application under this section, the Competition Appeal Tribunal may—

    (a)   quash the penalty;

    (b)   substitute a penalty of a different nature or of such lesser amount or amounts as the Competition Appeal Tribunal considers appropriate; or

    (c)   in a case falling within subsection (1)(c), substitute for the date or dates imposed by the Commission an alternative date or dates;

    if it considers it appropriate to do so.

(6)   The Competition Appeal Tribunal shall not substitute a penalty of a different nature under subsection (5)(b) unless it considers that the person on whom the penalty is imposed will, or is likely to, pay less under the substituted penalty than he would have paid under the original penalty.

(7)   Where an application has been made under this section—

    (a)   the penalty shall not be required to be paid until the application has been determined, withdrawn or otherwise dealt with; and

    (b)   the Commission may agree to reduce the amount or amounts of the penalty in settlement of the application.

(8)   Where the Competition Appeal Tribunal substitutes a penalty of a different nature or of a lesser amount or amounts it may require the payment of interest on the substituted penalty at such rate or rates, and from such date or dates, as it considers appropriate.

(9)   Where the Competition Appeal Tribunal specifies as a date by which the penalty, or a portion of the penalty, is to be paid a date before the determination of the application under this section it may require the payment of interest on the penalty, or portion, from that date at such rate as it considers appropriate.

(10)   An appeal lies to the appropriate court—
        (a)   on a point of law arising from a decision of the Tribunal in proceedings under this section; or
        (b)   from a decision of the Tribunal in such proceedings as to the amount or amounts of a penalty.

(11)   An appeal under subsection (10)—
        (a)   may be brought by a party to the proceedings before the Tribunal; and
        (b)   requires the permission of the Tribunal or the appropriate court.

(12)   In this section "the appropriate court" means the Court of Appeal or, in the case of Tribunal proceedings in Scotland, the Court of Session.

115.   Recovery of penalties

Where a penalty imposed under section 110(1) or (3), or any portion of such a penalty, has not been paid by the date on which it is required to be paid and—
        (a)   no application relating to the penalty has been made under section 114 during the period within which such an application may be made, or
        (b)   any such application which has been made has been determined, withdrawn or otherwise dealt with,
the Commission may recover from the person on whom the penalty was imposed any of the penalty and any interest which has not been paid; and in England and Wales and Northern Ireland such penalty and interest may be recovered as a civil debt due to the Commission.

116.   Statement of policy

(1)   The Commission shall prepare and publish a statement of policy in relation to the enforcement of notices under section 109.

(2)   The statement shall, in particular, include a statement about the considerations relevant to the determination of the nature and amount of any penalty imposed under section 110(1) or (3).

(3)   The Commission may revise its statement of policy and, where it does so, it shall publish the revised statement.

(4)   The Commission shall consult such persons as it considers appropriate when preparing or revising its statement of policy.

117.   False or misleading information

(1)   A person commits an offence if—
        (a)   he supplies any information to the OFT, OFCOM, the Commission or the Secretary of State in connection with any of their functions under this Part;
        (b)   the information is false or misleading in a material respect; and
        (c)   he knows that it is false or misleading in a material respect or is reckless as to whether it is false or misleading in a material respect.

(2)   A person commits an offence if he—
        (a)   supplies any information to another person which he knows to be false or misleading in a material respect; or
        (b)   recklessly supplies any information to another person which is false or misleading in a material respect;
knowing that the information is to be used for the purpose of supplying information to the OFT, OFCOM, the Commission or the Secretary of State in connection with any of their functions under this Part.

(3)   A person who commits an offence under subsection (1) or (2) shall be liable—

(a)   on summary conviction, to a fine not exceeding the statutory maximum;

(b)   on conviction on indictment, to imprisonment for a term not exceeding two years or to a fine or to both.

Reports

118.   Excisions from reports

(1)   Subsection (2) applies where the Secretary of State is under a duty to publish—

(a)   a report of the OFT under section 44 or 61; or

(aa)   a report of OFCOM under section 44A or 61A;

(b)   a report of the Commission under section 50 or 65.

(2)   The Secretary of State may exclude a matter from the report concerned if he considers that publication of the matter would be inappropriate.

(3)   In deciding what is inappropriate for the purposes of subsection (2) the Secretary of State shall have regard to the considerations mentioned in section 244.

(4)   The body which has prepared the report shall advise the Secretary of State as to the matters (if any) which it considers should be excluded by him under subsection (2).

(5)   References in sections 38(4) and 107(11) to the giving or laying of a report of the Commission shall be construed as references to the giving or laying of the report as published.

119.   Minority reports of Commission

(1)   Subsection (2) applies where, on a reference to the Commission under this Part, a member of a group constituted in connection with the reference in pursuance of paragraph 15 of Schedule 7 to the Competition Act 1998 (c. 41), disagrees with any decisions contained in the report of the Commission under this Part as the decisions of the Commission.

(2)   The report shall, if the member so wishes, include a statement of his disagreement and of his reasons for disagreeing.

Further provision about media mergers

119A.   Other general functions of OFCOM in relation to this Part

(1)   OFCOM have the function of obtaining, compiling and keeping under review information about matters relating to the carrying out of their functions under this Part.

(2)   That function is to be carried out with a view to (among other things) ensuring that OFCOM have sufficient information to take informed decisions and to carry out their other functions effectively.

(3)   In carrying out that function OFCOM may carry out, commission or support (financially or otherwise) research.

(4)   Section 3 of the Communications Act 2003 (general duties of OFCOM) shall not apply in relation to functions of OFCOM under this Part.

119B.   Monitoring role for OFT in relation to media mergers

(1)   The OFT has the function of obtaining, compiling and keeping under review information about matters which may be relevant to the Secretary of State in deciding whether to give a special intervention notice mentioning a consideration specified in section 58(2A) to (2C).

(2)   That function is to be carried out with a view to (among other things) ensuring that the Secretary of State is aware of cases where, in the opinion of the OFT, he might wish to consider giving such a notice.

(3)   That function does not extend to obtaining, compiling or keeping under review information with a view to carrying out a detailed analysis in each case of the operation in relation to that case of the consideration specified in section 58(2A) to (2C).

120.   Review of decisions under Part 3

(1)   Any person aggrieved by a decision of the OFT, OFCOM, the Secretary of State or the Commission under this Part in connection with a reference or possible reference in relation to a relevant merger situation or a special merger situation may apply to the Competition Appeal Tribunal for a review of that decision.

(2)   For this purpose "decision"—

(a)   does not include a decision to impose a penalty under section 110(1) or (3); but

(b)   includes a failure to take a decision permitted or required by this Part in connection with a reference or possible reference.

(3)   Except in so far as a direction to the contrary is given by the Competition Appeal Tribunal, the effect of the decision is not suspended by reason of the making of the application.

(4)   In determining such an application the Competition Appeal Tribunal shall apply the same principles as would be applied by a court on an application for judicial review.

(5)   The Competition Appeal Tribunal may—

(a)   dismiss the application or quash the whole or part of the decision to which it relates; and

(b)   where it quashes the whole or part of that decision, refer the matter back to the original decision maker with a direction to reconsider and make a new decision in accordance with the ruling of the Competition Appeal Tribunal.

(6)   An appeal lies on any point of law arising from a decision of the Competition Appeal Tribunal under this section to the appropriate court.

(7)   An appeal under subsection (6) requires the permission of the Tribunal or the appropriate court.

(8)   In this section—

"the appropriate court" means the Court of Appeal or, in the case of Tribunal proceedings in Scotland, the Court of Session; and

"Tribunal rules" has the meaning given by section 15(1).

121.   Fees

(1)   The Secretary of State may by order require the payment to him or the OFT of such fees as may be prescribed by the order in connection with the exercise by the Secretary of State, the OFT, OFCOM and the Commission of their functions under or by virtue of this Part ... and sections 32 to 34 of, and Schedule 4ZA to, the Water Industry Act 1991 (c. 56).

(2)   An order under this section may, in particular, provide for fees to be payable—

(a)   in respect of a merger notice; or

(b)   ...

(c)   on the occurrence of any event specified in the order.

(3)   The events that may be specified in an order under this section by virtue of subsection (2)(c) include, in particular—

(a)   the decision by the OFT in relation to a possible reference under section 22 or 33 that it is or may be the case that a relevant merger situation has been created or (as the case may be) that arrangements are in progress or in contemplation which, if carried into effect, will result in the creation of a relevant merger situation;

(b)   the decision by the Secretary of State in relation to a possible reference under section 45 that it is or may be the case that a relevant merger situation has been created or (as the case may be) that arrangements are in progress or in contemplation which, if carried into effect, will result in the creation of a relevant merger situation;

(c)   the decision by the Secretary of State in relation to a possible reference under section 62 that—

(i)   it is or may be the case that a special merger situation has been created or (as the case may be) that arrangements are in progress or in contemplation which, if carried into effect, will result in the creation of a special merger situation; and

       (ii)   one or more than one consideration mentioned in the special intervention notice is relevant to a consideration of the special merger situation concerned; and

(d)   the decision by the OFT in relation to a possible reference under section 32 of the Act of 1991 that it is or may be the case that arrangements are in progress which, if carried into effect, will result in a merger of any two or more water enterprises or that such a merger has taken place otherwise than as a result of the carrying into effect of arrangements that have been the subject of a reference by virtue of paragraph (a) of that section.

(4)   An order under this section may, in particular, contain provision—

(a)   for ascertaining the persons by whom fees are payable;

(b)   specifying whether any fee is payable to the Secretary of State or the OFT;

(c)   for the amount of any fee to be calculated by reference to matters which may include—

       (i)   …

       (ii)   … the value of the turnover of the enterprises concerned;

(d)   as to the time when any fee is to be paid; and

(e)   for the repayment by the Secretary of State or the OFT of the whole or part of any fee in specified circumstances.

(5)   For the purposes of subsection (4)(c)(ii) the turnover of an enterprise shall be determined in accordance with such provisions as may be specified in an order under this section.

(6)   Provision made by virtue of subsection (5) may, in particular, include provision—

(a)   as to the amounts which are, or which are not, to be treated as comprising an enterprise's turnover;

(b)   as to the date or dates by reference to which an enterprise's turnover is to be determined;

(c)   restricting the turnover to be taken into consideration to turnover which has a connection of a particular description with the United Kingdom.

(7)   An order under this section may, in particular, in connection with provisions of the kind mentioned in subsection (5) make provision enabling the Secretary of State or the OFT to determine matters of a description specified in the order (including any of the matters mentioned in paragraphs (a) to (c) of subsection (6)).

(8)   In determining the amount of any fees to be prescribed by an order under this section, the Secretary of State may take into account all costs incurred by him and by the OFT in respect of the exercise by him, the OFT, OFCOM and the Commission of their respective functions under or by virtue of this Part … and sections 32 to 34 of, and Schedule 4ZA to, the Act of 1991.

(9)   Fees paid to the Secretary of State or the OFT under this section shall be paid into the Consolidated Fund.

(10)   …

122.   Primacy of Community law

(1)   Advice and information published by virtue of section 106(1) or (3) shall include such advice and information about the effect of Community law, and anything done under or in accordance with it, on the provisions of this Part as the OFT or (as the case may be) the Commission considers appropriate.

(2)   Advice and information published by the OFT by virtue of section 106(1) shall, in particular, include advice and information about the circumstances in which the duties of the OFT under sections 22 and 33 do not apply as a result of the EC Merger Regulation or anything done under or in accordance with them.

(3)   The duty or power to make a reference under section 22 or 45(2) or (3), and the power to give an intervention notice under section 42, shall apply in a case in which the relevant enterprises ceased to be distinct enterprises at a time or in circumstances not falling within section 24 if the condition mentioned in subsection (4) is satisfied.

(4)   The condition mentioned in this subsection is that, because of the EC Merger Regulation or anything done under or in accordance with them, the reference, or (as the case may be) the reference under section 22 to which the intervention notice relates, could not have been made earlier than 4 months before the date on which it is to be made.

(5)   Where the duty or power to make a reference under section 22 or 45(2) or (3), or the power to give an intervention notice under section 42, applies as mentioned in subsection (3), references in this Part to the creation of a relevant merger situation shall be construed accordingly.

123.   Power to alter share of supply test

(1)   The Secretary of State may by order amend or replace the conditions which determine for the purposes of this Part whether a relevant merger situation has been created.

(2)   The Secretary of State shall not exercise his power under subsection (1)—

(a)   to amend or replace the conditions mentioned in paragraphs (a) and (b) of subsection (1) of section 23;

(b)   to amend or replace the condition mentioned in paragraph (a) of subsection (2) of that section.

(3)   In exercising his power under subsection (1) to amend or replace the condition mentioned in paragraph (b) of subsection (2) of section 23 or any condition which for the time being applies instead of it, the Secretary of State shall, in particular, have regard to the desirability of ensuring that any amended or new condition continues to operate by reference to the degree of commercial strength which results from the enterprises concerned having ceased to be distinct.

(4)   Before making an order under this section the Secretary of State shall consult the OFT and the Commission.

(5)   An order under this section may provide for the delegation of functions to the decision-making authority.

Other

124.   Orders and regulations under Part 3

(1)   Any power of the Secretary of State to make an order or regulations under this Part shall be exercisable by statutory instrument.

(2)   Any power of the Secretary of State to make an order or regulations under this Part—

(a)   may be exercised so as to make different provision for different cases or different purposes; and

(b)   includes power to make such incidental, supplementary, consequential, transitory, transitional or saving provision as the Secretary of State considers appropriate.

(3)   The power of the Secretary of State under section 34, 59(6A) or 123 (including that power as extended by subsection (2) above) may be exercised by modifying any enactment comprised in or made under this Act, or any other enactment.

(4)   The power of the Secretary of State under section 40(8), 44(11), 52(8) (including that enactment as applied by section 65(3)), 58(3), 68 or 102 as extended by subsection (2) above may be exercised by modifying any enactment comprised in or made under this Act, or any other enactment.

(5)   An order made by the Secretary of State under section 28 (including that enactment as applied by section 42(5), 59(5) and 67(7)), 40(8), 52(8) (including that enactment as applied by section 65(3)), 111(4) or (6), 114(3)(b) or (4)(b) or 121 or Schedule 7 shall be subject to annulment in pursuance of a resolution of either House of Parliament.

(6)   No order shall be made by the Secretary of State under section 34, 44(11), 59(6A), 68, 102, 123 or 128(6) unless a draft of it has been laid before, and approved by a resolution of, each House of Parliament.

(7)   An order made by the Secretary of State under section 58(3) shall be laid before Parliament after being made and shall cease to have effect unless approved, within the period of 28 days beginning with the day on which it is made, by a resolution of each House of Parliament.

(8)   In calculating the period of 28 days mentioned in subsection (7), no account shall be taken of any time during which Parliament is dissolved or prorogued or during which both Houses are adjourned for more than four days.

(9)   If an order made by the Secretary of State ceases to have effect by virtue of subsection (7), any modification made by it of an enactment is repealed (and the previous enactment revived) but

without prejudice to the validity of anything done in connection with that modification before the order ceased to have effect and without prejudice to the making of a new order.

(10)   If, apart from this subsection, an order made by the Secretary of State under section 58(3) would be treated for the purposes of the standing orders of either House of Parliament as a hybrid instrument, it shall proceed in that House as if it were not such an instrument.

125.   Offences by bodies corporate

(1)   Where an offence under this Part committed by a body corporate is proved to have been committed with the consent or connivance of, or to be attributable to any neglect on the part of—

       (a)   a director, manager, secretary or other similar officer of the body corporate, or

       (b)   a person purporting to act in such a capacity,

he as well as the body corporate commits the offence and shall be liable to be proceeded against and punished accordingly.

(2)   Where the affairs of a body corporate are managed by its members, subsection (1) applies in relation to the acts and defaults of a member in connection with his functions of management as if he were a director of the body corporate.

(3)   Where an offence under this Part is committed by a Scottish partnership and is proved to have been committed with the consent or connivance of a partner, or to be attributable to any neglect on the part of a partner, he as well as the partnership commits the offence and shall be liable to be proceeded against and punished accordingly.

(4)   In subsection (3) "partner" includes a person purporting to act as a partner.

126.   Service of documents

(1)   Any document required or authorised by virtue of this Part to be served on any person may be served—

       (a)   by delivering it to him or by leaving it at his proper address or by sending it by post to him at that address;

       (b)   if the person is a body corporate other than a limited liability partnership, by serving it in accordance with paragraph (a) on the secretary of the body;

       (c)   if the person is a limited liability partnership, by serving it in accordance with paragraph (a) on a member of the partnership; or

       (d)   if the person is a partnership, by serving it in accordance with paragraph (a) on a partner or a person having the control or management of the partnership business.

(2)   For the purposes of this section and section 7 of the Interpretation Act 1978 (c. 30) (service of documents by post) in its application to this section, the proper address of any person on whom a document is to be served shall be his last known address, except that—

       (a)   in the case of service on a body corporate (other than a limited liability partnership) or its secretary, it shall be the address of the registered or principal office of the body;

       (b)   in the case of service on a limited liability partnership or a member of the partnership, it shall be the address of the registered or principal office of the partnership;

       (c)   in the case of service on a partnership or a partner or a person having the control or management of a partnership business, it shall be the address of the principal office of the partnership.

(3)   For the purposes of subsection (2) the principal office of a company constituted under the law of a country or territory outside the United Kingdom or of a partnership carrying on business outside the United Kingdom is its principal office within the United Kingdom.

(4)   Subsection (5) applies if a person to be served under this Part with any document by another has specified to that other an address within the United Kingdom other than his proper address (as determined under subsection (2)) as the one at which he or someone on his behalf will accept documents of the same description as that document.

(5)   In relation to that document, that address shall be treated as his proper address for the purposes of this section and section 7 of the Interpretation Act 1978 in its application to this section, instead of that determined under subsection (2).

(6)   Any notice in writing or other document required or authorised by virtue of this Part to be served on any person may be served on that person by transmitting the text of the notice or other document to him by means of an electronic communications network or by other means but while in electronic form provided the text is received by that person in legible form and is capable of being used for subsequent reference.

(7)   This section does not apply to any document if rules of court make provision about its service.

(8)   In this section references to serving include references to similar expressions (such as giving or sending).

127.   Associated persons

(1)   Associated persons, and any bodies corporate which they or any of them control, shall be treated as one person—

    (a)   for the purpose of deciding under section 26 whether any two enterprises have been brought under common ownership or common control;

    (aa) for the purposes of section 58(2C); and

    (b)   for the purpose of determining what activities are carried on by way of business by any one person so far as that question arises in connection with paragraph 13(2) of Schedule 8.

(2)   Subsection (1) shall not exclude from section 26 any case which would otherwise fall within that section.

(3)   A reference under section 22, 33, 45 or 62 (whether or not made by virtue of this section) may be framed so as to exclude from consideration, either altogether or for a specified purpose or to a specified extent, any matter which, apart from this section, would not have been taken into account on that reference.

(4)   For the purposes of this section—

    (a)   any individual and that individual's spouse, *civil partner* or partner and any relative, or spouse, *civil partner* or partner of a relative, of that individual or of that individual's spouse, *civil partner* or partner;

    (b)   any person in his capacity as trustee of a settlement and the settlor or grantor and any person associated with the settlor or grantor;

    (c)   persons carrying on business in partnership and the spouse, *civil partner* or partner and relatives of any of them; or

    (d)   two or more persons acting together to secure or exercise control of a body of persons corporate or unincorporate or to secure control of any enterprise or assets,

shall be regarded as associated with one another.

(5)   The reference in subsection (1) to bodies corporate which associated persons control shall be construed in accordance with section 26(3) and (4).

(6)   In this section "relative" means a brother, sister, uncle, aunt, nephew, niece, lineal ancestor or descendant (the stepchild of any person, or anyone adopted by a person, whether legally or otherwise, as his child being regarded as a relative or taken into account to trace a relationship in the same way as that person's child); and references to a spouse, *civil partner* or partner shall include a former spouse, *civil partner* or partner.

Note. The italicized words in subsections (4)(a), (c) and (6) are inserted by the Civil Partnership Act 2004, s. 261(1), Sch. 27, para. 168, as from a day to be appointed.

128.   Supply of services and market for services etc.

(1)   References in this Part to the supply of services shall be construed in accordance with this section; and references in this Part to a market for services and other related expressions shall be construed accordingly.

(2)   The supply of services does not include the provision of services under a contract of service or of apprenticeship whether it is express or implied and (if it is express) whether it is oral or in writing.

(3)   The supply of services includes—

    (a)   performing for gain or reward any activity other than the supply of goods;

    (b)   rendering services to order;

(c)   the provision of services by making them available to potential users.

(4)   The supply of services includes making arrangements for the use of computer software or for granting access to data stored in any form which is not readily accessible.

(5)   The supply of services includes making arrangements by means of a relevant agreement (within the meaning of paragraph 29 of Schedule 2 to the Telecommunications Act 1984) for sharing the use of telecommunications apparatus.

(6)   The supply of services includes permitting or making arrangements to permit the use of land in such circumstances as the Secretary of State may by order specify.

129.   Other interpretation provisions

(1)   In this Part, unless the context otherwise requires—

"action" includes omission; and references to the taking of action include references to refraining from action;

"agreement" means any agreement or arrangement, in whatever way and whatever form it is made, and whether it is, or is intended to be, legally enforceable or not;

"business" includes a professional practice and includes any other undertaking which is carried on for gain or reward or which is an undertaking in the course of which goods or services are supplied otherwise than free of charge;

"change of circumstances" includes any discovery that information has been supplied which is false or misleading in a material respect;

"Community law" means—

(a)   all the rights, powers, liabilities, obligations and restrictions from time to time created or arising by or under the Community Treaties; and

(b)   all the remedies and procedures from time to time provided for by or under the Community Treaties;

"consumer" means any person who is—

(a)   a person to whom goods are or are sought to be supplied (whether by way of sale or otherwise) in the course of a business carried on by the person supplying or seeking to supply them; or

(b)   a person for whom services are or are sought to be supplied in the course of a business carried on by the person supplying or seeking to supply them;

and who does not receive or seek to receive the goods or services in the course of a business carried on by him;

"customer" includes a customer who is not a consumer;

"the EC Merger Regulation" means Council Regulation (EC) No 139/2004 of 20th January 2004 on the control of concentrations between undertakings;

"enactment" includes an Act of the Scottish Parliament, Northern Ireland legislation and an enactment comprised in subordinate legislation, and includes an enactment whenever passed or made;

"enterprise" means the activities, or part of the activities, of a business;

…

"goods" includes buildings and other structures, and also includes ships, aircraft and hovercraft;

"modify" includes amend or repeal;

"notice" means notice in writing;

"price" includes any charge or fee (however described);

"subordinate legislation" has the same meaning as in the Interpretation Act 1978 (c. 30) and also includes an instrument made under an Act of the Scottish Parliament and an instrument made under Northern Ireland legislation;

"subsidiary" has the meaning given by section 736 of the Companies Act 1985 (c. 6);

"supply", in relation to the supply of goods, includes supply by way of sale, lease, hire or hire-purchase, and, in relation to buildings or other structures, includes the construction of them by a person for another person; and

"United Kingdom national" means an individual who is—

    (a)   a British citizen, a British overseas territories citizen, a British National (Overseas) or a British Overseas citizen;

    (b)   a person who under the British Nationality Act 1981 (c. 61) is a British subject; or

    (c)   a British protected person within the meaning of that Act.

(2)   For the purposes of this Part any two bodies corporate are interconnected if—

    (a)   one of them is a body corporate of which the other is a subsidiary; or

    (b)   both of them are subsidiaries of one and the same body corporate;

and in this Part "interconnected bodies corporate" shall be construed accordingly and "group of interconnected bodies corporate" means a group consisting of two or more bodies corporate all of whom are interconnected with each other.

(3)   References in this Part to a person carrying on business include references to a person carrying on business in partnership with one or more other persons.

(4)   Any duty to publish which is imposed on a person by this Part shall, unless the context otherwise requires, be construed as a duty on that person to publish in such manner as he considers appropriate for the purpose of bringing the matter concerned to the attention of those likely to be affected by it.

130.   Index of defined expressions

In this Part, the expressions listed in the left-hand column have the meaning given by, or are to be interpreted in accordance with, the provisions listed in the right-hand column.

Expression	Provision of this Act
Action (and the taking of action)	Section 129(1)
Adverse public interest finding	Section 54(3)
Agreement	Section 129(1)
Anti-competitive outcome	Section 35(2)
Broadcasting	Section 44(9)
Business (and carrying on business)	Section 129(1) and (3)
Change of circumstances	Section 129(1)
The Commission	Section 273
Community law	Section 129(1)
Consumer	Section 129(1)
Customer	Section 129(1)
Date of reference	Section 39(9)
The decision-making authority	Section 22(7)
EC Merger Regulation	Section 129(1)
Enactment	Section 129(1)
Enforcement order	Section 86(6)
Enforcement undertaking	Section 89(2)
Enterprise	Section 129(1)
Enterprises ceasing to be distinct	Section 26(1)
…	…
Final determination of matter to which intervention notice relates	Section 43(4) and (5)
Final determination of matter to which special intervention notice relates	Section 60(4) and (5)
Final determination of reference under section 22 or 33	Section 79(1) and (2)
Goods	Section 129(1)
Interconnected bodies corporate (and a group of interconnected bodies corporate)	Section 129(2)
Intervention notice	Section 42(2)
Market for goods or services	Section 22(6)

Market in the United Kingdom	Section 22(6)
Media public interest consideration	Section 44(8)
Merger notice	Section 96(2)
Modify	Section 129(1)
Newspaper	Section 44(10)
Newspaper enterprise	Section 58A(3)
Notice	Section 129(1)
Notified arrangements	Section 96(6)
OFCOM	Section 43(6)
The OFT	Section 273
Orders under section 81	Section 81(6)
Orders under paragraph 2 of Schedule 7	Paragraph 2(7) of Schedule 7
The period for considering a merger notice	Sections 97 and 98
Price	Section 129(1)
Public interest consideration	Sections 42(3) and 67(9)
Public interest consideration being finalised	Section 42(8)
Publish	Section 129(4)
References under section 22, 33, 45 or 62	Sections 37(2), 49(1), 56(8) and 64(2)
Relevant customer benefit	Section 30
Relevant merger situation	Section 23 (as read with other enactments)
Reports of the Commission	Section 118(5)
Special intervention notice	Section 59(2)
Special merger situation	Section 59(3)
Subordinate legislation	Section 129(1)
Subsidiary	Section 129(1)
Supply (in relation to the supply of goods)	Section 129(1)
The supply of services (and a market for services etc.)	Section 128
The turnover in the United Kingdom of an enterprise	Section 28(2)
Undertakings under section 80	Section 80(6)
Undertakings under paragraph 1 of Schedule 7	Paragraph 1(7) of Schedule 7
United Kingdom national	Section 129(1)

PART 4
MARKET INVESTIGATIONS

CHAPTER 1
MARKET INVESTIGATION REFERENCES

Making of references

131. Power of OFT to make references

(1)   The OFT may, subject to subsection (4), make a reference to the Commission if the OFT has reasonable grounds for suspecting that any feature, or combination of features, of a market in the United Kingdom for goods or services prevents, restricts or distorts competition in connection with the supply or acquisition of any goods or services in the United Kingdom or a part of the United Kingdom.

(2)   For the purposes of this Part any reference to a feature of a market in the United Kingdom for goods or services shall be construed as a reference to—

(a)   the structure of the market concerned or any aspect of that structure;

(b) any conduct (whether or not in the market concerned) of one or more than one person who supplies or acquires goods or services in the market concerned; or

(c) any conduct relating to the market concerned of customers of any person who supplies or acquires goods or services.

(3) In subsection (2) "conduct" includes any failure to act (whether or not intentional) and any other unintentional conduct.

(4) No reference shall be made under this section if—

(a) the making of the reference is prevented by section 156(1); or

(b) a reference has been made under section 132 in relation to the same matter but has not been finally determined.

(5) References in this Part to a market investigation reference being finally determined shall be construed in accordance with section 183(3) to (6).

(6) In this Part—

"market in the United Kingdom" includes—

(a) so far as it operates in the United Kingdom or a part of the United Kingdom, any market which operates there and in another country or territory or in a part of another country or territory; and

(b) any market which operates only in a part of the United Kingdom;

"market investigation reference" means a reference under this section or section 132;

and references to a market for goods or services include references to a market for goods and services.

132. Ministerial power to make references

(1) Subsection (3) applies where, in relation to any goods or services, the appropriate Minister is not satisfied with a decision of the OFT not to make a reference under section 131.

(2) Subsection (3) also applies where, in relation to any goods or services, the appropriate Minister—

(a) has brought to the attention of the OFT information which the appropriate Minister considers to be relevant to the question of whether the OFT should make a reference under section 131; but

(b) is not satisfied that the OFT will decide, within such period as the appropriate Minister considers to be reasonable, whether to make such a reference.

(3) The appropriate Minister may, subject to subsection (4), make a reference to the Commission if he has reasonable grounds for suspecting that any feature, or combination of features, of a market in the United Kingdom for goods or services prevents, restricts or distorts competition in connection with the supply or acquisition of any goods or services in the United Kingdom or a part of the United Kingdom.

(4) No reference shall be made under this section if the making of the reference is prevented by section 156(1).

(5) In this Part "the appropriate Minister" means—

(a) the Secretary of State; or

(b) the Secretary of State and one or more than one other Minister of the Crown acting jointly.

133. Contents of references

(1) A market investigation reference shall, in particular, specify—

(a) the enactment under which it is made;

(b) the date on which it is made; and

(c) the description of goods or services to which the feature or combination of features concerned relates.

(2) A market investigation reference may be framed so as to require the Commission to confine its investigation into the effects of features of markets in the United Kingdom for goods or services of a description specified in the reference to the effects of features of such of those markets as exist in connection with—

(a) a supply, of a description specified in the reference, of the goods or services concerned; or

    (b)   an acquisition, of a description specified in the reference, of the goods or services concerned.

(3)   A description of the kind mentioned in subsection (2)(a) or (b) may, in particular, be by reference to—

    (a)   the place where the goods or services are supplied or acquired; or

    (b)   the persons by or to whom they are supplied or by or from whom they are acquired.

Determination of references

134.   Questions to be decided on market investigation references

(1)   The Commission shall, on a market investigation reference, decide whether any feature, or combination of features, of each relevant market prevents, restricts or distorts competition in connection with the supply or acquisition of any goods or services in the United Kingdom or a part of the United Kingdom.

(2)   For the purposes of this Part, in relation to a market investigation reference, there is an adverse effect on competition if any feature, or combination of features, of a relevant market prevents, restricts or distorts competition in connection with the supply or acquisition of any goods or services in the United Kingdom or a part of the United Kingdom.

(3)   In subsections (1) and (2) "relevant market" means—

    (a)   in the case of subsection (2) so far as it applies in connection with a possible reference, a market in the United Kingdom—

        (i)   for goods or services of a description to be specified in the reference; and

        (ii)   which would not be excluded from investigation by virtue of section 133(2); and

    (b)   in any other case, a market in the United Kingdom—

        (i)   for goods or services of a description specified in the reference concerned; and

        (ii)   which is not excluded from investigation by virtue of section 133(2).

(4)   The Commission shall, if it has decided on a market investigation reference that there is an adverse effect on competition, decide the following additional questions—

    (a)   whether action should be taken by it under section 138 for the purpose of remedying, mitigating or preventing the adverse effect on competition concerned or any detrimental effect on customers so far as it has resulted from, or may be expected to result from, the adverse effect on competition;

    (b)   whether it should recommend the taking of action by others for the purpose of remedying, mitigating or preventing the adverse effect on competition concerned or any detrimental effect on customers so far as it has resulted from, or may be expected to result from, the adverse effect on competition; and

    (c)   in either case, if action should be taken, what action should be taken and what is to be remedied, mitigated or prevented.

(5)   For the purposes of this Part, in relation to a market investigation reference, there is a detrimental effect on customers if there is a detrimental effect on customers or future customers in the form of—

    (a)   higher prices, lower quality or less choice of goods or services in any market in the United Kingdom (whether or not the market to which the feature or features concerned relate); or

    (b)   less innovation in relation to such goods or services.

(6)   In deciding the questions mentioned in subsection (4), the Commission shall, in particular, have regard to the need to achieve as comprehensive a solution as is reasonable and practicable to the adverse effect on competition and any detrimental effects on customers so far as resulting from the adverse effect on competition.

(7)   In deciding the questions mentioned in subsection (4), the Commission may, in particular, have regard to the effect of any action on any relevant customer benefits of the feature or features of the market concerned.

(8)   For the purposes of this Part a benefit is a relevant customer benefit of a feature or features of a market if—

(a)   it is a benefit to customers or future customers in the form of—

    (i)   lower prices, higher quality or greater choice of goods or services in any market in the United Kingdom (whether or not the market to which the feature or features concerned relate); or

    (ii)   greater innovation in relation to such goods or services; and

(b)   the Commission, the Secretary of State or (as the case may be) the OFT believes that—

    (i)   the benefit has accrued as a result (whether wholly or partly) of the feature or features concerned or may be expected to accrue within a reasonable period as a result (whether wholly or partly) of that feature or those features; and

    (ii)   the benefit was, or is, unlikely to accrue without the feature or features concerned.

135.   Variation of market investigation references

(1)   The OFT or (as the case may be) the appropriate Minister may at any time vary a market investigation reference made by it or (as the case may be) him.

(2)   The OFT or (as the case may be) the appropriate Minister shall consult the Commission before varying any such reference.

(3)   Subsection (2) shall not apply if the Commission has requested the variation concerned.

(4)   No variation under this section shall be capable of altering the period permitted by section 137 within which the report of the Commission under section 136 is to be prepared and published or (as the case may be) the period permitted by section 144 within which the report of the Commission under section 142 is to be prepared and published or given.

136.   Investigations and reports on market investigation references

(1)   The Commission shall prepare and publish a report on a market investigation reference within the period permitted by section 137.

(2)   The report shall, in particular, contain—

(a)   the decisions of the Commission on the questions which it is required to answer by virtue of section 134;

(b)   its reasons for its decisions; and

(c)   such information as the Commission considers appropriate for facilitating a proper understanding of those questions and of its reasons for its decisions.

(3)   The Commission shall carry out such investigations as it considers appropriate for the purposes of preparing a report under this section.

(4)   The Commission shall, at the same time as a report under this section is published—

(a)   in the case of a reference under section 131, give it to the OFT; and

(b)   in the case of a reference under section 132, give it to the appropriate Minister and give a copy of it to the OFT.

(5)   Where a reference has been made by the OFT under section 131 or by the appropriate Minister under section 132 in circumstances in which a reference could have been made by a relevant sectoral regulator under section 131 as it has effect by virtue of a relevant sectoral enactment, the Commission shall, at the same time as the report under this section is published, give a copy of it to the relevant sectoral regulator concerned.

(6)   Where a reference has been made by a relevant sectoral regulator under section 131 as it has effect by virtue of a relevant sectoral enactment, the Commission shall, at the same time as the report under this section is published, give a copy of it to the OFT.

(7)   In this Part "relevant sectoral enactment" means—

(a)   ...

(b)   in relation to the Gas and Electricity Markets Authority, section 36A of the Gas Act 1986 (c. 44) or (as the case may be) section 43 of the Electricity Act 1989 (c. 29);

(c)   in relation to the *Director General of Water Services [the Water Services Regulation Authority]*, section 31 of the Water Industry Act 1991 (c. 56);

(d)   in relation to the Director General of Electricity Supply for Northern Ireland, article 46 of the Electricity (Northern Ireland) Order 1992 (S.I. 1992/231 (N.I. 1));

(e)   in relation to the Office of Rail Regulation, section 67 of the Railways Act 1993 (c. 43);

(f)   in relation to the Director General of Gas for Northern Ireland, article 23 of the Gas (Northern Ireland) Order 1996 (S.I. 1996/275 (N.I. 2)); ...

(g)   in relation to the Civil Aviation Authority, section 86 of the Transport Act 2000 (c. 38);

(h)   in relation to the Office of Communications, sections 370 and 371 of the Communications Act 2003.

(8)   In this Part "relevant sectoral regulator" means ... the Gas and Electricity Markets Authority, *the Director General of Water Services [the Water Services Regulation Authority]*, the Director General of Electricity Supply for Northern Ireland, the Office of Rail Regulation, the Director General of Gas for Northern Ireland, the Civil Aviation Authority or the Office of Communications.

(9)   The Secretary of State may by order modify subsection (7) or (8).

Note. The italicized words in subsections (7)(c) and (8) are substituted by the words in square brackets following them by the Water Act 2003, s. 101(1), Sch. 7, Pt. 2, para. 36(1), (2), as from a day to be appointed.

137.   Time-limits for market investigations and reports

(1)   The Commission shall prepare and publish its report under section 136 within the period of two years beginning with the date of the market investigation reference concerned.

(2)   Subsection (1) is subject to section 151(3) and (5).

(3)   The Secretary of State may by order amend subsection (1) so as to alter the period of two years mentioned in that subsection or any period for the time being mentioned in that subsection in substitution for that period.

(4)   No alteration shall be made by virtue of subsection (3) which results in the period for the time being mentioned in subsection (1) exceeding two years.

(5)   An order under subsection (3) shall not affect any period of time within which the Commission is under a duty to prepare and publish its report under section 136 in relation to a market investigation reference if the Commission is already under that duty in relation to that reference when the order is made.

(6)   Before making an order under subsection (3) the Secretary of State shall consult the Commission and such other persons as he considers appropriate.

(7)   References in this Part to the date of a market investigation reference shall be construed as references to the date specified in the reference as the date on which it is made.

138.   Duty to remedy adverse effects

(1)   Subsection (2) applies where a report of the Commission has been prepared and published under section 136 within the period permitted by section 137 and contains the decision that there is one or more than one adverse effect on competition.

(2)   The Commission shall, in relation to each adverse effect on competition, take such action under section 159 or 161 as it considers to be reasonable and practicable—

(a)   to remedy, mitigate or prevent the adverse effect on competition concerned; and

(b)   to remedy, mitigate or prevent any detrimental effects on customers so far as they have resulted from, or may be expected to result from, the adverse effect on competition.

(3)   The decisions of the Commission under subsection (2) shall be consistent with its decisions as included in its report by virtue of section 134(4) unless there has been a material change of circumstances since the preparation of the report or the Commission otherwise has a special reason for deciding differently.

(4)   In making a decision under subsection (2), the Commission shall, in particular, have regard to the need to achieve as comprehensive a solution as is reasonable and practicable to the adverse effect on competition concerned and any detrimental effects on customers so far as resulting from the adverse effect on competition.

(5)   In making a decision under subsection (2), the Commission may, in particular, have regard to the effect of any action on any relevant customer benefits of the feature or features of the market concerned.

(6)   The Commission shall take no action under subsection (2) to remedy, mitigate or prevent any detrimental effect on customers so far as it may be expected to result from the adverse effect on competition concerned if—

(a)   no detrimental effect on customers has resulted from the adverse effect on competition; and

(b)   the adverse effect on competition is not being remedied, mitigated or prevented.

CHAPTER 2
PUBLIC INTEREST CASES

Intervention notices

139.   Public interest intervention by Secretary of State

(1)   The Secretary of State may give a notice to the Commission if—

(a)   a market investigation reference has been made to the Commission;

(b)   no more than four months has passed since the date of the reference;

(c)   the reference is not finally determined; and

(d)   the Secretary of State believes that it is or may be the case that one or more than one public interest consideration is relevant to the case.

(2)   The Secretary of State may give a notice to the OFT if—

(a)   the OFT is considering whether to accept—

(i)   an undertaking under section 154 instead of making a reference under section 131; or

(ii)   an undertaking varying or superseding any such undertaking;

(b)   the OFT has published a notice under section 155(1) or (4); and

(c)   the Secretary of State believes that it is or may be the case that one or more than one public interest consideration is relevant to the case.

(3)   In this Part "intervention notice" means a notice under subsection (1) or (2).

(4)   No more than one intervention notice shall be given under subsection (1) in relation to the same market investigation reference and no more than one intervention notice shall be given under subsection (2) in relation to the same proposed undertaking or in relation to proposed undertakings which do not differ from each other in any material respect.

(5)   For the purposes of this Part a public interest consideration is a consideration which, at the time of the giving of the intervention notice concerned, is specified in section 153 or is not so specified but, in the opinion of the Secretary of State, ought to be so specified.

(6)   Where the Secretary of State has given an intervention notice mentioning a public interest consideration which, at that time, is not finalised, he shall, as soon as practicable, take such action as is within his power to ensure that it is finalised.

(7)   For the purposes of this Part a public interest consideration is finalised if—

(a)   it is specified in section 153 otherwise than by virtue of an order under subsection (3) of that section; or

(b)   it is specified in that section by virtue of an order under subsection (3) of that section and the order providing for it to be so specified has been laid before, and approved by, Parliament in accordance with subsection (6) of section 181 and within the period mentioned in that subsection.

Intervention notices under section 139(1)

140.   Intervention notices under section 139(1)

(1)   An intervention notice under section 139(1) shall state—

(a)   the market investigation reference concerned;

(b)   the date of the market investigation reference concerned;

(c)   the public interest consideration or considerations which are, or may be, relevant to the case; and

(d)   where any public interest consideration concerned is not finalised, the proposed timetable for finalising it.

(2)   Where the Secretary of State believes that it is or may be the case that two or more public interest considerations are relevant to the case, he may decide not to mention in the intervention notice such of those considerations as he considers appropriate.

(3)   The Secretary of State may at any time revoke an intervention notice which has been given under section 139(1) and which is in force.

(4)   An intervention notice under section 139(1) shall come into force when it is given and shall cease to be in force when the matter to which it relates is finally determined under this Chapter.

(5)   For the purposes of subsection (4) a matter to which an intervention notice under section 139(1) relates is finally determined under this Chapter if—

   (a)   the period permitted by section 144 for the preparation of the report of the Commission under section 142 and for action to be taken in relation to it under section 143(1) or (3) has expired and no such report has been so prepared or no such action has been taken;

   (b)   the Commission decides under section 145(1) to terminate its investigation;

   (c)   the report of the Commission has been prepared under section 142 and published under section 143(1) within the period permitted by section 144;

   (d)   the Secretary of State fails to make and publish a decision under subsection (2) of section 146 within the period required by subsection (3) of that section;

   (e)   the Secretary of State decides under section 146(2) that no eligible public interest consideration is relevant;

   (f)   the Secretary of State decides under section 147(2) neither to accept an undertaking under section 159 nor to make an order under section 161;

   (g)   the Secretary of State accepts an undertaking under section 159 or makes an order under section 161; or

   (h)   the Secretary of State decides to revoke the intervention notice concerned.

(6)   For the purposes of subsections (4) and (5) the time when a matter to which an intervention notice under section 139(1) relates is finally determined under this Chapter is—

   (a)   in a case falling within subsection (5)(a) or (d), the expiry of the period concerned;

   (b)   in a case falling within subsection (5)(b), (e), (f) or (h), the making of the decision concerned;

   (c)   in a case falling within subsection (5)(c), the publication of the report concerned; and

   (d)   in a case falling within subsection (5)(g), the acceptance of the undertaking concerned or (as the case may be) the making of the order concerned.

(7)   In subsection (6)(d) the reference to the acceptance of the undertaking concerned or the making of the order concerned shall, in a case where the enforcement action under section 147(2) involves the acceptance of a group of undertakings, the making of a group of orders or the acceptance and making of a group of undertakings and orders, be treated as a reference to the acceptance or making of the last undertaking or order in the group; but undertakings or orders which vary, supersede or revoke earlier undertakings or orders shall be disregarded for the purposes of subsections (5)(g) and (6)(d).

141.   Questions to be decided by Commission

(1)   This section applies where an intervention notice under section 139(1) is in force in relation to a market investigation reference.

(2)   The Commission shall decide whether any feature, or combination of features, of each relevant market (within the meaning given by section 134(3)) prevents, restricts or distorts competition in connection with the supply or acquisition of any goods or services in the United Kingdom or a part of the United Kingdom.

(3)   The Commission shall, if it has decided that there is an adverse effect on competition, decide the following additional questions—

   (a)   whether action should be taken by the Secretary of State under section 147 for the purpose of remedying, mitigating or preventing the adverse effect on competition concerned or any detrimental effect on customers so far as it has resulted from, or may be expected to result from, the adverse effect on competition;

(b)   whether the Commission should recommend the taking of other action by the Secretary of State or action by persons other than itself and the Secretary of State for the purpose of remedying, mitigating or preventing the adverse effect on competition concerned or any detrimental effect on customers so far as it has resulted from, or may be expected to result from, the adverse effect on competition; and

(c)   in either case, if action should be taken, what action should be taken and what is to be remedied, mitigated or prevented.

(4)   The Commission shall, if it has decided that there is an adverse effect on competition, also decide separately the following questions (on the assumption that it is proceeding as mentioned in section 148(1))—

(a)   whether action should be taken by it under section 138 for the purpose of remedying, mitigating or preventing the adverse effect on competition concerned or any detrimental effect on customers so far as it has resulted from, or may be expected to result from, the adverse effect on competition;

(b)   whether the Commission should recommend the taking of action by other persons for the purpose of remedying, mitigating or preventing the adverse effect on competition concerned or any detrimental effect on customers so far as it has resulted from, or may be expected to result from, the adverse effect on competition; and

(c)   in either case, if action should be taken, what action should be taken and what is to be remedied, mitigated or prevented.

(5)   In deciding the questions mentioned in subsections (3) and (4), the Commission shall, in particular, have regard to the need to achieve as comprehensive a solution as is reasonable and practicable to the adverse effect on competition concerned and any detrimental effects on customers so far as resulting from the adverse effect on competition.

(6)   In deciding the questions mentioned in subsections (3) and (4), the Commission may, in particular, have regard to the effect of any action on any relevant customer benefits of the feature or features of the market concerned.

142.   Investigations and reports by Commission

(1)   Where an intervention notice under section 139(1) is in force in relation to a market investigation reference, the Commission shall prepare a report on the reference and take action in relation to it under section 143(1) or (3) within the period permitted by section 144.

(2)   The report shall, in particular, contain—

(a)   the decisions of the Commission on the questions which it is required to answer by virtue of section 141;

(b)   its reasons for its decisions; and

(c)   such information as the Commission considers appropriate for facilitating a proper understanding of those questions and of its reasons for its decisions.

(3)   The Commission shall carry out such investigations as it considers appropriate for the purposes of preparing a report under this section.

143.   Publication etc. of reports of Commission

(1)   The Commission shall publish a report under section 142 if it contains—

(a)   the decision of the Commission that there is no adverse effect on competition; or

(b)   the decisions of the Commission that there is one or more than one adverse effect on competition but, on the question mentioned in section 141(4)(a) and in relation to each adverse effect on competition, that no action should be taken by it.

(2)   The Commission shall, at the same time as the report is published under subsection (1)—

(a)   in the case of a reference under section 131, give it to the OFT; and

(b)   in the case of a reference under section 132, give it to the appropriate Minister and give a copy of it to the OFT.

(3)   Where a report under section 142 contains the decisions of the Commission that there is one or more than one adverse effect on competition and, on the question mentioned in section 141(4)(a)

and in relation to at least one such adverse effect, that action should be taken by it, the Commission shall give the report to the Secretary of State.

(4)   The Secretary of State shall publish, no later than publication of his decision under section 146(2) in relation to the case, a report of the Commission given to him under subsection (3) and not required to be published by virtue of section 148(2).

(5)   The Secretary of State shall, at the same time as a report of the Commission given to him under subsection (3) is published under subsection (4), give a copy of it—

(a)   in the case of a reference under section 131, to the OFT; and

(b)   in the case of a reference under section 132, to any other Minister of the Crown who made the reference and to the OFT.

(6)   Where a reference has been made by the OFT under section 131 or by the appropriate Minister under section 132 in circumstances in which a reference could have been made by a relevant sectoral regulator under section 131 as it has effect by virtue of a relevant sectoral enactment, the relevant authority shall, at the same time as the report under section 142 is published under subsection (1) or (4), give a copy of it to the relevant sectoral regulator concerned.

(7)   Where a reference has been made by a relevant sectoral regulator under section 131 as it has effect by virtue of a relevant sectoral enactment, the relevant authority shall, at the same time as the report under section 142 is published under subsection (1) or (4), give a copy of it to the OFT.

(8)   In subsections (6) and (7) "the relevant authority" means—

(a)   in the case of a report published under subsection (1), the Commission; and

(b)   in the case of a report published under subsection (4), the Secretary of State.

144.   Time-limits for investigations and reports: Part 4

(1)   The Commission shall, within the period of two years beginning with the date of the reference, prepare its report under section 142 and publish it under subsection (1) of section 143 or (as the case may be) give it to the Secretary of State under subsection (3) of that section.

(2)   The Secretary of State may by order amend subsection (1) so as to alter the period of two years mentioned in that subsection or any period for the time being mentioned in that subsection in substitution for that period.

(3)   No alteration shall be made by virtue of subsection (2) which results in the period for the time being mentioned in subsection (1) exceeding two years.

(4)   An order under subsection (2) shall not affect any period of time within which, in relation to a market investigation reference, the Commission is under a duty to prepare its report under section 142 and take action in relation to it under section 143(1) or (3) if the Commission is already under that duty in relation to that reference when the order is made.

(5)   Before making an order under subsection (2) the Secretary of State shall consult the Commission and such other persons as he considers appropriate.

145.   Restrictions where public interest considerations not finalised: Part 4

(1)   The Commission shall terminate its investigation under section 142 if—

(a)   the intervention notice concerned mentions a public interest consideration which was not finalised on the giving of that notice or public interest considerations which, at that time, were not finalised;

(b)   no other public interest consideration is mentioned in the notice;

(c)   at least 24 weeks has elapsed since the giving of the notice; and

(d)   the public interest consideration mentioned in the notice has not been finalised within that period of 24 weeks or (as the case may be) none of the public interest considerations mentioned in the notice has been finalised within that period of 24 weeks.

(2)   Where the intervention notice concerned mentions a public interest consideration which is not finalised on the giving of the notice, the Commission shall not give its report under section 142 to the Secretary of State in accordance with section 143(3) unless the period of 24 weeks beginning with the giving of the intervention notice concerned has expired or the public interest consideration concerned has been finalised.

(3)   The Commission shall, in reporting on any of the questions mentioned in section 141(3), disregard any public interest consideration which has not been finalised before the giving of the report.

(4)   The Commission shall, in reporting on any of the questions mentioned in section 141(3), disregard any public interest consideration which was not finalised on the giving of the intervention notice concerned and has not been finalised within the period of 24 weeks beginning with the giving of the notice concerned.

(5)   Subsections (1) to (4) are without prejudice to the power of the Commission to carry out investigations in relation to any public interest consideration to which it might be able to have regard in its report.

146.   Decision of Secretary of State

(1)   Subsection (2) applies where the Secretary of State has received a report of the Commission which—

(a)   has been prepared under section 142;

(b)   contains the decisions that there is one or more than one adverse effect on competition and, on the question mentioned in section 141(4)(a) and in relation to at least one such adverse effect, that action should be taken by it; and

(c)   has been given to the Secretary of State as required by section 143(3).

(2)   The Secretary of State shall decide whether—

(a)   any eligible public interest consideration is relevant; or

(b)   any eligible public interest considerations are relevant;

to any action which is mentioned in the report by virtue of section 141(4)(a) and (c) and which the Commission should take for the purpose of remedying, mitigating or preventing any adverse effect on competition concerned or any detrimental effect on customers so far as it has resulted or may be expected to result from any adverse effect on competition.

(3)   The Secretary of State shall make and publish his decision under subsection (2) within the period of 90 days beginning with the receipt of the report of the Commission under section 142.

(4)   In this section "eligible public interest consideration" means a public interest consideration which—

(a)   was mentioned in the intervention notice concerned; and

(b)   was not disregarded by the Commission for the purposes of its report under section 142.

147.   Remedial action by Secretary of State

(1)   Subsection (2) applies where the Secretary of State—

(a)   has decided under subsection (2) of section 146 within the period required by subsection (3) of that section that an eligible public interest consideration is relevant as mentioned in subsection (2) of that section or eligible public interest considerations are so relevant; and

(b)   has published his decision within the period required by subsection (3) of that section.

(2)   The Secretary of State may, in relation to any adverse effect on competition identified in the report concerned, take such action under section 159 or 161 as he considers to be—

(a)   reasonable and practicable—

(i)   to remedy, mitigate or prevent the adverse effect on competition concerned; or

(ii)   to remedy, mitigate or prevent any detrimental effect on customers so far as it has resulted from, or may be expected to result from, the adverse effect on competition; and

(b)   appropriate in the light of the eligible public interest consideration concerned or (as the case may be) the eligible public interest considerations concerned.

(3)   In making a decision under subsection (2), the Secretary of State shall, in particular, have regard to—

(a)   the need to achieve as comprehensive a solution as is reasonable and practicable to the adverse effect on competition concerned and any detrimental effects on customers so far as resulting from the adverse effect on competition; and

(b)   the report of the Commission under section 142.

(4)   In having regard by virtue of subsection (3) to the report of the Commission under section 142, the Secretary of State shall not challenge the decision of the Commission contained in the report that there is one or more than one adverse effect on competition.

(5)   In making a decision under subsection (2), the Secretary of State may, in particular, have regard to the effect of any action on any relevant customer benefits of the feature or features of the market concerned.

(6)   The Secretary of State shall take no action under subsection (2) to remedy, mitigate or prevent any detrimental effect on customers so far as it may be expected to result from the adverse effect on competition concerned if—

(a)   no detrimental effect on customers has resulted from the adverse effect on competition; and

(b)   the adverse effect on competition is not being remedied, mitigated or prevented.

(7)   In this section "eligible public interest consideration" has the same meaning as in section 146.

148.   Reversion of the matter to the Commission

(1)   If—

(a)   the Secretary of State fails to make and publish his decision under subsection (2) of section 146 within the period required by subsection (3) of that section; or

(b)   the Secretary of State decides that no eligible public interest consideration is relevant as mentioned in subsection (2) of that section;

the Commission shall proceed under section 138 as if the report had been prepared and published under section 136 within the period permitted by section 137.

(2)   The Commission shall publish the report which has been prepared by it under section 142 (if still unpublished) as soon as it becomes able to proceed by virtue of subsection (1).

(3)   The Commission shall, at the same time as its report is published under subsection (2), give a copy of it—

(a)   in the case of a reference under section 131, to the OFT; and

(b)   in the case of a reference under section 132, to any Minister of the Crown who made the reference (other than the Secretary of State) and to the OFT.

(4)   Where a reference has been made by the OFT under section 131 or by the appropriate Minister under section 132 in circumstances in which a reference could have been made by a relevant sectoral regulator under section 131 as it has effect by virtue of a relevant sectoral enactment, the Commission shall, at the same time as its report is published under subsection (2), give a copy of it to the relevant sectoral regulator concerned.

(5)   Where a reference has been made by a relevant sectoral regulator under section 131 as it has effect by virtue of a relevant sectoral enactment, the Commission shall, at the same time as its report is published under subsection (2), give a copy of it to the OFT.

(6)   In relation to proceedings by virtue of subsection (1), the reference in section 138(3) to decisions of the Commission included in its report by virtue of section 134(4) shall be construed as a reference to decisions which were included in the report of the Commission by virtue of section 141(4).

(7)   Where the Commission, in proceeding by virtue of subsection (1), intends to proceed in a way which is not consistent with its decisions as included in its report by virtue of section 141(4), it shall not so proceed without the consent of the Secretary of State.

(8)   The Secretary of State shall not withhold his consent under subsection (7) unless he believes that the proposed alternative way of proceeding will operate against the public interest.

(9)   For the purposes of subsection (8) a proposed alternative way of proceeding will operate against the public interest only if any eligible public interest consideration or considerations outweigh the considerations which have led the Commission to propose proceeding in that way.

(10)   In deciding whether to withhold his consent under subsection (7), the Secretary of State shall accept the Commission's view of what, if the only relevant consideration were how to remedy, mitigate or prevent the adverse effect on competition concerned or any detrimental effect on

customers so far as resulting from the adverse effect on competition, would be the most appropriate way to proceed.

(11)   In this section "eligible public interest consideration" has the same meaning as in section 146.

Intervention notices under section 139(2)

149.   Intervention notices under section 139(2)

(1)   An intervention notice under section 139(2) shall state—

    (a)   the proposed undertaking which may be accepted by the OFT;

    (b)   the notice under section 155(1) or (4);

    (c)   the public interest consideration or considerations which are, or may be, relevant to the case; and

    (d)   where any public interest consideration concerned is not finalised, the proposed timetable for finalising it.

(2)   Where the Secretary of State believes that it is or may be the case that two or more public interest considerations are relevant to the case, he may decide not to mention in the intervention notice such of those considerations as he considers appropriate.

(3)   The Secretary of State may at any time revoke an intervention notice which has been given under section 139(2) and which is in force.

(4)   An intervention notice under section 139(2) shall come into force when it is given and shall cease to be in force on the occurrence of any of the events mentioned in subsection (5).

(5)   The events are—

    (a)   the acceptance by the OFT with the consent of the Secretary of State of an undertaking which is the same as the proposed undertaking mentioned in the intervention notice by virtue of subsection (1)(a) or which does not differ from it in any material respect;

    (b)   the decision of the OFT to proceed neither with the proposed undertaking mentioned in the intervention notice by virtue of subsection (1)(a) nor a proposed undertaking which does not differ from it in any material respect; or

    (c)   the decision of the Secretary of State to revoke the intervention notice concerned.

150.   Power of veto of Secretary of State

(1)   Where an intervention notice under section 139(2) is in force, the OFT shall not, without the consent of the Secretary of State, accept the proposed undertaking concerned or a proposed undertaking which does not differ from it in any material respect.

(2)   The Secretary of State shall withhold his consent if he believes that it is or may be the case that the proposed undertaking will, if accepted, operate against the public interest.

(3)   For the purposes of subsection (2) a proposed undertaking will, if accepted, operate against the public interest only if any public interest consideration which is mentioned in the intervention notice concerned and has been finalised, or any public interest considerations which are so mentioned and have been finalised, outweigh the considerations which have led the OFT to propose accepting the undertaking.

(4)   In making his decision under subsection (2) the Secretary of State shall accept the OFT's view of what undertakings, if the only relevant consideration were how to remedy, mitigate or prevent the adverse effect on competition concerned or any detrimental effect on customers so far as resulting from the adverse effect on competition, would be most appropriate.

(5)   Where a public interest consideration which is mentioned in the intervention notice concerned is not finalised on the giving of the notice, the Secretary of State shall not make his decision as to whether to give his consent under this section before—

    (a)   the end of the period of 24 weeks beginning with the giving of the intervention notice; or

    (b)   if earlier, the date on which the public interest consideration concerned has been finalised.

(6)   Subject to subsections (2) to (5), the Secretary of State shall not withhold his consent under this section.

Other

151.   Further interaction of intervention notices with general procedure

(1)   Where an intervention notice under section 139(1) comes into force in relation to a market investigation reference, sections 134(1), (4), (6) and (7), 136(1) to (6), 137(1) to (6) and 138 shall cease to apply in relation to that reference.

(2)   Where the Secretary of State revokes an intervention notice which has been given under section 139(1), the Commission shall instead proceed under sections 134 and 136 to 138.

(3)   Where the Commission is proceeding by virtue of subsection (2), the period within which the Commission shall prepare and publish its report under section 136 shall be extended by an additional period of 20 days.

(4)   Where the Commission terminates its investigation under section 145(1), the Commission shall proceed under sections 134 and 136 to 138.

(5)   Where the Commission is proceeding by virtue of subsection (4), the period within which the Commission shall prepare and publish its report under section 136 shall be extended by an additional period of 20 days.

(6)   In determining the period of 20 days mentioned in subsection (3) or (5) no account shall be taken of—

(a)   Saturday, Sunday, Good Friday and Christmas Day; and

(b)   any day which is a bank holiday in England and Wales.

152.   Certain duties of OFT and Commission

(1)   The OFT shall, in considering whether to make a reference under section 131, bring to the attention of the Secretary of State any case which it believes raises any consideration specified in section 153 unless it believes that the Secretary of State would consider any such consideration immaterial in the context of the particular case.

(2)   The Commission shall, in investigating any reference made to it under section 131 or 132 within the previous four months, bring to the attention of the Secretary of State any case which it believes raises any consideration specified in section 153 unless it believes that the Secretary of State would consider any such consideration immaterial in the context of the particular case.

(3)   The OFT and the Commission shall bring to the attention of the Secretary of State any representations about exercising his power under section 153(3) which have been made to the OFT or (as the case may be) the Commission.

153.   Specified considerations: Part 4

(1)   The interests of national security are specified in this section.

(2)   In subsection (1) "national security" includes public security; and in this subsection "public security" has the same meaning as in article 21(4) of Council Regulation (EC) No 139/2004 of 20th January 2004 on the control of concentrations between undertakings.

(3)   The Secretary of State may by order modify this section for the purpose of specifying in this section a new consideration or removing or amending any consideration which is for the time being specified in this section.

(4)   An order under this section may apply in relation to cases under consideration by the OFT, by the Secretary of State, by the appropriate Minister (other than the Secretary of State acting alone) or by the Commission before the making of the order as well as cases under consideration on or after the making of the order.

CHAPTER 3
ENFORCEMENT

Undertakings and orders

154. Undertakings in lieu of market investigation references

(1)   Subsection (2) applies if the OFT considers that it has the power to make a reference under section 131 and otherwise intends to make such a reference.

(2)   The OFT may, instead of making such a reference and for the purpose of remedying, mitigating or preventing—

(a)   any adverse effect on competition concerned; or

(b)   any detrimental effect on customers so far as it has resulted from, or may be expected to result from, the adverse effect on competition;

accept, from such persons as it considers appropriate, undertakings to take such action as it considers appropriate.

(3)   In proceeding under subsection (2), the OFT shall, in particular, have regard to the need to achieve as comprehensive a solution as is reasonable and practicable to the adverse effect on competition concerned and any detrimental effects on customers so far as resulting from the adverse effect on competition.

(4)   In proceeding under subsection (2), the OFT may, in particular, have regard to the effect of any action on any relevant customer benefits of the feature or features of the market concerned.

(5)   The OFT shall take no action under subsection (2) to remedy, mitigate or prevent any detrimental effect on customers so far as it may be expected to result from the adverse effect on competition concerned if—

(a)   no detrimental effect on customers has resulted from the adverse effect on competition; and

(b)   the adverse effect on competition is not being remedied, mitigated or prevented.

(6)   An undertaking under this section—

(a)   shall come into force when accepted;

(b)   may be varied or superseded by another undertaking; and

(c)   may be released by the OFT.

(7)   The OFT shall, as soon as reasonably practicable, consider any representations received by it in relation to varying or releasing an undertaking under this section.

(8)   This section is subject to sections 150 and 155.

155. Undertakings in lieu: procedural requirements

(1)   Before accepting an undertaking under section 154 (other than an undertaking under that section which varies an undertaking under that section but not in any material respect), the OFT shall—

(a)   publish notice of the proposed undertaking; and

(b)   consider any representations made in accordance with the notice and not withdrawn.

(2)   A notice under subsection (1) shall state—

(a)   that the OFT proposes to accept the undertaking;

(b)   the purpose and effect of the undertaking;

(c)   the situation that the undertaking is seeking to deal with;

(d)   any other facts which the OFT considers justify the acceptance of the undertaking;

(e)   a means of gaining access to an accurate version of the proposed undertaking at all reasonable times; and

(f)   the period (not less than 15 days starting with the date of publication of the notice) within which representations may be made in relation to the proposed undertaking.

(3)   The matters to be included in a notice under subsection (1) by virtue of subsection (2) shall, in particular, include—

(a)   the terms of the reference under section 131 which the OFT considers that it has power to make and which it otherwise intends to make; and

(b)   the adverse effect on competition, and any detrimental effect on customers so far as resulting from the adverse effect on competition, which the OFT has identified.

(4)   The OFT shall not accept the undertaking with modifications unless it—

(a)   publishes notice of the proposed modifications; and

(b)   considers any representations made in accordance with the notice and not withdrawn.

(5)   A notice under subsection (4) shall state—

(a)   the proposed modifications;

(b)   the reasons for them; and

(c)   the period (not less than 7 days starting with the date of the publication of the notice under subsection (4)) within which representations may be made in relation to the proposed modifications.

(6)   If, after publishing notice under subsection (1) or (4), the OFT decides—

(a)   not to accept the undertaking concerned; and

(b)   not to proceed by virtue of subsection (8) or (9);

it shall publish notice of that decision.

(7)   As soon as practicable after accepting an undertaking to which this section applies, the OFT shall—

(a)   serve a copy of the undertaking on any person by whom it is given; and

(b)   publish the undertaking.

(8)   The requirements of subsection (4) (and those of subsection (1)) shall not apply if the OFT—

(a)   has already published notice under subsection (1) but not subsection (4) in relation to the proposed undertaking; and

(b)   considers that the modifications which are now being proposed are not material in any respect.

(9)   The requirements of subsection (4) (and those of subsection (1)) shall not apply if the OFT—

(a)   has already published notice under subsections (1) and (4) in relation to the matter concerned; and

(b)   considers that the further modifications which are now being proposed do not differ in any material respect from the modifications in relation to which notice was last given under subsection (4).

(10) Paragraphs 6 to 8 (but not paragraph 9) of Schedule 10 (procedural requirements before terminating undertakings) shall apply in relation to the proposed release of undertakings under section 154 (other than in connection with accepting an undertaking under that section which varies or supersedes an undertaking under that section) as they apply in relation to the proposed release of undertakings under section 73.

156.   Effect of undertakings under section 154

(1)   No market investigation reference shall be made by the OFT or the appropriate Minister in relation to any feature, or combination of features, of a market in the United Kingdom for goods or services if—

(a)   the OFT has accepted an undertaking or group of undertakings under section 154 within the previous 12 months; and

(b)   the goods or services to which the undertaking or group of undertakings relates are of the same description as the goods or services to which the feature, or combination of features, relates.

(2)   Subsection (1) does not prevent the making of a market investigation reference if—

(a)   the OFT considers that any undertaking concerned has been breached and has given notice of that fact to the person responsible for giving the undertaking; or

(b)   the person responsible for giving any undertaking concerned supplied, in connection with the matter, information to the OFT which was false or misleading in a material respect.

157.   Interim undertakings: Part 4

(1)   Subsection (2) applies where—

      (a)   a market investigation reference has been made;

      (b)   a report has been published under section 136 within the period permitted by section 137 or (as the case may be) a report prepared under section 142 and given to the Secretary of State under section 143(3) within the period permitted by section 144 has been published; and

      (c)   the market investigation reference concerned is not finally determined.

(2)   The relevant authority may, for the purpose of preventing pre-emptive action, accept, from such persons as the relevant authority considers appropriate, undertakings to take such action as the relevant authority considers appropriate.

(3)   An undertaking under this section—

      (a)   shall come into force when accepted;

      (b)   may be varied or superseded by another undertaking; and

      (c)   may be released by the relevant authority.

(4)   An undertaking under this section shall, if it has not previously ceased to be in force, cease to be in force when the market investigation reference is finally determined.

(5)   The relevant authority shall, as soon as reasonably practicable, consider any representations received by the relevant authority in relation to varying or releasing an undertaking under this section.

(6)   In this section and section 158—

      "pre-emptive action" means action which might impede the taking of any action under section 138(2) or (as the case may be) 147(2) in relation to the market investigation reference concerned; and

      "the relevant authority" means—

      (a)   where an intervention notice is in force in relation to the market investigation reference, the Secretary of State;

      (b)   in any other case, the Commission.

158.   **Interim orders: Part 4**

(1)   Subsection (2) applies where—

      (a)   a market investigation reference has been made;

      (b)   a report has been published under section 136 within the period permitted by section 137 or (as the case may be) a report prepared under section 142 and given to the Secretary of State under section 143(3) within the period permitted by section 144 has been published; and

      (c)   the market investigation reference concerned is not finally determined.

(2)   The relevant authority may by order, for the purpose of preventing pre-emptive action—

      (a)   prohibit or restrict the doing of things which the relevant authority considers would constitute pre-emptive action;

      (b)   impose on any person concerned obligations as to the carrying on of any activities or the safeguarding of any assets;

      (c)   provide for the carrying on of any activities or the safeguarding of any assets either by the appointment of a person to conduct or supervise the conduct of any activities (on such terms and with such powers as may be specified or described in the order) or in any other manner;

      (d)   do anything which may be done by virtue of paragraph 19 of Schedule 8.

(3)   An order under this section—

      (a)   shall come into force at such time as is determined by or under the order; and

      (b)   may be varied or revoked by another order.

(4)   An order under this section shall, if it has not previously ceased to be in force, cease to be in force when the market investigation reference is finally determined.

(5)   The relevant authority shall, as soon as reasonably practicable, consider any representations received by the relevant authority in relation to varying or revoking an order under this section.

159.   **Final undertakings: Part 4**

(1)   The Commission may, in accordance with section 138, accept, from such persons as it considers appropriate, undertakings to take action specified or described in the undertakings.

(2)   The Secretary of State may, in accordance with section 147, accept, from such persons as he considers appropriate, undertakings to take action specified or described in the undertakings.

(3)   An undertaking under this section shall come into force when accepted.

(4)   An undertaking under subsection (1) or (2) may be varied or superseded by another undertaking under that subsection.

(5)   An undertaking under subsection (1) may be released by the Commission and an undertaking under subsection (2) may be released by the Secretary of State.

(6)   The Commission or (as the case may be) the Secretary of State shall, as soon as reasonably practicable, consider any representations received by it or (as the case may be) him in relation to varying or releasing an undertaking under this section.

160.   Order-making power where final undertakings not fulfilled: Part 4

(1)   Subsection (2) applies where the relevant authority considers that—

    (a)   an undertaking accepted by the relevant authority under section 159 has not been, is not being or will not be fulfilled; or

    (b)   in relation to an undertaking accepted by the relevant authority under that section, information which was false or misleading in a material respect was given to the relevant authority or the OFT by the person giving the undertaking before the relevant authority decided to accept the undertaking.

(2)   The relevant authority may, for any of the purposes mentioned in section 138(2) or (as the case may be) 147(2), make an order under this section.

(3)   Subsections (3) to (6) of section 138 or (as the case may be) 147 shall apply for the purposes of subsection (2) above as they apply for the purposes of that section.

(4)   An order under this section may contain—

    (a)   anything permitted by Schedule 8; and

    (b)   such supplementary, consequential or incidental provision as the relevant authority considers appropriate.

(5)   An order under this section—

    (a)   shall come into force at such time as is determined by or under the order;

    (b)   may contain provision which is different from the provision contained in the undertaking concerned; and

    (c)   may be varied or revoked by another order.

(6)   No order shall be varied or revoked under this section unless the OFT advises that such a variation or revocation is appropriate by reason of a change of circumstances.

(7)   In this section "the relevant authority" means—

    (a)   in the case of an undertaking accepted under section 159 by the Commission, the Commission; and

    (b)   in the case of an undertaking accepted under that section by the Secretary of State, the Secretary of State.

161.   Final orders: Part 4

(1)   The Commission may, in accordance with section 138, make an order under this section.

(2)   The Secretary of State may, in accordance with section 147, make an order under this section.

(3)   An order under this section may contain—

    (a)   anything permitted by Schedule 8; and

    (b)   such supplementary, consequential or incidental provision as the person making it considers appropriate.

(4)   An order under this section—

    (a)   shall come into force at such time as is determined by or under the order; and

    (b)   may be varied or revoked by another order.

(5)   No order shall be varied or revoked under this section unless the OFT advises that such a variation or revocation is appropriate by reason of a change of circumstances.

Enforcement functions of OFT

162. Duty of OFT to monitor undertakings and orders: Part 4

(1)   The OFT shall keep under review the carrying out of any enforcement undertaking or any enforcement order.

(2)   The OFT shall, in particular, from time to time consider—

(a)   whether an enforcement undertaking or enforcement order has been or is being complied with;

(b)   whether, by reason of any change of circumstances, an enforcement undertaking is no longer appropriate and—

(i)   one or more of the parties to it can be released from it; or

(ii)   it needs to be varied or to be superseded by a new enforcement undertaking; and

(c)   whether, by reason of any change of circumstances, an enforcement order is no longer appropriate and needs to be varied or revoked.

(3)   The OFT shall give the Commission or (as the case may be) the Secretary of State such advice as it considers appropriate in relation to—

(a)   any possible variation or release by the Commission or (as the case may be) the Secretary of State of an enforcement undertaking accepted by it or (as the case may be) him;

(b)   any possible new enforcement undertaking to be accepted by the Commission or (as the case may be) the Secretary of State so as to supersede another enforcement undertaking given to the Commission or (as the case may be) the Secretary of State;

(c)   any possible variation or revocation by the Commission or (as the case may be) the Secretary of State of an enforcement order made by the Commission or (as the case may be) the Secretary of State;

(d)   any possible enforcement undertaking to be accepted by the Commission or (as the case may be) the Secretary of State instead of an enforcement order or any possible enforcement order to be made by the Commission or (as the case may be) the Secretary of State instead of an enforcement undertaking; or

(e)   the enforcement by virtue of section 167(6) to (8) of any enforcement undertaking or enforcement order.

(4)   The OFT shall take such action as it considers appropriate in relation to—

(a)   any possible variation or release by it of an undertaking accepted by it under section 154;

(b)   any possible new undertaking to be accepted by it under section 154 so as to supersede another undertaking given to it under that section; or

(c)   the enforcement by it by virtue of section 167(6) of any enforcement undertaking or enforcement order.

(5)   The OFT shall keep under review the effectiveness of enforcement undertakings accepted under this Part and enforcement orders made under this Part.

(6)   The OFT shall, whenever requested to do so by the Secretary of State and otherwise from time to time, prepare a report of its findings under subsection (5).

(7)   The OFT shall—

(a)   give any report prepared by it under subsection (6) to the Commission;

(b)   give a copy of the report to the Secretary of State; and

(c)   publish the report.

(8)   In this Part—

"enforcement order" means an order made under section 158, 160 or 161; and

"enforcement undertaking" means an undertaking accepted under section 154, 157 or 159.

163. Further role of OFT in relation to undertakings and orders: Part 4

(1)   Subsections (2) and (3) apply where the Commission or the Secretary of State (in this section "the relevant authority") is considering whether to accept undertakings under section 157 or 159.

(2)   The relevant authority may require the OFT to consult with such persons as the relevant authority considers appropriate with a view to discovering whether they will offer undertakings which the relevant authority would be prepared to accept under section 157 or (as the case may be) 159.

(3)   The relevant authority may require the OFT to report to the relevant authority on the outcome of the OFT's consultations within such period as the relevant authority may require.

(4)   A report under subsection (3) shall, in particular, contain advice from the OFT as to whether any undertakings offered should be accepted by the relevant authority under section 157 or (as the case may be) 159.

(5)   The powers conferred on the relevant authority by subsections (1) to (4) are without prejudice to the power of the relevant authority to consult the persons concerned itself.

(6)   If asked by the relevant authority for advice in relation to the taking of enforcement action (whether or not by way of undertakings) in a particular case, the OFT shall give such advice as it considers appropriate.

Supplementary

164.   Enforcement undertakings and orders under this Part: general provisions

(1)   The provision which may be contained in an enforcement undertaking is not limited to the provision which is permitted by Schedule 8.

(2)   The following enactments in Part 3 shall apply in relation to enforcement orders under this Part as they apply in relation to enforcement orders under that Part—
        (a)   section 86(1) to (5) (enforcement orders: general provisions); and
        (b)   section 87 (power of directions conferred by enforcement order).

(3)   An enforcement order under section 160 or 161 or any explanatory material accompanying the order shall state—
        (a)   the actions that the persons or description of persons to whom the order is addressed must do or (as the case may be) refrain from doing;
        (b)   the date on which the order comes into force;
        (c)   the possible consequences of not complying with the order; and
        (d)   the section of this Part under which a review can be sought in relation to the order.

165.   Procedural requirements for certain undertakings and orders: Part 4

        Schedule 10 (procedural requirements for certain undertakings and orders), other than paragraph 9 of that Schedule, shall apply in relation to undertakings under section 159 and orders under section 160 or 161 as it applies in relation to undertakings under section 82 and orders under section 83 or 84.

166.   Register of undertakings and orders: Part 4

(1)   The OFT shall compile and maintain a register for the purposes of this Part.

(2)   The register shall be kept in such form as the OFT considers appropriate.

(3)   The OFT shall ensure that the following matters are entered in the register—
        (a)   the provisions of any enforcement undertaking accepted by virtue of this Part (whether by the OFT, the Commission, the Secretary of State or a relevant sectoral regulator);
        (b)   the provisions of any enforcement order made by virtue of this Part (whether by the Commission, the Secretary of State or a relevant sectoral regulator); and
        (c)   the details of any variation, release or revocation of such an undertaking or order.

(4)   The duty in subsection (3) does not extend to anything of which the OFT is unaware.

(5)   The Commission, the Secretary of State and any relevant sectoral regulator shall inform the OFT of any matters which are to be included in the register by virtue of subsection (3) and which relate to enforcement undertakings accepted by them or enforcement orders made by them.

(6)   The OFT shall ensure that the contents of the register are available to the public—
        (a)   during (as a minimum) such hours as may be specified in an order made by the Secretary of State; and
        (b)   subject to such reasonable fees (if any) as the OFT may determine.

(7)   If requested by any person to do so and subject to such reasonable fees (if any) as the OFT may determine, the OFT shall supply the person concerned with a copy (certified to be true) of the register or of an extract from it.

167.   Rights to enforce undertakings and orders under this Part

(1)   This section applies to any enforcement undertaking or enforcement order.

(2)   Any person to whom such an undertaking or order relates shall have a duty to comply with it.

(3)   The duty shall be owed to any person who may be affected by a contravention of the undertaking or (as the case may be) order.

(4)   Any breach of the duty which causes such a person to sustain loss or damage shall be actionable by him.

(5)   In any proceedings brought under subsection (4) against a person to whom an enforcement undertaking or enforcement order relates it shall be a defence for that person to show that he took all reasonable steps and exercised all due diligence to avoid contravening the undertaking or (as the case may be) order.

(6)   Compliance with an enforcement undertaking or an enforcement order shall also be enforceable by civil proceedings brought by the OFT for an injunction or for interdict or for any other appropriate relief or remedy.

(7)   Compliance with an undertaking accepted under section 157 or 159, or an order under section 158, 160 or 161, shall also be enforceable by civil proceedings brought by the relevant authority for an injunction or for interdict or for any other appropriate relief or remedy.

(8)   In subsection (7) "the relevant authority" means—

　　(a)   in the case of an undertaking accepted by the Commission or an order made by the Commission, the Commission; and

　　(b)   in the case of an undertaking accepted by the Secretary of State or an order made by the Secretary of State, the Secretary of State.

(9)   Subsections (6) to (8) shall not prejudice any right that a person may have by virtue of subsection (4) to bring civil proceedings for contravention or apprehended contravention of an enforcement undertaking or an enforcement order.

CHAPTER 4
SUPPLEMENTARY

Regulated markets

168.   Regulated markets

(1)   Subsection (2) applies where the Commission or the Secretary of State is considering for the purposes of this Part whether relevant action would be reasonable and practicable for the purpose of remedying, mitigating or preventing an adverse effect on competition or any detrimental effect on customers so far as resulting from such an effect.

(2)   The Commission or (as the case may be) the Secretary of State shall, in deciding whether such action would be reasonable and practicable, have regard to the relevant statutory functions of the sectoral regulator concerned.

(3)   In this section "relevant action" means—

　　(a)   ...

　　(b)   modifying conditions in force under Part 4 of the Airports Act 1986 (c. 31) other than any conditions imposed or modified in pursuance of section 40(3) or (4) of that Act;

　　(c)   modifying the conditions of a licence granted under section 7 or 7A of the Gas Act 1986 (c. 44);

　　(d)   modifying the conditions of a licence granted under section 6 of the Electricity Act 1989 (c. 29);

　　(e)   modifying networking arrangements (within the meaning given by section 290 of the Communications Act 2003);

   (f)   modifying the conditions of a company's appointment under Chapter 1 of Part 2 of the Water Industry Act 1991 (c. 56);

  (ff)   modifying the conditions of a licence granted under Chapter 1A of Part 2 of the Act of 1991 or modifying the terms and conditions of an agreement under section 66D of that Act;

   (g)   modifying the conditions of a licence granted under article 10 of the Electricity (Northern Ireland) Order 1992 (S.I. 1992/231 (N.I. 1));

   (h)   modifying the conditions of a licence granted under section 8 of the Railways Act 1993 (c. 43);

   (i)   modifying an access agreement (within the meaning given by section 83(1) of the Act of 1993) or a franchise agreement (within the meaning given by section 23(3) of that Act);

   (j)   modifying conditions in force under Part 4 of the Airports (Northern Ireland) Order 1994 (S.I. 1994/426 (N.I. 1)) other than any conditions imposed or modified in pursuance of article 40(3) or (4) of that Order;

   (k)   modifying the conditions of a licence granted under article 8 of the Gas (Northern Ireland) Order 1996 (S.I. 1996/275 (N.I. 2));

   (l)   modifying the conditions of a licence granted under section 11 of the Postal Services Act 2000 (c. 26); or

   (m)   modifying the conditions of a licence granted under section 5 of the Transport Act 2000 (c. 38).

(4)   In this section "relevant statutory functions" means—

   (a)   ...

   (b)   in relation to conditions in force under Part 4 of the Airports Act 1986 (c. 31) other than any conditions imposed or modified in pursuance of section 40(3) or (4) of that Act, the duties of the Civil Aviation Authority under section 39(2) and (3) of that Act;

   (c)   in relation to any licence granted under section 7 or 7A of the Gas Act 1986 (c. 44), the objectives and duties of the Gas and Electricity Markets Authority under section 4AA and 4AB(2) of that Act;

   (d)   in relation to any licence granted under section 6 of the Electricity Act 1989 (c. 29), the objectives and duties of the Gas and Electricity Markets Authority under section 3A and 3B(2) of that Act;

   (e)   in relation to any networking arrangements (within the meaning given by section 290 of the Communications Act 2003), the duty of the Office of Communications under subsection (1) of section 3 of that Act to secure the matters mentioned in subsection (2)(c) of that section;

   (f)   in relation to a company's appointment under Chapter 1 of Part 2 of the Water Industry Act 1991 (c. 56), the duties of the *Director General of Water Services [the Water Services Regulation Authority]* under section 2 of that Act;

  (ff)   in relation to a licence granted under Chapter 1A of Part 2 of the Act of 1991 or an agreement under section 66D of that Act, the duties of the Authority under section 2 of that Act or under that section and section 66D of that Act (as the case may be);

   (g)   in relation to any licence granted under article 10 of the Electricity (Northern Ireland) Order 1992 (S.I. 1992/231 (N.I. 1)), the duty of the Director General of Electricity Supply for Northern Ireland under article 6 of that Order;

   (h)   in relation to any licence granted under section 8 of the Railways Act 1993 (c. 43) where none of the conditions of the licence relate to consumer protection, the duties of the Office of Rail Regulation under section 4 of that Act;

   (i)   in relation to any licence granted under section 8 of the Act of 1993 where one or more than one condition of the licence relates to consumer protection, the duties of the the Office of Rail Regulation under section 4 of that Act and the duties of the Strategic Rail Authority under section 207 of the Transport Act 2000 (c. 38);

   (j)   in relation to any access agreement (within the meaning given by section 83(1) of the Act of 1993), the duties of the the Office of Rail Regulation under section 4 of the Act of 1993;

(k)   in relation to any franchise agreement (within the meaning given by section 23(3) of the Act of 1993), the duties of the Strategic Rail Authority under section 207 of the Act of 2000;

(l)   in relation to conditions in force under Part 4 of the Airports (Northern Ireland) Order 1994 (S.I. 1994/426 (N.I. 1)) other than any conditions imposed or modified in pursuance of article 40(3) or (4) of that Order, the duties of the Civil Aviation Authority under article 30(2) and (3) of that Order;

(m)   in relation to any licence granted under article 8 of the Gas (Northern Ireland) Order 1996 (S.I. 1996/275 (N.I. 2)), the duties of the Director General of Gas for Northern Ireland under article 5 of that Order;

(n)   in relation to any licence granted under section 11 of the Postal Services Act 2000 (c. 26), the duties of the Postal Services Commission under sections 3 and 5 of that Act; and

(o)   in relation to any licence granted under section 5 of the Transport Act 2000, the duties of the Civil Aviation Authority under section 87 of that Act.

(5)   In this section "sectoral regulator" means—
(a)   the Civil Aviation Authority;
(b)   the Director General of Electricity Supply for Northern Ireland;
(c)   the Director General of Gas for Northern Ireland;
(d)   ...
(e)   the Director General of Water Services;
[(e) the Water Services Regulation Authority;]
(f)   the Gas and Electricity Markets Authority;
(g)   the Office of Communications;
(h)   the Postal Services Commission;
(i)   the Office of Rail Regulation; or
(j)   the Strategic Rail Authority.

(6)   Subsection (7) applies where the Commission or the Secretary of State is considering for the purposes of this Part whether modifying the conditions of a licence granted under section 7 or 7A of the Gas Act 1986 (c. 44) or section 6 of the Electricity Act 1989 (c. 29) would be reasonable and practicable for the purpose of remedying, mitigating or preventing an adverse effect on competition or any detrimental effect on customers so far as resulting from such an effect.

(7)   The Commission or (as the case may be) the Secretary of State may, in deciding whether modifying the conditions of such a licence would be reasonable and practicable, have regard to those matters to which the Gas and Electricity Markets Authority may have regard by virtue of section 4AA(4) of the Act of 1986 or (as the case may be) section 3A(4) of the Act of 1989.

(8)   The Secretary of State may by order modify subsection (3), (4), (5), (6) or (7).

(9)   Part 2 of Schedule 9 (which makes provision for functions under this Part to be exercisable by various sectoral regulators) shall have effect.

Note. Subsections (3)(ff) and (4)(ff) are inserted, and subsection (5)(ee) and the italicized words in subsection (4)(f) are substituted by the words in square brackets following them, by the Water Act 2003, s. 101(1), Sch. 7, Pt. 2, para. 36, Sch. 8, para. 55, as from a day to be appointed.

Consultation, information and publicity

169.   Certain duties of relevant authorities to consult: Part 4

(1)   Subsection (2) applies where the relevant authority is proposing to make a relevant decision in a way which the relevant authority considers is likely to have a substantial impact on the interests of any person.

(2)   The relevant authority shall, so far as practicable, consult that person about what is proposed before making that decision.

(3)   In consulting the person concerned, the relevant authority shall, so far as practicable, give the reasons of the relevant authority for the proposed decision.

(4)   In considering what is practicable for the purposes of this section the relevant authority shall, in particular, have regard to—

(a) any restrictions imposed by any timetable for making the decision; and

(b) any need to keep what is proposed, or the reasons for it, confidential.

(5) The duty under this section shall not apply in relation to the making of any decision so far as particular provision is made elsewhere by virtue of this Part for consultation before the making of that decision.

(6) In this section—

"the relevant authority" means the OFT, the appropriate Minister or the Commission; and

"relevant decision" means—

(a) in the case of the OFT, any decision by the OFT—

(i) as to whether to make a reference under section 131 or accept undertakings under section 154 instead of making such a reference; or

(ii) to vary under section 135 such a reference;

(b) in the case of the appropriate Minister, any decision by the appropriate Minister—

(i) as to whether to make a reference under section 132; or

(ii) to vary under section 135 such a reference; and

(c) in the case of the Commission, any decision on the questions mentioned in section 134 or 141.

170. General information duties

(1) The OFT shall give the Commission—

(a) such information in its possession as the Commission may reasonably require to enable the Commission to carry out its functions under this Part; and

(b) any other assistance which the Commission may reasonably require for the purpose of assisting it in carrying out its functions under this Part and which it is within the power of the OFT to give.

(2) The OFT shall give the Commission any information in its possession which has not been requested by the Commission but which, in the opinion of the OFT, would be appropriate to give to the Commission for the purpose of assisting it in carrying out its functions under this Part.

(3) The OFT and the Commission shall give the Secretary of State or the appropriate Minister so far as he is not the Secretary of State acting alone—

(a) such information in their possession as the Secretary of State or (as the case may be) the appropriate Minister concerned may by direction reasonably require to enable him to carry out his functions under this Part; and

(b) any other assistance which the Secretary of State or (as the case may be) the appropriate Minister concerned may by direction reasonably require for the purpose of assisting him in carrying out his functions under this Part and which it is within the power of the OFT or (as the case may be) the Commission to give.

(4) The OFT shall give the Secretary of State or the appropriate Minister so far as he is not the Secretary of State acting alone any information in its possession which has not been requested by the Secretary of State or (as the case may be) the appropriate Minister concerned but which, in the opinion of the OFT, would be appropriate to give to the Secretary of State or (as the case may be) the appropriate Minister concerned for the purpose of assisting him in carrying out his functions under this Part.

(5) The Commission shall have regard to any information given to it under subsection (1) or (2); and the Secretary of State or (as the case may be) the appropriate Minister concerned shall have regard to any information given to him under subsection (3) or (4).

(6) Any direction given under subsection (3)—

(a) shall be in writing; and

(b) may be varied or revoked by a subsequent direction.

171. Advice and information: Part 4

(1) As soon as reasonably practicable after the passing of this Act, the OFT shall prepare and publish general advice and information about the making of references by it under section 131.

(2)   The OFT may at any time publish revised, or new, advice or information.

(3)   As soon as reasonably practicable after the passing of this Act, the Commission shall prepare and publish general advice and information about the consideration by it of market investigation references and the way in which relevant customer benefits may affect the taking of enforcement action in relation to such references.

(4)   The Commission may at any time publish revised, or new, advice or information.

(5)   Advice and information published under this section shall be prepared with a view to—

    (a)   explaining relevant provisions of this Part to persons who are likely to be affected by them; and

    (b)   indicating how the OFT or (as the case may be) the Commission expects such provisions to operate.

(6)   Advice and information published by virtue of subsection (1) or (3) shall include such advice and information about the effect of Community law, and anything done under or in accordance with it, on the provisions of this Part as the OFT or (as the case may be) the Commission considers appropriate.

(7)   Advice (or information) published by virtue of subsection (1) or (3) may include advice (or information) about the factors which the OFT or (as the case may be) the Commission may take into account in considering whether, and if so how, to exercise a function conferred by this Part.

(8)   Any advice or information published by the OFT or the Commission under this section shall be published in such manner as the OFT or (as the case may be) the Commission considers appropriate.

(9)   In preparing any advice or information under this section, the OFT shall consult the Commission and such other persons as it considers appropriate.

(10)   In preparing any advice or information under this section, the Commission shall consult the OFT and such other persons as it considers appropriate.

(11)   In this section "Community law" means—

    (a)   all the rights, powers, liabilities, obligations and restrictions from time to time created or arising by or under the Community Treaties; and

    (b)   all the remedies and procedures from time to time provided for by or under the Community Treaties.

172.   Further publicity requirements: Part 4

(1)   The OFT shall publish—

    (a)   any reference made by it under section 131;

    (b)   any variation made by it under section 135 of a reference under section 131;

    (c)   any decision of a kind mentioned in section 149(5)(b); and

    (d)   such information as it considers appropriate about any decision made by it under section 152(1) to bring a case to the attention of the Secretary of State.

(2)   The Commission shall publish—

    (a)   any decision made by it under section 138(2) neither to accept an undertaking under section 159 nor to make an order under section 161;

    (b)   any decision made by it that there has been a material change of circumstances as mentioned in section 138(3) or there is another special reason as mentioned in that section;

    (c)   any termination under section 145(1) of an investigation by it;

    (d)   such information as it considers appropriate about any decision made by it under section 152(2) to bring a case to the attention of the Secretary of State;

    (e)   any enforcement undertaking accepted by it under section 157;

    (f)   any enforcement order made by it under section 158; and

    (g)   any variation, release or revocation of such an undertaking or order.

(3)   The Secretary of State shall publish—

    (a)   any reference made by him under section 132;

    (b)   any variation made by him under section 135 of a reference under section 132;

    (c)   any intervention notice given by him;

(d)   any decision made by him to revoke such a notice;

(e)   any decision made by him under section 147(2) neither to accept an undertaking under section 159 nor to make an order under section 161;

(f)   any enforcement undertaking accepted by him under section 157;

(g)   any variation or release of such an undertaking; and

(h)   any direction given by him under section 170(3) in connection with the exercise by him of his functions under section 132(3).

(4)   The appropriate Minister (other than the Secretary of State acting alone) shall publish—

(a)   any reference made by him under section 132;

(b)   any variation made by him under section 135 of a reference under section 132; and

(c)   any direction given by him under section 170(3) in connection with the exercise by him of his functions under section 132(3).

(5)   Where any person is under an obligation by virtue of subsection (1), (2), (3) or (4) to publish the result of any action taken by that person or any decision made by that person, the person concerned shall, subject to subsections (6) and (7), also publish that person's reasons for the action concerned or (as the case may be) the decision concerned.

(6)   Such reasons need not, if it is not reasonably practicable to do so, be published at the same time as the result of the action concerned or (as the case may be) as the decision concerned.

(7)   Subsections (5) and (6) shall not apply in relation to any case falling within subsection (1)(d) or (2)(d).

(8)   The Secretary of State shall publish his reasons for—

(a)   any decision made by him under section 146(2); or

(b)   any decision to make an order under section 153(3) or vary or revoke such an order.

(9)   Such reasons may be published after—

(a)   in the case of subsection (8)(a), the publication of the decision concerned; and

(b)   in the case of subsection (8)(b), the making of the order or of the variation or revocation;

if it is not reasonably practicable to publish them at the same time as the publication of the decision or (as the case may be) the making of the order or variation or revocation.

(10)   Where the Secretary of State has decided under section 147(2) to accept an undertaking under section 159 or to make an order under section 161, he shall (after the acceptance of the undertaking or (as the case may be) the making of the order) lay details of his decision and his reasons for it, and the Commission's report under section 142, before each House of Parliament.

173.   Defamation: Part 4

For the purposes of the law relating to defamation, absolute privilege attaches to any advice, guidance, notice or direction given, or decision or report made, by the OFT, by the Secretary of State, by the appropriate Minister (other than the Secretary of State acting alone) or by the Commission in the exercise of any of their functions under this Part.

Investigation powers

174.   Investigation powers of OFT

(1)   The OFT may exercise any of the powers in subsections (3) to (5) for the purpose of assisting it in deciding whether to make a reference under section 131 or to accept undertakings under section 154 instead of making such a reference.

(2)   The OFT shall not exercise any of the powers in subsections (3) to (5) for the purpose of assisting it as mentioned in subsection (1) unless it already believes that it has power to make such a reference.

(3)   The OFT may give notice to any person requiring him—

(a)   to attend at a time and place specified in the notice; and

(b)   to give evidence to the OFT or a person nominated by the OFT for the purpose.

(4)   The OFT may give notice to any person requiring him—

(a)   to produce any documents which—

   (i)   are specified or described in the notice, or fall within a category of document which is
         specified or described in the notice; and
   (ii) are in that person's custody or under his control; and
   (b)   to produce them at a time and place so specified and to a person so specified.

(5)   The OFT may give notice to any person who carries on any business requiring him—
   (a)   to supply to the OFT such estimates, forecasts, returns or other information as may be
         specified or described in the notice; and
   (b)   to supply it at a time and place, and in a form and manner, so specified and to a person so
         specified.

(6)   A notice under this section shall include information about the possible consequences of not
      complying with the notice.

(7)   The person to whom any document is produced in accordance with a notice under this section
      may, for the purpose mentioned in subsection (1), copy the document so produced.

(8)   No person shall be required under this section—
   (a)   to give any evidence or produce any documents which he could not be compelled to give or
         produce in civil proceedings before the court; or
   (b)   to supply any information which he could not be compelled to supply in evidence in such
         proceedings.

(9)   No person shall be required, in compliance with a notice under this section, to go more than 10
      miles from his place of residence unless his necessary travelling expenses are paid or offered to
      him.

(10) Any reference in this section to the production of a document includes a reference to the
      production of a legible and intelligible copy of information recorded otherwise than in legible
      form.

(11) In this section "the court" means—
   (a)   in relation to England and Wales or Northern Ireland, the High Court; and
   (b)   in relation to Scotland, the Court of Session.

175.   Enforcement of powers under section 174: offences

(1)   A person commits an offence if he, intentionally and without reasonable excuse, fails to comply
      with any requirement of a notice under section 174.

(2)   A person commits an offence if he intentionally and without reasonable excuse alters, suppresses
      or destroys any document which he has been required to produce by a notice under section 174.

(3)   A person who commits an offence under subsection (1) or (2) shall be liable—
   (a)   on summary conviction, to a fine not exceeding the statutory maximum;
   (b)   on conviction on indictment, to imprisonment for a term not exceeding two years or to a fine
         or to both.

(4)   A person commits an offence if he intentionally obstructs or delays—
   (a)   the OFT in the exercise of its powers under section 174; or
   (b)   any person in the exercise of his powers under subsection (7) of that section.

(5)   A person who commits an offence under subsection (4) shall be liable—
   (a)   on summary conviction, to a fine not exceeding the statutory maximum;
   (b)   on conviction on indictment, to a fine.

176.   Investigation powers of the Commission

(1)   The following sections in Part 3 shall apply, with the modifications mentioned in subsections (2)
      and (3) below, for the purposes of references under this Part as they apply for the purposes of
      references under that Part—
   (a)   section 109 (attendance of witnesses and production of documents etc.);
   (b)   section 110 (enforcement of powers under section 109: general);
   (c)   section 111 (penalties);
   (d)   section 112 (penalties: main procedural requirements);
   (e)   section 113 (payments and interest by instalments);

(f)   section 114 (appeals in relation to penalties);

(g)   section 115 (recovery of penalties); and

(h)   section 116 (statement of policy).

(2)   Section 110 shall, in its application by virtue of subsection (1) above, have effect as if—

(a)   subsection (2) were omitted; and

(b)   in subsection (9) the words from "or section" to "section 65(3))" were omitted.

(3)   Section 111(5)(b)(ii) shall, in its application by virtue of subsection (1) above, have effect as if—

(a)   for the words "section 50 or 65, given" there were substituted "section 142, published or given under section 143(1) or (3)"; and

(b)   for the words "(or given)", in both places where they appear, there were substituted "(or published or given)".

Reports

177.   Excisions from reports: Part 4

(1)   Subsection (2) applies where the Secretary of State is under a duty to publish a report of the Commission under section 142.

(2)   The Secretary of State may exclude a matter from the report if he considers that publication of the matter would be inappropriate.

(3)   In deciding what is inappropriate for the purposes of subsection (2) the Secretary of State shall have regard to the considerations mentioned in section 244.

(4)   The Commission shall advise the Secretary of State as to the matters (if any) which it considers should be excluded by him under subsection (2).

(5)   References in sections 136(4) to (6), 143(2) and (5) to (7), 148(3) to (5) and 172(10) to the giving or laying of a report of the Commission shall be construed as references to the giving or laying of the report as published.

178.   Minority reports of Commission: Part 4

(1)   Subsection (2) applies where, on a market investigation reference, a member of a group constituted in connection with the reference in pursuance of paragraph 15 of Schedule 7 to the Competition Act 1998 (c. 41), disagrees with any decisions contained in the report of the Commission under this Part as the decisions of the Commission.

(2)   The report shall, if the member so wishes, include a statement of his disagreement and of his reasons for disagreeing.

Other

179.   Review of decisions under Part 4

(1)   Any person aggrieved by a decision of the OFT, the appropriate Minister, the Secretary of State or the Commission in connection with a reference or possible reference under this Part may apply to the Competition Appeal Tribunal for a review of that decision.

(2)   For this purpose "decision"—

(a)   does not include a decision to impose a penalty under section 110(1) or (3) as applied by section 176; but

(b)   includes a failure to take a decision permitted or required by this Part in connection with a reference or possible reference.

(3)   Except in so far as a direction to the contrary is given by the Competition Appeal Tribunal, the effect of the decision is not suspended by reason of the making of the application.

(4)   In determining such an application the Competition Appeal Tribunal shall apply the same principles as would be applied by a court on an application for judicial review.

(5)   The Competition Appeal Tribunal may—

(a)   dismiss the application or quash the whole or part of the decision to which it relates; and

(b)   where it quashes the whole or part of that decision, refer the matter back to the original decision maker with a direction to reconsider and make a new decision in accordance with the ruling of the Competition Appeal Tribunal.

(6)   An appeal lies on any point of law arising from a decision of the Competition Appeal Tribunal under this section to the appropriate court.

(7)   An appeal under subsection (6) requires the permission of the Tribunal or the appropriate court.

(8)   In this section—

"the appropriate court" means the Court of Appeal or, in the case of Tribunal proceedings in Scotland, the Court of Session; and

"Tribunal rules" has the meaning given by section 15(1).

180.   Offences

(1)   Sections 117 (false or misleading information) and 125 (offences by bodies corporate) shall apply, with the modifications mentioned in subsection (2) below, for the purposes of this Part as they apply for the purposes of Part 3.

(2)   Section 117 shall, in its application by virtue of subsection (1) above, have effect as if references to the Secretary of State included references to the appropriate Minister so far as he is not the Secretary of State acting alone and as if the references to OFCOM were omitted.

181.   Orders under Part 4

(1)   Any power of the Secretary of State to make an order under this Part shall be exercisable by statutory instrument.

(2)   Any power of the Secretary of State to make an order under this Part—
(a)   may be exercised so as to make different provision for different cases or different purposes;
(b)   includes power to make such incidental, supplementary, consequential, transitory, transitional or saving provision as the Secretary of State considers appropriate.

(3)   The power of the Secretary of State under section 136(9), 137(3), 144(2), 153(3) or 168(8) as extended by subsection (2) above may be exercised by modifying any enactment comprised in or made under this Act, or any other enactment.

(4)   An order made by the Secretary of State under section 137(3), 144(2), 158, 160 or 161, or under section 111(4) or (6) or 114(3)(b) or (4)(b) as applied by section 176, shall be subject to annulment in pursuance of a resolution of either House of Parliament.

(5)   No order shall be made by the Secretary of State under section 136(9) or 168(8), or section 128(6) as applied by section 183(2), unless a draft of it has been laid before, and approved by a resolution of, each House of Parliament.

(6)   An order made by the Secretary of State under section 153(3) shall be laid before Parliament after being made and shall cease to have effect unless approved, within the period of 28 days beginning with the day on which it is made, by a resolution of each House of Parliament.

(7)   In calculating the period of 28 days mentioned in subsection (6), no account shall be taken of any time during which Parliament is dissolved or prorogued or during which both Houses are adjourned for more than four days.

(8)   If an order made by the Secretary of State ceases to have effect by virtue of subsection (6), any modification made by it of an enactment is repealed (and the previous enactment revived) but without prejudice to the validity of anything done in connection with that modification before the order ceased to have effect and without prejudice to the making of a new order.

(9)   If, apart from this subsection, an order made by the Secretary of State under section 153(3) would be treated for the purposes of the standing orders of either House of Parliament as a hybrid instrument, it shall proceed in that House as if it were not such an instrument.

(10)   References in this section to an order made under this Part include references to an order made under section 111(4) or (6) or 114(3)(b) or (4)(b) as applied by section 176 and an order made under section 128(6) as applied by section 183(2).

182.   Service of documents: Part 4

Section 126 shall apply for the purposes of this Part as it applies for the purposes of Part 3.

183.   Interpretation: Part 4

(1)   In this Part, unless the context otherwise requires—

"action" includes omission; and references to the taking of action include references to refraining from action;

"business" includes a professional practice and includes any other undertaking which is carried on for gain or reward or which is an undertaking in the course of which goods or services are supplied otherwise than free of charge;

"change of circumstances" includes any discovery that information has been supplied which is false or misleading in a material respect;

"consumer" means any person who is—

(a)   a person to whom goods are or are sought to be supplied (whether by way of sale or otherwise) in the course of a business carried on by the person supplying or seeking to supply them; or

(b)   a person for whom services are or are sought to be supplied in the course of a business carried on by the person supplying or seeking to supply them;

and who does not receive or seek to receive the goods or services in the course of a business carried on by him;

"customer" includes a customer who is not a consumer;

"enactment" includes an Act of the Scottish Parliament, Northern Ireland legislation and an enactment comprised in subordinate legislation, and includes an enactment whenever passed or made;

"goods" includes buildings and other structures, and also includes ships, aircraft and hovercraft;

"Minister of the Crown" means the holder of an office in Her Majesty's Government in the United Kingdom and includes the Treasury;

"modify" includes amend or repeal;

"notice" means notice in writing;

"subordinate legislation" has the same meaning as in the Interpretation Act 1978 (c. 30) and also includes an instrument made under an Act of the Scottish Parliament and an instrument made under Northern Ireland legislation; and

"supply", in relation to the supply of goods, includes supply by way of sale, lease, hire or hire-purchase, and, in relation to buildings or other structures, includes the construction of them by a person for another person.

(2)   Sections 127(1)(b) and (4) to (6) and 128 shall apply for the purposes of this Part as they apply for the purposes of Part 3.

(3)   For the purposes of this Part a market investigation reference is finally determined if—

(a)   where no intervention notice under section 139(1) has been given in relation to it—

(i)   the period permitted by section 137 for preparing and publishing a report under section 136 has expired and no such report has been prepared and published;

(ii)   such a report has been prepared and published within the period permitted by section 137 and contains the decision that there is no adverse effect on competition;

(iii)   the Commission has decided under section 138(2) neither to accept undertakings under section 159 nor to make an order under section 161; or

(iv)   the Commission has accepted an undertaking under section 159 or made an order under section 161;

(b)   where an intervention notice under section 139(1) has been given in relation to it—

(i)   the period permitted by section 144 for the preparation of the report of the Commission under section 142 and for action to be taken in relation to it under section 143(1) or (3) has expired while the intervention notice is still in force and no such report has been so prepared or no such action has been taken;

(ii)   the Commission has terminated under section 145(1) its investigation and the reference is finally determined under paragraph (a) above (disregarding the fact that the notice was given);

(iii)   the report of the Commission has been prepared under section 142 and published under section 143(1) within the period permitted by section 144;

(iv)   the intervention notice was revoked and the reference is finally determined under paragraph (a) above (disregarding the fact that the notice was given);

(v)   the Secretary of State has failed to make and publish a decision under subsection (2) of section 146 within the period permitted by subsection (3) of that section and the reference is finally determined under paragraph (a) above (disregarding the fact that the notice was given);

(vi)   the Secretary of State has decided under section 146(2) that no eligible public interest consideration is relevant and the reference is finally determined under paragraph (a) above (disregarding the fact that the notice was given);

(vii)   the Secretary of State has decided under 146(2) that a public interest consideration is relevant but has decided under section 147(2) neither to accept an undertaking under section 159 nor to make an order under section 161; or

(viii)   the Secretary of State has decided under section 146(2) that a public interest consideration is relevant and has accepted an undertaking under section 159 or made an order under section 161.

(4)   For the purposes of this Part the time when a market investigation reference is finally determined is—

(a)   in a case falling within subsection (3)(a)(i) or (b)(i), the expiry of the time concerned;

(b)   in a case falling within subsection (3)(a)(ii) or (b)(iii), the publication of the report;

(c)   in a case falling within subsection (3)(a)(iv) or (b)(viii), the acceptance of the undertaking concerned or (as the case may be) the making of the order concerned; and

(d)   in any other case, the making of the decision or last decision concerned or the taking of the action concerned.

(5)   The references in subsection (4) to subsections (3)(a)(i), (ii) and (iv) include those enactments as applied by subsection (3)(b)(ii), (iv), (v) or (vi).

(6)   In subsection (4)(c) the reference to the acceptance of the undertaking concerned or the making of the order concerned shall, in a case where the enforcement action concerned involves the acceptance of a group of undertakings, the making of a group of orders or the acceptance and making of a group of undertakings and orders, be treated as a reference to the acceptance or making of the last undertaking or order in the group; but undertakings or orders which vary, supersede or revoke earlier undertakings or orders shall be disregarded for the purposes of subsections (3)(a)(iv) and (b)(viii) and (4)(c).

(7)   Any duty to publish which is imposed on a person by this Part shall, unless the context otherwise requires, be construed as a duty on that person to publish in such manner as that person considers appropriate for the purpose of bringing the matter concerned to the attention of those likely to be affected by it.

184.   Index of defined expressions: Part 4

In this Part, the expressions listed in the left-hand column have the meaning given by, or are to be interpreted in accordance with, the provisions listed in the right-hand column.

Expression	*Provision of this Act*
Action (and the taking of action)	Section 183(1)
Adverse effect on competition	Section 134(2)
Appropriate Minister	Section 132(5)

Expression	*Provision of this Act*
Business	Section 183(1)
Change of circumstances	Section 183(1)
The Commission	Section 273
Consumer	Section 183(1)
Customer	Section 183(1)
Date of market investigation reference	Section 137(7)
Detrimental effect on customers	Section 134(5)
Enactment	Section 183(1)
Enforcement order	Section 162(8)
Enforcement undertaking	Section 162(8)
Feature of a market	Section 131(2)
Final determination of market investigation reference	Section 183(3) to (6)
Goods	Section 183(1)
Intervention notice	Section 139(3)
Market for goods or services	Section 131(6)
Market in the United Kingdom	Section 131(6)
Market investigation reference	Section 131(6)
Minister of the Crown	Section 183(1)
Modify	Section 183(1)
Notice	Section 183(1)
The OFT	Section 273
Public interest consideration	Section 139(5)
Public interest consideration being finalised	Section 139(7)
Publish	Section 183(7)
Relevant customer benefit	Section 134(8)
Relevant sectoral enactment	Section 136(7)
Relevant sectoral regulator	Section 136(8)
Reports of the Commission	Section 177(5)
Subordinate legislation	Section 183(1)
Supply (in relation to the supply of goods)	Section 183(1)
The supply of services (and a market for services etc.)	Section 183(2)

PART 5

THE COMPETITION COMMISSION

185. The Commission

Schedule 11 (which amends provisions relating to the constitution and powers of the Commission under Schedule 7 to the 1998 Act) has effect.

186, 187....

PART 6

CARTEL OFFENCE

Cartel offence

188. Cartel offence

(1) An individual is guilty of an offence if he dishonestly agrees with one or more other persons to make or implement, or to cause to be made or implemented, arrangements of the following kind relating to at least two undertakings (A and B).

(2) The arrangements must be ones which, if operating as the parties to the agreement intend, would—

     (a)   directly or indirectly fix a price for the supply by A in the United Kingdom (otherwise than to B) of a product or service,

     (b)   limit or prevent supply by A in the United Kingdom of a product or service,

     (c)   limit or prevent production by A in the United Kingdom of a product,

     (d)   divide between A and B the supply in the United Kingdom of a product or service to a customer or customers,

     (e)   divide between A and B customers for the supply in the United Kingdom of a product or service, or

     (f)   be bid-rigging arrangements.

(3)   Unless subsection (2)(d), (e) or (f) applies, the arrangements must also be ones which, if operating as the parties to the agreement intend, would—

     (a)   directly or indirectly fix a price for the supply by B in the United Kingdom (otherwise than to A) of a product or service,

     (b)   limit or prevent supply by B in the United Kingdom of a product or service, or

     (c)   limit or prevent production by B in the United Kingdom of a product.

(4)   In subsections (2)(a) to (d) and (3), references to supply or production are to supply or production in the appropriate circumstances (for which see section 189).

(5)   "Bid-rigging arrangements" are arrangements under which, in response to a request for bids for the supply of a product or service in the United Kingdom, or for the production of a product in the United Kingdom—

     (a)   A but not B may make a bid, or

     (b)   A and B may each make a bid but, in one case or both, only a bid arrived at in accordance with the arrangements.

(6)   But arrangements are not bid-rigging arrangements if, under them, the person requesting bids would be informed of them at or before the time when a bid is made.

(7)   "Undertaking" has the same meaning as in Part 1 of the 1998 Act.

189.   **Cartel offence: supplementary**

(1)   For section 188(2)(a), the appropriate circumstances are that A's supply of the product or service would be at a level in the supply chain at which the product or service would at the same time be supplied by B in the United Kingdom.

(2)   For section 188(2)(b), the appropriate circumstances are that A's supply of the product or service would be at a level in the supply chain—

     (a)   at which the product or service would at the same time be supplied by B in the United Kingdom, or

     (b)   at which supply by B in the United Kingdom of the product or service would be limited or prevented by the arrangements.

(3)   For section 188(2)(c), the appropriate circumstances are that A's production of the product would be at a level in the production chain—

     (a)   at which the product would at the same time be produced by B in the United Kingdom, or

     (b)   at which production by B in the United Kingdom of the product would be limited or prevented by the arrangements.

(4)   For section 188(2)(d), the appropriate circumstances are that A's supply of the product or service would be at the same level in the supply chain as B's.

(5)   For section 188(3)(a), the appropriate circumstances are that B's supply of the product or service would be at a level in the supply chain at which the product or service would at the same time be supplied by A in the United Kingdom.

(6)   For section 188(3)(b), the appropriate circumstances are that B's supply of the product or service would be at a level in the supply chain—

     (a)   at which the product or service would at the same time be supplied by A in the United Kingdom, or

     (b)   at which supply by A in the United Kingdom of the product or service would be limited or prevented by the arrangements.

(7)   For section 188(3)(c), the appropriate circumstances are that B's production of the product would be at a level in the production chain—

          (a)   at which the product would at the same time be produced by A in the United Kingdom, or

          (b)   at which production by A in the United Kingdom of the product would be limited or prevented by the arrangements.

190.   Cartel offence: penalty and prosecution

(1)   A person guilty of an offence under section 188 is liable—

          (a)   on conviction on indictment, to imprisonment for a term not exceeding five years or to a fine, or to both;

          (b)   on summary conviction, to imprisonment for a term not exceeding six months or to a fine not exceeding the statutory maximum, or to both.

(2)   In England and Wales and Northern Ireland, proceedings for an offence under section 188 may be instituted only—

          (a)   by the Director of the Serious Fraud Office, or

          (b)   by or with the consent of the OFT.

(3)   No proceedings may be brought for an offence under section 188 in respect of an agreement outside the United Kingdom, unless it has been implemented in whole or in part in the United Kingdom.

(4)   Where, for the purpose of the investigation or prosecution of offences under section 188, the OFT gives a person written notice under this subsection, no proceedings for an offence under section 188 that falls within a description specified in the notice may be brought against that person in England and Wales or Northern Ireland except in circumstances specified in the notice.

191.   ...

Criminal investigations by OFT

192.   Investigation of offences under section 188

(1)   The OFT may conduct an investigation if there are reasonable grounds for suspecting that an offence under section 188 has been committed.

(2)   The powers of the OFT under sections 193 and 194 are exercisable, but only for the purposes of an investigation under subsection (1), in any case where it appears to the OFT that there is good reason to exercise them for the purpose of investigating the affairs, or any aspect of the affairs, of any person ("the person under investigation").

193.   Powers when conducting an investigation

(1)   The OFT may by notice in writing require the person under investigation, or any other person who it has reason to believe has relevant information, to answer questions, or otherwise provide information, with respect to any matter relevant to the investigation at a specified place and either at a specified time or forthwith.

(2)   The OFT may by notice in writing require the person under investigation, or any other person, to produce, at a specified place and either at a specified time or forthwith, specified documents, or documents of a specified description, which appear to the OFT to relate to any matter relevant to the investigation.

(3)   If any such documents are produced, the OFT may—

          (a)   take copies or extracts from them;

          (b)   require the person producing them to provide an explanation of any of them.

(4)   If any such documents are not produced, the OFT may require the person who was required to produce them to state, to the best of his knowledge and belief, where they are.

(5)   A notice under subsection (1) or (2) must indicate—

          (a)   the subject matter and purpose of the investigation; and

          (b)   the nature of the offences created by section 201.

194. **Power to enter premises under a warrant**

(1)　On an application made by the OFT to the High Court, or, in Scotland, by the procurator fiscal to the sheriff, in accordance with rules of court, a judge or the sheriff may issue a warrant if he is satisfied that there are reasonable grounds for believing—

(a)　that there are on any premises documents which the OFT has power under section 193 to require to be produced for the purposes of an investigation; and

(b)　that—

(i)　a person has failed to comply with a requirement under that section to produce the documents;

(ii)　it is not practicable to serve a notice under that section in relation to them; or

(iii)　the service of such a notice in relation to them might seriously prejudice the investigation.

(2)　A warrant under this section shall authorise a named officer of the OFT, and any other officers of the OFT whom the OFT has authorised in writing to accompany the named officer—

(a)　to enter the premises, using such force as is reasonably necessary for the purpose;

(b)　to search the premises and—

(i)　take possession of any documents appearing to be of the relevant kind, or

(ii)　take, in relation to any documents appearing to be of the relevant kind, any other steps which may appear to be necessary for preserving them or preventing interference with them;

(c)　to require any person to provide an explanation of any document appearing to be of the relevant kind or to state, to the best of his knowledge and belief, where it may be found;

(d)　to require any information which is stored in any electronic form and is accessible from the premises and which the named officer considers relates to any matter relevant to the investigation, to be produced in a form—

(i)　in which it can be taken away, and

(ii)　in which it is visible and legible or from which it can readily be produced in a visible and legible form.

(3)　Documents are of the relevant kind if they are of a kind in respect of which the application under subsection (1) was granted.

(4)　A warrant under this section may authorise persons specified in the warrant to accompany the named officer who is executing it.

(5)　…

195. **Exercise of powers by authorised person**

(1)　The OFT may authorise any competent person who is not an officer of the OFT to exercise on its behalf all or any of the powers conferred by section 193 or 194.

(2)　No such authority may be granted except for the purpose of investigating the affairs, or any aspect of the affairs, of a person specified in the authority.

(3)　No person is bound to comply with any requirement imposed by a person exercising powers by virtue of any authority granted under this section unless he has, if required to do so, produced evidence of his authority.

196. **Privileged information etc.**

(1)　A person may not under section 193 or 194 be required to disclose any information or produce any document which he would be entitled to refuse to disclose or produce on grounds of legal professional privilege in proceedings in the High Court, except that a lawyer may be required to provide the name and address of his client.

(2)　A person may not under section 193 or 194 be required to disclose any information or produce any document in respect of which he owes an obligation of confidence by virtue of carrying on any banking business unless—

(a)　the person to whom the obligation of confidence is owed consents to the disclosure or production; or

(b)   the OFT has authorised the making of the requirement.

(3)   In the application of this section to Scotland, the reference in subsection (1)—

     (a)   to proceedings in the High Court is to be read as a reference to legal proceedings generally; and

     (b)   to an entitlement on grounds of legal professional privilege is to be read as a reference to an entitlement by virtue of any rule of law whereby—

         (i)   communications between a professional legal adviser and his client, or

         (ii)   communications made in connection with or in contemplation of legal proceedings and for the purposes of those proceedings,

are in such proceedings protected from disclosure on the ground of confidentiality.

197.   Restriction on use of statements in court

(1)   A statement by a person in response to a requirement imposed by virtue of section 193 or 194 may only be used in evidence against him—

     (a)   on a prosecution for an offence under section 201(2); or

     (b)   on a prosecution for some other offence where in giving evidence he makes a statement inconsistent with it.

(2)   However, the statement may not be used against that person by virtue of paragraph (b) of subsection (1) unless evidence relating to it is adduced, or a question relating to it is asked, by or on behalf of that person in the proceedings arising out of the prosecution.

198–200....

201.   Offences

(1)   Any person who without reasonable excuse fails to comply with a requirement imposed on him under section 193 or 194 is guilty of an offence and liable on summary conviction to imprisonment for a term not exceeding six months or to a fine not exceeding level 5 on the standard scale or to both.

(2)   A person who, in purported compliance with a requirement under section 193 or 194—

     (a)   makes a statement which he knows to be false or misleading in a material particular; or

     (b)   recklessly makes a statement which is false or misleading in a material particular,

is guilty of an offence.

(3)   A person guilty of an offence under subsection (2) is liable—

     (a)   on conviction on indictment, to imprisonment for a term not exceeding two years or to a fine or to both; and

     (b)   on summary conviction, to imprisonment for a term not exceeding six months or to a fine not exceeding the statutory maximum, or to both.

(4)   Where any person—

     (a)   knows or suspects that an investigation by the Serious Fraud Office or the OFT into an offence under section 188 is being or is likely to be carried out; and

     (b)   falsifies, conceals, destroys or otherwise disposes of, or causes or permits the falsification, concealment, destruction or disposal of documents which he knows or suspects are or would be relevant to such an investigation,

he is guilty of an offence unless he proves that he had no intention of concealing the facts disclosed by the documents from the persons carrying out such an investigation.

(5)   A person guilty of an offence under subsection (4) is liable—

     (a)   on conviction on indictment, to imprisonment for a term not exceeding 5 years or to a fine or to both; and

     (b)   on summary conviction, to imprisonment for a term not exceeding six months or to a fine not exceeding the statutory maximum, or to both.

(6)   A person who intentionally obstructs a person in the exercise of his powers under a warrant issued under section 194 is guilty of an offence and liable—

     (a)   on conviction on indictment, to imprisonment for a term not exceeding 2 years or to a fine or to both; and

(b) on summary conviction, to a fine not exceeding the statutory maximum.

202. Interpretation of sections 192 to 201

In sections 192 to 201—

"documents" includes information recorded in any form and, in relation to information recorded otherwise than in a form in which it is visible and legible, references to its production include references to producing it in a form in which it is visible and legible or from which it can readily be produced in a visible and legible form;

"person under investigation" has the meaning given in section 192(2).

PART 7
MISCELLANEOUS COMPETITION PROVISIONS

203, 204....

Miscellaneous

205. Super-complaints to regulators other than OFT

(1) The Secretary of State may by order provide that section 11 is to apply to complaints made to a specified regulator in relation to a market of a specified description as it applies to complaints made to the OFT, with such modifications as may be specified.

(2) An order under this section—

(a) shall be made by statutory instrument, and

(b) shall be subject to annulment in pursuance of a resolution of either House of Parliament.

(3) In this section—

"regulator" has the meaning given in section 54(1) of the 1998 Act; and

"specified" means specified in the order.

206. Power to modify Schedule 8

(1) The Secretary of State may by order made by statutory instrument modify Schedule 8.

(2) An order under this section may make—

(a) different provision for different cases or different purposes;

(b) such incidental, supplementary, consequential, transitory, transitional or saving provision as the Secretary of State considers appropriate.

(3) An order under this section may, in particular, modify that Schedule in its application by virtue of Part 3 of this Act, in its application by virtue of Part 4 of this Act, in its application by virtue of any other enactment (whether by virtue of Part 4 of this Act as applied by that enactment or otherwise) or in its application by virtue of every enactment that applies it.

(4) An order under this section as extended by subsection (2) may modify any enactment comprised in or made under this Act, or any other enactment.

(5) No order shall be made under this section unless a draft of it has been laid before, and approved by a resolution of, each House of Parliament.

(6) No modification of Schedule 8 in its application by virtue of Part 3 of this Act shall be made by an order under this section if the modification relates to a relevant merger situation or (as the case may be) a special merger situation which has been created before the coming into force of the order.

(7) No modification shall be made by an order under this section of Schedule 8 in its application in relation to references made under section 22, 33, 45 or 62 before the coming into force of the order.

(8) No modification shall be made by an order under this section of Schedule 8 in its application in relation to references made under section 131 or 132 before the coming into force of the order (including references made under section 131 as applied by another enactment).

(9) Before making an order under this section, the Secretary of State shall consult the OFT and the Commission.

(10)   Expressions used in this section which are also used in Part 3 of this Act have the same meaning in this section as in that Part.

207, 208. . . . .

209.   Reform of Community competition law

(1)   The Secretary of State may by regulations make such modifications of the 1998 Act as he considers appropriate for the purpose of eliminating or reducing any differences between—

(a)   the domestic provisions of the 1998 Act, and

(b)   European Community competition law,

which result (or would otherwise result) from a relevant Community instrument made after the passing of this Act.

(2)   In subsection (1)—

"the domestic provisions of the 1998 Act" means the provisions of the 1998 Act so far as they do not implement or give effect to a relevant Community instrument;

"European Community competition law" includes any Act or subordinate legislation so far as it implements or gives effect to a relevant Community instrument;

"relevant Community instrument" means a regulation or directive under Article 83 of the Treaty establishing the European Community.

(3)   The Secretary of State may by regulations repeal or otherwise modify any provision of an Act (other than the 1998 Act) which excludes any matter from the Chapter I prohibition or the Chapter II prohibition (within the meaning of Part 1 of the 1998 Act).

(4)   The power under subsection (3) may not be exercised—

(a)   before the power under subsection (1) has been exercised; or

(b)   so as to extend the scope of any exclusion that is not being removed by the regulations.

(5)   Regulations under this section may—

(a)   confer power to make subordinate legislation;

(b)   make such consequential, supplementary, incidental, transitory, transitional or saving provision as the Secretary of State considers appropriate (including provision modifying any Act or subordinate legislation); and

(c)   make different provision for different cases or circumstances.

(6)   The power to make regulations under this section is exercisable by statutory instrument.

(7)   No regulations may be made under this section unless a draft of them has been laid before and approved by a resolution of each House of Parliament.

(8)   Paragraph 1(1)(c) of Schedule 2 to the European Communities Act 1972 (c. 68) (restriction on powers to legislate) shall not apply to regulations which implement or give effect to a relevant Community instrument made after the passing of this Act.

PART 8

ENFORCEMENT OF CERTAIN CONSUMER LEGISLATION

Introduction

210.   Consumers

(1)   In this Part references to consumers must be construed in accordance with this section.

(2)   In relation to a domestic infringement a consumer is an individual in respect of whom the first and second conditions are satisfied.

(3)   The first condition is that—

(a)   goods are or are sought to be supplied to the individual (whether by way of sale or otherwise) in the course of a business carried on by the person supplying or seeking to supply them, or

(b)   services are or are sought to be supplied to the individual in the course of a business carried on by the person supplying or seeking to supply them.

(4)   The second condition is that—

(a) the individual receives or seeks to receive the goods or services otherwise than in the course of a business carried on by him, or

(b) the individual receives or seeks to receive the goods or services with a view to carrying on a business but not in the course of a business carried on by him.

(5) For the purposes of a domestic infringement it is immaterial whether a person supplying goods or services has a place of business in the United Kingdom.

(6) In relation to a Community infringement a consumer is a person who is a consumer for the purposes of—

(a) the Injunctions Directive, and

(b) the listed Directive concerned.

(7) A Directive is a listed Directive—

(a) if it is a Directive of the Council of the European Communities or of the European Parliament and of the Council, and

(b) if it is specified in Schedule 13 or to the extent that any of its provisions is so specified.

(8) A business includes—

(a) a professional practice;

(b) any other undertaking carried on for gain or reward;

(c) any undertaking in the course of which goods or services are supplied otherwise than free of charge.

(9) The Secretary of State may by order modify Schedule 13.

(10) An order under this section must be made by statutory instrument subject to annulment in pursuance of a resolution of either House of Parliament.

211. Domestic infringements

(1) In this Part a domestic infringement is an act or omission which—

(a) is done or made by a person in the course of a business,

(b) falls within subsection (2), and

(c) harms the collective interests of consumers in the United Kingdom.

(2) An act or omission falls within this subsection if it is of a description specified by the Secretary of State by order and consists of any of the following—

(a) a contravention of an enactment which imposes a duty, prohibition or restriction enforceable by criminal proceedings;

(b) an act done or omission made in breach of contract;

(c) an act done or omission made in breach of a non-contractual duty owed to a person by virtue of an enactment or rule of law and enforceable by civil proceedings;

(d) an act or omission in respect of which an enactment provides for a remedy or sanction enforceable by civil proceedings;

(e) an act done or omission made by a person supplying or seeking to supply goods or services as a result of which an agreement or security relating to the supply is void or unenforceable to any extent;

(f) an act or omission by which a person supplying or seeking to supply goods or services purports or attempts to exercise a right or remedy relating to the supply in circumstances where the exercise of the right or remedy is restricted or excluded under or by virtue of an enactment;

(g) an act or omission by which a person supplying or seeking to supply goods or services purports or attempts to avoid (to any extent) liability relating to the supply in circumstances where such avoidance is restricted or prevented under an enactment.

(3) But an order under this section may provide that any description of act or omission falling within subsection (2) is not a domestic infringement.

(4) For the purposes of subsection (2) it is immaterial—

(a) whether or not any duty, prohibition or restriction exists in relation to consumers as such;

(b) whether or not any remedy or sanction is provided for the benefit of consumers as such;

(c) whether or not any proceedings have been brought in relation to the act or omission;

(d)   whether or not any person has been convicted of an offence in respect of the contravention mentioned in subsection (2)(a);

(e)   whether or not there is a waiver in respect of the breach of contract mentioned in subsection (2)(b).

(5)   References to an enactment include references to subordinate legislation (within the meaning of the Interpretation Act 1978 (c. 30)).

(6)   The power to make an order under this section must be exercised by statutory instrument.

(7)   But no such order may be made unless a draft of it has been laid before Parliament and approved by a resolution of each House.

212.   Community infringements

(1)   In this Part a Community infringement is an act or omission which harms the collective interests of consumers and which—

(a)   contravenes a listed Directive as given effect by the laws, regulations or administrative provisions of an EEA State, or

(b)   contravenes such laws, regulations or administrative provisions which provide additional permitted protections.

(2)   The laws, regulations or administrative provisions of an EEA State which give effect to a listed Directive provide additional permitted protections if—

(a)   they provide protection for consumers which is in addition to the minimum protection required by the Directive concerned, and

(b)   such additional protection is permitted by that Directive.

(3)   The Secretary of State may by order specify for the purposes of this section the law in the United Kingdom which—

(a)   gives effect to the listed Directives;

(b)   provides additional permitted protections.

(4)   References to a listed Directive must be construed in accordance with section 210.

(5)   An EEA State is a State which is a contracting party to the Agreement on the European Economic Area signed at Oporto on 2nd May 1992 as adjusted by the Protocol signed at Brussels on 17th March 1993.

(6)   An order under this section must be made by statutory instrument subject to annulment in pursuance of a resolution of either House of Parliament.

213.   Enforcers

(1)   Each of the following is a general enforcer—

(a)   the OFT;

(b)   every local weights and measures authority in Great Britain;

(c)   the Department of Enterprise, Trade and Investment in Northern Ireland.

(2)   A designated enforcer is any person or body (whether or not incorporated) which the Secretary of State—

(a)   thinks has as one of its purposes the protection of the collective interests of consumers, and

(b)   designates by order.

(3)   The Secretary of State may designate a public body only if he is satisfied that it is independent.

(4)   The Secretary of State may designate a person or body which is not a public body only if the person or body (as the case may be) satisfies such criteria as the Secretary of State specifies by order.

(5)   A Community enforcer is a qualified entity for the purposes of the Injunctions Directive—

(a)   which is for the time being specified in the list published in the Official Journal of the European Communities in pursuance of Article 4.3 of that Directive, but

(b)   which is not a general enforcer or a designated enforcer.

(6)   An order under this section may designate an enforcer in respect of—

(a)   all infringements;

(b)   infringements of such descriptions as are specified in the order.

(7) An order under this section may make different provision for different purposes.

(8) The designation of a body by virtue of subsection (3) is conclusive evidence for the purposes of any question arising under this Part that the body is a public body.

(9) An order under this section must be made by statutory instrument subject to annulment in pursuance of a resolution of either House of Parliament.

(10) If requested to do so by a designated enforcer which is designated in respect of one or more Community infringements the Secretary of State must notify the Commission of the European Communities—

    (a) of its name and purpose;

    (b) of the Community infringements in respect of which it is designated.

(11) The Secretary of State must also notify the Commission—

    (a) of the fact that a person or body in respect of which he has given notice under subsection (10) ceases to be a designated enforcer;

    (b) of any change in the name or purpose of a designated enforcer in respect of which he has given such notice;

    (c) of any change to the Community infringements in respect of which a designated enforcer is designated.

Enforcement procedure

214. Consultation

(1) An enforcer must not make an application for an enforcement order unless he has engaged in appropriate consultation with—

    (a) the person against whom the enforcement order would be made, and

    (b) the OFT (if it is not the enforcer).

(2) Appropriate consultation is consultation for the purpose of—

    (a) achieving the cessation of the infringement in a case where an infringement is occurring;

    (b) ensuring that there will be no repetition of the infringement in a case where the infringement has occurred;

    (c) ensuring that there will be no repetition of the infringement in a case where the cessation of the infringement is achieved under paragraph (a);

    (d) ensuring that the infringement does not take place in the case of a Community infringement which the enforcer believes is likely to take place.

(3) Subsection (1) does not apply if the OFT thinks that an application for an enforcement order should be made without delay.

(4) Subsection (1) ceases to apply—

    (a) for the purposes of an application for an enforcement order at the end of the period of 14 days beginning with the day after the person against whom the enforcement order would be made receives a request for consultation from the enforcer;

    (b) for the purposes of an application for an interim enforcement order at the end of the period of seven days beginning with the day after the person against whom the interim enforcement order would be made receives a request for consultation from the enforcer.

(5) The Secretary of State may by order make rules in relation to consultation under this section.

(6) Such an order must be made by statutory instrument subject to annulment in pursuance of a resolution of either House of Parliament.

(7) In this section (except subsection (4)) and in sections 215 and 216 references to an enforcement order include references to an interim enforcement order.

215. Applications

(1) An application for an enforcement order must name the person the enforcer thinks—

    (a) has engaged or is engaging in conduct which constitutes a domestic or a Community infringement, or

    (b) is likely to engage in conduct which constitutes a Community infringement.

(2)   A general enforcer may make an application for an enforcement order in respect of any infringement.

(3)   A designated enforcer may make an application for an enforcement order in respect of an infringement to which his designation relates.

(4)   A Community enforcer may make an application for an enforcement order in respect of a Community infringement.

(5)   The following courts have jurisdiction to make an enforcement order—

    (a)   the High Court or a county court if the person against whom the order is sought carries on business or has a place of business in England and Wales or Northern Ireland;

    (b)   the Court of Session or the sheriff if the person against whom the order is sought carries on business or has a place of business in Scotland.

(6)   If an application for an enforcement order is made by a Community enforcer the court may examine whether the purpose of the enforcer justifies its making the application.

(7)   If the court thinks that the purpose of the Community enforcer does not justify its making the application the court may refuse the application on that ground alone.

(8)   The purpose of a Community enforcer must be construed by reference to the Injunctions Directive.

(9)   An enforcer which is not the OFT must notify the OFT of the result of an application under this section.

216.   Applications: directions by OFT

(1)   This section applies if the OFT believes that an enforcer other than the OFT intends to apply for an enforcement order.

(2)   In such a case the OFT may direct that if an application in respect of a particular infringement is to be made it must be made—

    (a)   only by the OFT, or

    (b)   only by such other enforcer as the OFT directs.

(3)   If the OFT directs that only it may make an application that does not prevent—

    (a)   the OFT or any enforcer from accepting an undertaking under section 219, or

    (b)   the OFT from taking such other steps it thinks appropriate (apart from making an application) for the purpose of securing that the infringement is not committed, continued or repeated.

(4)   The OFT may vary or withdraw a direction given under this section.

(5)   The OFT must take such steps as it thinks appropriate to bring a direction (or a variation or withdrawal of a direction) to the attention of enforcers it thinks may be affected by it.

(6)   But this section does not prevent an application for an enforcement order being made by a Community enforcer.

217.   Enforcement orders

(1)   This section applies if an application for an enforcement order is made under section 215 and the court finds that the person named in the application has engaged in conduct which constitutes the infringement.

(2)   This section also applies if such an application is made in relation to a Community infringement and the court finds that the person named in the application is likely to engage in conduct which constitutes the infringement.

(3)   If this section applies the court may make an enforcement order against the person.

(4)   In considering whether to make an enforcement order the court must have regard to whether the person named in the application—

    (a)   has given an undertaking under section 219 in respect of conduct such as is mentioned in subsection (3) of that section;

    (b)   has failed to comply with the undertaking.

(5)   An enforcement order must—

    (a)   indicate the nature of the conduct to which the finding under subsection (1) or (2) relates, and

    (b)   direct the person to comply with subsection (6).

(6)   A person complies with this subsection if he—

    (a)   does not continue or repeat the conduct;

    (b)   does not engage in such conduct in the course of his business or another business;

    (c)   does not consent to or connive in the carrying out of such conduct by a body corporate with which he has a special relationship (within the meaning of section 222(3)).

(7)   But subsection (6)(a) does not apply in the case of a finding under subsection (2).

(8)   An enforcement order may require a person against whom the order is made to publish in such form and manner and to such extent as the court thinks appropriate for the purpose of eliminating any continuing effects of the infringement—

    (a)   the order;

    (b)   a corrective statement.

(9)   If the court makes a finding under subsection (1) or (2) it may accept an undertaking by the person—

    (a)   to comply with subsection (6), or

    (b)   to take steps which the court believes will secure that he complies with subsection (6).

(10)   An undertaking under subsection (9) may include a further undertaking by the person to publish in such form and manner and to such extent as the court thinks appropriate for the purpose of eliminating any continuing effects of the infringement—

    (a)   the terms of the undertaking;

    (b)   a corrective statement.

(11)   If the court—

    (a)   makes a finding under subsection (1) or (2), and

    (b)   accepts an undertaking under subsection (9),

it must not make an enforcement order in respect of the infringement to which the undertaking relates.

(12)   An enforcement order made by a court in one part of the United Kingdom has effect in any other part of the United Kingdom as if made by a court in that part.

218.   **Interim enforcement order**

(1)   The court may make an interim enforcement order against a person named in the application for the order if it appears to the court—

    (a)   that it is alleged that the person is engaged in conduct which constitutes a domestic or Community infringement or is likely to engage in conduct which constitutes a Community infringement,

    (b)   that if the application had been an application for an enforcement order it would be likely to be granted,

    (c)   that it is expedient that the conduct is prohibited or prevented (as the case may be) immediately, and

    (d)   if no notice of the application has been given to the person named in the application that it is appropriate to make an interim enforcement order without notice.

(2)   An interim enforcement order must—

    (a)   indicate the nature of the alleged conduct, and

    (b)   direct the person to comply with subsection (3).

(3)   A person complies with this subsection if he—

    (a)   does not continue or repeat the conduct;

    (b)   does not engage in such conduct in the course of his business or another business;

    (c)   does not consent to or connive in the carrying out of such conduct by a body corporate with which he has a special relationship (within the meaning of section 222(3)).

(4)   But subsection (3)(a) does not apply in so far as the application is made in respect of an allegation that the person is likely to engage in conduct which constitutes a Community infringement.

(5) An application for an interim enforcement order against a person may be made at any time before an application for an enforcement order against the person in respect of the same conduct is determined.

(6) An application for an interim enforcement order must refer to all matters—
   (a) which are known to the applicant, and
   (b) which are material to the question whether or not the application is granted.

(7) If an application for an interim enforcement order is made without notice the application must state why no notice has been given.

(8) The court may vary or discharge an interim enforcement order on the application of—
   (a) the enforcer who applied for the order;
   (b) the person against whom it is made.

(9) An interim enforcement order against a person is discharged on the determination of an application for an enforcement order made against the person in respect of the same conduct.

(10) If it appears to the court as mentioned in subsection (1)(a) to (c) the court may instead of making an interim enforcement order accept an undertaking from the person named in the application—
   (a) to comply with subsection (3), or
   (b) to take steps which the court believes will secure that he complies with subsection (3).

(11) An interim enforcement order made by a court in one part of the United Kingdom has effect in any other part of the United Kingdom as if made by a court in that part.

219. Undertakings

(1) This section applies if an enforcer has power to make an application under section 215.

(2) In such a case the enforcer may accept from a person to whom subsection (3) applies an undertaking that the person will comply with subsection (4).

(3) This subsection applies to a person who the enforcer believes—
   (a) has engaged in conduct which constitutes an infringement;
   (b) is engaging in such conduct;
   (c) is likely to engage in conduct which constitutes a Community infringement.

(4) A person complies with this subsection if he—
   (a) does not continue or repeat the conduct;
   (b) does not engage in such conduct in the course of his business or another business;
   (c) does not consent to or connive in the carrying out of such conduct by a body corporate with which he has a special relationship (within the meaning of section 222(3)).

(5) But subsection (4)(a) does not apply in the case of an undertaking given by a person in so far as subsection (3) applies to him by virtue of paragraph (c).

(6) If an enforcer accepts an undertaking under this section it must notify the OFT—
   (a) of the terms of the undertaking;
   (b) of the identity of the person who gave it.

220. Further proceedings

(1) This section applies if the court—
   (a) makes an enforcement order under section 217,
   (b) makes an interim enforcement order under section 218, or
   (c) accepts an undertaking under either of those sections.

(2) In such a case the OFT has the same right to apply to the court in respect of a failure to comply with the order or undertaking as the enforcer who made the application for the order.

(3) An application to the court in respect of a failure to comply with an undertaking may include an application for an enforcement order or for an interim enforcement order.

(4) If the court finds that an undertaking is not being complied with it may make an enforcement order or an interim enforcement order (instead of making any other order it has power to make).

(5) In the case of an application for an enforcement order or for an interim enforcement order as mentioned in subsection (3) sections 214 and 216 must be ignored and sections 215 and 217 or 218 (as the case may be) apply subject to the following modifications—

(a) section 215(1)(b) must be ignored;
(b) section 215(5) must be ignored and the application must be made to the court which accepted the undertaking;
(c) section 217(9) to (11) must be ignored;
(d) section 218(10) must be ignored.

(6) If an enforcer which is not the OFT makes an application in respect of the failure of a person to comply with an enforcement order, an interim enforcement order or an undertaking given under section 217 or 218 the enforcer must notify the OFT—
(a) of the application;
(b) of any order made by the court on the application.

221. Community infringements: proceedings

(1) Subsection (2) applies to—
(a) every general enforcer;
(b) every designated enforcer which is a public body.

(2) An enforcer to which this subsection applies has power to take proceedings in EEA States other than the United Kingdom for the cessation or prohibition of a Community infringement.

(3) Subsection (4) applies to—
(a) every general enforcer;
(b) every designated enforcer.

(4) An enforcer to which this subsection applies may co-operate with a Community enforcer—
(a) for the purpose of bringing proceedings mentioned in subsection (2);
(b) in connection with the exercise by the Community enforcer of its functions under this Part.

(5) An EEA State is a State which is a contracting party to the Agreement on the European Economic Area signed at Oporto on 2nd May 1992 as adjusted by the Protocol signed at Brussels on 17th March 1993.

222. Bodies corporate: accessories

(1) This section applies if the person whose conduct constitutes a domestic infringement or a Community infringement is a body corporate.

(2) If the conduct takes place with the consent or connivance of a person (an accessory) who has a special relationship with the body corporate, the consent or connivance is also conduct which constitutes the infringement.

(3) A person has a special relationship with a body corporate if he is—
(a) a controller of the body corporate, or
(b) a director, manager, secretary or other similar officer of the body corporate or a person purporting to act in such a capacity.

(4) A person is a controller of a body corporate if—
(a) the directors of the body corporate or of another body corporate which is its controller are accustomed to act in accordance with the person's directions or instructions, or
(b) either alone or with an associate or associates he is entitled to exercise or control the exercise of one third or more of the voting power at any general meeting of the body corporate or of another body corporate which is its controller.

(5) An enforcement order or an interim enforcement order may be made against an accessory in respect of an infringement whether or not such an order is made against the body corporate.

(6) The court may accept an undertaking under section 217(9) or 218(10) from an accessory in respect of an infringement whether or not it accepts such an undertaking from the body corporate.

(7) An enforcer may accept an undertaking under section 219 from an accessory in respect of an infringement whether or not it accepts such an undertaking from the body corporate.

(8) Subsection (9) applies if—
(a) an order is made as mentioned in subsection (5), or
(b) an undertaking is accepted as mentioned in subsection (6) or (7).

(9)   In such a case for subsection (6) of section 217, subsection (3) of section 218 or subsection (4) of section 219 (as the case may be) there is substituted the following subsection—

"( )   A person complies with this subsection if he—

     (a)   does not continue or repeat the conduct;

     (b)   does not in the course of any business carried on by him engage in conduct such as that which constitutes the infringement committed by the body corporate mentioned in section 222(1);

     (c)   does not consent to or connive in the carrying out of such conduct by another body corporate with which he has a special relationship (within the meaning of section 222(3))."

(10)   A person is an associate of an individual if—

     (a)   he is the spouse *or civil partner* of the individual;

     (b)   he is a relative of the individual;

     (c)   he is a relative of the individual's spouse *or civil partner*;

     (d)   he is the spouse *or civil partner* of a relative of the individual;

     (e)   he is the spouse *or civil partner* of a relative of the individual's spouse *or civil partner*;

     (f)   he lives in the same household as the individual otherwise than merely because he or the individual is the other's employer, tenant, lodger or boarder;

     (g)   he is a relative of a person who is an associate of the individual by virtue of paragraph (f);

     (h)   he has at some time in the past fallen within any of paragraphs (a) to (g).

(11)   A person is also an associate of—

     (a)   an individual with whom he is in partnership;

     (b)   an individual who is an associate of the individual mentioned in paragraph (a);

     (c)   a body corporate if he is a controller of it or he is an associate of a person who is a controller of the body corporate.

(12)   A body corporate is an associate of another body corporate if—

     (a)   the same person is a controller of both;

     (b)   a person is a controller of one and persons who are his associates are controllers of the other;

     (c)   a person is a controller of one and he and persons who are his associates are controllers of the other;

     (d)   a group of two or more persons is a controller of each company and the groups consist of the same persons;

     (e)   a group of two or more persons is a controller of each company and the groups may be regarded as consisting of the same persons by treating (in one or more cases) a member of either group as replaced by a person of whom he is an associate.

(13)   A relative is a brother, sister, uncle, aunt, nephew, niece, lineal ancestor or lineal descendant.

Note. The italicized words in subsection (10)(a), (c), (d) and (e) are inserted by the Civil Partnership Act 2004, s. 261(1), Sch. 27, para. 169, as from a day to be appointed.

223.   Bodies corporate: orders

(1)   This section applies if a court makes an enforcement order or an interim enforcement order against a body corporate and—

     (a)   at the time the order is made the body corporate is a member of a group of interconnected bodies corporate,

     (b)   at any time when the order is in force the body corporate becomes a member of a group of interconnected bodies corporate, or

     (c)   at any time when the order is in force a group of interconnected bodies corporate of which the body corporate is a member is increased by the addition of one or more further members.

(2)   The court may direct that the order is binding upon all of the members of the group as if each of them were the body corporate against which the order is made.

(3)   A group of interconnected bodies corporate is a group consisting of two or more bodies corporate all of whom are interconnected with each other.

(4)   Any two bodies corporate are interconnected—
        (a)   if one of them is a subsidiary of the other, or
        (b)   if both of them are subsidiaries of the same body corporate.

(5)   "Subsidiary" must be construed in accordance with section 736 of the Companies Act 1985 (c. 6).

Information

224.   OFT

(1)   The OFT may for any of the purposes mentioned in subsection (2) give notice to any person requiring the person to provide it with the information specified in the notice.

(2)   The purposes are—
        (a)   to enable the OFT to exercise or to consider whether to exercise any function it has under this Part;
        (b)   to enable a designated enforcer to which section 225 does not apply to consider whether to exercise any function it has under this Part;
        (c)   to enable a Community enforcer to consider whether to exercise any function it has under this Part;
        (d)   to ascertain whether a person has complied with or is complying with an enforcement order, an interim enforcement order or an undertaking given under section 217(9), 218(10) or 219.

225.   Other enforcers

(1)   This section applies to—
        (a)   every general enforcer (other than the OFT);
        (b)   every designated enforcer which is a public body.

(2)   An enforcer to which this section applies may for any of the purposes mentioned in subsection (3) give notice to any person requiring the person to provide the enforcer with the information specified in the notice.

(3)   The purposes are—
        (a)   to enable the enforcer to exercise or to consider whether to exercise any function it has under this Part;
        (b)   to ascertain whether a person has complied with or is complying with an enforcement order or an interim enforcement order made on the application of the enforcer or an undertaking given under section 217(9) or 218(10) (as the case may be) following such an application or an undertaking given to the enforcer under section 219.

226.   Notices: procedure

(1)   This section applies to a notice given under section 224 or 225.

(2)   The notice must—
        (a)   be in writing;
        (b)   specify the purpose for which the information is required.

(3)   If the purpose is as mentioned in section 224(2)(a), (b) or (c) or 225(3)(a) the notice must specify the function concerned.

(4)   A notice may specify the time within which and manner in which it is to be complied with.

(5)   A notice may require the production of documents or any description of documents.

(6)   An enforcer may take copies of any documents produced in compliance with such a requirement.

(7)   A notice may be varied or revoked by a subsequent notice.

(8)   But a notice must not require a person to provide any information or produce any document which he would be entitled to refuse to provide or produce—
        (a)   in proceedings in the High Court on the grounds of legal professional privilege;
        (b)   in proceedings in the Court of Session on the grounds of confidentiality of communications.

227.   Notices: enforcement

(1)   If a person fails to comply with a notice given under section 224 or 225 the enforcer who gave the notice may make an application under this section.

(2)   If it appears to the court that the person to whom the notice was given has failed to comply with the notice the court may make an order under this section.

(3)   An order under this section may require the person to whom the notice was given to do anything the court thinks it is reasonable for him to do for any of the purposes mentioned in section 224 or 225 (as the case may be) to ensure that the notice is complied with.

(4)   An order under this section may require the person to meet all the costs or expenses of the application.

(5)   If the person is a company or association the court in proceeding under subsection (4) may require any officer of the company or association who is responsible for the failure to meet the costs or expenses.

(6)   The court is a court which may make an enforcement order.

(7)   In subsection (5) an officer of a company is a person who is a director, manager, secretary or other similar officer of the company.

Miscellaneous

228.   Evidence

(1)   Proceedings under this Part are civil proceedings for the purposes of—
   (a)   section 11 of the Civil Evidence Act 1968 (c. 64) (convictions admissible as evidence in civil proceedings);
   (b)   section 10 of the Law Reform (Miscellaneous Provisions) (Scotland) Act 1968 (c. 70) (corresponding provision in Scotland);
   (c)   section 7 of the Civil Evidence Act (Northern Ireland) 1971 (c. 36 (N.I.)) (corresponding provision in Northern Ireland).

(2)   In proceedings under this Part any finding by a court in civil proceedings that an act or omission mentioned in section 211(2)(b), (c) or (d) or 212(1) has occurred—
   (a)   is admissible as evidence that the act or omission occurred;
   (b)   unless the contrary is proved, is sufficient evidence that the act or omission occurred.

(3)   But subsection (2) does not apply to any finding—
   (a)   which has been reversed on appeal;
   (b)   which has been varied on appeal so as to negative it.

229.   Advice and information

(1)   As soon as is reasonably practicable after the passing of this Act the OFT must prepare and publish advice and information with a view to—
   (a)   explaining the provisions of this Part to persons who are likely to be affected by them, and
   (b)   indicating how the OFT expects such provisions to operate.

(2)   The OFT may at any time publish revised or new advice or information.

(3)   Advice or information published in pursuance of subsection (1)(b) may include advice or information about the factors which the OFT may take into account in considering how to exercise the functions conferred on it by this Part.

(4)   Advice or information published by the OFT under this section is to be published in such form and in such manner as it considers appropriate.

(5)   In preparing advice or information under this section the OFT must consult such persons as it thinks are representative of persons affected by this Part.

(6)   If any proposed advice or information relates to a matter in respect of which another general enforcer or a designated enforcer may act the persons to be consulted must include that enforcer.

230.   Notice to OFT of intended prosecution

(1)   This section applies if a local weights and measures authority in England and Wales intends to start proceedings for an offence under an enactment or subordinate legislation specified by the Secretary of State by order for the purposes of this section.

(2)   The authority must give the OFT—
   (a)   notice of its intention to start the proceedings;

(b) a summary of the evidence it intends to lead in respect of the charges.

(3) The authority must not start the proceedings until whichever is the earlier of the following—

    (a) the end of the period of 14 days starting with the day on which the authority gives the notice;

    (b) the day on which it is notified by the OFT that the OFT has received the notice and summary given under subsection (2).

(4) The authority must also notify the OFT of the outcome of the proceedings after they are finally determined.

(5) But such proceedings are not invalid by reason only of the failure of the authority to comply with this section.

(6) Subordinate legislation has the same meaning as in section 21(1) of the Interpretation Act 1978 (c. 30).

(7) An order under this section must be made by statutory instrument subject to annulment in pursuance of a resolution of either House of Parliament.

231. Notice of convictions and judgments to OFT

(1) This section applies if—

    (a) a person is convicted of an offence by or before a court in the United Kingdom, or

    (b) a judgment is given against a person by a court in civil proceedings in the United Kingdom.

(2) The court may make arrangements to bring the conviction or judgment to the attention of the OFT if it appears to the court—

    (a) having regard to the functions of the OFT under this Part or under the Estate Agents Act 1979 (c. 38) that it is expedient for the conviction or judgment to be brought to the attention of the OFT, and

    (b) without such arrangements the conviction or judgment may not be brought to the attention of the OFT.

(3) For the purposes of subsection (2) it is immaterial that the proceedings have been finally disposed of by the court.

(4) Judgment includes an order or decree and references to the giving of the judgment must be construed accordingly.

Interpretation

232. Goods and services

(1) References in this Part to goods and services must be construed in accordance with this section.

(2) Goods include—

    (a) buildings and other structures;

    (b) ships, aircraft and hovercraft.

(3) The supply of goods includes—

    (a) supply by way of sale, lease, hire or hire purchase;

    (b) in relation to buildings and other structures, construction of them by one person for another.

(4) Goods or services which are supplied wholly or partly outside the United Kingdom must be taken to be supplied to or for a person in the United Kingdom if they are supplied in accordance with arrangements falling within subsection (5).

(5) Arrangements fall within this subsection if they are made by any means and—

    (a) at the time the arrangements are made the person seeking the supply is in the United Kingdom, or

    (b) at the time the goods or services are supplied (or ought to be supplied in accordance with the arrangements) the person responsible under the arrangements for effecting the supply is in or has a place of business in the United Kingdom.

233. Person supplying goods

(1) This section has effect for the purpose of references in this Part to a person supplying or seeking to supply goods under—

(a) a hire-purchase agreement;

(b) a credit-sale agreement;

(c) a conditional sale agreement.

(2) The references include references to a person who conducts any antecedent negotiations relating to the agreement.

(3) The following expressions must be construed in accordance with section 189 of the Consumer Credit Act 1974 (c. 39)—

(a) hire-purchase agreement;

(b) credit-sale agreement;

(c) conditional sale agreement;

(d) antecedent negotiations.

234.   Supply of services

(1) References in this Part to the supply of services must be construed in accordance with this section.

(2) The supply of services does not include the provision of services under a contract of service or of apprenticeship whether it is express or implied and (if it is express) whether it is oral or in writing.

(3) The supply of services includes—

(a) performing for gain or reward any activity other than the supply of goods;

(b) rendering services to order;

(c) the provision of services by making them available to potential users.

(4) The supply of services includes making arrangements for the use of computer software or for granting access to data stored in any form which is not readily accessible.

(5) The supply of services includes making arrangements by means of a relevant agreement (within the meaning of paragraph 29 of Schedule 2 to the Telecommunications Act 1984) for sharing the use of telecommunications apparatus.

(6) The supply of services includes permitting or making arrangements to permit the use of land in such circumstances as the Secretary of State specifies by order.

(7) The power to make an order under subsection (6) must be exercised by statutory instrument.

(8) But no such order may be made unless a draft of it has been laid before Parliament and approved by a resolution of each House.

235.   Injunctions Directive

In this Part the Injunctions Directive is Directive 98/27/EC of the European Parliament and of the Council on injunctions for the protection of consumers' interests.

Crown

236.   Crown

This Part binds the Crown.

PART 9

INFORMATION

Restrictions on disclosure

237.   General restriction

(1) This section applies to specified information which relates to—

(a) the affairs of an individual;

(b) any business of an undertaking.

(2) Such information must not be disclosed—

(a) during the lifetime of the individual, or

(b) while the undertaking continues in existence,

unless the disclosure is permitted under this Part.

(3)   But subsection (2) does not prevent the disclosure of any information if the information has on an earlier occasion been disclosed to the public in circumstances which do not contravene—
    (a)   that subsection;
    (b)   any other enactment or rule of law prohibiting or restricting the disclosure of the information.

(4)   Nothing in this Part authorises a disclosure of information which contravenes the Data Protection Act 1998 (c. 29).

(5)   Nothing in this Part affects the Competition Appeal Tribunal.

(6)   This Part (except section 244) does not affect any power or duty to disclose information which exists apart from this Part.

238.   Information

(1)   Information is specified information if it comes to a public authority in connection with the exercise of any function it has under or by virtue of—
    (a)   Part 1, 3, 4, 6, 7 or 8;
    (b)   an enactment specified in Schedule 14;
    (c)   such subordinate legislation as the Secretary of State may by order specify for the purposes of this subsection.

(2)   It is immaterial whether information comes to a public authority before or after the passing of this Act.

(3)   Public authority (except in the expression "overseas public authority") must be construed in accordance with section 6 of the Human Rights Act 1998 (c. 42).

(4)   In subsection (1) the reference to an enactment includes a reference to an enactment contained in—
    (a)   an Act of the Scottish Parliament;
    (b)   Northern Ireland legislation;
    (c)   subordinate legislation.

(5)   The Secretary of State may by order amend Schedule 14.

(6)   The power to make an order under subsection (5) includes power to add, vary or remove a reference to any provision of—
    (a)   an Act of the Scottish Parliament;
    (b)   Northern Ireland legislation.

(7)   An order under this section must be made by statutory instrument subject to annulment in pursuance of a resolution of either House of Parliament.

(8)   This section applies for the purposes of this Part.

Permitted disclosure

239.   Consent

(1)   This Part does not prohibit the disclosure by a public authority of information held by it to any other person if it obtains each required consent.

(2)   If the information was obtained by the authority from a person who had the information lawfully and the authority knows the identity of that person the consent of that person is required.

(3)   If the information relates to the affairs of an individual the consent of the individual is required.

(4)   If the information relates to the business of an undertaking the consent of the person for the time being carrying on the business is required.

(5)   For the purposes of subsection (4) consent may be given—
    (a)   in the case of a company by a director, secretary or other officer of the company;
    (b)   in the case of a partnership by a partner;
    (c)   in the case of an unincorporated body or association by a person concerned in the management or control of the body or association.

240.   Community obligations

This Part does not prohibit the disclosure of information held by a public authority to another person if the disclosure is required for the purpose of a Community obligation.

241.   Statutory functions

(1)   A public authority which holds information to which section 237 applies may disclose that information for the purpose of facilitating the exercise by the authority of any function it has under or by virtue of this Act or any other enactment.

(2)   If information is disclosed under subsection (1) so that it is not made available to the public it must not be further disclosed by a person to whom it is so disclosed other than with the agreement of the public authority for the purpose mentioned in that subsection.

(3)   A public authority which holds information to which section 237 applies may disclose that information to any other person for the purpose of facilitating the exercise by that person of any function he has under or by virtue of—

(a)   this Act;

(b)   an enactment specified in Schedule 15;

(c)   such subordinate legislation as the Secretary of State may by order specify for the purposes of this subsection.

(4)   Information disclosed under subsection (3) must not be used by the person to whom it is disclosed for any purpose other than a purpose relating to a function mentioned in that subsection.

(5)   In subsection (1) the reference to an enactment includes a reference to an enactment contained in—

(a)   an Act of the Scottish Parliament;

(b)   Northern Ireland legislation;

(c)   subordinate legislation.

(6)   The Secretary of State may by order amend Schedule 15.

(7)   The power to make an order under subsection (6) includes power to add, vary or remove a reference to any provision of—

(a)   an Act of the Scottish Parliament;

(b)   Northern Ireland legislation.

(8)   An order under this section must be made by statutory instrument subject to annulment in pursuance of a resolution of either House of Parliament.

242.   Criminal proceedings

(1)   A public authority which holds information to which section 237 applies may disclose that information to any person—

(a)   in connection with the investigation of any criminal offence in any part of the United Kingdom;

(b)   for the purposes of any criminal proceedings there;

(c)   for the purpose of any decision whether to start or bring to an end such an investigation or proceedings.

(2)   Information disclosed under this section must not be used by the person to whom it is disclosed for any purpose other than that for which it is disclosed.

(3)   A public authority must not make a disclosure under this section unless it is satisfied that the making of the disclosure is proportionate to what is sought to be achieved by it.

243.   Overseas disclosures

(1)   A public authority which holds information to which section 237 applies (the discloser) may disclose that information to an overseas public authority for the purpose mentioned in subsection (2).

(2)   The purpose is facilitating the exercise by the overseas public authority of any function which it has relating to—

    (a)   carrying out investigations in connection with the enforcement of any relevant legislation by means of civil proceedings;

    (b)   bringing civil proceedings for the enforcement of such legislation or the conduct of such proceedings;

    (c)   the investigation of crime;

    (d)   bringing criminal proceedings or the conduct of such proceedings;

    (e)   deciding whether to start or bring to an end such investigations or proceedings.

(3)   But subsection (1) does not apply to any of the following—

    (a)   information which is held by a person who is designated by virtue of section 213(4) as a designated enforcer for the purposes of Part 8;

    (b)   information which comes to a public authority in connection with an investigation under Part 4, 5 or 6 of the 1973 Act or under section 11 of the Competition Act 1980 (c. 21);

    (c)   competition information within the meaning of section 351 of the Financial Services and Markets Act 2000 (c. 8);

    (d)   information which comes to a public authority in connection with an investigation under Part 3 or 4 or section 174 of this Act.

(4)   The Secretary of State may direct that a disclosure permitted by this section must not be made if he thinks that in connection with any matter in respect of which the disclosure could be made it is more appropriate—

    (a)   if any investigation is to be carried out, that it is carried out by an authority in the United Kingdom or in another specified country or territory;

    (b)   if any proceedings are to be brought, that they are brought in a court in the United Kingdom or in another specified country or territory.

(5)   The Secretary of State must take such steps as he thinks are appropriate to bring a direction under subsection (4) to the attention of persons likely to be affected by it.

(6)   In deciding whether to disclose information under this section a public authority must have regard in particular to the following considerations—

    (a)   whether the matter in respect of which the disclosure is sought is sufficiently serious to justify making the disclosure;

    (b)   whether the law of the country or territory to whose authority the disclosure would be made provides appropriate protection against self-incrimination in criminal proceedings;

    (c)   whether the law of that country or territory provides appropriate protection in relation to the storage and disclosure of personal data;

    (d)   whether there are arrangements in place for the provision of mutual assistance as between the United Kingdom and that country or territory in relation to the disclosure of information of the kind to which section 237 applies.

(7)   Protection is appropriate if it provides protection in relation to the matter in question which corresponds to that so provided in any part of the United Kingdom.

(8)   The Secretary of State may by order—

    (a)   modify the list of considerations in subsection (6);

    (b)   add to those considerations;

    (c)   remove any of those considerations.

(9)   An order under subsection (8) must be made by statutory instrument subject to annulment in pursuance of a resolution of either House of Parliament.

(10)   Information disclosed under this section—

    (a)   may be disclosed subject to the condition that it must not be further disclosed without the agreement of the discloser, and

    (b)   must not otherwise be used by the overseas public authority to which it is disclosed for any purpose other than that for which it is first disclosed.

(11)   An overseas public authority is a person or body in any country or territory outside the United Kingdom which appears to the discloser to exercise functions of a public nature in relation to any of the matters mentioned in paragraphs (a) to (e) of subsection (2).

(12) Relevant legislation is—

    (a) this Act, any enactment specified in Schedule 14 and such subordinate legislation as is specified by order for the purposes of section 238(1);

    (b) any enactment or subordinate legislation specified in an order under section 211(2);

    (c) any enactment or subordinate legislation specified in an order under section 212(3);

    (d) legislation in any country or territory outside the United Kingdom which appears to the discloser to make provision corresponding to this Act or to any such enactment or subordinate legislation.

244. Specified information: considerations relevant to disclosure

(1) A public authority must have regard to the following considerations before disclosing any specified information (within the meaning of section 238(1)).

(2) The first consideration is the need to exclude from disclosure (so far as practicable) any information whose disclosure the authority thinks is contrary to the public interest.

(3) The second consideration is the need to exclude from disclosure (so far as practicable)—

    (a) commercial information whose disclosure the authority thinks might significantly harm the legitimate business interests of the undertaking to which it relates, or

    (b) information relating to the private affairs of an individual whose disclosure the authority thinks might significantly harm the individual's interests.

(4) The third consideration is the extent to which the disclosure of the information mentioned in subsection (3)(a) or (b) is necessary for the purpose for which the authority is permitted to make the disclosure.

Offences

245. Offences

(1) A person commits an offence if he discloses information to which section 237 applies in contravention of section 237(2).

(2) A person commits an offence if he discloses information in contravention of a direction given under section 243(4).

(3) A person commits an offence if he uses information disclosed to him under this Part for a purpose which is not permitted under this Part.

(4) A person who commits an offence under this section is liable—

    (a) on summary conviction to imprisonment for a term not exceeding three months or to a fine not exceeding the statutory maximum or to both;

    (b) on conviction on indictment to imprisonment for a term not exceeding two years or to a fine or to both.

General

246. Subordinate legislation

In this Part "subordinate legislation" has the same meaning as in section 21(1) of the Interpretation Act 1978 (c. 30) and includes an instrument made under—

    (a) an Act of the Scottish Parliament;

    (b) Northern Ireland legislation.

247. …

PART 10
INSOLVENCY

Companies etc.

248. Replacement of Part II of Insolvency Act 1986

(1)–(3) …

(4) The Secretary of State may by order amend an enactment in consequence of this section.

(5)   An order under subsection (4)—

(a)   must be made by statutory instrument, and

(b)   shall be subject to annulment in pursuance of a resolution of either House of Parliament.

249.   Special administration regimes

(1)   Section 248 shall have no effect in relation to—

(a)   a company holding an appointment under Chapter I of Part II of the Water Industry Act 1991 (c. 56) (water and sewerage undertakers),

(aa)   a qualifying licensed water supplier within the meaning of subsection (6) of section 23 of the Water Industry Act 1991 (meaning and effect of special administration order),

(b)   a protected railway company within the meaning of section 59 of the Railways Act 1993 (c. 43) (railway administration order) (including that section as it has effect by virtue of section 19 of the Channel Tunnel Rail Link Act 1996 (c. 61) (administration)),

(c)   a licence company within the meaning of section 26 of the Transport Act 2000 (c. 38) (air traffic services),

(d)   a public-private partnership company within the meaning of section 210 of the Greater London Authority Act 1999 (c. 29) (public-private partnership agreement), or

(e)   a building society within the meaning of section 119 of the Building Societies Act 1986 (c. 53) (interpretation).

(2)   A reference in an Act listed in subsection (1) to a provision of Part II of the Insolvency Act 1986 (or to a provision which has effect in relation to a provision of that Part of that Act) shall, in so far as it relates to a company or society listed in subsection (1), continue to have effect as if it referred to Part II as it had effect immediately before the coming into force of section 248.

(3)   But the effect of subsection (2) in respect of a particular class of company or society may be modified by order of—

(a)   the Treasury, in the case of building societies, or

(b)   the Secretary of State, in any other case.

(4)   An order under subsection (3) may make consequential amendment of an enactment.

(5)   An order under subsection (3)—

(a)   must be made by statutory instrument, and

(b)   may not be made unless a draft has been laid before and approved by resolution of each House of Parliament.

(6)   An amendment of the Insolvency Act 1986 (c. 45) made by this Act is without prejudice to any power conferred by Part VII of the Companies Act 1989 (c. 40) (financial markets) to modify the law of insolvency.

Note. Subsection (1)(aa) is inserted by the Water Act 2003, s. 101(1), Sch. 8, para. 55(1), (3), as from a day to be appointed.

250–3.   ...

254.   Application of insolvency law to foreign company

(1)   The Secretary of State may by order provide for a provision of the Insolvency Act 1986 to apply (with or without modification) in relation to a company incorporated outside Great Britain.

(2)   An order under this section—

(a)   may make provision generally or for a specified purpose only,

(b)   may make different provision for different purposes, and

(c)   may make transitional, consequential or incidental provision.

(3)   An order under this section—

(a)   must be made by statutory instrument, and

(b)   shall be subject to annulment in pursuance of a resolution of either House of Parliament.

255.   Application of law about company arrangement or administration to non-company

(1)   The Treasury may with the concurrence of the Secretary of State by order provide for a company arrangement or administration provision to apply (with or without modification) in relation to—

        (a)   a society registered under the Industrial and Provident Societies Act 1965 (c. 12),

        (b)   a society registered under section 7(1)(b), (c), (d), (e) or (f) of the Friendly Societies Act 1974 (c. 46),

        (c)   a friendly society within the meaning of the Friendly Societies Act 1992 (c. 40), or

        (d)   an unregistered friendly society.

(2)   In subsection (1) "company arrangement or administration provision" means—

        (a)   a provision of Part I of the Insolvency Act 1986 (company voluntary arrangements),

        (b)   a provision of Part II of that Act (administration), and

        (c)   section 425 of the Companies Act 1985 (c. 6) (compromise or arrangement with creditors).

(3)   An order under this section may not provide for a company arrangement or administration provision to apply in relation to a society which is registered as a social landlord under Part I of the Housing Act 1996 (c. 52) or under Part 3 of the Housing (Scotland) Act 2001 (asp 10).

(4)   An order under this section—

        (a)   may make provision generally or for a specified purpose only,

        (b)   may make different provision for different purposes, and

        (c)   may make transitional, consequential or incidental provision.

(5)   Provision by virtue of subsection (4)(c) may, in particular—

        (a)   apply an enactment (with or without modification);

        (b)   amend an enactment.

(6)   An order under this section—

        (a)   must be made by statutory instrument, and

        (b)   shall be subject to annulment in pursuance of a resolution of either House of Parliament.

Individuals

256.   Duration of bankruptcy

(1)   …

(2)   Schedule 19 (which makes transitional provision in relation to this section)—

        (a)   shall have effect, and

        (b)   is without prejudice to the generality of section 276.

257–63. …

264.   Individual voluntary arrangement

(1)   Schedule 22 (which makes provision about individual voluntary arrangements) shall have effect.

(2)   The Secretary of State may by order amend the Insolvency Act 1986 so as to extend the provisions of sections 263B to 263G (which are inserted by Schedule 22 and provide a fast-track procedure for making an individual voluntary arrangement) to some or all cases other than those specified in section 263A as inserted by Schedule 22.

(3)   An order under subsection (2)—

        (a)   must be made by statutory instrument, and

        (b)   may not be made unless a draft has been laid before and approved by each House of Parliament.

(4)   An order under subsection (2) may make—

        (a)   consequential provision (which may include provision amending the Insolvency Act 1986 or another enactment);

        (b)   transitional provision.

265–6. …

267.   Disqualification from office: local government

(1)   The following shall be substituted for section 80(1)(b) of the Local Government Act 1972 (c. 70) (disqualification for membership of local authority: bankrupt)—

        "(b) is the subject of a bankruptcy restrictions order or interim order;".

(2)   Section 81(1) and (2) of that Act (which amplify the provision substituted by subsection (1) above) shall cease to have effect.

268.   Disqualification from office: general

(1)   The Secretary of State may make an order under this section in relation to a disqualification provision.

(2)   A "disqualification provision" is a provision which disqualifies (whether permanently or temporarily and whether absolutely or conditionally) a bankrupt or a class of bankrupts from—

   (a)   being elected or appointed to an office or position,

   (b)   holding an office or position, or

   (c)   becoming or remaining a member of a body or group.

(3)   In subsection (2) the reference to a provision which disqualifies a person conditionally includes a reference to a provision which enables him to be dismissed.

(4)   An order under subsection (1) may repeal or revoke the disqualification provision.

(5)   An order under subsection (1) may amend, or modify the effect of, the disqualification provision—

   (a)   so as to reduce the class of bankrupts to whom the disqualification provision applies;

   (b)   so as to extend the disqualification provision to some or all individuals who are subject to a bankruptcy restrictions regime;

   (c)   so that the disqualification provision applies only to some or all individuals who are subject to a bankruptcy restrictions regime;

   (d)   so as to make the application of the disqualification provision wholly or partly subject to the discretion of a specified person, body or group.

(6)   An order by virtue of subsection (5)(d) may provide for a discretion to be subject to—

   (a)   the approval of a specified person or body;

   (b)   appeal to a specified person or body.

(7)   An order by virtue of subsection (5)(d) made with the concurrence of the Lord Chancellor may provide for a discretion to be subject to appeal to a specified court or tribunal.

(8)   The Secretary of State may specify himself for the purposes of subsection (5)(d) or (6)(a) or (b).

(9)   In this section "bankrupt" means an individual—

   (a)   who has been adjudged bankrupt by a court in England and Wales or in Northern Ireland,

   (b)   whose estate has been sequestrated by a court in Scotland, or

   (c)   who has made an agreement with creditors of his for a composition of debts, for a scheme of arrangement of affairs, for the grant of a trust deed or for some other kind of settlement or arrangement.

(10)   In this section "bankruptcy restrictions regime" means an order or undertaking—

   (a)   under Schedule 4A to the Insolvency Act 1986 (c. 45) (bankruptcy restrictions orders), or

   (b)   under any system operating in Scotland or Northern Ireland which appears to the Secretary of State to be equivalent to the system operating under that Schedule.

(11)   In this section—

   "body" includes Parliament and any other legislative body, and

   "provision" means—

   (a)   a provision made by an Act of Parliament passed before or in the same Session as this Act, and

   (b)   a provision made, before or in the same Session as this Act, under an Act of Parliament.

(12)   An order under this section—

   (a)   may make provision generally or for a specified purpose only,

   (b)   may make different provision for different purposes, and

   (c)   may make transitional, consequential or incidental provision.

(13)   An order under this section—

   (a)   must be made by statutory instrument, and

(b) may not be made unless a draft has been laid before and approved by resolution of each House of Parliament.

(14) A reference in this section to the Secretary of State shall be treated as a reference to the National Assembly for Wales in so far as it relates to a disqualification provision which—

(a) is made by the National Assembly for Wales, or

(b) relates to a function of the National Assembly.

(15) Provision made by virtue of subsection (7) is subject to any order of the Lord Chancellor under section 56(1) of the Access to Justice Act 1999 (c. 22) (appeals: jurisdiction).

269–72. ….

PART 11
SUPPLEMENTARY

273. Interpretation

In this Act—

"the 1973 Act" means the Fair Trading Act 1973 (c. 41);

"the 1998 Act" means the Competition Act 1998 (c. 41);

"the Commission" means the Competition Commission;

"the Director" means the Director General of Fair Trading; and

"the OFT" means the Office of Fair Trading.

274. Provision of financial assistance for consumer purposes

The Secretary of State may give financial assistance to any person for the purpose of assisting—

(a) activities which the Secretary of State considers are of benefit to consumers; or

(b) the provision of—

(i) advice or information about consumer matters;

(ii) educational materials relating to consumer matters; or

(iii) advice or information to the Secretary of State in connection with the formulation of policy in respect of consumer matters.

275. Financial provision

There shall be paid out of money provided by Parliament—

(a) any expenditure incurred by the OFT, the Secretary of State, any other Minister of the Crown or a government department by virtue of this Act; and

(b) any increase attributable to this Act in the sums payable out of money so provided by virtue of any other Act.

276. Transitional or transitory provision and savings

(1) Schedule 24 (which makes transitional and transitory provisions and savings) has effect.

(2) The Secretary of State may by order made by statutory instrument make such transitional or transitory provisions and savings as he considers appropriate in connection with the coming into force of any provision of this Act.

(3) An order under subsection (2) may modify any Act or subordinate legislation.

(4) Schedule 24 does not restrict the power under subsection (2) to make other transitional or transitory provisions and savings.

277. Power to make consequential amendments etc.

(1) The Secretary of State may by order make such supplementary, incidental or consequential provision as he thinks appropriate—

(a) for the general purposes, or any particular purpose, of this Act; or

(b) in consequence of any provision made by or under this Act or for giving full effect to it.

(2) An order under this section may—

(a) modify any Act or subordinate legislation (including this Act);

(b) make incidental, supplementary, consequential, transitional, transitory or saving provision.

(3) The power to make an order under this section is exercisable by statutory instrument subject to annulment in pursuance of a resolution of either House of Parliament.

(4) The power conferred by this section is not restricted by any other provision of this Act.

278. ...

279. Commencement

The preceding provisions of this Act shall come into force on such day as the Secretary of State may by order made by statutory instrument appoint; and different days may be appointed for different purposes.

280. Extent

(1) Sections 256 to 265, 267, 269 and 272 extend only to England and Wales.

(2) Sections 204, 248 to 255 and 270 extend only to England and Wales and Scotland (but subsection (3) of section 415A as inserted by section 270 extends only to England and Wales).

(3) Any other modifications by this Act of an enactment have the same extent as the enactment being modified.

(4) Otherwise, this Act extends to England and Wales, Scotland and Northern Ireland.

281. Short title

This Act may be cited as the Enterprise Act 2002.

SCHEDULES

SCHEDULE 1

Section 1

THE OFFICE OF FAIR TRADING

Membership

1.— (1) The OFT shall consist of a chairman and no fewer than four other members, appointed by the Secretary of State.

(2) The Secretary of State shall consult the chairman before appointing any other member.

Terms of appointment, remuneration, pensions etc.

2.— (1) Subject to this Schedule, the chairman and other members shall hold and vacate office in accordance with the terms of their respective appointments.

(2) The terms of appointment of the chairman and other members shall be determined by the Secretary of State.

3.— (1) An appointment of a person to hold office as chairman or other member shall be for a term not exceeding five years.

(2) A person holding office as chairman or other member—

    (a) may resign that office by giving notice in writing to the Secretary of State; and

    (b) may be removed from office by the Secretary of State on the ground of incapacity or misbehaviour.

(3) A previous appointment as chairman or other member does not affect a person's eligibility for appointment to either office.

4.— (1) The OFT shall pay to the chairman and other members such remuneration, and such travelling and other allowances, as may be determined by the Secretary of State.

(2) The OFT shall, if required to do so by the Secretary of State—

    (a) pay such pension, allowances or gratuities as may be determined by the Secretary of State to or in respect of a person who holds or has held office as chairman or other member; or

      (b)   make such payments as may be so determined towards provision for the payment of a pension, allowances or gratuities to or in respect of such a person.

(3)   If, where any person ceases to hold office as chairman or other member, the Secretary of State determines that there are special circumstances which make it right that he should receive compensation, the OFT shall pay to him such amount by way of compensation as the Secretary of State may determine.

Staff

5.——   (1)   The Secretary of State shall, after consulting the chairman, appoint a person (who may, subject to sub-paragraph (2), also be a member of the OFT) to act as chief executive of the OFT on such terms and conditions as the Secretary of State may think appropriate.

(2)   A person appointed as chief executive after the end of the transitional period may not at the same time be chairman.

(3)   In sub-paragraph (2) "the transitional period" means the period of two years beginning with the day on which this paragraph comes into force.

6.   The OFT may, with the approval of the Minister for the Civil Service as to numbers and terms and conditions of service, appoint such other staff as it may determine.

Membership of committees or sub-committees of OFT

7.   The members of a committee or sub-committee of the OFT may include persons who are not members of the OFT (and a sub-committee may include persons who are not members of the committee which established it).

Proceedings etc.

8.——   (1)   The OFT may regulate its own procedure (including quorum).

(2)   The OFT shall consult the Secretary of State before making or revising its rules and procedures for dealing with conflicts of interest.

(3)   The OFT shall from time to time publish a summary of its rules and procedures for dealing with conflicts of interest.

9.   The validity of anything done by the OFT is not affected by a vacancy among its members or by a defect in the appointment of a member.

10.——   (1)   The application of the seal of the OFT shall be authenticated by the signature of—

      (a)   any member; or

      (b)   some other person who has been authorised for that purpose by the OFT, whether generally or specially.

(2)   Sub-paragraph (1) does not apply in relation to any document which is, or is to be, signed in accordance with the law of Scotland.

11.   A document purporting to be duly executed under the seal of the OFT, or signed on its behalf, shall be received in evidence and, unless the contrary is proved, be taken to be so executed or signed.

Performance of functions

12.——   (1)   Anything authorised or required to be done by the OFT (including exercising the power under this paragraph) may be done by—

      (a)   any member or employee of the OFT who is authorised for that purpose by the OFT, whether generally or specially;

      (b)   any committee of the OFT which has been so authorised.

(2)   Sub-paragraph (1)(b) does not apply to a committee whose members include any person who is not a member or employee of the OFT.

Supplementary powers

13.   The OFT has power to do anything which is calculated to facilitate, or is conducive or incidental to, the performance of its functions.

14–16.   …

SCHEDULE 2

THE COMPETITION APPEAL TRIBUNAL

Appointment, etc. of President and chairmen

1.— (1) A person is not eligible for appointment as President unless—

    (a) he has a 10 year general qualification;

    (b) he is an advocate or solicitor in Scotland of at least 10 years' standing; or

    (c) he is a member of the Bar of Northern Ireland or solicitor of the Supreme Court of Northern Ireland of at least 10 years' standing;

and he appears to the Lord Chancellor to have appropriate experience and knowledge of competition law and practice.

(2) A person is not eligible for appointment as a chairman unless—

    (a) he has a 7 year general qualification;

    (b) he is an advocate or solicitor in Scotland of at least 7 years' standing; or

    (c) he is a member of the Bar of Northern Ireland or solicitor of the Supreme Court of Northern Ireland of at least 7 years' standing;

and he appears to the Lord Chancellor to have appropriate experience and knowledge (either of competition law and practice or any other relevant law and practice).

(3) Before appointing an advocate or solicitor in Scotland under this paragraph, the Lord Chancellor must consult the Lord President of the Court of Session.

(4) In this paragraph "general qualification" has the same meaning as in section 71 of the Courts and Legal Services Act 1990 (c. 41).

2.— (1) The members appointed as President or as chairmen shall hold and vacate office in accordance with their terms of appointment, subject to the following provisions.

(2) A person may not be a chairman for more than 8 years (but this does not prevent a temporary re-appointment for the purpose of continuing to act as a member of the Tribunal as constituted for the purposes of any proceedings instituted before the end of his term of office).

(3) The President and the chairmen may resign their offices by notice in writing to the Lord Chancellor.

(4) The Lord Chancellor may remove a person from office as President or chairman on the ground of incapacity or misbehaviour.

3. If the President is absent or otherwise unable to act the Lord Chancellor may appoint as acting President any person qualified for appointment as a chairman.

Appointment, etc. of ordinary members

4.— (1) Ordinary members shall hold and vacate office in accordance with their terms of appointment, subject to the following provisions.

(2) A person may not be an ordinary member for more than 8 years (but this does not prevent a temporary re-appointment for the purpose of continuing to act as a member of the Tribunal as constituted for the purposes of any proceedings instituted before the end of his term of office).

(3) An ordinary member may resign his office by notice in writing to the Secretary of State.

(4) The Secretary of State may remove a person from office as an ordinary member on the ground of incapacity or misbehaviour.

Remuneration etc. for members

5.— (1) The Competition Service shall pay to the President, the chairmen and the ordinary members such remuneration (whether by way of salaries or fees), and such allowances, as the Secretary of State may determine.

(2)   The Competition Service shall, if required to do so by the Secretary of State—

(a)   pay such pension, allowances or gratuities as may be determined by the Secretary of State to or in respect of a person who holds or has held office as President, a chairman or an ordinary member; or

(b)   make such payments as may be so determined towards provision for the payment of a pension, allowance or gratuities to or in respect of such a person.

Compensation for loss of office

6.   If, where any person ceases to hold office as President, a chairman or ordinary member, the Secretary of State determines that there are special circumstances which make it right that he should receive compensation, the Competition Service shall pay to him such amount by way of compensation as the Secretary of State may determine.

Staff, accommodation and property

7.   Any staff, office accommodation or equipment required for the Tribunal shall be provided by the Competition Service.

Miscellaneous

8.   The President must arrange such training for members of the Tribunal as he considers appropriate.

9.   In this Schedule "chairman" and "ordinary member" mean respectively a member of the panel of chairmen, or a member of the panel of ordinary members, appointed under section 12.

10, 11.   …

SCHEDULE 3

Section 13

THE COMPETITION SERVICE

PART 1
CONSTITUTION ETC.

Membership of the Service

1.—   (1)   The Service shall consist of—

(a)   the President of the Competition Appeal Tribunal;

(b)   the Registrar of the Competition Appeal Tribunal; and

(c)   one or more appointed members.

(2)   An appointed member shall be appointed by the Secretary of State after consulting the President.

Chairman of Service

2.—   (1)   Subject to sub-paragraph (2), the members shall choose one of their number to be chairman of the Service.

(2)   The Secretary of State shall designate one of the members to be the first chairman of the Service for such period as the Secretary of State may determine.

Appointed members

3.   An appointed member shall hold and vacate office in accordance with the terms of his appointment (and is eligible for re-appointment).

Allowances, etc. for members

4.—   (1)   The Service shall pay—

(a)   such travelling and other allowances to its members, and

(b) such remuneration to any appointed member,

as may be determined by the Secretary of State.

(2) The Service shall, if required to do so by the Secretary of State—

(a) pay such pension, allowances or gratuities as may be determined by the Secretary of State to or in respect of a person who holds or has held office as an appointed member; or

(b) make such payments as may be so determined towards provision for the payment of a pension, allowances or gratuities to or in respect of such a person.

5.   If, where any person ceases to hold office as an appointed member, the Secretary of State determines that there are special circumstances which make it right that he should receive compensation, the Service shall pay to him such amount by way of compensation as the Secretary of State may determine.

Staff

6.— (1) The Service may, with the approval of the Secretary of State as to numbers and terms and conditions of service, appoint such staff as it may determine.

(2) The persons to whom section 1 of the Superannuation Act 1972 (c. 11) (persons to or in respect of whom benefits may be provided by schemes under that section) applies shall include the staff of the Service.

(3) The Service shall pay to the Minister for the Civil Service, at such times as he may direct, such sums as he may determine in respect of any increase attributable to sub-paragraph (2) in the sums payable out of money provided by Parliament under the Superannuation Act 1972.

Procedure

7.— (1) The Service may regulate its own procedure (including quorum).

(2) The validity of anything done by the Service is not affected by a vacancy among its members or by a defect in the appointment of a member.

8.— (1) The application of the seal of the Service shall be authenticated by the signature of—

(a) any member; or

(b) some other person who has been authorised for that purpose by the Service, whether generally or specially.

(2) Sub-paragraph (1) does not apply in relation to any document which is, or is to be, signed in accordance with the law of Scotland.

9.   A document purporting to be duly executed under the seal of the Service, or signed on its behalf, shall be received in evidence and, unless the contrary is proved, be taken to be so executed or signed.

The Service's powers

10.   The Service has power to do anything which is calculated to facilitate, or is conducive or incidental to, the performance of its functions.

Accounts

11.— (1) The Service shall keep proper accounts and proper records in relation to its accounts.

(2) In performing that duty the Service shall, in addition to accounts and records relating to its own activities (including the services provided to the Tribunal), keep separate accounts and separate records in relation to the activities of the Tribunal.

12.— (1) The Service shall—

(a) prepare a statement of accounts in respect of each of its financial years; and

(b) prepare a statement of accounts for the Tribunal for each of its financial years.

(2) The Service must send copies of the accounts required by sub-paragraph (1) to the Secretary of State and to the Comptroller and Auditor General before the end of August following the financial year to which they relate.

(3)   Those accounts must comply with any directions given by the Secretary of State with the approval of the Treasury as to—

    (a)   the information to be contained in them;

    (b)   the manner in which that information is to be presented; and

    (c)   the methods and principles according to which they are to be prepared.

(4)   The Comptroller and Auditor General shall—

    (a)   examine, certify and report on each statement of accounts received by him; and

    (b)   lay copies of each statement before Parliament.

(5)   In this paragraph "financial year" means the period of 12 months ending with 31st March.

PART 2
TRANSFERS OF PROPERTY ETC. BETWEEN THE COMMISSION AND THE SERVICE

13.—   (1)   The Secretary of State may make one or more schemes for the transfer to the Service of defined property, rights and liabilities of the Commission (including rights and liabilities relating to contracts of employment).

    (2)   A scheme may define the property, rights and liabilities to be transferred by specifying or describing them or by referring to all (or all except anything specified or described) of the property, rights and liabilities comprised in a specified part of the undertaking of the transferor.

    (3)   The property, rights and liabilities which may be transferred include any that would otherwise be incapable of being transferred or assigned.

    (4)   A scheme may include supplementary, incidental, transitional and consequential provision.

14.—   (1)   On the day appointed by a scheme under paragraph 13, the property, rights and liabilities which are the subject of the scheme shall, by virtue of this sub-paragraph, be transferred in accordance with the provisions of the scheme.

    (2)   If, after that day, the Commission and the Service so agree in writing, the scheme shall for all purposes be deemed to have come into force on that day with such modification as may be agreed.

    (3)   An agreement under sub-paragraph (2) may, in connection with giving effect to modifications to the scheme, include supplemental, incidental, transitional and consequential provision.

15.   The transfer by paragraph 14(1) of the rights and liabilities relating to an individual's contract of employment does not break the continuity of his employment and, accordingly—

    (a)   he is not to be regarded for the purposes of Part 11 of the Employment Rights Act 1996 as having been dismissed by virtue of the transfer; and

    (b)   his period of employment with the transferor counts as a period of employment with the transferee for the purposes of that Act.

16.—   (1)   Anything done by or in relation to the transferor for the purposes of or in connection with anything transferred by paragraph 14(1) which is in effect immediately before it is transferred shall be treated as if done by or in relation to the transferee.

    (2)   There may be continued by or in relation to the transferee anything (including legal proceedings) relating to anything so transferred which is in the process of being done by or in relation to the transferor immediately before it is transferred.

    (3)   A reference to the transferor in any document relating to anything so transferred shall be taken (so far as necessary for the purposes of or in consequence of the transfer) as a reference to the transferee.

    (4)   A transfer under paragraph 14(1) does not affect the validity of anything done by or in relation to the transferor before the transfer takes effect.

17, 18. ...

SCHEDULE 4

TRIBUNAL: PROCEDURE

PART 1
GENERAL

Decisions of the Tribunal

1.—   (1)   A decision of the Tribunal in any proceedings before it must—

(a)   state the reasons for the decision and whether it was unanimous or taken by a majority;

(b)   be recorded in a document signed and dated by the chairman of the Tribunal dealing with the proceedings.

(2)   In preparing that document the Tribunal shall have regard to the need for excluding, so far as practicable—

(a)   information the disclosure of which would in its opinion be contrary to the public interest;

(b)   commercial information the disclosure of which would or might, in its opinion, significantly harm the legitimate business interests of the undertaking to which it relates;

(c)   information relating to the private affairs of an individual the disclosure of which would, or might, in its opinion, significantly harm his interests.

(3)   But the Tribunal shall also have regard to the extent to which any disclosure mentioned in sub-paragraph (2) is necessary for the purpose of explaining the reasons for the decision.

(4)   The President shall make such arrangements for the publication of the decisions of the Tribunal as he considers appropriate.

Enforcement of decisions in Great Britain

2.   If a decision of the Tribunal is registered in England and Wales in accordance with rules of court or any practice direction—

(a)   payment of damages which are awarded by the decision;

(b)   costs or expenses awarded by the decision; and

(c)   any direction given as a result of the decision,

may be enforced by the High Court as if the damages, costs or expenses were an amount due in pursuance of a judgment or order of the High Court, or as if the direction were an order of the High Court.

3.   If a decision of the Tribunal awards damages, costs or expenses, or results in any direction being given, the decision may be recorded for execution in the Books of Council and Session and shall be enforceable accordingly.

4.   Subject to rules of court or any practice direction, a decision of the Tribunal may be registered or recorded for execution—

(a)   for the purpose of enforcing a direction given as a result of the decision, by the Registrar of the Tribunal or a person who was a party to the proceedings;

(b)   for the purpose of enforcing a decision to award damages, costs or expenses (other than a decision to which paragraph (c) applies), by the person to whom the sum concerned was awarded; and

(c)   for the purpose of enforcing a decision to award damages which is the subject of an order under section 47B(6) of the 1998 Act, by the specified body concerned.

Enforcement of decisions in Northern Ireland

5.—   (1)   A decision of the Tribunal may be enforced in Northern Ireland with the leave of the High Court in Northern Ireland—

(a)   in the case of a direction given as a result of the decision, by the Registrar of the Tribunal or a person who was a party to the proceedings;

(b)   for the purpose of enforcing a decision to award damages, costs or expenses (other than a decision to which paragraph (c) applies), by the person to whom the sum concerned was awarded; and

(c)   for the purpose of enforcing a decision to award damages which is the subject of an order under section 47B(6) of the 1998 Act, by the specified body concerned.

(2)   For the purpose of enforcing in Northern Ireland a decision to award damages, costs or expenses—

     (a)   payment may be enforced as if the damages, costs or expenses were an amount due in pursuance of a judgment or order of the High Court in Northern Ireland; and

     (b)   a sum equal to the amount of damages, costs or expenses shall be deemed to be payable under a money judgment within the meaning of Article 2(2) of the Judgments Enforcement (Northern Ireland) Order 1981 (S.I. 1981/226 (N.I. 6)) (and the provisions of that Order apply accordingly).

(3)   For the purpose of enforcing in Northern Ireland a direction given as a result of a decision of the Tribunal, the direction may be enforced as if it were an order of the High Court in Northern Ireland.

Miscellaneous

6.   A decision of the Tribunal in proceedings under section 47B of the 1998 Act which—

     (a)   awards damages to an individual in respect of a claim made or continued on his behalf (but is not the subject of an order under section 47B(6)); or

     (b)   awards costs or expenses to an individual in respect of proceedings in respect of a claim made under section 47A of that Act prior to its being continued on his behalf in the proceedings under section 47B,

may only be enforced by the individual concerned with the permission of the High Court or Court of Session.

7.   An award of costs or expenses against a specified body in proceedings under section 47B of the 1998 Act may not be enforced against any individual on whose behalf a claim was made or continued in those proceedings.

8.   In this Part of this Schedule any reference to damages includes a reference to any sum of money (other than costs or expenses) which may be awarded in respect of a claim made under section 47A of the 1998 Act or included in proceedings under section 47B of that Act.

PART 2

TRIBUNAL RULES

General

9.   In this Schedule "the Tribunal", in relation to any proceedings before it, means the Tribunal as constituted (in accordance with section 14) for the purposes of those proceedings.

10.   Tribunal rules may make different provision for different kinds of proceedings.

Institution of proceedings

11.—   (1)   Tribunal rules may make provision as to the period within which and the manner in which proceedings are to be brought.

     (2)   That provision may, in particular—

         (a)   provide for time limits for making claims to which section 47A of the 1998 Act applies in proceedings under section 47A or 47B;

         (b)   provide for the Tribunal to extend the period in which any particular proceedings may be brought; and

         (c)   provide for the form, contents, amendment and acknowledgement of the documents by which proceedings are to be instituted.

12.   Tribunal rules may provide for the Tribunal to reject any proceedings (other than proceedings under section 47A or 47B of the 1998 Act) if it considers that—

(a)   the person instituting them does not have a sufficient interest in the decision with respect to which the proceedings are brought; or

(b)   the document by which he institutes them discloses no valid grounds for bringing them.

13.   Tribunal rules may provide for the Tribunal—

(a)   to reject the whole of any proceedings under section 47B of the 1998 Act if it considers that the person bringing the proceedings is not entitled to do so or that the proceedings do not satisfy the requirements of section 47B(1);

(b)   to reject any claim which is included in proceedings under section 47B if it considers that—

(i)   the claim is not a consumer claim (within the meaning of section 47B(2)) which may be included in such proceedings; or

(ii)   the individual concerned has not consented to its being made or continued on his behalf in such proceedings; or

(c)   to reject any claim made under section 47A of the 1998 Act or included in proceedings under section 47B of that Act if it considers that there are no reasonable grounds for making it.

14.   Tribunal rules may provide for the Tribunal to reject any proceedings if it is satisfied that the person instituting the proceedings has habitually and persistently and without any reasonable ground—

(a)   instituted vexatious proceedings (whether against the same person or against different persons); or

(b)   made vexatious applications in any proceedings.

15.   Tribunal rules must ensure that no proceedings are rejected without giving the parties the opportunity to be heard.

Pre-hearing reviews and preliminary matters

16.—   (1)   Tribunal rules may make provision for the carrying out by the Tribunal of a preliminary consideration of proceedings (a "pre-hearing review").

(2)   That provision may include—

(a)   provision enabling such powers to be exercised on a pre-hearing review as may be specified in the rules;

(b)   provision for security and supplemental provision relating to security.

(3)   For the purposes of sub-paragraph (2)(b)—

(a)   "provision for security" means provision authorising the Tribunal, in specified circumstances, to order a party to the proceedings, if he wishes to continue to participate in them, to pay a deposit not exceeding such sum as may be specified or calculated in a specified manner; and

(b)   "supplemental provision", in relation to security, means provision as to—

(i)   the manner in which the amount of a deposit is to be determined;

(ii)   the consequences of non-payment of a deposit;

(iii)   the circumstances in which the deposit, or any part of it, may be refunded to the person who paid it or paid to another party to the proceedings.

Conduct of the hearing

17.—   (1)   Tribunal rules may make provision—

(a)   as to the manner in which proceedings are to be conducted, including provision for any hearing to be held in private if the Tribunal considers it appropriate because it is considering information of a kind mentioned in paragraph 1(2);

(b)   as to the persons entitled to appear on behalf of the parties;

(c)   for requiring persons to attend to give evidence and produce documents, and for authorising the administration of oaths to witnesses;

(d) as to the evidence which may be required or admitted and the extent to which it should be oral or written;

(e) allowing the Tribunal to fix time limits with respect to any aspect of proceedings and to extend any time limit (before or after its expiry);

(f) enabling the Tribunal, on the application of any party or on its own initiative, to order—

   (i)   the disclosure between, or the production by, the parties of documents or classes of documents; or

   (ii)   such recovery or inspection of documents as might be ordered by a sheriff;

(g) for the appointment of experts for the purposes of proceedings;

(h) for the award of costs or expenses, including allowances payable to persons in connection with attendance before the Tribunal;

(i) for taxing or otherwise settling any costs or expenses awarded by the Tribunal or for the enforcement of any order awarding costs or expenses.

(2) Rules under sub-paragraph (1)(h) may provide, in relation to a claim made under section 47A of the 1998 Act which is continued on behalf of an individual in proceedings under section 47B of that Act, for costs or expenses to be awarded to or against that individual in respect of proceedings on that claim which took place before it was included in the proceedings under section 47B of that Act.

(3) Otherwise Tribunal rules may not provide for costs or expenses to be awarded to or against an individual on whose behalf a claim is made or continued in proceedings under section 47B of the 1998 Act.

(4) Tribunal rules may make provision enabling the Tribunal to refer any matter arising in any proceedings (other than proceedings under section 47A or 47B of the 1998 Act) back to the authority that made the decision to which the proceedings relate, if it appears that the matter has not been adequately investigated.

(5) A person who without reasonable excuse fails to comply with—

(a) any requirement imposed by virtue of sub-paragraph (1)(c); or

(b) any requirement with respect to the disclosure, production, recovery or inspection of documents which is imposed by virtue of sub-paragraph (1)(f),

is guilty of an offence and liable on summary conviction to a fine not exceeding level 3 on the standard scale.

Quorum

18.— (1) Tribunal rules may make provision as to the consequences of a member of the Tribunal being unable to continue after part of any proceedings have been heard.

(2) The rules may allow the Tribunal to consist of the remaining members for the rest of the proceedings.

(3) The rules may enable the President, if it is the chairman of the Tribunal who is unable to continue—

(a) to appoint either of the remaining members to chair the Tribunal; and

(b) if that person is not a member of the panel of chairmen, to appoint himself or some other suitably qualified person to attend the proceedings and advise the remaining members on any questions of law arising.

(4) For the purpose of sub-paragraph (3) a person is "suitably qualified" if he is, or is qualified for appointment as, a member of the panel of chairmen.

Interest

19.— (1) Tribunal rules may make provision allowing the Tribunal to order that interest is payable on any sum awarded by the Tribunal or on any fees ordered to be paid under paragraph 20.

(2) That provision may include provision—

(a) as to the circumstances in which such an order may be made;

(b) as to the manner in which, and the periods in respect of which, interest is to be calculated and paid.

Fees

20.— (1) Tribunal rules may provide—

(a) for fees to be chargeable in respect of specified costs of proceedings; and

(b) for the amount of such costs to be determined by the Tribunal.

(2) Any sums received in respect of such fees shall be paid into the Consolidated Fund.

Withdrawal of proceedings

21.— (1) Tribunal rules may make provision—

(a) preventing a party who has instituted proceedings from withdrawing them without the permission of the Tribunal or, in specified circumstances, the President or the Registrar;

(b) for the Tribunal to grant permission to withdraw proceedings on such conditions as it considers appropriate;

(c) enabling the Tribunal to publish any decision which it would have made in any proceedings, had the proceedings not been withdrawn;

(d) as to the effect of withdrawal of proceedings; and

(e) as to the procedure to be followed if parties to proceedings agree to settle.

(2) Tribunal rules may make, in relation to a claim included in proceedings under section 47B of the 1998 Act, any provision which may be made under sub-paragraph (1) in relation to the whole proceedings.

Interim orders

22.— (1) Tribunal rules may provide for the Tribunal to make an order, on an interim basis—

(a) suspending the effect of any decision which is the subject matter of proceedings before it;

(b) in the case of an appeal under section 46 or 47 of the 1998 Act, varying the conditions or obligations attached to an exemption;

(c) granting any remedy which the Tribunal would have had power to grant in its final decision.

(2) Tribunal rules may also make provision giving the Tribunal powers similar to those given to the OFT by section 35 of the 1998 Act.

Miscellaneous

23.— (1) Tribunal rules may make provision enabling the Tribunal to decide where to sit for the purposes of, or of any part of, any proceedings before it.

(2) Tribunal rules may make provision enabling the Tribunal to decide that any proceedings before it are to be treated, for purposes connected with—

(a) any appeal from a decision of the Tribunal made in those proceedings; and

(b) any other matter connected with those proceedings,

as proceedings in England and Wales, Scotland or Northern Ireland (regardless of the decision made for the purposes of sub-paragraph (1)).

(3) For the purposes of sub-paragraph (2), Tribunal rules may provide for each claim made or continued on behalf of an individual in proceedings under section 47B of the 1998 Act to be treated as separate proceedings.

24. Tribunal rules may make provision—

(a) for a person who is not a party to be joined in any proceedings;

(b) for hearing a person who is not a party where, in any proceedings, it is proposed to make an order or give a direction in relation to that person;

(c) for proceedings to be consolidated on such terms as the Tribunal thinks appropriate in such circumstances as may be specified.

25. Tribunal rules may make provision for the Tribunal to transfer a claim made in proceedings under section 47A of the 1998 Act to—

   (a)   the High Court or a county court in England and Wales or Northern Ireland; or

   (b)   the Court of Session or a sheriff court in Scotland.

26. Tribunal rules may make provision in connection with the transfer of any proceedings from a court mentioned in paragraph 25 to the Tribunal under section 16.

SCHEDULE 5, 6

...

SCHEDULE 7

Section 85

ENFORCEMENT REGIME FOR PUBLIC INTEREST AND SPECIAL PUBLIC INTEREST CASES

Pre-emptive undertakings and orders

1.— (1) Sub-paragraph (2) applies where an intervention notice or special intervention notice is in force.

    (2) The Secretary of State may, for the purpose of preventing pre-emptive action, accept from such of the parties concerned as he considers appropriate undertakings to take such action as he considers appropriate.

    (3) Sub-paragraph (4) applies where an intervention notice is in force.

    (4) The Secretary of State may, for the purpose of preventing pre-emptive action, adopt an undertaking accepted by the OFT under section 71 if the undertaking is still in force when the Secretary of State adopts it.

    (5) An undertaking adopted under sub-paragraph (4)—

       (a) shall continue in force, in accordance with its terms, when adopted;

       (b) may be varied or superseded by an undertaking under this paragraph; and

       (c) may be released by the Secretary of State.

    (6) Any other undertaking under this paragraph—

       (a) shall come into force when accepted;

       (b) may be varied or superseded by another undertaking; and

       (c) may be released by the Secretary of State.

    (7) References in this Part to undertakings under this paragraph shall, unless the context otherwise requires, include references to undertakings adopted under this paragraph; and references to the acceptance or giving of undertakings under this paragraph shall be construed accordingly.

    (8) An undertaking which is in force under this paragraph in relation to a reference or possible reference under section 45 or (as the case may be) 62 shall cease to be in force if an order under paragraph 2 or an undertaking under paragraph 3 comes into force in relation to that reference.

    (9) An undertaking under this paragraph shall, if it has not previously ceased to be in force, cease to be in force when the intervention notice concerned or (as the case may be) special intervention notice concerned ceases to be in force.

   (10) No undertaking shall be accepted by the Secretary of State under this paragraph before the making of a reference under section 45 or (as the case may be) 62 unless the undertaking relates to a relevant merger situation which has been, or may have been, created or (as the case may be) a special merger situation which has been, or may have been, created.

(11) The Secretary of State shall, as soon as reasonably practicable, consider any representations received by him in relation to varying or releasing an undertaking under this paragraph.

(12) In this paragraph and paragraph 2 "pre-emptive action" means action which might prejudice the reference or possible reference concerned under section 45 or (as the case may be) 62 or impede the taking of any action under this Part which may be justified by the Secretary of State's decisions on the reference.

2.— (1) Sub-paragraph (2) applies where an intervention notice or special intervention notice is in force.

(2) The Secretary of State or the OFT may by order, for the purpose of preventing pre-emptive action—

    (a) prohibit or restrict the doing of things which the Secretary of State or (as the case may be) the OFT considers would constitute pre-emptive action;

    (b) impose on any person concerned obligations as to the carrying on of any activities or the safeguarding of any assets;

    (c) provide for the carrying on of any activities or the safeguarding of any assets either by the appointment of a person to conduct or supervise the conduct of any activities (on such terms and with such powers as may be specified or described in the order) or in any other manner;

    (d) do anything which may be done by virtue of paragraph 19 of Schedule 8.

(3) Sub-paragraph (4) applies where an intervention notice is in force.

(4) The Secretary of State or the OFT may, for the purpose of preventing pre-emptive action, adopt an order made by the OFT under section 72 if the order is still in force when the Secretary of State or (as the case may be) the OFT adopts it.

(5) An order adopted under sub-paragraph (4)—

    (a) shall continue in force, in accordance with its terms, when adopted; and

    (b) may be varied or revoked by an order under this paragraph.

(6) Any other order under this paragraph—

    (a) shall come into force at such time as is determined by or under the order; and

    (b) may be varied or revoked by another order.

(7) References in this Part to orders under this paragraph shall, unless the context otherwise requires, include references to orders adopted under this paragraph; and references to the making of orders under this paragraph shall be construed accordingly.

(8) An order which is in force under this paragraph in relation to a reference or possible reference under section 45 or (as the case may be) 62 shall cease to be in force if an undertaking under paragraph 1 or 3 comes into force in relation to that reference.

(9) An order under this paragraph shall, if it has not previously ceased to be in force, cease to be in force when the intervention notice concerned or (as the case may be) special intervention notice concerned ceases to be in force.

(10) No order shall be made by the Secretary of State or the OFT under this paragraph before the making of a reference under section 45 or (as the case may be) 62 unless the order relates to a relevant merger situation which has been, or may have been, created or (as the case may be) a special merger situation which has been, or may have been, created.

(11) The Secretary of State or (as the case may be) the OFT shall, as soon as reasonably practicable, consider any representations received by that person in relation to varying or revoking an order under this paragraph.

Undertakings in lieu of reference under section 45 or 62

3.— (1) Sub-paragraph (2) applies if the Secretary of State has power to make a reference to the Commission under section 45 or 62 and otherwise intends to make such a reference.

(2) The Secretary of State may, instead of making such a reference and for the purpose of remedying, mitigating or preventing any of the effects adverse to the public interest which have or may have resulted, or which may be expected to result, from the creation of the relevant merger situation concerned or (as the case may be) the special merger situation

concerned, accept from such of the parties concerned as he considers appropriate undertakings to take such action as he considers appropriate.

(3) In proceeding under sub-paragraph (2), the Secretary of State shall, in particular—
   (a) accept the decisions of the OFT included in its report under section 44 so far as they relate to the matters mentioned in subsections (4) and (5) of that section; or
   (b) (as the case may be) accept the decisions of the OFT included in its report under section 61 so far as they relate to the matters mentioned in subsections (3)(a) and (4) of that section.

(4) In proceeding under sub-paragraph (2) in relation to an anti-competitive outcome, the Secretary of State may, in particular, have regard to the effect of any action on any relevant customer benefits in relation to the creation of the relevant merger situation concerned.

(5) No undertaking shall be accepted by the Secretary of State under this paragraph in connection with a possible reference under section 45 if a public interest consideration mentioned in the intervention notice concerned has not been finalised and the period of 24 weeks beginning with the giving of that notice has not expired.

(6) The Secretary of State may delay making a decision as to whether to accept any such undertaking (and any related decision as to whether to make a reference under section 45) if he considers that there is a realistic prospect of the public interest consideration being finalised within the period of 24 weeks beginning with the giving of the intervention notice concerned.

(7) A delay under sub-paragraph (6) shall not extend beyond—
   (a) the time when the public interest consideration is finalised; or
   (b) if earlier, the expiry of the period of 24 weeks mentioned in that sub-paragraph.

(8) An undertaking under this paragraph—
   (a) shall come into force when accepted;
   (b) may be varied or superseded by another undertaking; or
   (c) may be released by the Secretary of State.

(9) An undertaking under this paragraph which is in force in relation to a relevant merger situation or (as the case may be) a special merger situation shall cease to be in force if an order comes into force under paragraph 5 or 6 in relation to that undertaking.

(10) The Secretary of State shall, as soon as reasonably practicable, consider any representations received by him in relation to varying or releasing an undertaking under this section.

4.— (1) The relevant authority shall not make a reference under section 22, 33 or 45 in relation to the creation of a relevant merger situation or (as the case may be) a reference under section 62 in relation to the creation of a special merger situation if—
   (a) the Secretary of State has accepted an undertaking or group of undertakings under paragraph 3; and
   (b) the relevant merger situation or (as the case may be) the special merger situation is the situation by reference to which the undertaking or group of undertakings was accepted.

(2) In sub-paragraph (1) "the relevant authority" means—
   (a) in relation to a possible reference under section 22 or 33, the OFT; and
   (b) in relation to a possible reference under section 45 or 62, the Secretary of State.

(3) Sub-paragraph (1) does not prevent the making of a reference if material facts about relevant arrangements or transactions, or relevant proposed arrangements or transactions, were not notified (whether in writing or otherwise) to the Secretary of State or the OFT or made public before any undertaking concerned was accepted.

(4) For the purposes of sub-paragraph (3) arrangements or transactions, or proposed arrangements or transactions, are relevant if they are the ones in consequence of which the enterprises concerned ceased or may have ceased, or may cease, to be distinct enterprises.

(5) In sub-paragraph (3) "made public" means so publicised as to be generally known or readily ascertainable.

5.— (1) Sub-paragraph (2) applies where the Secretary of State considers that—

(a) an undertaking accepted by him under paragraph 3 has not been, is not being or will not be fulfilled; or

(b) in relation to an undertaking accepted by him under that paragraph, information which was false or misleading in a material respect was given to him or the OFT by the person giving the undertaking before he decided to accept the undertaking.

(2) The Secretary of State may, for any of the purposes mentioned in paragraph 3(2), make an order under this paragraph.

(3) Sub-paragraphs (3) and (4) of paragraph 3 shall apply for the purposes of sub-paragraph (2) above as they apply for the purposes of sub-paragraph (2) of that paragraph.

(4) An order under this paragraph may contain—

(a) anything permitted by Schedule 8; and

(b) such supplementary, consequential or incidental provision as the Secretary of State considers appropriate.

(5) An order under this paragraph—

(a) shall come into force at such time as is determined by or under the order; and

(b) may contain provision which is different from the provision contained in the undertaking concerned.

(6) No order shall be varied or revoked under this paragraph unless the OFT advises that such a variation or revocation is appropriate by reason of a change of circumstances.

6.— (1) Sub-paragraph (2) applies where—

(a) the Secretary of State has the power to make an order under paragraph 5 in relation to a particular undertaking and intends to make such an order; or

(b) the Secretary of State has the power to make an order under paragraph 10 in relation to a particular undertaking and intends to make such an order.

(2) The Secretary of State may, for the purpose of preventing any action which might prejudice the making of that order, make an order under this paragraph.

(3) No order shall be made under sub-paragraph (2) unless the Secretary of State has reasonable grounds for suspecting that it is or may be the case that action which might prejudice the making of the order under paragraph 5 or (as the case may be) 10 is in progress or in contemplation.

(4) An order under sub-paragraph (2) may—

(a) prohibit or restrict the doing of things which the Secretary of State considers would prejudice the making of the order under paragraph 5 or 10;

(b) impose on any person concerned obligations as to the carrying on of any activities or the safeguarding of any assets;

(c) provide for the carrying on of any activities or the safeguarding of any assets either by the appointment of a person to conduct or supervise the conduct of any activities (on such terms and with such powers as may be specified or described in the order) or in any other manner;

(d) do anything which may be done by virtue of paragraph 19 of Schedule 8.

(5) An order under this paragraph shall come into force at such time as is determined by or under the order.

(6) An order under this paragraph shall, if it has not previously ceased to be in force, cease to be in force on—

(a) the coming into force of an order under paragraph 5 or (as the case may be) 10 in relation to the undertaking concerned; or

(b) the making of the decision not to proceed with such an order.

(7) The Secretary of State shall, as soon as reasonably practicable, consider any representations received by him in relation to varying or revoking an order under this paragraph.

Statutory restrictions following reference under section 45 or 62

7.— (1) Sub-paragraphs (2) and (3) apply where—

(a) a reference has been made under section 45(2) or (3) or 62(2) but not finally determined; and

(b) no undertakings under paragraph 1 are in force in relation to the relevant merger situation concerned or (as the case may be) the special merger situation concerned and no orders under paragraph 2 are in force in relation to that situation.

(2) No relevant person shall, without the consent of the Secretary of State—

(a) complete any outstanding matters in connection with any arrangements which have resulted in the enterprises concerned ceasing to be distinct enterprises;

(b) make any further arrangements in consequence of that result (other than arrangements which reverse that result); or

(c) transfer the ownership or control of any enterprises to which the reference relates.

(3) No relevant person shall, without the consent of the Secretary of State, assist in any of the activities mentioned in paragraphs (a) to (c) of sub-paragraph (2).

(4) The prohibitions in sub-paragraphs (2) and (3) do not apply in relation to anything which the person concerned is required to do by virtue of any enactment.

(5) The consent of the Secretary of State under sub-paragraph (2) or (3)—

(a) may be general or specific;

(b) may be revoked by the Secretary of State; and

(c) shall be published in such manner as the Secretary of State considers appropriate for bringing it to the attention of any person entitled to the benefit of it.

(6) Paragraph (c) of sub-paragraph (5) shall not apply if the Secretary of State considers that publication is not necessary for the purpose mentioned in that paragraph.

(7) Sub-paragraphs (2) and (3) shall apply to a person's conduct outside the United Kingdom if (and only if) he is—

(a) a United Kingdom national;

(b) a body incorporated under the law of the United Kingdom or of any part of the United Kingdom; or

(c) a person carrying on business in the United Kingdom.

(8) For the purpose of this paragraph a reference under section 45(2) or (3) is finally determined if—

(a) the time within which the Commission is to prepare a report under section 50 in relation to the reference and give it to the Secretary of State has expired and no such report has been so prepared and given;

(b) the Commission decides to cancel the reference under section 53(1);

(c) the time within which the Secretary of State is to make and publish a decision under section 54(2) has expired and no such decision has been made and published;

(d) the Secretary of State decides under section 54(2) to make no finding at all in the matter;

(e) the Secretary of State otherwise decides under section 54(2) not to make an adverse public interest finding;

(f) the Secretary of State decides under section 54(2) to make an adverse public interest finding but decides neither to accept an undertaking under paragraph 9 of this Schedule nor to make an order under paragraph 11 of this Schedule; or

(g) the Secretary of State decides under section 54(2) to make an adverse public interest finding and accepts an undertaking under paragraph 9 of this Schedule or makes an order under paragraph 11 of this Schedule.

(9) For the purpose of this paragraph a reference under section 62(2) is finally determined if—

(a) the time within which the Commission is to prepare a report under section 65 in relation to the reference and give it to the Secretary of State has expired and no such report has been so prepared and given;

(b) the time within which the Secretary of State is to make and publish a decision under section 66(2) has expired and no such decision has been made and published;

      (c)   the Secretary of State decides under subsection (2) of section 66 otherwise than as mentioned in subsection (5) of that section;

      (d)   the Secretary of State decides under subsection (2) of section 66 as mentioned in subsection (5) of that section but decides neither to accept an undertaking under paragraph 9 of this Schedule nor to make an order under paragraph 11 of this Schedule; or

      (e)   the Secretary of State decides under subsection (2) of section 66 as mentioned in subsection (5) of that section and accepts an undertaking under paragraph 9 of this Schedule or makes an order under paragraph 11 of this Schedule.

(10) For the purposes of this paragraph the time when a reference under section 45(2) or (3) or (as the case may be) 62(2) is finally determined is—

      (a)   in a case falling within sub-paragraph (8)(a) or (c) or (as the case may be) (9)(a) or (b), the expiry of the time concerned;

      (b)   in a case falling within sub-paragraph (8)(b), (d) or (e) or (as the case may be) (9)(c), the making of the decision concerned;

      (c)   in a case falling within sub-paragraph (8)(f) or (as the case may be) (9)(d), the making of the decision neither to accept an undertaking under paragraph 9 of this Schedule nor to make an order under paragraph 11 of this Schedule; and

      (d)   in a case falling within sub-paragraph (8)(g) or (as the case may be) (9)(e), the acceptance of the undertaking concerned or (as the case may be) the making of the order concerned.

(11) In this paragraph "relevant person" means—

      (a)   any person who carries on any enterprise to which the reference relates or who has control of any such enterprise;

      (b)   any subsidiary of any person falling within paragraph (a); or

      (c)   any person associated with any person falling within paragraph (a) or any subsidiary of any person so associated.

8.— (1) Sub-paragraph (2) applies where—

      (a)   a reference has been made under section 45(4) or (5) or 62(3); and

      (b)   no undertakings under paragraph 1 are in force in relation to the relevant merger situation concerned or (as the case may be) special merger situation concerned and no orders under paragraph 2 are in force in relation to that situation.

(2) No relevant person shall, without the consent of the Secretary of State, directly or indirectly acquire during the relevant period an interest in shares in a company if any enterprise to which the reference relates is carried on by or under the control of that company.

(3) The consent of the Secretary of State under sub-paragraph (2)—

      (a)   may be general or specific;

      (b)   may be revoked by the Secretary of State; and

      (c)   shall be published in such manner as the Secretary of State considers appropriate for bringing it to the attention of any person entitled to the benefit of it.

(4) Paragraph (c) of sub-paragraph (3) shall not apply if the Secretary of State considers that publication is not necessary for the purpose mentioned in that paragraph.

(5) Sub-paragraph (2) shall apply to a person's conduct outside the United Kingdom if (and only if) he is—

      (a)   a United Kingdom national;

      (b)   a body incorporated under the law of the United Kingdom or of any part of the United Kingdom; or

      (c)   a person carrying on business in the United Kingdom.

(6) In this paragraph—

      "company" includes any body corporate;

      "relevant period" means the period beginning with the publication of the decision of the Secretary of State to make the reference concerned and ending when the reference is finally determined;

"relevant person" means—

(a) any person who carries on any enterprise to which the reference relates or who has control of any such enterprise;

(b) any subsidiary of any person falling within paragraph (a); or

(c) any person associated with any person falling within paragraph (a) or any subsidiary of any person so associated; and

"share" means share in the capital of a company, and includes stock.

(7) For the purposes of the definition of "relevant period" in sub-paragraph (6), a reference under section 45(4) or (5) is finally determined if—

(a) the Commission cancels the reference under section 48(1) or 53(1);

(b) the time within which the Commission is to prepare a report under section 50 in relation to the reference and give it to the Secretary of State has expired and no such report has been so prepared and given;

(c) the time within which the Secretary of State is to make and publish a decision under section 54(2) has expired and no such decision has been made and published;

(d) the Secretary of State decides under section 54(2) to make no finding at all in the matter;

(e) the Secretary of State otherwise decides under section 54(2) not to make an adverse public interest finding;

(f) the Secretary of State decides under section 54(2) to make an adverse public interest finding but decides neither to accept an undertaking under paragraph 9 of this Schedule nor to make an order under paragraph 11 of this Schedule; or

(g) the Secretary of State decides under section 54(2) to make an adverse public interest finding and accepts an undertaking under paragraph 9 of this Schedule or makes an order under paragraph 11 of this Schedule.

(8) For the purposes of the definition of "relevant period" in sub-paragraph (6), a reference under section 62(3) is finally determined if—

(a) the Commission cancels the reference under section 64(1);

(b) the time within which the Commission is to prepare a report under section 65 in relation to the reference and give it to the Secretary of State has expired and no such report has been so prepared and given;

(c) the time within which the Secretary of State is to make and publish a decision under section 66(2) has expired and no such decision has been made and published;

(d) the Secretary of State decides under subsection (2) of section 66 otherwise than as mentioned in subsection (5) of that section;

(e) the Secretary of State decides under subsection (2) of section 66 as mentioned in subsection (5) of that section but decides neither to accept an undertaking under paragraph 9 of this Schedule nor to make an order under paragraph 11 of this Schedule; or

(f) the Secretary of State decides under subsection (2) of section 66 as mentioned in subsection (5) of that section and accepts an undertaking under paragraph 9 of this Schedule or makes an order under paragraph 11 of this Schedule.

(9) For the purposes of the definition of "relevant period" in sub-paragraph (6) above, the time when a reference under section 45(4) or (5) or (as the case may be) 62(3) is finally determined is—

(a) in a case falling within sub-paragraph (7)(a), (d) or (e) or (as the case may be) (8)(a) or (d), the making of the decision concerned;

(b) in a case falling within sub-paragraph (7)(b) or (c) or (as the case may be) (8)(b) or (c), the expiry of the time concerned;

(c) in a case falling within sub-paragraph (7)(f) or (as the case may be) (8)(e), the making of the decision neither to accept an undertaking under paragraph 9 of this Schedule nor to make an order under paragraph 11 of this Schedule; and

(d) in a case falling within sub-paragraph (7)(g) or (as the case may be) (8)(f), the acceptance of the undertaking concerned or (as the case may be) the making of the order concerned.

(10) Section 79 shall apply for the purposes of paragraph 7 and this paragraph in relation to a reference under section 45 or 62 as it applies for the purposes of sections 77 and 78 in relation to a reference under section 22 or 33.

(11) In its application by virtue of sub-paragraph (10) section 79 shall have effect as if—

(a) subsections (1) and (2) were omitted; and

(b) for the reference in subsection (4) to the OFT there were substituted a reference to the Secretary of State.

Final undertakings and orders

9.— (1) The Secretary of State may, in accordance with section 55 or (as the case may be) 66(5) to (7), accept, from such persons as he considers appropriate, undertakings to take action specified or described in the undertakings.

(2) An undertaking under this paragraph—

(a) shall come into force when accepted;

(b) may be varied or superseded by another undertaking; and

(c) may be released by the Secretary of State.

(3) An undertaking which is in force under this paragraph in relation to a reference under section 45 or 62 shall cease to be in force if an order under paragraph 6(1)(b) or 10 comes into force in relation to the subject-matter of the undertaking.

(4) No undertaking shall be accepted under this paragraph in relation to a reference under section 45 or 62 if an order has been made under—

(a) paragraph 6(1)(b) or 10 in relation to the subject-matter of the undertaking; or

(b) paragraph 11 in relation to that reference.

(5) The Secretary of State shall, as soon as reasonably practicable, consider any representations received by him in relation to varying or releasing an undertaking under this section.

10.— (1) Sub-paragraph (2) applies where the Secretary of State considers that—

(a) an undertaking accepted by him under paragraph 9 has not been, is not being or will not be fulfilled; or

(b) in relation to an undertaking accepted by him under that paragraph, information which was false or misleading in a material respect was given to him or the OFT by the person giving the undertaking before he decided to accept the undertaking.

(2) The Secretary of State may, for any purpose mentioned in section 55(2) or (as the case may be) 66(6), make an order under this paragraph.

(3) Subsections (3) and (4) of section 55 or (as the case may be) subsection (7) of section 66 shall apply for the purposes of sub-paragraph (2) above as they or it applies for the purposes of section 55(2) or (as the case may be) 66(6).

(4) An order under this paragraph may contain—

(a) anything permitted by Schedule 8; and

(b) such supplementary, consequential or incidental provision as the Secretary of State considers appropriate.

(5) An order under this paragraph—

(a) shall come into force at such time as is determined by or under the order; and

(b) may contain provision which is different from the provision contained in the undertaking concerned.

(6) No order shall be varied or revoked under this paragraph unless the OFT advises that such a variation or revocation is appropriate by reason of a change of circumstances.

11.— (1) The Secretary of State may, in accordance with section 55 or (as the case may be) 66(5) to (7), make an order under this paragraph.

(2) An order under this paragraph may contain—

(a) anything permitted by Schedule 8; and

(b)   such supplementary, consequential or incidental provision as the Secretary of State considers appropriate.

(3)   An order under this paragraph shall come into force at such time as is determined by or under the order.

(4)   No order shall be made under this paragraph in relation to a reference under section 45 or (as the case may be) 62 if an undertaking has been accepted under paragraph 9 in relation to that reference.

(5)   No order shall be varied or revoked under this paragraph unless the OFT advises that such a variation or revocation is appropriate by reason of a change of circumstances.

SCHEDULE 8

Section 86(4)

PROVISION THAT MAY BE CONTAINED IN CERTAIN ENFORCEMENT ORDERS

Introductory

1.   This Schedule applies in relation to such orders, and to such extent, as is provided by this Part and Part 4 and any other enactment; and references in this Schedule to an order shall be construed accordingly.

General restrictions on conduct

2.—   (1)   An order may—
        (a)   prohibit the making or performance of an agreement;
        (b)   require any party to an agreement to terminate the agreement.

        (2)   An order made by virtue of sub-paragraph (1) shall not—
        (a)   prohibit the making or performance of; or
        (b)   require any person to terminate,
        an agreement so far as, if made, the agreement would relate, or (as the case may be) so far as the agreement relates, to the terms and conditions of employment of any workers or to the physical conditions in which any workers are required to work.

3.—   (1)   An order may prohibit the withholding from any person of—
        (a)   any goods or services;
        (b)   any orders for any such goods or services.

        (2)   References in sub-paragraph (1) to withholding include references to—
        (a)   agreeing or threatening to withhold; and
        (b)   procuring others to withhold or to agree or threaten to withhold.

4.   An order may prohibit requiring as a condition of the supply of goods or services to any person—
        (a)   the buying of any goods;
        (b)   the making of any payment in respect of services other than the goods or services supplied;
        (c)   the doing of any other such matter or the refraining from doing anything mentioned in paragraph (a) or (b) or any other such matter.

5.   An order may prohibit—
        (a)   discrimination between persons in the prices charged for goods or services;
        (b)   anything which the relevant authority considers to be such discrimination;
        (c)   procuring others to do anything which is such discrimination or which the relevant authority considers to be such discrimination.

6.   An order may prohibit—
        (a)   giving, or agreeing to give in other ways, any preference in respect of the supply of goods or services or in respect of the giving of orders for goods or services;
        (b)   giving, or agreeing to give in other ways, anything which the relevant authority considers to be a preference in respect of the supply of goods or services or in respect of the giving of orders for goods or services;

(c) procuring others to do anything mentioned in paragraph (a) or (b).

7. An order may prohibit—

    (a) charging, for goods or services supplied, prices differing from those in any published list or notification;

    (b) doing anything which the relevant authority considers to be charging such prices.

8.— (1) An order may regulate the prices to be charged for any goods or services.

    (2) No order shall be made by virtue of sub-paragraph (1) unless the relevant report in relation to the matter concerned identifies the prices charged for the goods or services as requiring remedial action.

    (3) In this paragraph "the relevant report" means the report of the Commission which is required by the enactment concerned before an order can be made under this Schedule.

9. An order may prohibit the exercise of any right to vote exercisable by virtue of the holding of any shares, stock or securities.

General obligations to be performed

10.— (1) An order may require a person to supply goods or services or to do anything which the relevant authority considers appropriate to facilitate the provision of goods or services.

    (2) An order may require a person who is supplying, or is to supply, goods or services to supply such goods or services to a particular standard or in a particular manner or to do anything which the relevant authority considers appropriate to facilitate the provision of such goods or services to that standard or in that manner.

11. An order may require any activities to be carried on separately from any other activities.

Acquisitions and divisions

12.— (1) An order may prohibit or restrict—

    (a) the acquisition by any person of the whole or part of the undertaking or assets of another person's business;

    (b) the doing of anything which will or may result in two or more bodies corporate becoming interconnected bodies corporate.

    (2) An order may require that if—

    (a) an acquisition of the kind mentioned in sub-paragraph (1)(a) is made; or

    (b) anything is done which results in two or more bodies corporate becoming interconnected bodies corporate;

the persons concerned or any of them shall observe any prohibitions or restrictions imposed by or under the order.

    (3) This paragraph shall also apply to any result consisting in two or more enterprises ceasing to be distinct enterprises (other than any result consisting in two or more bodies corporate becoming interconnected bodies corporate).

13.— (1) An order may provide for—

    (a) the division of any business (whether by the sale of any part of the undertaking or assets or otherwise);

    (b) the division of any group of interconnected bodies corporate.

    (2) For the purposes of sub-paragraph (1)(a) all the activities carried on by way of business by any one person or by any two or more interconnected bodies corporate may be treated as a single business.

    (3) An order made by virtue of this paragraph may contain such provision as the relevant authority considers appropriate to effect or take account of the division, including, in particular, provision as to—

    (a) the transfer or creation of property, rights, liabilities or obligations;

    (b) the number of persons to whom the property, rights, liabilities or obligations are to be transferred or in whom they are to be vested;

    (c) the time within which the property, rights, liabilities or obligations are to be transferred or vested;

(d)   the adjustment of contracts (whether by discharge or reduction of any liability or obligation or otherwise);

(e)   the creation, allotment, surrender or cancellation of any shares, stock or securities;

(f)   the formation or winding up of any company or other body of persons corporate or unincorporate;

(g)   the amendment of the memorandum and articles or other instruments regulating any such company or other body of persons;

(h)   the extent to which, and the circumstances in which, provisions of the order affecting a company or other body of persons corporate or unincorporate in its share capital, constitution or other matters may be altered by the company or other body of persons concerned;

(i)   the registration of the order under any enactment by a company or other body of persons corporate or unincorporate which is affected by it as mentioned in paragraph (h);

(j)   the continuation, with any necessary change of parties, of any legal proceedings;

(k)   the approval by the relevant authority or another person of anything required by virtue of the order to be done or of any person to whom anything is to be transferred, or in whom anything is to be vested, by virtue of the order; or

(l)   the appointment of trustees or other persons to do anything on behalf of another person which is required of that person by virtue of the order or to monitor the doing by that person of any such thing.

14.   The references in paragraph 13 to the division of a business as mentioned in sub-paragraph (1)(a) of that paragraph shall, in the case of an order under section 75, 83, 84, 160 or 161, or an order under paragraph 5, 10 or 11 of Schedule 7, be construed as including references to the separation, by the sale of any part of any undertaking or assets concerned or other means, of enterprises which are under common control (within the meaning of section 26) otherwise than by reason of their being enterprises of interconnected bodies corporate.

Supply and publication of information

15.— (1)   An order may require a person supplying goods or services to publish a list of prices or otherwise notify prices.

(2)   An order made by virtue of this paragraph may also require or prohibit the publication or other notification of further information.

16.   An order may prohibit any person from notifying (whether by publication or otherwise) to persons supplying goods or services prices recommended or suggested as appropriate to be charged by those persons for those goods or services.

17.— (1)   An order may require a person supplying goods or services to publish—

(a)   accounting information in relation to the supply of the goods or services;

(b)   information in relation to the quantities of goods or services supplied;

(c)   information in relation to the geographical areas in which they are supplied.

(2)   In sub-paragraph (1) "accounting information", in relation to a supply of goods or services, means information as to—

(a)   the costs of the supply, including fixed costs and overheads;

(b)   the manner in which fixed costs and overheads are calculated and apportioned for accounting purposes of the supplier; and

(c)   the income attributable to the supply.

18.   An order made by virtue of paragraph 15 or 17 may provide for the manner in which information is to be published or otherwise notified.

19.   An order may—

(a)   require any person to supply information to the relevant authority;

(b)   where the OFT is not the relevant authority, require any person to supply information to the OFT;

(c)   provide for the publication, by the person who has received information by virtue of paragraph (a) or (b), of that information.

National security

20.— (1) An order may make such provision as the person making the order considers to be appropriate in the interests of national security (within the meaning of section 58(1)).

(2) Such provision may, in particular, include provision requiring a person to do, or not to do, particular things.

Newspaper mergers

20A.— (1) This paragraph applies in relation to any order—
   (a) which is to be made following the giving of—
       (i)   an intervention notice which mentions a newspaper public interest consideration;
       (ii) an intervention notice which mentions any other media public interest consideration in relation to a relevant merger situation in which one of the enterprises ceasing to be distinct is a newspaper enterprise;
       (iii) a special intervention notice which mentions a consideration specified in section 58(2A) or (2B); or
       (iv) a special intervention notice which, in relation to a special merger situation in which one of the enterprises ceasing to be distinct is a newspaper enterprise, mentions a consideration specified in section 58(2C); and
   (b) to which the consideration concerned is still relevant.

(2) The order may make such provision as the person making the order considers to be appropriate in all circumstances of the case.

(3) Such provision may, in particular, include provision requiring a person to do, or not to do, particular things.

(4) Provision made by virtue of this paragraph may, in particular, include provision—
   (a) altering the constitution of a body corporate (whether in connection with the appointment of directors, the establishment of an editorial board or otherwise);
   (b) requiring the agreement of the relevant authority or another person before the taking of particular action (including the appointment or dismissal of an editor, journalists or directors or acting as a shadow director);
   (c) attaching conditions to the operation of a newspaper;
   (d) prohibiting consultation or co-operation between subsidiaries.

(5) In this paragraph "newspaper public interest consideration" means a media public interest consideration other than one which is such a consideration—
   (a) by virtue of section 58(2C); or
   (b) by virtue of having been, in the opinion of the Secretary of State, concerned with broadcasting and a consideration that ought to have been specified in section 58.

(6) This paragraph is without prejudice to the operation of the other paragraphs of this Schedule in relation to the order concerned.

Supplementary

21.— (1) An order, as well as making provision in relation to all cases to which it may extend, may make provision in relation to—
   (a) those cases subject to specified exceptions; or
   (b) any particular case or class of case.

(2) An order may, in relation to the cases in relation to which it applies, make the full provision which may be made by it or any less provision (whether by way of exception or otherwise).

(3) An order may make provision for matters to be determined under the order.

(4) An order may—
   (a) make different provision for different cases or classes of case or different purposes;
   (b) make such transitional, transitory or saving provision as the person making it considers appropriate.

22.— (1) An order which may prohibit the doing of anything (or the refraining from doing anything) may in particular by virtue of paragraph 21(2) prohibit the doing of that thing (or the refraining from doing of it) except to such extent and in such circumstances as may be provided by or under the order.

(2) Any such order may, in particular, prohibit the doing of that thing (or the refraining from doing of it)—

(a) without the agreement of the relevant authority or another person; or

(b) by or in relation to a person who has not been approved by the relevant authority or another person.

Interpretation

23. References in this Schedule to the notification of prices or other information are not limited to the notification in writing of prices or other information.

24. In this Schedule "the relevant authority" means—

(a) in the case of an order to be made by the OFT, the OFT;

(b) in the case of an order to be made by the Commission, the Commission; and

(c) in the case of an order to be made by the Secretary of State, the Secretary of State.

SCHEDULE 9

...

SCHEDULE 10

Section 90

PROCEDURAL REQUIREMENTS FOR CERTAIN ENFORCEMENT UNDERTAKINGS AND ORDERS

Requirements for accepting undertakings and making orders

1. Paragraph 2 applies in relation to—

(a) any undertaking under section 73 or 82 or paragraph 3 or 9 of Schedule 7 (other than an undertaking under the enactment concerned which varies an undertaking under that enactment but not in any material respect); and

(b) any order under section 75, 83 or 84 or paragraph 5, 10 or 11 of Schedule 7 (other than an order under the enactment concerned which is a revoking order of the kind dealt with by paragraphs 6 to 8 below).

2.— (1) Before accepting an undertaking to which this paragraph applies or making an order to which this paragraph applies, the OFT, the Commission or (as the case may be) the Secretary of State (in this Schedule "the relevant authority") shall—

(a) give notice of the proposed undertaking or (as the case may be) order; and

(b) consider any representations made in accordance with the notice and not withdrawn.

(2) A notice under sub-paragraph (1) shall state—

(a) that the relevant authority proposes to accept the undertaking or (as the case may be) make the order;

(b) the purpose and effect of the undertaking or (as the case may be) order;

(c) the situation that the undertaking or (as the case may be) order is seeking to deal with;

(d) any other facts which the relevant authority considers justify the acceptance of the undertaking or (as the case may be) the making of the order;

(e) a means of gaining access to an accurate version of the proposed undertaking or (as the case may be) order at all reasonable times; and

(f) the period (not less than 15 days starting with the date of publication of the notice in the case of an undertaking and not less than 30 days starting with that date in the case of an order) within which representations may be made in relation to the proposed undertaking or (as the case may be) order.

(3) A notice under sub-paragraph (1) shall be given by—

(a) in the case of a proposed order, serving on any person identified in the order as a person on whom a copy of the order should be served a copy of the notice and a copy of the proposed order; and

(b) in every case, publishing the notice.

(4) The relevant authority shall not accept the undertaking with modifications or (as the case may be) make the order with modifications unless the relevant authority—

(a) gives notice of the proposed modifications; and

(b) considers any representations made in accordance with the notice and not withdrawn.

(5) A notice under sub-paragraph (4) shall state—

(a) the proposed modifications;

(b) the reasons for them; and

(c) the period (not less than 7 days starting with the date of the publication of the notice under sub-paragraph (4)) within which representations may be made in relation to the proposed modifications.

(6) A notice under sub-paragraph (4) shall be given by—

(a) in the case of a proposed order, serving a copy of the notice on any person identified in the order as a person on whom a copy of the order should be served; and

(b) in every case, publishing the notice.

3.— (1) If, after giving notice under paragraph 2(1) or (4), the relevant authority decides—

(a) not to accept the undertaking concerned or (as the case may be) make the order concerned; and

(b) not to proceed by virtue of paragraph 5;

the relevant authority shall give notice of that decision.

(2) A notice under sub-paragraph (1) shall be given by—

(a) in the case of a proposed order, serving a copy of the notice on any person identified in the order as a person on whom a copy of the order should be served; and

(b) in every case, publishing the notice.

4. As soon as practicable after accepting an undertaking to which paragraph 2 applies or (as the case may be) making an order to which that paragraph applies, the relevant authority shall (except in the case of an order which is a statutory instrument)—

(a) serve a copy of the undertaking on any person by whom it is given or (as the case may be) serve a copy of the order on any person identified in the order as a person on whom a copy of the order should be served; and

(b) publish the undertaking or (as the case may be) the order.

5.— (1) The requirements of paragraph 2(4) (and those of paragraph 2(1)) shall not apply if the relevant authority—

(a) has already given notice under paragraph 2(1) but not paragraph 2(4) in relation to the proposed undertaking or order; and

(b) considers that the modifications which are now being proposed are not material in any respect.

(2) The requirements of paragraph 2(4) (and those of paragraph 2(1)) shall not apply if the relevant authority—

(a) has already given notice under paragraphs 2(1) and (4) in relation to the matter concerned; and

(b) considers that the further modifications which are now being proposed do not differ in any material respect from the modifications in relation to which notice was last given under paragraph 2(4).

Termination of undertakings and orders

6. Paragraph 7 applies where the relevant authority is proposing to—

(a) release any undertaking under section 73 or 82 or paragraph 3 or 9 of Schedule 7 (other than in connection with accepting an undertaking under the enactment concerned which varies or supersedes an undertaking under that enactment); or

(b)   revoke any order under section 75, 83 or 84 or paragraph 5, 10 or 11 of Schedule 7 (other than in connection with making an order under the enactment concerned which varies or supersedes an order under that enactment).

7.—   (1)   Before releasing an undertaking to which this paragraph applies or (as the case may be) revoking an order to which this paragraph applies, the relevant authority shall—

(a)   give notice of the proposed release or (as the case may be) revocation; and

(b)   consider any representations made in accordance with the notice and not withdrawn.

(2)   A notice under sub-paragraph (1) shall state—

(a)   the fact that a release or (as the case may be) revocation is proposed;

(b)   the reasons for it; and

(c)   the period (not less than 15 days starting with the date of publication of the notice in the case of an undertaking and not less than 30 days starting with that date in the case of an order) within which representations may be made in relation to the proposed release or (as the case may be) revocation.

(3)   If after giving notice under sub-paragraph (1) the relevant authority decides not to proceed with the release or (as the case may be) the revocation, the relevant authority shall give notice of that decision.

(4)   A notice under sub-paragraph (1) or (3) shall be given by—

(a)   serving a copy of the notice on the person who gave the undertaking which is being released or (as the case may be) on any person identified in the order being revoked as a person on whom a copy of the order should be served; and

(b)   publishing the notice.

8.   As soon as practicable after releasing the undertaking or making the revoking order, the relevant authority shall (except in the case of an order which is a statutory instrument)—

(a)   serve a copy of the release of the undertaking on the person who gave the undertaking or (as the case may be) serve a copy of the revoking order on any person identified in the order being revoked as a person on whom a copy of that order should be served; and

(b)   publish the release or (as the case may be) the revoking order.

Power to dispense with the requirements of the Schedule

9.   The relevant authority may dispense with any or all of the requirements of this Schedule if the relevant authority considers that the relevant authority has special reasons for doing so.

SCHEDULES 11, 12

...

SCHEDULE 13

Section 210

LISTED DIRECTIVES

PART 1
DIRECTIVES

1.   Council Directive 84/450/EEC of 10 September 1984 relating to the approximation of the laws, regulations and administrative provisions of the Member States concerning misleading advertising.

2.   Council Directive 85/577/EEC of 20 December 1985 to protect the consumer in respect of contracts negotiated away from business premises.

3.   Council Directive 87/102/EEC of 22 December 1986 for the approximation of the laws, regulations and administrative provisions of the Member States concerning consumer credit as last amended by Directive 98/7/EC.

4. Council Directive 90/314/EEC of 13 June 1990 on package travel, package holidays and package tours.

5. Council Directive 93/13/EEC of 5 April 1993 on unfair terms in consumer contracts.

6. Directive 94/47/EC of the European Parliament and of the Council of 26 October 1994 on the protection of purchasers in respect of certain aspects of contracts relating to the purchase of the right to use immovable properties on a timeshare basis.

7. Directive 97/7/EC of the European Parliament and of the Council of 20 May 1997 on the protection of consumers in respect of distance contracts.

8. Directive 1999/44/EC of the European Parliament and of the Council of 25 May 1999 on certain aspects of the sale of consumer goods and associated guarantees.

9. Directive 2000/31/EC of the European Parliament and of the Council of 8 June 2000 on certain legal aspects of information society services, in particular electronic commerce, in the Internal Market ("Directive on electronic commerce").

9A. Directive 2002/65/EC of the European Parliament and of the Council of 23 September 2002 concerning the distance marketing of consumer financial services and amending Council Directive 90/619/EEC and Directives 97/7/EC and 98/27/EC.

PART 2
PROVISIONS OF DIRECTIVES

10. Articles 10 to 21 of Council Directive 89/552/EEC of 3 October 1989 on the co-ordination of certain provisions laid down by law, regulation or administrative action in Member States concerning the pursuit of television broadcasting activities as amended by Directive 97/36/EC.

11. Articles 86 to 100 of the Directive 2001/83/EC of the European Parliament and of the Council of 6 November 2001 on the Community code relating to medicinal products for human use.

SCHEDULE 14

Sections 238 and 243

SPECIFIED FUNCTIONS

Parts 1, 2, 3, 4, 5, 6, 7, 8 and 11 of the Fair Trading Act 1973 (c. 41).
Trade Descriptions Act 1968 (c. 29).
Hallmarking Act 1973 (c. 43).
Prices Act 1974 (c. 24).
Consumer Credit Act 1974 (c. 39).
Customs and Excise Management Act 1979 (c. 12).
Estate Agents Act 1979 (c. 38).
Competition Act 1980 (c. 21).
Video Recordings Act 1984 (c. 39).
Consumer Protection Act 1987 (c. 43).
Consumer Protection (Northern Ireland) Order 1987 (S.I. 1987/2049 (N.I. 20)).
Copyright, Designs and Patents Act 1988 (c. 48)
Property Misdescriptions Act 1991 (c. 29).
Timeshare Act 1992 (c. 35).
Clean Air Act 1993 (c. 11).
Value Added Tax Act 1994 (c. 23).
Trade Marks Act 1994 (c. 26).
Competition Act 1998 (c. 41).
Chapter 3 of Part 10 and Chapter 2 of Part 18 of the Financial Services and Markets Act 2000 (c. 8).
An order made under section 95 of that Act.
Fireworks Act 2003.

SCHEDULE 15

Section 241

ENACTMENTS CONFERRING FUNCTIONS

Gun Barrel Proof Act 1868 (cap 113).
Gun Barrel Proof Act 1950 (cap 3).
Trade Descriptions Act 1968.
Unsolicited Goods and Services Act 1971 (c. 30).
Fair Trading Act 1973.
Hallmarking Act 1973 (c. 43).
Prices Act 1974.
the relevant statutory provisions within the meaning of Part I of the Health and Safety at Work etc. Act 1974 (c. 37).
Consumer Credit Act 1974.
Unsolicited Goods and Services (Northern Ireland) Order 1976 (S.I. 1976/57 (N.I. 1).
Gun Barrel Proof Act 1978 (c. 9).
the relevant statutory provisions within the meaning of the Health and Safety at Work (Northern Ireland) Order 1978 (S.I. 1978/1039 (N.I. 9)).
Estate Agents Act 1979.
Competition Act 1980.
Weights and Measures (Northern Ireland) Order 1981 (S.I. 1981/231 (N.I. 10)).
National Audit Act 1983 (c. 44).
Telecommunications Act 1984 (c. 12).
Video Recordings Act 1984 (c. 39).
Companies Act 1985 (c. 6).
Weights and Measures Act 1985 (c. 72).
Airports Act 1986 (c. 31).
Gas Act 1986 (c. 44).
Insolvency Act 1986 (c. 45).
Company Directors Disqualification Act 1986 (c. 46).
Financial Services Act 1986 (c. 60).
Companies (Northern Ireland) Order 1986 (S.I. 1986/1032 (N.I. 6))
Consumer Protection Act 1987 (c. 43).
Consumer Protection (Northern Ireland) Order 1987 (S.I. 1987/2049 (N.I. 20)).
Banking Act 1987 (c. 22).
Education Reform Act 1988 (c. 40).
Copyright, Designs and Patents Act 1988 (c. 48).
The Education (Unrecognised Degrees) (Northern Ireland) Order 1988 (S.I. 1988/1989 (N.I. 22))
Water Act 1989 (c. 15).
Electricity Act 1989 (c. 29).
Companies Act 1989 (c. 40).
Companies (Northern Ireland) Order 1989 (S.I. 1989/2404 (N.I. 18)).
Insolvency (Northern Ireland) Order 1989 (S.I. 1989/2405 (N.I. 19)).
Companies (Northern Ireland) Order 1990 (S.I. 1990/593 (N.I. 5)).
Companies No. 2 (Northern Ireland) Order 1990 (S.I. 1990/1504 (N.I. 10)).
Companies Act 1989 (c. 40).
Companies (Northern Ireland) Order 1989 (S.I. 1989/2404 (N.I. 18)).
Insolvency (Northern Ireland) Order 1989 (S.I. 1989/2405 (N.I. 19)).
Companies (Northern Ireland) Order 1990 (S.I. 1990/593 (N.I. 5)).
Companies No. 2 (Northern Ireland) Order 1990 (S.I. 1990/1504 (N.I. 10)).
Courts and Legal Services Act 1990 (c. 41).

Broadcasting Act 1990 (c. 42).
Property Misdescriptions Act 1991 (c. 29).
Water Industry Act 1991 (c. 56).
Water Resources Act 1991 (c. 57).
Statutory Water Companies Act 1991 (c. 58).
Land Drainage Act 1991 (c. 59).
Water Consolidation (Consequential Provisions) Act 1991 (c. 60).
Timeshare Act 1992 (c. 35).
Electricity (Northern Ireland) Order 1992 (S.I. 1992/231 (N.I. 1)).
Clean Air Act 1993 (c. 11).
Railways Act 1993 (c. 43).
Coal Industry Act 1994 (c. 21).
Trade Marks Act 1994 (c. 26).
Part IV of the Airports (Northern Ireland) Order 1994 (S.I. 1994/426 (N.I. 1)).
Gas Act 1995 (c. 45).
Broadcasting Act 1996 (c. 55).
Gas (Northern Ireland) Order 1996 (S.I. 1996/275 (N.I. 2)).
Competition Act 1998 (c. 41).
Financial Services and Markets Act 2000 (c. 8).
Government Resources and Accounts Act 2000 (c. 20).
Postal Services Act 2000 (c. 26).
Utilities Act 2000 (c. 27).
Transport Act 2000 (c. 38).
Company Directors Disqualification (Northern Ireland) Order 2002 (S.I. 2002/3150 (N.I. 4)).
Communications Act 2003.
Fireworks Act 2003.
Water Act 2003 (c. 37).

SCHEDULES 16–18

...

SCHEDULE 19

Section 256

DURATION OF BANKRUPTCY: TRANSITIONAL PROVISIONS

Introduction

1. This Schedule applies to an individual who immediately before commencement—
    (a) has been adjudged bankrupt, and
    (b) has not been discharged from the bankruptcy.
2. In this Schedule—
    "commencement" means the date appointed under section 279 for the commencement of section 256, and
    "pre-commencement bankrupt" means an individual to whom this Schedule applies.

Neither old law nor new law to apply

3. Section 279 of the Insolvency Act 1986 (c. 45) (bankruptcy: discharge) shall not apply to a pre-commencement bankrupt (whether in its pre-commencement or its post-commencement form).

General rule for discharge from pre-commencement bankruptcy

4.— (1) A pre-commencement bankrupt is, subject to sub-paragraphs (2) and (3), discharged from bankruptcy at whichever is the earlier of—

    (a)   the end of the period of one year beginning with commencement, and

    (b)   the end of the relevant period applicable to the bankrupt under section 279(1)(b) of the Insolvency Act 1986 (duration of bankruptcy) as it had effect immediately before commencement.

  (2)   An order made under section 279(3) of that Act before commencement—

    (a)   shall continue to have effect in respect of the pre-commencement bankrupt after commencement, and

    (b)   may be varied or revoked after commencement by an order under section 279(3) as substituted by section 256 of this Act.

  (3)   Section 279(3) to (5) of that Act as substituted by section 256 of this Act shall have effect after commencement in relation to the period mentioned in sub-paragraph (1)(a) or (b) above.

Second-time bankruptcy

5.—— (1)   This paragraph applies to a pre-commencement bankrupt who was an undischarged bankrupt at some time during the period of 15 years ending with the day before the date on which the pre-commencement bankruptcy commenced.

  (2)   The pre-commencement bankrupt shall not be discharged from bankruptcy in accordance with paragraph 4 above.

  (3)   An order made before commencement under section 280(2)(b) or (c) of the Insolvency Act 1986 (c. 45) (discharge by order of the court) shall continue to have effect after commencement (including any provision made by the court by virtue of section 280(3)).

  (4)   A pre-commencement bankrupt to whom this paragraph applies (and in respect of whom no order is in force under section 280(2)(b) or (c) on commencement) is discharged—

    (a)   at the end of the period of five years beginning with commencement, or

    (b)   at such earlier time as the court may order on an application under section 280 of the Insolvency Act 1986 (discharge by order) heard after commencement.

  (5)   Section 279(3) to (5) of the Insolvency Act 1986 as substituted by section 256 of this Act shall have effect after commencement in relation to the period mentioned in sub-paragraph (4)(a) above.

  (6)   A bankruptcy annulled under section 282 shall be ignored for the purpose of sub-paragraph (1).

Criminal bankruptcy

6.   A pre-commencement bankrupt who was adjudged bankrupt on a petition under section 264(1)(d) of the Insolvency Act 1986 (criminal bankruptcy)—

    (a)   shall not be discharged from bankruptcy in accordance with paragraph 4 above, but

    (b)   may be discharged from bankruptcy by an order of the court under section 280 of that Act.

Income payments order

7.—— (1)   This paragraph applies where—

    (a)   a pre-commencement bankrupt is discharged by virtue of paragraph 4(1)(a), and

    (b)   an income payments order is in force in respect of him immediately before his discharge.

  (2)   If the income payments order specifies a date after which it is not to have effect, it shall continue in force until that date (and then lapse).

  (3)   But the court may on the application of the pre-commencement bankrupt—

    (a)   vary the income payments order;

    (b)   provide for the income payments order to cease to have effect before the date referred to in sub-paragraph (2).

Bankruptcy restrictions order or undertaking

8.   A provision of this Schedule which provides for an individual to be discharged from bankruptcy is subject to—

(a) any bankruptcy restrictions order (or interim order) which may be made in relation to that individual, and

(b) any bankruptcy restrictions undertaking entered into by that individual.

SCHEDULES 20–3

...

SCHEDULE 24

Section 276

TRANSITIONAL AND TRANSITORY PROVISIONS AND SAVINGS

Operation of references to OFT before commencement of section 2(3)

1.— (1) This paragraph applies to any provision contained in this Act, or made by virtue of this Act, which contains a reference to the OFT but comes into force before the time at which section 2(3) comes into force.

(2) Until that time any reference to the OFT is to be taken as a reference to the Director.

Pensions etc. of former Directors

2.   In the case of any such person who has held the office of the Director as may be determined by the Secretary of State with the approval of the Minister for the Civil Service—

(a) such pension, allowance or gratuity shall be paid to or in respect of him on his retirement or death, or

(b) such contributions or payments shall be paid towards provision for such a pension, allowance or gratuity,

as may be so determined.

First financial year of the OFT

3.— (1) If the period beginning with the day on which the OFT is established and ending with the next 31st March is six months or more, the first financial year of the OFT is that period.

(2) Otherwise the first financial year of the OFT is the period beginning with the day on which it is established and ending with 31st March in the following year.

First annual plan of the OFT

4.— (1) The OFT's first annual plan (as required by section 3(1)) shall be published within the period of three months beginning with the day on which it is established.

(2) Subject to sub-paragraph (3), that annual plan shall relate to the period beginning with the date of publication and ending with the next 31st March.

(3) If the period mentioned in sub-paragraph (2) is three months or less, that annual plan shall relate to the period beginning with the date of publication and ending with the 31st March in the following year.

Last annual report of the Director General of Fair Trading

5.— (1) After the abolition of the office of the Director, any duty of his to make an annual report, in relation to any calendar year for which such a report has not been made, shall be performed by the OFT.

(2) The period between the abolition of that office and the end of the preceding calendar year (if less than 12 months) shall be treated as the calendar year for which the last annual report is required.

(3)   If that period is nine months or more, the OFT shall make the last annual report as soon as practicable after the end of that period.

(4)   Otherwise the OFT shall make the last annual report no later than the making of its first report under section 4(1).

(5)   In this paragraph "annual report" means a report required by section 125(1) of the 1973 Act.

Effect of transfers under section 2

6.— (1)   In this paragraph—

"commencement" means the commencement of section 2(1);

"transferred" means transferred by section 2(1).

(2)   Anything which—

(a)   has been done by or in relation to the Director for the purposes of or in connection with anything transferred; and

(b)   is in effect immediately before commencement,

shall be treated as if done by or in relation to the OFT.

(3)   Anything (including legal proceedings) which—

(a)   relates to anything transferred; and

(b)   is in the process of being done by or in relation to the Director immediately before it is transferred,

may be continued by or in relation to the OFT.

(4)   Nothing in section 2 or this paragraph affects the validity of anything done by or in relation to the Director before commencement.

First President and Registrar of the Competition Appeal Tribunal

7.   The person who is President of the Competition Commission Appeal Tribunals (under paragraph 4 of Schedule 7 to the 1998 Act) immediately before the commencement of section 12 is on that date to become the President of the Competition Appeal Tribunal as if duly appointed under that section, on the same terms.

8.   The person who is Registrar of Appeal Tribunals (under paragraph 5 of Schedule 8 to the 1998 Act) immediately before the commencement of section 12 is on that date to become the Registrar of the Competition Appeal Tribunal as if duly appointed under that section, on the same terms.

9.   Any person who is a member of the Competition Commission appeal panel (but not a member of the panel of chairmen) immediately before the commencement of section 12 is on that date to become a member of the Competition Appeal Tribunal, on such terms and for such a period as the Secretary of State may determine.

10.   Any member of the Competition Commission appeal panel who is, immediately before the commencement of section 12, a member of the panel of chairmen under paragraph 26 of Schedule 7 to the 1998 Act is on that date to become a chairman of the Competition Appeal Tribunal, on such terms and for such a period as the Lord Chancellor may determine.

11.   Nothing in paragraph 7, 8, 9 or 10 applies to any person who, before the commencement of section 12, gives notice to the Secretary of State stating that he does not wish that paragraph to apply to him.

Tribunal rules

12.— (1)   Any rules made under section 48 of the 1998 Act which are in force immediately before the commencement of section 15 above shall be treated after that commencement as having been made under section 15.

(2)   The Secretary of State may treat any consultation carried out with the President of the Competition Commission Appeal Tribunals (before the appointment of the President of the Competition Appeal Tribunal) as being as effective for the purposes of section 15(1) as if it had been carried out with the President of the Competition Appeal Tribunal.

Merger references

13.— (1)   Subject to paragraphs 15 to 18, the old law shall continue to apply where—

    (a)   two or more enterprises have ceased to be distinct enterprises (within the meaning of Part 5 of the 1973 Act); and

    (b)   the cessation has occurred before the appointed day.

(2)   Subject to sub-paragraphs (3), (4) and (5) and paragraphs 15 to 18, the old law shall continue to apply in relation to any relevant arrangements which were in progress or in contemplation before the appointed day and are in progress or in contemplation on that day and (if events so require) the actual results of those arrangements where, before the appointed day—

    (a)   a merger notice was given, and not rejected under section 75B(7) of the 1973 Act or withdrawn, in relation to the arrangements;

    (b)   no merger notice was so given but, in relation to the arrangements—

        (i)   a reference was made under section 75 of the 1973 Act;

        (ii)   undertakings were accepted under section 75G of that Act; or

        (iii) a decision was made by the Secretary of State neither to make a reference under section 75 of that Act nor to accept undertakings under section 75G of that Act; or

    (c)   a merger notice was so given, was rejected under section 75B(7) of the 1973 Act or withdrawn, paragraph (a) does not apply in relation to a different merger notice given in relation to the arrangements and, in relation to the arrangements, paragraph (b)(i), (ii) or (iii) applies.

(3)   Subject to sub-paragraph (8), the new law shall, in a case of the kind mentioned in sub-paragraph (2)(a), apply in relation to any relevant arrangements and (if events so require) the actual results of those arrangements if, on or after the appointed day, a merger notice is rejected under section 75B(7) of the 1973 Act or withdrawn in relation to the arrangements.

(4)   Subject to sub-paragraph (8), the new law shall, in a case of the kind mentioned in sub-paragraph (2)(a), apply in relation to any relevant arrangements and (if events so require) the actual results of those arrangements if—

    (a)   the making of a reference under section 64 or 75 of the 1973 Act in relation to those arrangements and (if events so require) the actual results of those arrangements was, immediately before the appointed day and by virtue of section 75C(1)(c), (e) or (g) of that Act, not prevented;

    (b)   the period for considering the merger notice has expired (whether before, on or after the appointed day); and

    (c)   no reference has been made under section 64 or 75 of the 1973 Act and no undertakings have been accepted under section 75G of that Act.

(5)   Subject to sub-paragraph (8), the new law shall, in a case of the kind mentioned in sub-paragraph (2)(a), apply in relation to any relevant arrangements and (if events so require) the actual results of those arrangements if—

    (a)   the making of a reference under section 64 or 75 of the 1973 Act in relation to those arrangements and (if events so require) the actual results of those arrangements becomes, on or after the appointed day and by virtue of section 75C(1)(b), (c), (d), (e) or (g) of that Act, not prevented;

    (b)   the period for considering the merger notice has expired (whether before, on or after the appointed day); and

    (c)   no reference has been made under section 64 or 75 of the 1973 Act and no undertakings have been accepted under section 75G of that Act.

(6)   Subject to sub-paragraph (8), the new law shall apply in relation to relevant arrangements and (if events so require) the actual results of those arrangements if—

    (a)   the arrangements were in progress or in contemplation before the appointed day and are in progress or in contemplation on that day;

(b) before the appointed day and in relation to the arrangements—
    (i) no reference was made under section 75 of the 1973 Act;
    (ii) no undertakings were accepted under section 75G of that Act; and
    (iii) a decision neither to make a reference under section 75 of that Act nor to accept undertakings under section 75G of that Act was not made by the Secretary of State; and
(c) no merger notice was given to the Director or the OFT before that day in relation to the arrangements.

(7) Subject to sub-paragraph (8), the new law shall, in a case of the kind mentioned in sub-paragraph (2)(c) (excluding the words from "and" to the end), apply in relation to any relevant arrangements and (if events so require) the actual results of those arrangements if, in relation to the arrangements, sub-paragraph (2)(b)(i), (ii) and (iii) do not apply.

(8) Subject to paragraphs 15 to 18, the old law shall continue to apply in relation to concentrations with a Community dimension (within the meaning of the European Merger Regulations) notified before the appointed day to the European Commission under article 4 of those Regulations.

(9) In this paragraph references to relevant arrangements which are in progress or in contemplation on the appointed day include references to the actual results of those arrangements if the arrangements were in progress or in contemplation immediately before the appointed day and have, at the beginning of the appointed day, resulted in two or more enterprises ceasing to be distinct enterprises (within the meaning of Part 5 of the 1973 Act).

(10) In this paragraph—
"the European Merger Regulations" has the meaning given by section 129(1);
"merger notice" means a notice under section 75A(1) of the 1973 Act;
"the new law" means Part 3 of this Act and any related provision of law (including, in particular, any modification made under section 276(2) to that Part or any such provision);
"the old law" means sections 64 to 75K of the 1973 Act and any related provision of law (including, in particular, any modification made under section 276(2) to those sections or any such provision); and
"relevant arrangements" means arrangements which might result in two or more enterprises ceasing to be distinct enterprises (within the meaning of Part 5 of the 1973 Act).

Monopoly references

14.— (1) Subject to paragraphs 15 to 18, the old law shall continue to apply in relation to any monopoly reference made before the appointed day under section 50 or 51 of the 1973 Act.

(2) No person has to comply on or after the appointed day with a requirement imposed before that day under section 44 of the 1973 Act.

(3) In this paragraph—
"monopoly reference" has the meaning given by section 5(3) of the 1973 Act; and
"the old law" means Part 4 of the 1973 Act and any related provision of law (including, in particular, any modification made under section 276(2) to that Part or any such provision).

Enforcement undertakings and orders

15.— (1) Section 94(1) to (6) shall apply in relation to any undertaking—
(a) accepted (whether before, on or after the appointed day) by a Minister of the Crown—
    (i) in pursuance of a proposal under section 56A of the 1973 Act; or
    (ii) under section 56F, 75G or 88 of that Act; and
(b) of a description specified in an order made by the Secretary of State under this paragraph;
as it applies in relation to enforcement undertakings under Part 3.

(2) Section 94(1) to (6) shall apply in relation to any order made by a Minister of the Crown under section 56, 73, 74, 75K or 89 of the 1973 Act (whether before, on or after the appointed day) and of a description specified in an order made by the Secretary of State under this paragraph as it applies in relation to enforcement orders under Part 3.

(3) Compliance with—

(a) an undertaking accepted by a Minister of the Crown under section 88 of the 1973 Act (whether before, on or after the appointed day) and of a description specified in an order made by the Secretary of State under this paragraph; or

(b) an order made by a Minister of the Crown under section 56, 73, 74 or 89 of the 1973 Act (whether before, on or after the appointed day) and of a description specified in an order made by the Secretary of State under this paragraph;

shall also be enforceable by civil proceedings brought by the Commission for an injunction or for interdict or for any other appropriate relief or remedy.

(4) Sub-paragraph (3) and section 94(6) as applied by virtue of sub-paragraph (1) or (2) shall not prejudice any right that a person may have by virtue of section 94(4) as so applied to bring civil proceedings for contravention or apprehended contravention of an undertaking or order.

(5) Sections 93 and 93A of the 1973 Act shall accordingly cease to apply in relation to undertakings and orders to which sub-paragraphs (1) to (3) above apply.

16.— (1) Sub-paragraph (2) applies to any undertaking—

(a) accepted (whether before, on or after the appointed day) by a Minister of the Crown—

(i) in pursuance of a proposal under section 56A of the 1973 Act; or

(ii) under section 56F, 75G or 88 of that Act; and

(b) of a description specified in an order made by the Secretary of State under this paragraph.

(2) An undertaking to which this sub-paragraph applies may be—

(a) superseded by a new undertaking accepted by the relevant authority under this paragraph;

(b) varied by an undertaking accepted by the relevant authority under this paragraph; or

(c) released by the relevant authority.

(3) Subject to sub-paragraph (4) and any provision made under section 276(2), the power of the relevant authority under this paragraph to supersede, vary or release an undertaking is exercisable in the same circumstances, and on the same terms and conditions, as the power of the Minister concerned to supersede, vary or release the undertaking would be exercisable under the 1973 Act.

(4) The duty under section 75J(b) of the 1973 Act to give advice shall be a duty of the OFT to consider what action (if any) it should take.

(5) Where the relevant authority has the power by virtue of this paragraph to supersede, vary or release an undertaking accepted by a Minister of the Crown—

(a) in pursuance of a proposal under section 56A of the 1973 Act; or

(b) under section 56F, 75G or 88 of that Act;

the Minister concerned shall accordingly cease to have the power under that Act to supersede, vary or release the undertaking.

(6) In this paragraph "the relevant authority" means—

(a) in the case of an undertaking accepted in pursuance of a proposal under section 56A of the 1973 Act or an undertaking under section 56F or 75G of that Act, the OFT; and

(b) in the case of an undertaking accepted under section 88 of that Act, the Commission.

17.— (1) Any order made by a Minister of the Crown under section 56, 73, 74 or 89 of the 1973 Act (whether before, on or after the appointed day) and of a description specified in an order made by the Secretary of State under this paragraph may be varied or revoked by an order made by the Commission under this paragraph.

(2)   Any order made by a Minister of the Crown under section 75K of the 1973 Act (whether before, on or after the appointed day) and of a description specified in an order made by the Secretary of State under this paragraph may be varied or revoked by an order made by the OFT under this paragraph.

(3)   Subject to sub-paragraph (4) and any provision made under section 276(2), the power of the Commission to make an order under sub-paragraph (1), and the power of the OFT to make an order under sub-paragraph (2), is exercisable in the same circumstances, and on the same terms and conditions, as the power of the Minister concerned to make a corresponding varying or revoking order under the 1973 Act would be exercisable.

(4)   The power of the Commission to make an order under sub-paragraph (1), and the power of the OFT to make an order under sub-paragraph (2), shall not be exercisable by statutory instrument and shall not be subject to the requirements of section 134(1) of the 1973 Act.

(5)   Where the Commission or the OFT has the power by virtue of this paragraph to vary or revoke an order made by a Minister of the Crown under section 56, 73, 74, 75K or 89 of the 1973 Act, the Minister concerned shall accordingly cease to have the power to do so under that Act.

18.— (1)   Section 94(1) to (6) shall apply in relation to undertakings accepted under paragraph 16 and orders made under paragraph 17 as it applies in relation to enforcement undertakings and enforcement orders under Part 3.

(2)   Compliance with an undertaking accepted by the Commission under paragraph 16 or an order made by it under paragraph 17 shall also be enforceable by civil proceedings brought by the Commission for an injunction or for interdict or for any other appropriate relief or remedy.

(3)   Sub-paragraph (2) and section 94(6) as applied by virtue of sub-paragraph (1) shall not prejudice any right that a person may have by virtue of section 94(4) as so applied to bring civil proceedings for contravention or apprehended contravention of an undertaking or order.

Paragraphs 13 to 18: supplementary provision

19.— (1)   In paragraphs 13 to 18 "the appointed day" means such day as the Secretary of State may by order made by statutory instrument appoint; and different days may be appointed for different purposes.

(2)   An order made by the Secretary of State under paragraph 15, 16 or 17—

(a)   may make different provision for different purposes; and

(b)   shall be made by statutory instrument which shall be subject to annulment in pursuance of a resolution of either House of Parliament.

Designation orders under Schedule 4 to the 1998 Act

20.— (1)   Subject to sub-paragraph (2), the repeals made by section 207 do not affect—

(a)   the operation of Schedule 4 to the 1998 Act in relation to any application for designation of a professional rule which is made before the commencement date;

(b)   the operation of section 3(1)(d) of and Schedule 4 to the 1998 Act in relation to any designation effected by an order made before the commencement date or on an application mentioned in paragraph (a).

(2)   No designation order (whenever made) shall have any effect in relation to any period of time after the end of the transitional period.

(3)   Subject to sub-paragraph (2) a designation order may be made after the end of the transitional period on an application mentioned in sub-paragraph (1)(a).

(4)   For the purposes of this paragraph—

"commencement date" means the day on which section 207 comes into force;

"designation" means designation under paragraph 2 of Schedule 4 to the 1998 Act; and "the transitional period" means the period of three months beginning with the commencement date.

Proceedings under Part 3 of the 1973 Act

21. The repeal of section 133(3) of the 1973 Act does not affect any right to disclose information for the purposes of any proceedings before the Restrictive Practices Court to which paragraph 42 of Schedule 13 to the 1998 Act applies.

Supplementary

22. Any provision made by any of paragraphs 1 to 21 shall not apply if, and to the extent that, an order under section 276(2) makes alternative provision or provides for it not to apply.

SCHEDULES 25, 26

...

Council Regulation (EC) of 20 January 2004 on the control of concentrations between undertakings (the EC Merger Regulation)

No. 139/2004

THE COUNCIL OF THE EUROPEAN UNION,

Having regard to the Treaty establishing the European Community, and in particular Articles 83 and 308 thereof,

Having regard to the proposal from the Commission,

Having regard to the opinion of the European Parliament,

Having regard to the opinion of the European Economic and Social Committee,

Whereas:

(1)   Council Regulation (EEC) No 4064/89 of 21 December 1989 on the control of concentrations between undertakings has been substantially amended. Since further amendments are to be made, it should be recast in the interest of clarity.

(2)   For the achievement of the aims of the Treaty, Article 3(1)(g) gives the Community the objective of instituting a system ensuring that competition in the internal market is not distorted. Article 4(1) of the Treaty provides that the activities of the Member States and the Community are to be conducted in accordance with the principle of an open market economy with free competition. These principles are essential for the further development of the internal market.

(3)   The completion of the internal market and of economic and monetary union, the enlargement of the European Union and the lowering of international barriers to trade and investment will continue to result in major corporate reorganisations, particularly in the form of concentrations.

(4)   Such reorganisations are to be welcomed to the extent that they are in line with the requirements of dynamic competition and capable of increasing the competitiveness of European industry, improving the conditions of growth and raising the standard of living in the Community.

(5)   However, it should be ensured that the process of reorganisation does not result in lasting damage to competition; Community law must therefore include provisions governing those concentrations which may significantly impede effective competition in the common market or in a substantial part of it.

(6)   A specific legal instrument is therefore necessary to permit effective control of all concentrations in terms of their effect on the structure of competition in the Community and to be the only instrument applicable to such concentrations. Regulation (EEC) No 4064/89 has allowed a Community policy to develop in this field. In the light of experience, however, that Regulation should now be recast into legislation designed to meet the challenges of a more integrated market and the future enlargement of the European Union. In accordance with the principles of subsidiarity and of proportionality as set out in Article 5 of the Treaty, this Regulation does not go beyond what is necessary in order to achieve the objective of ensuring that competition in the common market is not distorted, in accordance with the principle of an open market economy with free competition.

(7)   Articles 81 and 82, while applicable, according to the case-law of the Court of Justice, to certain concentrations, are not sufficient to control all operations which may prove to be incompatible with the system of undistorted competition envisaged in the Treaty. This Regulation should therefore be based not only on Article 83 but, principally, on Article 308 of the Treaty, under which the Community may give itself the additional powers of action necessary for the attainment of its objectives, and also powers of action with regard to concentrations on the markets for agricultural products listed in Annex I to the Treaty.

(8)   The provisions to be adopted in this Regulation should apply to significant structural changes, the impact of which on the market goes beyond the national borders of any one Member State. Such concentrations should, as a general rule, be reviewed exclusively at Community level, in application of a 'one-stop shop' system and in compliance with the principle of subsidiarity. Concentrations not covered by this Regulation come, in principle, within the jurisdiction of the Member States.

(9)   The scope of application of this Regulation should be defined according to the geographical area of activity of the undertakings concerned and be limited by quantitative thresholds in order to cover those concentrations which have a Community dimension. The Commission should report to the Council on the implementation of the applicable thresholds and criteria so that the Council, acting in accordance with Article 202 of the Treaty, is in a position to review them regularly, as well as the rules regarding pre-notification referral, in the light of the experience gained; this requires statistical data to be provided by the Member States to the Commission to enable it to prepare such reports and possible proposals for amendments. The Commission's reports and proposals should be based on relevant information regularly provided by the Member States.

(10)   A concentration with a Community dimension should be deemed to exist where the aggregate turnover of the undertakings concerned exceeds given thresholds; that is the case irrespective of whether or not the undertakings effecting the concentration have their seat or their principal fields of activity in the Community, provided they have substantial operations there.

(11)   The rules governing the referral of concentrations from the Commission to Member States and from Member States to the Commission should operate as an effective corrective mechanism in the light of the principle of subsidiarity; these rules protect the competition interests of the Member States in an adequate manner and take due account of legal certainty and the 'one-stop shop' principle.

(12)   Concentrations may qualify for examination under a number of national merger control systems if they fall below the turnover thresholds referred to in this Regulation. Multiple notification of the same transaction increases legal uncertainty, effort and cost for undertakings and may lead to conflicting assessments. The system whereby concentrations may be referred to the Commission by the Member States concerned should therefore be further developed.

(13)   The Commission should act in close and constant liaison with the competent authorities of the Member States from which it obtains comments and information.

(14)   The Commission and the competent authorities of the Member States should together form a network of public authorities, applying their respective competences in close cooperation, using efficient arrangements for information- sharing and consultation, with a view to ensuring that a case is dealt with by the most appropriate authority, in the light of the principle of subsidiarity and with a view to ensuring that multiple notifications of a given concentration are avoided to the greatest extent possible. Referrals of concentrations from the Commission to Member States and from Member States to the Commission should be made in an efficient manner avoiding, to the greatest extent possible, situations where a concentration is subject to a referral both before and after its notification.

(15)   The Commission should be able to refer to a Member State notified concentrations with a Community dimension which threaten significantly to affect competition in a market within that Member State presenting all the characteristics of a distinct market. Where the concentration affects competition on such a market, which does not constitute a substantial part of the common market, the Commission should be obliged, upon request, to refer the whole or part of the case to the Member State concerned. A Member State should be able to refer to the Commission a concentration which does not have a Community dimension but which affects trade between Member States and threatens to significantly affect competition within its territory. Other Member States which are also competent to review the concentration should be able to join the request. In such a situation, in order to ensure the efficiency and predictability of the system, national time limits should be suspended until a decision has been reached as to the referral of the

case. The Commission should have the power to examine and deal with a concentration on behalf of a requesting Member State or requesting Member States.

(16)   The undertakings concerned should be granted the possibility of requesting referrals to or from the Commission before a concentration is notified so as to further improve the efficiency of the system for the control of concentrations within the Community. In such situations, the Commission and national competition authorities should decide within short, clearly defined time limits whether a referral to or from the Commission ought to be made, thereby ensuring the efficiency of the system. Upon request by the undertakings concerned, the Commission should be able to refer to a Member State a concentration with a Community dimension which may significantly affect competition in a market within that Member State presenting all the characteristics of a distinct market; the undertakings concerned should not, however, be required to demonstrate that the effects of the concentration would be detrimental to competition. A concentration should not be referred from the Commission to a Member State which has expressed its disagreement to such a referral. Before notification to national authorities, the undertakings concerned should also be able to request that a concentration without a Community dimension which is capable of being reviewed under the national competition laws of at least three Member States be referred to the Commission. Such requests for pre-notification referrals to the Commission would be particularly pertinent in situations where the concentration would affect competition beyond the territory of one Member State. Where a concentration capable of being reviewed under the competition laws of three or more Member States is referred to the Commission prior to any national notification, and no Member State competent to review the case expresses its disagreement, the Commission should acquire exclusive competence to review the concentration and such a concentration should be deemed to have a Community dimension. Such pre-notification referrals from Member States to the Commission should not, however, be made where at least one Member State competent to review the case has expressed its disagreement with such a referral.

(17)   The Commission should be given exclusive competence to apply this Regulation, subject to review by the Court of Justice.

(18)   The Member States should not be permitted to apply their national legislation on competition to concentrations with a Community dimension, unless this Regulation makes provision therefor. The relevant powers of national authorities should be limited to cases where, failing intervention by the Commission, effective competition is likely to be significantly impeded within the territory of a Member State and where the competition interests of that Member State cannot be sufficiently protected otherwise by this Regulation. The Member States concerned must act promptly in such cases; this Regulation cannot, because of the diversity of national law, fix a single time limit for the adoption of final decisions under national law.

(19)   Furthermore, the exclusive application of this Regulation to concentrations with a Community dimension is without prejudice to Article 296 of the Treaty, and does not prevent the Member States from taking appropriate measures to protect legitimate interests other than those pursued by this Regulation, provided that such measures are compatible with the general principles and other provisions of Community law.

(20)   It is expedient to define the concept of concentration in such a manner as to cover operations bringing about a lasting change in the control of the undertakings concerned and therefore in the structure of the market. It is therefore appropriate to include, within the scope of this Regulation, all joint ventures performing on a lasting basis all the functions of an autonomous economic entity. It is moreover appropriate to treat as a single concentration transactions that are closely connected in that they are linked by condition or take the form of a series of transactions in securities taking place within a reasonably short period of time.

(21)   This Regulation should also apply where the undertakings concerned accept restrictions directly related to, and necessary for, the implementation of the concentration. Commission decisions declaring concentrations compatible with the common market in application of this Regulation should automatically cover such restrictions, without the Commission having to assess such

restrictions in individual cases. At the request of the undertakings concerned, however, the Commission should, in cases presenting novel or unresolved questions giving rise to genuine uncertainty, expressly assess whether or not any restriction is directly related to, and necessary for, the implementation of the concentration. A case presents a novel or unresolved question giving rise to genuine uncertainty if the question is not covered by the relevant Commission notice in force or a published Commission decision.

(22)   The arrangements to be introduced for the control of concentrations should, without prejudice to Article 86(2) of the Treaty, respect the principle of non-discrimination between the public and the private sectors. In the public sector, calculation of the turnover of an undertaking concerned in a concentration needs, therefore, to take account of undertakings making up an economic unit with an independent power of decision, irrespective of the way in which their capital is held or of the rules of administrative supervision applicable to them.

(23)   It is necessary to establish whether or not concentrations with a Community dimension are compatible with the common market in terms of the need to maintain and develop effective competition in the common market. In so doing, the Commission must place its appraisal within the general framework of the achievement of the fundamental objectives referred to in Article 2 of the Treaty establishing the European Community and Article 2 of the Treaty on European Union.

(24)   In order to ensure a system of undistorted competition in the common market, in furtherance of a policy conducted in accordance with the principle of an open market economy with free competition, this Regulation must permit effective control of all concentrations from the point of view of their effect on competition in the Community. Accordingly, Regulation (EEC) No 4064/89 established the principle that a concentration with a Community dimension which creates or strengthens a dominant position as a result of which effective competition in the common market or in a substantial part of it would be significantly impeded should be declared incompatible with the common market.

(25)   In view of the consequences that concentrations in oligopolistic market structures may have, it is all the more necessary to maintain effective competition in such markets. Many oligopolistic markets exhibit a healthy degree of competition. However, under certain circumstances, concentrations involving the elimination of important competitive constraints that the merging parties had exerted upon each other, as well as a reduction of competitive pressure on the remaining competitors, may, even in the absence of a likelihood of coordination between the members of the oligopoly, result in a significant impediment to effective competition. The Community courts have, however, not to date expressly interpreted Regulation (EEC) No 4064/89 as requiring concentrations giving rise to such non-coordinated effects to be declared incompatible with the common market. Therefore, in the interests of legal certainty, it should be made clear that this Regulation permits effective control of all such concentrations by providing that any concentration which would significantly impede effective competition, in the common market or in a substantial part of it, should be declared incompatible with the common market. The notion of 'significant impediment to effective competition' in Article 2(2) and (3) should be interpreted as extending, beyond the concept of dominance, only to the anti-competitive effects of a concentration resulting from the non-coordinated behaviour of undertakings which would not have a dominant position on the market concerned.

(26)   A significant impediment to effective competition generally results from the creation or strengthening of a dominant position. With a view to preserving the guidance that may be drawn from past judgments of the European courts and Commission decisions pursuant to Regulation (EEC) No 4064/89, while at the same time maintaining consistency with the standards of competitive harm which have been applied by the Commission and the Community courts regarding the compatibility of a concentration with the common market, this Regulation should accordingly establish the principle that a concentration with a Community dimension which would significantly impede effective competition, in the common market or in a substantial part

thereof, in particular as a result of the creation or strengthening of a dominant position, is to be declared incompatible with the common market.

(27) In addition, the criteria of Article 81(1) and (3) of the Treaty should be applied to joint ventures performing, on a lasting basis, all the functions of autonomous economic entities, to the extent that their creation has as its consequence an appreciable restriction of competition between undertakings that remain independent.

(28) In order to clarify and explain the Commission's appraisal of concentrations under this Regulation, it is appropriate for the Commission to publish guidance which should provide a sound economic framework for the assessment of concentrations with a view to determining whether or not they may be declared compatible with the common market.

(29) In order to determine the impact of a concentration on competition in the common market, it is appropriate to take account of any substantiated and likely efficiencies put forward by the undertakings concerned. It is possible that the efficiencies brought about by the concentration counteract the effects on competition, and in particular the potential harm to consumers, that it might otherwise have and that, as a consequence, the concentration would not significantly impede effective competition, in the common market or in a substantial part of it, in particular as a result of the creation or strengthening of a dominant position. The Commission should publish guidance on the conditions under which it may take efficiencies into account in the assessment of a concentration.

(30) Where the undertakings concerned modify a notified concentration, in particular by offering commitments with a view to rendering the concentration compatible with the common market, the Commission should be able to declare the concentration, as modified, compatible with the common market. Such commitments should be proportionate to the competition problem and entirely eliminate it. It is also appropriate to accept commitments before the initiation of proceedings where the competition problem is readily identifiable and can easily be remedied. It should be expressly provided that the Commission may attach to its decision conditions and obligations in order to ensure that the undertakings concerned comply with their commitments in a timely and effective manner so as to render the concentration compatible with the common market. Transparency and effective consultation of Member States as well as of interested third parties should be ensured throughout the procedure.

(31) The Commission should have at its disposal appropriate instruments to ensure the enforcement of commitments and to deal with situations where they are not fulfilled. In cases of failure to fulfil a condition attached to the decision declaring a concentration compatible with the common market, the situation rendering the concentration compatible with the common market does not materialise and the concentration, as implemented, is therefore not authorised by the Commission. As a consequence, if the concentration is implemented, it should be treated in the same way as a non-notified concentration implemented without authorisation. Furthermore, where the Commission has already found that, in the absence of the condition, the concentration would be incompatible with the common market, it should have the power to directly order the dissolution of the concentration, so as to restore the situation prevailing prior to the implementation of the concentration. Where an obligation attached to a decision declaring the concentration compatible with the common market is not fulfilled, the Commission should be able to revoke its decision. Moreover, the Commission should be able to impose appropriate financial sanctions where conditions or obligations are not fulfilled.

(32) Concentrations which, by reason of the limited market share of the undertakings concerned, are not liable to impede effective competition may be presumed to be compatible with the common market. Without prejudice to Articles 81 and 82 of the Treaty, an indication to this effect exists, in particular, where the market share of the undertakings concerned does not exceed 25% either in the common market or in a substantial part of it.

(33) The Commission should have the task of taking all the decisions necessary to establish whether or not concentrations with a Community dimension are compatible with the common market, as

well as decisions designed to restore the situation prevailing prior to the implementation of a concentration which has been declared incompatible with the common market.

(34) To ensure effective control, undertakings should be obliged to give prior notification of concentrations with a Community dimension following the conclusion of the agreement, the announcement of the public bid or the acquisition of a controlling interest. Notification should also be possible where the undertakings concerned satisfy the Commission of their intention to enter into an agreement for a proposed concentration and demonstrate to the Commission that their plan for that proposed concentration is sufficiently concrete, for example on the basis of an agreement in principle, a memorandum of understanding, or a letter of intent signed by all undertakings concerned, or, in the case of a public bid, where they have publicly announced an intention to make such a bid, provided that the intended agreement or bid would result in a concentration with a Community dimension. The implementation of concentrations should be suspended until a final decision of the Commission has been taken. However, it should be possible to derogate from this suspension at the request of the undertakings concerned, where appropriate. In deciding whether or not to grant a derogation, the Commission should take account of all pertinent factors, such as the nature and gravity of damage to the undertakings concerned or to third parties, and the threat to competition posed by the concentration. In the interest of legal certainty, the validity of transactions must nevertheless be protected as much as necessary.

(35) A period within which the Commission must initiate proceedings in respect of a notified concentration and a period within which it must take a final decision on the compatibility or incompatibility with the common market of that concentration should be laid down. These periods should be extended whenever the undertakings concerned offer commitments with a view to rendering the concentration compatible with the common market, in order to allow for sufficient time for the analysis and market testing of such commitment offers and for the consultation of Member States as well as interested third parties. A limited extension of the period within which the Commission must take a final decision should also be possible in order to allow sufficient time for the investigation of the case and the verification of the facts and arguments submitted to the Commission.

(36) The Community respects the fundamental rights and observes the principles recognised in particular by the Charter of Fundamental Rights of the European Union. Accordingly, this Regulation should be interpreted and applied with respect to those rights and principles.

(37) The undertakings concerned must be afforded the right to be heard by the Commission when proceedings have been initiated; the members of the management and supervisory bodies and the recognised representatives of the employees of the undertakings concerned, and interested third parties, must also be given the opportunity to be heard.

(38) In order properly to appraise concentrations, the Commission should have the right to request all necessary information and to conduct all necessary inspections throughout the Community. To that end, and with a view to protecting competition effectively, the Commission's powers of investigation need to be expanded. The Commission should, in particular, have the right to interview any persons who may be in possession of useful information and to record the statements made.

(39) In the course of an inspection, officials authorised by the Commission should have the right to ask for any information relevant to the subject matter and purpose of the inspection; they should also have the right to affix seals during inspections, particularly in circumstances where there are reasonable grounds to suspect that a concentration has been implemented without being notified; that incorrect, incomplete or misleading information has been supplied to the Commission; or that the undertakings or persons concerned have failed to comply with a condition or obligation imposed by decision of the Commission. In any event, seals should only be used in exceptional circumstances, for the period of time strictly necessary for the inspection, normally not for more than 48 hours.

(40) Without prejudice to the case-law of the Court of Justice, it is also useful to set out the scope of the control that the national judicial authority may exercise when it authorises, as provided by national law and as a precautionary measure, assistance from law enforcement authorities in order to overcome possible opposition on the part of the undertaking against an inspection, including the affixing of seals, ordered by Commission decision. It results from the case-law that the national judicial authority may in particular ask of the Commission further information which it needs to carry out its control and in the absence of which it could refuse the authorisation. The case-law also confirms the competence of the national courts to control the application of national rules governing the implementation of coercive measures. The competent authorities of the Member States should cooperate actively in the exercise of the Commission's investigative powers.

(41) When complying with decisions of the Commission, the undertakings and persons concerned cannot be forced to admit that they have committed infringements, but they are in any event obliged to answer factual questions and to provide documents, even if this information may be used to establish against themselves or against others the existence of such infringements.

(42) For the sake of transparency, all decisions of the Commission which are not of a merely procedural nature should be widely publicised. While ensuring preservation of the rights of defence of the undertakings concerned, in particular the right of access to the file, it is essential that business secrets be protected. The confidentiality of information exchanged in the network and with the competent authorities of third countries should likewise be safeguarded.

(43) Compliance with this Regulation should be enforceable, as appropriate, by means of fines and periodic penalty payments. The Court of Justice should be given unlimited jurisdiction in that regard pursuant to Article 229 of the Treaty.

(44) The conditions in which concentrations, involving undertakings having their seat or their principal fields of activity in the Community, are carried out in third countries should be observed, and provision should be made for the possibility of the Council giving the Commission an appropriate mandate for negotiation with a view to obtaining non-discriminatory treatment for such undertakings.

(45) This Regulation in no way detracts from the collective rights of employees, as recognised in the undertakings concerned, notably with regard to any obligation to inform or consult their recognised representatives under Community and national law.

(46) The Commission should be able to lay down detailed rules concerning the implementation of this Regulation in accordance with the procedures for the exercise of implementing powers conferred on the Commission. For the adoption of such implementing provisions, the Commission should be assisted by an Advisory Committee composed of the representatives of the Member States as specified in Article 23,

HAS ADOPTED THIS REGULATION:

Article 1

Scope

1. Without prejudice to Article 4(5) and Article 22, this Regulation shall apply to all concentrations with a Community dimension as defined in this Article.

2. A concentration has a Community dimension where:

    (a) the combined aggregate worldwide turnover of all the undertakings concerned is more than EUR 5 000 million; and

    (b) the aggregate Community-wide turnover of each of at least two of the undertakings concerned is more than EUR 250 million,

unless each of the undertakings concerned achieves more than two-thirds of its aggregate Community-wide turnover within one and the same Member State.

3. A concentration that does not meet the thresholds laid down in paragraph 2 has a Community dimension where:

(a)   the combined aggregate worldwide turnover of all the undertakings concerned is more than EUR 2 500 million;

(b)   in each of at least three Member States, the combined aggregate turnover of all the undertakings concerned is more than EUR 100 million;

(c)   in each of at least three Member States included for the purpose of point (b), the aggregate turnover of each of at least two of the undertakings concerned is more than EUR 25 million; and

(d)   the aggregate Community-wide turnover of each of at least two of the undertakings concerned is more than EUR 100 million,

unless each of the undertakings concerned achieves more than two-thirds of its aggregate Community-wide turnover within one and the same Member State.

4.   On the basis of statistical data that may be regularly provided by the Member States, the Commission shall report to the Council on the operation of the thresholds and criteria set out in paragraphs 2 and 3 by 1 July 2009 and may present proposals pursuant to paragraph 5.

5.   Following the report referred to in paragraph 4 and on a proposal from the Commission, the Council, acting by a qualified majority, may revise the thresholds and criteria mentioned in paragraph 3.

Article 2

Appraisal of concentrations

1.   Concentrations within the scope of this Regulation shall be appraised in accordance with the objectives of this Regulation and the following provisions with a view to establishing whether or not they are compatible with the common market.

In making this appraisal, the Commission shall take into account:

(a)   the need to maintain and develop effective competition within the common market in view of, among other things, the structure of all the markets concerned and the actual or potential competition from undertakings located either within or outwith the Community;

(b)   the market position of the undertakings concerned and their economic and financial power, the alternatives available to suppliers and users, their access to supplies or markets, any legal or other barriers to entry, supply and demand trends for the relevant goods and services, the interests of the intermediate and ultimate consumers, and the development of technical and economic progress provided that it is to consumers' advantage and does not form an obstacle to competition.

2.   A concentration which would not significantly impede effective competition in the common market or in a substantial part of it, in particular as a result of the creation or strengthening of a dominant position, shall be declared compatible with the common market.

3.   A concentration which would significantly impede effective competition, in the common market or in a substantial part of it, in particular as a result of the creation or strengthening of a dominant position, shall be declared incompatible with the common market.

4.   To the extent that the creation of a joint venture constituting a concentration pursuant to Article 3 has as its object or effect the coordination of the competitive behaviour of undertakings that remain independent, such coordination shall be appraised in accordance with the criteria of Article 81(1) and (3) of the Treaty, with a view to establishing whether or not the operation is compatible with the common market.

5.   In making this appraisal, the Commission shall take into account in particular:

—   whether two or more parent companies retain, to a significant extent, activities in the same market as the joint venture or in a market which is downstream or upstream from that of the joint venture or in a neighbouring market closely related to this market,

—   whether the coordination which is the direct consequence of the creation of the joint venture affords the undertakings concerned the possibility of eliminating competition in respect of a substantial part of the products or services in question.

Article 3

Definition of concentration

1. A concentration shall be deemed to arise where a change of control on a lasting basis results from:
   (a) the merger of two or more previously independent undertakings or parts of undertakings, or
   (b) the acquisition, by one or more persons already controlling at least one undertaking, or by one or more undertakings, whether by purchase of securities or assets, by contract or by any other means, of direct or indirect control of the whole or parts of one or more other undertakings.

2. Control shall be constituted by rights, contracts or any other means which, either separately or in combination and having regard to the considerations of fact or law involved, confer the possibility of exercising decisive influence on an undertaking, in particular by:
   (a) ownership or the right to use all or part of the assets of an undertaking;
   (b) rights or contracts which confer decisive influence on the composition, voting or decisions of the organs of an undertaking.

3. Control is acquired by persons or undertakings which:
   (a) are holders of the rights or entitled to rights under the contracts concerned; or
   (b) while not being holders of such rights or entitled to rights under such contracts, have the power to exercise the rights deriving therefrom.

4. The creation of a joint venture performing on a lasting basis all the functions of an autonomous economic entity shall constitute a concentration within the meaning of paragraph 1(b).

5. A concentration shall not be deemed to arise where:
   (a) credit institutions or other financial institutions or insurance companies, the normal activities of which include transactions and dealing in securities for their own account or for the account of others, hold on a temporary basis securities which they have acquired in an undertaking with a view to reselling them, provided that they do not exercise voting rights in respect of those securities with a view to determining the competitive behaviour of that undertaking or provided that they exercise such voting rights only with a view to preparing the disposal of all or part of that undertaking or of its assets or the disposal of those securities and that any such disposal takes place within one year of the date of acquisition; that period may be extended by the Commission on request where such institutions or companies can show that the disposal was not reasonably possible within the period set;
   (b) control is acquired by an office-holder according to the law of a Member State relating to liquidation, winding up, insolvency, cessation of payments, compositions or analogous proceedings;
   (c) the operations referred to in paragraph 1(b) are carried out by the financial holding companies referred to in Article 5(3) of Fourth Council Directive 78/660/EEC of 25 July 1978 based on Article 54(3)(g) of the Treaty on the annual accounts of certain types of companies provided however that the voting rights in respect of the holding are exercised, in particular in relation to the appointment of members of the management and supervisory bodies of the undertakings in which they have holdings, only to maintain the full value of those investments and not to determine directly or indirectly the competitive conduct of those undertakings.

Article 4

Prior notification of concentrations and pre-notification referral at the request of the notifying parties

1. Concentrations with a Community dimension defined in this Regulation shall be notified to the Commission prior to their implementation and following the conclusion of the agreement, the announcement of the public bid, or the acquisition of a controlling interest.

   Notification may also be made where the undertakings concerned demonstrate to the Commission a good faith intention to conclude an agreement or, in the case of a public bid, where they have publicly announced an intention to make such a bid, provided that the intended agreement or bid would result in a concentration with a Community dimension.

For the purposes of this Regulation, the term 'notified concentration' shall also cover intended concentrations notified pursuant to the second subparagraph. For the purposes of paragraphs 4 and 5 of this Article, the term 'concentration' includes intended concentrations within the meaning of the second subparagraph.

2.   A concentration which consists of a merger within the meaning of Article 3(1)(a) or in the acquisition of joint control within the meaning of Article 3(1)(b) shall be notified jointly by the parties to the merger or by those acquiring joint control as the case may be. In all other cases, the notification shall be effected by the person or undertaking acquiring control of the whole or parts of one or more undertakings.

3.   Where the Commission finds that a notified concentration falls within the scope of this Regulation, it shall publish the fact of the notification, at the same time indicating the names of the undertakings concerned, their country of origin, the nature of the concentration and the economic sectors involved. The Commission shall take account of the legitimate interest of undertakings in the protection of their business secrets.

4.   Prior to the notification of a concentration within the meaning of paragraph 1, the persons or undertakings referred to in paragraph 2 may inform the Commission, by means of a reasoned submission, that the concentration may significantly affect competition in a market within a Member State which presents all the characteristics of a distinct market and should therefore be examined, in whole or in part, by that Member State.

The Commission shall transmit this submission to all Member States without delay. The Member State referred to in the reasoned submission shall, within 15 working days of receiving the submission, express its agreement or disagreement as regards the request to refer the case. Where that Member State takes no such decision within this period, it shall be deemed to have agreed.

Unless that Member State disagrees, the Commission, where it considers that such a distinct market exists, and that competition in that market may be significantly affected by the concentration, may decide to refer the whole or part of the case to the competent authorities of that Member State with a view to the application of that State's national competition law.

The decision whether or not to refer the case in accordance with the third subparagraph shall be taken within 25 working days starting from the receipt of the reasoned submission by the Commission. The Commission shall inform the other Member States and the persons or undertakings concerned of its decision. If the Commission does not take a decision within this period, it shall be deemed to have adopted a decision to refer the case in accordance with the submission made by the persons or undertakings concerned.

If the Commission decides, or is deemed to have decided, pursuant to the third and fourth subparagraphs, to refer the whole of the case, no notification shall be made pursuant to paragraph 1 and national competition law shall apply. Article 9(6) to (9) shall apply mutatis mutandis.

5.   With regard to a concentration as defined in Article 3 which does not have a Community dimension within the meaning of Article 1 and which is capable of being reviewed under the national competition laws of at least three Member States, the persons or undertakings referred to in paragraph 2 may, before any notification to the competent authorities, inform the Commission by means of a reasoned submission that the concentration should be examined by the Commission.

The Commission shall transmit this submission to all Member States without delay.

Any Member State competent to examine the concentration under its national competition law may, within 15 working days of receiving the reasoned submission, express its disagreement as regards the request to refer the case.

Where at least one such Member State has expressed its disagreement in accordance with the third subparagraph within the period of 15 working days, the case shall not be referred. The Commission shall, without delay, inform all Member States and the persons or undertakings concerned of any such expression of disagreement.

Where no Member State has expressed its disagreement in accordance with the third subparagraph within the period of 15 working days, the concentration shall be deemed to have a Community dimension and shall be notified to the Commission in accordance with paragraphs 1 and 2. In such situations, no Member State shall apply its national competition law to the concentration.

6. The Commission shall report to the Council on the operation of paragraphs 4 and 5 by 1 July 2009. Following this report and on a proposal from the Commission, the Council, acting by a qualified majority, may revise paragraphs 4 and 5.

Article 5

Calculation of turnover

1. Aggregate turnover within the meaning of this Regulation shall comprise the amounts derived by the undertakings concerned in the preceding financial year from the sale of products and the provision of services falling within the undertakings' ordinary activities after deduction of sales rebates and of value added tax and other taxes directly related to turnover. The aggregate turnover of an undertaking concerned shall not include the sale of products or the provision of services between any of the undertakings referred to in paragraph 4.

Turnover, in the Community or in a Member State, shall comprise products sold and services provided to undertakings or consumers, in the Community or in that Member State as the case may be.

2. By way of derogation from paragraph 1, where the concentration consists of the acquisition of parts, whether or not constituted as legal entities, of one or more undertakings, only the turnover relating to the parts which are the subject of the concentration shall be taken into account with regard to the seller or sellers.

However, two or more transactions within the meaning of the first subparagraph which take place within a two-year period between the same persons or undertakings shall be treated as one and the same concentration arising on the date of the last transaction.

3. In place of turnover the following shall be used:

(a) for credit institutions and other financial institutions, the sum of the following income items as defined in Council Directive 86/635/EEC, after deduction of value added tax and other taxes directly related to those items, where appropriate:

    (i) interest income and similar income;

    (ii) income from securities:

      — income from shares and other variable yield securities,

      — income from participating interests,

      — income from shares in affiliated undertakings;

    (iii) commissions receivable;

    (iv) net profit on financial operations;

    (v) other operating income.

The turnover of a credit or financial institution in the Community or in a Member State shall comprise the income items, as defined above, which are received by the branch or division of that institution established in the Community or in the Member State in question, as the case may be;

(b) for insurance undertakings, the value of gross premiums written which shall comprise all amounts received and receivable in respect of insurance contracts issued by or on behalf of the insurance undertakings, including also outgoing reinsurance premiums, and after deduction of taxes and parafiscal contributions or levies charged by reference to the amounts of individual premiums or the total volume of premiums; as regards Article 1(2)(b) and (3)(b), (c) and (d) and the final part of Article 1(2) and (3), gross premiums received from Community residents and from residents of one Member State respectively shall be taken into account.

4.   Without prejudice to paragraph 2, the aggregate turnover of an undertaking concerned within the meaning of this Regulation shall be calculated by adding together the respective turnovers of the following:

(a)   the undertaking concerned;

(b)   those undertakings in which the undertaking concerned, directly or indirectly:

    (i)   owns more than half the capital or business assets, or

    (ii) has the power to exercise more than half the voting rights, or

    (iii) has the power to appoint more than half the members of the supervisory board, the administrative board or bodies legally representing the undertakings, or

    (iv) has the right to manage the undertakings' affairs;

(c)   those undertakings which have in the undertaking concerned the rights or powers listed in (b);

(d)   those undertakings in which an undertaking as referred to in (c) has the rights or powers listed in (b);

(e)   those undertakings in which two or more undertakings as referred to in (a) to (d) jointly have the rights or powers listed in (b).

5.   Where undertakings concerned by the concentration jointly have the rights or powers listed in paragraph 4(b), in calculating the aggregate turnover of the undertakings concerned for the purposes of this Regulation:

(a)   no account shall be taken of the turnover resulting from the sale of products or the provision of services between the joint undertaking and each of the undertakings concerned or any other undertaking connected with any one of them, as set out in paragraph 4(b) to (e);

(b)   account shall be taken of the turnover resulting from the sale of products and the provision of services between the joint undertaking and any third undertakings. This turnover shall be apportioned equally amongst the undertakings concerned.

Article 6

Examination of the notification and initiation of proceedings

1.   The Commission shall examine the notification as soon as it is received.

(a)   Where it concludes that the concentration notified does not fall within the scope of this Regulation, it shall record that finding by means of a decision.

(b)   Where it finds that the concentration notified, although falling within the scope of this Regulation, does not raise serious doubts as to its compatibility with the common market, it shall decide not to oppose it and shall declare that it is compatible with the common market.

A decision declaring a concentration compatible shall be deemed to cover restrictions directly related and necessary to the implementation of the concentration.

(c)   Without prejudice to paragraph 2, where the Commission finds that the concentration notified falls within the scope of this Regulation and raises serious doubts as to its compatibility with the common market, it shall decide to initiate proceedings. Without prejudice to Article 9, such proceedings shall be closed by means of a decision as provided for in Article 8(1) to (4), unless the undertakings concerned have demonstrated to the satisfaction of the Commission that they have abandoned the concentration.

2.   Where the Commission finds that, following modification by the undertakings concerned, a notified concentration no longer raises serious doubts within the meaning of paragraph 1(c), it shall declare the concentration compatible with the common market pursuant to paragraph 1(b).

The Commission may attach to its decision under paragraph 1(b) conditions and obligations intended to ensure that the undertakings concerned comply with the commitments they have entered into vis-à-vis the Commission with a view to rendering the concentration compatible with the common market.

3.   The Commission may revoke the decision it took pursuant to paragraph 1(a) or (b) where:

(a)   the decision is based on incorrect information for which one of the undertakings is responsible or where it has been obtained by deceit, or

(b)   the undertakings concerned commit a breach of an obligation attached to the decision.

4.   In the cases referred to in paragraph 3, the Commission may take a decision under paragraph 1, without being bound by the time limits referred to in Article 10(1).

5.   The Commission shall notify its decision to the undertakings concerned and the competent authorities of the Member States without delay.

Article 7

Suspension of concentrations

1.   A concentration with a Community dimension as defined in Article 1, or which is to be examined by the Commission pursuant to Article 4(5), shall not be implemented either before its notification or until it has been declared compatible with the common market pursuant to a decision under Articles 6(1)(b), 8(1) or 8(2), or on the basis of a presumption according to Article 10(6).

2.   Paragraph 1 shall not prevent the implementation of a public bid or of a series of transactions in securities including those convertible into other securities admitted to trading on a market such as a stock exchange, by which control within the meaning of Article 3 is acquired from various sellers, provided that:

(a)   the concentration is notified to the Commission pursuant to Article 4 without delay; and

(b)   the acquirer does not exercise the voting rights attached to the securities in question or does so only to maintain the full value of its investments based on a derogation granted by the Commission under paragraph 3.

3.   The Commission may, on request, grant a derogation from the obligations imposed in paragraphs 1 or 2. The request to grant a derogation must be reasoned. In deciding on the request, the Commission shall take into account inter alia the effects of the suspension on one or more undertakings concerned by the concentration or on a third party and the threat to competition posed by the concentration. Such a derogation may be made subject to conditions and obligations in order to ensure conditions of effective competition. A derogation may be applied for and granted at any time, be it before notification or after the transaction.

4.   The validity of any transaction carried out in contravention of paragraph 1 shall be dependent on a decision pursuant to Article 6(1)(b) or Article 8(1), (2) or (3) or on a presumption pursuant to Article 10(6).

This Article shall, however, have no effect on the validity of transactions in securities including those convertible into other securities admitted to trading on a market such as a stock exchange, unless the buyer and seller knew or ought to have known that the transaction was carried out in contravention of paragraph 1.

Article 8

Powers of decision of the Commission

1.   Where the Commission finds that a notified concentration fulfils the criterion laid down in Article 2(2) and, in the cases referred to in Article 2(4), the criteria laid down in Article 81(3) of the Treaty, it shall issue a decision declaring the concentration compatible with the common market.

A decision declaring a concentration compatible shall be deemed to cover restrictions directly related and necessary to the implementation of the concentration.

2.   Where the Commission finds that, following modification by the undertakings concerned, a notified concentration fulfils the criterion laid down in Article 2(2) and, in the cases referred to in Article 2(4), the criteria laid down in Article 81(3) of the Treaty, it shall issue a decision declaring the concentration compatible with the common market.

The Commission may attach to its decision conditions and obligations intended to ensure that the undertakings concerned comply with the commitments they have entered into vis-à-vis the Commission with a view to rendering the concentration compatible with the common market.

A decision declaring a concentration compatible shall be deemed to cover restrictions directly related and necessary to the implementation of the concentration.

3.   Where the Commission finds that a concentration fulfils the criterion defined in Article 2(3) or, in the cases referred to in Article 2(4), does not fulfil the criteria laid down in Article 81(3) of the Treaty, it shall issue a decision declaring that the concentration is incompatible with the common market.

4.   Where the Commission finds that a concentration:

(a)   has already been implemented and that concentration has been declared incompatible with the common market, or

(b)   has been implemented in contravention of a condition attached to a decision taken under paragraph 2, which has found that, in the absence of the condition, the concentration would fulfil the criterion laid down in Article 2(3) or, in the cases referred to in Article 2(4), would not fulfil the criteria laid down in Article 81(3) of the Treaty,
        the Commission may:

—   require the undertakings concerned to dissolve the concentration, in particular through the dissolution of the merger or the disposal of all the shares or assets acquired, so as to restore the situation prevailing prior to the implementation of the concentration; in circumstances where restoration of the situation prevailing before the implementation of the concentration is not possible through dissolution of the concentration, the Commission may take any other measure appropriate to achieve such restoration as far as possible,

—   order any other appropriate measure to ensure that the undertakings concerned dissolve the concentration or take other restorative measures as required in its decision.

        In cases falling within point (a) of the first subparagraph, the measures referred to in that subparagraph may be imposed either in a decision pursuant to paragraph 3 or by separate decision.

5.   The Commission may take interim measures appropriate to restore or maintain conditions of effective competition where a concentration:

(a)   has been implemented in contravention of Article 7, and a decision as to the compatibility of the concentration with the common market has not yet been taken;

(b)   has been implemented in contravention of a condition attached to a decision under Article 6(1)(b) or paragraph 2 of this Article;

(c)   has already been implemented and is declared incompatible with the common market.

6.   The Commission may revoke the decision it has taken pursuant to paragraphs 1 or 2 where:

(a)   the declaration of compatibility is based on incorrect information for which one of the undertakings is responsible or where it has been obtained by deceit; or

(b)   the undertakings concerned commit a breach of an obligation attached to the decision.

7.   The Commission may take a decision pursuant to paragraphs 1 to 3 without being bound by the time limits referred to in Article 10(3), in cases where:

(a)   it finds that a concentration has been implemented

        (i)   in contravention of a condition attached to a decision under Article 6(1)(b), or

        (ii)   in contravention of a condition attached to a decision taken under paragraph 2 and in accordance with Article 10(2), which has found that, in the absence of the condition, the concentration would raise serious doubts as to its compatibility with the common market; or

(b)   a decision has been revoked pursuant to paragraph 6.

8.   The Commission shall notify its decision to the undertakings concerned and the competent authorities of the Member States without delay.

Article 9

Referral to the competent authorities of the Member States

1. The Commission may, by means of a decision notified without delay to the undertakings concerned and the competent authorities of the other Member States, refer a notified concentration to the competent authorities of the Member State concerned in the following circumstances.

2. Within 15 working days of the date of receipt of the copy of the notification, a Member State, on its own initiative or upon the invitation of the Commission, may inform the Commission, which shall inform the undertakings concerned, that:

   (a) a concentration threatens to affect significantly competition in a market within that Member State, which presents all the characteristics of a distinct market, or

   (b) a concentration affects competition in a market within that Member State, which presents all the characteristics of a distinct market and which does not constitute a substantial part of the common market.

3. If the Commission considers that, having regard to the market for the products or services in question and the geographical reference market within the meaning of paragraph 7, there is such a distinct market and that such a threat exists, either:

   (a) it shall itself deal with the case in accordance with this Regulation; or

   (b) it shall refer the whole or part of the case to the competent authorities of the Member State concerned with a view to the application of that State's national competition law.

   If, however, the Commission considers that such a distinct market or threat does not exist, it shall adopt a decision to that effect which it shall address to the Member State concerned, and shall itself deal with the case in accordance with this Regulation.

   In cases where a Member State informs the Commission pursuant to paragraph 2(b) that a concentration affects competition in a distinct market within its territory that does not form a substantial part of the common market, the Commission shall refer the whole or part of the case relating to the distinct market concerned, if it considers that such a distinct market is affected.

4. A decision to refer or not to refer pursuant to paragraph 3 shall be taken:

   (a) as a general rule within the period provided for in Article 10(1), second subparagraph, where the Commission, pursuant to Article 6(1)(b), has not initiated proceedings; or

   (b) within 65 working days at most of the notification of the concentration concerned where the Commission has initiated proceedings under Article 6(1)(c), without taking the preparatory steps in order to adopt the necessary measures under Article 8(2), (3) or (4) to maintain or restore effective competition on the market concerned.

5. If within the 65 working days referred to in paragraph 4(b) the Commission, despite a reminder from the Member State concerned, has not taken a decision on referral in accordance with paragraph 3 nor has taken the preparatory steps referred to in paragraph 4(b), it shall be deemed to have taken a decision to refer the case to the Member State concerned in accordance with paragraph 3(b).

6. The competent authority of the Member State concerned shall decide upon the case without undue delay.

   Within 45 working days after the Commission's referral, the competent authority of the Member State concerned shall inform the undertakings concerned of the result of the preliminary competition assessment and what further action, if any, it proposes to take. The Member State concerned may exceptionally suspend this time limit where necessary information has not been provided to it by the undertakings concerned as provided for by its national competition law.

   Where a notification is requested under national law, the period of 45 working days shall begin on the working day following that of the receipt of a complete notification by the competent authority of that Member State.

7. The geographical reference market shall consist of the area in which the undertakings concerned are involved in the supply and demand of products or services, in which the conditions of competition are sufficiently homogeneous and which can be distinguished from neighbouring

areas because, in particular, conditions of competition are appreciably different in those areas. This assessment should take account in particular of the nature and characteristics of the products or services concerned, of the existence of entry barriers or of consumer preferences, of appreciable differences of the undertakings' market shares between the area concerned and neighbouring areas or of substantial price differences.

8. In applying the provisions of this Article, the Member State concerned may take only the measures strictly necessary to safeguard or restore effective competition on the market concerned.

9. In accordance with the relevant provisions of the Treaty, any Member State may appeal to the Court of Justice, and in particular request the application of Article 243 of the Treaty, for the purpose of applying its national competition law.

Article 10

Time limits for initiating proceedings and for decisions

1. Without prejudice to Article 6(4), the decisions referred to in Article 6(1) shall be taken within 25 working days at most. That period shall begin on the working day following that of the receipt of a notification or, if the information to be supplied with the notification is incomplete, on the working day following that of the receipt of the complete information.

   That period shall be increased to 35 working days where the Commission receives a request from a Member State in accordance with Article 9(2)or where, the undertakings concerned offer commitments pursuant to Article 6(2) with a view to rendering the concentration compatible with the common market.

2. Decisions pursuant to Article 8(1) or (2) concerning notified concentrations shall be taken as soon as it appears that the serious doubts referred to in Article 6(1)(c) have been removed, particularly as a result of modifications made by the undertakings concerned, and at the latest by the time limit laid down in paragraph 3.

3. Without prejudice to Article 8(7), decisions pursuant to Article 8(1) to (3) concerning notified concentrations shall be taken within not more than 90 working days of the date on which the proceedings are initiated. That period shall be increased to 105 working days where the undertakings concerned offer commitments pursuant to Article 8(2), second subparagraph, with a view to rendering the concentration compatible with the common market, unless these commitments have been offered less than 55 working days after the initiation of proceedings.

   The periods set by the first subparagraph shall likewise be extended if the notifying parties make a request to that effect not later than 15 working days after the initiation of proceedings pursuant to Article 6(1)(c). The notifying parties may make only one such request. Likewise, at any time following the initiation of proceedings, the periods set by the first subparagraph may be extended by the Commission with the agreement of the notifying parties. The total duration of any extension or extensions effected pursuant to this subparagraph shall not exceed 20 working days.

4. The periods set by paragraphs 1 and 3 shall exceptionally be suspended where, owing to circumstances for which one of the undertakings involved in the concentration is responsible, the Commission has had to request information by decision pursuant to Article 11 or to order an inspection by decision pursuant to Article 13.

   The first subparagraph shall also apply to the period referred to in Article 9(4)(b).

5. Where the Court of Justice gives a judgment which annuls the whole or part of a Commission decision which is subject to a time limit set by this Article, the concentration shall be reexamined by the Commission with a view to adopting a decision pursuant to Article 6(1).

   The concentration shall be re-examined in the light of current market conditions.

   The notifying parties shall submit a new notification or supplement the original notification, without delay, where the original notification becomes incomplete by reason of intervening changes in market conditions or in the information provided. Where there are no such changes, the parties shall certify this fact without delay.

The periods laid down in paragraph 1 shall start on the working day following that of the receipt of complete information in a new notification, a supplemented notification, or a certification within the meaning of the third subparagraph.

The second and third subparagraphs shall also apply in the cases referred to in Article 6(4) and Article 8(7).

6.   Where the Commission has not taken a decision in accordance with Article 6(1)(b), (c), 8(1), (2) or (3) within the time limits set in paragraphs 1 and 3 respectively, the concentration shall be deemed to have been declared compatible with the common market, without prejudice to Article 9.

Article 11

Requests for information

1.   In order to carry out the duties assigned to it by this Regulation, the Commission may, by simple request or by decision, require the persons referred to in Article 3(1)(b), as well as undertakings and associations of undertakings, to provide all necessary information.

2.   When sending a simple request for information to a person, an undertaking or an association of undertakings, the Commission shall state the legal basis and the purpose of the request, specify what information is required and fix the time limit within which the information is to be provided, as well as the penalties provided for in Article 14 for supplying incorrect or misleading information.

3.   Where the Commission requires a person, an undertaking or an association of undertakings to supply information by decision, it shall state the legal basis and the purpose of the request, specify what information is required and fix the time limit within which it is to be provided. It shall also indicate the penalties provided for in Article 14 and indicate or impose the penalties provided for in Article 15. It shall further indicate the right to have the decision reviewed by the Court of Justice.

4.   The owners of the undertakings or their representatives and, in the case of legal persons, companies or firms, or associations having no legal personality, the persons authorised to represent them by law or by their constitution, shall supply the information requested on behalf of the undertaking concerned. Persons duly authorised to act may supply the information on behalf of their clients. The latter shall remain fully responsible if the information supplied is incomplete, incorrect or misleading.

5.   The Commission shall without delay forward a copy of any decision taken pursuant to paragraph 3 to the competent authorities of the Member State in whose territory the residence of the person or the seat of the undertaking or association of undertakings is situated, and to the competent authority of the Member State whose territory is affected. At the specific request of the competent authority of a Member State, the Commission shall also forward to that authority copies of simple requests for information relating to a notified concentration.

6.   At the request of the Commission, the governments and competent authorities of the Member States shall provide the Commission with all necessary information to carry out the duties assigned to it by this Regulation.

7.   In order to carry out the duties assigned to it by this Regulation, the Commission may interview any natural or legal person who consents to be interviewed for the purpose of collecting information relating to the subject matter of an investigation. At the beginning of the interview, which may be conducted by telephone or other electronic means, the Commission shall state the legal basis and the purpose of the interview.

Where an interview is not conducted on the premises of the Commission or by telephone or other electronic means, the Commission shall inform in advance the competent authority of the Member State in whose territory the interview takes place. If the competent authority of that Member State so requests, officials of that authority may assist the officials and other persons authorised by the Commission to conduct the interview.

Article 12

Inspections by the authorities of the Member States

1. At the request of the Commission, the competent authorities of the Member States shall undertake the inspections which the Commission considers to be necessary under Article 13(1), or which it has ordered by decision pursuant to Article 13(4). The officials of the competent authorities of the Member States who are responsible for conducting these inspections as well as those authorised or appointed by them shall exercise their powers in accordance with their national law.

2. If so requested by the Commission or by the competent authority of the Member State within whose territory the inspection is to be conducted, officials and other accompanying persons authorised by the Commission may assist the officials of the authority concerned.

Article 13

The Commission's powers of inspection

1. In order to carry out the duties assigned to it by this Regulation, the Commission may conduct all necessary inspections of undertakings and associations of undertakings.

2. The officials and other accompanying persons authorised by the Commission to conduct an inspection shall have the power:

    (a) to enter any premises, land and means of transport of undertakings and associations of undertakings;

    (b) to examine the books and other records related to the business, irrespective of the medium on which they are stored;

    (c) to take or obtain in any form copies of or extracts from such books or records;

    (d) to seal any business premises and books or records for the period and to the extent necessary for the inspection;

    (e) to ask any representative or member of staff of the undertaking or association of undertakings for explanations on facts or documents relating to the subject matter and purpose of the inspection and to record the answers.

3. Officials and other accompanying persons authorised by the Commission to conduct an inspection shall exercise their powers upon production of a written authorisation specifying the subject matter and purpose of the inspection and the penalties provided for in Article 14, in the production of the required books or other records related to the business which is incomplete or where answers to questions asked under paragraph 2 of this Article are incorrect or misleading. In good time before the inspection, the Commission shall give notice of the inspection to the competent authority of the Member State in whose territory the inspection is to be conducted.

4. Undertakings and associations of undertakings are required to submit to inspections ordered by decision of the Commission. The decision shall specify the subject matter and purpose of the inspection, appoint the date on which it is to begin and indicate the penalties provided for in Articles 14 and 15 and the right to have the decision reviewed by the Court of Justice. The Commission shall take such decisions after consulting the competent authority of the Member State in whose territory the inspection is to be conducted.

5. Officials of, and those authorised or appointed by, the competent authority of the Member State in whose territory the inspection is to be conducted shall, at the request of that authority or of the Commission, actively assist the officials and other accompanying persons authorised by the Commission. To this end, they shall enjoy the powers specified in paragraph 2.

6. Where the officials and other accompanying persons authorised by the Commission find that an undertaking opposes an inspection, including the sealing of business premises, books or records, ordered pursuant to this Article, the Member State concerned shall afford them the necessary assistance, requesting where appropriate the assistance of the police or of an equivalent enforcement authority, so as to enable them to conduct their inspection.

7. If the assistance provided for in paragraph 6 requires authorisation from a judicial authority according to national rules, such authorisation shall be applied for. Such authorisation may also be applied for as a precautionary measure.

8. Where authorisation as referred to in paragraph 7 is applied for, the national judicial authority shall ensure that the Commission decision is authentic and that the coercive measures envisaged are neither arbitrary nor excessive having regard to the subject matter of the inspection. In its control of proportionality of the coercive measures, the national judicial authority may ask the Commission, directly or through the competent authority of that Member State, for detailed explanations relating to the subject matter of the inspection. However, the national judicial authority may not call into question the necessity for the inspection nor demand that it be provided with the information in the Commission's file. The lawfulness of the Commission's decision shall be subject to review only by the Court of Justice.

Article 14

Fines

1. The Commission may by decision impose on the persons referred to in Article 3(1)b, undertakings or associations of undertakings, fines not exceeding 1% of the aggregate turnover of the undertaking or association of undertakings concerned within the meaning of Article 5 where, intentionally or negligently:

    (a) they supply incorrect or misleading information in a submission, certification, notification or supplement thereto, pursuant to Article 4, Article 10(5) or Article 22(3);

    (b) they supply incorrect or misleading information in response to a request made pursuant to Article 11(2);

    (c) in response to a request made by decision adopted pursuant to Article 11(3), they supply incorrect, incomplete or misleading information or do not supply information within the required time limit;

    (d) they produce the required books or other records related to the business in incomplete form during inspections under Article 13, or refuse to submit to an inspection ordered by decision taken pursuant to Article 13(4);

    (e) in response to a question asked in accordance with Article 13(2)(e),
    — they give an incorrect or misleading answer,
    — they fail to rectify within a time limit set by the Commission an incorrect, incomplete or misleading answer given by a member of staff, or
    — they fail or refuse to provide a complete answer on facts relating to the subject matter and purpose of an inspection ordered by a decision adopted pursuant to Article 13(4);

    (f) seals affixed by officials or other accompanying persons authorised by the Commission in accordance with Article 13(2)(d) have been broken.

2. The Commission may by decision impose fines not exceeding 10% of the aggregate turnover of the undertaking concerned within the meaning of Article 5 on the persons referred to in Article 3(1)b or the undertakings concerned where, either intentionally or negligently, they:

    (a) fail to notify a concentration in accordance with Articles 4 or 22(3) prior to its implementation, unless they are expressly authorised to do so by Article 7(2) or by a decision taken pursuant to Article 7(3);

    (b) implement a concentration in breach of Article 7;

    (c) implement a concentration declared incompatible with the common market by decision pursuant to Article 8(3) or do not comply with any measure ordered by decision pursuant to Article 8(4) or (5);

    (d) fail to comply with a condition or an obligation imposed by decision pursuant to Articles 6(1)(b), Article 7(3) or Article 8(2), second subparagraph.

3. In fixing the amount of the fine, regard shall be had to the nature, gravity and duration of the infringement.

4. Decisions taken pursuant to paragraphs 1, 2 and 3 shall not be of a criminal law nature.

Article 15

Periodic penalty payments

1.   The Commission may by decision impose on the persons referred to in Article 3(1)b, undertakings or associations of undertakings, periodic penalty payments not exceeding 5% of the average daily aggregate turnover of the undertaking or association of undertakings concerned within the meaning of Article 5 for each working day of delay, calculated from the date set in the decision, in order to compel them:

    (a)   to supply complete and correct information which it has requested by decision taken pursuant to Article 11(3);

    (b)   to submit to an inspection which it has ordered by decision taken pursuant to Article 13(4);

    (c)   to comply with an obligation imposed by decision pursuant to Article 6(1)(b), Article 7(3) or Article 8(2), second subparagraph; or;

    (d)   to comply with any measures ordered by decision pursuant to Article 8(4) or (5).

2.   Where the persons referred to in Article 3(1)(b), undertakings or associations of undertakings have satisfied the obligation which the periodic penalty payment was intended to enforce, the Commission may fix the definitive amount of the periodic penalty payments at a figure lower than that which would arise under the original decision.

Article 16

Review by the Court of Justice

The Court of Justice shall have unlimited jurisdiction within the meaning of Article 229 of the Treaty to review decisions whereby the Commission has fixed a fine or periodic penalty payments; it may cancel, reduce or increase the fine or periodic penalty payment imposed.

Article 17

Professional secrecy

1.   Information acquired as a result of the application of this Regulation shall be used only for the purposes of the relevant request, investigation or hearing.

2.   Without prejudice to Article 4(3), Articles 18 and 20, the Commission and the competent authorities of the Member States, their officials and other servants and other persons working under the supervision of these authorities as well as officials and civil servants of other authorities of the Member States shall not disclose information they have acquired through the application of this Regulation of the kind covered by the obligation of professional secrecy.

3.   Paragraphs 1 and 2 shall not prevent publication of general information or of surveys which do not contain information relating to particular undertakings or associations of undertakings.

Article 18

Hearing of the parties and of third persons

1.   Before taking any decision provided for in Article 6(3), Article 7(3), Article 8(2) to (6), and Articles 14 and 15, the Commission shall give the persons, undertakings and associations of undertakings concerned the opportunity, at every stage of the procedure up to the consultation of the Advisory Committee, of making known their views on the objections against them.

2.   By way of derogation from paragraph 1, a decision pursuant to Articles 7(3) and 8(5) may be taken provisionally, without the persons, undertakings or associations of undertakings concerned being given the opportunity to make known their views beforehand, provided that the Commission gives them that opportunity as soon as possible after having taken its decision.

3.   The Commission shall base its decision only on objections on which the parties have been able to submit their observations. The rights of the defence shall be fully respected in the proceedings. Access to the file shall be open at least to the parties directly involved, subject to the legitimate interest of undertakings in the protection of their business secrets.

4.   In so far as the Commission or the competent authorities of the Member States deem it necessary, they may also hear other natural or legal persons. Natural or legal persons showing a sufficient interest and especially members of the administrative or management bodies of the undertakings concerned or the recognised representatives of their employees shall be entitled, upon application, to be heard.

Article 19

Liaison with the authorities of the Member States

1.   The Commission shall transmit to the competent authorities of the Member States copies of notifications within three working days and, as soon as possible, copies of the most important documents lodged with or issued by the Commission pursuant to this Regulation. Such documents shall include commitments offered by the undertakings concerned vis-à-vis the Commission with a view to rendering the concentration compatible with the common market pursuant to Article 6(2) or Article 8(2), second subparagraph.

2.   The Commission shall carry out the procedures set out in this Regulation in close and constant liaison with the competent authorities of the Member States, which may express their views upon those procedures. For the purposes of Article 9 it shall obtain information from the competent authority of the Member State as referred to in paragraph 2 of that Article and give it the opportunity to make known its views at every stage of the procedure up to the adoption of a decision pursuant to paragraph 3 of that Article; to that end it shall give it access to the file.

3.   An Advisory Committee on concentrations shall be consulted before any decision is taken pursuant to Article 8(1) to (6), Articles 14 or 15 with the exception of provisional decisions taken in accordance with Article 18(2).

4.   The Advisory Committee shall consist of representatives of the competent authorities of the Member States. Each Member State shall appoint one or two representatives; if unable to attend, they may be replaced by other representatives. At least one of the representatives of a Member State shall be competent in matters of restrictive practices and dominant positions.

5.   Consultation shall take place at a joint meeting convened at the invitation of and chaired by the Commission. A summary of the case, together with an indication of the most important documents and a preliminary draft of the decision to be taken for each case considered, shall be sent with the invitation. The meeting shall take place not less than 10 working days after the invitation has been sent. The Commission may in exceptional cases shorten that period as appropriate in order to avoid serious harm to one or more of the undertakings concerned by a concentration.

6.   The Advisory Committee shall deliver an opinion on the Commission's draft decision, if necessary by taking a vote. The Advisory Committee may deliver an opinion even if some members are absent and unrepresented. The opinion shall be delivered in writing and appended to the draft decision. The Commission shall take the utmost account of the opinion delivered by the Committee. It shall inform the Committee of the manner in which its opinion has been taken into account.

7.   The Commission shall communicate the opinion of the Advisory Committee, together with the decision, to the addressees of the decision. It shall make the opinion public together with the decision, having regard to the legitimate interest of undertakings in the protection of their business secrets.

Article 20

Publication of decisions

1.   The Commission shall publish the decisions which it takes pursuant to Article 8(1) to (6), Articles 14 and 15 with the exception of provisional decisions taken in accordance with Article 18(2) together with the opinion of the Advisory Committee in the Official Journal of the European Union.

2.   The publication shall state the names of the parties and the main content of the decision; it shall
        have regard to the legitimate interest of undertakings in the protection of their business secrets.

Article 21

Application of the Regulation and jurisdiction

1.   This Regulation alone shall apply to concentrations as defined in Article 3, and Council
        Regulations (EC) No 1/2003, (EEC) No 1017/68, (EEC) No 4056/86 and (EEC) No 3975/87 shall
        not apply, except in relation to joint ventures that do not have a Community dimension and which
        have as their object or effect the coordination of the competitive behaviour of undertakings that
        remain independent.

2.   Subject to review by the Court of Justice, the Commission shall have sole jurisdiction to take the
        decisions provided for in this Regulation.

3.   No Member State shall apply its national legislation on competition to any concentration that has
        a Community dimension.
        The first subparagraph shall be without prejudice to any Member State's power to carry out any
        enquiries necessary for the application of Articles 4(4), 9(2) or after referral, pursuant to Article
        9(3), first subparagraph, indent (b), or Article 9(5), to take the measures strictly necessary for the
        application of Article 9(8).

4.   Notwithstanding paragraphs 2 and 3, Member States may take appropriate measures to protect
        legitimate interests other than those taken into consideration by this Regulation and compatible
        with the general principles and other provisions of Community law.
        Public security, plurality of the media and prudential rules shall be regarded as legitimate interests
        within the meaning of the first subparagraph.
        Any other public interest must be communicated to the Commission by the Member State
        concerned and shall be recognised by the Commission after an assessment of its compatibility
        with the general principles and other provisions of Community law before the measures referred
        to above may be taken. The Commission shall inform the Member State concerned of its decision
        within 25 working days of that communication.

Article 22

Referral to the Commission

1.   One or more Member States may request the Commission to examine any concentration as
        defined in Article 3 that does not have a Community dimension within the meaning of Article 1
        but affects trade between Member States and threatens to significantly affect competition within
        the territory of the Member State or States making the request.
        Such a request shall be made at most within 15 working days of the date on which the
        concentration was notified, or if no notification is required, otherwise made known to the
        Member State concerned.

2.   The Commission shall inform the competent authorities of the Member States and the
        undertakings concerned of any request received pursuant to paragraph 1 without delay.
        Any other Member State shall have the right to join the initial request within a period of 15
        working days of being informed by the Commission of the initial request.
        All national time limits relating to the concentration shall be suspended until, in accordance with
        the procedure set out in this Article, it has been decided where the concentration shall be
        examined. As soon as a Member State has informed the Commission and the undertakings
        concerned that it does not wish to join the request, the suspension of its national time limits shall
        end.

3.   The Commission may, at the latest 10 working days after the expiry of the period set in paragraph
        2, decide to examine, the concentration where it considers that it affects trade between Member
        States and threatens to significantly affect competition within the territory of the Member State or
        States making the request. If the Commission does not take a decision within this period, it shall

be deemed to have adopted a decision to examine the concentration in accordance with the request.

The Commission shall inform all Member States and the undertakings concerned of its decision. It may request the submission of a notification pursuant to Article 4.

The Member State or States having made the request shall no longer apply their national legislation on competition to the concentration.

4. Article 2, Article 4(2) to (3), Articles 5, 6, and 8 to 21 shall apply where the Commission examines a concentration pursuant to paragraph 3. Article 7 shall apply to the extent that the concentration has not been implemented on the date on which the Commission informs the undertakings concerned that a request has been made.

Where a notification pursuant to Article 4 is not required, the period set in Article 10(1) within which proceedings may be initiated shall begin on the working day following that on which the Commission informs the undertakings concerned that it has decided to examine the concentration pursuant to paragraph 3.

5. The Commission may inform one or several Member States that it considers a concentration fulfils the criteria in paragraph 1. In such cases, the Commission may invite that Member State or those Member States to make a request pursuant to paragraph 1.

Article 23

Implementing provisions

1. The Commission shall have the power to lay down in accordance with the procedure referred to in paragraph 2:
   (a) implementing provisions concerning the form, content and other details of notifications and submissions pursuant to Article 4;
   (b) implementing provisions concerning time limits pursuant to Article 4(4), (5) Articles 7, 9, 10 and 22;
   (c) the procedure and time limits for the submission and implementation of commitments pursuant to Article 6(2) and Article 8(2);
   (d) implementing provisions concerning hearings pursuant to Article 18.
2. The Commission shall be assisted by an Advisory Committee, composed of representatives of the Member States.
   (a) Before publishing draft implementing provisions and before adopting such provisions, the Commission shall consult the Advisory Committee.
   (b) Consultation shall take place at a meeting convened at the invitation of and chaired by the Commission. A draft of the implementing provisions to be taken shall be sent with the invitation. The meeting shall take place not less than 10 working days after the invitation has been sent.
   (c) The Advisory Committee shall deliver an opinion on the draft implementing provisions, if necessary by taking a vote. The Commission shall take the utmost account of the opinion delivered by the Committee.

Article 24

Relations with third countries

1. The Member States shall inform the Commission of any general difficulties encountered by their undertakings with concentrations as defined in Article 3 in a third country.
2. Initially not more than one year after the entry into force of this Regulation and, thereafter periodically, the Commission shall draw up a report examining the treatment accorded to undertakings having their seat or their principal fields of activity in the Community, in the terms referred to in paragraphs 3 and 4, as regards concentrations in third countries. The Commission shall submit those reports to the Council, together with any recommendations.
3. Whenever it appears to the Commission, either on the basis of the reports referred to in paragraph 2 or on the basis of other information, that a third country does not grant undertakings having

their seat or their principal fields of activity in the Community, treatment comparable to that granted by the Community to undertakings from that country, the Commission may submit proposals to the Council for an appropriate mandate for negotiation with a view to obtaining comparable treatment for undertakings having their seat or their principal fields of activity in the Community.

4.   Measures taken under this Article shall comply with the obligations of the Community or of the Member States, without prejudice to Article 307 of the Treaty, under international agreements, whether bilateral or multilateral.

Article 25

Repeal

1.   Without prejudice to Article 26(2), Regulations (EEC) No 4064/89 and (EC) No 1310/97 shall be repealed with effect from 1 May 2004.

2.   References to the repealed Regulations shall be construed as references to this Regulation and shall be read in accordance with the correlation table in the Annex.

Article 26

Entry into force and transitional provisions

1.   This Regulation shall enter into force on the 20th day following that of its publication in the Official Journal of the European Union.

It shall apply from 1 May 2004.

2.   Regulation (EEC) No 4064/89 shall continue to apply to any concentration which was the subject of an agreement or announcement or where control was acquired within the meaning of Article 4(1) of that Regulation before the date of application of this Regulation, subject, in particular, to the provisions governing applicability set out in Article 25(2) and (3) of Regulation (EEC) No 4064/89 and Article 2 of Regulation (EEC) No 1310/97.

3.   As regards concentrations to which this Regulation applies by virtue of accession, the date of accession shall be substituted for the date of application of this Regulation.

This Regulation shall be binding in its entirety and directly applicable in all Member States.

ANNEX
CORRELATION TABLE

Regulation (EEC) No 4064/89	This Regulation
Article 1(1), (2) and (3)	Article 1(1), (2) and (3)
Article 1(4)	Article 1(4)
Article 1(5)	Article 1(5)
Article 2(1)	Article 2(1)
—	Article 2(2)
Article 2(2)	Article 2(3)
Article 2(3)	Article 2(4)
Article 2(4)	Article 2(5)
Article 3(1)	Article 3(1)
Article 3(2)	Article 3(4)
Article 3(3)	Article 3(2)
Article 3(4)	Article 3(3)
—	Article 3(4)
Article 3(5)	Article 3(5)

Article 4(1) first sentence	Article 4(1) first subparagraph
Article 4(1) second sentence	—
—	Article 4(1) second and third subparagraphs
Article 4(2) and (3)	Article 4(2) and (3)
—	Article 4(4) to (6)
Article 5(1) to (3)	Article 5(1) to (3)
Article 5(4), introductory words	Article 5(4), introductory words
Article 5(4) point (a)	Article 5(4) point (a)
Article 5(4) point (b), introductory words	Article 5(4) point (b), introductory words
Article 5(4) point (b), first indent	Article 5(4) point (b)(i)
Article 5(4) point (b), second indent	Article 5(4) point (b)(ii)
Article 5(4) point (b), third indent	Article 5(4) point (b)(iii)
Article 5(4) point (b), fourth indent	Article 5(4) point (b)(iv)
Article 5(4) points (c), (d) and (e)	Article 5(4) points (c), (d) and (e)
Article 5(5)	Article 5(5)
Article 6(1), introductory words	Article 6(1), introductory words
Article 6(1) points (a) and (b)	Article 6(1) points (a) and (b)
Article 6(1) point (c)	Article 6(1) point (c), first sentence
Article 6(2) to (5)	Article 6(2) to (5)
Article 7(1)	Article 7(1)
Article 7(3)	Article 7(2)
Article 7(4)	Article 7(3)
Article 7(5)	Article 7(4)
Article 8(1)	Article 6(1) point (c), second sentence
Article 8(2)	Article 8(1) and (2)
Article 8(3)	Article 8(3)
Article 8(4)	Article 8(4)
—	Article 8(5)
Article 8(5)	Article 8(6)
Article 8(6)	Article 8(7)
—	Article 8(8)
Article 9(1) to (9)	Article 9(1) to (9)
Article 9(10)	—
Article 10(1) and (2)	Article 10(1) and (2)
Article 10(3)	Article 10(3) first subparagraph, first sentence
—	Article 10(3) first subparagraph, second sentence
—	Article 10(3) second subparagraph
Article 10(4)	Article 10(4) first subparagraph
—	Article 10(4), second subparagraph

Article 10(5)	Article 10(5), first and fourth subparagraphs
—	Article 10(5), second, third and fifth sub-paragraphs
Article 10(6)	Article 10(6)
Article 11(1)	Article 11(1)
Article 11(2)	—
Article 11(3)	Article 11(2)
Article 11(4)	Article 11(4) first sentence
—	Article 11(4) second and third sentences
Article 11(5) first sentence	—
Article 11(5) second sentence	Article 11(3)
Article 11(6)	Article 11(5)
—	Article 11(6) and (7)
Article 12	Article 12
Article 13(1) first subparagraph	Article 13(1)
Article 13(1) second subparagraph, introductory words	Article 13(2) introductory words
Article 13(1) second subparagraph, point (a)	Article 13(2) point (b)
Article 13(1) second subparagraph, point (b)	Article 13(2) point (c)
Article 13(1) second subparagraph, point (c)	Article 13(2) point (e)
Article 13(1) second subparagraph, point (d)	Article 13(2) point (a)
—	Article 13(2) point (d)
Article 13(2)	Article 13(3)
Article 13(3)	Article 13(4) first and second sentences
Article 13(4)	Article 13(4) third sentence
Article 13(5)	Article 13(5), first sentence
—	Article 13(5), second sentence
Article 13(6) first sentence	Article 13(6)
Article 13(6) second sentence	—
—	Article 13(7) and (8)
Article 14(1) introductory words	Article 14(1) introductory words
Article 14(1) point (a)	Article 14(2) point (a)
Article 14(1) point (b)	Article 14(1) point (a)
Article 14(1) point (c)	Article 14(1) points (b) and (c)
Article 14(1) point (d)	Article 14(1) point (d)
—	Article 14(1) points (e) and (f)
Article 14(2) introductory words	Article 14(2) introductory words
Article 14(2) point (a)	Article 14(2) point (d)
Article 14(2) points (b) and (c)	Article 14(2) points (b) and (c)
Article 14(3)	Article 14(3)
Article 14(4)	Article 14(4)

Article 15(1) introductory words	Article 15(1) introductory words
Article 15(1) points (a) and (b)	Article 15(1) points (a) and (b)
Article 15(2) introductory words	Article 15(1) introductory words
Article 15(2) point (a)	Article 15(1) point (c)
Article 15(2) point (b)	Article 15(1) point (d)
Article 15(3)	Article 15(2)
Articles 16 to 20	Articles 16 to 20
Article 21(1)	Article 21(2)
Article 21(2)	Article 21(3)
Article 21(3)	Article 21(4)
Article 22(1)	Article 21(1)
Article 22(3)	—
—	Article 22(1) to (3)
Article 22(4)	Article 22(4)
Article 22(5)	—
—	Article 22(5)
Article 23	Article 23(1)
—	Article 23(2)
Article 24	Article 24
—	Article 25
Article 25(1)	Article 26(1), first subparagraph
—	Article 26(1), second subparagraph
Article 25(2)	Article 26(2)
Article 25(3)	Article 26(3)
—	Annex

EC Treaty

(Articles 28, 30, 39, 43, 49, 81, 82)

PART THREE
COMMUNITY POLICIES

TITLE I
FREE MOVEMENT OF GOODS

CHAPTER 2
PROHIBITION OF QUANTITATIVE RESTRICTIONS BETWEEN MEMBER STATES

Article 28

Quantitative restrictions on imports and all measures having equivalent effect shall be prohibited between Member States.

Article 30

The provisions of Articles 28 and 29 shall not preclude prohibitions or restrictions on imports, exports or goods in transit justified on grounds of public morality, public policy or public security; the protection of health and life of humans, animals or plants; the protection of national treasures possessing artistic, historic or archaeological value; or the protection of industrial and commercial property. Such prohibitions or restrictions shall not, however, constitute a means of arbitrary discrimination or a disguised restriction on trade between Member States.

TITLE III
FREE MOVEMENT OF PERSONS, SERVICES AND CAPITAL

CHAPTER 1
WORKERS

Article 39

1. Freedom of movement for workers shall be secured within the Community.
2. Such freedom of movement shall entail the abolition of any discrimination based on nationality between workers of the Member States as regards employment, remuneration and other conditions of work and employment.
3. It shall entail the right, subject to limitations justified on grounds of public policy, public security or public health:
   (a) to accept offers of employment actually made;
   (b) to move freely within the territory of Member States for this purpose;
   (c) to stay in a Member State for the purpose of employment in accordance with the provisions governing the employment of nationals of that State laid down by law, regulation or administrative action;
   (d) to remain in the territory of a Member State after having been employed in that State, subject to conditions which shall be embodied in implementing regulations to be drawn up by the Commission.
4. The provisions of this article shall not apply to employment in the public service.

CHAPTER 2
RIGHT OF ESTABLISHMENT

Article 43

Within the framework of the provisions set out below, restrictions on the freedom of establishment of nationals of a Member State in the territory of another Member State shall be prohibited. Such prohibition shall also apply to restrictions on the setting-up of agencies, branches or subsidiaries by nationals of any Member State established in the territory of any Member State.

Freedom of establishment shall include the right to take up and pursue activities as self-employed persons and to set up and manage undertakings, in particular companies or firms within the meaning of the second paragraph of Article 48, under the conditions laid down for its own nationals by the law of the country where such establishment is effected, subject to the provisions of the chapter relating to capital.

CHAPTER 3
SERVICES

Article 49

Within the framework of the provisions set out below, restrictions on freedom to provide services within the Community shall be prohibited in respect of nationals of Member States who are established in a State of the Community other than that of the person for whom the services are intended.

The Council may, acting by a qualified majority on a proposal from the Commission, extend the provisions of the Chapter to nationals of a third country who provide services and who are established within the Community.

TITLE VI
COMMON RULES ON COMPETITION, TAXATION AND APPROXIMATION OF LAWS

CHAPTER 1
RULES ON COMPETITION

SECTION 1
RULES APPLYING TO UNDERTAKINGS

Article 81

1.   The following shall be prohibited as incompatible with the common market: all agreements between undertakings, decisions by associations of undertakings and concerted practices which may affect trade between Member States and which have as their object or effect the prevention, restriction or distortion of competition within the common market, and in particular those which:
   (a)   directly or indirectly fix purchase or selling prices or any other trading conditions;
   (b)   limit or control production, markets, technical development, or investment;
   (c)   share markets or sources of supply;
   (d)   apply dissimilar conditions to equivalent transactions with other trading parties, thereby placing them at a competitive disadvantage;
   (e)   make the conclusion of contracts subject to acceptance by the other parties of supplementary obligations which, by their nature or according to commercial usage, have no connection with the subject of such contracts.
2.   Any agreements or decisions prohibited pursuant to this article shall be automatically void.
3.   The provisions of paragraph 1 may, however, be declared inapplicable in the case of:
   —   any agreement or category of agreements between undertakings,
   —   any decision or category of decisions by associations of undertakings,
   —   any concerted practice or category of concerted practices,

which contributes to improving the production or distribution of goods or to promoting technical or economic progress, while allowing consumers a fair share of the resulting benefit, and which does not:

(a)   impose on the undertakings concerned restrictions which are not indispensable to the attainment of these objectives;

(b)   afford such undertakings the possibility of eliminating competition in respect of a substantial part of the products in question.

Article 82

Any abuse by one or more undertakings of a dominant position within the common market or in a substantial part of it shall be prohibited as incompatible with the common market in so far as it may affect trade between Member States.

Such abuse may, in particular, consist in:

(a)   directly or indirectly imposing unfair purchase or selling prices or other unfair trading conditions;

(b)   limiting production, markets or technical development to the prejudice of consumers;

(c)   applying dissimilar conditions to equivalent transactions with other trading parties, thereby placing them at a competitive disadvantage;

(d)   making the conclusion of contracts subject to acceptance by the other parties of supplementary obligations which, by their nature or according to commercial usage, have no connection with the subject of such contracts.

Commission Regulation (EC) of 22 December 1999 on the application of Article 81(3) of the Treaty to categories of vertical agreements and concerted practices

No. 2790/1999

THE COMMISSION OF THE EUROPEAN COMMUNITIES,

Having regard to the Treaty establishing the European Community,

Having regard to Council Regulation No 19/65/EEC of 2 March 1965 on the application of Article 85(3) of the Treaty to certain categories of agreements and concerted practices, as last amended by Regulation (EC) No 1215/1999, and in particular Article 1 thereof,

Having published a draft of this Regulation,

Having consulted the Advisory Committee on Restrictive Practices and Dominant Positions,

Whereas:

(1)   Regulation No 19/65/EEC empowers the Commission to apply Article 81(3) of the Treaty (formerly Article 85(3)) by regulation to certain categories of vertical agreements and corresponding concerted practices falling within Article 81(1).

(2)   Experience acquired to date makes it possible to define a category of vertical agreements which can be regarded as normally satisfying the conditions laid down in Article 81(3).

(3)   This category includes vertical agreements for the purchase or sale of goods or services where these agreements are concluded between non-competing undertakings, between certain competitors or by certain associations of retailers of goods; it also includes vertical agreements containing ancillary provisions on the assignment or use of intellectual property rights; for the purposes of this Regulation, the term 'vertical agreements' includes the corresponding concerted practices.

(4)   For the application of Article 81(3) by regulation, it is not necessary to define those vertical agreements which are capable of falling within Article 81(1); in the individual assessment of agreements under Article 81(1), account has to be taken of several factors, and in particular the market structure on the supply and purchase side.

(5)   The benefit of the block exemption should be limited to vertical agreements for which it can be assumed with sufficient certainty that they satisfy the conditions of Article 81(3).

(6)   Vertical agreements of the category defined in this Regulation can improve economic efficiency within a chain of production or distribution by facilitating better coordination between the participating undertakings; in particular, they can lead to a reduction in the transaction and distribution costs of the parties and to an optimisation of their sales and investment levels.

(7)   The likelihood that such efficiency-enhancing effects will outweigh any anti-competitive effects due to restrictions contained in vertical agreements depends on the degree of market power of the undertakings concerned and, therefore, on the extent to which those undertakings face competition from other suppliers of goods or services regarded by the buyer as interchangeable or substitutable for one another, by reason of the products' characteristics, their prices and their intended use.

(8)   It can be presumed that, where the share of the relevant market accounted for by the supplier does not exceed 30%, vertical agreements which do not contain certain types of severely anti-competitive restraints generally lead to an improvement in production or distribution and allow consumers a fair share of the resulting benefits; in the case of vertical agreements containing exclusive supply obligations, it is the market share of the buyer which is relevant in determining the overall effects of such vertical agreements on the market.

(9)   Above the market share threshold of 30%, there can be no presumption that vertical agreements
         falling within the scope of Article 81(1) will usually give rise to objective advantages of such a
         character and size as to compensate for the disadvantages which they create for competition.

(10)   This Regulation should not exempt vertical agreements containing restrictions which are not
         indispensable to the attainment of the positive effects mentioned above; in particular, vertical
         agreements containing certain types of severely anti-competitive restraints such as minimum and
         fixed resale-prices, as well as certain types of territorial protection, should be excluded from the
         benefit of the block exemption established by this Regulation irrespective of the market share of
         the undertakings concerned.

(11)   In order to ensure access to or to prevent collusion on the relevant market, certain conditions are
         to be attached to the block exemption; to this end, the exemption of non-compete obligations
         should be limited to obligations which do not exceed a definite duration; for the same reasons,
         any direct or indirect obligation causing the members of a selective distribution system not to sell
         the brands of particular competing suppliers should be excluded from the benefit of this
         Regulation.

(12)   The market-share limitation, the non-exemption of certain vertical agreements and the conditions
         provided for in this Regulation normally ensure that the agreements to which the block exemption
         applies do not enable the participating undertakings to eliminate competition in respect of a
         substantial part of the products in question.

(13)   In particular cases in which the agreements falling under this Regulation nevertheless have effects
         incompatible with Article 81(3), the Commission may withdraw the benefit of the block
         exemption; this may occur in particular where the buyer has significant market power in the
         relevant market in which it resells the goods or provides the services or where parallel networks
         of vertical agreements have similar effects which significantly restrict access to a relevant market
         or competition therein; such cumulative effects may for example arise in the case of selective
         distribution or non-compete obligations.

(14)   Regulation No 19/65/EEC empowers the competent authorities of Member States to withdraw the
         benefit of the block exemption in respect of vertical agreements having effects incompatible with
         the conditions laid down in Article 81(3), where such effects are felt in their respective territory,
         or in a part thereof, and where such territory has the characteristics of a distinct geographic
         market; Member States should ensure that the exercise of this power of withdrawal does not
         prejudice the uniform application throughout the common market of the Community competition
         rules or the full effect of the measures adopted in implementation of those rules.

(15)   In order to strengthen supervision of parallel networks of vertical agreements which have similar
         restrictive effects and which cover more than 50% of a given market, the Commission may
         declare this Regulation inapplicable to vertical agreements containing specific restraints relating
         to the market concerned, thereby restoring the full application of Article 81 to such agreements.

(16)   This Regulation is without prejudice to the application of Article 82.

(17)   In accordance with the principle of the primacy of Community law, no measure taken pursuant to
         national laws on competition should prejudice the uniform application throughout the common
         market of the Community competition rules or the full effect of any measures adopted in
         implementation of those rules, including this Regulation,

HAS ADOPTED THIS REGULATION:

Article 1

For the purposes of this Regulation:

(a)   'competing undertakings' means actual or potential suppliers in the same product market; the,
         product market includes goods or services which are regarded by the buyer as interchangeable
         with or substitutable for the contract goods or services, by reason of the products' characteristics,
         their prices and their intended use;

(b)   'non-compete obligation' means any direct or indirect obligation causing the buyer not to
         manufacture, purchase, sell or resell goods or services which compete with the contract goods or

services, or any direct or indirect obligation on the buyer to purchase from the supplier or from another undertaking designated by the supplier more than 80% of the buyer's total purchases of the contract goods or services and their substitutes on the relevant market, calculated on the basis of the value of its purchases in the preceding calendar year;

(c) 'exclusive supply obligation' means any direct or indirect obligation causing the supplier to sell the goods or services specified in the agreement only to one buyer inside the Community for the purposes of a specific use or for resale;

(d) 'Selective distribution system' means a distribution system where the supplier undertakes to sell the contract goods or services, either directly or indirectly, only to distributors selected on the basis of specified criteria and where these distributors undertake not to sell such goods or services to unauthorised distributors;

(e) 'intellectual property rights' includes industrial property rights, copyright and neighbouring rights;

(f) 'know-how' means a package of non-patented practical information, resulting from experience and testing by the supplier, which is secret, substantial and identified: in this context, 'secret' means that the know-how, as a body or in the precise configuration and assembly of its components, is not generally known or easily accessible; 'substantial' means that the know-how includes information which is indispensable to the buyer for the use, sale or resale of the contract goods or services; 'identified' means that the know-how must be described in a sufficiently comprehensive manner so as to make it possible to verify that it fulfils the criteria of secrecy and substantiality;

(g) 'buyer' includes an undertaking which, under an agreement falling within Article 81(1) of the Treaty, sells goods or services on behalf of another undertaking.

Article 2

1. Pursuant to Article 81(3) of the Treaty and subject to the provisions of this Regulation, it is hereby declared that Article 81(1) shall not apply to agreements or concerted practices entered into between two or more undertakings each of which operates, for the purposes of the agreement, at a different level of the production or distribution chain, and relating to the conditions under which the parties may purchase, sell or resell certain goods or services ('vertical agreements'). This exemption shall apply to the extent that such agreements contain restrictions of competition falling within the scope of Article 81(1) ('vertical restraints').

2. The exemption provided for in paragraph 1 shall apply to vertical agreements entered into between an association of undertakings and its members, or between such an association and its suppliers, only if all its members are retailers of goods and if no individual member of the association, together with its connected undertakings, has a total annual turnover exceeding EUR 50 million; vertical agreements entered into by such associations shall be covered by this Regulation without prejudice to the application of Article 81 to horizontal agreements concluded between the members of the association or decisions adopted by the association.

3. The exemption provided for in paragraph 1 shall apply to vertical agreements containing provisions which relate to the assignment to the buyer or use by the buyer of intellectual property rights, provided that those provisions do not constitute the primary object of such agreements and are directly related to the use, sale or resale of goods or services by the buyer or its customers. The exemption applies on condition that, in relation to the contract goods or services, those provisions do not contain restrictions of competition having the same object or effect as vertical restraints which are not exempted under this Regulation.

4. The exemption provided for in paragraph 1 shall not apply to vertical agreements entered into between competing undertakings; however, it shall apply where competing undertakings enter into a non-reciprocal vertical agreement and:
   (a) the buyer has a total annual turnover not exceeding EUR 100 million, or
   (b) the supplier is a manufacturer and a distributor of goods, while the buyer is a distributor not manufacturing goods competing with the contract goods, or

(c)   the supplier is a provider of services at several levels of trade, while the buyer does not provide competing services at the level of trade where it purchases the contract services.

5.   This Regulation shall not apply to vertical agreements the subject matter of which falls within the scope of any other block exemption regulation.

Article 3

1.   Subject to paragraph 2 of this Article, the exemption provided for in Article 2 shall apply on condition that the market share held by the supplier does not exceed 30% of the relevant market on which it sells the contract goods or services.

2.   In the case of vertical agreements containing exclusive supply obligations, the exemption provided for in Article 2 shall apply on condition that the market share held by the buyer does not exceed 30% of the relevant market on which it purchases the contract goods or services.

Article 4

The exemption provided for in Article 2 shall not apply to vertical agreements which, directly or indirectly, in isolation or in combination with other factors under the control of the parties, have as their object:

(a)   the restriction of the buyer's ability to determine its sale price, without prejudice to the possibility of the supplier's imposing a maximum sale price or recommending a sale price, provided that they do not amount to a fixed or minimum sale price as a result of pressure from, or incentives offered by, any of the parties;

(b)   the restriction of the territory into which, or of the customers to whom, the buyer may sell the contract goods or services, except:
  —   the restriction of active sales into the exclusive territory or to an exclusive customer group reserved to the supplier or allocated by the supplier to another buyer, where such a restriction does not limit sales by the customers of the buyer,
  —   the restriction of sales to end users by a buyer operating at the wholesale level of trade,
  —   the restriction of sales to unauthorised distributors by the members of a selective distribution system, and
  —   the restriction of the buyer's ability to sell components, supplied for the purposes of incorporation, to customers who would use them to manufacture the same type of goods as those produced by the supplier;

(c)   the restriction of active or passive sales to end users by members of a selective distribution system operating at the retail level of trade, without prejudice to the possibility of prohibiting a member of the system from operating out of an unauthorised place of establishment;

(d)   the restriction of cross-supplies between distributors within a selective distribution system, including between distributors operating at different level of trade;

(e)   the restriction agreed between a supplier of components and a buyer who incorporates those components, which limits the supplier to selling the components as spare parts to end-users or to repairers or other service providers not entrusted by the buyer with the repair or servicing of its goods.

Article 5

The exemption provided for in Article 2 shall not apply to any of the following obligations contained in vertical agreements:

(a)   any direct or indirect non-compete obligation, the duration of which is indefinite or exceeds five years. A non-compete obligation which is tacitly renewable beyond a period of five years is to be deemed to have been concluded for an indefinite duration. However, the time limitation of five years shall not apply where the contract goods or services are sold by the buyer from premises and land owned by the supplier or leased by the supplier from third parties not connected with the buyer, provided that the duration of the non-compete obligation does not exceed the period of occupancy of the premises and land by the buyer;

(b) any direct or indirect obligation causing the buyer, after termination of the agreement, not to manufacture, purchase, sell or resell goods or services, unless such obligation:
— relates to goods or services which compete with the contract goods or services, and
— is limited to the premises and land from which the buyer has operated during the contract period, and
— is indispensable to protect know-how transferred by the supplier to the buyer,

and provided that the duration of such non-compete obligation is limited to a period of one year after termination of the agreement; this obligation is without prejudice to the possibility of imposing a restriction which is unlimited in time on the use and disclosure of know-how which has not entered the public domain;

(c) any direct or indirect obligation causing the members of a selective distribution system not to sell the brands of particular competing suppliers.

Article 6

The Commission may withdraw the benefit of this Regulation, pursuant to Article 7(1) of Regulation No 19/65/EEC, where it finds in any particular case that vertical agreements to which this Regulation applies nevertheless have effects which are incompatible with the conditions laid down in Article 81(3) of the Treaty, and in particular where access to the relevant market or competition therein is significantly restricted by the cumulative effect of parallel networks of similar vertical restraints implemented by competing suppliers or buyers.

Article 7

Where in any particular case vertical agreements to which the exemption provided for in Article 2 applies have effects incompatible with the conditions laid down in Article 81(3) of the Treaty in the territory of a Member State, or in a part thereof, which has all the characteristics of a distinct geographic market, the competent authority of that Member State may withdraw the benefit of application of this Regulation in respect of that territory, under the same conditions as provided in Article 6.

Article 8

1. Pursuant to Article 1 a of Regulation No 19/65/EEC, the Commission may by regulation declare that, where parallel networks of similar vertical restraints cover more than 50% of a relevant market, this Regulation shall not apply to vertical agreements containing specific restraints relating to that market.

2. A regulation pursuant to paragraph 1 shall not become applicable earlier than six months following its adoption.

Article 9

1. The market share of 30% provided for in Article 3(1) shall be calculated on the basis of the market sales value of the contract goods or services and other goods or services sold by the supplier, which are regarded as interchangeable or substitutable by the buyer, by reason of the products' characteristics, their prices and their intended use; if market sales value data are not available, estimates based on other reliable market information, including market sales volumes, may be used to establish the market share of the undertaking concerned. For the purposes of Article 3(2), it is either the market purchase value or estimates thereof which shall be used to calculate the market share.

2. For the purposes of applying the market share, threshold provided for in Article 3 the following rules shall apply:
(a) the market share shall be calculated on the basis of data relating to the preceding calendar year;
(b) the market share shall include any goods or services supplied to integrated distributors for the purposes of sale;
(c) if the market share is initially not more than 30% but subsequently rises above that level without exceeding 35%, the exemption provided for in Article 2 shall continue to apply for

a period of two consecutive calendar years following the year in which the 30% market share threshold was first exceeded;

(d)   if the market share is initially not more than 30% but subsequently rises above 35%, the exemption provided for in Article 2 shall continue to apply for one calendar year following the year in which the level of 35% was first exceeded;

(e)   the benefit of points (c) and (d) may not be combined so as to exceed a period of two calendar years.

Article 10

1.   For the purpose of calculating total annual turnover within the meaning of Article 2(2) and (4), the turnover achieved during the previous financial year by the relevant party to the vertical agreement and the turnover achieved by its connected undertakings in respect of all goods and services, excluding all taxes and other duties, shall be added together. For this purpose, no account shall be taken of dealings between the party to the vertical agreement and its connected undertakings or between its connected undertakings.

2.   The exemption provided for in Article 2 shall remain applicable where, for any period of two consecutive financial years, the total annual turnover threshold is exceeded by no more than 10%.

Article 11

1.   For the purposes of this Regulation, the terms 'undertaking', 'supplier' and 'buyer' shall include their respective connected undertakings.

2.   'Connected undertakings' are:

(a)   undertakings in which a party to the agreement, directly or indirectly:
— has the power to exercise more than half the voting rights, or
— has the power to appoint more than half the members of the supervisory board, board of management or bodies legally representing the undertaking, or
— has the right to manage the undertaking's affairs;

(b)   undertakings which directly or indirectly have, over a party to the agreement, the rights or powers listed in (a);

(c)   undertakings in which an undertaking referred to in (b) has, directly or indirectly, the rights or powers listed in (a);

(d)   undertakings in which a party to the agreement together with one or more of the undertakings referred to in (a), (b) or (c), or in which two or more of the latter undertakings, jointly have the rights or powers listed in (a);

(e)   undertakings in which the rights or the powers listed in (a) are jointly held by:
— parties to the agreement or their respective connected undertakings referred to in (a) to (d), or
— one or more of the parties to the agreement or one or more of their connected undertakings referred to in (a) to (d) and one or more third parties.

3.   For the purposes of Article 3, the market share held by the undertakings referred to in paragraph 2(e) of this Article shall be apportioned equally to each undertaking having the rights or the powers listed in paragraph 2(a).

Article 12

1.   The exemptions provided for in Commission Regulations (EEC) No 1983/83, (EEC) No 1984/83 and (EEC) No 4087/88 shall continue to apply until 31 May 2000.

2.   The prohibition laid down in Article 81(1) of the EC Treaty shall not apply during the period from 1 June 2000 to 31 December 2001 in respect of agreements already in force on 31 May 2000 which do not satisfy the conditions for exemption provided for in this Regulation but which satisfy the conditions for exemption provided for in Regulations (EEC) No 1983/83, (EEC) No 1984/83 or (EEC) No 4087/88.

Article 12a

The prohibition in Article 81(1) of the Treaty shall not apply to agreements which were in existence at the date of accession of the Czech Republic, Estonia, Cyprus, Latvia, Lithuania, Hungary, Malta, Poland, Slovenia and Slovakia and which, by reason of accession, fall within the scope of Article 81(1) if, within six months from the date of accession, they are so amended that they comply with the conditions laid down in this Regulation.

Article 13

This Regulation shall enter into force on 1 January 2000.

It shall apply from 1 June 2000, except for Article 12(1) which shall apply from 1 January 2000.

This Regulation shall expire on 31 May 2010.

This Regulation shall be binding in its entirety and directly applicable in all Member States.

Council Regulation (EC) of 16 December 2002 on the implementation of the rules on competition laid down in Articles 81 and 82 of the Treaty

No. 1/2003

THE COUNCIL OF THE EUROPEAN UNION,

Having regard to the Treaty establishing the European Community, and in particular Article 83 thereof,

Having regard to the proposal from the Commission,

Having regard to the opinion of the European Parliament,

Having regard to the opinion of the European Economic and Social Committee,

Whereas:

(1)   In order to establish a system which ensures that competition in the common market is not distorted, Articles 81 and 82 of the Treaty must be applied effectively and uniformly in the Community. Council Regulation No 17 of 6 February 1962, First Regulation implementing Articles 81 and 82 of the Treaty, has allowed a Community competition policy to develop that has helped to disseminate a competition culture within the Community. In the light of experience, however, that Regulation should now be replaced by legislation designed to meet the challenges of an integrated market and a future enlargement of the Community.

(2)   In particular, there is a need to rethink the arrangements for applying the exception from the prohibition on agreements, which restrict competition, laid down in Article 81(3) of the Treaty. Under Article 83(2)(b) of the Treaty, account must be taken in this regard of the need to ensure effective supervision, on the one hand, and to simplify administration to the greatest possible extent, on the other.

(3)   The centralised scheme set up by Regulation No 17 no longer secures a balance between those two objectives. It hampers application of the Community competition rules by the courts and competition authorities of the Member States, and the system of notification it involves prevents the Commission from concentrating its resources on curbing the most serious infringements. It also imposes considerable costs on undertakings.

(4)   The present systemshould therefore be replaced by a directly applicable exception systemin which the competition authorities and courts of the Member States have the power to apply not only Article 81(1) and Article 82 of the Treaty, which have direct applicability by virtue of the case-law of the Court of Justice of the European Communities, but also Article 81(3) of the Treaty.

(5)   In order to ensure an effective enforcement of the Community competition rules and at the same time the respect of fundamental rights of defence, this Regulation should regulate the burden of proof under Articles 81 and 82 of the Treaty. It should be for the party or the authority alleging an infringement of Article 81(1) and Article 82 of the Treaty to prove the existence thereof to the required legal standard. It should be for the undertaking or association of undertakings invoking the benefit of a defence against a finding of an infringement to demonstrate to the required legal standard that the conditions for applying such defence are satisfied. This Regulation affects neither national rules on the standard of proof nor obligations of competition authorities and courts of the Member States to ascertain the relevant facts of a case, provided that such rules and obligations are compatible with general principles of Community law.

(6)   In order to ensure that the Community competition rules are applied effectively, the competition authorities of the Member States should be associated more closely with their application. To this end, they should be empowered to apply Community law.

(7)   National courts have an essential part to play in applying the Community competition rules. When deciding disputes between private individuals, they protect the subjective rights under Community law, for example by awarding damages to the victims of infringements. The role of

the national courts here complements that of the competition authorities of the Member States. They should therefore be allowed to apply Articles 81 and 82 of the Treaty in full.

(8) In order to ensure the effective enforcement of the Community competition rules and the proper functioning of the cooperation mechanisms contained in this Regulation, it is necessary to oblige the competition authorities and courts of the Member States to also apply Articles 81 and 82 of the Treaty where they apply national competition law to agreements and practices which may affect trade between Member States. In order to create a level playing field for agreements, decisions by associations of undertakings and concerted practices within the internal market, it is also necessary to determine pursuant to Article 83(2)(e) of the Treaty the relationship between national laws and Community competition law. To that effect it is necessary to provide that the application of national competition laws to agreements, decisions or concerted practices within the meaning of Article 81(1) of the Treaty may not lead to the prohibition of such agreements, decisions and concerted practices if they are not also prohibited under Community competition law. The notions of agreements, decisions and concerted practices are autonomous concepts of Community competition law covering the coordination of behaviour of undertakings on the market as interpreted by the Community Courts. Member States should not under this Regulation be precluded from adopting and applying on their territory stricter national competition laws which prohibit or impose sanctions on unilateral conduct engaged in by undertakings. These stricter national laws may include provisions which prohibit or impose sanctions on abusive behaviour toward economically dependent undertakings. Furthermore, this Regulation does not apply to national laws which impose criminal sanctions on natural persons except to the extent that such sanctions are the means whereby competition rules applying to undertakings are enforced.

(9) Articles 81 and 82 of the Treaty have as their objective the protection of competition on the market. This Regulation, which is adopted for the implementation of these Treaty provisions, does not preclude Member States from implementing on their territory national legislation, which protects other legitimate interests provided that such legislation is compatible with general principles and other provisions of Community law. In so far as such national legislation pursues predominantly an objective different from that of protecting competition on the market, the competition authorities and courts of the Member States may apply such legislation on their territory. Accordingly, Member States may under this Regulation implement on their territory national legislation that prohibits or imposes sanctions on acts of unfair trading practice, be they unilateral or contractual. Such legislation pursues a specific objective, irrespective of the actual or presumed effects of such acts on competition on the market. This is particularly the case of legislation which prohibits undertakings from imposing on their trading partners, obtaining or attempting to obtain from them terms and conditions that are unjustified, disproportionate or without consideration.

(10) Regulations such as 19/65/EEC, (EEC) No 2821/71, (EEC) No 3976/87, (EEC) No 1534/91, or (EEC) No 479/92 empower the Commission to apply Article 81(3) of the Treaty by Regulation to certain categories of agreements, decisions by associations of undertakings and concerted practices. In the areas defined by such Regulations, the Commission has adopted and may continue to adopt so called 'block' exemption Regulations by which it declares Article 81(1) of the Treaty inapplicable to categories of agreements, decisions and concerted practices. Where agreements, decisions and concerted practices to which such Regulations apply nonetheless have effects that are incompatible with Article 81(3) of the Treaty, the Commission and the competition authorities of the Member States should have the power to withdraw in a particular case the benefit of the block exemption Regulation.

(11) For it to ensure that the provisions of the Treaty are applied, the Commission should be able to address decisions to undertakings or associations of undertakings for the purpose of bringing to an end infringements of Articles 81 and 82 of the Treaty. Provided there is a legitimate interest in doing so, the Commission should also be able to adopt decisions which find that an infringement has been committed in the past even if it does not impose a fine. This Regulation should also

make explicit provision for the Commission's power to adopt decisions ordering interim measures, which has been acknowledged by the Court of Justice.

(12) This Regulation should make explicit provision for the Commission's power to impose any remedy, whether behavioural or structural, which is necessary to bring the infringement effectively to an end, having regard to the principle of proportionality. Structural remedies should only be imposed either where there is no equally effective behavioural remedy or where any equally effective behavioural remedy would be more burdensome for the undertaking concerned than the structural remedy. Changes to the structure of an undertaking as it existed before the infringement was committed would only be proportionate where there is a substantial risk of a lasting or repeated infringement that derives from the very structure of the undertaking.

(13) Where, in the course of proceedings which might lead to an agreement or practice being prohibited, undertakings offer the Commission commitments such as to meet its concerns, the Commission should be able to adopt decisions which make those commitments binding on the undertakings concerned. Commitment decisions should find that there are no longer grounds for action by the Commission without concluding whether or not there has been or still is an infringement. Commitment decisions are without prejudice to the powers of competition authorities and courts of the Member States to make such a finding and decide upon the case. Commitment decisions are not appropriate in cases where the Commission intends to impose a fine.

(14) In exceptional cases where the public interest of the Community so requires, it may also be expedient for the Commission to adopt a decision of a declaratory nature finding that the prohibition in Article 81 or Article 82 of the Treaty does not apply, with a view to clarifying the law and ensuring its consistent application throughout the Community, in particular with regard to new types of agreements or practices that have not been settled in the existing case-law and administrative practice.

(15) The Commission and the competition authorities of the Member States should form together a network of public authorities applying the Community competition rules in close cooperation. For that purpose it is necessary to set up arrangements for information and consultation. Further modalities for the cooperation within the network will be laid down and revised by the Commission, in close cooperation with the Member States.

(16) Notwithstanding any national provision to the contrary, the exchange of information and the use of such information in evidence should be allowed between the members of the network even where the information is confidential. This information may be used for the application of Articles 81 and 82 of the Treaty as well as for the parallel application of national competition law, provided that the latter application relates to the same case and does not lead to a different outcome. When the information exchanged is used by the receiving authority to impose sanctions on undertakings, there should be no other limit to the use of the information than the obligation to use it for the purpose for which it was collected given the fact that the sanctions imposed on undertakings are of the same type in all systems. The rights of defence enjoyed by undertakings in the various systems can be considered as sufficiently equivalent. However, as regards natural persons, they may be subject to substantially different types of sanctions across the various systems. Where that is the case, it is necessary to ensure that information can only be used if it has been collected in a way which respects the same level of protection of the rights of defence of natural persons as provided for under the national rules of the receiving authority.

(17) If the competition rules are to be applied consistently and, at the same time, the network is to be managed in the best possible way, it is essential to retain the rule that the competition authorities of the Member States are automatically relieved of their competence if the Commission initiates its own proceedings. Where a competition authority of a Member State is already acting on a case and the Commission intends to initiate proceedings, it should endeavour to do so as soon as possible. Before initiating proceedings, the Commission should consult the national authority concerned.

(18)   To ensure that cases are dealt with by the most appropriate authorities within the network, a general provision should be laid down allowing a competition authority to suspend or close a case on the ground that another authority is dealing with it or has already dealt with it, the objective being that each case should be handled by a single authority. This provision should not prevent the Commission from rejecting a complaint for lack of Community interest, as the case-law of the Court of Justice has acknowledged it may do, even if no other competition authority has indicated its intention of dealing with the case.

(19)   The Advisory Committee on Restrictive Practices and Dominant Positions set up by Regulation No 17 has functioned in a very satisfactory manner. It will fit well into the new system of decentralised application. It is necessary, therefore, to build upon the rules laid down by Regulation No 17, while improving the effectiveness of the organisational arrangements. To this end, it would be expedient to allow opinions to be delivered by written procedure. The Advisory Committee should also be able to act as a forum for discussing cases that are being handled by the competition authorities of the Member States, so as to help safeguard the consistent application of the Community competition rules.

(20)   The Advisory Committee should be composed of representatives of the competition authorities of the Member States. For meetings in which general issues are being discussed, Member States should be able to appoint an additional representative. This is without prejudice to members of the Committee being assisted by other experts from the Member States.

(21)   Consistency in the application of the competition rules also requires that arrangements be established for cooperation between the courts of the Member States and the Commission. This is relevant for all courts of the Member States that apply Articles 81 and 82 of the Treaty, whether applying these rules in lawsuits between private parties, acting as public enforcers or as review courts. In particular, national courts should be able to ask the Commission for information or for its opinion on points concerning the application of Community competition law. The Commission and the competition authorities of the Member States should also be able to submit written or oral observations to courts called upon to apply Article 81 or Article 82 of the Treaty. These observations should be submitted within the framework of national procedural rules and practices including those safeguarding the rights of the parties. Steps should therefore be taken to ensure that the Commission and the competition authorities of the Member States are kept sufficiently well informed of proceedings before national courts.

(22)   In order to ensure compliance with the principles of legal certainty and the uniform application of the Community competition rules in a system of parallel powers, conflicting decisions must be avoided. It is therefore necessary to clarify, in accordance with the case-law of the Court of Justice, the effects of Commission decisions and proceedings on courts and competition authorities of the Member States. Commitment decisions adopted by the Commission do not affect the power of the courts and the competition authorities of the Member States to apply Articles 81 and 82 of the Treaty.

(23)   The Commission should be empowered throughout the Community to require such information to be supplied as is necessary to detect any agreement, decision or concerted practice prohibited by Article 81 of the Treaty or any abuse of a dominant position prohibited by Article 82 of the Treaty. When complying with a decision of the Commission, undertakings cannot be forced to admit that they have committed an infringement, but they are in any event obliged to answer factual questions and to provide documents, even if this information may be used to establish against them or against another undertaking the existence of an infringement.

(24)   The Commission should also be empowered to undertake such inspections as are necessary to detect any agreement, decision or concerted practice prohibited by Article 81 of the Treaty or any abuse of a dominant position prohibited by Article 82 of the Treaty. The competition authorities of the Member States should cooperate actively in the exercise of these powers.

(25)   The detection of infringements of the competition rules is growing ever more difficult, and, in order to protect competition effectively, the Commission's powers of investigation need to be supplemented. The Commission should in particular be empowered to interview any persons who

may be in possession of useful information and to record the statements made. In the course of an inspection, officials authorised by the Commission should be empowered to affix seals for the period of time necessary for the inspection. Seals should normally not be affixed for more than 72 hours. Officials authorised by the Commission should also be empowered to ask for any information relevant to the subject matter and purpose of the inspection.

(26)   Experience has shown that there are cases where business records are kept in the homes of directors or other people working for an undertaking. In order to safeguard the effectiveness of inspections, therefore, officials and other persons authorised by the Commission should be empowered to enter any premises where business records may be kept, including private homes. However, the exercise of this latter power should be subject to the authorisation of the judicial authority.

(27)   Without prejudice to the case-law of the Court of Justice, it is useful to set out the scope of the control that the national judicial authority may carry out when it authorises, as foreseen by national law including as a precautionary measure, assistance from law enforcement authorities in order to overcome possible opposition on the part of the undertaking or the execution of the decision to carry out inspections in non-business premises. It results from the case-law that the national judicial authority may in particular ask the Commission for further information which it needs to carry out its control and in the absence of which it could refuse the authorisation. The case-law also confirms the competence of the national courts to control the application of national rules governing the implementation of coercive measures.

(28)   In order to help the competition authorities of the Member States to apply Articles 81 and 82 of the Treaty effectively, it is expedient to enable them to assist one another by carrying out inspections and other fact-finding measures.

(29)   Compliance with Articles 81 and 82 of the Treaty and the fulfilment of the obligations imposed on undertakings and associations of undertakings under this Regulation should be enforceable by means of fines and periodic penalty payments. To that end, appropriate levels of fine should also be laid down for infringements of the procedural rules.

(30)   In order to ensure effective recovery of fines imposed on associations of undertakings for infringements that they have committed, it is necessary to lay down the conditions on which the Commission may require payment of the fine from the members of the association where the association is not solvent. In doing so, the Commission should have regard to the relative size of the undertakings belonging to the association and in particular to the situation of small and medium-sized enterprises. Payment of the fine by one or several members of an association is without prejudice to rules of national law that provide for recovery of the amount paid from other members of the association.

(31)   The rules on periods of limitation for the imposition of fines and periodic penalty payments were laid down in Council Regulation (EEC) No 2988/74, which also concerns penalties in the field of transport. In a system of parallel powers, the acts, which may interrupt a limitation period, should include procedural steps taken independently by the competition authority of a Member State. To clarify the legal framework, Regulation (EEC) No 2988/74 should therefore be amended to prevent it applying to matters covered by this Regulation, and this Regulation should include provisions on periods of limitation.

(32)   The undertakings concerned should be accorded the right to be heard by the Commission, third parties whose interests may be affected by a decision should be given the opportunity of submitting their observations beforehand, and the decisions taken should be widely publicised. While ensuring the rights of defence of the undertakings concerned, in particular, the right of access to the file, it is essential that business secrets be protected. The confidentiality of information exchanged in the network should likewise be safeguarded.

(33)   Since all decisions taken by the Commission under this Regulation are subject to review by the Court of Justice in accordance with the Treaty, the Court of Justice should, in accordance with Article 229 thereof be given unlimited jurisdiction in respect of decisions by which the Commission imposes fines or periodic penalty payments.

(34)   The principles laid down in Articles 81 and 82 of the Treaty, as they have been applied by
        Regulation No 17, have given a central role to the Community bodies. This central role should be
        retained, whilst associating the Member States more closely with the application of the
        Community competition rules. In accordance with the principles of subsidiarity and
        proportionality as set out in Article 5 of the Treaty, this Regulation does not go beyond what is
        necessary in order to achieve its objective, which is to allow the Community competition rules to
        be applied effectively.

(35)   In order to attain a proper enforcement of Community competition law, Member States should
        designate and empower authorities to apply Articles 81 and 82 of the Treaty as public enforcers.
        They should be able to designate administrative as well as judicial authorities to carry out the
        various functions conferred upon competition authorities in this Regulation. This Regulation
        recognises the wide variation which exists in the public enforcement systems of Member States.
        The effects of Article 11(6) of this Regulation should apply to all competition authorities. As an
        exception to this general rule, where a prosecuting authority brings a case before a separate
        judicial authority, Article 11(6) should apply to the prosecuting authority subject to the conditions
        in Article 35(4) of this Regulation. Where these conditions are not fulfilled, the general rule
        should apply. In any case, Article 11(6) should not apply to courts insofar as they are acting as
        review courts.

(36)   As the case-law has made it clear that the competition rules apply to transport, that sector should
        be made subject to the procedural provisions of this Regulation. Council Regulation No 141 of 26
        November 1962 exempting transport from the application of Regulation No 17 should therefore
        be repealed and Regulations (EEC) No 1017/68, (EEC) No 4056/86 and (EEC) No 3975/87
        should be amended in order to delete the specific procedural provisions they contain.

(37)   This Regulation respects the fundamental rights and observes the principles recognised in
        particular by the Charter of Fundamental Rights of the European Union. Accordingly, this
        Regulation should be interpreted and applied with respect to those rights and principles.

(38)   Legal certainty for undertakings operating under the Community competition rules contributes to
        the promotion of innovation and investment. Where cases give rise to genuine uncertainty
        because they present novel or unresolved questions for the application of these rules, individual
        undertakings may wish to seek informal guidance from the Commission. This Regulation is
        without prejudice to the ability of the Commission to issue such informal guidance,

HAS ADOPTED THIS REGULATION:

CHAPTER I
PRINCIPLES

Article 1

Application of Articles 81 and 82 of the Treaty

1.   Agreements, decisions and concerted practices caught by Article 81(1) of the Treaty which do not
        satisfy the conditions of Article 81(3) of the Treaty shall be prohibited, no prior decision to that
        effect being required.

2.   Agreements, decisions and concerted practices caught by Article 81(1) of the Treaty which satisfy
        the conditions of Article 81(3) of the Treaty shall not be prohibited, no prior decision to that effect
        being required.

3.   The abuse of a dominant position referred to in Article 82 of the Treaty shall be prohibited, no
        prior decision to that effect being required.

Article 2

Burden of proof

In any national or Community proceedings for the application of Articles 81 and 82 of the Treaty, the burden of proving an infringement of Article 81(1) or of Article 82 of the Treaty shall rest on the party or the

authority alleging the infringement. The undertaking or association of undertakings claiming the benefit of Article 81(3) of the Treaty shall bear the burden of proving that the conditions of that paragraph are fulfilled.

Article 3

Relationshipbetween Articles 81 and 82 of the Treaty and national competition laws

1.   Where the competition authorities of the Member States or national courts apply national competition law to agreements, decisions by associations of undertakings or concerted practices within the meaning of Article 81(1) of the Treaty which may affect trade between Member States within the meaning of that provision, they shall also apply Article 81 of the Treaty to such agreements, decisions or concerted practices. Where the competition authorities of the Member States or national courts apply national competition law to any abuse prohibited by Article 82 of the Treaty, they shall also apply Article 82 of the Treaty.

2.   The application of national competition law may not lead to the prohibition of agreements, decisions by associations of undertakings or concerted practices which may affect trade between Member States but which do not restrict competition within the meaning of Article 81(1) of the Treaty, or which fulfil the conditions of Article 81(3) of the Treaty or which are covered by a Regulation for the application of Article 81(3) of the Treaty. Member States shall not under this Regulation be precluded from adopting and applying on their territory stricter national laws which prohibit or sanction unilateral conduct engaged in by undertakings.

3.   Without prejudice to general principles and other provisions of Community law, paragraphs 1 and 2 do not apply when the competition authorities and the courts of the Member States apply national merger control laws nor do they preclude the application of provisions of national law that predominantly pursue an objective different fromthat pursued by Articles 81 and 82 of the Treaty.

CHAPTER II
POWERS

Article 4

Powers of the Commission

For the purpose of applying Articles 81 and 82 of the Treaty, the Commission shall have the powers provided for by this Regulation.

Article 5

Powers of the competition authorities of the Member States

The competition authorities of the Member States shall have the power to apply Articles 81 and 82 of the Treaty in individual cases. For this purpose, acting on their own initiative or on a complaint, they may take the following decisions:

—   requiring that an infringement be brought to an end,

—   ordering interimm easures,

—   accepting commitments,

—   imposing fines, periodic penalty payments or any other penalty provided for in their national law.

Where on the basis of the information in their possession the conditions for prohibition are not met they may likewise decide that there are no grounds for action on their part.

Article 6

Powers of the national courts

National courts shall have the power to apply Articles 81 and 82 of the Treaty.

CHAPTER III
COMMISSION DECISIONS

Article 7

Finding and termination of infringement

1. Where the Commission, acting on a complaint or on its own initiative, finds that there is an infringement of Article 81 or of Article 82 of the Treaty, it may by decision require the undertakings and associations of undertakings concerned to bring such infringement to an end. For this purpose, it may impose on them any behavioural or structural remedies which are proportionate to the infringement committed and necessary to bring the infringement effectively to an end. Structural remedies can only be imposed either where there is no equally effective behavioural remedy or where any equally effective behavioural remedy would be more burdensome for the undertaking concerned than the structural remedy. If the Commission has a legitimate interest in doing so, it may also find that an infringement has been committed in the past.

2. Those entitled to lodge a complaint for the purposes of paragraph 1 are natural or legal persons who can show a legitimate interest and Member States.

Article 8

Interim measures

1. In cases of urgency due to the risk of serious and irreparable damage to competition, the Commission, acting on its own initiative may by decision, on the basis of a prima facie finding of infringement, order interimm easures.

2. A decision under paragraph 1 shall apply for a specified period of time and may be renewed in so far this is necessary and appropriate.

Article 9

Commitments

1. Where the Commission intends to adopt a decision requiring that an infringement be brought to an end and the undertakings concerned offer commitments to meet the concerns expressed to them by the Commission in its preliminary assessment, the Commission may by decision make those commitments binding on the undertakings. Such a decision may be adopted for a specified period and shall conclude that there are no longer grounds for action by the Commission.

2. The Commission may, upon request or on its own initiative, reopen the proceedings:
   (a) where there has been a material change in any of the facts on which the decision was based;
   (b) where the undertakings concerned act contrary to their commitments; or
   (c) where the decision was based on incomplete, incorrect or misleading information provided by the parties.

Article 10

Finding of inapplicability

Where the Community public interest relating to the application of Articles 81 and 82 of the Treaty so requires, the Commission, acting on its own initiative, may by decision find that Article 81 of the Treaty is not applicable to an agreement, a decision by an association of undertakings or a concerted practice, either because the conditions of Article 81(1) of the Treaty are not fulfilled, or because the conditions of Article 81(3) of the Treaty are satisfied.

The Commission may likewise make such a finding with reference to Article 82 of the Treaty.

CHAPTER IV
COOPERATION

Article 11

Cooperation between the Commission and the competition authorities of the Member States

1. The Commission and the competition authorities of the Member States shall apply the Community competition rules in close cooperation.

2. The Commission shall transmit to the competition authorities of the Member States copies of the most important documents it has collected with a view to applying Articles 7, 8, 9, 10 and Article 29(1). At the request of the competition authority of a Member State, the Commission shall provide it with a copy of other existing documents necessary for the assessment of the case.

3. The competition authorities of the Member States shall, when acting under Article 81 or Article 82 of the Treaty, inform the Commission in writing before or without delay after commencing the first formal investigative measure. This information may also be made available to the competition authorities of the other Member States.

4. No later than 30 days before the adoption of a decision requiring that an infringement be brought to an end, accepting commitments or withdrawing the benefit of a block exemption Regulation, the competition authorities of the Member States shall inform the Commission. To that effect, they shall provide the Commission with a summary of the case, the envisaged decision or, in the absence thereof, any other document indicating the proposed course of action. This information may also be made available to the competition authorities of the other Member States. At the request of the Commission, the acting competition authority shall make available to the Commission other documents it holds which are necessary for the assessment of the case. The information supplied to the Commission may be made available to the competition authorities of the other Member States. National competition authorities may also exchange between themselves information necessary for the assessment of a case that they are dealing with under Article 81 or Article 82 of the Treaty.

5. The competition authorities of the Member States may consult the Commission on any case involving the application of Community law.

6. The initiation by the Commission of proceedings for the adoption of a decision under Chapter III shall relieve the competition authorities of the Member States of their competence to apply Articles 81 and 82 of the Treaty. If a competition authority of a Member State is already acting on a case, the Commission shall only initiate proceedings after consulting with that national competition authority.

Article 12

Exchange of information

1. For the purpose of applying Articles 81 and 82 of the Treaty the Commission and the competition authorities of the Member States shall have the power to provide one another with and use in evidence any matter of fact or of law, including confidential information.

2. Information exchanged shall only be used in evidence for the purpose of applying Article 81 or Article 82 of the Treaty and in respect of the subject-matter for which it was collected by the transmitting authority. However, where national competition law is applied in the same case and in parallel to Community competition law and does not lead to a different outcome, information exchanged under this Article may also be used for the application of national competition law.

3. Information exchanged pursuant to paragraph 1 can only be used in evidence to impose sanctions on natural persons where:
   — the law of the transmitting authority foresees sanctions of a similar kind in relation to an infringement of Article 81 or Article 82 of the Treaty or, in the absence thereof,
   — the information has been collected in a way which respects the same level of protection of the rights of defence of natural persons as provided for under the national rules of the

receiving authority. However, in this case, the information exchanged cannot be used by the receiving authority to impose custodial sanctions.

Article 13

Suspension or termination of proceedings

1. Where competition authorities of two or more Member States have received a complaint or are acting on their own initiative under Article 81 or Article 82 of the Treaty against the same agreement, decision of an association or practice, the fact that one authority is dealing with the case shall be sufficient grounds for the others to suspend the proceedings before them or to reject the complaint. The Commission may likewise reject a complaint on the ground that a competition authority of a Member State is dealing with the case.

2. Where a competition authority of a Member State or the Commission has received a complaint against an agreement, decision of an association or practice which has already been dealt with by another competition authority, it may reject it.

Article 14

Advisory Committee

1. The Commission shall consult an Advisory Committee on Restrictive Practices and Dominant Positions prior to the taking of any decision under Articles 7, 8, 9, 10, 23, Article 24(2) and Article 29(1).

2. For the discussion of individual cases, the Advisory Committee shall be composed of representatives of the competition authorities of the Member States. For meetings in which issues other than individual cases are being discussed, an additional Member State representative competent in competition matters may be appointed. Representatives may, if unable to attend, be replaced by other representatives.

3. The consultation may take place at a meeting convened and chaired by the Commission, held not earlier than 14 days after dispatch of the notice convening it, together with a summary of the case, an indication of the most important documents and a preliminary draft decision. In respect of decisions pursuant to Article 8, the meeting may be held seven days after the dispatch of the operative part of a draft decision. Where the Commission dispatches a notice convening the meeting which gives a shorter period of notice than those specified above, the meeting may take place on the proposed date in the absence of an objection by any Member State. The Advisory Committee shall deliver a written opinion on the Commission's preliminary draft decision. It may deliver an opinion even if some members are absent and are not represented. At the request of one or several members, the positions stated in the opinion shall be reasoned.

4. Consultation may also take place by written procedure. However, if any Member State so requests, the Commission shall convene a meeting. In case of written procedure, the Commission shall determine a time-limit of not less than 14 days within which the Member States are to put forward their observations for circulation to all other Member States. In case of decisions to be taken pursuant to Article 8, the time-limit of 14 days is replaced by seven days. Where the Commission determines a time-limit for the written procedure which is shorter than those specified above, the proposed time-limit shall be applicable in the absence of an objection by any Member State.

5. The Commission shall take the utmost account of the opinion delivered by the Advisory Committee. It shall inform the Committee of the manner in which its opinion has been taken into account.

6. Where the Advisory Committee delivers a written opinion, this opinion shall be appended to the draft decision. If the Advisory Committee recommends publication of the opinion, the Commission shall carry out such publication taking into account the legitimate interest of undertakings in the protection of their business secrets.

7. At the request of a competition authority of a Member State, the Commission shall include on the agenda of the Advisory Committee cases that are being dealt with by a competition authority of a

Member State under Article 81 or Article 82 of the Treaty. The Commission may also do so on its own initiative. In either case, the Commission shall inform the competition authority concerned. A request may in particular be made by a competition authority of a Member State in respect of a case where the Commission intends to initiate proceedings with the effect of Article 11(6).

The Advisory Committee shall not issue opinions on cases dealt with by competition authorities of the Member States. The Advisory Committee may also discuss general issues of Community competition law.

Article 15

Cooperation with national courts

1. In proceedings for the application of Article 81 or Article 82 of the Treaty, courts of the Member States may ask the Commission to transmit to them information in its possession or its opinion on questions concerning the application of the Community competition rules.

2. Member States shall forward to the Commission a copy of any written judgment of national courts deciding on the application of Article 81 or Article 82 of the Treaty. Such copy shall be forwarded without delay after the full written judgment is notified to the parties.

3. Competition authorities of the Member States, acting on their own initiative, may submit written observations to the national courts of their Member State on issues relating to the application of Article 81 or Article 82 of the Treaty. With the permission of the court in question, they may also submit oral observations to the national courts of their Member State. Where the coherent application of Article 81 or Article 82 of the Treaty so requires, the Commission, acting on its own initiative, may submit written observations to courts of the Member States. With the permission of the court in question, it may also make oral observations.

   For the purpose of the preparation of their observations only, the competition authorities of the Member States and the Commission may request the relevant court of the Member State to transmit or ensure the transmission to them of any documents necessary for the assessment of the case.

4. This Article is without prejudice to wider powers to make observations before courts conferred on competition authorities of the Member States under the law of their Member State.

Article 16

Uniform application of Community competition law

1. When national courts rule on agreements, decisions or practices under Article 81 or Article 82 of the Treaty which are already the subject of a Commission decision, they cannot take decisions running counter to the decision adopted by the Commission. They must also avoid giving decisions which would conflict with a decision contemplated by the Commission in proceedings it has initiated. To that effect, the national court may assess whether it is necessary to stay its proceedings. This obligation is without prejudice to the rights and obligations under Article 234 of the Treaty.

2. When competition authorities of the Member States rule on agreements, decisions or practices under Article 81 or Article 82 of the Treaty which are already the subject of a Commission decision, they cannot take decisions which would run counter to the decision adopted by the Commission.

CHAPTER V
POWERS OF INVESTIGATION

Article 17

Investigations into sectors of the economy and into types of agreements

1. Where the trend of trade between Member States, the rigidity of prices or other circumstances suggest that competition may be restricted or distorted within the common market, the Commission may conduct its inquiry into a particular sector of the economy or into a particular

type of agreements across various sectors. In the course of that inquiry, the Commission may request the undertakings or associations of undertakings concerned to supply the information necessary for giving effect to Articles 81 and 82 of the Treaty and may carry out any inspections necessary for that purpose.

The Commission may in particular request the undertakings or associations of undertakings concerned to communicate to it all agreements, decisions and concerted practices. The Commission may publish a report on the results of its inquiry into particular sectors of the economy or particular types of agreements across various sectors and invite comments from interested parties.

2.   Articles 14, 18, 19, 20, 22, 23 and 24 shall apply mutatis mutandis.

Article 18

Requests for information

1.   In order to carry out the duties assigned to it by this Regulation, the Commission may, by simple request or by decision, require undertakings and associations of undertakings to provide all necessary information.

2.   When sending a simple request for information to an undertaking or association of undertakings, the Commission shall state the legal basis and the purpose of the request, specify what information is required and fix the time-limit within which the information is to be provided, and the penalties provided for in Article 23 for supplying incorrect or misleading information.

3.   Where the Commission requires undertakings and associations of undertakings to supply information by decision, it shall state the legal basis and the purpose of the request, specify what information is required and fix the time-limit within which it is to be provided. It shall also indicate the penalties provided for in Article 23 and indicate or impose the penalties provided for in Article 24. It shall further indicate the right to have the decision reviewed by the Court of Justice.

4.   The owners of the undertakings or their representatives and, in the case of legal persons, companies or firms, or associations having no legal personality, the persons authorised to represent them by law or by their constitution shall supply the information requested on behalf of the undertaking or the association of undertakings concerned. Lawyers duly authorised to act may supply the information on behalf of their clients. The latter shall remain fully responsible if the information supplied is incomplete, incorrect or misleading.

5.   The Commission shall without delay forward a copy of the simple request or of the decision to the competition authority of the Member State in whose territory the seat of the undertaking or association of undertakings is situated and the competition authority of the Member State whose territory is affected.

6.   At the request of the Commission the governments and competition authorities of the Member States shall provide the Commission with all necessary information to carry out the duties assigned to it by this Regulation.

Article 19

Power to take statements

1.   In order to carry out the duties assigned to it by this Regulation, the Commission may interview any natural or legal person who consents to be interviewed for the purpose of collecting information relating to the subject-matter of an investigation.

2.   Where an interview pursuant to paragraph 1 is conducted in the premises of an undertaking, the Commission shall inform the competition authority of the Member State in whose territory the interview takes place. If so requested by the competition authority of that Member State, its officials may assist the officials and other accompanying persons authorised by the Commission to conduct the interview.

Article 20

The Commission's powers of inspection

1.   In order to carry out the duties assigned to it by this Regulation, the Commission may conduct all necessary inspections of undertakings and associations of undertakings.

2.   The officials and other accompanying persons authorised by the Commission to conduct an inspection are empowered:

    (a)   to enter any premises, land and means of transport of undertakings and associations of undertakings;

    (b)   to examine the books and other records related to the business, irrespective of the medium on which they are stored;

    (c)   to take or obtain in any formcopies of or extracts fromsuch books or records;

    (d)   to seal any business premises and books or records for the period and to the extent necessary for the inspection;

    (e)   to ask any representative or member of staff of the undertaking or association of undertakings for explanations on facts or documents relating to the subject-matter and purpose of the inspection and to record the answers.

3.   The officials and other accompanying persons authorised by the Commission to conduct an inspection shall exercise their powers upon production of a written authorisation specifying the subject matter and purpose of the inspection and the penalties provided for in Article 23 in case the production of the required books or other records related to the business is incomplete or where the answers to questions asked under paragraph 2 of the present Article are incorrect or misleading. In good time before the inspection, the Commission shall give notice of the inspection to the competition authority of the Member State in whose territory it is to be conducted.

4.   Undertakings and associations of undertakings are required to submit to inspections ordered by decision of the Commission. The decision shall specify the subject matter and purpose of the inspection, appoint the date on which it is to begin and indicate the penalties provided for in Articles 23 and 24 and the right to have the decision reviewed by the Court of Justice. The Commission shall take such decisions after consulting the competition authority of the Member State in whose territory the inspection is to be conducted.

5.   Officials of as well as those authorised or appointed by the competition authority of the Member State in whose territory the inspection is to be conducted shall, at the request of that authority or of the Commission, actively assist the officials and other accompanying persons authorised by the Commission. To this end, they shall enjoy the powers specified in paragraph 2.

6.   Where the officials and other accompanying persons authorised by the Commission find that an undertaking opposes an inspection ordered pursuant to this Article, the Member State concerned shall afford themthe necessary assistance, requesting where appropriate the assistance of the police or of an equivalent enforcement authority, so as to enable them to conduct their inspection.

7.   If the assistance provided for in paragraph 6 requires authorisation froma judicial authority according to national rules, such authorisation shall be applied for. Such authorisation may also be applied for as a precautionary measure.

8.   Where authorisation as referred to in paragraph 7 is applied for, the national judicial authority shall control that the Commission decision is authentic and that the coercive measures envisaged are neither arbitrary nor excessive having regard to the subject matter of the inspection. In its control of the proportionality of the coercive measures, the national judicial authority may ask the Commission, directly or through the Member State competition authority, for detailed explanations in particular on the grounds the Commission has for suspecting infringement of Articles 81 and 82 of the Treaty, as well as on the seriousness of the suspected infringement and on the nature of the involvement of the undertaking concerned. However, the national judicial authority may not call into question the necessity for the inspection nor demand that it be provided with the information in the Commission's file. The lawfulness of the Commission decision shall be subject to review only by the Court of Justice.

Article 21

Inspection of other premises

1.   If a reasonable suspicion exists that books or other records related to the business and to the subject-matter of the inspection, which may be relevant to prove a serious violation of Article 81 or Article 82 of the Treaty, are being kept in any other premises, land and means of transport, including the homes of directors, managers and other members of staff of the undertakings and associations of undertakings concerned, the Commission can by decision order an inspection to be conducted in such other premises, land and means of transport.

2.   The decision shall specify the subject matter and purpose of the inspection, appoint the date on which it is to begin and indicate the right to have the decision reviewed by the Court of Justice. It shall in particular state the reasons that have led the Commission to conclude that a suspicion in the sense of paragraph 1 exists. The Commission shall take such decisions after consulting the competition authority of the Member State in whose territory the inspection is to be conducted.

3.   A decision adopted pursuant to paragraph 1 cannot be executed without prior authorisation from the national judicial authority of the Member State concerned. The national judicial authority shall control that the Commission decision is authentic and that the coercive measures envisaged are neither arbitrary nor excessive having regard in particular to the seriousness of the suspected infringement, to the importance of the evidence sought, to the involvement of the undertaking concerned and to the reasonable likelihood that business books and records relating to the subject matter of the inspection are kept in the premises for which the authorisation is requested. The national judicial authority may ask the Commission, directly or through the Member State competition authority, for detailed explanations on those elements which are necessary to allow its control of the proportionality of the coercive measures envisaged.

However, the national judicial authority may not call into question the necessity for the inspection nor demand that it be provided with information in the Commission's file. The lawfulness of the Commission decision shall be subject to review only by the Court of Justice.

4.   The officials and other accompanying persons authorised by the Commission to conduct an inspection ordered in accordance with paragraph 1 of this Article shall have the powers set out in Article 20(2)(a), (b) and (c). Article 20(5) and (6) shall apply mutatis mutandis.

Article 22

Investigations by competition authorities of Member States

1.   The competition authority of a Member State may in its own territory carry out any inspection or other fact-finding measure under its national law on behalf and for the account of the competition authority of another Member State in order to establish whether there has been an infringement of Article 81 or Article 82 of the Treaty. Any exchange and use of the information collected shall be carried out in accordance with Article 12.

2.   At the request of the Commission, the competition authorities of the Member States shall undertake the inspections which the Commission considers to be necessary under Article 20(1) or which it has ordered by decision pursuant to Article 20(4). The officials of the competition authorities of the Member States who are responsible for conducting these inspections as well as those authorised or appointed by themshall exercise their powers in accordance with their national law.

If so requested by the Commission or by the competition authority of the Member State in whose territory the inspection is to be conducted, officials and other accompanying persons authorised by the Commission may assist the officials of the authority concerned.

CHAPTER VI
PENALTIES

Article 23

Fines

1.   The Commission may by decision impose on undertakings and associations of undertakings fines not exceeding 1% of the total turnover in the preceding business year where, intentionally or negligently:

(a)   they supply incorrect or misleading information in response to a request made pursuant to Article 17 or Article 18(2);

(b)   in response to a request made by decision adopted pursuant to Article 17 or Article 18(3), they supply incorrect, incomplete or misleading information or do not supply information within the required time-limit;

(c)   they produce the required books or other records related to the business in incomplete form during inspections under Article 20 or refuse to submit to inspections ordered by a decision adopted pursuant to Article 20(4);

(d)   in response to a question asked in accordance with Article 20(2)(e),

— they give an incorrect or misleading answer,

— they fail to rectify within a time-limit set by the Commission an incorrect, incomplete or misleading answer given by a member of staff, or

— they fail or refuse to provide a complete answer on facts relating to the subject-matter and purpose of an inspection ordered by a decision adopted pursuant to Article 20(4);

(e)   seals affixed in accordance with Article 20(2)(d) by officials or other accompanying persons authorised by the Commission have been broken.

2.   The Commission may by decision impose fines on undertakings and associations of undertakings where, either intentionally or negligently:

(a)   they infringe Article 81 or Article 82 of the Treaty; or

(b)   they contravene a decision ordering interimm easures under Article 8; or

(c)   they fail to comply with a commitment made binding by a decision pursuant to Article 9.

For each undertaking and association of undertakings participating in the infringement, the fine shall not exceed 10% of its total turnover in the preceding business year.

Where the infringement of an association relates to the activities of its members, the fine shall not exceed 10% of the sum of the total turnover of each member active on the market affected by the infringement of the association.

3.   In fixing the amount of the fine, regard shall be had both to the gravity and to the duration of the infringement.

4.   When a fine is imposed on an association of undertakings taking account of the turnover of its members and the association is not solvent, the association is obliged to call for contributions from its members to cover the amount of the fine.

Where such contributions have not been made to the association within a time-limit fixed by the Commission, the Commission may require payment of the fine directly by any of the undertakings whose representatives were members of the decision-making bodies concerned of the association.

After the Commission has required payment under the second subparagraph, where necessary to ensure full payment of the fine, the Commission may require payment of the balance by any of the members of the association which were active on the market on which the infringement occurred.

However, the Commission shall not require payment under the second or the third subparagraph from undertakings which show that they have not implemented the infringing decision of the association and either were not aware of its existence or have actively distanced themselves from it before the Commission started investigating the case.

The financial liability of each undertaking in respect of the payment of the fine shall not exceed 10% of its total turnover in the preceding business year.

5.   Decisions taken pursuant to paragraphs 1 and 2 shall not be of a criminal law nature.

Article 24

Periodic penalty payments

1.   The Commission may, by decision, impose on undertakings or associations of undertakings periodic penalty payments not exceeding 5% of the average daily turnover in the preceding business year per day and calculated from the date appointed by the decision, in order to compel them:

(a)   to put an end to an infringement of Article 81 or Article 82 of the Treaty, in accordance with a decision taken pursuant to Article 7;

(b)   to comply with a decision ordering interim measures taken pursuant to Article 8;

(c)   to comply with a commitment made binding by a decision pursuant to Article 9;

(d)   to supply complete and correct information which it has requested by decision taken pursuant to Article 17 or Article 18(3);

(e)   to submit to an inspection which it has ordered by decision taken pursuant to Article 20(4).

2.   Where the undertakings or associations of undertakings have satisfied the obligation which the periodic penalty payment was intended to enforce, the Commission may fix the definitive amount of the periodic penalty payment at a figure lower than that which would arise under the original decision. Article 23(4) shall apply correspondingly.

CHAPTER VII
LIMITATION PERIODS

Article 25

Limitation periods for the imposition of penalties

1.   The powers conferred on the Commission by Articles 23 and 24 shall be subject to the following limitation periods:

(a) three years in the case of infringements of provisions concerning requests for information or the conduct of inspections;

(b) five years in the case of all other infringements.

2.   Time shall begin to run on the day on which the infringement is committed. However, in the case of continuing or repeated infringements, time shall begin to run on the day on which the infringement ceases.

3.   Any action taken by the Commission or by the competition authority of a Member State for the purpose of the investigation or proceedings in respect of an infringement shall interrupt the limitation period for the imposition of fines or periodic penalty payments. The limitation period shall be interrupted with effect fromthe date on which the action is notified to at least one undertaking or association of undertakings which has participated in the infringement. Actions which interrupt the running of the period shall include in particular the following:

(a)   written requests for information by the Commission or by the competition authority of a Member State;

(b)   written authorisations to conduct inspections issued to its officials by the Commission or by the competition authority of a Member State;

(c)   the initiation of proceedings by the Commission or by the competition authority of a Member State;

(d)   notification of the statement of objections of the Commission or of the competition authority of a Member State.

4.   The interruption of the limitation period shall apply for all the undertakings or associations of undertakings which have participated in the infringement.

5.   Each interruption shall start time running afresh. However, the limitation period shall expire at the latest on the day on which a period equal to twice the limitation period has elapsed without the Commission having imposed a fine or a periodic penalty payment. That period shall be extended by the time during which limitation is suspended pursuant to paragraph 6.

6.   The limitation period for the imposition of fines or periodic penalty payments shall be suspended for as long as the decision of the Commission is the subject of proceedings pending before the Court of Justice.

Article 26

Limitation period for the enforcement of penalties

1.   The power of the Commission to enforce decisions taken pursuant to Articles 23 and 24 shall be subject to a limitation period of five years.

2.   Time shall begin to run on the day on which the decision becomes final.

3.   The limitation period for the enforcement of penalties shall be interrupted:

   (a)   by notification of a decision varying the original amount of the fine or periodic penalty payment or refusing an application for variation;

   (b)   by any action of the Commission or of a Member State, acting at the request of the Commission, designed to enforce payment of the fine or periodic penalty payment.

4.   Each interruption shall start time running afresh.

5.   The limitation period for the enforcement of penalties shall be suspended for so long as:

   (a)   time to pay is allowed;

   (b)   enforcement of payment is suspended pursuant to a decision of the Court of Justice.

CHAPTER VIII
HEARINGS AND PROFESSIONAL SECRECY

Article 27

Hearing of the parties, complainants and others

1.   Before taking decisions as provided for in Articles 7, 8, 23 and Article 24(2), the Commission shall give the undertakings or associations of undertakings which are the subject of the proceedings conducted by the Commission the opportunity of being heard on the matters to which the Commission has taken objection. The Commission shall base its decisions only on objections on which the parties concerned have been able to comment. Complainants shall be associated closely with the proceedings.

2.   The rights of defence of the parties concerned shall be fully respected in the proceedings. They shall be entitled to have access to the Commission's file, subject to the legitimate interest of undertakings in the protection of their business secrets. The right of access to the file shall not extend to confidential information and internal documents of the Commission or the competition authorities of the Member States. In particular, the right of access shall not extend to correspondence between the Commission and the competition authorities of the Member States, or between the latter, including documents drawn up pursuant to Articles 11 and 14. Nothing in this paragraph shall prevent the Commission from disclosing and using information necessary to prove an infringement.

3.   If the Commission considers it necessary, it may also hear other natural or legal persons. Applications to be heard on the part of such persons shall, where they show a sufficient interest, be granted. The competition authorities of the Member States may also ask the Commission to hear other natural or legal persons.

4.   Where the Commission intends to adopt a decision pursuant to Article 9 or Article 10, it shall publish a concise summary of the case and the main content of the commitments or of the proposed course of action. Interested third parties may submit their observations within a time limit which is fixed by the Commission in its publication and which may not be less than one

month. Publication shall have regard to the legitimate interest of undertakings in the protection of their business secrets.

Article 28

Professional secrecy

1.   Without prejudice to Articles 12 and 15, information collected pursuant to Articles 17 to 22 shall be used only for the purpose for which it was acquired.

2.   Without prejudice to the exchange and to the use of information foreseen in Articles 11, 12, 14, 15 and 27, the Commission and the competition authorities of the Member States, their officials, servants and other persons working under the supervision of these authorities as well as officials and civil servants of other authorities of the Member States shall not disclose information acquired or exchanged by them pursuant to this Regulation and of the kind covered by the obligation of professional secrecy. This obligation also applies to all representatives and experts of Member States attending meetings of the Advisory Committee pursuant to Article 14.

CHAPTER IX
EXEMPTION REGULATIONS

Article 29

Withdrawal in individual cases

1.   Where the Commission, empowered by a Council Regulation, such as Regulations 19/65/EEC, (EEC) No 2821/71, (EEC) No 3976/87, (EEC) No 1534/91 or (EEC) No 479/92, to apply Article 81(3) of the Treaty by regulation, has declared Article 81(1) of the Treaty inapplicable to certain categories of agreements, decisions by associations of undertakings or concerted practices, it may, acting on its own initiative or on a complaint, withdraw the benefit of such an exemption Regulation when it finds that in any particular case an agreement, decision or concerted practice to which the exemption Regulation applies has certain effects which are incompatible with Article 81(3) of the Treaty.

2.   Where, in any particular case, agreements, decisions by associations of undertakings or concerted practices to which a Commission Regulation referred to in paragraph 1 applies have effects which are incompatible with Article 81(3) of the Treaty in the territory of a Member State, or in a part thereof, which has all the characteristics of a distinct geographic market, the competition authority of that Member State may withdraw the benefit of the Regulation in question in respect of that territory.

CHAPTER X
GENERAL PROVISIONS

Article 30

Publication of decisions

1.   The Commission shall publish the decisions, which it takes pursuant to Articles 7 to 10, 23 and 24.

2.   The publication shall state the names of the parties and the main content of the decision, including any penalties imposed. It shall have regard to the legitimate interest of undertakings in the protection of their business secrets.

Article 31

Review by the Court of Justice

The Court of Justice shall have unlimited jurisdiction to review decisions whereby the Commission has fixed a fine or periodic penalty payment. It may cancel, reduce or increase the fine or periodic penalty payment imposed.

Article 32

Exclusions

This Regulation ... not apply to:

(a)   ...al tramp vessel services as defined in Article 1(3)(a) of Regulation (EEC) No 4056/86;

(b)   ...e transport service that takes place exclusively between ports in one and the same ... State as foreseen in Article 1(2) of Regulation (EEC) No 4056/86.

(c)

Article 33

...ding provisions

.he Commission shall be authorised to take such measures as may be appropriate in order to apply this Regulation. The measures may concern, inter alia:

(a)   the form, content and other details of complaints lodged pursuant to Article 7 and the procedure for rejecting complaints;

(b)   the practical arrangements for the exchange of information and consultations provided for in Article 11;

(c)   the practical arrangements for the hearings provided for in Article 27.

2.   Before the adoption of any measures pursuant to paragraph 1, the Commission shall publish a draft thereof and invite all interested parties to submit their comments within the time-limit it lays down, which may not be less than one month. Before publishing a draft measure and before adopting it, the Commission shall consult the Advisory Committee on Restrictive Practices and Dominant Positions.

CHAPTER XI
TRANSITIONAL, AMENDING AND FINAL PROVISIONS

Article 34

Transitional provisions

1.   Applications made to the Commission under Article 2 of Regulation No 17, notifications mad... under Articles 4 and 5 of that Regulation and the corresponding applications and notificati... made under Regulations (EEC) No 1017/68, (EEC) No 4056/86 and (EEC) No 3975/87 s... lapse as from the date of application of this Regulation.

2.   Procedural steps taken under Regulation No 17 and Regulations (EEC) No 1017/68, (EE... 4056/86 and (EEC) No 3975/87 shall continue to have effect for the purposes of apply... Regulation.

Article 35

Designation of competition authorities of Member States

1.   The Member States shall designate the competition authority or authorities resp... application of Articles 81 and 82 of the Treaty in such a way that the provisions o... are effectively complied with. The measures necessary to empower those aut... those Articles shall be taken before 1 May 2004. The authorities designated m...

2.   When enforcement of Community competition law is entrusted to national... judicial authorities, the Member States may allocate different powers and... different national authorities, whether administrative or judicial.

3.   The effects of Article 11(6) apply to the authorities designated by the M... courts that exercise functions regarding the preparation and the adoption... foreseen in Article 5. The effects of Article 11(6) do not extend to cou... review courts in respect of the types of decisions foreseen in Article 5...

4.   Notwithstanding paragraph 3, in the Member States where, for the ... decisions foreseen in Article 5, an authority brings an action befor...

separate and different from the prosecuting authority and provided t̶ terms of this
paragraph are complied with, the effects of Article 11(6) shall be limi̶te the authority
prosecuting the case which shall withdraw its claim before the judicial a̶ when the
Commission opens proceedings and this withdrawal shall bring the natio̶ ...eedings
effectively to an end.

Article 36

Amendment of Regulation (EEC) No 1017/68

Regulation (EEC) No 1017/68 is amended as follows:

1.   Article 2 is repealed;
2.   In Article 3(1), the words 'The prohibition laid down in Article 2' are replaced by the words '
        prohibition in Article 81(1) of the Treaty';
3.   Article 4 is amended as follows:
        (a)   In paragraph 1, the words 'The agreements, decisions and concerted practices referred to in
                Article 2' are replaced by the words 'Agreements, decisions and concerted practices
                pursuant to Article 81(1) of the Treaty';
        (b)   Paragraph 2 is replaced by the following:
                '2.   If the implementation of any agreement, decision or concerted practice covered by
                        paragraph 1 has, in a given case, effects which are incompatible with the requirements
                        of Article 81(3) of the Treaty, undertakings or associations of undertakings may be
                        required to make such effects cease.'
4.   Articles 5 to 29 are repealed with the exception of Article 13(3) which continues to apply to
        decisions adopted pursuant to Article 5 of Regulation (EEC) No 1017/68 prior to the date of
        application of this Regulation until the date of expiration of those decisions;
        In Article 30, paragraphs 2, 3 and 4 are deleted.

Article 37

ˮ Regulation (EEC) No 2988/74

...C) No 2988/74, the following Article is inserted:

'Article 7a

...all not apply to measures taken under Council Regulation (EC) No 1/2003 of
...on the implementation of the rules on competition laid down in Articles 81

Article 38

No 4056/86

...nded as follows:

...s:

...the following:

...on

...rned are in breach of an obligation which, pursuant to Article
...n provided for in Article 3, the Commission may, in order to
...nd under the conditions laid down in Council Regulation
...ber 2002 on the implementation of the rules on competi-
...d 82 of the Treaty adopt a decision that either prohibits
...s themto performcertain specific acts, or withdraws
...which they enjoyed.'

...nditions laid down in Section II' are replaced by
...id down in Regulation (EC) No 1/2003';

    (ii)   The second sentence of the second subparagraph of point (c)(i) is replaced by the following:

> 'At the same time it shall decide, in accordance with Article 9 of Regulation (EC) No 1/2003, whether to accept commitments offered by the undertakings concerned with a view, inter alia, to obtaining access to the market for non-conference lines.'

2.   Article 8 is amended as follows:

    (a)   Paragraph 1 is deleted.

    (b)   In paragraph 2 the words 'pursuant to Article 10' are replaced by the words 'pursuant to Regulation (EC) No 1/2003'.

    (c)   Paragraph 3 is deleted;

3.   Article 9 is amended as follows:

    (a)   In paragraph 1, the words 'Advisory Committee referred to in Article 15' are replaced by the words 'Advisory Committee referred to in Article 14 of Regulation (EC) No 1/2003';

    (b)   In paragraph 2, the words 'Advisory Committee as referred to in Article 15' are replaced by the words 'Advisory Committee referred to in Article 14 of Regulation (EC) No 1/2003';

4.   Articles 10 to 25 are repealed with the exception of Article 13(3) which continues to apply to decisions adopted pursuant to Article 81(3) of the Treaty prior to the date of application of this Regulation until the date of expiration of those decisions;

5.   In Article 26, the words 'the form, content and other details of complaints pursuant to Article 10, applications pursuant to Article 12 and the hearings provided for in Article 23(1) and (2)' are deleted.

Article 39

Amendment of Regulation (EEC) No 3975/87

Articles 3 to 19 of Regulation (EEC) No 3975/87 are repealed with the exception of Article 6(3) which continues to apply to decisions adopted pursuant to Article 81(3) of the Treaty prior to the date of application of this Regulation until the date of expiration of those decisions.

Article 40

Amendment of Regulations No 19/65/EEC, (EEC) No 2821/71 and (EEC) No 1534/91 Article 7 of Regulation No 19/65/EEC, Article 7 of Regulation (EEC) No 2821/71 and Article 7 of Regulation (EEC) No 1534/91 are repealed.

Article 41

Amendment of Regulation (EEC) No 3976/87

Regulation (EEC) No 3976/87 is amended as follows:

1.   Article 6 is replaced by the following:

'Article 6

> The Commission shall consult the Advisory Committee referred to in Article 14 of Council Regulation (EC) No 1/2003 of 16 December 2002 on the implementation of the rules on competition laid down in Articles 81 and 82 of the Treaty before publishing a draft Regulation and before adopting a Regulation.'

2.   Article 7 is repealed.

Article 42

Amendment of Regulation (EEC) No 479/92

Regulation (EEC) No 479/92 is amended as follows:

1.   Article 5 is replaced by the following:

'Article 5

Before publishing the draft Regulation and before adopting the Regulation, the Commission shall consult the Advisory Committee referred to in Article 14 of Council Regulation (EC) No 1/2003 of 16 December 2002 on the implementation of the rules on competition laid down in Articles 81 and 82 of the Treaty.'

2.   Article 6 is repealed.

Article 43

Repeal of Regulations No 17 and No 141

1.   Regulation No 17 is repealed with the exception of Article 8(3) which continues to apply to decisions adopted pursuant to Article 81(3) of the Treaty prior to the date of application of this Regulation until the date of expiration of those decisions.

2.   Regulation No 141 is repealed.

3.   References to the repealed Regulations shall be construed as references to this Regulation.

Article 44

Report on the application of the present Regulation

Five years from the date of application of this Regulation, the Commission shall report to the European Parliament and the Council on the functioning of this Regulation, in particular on the application of Article 11(6) and Article 17.

On the basis of this report, the Commission shall assess whether it is appropriate to propose to the Council a revision of this Regulation.

Article 45

Entry into force

This Regulation shall enter into force on the 20th day following that of its publication in the Official Journal of the European Communities.

It shall apply from 1 May 2004.

This Regulation shall be binding in its entirety and directly applicable in all Member States.

Commission Notice
on agreements of minor importance which do not appreciably restrict competition under Article 81(1) of the Treaty establishing the European Community (*de minimis*)

(2001/C 368/07)

I

1. Article 81(1) prohibits agreements between undertakings which may affect trade between Member States and which have as their object or effect the prevention, restriction or distortion of competition within the common market. The Court of Justice of the European Communities has clarified that this provision is not applicable where the impact of the agreement on intra-Community trade or on competition is not appreciable.

2. In this notice the Commission quantifies, with the help of market share thresholds, what is not an appreciable restriction of competition under Article 81 of the EC Treaty. This negative definition of appreciability does not imply that agreements between undertakings which exceed the thresholds set out in this notice appreciably restrict competition. Such agreements may still have only a negligible effect on competition and may therefore not be prohibited by Article 81(1).

3. Agreements may in addition not fall under Article 81(1) because they are not capable of appreciably affecting trade between Member States. This notice does not deal with this issue. It does not quantify what does not constitute an appreciable effect on trade. It is however acknowledged that agreements between small and medium-sized undertakings, as defined in the Annex to Commission Recommendation 96/280/EC, are rarely capable of appreciably affecting trade between Member States. Small and medium-sized undertakings are currently defined in that recommendation as undertakings which have fewer than 250 employees and have either an annual turnover not exceeding EUR 40 million or an annual balance-sheet total not exceeding EUR 27 million.

4. In cases covered by this notice the Commission will not institute proceedings either upon application or on its own initiative. Where undertakings assume in good faith that an agreement is covered by this notice, the Commission will not impose fines. Although not binding on them, this notice also intends to give guidance to the courts and authorities of the Member States in their application of Article 81.

5. This notice also applies to decisions by associations of undertakings and to concerted practices.

6. This notice is without prejudice to any interpretation of Article 81 which may be given by the Court of Justice or the Court of First Instance of the European Communities.

II

7. The Commission holds the view that agreements between undertakings which affect trade between Member States do not appreciably restrict competition within the meaning of Article 81(1):

   (a) if the aggregate market share held by the parties to the agreement does not exceed 10% on any of the relevant markets affected by the agreement, where the agreement is made between undertakings which are actual or potential competitors on any of these markets (agreements between competitors); or

   (b) if the market share held by each of the parties to the agreement does not exceed 15% on any of the relevant markets affected by the agreement, where the agreement is made between undertakings which are not actual or potential competitors on any of these markets (agreements between non-competitors).

In cases where it is difficult to classify the agreement as either an agreement between competitors or an agreement between non-competitors the 10% threshold is applicable.

8.   Where in a relevant market competition is restricted by the cumulative effect of agreements for the sale of goods or services entered into by different suppliers or distributors (cumulative foreclosure effect of parallel networks of agreements having similar effects on the market), the market share thresholds under point 7 are reduced to 5%, both for agreements between competitors and for agreements between non-competitors. Individual suppliers or distributors with a market share not exceeding 5% are in general not considered to contribute significantly to a cumulative foreclosure effect (1). A cumulative foreclosure effect is unlikely to exist if less than 30% of the relevant market is covered by parallel (networks of) agreements having similar effects.

9.   The Commission also holds the view that agreements are not restrictive of competition if the market shares do not exceed the thresholds of respectively 10%, 15% and 5% set out in point 7 and 8 during two successive calendar years by more than 2 percentage points.

10.   In order to calculate the market share, it is necessary to determine the relevant market. This consists of the relevant product market and the relevant geographic market. When defining the relevant market, reference should be had to the notice on the definition of the relevant market for the purposes of Community competition law. The market shares are to be calculated on the basis of sales value data or, where appropriate, purchase value data. If value data are not available, estimates based on other reliable market information, including volume data, may be used.

11.   Points 7, 8 and 9 do not apply to agreements containing any of the following hardcore restrictions:

     (1)   as regards agreements between competitors as defined in point 7, restrictions which, directly or indirectly, in isolation or in combination with other factors under the control of the parties, have as their object:

         (a)   the fixing of prices when selling the products to third parties;

         (b)   the limitation of output or sales;

         (c)   the allocation of markets or customers;

     (2)   as regards agreements between non-competitors as defined in point 7, restrictions which, directly or indirectly, in isolation or in combination with other factors under the control of the parties, have as their object:

         (a)   the restriction of the buyer's ability to determine its sale price, without prejudice to the possibility of the supplier imposing a maximum sale price or recommending a sale price, provided that they do not amount to a fixed or minimum sale price as a result of pressure from, or incentives offered by, any of the parties;

         (b)   the restriction of the territory into which, or of the customers to whom, the buyer may sell the contract goods or services, except the following restrictions which are not hardcore:

            —   the restriction of active sales into the exclusive territory or to an exclusive customer group reserved to the supplier or allocated by the supplier to another buyer, where such a restriction does not limit sales by the customers of the buyer,

            —   the restriction of sales to end users by a buyer operating at the wholesale level of trade,

            —   the restriction of sales to unauthorised distributors by the members of a selective distribution system, and

            —   the restriction of the buyer's ability to sell components, supplied for the purposes of incorporation, to customers who would use them to manufacture the same type of goods as those produced by the supplier;

         (c)   the restriction of active or passive sales to end users by members of a selective distribution system operating at the retail level of trade, without prejudice to the possibility of prohibiting a member of the system from operating out of an unauthorised place of establishment;

(d) the restriction of cross-supplies between distributors within a selective distribution system, including between distributors operating at different levels of trade;

(e) the restriction agreed between a supplier of components and a buyer who incorporates those components, which limits the supplier's ability to sell the components as spare parts to end users or to repairers or other service providers not entrusted by the buyer with the repair or servicing of its goods;

(3) as regards agreements between competitors as defined in point 7, where the competitors operate, for the purposes of the agreement, at a different level of the production or distribution chain, any of the hardcore restrictions listed in paragraph (1) and (2) above.

12.— (1) For the purposes of this notice, the terms "undertaking", "party to the agreement", "distributor", "supplier" and "buyer" shall include their respective connected undertakings.

(2) "Connected undertakings" are:

(a) undertakings in which a party to the agreement, directly or indirectly:
— has the power to exercise more than half the voting rights, or
— has the power to appoint more than half the members of the supervisory board, board of management or bodies legally representing the undertaking, or
— has the right to manage the undertaking's affairs;

(b) undertakings which directly or indirectly have, over a party to the agreement, the rights or powers listed in (a);

(c) undertakings in which an undertaking referred to in (b) has, directly or indirectly, the rights or powers listed in (a);

(d) undertakings in which a party to the agreement together with one or more of the undertakings referred to in (a), (b) or (c), or in which two or more of the latter undertakings, jointly have the rights or powers listed in (a);

(e) undertakings in which the rights or the powers listed in (a) are jointly held by:
— parties to the agreement or their respective connected undertakings referred to in (a) to (d), or
— one or more of the parties to the agreement or one or more of their connected undertakings referred to in (a) to (d) and one or more third parties.

(3) For the purposes of paragraph 2(e), the market share held by these jointly held undertakings shall be apportioned equally to each undertaking having the rights or the powers listed in paragraph 2(a).

Index

Insolvency

Test for fraudulent trading is a subjective test.

Wrongful trading test is an objective test.